Encyclopedia of American Quaker Genealogy

[Volume VII]

# ABSTRACTS OF THE RECORDS OF THE SOCIETY OF FRIENDS IN INDIANA

PART FOUR

*Edited by*

Willard Heiss

Indiana Historical Society
Indianapolis
1972

# Preface

Considerable time has elapsed since publication of the previous volume. Work on Part Four has started and stopped many times. In the course of these years I moved and all the material was packed away in storage for nearly eighteen months.

At least four typists have worked on the composition. This will be noted in some variation of type, format and style. The editorial work done on meeting records varies as years have separated time spent on different meetings. The form generally follows that of the previous publications.

The introductory sketch of each meeting should be read. This may help you to understand why information may be lacking. For example, Duck Creek Meeting was laid down and attached for some time to Spiceland Meeting.

Much help has been given to this project by Ruth Slevin and Imogene Brown who have searched, rechecked and organized many of the records. Mrs. Brown has added several notations to help identify persons. In these cases the information should be in parentheses.

As this volume goes to the printer Part Five is already well along. Hopefully, the end of the tunnel can dimly be seen.

It should be restated here that records of monthly meetings established after 1875 have not been included in this series. Records of these meetings may be found in the William Wade Hinshaw Index to Quaker Meeting Records. This index is in the Friends Historical Library of Swarthmore College, Pennsylvania. A typescript is in the Library of the Indiana Historical Society.

Indianapolis, Twelfth 1972
Willard Heiss

# Contents

| | |
|---|---|
| Preface | iii |
| Annotated Abbreviations | vii |
| West Grove Meeting (Wayne Co.) | 1 |
| Milford Meeting (Wayne Co.) | 37 |
| Milford (Hicksite) Meeting (Wayne Co.) | 97 |
| Fall Creek (Hicksite) Meeting (Madison Co.) | 121 |
| Duck Creek Meeting (Henry Co.) | 153 |
| Duck Creek (Anti-Slavery) Meeting (Henry Co.) | 215 |
| Spiceland Meeting (Henry Co.) | 221 |
| Walnut Ridge Meeting (Rush Co.) | 327 |
| Hopewell Meeting (Henry Co.) | 389 |
| Raysville-Knightstown Meeting (Henry Co.) | 435 |
| Carthage Meeting (Rush Co.) | 489 |

# Annotated Abbreviations

The user of these abstracts of Quaker records will find some inconsistency in use of terms and abbreviations. As this work has been done at different times by different people, it is inevitable that there is an inconsistency in form. To revise the material to make it uniform would have required time which could best be used in other areas. The editor feels that the substance of the information that is supplied is consistent.

The editor has generally followed the pattern of abbreviations established in the Hinshaw volumes. In some instances there are improvements and in others it may be worse. Some may wish that no abbreviations had been used, but by so doing the copy has been reduced more than half.

| | | |
|---|---|---|
| **acc** | accept(ed) | Used in reference to any matter which was acceptable to the monthly meeting; for example, when a member would bring or send a statement to the monthly meeting condemning or acknowledging a wrong-doing the meeting would (or would not) accept it. |
| **acc** | accomplish(ed) | Used ordinarily when the committee having the care of a marriage would report back to the monthly meeting that it "had been orderly accomplished." |
| **altm** | at liberty to marry | When a couple would announce at monthly meeting their intention of marriage, a committee was appointed to investigate "their clearness" and report back to the next monthly meeting, after which time the couple were "left at liberty to marry." |
| **apd** | attending places of diversion | "Friends are fervently exhorted to watch carefully over [members] to prevent them...from frequenting stage-plays, horse-races, music, dancing, and other vain sports and amusements; also, in a particular manner, from being concerned in lotteries, wagering, or any kind of gaming; it being abundantly obvious, that those practices have a tendency to alienate the mind from the counsel of divine wisdom...If...any of our members fall into either of these practices...and cannot be reclaimed by further labour [The monthly meeting] should proceed to disown them." *Discipline (1819)* |

| | | |
|---|---|---|
| **appt** | appointed | as a clerk, committee and the like are appointed. The editor has used *appt comm* as a device to indicate the first mention of an individual in the minutes. It would be apparent that a person could serve on hundreds of committees over a period of years. |
| **att** | attend(ed)(ing) | |
| **b** | born | |
| **bur** | buried | |
| **cert** | certificate | a statement issued by a monthly meeting to a person (or persons) transferring their membership to another monthly meeting. Also a marriage certificate. |
| **ch** | children | |
| **chm** | condemned his (or her) misconduct | "It is the judgment of the Yearly Meeting, that offenders, whether under dealing, or disowned, who incline to make acknowledgment of their offences, shall prepare the same in writing; which ought to be shewn, if under dealing, to the committee appointed in their case; or if disowned, to the overseers. And if the purport is judged to be suitable to the occasion, the party may present it to the Monthly Meeting, and stay till it is read; and after time given for a solid pause, should withdraw, before either that, or any other business, is proceeded upon. The meeting is then to consider the case, and appoint two or more Friends to inform the party of the result." *Discipline (1819)* |
| **comm** | committee | |
| **compl** | complained of | A person could be complained of for an act which was contrary to the rules and advices as outlined in the *Discipline*. |
| **con** | condemned | see chm |
| **d** | died | |
| **dec** | deceased | |
| **dis** | disowned | "Such are to be treated with, as are guilty of lying, drunkenness, swearing, cursing; together with every other immoral or scandalous practice: and when persons are guilty in these respects, or |

any of them, after being treated with by the overseers or other concerned Friends, if they be brought to a sense of the iniquity thereof, such offenders are without improper delay, to remove the scandal, and clear, as much as possible, our holy profession therefrom, by acknowledging and condemning the offence, in writing, under their hands, to the satisfaction of the Monthly Meetings, to which they belong. And if any such offenders refuse so to acknowledge and condemn their faults, the said meetings, ought speedily to testify against them." *Discipline (1819)*

**dp**     deviation from plainness of dress and address

"Upon the first of these subjects, our principle is, to let decency, simplicity and utility, be our principal motives, and not to conform to the vain and changeable fashions of the world . . .

"In our address also, we are bound to differ from the world in several respects; such as our using the singular number in speaking to a single person; our disuse of the appellation of Master, Mistress, &c . . . and our calling the months and days of the week by their numerical names, instead of those which are derived from the heathen dieties . . ." *Discipline (1819)*

**dr**     drinking spiritous liquor to excess

**drpd**     dropped     as dropped from membership. A practice employed for the past seventy-five years in revising the membership list. This action would be taken if the member had ceased to attend meetings for a long period of time.

**dt**     daughter(s)

**end**     endorsed     as a certificate which was addressed to one monthly meeting would be endorsed and forwarded to another.

**fam**     family

**form**     formerly

**gct**     granted a certificate to

"All members removing beyond the limits of their Monthly Meetings . . . are to apply to their respective meetings for certificates [of memberships] directed to [the monthly meeting] within the limits of which they propose to sojourn or settle. But if any shall remove without so applying, the Monthly Meeting of which they are members, after

> making the usual inquiry, and finding no obstruction, should without improper delay, send certificates for them . . . but if their previous conduct require that they be treated with, and the distance be such as to render it inconvenient for the meetings they removed from, the Monthly Meetings, within the verge of which they are, should be requested to treat with them, and report the effect of their care: on which, if it prove satisfactory, certificates of removal may be directed; but if otherwise . . . testimonies of [disownment should] issued..." *Discipline (1819)*

| | | |
|---|---|---|
| **glt** | given a letter to | After about 1875 letters of membership were granted to and received from most other Protestant bodies. |
| **grdt** | granddaughter | |
| **grs** | grandson | |
| **h** | husband | |
| **inf** | informed | see rpt |
| **j** | joined | |
| **jas** | joined another society | that is, another religious group |
| **jASF** | joined Anti-Slavery Friends | from 1843 and the decade following, where the minutes say joined with "Separatists" or joined in "setting up a meeting contrary to discipline," this has been interpreted to mean joining Anti-Slavery Friends and is thus: j [ASF] |
| **jC** | joined Conservative Friends | |
| **jH** | joined Hicksite Friends | |
| **jMeth** | joined Methodists | |
| **m** | marry(ied) | |
| **mbr** | member | |
| **mbrp** | membership | |
| **mcd** | married contrary to discipline | Both parties were members of the Society of Friends and were married by a civil ceremony. |
| **MH** | meetinghouse | |

| | | |
|---|---|---|
| **MM** | monthly meeting | Where the name of a state is not given, it is to be assumed the meeting is located in Indiana. |
| **mou** | married out of unity | One of the parties was not a member of the Society of Friends. |
| **mtg** | meeting | |
| **na** | neglected attendance of meeting | |
| **PM** | preparative meeting | |
| **prc** | produced certificate | |
| **QM** | quarterly meeting | |
| **rec** | receive(d) | |
| **rec** | recorded | as the gift of the ministry was recorded |
| **rel** | released | |
| **rem** | removed | |
| **req** | request | |
| **res** | residence | |
| **ret** | retained | |
| **ret** | returned | |
| **rocf** | received on certificate from | A certificate of membership was received from another monthly meeting. Usually (but not always) where no state follows the name of the monthly meeting it is to be assumed that the meeting is located in Indiana. |
| **rolf** | received on letter from | After about 1875 letters of membership were accepted from most Protestant bodies. |
| **rpt** | report(ed) | When a member was found to have acted contrary to the rules and advices as outlined in the Discipline, he was reported to (or complained of for) the monthly meeting. The meeting then appointed a committee to treat with him and report their findings. Usually they reported "treated with satisfaction," and he condemned his misconduct. If not it was reported "treated without satisfaction" and he was disowned. Any one disowned had the right of appeal to the Quarterly Meeting and the Yearly Meeting. |

| | | |
|---|---|---|
| rst | re-instated in membership | After a disownment the member could still condemn his misconduct and be re-instated in membership. |
| tr | treated | When a complaint was made against a member, he was treated or dealt with for the offence by a committee to endeavor to have him acknowledge his error. |
| s | son(s) | |
| us | under care of | |
| unm | unmarried | |
| upl | using profane language | |
| w | wife | |
| w/c | with consent of | |
| wid | widow | |

# WEST GROVE MONTHLY MEETING
## Wayne County, Indiana

West Grove Monthly Meeting was set-off from Whitewater Monthly Meeting and first held, probably, in the second month 1818. [Records to establish the exact date are lacking.]

In 1821 **Milford** Preparative was established under West Grove. Two years later Milford was set-off as a monthly meeting.

In 1826 Fairfield (formerly known as Greensfork) was established as a preparative. The monthly meeting was composed of but two preparatives until the 1880s when **Centerville** was established. In 1905 Fairfield was set-off as a monthly meeting and its name changed to Greensfork.

By 1922 it would appear that the monthly meeting was held at Centerville and the name was changed to Centerville Monthly Meeting.

The West Grove meetinghouse and burying ground were located 2½ miles northwest of Centerville. Caleb W. King wrote in 1893: "The first meetings were held in the home of James Townsend, but soon a regular place of worship was built, this was a little to the north and west of the present site of the one now used. This of course was built of logs and had a partition as the men occupied a separate room from that of the women. This was about the year 1815, and served about 12 years, till the present frame structure was built in 1827.

"Just why this particular place was selected the writer is unable to tell for it could not have been so very inviting in the midst of an unbroken forest, but suppose its location was near the center of settlement. Its situation [was on the brow of a hill separating the Nolands fork bottoms facing them to the south and east, away from the more hilly country in the rear to the north and west . . . "

## Monthly Meeting Records

Some West Grove records are thought to be in the private collection of a resident of Centerville, Indiana. They were not made available for copying. Among them is the Marriage Record. Most fortunately the editor located abstracts of the marriage records made several years ago by Webster Parry. Information concerning removals has been culled from other monthly meeting records. This supplants in part the lost records.

The following volumes are in the vault of Indiana Yearly Meetinghouse. They have been microfilmed. Those searched for this publication are marked (*). The Hinshaw abstracts have been used for later dates (to 1932).

Men's Minutes

(lacking)
3-11-1837 : 3- 9-1850*
4-13-1850 : 6- 9-1866
7-14-1866 : 8-11-1894
(joint after 1884)

Women's Minutes

(lacking)
7-10-1847 : 3-8-1884*

Joint Minutes 9-18-1894 : 11-2-1950*
Marriage Record (see above)
Birth and Death Record - Books A and B*

WEST GROVE MONTHLY MEETING
WAYNE COUNTY, INDIANA
BIRTH AND DEATH RECORD

ALBERTSON
Jesse             b 3-23-1788, s Josiah & Sarah
                          d 12- 3-1879
Ann               b 1-13-1792, dt John & Alice Bailey
                          d 11-28-1876
Ch: Sarah         b 6-14-1811   d 11-17-1882
    Bailey        b 3-20-1813   d 9- 1-1839
    Maryann       b 8- 1-1815   d 11-22-1891
    Elwood        b 12- 9-1817  d 11-30-1885
    William       b 7-10-1822

Elwood            b 12- 9-1817, s Jesse & Anna
Mary              b 4- 7-1821, dt Daniel & Margaret
Ch: Oliver        b 11- 1-1847
    Hannah J      b 2-18-1856
    Albert        b 11-21-1858
    Bailey        b 12-30-1859

Martha J                        d 1888 ae 32y

BALDWIN
Asa W             b 7- 6-1812, s Uriah & Hannah
Mary              b 5- ?-1812, dt Jacob & Catharine Hoover
Ch: Nancy         b 4-23-1832
    Wm. H         b 4-23-1834
    Sarah         b 2-11-1837
    Jesse         b 2-11-1837
    Eli           b 6-12-1838
    Nathan        b 7-15-1841
    Hannah        b 5- 5-1844   d 7-19-1844, bur West Grove

Bailey            b 7-31-1840, s Jonathan & Mary Ann
Elizabeth J       b 11-15-1842, dt Samuel C. & Sarah Pollard
Ch: Albert        b 3- 5-1866

Caleb             b 2-11-1819, Guilford Co. N.C.
                          s John & Charlotte
Matilda           b 11-24-1822, N.C.
                          dt David & Mary Lindley
Ch: Asenath       b 9- 2-1844, White Lick
    Martha        b 1-28-1846, Wayne Co.
    Mary          b 5- 2-1849
    Caroline      b 2-28-1851

Cyrus             b 6- 3-1837, s Jonathan & Mary Ann
Barbara           b 1- 5-1843, dt Jacob & Catherine Sherrick
Ch: Luella        b 10-28-1860
    Ednie         b 10-30-1862
    Florence      b 3-18-1869
    Lodosca       b 3-19-1877

Isaac             b 11-16-1805, s John & Charlotte
Sarah             b 1-26-1805, dt Joshua & Margaret Murphey
                          d 7-11-1830, bur Fairfield
Ch: William       b 7-25-1828
    Margaret A    b 2- 6-1830

John              b 11- 4-1781, s John & Jemima
                          d 3- ?-1856
Charlotte         b 8- 4-1778, dt John & Margaret Pain
                          d 6- ?-1858
Ch: Jesse         b 7- 8-1804
    Isaac         b 11-16-1805
    Margaret      b 3- 3-1807
    Jemima        b 1-12-1809
    David         b 2- 2-1811
    Hezekiah      b 12-12-1812  d 2-18-1821, bur Deep River, N.C.
    Jonathan      b 12- 4-1815  d 3-13-1896
    Caleb         b 2-11-1819
    John C        b 1-19-1821   d 1-23-1900
    Charlotte     b 5-11-1823

Jonathan          b 12- 4-1815, s John & Charlotte
Mary Ann          b 8-11-1815, dt Jesse & Ann Albertson
Ch: Cyrus A       b 6- 3-1837
    Baily P       b 7-31-1840
    Albert C      b 2-24-1844   d 12- 2-1864

    Jane D        b 1- 8-1848
    James A       b 4-25-1854

Josiah            b 5-12-1791, Guilford Co. N.C.
                          s Uriah & Hannah
Lyda
Ch: Thomas        b 12-13-1814, Guilford Co. N.C.
    Simeon        b 1- 8-1820
    Betsey        b 4- 2-1822
    Hannah        b 7-13-1824

Rachel A          b 10-17-1863, dt Eli

Uriah             b 3-19-1764, s Wm. & Elizabeth
                          d 11-15-1844, bur West Grove
Hannah            b 1-26-1767, dt Wm. & Sarah Hunt
                          d 11-11-1831, bur West Grove
Ch: Asa W         b 7- 6-1812

William, s Asia W              d 1- 9-1838, bur West Grove
Sarah, dt Asia W               d 1-13-1838, bur West Grove

BARNARD
Obed              b 8-21-1759   d 3-17-1842, bur West Grove
1st w Margaret    b 12- 7-1766  d 11-30-1825, bur West Grove
2nd w Sophia      b 11- 3-1781

BELL
John              b 2- 6-1768, s Lancelot & Miriam
                          near West Union
Sarah             b 4-24-1780, dt Jesse & Sarah Symons
Ch: Lancelot      b 11- 3-1790
    Mary          b 3- 3-1792
    Miriam        b 8- 5-1795
    Josiah        b 1-11-1798
    Sarah         b 1-16-1800
    Thomas        b 4-17-1802
    Rebekah       b 4-21-1804

John
2nd w Lydia
Ch: Margaret      b 5- 6-1810
    Jesse         b 4-26-1812
    Abigail       b 1-14-1814
    Lydia         b 3-11-1816
    Martha        b 1-29-1818

Lancelot
Mary
Ch: Daniel        b 9-25-1819
    Sarah         b 3-14-1821

BENBOW
Edward, Sr.                    d 4-12-1829, ae 67y7m20d
                                      bur West Grove

BLACK
Alonzo
Sadie
Ch: Blanch        b 9-27-1890   d 1- 3-1892

BOND
Jesse             b 10- 7-1808, s Thomas
Anna              b 2- 4-1811, dt Joseph & Lydia Cook
                          d 12- 6-1846, bur West Grove
Ch: Calvin        b 4-22-1830
    Mahala        b 7-31-1832
    William       b 10-13-1834
    Lydia         b 9- 1-1837
    Oliver        b 1-23-1840   d 9- 3-1847
    Emily         b 11-25-1842  d 9-10-1847
    Rhoda         b 9-14-1845   d 8-15-1847

Jesse
Phebe
Ch: Nathan        b 8-16-1803
    Robert        b 12-23-1804
    John          b 7-24-1806
    William       b 8-23-1808
    Enos          b 7-22-1810
    Isom          b 8-29-1813
    Ruth          b 5-12-1815

WEST GROVE

BOND (Cont)
Jesse & Phebe
    Hannah      b  1-27-1818
    Isaac       b  2-27-1820
    Jesse
    Lydia

John           b  7-24-1806, s Jesse & Phebe
Mary          b 11-26-1811, dt Obed & Margaret Barnard
Ch: Margaret   b 11-22-1828

John
------
Ch: Marce     b 10-19-1891

Nathan
Tamer
Ch: Jonathan

Robert
Rachel
Ch: Henry
    John

BOWMAN
Richard      b  1-18-1807, Guilford Co. N.C.
                      s Wm. & Anna
Phebe        b 11-30-1805, Stokes Co. N.C.
                      dt Jonathan & Ann Mendenhall
Ch: Sarah A    b  1-30-1826
    Elvira     b 10-24-1827
    Susanna    b 10-10-1829
    William    b  8- 4-1831   d 12-12-1832, bur West Grove
    Jonathan   b  8-30-1833

BRANSON
Owen
Hannah
Ch: Hannah
    Susannah
    Margaret
    Owen

BROOKS
David        b  9-12-1803, s Jesse & Judith
                      d 1886, bur Fairfield
Lydia        b 12-29-1803, dt Daniel & Deborah Mendenhall
Ch: Pamela     b  5-27-1825
    Deborah    b 11-22-1826
    John       b  4-11-1828
    Edmund M   b 11- 6-1829
    Judith     b  2- 1-1832
    Eliza      b  2-20-1835
    Joel       b 12- 4-1836
    Emily      b  3- 7-1840
    Arthur     b  2-10-1848

Emanuel Milton b 11- 6-1829
Amanda       b  1-14-1835   d 1888
Ch: Ada M      b  7-31-1857
    Eliza D    b 12-27-1859
    David      b  8-18-1862
    Charles    b 10-17-1865

John         b  2-24-1765, s David & Sarah
                      d  9-13-1838, bur Fairfield
Deborah      b  4-14-1779   d 11-26-1844, bur Fairfield

BROOK
Olive, w Arthur          d 12-26-1869, ae 21y2m16d
                                    bur Fairfield

Milton                   d 10- ?-1881, ae 54y1m

BROWN
George W     b 11-11-1825
Mary Jane    b  1-11-1831
Ch: Marah      b  3- 8-1855
    John A.    b  5- 7-1858
    Grace
    Nancy A    b  9-15-1861
    Martha J   b  5-22-1863
    Elizabeth K b 12- 5-1865

    William E  b  7-30-1867
    George W   b  6-17-1869
    Emma A     b  2- 5-1872

BUNDY
Benjamin
Sarah
Ch: Jonathan   b  1-13-1797
    Jesse      b  8- 5-1803

George        b 11-16-1781, s Josiah & Mary
Sarah
Ch: Samuel M   b  9- 2-1808
    Sarah      b  4-24-1811
    George     b  4-24-1811

George
Keren        b  3-15-1788, dt Abraham & Julianna Elliott
Ch: Mary      b  8-23-1819
    Josiah     b  4-21-1823

Josiah        b  4-12-1748, s Josiah & Elizabeth
                      d  3- 4-1819, ae 70y10mo23d
                      bur West Union

William
Leah
Ch: Diana
    Elvira Ann
    Polly Witten
    Luzena
    Peggy J
    Sinthy E
    Franklin A

CANADAY
Boater        b  5-14-1768, s John & Margaret
Mary          b 10- 1-1772, dt William & Mary Russell
Ch: John      b 10-16-1797   d  9- 3-1822
    William    b  4-19-1799
    Sarah      b  2- 6-1801   d 12-13-1823
    Jane       b  3-21-1803
    Margaret   b  7- 7-1805
    Walter     b  9-16-1807   d  9- 6-1824
    Anna       b 11-22-1809
    Boater     b  7-25-1812
    Russell    b  6- 4-1815

Charles       b  4-18-1770, s John & Margaret
                      d  5-20-1851
Sarah        b  2- 4-1776   d  3-14-1850
Ch: William   b  4-14-1795
    Margaret   b  8-22-1797
    Mary       b  2- 6-1800
    Phebe      b  5- 7-1802
    Sarah      b  7-25-1804
    Nathan     b  4- 9-1807
    Charity    b  9- 6-1809
    Matilda    b  2-27-1812
    Charles    b 10-28-1814
    Malinda    b  5-25-1817

John, Sr.               d  3- 2-1830, ae 88y10mo26d
                                    bur West Grove
Margaret               d  3-12-1819

CHAPPELL
Reuben        b  8- 1-1810, Perq.Co. N.C.
                      s Gabriel & Lydia
Mary Ann      b 12-30-1813, Bedford Co. Va.
                      dt Nicholas & Caty Johnson
                      d 10-26-1849
Ch: John N    b  2-16-1838
    Griffin A  b  4-26-1839
    Milton H   b  8-24-1841
    Lydia M    b  8-26-1844

CLARK
Loke H                   d 10-24-1862, ae 19y
                                    bur Richmond, Ky.

WEST GROVE

CLAWSON
Josiah          b  4-28-1819
Sarah N         b 11- 9-1825
Ch: William F   b 12-28-1849
    Samuel      b  5- 4-1852
    Margaret    b  8-18-1854
    Isabella    b 12-20-1856
    Edna        b  2-13-1859
    Francis     b  7-19-1861
    Fletcher    b 10-12-1863
    Richard W   b  5- 9-1866

CLOUD
Joel            b  5-23-1800, s Jonathan & Elizabeth
Anna            b  8-28-1798, dt Charles & Ruth Gordon
Ch: Asenith     b  9-25-1822
    Ruth        b 12- 7-1824
    William     b  7- 5-1827
    Seth        b 11- 5-1829

Jonathan        b  1- 5-1772, s Joseph & Mary
                d  7- 5-1850
Elizabeth       b  8-18-1776, dt Ellick & Margaret Campbell
Ch: Anne        b 11-26-1797
    Joel        b  5-23-1800
    Elizabeth   b  6-29-1802   d 10- 5-1805
    William     b  7-14-1805
    Mordecai    b  8- 2-1808
    Metilda     b 10-18-1812
    Mary        b  8-19-1815
    Joseph      b  5-23-1818
    Rachel      b 10- 7-1821

Joseph          b  5-23-1818, s Jonathan & Elizabeth
Elenora         b  2-10-1821, dt Thomas & Mary Edgerton
                d 1892
Ch: Stephen     b 10- 8-1838
    William     b  4-30-1842
    Jonathan    b  5- 9-1847
    Mary E      b 12-25-1850
    Martha J    b  8- 8-1856
    Emily A     b  2- 3-1864

Rachel E, w Jonathan     d  2- 3-1876, bur West Grove

COFFIN
Joseph, Sr.     b  1-12-1774, s Barnabas & Phebe
Hannah          b 10-13-1774, dt John & Catharine Ballinger
                d  2-22-1845, bur Fairfield
Ch: Stephen     b  5- 6-1816
    William                  d  6- 5-1862, ae 50y5mo25d

Moses           b  3- 8-1800, s Adam & Anna
Margaret        b  7- 8-1809, dt Jonathan & Ann Mendenhall
Ch: Levi        b 11- 2-1829

Stephen         b  5- 6-1816, s Joseph & Hannah
Exaline         b  1- 3-1820, dt James Price
                d  6-18-1845, bur Fairfield
Ch: James A.    b  8-30-1840
    Oliver O    b  1-31-1845
Martha Ann, 2nd w  b 2-18-1823, dt Samuel & Rhoda Nixon
Ch: Leander W   b 10-23-1847
    Charles W   b  9-12-1849

William         b  9-26-1825
Sarah           b  8- 8-1824
Ch: John W      b  8-20-1848
    William H   b  4-29-1850
    Albert      b 11-24-1851
    Robert      b  2-19-1853
    Frank       b 10-27-1860

William H       b  4-29-1850, s Wm. H Sr.
Josephine       b  5- 7-1856, dt Allen Harris
Ch: Allen M     b  5-20-1873
    Eddie S     b  9-26-1875   d  3-20-1876
    Rosie M     b  1-15-1877

COMMONS
Robert D        b  4-10-1839   d  5-14-1879
Ollie J         b  9-19-1845

Ch: Lillia A    b  2-26-1870   d  2-21-1879
    Harry D     b  6-30-1873
    Ada M       b 10- 4-1876

Philip          b 12-15-1825, s David & Rachel
Hannah          b 10-14-1831, dt John & Hannah Maxwell
Ch: Thomas L    b  1- 5-1851

William
Sarah
Ch: Ruth
    David
    Rebecca
    Resin
    Charity
    Eliza
    Elener
    Nathan

COOK
Abraham         b  7-31-1769, s Abraham & Phebe
                (sic)        d  3-22-1842, ae 72y5mo22d
                bur West Grove
Elizabeth       b  3-15-1797, dt Uriah & Hannah Baldwin
                d  6-22-1859
Ch: William     b  7-13-1817, Guilford Co. N.C.
    Eli         b 12- 1-1821, Wayne Co. Ind
    Mary        b 12-19-1823
    Nathan      b  1-24-1826
    Jesse       b  5- 5-1828   d  7-28-1881, bur West Grove
    Isaac       b  3- 5-1832   d  5-30-1851
    Aaron       b  3-30-1835   d 12- ?-1894
    Margaret    b  8- 3-1837   d  4-28-1880

Cyrus           b  9- 4-1818
Phebe           b  3-30-1820
Ch: Jesse       b  2-13-1856

Eli             b 12- 1-1821
Emily           b  1-12-1824

Jehu            b  6-23-1806, Guilford N.C.
                s Joseph & Lydia
                d  9- 6-1859
Mary            b  5-26-1812, Wayne Co.
                dt William & Rachel Pike
                d 11-11-1862
Ch: Marinda     b 12-24-1831
    Rachel      b  7-29-1833
    Isom        b  4-14-1835   d  8- 5-1869
    Lydia       b  1-21-1837
    Temple      b  3- 2-1839
    John        b  3-19-1841   d  3-31-1872
    Priscilla   b  4- 1-1843
    Anna        b  7-23-1845
    Elizabeth   b  3-30-1848   d  3-26-1870
    William     b  7-14-1850   d  9- 5-1869
    Joseph      b  5- 6-1853   d  4- 8-1876
    Emily J     b  8- 9-1858

Joseph          b  5-28-1775, s Thomas & Mary
                d  9-16-1854 bur West Grove
Lydia           b  3- 4-1777, dt Jehu & Mary Wickersham
                d  8-10-1834 bur West Grove
Ch: Mary        b 11-30-1799
    Charity     b  7-14-1801   d  4-18-1802 bur Deep River
    William     b  6-20-1803                            N.C.
    Jehu        b  6-23-1806
    Fimri       b  9-26-1808   d  ?- ?-1892
    Anna        b  2- 4-1811
    Rachel      b  8-24-1814

Nathan          b  5-17-1795, s Thomas & Mary
Anna            b  9- 1-1797, dt Jehu & Mary Wickersham
Ch: Louisa      b  8-12-1816
    Sarah       b  1-18-1818
    Mary        b  2-19-1820   d  3- 7-1820
    Solomon     b  8-20-1821
    Emily       b  1-12-1824
    Eliha       b 11-22-1826
    Ascenith    b 12- 5-1828
    Eunice      b  9-12-1831
    Hiram       b  2- 2-1834

WEST GROVE

COOK (Cont)

|  | |  |  |
|---|---|---|---|
| Nathan | b | 1-24-1826 | |
| Sarah Jane | b | 1-29-1831 | |

William      b  6-20-1803, s Joseph & Lydia
Ruth         b  5-18-1804, dt Gideon & Sarah Small
Ch: Sarah A  b  8-23-1827
    Charity  b  1-12-1829
    Joseph   b 11-25-1830
    Jacob G  b  3-22-1832
    Jesse B  b  1-30-1836
    Hannah M b  7-10-1838
    Jonathan S b 5-12-1841
    Thomas   b  2- 4-1844

William
Anna
Ch: Martin
    Jabez
    Dayton

Lydia        d 12- ?-1890, ae 53 y

COPELAND
John         b  7-18-1784, s Joshua & Susannah
Susannah     b  1-10-1781, dt John & Winniford Pirvis
Ch: Winniford b 5-12-1807
    Jonathan b  8-15-1809
    Leah     b  7-11-1811
    Rachel   b  5-24-1813   d 10- 2-1814, bur West Grove
    Jesse    b  2-24-1815
    Joshua   b 12- 1-1816
    Samuel   b  8-19-1818
    John     b 11- 6-1820
    Susannah b  4-29-1822

Susannah     b  5-23-1752, dt Samuel & Sarah Pike

COX
Dinah, w Joseph    d 4- 5-1826, ae 66y5mo22d
                   bur West Grove
Joseph             d 8-18-1828, ae 68y6mo9d
                   bur West Grove

DAVIS
Elijah       b  9- 9-1798, Va., s John & Lyda
Margaret     b  3- 3-1807, Guilford Co. N.C.
                dt John & Charlotte Baldwin
Ch: Phebe E  b 10-28-1825
    Nancy L  b  6- 9-1827
    Charlotte A b 12-19-1828
    Lydia J  b  9-19-1830

Harmon       b  ?- ?-1774, s Thomas & Elizabeth
                d  9-14-1838
Hannah       b 12- 7-1778, dt Joseph & Phebe Middleton

Jehu
Rebecca
Ch: Oliver   b  8- 9-1833
    Alpheus  b  1- 9-1837
    Mary E   b  4- 6-1838
    Albert   b  5- 1-1841

Joseph       b  3-28-1800, s Harmon & Hannah
Hannah       b  4-24-1814, dt Benjamin & Elizabeth Morgan
Ch: Eliza    b  7- 9-1831
    George   b 10-13-1833
    Benjamin b  5- 1-1836
    William  b  9-22-1838
    Charles  b  1- 6-1841
    Harmon   b  7-31-1843
    Isaac    b 11-13-1847

Thomas       b 11- 3-1807, s Harmon & Hannah
                d  4- ?-1893
Hannah T     b  3-18-1812, dt Abraham & Susanna Moore
Ch: Susanna  b  3-29-1831
    Abraham  b  2-16-1833   d 8-31-1833
    Pierce   b  3-29-1835
    Tacy     b  4-18-1838
    Samuel   b  1-20-1841   d 10-10-1844

    Rachel   b 12- 8-1843
    Naomi    b 12- 1-1848
    William T b 5- 4-1851

Rachel R             d 1888
Mary                 d 1888

DENNIS
Thomas       b 11- 4-1791,     N.C.
                s Wm. & Delilah
Elizabeth    b 10-12-1794, dt Jesse & Elizabeth Wilson
Ch: Wilson   b  6- 1-1814,     N.C.
    Lucinda  b  1-14-1816      "
    Branson  b  5-10-1818      "
    Cyntha   b  3-21-1820      "
    Lyndsey  b  3- 8-1822      "
    Mariam   b  8-10-1824, Ind.
    William  b  8- 8-1826, Ind. d 7-28-1827, bur Fairfield
    Elizabeth b 6- 2-1828, Ind.

EDGERTON
Joseph
Ellen
Ch: Joseph   b  1-15-1839
    Elven    b  5- 3-1846
    Lydia J  b 12- 8-1862
    Laura A  b  1- 2-1865
    Oliver M b 12-13-1866

EDGINGTON
Samuel       b  9-13-1802

ELLIOTT
Able               s Axion & Cathrine
Sarah              dt Nathan & Anna Cook
Ch: Mary     b 10-19-1837

Absalom      b  6-18-1813, s Jacob & Mary
Polly M      b  9- 5-1816, dt John & Hannah Maxwell
Ch: Emily P  b  4-14-1840
    Maria M  b  4-25-1842
    Oliver   b  9-12-1844
    Mary Jane b 4- 7-1849

Exum         b  4-10-1765, Perq.Co. N.C.
                s Jacob & Filpah
                d 10- 8-1841, bur West Grove
Catharine    b  6- 8-1774, Ra Co. N.C.,
                dt Jacob & Sarah Lamb
Ch: Filpah   b  3-15-1792, Ra Co. N.C.
    Jacob    b  8-22-1793      "
    Huldah   b  6-24-1795      "
    John     b  2-12-1797      "
    Elwood   b  2-16-1799      "
    Isaac    b  3-16-1801      "
    Rebecca  b  1-31-1803      "
    Ursula   b  7- 7-1805      "
    Exum     b  3- 7-1808, Sury Co. N.C.
    Nathan   b  3-15-1810      "
    Sarah    b 10-28-1811      "
    Mark     b 12-28-1813
    Abel     b  7-26-1818, Wayne Co.

Jacob        b  8-22-1793, s Axum & Katharine
Mary         b 12-17-1790, dt Reuben & Rhoda Peel
Ch: Jonathan b  8-31-1811
    Absolem  b  6-18-1813
    Gulany   b 10- 4-1814
    Rhoda    b  4- 8-1818
    Solomon  b 12- 2-1819

Mark         b 12-28-1813, s Exum & Catharine
                d  4- 6-1858 bur West Grove
Mary         b 12- 2-1813, dt Joel & Elizabeth Haworth
Ch: William  b  2-18-1837
    Hannah   b  8-14-1838
    Joel H   b 10-27-1840
    Permelia b 10-12-1842
    Elton B  b  4-13-1845
    Sarah E  b  4-28-1850
    Louis C  b  5- 2-1855

## WEST GROVE

ELLIOTT (cont)
Nathan          b  3-15-1810, Sury Co. N.C.
                   s Exum & Cathrine
Betsy           b 11-18-1814, Wayne Co., dt John Maxwell
                   d  5-17-1841, ae 26y6mold
                   bur West Grove
Ch: Jane        b  8- 1-1835
    Sarah       b  4- 3-1837
    John M      b 12-22-1839

Nathan
2nd w Naomi     b 10-28-1818, Stokes Co., N.C.
                   dt Jonathan & Ann Mendenhall
Ch: Henry       b  8- 1-1843
    Anna E      b  9-14-1844
    David       b  9-21-1846  d  8-18-1853
    Wesley      b 11-12-1848
    Alvin       b  6-17-1850
    Elton B     b  3-10-1854

James Cassius              d  5-24-1860

ELLIS
Thomas
Lyda
Ch: Sophia      b 11- 2-1817
    Margaret A  b  1-24-1819
    Emily       b 11-14-1820
    Eleanor     b  1-23-1822
    Morris R    b 12-20-1823
    Rachel      b  1-24-1826
    Larkin T    b  5-15-1828

EVANS
William
Mary
Ch: Charles
    William
    Henry

FAUCET
Elvira, w George           d  6- 2-1878

FIFER
Ora             b  7-29-1891

GORDON
Charles         b  1-11-1766
Ruth            b  2- 8-1768
Ch: Sarah       b  4- 7-1789
    Mary        b 12-11-1794
    Richard     b  8-22-1796
    Anna        b  8-28-1798
    James       b  8- 6-1800
    Seth        b  9-28-1802
    Charles     b 11- 3-1804
    Ruth        b  5-17-1807
    Esther      b  7-15-1810  d  8-31-1830, bur West Grove

GRIFFIN
Jacob           b  5- 2-1776, s James & Hannah
                   d  1-14-1845, bur West Grove
Mary            b  8-28-1776, dt Joshua & Susanna Copeland
                   d  4- 4-1823, bur West Grove
Ch: John        b 11- 5-1801  d  3-18-1802
    James       b 11- 5-1801
    Samuel      b  1-22-1804
    Joseph      b  7-26-1806
    Joshua      b  4-15-1808
    Jacob       b 12-20-1810
    William     b  7-12-1813
    Mary        b  4-16-1816

Jacob
2nd w Sarah     b 12- 9-1782, dt Jehu & Mary Wickersham
                   d  2- 5-1870

Jacob           b 12-20-1810, s Jacob
Rebecca         b  5-19-1815, dt Wm. & Rachel Harvey
Ch: Eliza       b  5-19-1835
    Rachel      b  9-15-1837
    Mary        b  1-28-1840
    Joseph      b  2-12-1842

    Sarah       b  3- 9-1845  d  4-28-1845
    Elvira      b  3-22-1846
    Enos P      b  7- 9-1848
    Jacob H     b 10-19-1850

Jeremiah        b 12-25-1823, s Samuel & Lydia
Ann             b  9- 4-1828, dt Amos Kenworthy
Ch: Mary        b  1- 1-1849
    Charles     b 11- 3-1850

Joel            b  6- 4-1847
Mary E          b  5-27-1855
Ch: Minnia      b  1-10-1873
    Idora E

Joshua          b  4-15-1808, s Jacob & Mary
                   d  1-29-1881
Matilda         b 10-18-1812, dt Jonathan & Elizabeth Cloud
                   d  1892
Ch: Mordica     b 11-23-1832
    Jonathan    b  6- 1-1834
    Mary        b  4-14-1836
    Rachel      b  3-26-1838
    Jacob       b 10-10-1840
    Elizabeth A b  5-23-1843
    Joel        b  6- 4-1847
    Calvin W    b  8-23-1849

HARRIS
George B
Priscilla       b  4- 1-1843
Ch: Mary J      b  3-12-1862
    Louis B     b  2-28-1865
    Wilson A    b  1-14-1867
    Milo J      b  4-13-1869
    Willis B    b  9- 3-1871
    George D    b 12-12-1873
    Charles L   b  2- 3-1876
    Martha H    b  5-15-1878

Willis L        b  1-15-1806  d  4-19-1883
Hannah B        b  6-12-1811  d 11-21-1877, bur West Grove
Ch: Naomi L     b 10-22-1829  d 12-30-1880
    George B    b  9-29-1836
    Elizabeth   b  5-10-1838  d  1-28-1860
    Milton      b  3-30-1840
    Jesse D     b 12-25-1842
    Talitha A   b  1-11-1844
    Sophia C    b  1-19-1847
    James       b  4-18-1849
    Alice J     b  5- 5-1851
    Lavina L    b 10-10-1853

HARVEY
John            b  5- 4-1779, s Wm. & Jemima
Jane            b  3- 3-1782, dt Benj. & Rebecca Cox
                   d  4-16-1854, bur West Grove
Ch: Rebecca     b 11- 1-1804
    Isom        b  3- 7-1806
    Benjamin    b  5-15-1808
    Aaron       b 12-21-1810
    Nathan      b 11-21-1813
    William C   b  3- 1-1816
    John P      b  4-16-1819
    Mary        b  9- 7-1821
    Jane        b  1-24-1823

Samuel          b 10-11-1780, s of Caleb
                   d  9- 9-1822, bur White Water
Rebecca         b  4- 4-1790
Ch: Margaret    b  8-26-1811
    Mary        b  3-29-1813
    Sarah       b 10-19-1815
    Isaac       b  9- 8-1818
    Davis       b 10-17-1820

William         b  9-17-1782, s Caleb & Mary
Rachel          b 10-29-1790, dt John & Elvira Townsend
Ch: John        b  7- 9-1810
    Caleb       b 11- 9-1812
    Rebecca     b  5-19-1815
    Mary M      b  6- 7-1818
    Elvirah     b 12-15-1822  d  2-15-1823, bur West Grove

WEST GROVE

## HARVEY (Cont)
**William & Rachel (Cont)**
Ch: Sarah     b 12-12-1823
    William   b 3- 3-1826   d 5-10-1826, bur West Grove
    Rachel    b 4-24-1828

## HASTINGS
Aaron       b 5- 2-1802, s Wm. & Sarah
Margaret              dt Uriah & Hannah Baldwin
Ch: Solomon  b 10-10-1822

William     b 1-31-1773, s Joshua & Ann
                d 8-30-1845, bur West Grove
Sarah       b 8-23-1781, dt Katharine Evans
                d 1-16-1841, bur West Grove
Ch: Nancy    b 8-23-1799, Randolph Co. N.C.
    Catharine  b 7-30-1801     "
    Eunice    b 12- 1-1803     "
    Welmet    b 12- 7-1805     "
                d 9-26-1809, bur White Water
    Aaron     b 5- 2-1808, Wayne Co., Ind.
    Mary      b 9-26-1810
    William   b 3-10-1813
    Daniel C  b 2-19-1815
    Sarah     b 4- 8-1817
    Hannah    b 8-28-1819
    David     b 3- 5-1822  d 11- 4-1840, bur West Grove
    Rebekah   b 8-26-1824

## HAWORTH
Dillen      b 11-18-1806, Jefferson Co., Tenn.
                s Richard & Hannah
Sarah       b 3-10-1809, dt Benjamin & Leah Maudlin
Ch: James B   b 12-14-1826
    Benjamin  b 4-11-1828, Walnut Ridge, Rush Co.
    Solomon   b 8-28-1829,     "
    Calvin    b 4-26-1831,     "
    Cynchiann  b 5-10-1833,     "
    Maria     b 2- 5-1835,     "
    Hannah    b 2-21-1837, near West Grove
    Richard   b 10-17-1838
    Esther    b 9-20-1841
    Emily     b 7-16-1843
    Sarah     b 6-14-1845
    Bathena J  b 5- 3-1849

James       b 3-25-1805, s Richard & Hannah
Penninah    b 11- 2-1801, dt Benjamin & Leah Modlin
Ch: Ira      b 8- 5-1827

Richard
Hannah
Ch: James    b 3-25-1805
    Dillen    b 11-18-1806, Jefferson Co. Tenn.
    Richard   b 4-12-1809,     "

## HILL
John
Dinah
Ch: Joseph    b 2-19-1818
    Martha    b 1- 8-1819
    Benjamin C b 4-19-1820
    Nathan C  b 12- 3-1821
    Ervin     b 4-29-1823
    Sarah A   b 8- 7-1824

## HOOVER
Sarah                  d 10-28-1891, ae 40y

## HORNEY
Stephen     b 5-10-1797, s John & Mary
Nancy       b 8-14-1802, dt Absalom & Sarah Williams(?)
Ch: Rebecca  b 2-12-1827
    John      b 2- 4-1829
    Absalom   b 2-20-1831
    Sarah     b 8- 1-1833
    Andrew    b 12-20-1835
    Esther    b 3-20-1838
    Maryann   b 7- 6-1840
    Jesse     b 7-29-1843
    Martha    b 11- 3-1845

## HORNISH
Jacob       b 10-22-1794
Tamer       b 9-24-1792
Ch: Bazeleel B b 7-24-1820
    William W  b 4-14-1822
    Sarah A    b 5-27-1824
    Sophia     b 11-30-1826
    Ruth A     b 5- 2-1829

## HOUGH
Rachel                d 12-24-1831

## HOSIER
Ellen                 d 5-31-1890, ae 71y

## HUNT
John
Caty
Ch: Irena     b 1- 7-1820
    Lucinda   b 4-28-1821
    Calvin    b 2-11-1823
    Franklin B b 6-16-1824
    Melinda   b 5-18-1827
    Milton    b 7-24-1828

## JONES
Lewis       b 3-25-1807  d 4- 3-1877, bur Centerville
Ruth        b 9- 8-1816

Sophia C, w John        d ae 28y9mo21d

## JOHNSON
Charles     b 7- 8-1797, s James & Ruth
Nancy       b 12-14-1804, dt Amaziah & Isabel Beeson
Ch: Caleb    b 4- 8-1819, s Charles & Mary
    Martha    b 10-12-1820, dt     "
    Betsy A   b 4-13-1823, dt     "
    Charles A b 12-25-1827, s Charles & Nancy
    Isaac K   b 7-24-1829, s     "

## KINLEY
Nathaniel   b 9-15-1817
Ch: China A  b 8-12-1859
    Daniel P  b 7-15-1861

## KIRK
William     b 7- 6-1793, s Ezekiel & Hannah
                d 3-31-1858, ae 62y8mo25d
Rachel      b 10-18-1792, dt Jehu & Mary Wickersham
                d 4-10-1869

## LACEY
John        b 4-22-1789, s Peter & Susannah
                West Union
Penninah    b 9-30-1791, dt Thomas & Ann Hill
Ch: Samuel   b 9-29-1815
    Susanna   b 10-24-1817
    Jesse     b 3-24-1820
    Thomas    b 1-25-1822
    Phebe     b 12- 1-1824

## LUNDY
William
Rachel
Ch: Sarah A
    Hannah
    Martha

Jackson               d 9- 1-1884, ae 49y

William L             d 11-14-1884, ae 26y2mo17d

## MARTIN
James      b 4-22-1795, s John & Rachel
Sarah                dt Edward & Mary Beeson
Ch: John     b 9- 7-1819
    Mary Ann  b 7-27-1822
    David M   b 11-26-1825
    Elizabeth M 3- 6-1828
    James B   b 6-20-1831
    Edward B  b 2-16-1834

MARTIN (Cont)
John                                    d 2-13-1837
Elizabeth                               d 9-27-1844

MARTINDALE
Eden
Sally
Ch: Voyle       b 11-31-1891

James
Lydia
Ch: Lydia       b  8-13-1830
    John        b 10-10-1849
    Emma        b  6-10-1852
    Eden        b  7-27-1857

MAUDLIN
Benjamin        b 12-10-1771, s Edmond & Sarah
Leah
Ch: Wright      b  3-26-1797
    Samuel      b  3-12-1799  d 5-26-1813, bur White Water
    Peninnah    b 11- 2-1801
    Thomas      b  1-23-1804
    John        b  1-18-1806
    Sarah       b  3-10-1809
    Rachel      b 12-16-1812
    Susanna     b  2-14-1816
    Leah        b  8- 4-1818
    Anna        b  8- 5-1820
    Benjamin    b  1-23-1823

Mary

John            b  6-12-1806, s Benjamin & Leah
                              d 1892
Rebecca         b  1-31-1803, dt Exum & Catharine Elliott
                              d 5-10-1875, bur West Grove
Ch: Mark        b  9- 6-1826, d 1892
    Nathan      b 12-23-1827
    Exum        b 10-11-1829
    Eliza Ann   b  2- 1-1831
    Catharine J 11-26-1832
    Sarah       b  3-12-1835
    John, Jr.   b  5- 8-1837
    Rachel      b 12-27-1839

Nathan          b  9-17-1823, s Wright & Mary
Sarah G         b  7-15-1826, dt Wm. & Mary Gardener

Wright
Mary
Ch: Thomas      b  8-23-1818
    Rachel      b 10- 8-1819
    Sidney      b 11-21-1821
    Nathan      b  9-17-1823
    Lucinda     b 12-22-1825

MAXWELL
Hugh            b 11- 8-1820, s John & Hannah
Ruth A          b 10-17-1823, dt David & Mary James
Ch: Mary        b  3- 8-1841
    Sarah       b  2-15-1843
    Caroline    b  5-22-1845
    Emeline     b  5- 3-1847
    Ann         b 10-17-1849

John            b  5-10-1789, s Hugh & Elizabeth
                              d 9-13-1860, bur West Grove
Hannah          b  7-30-1787, dt James & Mary Whitlock
                              d 3-29-1857, bur West Grove
Ch: Betsy       b 11-18-1814
    Polly       b  9- 5-1816
    Maria       b  9-14-1818
    Hugh W      b 11- 8-1820
    Milton      b 10-15-1822  d 6-20-1823, bur West Grove
    Sarah       b  5-18-1824
    John M      b  8-17-1826
    Hannah Ann  b 10-14-1831

John M          b  8-17-1826, s John & Hannah
Nancy Jane      b  6- 2-1829  d 1-31-1859
Ch: Ann Elizabeth 9-10-1850
    Albert      b 10-17-1851

WEST GROVE

    King M      b 10- 6-1853  d 6- 5-1866, bur West Grove
    Elma J      b 10-25-1855  d 1- 5-1856
    Emily P     b  1-27-1857
Ann Elizabeth, 2nd w
                b  1-16-1834  d 8- 2-1868, bur West Grove
    Robert M    b  7-23-1865
    Sallie H    b 12-26-1866

MENDENHALL
Elijah          b  2- 6-1797, Guilford Co. N.C.
                              s Daniel & Deborah
Huldah          b  6- 6-1799, dt Joseph & Hannah Coffin
Ch: Joseph C    b  2-10-1818, Guilford Co. N.C.
    Daniel      b 12-12-1819,        "
    Anderton    b  6-26-1823,        "
    John B      b  6- 3-1825,        "
    William     b  9- 3-1827, Wayne Co. Ind.

Isaiah          b  7- 6-1778, s Elijah & Mary
Christiana      b  2- 5-1783, dt John & Margaret Clark
Ch: Elijah T    b 12-29-1806
    Enoch       b 10- 2-1808
    John        b  3-12-1810
    Margaret    b  1- 9-1812
    Solomon     b  1-12-1814
    Mary        b 12-29-1815
    Hannah      b  1-16-1818
    Sarah       b 12-11-1819
    Caleb C     b 11-21-1821
    Elem        b  3-23-1824

James           b  1- 2-1806, Guilford Co. N.C.
                              s Daniel & Deborah
Milicent        b 11- 5-1810, dt Joseph & Hannah Coffin
Ch: Stephen C   b 11-25-1828, Wayne Co. Ind.
    Rebecca A   b  2-25-1831
    Susan B     b  4-20-1833
    Olinda B    b  8-22-1836
    Sarah E     b  6- 4-1839
    Hannah B    b 12- 4-1841
    Joseph C    b  2-20-1845

Jonathan        b  5- 6-1782, Wrightsboro, Ga.
                              s Joseph & Elizabeth
Ann             b  3-28-1786, Buck Co. Penna.
                              dt John & Ann Phillips
Ch: Elizabeth   b  8-21-1804, Stokes Co. N.C.
    Phebe       b 11-30-1805,        "
    Mary        b  3-27-1807,        "
    Margaret    b  7- 8-1809,        "
    Robert      b  3-13-1811,        "
    John        b  1- 2-1813,        "
    Joseph      b 12- 6-1814,        "
    Rebecca     b 10-10-1816,        "
    Naomi       b 10-28-1818,        "
    Nathan      b 10- 4-1820,        "
    Anna        b  9-30-1822,        "
    Sally       b  2-20-1825,        "
    Keziah      b  7- 1-1827, Wayne Co. Ind.

Mary, w Elijah T.             d 5-12-1840, ae 24y8mo22d
                              bur Fairfield

MILLER
Permelia        b 10-12-1832

MORGAN
Elizabeth, w Benjamin, dt James & Ruth Johnson
                b  2-28-1782  d 3-13-1821, ae 39y0mo15d
                              bur West Union

MORRIS
Isaac           b  4-20-1780, s Aaron & Margaret
                              West Union
Pharba          b  3-31-1784, dt Josiah & Mary Bundy
Ch: Margaret    b 10- 5-1803
    George      b 10- 7-1805  d 12-20-1823, bur West Union
    Ruth        b 12-11-1807  d 1-21-1818, bur West Union
    Elizabeth   b 10-13-1809
    Gulielma    b  4-17-1812
    Christopher   6-28-1814
    Edward      b  8-10-1816

WEST GROVE

## MORRIS (Cont)
**Jehosophat**
**Sarah**
Ch: James    b 10- 6-1817
     Mary    b 12- 1-1818
     Joel    b 4-28-1820

**Jehosophat**
**Mary**
Ch: Sarah    b 9-10-1824

**Jonathan**
**Abigail**
Ch: Elias    b 11- 6-1817
     Phinas    b 2-25-1820
     Rebecca    b 9-19-1821

**Joshua**    b 4-29-1785, s Nathan & Mary
**Mary**    b 1-16-1788, dt Charles & Lydia Morgan
Ch: Charles    b 4- 5-1807
     Lydia    b 1-15-1809
     Susannah    b 11-16-1810
     Samuel    b 1- 7-1813
     John    b 4-17-1815
     Mary    b 2-11-1817
     Jesse    b 9-24-1819
     Priscilla    b 12- 6-1821
     Ruth    b 2-17-1824

**Sarah**    d 11-20-1820, bur West Union

**Benoni**    d 11-14-1820, bur West Union

## MUNDON
**Jesse**    b 9-10-1779, s Wm. & Ruth
**Mary**    b 11-20-1785, dt John & Jane Nixon
Ch: Ruth E    b 9-22-1809
     Sarah    b 1- 4-1812
     William    b 1- 2-1814
     Abigail    b 11-12-1815
     Aseanath    b 2- 1-1818
     Nixon    b 2-20-1820

## MURPHY
**John**    b 1-24-1817, s Joshua & Margaret
**Susanna**    b 2-16-1818, dt Daniel & Margaret Williams
Ch: Lydia J    b 7-21-1840
     Albert H    b 2-15-1842
     Caroline    b 12-23-1843
     William    b 10- 4-1845

**Joshua**    b 4-26-1782    d 4- 1-1840, bur Fairfield
**Margaret**    b 9- 2-1784, dt Joshua & Rachel Chamness
Ch: Sarah    b 1-26-1805    (d 2-9-1854)
     William    b 4-30-1806
     Rachel    b 1-26-1808
     Amos    b 11-27-1812
     Rebecca    b 4-30-1815
     John    b 1-24-1817
     Joshua    b 1-22-1820
     Jesse    b 8-14-1821
     Milton    b 11-14-1823    d 9-29-1841
     Margaret    b 7-21-1825
     Polly    b 1-27-1828
     Betsy    b 1-27-1828

**Joshua**
**Tacy**
Ch: Susanna    b 12- 4-1837
     Martha Ann    b 12- 6-1839    d 10-29-1845
     Emily    b 10-30-1841
     Milton    b 8-15-1844
     Amos    b 2- 4-1846

**William**    b 4-30-1806, s Joshua & Margaret
**Betsey**    b 12-26-1806, dt Peter & Margaret Cox

## NORTH
**Daniel**    b 8- ?-1769
**Keziah**    b 6-26-1767    d 7-26-1843, bur Fairfield

## NIXON
**Gabriel**    b 10-25-1801, Ra Co. N.C.
     s Phineas & Milicent
**Mary**    b 2-28-1808, Guilford Co. N.C.
     dt Daniel & Deborah Mendenhall
Ch: Letitia    b 5- 3-1830, Richmond
     Phineas    b 4-18-1833, near Milford
     Daniel M    b 1- 2-1835,    "    "
     Milicent    b 5-10-1837,    "    Fairfield
     Albert W    b 8-17-1840,    "    West Grove
     Stephen    b 10- 4-1842

**John**    d 7-20-1824, bur West Union
**Jane, w**    d 10-19-1824,    "    "    "

## OGBORN
**Samuel**    b 3-14-1788, N.J., s Caleb & Ann
     d 7-14-1839, bur Fairfield
**Esther**    b 11-18-1784, dt Isaac & Rebecca Andrews
Ch: Joseph    b 2- 9-1812, N.J.
     Mary    b 9- 9-1814, "    d 1-2-1836, bur Fairfield
     Allen    b 8-25-1816, "
     Edwin    b 8-25-1816, "
     Evan    b 3-20-1819, "
     Lyda    b 1- 3-1821, "
     Ezra    b 11-25-1823, Warren Co. O.
     Ann    b 10- 2-1825, Wayne Co. Ind.
     Joel    b 3-17-1828,    "    "

## OSBORN
**James**    b 11-10-1798, Knox Co., Tenn.
     s Charles & Sarah
**Catharine**    b 7-30-1801, Ra Co. N.C.
     dt Wm. & Sarah
     d 12-11-1838, bur West Grove
Ch: Enos    b 10-20-1827    d 7- 2-1893
     Sarah    b 5-11-1829

**William**
Ch: Charles
     Lemuel

**William**
**Anne**
Ch: Jeremiah
     Catharine
     William D

## OVERMAN
**Nathan**    b 2- 8-1777, s Isaac & Sarah
**Elizabeth**    b 3-10-1785, dt Cornelius & Elizabeth Ratliff
     d 4-23-1837, bur West Grove
Ch: Cornelius    b 9-11-1805
     Isaac    b 8- 8-1807
     Sarah    b 10-11-1809
     Cyrus    b 5-18-1812
     Nathan    b 11-18-1814
     Joseph    b 4- 7-1817
     Charles    b 8-28-1819
     Enoch    b 9-25-1821    d 8- 9-1823, bur West Grove
     Elizabeth    b 9-24-1824
     John H    b 7- 7-1827

## PEELLE
**John**    b 3-27-1791

## PERSONETTE
**Luke, s William**    d 1875
**Mary**    d 2-28-1879, ae 42y8mo14d

## PIKE
**Rachel**    b 9-19-1785, dt John & Mary Davis
     d 12- 5-1857, ae 72y2mo16d

## PITTS
**William, s Calvin**    d 1878, bur West Grove
**Elizabeth**    d 1892, ae 47y, bur Jay Co.

## ROBENSON
**Thomas**
**Rebecca**
Ch: Martha Ann    12-14-1844
     Isaac    b 9-18-1846

## ROBENSON (Cont)
**Thomas & Rebecca (Cont)**
Ch: Harmon    b 2-19-1848
    William H   b 8- 2-1851
    Emma C    b 4-19-1857

Clarkson E              d 8- 3-1855
Lorezzo Dow            d 7- 6-1857

## ROBERTS
Henry       b 8- 8-1817, near Richmond, s Walter & Mary
Elizabeth   b 10-12-1822
Ch: Matilda    b 9- 6-1839
    Mary       b 1-10-1842
    Ruth       b 7-31-1844    d 7-15-1845
    Maria      b 8-20-1846
    Thomas     b 7-14-1850

## RUSSELL
George      b 8-19-1782, s Timothy & Sarah
Judith      b 5-15-1787, dt James & Ruth Johnson
                 d 4-18-1833, bur West Grove
Ch: Ruth       b 4- 8-1810    d 8- 9-1830, " "
    Sarah      b 8-10-1812
    Sinah      b 2-19-1814
    Timothy    b 4-30-1816
    Josiah     b 12-23-1817
    George     b 3- 2-1820
    James      b 3-25-1823

George      b 8-19-1782, s Timothy & Sarah
                 d 6-20-1841, bur West Grove
Susannah, 2nd w   b 2-10-1797
Ch: Mary       b 8-30-1835
    Judith     b 7-25-1837
    Calvin W    b 8-23-1838

George      b 3- 2-1820, s George & Judith
Clarissa    b 4-26-1821, dt Robert & Lydia Franklin
Ch: William    b 7-16-1842
    Franklin    b 8-20-1843
    Lydia      b 8-22-1845

James J     b 3-25-1823    d 1837
Rachel      b 7-17-1825    d 1888
Ch: Elvia     b 9-22-1847
    Edam J     b 12-25-1849
    Ruth A     b 10-17-1851
    Joseph P   b 1-27-1858

## SAINT
William
Aohsah
Ch: Exum Ely   b 9-10-1808, Perq. Co. N.C.
    Juliana    b 8- 8-1811,    "
    Alpheus    b 2-21-1813,    "
    Jennet     b 2- 8-1816,    "
    Daughty    b 8- 7-1818, Wayne Co. Ind.
    Joseph     b 3-21-1820,    "
    Jonathan   b 1-26-1822,    "
    Daniel     b 11-24-1823,   "

## SHOEMAKER
Charles     b 8-18-1818, s Ezekiel & Margaret
Margaret A   b 1-24-1819, dt Thomas & Lydia Ellis
Ch: Ezekial    b 10- 2-1840
    Elijah     b 10- 3-1842
    Tacy       b 4-11-1844
    Sophia     b 9-11-1845

Ezekial
Margaret (now wife of Daniel Williams)
Ch: Tacy       b 1-29-1817, Montgomery Co. Penna.
    Charles    b 8-18-1818,         "

## SMALL
Josiah      b 10-16-17--
Jane        b 5-16-1796
Ch: Thomas    b 9-27-1816
    Sarah      b 12- 2-1818

WEST GROVE

## SMITH
Albert      b 5-18-1841, s John P.
               d 8-22-1874

Freeman     b 6-26-1834, s John P.
Emily       b 2-22-1838
Ch: Katie     b 8-19-1865
    Nellie     b 12-25-1869

Nicholas
Flora
Ch: Fleecy M   b 4-13-1889
    Cyrus K    b 1- 5-1892

## STAFFORD
Samuel
Nancy                d 2- 7-1819, ae 19y5mo14d
                   bur West Grove
Ch: Daniel     b 8-30-1818, Wayne Co. Ind.

Eli         b 11-19-1797, s Samuel & Abigail
Elizabeth   b 12-11-1799, dt John & Miriam Pritchard
Ch: John       b 7- 1-1821
    Cynthia    b 2-10-1823

## STEVENSON
Samuel
Hepsebeth
Ch: Thomas
    Mary
    Amos
    Rebecca
    Abigail

## STRATTON
Hannah      b 9- 5-1808
Ch: Ella M    b 6-27-1835
    Charles W   b 11- 9-1837

## STRATTAIN
Joseph      b 9- 2-1811, s Eli & Eunice
Nancy M     b 10- 5-1813, dt John & Mary Morrow
                 d 11-21-1843, bur Fairfield
Ch: Edward D   b 8-11-1839
    Caroline E   b 3-23-1841
    Charles W   b 2-10-1843

## SYMONS
Thomas      b 2-17-1782, s Jesse & Sarah
Hannah      b 5-15-1788, dt Bethuel & Hannah Coffin
Ch: Josiah     b 6-10-1812
    Bethuel    b 2- 7-1814
    Elijah     b 8-17-1816
    Nathan D    b 4-19-1818
    Rebecca    b 2-10-1820
    Thomas     b 1-23-1822

## THOMPSON
James
Catharine
Ch: William
    Margaret
    Dunham
    Hedge

## TOWNSEND
James       b 12-17-1787, s John & Elvira
Rosanna     b 9-16-1787    d 1-23-1854, bur West Grove
Ch: Thomas    b 12- 3-1808
    Rachel     b 3- 7-1810    d 2-22-1811
    Celah      b 11-10-1811
    Charlotta   b 7-27-1813
    Isaac      b 8- 4-1815
    Hannah     b 3- 8-1817
    David      b 2-25-1819
    Rachel     b 10- 5-1820
    Elizabeth   b 6- 1-1823    d 7- 3-1825, bur West Grove
    Esther     b 7-10-1825
    Elvira     b 5-27-1827

WEST GROVE

TOWNSEND (Cont)
John          b 11- 6-1763
Elvinah       b  3- 7-1769
Ch: Barbary   b  2- 6-1807

John M        b 10- 7-1825    d 1894
Elizabeth     b  7-19-1829
Ch: Albert    b  7-1-1853
    Joel      b 11-17-1854
    Rawly     b  1-13-1856
    William C b 10-20-1857
    Emily Jane b 1-31-1861
    Francis   b  2-26-1865
    Rosa E    b  8-25-1866
    Oliver    b  1-15-1868
    Elmer     b 12- 7-1869
    Melissa   b  3-13-1872
    Harvy     b 11-11-1873

Stephen       b 12-31-1810, s John & Elvirah
Barbara       b  2- 6-1807

Stephen       b 12-31-1810, near Richmond, s John & Elvira
Mary          b  4-16-1816, dt Jacob & Mary Griffin
Ch: Elvira    b 10-23-1836, Ra Co. Ind
    Sarah G   b  2-16-1839, Wayne Co.
    James     b  3-27-1841,      "
    Jacob     b  1-25-1844,      "
    Lydia E   b 11- 4-1847,      "
    Lindley H b  6-24-1850,      "

Thomas        b 12- 3-1808, s James & Rosanna
Mary          b  9-26-1810, dt Wm. & Sarah Hastings
Ch: Nancy     b  1-30-1830
    William H b 11-27-1832  d  6-28-1833, bur West Grove
    Elisha    b 10-15-1834
    Hannah    b  4-16-1837  d  8-24-1837
    James     b 10- 6-1838
    Richard   b 12-24-1841  d  8- 2-1842
    Isaac     b  6- 5-1843

William       b  4-10-1795, s John & Elvira
                           d  2-29-1848, bur West Grove
Elizabeth     b  9-12-1795, dt John & Mary Morrow
                           d 10-11-1838, bur West Grove
Ch: Eli       b  4-20-1817
    Mary      b 11-10-1818  d  8-10-1843
    Sarah     b  7-24-1820
    Elvira    b  6- 5-1822
    Lydia     b 12- 1-1823
    John M    b 10- 7-1825
    Eliza A   b  1- 8-1828
    Esther    b  1- 4-1830
    Joel      b  6-19-1832
    James     b  9- 1-1834

William
Lydia
Ch: Elizabeth b  5-11-1846  d  8-29-1848

James                       d 12- 2-1839
Esther                      d 10- ?-1847, bur West Grove

UNDERHILL
Alfred        b  5- 2-1811, s John & Jane
                           d  7- 7-1876, bur Fairfield
Hannah        b 12- 1-1815, dt Joel & Elizabeth Haworth
                           d  2-19-1892
Ch: Elizabeth b  9-21-1837
    Anna M    b  6-14-1840
    Mary      b  3-15-1843
    Sarah     b  3-15-1843
    Olive     b 10-10-1848

UNTHANK
John          b  6-29-1780
Mary          b 12-15-1782
Ch: Leveicy   b 10- 4-1804
    Ann       b  3-18-1806
    Jonathan  b 12-21-1807
    Sarah     b 12-12-1809
    Elizabeth b 11- 4-1811
    Mary      b  8-17-1813

    Joseph    b 11-10-1815
    Rebecca   b 10- 6-1817
    John A    b 12-18-1819
    Beulah    b 12-28-1821  d  7-22-1823, bur Woodbury
    William   b  9- 6-1824

WARD
John
Hannah
Ch: William E b  4-29-1821

WEAMER
Talitha, dt Willis & Hannah Harris
                           d  8-21-1879, ae 35y7mo10d
                           bur Ioway

WHITE
Exum          b 11-24-1799, near Pineywoods, N.C.
              s Thomas & Jemima
                           d  2- 4-1843, bur West Grove
Ann           b  8-15-1803, near Somerton, Va.
              dt Jesse & Sarah Hare
Ch: Sarah Ann b  1-24-1826, Perquimmons Co. N.C.
    Margaret Susan b 3-28-1827      "
    Joseph H  b  2- 7-1830, Nansemond Co. N.C.
    Jesse Thomas b 9-20-1832, Henry Co. Ind.
    Harriet   b  4-19-1835,      "
    John Gurney b 3-15-1838,     "
    Elizabeth b 12-1-1840, Wayne Co. Ind.

WICKERSHAM
Jehu          b  5-30-1746  d  4-27-1838, bur West Grove
Mary          b  1- 1-1751  d 10- 6-1837,      "

William       b  3-16-1809  d  6-30-1855, bur West Grove
Idema         b  6-25-1809
Ch: Calvin    b  4-15-1828
    Eliza     b 10- 3-1830
    Isom      b  1- 3-1833
    Eli       b  7-13-1835
    Sarah J   b  7-16-1837
    John      b  1-20-1840
    Mary K    b 11-21-1842
    Elihu     b  4-24-1847  d 12-21-1849
    Alpheus   b 11-20-1849

WILLIAMS
Absalom       b  1-12-1775, s John & Mary
Mary          b 11-30-1799, dt Joseph & Lydia Cook
                           d  8-20-1879, near Winchester
Ch: Henry
    Sarah J

Achilles      b  9-23-1795, s Jesse & Sarah
Beulah        b 11- 2-1795, dt Joseph & Rebecca Unthank
Ch: Robert    b  2-18-1828
    Sarah     b  4-10-1835
    Caroline  b  7-21-1839

Daniel
Margaret (former wife)
Ch: Lydia     b  1-21-1815, Penna.
    Rebecca   b  9-13-1816,      "
    Susanna   b  2-16-1818,      "
    Nathan    b  1- 5-1820,      "
    Mary      b  4- 7-1821,      "

Daniel        b  8-23-1792, Guilford Co. N.C.,
              s Richard & Sarah
                           d  8-14-1873, bur Fairfield
Margaret      b  6-24-1790, Montgomery Co., Penna.
              dt Jacob & Tacy Weber
                           d 10-23-1846, bur Fairfield
Ch: Solomon   b  5- 7-1824, Montgomery Co. Penna.
    Jesse B   b  9-22-1825,      "
    Jacob     b  3- 3-1827,      "
    Sarah     b  8-23-1829,      "
    Margaretta 10-27-1831,       "
    Daniel    b  4- 7-1834, Wayne Co. Ind.
Lydia R. 3rd w b 4- 4-1808, Cornwall Co. N.Y.
              dt King & Rosanna Rider
Ch: King R    b 11-27-1850

WEST GROVE

```
WILLIAMS (Cont)
Daniel          b  4- 7-1834, s Daniel & Margaret
                           d  1- 3-1865
Synthia Ann     b  5-10-1833, dt Dillan & Sarah Hayworth
Ch: Dillin      b  9- 5-1854
    Alonzo      b 11-27-1857  d 12- ?-1889

James E         b  5-17-1892, s King

Jesse           b  9-22-1825, s Daniel & Margaret
Mary Ann        b  2- 6-1829, dt Wm. & Rebecca Mendenhall
Ch: Caroline    b  6- 9-1847
    Daniel B    b  8-19-1849

John
Mary
Ch: Lydia       b  9-19-1817
    Matilda     b  9-13-1819
    Jehiel      b 10- 5-1821
    Nancy       b  1-15-1824
    John        b  4-15-1826

Joshua          b 10-13-1798, s Wm. & Rachel
                           d  5-24-1831, bur West Grove
Hannah *        b 11-12-1798, dt John & Hannah Copeland
*widow of Joshua & w Absalom  d  9-21-1835, ae 37y8mo9d
                           bur West Grove

Solomon         b  5- 7-1824, s Daniel & Margaret
Margaret        b  7-21-1825, dt Joshua & Margaret Murphy
Ch: Ellen       b  5- 3-1846
    Emeline     b 12- 6-1847
    Charles     b  6-14-1849
    Alpheus     b  4- 5-1851
    Oliver      b  1-25-1853
    Margaret    b 10-13-1854
    Mary E      b  1-16-1857
    Eva         b  9-25-1859
    George B    b  9-15-1861
    Olive       b  5-12-1864

Anna, w John               d  6- 2-1863, ae 22y10mo10d

WILLITS
Brady
Susanna
Ch: Augustus W  b  4-17-1820

WILLITTS
Henry           b 10-11-1803, Stokes Co. N.C.
                           s Gabriel & Priscilla
Mary            b  8-27-1807, dt Jonathan & Ann Mendenhall
                           d  4- 1-1830, bur Fairfield
Ch: Jonathan    b  2- 6-1826
    Mailen      b 10-13-1827
    Mary        b  3-16-1830  d  9-17-1830, bur Fairfield

WILLITS
Isaac           b 10-20-1772, s Isaiah & Susannah
Rachel          b  1- 9-1777, dt Isaac & Elizabeth Willits
                                              (sic)
                           d  9- 9-1816, bur West Union
Ch: Brady       b  7- 3-1794
    Harriet     b  6-22-1797
    Mark        b 11-29-1800
    Joshua      b  4- 5-1803
    Reuben      b  5- 2-1805
    Belinda     b 11-16-1807
    Maria       b  4-16-1810
    Newton Q    b  8-12-1812
Miriam 2nd w    b  8- 9-1777, dt Joseph & Mary Jones
Ch: Henry       b  5-12-1823  d  6-28-1823 (sic)

WILSON
Samuel
Keziah
Ch: Elizabeth
    John
    Nathan
    Lyda
    Martha
    James
    Mary
```

```
WRIGHT
William
Selah
Ch: Peter
    James
    Rhoda
    Celah
    Wm.
    Edward
    Jacob
    Mary E
```

## WEST GROVE MONTHLY MEETING
## MINUTES AND MARRIAGES

**ADAIR**
1-13-1906 William rec in mbrp

**ADDINGTON**
1- 2-1841 Celah & s David rocf White River MM
11-13-1841 Celah & s gct Sparrow Creek MM

**ADKINSON**
3-14-1896 Isadora rec in mbrp

**AGLE**
2-10-1894 William, Josie & Mary E rec in mbrp

**ALBERT**
12-14-1889 Maggie & Nellie rec in mbrp
4-12-1890 Eva rec in mbrp

**ALBERTSON**
( 8 mo-1823 Benjamin & w Millicent & s Alfred & James rocf Whitewater MM)
( 8 mo-1823 Joshua & w Abigail & ch Eli, Eliza & Milton rocf Whitewater MM)
( 3 mo-1824 Benjamin & w Millicent & s Alfred & James gct Whitewater MM)
( 3 mo-1824 Joshua & s Eli & William Milton gct Whitewater MM)
6-22-1836 Mary Ann dt Jesse & Ann m Jonathan Baldwin at Fairfield MH
9- 8-1838 Eli, Milton & Benjamin rocf Whitewater MM
12-12-1838 Bailey s Jesse & Ann m Rebecca Murphy at Fairfield MH
4-11-1840 Eliza (now Summers) mcd dis
2- 8-1845 Eli, Fairfield PM compl of for neg att & att mcd & mcd
4-12-1845 Eli mcd dis
11- 8-1845 William, Fairfield PM compl for mcd
2-14-1846 William mcd dis
2-17-1847 Elwood s Jesse & Ann m Mary Williams at Fairfield MH
5-12-1849 Benjamin, Fairfield compl of for neg att, use profane lang & offering to fight
8-11-1849 Benjamin dis
3-11-1893 John rocf Timber Hill MM, KS
3-11-1893 Mary rec in mbrp
6-10-1893 Albert R rel fr mbrp
12-14-1895 John jas drpd fr mbrp
7-10-1897 Baily drpd fr mbrp
10- 9-1897 Mary gct New London MM
6-10-1899 John M & May rocf New London MM

**ALLEN**
11-10-1838 Harmon & w Nancy & ch John Philander, Joseph Milton, Samuel S, Harmon H, Juliann, Mary S, Nancy C, Jonathan T, Sibba J & Nathan H, rocf Dover MM
8-10-1839 Harmon & fam gct Walnut Ridge MM
4-11-1874 Rachel rec in mbrp
1- 9-1875 Rachel rel fr mbrp
2-11-1882 James rec in mbrp
12-11-1915 Mildred B rocf Duck Creek MM
3- 8-1919 Mildred B gct Fairmount MM
8- 6-1921 Callie F (Tremp) gct Fairmount MM

**AMMERMAN**
2-11-1911 Dorothy rec in mbrp
7-13-1918 Dorothy drpd fr mbrp

**ANDERSON**
(5 mo-1819 Leah rocf Whitewater MM)
10-13-1906 Mary Townsend glt Presby Ch, Twin Falls, Idaho

**ANTRIM**
(12 mo-1823 James P rocf Whitewater MM)
( 3 mo-1824 Daniel rocf Whitewater MM)
( 7-16-1825 James gct Whitewater MM)

**APPLEGATE**
11-10-1923 A Ward & w Lena G & ch Kenneth & Esther rocf Hinkles Creek MM
8 mo-1929 A Ward & fam gct Kokomo MM

**ARMENT**
7-10-1852 Sarah R gct Whitewater MM

**ARNETT**
11-12-1887 Addison & ch Sarah W, Edgar & Marcus rocf Dale MM, Kansas
8-11-1886 Addison drpd frm mbrp

**ATKINSON**
5-11-1844 Rachel (form Ellis) mcd dis
10- 9-1847 Mary (form Murphy) mcd dis
2- 9-1884 Henry, Emma, Wm. Henry, David L & Larkin rec in mbrp
4-12-1884 Rachel rec in mbrp
7-14-1888 Wm H gct White River MM
8-11-1888 D Luther & Larkin drpd fr mbrp
9- 8-1888 Rachel rel frm mbrp

**AXTON**
11-11-1899 Charles R & w Malinda & ch Oakie E & Victor L gct Amboy MM

**AYDELOT**
(11 mo-1832 Rebecca rocf Whitewater MM)
12- 9-1843 Rebecca rocf Whitewater MM

**BAKER**
5-11-1895 Iva E rec in mbrp

**BAILY (BAILEY)**
( 8 mo-1823 Sarah rocf Whitewater MM)

**BALDRIDGE**
2-14-1885 George & Julia rec in mbrp
8-15-1899 Julia & Frank drpd

**BALDWIN**
(11 mo-1822 Isaiah & fam rocf New Garden MM)
( 6 mo-1824 Isaiah & ch Wm, Elwood & Uriah gct New Garden MM)
( 6 mo-1824 Sarah gct New Garden MM)
( 7 mo-1824 Margaret rocf New Garden MM)
( 7 mo-1824 Uriah & fam rocf New Garden MM, NC)
( 7 mo-1824 Hannah w/h & fam rocf New Garden MM, NC)
( 4 mo-1827 Wm, Elwood, Louisa, Uriah, Hannah & Mary rocf New Garden MM)
8-16-1827 Margaret dt Uriah & Hannah m Aaron Hastings at West Grove MH
10-27-1827 Isaac s John & Charlotte m Sarah Murphy at Fairfield MH
9-18-1828 Uriah Jr s Uriah & Hannah m Lydia Pickett at West Grove MH
9-13-1829 Jesse s John & Charlotte of West Grove MM m Priscilla Johnson at Whitewater MH
(11 mo-1829 Josiah & fam rocf Hopewell MM, NC)
( 3 mo-1830 Priscilla rocf Whitewater MM)
( 3 mo-1832 Sarah rocf New Garden MM)
12-12-1832 Jemima dt John & Charlotte m Mordecai Cloud at Fairfield MH
( 3-12-1836 David gct Westfield MM)
6-22-1836 Jonathan s John & Charlotte m Mary Ann Albertson at Fairfield MH
( 9-10-1836 Jonathan gct Westfield MM)
( 9-10-1836 Mary Ann gct Westfield MM)
12- 8-1838 Jonathan & w Mary Ann & s Cyrus A rocf Westfield MM
9-14-1839 Enos & w Elizabeth & ch gct Back Creek MM
12-15-1841 Charlotte dt John & Charlotte m George Davis at Fairfield MH
11-12-1842 Caleb gct White Lick MM
9-14-1844 John C, Fairfield PM compl for mcd. He now resides in limits of Westfield MM. That mtg req to treat with him.
12-12-1844 John C, Westfield MM inf that he con his misconduct
1-14-1845 John C gct Westfield MM
1-11-1845 Caleb & w Matilda & dt Asenith rocf White Lick MM
4- 8-1848 Asa W & fam gct Westfield MM
11- 8-1851 John & w gct Westfield MM
11-13-1852 Caleb & fam gct West Union MM

WEST GROVE

BALDWIN (Cont)
11-12-1859  Cyrus mcd chm
6- 9-1860  Barbara Ann rec in mbrp
5-14-1864  Baily mcd chm
2-28-1866  Jane D dt Jonathan & Mary Ann m Rees D Loughman at Fairfield MH
4-13-1867  Elizabeth Ann rec in mbrp
6-11-1870  Cyrus A & fam gct Westfield MM
3-14-1874  Rachel Ann rec in mbrp
7- 8-1876  Bailey P & fam gct Whitewater MM
7-13-1878  Cyrus A & w Barbary & ch Luella, Edna, Florence & Lodocia rocf Westfield MM
8-10-1878  Jonathan & w Mary Ann gct Whitewater MM
5-14-1881  Alpheus & w Emma gct Whitewater MM
10-14-1893  Marilla C gct Whitewater MM
4-14-1894  Cyrus A, Barbary & Lodocia rel frm mbrp
3-11-1899  Cyrus A rec in mbrp

BALLARD
( 8 mo-1822  Joseph & fam rocf Elk MM, Ohio)

BARNARD
(     1822  Obed & w Margaret & dt Mary rocf Center MM, NC)
1-17-1828  Mary dt Obed & Margaret m John Bond at West Grove MH
(12 mo-1830  John & w Elizabeth & dt Amy, Lucinda & Phebe rocf Center MM, NC)

BARNES
6-11-1870  Ann Elizabeth (form Maxwell) mcd chm
7-14-1877  Ann Elizabeth gct New Garden MM
12- 8-1900  Elizabeth rec in mbrp
2- 9-1907  Elizabeth gct Whitewater MM

BARR
8-14-1869  Sarah E (form Elliott) mcd chm
6-14-1873  Sarah & ch Mary Evaline & Martha gct Indianapolis MM

BEAMAN
( 8-19-1819  Cornelius gct Blue River MM)
(12 mo-1822  Cornelius rocf Blue River MM)

BEAUCHAMP
(     1821  Elizabeth & s Caleb (mother of Elleck) rocf Whitewater MM)
(12 mo-1823  Jesse, Miles, Wilson & Wm., ch of Ellick, dec, & Alice (Mendenhall) Beauchamp, now the wife of ------ Jessop, gct Milford MM)

BEESON
4-14-1888  Sadie rec in mbrp
6- 9-1888  Laura Frances rec in mbrp
5-11-1889  Olive R rec in mbrp
10-12-1889  Rebecca E rec in mbrp
12-14-1889  Robert rec in mbrp
4-14-1917  Claud & Bertha drpd fr mbrp
7-13-1918  Robert & Ollie drpd fr mbrp

BELL
12-16-1818  Lancelot s John & Sarah, decd, m Mary Justice at West Union MH
2-17-1820  Sarah dt John & Sarah, decd, m John Morris at Milford MH
5- 2-1821  Josiah of West Grove MM, s John & Sarah, decd, m Abigail Charles at Whitewater MH
( 9 mo-1821  Abigail rocf Whitewater MM)
5-23-1822  Rebecca dt John & Sarah, decd, m John Symons at Milford MH
1-23-1823  Mary dt John & Sarah, decd, m Jehosephat Morris at Milford MH
2-14-1848  Margaret (form Bond) mcd dis

BENBOW
( 2 mo-1815  Edward & s Evan, Edward, Benjamin & Powel rocf Miami MM, Ohio)
( 2 mo-1815  Mary & dt Elizabeth rocf Miami MM, Ohio)
(10 mo-1819  Evan gct Miami MM, Ohio to m Maria Venable dt Wm. & Rachel of Warren Co. Ohio)
7-11-1846  Harriett (now Veal) mcd & jas UB ch. Dis
12- 9-1848  Ann mcd chm
10-14-1848  Evan con that for which he was dis & req to be rec in mem again
11-11-1848  Evan not rec
12- 5-1849  Evan rec in mbrp again
10-12-1850  Elizabeth Ann White whose mth is now Ann Benbow, w of Evan, rec in mbrp on req of her parent
11- 8-1851  Evan & w Ann & her dt Elizabeth Ann White gct Honey Creek MM

BENNER
9-16-1897  Susan rocf New Garden MM

BETTS
4- 8-1899  Charles, Gertrude & Ora rec in mbrp
6-10-1899  Josie rolf Meth Ch Greensfork, IN

BIRD
6- 8-1844  Ann (form Ogborn) mcd & j UB Ch, dis

BISHOP
1- 8-1842  Sarah dis "for leaving & joining the mormons"

BLACK
2- 9-1856  Rachel (form Griffith) mcd dis
1-10-1885  Lycurgus, Lorinda & Mary Catharine rec in mbrp
2-12-1887  Wm A & Mary Catharine rel on req
8-11-1888  Laurinda drpd fr mbrp
9- 8-1888  Minnie rec in mbrp
7-10-1897  Lycurgus drpd fr mbrp
2-10-1900  Newton rolf Meth Ch, Centerville, IN
8-10-1901  Cordelia rel on req

BLISS
1-14-1922  Mildred rec in mbrp

BLIZZARD
( 4 mo-1831  Charlotte, minor in care of Caleb Reece fam rocf Cherry Grove MM)

BLUE
2-14-1891  Melvina rocf Whitewater MM

BOGUE
( 7 mo-1822  Benjamin & Joseph rocf Westfield MM, Ohio)
( 7 mo-1822  Elizabeth & minor ch Mary, Newby, Sarah, Elizabeth & Miriam rocf Westfield MM Ohio)
(     1822  Joseph gct Milford MM)
(     1824  Benjamin, Mary, Newby, Sarah, Elizabeth & Miriam (ch of Samuel, dis, & Elizabeth) gct Milford MM)

BOND
(12- 2-1820  John & w Rebecca & fam rocf Blue River MM)
1-17-1828  John s Jesse & Phebe m Mary Barnard at West Grove MH
6-18-1829  Jesse s Thomas & Mary m Anna Cook at West Grove MH
12-20-1834  Silas rocf New Garden MM to m Rebecca Williams
1-14-1835  Silas W s Silas & Hannah m Rebecca Williams at Fairfield MH
3-14-1835  Rebecca gct New Garden MM
5-16-1835  Silas W & w Rebecca rocf New Garden MM
6- 9-1838  Hannah (now Wilson) mcd & na, dis
7-17-1839  Silas W & w Rebecca & ch Daniel & Josiah gct New Garden MM
6-21-1841  Hiram & w Lydia & ch Lucinda, Henry & Elam rocf Dover MM
10-14-1843  Hiram & w jasf
6- 8-1844  Hiram & Lydia gct Salem MM, Iowa
7-13-1844  Jesse & w Anna & ch Calvin, Mahala, William, Lydia, Oliver & Emily rocf Dover MM
8-10-1844  Lydia (now Mendenhall) mcd & na, dis
6- 8-1844  Isaac, Fairfield PM compl na & mcd & att mcd
9-14-1844  Isaac dis
3 mo-1845  Rhoda of Dover MM rmt Nathan Mendenhall
2-14-1846  Margaret (now Bell) mcd Dis
8- 9-1845  Jesse Jr, Fairfield compl for neg att & mcd. Comm appt to communicate with him "as he resides at a considerable distance from a settlement of Friends." 5-9-1846 dis
11-14-1846  Jonathan mcd & na  dis

WEST GROVE

## BOND (Cont)
| | |
|---|---|
| 11-14-1846 | Ellen (form Commons) mcd & na dis |
| 1- 8-1848 | Jesse gct Spiceland MM to m Delana Stanley, wid |
| 6-10-1848 | Delana & her ch Mordecai & Susan Stanley rocf Spiceland MM |
| 7-14-1849 | Calvin gct Richland MM |
| 8-11-1849 | Jesse & fam gct Spiceland MM |
| 12- 8-1855 | John mcd dis |
| 9-14-1861 | Henry T mcd dis |
| 8-14-1869 | Rachel rec in mbrp |
| 7- 8-1871 | John & w Tansy Ann & ch Louisa C, Arthur D, Rachel R & Oliver G rec in mbrp |
| 3-14-1885 | Ella rec in mbrp |
| 4-11-1885 | Nathan I rec in mbrp |
| 4- 9-1887 | Henry & Mary rec in mbrp |
| 4-14-1888 | Edward, Emma & Malissa rec in mbrp |
| 4-14-1888 | Claudie E, Lawrence C, Myrtle E, & Jesse ch John & w, rec in mbrp |
| 5-12-1894 | Henry T, Mary A, Ed & Emma rel fr mbrp |
| 6- 9-1894 | Lindley & w Sarah G & dt Emma rocf Whitewater MM |
| 3-10-1895 | Lindley & w Sarah & dt Emma gct Dover MM |
| 6-12-1897 | Lindley & w Sarah & dt Emma rocf Dover MM |

## BONINE
| | |
|---|---|
| ( 5 mo-1823 | David & w Prudence & minor ch William, Isaac, Rachel, Clark, John & Betsey rocf Whitewater MM) |
| ( 8 mo-1825 | David & w Prudence & ch Isaac, Wm, Clark, John Joshua, Rachel & Betsey gct Whitewater MM) |

## BOSWELL
| | |
|---|---|
| 4-27-1833 | Wm & w Rachel & ch Ruth, Elizabeth, Asenith, Rebecca, Joseph, Milisent & Elihu rocf Milford MM |

## BOUSMAN
| | |
|---|---|
| 3-14-1870 | Alice (form Harris) mcd chm |
| 7- 9-1870 | Alice gct Oak Ridge MM |
| 4-12-1884 | Alice & ch Bertha L, Clara B & Francis F rocf Oak Ridge MM |

## BOWLES
| | |
|---|---|
| ( 2 mo-1837 | George & w Elizabeth & ch Ephraim, Edith, Bathsheba, Penniah, Anna, Rebecca & Rachel gct Cherry Grove MM) |

## BOWMAN
| | |
|---|---|
| 3-27-1833 | Wm & w Elvira & minor ch Milton H, Martha Ann, Edmund F, Sally Jane, Emmaline & Calvin W rocf Whitewater MM |
| 3- 4-1844 | Phebe & ch Susannah, Edmond, Louisa, Oliver & Robert Barklay rocf Duck Creek MM |
| 3-17-1847 | Phebe, wid of Richard & dt of Jonathan & Anna Mendenhall m John Hutton at Fairfield MH |
| 4-14-1849 | Susanna M dis for att mcd (now at Duck Creek) |
| 11- 9-1850 | Edmund, Louisa & Oliver, ch of Phebe (now Hutton) gct Duck Creek MM |

## BOYD
| | |
|---|---|
| 4-14-1888 | Neva rec in mbrp |
| 5-12-1894 | Genevia rel fr mbrp |
| 4-10-1897 | Harry rec in mbrp |
| 4- 6-1899 | Calvin rec in mbrp |
| 2-10-1900 | H.L. & w glt UB Ch |
| 8-10-1901 | Dorothy jas |
| 8- 9-1902 | Calvin rel on req |

## BRADY
| | |
|---|---|
| 9-11-1830 | Mary (form Thornton) gct Vermilion MM, Ill. |

## BRADLEY
| | |
|---|---|
| 10-13-1888 | Mary rec in mbrp |
| 4-11-1891 | Mary gct Dublin MM |

## BRASHIER
| | |
|---|---|
| 7-14-1838 | Nathan, Fairfield PM na, dp & "drinking ardent spirits unnecessarily" dis |
| 1-11-1840 | Priscilla not rec in mbrp |
| 12-12-1868 | Nathan rec in mbrp |
| 3-11-1871 | Nathan gct New Garden MM |
| 1- 9-1875 | Nathan rocf New Garden MM |
| 6-14-1879 | Nathan rel on req |

## BRAZINGTON
| | |
|---|---|
| 3-11-1837 | Samuel & fam rocf White Water end to Duck Creek |

## BREWER
| | |
|---|---|
| 9- 9-1837 | John & s William rocf Milford MM |
| 5-12-1838 | John & ch gct Spiceland MM |
| 4- 9-1842 | Sarah & ch rocf Duck Creek MM |
| 4- 9-1842 | Elizabeth rocf Duck Creek MM |
| 8-14-1852 | Mary, Morris W, Jason W, Susannah & Rebecca H, ch of Sarah (now Cox) rocf Whitewater MM |
| 1-10-1857 | Mary (now Leonard) mcd drpd |
| 2-13-1858 | Morris W, Jason W, Susanna & Rebecca H, ch of John, dec, gct Duck Creek MM |

## BRITTAIN
| | |
|---|---|
| 2- 9-1884 | William L rec in mbrp |
| 4-10-1886 | Wm L rel fr mbrp |
| 3-12-1887 | Wm rec in mbrp |
| 10-13-1894 | Lincoln gct Dover MM |

## BROOKS
| | |
|---|---|
| 5-11-1844 | Sarah jas UB Ch dis |
| 4-10-1847 | Jesse rec in mbrp |
| 6- 8-1850 | John of Fairfield PM mcd dis |
| 7-11-1855 | E. Milton mcd dis |
| 2-14-1857 | Emily (now Patty) mcd drpd |
| 4-12-1867 | Emanuel Milton & w Amanda & ch Ada, Marion Eliza, Ellen, David & Charles rec in mbrp |
| 10-14-1868 | Arthur s Isaac & Lydia m Olive Underhill at Fairfield MH (West Grove MM) |
| 5-14-1870 | Joel mcd chm |
| 1-14-1871 | John & w Mary Ann rec in mbrp |
| 11-11-1882 | Arthur dis for "taking the life of a fellowman" |
| 2-14-1885 | Alice rec in mbrp |
| 4-10-1897 | Clara M rec in mbrp |
| 7-10-1897 | Charles drpd |
| 11-13-1897 | Clara gct Elm Grove MM |

## BROWN
| | |
|---|---|
| (10 mo-1822 | Mary rocf Marlborough MM, NC) |
| (10 mo-1822 | Hannah rocf Union MM, Ohio) |
| ( 4 mo-1834 | Mary rocf Deep Creek MM, NC) |
| ( 5 mo-1834 | Isaac & w Sarah & dt Martha rocf Milford MM) |
| ( 3 mo-1835 | Samuel & w Margaret & ch Keziah, Mary, Eli, Rachel, Robert, Jane, Israel & Samuel Jr, rocf Elk MM, Ohio) |
| 10-22-1835 | Keziah dt Samuel & Margaret m Daniel C Hastings at Fairfield MH |
| ( 8 mo-1837 | John & ch Elizabeth & Wm rocf Milford MM) |
| 4-13-1839 | Isaac & w Sarah & ch gct Sugar River MM |
| 5- 4-1864 | Mary (form Underhill) mcd chm |
| 5-13-1865 | Mary U gct White River MM |
| 3-13-1869 | Mary U & s Alfred rocf White River MM |
| 3-14-1874 | George & w Mary Jane & ch Mary Alice & John rec in mbrp |
| 4-11-1874 | Nancy Irena, Martha Jane, Katie E, Wm Elmer, George Jr, & Emily A, ch of Geo & w, rec in mbrp |
| 4-10-1875 | Grace, dt of George rec in mbrp |
| 6- 9-1877 | Mary U relt Meth Ch |
| 4-12-1879 | Sarah gct Salem MM |
| 5- 8-1880 | Eli & w Phebe & ch Sarah rocf Caesars Creek MM, Ohio |
| 5-13-1882 | Eli & fam gct Elk MM, Ohio |
| 11- 8-1884 | Benjamin F & w Sarah U & dt Bertha rocf Salem MM |
| 12-14-1889 | Zeri & Mattie rec in mbrp |
| 7-10-1897 | Zeri & w Mattie gct Dover MM |
| 8-14-1897 | Wm & Irena drpd fr mbrp |
| 5-13-1899 | Benjamin F, a trustee, deceased |

## BRUMFIELD
| | |
|---|---|
| 11-11-1837 | William dis for na dp |
| 10-13-1894 | Mary A gct Dover MM |
| 10-13-1894 | Emma gct Whitewater MM |

## BUNDY
| | |
|---|---|
| ( 2 mo-1825 | Thomas s Nathan & Ruth, dec, rocf Pasquotank MM, NC) |
| ( 8 mo-1825 | Thomas gct Milford MM) |
| 8-11-1838 | Luzena Jane (now Thomas) mcd dis |

## BUNDY (Cont)
- 8- 9-1845 Cynthia Elmy dis for na & dp
- 8-13-1853 Benjamin mcd chm

## BUNKER
- ( 4 mo-1821 Phebe cert rec from West Branch MM, Ohio at Whitewater MM, Ind & end to West Grove MM)

## BUTLER
- (10 mo-1822 Michal rocf Center MM, Ohio)
- (11 mo-1822 David & w Mary rocf Center MM, Ohio)
- (12 mo-1822 William & w Esther & ch Jonathan, Elizabeth, Wm Jr, Joseph, Lydia, Priscilla & Edwin, rocf Center MM, Ohio)
- ( 6 mo-1823 Wm & w Esther & fam gct Milford MM)

## CAMMACK
- 2-19-1825 Samuel & w Hannah & minor ch Nathan H & David rocf Whitewater MM
- 12-23-1826 Samuel & w Hannah & ch Nathan, David & Eli gct Milford MM

## CANADAY
- 1815 Charles & w Sarah & ch Nathan, Charles Jr, Margaret, Mary, Phebe, Sarah, Charity & Matilda rocf Lost Creek MM Tenn (lived in the area that became West Grove MM, Ind in 1818)
- 1816 Bowater & w Mary & ch John, Wm, Sarah, Jane, Margaret, Walter, Anna, Bowater Jr & Russell rocf Lost Creek MM, Tenn (lived in the area that became West Grove MM, Ind in 1818)
- 1817 John Sr & w Margaret rocf Lost Creek MM, Tenn (lived with their 2 sons in the area that became West Grove MM, Ind in 1818)
- ( 7 mo-1820 John gct Fall Creek MM, Ohio)
- 2-14-1822 Phebe dt Charles & Sarah m Jacob Hill at West Grove MH, West Grove MM
- 5-13-1830 Charity dt Charles & Sarah m William Milliken of Springfield MM, Ohio at West Grove MH
- 7-14-1833 Malinda dt Charles & Sarah m John Harvey at West Grove MH
- 11-14-1835 Bowater & w Mary & ch Margaret & Russell gct Vermilion MM, Ill.
- 4-14-1838 Walter & s Enos, Jonathan, David & Wm rocf Cherry Grove MM
- 12- 8-1838 Charles Jr mcd dis
- 1-12-1839 Mary dis for unchastity
- 8-13-1842 Walter & fam gct Springfield MM
- 3-11-1843 Enos mcd dis

## CAREY
- ( 1822 Thomas & w Rhoda & ch Elizabeth B, Joseph & Rachel D rocf Elk MM, Ohio)

## CARLSON
- 8-11-1917 Anna rocf Dublin MM
- 11-13-1920 Nels rec in mbrp

## CARR
- 10-10-1885 Virginia rec in mbrp
- 12-10-1886 Virginia rel on req
- 10-13-1888 Joseph & Elmira rec in mbrp
- 6-10-1895 Joseph & fam gct Hopewell MM

## CARTER
- 1-10-1885 Lutie rec in mbrp
- 2-14-1885 Nathan P rec in mbrp
- 7-10-1886 Nathan P & Alice gct Whitewater MM

## CHAMBERLAIN
- 1-18-1910 Rosaltha rolf Meth Ch, Centerville
- 1-11-1913 Minnie rec in mbrp

## CHAMNESS
- (10 mo-1820 Martha rocf Blue River MM)

## CHAPMAN
- 1-10-1885 John rec in mbrp
- 12-10-1886 John dis
- 3-14-1896 Harry rec in mbrp

## CHAPPEL
- (10 mo-1847 Reuben & w Mary Ann & ch John N, Griffith A, Milton H & Lydia M rocf Silver Creek MM)
- 4-12-1851 Reuben gct Spiceland MM to m Martha N. White
- 9-13-1851 Reuben & ch gct Spiceland MM

## CHARLES
- ( 1 mo-1820 Joseph rocf Blue River MM)

## CHARMAN
- 7-11-1891 Martha rec in mbrp
- 2-13-1892 Arthur rec in mbrp
- 5-14-1892 Jennette & L Myrtie rec in mbrp

## CLARK
- 9-12-1846 Malinda & ch Wm Edward, Margaret A, & John Harmon rocf Hopewell MM, NC
- 11-14-1858 Margaret A (now Saintmires) mcd dis
- 2-12-1859 Edward (? Elwood) mcd dis
- 4- 8-1865 Eli rec in mbrp again
- 12-12-1874 John & Elizabeth rec in mbrp
- 4-10-1886 Eli & w Malinda gct Dover MM
- 7-14-1888 John gct Verm MM, Ill
- 8-11-1888 George drpd frm mbrp
- 1- 9-1904 Thomas & ch Daniel & Anna rocf Whitewater MM

## CLAWSON
- 8-13-1853 Matilda rocf New Garden MM
- 3-10-1855 Thomas B rocf Whitewater MM
- 6- 9-1855 Josiah & w Sarah W & ch Wm Foster, Samuel & Margaret A rocf Chester MM
- 8-13-1859 Thomas mcd & j Free Masons dis
- 3- 9-1861 Matilda gct New Garden MM
- 5- 9-1874 Adaline R, Mary, Louisa & Edgar Parker, ch of Wm, & Matilda rec in mbrp
- 6-13-1874 William rec in mbrp
- 6- 9-1877 William, dis for striking a man in anger
- 8-11-1877 Josiah dis for not complying with his contracts, engagements & causing financial loss to creditors
- 1-10-1885 Lenora rec in mbrp
- 4-28-1886 Margaret Ann dt Josiah & Sarah m Robert Fisk Taggart at the residence of Jonathan Clawson in Tennessee
- 4- 9-1887 Nora rel fr mbrp
- 9-14-1889 Mary gct New Garden MM
- 9-14-1889 Matilda gct New Garden MM
- 7-10-1897 Edgar drpd fr mbrp
- 8-15-1899 Samuel, Edna, Frank, Fletcher, Richard & Ella drpd frm mbrp

## CLEARWATER
- 4- 9-1887 Laura rec in mbrp

## CLEVELAND
- 3-10-1894 Maggie rec in mbrp

## CLOUD
- 12-13-1821 Joel s Jonathan & Elizabeth m Anna Gordon at West Grove MH
- 5-13-1830 Mary dt Jonathan & Elizabeth m Elijah T Mendenhall at West Grove MH
- 7-15-1830 Matilda dt Jonathan & Elizabeth m Joshua Griffin at West Grove MH
- 12-12-1832 Mordecai s Jonathan & Elizabeth m Jemima Baldwin at Fairfield MH
- 4-17-1837 Anna dt Jonathan & Elizabeth m Isaac Williams at West Grove MH
- 12-14-1837 Joseph s Jonathan & Elizabeth m Elenora Edgerton at West Grove MH
- 6-12-1858 Rachel (now Scott) mcd chm
- 8-11-1860 Stephen dis for "grand larceny"
- 1- 8-1870 Jonathan mcd chm
- 7- 9-1870 Rachel rocf Oak Ridge MM
- 7-14-1883 Esther rocf Springfield MM
- 2-11-1888 Alice rel fr mbrp
- 6-14-1890 Linnie rel fr mbrp
- 12- 9-1899 Alonzo E & w Bertha & ch gct Salem MM

## COFFIN
- ( 3 mo-1822 Mary rocf New Garden MM, NC)

WEST GROVE

## COFFIN (Cont)
( 3 mo-1822   Paul & w Elizabeth & dt Louisa rocf Deep River MM, NC)
( 6 mo-1828   Moses rocf Whitewater MM)
12-17-1828   Moses s Adam & Ann m Margaret Mendenhall at Fairfield MH
( 4-11-1835   Susannah & dt Alladelphia & Margaret gct White River MM)
12-12-1840   Joseph & w Hannah rocf Springfield MM
9-11-1841   Stephen & w Exaline & ch James Alpheus rocf Springfield MM
2-12-1842   Joseph & w Hannah appt elders
9-12-1846   Stephen gct New Garden MM to m Martha Ann Nixon
6-12-1847   Martha Ann rocf New Garden
11- 8-1851   Jeremiah & fam gct Spiceland MM
2-12-1853   Stephen & fam gct Philadelphia MM, Pa
8-13-1853   Joseph gct Springfield MM
11-12-1864   Wm H & Sarah & ch John W, Wm Henry, Albert, Robert & Frank rocf Kansas MM, Kansas
8-11-1866   Jonathan B rec in mbrp
5-11-1872   John chm
3-14-1874   Wm H & fam gct Whitewater MM
12-12-1874   Josephine rec in mbrp
5-11-1878   Josephine rel fr mbrp
6- 8-1878   John W gct Lawrence MM, Kansas
3-10-1883   Wm H & s Allen M rris gct Spiceland MM
8- 8-1885   Albert rel fr mbrp
1-11-1902   Walter gct Spiceland MM
2-13-1904   Wm H & fam gct Spiceland MM

## COFFMAN
1- 8-1927   Frank & Leona rocf Williamsburg MM

## COLTER
2-15-1865   Susan & dt Lucy Ellen rec in mbrp

## COMMONS
4- 4-1816   Ezekial s Robert & Ruth m Sarah Julian dt Isaac C & Sarah at West Grove MH
( 2-13-1819   John & w Elizabeth & dt Rachel gct West Branch MM, Ohio)
( 4 mo-1822   Abraham & fam rocf Whitewater MM)
( 6 mo-1822   Anna w Wm Jr & ch rocf Whitewater MM)
( 8 mo-1822   William rocf Whitewater MM)
( 6 mo-1824   Rachel rocf West Branch MM, Ohio)
6- 8-1839   David mcd & na dis
11-13-1841   Charity (now Wolfe) mcd dis
9-10-1842   Eliza (now Henderson) mcd & na dis
12- 9-1843   Reason mcd & na dis
11-14-1846   Ellen (now Bond) mcd & na dis
12-11-1847   John M mcd
9- 8-1849   Fancena dis for att mcd & na
12-13-1849   Philip S s David & Rachel m Hannah Ann Maxwell at West Grove MH
2-13-1858   Philip S & family gct Vermilion MM, Ill
3-14-1874   Robert D & w Olive Jane & ch Lillie A & Harvey D rec in mbrp
3- 9-1877   Berthena rec in mbrp
4-14-1894   Mattie E rocf Dublin MM
9-12-1914   Mattie B & Robert D drpd fr mbrp

## COOK
( 4- -1822   Abraham & w Elizabeth & s William & Eli rocf Whitewater MM)
( 6- -1822   Anna w of Wm Jr & ch rocf Whitewater MM)
( 8- -1822   William rocf Whitewater MM)
( 9- -1822   John & w Mary & ch Robert & Joshua rocf Caesars Creek MM, Ohio)
11-16-1826   William s Joseph & Lydia m Ruth Small at West Grove MH
6-18-1829   Anna dt Joseph & Lydia m Jesse Bond at West Grove MH
2-17-1831   Louisa dt Nathan & Anna m Caleb Harvey at West Grove MH
4-14-1836   Sarah dt Nathan & Anna m Abel Elliott at West Grove MH
4-14-1838   Nathan & s Solomon, Elihu & Hiram gct Westfield MM
4-14-1838   Anna & dts Emily, Asenath & Eunice gct Westfield MM
3- 9-1839   Joseph gct Spiceland MM to m Rachel Potter
4-11-1840   Wm Jr con mcd
7-10-1841   William s Abraham gct Walnut Ridge MM
8- 8-1846   Nathan comp dev plan, j military company & used profane language 12-12-1846 chm
8-12-1848   Emily rocf Westfield MM
2-10-1849   Nathan dis mcd rpt removed out of the limits of this meeting & remote from any other.
2-10-1849   William & fam gct Mississinewa MM
3-13-1850   Miranda dt Jehu & Mary m Eli Ratliff at West Grove MH
2-11-1854   Nathan B rst in mbrp at Walnut Ridge MM
10-19-1854   Rachel dt Jehu & Mary m Amos Easterling at West Grove MH
11-10-1855   Rachel P gct Spiceland MM
5-10-1856   Peter H rst at New Garden MM w/c of West Grove MM
5-15-1856   Eli s Abraham, decd, & Elizabeth m Emily Cook dt Nathan & Anna, decd, at West Grove MH
8- 9-1856   Eli & fam gct Walnut Ridge MM
3- 8-1856   Rachel (now Jones) mcd drpd from mbrp
6-13-1857   Eli & Emily rocf Walnut Ridge MM
12-11-1858   Anna rst at Westfield MM w/c of West Grove MM
2-14-1861   Priscilla dt Jehu, decd & Mary m George B Harris at West Grove MH
3- 8-1862   Temple con mcd
3-10-1866   Anna (now Williams) con mcd
4-14-1866   Cyrus & w Phebe & s Jesse rocf Greenwood MM
5-12-1866   Nathan R & w Sarah J rocf Pipe Creek MM
7-13-1867   Gulielma (form Harvey) con mcd
9-14-1867   Cynthia Ann rocf Greenwood MM
11- 9-1867   Cyrus & fam gct Richland MM
11- 9-1867   Isom con mcd
4-11-1868   Mary rocf New Garden MM
3-13-1869   Gulielma gct Richland MM
7- 9-1870   Mary gct New Garden MM
1-12-1895   Alva glt Meth Ch, Hewanna
2-14-1914   Lydia & Arthur rec in mbrp

## COPE
( 5- -1819   Caleb & w Rebecca & dt Ruth rocf Middleton MM, Ohio)
11- -1831   Rebecca & ch Ruth, Simeon, Luann, Eliza, Lydia & Lemuel gct Milford MM

## COPELAND
( 2- -1814   John & fam rocf Back Creek MM, NC at Whitewater MM, Indiana Territory but they lived in the area which became West Grove Mtg as a dt was bur at West Grove Mtg in 1814)
( 7- -1815   Susannah gct "cert to MM NEAR Whitewater MM, Ind.," from Contentnea MM, NC (she probably was the mother of John and the widow of Joshua of NC)
3-13-1847   Hannah rocf Birch Lake MM, Mich
7-10-1847   Hannah gc

## CORNELIUS
11-11-1843   Permelia jas UB Ch

## COULTER
8- 9-1873   Susanna & dt Lucy Ellen gct Milford MM

## COX
(   1816   Joseph & w Dinah & ch Joseph, Nathan, Dinah & Martha rocf Cane Creek MM, NC (lived in area that became West Grove mtg.)
2-22-1817   Dinah, dt Joseph & Dinah m at West Grove MH to John Hill
( 8-28-1819   Martha gct Whitewater MM)
( 9- -1821   Joshua & s Benjamin & Solomon rocf Monellan MM, Pa at New Garden MM & end to West Grove MM)
( 9 mo-1821   Joshua Jr rocf Monellan MM, Pa at New Garden MM & end to West Grove MM)
(10 mo-1821   Ruth & dt Rebecca & Amy rocf Warrington MM, Pa at New Garden MM & end to West Grove MM
12-19-1822   Joseph s Joseph Sr & Dinah m Mary Hosier at West Grove MH
(11- -1824   Solomon gct White River MM)
3-10-1838   Peter & fam gct Springfield MM
4-12-1856   Abigail (form Hinshaw) mcd dis
12-14-1874   Martin & w Sarah rec in mbrp
12-12-1874   John & Elizabeth rec in mbrp

WEST GROVE

CRAIG
- 2-11-1882  Emma rec in mbrp
- 5- 8-1886  Robert & Julia rec in mbrp
- 5- 8-1886  Jennie Bell & ch Robert & Julia rec in mbrp
- 1-13-1894  Emma gct Whitewater MM
- 8-15-1899  Robert drpd frm mbrp

CRAMOR
- 10- 8-1904  Albert & w Adaline & s Chauncy rocf Cherry Grove MM

CROCKER
- 10-13-1888  Sally B rec in mbrp

CROOK
- 12-12-1874  William rec in mbrp

CULBERTSON
- 6-12-1886  Ray & w Emma rocf Long Lake MM, Mich
- 6-10-1899  Fay rel fr mbrp
- 3- 9-1901  Emma rocf Matamora MM, Mexico
- 9-13-1913  Robert rec in mbrp
- 2-14-1914  Karl rec in mbrp
- 6- 9-1917  Robert gct Norwalk MM, Ohio

CURTICE
- 2-14-1885  Joseph rec in mbrp

CURTS
- 12-11-1920  Harry rec in mbrp

DAGGETT
- 2- 8-1896  Earl rec in mbrp
- 10-10-1908  Earl drpd frm mbrp

DAUGHERTY
- 9-12-1891  Alice S rec in mbrp
- 9- 9-1893  Frances & fam gct Whitewater MM
- 9- 9-1893  Charles gct Whitewater MM
- 2- 8-1902  Mary Ann rec in mbrp

DAVIS
- ( 4 mo-1822  Nathan & w Lydia & dt Elizabeth rocf Miami MM, Ohio)
- ( 4 mo-1826  Elijah & w Margaret rocf Deep River MM, NC)
- ( 2 mo-1832  Joseph & w Hannah & dt Eliza rocf Milford MM)
- 8-17-1836  Eunice dt Harmon & Hannah m Joseph Mendenhall at Fairfield MH
- 5-12-1838  Jehu & s rocf Walnut Ridge MM
- 4-13-1839  Thomas & w Hannah & ch gct Sugar River MM
- 11-14-1840  Jehu & fam gct Sugar River MM
- 12-15-1841  George s Joseph & Catherine m Charlotte Baldwin at Fairfield MH
- 1-14-1843  Hannah rocf Sugar Plain MM
- 10-14-1843  Thomas & w Hannah & ch Susannah, Pearson, & Tacy rocf Sugar River MM
- 4-13-1844  Thomas & fam gct Dover MM
- 1-11-1845  Thomas & w Hannah & ch Susannah, Pierce, Tacy & Rachel rocf Dover MM
- 1-22-1845  Rebecca & ch Oliver, Alpheus, Mary Elizabeth & Albert rocf Sugar Plain MM
- 5-12-1849  Joseph, Fairfield compl of for "giving way to passion, so far as to strike a fellow being" 6-9-1849 chm
- 2- 9-1850  Rebecca & ch Oliver, Alpheus, Mary & Albert gct Honey Creek MM (Howard Co)
- 2- 9-1850  Hannah gct Sugar Plain MM
- 11- 9-1850  Thomas & w Hannah & ch Susannah, Pierce, Tacy, Rachel & Naomi gct Honey Creek (Howard Co)
- 11-13-1852  Allen & rocf Nine Partners MM, NY
- 2-11-1854  Allen & w gct Centre MM, Ohio
- 12- 8-1855  George mcd dis
- 12-12-1857  Benjamin mcd dis
- 8- 8-1857  Deborah D (form Hare) mcd dis
- 3- 9-1861  Hannah T & ch Tacy B, Rachel M, Naomi & Wm rocf Plainfield MM
- 3- 9-1861  Pierce & w Mahala & ch Viola Ellin, Mary Hannah rocf White Lick MM
- 12-14-1861  Thomas rocf Honey Creek MM
- 7-11-1863  Joseph mcd less than 5 months after the death of his 1st wife drpd frm mbrp
- 2-13-1864  Pierce & fam gct Hinkles Creek MM
- 2-11-1865  Louisa rec in mbrp
- 3-11-1865  Wm Elvin rec in mbrp on req of parents Alpheus & Louisa
- 5-13-1865  Alpheus rocf Honey Creek MM
- 7-13-1867  Alpheus & fam gct Milford MM
- 10-12-1867  Tacy (now Lee) mcd chm
- 4-11-1868  Naomi Jane (now Nicholson) mcd drpd fr mbrp
- 8-14-1869  William mcd chm
- 8-14-1869  Charles mcd drpd frm mbrp
- 8-14-1869  Harmon mcd drpd frm mbrp
- 4- 9-1870  Rachel (now Frazier) mcd chm
- 6-14-1873  Thomas gct Hinkles Creek MM
- 6-14-1873  William gct Milford MM
- 1-10-1885  Mary, Fannie, Francis, Elizabeth, Sarah, & Harry Lawrence rec in mbrp
- 8-11-1888  Thomas & w Rachel rec in mbrp
- 5-11-1889  Sarah Jane rec in mbrp
- 12-14-1889  Frederick & Jesse rec in mbrp
- 3-10-1894  Nathan rec in mbrp
- 3-14-1896  Morton rec in mbrp
- 1- 9-1897  Susan rec in mbrp
- 4-10-1897  William O rec in mbrp
- 1-11-1902  Louisa gct Whitewater MM

DAVISEN
- 2- 9-1850  Hannah gct Sugar Plain MM

DEAN
- 2-14-1885  Davis B rec in mbrp
- 12-14-1889  Frank rec in mbrp
- 7-10-1897  Frank gct Whitewater MM
- 2-14-1914  Clarence rec in mbrp

DEARTH
- 6- 9-1894  Alice rec in mbrp
- 9- 8-1894  James C & dt Laura rec in mbrp
- 9-12-1914  Laura drpd frm mbrp
- 7-13-1918  Alice Brooks drpd frm mbrp

DECK
- 4-11-1891  Mary rec in mbrp

DELLHEIGHAN
- 4-11-1891  Daniel rec in mbrp

DEMAREE
- 3-14-1874  Eliza rec in mbrp

DENNIS
- ( 4 mo-1822  Benjamin & fam rocf Whitewater MM)
- ( 8 mo-1830  Elisha & w Ruth & fam rocf Marlborough MM, NC)

DEWEESS
- 8-14-1886  Ada rec in mbrp

DOUGHERTY
- 1-10-1885  Allen, Martha, Francis Layton & Charley rec in mbrp

DOHERTY
- 9-13-1933  Mabel rolf St Omer U B Ch

DORSEY
- 4-14-1894  James R & w Josephine rocf Whitewater MM
- 8- 8-1896  Josephine gct Whitewater MM

DOUGHITT
- 1-10-1885  John rec in mbrp
- 8-11-1889  John drpd frm mbrp

DOUGLASS
- 1-11-1896  Anna rec in mbrp

DRAPER
- ( 4 mo-1822  Josiah Jr rocf Whitewater MM)
- ( 5 mo-1822  Josiah & fam rocf Whitewater MM)
- ( 5 mo-1825  Catharine & dt Huldah restored)
- 2-14-1891  Sarah rocf Whitewater MM

WEST GROVE

**DUDLEY**
| | |
|---|---|
| 9-14-1839 | Ruth Thorn rocf Chester MM, NJ |
| 3-14-1840 | Ruth (form Thorn) mcd dis |

**DUNBAR**
| | |
|---|---|
| 12-8-1883 | Almeda rocf Vermilion MM, Ill |

**DYNES**
| | |
|---|---|
| 5-8-1909 | Wm & Nora E rec in mbrp |
| 7-10-1920 | William rel frm mbrp |

**EAGLE**
| | |
|---|---|
| 10-15-1887 | George, Jennie, Willis, Clarence & Verlin rec in mbrp |
| 1-8-1887 | George & Jennie rel frm mbrp |
| 8-11-1888 | Ch of George & Jane drpd frm mbrp |

**EARLY**
| | |
|---|---|
| 5-9-1914 | George & w Carrie rolf Bapt Ch, Shady Grove, Tenn |

**EASTERLING**
| | |
|---|---|
| 10-19-1854 | Amos s Enoch & Hannah m Rachel Cook at West Grove MH |
| 12-9-1854 | Rachel gct Honey Creek (Howard Co) |

**EDGERTON**
| | |
|---|---|
| (12 mo-1835 | Thomas & w Mary & ch Eleanor, Mary Ann, Samuel, Martha Ann, Thomas & Richard rocf Milford MM) |
| 12-15-1836 | William s Thomas & Mary m Hannah Hastings at West Grove MH |
| 2-10-1837 | Thomas compl of for drinking ardent spirits unnecessarily & for admitting it used about his house improperly which he adknowledges & condemns |
| 12-14-1837 | Eleanor dt Thomas & Mary m Joseph Cloud at West Grove MH |
| 11-10-1838 | Thomas dis for slandering an individual & making contradictory statements & for drinking unnecessarily |
| 2-19-1839 | William gct Walnut Ridge MM |
| 10-9-1841 | Mary & ch gct Bear Creek MM |
| 2-12-1842 | William & w Hannah & dt Mary Jane rocf Walnut Ridge MM |
| 3-11-1843 | William & fam gct Walnut Ridge MM |
| 5-10-1845 | Samuel rec in mbrp w/c of Whitewater MM |
| 4-9-1853 | Nathan rec in mbrp |
| 9-10-1853 | Nathan gct New Garden MM to m Ruth Annie Roberts |
| 1-14-1854 | John rocf Back Creek |
| 5-29-1854 | Nathan gct New Garden MM |
| 7-12-1862 | Ellen (form Williams) mcd chm |
| 11-9-1860 | Samuel dis |
| 4-14-1866 | Joseph W & ch Lydia Josephine, & Laura rec in mbrp |
| 3-9-1872 | Joseph & fam gct Sugar Plain MM |

**EDWARDS**
| | |
|---|---|
| 2-13-1841 | Ira rocf Hopewell MM, NC, end by Milford to Whitewater MM to this mtg. 3-13-1841 rpt he has left the neighborhood |

**ELIASON**
| | |
|---|---|
| 2-25-1891 | Nellie Smith dt Freeman & Ann Smith m ? Eliason at West Grove mtg |

**ELLIOTT**
| | |
|---|---|
| ( 1815 | John & w Mary rocf Deep Creek MM, NC at Whitewater MM (they lived in the area that became West Grove MM in 1818) |
| ( 1816 | Exum & s Elwood, Isaac, Exum Jr, Nathan & Mark rocf Deep Creek MM, NC at Whitewater MM but lived in that area that became West Grove MM) |
| ( 1816 | Catherine & dt Rebekah, Ursula & Sarah rocf Deep Creek MM, NC at Whitewater MM but lived in the area that became West Grove MM) |
| ( 3 mo-1822 | Isaac gct New Garden MM) |
| ( 3 mo-1822 | Catharine gct New Garden MM) |
| 11-17-1825 | Rebecca dt Exum & Catherine m John Maudlin at West Grove MH |
| ( 6 mo-1828 | Exum Jr gct Milford MM to m Hannah Smith) |
| (10 mo-1829 | Exum Jr gct Milford MM) |
| 8-14-1834 | Nathan s Exum Sr & Catherine m Betsy Maxwell at West Grove MH |
| ( 8 mo-1835 | Mark gct Silver Creek MM to m Mary Haworth) |
| (11 mo-1835 | Mary rocf Silver Creek MM) |
| (12 mo-1835 | Absalom rocf Milford MM to m Polly Maxwell) |
| 1-14-1836 | Absalom s Jacob & Mary m Polly Maxwell at West Grove MH |
| ( 3 mo-1836 | Absalom rocf Milford MM) |
| 4-14-1836 | Abel s Exum Sr & Catherine m Sarah Cook at West Grove MH |
| 7-11-1840 | Abel & w Sarah & ch Mary & Lutitia gct Westfield MM |
| 9-14-1842 | Nathan s Exum Sr, decd & Catherine m Naomi Mendenhall at Fairfield MH |
| 4-12-1845 | Lydia (form Ogborn) mcd dis |
| 8-17-1848 | Jonathan s Jacob & Mary m Maria Maxwell at West Grove MH |
| 11-11-1848 | Maria M gct Milford MM |
| 11-8-1851 | Elwood gct Mississinewa MM |
| 2-10-1855 | Nathan & fam gct Vermilion MM, Ill |
| 3-6-1856 | Absalom & fam gct Vermilion MM, Ill |
| 10-16-1856 | Hannah dt Mark & Mary m Isaiah H Sleeper at West Grove MH |
| 4-9-1859 | William mcd dis |
| 3-10-1860 | Parmelia (now Miller) con mcd |
| 12-14-1865 | Sarah dt Exum & Catherine, both decd, m Davis Meeker at West Grove MH |
| 4-13-1867 | Joel dis for serving in the army and accepting an office in the army |
| 7-11-1868 | Elton mcd chm |
| 8-14-1869 | Sarah E (now Barr) mcd chm |
| 3-11-1871 | Rebecca Jane rec in mbrp |
| 9-9-1871 | William rec in mbrp |
| 3-14-1874 | Joseph & Salena rec in mbrp |
| 9-12-1874 | William & fam gct Toleda MM, Kansas |
| 12-11-1875 | Mary S gct Peace MM, Kansas |
| 7-14-1877 | Elton & s Clifford gct Indianapolis, MM |

**ELLIS**
| | |
|---|---|
| 11-22-1823 | Thomas & w Lydia & ch Sophia, Margaret Ann, Emely & Eleanor rocf Greenplain MM, Ohio |
| 10-16-1839 | Margaret Ann, dt Thomas & Lydia m Charles Shoemaker at Fairfield MH |
| 12-9-1843 | Thomas & Lydia of Fairfield PM dis for j (ASF) |
| 5-11-1844 | Rachel (now Atkinson) mcd dis |
| 12-14-1844 | Sophia gct Fairfield MM Ohio |
| 10-16-1848 | Rebecca, dt Thomas & Lydia m Alvin C Talbert at Fairfield MH |
| 8-11-1849 | Larkin dis att mcd |
| 6-11-1853 | Morris R & David ch of Thomas gct Vermilion MM Ill |
| 6-11-1853 | Henry & Thomas E ch of Thomas gct Vermilion MM, Ill |
| 7-9-1853 | Emily gct Vermilion MM, Ill |
| 8-13-1859 | Thomas rec in mbrp |
| 11-12-1859 | Thomas gct Vermilion MM, Ill |
| 11-10-1888 | Elizabeth C & ch Edith V, Mary E, Leonidas F rocf Miami MM, Ohio |

**ELWOOD**
| | |
|---|---|
| 8-13-1892 | Jackson rec in mbrp |
| 7-11-1896 | Mary gct Whitewater MM |

**ELZEY**
| | |
|---|---|
| 11 mo-1822 | Priscilla, dt Wm & Agatha, dec, rocf Fairfield MM, Ohio |
| 2 mo-1823 | William & ch Keziah, Garrard & Esther rocf Fairfield MM, Ohio |

**ENDSLEY**
| | |
|---|---|
| 5-14-1892 | Sarah rocf Whitewater MM, |
| 2-10-1894 | Jane rec in mbrp |

**EVANS**
| | |
|---|---|
| (11 mo-1820 | Samuel rocf Miami MM, Ohio at New Garden MM and end to West Grove MM) |
| (11 mo-1824 | Mary, w William & ch Abel, Lydia, Charles, Martha, Wm Jr & Henry Emmor rocf Miami MM, Ohio) |
| (11 mo-1824 | Mary dt Wm & Mary rocf Miami MM, Ohio) |

## EVANS (Cont)
( 1 mo-1827  Martha w Jonathan & dt Eliza Ann & Juletta gct Milford MM
( 4 mo-1834  Jonathan P rocf New Garden MM, NC)
(11 mo-1834  Jonathan P gct Milford MM
8-12-1837  Henry B dis for na & "using unbecoming language"

## FAWCETT
12-14-1889  Alice rec in mbrp

## FENNEL
5-12-1855  Elizabeth (form Murphy) mcd chm
12-11-1859  Elizabeth gct New Garden MM

## FERREL
4- 9-1887  Jennie rec in mbrp

## FIFER
10-13-1888  Henry & Mary rec in mbrp
11-10-1888  Rosa & Ora rec in mbrp
3-14-1896  Laura D rec in mbrp

## FILBY
9-10-1910  Elworth & w Martha & ch Naomi, Emil & Monroe rocf Whitewater MM
4-14-1917  Naomi, Monroe & Emil drpd frm mbrp
7-13-1918  Martha drpd frm mbrp

## FINK
2-10-1894  Jacob W rec in mbrp
9-12-1914  Jacob & Martha drpd frm mbrp

## FLOYD
3-14-1896  Mary O rec in mbrp
3-14-1896  Horace rec in mbrp
2- 8-1902  Joseph & Lizzie rec in mbrp

## FODREA
( 1-10-1835  William gct New Garden MM)

## FORT
12-14-1918  Laura E rolf Meth Ch, Olathe, Kansas
12-13-1919  Mary Francis & Ivan rec in mbrp

## FOX
12-14-1889  John & Maggie rec in mbrp
2-10-1894  John A rec in mbrp
5-12-1894  Jonnie & Maggie rel frm mbrp
4-14-1917  John drpd frm mbrp

## FRAME
7-31-1867  Nathan rocf ------
12-14-1867  Esther Ellen rocf Salem MM, Ia
3-14-1868  Itasca M & Hettie C rec in mbrp on req of parents Nathan & Esther
6-13-1868  Nathan T & fam gct Dover MM

## FRAZIER
4- 9-1870  Rachel (form Davis) mcd chm
8- 9-1873  Rachel gct Milford MM
1-10-1885  Luther & Rachel & Burney Clifton & Jennie Pearl rec in mbrp
8-15-1899  Martin & Jennie Pearl drpd frm mbrp

## FRENCH
3-12-1887  Miriam, Henry, Samuel & Luke rec in mbrp
7-10-1897  Samuel drpd frm mbrp

## FROST
12-30-1825  Phebe (form Cook) rocf Caesars Creek MM, Ohio

## GAILOR
4-10-1897  Narcisa P rec in mbrp

## GAILENGER
8-10-1901  William gct Whitewater MM

## GAMBER
12-14-1889  Nicholas & Sarah rec in mbrp

## GARNER
10 mo-1820  Elizabeth rocf Newberry MM, Ohio

## GARRETT
1-13-1912  Nora M rolf Meth Ch, Doddridge Chapel, Wayne Co
2-14-1914  Mary rec in mbrp
3-11-1916  Ethel rec in mbrp

## GAUSE
12- 9-1876  Thomas & w Christianna & s Clarrentz rocf Spiceland MM
9- 8-1883  Christina B & ch gct Spiceland MM

## GEORGE
2-13-1892  Ora rec in mbrp

## GILBERT
( 9 mo-1821  Aaron L & w Jemima & ch Rebecca, Elizabeth, Anna & Asenath rocf Springfield MM, NC)

## GORDON
( 5 mo-1818  Charles & w Ruth & ch James, Seth & Charles Jr rocf Whitewater MM)
( 5 mo-1818  Mary & Anna dt Charles & Ruth, rocf Whitewater MM)
(10 mo-1824  Richard & w Susannah & ch Rebecca, Alfred & Edwin rocf New Garden MM, NC endorsed to Milford MM by West Grove MM)
( 5 mo-1825  James gct Milford MM)
( 2 mo-1826  Seth gct Whitewater MM)
( 2 mo-1827  Charles gct Milford MM to m Lydia R Jessop)
( 6 mo-1827  Lydia R rocf Milford MM)
( 7 mo-1828  Charles Jr & w Lydia & s Micajah C gct Milford MM)
1-15-1829  Ruth dt Charles & Ruth m Josiah Lacy of Milford MM at West Grove MH

## GOULD
3-11-1911  Marie rec in mbrp
10-12-1912  Alice rec in mbrp

## GREEN
12-11-1852  Polly rocf Nine Partners MM, NY
2-11-1854  Polly gct Centre MM, Ohio
4-12-1890  Edward F & w Martha rocf Dover MM
4-12-1890  Edward Sr rocf Dover MM
6-11-1910  Martha J rec in mbrp

## GREGG
4- 6-1876  Harriet rec in mbrp

## GRIFFIN
( 2 mo-1822  James s Jacob & Mary gct Whitewater MM to m Ann Weeks at Middle Fork MH)
( 1 mo-1823  Ann rocf Whitewater MM)
( 3 mo-1823  Samuel gct Springfield MM, Ohio to m Lydia Reynard)
(11 mo-1823  Lydia rocf Springfield MM, Ohio)
5-20-1824  Jacob s James & Hannah m Sarah Wickersham at West Grove MH
( 6 mo-1824  Samuel & w Lydia & s Jeremiah gct Milford MM)
2-18-1830  Jacob s Jacob Sr & Mary, decd, m Rebecca Harvey at West Grove MH
7-15-1830  Joshua s Jacob & Mary, decd, m Matilda Cloud at West Grove MH
11-19-1835  Mary dt Jacob & Mary, decd, m Stephen Townsend at West Grove MH
( 3 mo-1836  Jacob Jr & w Rebecca & dt Eliza gct Westfield MM)
11-10-1838  Joseph rst at Spiceland MM w/c of West Grove MM
6- 8-1839  William mcd dis (lives in limits of Spiceland MM)
1-11-1845  Jacob & w Rebecca & ch Eliza, Rachel, Mary M & Joseph rocf Westfield MM
6- 8-1850  Jeremiah & w Ann & ch Mary Emily rocf Spiceland MM
4-17-1851  Eliza dt Jacob Jr & Rebecca m George B. White at West Grove MH
2- 9-1856  Rachel (now Black) mcd dis
11- 8-1856  Jacob & fam gct East Grove MM, Iowa
3- 9-1861  Mordecai mcd drpd frm mbrp
10-10-1863  Jacob mcd drpd frm mbrp
3-10-1866  Elizabeth (now Pitts) mcd chm
7-14-1866  Mary (now Pereonnette) mcd chm
8-10-1872  Joel mcd chm

WEST GROVE

**GRIFFIN (Cont)**
- 2- 8-1873 Calvin mcd
- 6-14-1873 Mary Elizabeth rec in mbrp

**GRISSELL**
- 9-14-1872 Annie rocf Adrian MM, Mich
- 5-10-1873 Anna gct Alum Creek MM, Ohio

**GROVE**
- 5-11-1895 Henrietta rec in mbrp

**HAISLEY**
- 12-21-1850 Eli rocf New Garden MM to m Sally Ann Mendenhall
- 1-15-1851 Eli, s Jesse & Ruth m Sally Ann Mendenhall at Fairfield MH
- 3- 8-1851 Sally Ann gct New Garden MM
- 5- 9-1896 Lizzie & ch Edith, Vestel, Mary, Ethel & Frances L gct Oak Ridge MM

**HALE**
- 3-13-1897 Joseph gct Springfield MM
- 12-11-1915 Elmer E & w Lizzie J & dt Esther F rocf Whitewater MM

**HALER**
- 1-10-1885 David rec in mbrp
- 2-14-1885 Lulu rec in mbrp
- 3-12-1887 Charles, Joseph & Martha & John rec in mbrp
- 2-11-1888 Wm V & w Mary Ann rec in mbrp
- 3-13-1892 Martha dis
- 3-13-1896 Martin rec in mbrp
- 7-10-1897 Martin, David, Retta, Lula, John, Nettia & Charles drpd from mbrp
- 12-11-1897 Joseph & Maggie rocf Springfield MM

**HAMBLETON**
- 4-14-1849 Hannah (form King) mcd dis
- 3-11-1882 Oscar & w Sarah Alice rec in mbrp
- 1-10-1885 J. M. rec in mbrp
- 3-14-1885 George rec in mbrp
- 2-13-1886 Norval rec in mbrp
- 8-11-1888 Joseph drpd frm mbrp

**HARDWICK**
- 8-11-1888 Samantha drpd from mbrp

**HARE**
- 3- 9-1839 Harmon & w Mary & ch Deborah D, Mariah J, Sarah E & Rebecca Ann rocf Milford MM
- 1- 8-1842 Harmon & fam gct Hopewell MM
- 9-14-1850 Deborah D rocf Hopewell MM
- 8- 8-1857 Deborah D (now Davis) mcd drpd from mbrp

**HARRIS**
- ( 5 mo-1833 Zemeriah rocf Whitewater MM)
- ( 5 mo-1835 Zemeriah gct New Garden MM)
- 4- 9-1859 Willis L & w Hannah B & ch Milton M, Jesse, Tabitha Ann, Sophia C, James Sanders, Alice Jane, Lavina rocf Dover MM
- 7- 9-1859 George rocf Dover MM
- 12-10-1859 Naomi & Elizabeth rocf Dover MM
- 2-14-1861 George B s Willis L & Hannah m Priscilla Cook at West Grove MH
- 11- 9-1861 Milton dis for na, dr & upl & offering to fight
- 8-11-1866 George B & fam gct Wabash MM
- 11- 9-1867 Jesse dis for "grand larceny"
- 3-14-1870 Alice Jane (now Bousman) mcd chm
- 6-14-1873 Tabitha Ann (now Wimmer) mcd chm
- 3-14-1874 Jesse B rec in mbrp
- 12-12-1874 James M rec in mbrp
- 5- 8-1875 George B & w Priscilla & ch Mary Josephine, Lewis B, Wilson A, Miles J, Willis & George Jr rocf Onarga MM, Ill
- 12-11-1875 Augusta F rec in mbrp
- 4-13-1878 Esther rec in mbrp
- 2-11-1882 Judy M rec in mbrp
- 5-13-1882 Jesse D & w Judith gct Dover MM
- 8- 2-1883 Josie dt George & Priscilla m James B Lybolt (by civil ceremony)
- 8-11-1888 Augusta & James drpd from mbrp
- 12-14-1889 Lawson & Alice rec in mbrp

- 4-14-1894 L. L. & Alice rel from mbrp
- 2-14-1914 Howard rec in mbrp
- 2-14-1914 Paul E rec in mbrp
- 3-11-1916 Anna rec in mbrp

**HART**
- 4- 8-1876 Laura rec in mbrp

**HARTER**
- 8-10-1901 Morton & Emma gct Springfield MM

**HARTLEY**
- 1- 8-1916 Emma Woolman gct New Garden MM

**HARVEY**
- ( -1817 John & w Jane & ch Rebecca, Isom, Benjamin, Aaron, Nathan & William rec in mbrp at Whitewater MM (however they lived in the area that became West Grove mtg in 1818) )
- ( 9 mo-1817 Henry gct Center MM, Ohio to m Ann Madden)
- ( 4 mo-1818 Ann rocf Center MM, Ohio)
- ( 6 mo-1818 Samuel & w Rebecca & dt Margaret, Mary & Sarah rocf Whitewater MM)
- ( 7 mo-1818 Henry rocf Whitewater MM)
- ( 9 mo-1819 Henry & w Ann & s George Madden gct Springfield MM, Ohio)
- 4-17-1823 Rebecca dt John & Jane m Gabriel Newby at West Grove MH
- 4-15-1828 Rebecca wid of Samuel & dt of Edward & Margaret Kindley m Joseph Stratton at West Grove MH
- (12 mo-1828 Mary, Sarah, Isaac & Davis, ch Samuel decd, & Rebecca (now w of Joseph Stratton) gct Springfield MM, Ohio)
- 2-18-1830 Rebecca dt William & Rachel m Jacob Griffin at West Grove MH
- 2-17-1831 Caleb s William & Rachel m Louisa Cook at West Grove MH
- 7-14-1833 John s William & Rachel m Malinda Canaday at West Grove MH
- ( 7 mo-1836 John & w Malinda & dt Rachel gct Westfield MM)
- 7 mo-1836 Caleb & w Louisa & dt Beulah gct Westfield MM
- ( 7 mo-1836 Mary M dt William & Rachel m Laban Haworth at West Grove MH)
- 6-10-1837 Wm & w Rachel & ch Wm Jr, Sarah & Rachel gct Westfield MM
- 2-10-1838 Mary (now Jackson) mcd & dp dis
- 4-10-1841 Jane (now Ray) mcd & na dis
- 7-10-1841 John Jr compl of for ng att & mcd  9-11-1841 dis
- 2-11-1865 Elijah & w Ann & ch Gulielma, Elizabeth Ann, Abner C, William F, Alfred H & Mahlon C rocf Whitewater MM
- 7-13-1867 Gulielma (now Cook) mcd chm
- 3-13-1869 Elijah & fam gct Dover MM
- 4-11-1908 William rocf Dover MM

**HASTINGS**
- ( -1809 William & w Sarah & ch Nancy Ann, Catharine, Eunice, Welmett (Millicent) & Aaron rocf West Branch MM, Ohio, at Whitewater MM (they lived in the area that became West Grove MM in 1818)
- ( -1815 Joshua Sr & w Ann rocf Back Creek MM, NC at Whitewater MM (they lived in the area that became West Grove MM in 1818)
- 7-31-1817 Nancy dt William & Sarah m Samuel Stafford at West Grove MH
- 8-17-1820 Eunice dt William & Sarah m Peter Pearson at West Grove MH
- 7-13-1826 Catherine dt William & Sarah m James Osborn at West Grove MH
- 8-16-1827 Aaron s William & Sarah m Margaret Baldwin at West Grove MH
- 7-17-1828 Mary dt William & Sarah m Thomas Townsend at West Grove MH
- 9-22-1831 Sarah dt William & Sarah m Daniel Reese at West Grove MH
- 10-22-1835 Daniel C s William & Sarah m Keziah Brown at Fairfield MH

WEST GROVE

HASTINGS (Cont)
- 12-15-1836  Hannah dt William & Sarah m William Edgerton at West Grove MH
- 10- 9-1841  William gct Hopewell MM
- 1-14-1843  William rocf Hopewell MM

HATFIELD
- 5- 8-1841  Jehu (John?) Fairfield PM compl na & mcd dis
- 1-12-1842  Matilda j Mormons  dis
- 7- 8-1843  Sarah na & att mcd  dis
- 7- 8-1843  Mary na & att mcd  dis

HAWKINS
- 3-11-1911  Emily gct Whitewater MM

HAWLEY
- ( 4 mo-1820  Richard & w Rachel & dt Ann rocf Plainfield MM, Ohio)

HAWORTH
- ( 1815  James, Dillin & Richard, ch Richard Sr, dec, & Hannah, now w of John Maxwell, rocf Lost Creek MM, Tenn at Whitewater MM, Ind (they lived in the area that became West Grove MM, Ind)
- 12-23-1824  James s Richard, dec, & Hannah m Penninah Maudlin at West Grove MH
- 12-15-1825  Dillon s Richard, dec, & Hannah m Sarah Maudlin at West Grove MH
- 8-27-1835  Mary dt Joel & Elizabeth m Mark Elliott at New Hope MH
- (12 mo-1835  Mary rocf Silver Creek MM)
- ( 6 mo-1836  Laban rocf Silver Creek MM to m Mary M Harvey)
- 7-14-1836  Laban s Joel & Elizabeth m Mary M Harvey at West Grove MH
- (12 mo-1836  Mary gct Silver Creek MM)
- 3-10-1838  Richard & s Benjamin H & James W rocf Walnut Ridge MM
- 4- 9-1842  Richard & fam gct Salem MM, Iowa Terr
- 4- 9-1842  Peninah & ch gct Salem MM, Iowa Terr
- 3-13-1847  Richard & w Mary & ch Benjamin, James W, Mary J & Richard D rocf Salem MM, Iowa
- 8-12-1848  Peninah & ch Ira, Emily, Lot & Hannah rocf Salem MM, Iowa
- 12- 9-1848  Richard & fam gct Salem MM, Iowa
- 6- 9-1849  Ira gct Whitewater MM
- 7-14-1849  Peninah & ch gct Whitewater MM
- 6 mo-1850  Ira & Asenath rocf Whitewater MM
- 3- 9-1850  Dillon compl of for "dealing for a certificate issued by general government as a compensation for service in war..."
- 9-18-1850  Solomon s of Dillon & Sarah m Keziah Mendenhall at Fairfield MH
- 11- 9-1850  Benjamin mcd dis
- 3- 8-1851  Ira & fam gct Duck Creek MM
- 6-14-1852  Peninah & ch Emily, Lot & Hannah rocf Whitewater MM
- 10-13-1853  Cynthia Ann dt Dillon & Sarah m Daniel Williams at West Grove MH
- 2-11-1854  Solomon & fam gct Vermilion MM, Ill
- 5-29-1854  Peninah & ch gct Vermilion MM, Ill
- 10-14-1854  James B mcd chm
- 11-11-1854  Esther (form Townsend) mcd chm
- 6- 9-1855  Dillon & fam gct Vermilion MM, Ill
- 11-14-1857  James B & w gct Vermilion MM, Ill
- 4- 9-1859  Benjamin rst at Vermilion MM, Ill w/c of West Grove MM
- 7-13-1861  Calvin mcd chm
- 1-11-1862  Calvin gct Elwood MM, Ill
- 12-14-1912  Benjamin rocf Georgetown MM, Ill
- 12-15-1917  Benjamin gct Georgetown MM, Ill

HELMS
- 11- 8-1919  Cora M glt Doddridge Chapel Meth Ch, Wayne Co
- 3- 8-1933  Wanetta rec in mbrp

HENDERSON
- 9-10-1842  Eliza (form Commons) mcd & na  dis
- 3-13-1892  M  rec in mbrp
- 8-13-1892  F S  rec in mbrp
- 1-14-1893  W C & w Martha B & ch Arthur N, Samuel B, Lida J, Thomas M & Horace E rec in mbrp
- 10-10-1908  Sammy drpd from mbrp
- 9-12-1914  Arthur drpd from mbrp

HENLEY
- ( 1 mo-1826  Jordan & w Elizabeth & ch Joseph, Charles, Margaret, David, Jonathan, Samuel & Thomas Elwood rocf Blue River MM)

HIATT
- ( 4 mo-1821  Silas & w Ann & ch Jordon, Armelia, Asenath, Irena, Henry & Benajah rocf Caesars Creek MM, Ohio)
- ( 8 mo-1822  Jesse rocf Caesars Creek MM, Ohio)
- ( 4 mo-1824  Mary & ch Margaret & Samuel gct Springfield MM Ohio)
- 11-12-1834  Joel W s Joel Sr & Mary m Lydia Williams at Fairfield MH
- ( 2 mo-1835  Lydia gct New Garden MM,)
- ( 5 mo-1835  Sarah (aged mother of Eleazer) rocf New Garden MM)
- ( 7 mo-1835  Eleazer & w Gulielma & ch Daniel, Anna & Mariah rocf New Garden MM)
- 3- 4-1841  Daniel W s Eleazer & Ann, dec, gct Springfield MM to m Malinda Mendenhall
- 12-10-1842  Daniel W & w Malinda & s Edwin W gct Dover MM
- 5-13-1843  Eleazer & w Gulielma & dt Anna Mariah & their aged mother Sarah Hiatt, gct Chester MM
- 5-14-1892  Charles E & w Hannah & ch Hazel & Murray rocf Amboy MM
- 5-11-1895  Charles E & fam gct White River MM

HILDEBRAND
- 12- 9-1905  Edward rolf Evansville Evang Luthern Ch, East Salem
- 12- 9-1905  Sarah C w Edward rec in mbrp
- 3-11-1916  Glen rec in mbrp

HILL
- 2-14-1822  Jacob s Benjamin & Mary dec, m Phebe Canaday at West Grove MH

HINSHAW
- ( 6 mo-1832  Hannah w Wm B Hinshaw rocf Deep River MM, NC)
- ( 6 mo-1832  Wm B rocf Marlborough MM, NC)
- (12 mo-1832  Sarah & ch Ruth rocf Marlborough MM, NC at New Garden MM & end to West Grove MM)
- ( 1 mo-1833  John & s Quinton rocf Marlborough MM, NC at New Garden MM & end to West Grove MM)
- ( 9 mo-1833  Wm B & w Hannah & s James Madison gct New Garden MM)
- (12 mo-1833  John & s Quinton gct New Garden MM)
- ( 4 mo-1834  Edmond B rocf New Garden MM)
- 8-12-1848  Abigail rocf Cane Creek MM, NC
- 4-12-1856  Abigail (now Cox) mcd dis

HOBBS
- ( 9 mo-1846  Wilson rocf Springfield MM, Ohio to m Zalinda Williams)
- 10-12-1846  Wilson s Samuel & Ruth m Zalinda Williams at West Grove MH
- 7- 8-1848  Zalinda & s Orville A gct Springfield MM, Ohio

HOBSON
- (11 mo-1820  Aaron rocf Springfield MM, Ohio)
- ( 2 mo-1821  Jane & ch Evan, Elizabeth, Mary, John, David, & Allen rocf Springfield MM, Ohio)

HOCKET
- ( 3 mo-1821  Leah rocf Newberry MM, Ohio)

HODSON
- ( 3 mo-1833  Enos & fam rocf Cherry Grove MM)
- 5-12-1834  Mary dt Enos & Lavinia m Solomon Way at Fairfield MH
- 4-14-1838  Levina w Enos & ch Jonathan, Susannah, Lavina, Cynthia Ann, Elizabeth & Sarah gct Westfield MM  (Enos not gc because of "obstruction")
- 10-21-1839  Enos gct Westfield MM
- 12-11-1841  Henry & fam gct Springfield MM
- 2- 9-1867  William & w Rachel & ch George, Anna Evaline, Mary Juliana & Wm Sheels rocf Center MM, NC
- 4-10-1886  William & w Rachel gct Dover MM

# WEST GROVE

## HODSON (Cont)
- 4-10-1886  George gct Dover MM
- 8-11-1888  Alpheus & Wm drpd from mbrp
- 12-14-1889  Olive rec in mbrp

## HOLDER
- 2-13-1892  John & Mary rec in mbrp

## HOLLINGSWORTH
- ( 5 mo-1823  Nathan & fam rocf Whitewater MM)
- ( 2 mo-1825  Joseph rocf Whitewater MM)
- ( 4 mo-1827  Nathan & w Elizabeth & ch Jemima & John gct Milford MM)
- 4-12-1845  Jemima, John & Mary, ch of Nathan rocf Milford MM
- 9-13-1845  Mary Jane dt Nathan Milford MM informs that it finds she was not a mem, therefore not a member of this mtg.
- 6-13-1846  Jemima mcd & na dis
- 11-10-1849  Lucinda (form Maudlin) mcd  chm
- 4-13-1850  Christopher, s Thomas & Joann of Silver Creek MM m Deborah King at West Grove MH
- 6-11-1853  Lucinda gct Red Cedar MM, Iowa
- 2-11-1854  Rebecca gct Red Cedar MM, Iowa
- 3- 9-1867  John gct Milford MM
- 12-11-1920  Ruby rec in mbrp
- 9-10-1926  Ruby drpd from mbrp

## HONN
- 5-14-1842  Martha (form Wilson) mcd & jas U B Ch  dis

## HOOD
- 4- 8-1911  Leona rocf Dublin MM
- 4-12-1913  Ellen rolf Meth Ch, Milton
- 2-14-1914  Agnes rec in mbrp
- 12- 9-1922  Leona drpd from mbrp

## HOOVER
- 10-10-1840  Allen, Daniel C & William H (ch of Henry & Susannah, dec,) rocf Whitewater MM
- 7-12-1845  Allen, Fairfield PM compls of j Meth Ch  dis
- 5-14-1887  Charles & Hattie rec in mbrp
- 12-14-1889  Maggie, Lettie & George rec in mbrp
- 12-14-1889  John rec in mbrp
- 11- 8-1890  Sarah & Gaddy rec in mbrp
- 10-10-1908  Harrison drpd from mbrp

## HORNEY
- 11-14-1857  Stephen, Absalom & Andrew na dis
- 11-14-1857  Nancy & dt Sarah, Esther, Rebecca & Mary na dis
- 11-14-1857  James B & Esther gct Vermilion MM, Ill
- 8- 8-1885  Jesse drpd from mbrp
- 12-14-1889  Catherine rec in mbrp
- 3-14-1896  Kate glt Meth Ch Olive Hill

## HOSIER
- 12-19-1822  Mary dt William & Milicent m Joseph Cox at West Grove MH
- 2-14-1885  Ellen rec in mbrp
- 5-11-1889  Hester rec in mbrp
- 5-11-1889  Rebecca E rec in mbrp
- 12-14-1889  Vernon & Clary E rec in mbrp
- 12-14-1889  Lewis rec in mbrp
- 7-11-1914  Lewis & Hettie rel frm mbrp
- 9-12-1914  Verne & Rebecca drpd from mbrp

## HORNISH
- (10 mo-1827  Jacob & w Tamer & ch Bazalleel, Wm & Sophia rocf Chester MM)

## HOUGH
- 10-13-1888  Hiram & Rachel rec in mbrp
- 4-14-1894  Miriam rel from mbrp

## HUNT
- 3-16-1820  Rachel dt John & Rachel m Samuel Stafford at West Grove MH
- ( 7 mo-1820)  John & Catharine & dt Irena rocf Whitewater MM
- (11 mo-1822)  John & w Catharine & dt Irena & Lucinda gct Whitewater MM
- ( 1 mo-1823  Allen & w Huldah & fam rocf New Garden MM, NC)
- ( 2 mo-1823  Nathan rocf New Garden MM, NC)
- ( 4 mo-1824  Allen & w Huldah & ch Nancy, Lucinda, Rachel & Abel gct Milford MM)
- ( 4 mo-1824  Nathan gct Milford MM)
- (11 mo-1828  Thomas & w Sarah & ch Delila, John, Cela, Elam & Eunice, Jacob & Sally A rocf New Garden MM, NC)
- ( 5 mo-1830  Irena, Lucinda, Calvin, Franklin B, Melinda & Milton, ch of John Hunt rocf Whitewater MM)
- ( 9 mo-1830  Mourning, w of Jesse & ch Wilson, Miriam, Elizabeth, Jonathan, Phanuel & Mary rocf New Garden MM, NC)
- 4- 8-1837  Irena, Lucinda, Calvin, Franklin B, Melinda & Milton ch of John gct Westfield MM
- 12-11-1847  Charlotte (form Towsend) mcd  chm
- 8-12-1848  Charlotte gct Elk MM, Ohio
- 10-15-1849  William of Bloomfield MM s George & Dorcas m Sarah Williams at Fairfield MH
- 12- 3-1849  Sarah gct Bloomfield MM
- 8- 9-1873  David & w Martha rocf Whitewater MM
- 1-10-1874  David W & w Martha N gct Indianapolis MM
- 2-10-1894  Jabez & w Martha B & ch Ira, French & Rex H rec in mbrp
- 2-11-1899  Martha B rec in mbrp
- 10-10-1908  Ira & Rex drpd from mbrp
- 3-11-1911  Geneva rec in mbrp
- 9-12-1914  French drpd frm mbrp
- 11-13-1915  Paul rec in mbrp

## HUTCHENS
- 11-11-1899  Benjamin & w Emma rocf Amboy MM
- 10-12-1901  Benjamin & w gct Walnut Ridge MM

## HUTTON
- ( 1 mo-1831  John rocf Middleton MM, Ohio)
- ( 6 mo-1845  John & ch Samuel W, Margaret Jane & Wm H rocf Whitewater MM)
- 3-17-1847  John s John & Jane, dec, m Phebe Bowman, wid, at Fairfield MH
- 5-11-1850  John & fam gct Richland MM, Ind (Phebe's own ch gct Duck Creek MM)

## IDDINGS
- 11- 9-1839  Ruth rocf Union MM, Ohio  (wid of Benjamin Iddings & mother of Benjamin D Peirce)

## ISENHOUR
- 12-11-1909  Bessie rec in mbrp

## JACKSON
- 2-10-1838  Mary (form Harvey) mcd & dp  dis
- 3-11-1911  Alonzo rolf Christian Ch, Centerville
- 4- 8-1911  Andrew rec in mbrp
- 12-13-1919  Mrs. Alonzo rec in mbrp

## JAMES
- 6- 9-1838  David & w Mary & ch Ruthann, Mary, Levi C, Atticus S, Alfred P, Jonathan H & Lindley M rocf Spiceland MM
- 2-14-1839  Ruthann, dt David & Mary m Hugh W Maxwell at West Grove MM
- 6-13-1840  Isaac Sr & w Leah rocf Whitewater MM
- 11-14-1840  Daniel, cert rec from Spiceland MM "being informed he was an idiot" comm appt to inspect his case  5-8-1841 rec an article of agreement from his father securing his maintenance.  His cert is now rec.
- 5- 8-1841  David & w Mary & ch Mary, Levi C, Atticus, Alfred P, Jonathan H, Lindley M, Sarah & Dillin H gct Clear Creek MM, Ohio
- 4- 9-1842  Isaac Sr & w Leah gct Whitewater MM

## JARRETT
- 1-11-1933  Rexeen rec in mbrp

## JAY
- 9- 8-1883  Hannah gct Dover MM

## JENKINS
- ( 9 mo-1840  Samuel rocf Mill Creek MM, Ohio to m Sarah Russell)

WEST GROVE

JENKINS (Cont)
10-12-1840  Samuel s Amos dec & Elizabeth m Sarah Russell at West Grove MH

JESSOP
( 9 mo-1823  Enoch & w Ann & fam rocf New Garden MM, NC)
( 2 mo-1824  Alice Jessop & her ch by previous m, Jesse, Miles, Wilson & Wm Beauchamp, ch of Elleck, dec, rocf Milford MM)
( 5 mo-1825  Alice & dt Betty B gct Milford MM)
( 5 mo-1826  Elizabeth, w Jonathan & ch Mary, Peninah, Thomas, Ludia, Nancy, Miriam, Jacob & Huldah gct Milford MM)
( 6 mo-1830  Jacob Jr & w Elizabeth & minor ch Elihu, James, Mahlon & Rachel rocf Whitewater MM)
( 1 mo-1832  Sarah rocf Milford MM)
( 2 mo-1832  Evan rocf Milford MM)
( 5 mo-1836  Eli rocf New Garden MM)
8-12-1837  Eli gct New Garden MM
12-12-1874  David B & Sarah rec in mbrp
7-14-1877  David & Sarah gct Whitewater MM

JOHNSON
(11 mo-1820  Isaac rocf Silver Creek MM)
( 6 mo-1836  Charles Sr rocf New Garden MM)
5- 8-1841  Charles gct Chester MM
8-11-1888  Lina drpd from mbrp

JOICE
12-14-1889  Hattie rec in mbrp

JONES
(11 mo-1826  Lydia rocf Springfield MM, NC)
( 2 mo-1827  Lydia gct Milford MM)
2- 8-1856  Rachel (form Cook) mcd dis
3-14-1874  Lewis & w Ruth & s Albert rec in mbrp
2-10-1885  Isaac rec in mbrp
8-11-1888  Albert drpd from mbrp
11-14-1896  Isaac gct Whitewater MM
1- 9-1897  Emma rec in mbrp
10-10-1908  Emma drpd from mbrp

JOSLIN (Joslyn)
3-11-1911  Rhoma rec in mbrp
4- 8-1911  Ira rec in mbrp
9-12-1914  Ira drpd from mbrp
12-13-1919  Wina rec in mbrp

JULIAN
(      1816  Sarah dt Isaac & Sarah of Whitewater MM m Ezekiel Commons at West Grove MH)
( 5 mo-1826  Rebecca gct Whitewater MM)
( 7 mo-1827  Rebecca rocf Whitewater MM)
4-14-1894  Lily gct Raysville MM

JUSTICE
12-16-1818  Mary dt Jonathan & Elizabeth m Lancelot Bell at West Union MH

KANCHER
1-10-1885  Ceno rec in mbrp
12-14-1889  Mary rec in mbrp
4-14-1894  Marah (Mary) & Seno rel from mbrp
3-14-1896  Mary rec in mbrp
3-14-1896  Ceno rolf Greenfork U B Ch

KARCH
10-10-1885  Peter & Nancy rec in mbrp

KEEVER
9-14-1889  Mary Louisa gct New Garden MM

KEMM
2- 8-1845  Celia Ann (form Wright) mcd & na dis
12-14-1889  Ethel rec in mbrp
12-14-1889  John rec in mbrp
7-10-1897  John drpd from mbrp

KELLUM
( 3 mo-1822  Jesse rocf Newberry MM, Ohio)
( 4 mo-1822  Christopher & fam rocf Newberry MM, Ohio)

KEMPTON
3-10-1900  Sarah J & Alice rec in mbrp
3-11-1911  Sarah J gct Whitewater MM
3-11-1911  Alice G gct Whitewater MM

KEPLER
4-14-1888  Carrie rec in mbrp
3-10-1895  Charles P & w Hattie rec in mbrp
11-10-1900  Mable C rec in mbrp
2-12-1916  Charles B rel from mbrp

KEPLINGER
11-14-1914  Nettie glt ------

KERR
1-10-1885  James rec in mbrp
12-10-1886  James dis for dr & selling liquors
4- 9-1887  Eva rel from mbrp
3-11-1911  Maud rec in mbrp
9-12-1914  Maud drpd from mbrp

KEY
3-10-1877  Hamilton & w Margaret & ch John, Mary, Joseph, Charles, Martha & James rec in mbrp
5-11-1877  Hamilton & fam gct Hickory Valley MM, Tenn

KINDLY (Kinley)
( 8 mo-1819  Isaac & w Ann & ch Caleb, Edward & Frederick rocf New Garden MM)
(11 mo-1820  Isaac & w Ann & ch Caleb, Edward & Frederick gct New Garden MM)
( 5 mo-1821  John & w Ann & ch Jonathan, Joel, Sarah, Elizabeth, Ruth & John W rocf Mill Creek MM, Ohio)
11-10-1838  Caleb jH dis
6-12-1841  Frederick Jr mcd & na dis
11-13-1841  Edward mcd & na dis
8-12-1843  Anna na & dp dis
5-11-1850  Isaac Jr mcd na dis
3-14-1874  Nathaniel rec in mbrp
6-13-1874  Daniel & Dinah Ann, ch Nathaniel, rec in mbrp

KING
9-11-1847  Harmon, Walnut Ridge MM req this to treat for mcd. 10-9-1847 Tr without sat. Walnut Ridge inf. 1- 8-1848 Dis rec from Walnut Ridge MM.
2-12-1848  Lydia & Deborah & mother Ann White rocf Walnut Ridge MM
5-13-1848  Hannah rocf Spiceland MM
4-14-1849  Hannah (now Hambleton) mcd dis
5- 9-1849  Lydia (now Martindale) mcd chm
4-18-1850  Deborah, dt Isaac, dec, & Ann m Christopher Hollingsworth of Silver Creek MM at West Grove MH
12-12-1885  Alice rec in mbrp
7-11-1891  Alice drpd from mbrp
2-13-1892  John E & Emma rec in mbrp
2-10-1894  Miriam & Daisy rec in mbrp
3-14-1896  Etta glt -----
9-12-1914  Mariam drpd from mbrp
4-14-1917  John E & Emma drpd from mbrp

KIRK
(10 mo-1824  William of Center MM, Ohio roc to m Rachel Wickersham)
10-28-1824  William s Ezekiel & Hannah m Rachel Wickersham at West Grove MH
( 1 mo-1826  William Kirk rocf Center MM, Ohio)
2-10-1843  Rachel appt elder
2- 9-1850  William appt elder

KITTERMAN
2- 9-1858  Sarah Jane (form Wickersham) mcd drpd from mbrp
11-10-1888  Emma rec in mbrp
12-14-1889  Mary Ann rec in mbrp

LACY
(      1815  Peter & w Susanna & ch John, Pearson, Susannah, Ruth & Josiah rocf Back Creek MM, NC at Whitewater MM, Ind Territory (they lived in the West Union PM area which was under West Grove MM when that was set up in 1818)

WEST GROVE

26

LACY (Cont)
  4-14-1819  Susannah dt Peter & Susannah m Brady M Willets at West Union MH
  12-13-1820  Ruth dt Peter & Susannah m Matthew Symons at West Union MH
  (12 mo-1828  Josiah rocf Milford MM to m Ruth Gordon)
  1-15-1829  Josiah s Peter & Susannah m Ruth Gordon at West Grove MH
  5 mo-1829  Ruth gct Milford MM

LAIRD
  10-14-1893  Carrie gct Van Wert MM, Ohio

LAMB
  1-10-1885  Abiather rec in mbrp
  2-10-1900  James M & w Mary rec in mbrp
  7-13-1918  Verla Stoffer drpd from mbrp

LAMMOTT
  10-11-1905  William A & w gct Muncie MM
  10- 9-1909  W. L rec in mbrp
  2-14-1914  Belva, Rosetta & Omer rec in mbrp
  2- 4-1929  Omer & Rosetta jas drpd from mbrp

LANE
  11-10-1838  Ira & w Hannah & ch Levi, Lydia, Martha, Esther & Robert Barclay rocf Elk MM, Ohio
  6-10-1843  Hannah dis for unbecoming conduct and conversation
  7- 8-1843  Ira j U B Ch dis
  9-14-1850  Martha (now Ogborn) mcd, na & j U B Ch dis
  10- 9-1852  Lydia j U B Ch dis

LAWRENCE
  2- 4-1914  Grover rec in mbrp
  11-13-1915  Thomas rec in mbrp
  4-14-1917  Grover drpd from mbrp

LEASURE
  5- 8-1909  Harry rec in mbrp

LEE
  10-12-1867  Tacy (form Davis) mcd chm

LEESON
  2-11-1860  Rachel (form Maudlin) mcd "has forfeited right of mbrp"

LEONARD
  1-10-1857  Mary (form Brewer) mcd drpd from mbrp

LEWELLIN
  (10 mo-1822  Certificate for Meshack & ch Jane, Henry, Henderson, John, Seth & William rocf Back Creek MM, NC at Whitewater MM & end to West Grove MM)

LEWIS
  1- 9-1858  Rebecca rst at Bloomfield MM w/c of West Grove MM
  12- 8-1883  Addie Lewis, a minor in care of William & Mary Ann West, rocf Caesars Creek MM, Ohio
  9-10-1887  Addie rel on req

LINDERMAN
  5-10-1856  Sarah mcd on 8-11-1855 dis
  5-11-1889  Louella rec in mbrp
  12-14-1889  Frank rec in mbrp
  7-10-1909  Frank & Ella drpd from mbrp

LINDLEY
  ( 9 mo-1865  Aaron rocf West Union MM (Morgan Co) to m Sarah Maxwell)
  9-11-1865  Aaron s David & Mary m Sarah Maxwell at West Grove MH
  2-10-1866  Sarah gct West Union MM

LINKENFELTER
  9-14-1918  Iva rec in mbrp

LIVINGOOD
  1-11-1840  Margaret Jerusia mcd dis (Margaret Bundy m 1839 by civil ceremony Jonathan Livingood)

LONG
  8-12-1837  Rachel gct Westfield MM

LOOTZ
  2-13-1915  Maud rec in mbrp

LOUGHMAN
  2-28-1866  Rees D s John & Mary, dec, m Jane D Baldwin at Fairfield MH
  3-13-1875  Jane rel to j Meth Ch

LUNDY
  1-10-1880  William & w Rachel rec in mbrp
  1-10-1880  Mordecai, Mary K & Sarah A rec in mbrp
  2-11-1882  Leroy, Andrew J, Malissa, Hannah & Martha rec in mbrp
  3-11-1882  Mary Orlena rec in mbrp
  4- 8-1882  Elizabeth rocf Springfield
  4-12-1884  Mordecai & fam gct Springfield MM
  12-14-1889  William drpd from mbrp
  7-11-1896  Mattie gct Whitewater MM
  9-12-1914  Laura drpd from mbrp
  11-13-1915  Oscar rec in mbrp
  7-13-1918  Oscar drpd from mbrp

LYBOLT
  8- 2-1883  James B m Josie Harris, dt George & Priscilla Harris (a civil ceremony)

LYKENS
  12- 8-1877  Sarah Jane gct Spiceland MM

LYTLE
  10-10-1885  Martha rec in mbrp
  11-12-1887  Mattie drpd from mbrp

McCONNAHA
  10-10-1908  Minnie A & Carrie drpd from mbrp
  3-11-1916  Omer rec in mbrp
  12-13-1919  Martha & Mildred rec in mbrp

McDANIEL
  6-14-1885  Hattie rel on req

McGATHE
  8-11-1888  Eliza drpd from mbrp

McKINLEY
  1- 9-1897  Henry & fam rocf Olive Branch MM (Blackford Co)
  1- 8-1898  Henry & fam gct Olive Branch MM

McKINNEY
  6-11-1927  Donald rec in mbrp
  9 mo-1931  Donald gct Economy MM

McLAUGHLIN
  4-14-1888  Asenath rec in mbrp

McNUTT
  4-13-1878  Emily rec in mbrp
  3-11-1882  Harmon rec in mbrp
  4- 9-1887  Cassie rec in mbrp
  12-14-1889  Alice rec in mbrp
  9-12-1914  Harmon, Orlena, Ola, George, Cassie, Flossie, Bert, Clayborn & Irene drpd from mbrp

MACE
  ( 2 mo-1833  Nathan rec cert from Core Sound MM, NC to West Grove MM (a cert he had req for New Garden MM got lost)
  ( 2 mo-1835  Nathan gct New Garden MM)

MACY
  ( 5 mo-1821  Cert rec for William & w Phebe from New Garden MM, NC at Whitewater MM & end to West Grove MM)

MADDEN
  4- 9-1864  Sarah gct Bear Creek MM, Iowa

MANLY
  5-13-1899  Estella rocf Sanford MM, NY
  2-10-1900  Estella m Fred A Tear at home of Wm F Manley

WEST GROVE

26a

MARADETH (Meridith)
 8-12-1837 David rocf Gwyned MM, Pa

MARKINS
 4- 9-1887 Mary rec in mbrp

MARTIN
( 4 mo-1823 James & w Sarah & ch John & Mary rocf Whitewater MM)
10- 9-1841 Mary Ann dis for na & dp
3- 3-1846 David mcd dis
6-14-1851 James mcd dis
3-14-1885 Sue A rec in mbrp
8-11-1888 Sue drpd from mbrp
7-10-1909 Minnie drpd from mbrp
2-14-1914 Edna & Ethel rec in mbrp
7-13-1918 Edna & Ethel drpd from mbrp
3- 8-1933 Minnie rec in mbrp

MARTINDALE
5- 9-1849 Lydia (form King) mcd chm
3-14-1863 John, Emily & Eden ch of James M & Lydia rec in mbrp
4- 9-1887 John gct Cherry Grove MM
12-10-1887 Eden gct Cherry Grove MM
10-12-1889 John & w Amanda rocf Cherry Grove MM
10-12-1889 Eden rocf Cherry Grove MM
12-14-1889 Sarah rec in mbrp
10-13-1894 John & w gct Whitewater MM
3-14-1896 Bessie rec in mbrp
4- 8-1899 James & Esther rec in mbrp
12-14-1901 John & Amanda rocf Whitewater MM
4-10-1915 Henry & Eva rec in mbrp
7-12-1918 Henry & Eva drpd from mbrp

MASON
4- 8-1911 Eva rec in mbrp

MATHEWS
6-12-1909 Hannah rocf Chester MM

MAUDLIN
( 1809 Benjamin & Leah were appt to comm in Whitewater MM (they lived in the area that became West Grove MM in 1818) They came from Back Creek MM, NC to West Branch MM, Ohio in 1807 and were in Ind by 1809)
12- 4-1817 Wright s of Benjamin & Leah m Mary Wickersham dt Jehu & Mary at West Grove MH
11-21-1822 Thomas s Benjamin & Sarah m Hannah Sheridan at West Grove MH
12-23-1824 Penninah dt Benjamin & Leah m James Haworth at West Grove MH
( 4 mo-1825 Thomas & w Hannah gct Milford MM)
11-17-1825 John s Benjamin & Leah m Rebecca Elliott at West Grove MH
12-15-1825 Sarah dt Benjamin & Leah m Dillon Haworth at West Grove MH
9- 8-1838 Thomas con mcd & dp
5-16-1839 Sydney dt Wright & Mary m David Townsend at West Grove MH
4-15-1844 Rachel dt Wright & Mary m Robert Stuart at West Grove MH
10-12-1844 John dis for na & dr
7-12-1845 Nathan mcd chm
12-13-1845 Rebecca na dis
12-13-1845 Thomas & Rachel & ch gct Westfield MM
12-13-1845 Sarah rocf Salem MM
9- 9-1848 Mark na dp upl dis
1-13-1849 Nathan compl of for neg att, dev plain, att places of diversion, danced, & assisted in obtaining marriage licenses for parties who are mem. 3-10-1849 dis
3-10-1849 Eliza Ann (now Newby) mcd dis
11-10-1849 Lucinda (now Hollingsworth) mcd chm
6-13-1852 Nathan & fam gct Salem MM, Iowa
7-10-1852 Catherine Jane na dp & dancing dis
2-11-1860 Rachel (now Leeson) mcd "forfeited her right to mbrp"
3-10-1860 Mary H (form Wickersham) mcd chm
6- 9-1860 John Jr mcd "and right to mbrp ceases"
2- 8-1868 Elizabeth Adaline rec in mbrp
2- 8-1868 Elizabeth (now Scates) mcd drpd from mbrp
3-14-1872 Mark rec in mbrp
3-14-1874 John & Rebecca rec in mbrp
2-11-1882 Nettie rec in mbrp
4- 9-1887 Nathan rocf Whitewater MM
1-14-1893 Frank Burton, Nancy D & Sarah E rec in mbrp
2-10-1894 James Alpheus rec in mbrp
12- 9-1911 Sarah gct Whittier MM, Calif
9-12-1914 Bert & Murray drpd from mbrp

MAXWELL
( 1814 John & w Hannah (Whitlock) and his stepsons, James, Dillon & Richard Haworth, rocf Lost Creek MM, Tenn (They lived in the area that became West Grove MM, Ind in 1818)
8-14-1834 Betsey dt John & Hannah m Nathan Elliott at West Grove MH
1-14-1836 Polly dt John & Hannah m Absolom Elliott at West Grove MH
2-14-1839 Hugh W s John & Hannah m Ruth Ann James at West Grove MH
8-10-1846 John M con mcd
8-17-1848 Maria dt John & Hannah m Jonathan Elliott at West Grove MH
12-13-1849 Hannah Ann dt John & Hannah m Philip S Commons at West Grove MH
9- 9-1854 Nancy Jane rec in mbrp
4-14-1855 Ann Elizabeth, Albert & King, ch of John M & Nancy Jane, rec in mbrp on req of parents
4-10-1858 Hugh W & fam gct Whitewater MM
1-12-1861 Sarah Sylvania rocf Whitewater MM
3- 9-1861 Benjamin F rocf Salem MM (Silver Creek)
10-10-1863 Benjamin F & w Sarah Sylvania gct Salem MM (Silver Creek)
5-14-1864 John M mcd chm
1-14-1865 Ann Elizabeth rocf Whitewater MM
9-11-1865 Sarah, dt John & Hannah m Aaron Lindley at West Grove MH
8-14-1869 John M rel from mbrp
6-11-1870 Ann Elizabeth (now Barnes) mcd chm
8-11-1877 Emily gct Whitewater MM
9- 3-1877 Robert & Sarah & s John M gct Whitewater MM
2-14-1885 Albert gct Cottonwood MM, Kansas

MEANS
3-11-1916 Harry C rec in mbrp

MEDEARIS
5- 8-1909 Ora B & Henrietta rec in mbrp
5-10-1913 Alice rolf Central Christian Ch, Indianapolis

MEEKER
12-14-1865 Davis a widower m Sarah Elliott at West Grove MH
9- 8-1866 Sarah gct Plainfield MM

MENDENHALL
( 6 mo-1818 Stephen rocf New Garden MM)
(10 mo-1818 Cert rec for Mordecai & w from Miami MM, Ohio at Whitewater MM and end to West Grove MM)
( 5 mo-1826 Elijah & w Huldah & ch Joseph C, Daniel, Anderson & John B rocf Whitewater MM)
( 4 mo-1826 Samuel's mbrp in West Grove MM ret by Milford MM for mcd & training with militia)
(11 mo-1826 Jonathan & w Ann & ch rocf Union MM, NC at New Garden MM & end to West Grove MM)
( 2 mo-1827 Cert rec for Wm & s Oliver L from Deep River MM, NC at Whitewater MM & end to West Grove MM)
12-17-1828 Margaret dt Jonathan & Ann m Moses Coffin at Fairfield MH
5-13-1830 Elijah T s Isaiah & Christiana m Mary Cloud at West Grove MH
( 5 mo-1831 Elijah & Mary gct New Garden MM)
( 2 mo-1832 Robert s Jonathan & Ann gct New Garden MM to m Mary Jessop)
( 4 mo-1832 Mary rocf New Garden MM)
( 4 mo-1832 John s Jonathan & Ann gct New Garden MM to m Eunice Haisley)
( 7 mo-1832 Robert & w Mary gct New Garden MM)
8-17-1836 Joseph s Jonathan & Ann m Eunice Davis at Fairfield MH
4- 8-1837 Jonathan & w Phebe & dt Abigail, Permelia, Rhoda, Eunice & Mary Jane rocf Deep River MM, NC & end to Mill Creek MM

## MENDENHALL (Cont)
| | |
|---|---|
| 5-13-1837 | Elijah & w Huldah & ch gct Springfield MM |
| ( 5 mo-1837 | Mary & s rocf Westfield MM |
| 7- 8-1837 | Robert & s Nathan & Jonathan rocf Dover MM |
| 7- 8-1837 | William, a minor, rocf Westfield MM |
| 9- 9-1837 | Mary dis for being guilty of unchastity |
| 1-13-1838 | Robert gct Westfield to m Anna Smith |
| 2 mo-1838 | Robert & s Nathan & Jonathan gct Westfield MM |
| 8-11-1838 | Solomon Fairfield PM mcd dis |
| 10-13-1838 | Rebecca dt Jonathan & Ann m John Smith at Fairfield MH |
| 3-14-1840 | Eunice jas dis |
| 1-11-1840 | Joseph gct Spiceland MM |
| 10-10-1840 | Elijah T rec in mbrp w/c of New Garden MM |
| 9-14-1842 | Naomi dt Jonathan & Ann m Nathan Elliott at Fairfield MH |
| 7- 8-1843 | Elijah T Fairfield PM compl mcd chm |
| 8-10-1844 | Lydia (form Bond) mcd & na dis |
| 3- 8-1845 | Nathan gct Dover MM to m Rhoda Bond |
| 8- 9-1845 | Rhoda rocf Dover MM |
| 1-10-1846 | Nathan & w Rhoda gct Dover MM |
| 1- 9-1847 | Caleb C Fairfield PM compl mcd & na dis |
| 2-16-1848 | Ann M dt Jonathan & Ann m Jonathan Osborn at Fairfield MH |
| 7- 8-1848 | Rebecca Ann (now Murphy) mcd dis |
| 11-11-1848 | James & fam gct Sugar Plain MM |
| 3- 9-1850 | Stephen rocf Sugar Plain MM |
| 9-18-1850 | Keziah dt Jonathan & Ann m Solomon Haworth at Fairfield MH |
| 1-15-1851 | Sally Ann dt Jonathan & Ann m Eli Haisley at Fairfield MH (West Grove MM) |
| 3-11-1854 | Margaret E gct New Garden MM |
| 3- 8-1856 | Jonathan & w Ann gct Dover MM |
| 3-13-1915 | Dora rolf Meth Ch Centerville |

## MERIDITH
| | |
|---|---|
| 8-12-1837 | David, a minor, rocf Gwynned MM Montgomery Co Penn & end by Whitewater MM |
| 12-14-1889 | Joseph, Charles & Anna Louisa rec in mbrp |

## MILLER
| | |
|---|---|
| 3-10-188? | Parmelia (form Elliott) mcd chm |
| 4-14-1888 | Indiana & Martha rec in mbrp |
| 2-10-1894 | Isaac N & M Ann rec in mbrp |
| 3-10-1906 | Permelia gct Whitewater MM |

## MILLIKAN (Millican)
| | |
|---|---|
| ( 5 mo-1820 | Mary rocf Whitewater MM) |
| ( 6 mo-1824 | Mary gct Lost Creek MM, Tenn) |
| 5-13-1830 | William s Eli & Mary of Springfield MM, Ohio m Charity Canaday at West Grove MH |
| (10 mo-1830 | Charity gct Springfield MM, Ohio) |
| 8-10-1901 | Susan gct Marion MM |

## MILLS
| | |
|---|---|
| (12 mo-1822 | Daniel & w Esther & dt Hannah rocf Caesars Creek MM, Ohio) |
| 4- 9-1887 | Thomas rocf Whitewater MM |
| 1-10-1891 | Susan rocf Whitewater MM |
| 1-12-1901 | Jonathan B & w Rebecca E & ch Lovel & Anna rocf Anderson MM |
| 2- 8-1902 | Benjamin J & fam gct Westland MM |

## MOFFITT
| | |
|---|---|
| 2-10-1883 | Charles & w Lucinda & ch Oliver, Eunice E, Arthur C & Hugh C rocf Sugar Plain MM |
| 10-10-1891 | Charles & fam gct Whitewater MM |

## MOON
| | |
|---|---|
| ( 3 mo-1821 | Rachel, nee Hockett, rocf Newberry MM, Ohio) |
| ( 1 mo-1823 | Rachel gct Newberry MM, Ohio) |

## MOORE
| | |
|---|---|
| 3-12-1885 | John D rec in mbrp |
| 8-11-1888 | John D drpd from mbrp |

## MORGAN
| | |
|---|---|
| ( 7 mo-1820 | Benjamin & dts rocf Whitewater MM) |
| (11 mo-1823 | Ruth rocf Whitewater MM) |
| ( 2 mo-1824 | Charles gct Milford MM) |
| 10-10-1908 | Katie Smith drpd from mbrp |
| 2- 8-1913 | John & w Sarah rolf Locust Grove Meth Ch |
| 1- 8-1916 | John & Sarah rel on req |

## MORRIS
| | |
|---|---|
| ( 1815 | Isaac & w Pharaby & ch Margaret, George, Ruth, Elizabeth, Gulielma & Christopher rocf Springfield MM, NC at Whitewater MM Ind Territory (They lived in the area that West Union MH of West Grove MM) |
| ( 1815 | Josiah rocf Springfield MM, NC) |
| 2-17-1820 | John s Aaron & Lydia m Sarah Bell at Milford MH |
| (12 mo-1821 | Josiah gct Whitewater MM to m Abigail Symons) |
| ( 8 mo-1822 | Abigail rocf Whitewater MM) |
| 1-23-1823 | Jehosephat s Jonathan & Penelope, both dec, m Mary Bell at Milford MH |
| ( 1823 | Josiah & w Abigail gct Milford MM) |
| 7-21-1830 | Mary gct Arba MM |

## MULL
| | |
|---|---|
| 12-14-1889 | Laura rec in mbrp |
| 7-10-1909 | Laura drpd from mbrp |

## MURDOCK (Mardock)
| | |
|---|---|
| ( 5 mo-1826 | Rachel gct Whitewater MM) |

## MURPHY
| | |
|---|---|
| ( 1814 | Margaret w of Joshua Sr & ch Sarah, William, Rachel & Amos rocf Miami MM, Ohio at Whitewater MH (They lived in the area of Fairfield MH in the area that became West Grove MM in 1818) |
| 10-27-1827 | Sarah dt Joshua & Margaret m Isaac Baldwin at Fairfield MH |
| 5-18-1831 | Rachel dt Joshua & Margaret m Henry Willets at Fairfield MH |
| 6-11-1836 | William & w Betsey & ch Martin, Sarah & Margaret Ann gct Westfield MM |
| 10-19-1836 | Joshua s Joshua Sr & Margaret m Tacy Shoemaker at Fairfield MH |
| 12-12-1838 | Rebecca dt Joshua Sr & Margaret m Bailey Albertson at Fairfield MH |
| 10-16-1839 | John s Joshua & Margaret m Susannah Williams at Fairfield MH |
| 10-10-1840 | Jesse Fairfield PM compl for "calling an individual a liar, and saying he could prove it, and failed to do it, and offered to fight him and also manifested a disposition to fight another person." 11-14-1840 chm |
| 11-13-1844 | Margaret dt Joshua, dec, & Margaret m Solomon Williams at Fairfield MH |
| 9-13-1845 | Jesse Fairfield PM dis for "wagering" |
| 10- 9-1847 | Mary (now Atkinson) dis for "being unchaste" & mcd |
| 7- 8-1848 | Rebecca (form Mendenhall) mcd dis |
| 8- 9-1851 | Joshua Jr & w Tacy & fam gct Wabash MM |
| 10- 9-1852 | John & fam gct Wabash MM |
| 5-12-1855 | Elizabeth (now Fennel) mcd chm |

## MYERS
| | |
|---|---|
| 2- 8-1913 | Catherine rec in mbrp |

## NAPIER
| | |
|---|---|
| 6-10-1905 | Nora glt Christian Ch Elwood |
| 12- 8-1906 | Aaron & w Jennie rocf Salem MM |

## NELSON
| | |
|---|---|
| 4-19-1927 | Leslie N & w Emma Elizabeth & ch Margaret, Raymond, Robert, Jack, Charles Eugene & Emma Jane rocf Whitewater MM |

## NEWBORN
| | |
|---|---|
| 2-10-1894 | Henry rec in mbrp |

## NEWBY
| | |
|---|---|
| ( 9 mo-1819 | William & w Elizabeth & fam rocf New Garden MM |
| ( 3 mo-1822 | Micah of West Grove MM rpt mcd) |
| 8-13-1822 | Mary D gct Blue River MM |
| ( 1823 | Gabriel rocf Driftwood MM & end to Milford MM) |
| 4-17-1823 | Gabriel s Thomas & Mary m Rebecca Harvey at West Grove MH |
| ( 8-1823 | Joseph rocf Driftwood MM & end to Milford MM) |
| ( 8-1823 | Elizabeth rocf Driftwood MM & end to Milford MM) |
| (10 mo-1824 | Rebecca gct Milford MM) |
| 3-10-1849 | Eliza Ann (form Maudlin) mcd dis |
| 2-13-1875 | Rebecca Ann rec in mbrp |

WEST GROVE

NEWMAN
- 2-13-1915  Eugene & w Trevia rec in mbrp
- 3-11-1916  Eugene & w Trevia glt U B Ch, Eaton, Ohio

NICHOLSON
- 4-11-1868  Naomi Jane (form Davis) mcd dis
- 1-10-1865  Rhodes rec in mbrp
- 2-14-1885  George & Naomi J rec in mbrp
- 4- 9-1887  Etta rec in mbrp
- 4-14-1888  George L, Clary A, Rhoda M, Verling, Charles, Frank P & Benton R ch of Rhodes & w rec in mbrp
- 12-14-1888  Flora rec in mbrp
- 6-12-1897  Elzena J rec in mbrp
- 7-10-1897  Clara, May, Verling, Charles, Ray Oliver & Omer drpd from mbrp
- 6-13-1903  George, Naomi & Jennie drpd from mbrp

NISLER
- 3- 8-1924  Lawrence & w Stella & ch rec in mbrp

NIXON
- (     1811  John & w Jane & fam rocf Springfield MM, NC at Whitewater MM (Lived in the area that became West Grove MM in 1818)
- ( 5 mo-1836  Gabriel & w Mary & ch Letitia Ann, Phineas H, & Daniel M rocf Milford MM)
- 3- 4-1844  Gabriel & fam gct Salem MM, Iowa

NORMAN
- 11-10-1849  Eliza Ann (form Wickersham) mcd dis

NORTH
- (10 mo-1821  Keziah (form Bond) rocf Whitewater MM)
- ( 1 mo-1824  Daniel gct Chester MM)
- 10-14-1837  Daniel rocf Springfield MM

ODLE (Odell)
- ( 4 mo-1827  Daniel & w Betty & ch Polly rocf Whitewater MM)
- (12 mo-1827  Daniel & w Betty & Polly gct Whitewater MM)

OGBORN
- ( 6 mo-1825  Samuel & w Esther & ch Joseph, Mary, Allen, Edwin, Evan, Lydia & Ezra rocf Miami MM, Ohio)
- ( 8-12-1837  Joseph P & w Elizabeth & minor ch Ann E & Sarah B rocf Whitewater MM)
- 4-14-1838  Edwin Fairfield PM mcd & na dis
- 8- 8-1840  Joseph dis for permitting a mcd & entertainment in his house
- 5-14-1842  Evan dis for att mcd & j U B Ch
- 11-12-1842  Allen W dis for mcd & dp (living in limits of Caesar's Creek MM)
- 6- 8-1844  Ann (now Bird) mcd & j U B Ch dis
- 8-10-1844  Ezra j U B Ch dis
- 4-12-1845  Lydia (now Elliott) mcd dis
- 7-12-1845  Ann (now Personett) mcd & na dis
- 1- 8-1848  Elizabeth gct Whitewater MM
- 4- 8-1848  Anna gct Cherry Grove MM
- 5-17-1848  Esther (Andrews) wid of Samuel m William Widows at Fairfield MH
- 8-11-1849  Joel j U B Ch dis
- 9-14-1850  Martha (form Lane) mcd & na & j U B Ch dis
- 11- 8-1856  Joseph rst at Chester MM w/c of West Grove MM
- 6- 8-1889  Daniel B & w Lizzie G rocf Spiceland MM
- 3-14-1891  Daniel B & w Lizzie rel from mbrp

OSBORN
- ( 3 mo-1820  William & (2nd w) Amy & his ch Daniel, Allen, Wilfing, Elizabeth, Charles, Lemuel & Jeremiah & Elizabeth rocf Lost Creek MM, Tenn)
- ( 9 mo-1822  Elizabeth Sr rocf Springfield MM, Ohio (wid of Thomas & mother of Wm, b 8-1-1778)
- ( 5 mo-1824  William & w Anna & ch Ambrose, Rachel, Anna, Elizabeth, William Jr, Tamer, Jemima & Daniel rocf Whitewater MM)
- ( 5 mo-1825  William & w Anna & ch gct New Garden MM)
- 7-13-1826  James s Charles & Sarah m Catherine Hastings at West Grove MH
- 3-11-1837  Narcissa Memorial recd
- 11-11-1843  James j (ASF) dis
- 2-16-1848  Jonathan s John & Rebecca, dec, m Anna M Mendenhall at Fairfield MH
- 3-13-1852  Enos con mcd
- 6- 8-1861  Enos dis for na
- 3-10-1877  Enos & w Mary Ann rec in mbrp
- 1-10-1880  James N, Alvina & Orlena rec in mbrp
- 3-10-1900  Emma rec in mbrp
- 8-10-1901  Christian M gct Danville MM
- 10-14-1905  Anna, Martha & Florence, ch Christena gct Mill Creek MM

OUTLAND
- 12- 9-1893  Joseph W rocf Westland MM

OVERMAN
- 7-14-1838  Nathan & dt gct Walnut Ridge MM
- 10-21-1839  Cyrus dis for mcd & na (living in limits of Walnut Ridge MM)
- 4- 9-1853  Ephraim rocf Whitewater MM
- 2-13-1858  Ephraim gct Whitewater MM

PALMER
- ( 6 mo-1821  Sarah rocf Whitewater MM)

PARKER
- 1 mo-1904  Ida B & dt Margaret Ruth roc

PATTY (Petty)
- (     1821  Elizabeth gct New Garden MM)
- 2-14-1857  Emily (form Brooks) mcd drpd from mbrp

PAXTON (Paxson - Paxon)
- (12 mo-1822  John rocf Plainfield MM, Ohio)
- ( 8 mo-1830  The cert for Sarah, a mbr at West Grove was returned by Milford MM. She was dis for mcd)

PEACOCK
- 7-11-1840  Rachel rocf Whitewater MM
- 4- 9-1887  Ida May rec in mbrp
- 4- 8-1899  Lewis rec in mbrp

PEARCE
- 11- 9-1839  Benjamin D & w Rachel rocf Union MM
- 8-13-1842  Rachel gct Salem MM, Iowa Terr, Benjamin's withheld
- 8-13-1842  Benjamin D, Union MM informs this that he has applied to law to collect a debt from one of our members, when all reasonable exertions were made to give satisfaction & where there was not a prospect of bankruptcy (to save sheriff's fees), the member went forward & complyed judgement. This will inform you we had not an opportunity to enter a complaint against him. The forgoing transmitted to Salem MM, Iowa Terr that they might treat with him.
- 3-11-1843  Salem MM, Iowa rpt he was tr w/out satisfaction. Disownment sent to Salem MM.

PEARSON
- (     1815  Jesse & s Jonathan & Jesse rocf Back Creek MM, NC at Whitewater MM (They lived in the area that became West Grove MM in 1818)
- (     1815  Polly & dt Sarah, Rachel, Elizabeth, Susannah & Rebecca rocf Back Creek MM, NC at Whitewater MM (They lived in the area that became West Grove MM in 1818)
- (12 mo-1818  Nathan & s Zeno, William, Aaron & Joseph rocf Whitewater MM)
- (12 mo-1818  Huldah rocf Whitewater MM)
- ( 2 mo-1819  Jesse & s Jesse & James gct Blue River MM)
- ( 2 mo-1819  Mary & dt Mary Elizabeth, Susannah & Rebecca gct Blue River MM)
- 8-17-1820  Peter s Nathan & Mary m Eunice Hastings at West Grove MH
- ( 5 mo-1821  Peter gct New Garden MM)
- ( 5 mo-1821  Eunice gct New Garden MM)
- 12- 9-1843  Elizabeth rst at Duck Creek MM w/c of West Grove MM
- 6- 5-1895  Morton C & w Cora & dt rocf Amboy MM
- 10-10-1896  Morton C & fam gct Sabina MM
- 11-13-1915  John L rolf Meth Ch, Centerville

WEST GROVE

PEELE
( 5 mo-1818   Reuben & w Rhoda rocf Deep Creek MM, NC end
              by Whitewater MM)
( 5 mo-1820   Reuben & Rhoda gct New Garden MM)
(12 mo-1835   Zilpha rocf Chester MM)
 4- 8-1837    Zilpha gct New Garden MM
 9-11-1841    Mary rocf Dover MM
 3-12-1843    Mary gct New Garden MM
 7-14-1866    John rec in mbrp

PEIRCE
(11 mo-1839   Benjamin D & w Rachel rocf Union MM, Ohio)

PENNINGTON
 12- 8-1877   Eli rec in mbrp
 5-10-1879    Eli rel on req

PERSONET
 7-12-1845    Ann (form Ogborn) mcd & na dis
 7-14-1866    Mary (form Griffin) mcd chm
 6-13-1868    William rec in mbrp
 7-14-1877    William & w Mary gct White River MM

PICKETT
( 2 mo-1818   Joseph & s Joseph rocf Center MM, Ohio at
              Whitewater MM (Lived in the area that became
              West Grove MM in 1818.)
( 2 mo-1818   Priscilla & dt Tamar, Anne, Lydia, Mary &
              Sarah rocf Center MM, Ohio at Whitewater MM
              (They lived in the area that became West
              Grove MM in 1818)
( 9 mo-1823   Joseph & w Priscilla & ch Tamar, Anna, Lydia,
              Mary, Sarah & Joseph gct Milford MM)
 9-13-1828    Lydia dt Joseph & Priscilla m Uriah Baldwin at
              West Grove MH

PIKE
 1-10-1885    Elizabeth, Flora & Etta rec in mbrp
 8-15-1899    Elizabeth drpd from mbrp
 8-11-1900    Elizabeth rec in mbrp
10-10-1908    Sallie W drpd from mbrp

PITTS
 3-10-1866    Elizabeth (form Griffin) mcd chm
 5-11-1867    Calvin rocf Dover MM

POLLARD
 8-14-1869    Emmaline (form Williams) mcd chm

POTTER
 2-11-1899    Elizabeth rolf Presby Ch, Haggerstown

PRESNALL
( 9 mo-1823   Daniel & w Christianna rocf Back Creek MM, NC)
( 2 mo-1824   Daniel & w Christiana gct Milford MM)
( 9 mo-1828   Nathan & w Rebecca & ch Elisha & Julia rocf
              Back Creek MM, NC)

PROBST
10-11-1913    Jacob F & w Ethel Jay & s Paul rocf -----
              (Montgomery Co, Ohio)
 9- 9-1916    Jacob F & w Ethel Jay & s Paul gct Whitewater
              MM

PUCKETT
( 3 mo-1824   Leah gct Newberry MM, Ohio)
( 8 mo-1831   Thomas rocf New Garden MM)
(12 mo-1832   Lavina rocf New Garden MM)
(     1832    Daniel, a minister, & s Greenley & Henry roc)
(     1832    Beulah & dt Anna, Celia & Beulah roc)
(12 mo-1835   Mary gct Chester MM)
( 5 mo-1836   Daniel, a minister, & s Henry gct New Garden
              MM)
( 5 mo-1836   Beulah & dt Anna, Celia & Beulah gct New
              Garden MM)
( 9 mo-1837   Greenlee gct Milford MM to m Margaret A
              Heavenridge)
 2-10-1838    Greenley gct Cherry Grove MM

PURVIS
 4- 8-1848    Sarah rocf Pennsville MM
 9- 8-1848    Sarah gct Walnut Ridge MM

QUATE
 1- 9-1886    Clara rec in mbrp
 8-11-1888    Nancy Clara drpd from mbrp

RATLIFF (Ratcliff)
(     1815    Richard & w Elizabeth & ch Richard, Gabriel,
              Cornelius & Elizabeth rocf Deep Creek MM, NC
              at Whitewater MM (They probably lived in the
              area that became West Grove MM in 1818)
(     1820    Richard gct Whitewater MM to m Caroline
              Bailey)
( 3 mo-1821   Caroline rocf Whitewater MM)
(     1823    Richard Sr & fam gct Milford MM)
(     1823    Richard Jr & w gct Milford MM)
 3-13-1850    Eli of Honey Creek MM s Elias & Achsah
              m Marinda Cook at West Grove MH
 7-13-1850    Marinda gct Honey Creek MM
 3-14-1874    Abbie rec in mbrp

RATHFROW (Rathfrom)
 2- 9-1889    Hershel rec on req of parents John D & Luella
 4-14-1894    Luella & Hershel E rel from mbrp

RAUCHER
 2-14-1885    Marilla C rec in mbrp

RAY
 4-10-1841    Jane (form Harvey) mcd & na dis

REAGAN
(10 mo-1820   Reason & w Mary & ch John rocf Caesars
              Creek MM, Ohio)
( 1 mo-1821   Thomas & w Rachel & s John, Wiley & Thomas Jr
              rocf Caesars Creek MM, Ohio)
 5-23-1822    Wiley s Thomas & Rachel m Ruth Wilson at
              Milford MH
       1823   Reason & w Mary & ch John & Dinah gct Milford
              MM

RECKNER
 2-13-1892    George F rec in mbrp
 3-13-1892    Mary rec in mbrp

REESE (Reece)
(     1823    Cert rec for John & w Ann & fam from Back
              Creek MM, NC at Whitewater MM end to West
              Grove MM)
( 5 mo-1824   John & w (Nancy) Ann & ch Nathan, Needham,
              Millicent, Daniel, Elias, Christiana, Jane
              & John Jr gct Milford MM)
( 4 mo-1831   Needham rocf Milford MM to m Celia Towsend)
 4-14-1831    Needham s John & Ann m Celia Townsend at
              West Grove MH
( 5 mo-1831   Caleb & w Sarah & a minor Charlotte Blizzard,
              rocf Cherry Grove MM)
( 9 mo-1831   Daniel rocf Milford MM to m Sarah Hastings)
 9-22-1831    Daniel s John, dec, & Ann m Sarah Hastings at
              West Grove MH
(10 mo-1831   Celia gct Milford MM)
(     1832    Sarah gct Milford MM)

REEVES
 7-12-1845    Julietta (form Pretlow) rocf Whitewater MM

REINHEIMER
 1-10-1885    Eva rec in mbrp
 2-14-1885    Wm H & Jennie rec in mbrp
 4-14-1888    Wm & Jennie drpd from mbrp

REVALREE
 2-14-1891    Catharine rocf Whitewater MM

REYNOLDS
 1-19-1839    Jesse & w Eliza W & ch Anna Jane rocf New
              Garden MM
12-12-1840    Jesse & w Eliza & ch Anna Jane & Addison gct
              New Garden MM
 1- 9-1915    Alden & Bertha rec in mbrp

RHINARD
( 5 mo-1822   Jacob & w Elizabeth rocf Springfield MM, Ohio)
(11 mo-1825   Jacob & w Elizabeth & dt Margaret & Katharine
              gct Milford MM)

WEST GROVE

RICHARDSON
  12-13-1919  Russell, Sherman & Frances rec in mbrp
  8- 6-1921   Harry & Ruth Tremps req l to -----
  1-13-1923   Francis gct West Richmond MM

RIDENOUR
  4-14-1888   Lot & w Lizzie & ch Minnie, Stella, Hattie & Harry rec in mbrp
  11-14-1891  Lot & fam gct Dublin MM
  4- 8-1911   Lola rec in mbrp
  2-14-1914   Charles & Mary rec in mbrp
  7-13-1918   Charles & Mary drpd from mbrp

RIDER
  ( 7- 8-1848  Lydia of Cornwall MM m Daniel Williams of West Grove MM at Cornwall mtg)

RIGLEY
  2-10-1894   Ida May rec in mbrp

RIVERS
  8- 8-1896   Minnie gct Dublin MM

ROBBINS
  10-10-1885  Sarah rec in mbrp
  1-10-1925   J Earl & w Caroline & ch John, Kenneth & Edwin rocf Lynn MM

ROBERTS
  (     1815  Amy con her mcd (at Whitewater MM, but she probably lived in the area that became West Grove in 1818)
  ( 7 mo-1818  Amy gct New Garden MM)
  (11 mo-1838  Henry & w Elizabeth rocf Dover MM)
  8-10-1853   Henry & fam gct Richland MM
  2-10-1894   Nancy rec in mbrp
  3-11-1911   Roscoe & Grace rec in mbrp
  3-11-1916   Lora rec in mbrp
  9- 9-1916   Glenna M rocf Dublin MM
  7-13-1918   Grace drpd from mbrp
  3- 8-1924   Carrie M rocf Greensfork MM
  1-10-1925   Roscoe & Glenna gct Dublin MM

ROBINSON
  9- 8-1849   Thomas & w Rebecca & ch Martha Ann, Isaac & Harmon rocf Duck Creek MM
  3-11-1854   Thomas & w Rebecca & ch Martha Ann, Isaac, Harmon & Wm Henry gct Honey Creek MM
  10 mo-1861  Thomas & w Rebecca & ch Martha Ann, Isaac King, Harmon, Wm Henry & Lorenzo Dow rocf Whitewater MM
  5-14-1864   Thomas & family gct Wabash MM
  1-14-1882   Thomas & w Rebecca & ch Elizabeth & Lemuel rocf Whitewater MM
  5-14-1887   Thomas & fam gct Whitewater MM

ROCKHILL
  3-11-1865   Calvin & w Lydia rocf Greenwood MM
  5-11-1867   Calvin & w Lydia gct Center MM, Ohio

ROGERS
        1872  Ansel & w Priscilla & s Arthur rocf Rasin MM, Mich
  5-10-1873   Priscilla gct Alum Creek MM, Ohio
  6-14-1885   Jonathan C & w Anna V & ch Christine M, Jacob Edward & John V rocf New Garden MM
  5- 8-1915   Herbert rec in mbrp
  7-13-1918   Herbert drpd from mbrp

ROLLER
  4- 8-1899   Frank M rec in mbrp
  6-10-1901   Frank & Lizzie gct Indianapolis MM

ROMICK
  9-14-1872   Lydia G rocf Adrian MM, Mich
  5-10-1873   Lydia G gct Alum Creek MM, Ohio

ROOKER
  ( 6 mo-1826  Phebe gct White Lick MM)

RUSSELL
  (11 mo-1824  George & w Judith & ch Ruth, Sarah, Sina, Timothy, Josiah, George Jr & James rocf Whitewater MM)

  (11 mo-1834  Susanna rocf Whitewater MM)
  2-16-1837   Sinah dt George & Judith, dec, m John Witson at West Grove MH
  9- 9-1837   Josiah, living in the limits of Dover MM which is req to treated with him because of associating with evil companions.
              11-11-1837 Dover MM rpt he chm
              4-14-1837 gct Dover
  10-12-1840  Sarah dt George & Judith, dec, m Samuel Jenkins at West Grove MH
  11-13-1841  George Jr mcd chm
  12-14-1844  George & w Clarissa & ch William & Franklin rec in mbrp
  12-14-1844  James J mcd chm
  4-13-1850   George Jr & fam gct Dover MM
  11- 8-1856  Susannah & fam gct Fairfield MM
  8- 9-1862   Rachel rec in mbrp
  1- 8-1870   Elam & Ruth rec in mbrp
  3- 8-1873   Ruth Ann (now Williams) mcd chm
  7-12-1873   Elvira rec in mbrp
  7-12-1873   Joseph Perry rec in mbrp
  8- 9-1884   Elam gct Indianapolis MM
  5- 9-1885   Perry M rec in mbrp
  11-12-1892  Perry & w Anna rocf Hopewell MM
  3-11-1911   Anna glt U B Ch New Madison, Ohio
  4-14-1917   Oscar drpd from mbrp

SAINTMIRES
  11-14-1857  Margaret Adpline (form Clark) mcd dis

SAMPLE
  4-13-1889   Samuel D & w Mary rec in mbrp
  4-14-1894   Samuel D & w Mary F rel from mbrp

SANDERS
  ( 3 mo-1822  Martha (w Joseph, dis) & ch Elizabeth, Miriam, Hannah, Thomas & Joseph Wills, rocf Westfield MM, Ohio)
  ( 3 mo-1822  Nancy & Mary rocf Westfield MM, Ohio)
  1-10-1885   Samantha & Rette rec in mbrp
  2-10-1894   George & Sarah J rec in mbrp
  9-12-1914   George & Sarah J drpd from mbrp

SARBER
  10-10-1906  Sadie drpd from mbrp

SAVAGE
  7-11-1891   Sarah Jane rec in mbrp
  2-10-1894   Nola rec in mbrp
  1-10-1914   Nola glt U B Ch, Muncie

SCATES
  2- 8-1868   Elizabeth (form Maudlin) mcd dis

SCHLEGEL
  2- 8-1933   Minnie & Luther rol
  3- 8-1933   Glen rec in mbrp

SCOTT
  6-12-1858   Rachel (form Cloud) mcd chm
  12-11-1858  Rachel gct Oak Ridge MM
  5-13-1884   John L rocf Oak Ridge MM

SEYMOUR
  10-10-1885  Catharine & Clara rec in mbrp
  8-11-1888   Catharine & Clara drpd from mbrp
  2-10-1894   Henry & Margaret rec in mbrp

SHANK
  4-10-1875   Daniel rec in mbrp
  2-14-1885   Enos rec in mbrp
  8-11-1888   Enos drpd from mbrp

SHARP
  2-14-1885   William & Melissa rec in mbrp
  8-11-1888   William & Melissa drpd from mbrp

SHAWLEY
  5- 9-1903   Daniel C rocf Dover MM

SHERIDAN
  ( 5 mo-1822  John & fam rocf Springfield MM, Ohio)
  11-21-1822  Hannah dt John & Margaret m Thomas Maudlin at West Grove MH

WEST GROVE

## SHERIDAN (Cont)
( 7 mo-1825  John & w Margaret & ch William, Rachel, George, John Jr, Hannah, Abner, Susanna & Thomas gct Milford MM)

## SHIELDS
( 8 mo-1820  Sarah (form Sanders) rocf Whitewater MM)

## SHOEMAKER
(11 mo-1833  Tacy & Charles, minor ch of Margaret Shoemaker wid (now m to Daniel Williams) rocf New Garden MM)
( 8 mo-1834  Charles, a minor, gct Milford MM)
10-19-1836  Tacy dt Ezekiel, dec, & Margaret m Joshua Murphy at Fairfield MH
6- 9-1838  Charles, a minor, rocf Milford MM
10-16-1839  Charles s Ezekiel, dec, & Margaret m Margaret Ann Ellis at Fairfield MH
3-13-1841  Charles & fam gct Springfield MM
11- 9-1844  Charles & w Margaret Ann & ch Ezekiel, Elijah & Tacy rocf Springfield MM
4- 8-1848  Charles & fam gct Springfield MM
( 4 mo-1887  Amos rocf Springfield MM, Ohio)

## SHOLTY
8-11-1888  Anna drpd from mbrp

## SHOOP
1-10-1885  Menter K rec in mbrp
10-10-1885  Mentor drpd from mbrp

## SIMMONS (Simon)
( 8 mo-1821  William & w Rebekah & dts rocf Lost Creek MM Tenn)
( 9 mo-1824  William & s Solomon & Wm Jr gct Lost Creek MM Tenn)
( 9 mo-1824  Rebekah & dt Mary, Susanna & Elizabeth gct Lost Creek MM, Tenn)
9-13-1913  Mabel rec in mbrp
2-14-1914  Marshal rec in mbrp
2-14-1920  Marshall rel from mbrp
7- 8-1922  Marshall gc

## SLEEPER
10-16-1856  Isaiah H s Jacob & Sarah m Hannah Elliott at West Grove MH
7-11-1857  Hannah E gct Greenfield MM

## SMALL
11-16-1826  Ruth dt Gideon, dec, & Sarah m William Cook at West Grove MH

## SMITH
( 4 mo-1822  Ann rocf Springfield MM, Ohio)
10-18-1838  John s Jirah & Avis m Rebecca Mendenhall at Fairfield MH
12- 8-1838  Rebecca gct Westfield MM
3-11-1848  John & w Rebecca & ch Elihu, Ruthann & Barclay rocf Richland MM
7- 8-1848  John & fam gct Richland MM
3-14-1874  Freeman & w Emily & ch Katy & Nellie rec in mbrp
5- 9-1874  Albert M rec in mbrp
3-11-1882  Amos, Rhoema & Wm rec in mbrp
4- 9-1887  Lewis & Martha J rec in mbrp
4- 9-1887  John & w Mary & ch Catherine, Carrie & Minnie rocf Whitewater MM
5-14-1887  Nicholas rec in mbrp
4-14-1888  Jennie rec in mbrp
3- 9-1889  Lewis & Martha J rel from mbrp
12-14-1889  George & William rec in mbrp
2-14-1891  Mary Ann rocf Whitewater MM
4-14-1894  Nicholas & Florence rel from mbrp
5-12-1894  George & Mattie rel from mbrp
12-12-1896  Fred E rocf Ypsilanti MM, Mich
1- 9-1897  Alice Rays rocf Van Wert MM, Ohio
6- 9-1900  Amanda rocf Whitewater MM
5- 9-1909  Katie rel from mbrp

## SOPER
1- 9-1886  Franklin & Mary rec in mbrp
2-11-1888  Franklin & Mary drpd from mbrp
2-14-1914  Verla rec in mbrp

## SPARROW
5-11-1895  W B & Mary E rec in mbrp
1- 9-1897  Grace rec in mbrp

## SPEEKS
12-11-1897  Margaret rec in mbrp

## SPOTTS
5-10-1919  William & fam rocf West Richmond MM
9-13-1919  William's cert to be returned
5- 8-1920  William & fam cert to be recalled from West Richmond MM
6-12-1920  William & w Sarah Elizabeth & ch Ida M, George W, Edna G, Edith E, Allen F, Lawrence E, Robert V, Mary J & Lola May rocf West Richmond MM
3-14-1925  Sarah & ch gct New Westville MM
2-13-1926  Sarah & ch rocf New Westville MM

## SPRAKER
12-13-1919  Ruby rec in mbrp
4-19-1924  Claud rec in mbrp
11- 4-1928  Ruby glt Cresent Ave Evangelical Ch, Fort Wayne

## SQUIRES
5- 8-1886  Rebecca gct Springfield MM

## STACKHOUSE
2- 9-1884  Samuel rec in mbrp
1-10-1885  Erastus rec in mbrp
2-14-1885  Lucius rec in mbrp
4-14-1888  Philatha rec in mbrp
8-11-1888  Lucius drpd from mbrp
3-14-1896  Maud rec in mbrp
8-14-1897  Erastus drpd from mbrp

## STAFFORD
( 7-31-1817  Samuel s Samuel Sr & Abigail of Whitewater MM m Nancy Hastings dt Wm & Sarah at West Grove MH Whitewater Records)
(11 mo-1818  Certificate for Eli rocf Back Creek MM, NC at Whitewater MM and end to West Grove MM)
3-16-1820  Samuel s Samuel Sr & Abigail m Rachel Hunt at West Grove MH
( 9 mo-1824  Eli & w Elizabeth & ch John & Cynthia gct Milford MM)

## STANLEY
6-10-1848  Delana (now Bond) & ch Mordecai & Susan Stanley rocf Spiceland MM
2- 8-1902  Frank C & w rocf Van Wert MM, Ohio
1-10-1903  Francis & w Sarah A gct West Branch MM, Ohio

## STATTS
2- 8-1890  Oliver & w Mary Ann rocf Dover MM

## STANBROUGH
(11 mo-1821  James & w Mary & ch Isaac, Jonathan & Phebe rocf Center MM, Ohio)

## STEEL
1-10-1885  Clarence, Emma & John rec in mbrp
8- 8-1885  Clarence drpd from mbrp
8-11-1888  Emma drpd from mbrp
8-15-1899  Clara & Emma rec in mbrp
2-10-1900  Clarence & w Emma & ch Earl, Walter & Essie rec in mbrp
3-14-1908  Essie rec in mbrp
9-12-1914  Clara, Essie, Earl & Walter drpd from mbrp

## STEPHENS
3- 9-1877  Walter & w Martha Ann rec in mbrp
12- 9-1899  Belle drpd from mbrp

## STIGLEMAN
12-14-1889  Lafayette rec in mbrp
5-12-1894  Lafayette rel from mbrp

## STOCKWELL
2-13-1892  Edithe rec in mbrp
8-13-1892  John Franklin rec in mbrp

## WEST GROVE

**STRATTON**
( 5 mo-1819  Benjamin & w Amy & ch Levi, Ephraim, Benjamin Jr, Jerusha, Martha, Mary, Joseph & Samuel rocf Middleton MM, Ohio)
( 5 mo-1819  Naomi rocf Middleton MM, Ohio)
( 8 mo-1819  Naomi gct Whitewater MM)
( 8 mo-1821  John rocf Caesars Creek MM, Ohio)
(10 mo-1825  Sarah rocf Goshen MM, Ohio)
( 4 mo-1828  Joseph rocf Springfield MM, Ohio to m Rebecca Harvey)
4-15-1828  Joseph s Joseph & Naomi m Rebecca Harvey, wid of Samuel, & dt of Edward & Margaret Kindley at West Grove MH
( 6 mo-1828  Rebecca with her ch Margaret, Mary, Sarah, Isaac & Davis Harvey gct Springfield MM, Ohio)
2-11-1837  Eli rocf Walnut Ridge MM
3-11-1837  Joseph E rocf Walnut Ridge MM
10-17-1838  Jonathan gct Whitewater MM to m Nancy Morrow
1-12-1839  Eli & w gct Spiceland MM
4-13-1839  Nancy rocf Whitewater MM
5 mo-1839  Whitewater MM granted permission to rst Hannah (Ogborn) Stratton, dis by Whitewater MM 1834
9-12-1840  Ella Maria & Charles Henry ch of Hannah rec in mbrp "with consent of her husband"
4-13-1844  Joseph E gct Whitewater MM
11-14-1846  Joseph E & w Martha H & ch Edward D, Caroline E, & Charles W rocf Whitewater MM
10- 9-1847  Hannah & 2 ch gct Whitewater MM
4-14-1849  Joseph E & fam gct Whitewater MM

**STRAWSER**
8-14-1875  Henry rec in mbrp
8-11-1888  Henry drpd from mbrp

**STRAYER**
10-10-1885  William Jackson rec in mbrp
11-12-1887  Wm Jackson drpd from mbrp

**STUART**
4-15-1844  Robert s Jehu & Sarah m Rachel Maudlin at West Grove MH

**STUBBS**
2- 9-1878  Alvin rocf Spiceland MM
8-11-1883  Alvin gct Dublin MM

**STUTSON**
12-14-1889  Charles & Sarah rec in mbrp

**SULTINE**
5- 8-1886  Carrie & s Rollie rec in mbrp

**SUMNERS**
3-14-1840  Eliza (form Albertson) mcd & j (H) dis

**SWAIN**
8- 9-1902  Jeb rocf Cherry Grove MM

**SYMONS**
( 1 mo-1819  Cert rec for Mathew & w Sarah & s Mathew Jr & dts from Marlborough MM, NC rec at Whitewater MM & end to West Grove MM)
( 1 mo-1819  Cert for Thomas & w Abigail rec from Marlborough MM, NC at Whitewater MM & end to West Grove MM)
( 4 mo-1820  Abraham & w Mary & fam rocf Whitewater MM)
12-13-1820  Matthew s Matthew Sr & Sarah m Ruth Lacey at West Union MH
5-23-1822  John s Abraham & Mary m Rebecca Bell at Milford MH
( 1823  Thomas & w Abigail & ch Rebecca & Henry W gct Milford MM)

**SYMORE**
8-11-1895  Wallace rec in mbrp

**TAGGART**
4-28-1836  Robert Fisk s Ebenezer F & Mary Ann m Margaret Ann Clawson at the residence of Jonathan Clawson in Tennessee
8-15-1899  Maggie drpd from mbrp

**TAGUE**
2-14-1914  Gertrude rec in mbrp
7-15-1918  Gertrude drpd from mbrp

**TALBERT**
8 mo-1848  Alvan rocf Silver Creek MM to m Rebecca Ellis
10-16-1848  Alvan C s William & Miriam m Rebecca Ellis at Fairfield MH
2-10-1849  Rebecca gct Silver Creek MM

**TAYLOR**
9-12-1891  Elizabeth rocf Whitewater MM
8-13-1892  Charles rec in mbrp
2-13-1897  Elizabeth gct Whitewater MM

**TEAS**
8-15-1899  Sarah A & Fred E rocf Indianapolis MM
2-10-1900  Fred E m Estele Manley at the home of Wm F Manley
7-12-1902  Sarah A gct 8th Street Ch, Richmond
10- 8-1904  Fred E & Estelle & s Amos H gct Dublin MM
9-10-1910  Fred E & w Estelle & s Amos rocf Dublin MM
5-14-1921  Fred E & fam gct Memorial Friends Ch, Seattle, Washington

**TERRY**
1-11-1913  Eva rolf Christian Ch Centerville

**THOMAS**
8-11-1838  Luzena Jane (form Bundy) mcd dis
4- 9-1842  Levi, a minor, rocf West Branch MM, Ohio

**THORN**
( 5 mo-1835  Ezra & Benjamin, ch Benjamin Sr rocf Whitewater MM)
9- 8-1838  Ezra mcd dis
9-14-1839  Ruth rocf Chester MM, NJ & end by Whitewater MM
3-14-1840  Ruth (now Dudley) mcd dis
11-13-1841  Benjamin mcd & na dis
9 mo-1843  Mary dt Benjamin Sr rocf Whitewater MM
7-11-1855  Jonathan J rocf Cornwall MM
8-15-1855  Jonathan J s Jonathan Sr & Cornelia m Margaretta Williams at Fairfield MH
12-11-1858  Jonathan J & fam gct Dover MM
1-10-1885  Salina rec in mbrp

**THORNBERRY**
(11 mo-1822  Clarissa rocf Union MM, Ohio)
( 6 mo-1833  Clarissa gct White Lick MM)

**THORNBURGH**
( 6 mo-1820  Henry & w Rebecca & ch John, Elizabeth, Milton, Eunice & Hannah rocf Whitewater MM)
( 1822  Henry & w Rebecca & ch John, Elizabeth, Milton, Eunice & Hannah gct Milford MM)
2-20-1839  Ezekiel rocf Spiceland MM
3-14-1840  Ezekiel mcd chm
10-14-1843  Ezekiel & fam gct Richland MM
2-14-1885  Martin rec in mbrp
8-13-1887  Martin L rel from mbrp
4- 8-1899  James rec in mbrp

**TIBBITS**
1-11-1896  Ina rec in mbrp

**TIMBERLAKE**
8- 9-1902  Mary O & dt Martha Helen gct Whitewater MM

**TIPIN**
5- 8-1886  Kate rel from mbrp

**TOMLINSON**
( 3 mo-1822  Robert & w Lydia & s Milton rocf Springfield MM, NC & end by Newberry MM, Ohio)
( 1823  Robert & fam gct White Lick MM)

**TOMS**
11- 9-1895  Anderson & w Mary & ch Joseph, Leland & Eva rocf Bloomingdale MM

TOWNSEND
(prior to 1823) James & w Rosannah & ch Thomas, Celah, Charlotte, Isaac, Hannah, David & Rachel rocf -------, Ohio (In 1823 a dt Elizabeth was b & died & was buried in West Grove burying ground)
(12 mo-1826) John & Elvira & ch Barbara & Stephen rocf Whitewater MM)
7-17-1828 Thomas s James & Rosannah m Mary Hastings at West Grove MH
4-14-1831 Celia dt James & Rosannah m Needham Reece at West Grove MH
( 4 mo-1831) Jonathan & w Mary & ch Daniel, Mahlon, Amos, Stephen, Rebecca & William rocf Whitewater MM)
( 4 mo-1832) William & w Elizabeth & ch Eli, Mary, Sarah, Elvira, Lydia, John M, Eliza Ann & Esther rocf Whitewater MM)
11-19-1835 Stephen s John & Elvirah m Mary Griffin at West Grove MH
( 4 mo-1836) John & w Elvira & dt Barbara gct Chester MM)
10-14-1837 Isaac con mcd da upl
5-12-1838 Thomas & fam gct Walnut Ridge MM
2- 9-1839 John & w Elvira & dt Barbara rocf Chester MM
3- 9-1839 Eli mcd dis
4-13-1839 Stephen & w Mary & dt Elvira rocf White River MM
5-16-1839 David s James & Rosannah m Sydney Maudlin at West Grove MH
1-11-1840 Isaac dis for dp & upl
8- 8-1840 Rachel (form Moore) rocf Chester MM
2-11-1843 David & fam gct Westfield MM
6-10-1843 Eli & w Rachel & ch Hiram & Elizabeth gct Chester MM
1-18-1844 William s John & Elvira m Lydia Wickersham at West Grove MH, West Grove MM
2- 8-1845 Thomas & w Mary & ch Nancy, Elisha James & Isaac rocf Walnut Ridge MM
4- 8-1848 Thomas & fam gct Westfield MM
12-11-1847 Charlotte (now Hunt) mcd chm
6-10-1848 John Sr & fam gct Chester MM
9- 9-1848 Elvirah Jr gct Chester MM
2-10-1849 Lydia W gct Milford MM
7-14-1849 Lydia & Eliza Ann gct Elk MM, Ohio
4-14-1853 Elvira dt Stephen & Mary m Luke Woodard at West Grove MH
8-13-1853 John M mcd chm
11-11-1854 Esther (now Haworth) mcd chm
8- 9-1856 James mcd dis
9-13-1856 Stephen & fam gct East Grove MM, Iowa
11-14-1857 Elvira Sr gct West Branch MM, Ohio
11-14-1857 Hannah gct Vermilion MM, Ill
10-19-1858 Elizabeth rec in mbrp
11-13-1858 Albert, Joel, Rawley (Raleigh) & Wm C ch John M & Elizabeth rec in mbrp
4-12-1873 Albert gct Sugar Plain MM
1875 Joel gct Sugar Plain MM to m Abigail Albertson
6-10-1876 Joel gct Sugar Plain MM
7-14-1877 Raleigh W & w Dina Ann gct Springdale MM, Iowa
12-14-1889 Frank drpd from mbrp
9-12-1891 Oliver gct Poplar Run MM
8- 8-1896 Ellen gct New Garden MM
3-10-1906 Albert & s Murray gct Gate MM, Oklahoma
11-12-1910 Harvey gct Springfield MM
3- 8-1924 Olive & dt Nellie & minor ch Mary Elizabeth & Robert rocf Economy MM

TREMPS
2-10-1894 Andy & w Mary rec in mbrp
5-11-1895 Laura, Dora & Earnest rec in mbrp
11-10-1900 Callie & Cora rec in mbrp
12- 8-1905 Mary R & Nellie R rec in mbrp
10-12-1907 Lois Cramer rolf Locust Grove Meth Ch
12-12-1908 Laura E glt Meth Ch Olathe, Kansas
3-11-1911 Floyd rec in mbrp
2- 8-1919 A C & Mary rel from mbrp
12-13-1919 Ethel & Harold rec in mbrp

TULL
2-13-1892 Hiram W & Minnie rec in mbrp

TURNER
7-14-1888 Emma gct White River MM

UNDERHILL
1 mo-1837 Hannah rocf Silver Creek MM
5- 4-1864 Mary (now Brown) mcd chm
10-14-1868 Olive dt Alfred & Hannah m Arthur Brooks at Fairfield MH
5- 8-1886 Rebecca Ann gct Dover MM
3-13-1897 Iva Lee rolf Presby Ch, Hagerstown
8-12-1805 India rel from mbrp

UNTHANK
1- 9-1904 Anna R C rocf Whitewater MM
4-14-1917 Anna R drpd from mbrp

VEAL
7-11-1846 Harriett (form Benbow) mcd & j U B dis

VENARD
4- 9-1887 Ruth rocf Whitewater MM
2-14-1891 Ruth rocf Whitewater MM

VORIS
9-10-1892 Oliver L rec in mbrp
10- 8-1892 Carrie rocf Chester MM

WAGNER
2-10-1894 Alfred N & Cora rec in mbrp
1-11-1896 Alphius & w gct Anderson MM

WALTERS
9-12-1885 John rocf New Garden MM
5-15-1912 John R s --------- m Louie Pearl Williams West Grove MM
7-13-1912 Walter & Pearl W gct Scipio MM, NY

WANN
10-10-1885 Ferdinan rec in mbrp
7-11-1891 Ferdinan drpd from mbrp

WARD
( 3 mo-1821) John & w Hannah Ann rocf Miami MM, Ohio)
( 9 mo-1822) Obed & w Mary & ch Susanna, Timothy, George & Rachel rocf Clear Creek MM, Ohio)
(12 mo-1822) Grace, step-mother of Obed, rocf Clear Creek MM, Ohio)
3- 5-1878 Emanuel rocf Poplar Run MM

WARMSLEY
8- 8-1896 Grace glt Meth Ch, Whitcomb

WASSON
7-14-1838 Calvin & s Nathan, William & Calvin Jr rocf Spiceland MM
8- 8-1840 Calvin & w Mary & ch gct Clear Creek MM, Ohio

WAY
5-12-1834 Solomon s Paul & Lavina m Mary Hodson at Fairfield MH

WEDDELL
12-12-1874 Rebecca rec in mbrp

WEISER
3-11-1911 Esther & Marion rec in mbrp
10-12-1912 Esther glt Meth Ch, Centerville
2-14-1914 Esther rolf Meth Ch, Centerville
2-14-1914 Florence rec in mbrp

WEST
12- 8-1883 William & w Mary Ann & ch Enos & Caroline, also Addie Lewis, a minor in their care, rocf Caesars Creek MM, Ohio
4- 9-1892 William & w Mary Ann gct Van Wert MM, Ohio
12- 8-1894 William & w Mary rocf Van Wert MM, Ohio
12-12-1896 William & w Mary gct Whitewater MM
4- 8-1899 Enos D glt Edward Ray Meth Ch, Indianapolis

WELCH
11-12-1832 Samuel Sr s John & Mary, dec, m Rachel Williams dt Richard & Susannah Kemp at West Grove MH
5-11-1833 Rachel gct Miami MM, Ohio

WEST GROVE

34

## WHITACRE (Whitaker)
| | |
|---|---|
| 1- 9-1841 | John rocf White River MM |
| 2-13-1841 | Bethula & ch Christopher, Susannah, Mary, Martha, Calvin & Rachel rocf White River MM |
| 3-13-1841 | Ephraim, White River MM rq this to treat for att places of diversion & dancing. 4-10-1841 con his misc, White River inf. 8-14-1841 rocf White River MM |
| 4- 8-1843 | Ephraim dis for na, dp & shooting for property at stake (1842 resided limits of Elk MM, Ohio. 1843 rpt moved to Iowa) |
| ( 1-14-1843 | John h of Bethula gct Elk MM, Ohio) |
| ( 1-14-1843 | Bethula & ch Christopher, Susanna, Mary, Martha, Calvin & Rachel gct Elk MM, Ohio) |

## WHITE
| | |
|---|---|
| ( 8 mo-1822 | Rebecca & ch rocf Hopewell MH, New Garden MM, NC) |
| 3- 9-1839 | Exum & w Ann & ch Margaret S, Joseph, Jesse T, Harriet & John G & also Thomas White, a minor in their care, rocf Spiceland MM |
| 8- 8-1840 | Thomas N gct Spiceland MM |
| 5-13-1843 | Ann & fam gct Hopewell MM |
| 2-12-1848 | Ann & dt Lydia & Deborah King rocf Walnut Ridge MM |
| 10-12-1850 | Elizabeth Ann dt Ann Benbow, rec in mbrp at req of parent |
| 4-17-1851 | George B s Robert & Rebecca, both dec, m Eliza Griffin at West Grove MM |
| 4 mo-1851 | Martha N wid, m Reuben Chappell of West Grove MM at Spiceland MM |
| 11- 8-1851 | Elizabeth Ann, minor dt of Ann Benbow, now the w of Evan Benbow, gct Honey Creek MM |
| 8-14-1852 | George B rocf Walnut Ridge MM |
| 8- 8-1857 | George B & fam gct East Grove MM, Iowa |
| 3-14-1885 | William rec in mbrp |
| 8-11-1888 | William drpd from mbrp |
| 11- 9-1889 | Elihu & w Rebecca & ch Ross & Pearl rocf Dover MM |
| 2-14-1891 | Rebecca & ch Ross & Pearl rel from mbrp |
| 3-14-1891 | Elihu dis for procuring property under false pretenses |
| 4-11-1891 | John rec in mbrp |
| 7-10-1897 | David drpd from mbrp |

## WHITSON
| | |
|---|---|
| 2-16-1837 | John s Willis, dec, & Rebecca m Sinah Russell at West Grove MH |
| 1837 | Sinah gct Dover MM) |

## WICKERSHAM
| | |
|---|---|
| (12- 4-1817 | Mary dt Jehu & Mary m Wright Maudlin at West Grove MH, Whitewater MM records) |
| 5-22-1824 | Sarah dt Jehu & Mary m Jacob Griffin at West Grove MH |
| 10-28-1824 | Rachel dt Jehu & Mary m William Kirk at West Grove MH |
| 1-14-1843 | Lydia rocf Deer Creek MM |
| 1-18-1844 | Lydia dt Jesse, dec, & Phebe m William Townsend at West Grove MH |
| 9- 8-1849 | Calvin dis for dp att mcd |
| 11-10-1849 | Eliza Ann (now Norman) mcd dis |
| 4- 8-1854 | Isom mcd chm |
| 2- 9-1856 | Sarah Jane (now Kitterman) mcd dis |
| 1-10-1857 | Eli mcd dis |
| 12-12-1857 | Isom gct Richland MM |
| 3-10-1860 | Mary H (now Maudlin) mcd chm |
| 4-14-1860 | Isom rocf Richland MM |
| 5-10-1862 | John mcd dis |
| 7-11-1863 | Isom dis for na, pl & att pd |
| 3-11-1871 | Alpheus G mcd dis |
| 7-10-1875 | Isom rst in mbrp |
| 8-14-1875 | Isom gct Richland MM (cert ret because he was a member of ODD FELLOWS) |
| 3-10-1877 | Isom gct Richland MM |

## WIDOWS
| | |
|---|---|
| 10- 9-1847 | William Sr rec in mbrp |
| 5-17-1848 | William Sr m Esther Ogborn at Fairfield MH |

## WILLETS
| | |
|---|---|
| 4-14-1819 | Brady M s Isaac & Rachel, dec, m Susannah Lacey at West Union MH |
| (11 mo-1828 | Henry & w Mary & ch Jonathan & Mary rocf Chester MM) |
| 5-18-1831 | Henry s Gabriel & Priscilla, dec, m Rachel Murphy at Fairfield MH |

## WILLIAMS
| | |
|---|---|
| ( 7 mo-1823 | Jesse & w Sarah & minor s Jesse rocf Whitewater MM) |
| ( 7 mo-1823 | Sarah T & Elizabeth D rocf Whitewater MM) |
| (11 mo-1825 | Matilda w of Caleb & ch Henry, Luzena, Salina & Merchant rocf Whitewater MM) |
| ( 1 mo-1825 | Joshua & w Hannah rocf Whitewater MM) |
| ( 3 mo-1826 | Jesse gct Whitewater MM) |
| ( 5 mo-1827 | Mary w of John & ch Jehiel, John, Lillian rocf Whitewater MM) |
| (10 mo-1831 | Rachel rocf Dover MM, Ohio) |
| 11-12-1832 | Rachel dt Richard & Susannah Kemp m Samuel Welch at West Grove MH |
| (11 mo-1833 | Daniel & w Margaret & ch Lydia, Rebecca, Nathan H, Solomon, Jesse B, Jacob & Margaret Williams & Tacy & Charles Shoemaker rocf New Garden MM) |
| 11-12-1834 | Lydia dt Daniel & Margaret m Joel W Hiatt at Fairfield MH |
| 1-14-1835 | Rebecca dt Daniel & Margaret m Silas W Bond at Fairfield MH |
| 12-15-1836 | Absalom s John & Mary m Mary Williams at West Grove MH |
| 12-15-1836 | Mary, wid of John & dt of Joseph & Lydia Cook m Absalom Williams at West Grove MH |
| 4-17-1837 | Isaac s Owen & Catherine, dec, m Anna Cloud at West Grove MH |
| (10 mo-1837 | Ann gct New Garden MM) |
| 10-16-1839 | Susannah dt Daniel & Margaret m John Murphy at Fairfield MH |
| 10-10-1840 | Matilda dis |
| 11-14-1840 | Jehiel gct Westfield MM |
| 6-11-1842 | Nathan H dis for mcd & j Meth Ch |
| 11-13-1844 | Solomon s Daniel & Margaret m Margaret Murphy at Fairfield MH |
| 7-12-1845 | Achilles & w Beulah & ch Robert, Martha Ann, Sarah & Caroline rocf Whitewater MM |
| 7-12-1845 | Zalinda rocf Whitewater MM |
| 8- 9-1845 | Jesse H gct Springfield MM to m Mary Ann Mendenhall |
| 5- 9-1846 | Mary Ann rocf Springfield MM |
| 10-12-1846 | Zalinda dt Achilles & Beulah m Wilson Hobbs at West Grove MH, West Grove MM |
| 2-17-1847 | Mary dt Daniel & Margaret m Elwood Albertson at Fairfield MH (West Grove MM) |
| 12-11-1847 | Nancy dis for unchastity |
| 7- 8-1848 | Daniel gct Cornwall MM, NY to m Lydia Rider |
| 11-11-1848 | Lydia R rocf Cornwall MM, NY |
| 5-12-1849 | Jacob gct New Garden MM |
| 10-15-1849 | Sarah dt Daniel & Margaret, dec, m William Hunt at Fairfield MH |
| 6-14-1851 | John gct Spiceland MM to m Eunice Street |
| 11- 8-1851 | Martha Ann (now Yoe) mcd chm |
| 5- 8-1852 | Jesse B & fam gct Poplar Run MM |
| 10-13-1853 | Daniel Jr s Daniel & Margaret, dec, m Cynthia Ann Haworth at West Grove MH |
| 11-10-1855 | Achilles & fam gct Whitewater MM |
| 8-15-1855 | Margaretta, dt Daniel & Margaret, dec, m Jonathan Thorn at Fairfield MH |
| 2-12-1856 | Robert gct Whitewater MM |
| 7-12-1862 | Ellen (now Edgerton) mcd chm |
| 4- 8-1865 | Cynthia Ann & fam gct Plainfield MM |
| 3-10-1866 | Ann (form Cook) mcd chm |
| 2- 9-1868 | Cynthia Ann & fam rocf Plainfield MM |
| 8-14-1869 | Emmaline (now Pollard) mcd chm |
| 5-13-1871 | Charles mcd chm |
| 7- 8-1871 | Mary E rec in mbrp |
| 5-11-1872 | Solomon & fam gct Hinkles Creek MM |
| 3- 8-1873 | Alpheus mcd chm |
| 3- 8-1873 | Ruthann (form Russell) mcd chm |
| 6-14-1873 | Alpheus & w Ruthann gct Hinkles Creek MM |
| 3-14-1874 | Charles & fam gct Sugar Plain MM |
| 12-12-1874 | Elizabeth H rec in mbrp |
| 5- 8-1880 | Ruthann & ch Perry, Mertie & Alonzo rocf Sugar River MM |
| 10- 8-1881 | Charles & dt gct Richland MM |
| 10-13-1883 | Alpheus rec in mbrp |
| 12- 8-1883 | Louella, a minor under the care of Enos Wilson, rocf Caesars Creek MM, Ohio |
| 8-11-1888 | Alpheus & w Ruthann & ch drpd from mbrp |

WEST GROVE

WILLIAMS (Cont)
- 7-11-1891  Lafayette rec in mbrp
- 8- 8-1891  Lizzie rocf Carthage MM
- 11-14-1891  Emma rocf Whitewater MM
- 2-13-1892  Albert, Nettie, Josie & Sallie rec in mbrp
- 2-13-1892  Arthur H, Wistar H & Albert Ross ch Albert & Lizzie rec in mbrp
- 2-13-1892  Robert E & Mildred S ch Lafayette & Emma rec in mbrp
- 11-12-1892  Albert F & w Lizzie & ch Arthur H, Wistar P & Albert Ross gct Spiceland MM
- 10-13-1894  King R & fam gct Whitewater MM
- 9- 9-1899  Lafayette & fam gct Marion MM
- 10-13-1906  Dillon H gct Georgetown MM, Ill
- 11-12-1910  Pearl rocf Marion MM
- 5-15-1912  Louella m John R Walter at West Grove MM

WILSON
- 5-23-1822  Ruth dt John & Dinah m Wiley Reagan at Milford MH
- (11 mo-1825  Samuel & w Keziah & ch Sarah, Millicent, Elizabeth, John, Lydia, Nathan, Martha & James rocf Whitewater MM)
- (12 mo-1825  Joseph rocf Whitewater MM)
- 10-14-1837  John dis for na & mcd at a Hicksite mtg
- 6- 9-1838  Hannah (form Bond) dis for mcd & na
- 8-14-1841  Nathan dis for mcd & na
- 5-14-1842  Martha (now Honn) dis for mcd & jas
- 5-11-1844  James mcd & na dis
- 5- 8-1880  Amos rocf Caesars Creek MM, Ohio
- 12- 8-1883  Enos rocf Caesars Creek MM, Ohio with a minor, Louella Williams, under his care

WIMMER
- 8-14-1873  Tabitha Ann (form Harris) mcd chm
- 9-13-1873  Tabitha Ann gct Oak Ridge MM

WINSLOW
- ( 4 mo-1822  Sarah rocf Blue River MM)
- (12 mo-1826  Sarah gct Blue River MM)

WISE
- 4-14-1888  John rec in mbrp
- 5-12-1894  John & Jessie rel in mbrp

WISEHART
- 12-14-1859  James P rec in mbrp

WISER
- 12- 9-1911  Marion F rel from mbrp

WISSLER
- ?  Laurence & w Stella rec in mbrp

WOLF
- 11-13-1841  Charity (form Commons) mcd dis

WOLLAM
- 9-12-1909  Hiram S & w Emma & s Roy rocf Union MM
- 8-10-1912  Hiram S a memorial read
- 9- 9-1918  Roy H gct Spiceland MM

WOOD
- 8-11-1888  Emma rec in mbrp
- 3-11-1916  Alonzo H & Ethel rec in mbrp
- 9-10-1926  Alonzo drpd from mbrp
- 9-10-1926  Ethel drpd from mbrp

WOODARD
- 4-14-1853  Luke s Cader & Rachel, dec, m Elvira Townsend at West Grove MH
- 8-13-1853  Elvira gct New Garden MM

WORL
- 8-11-1888  Miriam drpd from mbrp

WRIGHT
- 4-13-1844  William Jr of Fairfield PM mcd chm
- 2- 8-1845  Celia Ann (now Kem) mcd & na dis
- 6-13-1846  Edward mcd & na dis
- 5-14-1853  Jacob mcd chm
- 4- 9-1864  Jacob rocf Whitewater MM
- 7-10-1875  Jacob rel from mbrp
- 12-10-1930  Paul K & w LaVerne & ch rocf Walnut Ridge MM
- 11- 9-1932  Paul K & fam gc

WRIGLEY
- 7-11-1908  Lorena rec in mbrp

WYCOFF
- 3-11-1916  Samuel rec in mbrp

YATES
- ( 9 mo-1818  Patrick & Enos, minors gct New Garden MM)
- ( 9 mo-1818  Mary & ch Charles, Elizabeth & Caroline gct New Garden MM)
- ( 6 mo-1820  Mary & ch Charles, Elizabeth & Caroline rocf New Garden MM)

YOE
- 11- 8-1851  Martha Ann (form Williams) con mcd
- 5- 8-1852  Martha Ann gct Caesars Creek MM, Ohio

ZERING
- 8-10-1895  Edward B & w Mary E & ch Dora L, Frank H, Earl L, Ira E & Glen E rocf Knightstown MM
- 5-12-1900  Edward & fam gct Farmland MM

ZOOK
- 4- 8-1865  Achsah rocf New Garden MM

# MILFORD MONTHLY MEETING
## Wayne County, Indiana

Milford Monthly Meeting was set-off from West Grove Monthly Meeting and first held on the 17th of Seventh Month 1823.

William H. Coffin wrote in the Milton News, February 5, 1903: "Thomas Symons, of Symons Creek, North Carolina, married my aunt, Hannah Coffin, and removed to the Whitewater country, Indiana Territory, in 1811, stopping a short time at the Cox settlement where Richmond now is.

"The Twelve Mile Purchase having just come in, he cut his way through the woods 15 miles west, and was the first settler on West River, one-half mile north of where Milton now is . . .

"They . . . built a hewed log meeting house on the southeast part of Symons' land, which soon after became the center of a large body of Friends . . . "

A few years later a frame house was built. All that now remains (1972) are a few foundation stones. As is indicated above the meeting was located one-half mile north of the village of Milton.

The monthly meeting consisted of several preparative meetings, namely, Milford; West Union laid down in 1829; Bethel established 1825 and laid down 1878 and the following were established and later set-off as monthly meetings **Duck Creek** (1826); **Hopewell** (1841); **Rich Square** (set-off with Hopewell in 1841); and **Dublin** (1874).

The center of the meeting moved to Dublin and by 1882 monthly meeting was regularly held there and the name was changed to Dublin Monthly Meeting. Meetings at Milford had been discontinued for sometime prior to that date.

## Monthly Meeting Records

The volumes listed below are in the vault of the Indiana Yearly Meetinghouse in Richmond. The material searched for this publication is marked (*). They have been microfilmed. It is assumed later records are in the care of Dublin Monthly Meeting.

Men's Minutes

7-17-1823 :  6-27-1835*
7-25-1835 :  3-22-1845*
4-26-1845 : 11-26-1864*
12-24-1864 : 1-25-1894*

Women's Minutes

7-17-1823 :  9-24-1842*
10-22-1842 : 12-24-1864*
1-28-1865 : 12-25-1890*
(from 1890 meetings were held jointly)

1 Volume of Birth & Death Records*
Marriage Record 1823 - 1881*
Removal Certificates 1832-1888*

MILFORD MONTHLY MEETING
BIRTH AND DEATH RECORD

ADAMSON
Mordecai      b 1-30-1798    -s John & Mary
Susan (form Peck) of Tenn
Ch: Adam              b 10-23-1823
    Peter             b  1- 7-1828
    Catharine         b  6-13-1830
    John              b  6- 8-1832
    Eliza             b  5-30-1835

ALLEN
James L       b  6-11-1824
Lucy          b  9-18-1824    -dt Joshua & Margaret Waring
Ch: Maria Jane        b 12-14-1845
    Anna Rosella      b  6-14-1847
    Margaret          b  6- 3-1849
    Joseph P          b  1-16-1852
    Hiram             b  7-14-1854

John          b 11- 5-1809    -s Hugh & Frances
Rachel        b  6-16-1809    -dt Esther Newby
Ch: Esther            b 11- 8-1831
    Mary              b  4- 2-1833
    Elizabeth         b  4-12-1835

BALES
Thomas                        -s John & Mary (dec)
Nancy                         -dt Samuel & Susannah Stanley
Ch: Lemuel            b 12-29-1822
    Mary              b  6-21-1828
    Daniel            b 12- 5-1830

BELL
Jesse         b  3-26-1812    d 11- 3-1839
              -s John & Lydia
Penelope      b  8-10-1814    d  8-24-1867
              -dt Elias & Jane Henley of Duck Creek MM
Ch: Jephthah          b 10-22-1834    d  3- 9-1862
    Lydia Jane        b  6-15-1836
    Mary Ann          b 10-11-1838    d  1-10-1840

John          b  2- 7-1768    -s Lancelot & Miriam (Nichol-
              d 12- 2-1839, Milford MM, Ind       son)
              m 12-30-1789, Pasquotauk MM, N C
Sarah (1st w) b  6-17-1770    d  6-11-1806, Pasquotauk MM,
              -dt Josiah & Mary (Symons) Bundy     N C
Ch: Lancelot          b 11- 3-1790
    Miriam            b  8- 5-1795
    Josiah            b  1-11-1798
    Sarah             b  1-16-1800
    Thomas            b  4-17-1802
    Rebecca           b  4-27-1804
Lydia (2nd w) b 4-24-1780  d 9-26-1843, Milford MM, Ind
              -dt Jesse & Sarah (Bundy) Symons
              m 2-19-1809, Pasquotauk MM, N C
Ch: Margaret          b  5- 6-1810
    Jesse             b  3-26-1812
    Abigail           b  1-14-1814
    Lydia             b  3-11-1816
    Martha            b  1-29-1818

John C        b  7- 7-1827    d 11-21-1885
              -s Jonah & Abigail
Eliza         b  7-23-1835    m 12-31-1851
              -dt Jonathan & Amelia Elliott
Ch: Charles W         b  2-23-1853    d  3-18-1854
    Mary J            b  5-11-1856
    Alfred W          b  8-11-1858
    Samuel C          b  6-26-1861
    Oliver C          b  9-29-1864
    Anna              b  2- 5-1867    d 1879
    Emma              b 10-16-1869
    Harriett A        b  6-24-1872
    Abigail O         b 10-24-1874    d 1879
    Eliza Ellen       b 10-30-1880

MILFORD

Josiah        b  1-11-1798    d  9-10-1886
              -s John & 1st wife, Sarah
Abigail       b  1- 5-1801    d 12- 8-1889
              -dt Samuel & Gulielma Charles
Ch: Gulielma          b  9-27-1825
    John              b  7- 7-1827
    Rebecca           b  3- 5-1830
    Caroline          b  8- 8-1832

Lancelot      b 11- 3-1790    d 10-19-1875
              -s John & 1st wife, Sarah
Mary          b  7- 7-1802    d  8- 4-1837
              -dt Jonathan & Elizabeth Justice
Ch: Daniel            b  9-25-1819    d  6-11-1860
    Sarah             b  3-24-1821    d 11-12-1893
    Stephen           b  3-30-1823    d 12-29-1823
    John J            b  3-30-1825    d  3-17-1879
    Irena             b 11-18-1827    d  5- 8-1853
    David             b  9-21-1833    d  7-23-1884

Thomas        b  4-17-1802    d 11-24-1878
              -s John & 1st wife, Sarah
Jerusha       b  1-25-1808    d  7-26-1837
              -dt Benjamin & Anny Stratton
Ch: Martha            b 11-25-1829
    Sarah             b  2-20-1832    d  1-22-1880
    Margaret          b  7- 8-1834    d  2- 7-1865
    Eliza             b  9-26-1836    d  1- 5-1838

BENNETT
Solomon                       -s Matthew (dec) & Ruth ( now Ruth Hester
                                                          by 2nd m)
Mary                          -dt Evan & Elizabeth Stambaugh
Ch: Elizabeth         b  8-13-1834

BINFORD
James                         -s Joshua & Lydia (both dec)
Rachel                        -dt Joseph & Elizabeth Cox
                              (Widow of a Patterson)
Ch: Joseph C          b  5-28-1861    d  7- 4-1862
    Elizabeth A       b  1-12-1863

Samuel B                      -s Samuel & Mary (both dec) of Va
Ann J         b 11-13-1813    m  3-28-1833
              -dt James S & Deborah Butler
Ch: Deborah Ann       b 12-23-1833    d  9-15-1838
    Mary S            b  8-25-1835
    William P         b  9-17-1837

BOGUE
Aaron         b 1790          d 1855  -s Job (dec) & Elizabeth
Elizabeth     b 1797          d 1879  -dt ... Evans
Ch: Benjamin          b  8-19-1821
    William O         b 12-28-1825
    Sarahann          b  5-17-1829

Benjamin                      -s Samuel & Elizabeth
Milly
Ch: Anna              b  6-27-1829    d  9-14-1850
    Silas             b  7-31-1830
    Huldah            b 10- 3-1831
    Samuel            b  1- 3-1834
    Joshua            b  7- 3-1838
    Allen             b  2- 1-1840
    Asenath           b 11-27-1841
    Newby             b 10-14-1845
    Mary E            b  6-15-1848
    Joseph D          b  4-20-1850

BOND
Edward        b  3- 8-1800    -s Benjamin & Mary
Ann           b 10-21-1803    -dt Henry & Elizabeth
                                  Hayworth
Ch: Lucinda           b  8- 8-1828
    Athlinda          b  6- 6-1830
    Jediah            b  4-16-1832
    Benjamin Frank    b  1-30-1834 (or 2-30-1836)

MILFORD

BOON
Driver           =s John Sr & Dorcas
                 m 4-22-1819, Springfield MM, N C
Anna (Kersey)    =a widow
Ch: Rachel
    Rhoda
    Rebecca
    Sampson
    Irena

BOSWELL
Ruth       =a minister    d 1-21-1833, =ae 81yr,3mo
           (Widow of Zadock Boswell)

BROTHERS
Nathan     =s Durent & Sarah   m 3-14-1844, Deep River
Abagail    b 9- -1816                     MM, N C
           =dt Jesse & Mary Moore
Ch: Mary Ann          b 1- 8-1845
    Sarah Roxanna     b 2- 9-1847
    Rebecca Amanda    b 7- 9-1849
    Melissa Jane      b 1-18-1852
    Mariah Elma       b 3-26-1854
    Joel G            b 7- 4-1857
    Ira S             b 9-19-1859

BROWN
Isaac      b 2-16-1809   =s James & Mary
Sarah      b 2-11-1812   =dt Harmon & Hannah Davis
Ch: Martha           b 6-28-1832

James J    b 2-14-1776   =s James Sr & Martha
Mary       b 7- 2-1780   =dt Seth & Lydia Huddleston
Ch: Rebecca          b 12-22-1802
    John             b 4-15-1804
    Sarah            b 3- 2-1806
    Isaac            b 2-16-1809
    Phebe            b 10-16-1811
    James            b 8-19-1813
    Seth             b 3-28-1815
    Eli              b 12- 5-1816
    Mary             b 2-28-1819
    William          b 4-30-1821    d 7-19-1836

James Jr   b 8-19-1813   =s James & Mary
Ruth       b 4-15-1810   =dt Jeremiah & Deborah Mills
Ch: Deborah          b 1-18-1836
    John             b 3-24-1837

BUNDY
George     =s Josiah & Mary   b 8-16-1781   d 1837
           m 10- 6-1804, Perquimans MM, N C
Sarah (1st w) =dt ... Moore   d 5- 1-1811, N C
Ch: Margaret         b 6-29-1805    d 6-14-1857
    Samuel Moore     b 9- 2-1808
    Sarah            b 4-24-1811
    George           b 4-24-1811
Keron (2nd w) b 3-15-1788 =dt Abraham & Julia Elliott
           m 7- 1-1815, Perquimans MM, N C
Ch: Mary             b 8-23-1819
    Josiah           b 4-21-1823
    Catharine        b 7-23-1826

Jesse      b 8- 5-1803   d 9-16-1873
           =s Benjamin (dec) & Sarah
Rachel     =dt Francis & Mary (dec) Hester
           b 1- 4-1807   d 12- 2-1872
Ch: Benjamin         b 4-25-1826
    Martha           b 4-16-1828
    Mary             b 3-17-1830
    Sarah            b 4-30-1832
    Jonathan         b 6-24-1834
    William H        b 10- 7-1836
    Francis          b 4-22-1839
(There were 5 more ch)

Josiah Jr  b 11-11-1786   =s Josiah & Mary
Huldah (1st w) b 11-15-1779 d 2- 1-1811, Perquimans MM,
           =dt Joseph & Mary Jones            N C
Ch: Huldah           b 1-17-1811

Mary (2nd w) b 9-28-1794  =dt Nathan & Mary Morris
           m 9-22-1813, Perquimans Co, N C
Ch: Miriam           b 6-30-1816
    Susannah         b 2-24-1818
    Nathan           b 3-20-1820
    Ruth             b 8- 3-1822
    Henry            b 9-21-1825
    Mary             b 4- 4-1828
    Caleb            b 7-20-1830
    Josiah           b 4-25-1833    d 11-15-1881

Samuel M   b 9- 2-1808   d prior to 1846
           =s George & Sarah (dec)
           m 9-29-1830, Milford MM, Ind
Priscilla  b 5- 5-1810   =dt Joseph & Elizabeth Cox
           (she m 2nd time to David Butler)
Ch: Joseph
    Rachel
    Sarah

Thomas
Mary
Ch: Abigail          b 8-12-1825
    Nathan           b 12- 1-1828
    Morgan           b 7- 2-1830
    Sarah            b 5- 9-1832
    Charles          b 7-24-1834
    Mariah           b 7-21-1837

BUTLER
Ansolem    b 10-24-1811   =s Stephen & Matilda
Ruth       b 1-14-1813    =dt Isaac & Elizabeth Cook
Ch: Benjamin         b 12- 6-1833
    Joel             b 3- 1-1836
    Charles          b 12-26-1838   d 7-27-1839
    Emily            b 10-29-1840
    Theodore         b 9-27-1843

David      =s William & Mary (dec)
Mary (1st w)
Ch: Mary             b 11- 6-1826
    Esther           b 10-31-1835
Priscilla (2nd w)    b 5- 5-1810
           =dt Joseph & Elizabeth Cox
           (a widow with ch of Samuel)
Ch: Cyrus            b 1-24-1847

James S    b 7-31-1782   =s Stephen & Mary
Debora     b 6-21-1791   =dt Say & Mary Johnson
Ch: Ann J            b 11-13-1814
    Martha           b 8-27-1816
    William          b 9-19-1818
    James E          b 9-17-1820
    Alfred           b 5-29-1822
    Joseph           b 5- 6-1824    d 4- 9-1881
    Robert           b 3-29-1827
    Deborah J        b 2- 2-1830
    Mary E           b 10-14-1833

Joshua     b 10- 3-1830   d 1-17-1877
           =s William & Susannah
Diza       =dt Thomas & Sarah Thornburgh
Ch: William G        b 4-30-1854    d 8-19-1855
    Rollins          b 3- 2-1856
    Barton L         b 7-24-1858
    Orville J        b 1-15-1861
    Laura M          b 8-28-1863
    Christopher W    b 7-16-1867

Lemuel Sr   From Va & Whitewater MM, Ind
Jane
Ch: Thomas Durham
    Mary
    Lemuel Jr
    Jane
    Tacy
    Pleasant
    Martha
    Mahlon
    Joseph Fleming

MILFORD

BUTLER (Cont)
Lemuel     -s Lemuel Sr & Jane
Hannah
Ch: Milton           b 4-18-1834

Stanton
Elizabeth  -dt ... Binford
Ch: Mary             b 3-13-1836

William    -s Joseph & Miriam
Esther     -dt Garrard & Sarah Ladd
Ch: Robert T         b 8-13-1824

William    b 1806    d 4- 1-1862  -s William & Mary (dec)
Susanna    b 10-16-1810   d 9- 4-1874
           -dt Joshua & Mary Morris
Ch: Joshua          b 10- 3-1830    d 1-17-1873
    Mary            b 6-25-1832     d 4- 5-1841
    Margaret        b 5-13-1834     d 5-16-1865
    Charles M       b 1-27-1837
    Melissa         b 1-15-1839
    Mariah          b 3- 1-1841     d 3- 8-1841

CAIN
James
Axelina
Ch: Mary E           b 12-11-1872

CAMMACK
Amos       b 12- 9-1798    -s James & 2nd wife, Rachel
Ruth
Ch: Joseph           b 8-15-1823    d 9-16-1847

John       b 7- 7-1789    -s James & 1st wife, Joanna
Jane       -dt ... Hollingsworth
Ch: Mary             b 9-21-1828    d 11-17-1849

Nathan H   b 8-19-1821    -s Samuel & Hannah
Priscilla  b 12- 6-1821   d 11- 8-1894
           -dt Joshua & Mary Morris
Ch: Adeline          b 12-22-1843
    David            b 1-25-1846
    Charles          b 1- 6-1848
    Laura            b 3- 9-1851

James
Rachel (2nd w)       -dt ... Compton
           b 12-19-1764   d 3-11-1844
Ch: Amos
    Samuel           b 1-12-1796

Samuel     b 1-12-1796    -s James & 2nd wife, Rachel
Hannah     b 3-18-1803    -dt John & Rachel Hollingsworth
Ch: Nathan H         b 8-19-1821
    David            b 9-16-1823    d 6-15-1845
                                    Milford MM
    Eli              b 10-10-1825
    Rachel           b 6-21-1827

CHAPPELL
Reuben     b 10- 1-1810   -s Gabriel & Lydia d 1882
Mary Ann   b 12-30-1813   -dt Nicholas & Catharine
           d 1849                      Johnson
Ch: Milton H         b 8-23-1841

William
Christian Ann (1st w)  d 3-24-1858
Ch: Missouri C       b 7-12-1854
    Alice Isabella   b 1-24-1857
Martha Ann (2nd w)
Ch: Anna Phebe       b 6- 3-1868

COFFIN
Elijah     b 11-17-1798   -s Bethuel & Hannah
           d 1-22-1862
Naomi      b 11-15-1797   -dt Benajah & Elizabeth Hiatt
           d 6-14-1866
Ch: Miriam           b 1- 9-1821, N C
    Charles F        b 4- 3-1823, N C

William H            b 9-26-1825, Washington Co, Ind
Eliphalet            b 8-25-1828, Washington Co, Ind
                     d 5- 5-1831
Caroline E           b 6-20-1831

COGGSHALL
John M     -s T.... & Millicent
Mary Jane  -dt .. Elliott
Ch: Olan             b 3-23-1862
    George W         b

Peter      -s Gayer & Hannah (both dec)
Jane       -dt Josiah & Mary (dec)  b 2-24-1825
                                    (Nixon)
Ch: Mary Ellen       b
    Margaret Susan   b 1-24-1857

COOK
John       b 5- 2-1809  d 5-2-1839
           -s Isaac & Elizabeth
Mary       b 2-15-1805  -dt Josiah & Dorothy Gilbert
Ch: Martha           b 10-11-1831
    Josiah           b 12-10-1833
    William          b 7- 9-1836
    Samuel           b 11- 7-1838

COX
Bennett    b 1-25-1817   -s Joseph & Elizabeth
Elizabeth  b 4-26-1815   -dt John & Betty Kindley
Ch: Ruth Ann         b 2-27-1839    d 3-12-1862
    Melissa          b 2-15-1841    d 1- 9-1865
    Lindley H        b 3-11-1852
    Elizabeth E      b 5- 9-1854
    Marietta         b 2- 3-1858

Joel M     b 6- 2-1805  d 10-17-1883
           -s Joseph & Elizabeth
Catharine  b 6-23-1805  -dt Jeremiah & Catherine Cox
Ch: Elizabeth        b 2-20-1829
    Jeremiah         b 7- 8-1830
    Joseph           b 3-11-1832
    William B        b 4-27-1834
    Rebecca          b 12-21-1836
    Samuel           b 1-11-1839
    Jane M           b 9-20-1841
    Daniel W         b 12-28-1848

Joseph     b 1-21-1779  d 12-30-1872
Elizabeth  b 3-24-1789  d 7- 6-1873
           -dt .. Musgrave
Ch: Joel M           b 6- 2-1805
    Rebecca          b 2-23-1807
    Elizabeth        b 10-16-1808   d 9-21-1809
    Priscilla        b 5- 5-1810
    Marmaduke        b 1- 3-1812    d 2-28-1812
    Elizabeth        b 5-22-1813
    Drusilla         b 5-23-1815
    Bennett          b 1-25-1817
    Seth             b 4-19-1819
    William          b 5-28-1821
    Mariah           b 9-15-1822
    Rachel           b 3-27-1825
    Joseph M         b 4- 2-1827
    Ann              b 11-30-1829

Joseph M   -s Joseph & Elizabeth  b 4- 2-1827
                                  d 4-17-1894
Rachel M   b 5- 1-1831  -dt Clark & Mary Terrell
Ch: William          b 6-13-1856
    George T         b 12-19-1857
    Joseph           b 3-21-1860
    Mary E           b 3-21-1860
    Hannah A         b 1-21-1862
    Sarah J          b 8-15-1863    d 1- 1-1865
    Rachel           b 2- 4-1871
    Thomas           b 8-21-1872

Seth       b 4-19-1819  -s Joseph & Elizabeth
Ruth       b 4-29-1817  -dt John & Betty Kindley
Ch: John             b 5- 2-1841

MILFORD

COX (Cont)
Ch of Seth & Ruth (Cont)
    Amos                b  5- 6-1844
    Sarah              b 12-19-1847
    Milton             b  8-16-1852

William
Martha       -dt ... Jessup    d 6-20-1859
Ch: Arthur          b 6-19-1857

DAVIS
Harmon      b 11-11-1773    -s Thomas & Elizabeth
Hannah      b 12- 7-1778    -dt Joseph & Phebe Middleton
Ch: Rachel    b    ca1798
    Joseph    b  3-28-1800
    Isaac     b  4-24-1802
    Anne      b 10-21-1804
    Thomas    b 11-30-1806
    Sarah     b  2-11-1812
    Jehu      b  6-11-1814
    Hannah    b 12-28-1816
    Eunice    b  6-30-1819

Isaac       b  4-24-1802    -s Harmon & Hannah
Phoebe      b 10-16-1811    -dt James & Mary Brown
Ch: Louisa     b  5- 6-1834

Joseph B
Parthenia
Ch: Margaret A    b  5-13-1847
    Rebecca Jane   b  4-22-1849
    Martha Kaloolah b  1- 3-1853

DENNIS
Benjamin    -s John & Hannah
Clarky      -dt John & Elizabeth Pool
Ch: John         b  3- 3-1821
    Gulielma     b 12- 5-1822
    Priscilla    b 10- 2-1824
    Elizabeth    b 12-24-1826
    Eunice      b  7-19-1829
    William Clark b  2- 9-1832
    Jethro      b  9- 2-1834
    Benjamin S   b  8-10-1837

DICKINSON
Jonathan (of England)  d 10-19-1863 -bur Earlham Cem
Alice       b  3-15-1784   d 4-20-1862
           -dt ... Hunt
Ch: Joseph     b           d 8- 5-1895
    Charles     b  9-27-1816
    Jane        b  6-11-1818
    George      b  5- 5-1822
    Henry       b
    Jonathan    b  9-30-1828
    Alice       b 12-  -1830
    James H     b 12-15-1834

Charles     b  9-27-1816    -s Jonathan & Alice
Hannah      b 12- 4-1818    d 10-11-1894
          -dt Benajah & Elizabeth Hiatt
Ch: Henry      b  6- 1-1847
    Benajah    b 11-20-1851

Joseph     -s Jonathan & Alice    d 8- 5-1895
Esther G    b  3- 2-1816    d 2- 2-1891
         -dt Benajah & Elizabeth Hiatt & widow of
         Josiah White
Ch: Hannah     b 11-15-1845
    Samuel      b  5-29-1848

EDGERTON
Thomas     -s Joseph & Martha
Mary       b 7-24-1794    -dt William & Mary Osborn
Ch: William Osborn
    Eleanor
    Mary Ann
    Samuel
    Martha

    Thomas      b 12- 5-1831
    Richard     b 12- 5-1835

Thomas      b  2- 2-1813  -s Samuel & Elizabeth
          m 1-23-1834, Elk MM, Ohio
Mary        b  4-15-1815  -dt George & Elizabeth Taylor
Ch: William T    b  4-24-1835
    Elizabeth A   b  9- 5-1836
    Samuel      b  6- 5-1839
    Sarah J     b  7-23-1841
    Susan       b  1-15-1844

Walter      b  8- 6-1806  -s James & Sarah
Rebecca     b  2-23-1807  -dt Joseph & Elizabeth Cox
Ch: William     b 11- 4-1827
    Sarah       b  8- 5-1830

William     -s Joseph & Martha
         m 7-31-1817, Stillwater MM, Ohio
Nelly       -dt Daniel & Nelly Frazier
Ch: Eli
    Owen
    Ruthanna
    Eliza Ann
    William Penn

ELLIOTT
Exum Jr     b  1- 7-1808  -s Exum & Catharine
Hannah      b  4-14-1809  -dt Benjamin & Tamar Smith
Ch: John W      b  9-18-1829
    Thomas H    b  8-22-1831
    Hiram       b 12-11-1834
    Emeline     b  4-16-1837
    Sarah C     b  3-29-1842

Jacob       b  8-22-1793  d 10-27-1868
         -s Exum Sr & Catharine
Mary (1st w) b 12-17-1790  d 12-18-1853
         -dt Reuben & Rhoda Peal
Ch: Jonathan    b  8-31-1811
    Absolem     b  6-18-1813
    Gulana      b 10- 4-1814
    Rhoda       b  4- 8-1818
    Solomon     b  2-12-1819
    Catharine   b 10-12-1821
    Exum        b 11- 5-1823
    Rachel      b  1- 8-1826
    Mark        b  2- 9-1829
    Mary        b  8- 4-1832
    Ruth        b 11-10-1835
Isabella M (2nd w)   -a widow of .. Hawkins
         -dt ... Powel

John        b  2-17-1797  d 8-23-1839
         -s Exum & Catharine
Mary b ca 1797    (m 2nd to David Palmer in 1842)
    -dt Richard & Betty Ratliff
Ch: Elizabeth   b  3- 9-1819
    Sarah       b  7-13-1821
    Richard T   b 11-21-1823
    Isaac       b  2-26-1827
    Katherine   b 10- 4-1829
    Maryann     b 11-19-1831
    Martha      b  5- 3-1834
    Melissa     b 11-15-1836
    John Jr     b 12- 5-1838

Jonathan    b  8-31-1811  -s Jacob & Mary
Amelia (1st w) b  8- 1-1815  d 6-26-1847
         -dt John Huff
Ch: Eliza      b  7-23-1835
    William B   b 10-13-1837
    Jacob C     b 10-20-1840
    Mary        b  9-23-1842
    Matilda     b  1- 5-1845    d 1-10-1845
    Jane        b  5-22-1847
    James       b  5-22-1847    d 6- 4-1847
Mariah (2nd w)    -dt John & Hannah Maxwell
     of West Grove MM, Ind

## ELLIOTT (Cont)
Ch of Jonathan & Mariah:
```
    John M              b  6-15-1849
    Achilles W          b  1-28-1851
    Albert              b  1-25-1853
    Linus M             b  6-26-1855

Solomon         b 2-12-1819    -s Jacob & Mary
Penelope (1st w) b 12- 8-1823  d 12-26-1883
                -dt Jonathan & Abigail Morris
Ch: Franklin            b  7-13-1842
    Martin L            b  4-18-1847
    Emma F              b  7-19-1849
    Charles M           b  3-22-1852    d 2-16-1854
    Lindley M           b  9-  -1854
    Laura C             b 11-13-1856
    Amanda              b 12- 5-1858
    Anna M              b  2-22-1861
    Milo P              b  5-25-1865
Emily J (2nd w)         -dt Henry & Huldah Davis of Union
                                           Co, Ind
```

## FLETCHER
```
Albert White    b 1- 2-1841   -s Samuel Frances &
                                          Elizabeth
Elizabeth       b 2-19-1846   -dt Henry & Mary Peelle
Ch: Wilfred             b  7- 4-1872

William of N C          -s John & Margaret
Sarah      b 11-10-1795  d 12-11-1825  -dt .. Nixon
Ch: Samuel F            b  6- 7-1818
    Margaret A          b  2-29-1820
    Sarah N             b 11- 9-1825
NOTE: These ch were orphans u/c Aaron & Margaret White
                        in 1831

Zachariah       -s Joshua & Margaret
Anna       b 2- 6-1813   -dt James & Mary Johnson
Ch: Henry F             b 12-10-1836
    William A           b  3- 4-1843    d 2-16-1847
    Margaret            b 10-26-1844
    James J             b 11-  -1848
```

## FLORA
```
J D
Sarah Elvira            b  9- 9-1842   d 7-14-1874
                    -dt Gideon & Margaret Wilson
Ch: Charles D           b  1-23-1866
    Frank L             b 10-26-1867
    Lillian             b  9- 1-1869
```

## FRAZIER
```
Daniel              -s Daniel & Elenor (dec)
Martha              -dt Joseph & Martha Edgerton
Ch: Sarah               b  7- 3-1826
    Ann                 b  4- 8-1828
    Thomas              b 10-30-1829
    Rachel              b 11-29-1831
    Joseph              b

James G
Rachel L        -dt Willets
Ch: Joseph B            b  4- 5-1869
```

## GARRETT
```
William    b 2-28-1801   -s Abigail (Gilbert) Garrett
Anna
Ch: Mary Ann            b 10-16-1828
    Madison             b  2- 8-1830
    Daniel B            b 10- 4-1833
```

## GAUSE
```
Nathan Jr  b 10- 5-1824   -s Nathan Sr & Martha
Ann        b 11-30-1829   -dt Joseph & Elizabeth Cox
Ch: Thomas              b  2- 2-1846   d 8-29-1882
    Clarkson            b 12-19-1848
    Sylvester           b 12-13-1855
    Oscar               b  9-26-1859
```

## GILBERT
```
Aaron L    b 1-25-1785  -s Jeremiah & Rebecca
Jemima     b 1-20-1791  -dt William & Elizabeth Newby
Ch: Rebecca             b  1-25-1810   d 7-31-1828
    Elizabeth           b  3- 4-1813
    Anna                b 12- 2-1816   d 8- 1-1841
    Asenath             b  2-24-1819
    Sarah               b 10-27-1823
    Miriam              b  1-16-1826

Aaron           b 12- 8-1804   d 3- 7-1877
                -s Joel & Lydia
Margaret        b 5- 6-1810   -dt John & Lydia Bell
Ch: John B              b 10-24-1828
    Joel M              b 10-14-1830
    Jesse               b  4- 2-1834   d 4- 1-1892
    Martha              b  6-26-1836
    Lydia               b  2-28-1838
    Peninnah            b  5-20-1841   d 2-26-1871
    Sarah               b  4-25-1843
    Margaret            b  3-16-1845
    Aaron               b  4-17-1849

Joel       b 10-14-1783   d 2-12-1870
           -s Jeremiah & Rebecca
Lydia      b 11- 1-1786   -dt James & 2nd w, Millisant
                                         Morgan
Ch: Aaron               b 12- 8-1804
    Abigail             b  9-25-1806
    Millicent           b 10- 7-1808   d 5-22-1839
    Peninah             b 10-11-1815
    Nathan H            b  9-22-1817
    Joel                b  8-15-1820
    Lydia               b  5-29-1822
    Mordecai            b  9- 5-1824
    Jeremiah            b 10-13-1826

Jonathan N              -s Thomas & Catharine
Catherine               -dt ... Pike
Ch: Hortense            b 10-21-1873
    Thomas L

Josiah Sr  b 8-20-1773  -s Jeremiah & Miriam
Dorothy    b 4-17-1777  -dt John & Jane Nixon
Ch: Elizabeth           b  8- 3-1802
    Mary                b  2-15-1805
    Dorothy             b 12-29-1807
    Josiah              b 11-30-1809
    Lydia               b  4-22-1812
    Achsah              b  3-28-1815
    Maurice             b  7-10-1817
    Thomas              b  8-18-1818

Josiah Jr  b 11-30-1809  d 1-26-1839
           -s Josiah Sr & Dorothy
Abigail    b  1-14-1814  d 8-31-1889
           -dt John & Lydia Bell
Ch: Josiah              b 10-23-1834
    John                b  2-12-1837
    Dorothy J           b  4-18-1839   d 5- 7-1862

Maurice Morris   -s Josiah & Dorothy  b 7-10-1817
Elizabeth   b 3- 9-1819  -dt John & Mary Elliott
Ch: Sarah Ann           b  1- 2-1838
    Josiah B            b

Oliver          -s Thomas & Catharine
Nancy           -dt .. McTaggart
Ch: Ross E              b  3-15-1870
    Thomas H            b  5- 1-1872
    Kenneth             b

Thomas     b 2-20-1779  -s Jeremiah & Miriam
Sarah      b 4-14-1788  -dt Aaron & Sarah Hill
Ch: Phebe               b  4- 2-1811
    Miriam              b  3- 7-1813
    Hannah              b  3-14-1815
    Mary                b  6- 8-1817
    Jeremiah            b 10-17-1819
```

MILFORD

## GILBERT (Cont)
Ch of Thomas & Sarah (Cont)
```
    Gulielma            b 12- 7-1821
    George H            b  5-29-1825
    Thomas              b 11-29-1827
    Aaron               b  8-29-1833
```

## GOLDSMITH
```
Daniel                  b 7-30-1772    -s Daniel & Susanna of N Y
Hannah                  -dt Sylvanus & Ann Gardner of Nantucket
                        d  8- 8-1833
Ch: Ellen               b  1-26-1802
    Benjamin            b  2- 7-1804      d 9-23-1822
    Anna                b  6- 8-1806
    Joseph              b  8-13-1810
    Gardner             b 11-16-1812
```

## GORDON
```
Parker                  -s Charles   d 3- 8-1850, -ae 19-1/2 yrs
                                                -bur Milton

Richard                 b  8-22-1796    -s Charles & Ruth
Susanna                 b 10-18-1797    d  4- 2-1869
                        -dt George & Sarah Hiatt
Ch: Rebecca             b  7- 2-1819
    Alfred              b  1- 7-1821
    Edwin               b 10-25-1823
    Mahala              b  2-21-1826
    Sarahann            b  9-18-1828
    Seth                b  7-14-1831
    Nathan              b  8-31-1833
```

## GRESS
```
Hervey
Eliza Ann               b  2- 2-1846  -dt William & Abigail Edgerton
Ch: Rosa M              b  2- 4-1866
    Florella D          b  9- 9-1869
```

## GRIFFIN
```
James                   b  4-21-1781   d 12-16-1855
                        -s James Sr & Hannah of N C
Priscilla
Ch: Benjamin
```

## HALL
```
Benjamin
Esther
Ch: Agatha              b  6-15-1836

John                    b 11-23-1792   -s John & Miriam
Sarah                   b  1-10-1790   -dt Jeremiah & Keron Parker
Ch: Martha              b 11- 9-1812
    Phineas             b  9-24-1814
    Robert              b  1-19-1817
    Moses               b  6-18-1819
    Sarah               b  1- 8-1826
    John                b  1-19-1828
    Joseph              b  9-11-1831
```

## HANNAH
```
James                   b  8- 9-1760   d  4- 3-1846
                                        -ae 85yrs and about 7 mo
```

## HARVEY
```
Isaac (not mbr)
Rachel                  -dt ... Elliott
Ch: Henry H             b  5-19-1849

Ruth      -w of N       d  2- 6-1865, -ae 26yrs
```

## HASKET
```
Thomas (dec)
Ann          (now m to Levi Cook)
Ch: Charity             b 12-17-1804
    Thomas Jr           b  9-21-1807
    Ann                 b  4- 2-1810
    William             b  6-20-1813
```

## HASTINGS
```
Aaron                   b  5- 2-1808   -s William & Sarah
Margaret (1st w)        b  5-16-1801   -dt Uriah & Hannah Baldwin
                        d at Duck Creek MM, Ind
Ch: Solomon             b 10-10-1828
Christiana (2nd w)      b  5-29-1813   -dt John & Ann Reece
Ch: Sarah               b  9-19-1831   d 12- 7-1832
    William             b  7-12-1833
    Elias R             b  6-25-1835
    Eunice              b 11-19-1837   d 10-22-1838
    Letitia A           b  9-14-1839
    Joshua              b 12-19-1841   d  7- 2-1868
    Margaret J          b  3-22-1844
    John N              b  9- 8-1846
    Henry H             b 12- 2-1848
    Emily E             b  9-29-1851   d  8-22-1851 (?)
    Mary E              b  6-28-1854   d 10-22-1856

Elias R                 b  6-25-1835  -s Aaron & Christiana
Sarah                   b  6-26-1837  -dt William & Abigail
                                                Edgerton
Ch: William E           b  5- 4-1859
    Charles F           b 10- 5-1862   d  8-25-1863
    Mary Emma           b
    Anna Letitia        b

William                 b 10- 3-1813   -s William Sr & Sarah
Jane                    b  1- 1-1815   -dt John & Ann Reece
Ch: David               b  9- 4-1832
    John R              b  1-15-1834
    Rebecca             b  9-24-1837
```

## HAWKINS
```
Jonathan                b  9-24-1792   d  4-21-1863
                        -s Amos & Phebe
Sarah
Ch: Isaac               b 10-31-1818   d  8-15-1841

Lemuel                  b  8- 5-1844  -s William & Isabel
Caroline (form Brown)
Ch: Norah               b  5-10-1866   d  9- 1-1866
    Martha Bell         b  2- 3-1868
    Tamer               b 12-15-1870

William                 d  5- 8-1851  -s John & Mary
Isabel                  -dt Simon & Jane Powell of Ky
Ch: Jane                b  7-18-1821
    John                b  5-11-1823
    Mary                b 10-30-1825
    Simon               b 11-20-1827
    Nathan              b 10-12-1829
    Tamar               b  3-19-1833
    William             b  3- 5-1835
    Amos                b 12- 6-1837   d  2-26-1848
    Isabel              b  6-30-1841   d  5-25-1843
    Lemuel              b  8- 5-1844
```

## HAWLEY
```
Richard                 -s Caleb & Hannah
                        m 12- 3-1818, Plainfield MM, Ohio
Rachel                  -dt Benjamin & Ruth (dec) Paxson
Ch: Ann
    Eli
```

## HENBY
```
Eli                     -s John (dec) & Mary
Gulielma                b  9-27-1825  -dt Josiah & Abigail Bell
Ch: Sarah               b  2- 8-1847   d  2-11-1847
    Mary Ann            b  5-15-1848   d  4-29-1855
    Abigail E           b 10- 9-1850
    Achsah              b  6-22-1853
    Jesse B             b 10-13-1856
    Thomas O            b  9- 4-1858

Elias                   -s John (dec) & Mary
Phebe (1st w)           b  4- 2-1813  -dt Abraham & Mary Symons
                                                (both dec)
```

MILFORD

HENBY (Cont)
Ch of Elias & Phebe:
    Martha Ann     b
    John     b
    Sarah     b
    Phebe E     b
    Elizabeth W     b
Elizabeth L (Henby) (2nd w)

John
Rebecca     (form Hastings)
Ch: Franklin C     b  8- 4-1870
    William H     b
    Arthur     b
    Anna     b

HENLEY
Jordan     b 12-10-1793     -s Joseph & Mourning
Elizabeth     b 9-25-1793     -dt Charles & Lydia Morgan
Ch: Joseph     b
    Charles     b
    Margaret     b
    David     b
    Jonathan     b
    Samuel     b
    Thomas Elwood     b

HERBST
David (not mbr)
Abigail     (form Symons)
Ch: Clara     b 10-25-1870
    Clarence     b 10-25-1870
    John H     b 10-23-1872

HESTER
Francis     b 2-13-1767     d 1-31-1848     -bur Milford
    -s Robert & Elizabeth
Mary (1st w) b 5-19-1769     d 1824
    -dt John & Mary Hodson
Ch: Elizabeth     b  5- 2-1795
    Thomas     b  1-11-1797
    Ruth     b  9-25-1799
    John     b  8-28-1801
    Robert     b  2-14-1803
    Rachel     b  1- 4-1807
    Henry     b  1-15-1809
    William     b  2- 9-1811
    Isaac     b 12- 9-1812
Ruth (2nd w) (form Bennet)
    -widow of Matthew of Cherry Grove MM, Ind

HIATT
Absolom     -s Joseph Sr & Hannah of N C
    m 2-20-1793 at Westfield MM, N C
Ann     -dt David & Elizabeth Reece
Ch: David     b 10-6-1793
    Aaron     b 11-2-1795
    James     b
    Hiram     b     NOTE:
    Joseph     b     Order of births
    Phebe     b     not known
    Absolom Jr     b
    Cornelius     b
    Hannah     b
    Anthony     b
    Jane     b
    Daniel     b

Allen     b 6- 6-1795     -s Joel & Mary
Rhoda     -from New Garden MM, N C
Ch: Susanna     b 9-22-1819     d 8-13-1827
    Gulielma     b 11-19-1821
    John Milton     b 1-20-1824
    Addison     b 1-16-1826     d 2- 3-1826
    Anna M     b 2- 3-1835
    Minerva     b 11-23-1839

Abner     m 6-12-1816 at New Garden MM, N C
Achsah     b 11-28-1799     -dt Joel & Hannah Willis
Ch: Jane     b  6- 3-1817
    Herman     b  1-20-1819
    Elim     b
    Alfred     b
    Jesse W     b
    Elizabeth W     b

Aseph     b 8-30-1789     -s Asher (dec) & Mary
Rebecca (1st w)     -dt Abner & Mary (Pope) Hunt
    d 6-28-1829     -bur Newberry MM, Ohio
Ch: Asher     b  6-15-1816
    Zimri     b  6-13-1819     d 1820
                                                      -bur Newberry
    Mahala     b  1-13-1821
    Caleb     b 12- 8-1824
Sarah (2nd w) b 3-19-1802     -dt Jirah & Avis Smith

Benajah     b 7-17-1773     d 10-14-1847
    -s William & Charity
Elizabeth     b 12-24-1770     d 11-11-1862
    -dt Isaac & Catharine White
Ch: Naomi     b 11-15-1797
    Mordecai     b 11-13-1799
    Anna     b 10-10-1801
    John     b  7- 9-1804
    Joel     b  7-17-1807
    David     b  2- 8-1810
    Abigail     b  2- 8-1810
    Benjah     b  7- 8-1812
    Esther G     b  3- 2-1816
    Hannah F     b 12-24-1818

Benajah W     b 12- 4-1824     -s Mordecai & Rhoda
Martha Ann     b 2-18-1827     -dt John & Ann (dec) Wilson
Ch: Edward     b  7-23-1847
    Sarah     b  6-11-1849
    Anna     b 11-14-1852     d 12-22-1854
    Oliver     b  8-24-1854
    Mordecai     b  5-20-1856

Christopher     -s Amos & Priscilla of Clinton Co, Ohio
    m 4- 1-1824, Newberry MM, Ohio
Martha     -dt Samuel & Susannah Stanley of Ohio
Ch: Amos     b  1- 8-1825
    Susannah     b  7-21-1826
    Lydia     b 10-16-1828
    Emily     b 11-18-1830
    Samuel     b  9-16-1833
    Priscilla     b  3-17-1836

Elijah     b 9-11-1805     -s Jehu & 1st wife, Tamar
Ann     -dt Dempsey & Mary Boswell
Ch: Dempsey     b 11-12-1826
    Jehu     b 12- 2-1828
    Joseph     b  5-30-1831

Jesse     b 9-30-1814     -s Eleazer & Anna (dec)
Margaret Ann     b 8-29-1820     -dt William & Sarah (dec)
                                                        Fletcher
Ch: Emaline     b  8-25-1841     d 7-28-1859
    William F     b  1-21-1844
    Charles E     b  6-22-1847
    Mary     b 10-30-1849     d 12- 6-1862
    Francis F     b 12-11-1850
    Robert L     b  7- 2-1852     d 6-17-1863
    Sarah Ann     b  4- 9-1861

Mordecai     b 11-13-1799     d 11-24-1873
    -s Benajah & Elizabeth
Rhoda     b 5-28-1802     d 12-18-1881
    -dt Joshua & Elizabeth Dix
Ch: Elizabeth D     b 12-10-1820
    Henry W     b  1- 4-1823     d 7- 4-1824
    Benajah     b 12- 4-1824
    Luvisa     b  7-22-1827
    Martha W     b  2-17-1830

MILFORD

HIATT (Cont)
Ch of Mordecai & Rhoda (Cont)
  Mary T              b 6-22-1832    d 9-13-1833
  Jesse D             b 7-23-1834
  Samuel F           b 8- 4-1837    d 7-31-1844
  William J          b 12- 3-1839
  Francis H          b 1-23-1846

William F  b 1-21-1844    -s Jesse & Margaret
Frances
Ch: Harry F           b 6-25-1871    d 3-27-1872
    Laura Alice       b

HOSKINS
Joseph W  b 12-28-1806    -s John & Mary
Susanna (1st w) b ca 1828-1830
Ch: Gulielma M       b 11-14-1825
    Amanda M          b 11-21-1826
    John Q            b 10-30-1828
Anne (2nd w) b 12-24-1812    -dt Thomas & Anne Moore
Ch: George F          b 4- 2-1835
    Rowland G         b 1-24-1837
    Mary Anna         b 7- 3-1839
    Stephen M         b 9-29-1841
    Samuel H          b 9- 1-1843
    Elizabeth        b 2-14-1846

HUBBARD
Richard J  b 11- 2-1807    -s Jeremiah & Margaret (dec)
Sarah (1st w) (form Swain)    d 2-20-1860
Ch: W Edwin          b 10-24-1827
    Charles S         b 9- 7-1829
    Margaret          b 8- 3-1831
    Caroline          b 10- 6-1833
    Phebe Ann         b 10-17-1835
    Harriet P         b 12-22-1837
    Julinetta        b 6- 5-1845    d 12-20-1861
    Henry             b               d 12-17-1864
    Joseph            b               d 5-26-1865
    George            b
Abigail (2nd w)    -widow of ... Edgerton
                   -dt Job & Letitia Stratton

HUNT
Allen      b 3- 6-1783    -s Isom & Ann (dec) (1st w)
Huldah
Ch: Nathan            b
    Nancy             b
    Lucinda          b
    Rachel           b
    Abel             b

Ezra       b 7-17-1797    -s Asa & 2nd w, Sarah
Rebecca    b 11-29-1799    -dt Pheraby Griffin Albertson
Ch: James             b 8-18-1822
    Eunice            b 11- 2-1824
    Asenath          b 11-22-1825
    Asa               b 9-17-1828
    Priscilla        b 5-17-1829
    Pheraby          b 3-23-1836    d 3-26-1836
    Benjamin         b 6-27-1837

Hanuel     b 1-31-1799    -s Asa & 2nd w, Sarah
Eleanor (1st w) b ca 8-13-1805    d 1-26-1835
              -dt William & Sarah (Overman) Newby
Ch: Sarah             b 8-12-1824
    Asenath          b 6-15-1827
    Ezra             b 1-12-1829
    Nancy Jane        b 1-11-1831
Lucinda (2nd w) b 1-14-1815 -dt Nimrod & Anna Dickey
Ch: James             b 7-19-1836
    Cyrus             b

Isom Jr    -s Isom (dec) & 2nd w, Margaret of N C & Ind
Susanna    -dt Samuel & Susanna Stanley
Ch: Calvin J          b 1-15-1835
    Margaret A        b 7-17-1836
    William A         b 5- 1-1838

Jonathan     b 3-17-1780  d 3-10-1846
               -s John & Rachel
Phebe        b 3-11-1783  d 11-29-1860
               -dt Barnabas & Phebe Coffin
Ch: Barnabas         b 12-21-1798
    Margaret          b 4-19-1801
    John             b 10-16-1803
    Huldah           b 12-17-1805
    Jesse            b 1-16-1808
    Phebe            b 10-20-1809
    Elizabeth        b 9-10-1811
    Rachel           b 8- 7-1813
    Mary             b 5- 2-1815
    Beulah           b 11-28-1816
    Celia            b 11-29-1818
    Lydia            b 1- 1-1821
    Joseph           b 1-23-1823
    Abijah           b 8-29-1824    d 12- 5-1839
    Hannah           b 3- 2-1826
    Jonathan         b 2-11-1831

Thomas       b 5-23-1784  -s Jacob & Hannah of N C
Sarah        b 1-19-1794
Ch: Delila            b 4-12-1813
    John             b 3-23-1815
    Celia            b 7-25-1817
    Elam             b 11- 9-1819
    Eunice           b 1-11-1824
    Jacob            b 10-25-1825
    Sally A           b 8-29-1827
    William C         b 9-26-1831
    Elmina           b 10-20-1836

Eleazer
Susannah    b 11-15-1775  d 8- 9-1848 -bur Milford
            -dt Peter & Comfort Clemons

Thomas T    b 7- 5-1800    -s Nathan & Prudence (2nd w)
               of N C
Nancy D    b 4-30-1800    -dt Doughty & Elizabeth
               Stockton of Deep River, N C
Ch: Felix            b 9-10-1823
    David W           b 3-28-1825
    Samuel E          b 5-29-1827
    Henry            b 10-15-1829
    Elen Prudence     b 10- 9-1831    d 1-14-1834
    Hannah B          b 2-10-1835
    Eliza K           b 10- 5-1837
    Laura            b
    Mary J            b
    Margaret P        b

JESSOP
Nathan
Alice
Ch: Evan             b 11- 7-1823
    John             b 3-24-1825
    Mary             b 7- 9-1827    d 12-21-1840
    Jehial           b 10- 9-1833

William T    b 11-17-1833  d 12-22-1863
               -s Jesse & 3rd w, Eliza E (White)
Mary A      b 1- 1-1837    -dt William & Jane Brown
Ch: Jesse William     b
    James Henry       b 9-12-1862

JOHNSON          -s Zachariah
Jervis    From Isle of Wight, Va  b 2-18-1804
Melissa    b 6- 2-1807    -dt Joseph
Ch: Joseph           b 5-17-1832

Richard    -s Zachariah (dec) & Susannah
Edna       b 3-16-1813  d 12- 5-1836
               -bur Silver Creek MM, Ind
               -dt Stephen & Matilda (dec) Butler
Ch: William S         b 4-15-1835

MILFORD

## KENNEDY
Thomas      m 1853
Isabella    -dt George & Elizabeth Walton (both dec) of
            Chowan Co, N C
            (m 1st to Exum Elliott of N C) m ca 1844
Ch: Jane Elliott (dt of Exum)  b ca 1847  d 10-27-1898
            -ae 51, -bur Earlham Cem
            (m 3rd to Caleb Hall of Spiceland MM, Ind)
            (m 1866) - Isabella

## KERSEY
James C     b 2- 2-1801   -s Amos & Elizabeth (2nd w)
Elizabeth   b 1-19-1805   -dt Jesse & Mary Hodson
Ch: Jesse           b 10- 6-1827
    Abigail         b  9-14-1829
    James           b 10-15-1831

Verling     b 9- 8-1809   -s William & Rachel
Mary Emily  (form Butler)
Ch: Anna Maria      b  8-22-1840
    Richard W       b 11- 6-1842
    Charles A       b 12-22-1845
    Ellen H         b  2- 9-1848   d 11-20-1848
    Pliny E         b  1-13-1850
    Margaret W      b  5-31-1852
    Virginia        b
    Verling Jr      b
    Robert B        b

William     b 8-27-1781   -s Daniel & Mary (dec)
Rachel      b 3-30-1781   -dt William & Charity Hiatt
Ch: Anna            b  6-17-1802
    Eli             b  3- 6-1804
    Asher           b  4-22-1807
    Verling         b  9- 8-1809
    Silas H         b 12- 9-1818
    Mary C          b 11-11-1820
    Charity W       b  8-20-1822

## KINDLEY
Joel        b 1-16-1811   -s John & Elizabeth
Rachel      b 8- 7-1813   -dt Jonathan & Phebe Hunt
Ch: Charles         b  8-25-1833
    Margaret        b  3- 2-1835
    Lydia H         b 10-31-1836
    Joseph J        b  5-13-1839
    Rebecca         b  2-28-1842

John        b 4-20-1788   d 11- 4-1839, Milford MM, Ind
            -s Edward & Margaret
Elizabeth   b 10-10-1791  -dt John & Sarah Wilson
Ch: Jonathan        b  9-28-1808
    Joel            b  1-16-1811
    Sarah           b 12- 7-1813
    Elizabeth       b  4-26-1815
    Ruth            b  4-29-1817
    John W          b  7-24-1820
    Seth            b 10-29-1822

## LINDLEY
Osmond      -s James & Ruth of Howard Co, Ind
Achsah W    b 11-10-1836  -dt John W & Margaret Wilson
Ch: Sylvia A        b  4-10-1854
    Alfred W        b  9- 7-1856
    Franklin        b  3-10-1858
    Gurney          b  2- 7-1860
    John W          b 12- 4-1861
    Charles         b 11- 2-1863
    James H         b  3-   -1865
    Joel F          b  1-31-1869
    Erasmas         b 10-23-1870

## LUPTON
David W     -s Joseph & Esther of Hopewell MM, Va
            m 1-29-1835, Sugar Creek MM, Montgomery Co, O
            (Springborough MM, Ohio)
Ann         -dt Solomon & Ruth Miller
Ch: Ruth E          b  8-14-1837
    Beulah E        b 10-24-1842
    Richard P       b  2-12-1845

## McCOY
Henry C
Rachel      (form Wilson)
Ch: William Rufus   b 7-18-1865
    Edwin Everett   b 1- 3-1867   d 8- 7-1867
    John
    James

## MACY
James       b 8-29-1805   -s Zacheus & Sarah
Anna        b 3-10-1805   d 8- 8-1881
            -dt Joseph & Rachel Mendenhall of Ohio
Ch: Lydia Ann       b  6- 7-1824
    Eunice          b  1- 4-1826
    Rachel          b 11- 3-1829
    Phineas         b  8-19-1833
    Mary            b 10- 2-1835
    Avis            b  7-14-1838

John H      b 12-28-1806  -s Stephen & Rebecca
Beulah (1st w)   -dt Isom (dec) & Margaret Hunt
Betsy Ann (2nd w) -dt Thomas & Jemima (dec) White
Ch: Henrietta M     b         of Spiceland MM
    Margaret W      b
    William         b

Nathan      b 8- 8-1802   -s Zacheus & Sarah
Catharine (1st w) b 6-28-1800  d 2-18-1838
            -dt Jeremiah & Keron Parker
Ch: Pemberton       b 1-29-1825 d 1-22-1863 Union Co
    Sarah           b 6- 3-1826 d 5-4-1849 Westfield
    Jemima          b 4-12-1828
    Lydia           b 5- 4-1830
    Hepsebah        b 4- 7-1832
    Miriam          b 5-20-1835
    Nathan P        b 3- -1837 d 11-8-1838, Hopewell
Lydia (2nd w) b 10- 5-1799 -a min -wid Obed Macy
Ch: Anna Maria      b         -dt Tristrum & Love
    Nathan          b                      Davis
    Susanna         b

Thaddeus b 2-25-1775  d 10-8-1814, N C -s Enoch & Ann
Catharine b 1-4-1776  -dt Isaac & Catharine White
            (later w of Bethuel Coffin)
Ch: (Minors - to Ind)
    Jonathan W      b 10-10-1808
    Anna            b  6- 2-1814

Zachaeus    b 10-18-1773  -s Nathaniel & Hepzebeth
Sarah       b  5-15-1775  -dt Seth & Lydia Huddleston
Ch: Lydia           b  9-17-1800   d 9-14-1836
    Nathan          b  8- 8-1802
    James           b  8-29-1805

## MAUDLIN (MODLIN)
William     b 10-10-1782  -s John & Ann
Anna        -dt Richard & Betty Ratliff  b 3-4-1786
Ch: Elizabeth       b
    John            b
    Levi            b 12-23-1811
    Richard         b 10-10-1813
    William         b  9- 2-1815
    Rebecca         b 10-19-1817
    Joseph          b  3-21-1829 (sic)

William Jr  b 9- 2-1815   -s William & Ann
Elizabeth Ann    -dt Daniel & Mary Hunnicut
Ch: Oliver H        b 1-21-1835

## MAXWELL
Benjamin F  -s Hugh & Anna
Sarah Sylvania  -dt William A & Sarah M Rambo (both dec)
Ch: Lanetta         b
    Naomi           b
    Perry           b 12-31-1872

## MENDENHALL
Miles       b 3-13-1799   -s Isaac & Rachel
Margaret    b ca 1799-1800 -dt Moses & Elizabeth (dec) Bundy
Ch: Sina            b  1- 2-1822
    Jacob           b 11-27-1822
    Eli             b  3-15-1824

MILFORD

MENDENHALL (Cont)
Ch of Miles & Margaret (Cont):
   Demcy B         b  4-15-1825
   Nathan C        b  8- 5-1827
   Isaac            b  6-11-1830
   Mary Ann       b  7-11-1832
   Rachel         b

Nathan M
Susannah
Ch: George C       b  3-21-1866, near Terre Haute, Ind
   Phebe J        b 10- 5-1867, near Terre Haute, Ind
   Delana         b 12-12-1869, near Dublin, Ind
   Nathan         b  8-20-1873    d  9-20-1873

MEREDITH
James Jr of Dover MM, N C
Mary
Ch: Joanna         b  6-27-1816
   Jefferson      b  6-30-1817
   Hervey         b  4-15-1819
   Jabez           b
   Rosanna        b
   Jesse           b
   Susanna        b
   William         b

MILES
John         b 11-23-1802   d  8- 4-1882  -s William &
                                                                 Rachel
Rebecca (1st w) b 5-15-1806  d  8-26-1872
    -dt Thomas (dec) & Mary Jay
Ch: Thomas F      b  5- 9-1827    d  5-21-1838, Ohio
   Lindley        b  3- 1-1829
   Mary           b  4-11-1831
   Rachel         b  4-30-1833    d  3-26-1852, Ohio
   Joanna         b  2-14-1835
   Rebecca Jane    b  5- 9-1840    d  8-14-1841, Ohio
Dorcas (2nd w) b  2-24-1814    -dt John & Sarah Jones
(Hutchens)

Lindley      b  3- 1-1829    -s John & Rebecca
Lidia        b 12-13-1830   -dt Ellis & Rachel Willets
Ch: Rachel W      b
   Rhoda Ellen    b
   Thomas Elwood  b
   John Ellis     b
   Rebecca J      b 11-26-1863
   Martha A       b 10- 5-1865

MILLS
Jeremiah    (Dis 1807 in Deep River MM, N C)
Deborah
Ch: Ruth          b  4-15-1810

Hugh         b  2-23-1795  -s Marmaduke & Patience
Lidia        b  1-14-1796  -dt Thomas & Nancy Ann Hasket
Ch: Thomas H      b 10-30-1819
   Jerusha        b
   Peninah        b
   Priscilla      b

MOON
Simon        b  4- 9-1784    d  1- 1-1873
    -s John & Rachel
Hannah       b  3-12-1788  -dt Joseph & Hannah Stout
Ch: Joseph        b
   Mary           b
   William         b
   John Riley     b
   Sibbinah       b
   Simon Jr       b
   Hannah         b

MOORE
Charles Hubbard b 10-24-1806  d  1- 1-1873
    -s Thomas & Ann
Marcia       b  9-13-1823   -dt Aaron & Margaret White
Ch: Aaron W       b  9-27-1840    d  7-13-1842

   Thomas A      b  9- 4-1842
   Margaret      b 12-16-1843   d  1-31-1848
   Mary           b 12- 6-1846
   Anne           b  7-26-1849
   Morris H       b 10-16-1851
   Deborah W     b 12- 5-1855
   Elizabeth W    b  1- 7-1861
   Marcia F       b 10- 9-1867

Hannah               d  2- 2-1865, -ae 77yrs

Richard Woodson   b  8-15-1813  -s Thomas & Anne
Anna         b 11-10-1818  d  2-20-1847
   (of Whitewater MM, Ind
Ch: Marcus H      b  9- 3-1843
   Albert         b  6- 5-1846    d 12-29-1846

Thomas       b  2- 4-1770, Peck's Hill, N Y
              d  3- 4-1846, Milford MM, Ind
              m 12-24-1801
Anne         b  5-15-1781  d  3- 3-1855, Milford MM, Ind
   -dt ... Hubbard
Ch: (to Ind)
   Charles Hubbard  b 10-24-1806
   T Clarkson     b  9- 9-1810    d 10-25-1839
   Richard Woodson  b  8-15-1813
   Elizabeth Walker b  8-30-1818
   Jacob Hubbard    b  4-26-1820    d  7-28-1852
                                         Cincinnati
   John Thomas    b  1-28-1822    d 11-18-1844, N C
   William Henry   b  9-26-1823

William H      b  9-26-1823   -s Thomas & Anne
Mahala J      (form Petty)
Ch: William A     b  7-22-1867
   Thomas F       b  9-27-1869

MORGAN
Benjamin     b  7- 1-1772   d 11- 1-1859
          (Prob Walnut Ridge MM, Ind)
    -s Charles & Susanna
Naomi (1st w) b 7-24-1773   d  7- 8-1811, Whitewater MM
Ch: Micajah       b 11-10-1798   d  9-12-1860
                                   Whitewater MM, Ind
   Charles        b  2-18-1801
   Susannah       b 11- 6-1809
Elizabeth (2nd w) b 2-28-1782  d ca 1821-1822
    -dt James & Ruth  at West Grove MM, Ind
    Johnson (dec)
Ch: Hannah        b  4-24-1814
Ruth (3rd w) b  9-16-1780  d  1- 9-1852, Milford MM, Ind
    -dt Hugh (dec) & Hannah Moffitt
Sarah (4th w)  -dt of ... Hill of New Garden MM, Ind

Charles       b  2-18-1801   d  8- 7-1864
                                 -bur Earlham Cem
    -s Benjamin & Naomi
Michal        b  4-10-1802  d  8-19-1888 -bur Earlham
    -dt William & Mary  Butler
Ch: Edward        b 11-19-1826
   Elizabeth     b 10-20-1828
   William B      b 12- 2-1830
   Benjamin F     b  3-29-1834
   Naomi W        b

MORRIS
Aaron        b  9- 6-1776   -s John (dec) & Ruth (2nd w)
Lydia        b  1-23-1781   -dt William (dec) & Lydda
                                     Davis
Ch: John          b
   Samuel         b
   Elizabeth     b
   George         b

Caleb        b 10-23-1790  d  2-19-1835, Milford MM, Ind
    -s Nathan & Mary
Margaret     b  3-27-1784  d  2-13-1860, Milford MM, Ind
    -dt Aaron & Miriam (dec) Morris
Ch: Stephen       b  5- 3-1818

MILFORD

MORRIS (Cont)
Ch of Caleb & Margaret (Cont)
 Ann     b 2-26-1822 d 2- 7-1846
 Mary    b 1-24-1825

Christopher b 10-18-1771 d 10-24-1811
    (drowned in river in N C)
 -s Aaron & Margaret
Gulielma b 8-23-1779 d 1-24-1808 in N C
 -dt Josiah & Mary Bundy
Ch: (those who came to Ind)
 Mary    b 10-12-1798
 Josiah   b 8-22-1799
 Margaret  b 5-12-1806
 Aaron   b 8-30-1807

Christopher b 9- 3-1826 -s Josiah & Abigail
Margaret (1st w) b 7- 8-1834 d 2- 7-1865
 -dt Thomas & Jerusha Bell
Ch: Martha E  b 9- 8-1853 d 2-25-1864
 William L  b 7-20-1863
Prudence (2nd w) b 2-26-1838 -dt Thomas & Esther
           Stanley
Ch: Oliver H  b 5-25-1870
 Nellie G  b

David W b d 6-29-1895 -s John & Martha
Elizabeth b 9-27-1842 d 12- 7-1871 -dt Samuel M ...
Ch: Anna M  b 9-18-1865
 Elmore E  b 6-11-1867
 Samuel F  b 11-23-1871

Jehosaphat b 11-12-1787 -s Jonathan & Penelope
Peninah (1st w) -widow of Caleb Symons
 -dt Benjamin & Sarah Bundy
      b 3-27-1787 d 7-23-1813, Whitewater MM, Ind
Ch: Benoni  b 2-18-1813 d when young
Sarah (2nd w) b 6-17-1798 -dt Benjamin & Mary (dec) Hill
Ch: James  b 10- 6-1817 d 8-27-1838
 Joel   b 4-28-1820

Joel b 4-28-1820 -s Jehosaphat & Sarah
Ruth b 2-17-1824 -dt Joshua (dec) & Mary Morris
Ch: Theodosia  b 6-13-1844
 Sarah H  b 7-23-1846
 T Augustus  b 3- 9-1851
 Joshua L  b 1-16-1856

Jonathan b 2- 1-1807 -s William & Susanna
Theodate b 7-11-1804 -dt Amos & Mary Vernon of Ohio
Ch: Ruthanna V b 1-23-1831
 William R b

Jonathan b 6-16-1829 -s Jonathan & Abigail
Patience b 9-30-1828 d 11-13-1886
 -dt John & Elizabeth Hall of Driftwood MM, Ind
Ch: Albert H  b 8- 8-1856
 Elizabeth  b 12-10-1857 d 10-29-1864
 Alida   b 5- 4-1860
 Margaret H  b 8-10-1863
 Oliver M  b 5-21-1866
 Joseph C  b 6- 4-1868

Joshua b 4-29-1785 d 10-16-1823, Pasquotauk MM,
 -s Nathan Sr & Mary      N C
Mary b 4-16-1788 -dt Charles & Lydia Morgan
 (Married 2nd Abraham Symons Sr at Milford MM, Ind)
Ch: (by 1st h) (ch who came to Ind with their mother)
 Charles  b 4- 5-1807
 Lydia   b 1-15-1809
 Susanna  b 11-16-1810
 John   b 4-17-1815
 Mary   b 2-16-1817
 Jesse   b 9-24-1819
 Priscilla  b 12- 6-1821
 Ruth   b 2-17-1824

Josiah b 8-22-1799 d 12-10-1881
 -s Christopher & Gulielma (both dec)
Abigail b 5- 2-1797 d 2- 4-1868
 -dt Abraham & 1st w, Mary (Charles) Symons
Ch: Henry  b 7- 7-1824 d 9- 6-1849
 Christopher b 9- 3-1826

Nathan O b 12-14-1834 -s Joseph H & Martha
Phariba b 6-19-1841 -dt Christopher & Elizabeth
           Wilson
Ch: Joseph C  b 10- 5-1866
 Edith E  b 6-16-1868
 Francis  b 6-25-1870

Stephen b 5- 3-1818 d 10-12-1844
 -s Caleb (dec) & Margaret
Elizabeth W b 8-30-1818 -dt Thomas & Ann Moore
Ch: Margaret Ann b 5-13-1840 d 11-15-1860, Milford
 Susan   b 12-20-1841
 Ellen   b 8- 4-1844

William b 10-13-1781 -s Benjamin & Lydia
Susan b 9-30-1779 -dt Joshua & Susannah
         Copeland
Ch: Benjamin  b 4-19-1800
 Ava   b 9-21-1801
 Mordecai  b 12-21-1802
 Jonathan  b 2- 1-1807
 Susanna  b 2-23-1812
 Lydia   b 5-21-1814
 Ruth   b 9-22-1818
 Rachel  b 1-15-1824

NEWBY
Gabriel b 2-14-1773
 -s William & 1st w, Elizabeth (Ratliff)
Elizabeth -dt Jonathan Phelps of Randolph Co, N C
Ch: Elkanah  b 7-23-1797
 Jonathan  b 3- 1-1799 d 4- 7-1839
         Hopewell MM, Ind
 Miriam  b 1- 7-1801
 William  b 7-22-1803

Gabriel b 12-30-1799 -s Thomas & Mary
Rebecca b 11- 1-1804 -dt John & Jane Harvey
Ch: Mary Ann  b 7-25-1825
 Isom H  b 5-17-1827
 Elizabeth M  b 1- 5-1830
 Thomas J  b 5- 1-1832
 Jane Amanda b 12-18-1834
 Sarah E  b
 John F  b

Henry
Mary
Ch: Mildred  b 9- 7-1828
 William  b 7-15-1831
 Nathan  b 9-10-1834
 Matilda  b 12-22-1842

James W
Mary (form Moore)
Ch: William O  b 4-30-1868 d 8-11-1868
 Richard R  b 12-12-1870
 Annie P  b 2-18-1873
 Elizabeth  b

John b 1801 d 10- 7-1870, Milford MM, Ind
 -s Thomas & Mary of Jackson Co, Ind
Rebecca (1st w) b 4- 2-1804 d 12- 3-1841, Milford MM
Ch: Sarah R  b 7-19-1822
 Katharine R  b 11- 3-1824
 Henry   b 12-28-1826
 Thomas  b 9-21-1829
 John L  b 3- 5-1832
 Gabriel  b 3- 4-1835
 Mary   b 10-18-1837
 Jeremiah L  b 3-11-1841
Rachel (2nd w) b 3-23-1807 d 7- 3-1853, Milford MM
Ch: Abigail  b 12- 5-1843 d 12-12-1843
Mary B (3rd w) -dt Daniel (dec) & Jane Hunnicut
Ch: Rebecca J  b 6-14-1856

MILFORD

NEWBY (Cont)
Jonathan     b 3-1-1799      -s Gabriel & Elizabeth (Phelps)
Elizabeth    b 8-3-1802      -dt Josiah & Dorothy Gilbert

Joseph
Elizabeth
Ch: Charles      b 9-22-1823    d 11-25-1843
    Mary         b 6-19-1826    d 9-8-1826
    Margaret     b 9-10-1827
    Elijah       b 2-7-1829
    Caroline     b 8-12-1830
    Joshua       b 3-28-1832
    Aaron        b 6-14-1835
    Susan        b 11-14-1836
    Abigail      b 8-28-1838
    William      b 1-4-1840
    Hannah       b 7-31-1841

Thomas       b 12-13-1802    d 10-11-1872
                -s Jesse & Elizabeth
Nancy (1st w)  b 8-6-1833 in N C
                -dt Christopher & Phariba Wilson
Ch: (2 died at age of 3yrs & 6 yrs)
    Margaret Ann   b 7-3-1830
                (m in N C & remained there)
Margaret (2nd w)   b 8-28-1807
                -dt Joseph & Elizabeth Parker
                -widow of Elias White
Ch: James          b 6-10-1836
    William C      b 9-19-1837
    Martha P       b 4-9-1839
    Sarah Isabella b 2-7-1841
    Joseph P       b 10-8-1842    d 11- -1853
    Thomas R       b 5-28-1846
    Jane           b 2-24-1848
    Annie E        b 11-5-1849    d 7-8-1865
                                   Bethany MM

Thomas        -s Thomas & Mary
Rebecca       b 2-18-1814   d 1-26-1843, Milford MM
              -dt Benjamin (dec) & Martha Hill
Ch: Benjamin H  b 8-15-1839   d 9-1-1839
    James       b 11-14-1840
    Franklin    b 3-25-1842

Thomas    b 9-21-1829    -s John & Rebecca (dec)
Alice     b 12- -1830    -dt Jonathan & Alice Dickinson
Ch: William H    b 9-25-1850    d 1-12-1858
    Jonathan N   b

Thomas         b 3-11-1807    -s William & Elizabeth
Susannah (1st w)   -dt Jesse & Polly Pearson
Millicent (2nd w)  -dt John (dec) & Ann Reece

William      m 10-8-1766, Center MM, N C  -s Samuel
Elizabeth (1st w)   -dt Joseph & Mary Ratliff
              d 8-25-1803, Back Creek, N C
Elizabeth (2nd w)   -dt Thomas (dec) & Jane Symons
                    -widow of Obadiah Small
              b 4-5-1768
Ch: Nathan    b 12-22-1805    d 8-27-1806
    Thomas    b 3-11-1807
    Cyrus     b 10-30-1809
    Joseph    b

William C   b 9-19-1837    -s Thomas & Margaret
Olive P     b 5-18-1842    -dt Matthew & Elizabeth
                                   Terrell
Ch: Margaret T   b 8-9-1870

NIXON
Gabriel     b 10-25-1801   -s Phineas & Millicent
Mary        b 2-28-1808    -dt Daniel & Deborah
                                   Mendenhall
Ch: J Ann        b 5-4-1830
    Phenias H    b 4-18-1833
    Daniel M     b 1-2-1835

Josiah       b 2-23-1783    -s John & Jane
Mary         b 6-17-1788    d 6-7-1841, Milford MM, Ind
             -dt William & Elizabeth (Ratliff) Newby
Ch: William      b 4-6-1811
    John         b 7-27-1813
    Lydia        b 11-3-1815
    Elizabeth    b 3-7-1818
    Josiah       b 4-30-1820
    Nancy        b 12-1-1822
    Jane         b 2-24-1825
    Zachariah    b 4-4-1828
    Mary         b 10-19-1830
    Margaret     b 9-6-1833

Samuel R     b 2-24-1799    -s John & Ann (both dec)
Martha N     -dt Isaac (dec) & Jane Pleas
Ch: Margaret J   b 1-8-1831
    Ann          b 3-3-1833
    Alfred       b 6-27-1835
    James S      b 8-3-1838
    Samuel R     b 3-25-1840

William Muse  b 12-29-1800   -s John & Ann (both dec)
Achsah        b 6-12-1806    -dt Jonathan & Rachel White

PALIN
Exum         b 1-8-1808     -s Henry & Sarah
Elizabeth    -dt ... Bond of Duck Creek MM, Ind
Ch: Thomas       b 4-7-1828
    Henry        b 9-18-1829
    Gulielma     b 5-22-1831

                              -s Henry & Mary
Henry        b 12-6-1776    d 9-4-1848, Milford MM, Ind
Sarah (1st w) b 3-17-1774   d ca 1839-1840
             -dt John & Jane Nixon
Ch: Nixon        b 4-3-1800
    Henry Jr     b 1-12-1802
    Exum         b 1-8-1808
    Mary         b 12-6-1810
Miriam (2nd w)  -widow of .. Pike, widow w/ch of
                    Hopewell MM, Ind
        (After d of Henry, Miriam m .. Wickersham)

PARKER
Isaac        b 9-22-1806    -s Jeremiah & Keren
Mary         b ca 1813      -dt Benjamin & Anny Stratton
Ch: Benjamin     b 2-10-1833
    Robert       b 3-8-1835    d 10-2-1835
                                   Rich Square MM
    Rebecca      b 8-12-1836
    Edwin E      b 12-11-1840
                              -s Joseph & Sarah
Jeremiah     b 11-22-1767   d 2-12-1837, Rich Sq MM
Keren        b 2-27-1767    -dt Robert & Jemima Newby

Robert       b 3-14-1793    d 3-8-1838, Hopewell MM
                -s Jeremiah & Keren
Miriam       b 8-5-1795     -dt John & Sarah Bell
Ch: Mary         b 3-19-1826
    Lydia        b 4-15-1827
    Abigail      b 7-22-1829
    William      b 12-30-1830
    Michael      b 4-12-1833    d 1-24-1838
                                   Hopewell MM
    John         b 6-6-1835

PATTERSON
Elihu        d ca 1843      -s Jared & Angeline of
                                   Walnut Ridge MM, Ind
Rachel       b 3-27-1825    -dt Joseph & Elizabeth Cox
             (Rachel m 2nd James Binford at Bethel MM-
              he of Walnut Ridge MM)

PEARSON
Thomas B     b 2-19-1835
Mary         b 4-18-1832    -dt .. Elliott
Ch: Charles Exum    b 5-1-1855
    Margaret S      b 3-3-1858

MILFORD

PEELE
Caleb M        b  6-12-1843    -s Henry E & Mary
Maria          b 10- 7-1842    -dt James & Sarah Smith
Ch: James R                b  9-15-1868    d 11-22-1868
    Frances H              b  4-15-1870
    Walter                 b  3-26-1872

Henry E        b  9- 1-1816    -s James & Ruth   d 10- 3-1895
Mary           b  1-24-1825    -dt Caleb & Margaret Morris
Ch: Caleb M                b  6-12-1843
    James                  b  4-21-1845
    Elizabeth              b  2-19-1847    d  3-20-1891
    Edward                 b  3-16-1849
    Isabella               b 11- 6-1850
    Stephen                b  8-24-1852
    John                   b 11- 7-1854
    Charles F              b 10-28-1856
    Margaret M             b 12- 3-1858
    Deborah                b 11-22-1860
    Henry                  b 10- 7-1862
    Walter C               b 10- 7-1864    d  6- 6-1866
    Mary Olive             b  7-19-1868

PENNINGTON
Josiah         (Of Ohio & Center MM, Pa)
Deborah        (Of Ohio & Pipe Creek MM, Pa)
Ch: Leroy Talbott          b  4-30-1812
    Mary                   b 10- 9-1813
    Susannah               b  7-18-1815
    John P                 b  3-11-
    Eliza                  b 11-30-1818
    Rachel                 b  3- 8-1821

PERISHO
Nathan         b  9-29-1800    -s Joshua Jr & Elizabeth
Mary           -dt Joseph (dec) Lamb
Ch: Elizabeth              b 10-21-1820    d  1- 4-1823, N C
    Mary Elma              b 12-26-1824
    John                   b  7-11-1826
    Joshua Morris          b  3- 5-1829
    Martha                 b  1-18-1831

PICKERING
Jonas          -s Samuel & Phebe of Concord MM, Ohio
Ruth           -dt Abner & Sarah Gregg of Concord MM, Ohio
Ch: Abner                  b  3- 9-1805
    Abigail                b  8-25-1806
    Samuel                 b 11-30-1807
    Sarah                  b  4- 7-1809
    Phebe                  b  6-30-1811
    Jonas Jr               b  9- 8-1812
    Mahlon                 b  6-15-1814
    Ruthanna               b  2-25-1816
    Joseph                 b  1-27-1818
    Jordan                 b  5-31-1820

Samuel Jr      -s Samuel Sr & Phebe
Phebe          -dt Adam (dec) & Esther Kirk of Kenneth MM, Pa
               & Redstone MM, Pa & Ohio
Ch: Rebecca                b
    James                  b
    Hiram                  b
    Esther                 b
    Susanna                b
    Samuel                 b

PIERCE
Samuel         b  6- 3-1790    -s Caleb & Priscilla of
                                Cincinnati, Ohio
Lydia          b 12-15-1796    -dt David & Hannah Holloway
                                of Highland Co, Ohio
Ch: Gideon                 b 11-30-1819
    Kersey                 b 11-20-1821
    David                  b

Samuel         b  9-12-1822    -s Samuel & Milly of Union MM,
                                                        Ohio
Elizabeth (1st w) b 10-12-1825  d 10-27-1852, Union MM,
               (Most of ch died young)                  Ohio
               -dt Enos & Margaret Elleman

Ann (2nd w)    -widow of Lyman W Jones, Dover MM, Ind
Ch: Esther                 b 10-22-1855
    Milly                  b  4-17-1860
    John Paine             b  3-14-1863
    Sophia P               b

PIKE
Wilson         b  1- 5-1798    -s John & Fanny (dec) of N C
Miriam
Ch: Milah                  b  1-25-1818
    Peninah                b  3- 6-1820
    Jordan                 b 11-21-1823
    Mary Ann               b
    Stanford               b

PITMAN
Robert         d  2-11-1872
Mary
Ch: Milton                 b 10- 9-1821
    Mary                   b  8-12-1824

PLEAS - PLACE
Aaron L        b 10-29-1805    -s Isaac (dec) & Jane
                                in N C
Lydia          b  2-22-1812    d  5-18-1839, Hopewell MM, Ind
                               -dt Josiah & Dorothy Gilbert
Ch: Elwood                 b  4- 5-1831
    Maurice                b  9-10-1833
    Dorothy J              b  4-17-1836
    Achsah                 b 12-28-1838

PRAY
Enos           b ca 1812    -s William (dec) & Mary,
                                of Preble Co, Ohio
                             (Mary of Redstone MM, Pa)
Elvira         b 12-29-1815 -dt William & Esther (dec)
                             Stubbs of Elk MM, Ohio
                             Elvira of Butler Co, Ohio
Ch: Esther                 b  8-30-1834    d 1835
    William S              b  2- 2-1836
    Elizabeth M            b
    Martha                 b              d 1866
    Rachel                 b
    Sibil                  b
    Rhoda J                b
    Joseph J               b
    Anna Maria             b
    Samuel Dilwin          b
    Enos Edwin             b
    Walter C               b  4-27-1858    d  9- 8-1860

William S      b 2- 2-1836     -s Enos & Elvira
Nancy H
Ch: Charles                b  5-15-1862    d 12-29-1862
    Clara Ellen            b  4-12-1864

PRETLOW
Robert S
Isabella H
Ch: James Thomas           b
    Deborah H              b
    Sarah Isabella         b
    Chlotilda L            b
    Robert E               b  7-15-1862
    Elizabeth              b 11-27-1869

RATLIFF
Cornelius      b ca 1805    -s Richard (dec) & Elizabeth
                                            (Pierson)
Abigail        b  9-25-1806 -dt Joel & Lydia Gilbert
Ch: Richard                b 10- 7-1828
    Betsy                  b 12-16-1830
    Calvin                 b 10-25-1832
    Reuben                 b  3- 6-1834

Elias          b ca 1814    -s Jonathan & Sarah (dec)
                                (1st w)
Miriam         -dt Samuel & Elizabeth Bogue Of Hopewell MM
                                (Elizabeth dec)
Ch: Eliza Jane             b 10- 5-1838

MILFORD

RATLIFF (Cont)
Jonathan        b 2- 8-1791    -s Richard & Elizabeth (Pearson)
Sarah (1st w)              m 1813, N C  d in Ind between 1815
                                                    & 1827
Ch: Elias              b ca 1814 in N C
    John P             b ca 1816 in Ind
Sarah (2nd w)   -dt Samuel & Elizabeth Bogue of Milford MM
Ch: Mary               b 7- 6-1827
    Samuel             b 8- 2-1828
    Sally              b 8-28-1829
    Miriam             b 8-12-1831

Nathan          b 9- 6-1793    -s Richard & Elizabeth
Lydia           Of Deep Creek MM, N C   (Pearson)
Ch: Mary               b 4-27-1817
    Alfred             b 4-17-1819
    Martha             b 5-11-1820
    Joseph             b 5- 4-1825
    Tom                b 5- 4-1825
    Ann                b 3- 4-1828
    Levi               b 9-19-1832

Richard S  b ca 1759  d ca 1827  -s Joseph & Mary of N C
Elizabeth       -dt Jonathan Pearson of N C
Ch: Ann                b 3- 4-1786
    Joseph             b 8- 3-1788
    Jonathan           b 2- 8-1791
    Nathan             b 9- 6-1793
    Mary               b    ca1797
    Richard Jr         b
    Gabriel            b
    Cornelius          b
    Elizabeth          b

REAGAN
Reason     b 10-13-1797   -s Thomas & Rachel of Caesars
           d 1- 5-1864                 Creek MM, Ohio
Mary       b 6-30-1798   d 3-17-1852, Caesars Creek
                                      MM, Ohio
           -dt Samuel & Mary Spray of Clinton Co, Ohio
Ch: John               b 12-31-1819
    Dinah              b 1-22-1821
    Rachel             b 2-22-1825   d 4-26-1848, Ohio
    Mary               b 1- 5-1829   d 8- 7-1847, Ohio

Wiley      -s Thomas & Rachel of Ohio & West Grove MM, Ind
Ruth       -dt John & Dinah Wilson
Ch: Thomas             b 11- 9-1822
    Louisa             b 3- 4-1825
    Anna M             b 8-15-1827
    Sarah              b 8-15-1830
    Wilson             b 4-29-1832   d 2-14-1835

REECE
John       b 2-18-1780     -s Francis & Christiana (Stone)
                              of Center MM, N C
Ann        -dt ... Needham of Back Creek MM, N C
Ch: Nathan             b 5-23-1806
    Needham            b 10- 2-1807
    Millicent          b 4- 8-1809
    Daniel             b 7- 8-1810
    Elias              b 11-16-1811
    Christiana         b 5-29-1813
    Jane               b 1- 1-1815
    John Jr            b 4- 7-1817

Nathan     b 5-23-1806   -s John & Ann
Susanna    -of Duck Creek MM, Ind
Ch: Charles            b 2- 9-1829
    Susannah           b 4- 8-1832
    Ann                b 11-19-1834
    Jane               b 11-11-1835
    Mary               b 5-31-1838

Needham    b 10- 2-1807  -s John & Ann (Needham)
Celia      b 11-10-1812  d 9-10-1838, Rich Sq MM
           -dt James & Rosanna Townsend of West Grove MM,
                                                      Ind

Ch: John               b 3-12-1832
    James T            b 10-25-1834   d 9-25-1886
REYNOLDS
Benjamin   -from Cincinnati, Ohio & Cornwall MM, N Y
Ann (form Cowell)
Ch: Daniel             b 10-13-1805
    Elizabeth          b
    Phebe              b 6-12-1808
    Josiah             b
    David              b
    Rueben             b
    Stephen            b
    Hannah             b
    Sarah              b
    Benjamin C         b
    Amos B             b
    Anna               b 9- 1-1823
    Jonathan           b 4-11-1824

Daniel     -s Benjamin & Ann    b 10-13-1805
Margaret   b 5-12-1806  -dt Christopher & Gulielma
                                            Morris
Ch: Mary               b 12- 3-1828
    Milton             b 11- 1-1830
    Morris             b 10-11-1832
    Thomas             b 8-15-1834
    Phebe              b 9- 5-1836
    Josiah             b 9-29-1838

RIDGEWAY
John       -s Timothy & Michel (fr Little Eggharbour MM
            of Harrison Co, Ohio - Flushing MM, Ohio
Ruth       -dt Isaac & Rachel Nevit of Harrison Co,
            Ohio - fr Hopewell MM, Va
Ch: Abijah J           b 3- 8-1819
    Lydia              b 12-10-1820
    Daniel             b 11-26-1822
    Jane               b 2-23-1825
    Catharine          b 2- 4-1827   d 8- 9-1832, Ohio
    Richard            b 6-10-1829
    Ruthanna           b 8-21-1831
    John               b 6-28-1838

ROBERTS
Hannah     b 1792   d 1-12-1841, Milford MM, Ind

SAINT
Thomas     b 10-19-1790  -s Daniel (dec) & Margaret
                                          (Jones)
Margaret (1st w) b 3-24-1798   d 5- 3-1837
           -dt Joseph & Margaret (Jordan) Trueblood
Ch: William            b 5-20-1815
    Joseph             b 9-16-1817
    Thomas             b 5- 6-1820
    Samuel T           b 12- 6-1822
    Daniel             b 10-13-1825  d 4- -1892
    Sarah              b 4- 3-1829
    John               b 11-28-1833
    Richard J          b 4-14-1837
Mary (2nd w) (form Pritchard - a widow with ch)
Ch: George S           b

William    b 1781  d 1- 2-1871
           -s Hercules & Sarah of Piney Woods MM, N C
Achsah     b 1786  d 11-29-1839
           -dt .. Elliott of Piney Woods MM, N C
Ch: Exum               b 9-10-1808
    Julianna           b 8- 8-1811
    Alpheus            b 2-21-1813
    Jenette            b 2-16-1816
    Doughty            b 8- 7-1818
    Joseph             b 3-23-1820
    Jonathan           b 1-26-1822
    Daniel             b 11-24-1823
    Milton             b 1-13-1826
    William            b 11-30-1828
    Cynthia            b 12-28-1830

MILFORD

SHARP
William Henry        -s Samuel T & Mary V, Cedar Co,
                        Ohio - Plainfield MM, Ohio
Rebecca      -dt Jesse & Lydia Roberts, Belmont Co, Ohio
Ch: Samuel T           b 12-30-1857    d 11-15-1865
    Jesse Robert       b 10-27-1860
    Mary Caroline      b 11-10-1865

SMALL
Samuel       b  3- 2-1800   -s Gideon & Sarah
Abigail      b  8-20-1799   -dt Samuel & Abigail Stafford
                               of Back Creek MM, N C
Ch: Jesse              b  9-29-1820
    Louisa             b  5- 1-1823    d 10-15-1826
    Eli                b 12-15-1825
    James G            b  3- 6-1828


Josiah       b 10-18-1790
                -s Obadiah Jr & Elizabeth (Symons)
Jane         -dt Thomas & 2nd w, Abigail Moore
Ch: Thomas             b
    Sarah              b
    Elizabeth          b
    Abigail            b

SMITH
Benjamin     b  6-23-1787   -s Joseph & Hannah (dec)
Tamar        b 10-19-1784   -dt John & Mary Hawkins
Ch: Hannah             b  4- 4-1809
    Mary               b  7- 8-1811
    John               b  6-26-1813
    William            b 11-20-1814
    Sarah              b  1-22-1818
    Lydia              b  3- 4-1819
    Amos               b  2-25-1822
    Tamar              b  2- 2-1824
    Martha             b  9- 3-1825
    Patience           b 10-17-1827

James        b  4- 3-1805   d  1- 4-1885
                -s Joseph & Elizabeth
                (Formerly of Sheffield, York Co, England
Sarah        b 10-31-1814   d 12-17-1885
                -dt James & Elizabeth Williams
Ch: Joseph             b 10- 3-1837
    Eliza              b  4- 8-1839
    Maria              b 10- 7-1842

STANBROUGH
Evan         b  5-17-1790   -s Solomon & Tabitha of Ohio
Elizabeth    b  2- 5-1795   -dt Francis & Mary Hester of
                               Ohio
Ch: Mary               b  1-14-1814
    Solomon            b  6-15-1815
    Tabitha            b  1-11-1817
    Rachel             b 12- 7-1818
    John               b 11-18-1820
    Francis H          b 12-19-1822
    William            b 12-13-1824
    Elizabeth          b  1- 1-1827

James        b  5-25-1793   d 11-22-1831
                -s Solomon & Tabitha of Ohio
Mary         b  7- 2-1790
                -dt Hurr & Elizabeth Hodgson of Ohio
Ch: Isaac              b 12- 9-1814    d  9- 4-1823
    Jonathan           b  4-13-1817    d  9- 4-1869
    Phebe              b  8-10-1818
    Elizabeth          b  7-12-1822
    Rebecca            b  9-27-1826    d  9- 6-1827
    Solomon            b  7- 9-1828    d 11-10-1835

Nehemiah     b  3-23-1792   -s Solomon & Tabitha of Ohio
Ruth         b  9-25-1798   -dt Francis & Mary Hester of
                               Ohio
Ch: Ann                b  3- 3-1816
    Thomas             b
    Francis            b
    James              b

    Solomon            b 11-19-1823
    Mary H             b 11-26-1825
    Levi               b  2-17-1828
    Tabitha            b  6- 7-1831

STANLEY
Daniel W     b 11-21-1835   d  5- 4-1865
                -s Ira & Betsy
Sarah H      b  7-12-1840   -dt Matthew & Elizabeth D
                               Terrell of Short Creek MM, Ohio
Ch: Elizabeth Ann      b 10- 8-1861
    Oliver T           b  7- 4-1864

George       -s Samuel & Susannah of N C & Ohio
Jemima       b  1-27-1795
                -dt Jeremiah & Keren Parker of Whitewater
                    MM, Ind
Ch: Samuel             b 12-12-1822
    Jeremiah           b  7-13-1824
    Isaac              b 12-15-1825
    Keren              b  2-11-1828
    John T             b 10-14-1829
    Elizabeth          b  9-25-1831
    Elam               b  7- 5-1834
    James M            b  4-16-1838

Ira   b 12- 1-1808   -s Michael & Mary (Gurley)
Elizabeth    b  4-30-1814   -dt Mathew & Ruth Bennett
Ch: Daniel W           b 11-21-1835    d  5- 4-1865
    Josiah             b  8- 8-1837
    Ruthann            b  8-11-1839
    Abagail            b  7-30-1841    d  6-30-1842
    Priscilla          b  6- 4-1843    d  9-21-1844
    Oliver             b  6-16-1845    d  3-25-1846
    William B          b  1-11-1847
    Lucinda            b 11- 3-1848
    Emily              b  3-22-1851
    John               b  5- 3-1854    d  8-21-1855
    Isabella           b 10-27-1856    d  5- 6-1873
    Charles H          b  9- 3-1858

William      b  7-18-1799   -s Samuel & Sarah
Susannah     b  2-17-1808   -dt Thomas & Ann Moore
             d 11-19-1857
Ch: Jesse C            b 12-21-1826
    Sarah C            b  4-10-1829
    Eliza A            b  8-25-1831
    William C          b  9- 2-1833

William C    b  9- 2-1833   -s William & Susannah
Mary Maria (1st w)  b  7-20-1836   d  6-25-1861
                -dt Jonathan & Abigail Morris
Miriam (2nd w) -dt .. King of Spiceland MM, Ind
Sarah H (3rd w)     b  7-12-1840
                -dt Mathew & Elizabeth Terrell
                -widow of Daniel Stanley

STEWART
Samuel W     b 1798   d 4-26-1872
                (from Greenwich MM, N J)
Hannah       d 1855   -dt ... Jeffries, Greenwich MM, N J
Ch: Mary               b 10-25-1823
    Elizabeth          b  7- 7-1825
    James              b  1-10-1827
    Beulah             b  8- 4-1828
    Charles            b 12-25-1829
    John               b 10-18-1831
    William            b  9-10-1833
    Edwin              b  8- 5-1835
    Samuel             b  5-10-1838

STOKES
Samuel       b  6- 2-1788   d 11- 4-1858
                -s .. From Philadelphia MM, Pa
Jane         b           d  6-16-1863
                -dt ... Burson from Philadelphia MM, Pa
Ch: Isabella           b           d  7-12-1854
    Elizabeth          b  4- 9-1818
    Hannah R           b

MILFORD

STOKES (Cont)
Ch of Samuel & Jane (Cont)
  Edwin         b
  Henry         b
  Susan         b 5- 6-1829    d 1-29-1863
  Albert J      b

STRATTON
Benjamin    -From South River MM, Va & Middleton MM,
                             Columbiana Co, Ohio
Anny
Ch: Rebecca       b ca 1797
    Naomi         b
    Levi          b
    Ephraim       b
    Benjamin Jr   b
    Jerusha       b 1-22-1808   d 7-23-1837
    Martha        b 4- 2-1810   d 10- 8-1885
    Mary          b
    Joseph        b 2- 5-1815
    Samuel        b 9- 1-1817   d 11-11-1837
    Luanna        b 3-23-1820   d 9- 8-1841

STRAUGHN
Merriman
Hannah       (form Vickery)
Ch: John          b 3- 6-1820
    Jonathan      b 7-26-1821
    Jehu          b 5-13-1823
    James         b 10-23-1824
    Milton        b 7- 4-1826

STREET
John       b 11- 9-1804   -s Aaron & Mary
Dorothy (1st w) b 12-29-1807   d 1- 6-1839, Hopewell
    -dt Josiah & Dorothy Gilbert
Ch: Eunice       b 5-21-1828
    Emily         b 8- 7-1830
    Mary          b 11-28-1832
    Josiah        b 9-12-1835   d 1-11-1836
    John          b
Agatha (2nd w)   -dt .. Hussey of Walnut Ridge MM,
                                      Ind

STUART
John       b 10-22-1802   d 4-17-1885
    -s Jehu & Sarah
Martha     b 4- 2-1810   d 10- 8-1885
    -dt Benjamin & Anny Stratton
Ch: Benjamin     b 10-30-1828
    John          b 3-21-1830
    Anny          b 1-19-1833
    Levi          b 7- 8-1836

STUBBS
Jonathan   b 1- 8-1823
    -s William & Esther (dec) of Elk MM, Ohio
Rachel     b 1- 9-1823   -dt Jesse & Hannah (dec) Lane
Ch: Susan L      b 7-21-1845
    Alvan         b 1-24-1847
    Enoch         b 2-18-1848
    Albert        b 8-30-1850
    Elvira        b 3- 8-1853
    Mary Emma    b 12-27-1857

Joseph    b 11-12-1799   d 9-15-1839, Milford MM, Ind
    -s Nathan & Elizabeth of Butler Co, Ohio
Sarah     b ca 1801   -dt John & Elvira Townsend of
                              Whitewater MM, Ind
Ch: Celia        b 4- 9-1819
    Daniel        b 8-16-1820   d 12- 7-1839
    Jemima        b 9-24-1821
    Elisha        b 7-15-1823   d 4-30-1824
    Mahlon        b 2- 2-1825
    Amy           b 3- 1-1827
    Stephen       b 12-10-1828
    Jacob         b 7-18-1831
    Martha        b 7- 5-1833   d 7-29-1833
    Mary          b 7- 5-1833

  John T       b 7-23-1835
  Margaret M   b 5- 7-1839

SUTTON
Aaron F     -s Aaron & Mary H of Ulster Co, N Y
Anne       b 7-26-1849   -dt Charles H & Marcia Moore
                          of Milford MM, Ind
Ch: Mary B      b 12-17-1872
    Marcia E     b
    Caroline     b

David      b 4-26-1827   -s Isaac & Sarah of Adrian,
                                     Mich
Deborah   b 10- 2-1834   d 1-29-1884
    -dt Aaron & Margaret White
Ch: Marcia E     b 12-28-1860
    Aaron W      b 5-23-1862   d 10-22-1874
    Howard       b 12-16-1868

SWAIN
Anna Jane  -widow of Dr George Swain of New Garden
                                  MM, N C

David      b 5-25-1790   m 6- 8-1815, New Garden MM
    -s Sylvanus & Miriam (Gardner)
Phebe (1st w) b 3-10-1789   d 1- 8-1842, Poplar Ridge
                          -ae 52yrs,10mo,12da
Ch: Ruth          b
    Eunice    b ca 3-1-1818   d 2-19-1844, Poplar Ridge
                            -ae 25yrs,11mo,19da
Ruth (2nd w)   d 8- 7-1852, Milford MM, Ind
    -of Walnut Ridge MM, Ind   -dt ... Coffin
Phebe (3rd w) -dt .. Weisner of Walnut Ridge MM, Ind

George R   b 4-25-1817   d 7-12-1871
    -s Reul & Miriam of New Garden MM, N C
Luzena     b 1-23-1824   d 8-29-1871
    -dt Israel & Elizabeth Stanley of Hopewell
                                   MM, N C
Ch: Miriam       b
    Sarah A      b 3-20-1867   d 2- 6-1873

Jonathan   d 10-18-1859 (husband of Lydia)

Shubal     b 1-26-1810   -s Sylvanus (dec) & Miriam
                          of Silver Creek MM, Ind
Mary       b 1- 1-1812   -dt William & Matilda Barnard
                          of Silver Creek MM, Ind
Ch: Florella     b 6-25-1838   d 1- 2-1853
                                    Milford MM
    Calvin        b 2-18-1840
    Louisa        b 3-17-1842
    Matilda B    b 11-14-1843
    Byron         b 12- 4-1845
    Barclay       b 10- 3-1847
    Sophia        b 10- 7-1849
    Sylvanus     b 6-12-1852
    Herschel     b 11- 8-1857

SYMONS
Abraham   b 4- 7-1769   d 9-20-1836
    -s John & Anna
Mary (1st w)  d prior to 1828
    -dt Samuel & Abigail Charles
Ch: (brought to Ind)
    Samuel        b 1- 6-1794
    Henry         b            Died young
    Abigail       b 5- 2-1797
    Sarah         b 8- 5-1799
    John          b 9- 2-1801
    Margaret     b 4-11-1803
    Gulielma     b 2- 8-1805
    Abraham      b 10-17-1809
    Matthew      b 7-15-1811
    Phebey        b 4- 2-1813
    Thomas        b 3-18-1815
Mary (2nd w)  b 4-16-1788   -widow of Joshua Morris
    -dt Charles & Lydia Morgan
Ch: Eunice       b 2-27-1829   d 12-24-1860

MILFORD

SYMONS (Cont)
Abraham      b 10-17-1809    d 10- 8-1838, Hopewell MM, Ind
             -s Abraham Sr & Mary (Charles)
Achsah       b 3-28-1815     d 11- 9-1838, Hopewell MM, Ind
             -dt Josiah & Dorothy Gilbert
Ch: Matilda           b 4- 2-1836    d 12-28-1838
                                     Hopewell MM, Ind
    Benjamin F        b 12-16-1837

John         b 9- 2-1801     -s Abraham & Mary (dec)
Rebecca      b 4-27-1804     -dt John & Sarah Bell
Ch: Charles           b 11- 8-1823   d 8-19-1840
    Daniel            b 6-11-1827    d 5-10-1880
    Abraham           b 11- 3-1828
    Sarah             b 12-14-1830
    Joel              b 7-18-1833    d 2-16-1863
    Mary              b 10-22-1835   d 5- 5-1865
    Abigail           b 7-26-1839
    Benjamin F        b 8-28-1842    d 3- 7-1863

Josiah       b 6-10-1812     d 7-24-1879
             -s Thomas & Hannah
Sarah        b 1- 7-1813     d 10- 3-1893
             -dt John & Betty Kindley
Ch: Jehu              b 7-16-1832
    Joel              b

Matthew      b 12- 7-1766    -s John & Ann (Morris)
Sarah
Ch: Thomas            b 3-25-1794
    Matthew Jr        b 2-11-1798
    Ann               b 4-23-1800
    Mary              b
    Sarah             b 10- 6-1812

Nathan       b 10-15-1786    -s Jesse & Sarah
Jane         b 12-28-1793    -dt Obediah & Elizabeth Small
Ch: Rebecca           b 9-11-1823
    Jane              b 3-16-1826
    Ruth              b 7-23-1828
    Nathan            b 10-27-1830

Samuel       b 1- 6-1794     -s Abraham & Mary (dec)
Ann          b 5-13-1794     -dt Daniel (dec) & Mary Bonine
Ch: Lydia             b 6-22-1825
    James             b 1- 7-1828
    John              b 10-18-1830
    Abraham           b 8-31-1832
    Henry             b 12-22-1834

Thomas       b 3-25-1794     d 9-20-1839
             -s Matthew & Sarah
Abigail      b 3-22-1796     d 5-17-1875
             -dt Joseph & Sarah (both dec) Wilson
Ch: Rebecca           b 4- 5-1819    d 4-16-1835
    Henry W           b 8-13-1821
    Mary              b 6-21-1824
    Milton            b 9-13-1826    d 8-14-1856
    Nathan M          b 12- 4-1828
    Mahlon            b 4- 5-1831    d 9-24-1839
    Samuel C          b 11-12-1832

Thomas       b 2-17-1782     -s Jesse & Sarah
Hannah       b 5-15-1788     -dt Bethuel & Hannah Coffin
Ch: Josiah            b 6-10-1812
    Bethuel           b 2- 7-1814
    Elijah            b 8-17-1816
    Nathan            b 4-19-1818
    Rebecca           b 2-10-1820
    Thomas            b 1-23-1822
    Abel              b 2-17-1827
    Daniel            b 5-15-1829
    Aaron             b 2- 2-1832

TALBERT
Elihu        b 3-31-1812     -s William & Miriam of Union
                                                  Co, Ind
Lucretia C   b 3-26-1814     -dt Samuel & Deborah Paddock

Ch: Louisa            b 4- 2-1834
    Emily C           b 1- 8-1836
    Ann M             b 6- 5-1839
    Avis P            b 9-12-1845
    Lindley H         b 2-12-1848
    Mary Florence     b 1- 8-1851

THATCHER
Joseph       From Ohio       d 5- 3-1857
Deborah      (Form Hadley)   d 9- 1-1862
Ch: Mary Ellen        b 9-24-1834
    William H         b 10-30-1837
    Susan             b 7-29-1840
    Sarah             b 9- 4-1843
    Lydia Mariah      b 7-20-1846
    Anna J            b 5- 2-1849

TOMS
Anderson     b 2-27-1842     -s Joseph & Phariba
Mary M       -dt ... Johnson of Kokomo MM, Ind
Ch: Laura E           b 11- 3-1869
    Margaret          b 6-27-1872
    Joseph            b
    Jesse             b

Joseph       b 12-29-1814    d 3-27-1891
             -s Anderson (dec) & Mary of N C
Phariba      b 12-14-1818
             -dt William & Sarah (White) Wilson of N C
Ch: William           b 1-23-1838
    Mary              b 7-19-1839
    Anderson          b 2-27-1842
    Joseph            b
    John              b
    Benjamin W        b 5-23-1856
    Sarah I           b 6-25-1858
    Pharaba           b 6-25-1860

William      b 1-23-1838     -s Joseph & Phariba
Phebe Ann (1st w) b 4-17-1836    d 6-29-1865
             -dt Matthew & Susan Symons
Ch: Edgar V           b 6-19-1865
Charity (2nd w)       -dt ... Hill of Walnut Ridge

VICKERY
Elizabeth    (form Newby)    d 6- 9-1852

WALTON
Joseph
Caroline     b 5-15-1850     -dt Silas & Emily Huddleston
Ch: Anna B            b 7-11-1868
    George F          b
    Sarah Estelle     b

WARING
Joshua
Margaret
Ch: William P         b 4-18-1827
    Abigail           b 7- 9-1832

WASSON
Calvin       b 2-14-1798
             -s Archibald & Elizabeth of Whitewater MM, Ind
Mary         b 5- 9-1795     -dt William & Charlotte Bond
Ch: William           b 6-20-1819
    Nathan            b 3-14-1821
    Elizabeth         b 1-30-1824
    Sarah             b 5-16-1826

Jehiel       b 1-16-1800     -s Archibald & Elizabeth
Lydia        b 2- 3-1800     -dt William & Charlotte Bond
Ch: Jesse             b ca 1821-1822
    Charlotte         b

Nathan       b 3-14-1821     -s Calvin & Mary
Maria (1st w) b 9-15-1822    d 7- 6-1844, Bethel MM, Ind
             -dt Joseph & Elizabeth Cox
Ch: Margaret          b 10-13-1843   d 12-25-1856
Elizabeth (2nd w)     b 8-30-1818    -widow of Stephen
             -dt Thomas (dec) & Anne Moore        Morris

MILFORD

WASSON (Cont)
Ch of Nathan & 2nd w, Elizabeth:
    Oliver          b 12- 4-1849    d 11-16-1850
    Mary            b 10-23-1851
    Henry          b 10-31-1853
    Charles        b 9- 6-1856

WAY
Robert         b 6-29-1804    -s David & Ann of Monroe Co, Ohio
Lydia          b 4-12-1807
                -dt Dempsey & Mary Boswell of Belmont Co, Ohio
Ch: Milicent       b 2-19-1827
    Mary Ann       b 5-25-1828
    David L        b 12-15-1830
    Sarah          b 10-22-1833

WESTCOMBE
Charles F   d 3- -1881
                -s Samuel T & Elizabeth of Worcestershire MM, England
Isabella    b ca 1816   d 7-12-1854
                -dt Samuel & Jane Stokes of Milford MM, Ind

WHITE
Aaron          b 9-27-1793   d 10-22-1863
                -s Edmund & Mary of N C
Margaret (1st w)  b 11-14-1796  d 8-20-1854
                -dt Joshua & Margaret Fletcher of N C
Ch: Albert         b 4-26-1817   d 12-22-1840
    Marcia         b 9-13-1823
    Susannah       b 5- 9-1828   d Milford MM, Ind
    Richard        b 7-11-1829
    Augustus       b 10-30-1832  d 7-31-1833 Milford MM, Ind
    Deborah        b 10- 2-1834  d 4-29-1888
    Lemuel         b 6-21-1838   d 9- 9-1838

Daniel T    b 2-23-1835   (an orphan in 1850 u/c of Aaron & Margaret White)
Sarah       b 4-25-1843   Of Hopewell MM, Ind
Ch: Annie S       b 8-27-1865
    Olive B        b 1-16-1868
    Arthur S       b 8-24-1869

Josiah         b 3- 7-1811   d 1-17-1837, Milford MM, Ind
                -s Thomas & Jemima (both dec) of N C
Esther G    b 3- 2-1816   -dt Benajah & Elizabeth Hiatt
           d 2- 2-1891   of Milford MM
           (m 2nd to Joseph Dickinson
Ch: Oliver         b 8-21-1836

Josiah T    b 4- 3-1824   d 6- 7-1915
            -s David & Elizabeth of N C
Elizabeth   b 11-22-1825
            -dt William & Mary Wilson of N C (Mary dec)
Ch: William W     b 11- 2-1846   d 6-24-1891
    Mary Isabella  b 1- 9-1849
    David F        b 10- 7-1850
    Oliver         b 10- 9-1852
    Delphina       b 7- 7-1855
    Phariba W      b 6-24-1857
    Julia E        b 5- 7-1860   d 10- 2-1861
    Jeptha         b 3-17-1862
    Josiah T Jr    b 9-25-1867

Robert         b 6-18-1789   d 6-25-1830, Suttons Creek NC
                -s John & Mourning
Rebecca    -dt Francis (dec) & Caroline (Bell) Albertson
    m 9-16-1819, Suttons Creek, N C
Ch: (Brought to Ind with widowed mother)
    Lucinda        b
    William Albertson  b

Richard       b 7-11-1829   -s Aaron & Margaret
Mary A        b 4-29-1836   -dt Jacob & Sarah Underhill of Miami MM, Ohio
Ch: Charles A     b 6-28-1856
    Sarah C        b 10-18-1862
    William A      b 10- 9-1864
    Anna A         b 2- 9-1868

William W     b 11- 2-1846   d 6-24-1891
           -s Josiah T & Elizabeth
Mary A        b 11-29-1848
           -dt Thomas N & Lydia White of Hopewell MM, Ind
Ch: Roy W         b 6- 6-1872
    Thomas K      b 8-30-1875
    Marian E       b 12-28-1877

WICKERSHAM
Caleb          b 2-10-1780   -s John Sr & Mary of N C
Lydia (1st w)  b 10- 6-1782   d 1- 9-1820 at Silver Creek
            -dt Eliab & Sarah Gardner of N C   MM, Ind
Ch: Abel          b 1- 8-1804
    Miriam         b 9-30-1805
    John           b 9-18-1807
    Mary           b 3-23-1810
    Sarah          b 12-28-1811
    Anna           b 4-28-1814
    Huldah         b 11-28-1815
    Jehu           b 12- 9-1817
    Oliver         b 12- 9-1817
Eunice (2nd w)  b ca 1797-1799
            -dt Latham & Matilda Folger of Union MM, N C
m 5-22-1822 at Silver Creek MM, Ind
Ch: Jethro         b 4- 9-1823
    David          b 1- 4-1825

Gurney
......
Ch: Rollin         b 8- 2-1867

Jehu Jr     b 12-28-1787  -s Jehu Sr & Mary of N C &
Mary        (mou 1813 N C)       Ind
           (Mary & ch rec in mbrp 1825 - Milford MM)
Ch: Moses          b
    Price          b   Order of birth not known
    Asenath        b
    Jemima         b

WILLETS
Jehu L    (Jehu & wife from Legrand, Ia)
Mary J    -dt John & Rebecca Miles
Ch: Walter D      b 2-15-1865   d 5-15-1866
    Van Burton    b 9-22-1867
    Lydia M        b 8-10-1869

William    d 10-12-1858, Milford MM

WILLIAMS
Jesse         b 6-26-1804  -s Rev William Williams &
    wife, Rachel (Kemp) of Tenn & Whitewater MM, Ind
Elizabeth N  b 11-27-1809  -dt Samuel & Rachel Crampton
              of Whitewater MM, Ind
Ch: William        b 10- 6-1830  d 5- 2-1848, Milford MM
    Phebe Ann      b 3-11-1832
    Malinda        b 7-26-1837
    Casandra       b 11- 5-1839
    Mary E         b 3-10-1841
    Ruth A         b 12-11-1844
    William A      b 12-25-1848

WILSON
Charles     b 11- 6-1835  -s Gideon & Margaret (Charles)
Susan J    (form Whisler)
Ch: Albert         b 7-12-1859
    Adda           b 9- 3-1861
    Emma           b 11-21-1868

Christopher   b 5- 4-1834   d 6-27-1870
              -s John W & Margaret
Margaret (1st w) b 5-13-1834   d 5-16-1865
            -dt William & Susannah Butler
Ch: Emma T        b 1-21-1858
    Delphina M    b 4-19-1860
    Melissa E      b 12-19-1861
Mary (2nd w)  b 7- 9-1839   -dt Joseph & Phariba Toms
Ch: John A         b 5-22-1868
    Anna N         b 10-14-1869

MILFORD

WILSON (Cont)
Franklin (Benjamin)   -s John W & Margaret of Wayne Co,
Lucy W    b 4-15-1838    d 5-29-1864           Ind
-dt Terrell, - Matthew & Elizabeth of Short Creek MM, O
Ch: Hester         b  9-27-1861
    Lucy E         b  4- 5-1864

Gideon         b  3- 3-1812   d 11-27-1850, Milford MM, Ind
               -s Jehu & Sarah
Margaret       b  8- 5-1815   d 11-11-1864
               -dt John & Elvira Charles
Ch: Charles        b 11- 6-1835
    Mary           b  1-18-1837    d  1-19-1844
                                      Milford
    Isaac          b  7-15-1838
    John C         b  9-15-1840    d 10- 4-1846
                                      Milford
    Sarah E        b  9- 9-1842    d  7-14-1874
    Amos           b  2-15-1845    d  9- 9-1853
                                      Milford
    Jehu H         b  3-19-1848    d  8-30-1853
                                      Milford
    Emaline        b  9-17-1849

Gideon         b  8- 8-1825   -s John & Ann (Calloway)
Susan          b  5- 6-1829   d  1-29-1863
               -dt Samuel & Susan Stokes
Ch: Anna J         b  2- 6-1858
    John S         b  2-19-1859
    Albert J       b 12-26-1860   d  1-18-1864
    Francis        b  4- 5-1862

Isaac          b  7-15-1838  -s Gideon & Margaret (Charles)
Susan M        (form Edgerton)
Ch: William Gideon  b  1-30-1865
    Ina M          b  9- 4-1867

Jehu           b  1- 1-1763   d  6-27-1848, Milford MM, Ind
               -s John & Dinah (Cook) of Cane Creek MM, S C
Sarah          b ca 12-14-1773  d  3-13-1850 -ae 77yrs,2mo,
               -dt Isaac & Margaret Hawkins of N C        30da
Ch: (from Cane Creek MM, S C)
    Betty          b 10-10-1791
    Dinah          b  3-14-1794
    John           b 12-17-1796
    Isaac          b  7-26-1799
    Seth           b  7-23-1801
    Amos           b  1-10-1803
    Ruth           b  9-17-1806
    Gideon         b  3- 3-1812

John           b 12-17-1796   -s Jehu & Sarah
Ann (1st w)    b 11-26-1801   -dt ... Calloway
                                 (perhaps of Ohio)
Ch: Sarah          b  8- 8-1824
    Gideon         b  8- 8-1825
    Martha A       b  2-18-1827
    Jehu           b  1-16-1829   d  7-20-1829
Eliza (2nd w) -dt Isaac & Elizabeth Burson (both dec) of
                                                      Pa

John           m 11- 1-1828, Perquimans MM, N C
               -s Christopher & Phariba (Sanders) of Suttons
                                          Creek MM, N C
Margaret Winslow (White) of Perquimans Co, N C
Ch: Alfred         b  1- 9-1830   d  6-27-1852
    Timothy        b  1-20-1832
    Christopher    b  5- 4-1834   d  6-27-1870
    Achsah         b 11-10-1836
    Benjamin F     b  5-14-1840
    Margaret W     b 12- 9-1842
    Mary Ann       b  1- 9-1845
    Rachel         b 12- 5-1846
    Jane H         b  8- 7-1850
    Phariba        b 10-22-1852

John C         b  1- 5-1799   -s Israel & Martha of
                                 Harrison Co, Flushing MM, Ohio
Amelia         -dt Judah & Sarah Foulks, Plainfield MM, Ohio

Ch: Edith          b 10-13-1823
    Mary           b  2- 5-1825
    Ann            b

Jonathan       b  8-12-1809
               -s Israel & Martha of Flushing MM, Ohio
Druscilla      b  5-23-1815
               -dt Joseph & Elizabeth Cox of Milford MM
Ch: Anna           b 10-26-1834
    Elizabeth      b  8- 1-1836
    Margaret       b  5- 2-1838   d 10- 6-1839
    Israel         b  3-21-1840
    Martha         b  7- 1-1842
    Joseph C       b 10-29-1844

Joseph         b 12-16-1809  d  3-31-1854
               -s Samuel & Ruth of Whitewater MM, Ind
Elizabeth      b  4- 9-1818  -dt Samuel & Jane Stokes
Ch: Sarah S        b 11-24-1839
    Samuel S       b 12- 7-1840
    Ruth A         b  2-20-1842
    Eliza J        b 12-13-1843   d  8- 4-1844
    Mary A         b  2-12-1847

Seth           b  7-23-1801  -s Jehu & Sarah
Elizabeth      b  1- 3-1806
               -dt Henry & Rebecca Thornburgh of West
                                          Grove MM, Ind
Ch: Milton         b 12-11-1825
    Elizann        b  8-14-1827
    Caroline       b  9- 5-1830
    Henry          b  8-25-1833   d 12- 3-1837,
                                      Milford MM
    Eunice         b  2- 4-1837
    Rebecca T      b 10-19-1840
    Sarah H        b 12-17-1843
    Maria          b 11-25-1846

Timothy        b  1-20-1832  -s John & Margaret W (White)
Elizabeth Ann  b  3- 6-1832  d  4-24-1865
               -dt Matthew & Elizabeth D Terrell of
                                    Upper Springfield MM, Ohio
Ch: Alfred         b  1-19-1855   d  3-24-1855
    Charles M      b  2-26-1856   d  1-12-1858
    Olive B        b  6-30-1858
    Terrell        b 10-24-1860
    Matthew        b  1-29-1863
    William N      b

WINSLOW
Jacob          b 12-25-1793  d  4- 8-1857
               -s William & Pleasant
Martha         b  3-26-1800  d  5- 1-1864
               -dt Jesse & Elizabeth Newby
Ch: Edmund W       b  1- 8-1850
    Margaret Ann   b

MILFORD

## MILFORD MONTHLY MEETING
## MINUTES AND MARRIAGES

ADAMSON
12-26-1829  Mordecai & w Susannah & ch Adam & Peter rocf Newberry MM, Tenn
8-25-1838   Mordecai & w Susannah & ch Adam, Peter, Catharine, John, Mary & Eliza gct White Lick MM, Ind

ADDISON
7-23-1825   Susannah, Duck Creek rpt mcd
9-24-1825   Susannah dis for mcd

ALBERTSON
5-26-1832   Nathan & s Benjamin & Alpheus rocf Suttons Creek MM, N C
5-26-1832   Pheriba & dt Sarah rocf Suttons Creek MM, N C
6-23-1832   Thomas Parker, a minor, rocf Blue River MM, Ind
10-27-1832  Thomas P gct Springfield MM, Ind
6-22-1833   Jordan rocf Suttons Creek MM, N C
8-24-1833   Thomas P & w Hannah rocf Springfield MM, Ind
8-23-1834   Nathan & w Fereba & ch Benjamin, Sarah, Alpheus & George J gct Duck Creek MM, Ind
3-28-1835   Thomas P & w Hannah & s Nixon gct Duck Creek MM, Ind
2-27-1836   Jordan gct Spiceland MM, Ind
7-23-1836   William rocf Symons Creek MM, N C
7-23-1836   Margaret & dt Margaret rocf Little River MM, N C
1-23-1841   William gct Spiceland MM, Ind
10-23-1841  William Saint Jr gct Blue River MM to m Mary Ann Albertson
10-22-1842  Margaret & dt Margaret gct Back Creek MM, Ind
11-27-1847  Benjamin rocf Blue River MM, Ind
1-25-1851   Benjamin gct Spiceland MM, Ind
4-24-1875   Edward rec in mbrp
9-21-1893   Edward rel fr mbrp

ALCORN
3-29-1888   William & w Amanda rocf New Castle MM
2-26-1891   William rel fr mbrp

ALLEN
11-27-1830  Rachel (form Newby) rpt mcd
12-25-1830  Rachel chm of mcd
8-27-1831   William rec in mbrp
12- 1-1831  William, -s Hugh & Frances of Wayne Co, Ind, m Sarah Symons at Milford MH
12-24-1831  Hugh rocf Bloomfield MM
2-25-1832   John rec in mbrp
2-23-1833   Elizabeth rec in mbrp
10-26-1833  Elizabeth Morris (form Allen) rpt mcd by Bethel MM
1-25-1834   Elizabeth Morris (form Allen) chm of mcd
10-26-1833  Hugh rpt "for encouraging his dt, Elizabeth, in accomplishing her mcd, so far as to send for a justice of peace for that purpose & have the m accomplished in his own house"
1-25-1834   Hugh dis
11-22-1834  William & w Sarah & ch Martha & Nathan gct Mississinewa MM, Ind
4-25-1835   James rec in mbrp
11-28-1835  John & w Rachel & ch Mary & Elizabeth gct Mississinewa MM, Ind
9-24-1836   James gct Mississinewa MM, Ind
7-22-1848   James & w Lucy & ch Maria Jane, Anna & Rosella rocf Salem MM, Ind
3-24-1855   James L & w Lucy & ch Maria Jane, Anna, Rosella, Margaret Ann, Joseph Percival & Hiram gct Honey Creek MM, Ind

ALLINSON
10-29-1891  Alonzo & w Annie B rec in mbrp
11-28-1891  Gertrude, Jessie & Bertha rec in mbrp

2-25-1892   James A rec in mbrp
9-22-1892   Cyrus & Ruth rec in mbrp

ALSPAUGH
12-26-1829  Elizabeth (form Beason) rpt mcd
3- 9-1830   Elizabeth (form Beason) dis

ANDERSON
5-28-1859   Mary rec in mbrp w/c Sugar River MM

ANTRIM
8-26-1826   James P rocf Whitewater MM, Ind
9-22-1827   James P rpt mcd; chm 10-27-1827
12-22-1838  James P gct Westfield MM, Ind

BACON
10-25-1835  Beulah Shipley (form Bacon), mbr Greenwich MM, N J, rpt mcd
6-25-1836   Beulah Shipley (form Bacon) dis for mcd

BAILEY
9-18-1823   Sarah appt Overseer at Duck Creek PM
12-18-1823  David rocf Whitewater MM, Ind
5-25-1833   Mary rocf Silver Creek MM, Ind

BALDWIN
5-28-1825   Jesse rocf Whitewater MM, Ind
7- 7-1825   Jesse, a widower from Wayne Co, Ind & Fall Creek MM, Ohio, m Miriam Macy of Milford MM & New Garden MM, N C, at Milford MH
8-27-1825   Jesse & w Miriam gct Springfield MM, Ind
4-25-1835   Simeon, a minor, rocf West Grove MM, Ind

BALES
7-26-1828   John rocf Duck Creek MM, Ind
3- 9-1830   John rpt dr
3-27-1830   John chm for dr
2-26-1831   Thomas & w Nancy & ch Lemuel & Mary rocf Newberry MM, Ohio
12-24-1831  John gct Duck Creek MM, Ind

BAKER
2-28-1880   Mary Ella gct Whitewater MM, Ind
1-28-1886   Leopold rec in mbrp
11-27-1890  Leopold rel fr mbrp

BALLARD
4-23-1885   Mary & Lauretta rocf Raysville MM, Ind
9-23-1886   Mary & Lauretta gct Indianapolis MM, Ind

BARKER
1-25-1894   Orville E rocf Duck Creek MM, Ind

BARNARD
8-22-1835   Obed rpt na, dp & mcd by Salem MM
12-26-1835  Obed - rpt dis by Salem MM, Ind
5-23-1846   Paul & w Martha & dt Susan rocf Salem MM
11-24-1855  Paul & w Martha & dt Susan gct Whitewater MM, Ind
2-22-1868   Paul & w Martha rocf Whitewater MM, Ind
3-26-1870   Paul & w Martha gct Whitewater MM, Ind

BARTLETT
4-24-1884   Jennie Reynolds (form Bartlett) rel fr mbrp

BEAMAN
9-16-1824   Betty, mbr of Blue River MM, rpt mcd
8-27-1825   Betty- Blue River rpt dis for mcd
7-23-1825   Cornelius rocf Blue River MM, Ind

BEARD
9-27-1828   Abraham, rpt by West Union MM for mcd & na
12-27-1828  Abraham dis
12-27-1828  Patrick rpt jH
2-28-1829   Patrick dis
8-22-1829   Elizabeth rpt dp & na
10-24-1829  Elizabeth dis

MILFORD

**BEARD (Cont)**
| | |
|---|---|
| 3- 9-1830 | Alice rpt na |
| 3-27-1830 | Patrick Jr rpt dp & na |
| 4-24-1830 | Alice dis for na |
| 5-22-1830 | Patrick Jr dis for dp & na |
| 11-24-1832 | Woodard rpt na & dp |
| 11-24-1832 | Rachel rpt jH |
| 2-23-1833 | Woodard dis for na & dp |
| 2-23-1833 | Rachel dis for jH |
| 4-24-1833 | Susannah (form Winslow), mbr Blue River MM, rpt mcd; Blue River inf |

**BEAUCHAMP**
| | |
|---|---|
| 12-18-1823 | Jesse, Miles, Wilson & William, minor ch of Alice Jessop, rocf New Garden MM, -end by West Grove MM, Ind |
| 4-27-1839 | Jesse rpt na & dp |
| 7-27-1839 | Jesse dis for na & dp |
| 2-27-1841 | Wilson rpt mcd by Mississinewa MM, Ind |
| 5-22-1841 | Wilson dis for mcd |
| 6-26-1841 | William gct Mississinewa MM, Ind |
| 6-26-1841 | Miles gct Mississinewa MM, Ind |

**BEESON**
| | |
|---|---|
| 12-27-1828 | Isabel & ch Elmaward, Samuel & Isabel rocf Springfield MM, -end by White Lick MM, Ind |
| 4-25-1829 | Sally & ch Betsy, Absalom, Mahlon, John & Nancy rocf Whitewater MM, Ind |
| 5-23-1829 | Samuel rq mbrp |
| 6-27-1829 | Samuel - 'time not come' rpt by Society |
| 12-26-1829 | Elizabeth Alspaugh (form Beason) rpt mcd |
| 3- 9-1830 | Elizabeth Alspaugh (form Beason) dis for mcd |
| 5-22-1830 | Sarah & ch Absalom, Mahlon, Job & Nancy gct New Garden MM, Ind |
| 5-26-1832 | Isabel & ch Gulielma, Wade, Samuel & Isabel gct Springfield MM, Ind |
| 10- 2-1856 | Thomas E of Springfield MM, Wayne Co, Ind, -s Isaac & Hannah (dec), m Celia Hunt at Milford MH |
| 4-25-1857 | Celia gct Springfield MM, Ind |
| 7-22-1882 | John W & w Martha & ch William & Jesse F rocf Spiceland MM, Ind |
| 7-22-1882 | Samuel W & w Julia & ch Lawrence & Linnie & niece Josephine rocf Spiceland MM, Ind |
| 2-25-1886 | S W, Julia, J W, Hattie E, Flora H & Frank rel fr mbrp |
| 2-25-1886 | Fred, Laura C, Linnie C & Josephine rel fr mbrp |

**BELL**
| | |
|---|---|
| 7-17-1823 | John appt Clerk |
| 7-17-1823 | Lancelot appt Overseer |
| 7-17-1823 | Lydia appt Clerk |
| 8-14-1823 | Abigail appt Clerk |
| 8-14-1823 | Mary appt Asst-Clerk |
| 1-22-1824 | Miriam, -dt John & Sarah (dec), Wayne Co, Ind, m Robert Parker at Milford MH |
| 4- 5-1827 | Margaret, -dt John & Lydia of Wayne Co, Ind, m Aaron Gilbert of Henry Co, Ind, -s Joel & Lydia, at Milford MH |
| 10-29-1828 | Thomas of Wayne Co, Ind, -s John & Sarah (dec) m Jerusha Stratton at Hopewell MH |
| 10-25-1828 | Lancelot rpt jH |
| 10-25-1828 | Mary rpt jH |
| 12-27-1828 | Lancelot dis for jH |
| 12-27-1828 | Mary dis for jH |
| 5-10-1832 | Abigail, -dt John & Lydia, all of Wayne Co, Ind, m Josiah Gilbert of same place, at Milford MH |
| 10-26-1833 | Jesse gct Duck Creek MM to m Penelope N Henley |
| 3-22-1834 | Penelope N rocf Duck Creek MM, Ind |
| 6-23-1838 | Sarah Frampton (form Bell) rpt mcd & jH |
| 8-25-1838 | Sarah Frampton (form Bell) dis for mcd & jH |
| 3-31-1841 | Thomas, Henry Co, Ind, -s John & Sarah (both dec), m Hannah Mendenhall at Bethel MH |
| 2-25-1843 | Daniel rpt jH |
| 4-22-1843 | Daniel dis for jH |
| 10-16-1845 | Martha, -dt John & Lydia (both dec), m Thomas E Henly at Milford MH |
| 1-28-1846 | Gulielma, -dt Josiah & Abigail, Wayne Co, Ind, m Eli Henby at Bethel MH |
| 3-28-1846 | Lydia gct Hopewell MM, Ind |
| 6-27-1846 | Jepthah, a minor, gct Duck Creek MM, Ind |
| 6-27-1846 | Penelope & dt Lydia Jane gct Walnut Ridge MM, Ind |
| 9-23-1848 | Penelope N & dt Lydia Jane rocf Walnut Ridge MM, Ind |
| 5-30-1850 | Penelope N, widow of Jesse Bell & dt of Elias & Jane Henley (both dec), of Rush Co, Ind, m Reuben Ratliff at Milford MH |
| 8-24-1850 | Lydia Jane gct Duck Creek MM, Ind |
| 1- 1-1851 | Rebecca, -dt Josiah & Abigail of Wayne Co, Ind, m Ansalem Johnson at Bethel MH |
| 8-24-1851 | Lydia Jane & mother, Penelope N Ratliff gct Duck Creek MM, Ind |
| 12-31-1851 | John C, of Wayne Co, Ind, -s Josiah & Abigail, m Eliza Elliott at Bethel MH |
| 5-27-1886 | Mary rocf Hopewell MM, Ind |
| 11-28-1889 | Enos rocf Hopewell MM, Ind |
| 11-28-1889 | Lydia rocf Hopewell MM, Ind |
| 7-23-1890 | Julia rec in mbrp |
| 11-24-1892 | Alfred & w Mary E & fam gct Westland MM |

**BELLIS**
| | |
|---|---|
| 7-22-1848 | Edward & Samuel rocf Balby MM, England, -end to Whitewater MM, Ind |

**BENBOW**
| | |
|---|---|
| 1-28-1865 | Sarah rocf Wabash MM, Ind |
| 9-25-1869 | Sarah M Mills (form Benbow) rpt mcd; chm |

**BENNETT**
| | |
|---|---|
| 2-27-1830 | Zechariah, Solomon & Elizabeth, ch of Ruth Hester, rocf Cherry Grove MM, Ind |
| 10-31-1833 | Solomon of Wayne Co, Ind, -s Matthew & Ruth, m Mary Stanbrough at Milford MH |
| 3- 4-1835 | Betsy, -dt Matthew & Ruth of Wayne Co, Ind, m Ira Stanley at Bethel MH |
| 9-24-1835 | Solomon & w Mary & ch Elizabeth & Ruth gct Westfield MM, Ind |
| 1-28-1843 | Elizabeth, Ruth, Matthew & Joseph W, ch of Solomon, rocf Westfield MM, Ind |
| 9-23-1843 | Anna (form Stout), mbr of Westfield, rpt mcd |
| 5-25-1844 | Anna (form Stout) dis |
| 2-23-1850 | Elizabeth, Ruth, Matthew & Joseph, minor ch of Solomon, gct Westfield MM, Ind |
| 3-23-1850 | Zachariah gct Westfield MM, Ind |

**BENSON**
| | |
|---|---|
| 3-26-1885 | Anna S W gct New Garden MM, Ind |

**BERRY**
| | |
|---|---|
| 3-24-1832 | Prunell, mbr Wilmington MM, Dela, rpt jH |
| 7-28-1832 | Prunell dis for jH |

**BINFORD**
| | |
|---|---|
| 3-28-1833 | Samuel B of Hancock Co, Ind, -s Samuel & Mary (both dec), of Prince George Co, Va, m Ann Butler at Rich Square MH |
| 7-26-1834 | Samuel B rocf Duck Creek MM, Ind |
| 2- 8-1837 | Ashbel of Rush Co, Ind, -s Joshua & Lydia, m Gulielma Symons at Bethel MH |
| 8-26-1837 | Gulielma gct Walnut Ridge MM, Ind |
| 2-26-1845 | James of Rush Co, Ind, -s Joshua & Lydia, (both dec), m Rachel Patterson at Bethel MH |
| 2-28-1846 | Rachel gct Walnut Ridge MM, Ind |
| 12-30-1852 | David of Boone Co, Ind, -s Peter & Martha (both dec), m Tamar Ann Hawkins at Milford MH |
| 5-28-1853 | Tamar Ann gct Sugar Plain MM, Ind |
| 4-26-1856 | James & w Rachel rocf Walnut Ridge MM, Ind |
| 4-26-1856 | Mary Ann, a minor, rocf Spiceland MM, Ind |
| 8-23-1862 | James, rpt by Bethel MM "he has jFreeMasons & having been associated with them for some time, which he repeatedly denies" |

MILFORD

**BINFORD (Cont)**
| | |
|---|---|
| 11-22-1862 | James dis for jFreemasons |
| 12-27-1862 | James appeals to QM |
| 10-25-1862 | Mary Ann Gard (form Binford) rpt mcd by Spiceland MM |
| 6-27-1863 | James - QM reverses dis |
| 5-23-1863 | Mary Ann Gard (form Binford) dis for mcd |
| 3-23-1872 | James & w Rachel & dt Elizabeth Ann gct Marysville MM, Tenn |

**BISHOP**
| | |
|---|---|
| 4-23-1842 | Rebecca (form Butler) rpt mcd by Bethel MM |
| 6-25-1842 | Rebecca (form Butler) dis for mcd |

**BITNER**
| | |
|---|---|
| 12-25-1890 | Benjamin rec in mbrp |
| 4-27-1893 | Benjamin rel fr mbrp |

**BLACKMAN**
| | |
|---|---|
| 4-25-1874 | Mary M rec in mbrp |

**BOGUE**
| | |
|---|---|
| 11-13-1823 | Joseph rpt mcd |
| 5-13-1824 | Joseph dis for mcd |
| 10-23-1824 | Mary Bundy (form Bogue) rpt mcd |
| 12-25-1824 | Mary Bundy (form Bogue) chm of mcd |
| 6-25-1825 | Newby rpt "training with the Militia" |
| 8-27-1825 | Newby dis for "training with the Militia" |
| 2-16-1826 | Sarah, -dt Samuel & Elizabeth, m Jonathan Ratliff at Milford MH |
| 2-28-1829 | Benjamin rpt mcd by Bethel MM |
| 3-28-1829 | Benjamin chm of mcd |
| 2-27-1830 | Aaron & w Elizabeth & ch Benjamin Evans, William Osborn & Sarah Ann rocf Blue River MM, Ind |
| 4-25-1836 | Elizabeth rpt na & dp; dis |
| 11-29-1837 | Miriam, -dt Samuel & Elizabeth (dec), of Madison Co, Ind, m Elias Ratliff at Hopewell MH |
| 8-28-1841 | Benjamin gct Salem MM, Iowa Terr |
| 6-25-1842 | Milly rst in mbrp by Salem MM, Iowa Terr |
| 2-27-1847 | Benjamin & w Milly & ch Anna, Silas, Huldah, Samuel, Joshua, Allen, Asenith & Newby rocf Salem MM, Ia |
| 3-24-1849 | Benjamin & w Milly & ch Huldah, Samuel, Joshua, Asenith, Newby & Mary Ellen gct Hopewell MM, Ind |
| 8-26-1849 | Silas gct Salem MM, Ia |
| 6-22-1850 | William, Bethel MM rpt na & mcd |
| 8-24-1850 | William dis for na & mcd |
| 12-28-1850 | Benjamin & w Milly & ch Huldah, Samuel, Joshua, Allen, Asenith, Newby, Mary E & Joseph D rocf Hopewell MM, Ind |
| 1-25-1851 | Benjamin, Bethel MM rpt dp & mcd |
| 3-22-1851 | Benjamin dis for dp & mcd |
| 5-24-1851 | Sarah Ann Puntney (form Bogue), Bethel MM rpt mcd & na |
| 9-21-1851 | Sarah Ann Puntney (form Bogue) dis for mcd & na |
| 8-23-1851 | Benjamin & w Milly & ch Huldah, Samuel, Joshua, Asenith, Newby, Mary Ellen & Joseph D gct Salem MM, Ia |
| 7-10-1860 | Elizabeth gct Winnesheik MM, Ia |
| 4-25-1874 | William O & Mary rec in mbrp |
| -  -1888 | Oliver gct Wabash MM, Ind |

**BOND**
| | |
|---|---|
| 8-12-1824 | William & w Charlotte & ch Charlotte, William, John & Ira rocf Chester MM, Ind |
| 8-12-1824 | Jesse & w Mary & ch Lydia & Sarah rocf Chester MM, Ind |
| 6-25-1825 | Charlotte appt Overseer at Flatrock MM |
| 7-23-1825 | Thomas & w Mary & ch Amer, Betsy, Jesse, Thomas, Hiram, Pleasant, Asenith & Phebe rocf New Garden MM, Ind |
| 4-26-1828 | Ellen (form Goldsmith), Bethel MM rpt mcd |
| 8-23-1828 | Ellen (form Goldsmith) dis for mcd |
| 6-27-1829 | Edward & w Ann & ch Lucinda rocf Duck Creek MM, Ind |
| 7-25-1829 | John & w Rebecca & ch Lavina, Hannah, Abigail, Jacob, William, Elias, Albertson, Aaron, Mannon, Sarah & Anna gct Duck Creek MM, Ind |
| 12-28-1833 | Benjamin rocf New Garden MM, Ind |
| 12-28-1833 | Tabitha rocf New Garden MM, Ind |
| 2- 3-1836 | John of Henry Co, Ind, -s William (dec) of Perquimans MM, N C & Abigail, m Mary (Hodgson) Stanbrough, a widow, at Bethel MH |
| 3-26-1836 | Mary & dt Phebe & Elizabeth gct Spiceland MM Ind |
| 11-25-1837 | Jonathan W rocf Whitewater MM, Ind |
| 5-28-1840 | Tabitha of Henry Co, Ind, -dt Benjamin & Mary (both dec), m Elias Newby at Rich Square MH |
| 5-23-1840 | Elam, a minor, u/c Jonathan Bond, rec in mbrp |
| 7-24-1841 | Cyrus, a minor, rocf Sparrow Creek, -end to Hopewell MM, Ind |

**BOON**
| | |
|---|---|
| 1-22-1825 | Driver & w Anna & ch Rachel & Rhoda rocf Springfield MM, N C |
| 2-25-1826 | John & w Dorcas & ch Charles, Betsy, Stephen & Dorcas rocf Cherry Grove MM, Ind |
| 5-27-1826 | John & w Sarah & ch William, Rachel & Betsy rocf Cherry Grove MM, Ind |
| 1-27-1827 | John & w Sarah & ch William, Rachel, Betsy & Joseph gct Cherry Grove MM, Ind |
| 10-23-1830 | John & w Dorcas & ch gct Duck Creek MM, Ind |
| 6-25-1831 | Driver & w Ann & ch Rachel, Rhoda, Rebecca, Sampson & Irena gct Duck Creek MM, Ind |

**BOSWELL**
| | |
|---|---|
| 4-24-1830 | William & w Rachel & ch Ruth, Elizabeth, Asenith, Rebecca, Isaac & Joseph rocf Whitewater MM, Ind |
| 8-28-1830 | Ruth, a minor, rocf Whitewater MM, Ind |
| 8-28-1830 | Dempsey & w & ch rocf Whitewater MM, Ind |
| 7-23-1831 | John, Bethel MM rpt "guilty of fornication" |
| 9-24-1831 | John dis for fornication |
| 1-28-1832 | John chm for fornication but MM not free to rec him |
| 4-26-1832 | Mary (form Smith), Bethel MM rpt mcd |
| 6-23-1832 | Mary (form Smith) dis for mcd |
| 12-22-1832 | Jesse gct Somerset MM, Ohio to m Eliza Patterson |
| 4-27-1833 | William & w Rachel & ch Ruth, Elizabeth, Asenith, Rebecca, Joseph, Milisent & Elihu gct West Grove MM, Ind |
| 8-24-1833 | Jesse gct Deerfield MM, Ohio |
| 5-24-1834 | Dempsy & w Mary & dt Phebe gct Deerfield MM, Ohio "not withstanding his failure in circumstances is such that there are unsettled demands standing against him, yet he having made a surrender of his effects to his Creditors as far as appears, so that nothing more at present can be expected..." |

**BOWIE**
| | |
|---|---|
| 9-25-1859 | Lucinda (form Stanley) rpt mcd; chm |

**BRADBURY**
| | |
|---|---|
| 7-22-1865 | Sarah rocf New Garden MM, Ia |

**BRADDOCK**
| | |
|---|---|
| 11-28-1891 | William, Adella & Jesse H rec in mbrp |

**BRADLEY**
| | |
|---|---|
| 4-23-1891 | Mary B rocf West Grove MM, Ind |
| 1-29-1891 | Benjamin rec in mbrp |

**BRATTAIN**
| | |
|---|---|
| 11-26-1825 | Hannah rocf Whitewater MM, Ind |
| 4-22-1886 | Rosetta gct Sugar Plain MM, Ind |

MILFORD

### BREWER
|  |  |
|---|---|
| 10-23-1830 | Mary (form Morris) rpt mcd |
| 12-25-1830 | Mary (form Morris) dis for mcd |
| 6-22-1833 | Rachel (form Jessop), Blue River MM rpt mcd |
| 10-26-1833 | Rachel (form Jessop), Blue River MM rpt she chm of mcd |
| 11-22-1834 | John rocf Flushing MM, Ohio, -end by Blue River MM, Ind |
| 2-28-1835 | Elizabeth, Rachel, William & Elias, ch of John, rec in mbrp |
| 4-25-1835 | Rachel, -dt of John & 1st w (dec), gct Spiceland MM, Ind, u/c Zachariah & Ann Johnson |
| 1-28-1837 | John rpt mcd |
| 4-22-1837 | John chm of mcd |
| 8-26-1837 | John & ch William & Elizabeth gct West Grove MM, Ind |
| 9-28-1839 | Sarah & ch Elizabeth, William & Mary Morris rocf Spiceland MM, but as they were about to ret, cert was end back to same MM |
| 1-25-1840 | Elias, a minor, gct Spiceland MM, Ind |
| 12-24-1877 | Ellen Jane rocf Duck Creek MM, Ind |
| 4-27-1878 | Mattie rocf Fairmount MM, Ind |
| 11-23-1878 | Jason & w Frances rec in mbrp |
| 6-25-1881 | Susan & s Jason rocf Spiceland MM, Ind |

### BRIGHT
|  |  |
|---|---|
| 2-26-1825 | Abigail rocf New Garden MM, Ind |
| 11-21-1827 | Abigail gct Whitewater MM, Ind |

### BROTHERS
|  |  |
|---|---|
| 7-25-1857 | Nathan & w Abigail & ch Mary Ann, Sarah Roxana, Rebecca Amanda, Malissa Jane, Maria Ellen & Joel G rocf Deep River MM, N C |
| 9-22-1860 | Nathan & w Abigail & ch Mary Ann, Sarah R, Rebecca A, Malissa J, Maria E, Joel G & Ira S gct Hopewell MM, Ind |

### BROWN
|  |  |
|---|---|
| 10-24-1829 | James & w Mary & ch Isaac, Phebe, James, Seth, Eli, Mary & William rocf Deep River MM, N C |
| 10-24-1829 | John rocf Deep River MM, N C |
| 10-24-1829 | Rebeckah rocf Deep River MM, N C |
| 9-29-1830 | Isaac of Henry Co, Ind, m Sarah Davis at Bethel MH |
| 12- 1-1830 | Phebe, -dt James & Mary of Henry Co, Ind, m Isaac Davis at Bethel MH |
| 4-23-1831 | Rebecca declared int to m Jehu Davis, but there was some objection |
| 6-25-1831 | Rebecca rpt mcd |
| 7-23-1831 | Rebecca chm of mcd |
| 7-23-1831 | John gct Deep River MM, N C to m Cyrena Coffin |
| 7-23-1831 | Rebecca Davis (form Brown) rpt mcd |
| 10-21-1831 | Rebecca Davis (form Brown) chm of mcd |
| 1-28-1832 | Cyrena rocf Deep River MM, N C |
| 5-25-1833 | John & w Cyrena gct Duck Creek MM |
| 5-24-1834 | Isaac & w Sarah & dt Martha gct West Grove MM, Ind |
| 8-23-1834 | Ruth (form Cadwallader), mbr of Blue River MM, rpt mcd; Blue River MM, inf |
| 11-22-1834 | Ruth (form Cadwallader) dis for mcd |
| 4- 1-1835 | James of Henry Co, Ind, -s James & Mary, m Ruth Mills at Bethel MH |
| 12-26-1835 | Virgin, -w of William, & ch Keziah, Isaac, Elisha & Rhoda rocf Elk MM, Ohio |
| 8-26-1837 | John & ch Elizabeth & William gct West Grove MM, Ind |
| 4-27-1839 | James & w Mary gct Sugar River MM, Ind |
| 8-22-1840 | Keziah, Isaac, Elisha, Rhoda & Lydia Jane, minor ch of William (dec), gct Elk MM, Ohio |
| 9-26-1840 | Virgin - Obstruction rpt to gct Elk MM, Ohio |
| 4-24-1841 | Virgin - MM "could not consistantly grant her a cert"; subject dismissed |
| 11-28-1840 | Seth gct Sugar River MM, Ind |
| 9-25-1841 | James & w Ruth & ch Deborah, John, Mary E & William gct Sugar River MM, Ind |
| 3-23-1850 | Virgin Shaner (form Brown), Dover MM, Ohio rpt her mcd |
| 1-25-1851 | Virgin Shaner (form Brown), Dover MM, Ohio rpt she has dec |
| 11-22-1851 | James, mbr Springfield MM, rpt mcd & na, Springfield MM, informed |
| 6-26-1852 | James rpt dis |
| 8-24-1861 | Sarah Catharine (form Elliott), Bethel MM rpt mcd; chm |
| 5-25-1878 | Catherine rel fr mbrp |
| 11-27-1890 | William rec in mbrp |

### BUDD
|  |  |
|---|---|
| 3-26-1836 | Elizabeth (form Hunt) rpt mcd |
| 7-23-1836 | Elizabeth (form Hunt) dis for mcd |
| 3-23-1839 | Elizabeth rec in mbrp |
| 11-23-1839 | Elizabeth gct Whitewater MM, Ind |

### BUNDRANT
|  |  |
|---|---|
| 4-28-1849 | Adaline, a minor u/c Daniel Swain, rocf Salem MM, Ind |
| 8-23-1856 | Adaline Jordan (form Bundrant) rpt mcd; dis |

### BUNDY
|  |  |
|---|---|
| 10-23-1824 | Mary (form Bogue) rpt mcd |
| 12-25-1824 | Mary (form Bogue) chm of mcd |
| 8-27-1825 | Thomas rocf Symons Creek MM, N C; -end by West Grove MM, Ind |
| 8- 4-1825 | Jesse of Wayne Co, Ind, -s Benjamin (dec) & Sarah, m Rachel Hester at Milford MH |
| 12-24-1825 | Thomas rpt retailing spirituous liquors |
| 2-25-1826 | Thomas dis for retailing spirituous liquors |
| 1-28-1826 | Josiah appt Clerk |
| 6-24-1826 | George appt Elder |
| 9-29-1830 | Samuel of Wayne Co, Ind, -s George & Sarah (dec), m Priscilla Cox at Bethel MH |
| 11-27-1830 | Karen appt Elder |
| 12-25-1830 | Samuel & w Ruth gct Duck Creek MM, Ind |
| 6- 2-1831 | Sarah, -dt George & Sarah of Wayne Co, Ind, m Phineas White at Milford MH |
| 5-28-1831 | Sarah altm Phineas White |
| 3-24-1832 | Mary gct Duck Creek MM, Ind |
| 5-26-1832 | Elias & w Sarah & ch Ellen, Mary, Penninah & Martha rocf Symons Creek MM, N C |
| 8-24-1833 | Elias & w Sarah & ch Ellen, Mary, Penninah, Martha & Ann gct Duck Creek MM, Ind |
| 10-26-1833 | George Jr gct Duck Creek MM, Ind |
| 10-26-1833 | Mary rocf Duck Creek MM, Ind |
| 11-22-1834 | Josiah & w Mary & ch Huldah, Susannah, Nathan, Ruth, Henry, Mary, Caleb & Josiah gct Duck Creek MM, Ind |
| 2-28-1835 | Phineas Lamb gct Duck Creek MM to m Huldah Bundy |
| 2-27-1836 | George & w Keran & ch Mary, Josiah & Catharine & Anthony Hasket, a minor, gct Duck Creek MM, Ind |
| 4-26-1845 | Priscilla & ch Joseph, Rachel & Sarah rocf Walnut Ridge MM, -end to Hopewell MM, Ind |
| 6-28-1845 | Mary rpt jas by Spiceland MM |
| 12-27-1845 | Mary treated without satisfaction; dis |
| 6-28-1845 | Abigail Hall (form Bundy) rpt jas & mcd by Spiceland MM |
| 1-24-1846 | Abigail Hall (form Bundy) dis |
| 9-27-1845 | Sarah, Morgan, Charles & Mariah gct Spiceland MM, Ind (Ch of Thomas & Mary) |
| 3- 4-1846 | Priscilla, a widow, -dt Joseph & Elizabeth Cox of Wayne Co, Ind, m David Butler at Bethel MH |
| 2-23-1850 | Joseph, Rachel & Sarah, ch of Priscilla Butler, gct Walnut Ridge MM, Ind |
| 1-26-1888 | Annie B W gct Sterling MM, Kans |
| 10-29-1891 | Henry C & w Mary E & ch Nellie, Elsie, Myrtle & Oral H rocf Raysville MM, Ind |

### BURGESS
|  |  |
|---|---|
| 4-22-1837 | Sarah (form Reynolds), Bethel MM rpt mcd & na |
| 6-24-1837 | Sarah (form Reynolds) dis for mcd & na |

MILFORD

BURKETT
5-28-1842    Lucinda (form Huddleston) rpt mcd by Bethel MM
7-23-1842    Lucinda (form Huddleston) dis for mcd
3-26-1881    Mary rec in mbrp

BURR
10-25-1828   Joseph, mbr of Short Creek MM, Ohio, rpt mcd
7-25-1829    Joseph chm of mcd; Short Creek MM inf
3-27-1830    Joseph S rocf Short Creek MM, Ohio
1-28-1832    Joseph S rpt dp & jMeth
3-24-1832    Joseph S dis for dp & jMeth

BURSON
11-2-1854    Eliza of Wayne Co, Ind, -dt Isaac & Elizabeth (both dec), of Bucks Co, Pa, m John Wilson at Milford MH

BUTLER
8-14-1823    William appt Clerk
9-16-1824    William & Esther appt Elders
5-28-1825    Lemuel & w Jane & ch Thomas Durham, Mary, Lemuel, Jane, Tacy, Pleasant, Martha, Mahlon & Joseph Fleming rocf Whitewater MM, Ind
9-1-1825     Michal, -dt William & Mary (dec), of Wayne Co, Ind, m Charles Morgan at Milford MH
2-1-1826     Mary, -dt Lemuel & Jane of Fayette Co, Ind, m John Thornburgh at Bethel MH
4-27-1826    Jonathan of Wayne Co, Ind, -s William & Mary (dec), m Abigail Pickering at Duck Creek MH
1-13-1828    Thomas of Fayette Co, Ind, -s Lemuel & Jane, m Amelia Charles at Bethel MH
11-22-1828   David rpt jH by Bethel MM
11-22-1828   Mary rpt jH by Bethel MM
11-22-1828   Armelia rpt jH by Bethel MM
1-24-1829    David dis for jH
1-24-1829    Mary dis for jH
1-24-1829    Armelia dis for jH
3-28-1829    Thomas rpt jH by Bethel MM
5-23-1829    Thomas dis for jH
11-28-1829   Robert, Joseph & Susannah, ch of Rhoda Nixon, rocf Deep River MM, N C
1-7-1830     William Jr of Wayne Co, Ind, -s William & Mary (dec), m Susannah Morris at Milford MH
2-27-1830    Jonathan & dt Sarah Ann gct Duck Creek MM, Ind
1-6-1831     Jonathan of Henry Co, Ind, -s William of Wayne Co, Ind & Mary (dec), formerly of Clinton Co, Ohio, m Sarah P Hubbard at Milford MH
8-25-1832    James S & w Deborah & ch Ann J, Martha, William, James E, Joseph, Robert J & Deborah rocf Western Branch, Va, -end by Silver Creek MM, Ind
9-22-1832    Charlotte & ch Gulia M, Oliver, Benjamin P, Edna & Joseph rocf Western Branch MM, Va
12-22-1832   William Jr, Bethel MM rpt for violating a verbal contract for taking a small quantity of his neighbors (corn) without leave & for going to law with a mbr of our Society
3-23-1833    William Jr dis
1-26-1833    Lemuel gct Duck Creek MM, Ind
3-28-1833    Ann J, -dt James S & Deborah of Henry Co, Ind, m Samuel B Binford at Rich Square MH
3-23-1833    Stanton & w Elizabeth & ch John Chappel, Martha Ann, Elizabeth Stanton, James, Robert Binford & Rebecca Jane rocf Western Branch MM, Va
7-27-1833    Stanton rpt dr by Hopewell MM
11-27-1833   Gulielma M, -dt Joseph, (dec) of Va & Henry Co, Ind, m Richard Maudlin (Modlin) at Hopewell MH
12-28-1833   Stanton dis for dr
4-26-1834    Lemuel & w Jane, ch Jane, Tacy, Pleasant, Martha, Mahlon & Joseph Fleming gct Sugar River MM, Ind
7-26-1834    Lemuel & w Hannah rocf Duck Creek MM, Ind
10-25-1834   Charlotte & ch Oliver, Benjamin Pretlow, Edna & Joseph gct Duck Creek MM, Ind
11-22-1834   Joseph rpt mcd by Duck Creek MM
2-28-1835    Joseph rpt dis by Duck Creek MM
12-27-1834   Robert gct Duck Creek MM, Ind
3-28-1835    Lemuel & w Hannah & Milton gct Sugar River MM, Ind
1-23-1836    William & Esther & ch Elizabeth, Lydia, Priscilla, Edward & Robert T gct Spiceland MM, Ind
1-28-1837    John & w Isley & ch William Henry, John Stanton & Elizabeth rocf Marlborough MM, Ohio, -end by Walnut Ridge MM, Ind
3-30-1837    Martha, -dt James S & Deborah of Henry Co, Ind, m Ellwood Stanley at Rich Square MH
4-22-1837    Joseph J gct Walnut Ridge MM, Ind
5-27-1837    Ansalem & w Ruth & ch Benjamin & Joel rocf Salem MM, Ind
9-26-1840    William Jr rec in mbrp
4-23-1842    Rebecca Bishop (form Butler) rep mcd by Bethel MM
6-25-1842    Rebecca Bishop (form Butler) dis for mcd
4-27-1844    William Jr & w Susan & ch Joshua, Margaret, Charles & Melissa rocf Hopewell MM, Ind
9-28-1844    Mary Jane, minor dt of Thomas & Amelia, gct Sugar River MM, Ind
4-26-1845    Thomas & Amelia rst in mbrp at Sugar River MM, Ind
6-28-1845    David rst in mbrp
7-26-1845    Anslem rpt na by Bethel MM
9-27-1845    Anslem dis for na
3-4-1846     David of Henry Co, Ind, -s William & Mary (dec) of Hancock Co, Ind, m Priscilla Bundy at Bethel MH
7-25-1846    Esther rec in mbrp
4-22-1848    William Exum rocf Salem MM, Ind
8-25-1849    William E gct Hopewell MM to m Sarah Foulk
2-23-1850    David & w Priscilla & ch Joseph, Rachel & Sarah Bundy & Esther & Cyrus Butler gct Walnut Ridge MM, Ind
2-23-1850    William E gct Whitewater MM, Ind
12-25-1852   Mary T Treadway (form Butler) rpt mcd by Spiceland MM
3-26-1853    Mary T Treadway (form Butler) dis for mcd
4-24-1853    Joshua M gct Walnut Ridge MM to m Diza Thornburgh
1-28-1854    Diza rocf Walnut Ridge MM, Ind
5-24-1856    Charles M gct Blue River to m Miriam E White
11-22-1856   Miriam rocf Blue River MM, Ind
3-4-1857     Margaret, -dt William & Susanna of Wayne Co, Ind, m Christopher Wilson at Bethel MH
4-25-1857    Benjamin gct Hopewell MM, Ind
9-25-1858    Emily Griffy (form Butler) rpt mcd by Bethel MM; dis
9-24-1859    Charles M & w Miriam E & dt Elenora gct Raysville MM, Ind
1-28-1860    Joel rpt mcd; chm
7-25-1868    Olive Wilson (form Butler) rpt mcd; chm
8-22-1868    Joel dis for "bearing arms in Civil War"
7-28-1883    William & w Priscilla & s James rocf White Lick MM, Ind
7-28-1883    William T rocf White Lick MM, Ind
4-24-1884    Martha & ch Mary Estella, Nellie M & Diza L rec in mbrp
3-26-1891    James E rocf Westland MM
9-21-1893    Diza rel fr mbrp

CAIN
7-27-1872    Exalina & ch Everett, Orville & Claude rocf Duck Creek MM, Ind
2-24-1883    Exalina rel fr mbrp
2-21-1889    Orville & Mary Edna rel fr mbrp

CALDWELL
1-15-1824    Joseph & w Miriam & ch Joseph & Lydia rocf Elk MM, Ohio
6-27-1829    James rocf Westfield MM, Ind
9-25-1830    Joseph rpt jH
11-27-1830   Joseph dis for jH
5-24-1834    Lydia rpt na & dp & jH
8-23-1834    Lydia dis for na, dp & jH

MILFORD

**CALDWELL (Cont)**
9-17-1840 (Colwell) Joseph chm of mcd
1-28-1886 Amos & Catherine rec in mbrp
4-25-1889 Hester rel fr mbrp
11-27-1890 Amos rel fr mbrp

**CALLOWAY**
1-15-1824 Ann Wilson (form Calloway) rpt mcd
2-12-1824 Ann Wilson (form Calloway) chm of mcd
3-18-1824 John rpt "getting in a passion & abusing his wife"
5-13-1824 John dis
5-22-1847 Ann Maria (form Reagan) rpt mcd by Bethel MM
7-29-1847 Ann Maria (form Reagan) dis for mcd

**CAMMACK**
12-23-1826 Samuel & w Hannah & ch Nathan, David & Eli rocf West Grove MM, Ind
4-28-1832 Samuel & w Hannah & ch Nathan, David, Eli & Rachel gct Arba MM, Ind
12-28-1833 Samuel & w Hannah & ch Nathan, David, Eli & Rachel rocf Arba MM, Ind
7-25-1840 Joanna rocf New Garden MM, Ind
7-25-1840 Mary, a minor, rocf New Garden MM, Ind
5-6-1841 Nathan H of Wayne Co, Ind, -s Samuel & Hannah, m Priscilla Morris at Milford MH
6-21-1841 Joseph & Sally, minors, rocf New Garden MM, Ind
10-7-1841 Joanna, -dt John (dec) & Jane, m Jesse Morris at Milford MH
12-23-1843 Rachel rocf Sugar Plain MM, Ind
1-24-1846 Eli rpt mcd
2-28-1846 Eli chm of mcd
12-26-1846 James, mbr New Garden, rpt "striking a fellow being with a weapon in anger
3-27-1847 James chm; New Garden inf
7-24-1847 James rocf New Garden MM, Ind
11-27-1847 Samuel appt an Elder
1-22-1848 Rachel Robinson (form Cammack) rpt mcd
4-22-1848 Rachel Robinson (form Cammack) chm of mcd
9-23-1848 Sarah rocf Cherry Grove MM, Ind
7-27-1850 Sally gct Chester MM, Ind
7-24-1852 Sarah gct Back Creek MM, Ind
7-26-1856 Eli gct Red Cedar MM, Ia
11-27-1858 Eli rocf Red Cedar MM, Ia
4-26-1862 Edwin S, Enos M, Eva Jane, Elmer D, Elma H & Edna Ann, ch of Eli, rec in mbrp
5-24-1862 Eli & ch Edwin S, Enos M, Eva Jane, Elmer D, Elma H & Edna Ann gct Mississinewa MM, Ind
3-25-1865 Samuel & w Hannah gct Back Creek MM, Ind
2-22-1868 Adaline Peelle (form Cammack) rpt mcd; chm
1-22-1870 Charles rpt mcd; rel fr mbrp
11-25-1871 Eli & ch Eva J, Elmer D, Elma H & Enos M rocf Spring River MM, Kans
5-25-1872 Edwin rocf Spring River MM, Kans
10-23-1873 David rpt mcd; chm
6-26-1875 Hannah rocf New Garden MM, Ind
5-25-1878 Eli & ch Edna Ann & Elmer D gct Lowell MM, Kans

**CANADAY**
10-23-1852 Mary (form Nixon) rpt mcd
4-23-1853 Mary (form Nixon) dis for mcd
4-28-1866 George Fox rocf Neuse MM, N C

**CARTER**
1-29-1885 Daniel rocf West Union MM, Ind
3-25-1886 Joseph rocf West Union MM, Ind
2-21-1889 Joseph gct Plainfield MM, Ind
2-21-1889 Daniel M gct Cottonwood MM, Kans

**CHADWICK**
2-28-1829 Anna rocf Silver Creek MM, Ind
6-25-1831 Ann gct Silver Creek MM, Ind

**CHAPPELL**
9-26-1829 .......... rocf Piney Woods, N C, -end by Whitewater MM, Ind
3-24-1832 Reuben rocf Suttons Creek MM, N C
8-24-1833 Mary & Lydia rocf Suttons Creek MM, N C
12-31-1835 Martha, -dt Gideon & Mary of Perquimans MM, N C, m John Morris at Milford MH
6-25-1836 Reuben gct Salem MM to m Mary Ann Johnson
10-22-1836 Mary Ann rocf Salem MM, Ind
11-26-1836 Lydia rpt na, dp & apd & dancing
1-28-1837 Lydia dis
12-22-1838 Reuben & w Mary & s Benjamin Albertson gct Salem MM, Ind
3-27-1858 William H & w Christian Ann & ch Missouri C & Allice J rocf Piney Woods MM, N C
3-23-1867 William H rpt mcd; chm
3-23-1867 Mary Ann chm of mcd
9-23-1871 William H & w Martha Ann & ch Alice J & Anna Phebe gct Deer Creek MM, N C
4-25-1874 Jeptha & w Josephine & s Charles rec in mbrp
3-26-1881 Jeptha & w & ch Charles F, Christopher C & Mary F gct Piney Woods MM, N C
6-26-1884 Sophronia rocf Piney Woods MM, N C
6-23-1887 Sophronia (Chappell) White gct Hopewell MM, Ind

**CHARLES**
12-23-1826 Amelia, a minor, u/c Hatfield Wright & w, rocf Northwest Fork, Caroline Co, Md
1-27-1827 Levicia rocf Northwest Fork MM, Md
10-27-1827 Leven rocf Northwest Fork MM, Md
11-8-1827 Nathan of Whitewater MM, -s Samuel & Gulielma, m Mary Symons at Milford MH
1-13-1828 Amelia of Henry Co, Ind, -dt Henry & Mary, (dec) of Dorchester Co, Md, m Thomas Butler at Bethel MH
4-25-1828 Mary gct Whitewater MM, Ind
9-27-1828 William, rpt mcd by Hopewell MM
9-27-1828 Lovisa rpt jH by Bethel MM
11-22-1828 William dis
11-22-1828 Lovisa dis
11-22-1828 Joseph rpt jH by Bethel MM
1-24-1829 Joseph dis
3-28-1829 Levan rpt jH
6-27-1829 Levan dis
9-26-1829 Samuel rpt jH by Hopewell MM
11-28-1829 Samuel dis
12-26-1829 Sarah Sr rpt jH by Bethel MM
2-27-1830 Sarah Sr dis
7-23-1831 Margaret, a minor, rocf Whitewater MM, Ind
10-1-1834 Margaret, -dt John & Elvira, Wayne Co, Ind, m Gideon Wilson at Bethel MH
4-27-1844 Elizabeth Heavenridge (form Charles) rpt mcd by Bethel MM
6-22-1844 Elizabeth Heavenridge (form Charles) chm of mcd
1-27-1849 Rebecca Savage (form Charles) rpt mcd by Mississinewa MM
7-28-1849 Rebecca Savage (form Charles), Mississinewa MM rpt they do not know where she lives
2-22-1851 Rebecca Savage (form Charles) dis with comment "she lives remote from this mtg"
12-22-1855 Abigail Parks (form Charles) rpt mcd by Wabash MM
11-22-1873 Josiah Morris gct Whitewater MM to m Mary Charles
11-23-1878 Caroline rec in mbrp

**CLAMPET**
11-24-1832 Mary rec in mbrp
5-25-1833 Mary gct Duck Creek MM, Ind
10-22-1836 Mary rocf Duck Creek MM, Ind
2-25-1837 William & ch Herman, Emila, Cyrus, Phebe & Jesse rec in mbrp
8-25-1838 William & w Mary & ch Herman, Emila, Cyrus, Phebe, Jesse & Joel gct Westfield MM, Ind

**CLARK**
12-28-1867 Martha (form Reynolds) rpt mcd; rel fr mbrp
4-26-1888 Ellen Henby gct Springfield MM, Ind
4-26-1888 Charles T & w Emma J & s Earl C rec in mbrp

MILFORD

CLARK (Cont)
7-25-1889  Charles T & w Emma J & s Earl rel fr mbrp

CLARY
12-25-1824  Barnes rpt dr & upl
2-26-1825   Barnes chm for dr & upl
2-25-1826   Barnes rpt dr
4-22-1826   Barnes dis
6-28-1828   Rebecca rpt apd by Bethel MM
8-23-1828   Rebecca dis

CLAWSON
9- 7-1848   Josiah of Wayne Co, Ind, -s Wilson & Keziah (dec), m Sarah N Fletcher at Milford MH
2-24-1849   Sarah N gct Chester MM, Ind

CLAYTON
3- 9-1830   Thomas rocf New Garden MM, N C, -end to New Garden MM, Ind

COFFIN
8-14-1823   Paul appt to a comm
11-27-1824  Bethuel & w Katharine, a min, & her ch Jonathan & Anna Macy rocf New Garden MM, N C
12-25-1824  Elijah & w Naomi & ch Miriam & Charles rocf Hopewell MM, N C
7-26-1828   Paul rpt jH
7-26-1828   Elizabeth rpt jH
10-25-1828  Paul dis
10-25-1828  Elizabeth dis
10-25-1828  Bethuel rpt jH
12-27-1828  Bethuel dis for jH
10-24-1829  Elihu & w Sarah & ch Isaac & William Starbuck rocf Deep River MM, N C
1-28-1832   Harvey & w Rachel & dt Ruth rocf Deep River MM, N C
4-28-1832   Alfred rocf Deep River MM, N C, -end to Duck Creek MM, Ind
1-26-1833   Elihu rpt "he has threatened one of his fellow creatures with violence" by Duck Creek MM
4-27-1833   Elihu chm of (he has threatened one of his fellow creatures with violence)
7-27-1833   Elijah & w Naomi & ch Mariam A, Charles F, William H & Caroline E gct Cincinnati MM, Ohio
7-27-1833   Elihu & w Sarah & ch Isaac Newton, William Starbuck, Alfred & Phebe gct Duck Creek MM, Ind
5-23-1835   Catharine gct Duck Creek MM, Ind
2-27-1836   Louisa Paxton (form Coffin) rpt mcd by Hopewell MM
4-23-1836   Louisa Paxton (form Coffin) dis for mcd
8-26-1837   Harvey & w Rachel & ch Ruth, Nathan Dix, William & Sarah gct Westfield MM, Ind
10-16-1845  William H of Richmond, Ind, -s Elijah & Naomi, m Sarah Wilson at Milford MH
1-24-1846   Sarah gct Whitewater MM, Ind
6-24-1854   William & w Sarah & ch John, Wilson, William, Henry, Albert & Robert B rocf Whitewater MM, Ind
7-27-1858   William H & Sarah W set-off to Kansas MM, Kans
1-27-1887   Malissa E gct Spiceland MM, Ind

COGGSHALL
10-24-1829  Gayer rocf Springfield MM, Ind
1-22-1831   Gayer rpt mcd
2-26-1831   Gayer chm of mcd
4-28-1838   Peter, u/c Margaret Morris, rec in mbrp
4- 2-1846   Peter, of Wayne Co, Ind, -s Gayer & Hannah, (both dec), m Jane Nixon at Milford MH
9-25-1847   Peter & w Jane gct Westfield MM, Ind
4-22-1848   Milton rocf Walnut Ridge MM, Ind
2-24-1855   Peter & w Jane & dt Mary Ellen rocf Hinkles Creek MM, Ind
3-27-1858   John Milton rpt mcd
4-24-1858   John Milton chm of mcd
8-24-1861   Mary Jane rec in mbrp
5-23-1868   Peter & w Jane & ch Mary Ellen & Margaret Susan gct Walnut Ridge MM, Ind
11-26-1870  John Milton & w Mary Jane & ch Olan T & George W gct Greenwood MM, Ia
11-26-1881  Mary gct Deer Creek MM

COLLINS
5-23-1854   Lewis G & w Sarah D & dt Jane rocf Springfield MM, Ohio, -end to Sugar River MM, Ind

CONLEY
2-25-1886   Franklin M rec in mbrp
2-21-1889   Franklin M rel fr mbrp

COOK
12-25-1824  John, w Mary & ch Nancy, Robert, Joshua & Joseph gct White Lick MM, Ind
8-27-1825   Levi & w Ann & ch Isaac & John Cook & Thomas, Ann & William Hasket rocf Miami MM, Ohio
6-24-1826   Ann appt an Elder
11-28-1827  John of Henry Co, Ind, -s Levi & Ann (dec), m Juliana Saint at West Union MH
2-23-1828   Julia Ann gct Duck Creek MM, Ind
5-24-1828   Eli & dt Martha rocf Silver Creek MM, Ind
5-25-1830   Eli rpt jH
7- 4-1830   Eli dis for jH
10-22-1836  Thomas, Henderson, Everet & Riley, ch of Zimri, rocf Salem MM, Ind
12-24-1836  John & w Mary & ch Martha, Josiah & William rocf Salem MM, Ind
12-24-1836  Isaac & w Elizabeth & ch Mary, James & Susanna rocf Salem MM, Ind
5-27-1837   Thomas rpt dp & na
8-28-1837   Thomas dis for dp & na
7- 1-1840   John of Henry Co, Ind, -s Israel & Elizabeth, m Peninah Gilbert at Hopewell MH
8-28-1841   Henderson rpt na & dp
10-23-1841  Henderson dis for na & dp
5-27-1843   Everit, rpt na & mcd by Vermillion MM, Ill
12-23-1843  Everit dis for na & mcd
3-22-1845   Riley gct Vermillion MM, Ill
3-27-1869   Hannah & ch Sarah, Ann, Isaac & Dorinda rocf Plainfield MM, Ind
6-24-1871   Hannah & ch Sarah, Ann, Isaac & Dorinda gct Mill Creek MM, Ind

COONEY
11-27-1890  John rec in mbrp

COOPER
12-24-1825  James rocf Whitewater MM, Ind
12-24-1825  Katharine & ch Joshua, Josiah, Rachel, John, Arthur & William rocf Whitewater MM, Ind
5-22-1830   John rpt dp, aiding in distilling spiritous liquors, jMeth, training with the Militia & mcd
5-22-1830   Joshua rpt mcd, dp, na & aiding in distilling spirituous liquors
5-22-1830   Joseph rpt mcd & jMeth  He lives in Clinton Co, in the Two mile Prairie, 15 miles below Lafayette; White Lick rq to tr w/h
5-22-1830   Catharine rpt na
5-22-1830   Rachel rpt na
7-24-1830   John dis
7-24-1830   Joshua dis
7-24-1830   Rachel dis
10-23-1830  Catharine chm for na
3-26-1831   Joseph - White Lick infs they cannot ascertain where he lives
8-27-1831   Joseph - it is now understood that he lives on Wild Cat Prairie, called Two Mile Prairie; Sugar River rq to tr w/h
5-26-1832   Joseph - Sugar River rpt; dis
1-23-1836   William rpt mcd
3-26-1836   William dis - the remoteness of his situation is referred to

MILFORD

## COOPER (Cont)
| | |
|---|---|
| 5-24-1845 | Martha (form Smith) rpt mcd by Bethel MM |
| 7-26-1845 | Martha (form Smith) dis for mcd |

## COPE
| | |
|---|---|
| 11-26-1831 | Rebecca & ch Ruth Luann, Simeon, Eliza, Lydia & Lemuel rocf West Grove MM, Ind |
| 3-22-1845 | Rebecca & ch Ruth Luann, Eliza, Lydia & Samuel gct Mississinewa MM, Ind |

## COPELAND
| | |
|---|---|
| 11-13-1823 | John appt to a comm |
| 11-17-1823 | Winnifred, -dt John & Susannah of Henry Co, Ind, m Benjamin Weeks at Duck Creek MH |
| 8-25-1832 | Jesse, Joshua, Samuel, John & Nathan, ch of John, rocf Duck Creek MM, Ind |
| 12-28-1833 | Jesse rpt mcd & jH |
| 2-28-1834 | Joshua, Samuel, John & Nathan, ch of John & Susannah, gct Duck Creek MM, Ind |
| 3-22-1834 | Jesse dis for mcd & jH |
| 5-27-1837 | Charlotte (form Taylor), mbr Chester MM, rpt mcd |
| 9-23-1837 | Charlotte (form Taylor) rpt dis by Chester MM |

## COPPOCK
| | |
|---|---|
| 7-25-1874 | Isaac C & w Martha E rocf West Grove MM, Ind |
| 1-23-1875 | Isaac & w Martha gct West Branch MM, Ohio |

## CORNETTA
| | |
|---|---|
| 11-27-1890 | Charles P rec in mbrp |

## COSAND
| | |
|---|---|
| 4-23-1825 | Mary & s John, Nathan & Elias rocf Chester MM, Ind |
| 11-24-1832 | John rocf Duck Creek MM, Ind |
| 11-24-1832 | Mary & s Elias rocf Duck Creek MM, Ind |
| 3-23-1833 | Elias rpt dp & upl by Hopewell MM |
| 6-22-1833 | Elias - the matter of dp & upl discontinued |
| 3-22-1834 | Sarah (form Wickersham) rpt mcd by Hopewell MM |
| 7-26-1834 | Sarah (form Wickersham) dis for mcd |
| 5-28-1864 | Sarah rst at Hopewell MM, Ind |
| 2-26-1885 | Emma rec in mbrp |

## COUCH
| | |
|---|---|
| 8-26-1848 | Elizabeth rocf Deep River MM, N C, "she living quite remote from mtg and a stranger amongst us" |

## COULTER
| | |
|---|---|
| 5-22-1875 | Susan T rel fr mbrp |
| 5-22-1875 | Lucy E rel fr mbrp |

## COX
| | |
|---|---|
| 4-22-1826 | Benjamin & w Mary & ch Sarah, Katharine, Levina, Zilpha, Mahlon & Rice Price rocf Chester MM, Ind |
| 5-27-1826 | Joel rocf Somerset MM, Ohio, -end by Whitewater MM, Ind |
| 7-28-1827 | Joel gct White River MM to m Catharine Cox |
| 8-25-1827 | Jacob rocf Blue River MM, Ind |
| 1-26-1828 | Catharine rocf White River MM, Ind |
| 10-24-1829 | Joseph & w Elizabeth & ch Priscilla, Drucilla, Bennet, Seth, William, Mariah, Rachel & Joseph rocf Somerset MM, Ohio |
| 9-29-1830 | Priscilla, -dt Joseph & Elizabeth of Wayne Co, Ind, m Samuel Bundy at Bethel MH |
| 10-30-1830 | Drucilla, -dt Joseph & Elizabeth, Wayne Co, Ind, m Jonathan Wilson at Bethel MH |
| 9-29-1836 | Bennett of Wayne Co, Ind, -s Joseph & Elizabeth, m Elizabeth Kindley at Milford MH |
| 11-26-1836 | Elizabeth appt an Elder |
| 5-27-1837 | Joseph appt an Elder |
| 6-24-1837 | Bennett & w Elizabeth gct Walnut Ridge MM, Ind |
| 2-23-1839 | Jacob gct Blue River MM, Ind |
| 11-14-1839 | Seth of Wayne Co, Ind, -s Joseph & Elizabeth, m Ruth Kindley at Milford MH |
| 3-31-1841 | Maria, -dt Joseph & Elizabeth of Wayne Co, Ind, m Nathan Wasson at Bethel MH |
| 3- 2-1842 | Elijah, -s Jeremiah & Jemima (both dec), m Esther Hollowell, a widow, at Bethel MH |
| 3-30-1842 | Rachel, -dt Joseph & Elizabeth of Wayne Co, Ind, m Elihu Patterson at Bethel MH |
| 8-27-1842 | Esther & ch Mary Jane & Nathan Hollowell gct Sugar River MM, Ind |
| 3- 2-1843 | William of Wayne Co, Ind, -s Joseph & Elizabeth, m Hannah R Stokes at Milford MH |
| 4-26-1845 | William & w Hannah & s Albert gct Hopewell MM, Ind |
| 4-30-1845 | Ann, -dt Joseph & Elizabeth of Wayne Co, Ind, m Nathan Gause Jr at Bethel MH |
| 8-30-1848 | Elizabeth, -dt Joel & Catherine of Henry Co, Ind, m David W Farquhar at Bethel MH |
| 12-22-1849 | Bennett & w Elizabeth & ch Albert, Ruth Ann, Melissa, John K, Seth, Eliza B & Caroline rocf Walnut Ridge MM, Ind |
| 2-28-1852 | Jeremiah rpt mcd by Bethel MM |
| 4-24-1852 | Jeremiah dis for mcd |
| 5-29-1853 | Joseph J rpt mcd by Bethel MM |
| 6-25-1853 | Joseph J chm of mcd |
| 8-27-1853 | Joseph M gct Short Creek MM, Ohio to m Rachel M Terril |
| 12-24-1853 | Lydia Ann rec in mbrp |
| 1-28-1854 | Joseph M gct Walnut Ridge MM, Ind |
| 6-24-1854 | Jeremiah rst at Richland MM, Ind |
| 4-26-1856 | Joseph M & w Rachel rocf Walnut Ridge MM, Ind |
| 6-28-1856 | Joseph J & w Lydia Ann gct Spiceland MM, Ind |
| 7-26-1856 | William gct Richland MM to m Martha Jessup |
| 7-25-1857 | Martha rocf Richland MM, Ind |
| 1-23-1858 | Seth, Bethel MM rpt that "he has made and put in circulation charges and assertions against a friend, tending to slander his character" |
| 4-17-1858 | Seth - Comm rpt "that he is not entirely clear of the charges" however matter is discontinued |
| 10-22-1859 | Joel & w Catharine & ch Rebecca E, Samuel, Jane M & Daniel W gct Bridgeport MM, Ind |
| 6-28-1860 | Thomas of Bartholomew Co, Ind, -s Isaac & Millicent, (both dec), m Mary Newby at Milford MH |
| 8-25-1860 | Mary N gct Driftwood MM, Ind |
| 9-22-1860 | William gct Spiceland MM to m Elvira T Gause |
| 12-22-1860 | William rpt mcd by Spiceland MM, but now lives in limits of Bridgeport |
| 5-25-1860 | William chm of mcd |
| 6-22-1861 | William & s Arthur gct Bridgeport MM, Ind |
| 1-25-1862 | Albert rpt mcd by Bethel MM; chm |
| 6-24-1866 | Seth & w Ruth & ch Sarah & Milton gct Spring Creek MM, Ia |
| 5-26-1866 | John rpt mcd; chm |
| 6-23-1866 | John gct Spring Creek MM, Ia |
| 10-27-1866 | Amos rpt mcd; chm |
| 11-24-1866 | Amos gct Bear Creek MM |
| 4-27-1867 | Eliza B Perkins (form Cox) rpt mcd; chm |
| 1-22-1870 | Seth rpt mcd; chm |
| 2-26-1870 | Caroline Edwards (form Cox) rpt mcd; chm |
| 2-26-1870 | Seth rel fr mbrp |
| 4-26-1873 | Henry & w Malinda & s Willis T rocf Hopewell MM, Ind |
| 6-28-1873 | Elizabeth rpt separated fr her h; dis |
| 7-26-1873 | Bennett rpt separated fr his w; dis |
| 8-23-1873 | Henry & w Malinda & s Willis gct Hopewell MM, Ind |
| 1-27-1877 | Bennett & w Elizabeth rec in mbrp |
| 3-24-1883 | Sarah rec in mbrp |
| 10-27-1883 | Rachel D & dt Lulu rec in mbrp |
| 2-23-1884 | William E & w Rachel D & ch Hannah Lulu gct Portland MM, Ind |
| 1-23-1890 | Harriet rocf Hopewell MM, Ind |

MILFORD

COX (Cont)
3-26-1891  J Clark & w Hattie gct Denver MM
11-23-1893  Charles S & w Eliza & ch Maude L, Cora S, Charlie E & Otto Z gct Raysville MM, Ind

CRAFT
10-26-1844  Thomas Fairbank - a cert rec in the course of the year from Balby MM, England, but his residence not being known it is ret to same MM

CRAIG
4-28-1892  George, Leroy & Fannie rec in mbrp

CRAMER
3-23-1893  Sylvester rec in mbrp

CRANE
10-23-1830  Sarah, mbr Cincinnati MM, rpt mcd
1-22-1831  Sarah dis by Cincinnati MM for mcd

CROOK
2-22-1845  Eliza Ann (form Newby), mbr Duck Creek MM, rpt for na, jMeth & mcd
4-26-1845  Eliza Ann (form Newby) dis by Duck Creek MM, Ind

CRULL
8-26-1888  Daniel rec in mbrp
9-21-1893  Daniel rel fr mbrp

CULBERTSON
12-27-1856  Eliza K (form Hunt) rpt mcd by Bethel MM; dis

DARAN
2-21-1889  Maggie rel fr mbrp

DAVIS
4-22-1826  Harmon & w Hannah & ch Thomas, Sarah, Jehu, Hannah & Eunice rocf Stillwater MM, Ohio
5-27-1826  Love & ch Alexander, Rhosanna, Allen W, Zeno, Edwin & Eliza Jane rocf Springfield MM, Ind
12-22-1827  Isaac rocf Stillwater MM, Ohio
5-23-1829  Harmon rpt he told an untruth
6-27-1829  Harmon chm for telling an untruth
1-23-1830  Thomas gct Duck Creek MM to m Hannah Moore
3- 9-1830  Joseph rocf Whitewater MM, Ind
5-22-1830  Hannah T rocf Duck Creek MM, Ind
5-26-1830  Joseph of Wayne Co, Ind, -s Harmon & Hannah, m Hannah Morgan at West Union MH
9-29-1830  Sarah, -dt Harmon & Hannah of Wayne Co, Ind, m Isaac Brown at Bethel MH
12- 1-1830  Isaac of Wayne Co, Ind, -s Harmon & Hannah, m Phebe Brown at Bethel MH
12-25-1830  Thomas & w Hannah T gct Duck Creek MM, Ind
4-23-1831  Jehu dec int to m Rebecca Brown, but there was some objection
6-25-1831  Jehu rpt mcd
9-10-1831  Jehu chm of mcd
7-23-1831  Rebecca (form Brown) rpt clm of mcd
10-21-1831  Rebecca (form Brown) clm of mcd
1-28-1832  Thomas & w Hannah T & dt Susanna rocf Duck Creek MM, Ind
2-25-1832  Joseph & w Hannah & dt Eliza gct West Grove MM, Ind
10-27-1832  Harmon & w Hannah & ch Hannah & Eunice gct Springfield MM, Ind
6-22-1833  Thomas & w Hannah & ch Susannah & Abraham gct Duck Creek MM, Ind
9-27-1834  Isaac & w Phebe & dt Louiza gct Duck Creek MM, Ind
5-23-1835  Jehu & w Rebecca & s Oliver gct Duck Creek MM, Ind
8-22-1835  James rocf Spiceland MM, Ind
11-26-1836  Frances rocf Spiceland MM, Ind
3-25-1837  Jonah M, a minor, rocf Dover MM (-s of Jesse, probably 'bound out')
2-22-1840  Francis gct White River MM, Ind
4-24-1841  James gct Spiceland MM, Ind
1-24-1846  Joseph B & w Parthenia rocf Spiceland MM, Ind
6-24-1848  Sarah rocf Whitewater MM, Ind
7-22-1848  Jonah M gct Spiceland MM, Ind
10-25-1851  Joseph B rpt "being engaged in a fight in anger with one of his fellow beings"
11-22-1851  Joseph B chm of "being in a fight in anger with one of his fellow beings"
5-23-1854  Parthenia, -w Joseph, & ch Margaret A, Rebecca Jane & Martha Kaloolah gct Pipe Creek MM, Ind
6-24-1854  Joseph B rpt by Pipe Creek MM for "fighting a fellow man, for upl, & for refusing to have an accout in dispute arbitrated, having been issued a cert at last mtg, but not forwarded, Pipe Creek MM returned
1-27-1855  Joseph B - Pipe Creek MM rpt the disputed account settled & other charge changed to laying violent hands on a fellow creature & upl, but he failed to make satisfaction; dis
4-25-1857  Sarah gct Philadelphia MM, Pa
3-27-1858  Edwin & w Rebecca & s Lindley Albert rocf Wabash MM, Ind
2-26-1859  Edwin & w Rebecca Jane & ch Albert L gct Wabash MM, Ind
7-27-1867  Alpheus & w Luiza & s Walter Elvin rocf West Grove MM, Ind
5-22-1869  Alpheus & w Luiza & s Alvin gct Sugar Plain MM, Ind
6-22-1872  Joseph rec in mbrp
7-26-1873  William rocf West Grove MM, Ind
5-22-1875  William rel fr mbrp
9-24-1885  Solomon Elliot gct Salem MM to m Emily J Davis

DAWES
3-27-1858  Edwin & w Rebecca & ch Lindley Albert rocf Wabash MM, Ind
2-26-1859  Edwin & w Rebecca Jane & ch Albert Lindley gct Wabash MM, Ind

DAWSON
12-27-1827  James H rocf Whitewater MM, Ind
1-24-1829  James H rpt jH
3-28-1829  James H dis for jH

DENNIS
8-14-1823  Benjamin appt Clerk
7-31-1839  Gulielma, -dt Benjamin & Clarky of Henry Co, Ind, m John Reece at Hopewell MH

DERBYSHIRE
8-24-1867  Ann (form Willetts) rpt mcd; chm

DICKEY
2-28-1846  Mary Ann, mbr Duck Creek MM, jMeth
3-28-1846  Mary Ann - Duck Creek MM inf of her jMeth
1-26-1850  Jane rocf Duck Creek MM, Ind
9-28-1850  Jane gct Richland MM, Ind
2-22-1851  Asenith rocf Duck Creek MM, Ind
9-25-1858  Asenith rpt na & guilty of unchaste conduct by Duck Creek MM
1-22-1859  Asenith dis by Duck Creek MM for na & unchaste conduct

DICKINSON
5-25-1839  Sarah (form Smith) rpt mcd by Bethel MM
7-27-1839  Sarah (form Smith) dis for mcd
8-24-1839  Isaac, mbr Whitewater MM, rpt mcd
11-26-1842  Joseph rocf Balby, held at Thorne, Eng, -end by Whitewater MM, Ind
6-24-1843  Charles rocf Balby, Sheffield, Eng
9-28-1844  Alice & ch Alice & James H rocf Balby MM, Sheffield, Eng
10-17-1844  Joseph of Wayne Co, Ind, -s Jonathan (dec) & Alice of Eng, m Esther G White at Milford MH

MILFORD

**DICKINSON (Cont)**

10-26-1844 Jane rocf Brighouse MM, held at Leeds, Co of York
4-26-1845 Jonathan rocf Balby MM, Eng
7-2-1846 Charles of Wayne Co, Ind, -s Jonathan (dec) & Alice of Eng, m Hannah F Hiatt at Milford MH
7-22-1848 Henry & w Grace rocf Balby MM, Sheffield, Eng
3-27-1849 Jane of Wayne Co, Ind, -dt Jonathan (dec) & Alice of England, m James Trueblood at Milford MH
9-6-1849 Alice of Wayne Co, Ind, -dt Jonathan (dec) & Alice of England, m Thomas Newby at Milford MH
12-28-1850 Joseph & w Esther & ch Oliver White, Hannah & Samuel gct Whitewater MM, Ind
3-27-1852 Charles & w Hannah & ch Henry & Benajah gct Whitewater MM, Ind
3-27-1852 Jonathan gct Whitewater MM, Ind
3-27-1852 James H, a minor, gct Whitewater MM, Ind
6-26-1852 Alice gct Whitewater MM, Ind

**DICKS**

3-28-1835 Elizabeth rocf Bloomfield MM, Ind

**DILLON**

11-26-1825 Gulielma rocf Springfield MM, Ohio, -end to Honey Creek MM, Ind
3-23-1850 Isaiah, mbr Deep River MM, N C, rec, but he has returned to N C
1-26-1888 John rec in mbrp

**DIXON**

1-22-1881 Calvin & w Mary & ch Keziah Jenneate, Rosa Jane & Rustitia Ann rocf Walnut Ridge MM
10-27-1883 Joel & s Lewis rocf White Lick MM, Ind
2-23-1884 Calvin & w Mary M & ch Keziah J, Rosa J, Rustitia Ann, Elmer P & Harley G gct Hopewell MM, Ind

**DORAN**

1-28-1886 Margaret rec in mbrp

**DOTY**

1-28-1886 Frank & Laura rec in mbrp
2-21-1889 Frank & Laura rel fr mbrp

**DRAPER**

11-27-1824 Josiah appt Clerk
5-28-1825 Catharine & dt Huldah rst in mbrp w/c of West Grove MM, Ind
5-28-1825 Huldah Draper (form Pearson) rpt mcd
5-28-1825 Joshua rpt mcd
7-23-1825 Joshua chm of mcd
8-27-1825 Huldah Draper (form Pearson) chm of mcd
10-22-1825 Mary rocf Whitewater MM, -end to Driftwood MM, Ind
9-22-1827 Josiah Jr & fam gct Duck Creek MM, Ind
1-26-1828 Joshua rpt "gitting in a passion & fiting"
2-23-1828 Joshua chm of "gitting in a passion & fiting"
3-27-1830 Joshua & w Huldah & dt Millicent gct Duck Creek MM, Ind
7-28-1832 Josiah & w Jemima & dt Mary Ann gct Duck Creek MM, Ind

**DUBOIS**

3-29-1888 Dora rec in mbrp
4-26-1888 Katie May & Martie rec in mbrp

**DUNLAP**

5-25-1844 Phebe (form Gray) rpt mcd & jMeth by Duck Creek MM
9-28-1844 Phebe (form Gray) dis for mcd & jMeth

**EARL**

2-28-1874 Phebe R rec in mbrp
3-28-1874 Isaac H rec in mbrp
9-21-1893 Isaac rel fr mbrp

**ECLES**

12-22-1860 Rachel rocf Elk MM, Ohio, -end to Walnut Ridge MM
2-23-1861 Rachel - cert ret here but as she does not reside here, it is ret to Elk MM, Ohio

**EDGERTON**

4-25-1829 Nelly & ch Eli, Owen, Ruthanna, Eliza Ann & William P rocf Whitewater MM, Ind
10-24-1829 Walter & w Rebeccah & s William rocf Somerset MM, Ohio
2-27-1830 Thomas & w Mary & ch William Osborn, Elenor, Mary Ann, Samuel & Martha rocf Whitewater MM, Ind
11-26-1831 Nelly rpt jH; dis
11-28-1835 Thomas & w Mary & ch Eleanora, Mary Ann, Samuel, Martha Ann, Thomas & Richard gct West Grove MM, Ind
12-24-1836 Walter & w Rebecca & ch William & Sarah gct Spiceland MM, Ind
12-22-1838 Owen, Ruthanna, Eliza Ann & William P, ch of Nelly, gct Back Creek MM, Ind
3-23-1839 Thomas & w Mary & ch William T & Elizabeth Ann & George Taylor, a minor, rocf Salem MM, Ind
2-27-1841 Rachel & ch Calvin, Mary, Margaret & Daniel rocf Whitewater MM, Ind
2-25-1843 Thomas & w Mary & ch Eliza Ann, Samuel & Sarah Jane rocf Hopewell MM, Ind
1-27-1844 Thomas rpt jASF
3-23-1844 Thomas dis for jASF
3-23-1844 Rachel & ch Calvin, Mary & Margaret gct New Garden MM, Ind
4-27-1844 Mary rpt jASF
7-27-1844 Mary dis for jASF
6-26-1852 William T, Elizabeth Ann, Samuel, Sarah Jane & Susan, ch of Thomas & Mary, gct Whitewater MM, Ind
7-28-1855 Thomas & Mary rst in mbrp at Whitewater MM, Ind
1-28-1860 Abigail & dt Susan M, Eliza Ann & Emily C rocf Whitewater MM, Ind
10-2-1862 Abigail, a widow, -dt Job & Letitia Stratton, m Richard J Hubbard at Milford MH
11-28-1863 Susan Wilson (form Edgerton) rpt mcd; chm
11-23-1867 Eliza Ann Gresh (form Edgerton) rpt mcd; chm

**EDWARDS**

10-24-1840 Ira rocf Hopewell MM, N C, -end to Whitewater MM, Ind
2-26-1870 Caroline (form Cox) rpt mcd; chm

**EIDSON**

9-23-1854 Ruth (form Elliott) rpt mcd by Bethel MM
11-25-1854 Ruth (form Elliott) dis for mcd
6-23-1866 Charles & w Ruth & ch Alice, Oliver, Wynona, Elmer & Mary rec in mbrp
3-23-1867 Charles & w Ruth & ch Alice, Oliver, Wynona, Elmer & Mary gct Poplar Ridge MM, Ind

**ELLENBARGER**

8-24-1893 Alfred L & Agnes rec in mbrp

**ELLIOTT**

11-25-1815 John & w Mary rocf Deep Creek MM, N C at Whitewater MM, Ind Territory (they settled in the area that became Milford MM, Ind)
12-30-1815 Jacob & w Mary & ch Jonathan, Absolem & Gulielma rocf Deep Creek MM, N C at Whitewater MM, Ind Terr (they settled in area that became Milford MM, Ind)
3-13-1823 Jacob appt to a comm
12-25-1824 Ann & ch Olive, Alice, Welmet, Susannah, Elvina, Melinda, Anna & Israel rocf Whitewater MM, Ind

MILFORD

## ELLIOTT (Cont)

|  |  |
|---|---|
| 9- 1-1825 | Olive, -dt Jacob & Anna of Henry Co, Ind, m Simeon Thomas at Duck Creek MH |
| 9-29-1825 | Alice, -dt Jacob & Anna of Henry Co, Ind, m Nathan Hosier at Duck Creek MH |
| 7- 2-1828 | Exum of Wayne Co, Ind, -s Exum Sr & Katharine, m Hannah Smith at Bethel MH |
| 10-24-1829 | Exum Jr rocf West Grove MM, Ind |
| 11-26-1831 | Ruth gct Duck Creek MM, Ind |
| 11-28-1832 | Gulielma, -dt Jacob & Mary of Wayne Co, Ind, m Stephen Marshall at Bethel MH |
| 3-22-1834 | Jonathan gct New Garden MM to m Amelia Huff |
| 6-28-1834 | Amelia rocf New Garden MM, Ind |
| 12-26-1835 | Absalom gct West Grove MM to m Polly Maxwell |
| 3-26-1836 | Absalom gct West Grove MM, Ind |
| 9-24-1836 | Jonathan & w Amelia & dt Eliza gct Walnut Ridge MM, Ind |
| 12-26-1836 | Exum & w Hannah & ch John, Thamer & Hiram gct Sugar River MM, Ind |
| 12-28-1836 | Sarah M, -dt John & Mary of Wayne Co, Ind, m Asher Hiatt at Bethel MH |
| 3- 1-1837 | Elizabeth, -dt John & Mary of Wayne Co, Ind, m Morris Gilbert at Bethel MH |
| 6-28-1837 | Catherine W, -dt Jacob & Mary of Wayne Co, Ind m Thomas Gilbert at Bethel MH |
| 12-28-1839 | Exum S & w Hannah & ch John W, Thamer H, Hiram & Emeline rocf Sugar River MM, Ind |
| 1- 1-1840 | Rhoda, -dt Jacob & Mary of Wayne Co, Ind, m Nathan Gilbert at Bethel MH |
| 4- 3-1841 | Jonathan & w Amelia & ch Eliza, William B & Jacob C rocf Walnut Ridge MM, Ind |
| 9-30-1841 | Solomon of Wayne Co, Ind, -s Jacob & Mary, m Penelope Morris at Milford MH |
| 11-30-1842 | Mary, widow of John, -dt Richard & Betty Ratliff (both dec), m David Palmer at Bethel MH |
| 1-28-1843 | Mary Palmer & ch Isaac, Mary Ann, Martha, Melissa J & John gct Duck Creek MM, Ind |
| 5-23-1846 | Catharine W gct Duck Creek MM, Ind |
| 2-27-1847 | Richard P gct Duck Creek MM, Ind |
| 5-22-1847 | Sarah & ch Mary, Lutitia, Solomon & Hannah rocf Westfield MM, Ind |
| 5-22-1847 | Abel, mbr Westfield MM, rpt for not settling his outward affairs to satisfaction before moving from their limits & for j United Brethren |
| 6-26-1847 | Abel - Westfield MM, informed |
| 5-27-1848 | Rachel Harvey (form Elliott) rpt mcd by Bethel MM to Duck Creek MM |
| 11-25-1848 | Rachel Harvey (form Elliott), Duck Creek MM rpt she chm |
| 8-26-1848 | Sarah rpt na by Bethel MM |
| 7-22-1848 | Jonathan gct West Grove MM to m Maria Maxwell |
| 10-28-1848 | Sarah dis for na |
| 11-28-1848 | Mariah M rocf West Grove MM, Ind |
| 12-31-1851 | Eliza, -dt Jonathan & Amelia (dec), of Wayne Co, Ind, m John C Bell at Bethel MH |
| 3-27-1852 | Exum rpt mcd |
| 5-22-1852 | Exum dis for mcd |
| 8-28-1852 | Penelope rpt mcd with a mbr |
| 8-28-1852 | Solomon rpt mcd & na |
| 9-25-1852 | Penelope chm of mcd with a mbr |
| 9-25-1852 | Solomon chm of mcd & na |
| 9-23-1854 | Ruth Eidson (form Elliott) rpt mcd |
| 11-25-1854 | Ruth Eidson (form Elliott) dis for mcd |
| 2- 1-1855 | Jacob of Wayne Co, Ind, -s Exum (dec) & Catharine, m Isabella M Hawkins, widow of William & dt of Simon & Jane Powel (both dec) of Ky, m at Milford MH |
| 3-24-1855 | Mary E Pearson (form Elliott) rpt mcd |
| 4-28-1855 | Mary E Pearson (form Elliott) chm of mcd |
| 6-23-1855 | Mark rpt mcd; dis |
| 4-25-1857 | Exum rec in mbrp again |
| 5-23-1857 | Mary M rec in mbrp |
| 8-22-1857 | Isabella M appt an Elder |
| 3-25-1860 | Jonathan & w Maria & ch Mary, John, Achilles, Albert, David & Linus gct Chester MM, Ind |
| 10-27-1860 | Hiram rpt mcd; dis |
| 8-24-1861 | Sarah Catharine Brown (form Elliott) rpt mcd; chm |
| 3-25-1865 | Jonathan & w Maria & ch Mary, John M, Achilles W, Albert & David gct Chester MM, Ind |
| 8-25-1866 | Isabella K Hall & dt Margaret Jane Elliott gct Spiceland MM, Ind |
| 11-24-1866 | Jacob rpt mcd; chm |
| 1-26-1867 | Jacob gct Chester MM, Ind |
| 2-27-1869 | M Jane Hastings (form Elliott) rpt mcd; chm |
| 7-24-1869 | Martin L gct Union MM, Mo |
| 2-26-1870 | Malissa J rocf Hopewell MM, Ind |
| 7-23-1870 | Franklin gct Springdale MM, Ia to m Eliza Grinnell |
| 1-16-1871 | Melissa J, -dt John & Mary of Wayne Co, Ind, m John P Pennington at res of Melissa Elliott |
| 9-23-1871 | Franklin gct Marysville MM, Tenn |
| 12-27-1873 | Elias & w Jane & s John & gr-ch Delphina & Hettie rocf Whitewater MM, Ind |
| 9-26-1874 | Martin Luther & w Sarah Ellen rocf Union MM, Mo |
| 11-27-1874 | Mary Jane rocf Whitewater MM, Ind |
| 1-22-1876 | William rel fr mbrp |
| 10-28-1876 | Martin L & w Sarah E gct Union MM, Mo |
| 7-28-1877 | Lindley M H rec in mbrp |
| 7-26-1881 | Jane, widow of Elias, -dt William & Sarah Cain (both dec), m Jacob Moore |
| 9-24-1881 | Hattie A, -dt Jane E Moore, gct Whitewater MM, Ind |
| 4-28-1883 | John C rel fr mbrp |
| 4-24-1884 | John B gct Spiceland MM, Ind |
| 2-26-1885 | Lizzie Miller rec in mbrp |
| 9-24-1885 | Solomon gct Salem MM to m Emily J Davis |
| 12-24-1885 | Emily Davis rocf Salem MM, Ind |
| 5-25-1887 | Ann Hill gct Walnut Ridge MM, Ind |
| 1-24-1889 | Amanda rel fr mbrp |
| 12-24-1891 | Olive rocf Hopewell MM, Ind |
| 4-28-1892 | Alice rec in mbrp |
| 9-21-1893 | Solomon, John, Tamar & Emeline rel fr mbrp |

## ELZEY

|  |  |
|---|---|
| 12-18-1823 | Garnet rpt mcd; chm |
| 1-15-1824 | Keziah Holtsclaw (form Elzey) rpt mcd |
| 3-18-1824 | Keziah Holtsclaw (form Elzey) chm of mcd |
| 11-22-1828 | Esther rpt guilty of fornication by Bethel MM |
| 1-24-1829 | Esther dis for fornication |
| 1-24-1829 | Priscilla Hall (form Elzey) rpt mcd |
| 3-28-1829 | Priscilla Hall (form Elzey) chm of mcd |
| 3-24-1832 | James gct Duck Creek MM, Ind |

## ENGLE

|  |  |
|---|---|
| 7-23-1825 | Phebe rocf Flushing MM, Ohio, -end from Whitewater MM, Ind |

## EVANS

|  |  |
|---|---|
| 8-26-1826 | George & w Mary & dt Asenath & John Van Horn, a minor u/c of George & Mary, rocf Miami MM, Ohio, -end to Duck Creek MM, Ind |
| 1-27-1827 | Rebecca Wright (form Evans) rpt mcd |
| 4-28-1827 | Rebecca Wright (form Evans) chm of mcd |
| 9-27-1834 | Martha & dt Eliza Ann & Juretta rocf West Grove MM, Ind |
| 11-22-1834 | Jonathan P rocf West Grove MM, Ind |
| 3-26-1836 | Jonathan & w Martha & ch Eliza Ann & Juretta Jane gct Westfield MM, Ind |
| 2-28-1857 | Christian rocf Rich Square MM, N C |
| 5-23-1863 | Christiana gct Miami MM, Ohio |

## FARQUHAR

|  |  |
|---|---|
| 7-25-1846 | David rocf Stillwater MM, Ohio |
| 8-30-1848 | David W of Wayne Co, Ind, -s Allen & Edith (both dec), of Harrison Co, Ohio, m Elizabeth Cox at Bethel MH |
| 12-23-1848 | David W & w Elizabeth gct Hopewell MM, Ind |
| 6-22-1850 | David & w Elizabeth rocf Hopewell MM, Ind |
| 3-22-1851 | David & w Elizabeth gct Richland MM, Ind |

## FERGUSON

|  |  |
|---|---|
| 2-22-1873 | Emma (form Wilson) rpt mcd; chm |
| 2-21-1889 | Emma & Daisy rel fr mbrp |

MILFORD

FERGUSON (Cont)
4-28-1892   Lulu rec in mbrp

FERRIS
5-22-1830   John, mbr Wilmington MM, Dela, rpt jH
5-22-1830   Ann, -w of John, & dt Edith, mbr Wilmington MM, Dela, rpt jH
6-26-1830   Matthew, William & Joseph, ch of John, rocf Wilmington MM, Dela
11-27-1830  John rpt dis by Wilmington MM, Dela
12-25-1830  Ann, -w of John, & dt Edith dis by Wilmington MM, Dela
11-26-1831  Matthew rpt jH
11-26-1831  William rpt jH
1-28-1832   Matthew dis for jH
1-28-1832   William dis for jH
10-27-1832  Joseph rpt jH & mcd
12-22-1832  Joseph dis for jH & mcd

FILBY
1-28-1886   Ellsworth & Flora rec in mbrp
3-28-1889   Mary Jane rec in mbrp
4-28-1892   George B, Annie B & Mattie rec in mbrp

FITCH
1-24-1852   Asenith (form Smith), rpt mcd by Bethel MM
3-27-1852   Asenith (form Smith) dis for mcd

FLETCHER
11-28-1829  Zachariah rocf Suttons Creek MM, N C
10-28-1830  Zachariah of Wayne Co, Ind, -s Joshua & Margaret, m Anna Johnson at Milford MH
4-23-1831   Samuel Francis, Margaret Ann & Sarah Nixon, orphan ch of William & Sarah (Nixon), u/c Aaron & Margaret White, rec in mbrp
4-25-1835   Zachariah & w Anna & Rachel Brewer, a minor, -dt John Brewer & 1st w (dec), u/c Zachariah & Ann Fletcher
4-25-1840   Samuel Francis altm Elizabeth D Hiatt
6-27-1840   Margaret Ann altm Jesse Hiatt
11-28-1840  Samuel F & w Elizabeth D gct Whitewater MM, Ind
2-27-1847   Zachariah & w Anna & ch Henry Francis, Augustus & Margaret A & Mary Johnson, a minor, rocf Spiceland MM
8-27-1853   Zachariah & w Anna & ch Henry, Margaret A & James J gct Spiceland MM, Ind

FRAZIER
10-25-1834  Daniel & w Martha & ch Sarah Ann, Anna, Thomas, Rachel & Joseph gct Mississinewa MM, Ind
9-24-1870   Rachel & ch Joseph B gct Wilmington MM, Ohio
9-25-1884   Rachel gct West Grove MM, Ind

GARD
10-25-1862  Mary Ann (form Binford) rpt mcd by Spiceland MM
5-23-1863   Mary Ann (form Binford) dis for mcd
1-28-1886   Daniel, Stephen & Frank rec in mbrp
2-25-1886   Sophronia rec in mbrp
10-27-1887  Harriet rec in mbrp
2-23-1893   Sophronia rel fr mbrp
11-23-1893  Frank rel fr mbrp

GARDNER
2-23-1850   Joseph, mbr Salem MM, rpt for m too soon after death of former w
10-26-1850  Joseph - Salem MM inf
3-22-1862   Esther rocf Elk MM, Ohio
6-22-1872   Esther Hayhurst (form Gardner) rpt mcd

GARNER
11-27-1890  Marie E rec in mbrp

GARRET
12-27-1834  William & w Anna & ch Mary Ann, Madison, Daniel B & John M rocf Whitewater MM, Ind
8-22-1835   William & w Anna & ch Mary Ann, Madison, Daniel Burgess & John Milton gct White Lick MM

8-28-1841   William & fam rocf White Lick MM, -end to Hopewell MM, Ind

GATES
7-27-1833   Caroline, Needham & William gct Spiceland MM, Ind

GAUSE
8-31-1837   Solomon of Henry Co, Ind, -s Nathan & Mary, m Celia Stubbs at Milford MH
11-25-1837  Celia gct Spiceland MM, Ind
4-30-1845   Nathan Jr of Henry Co, Ind, -s Nathan & Martha, m Ann Cox at Bethel MH
7-26-1845   Ann gct Spiceland MM, Ind
3-28-1846   Nathan Jr & w Ann & infant ch rocf Spiceland MM, Ind
6-23-1860   Nathan & w Ann & ch Thomas Clarkson, Sylvester & Oscar gct Bridgeport MM, Ind
4-24-1875   Nathan & w Ann & ch Sylvester, Oscar & Joseph rocf Spiceland MM, Ind

GEORGE
7-23-1836   Caleb rocf New Garden MM, Ind

GILBERT
12-25-1824  Joel & w Lydia & ch Aaron, Abigail, Millicent, Penninah, Nathan H, Joel, Lydia & Mordecai M rocf Springfield MM, N C
12-25-1824  Thomas & w Sarah & ch Phebe, Miriam, Hannah, Mary, Jeremiah & Gulielma rocf Whitewater MM, Ind
4-5-1827    Aaron of Henry Co, Ind, -s Joel & Lydia, m Margaret Bell at Milford MH
8-29-1827   Abigail, -dt Joel & Lydia, m Cornelius Ratliff at Hopewell MH
2-28-1831   Phebe, -dt Thomas & Sarah of Henry Co, Ind, m Nehemiah Thomas at Hopewell MH
1-28-1832   Josiah Jr rocf Whitewater MM, Ind
5-10-1832   Josiah Jr, -s Josiah Sr & Dorothy, m Abigail Bell at Milford MH
9-22-1832   Josiah Sr & w Dorothy & ch Elizabeth, Achsah, Morris & Thomas rocf Whitewater MM, Ind
3-27-1833   Elizabeth, -dt Josiah Sr & Dorothy of Henry Co, Ind, m Jonathan Newby at Hopewell MH
5-24-1834   Miriam Thomas (form Gilbert) rpt mcd by West Branch MM, Ohio
9-24-1834   Miriam Thomas (form Gilbert), West Branch rpt chm of mcd
12-27-1834  Elizabeth Morris (form Gilbert) rpt mcd
3-28-1835   Elizabeth Morris (form Gilbert) dis for mcd
5-27-1835   Achsah, -dt Josiah Sr & Dorothy of Henry Co, Ind, m Abraham Jr at Hopewell MH
3-1-1837    Morris of Henry Co, Ind, -s Josiah Sr & Dorothy, m Elizabeth Elliott at Bethel MH
6-28-1837   Thomas of Henry Co, Ind, -s Josiah Sr & Dorothy, m Catharine W Elliott at Bethel MH
4-27-1839   Millicent & Nathan Macy dec m int
5-25-1839   Rpt "the young woman has dec" - Millicent
1-1-1840    Nathan of Henry Co, Ind, -s Joel & Lydia, m Rhoda Elliott at Bethel MH
3-28-1840   Jeremiah rpt mcd by Hopewell MM
4-25-1840   Jemima rpt for disunity; matter dismissed
5-23-1840   Jeremiah chm of mcd
7-1-1840    Peninah, -dt Joel & Lydia of Henry Co, Ind, m John Cook at Hopewell MH
12-2-1840   Hannah, -dt Thomas & Sarah of Henry Co, Ind, m John P Ratliff at Hopewell MH
5-22-1841   Eunice rocf West Branch MM, Ohio; -end to Hopewell MM, Ind
5-28-1842   Asenath Showalter (form Gilbert) rpt mcd by Duck Creek MM
8-27-1842   Asenath Showalter (form Gilbert) dis by Duck Creek MM for mcd
3-28-1846   Abigail & ch John & Dorothy gct Hopewell MM, Ind
11-28-1846  Miriam rpt na & dp
11-28-1846  Sarah rpt na & dp

MILFORD

**GILBERT (Cont)**
| | |
|---|---|
| 1-23-1847 | Miriam dis for na & dp |
| 1-23-1847 | Sarah dis for na & dp |
| 12-27-1856 | Thomas & w Catharine & ch Jonathan, Oliver & Ann rocf Hopewell MM, Ind |
| 4-23-1859 | Joel M & w Phebe J rocf Hopewell MM, Ind |
| 2-25-1860 | Aaron L gct Duck Creek MM, Ind |
| 4-27-1867 | Oliver rpt mcd; chm |
| 8-23-1873 | Jonathan N mcd; chm |
| 8-23-1873 | Anna Moore (form Gilbert) rpt mcd; chm |
| 4-25-1874 | Nancy J rec in mbrp |
| 5-27-1876 | Oliver & w Nancy & ch Ross & Thomas H gct New Hope MM, Ind |
| 4-26-1879 | Mary rocf New Hope MM, Ind |
| 4-27-1881 | Mordecai M of Henry Co, Ind, -s Joel & Lydia, m Catharine Gilbert, widow of Thomas & -dt Jacob & Mary Elliott, at Dublin MH |
| 6-25-1881 | Catharine gct Hopewell MM, Ind |
| 1-28-1886 | Oliver & w Nancy & ch Ross, Thomas Elwood & Kenneth gct Liberty MM, Kans |

**GOLDSMITH**
| | |
|---|---|
| 8-12-1824 | Daniel appt to a comm |
| 8-12-1824 | Ellen appt to a comm |
| 4-26-1828 | Ellen Bond (form Goldsmith) rpt mcd by Bethel MM |
| 8-23-1828 | Ellen Bond (form Goldsmith) dis for mcd |
| 10-25-1828 | Anna rpt jH |
| 11-22-1828 | Daniel rpt jH |
| 1-27-1829 | Anna dis for jH |
| 1-24-1829 | Daniel dis for jH |
| 8-27-1831 | Joseph rpt na & dp by Bethel MM |
| 9-24-1831 | Joseph dis for na & dp |

**GORDON**
| | |
|---|---|
| 10-23-1824 | Richard & w Susannah & ch Rebecca, Alfred & Edwin rocf New Garden MM, N C, -end from West Grove MM, Ind |
| 6-25-1825 | James rocf West Grove MM, Ind |
| 10-22-1825 | James gct Silver Creek MM to m Ruth Maxwell |
| 5-27-1826 | James gct Silver Creek MM |
| 3- 1-1827 | Charles Jr of Wayne Co, Ind, -s Charles Sr & Ruth, m Lydia R Jessop at Milford MH |
| 6-23-1827 | Lydia R gct West Grove MM, Ind |
| 7-26-1828 | Charles Jr & w Lydia & s Micajah C rocf West Grove MM, Ind |
| 12-27-1828 | Josiah Lacy gct West Grove MM to m Ruth Gordon |
| 8-22-1829 | Charles & w Lydia & s Micajah Collons gct New Garden MM, Ind |
| 3-26-1831 | Charles & w Ruth rocf West Grove MM, Ind |
| 3-26-1831 | Mary rocf West Grove MM, Ind |
| 4-28-1832 | Charles & w Ruth & dt Mary gct New Garden MM, Ind |
| 10-24-1835 | Richard & w Susannah & ch Rebecca, Alfred, Edwin, Mahala, Sarah Ann, Seth & Nathan gct Spiceland MM, Ind |

**GRAY**
| | |
|---|---|
| 7-26-1834 | Phebe rocf Spiceland MM, Ind |
| 5-25-1844 | Phebe Dunlap (form Gray) rpt mcd & jMeth by Duck Creek MM |
| 9-28-1844 | Duck Creek MM tr w/h without success |
| 2-26-1881 | Hugh & w Rebecca & ch Rosetta & Flora rocf Raysville MM, Ind |
| 1-28-1886 | James rec in mbrp |
| 2-25-1886 | Mary rec in mbrp |

**GRESH**
| | |
|---|---|
| 11-23-1867 | Eliza Ann (form Edgerton) rpt mcd; chm |
| 1-28-1886 | Leroy rec in mbrp |

**GRIFFIN**
| | |
|---|---|
| 7-17-1823 | James appt to a comm |
| 7-17-1823 | Priscilla appt to a comm |
| 7-15-1824 | Samuel & w Lydia & s Jeremiah rocf West Grove MM, Ind |
| 12- 1-1825 | Benjamin of Wayne Co, Ind, -s James & Pharaby m Sarah Justice at Milford MH |
| 2-28-1829 | James appt an Elder |
| 7-25-1829 | Sarah rpt jH |
| 9-26-1829 | Sarah dis for jH |
| 9-26-1829 | Benjamin rpt jH |
| 11-28-1829 | Benjamin dis for jH |
| 9-24-1836 | James dismissed as an Elder |
| 9-28-1850 | Eliza Ann (form Wilson) rpt mcd |
| 10-26-1850 | Cyrus rpt mcd by Mississinewa MM |
| 11-23-1850 | Eliza Ann (form Wilson) - notice of dis sent to Mississinewa MM to be given to her |
| 11-27-1852 | Jonathan rpt mcd & na |
| 1-22-1853 | Jonathan dis for mcd & na |
| 2-28-1857 | Priscilla gct Walnut Ridge MM, Ind |
| 9-30-1863 | William of Henry Co, Ind, -s Samuel & Lydia, m Margaret Wilson at Bethel MH |
| 9-23-1865 | Lydia (form Hunt) rpt mcd with a divorced man; dis |
| 8-26-1885 | Isabella & ch Alice K gct Indianapolis MM, Ind |
| 1-28-1886 | Alonzo, Mary & Elizabeth rec in mbrp |
| 12-23-1886 | Mary & dt Susan Leonard gct New Castle MM, Ind |
| 2-21-1889 | Alonzo rel fr mbrp |

**GRIFFY**
| | |
|---|---|
| 9-25-1858 | Emily (form Butler) rpt mcd; dis |

**GUNNING**
| | |
|---|---|
| 10-26-1833 | Mary (form Wickersham) rpt mcd by Silver Creek MM |
| 5-28-1836 | Mary (form Wickersham) rpt dis by Silver Creek MM |

**GUYER**
| | |
|---|---|
| 4-23-1825 | Rachel rocf Driftwood, -end fr New Garden MM, Ind |
| 11-21-1827 | Rachel gct New Garden MM, Ind |

**HADLEY**
| | |
|---|---|
| 8-23-1851 | Alfred Wilson gct Springfield MM, Ohio to m Almira Hadley |
| 2-25-1871 | James rocf Fairfield MM, Ohio |
| 2-25-1871 | Emily G & dt Mary Ellen Saint rocf Duck Creek MM, Ind |
| 1-22-1876 | James A rocf Springfield MM, Kans |
| 1-22-1876 | Lydia T rocf New Garden MM, Ind |
| 10-25-1876 | James A rpt "striking & assulting a fellowman after premeditation"; dis |
| 3-27-1880 | Lydia F gct New Garden MM, Ind |
| 10-27-1892 | Emily G gct Whitewater MM, Ind |

**HALL**
| | |
|---|---|
| 2-12-1824 | Benjamin Jr rpt upl & na |
| 4-15-1824 | Benjamin Jr dis for upl & na |
| 4-23-1825 | Rhoda rocf Chester MM, Ind |
| 1-24-1829 | Priscilla (form Elzey) rpt mcd |
| 3-28-1829 | Priscilla (form Elzey) chm for mcd |
| 4-24-1830 | William rpt att mcd of a mbr at a Hicksite mtg |
| 6-26-1830 | William dis |
| 9-25-1830 | John & w Sarah & ch Martha, Phineas, Robert, Moses, Sarah & John rocf Whitewater MM, Ind |
| 12-25-1830 | Benjamin & w Elizabeth & ch Chalkley gct Duck Creek MM, Ind |
| 1-22-1831 | Stephen rpt mcd |
| 2-26-1831 | Stephen chm of mcd |
| 1- 4-1832 | Caleb of Wayne Co, Ind, -s Benjamin & Elizabeth, m Hannah Sanders at Bethel MH |
| 4-28-1832 | Caleb & w Hannah gct Duck Creek MM, Ind |
| 6-23-1832 | Rhoda gct Duck Creek MM, Ind |
| 12-22-1832 | Esther - Hopewell MM rpt she rq rst; rq denied |
| 6-28-1834 | Esther chm & rq rst |
| 7-26-1834 | Esther rst in mbrp |
| 10-25-1834 | Benjamin rst in mbrp |
| 12-27-1834 | Stephen gct Spiceland MM, Ind |
| 8-27-1836 | Benjamin rpt for "telling an untruth" |
| 10-22-1836 | Benjamin - rpt not substantiated; dismissed |

MILFORD

## HALL (Cont)
| | |
|---|---|
| 5-27-1837 | Hannah (form Stanfield), mbr Duck Creek MM, rpt mcd |
| 6-24-1837 | Hannah (form Stanfield), Duck Creek inf; dis |
| 10-27-1838 | Benjamin & w Esther & dt Agatha gct Westfield MM, Ind |
| 4-27-1839 | Phineas rpt mcd by Hopewell MM |
| 7-27-1839 | Phineas dis for mcd |
| 10- 2-1839 | Robert, -s John & Sarah of Henry Co, Ind, m Luanna Stratton at Hopewell MH |
| 6-28-1845 | Abigail (form Bundy) rpt mcd & jas by Spiceland MM |
| 1-23-1846 | Abigail (form Bundy) dis for mcd & jas |
| 6-25-1853 | Phineas rst in mbrp at Hopewell MM, Ind |
| 4-25-1863 | Sarah E, mbr of Rich Square MM, N C, being for quite some time among us & unable to secure a cert (on account of war) is rec in mbrp |
| 12-24-1864 | Sarah gct Hopewell MM, Ind |
| 6-27-1866 | Caleb of Henry Co, Ind, -s Benjamin & Elizabeth (both dec), m Isabella Kenneday, -widow of Thomas, Neuse MM, N C, & widow of Exum Elliott (dis), Pasquotauk MM, N C, -dt George Jr & Isabella (Scott) Walton, (both dec) (form of Chowan Co, N C), at Bethel MH, Ind |
| 8-25-1866 | Isabella K & dt Margaret Jane Elliott gct Spiceland MM, Ind |
| 1-22-1870 | Charles A mcd; chm |
| 4-24-1875 | John W rocf Indianapolis MM, Ind |
| 9-25-1875 | Mary Jane gct Spiceland MM, Ind |
| 4-28-1883 | John W rel fr mbrp |
| 4-28-1883 | Alice W gct Hopewell MM, Ind |
| 6-25-1885 | Martha rec in mbrp |
| 2-23-1886 | Leona Hortense gct Hopewell MM, Ind |
| 3-27-1890 | Martha rel fr mbrp |

## HAMM
| | |
|---|---|
| 9-26-1829 | Elizabeth & fam, Martha, Priscilla, Jane, Hezekiah & Elizabeth rocf New Garden MM, N C, -end by Whitewater MM, Ind |
| 12- 2-1830 | Priscilla, -dt John (dec) & Elizabeth, m Solomon Macy at Milford MH |
| 6-25-1831 | Elizabeth & ch Martha, Hezekiah & Elizabeth gct Duck Creek MM, Ind |
| 12-30-1833 | Jane gct Duck Creek MM, Ind |

## HAMMER
| | |
|---|---|
| 9-26-1829 | Elisha & w Nancy & ch Newton rocf Holly Springs MM, N C |
| 2-25-1832 | Elisha & w Nancy & ch Newton, Abigail & Catharine gct Duck Creek MM, Ind |

## HANNAH
| | |
|---|---|
| 6-22-1833 | James rec in mbrp |
| 11-27-1847 | Rebecca (form Jackson), mbr Providence MM, Pa, rpt mcd |
| 12-25-1847 | Rebecca (form Jackson), Providence MM, Pa, inf of mcd; dis |

## HARE
| | |
|---|---|
| 10-28-1837 | Herman & w Mary & ch Deborah D, Maria J, Sarah E & Rebecca A rocf Western Branch MM, Va |
| 2-23-1839 | Herman & w Mary & ch Deborah D, Maria J, Sarah E & Rebecca Ann gct West Grove MM, Ind |

## HARRIS
| | |
|---|---|
| 4-26-1879 | James Freemont rec in mbrp |
| 9-27-1879 | J Freemont & w Lizzie gct Spiceland MM, Ind |
| 10-27-1883 | Freemont & w Lizzie & ch George C & Mary E rocf Spiceland MM, Ind |
| 10-26-1893 | Freemont & w Mary & fam gct Raysville MM, Ind |

## HARRISON
| | |
|---|---|
| 7-28-1832 | Robert rocf Balby MM, England, -end by Philadelphia MM, Pa |
| 9-28-1833 | Robert gct Cincinnati MM, Ohio |
| 3-22-1834 | Robert rocf Cincinnati MM, Ohio |
| 5-28-1836 | Robert gct Spiceland MM, Ind |

## HARVEY
| | |
|---|---|
| 1-27-1827 | Elizabeth rocf New Garden MM, -end to Duck Creek MM, Ind |
| 12-28-1833 | Mildred, mbr Driftwood MM, rpt mcd |
| 2-22-1834 | Mildred, Driftwood MM inf of mcd |
| 5-27-1848 | Rachel (form Elliott) rpt mcd by Duck Creek MM |
| 11-25-1848 | Rachel (form Elliott), rpt chm of mcd by Duck Creek MM |
| 12-23-1848 | Rachel & h Isaac gct Duck Creek MM, Ind |
| 11-24-1849 | Rachel & s Henry H rocf Duck Creek MM, Ind |
| 4-28-1855 | Rachel Johnson (form Harvey) rpt mcd; dis |
| 12-24-1864 | Ruth Ann (form Stanley) rpt mcd; chm |
| 4-24-1880 | James W & w Ann H & ch Elva rocf White Lick MM, Ind |
| 9-25-1884 | Edith rocf White Lick MM, Ind |

## HASHOUR
| | |
|---|---|
| 1-28-1886 | Samuel rec in mbrp |

## HASKET
| | |
|---|---|
| 8-27-1825 | Thomas, Ann & William rocf Miami MM, Ohio with their mother, Ann Cook, now wife of Levi Cook |
| 8-27-1825 | Charity rocf Miami MM, Ohio |
| 10-22-1831 | Palin rocf Whitewater MM, Ind |
| 5-24-1834 | Palin rpt mcd with 1st cousin |
| 5-24-1834 | Mary (form Palin) rpt mcd with 1st cousin |
| 7-26-1834 | Mary (form Palin) dis for mcd |
| 8-23-1834 | Palin dis for mcd |
| 10-25-1834 | Rebecca (form Maudlin) rpt mcd by Hopewell MM, Ind |
| 2-28-1835 | Rebecca (form Maudlin) dis for mcd |
| 9-26-1835 | Daniel G, William H & Anthony rocf Suttons Creek MM, N C |
| 2-27-1836 | Anthony, a minor, with George Bundy & fam, gct Duck Creek MM, Ind |
| 12-23-1837 | Morgan rocf Spiceland MM, Ind |
| 6-27-1840 | Martha & Allen, ch of Joseph (dec), rocf Symons Creek MM, N C |
| 9-25-1841 | Morgan rpt jMeth by Duck Creek MM |
| 2-26-1842 | Morgan rpt dis by Duck Creek MM for jMeth |
| 3-27-1843 | Daniel rpt mcd; chm |
| 8-27-1842 | Allen rpt mcd by Symons Creek MM, N C |
| 5-27-1843 | Allen rpt dis by Symons Creek MM, N C for mcd |
| 1-27-1844 | Martha Wright (form Hasket) rpt mcd |
| 3-23-1844 | Martha Wright (form Hasket) dis for mcd |
| 6-22-1844 | Daniel G gct Hopewell MM, Ind |

## HASTINGS
| | |
|---|---|
| 9- 1-1830 | Aaron of Henry Co, Ind, -s William & Sarah of Wayne Co, Ind, m (2nd w) Christian Reece at Hopewell MH |
| 12-25-1830 | Aaron & s Solomon rocf Duck Creek MM, Ind |
| 11-31-1831 | William Jr of Wayne Co, Ind, -s William Sr & Sarah, m Jane Reece at Hopewell MH |
| 12-22-1832 | William rocf West Grove MM, Ind |
| 6-26-1852 | Aaron & w Christiana & ch Elias, Letitia Ann, Joshua, Margaret Jane, John & Emily rocf Hopewell MM, Ind |
| 10-27-1855 | William P & w Luzena & dt Elmira Jane rocf Hopewell MM, Ind |
| 8-22-1857 | Elias R gct Whitewater MM to m Sarah Edgerton |
| 5-28-1859 | Elias R & w Sarah E rocf Whitewater MM, Ind |
| 6-23-1860 | Solomon rst w/c Hopewell MM, Ind |
| 8-25-1860 | Solomon gct Honey Creek MM to m Hannah George |
| 5-25-1861 | Letitia Johnson (form Hastings) rpt mcd; chm |
| 9-28-1861 | Solomon gct Hopewell MM, Ind |
| 4-22-1865 | Elias P & w Sarah E & ch William E & Mary E gct Whitewater MM, Ind |
| 11-23-1867 | Margaret Johnson (form Hastings) rpt mcd & jBaptists; dis |
| 11-23-1867 | William & w Luzena & ch Elmira Jane, Nathan, Lineous, Letitia, Angeline & Willie gct Bear Creek MM, Ia |

MILFORD

## HASTINGS (Cont)

|  |  |
|---|---|
| 11-28-1868 | Jane & ch Seth, Aaron, Rebecca J & William C (wife & ch of William Jr), rocf Whitewater MM, Ind |
| 2-27-1869 | Margaret Jane (form Elliott) rpt mcd; chm |
| 5-22-1869 | John N rpt mcd; chm |
| 5-22-1869 | Elias R & w Sarah & ch William Edward, Mary Emma & Anna Letitia rocf Whitewater MM, Ind |
| 1-22-1870 | Seth gct Bloomfield MM, Ind |
| 2-26-1870 | Rebecca Henby (form Hastings) rpt mcd; chm |
| 3-23-1872 | Aaron rpt mcd; chm |
| 4-27-1872 | Aaron gct Richland MM, Ind |
| 5-25-1872 | John N & w Margaret Jane E & ch Ellen, Otis & Luther gct Vermillion MM, Ill |
| 4-24-1875 | Annie G rec in mbrp |
| 6-25-1881 | William E & w Flora & ch rel fr mbrp |
| 7-23-1881 | William C & w Anna & ch Albert Carrel gct Van Wert MM, Ohio |
| 1-28-1886 | John N & w Margaret Jane E & ch Ellen, Otis & Gertrude rocf Vermillion MM, Ill |
| 2-21-1889 | Eva rel fr mbrp |
| 3-26-1891 | John N & fam gct Whitewater MM, Ind |

## HATTERSLEY

|  |  |
|---|---|
| 4-27-1850 | John rocf Marlborough MM |
| 12-26-1857 | John rpt "contracting debts without paying them, soliciting subscriptions on a periodical, receiving money thereon which he did not apply to the object for which he obtained it, & has left this part of the country" |
| 2-27-1858 | John - his present place of res unknown |
| 3-27-1858 | John dis |

## HAWKINS

|  |  |
|---|---|
| 2-12-1824 | Jonathan & w Sarah & s Isaac rocf Back Creek MM, -end by Whitewater MM, Ind |
| 6-25-1825 | John (s of William) rec in mbrp |
| 7-23-1825 | Isabella & dt Jane rec in mbrp |
| 5-23-1840 | Jane Williams (form Hawkins) rpt dp & mcd |
| 7-25-1840 | Jane Williams (form Hawkins) dis for dp & mcd |
| 3-23-1844 | John rpt jas |
| 9-28-1844 | John dis for jas |
| 5-27-1848 | Simon rpt striking a fellow being in anger |
| 7-22-1848 | Simon chm of striking a fellow geing in anger |
| 6-22-1850 | Mary Woodward (form Hawkins) rpt mcd |
| 7-27-1850 | Mary Woodward (form Hawkins) chm of mcd |
| 4-24-1852 | Nathan rpt na, dp & "att dances & has caused a disturbance between a man & his wife by improper conduct toward her" |
| 6-26-1852 | Nathan dis |
| 12-30-1852 | Tamar Ann, -dt William (dec) & Isabel of Wayne Co, Ind, m David Binford at Milford MH |
| 2-1-1855 | Isabel, widow of William Hawkins & dt of Simon & Jane Power (both dec) of Ky, m Jacob Elliott at Milford MH |
| 12-27-1856 | Simon P rpt na & bearing arms |
| 2-28-1857 | Simon P dis for na & bearing arms |
| 5-28-1859 | William rpt mcd; chm; has removed to Kansas |
| 4-28-1866 | Lemuel rpt mcd; chm |
| 4-25-1874 | Caroline E rec in mbrp |
| 7-28-1883 | Cornelia rec in mbrp |
| 4-28-1883 | Lemuel & w Caroline & ch Martha B & Thamer A gct Sterling MM, Kans |
| 2-26-1885 | Belle, Kathie & Pearl rec in mbrp |
| 11-23-1893 | Cornelia & dt Belle J & Cora Pearl gct Spiceland MM, Ind |

## HAWLEY

|  |  |
|---|---|
| 12-18-1823 | Richard & w Rachel & s Eli rocf Whitewater MM, Ind |
| 12-27-1828 | Richard & w Rachel rpt "denying the divinity of our Lord & Savior, for being out of unity with friends, for allowing a m of a mbr of our Society to be accomplished in their home before a justice of the peace & giving a m entertainment" |
| 2-28-1829 | Richard & w Rachel dis |
| 9-26-1838 | Ann, -dt Richard & Rachel of Henry Co, Ind, m Joseph Stratton at Hopewell MH |

## HAYHURST

|  |  |
|---|---|
| 6-22-1872 | Esther (form Gardner) rpt mcd |

## HEACOCK

|  |  |
|---|---|
| 2-22-1840 | Rachel & Jesse, ch of John, rocf Gwynedd, Pa |

## HEAVENRIDGE

|  |  |
|---|---|
| 9-27-1807 | Margaret, -dt Samuel & Elizabeth of Henry Co, Ind, m Greenly Puckett at Hopewell MH |
| 10-25-1834 | Margaret rocf Salem MM, Ind |
| 5-25-1838 | Elizabeth rst in mbrp w/c Salem MM, Ind |
| 3-23-1839 | Mary & ch John Calvin, Elvin, Edmund, Allen, Dicey, William & Gideon rocf Salem MM, Ind |
| 3-23-1839 | Elizabeth rocf Salem MM, Ind |
| 11-28-1840 | Mary rpt na by Hopewell MM |
| 3-27-1841 | Mary dis for na |
| 4-27-1844 | Elizabeth (form Charles) rpt mcd |
| 6-22-1844 | Elizabeth (form Charles) chm of mcd |

## HENBY

|  |  |
|---|---|
| 5-28-1836 | William, Eli & Elias rocf Suttons Creek MM, N C |
| 2-28-1838 | Elias of Wayne Co, Ind, -s John (dec) & Mary of Perquimans MM, N C, m Phebe Symons at Bethel MH |
| 5-25-1839 | Elias & w Phebe gct Walnut Ridge MM, Ind |
| 1-28-1846 | Eli of Wayne Co, Ind, -s John (dec) & Mary of N C, m Gulielma Bell at Bethel MH |
| 4-26-1856 | Elias & ch Martha Ann, John, Sarah, Phebe E & Elizabeth W rocf Walnut Ridge MM, Ind |
| 2-28-1857 | Elias gct Walnut Ridge to m Elizabeth T Henby |
| 10-24-1857 | Elizabeth T rocf Walnut Ridge MM, Ind |
| 1-22-1870 | John rpt mcd; chm |
| 2-26-1870 | Rebecca (form Hastings) rpt mcd; chm |
| 2-22-1879 | Elias & w Elizabeth gct Wabash MM, Ind |
| 4-24-1880 | Sarah gct Wabash MM, Ind |

## HENDRICKS

|  |  |
|---|---|
| 5-25-1835 | Peninnah rocf Suttons Creek MM, N C |

## HENLEY

|  |  |
|---|---|
| 2-25-1826 | Jordan & w Elizabeth & ch Joseph, Charles, Margaret, David, Jonathan, Samuel & Thomas Elwood rocf Blue River MM, -end fr West Grove MM, Ind |
| 12-27-1828 | Jordan rpt jH |
| 12-27-1828 | Elizabeth rpt jH |
| 1-24-1829 | Jordan intrudes himself on the mtg after being rq to withdraw |
| 2-28-1829 | Jordan dis |
| 3-28-1829 | Elizabeth dis |
| 3-28-1840 | Margaret rpt na & dp |
| 5-23-1840 | Margaret dis for na & dp |
| 2-27-1841 | John, mbr of Walnut Ridge MM, rpt na |
| 9-24-1841 | John dis by Walnut Ridge MM, Ind |
| 3-25-1843 | Jonathan rpt na |
| 3-25-1843 | David rpt na |
| 5-27-1843 | Jonathan dis for na |
| 6-24-1843 | David dis for na |
| 3-22-1845 | James gct Walnut Ridge MM, Ind |
| 10-16-1845 | Thomas E of Wayne Co, Ind, -s Jordan & Elizabeth, (both dec), m Martha Bell at Milford MH |
| 2-28-1846 | Thomas E & w Martha gct Hopewell MM, Ind |
| 12-23-1848 | James rocf Walnut Ridge MM, Ind |
| 5-26-1849 | James rpt mcd by Walnut Ridge MM |
| 8-25-1849 | James dis by Walnut Ridge MM for mcd |
| 9-26-1863 | Thomas E & w Martha & s Isaac rocf Hopewell MM, Ind |
| 10-22-1864 | Thomas E & w Martha & s Isaac F gct Hopewell MM, Ind |
| 5-27-1886 | Walter C & w Caroline B rocf Carthage MM, Ind |

## HERBST

|  |  |
|---|---|
| 6-25-1870 | Abigail (form Symons) rpt mcd; chm |

## HERBST (Cont)
| | |
|---|---|
| 3-26-1891 | Sarah gct Denver MM, Colo |
| 7-23-1891 | Sarah rel fr mbrp |

## HESS
| | |
|---|---|
| 1-28-1886 | Daniel Sr & Lydia A rec in mbrp |
| 1-28-1886 | Daniel Jr & Emma rec in mbrp |
| 2-25-1886 | Mattie rec in mbrp |

## HESTER
| | |
|---|---|
| 7-17-1823 | Francis appt to a comm |
| 9-16-1824 | Ann rocf Whitewater MM, Ind |
| 8-4-1825 | Rachel, -dt Francis & Mary, (dec), Wayne Co, Ind, m Jesse Bundy at Milford MH |
| 6-24-1826 | Mary & Mercy rec in mbrp |
| 8-26-1826 | Robert gct Dover MM, Ohio to m Mary Starbuck |
| 9-26-1827 | Henry of Wayne Co, Ind, -s Francis & Mary (dec), m Elizabeth Reynolds at Bethel MH |
| 4-26-1828 | Henry rpt committing fornication with her who is now his wife & for talebearing |
| 4-26-1828 | Elizabeth rpt for unchastity |
| 5-24-1828 | Robert rpt na & training with the Militia |
| 6-28-1828 | Henry dis for fornication & talebearing |
| 6-28-1828 | Elizabeth dis for unchastity |
| 8-23-1828 | Robert dis for na & training with militia |
| 11-22-1828 | Mary rocf Dover MM, Ind |
| 9-26-1829 | Francis gct Cherry Grove MM to m Ruth Bennet |
| 7-25-1829 | William rpt upl & offering to fight |
| 11-28-1829 | William dis for upl & offering to fight |
| 2-27-1830 | Ruth & ch Zechariah, Solomon & Elizabeth Bennet rocf Cherry Grove MM, Ind |
| 11-27-1830 | John rpt mcd by Vermillion MM, Ill |
| 9-24-1831 | John dis for mcd |
| 10-27-1832 | Mary & ch Amos, Zimri & Louisa gct Duck Creek MM, Ind |
| 1-29-1834 | Isaac, -s Francis & Mary (dec), Wayne Co, Ind m Hannah Reynolds at Bethel MH |
| 8-22-1835 | Hannah rpt jH |
| 8-22-1835 | Mary & ch Amos, Zimri & Joel rocf Spiceland MM, Ind |
| 11-28-1835 | Hannah dis for jH |
| 11-28-1835 | Mary & s Amos, Zimri & Joel gct Dover MM, Ohio |
| 2-27-1836 | Mary gct Duck Creek MM, Ind |
| 8-27-1836 | Isaac rpt na |
| 10-22-1836 | Isaac dis for na |
| 11-24-1838 | Mary rocf Spiceland MM, Ind |
| 2-23-1850 | Ruth gct Westfield MM, Ind |

## HEWITT
| | |
|---|---|
| 11-27-1890 | Lessie rel fr mbrp |

## HIATT
| | |
|---|---|
| 7-17-1823 | Anna appt to a comm |
| 8-14-1823 | Absalem & s Hiram, Joseph, Absalem, Cornelius, Anthony & Daniel rocf Fall Creek MM, Ohio |
| 8-14-1823 | Ann & dt Hannah & Jane rocf Fall Creek MM, Ohio |
| 9-18-1823 | Silas appt an Overseer |
| 12-18-1823 | James rocf Fall Creek MM, Ohio |
| 3-18-1824 | Amer & w Achsah & ch Jane, Harman & Elam rocf New Garden MM, N C |
| 3-18-1824 | Jesse rpt "being father of illegitimate ch" & mcd |
| 4-15-1824 | Milla rpt guilty of unchastity |
| 5-13-1824 | Jesse dis |
| 6-17-1824 | Milla dis |
| 10-23-1824 | Benajah, a min, & w Elizabeth & ch Joel G & Hannah F rocf New Garden MM, N C |
| 10-23-1824 | John & w Rebecca rocf New Garden MM, N C |
| 10-23-1824 | Richard & w Sarah & ch David, Susannah, Elizabeth, Jesse, Joel & James rocf Fall Creek MM, Ohio |
| 10-23-1824 | Catharine, mbr of Fall Creek MM, Ohio, rpt for unchastity |
| 10-23-1824 | William rocf Hopewell MM, N C, -end by Whitewater MM |
| 11-27-1824 | Fall Creek MM, Ohio, infs Catharine dis |
| 11-27-1824 | Charity rocf New Garden MM, N C |
| 4-23-1825 | Allen & w Rhoda & ch Susanna, Gulielma & Milton rocf Springfield MM, Ohio |
| 5-28-1825 | Elizabeth appt an Elder |
| 2-26-1825 | William, mbr Fall Creek MM, Ohio, rpt for fornication |
| 7-23-1825 | David rpt mcd |
| 8-27-1825 | William dis |
| 8-27-1825 | John rst in mbrp w/c of Fall Creek MM, Ohio |
| 8-27-1825 | Aaron & s Amos rst in mbrp w/c Fall Creek MM, Ohio |
| 10-22-1825 | David chm of mcd |
| 10-22-1825 | Samuel, a minor, rocf Goshen MM, Ohio |
| 2-25-1826 | Elizabeth rst in mbrp w/c Fairfield MM, Ohio |
| 3-24-1826 | Joel & fam rocf Springfield MM, Ohio, -end to Honey Creek MM, Ind |
| 4-22-1826 | Eunice, -dt Elizabeth, rec in mbrp |
| 4-22-1826 | George & w Sarah rocf Whitewater MM, Ind |
| 6-24-1826 | Ruth, mbr Whitewater MM, rpt mcd; chm |
| 1-27-1827 | Ruth rocf Whitewater MM, -end to Duck Creek MM, Ind |
| 1-27-1827 | Mordecai & w Rhoda & ch Elizabeth & Benajah rocf New Garden MM, N C |
| 7-28-1827 | Allen & w Rhoda & ch Susanna, Gulielma & Milton gct Duck Creek MM, Ind |
| 10-25-1828 | Anne rpt jH |
| 11-22-1828 | Samuel gct Goshen MM, Ohio |
| 11-22-1828 | Silas rpt jH |
| 12-27-1828 | Anne dis for jH |
| 1-24-1829 | Silas dis for jH |
| 1-24-1829 | Joel rpt dp, na & j a singing school |
| 3-29-1829 | Joel dis |
| 10-24-1829 | Jordan rpt jH; dis |
| 5-22-1830 | William rst in mbrp at Duck Creek MM, Ind |
| 8-28-1830 | Elijah & w Anne & ch Demsey & Jehu rocf Stillwater MM, Ohio, -end by Whitewater MM, Ind |
| 9-24-1831 | Amer & w Achsah & ch Jane, Herman, Elim, Alfred, Jesse W & Elizabeth W gct Cherry Grove MM, Ind |
| 1-28-1832 | Joel & s Joel & Joshua gct New Garden MM (He previously gct Honey Creek MM but record was lost) |
| 3-24-1832 | John & w Rebecca & ch Anna Jane, Alfred & Josiah gct Duck Creek MM, Ind |
| 12-28-1833 | Aseph & w Sarah & ch Asher, Mahalah & Caleb rocf Newberry MM, Ind |
| 3-22-1834 | Elijah & w Anna & ch Demsey, Jehu & Joseph gct Deerfield MM, Ohio |
| 11-27-1834 | Irena, -dt Silas & Ann of Wayne Co, Ind, m Alpheus Saint at Milford MH |
| 10-1-1835 | Esther G, -dt Benajah & Elizabeth, m Josiah White at Milford MH |
| 10-22-1836 | Rhoda & ch Gulielma, Milton & Anna rocf White River MM, Ind |
| 12-28-1836 | Asher, Fayette Co, Ind, -s Asaph & Rebecca (dec), m Sarah M Elliott at Bethel MH |
| 1-28-1837 | Asaph & w Sarah & ch Mahala, Caleb & Mary Johnson gct Westfield MM, Ind |
| 8-28-1837 | Jesse rocf New Garden MM, Ind |
| 1-27-1838 | Asher & w Sarah M gct Westfield MM, Ind |
| 7-28-1838 | Elda Ann Smith (form Hiatt) rpt mcd |
| 9-22-1838 | Elda Ann Smith (form Hiatt) dis for mcd |
| 1-26-1839 | Henry rpt jH |
| 2-23-1839 | Benajah Jr rpt jH |
| 3-23-1839 | Henry dis for jH |
| 5-25-1839 | Benajah Jr dis for jH |
| 4-30-1840 | Elizabeth D, -dt Mordecai & Rhoda of Wayne Co, Ind, m Samuel F Fletcher at Milford MH |
| 7-2-1840 | Jesse of Wayne Co, Ind, -s Eleazar & Anna, (dec), m Margaret Ann Fletcher at Milford MH |
| 8-22-1840 | Mordecai appt an Elder |
| 10-29-1840 | Gulielma, -dt Allen & Rhoda of Wayne Co, Ind, m Albert White at Milford MH |
| 2-25-1843 | Asher & w Sarah & ch Eleazer B rocf Westfield MM, Ind |
| 11-25-1843 | Sarah rec a minister |
| 1-25-1845 | John Milton rpt na; dis |

MILFORD

## HIATT (Cont)
|  |  |
|---|---|
| 1-25-1845 | Edward rpt na & mcd |
| 5-24-1845 | Edward dis for na & mcd |
| 6-28-1845 | Louisa Spencer (form Hiatt) rpt mcd by Duck Creek MM |
| 9-27-1845 | Lydia rpt jH |
| 10-16-1845 | Benajah W of Wayne Co, Ind, -s Mordecai & Rhoda, m Martha Ann Wilson at Milford MH |
| 11-22-1845 | Louisa Spencer (form Hiatt) dis for mcd |
| 11-22-1845 | Lydia dis for jH |
| 7-2-1846 | Hannah F, -dt Benajah & Elizabeth, m Charles Dickinson at Milford MH |
| 11-28-1846 | Asher & w Sarah M, a min, & ch Eleazar B & Clarkson gct White.. |
| 2-22-1851 | Allen rst in mbrp w/c Duck Creek MM |
| 4-26-1851 | Jesse rst in mbrp at Goshen MM, Ohio |
| 7-1-1852 | Semira, -dt Mordecai & Rhoda, m William P Waring at Milford MH |
| 5-28-1853 | Allen & w Rhoda & dt Gulielma White & Anna Mary gct Salem MM, Ind |
| 5-23-1857 | Jesse D gct Whitewater MM, Ind |
| 7-27-1858 | Benajah & Martha set-off with Kans |
| 5-26-1860 | Martha W Moffatt (form Hiatt) rpt mcd; chm |
| 12-26-1865 | William J of Wayne Co, Ind, -s Mordecai & Rhoda, m Elizabeth Smith at res of James Smith at Cambridge City, Ind |
| 10-27-1866 | William J & w Elizabeth gct Whitewater MM, Ind |
| 4-27-1867 | Francis Henry rel fr mbrp |
| 2-27-1869 | William F rpt mcd; chm |
| 11-27-1869 | Eleazar rocf West Union MM, Ind |
| 11-27-1870 | Mordecai & Rhoda gct Whitewater MM, Ind |
| 2-24-1872 | Charles mcd; chm |
| 3-22-1878 | William F & dt Laura Alice gct Whitewater MM, Ind |
| 3-22-1878 | Francis F gct Whitewater MM, Ind |
| 5-25-1878 | Jesse & w Margaret Ann & dt Sarah Ann gct Whitewater MM, Ind |
| 6-26-1883 | Charles E & s Burton LeRoy gct Indianapolis MM, Ind |
| 6-26-1884 | Charles E & s Burton L rocf Indianapolis MM, Ind |
| 3-26-1885 | William & w Eliza & ch Edgar F & James rocf Whitewater MM, Ind |
| 6-25-1885 | Jesse & w Margaret Ann rocf Fairmount MM, Ind |
| 6-25-1885 | Sarah Ann rocf Fairmount MM, Ind |
| 4-26-1888 | Albert & w Margaret & dt Ore Anna rec in mbrp |
| 4-24-1890 | William G & fam gct Whitewater MM, Ind |
| 1-29-1891 | Albert & w Margaret Ann & dt Ore Anna gct Indianapolis MM, Ind |

## HILL
|  |  |
|---|---|
| 12-18-1823 | Jonathan & w Zilphy & dt Anna rocf Whitewater MM, Ind |
| 12-18-1823 | Thomas & w Tamer & s Milton rocf Whitewater MM, Ind |
| 11-22-1825 | Jesse rst in mbrp w/c Whitewater MM, Ind |
| 12-27-1826 | Ann, -dt Thomas & Ann (dec), m Charles Morris at West Union MH |
| 6-23-1827 | Thomas & w Tamer & ch Milton, John Clark & Sarah Ann gct Duck Creek MM, Ind |
| 9-22-1832 | Penninah rocf White River MM, Ind |
| 4-26-1834 | Penninah gct Duck Creek MM, Ind |
| 5-23-1863 | Charles A gct Whitewater MM, Ind |
| 11-26-1885 | Charles A gct Hesper MM, Kans |
| 5-26-1887 | Anna Elliott gct Walnut Ridge MM, Ind |
| 12-26-1889 | Rosetta gct Marysville MM, Tenn |
| 10-27-1892 | Charles R & w Rosetta & s Leroy rocf Maryville MM, Tenn |

## HINSHAW
|  |  |
|---|---|
| 1-27-1883 | Philander & w Emma & ch Edwin M, Elbert R, Carrie Iona, Laura May, Franklin B & Mary J rocf Sterling MM, Kans |
| 1-28-1886 | Philander & w Emma & ch Edwin, Elbert, Carrie, Olla, Laura, Franklin, Mary & Walter gct Whitewater MM, Ind |

## HOBSON
|  |  |
|---|---|
| 2-25-1826 | Evan rpt dp, training with Militia & mcd |
| 4-22-1826 | Evan dis |

## HOCKETT - HOGGATT
|  |  |
|---|---|
| 5-26-1827 | Miriam rocf New Garden MM, Ind |
| 12-22-1827 | Philip rst w/c Goshen MM, Ohio |
| 4-26-1828 | Philip & w Eunice & ch Elijah, Elizabeth & Eunice rocf New Garden MM, Ind |
| 7-25-1829 | Philip Jr rpt dr; chm |
| 1-23-1830 | Philip gct Cherry Grove MM, Ind |
| 3-27-1830 | Philip rpt leaving this part of the country without complying with his contracts & for dancing; dis |
| 3-26-1831 | Eunice & ch Elijah, Elizabeth, Joseph & Daniel gct White River MM, Ind |
| 4-23-1859 | Benjamin rq rst; (dis by Raysville); rq not granted |

## HODSON
|  |  |
|---|---|
| 2-25-1832 | Aaron & w Mary & ch Lydia, Ners, Seth, Anna, Robert B, Reuben & Sarah rocf Springfield MM, N C, -end to Duck Creek MM, Ind |
| 3-23-1878 | Lewis N & w Rebecca M & Casper, Olive & Eunice rec in mbrp |
| 4-27-1878 | Casper, Olive & Eunice, ch of Lewis & Rebecca, rocf Walnut Ridge MM, Ind |
| 1-25-1879 | Lewis N & w Rebecca & ch Casper, Olive & Eunice gct Cherry Grove MM, Ind |

## HOLLAND
|  |  |
|---|---|
| 4-25-1874 | Elizabeth Jane rec in mbrp |

## HOLLINGSWORTH
|  |  |
|---|---|
| 5-26-1827 | Nathan & w Elizabeth & ch Jemima & John rocf West Grove MM, Ind |
| 1-22-1831 | Nathan rpt jH; dis |
| 7-23-1831 | Elizabeth rpt jH; dis |
| 3-23-1839 | Hepsabah rocf Salem MM, Ind |
| 3-22-1845 | Jemima & John, ch of Nathan, gct West Grove MM, Ind |
| 8-23-1845 | Jane, -dt Nathan, gct West Grove MM, found not to be mbr, name removed from cert |
| 9-28-1861 | Thomas rocf Salem, but appears his affairs not settled; cert ret |
| 3-23-1867 | John rocf West Grove MM, Ind |

## HOLLOWAY
|  |  |
|---|---|
| 1-28-1886 | Ithamel & Maggie rec in mbrp |

## HOLLOWELL
|  |  |
|---|---|
| 5-23-1840 | Esther & ch rocf Piney Woods MM, N C, -end to Spiceland MM, Ind |
| 11-28-1840 | Esther & ch Nathan & Mary Jane rocf Spiceland MM, Ind |
| 3-2-1842 | Esther, widow of Aaron Hollowell of N C & -dt Jesse & Elizabeth Newby of Fayette Co, Ind, m Elijah Cox at Bethel MH |
| 8-27-1842 | Mary Jane & Nathan, with mother, Esther Cox, gct Sugar River MM, Ind |
| 1-28-1886 | Sarah rec in mbrp |
| 5-27-1886 | James S rocf Indianapolis MM, Ind |
| 3-28-1889 | James S & fam gct Westfield MM, Ind |

## HOLTSCLAW
|  |  |
|---|---|
| 1-15-1824 | Keziah (form Elzey) rpt mcd; chm |
| 8-25-1827 | Nancy rpt mcd |
| 9-22-1827 | Nancy chm of mcd |
| 4-25-1835 | Keziah gct Bloomfield MM, Ind |
| 10-22-1836 | Nancy gct Spiceland MM, Ind |

## HOOPS
|  |  |
|---|---|
| 7-28-1832 | Ellis & ch Margaret, Elizabeth & Sarah rocf Somerset MM, Ohio |
| 2-22-1834 | Ellis & ch Margaret, Elizabeth, Sarah & Susan gct Duck Creek MM, Ind |

## HOPKINS
|  |  |
|---|---|
| 7-25-1874 | Sarah A rocf Whitewater MM, Ind |

## HOPPER
|  |  |
|---|---|
| 1-28-1886 | Robert & Fannie rec in mbrp |

MILFORD

**HORNEY**
12- 3-1846  Solomon of Wayne Co, Ind, -s John & Mary (both dec), m Deborah D Roberts at Milford MH
3-27-1847   Deborah D gct Whitewater MM, Ind
1-25-1868   Deborah D rocf Whitewater MM, Ind

**HOSIER**
9-18-1823   William appt an Overseer
9-29-1825   Nathan of Henry Co, Ind, -s William & Millicent, m Alice Elliott at Duck Creek MH
12-17-1826  Lewis appt to a comm
1-28-1832   Lewis rpt na; dis

**HOSKINS**
1-23-1847   Joseph & w Anna & ch Gulielma, Amanda M, John Quincy, George Rowland, Green, Mary A, Stephen M & Samuel rocf New Garden MM, N C
10-23-1847  Joseph W & w Anna M & ch Gulielma Mariah, Amanda Malinda, John Quincy, George Fox, Rowland Green, Mary Anna, Stephen Moore, Samuel Hill & Elizabeth gct Westfield MM, Ind

**HOWARD**
12-25-1884  David rec in mbrp

**HOWEL**
9-18-1823   Rachel rocf Driftwood MM, -end by Whitewater & -end to New Garden MM, Ind

**HUBBARD**
11-26-1825  Hardy & w Mary & ch Anna, Joseph, Sarah, Simeon, Martha, Susannah, Richard, Mary & Caleb rocf New Garden MM, N C
1-24-1829   Joseph gct New Garden MM, Ind
10-24-1829  Joseph Butler rocf Deep River MM, N C
2-27-1830   Joseph Butler chm of dr
1-23-1830   Anna rocf Deep River MM, N C
1- 6-1831   Sarah P, -dt Hardy & Mary of Wayne Co, Ind, m Jonathan Butler at Milford MH
1-22-1831   Sally rst in mbrp w/c New Garden MM, N C
2-26-1831   Richard J & ch William Edwin & Charles Swain rst in mbrp w/c Deep River MM, N C
3-23-1833   Hardy & w Mary & ch Anna, Susanna, Mary & Caleb gct Duck Creek MM, Ind
1-25-1834   Simeon rpt mcd; dis
7-26-1834   Martha gct Duck Creek MM, Ind
11-28-1835  Anna C gct Duck Creek MM, Ind
8-27-1836   Richard Jr rpt na & dp; dis
12-24-1836  Butler rpt mcd by Hopewell MM
5-27-1837   Butler, Hopewell MM inf he is dis
12-28-1839  Richard J & w Sarah & ch Edwin, Charles J, Margaret, Caroline, Phebe Ann & Harriet P gct Spiceland MM, Ind
1-23-1841   Joseph rocf New Garden MM, Ind
7-24-1847   Jacob & ch rocf New Garden MM, N C, but as his affairs not settled it is not received
11-24-1855  Richard J & w Sarah & ch Harriet P, Emily, Henry, Joseph B, George, Julinetta & Anna rocf Spiceland MM, Ind
6-27-1857   Richard J & w Sarah & ch Emily, Henry, George, Joseph B, Julinetta & Anna M gct Whitewater MM, Ind
12-26-1857  Harriet P gct Whitewater MM, Ind
6-26-1858   Richard J & w Sarah & ch Harriet P, Emily, Henry, Joseph B, George, Julinetta & Anna rocf Whitewater MM, Ind
3-24-1860   Harriet P Waters (form Hubbard) rpt mcd; chm
10- 2-1862  Richard J of Wayne Co, Ind, -s Jeremiah & Margaret (both dec) m Abigail Edgerton, widow of William at Milford MH

**HUDDLESTON**
5-28-1836   Levenia rocf Salem MM, Ind
3-24-1838   Stephen rocf Salem MM, Ind
3-24-1838   Anna rocf Salem MM, Ind
3-24-1838   Nathan, Lucinda, Mary & Solomon, ch of Jonathan & Phebe, rocf Salem MM, Ind
8-25-1838   Stephen rpt jH by Bethel MM; dis
3-23-1839   Phebe rq mbrp
5-25-1839   Phebe - rq for mbrp denied
10-26-1839  Mary rpt jH; dis
7-27-1840   Phebe rq rst in mbrp; Salem MM does not consent that she be rst in mbrp
12-25-1841  Nathan rpt na; dis
5-28-1842   Lucinda Burkett (form Huddleston) rpt mcd; dis
1-27-1844   Anna (form Reynolds) rpt mcd; dis
8-28-1847   Phebe rst in mbrp w/c Salem MM, Ind
8-27-1854   Phebe na for a long time & refuses to live with her husband without giving any substantial reason; dis
5-26-1866   Aaron & w Emily & ch Clayton & Lindley rocf Alum Creek MM, Ohio
3-23-1867   Silas & w Emily Ann & ch Caroline, Hiram, Albert & Rosetta rocf Salem MM, Ind
11-23-1867  Caroline Walton (form Huddleston) rpt mcd; chm
12-28-1867  Sophia (form Pemberton) rel fr mbrp
11-24-1868  Aaron & w Emily & ch Clayton, Lindley & Ellen gct Kansas MM, Kans
4-24-1869   David & w Elizabeth rocf Salem MM, Ind
11-24-1877  Hiram gct Mississinewa MM, Ind
4-23-1881   Hiram rocf Mississinewa MM, Ind
6-25-1881   Hiram P & w Elizabeth & ch Oliver gct White River MM, Ind
9-24-1881   Albert F gct White River MM, Ind
6-26-1884   Hiram & w Lizzie & s Oliver rocf White River MM, Ind
6-26-1884   Albert F & w Laura & dt Ina P rocf White River MM, Ind
6-25-1885   William F & w Elizabeth & s Oliver gct Maryville MM, Tenn
2-25-1886   Albert & w Laura & dt Ina Pansy gct Whitewater MM, Ind
11-28-1888  Rosetta rocf Sugar Plain MM, Ind
11-27-1890  Elizabeth gct Thorntown MM, Ind

**HUNNICUTT**
5-24-1828   Daniel & w Jane & ch James B, Jemima W, Mary B, John T, Jane & Daniel rocf Upper MM, Va
2-28-1829   Daniel & w Jane & ch Jemima W, Mary Jane, John T & Daniel gct Springfield MM, Ind
6-22-1833   Elizabeth Ann rocf Western Branch MM, Va
11-23-1833  James B gct Duck Creek MM, Ind
5- 1-1834   Elizabeth A, -dt Daniel & Mary of Wayne Co, Ind, m William Modlin (Maudlin) at Milford MH
6-24-1848   Mary rocf Springfield MM, Ind
8-31-1854   Mary B, -dt Daniel (dec) & Jane, m John Newby at Milford MH

**HUNT**
8-14-1823   John appt an Overseer
3-18-1824   Jonathan & w Phebe & ch Huldah, Jesse, Phebe, Elizabeth, Rachel, Mary, Bulah, Selah & Lydia rocf New Garden MM, Ind
5-13-1824   Allen & w Huldah & ch Nancy, Lucinda, Rachel & Abel rocf New Garden MM, N C, -end fr West Grove MM, Ind
5-13-1824   Nathan rocf New Garden MM, N C, -end fr West Grove MM, Ind
10-23-1824  Huldah Palin (form Hunt) rpt mcd; chm
8-26-1826   Ezra & w Rebecca & ch James & Asenath rocf White River MM, Ind
9-22-1827   Jesse rpt dp; dis
2-28-1829   Phebe appt an Elder
3- 8-1832   Rachel, -dt Jonathan & Phebe, Wayne Co, Ind, m Joel Kindley at Milford MH
3-26-1834   Isom of Henry Co, Ind, -s Isom Sr (dec) late of Guilford Co, N C & wife, Margaret of Wayne Co, Ind, m Susanna Stanley at Hopewell MH
7-26-1834   Isom rocf Spiceland MM, Ind
9-27-1834   Ezra rpt "unbecoming behavior toward a young woman" by Bethel MM; chm
3-26-1836   Elizabeth Budd (form Hunt) rpt mcd; dis

MILFORD

## HUNT (Cont)
|  |  |
|---|---|
| 3-26-1836 | Lucinda rocf Newberry MM, Ohio |
| 10-22-1836 | George & w Dorcas & ch rocf New Garden MM & end to Bloomfield MM, Ind |
| 3-25-1837 | Hanuel & ch Sarah, Aseneth, Ezra, Nancy, Jane & James rocf Clear Creek MM, Ohio |
| 3-27-1837 | Lucinda rocf Newberry MM, Ohio |
| 11-30-1837 | Mary, -dt Jonathan & Phebe, m Solomon Stanbrough at Milford MH |
| 2-1-1838 | Lydia, -dt Jonathan & Phebe of Wayne Co, Ind, m John Stanbrough at Milford MH |
| 4-28-1838 | Ezra & w Rebecca & ch James, Aceneth, Asa, Priscilla & Benjamin gct Walnut Ridge MM, Ind |
| 4-27-1839 | Hanuel & w Lucinda & ch Sarah, Aseneth, Ezra, Nancy, Jane, James & Cyrus gct Walnut Ridge MM, Ind |
| 8-22-1846 | Phebe & s Jonathan gct Springfield (he ret before cert was sent) |
| 10-24-1846 | Sarah & ch Jacob, Sarah, William & Elmina rocf Hopewell MM, N C |
| 7-23-1853 | Thomas T & w Nancy D & ch Hannah B, Eliza K, Laura, Mary J & Margaret rocf Newberry MM, Ohio |
| 7-23-1853 | Lydia rst in mbrp w/c Hopewell MM, N C |
| 5-29-1853 | Jonathan rpt na, dp & participating in dances; chm |
| 7-22-1854 | Thomas T, rpt na & jFreemasons by Bethel MM; dis |
| 7-22-1854 | Nancy D rpt na; dis |
| 11-25-1854 | Jonathan rpt na; dis |
| 10-2-1856 | Celia, -dt Jonathan (dec) & Phebe of Wayne Co, Ind, m Thomas E Beeson at Milford MH |
| 12-27-1856 | Eliza K Culbertson (form Hunt) rpt mcd; dis |
| 8-22-1857 | James rec in mbrp |
| 9-23-1865 | Lydia Griffith (form Hunt) rpt mcd with a divorced man; dis |
| 12-24-1870 | Martha N rocf Spring River MM, Kans |
| 1-28-1871 | David rocf Springfield MM, N C |
| 11-25-1871 | David & w Martha gct Whitewater MM, Ind |
| 1-28-1886 | Edward I rec in mbrp, also Jonathan C |
| 2-25-1886 | Sarah E rec in mbrp |
| 2-21-1889 | Edward I rel fr mbrp |
| 2-23-1893 | Jonathan C rel fr mbrp |

## HUSSEY
|  |  |
|---|---|
| 5-23-1840 | Joseph, mbr Deep River MM, N C, rpt mcd |
| 6-27-1840 | Jonathan, a min, rpt residing within our limits & has cert fr Deep River MM, N C directed to Milford & withholds it & has entirely declined attendance of our mtgs - rpt by Bethel MM |
| 11-26-1862 | Asahel H of Jefferson Co, Ohio, -s Penrose & Susanna, m Martha P Newby at Bethel MH |
| 4-25-1863 | Martha gct Short Creek MM, Ohio |

## HUTSON
|  |  |
|---|---|
| 2-12-1824 | Lydia & dt Sarah, Huldah, Nancy, Penelope & Lydia rocf Back Creek MM, N C, -end by Whitewater MM, Ind |
| 4-22-1824 | Daniel of Henry Co, Ind, -s Nathan & Lydia m Elizabeth Maudlin at Milford MH |
| 5-27-1826 | John rpt mcd by Newberry MM; Newberry MM reports dis |
| 1-28-1886 | Grant rec in mbrp |

## HUTTON
|  |  |
|---|---|
| 8-27-1853 | William H, a minor, rocf Richland MM, Ind |
| 10-27-1855 | William H rpt mcd; dis; Richland MM inf |

## INGERSOLL
|  |  |
|---|---|
| 7-28-1883 | Josephine gct Hopewell MM, Ind |

## JACKSON
|  |  |
|---|---|
| 4-22-1837 | Elanor a mbr of Salem MM, Ind, dis |
| 10-27-1883 | Mary M rel fr mbrp |

## JAMES
|  |  |
|---|---|
| 12-25-1824 | Evan & w Rebecca & ch Hannah, Phebe, Jonas, Jesse, Joshua & Mary rocf Whitewater MM, Ind |
| 8-27-1825 | Rebecca appt an Overseer at Duck Creek MM, Ind |
| 6-22-1838 | Hannah rec in mbrp |

## JAY
|  |  |
|---|---|
| 5-22-1858 | Mary & ch Henry, William H, Mary & Ann Elizabeth rocf Union MM |
| 3-28-1868 | William rpt bearing arms in war; dis |
| 3-28-1868 | Mary E rpt jas; dis |
| 12-30-1880 | Walter Denny of Wayne Co, Ind, -s John & Mary, (both dec), m Margaret A Shekel, a widow, at Dublin MH |
| 7-23-1881 | Walter D & ch William & Allie rocf Chester MM, Ind |

## JELLISON
|  |  |
|---|---|
| 2-27-1836 | Priscilla (form Marmon), mbr Whitewater MM, mcd; dis |

## JENKINS
|  |  |
|---|---|
| 12-31-1878 | William M of Alliance, Stark Co, Ohio, -s William & Lydia, m Delphina White at res of her father, Josiah White |
| 7-26-1879 | Delphina gct Alliance MM, Ohio |
| 11-27-1884 | Mary J rel fr mbrp |

## JESSOP
|  |  |
|---|---|
| 12-18-1823 | Alice Jessop & ch Jesse, Miles, Wilson & William Beauchamp rocf New Garden MM, -end by West Grove MM, Ind |
| 6-25-1825 | Alice Jessop & dt Betty Beauchamp rocf West Grove MM, Ind |
| 11-26-1825 | Lydia R rocf New Garden MM, N C |
| 1-28-1826 | Tidamon rocf Whitewater, -end fr White Lick to West Grove & thence to our mtg |
| 2-1-1826 | Tidamon of Wayne Co, Ind, -s Pratt & Hope, m Lydia Morris at West Union MH |
| 6-24-1826 | Elizabeth & ch Mary, Peninah, Thomas, Lydia, Nancy, Miriam, Jacob & Huldah rocf West Grove MM, Ind |
| 11-25-1826 | Tidamon & fam gct Duck Creek MM, Ind |
| 3-1-1827 | Lydia R, -dt William & Ruth (dec) of Wayne Co, Ind, m Charles Gordon at Milford MH |
| 6-25-1831 | Joseph & w Mary & ch Jacob & Jonathan rocf New Garden MM, N C |
| 6-25-1831 | Sarah & sister, Rachel, rocf New Garden MM, N C |
| 8-27-1831 | Evan rocf New Garden MM, N C |
| 12-24-1831 | Sarah gct West Grove MM, Ind |
| 1-28-1832 | Evan gct West Grove MM, Ind |
| 10-27-1832 | Nathan rpt na & furnishing hands in his employ with spirituous liquors; chm |
| 6-22-1833 | Rachel Brewer (form Jessop), mbr Blue River MM, rpt mcd; chm |
| 7-27-1833 | Joseph & w Mary & ch Jacob & Jonathan gct Fairfield MM, Ind |
| 5-27-1837 | Evan rocf Spiceland MM, Ind |
| 9-28-1839 | Jacob, mbr Fairfield MM, rpt mcd; dis |
| 11-28-1840 | Evan gct Westfield MM, Ind |
| 4-22-1843 | Nathan, rpt na "for several yrs & hath not complyed with his promises in payment of money, when he had it in his possession;" dis |
| 3-22-1845 | Alice & s Evan, John & Jehiel gct Mississinewa MM, Ind |
| 6-28-1845 | Jonathan rocf Richland MM, Ind |
| 3-28-1846 | Jonathan rpt dp & na; dis |
| 4-25-1863 | William T & w Mary Ann & ch Jesse William & James Henry rec in mbrp — William of Piney Woods, N C & Mary Ann of Rich Square MM, N C, having removed & being unable to secure cert due to the State of Public affairs |
| 3-2-1871 | Levi of Richmond, Wayne Co, Ind, -s Isaac & Ann (both dec) m Rachel M White, widow of Aaron White, at Milford MH |
| 4-22-1871 | Rachel gct Whitewater MM, Ind |
| 12-23-1882 | Wilford, -s Thomas rocf Mill Creek MM, Ind |

MILFORD

JESSOP (Cont)
6-23-1883  Wilfred rel fr mbrp

JOHNS
5-28-1881  Percy rec in mbrp
5-28-1885  Mary J rel fr mbrp

JOHNSON
6-30-1830  James & w Mary & ch Anne, Rachel, Elizabeth, Caleb, Emily, Grace & John Warner rocf Whitewater MM, Ind
10-28-1830  Anna, -dt James & Mary of Wayne Co, Ind, m Zachariah Fletcher at Milford MH
5-28-1831  Sookey & dt Almeda rocf Western Branch, Isle of Wight Co, Va
6-25-1831  James & w Mary & ch Rachel, Elizabeth, Emily Grace, Caleb & John Warner gct Duck Creek MM
2-25-1832  Jervis & w Melissa rocf Western Branch MM, Va
2-25-1832  William rocf Western Branch MM, Va
8-30-1832  Almeda, -dt Zachariah (dec) of Isle of Wight Co, Va, & w Sukey of Henry Co, Ind, m William Parker at Rich Square MH
1-26-1833  Richard rocf Short Creek MM, Ohio
3-23-1833  Sarah & ch Eliza, Joel, Robert, Ansalem & Elijah rocf West Branch MM, Va
3-23-1833  Daniel & w Maria rocf Western Branch MM, Va
3-23-1833  Lazarus & w Mary rocf Western Branch MM, Va
3-22-1834  Richard gct Salem MM to m Edna Butler
10-25-1835  Sookey gct Duck Creek MM, Ind
11-22-1834  Edna rocf Salem MM, Ind
3-25-1837  Jervis & w Melissa & minor s Joseph gct Sugar River MM, Ind
11-25-1837  Richard & s William S gct Walnut Ridge MM, Ind
3-24-1838  Sylvester, Dorinda, Martha & Edward, ch of Pleasant & Sarah, rocf Salem MM, Ind
5-25-1839  William gct Walnut Ridge MM, Ind
9-23-1839  Joel gct Spiceland MM to m Elizabeth Davis
4-25-1840  Joel gct Spiceland MM, Ind
12-25-1841  Dorinda King (form Johnson) rpt mcd; dis
7-26-1845  Sylvester rpt na & mcd; dis
2-27-1847  Mary, a minor, with the Zachariah Fletcher fam, rocf Spiceland MM, Ind
1- 1-1851  Ansalem of Henry Co, Ind, -s Laban (dec) & Sarah of Isle of Wight Co, Va, m Rebecca Bell at Bethel MH
8-23-1851  Rebecca gct Hopewell MM, Ind
7-23-1853  Mary Saint (form Johnson) rpt mcd by Duck Creek MM; chm
4-25-1855  Rachel (form Harvey) rpt mcd; dis
5-25-1861  Letitia (form Hastings) rpt mcd; chm
7-27-1867  Edwin & w Eliza S & dt Emily H rocf Cincinnati MM, Ohio
11-23-1867  Margaret (form Hastings) rpt jBaptists; dis
7-24-1869  Edwin & w Eliza & dt Emily gct Raysville MM, Ind
11-25-1871  Horace Bucker rec in mbrp
4-27-1872  Sylvia A (form Lindley) rpt mcd; chm
10-28-1872  Sylvia gct Hopewell MM, Ind
1-28-1886  William rec in mbrp
3-24-1887  Lulu rec in mbrp
12-28-1887  Matilda gct Hopewell MM, Ind

JONES
9-16-1824  Polly, mbr Blue River MM, rpt mcd
8-27-1825  Polly, rpt of dis received
3-24-1827  Lydia rocf Springfield MM, N C, -end by West Grove MM, Ind
4-26-1828  Lydia gct Duck Creek MM, Ind
5-26-1832  Mary rocf Suttons Creek MM, N C
6-22-1833  Mary rpt jH; dis
9-26-1846  Margaret rocf Spiceland MM, Ind
5-23-1854  Margaret gct Pipe Creek MM, Ind
7-28-1877  James R & w Achsah & ch Anna & Mary rocf Spiceland MM, Ind
6-28-1880  James R & w Achsah & ch Anna L & Mary F gct New Garden MM, Ind
6-25-1881  Sylvester & w Mary & ch William & Maud rocf Spiceland MM, Ind
4-28-1883  Sylvester & w Mary & ch William & Maud gct Whitewater MM, Ind

JORDAN
6-23-1849  Margaret (form Weisner), mbr Walnut Ridge MM, rpt mcd; dis
8-23-1856  Adaline (form Bundrant) rpt mcd; dis
10-24-1874  Melville rec in mbrp
1-24-1880  Melville M gct Piney Woods MM, N C

JUSTICE
7-17-1823  Jonathan appt to a comm
1-15-1824  Elizabeth appt an Elder
12- 1-1825  Sarah, -dt Jonathan & Elizabeth of Wayne Co, Ind, m Benjamin Griffin at Milford MH
11-30-1826  Elizabeth, -dt Jonathan & Elizabeth, m William Wright at Milford MH
6-28-1828  Jonathan rpt reading Hicksite books & papers; dis
8-23-1828  Elizabeth rpt jH; dis
12-28-1839  Anna rpt jH; dis
1-23-1841  Henry rpt jH; dis
1-23-1841  Enoch P rpt jH; dis
6-23-1845  Martha rpt jH; dis

KEMPER
1-26-1888  Mary Maud rec in mbrp
3-28-1889  Ernest O rec in mbrp
11-27-1890  William L rec in mbrp

KENDALL
6-28-1828  James G rocf Springfield MM, -end to White Lick MM, Ind

KENNEDAY
4-28-1866  Isabella & dt Margaret Jane Elliott rocf Neuse MM, N C
6-27-1866  Isabella, widow of Thomas Kenneday of N C, (her 2nd h), & dt of George & Isabella (Scott) Walton, (all dec), m Caleb Hall at Bethel MH
8-25-1866  Isabella Hall & dt Margaret Jane Elliott gct Spiceland MM, Ind

KERSEY
11-26-1825  William & w Rachel & ch Asher, Verling, Silas H, Mary C & Charity W rocf Springfield MM, N C
8-25-1827  Eli rocf Springfield MM, N C
1-26-1828  Asher rpt upl; chm
8- 5-1829  Asher of Wayne Co, Ind, -s William & Rachel, m Susannah Morgan at West Union MH
12-24-1831  Asher & w Susannah & s Benjamin Veirlin gct Duck Creek MM, Ind
6-23-1832  James & Elizabeth & ch Jesse & Abigail rocf Springfield MM, N C
11-24-1832  Daniel rocf Cherry Grove MM, Ind
3-23-1833  James & Elizabeth & ch Jesse, Abigail & James gct White Lick MM, Ind
4-26-1834  Daniel gct Cherry Grove MM, Ind
11-22-1834  Verling gct Spiceland MM, Ind
12-24-1836  William & w Rachel & ch Silas H, Mary C & Charity gct Spiceland MM, Ind
7-25-1840  Eli gct Spiceland MM, Ind
8-23-1845  Mary Emily & ch Ann Maria & Richard W rocf Spiceland MM, Ind
8-20-1852  Mary Emily rpt in "disunity with Friends doctrines & saying that she did not think that a belief in the divinity of Christ essential to salvation" & na; complaint dismissed
12-25-1852  Mary Emily rpt na for some considerable time; dis
1-24-1863  Richard W, Charles A, Pliny Earl & Margaret, ch of Vierling & Mary E, gct Whitewater MM, Ind

KIMMER
4-26-1879  William & w Charlotte rec in mbrp

MILFORD

## KIMMEY
7-17-1823  William M appt Asst-Clerk

## KINDLEY
5-27-1826  John rec a min
5-26-1827  Betty appt an Elder
5-28-1831  Jonathan gct Chester MM to m Hannah Picket
9- 8-1831  Sarah, -dt John & Betty, Wayne Co, Ind, m Josiah Symons at Milford MH
9-24-1831  Hannah rocf Chester MM, -but she having ret the cert was -end back
9-24-1831  Jonathan rq cert to Chester MM, Ind
3- 8-1832  Joel of Wayne Co, Ind, -s John & Betty, m Rachel Hunt at Milford MH
11-27-1832  Joel & w Rachel gct Duck Creek MM, Ind
12-22-1832  Jonathan & w Hannah rocf Chester MM, Ind
8-23-1834  Joel & w Rachel & s Charles rocf Spiceland MM, Ind
10-24-1835  Jonathan & w Hannah & dt Elizabeth gct White River MM, Ind
9-29-1836  Elizabeth, -dt John & Betty of Wayne Co, Ind, m Bennett Cox at Milford MH
1-28-1837  Jonathan & dt Elizabeth rocf White River MM, Ind
6-24-1837  Jonathan rpt mcd; dis
11-14-1839  Ruth, -dt John (dec) & Betty of Wayne Co, Ind, m Seth Cox at Milford MH
4-23-1842  Joel & w Rachel & ch Charles, Margaret, Lydia, Joseph, John & Rebecca gct Westfield MM, Ind
1-28-1843  Joel & w Rachel & ch Charles, Margaret, Lydia, Joseph & Rebecca rocf Westfield MM, Ind
8-23-1845  Joel & w Rachel & ch Charles, Margaret, Lydia, Joseph, John & Rebecca gct Springfield MM, Ind
4-25-1846  Seth rpt mcd; dis
2-22-1851  John W rpt dp & na
6-28-1851  John W dis for dp & na
3-27-1858  Elizabeth Tingle (form Kindley) rpt mcd; dis
3-22-1884  John W rec in mbrp

## KING
10-22-1826  Isaac & w Ann & ch Harmon, Hannah & Phebe rocf Stillwater MM, Ohio
11-22-1828  Isaac rpt dr; chm
3-23-1833  Isaac & w Ann & ch Harmon, Hannah, Phebe, Rebecca, Lydia & Deborah gct Duck Creek MM, Ind
12-25-1841  Dorinda (form Johnson) rpt mcd
2-26-1841  Dorinda (form Johnson) dis for mcd
6-28-1879  Dorinda & Sarah rec in mbrp
2-23-1884  Jennie rec in mbrp
2-25-1886  Emma T rec in mbrp

## KINSEY
6-22-1833  Joseph rocf Westland MM, Pa
6-22-1833  Eliza Ann rocf Westland MM, Pa
1-23-1836  Eliza McKey (form Kinsey) rpt mcd; dis
5-25-1844  Joseph gct Duck Creek MM, Ind

## KIRK
7-25-1835  Mahlon & ch Isaiah & Sarah rocf Whitewater MM, Ind
11-27-1891  Ella rec in mbrp
2-25-1892  Mary Ann & s Riley rec in mbrp
6- -1892  Josephine rec in mbrp

## KITHCART
4-22-1876  Jane N gct Short Creek MM, Ohio

## KOUTNEY
1-28-1886  Earl rec in mbrp

## KUHNS
10-27-1887  Alice A rec in mbrp

## LACY
1-27-1828  Josiah gct West Grove MM to m Ruth Gordon
6-27-1829  Ruth rocf West Grove MM, Ind
3-27-1830  John rpt na; dis
4-24-1830  Penninah rpt na; dis
2-28-1835  Josiah & w Ruth & s Lowring gct Duck Creek MM, Ind
10-28-1837  Samuel rpt na & training with Militia by Walnut Ridge MM
12-23-1837  Walnut Ridge MM rpt Samuel is dis
5-23-1840  Susannah Overman (form Lacey) rpt mcd by Westfield MM
6-26-1840  Susannah Overman (form Lacey) dis; rpt by Westfield MM
7-23-1842  Jesse gct Walnut Ridge MM, Ind
1-24-1846  Jesse, mbrp Walnut Ridge MM, rpt na & guilty of fornication
5-23-1846  Jesse - rpt of dis rec fr Walnut Ridge MM
4-24-1847  Naomi Newby (form Lacey) rpt mcd; dis
5-26-1849  Thomas gct Walnut Ridge MM, Ind

## LAMB
2-12-1824  Martha rocf Back Creek MM, N C, -end by Whitewater MM, Ind
4-28-1832  Sarah rocf Symons Creek MM, N C, -end to Duck Creek MM, Ind
10-27-1832  Phineas rocf Piney Woods MM, N C
12-28-1833  Phineas dec int to m Mary Palin
1-25-1834  Phineas & Mary Palin dincontinue m int
2-28-1835  Phineas gct Duck Creek MM to m Huldah Bundy
7-25-1835  Huldah rocf Duck Creek MM, Ind
6-25-1836  Caleb & fam rocf Symons Creek MM, N C, -end to Walnut Ridge MM, Ind
3-24-1838  Phineas & w Huldah & dt Martha gct Walnut Ridge MM, Ind
2-26-1870  Benjamin rocf Piney Woods MM, N C
2-26-1870  Vashti rocf Whitewater MM, Ind
4-24-1875  Benjamin & w Vashti & ch Algernon Thycle, Benjamin & Galen gct PineyWoods MM, N C
3-26-1885  Emily rocf Springfield MM, Ind

## LATHRUM (Lotham)
7-23-1825  Ruth rpt mcd; dis

## LAUNIS
1-28-1886  Jacob & Rebecca rec in mbrp

## LAWRENCE
10-24-1829  Jonathan - "a few lines .. from Holly Springs MM N C, .. that he is mbr of their mtg"
4-24-1830  Jonathan rocf Holly Springs MM, N C
6-26-1830  Jonathan rpt dp & mcd by Hopewell MM
8-28-1830  Jonathan dis for dp & mcd
3-27-1847  Thomas H rocf Spiceland MM, Ind
6-22-1850  Thomas H gct Back Creek MM, Ind
5-27-1886  Annie rocf West Union MM, Ind

## LEEDS
9-23-1843  William rocf Whitewater MM, Ind
4-26-1845  William, -s Noah, gct Philadelphia MM, Pa

## LEIBHARDT
1-29-1891  Mary rec in mbrp
2-23-1893  Mary rel fr mbrp

## LEONARD
2-24-1883  Mary Shaw & ch Sarah & Ora rec in mbrp
12-23-1886  Mary Griffith & dt Susan gct New Castle MM, Ind
2-21-1888  Laurah gct Indianapolis MM, Ind

## LEVERTON
1-28-1886  William & Jane rec in mbrp

## LEWELLEN
8-12-1824  Meschach appt Clerk
8-12-1824  Jane appt Clerk

## LEWIS
1-28-1886  Henry rec in mbrp

MILFORD

LILLEY
11-28-1840    Margaretta (form Foulke) rpt mcd by Hopewell MM
1-23-1841     Margaretta (form Foulke) dis for mcd

LINDLEY
3-28-1853     Osmond of White Lick MM, Ind, -s James & Ruth of Howard Co, Ind, m Achsah W Wilson at Bethel MH
10-22-1853    Achsah gct Honey Creek MM, Ind
1-27-1855     Osmond & w Achsah rocf Honey Creek MM, Ind
3-25-1865     Joshua gct Sugar Plain MM, Ind
4-27-1872     Sylvia A Johnson (form Lindley) rpt mcd; chm
11-23-1872    Osmond & w Achsah & Alfred, Franklin, Gerney, John, Charles, James, Horace, Fletcher & Christopher Erasmus gct Fairview MM, Ill

LOW
10-23-1830    Miriam (form Saunders), living in the limits of Westfield MM, rpt mcd; dis

LUPTSON
7-24-1847     David W & w Ann & ch Ruth, Emma & Richard rocf Walnut Ridge MM, Ind
8-26-1848     David W & w Ann & ch Ruth, Esther, Beulah & Richard P gct Chester MM, Ind

LYNN
2-25-1892     Frank rec in mbrp

LYONS
1-28-1886     Andrew J & Carrie rec in mbrp

McCOY
12-24-1864    Rachel (form Wilson) rpt mcd by Bethel MM; chm
1-25-1868     Henry & w Rachel & s William gct Spiceland MM, Ind
11-25-1871    James W & w Rachel & ch Alice A, Dorinda E & Flora B rec in mbrp
5-25-1873     Henry C & w Rachel & ch William, John & James rocf Spiceland MM, Ind
6-28-1879     Rachel W rel fr mbrp

McKEY
1-23-1836     Eliza (form Kinsey) rpt mcd
4-25-1836     Eliza (form Kinsey) dis for mcd

McIMMEY
6-27-1829     William rpt jH
8-22-1829     William dis for jH

MACY
10-23-1824    Miriam rocf New Garden MM, N C
11-27-1824    Jonathan & Anna, ch of Katherine Coffin, rocf New Garden MM, N C
7- 7-1825     Miriam, -dt John (dec) & Rhoda (Gardner) Macy (dec) of N C, m Jesse Baldwin of N C & Ohio, (his 3rd wife) at Milford MH
8-26-1826     Nathan rocf Hopewell MM, N C, -end to Duck Creek MM
7-28-1827     Solomon rocf Hopewell MM, N C
9-27-1828     Nathan & w Catharine & ch Pemberton, Sarah & Jemima rocf Silver Creek MM, Ind
12- 2-1830    Solomon of Henry Co, Ind, -s Thaddeus (dec) & Catharine, m Priscilla Hamm at Milford MH
1-25-1831     Solomon & w Priscilla gct Duck Creek MM, Ind
1-25-1834     Hannah (form Thornburg) rpt mcd & jH; dis
5-23-1835     Anna gct Duck Creek MM, Ind
12-26-1835    James & w Anna & ch Lydia Ann, Eunice, Rachel, Phineas & Mary rocf Salem MM, Ind
12-26-1835    Zachaeus & w Sarah & dt Lydia rocf Salem MM, Ind
2-27-1836     Jonathan rpt na & mcd by Bethel MM; dis
3-24-1838     John rocf Salem MM, -end fr Spiceland MM, Ind
4-27-1839     Nathan dec int to m Millicent Gilbert
5-25-1839     Millicent Gilbert rpt dec
3-28-1840     Nathan gct Salem MM to m Lydia Macy
5- 7-1840     John M of Wayne Co, Ind, -s Stephen & Rebecca of Henry Co, Ind, m Betsy Ann White at Milford MH
10-24-1840    Lydia & ch Ann Maria, Nathan & Susanna rocf Salem MM, Ind
9-24-1842     John M & w Betsy Ann & dt Henrietta gct Spiceland MM, Ind
12-28-1844    John M & w Betsey Ann & ch Henrietta Maria & Margaret W rocf Spiceland MM, Ind
10-24-1846    John M & w Betsey Ann & ch Henrietta Maria, Margaret W & William gct Spiceland MM, Ind
8-28-1880     Larkin rocf Springfield MM, Ind

MALES
3-24-1887     William F & w Mary L ....

MARMON
5-27-1837     James, Benjamin Franklin & Malinda, ch of Rachel Shank, rocf Whitewater MM, Ind

MARSHALL
11-28-1832    Stephen of Henry Co, Ind, -s John & Anna, m Gulana Elliott at Bethel MH
3-23-1833     Gulana gct Springfield MM, Ind

MATTHEWS
7-28-1827     Susannah rocf Springborough MM, Ohio
12-22-1827    Susan gct Cincinnati MM, Ohio

MAUDLIN -(Modlin)
4-22-1824     Elizabeth, -dt William & Anna of Henry Co, Ind, m Daniel Hutson at Milford MH
5-13-1824     John rpt mcd; dis
12-25-1824    Enoch & w Miriam & ch Eliza & Henry rocf Whitewater MM, Ind
4-23-1825     Thomas & w Hannah rocf West Grove MM, Ind
7-23-1825     George & ch Rhoda, Nancy, Dillon, Reuben, Elias, Mark, Leah & Jacob rocf New Garden MM, Ind
7-23-1825     Ann rocf New Garden MM, Ind
11-22-1828    Miriam rpt jH; dis
1-24-1829     Enoch rpt jH; dis
8-25-1832     Levi rpt mcd with 1st cousin
8-25-1832     Elizabeth (form Ratliff) rpt mcd with her 1st cousin; dis
10-27-1832    Levi dis for mcd with his 1st cousin
11-27-1833    Richard, -s William & Ann of Henry Co, Ind, m Gulielma M Butler at Hopewell MH
5- 1-1834     William of Henry Co, Ind, -s William & Ann, m Elizabeth A Hunnicutt at Milford MH
10-25-1834    Rebecca Hasket (form Maudlin) rpt mcd
2-28-1835     Rebecca Hasket (form Maudlin) dis for mcd
3-25-1835     Richard & w Guly gct Buck Creek MM, Ind
6-12-1835     William & w Elizabeth & s Oliver gct Duck Creek MM, Ind
5-23-1840     Eliza Wiley (form Modlin) rpt mcd; dis
10-23-1841    Anna gct Duck Creek MM, Ind
12-25-1847    Elvira rpt na & dp
2-26-1848     Elvira dis for na & dp
7-22-1882     Mahlon & w Margaret & ch Nathan L, Louisa, Eliza, Sarah & John Sherman rocf Springfield MM, Ind
2-25-1886     Margaret, Alonzo, Clara, Laura & Jennie rel fr mbrp

MAXWELL
12-13-1871    Benjamin & w Sarah S & ch Lanetta & Naomi rocf Salem MM, Ind
4-25-1874     Hugh & w Anna rocf Salem MM, Ind
4-25-1874     Sarah rocf Salem MM, Ind
7-24-1884     Anna gct Salem MM, Ind
7-28-1892     Benjamin F & w Sylvania & ch Perry F Maxwell, Lenneta Vixler & Naomi See rel fr mbrp

MENDENHALL
3-25-1826     Samuel, mbr West Grove MM, rpt for mcd & training with the militia; West Grove inf not satisfactory results

MILFORD

## MENDENHALL (Cont)
| | |
|---|---|
| 10-27-1832 | Miles & w Margaret & ch Sina, Jacob, Eli, Dempsey, Nathan & Isaac rocf Springfield MM, N C |
| 4-26-1834 | Mary B rocf Salem MM, Ind |
| 9-27-1834 | Mary gct White Lick MM, Ind |
| 11-24-1835 | Miles & w Margaret & ch Sina, Jacob, Eli B, Dempsey B, Nathan C, Isaac, Mary Ann & Rachel gct Mill Creek MM, Ind |
| 10-28-1837 | Hannah rocf White Lick MM, Ind |
| 3-31-1841 | Hannah, -dt Enos & Lydia of Henry Co, Ind, m Thomas Bell at Bethel MH |
| 7-23-1864 | Susan C (form Stanley), mbr Spiceland MM, rpt mcd; chm |
| 10-22-1864 | Susan rocf Spiceland MM, Ind |
| 1-22-1876 | Susannah & ch George, Phebe, Jane & Delana gct Spiceland MM, Ind |

## MEREDITH
| | |
|---|---|
| 6-27-1835 | Mary & ch Jabez, Jesse, Joanna, Rosanna, Susanna & William rocf Whitewater MM, Ind |
| 3-26-1836 | Joanna rpt na & dp; dis |
| 4-22-1843 | Mary & ch Jabez, Jesse, Susanna & William gct Spiceland MM, Ind |
| 4-22-1843 | Rosanna rpt for unchastity; dis |

## MICHAEL
| | |
|---|---|
| 1-28-1886 | Sarah rec in mbrp |

## MILES
| | |
|---|---|
| 3-27-1858 | Lindley M & w Lydia & ch Rachel W, Rhoda Ellen & Thomas Elwood rocf Wabash MM, Ind |
| 3-27-1858 | John, a min, & w Rebecca rocf Wabash MM, Ind |
| 9-24-1859 | John, a min, & w Rebecca gct Wabash MM, Ind |
| 9-24-1859 | Lindley M & w Lydia & ch Rachel W, Rhoda & Thomas Elwood gct Wabash MM, Ind |
| 11-23-1861 | John, a min, & w Rebecca rocf Wabash MM, Ind |
| 11-23-1861 | Lindley M & w Lydia & ch Rachel, Rhoda Ellen, Thomas Elwood & John Ellis rocf Wabash MM, Ind |
| 12-27-1873 | John gct West Branch MM, Ohio to m Dorcas Hutchens |
| 7-25-1875 | Dorcas rocf West Branch MM, Ohio |
| 7-27-1875 | Dorcas rpt separated fr her h; dis |
| 2-28-1883 | Rhoda E, -dt Lindley & Lydia G of Dublin, Wayne Co, Ind, m David A Outland at father's res |
| 10-18-1883 | Thomas E of Dickey Co, Dakota Terr, -s Lindley & Lydia of Wayne Co, Ind, m Sarah C White at the home of her parents, Ellendale, Dakota Terr |

## MILLER
| | |
|---|---|
| 10-23-1847 | Phebe rocf Walnut Ridge MM, Ind |
| 10-26-1850 | Phebe Ann gct Chester MM, Ind |
| 2-25-1871 | William R rocf Wabash MM, Ind |
| 2-26-1885 | Lizzie Miller Elliott rec in mbrp |
| 4-28-1892 | Foster & w Olive rocf Walnut Ridge MM, Ind |

## MILLS
| | |
|---|---|
| 1-22-1825 | Daniel & fam gct White Lick MM, Ind |
| 7-22-1826 | Hugh & w Lydia & ch Thomas, Jerusha, Peninah & Priscilla rocf Miami MM, Ohio |
| 6-28-1834 | Ruth rocf Deep River MM, N C |
| 6-28-1834 | Deborah rocf Deep River MM, N C |
| 4- 1-1835 | Ruth, -dt Jeremiah & Deborah of Henry Co, Ind, m James Brown at Bethel MH |
| 8-26-1837 | Deborah gct Westfield MM, Ind |
| 11-26-1837 | Tabitha (form Stanbrough) rpt mcd; dis |
| 10-22-1853 | Tabitha rst in mbrp at Sugar Plain MM, Ind |
| 9-25-1869 | Sarah M (form Benbow) rpt mcd; chm |
| 11-27-1869 | Sarah M gct Pipe Creek MM, Ind |
| 2-28-1880 | Laura E gct Hopewell MM, Ind |

## MILLSPAUGH
| | |
|---|---|
| 3-23-1893 | William rec in mbrp |

## MISENER
| | |
|---|---|
| 11-23-1867 | Margaret rpt mcd; dis |

## MOFFITT
| | |
|---|---|
| 6-22-1850 | Exalina (form Cox), mbr Spiceland MM, rpt mcd |
| 10-26-1850 | Exalina (form Cox) dis for mcd |
| 5-26-1860 | Martha W (form Hiatt) rpt mcd; chm |
| 11-28-1863 | Martha W gct Sugar Plain MM, Ind |

## MOON
| | |
|---|---|
| 3-31-1825 | Samuel of Clinton Co, Ohio, -s Daniel & Ruth of same place, m Mary Presnall at Duck Creek MH |
| 4-22-1826 | Samuel rocf Whitewater MM, Ind |
| 10-22-1826 | Simon & w Hannah & ch Joseph, Mary, William, John Riley, Sibina & Simon rocf Whitewater MM, Ind |
| 2-28-1829 | Simon & w Hannah & ch Joseph, Mary, John, William Riley, Sibina, Simon & Hannah gct White Lick MM, Ind |
| 3-28-1840 | Samuel rpt telling a willful untruth & jMeth; dis |

## MOORE
| | |
|---|---|
| 4-22-1826 | Belina (form Willets) rpt mcd; dis |
| 11-25-1826 | Rebecca rst in mbrp (form mbr of Piney Woods MM, N C) |
| 2-28-1829 | Hariet rpt jH; dis |
| 12-25-1830 | Charles H rocf New Garden MM, N C |
| 1-26-1833 | Smith rocf New Garden MM, N C |
| 5-27-1837 | Thomas & w Anna & ch Elizabeth Walker, Jacob Hubbard, John Thomas & William Henry "now on a visit to this country from New Garden MM, N C, were in attendance" |
| 3-24-1838 | Thomas & w Anna & ch Elizabeth Walker, Jacob Hubbard, John Thomas & William Henry rocf New Garden MM, N C |
| 5- 2-1839 | Elizabeth W, -dt Thomas & Ann of Wayne Co, Ind, m Stephen Morris at Milford MH |
| 8-24-1839 | Charles H rocf Spiceland MM, Ind |
| 8-29-1839 | Charles H of Wayne Co, Ind, -s Thomas & Ann, m Marcia White at Milford MH |
| 9-23-1843 | Richard W & w Anna rocf Whitewater MM, Ind |
| 11-25-1848 | Richard W rpt mcd; dis |
| 2-22-1851 | Charles H appt an Elder |
| 12-22-1855 | Hannah & Rachel rocf Poplar Run MM, Ind |
| 11-22-1856 | Hannah Eliza & ch Mary Jane, Thomas Clarkson, Joseph Wilson & Theodore Adolphus rocf Poplar Run MM, Ind |
| 4-24-1858 | Marcus Henry, a minor, gct Richland MM, Ind |
| 4-28-1858 | Rachel P, -dt Abraham (dec) & Hannah of Wayne Co, Ind, m Aaron White at Bethel MH |
| 5-22-1858 | Joshua Jr rocf Springfield MM, Ohio |
| 7-24-1858 | Richard W rst in mbrp at Richland MM, Ind |
| 8-27-1859 | William H rpt mcd; chm |
| 8-27-1859 | Joshua gct Hopewell MM, Ind |
| 3- 9-1871 | Anne, -dt Charles H & Marcia of Wayne Co, Ind, m Aaron Franklin Sutton at Milford MH |
| 7-26-1873 | Mary Moore Newby rec in mbrp |
| 8-23-1873 | Anna (form Gilbert) rpt mcd; chm |
| 1-24-1874 | Anne gct Whitewater MM, Ind |
| 4-24-1875 | Mahala J rec in mbrp |
| 7-26-1879 | Thomas Albert gct Windham MM, Me, to m Martha G Read |
| 1- 1-1880 | Deborah W, -dt Charles H & Marcia of Wayne Co, Ind, m William Furnas at Milford MH |
| 3-26-1881 | Alice W rec in mbrp |
| 7-26-1881 | Jacob of Richmond, Wayne Co, Ind, -s Abraham & Susannah (both dec) m Jane Elliott, widow of Elias Elliott |
| 9-24-1881 | Jane & -dt Hettie A Elliott gct Whitewater MM, Ind |
| 12-23-1882 | Theodore W gct Lawrence MM, Kans |
| 4-28-1883 | Thomas C rel fr mbrp |
| 7-17-1884 | Florence (form Morris) rpt mcd; chm |
| 1-28-1886 | Marcus H rec in mbrp |
| 2-24-1887 | Morris & w Alice gct Cottonwood MM, Kans |
| 3-29-1888 | Mary gct Whitewater MM, Ind |
| 5-23-1889 | William H, Mahala J & Thomas Franklin gct Green River MM, Ia |
| 5-23-1889 | Albert & w Martha H & fam gct Grand River MM, Kans |

MILFORD

MOORE (Cont)
11-27-1890 Melvin rec in mbrp
11-27-1890 Marcus rel fr mbrp
2-25-1892 Marcia Frances gct Whitewater MM, Ind

MOORMAN
10-28-1886 Mary P rel fr mbrp

MORGAN
3-18-1824 Charles rocf West Grove MM, Ind
9- 1-1825 Charles of Wayne Co, Ind, -s Benjamin & Naomi (dec), m Michel Butler at Milford MH
11-25-1825 Benjamin appt an Elder
8- 5-1829 Susanna, -dt Benjamin & Naomi (dec), m Asher Kersey at West Union MH
5-26-1830 Hannah, -dt Benjamin & 2nd w Elizabeth (dec) of Wayne Co, Ind, m Joseph Davis at West Union MH
1-23-1836 Charles & w Michal & ch Edward, Elizabeth, William & Benjamin gct Spiceland MM, Ind
5-28-1853 Benjamin gct New Garden MM to m Sarah Hill
2-25-1854 Sarah rocf New Garden MM, Ind
3-25-1854 Benjamin & w Sarah gct Walnut Ridge MM, Ind
1-28-1886 John J & Sarah rec in mbrp

MORRIS
7-17-1823 Lydia appt to a comm
7-17-1823 Abigail appt to a comm
7-17-1823 Sarah appt to a comm
12-18-1823 Josiah appt to a comm
2-12-1824 John appt to a comm
9-16-1824 Margaret rocf Symons Creek MM, N C, -end from Whitewater MM, Ind
2- 1-1826 Lydia, -dt Joshua, (dec) & Mary of Wayne Co, Ind, m Tidaman Jessop at West Union MH
12-27-1826 Charles of Wayne Co, Ind, -s Joshua (dec) & Mary, m Ann Hill at West Union MH
12- 6-1827 Samuel of Wayne Co, Ind, -s Aaron & Lydia, m Sarah Symons at Milford MH
1- 2-1828 Mary, widow of Joshua &-dt of Charles & Lydia (dec), m Abraham Symons at Hopewell MH
1- 2-1828 Margaret of Henry Co, Ind, -dt Christopher & Gulielma (both dec) of N C, m Daniel Reynolds at Bethel MH
10-25-1828 John rpt jH; dis
11-22-1828 Sarah rpt jH; dis
12-27-1828 Jehoshaphat rpt jH; dis
12-27-1828 Charles rpt jH; dis
12-27-1828 Sarah rpt jH; dis
12-27-1828 Margaret rpt jH; dis
12-27-1828 Elizabeth rpt jH; dis
1-24-1829 Jonathan rpt jH; dis
1-24-1829 Pharaba rpt jH; dis
1-24-1829 Isaac rpt jH; dis
3-28-1829 Samuel rpt jH; dis
3-28-1829 George rpt jH; dis
7-25-1829 Lydia rpt jH; dis
7-25-1829 Elizabeth S rpt jH; dis
8-22-1829 Aaron rpt jH
10-24-1829 Aaron dis for jH
1- 7-1830 Susannah, -dt Joshua (dec) & Mary of Wayne Co, Ind, m William Butler at Milford MH
1-23-1830 Mary rpt jH
3-27-1830 Mary dis for jH
6-26-1830 Caleb & w Margaret & s Stephen & dt Mary rocf Symons Creek MM, N C
10-23-1830 Mary Brewer (form Morris) rpt mcd
12-25-1830 Mary Brewer (form Morris) dis
3-26-1831 Gulielma rpt na & jH; dis
2-25-1832 Caleb appt an Elder
2-25-1832 Abigail appt an Elder
4-26-1832 Rhoda (form Frampton) rpt jH; dis
11-24-1832 Margaret appt an Elder
10-26-1833 Elizabeth (form Allen) rpt mcd; chm
11-23-1833 John, minor s of Joshua (dec), gct Duck Creek MM, Ind
6-28-1834 William rst in mbrp with consent of Somerset MM, Ohio
7-26-1834 William & w Susannah rocf Deerfield MM, Ohio
7-26-1834 Lydia rocf Deerfield MM, Ohio
9-27-1834 Jonathan & w Theodate & ch Ruth Anna & William R rocf Duck Creek MM, Ind
11-22-1834 William & w Susanna & ch Ruth & Rachel gct Duck Creek MM, Ind
12-27-1834 Elizabeth (form Gilbert) rpt mcd; dis
2-28-1835 William & w Elizabeth & s Benjamin gct Mississinewa MM, Ind
2-28-1835 Lydia gct Duck Creek MM, Ind
3-28-1835 Jonathan rpt jH; chm
7-25-1835 John rocf Duck Creek MM, Ind
8-22-1835 Christopher rpt jH; dis
12-31-1835 John, Wayne Co, Ind, -s Joshua & Mary of Pasquotauk MM, N C, m Martha Chappel at Milford MH
7-23-1836 William & w Susannah & ch Lydia, Ruth & Rachel rocf Duck Creek MM, Ind
7-22-1837 William rpt na; dis
4-28-1838 John & w Martha & s Francis M gct Walnut Ridge MM, Ind
6-23-1838 Theodate & ch Ruthanna, William W & Benajah gct Chesterfield MM, Ohio
10-27-1838 Jonathan rpt for withholding a just debt, after having been advised to settle it, rpt by Chesterfield MM, Ohio-Dis 4-27-1839
2-23-1839 Comm on Education rpts the school house near Isaiah Nixon's, known by the name of New Hope, as an inconvenient place for Friends to hold a school under the control of the comm. The lot of ground was conveyed to the mtg by Caleb Morris (dec) & in his will & testament, the remaining part to his son Stephen Morris. The mtg comes to the judgement to transfer that lot of land to Stephen Morris, retaining the right to the school house
5- 2-1839 Stephen of Wayne Co, Ind, -s Caleb (dec) & Margaret, m Elizabeth W Moore at Milford MH
10-26-1839 Susannah rpt na; dis
11-23-1839 Lydia rpt na; dis
11-23-1839 Ruth rpt na; dis
5- 6-1841 Priscilla of Wayne Co, Ind, -dt Joshua (dec) & Mary, m Nathan H Cammack at Milford MH
9-30-1841 Penelope, -dt Jonathan & Abigail of Wayne Co, Ind, m Solomon Elliott at Milford MH
10- 7-1841 Jesse of Wayne Co, Ind, -s Joshua (dec) & Mary, m Joanna Cammack at Milford MH
11-27-1841 Josiah appt an Elder
12- 6-1841 Ruth, -dt Joshua (dec) & Mary of N C, m Joel Morris at Milford MH
12- 6-1841 Joel, Wayne Co, Ind, -s Jehosaphat & Sarah (dec), m Ruth Morris at Milford MH
4-23-1842 Jesse & w Joanna gct Walnut Ridge MM, Ind
4-23-1842 Joel rpt guilty of fornication with her who is now his w; chm
6- 2-1842 Mary, -dt Caleb (dec) & Margaret, m Henry E Peelle at Milford MH
5-28-1842 Ruth rpt becoming a mother of an infant in less than 5 mo after m; chm
4-26-1845 Elias rpt mcd; dis
6-28-1845 Tombs A & Nathan O rocf Symons Creek MM, N C
8-28-1847 Nathan O, a minor, gct Spiceland MM, Ind
10-28-1848 Joshua gct Hopewell MM, Ind
11-30-1848 Elizabeth W, widow of Stephen Morris, & -dt Thomas (dec) & Anne Moore, Wayne Co, Ind, m Nathan Wasson at Milford MH
12-23-1848 Rachel rpt na; dis
5-28-1853 John & w Martha & ch Francis, David, Caleb & Ann rocf Walnut Ridge MM, Ind
10-22-1853 Rebecca Mundell (form Morris) rpt mcd by Hinkles Creek MM; dis - Hinkles Creek MM inf
11-25-1853 Rebecca Mundell (form Morris) - Dis ret by Hinkles Creek MM with rpt that she has dec
2-25-1854 Christopher gct Hopewell MM to m Margaret Bell

MILFORD

**MORRIS (Cont)**

|  |  |
|---|---|
| 9-23-1854 | Margaret B rocf Hopewell MM, Ind |
| 1-27-1855 | Jonathan gct Driftwood MM to m Patience Hall |
| 7-28-1855 | Patience rocf Driftwood MM, Ind |
| 5-24-1856 | Sarah gct Hopewell MM, Ind |
| 10-30-1856 | Abigail C of Wayne Co, Ind, -dt Jonathan & Abigail (both dec), m Calvin H Wasson at Milford MH |
| 11-28-1857 | Thomas B rpt mcd; dis |
| 4-29-1858 | Mary M, -dt Jonathan & Abigail (both dec), Wayne Co, Ind, m William C Stanley at Milford MH |
| 1-28-1860 | Francis W rpt mcd; chm |
| 10-26-1864 | Nathan O of Rush Co, Ind, -s Joseph H (dec), & Martha, m Pharaba A Wilson at Bethel MH |
| 3-25-1865 | Joel H & w Ruth & ch Theodocia Sarah & Theodore Augustus gct Spiceland MM, Ind |
| 6-24-1865 | David W rpt mcd; chm |
| 10-12-1865 | Ellen, -dt Stephen (dec) & Elizabeth of Cambridge City, Ind, m Caleb J Morris at Milford MH |
| 10-12-1865 | Caleb J of Cambridge City, Wayne Co, Ind, -s John & Martha, m Ellen Morris at Milford MH |
| 6-23-1866 | Christopher rpt mcd; chm |
| 6-23-1866 | Prudence rec in mbrp |
| 10-27-1866 | Pharaba gct Kansas MM, Kans |
| 1-25-1868 | Nathan O rocf Raysville MM, Ind |
| 1-25-1868 | Pharaba & s John C rocf Kansas MM, Kans |
| 3-27-1869 | Jonathan & w Patience & ch Albert, Olida, Oliver, Margaret & Joseph gct Driftwood MM, Ind |
| 2-26-1870 | Susanna Scofield (form Morris) rpt mcd; dis |
| 10-28-1871 | Susan rpt mcd; chm |
| 9-21-1872 | Susan gct Westfield MM, Ind |
| 11-22-1873 | Josiah gct Whitewater MM, Ind |
| 5-23-1874 | Mary C rocf Whitewater MM, Ind |
| 6-24-1876 | Francis B rel fr mbrp |
| 4-24-1880 | Albert C & w Esther & s Arthur rocf White Lick MM, Ind |
| 10-23-1880 | Nathan O & w Pharaba & ch Joseph C, Edith E, Franklin gct Spiceland MM, Ind |
| 5-27-1882 | Mary C gct Whitewater MM, Ind |
| 7-17-1884 | Florence Moore (form Morris) rpt mcd; chm |
| 7-17-1884 | Naomi C & ch Albert F, John B & Martha E rec in mbrp |

**MUNDELL**

|  |  |
|---|---|
| 10-22-1853 | Rebecca (form Morris) rpt mcd by Hinkles Creek MM |
| 3-25-1853 | Rebecca rpt dis by Hinkles Creek MM Rpt of dis ret with rpt of dec |

**MUNDEN**

|  |  |
|---|---|
| 12-18-1823 | Jesse rpt taking an affirmation to what he could not afterward make appear |
| 3-18-1824 | Jesse dis |
| 9-16-1824 | Jane appt to a comm |
| 6-25-1836 | Jesse & w Mary & ch Aseneth, Margaret & Calvin A rocf Symons Creek MM, N C |
| 8-26-1837 | Jesse & w Mary & ch Aseneth, Margaret & Calvin gct Duck Creek MM, Ind |

**MURLEY**

|  |  |
|---|---|
| 1-29-1891 | Alice C rec in mbrp |

**MURPHY**

|  |  |
|---|---|
| 11-27-1824 | Miles appt to a comm |

**MYERS**

|  |  |
|---|---|
| 1-24-1846 | Louisa (form Reagan) rpt mcd; dis |

**NEWBY**

|  |  |
|---|---|
| 8-14-1823 | Joseph rocf Driftwood MM, -end fr West Grove MM, Ind |
| 8-14-1823 | Elizabeth rocf Driftwood MM, -end fr West Grove MM, Ind |
| 1-15-1824 | Gabriel rocf Driftwood MM, Ind |
| 6-17-1824 | Esther & ch Rachel, Robert & Nathan rocf Driftwood MM, Ind |
| 10-23-1824 | Rebecca rocf West Grove MM, Ind |
| 8-2-1827 | Thomas, Wayne Co, Ind, -s William & Elizabeth, m Susannah Pearson at Milford MH |
| 11-24-1827 | Thomas & w gct Duck Creek MM, Ind |
| 3-9-1830 | Nathan rpt dp & na; dis |
| 6-26-1830 | William & w Elizabeth & s Cyrus & Joseph gct Duck Creek MM, Ind |
| 11-27-1830 | Rachel Allen (form Newby) rpt mcd; chm |
| 9-24-1831 | Joseph rpt jH; dis |
| 10-27-1832 | Joseph rocf Driftwood MM, Ind |
| 1-26-1833 | Thomas rocf Duck Creek MM, Ind |
| 2-23-1833 | Joseph gct Driftwood MM, Ind |
| 3-27-1833 | Jonathan, Henry Co, Ind, -s Gabriel & Elizabeth (dec), m Elizabeth Gilbert at Hopewell MH |
| 1-2-1834 | Thomas of Henry Co, Ind, -s William (dec) & Elizabeth, m Milicent Reece at Rich Square MH |
| 4-26-1834 | Thomas & w Millicent gct Spiceland MM, Ind |
| 2-28-1835 | Mary & dt Mildred rocf Driftwood MM, Ind |
| 2-28-1835 | Mary, -w of Joseph, rocf Driftwood MM, Ind |
| 5-25-1835 | Henry & s William & Nathan rocf Driftwood MM, Ind |
| 8-22-1835 | Thomas & w Millicent & dt Huldah rocf Spiceland MM, Ind |
| 11-28-1835 | Esther gct Mississinewa MM, Ind |
| 5-28-1836 | John & w Rebecca & ch Sarah, Roberson, Catharine, Reese, Henry, Thomas, John Letters & Gabriel rocf Suttons Creek MM, N C |
| 6-25-1836 | Frederick & w Sarah & ch William T, John T Albert, Oliver, Eliza, Lydia, Exum & Henry F rocf Piney Woods MM, N C |
| 9-24-1836 | Frederick & w Sarah & ch William J, John T, Albert, Oliver, Eliza, Lydia, Exum & Henry F gct Spiceland MM, Ind |
| 1-27-1837 | Thomas rpt apd & dancing; chm |
| 2-25-1837 | Robert gct Mississinewa MM, Ind |
| 6-24-1837 | Thomas rocf Driftwood MM, Ind |
| 8-28-1837 | Gabriel rpt dr; dis |
| 10-28-1837 | Sarah Thomson (form Newby) rpt mcd; dis |
| 5-26-1838 | Thomas gct Whitewater MM to m Rebecca Hill |
| 5-26-1838 | Jonathan rpt suing a mbr; chm |
| 1-26-1839 | Rebecca rocf Whitewater MM, Ind |
| 2-23-1839 | Thomas & w Mary & ch Sarah & Nathan rocf Driftwood MM, Ind |
| 2-23-1839 | Millicent rocf Driftwood MM, Ind |
| 6-27-1839 | Sarah, -dt Thomas & Mary of Wayne Co, Ind, m William Saint at Milford MH |
| 10-21-1839 | Thomas & w Mary & s Nathan gct Driftwood MM, Ind |
| 3-28-1840 | Millicent gct Driftwood MM, Ind |
| 5-28-1840 | Elias of Henry Co, Ind, -s Joseph & Penelope (both dec), m Tabitha Bond at Rich Square MH |
| 8-22-1840 | Tabitha gct Spiceland MM, Ind |
| 4-23-1842 | Rebecca, -w of Gabriel, & ch Mary Ann, Isam H, Elizabeth Melissa, Thomas Jefferson, Jane Amanda, Sarah Ellen & John Franklin gct Salem MM, Ia Terr |
| 12-24-1842 | John gct Duck Creek MM to m Rachel Brown |
| 6-24-1843 | Rachel & s Reuben Pearson rocf Duck Creek MM, Ind |
| 8-26-1843 | Mary, -w of Joseph, rpt jas; dis |
| 6-22-1844 | Thomas rpt jCampbellites; dis |
| 4-28-1845 | Catherine R, -dt John & Rebecca of Wayne Co, Ind, m Benjamin A Parker at Milford MH |
| 4-25-1846 | Henry & w Mary & ch Mildred, William Nathan & Matilda gct Walnut Ridge MM, Ind |
| 4-24-1847 | Naomi (form Lacy) rpt mcd; dis |
| 5-22-1847 | Henry rpt dis |
| 5-26-1849 | Caroline Vicory (form Newby) rpt mcd; dis |
| 9-6-1849 | Thomas, Wayne Co, Ind, -s John & Rebecca (dec), m Alice Dickinson at Milford MH |
| 2-23-1850 | Elizabeth Vicory (form Newby) rpt mcd; chm |
| 5-24-1851 | John L rpt indulging in fashions of the world by Driftwood MM |
| 8-23-1851 | John L chm for dp |

NEWBY (Cont)
4-26-1851    Elijah rpt apd by Driftwood MM; dis
5-24-1851    Aaron, a minor, gct Driftwood MM, Ind
9-27-1851    John L gct Driftwood MM, Ind
9-25-1852    Thomas & w Alice & ch William H & Jonathan N gct Whitewater MM, Ind
2-26-1853    Abigail gct Richland MM (-end by Richland MM & ret)
3-25-1854    Margaret gct Salem MM, Ia
3-25-1854    Susan, William & Hannah, ch of Joseph & Elizabeth (dec), gct Salem MM, Ia
8-31-1854    John, Wayne Co, Ind, -s Thomas (dec) & Mary, m Mary Hunnicutt at Milford MH
5-24-1855    Thomas & w Margaret P & ch James, William Charles, Martha Parker, Sarah Isabella, Thomas Richard, Jane & Annie rocf Piney Woods MM, N C
6-28-1856    Gabriel rpt mcd; dis sent to East Grove MM, Ia
6-28-1860    Mary, -dt John & Rebecca (dec), Wayne Co, Ind, m Thomas Cox at Milford MH
10-27-1860   Abigail rpt na & att dances by Salem MM, Ia; dis
11-26-1862   Martha P, -dt Thomas & Margaret of Henry Co, Ind, m Asahel H Hussey at Bethel MH
6- 1-1864    Isabel, -dt Thomas & Margaret P of Wayne Co, Ind, m Mathew Terrell at Bethel MH
5-28-1864    Jeremiah L gct Kansas MM, Kans
3-25-1865    Franklin rpt mcd; dis
5-27-1865    James rpt mcd & has had Military Serv; dis
7-22-1865    William C gct Short Creek MM, Ohio to m Olive B Terril
8-25-1866    Olive T rocf Short Creek MM, Ohio
4-22-1867    James rpt mcd; chm
7-26-1873    Mary Moore rec in mbrp
11-28-1874   William C & w Olive & ch Margaret T & William Stanley gct Fountain MM, Colo
6-23-1877    James W & w Mary & ch Richard, Annie & Elizabeth gct Maryville MM, Tenn
5-28-1881    William C & w Olive & ch Margaret, William Stanley & Edward C rocf Fountain MM, Colo
8-28-1881    Margaret R gct Maryville MM, Tenn
2-25-1882    William & w Olive & ch Margaret, William & Edward gct Maryville MM, Tenn
4-23-1885    Ella rel fr mbrp

NEWLIN
7-22-1882    John & w Lucinda & ch Matilda & Luther rocf Mill Creek MM
1-29-1891    Luther G rel fr mbrp
5-28-1891    Edgar S rocf Whitewater MM, Ind

NEWMAN
1-28-1886    Virgil rec in mbrp

NEWSOM
7-26-1828    Luke & w Elizabeth & dt Martha rocf Back Creek MM, N C
7-25-1829    Luke & w Elizabeth & ch Martha & Henry gct Duck Creek MM, Ind

NICHOLSON
5-26-1832    Peninah & dt Peninah rocf Suttons Creek MM, N C
5-26-1832    George, Nathan & Parker, minors, rocf Suttons Creek MM, N C
8-24-1833    Peninah & ch Nathan, Parker & Peninah gct Duck Creek MM, Ind
8-24-1835    George gct Duck Creek MM to m Mary Hill
2-27-1836    George gct Walnut Ridge MM, Ind
7-25-1857    John H rst in mbrp w/c Salem MM, N J
2-25-1860    Anna rocf Piney Woods MM, N C
8-25-1860    John H gct Bridgeport MM, Ind
5-25-1866    Anna gct Piney Woods MM, N C

NIXON
11-28-1829   Samuel & w Rhoda & ch Robert, Joseph & Susanna Butler & Emily & Oliver Nixon, rocf Deep River MM, N C
7-24-1830    Samuel & w Rhoda & ch Susannah H Butler & Emily Jane, Martha Ann & Oliver W Nixon gct New Garden MM, Ind

11-27-1830   Miriam rpt na & making her home at a place that is not commendable; dis
5-28-1831    Samuel R & w Martha & dt Jane rocf Whitewater MM, Ind
3-23-1833    Gabriel & w Mary & dt Letica Ann rocf Whitewater MM, Ind
9-27-1834    Lydia rpt unchaste; dis
1-24-1835    John rpt mcd
5-25-1835    John dis for mcd
6-27-1835    William & w Achsah rocf Suttons Creek MM, N C
3-23-1836    Gabriel & w Mary & ch Letica Ann, Pheneas & Daniel M gct West Grove MM, Ind
5-28-1836    William rpt upl & na; dis
10-28-1837   Sarah A rocf Western Branch MM
1-26-1839    Elizabeth rpt na & dp
3-23-1839    Elizabeth dis for na & dp
6-22-1839    Sarah gct Whitewater MM, Ind
9-25-1839    Samuel R & w Martha & ch Margaret Jane, Ann, Alfred & James gct Salem MM, Ia Terr
4-25-1840    Martha & ch Margaret J, Ann, Alfred & James rocf Salem MM, Ia
6-27-1840    Benjamin & Lydia, ch of John (dec), rocf Symons Creek MM, N C
8-22-1840    Benjamin & Lydia, minors, gct Walnut Ridge MM, Ind
10-24-1840   Huldah, a minor u/c Benjamin & Amy Stratton, rec in mbrp
4- 2-1846    Jane, -dt Josiah & Mary (dec) of Wayne Co, Ind, m Peter Coggshall at Milford MH
7-25-1846    Josiah Jr rpt dp & na
10-24-1846   Josiah Jr dis for dp & na
5-26-1849    Martha N & ch Margaret Jane, Ann, Alfred, James Smith & Samuel Robinson gct Salem MM, Ia
10-26-1850   Nancy Pumphrey (form Nixon) rpt mcd; dis
8-28-1852    Zachariah rpt na & jMeth; dis
10-23-1852   Mary Canaday (form Nixon) rpt mcd; dis
11-25-1854   Margaret Stonebraker (form Nixon) rpt mcd by Hinkles Creek MM, Ind
4-28-1855    Margaret Stonebraker (form Nixon) rpt dis by Hinkles Creek MM, Ind
3-28-1868    Josiah gct Spiceland MM, Ind

NOLL
12-25-1884   Jacob rec in mbrp

NORTHERN
11-28-1891   Isa Dora & Daisy rec in mbrp

ODEM
4-26-1832    Lydia (form Roberts) rpt mcd ( a mbr of our Society & living some distance away)
7-28-1832    Lydia dis for mcd

OFTERDINGER
4-28-1838    Hannah rocf West Grove MM, Ind
10-22-1842   Hannah gct Springfield MM, Ind

OUTLAND
2-28-1883    David A, Henry Co, Ind, -s David & Margaret C (dec), of Hancock Co, Ind, m Rhoda E Miles at res of Lindley Miles
10-27-1883   Amos rocf Walnut Ridge MM

OVERMAN
5-23-1840    Susannah (form Lacy) rpt mcd by Westfield MM; dis

PADDOCK
11-27-1890   John C rec in mbrp
2-23-1893    John rel fr mbrp

PALIN
10-23-1824   Huldah (form Hunt) rpt mcd; chm
6-23-1827    Exum gct Duck Creek MM to m Elizabeth Bond
6-27-1829    Exum & w Betsey & s Thomas rocf Duck Creek MM, Ind
12-28-1833   Mary dec m int with Phineas Lamb

MILFORD

PALIN (Cont)
1-25-1834  Mary & Phineas Lamb - m int discontinued
5-24-1834  Mary Hasket (form Palin) rpt mcd to 1st cousin; dis
12-27-1834 Sarah rpt for unbecoming conduct & abusive language
4-25-1835  Sarah dis
10-24-1835 Exum N rpt apd & na; dis
12-26-1835 Betsey rpt na & disunity; dis
8-24-1839  Penninah & ch Lucinda, William, Irena & Sylvanus rocf Spiceland MM, Ind
12-25-1841 Henry gct Hopewell MM to m Miriam Pike, a widow
7-23-1842  Miriam & ch Mary & Stanford Pike rocf Hopewell MM, Ind
5-24-1845  Henry & Gulielma, ch of Exum, gct Sugar River MM, Ind
2-28-1846  This mtg inf by Sugar River MM that they had rec cert for ch of Exum, but they lived about 30 miles distant in Shawnee Prairie, Sugar River is rq to forward
4-25-1846  Sugar River infs cert for Henry & Gulielma, ch of Exum, forwarded to Greenfield MM, Ind
1-23-1847  Mary (form Pike) rpt mcd by Spiceland MM; chm
7-24-1847  Mary gct Spiceland MM, Ind
1-27-1849  Miriam Wickersham (form Palin) rpt mcd within 5 mo after dec of husband; dis

PALMER
11-30-1842 David, Henry Co, Ind, -s John & Ann, m Mary Elliott, widow of John Elliott, at Bethel MH
1-28-1843  Mary, -w of David, & ch Isaac, Mary Ann, Martha, Melissa J & John Elliott gct Duck Creek MM

PARKER
1-22-1824  Robert of Whitewater MM, -s Jeremiah & Keren, m Miriam Bell at Milford MH
4-15-1824  Miriam appt to a comm
6-17-1824  Robert rocf Whitewater MM, Ind
2-28-1829  William rocf Rich Square MM, N C, -end to Duck Creek MM, Ind
11-27-1830 Jeremiah & w Keren rocf Whitewater MM, Ind
11-27-1830 Isaac rocf Whitewater MM, Ind
3-30-1831  Isaac, -s Jeremiah & Keren of Henry Co, Ind, m Mary Stratton at Hopewell MH
8-30-1832  William of Rush Co, Ind, -s Josiah & Martha of Northampton Co, N C, m Almeda Johnson at Rich Square MH
2-23-1833  Almeda gct Duck Creek MM, Ind
10-26-1844 Joseph R rocf Dartmouth MM, Mass, -end to Symons Creek MM, N C
4-28-1845  Benjamin A, -s William & Elizabeth (dec), m Catharine R Newby at Milford MH
6-28-1845  Catharine R gct Driftwood MM, Ind
12-22-1855 Abigail (form Charles) rpt mcd by Wabash MM
9-24-1864  George H rec in mbrp
7-22-1865  George H gct Rich Square MM, N C
2-25-1871  Robert J rocf Walnut Ridge MM, Ind
1-24-1874  Robert J gct Duck Creek MM, Ind
3-24-1877  James B & w Hannah & s Charles rocf Walnut Ridge MM, Ind
12-28-1878 Mary B rocf Deer Creek MM
2-28-1880  James B & w Hannah & s Charles gct Walnut Ridge MM, Ind

PARKS
1-26-1856  Abigail (form Charles) rpt mcd; dis

PATTERSON
6-25-1831  William & w Elizabeth, a min, rocf Somerset MM, Ohio
7-28-1832  William & w Elizabeth, a min, gct Somerset MM, Ohio
12-22-1832 James Boswell gct Somerset MM, Ohio to m Eliza Patterson
3-30-1842  Elihu, Rush Co, Ind, -s Jared & Angeline, m Rachel Cox at Bethel MH

1-28-1843  Rachel, -w of Elihu, gct Walnut Ridge MM, Ind
11-23-1844 Rachel rocf Walnut Ridge MM, Ind
2-26-1845  Rachel, widow of Elihu Patterson & -dt Joseph & Elizabeth Cox of Wayne Co, Ind, m James Binford at Bethel MH

PAXTON
5-22-1830  Sarah, mbr West Grove MM, rpt mcd; dis by West Grove on 8-28-1830
12-24-1831 Charles, mbr Stillwater MM, Ohio, rpt jH; dis
3-23-1833  Ruth, Lydia, Aaron & Webster, minor ch of Benjamin, rocf Stillwater MM, Ohio
10-24-1835 Ruth rpt na & dp; dis
2-27-1836  Louisa (form Coffin) rpt mcd; dis
1-27-1838  Aaron rpt na & mcd; dis
1-28-1886  James W rec in mbrp
2-21-1889  James W & Mattie rel fr mbrp

PEARSON
10-16-1823 Nathan appt to a comm
12-18-1823 Catharine rocf Whitewater MM, Ind
12-25-1823 Catharine, -dt Nathan & Mary (dec), Henry Co, Ind, m Gabriel Ratliff at Duck Creek MH
2-12-1824  Jonathan Jr rpt getting angry & offering to fight; chm
11-20-1824 Peter & w Eunice & ch Enoch & Isom rocf New Garden MM, Ind
5-28-1825  Huldah Draper (form Pearson) rpt mcd; chm
6-25-1825  Jonathan, the Younger, rpt training in the Militia; dis
6-25-1825  Levi rocf Whitewater MM, Ind
7-23-1825  Jesse & w Mary & ch Jesse, James, Susanna & Rebecca rocf Blue River MM, Ind
9-24-1825  Levi gct New Garden MM to m Huldah Thomas
9-24-1825  John & w Lydia & dt Huldah rocf New Garden MM, Ind
9-24-1825  Elliott rocf Whitewater MM
           Note: Not given in WW, but gives Bailey & William
8- 2-1827  Susannah, -dt Jesse & Polly of Henry Co, Ind, m Thomas Newby at Milford MH
3-27-1830  Nancy & ch - way not clear to get Duck Creek MM, Ind
3-27-1830  Jonathan gct Duck Creek MM, Ind
4-24-1830  Nancy rpt dp & na by Duck Creek MM; dis
7-24-1830  David, Lydia Jane, Eli, Zeno, Moses & Sarah, ch of Nancy, gct Duck Creek MM, Ind
5-26-1832  Jesse & w Polly & ch Rebecca, Jesse & James gct Duck Creek MM, Ind
7-26-1834  Exum rst in mbpr w/c Whitewater MM, Ind
3-28-1835  Exum gct Duck Creek MM, Ind
12-26-1840 Lydia rocf Spiceland MM, Ind
6-24-1843  Rachel Newby & s Reuben Pearson rocf Duck Creek MM, Ind
6-27-1846  Sarah rocf Mississinewa MM, Ind
4-22-1848  Sarah gct Mississinewa MM, Ind
12-25-1852 Reuben rpt att mcd of a mbr; dis
3-24-1855  Mary E (form Elliott) rpt mcd; chm
5-26-1855  Mary E gct Dover MM, Ohio
12-27-1856 Thomas B & w Mary & s Charles E rocf Hopewell MM, Ind
10-22-1859 Eliza Ann (form Stanley) rpt mcd by Honey Creek MM, Ind; chm
2-25-1860  Eliza Ann gct Honey Creek MM, Ind
4-28-1860  Thomas B & w Mary E & ch Exum & Margaret Susan gct Dover MM, Ohio
7-22-1876  Thomas & w Mary & ch Gilbert, Susan, Elizabeth & Flety rocf Chestnut Hill MM, Ia
2-28-1880  Rebecca Jane rec in mbrp

PEAS
2-25-1892  Isaac W rec in mbrp
7-28-1892  Sarah L & ch Charles Franklin, Clarence Earl & Laura P rec in mbrp

MILFORD

## PEEBLES
| | |
|---|---|
| 10-25-1845 | Elijah rocf Newberry MM, Ohio |
| 12-28-1850 | Elijah gct Whitewater MM, Ind |

## PEELLE
| | |
|---|---|
| 7-27-1839 | Henry Edward rocf Rich Square MM, N C |
| 6- 2-1842 | Henry E of Wayne Co, Ind, -s James & Ruth of Northampton Co, N C, m Mary Morris at Milford MH |
| 2-27-1858 | Mary appt an Elder |
| 5-28-1859 | Henry E appt an Elder |
| 2-22-1862 | William rst in mbrp (mbr Rich Square MM, N C) |
| 12-27-1862 | William rocf Richland MM, Ind |
| 12-26-1865 | Caleb M of Wayne Co, Ind, -s Henry & Mary, m Maria Smith at res of James Smith |
| 2-22-1868 | James rpt mcd; clm |
| 2-22-1868 | Adaline (form Cammack) rpt mcd; chm |
| 9-10-1868 | Elizabeth, -dt Henry & Mary of Wayne Co, Ind, m Albert W Fletcher at Milford MH |
| 4-24-1875 | Caleb & w Maria & ch Frank Henry, Walter & Louisa gct Raysville MM, Ind |
| 10-27-1877 | Stephen gct Westfield MM, Ind |
| 5-24-1879 | James & w Adeline gct Hopewell MM, Ind |
| 7-26-1879 | Emma F E gct Dover MM, Ohio |
| 11-27-1884 | Charles gct Whitewater MM, Ind |
| 3-26-1885 | Henry E & w Mary & ch Mary Olive gct Spicewood MM, Ind |
| 11-24-1887 | John gct Westfield MM, Ind |
| 11-24-1887 | Deborah gct Whitewater MM, Ind |

## PEGG
| | |
|---|---|
| 3- 9-1830 | Sarah rocf Whitewater MM, Ind |
| 8-24-1833 | Sarah gct Spiceland MM, Ind |

## PEMBERTON
| | |
|---|---|
| 12-28-1867 | Sophia Huddleston (form Pemberton) rpt mcd; rel fr mbrp |

## PENNINGTON
| | |
|---|---|
| 12-25-1824 | Josiah & w Deborah & ch Levi, Talbot, Mary, Susannah, John, Eliza & Rachel rocf Miami MM, Ohio, -end fr Whitewater MM, Ind |
| 7-22-1826 | Ann rocf Springboro MM, Ohio |
| 1-23-1830 | Ann rpt att a ball & jH; dis |
| 1-16-1871 | John P of Henry Co, Ind, -s Josiah & Deborah, m Melissa J Elliott at res of Melissa Elliott |
| 4-22-1871 | Melissa gct Spiceland MM, Ind |

## PERISHO
| | |
|---|---|
| 4-28-1832 | Nathan & fam rocf Symons Creek MM, N C |

## PERKINS
| | |
|---|---|
| 4-27-1867 | Eliza B (form Cox) rpt mcd; chm |
| 5-28-1885 | Elizabeth rel fr mbrp |

## PICKERING
| | |
|---|---|
| 9-18-1823 | Jonas & w Ruth & ch Abner, Abigail, Sarah, Samuel, Phebe, Jonas, Mahlon, Ruthanna & Jordan rocf Flushing MM, Ohio |
| 9-18-1823 | Samuel & w & fam rocf Flushing MM, Ohio |
| 4-27-1826 | Abigail, -dt Jonas & Ruth of Henry Co, Ind, m Jonathan Butler at Duck Creek MH |
| 4-24-1826 | Samuel appt an Elder |
| 9-27-1834 | James, Samuel, Esther, Susanna, Phebe Ann, Mary & Leah, ch of Phebe, rocf Duck Creek MM, Ind |
| 9-24-1836 | Susannah Smith (form Pickering) rpt mcd; dis |
| 3-24-1838 | James gct Spiceland MM to m Ann Pitts |
| 10-24-1840 | Sarah Ann (form Smith), mbr of Plainfield MM, Ohio, mcd; dis |
| 10-25-1845 | Mary rpt guilty of unchastity by Duck Creek MM; dis |
| 11-22-1845 | Leah Stanley (form Pickering) rpt mcd by Duck Creek MM; - now resides at Back Creek MM |
| 9-26-1846 | Leah Stanley (form Pickering) - dis - dis sent to Mississinewa MM, Ind |

## PICKETT - PIGGOTT
| | |
|---|---|
| 10-16-1823 | Joseph & Priscilla & ch Tamer, Anna, Lydia, Mary, Sarah & Joseph rocf West Grove MM, Ind |
| 5-28-1831 | Jonathan Kindley gct Chester MM to m Hannah Pickett |
| 12-22-1832 | Joshua & w Sarah rocf Chester MM, Ind |
| 2-22-1834 | Anna & ch Esther T, Rhoda H, Benjamin N & Elizabeth Hane rocf Spiceland MM, Ind |
| 12-27-1834 | Sarah gct White River MM, Ind |
| 12-27-1834 | Ann & ch Rhoda, Benjamin, Esther & Betsy gct Spiceland MM, Ind (Was not rec & cert was ret) |
| 8-26-1854 | Suanna, a minor, gct Westfield MM, Ind |
| 8-26-1854 | Benjamin N rpt na by Chester MM |
| 12-23-1854 | Benjamin N - Chester rpts dis |

## PIERCE
| | |
|---|---|
| 8-27-1825 | Samuel & w Lydia & ch Gideon, Kersy & David rocf Cincinnati MM, Ohio |
| 11-22-1828 | Lydia rpt jH; dis |
| 1-24-1829 | Samuel rpt jH; dis |
| 12-22-1866 | Samuel & w Ann & ch Esther Milly, John Paine & Sophia Pemberton rocf Dover MM, Ohio |
| 5-22-1869 | Samuel & w Ann & ch Esther Milly & John gct Whitewater MM, Ind |

## PIKE
| | |
|---|---|
| 5-24-1834 | Wilson & w Miriam & ch Milah, Penninah, Jordon & Mary Ann rocf Symons Creek MM, N C |
| 12-25-1841 | Henry Palin gct Hopewell MM to m Miriam Pike |
| 7-23-1842 | Mary & Stanford, ch of Miriam Pike Palin, rocf Hopewell MM, Ind |
| 12-27-1845 | Jordan rocf Hopewell MM, Ind |
| 1-23-1847 | Mary Palin (form Pike) rpt mcd by Spiceland MM ; chm on 6-26-1847 |
| 7-29-1847 | Mila Ann rpt unchaste; dis |
| 5-26-1849 | Jordan rpt mcd by Mississinewa MM; dis |
| 5-25-1850 | Stanford, a minor, gct Hopewell MM, Ind |

## PITMAN
| | |
|---|---|
| 7-25-1835 | Robert rocf Deep River MM, N C |
| 8-26-1837 | Robert & w Mary & ch Milton & Mary gct Duck Creek MM, Ind |
| 2-26-1842 | Robert & w Mary & ch Milton & Mary rocf Spiceland MM, Ind |
| 2-28-1852 | Milton rpt na & dp; dis |
| 4-28-1883 | Mary rel fr mbrp |

## PLACE - PLEAS
| | |
|---|---|
| 1-27-1827 | Maurice rocf Whitewater MM, Ind |
| 4-26-1828 | Maurice gct Miami MM, Ohio |
| 4-28-1827 | Ruth rec in mbrp |
| 9-24-1831 | Aaron & w Lydia & s Elwood rocf Whitewater MM, Ind |
| 12-28-1833 | Ruth rpt "leaving the necessary care of her fam & travelling about in an unbecoming manner making some appearance in the Ministry contrary to the order of Friends & for telling untruths.." Comm appt to tr w/h |
| 1-24-1834 | Ruth - Comm rpt "they did not find her in a suitable disposition of mind to make satisfaction for her misconduct, & they thought her partially deranged" |
| 5-24-1834 | Ruth dis |

## POWELL
| | |
|---|---|
| 8-25-1883 | James C rocf Hopewell MM, Ind |
| 2-21-1889 | James C gct Hopewell MM, Ind |
| 2-26-1891 | James C rel fr mbrp |

## PRAY
| | |
|---|---|
| 12-25-1824 | Enos, a minor, rocf Whitewater MM, Ind |
| 8-25-1827 | Enos, a minor, gct Elk MM, Ohio |

MILFORD

## PRAY (Cont)

4-25-1857 Enos G, a min, & w Elvira & ch Martha Rachel, Sybil J, Rhoda J, Joseph J, Anna Maria, Samuel Dilwin & Enos Edwin rocf Springfield MM, Ohio

4-25-1857 William S rocf Springfield MM, Ohio

4-25-1857 Elizabeth M rocf Springfield MM, Ohio

8-26-1857 Elizabeth M, -dt Enos G & Elvira of Wayne Co, Ind, m Zacheus Test at Bethel MH

10-26-1861 William rpt mcd; chm

11-23-1861 Nancy H rec in mbrp

10-22-1864 William & w Nancy H gct Bridgeport MM, Ind

11-24-1866 Enos G & w Elvira & ch Rachel, Sylvia, Rhoda, Joseph, Anna Maria, Samuel & Enos gct Indianapolis MM, Ind

## PRESNELL

3-18-1824 Daniel & w Christena rocf Back Creek MM, N C, -end fr West Grove MM, Ind

2-26-1825 Mary rocf New Garden MM, Ind

3-31-1825 Mary, -dt Daniel & Pleasant of Henry Co, Ind, m Samuel Moon at Duck Creek MH

3-26-1825 Daniel Sr & wife - a comm appt "to inspect the situation of- & devise such methods for their relief as may appear necessary"

7-23-1825 Daniel Sr & wife - Comm rpt "that the matter be discontinued and be no longer a Mtg concern"

2-25-1826 Daniel & w Pleasant & ch Benoni, Sarah, Daniel, John, Henry & Nathan rocf New Garden MM, Ind

3-25-1826 Daniel Sr & wife rpt that they need immediate assistance of friends

4-22-1826 $20 raised for relief (Daniel Sr & fam)

## PRETLOW

3-21-1861 Robert S & w Isabella & ch James Thomas, Deborah Harris, Sarah Isabella & Chlotilda Ladd rocf Lower MM, Va

2-26-1870 James gct Lower MM, Va

10-23-1875 James & w Maria & ch Gertrude E & Joel C rec in mbrp

12-24-1881 Joseph J gct Poplar Run MM, Ind

1-28-1882 James L & w Maria & ch Gertrude E, Joel C & John gct Lower MM, Va

10-23-1890 Isabella gct Minneapolis MM, Minn

11-28-1891 Deborah H, Chlotilda & Elizabeth gct Minneapolis MM, Minn

1-28-1892 Isabella gct Minneapolis MM, Minn

3-23-1893 Robert E & w Emma & fam gct Sugar Plain MM, Ind

## PRICE

12-18-1823 Rice rocf Whitewater MM, Ind

7-15-1824 Katharine & s Robert rocf Whitewater MM, Ind

2-26-1825 Susanna & dt Sally rec in mbrp

## PRITCHARD

1-22-1842 William B H, -s William (dec) & Mary (now Mary Saint) rec in mbrp at Milford MM, Ind

6-24-1843 Calvin W, -s William (dec) rocf Spiceland MM, Ind

11-25-1843 Calvin W & William B H, minor ch of William (dec) & Mary (now Mary Saint), gct Salem MM, Ia Terr

## PUCKETT

9-27-1837 Greenly of Wayne Co, Ind, -s Daniel & Celia (dec), m Margaret A Heavenridge at Hopewell MH

6-23-1838 Margaret A gct New Garden MM, Ind

7-25-1840 Greenly & w Margaret & s Samuel rocf New Garden MM, Ind

## PUGH

5-26-1832 Rachel rocf Cincinnati MM, Ohio

## PUMPHREY

10-26-1850 Nancy (form Nixon) rpt mcd

12-28-1850 Nancy (form Nixon) dis for mcd

## PUNTENEY

5-24-1851 Sarah Ann (form Bogue) rpt mcd; dis

## PUSEY

8-24-1844 Jesse & w Jane & s William B rocf Spiceland MM, Ind

8-24-1844 Joel & w Hannah & dt Rachel rocf Spiceland MM, Ind

3-22-1845 Jesse F & w Jane & s William B gct Walnut Ridge MM, Ind

7-27-1850 Joel & w Hannah & dt Rachel gct Spiceland MM, Ind

## RATLIFF

8-14-1823 Richard appt to a comm

12-18-1823 Richard Jr appt to a comm

12-25-1823 Gabriel, Henry Co, Ind, -s Richard & Elizabeth, m Catharine Pearson at Duck Creek MH

6-17-1824 Joseph & w Rebeckah & ch Jane, Reubin, Huldah, Anna, Elizabeth, Jesse & Eli rocf Chester MM, Ind

11-27-1824 Phineas rocf Whitewater MM, Ind

12-25-1824 Hannah & dt Achsah rocf Whitewater MM, Ind

12-25-1824 Benjamin rocf Whitewater MM, Ind

11-26-1825 Joshua & Letitia & ch Mary, Thomas, Samuel, Ephraim, Joseph, Branson & Amelia rocf Whitewater MM, Ind

2-16-1826 Jonathan of Henry Co, Ind, -s Richard & Elizabeth, m Sarah Bogue at Milford MH

8-26-1826 Nathan & w Lydia & ch Polly, Alfred, Patsy, Joseph & Jane rocf Deep Creek MM, N C

8-29-1827 Cornelius of Henry Co, Ind, -s Richard (dec) & Elizabeth, m Abigail Gilbert at Hopewell MH

8-25-1832 Elizabeth Maudlin (form Ratliff) rpt mcd with 1st cousin

10-27-1832 Elizabeth Maudlin (form Ratliff) dis for mcd with 1st cousin

5-25-1833 Nathan & w Lydia & ch Mary, Alfred, Joseph, Levi, Martha, Anna & Nathan gct Duck Creek MM, Ind

11-29-1837 Elias, Henry Co, Ind, -s Jonathan & Sarah (dec), m Miriam Bogue at Hopewell MH

12-2-1840 John P, Henry Co, Ind, -s Jonathan & Sarah (dec), m Hannah Gilbert at Hopewell MH

5-30-1850 Reuben, Henry Co, Ind, -s Joseph (dec) & Rebecca, m Penelope N Bell, a widow, at Milford MH

8-24-1850 Penelope N & her dt Lydia Jane Bell gct Duck Creek MM, Ind

9-4-1886 Annie M gct New Castle MM, Ind

## RAYLE

9-22-1860 Mary & dt Isabella rec in mbrp

6-22-1861 Mary & dt Isabella gct Greenwood MM, Ind

1-26-1884 Lafayette rec in mbrp

## REAGAN

11-13-1823 Reason appt to a comm

3-26-1825 John rpt "being lawfully charged with being the father of an illegitimate ch, absconding to avoid the penalty of the law & for having been intoxicated"

4-23-1825 John - Caesars Creek MM, Ohio rq to tr w/h

7-23-1825 Thomas rpt na & dp; dis

9-23-1825 John - Comm rpt no success in tr w/h; dis

1-24-1829 William rpt na, dp & upl; dis

11-28-1829 Reason & w Mary & ch John, Dinah, Rachel & Mary gct Caesars Creek MM, Ohio

2-23-1829 Ruth rpt na; dis

4-27-1839 Wiley rpt na; dis

1-24-1846 Louisa Meyers (form Reagan) rpt mcd; dis

5-22-1847 Thomas rpt dp & na

MILFORD

REAGAN (Cont)
5-22-1847    Ann Maria Calaway (form Reagan) rpt mcd; dis
6-26-1847    Thomas rpt dp & na - Comm rpt he was in school at Greencastle
9-25-1847    Thomas - Case dismissed
11-23-1850   Sarah Frazier (form Reagan) rpt mcd; dis
9-25-1852    Thomas rpt na & mcd by Duck Creek MM; dis rpt by Duck Creek MM on 2-26-1853

REECE
7-15-1824    John & w Nancy & ch Nathan, Needham, Millicent, Daniel, Elias, Christian, Jane & John rocf West Grove MM, Ind
3-22-1828    John & w Ann & ch Needham, Millicent, Daniel, Elias Christian, Jane & John rocf Duck Creek MM, Ind
6-27-1829    Nathan & w Susanna & s Charles rocf Duck Creek MM, Ind
9- 1-1830    Christiana, -dt John & Ann of Henry Co, Ind, m Aaron Hastings at Hopewell MH
8-27-1831    Daniel gct West Grove MM to m Sarah Hastings
10-22-1831   Celia rocf West Grove MM, Ind
11-13-1831   Jane, -dt John (dec) & Anna of Henry Co, Ind, m William Hastings at Hopewell MH
1- 2-1834    Millicent, -dt John (dec) & Ann of Henry Co, Ind, m Thomas Newby at Rich Square MH
3-26-1836    Needham gct West Grove MM to m Celia Townsend
12-24-1836   Daniel & w Sarah & s David gct Walnut Ridge MM, Ind
7-31-1839    John of Henry Co, Ind, -s John (dec) & Ann, m Gulielma Dennis at Hopewell MH
5-23-1840    John & w Gulielma gct Walnut Ridge MM, Ind

REYNOLDS
9-18-1823    Benjamin appt to a comm
12-18-1823   Ann appt to a comm
9-26-1827    Elizabeth, -dt Benjamin & Anna of Wayne Co, Ind, m Henry Hester at Bethel MH
1- 2-1828    Daniel of Wayne Co, Ind, -s Benjamin & Ann, m Margaret Morris at Bethel MH
6-28-1828    Benjamin rpt "opposing the proceedings of the YM"; dis
11-22-1828   Ann rpt jH; dis
4-25-1829    Phebe rpt jH; dis
11-27-1830   Josiah rpt jH; dis
2-26-1831    Daniel rpt na & att mcd; chm
2-23-1833    Reuben rpt na & mcd; dis
4-27-1833    David rpt na; dis
1-29-1834    Hannah, -dt Benjamin & Ann of Wayne Co, Ind, m Isaac Hester at Bethel MH
4-22-1837    Sarah Burgess (form Reynolds) rpt na & mcd; dis
8-28-1837    Stephen, rpt jH
10-28-1837   Stephen dis for jH
9-22-1838    Benjamin rpt mcd & jMeth; dis
12-28-1839   Amos rpt na & mcd; dis
1-27-1844    Anna Huddleston (form Reynolds) rpt mcd
3-23-1844    Anna Huddleston (form Reynolds) dis for mcd
3-25-1865    Daniel & w Margaret & dt Martha rocf Hopewell MM, Ind
11-23-1867   Martha Clark (form Reynolds) rpt mcd; rel fr mbrp
12-26-1874   Josiah & w Lucretia & s William H & adopted dt Jennie rocf Hopewell MM, Ind
7-24-1884    Jennie (form Bartlett) rel fr mbrp

RHINARD
12-24-1825   Jacob & w Elizabeth & dt Margaret & Katharine rocf West Grove MM, Ind

RIDGEWAY
7-26-1834    John & w Ruth & ch Abijah, Lydia, Daniel, Jane, Richard, Ruth Anna & John rocf Flushing MM, Ohio
8-25-1838    John & w Ruth & ch Elijah, Lydia, Jane, Ruth Anna, Richard & John gct Westfield MM, Ind

ROBERTS
10-22-1825   Mary rst in mbrp w/c New Garden MM, N C

2-24-1827    Lydia, -dt Mary, rec in mbrp
6-25-1831    Amy rocf White River MM, Ind
4-26-1832    Lydia Odem (form Roberts) rpt mcd 'living at some distance'; dis
5-26-1832    Mary rpt "assisting in preparing the entertainment & being present at the m of her dt"
8-25-1832    Mary chm
10-27-1838   Mary & her sisters Sarah, Hannah & Deborah D rocf Philadelphia MM, Pa
12- 3-1846   Deborah D, -dt Daniel & Hannah (both dec), m Solomon Horney at Milford MH
4-25-1857    Sarah gct Whitewater MM, Ind

ROBEY
4-25-1874    Mary J & ch Emma & Oscar rec in mbrp

ROBINSON
1-22-1848    Rachel (form Cammack) rpt mcd; chm
4-22-1854    Rachel gct Red Cedar MM, Ia
5-24-1873    Rachel gct Chester MM, Ind

ROCKAFELLOW
9-22-1883    Charles W & w Minnie W rocf Raysville MM, Ind
10-27-1887   Minnie H gct Indianapolis MM, Ind

ROTHERMILL
1-28-1886    Grant & Mary rec in mbrp
1-28-1886    Harry rec in mbrp

RUMLEY
8-22-1829    Maria (form Willets) rpt mcd
10-24-1829   Maria (form Willets) dis for mcd

SAINT
1-28-1826    William appt to a comm
12-23-1826   Thomas & w Margaret & ch William, Joseph Thomas, Samuel & Daniel rocf Blue River MM, Ind
11-28-1827   Julianna, -dt William & Achsah of Wayne Co, Ind, m John Cook at West Union MH
6-26-1830    Exum gct Duck Creek MM
11-27-1834   Alpheus, -s William & Achsah, m Irena Hiatt at Milford MH
5-23-1835    Alpheus & w Irena gct Duck Creek MM, Ind
6-27-1835    Alpheus & w Irena rocf Duck Creek MM, Ind
4-23-1836    Alpheus & w Irena gct Duck Creek MM, Ind
10-23-1836   William & w Achsah & ch Jennet, Doughty, Joseph, Jonathan, Daniel, Milton, William & Cynthia gct Duck Creek MM, Ind
2-24-1838    Thomas rpt mcd within a yr after dec of former w
4-28-1838    Thomas chm for mcd
6-27-1839    William of Wayne Co, Ind, -s Thomas & Margaret (dec), m Sarah Newby at Milford MH
11-23-1839   William & w Sarah gct Driftwood MM
1-25-1840    Sarah & Richard, ch of Thomas, gct Whitewater MM
8-28-1841    Mary rst in mbrp w/c Blue River MM, Ind
10-23-1841   Thomas Jr gct Blue River MM to m Mary Ann Albertson
1-22-1842    William Barnabas Hobbs Pritchard, -s Mary Pritchard (now Mary Saint) rec in mbrp
1-22-1842    George, -s Thomas & Mary Saint, rec in mbrp
12-24-1842   Sarah, -dt Thomas, rocf Whitewater MM
12-24-1842   Thomas Jr gct Back Creek MM, Ind
11-25-1843   Thomas & w Mary & ch Samuel T, Daniel, Sarah, John & George S & Calvin W & William B H Pritchard gct Salem MM, Ia Terr
11-25-1843   Joseph gct Salem MM, Ia Terr
2-22-1845    Joseph & Samuel rocf Salem MM, Ia
8-23-1845    Joseph rpt dp & mcd; chm
3-26-1846    Samuel T gct Salem MM, Ia
4-25-1846    Daniel rocf Salem MM, Ia, -end fr Driftwood MM, Ind
2-27-1847    Joseph gct Salem MM, Ia

MILFORD

SAINT (Cont)
4-26-1851   Daniel rpt having sued at law a mbr; chm
5-22-1852   Daniel gct Whitewater MM, Ind
7-23-1853   Mary (form Johnson) rpt mcd by Duck Creek MM
10-26-1853  Mary (form Johnson) rpt chm by Duck Creek MM
12-24-1853  Mary gct Duck Creek MM, Ind
2-25-1871   Emily J Hadley & dt Mary Ellen Saint gct Duck Creek MM, Ind

SAUNDERS - SANDERS
5-13-1824   John rec in mbrp
6-25-1825   Elizabeth Foreman (form Sanders) rpt mcd; chm
10-23-1830  Miriam Low (form Sanders) rpt mcd by Westfield MM
6-25-1831   Miriam Low (form Sanders) dis for mcd
1- 4-1832   Hannah of Fayette Co, Ind, -dt Joseph & Martha m Caleb Hall at Bethel MH
1-23-1836   Martha & s Joseph gct Spiceland MM, Ind
10-22-1836  Thomas gct Spiceland MM, Ind
6-27-1874   Romulus W rec in mbrp
3-27-1875   Romulus gct Deer Creek MM

SAVAGE
1-27-1849   Rebecca (form Charles) rpt mcd by Mississinewa MM
7-28-1849   Rebecca - Mississinewa MM rpts they do not know where she lives
2-22-1851   Rebecca (form Charles) - dis with note that she lives remote from this mtg

SCOFIELD
2-26-1870   Susanna (form Morris) rpt mcd; dis

SCHOOLEY
9-23-1843   Susan (form Taylor) rpt mcd; dis
7-27-1844   Wilson, mbr Spiceland MM, rpt mcd
8-24-1844   Wilson - Spiceland infs they tr w/h without success
10-27-1860  Thomas & w Elizabeth & ch Rebecca Jane & Emma gct Mississinewa MM, Ind
2-21-1889   Elizabeth C & dt Emma & Adaline gct Back Creek MM, Ind

SEXTON
12-23-1826  Hannah rocf Miami MM, Ohio, -end to Duck Creek MM, Ind

SHANER
3-23-1850   Virginia (form Brown) rpt mcd by Dover MM, Ohio
1-25-1851   Virginia (form Brown) - Dover rpts she has dec

SHANK
2-27-1836   Rachel (form Clark), mbr Whitewater MM, rpt mcd
8-27-1836   Rachel (form Clark) dis by Whietwater MM
2-27-1837   James, Benjamin & Malinda Morman, ch of Rachel, rocf Whitewater MM, Ind

SHARP
11-26-1859  William Henry & w Rebecca & s Samuel T rocf Short Creek MM, Ohio
5-23-1867   William Henry & w Rebecca R & ch Jesse & Mary gct Chicago MM, Ill

SHAW
2-24-1883   Mary & ch Sarah & Ora Leonard rec in mbrp

SHECKEL
4-27-1867   Margaret Ann (form Winslow) rpt mcd; chm
12-30-1880  Margaret Ann, a widow, -dt Jacob & Martha Winslow (both dec), m Walter Denny Jay at Dublin MH

SHERIDAN
8-27-1825   John & w Margery & ch William, Rachel, George, John, Hannah, Abner, Susanna & Isaac rocf West Grove MM, Ind

SHIPLEY
10-24-1835  Beulah (form Bacon), mbr Greenwich MM, N J, rpt mcd
6-25-1836   Beulah (form Bacon), dis by Greenwich MM, N J

SHISTLER
2-25-1886   Philip & Laura rec in mbrp

SHOEMAKER
9-27-1834   Charles, a minor, rocf West Grove MM, Ind
4-28-1838   Charles, a minor, gct West Grove MM, Ind

SHOWALTER
5-28-1842   Acenath (form Gilbert) rpt mcd by Duck Creek MM
8-27-1842   Acenath (form Gilbert) dis for mcd

SMALL
7-23-1825   Samuel & w Abigail & ch Jesse & Louisa rocf Chester MM, Ind
3-24-1827   Josiah & w Jane & ch Thomas, Sarah, Elizabeth & Abigail gct Duck Creek MM, Ind
6-28-1828   Abraham gct Duck Creek MM, Ind
8-26-1837   Susannah rocf New Garden MM, Ind
11-24-1838  Samuel & w Abigail & ch Jesse, Eli & James gct Westfield MM, Ind
9-26-1840   Susan gct Spiceland MM, Ind

SMITH
8-27-1825   Benjamin & w Tamer & ch Hannah, Mary, John, William, Sarah, Lydia, Amos & Tamar rocf Chester MM, Ind
11-26-1825  Sarah, Ira, Millicent, Abigail & Mary, ch of Robert, rocf Whitewater MM, Ind
7- 2-1828   Hannah, -dt Benjamin & Tamar of Wayne Co, Ind, m Exum Elliott at Bethel MH
5-22-1830   Mary rpt na & dp; dis
4-26-1832   Mary Boswell (form Smith) rpt mcd; dis
4-25-1835   John rpt na; dis
8-27-1836   William rpt dp & mcd; dis
9-24-1836   Susannah (form Pickering) rpt mcd; dis
9-23-1837   Benjamin rpt for conveying spirituous liquor to market
10-28-1837  Benjamin chm
7-28-1838   Elda Ann (form Hiatt) rpt mcd; dis
4-27-1839   Thomas Wilkinson rocf Plainfield MM, Ohio
5-25-1839   Sarah Dickinson (form Smith) rpt mcd; dis
11-28-1840  Amos rpt na & dp; dis
5-24-1845   Martha Cooper (form Smith) rpt mcd; dis
4-25-1846   James & w Sarah & ch Joseph, Elizabeth & Maria rocf Balby MM, England
4-27-1850   Tamar & Patience rpt na & att a dancing school; dis
5-24-1851   Sarah rec a min
1-24-1852   Asenith Fitch (form Smith) rpt mcd; dis
2-25-1865   Joseph M rpt mcd; rel fr mbrp
12-26-1865  Eliza, -dt James & Sarah of Cambridge City, Ind, m William J Hiatt at res of James Smith
12-26-1865  Maria, -dt James & Sarah of Cambridge City, m Caleb M Peele at res of James Smith
11-26-1870  James & w Sarah gct Indianapolis MM, Ind
11-23-1872  Thoburn Wayne & w Mary rec in mbrp
2-28-1874   Thomas P & Sarah rec in mbrp
4-26-1879   Laura rec in mbrp
3-26-1885   Sarah J rocf Whitewater MM, Ind
10-28-1886  Mary Alice rec in mbrp

SPANGLER
2-23-1884   John S & w Katie rec in mbrp

SPENCER
6-28-1845   Louisa (form Hiatt) rpt mcd & jH by Duck Creek MM
11-22-1845  Louisa (form Hiatt) dis for mcd & jH

SPRINGER
3-25-1836   Sarah rocf Whitewater MM, Ind

MILFORD

STAFFORD
7-17-1823    Samuel appt to comm
10-23-1824   Eli & w Elizabeth & ch John & Cynthia rocf
             West Grove MM, Ind
12-23-1837   Daniel rocf Spiceland MM, Ind
8- 2-1838    Daniel H of Henry Co, Ind, -s Samuel & Nancy
             (dec), Hamilton Co, Ind, m Sarah G Stretch
             at Rich Square MH

STANBROUGH
12-18-1823   James appt to comm
1-15-1824    Nehemiah & w Ruth & ch Ann, Thomas, Francis
             & James rocf Centre MM, Ohio
4-15-1824    Mary appt to comm
8-23-1828    James rec a min
2-26-1831    Evan & w Elizabeth & ch Mary, Solomon,
             Tabitha, Rachel, John, Frances Hester,
             William, Elizabeth & James rocf Center MM,
             Ohio
10-31-1833   Mary, -dt Evan & Elizabeth of Wayne Co, Ind,
             m Solomon Bennett at Milford MH
12-28-1833   Nehemiah & w Ruth & ch Ann, Thomas, Francis,
             James, Solomon, Mary F, Levi, Tabitha &
             Malinda gct Duck Creek MM, Ind
2- 3-1836    Mary, widow of James Stanbrough, -dt Hurr
             & Elizabeth Hodgson, Clinton Co, Ohio, m
             John Bond at Bethel MH
11-26-1836   Tabitha Mills (form Stanbrough) rpt mcd; dis
7-22-1837    Jonathan rocf Westfield MM, Ind
11-30-1837   Solomon of Wayne Co, Ind, -s Evan & Elizabeth,
             m Mary Hunt at Milford MH
2- 1-1838    John, Wayne Co, Ind, -s Evan & Elizabeth, m
             Lydia Hunt at Milford MH
1-27-1838    Solomon & w Mary gct Westfield MM, Ind
3-24-1838    Evan & w Elizabeth & ch Rachel, Frances
             Hester, William, Elizabeth, James, Ruth &
             Rhoda gct Westfield MM, Ind
6-23-1838    John & w Lydia D gct Westfield MM, Ind

STANLEY
7-28-1827    Aaron & w Mahala rocf Honey Creek MM, Ind
6-27-1829    George & w Jemima & ch Samuel, Jeremiah
             Parker, Isaac, Keren  Newby rocf Newberry
             MM, Ohio
6-26-1830    Samuel & w Susanna & ch Elizabeth & Susanna
             rocf Newbery MM, Ohio
7-24-1830    Aaron & w Mahala & ch Eliza Jane & Michael
             gct Duck Creek MM, Ind
1-22-1831    Nathan rocf Dover MM, N C, -end fr Duck
             Creek MM, Ind
11-26-1831   Nathan gct Duck Creek MM, Ind
6-22-1833    William rocf New Garden MM, N C
12-28-1833   Ira rocf Dover MM, N C
3-26-1834    Susannah, -dt Samuel & Susanna of Henry Co,
             Ind, m Isom Hunt at Hopewell MH
11-22-1834   William rpt dr & dp & (rpt to have left the
             country); dis
3- 4-1835    Ira of Wayne Co, Ind, -s Michael & Mary, m
             Betsey Bennet at Bethel MH
11-28-1835   Sarah rocf Dover MM, N C
6-25-1836    Nathan rocf Centre MM, N C
3-30-1837    Ellwood of Henry Co, Ind, -s Richard &
             Abigail, m Martha Butler at Rich Square MH
3-24-1838    Martha gct Spiceland MM, Ind
4-25-1840    Elwood & w Martha & ch William & Emaline rocf
             Spiceland MM, Ind
1-25-1845    Susan & ch Jesse Collins, Sarah Caroline,
             Eliza Ann & William Charles rocf New Garden
             MM, Ind
3-22-1845    Nathan gct Spiceland MM, Ind
11-22-1845   Leah (form Pickering) rpt mcd by Duck Creek
             MM, but she now resides in limits of Back
             Creek MM
9-26-1846    Dis sent to Mississinewa MM, Ind for Leah
3-25-1848    Samuel & w Mary rocf Westfield MM - he having
             dec, she has ret; cert ret to Westfield MM,
             Ind
11- 2-1848   Caroline, -dt William (dec) & Susannah, m
             Benjamin A Wilson at Milford MH

1-25-1851    Jesse C gct Bloomfield MM, Ind
12-27-1856   Michael & w Lydia Jane & ch Eliza Ellen
             rocf Spiceland MM, Ind
4-29-1858    William C of Wayne Co, Ind, -s William &
             Susanna (both dec) of Guilford Co, N C,
             m Mary M Morris at Milford MH
10-22-1859   Eliza Ann Pearson (form Stanley) rpt mcd
             by Honey Creek MM
12-24-1859   Michael & w Lydia Jane & ch Eliza Ellen &
             Charles Henly gct Lynn Grove MM
1-28-1860    Eliza Ann Pearson (form Stanley) chm for
             mcd - rpt by Honey Creek MM
7-28-1860    Daniel gct Short Creek MM, Ohio to m
             Sarah H Terrell
2-23-1861    Sarah T rocf Short Creek MM, Ohio
2-22-1862    Josiah rpt mcd by Bear Creek MM, Ia; chm
2-22-1862    Sarah H (form Wilson) rpt mcd by Bear
             Creek MM, Ia, chm
9-27-1862    Josiah & w Sarah H gct Bear Creek MM, Ia
7-25-1863    William C gct Spiceland MM to m Miriam
             King
11-28-1863   William C rpt mcd; chm
2-27-1864    Miriam (form King), (mbr Spiceland MM)
             rpt mcd; chm
6-25-1864    Miriam rocf Spiceland MM, Ind
12-24-1864   Ruth Ann Harvey (form Stanley) rpt mcd;
             chm
8-28-1867    William C of Wayne Co, Ind, -s William &
             Susan (both dec), Guilford Co, N C, m
             Sarah T Stanley, widow of Daniel Stanley,
             at Bethel MH
8-28-1867    Sarah T, widow of Daniel Stanley, & -dt
             Mathew & Elizabeth D Terrell of Jefferson
             Co, Ohio, m William C Stanley at Bethel
             MH
9-25-1869    Lucinda Bowie (form Stanley) rpt mcd; chm
4-25-1874    Ira Jr & w Hannah & ch Leora & Laina rec
             in mbrp
3-27-1875    Delphina & Elmina rec in mbrp
3-24-1877    Ira & w Hannah & ch Lasea Ann, Mary Laura,
             Roy Franklin & William Gurley gct Union MM,
             Mo
1-28-1882    Hannah rec in mbrp
5-27-1882    William C & w Sarah gct White River MM,
             Ind
4-28-1883    Bennet rel fr mbrp
3-24-1883    Oliver gct White River MM, Ind

STANTON
9-24-1825    Bailey William, a minor, rocf Whitewater
             MM, Ind
8-25-1827    Peter & s Isaac W & James B rocf North-
             east Fork MM, Md
8-25-1827    Cela rocf Northeast Fork MM, Md
11-22-1828   Peter rpt jH; dis
12-27-1828   Cela rpt jH; dis
6-26-1847    Ann B rocf New Garden MM, Ind
9-25-1847    Isaac W gct Richland MM, Ind
6-24-1848    Ann B gct White Lick MM, Ind

STETAN
1-28-1886    William rec in mbrp
2-21-1889    William (Stotan) rel fr mbrp

STEWART
6-26-1830    Samuel & w Hannah & ch Mary, Elizabeth,
             James, Beuley & Charles rocf White-
             water MM, Ind
10-26-1861   Edmond & Albert, ch of Samuel W, rocf
             Hopewell MM, Ind
2-27-1875    Edmund gct Spiceland MM, Ind
2-27-1875    Albert gct Indianapolis MM, Ind

STILES
10-23-1847   Robert rocf Adrian MM, Mich
10-28-1848   Robert gct West Branch MM, Ohio

STITES
1-28-1886    Clem rec in mbrp

MILFORD

## STOKES
| | |
|---|---|
| 7-25-1835 | Samuel & w Jane & ch Isabella, Elizabeth, Hannah R, Edwin, Henry, Susan & Albert rocf Whitewater MM, Ind |
| 1-31-1839 | Elizabeth, -dt Samuel & Jane, Wayne Co, Ind, m Joseph Wilson at Milford MH |
| 3- 2-1843 | Hannah R, -dt Samuel & Jane of Wayne Co, Ind, m William Cox at Milford MH |
| 10-28-1847 | Isabella, -dt Samuel & Jane of Wayne Co, Ind, m Charles F Westcombe at Milford MH |
| 2-24-1849 | Edwin rpt att a dancing school |
| 5-24-1849 | Edwin dis for att a dancing school |
| 9-24-1853 | Henry rpt na "particularly the mid-week mtg", dp & mcd; 12-24-1853 - chm |
| 11-25-1854 | Albert J gct Richland MM, Ind |
| 9-27-1855 | Susan, -dt Samuel & Jane of Wayne Co, Ind, m Gideon C Wilson at Milford MH |

## STONEBRAKER
| | |
|---|---|
| 11-25-1854 | Margaret (form Nixon) rpt mcd by Hinkles Creek |
| 4-28-1855 | Margaret (form Nixon), Hinkles Creek rpts they tr w/h without success; dis |

## STRATTON
| | |
|---|---|
| 9-24-1825 | Benjamin & w Anny & ch Benjamin, Jerusha, Martha, Mary, Joseph, Samuel & Lusamy rocf Whitewater MM, Ind |
| 3-25-1826 | Ephraim, mbr Whitewater, rpt dr |
| 6-24-1826 | Ephraim - Whitewater rpts they tr w/h without success |
| 8-29-1827 | Martha, -dt Benjamin & Anny of Henry Co, Ind, m John Stuart at Hopewell MH |
| 10-29-1828 | Jerusha, -dt Benjamin & Anny of Henry Co, Ind, m Thomas Bell at Hopewell MH |
| 3-30-1831 | Mary, -dt Benjamin & Anny of Henry Co, Ind, m Isaac Parker at Hopewell MH |
| 4-23-1831 | Benjamin Jr rpt dp, na & offering to fight; dis |
| 9-26-1838 | Joseph of Henry Co, Ind, -s Benjamin & Anny, m Ann Hawley at Hopewell MH |
| 10-29-1839 | Lusanna, -dt Benjamin & Anny of Henry Co, Ind, m Robert Hall at Hopewell MH |

## STRAUGHN
| | |
|---|---|
| 12-27-1828 | Hannah rpt att mcd; dis |
| 12-27-1828 | Merriman rpt na & att mcd of a mbr; dis |

## STREET
| | |
|---|---|
| 6-23-1832 | John & w Dorothy & dt Eunice rocf Silver Creek MM, Ind |
| 4-24-1841 | John gct Walnut Ridge MM to m Agatha Hussey |

## STRETCH
| | |
|---|---|
| 1-23-1836 | James & w Ann & ch Elizabeth, James A, Sarah G & Hannah Ann rocf Whitewater MM, Ind |
| 8- 2-1838 | Sarah G, -dt James & Ann of Henry Co, Ind, m Daniel H Stafford at Rich Square MH |
| 12-22-1838 | James A rpt mcd; dis |

## STUART
| | |
|---|---|
| 8-29-1827 | John, -s Sarah & Jehu of Wayne Co, Ind, m Martha Stratton at Hopewell MH |
| 8-23-1828 | John rocf Whitewater MM, Ind |

## STUBBS
| | |
|---|---|
| 10-25-1834 | Joseph & w Sarah & ch Celia, Daniel, Jeremiah, Mahlon, Amy, Stephen, Jacob & Mary rocf Elk MM, Ohio |
| 8-31-1837 | Celia, -dt Joseph & Sarah of Wayne Co, Ind, m Solomon Gause at Milford MH |
| 4-23-1842 | Sarah & ch Jemima, Mahlon, Amy, Stephen, Jacob, Mary, John T & Margaret M gct New Garden MM, Ind |
| 6-25-1859 | Jonathan & w Rachel & ch Alvan, Enoch, Albert, Elvira, Elizabeth & Mary Emma rocf Whitewater MM, Ind |
| 8-25-1883 | Alvan rocf West Grove MM, Ind |
| 11-24-1887 | Alvan gct Lawrence MM, Kans |

## SUMNER
| | |
|---|---|
| 3-22-1834 | Samuel rocf Fall Creek MM, Ohio |
| 3-25-1837 | Samuel gct Westfield MM, Ind |

## SUTTON
| | |
|---|---|
| 12-29-1859 | David of Chenoa, McLean Co, Ill, -s Isaac & Sarah of Battle Creek, Calhoun Co, Mich, m Deborah White at Milford MH |
| 6-28-1862 | David rocf Adrain MM, Mich |
| 3-26-1870 | Aaron Franklin rocf Marlborough MM, N Y |
| 3- 9-1871 | Aaron F of Wayne Co, Ind, -s Aaron & Mary H of Ulster Co, N Y, m Anne Moore at Milford MH |
| 9-26-1874 | Mary H & ch John G, Mary W & Sarah Helena rocf Providence MM, R I |
| 7-22-1876 | Mary H & ch Mary W & Sarah H gct Providence MM, R I |
| 2-24-1877 | Aaron Franklin & w Annie & ch Mary R, Marcia E & Caroline gct Whitewater MM, Ind |
| 4-22-1882 | John G gct Whitewater MM, Ind |

## SWAIN
| | |
|---|---|
| 8-24-1833 | Shubal rocf Silver Creek MM, Ind |
| 9-26-1835 | Shubal gct Salem MM to m Mary B Barnard |
| 6-25-1836 | Mary B rocf Salem MM, Ind |
| 4-28-1849 | David & w Ruth & ch Ruth & Adaline Bundrant, a minor, rocf Salem MM, Ind |
| 12-24-1853 | David gct Walnut Ridge MM to m Phebe Weisner |
| 8-26-1854 | Phebe rocf Walnut Ridge MM, Ind |
| 1-22-1859 | Jonathan & w Lydia & ch Cyrus S & Martha H rocf Elk MM, Ohio |
| 3-25-1865 | David & w Phebe & dt Ruth gct Walnut Ridge MM, Ind |
| 10-27-1866 | George R & w Luzena & dt Miriam rocf New Garden MM, Ind |
| 3-28-1868 | Cyrus rpt bearing arms in Civil War & mcd; dis |
| 12-25-1869 | Anna J rocf New Garden MM, N C |

## SWIGETT
| | |
|---|---|
| 1-27-1827 | Solomon & w Euphamia,-dt Jane rocf Northwest Fork MM, Md |
| 9-27-1828 | Solomon rpt jH; dis |
| 9-27-1828 | Euphamia rpt jH; dis |
| 5-28-1842 | Jane rpt na & jH; dis |

## SWISHER
| | |
|---|---|
| 11-24-1827 | Amelia (form Wright) rpt mcd; chm |

## SYMONS
| | |
|---|---|
| 7-13-1823 | Thomas appt to a comm |
| 7-13-1823 | Mathew appt to a comm |
| 7-13-1823 | Jane appt to a comm |
| 7-13-1823 | Hannah appt to a comm |
| 8-14-1823 | Nathan appt to a comm |
| 8-14-1823 | Sarah Jr appt to a comm |
| 3-18-1824 | Martha appt to be an Elder |
| 3-18-1824 | Mathew appt to be an Elder |
| 11- 8-1827 | Mary, -dt Matthew & Sarah of Wayne Co, Ind, m Nathan Charles at Milford MH |
| 12- 6-1827 | Sarah, -dt Abraham & Mary of Wayne Co, Ind, m Samuel Morris at Milford MH |
| 1-2- 1828 | Abraham of Wayne Co, Ind, -s John & Ann, (dec), m Mary Morris, widow of Joshua Morris, at Hopewell MH |
| 10-25-1828 | Matthew rpt jH; dis |
| 4-25-1829 | Matthew Jr rpt jH; dis |
| 6-27-1829 | Thomas Jr rpt jH; dis |
| 7-25-1829 | Ruth rpt jH; dis |
| 3-27-1830 | Abigail rpt jH; dis |
| 8-27-1831 | Sarah rpt jH & att a dance; dis |
| 9- 8-1831 | Josiah, Wayne Co, Ind, -s Thomas & Hannah, m Sarah Kindley at Milford MH |
| 12- 1-1831 | Sarah, -dt Nathan & Jane of Wayne Co, Ind, m William Allen at Milford MH |
| 5-24-1834 | Margaret rpt jH; dis |
| 7-26-1834 | Thomas & w Hannah & ch Bethuel, Elijah, Nathan, Rebecca, Thomas & Abel gct Mississinewa MM, Ind |

MILFORD

**SYMONS (Cont)**

|  |  |
|---|---|
| 10-25-1834 | Matthew gct Duck Creek MM, Ind |
| 10-25-1834 | Nathan & w Jane & ch Elizabeth, Jesse, Lydia, Anna, Pheraba, Rebecca Jane, Ruth, Nathan & Abigail gct Mississinewa MM, Ind |
| 2-20-1835 | Josiah & w Sarah & ch Jehu & Joel gct Mississinewa MM, Ind |
| 5-27-1835 | Abraham Jr, -s Abraham & Mary (dec) of Wayne Co, Ind, m Achsah Gilbert at Hopewell MH |
| 8-27-1836 | Hannah & dt Malinda, Sarah Jane & Martha Ann rocf Driftwood MM, Ind |
| 2-8-1837 | Gulielma of Henry Co, Ind, -dt Abraham Sr & Mary (both dec), m Ashbel Binford at Bethel MH |
| 3-25-1837 | Hannah & dt Malinda, Sarah Jane & Martha Ann gct Spiceland MM, Ind |
| 2-28-1838 | Phebe, -dt Abraham Sr & Mary (both dec), of Wayne Co, Ind, m Elias Henby at Bethel MH |
| 9-28-1839 | Samuel & w Ann & ch Lydia, James, John, Abraham & Henry rocf Whitewater MM, Ind |
| 4-24-1841 | Abigail & s Samuel rec in mbrp |
| 4-22-1848 | Mary Waddle (form Symons) rpt mcd; dis |
| 12-23-1848 | Milton rpt mcd; dis |
| 8-25-1849 | Henry W rpt mcd; dis |
| 11-26-1850 | Mary & dt Eunice gct Walnut Ridge MM, Ind |
| 9-23-1854 | Nathan M gct Richland MM, Ind |
| 8-27-1864 | Rebecca, Mary & Abigail rocf Hopewell MM, Ind |
| 10-27-1866 | Abraham & ch Julian O, Wilson E & Luther R rocf Poplar Run MM, Ind |
| 6-27-1868 | Abigail gct Poplar Run MM, Ind |
| 7-25-1868 | Samuel gct Poplar Run MM, Ind |
| 8-28-1869 | Abraham gct Poplar Run to m Mary Elizabeth Townsend |
| 4-23-1870 | Abraham & ch Julian & Wilson gct Poplar Run MM, Ind |
| 6-25-1870 | Abigail Herbts (form Symons) rpt mcd; chm |
| 7-24-1875 | Rebecca gct Hopewell MM, Ind |

**TALBERT**

|  |  |
|---|---|
| 4-28-1849 | Elihu & w Lucretia & ch Louisa, Emily, Ann, Mercy Bell, Avis R & Lindley H rocf Salem MM, Ind |
| 1-24-1852 | Elihu & w Lucretia & ch Louisa, Emily, Ann, Mercy Bell, Avis Paddock, Lindley Hoagg & Mary Florence gct Honey Creek MM, Ind |

**TAYLOR**

|  |  |
|---|---|
| 12-25-1824 | Polly B rocf Springfield MM, N C |
| 11-25-1826 | Stephen rocf Blue River MM, Ind |
| 9-22-1827 | Ann & dt Lydia & Elizabeth rq mbrp; rq denied |
| 9-27-1828 | Stephen rpt jH; dis |
| 3-23-1839 | Susan rocf Salem MM, Ind |
| 3-23-1839 | George, a minor u/c Thomas & Mary Edgerton, rocf Salem MM, Ind |
| 8-27-1842 | George rpt na & has taught singing; dis |
| 9-23-1843 | Susan Schooley (form Taylor) rpt mcd; dis |
| 10-27-1883 | John W rocf Walnut Ridge MM |

**TEAGUE**

|  |  |
|---|---|
| 4-27-1833 | Samuel & w Prudence & ch Isaac Cooper, Joseph C, Abijah & Moses Furnace Teague rocf Mill Creek MM, Ohio |
| 1-25-1834 | Samuel & w Prudence & ch Isaac, Joseph, Abigail & Moses Furnace gct Union MM, Ind |

**TERRELL**

|  |  |
|---|---|
| 6-1-1864 | Mathew of Oskaloosa, Mahaskia Co, Iowa, -s Clark & Mary of Short Creek MM, Ohio, m Isabel Newby at Bethel MH |

**TEST**

|  |  |
|---|---|
| 7-28-1849 | Mark rocf Salem MM, Ind |
| 8-26-1857 | Zacheus of Wayne Co, Ind, -s Samuel (dec) & Hannah, m Elizabeth M Pray at Bethel MH |
| 1-22-1859 | Elizabeth M gct Whitewater MM, Ind |

**THATCHER**

|  |  |
|---|---|
| 8-25-1849 | Joseph & w Deborah & ch Mary Ellen, William, Susannah, Sarah, Lydia & Anna J rocf Springfield MM, Ohio |
| 4-24-1852 | Deborah & ch Mary E, William, Susan, Sarah, Lydia Maria & Anna G gct Springfield MM, Ohio |
| 1-28-1854 | Joseph gct Springfield MM, Ohio |

**THOMAS**

|  |  |
|---|---|
| 8-12-1824 | Isaac rpt na, dp & for administering oaths as a justice of the peace & for erecting a distillery; dis |
| 8-12-1824 | Lydia rpt jas; dis |
| 9-1-1825 | Simeon, Wayne Co, Ind, -s Elijah & Susannah, m Olive Elliott at Duck Creek MH |
| 2-25-1826 | Simeon rocf New Garden MM, Ind |
| 5-22-1830 | Levi rpt dp, training with Militia & mcd; dis |
| 5-22-1830 | Serepta Wherit (form Thomas) rpt mcd; dis |
| 6-26-1830 | Edward rpt out of unity, na & dp; dis |
| 2-28-1831 | Nehemiah of West Branch MM, Ohio, -s Thomas & Sarah of Montgomery Co, Ohio, m Phebe Gilbert at Hopewell MH |
| 5-28-1831 | Phebe gct West Branch MM, Ohio |
| 5-24-1834 | Miriam (form Gilbert) West Branch MM, Ohio, rpt mcd; West Branch MM inf she chm |
| 12-23-1837 | Miriam - cert issued to West Branch, but as she now lives in these limits she is a mbr with us at Milford MM, Ind |
| 6-22-1839 | James rpt mcd by Mississinewa MM |
| 7-27-1839 | Mariam, a min, gct White River MM, Ind |
| 11-23-1839 | James - Mississinewa MM rpts dis |

**THOMPSON**

|  |  |
|---|---|
| 10-28-1837 | Sarah (form Newby) rpt mcd; dis |
| 2-27-1869 | Emily (form Hubbard) rpt mcd; chm |

**THORNBURG**

|  |  |
|---|---|
| 7-17-1823 | Henry appt to a comm |
| 8-14-1823 | Rebecca appt a Clerk |
| 2-3-1825 | Elizabeth of Fayette Co, Ind, -dt Henry & Rebecca, m Seth Wilson at Milford MH |
| 2-1-1826 | John of Fayette Co, Ind, -s Henry & Rebecca, m Mary Butler at Bethel MH |
| 6-28-1828 | Henry rpt reading Hicksite books & papers; dis |
| 11-22-1828 | John rpt jH; dis |
| 11-22-1828 | Rebecca rpt jH; dis |
| 11-22-1828 | Eunice rpt jH; dis |
| 3-28-1829 | Mary rpt jH; dis |
| 1-25-1834 | Milton rpt jH; dis |
| 1-25-1834 | Hannah Macy (form Thornburg) rpt mcd & jH |
| 9-26-1835 | Hannah Macy (form Thornburg) dis for mcd & jH |
| 9-26-1835 | Sarah (form Charles), mbr Whitewater MM, rpt mcd |
| 3-26-1836 | Sarah (form Charles) rpt dis |

**TINGLE**

|  |  |
|---|---|
| 3-27-1858 | Elizabeth (form Kindley) rpt mcd; dis |

**TOMS**

|  |  |
|---|---|
| 10-28-1854 | Pheriba, a min, & ch William, Mary, Anderson, Joseph & John rocf Piney Woods MM, N C |
| 9-26-1857 | Joseph rst in mbrp (form mbr of Symons Creek MM, N C) |
| 8-27-1864 | William rpt mcd; chm |
| 9-24-1864 | Phebe Ann (form Symons), of Duck Creek MM, rpt mcd; chm |
| 12-24-1864 | Phebe Ann rocf Duck Creek MM, Ind |
| 12-26-1866 | Mary, -dt Joseph & Phariba of Fayette Co, Ind, m Christopher Wilson at Bethel MH |
| 9-26-1868 | Anderson gct Kokomo MM to m Mary M Johnson |
| 8-28-1869 | Mary J rocf Kokomo MM, Ind |
| 5-25-1872 | William gct Walnut Ridge MM to m Charity Hill |
| 4-24-1875 | Anderson & w Mary & ch Laura Margaret, Joseph & Jesse gct Deer Creek MM, Ind |
| 4-23-1881 | Joseph & w Elizabeth W & ch Maude & William Henry gct Whitewater MM, Ind |
| 3-24-1883 | William & w Charity & ch Edgar V gct Westland MM, Ind |

MILFORD

**TOWNSEND**
2-24-1849   Lydia W rocf West Grove MM, Ind
10-25-1851  Lydia W gct Salem MM, Ia Terr

**TREADWAY**
12-25-1852  Mary T (form Butler) rpt mcd by Spiceland MM
3-26-1853   Mary T (form Butler) dis for mcd

**TRUEBLOOD**
3-27-1849   James of Blue River MM, Ind, -s William & Margaret, (both dec), of Orange Co, Ind, m Jane Dickinson of Wayne Co, Ind, -dt Jonathan (dec) & Alice, at Milford MH
5-26-1849   Jane gct Blue River MM, Ind

**TUCKER**
6-23-1877   Lincoln & Emma rocf Westland MM, Ind

**TYLER**
3-24-1832   John, mbr Wilmington MM, Dela, rpt jH; dis

**UNTHANK**
11-26-1825  William & w Rebecca & ch Drusilla, Samuel N & Naomi J rocf New Garden MM, Ind
6-23-1827   Josiah & Anna, a min, rocf New Garden MM, Ind
4-26-1828   Josiah & Anna, having sojourned with us for several months past, now being about to ret to New Garden MM, Ind
12-25-1830  William B & w Rebecca & ch Drusilla, Samuel & Addison gct Duck Creek MM, Ind
1-24-1835   Eli & fam rocf New Garden MM, N C, -end to Spiceland MM, Ind

**VANHORN**
8-26-1826   John, a minor u/c George & Mary Evans, rocf Miami MM, Ohio -- -end to Duck Creek MM, Ind

**VICORY - VICKERY**
5-26-1849   Caroline (form Newby) rpt mcd; dis
2-23-1850   Elizabeth (form Newby) rpt mcd; chm

**WADDLE**
4-22-1848   Mary (form Symons) rpt mcd; dis

**WALTERS**
12-23-1886  Sarah R gct Spiceland MM, Ind

**WALTON**
11-23-1867  Joseph P rpt mcd; chm
11-23-1867  Caroline (form Huddleston) rpt mcd; chm
11-22-1879  Joseph P & w Caroline & ch Anna Belle, George Franklin & Sarah Estella gct Spiceland MM, Ind

**WARD**
2-25-1886   Louie rec in mbrp

**WARING**
7-28-1849   Margaret & dt Abigail rocf Salem MM, Ind
7- 1-1852   William P of Wayne Co, Ind, -s Joshua (dec) & Margaret of Fayette Co, Ind, m Semira Hiatt at Milford MH
1-22-1853   Semira gct Whitewater MM, Ind
3-24-1855   Margaret gct Honey Creek MM, Ind
8-25-1855   Abigail gct Honey Creek MM, Ind

**WARREN**
1-28-1886   Morton, Jesse & Clayton C rec in mbrp

**WASHUM**
10-22-1836  Rebecca (form Marmon), mbr Whitewater MM, rpt mcd

**WASSON**
8-12-1824   Jehial & w Lydia & ch Jesse & Charlotte rocf Chester MM, Ind
5-28-1825   Calvin & w Mary & ch William, Nathan & Elizabeth rocf Chester MM, Ind
3-31-1841   Nathan of Highland Co, Ohio, -s Calvin & Mary of same place, m Maria Cox at Bethel MH
10-23-1841  Nathan rocf Clear Creek MM, Ohio
11-30-1848  Nathan of Wayne Co, Ind, -s Calvin & Mary of Clinton Co, Ohio, m Elizabeth W Morris, widow of Stephen Morris, at Milford MH
7-26-1851   Mahlon rocf Chester MM, Ind
4-24-1852   Mahlon rpt na & j Meth by Spiceland MM; dis
10-30-1856  Calvin H of Wayne Co, Ind, -s Calvin & Mary of Clinton Co, Ohio, m Abigail C Morris at Milford MH
12-26-1857  Abigail C gct Hopewell MM, Ind
11-24-1866  Nathan & w Elizabeth & ch Mary, Henry & Charles gct Poplar Ridge MM, Ind
5-22-1875   Jehiel & w Sydney rel fr mbrp
1-28-1886   John, Anne, Harry, Edgar & Mary rec in mbrp

**WATERS**
3-24-1860   Harriett P (form Hubbard) rpt mcd; chm

**WAY**
6-23-1827   Phebe rocf Cherry Grove MM, Ind
5-28-1831   Lydia & ch Millicent, Mary Ann & Daniel L rocf Whitewater MM, Ind
6-25-1831   Robert rocf Whitewater MM, Ind
12-24-1831  Phebe gct Cherry Grove MM, Ind
4-28-1832   Robert rpt dr; chm
5-24-1834   Robert & w Lydia & ch Millicent, Mary Ann, David L & Sarah gct Stillwater MM, Ohio, "not withstanding his failure in circumstances is such that they are unsettled demands standing against him; yet he having made a surrender of his effects to his creditors, as far as appears, so that nothing more for the present can be expected"
4-23-1842   William & w Betty & ch Achsah Ann, Lydia, Abigail & Mary Jane rocf New Garden MM, Ind
12-23-1843  William rpt na & jASF; dis
4-27-1844   Betty rpt jASF; dis
3-22-1845   Achsah Ann, Abigail, Lydia & Mary Jane gct New Garden MM, Ind

**WEAVER**
7-22-1882   Rachel & Emma rocf Springfield MM, Ind

**WEEKS**
11-17-1823  Benjamin of Wayne Co, Ind, -s John & Jane of same county, m Wineford Copeland at Duck Creek MH
12-25-1824  Benjamin rocf Whitewater MM, Ind

**WEISNER**
11-27-1824  Michael rocf Union MM, N C, -end to Chester MM, Ind

**WEST**
8-26-1886   Thomas & Marjorie rec in mbrp
4-26-1888   Thomas rel fr mbrp

**WESTCOMBE**
12-28-1844  Charles F rocf Cincinnati MM, Ohio
10-28-1847  Charles F of Henry Co, Ind, -s Samuel T & Elizabeth (both dec), of Worcester Co, England, m Isabella Stokes at Milford MH
2-22-1862   Charles gct Worcestershire Co, Shropshire, England

**WHERIT**
5-22-1830   Serepta (form Thomas) rpt mcd
8-28-1830   Serepta (form Thomas) dis for mcd

**WHITE**
4-22-1826   Robert rec in mbrp
7-28-1827   William rq mbrp; denied
10-27-1827  Stanton & fam rocf Hopewell MM, N C, -end to Duck Creek MM, Ind
10-27-1827  Jesse rocf Hopewell MM, N C, -end to Duck Creek MM, Ind

MILFORD

**WHITE (Cont)**

|  |  |
|---|---|
| 10-27-1827 | Isaac & fam rocf New Garden MM, N C, -end to Duck Creek MM, Ind |
| 4-28-1828 | Phineas rocf Piney Woods MM, N C |
| 9-26-1829 | Aaron & w Margaret & ch Albert, Marcia, Susannah & Richard rocf Symons Creek MM, N C, - Aaron infs that his dt Susannah has dec since he came to this settlement |
| 6-26-1830 | Robert & w Rebecca rocf Duck Creek MM, Ind |
| 6-26-1830 | Eli rocf Duck Creek MM, Ind |
| 1-22-1831 | Robert & w Rebecca & ch Harriet, Thomas, Thaddeus, Isaac & George gct Duck Creek MM, Ind |
| 1-22-1831 | Eli gct Duck Creek MM, Ind |
| 4-23-1831 | Aaron & Margaret rq mbrp for Samuel Frances, Margaret Ann & Sarah Nixon Fletcher, orphans under their care |
| 6- 2-1831 | Phineas, Rush Co, Ind, -s Jesse & Mary, m Sarah Bundy at Milford MH |
| 9-24-1831 | Sarah gct Duck Creek MM, Ind |
| 3-23-1833 | Lydia rocf Western Branch MM, Va |
| 3-23-1833 | Exum & fam rocf Western Branch MM, Va |
| 5-25-1833 | Rebecca & ch Lucinda & William A rocf Suttons Creek MM, N C |
| 12-28-1833 | Josiah rocf Piney Woods MM, N C |
| 9-26-1835 | Caleb & w Mary & ch Jane, Charles, James, Joseph & Margaret rocf Suttons Creek MM, N C |
| 10- 1-1835 | Josiah of Wayne Co, Ind, -s Thomas & Jemimah, (both dec), m Esther G Hiatt at Milford MH |
| 11-28-1835 | Caleb & w Mary & ch Jane, Charles, James, Joseph & Margaret gct Spiceland MM, Ind |
| 3-26-1836 | Rebecca & ch Lucinda & William gct Spiceland MM, Ind |
| 3-26-1836 | Betsey Ann rocf Spiceland MM, Ind |
| 8-29-1839 | Marcia, -dt Aaron & Margaret of Wayne Co, Ind, m Charles H Moore at Milford MH |
| 5- 7-1840 | Betsey Ann of Wayne Co, Ind, -dt Thomas & Jemima (dec), m John M Macy at Milford MH |
| 10-29-1840 | Albert, -s Aaron & Margaret of Wayne Co, Ind, m Gulielma Hiatt at Milford MH |
| 4-24-1841 | Thomas N rocf Spiceland MM, -end to Hopewell MM, Ind |
| 6-25-1842 | Priscilla rocf Piney Woods MM, N C |
| 8-27-1842 | Margaret rec a min |
| 10-17-1844 | Esther G, widow of Josiah White, Wayne Co, Ind, & -dt Benajah & Elizabeth Hiatt, m Joseph Dickinson at Milford MH |
| 6-28-1845 | Edmund rocf Symons Creek MM, N C |
| 6-26-1847 | Oliver, a minor, rocf Hopewell MM, Ind |
| 8-28-1847 | Edmund, a minor, gct Spiceland MM, Ind |
| 3-23-1850 | Daniel T, a minor residing with Aaron & Margaret White, rec in mbrp |
| 7-23-1853 | Richard gct Miami MM, Ohio, to m Mary A Underhill |
| 7-22-1854 | Mary N rocf Miami MM, Ohio |
| 6-27-1857 | Priscilla gct Whitewater MM, Ind |
| 4-28-1858 | Aaron of Wayne Co, Ind, -s Edmund & Mary of N C, (both dec), m Rachel P Moore at Bethel MH |
| 5-28-1859 | Josiah T & w Elizabeth & ch William Wilson, Mary Isabella, David Francis, Oliver, Delphina & Priscilla rocf Piney Woods MM, N C |
| 5-28-1859 | Francis F rec in mbrp |
| 6-25-1859 | Sarah rocf Deep River MM, N C |
| 12-29-1859 | Deborah, -dt Aaron & Margaret (dec) of Wayne Co, Ind, m David Sutton at Milford MH |
| 8-25-1860 | William E rec in mbrp |
| 5-25-1861 | Sarah gct Hopewell MM, Ind |
| 11-23-1861 | Daniel gct Hopewell MM, Ind |
| 3-25-1865 | John W rec in mbrp |
| 11-25-1865 | John gct Pine Woods MM, N C |
| 6-26-1869 | Daniel T & w Sarah & ch Anna S, Olive B rocf Hopewell MM, Ind |
| 9-24-1870 | Francis T rpt mcd; chm |
| 11-26-1870 | William W gct Hopewell MM to m Mary A White |
| 3- 2-1871 | Rachel M, widow of Aaron White, & -dt Abraham & Hannah Moore (both dec), m Levi Jessup at Milford MH |
| 10-28-1871 | Mary A rocf Hopewell MM, Ind |
| 5-25-1872 | Francis gct Back Creek MM, Ind |
| 5-25-1872 | William E gct Back Creek MM, Ind |
| 5-25-1872 | Daniel & w Sarah & ch Anna, Oliver & Arthur gct Hopewell MM, Ind |
| 3-25-1876 | David gct New Garden MM to m Angelina Hough |
| 2-24-1877 | Levinia rec in mbrp |
| 5-25-1877 | Francis & Peninah rocf Hopewell MM, Ind |
| 6-23-1877 | Oliver & fam rocf Whitewater MM, Ind |
| 2-23-1878 | Joseph rec in mbrp |
| 4-27-1878 | Abigail & ch Mary L, Ella Ann, William T & Ann L rec in mbrp |
| 12-31-1878 | Delphina, -dt Josiah T & Elizabeth W of Wayne Co, Ind, m William M Jenkins at res of Josiah White |
| 8-28-1880 | William & w Mary A & ch Roy, Thomas, Reaborn & Miriam gct Whitewater MM, Ind |
| 11-27-1880 | Oliver H gct Walnut Ridge MM to m Caroline Hill |
| 4- 2-1881 | Oliver H gct Piney Woods MM, N C |
| 9-24-1881 | Josiah & ch Josiah, Mary J & Pharaba W gct Maryville MM, Tenn |
| 10-18-1883 | Sarah C, -dt Richard & Mary W of Ellendale MM, Dakota Terr, m Thomas E Miles at home of her parents |
| 3-26-1885 | Winnifield gct Whitewater MM, Ind |
| 4-23-1885 | Charles A gct Whitewater MM to m Annie Ritchie |
| 4-23-1886 | Oliver & w Caroline & ch Esther G, Raymond T & Robert F gct Whitewater MM, Ind |
| 1-27-1887 | Joseph & w Abigail & ch Mary W, Ella Ann, William T, Annie & Elizabeth gct Hopewell MM, Ind |

**WHITELY**

|  |  |
|---|---|
| 1-27-1877 | Alexander rocf Spiceland MM, Ind |

**WHITLOCK**

|  |  |
|---|---|
| 1-28-1886 | John R, William & Dollie rec in mbrp |
| 2-21-1889 | John & William rel fr mbrp |

**WICKERSHAM**

|  |  |
|---|---|
| 3-18-1824 | Jehu rocf Springfield MM, N C |
| 4-23-1825 | Moses & Price, -s Jehu, rec in mbrp |
| 4-23-1825 | Mary & dt Asenath & Jemima rec in mbrp |
| 1-28-1832 | Caleb & w Eunice & ch Miriam, Mary, Sarah, Anna, Huldah, Jehu, Oliver, Jethro & David rocf Silver Creek MM, Ind |
| 2-23-1833 | Miriam Fosdick (form Wickersham) rpt mcd by Silver Creek MM; dis |
| 3-23-1833 | Mary, having removed here fr Silver Creek MM but since declined coming - cert to be sent back |
| 4-27-1833 | Mary, -dt of Caleb, gct Silver Creek MM (Note says: "ret to this") |
| 7-27-1833 | Abel & w Eliza Ann & dt Caroline Meader rocf Silver Creek MM, Ind |
| 10-26-1833 | Mary Gunning (form Wickersham) rpt mcd by Silver Creek MM; dis |
| 3-22-1834 | Sarah Cosand (form Wickersham) rpt mcd; dis |
| 7-28-1838 | Jehu, rpt dp & apd; dis |
| 1-25-1840 | Anna rpt mcd; dis |
| 6-27-1840 | Anna Eliza (form Dillhorn), mbr Whitewater MM, rpt mcd; dis |
| 1-27-1849 | Miriam (form Palin) rpt mcd within 5 mo after dec of her former h; dis |
| 1-27-1855 | Jehu rst in mbrp at Honey Creek MM, Ind |
| 3-26-1864 | Joshua & w Elizabeth W & dt Elnorah rocf Hopewell MM, Ind |
| 4-27-1867 | Joshua rpt mcd; chm |

**WIGGIN**

|  |  |
|---|---|
| 1-28-1886 | John A rec in mbrp |

**WILEY**

|  |  |
|---|---|
| 5-23-1840 | Eliza (form Modlin) rpt mcd; dis |

**WILLETS**

|  |  |
|---|---|
| 10-23-1824 | Mark rocf West Grove MM, Ind |
| 11-27-1824 | Mark rpt dp & na; dis |

MILFORD

WILLETS (Cont)
1-28-1826　Reuben gct Springfield MM to m
4-22-1826　Belinda Moore (form Willets) rpt mcd; dis
6-24-1826　Joshua, mbr Whitewater MM, rpt dp, upl & dancing
7-22-1826　Joshua rqs complaint be ret to Whitewater MM that they may deal with him
6-23-1827　Mary rocf Springfield MM, Ind
12-27-1828　Isaac rpt jH; dis
12-27-1828　Miriam rpt jH; dis
1-24-1829　Brady M rpt jH; dis
1-24-1829　Susannah rpt jH; dis
8-22-1829　Maria Rumbly (form Willets) rpt mcd; dis
12-26-1829　Reuben rpt jH
3- 9-1830　Reuben dis for jH
2-23-1833　Isaac Newton rpt na & dp; dis
2-24-1838　Lydia & dt Eliza Ann & Lucinda rocf Springfield MM, Ind
5-22-1841　William rec in mbrp
12-23-1865　Jehu & w Mary J & ch Rebecca Ann, Ellis J & Walter D rocf LeGrand MM, Ia
5-26-1866　Ellis & w Rachel & ch Ann & Robert rocf Alum Creek MM, Ohio
8-24-1867　Ann Derbyshire (form Willets) rpt mcd; chm
1-25-1868　Rachel Frazier (form Willets) rpt mcd; chm
3-28-1868　Ellis & w Rachel gct Alum Creek MM, Ohio
5-27-1871　Jehu & Mary & ch Rebecca, Ellis, Van Burton & Lydia gct Poplar Ridge MM, Ind

WILLIAMS
5-27-1826　Jesse, a minor, rocf Goshen MM, Ohio
7-28-1827　Jesse rpt mcd; dis
5-23-1840　Jane (form Hawkins) rpt mcd; dis
5-25-1844　Jesse & w Elizabeth & ch William, Phebe Ann, Malinda, Cassander & Mary Elizabeth rocf Chester MM, Ind
6-26-1847　Jesse rpt dr; chm
8-26-1849　Jesse & w Elizabeth & ch Phebe Ann, Malinda, Cassander, Mary Elizabeth & William Albert gct Whitewater MM, Ind
4-22-1876　Sarah gct Salem MM, Ind

WILLIS
2-24-1838　Lydia & Eliza Ann & Lorinda rocf Springfield MM, Ind
6-24-1843　Lydia rpt na & jas by Springfield MM
7-22-1843　Eliza Ann, Laurenda & Sarah Lavina, ch of John & Lydia, gct Springfield MM, Ind

WILSON
7-17-1823　Jehu appt to a comm
7-17-1823　Sarah appt to a comm
12-18-1823　John rpt mcd; chm
1-15-1824　Ann (form Calloway) rpt mcd; chm
2- 3-1825　Seth of Wayne Co, Ind, -s Jehu & Sarah, m Elizabeth Thornburg at Milford MH
2-23-1828　John C & w Amelia & ch Edith Mary & Ann rocf Flushing MM, Ohio
7-26-1828　John C rpt jH; dis
7-26-1828　Amelia rpt jH; dis
11-26-1831　John & w Anna & ch Sarah, Gideon & Martha Ann gct Caesars Creek MM, Ohio
11-24-1832　Elizabeth rpt jH; dis
10-30-1833　Jonathan of Henry Co, Ind, -s Israel & Martha of Belmont Co, Ohio, m Drusilla Cox at Bethel MH
4-26-1834　Jonathan rocf Duck Creek MM, Ind
10- 1-1834　Gideon of Wayne Co, Ind, -s Jehu & Sarah, m Margaret Charles at Bethel MH
6-27-1835　John & w Margaret & s Alfred, Timothy & Christopher rocf Suttons Creek MM, N C
9-26-1835　John & w Anna & ch Sarah, Gideon & Martha Ann rocf Caesars Creek MM, Ohio
5-27-1837　Joseph rocf Whitewater MM, Ind
1-31-1839　Joseph of Wayne Co, Ind, -s Samuel & Ruth of Hamilton Co, Ind, m Elizabeth Stokes at Milford MH
3-22-1845　Oliver, -s Esther Dickinson, gct Hopewell MM, Ind

10-16-1845　Sarah, -dt John & Anna (dec) of Wayne Co, Ind, m William H Coffin at Milford MH
10-16-1845　Martha Ann, -dt John & Ann (dec) of Wayne Co, Ind, m Benajah W Hiatt at Milford MH
9-27-1845　John C & w Amelia rst in mbrp at Hopewell MM, Ind
5-22-1847　Joseph & w Elizabeth & ch Sarah, Samuel, Ruthanna, Isabella & Mary Abigail gct Walnut Ridge MM, Ind
11-27-1847　Benjamin rocf Blue River MM, Ind
11- 2-1848　Benjamin A, Henry Co, Ind, -s Reuben (dec) & Miriam of Washington Co, Ind, m Caroline Stanley at Milford MH
2-24-1849　Benjamin A & w Caroline gct Spiceland MM, Ind
2-23-1850　Jonathan & w Drusilla & ch Ann, Elizabeth, Israel, Martha & Joseph C gct Westfield MM, Ind
4-27-1850　Benjamin A & w Caroline & s William Albert rocf Spiceland MM, Ind
9-28-1850　Eliza Ann Griffin (form Wilson) rpt mcd; dis
8-23-1851　Alfred gct Springfield MM, Ohio, to m Almira Hadley
12-27-1851　Alfred gct Honey Creek MM, Ind
12-27-1851　Benjamin A & w Sarah Caroline & s William Albert gct Duck Creek MM, Ind
7-24-1852　Timothy gct Short Creek MM, Ohio, to m Elizabeth Ann Terril
3-28-1853　Achsah W, -dt John W & Margaret of Wayne Co, Ind, m Osmund Lindley at Bethel MH
3-26-1853　Milton rpt mcd; dis
3-26-1853　Timothy gct Honey Creek MM, Ind
11- 2-1854　John, Wayne Co, Ind, -s Jehu & Sarah, (both dec), m Eliza Burson at Milford MH
10-28-1854　Elizabeth & ch Phariba A & William R rocf Piney Woods MM, N C
1-27-1855　Timothy & w Elizabeth Ann & s William N rocf Honey Creek MM, Ind
9-27-1855　Gideon C, Wayne Co, Ind, -s John (dec) & Ann, m Susan Stokes at Milford MH
5-24-1856　Margaret M rec a min
3- 4-1857　Christopher, -s John W & Margaret W of Wayne Co, Ind, m Margaret Butler at Bethel MH
11-27-1858　Charles rpt mcd; chm
8-27-1859　Benjamin gct Short Creek MM, Ohio, to m Lucy W Terril
1-28-1860　Lucy T rocf Short Creek MM, Ohio
2-22-1862　Seth & dt Eunice S, Rebecca T & Maria E gct Bear Creek, Ia
2-22-1862　Sarah H Stanley (form Wilson) rpt mcd; rpt by Bear Creek MM, Ia
9-30-1863　Margaret, -dt John W & Margaret W of Wayne Co, Ind, m William Griffin at Bethel MH
11-28-1863　Susan (form Edgerton) rpt mcd; chm
12-26-1863　Isaac rpt mcd; chm
2-27-1864　Sarah Flora (form Wilson) rpt mcd; chm
10-26-1864　Pharaba A, -dt Christopher (dec) & Elizabeth of Fayette Co, Ind, m Nathan O Morris at Bethel MH
12-24-1864　Rachel McCoy (form Wilson) rpt mcd; chm
5-26-1866　Timothy & ch William, Olive B, Terril & Mathew gct Spiceland MM, Ind
10-27-1866　William P gct Kansas MM, Kans
10-27-1866　Elizabeth gct Kansas MM, Kans
12-26-1866　Christopher, Wayne Co, Ind, -s John W & Margaret, m Mary Toms at Bethel MH
7-25-1868　Olive (form Butler) rpt mcd; chm
10-24-1868　Olive gct Spiceland MM, Ind
2-22-1873　Emma Ferguson (form Wilson) rpt mcd; chm
5-23-1874　Henry H & w Martha M rec in mbrp
3-25-1876　Mananna rel fr mbrp
11-23-1878　Pharaba rel fr mbrp
1-28-1886　Fannie rec in mbrp
5-27-1886　James & w Grizella & ch Dayton, Norah, Hattie, Henry & Susanna rocf Walnut Ridge MM, Ind
5-24-1888　Ann gct Pasadena MM, Calif
3-28-1889　Martha C & Hannah J rocf Hopewell MM, Ind

MILFORD

WILTSE
1-22-1876    Josiah & w Susan & ch Theodore, Elistus &
             David rocf Kokomo MM, Ind
4-24-1880    Susan M & ch Theodore C, Elistus L, David &
             Lizzie gct Peace MM, Kans

WINSLOW
5-23-1840    Jacob W & fam rocf Piney Woods MM, N C; -end
             to Spiceland MM, Ind
11-28-1840   Jacob W & w Martha & ch Margaret Ann & Ed-
             mund rocf Spiceland MM, Ind
2-27-1858    Theopholus rq mbrp
4-24-1858    Theopholus, - "there was hardly that stability
             of mind & firmness of purpose, that would
             justify his being rec"

WOOD
9-18-1823    Phebe appt to a comm
12-23-1826   Jesse M rocf Flushing MM, Ohio, -end to Miami
             MM, Ohio

WOODWARD
6-22-1850    Mary (form Hawkins) rpt mcd; chm
10-26-1850   Mary gct Duck Creek MM, Ind

WRIGHT
4-22-1826    William rocf Whitewater MM, Ind
11-30-1826   William of Wayne Co, Ind, -s John & Esther,
             m Elizabeth Justice at Milford MH
12-23-1826   Hatfield & w Mary & ch Isaac, Hatfield K,
             Levin, Mary, Amelia & Lucretia & Amelia
             Charles, a minor u/c of Hatifled & w Mary,
             rocf Northwest Fork MM, Md
12-23-1826   Edward rocf Northwest Fork MM, Md
1-27-1827    John & Esther rocf Whitewater MM, Ind
1-27-1827    Rebecca (form Evans) rpt mcd; chm
4-28-1827    Isaac gct Whitewater MM to m Mary Wright
4-28-1827    Charles rec in mbrp
6-23-1827    Rebecca gct Whitewater MM, Ind
9-22-1827    Mary H rocf Whitewater MM, Ind
10-27-1827   Hatfield rpt "for consenting to dt's accomp-
             lishing her m at his house in his presence
             contrary to our rules"; he appeared & chm
11-24-1827   Amelia Swisher (form Wright) rpt mcd; chm
6-28-1828    John rpt "reading such books & papers as the
             YM has set apart as 'pernicious' & acknowledg-
             ing the doctrines they contain & for being
             out of unity with friends"; dis
10-25-1828   Esther rpt jH; dis
11-22-1828   Hatfield rpt jH; dis
11-22-1828   Elizabeth rpt jH; dis
11-22-1828   Mary H rpt jH; dis
12-27-1828   Mary rpt jH; dis
12-27-1828   Mary Jr rpt jH; dis
1-24-1829    Isaac rpt jH; dis
1-24-1829    William rpt jH; dis
10-24-1829   Charles rpt jH; dis
9-23-1837    Willis rocf Wilmington MM, Dela
5-22-1841    Willis W rpt mcd by Fairfield MM; dis
6-26-1841    Levin rpt jH; dis
1-27-1844    Martha (form Hasket) rpt mcd; dis
2-22-1845    Edward rpt mcd; dis
3-22-1845    Sarah & Benjamin, ch of William & Elizabeth,
             rocf Duck Creek MM, Ind
4-26-1845    Charles gct Philadelphia MM, Pa
6-28-1845    Thaddeus & w Rebecca & dt Mary rocf White-
             water MM, Ind
8-28-1847    Thaddeus & w Rebecca gct Whitewater MM, Ind
3-24-1849    Susanna rocf Salem MM, -end to Whitewater MM,
             Ind
2-27-1875    Thaddeus & ch Mary R & Hannah P rocf White-
             water MM, Ind
3-22-1879    Thaddeus & ch Mary R & Hannah P gct White-
             water MM, Ind

YATES
9-16-1824    Patrick rpt upl & offering to fight; dis
10-25-1825   William rq mbrp; dis by Lost Creek, Tenn:
             rq denied
11-27-1830   Elizabeth & Clarky, -dt Mary, rpt na & dp;
             dis
11-27-1830   Mary rpt jH; dis
3-26-1831    Enoch rpt na & dp; dis
7-27-1833    Caroline Needham Yates & William Yates, a
             minor, gct Spiceland MM, Ind

YOUNG
7-25-1889    Lucy Ellen rel fr mbrp

ZEIGLER
2-26-1885    William H & w Mattie V & s Charles rec in
             mbrp

# MILFORD MONTHLY MEETING
## (Hicksite)
### Wayne County, Indiana

Milford Monthly Meeting (Hicksite) existed from 22nd of 10th Month 1828. The monthly meeting was comprised of Milford, Bethel and Duck Creek Preparatives. Fall Creek was established as a preparative in 1838.

**Duck Creek** and **Fall Creek** were set-off as a monthly meeting in 1840. Bethel was discontinued in 1878. Milford Monthly Meeting was laid down in 1911. Its membership was attached to Whitewater Monthly Meeting.

The Milford meetinghouse was located in the south edge of Milton. It was a frame built in 1829 and was torn down soon after 1911.

### Monthly Meeting Records

The volumes listed below are in a vault in the Miami meetinghouse in Waynesville, Ohio. These records have been microfilmed. The material searched for this publication is marked (*).

| Men's Minutes | Women's Minutes |
|---|---|
| 10-22-1828 : 2-21-1850* | 10-22-1828 : 2-19-1857* |
| 3-21-1850 : 7-20-1899* | 3-18-1857 : 8-18-1892* |
|  | 9-15-1892 : 1-17-1895* |
|  | (joint after 1895) |

Joint Minutes 8-17-1899 : 4-15-1911*

1 Volume Births & Deaths*
Marriage Record 1829-1899*

MILFORD (Hicksite)

## MILFORD MONTHLY MEETING
## (Hicksite)
## BIRTH AND DEATH RECORD

ADAMS
Samuel
Elizabeth

ALBERTSON
Joshua
Abigail
Ch: Rebecca        b 12- 1-1843
    Eli
    Benjamin
    William
    Cyrus
    Ellen
    Elizabeth

Milton      d 7- 7-1843

ANDERSON
Wright
Mary
Ch: William W      b 6- 4-1821
    Mary E         b 11-24-1822
    Ann Jane      b 12-28-1824
    John A        b 11-10-1826
    Margaret      b 12- 1-1828
    Celia D       b 2- 8-1834    d 10- 4-1835
    Martha        b 12-21-1835
    Benjamin F    b 4- 1-1838
    Lydia W       b 1-21-1840
    Sarah P       b 1- 7-1842
    James E       b 1- 7-1845
    Joseph        b 12-20-1847

ANTRAM
Thomas
Rachel
Ch: John          b 4-24-1809
    Thomas Jr     b 6-30-1814
    Euphonia      b 12-24-1816
    Sarah         b 3- 2-1819

BABB
Joseph W
Mary A

BELL
Lancelot      b 11- 3-1790     d 10- 8-1875
Mary          b 7- 7-1802      d 8- 4-1837
Ch: Daniel        b 9-25-1819    d 6-10-1860
    Sarah         b 3-14-1821
    John          b 3-30-1825
    Irena         b 11-18-1827   d 5- 8-1863
    David         b 9-21-1833

BERRY
William
Sarah
Ch: Elizabeth
    James
    Mary Jane
    Esther Ann
    Sarah C
    Susan
    William H
    Margaret
    Lydia Ann      b 6-11-1845

BOND
Jesse
Phebe                   d 6-30-1845

Enos
Susanna

Ch: Calvin
    William C      d 3-12-1856
    Hannah
    Catharine
    Isam
    Eli
    Jesse
    Phebe

Nathan
Tamar
Ch: Ruth (Exum in other records)
    Mary Jane
    Jonathan

Robert
Rachel
Ch: Henry T       b 7-10-1827
    John          b 3- 8-1829
    Emily         b 11-22-1830    d 4-19-1855
    Milton        b 10-20-1832
    Abner L       b 4-19-1836
    Lewis T       b 5-30-1839
    Lydia Ellen    b 7-10-1842
    Larkin T      b 3-10-1847

William
Hannah
Ch: Oliver        b 6-29-1831
    Damaris S     b 9-29-1833
    Larkin T      b 12- 6-1835
    Francinia T    b 12-10-1837

BUTLER
David
Mary              d 10-14-1843
Ch: Rebecca
    Mary
    Esther

Stephen
Mary            b 3-17-1840

Thomas          b 3-28-1806
Amelia          b 3-13-1811

CARR
Lydia             d 2-28-1899

CAVENDER
Abraham
Rebecca
Ch: William
    Hannah

CHARLES
Joseph         d 6- 1-1853
Phebe          b 6-12-1808    d 1- 7-1894
Ch: Mary         b 10-30-1831
    John E        b 11-21-1833
    Levi          b 2- 2-1839
    Henry         b 3- 4-1840
    Sarah         b 9-18-1842
    Luther                   d 1-28-1865

Levin             d 10- 6-1853
Anna

Phebe            d 1- 7-1896

COFFIN
Paul             b 3-23-1784
Elizabeth      b 11-15-1783
Ch: Louisa        b 11-19-1817
    Cyrus         b 5- 5-1820

COOK
. . .
Ann              b 11-14-1784

MILFORD (Hicksite)

COOK (Cont.)
Ch of ... & Ann:
    Angeline           b  8-28-1812
    Martin             b  6-25-1815
    Jabez W           b 12-25-1818
    Dayton C          b 10-20-1823

Levi        b  1-16-1776
Ann         b  3-10-1772
Ch:  Isaac          b 12- 8-1801
    Anna           b 11-22-1803
    Eliza          b  2- 6-1829
    Nancy          b 10-12-1830
    Mary           b  2-10-1833

COPELAND
Charlotte

Jesse

DAWSON
James H                        d 10-20-1850
Lydia
Ch:  Sarah Ann
    Celia A
    Deborah
    Rhoda

DORAN
Jennie      b  3-28-1851     d 2- -1894
                            -bur Friends ground, Milton

ENGLE
Job
Sarah                      d 10- 1-1854

FERRIS
Charles     b 12-24-1856
Mary        b 10-16-1856
Ch:  Elizabeth     b  9-25-1884    m ..Mills
    Albert E      b  2-22-1897

Elwood      b  1- 8-1862
Barbara    -dt .. Shank
Ch:  Eva           b 11-12-1883
    Paul          b 12-22-1886
    Elizabeth     b  4-25-1884
    Albert Elwood  b  2-22-1897

John        b  3-14-1773     d  7-19-1853
Anna                      d  3-20-1856

Joseph                    d  5- 9-1902
Deborah                 d  3-22-1895
Ch:  William       b  3-11-1832
    Elizabeth A   b  9-23-1833

Mathew      b  -  -1805     d 12-28-1866
Elizabeth   b  5-31-1811

William Sr
..
Ch:  Ann Eliza     b  6- 7-1836
    Gulielma A    b  6- 4-1839
    Alytha E      b  8-29-1844
    Hannah K      b  2-19-1847
    Elizabeth H   b  6-25-1849

William Jr   b  3-11-1832
Lydia Ann    b  8-23-1832
Ch:  Charles      b 12-24-1856
    Ellwood      b  1-18-1862    d  4-19-1890
               m Barbara Shank    -bur West Side, Milton

FOULKE
Thomas E
Hannah

Ch:  Ellis
    Ira
    Sarah
    William

William                   d 11- 4-1851

FRAMPTON
Isaac       b  7-28-1782    d 11-28-1847
Deborah     b  9-22-1789    d  1-11-1856
Ch:  William D     b 10-26-1811
    Rhoda A      b  6- 3-1814

William D
Sarah B
Ch:  Henry J      b 12-24-1838    d  6-26-1843
    Isaac B      b  8-20-1840    d  3-24-1841
    William C    b 10-16-1842
    Elisha D     b  4-24-1844
    Arthur E     b  6-12-1847
    George M     b  4-11-1849
    Charles S    b 12-26-1851
    Mary D       b  1-10-1854
    Anna M       b  4-15-1856
    Joseph Justice b  7- 4-1858

FUSSELL
Edwin
Rebecca

GOLDSMITH
Anna        b  6- 8-1806

GRAY
James       b 11- 6-1823
Esther      b  9-14-1821    d  1- 5-1882
Ch:  Lydia Ann    b 10-12-1845
    Mary Alice   b  7- 1-1847
    Sarah Elen   b 11-10-1848
    Caroline Elizabeth b 8- 6-1853
    Elmira Emma  b  2-21-1857
    William Henry b  7-28-1859    d  7-27-1860
    Charles F    b

Joseph         d  4- 2-1843
Mary           d  4-21-1876
Ch:  Elizabeth
    William
    James
    Joseph
    Mary
    Lydia Ann    d  3-31-1843

GRAYLESS
Elizabeth            d  8-  -1839

GREGG
Eli          d  9-27-1852
Martha       d 11-27-1851
Ch:  Ann
    William
    Alma
    Eli
    Edgar
    Salathiel
    Elen

GRIFFIN
Benjamin
Sarah         d  2-11-1863
Ch:  Cyrus        b  5-30-1827
    Jonathan J   b  2- 8-1829
    Elizabeth    b  9-29-1830    d  5- 9-1864
    Mary B       b  8- 1-1832    d  8-18-1835
    James        b  4-12-1835    d  8- 8-1838
    Priscilla    b  5-30-1837    d  7- 5-1837
    Charles      b  9- 2-1838    d 11-24-1839
    Martha Ann   b  5-16-1840
    Sarah Jane   b  7-24-1842
    Henry J      b  4-15-1848    d  6-24-1849

MILFORD (Hicksite)

HAGUE
Samuel
Eleanor

HEACOCK
Daniel T                              d  8- 3-1892
Edna Ann      b 9-11-1819
Ch:  Alice J          b  2-24-1850    d  6-24-1854
     Maryetta         b  1-20-1853
     Caroline         b  5- 7-1856
     Abel Strawn      b  2- 3-1860

Enos          b 12-20-1802
Sarah         b  1-26-1807
Ch:  Hannah F         b  3-17-1828
     Hugh F           b  1-29-1831
     William          b 12- 2-1833    d  2-21-1856
     Enos Ellwood     b  6- 5-1843

Jesse
Mary E
Ch:  Sarah J          b 12- 8-1843
     Joseph Howard    b 10-17-1847

John          b  8-28-1786
Christiana    b 12-27-1784
Ch:  Jesse            b  6- 6-1819
     Rachel                           d  8-18-1864

Nathan        b  4- 9-1806
Eliza         b  4- 9-1809
Ch:  Mary Ann         b 12- 4-1831
     Elizabeth        b  3-27-1837
     Jonah            b  7-22-1840
     Sarah Jane       b  1-25-1843

HIATT
Benajah       b  5-30-1817
Mary          b  4- 6-1820    d  1-18-1839
Ch:  Mary Jane        b  1- 1-1839

Grayson       b  3- 7-1866    d 10- 4-1893
                              -bur Riverside Cem,
                              Cambridge City

Hannah                        d  4-27-1871

Jordan
Edith
Ch:  Anna Maria       b  3-31-1830
     Edward           b  9-15-1831
     John             b 11- 9-1833
     Elda             b 11- 9-1833
     Franklin         b 12- 1-1835
     Albert           b  9-19-1837
     Oliver           b  1-29-1840
     Silas            b  7-15-1843

Oliver        b  1-29-1840
Ellen P       b  9- 2-1841
Ch:  Samuel Grayson   b  3- 7-1866    d 10- 4-1893
     George E         b  4-30-1870
     Martha E         b  7-17-1872
     Cassius F        b  6- 2-1874
     William E        b  7-28-1876
     Olive            b 11-12-1877
     Edith F          b  5- 2-1880
     Olin T           b 12-15-1882
     Margorie S       b  8-20-1884

Silas         b 11- 7-1787
Anna          b  2-22-1784    d  8- 2-1838
Ch:  Ascenith         b  5- 5-1811
     Henry            b 12-30-1815
     Benajah          b  5-30-1817
     Elda Ann         b 11-27-1819
     Louisa           b 10-29-1822
     Lydia            b  1-13-1826

HUSSEY
Lindley
Mary          b  2- 3-1861

HUSTON
Paul
R Anna        b  8-13-1840

JAMES
Even          b 10-11-1784
Rebecca       b  4-21-1789
Ch:  Jonas            b  5-31-1812
     Jesse            b  5-30-1814
     Joshua           b  6-11-1818
     Mary C           b  8- 6-1820
     Joel E           b  8-23-1826
     John             b  6-24-1829

JONES
Aquilla       b  9- 9-1796    d  6-12-1880
Ann H         b  5-28-1803
Ch:  Hannah Y         b  7- 8-1827    d  9-21-1893

Hannah        b  7- 8-1827    d  9-21-1893
              -bur Spring Grove, Cincinnati

JOHNSON
Pleasant      b 10- 4-1795
Sarah         b  6-24-1800
Ch:  Dorinda          b  7-28-1823
     Sylvester        b  1-31-1822
     Martha           b  9-14-1825    d  7-24-1843
     Ellwood          b  1-14-1828
     Timothy          b  3-31-1832
     Elvira           b  1-23-1830
     Milo             b 10-23-1834
     Mary Ann         b  4-10-1839
     Eliza Elen       b  1-16-1843
     John Ashley      b  8-30-1846

JUSTICE
Jonathan      b  8-18-1775    d  1-18-1844
Elizabeth     b  3-15-1783    d  5-17-1851
Ch:  Benjamin         b  9-13-1810    d 11-17-1864
     John             b  1- 4-1813
     Anna             b  5-15-1815    d 11-14-1854
     Enoch            b  7-15-1817
     Henry            b  3-29-1820
     Martha           b  4-13-1822
     Jesse B          b  9-11-1826

KELLY
Rachel        b 11- 6-1790

KENDAL
Jesse         b  9-24-1790    d  5- 8-1857
Maria G       b  3-12-1801
Ch:  John             b  7-31-1827
     Eliza            b  7-23-1825
     Mary             b  6- 7-1829
     James            b 10-25-1831

John
Mary
Ch:  Jesse G          b 10- 1-1852
     Charles H        b 12-26-1854

KING
Thomas
Sally
Ch:  Mary
     Henry
     Zady Ann

KINSEY
Isaac         b  5-19-1821    d  4-18-1896  -bur Spring Grove
                                            Cem, Cincinnati, O
Mary          b  5-26-1826    d  3-26-1889

MILFORD (Hicksite)

**KIRK**
Benjamin M  b 4- 4-1780   d 3-24-1857
Mary        b 2-13-1788   d 11-28-1862

Isaiah      b 3-30-1801   d 1-17-1868
Sarah W     b 10-22-1798
Ch: Mahlon C      b 6-17-1825
    Hannah Jane   b 4-14-1829

Sarah       b 6- 5-1811

**LEVERTON**
Arthur W              d 7- 4-1880
Margaret              d 3- 6-1891
Ch: Baynard T    b 5-24-1840
    Francis M    b 1-16-1843
    Anthony W    b 9-27-1846
    Mary W       b 12-17-1848
    Hannah V     b 3-28-1851   d 2- -1894
                 -bur Friends Cem, Milton, Ind
    Arthur L     b 6-20-1853
    Willis W     b 3-30-1855

Charles
...
Ch: Louisa      b 10- 4-1843
    Rachel      b 3- 1-1835
    Arthur      b 3-31-1846   d 3-27-1863
    Thomas F    b 3- 4-1837
    John E      b 11-19-1839
    Ann J       b 2- 2-1841
    Samuel      b 4-14-1843   d 10-10-1857
    Willis      b 10-16-1844  d 3-13-1851
    Oliver      b 2-25-1849   d 7-19-1849

**MASON**
Alice L     b 3-28-1838   m James Davis

**MATTHEWS**
Oliver              d 1- 1-1854
Phebe               d 7- 6-1857

**MILLS**
Hugh
Lydia
Ch: Thomas H    b 8-30-1819
    Jerusha     b 9- 5-1821
    Peninah     b 3-27-1823
    Priscilla   b 12- 1-1825   d 1-14-1831
    Eber        b 8-22-1828
    Rhoda       b 2-14-1831
    Ruth        b 8-27-1833
    Joel        b 4-16-1836

**MOORE**
Elias           b 4-27-1820   d 3-23-1900
Jane (Whitely)  b 1-4-1824    d 12-17-1879
Ch: William P    b 7-12-1846
    Esther       b 12- 3-1849
    Ellwood      b 5- 9-1855
    Joseph H     b 9-15-1856
    George F     b 10-12-1858
    Jesse E      b 9-16-1861
    Oliver C     b 3- 3-1865

Josiah              d 10- 9-1855

William P    b 7-12-1846
Theresa      b 12-18-1845
Ch: Anna         b 9- 3-1869   d 11-11-1870
    Henry Isaac  b 11- 2-1874

William P
Jemima

**MORRIS**
Aaron    b 9- 6-1776   d 9-20-1845
Lydia    b 1-23-1781   d 10-22-1839

Aaron       b 11-23-1834   d 2-15-1907
Martha M    b 2- 3-1839
Ch: Luella      b 7-30-1867
    William F   b 4-18-1871
    Robert A    b 5-16-1877
    Elizabeth   b 1- 4-1880

Eli
Eliza
Ch: Jeheil Wasson   b 4-23-1866
    William Edwin   b 8-28-1868
    Annie E         b 5-21-1875
    Martha E        b 2- 5-1876

George L    b 9-12-1808   d 9-23-1843
Rhoda A     b 6- 3-1814   d 8- 7-1904
Ch: William F    b 12- 9-1832
    Aaron        b 11-23-1834  d 2-15-1907
    Mary E       b 7-20-1837   m D Tatman
    Ruth Ann     b 8-13-1840
    Elmira Jane  b 4- 8-1843

Isaac       b 4-20-1780
Pharaby     b 3-31-1784
Ch: Margaret     b 10- 5-1803
    Elizabeth    b 10-13-1809
    Gulielma     b 4-17-1812
    Christopher  b 6-28-1814
    Edward       b 8-10-1816

Jason       b 6-18-1830
Ruth        b 8-27-1833
Ch: Jerusha   b 7- 4-1853
    Florence  b 8- 8-1857
    Hugh G    b 2-14-1860   d 10-17-1860
    Sarah A   b 10-26-1861

Jehoshaphat
Mary
Ch: Sarah     b 9-10-1824
    Mordacai  b 6-20-1830

John    b 9- 2-1800   d 10-25-1854
Sarah   b 1-15-1800   d 11- 8-1854
Ch: Susanna   b 12-26-1822
    Thomas B  b 12-10-1824
    Lydia     b 12-10-1826  d 11- 9-1854
    Martha    b 5-25-1834   d 11-29-1854
    Eli       b 9-26-1838

Mordacai    b 6-20-1830
Mary        b 12- 4-1831
Ch: Sarah H    b 10- 5-1854

Samuel    b 3-12-1804   d 8-20-1888
Sarah     b 8- 5-1799   d 6-24-1871
Ch: Cyrus    b 8-23-1828   d 10- 9-1841
    Jason    b 6-18-1830
    Lydia    b 7-11-1838   d 7-21-1839
    Mary     b 3-17-1840
    Charles  b 10-27-1843

Rebecca J         d 1-27-1884

Thomas B   b 12-10-1824
Susan H    b 3-25-1832
Ch: John E         b 1-24-1859   d 10-12-1902
    James M        b 7-12-1862
    Ellwood Thomas b 4-27-1867   d 3- -1869
    Lydia Ann      b 12-31-1869

William F   b 12- 9-1832
Mary E      b 5-29-1836
Ch: Lizzie E    b 7-12-1858
    Emma C      b 9-20-1860

MILFORD (Hicksite)

PICKERING
...
Phebe
Ch: James
    Hiram
    Esther
    Susanna
    Samuel
    Phebe Ann
    Mary
    Leah

PLEASANTS
Elizabeth J    b  3-22-1837
Ch: Ann Howard        b  6- 5-1859    d  1-28-1866

REYNOLDS
Benjamin    b  1- 1-1779
Anna        b  5- 9-1786
Ch: Elizabeth      b
    Phebe          b  6-12-1808
    Josiah         b  3-20-1810
    David          b 11-20-1811
    Reuben         b  4- 1-1813
    Stephen        b 12-18-1814
    Hannah         b  4-19-1816
    Sarah          b 11-21-1817
    Benjamin       b  7-19-1819
    Amos           b  3- 2-1821
    Anna           b  1- 9-1823
    Jonathan       b  8- 7-1824    d  8-11-1829
    Silas          b  8- 6-1826
    Nathan         b  8-21-1828    d  7-24-1829
    William        b  2-28-1830

RIDGEWAY
Reese
Mary        b  2- 1-1801    d 12-19-1832
Ch: Job            b  6- 5-1832
    Lucretia       b  2-15-1834
    Henry          b  7- 3-1835

ROSE
Mary        d  8-23-1846

ROWLET
David
Ann
Ch: Jesse
    Susanna
    David

Edwin
Mary E
Ch: David E        b  6-28-1849
    William W      b  2- 8-1851

RULON
Daniel      b  6-25-1800    d 10-28-1874
Eleanor     b  9-20-1823    d  9- 6-1870

SINKS
Mary                        d 10-10-1846
Catharine   b  4-23-1821    d 10-12-1838

SLEETH
Jerusha     b  7- 4-1853

SPENCER
David       b  4-19-1791    d  9-25-1858
...
David Jr

Louisa      d 11-15-1899    -bur West Side Cem, Milton

Nathan      b  4-20-1820
Louisa      b 10-29-1822
Ch: Benajah N      b  3-25-1845
    Joseph H       b  9-27-1847

Viola           b  4-13-1849
Lexemuel        b  6-21-1851    d 1870
Grome           b  1- 6-1854
Alvaretta       b  7-22-1857
Charley         b  7-17-1859

STRATTON
Joseph P    b  1- 9-1800
Martha W    b  9-20-1806
Ch: Ann J          b  4- 2-1831
    Benjamin W     b  7-13-1834
    Ellwood L      b  7- 8-1838
    Theodosia      b 12-17-1839
    Abram S        b  5- 8-1841
    Lydia J        b 11-17-1842
    Emily          b  7-31-1844
    Joseph M       b 12- 8-1846

STANTON
Peter       b  8-30-1794
Cecilia     b  1-28-1803
Ch: Isaac          b  3-25-1823
    James          b 10- 1-1826
    Edward         b  6- 6-1828    d  7-27-1829
    Mary E         b  4-24-1830
    Ann M          b  9- 2-1832

SWAIN
Charles W   b  7-30-1808
Sarah Ann   b  3-24-1810
Ch: Mary Elen      b  5-29-1836
    Caroline       b  1-15-1838
    Anna           b  9-26-1839
    Joseph S       b 10-10-1841
    Charles        b  4-28-1844

SWIGGETT
Solomon                     d  5-31-1864
Euphemia                    d  8-16-1873
Ch: Jane

SYMONS
Mathew J    b  2-11-1798    d 11-19-1859
Ruth        b     1800
Ch: Jehiel         b  1- 8-1828
    Elias          b  3-26-1831
    Phebe Ann      b  5- 6-1838

Matthew     b 12- 7-1766
...
Ch: Sarah          b 10- 6-1812
    Margaret       b  2-15-1815
    Ann            b  4-23-1800

TAYLOR
John                        d  8-23-1846
Phebe
Ch: Mary
    Sarah
    Martha         b 12-15-1845

THORNBURGH
John        b  8-16-1803
Mary        b  1-28-1808
Ch: Rebecca        b  1-13-1827
    Henry          b 10-30-1828
    John M         b  8-30-1831

THORNE
Joseph      b 11-16-1808
Edith A     b  9-28-1809
Ch: Ellwood E      b 10- 2-1831
    Joseph H       b 10-30-1837

Josiah
Hannah
Ch: Esther Ann                d  8- 9-1846
    Barclay
    Josiah

MILFORD (Hicksite)

THORNE (Cont)
Ch of Josiah & Hannah (cont):
    Rachel
    Jane

TRIMBLE
Joseph
Sarah
Ch: William
    Eliza V    b  1-15-1856

TYSON
William
Mary Jane
Ch: Robert
    Lewis
    Elizabeth
    Samuel
    Elisha

VORE
Isaac    b  4- 3-1783    d  2-24-1862
Ruth    b 12-15-1787    d  8- 2-1878

Jacob    b 10- 5-1808
Sarah    b  6- 5-1811    d  4-21-1877
Ch: Elizabeth R    b 12-11-1834    d  3-25-1835
    Mary    b 10- 1-1839
    William    b 12-24-1842
    James    b  5- 7-1846

WALTON
Ezra    b  7-27-1803    d  2- 5-1883
Deborah    b  4-29-1806

WASSON
Jehiel    b  1-16-1800    d  6-29-1878
Sidney    b  9-17-1802
Ch: Martha A
    Eliza
    Lydia E

WETHERALD
Henry L
Ann
Ch: Mary E
    Edgar
    Amanda
    Henry
    Newton T
    Oscar C
    Charlie M
    Franklin T

WILSON
John C    b  1- 5-1799
Amelia    b  6-30-1801
Ch: Edith    b 10-13-1823
    Mary    b  2- 5-1825
    Ann    b 10- 8-1826
    Martha
    Sarah
    Hannah

Mark L    b  8-27-1802
Mary W    b  7- 1-1807
Ch: Stephen B    b  3- 3-1829
    Shipley F    b  1- 3-1831
    Elizabeth M    b 10-22-1833
    Hannah J    b  1-27-1836
    Massey A    b 11- 3-1839
    Charles B    b  3-24-1842    d  8- 9-1843
    Mark    b  3-30-1844

Moses    b  3-24-1773    d  1-19-1865
Jane    b  8- 8-1771

Samuel
Kezia

Ch: Lydia    b  3-14-1837
    Olivia    b  2- 3-1839
    Martha Elen    b  9-21-1840
    Phebe B    b  9-21-1842
    Adaline    b  1-18-1844
    Jesse B    b  1-29-1847
    Eliza Ann
    James A

Stephen B    b  3- 3-1829
Ann J    b  4- 2-1831
Ch: Charles Ellwood    b  6- 3-1853
    Adaline M    b  4- 7-1856
    Francis L    b  7-31-1864

WINDER
Joseph
Rebecca
Ch: Mary Jane
    Alfred
    Caroline
    Sarah Elen
    Anna Mariah
    Joseph Henry

WOOD
Jacob
Phebe
Ch: Hannah
    Simeon
    Levi
    Seth
    Sarah
    Rebecca

WOOLMAN
Uriah J
...
Ch: Anna
    Mary Elsa
    Mattie Ettie    b 11-25-1866

WRIGHT
Hatfield    d  4- 3-1839
Mary    d  8-18-1848
Ch: Mary    b  2- 1-1801
    Cecelia    b  1-28-1803
    Isaac    b
    Hatfield V    b  6-27-1810
    Lucretia    b  2-15-1814
    Leven    b  2-22-1818

John    d  1- 1-1839
Esther    d  3- 6-1837

Mary Elizabeth    b  3-10-1827
Samuel    b  9-12-1829
Elisha    b 12-25-1831
Lydia Elen    b 10-18-1835

William
Elizabeth

WHITELY
Daniel    b  9-24-1788    d  8-15-1876
Cecelia    b 11- 8-1800    d  3- 5-1866
Ch: Mary C    b  4- 6-1820
    Elizabeth A    b  1- 5-1822    d 11- 8-1826
    Jane S    b  1- 4-1824    d 12-17-1879
    Sarah Ann    b  7-12-1826
    Henry A    b  4-23-1828
    Daniel    b  3-13-1830    d  5-30-1882
    Cecelia M    b  5-18-1832
    Elizabeth G    b  8-30-1834
    William P    b  5-27-1837    d 10-14-1843
    Anna W    b  5-27-1837
    Martha    b  6-19-1840
    Ruth    b  8- 5-1842    d 10- 3-1843

MILFORD (Hicksite)

WHITELY (Cont)
Daniel Jr      b  3-13-1830        d  5-30-1882
Anna Maria     b  6-27-1835
Ch: Edgar D            b  6- 5-1856
    Mary A             b  2- 3-1861
    Ella Anna          b 12- 4-1863
    Byron Alfred       b  3-17-1876
    Benjamin Snow      b 10-21-1877

Edgar          b  6- 5-1856
Alice
Ch: Anna M
    Emma T
    Lewis D
    Emory E

Edward H       b 12-18-1823
Anna E         b  6- 7-1836
Ch: William W          b  1-22-1859
    Lydia Margaret     b  9-12-1861

Henry          b  4-23-1828
Rachel                           d  6-19-1904 -bur Milford
Ch: Alice H            b  8-20-1855   d  1- 9-1863
    Jesse              b  2-23-1858
    Cyrus              b  6- 5-1862

Howard A       b 12-20-1856
Lora R         b 11-13-1862
Ch: Frank M            b 12-16-1883   d  3- 6-1894
    Carlisle K         b 11-14-1885
    Audra              b  6-14-1897

Isaac                            d  8-18-1867
Lydia                            d  4-23-1875
Ch: James A            b 10- 8-1821   d  8- 4-1836
    Edward H           b 12-18-1823
    Frances H          b 10-13-1827   d 11- 5-1862
    Isaac L            b  4- 4-1830
    Lydia A            b  8-23-1832
    Peter A            b 10-23-1834   d  2-24-1835
    Mary Jane          b  1-17-1836

Isaac L        b  4- 4-1830      d 11- 7-1908
                                 -bur Riverside, Milford
Sarah Ann      b  7-12-1826
Ch: Norwood P          b 11-17-1852   d  3-26-1877
    Howard A           b 12-20-1856   m Lora King

MILFORD (Hicksite)

MILFORD MONTHLY MEETING
(Hicksite)
MINUTES AND MARRIAGES

ADAMS
10- 2-1847  Solomon W, -s Thomas & Ann of Wayne Co, Ind, m Susanna W Rowlett, -dt David E & Ann of Wayne Co, Ind, at Fairfield MH
9-16-1847  Solomon W rocf Whitewater MM
10-21-1847  Samuel C rocf Westfield MM
8-17-1848  Elizabeth J & s Isaac H rec in mbrp
12-21-1848  Solomon W & w Susanna gct Whitewater MM
9-18-1862  Elizabeth Edgerton (form Adams) dis for m within a shorter time than allowed after d of a former h

ALBERTSON
9-21-1843  Joshua & w Abigail & ch Benjamin, Martha Sarah, William, Cyrus, Ellen & Elizabeth rocf Whitewater MM
9-21-1843  Eli rocf Whitewater MM
1-21-1847  Eli rpt for mcd with a non-mbr by Fairfield PM
3-18-1847  Eli chm
3-18-1847  Martha Ann Bond (form Albertson) chm; ret mbrp
8-19-1847  Sarah Ann Shafer (form Albertson) rpt mcd
11-18-1847  Sarah Ann Shafer (form Albertson) dis
7-21-1853  William rpt mcd
10-20-1853  William dis
4-20-1854  Elizabeth Shafer (form Albertson) rpt mcd
7-20-1854  Elizabeth Shafer (form Albertson) dis
7-20-1854  Ellen McCullough (form Albertson) mcd
10-19-1854  Ellen McCullough (form Albertson) dis
10-16-1862  Rebecca rel fr mbrp
10-16-1862  Joshua rel fr mbrp
10-16-1862  Eli rel fr mbrp
10-16-1862  Cyrus rel fr mbrp

ALLEN
10-17-1839  Daniel H, w Eliza & ch Amos G, Benjamin, Lindley, Mary Ann, Narcissa & Louisa rocf Plainfield MM
10-17-1839  Jehu, w Mary Ann & ch Mary & Rebecca rocf Plainfield MM

ANDERSON
3-18-1830  Wright & ch William, Mary Elizabeth, Ann Jane, John & Margaret rocf Third Haven MM
11-18-1830  Peter rocf Northwest Fork MM, Caroline Co, Md
9-19-1833  Wright rpt mcd by Bethel PM; ret mbrp
9-19-1833  Mary (form Thornburgh) rpt mcd; chm & ret mbrp
5-17-1838  Peter rpt mcd
10-18-1838  Peter dis
10-28-1841  Mary Elizabeth, -dt Wright & Margaret (dec) of Fayette Co, Ind, m Jesse Heacock, -s John & Christiana of Henry Co, Ind, at Milford MH
2-19-1846  Margaret Haines (form Anderson) rpt mcd; Springborough MM rq to tr w/h & rpt
8-20-1846  Margaret Haines (form Anderson); Springborough MM rpt they tr w/h; she chm; ret mbrp
4-17-1851  Ann Jane Shafer (form Anderson) dis for mou
8-18-1853  Elda Ann (form Hiatt) rpt mcd
11-17-1853  Elda Ann (form Hiatt) dis
8-18-1853  John rpt mcd
11-17-1853  John dis
11-17-1853  Elda dis for mou
10-19-1858  Martha Mendenhall (form Anderson) rpt mcd
4-21-1859  Martha Mendenhall (form Anderson) dis
1-19-1860  William rpt for mcd & na
9-20-1860  William dis
4-19-1860  Wright rpt for jas
9-20-1860  Wright & Mary dis
10-16-1862  James E rel fr mbrp
10-16-1862  Joseph rel fr mbrp

2-19-1863  Sarah rel fr mbrp
3- 2-1879  Caroline J (form Heacock) rpt mcd; ret mbrp
4-19-1888  Caroline J gct Fall Creek MM

ANTRIM
9-20-1838  Fanny Kever (form Antrim) rpt mcd
9-20-1838  John rpt mcd
12-20-1838  Fanny Kever (form Antrim) dis
12-20-1838  John dis

ARNOLD
10-19-1850  Eliza (form Wiley) dis for mou

ATWELL
4-28-1831  Deborah, -dt John & Anna (dec) of Fayette Co, Ind, m Joseph Ferris, -s John & Anna of Wayne Co, Ind, at Milford MH
7-25-1831  Deborah rocf Third Haven MM, Talbot Co, Md

BABB
6-20-1839  Mary Ann rec in mbrp
6-20-1839  Joseph W rec in mbrp

BALLARD
10-16-1865  Penninah & Anna rocf East Hamburgh MM
6-18-1868  Achilles & w Penninah gct Whitewater MM
12-17-1868  Anna gct Whitewater MM

BELL
10-22-1828  Lancelot appt Overseer
11-19-1828  Mary appt to comm
8-19-1830  Mary appt Elder
1-25-1838  Sarah, -dt Lancelot & Mary (dec), of Milton, Wayne Co, Ind, m William D Frampton, -s Isaac & Deborah of Milton, Wayne Co, Ind, at Milford MH
10-21-1847  Margaret (form Bond) dis for mou

BERRY
2-18-1830  William, w Sarah & ch Elizabeth, James, Mary Jane rocf Northwest Fork, Caroline Co, Md
11-18-1830  John & s Christopher G W rocf Northwest MM, Caroline Co, Md
11-18-1830  Purnel rocf Northwest Fork MM, Caroline Co, Md
11-18-1830  Mary & Sarah rocf Northwest Fork MM, Caroline Co, Md
5-16-1833  Sarah Tomlinson (form Berry) rpt mcd
7-18-1833  Sarah Tomlinson (form Berry) dis
5-15-1834  Purnel rpt mcd
9-18-1834  Purnel dis
1-18-1838  Christopher G W rpt na & jas
2-15-1838  Christopher G W dis
4-15-1847  James rpt for na & apd & participating therein
11-18-1847  James dis
1-19-1850  Mary Jane dis for apd & na
3-20-1851  William rpt for na & att mcd at his own house
6-19-1851  William dis
3-18-1852  Sarah Catharine Kirkwood (form Berry) dis for mou
7-19-1855  Hester Ann dis for jas
4-17-1856  Susan Smith (form Berry) dis for mcd
5-15-1862  Margaret Weaver (form Berry) rpt mcd
7-17-1862  Margaret Weaver (form Berry) chm of mcd
8-18-1864  Lydia Ann dis for na & att dancing parties
6-16-1870  Margaret S Weaver (form Berry) rpt mcd; dis

BINGHAM
8-17-1848  Elvira (form Maudlin) dis for mou

BISHOP
5-19-1842  Rebecca (form Butler) rpt mcd
6-16-1842  Rebecca (form Butler) chm; ret mbrp
8-21-1851  Rebecca gct Fall Creek MM

MILFORD (Hicksite)

BOND
2- 1-1829    Phebe appt Overseer
11-18-1829   Charlotte appt to comm
2-18-1830    Jesse appt to comm
8-19-1830    Robert appt to comm
9-23-1830    William, -s Jesse & Phebe of Wayne Co, Ind, m Hannah Lock, -dt William & Demaris of Wayne Co, Ind, at Fairfield MH
3-17-1831    William & s Jesse gct..
10-24-1833   Isom, -s Jesse & Phebe of Wayne Co, Ind, m Dinah Kenworthy, -dt Robert & Ann of Tippecanoe Co, Ind, at Fairfield MH
6-18-1835    Ruth Nicholson (form Bond) rpt mcd
8-20-1835    Ruth Nicholson (form Bond chm for mcd; ret mbrp
12-17-1835   William appt to comm
4-28-1836    Hannah, -dt Jesse & Phebe of Wayne, Ind, m John Wilson, -s Samuel & Keziah of Wayne Co, Ind, at Fairfield MH
1-21-1836    William & w Charlotte & Ira, a minor & William Jr gct Whitewater MM
10-18-1838   Susannah & ch Calvin, Maryann, William & Hannah rec in mbrp
10-20-1842   Jesse Jr rpt mcd by Fairfield PM; chm of mcd
8-15-1844    Lydia Mendenhall (form Bond) chm of mcd; ret mbrp
10-17-1844   Isaac rpt mcd; ret mbrp
3-18-1847    Ruth Ann Shafer (form Bond) chm of mcd; ret mbrp
3-18-1847    Martha Ann (form Albertson) chm; ret mbrp
3-18-1847    Jonathan chm of mcd; not accepted
7-13-1847    Jonathan dis
10-21-1847   Margaret Bell (form Bond) dis for mou
2-22-1850    Demaris, -dt William C & Hannah L of Wayne Co, Ind, m Elias H Wright, -s Isaac & Mary of Madison Co, Ind, at Fairfield MH
11-21-1850   Jesse rpt mcd
2-20-1851    Jesse dis
8- 1-1855    Hannah, -dt Enos & Susan of Henry Co, Ind, m Edward K Stratton, -s Joseph (dec) & Rebecca of Henry Co, Ind, at Bethel MH
4-17-1856    Oliver S gct New York MM
12-17-1857   Calvin rpt mcd
2-18-1858    Calvin chm; ret mbrp
3-18-1858    Isaac rpt for mcd
10-21-1858   Isaac dis
3-18-1858    Jesse Jr rpt for mcd
10-21-1858   Jesse Jr dis
5-20-1858    Francinia Snyder (form Bond) rpt mcd
11- 3-1858   Francinia Snyder (form Bond) dis
11-18-1858   Mary Jane Draper (form Bond) rpt mcd
1-20-1859    Mary Jane Draper (form Bond) dis
1-17-1861    Larkin rpt jas & na
3-21-1861    Larkin dis
10-16-1862   Oliver rel fr mbrp
2-19-1863    Henry rpt mcd
2-19-1863    John rpt mcd
2-19-1863    Milton rpt mcd
2-19-1863    Abner rpt for mcd
7-16-1863    Henry chm of mcd; ret mbrp
8-20-1863    John dis for mcd
8-20-1863    Milton chm of mcd; ret mbrp
8-20-1863    Abner chm of mcd; ret mbrp
8-20-1863    Mary Ann Wickersham (form Bond) rpt mcd & na by Bethel PM
10-19-1863   Mary Ann Wickersham (form Bond) chm of mcd & na
2-17-1876    Mary Ann Garretson (form Bond) rpt mcd by availing herself of the privilege of a divorce & m again by the aid of a hired min
4-20-1876    Mary Ann Garretson (form Bond) rel fr mbrp

BONSAL
2-19-1863    Lydia rel fr mbrp

BRAG
9-15-1864    Lydia Ann (form Gray) dis for mcd

BRANSON
11-19-1835   Sarah rocf Flushing MM, Belmont Co, O

BREWER
4-22-1830    Mary (form Morris) rpt mcd
8-18-1831    Mary (form Morris) chm of mcd; ret mbrp
4-16-1846    Mary dis for na & jas

BROWN
10-16-1834   Ruth (form Cadwallader) rpt mcd
12-10-1834   Ruth (form Cadwallader) dis

BUNDY
11-16-1836   July Elma (form Morris) rpt mcd
1-19-1837    July Elma (form Morris) dis
12-18-1862   Hester L rel fr mbrp

BURDSALL
1-18-1894    Luella (form Morris) gct Purchase MM, N Y
10- 4-1893   Ellwood, -s Ellwood (dec) & Hannah O of Harrison, Westchester Co, N Y, m Luella T Morris, -dt Aaron & Martha M Morris of Milton, Wayne Co, Ind, at residence of Aaron Morris in Milton, Wayne Co, Ind

BURGESS
5-17-1838    Sarah (form Reynolds) rpt mcd
8-16-1838    Sarah (form Reynolds) chm; ret mbrp

BURKSHIRE
8-18-1842    Mary (form Paxton) rpt mcd & na
10-20-1842   Mary (form Paxton) dis

BURT
9-16-1841    Tacy H (form Foulke) rpt mcd
10-21-1841   Tacy H (form Foulke) dis

BUTLER
5-19-1842    Rebecca Bishop (form Butler) rpt mcd
6-16-1842    Rebecca Bishop (form Butler) chm of mcd; ret mbrp
5-21-1846    David rpt for na & jas
7-16-1846    David dis
4-20-1848    Amelia dis for jas
10-21-1847   Thomas rpt for jas
1-20-1848    Thomas dis
11-20-1851   Eliza Jane (form Davis) dis for mou
5-20-1852    Sarah dis for jas
3-16-1854    Mary Treadway (form Butler) rpt for mou
5-18-1854    Mary Treadway (form Butler) dis

CADWALLADER
6-21-1832    Ruth rocf Whitewater MM
10-16-1834   Ruth Brown (form Cadwallader) rpt mcd
10-16-1834   Joseph & ch Joseph Jr & Rebecca rq cert to Blue River MM
12-10-1834   Ruth Brown (form Cadwallader) dis
12-18-1834   Joseph Jr & Rebecca, minor ch of Joseph, gct Blue River MM
3-17-1836    Joseph, a min, dis because "his ministry is no longer edifying nor satisfactory"
6-21-1836    Joseph, a min, & ch Joseph & Rebecca rocf Blue River MM
12-20-1832   Joseph appt to comm

CAIN
2-15-1838    Mary Ann & dt Hannah C rocf Whitewater MM
9-24-1856    Thornton P, -s William & Mary B (dec) of Richmond, Wayne Co, Ind, m Caroline Winder -dt Joseph & Rebecca, at Bethel MH
4-16-1857    Caroline W gct Whitewater MM

CALDWELL
10-22-1828   Joseph appt to comm
2-17-1831    Joseph appt to comm

CAMPBELL
No date      Lydia (form Wilson) dis for mcd & na

MILFORD (Hicksite)

**CANBY**
5-19-1881 — Evan, w Anna & ch Oliver & Herbert rocf Prairie Grove MM, Henry Co, Ia

**CARR**
2-15-1838 — Hannah W rocf Whitewater MM
2-15-1838 — Job, w Ruth & s Vincent rocf Whitewater MM
4-16-1840 — Hannah gct Whitewater MM
6-18-1840 — Job & w Ruth gct Whitewater MM
6-19-1845 — Vincent gct Green Street MM, Philadelphia, Pa
12-16-1847 — John M & w Rachel T & ch Oliver H & Ruthanna rocf Whitewater MM
3-19-1857 — John, w Rachel & ch Ruthann & Oliver gct New York MM
5-19-1864 — Lydia E gct Prairie Grove MM, Ia
10-21-1880 — John W & w Rachel rocf Prairie Grove MM, Henry Co, Ia
5-21-1885 — John M & w Rachel gct Marietta MM, Ia

**CATREN**
4-18-1839 — Rebecca rocf Whitewater MM

**CAVENDER**
8-17-1854 — Abraham, w Rebecca & dt Hannah rocf Whitewater MM
5-19-1859 — Abraham, w Rebecca & s William gct Whitewater MM
11-17-1859 — Anthony rpt mcd by Cincinnati MM; that mtg rq this to tr w/h & rpt
1-19-1860 — Anthony chm; Cincinnati inf
11- -1860 — Hannah Patterson (form Cavender) rpt for mcd
12-20-1860 — Hannah Patterson (form Cavender) chm

**CHARLES**
11-19-1828 — Levicey appt to comm
4-15-1830 — Leven appt to comm
1-18-1838 — Joseph rec in mbrp
8-18-1831 — Eunice (form Thornburgh) rpt mcd
11-17-1831 — Eunice (form Thornburgh) chm; ret mbrp
3-21-1838 — Joseph of Wayne Co, Ind, m Phebe Reins of Wayne Co, Ind, at Bethel MH
5-23-1839 — Levin of Fayette Co, Ind, -s Henry & Mary (both dec), of Dorchester Co, Md, m Anna Williams, -dt William & Hannah of Madison Co, Ind, at Milford MH
12-21-1854 — Anna gct Fall Creek MM
9-18-1862 — Mary Farrington (form Charles) dis for mcd
10-16-1862 — Joseph Evan rel fr mbrp
10-16-1862 — Levi rel fr mbrp
5-21-1863 — Sarah Williams (form Charles) rpt mcd & na
9-17-1863 — Sarah Williams (form Charles) chm

**CLARK**
6-16-1842 — Sarah dis for na & dr

**COCKAYNE**
1-18-1838 — Thomas, w Martha & ch Sarah, Benjamin & Nathan Wilson rocf Whitewater MM

**COFFIN**
6-21-1838 — Paul rpt for allowing his dt mcd - by Bethel PM
8-16-1838 — Paul dis
6-21-1838 — Louisa Paxton (form Coffin) rpt mcd
11-15-1838 — Louisa Paxton (form Coffin) dis
6-21-1838 — Elizabeth rpt for na & promoting m of dt in her own house
12-20-1838 — Elizabeth dis
6-19-1845 — Cyrus rpt mcd by Bethel PM
8-21-1845 — Cyrus dis

**COGSHALL**
5-20-1858 — Mary Jane (form Whiteley) rpt for mcd
9-16-1858 — Mary Jane (form Whiteley) dis

**COLE**
1-21-1830 — Mary Willets (form Cole) rpt mcd by Springborough; that mtg rq this to tr w/h & rpt
8-18-1831 — Mary Willets (form Cole) chm of mcd; ret mbrp; Springborough MM inf
2-15-1838 — Anna & dt Sarah Jane rocf Pipe Creek MM
7-26-1838 — Ann of Wayne Co, Ind, m John Wright of Milton, Wayne Co, Ind, at Milford MH

**COLWELL**
9-17-1840 — Joseph rpt for mcd; ret mbrp

**COALE**
9-24-1840 — Sarah Jane, -dt William (dec) & Ann of Wayne Co, Ind, m Henry Justice, -s Jonathan & Elizabeth of Wayne Co, Ind, at Milford MH

**COFFIN**
10-22-1828 — Bethuel appt to comm
11-19-1828 — Elizabeth appt to comm
11-19-1828 — Paul appt to comm

**COMPTON**
4-21-1870 — Eliza Ellen rpt mcd & guilty of illigitimacy
5-19-1870 — Eliza Ellen dis

**COOK**
2- 1-1829 — Anna appt to comm
1-21-1830 — Levi appt to comm

**COOPER**
11-19-1835 — Letisha E rocf Horseham MM, Pa
10-16-1862 — Letitia rel fr mbrp
12-20-1877 — Emma F (form Gray) rpt mcd; rel fr mbrp

**COPELAND**
6-17-1830 — John appt to comm
10-18-1832 — John appt Overseer
2-21-1833 — Ephriam, w Leah & ch Abigail & Louisa rec in mbrp
7-18-1833 — Jesse rpt mcd
11-25-1833 — Jesse dis
6-16-1836 — Charlotte rocf Whitewater MM
8-24-1836 — John, -s .. of Bethel, Wayne Co, Ind, m Phebe Pickering of Wayne Co, Ind, at Bethel MH
5-18-1837 — John & fam gct Honey Creek MM
6-15-1837 — Samuel rq cert to Whitewater MM to m
7-20-1837 — Samuel gct Whitewater MM to m
2-15-1838 — Martha rocf Whitewater MM
5-17-1838 — Joshua rpt by Duck Creek, PM for att mcd & mcd; Hoeny Creek MM asked to tr w/h
11-15-1838 — Joshua dis
2-21-1839 — Charlotta gct Honey Creek MM
4-16-1846 — Charlotte rocf Honey Creek MM
7-16-1846 — Samuel, w Martha & minor ch, Margaret & Ellen gct Whitewater MM
10-19-1848 — Samuel, w Martha & ch Margaret M & Ellen P gct Whitewater MM

**DAVIS**
1-16-1834 — Rachel, w of Thomas, rocf Center MM, Clinton Co, O
1-16-1834 — Elisha rocf Center MM, Clinton Co, O
5-21-1835 — Elisha rpt by Duck Creek PM for mcd
7-16-1835 — Elisha dis
6-21-1838 — Eliza Jane, a minor, rocf Center MM, O
10-17-1839 — Anna rocf Horseham MM, Mont Co, Pa
11-20-1851 — Eliza Jane Butler (form Davis) dis for mou
6-19-1862 — Martha W gct Whitewater MM
10-16-1862 — Eliza Jane rel fr mbrp
1-19-1865 — James rocf Whitewater MM
11-28-1861 — James, Wayne Co, Ind, -s Joseph & Rebecca Davis of Clearfield Co, Pa, m Martha Whiteley, -dt Daniel & Cecelia of Fayette Co, Ind, at Milford MH
5-25-1865 — James, Wayne Co, Ind, -s Joseph & Rebecca of Clearfield Co, Pa, m Alice L Mason, -dt Howard (dec) & Sydney of Laporte Co, Ind, at Milford MH

MILFORD (Hicksite)

## DAVIS (Cont)
5-16-1867 — James, w Alice & infant s, Howard, gct Whitewater MM, Ind

## DAWSON
2-22-1830 — James H of Wayne Co, Ind, -s Elisha & Lydia (dec) of Caroline Co, Md, m Anna Wright, -dt William & Celia of Wayne Co, Ind, at Fairfield MH
10-17-1844 — James H rpt mcd; Fall Creek MM asked to tr with him & rpt
1-16-1845 — Fall Creek MM rpt James H chm of mcd
3-20-1847 — Lydia, Sarah Ann & Ceilia Ann, ch of James, gct Fall Creek MM
4-19-1849 — James & ch Lydia, Sarah Ann, Celiann & Rhoda rocf Fall Creek MM
5-19-1859 — Sarah Thomas (form Dawson) dis for mcd
10-20-1859 — Sarah refused mbrp because she availed herself of the privilege of a divorce by law
10-20-1859 — Celia Ann gct Whitewater MM, already removed
2-21-1861 — Lydia gct Whitewater MM

## DORON
7-17-1873 — Jennie (form Leverton) rpt mcd by a hireling min; chm; ret mbrp

## DRAPER
11-18-1858 — Mary Jane (form Bond) rpt mcd
1-20-1859 — Mary Jane (form Bond) dis

## EDGERTON
9-18-1862 — Elizabeth (form Adams) dis for m within a shorter time than allowed after d of a form husband

## EDMONDSON
9-21-1843 — Samuel & w Martha R & ch Mary Ann, Rebecca R, Susanna & Samuel Arthur rocf Whitewater MM
5-21-1846 — Samuel & fam gct Whitewater MM

## ENGLE
6-14-1847 — Sarah, a min, rocf Evesham MM
7-20-1848 — Sarah, a min, given permission to visit Whitewater & Miami mtgs
11-16-1854 — Sarah, a min reported dec Oct 1, 1854, ae 72yrs, 2mo, 7da
4-19-1855 — Job gct visit relatives & friends in & near Gwynned MM, Pa
3-19-1857 — Job gct Gwyned MM, Pa

## EVANS
3- 2-1879 — Marietta rpt mcd; ret mbrp

## FARQUAR
3-19-1846 — Elma A chm of mcd; ret mbrp

## FARR
10-19-1837 — Isaac rocf Green Plain MM
3-15-1855 — Isaac gct Maple Grove MM
7-19-1855 — Isaac charged by Maple Grove MM of immoral conduct; that mtg ret his cert; that mtg asked to tr w/h & report
1-17-1856 — Isaac - Maple Grove MM rpts no satisfaction
2-21-1856 — Isaac dis

## FARRINGTON
9-18-1862 — Mary (form Charles) dis for mcd

## FERAN
11-19-1835 — Daniel rocf Gwyned MM, Montgomery Co, Pa

## FERRIS
3-18-1829 — Edith rocf Wilmington MM, Wilmington, Dela
3-18-1829 — John, w Anna & ch Joseph rocf Wilmington MM, Wilmington, Dela
3-18-1829 — John appt to comm
3-18-1829 — Matthew rocf Wilmington MM, Wilmington, Dela
4-29-1829 — Edith, -dt John & Anna of Wayne Co, m Jordan Hiatt, -s Silas & Ann of same place, at Milford MH
3-18-1829 — William rocf Wilmington MM, Wilmington, Dela
4-28-1831 — Joseph, -s John & Anna, Wayne Co, Ind, m Deborah Atwell, -dt John & Anna (dec) of Fayette Co, Ind, at Milford MH
4-18-1833 — William chm of mou
11-28-1833 — Mathew, -s John & Anna of Wayne Co, Ind, m Elizabeth Morris, -dt Aaron & Lydia, Wayne Co, Ind, at Milford MH
12-17-1846 — William rpt mcd
2-18-1847 — William chm of mcd
8-16-1849 — Anna Eliza, Gulielma, Alytha Hannah & infant dt Elizabeth, ch of William, rec in mbrp
11-17-1853 — William & dt Anna, Eliza, Gulielma, Alitha E, Hannah K & Elizabeth H gct Fall Creek MM
1-19-1854 — Elizabeth Myers (form Ferris) dis for mcd
10-25-1855 — William, -s Joseph & Deborah, Milton, Wayne Co, Ind, m Lydia Ann Whiteley, -dt Isaac & Lydia A, Fayette Co, Ind, at Milford MH
6-18-1868 — William chm of violating this mtg's testimony against war

## FOULK
12-20-1838 — Samuel M, w Ann H & ch Tacy H, Margaret H, Jesse H, Sarah, Joseph & Edith rocf Richland MM
12-17-1840 — Margareta Lilly, (form Foulk) dis for mcd
9-16-1841 — Tacy H Burt (form Foulk) rpt mcd
10-21-1841 — Tacy H dis

## FOULKE
2-17-1848 — William E rpt for m a mbr not in mbrp with us, by Richland MM; that mtg asks this to tr w/h; this mtg inf Richland MM it could not act thereon
7-20-1848 — Ann dis for jas
10-19-1848 — William E rocf Richland MM
2-19-1857 — Thomas E, w Hannah & ch Ellis, Ira, Sarah & William rocf Whitewater MM

## FRAMPTON
10-27-1828 — Deborah H appt Clerk
5-20-1829 — Isaac appt to comm
8-19-1830 — Deborah appt Elder
12-22-1831 — Rhoda A, -dt Isaac & Deborah, Wayne Co, Ind, m George Morris, -s Aaron & Lydia, Wayne Co, Ind, at Milford MH
3-20-1834 — Isaac appt Clerk
1-25-1838 — William D, -s Isaac & Deborah, Milton, Wayne Co, Ind, m Sarah Bell, -dt Lancelot & Mary (dec), Milton, Wayne Co, Ind, at Milford MH
10-18-1838 — Isaac appt Asst Clerk
5-16-1839 — William appt Recorder
11-21-1839 — William D appt Clerk
3-16-1843 — William D rpt to have introduced conversation to his neighbor's wife which was calculated to lead to unchastity & in defending himself against this charge, used language that would reflect upon her character
8-17-1843 — William D chm
10-18-1860 — William D, w Sarah & ch William E, Elisha D, Arthur E, George M, Charles L, Mary, Anna M, Joseph J gct Fall Creek MM

## FUSSELL
12- 1-1836 — Solomon of Fall Creek, Madison Co, Ind, -s Bartholomew & Rebecca of Chester Co, Pa, m Hannah Lewis, -dt Joseph (dec) & Lydia of Fall Creek, Madison Co, Ind at Fall Creek MH
2-23-1837 — Priscilla M, -dt Solomon & Martha (dec), of Madison Co, Ind, m Lewis W Thomas, -s of Jonathan & Ann of Madison Co, Ind, at Fall Creek MH
12-20-1838 — Edwin & w Rebecca rec in mbrp

## GARRETSON
10-17-1839 — Peggy rocf Flushing MM
10-17-1839 — Angelina rocf Flushing MM
2-17-1876 — Mary Ann (form Bond) rpt mcd by availing herself of the privilege of a divorce & m again by the aid of a hireling min
4-20-1876 — Mary Ann (form Bond) rel fr mbrp

MILFORD (Hicksite)

GARST
5-  -1843   Anna (form Justice) rpt mcd; chm; ret mbrp

GARTMAN
3-15-1855   Elvira (form Johnson) rpt mcd
5-17-1855   Elvira (form Johnson) dis

GATCHELL
6-18-1840   Sarah S rocf Little Britain MM
2-18-1841   Sarah S gct Whitewater MM

GILBERT
12-18-1862  Sarah (form Morris) dis for mcd with a man not in mbrp with us

GIVORD
10-17-1833  Daniel E produced a minute of approbation fr Oblong MM

GOLDSMITH
5-20-1829   Anna appt to comm
2-17-1831   Daniel app to comm

GOODENOUGH
11- 3-1841  Elizabeth Hester (form Goodenough) rpt mcd
1-20-1842   Elizabeth Hester, (form Goodenough) chm; ret mbrp

GOODRICH
11-15-1866  Rachel (form Leverton) dis for mcd

GORDON
10-16-1862  Amanda (form Wetherald) dis for mcd

GRAY
11-15-1832  Joseph & w Mary & ch William, James, Josephine & Mary rocf Northwest Fork MM, Caroline Co, Md
11-15-1832  Perry rocf Northwest Fork, Caroline Co, Md
11-15-1832  Elizabeth Ann rocf Northwest Fork MM, Caroline Co, Md
7-24-1834   Elizabeth Ann, -dt Joseph & Mary of Wayne Co Ind, m Enoch Maudlin, Wayne Co, Ind, -s of Jesse & Huldah of Henry Co, at Milford MH
11-19-1835  Joseph appt to comm
6-16-1836   Enoch, w Mary & ch Dennis, Sarah Ann, Edmond, Connard & Susannah rocf Bradford MM
11-16-1837  William rpt father of illegitimate ch; ret mbrp
11-18-1841  William F gct Whitewater MM to m Isabella Moore
10-20-1842  Isabel rocf Whitewater MM
1-15-1846   James rpt for mcd; ret mbrp
4-15-1847   Joseph rpt for apd & participating there in
6-17-1847   Joseph chm; ret mbrp
12-16-1847  James rpt for upl & going to law with a mbr
3-16-1848   James chm; ret mbrp
4-17-1851   Mary Long (form Gray) dis for mou & jas
11-20-1853  William & w Isabel gct Whitewater MM
1-20-1853   Joseph rpt mou; chm; ret mbrp
3-17-1853   William & wife gct Whitewater MM
3-15-1855   Esther, w of James, & their dt Lydia Ann, Mary Alice, Sarah Ellen & Caroline Elizabeth rec in mbrp
7-17-1856   Joseph rpt mcd
9-18-1856   Joseph chm; ret mbrp
10-16-1862  Enoch rel fr mbrp
12-18-1862  James rpt for offering violence to his fellow man & na
4-16-1863   James dis
9-15-1864   Lydia Ann Brag (form Gray) dis for mcd
11-16-1871  Sarah C Stonecypher (form Gray) rpt mcd; rel fr mbrp
12-20-1877  Emma F Cooper (form Gray) rpt mcd; rel fr mbrp
4-17-1887   Joseph rel fr mbrp; jas

GRAYLESS
12-17-1828  Elizabeth rocf Northwest MM, Caroline Co, Md

GREGG
9-24-1834   Hannah, -dt Stephen & Hannah of Henry Co, Ind, m Caleb Williams, -s William & Hannah of Madison Co, Ind, at Duck Creek MH
9-21-1837   Eli, w Martha & ch Anna, Alma A, William W, Eli, Edgar A & Salathiel L rocf Miami MM
9-21-1837   Phebe H rocf Miami MM
8-16-1838   Phebe Sweem (form Gregg) rpt mcd & na
10-10-1838  Phebe Sweem (form Gregg) dis
2-19-1846   Anne E Izor (form Gregg) chm of mcd; ret mbrp
4-18-1850   William rpt mcd & na by Bethel PM
6-20-1850   William dis
5-15-1856   Edgar rpt for mcd
7-17-1856   Edgar dis
1-16-1862   Salathiel rpt for participating in Military Service & na
5-17-1866   Salathiel not within knowledge of this mtg; rel fr mbrp
10-16-1862  Eli rel fr mbrp

GRIFFIN
11-18-1830  Benjamin appt to comm
3-18-1852   Elizabeth Newman (form Griffin) rpt mcd
4-15-1852   Elizabeth Newman (form Griffin) chm; ret mbrp
12-16-1852  Cyrus rpt mcd by Bethel PM
10-20-1853  Cyrus dis
12-15-1853  Jonathan rpt mcd by Bethel PM
4-20-1854   Jonathan dis
5-19-1859   Benjamin rpt for unchaste conduct by Bethel PM
7-21-1859   Benjamin dis
12-21-1865  Martha Ann Orr (form Griffin) dis for unchastity & mcd by a hireling minister
12-20-1865  Sarah Jane dis for using secret means in order to secrete a sister's unlawful ch & na

GRIFFITH
6-16-1859   Allen, w Sarah & dt Rachel J rocf Whitewater MM
2-21-1861   Rachel Josephine Mason (form Griffith) rpt for mcd
5-16-1861   Rachel Josephine Mason (form Griffith) dis
12-16-1880  Viola (form Spencer) rpt mcd with one not a mbr; ret mbrp
7-16-1891   Viola (form Spencer) rel fr mbrp

GUYTON
1-20-1870   Alice (form Gray) dis

HAINES
2-15-1838   Isaac B, w Mary Ann & ch Edwin & Hannah C rocf Whitewater MM
11-18-1842  Isaac B & w Mary Ann & ch gct Camden MM
2-19-1846   Margaret (form Anderson) rpt mcd; Springborough MM rq to tr w/h & rpt
8-20-1846   Margaret (form Anderson); Springborough MM rpt tr w/h; she chm; ret mbrp
9-17-1846   Margaret gct Springborough MM

HARDY
12-18-1834  Elizabeth R rocf Green Street MM, Philadelphia, Pa
6-20-1839   Mary Jane, & dt Elizabeth R, rec in mbrp
9-19-1839   Neal & fam rec in mbrp

HEACOCK
11-17-1836  John, w Christiana & ch Rachel W & Jesse rocf Richland MM, Pa
6-21-1838   Aaron rocf Abington MM, Montgomery Co, Pa

HASKIT
-  -1829    Thomas, Henry Co, Ind, -s Thomas (dec) & Ann of Warren Co, O, m Sarah Pickering, -dt Jonas & Ruth of Henry Co, Ind, at residence of Levi Cook, Duck Creek

## HASKET
| | |
|---|---|
| 7-15-1830 | Thomas appt to comm |

## HATFIELD
| | |
|---|---|
| 10-22-1828 | Wright appt to comm |
| 2-21-1833 | Mary appt Elder |
| 2-21-1833 | Wright appt Elder |

## HEACOCK
| | |
|---|---|
| 2-27-1839 | Aaron, Rush Co, Ind, -s Jesse & Tacy (dec), Bucks Co, Pa, m Hannah M Wood, -dt Jacob & Phebe of Henry Co, Ind, at Duck Creek MH |
| 10-28-1841 | Jesse, -s John & Christiana, Henry Co, Ind, m Mary Elizabeth Anderson, -dt Wright & Margaret (dec) of Fayette Co, Ind, at Milford MH |
| 4-17-1845 | Enos, w Sarah & ch Hannah F, Hugh F, William & Enos Elwood rocf Richland MM, Pa |
| 4-16-1846 | Edna Ann (form Hiatt) rpt mcd |
| 5-21-1846 | Edna Ann (form Hiatt) chm; ret mbrp |
| 2-21-1849 | Hannah F, -dt Enos & Sarah, Henry Co, Ind, m Levi P Wood, -s Jacob & Phebe, Henry Co, Ind, at Bethel MH |
| 1-24-1850 | John, Henry Co, Ind, -s Jesse & Tacy, (both dec), of Pa, m Rachel Kelly, -dt Henry & Mary Ward (both dec) of Md, at Milford MH |
| 9-18-1851 | Mary Ann rec in mbrp |
| 9-18-1851 | Nathan, w Eliza & ch Elizabeth, Sarah Jane, & Jonah rec in mbrp |
| 9-18-1851 | Mary Ann rec in mbrp |
| 9-16-1852 | Jesse, w Mary Elizabeth & ch Sarah Jane & Jesse Howard gct Fall Creek MM |
| 9-22-1852 | Mary Ann, -dt Nathan & Eliza of Henry Co, Ind m Mordecai, -s Jehoshaphat & Mary (both dec) of Wayne Co, Ind, at Bethel MH |
| 2-16-1854 | Nathan & fam gct Fall Creek MM |
| 11- 2-1854 | Rachel W, -dt John & Christiana (dec) of Henry Co, Ind, m Henry A Whiteley, -s of Daniel & Cecelia of Fayette Co, Ind, at Bethel MH |
| 1-21-1858 | Hugh rpt mcd |
| 2-18-1858 | Hugh chm, ret mbrp |
| 10-20-1864 | Rachel (dec); her will leaves $50.00 to each PM |
| 3-19-1868 | Daniel chm of violating testamony against war |
| 5-21-1874 | Edward rel fr mbrp |
| 3- 2-1879 | Caroline J Anderson (form Heacock) rpt mcd; ret mbrp |
| 11-20-1884 | Ella (form Whitely) rpt mcd; ret mbrp |
| 8-20-1891 | Hugh rel fr mbrp for jas |
| 1-19-1893 | Edna Ann gct Fall Creek MM |

## HERRINGTON
| | |
|---|---|
| 8-15-1861 | Mary Ann (form Johnson) rpt mcd by Bethel PM |
| 12-19-1861 | Mary Ann (form Johnson) dis |

## HESTER
| | |
|---|---|
| 11-15-1832 | Elizabeth rec in mbrp |
| 11- 1841 | Elizabeth (form Goodenough) rpt mcd |
| 1-20-1842 | Elizabeth (form Goodenough) chm; ret mbrp |
| 11-20-1851 | Hannah dis for jas |

## HIATT
| | |
|---|---|
| 4-29-1829 | Jordan, Wayne Co, Ind, -s Silas & Ann, Wayne Co, Ind, m Edith Ferris, -dt John & Anna of Wayne Co, at Milford MH |
| 10-22-1828 | Silas appt to comm |
| 10-27-1828 | Anna appt Overseer |
| 8-19-1829 | Jordan appt to comm |
| 8-19-1829 | Joseph appt to comm |
| 12-16-1829 | Edith appt to comm |
| 7-15-1830 | Silas appt Overseer |
| 12-28-1837 | Benajah, -s Silas & Anna of Milford, Wayne Co, Ind, m Mary C Whitely, -dt Daniel & Celia of Fayette Co, Ind, at Milford MH |
| 12-20-1838 | Elda Ann Smith (form Hiatt) rpt mcd |
| 2-21-1839 | Elda Ann Smith (form Hiatt) chm; ret mbrp |
| 9-19-1839 | Silas rq cert to Whitewater MM to m Hannah Erwin |
| 10-17-1839 | Silas gct Whitewater MM to m Hannah Erwin |
| 11-21-1839 | Henry appt asst Clerk |
| 1-16-1840 | Hannah rocf Whitewater MM |
| 6-25-1840 | Benajah, -s Silas & Anna (dec), Wayne Co, Ind, m Edna Ann Jones, -dt Henry (dec) & Margaret of same place at Milford MH |
| 6-15-1843 | Henry rpt for mcd; chm of mcd |
| 3-28-1844 | Louisa, -dt Silas & Anna (dec) of Wayne Co, Ind, m Nathan Spencer, -s David & Leah, of Henry Co, Ind, at Milford MH |
| 4-16-1846 | Edna Ann Heacock (form Hiatt) rpt mcd |
| 5-21-1846 | Edna Ann Heacock (form Hiatt) chm; ret mbrp |
| 6-20-1850 | Henry rpt for na & denying authenticity of the Scriptures |
| 9-19-1850 | Henry dis |
| 3-18-1852 | Silas rpt for na & being out of unity with Friends |
| 8-19-1852 | Silas dis |
| 8-18-1853 | Elda Ann Anderson (form Hiatt) rpt mcd |
| 11-17-1853 | Elda Ann Anderson (form Hiatt) dis |
| 8-18-1853 | Jordan rpt for allowing a dt to mcd & na |
| 11-17-1853 | Jordan dis |
| 4-20-1854 | Edward rpt mcd |
| 7-20-1854 | Edward dis |
| 7-15-1858 | John rpt for mcd |
| 9-16-1858 | John dis |
| 12-16-1858 | Franklin rpt for mcd |
| 2-17-1859 | Franklin dis |
| 5-18-1865 | Oliver rq cert to Maple Grove MM to m Ellen P Copeland |
| 6-15-1865 | Oliver gct Maple Grove MM to m Ellen P Copeland |
| 10-19-1865 | Albert rpt for mcd |
| 3-15-1866 | Albert dis |
| 5-16-1867 | Silas rpt mcd & na by Milford PM; case ordered back to Milford PM |
| 11-21-1867 | Hannah gct Whitewater MM |
| 2-18-1869 | Ellen P & minor s Samuel Graston Hiatt rocf Maple Grove MM |
| 7-21-1870 | Silas rpt for mcd by aid of a hireling min & na |
| 12-15-1870 | Silas dis |
| 6-10-1880 | Anna M rpt jas; rel fr mbrp |
| 8-21-1890 | Ellen rpt jas; rel fr mbrp |
| 6-16-1892 | Martha rpt jas; rel fr mbrp |
| 7-21-1892 | Oliver jas; rel fr mbrp |
| 7-21-1892 | George jas; rel fr mbrp |

## HIBLERT
| | |
|---|---|
| 2-19-1835 | Benjamin appt to comm |

## HISTIN
| | |
|---|---|
| 11-15-1832 | Elizabeth rec in mbrp |

## HOLLAND
| | |
|---|---|
| 9-20-1849 | Jane (form Swigget) dis for mcd |

## HOLLINGSWORTH
| | |
|---|---|
| 4-18-1833 | Nathan & w Elizabeth & ch Jemima & John gct Whitewater MM |

## HOLLOWAY
| | |
|---|---|
| 2-15-1838 | Jason, w Jane & ch Edward, Jesse, Edna, Job, Nathan & Israel rocf Marlborough MM |

## HOPKINS
| | |
|---|---|
| 1-10-1832 | George rocf Third Haven MM -end by Whitewater MM |
| 2-16-1854 | George gct Burlington MM, N J |

## HUDDLESTON
| | |
|---|---|
| 8-15-1844 | Ann (form Reynolds) rpt mcd; chm; ret mbrp |
| 10-16-1845 | Jonathan rpt for na & being out of unity by Bethel PM |
| 1-15-1846 | Jonathan dis |
| 10-16-1862 | Anna rel fr mbrp |

## HUNT
| | |
|---|---|
| 9-19-1850 | Sarah (form Wright) dis for mou |

MILFORD (Hicksite)

HUSSEY
2-15-1883   Mary (form Whitely) rpt mcd with one not a mbr; ret mbrp

HUSTON
1-21-1869   Ruth Ann, (form Morris) rpt mcd; chm

IZOR
2-19-1846   Ann E (form Gregg) chm of mcd; ret mbrp
8-16-1860   Ann dis for na & encouraging a Hireling ministry

JAMES
1-27-1836   Jonas, Duck Creek, Henry Co, Ind, -s Evan & Rebecca, m Rachel Kennard, -dt Thomas & Elizabeth of Henry Co, Ind, at Duck Creek MH

JENNINGS
2-20-1851   Rachel (form Thorne) rpt mcd
6-19-1851   Rachel (form Thorne) chm; ret mbrp
10-16-1851  Rachel gct Fall Creek MM

JOHNSON
5-17-1838   Pleasant, w Sarah & ch Sylvester, Dorinda, Martha, Ellwood, Elvira, Timothy, Milo & Mary Ann rocf Westfield MM
4-21-1842   Dorinda King (form Johnson) rpt mcd
11-17-1842  Dorinda King (form Johnson) dis
2-19-1846   Sylvester rpt mcd by Bethel PM; ret mbrp
7-20-1848   Sylvester rpt jas by Bethel PM
10-19-1848  Sylvester dis
4-18-1850   Pleasant rpt na by Bethel PM
6-20-1850   Pleasant dis
3-15-1855   Elvira Gartman (form Johnson) rpt mcd
5-17-1855   Elvira Gartman (form Johnson) dis
11-15-1855  Elwood rpt for na by Bethel PM
2-21-1856   Elwood dis
8-15-1861   Mary Ann Herrington (form Johnson) rpt mcd by Bethel PM
12-19-1861  Mary Ann Herrington (form Johnson) rpt mcd by Bethel PM
8-15-1861   Milo rpt for mcd by Bethel PM, also na
12-19-1861  Mary Ann Herrington (form Johnson) dis
12-24-1861  Milo dis
5-21-1863   Timothy rpt for mcd
7-16-1863   Timothy dis

JONES
7-20-1837   Edney Ann rec in mbrp
6-25-1840   Edna Ann, -dt Henry (dec) & Margaret, of Wayne Co, Ind, m Benajah Hiatt, -s Silas & Anna (dec) of Wayne Co, Ind, at Milford MH
1-18-1866   Aquilla & w Ann W & dt Hannah Y Jones & Elizabeth S Pleasants rocf Cincinnati MM

JUSTICE
10-22-1828  Jonathan appt Treasurer
2- 1-1829   Elizabeth appt to comm
8-19-1830   Benjamin appt Elder
9-24-1840   Henry, -s Jonathan & Elizabeth, Milton, Wayne Co, Ind, m Sarah Jane Coale, -dt William (dec) & Ann, Wayne Co, Ind, at Milford MH
5-  -1843   Anna Garst (form Justice) rpt mcd; chm; ret mbrp
6-20-1844   Henry & w Sarah Jane gct Cincinnati MM
6-19-1845   Enoch P rpt for offering violence to a fellow being & greatly dp
11-20-1845  Enoch dis
11-15-1849  Martha Lynch (form Justice) rpt mcd
12-20-1849  Martha Lynch (form Justice) chm; ret mbrp

KELLY
8-19-1847   Rachel rec in mbrp
1-24-1850   Rachel, -dt Henry & Mary Ward (both dec) of Md, m John Heacock, of Henry Co, Ind, -s of Jesse & Tacy (both dec) of Pa, at Milford MH

KENDAL - KENDALL
2-17-1848   Jesse & w Maria & ch Mary & James rocf Wilmington MM

10-19-1848  John rocf Wilmington MM
5-18-1850   Mary, -dt Jesse & Maria G, Wayne Co, Ind m David R Shinn, -s David & Susan, Huntington, Ind, at Milford MH
9-18-1851   John rq cert to Whitewater MM to m Mary Willetts
10-16-1851  John gct Whitewater MM to m Mary Willetts
4-17-1852   Eliza, -dt Jesse & Maria, Wayne Co, Ind, m Samuel B Moore, -s David & Mary (dec) of Preble Co, O, at Milford MH
5-19-1853   John gct Whitewater MM
8-17-1854   John & w Mary & s Jesse G rocf Whitewater MM
11-17-1859  John, w Mary & ch Jessy G, Charles H & John A, residing within limits of Maple Grove, gct that mtg
12-15-1860  Maria G gct Maple Grove MM
12-15-1860  James gct Maple Grove MM

KENNARD
10-16-1834  Thomas & w Elizabeth & ch Rachel, Levi, John, Jacob Jenkins, Thomas, Joseph & Michael rocf Flushing MM
1-27-1836   Rachel, -dt Thomas & Elizabeth, Henry Co, Ind m Jonas James, -s Evan & Rebecca of Duck Creek Henry Co, Ind, at Duck Creek MH

KENNEY
10-17-1839  Daniel & w Anna & ch Hannah L & Daniel Lukins, fr Horsham MM, Montgomery Co, Pa

KENWORTHY
10-24-1833  Dinah, -dt Robert & Ann of Tippecanoe Co, Ind, m Isom Bond, -s Jesse & Phebe, Wayne Co, Ind, at Fairfield MH

KEVER
9-20-1838   Fanny (form Antrim) rpt mcd
12-20-1838  Fanny (form Antrim) dis

KIMBLE
5-17-1855   Susanna rocf Whitewater MM
7-19-1860   Susan gct Whitewater MM

KINDLEY
3-15-1832   Isaac rec in mbrp
6-15-1837   Frederick & w Mary & ch Edward, Asa, Sarah & Davies rocf Miami MM
3-17-1842   Frederic rpt for refusing to pay a just debt & telling an untruth
3-16-1843   Frederic dis
4-16-1846   Mary & ch Asa, Sarah, Levi, Tamar & Margaret gct Fall Creek MM
10-21-1847  Margaret (form Maudlin) dis for mou
12-20-1851  Frederick rq mbrp in Fall Creek MM, that mtg asks our consent
2-19-1852   Frederick had not settled his affairs, for which he was dis by this mtg; info frowarded to Fall Creek MM

KING
5-21-1835   Thomas W, w Sally & ch Mary Eliza, John T, Henry D rocf Whitewater MM
11-19-1835  Thomas appt to comm
4-21-1836   Thomas & fam gct Whitewater MM
4-21-1836   Mary Eliza gct Whitewater MM
8-15-1839   Thomas, w Sally & ch John T, Henry D & Zada Ann rocf Whitewater MM
8-15-1839   Mary Eliza rocf Whitewater MM
4-21-1842   John T rpt mcd by Bethel PM
10-20-1842  John T dis
8-18-1842   Mary E rpt for att mcd of John T King & Dorinda Johnson
10-20-1842  Mary E dis
4-21-1842   Dorinda (form Johnson) rpt mcd
11-17-1842  Dorinda (form Johnson) dis
3-15-1849   Henry D rpt for na, apd & participating therein by Bethel PM
6-21-1849   Henry D drpd fr mbrp
2-15-1855   Thomas & w Sally & dt Zady Ann gct Maple Grove MM

MILFORD (Hicksite)

**KINNEY**
11-16-1854  Isaac & w Mary P rocf Cincinnati MM

**KINSEY**
6-18-1868  Isaac chm of violating this mtg's testimony against war

**KIRK**
12-20-1832  Isaiah, w Sarah & ch Mahlon & Hannah Jane rocf Whitewater MM
1-17-1833  Leven rocf Whitewater MM
8-22-1833  Sarah, -dt Benjamin & Elizabeth (dec), Wayne Co, Ind, m Jacob Vore, -s Isaac & Ruth, Wayne Co, Ind, at Milford MH
5-21-1835  Sarah & dt Mary Eliza rocf Whitewater MM
11-19-1835  Isaiah appt to comm
1-18-1844  Benjamin Jr rpt for mou by a priest, by Whitewater MM; that mtg asks this to tr w/h & rpt; did not make satisfaction; Whitewater notified
9-18-1845  Mary rec in mbrp
9-18-1845  Benjamin rec in mbrp
8-18-1853  Mahlon rpt mcd & na by Bethel PM
9-15-1853  Mahlon chm
4-13-1854  Hannah Jane Sharpe (form Kirk) rpt mcd
5-18-1854  Hannah Jane Sharpe (form Kirk) chm; ret mbrp
8-20-1857  Mahlon C rpt for mcd by Bethel PM
3-18-1858  Mahlon C dis

**KIRKWOOD**
3-18-1852  Sarah Catharine (form Berry) dis for mou

**KNIGHT**
4-15-1829  William rec in mbrp

**LACY**
2-16-1832  John appt to comm
12-20-1832  John appt asst Clerk
1-15-1852  John rpt for na & being out of unity with some mbrs
6-17-1852  John dis

**LANTZ**
2-4-1909  Elizabeth (from Morris) gct Fall Creek MM

**LEEDS**
10-20-1842  Noah, w Ann L & s William C rocf Whitewater MM
4-18-1844  Noah, w Ann L & minor s William Craig gct Cherry Street MM, Philadelphia, Pa

**LESTER**
5-19-1836  Ann rocf Richland MM, Bucks Co, Pa
11-20-1853  Elizabeth (form Wilson) rpt mcd
1-19-1854  Elizabeth (form Wilson) dis
7-20-1854  Elizabeth gct Whitewater MM
6-15-1854  Ann Ogle (form Lester) rpt m by a hireling min
8-17-1854  Ann Ogle (form Lester) dis

**LEVERTON**
6-17-1830  Rebecca rocf Northwest Fork MM, Caroline Co, Md
11-15-1832  Charles & w Lydia rocf Northwest Fork, Caroline Co, Md
2-21-1833  Rebecca Wright (form Leverton) rpt mcd; Whitewater MM rq to tr w/h
7-14-1833  Rebecca Wright (form Leverton) - Whitewater MM rpt she chm; ret mbrp
11-25-1833  Charles rpt mcd & guilty in a case of illegitimacy
5-20-1847  Thomas, John Edward, Lemuel, Willis & Arthur, ch of Charles, rec in mbrp
6-16-1859  Nannah W rocf Northwest Fork MM, Md
7-18-1861  Arthur W, w Margaret A & ch Baynard T, Francis M, Anthony W, Mary W, Hannah V, Arthur L & Willis W rocf Northwest Fork MM, Md
1-21-1864  Thomas rpt for na
6-16-1864  Thomas dis
2-16-1865  Hannah W gct Fall Creek MM
5-17-1866  Anthony rpt for misconduct & na
7-18-1866  Anthony dis
11-15-1866  Ann Jane Thomas (form Leverton) dis for mcd
11-15-1866  Rachel Goodrich (form Leverton) dis for mcd
11-15-1866  Louisa McNemor (form Leverton) dis for mcd
5-16-1867  Mary W dis for jas & na
7-17-1873  Jennie Doron (form Leverton) rpt mcd by a hireling minister; chm; ret mbrp
8-19-1880  Willis rpt for intemperate habits & na
1-20-1881  Willis dis

**LEWIS**
6-19-1834  Rebecca T rocf Exeter MM
7-16-1835  Able & w Mary rocf Goshen MM, Pa
8-20-1835  Lydia rocf Goshen MM, Pa
8-18-1836  Hannah rec in mbrp
12-1-1836  Hannah, -dt Joseph (dec) & Lydia, Fall Creek, Madison Co, Ind, m Solomon Fussell, Fall Creek, Madison Co, Ind, -s Bartholomew & Rebecca, Chester Co, Pa, at Fall Creek MH

**LILLEY**
12-17-1840  Margaretta (form Foulk) dis for mcd

**LINDLEY**
4-15-1841  Ann L rocf Whitewater MM

**LOCK**
9-23-1830  Hannah, -dt William & Demaris, Wayne Co, Ind, m William Bond, -s Jesse & Phebe, Wayne Co, Ind, at Fairfield MH

**LONG**
4-17-1851  Mary (form Gray) dis for mou & jas

**LUPTON**
5-16-1850  Joseph A rocf Whitewater MM
4-17-1851  Joseph A gct Whitewater MM

**LUKINS**
10-17-1839  William, w Lydia Ann & ch Martha & Rebecca rocf Horsham MM, Montgomery Co, Pa

**LYKINS**
7-17-1834  Allen rocf Guynned MM, Montgomery Co, Pa

**LYNCH**
11-15-1849  Martha (form Justice) rpt mcd
12-20-1849  Martha (form Justice) chm; ret mbrp
10-17-1850  Martha gct Whitewater MM

**McCULLOUGH**
7-20-1854  Ellen (form Albertson) rpt mcd
10-19-1854  Ellen (form Albertson) dis

**McKIMMEY**
9-21-1843  Mary rec in mbrp
6-18-1846  William rec a min
7-16-1846  William, w Mary & s Cyrus gct Fall Creek MM

**McKINNEY**
5-20-1829  William appt to comm
8-19-1829  William appt asst Clerk
2-21-1833  William appt Elder

**McNEMOR**
11-15-1866  Louisa (form Leverton) dis for mcd

**MACY**
11-19-1835  Jonathan rpt mcd
2-18-1836  Jonathan dis
4-21-1836  Hannah (form Thornburgh) rpt mcd
5-19-1836  Hannah (form Thornburgh) dis

**MASON**
4-19-1860  Joseph gct Maple Grove MM

MILFORD (Hicksite)

MASON (Cont)
5-17-1860  Joseph's cert ret to Maple Grove MM (it having been ret 2nd time) & inf it that this mtg is unwilling to rec his cert for reasons already given (ie for mcd)
2-21-1861  Rachel Josephine (form Griffith) rpt for mcd
5-16-1861  Rachel Josephine (form Griffith) dis
3-18-1861  Martha A (form Wasson) rpt mcd by assistance of a hireling min
4-18-1861  Martha A (form Wasson) chm
2-18-1864  Ellwood rpt for mcd
5-19-1864  Ellwood chm
5-25-1865  Alice L, -dt Howard (dec) & Sydney of Laporte Co, Ind, m James Davis, Wayne Co, Ind, -s Joseph & Rebecca, Clearfield Co, Pa, at Milford MH
4-16-1874  Rebecca J, a min, rocf Maple Grove MM
2-19-1880  Rebecca J rocf Maple Grove MM
1-17-1895  Rebecca F gct Chicago Executive Mtg

MATTHEWS
9-17-1846  Phebe rocf Cincinnati MM
7-20-1848  Oliver rocf Springborough MM

MAUDLIN
11-19-1828  Enoch appt to comm
7-24-1834  Enoch, Wayne Co, Ind, -s Jesse & Huldah, Henry Co, Ind, m Elizabeth Ann Gray, -dt Joseph & Mary, Wayne Co, Ind, at Milford MH
4-23-1840  Eliza, -dt Enoch & Miriam (dec), m Isaac Wiley, -s Thomas & Ann, Milton, Wayne Co, Ind, at Milford MH
12-21-1843  Enoch rpt for using abusive language toward his neighbor & being out of unity
2-15-1844  Enoch dis
10-21-1847  Margaret Kindley (form Maudlin) dis for mou
8-17-1848  Elvira Bingham (form Maudlin) dis for mou
10-19-1854  Elizabeth dis for jas

MEAD
9-20-1883  Alfaretta (form Spencer) rpt mcd & jMeth; rel fr mbrp

MENDENHALL
1-16-1834  Alice rocf Center MM, Clinton Co, Ohio
12-17-1835  Alice gct
8-15-1844  Lydia (form Bond) chm of mcd; ret mbrp
10-19-1858  Martha (form Anderson) rpt for mcd
4-21-1859  Martha (form Anderson) dis

MESSICKS
6-20-1839  Elizabeth & Ann, -dt George, rocf Cecil MM, Kent Co, Md
6-20-1839  Sarah Smith (form Messicks) rpt mcd by Cecil MM, Kent Co, Md, that mtg rq this to tr w/h & rpt
10-17-1839  Sarah Smith (form Messicks) dis

MIDDLETON
8-21-1834  Jehu & w Mary & ch Hannah, Richard & Rachel rocf Miami MM
1-15-1835  Phebe rocf Miami MM
5-25-1837  Phebe, -dt John & Mary, Fall Creek, Madison Co, Ind, m John Tyler, -s Thomas & Mary (dec) of Bethel, Wayne Co, Ind, at Fall Creek MH

MILLS
11-18-1829  Hugh appt to comm
7-15-1830  Hugh appt Overseer
11-21-1838  Jerusha, -dt Hugh & Lydia, Henry Co, Ind, m Joseph Sanders, -s Joseph & Martha, Henry Co, Ind, at Duck Creek MH

MITCHELL
3-17-1836  John gct Whitewater MM

MOONEY
6-15-1837  Rebecca rocf Sadsbury MM, Lancaster Co, Pa

4-21-1859  Esther, rocf Solsbury MM, Bucks Co, Pa
10-16-1865  Rebecca gct Whitewater MM

MOORE
5-29-1829  Thomas, -s Thomas & Abigail (dec), Wayne Co, Ind, m Elizabeth Morris, -dt Isaac & Pharabe, Wayne Co, Ind, at Milford MH
8-19-1829  Elizabeth gct Whitewater MM
9-23-1829  Jonathan, -s Josiah & Elizabeth, Wayne Co, Ind, m Margaret Morris, -dt Isaac & Pharabe of same place, at Milford MH
11-20-1829  William rpt mcd; ret mbrp
12-16-1829  Margaret gct Whitewater MM
7-21-1842  Anna (form Sinks) rpt mcd
9-15-1842  Anna (form Sinks) dis
11-2-1843  Elias, -s Josiah & Elizabeth, Richmond, Wayne Co, Ind, m Jane Whiteley, -dt Daniel & Cecilia, Fayette Co, Ind, at Milford MH
3-21-1844  Jane gct Whitewater MM
9-18-1845  Elias & w Jane rocf Whitewater MM
4-17-1852  Samuel B, -s David & Mary (dec), Preble Co, Ohio, m Eliza Kendall, -dt Jesse & Maria, Wayne Co, Ind, at Milford MH
8-9-1852  Eliza K gct Westfield MM, O
3-15-1855  Josiah rocf Whitewater MM
7-16-1857  Jane rpt guilty of taking goods not her own & departing fr the truth relating thereto
10-15-1857  Jane dis
8-20-1857  Massa Ann (form Wilson) rpt mcd
10-15-1857  Massa Ann (form Wilson) dis
5-21-1863  Jane rec in mbrp
7-16-1868  William P rq cert to Green Plain MM to m Terricia E Myers
8-21-1868  William P gct Green Plain MM to m Terricia E Myers
8-19-1869  Therisia E rocf Green Plain MM
6-19-1879  Jemima rocf Whitewater MM

MORRIS
10-27-1828  Elizabeth appt asst Clerk
10-22-1828  Samuel appt Clerk
11-19-1828  Sarah appt to comm
3-18-1829  Isaac appt to comm
3-18-1829  Pheby appt to comm
5-29-1829  Elizabeth, -dt Isaac & Pharabe, Wayne Co, Ind, m Thomas Moore, -s Thomas & Abigail (dec), Wayne Co, Ind, at Milford MH
9-23-1829  Margaret, -dt Isaac & Pharabe, Wayne Co, Ind, m Jonathan Moore, -s Josiah & Elizabeth, Wayne Co, Ind, at Milford MH
8-19-1829  Lydia appt to comm
11-18-1829  Guly E appt to comm
4-22-1830  Mary Brewer (form Morris) rpt mcd
8-18-1831  Mary Brewer (form Morris) chm; ret mbrp
12-22-1831  George, -s Aaron & Lydia, Wayne Co, Ind, m Rhoda A Frampton, -dt Isaac & Deborah, Wayne Co, Ind, at Milford MH
7-18-1833  Charles rpt mcd
10-17-1833  Charles dis
11-28-1833  Elizabeth, -dt Aaron & Lydia, Wayne Co, Ind, m Matthew Ferris, -s John & Anna, Wayne Co, Ind, at Milford MH
4-16-1835  Isaac rpt for na
8-21-1835  Isaac dis
11-16-1835  July Elma Bundy (form Morris) rpt mcd
1-19-1837  July Elma Bundy (form Morris) dis
11-19-1835  Jonathan rpt na by Bethel PM
1-21-1836  Jonathan dis
7-21-1836  Christopher rpt for na & dp
10-20-1836  Christopher dis
8-17-1837  Samuel appt Clerk
10-18-1838  Samuel appt Clerk
9-22-1852  Mordecai, -s Jehoshaphat & Mary, (both dec) Wayne Co, Ind, m Mary Ann Heacock, -dt Nathan & Eliza, Henry Co, Ind, at Bethel MH
4-20-1854  Ruth J rocf Fall Creek MM
1-18-1855  Mordacai, w Mary Ann & dt Sarah H gct Maple Grove MM

MILFORD (Hicksite)

MORRIS (Cont)
11-20-1856  William F gct Fall Creek MM to m Mary Ellen Swain
8-20-1857  Thomas B gct Whitewater MM to m Susan H Shute
12-17-1857  Susan H rocf Whitewater MM
12-18-1862  Sarah Gilbert (form Morris) dis for mcd with a man not in mbrp with us
5-25-1865  Eli, -s John & Sarah (both dec), Wayne Co, Ind, m Eliza Wasson, -dt Jehiel & Lydia (dec) of Milton, Wayne Co, Ind, at Milford MH
10-19-1865  Aaron rq cert to Fall Creek MM to m Martha M Thomas
11-16-1865  Aaron gct Fall Creek MM to m Martha M Thomas
3-15-1866  Martha M rec in mbrp
7-20-1866  William F & w Mary Ellen & ch Emma Caroline & George D gct Fall Creek MM
7-24-1867  Susanna, -dt John & Sarah, (both dec), Wayne Co, Ind, m William A Schofield, -s Jonathan & Elenor, Marion Co, Ind, at Bethel MH
6-18-1868  Charles chm of violating this mtg's testamony against war
6-18-1868  Aaron chm of violating testamony against war
7-16-1868  Susannah M Schofield, (from Morris) gct Fall Creek MM
1-21-1869  Ruth Ann Huston (form Morris) rpt mcd; chm
3-21-1872  Mary E Tatman (form Morris) rpt mcd by a hireling min; chm; ret mbrp
10-17-1872  Esther Whitely (form Morris) rpt mcd with one not a mbr; ret mbrp
12-18-1873  Samuel rq cert to Maple Grove MM to m Rebecca J Mason
1-15-1874  Samuel gct Maple Grove MM to m Rebecca J Mason
5-21-1874  Rebecca J rocf Maple Grove MM (she being an acknowledged min)
9-19-1878  Thomas B, w Susan H & ch John C, James M & Lydia A gct Whitewater MM
1-15-1880  Eli & w Eliza & ch Jehiel W, William Edwin, Annie Elizabeth & Martha Ellen gct Whitewater MM
4-17-1884  Jerusha Sleeth (form Morris) rpt mcd; ret mbrp
5-15-1884  Rebecca J, a min, dec 1-27-1884, ae 82yrs
5-21-1891  John C rocf Whitewater MM
10-4-1893  Luella T, -dt Aaron & Martha M, Milton, Wayne Co, Ind, m Ellwood Burdsall, -s Ellwood (dec) & Hannah O, Harrison, Westchester Co, New York, at residence of Aaron Morris in Milton, Wayne Co, Ind
6-12-1899  William F, Pendleton, Madison Co, Ind, -s Aaron & Martha M, Milton, Wayne Co, Ind, m Lyle Zenblin, -dt Jonathan W & Marietta R of Pendleton, Madison Co, Ind, at residence of Jonathan W Morris
2-4-1909  Martha M gct Fall Creek MM
2-4-1909  William F gct Fall Creek MM
2-4-1909  Robert A gct Fall Creek MM

MYERS
1-19-1854  Elizabeth (form Ferris) dis for mcd

NEWBY
2-16-1832  Joseph appt to comm

NEWMAN
3-18-1852  Elizabeth (form Griffin) rpt mcd
4-15-1852  Elizabeth (form Griffin) chm; ret mbrp

NICHOLSON
8-15-1833  Daniel & w Elizabeth rocf Miami MM, O
6-18-1835  Ruth (form Bond) rpt mcd
8-20-1835  Ruth (form Bond) chm; ret mbrp
10-20-1836  Mary rocf Center MM
9-18-1845  John H rocf Salem MM
9-18-1845  William, a minor, rocf Salem MM
12-16-1847  John rpt for na, upl & wilfully striking a neighbor
2-17-1848  John dis

12-20-1855  William rpt for mcd; Salem MM, N J, rq to tr w/h & report
4-17-1856  William - Salem MM, N J, rpt that they tr with William with no satisfaction
5-15-1856  William dis; Salem MM informed
10-16-1862  Mary rel fr mbrp

NIELESON
5-21-1835  Ruth rpt mou; ret mbrp

NUCHOLS
5-19-1836  Rebecca dis for mou

OGLE
8-17-1854  Ann (form Lester) dis for mcd

ORR
12-21-1865  Martha Ann (form Griffin) dis for unchastity, mcd by a hireling min

OWEN
4-15-1829  Branson appt to comm

PACKER
6-20-1867  Aaron, an Elder, & Ann, a min, produced a minute of concurrance fr Green Plain MM

PANCOAST
9-20-1832  Sevier rocf Goose Creek MM

PARRY
10-24-1839  Robert, -s Joseph & Sarah, Richmond, Wayne Co, Ind, m Esther Vernon, -dt Abraham & Mary, Madison Co, Ind, at Fall Creek MH
12-15-1841  Esther gct Whitewater MM

PATTERSON
11- -1860  Hannah (form Cavender) rpt for mcd
12-20-1860  Hannah (form Cavender) chm

PAUL
3-21-1844  William, w Mary & ch Abigail R, Hannah T, Sarah Michel, Thomas C & Mary rocf Camden MM
7-20-1845  William M, w Mary Ann & ch Abigail R, Hannah T, Sarah, Mickel & Mary gct Chester MM, N J

PAXSON - PAXTON
8-21-1834  Benjamin & w Mary & ch Ruth, Aaron, Lydia & Webster rocf Plainfield MM
8-16-1838  Aaron rpt for na & mcd by Bethel PM
10-18-1838  Aaron dis
6-21-1838  Louisa (form Coffin) rpt mcd
11-15-1838  Louisa (form Coffin) dis
6-21-1838  Ruth Puntney (form Paxton) rpt mcd
9-20-1838  Ruth Puntney (form Paxton) dis
4-18-1839  Lydia rpt for na & jas; dis
9-15-1842  Mary Burkeshire (form Paxson) rpt mcd & na
10-20-1842  Mary dis

PEARCE
11-19-1828  Lydia appt to comm

PENNINGTON
4-18-1839  Paul rocf Center MM, Kent Co, Md
1-18-1844  Ann dis for jas

PICKERING
About-1829  Sarah, -dt Jonas & Ruth, Henry Co, Ind, m Thomas Haskit, Henry Co, -s Thomas (dec) & w of Warren Co, Ohio (w-Ann), at the residence of Levi Cook, at Duck Creek MH
1-21-1830  Phebe appt to comm
2-24-1830  Rebecca, -dt Samuel (dec) & Phebe, Henry Co, Ind, m Nathan Smith, Henry Co, Ind, -s Jacob & Sarah (dec), Preble Co, Ohio, at Milford MH

MILFORD (Hicksite)

PICKERING (Cont)
8-24-1836 Phebe, Wayne Co, Ind, m John Copeland of Bethel, Wayne Co, Ind, at Bethel MH
9-21-1837 Susan Smith (form Pickering) rpt mcd
11-16-1837 Susan Smith (form Pickering) dis
6-21-1838 Hiram K rpt mcd by Bethel PM
8-16-1838 Hiram K dis
7-19-1838 James rpt na & mcd by Bethel PM
11-15-1838 James dis
2-16-1843 Sarah Ann (form Smith) rpt mcd by Plainfield MM, that mtg rq this to tr w/h
3-16-1843 Sarah Ann (form Smith) - comm rpt no satisfaction
9-21-1843 Sarah Ann (form Smith) dis by Plainfield MM

PIERCE
10-22-1828 Samuel, appt recorder of births & deaths & marriages
2-20-1834 Samuel & fam gct Whitewater MM

PLEASANTS
1-18-1866 Annie H, -dt Elizabeth S, rec in mbrp
5-24-1868 Elizabeth J Wright (form Pleasants) rpt mcd; chm

PONTENAY
8-16-1838 Ruth dis

POTTS
11-25-1833 Edward & w Abigail & ch Alfred Oliver, G Franklin, Mary & Lindley rocf Springborough MM
4-16-1835 Edward & fam gct Springborough MM

PUNTNEY
5-21-1838 Ruth (form Paxton) rpt mcd
9-20-1838 Ruth (form Paxton) dis

RAINS
10-20-1831 Phebe (form Reynolds) rpt mcd
11-18-1831 Phebe chm; ret mbrp

REINS
3-21-1838 Phebe, Wayne Co, Ind, m Joseph Charles, Wayne Co, Ind, at Bethel MH

REECE
1-17-1833 Francis rec in mbrp
10-16-1862 Francis rel fr mbrp

REYNOLDS
10-20-1831 Phebe Rains (form Reynolds) rpt mcd
11-18-1831 Phebe Rains (form Reynolds) chm; ret mbrp
12-20-1832 Josiah rpt by Bethel PM for mou
2-21-1833 Josiah dis
10-22-1828 Benjamin appt to comm
7-15-1830 Anna appt to comm
12-24-1833 Reuben rpt mcd
2-20-1834 Reuben dis
7-17-1834 David rpt mcd
10-16-1834 David dis
5-17-1838 Sarah Burgess (form Reynolds) rpt mcd
8-16-1838 Sarah Burgess (form Reynolds) chm; ret mbrp
7-19-1838 Benjamin Jr rpt jas & mcd by Bethel PM
9-20-1838 Benjamin Jr dis
12-19-1839 Amos rpt na & mcd by Bethel PM
2-20-1840 Amos dis
8-15-1844 Ann Huddleston (form Reynolds) rpt mcd; chm & ret mbrp
12-21-1848 Silas rpt mcd by Bethel PM
3-15-1849 Silas dis
1-15-1851 William rpt mcd & jas by Bethel PM
3-20-1851 William dis

RIDGEWAY
10-21-1829 Rees rocf Concord MM, Belmont Co, O
12-23-1830 (Ridgway) Reece, Henry Co, Ind, -s Job & Rebecca, Belmont Co, O, m Mary Wright, -dt Hatfield & Lucretia (dec), Wayne Co, Ind, at Milford MH
2-27-1834 (Ridgway) Rees, -s Job (dec) & Rebecca, Belmont Co, O, m Lucretia Wright, -dt Hatfield & Lucretia, Wayne Co, Ind, at Milford MH

ROBERTS
2-18-1847 Joshua & fam rocf Evesham MM N J & -end to Whitewater MM
10-19-1848 Joshua & w Hannah & ch William W, Hester Ann & Joseph T rocf Whitewater MM
4-19-1849 Joshua & fam gct Fall Creek MM

ROGERS
12-18-1834 Joseph, w Elizabeth & ch Charles J, Sarah Ann, Hannah, Mary Ann, Joseph R, Elizabeth Ann & Margaret W rocf Unchland MM, Pa
8-21-1835 Benjamin rocf Goshen MM, Pa
9-20-1838 Charles rpt mcd by Fall Creek PM
11-15-1838 Charles chm of mcd
5-16-1839 Jonathan J rec in mbrp
9-26-1839 Jonathan J, -s Benjamin & Elizabeth, Madison Co, Ind, m Hannah Weeks, -dt Joseph & Susanna (dec) of same place, at Fall Creek MH

ROSE
8-20-1846 Mary rec in mbrp

ROTHERMEL
4-17-1834 Nancy rec in mbrp
12-16-1847 Nancy gct Cincinnati MM

ROWLET
11-20-1845 George, w Lydia & ch Joseph F, Elizabeth V & Jacob V rq to be rec in mbrp
12-18-1845 Rq refused because he has availed himself of privilege of the law of divorcement
5-21-1846 David E, w Ann & ch Edwin, Jesse, Ezekiel & Susannah rocf Whitewater MM
8-26-1847 Edwin, -s David E & Ann, Wayne Co, Ind, m Mary Elizabeth Wright, -dt William & Celia, Wayne Co, Ind, at Fairfield MH
10-28-1847 Susanna W, -dt David E & Ann, Wayne Co, Ind, m Solomon W Adams, -s Thomas & Ann, Wayne Co, Ind, at Fairfield MH
12-21-1848 David E, w Ann & ch Jesse & Ezekiel gct Whitewater MM
7-7-1851 Edwin, w Mary Elizabeth & ch David E & William W gct Whitewater MM

RULEN - RULON
6-27-1849 Daniel, Wayne Co, Ind, -s Moses & Suanna of N J, (both dec), m Phebe M Tyler, -dt Jehu & Mary Middleton, Madison Co, Ind, at Bethel MH
10-18-1849 Phebe M & dt Mary, Sarah & Martha J Tylor gct Whitewater MM
10-21-1852 Daniel rocf Whitewater MM
2-21-1855 Daniel, Wayne Co, -s Moses & Susanna, (both dec), of N J, m Eleanor Spencer, -dt David & Leah (dec), Wayne Co, Ind, at Bethel MH

SACKETT
4-15-1830 Martha appt to comm

SANDERS
10-18-1838 Joseph rec in mbrp
11-21-1838 Joseph, -s Joseph & Martha, Henry Co, Ind, m Jerusha Mills, -dt Hugh & Lydia, Henry Co, Ind, at Duck Creek MH

SATTERWAITE
3-18-1830 Benjamin L & w Ruth & ch Sarah Ann & Samuel rocf Miami MM
4-15-1830 Ruth appt to comm
6-21-1832 Benjamin & ch Sarah Ann & Samuel gct Miami MM

MILFORD (Hicksite)

## SCHOFIELD
| | |
|---|---|
| 7-16-1835 | Elleanor & ch Mary Eliza, William A, David B, Margaret A, Joseph, Maria P & Susanna rocf Alexandria MM, Dist of Columbia |
| 7-16-1835 | Jonathan rpt by Alexandria PM, Dist of Columbia, to have absconded after being sued, leaving the officer who served the notice, accountable for the amt sued for, Jonathan now living in limits of Milford MM |
| 7-16-1835 | Phebe Ellen rocf Alexandria MM, Dist of Columbia |
| 7-16-1835 | Samuel rocf Alexandria MM, Dist of Columbia |
| 7-24-1867 | William A, -s Jonathan & Ellenor, Marion Co, Ind, m Susanna Morris, -dt John & Sarah, (both dec), Wayne Co, Ind, at Bethel MH |
| 7-16-1868 | Susannah M (form Morris) gct Fall Creek MM |

## SHAFER
| | |
|---|---|
| 3-18-1847 | Ruth Ann (form Bond) chm of mcd; ret mbrp |
| 10-21-1847 | Sarah dis for mou |
| 4-17-1851 | Ann Jane (form Anderson) dis for mou |
| 7-20-1854 | Elizabeth dis for mcd |
| 8-19-1847 | Sarah Ann (form Albertson) rpt mcd |
| 11-18-1847 | Sarah Ann (form Albertson) dis |
| 4-20-1854 | Elizabeth (form Albertson) rpt mcd |
| 7-20-1854 | Elizabeth (form Albertson) dis |

## SHARPE
| | |
|---|---|
| 4-13-1856 | Hannah Jan (form Kirk) rpt mcd |
| 5-18-1854 | Hannah Jan (form Kirk) chm; ret mbrp |

## SHAW
| | |
|---|---|
| 6-18-1835 | Sarah (form Wright) rpt mcd |
| 12-17-1835 | Sarah (form Wright) dis |

## SHINN
| | |
|---|---|
| 5-18-1850 | David R, -s David & Susan, Huntington Co, Ind, m Mary Kendall, -dt Jesse & Maria G, Wayne Co, Ind, at Milford MH |
| 11-21-1850 | Mary K gct Whitewater MM |

## SIMMONS
| | |
|---|---|
| 5-23-1839 | Joshua, Madison Co, Ind, -s Joseph & Sarah, Kent Co, Md, (both dec), m Elizabeth Weeks, -dt Joseph & Susanna (dec), at Fall Creek MH |

## SINGLEY
| | |
|---|---|
| 6-17-1841 | Edward, w Anne & ch Jesse I rocf Whitewater MM |
| 4-18-1843 | Edward, w Ann L & ch Jesse Iden & Mary gc.. |

## SINKS
| | |
|---|---|
| 6-19-1834 | Mary & ch Anna & Catharine rec in mbrp |
| 7-21-1842 | Anna Moore (form Sinks) rpt mcd |
| 9-15-1842 | Anna Moore (form Sinks) dis |

## SLEETH
| | |
|---|---|
| 4-17-1884 | Jerusha (form Morris) rpt mcd; ret mbrp |

## SMITH
| | |
|---|---|
| 2-24-1830 | Nathan, Henry Co, Ind, -s Jacob & Sarah (dec) of Preble Co, O, m Rebecca Pickering, -dt Samuel (dec) & Phebe, Henry Co, Ind, at Milford MH |
| 3-18-1830 | Nathan rocf Whitewater MM |
| 7- 5-1832 | Nathan & w Rebecca gct Whitewater MM |
| 8-16-1832 | Henry T & w Phebe rocf Springborough MM |
| 4-16-1835 | Henry T & fam gct Whitewater MM |
| 3-17-1836 | Nathan, w Rebecca & ch Eliza Anna & Milton rocf Whitewater MM |
| 9-21-1837 | Susan (form Pickering) rpt mcd |
| 11-16-1837 | Susan (form Pickering) dis |
| 12-20-1838 | Elda Ann (form Hiatt) rpt mcd |
| 2-21-1839 | Elda Ann (form Hiatt) chm; ret mbrp |
| 9-19-1839 | Eliza Ann gct Whitewater MM |
| 9-19-1839 | Isaac & dt Elizabeth P & Margaret rocf Whitewater MM |
| 6-20-1839 | Sarah (form Messicks) rpt mcd by Cecil MM, Kent Co, Md, that mtg rq this to tr w/h & rpt |
| 10-17-1839 | Sarah (form Messicks) dis |
| 11-15-1840 | Isaac gct Bradford MM, Chester Co, Pa |
| 11-18-1841 | Edwin rocf Whitewater MM |
| 2-16-1843 | Sarah Ann (form Pickering) rpt mcd by Plainfield MM, that mtg rq this to tr w/h |
| 3-16-1843 | Sarah Ann (form Pickering), comm rpt no satisfaction |
| 9-21-1843 | Plainfield MM dis Sarah Ann (form Pickering) |
| 5-18-1843 | Alice rocf Plainfield MM |
| 4-18-1844 | Margaret gct Bradford MM, Pa |
| 4-18-1844 | Edward (or Edwin) gct Bradford MM, Pa |
| 6-19-1845 | Wilkinson rpt mcd by Bethel PM |
| 8-21-1845 | Wilkinson dis |
| 9-18-1845 | Alice dis |
| 9-17-1846 | Elizabeth gct Whitewater MM |
| 12-21-1848 | Lydia C gct Bradford MM, Pa |
| 8-15-1850 | Elda Ann dis for na & jas |
| 4-17-1856 | Susan (form Berry) dis for mcd |

## SNYDER
| | |
|---|---|
| 5-20-1858 | Francinia (form Bond) rpt mcd |
| 11-18-1858 | Francinia (form Bond) dis |

## SOOY
| | |
|---|---|
| 8-20-1863 | Thomas & w Elma rocf Whitewater MM |
| 5-17-1866 | Thomas & w Elma gct Whitewater MM |

## SPENCER
| | |
|---|---|
| 3-28-1844 | Nathan, -s David & Leah, Henry Co, Ind, m Louisa Hiatt, -dt Silas & Anna (dec), Wayne Co, Ind, at Milford MH |
| 11-21-1844 | Louisa gct Fall Creek MM |
| 6-15-1848 | Nathan & w Louisa & ch Benajah H & Joseph Henry rocf Fall Creek MM |
| 8-17-1854 | Ellen rocf Whitewater MM |
| 2-21-1855 | Eleanor, -dt David & Leah, (dec), Wayne Co, Ind, m Daniel Rulen, Wayne Co, Ind, -s Moses & Susanna (both dec) of N J, at Bethel MH |
| 3-15-1855 | David & s David P rocf Whitewater MM |
| 1-16-1862 | David rpt mcd |
| 5-17-1866 | David rpt dec |
| 12-16-1880 | Viola Griffith (form Spencer) rpt mcd, with one not a mbr; ret mbrp |
| 7-16-1891 | Viola Griffith (form Spencer) rel fr mbrp |
| 9-20-1883 | Alfaretta Mead (form Spencer) rpt mcd & jMeth; rel fr mbrp |

## STANTON
| | |
|---|---|
| 12-20-1832 | Peter dis for conducting himself unbecomingly toward a young woman & not denying the charge |
| 5-18-1843 | Celia & ch Isaac, James, Mary & Lucrecia, gct Fall Creek MM |

## STEWART
| | |
|---|---|
| 5-20-1869 | Mary W rocf Green Street MM, Philadelphia, Pa |
| 6-15-1876 | Mary W gct Woodberry MM, N J |

## STONESYPHER
| | |
|---|---|
| 11-16-1871 | Sarah C (form Gray) rpt mcd; rel fr mbrp |

## STRATTON
| | |
|---|---|
| 2-19-1846 | Joseph P, w Martha & ch Ann P, Benjamin W, Elwood, Theodocia, Abram, Lydia & Emily rocf Whitewater MM |
| 9-24-1851 | Ann J, -dt Joseph P & Martha, of Dublin, Wayne Co, Ind, m Stephen B Wilson, -s Mark L & Mary W, at Bethel MH |
| 8- 1-1855 | Edward K, -s Joseph (dec) & Rebecca, Henry Co, Ind, m Hannah Bond, -dt Enos & Susan, Henry Co, Ind, at Bethel MH |
| 4-17-1856 | Hannah gct Fall Creek MM |
| 5-19-1859 | Joseph P, w Martha W & ch Abraham S, Lydia J, Mary Emily & Joseph M gct Whitewater MM |
| 5-19-1859 | Theodocia M gct Whitewater MM |
| 12-15-1859 | Elwood gct Whitewater MM, already removed |
| 12-15-1859 | Benjamin - cert not granted to Whitewater MM |
| 2-16-1860 | Elwood - cert ret fr Whitewater MM, he will reside in limits of this mtg another yr |

MILFORD (Hicksite)

STRATTON (Cont)
4-19-1860  Elwood gct Whitewater MM
7-21-1864  Benjamin W gct New York MM

SWAIM
9-20-1838  Phebe (form Gregg) dis for mcd

SWAIN
6-14-1847  Sarah Ann, a min, & ch Mary Ellen, Caroline & Anna rocf Fall Creek MM
5-20-1852  Charles, w Sarah Ann & ch Mary Ellen, Caroline, Anna, Joseph & Charles gct Fall Creek MM

SWIGGET
7-20-1848  Euphemia, an Elder, gr permission to accompany Sarah Engle on her visit to Friends mtgs
2-18-1830  Euphemia appt to comm
11-17-1831 Solomon appt Overseer
9-20-1849  Jane Holland (form Swigget) dis for mcd

SWISHER
11-21-1844 Amelia rpt jas
12-19-1844 Amelia dis

SYMONDS
3-15-1849  Jehiel rpt mcd
7-19-1849  Jehiel dis

SYMONS
10-22-1828 Mathew appt to comm

TALBOT
7-19-1838  John, w Mary & ch Anna Elizabeth & Mary Roberts rocf Baltimore MM
7-18-1844  John, w Mary & minor ch Ann E, Mary K, Ruth A, William H, John L & Elisha P gct Cincinnati MM

TATMAN
3-21-1872  Mary E (form Morris) rpt mcd by a hireling min; chm; ret mbrp

TAYLOR
11-19-1828 Stephen appt to comm
4-19-1832  John rocf Northwest Fork MM, Caroline Co, Md
1-15-1835  Stephen rpt na & jas
2-19-1835  Stephen dis
9-17-1835  Stephen dis
11-16-1865 Mary V (form Vore) rpt mcd by Bethel PM
1- 8-1866  Mary V chm
3-15-1894  Mary V gct Lincoln executive Mtg, Nebraska

THOMAS
12-18-1834 Jonathan, w Ann & dt Mary Ann rocf Unchland MM
2-23-1837  Lewis W, -s Jonathan & Ann, Madison Co, Ind, m Priscilla M Fussell, -dt Solomon & Martha (dec), Madison Co, Ind, at Fall Creek MH, Madison Co, Ind
11-21-1844 Thomas rpt for reproachful conduct by Richland MM, Pa; that mtg rq the aid of this in tr w/h & rpt
12-19-1844 Thomas removed from limits of this mtg; Richland inf
5-18-1848  Mary (form Witchell) dis for mou
5-19-1859  Sarah (form Dawson) dis for mcd
10-20-1859 Sarah refused mbrp because she availed herself of the privilege of a divorce law
11-15-1866 Ann Jane, (form Leverton) dis for mcd

TOMLINSON
5-16-1833  Sarah (form Berry) rpt mcd
7-18-1833  Sarah (form Berry) dis

THORNBURGH
10-22-1828 Henry appt to comm

10-27-1828 Rebecca appt Overseer
8-18-1831  Eunice Charles (form Thornburgh) rpt mcd
11-17-1831 Eunice Charles (form Thornburgh) chm; ret mbrp
9-19-1833  (Thornburg) Mary Anderson (form Thornburg) rpt mcd; chm; ret mbrp
11-19-1835 (Thornburg) Milton rpt mcd by Bethel PM
1-21-1836  Milton dis (Thornburg)
4-21-1836  Hannah Macy (form Thornburgh) rpt mcd
5-19-1836  Hannah Macy (form Thornburgh) dis
6-21-1849  Henry rpt for na & being out of unity with Friends
8-16-1849  Henry dis
12-25-1851 Henry, -s John (dec) & Mary of Fayette Co, Ind, m Maria Whiteley, -dt Daniel & Cecelia, Fayette Co, Ind, at Milford MH
8-19-1852  (Thornburg) Henry H & w Celia Maria gct Fall Creek MM
11-20-1856 (Thornburg) Elizabeth (form Whitely) rpt mcd
12-18-1856 (Thornburg) Elizabeth (form Whitely) chm; ret mbrp
8-20-1863  (Thornburg) Phebe Ann (form Symons) dis for mcd & na
11-19-1874 (Thornburg) Elizabeth G rpt jas
12-17-1874 (Thornburg) Elizabeth G dis

THORNE
9-19-1844  Joseph produced a cert of concurrance fr Horsham MM, Pa; -end by Abington QM
5-15-1845  Joseph, w Edith Ann & s Elwood & Joseph Howard rocf Horsham MM, Pa
6-18-1846  Josiah, w Hannah B & ch Barclay, Josiah B, Rachel B & Eliza Jane rocf Chester MM
6-18-1846  Esther Ann rocf Chester MM
10-19-1848 Joseph, w Edith Ann & ch Elwood E & Joseph Howard gct Cincinnati MM, O
10-17-1850 Josiah, w Hannah B & dt Eliza Jane gct Fall Creek MM
2-20-1851  Rachel Jennings (form Thorne) rpt mcd
4-17-1851  Barclay gct Fall Creek MM
12-18-1851 Barclay rpt mcd; his cert ret fr Fall Creek MM
12-20-1851 Josiah Jr rpt mcd by Bethel PM
3-18-1852  Josiah Jr gct Fall Creek MM
5-20-1852  Barclay chm; gct Fall Creek MM

TINGLEY
4-18-1844  Edward & w ch Jesse Iden & Mary Singley gct Cherry Street MM, Philadelphia

TOMLINSON
4-18-1833  Sarah rpt mou by Bethel PM
7-18-1833  Sarah dis

TREADWAY
3-16-1854  Mary (form Butler) rpt for mou
5-18-1854  Mary (form Butler) dis

TRIMBLE
5-20-1852  Sarah G rocf Cincinnati MM
8-20-1857  Joseph M & w Sarah G, ch William & Eliza V gct Whitewater MM

TYLER
5-25-1837  John, -s Thomas & Mary (dec), Bethel, Wayne Co, Ind, m Phebe Middleton, -dt John & Mary, Fall Creek, Madison Co, Ind, at Fall Creek MH
10-21-1841 John, dec, a memorial prepared of his exemplary life

TYSON
6-27-1849  Phebe M, -dt Jehu & Mary, Middleton, Madison Co, Ind, m Daniel Rulen, Wayne Co, Ind, -s Moses & Susanna (both dec), of N J, at Bethel MH
9-21-1854  William & w Mary, a min, & ch Robert A, Lewis A, Elizabeth, Samuel E & Elisha E rocf Whitewater MM
1-17-1859  Mary Jane removed from the station of a minister because of a want of sufficient depth in Gospel experience

MILFORD (Hicksite)

**TYSON (Cont)**
- 8-16-1860  William, w Mary Jane & ch Robert A, Lewis A, Elizabeth, Samuel E & Elisha gct Maple Grove MM
- 10-16-1862  Daniel rel fr mbrp

**VERNON**
- 4-18-1839  Esther rocf Whitewater MM
- 4-18-1839  Abram, w Mary & dt Esther rocf Whitewater MM
- 4-18-1839  Edward B rocf Whitewater MM
- 10-24-1839  Esther, -dt Abraham & Mary, Madison Co, Ind, m Robert Parry, -s Joseph & Sarah, Richmond, Wayne Co, Ind, at Fall Creek MH

**VORE**
- 4-19-1832  Jacob Jr rocf Whitewater MM
- 8-22-1833  Jacob, -s Isaac & Ruth, Wayne Co, Ind, m Sarah Kirk, -dt Benjamin & Elizabeth (dec), Wayne Co, Ind, at Milford MH
- 1-21-1847  Isaac & w Ruth rocf Whitewater MM
- 9-19-1850  Mary rocf Pipe Creek MM, Md, -end by Whitewater MM
- 2-19-1863  Ruth gct Whitewater MM
- 11-16-1865  Mary V Taylor (form Vore) rpt mcd by Bethel PM
- 1-8-1866  Mary V Taylor (form Vore) chm
- 4-18-1889  Jacob gct Lincoln Executive MM, Nebr

**WALTON**
- 10-19-1837  Ezra & w Deborah rocf Chester MM, N J
- 7-19-1883  Deborah L gct Chester MM, N J

**WASSON**
- 10-19-1855  Jehiel, w Sidney & ch Martha A, Lydia E, Eliza & Alice rocf Whitewater MM
- 5-25-1865  Eliza, -dt Jehiel & Lydia (dec), Milton, Wayne Co, Ind, m Eli Morris, -s John & Sarah (both dec), Wayne Co, Ind, at Milford MH

**WATSON**
- 4-19-1855  Hannah Jane (form Wilson) rpt mcd
- 5-17-1855  Hannah Jane (form Wilson) chm; ret mbrp
- 4-21-1859  Hannah Jane rpt jas
- 7-21-1859  Hannah Jane dis

**WEAVER**
- 5-15-1862  Margaret (form Berry) rpt mcd
- 7-17-1862  Margaret (form Berry) chm
- 6-16-1870  Margaret S (form Berry) dis for mcd

**WEEKS**
- 3-20-1824  Anna rocf Cornwall MM
- 3-20-1834  Joseph, w Lydia & ch Sarah, Charles, Hanna, Maria Ann, Eliza, Rebecca & John rocf Cornwall MM
- 11-17-1836  Joseph, w Susanna & ch Elizabeth, Susan, Hannah, Samuel, Joseph, Thomas & Abraham, (the four latter minors), rocf Cornwall MM, held at Smith Cove
- 5-23-1839  Elizabeth, -dt Joseph & Susanna (dec), m Joshua Simmons, Madison Co, Ind, -s Joseph & Sarah, (both dec), Kent Co, Md, at Fall Creek MH
- 6-20-1839  Phebe rec in mbrp
- 9-26-1839  Hannah, -dt Joseph & Susanna (dec), Madison Co, Ind, m Jonathan J Rogers, -s Benjamin & Elizabeth, of same place, at Fall Creek MH

**WETHERALD**
- 11-19-1846  Henry L, w Ann & ch Mary E, Edgar, Amanda, Henry & Newton rocf Whitewater MM
- 10-16-1862  Amanda Gordon (form Wetherald) dis for mcd
- 10-16-1862  Henry rel fr mbrp
- 10-15-1863  Ann H & minor s Newton T, Oscar C, Charlie M & Franklin T gct Whitewater MM

**WHIPPO**
- 9-21-1837  Hannah rocf Rochester MM, N Y

**WHITE**
- 4-18-1839  Lewis rocf Whitewater MM

**WHITELEY - WHITELY**
- 12-17-1828  Daniel, w Celia & ch Mary C, Jane, Sarah Ann & Henry A rocf Northwest Fork MM, Caroline Co, Md
- 12-17-1828  Isaac, w Lydia & ch James Anthony, Edmond Hicks & Francis Henry rocf Northwest MM Caroline Co, Md
- 8-19-1829  Daniel appt to comm
- 10-21-1829  Celia appt to comm
- 9-20-1832  Isom appt to comm
- 11-15-1832  Daniel appt Overseer
- 9-20-1834  Daniel appt Clerk
- 8-17-1837  Isaac appt asst Clerk
- 12-28-1837  Mary C, -dt Daniel & Celia, Fayette Co, Ind, m Benajah Hiatt, -s Silas & Anna, Milford, Wayne Co, Ind, at Milford M
- 11-2-1843  Jane, -dt Daniel & Cecilia, Fayette Co, Ind, m Elias Moore, -s Josiah & Elizabeth, of Richmond, Wayne Co, Ind, at Milford MH
- 12-25-1851  Maria, -dt Daniel & Cecelia, Fayette Co, Ind, m Henry Thornburgh, -s John (dec) of same place, at Milford MH
- 2-19-1852  Isaac Jr rpt mcd to one too nearly related to him
- 3-18-1852  Isaac Jr, ret mbrp
- 1-15-1852  Sarah Ann rpt mcd with a near relative
- 2-19-1852  Sarah Ann chm; ret mbrp
- 11-2-1854  Henry A, -s Daniel & Cecilia, Fayette Co, Ind, m Rachel W Heacock, -dt John & Christiana (dec) of Henry Co, Ind, at Bethel MH
- 10-25-1855  Lydia Ann, -dt Isaac & Lydia A of Fayette Co, Ind, m William Ferris, -s Joseph & Deborah of Milton, Wayne Co, Ind, at Milford MH
- 5-15-1856  Daniel Jr rpt for mcd
- 7-17-1856  Daniel Jr chm
- 11-20-1856  Elizabeth Thornburg (form Whitely) rpt mcd
- 12-18-1856  Elizabeth Thornburg (form Whitely) chm; ret mbrp
- 2-19-1857  (Whitely) Edward H rpt for mcd; Maple Grove MM asked to tr w/h
- 6-18-1857  Edward H Whitely, Maple Grove inf that Edward chm; ret mbrp
- 4-16-1857  Anna Maria rec in mbrp
- 4-16-1857  (Whitely) Edgar D infant s of Daniel Jr & Mariah, rec in mbrp
- 8-20-1857  Edward H gct Maple Grove MM
- 5-20-1858  Mary Jane Cogshall (form Whiteley) rpt for mcd
- 9-16-1858  Mary Jane Cogshall (form Whiteley) dis
- 8-19-1858  Mary Jane Cogshall (form Whiteley) rpt mcd
- 9-16-1858  Mary Jane Cogshall (form Whiteley) dis
- 1-19-1860  Edward H, w Anna Eliza & s William rocf Maple Grove MM
- 1-26-1860  Annie, -dt Daniel & Celia of Fayette Co, Ind, m Uriah Woolman, -s Uriah & Mary (dec), of Preble Co, O, at Milford MH
- 11-28-1861  Martha, -dt Daniel & Cecelia of Fayette Co, Ind, m James of Wayne Co, Ind, -s Joseph & Rebecca of Clearfield Co, Pa, at Milford MH
- 7-15-1869  Ann Eliza rpt jas; chm
- 10-17-1872  (Whitely) Esther (form Morris) rpt mcd with one not a mbr; ret mbrp
- 2-20-1873  Edward H & w Ann Eliza & ch William & Lydia Margaretta gct Maple Grove MM
- 1-17-1878  Henry appt Elder
- 8-21-1879  Edgar D rq cert to Fall Creek MM to m Alice G Thomas
- 10-21-1880  Alice T rocf Fall Creek MM
- 2-15-1883  Mary Hussey (form Whitely) rpt mcd with one not a mbrp; ret mbrp
- 4-17-1884  Lora R rec in mbrp
- 11-20-1884  Ella Heacock (form Whiteley) rpt mcd; ret mbrp
- 6-17-1886  Alexander rec in mbrp
- 2-18-1892  Edgar D, w Alice G & ch Anna M, Emma L, Lewis D & Emory E gct Fall Creek MM
- 3-15-1894  Sarah Ann rel fr mbrp
- 10-17-1895  Alexander & w Esther gct Whitewater MM

MILFORD (Hicksite)

WITCHEL
6-18-1835  John, w Barsheba & ch Jane, Isaac & Mary rocf Flushing MM, Belmont Co, O
5-21-1840  John & w Barsheba rocf Whitewater MM
5-21-1840  Mary rocf Whitewater MM
12-16-1841 Isaac rpt for being father of an illegitimate ch & using abusive language to his neighbors by Bethel PM
8-18-1842  Isaac dis
2-15-1844  John rpt for allowing his dt to mcd also for na by Bethel PM
4-18-1844  John dis
1-20-1848  Mary Thomas (form Witchel) rpt mcd
5-18-1848  Mary Thomas (form Witchel) dis
1-20-1848  Barsheba rpt for manifesting disunity and promoting m of dt in her own home
5-18-1848  Barsheba dis

WICKERSHAM
6-21-1838  Edward, w Susanna & ch Rebecca, Jesse, Jane, Susan & Edward rocf Center MM, O
5-18-1848  Edward rpt for na & being out of unity with Friends
8-17-1848  Edward dis
8-17-1848  Susanna dis for na & being out of unity with Friends
8-20-1863  Mary Ann (form Bond) rpt mcd & na by Bethel PM
10-19-1863 Mary Ann (form Bond) chm

WILEY
4-16-1840  Isaac rocf Whitewater MM
4-23-1840  Isaac, -s Thomas & Ann of Milton, Wayne Co, Ind, m Eliza Maudlin, -dt Enoch & Miriam (dec) at Milford MH
10-20-1850 Eliza Arnold (form Wiley) dis for mou
6-17-1852  Mary Ann gct Fall Creek MM; rq by Edward & Hannah Kirby

WILLITTS
11-19-1828 Isaac appt to comm
3-18-1829  Brady appt Overseer
5-20-1829  Miriam appt to comm

WILLETS
1-21-1830  Mary (form Cole) rpt by Springborough MM for mcd; that mtg rq this to tr w/h & rpt
8-18-1831  Mary (form Cole) chm; ret mbrp; Springborough MM inf
10-15-1835 Taylor rocf Alum Creek MM
5-17-1838  Isaac rpt mcd
11-15-1838 Isaac dis
10-16-1862 Taylor rel fr mbrp

WILLIAMS
1-17-1833  Caleb rec in mbrp
9-24-1834  Caleb, -s William & Hannah of Madison Co, Ind, m Hannah Gregg, -dt Stephen & Hannah of Henry Co, Ind at Duck Creek MH
5-23-1839  Anna, -dt William & Hannah of Madison Co, Ind, m Levin Charles of Fayette Co, Ind, -s Henry & Mary (both dec) of Dorchester Co, Md, at Milford MH
1-18-1844  Alfred rpt mou by Whitewater MM; that mtg ask this to tr w/h & rpt; did not make satisfaction; Whitewater MM notified
6-18-1846  Alfred rpt for na & j a musical band
10-15-1846 Alfred chm
10-19-1848 Alfred gct Cincinnati MM, already removed
10-18-1849 Alfred rpt na; Cincinnati MM rq to tr w/h
5-16-1850  Alfred dis
5-21-1863  Sarah (form Charles) rpt mcd & na
9-17-1863  Sarah (form Charles) chm

WILSON
10-22-1828 John appt asst Clerk
2-18-1829  Samuel appt to comm
9-20-1832  Hannah P rec on cert of concurrence fr Goose MM, -end by Fairfield MM
9-19-1835  Jane rocf Richland MM, Pa
2-19-1835  Mark L & w Mary W & ch Stephen B, Shipley & Elizabeth rocf Richland MM, Pa
2-19-1835  Moses, w Jane rocf Richland MM, Pa
4-28-1836  John, -s Samuel & Keziah of Wayne Co, Ind, m Hannah Bond, -dt Jesse & Phebe of Wayne Co, Ind, at Fairfield MH
7-16-1840  John C rpt for na & jas by Bethel PM
12-17-1840 John C dis
3-20-1845  Joseph F gct Cincinnati MM
9-21-1848  Amelia dis for jas
9-24-1851  Stephen B, -s Mark L & Mary W m Ann J Stratton, -dt Joseph P & Martha of Dublin, Wayne Co, Ind, at Bethel MH
4-21-1853  Samuel dis for na
11-20-1853 Elizabeth Lester (form Wilson) rpt mcd
1-19-1854  Elizabeth Lester (form Wilson) dis
4-15-1855  Hannah Jane Watson (form Wilson) rpt mcd
5-17-1855  Hannah Jane Watson (form Wilson) chm; ret mbrp
2-19-1857  Shipley rpt for mcd & j a secret Society
4-16-1857  Shipley dis
8-20-1857  Massa Ann Moore (form Wilson) rpt mcd
10-15-1857 Massa Ann Moore (form Wilson) dis
8-2-1862   Mary, Martha, Sarah & Hannah dis for na & jOrth MM
1-16-1873  Ann rpt jas & na
5-15-1873  Ann dis

WINDER
10-21-1847 Joseph & w Rebecca H & ch Mary Jane, Alfred, Caroline, Sarah Ellen, Anna Maria & Joseph Henry rocf Upper Evesham MM
1-19-1850  Joseph & fam gct Fall Creek MM - Joseph already removed
8-17-1854  Joseph, w Rebecca & ch Alfred, Caroline, Sarah Ellen, Anna Maria & Joseph Henry rocf Whitewater MM
11-16-1854 Mary Jane rocf Whitewater MM
9-24-1856  Caroline Winder, -dt Joseph & Rebecca, m Thornton P Cain, -s William & Mary B (dec), of Richmond, Wayne Co, Ind, at Bethel MH
12-20-1860 Joseph Henry, minor s of Joseph, gct Whitewater MM
1-17-1861  Mary J gct Whitewater MM
5-19-1864  Rebecca rq cert to take to her native state of N J to visit friends; cert gr
5-18-1865  Sarah Ellen & Anna Maria gct Whitewater MM
6-15-1865  Joseph, w Rebecca H gct Whitewater MM
4-18-1867  Alfred chm of mcd; ret mbrp
5-21-1868  Alfred gct Whitewater MM

WOOD
2-27-1839  Hannah M, -dt Jacob & Phebe of Henry Co, Ind, m Aaron Heacock, Rush Co, Ind, -s Jesse & Tacy (dec) of Bucks Co, Pa, at Duck Creek MH
7-15-1830  Jacob appt to comm
12-17-1835 Jacob appt to comm
2-21-1849  Levi P, -s Jacob & Phebe of Henry Co, Ind, m Hannah F Heacock, -dt Enos & Sarah of Henry Co, Ind, at Bethel MH
6-20-1850  Hannah F gct Fall Creek MM

WOOLMAN
9-16-1847  William rocf Westfield MM
12-19-1850 William gct Westfield MM
1-26-1860  Uriah, -s Uriah & Mary (dec) of Preble Co, Ohio, m Annie Whiteley, -dt Daniel & Celia of Fayette Co, Ind, at Milton MH
7-19-1860  Annie gct Westfield MM
6-16-1864  Uriah Jr, w Anna & dt Mary Elsa rocf Westfield MM
4-15-1875  Uriah & fam gct Westfield MM

WRIGHT
2-22-1830  Anna, -dt William & Celia of Wayne Co, Ind, m James H Dawson of Wayne Co, Ind, -s Elisha & Lydia (dec) of Caroline Co, Md, at Fairfield MH

MILFORD (Hicksite)

WRIGHT (Cont)
|  |  |
|---|---|
| 11-19-1828 | John appt to comm |
| 11-19-1828 | Mary Sr, appt to comm |
| 2- 1-1829 | Esther appt to comm |
| 8-19-1829 | William appt to comm |
| 12-16-1829 | Mary Jr appt to comm |
| 12-23-1830 | Mary, -dt Hatfield & Lucretia (dec) of Wayne Co, Ind, m Reece Ridgway of Henry Co, Ind -s Job & Rebecca of Belmont Co, O, at Milford MH |
| 2-21-1833 | Rebecca (form Leverton) rpt mcd; Whitewater MM rq to tr w/h |
| 7-14-1833 | Rebecca (form Leverton) - Whitewater MM rpt she chm; ret mbrp |
| 7-18-1833 | Charles rpt mcd |
| 12-19-1833 | Charles dis |
| 2-27-1834 | Lucretia, -dt Hatfield & Lucretia of Wayne Co, Ind, m Rees Ridgway, -s Job (dec) & Rebecca of Belmont Co, O, at Milford MH |
| 6-18-1835 | Sarah Shaw (form Wright) rpt mcd |
| 12-17-1835 | Sarah Shaw (form Wright) dis |
| 11-19-1835 | John H rocf Whitewater MM |
| 1-19-1837 | John H rpt dealing in spirituous liquors & dp |
| 8-17-1837 | John H dis |
| 7-19-1838 | Hatfield B rpt mcd |
| 11-17-1839 | Hatfield B dis |
| 7-26-1838 | John of Milton, Wayne Co, Ind, m Ann Cole of same place, at Milford MH |
| 6-20-1844 | Anna C gct Cincinnati MM |
| 6-18-1846 | Leven rpt for mcd |
| 9-17-1846 | Leven dis |
| 7-16-1846 | Elizabeth & dt Sarah, Mary Jane & Ann Elizabeth rocf Fall Creek MM |
| 8-26-1847 | Mary Elizabeth, -dt William & Celia, Wayne Co, Ind, m Edwin Rowlett, -s David E & Ann of Wayne Co, Ind, at Fairfield MH |
| 12-16-1847 | Rebecca gct Whitewater MM |
| 2-22-1850 | Elias H, -s Isaac & Mary of Madison Co, Ind, m Demaris L Bond, -dt William C & Hannah of Wayne Co, Ind, at Fairfield MH |
| 6-20-1850 | Sarah Hunt (form Wright) rpt mcd |
| 9-19-1850 | Sarah Hunt (form Wright) dis |
| 2-19-1852 | Demaris L gct Fall Creek MM |
| 2-17-1853 | Jacob rpt mcd |
| 5-19-1853 | Jacob dis |
| 1-18-1855 | William & dt Mary Jane, Ann Elizabeth gct Green Street MM |
| 2-21-1856 | David rec in mbrp |
| 5-20-1858 | David rpt for jas |
| 9-16-1858 | David dis |
| 2-16-1860 | Isaac, w Mary & dt Mary Ellen rocf Fall Creek MM |
| 2-21-1861 | Jonathan J gct Whitewater MM |
| 5-24-1868 | Elizabeth J (form Pleasants) rpt mcd; chm |
| 10-15-1868 | Isaac & w Mary H & dt Mary Ellen gct Fall Creek MM |
| 9-21-1871 | Demaris rpt jas |
| 1-18-1872 | Demaris dis |
| 8-21-1879 | Elizabeth J gct Whitewater MM |
| 9-16-1880 | Elizabeth J rel fr mbrp; jas |

ZENBLIN
|  |  |
|---|---|
| 6-12-1899 | Lyle, -dt Jonathan W & Marietta R of Pendleton, Madison Co, Ind, m William F Morris of Pendleton, Madison Co, Ind, -s Aaron & Martha M of Milton, Wayne Co, Ind, at residence of Jonathan W Morris |

# FALL CREEK MONTHLY MEETING
## (Hicksite)
### Madison County, Indiana

Fall Creek Monthly Meeting was set-off from Milford Monthly Meeting and first held on the 14th of Eleventh Month 1839. Its limits encompassed Duck Creek Preparative Meeting in Henry County. In 1848 Maple Grove Preparative Meeting was established in Huntington County. It was set-off as a monthly meeting in 1854. Duck Creek meeting, Greensboro, Henry County was laid down circa 1915.

Fall Creek meeting is located two and one-quarter miles east of Pendleton in Fall Creek Township.

Jonathan Thomas of Chester Co., Pa. was a man sixty-six years of age when in 8 mo 1833 he visited in the home of John J. Lewis who had married his daughter, Rebecca. . . On the morning of 8 mo 3rd he and his daughter, Rebecca Lewis, and children went to the village of Huntsville then a more thriving center than Pendleton. They followed an Indian trail leading over the hill back of the meeting house. When he reached a point where his grave now lies, the incident occured of which he later (in 1839) wrote to his friend, Rachel Hicks . . .

> ". . . As I was walking the road where the meetinghouse and graveyard are, I felt a remarkable stoppage in mind on which I turned half around. I then had a full view of the ground where they are. The language, distinctly to the inner man, passed through my mind, 'Now, buy this place and give Friends a lot for a meeting house and a graveyard . . .

> "But the above language followed me to Pennsylvania as a duty to perform and in one year and one day I was here again with my family, having in the fall of 1833 instructed my son-in-law, J. J. Lewis to purchase the place having sent money for that purpose. I remembered that there were three or four families of Friends here and I felt that I ought to be one of their number . . ." *

### Monthly Meeting Records

The first volume of Men's Minutes and the Marriage Register have been lost. Fortunately they had been abstracted by Hinshaw, which with his other abstracts to 1929 comprise this record. The volumes listed below are in a vault in the Miami meetinghouse, Waynesville, Ohio. These records have been microfilmed. Current records are in the hands of the clerk.

| Men's Minutes | Women's Minutes |
|---|---|
| first volume lost | 11-14-1839 : 1-10-1895 |
| 1-21-1888 : 1-10-1895 | |

Joint Minutes
2-14-1895 : 12-12-1895
1- 9-1896 : 12-12-1918
1- 8-1920 : 12-19-1920
1-16-1921 : 12-19-1943 (abstracted to 1929)

1 Volume Removal Certificates 1870-1916
1 Volume Births and Deaths
1 Volume Membership Record

* From a paper read by Rebecca L. Swain and prepared by Evangeline E. Lewis for the Pendleton Art Association June 26, 1923.

As this page was going to press the Marriage Register beginning in 1840 was found. It will be microfilmed and added to the Society's collection. It should be consulted as there is some additional data to be found therein.

FALL CREEK MONTHLY MEETING
( Hicksite )
BIRTH AND DEATH RECORDS

ALLEN
Daniel H      b 2-24-1800     d 11- 3-1859
Eliza G                       d 4-12-1879 ae 73 yrs
Ch: Reuben W  b 4-12-1840     d 3- 3-1863
    Hannah    b 8- 3-1842
    Thomas C  b 9- 1-1844
    Elmira    b 9-18-1846
    Tamson    b 9-26-1849

Elwood        b 10-20-1861
...
Ch: Esther           b 9-13-1901
    John Stuart      b 5-13-1907
    William Anderson b 2-27-1910  d 8- 4-1910
    Frank Dixon      b 12-24-1913
    Virginia C       b 3-29-1917

John
Mary Ann
Ch: Mary        b 7-18-1836
    Rebecca     b 10-15-1838
    Elizabeth   b 8-10-1842   d 12-17-1863
    Alcinda     b 12-15-1844
    Edward W C  b 9-26-1848

AMIAN
Barbara       b 9-17-1888

ANDERSON
Archie        b 9- 7-1855   -s John A & w  d 11-27-1930
Caroline      b 5- 7-1856   -dt ... Heacock

Chester H     b 11-25-1885
Lula          b 10-20-1886
Ch: Mary Elizabeth b 5- 4-1910
    Paul Clark     b 7-22-1913

Daniel
Edna Ann
Ch: Stella    b 7- 4-1880
    Chester   b 11-25-1885

John A        b 11-10-1826
Elda                        -dt ... Hiatt       d 9-28-1917
Ch: Archie C    b 7- 7-1855
    Caroline J  b 5- 7-1856

BABB
Joseph W
Mary Ann
Ch: Susan Elizabeth b 1-14-1841
    Joseph J        b 3-25-1844  d 9- 9-1845
    Mary Alice      b 7-28-1846
    .... J (torn)   b 9-27-1850

BAKER
Amasa         d 8-10-1874 ae 93yrs, 7mo

Elsie         d -29-1895 ae 70yrs (not a mbr)

BESS
Esther (not a mbr)  d 2- 4-1881 ae 32yrs, 8mo, 24da

BLAKELY
Forest Raymond  b 2- 5-1890  -s William R & Rosa B
                m 12-18-1913
Edith Mary      b 4-27-1891  -dt William H & Mary S
                                Kinnard
Ch: Murril Frances  b 11- 9-1914
    Mary Marjorie   b 2-25-1918
    Priscilla M     b 5-12-1924

BLOOM
Matthew E     b 7-12-1882
Lora          b 3-25-1886   -dt .. Boram

Ch: Rebecca Mary   b 11-24-1919
    Laura Matthews b 10- 6-1921
    Mathew Andrew  b 5-23-1923

BOND
Dora May      d 8-31-1872  -dt Elias Bond (not a mbr)
              -bur Fall Cr

Lydia         d 8- 7-1871 (not a mbr)

Robert        b 9-27-1842  -s Jesse & Elizabeth J of
                              Miami Co, Ind
S Lucretia M  b 7- 6-1844  -dt Lewis W & Priscilla M
                              Thomas
Ch: Oscar L        b 5-11-1876

BORAM
Allen         b 6-29-1847
Jennie A      b 8- 2-1852
Ch: Elsie Vance    b 4- 4-1877
    Rolla Kirk     b 8-24-1880
    Laura Allen    b 3-25-1886  m Matthew E Bloom
    Emmette        b 12-20-1891 m Blanche Rogers

Emmet         b 12-20-1891
Blanche       b 10-20-1892  -dt ..... Rogers
Ch: Robert Allen
    Emmet Ward
    Dorcas
    Aleda Jane     b 3- 7-1917

BOSTON
Eliza Ann     b 10-13-1843  d 7-26-1922 -bur Pendleton,Ind
James Gray
Mary Emma     b 12-19-1861

Mary          b 5-13-1871

Benjamin Wright  d 10-11-1880 ae 1yr,7mo,3da
                 (not a mbr)

BRADLEY
Priscilla     d 11-14-1881 (not a mbr)

BRANSON
Nathan        -s Thomas & Anna of Clark Co, O
              m 11-18-1858
Anna          -dt Charles & Sarah Ann Swain
Ch: Evelyn         b 9- 2-1864
    Thomas Swain   b 6-13-1866
    Luella         b 2- 1-1869

BRECKENRIDGE
Maggie M      b 12- 4-1871

BROWN
Alonzo Scott  d 7-19-1884 ae 1yr, 4da

Elizabeth     b 10- 2-1822  d 8-16-1911 -bur Pendleton

Elwood        d 2-23-1883 ae 66yrs, 4mo, 16da
Mary Ann      b 10-30-1813 d 2- 6-1902 -bur Fall Cr
Ch: Mary Ellen     b 12- 4-1855
    Anna E         b 8- 4-1857  d 11-21-1874
                                -bur Fall Cr
...
...
Ch: George Henry   b 2-29-1840
    Isaac Smith    b 2- 7-1843
    Charles Bowman b 2-24-1853  d 7- 9-1932
                                -bur Mexico, Ind

Joseph E      d 2-25-1887 ae 36yrs, 3mo, 10da

Olive         d 9- 1-1877 ae 2yrs, 24da -bur Fall Cr

Samuel        d 5-15-1854 ae 4yrs, 1mo -bur Fall Cr

FALL CREEK

BURDSALL
Richard H      =s Elwood & Sarah E of Harrison Co, N Y
               m 11- 3-1898
Mary T         -dt Benjamin & Annie L Rogers

CAMPLIN
Thomas Henry   b 4- 7-1847
Rebecca E
Ch: James Floyd       b 10- 2-1872
    Orlando Perry     b 11-25-1874
    Forest Clifford   b 8-20-1877   d 4-18-1895
    Harry Lincoln     b 5-16-1881

CATREN
David          d 11-18-1894 ae 86yrs, 9mo, 8da -bur Fall Cr
               (not a mbr)

....
Josephine M    b 8-17-1847   d 3-25-1926 -bur Pendleton
Ch: Edwin              b 12-28-1876
    Lillian Vernon     b 10-18-1880

Mary Jane      b 6- 5-1848   m .... Tunis

William H      b 2-27-1841   d 6-12-1909 -bur Pendleton

CHAMBERLAIN
Bessie         b 1-17-1891

CHENEY
Mary E         b 2-14-1878

CHILD
James W        d 12-21-1893 ae 42yrs, 6mo, 6 da

Jane           d 2-23-1885 ae 64 yrs, 7mo, 7da (not mbr)

William        d 11- 7-1887 ae 70yrs

Mary A (Childs) b 3-13-1882   w of Herman

COCKAYNE
James          b 4-23-1844   d 2-10-1907 =s Thomas & Martha
Philena        b 5-20-1846   d 5-12-1928 -dt Elwood & Mary
                                         Ann Brown
Ch: Martha         b 11- 5-1867
    Retta May      b 6-24-1872
    Emma Pearl     b 6- 4-1875   d 10-10-1877
                   -bur Fall Cr ae 2yrs, 4mo, 6da
    Bertha         b 10- 5-1877

Benjamin T     =s Thomas & Martha
Mariah Jane    b 12-24-1834 -dt George & Elizabeth Cook
Ch: Ida            b 8-11-1860   d 12-14-1863
                                 -bur Fall Creek
    Thomas         b 11-17-1863  d 2-18-1866
    Mary E         b 1-18-1867
    Georgianna C   b 9-10-1869

Elizabeth      b 1839

Nathan         b 1834   d 1920   =s Thomas & Martha
Margaret W             d 2- 4-1864 ae 32yrs, 6mo
               --dt John & Anna Oldham
Ch: Martha E       b 5-10-1864   d 10-16-1864

Thomas         d 9- 4-1865 ae 69yrs -bur Fall Creek Cem
Martha         d 10-21-1865 ae 63yrs -bur Fall Creek Cem
Ch: Sarah
    Benjamin
    Nathan         b  - -1834
    Elizabeth      b 8-18-1838
    Ann            b 2-28-1842
    James          b 4-23-1844

COFFIN
Olen W         b 11- 1-1895 =s Claudius & Cora

COOK
Asahel W       b 6-17-1833 =s George & Elizabeth
               d 4- 1-1916 -bur Grovelawn Cem, Pendleton
Hannah         d 9- 5-1910
Ch: Theresa Caroline  b 8- 5-1855   m .... Michel
    Anna E            b 6-24-1857   m .... Jones
    George W          b 10-20-1859
    Mary E            b 12-30-1861  m .... Hedrick
    Ida Jane          b 12-27-1864  m .... Hileman
    Malissa G         b 12- 3-1866  m .... Rogers

George W       d 10-17-1860 ae 49yrs, 4mo
Elizabeth      d 2-18-1891
Ch: Asahel W       b 6-17-1833
    Mariah Jane    b 11-24-1834  m .... Cockayne
    Samuel         b 10-24-1836
    Sarah Ann      b 9-10-1839   m .... Williams
    Mary Elizabeth b 4- 9-1842   m .... Cox
    Georgianna     b 1-10-1845   m .... Lukens
    Jesse G        b 6- 8-1847
    Ruth Emma      b 3-23-1851   m .... Vanwinckle

Isaac          d 3-27-1857 ae 49yrs, 3mo, 19da -bur Fall
                                              Creek
Anna           -bur Duck Creek, Henry Co, Ind
Ch: Eliza          b 2- 6-1829
    Nancy          b 10-12-1830
    Mary           b 2-10-1833
    Jason          b 12- 5-1834  d 2-21-1855
                                 -bur Duck Creek, Ind
    Jane           b 6-13-1837
    Levi           b 12-21-1839  d 4-18-1844
                                 -bur Duck Creek, Ind
    Oliver         b 5-20-1844
    Emily          b 10-15-1846

John           d 4-10-1896 ae 92yrs
Julianne       d 1-12-1864 -bur Duck Creek, Henry Co
Ch: Cynthia        b 8- 6-1830
    Ann            b 4-18-1838
    Seth           b 12-21-1840
    Rhoda          b 4-25-1843
    Levi           b 6-13-1845
    Eleanor        b 11-26-1847  d 9- 4-1850
                                 -bur Duck Creek
    Milton         b 1-21-1852
    Susan          b 12- 3-1853

John A         b 11- 4-1865
Essie          b 1870  -dt ... Camplin
Ch: Vivian Bernice    b 4-20-1900
    Persival Hunt     b 6-15-1901
    Julian Leslie     b 5-11-1905

Julianne       d 1-29-1864 -bur Duck Creek Cem

Levi           b 6-13-1845  =s John & Juliann
Mary E         b 4-15-1846  d 6- 6-1928
               -dt Simeon & Margaret Wood
Ch: Arthur J       b 11- 4-1865
    Herbert C      b 12-21-1869
    Maggie May     b 12- 4-1871

Leah           d 2-19-1893 ae 81yrs, 8da

Marcellius
Eliza B        d 11-27-1857
Ch: Anna B         b 9- 3-1851
    Hadley S       b 8-26-1854   d 4-29-1860
    Elizabeth      b 2-11-1857   d 8-25-1859
    Tamzen         b 2-11-1857

....
Viola B        b 10-14-1864
Ch: Morris         b 4-24-1885

COOPER
Elizabeth R    d 4-25-1833 ae 32yrs, 8mo, 23da

FALL CREEK

## COOPER (Cont)
Charles E    b 9-30-1878  
Cora B    b 12-20-1879  
Ch: William P    b 7-10-1881  
    Woody A    b 11-12-1882  
    Harley R    b 7-28-1894  

Elwood P    b 6-13-1849   d 10-24-1920  
Sarah E    b 8-26-1846  
Ch: Ida May    b 4-25-1877  
    Charles Elwood    b 9-30-1878  
    Cora Belle    b 12-20-1879  
    William Penn    b 7-10-1881  
    Woody Averill    b 11-12-1882  
    Harriet Martha    b 10-12-1884   d 9-7-1911  
        -bur Pendleton  
    Ermile Ina    b 8-5-1886  
    Harley Reece    b 7-28-1894  

Pha  
Martha Gertrude    b 9-1-1900  
Ch: Pha Russell    b 1-31-1919  
    Nancy Mae    b 1-9-1921  

## COPELAND
Anna M    b 2-27-1867   d 4-2-1892  

Ephriam    d 9-1-1860   ae 58yrs, 1mo, 1da  
Leah  
Ch: Abigail    b 9-10-1828  
    Louisa    b 11-13-1830  
    John Wright    b 5-24-1832   d 10-15-1849  
    Rebecca    b 9-14-1834  
    Lewis    b 3-23-1836  
    Simeon    b 10-12-1837   d 10-9-1844  
    Seth    b 7-18-1840  
    Jesse S    b 7-3-1842   d 8-20-1860  
    Mary Ann    b 12-10-1848  
    Samirah Ellen    b 4-8-1858  

Floie E    b 1-30-1887  

John    d 2-3-1870   ae 85yrs, 6mo, 25da  
    -bur Duck Creek  
Phebe    d 6-11-1875   ae 82yrs, 1mo, 17da  
    -bur Duck Creek  

Seth    -s Ephriam & Leah   m 11-18-1863  
Elizabeth    b 7-6-1845   -dt John & Martha Kennard  
Ch: Glen S    b 4-20-1866  
    Earl W    b 3-15-1871  
    Ethel M    b 10-18-1872  

## CORBIN
Vora    b 10-1-1897   w of Harry I  

## COX
Mary    b 1842   d 10-7-1912   -bur Pendleton  

## DARLINGTON
Annis P    b 2-12-1846  

Charles R    b 12-11-1867   -s Ziba & Elmira  
Martha J    b 1-19-1869   d 5-26-1918   -dt .. Lukens  
Ch: Annis E    b 11-4-1891  

Helen Irene    b 12-7-1901  

Ziba    b 5-28-1838   d 12-23-1918   -bur Pendleton  
    -s Amos & Jane   m 3-21-1867  
Elmira    b 1-13-1843   d 7-8-1916   -bur Pendleton  
    -dt Charles J & Sarah D Rogers  
Ch: Charles R    b 12-11-1867  
    Harry G    b 2-31-1872  
    Sarah R    b 7-31-1876  
    Elizabeth L    b 3-12-1879  

## DARNELL
Charles    b 7-21-1827   -s Isaiah & Mary L  
Mary W (1st w)    d 4-27-1865   ae 34yrs, 5mo, 11da  
    -bur Fall Creek  
Ch: Clayton H    b 9-13-1858   d 2-29-1880  
    Mary Ida    b 10-15-1862   m ... Parsons  
Sarah L (2nd w)    b 9-13-1831   d 12-21-1907   -bur Fall Cr  
    m 1-16-1868   -dt Thomas & Rachel Davis  
Ch: Thomas D    b 10-5-1869  
    Arie Anna    b 6-14-1872   d 2-19-1893  
        -bur Fall Cr  

## DAVIS
Earl Leroy    b 12-9-1894  

Louella    d 3-1-1891   ae 29yrs, 5da  

Margaret    d 4-9-1857   ae 45yrs, 1mo, 1da   -bur Fall Cr  

Martha    b 10-9-1841   m ... Dickinson  

Pennington    -s Caleb & Ann  
Hannah (Margaret ?)    d 4-9-1857   ae 45yrs, 1mo, 1da  
    -dt Jehu & Mary Middleton  
Ch: Charles    b 9-27-1841   d 2-6-1863 Ia  
    William    b 11-8-1843  
    Elizabeth Ann    b 8-11-1846   d 8-25-1861 Ia  
    Edwin    b 2-14-1849   d 6-24-1849  
        -bur Fall Creek  
    Andrew M    b 4-18-1850  
    Mary Margaret    b 5-17-1853  
    Hannah Ellen    b 9-18-1857   d 8-30-1861 Ia  

Rachel    d 2-6-1877   ae 75 yrs  

Ruby Eva    b 1-17-1907  

Susannah T    d 5-22-1888   ae 52yrs, 3mo, 6da  

Thomas    d 11-17-1867   ae 71yrs, 3mo, 13da  
    -bur Fall Creek  

Washington    b 7-26-1833   d 5-23-1912   -bur Fall Creek  
Mary    b 11-8-1841   d 9-8-1932   -dt ..Garretson  
Ch: Louiza    b 2-14-1862  
    Alice M    b 2-28-1865  
    Thomas    b 10-13-1866  
    Isaac    b 12-22-1878   d 1-1-1930  
        -bur West Grove Lawn Cem, Pendleton  

## DICKS
Sally    d 5-10-1859   -bur Green Rusk Cem, Lafayette, Ind  

## DIX
Gertrude    d 4-9-1883   -bur Fall Creek  

## DOAN
Wilson Spray    b 11-22-1863   d 4-25-1930  
    -bur Crown Hill, Indianapolis  
Myra H    b 2-14-1869   -dt .. Holbrook  
Ch: Florence Holbrook    b 4-10-1893  
    Marcia Sibyl    b 9-15-1894  
    Dorothy    b 8-30-1896   d 3-18-1899  
        -bur Crown Hill, Indianapolis  

## DOWNS
Isaac    b 2-7-1823   d 8-18-1894  
Jane G    b 10-7-1830   d 1-24-1914   -bur Pendleton  

## DUNWOODY
Eleanor P    d 10-26-1876   ae 79yrs, 5mo, 22da  

## ELLIOTT
Jesse H  
Rachel  
Ch: Loretta    b 5-14-1848  
    Lorenzo    b 5-14-1848  

## ESTELL
Margaret    b 8-9-1895   w of Harless  

## FENTRESS
Martha J    b 9-1-1900

FALL CREEK

## FENTRESS (Cont)
Mary C           b  2-14-1878

William A        b  7- 8-1880
Gertrude         b  6-10-1881
Ch: Herman M         b  3-27-1906
    Donald E         b  3-27-1907

## FOULKE - FOULK
Amos             d  4-27-1840

Arthur           b  1-19-1894

Francis          b  1- 6-1859

George           b  6- 7-1845

Jesse            d  2-18-1876  ae 70yrs, -bur Fall Creek

Mary G           b 11- 2-1875  -dt William & Caroline
                               (Garretson)

William          d  6-28-1877  ae 29yrs, 7mo, 11da
Caroline
Ch: Mary G           b 11- 2-1875

## FOUST
Rachel           b 12-19-1864  w of Henry

## FRAMPTON
Annie            b  1856  d  1923

Elishua D        d  9-26-1864  ae 20yrs, 5mo, 4da -bur Fall Cr

Justine          b  1858

...
...
Ch: William          b 1848  d  1-21-1929
                         -bur Grovelawn, Pendleton, Ind
    George           b 1850
    Charles          b 1851  d  9-17-1926
                         -bur Mechanicsburg, Ind
    Arthur           b 1857  d 12-  -1930 -bur Calif

William C        -s William & Sarah
Annie S          b  2-28-1842  d  9-25-1887 ae 45yrs,6mo,27da
                 -dt Thomas & Martha Cockayne
Ch: Martha C         b  2- 3-1871
    Walter Henry     b  1- 1-1873  d 10-28-1873
    Edward S         b  7-12-1875
    Arthur T         b  6-19-1879

William D        d  8-11-1877  ae 65yrs, 9mo, 15da
                     -bur Fall Creek
Sarah B          d 11-11-1893  ae 72yrs, 7mo, 27da
Ch: Mary D           b  1-10-1854  m .. Trump
    John Edgar       b 10-14-1861
    William C

## FUSSEL
Benjamin Sunday  b  3-27-1840  -bur Fall Creek

Charles R        b 10- 5-1862  d  6-26-1922 -bur Fall Creek
Mariam           b 11-20-1865
Ch: Leona Bell       b  7- 8-1889
    Della Frances    b  6-21-1898

Edwin
Rebecca L
Ch: Emma J           b  6- 1-1839
    Charles          b 10-26-1840
    Linneas          b  9- 2-1842

John L           b  8- 8-1830  d  4-30-1908 -bur Fall Creek
Mary Jane        b  6-19-1834  d  5-18-1913
                     -bur Friends Cem, Pendleton
Ch: Ella J           b 11-28-1856  d  2-27-1930
                         -bur Friends Cem, Pendleton
    Mary E           b  2- 5-1865

Joseph B         d 10-15-1855  ae 68yrs, 5mo, 15da
                     -bur Fall Creek
Elizabeth        d  2-19-1866  ae 76yrs -bur Fall Creek
Ch: John L           b  8- 8-1830  d  4-30-1908
                         -bur Fall Creek

Joshua L         b  6- 9-1827  d  3- 1-1915

Mary M           d  4-17-1856

Samuel           d  4-15-1876  ae 56yrs, 8mo, 17da
                 -s Joseph & Elizabeth
Annie E          d  8-22-1896  ae 55yrs, 8mo, 7da,
                 -dt Charles & Sarah Rogers  -bur Fall Creek
Ch: Charles R        b 10- 5-1862
    Mary Matilda     b  2- 9-1865
    Sarah Rebecca    b  7-21-1868  d  3-25-1874
    Solomon H        b  1-31-1873  d 11- 1-1890

Solomon          d  3- 1-1849  ae 59yrs, 8mo, 2da -bur Fall
                                                     Creek
Milcha Martha    d  8-16-1833  ae 42yrs, 7mo, 16da
                     -bur Fall Creek
Ch: Milcha Martha    b 10-19-1825
    Marion W (dt)    d  9-18-1833  ae 1mo, 4da
                         -bur Fall Creek
    Esther L         d  8-20-1835  ae 6yrs, 1mo, 15da
                         -bur Fall Creek
    Sarah J          d  8-21-1835  ae 15yrs, 5da
                         -bur Fall Creek
    Bartholomew B    d  8-24-1835  ae 12yrs,10mo, 9da
                         -bur Fall Creek
Hannah L (2nd w)     d  9- 8-1874  ae 74yrs, 1mo, 17da
Ch: Lydia J          b  8- 9-1838
    Anna W           b 11-12-1841

William          d  8- 4-1856  ae 73yrs, 11mo, 4da
Jane             d  5- 9-1857  ae 75yrs, 1mo, 19da
Ch: Howard           d  8-19-1880  ae 57yrs, 3mo, 3da
    Susan M      d  7-19-1889  ae 57yrs, 3mo, 3da

## GARRETSON
Amos             d  2-28-1864  ae 86yrs, 3mo, 23da
                     -bur Fall Creek
Mary
Ch: Peggy            d  3- 2-1849  ae 35yrs, 6mo, 11da
                         -bur Duck Creek
    Joel             b  2- 6-1818  d  7- 8-1892

Amos             b 12-19-1848  d  4- 7-1882 -bur Pendleton
Florence         b 12-24-1851  d  4-20-1916 -bur Pendleton
Ch: Sarah Jane       b  7-25-1871
    Margaret May     b 11-20-1872
    Laura C          b 12-12-1876
    Mary Ada         b  4-14-1882
    Chester A        b 12-25-1884

Chester A        b 12-25-1884
Gladys M         b 12- 5-1888  -dt .. Fisher
Ch: George L         b 10- 3-1908
    Elenore M        b  4-13-1911
    Esther Ruth      b 10-27-1914

Joel             b  2- 6-1818  d  7- 8-1892 ae 58yrs,2mo,5da
                 -s Amos & Mary
Sarah            -dt Samuel & Rebecca  d  1-14-1874
Ch: Mary         b12-31-1844  d  5- 3-1854 -bur Fall Creek
    Amos         b12-19-1848
    Caroline     b  2-1-1851
    Harvey       b  4-20-1853
    Nathan       b 12-18-1856
    Levi         b  6-27-1858  d  9-10-1858
    Harvey       b  4-20-1863
Mary Ann (2nd w) b 11-25-1833  d 1914

Nathan           b 12-18-1856  -s Joel & Sarah
Mary E           b  2- 3-1857  d  9- -1913
Ch: Margaret A       b  9-24-1882
    Davis R          b  7-25-1885
    Joel C           b 10-30-1887

FALL CREEK

**GARRETSON (Cont)**
Ch of Nathan & Mary E (Cont):
Lester E           b 2-10-1891
Ray William        b 2-27-1894
Nellie Emma        b 12-22-1896

**GARRIATT**
Addie R    b 10-4-1867  d 1918  w of Charles

**GEORGE**
Ellis              d 12-26-1863

Evan               d 12-22-1865

Ruth               d 8-30-1868  ae 78yrs

Sarah              d 11-7-1864  ae 59yrs

..
..
Ch: Richard        b 7-26-1861
    Charles W      b 9-27-1863
    Joseph C       b 3-10-1866

**GOOD**
Charles    d 8-7-1856  -s John & Sarah of Marion
           -bur Indianapolis
Margaret A  d 7-11-1855 ae 34yrs, 8mo, 15da
           -dt Jonathan & Eleanor  -bur Indianapolis
Ch: John Pearson   b 2-19-1849
    Sarah Ellen    b 6-17-1851  m .. Jones
    James William  b 4-28-1853  d 10-6-1868

**GOUL**
Alice Edna   b 3-4-1891  w of Jesse

**GRAY**
Enoch   d 1-17-1868  ae 71yrs, 4mo, 1da
Mary    d 10-4-1846  ae 40yrs, 7mo, 1da -bur Fall Cr
Ch: Dennis
    Sarahann
    Edmund         d 4-14-1844  ae 36yrs, 1mo, 11da
    Connard
    Susannah       b 11-18-1837
    Franklin       b 2-22-1840
    Joseph B       b 6-21-1843
    Mary Elizabeth

**GRISSOM**
Vivian B   b 4-20-1900

**GWINN**
Edith M    b 2-17-1886

**HAINES**
Aaron       b 10-20-1839  -s Charles & Ann
Sarah Jane  b 12-8-1843   -dt Jesse & Mary Heacock
Ch: Anna Mary      b 7-1-1864
    Charles J      b 5-28-1869  d 8-12-1887
    Adaline        b 10-21-1871 d 5-24-1874
    Oscar W        b 6-19-1881

Charles    -s John & Jemima  d 2-17-1889
           ae 79yrs, 7mo, 30da
Mary       -dt Solomon & Elizabeth Roberts
           d 11-21-1895  ae 75yrs, 1mo, 26da

Clark      d 10-17-1874  ae 61yrs, 3mo, 20da
           -s John & Jemima
Margaret F d 6-13-1863  ae 34yrs, 8mo
Ch: Alice E        b 3-13-1846  m .. Watkins
    Sarah Belle    b 1-1-1855   d 9-10-1855
    Mary Belle     b 1-1-1855   d 9-30-1898
                   m .. Kinnard
    Albert         b 11-26-1858
    Annie Grace    b 11-26-1858
    Oscar          d 2-13-1872  ae 23yrs, 2mo, 17da
                   -bur Fall Creek
Mary B (2nd w)     d 9-20-1898  -dt Joseph & Eleanor
                                Dunwoody

Edward Vernon      b 2-20-1875  -s Noah C & Mary E
Elizabeth Clay     b 6-22-1877  -dt William H &
                                Mary Kinnard
Ch: Herman Kinnard  b 2-13-1909
                    d 6-23-1911  -bur Pendleton

Isaiah    d 8- -1856  ae 21yrs, -s Charles & Anna
          -bur Fall Creek

Noah   b 4-9-1842   d 12-30-1910
Mary   b 12-31-1849 d 6-9-1911  -bur Pendleton
Ch: John           b 9-15-1867  d 7-31-1933
    Sarah Ellen    b 12-4-1868
    Edward V       b 2-20-1875
    Olive May      b 5-10-1881

Oscar William  b 6-19-1881  -s Aaron M & Sarah Jane
Bessie Lee     b 1-27-1891  -dt Elmer C & Eliza Chamber-
                            lain
Ch: Kenneth A      b 3-27-1907
    Anna Louise    b 9-26-1911

**HARDIN**
Helen J    b 12-7-1901  w of Herman

**HARDY**
Horace
Florence   b 8-19-1877
Ch: Merrill Burke   b 9-22-1904  d 4-20-1930
                    -bur Fall Creek
    Horace Franklin b 6-20-1908
    Ralph Charles   b 3-30-1910

Anna       b  d 10-15-1879  ae 13yrs, 11mo, 22da

Neal        d 11-16-1869  ae 66yrs  -bur Fall Creek
Elizabeth R d 6-10-1888   ae 77yrs, 10mo, 10da
Ch: Mary Jane      b 6-19-1834
    William F      b 2-7-1836
    Solomon F      b 10-19-1838

Roscoe W   b 11-13-1883
Nellie     b 1-14-1887  -dt .. Mingle
Ch: Susan Virginia  b 7-4-1914
    (Jeanne in another record)

Solomon F  b 10-19-1838  d 6-29-1909
           -s Neal & Elizabeth R
Rebecca P  b 11-19-1868  d 6- -1922
           -dt Joshua P & Sarah A James
Ch: Charles N      b 9-10-1869
    John           b 4-10-1872  d 12-31-1873
                   -bur Fall Creek
    Horace G       b 3-25-1874
    Joseph J       b 5-1-1876   d 3-25-1882
                   -bur Fall Creek
    Elizabeth R    b 7-5-1878
    Thomas Maris   b 2-19-1881
    Roscoe W       b 11-13-1883
    Solomon Frank  b 8-26-1886

S Frank      b 8-26-1886  -s Solomon & Rebecca P
Myrtle Sarah b 2-27-1886  -dt ... Long
Ch: Richard Frank   b 4-1-1911

Thomas M    b 2-4-1840   d 5-31-1915  -bur Fall Creek
Margaret W  b 11-20-1839 d 8-22-1909

Thomas Morris Jr  b 2-19-1881  -s Solomon & Rebecca P
Georgia           b 10-26-1884 -dt Millikin
Ch: Robert Millikin b 11-28-1908
    Hugh Morris     b 12-3-1912  d 1913
    Susan W         b 7-4-1914

**HARLAN**
Abner V    d 11-22-1889  ae 87yrs
Rachel C   d 8-13-1882   -bur Fall Creek

Clarence   b 7-22-1898

FALL CREEK

**HARLAN (Cont)**
Earl S           b  1-30-1888

George           b  5- 3-1896
Nina             b 12-13-1897
Ch: Donald M         b 12-22-1919

Mary E           b  7-30-1889   w of Walter

Mary E           d  3- 4-1879   ae 70yrs, 2mo -bur Fall Creek

Matilda          b  2- 9-1865   d  4-14-1923 -bur Fall Creek
                 w of George

Susan            d  5- 9-1882   ae 77yrs, 3mo, 28da -bur Fall
                                                         Creek

Thompson         b 10- 5-1834   d  5- 3-1890
Sarah            b  1-18-1832   d  9- 7-1906 -bur Pendleton
Ch: Rebecca          b  9-28-1864
    Elizabeth        b 10-12-1865
    William          b  3- 2-1871   d  2-12-1887

**HASKET**
Thomas
Sarah
Ch: Rachel           b 11- 3-1830
    William Irving   b  2- 8-1833
    Jonas P          b  4- 2-1835
    Emiley           b 10- 1-1837
    Ann              b 10-25-1840

**HAYS**
Hannah V         d  3-25-1885   ae 83yrs, 4mo, 26da (not mbr)

**HAYES**
Seth             d  7- 3-1870   ae 40yrs, 4mo, 5da (not a mbr)
                 h of Marietta

**HEACOCK**
Aaron
Hannah M
Ch: Margaret         b  1-15-1840
    Sarah            b  9-25-1841   d  7- 1-1846
                                    -bur Duck Creek, Ind
    Phebe            b  7-18-1843
    Deborah          b  8- 1-1846

Edna Ann         b  9-11-1821   d  1- 8-1901 -bur Milton, Ind
                 w of Daniel

Jacob            d  8-11-1851   -bur Duck Creek, Ind

Jesse            b  6- 6-1819   d  6-23-1910 -bur Pendleton
Mary E           b 11-24-1822   d 10-25-1900
Ch: Jesse Howard     b   -1848   d  5-26-1882
                                 ae 34yrs, 7mo, 9da
    William Arthur   b  1- 5-1857  (or 5-6-1859)
    Emma             b 12-19-1861  m James Boston

**HEDRICK**
Mary E           b 12-30-1861   w of Charles

**HIATT**
Esther           d  9-21-1894   ae 54yrs,  -bur Duck Creek, Ind

James            d  9-29-1841   ae 41yrs, 9mo, 5da
Betty            d  3-10-1848   ae 48yrs
Ch: Job              b  7-29-1829
    Levi             b 10-29-1831
    Seth             b  5-29-1833
    Isaac            b 11-23-1835
    Abigail          b  6-23-1838   d  4-15-1855
    Ann              b  4-14-1840

Seth             b  5-29-1833   -s James & Betty
Zalinda A        -dt Jonas & Rachel James
Ch: Alveretta Ann    b  9- 6-1856
    Rachel Eva       b  3-10-1860   d  8-25-1863
                                    -bur Duck Creek

Orlando V        b  6-29-1862   d  5-10-1867
                                -bur Duck Creek
James S          b  3-31-1864

**HIBBERD**
Alice A          d  9-21-1874   ae 52yrs, 3mo, 26da
                                -bur Fall Creek

**HILEMAN**
Ada J            d  6-30-1886   ae 21yrs, 5mo, 27da

Lena H           b  2- 1-1885   d  4-27-1917 -bur Pendleton

**HILL**
Alice            b  7- 6-1854   m .. Dilts

**HINSHAW**
Warren           b 11-29-1863
Della (Cordelia) b  4-16-1859 -dt John & Martha Kennard

**HODGES**
Edward W         b 10-14-1849   d 11-26-1920 -bur Pendleton Cem
Elizabeth Arissa b 12-28-1861   d  3-24-1926
                                -bur Spring Valley
Ch: Mary J           b 12-28-1893   d  1-23-1900 -bur Fall Creek
    Margaret         b  8- 9-1895
    Richard          b  8-17-1898

Mary Jane        d  8-20-1854   -dt Joseph & Elizabeth Fensell
                                -bur Fall Creek

**HODSON**
Ella             b 10-22-1864   w of Alonzo

**HOLLOWAY**
Jason
Jane
Ch: Edna
    Jesse
    Job H
    Israel
    Nathan
    John             b  7- 2-1837
    Amos             b  6-29-1839
    Silas            b 10-29-1842
    Nancy Jane       b  3-23-1845
    Zilpha           b  8-29-1848
    Mary             b  2- 8-1851

**HOLLOWELL**
Essie V          b  7-28-1889

Nixon            -s Thomas & Achsah, Huntington
Edna             -dt Jason & Jane Holloway of Wabash
Ch: Mary Jane        b  9-15-1846
    Zeruah           b  6- 8-1848
    William McKinney b  4-23-1850
    John Nixon       b  1- 5-1852

Anna Mary        d  9-20-1878   ae 2yrs, 9mo, 20da

**HOOVER**
Henry T          b 11- 1831   d  9-22-1911 -s Levi & Margaret
Ann              d  4-10-1863   ae 24yrs, 11mo, 22da
                                -dt John & Juliann Cook
Ch: Levi             b  9-28-1857
    Ellen            b  4-22-1859
    John             b  9-20-1860
    William H        b  1-18-1863

Margaret         d  4-23-1888   ae 77 yrs  -bur Duck Creek

William F        b  1-18-1863
Phoebe A         b  9-30-1863
Ch: George E         b  2- 3-1885
    Mildred Marie    b  4-12-1894

Samuel           b  1- 5-1829   d  3-25-1913
Anna             b  3-14-1842   d  2-  -1914 -dt ... Hill

FALL CREEK

## HOSS
Dewey S    b 5- 3-1898
Della    b 6-21-1898 -dt .. Fussell
Ch: Mirriam Lillian    b 7-29-1920
     Dewey Fussell    b 8-19-1923

## HUNT
Rebecca (form Hiatt)    d 5-15-    ae 85yrs, 4mo, 22da

## IFORT or IFORD
Henry
Mary A    b 4-27-1864    d 9-13-1908 -bur Pendleton Cem
Ch: Anna S    b 1- 8-1891

## JACOBS
Cassius    b 9- 1-1845    d 1-26-1920
Sarah Ann    b 1-22-1850

Charles
Esther Ann    b 2-22-1818    d 1901, 4th mo

## JAMES
Asa    b 10-11-1838 -s Jonas & Rachel
Jane    b 6-13-1837 -dt Isaac & Anna Cook
Ch: Arthur L    b 9-14-1859
     Charles L    b 6- 1-1863    d 9-16-1882
                      -bur Duck Creek
     Rachel Addie    b 10- 4-1867
     Anna E    b 1-11-1871    d 12-18-1874
                      -bur Fall Creek
     Arlington    b 11-21-1878    d 5- 4-1883
                      -bur Duck Creek

Charles R    b 5-18-1864    d 11-22-1889    ae 25yrs, 7mo,4da
     -s Joel & Elizabeth Ann

Elizabeth
Ch: Joseph    d 5-29-1878 in 10th yr
     Benjamin    d 5-27-1878    ae 16mo
     Evan    b 12-12-1887

Evan    d 8-25-1844    ae 59yrs, 10mo, 14da
     -bur Duck Creek
Rebecca    d 1- 8-1848    ae 58yrs, 8mo, 17da
Ch: Mary C
     Joab
     Jehu
     Joel E
     Jesse
     Joshua P

Hannah P    d 10-12-1893    ae 70yrs, 7mo, 5da

J Kerwin    b 3-27-1853
Elizabeth H    b 12-10-1865
Ch: Evan W    b 12-12-1887
     Vora    b 10- 1-1897
     Charles K    b 3-10-1901
     Ada M    b 4-29-1903
     Jonas    b    d 8- 5-1905

Jesse    -s Evan & Rebecca of Henry Co, Ind
Mary    -dt Samuel & Rebecca Harvey
Ch: Henry    b 10- 7-1840
     Evan    b 5-13-1842
     Samuel    b 2- 5-1844
     Malissa    b 10-19-1845
     David R    b 12-20-1847
     Robert Owen    b 3-18-1852 (or 3-19)

Joel E    -s Evan & Rebecca
Elizabeth Ann    d 1-22-1865    ae 35yrs, 11da
     -bur Iowa -dt Joseph & Elizabeth Rodgers
Ch: Jesse R    b 7- 1-1849
     Joseph Reese    b 3-12-1852
     Chalkley    b 8- 8-1856
     Jehu Wilks    b 12-15-1859
     Elizabeth A    b 12-28-1861
     Charles R    b 5-18-1864    d 11-22-1889

Robert O    b 3-19-1850    (Parents ?)
John H    b 1852

Jonas
Rachel
Ch: Zelinda Ann    b 11-13-1836
     Asa    b 10-11-1838
     Esther    b 12- 3-1840
     Elizabeth    b 11-30-1842
     Rebecca    b 12- 4-1844
     Thomas R    b 12-20-1848
     Jesse    b 2-10-1852

Joshua P    b 6-11-1818    d 2- 3-1900 -s Evan & Rebecca
Sarah Ann    d 12- 6-1857    ae 31yrs, 4mo, 24 da
     -dt Joseph & Elizabeth Rodgers
Ch: Joseph Evan    b 6-16-1842    d 7- 9-1863
                      -bur Fall Creek
     Charles R    b 1-13-1844    d 7-29-1906
                      -bur Fall Creek
     Rebecca P    b 4- 5-1846
     Mary Margaret    b 3- 2-1848
     Elizabeth R    b 8- 2-1850

Rees    d 4-22-1854 -bur Fall Creek

Thomas R    b 10-20-1848 (or 12-20-1848)
     -s Jonas & Rachel
Eva E    b 12-14-1851
Ch: Lester Warren    b 9- 9-1872
     Asa Gilbert    b 4-23-1877
     Walter Irvin    b 5- 9-1889

## JANNEY
Ruth D    d 1-30-1892    ae 76yrs, 4mo, 28da

Elouise    d 8-24-1887    ae 52yrs, 11mo, 10da

## JOHNSON
J Anthony    d 5-26-1878    ae 63yrs, 8mo, 1da

Joseph M    b 12-26-1859    d 8-16-18.. -s Meredith H
     -bur Pendleton, Ind & Winifred J
Frances L    b 9-10-1860 -dt Woolston & Mary A Swaim

Joshua    d 8-24-1850    ae 11yrs, 11da

Lydia    d 12-23-1851    ae 67yrs, 9mo, 18da

Miller    d 1-17-1864

Sarah    b 1-13-1841

## JONES
John Willets    b 12-22-1865
Sarah Ellen    b 12- 4-1868

Edward    b 7- 5-1874
Margaret T    b 9-17-1875
Ch: George J    b 12-31-1895
     Edward Jr    b 9- 1-1897
     (given as Roger C in another record)

Elihu    d 11-19-1850    ae 32yrs, 6mo, 1da

## JORDAN
Arthur
Leona B    b 7- 8-1889
Ch: Charles R    b 6- 9-1909

## KENDALL
John
Mary
Ch: Jessie G
     Charles Henry
     John Albert
     Lilly May
     Sarah Maria

FALL CREEK

**KENNARD**
Albert Franklin  b 5-26-1853  -s John & Elizabeth
                 d 12- 8-1919  -bur Greensboro, Ind
Louella     b 3-14-1857  d 8-25-1913
Ch: Mary E           b 10- 6-1878
    Elva M           b 10-13-1887
Rebecca U (2nd w) b 4-28-1867

Clarence    b 6-24-1895

Elizabeth C  b 12- 8-1821  d 1-16-1892

Everette    b 5- 3-1890

Jacob       b 2- 3-1825  d 9- 4-1904  -bur Knightstown,
Rebecca                                           Ind
Ch: Mary Jane       b 10-19-1850  m William A Gray

John        d 3-17-1891  ae 70yrs  -s Thomas & Elizabeth
            m 11-20-1844
Martha J    b 2-22-1821  -dt Amos & Martha Garretson of
                         Belmont Co, O
Ch: Elizabeth J      b 9- 6-1845
    Marcellus        b 2-14-1847  d 5- 3-1847
    Mary Ellen       b 4-24-1848  d 9-15-1858
                     -bur Duck Creek
    Rachel Ann       b 6-23-1851  m... Maudlin
    Albert Franklin  b 5-26-1853
    Cordelia E       b 4-16-1859  m Warren Hinshaw

Lewis D     b 9-17-1865
Della       b 3- 5-1870  -dt .. Downs
Ch: Charles Downs    b 9-14-1891
    Helen Josephine  b 1-20-1899
    Hugh Hannum      b 2- 3-1902

Marietta (Kinnard) b 12- 6-1863  w of George

Mary        b 10-16-1818  d 12-17-1910
                         -bur Greensboro, Ind

Ruth        b 1- 2-1833  d 11-10-1908
                         -bur Knightstown, Ind

Thomas      d 4-11-1863  ae 78yrs, 3mo, 18da
            -bur Duck Creek
Elizabeth   d 5- 5-1879  ae 85yrs, 10mo, 29da
            -bur Duck Creek
Ch: Levi
    John
    Jacob            b 2- 3-1825  d 9- 4-1904
    Jenkins          b 4-12-1826
    Thomas
    Joseph
    Michael

William R   b 12- 7-1848  d 1- 7-1930
Mary S      b 1- 8-1850  d 10-11-1915  -bur Pendleton
Ch: Alice T          b 12-10-1874
    Elizabeth C      b 6-22-1877
    Lyman            b 3- 8-1887  d 9- 8-1902
    Edith M          b 4-27-1891  d 6-21-1932
                     m Ray Blakely

**KENNEY**
Daniel      d 4- 3-1844  ae 49yrs, 6mo, 20da
            -bur Fall Creek
Ann         d 4-22-1870  -bur Fall Creek
Ch: Hannah L         b 6-25-1835
    Daniel Lukens    b 9-10-1838
    Susanna L        b 2-22-1842

**KERN**
Charles C   b 7-24-1882
Bertha      b 10- 5-1877  -dt .. Cockayne

**KINDLEY**
Edward P    d 3- 9-1843  ae 11yrs, 8mo, 28da

...
Mary
Ch: Tamur            b 2-21-1842
    Margaret         b 2-10-1845

**KIRK**
William     d 11-22-1875  ae 60yrs, 11mo, 3da
            -bur Fall Creek
Jane H      d 1-17-1872  ae 54yrs, 11mo, 29da
            -bur Fall Creek
Ch: Jane Augusta     b 2- 8-1852
    Esther Ilena     b 3- 7-1857  d 12-30-1867

**LANTZ**
Fred        b 2-26-1883
Elizabeth M b 1- 4-1880
Ch: Deborah          b 3- 1-1907

**LEVERTON**
Hannah      d 5-12-1866  ae 66yrs    A minister

**LEWIS**
Abel        d 10-  -1867  ae 81yrs
Mary G      d 2-23-1845  ae 51yrs, 4mo, 5da

...
Emily       b 12- 5-1845  d 11-11-1891
Ch: Margaret H       b 8- 4-1877
    Emily Grace      b 6-23-1881

Evan        d 6-15-1862  ae 46yrs, 9mo, 28da
            -s Abner & Susanna   -bur Fall Creek
Sarah C     -dt Thomas & Martha Cockayne -bur Fall Creek
Ch: Thomas C         b 3-18-1857
    Anna             b 2-28-1859

Horace F    b 2-25-1852  d 6-24-1912 -bur Pendleton
Eleanor D   b 9-16-1860

John        d 8- 2-1859  ae 46yrs
Margaret T  d 1-11-1861  ae 33yrs, 11mo, 9da

John J      d 2- 9-1880  ae 76yrs, 11mo, 7da
Rebecca T   d 7- 2-1865  ae 57yrs, 5mo, 24da
Ch: Joseph Baldwin   b 3- 8-1830
    Jonathan Watson  b 9-24-1832  d 2-24-1871
                     -bur Fall Creek
    Albert G         b 5-14-1848

John Joseph b 2-10-1857  d 3-28-1916 -bur Pendleton
Josephine D b 4-23-1862  -dt ... Downs
Ch: Floyd (or Lloyd) b 5- 2-1891
    Louise           b 6-11-1895

Joseph B    d 5-29-1907
Elizabeth   b 3-18-1827  d 3-26-1903 -dt ..Deweese
Ch: Maude Mary       b 10- 1-1859
    Josephine        b 4-23-1862
    Evangeline Elizabeth b 4-27-1865

Lydia       d 11- 6-1842  ae 77yrs, 2mo, 21da

Samuel      d 9-11-1889  ae 81yrs, 3mo, 21da

Sarah Rogers b 11-  -1851  d 6-28-1917 -bur Pendleton
             w of Albert G

Simeon M    d 4-11-1877  ae 71yrs
Milcah Martha b 10-19-1825  d 3-29-1900 -bur Fall Cr
Ch: Walter Hibbard   b 12-25-1849
    Horace Fussell   b 2-25-1852  d 6-24-1912
                     -bur Pendleton
    Susan M          b 11-29-1853  d 11-16-1858
                     -bur Pendleton

Susannah M  d 8-10-1857  ae 73yrs, 11mo, 1da
            -bur Fall Creek

Thomas C    b 1857

## FALL CREEK

### LEWIS (Cont)
Walter L          b 10-23-1884
Helen Faye        b 6-22-1884  -dt ,, Bennet
Ch: Helen Faye    b 7-13-1913
    Eleanor K     b 6-21-1915

### LITTLER
Emma Williams     b 4-15-1874  w Willis B

### LIVEZEY
Nathan            d 9-10-1858  ae 83yrs, 5mo, 14da

### LUKENS
Allen             b 9- 3-1821  d 6-28-1900
Mary Ann          d            ae 41yrs, 2mo, 7da
Ch: William A     b 4-28-1844  d 1- 5-1866
                              -bur Fall Creek
    Elizabeth R   b 1-13-1846
    Perry         b 12-14-1847 d 8-11-1914
                              -bur Pendleton
    Mary Ann      b 5- 3-1850  d 3-21-1851
                              -bur Pendleton
    Margaret      b 9- 9-1852
    Solomon F     b 9- 4-1855
    Evaline       b 11-14-1857 d 12- 6-1865
                              -bur Fall Creek
Ann G (2nd w) b 4-21-1825 d 7- 7-1899 -bur Fall Creek

Bessie S          d 2- 5-1894  ae 19yrs, 1mo, 21da -bur Fall Creek

Frank D           b 1903

Isaac
Edith
Ch: Eliza S       b 9-30-1867
    Hannah T      b 9-16-1870
    David B       b 5-27-1872

Isaac A           b 1-17-1869
Cora              b 2-23-1899
Ch: Kenneth
    Raymond
    Ralph

Jane D            d 6-17-1925  -bur Pendleton

Juliema P         d 8-25-1872  -dt Charles A & Mary Ellen
                              (not mbr)

Martha            d 5- 3-1894  ae 35yrs, 14da -bur Fall Creek

Mary              d 12-11-1874 ae 16yrs -bur Fall Creek

Matilda           d 9- 1-1885  ae 48yrs, 1mo

Perry             b 12-14-1847 d 8-11-1914 -bur Pendleton
Mary              b 9- 9-1850  d 2- 6-1929 -bur Pendleton
Ch: William       b 3-17-1875
    Evaline       b 5-23-1881

Richard M
Caroline
Ch: Mary Moore    b 4-14-1838
    Hannah T      d 2- 2-1865  ae 13yrs, 10mo, 20da
                              -bur Fall Creek

Rita (Lukins)     b 12-28-1898

Robert            b 10-28-1840 d 1-22-1905
Elizabeth         b 1841
Ch: Anna Jane     b 2-19-1863  d 9- 7-1864
                              -bur Fall Creek
    Lydia Ellen   b 1-23-1865
    Isaac A       b 1-17-1869
    Abner Warner  b 4- 9-1877  d 8-28-1877
    Maud E        b 12-14-1879 d 10-23-1916
                              -bur Pendleton
    Howard R      b 9- 1-1882

Susan             d            ae 29yrs, 10mo, 11da
                  w of Benjamin Lukens

William           d 6-11-1881  ae 72yrs, 11mo, 28da (not mbr)
Lydia Ann         d 3-13-1896  ae 85yrs, 11mo, 12da
Ch: Martha C      b 6- 6-1836
    Benjamin      b 4- 2-1838
    Robert Austin b 10-28-1840
    Elizabeth A   b 11-24-1842
    William J     b 2-24-1846  d 4- 6-1889
                              -bur Fall Creek
    Mary Lusana   b 4-14-1850  d 4- 4-1854
                              -bur Fall Creek
    Hannah        b 4-30-1854

William J         d 4- 6-1889  ae 43yrs, 1mo, 10da
Georgianna C      b 1-10-1845  -dt George & Elizabeth Cook
                  d 6-29-1906
Ch: Lydia Ann     b 9-27-1873
    Asahel C      b 10-15-1874
    Louie Estilla b 4-26-1879
    Maria Edith   b 2-17-1886

### McCURDY
William
Alice Lewis       b 9- 8-1872
Ch: Emily Dean    b 4- 3-1890  d 8-10-1912
    Margaret Lois b 12-16-1891 d 12-19-1918
                              -bur Pendleton
    Helen         b 2- 7-1896  d 12-  -1918
                              -bur Pendleton
    Harold Lewis  b 7-20-1903
    Robert Morris b 9-17-1912

### MASON
George            b 5-21-1866
Margaret          b 9-14-1864
Ch: Johnson G     b 4- 9-1890
    Alice H       b 6-17-1892
    Henry W       b 12-23-1893
    David P       b 5-30-1895
    James G       b 2-10-1896
    Emily O       b 7- 1-1898
    Albert E      b 12-24-1900
    Edith M       b 10-14-1902
    Charles Ray   b 1904
    Lillian Gertrude b 3-25-1905
    William Howard b 5- 7-1906  d 7-29-1906
    Raymond H     b 10-28-1909

### MARRANVILLE
Margaret P        b 12-24-1902 w of Charles

Robert E Sr       b 8-28-1867
...
Ch: Robert M Jr   b 9- 1-1889
    Charles       b 7-27-1901

### MANNON
Martha C          b 2- 3-1871  w of Fulton

### McLELAND
Alice             b 11-15-1858 w of Seth

### McKINLEY
Minnie May        b 6-16-1888

### McKINNEY
Cyrus             b 9- 7-1844  -s William & Mary

### McGRIFF
Mary Ellen        b 12- 4-1855 w of William

### MATHEWS
Samuel
Esther            d 5-12-1864  ae 32yrs, 9mo, 28da
                              -bur Blue Grass Cem near Rossville, Va
Ch: Lizzie Anna   b 5-23-1851
    Edgar R       b 12-20-1854

FALL CREEK

MATHEWS (Cont)
Samuel & Esther
Ch: (Cont):
   Thomas Branson   b  6-29-1857
   Charles William  b  5-19-1861
   Joseph S   b  3-29-1863  d  9-3-1864  -bur Ill

MEALEY
Ritta May   b  6-24-1872  w of George

MICHAEL
Joseph H
Theresa   b  8-12-1855  d  2-17-1929
        -bur Grove Lawn Cem, Pendleton, Ind
Ch:  Howard   b  7-15-1887
    Edith M   b  1-19-1891
    Charles A   b  5-26-1894
    Annie R   b  4-5-1897
    Ruth Emma   b  4-5-1897

MIDDLETON
John   d  7-5-1854  ae 77yrs, 2mo, 11da
Mary   d  4-10-1858  ae 78yrs, 10mo, 28da
Ch:  Hannah
    Richard
    Rachel

MILLER
John Bishop  b  8-26-1901

Helen J   b  1-20-1899  w Paul Gregory Miller

Helen Roena  b  7-2-1903

MILLS
Hugh   d  1-16-1857  -bur Duck Creek
Lydia   d  1-11-1870  ae 74yrs  -bur Duck Creek
Ch:  Thomas H   b  8-30-1819
    Jerusha   b  9-5-1821
    Peninnah   b  3-27-1823
    Priscilla   b  12-1-1825  d  1-14-1831
    Eber   b  8-22-1828
    Rhoda   b  2-14-1831
    Ruth   b  8-27-1833
    Joel   b  4-16-1836

MOORE
James
Phebe
Ch:  Edward A   b  1-28-1861
    Mary E   b  3-28-1863
    Albert U   b  8-6-1864

MOREHEAD
Martha   b  11-5-1867  w of George

MORRIS
Aaron   b  11-28-1834  m  12-21-1865
Martha M
Ch:  Louie   b  7-30-1867
    William F   b  4-18-1871
    Robert A   b  5-16-1877
    Elizabeth   b  1-4-1880

William F   b  2-9-1832  -s George & Rhoda
Mary Ellen   b  5-29-1836  -dt Charles & Sarah Swaim
Ch:  Lizzie Ellen  b  7-12-1858  d  8-4-1883
        -bur Fall Creek
    Emma Caroline  b  9-20-1860
    George D   b  5-25-1864
    Anna P   b  9-5-1866
    Charles W   b  12-29-1870  d  3-11-1871
        -bur Fall Creek
    Sarah Ellen  b  9-12-1872  d ae 2mo, 13da

MORRISON
James   d  10-10-1873  ae 69yrs, 6mo  -bur Fall Cr
Ellen   d  6-6-1889  ae 83yrs

NICHOLSON
Elizabeth   d  10-9-1846  ae 69yrs, 8mo, 2da
    -bur Fall Creek

OLDHAM
Abner W   b  1843  d  5-8-1932  -bur Pendleton Cem

Della M   b  6-18-1883

Herman A   d  1-24-1894  ae 1mo  -bur Pendleton Cem

Lenna M   b  8-5-1876

PARDUE
Margaret   d  6-14-1873  ae 20yrs, 8mo, 29da
Ch:  William   d  9-7-1873  ae 3mo, 5da

PARKER
J Allen   b  11-10-1875
Lillian W   b  10-18-1880  -dt .. Catren
Ch:  William C   b  6-3-1909
    Mary Louise  b  5-3-1915
    Jean   b  10-11-1919

Sarah   d  11-9-1859

PARSONS
Mary Ida   b  10-15-1862

PENNY
Margaret B   b  10-2-1877  w of Perry

POPE
Abner   d  12-6-1874  ae 82yrs
Maria   d  5-31-1878  ae 83yrs, 4mo, 26da

Abner James   -s Abner & Maria
Peninnah   -d Hugh & Lydia Mills
Ch:  Lydia Mills  b  9-1-1847
    George F   b  8-22-1850  d  12-8-1853
        -bur Indianapolis
    Daniel   b  7-30-1853  d  12-7-1853
    Charles   b  8-24-1855
    Anna   b  8-17-1858
    Mary   b  3-23-1861
    Julia   b  3-2-1864

Edward   -s Abner & Maria
Susana E (1st w)  d  2-28-1844  ae 18yrs, 7mo, 2da
    -dt Jonathan & Eleanor Schofield, Marion, Ind
Ch:  David Edward  b  2-28-1844  d  4-8-1844
Mary (2nd w)
Ch:  Anna Maria  b  4-11-1852  d  9-15-1853
    Robert Abner  b  3-20-1854
    George K   b  6-10-1857
    Mary Ellen  b  8-25-1860

POWERS
Richard Lyle
Florence   b  4-10-1893  -dt .. Doan
Ch:  Marcia Catharine  b  6-22-1906
    Richard Wilson  b  11-28-1907

PRIDDY
Haviland   d  11-18-1873  ae nearly 1yr

RAGSDALE
Anna P   b  9-5-1866  w of J F

RANDALL
Elizabeth   b  1-18-1867  w of Phillip

REID
Clara   d  8-23-1880  ae 3mo, 7da

RIDGWAY
Reese   d  8-22-1848  ae 39yrs, 3mo, 7da
Lucretia
Ch:  Henry   b  7-3-1835

FALL CREEK

RIDGWAY (Cont)
Reese & Lucretia
Ch: (Cont):
 Mary    b 10- -1838
 Viola    b 3- 6-1840
 Ann    b 3- 1-1842 d 9- 2-1846
        -bur Rush Creek Cem
 Edward   b 9-29-1844 d 8- 8-1846
        -bur Milford Cem

ROBERTS
..
Anna  d 12-10-1876 ae 69yrs, 7mo, 1 da
Ch: Eunice  d 1- -1869 ae 35yrs
  Elihu   d 6- 8-1858
  Anna   d 4-29-1853

Jesse  d 11-26-1876 ae 67yrs, 9mo, 9da
Hannah d 4-13-1853
Ch: Priscilla S b 1-21-1841 d 3- 6-1844
  John S  b 2- 9-1843 d 3- 4-1844
     -bur Nathan Livezey's Burial Gr
  James L  b 2-18-1845
  Infant dt  b 2-31-1847
  Rebecca Ann b 4- 2-1850
  Mary Ann  b d 3- 4-1844 ae 6yrs,9mo,19da
  Nathan L  b d 3-11-1844 ae 8yrs,5mo,14da

Joshua
Hannah L d 8-24-1869 ae 67yrs, -bur Fall Creek
Ch: Joseph T d 8-30-1849 ae 1yr, 11mo, 9da
  Sarah B  b 8-10-1851
  William W
  Hester Ann

Solomon d 4- 6-1857 ae 61yrs, 11mo, 24da
Elizabeth d 11- 8-1884 ae 85rs, 5mo, 3da
Ch: Mary
  Elihu
  Hannah
  Artemus

ROGERS
Annie Thomas b 1-25-1876 d 10-31-1931 -bur Pendleton
 w of Arthur

Arthur Frank b 5-26-1902

Benjamin Sr d 9-15-1872 ae 82yrs, -bur Fall Creek

Benjamin b 3-30-1843 d 6-7-1929 -s Jonathan & Hannah
Ann L  b 11- 4-1841 d 3- 9-1904
  -dt Lewis & Priscilla Thomas
Ch: Jonathan  b 10-24-1867
  Mary T   b 6-30-1876
  Esther L  b 8- 3-1882

B Franklin d 8-28-1878 ae 39yrs, 7mo, 28da (not mbr)

Blanch A  b 9-29-1892
Mabel Emily b 10- 4-1894

Charles J d 4- 1-1882 ae 83yrs, 11mo, 25da
 -s Joseph & Elizabeth
......... (1st w)
Ch: Susannah W b 3-22-1838 d 10- 3-1853
  Joseph M  b 4-23-1839
  Ann Elizabeth b 12-15-1840
  Elmina Francina b 1-13-1843
  John U  b 3-20-1845
Rebecca B (2nd w) b d 8-14-1880 ae 64yrs, 1mo
 m 11-22-1849 -dt Joseph & Elizabeth Fussell
Ch: Sarah D  b 11-19-1851
  Charles H  b 1-21-1853 d 1-13-1854
  Solemon Fussell b 5-12-1855 d 5-12-1855
  Charles Fussell b 5-12-1855 d 5-24-1855

Charles J b 12-30-1858 d 5-16-1921 -bur Pendleton
Sarah R  b 5- 6-1864 d 9- 8-1922
Ch: William N  d 3- 6-1885 ae 3yrs, 4mo, 7da
  Chester C  d 1-20-1896 ae 3yrs, 11mo, 12da
  Nina   b or d (?) 12-13-1897

Edward  b 2- 4-1830 d 2-15-1905 -bur Fall Creek
Mary A  b 3- 4-1833 d 2-15-1905 -bur Fall Creek

Elijah P  b 4-17-1833 d 12-27-1899 -bur Friends
           Burial Ground
Ellen P  b 5- 5-1832 d 2-27-1908

Elizabeth d 11- 8-1842 ae 43yrs, 7mo, 15da

George C  b 4-13-1866
Melissa G  b 12- 3-1866
Ch: Raymond J  b 5- 1-1890
  Noland Asahel b 1- 5-1894
  Clarence Cook b 2- 1-1903

George Willis  b 3-10-1929

Jonathan J d 10-23-1886 ae 68yrs, 10m, 7 da
 -s Benjamin & Elizabeth
Hannah (1st w) d 10-15-1848 ae 36yrs, 1mo, 25da
Ch: Joshua W  b 1-12-1841 d 3-22-1849
        -bur Fall Creek
  Benjamin  b 3-30-1843
Louisa (2nd w) b 11-13-1830 -dt Ephriam & Leah Copeland
John J  b 4-13-1866

John U  b 3-20-1845 d 8- 3-1905 -bur Fall Creek
Elizabeth H b 10- 3-1845 d 6- 5-1929 -bur Pendleton
Ch: Jonathan T b 6-14-1869
  Alice E  b 3-28-1871
  Charles W  b 3-10-1873 d 9- 3-1886
  Sarah Lydia b 2- 6-1875
  Ellen P  b 3-18-1878 d 3-15-1907
        -bur Fall Creek

Joseph M b 4-23-1839 d 1-26-1916 -bur Pendleton
Rebecca J b 10- 9-1844 d 3-26-1927 -bur Pendleton
Ch: James Ernest b 9- 8-1866 d 9-29-1911
  Walter C  b 2-23-1870 d 9- 9-1870
        -bur Fall Creek
  Margaret T b 9-17-1875

Joseph  d 8-22-1840 ae 50yrs, 2da -bur Fall Cr
Elizabeth d 6-16-1851 ae 62yrs, 5mo, 26da
  -bur Fall Creek
Ch: Charles J
  Sarah Ann
  Hannah
  Mary Ann
  Joseph Reese d 8-22-1872 ae 44yrs, 8mo
   (not a mbrp)  -bur Fall Creek
  Elizabeth
  Margaret  m .. Tyson

Joseph Thomas d 1-29-1895 ae 19yrs, 15mo, 18da
 (not a mbr)

Lester Charles b 6-10-1890
Vadia Ethel  b 9-12-1889 -dt .. Linkinfelter
Ch: Lois Eunice b 8-18-1916
  Elizabeth Jean b 6-10-1922

Mary J b 11-25-1853 d 5-15-1922 -bur Fall Creek

Roland C
Lula  b 2-11-1898 -dt Richardson
Ch: Gerald
  Katherine Louella b 11-15-1918
  Carolyn Jane b 1924 d 1- 8-1929
        -bur Fall Creek
  Asahel
  Mary Ilene b 12- 8-1927
  Roland Edward b 8- 9-1930

William d 2- 5-1873 Infant s of William & Anna

William d 3-22-1872 (not a mbr)

FALL CREEK

## SANDERS
Joseph W  
Jerusha  
Ch: Lydia Ann　　　　b 10- 3-1839  
　　Margaret E　　　b 8- 8-1841  
　　Priscilla　　　　b 2-12-1844  
　　Mary　　　　　　b 8-21-1846  
　　Thomas E　　　　b 2-12-1849  

## SCHOFIELD
Anna Mary　　b 1856  

Jonathan　　d 11-16-1863　ae 87yrs,　-bur Indianapolis  
Eleanor　　 d 3-28-1858　 ae 72yrs,　-bur Indianapolis  
Ch: Samuel W　　　　b 8-16-1808　d 1- 2-1867  
　　Sarah Ann　　　 b 3-24-1810  
　　William A　　　 b 11- 3-1812　d 1-21-1893  
　　Phebe Ellen　　 b 11-15-1814　m .. Hunter  
　　Mary Eliza　　　b 2- 9-1816　m .. Sutherland  
　　David Brown　　 b 9-30-1819  
　　Margaret Allison　b 11-26-1821  
　　Maria Pope　　　b 5-15-1823  
　　Susan Elizabeth　b 7-23-1825  
　　Joseph Fell　　 b 6- 7-1828　d 3-30-1910  

Lydia　　d 10- 3-1886　ae 82yrs, 11mo, 8da  

## SCHOOLEY
James  
Sarah J　　b 1-13-1841　-dt Johnson  
Ch: Benjamin Anthony　b 6-23-1871  
　　William　　　　b  d 10-14-1872　ae 3mo, 11da  
　　　　　　　　　　　-bur Fall Creek  
　　Charles Edward　b 12-22-1875  

## SHANNON
Joseph Barnett　　b 12-27-1877  
Mabel Marie　　　 b 5- 1-1881  
Ch: Anna Marie　　b 7-11-1900  
　　Marion Ellen　b 4-20-1903  
　　Elizabeth Adelaide b 3-28-1908  

## SHARP
Lydia J　　d 2-29-1872　ae 33yrs, 6mo, 20da -bur Fall Cr  

## SHAUL
Anna J　　d 9-13-1882　ae 51yrs, 5da (not a mbrp)  

## SIMMONDS
Elizabeth W　d 5-30-1831　ae 75yrs, 9mo, 7da  
　　　　　　-bur Pleasanton, Linn Co, Kans  

Samuel  
Rachel  
Ch: Philip T　　b 7-27-1847  
　　Joshua　　　b 9-12-1850  
　　Ellwood　　b 9-17-1853  
　　Mary E　　　b 5-10-1859  

## SMITH
Maria P　　d 9-19-1858　-dt Jonathan & Eleanor  
　　　　　　-bur near Indianapolis  

Milton  
Mary Ann  
Ch: Alva Charles　b 5-19-1858  
　　Edgar Julian　b 1-14-1861  

Nathan  
Rebecca　　b　　d 1- 4-1876 ae 63yrs, 9mo, 14da  
Ch: Eliza Ann　b 2- 9-1832　d 9- 5-1847  
　　Ezra　　　 b 9-13-1833　d 1-21-1835  
　　　　　　　　　　　　-bur Whitewater  
　　Milton　　b 8-18-1835  
　　Hiram　　 b 12-15-1837  
　　Martha　　b 6-12-1840　d 5-20-1868  
　　Jacob　　 b 5- 4-1842  
　　Margaret　b 8-27-1845  
　　Samuel　　b 4-19-1849  
　　Phebe　　 b 11-13-1851  
　　Mary　　　b 5-13-1854  

T  
Phebe  
Ch: Caroline　b 11-27-1836  
　　Albert　　b 2-21-1839  

## STAFFORD
Minnie　　b 4- 4-1879　w of Milton  

## STANLEY
Christian　d 7-10-1873　ae 72yrs, 3mo, 8da  

## STRADLING
George　　　b 1- 8-1846　d 5- 3-1928  
Martha Ellen b 1-20-1851  
Ch: Emma C　b 7- 3-1873  

## STRATTON
Edward　　b 4-19-1831  
Hannah B　b 1- 4-1838  
Ch: Albert　　b 9-15-1856  
　　William E　b 12- 9-1857　d 9-13-1857  
　　　　　　　　　(?)　-bur Duck Creek  
　　Arthur J　b 8- 7-1860　d 1-22-1882  
　　　　　　　　　　-bur Duck Creek  
　　Ella　　　b 10-25-1864  
　　Benjamin　b 1- 6-1866  
　　Minnie B　b 4- 4-1879  

Rebecca　　d 9-10-1849　ae 20yrs, 10da -bur Duck Cr  

## SWAIN
Beaulah Ann　　d 3- 8-1908  

Charles　　b 7-31-1808　d 3- 2-1867 -bur Fall Creek  
Sarah Ann　b 3-24-1810　d 7- 9-1868 -bur Fall Creek  
(a min)  

Charles W　b 8-25-1878  
Mattie　　 b 4-28-1879　-dt .. Stephens  

Charles E　b 1-28-1844　-s Charles & Sarah Ann  
　　　　　　m 11-16-1865  
Margaret S　b 4-29-1845　d 12-22-1927  
　　　　　　-dt Elwood & Mary Ann Brown  
Ch: Edwin Howard　b 9-16-1866　d 1-14-1912  
　　　　　　　　　　-bur Pendleton  
　　Elwood Brown　　b 11- 8-1868  
　　Elnora Beatrice　b 7- 4-1871  
　　Walter Anthony　 b 12-15-1874  
　　George Henry　　 b 2- 8-1878  
　　William M　　　　b 2- 8-1878  

Estella M　d 8-18-1893　ae 9mo, 22da  
　　　　　　-dt Allen L & Alice  

Frances M (Morgan)　b 5-22-1860　w of Joseph  

George H　　b 2- 8-1878  
Elizabeth　 b 7- 5-1878　-dt .. Hardy  
Ch: C Edwin　　　b - -1906  
　　Ruth Jean　　b 8- 3-1914  
　　Walter D　　 b 12-20-1915  
　　Joseph Hugh　b 11-22-1916  
　　George Henry Jr b 2- 4-1918  

Horace　　b 12-12-1894  

Joseph S　　b 10-10-1841　d 9- 8-1912  
　　　　　　-s Charles & Sarah Ann  
Elizabeth　 b 1-13-1846　d 6- 9-1912  
　　　　　　-dt Alben & Mary Ann Lukens  
Ch: Marietta　　b 12- 6-1865 (or Marilla)  
　　Allen L　　b 12-25-1866  
　　Sarah Ann　b 8-29-1868  
　　Charles W　b 8-25-1878  
　　Mattie Delia　b 4- 2-1879  

Martha　　d 8-28-1853　ae 21da　-bur Fall Creek

FALL CREEK

SWAIN (Cont)
Walter          b 12-15-1874  =s Charles E & Margaret B
Elizabeth Belle b 11-3-1877   d 2-  -1911
                -Protogee of Thomas & Margaret Hardy
Ch: Helen Hardy     b  6- 2-1903

William E       b  2- 8-1878
Etta Louise     b  5-23-1878
Ch: Frederick William  b 12-22-1905
    Morris Stanley     b 10-20-1909
    Ruth J             b  8- 3-1914
    Joseph H           b 11-24-1916

Woolston        b  2-20-1822  d 12-21-1899 -bur Fall Creek
                -s Samuel & Martha, Marion, Ind
Mary Ann        b  7-22-1818  d  8-17-1908 -bur Fall Creek
                -dt Jonathan & Ann Thomas
Ch: Anna Mary       b 12- 7-1844    d  7-20-1913
                                    -bur Pendleton
    Samuel          b  2-14-1848    d  9- 9-1913
                                    -bur Fall Creek
    Rebecca L       b  7-11-1852
    Joseph L        b  6-16-1857    d  5-19-1927
                                    -bur Fall Creek
    Frances L       b  9-10-1860

SUTHERLAND
Mary E          d  3-17-1859  ae 43yrs, 1mo, 1da
                -bur near Indianapolis

TAYLOR
Joseph W        d 10-14-1857  ae 49yrs, 8mo, 26da -bur Fall Cr
Susanna         d  4-29-1878  ae 71yrs, 1mo, 9da (not a mbr)

THOMAS
Esther S        d  9-11-1894  ae 46yrs, 2mo, 7da

Hannah          d  3- 4-1868  ae 78yrs -bur Fall Creek

Lewis W         d  1-12-1864  ae 50yrs, 7mo, 15da
                -bur Fall Creek
Priscilla M  b           d  8- 6-1886 ae 67yrs, 10mo, 11da
                -bur Fall Creek
Ch: John L          b 11-30-1837   d 12-12-
    Martha M        b  2- 3-1839
    Ann L           b 11- 4-1841
    Lucretia M      b  7- 6-1844
    Jonathan        b  2-25-1846
    Esther Lewis    b  7- 4-1848   d  9-11-1894
    Mary S          b  1- 8-1850   m .. Kinnard
    Solomon Fussell b  9-28-1852
    Rebecca L       b  7-30-1854   d  1-12-1864
                                   -bur Fall Creek
    Priscilla M     b  1- 6-1856   d 10- 8-1858
                                   -bur Fall Creek
    Alice Grace     b  8-16-1857 m .. Whitely

Jonathan     b  2-25-1846  =s Lewis W & Priscilla
             d  4-22-1931  -bur Pendleton
Emily        b 11-23-1856
Ch: Ann R           b  1-25-1876   d 10-31-1931
                                   -bur Pendleton
    Joseph R        b  4- 8-1879   d  4-14-1882
                                   -bur Fall Creek
    Josephine       b  4-29-1882   d  9- 2-1882
                    (not a mbr) -bur Fall Creek
    John L          b 12-22-1883

Jonathan        d  9- 6-1839  ae 72yrs, 11mo -bur Fall Creek
Ann             d  2-21-1867  ae 90yrs, 5mo, 21da
Ch: Mary Ann        b  7-22-1818

    Solomon Fussell b  9-28-1852   d  4- 2-1923
                                   -bur Spring Valley
    Caroline L      b  9-13-1854   d 12-15-1901
                                   -bur Fall Creek
Ch: Muriel F        b  1- 7-1888

John L          b 11-20-1837  d 12-12-    -bur Pendleton
                =s Lewis & Priscilla
Caroline L      b  1-13-1838  d  3-13-1915 -bur Pendleton
                -dt Charles & Sarah Ann Swain
Ch: Emma Fussell    b 11-21-1864
    Lewis W         b  1- 1-1866   d  3- 1-1867
                                   -bur Fall Creek
    Charles W       b 12-29-1868
    Lewis W         b  5- 5-1876

Lewis W         b  5- 5-1876  d 11-27-1932
                =s John L & Caroline L
Margaret        b 12-28-1875 -dt Samuel E & Virginia Hardy
Ch: Virginia        b  3-  -1913
    Swain           b       1915
    James M         b  8-28-1916

THURSTON
Ida M           b  8-12-1875

TRUMP
William H       d  8-29-1885  ae 2-1/2 mo -bur Greenfield
Mary F          d 11-17-1890  ae 36yrs, 10mo, 7da
                Mother of William

TURNER
Eliza Ann       b  9-25-1852  w of John

TUNES
Charley         b 11-18-1882  d  5-16-1917 -bur Spring Valley
Mary Alice      b  3- 3-1882

Mary J          b  5- 6-1843  d 11-22-1928  w of William

Omer            =s William H & Sarah B
Sarah F         b  7-31-1876  -dt Ziba & Elmina Darlington
Ch: Horace Glenn    b  1-25-1905
    Hazel May       b  9-10-1909

TYSON
Davis           d 10- 6-1879  ae 23yrs, 4mo

Margaret        b 10-13-1832  d 11-27-1907 -bur Fall Creek

ULEN
Jerry           b 12-25-1885

UNDERWOOD
Lewis           d  2-27-1887  ae 62yrs
Sarah B
Ch: William E       b  7-11-1855
    Charles A       b  5-29-1858
    Caroline M      b 12- 5-1859   d 12-19-1880
    Alveretta E     b  5-15-1861
    Laura B         b  9-14-1863   m .. Owens
    Elmer E         b  7-28-1865
    Asenath         b  7-23-1867   d  3-25-1868
                                   -bur Hamilton Co, Ind

Amos
Alice           b  2-28-1865
Ch: John            b
    Mary Catharine  b  2-24-1895

Catharine       b  4-19-1834

Charles A       b  5-29-1858

Isaac           d 11-13-1878  ae 68yrs, 1mo, 14da
                =s Amos & Mary

VERNON
Abner           b 12-28-1843  d  3-  -1900 -bur Menden Cem
Jemima          b  8-15-1847
Ch: Noah H          b  2-20-1872

Fannie T        d  8-28-1872  ae 9mo

Abraham         d  7- 3-1867  ae 84yrs -bur Fall Creek

FALL CREEK

VERNON (Cont)
Abram
Mary
Ch: Edward B
Esther

Edward
Hannah          d 10-24-1851  ae 28yrs, 11mo, 6da -bur Fall Creek
Ch: Elizabeth R    b  9- 1-1840  d  9- 1-1840
    Abner R        b 12-28-1843
    Mary E         b 12-31-1847  m Noah C Haines
    Sarah Ann      b  1-22-1850  m .. Jacobs

Noah R         b  2-20-1872  -s Abner & Jemima
Anna M         b 12- 5-1877
Ch: Geneva Elizabeth  b  8-10-1907

Rachel         b 12-19-1863  m .. Foust

Ruth Anna      d  3-17-1877  (a baby - not a mbr)

Ruth Anna      d  3-21-1877  ae 47yrs, 7mo, 24da (not mbr)

WALKER
Margaret S     b  6-28-1886

WATSON
Cervantes L    b   - -1829
Hannah         b   - -1828  d  8-16-1908 -bur Fall Creek

WARD
Maud Anna                b 10-28-1903  w of Walter D

WEEKS
Jacob
Lydia
Ch: Anna
    Sarah
    Charles
    Hannah
    Maria
    Eliza
    Rebecca
    John
    Aaron

Joseph         b   - -1820  d 11-13-1908 -bur Fall Creek
..
Ch: Susan
    Phebe
    Samuel
    Joseph
    Thomas
    Abram

Joseph         d 11-22-1857  ae 66yrs, 7mo, 14da, -bur Fall Creek

Samuel         -s Joseph & Susannah
Elizabeth Ann  b           -dt Jacob & Elizabeth Styler of Wabash Co, Ind
Ch: Stephen         b 12- 5-1847
    Thomas C        b 12-25-1849
    William Henry   b  9- 1-1852

WEESNER
Louisa Wood   b 11-22-1852  -bur Wabash, Ind
              -dt           w of Robert Ed

WENE
Elizabeth C   b 12- 7-1865  w of Lee

WHITE
Lewis         d 10- 9-1840  ae 53yrs, 3mo, 17da
              -bur Crown Hill, vicinity of Fall Creek Mtg

Sophia        d  5- 4-1855  ae 36yrs

WHITELY
Edgar         b  6- 5-1856  d  8- 5-1918
              -s Daniel & Anna M
Alice G       b  8-16-1857  -dt Lewis G & Priscilla Thomas
Ch: Anna M        b 11-24-1880
    Emma T        b  5-28-1883
    Lewis D       b  4-29-1886
    Emory E       b  2-19-1888
    Ina H         b 10-29-1891
    Walter Byron  b 12- 4-1895

Lewis D       b 4-28-1886
Anna (Divon)  b 11-15-1885
Ch: Daniel Diven     b  3- 7-1914  d  3- 9-1914
                     -bur Pendleton
    Mary Ruth        b 10- 8-1916

WILDRIDGE
Hilda Elizabeth       b 10-24-1907

WILLIAMS
Caleb
Hannah        d  7- 6-1855  ae 39yrs
Ch: Milton        b  9- 1-1835
    Stephen       b 11-16-1836
    Silas         b  3-26-1838
    Lydia Ann     b  8- 7-1840
    Elizabeth     b 11- 6-1842

Charles C     d 12- 5-1870  ae 13mo, 12da -bur Urbana, Ill

Jesse         d  2-17-1858  ae 62yrs, 10mo, 5da
Sarah         d  9-30-1873  ae 82yrs, 8mo, 9da
Ch: Davis     d  1-17-1847  ae 27yrs, 7mo, 2da
    Oliver R  d  3- 1-1852  ae 21yrs, 8mo, 24da

Silas         b  3-26-1838  -s Caleb & Hannah
              d  7-15-1904  -bur Huntsville Cem
Sarah Ann     b  9-10-1839  d 1921  -bur Huntsville Cem
              -dt George & Elizabeth Cook
Ch: William A     b 12-20-1863
    Elizabeth C   b 12- 7-1865
    Caleb S       b  3- 2-1869
    Ruth Emma     b  4-15-1874

Stephen       b  3-12-1862  d  3-30-1903
Masse         b  3- 6-1836  d 10- 3-1916 -bur Huntsville Cem
Ch: Emma J         b  1-29-1863  d  9-24-1864
    Mariam Fussell b 11-20-1865
    Jason S        b 10-24-1871
    Olive H        b  8-16-1876

William       d 11-18-1847  ae 72yrs, 4mo, 23da
              -bur Huntsville Cem

WILLITS
Margaret M    b 11-20-1872  w of Orlin

WILSON
Nathan        d  3-12-1860  ae 60yrs, 2mo, 8da
              -bur Fall Creek

Ralph         b  3-13-1870  -s David & Zerilda of Hancock Co, Ind
Victoria B    b  2-28-1871  -dt Warner M & Narcissa A Trueblood of Washington Co
Ch: Ralph         b 10-31-1902
    Max Maurice   b 11-13-1911

Sarah L       d  9-17-1849  ae 53yrs, 3mo, 10da
              -bur Fall Creek

WINDLE
Evaline       b  5-23-1881  w of Dory

WING
DeWitt C      b  2-18-1878

FALL CREEK

WISEHART
Benjamin F    b  1-12-1883
Grace E       b  10-21-1884  -dt ... Rogers
Ch: Charles           b  4- 3-1913

WOOD
Albert C      b  1-19-1849  d  5-29-1930
              -s Simeon F & Margaret H
Eva M         b  5-27-1851  -dt Clark C & Margaret F
                             Haines
Ch: Wilbur Clifford   b  6-22-1874
    Walter B          b  8-13-1875  d  9-10-1910
                                    -bur Pendleton
    Margaret          b  10- 2-1877

Ida M         b  4-26-1877

Jacob         b            d  3-27-1872 ae 79yrs, 1mo, 23da
Phebe         b            d  8-23-1866 ae 69yrs, 10mo, 28da
Ch: Levi P            b  4- 5-1823
    Rebecca           b  3-24-1830  d  3-13-1834
                                    -bur Duck Creek
    Owen              b  3- 8-1833  d  2-17-1847
                                    -bur Duck Creek
    Jesse M           b  8-25-1836  d  5-20-1839
                                    -bur Duck Creek
    Aseneth           b  11-20-1838

James         d  5-21-1885 ae 7yrs, 20 da -bur Fall Creek
              -s Peter & Esther
Sarah E       d  9- 4-1882 ae 10yrs, 7mo, 13da
              -dt Peter & Esther   -bur Fall Creek

John Arthur   b  1-23-1921

Levi          b  4- 5-1823  -s Jacob & Phebe
              d  8-24-1910  -bur Greensboro, Ind
Hannah F      b  3-17-1828  d  10- 2-1916 -bur Greensboro
Ch: Joseph Hugh       b  11-29-1849
    Louiza            b  11-22-1851
    Sarah H           b  11- 5-1852    d  9-27-1878
                        Widow of Homer
    William Owen      b  2-20-1856    d  7-31-1879
    Phebe Alice       b  1-15-1858
    Chalkley Enos     b  11-15-1860
    Charles Sumner    b  11- 3-1865

Margaret K    b  10-12-1924  d  9-30-1822 (sic)
              -bur Greensburg

Pearl         b  4-25-1893

Simeon        d  1-29-1887 ae 66yrs, 6mo, 27da
              -bur Greensboro, Ind
Margaret      b  4-18-1825
Ch: John R            b  11-17-1843   d  6-15-1857
                                      -bur Fall Creek
    Mary Elizabeth    b  4-18-1846
    Albert C          b  1-19-1849
    Louisa            b  11-22-1852
    Arthur J          b  3- 4-1854    d  12- 3-1860
                                      -bur Fall Creek
    Phebe E           b  5- 2-1857
    Sarah Emma        b  9-18-1859
    Corie Anna        b  4-15-1862
    William C         b  4- 8-1865
    Oscar             b  5-28-1868

Wilbur Clifford    b  6-22-1874  -s Albert C & Eva M
Laura Belle        b  11-19-1882
              -dt Benten L & Sarah Elizabeth Barrett
                  of Hancock Co, Ind
Ch: Lillian B         b  9-16-1903
    Ruth Holloway     b  11- 7-1910
    Esther Haines     b  6- 6-1912
    Wilbur Clifford Jr b 12-29-1914
    Laura B           b  4- 9-1916

William Elmer      b  10-28-1925

WOOLMAN
Clara         d  11-12-1884 ae 23yrs, 11mo, 14da
              (or 1-12-1884)

Isaac C
Esther P      b  1862
Ch: Walter B          b  6-29-1882
    Ruth E            b  10-26-1886
    Benjamin H        b  8-21-1889
    Anna Ray          b  4-18-1891

John
Asenath
Ch: Phebe A           b  7- 2-1852
    Charles Aaron     b  3-11-1855
    Mary E            b  2-26-1858
    Thomas D          b  6-20-1862
    William Parry     b  8-25-1864  d  2-11-1865
                                    -bur Fall Creek
    John C            b  1-16-1866
    Florence M        b  9-22-1869
    Warner Ortis      b  9-21-1871

Joseph B      d  10- 3-1876 ae 60yrs, 20da  -s Uriah &
              Prebble Co, O                  Mary
Eliza         d  5-14-1866  -dt Isaac & Anna -bur Fall Cr
Ch: Isaac C           b  10-17-1854
    William V         b  9-18-1856
    Julietha          b  6-29-1858  d  12-26-1865
    Mary A            b  1-20-1864

WRIGHT
Elias         b  4- 1-1828  -s Isaac & Mary
Damareas L
Ch: William Arthur    b  6-10-1852

Isaac         d  2-27-1875 ae 70yrs, 3mo, 16da
Mary H        d  6-19-1869 -bur Fall Creek
Ch: Elias H           b  4- 1-1828
    Peter             b  2-12-1830  d  7-25-1836
                                    -bur Milton, Wayne Co
    Basil B           b  8-25-1831  d  7- 5-1833
                                    -bur Milton, Wayne Co
    Francis Henry     b  1-29-1833
    Arthur T          b  3-21-1835
    Martha Ann        b  12-15-1837 d  2- 1-1838
                                    -bur Fall Creek
    Hannah Ann        b  2- 1-1839  d  9- 5-1839
                                    -bur Fall Creek
    Mary Caroline     b  11-21-1840 d  8-19-1841
                                    -bur Fall Creek
    Mary Ellen        b  3-28-1842  d  6-29-1871
                                    -bur Indianapolis, Crown Hill

William
Elizabeth
Ch: Sarah             b  8- 9-1827
    Benjamin          b  4- 7-1829
    Lydia             b  1- 6-1831  d  9-24-1836
                                    -bur Huntsville, Ind
    William Henry     b  12- 5-1832
    John              b  12-29-1834
    Mary Jane         b  1- 9-1837
    Jonathan J        b  7- 4-1839
    Ann Elizabeth     b  6- 1-1842
    Albert            b  12-28-1844

YATES
William       d  9-13-1841 ae "near 61" -bur Duck Cr

FALL CREEK

## FALL CREEK MONTHLY MEETING
### MINUTES AND MARRIAGES

ALLEN
11-14-1839  Eliza appt on comm
12-10-1840  Mary Ann appt asst clerk
6-10-1847   Aaron, Sarah Hannah, Eunice & Isaac, ch of Moses & Jane, rocf Whitewater MM, Ind
4-12-1849   Ch of Moses & Jane gct Milford MM
8-12-1852   Amos dis for mcd
9- 8-1853   Lindley dis for mcd
11-10-1853  Benjamin dis for att mcd
9-17-1856   Mary Ann, -dt Daniel & Eliza, m Edward Roberts, -s Solomon & Elizabeth, at Duck Creek MH
4-15-1857   Mary G, -dt Jehu & Mary Ann, m Milton Smith, -s Nathan & Rebecca, at Duck Creek MH
10-15-1859  Narcissa, -dt Daniel & Eliza, m Warner Trueblood, -s James & Elizabeth of Washington Co, Ind, at Duck Creek MH
3-14-1861   Louisa Copeland (form Allen) dis for mcd
9-14-1865   Rebecca & Alcinda gct Clear Creek MM, Ill
9-14-1865   Jehu & w Mary Ann & s Edward W gct Clear Creek MM, Ill
7-11-1872   Tamson E Walker (form Allen) chm of mcd
1-13-1873   Elmira Priddy (form Allen) chm of mcd
4-12-1888   Hannah rec in mbrp
6- 9-1904   Esther, -dt Elwood D & Stella, rec in mbrp
8-11-1923   Esther, -dt Elwood & Stella A, m Chas Merwin Palmer, -s Charles & Arletta C of Redley Park, Pa, at Pendleton MH

ALLISON
8-10-1876   Susan (form Cook) chm of mcd

ANDERSON
5-10-1888   Caroline J rocf Milford MM
2-14-1889   Archibald & ch Estella & Chester rst
2-14-1889   John rst
11-11-1915  Mrs Chester & ch Mary Elizabeth & Paul Clark rolf M E Ch, Pendleton, Ind

AXMAN
9-13-1889   Lillian Kendall rel fr mbrp

BABB
1- 8-1846   Joseph dis for att mcd

BAKER
6-10-1852   George & w Margaret & ch Lydia A & Mary rocf Fall Creek MM, O
8-13-1854   Amasa & w Sarah rocf Clear Creek MM, O
10-11-1855  Amy (form George) dis for mcd
3-11-1858   Sarah (form George) dis for mcd

BALDWIN
3-10-1877   Virgil F rec in mbrp
10-10-1878  Virgil rel fr mbrp

BARRETT
6-12-1902   Laura Belle, -dt Benton L & Sarah Elizabeth of Hancock Co, Ind, m Wilbur Clifford Wood, -s Albert C & Eva, in Barrett Residence

BARRICKMAN
12- 9-1841  Nancy (form Batty) dis for mcd

BATTY
8-13-1840   Nancy rocf Hamburgh MM, N Y
8-13-1840   David & ch Marmaduke & Richard rocf Hamburgh MM, N Y
12- 9-1841  Nancy Barrickman (form Batty) dis for mcd
8-14-1845   Marmaduke dis for mcd
8-14-1851   David chm of mcd

BELL
12-30-1897  Elizabeth, protegee of Thomas & Margaret W Hardy m Walter Swain, -s Charles E & Margaret B, in Swain Residence

BISHOP
10- 9-1851  Rebecca rocf Milford MM, Ind

BLAKELY
10- 8-1914  Ray rolf M E Ch, Pendleton, Ind
12-18-1913  Forrest Raymond, -s William R & Rosa B, m Edith Mary Kinnard, -dt William R & Mary S, at Kinnard Residence

BLOOM
1-14-1915   Matthew E rec in mbrp (Aberdeen Wash)

BOND
2-14-1850   Elias M Wright gct Milford MM, Ind to m Damarias S Bond
12-12-1850  Isaac & w Sarah & ch Lydia, Emily, Susannah, Rosanna & Mary rocf Whitewater MM, Ind
1- 9-1851   Aaron & w Amy & ch Louisa, Mary Jane, Zilpha Ann, Malissa Ellen, Ursula & Harriet rocf Whitewater MM, Ind
7-12-1855   Edward H Stratton gct Milford MM to m Hannah Bond
8-14-1856   Sarah Johnson (form Bond) chm of mcd
9- 3-1874   Robert, -s Jesse & Elizabeth J of Miami Co, Ind, m Lucretia M Thomas, -dt Lewis & Priscilla M, at Residence of Priscilla M Thomas
8- 8-1889   Robert rec in mbrp

BOSTON
9-13-1849   Margaret (form Rogers) chm of mcd
8-11-1881   Emma (form Heacock) mcd
4-11-1886   Eliza Ann rec in mbrp
12-13-1900  Mary rec in mbrp

BOWMAN
7-10-1862   Rhoda (form Cook) chm of mcd

BURCH
10-14-1869  Anna (form Sattethwait) dis for mcd

BURDSALL
11- 3-1898  Richard S, -s Elwood & Sarah E of Harrison Co, N Y, m Mary T Rogers, -dt Benjamin & Annie, at Rogers Residence
9-14-1899   Mary Rogers gct Purchas MM, N Y

BUTLER
11-14-1844  Hannah (form Weeks) dis for mcd

BRANSON
11-14-1839  Sarah appt on comm
11-18-1858  Nathan, -s Thomas & Annie, Clark Co, O, m Anna Swain, -dt Charles & Sarah Ann, at Fall Creek MH
3-10-1859   Anna S gct Green Plain MM, O

BRECKENRIDGE
12- 9-1909  Margaret gct Whitewater MM

BROOKS
8- 8-1895   Deborah Moore (form Watson) mcd; ret mbrp

BROWN
1-12-1854   Elwood & w Mary Ann & ch George, Henry, Isaac S, Margaret S, Philena, Samuel C, Joseph, Elwood & Charles rocf Whitewater MM, Ind
2- 9-1854   Charles rec in mbrp
11-16-1865  Margaret S, -dt Elwood & Mary Ann, m Charles Swain, -s Charles & Sarah Ann, at Fall Creek MH
10-12-1865  George H chm of mcd
9-20-1866   Philena, -dt Elwood & Mary Ann, m James Cockayne, -s Thomas & Martha, at Fall Creek MH

FALL CREEK

**BROWN (Cont)**
- 4-11-1872  Isaac chm of mcd
- 2- 8-1883  Joseph chm of mcd
- 8-20-1887  Charles chm of mcd
- 5- 8-1890  Isaac dis
- 12-18-1904 George H rel fr mbrp

**BUNKER**
- 2- 8-1849  Milia rocf Alum Creek MM, O

**CAMPLIN**
- 4-13-1871  Rebecca (form James) mcd
- 6-14-1888  Henry & ch James Floyd, Orlando Perry, Forrest Clifford & Harry Lincoln rec in mbrp
- 11-11-1897 Essiel L rec in mbrp
- 5-11-1905  Carrie F rel fr mbrp
- 6-12-1884  Caroline (form Foulke) chm of mcd

**CARPENTER**
- 9-17-1907  Howard H, -s John E & Mary H, Boulder, Colo m Esther L Rogers, -dt Benjamin & Annie L at Rogers Residence
- 11-14-1912 Esther & ch Mary E & Margery gct Orange Grove MM, Pasadena, Calif

**CARTER**
- 8-14-1913  Margaret gct Newark MM, Calif

**CATREN**
- 6-10-1886  Josephine & ch Edwin, Estilla & Lillian U rec in mbrp
- 5-11-1905  William H rec in mbrp

**CHAMBERLAIN**
- 2-23-1921  Bessie Lee, -dt Elmer C & Eliza, m Oscar M Haines, -s Aaron & Sarah Jane, in the Chamberlain Residence

**CHARLES**
- 2- 8-1855  Anna rocf Milford MM, Ind
- 7-16-1872  Anna, -dt William & Hannah Williams, m Jesse W Roberts, -s Samuel & Priscilla, at Anna Charles Residence, Huntsville

**CHENEY**
- 2- 8-1912  Mary F gct Pasadena MM, Calif

**CHURCHMAN**
- 8- 9-1849  William rocf Whitewater MM, Ind

**CLANTON**
- 5-12-1842  Sarah (form Weeks) dis for mcd

**CLARK**
- 8-12-1885  Ella McGriff (form Clark) mcd; rel fr mbrp

**COCKAYNE**
- 11-14-1839 Martha appt on comm
- 12-12-1839 Martha appt Clerk
- 3-15-1856  Sarah, -dt Thomas & Martha, m Evan Lewis, -s Abner & Susan, at Fall Creek MH
- 10-20-1859 Benjamin, -s Thomas & Martha, m Maria Jane Cook, -dt George & Elizabeth, at Fall Creek MH
- 12-15-1859 Nathan, -s Thomas & Martha, m Margaret Oldham, -dt John & Ann, at Fall Creek MH
- 9-20-1866  James, -s Thomas & Martha, m Philena Brown, -dt Elwood & Mary Ann
- 2-18-1869  Annie S, -dt Thomas & Martha, m William Frampton, -s William D & Sarah B, at Fall Creek MH

**COFFIN**
- 9-17-1887  Cora (form Wood) mcd; ret mbrp
- 7-12-1894  Claudius rec in mbrp
- 2- 8-1912  Claud, Cora, Glenn & Birdia gct Pasadena MM, Calif

**COLLINS**
- 4-14-1887  Hannah (form Lukens) mcd; ret mbrp

- 7- 9-1891  Hannah L gct Whitewater MM, Ind

**CONNOR**
- 3-15-1925  Ida Thurston glt 1st M E Ch, New Castle, Ind

**CONRAD**
- 10-14-1897 Lydia (form Lukens) mcd; ret mbrp

**COOK**
- 11-14-1839 Juliann appt on comm
- 12-12-1839 Juliann appt Asst-Clerk
- 4-19-1849  Nancy dis
- 11-11-1852 Cynthia Fenters (form Cook) chm of mcd
- 10-13-1853 Mary Macy (form Cook) dis for mcd
- 10-13-1853 Marcellius & w Eliza W & ch Esther Jane, Harriet E & Anna B rocf Green Plain MM, O
- 12-10-1853 Eliza, -dt Isaac & Anna, m Joseph B Woolman, -s Uriah & Mary of Preble Co, O, at Duck Creek MH
- 11-19-1856 Ann, -dt John & Juliann, m Henry Hoover, -s Levi & Margaret, at Duck Creek MH
- 2-11-1858  Jesse Jr rocf Green Plain MM, O
- 2-11-1858  George & w Elizabeth & ch Maria Jane, Samuel, Sarah Ann, Mary Elizabeth, Georgiana, Jesse C & Ruth Emma rocf Warrington MM, Pa
- 9-15-1858  Jane, -dt Isaac & Anna, m Asa James, -s Jonas & Rachel, at Duck Creek MH
- 8- 8-1859  Susan G & ch Bowen M & Eloise rec in mbrp
- 10-20-1859 Maria Jane, -dt George & Elizabeth, m Benjamin Cockayne, -s Thomas & Martha, at Fall Creek MH
- 11-14-1861 Marcellas S gct Medford MM, N J to m Esther Hollingshead
- 4-10-1862  Marcellias S & ch Esther Jane, Harriet, Anna & Tamzen gct New Garden MM, Pa
- 7-10-1862  Rhoda Bowman (form Cook) chm of mcd
- 2-19-1863  Sarah Ann, -dt George & Eliza, m Silas Williams, -s Caleb & Hannah, in Fall Creek MH
- 5-14-1863  Jesse M & w Susan & fam gct Green Plain MM, O
- 8-13-1863  Samuel chm of mcd
- 4-14-1864  Ashael W & w Hannah C & ch Theresa Caroline, Ann Elizabwth, George W, & Mary Ellen rocf Monallen MM, Pa
- 1-18-1865  Levi, -s John & Juliann, m Mary E Wood, -dt Simeon & Margaret, at Duck Creek MH
- 3-15-1865  John, -s Levi & Ann, m Leah Copeland, -dt John & Susana at Duck Creek MH
- 8- 8-1867  Emily Saint (form Cook) dis for mcd
- 4- 9-1869  John chm of "serving in the army"
- 1-13-1876  Georgiana Lukens (form Cook) chm of mcd
- 7- 9-1874  Mary Cocks (form Cook) chm of mcd
- 6- 8-1876  Milton chm of mcd
- 8-10-1876  Susan Allison (form Cook) chm of mcd
- 9-14-1876  Ruth Emma VanWinkle (form Cook) chm of mcd
- 2-13-1879  Annie Jones (form Cook) chm of mcd
- 4-10-1879  Jesse W dis for mcd
- 2- 8-1883  George chm of mcd
- 8-12-1885  Ida J Hileman (form Cook) chm of mcd
- 4-12-1888  Viola B & dt Mansialine rec in mbrp
- 5-10-1888  Theresa Michell (form Cook) rst
- 11-14-1889 Melissa G Rogers (form Cook) chm of mcd
- 6- 9-1904  Clarence, -s George & Melissa, rec in mbrp
- 4-11-1918  Edith M glt M E Ch, Anderson, Ind

**COOPER**
- 1- 9-1868  Sallie (form Dix) dis for mcd
- 2-12-1880  Elizabeth (form James) chm of mcd
- 10-11-1894 Sallie Swain ret mbrp
- 5-13-1897  Sarah Swain rel fr mbrp
- 7-12-1900  Elwood & w Sarah & ch Ida M, Charles Elwood, Cora Bell, William Penn, Woody Avril, Harriet Martha, Ermil Ione & Harley Reece rocf Marietta MM
- 11-20-1921 Nancy Mae, -dt Pha R & Gertrude, rec in mbrp

FALL CREEK

## COPELAND
| | |
|---|---|
| 11-14-1839 | Leah appt on comm |
| 11-14-1839 | Ephriam appt Overseer for Duck Creek |
| 8-13-1846 | John dis at Honey Creek MM |
| 5- 9-1851 | Abigail, -dt Ephriam & Leah, m Jesse Holloway, -s Jason & Jane, Wabash, in Duck Creek MH |
| 2-15-1853 | Louisa, -dt Ephriam & Leah, m Jonathan J Rodgers, -s Benjamin & Elizabeth |
| 6-10-1858 | John rec in mbrp |
| 9-26-1855 | Rebecca, -dt Ephriam & Leah, m Job Holloway, -s Jason & Jane of Wabash, at Duck Creek MH |
| 11-10-1858 | Phebe dis for na |
| 2-10-1859 | Phebe rec in mbrp |
| 2-10-1859 | Semira Ellen, adopted dt of Ephriam & Leah, rec in mbrp |
| 3-14-1861 | Louisa (form Allen) dis for mcd |
| 11-18-1863 | Seth, -s Ephriam & Leah, m Elizabeth Kennard, -dt John & Martha, at Duck Creek MH |
| 3-15-1865 | Leah, -dt John & Susana, m John Cook, -s Levi & Ann at Duck Creek MH |
| 10-12-1871 | Mary Ann Reed (form Copeland) chm of mcd |
| 10-12-1871 | Lewis rec in mbrp |
| 4-10-1879 | Ellen Mills (form Copeland) chm of mcd |
| 1-14-1892 | Anna M & s Floie rec in mbrp |
| 11-12-1903 | Earl rel fr mbrp |

## COX
| | |
|---|---|
| 3-11-1858 | Huldah (form Wildon) chm of mcd |
| 7- 9-1874 | Mary (form Cook) chm of mcd |

## CUMMINS
| | |
|---|---|
| 6-10-1858 | Phebe (form Sisson) dis for mcd |

## DALE
| | |
|---|---|
| 1-14-1841 | Mary dis for mcd & jas |

## DARLINGTON
| | |
|---|---|
| 8-11-1859 | Benjamin rocf Birmingham MM, Pa |
| 2-19-1862 | Ziba rocf Birmingham MM, Pa |
| 3-21-1867 | Ziba, -s Amos & Jane, m Elmira Rogers, -dt Charles J & Sarah D, at Fall Creek MH |
| 4- 9-1868 | Ziba chm of "serving in the army" |
| 4-11-1872 | Benjamin chm of mcd |
| 4- 9-1891 | Mattie J rec in mbrp |
| 11- 8-1894 | Annis rocf Birmingham MM, Pa |
| 1-17-1900 | Sarah F, -dt Elba & Elmina, m Omer Tunes, -s William H & Sarah B, at residence of bride |
| 5- 9-1901 | Annis P gct Birmingham MM, Pa |

## DARNELL
| | |
|---|---|
| 7- 8-1858 | Mary rocf Westfield MM |
| 11-14-1858 | Charles rocf Chester MM, N J |
| 1-16-1868 | Charles, -s Isaiah & Mary L, m 2nd time, Sarah L Davis, -dt Thomas & Rachel, at Fall Creek MH |
| 4- 9-1868 | Charles chm of "serving in the army" |
| 6-12-1884 | Mary Ida Parsons (form Darnell) chm of mcd |

## DAVIS
| | |
|---|---|
| 8-13-1840 | Sarah Ann rocf Center MM, O |
| 8-13-1840 | Margaret rocf Center MM, O |
| 8-13-1840 | Elizabeth rocf Center MM, O |
| 9-24-1840 | Pennington, -s Caleb & Ann, m Hannah Middleton, -dt Jehu & Mary at Duck Creek MH |
| 11- 9-1843 | Harvey dis for mcd |
| 12-14-1848 | Thomas & ch Sarah S, Noble Washington, Susan P & Martha rec in mbrp |
| 8-10-1848 | Sarah Ann dis for na & jas |
| 11-11-1852 | Martha (form Place) chm of mcd |
| 3-14-1861 | Washington gct East Branch MM, Pa to m Mary C Garretson |
| 12-11-1862 | Mary E rocf East Branch MM, Pa |
| 1-16-1868 | Sarah L, -dt Thomas & Rachel, m Charles Darnell (his 2nd w), at Fall Creek MH |
| 4- 9-1868 | Washington chm of "serving in the army" |
| 4-11-1872 | Martha Dickenson (form Davis) mcd |
| 6-11-1874 | Andrew M gct Marietta MM |
| 8-11-1881 | Mary Eveline (form Woolman) chm of mcd |
| 2-11-1909 | Earl rec in mbrp |
| 7-16-1922 | Ruby rec in mbrp |

## DAWSON
| | |
|---|---|
| 10-10-1844 | James chm of mcd |
| 8-14-1845 | James & ch Lydia, Sarah Ann & Calla Ann rocf Milford MM |
| 4-12-1849 | James & ch Lydia, Sarah Ann, Callie Ann & Rhoda gct Milford MM |

## DELONG or DAYLONG
| | |
|---|---|
| 4-10-1856 | Susannah (form Gray) dis for mcd |

## DICKENSON
| | |
|---|---|
| 4-11-1872 | Martha (form Davis) mcd |

## DICKS - DIX
| | |
|---|---|
| 10-14-1852 | Sally & ch James B & Sarah M rocf Miami MM, O (Hicksites); Ohio cert ret with info they lived too remote for mtg |
| 7-14-1853 | Sally & ch James B & Sarah M rocf Miami MM, O |
| 1- 9-1868 | Sallie Cooper (form Dix) dis for mcd |

## DILKS
| | |
|---|---|
| 3-14-1878 | Alice gct Whitewater MM |

## DOAN
| | |
|---|---|
| 4-11-1901 | Wilson S & w Myra H & ch Florence H & Marcia S rocf Miami MM, O |

## DOBSON
| | |
|---|---|
| 4-25-1866 | Sarah (form Snyder) dis for mcd |

## DORLAN
| | |
|---|---|
| 10- 4-1866 | Andrew rocf Saratoga MM |

## DOWNS
| | |
|---|---|
| 2- 9-1888 | Jane B rocf Green Plain MM, O |
| 5-10-1888 | Isaac rec in mbrp |
| 2- 9-1911 | Charles rec in mbrp |

## DUNWOODY
| | |
|---|---|
| 7- 8-1858 | Eleanor rocf Birmingham MM, Pa |
| 12-13-1860 | Mary B rec in mbrp |
| 8-23-1866 | Mary B, -dt Joseph & Eleanor, m Clark Hains -s John & Jemimah, at Fall Creek MH |

## ELLIOTT
| | |
|---|---|
| 10- 9-1845 | Maria (form Weeks) dis for mcd |
| 6-10-1847 | Jesse H & w Rachel & ch Elizabeth, Mary, Laura & Lydia Ellen rocf Deerfield MM, O |
| 9-11-1862 | Emily (form Hasket) chm of mcd |

## FENTRESS
| | |
|---|---|
| 11-11-1852 | Cynthia (form Cook) chm of mcd |
| 11- 8-1866 | Cynthia Jessup (form Fentress) dis for mcd |
| 1- 8-1903 | William A rec in mbrp |
| 9-10-1903 | Mary C rec in mbrp |
| 11- 8-1906 | Gertrude & s Hermon rec in mbrp |
| 2- 8-1912 | Ella gct Pasadena MM, Calif |

## FERRIS
| | |
|---|---|
| 8-12-1853 | William & dt Anna, Eliza, Gulielma, Mitha, Hannah K & Elizabeth H rocf Milford MM |

## FOULKE
| | |
|---|---|
| 2-13-1840 | Amos & w Mary G rocf Darby MM, Delaware Co, Pa |
| 11-12-1840 | Mary G gct Concord MM, Pa |
| 10-14-1847 | Samuel W & dt Mary Jane rec in mbrp |
| 8-12-1852 | Jesse M & w Mary & ch John B, George, Sarah Ann, William & Amasa rocf Short Creek MM, O |
| 5-12-1859 | Samuel N gct Whitewater MM, Ind |
| 11-11-1875 | William chm of mcd |
| 1-13-1876 | Caroline (form Garretson) chm of mcd |
| 6-12-1884 | Caroline Champlin (form Foulke) chm of mcd |

## FOUST
| | |
|---|---|
| 6- 9-1892 | Rachel Vernon ret mbrp |

FALL CREEK

**FOUST (Cont)**
2-11-1909 Rachel glt Christian Ch, Pendleton, Ind

**FRAME**
2-14-1889 Sallie (form Swain) ret mbrp

**FRAMPTON**
12-13-1860 William & w Sarah & ch William C, Elisha, Arthur E, George M, Charles, Mary, Anna M & Joseph rocf Milford MM, Ind
4- 9-1868 William chm of "serving in the army"
2-18-1869 William, -s William D & Sarah B, m Annie S Cockayne, -dt Thomas & Martha, at Fall Creek MH
8-10-1882 Mary D Trump (form Frampton) chm of mcd
8-20-1887 George chm of mcd
8-20-1887 Charles chm of mcd
1- 8-1903 Arthur J rel fr mbrp

**FUSSELL**
9-13-1840 Mary Jane Hodges (form Fussell) chm of mcd
2- 9-1843 Edwin dis for dis-unity
3-12-1846 Rebecca L & ch Emma, Charles & Lynieus gct Unchland MM, Pa
6-10-1847 Mary Jane rocf Radnor MM, Pa
6-10-1847 Joseph & w Elizabeth & ch John L rocf Radnor MM, Pa
7-15-1847 Milcha Martha, -dt Solomon & Milcha Martha m Simeon Lewis, -s Abner & Susannah, at Fall Creek MH
11-22-1849 Rebecca, -dt Joseph & Elizabeth, m Charles Rodgers, -s Joseph & Elizabeth, at Fall Creek MH
10- 9-1856 Samuel rocf Green St MM, Philadelphia, Pa
2-12-1857 Mary Jane (form Hardy) chm of mcd
2-12-1857 John L dis for mcd
10-11-1860 Joseph L rocf Kennet MM, Pa
10-16-1861 Samuel, -s Joseph & Elizabeth, m Ann Rogers, -dt Charles & Sarah at Fall Creek MH
8-12-1862 Bartholomew & w Rebecca A & s Edward C rocf Unchland MM, Pa
6-13-1867 Anna W dis for dancing
4- 9-1868 Joshua L chm of "serving in the army"
2-10-1870 Susan rocf Unchland MM, Pa
4-13-1871 Benjamin Bunday, rocf Unchland MM, Pa
2-12-1885 John L rst
8-12-1886 Ella & Mary rec in mbrp
2-13-1890 Merriam rocf Benjaminville MM, Ill
5- 2-1901 Mary Elizabeth, -dt John L & Mary m Finley Tomlinson, -s Noah & Abigail, Hamilton Co, Ind, at Fussell Residence
12-12-1907 Lewis gct Middletown MM, Pa
12-28-1907 Lewis, -s Henry M & Mary F of Media Co, Pa, m Margaret Hardy Lewis, -dt Albert G & Emily H, at Pendleton MH
5-13-1909 Margaret Lewis gct Chester MM, Pa

**GARRETSON**
1-11-1844 Angelina Harvey (form Garretson) dis for mcd
1-11-1844 Joel rocf Freeport MM
3-27-1844 Joel, -s Amos & Mary, m Sarah Harvey, -dt Samuel & Rebecca, at Duck Creek MH
10-10-1844 Martha rocf Plainfield MM, O
11-20-1844 Martha, -dt Amos & Mary, Belmont Co, O, m John Kennard, -s Thomas & Elizabeth, at Duck Creek MH
6-11-1857 Amos & w Hannah T rocf Plainfield MM, O
3-14-1861 Washington Davis gct West Branch MM, Pa, to m Mary E Garretson
4- 9-1868 Joel chm of "serving in the army"
5-14-1868 Hannah P gct Benjaminville MM, Ill
4-11-1872 Amos chm of mcd
7- 8-1875 Florence & dt Sarah Jane & Margaret May rec in mbrp
1-13-1876 Caroline Foulk (form Garretson) chm of mcd
5-11-1876 Joel chm of mcd
6- 8-1882 Joel rel fr mbrp
9-17-1887 Joel & Mary Ann rst

11- 8-1894 Mary E & ch Margaret A, Davis R, Joel C, Lester E & Mary W rec in mbrp
12-14-1911 Davis, Lester, Ray & Nellie gct Friendswood MM, Texas
7-13-1916 Gladys & ch George L, Eleanor M & Esther Ruth rec in mbrp

**GAUSE**
2- 8-1855 William M rocf Whitewater MM, Ind

**GEORGE**
4- 8-1852 John & w Leah & ch Sarah L, Isaac C, Abner B, Anne, David, Cyrus, Mary R, Leah & John Lewis rocf Fall Creek MM, O
2-10-1853 Evan & w Hannah & ch Margaret, Rachel, Mary C, Ellis & Enos rocf Fall Creek MM, O
2-10-1853 John B rocf Fall Creek MM, O
5- 8-1856 Isaac C dis for mcd
5- 8-1856 Abner B dis for mcd
3-11-1858 Sarah Baker (form George) dis for mcd
11-14-1861 John chm of mcd
1- 9-1862 Hannah E chm of mcd
4- 8-1862 Sarah & Mary rocf Fall Creek MM, O
6- 8-1876 Hannah dis for jas

**GILLINGHAM**
4-13-1854 Lucus & ch Theodore T, Emma J, Elwood W & Ellen R rocf Cherry St MM, Philadelphia, Pa

**GLENN**
-18-1903 Oliver Edmund, -s James D & Jinnie H of Switzerland Co, Ind, m Alice Thomas Kennard, -dt William R & Mary S, at the Kennard Residence
6-10-1909 Alice K gct Landsdown MM, Pa

**GLOVER**
12-13-1849 Josiah rocf Miami MM, O

**GOOD**
2-12-1846 Charles rocf Buckingham MM, Pa
3-13-1846 Charles, -s John & Sarah of Marion, Ind, m Margaret Schofield, -dt Jonathan & Eleanor of Marion, Ind, at Duck Creek MH

**GOUL**
8-13-1901 Alice E rel fr mbrp

**GRAY**
11-14-1844 Enoch dis for att mcd
11-11-1847 Dennis dis for mcd
12- 9-1847 Sarah Ann McCarty (form Gray) dis for mcd
7-10-1856 Susana Delong (form Gray) dis for mcd
3-12-1868 Conrad & Franklin dis for "having removed beyond the care of the Society"
12-10-1868 Mary E Walker (form Gray) chm of mcd
3-11-1869 Joseph dis for mcd
4- 8-1880 Mary Jane (form Kennard) chm of mcd
10-13-1892 Mary Jane (form Kennard) rel fr mbrp

**HAGGARTY**
4-14-1904 Laura C S rel fr mbrp

**HAINES**
12- 9-1852 Clark C & w Margaret & ch Alice E, Oscar & Eva rocf Springborough MM
6-12-1856 Charles & ch Isaac, Sarah, Susan, Noah & Jemima rocf Springborough MM
2-17-1859 Charles, -s John & Jemima, m Mary Roberts -dt Solomon & Elizabeth, at Fall Creek MH
8-11-1859 Jane Lukens (form Haines) chm of mcd
9-17-1863 Aaron, -s Charles & Ann, m Sary Jane Heacock, -dt Jesse & Mary, at Fall Creek MH
2-13-1868 Mary (form Vernon) chm of mcd
4- 9-1868 Clark chm of "serving in the army"
4- 9-1868 Aaron chm of "serving in the army"
5-14-1868 Alice Watkins (form Haines) chm of mcd
7- 9-1868 Noah chm of mcd
8-23-1866 Clark, -s John & Jemima, m Mary B Dunwoody, -dt Joseph & Eleanor, at Fall Creek MH

FALL CREEK

### HAINES (Cont)
| | |
|---|---|
| 1-17-1872 | Eva, -dt Clark C & Margaret F, m Albert Wood, -s Simeon & Margaret H |
| 2-14-1878 | Mary Belle Kinnard (form Haines) chm of mcd |
| 10-14-1886 | Annie G Woollett (form Haines, ret mbrp |
| 2-21-1899 | (Hains) Edward Vernon, -s Noah C & Mary E, m Elizabeth Clay Kennard, -dt William H & Mary S, at Kennard residence |
| 2-23-1921 | Oscar M, -s Aaron M & Sarah Jane, m Bessie Lee Chamberlain, -dt Elmer C & Eliza at Chamberlain residence |

### HARDEN
| | |
|---|---|
| 8- 9-1860 | Ann (form Hiatt) chm of mcd |
| 4-10-1884 | Mary (form James) chm of mcd |
| 9-12-1889 | Mary gct Maple Grove MM, Ind |

### HARDY
| | |
|---|---|
| 12-28-1898 | Elizabeth F, -dt Solomon F & Rebecca m George H Swain, -s Charles E & Margaret S, at Hardy residence, Markleville, Ind |
| 2-12-1857 | Mary Jane Fussell (form Hardy) chm of mcd |
| 6-11-1857 | William F dis for mcd |
| 11- 8-1866 | Esther (form Satterthwait) chm of mcd |
| 11-19-1868 | Solomon, -s Neal & Elizabeth, m Rebecca P James, -dt Joshia P & Sarah A at Fall Creek MH |
| 8-12-1880 | Esther rel fr mbrp |
| 2-27-1886 | Frank m Myrtle Sarah Long |
| 3-11-1886 | F M & w Maggie (Margaret) rec in mbrp |
| 2- 9-1905 | Florence & s Merrill rec in mbrp |
| 8-14-1913 | Nellie rec in mbrp |
| 10- 9-1913 | Mrs Georgia & her ch Robert & Hugh Morris rolf Spiceland M E Ch |

### HARLAN
| | |
|---|---|
| 6-14-1860 | Abner V & w Rachel C rocf Fallowfield MM, Pa |
| 8- 9-1860 | Susan rocf Fallowfield MM, Pa |
| 8- 9-1860 | Mary E rocf Fallowfield MM, Pa |
| 6-13-1867 | Osborn & w Mary P rocf Fallowfield MM, Pa |
| 6-11-1868 | Samuel T & w Sarah M & ch George M, Mary Rebecca & Elizabeth rocf Fallowfield MM, Pa |
| 4-11-1871 | Osborn & Mary gct Fallowfield MM, Pa |
| 11- 8-1871 | Samuel T & w Sarah M & ch George M, Mary Rebecca, Hannah Elizabeth & Curtis W gct Fallowfield MM, Pa |
| 8-12-1886 | Samuel T, w Sarah M & ch Mary M, Hannah Elizabeth & Curtis William rocf Fallowfield MM, Pa |
| 12- 9-1886 | Lizzie James (form Harlan) chm of mcd |

### HARPER
| | |
|---|---|
| 11-14-1844 | Nathan dis for na & att mcd |

### HARVEY
| | |
|---|---|
| 1- 9-1840 | Mary & Sarah rocf Miami MM, O (Another record says Concord MM, O) |
| 1-15-1840 | Mary, -dt Samuel & Rebecca m Jesse James, -s Evan & Rebecca at Duck Creek MH |
| 1-11-1844 | Angelina (form Garretson) dis for mcd |
| 3-27-1844 | Sarah, -dt Samuel & Rebecca, m Joel Garretson, -s Amos & Mary, at Duck Creek MH |
| 8-10-1848 | Isaac dis for mcd |

### HASKET
| | |
|---|---|
| 7- 9-1857 | William L dis for mcd |
| 9-11-1862 | Emily (form Elliott) (form Cook) chm of mcd |
| 3-11-1869 | Thomas & w Sarah gct Wapsinodoc MM, Ia |

### HAYCOCK - HEACOCK
| | |
|---|---|
| 3-14-1844 | Anna (form Weeks) chm of mcd |
| 1-11-1849 | Levi P Wood gct Milford MM, Ind to m Hannah F Haycock |
| 11-16-1850 | Mary rocf Radnor MM, Pa |
| 10-14-1852 | Jesse & w Mary Elizabeth & ch Sarah Jane & Jesse R rocf Milford MM |
| 3- 9-1854 | Nathan & w Eliza & ch Elizabeth, Jonah & Sarah Jane rocf Milford MM, Ind |
| 7-12-1855 | Mary gct Blue River MM, Ind |
| 8-12-1858 | Hannah's ch, Phebe W & Deborah F, gct Maple Grove MM, Ind |
| 11-11-1858 | Margaret gct Maple Grove MM |
| 9-17-1863 | Sary Jane, -dt Jesse & Mary m Aaron Hains, -s Charles & Ann at Fall Creek MH |
| 8-11-1881 | Emma Boston (form Haycock) mcd |
| 3- 9-1898 | Edna Ann rocf Milford MM |

### HEIFLER
| | |
|---|---|
| 7-14-1864 | Maria (form Rogers) rpt mcd by Unchland MM, Pa, rel fr mbrp |

### HENRY
| | |
|---|---|
| 6-11-1853 | Hannah Watson (form Henry) dis for mcd & jas |

### HESTON
| | |
|---|---|
| 10-14-1852 | Mary S rocf Whitewater MM, Ind |
| 10-14-1852 | Samuel & w Susan & ch Letitia Jane & William Henry rocf Whitewater MM, Ind |

### HIATT
| | |
|---|---|
| 1- 9-1840 | Betty appt to comm |
| 8- 9-1860 | Ann Harden (form Hiatt) chm of mcd |
| 11-14-1839 | James appt Overseer for Duck Creek |
| 3-14-1844 | Nathan Spencer gct Milford MM to m Louisa Hiatt |
| 4-11-1844 | John dis for na & jas |
| 4-29-1854 | Job chm of mcd |
| 12-18-1855 | Seth, -s James & Betty, m Zalinda James, -dt Jonas & Rachel, at Duck Creek MH |
| 7-14-1859 | Esther (form James) chm of mcd |
| 4-12-1860 | Levi dis for att mcd & na |
| 7-12-1891 | Daniel rec in mbrp |

### HIBBARD
| | |
|---|---|
| 11-18-1866 | Jane rocf Whitewater MM, Ind |
| 11- 8-1868 | Alice N rocf Whitewater MM, Ind |
| 5-11-1882 | Jane gct Whitewater MM, Ind |

### HILEMAN
| | |
|---|---|
| 11- 9-1865 | Emeline (form Kirk) dis |
| 8-12-1885 | Ida J (form Cook) chm of mcd |

### HILL
| | |
|---|---|
| 6-14-1866 | George & w Tacy B & ch Alice J, Theodore H, Benjamin Hubbard & Ann Elizabeth rocf Whitewater MM, Ind |
| 3- 8-1877 | George H appt trustee of Indianapolis prop in place of Abner Pope who has dec |
| 5-11-1882 | George & w Tacy gct Whitewater MM, Ind |
| 5-11-1882 | Ann gct Whitewater MM, Ind |
| 8- 8-1889 | Theodore rel fr mbrp |

### HINSHAW
| | |
|---|---|
| 6-13-1901 | Warren rec in mbrp |

### HODGES
| | |
|---|---|
| 9-13-1849 | Mary Jane (form Fussell) chm of mcd |
| 2- 8-1894 | Mary J & dt Mary J enrolled on record |
| 4-18-1905 | Edward W rec in mbrp |

### HODSON
| | |
|---|---|
| 7- 8-1897 | Ella Stratton ret mbrp |
| 4-17-1927 | Ella rel fr mbrp |

### HOLLINGSHEAD
| | |
|---|---|
| 11-14-1861 | Marcellus S Cook gct Medford MM, N J to m Esther Hollingshead |

### HOLLOWAY
| | |
|---|---|
| 8- 1-1845 | Edna, -dt Jason & Jane, Wabash, Ind, m Nixon Hollowell, -s Thomas & Achsah, Huntington, Ind, at Fall Creek MH |
| 5- 9-1851 | Jesse, -s Jason & Jane, Wabash, Ind, m Abigail Copeland, -dt Ephriam & Leah |
| 9-26-1855 | Job, -s Jason & Jane, Wabash, Ind, m Rebecca Copeland, -dt Ephriam & Leah at Duck Creek MH |

FALL CREEK

## HOLLOWAY (Cont)
12-11-1856 Rebecca gct Maple Grove MM
6-11-1903 Louisa Rogers gct Maple Grove MM

## HOLLOWELL
8- 1-1845 Nixon, -s Thomas & Achsah, Huntington, Ind, m Edna Holloway, -dt Jason & Jane, Wabash, Ind, at Fall Creek MH
2- -1915 Mary E rec in mbrp
12- 9-1915 Essie V rec in mbrp

## HOOVER
3-11-1841 Margaret rec in mbrp
2-11-1847 Margaret & ch Henry, Sarah, John & Elizabeth rec in mbrp
11-19-1856 Henry, -s Levi & Margaret, m Ann Cook, -dt John & Juliann, at Duck Creek MH
4- 9-1868 Mary T (form Taylor) chm of mcd
3- 8-1883 Anna Hill rocf Whitewater MM, Ind
5-10-1888 Margaret, an elder, has dec
5-14-1896 Phebe A & ch George & Mildred rec in mbrp
4-10-1851 Sarah Phelps (form Hoover) chm of mcd
12-17-1922 William F & Phebe gct Orange Grove MM, Pasadena, Calif

## HOWARD
4- 9-1868 Elizabeth (form Wilson) chm of mcd

## HULSE
2-20-1921 Ruth Michael glt M E Ch, Anderson, Ind

## HUNTER
8-14-1851 Ellen Williams (form Hunter) dis for mcd

## IFORD - IFORT
6-13-1889 Mary A rocf Green Plain MM, O
10-13-1910 Anna rel fr mbrp

## JACOBS
2- 9-1854 Ann rocf Richland MM
4- 9-1874 Sarah (form Vernon) mcd
7-13-1916 Cassius rec in mbrp

## JAMES
1-15-1840 Jesse, -s Evan & Rebecca, Henry Co, Ind, m Mary Harvey, -dt Samuel & Rebecca, at Duck Creek MH
10- 8-1840 Rebecca appt to comm
10-15-1840 Joshua P, -s Evan & Rebecca, m Sarah Rodgers, -dt Joseph & Elizabeth, at Fall Creek MH
5-14-1846 Mary Jones (form James) dis for mcd
8-24-1849 Joel E, -s Evan & Rebecca, m Elizabeth Ann Rodgers, -dt Joseph & Elizabeth, at Fall Creek MH
11-13-1851 Jehu dis for mcd
6-16-1853 Joshua P, -s Evan & Rebecca, m 2nd time, Hannah P Lewis, -dt Abner & Susannah of Delaware Co, Ind, at Fall Creek MH
12-18-1855 Zalinda, -dt Jonas & Rachel, m Seth Hiatt, -s James & Betty, at Duck Creek MH
9-15-1858 Asa, -s Jonas & Rachel, m Jane Cook, -dt Isaac & Anna, at Duck Creek MH
7-14-1859 Esther Hiatt (form James) chm of mcd
1- 9-1862 Elizabeth Wilson (form James) chm of mcd
4- 9-1868 Charles R chm of "serving in the army"
11-19-1868 Rebecca P, -dt Joshua P & Sarah A, m Solomon Hardy, -s Neal & Elizabeth, at Fall Creek MH
4-13-1871 Rebecca Camplin, (form James) mcd
2-12-1880 Elizabeth Cooper (form James) chm of mcd
4-10-1884 Mary Harden (form James) chm of mcd
4-12-1886 Eva E & s Asa Gilbert rec in mbrp
12- 9-1886 Lizzie (form Harlan) chm of mcd
11-10-1898 Anna rec in mbrp
5- 8-1902 Edward P rec in mbrp
4-18-1905 Kenvin rec in mbrp
4-18-1905 Vora, Charles K & Ada rec in mbrp
5-11-1905 John H rec in mbrp
12-12-1907 Robert C rocf Maple Grove MM, Huntington Co, Ind

## JANNEY
10-12-1882 Jones, w Ruth & ch Nancy rocf Miami MM, O

## JENKINS
11-13-1851 Rachel rocf Milford MM, Ind
9- 8-1853 Kennard chm of mcd

## JESSUP
11- 8-1866 Cynthia (form Fentress) dis for mcd
11- 8-1866 Cynthia (form Winters) dis for mcd

## JOHNSON
4-12-1849 Joshua & w Lydia rocf Hopewell MM, Va
10-14-1850 Miller rocf Fall Creek MM, O
10-14-1852 Polly rocf Miami MM, O
10-14-1852 Benjamin B rocf Miami MM, O
3-10-1853 Benjamin & w Susanna & ch Anna, Joseph, Deborah & Enos rocf Miami MM, O
8-13-1854 Mariam (form Williams) chm of mcd
9-13-1855 Miller chm of mcd
8-14-1856 Sarah (form Bond) chm of mcd
2-12-1857 Sarah S rocf Hopewell MM, Va
2-12-1857 James A & w Rebecca & ch Hannah E, Sarah E & Clark rocf Center MM, O
6-13-1861 Miriam Tillson (form Johnson) mcd
1- 9-1868 Benjamin & Susannah dis for disunity
9-10-1868 J Anthony chm of "hiring a substitute for the army"
5-11-1871 Sarah Schooley (form Johnson) mcd
1- 8-1874 Clark gct Benjaminville MM, Ill
1- 8-1874 James Anthony & w Rebecca gct Benjaminville MM, Ill
8-12-1886 Joseph rec in mbrp

## JOHNSTON
7-10-1893 Joseph H, -s Meredith H & Winifred J, m Fannie L Swain, -dt Woolston & Mary A, at Swain Residence

## JONES
5-14-1848 Mary (form James) dis for mcd
12-12-1850 Micajah & w Sarah rocf Whitewater MM, Ind
12-12-1850 Elihu & w Ann & dt Martha rocf Whitewater MM, Ind
NOTE: Whitewater records list ch as Jesse, Martha, Amos & Joseph in this cert
7-14-1864 Elihu mcd
2-13-1879 Annie (form Cook) chm of mcd
6-12-1884 Sarah E rel fr mbrp
6-10-1886 Ellen (form Lukens) rel fr mbrp
3-14-1893 Sarah Ellen Haines ret mbrp
4-12-1894 Annie rel fr mbrp
10-14-1897 Margaret Rogers ret mbrp
10-14-1897 George, Joseph & Claud Rogers, ch of Margaret Rogers Jones, rec in mbrp
5-13-1909 Edmond rec in mbrp

## JORDAN
11- 9-1843 Mary Ann dis for mcd thru Baltimore MM, Md

## KENDALL
10-14-1869 Mary & ch Jesse G, Charles Henry, John Albert, Lilly Mary & Sarah Mariah rocf Maple Grove MM
3-10-1870 John rec in mbrp
11-14-1872 Jesse dis for jas
6- 9-1875 Mary dis
8- 8-1882 Jesse, Charles & Albert rel fr mbrp
10-10-1889 Sada rel fr mbrp

## KENNARD
11-14-1839 Elizabeth appt on comm
11-20-1844 John, -s Thomas & Elizabeth, m Martha Garritson, -dt Amos & Mary, Belmont Co, O, at Duck Creek MH
11-11-1847 Jacob mcd
12- 9-1847 Levi dis for mcd
7-12-1849 Joseph gct Whitewater MM, Ind
9- 9-1852 Thomas Jr dis for mcd

FALL CREEK

KENNARD (Cont)
11-18-1863  Elizabeth, -dt John & Martha, m Seth Copeland, -s Ephriam & Leah, at Duck Creek MH
4- 9-1868  John chm of "serving in the army"
1-13-1873  Mary (form Thomas) chm of mcd
4- 9-1874  Mary Jane rec in mbrp
6- 8-1876  Rachel Maudlin (form Kennard) chm of mcd
2-14-1878  Mary Belle (form Haines) chm of mcd
4- 8-1880  Mary Jane Gray (form Kennard) chm of mcd
4-14-1887  Mary Etta (form Swain) ret mbrp
4-12-1888  Ruth rec in mbrp
4-12-1888  Luella & ch Mary E & Elva M rec in mbrp
4-11-1889  William R rec in mbrp
8-12-1891  Elizabeth rec in mbrp
7-12-1894  Mary Belle rel fr mbrp
2-21-1899  Elizabeth Clay, -dt William H & Mary S, m Edward Vernon Hains, -s Noah C & Mary E, at Kennard residence
11-18-1903  Alice Thomas, -dt William R & Mary S, m Oliver Edmund Gleen, -s James D & Jennie H of Switzerland Co, Ind, at Kennard residence
5-11-1905  Clarence H rec in mbrp
4-19-1906  Lewis D & w Della rec in mbrp
2- 9-1911  Helen Josephine & Hugh Mannum rec in mbrp
12-18-1913  Edith Mary, -dt William R & Mary S, m Forrest Raymond Blakly, -s William R & Rosa B, at Kennard residence
8-10-1916  Rebecca D rocf Spiceland MM, Ind

KENNEMAN
6-13-1861  Susanna (form Kenny) chm of mcd
9- 8-1870  (Kinneman) Susan dis

KENNY
6-13-1861  Susanna Kenneman (form Kenny) chm of mcd

KENWORTHY
9-10-1846  Rebecca (form Spencer) dis for mcd
6-12-1845  Mary Ann (form Spencer) dis for mcd
1- 9-1862  Lydia (form Williams) dis for mcd & jas

KERN
8-15-1926  Charles rec in mbrp

KINDLEY
12-22-1840  Daniel, -s Edward & Margaret, Preble Co, O, m Susan Weeks, -dt Joseph & Susannah, at Fall Creek MH
2-11-1841  Susan E gct Westfield MM, O
5-11-1846  Mary & ch Asa, Sarah, Levi, Tamer & Margaret rocf Milford MM, Ind
3-13-1852  Fredrick refused rst by Milford MM, Ind

KINNEY
4-13-1848  Ann dis for "distraction"

KIRK
10-10-1861  William A & w Jane & ch Eunice Elizabeth, Jane Augusta, Lester Allen & Esther Ilena rocf Nottingham MM, Pa
10- 9-1862  Mary Emmaline & Rachel Lewis rocf Nottingham MM, Pa
11- 9-1865  Emmaline Hileman (form Kirk) dis
4-11-1867  Rachel Swain (form Kirk) dis for mcd
11- 8-1877  Jane A chm of mcd

LANTZ
4- 6-1909  Elizabeth Morris rocf Milford MM, Ind
6- 8-1916  Fred rolf M E Ch, Milton, Ind
12-16-1923  Elizabeth & dt Deborah gct Purchase MM, N Y

LEE
7- 8-1898  Ethel Copeland ret mbrp
4- 8-1915  Ethel M C gct Park Ave Congregational Ch, Meadville, Pa

LEVERTON
3- 9-1865  Hannah rocf Milford MM, Ind

LEWIS
11-14-1839  Thomas appt Clerk
4- 9-1840  Rebecca I appt to comm
9-14-1843  William dis for apd & dancing
9-11-1845  Phebe (form Smith) dis for mcd
2-11-1847  Simeon rocf Goshen MM, Pa
7-15-1847  Simeon, -s Abner & Susannah, m Milcha Martha Fussell, -dt Solomon & Milcha Martha, at Fall Creek MH
10-14-1852  Susannah M rocf Radnor MM, Pa
10-14-1852  Hannah P rocf Radnor MM, Pa
2-10-1853  Evan rocf Radnor MM, Pa
6-16-1853  Hannah P, -dt Abner & Susannah, Delaware Co, Ind, m (his 2nd w) Joshua P James, -s Evan & Rebecca, at Fall Creek MH
1-12-1854  Joseph B dis for upl & na
2- 9-1854  Jonathan W dis for mcd
4-13-1854  John rocf Radnor MM, Pa
3-15-1855  Evan, -s Abner & Susan, m Sarah Cockayne, -dt Thomas & Martha, at Fall Creek MH
12-13-1860  Abner rocf Radnor MM, Pa
8-10-1882  Walter H mcd
8-20-1887  Horace chm of mcd
2- 9-1888  Emily H rec in mbrp
11-13-1890  Margaret H & Emily Grace, ch of Emily H, rec in mbrp
4- 9-1891  Josephine & Evangeline rec in mbrp
5-14-1896  Sarah Rogers ret mbrp
4-18-1905  Joseph B, Jan J, Lloyd D & Louisa E rec in mbrp
9-13-1906  Elinor rec in mbrp
12-28-1907  Margaret Hardy, -dt Albert & Emily H, m Lewis Fussell, -s Henry M & Mary F of Media Co, Pa, at Pendleton MH

LINDSEY
7-14-1853  Mahala rocf Miami MM, O

LITTLER
10-  -1898  Eunice Williams ret mbrp
6- 9-1904  Emma W rec in mbrp

LIVEZEY
12-10-1840  Anthony mcd at Springborough MM, this mtg asked to tr w/h
7- 8-1841  Isaac & w Margaret & ch Thomas, Elizabeth, Rebecca Ann, Deborah & Martha rocf Springborough MM
7- 8-1841  Nathan & w Rebecca rocf Springborough MM

LONG
2-27-1886  Myrtle Sarah m Frank S Hardy

LUKENS
10-19-1843  Allen, -s Perry & Mary, m Mary Ann Rodgers, -dt Joseph & Elizabeth, at Fall Creek MH
9-13-1849  Benjamin mcd at Horsham MM, Pa; chm of mcd
8-13-1854  Richard & w Caroline & ch Charles Abel, Isaac Thomas, Horace & Hannah Thomas rocf Springborough MM
4- 9-1857  Benjamin dis for mcd
8-11-1859  Susan Jane (form Haines) chm of mcd
8-11-1859  Benjamin Jr dis for mcd
5-14-1863  Robert chm of mcd
5-14-1863  Elizabeth (form Oldham) chm of mcd
12-15-1864  Elizabeth R, -dt Allen & Mary Ann, m Joseph Swain, -s Charles & Sarah Ann, at Fall Creek MH
5-17-1866  Isaac, -s Richard & Caroline, m Edith Satterthwait, -dt Joseph M & Eliza, at Fall Creek MH
4- 9-1868  Richard M chm of "serving in the army"
4- 9-1868  Allen chm of "serving in the army"
11-13-1868  Allen chm of mcd
2-10-1870  Ann C rocf Unchland MM, Pa
4-11-1872  Charles A chm of mcd
7-11-1872  Margaret Pardee (form Lukens) chm of mcd
1-13-1873  Georgiana (form Cook) chm of mcd
12-11-1873  Charles A gct Benjaminville MM, Ill

FALL CREEK

## LUKENS (Cont)
- 12-11-1873    Horace gct Benjaminville MM, Ill
- 12-11-1873    Richard & w Caroline & dt Mary M gct Benjaminville MM, Ill
- 12-11-1873    Isaac T & w Edith & ch Eliza S & Hannah T gct Benjaminville MM, Ill
- 2-12-1874    William chm of mcd
- 10-8-1874    Martha Riley (form Lukens) chm of mcd
- 10-10-1876    Solomon F mcd; rel fr mbrp
- 6-10-1886    Ellen Jones (form Lukens) rel fr mbrp
- 4-14-1887    Hannah Collins (form Lukens) ret mbrp
- 6-10-1887    Mary & ch William A & Eva rec in mbrp
- 7-9-1891    Elizabeth A gct Whitewater MM, Ind
- 4-12-1906    Cora rec in mbrp
- 2-11-1909    Cora rel fr mbrp
- 11-12-1914    Kenneth, Raymond & Ralph, ch of Isaac, rec in mbrp
- 1-21-1923    Beta rec in mbrp
- 3-18-1923    Frank & Jennie rec in mbrp

## McCARTY
- 12-9-1847    Sarah Ann (form Gray) dis for mcd
- 4-3-1908    Ada rec in mbrp

## McCULLOCK
- 6-7-1904    Alva Wright, -s William & Sarah L, Warren Co, Ind, m Elizabeth Rogers, -dt John M & Elizabeth H, at McCullock residence
- 10-9-1913    Sarah Rogers rel fr mbrp

## McCURDY
- 6-14-1894    Alice Lewis & dt Emily Dean & Margaret rec in mbrp

## McGRIFF
- 8-12-1885    Ella Clark mcd; rel fr mbrp
- 2-13-1913    (McGriffe) Ella Brown rec in mbrp

## McKINLEY
- 12-14-1905    Minnie rec in mbrp

## McKINNEY
- 8-13-1846    William & w Mary & s Cyrus rocf Milford MM, Ind

## McLELLAND
- 7-8-1886    Alice (form Wood) ret mbrp; she "has not violated our testamonies"

## McNEW
- 12-14-1871    Elizabeth (form Wilson) mcd; rel fr mbrp

## MACY
- 2-10-1853    Mary (form Cook) dis for mcd

## MARANVILLE
- 4-12-1906    Robert E & s Robert Jr & Charles S rec in mbrp
- 6-10-1915    Elnora B rel fr mbrp

## MASON
- 4-9-1903    George & w Margaret & ch John J, Emily O, Albert E & Edith M rec in mbrp
- 6-13-1912    George & fam gct Camden MM, N J

## MATHEWS
- 2-8-1855    Samuel & w Esther & dt Lizzie Ann rocf Whitewater MM, Ind
- 5-13-1875    (Matthews) Edgar R, Thomas B & Charles W gct Benjaminville MM, Ill

## MAUDLIN
- 6-8-1876    Rachel (form Kennard) chm of mcd

## MICHEL
- 5-10-1888    Theresa (form Cook) ret mbrp

## MIDDLETON
- 12-12-1839    Richard chm of mcd
- 9-24-1840    Hannah, -dt Jehu & Mary, m Pennington Davis, -s Caleb & Ann, at Duck Creek MH
- 8-8-1844    Jehu dis for refusing to settle difficulty with a friend
- 7-10-1845    Rachel Simmons (form Middleton) chm of mcd
- 11-11-1852    Richard dis
- 1-13-1853    Jehu rst

## MILLER
- 9-1-1897    Frank B, -s Charles D & Isabell, Clark Co, Ohio, m Emma F Thomas, -dt John & Caroline, at home of bride

## MILLS
- 11-14-1839    Lydia appt on comm
- 5-14-1846    Penninah, -dt Hugh & Lydia, m Abner Pope, -s Abner & Maria, Marion, Ind, at Duck Creek MH
- 2-8-1849    Thomas chm of mcd
- 10-13-1854    Eber dis for mcd
- 6-11-1868    Joel chm of mcd
- 4-10-1879    Ellen (form Copeland) chm of mcd

## MOORE
- 9-11-1851    Mary C rpt mcd
- 9-12-1851    Mary (form Stanton) dis for mcd
- 1-12-1860    James gct Westfield MM, O to m Phebe Woolman
- 11-14-1867    James & ch Edward A, Mary E & Albert U gct Westfield MM, O
- 9-17-1868    Jehiel F, -s Jonathan & Eliza m Sarah Tyler, -dt John & Phebe, Fayette Co, Ind, at Fall Creek MH
- 1-14-1869    Hiram T gct Whitewater MM, Ind

## MORRIS
- 9-14-1853    Ruth, -dt Hugh & Lydia, m Jason Morris, -s Samuel & Sarah, at Duck Creek MH
- 9-14-1853    Jason, -s Samuel & Sarah, m Ruth Mills, -dt Hugh & Lydia, at Duck Creek MH
- 4-13-1854    Ruth J gct Milford MM, Ind
- 12-25-1856    William F, -s George & Rhoda, m Mary Ellen Swain, -dt Charles & Sarah Ann, at Fall Creek MH
- 11-12-1857    Mary Ellen gct Milford MM, Ind
- 12-21-1865    Aaron, -s George & Rhoda A, m Martha M Thomas, -dt Lewis W & Priscilla, at Fall Creek MH
- 3-8-1866    Martha M gct Milford MM, Ind
- 11-8-1866    William F & w Mary Ellen & ch Emma Caroline & George D rocf Milford MM, Ind
- 2-11-1904    William F rocf Milford MM, Ind
- 4-8-1909    Robert A rocf Milford MM, Ind
- 4-8-1909    Martha M rocf Milford MM, Ind

## MORRISON
- 12-8-1864    Ellen rocf Cincinnati MM, O

## MUELLER
- 3-21-1926    Elva Kennard gct Whitewater MM, Ind

## MULLIN
- 10-12-1871    Thomas Elwood rocf Horsham MM, Pa
- 12-11-1873    Edith gct Benjaminville MM, Ill
- 12-11-1873    Thomas Elwood gct Benjaminville MM, Ill

## MULLIS
- 2-8-1872    Edith rocf Chester MM, Pa

## NICHOLSON
- 12-12-1839    Elizabeth appt Overseer
- 8-8-1867    Edwin rocf Baltimore MM, Md

## OLDHAM
- 3-11-1858    Caleb Williams gct Green Plain MM, O
- 11-10-1859    Margaret W rocf Green Plain MM, O
- 11-10-1859    Massey rocf Green Plain MM, O
- 12-15-1859    Margaret, -dt John & Ann, m Nathan Cockayne, -s Thomas & Martha

FALL CREEK

OLDHAM (Cont)
5-14-1863  Massey W Williams (form Oldham) chm of mcd
5-14-1863  Elizabeth Lukens (form Oldham) chm of mcd
7- 9-1868  Abner chm of mcd
8-12-1875  James G chm of mcd
8-12-1875  Joseph chm of mcd
12- 9-1875  Joseph & James gct Benjaminville MM, Ill

OSBORN
5-12-1859  Ascenith (form Wood) chm of mcd
5-11-1893  Ann rel fr mbrp

PALMER
8-11-1923  Charles Merwin, -s Charles & Arletta of Ridley Park, Pa, m Esther Allen, -dt Elwood & Stella A, at Pendleton MH

PARDUE
7-11-1872  Margaret (form Lukens) chm of mcd

PARKER
5-13-1909  Allen rec in mbrp

PARSONS
6-12-1884  Mary Ida (form Darnell) chm of mcd

PHELPS
4-10-1851  Sarah (form Hoover) chm of mcd
10-12-1871  Sarah (form Hoover) dis for jas & na

PICKERING
2-11-1841  Phebe Ann & Mary rocf Honey Creek MM
9- 9-1841  Samuel dis for na & dp
10-13-1842  Mary gct Honey Creek MM
10-14-1847  Isaac & w Elizabeth & ch Lamira, Rachel, Ellen, John E & Charles Lewis rocf Plainfield MM, O
8-14-1845  Leah Stanley (form Pickering) mcd
11-11-1852  Isaac & w Elizabeth & ch Laura, Rachel Eleanor, John Ellis H & Charles Lewis gct Plainfield MM, O

PIKE
8-14-1851  Lucretia (form Ridgway) chm of mcd

PLACE
7- 9-1840  Maurice & w Mary & ch Martha, Elizabeth B & Sabina rocf Whitewater MM, Ind
10- 3-1853  Martha Davis (form Place) chm of mcd (Women's Minutes) - dis - (Men's Minutes)

POPE
3- 9-1843  Abner, w Maria & ch Abner Jr & Joseph rocf Baltimore MM, Md
4-14-1843  Edward, -s Abner & Maria, Marion, Ind, m Susan E Schofield, -dt Jonathan & Eleanor, Marion, Ind, at Fall Creek MH
5-14-1846  Abner, -s Abner & Maria, Marion, Ind, m Peninnah Mills, -dt Hugh & Lydia, at Duck Creek MH
11-11-1847  Edward S chm of mcd
2-10-1848  Mary rec in mbrp
10-11-1855  Joseph P dis for mcd
6-14-1866  Abner & w Peninah & ch Charles, Anna, Mary & Julia gct Wapsinodoc, MM, Ia
6- 8-1876  Abner J & w Peninah & ch Charles, Anna, Mary & Julia presented cert fr Wapsinodoc MM, Ia; which was not accepted due to his connection with so-called Spiritualists
9- 8-1881  Edward dis

POWER
8-19-1928  Richard & Maria Catharine, ch of Richard Lyle & Florence Doan rec in mbrp

PRIDDY
1-13-1873  Elmira (form Allen) chm of mcd
12-17-1887  Elmira A rel fr mbrp

RADNOR
12- 9-1852  Samuel rocf Radnor MM, Pa

RAGSDALE
12-12-1901  Anna Morris of Knoxville, Tenn, rel fr mbrp

RATLIFF
12- 8-1842  Simeon P Wood gct Whitewater MM to m Margaret Ratliff

RATCLIFF
1-14-1869  Elizabeth dis for jas

REGOR
6-13-1889  Florence Woolman rel fr mbrp

REED
10-12-1871  Mary Ann (form Copeland) chm of mcd

REEDE
6- 9-1910  Mary Adda Garretson glt M E Ch, Chicago

RIDGWAY
8-14-1851  Lucretia Pike (form Ridgway) chm of mcd

RILEY
10- 8-1874  Martha (form Lukens) chm of mcd
4- 9-1896  Martha gct Whitewater MM, Ind

RISK
8-12-1880  Emma (form Wood) mcd; rel fr mbrp

ROBERTS
3-11-1841  Jesse & w Hannah & ch Nathan L, Maryann W & William W rocf Springborough MM
5-10-1849  Joshua & w Hannah & ch William W, Hester Ann & Joseph S rocf Milford MM
2-10-1853  Solomon & w Elizabeth & ch Elihu, Hannah & Artemus rocf Whitewater MM
2-10-1853  Anna rocf Whitewater MM, Ind
11-10-1853  Mary rocf Whitewater MM, Ind
11-10-1853  Edward rocf Whitewater MM, Ind
11-10-1853  Eunice rocf Whitewater MM, Ind
9-17-1856  Edward, -s Solomon & Elizabeth, m Mary Ann Allen, -dt Daniel & Eliza, at Duck Creek MH
2-17-1859  Mary, -dt Solomon & Elizabeth, m Charles Hanes, -s John & Jemima, at Fall Creek MH
10-10-1867  Elizabeth gct Whitewater MM, Ind
3-12-1868  Eunice gct Whitewater MM, Ind
4- 9-1868  William W chm of "serving in the army"
8-12-1869  Elizabeth rocf Whitewater MM, Ind
10-14-1869  Artemus gct Whitewater MM, Ind
5-11-1871  James chm of mcd
7-16-1872  Jesse W, -s Samuel & Priscilla, m Anna Charles (form Williams), -dt William & Hannah, at residence of Anna Charles in Huntsville
5-13-1875  Elizabeth gct Maple Grove MM
9-12-1878  James chm of mcd
2-12-1885  Elizabeth, a min, memorial prepared & forwarded to QM
2-13-1890  James S dis

ROGERS
1- 9-1840  Elizabeth appt to comm
2-13-1840  Hannah appt to comm
10-15-1840  (Rodgers) Sarah, -dt Joseph & Elizabeth, m Joshua James, -s Evan & Rebecca, at Fall Creek MH
10-15-1840  (Rodgers) Hannah, -dt Joseph & Elizabeth, m Edward Vernon, -s Abraham & Mary, at Fall Creek MH
7-14-1842  Elizabeth & dt Margaret Ann rec in mbrp
10-19-1843  (Rodgers) Mary Ann, -dt Joseph & Elizabeth, m Allen Lukens, -s Perry & Mary, at Fall Creek MH
8-24-1849  (Rodgers) Elizabeth Ann, -dt Joseph & Elizabeth, m Joel E James, -s Evan & Rebecca, at Fall Creek MH
9-13-1849  Margaret Boston (form Rogers) chm of mcd
11-22-1849  (Rodgers) Charles, -s Joseph & Elizabeth, m Rebecca Fussell, -dt Joseph & Elizabeth, at Fall Creek MH

FALL CREEK

ROGERS (Cont)
4-10-1851  Susanna W, Joseph M, Ann E & Elmira F, ch of Charles J & Rebecca B, rec in mbrp
2-15-1853  (Rodgers) Jonathan J, -s Benjamin & Elizabeth m Louisa Copeland, -dt Ephriam & Leah
2- 9-1854  Joseph R dis for mcd
4- 9-1857  Sarah Snyder (form Rogers) chm of mcd
4- 9-1857  Rebecca rocf Unchland MM, Pa
4- 9-1857  Elijah P chm of mcd
10- 8-1857  Elijah P rocf Unchland MM, Pa
10-16-1861  Ann, -dt Charles & Sarah, m Samuel Fussell, -s Joseph & Elizabeth, at Fall Creek MH
4- 9-1863  Elijah P dis for att mcd
7-14-1864  Maria Heifler (form Rogers) rpt mcd by Unchland MM, Pa, "does not wish to ret mbrp"
8-17-1865  Benjamin, -s Jonathan & Hannah, m Ann Thomas -dt Lewis & Priscilla, at Fall Creek MH
3-21-1867  Elmira, -dt Charles J & Sarah D, m Ziba Darlington, -s Amos & Jane, at Fall Creek MH
1- 9-1868  Rebecca F (w of Joseph M) & s Earnest rec in mbrp
4- 9-1868  Joseph M chm of "serving in the army"
4- 9-1868  Charles chm of "serving in the army"
7- 9-1868  Joseph M chm of mcd
4-11-1872  John U chm of mcd
5-14-1874  Elizabeth, Jonathan Lewis, Alice Mina & Charles Wood rec in mbrp
12-13-1877  Ellen rec in mbrp
12-13-1877  Elijah P rec in mbrp
2-13-1879  Phebe Ann (form Woolman) chm of mcd
11-14-1889  Melissa G (form Cook) chm of mcd
11- 3-1898  Mary T, -dt Benjamin & Annie, m Richard S Burdsall, -s Elwood & Sarah E of Harrison Co, N Y
6- 7-1904  Elizabeth, -dt John M & Elizabeth H, m Alva Wright McCullock, -s William & Sarah L, Warren Co, Ind, at McCullock residence
4-12-1906  George A rec in mbrp
9-13-1906  Joseph S, Charles S & Sarah rec in mbrp
11- 8-1906  Nina, -dt Charles S & Sarah, rec in mbrp
12-12-1906  Mary Jane rec in mbrp
12-13-1906  Ch of Seth & Nora rec in mbrp
9-17-1907  Esther L, -dt Benjamin & Annie L, m Howard H Carpenter, -s John E & Mary H, Boulder, Colo, at Rogers residence
10-10-1907  John J rec in mbrp
8- 9-1917  Gerald Keith, -s Roland, rec in mbrp
8- 9-1917  Lula R rec in mbrp

ROSS
1-14-1841  Ann dis for mcd & jas

SAINT
8- 8-1867  Emily (form Cook) dis for mcd

SANDERS
8- -1850  Joseph dis for jas & na
9-12-1850  Jerusha dis for jas & na

SATTERTHWAIT
10-14-1852  Mary & dt Elizabeth rocf Miami MM, O
11-10-1853  Samuel rocf Miami MM, O
12-11-1856  Joseph & w Eliza & ch Esther, Edith & Anna rocf Miami MM, O
5-17-1866  Edith, -dt Joseph M & Eliza, m Isaac Lukens, -s Richard & Caroline, at Fall Creek MH
11- 8-1866  Esther Hardy (form Sattertwwait) chm of mcd
10-14-1869  Anna Burch (form Satterthwait) dis for mcd
12-11-1873  Joseph M & w Eliza gct Benjaminville MM, Ill

SAUNDERS
8- 8-1850  Sarah (form Wood) dis for mcd

SCHOFIELD
1-13-1842  Jonathan rec in mbrp
4-14-1843  Susan E, -dt Jonathan & Eleanor, Marion, Ind, m Edward Pope, -s Abner & Maria of Marion, Ind, at Fall Creek MH
8-14-1845  William A chm of mcd
3-13-1846  Margaret, -dt Jonathan & Eleanor, Marion, Ind m Charles Good, -s John & Sarah, Marion, Ind, at Duck Creek MH
9-19-1848  Maria, -dt Jonathan & Eleanor, Marion, Ind, m Isaac Smith, -s Jonathan & Martha, Laporte, Ind, at Indianapolis MH
9-13-1855  Samuel chm of mcd
6-14-1860  Joseph F chm of mcd
4-13-1865  William chm of mcd
6- 8-1865  Lydia rocf Haddonfield MM
6-13-1867  Amanda, w of Joseph & dt   Anna Mary, rec in mbrp
4- 9-1868  David chm of "serving in the army"
4- 9-1868  Joseph chm of "serving in the army"
8-13-1868  Susannah rocf Milford MM, Ind
11- 9-1893  Susannah gct Whitewater MM
7-14-1898  Joseph of Knoxville, Tenn, rocf purpose of m
4-11-1901  Joseph chm of mcd; ret mbrp

SCHOOLEY
5-11-1871  Sarah (form Johnson) chm of mcd
2-10-1881  Benjamin & Charles E, ch of Sarah, rec in mbrp
2- 8-1883  Sarah rel fr mbrp

SHANNON
5-11-1905  Mabel Maris rocf Maple Grove MM

SHUTE
6-10-1852  Eliza dis for mcd

SIMMONS
12-12-1839  Elizabeth appt Overseer
7-10-1845  Samuel chm of mcd (Simons)
7-10-1845  (Simmonds) Rachel (form Middleton) chm of mcd
12-11-1845  (Simmonds) Samuel rpt mcd by Baltimore MM, Md
8-12-1847  (Simmonds) Samuel rocf Cecil MM, Md
4-10-1851  (Simmonds) Samuel rec in mbrp
10-10-1867  (Simmonds) Joshua & w Elizabeth gct Cecil MM, Md
10-14-1875  (Simmonds) Joshua & Elizabeth rocf Cecil MM, Md

SISSON
6-10-1858  Phebe Cummins (form Sisson) dis for mcd

SLACK
4-13-1848  Hannah (form Williams) chm of mcd
1-11-1855  Hanna Wilson (form Slack) chm of mcd

SLYTER
8-12-1842  Elizabeth & ch Seth Thomas & Norton Edward rocf Whitewater MM, Ind
10-13-1842  Phebe rocf Whitewater MM, Ind
10-15-1842  Elizabeth Amm rocf Whitewater MM, Ind
11- 9-1843  Joseph rocf Whitewater MM, Ind
9-11-1845  Phebe Lewis (form Slyter) dis for mcd
5-11-1848  Thomas, dis for leaving neighborhood without paying his debts
11- 9-1848  Seth dis for mcd & na
10-13-1853  Horton dis for mcd

SMITH
4- 9-1840  Henry Taylor dis for dp & na
11- 9-1843  Phebe (form Spencer) dis for mcd
2-13-1845  Phebe T & ch Caroline, Albert Henry, Ellen & Henrietta gct Springborough MM
9-10-1848  Isaac, -s Jonathan & Martha, La Porte, Ind, m Maria Schofield, -dt Jonathan & Eleanor, Marion, Ind, at Indianapolis MH
4-15-1857  Milton, -s Nathan & Rebecca, m Mary G Allen, -dt Jehu & Mary Ann, at Duck Creek MH
2-14-1861  Hiram gct Maple Grove MM
10-12-1865  Milton & w Mary G & ch Ava C, Edgar J, Elizabeth Ann gct Clear Creek MM, Ill
4- 9-1868  Elizabeth (form Williams) chm of mcd

FALL CREEK

SMITH (Cont)
7- 2-1868  Jacob dis for mcd & Military Service
4-13-1871  Mary Stites (form Smith) mcd; rel fr mbrp
2- 8-1872  Phebe Yecco (form Smith) dis for mcd
           (Given as Yacan in Women's Min)
12- 9-1875 Elizabeth Williams gct Benjaminville MM, Ill
1- 8-1880  Nathan gct Benjaminville MM, Ill
10-12-1882 Nathan rocf Benjaminville MM, Ill
12-15-1903 Mary G rocf Hoopston MM, Ill

SNYDER
4- 9-1857  Sarah (form Rogers) chm of mcd
10- 4-1866 Sarah Dobson (form Snyder) dis for mcd

SPENCER
1- 9-1840  Mary Ann & Phebe rocf Concord MM, O, -end by Milford MM, Ind
1- 9-1840  David, w Leah & ch Nathan, Eleanor, Rebecca, Edwin & David P rocf Concord MM, O; -end by Milford MM, Ind
11- 9-1843 Phebe Smith (form Spencer) dis for mcd
3- 4-1844  Nathan gct Milford MM, Ind to m Louisa Hiatt
12-12-1844 Louisa rocf Milford MM, Ind
6-12-1845  Mary Ann Kenworthy (form Spencer) dis for mcd
2-10-1846  Rebecca Kenworthy (form Spencer) dis for mcd
11-11-1847 David & w Leah & ch Edward & David gct Whitewater MM, Ind
5-11-1848  Nathan & w Louisa & ch Banajah H & Joseph Henry gct Milford MM, Ind
1-10-1850  Eleanor gct Whitewater MM, Ind

STAFFORD
3- 8-1900  Emma rocf Whitewater MM, Ind

STANLEY
8-14-1845  Leah (form Pickering) chm of mcd

STANTON
6- 8-1843  Celia & ch Isaac W, James B, Mary Elizabeth & Lucretia rocf Milford MM, Ind

STARBUCK
7- 8-1841  Elizabeth (Edith in Women's Minutes) rocf Goshen MM, O

STITES
4-13-1871  Mary (form Smith) mcd; rel fr mbrp

STRADLING
9-12-1912  Emma rec in mbrp

STRATTON
1- 9-1840  Rebecca & ch Davis Harvey, Rebecca & Edwin rocf Miami MM, O
2-19-1840  Rebecca, -dt Edward & Penelope, m Joseph Weeks, -s Thomas & Penelope, at Duck Creek MH
7-12-1855  Edward H gct Milford MM, Ind to m Hannah Bond
6-12-1856  Hannah rocf Milford MM, Ind

STYLER
10-18-1842 Elizabeth Ann, -dt Joseph & Elizabeth, of Wabash Co, Ind, m Samuel Weeks -s Joseph & Susannah, at Salimony Mtg

SWAIN
10-12-1843 Woolston rocf Middleton MM, Pa
11- 3-1843 Woolston, -s Samuel & Martha, Marion, Ind, m Mary Ann Thomas, -dt Jonathan & Ann, at Fall Creek MH
10- 8-1846 Charles & w Sarah Ann & ch Mary Ellen, Caroline, Anna, Joseph S & Charles Jr rocf Wakefield MM, Pa
6-10-1847  Charles & w Sarah Ann & ch Mary Ellen, Anna, Caroline, Joseph S & Charles gct Milford MM, Ind

6-10-1852  Charles & w Sarah Ann & ch Mary Ellen, Caroline, Anna, Joseph & Charles Jr rocf Milford MM, Ind
12-25-1856 Mary Ellen, -dt Charles & Sarah Ann, m William F Morris, -s George & Rhoda, at Fall Creek MH
11-18-1858 Anna, -dt Charles & Sarah Ann, m Nathan Branson, -s Thomas & Anne, at Fall Creek MH
8-11-1859  Beulah rocf Buckingham MM, Pa
9-18-1862  Caroline, -dt Charles & Sarah Ann, m John L Thomas, -s Lewis & Priscilla, at Fall Creek MH
12-15-1864 Joseph, -s Charles & Sarah Ann, m Elizabeth R Lukens, -dt Allen & Mary Ann, at Fall Creek MH
11-16-1865 Charles, -s Charles & Sarah Ann, m Margaret S Brown, -dt Elwood & Mary Ann, at Fall Creek MH
4-11-1867  Rachel (form Kirk) dis for mcd
4- 8-1868  Chalres W & w Sarah Ann "Memorial Proposed"
7- 8-1869  Memorial for Charles W & Sarah Ann Swain read & forwarded to QM
4-14-1887  Mary Etta Kinnard (form Swain) ret mbrp
8-20-1887  Joseph chm of mcd
2-14-1889  Sallie Frank (form Swain) ret mbrp
6-11-1891  Fannie Morgan rec in mbrp
7-10-1893  Fannie L, -dt Woolston & Mary A, m Joseph M Johnston, -s Meredith H & Winifred J, at Swain residence
12-30-1897 Walter, -s Charles E S & Margaret B, m Elizabeth Bell, protegee of Thomas & Margaret W Hardy, at Swain residence
12-28-1898 George H, -s Charles F & Margaret S, m Elizabeth F Hardy, -dt Solomon & Rebecca at Hardy residence, Markleville, Ind
4-12-1900  Woolston Memorial produced & forwarded to QM
12-12-1901 Elizabeth Belle rec in mbrp
10- 9-1902 Joseph & w Frances gct Swarthmore MM, Pa
10- 9-1913 Etta Louise & ch Frederick William & Morris Stanley rec in mbrp

TAYLOR
12-10-1846 Joseph W rocf Green St MM, Philadelphia, Pa
4- 9-1868  Mary T Hoover (form Taylor) chm of mcd

THOMAS
11-14-1839 Mary Ann appt on comm
11- 3-1843 Mary Ann, -dt Jonathan & Ann, m Woolston Swain, -s Samuel & Martha, Marion, Ind, at Fall Creek MH
6-14-1860  Abner rocf Springborough MM, O
6-13-1861  Hannah rocf Springborough MM, O
9-18-1862  John L, -s Lewis & Priscilla, m Caroline Swain, -dt Charles & Sarah Ann, at Fall Creek MH
8-17-1865  Ann, -dt Lewis & Priscilla, m Benjamin Rogers, -s Jonathan & Hannah, at Fall Creek MH
12-21-1865 Martha M, -dt Lewis W & Priscilla, m Aaron Morris, -s George & Rhoda A, at Fall Creek MH
7-13-1871  Abner dis for jas
9- 3-1874  Lucretia M, -dt Lewis & Patricia, m Robert Bond, -s Jesse & Elizabeth J, Miami Co, Ind
9-12-1878  Jonathan mcd
10- 9-1879 Alice, -dt Lewis & Priscilla, m Edgar D Whitley, -s Daniel & Ann M at Residence of bride
6-10-1886  Emily S & ch Anna & John rec in mbrp
10-13-1892 Caroline L, ch Muriel F, rocf Bristol MM, Pa
9- 1-1897  Emma F, -dt John & Caroline, m Frank B Miller, -s Charles D & Isabell, Clark Co, Ohio, at home of bride

FALL CREEK

### THOMAS (Cont)
- 8- 9-1898    Charles gct Presby Ch, North
- 3-23-1910    Lewis W, -s John L & Caroline L, m Margaret Willets, -dt Samuel E & Virginia, at the residence of Thomas W Hardy
- 6- 9-1910    Margaret Willets rolf Hope Congregational Ch, Chicago, Ill
- 8-13-1926    James rec in mbrp

### THORN
- 11-14-1850    Nancy W rocf Green Plain MM, O
- 11-14-1850    Josiah & w Hannah B & dt Jane rocf Milford MM, Ind
- 4- 8-1852    Josiah Jr rocf Milford MM, Ind
- 6-10-1852    Barclay rocf Milford MM, Ind

### THORNBURGH
- 9- 9-1852    Henry & w Celia Maria rocf Milford MM, Ind

### THURSTON
- 12-12-1901    Ida M rec in mbrp

### TILLSON
- 6-13-1861    Miriam (form Johnson) chm of mcd

### TOMLINSON
- 5- 2-1901    Finley, -s Noah & Abigail, Hamilton Co, Ind, m Mary Elizabeth Fussell, -dt John L & Mary J, at Fussell residence
- 4-11-1907    Findley rec in mbrp

### TRUEBLOOD
- 10-15-1859    Warner, -s James & Elizabeth, m Narcissa Allen, -dt Daniel & Eliza, at Duck Creek MH
- 5-10-1860    Narcissa A gct Blue River MM
- 7- 8-1875    Allen D, Laura A, James E & Victoria B, ch of Warner & Narcissa, rocf Blue River MM
- 3- 8-1883    Thomas rocf Blue River MM, Ind
- 4-11-1889    Victoria B gct Clear Creek MM, Ill
- 8-11-1898    Victoria E rocf Clear Creek MM, Ill
- 9-20-1898    Victoria B, -dt Warner M & Narcissa A, Wash Co, Ind, m Ralph Wilson, -s David & Zerilda of Hancock Co, Ind, at residence of Edward Roberts

### TRUMP
- 8-10-1882    Mary D (form Frampton) chm of mcd

### TUNES
- 1-17-1900    Omer, -s William H & Sarah B, m Sarah F Darlington, -dt Elba & Elmina, at home of the bride

### TUNIS
- 10- 8-1891    Mary Jane (form Catrun) ret mbrp
- 2-11-1909    Charles & w Mary & s Horace rec in mbrp

### TURNER
- 4- 9-1891    Eliza Ann rec in mbrp
- 6-17-1928    Eliza Ann rec in mbrp

### TYLER
- 2- 9-1860    Mary rocf Whitewater MM, Ind
- 2- 9-1860    Sarah rocf Whitewater MM, Ind
- 9-17-1868    Sarah, -dt John & Phebe, Fayette Co, Ind, m Jehiel F Moor, -s Jonathan & Eliza, at Fall Creek MH

### TYSON
- 11-14-1844    Daniel dis for att mcd
- 4-13-1854    Sarah Ann rocf Cherry St MM, Philadelphia, Pa

### UNDERWOOD
- 8-13-1854    John rocf Centre MM, O
- 8-13-1854    Lewis rocf Centre MM, O
- 9-13-1855    Sarah B & dt Mary Frances rocf Westfield MM, O
- 8- 8-1882    Catharine rocf Miami MM, O
- 10-10-1889    Ava rel fr mbrp
- 5-12-1904    John & Mary, ch of Amos & Alice, rec in mbrp

### ULEN
- 10-13-1910    Jerry rec in mbrp

### VAN BRUNT
- 6-11-1846    Mary Ann rocf Whitewater MM, Ind

### VANWINKLE
- 9-14-1876    Ruth Emma (form Cook) chm of mcd
- 4- 9-1885    Emma (form Cook) rel fr mbrp

### VERNON
- 10- 8-1840    Mary appt to comm
- 10-15-1840    Edward, -s Abraham & Mary, m Hannah Rodgers, -dt Joseph & Elizabeth, at Fall Creek MH
- 12-12-1844    Edward dis for assisting to pull down a Mill dam without owner's consent
- 3-11-1869    Jemima chm of mcd
- 3-11-1869    Mary Haines (form Vernon) chm of mcd
- 4- 9-1874    Sarah Jacobs (form Vernon) rpt mcd
- 7-12-1888    Rachel D rec in mbrp
- 11-11-1915    Anna M & dt Geneva Louisa rec in mbrp

### VINTERS
- 11- 8-1866    Cynthia Jessup (form Vinters) dis for mcd

### WALKER
- 12-10-1868    Mary E (form Gray) dis for mcd
- 7-11-1872    Tamson (form Allen) chm of mcd
- 12-11-1873    Tamson E dis for stage playing
- 4-14-1904    Margaret F rec in mbrp

### WATKINS
- 5-14-1868    Alice (form Haines) chm of mcd
- 4-11-1886    Alice rel fr mbrp

### WATSON
- 6-11-1853    Hannah (form Henry) dis for mcd & jas
- 12-14-1882    Sylvanus & w Hannah & dt Deborah rec in mbrp
- 8- 8-1895    Deborah Moore Brooks (form Watson) mcd; ret mbrp

### WAY
- 11-11-1915    Anna Whitely gct Centre MM, Pa

### WEEKS
- 11-14-1839    Susan E appt on comm
- 2-19-1840    Joseph, -s Thomas & Penelope, m Rebecca Stratton, -dt Edward & Margaret Kinley, at Duck Creek MH
- 4- 9-1840    Rebecca appt on comm
- 12-22-1840    Susan, -dt Joseph & Susannah, m Daniel Kindley, -s Edward & Margaret, Preble Co, Ohio, at Fall Creek MH
- 5-12-1842    Charles dis for mcd
- 5-12-1842    Sarah Clanton (form Weeks) dis for mcd
- 10-18-1842    Samuel, -s Joseph & Elizabeth, m Elizabeth Ann Styler, -dt Jacob & Elizabeth, Wabash Co, Ind, at Salomony Mtg
- 3-14-1844    Anna Haycock (form Weeks) chm of mcd
- 11-14-1844    Hannah Butler (form Weeks) dis for mcd
- 2-13-1845    Jacob dis for na
- 10- 9-1845    Maria Elliott (form Weeks) dis for mcd
- 5- 9-1850    Joseph Jr chm of mcd
- 2-13-1851    Thomas chm of mcd
- 3-13-1852    Aaron dis for mcd
- 8-12-1852    Rebecca dis
- 4-12-1855    Lydia, Eliza & Rebecca gct Whitewater MM, Ind
- 4- 9-1857    Thomas dis for na
- 4- 8-1858    Abraham dis for na
- 6- 9-1863    Lydia & Rebecca dis for att mcd

### WEESNER
- 1-14-1875    Louisa (form Wood) chm of mcd

FALL CREEK

**WENE**
8- 8-1895  Elizabeth (form Williams) mcd; ret mbrp

**WHITACRE**
8- 8-1850  Samuel Kelly tr with at Miami MM, O for fiddleing & dancing

**WHITE**
11-14-1839  Lewis appt Overseer for Fall Creek
8-14-1845  Sophia rec in mbrp

**WHITLEY**
10- 9-1879  Edgar D, -s Daniel & Ann M, m Alice G Thomas, -dt Lewis & Priscilla, at residence of bride

**WHITELY**
11-11-1880  Alice T gct Milford MM, Ind
4-14-1892  Edgar & w Alice & ch Ann M, Emma T, Lewis D & Emory E rocf Milton MM
1- 8-1914  Anna Divin rec in mbrp

**WILLETS**
3-23-1900  Margaret,-dt Samuel E & Virginia, m Lewis Thomas, -s John L & Caroline L, at the Thomas W Hardy residence

**WILLIAMS**
11-14-1839  Hannah appt on comm
11-14-1839  William appt Overseer for Fall Creek
4-13-1848  Hannah Slack (form Williams) chm of mcd
6-14-1851  Phebe Ellen (form Hunter) dis for mcd
11- -1852  Phebe Ellen dis at Buckingham MM, Pa, this mtg to inf her
8-13-1854  Mariam Johnson (form Williams) chm of mcd
3-11-1856  Caleb gct Green Plains MM, O, to m Anna Oldham
12- 9-1858  Anna W & ch Elizabeth W, Abner W, Joseph W, & James C rocf Green Plains MM, O
1- 9-1862  Lydia Kenworthy (form Williams) dis for mcd & jas
2-19-1863  Silas, -s Caleb & Hannah, m Sarah Ann Cook, -dt George & Eliza, at Fall Creek MH
5-14-1863  Stephen chm of mcd
5-14-1863  Massy W (form Oldham) chm of mcd
4- 9-1868  Elizabeth Smith (form Williams) chm of mcd
5-13-1875  Caleb & Anna gct Benjaminville MM, Ill
5-13-1875  Stephen & Massie & ch Miriam J & Jason gct Benjaminville MM, Ill
2-13-1890  Stephen & Massey & ch Jason & Ollie rocf Benjaminville MM, Ill
8- 8-1895  Elizabeth Wene (form Williams) rpt mcd; ret mbrp
11-11-1897  Caleb ret mbrp
6-13-1912  Caleb glt M E Ch, Pendleton, Ind

**WILSON**
12- 9-1847  Nathan & w Sarah rocf Whitewater MM, Ind
4-14-1853  Nathan dis for dr
4-14-1853  Thomas rocf Miami MM, O
10-13-1853  Huldah, dt Ruth, rec in mbrp
10-13-1853  Ruth & ch Seth, Jesse, Barnett, Christopher, Charles, John, Martha & Ruth rec in mbrp
1-11-1855  Hannah (form Slack) chm of mcd
12-10-1857  Thomas & w Ruth & ch Seth, Jesse, Barnett, Christopher, Charles, John, Martha, Ruth & Jane gct Priaire Grove MM, Ia
3-11-1858  Huldah Cox (form Wilson) chm of mcd
1- 9-1862  Elizabeth (form James) chm of mcd
4- 9-1868  Elizabeth Howard (form Wilson) chm of mcd
2-11-1869  Lydia (form Pore) dis for mcd
12-14-1871  Elizabeth McNew (form Wilson) rpt mcd; rel fr mbrp
9-20-1898  Ralph, -s David & Zerilda, Hancock Co, m Victoria B Trueblood, -dt Warner M & Narcissa A, Washington Co, Ind, at Edward Roberts residence
8- 9-1917  Ralph & ch Ralph D & Max Maurice rec in mbrp
1-20-1929  Ralph rel fr mbrp

**WINDER**
3-14-1850  Joseph & w Rebecca & ch Mary Jane, Alfred, Caroline, Sarah Ellen, Anna Marie & Joseph Henry rocf Milford MM, Ind
2- 9-1854  Joseph & w Rebecca & ch Alfred, Caroline, Sarah Ellen, Maria & Joseph Henry gct Whitewater MM, Ind

**WING**
1-14-1915  DeWitt C (Chicago) rec in mbrp

**WISEMAN**
12-13-1906  Grace Emily rec in mbrp

**WOOD**
11-14-1839  Phebe appt on comm
12- 8-1842  Simeon P gct Whitewater MM to m Margaret Ratliff
11-13-1845  Simeon P gct Whitewater MM, Ind
7- 9-1846  Simeon & w Margaret H & s John R rocf Whitewater MM, Ind
1-11-1849  Levi P gct Milford MM, Ind to m Hannah F Haycock
5- 9-1850  Sarah Sanders (form Wood) dis for mcd
7-11-1850  Hannah F rocf Milford MM, Ind
10-13-1854  Seth dis for mcd
5-12-1859  Ascenith Osborn (form Wood) chm of mcd
1-18-1865  Mary E, -dt Simeon & Margaret, m Levi Cook, -s John & Juliann,at Duck Creek MH
1-17-1872  Albert, -s Simeon & Margaret H, m Eva Haines -dt Clark C & Margaret F
1-14-1875  Louisa Weesner (form Wood) rpt mcd; rel fr mbrp
8-12-1880  Emma Risk (form Wood) rpt mcd; rel fr mbrp
7- 8-1886  Alice Wood McLelland ret mbrp; "she not having violated our testimonies in performing her marriage
9-17-1887  Cora (form Coffin) ret mbrp
6-12-1902  Wilbur Clifford, -s Albert C & Eva, m Laura Belle Barrett, -dt Benton L & Sarah Elizabeth, at Barrett residence
5-16-1926  Pearl & ch John Arthur, Margaret E & William Elmer rec in mbrp

**WOOLLETT**
10-14-1888  Annie C (form Haines) chm of mcd
6-13-1901  Anna (form Haines) rel fr mbrp

**WOOLMAN**
12-10-1853  Joseph B, -s Uriah & Mary, Preble Co, O, m Eliza Cook, -dt Isaac & Anna, at Duck Creek MH
4-13-1854  Eliza gct Westfield MM
2-10-1859  Joseph B & w Elizabeth & ch Isaac C, William V & Julietta rocf Westfield MM
6- 9-1859  John A & w Ascenith & ch Phebe Ann, Charles, & an infant rocf Whitewater MM, Ind
1-12-1860  James Moore gct Westfield MM to m Phebe Woolman
2-13-1879  Phebe Ann Rogers (form Woolman) chm of mcd
4-10-1879  Charles A chm of mcd
2-10-1881  William chm of mcd
8-11-1881  Mary Eveline Davis (form Woolman) chm of mcd
4-13-1882  Isaac rpt mcd
1-13-1887  William rel fr mbrp
8-20-1887  Isaac chm of mcd
5-10-1888  Esther B & ch Walker B & Ruth E rec in mbrp
4-11-1889  Ascenith rec in mbrp

**WRIGHT**
11-14-1839  Mary appt on comm
10- 8-1840  Elizabeth J appt on comm
6-11-1846  William & w Elizabeth & ch Sarah, Benjamin, William Henry, John, Mary, Jean, Jonathan, Ann Elizabeth & Albert gct Milford MM, Ind
2-14-1850  Elias H gct Milford MM to m Demaries S Bond

FALL CREEK

WRIGHT (Cont)
5-23-1852  Demaries rocf Milford MM, Ind
3-14-1856  Elias H dis for sueing a fellow mbr
2- 9-1860  Isaac & w Mary H & dt Mary Ellen gct Milford MM, Ind
3-12-1868  Arthur F dis, having moved beyond the care of the Society
11-13-1868 Isaac & w Mary & dt Mary Ellen rocf Milford MM, Ind

WYATT
1- 8-1880  Seth dis for jas

YECCO (Yacan in Women's Minutes)
2- 8-1872  Phebe (form Smith) dis for mcd

# DUCK CREEK MONTHLY MEETING
## Henry County, Indiana

Duck Creek Monthly Meeting was set-off from Milford Monthly Meeting and first held on the 27th of Seventh Month 1826. The meetinghouse was located in or near Greensboro. Friends had settled here as early as 1823.

When established the monthly meeting's limits included all of Henry County and adjacent parts of Madison and Rush. **Walnut Ridge** was established as a Preparative in 1827 and set-off as a monthly meeting in 1836; **Spiceland** became a Preparative in 1829 and was set-off in 1833 as a monthly meeting; Clear Spring was established as a Preparative in 1833; Fall Creek (near Huntsville, Madison County) became a Preparative in 1834. [In 1838 while Duck Creek was a part of Spiceland Monthly, Friends on Killbuck (in Richland Township, Madison County) was established as a Preparative. Because of smallness in numbers Fall Creek Preparative was discontinued and same *"to be removed to Friends settlement of Killbuck to be held at that place where Friends of that settlement have agreed upon for meeting ground."* The 'place' was Sommerton and both groups of Friends joined to hold Sommerton Preparative Meeting. *"Because of distance and difficulty of crossing high waters"* Sommerton was attached to Back Creek Monthly Meeting in Grant County. The meeting is thought to have been discontinued in 1845]. Elm Grove was established as a Preparative in 1835 but was attached to Spiceland Monthly Meeting.

The Hicksite division affected Duck Creek in 1828 and the Anti-slavery controversy divided the meeting in 1843. There was another period of dissension of such difficulty that the Quarterly Meeting laid down Duck Creek Monthly Meeting 8-24-1837 and its membership was attached to Spiceland Monthly Meeting until it was re-established 10-20-1840.

The reason for this cantankerousness remains obscure. N. H. Ballanger writing in 1890 says that it was *"a contention over the Reserection doctrine. J J Gurneys visit & letter to that meeting had much to do in the matter. This contention waxed so hot that White Water Q M interfered . . ."*

The Duck Creek minutes do not shed much light. When Walnut Ridge requested to become a monthly meeting a committee was appointed to survey the situation. On 6mo 25, 1835 the committee reported in somewhat tortured prose, *"We have visited that Preparative and Duck Creek Monthly Meeting and notwithstanding on coming to the important consideration of the subject in its different bearings, we were introduced into something of a peculiar trial, yet we were united in believing it might be best to grant their request."* The monthly meeting did not concur. The following month Walnut Ridge again sent up a request that was then forwarded to the Quarterly Meeting.

On 8mo 24, 1837 *"Clear Spring Preparative meeting informs that Henry Lamb has regardless and in violation of the repeated advice and entreaties of Elders & overseers, continued to disturb our Religious meetings by a lifeless ministry or public communication. But the meeting believing it was not in a suitable situation to appoint a committee defers the case to next meeting."* The next meeting was three years later.

In the 1930s the name of Duck Creek was changed to Greensboro Monthly Meeting.

## Monthly Meeting Records

The volumes listed below are in the vault of the Indiana Yearly Meetinghouse in Richmond. The material searched for this publication is marked (*). These records have been microfilmed.

Men's Minutes
* 7-27-1826 : 11-20-1834
*11-20-1834 : 12-25-1851
* 1-22-1852 :  5-20-1875 (1)
* 6-24-1875 :  9-25-1884 (joint after 1882)

Women's Minutes
*7-27-1826 : 8-20-1846
*9-24-1846 : 2-23-1860

Joint Minutes
*10-23-1885 : 5-22-1890
* 6-26-1890 : 3-24-1910

*1 Volume Births and Deaths
*1 Marriage Register, 1827-1870

(1) pages for 9th and 10th months of 1873 are lacking.

DUCK CREEK

## DUCK CREEK MONTHLY MEETING

### BIRTH & DEATH RECORD

**ALLEN**
Herman H    b 2-28-1826
Lydia M    b 7- 6-1833
Ch: Elizabeth    b 10-24-1848
     Frank E    b 12-10-1853
     Linneus    b 1-14-1861

**ANDERSON**
John C    b 11-25-1835
Lydia    b 4-19-1841   dt Elias & Martha Modlin
Ch: Luther M    b 3-15-1861
     Martha J    b 3- 4-1863

**BAILEY**
David    b 1-24-1780 Randolph Co, N C s John & Dorcas   d 9-11-1843 bur Clear Springs
Sarah    b 8-31-1784 N C dt Rice & Catharine Price   d 2- 4-1871 bur Clear Springs

**BEALS**
(Abraham)
Mehitable    b 3- 4-1778 Randolph Co, N C
Ch: Bethiah    b 4-23-1806 Tenn
     Priscilla    b 11- 4-1807 Ohio
     Matilda    b 5- 3-1811 "

John H    b 8-16-1810 s Jesse & Ann b Guilford Co N C
Ann (Hasket)    b 4- 2-1810 Warren Co, Ohio dt Thomas & Ann Haskit
Ch: Emily    b 12-16-1832
          d 4-24-1834 bur Duck Creek Mtg

**BEARD**
Hannah    d 9-27-1857 age 65 yrs bur Duck Creek Mtg

**BEESON**
Edward    b 3-15-1766 Stokes Co, N C s Isaac & Phebe
Mary    b 9-15-1770 " " " dt David & Hannah Brooks
Ch: Martha    b 4-20-1814
     Benjamin    b 4-20-1817
     Jemima    b 5-18-1820

**BINFORD**
Avice (w of Asahel) b 6-13-1814 Belmont Co, Ohio d 11-24-1834 bur Walnut Ridge Mtg, Ind

Benajah
Judith
Ch: Jeremiah    b 2-11-1828
     Josiah    b 10-29-1830 d 1- 2-1832 bur Walnut Ridge Mtg
     Isaiah    b 2- 3-1833

William    b 11-27-1804 Northampton N C s of Micajah & Sarah
Mary    b 4- 5-1810 Wayne Co, N C
Ch: Eliza    b 7- 8-1828

**BOND**
Aaron M    b 5- 8-1825
Ann    b 4-11-1829 dt John & Sarah Ratliff
Ch: John R    b 2-28-1854
     Abner R    b 8-20-1855
     William    b 9-12-1857
     Sarah B    b 5-10-1859
     Ezra    b 9-11-1860
     Metilda A    b 11-16-1863
     Mary Etta    b 5-14-1867

Amor    b 9-22-1805 s Thomas & Mary
Mary    b 9-30-1808 dt Joseph & Priscilla Pickett
Ch: Priscilla    b 11- 1-1828
     Jonathan    b 11- 4-1831

Eliza A    d 2-25-1863 age 40 yrs bur Cadiz Mtg, Ind Henry Co

Mary    d 4- 3-1844 age 52 yrs 9 mo 1 day bur Clear Spring Mtg, Ind

Sarah Ann    d 2-22-1863 age 30 yrs bur Cadiz Mtg, Ind

Thomas    b 12- 5-1780
Mary    b 9-30-1782
Ch: Amor    b 9-22-1805
     Betsy    b 1- 4-1807
     Jesse    b 10- 7-1808
     Thomas    b 3- 4-1811
     Hiram    b 1- 7-1814
     Pleasant    b 3- 4-1817
     Asenath    b 3-26-1819
     Phebe    b 7-30-1821
     Mary    b 7-14-1826

William    b 9-17-1822 s John & Rebecca
Sarah    b 8-12-1824 Highland Co, Ohio dt Hanuel & Eleanor Hunt   d 12-23-1848
Ch: Lucinda H    b 10- 7-1844
     Josiah N    b 9- 5-1846 d 2-19-1849 bur Clear Springs Mtg, Ind

**BOWMAN**
Edmund    b 12-12-1792 Stokes Co, N C s of William & Anna
Sarah S    b 2- 8-1800 Guilford Co, N C dt Robert & Martha Stuart
Ch: Phebe S    b 4-27-1821 Randolph Co, N C
     Anna Mariah    b 10- 6-1823 " " "
     George Anson    b 3- 5-1826 Stokes Co N C
     Elizabeth Ann    b 3-21-1828 " "
     Martha Elma    b 5-26-1830 " "
     Mary    b 1- 4-1832 " "
     Rebecca    b 5-12-1835 " "
     Emily Jane    b 5-27-1838 Henry Co

Jesse    b 2-23-1811 Guilford Co, N C s William & Anna
Mary    b 5-28-1813 Guilford Co, N C dt Joseph & Mary Birchum
Ch: Lucinda    b 12-15-1833 Stokes Co, N C
     William    b 4- 5-1835 Henry Co
     Anna    b 10-14-1836
     Shepard    b 9- 8-1838
     Caroline    b 2-17-1840
     Lydia    b 5-26-1842

Richard    b 1-18-1807 Guilford Co, N C s William & Anna (d 6 or 7 mo 1843 at Duck Creek Mtg, Ind)
Phebe    b 11-30-1805 Stokes Co, N C dt Jonathan & Nancy Mendenhall
Ch: Sarah Ann    b 1-30-1826 Guilford Co, N C
     Elvira    b 10-28-1827 Wayne Co, Ind
     William    b 8- 4-1831 " " "
          d 12-12-1832 West Grove Mtg
     Jonathan M    b 8-30-1833 Wayne Co, Ind
     Edmund    b 7-26-1835 Henry Co, Ind

William
Elvira
Ch: Sarah    b 5-18-1827
     Emeline    b 10-10-1829
     Calvin W    b 5- 2-1831
     Buley    b 5- 7-1833
     William    b 9- 2-1835
     Jabez H    b 12-28-1837
     Levi    b 3- 7-1841
     Thomas C    b 5- 3-1843

William Sr    d 1-29-1840 age 72 yrs 6 mo 24 dys bur Duck Creek Mtg, Ind

**BRANSON**
John W    d 12-25-1859 bur Duck Creek Mtg
Hannah
Ch: Asa    b 10-28-1844
        d 2-12-1846 bur Duck Creek Mtg

**BRATTON**
Hannah    b 1- 7-1770 Perquimans Co, N C dt John & Ann Maudlin

DUCK CREEK

## BREWER
John
(Rachel)
Ch: Elizabeth    b  1- 5-1822  Ohio
    Rachel       b 11- 4-1823   "
    William H    b  4-19-1826   "
    Elias        b 10-24-1826   "
m 3rd
Sarah    b 12-27-1808  Indiana
Ch: Mary         b 11-18-1837  Ind
    Morris W     b  3- 6-1839   "
    Jason W      b  2-16-1841   "

## BROWN
Abigail  b 12-11-1833  dt John & Cyrene

## BUFKIN
John  b  9-12-1811  Belmont Co, Ohio  s Thomas & Ruth
  m 1st
Hannah  b 2-16-1817  Stokes Co, N C  dt Jesse & Lydia
           d 7- 9-1854  bur Cadiz, Ind
Ch: Eliza        b  5-18-1841
    Lindley      b 12- 8-1842
    Lydia        b 11-28-1844  d  8-28-1859
                 bur Cadiz, Ind
    Elizabeth    b  1-24-1847
    Sarah Elma   b  1- 8-1849
    Calvin W     b  4- 9-1851
    Martha E     b  5-13-1853  d 10-14-1867
                 bur Cadiz, Ind
  m 2nd
Abigail P  b  8-14-1822  Gurnsey Co, Ohio
Ch: Joshua Y     b  6- 4-1857  d  6- 8-1857
                 bur Cadiz, Ind
    Mary Alice   b  6-22-1858
    Asa E        b  2-27-1860
    Rachel E     b 11-27-1861

Samuel     b  5-31-1810  (Belmont Co, Ohio)  d  5-18-1850
(Catharine)                        bur Clear Springs Mtg
Ch: Sarah Ann    b  2-23-1833
    John C       b 10-28-1834
    Mary         b  6- 5-1837
    Oliver       b  7-20-1839
    Tirzah Jane  b  7- 3-1841
    Martha       b  2-12-1845
    Ezra         b  6-15-1847
    Samuel       b  5-16-1850

Ruth  (w of Thomas)  d 4- 1-1849  age 72-6-0  bur
         Clear Springs Mtg, Ind

## BUNDY
Elias
Sarah
Ch: Ellen        b  7-24-1824  Perquimans Co, N C
    Mary         b  9-28-1826      "      "   "
    Peninah      b  2-22-1829      "      "   "
    Martha       b  1-13-1831      "      "   "
    Ann          b  5- 7-1833  Henry Co

George  s Josiah & Mary  b 11-16-1781  Perquimans Co, N C
Karen (Elliott)  dt Abraham & Julian Elliott
     b 3-15-1788  N Car  d 4-21-1847  bur Duck Creek
        Mtg, Ind
Ch: Mary         b  8-23-1819  Wayne Co, Ind
    Josiah       b  4-21-1823   "    "   "
    Catharine    b  7-23-1826   "    "   "

## BURRIS
Daniel  s John & Esther  b 7-10-1771  Surry Co, N C
     d 6-13-1845  bur Duck Creek Mtg, Ind
Mary (Horton) dt William & Winnefred  b 3-25-1778
        Surry Co, N C
Ch: Rebecca      b  1-17-1821  Highland Co, Ohio

Stephen  s Daniel & Mary  b 11- 5-1797  Surry Co, N C
  m 1st
Hannah (Hiatt) dt Absalom & Ann  b 6-20-1806  Tazzes
     Valley, Va (another place gives Canowa Co, Va)
     d  8- 6-1841  bur Duck Creek Mtg, Ind
Ch: Absalom      b  2-27-1830  d  3- 3-1830
    Daniel       b  9- 7-1831

Ch: Cynthia      b  3-21-1833  d  8-11-1834
                 bur Duck Creek, Ind
    Nancy        b 10-11-1834
    Jacob        b  7-30-1836
    Pleasant     b  3-30-1838
    Joel         b  8- 9-1840  d  9-18-1841
                 bur Duck Creek, Ind
  m 2nd
Margaret  b 12-23-1809  d 11-15-1847  bur Duck Creek
Ch: Isaac Franklin   b 12- 5-1844
    Tabitha Ann      b  8-28-1846

## CAIN
(James)
(Exalina)
Ch: Emma B       b  1- 1-1866  d  5- 8-1866
                 bur Duck Creek Mtg
    Everett      b  2-14-1867

## CARPENTER
Penelope  w of John  d 12- 6-1846  age 18-6-20
     bur Clear Spring Mtg

## CLAMPET
Mary (Jones) dt William & Deborah Jones  b 2-24-1800
        Grayson Co, Va   (w of William)

## COGGSHALL
Tristram  b  9- 7-1797  Randolph Co, N C  s Peter &
     Pamelia
Milicent  b  1-24-1801    "     "    "   dt Joseph &
     Penelope Newby
Ch: Eunice Worth     b  8- 8-1826  Marlborough N C
    Thomas Elwood   b  3-24-1828       "       "  "
     d 4-21-1834  bur Walnut Ridge Mtg, Ind
    John Milton     b  6-10-1829  Back Creek N C
    Joseph Newby    b  9-28-1831   "    "    " "
    Penelope N      b  2-23-1833
    Oliver          b 10- 9-1834

## COOK
(James)
Eunice  b  6- 5-1808  Guilford Co, N C  dt William &
     Elizabeth Hunt
Ch: Manirva Ann  b  1-26-1828  Wayne Co, Ind
    Elizabeth A  b  1-24-1832  Madison Co
    James Allen  b 11- 6-1834     "      "

(Isaac)
Anne  b 11-22-1803  dt Joseph & Priscilla Pickett
Ch: Eliza        b  2- 6-1829
    Nancy        b 10-12-1830
    Mary         b  2-10-1833

John  b 12-25-1804  s Levi & (Ann)
Julian  b  8- 8-1811 (1801?) dt William & Achsah Saint

Jesse  b  8-29-1824  d  7- 7-1863  bur Clear Spring Mtg
Abigail (Stafford)  b 8-21-1826  dt Eli & Elizabeth
Ch: Ellen        b  7-28-1853
    Emma         b  6-16-1855
    Esther       b  3- 8-1858
    Albert       b  2- 3-1860
    John         b  1-10-1862

## COOPER
William T  b  3-13-1804  Pa
Anna S     b  2-28-1808  Pa
Ch: Levi         b  4-25-1831  Pa
    Elizabeth    b  9-19-1833   "
    Truman       b  5-28-1836  Indiana
    Jeremiah     b  3-21-1839    "
    Phebe R      b  6-23-1841    "
    Deborah      b 11-30-1843    "

## COX
William B
Elvira
Ch: Mary Elizabeth   b  2- 7-1867  d  3-16-1867
                     bur Duck Creek Mtg
    Margaret B       b 10-24-1868

## DAVIS

Elihu    d 4-10-1875   bur Springfield Mtg, Ind
Love (Barnard)   b 11-31-1788   Guilford Co, N C
    dt Uriah & Elizabeth
Ch:   Alexander       b 1-12-1813   Highland Co, Ohio
     Rosanna         b 11-18-1814     "     "     "
     Allen W          b 7-12-1816      "     "     "
     Zeno            b 6-22-1817   Wayne Co, Ind
     Alfred ?         b 7-15-1819      "     "     "
     Edwin           b 3-13-1822
     Eliza Jane       b 5-27-1824
     Elihu           b 2-9-1828

Nathan   s Elisha & Alice   b 4-12-1792, Pa
Lydia (Cleaver)   dt Ezekiel & Abigail   b 10-29-1801
    Warren Co, Ohio
Ch:   Elizabeth       b 7-19-1822   Warren Co, Ohio
     Mary             b 11-1-1824     "     "     "
     John             b 8-21-1826     "     "     "
     David            b 10-17-1828     "     "     "

Tristram   s Tristrim & Love   b 10-28-1794   Guilford Co, NC
Rebecca (Sumner)   dt Thomas & Hannah Sumner   b Stokes Co, N C
Ch:   Clarkson        b 9-5-1821
     Elwood          b 10-2-1823   Wayne Co, Ind
     Malinda         b 2-6-1826   Highland Co, Ohio
     Lucinda         b 1-11-1828   Union Co, Ind
     Leander         b 3-15-1830   Union Co, Ind
                    d 7-10-1834   bur Duck Creek Mtg
     Irena           b 5-1-1832
     Delana          b 3-3-1834

## DAWSON

Isaac
Sarah   d 4-13-1863   age 60 yrs   bur Cadiz, Ind
Ch:   William         b 4-3-1834   Stark Co, Ohio
     Anne W          b 7-31-1835
     Nathan          b 4-13-1837   Ind   d 5-7-1837
                    Duck Creek Mtg
     Ruth            b 4-24-1838
     Lydian          b 10-2-1839
     Robert          b 3-22-1841   d 4-30-1863
                    bur Cadiz, Ind
     Tobitha         b 5-4-1844
     Sina            b 4-18-1846

## DENNEY

Shubel   b 1-8-1810
Doritha H   dt William & Lydia Jenkins   b 2-18-1822
Ch:   Lewis Marion     b 6-29-1857
     Mary Lucinda     b 9-5-1859
     Phebe Melinda    b 2-9-1862   d 4-17-1864
                    bur Cadiz, Ind
     Charles Monroe   b 2-25-1865   d 3-1-1865
                    bur Cadiz, Ind
     Lydia Emela      b 7-27-1866

## DICKEY

Nimrod   b 3-1-1780   Guilford Co, N C
Ann   b 11-29-1779   Randolph Co, N C
Ch:   Jane            b 5-7-1808   Jefferson Co, Tenn
     Mary A          b 7-17-1817   Clinton Co, Ohio
     James           b 2-25-1820     "     "     "
     Asenath         b 11-20-1822    "     "     "

## DRAPER

(Joshua)
Huldah   b 3-1-1809   Surry Co, N C   dt Nathan & Huldah Pearson
Ch:   Milicent        b 6-8-1828   Wayne Co, Ind
     Lucinda         b 8-17-1830    "     "     "

Josiah Jr   b 1-14-1788   Perquimans Co, N C   s Josiah & Miriam
Catherine   b 10-12-1806   Surry Co, N C   dt Nathan & Huldah Pearson
Ch:   Huldah          b 10-23-1823
     Jane            b 9-1-1827
     Azzaal          b 7-18-1829   d 2-3-1835
                    bur at Josiah Draper's burying ground
     Rachel          b 4-22-1831
     Martha          b 4-26-1834
     Mary            b 6-11-1836
     Mariam          b 8-27-1838
     Catharine       b 4-18-1840   d 3-22-1846
                    bur at Josiah Draper's burying ground

Robert Linzy   b 1-21-1865   s of Noah & Lydia

## DULEA

Maxon
Lydia
Ch:   Eliza Jane       b 6-2-1827
     Thomas Elwood   b 5-31-1830
     Lydia            b 4-17-1832
     Mary            b 7-4-1834
     John            b 11-4-1837

## EDGERTON

Benajah   s Reuben & Patience   b 11-13-1816   d 11-2-1838
    Duck Creek Mtg, Ind

Joseph   s Thomas & Sarah   b 1-22-1762   N C   d 2-7-1841
    Duck Creek Mtg, Ind
Martha (Lamb)   dt Reuben & Martha   d 8-10-1844   aged 79 yrs 8 mo 12 days   Duck Creek Mtg, Ind

Reuben   s Joseph & Martha   b 4-17-1786   Wayne Co, N C
Patience   dt Elijah & Susanna Hanson   b 3-25-1787
    Wayne Co, N C   d 8-9-1844   Duck Creek Mtg, Ind
Ch:   Avice            b 6-13-1814   Belmont Co, Ohio
     Benajah         (b 11-13-1816)   d 11-2-1838
                    age 21-11-19   Duck Creek Mtg
     Louisa ?         b 11-13-1816
     Elizabeth       b 10-22-1818
     Susanna         b 12-25-1820   Logan Co, Ohio
     Elijah          b 10-24-1822   d 8-2-1841
                    bur Duck Creek
     Reuben jr       b 4-2-1825   d 8-2-1844
                    bur Duck Creek

## ELLIOTT

Isaac T   b 2-26-1827   s John & Mary
Mary E   b 4-22-1826   N C   dt Elias & Lydia Newby
Ch:   Elizabeth A      b 9-27-1850   Henry Co
     Martha J        b 10-11-1852    "     "
     John Charles     b 9-16-1854     "     "
     Lydia T         b 12-14-1857    "     "
     Naomi H         b 5-17-1861     "     "

(Jacob s Israel & Welmet)
Ann   b 1-4-1785   dt Salathiel & Susanna Stone
Ch:   Salathiel        b 11-14-1804
     Olive            b 4-10-1806
     Alce            b 5-7-1808
     Welmet          b 4-21-1810
     Susanna         b 2-29-1812
     Allen            b 4-23-1814
     Elvy            b 10-11-1815
     Melinda         b 4-7-1818

Obediah jr   b 3-28-1801   N C   s Obadiah & Sarah
Armela   b 6-14-1810   N C   dt Seth & Hannah Hinshaw
Ch:   Benjamin B       b 10-18-1828   Randolph Co, N C
     Seth H          b 2-18-1380      "     "     "
     Calvin          b 9-8-1831      "     "     "
     Clark            b 1-26-1833      "     "     "
                    2-20-(sic)

## ELLIS

Elizabeth   d 8-10-1855   age 21-10-21   bur Cadiz, Ind
Joshua   d 8-18-1855   age 54-2-1   bur Cadiz, Ind

## EVANS

George   b 2-25-1802   Newberry Dist, S C   s Benjamin & Hannah
Mary   b 3-6-1798   dt Thomas & Ann Haskit
Ch:   Asenath         b 10-14-1822   Warren Co, Ohio
     Owen            b 8-11-1826   Indiana
     Sarah            b 3-14-1829      "
     Richard         b 6-15-1832      "

## FENTRESS

Susanna   b 11-16-1811   Stokes Co, N C   dt Benjamin & Annes Hinshaw

## GAUSE

Lorenzo   b 3-27-1867   d 8-13-1868   bur Duck Creek Mtg
    s of Eli & Elva P

DUCK CREEK

## GAUSE (Cont)
Samuel
Mary J
Ch: Rhoda b 3-11-1867 d 2-13-1868
bur Spiceland Mtg
Elkannah B b 8-30-1869

## GIBBONS
Sophiah d 10-16-1843 age 79-4-2 bur Fall Creek Mtg, Ind

## GREGG
(Stephen)
Hannah (Pickering) dt Jacob & Hannah d 7-26-1847
Duck Creek Mtg, Ind
Ch: Ann b 9-10-1814
Hannah b 5-10-1816
Asahel b 2-28-1817 d 10-15-1840
Duck Creek Mtg
Sarah b 6-12-1819
Emily b 5-14-1821
Lydia b 10-23-1822 d 8-20-1840
age 16-9-28 Duck Creek Mtg
Eliza b 3-23-1824
Mary b 6-3-1826 d 10-22-1840
age 14-5-24 Duck Creek Mtg

## GRIFFIN
Samuel b 1-22-1804 s Jacob & Mary
Lydia b 2-7-1804 dt Adam & Catharine Rinard
Ch: Jeremiah b 12-25-1823
Jacob b 1-3-1826
Adam b 1-2-1828

## HAMMER
Elisha b 6-19-1805 Randolph Co, N C s Abraham & Catharine
Nancy b 2-22-1798 Randolph Co, N C dt Peter & Abigail Lawrence
Ch: Isaac N b 5-19-1826
Abigail b 9-26-1829
Catharine b 10-21-1831
Peter b 12-13-1833
Mary b 5-26-1836

John d 3-14-1836 bur Fall Creek Mtg, Ind

## HAWORTH
Irena dt Ira & Asenath (Hunt) d 10-1-1851 age 1-3-9
bur Duck Creek Mtg

## HENLEY
Jabez H s Elias & Jane b 7-23-1810 Randolph Co, N C
Margaret (Holloway) dt Joseph & Eleanor b 4-17-1813
Belmont Co, Ohio
Ch: Elen S b 1-28-1843
Albert b 10-28-1845
David H b 12-6-1848
Mary Jane b 12-4-1853
John Arthur b 11-4-1860

## HESTON
Lovernia b 10-3-1866 dt Amos & Elvira

## HIATT
Aaron b 11-mo-1795 Grayson Co, Va s Absalom & Anna
Elizabeth b 10-17-1804 dt Abraham & Mahitabel Beals
(b Surry Co, N Car)
Ch: Amos b 2-15-1823
Eunice b 5-17-1825
Belinda
or Melinda? b 6-15-1827
Sintha H b 1-9-1829
Allen b 7-2-1833

Absolom
Ann
Ch: Cornelius b 6-1-1810 Highland Co, Ohio
Daniel b 7-3-1818 " " "

(Anthony)
Rebekah b 12-23-1810
Ch: Calvin b 11-9-1830
Daniel b 9-21-1838
Thomas b 10-27-1840

David b 4-3-1806 Kanhaway Co, Va s Richard & Sarah
Ruth b 7-6-1805 Stokes Co, N C dt Joshua & Letitia
Ratliff
Ch: Joshua b 7-20-1826
Margaret b 3-1-1828
Harriet b 5-15-1830
Gulielma b 8-17-1833
Oliver S b 4-12-1837
Richard R b 10-9-1840

George b 6-22-1757 s John & Sarah
Sarah b 6-13-1765 dt William & Elizabeth Stanley
Ch: Phebe b 6-10-1801 N C
William b 9-18-1803 "

(James)
Sina Jane dt Maxon & Lydia Dulea b 3-9-1825
Ch: Susan Elizabeth b 2-25-1843

Jesse
Phebe b 3-26-1806 Sevier Co, Tenn dt Nimrod & Ann
Dickey
Ch: Sarah Ann b 8-13-1842
David b 5-28-1844
Jane b 9-18-1845
Mary Elizabeth b 9-24-1847

Joel b 8-7-1818 (s Richard & Sarah)
Anna b 4-3-1818
Ch: Jesse H b 2-2-1838
John H b 3-26-1840
Rebecca Jane b 10-7-1842
Robert C b 5-22-1847
Nancy M b 11-27-1849

(John)
Rachel b 2-16-1783 Grayson Co, Va dt David & Elizabeth Reece
Ch: Henry b 8-28-1806 Grayson Co, Va
Greenberry b 2-8-1810 Highland Co, Ohio
Lydia b 11-23-1817 " " "
Mary b 11-29-1824 " " "

Malinda b 6-15-1827 dt Aaron & Elizabeth

Richard b 1-5-1775 Surry Co, Va s William & Susannah
Sarah b 3-10-1782 Grayson Co, Va dt David & Elizabeth Reece
Ch: Elizabeth Ann b 12-20-1801
Jacob b 1-19-1812
Jesse b 10-12-1815
Joel b 8-17-1818
James b 10-18-1821

William b 5-28-1804 Grayson Co, Va s Richard & Sarah
Martha b 1-27-1805 Randolph Co, N C dt John & Hannah
Presnall
Ch: Julian b 9-24-1829 Henry Co
Abigail b 7-15-1831 " "
Richard b 11-9-1833 " "
Martha b 8-13-1836 " "
Mary b 5-8-1839 " "
John G b 8-16-1842 " "
William Penn b 3-30-1844 " "
Lydia J b 11-12-1846 " "
Elizabeth b 5-10-1851

## HILL
Henry B
Lucretia
Ch: William Penn b 12-19-1830
Allen b 12-15-1832

John b 2-20-1797 Randolph Co, N C s Benjamin & Mary
Dinah b 9-4-1792 " " " dt Joseph & Dinah Cox
Ch: Joseph b 2-19-1818 Wayne Co, Ind
Mary ) b 1-18-1819 d 2-16-1819
bur Walnut Ridge P M
twins
Martha) b 1-18-1819
Benjamin C b 4-19-1820 Wayne Co, Ind
Nathan C b 12-3-1821 " " "
Ervin b 4-29-1823 " " "

DUCK CREEK

## HILL (Cont)
John & Dinah Ch (Cont)
    Sarah Ann        b 8- 7-1824   Wayne Co, Ind
    William R        b 7-19-1827   Rush Co, Ind
    Miriam Jane      b 3-24-1831     "   "   "

Jonathan   b 11-21-1795   Randolph Co, N C   s Thomas & Anna
Zilpha   b 7-14-1799   Wayne Co, N C   dt Rice, decd &
    Catharine Price
Ch:    Anna             b 10-15-1822
     Calvin           b 2-14-1825
     Robert           b 9- 7-1826   d 9- 4-1833
                                age 6-11-28   bur Duck Creek Mtg
     Synthia          b 1- 8-1829
     Matilda          b 12- 9-1830
     Elisha           b 6- 9-1833

Nathan
Elizabeth
Ch:    Robert           b 3- 2-1813
     Mary             b 9-14-1814
     Thomas           b 11-11-1817
     Sarah            b 7-13-1819
     Henley?          b 11-17-1820
     Eliza            b 2-25-1823
     Nathan           b 4-14-1825
     William S        b 10-16-1827

## HINSHAW
Benjamin   b 12-14-1782   Stokes Co, N C   s John & Ruth
Annis    b 5- 3-1790   Stokes Co, N C   dt William & Anna
     Bowman   d 11-30-1865   bur Duck Creek Mtg
Ch:    Seth             b 4- 5-1818   Randolph Co, N C
     Benjamin F       b 8- 6-1820    "    "    "
     Cyrus C          b 3- 2-1823    "    "    "
     David F          b 9- 3-1826    "    "    "
     Mille Mariah     b 8- 8-1828    "    "    "
     Elias            b 11- 9-1830   "    "    "

Jabez   b 8-24-1814   Randolph Co, N C   s Seth & Abigail
Mary   b 9- 9-1817    "    "    "   dt Henry & Rebecca
     Lamb
Ch:    Henry            b 6-14-1835   Randolph Co, N C
     Seth             b 5- 3-1837    "    "
     Elkannah         b 4-13-1840
     Hannah Ellen     b

John   b 10-23-1807   Stoke Co, N C   s Benjamin & Annis
   m 1st
(Sarah)
Ch:    Quinton          b 9-12-1830   N C
     Ruth             b 1-12-1832    "
   m 2nd
Anna   b 6-25-1814   Surry Co, N C   dt Joseph & Rebecca
     Ratliff
Ch:    Nathan R         b 7-31-1838
     Rebecca Ann      b 3- 8-1841

Seth   b 4-14-1787   Stokes Co, N C   s John & Ruth
Abigail   b 12- 4-1791   Randolph Co, N C   dt Peter & Mary
     Rich
Ch:    Diana            b 8-30-1817
     Asenath          b 11-21-1819
     Hannah           b 12-15-1824
     Mary             b 12-17-1826
     Ruth             b 8- 5-1828

Seth
Sarah
Ch:    Asabel           b 4-11-1839
     Terresa          b 7-29-1841
     Martha Mariah    b 2-11-1843
     William Henry    b 1-29-1845

William B   b 11-29-1808   Stoke Co, N C   s Benjamin & Annis
Hannah    b 12- 3-1814   Guilford Co, N C   dt Joseph &
     Hannah Coffin
Ch:    James Madison    b 8- 8-1832   Wayne Co, Ind
     Emily Jane       b 6-10-1834        "
     Elmina Louisa    b 9- 3-1835   Henry Co, Ind

## HOBSON
(Joseph)
Jane   b 1-19-1771   Cumberland Co, N C

Ch:    John S           b 8-17-1811
     David            b 7- 9-1814
     Allen            b 4- 5-1816

## HOLLOWAY
David    b 9-19-1805   s Joseph & Eleanor
Mary S   b 1-23-1812   (Pa dt Joseph & Mary Williams)
Ch:    Joseph W         b 12-29-1834
     Asa              b 10-18-1836
     Eliza            b 8-23-1838
     Hannah Anna      b 11- 8-1840
     Mary Ellen       b 1- 1-1843
     Nancy            b 9-17-1846
     Lydia Maria      b 5-23-1849
     Jason W          b 11-10-1851

Joseph
Eleanor   b 8- 4-1777   dt Jacob & Hannah Pickering
     d 6-15-1845   age 68 yrs   bur Duck Creek Mtg

## HOSIER
Nathan   b 12-12-1805   s William & Milicent
Alce    b 3- 7-1808   dt Jacob & Ann Elliott
Ch:    Hannah           b 7-24-1826
     Huldah           b 7- 2-1828

## HUBBARD
Hardy   b 12-23-1777   Mecklenburg Co, N C   s Joseph & Ann
Mary
Ch:    Anna             b 7-23-1799   Pearson Co, N C
     Martha           b 2-19-1808    "
     Susanna          b 2-10-1810   Guilford Co, N C
     Mary             b 6-15-1816    "
     Caleb            b 6-13-1819    "

Mary    d 5- 3-1832   Duck Creek Mtg, Ind

## HUNT
Allen   b 3- 6-1783   Guilford Co, N C   s Isom & Nancy
Huldah   b 3- 3-1784    "    "    "   dt Abel & Hannah
     Knight
Ch:    Nancy            b 9-17-1807
     Lucinda          b 11- 5-1811
     Rachel           b 8-20-1813
     Abel             b 6- 8-1818

Hanuel
(Eleanor (Newby))
Ch:    Asenath          b 6-15-1827   Highland Co, Ohio
     Ezra             b 1-12-1829    "
     Nancy Jane       b 1-11-1832    "
   m 2nd
Lucinda Dickey   b 1-14-1815   dt Nimrod & Ann
Ch:    James D          b 1-13-1836
     Cyrus            b 2-11-1838
     Josiah           b 9-14-1839
     Eleanor          b 7- 9-1842
     Libni            b 7-10-1844
     Ann              b 10- 7-1846
     Hannah           b 4- 7-1851

John   b 10-30-1760   Guilford Co, N C   s William & Sarah
Rachel   b ca 1757    "    "    "   dt Stephanus &
     Rachel Hayworth

Margaret    wid of Isom Sr   d 4-30-1846   age 75-1-28
     bur Duck Creek Mtg

Nathan   b 11-10-1795   Guilford Co, N C   s Isom & Nancy
Tamer   b 2- 4-1802    "    "    "   dt Joseph &
     Priscilla Pickett   d 11-11-1850   bur Duck Creek Mtg
Ch:    Asenath          b 12-27-1827
     Margaret         b 8- 8-1830
     Lucinda          b 4-27-1832
     William          b 5-25-1834   d 5-15-1835
     Beulah           b 8- 9-1836   d 8- 7-1854
                                 bur Duck Creek Mtg
     Isom             b 11- 5-1838
     Louisa           b 3-20-1840
     Nathan jr        b 8- 9-1842

DUCK CREEK

## HUTSON
Daniel  b  3- 2-1803  Randolph Co, N C  s Nathan & Lydia
Elizabeth  b  5- 2-1807  Surry Co, N C  dt William & Anna Maudlin
Ch: Anna          b 12-22-1824  Henry Co
    Richard       b  7-17-1826     "
    Levi          b  3- 4-1828     "
    James P       b 11-19-1830     "
    William       b 10-15-1832  d 7-10-1849
                    bur Clear Spring Mtg
    Milton        b  1- 7-1834
    Joel R        b  5-25-1838
    Seth          b  4- 6-1840
    Daniel jr     b  5-25-1842
    Elizabeth R   b  1-18-1844
    Mary Helen    b 12- 6-1846
    Thomas C      b 12- 3-1848

(John)
Margaret  b 12- 5-1801  Chatham Co, NC  dt Abner & Sarah Ratliff
Ch: Sarah Ann     b 12-28-1826  Clinton Co, Ohio
                  d  9-27-1838  bur Clear Springs

Nathan  b  8- 1-1778  Randolph Co, N C  s Richard & Sarah
Lydia  b  6-13-1784     "         "    dt Daniel & Martha Presnall
Ch: Sarah         b  9-30-1805  Back Creek Mtg, NC
    James         b  2-25-1808       "
    Huldah        b  1-30-1810       "
    Nancy         b  3-14-1812       "
    Penelope      b  2- 9-1814       "
    Lydia         b  7-29-1816       "

## JAMES
Evan  b 10-11-1784  s of Samuel & Hannah
Rebeckah  b  4-21-1789  dt Samuel & Phebe Pickering
Ch: Hannah        b  5- 8-1808
    Phebe         b 12- 2-1809
    Jonas         b  5-31-1812
    Jesse K       b  5-30-1814
    Samuel        b  3-13-1817
    Joshua        b  6-11-1818
    Mary          b  8- 6-1820
    Joel E        b  8-23-1826
    Jehu          b  6-24-1829

Isaac  b  8-31-1763  York Co, Pa  s Thomas & Sarah
Leah (Webb)  b  8- 8-1786  Wayne Co, N C  dt Benjamin & Lydia Morris  (see also Webb)

## JESSOP
Elias  b  8-31-1794  Stokes Co, N C  s Pratt & Hope
Ann  b  7-10-1788  Guilford Co, NC  dt of Joseph & Hannah Haskins
Ch: Jesse B       b  1-19-1824

Tidamon  b  9-27-1800  s Pratt W & Hope
Lydia  b  1-15-1809  Pasquotank Co, NC  dt Joshua & Mary Morris
Ch: Morris        b  9- 4-1826  Wayne Co, Ind
    David         b  2- 1-1828
    Susanna       b  9-20-1829
    Mary          b  3-15-1830
    Ruth          b  2- 1-1833

## KENDALL
Cyrus  b  9-21-1821  s Thomas & Elizabeth
Lydia  b  5-29-1822  dt Joel & Lydia Gilbert
Ch: Marcus Ratliff  b 10- 2-1857  (s Millicent Ratliff)
    "a bound boy"

David  b 7-30-1815  Guilford Co, NC  d  8- 4-1866 bur
  m 1st                                      Cadiz, Ind
Charity  b 11-15-1812  Highland Co, Ohio  d 4- 6-1847
    Clear Springs Mtg - (Duck Creek MM, Ind)
Ch: Silas         b  7- 5-1840  Henry Co, Ind
    Elizabeth Ann b  9-15-1842       "
    Jane          b  5-25-1846       "
  m 2nd
Mary (Cook)  d  7-24-1849  (Harrison twp, Henry Co, Ind)
Ch: Isaac         b  1- 2-1849  d 1-15-1850
  m 3rd                 bur Clear Springs Mtg, Ind
Irena (Jessop)
Ch: Susannah      b  2-21-1853
    Priscilla L   b 12-18-1855  d  6- 3-1868
                    bur Cadiz, Ind
    Thomas C      b 10-27-1858

    Hannah Eliza  b  3- 3-1863

Dennis  b  6-23-1827  Wayne Co, Ind  s Thomas & Elizabeth
Rebecca Jane (Hill)  b 12- 9-1831  Wayne Co, Ind  dt
    Harmon & Mary (Henley)  d 10- 4-1866  bur Cadiz, Ind
Ch: Margaretta    b  1- 4-1850
    Albert        b  8- 6-1851
    Henry         b  5-31-1853
    Harmon H      b  7-22-1855
    Mary Elizabeth b  4-11-1858
    William Harvey b  1- 7-1860
    Micajah       b  2- 3-1862
    Joel Z        b  2-28-1864
    Rebecca J jr  b  9-27-1866  d 10- 5-1866
                    bur Cadiz, Ind

Thomas  d  8- 4-1862  age 76-7-3 at Duck Creek Mtg
    bur at Whitewater Mtg, Ind

## KENWORTHY
Jesse  b  8- 6-1822  Warren Co, Ohio  s Amos & Mary
Eliza (Gregg)  b  3-23-1824  Henry Co  dt Stephen & Hannah
Ch: Ambrose A     b  8- 6-1843
    Mary Elizabeth b  4-11-1845
    Emily J       b  5-16-1846
    Hannah Ann    b  3-31-1850
    Seth H        b  2-27-1854

## KIRK
Edith  d 10-26-1858  bur Clear Springs Mtg

Jesse W  b 11-29-1831  Ohio
Sarah M  b  8-10-1839
Ch: Cora M        b  5-29-1864
    Eva           b  6- 7-1866  d 8-12-1868
                    bur Duck Creek Mtg

Thomas  b  3-21-1781  Pa  s Thomas & Hannah
Sarah  b 10-17-1793  dt Jacob & Hannah Taylor
    d  9- 5-1837  (Duck Creek)
Ch: Israel        b 12-26-1810  Clearfield Co, Pa
    Hannah        b  2- 7-1813       "
    Elizabeth     b  4- 1-1815       "
    Mary Ann      b  8-26-1817  Clinton Co, Ohio
    Rachel H      b  1-20-1820
    Jacob         b  2-10-1822  d 9-mo-1823
                    Clinton Co, Ohio
    Thomas C      b  4-14-1825
    Naomi         b  6-19-1827
    Allen T       b 11-15-1829
    Jesse W       b 11- 9-1831

## LAMB
Martha  b 11-21-1798  Randolph Co, N C  dt Nathan & Lydia Hutson

## LEWELLING
Henderson  b 4-23-1809  Randolph Co, NC  s Meschach & Jane
Elizabeth  b  4- 8-1815     "       "   dt John & Hannah Presnall
Ch: Alfred        b 11-30-1831
    Mary          b  3-14-1833
    Asenath       b 12- 6-1834

Henry  b 10-14-1807  Randolph Co, NC  s Meschack & Jane
    (d 6-mo-1850  (see 1850 mortality census))
Rachel (Presnall)  b 12-31-1806  Randolph Co, N C
    dt John & Hannah
Ch: (Jonathan     b  1-14-1828)  d 5-10-1848
                    bur Clear Spring Mtg
    Jane B        b  2-27-1830
    John          b 12-14-1831
    Jehu          b  1-22-1834
    Meschach      b  9- 2-1836  d 5-18-1844
                    bur Duck Creek
    Elizabeth     b  5- 2-1839
    Hannah H      b  1- 5-1842
    Henry Clayton b 12-18-1843
    Martha Ann    b  8- 4-1846
    Rachel E      b  8- 8-1849

John  b  1-16-1811  Randolph Co, N C  s Meschach & Jane
Elvy  b 10-11-1815  dt Jacob & Ann Elliott
Ch: Sarah         b  6-29-1834

DUCK CREEK

## LEWELLING (Cont)
Meshack  b  1-29-1787  Randolph Co, N C   d 11-30-1840
    bur at Meshack Lewelling's burial place Henry Co, Ind
    s William & Mary
  m 1st
Jane (Brookshire) b 8-25-1789 Randolph Co, N C
    d 8-11-1835 bur at Meshack Lewelling's burial
    place, Henry Co, Ind  dt Thomas & Sarah
  Ch: Henry           b 10-14-1807  Randolph Co, N C
      Henderson       b  4-23-1809        "
      John            b  1-16-1811        "
      Mary            b  5-11-1815        "
      William         b  9-28-1817        "
      Seth            b  3- 6-1820        "
      Thomas          b  8-29-1822  Henry Co, Ind
      Jane            b  8-21-1825        "
  m 2nd
Margaret (Williams) b 12-23-1809 Deep River Mtg, N C
  Ch: Harrison        b  7-25-1838  Henry Co, Ind
      Jefferson W     b 12- 9-1839        "
      Meshack jr      b  2- 8-1841        "

## LOWDER
Samuel  b  1-26-1772  Orange Co, N C  s John & Hannah
Elizabeth
  Ch: Sarah           b 12-18-1809  Wilkes Co, N C
      Thomas          b  8-21-1811        "
      Miriam          b  1-19-1813        "
      Mary            b  3-13-1816        "
      Emily           b 12- 1-1819        "
      Phineas         b  4-16-1821        "
      Hiram           b 11-25-1823        "
      Elizabeth       b  8- 1-1826        "

## McGREW
Squire L   b  4-27-1836
Lucinda    b  5-22-1844
  Ch: Wilma Gertrude   b 3-15-1866

## MACY
Francis B  b  9-18-1810  Montgomery Co, Ohio  s Stephen
    & Rebecca
Huldah   b  5-28-1807  Guilford Co, N C  dt Isom &
    Margaret Hunt
  Ch: Rebecca Ann     b  6-20-1835
      Margaret Jane   b 10- 9-1836
      John Lilburn    b  9-27-1839
      Loretta Mariah  b  3- 2-1842

Gardner
Margaret (Wilson) b 7-28-1811  dt William
  Ch: Sally Ann       b  8-20-1835
      James           b 10-18-1837
      Lydia           b  3-23-1841
      Lurana          b  7-16-1843

Henry    b  5-31-1801  Guilford Co, N C  s Thaddeus &
    Catherine
Penninah   b  9-16-1811  dt Jonathan & Elizabeth Jessop
  Ch: Ann H           b  7-11-1831  Rush Co, Ind

Nathan   b  8-10-1803  s Thaddeus & Catherine
Jane A   b 10-22-1810  Jefferson Co, Tenn  dt Jacob & Jane
  Ch: Whitecel D      b 12-26-1833

Pemberton  b  1-29-1825  Union Co, Ind  s Nathan &
    Catharine
Nancy Ann  b 10-22-1824  Tenn  dt Thomas & Elizabeth
                                             Ellis
  Ch: Robert P        b  4-29-1846
      Catharine E     b 11-27-1847
      Nathan T        b  3-11-1850

Stephen  b 12- 4-1778  Guilford Co N C  s Enoch & Anna

William  b  1-20-1799  Guilford Co, N C  s Thaddeus &
    Catherine
Phebe  b  6-10-1801  Guilford Co, N C  dt George & Sarah
                                                  Hiatt
  Ch: Anna            b 11-27-1820
      Calvin          b 10- 3-1822
      Susanna         b  3-16-1824
      Luzena          b  8- 9-1825
      Jason           b  4-25-1827
      Terrel          b 12-24-1828
      Sarah Jane      b 12-12-1830
      Catharine       b  7-27-1832
      Rebecca         b  4- 9-1834
      Seth            b 11-24-1835

## MARSHALL
Joseph  b  8- 1-1818  d 9- 8-1843  s Isaac & Ruth
Elizabeth (Edgerton) (b 10-22-1818)
  Ch: Ruth J          b  1-17-1844  Henry Co, Ind

Thomas  b 10- 5-1795  Surry Co, N C  s Joseph & Ruth

## MAUDLIN - MODLIN
Ann  b  5-16-1750  Perquimans Co, N C  dt William &
    Jemima Newby

Elias  (b 5-10-1817 Wayne Co, Ind)  s George & Sarah
    ?
  Ch: Lydia           b  4-19-1841
      Seth     )      b 11-26-1843
      Sarah Ann) twins b 11-26-1843
  m 2nd
Martha (Ratliff) (b 5-11-1820 Wayne Co, Ind) dt Nathan
    & Lydia   d 11-25-1857  bur Duck Creek Mtg
  Ch: Rebecca P       b  3- 7-1854
      Huldah L        b 11- 8-1856
      Jason R         b 11-17-1857
  m 3rd
Ann (Dawson) (b 7-31-1835) d 4-22-1863 age ca 27 yrs
    bur Cadiz, Ind  (dt Isaac & Sarah)
  Ch: Minerva J       b  1-17-1860
      Emma T          b 11-30-1861
  m 4th
Emily Jane   b  2- 9-1829
  Ch: Mary Ann        b  - - - -

George
Sarah
  Ch: Dillon          b  5-12-1813  Wilkes Co, N C
      Reuben          b  5-29-1815        "
      Elias           b  5-10-1817  Wayne Co, Ind
      Mark            b 10-28-1819        "
      Leah            b  2-20-1821        "
      Jacob           b  1-13-1824        "

Joseph  b  5- 8-1775  s John & Ann
Vilet   d  6-16-1848  age 72-5-26  bur Clear Springs Mtg
  Ch: Nathan          b 10- 9-1801
      Ann             b  8-20-1803
      John            b  2-22-1805
      William         b  8-27-1806
      Thomas          b  8- 6-1808
      (Newby          b  ca   1810)
      Mark            b 10-26-1813
      Hannah          b 12- 1-1815
      Elwood          b  6- 3-1818
      Elias           b 11- 1-1823

Richard  b  5- 5-1841  s William jr & Elizabeth Ann
Mary Ann   b 11-29-1844
  Ch: Emma Ora        b  6-20-1864
      Laura Edith     b 10-27-1865
      Elizabeth       b 11- 5-1870
      Oliver W        b  7- 2-1872

Thomas  (s Benjamin & Leah) b 1-23-1804  N C
Hannah (Sheridan) b 2-24-1802
  Ch: Sarah           b  9- 1-1823
      Elizabeth       b  2-16-1825
      Benjamin        b  2-11-1827
      Margaret        b  2-18-1829
      John            b  3-25-1831  d 10-26-1831
           bur Spiceland Mtg, Ind

William jr
Elizabeth Ann
  Ch: Oliver H        b  1-21-1835  Henry Co, Ind
      Mary Margart    b  3-20-1837        "
      Albert D        b  3- 7-1839        "
      John     )      b  5- 5-1841        "
      Richard) twins  b  5- 5-1841        "
      Lindley M       b 10- 3-1847        "
      Minerva J       b  2- 3-1850        "

DUCK CREEK

MENDENHALL
Taylor W        b  5- 1-1836
Lydia Ann       b  4- 3-1840  dt Samuel & Cynthia Pickering
Ch:  Lelia A            b  8-24-1858
     Samuel P           b 10-27-1863

MEREDITH
James Harvey    b  4-15-1819  N C  s James & Mary
Eliza B         b  9-22-1823  dt John & Elizabeth Stanley
Ch:  Jane               b  7-15-1846
     Oliver             b 12-15-1847

Jesse
Luzena
Ch:  Charles O          b 10-16-1844
     Franklin           b 10- 4-1846
     Melissa Ann        b  4-12-1848
     Anne Jane          b  2- 7-1850
     John               b 12-16-1851
     James H            b  9- 1-1854

MILLS
Eber    b  8-22-1828  s Hugh & Lydia
Elizabeth  b 10-23-1833  Randolph Co, N C  dt Elizabeth
     & Eli Stafford
Ch:  Ada                b  5- 9-1856
     Alice              b  4-22-1859
     Eli                b  9-26-1862
     Seth               b  6-26-1865
     Anna               b  8-13-1868
     Owen               b  - - - - -

MOORE
Abraham        b  6- 2-1786  Chester Co, Pa  s of John & Mary
(Susannah)
Ch:  Hannah             b  3-18-1812  Chester Co, Pa
     Jacob              b  9-24-1816  Ohio
  m 2nd
Hannah   b  2- 9-1787  Pa  dt Ezekiel & Hannah Kirk
Ch:  Abraham jr         b  7-26-1824  Ohio
     Sarah              b  6-18-1826    "
     Rachel             b  3-22-1828    "

John  b  8-31-1798  Pa  d  9-17-1847  bur Clear Spring
     Mtg, Ind    s Thomas & Sarah
Ann (Moore)  b  7- 6-1805  Pa  dt Elijah & Sarah
Ch:  Sarah              b 11-30-1828  Clinton Co, Ohio
     Martha Ann         b 12-31-1830       "
     Thomas             b  2-19-1833
     Elizabeth          b  6- 5-1835
     Rebecca J          b  3- 1-1838
     Mary               b 11-10-1840
     John W             b 11-18-1842
     Nancy E            b  7- 6-1845

Samuel   b  6-21-1792  Perquimans Co, N C  s Samuel &
     Margaret
Rebecca  b  4- 5-1804     "         "   dt Jesse & Mary
                                            White
Ch:  Joshua             b 12- 2-1826
     Jesse W            b 10-18-1828  d 12- 4-1829  Rush
       Co, Ind    bur Walnut Ridge Mtg
     Mary               b  8-24-1830
     Margaret           b  8-11-1832

MORGAN
Hezekiah    b  2- 6-1796  Guilford Co, N C  s Thomas &
     d  8- 2-1836  bur Fall Creek Mtg, Ind    Ruth
Lydia (Hammer)  b  3-17-1799  Jefferson Co, Tenn
     dt Isaac & Hannah
Ch:  Obadiah            b  2-20-1817  Jefferson Co, Tenn
     Henry              b  4- 9-1818       "
     Thomas             b 12-24-1819       "
     Isaac              b  2- 3-1822       "
     James              b  4- 5-1824       "
     Hannah             b  7-13-1826       "
     Rebecca            b 11-24-1827       "
     Zeno               b 11-26-1829       "
     Nathan             b  9-25-1831       "
     Damarius           b  2-17-1834  Madison Co, Ind
     Hezekiah           b 11-10-1836       "

Obediah    b  2- 6-1796  Guilford Co, N C    s Thomas & Ruth

162

Ann (Jones)  b  7-21-1803  Blount Co, Tenn  dt Thomas &
                                                Margaret
Ch:  Hezekiah           b 11-23-1821  Tenn
     Margaret J         b  7-27-1823    "
     Thomas             b  5-11-1826    "
     Sophiah            b  7-27-1828    "
     Joseph             b 12-10-1830    "
     William T          b  1-13-1833    "
     Mary Ann           b  7-17-1835  Indiana

MORRIS
Reuben
Miriam
Ch:  Benjamin           b 10-29-1808
     John               b  2- 7-1811
     Joseph             b  9-22-1813
     Sarah              b 10-10-1816
     Levi               b  1-30-1819
     Samuel             b  7-29-1821
     Mary               b 12-21-1823

NEWBY
Elias  b 10-16-1798  N C  s Joseph & Penelope
Lydia  b  1-15-1803  N C  dt John & Hannah Presnall
     d  2- 6-1835  bur Clear Spring Mtg, Ind
Ch:  William P          b  1-11-1824
     Mary               b  4-22-1826
     Penelope           b  5-16-1828
     Lydia              b  3- 8-1830
     Jane               b  2-15-1834
  m 2nd
Tabitha
Ch:  Eliza Ann)         b  2-14-1841
     Elizabeth D) twins b  2-14-1841

Henry  b  8- 8-1795  N C  s Joseph & Penelope
Sarah  b  8-22-1800  N C  (dt Thomas & Miriam Thornburg)
Ch:  Penelope           b 10-23-1819  N C
     Abigail            b 10-30-1821    "
     Milly              b  4-20-1824    "
     Mary               b  8-13-1826    "
     William            b 10-28-1829    "
     Phebe              b  9-20-1831    "

Jesse  b 11-22-1828  s Thomas & Susanna

Joseph A  b  3-19-1869  s James & Delphina
Ettie R   b 10-16-1872

(Thomas)
Sarah  b 11-16-1798  Randolph Co, N C  dt Thomas &
     Sarah Brookshire
Ch:  Jane               b  6-22-1822  N C
     William            b  4-13-1824    "
     Alfred             b  4-29-1826    "
     Joshua             b  5- 1-1830    "
     Charity            b  1-26-1832  Henry Co, Ind
     John               b  4-11-1833    "
     James              b  1- 6-1835    "

William  d  5-30-1831  age 87-4-30 at Duck Creek Mtg
     bur Spiceland Mtg, Ind

William P
Louisa M
Ch:  Morton E           b 11-27-1864
     Cyrus K            b  3-19-1868  d 8-25-1868
                             bur Cadiz, Ind

NEWSOM
Luke  b 12-15-1802  Randolph Co, NC  s Ranson & Sarah
Elizabeth  b  9-24-1800  Randolph Co, N C  dt Jesse &
     Mary Hill
Ch:  Martha             b  7-24-1826
     Henry              b  9-22-1828
     Elizabeth          b  7-16-1833
     Jabez              b 12-25-1830

NIXON
Anna (Ratliff) Maudlin  d  6-12-1868  age 82-3-8
     bur Clear Springs Mtg

DUCK CREEK

## NORTON
Dennis   b 12-25-1805   Randolph Co, N C   s Richard & Elizabeth
Sarah   b 8-17-1805   Guilford Co, N C   d 9-23-1846 dt William & Anna Bowman
- Ch:
  - Anna Jane   b 4-19-1831   Stokes Co, N C
  - Elizabeth Caroline   6- 8-1833   "
  - Rebecca   b 5- 2-1835   Henry Co
  - Delphina   b 1-11-1840   "
  - Mary   b 3-10-1842
  - Nancy Mariah   b 11- 3-1845   d 1-14-1849

Edward   b 8-15-1808
Nancy   b 7-13-1810
- Ch:
  - Dennis K   b 12- 7-1833
  - Amy   b 8-17-1838

Richard   b 3-27-1784   Randolph Co, N C   d 6-27-1853 bur Clear Springs Mtg   age 69-3-0
Elizabeth   b 3-23-1773   Randolph Co, N C   d 12-21-1843 age 70-8-28   bur Duck Creek Mtg

## PALMER
David   b 9-20-1797   Stokes Co, N C   d 10- 7-1877 bur Clear Springs Mtg, Ind
m 1st
Sarah   (b 11-10-1799   Randolph Co, N C)   (dt Nathan & Huldah Pearson)   (d ca between 1836 & 1840   Henry Co, Ind)
- Ch:
  - Pearson   b 12-28-1822   Indiana
  - Nathan   b 2-11-1824   "
  - Elias   b 8-23-1827   "
  - Asenath   b 6-10-1830   "
  - John P   b 8- 1-1833   "
  - Hannah B   b 2-15-1836   "
m 2nd
Mary (Ratliff) Elliott   wid of John Elliott Sr
     b 5-22-1799   Randolph Co, N C   d 3- 5-1865
     bur Clear Springs Mtg, Ind

Elias   b 8-23-1827   Ind   s David & Sarah
(Eunice W (Coggeshall))
- Ch:
  - James O   b 1-11-1850   Ind
  - Harriett Ellen   b 5-18-1859   "

John P   b 8- 1-1835   s David & Sarah
Hannah L   b 6- 7-1836   dt Isaac & Mary Ratliff
- Ch:
  - William I   b 5-11-1859
  - Hannah E   b 7-31-1865

Pearson   b 12-28-1822   s David & Sarah
Lydia   b 3- 8-1830   dt Elias & Lydia Newby
- Ch:
  - William F   b 12-30-1845   d 1-25-1848 bur Clear Spring Mtg
  - Isaac E   b 1-20-1848
  - John M   b 8-21-1850   d 9-13-1851 bur Clear Spring Mtg
  - Asenath Jane   b 8-16-1852
  - Mary Louisa   b 10-27-1855
  - Joseph P   b 1- 9-1861

Sarah   b 11-10-1799   Randolph Co, N C   dt Nathan & Huldah

Sarah Ann   d 11- 1-1846   age 2-2-10   bur Clear Spring Mtg

## PATTERSON - PATTISON
Hezekiah   b 11- 6-1798   Tenn
Elizabeth   b 11-25-1802
- Ch:
  - Joseph   b 7-28-1824
  - Sarah E   b 9-25-1828
  - Eli   b 10-14-1830
  - Levi C   b 4-17-1834
  - Margaret   b 1- 5-1839
  - Milton   b 10-10-1842
  - John W   b 12- 4-1844

## PAYNE
Joel R   b 6-21-1835   d 9- 9-1865   bur Cadiz, Ind s John & Sarah
Martha C (Hastings)   b 4-30-1835   dt William & Jane
- Ch:
  - William H   b 7- 6-1856
  - John Clarkson   b 3- 6-1858   d 1-15-1861 bur Cadiz, Ind
  - Emma Jane   b 8- 6-1860
  - Rebecca E   b 3- 3-1863

John W
Eliza Ann (Newby)   b 2-14-1841   (d 5- 7-1915, drowned, see Spiceland records)   dt Elias & 2nd w Tabitha
- Ch:
  - Mary Elizabeth   b 2-18-1866

## PEARSON
Bailey   b 2-24-1807   Randolph Co, N C   s Nathan & Mary
Jane   b 10-28-1808   Randolph Co, N C   dt Joseph & Rebecca Ratliff
- Ch:
  - Asenath   b 8- 4-1828   Henry Co
  - Anna   b 2-13-1830   "
  - Calvin   b 5- 7-1831   "
  - Levi   b 12-12-1832   "

Enos   b 6- 1-1824   s Exum & Elizabeth
Anna   b 12-22-1824   dt Daniel & Elizabeth Hutson
- Ch:
  - Margaret H   b 9- 7-1845   d 9-17-1845 bur Clear Spring Mtg
  - Emery R   b 9-24-1846   d 1- 1-1851 bur Clear Spring Mtg
  - Alpheus W   b 2-21-1854   d 1-21-1860 bur Clear Spring Mtg
  - Cascius M Clay   b 3-15-1861

(Exum)   d 8-22-1875   bur Clear Spring Mtg, Ind
Elizabeth (Ratliff)   b 11-10-1805   N C   dt Richard & Elizabeth
- Ch:
  - Enos   b 6- 1-1824
  - Sarah   b 1-18-1830
  - Seth   b 2-27-1832
  - Mary   b 1- 8-1834
  - Margaret   b 4-24-1836
  - Abigail   b 8- 7-1842
  - Cornelius D   b 12-18-1844

Isaiah   b 5-19-1833   s Jonathan

Levi   b 4- 4-1803   Randolph Co, N C   s Nathan & Mary
   d 12-22-1832   bur Duck Creek Mtg, Ind
m 1st
Huldah (Thomas)   b 4- 7-1809   dt John & Lydia (d ca 1828   Duck Creek Mtg, Ind)
- Ch:
  - Hiram   b 10- 7-1826
  - Sarah   b 12- 7-1827
m 2nd
Rachel (Presnall)
- Ch:
  - Reuben   b 6-30-1830
  - Enos   b 9-30-1831

Nathan   b 10-25-1770   Perquimans Co, N C   d 11-13-1845 bur Clear Springs Mtg, Ind   s Jonathan & Sarah
Huldah (Lamb)   b 3- 9-1778   Randolph Co, N C dt Jacob & Sarah
- Ch:
  - Sarah   b 11-10-1799   Randolph Co, N C
  - Catharine   b 10-12-1806   Surry Co, N C
  - Huldah jr   b 3- 1-1809   "   "
  - Aaron   b 11-12-1811   "   "
  - Rhoda   b 3- 3-1814   Wayne Co, Ind
  - Joseph   b 11- 7-1816   "   "
  - Nathan jr   b 3- 2-1819   "   "
  - Zimri   b 3- 4-1821   "   "

Peter   b 4-19-1797   Randolph Co, N C   s Nathan & Mary
Eunice   b 12- 1-1803   "   "   "   dt William & Sarah Hastings
- Ch:
  - Enoch   b 6-18-1822   Wayne Co, Ind
  - Isom   b 6-30-1824   "   "   "
  - Nancy   b 4-29-1827
  - Aaron   b 4-26-1830

Seth
Sarah
- Ch:
  - Eliza Jane   b 7-15-1854

## PENNINGTON
Josiah   b 2-17-1780   Baltimore Co, Md   s (Daniel) or (David?) & Martha
Deborah   b 4- 9-1782   Brush Creek, Frederick Co, Md dt John & Mary Talbot
- Ch:
  - Levi T   b 4-30-1812   Belmont Co, Ohio
  - Mary   b 10- 9-1813   "
  - Susannah   b 7-18-1815   "
  - John   b 3-15-1817   "
  - Eliza   b 11-30-1818   "
  - Rachel   b 3- 8-1821   "

DUCK CREEK

## PHELPS
Frederick  b  7-11-1827  s Samuel & Sarah
    d  3- 7-1863  bur Cadiz Mtg, Ind
Elizabeth  b  2-14-1841  dt Elias & 2nd w Tabitha Newley
Ch:  Charles A  b  8- 3-1862

## PICKERING
Abner  b  3- 9-1805  Belmont Co, Ohio  s Jonas & Ruth
    d  9-23-1853  bur Duck Creek Mtg, Ind
  m 1st
Charity (Hasket)  b 12-17-1804  Ohio  d 5-26-1836
    bur Duck Creek Mtg, Ind  dt Thomas & Ann
Ch:  Sarah Ann          b  1-14-1829
    Calvin W           b 10-19-1830  d 9-10-1846
      bur Duck Creek Mtg
    Abagail            b  3-12-1833
    Charity jr         b  5-19-1836  d 10-19-1836
      bur Duck Creek Mtg
  m 2nd
Jennet (Saint)  b  2- 8-1816  dt William & Achsah
Ch:  Martha             b  8-15-1838
    Achsah             b  9-29-1840  d 1-20-1843
      bur Duck Creek Mtg
    Infant dt          b  7- 8-1842  d infant
    Thomas S           b 12-22-1843
    Infant son         b 11-10-1845  d infant
    Julia Ann          b 10-25-1846
    William Exum       b  8-27-1849

David  b  7-26-1788  d 6-25-1868  bur Cadiz Mtg, Ind

Jacob jr  b  5- 8-1786  Frederick Co, Va  s Jacob &
    Hannah
Rachel (Hurford)  b  9-20-1787  dt John & Sarah
Ch:  Sarah Ann     b  6-15-1817  Harrison Co, Ohio
    Aquilla       b 12-11-1820          "
    Elihu         b  8-24-1823          "
    Naomi         b  7- 7-1828          "

Jonas Sr
Ruth (Gregg)
Ch:  Abner         b  3- 9-1805  Belmont Co, Ohio
    Abigail       b  8-25-1806      "        "
    Samuel        b 11-30-1807      "        "
    Sarah         b  4- 7-1809      "        "
    Phebe         b  6-30-1811      "        "
    Jonas jr      b  9- 8-1812      "        "
    Mahlon        b  6-15-1814      "        "
    Ruthanna      b  2-25-1816      "        "
    Joseph        b  1-27-1818      "        "
    Jordon        b  5-31-1820      "        "

Jonas jr  b  9- 8-1812
Mary  b  3-23-1818
Ch:  Mary Ann           b  5-26-1845

Jonathan E  b  9- 5-1812  Ohio  s Jacob jr & Rachel
Tirzah (Cooper)  b  8- 4-1812  dt Caleb & Ruth
Ch:  Lindley M          b 10-18-1835  Henry Co, Ind

Margaret (form Reece)  is deceased; rptd by Cadiz Mtg
    11-25-1852

Samuel  b 11-30-1808  s Jonas & Ruth
Cynthia  b 11-23-1808  dt John jr & Elizabeth Maulsby
Ch:  Larkin             b 11-23-1830  d 8-16-1841
      bur Duck Creek Mtg
    Elizabeth          b  6-22-1833
    Lindley            b 12-16-1835
    Henry              b  2- 8-1838
    Lydia Ann          b  4- 5-1840
    Macy               b  6-10-1842

William  s John & Jane
Sarah (Willets)  b  7-17-1799  Stokes Co, N C
    d  1- 4-1851  bur Duck Creek Mtg, Ind
Ch:  Lucinda            b 11-15-1837
    Seth               b  9-23-1839
    Ida                b  1- 8-1841

## PICKETT - PIGGOTT
Joseph  b  2- 1-1778  d 4- 7-1846  bur Duck Creek Mtg
  s Jeremiah & Charity (Moon)

Priscilla (Wickersham)  b 10- 1-1773  d 11-11-1844
  bur Duck Creek Mtg, Ind  dt Jehu & Mary
Ch:  Tamar         b  2- 4-1802
    Anna          b 11-21-1803
    Lydia         b  3- 1-1806
    Mary          b  4-30-1808
    Sarah         b  2-24-1811
    Joseph        b  7-25-1814

## PITTS
Cadwallader  b  1-30-1787  Stokes Co, N C  d 12-16-1855
    bur Duck Creek Mtg, Ind
  m 1st
Elizabeth  b  3- 5-1788  Guilford Co, N C  d 12-27-1842
    bur Duck Creek Mtg, Ind
Ch:  Sarah Ann     b  8-18-1817  Stokes Co, N C
    Eliza Jane    b  7-23-1824      "        "
    (a motherless boy, under care of Cadwallader &
    Elizabeth Pitts) Nathan Pike  s Nathan jr
    b 12-29-1830  Union Mtg, N C
  m 2nd
Mary (Chamness)  b  2- 6-1800  Randolph Co, N C
  dt William & Isabel

## PRESNALL
Benoni
Jane (Moon)
Ch:  Jeremiah      b  3-11-1828  Ohio
    William       b  9-31-1829    "
    James         b  2- 4-1831    "
    Henry         b  5-17-1832    "
    Mary          b  3-16-1834  Ind
    Ruth          b  9- 1-1836    "
    Sarah Ann     b  7- 6-1838    "

Daniel Sr  b  3-15-1748  Va  s Jacob & Martha
    d 11-16-1830  bur Duck Creek Mtg, Ind
Christina (Stone)  b 11-16-1754  Perquimans Co, N C
  dt John & Catharine Stone

Daniel  b 11-29-1786  Randolph Co, N C  s Daniel &
            Martha
Pleasant (Maudlin)  b  6-13-1784  Perquimans Co, N C
  dt John & Ann
Ch:  Sarah            b 11-22-1811  Randolph Co, N C
    Daniel)          b  6- 4-1814      "        "
    John  ) twins   b  6- 4-1814      "        "
    Nathan)          b  2-25-1818      "        "
    Henry ) twins   b  2-25-1818      "        "

Daniel  b  2- 1-1810  Randolph Co, N C  s John & Hannah
Huldah (Ratliff)  b 11-30-1812  Surry Co, N C
  dt Joseph & Rebecca
Ch:  Rebecca J      b  3-11-1834
    Hannah L       b 12- 6-1835
    Joseph J G     b  4- 6-1838
    Lindley M      b  7- 5-1840
    Jesse R        b  1-12-1843
    Reuben         b  8- 7-1845  d 10-18-1846
      bur Clear Springs Mtg
    Cynthia        b  4- 7-1848
    Elizabeth      b  4-23-1850

Dempsey
Eliza
Ch:  John Temple    b  1- 7-1866
    William D      b 11- 9-1868

James
Anna (Brown)
Ch:  Alfred         b 10- 8-1847
    Martha         b 10-28-1848
    James L        b  6- 7-1850
    Maria          b  3- 7-1852
    Harvey         b 11- 3-1854
    Mary M         b  8-16-1857
    Asbery         b  6-26-1859  d 5-26-1860
    Sarah E        b  2-23-1861  d 3-15-1861
    Francis M      b 11- 6-1863

Jehu
Eliza Jane

DUCK CREEK

PRESNALL (Cont)
Ch: of Jehu & Eliza Jane
    Charles F    b 1- 4-1849
    Bowen B    b 10-15-1850
    Louisa S    b 12-19-1852
    John T    b 8-17-1855
    Phineas R    b 6-22-1858
    Eli A    b 9-15-1860
    Mary Ann    b 1-31-1863
    Martha Jane    b 1-31-1863
    Elizabeth    b 10-16-1866
    William Henry    b 5-31-1868

John b 2-17-1778 Dist 96, S C s Daniel Sr & Martha
Hannah (Littler) b 11-14-1784 Chatham Co, N C
    dt Mincher & Deborah d 1-10-1862 bur Clear
    Springs Mtg, Ind
Ch: Lydia    b 1-15-1803 Randolph Co, N C
    Martha    b 1-27-1805 "
    Rachel    b 12-26-1806 "
    Daniel    b 2- 1-1810 "
    Mary    b 7-23-1812 "
    Elizabeth    b 4- 8-1815 "
    Jeremiah    b 4-12-1818 "
    John M    b 1-24-1821 "
        d 6-29-1848 bur Clear Spring
    Jehu    b 4-18-1824 Randolph Co, N C
    Hannah    b 2-17-1828 "

Nathan b 12- 7-1802 Randolph Co, N C s Stephen & Hannah

Hannah b 9- 7-1812

Stephen b 9-11-1773 N C (d prior to 1829 probably in Henry Co, Ind but may have d before the fam left N C)
Hannah (Reece) b 12-10-1775 Guilford Co, N C dt Francis, decd & Christina
Ch: Nathan    b 12- 7-1802 Randolph Co, N C
    Elijah    b 5-27-1805 "
    Rachel    b 3-22-1807 "
    Absolom    b 10- 5-1809 "
    Christina    b 12-30-1812 "
    James)    b 7-29-1817 "
    Sarah) twins    b 7-29-1817 "
    Reuben    b 2- 2-1819

PRICE
Rice b 9-19-1794 Wayne Co, N C s Rice, decd & Catharine
Susanna (Keesling) b 2-mo-1802 Wythe Co, Va dt John & Eve
Ch: Sally    b 11-11-1822
    Martha Ann    b 7-29-1825
    Narcissa    b 4-26-1828
    James    b 4-19-1831 d 6- 4-1831
        bur Duck Creek Mtg
    Anna C    b 9-30-1832
    Charity    b 9-28-1834
    Robert B    b 11- 2-1837
    Rice Bryant    b 11- 3-1840
    Exalina C    b 11-20-1843
    Susanna    b 3-20-1846

Robert b 8-15-1804 Wayne Co, N C s Rice & Catharine
Mary (Ratliff) b 2- 8-1807 Randolph Co, N C dt Joshua & Letitia
Ch: Ann    b 11-24-1827 Henry Co, Ind
    Belinda    b 12-22-1829 "
    Zilpah    b 3-16-1832 "
    Sarah Jane    b 1-11-1835 "

RATLIFF - RATCLIFF
Eli
Jane (Draper)
Ch: Huldah P    b 1-20-1846
    Calvin W    b 10-27-1848

Gabriel b 5- 8-1802 Randolph Co, N C s Richard & Betty
Catharine (Pearson) b 1-31-1805 Randolph Co, N C dt Nathan & Mary
Ch: Mahlon    b 11- 2-1825
    Mary    b 12-16-1826
    Benajah    b 6-15-1828
    Huldah    b 12-25-1829
    Caroline    b 3-10-1831 d 8- 1-1833
        bur Duck Creek Mtg
    Sarah    b 10-10-1832
    Seth    b 9-29-1834
    Elizabeth    b 5-23-1836

Isaac
Mary (Presnall)
Ch: Hannah L    b 6- 7-1836
    Abner C    b 11-28-1837
    John P    b 6-10-1843

John M b 10- 7-1826 d 8-29-1854 bur Clear Springs Mtg, Ind s Joseph, decd & Rebecca
Asenath (Palmer) b 10- 6-1830 dt David & Sarah
Ch: Franklin J    b 3- 6-1849

Joseph b 8- 3-1788 Randolph Co, N C d 4-12-1837 bur Clear Spring Mtg, Ind s Richard & Betty
Rebecca (Lamb) b 4-19-1786 Randolph Co, N C dt Jacob & Sarah
Ch: Jane    b 10-28-1808 Surry Co, N C
    Reuben    b 3-19-1811 "
    Huldah    b 11-30-1812 "
    Anna    b 6-25-1814 "
    Sarah    b 7-12-1816 Wayne Co, Ind
    Elizabeth    b 2-23-1818 "
    Jesse    b 4-11-1820 "
        d 9-22-1839 bur Clear Spring
    Eli    b 10-11-1822 Wayne Co, Ind
    Nathan    b 12- 9-1824 Henry Co, Ind
    John M    b 10- 7-1826 "
        d 8-29-1854 bur Clear Spring

Joshua b 12-14-1779 Perquimans Co, N C d 9-17-1838 bur Clear Spring Mtg, Ind s Thomas & Hannah
Letitia b 7- 1-1777 Stokes Co, N C
Ch: Ruth    b 7- 6-1805 Randolph Co, N C
    Mary    b 2- 8-1807 "
    Margaret    b 7-14-1809 Wilkes Co, N C
    Thomas    b 1- 9-1811 "
    Samuel P    b 3-16-1813 "
    Ephraim B    b 9-30-1815 "
    Joseph Branson    b 4-20-1818 Surry Co, N C
    Amelia L    b 4- 7-1821 "

(Marcus s of Millicent Ratliff) (b 10- 2-1857)
(minor ch under care of Cyrus & Lydia Kendall)

Mary E d 9-17-1870 bur Clear Spring Mtg (no other inf)

Nathan (b 9- 6-1793) Randolph Co, N C s Richard & Betty
Lydia (Palmer) dt John & Anna
Ch: (Mary    b 4-27-1817 N Car)
    Alfred    b 4-17-1819 Wayne Co, Ind
    Martha    b 5-11-1820 "
    Tom )    b 5- 4-1825
    Joseph) twins    b 5- 4-1825
    (Anna    b 3- 4-1828)
    Levi    b 9-19-1830
    Nathan jr    b 9-28-1832
    David    b 8- 1-1834

Nathan b 12- 9-1824 s Joseph & Rebecca
m 1st
(Cynthia (Stafford) dt Eli & Elizabeth (Pritchard)
    b 2-10-1823 d 10-28-1850 bur Clear Spring Mtg)
Ch: Seth S    b 3-17-1850
m 2nd
Penelope N (Coggeshall) b 2-23-1833 d 2-23-1864 bur Clear Spring Mtg, Ind dt Tristrim & Millicent
Ch: Cynthia M    b 12-10-1852
    Barclay F    b 5- 4-1854
    William Henry    b 9-16-1856
    Milicent C    b 9-24-1858
    Ruth Ellen    b 1-13-1861

**DUCK CREEK**

RATLIFF - RATCLIFF (Cont)
(Phineas  s Thomas & Hannah  d  6-13-1870  bur Clear
    Spring Mtg, Ind)

Reuben  b  3-19-1811  s Joseph & Rebecca
  m 1st
Margaret (Kendall)  b  2-16-1812  d  7-25-1848
    bur Clear Spring Mtg    dt Thomas & Elizabeth
  m 2nd
Penelope (Henley wid of Jesse Bell)  b  8-10-1814
Ch:  Margaret          b  5-18-1852
     Jesse B           b  3-22-1855
     Elias H           b  6-12-1857

Reuben  d  4-17-1864  age 77-11-28  bur Spiceland Mtg

Richard jr  b  8-11-1796  Randolph Co, N C  d 12-22-1842
    bur Clear Spring Mtg  s Richard Sr & Betty
Caroline (Bailey)  b  9- 7-1791  Randolph Co, N C
    d  3- 3-1848  bur Clear Spring Mtg  dt John &
                                                Catharine
Ch:  Rebecca           b 12-21-1821  Wayne Co, Ind
     David             b  7-31-1823  d  5-21-1854
       bur in Asylum Graveyard, Indianapolis, Ind
     Levi              b  7-25-1825  d  7-15-1842
            bur Clear Spring Mtg

(Thomas)
Hannah b  9-15-1757  Perquimans Co, N C  dt Benjamin &
                                        Betty Maudlin
Ch:  Margaret          b 11- 8-1781
     Benjamin          b  5- 3-1787  d  8-24-1838
                          bur Clear Spring
     Phineas           b 12- 7-1798  d  6-13-1870
                          bur Clear Spring
     Achsah            b 11-22-1801

REECE
Abner
Sarah
Ch:  Margaret          b  9- 9-1852  Henry Co, Ind
     John Umphry       b 11-29-1854       "
     Rebecca A         b  5-17-1855       "
     Benjamin T        b  9-30-1858       "

Dempsey  b  2- 8-1796  N C  s Hannah Reece
  m 1st mou
Lydia (Hendricks)  b 12-25-1798  Guilford Co, N C
    (d ca 1829  Henry Co, Ind)  dt John & Mary
Ch:  Abner             b  2- 7-1822  Randolph Co, N C
     Mary              b  6-25-1825  Indiana
     John              b 10-16-1827       "
  m 2nd
Ann (Ratliff)
Ch:  Margaret          b  5-14-1832  Henry Co, Ind
     Christina         b  2-25-1834
     Dempsey jr        b  9-11-1835
     Thomas            b  3-25-1841

Margaret (form Reece) now Pickering  Cadiz compl for mcd
    8-26-1852; deceased   rptd by Cadiz Mtg 11-25-1852

RINARD
Jacob  b  1- 8-1802  N C
Elizabeth (Sheridan)  b  6-10-1804  Orange Co, N C
    dt John & Margaret
Ch:  Margaret          b  2-24-1823
     Catherine         b  8-30-1825
     Rachel            b 10-24-1827

SAINT
Exum  b  9-10-1808  Perquimans Co, N C  s William &
                                                Achsah
Phebe (Pickering)  b  6-30-1811  d  9-14-1836
    dt Jonas & Ruth
Ch:  Maria             b 11- 5-1831  Henry Co, Ind
     William M         b  3- 6-1834

Jabez
Margaret
Ch:  Ester             b  8-16-1850
     Semantha          b 12-31-1853
     Semira            b  5-17-1855

Jonathan E  b  1-13-1822  Indiana  d  9-18-1855  bur
    Duck Creek Mtg, Ind  s William & Achsah
Emily G (Johnson)  b 10-20-1823  dt James & Mary
Ch:  Excelina          b  3- 6-1843
     Martha E          b 11-14-1844
     John Quincy       b 12-19-1847

Achsah (wid of William)  d 11-29-1839  age 53-5-14
    bur at Duck Creek Mtg, Ind

Joseph B   d  4-14-1842  bur at Duck Creek Mtg

Milton  d 12-19-1855  bur at Duck Creek Mtg

William jr  b 11-29-1828  Wayne Co, Ind  s William Sr
  m 1st                                      & Achsah
Mary Ann (Elliott)  b 10-20-1831  d  8-16-1850
    dt John & Mary
Ch:  Esther            b  8-16-1850
  m 2nd
Mary Ann (Johnson)
Ch:  Semantha          b 12-31-1853
     Semira            b  5-17-1855

SANDERS - SAUNDERS
Tobias  b  5-16-1813
Anna (Wright)  b  7- 4-1820  (d ca 1866)
Ch:  Jonah W           b  8-16-1840
     Sarah Jane        b  1-21-1843
     Calvin            b  6-29-1845
     Seth              b  9-21-1847
     Eliza Ann         b  9- 4-1853
     Emma              b  1-29-1864

SHAFFER
Peter
Elizabeth (prob wid of Fredrick Phelps)
Ch:  Ruth Alice        b 10-11-1865
     Dora T            b  1- 3-1872

SHERIDAN
John  b  7-22-1775  Guilford Co, N C  s George & Hannah
Margaret (Osborn)  b  8-27-1780  Orange Co, N C
    dt Thomas & Elizabeth
Ch:  Hannah            b  2-24-1802  Guilford Co, N C
     Elizabeth         b  6-10-1804  Orange Co, N C
     William           b 10- 8-1806  Clinton Co, Ohio
     Rachel            b  5-26-1809       "
     George            b  4- 6-1811       "
     John              b  2- 7-1813       "
     Thomas            b  3-24-1815       "
     Abner             b  4-22-1817       "
     Susannah          b 11-15-1821       "
     Isaac             b 11- 9-1824

Mary  b  7-19-1800  Chatham Co, N C  dt John & Mary

SMALL
Benjamin
Rachel (Presnall)  b  1-29-1838  dt Nathan & Hannah
Ch:  Reuben            b  2-15-1858
     Elkanah           b 10-17-1859
     Mary              b 11-17-1865

Josiah  b 10-18-1790  Randolph Co, N C  s Obediah &
                                                Elizabeth
Jane (Moore)  b  5-18-1797  dt Thomas & his 2nd w
    Abigail (Albertson) Bond Moore
Ch:  Thomas            b  9-27-1816  Indiana
     Sarah             b 12- 2-1818       "
     Elizabeth         b  4-17-1822       "
     Abigail           b  5-22-1824       "
     William           b  1-15-1829

Obediah  b 10-13-1794  Randolph Co, N C  s Gideon & Sarah
Isabel  b  3-13-1787  Perquimans Co, N C  dt Thomas &
    his 1st w Isabel
Ch:  Mary              b  2-19-1819  Randolph Co, Ind

SPENCER
Ezra  b 12- 8-1827  s John & Elizabeth
  m 1st
Hannah B (Palmer)  b  2-15-1836  d 10- 5-1856  bur Clear
    Spring Mtg  dt David & Sarah

DUCK CREEK

SPENCER (Cont)
Ch: of Ezra & Hannah B
    Elvira Louisa    b  9- 3-1853
    Charles Burret    b  2-28-1855
m 2nd  (1859 Cadiz Mtg)
Eliza C
Ch: John Rollin    b  8- 8-1862  d  2- 2-1863
                    bur Cadiz Mtg
    William Penn    b  3-26-1864

John  b  5-22-1802  Frederick Co, Va  (d  8-16-1883
    Spiceland Mtg, bur Duck Creek Mtg )
Elizabeth (Deselms)  b  2-26-1805  in Va  (d ca  prior to
    1874 at Spiceland Mtg)  dt Jesse & Elizabeth
    from Flushing Mtg, Ohio
Ch: Ezra          b 12- 8-1827  Ohio
    Louisa        b  5- 6-1832    "
    Lindley H     b  8- 9-1835    "
    David         b  6- 1-1839  Indiana
    John A        b  1- 9-1842    "
    Milton M     b  2- 7-1845    "

STAFFORD
Eli  b 11-19-1797  Randolph Co, N C  d 11-22-1877
    bur Clear Spring Mtg  s Samuel & Abigail
Elizabeth (Pritchard)  b 12-11-1799  N C  d  1-24-1870
    bur Clear Spring Mtg  dt John & Mariam
Ch: John          b  7- 1-1821  d  2-mo-1834
                    bur Clear Spring Mtg
    Cynthia       b  2-10-1823
    Phineas       b  8-11-1825  d  9- 3-1845
    Abigail       b  8-21-1826
    Achsah        b  6- 2-1828  d 10-24-1840
                    bur Clear Spring Mtg
    Seth          b 11- 5-1830
    Elizabeth     b 10-23-1833
    Sarah         b  9- 4-1837

Samuel  b  9-21-1795  s Samuel Sr & Abigail
Nancy (Hastings)
Ch: Daniel        b  8-30-1818
m 2nd
Rachel (Hunt)
Ch: Asenath       b  3-16-1821
    William       b  9-26-1822
    Mahalia       b  6-22-1824
    Noah          b  7-13-1826

Seth  b 11- 5-1830  s Eli & Elizabeth
Rebecca Jane  b 12- 1-1843  (d  6-11-1924)  dt Joshua
                                     (Albertson?)
Ch: Julia         b  9-20-1862
    Charles       b 11-21-1867
    (Milton       b  9- 9-1872)
    (Merritt      b  7-28-1878)

STANBROUGH
Francis  b 11-26-1819  s Nehemiah & Ruth
Huldah  b 11-23-1823  dt Josiah & Catharine Draper
Ch: Louisa        b  5-14-1842
    Josiah        b 11-17-1843
    Nathaniel     b  3- 6-1846  d 1 month
                    bur Josiah Draper's graveyard

Thomas
Abigail
Ch: John          b 11- 7-1838
    Jehu          b  3-23-1840
    Eli           b  7- 6-1842

Sarah    b  1-23-1843  dt William & Rachel

STANLEY
John  b  3-16-1777  Stokes Co, N C  s Elijah & Hannah
Elizabeth (Dicks)  b 12- 5-1786  Stokes Co, N C
    d 10- 9-1852  bur Duck Creek Mtg  dt Joshua &
                                       Elizabeth
Ch: Wyatt         b 12-18-1813?  Stokes Co, N C
    Milton        b  6-13-1819    "
    Harmon        b  3-10-1821    "
    Eliza B       b  9-22-1823    "
    Maria Jane    b 11-14-1826  Sullivan Co, Ind

John jr  b 11-22-1799  Guilford Co, N C  d 10- 8-1841
    Henry Co, Ind  s Michael & Mary
Deborah (Weisner)  b  2-19-1807  Stokes Co, N C
    dt Jesse & Ann
Ch: Moses         b  4- 3-1826  Guilford Co, N C
    Elizabeth     b 12-13-1827    "
                    d  4-10-1844  Henry Co, Ind
    Ann           b  6- 2-1830  Guilford Co, N C
                    d  3-12-1832  Henry Co, Ind
    Aaron         b  2-15-1832  Guilford Co, N C
    Jesse         b  2- 9-1834  Henry Co, Ind
    Mary          b  5-13-1836    "
    Penina        b 12- 6-1839    "
                    d  9-26-1860  bur Cadiz, Ind
    Lydia         b  3- 2-1842

Joshua F
Mary
Ch: Jesse Clarkson  b  6- 6-1850
    Martha Ann     b  8- 5-1851
    Selina Jane    b  4-10-1853
    Rebecca Ellen  b 12-27-1854

Richard  b  1- 3-1782  Guilford Co, N C
Abigail (Foster)  b  2- 7-1789  Guilford Co, N C
Ch: (Temple        b 10-17-1810) Guilford Co, N C
    (Elmina       b  4-12-1812)    "
    Elwood        b 11-29-1814    "
    Rebecca       b  9- 3-1816    "
    Joshua F      b  1-29-1824    "
    Nathan Dicks   b  1- 8-1826    "

Sarah  b  6-10-1763  Guilford Co, N C

Temple  b 10-17-1810  Guilford Co, N C  s Richard &
                                     Abigail
Anna (Norton)  b  2-17-1811  Randolph Co, N C
Ch: Ellwood       b  7-17-1834  Henry Co, Ind
    Richard J     b 11- 7-1837
    David C       b  3-27-1840
    Abigail F     b  1- 7-1843
    Elizabeth P   b  5- 2-1845
    Martha E      b  6-12-1848
    Jasin C       b  3- 9-1851
    Ezra L        b  1-17-1854

Temple B  b 12-27-1802  Guilford Co, N C
Anna  b  8- 9-1808  N C
Ch: Mary          b  8- 1-1828
    Eliza Ann     b 11-18-1830
    Dianna        b  8-27-1832  d 10-21-1833
                    bur Duck Creek Mtg
    Joab G        b 12- 6-1833
    Henry C       b  5-21-1836
    Huldah Ellen   b 11-12-1837
    Oliver H S    b 12-24-1839
    Eunice        b  2- 3-1842  d  2-12-1846
                    bur Duck Creek Mtg
    Anna Marie    b  7-23-1844
    Martha Elmina b  7-10-1849
    Seth H        b 11-18-1851

STARBUCK
George W  (b  2-17-1842)  s Bezaleel & Jane
Sarah (Stafford)  b  4- 9-1837  dt Eli & Elizabeth
Ch: Frank         b 10-22-1866
    Orion         b  4-24-1872

Richard W  b  5-20-1853  (s of Bezaleel & Jane)

Thomas C  b  4- 8-1846  N C  s Bezaleel & Jane
Mary (Presnall)  b  3- 8-1852  dt Nathan & Hannah
Ch: Charles       b  9- 6-1868

STEWART - STUART
Jehu  b 11-10-1772  N C  s Jehu Sr & 1st w Sarah
Sarah (Cook)  b 12-12-1772  N C  dt Thomas & Mary
Ch: Beulah        b 10-14-1808  Guilford Co, N C
    (Sarah        b  7-14-1810)
    Anna          b  2- 9-1813  Warren Co, Ohio
    Robert        b  1- 7-1815  Wayne Co, Ind
    Cyrus         b  7-20-1817  d 10- 4-1832
                    bur Duck Creek Mtg
    Ithamer       b  5-18-1820

## STOUT
Solomon  b 3-13-1807  Orange Co, N C  d 1-5-1835
    bur Duck Creek Mtg   s Joseph & Naomi
Susanna  b 8-31-1796  Randolph Co, N C  dt Peter &
    Abigail Lawrence
Ch: Zeno            b 7-7-1828  Randolph Co, N C
                  d 1-12-1834  bur Duck Creek Mtg
    Isaac           b 4-4-1831  N C
    Joseph          b 6-24-1834  Indiana

## SWAIN
Howland  b 5-19-1793  Guilford Co, N C  s George &
    Deborah
Phebe (Kelley)  b 12-11-1796  Guilford Co, N C
    d 1-12-1852  bur Duck Creek Mtg  dt Isaac & Sarah
Ch: Susan E         b 11-30-1822  Guilford Co, N C
    Betsy Ann       b 4-15-1826       "
    Phebe E         b 3-29-1829       "
    George H)       b 1-14-1832       "
    William H) twins b 1-14-1832      "
    Thomas M        b 1-26-1834

Jesse F H  b 11-4-1820
Anna F     b 7-5-1824
Ch: William N F     b 10-29-1843
    John Henry      b 2-23-1845
    George Strether b 3-23-1847  d 5-25-1853
                  bur Duck Creek Mtg
    Thomas Howland  b 8-12-1849  d 7-17-1851
                  bur Duck Creek Mtg
    Mary Eliza      b 1-17-1852
    Jesse Clarkson  b 4-6-1854
    Charles Gregory b 7-6-1857

John  b 1-10-1784  Guilford Co, N C
Ann   b 7-31-1789  Jefferson Co, Tenn  dt Evan &
    Susannah Lewis
Ch: Lewis           b 6-21-1810  Jefferson Co, Tenn
    Huldah          b 3-20-1812       "
    Thomas Clarkson b 2-6-1814        "
    Elihu           b 4-21-1816       "
    William         b 10-14-1818      "
    Ezra            b 3-10-1822       "
    Susannah        b 9-20-1824       "
    Sally Ann       b 11-8-1826       "
                  d 10-23-1838 bur Fall Creek Mtg
                  (Madison Co, Ind)
    John            b 3-5-1830  Jefferson Co, Tenn
    Rachel          b 3-31-1832  Henry Co, Ind
        d 12-21-1840  bur Fall Creek Mtg (Madison Co, Ind)
    Rhoda           b 4-5-1836  Henry Co, Ind

## THOMAS
Elijah   b 2-19-1809  Richmond Co, N C  s Elijah &
    Susanna
Christian  b 12-30-1812  Randolph Co, N C  dt Stephen
    & Hannah Presnall
Ch: Elvy            b 2-9-1834

Simeon  b 7-29-1803  Marlborough Dist, S C  s Elijah
    & Susanna
Olive   b 4-10-1806  Knox Co, Tenn  dt Jacob & Ann
    Elliott
Ch: Ruth            b 10-14-1826
    Henry           b 4-30-1828
    Susannah        b 7-16-1830
    Elwood          b 2-26-1834  d 8-21-1835
                  bur Duck Creek Mtg
    Melinda         b 12-2-1835

## THORNBURGH
Joel  b 11-29-1789  Guilford Co, N C  s Joseph & Rachel
Ann J b 9-28-1794  Guilford Co, N C  dt Joel & Hannah
    Willis
Ch: Cyrus           b 3-15-1818  Highland Co, Ohio
    William W       b 7-9-1819        "
    Mary Ann        b 12-25-1822      "
    Lydia Jane      b 12-12-1827      "

## WALES
William W  b 3-14-1818  Iredell Co, N C  s Samuel & Mary
Catharine E  b 7-23-1826  Wayne Co, Ind  dt George &
    Karon Bundy
Ch: Maria E         b 2-20-1849
    William Henry   b 8-25-1855

## WEBB
John
Leah (Morris)
Ch: Peninah         b 10-21-1817  Cumberland Co, Ohio
    Benjamin        b 11-24-1820       "
    Lydia           b 11-12-1822       "

## WEISNER
Jesse  b (12-20)-1786  (d prior to 9-21-1848 after req
    cert to Walnut Ridge Mtg) (may be bur Walnut
    Ridge Mtg)
m 2nd
Lydia (Kendal)  b (2-25)-1788  (d ca 1844-1845 prob
    Duck Creek Mtg) dt John & Ann, decd
Ch: William         b 6-13-1814  Stokes Co, N C
    Jehu            b 11-6-1816        "
    Hannah          b 7-16-1817        "
    Cyrus           b 10-3-1818        "
    Anna            b 5-25-1820        "
    Seth            b 5-30-1824        "
    Nathan          b 7-20-1826        "
    Margaret        b 1-29-1829        "
    Jesse jr        b 10-8-1832  Wayne Co, Ind

Martha  b 8-4-1842

Michael  b 11-10-1811  Stokes Co, N C  s Jesse & Ann
Hannah   b 2-24-1812  Wayne Co  dt Isaac & Mary Barker

Phebe Ann  b 12-5-1847  dt of Nathan

Seth
Ann (Pike)
Ch: Jesse           b 11-7-1846
    Lydia Mariah    b 1-28-1850

William
Sarah
Ch: Elwood          b 12-18-1840
    Martha          b 8-4-1842

## WHITE
Anna  b 1772

Anna jr  b 1816

Bethuel C  b 9-7-1806  Guilford Co, N C  s Robert &
    Rebecca
Hannah  b 2-3-1806  Northampton Co, N C  dt Joshua
    & Lydia Binford
Ch: Elizabeth       b 9-7-1828  Henry Co, Ind
    Aaron           b 10-3-1830       "
    Ann             b 12-31-1832      "

Isaac   b 8-24-1798  Guilford Co, N C  s Stanton & Sarah
Louisa  b 9-26-1797  Randolph Co, N C  dt Nancy Bundren
Ch: Micajah C       b 5-29-1819  Guilford Co, N C
    Lilburn         b 3-21-1821       "
    Jesse S         b 11-19-1823      "
    Martha G        b 8-27-1826       "

Nathan    b  1801
Prudence  b  1806
Ch: William G       b 2-2-1846
    Moses H         b 9-7-1848
    Esther Ann      b 3-7-1850

Stanton  b 12-14-1767  s Isaac & Catherine
Sarah (Stanley) dt Micajah & Barbara  b 3-22-1771
Ch: Hannah          b 5-25-1796
    Isaac           b 8-24-1798
    Mary            b 4-6-1801
    Catharine       b 9-10-1803
    Jesse           b 12-14-1805
    Micajah         b 7-1-1808

## WICKERSHAM
Jehu  b 12-28-1787  Guilford Co, N C  s Jehu Sr & Mary
Mary (Robbins)  dt Moses & Alice  b 10-27-1793
    Randolph Co, N C
Ch: Moses           b 1-8-1815  Randolph Co, N C
    Price           b 9-28-1818  Wayne Co, Ind
    Asenath         b 1-2-1821         "
    Jemima          b 12-9-1824        "
    William         b 11-17-1828  Henry Co, Ind

## WILLETS
Gabriel  b 1-6-1771 Sussex Co, N J  s Henry & Charity
m 1st
Priscilla (Pike)
Ch: (Sarah         b  7-17-1799)
    (Abigail       b  9-15-1801)
    (Henry         b 10-11-1803)
    (Elizabeth     b  9-22-1805)
    Nathan         b  9- 2-1807
    (Charity       b 11-27-1809)
    Joseph         b  2-13-1812
    Phebe          b  5- 9-1814
    Susannah       b  6-24-1816
    Levi           b  2- 4-1819
    Jesse          b  3- 1-1822
m 2nd
Elizabeth  b 12-7-1793 Guilford Co, N C  dt Michael
                                    & Mary Stanley
Ch: Ruth           b  7- 1-1826  Stokes Co, N C
    Isaac          b  4-23-1831       "

## WILLIAMS
Darius  d 8-20-1844  age 23-0-12  bur Duck Creek Mtg

Jason  b 7- 5-1808 Chester Co, Pa  s Joseph & Mary
Abigail (Holloway)  b 8-18-1810 Belmont Co, Ohio
        dt Joseph & Eleanor
Ch: Sarah          b  8-17-1830  Belmont Co, Ohio
    Hannah         b  6-23-1832       "
    Joseph H       b  8-19-1834       "
    Mary Ellen     b  6-30-1836       "
    Martha Ann     b  3- 1-1839  Henry Co, Ind
                   d 11-26-1854  bur Duck Creek Mtg
    Samuel T S     b  7-14-1841  Henry Co, Ind
    William        b 11-22-1843       "
    John B         b  6- 6-1848  d 5-25-1851
                   bur Duck Creek Mtg
    Margaret Eliza b 12-24-1851  d 7-27-1857
                   bur Duck Creek Mtg

Margaret  b 12-23-1809  dt James & Julia Ann

## WILSON
Susan Caroline  b 2- 1-1852  d 5- 2-1852  bur Duck
    Creek         dt Benjamin & Caroline

David  b 12- 3-1802 Fayette Co, Pa
Esther (Barrett)  b 2-12-1801 Frederick Co, Va
Ch: Margaret      b 12-21-1827  Harrison Co, Ohio
    Isaac         b 12-25-1829       "
    Amy           b  7-31-1832  Guernsey Co, Ohio
    Rachel        b 10-22-1834       "

John jr  b 7-10-1796 Guilford Co, N C  s John &
                                        Elizabeth
Mary (Osborn)  b 3- 7-1795 Guilford Co, N C
        dt David & Lydia
Ch: David Franklin   b  6- 5-1819  Guilford Co, N C
    Thomas Arnett    b  2-13-1828       "
    Mary Ruhannah    b  1-28-1833       "
    Michael Clarkson b 10-25-1835       "

Joseph  b 1-28-1796  d 9-30-1832  bur Duck Creek Mtg
        s Michael & Esther
Phebe (Reece)  b 1- 5-1798  dt David & Susanna
Ch: Susanna       b  2-25-1819  Highland Co, Ohio
    Catherine     b 11-28-1820       "
    Abner         b  3- 1-1823       "
    Asenath       b 11-10-1824       "
    Henry         b 10-12-1827       "
    Calvin        b  8-12-1832       "

Michael jr  b 12-12-1789 Guilford Co, N C  s Michael Sr
                                            & Esther
Rebecca (Reece)  b 1- 5-1798 Grayson Co, Va  dt David
                                            & Susanna
Ch: Sirena        b 11-27-1817  Highland Co, Ohio
    David         b  2- 1-1821       "
    Esther        b 12-25-1822       "
    Jane          b 12-17-1824       "
    Elias         b  1-30-1827       "
    Rebecca       b  3-14-1831       "

William  b 4-17-1785 Guilford Co, N C  s Michael &
                                        Esther

## WILTSE
Elizabeth  b 3- 5-1834  dt of Simeon & Rachel

## WOOD
Jacob
    (m 1815 Plainfield Mtg, Ohio)
Phebe (Pickering)
Ch: Hannah        b  3- 7-1818
    Simeon P      b  7- 2-1820
    Levi P        b  4- 5-1823
    Seth          b 11-12-1825
    Sarah         b  4- 3-1828

## WORTH
Sarah E  d 4-30-1868  age 19-3-22  bur Cadiz, Ind

## WRIGHT
Jacob  d 6-20-1877  age 77-9-27  bur Clear Spring
                                    Mtg, Ind
Catharine (Reese)  d 10-16-1863  bur Clear Spring Mtg,
    Ind    dt Moses & Sarah of Tenn
Ch: Mary Ann      b  9-23-1836  Henry Co, Ind

(Jesse)
Anna (Clearwater)  b 7-27-1777
Ch: Joab          b  6-19-1815  Green Co, Tenn
    Joel          b 10-30-1817       "
    Anna          b  7- 4-1820       "

Joel  b 10-30-1817 (Green Co, Tenn)  s Jesse Sr & Ann
Eliza M  b 3-10-1823
Ch: Marilla E     b  4-28-1848
    Sylvannus J   b  2- 2-1850
    Cynthia Ann   b  8-19-1854
    Caroline J    b  7-11-1857
    Sumner S      b  9-25-1860
    Florence      b  7-26-1863

John  b 3-30-1799 Harrison Co, Tenn  s James &
                                        Catharine
Abigail (Pike)  b 7-14-1807 Grayson Co, Va
        dt John & Leah
Ch: Mary Jane     b  2-22-1836  Clinton Co, Ohio
    Nathan        b  5-28-1829       "
    Sarah         b  4-30-1835  Indiana

Sarah M  b 8-10-1839 Henry Co, Ind  dt Joel & Anna
(Anna, the mother of Sarah M)  (d 8-15-1840 age 20-5-10)
(bur Duck Creek Mtg)

DUCK CREEK

## DUCK CREEK MONTHLY MEETING
## MINUTES & MARRIAGES

**ABRAMS**
| | |
|---|---|
| 1-25-1894 | Mitchel rec in mbrp |

**ADAMS**
| | |
|---|---|
| 7-20-1922 | Hiram rec in mbrp |

**ADAMSON**
| | |
|---|---|
| 4-21-1831 | Seth & w Mary & ch Jacob & Huldah rocf Newberry MM, TN |
| 6-23-1831 | Abraham & w Eleanor & ch Evan, John, Benjamin, Elizabeth, Enos, Lewis & Henry rocf Newberry MM, TN |
| 6-23-1831 | Enos rocf Lost Creek MM, TN |
| 6-23-1831 | Mary rocf Newberry MM, TN |
| 6-23-1831 | Eleanor rocf Newberry MM, TN |
| 7-21-1831 | Isaac rocf Newberry MM, TN |
| 10-25-1832 | Solomon rocf Newberry MM, TN |
| 2-27-1833 | Elizabeth (form Nicholson) compl mcd dis 4-25-1833 |
| 6-26-1834 | Evan compl for att a mcd of a mbr dis 10-23-1834 |
| 5-24-1835 | Seth, Fall Creek Mtg compl of for mcd 8-20-1835 dis |
| 8-20-1835 | Enos, Fall Creek Mtg compl of for na, drinking & offering liquor to work hands dis 11-25-1835 |
| 8-24-1837 | Seth, Springfield MM is given consent to rec him in mbrp |
| 1-22-1852 | Isaac appt an Elder |
| 8-25-1864 | Isaac being on a visit in Iowa, req a minute showing his membrp at Duck Creek |
| 12-21-1865 | Isaac gct Walnut Ridge MM to m Catherine (Bufkin) Redding, a wid w/ch |
| 4-27-1870 | Catherine rocf Walnut Ridge MM |
| 10-23-1884 | Catherine gct Farmland MM |

**ADDINGTON**
| | |
|---|---|
| 5-22-1851 | John & w Rebecca "aged friends" rocf Chester MM |

**ADISON**
| | |
|---|---|
| 1-26-1837 | Elenor Thorp (form Adison) Fall Creek MM compl for mcd & dpl dis 5-21-1837 |

**ALBERTSON**
| | |
|---|---|
| 9-25-1834 | Nathan & w Fereba & ch Benjamin, Sarah, Alpheus & George rocf Milford MM |
| 5-24-1835 | Thomas P & w Hannah & s Nixon rocf Milford MM |

**ALISON**
| | |
|---|---|
| 3-24-1892 | Susan & ch Eva, Hattie, Julia & Horace L rec on req |

**ALLEE**
| | |
|---|---|
| 5-23-1844 | Melinda (form Hiatt) Duck Creek PM compl for mcd dis 9-26-1844 |

**ALLEN**
| | |
|---|---|
| 7-24-1862 | Harmon H & w Lydia & ch Elizabeth Ann, Frank Edgar & Lineas rocf Spiceland MM |
| 9-20-1866 | Herman H & w Lydia & ch gct Sugar Plain MM |
| 4-23-1915 | Mildred B rocf Fairmount MM |
| 11-25-1915 | Mildred B gct West Grove MM |
| 6-24-1926 | Helen McKee gct Spiceland MM |

**ANDERSON**
| | |
|---|---|
| 5-25-1859 | Lydia (form Maudlin) rpt mcd dis |
| 7-23-1868 | John C & w Lydia & ch Luther M & Martha Jane rec on req |
| 3-24-1881 | Sarah & dt Katie Bell rec on req |
| 6-23-1881 | Huldah & ch Lewis Swain & Naomi Myrtle rec on req |
| 1-21-1892 | Frank rec on req |
| 1-26-1899 | John rec on req |
| 12-21-1899 | Frank drpd from mbrp |
| 1-24-1901 | Sarah Catherine rel on req |
| 3-21-1901 | John drpd from mbrp |
| 8-22-1901 | Lavina rocf Spiceland MM |
| 4-24-1902 | Amos B & w Martha E & ch Raymond, Bernard & Paul rocf Knightstown MM |
| 3-22-1917 | Raymond & Bernard drpd from mbrp |
| 3-22-1917 | Paul rel on req |

**ANDREWS**
| | |
|---|---|
| 12-30-1832 | Joseph & w Anna Maria & ch William Edward, Pamela Jane, Mary Emily, Caroline Virginia & Joseph Oliver rocf Western Branch MM, Va |

**ANTRIM**
| | |
|---|---|
| 5-21-1835 | Hannah (form Maudlin) Clear Springs PM compl of for mcd Springfield MM, req to treat with her |

**APPLEGATE**
| | |
|---|---|
| 8-22-1907 | Terresse Walton gct Knightstown MM |
| 12-21-1921 | Mrs Ethel rec on req |

**AYDELOTTE**
| | |
|---|---|
| 8-23-1832 | Sarah (form Stuart) Spiceland inf she mcd chm |
| 6-20-1833 | Sarah gct Whitewater MM |

**BAILEY**
| | |
|---|---|
| 11-30-1826 | David appt to a comm |
| 10- 2-1826 | Sarah appt to comm on "poor" |
| 3-20-1828 | David, Duck Creek inf that he "hath been guilty of accusing a friend in an unbecoming manner and denies the charge" case discontinued |
| 4-25-1878 | Henry & w Ann rec on req |
| 7-24-1890 | Mary rocf Spiceland MM |
| 1-26-1899 | George rec on req |
| 4-23-1903 | Flossie Gray rocf Spiceland MM |
| 5-23-1907 | George, Flossie & Hershell rel on req |

**BAKER**
| | |
|---|---|
| 12-25-1851 | Mary (form Pearson) Clear Springs mtg compl for mcd chm |
| 2-22-1894 | Josephine rec on req |
| 4-23-1896 | Josie rel on req |

**BALDWIN**
| | |
|---|---|
| 6-24-1830 | Enos & w Elizabeth & ch Zeri & William rocf West Grove MM |
| 6-24-1830 | Uriah & w Lydia & s Milton rocf West Grove MM |
| 1-20-1831 | Isaiah & w Elizabeth & ch William, Elwood, Louisa, Uriah jr, Hannah, Mary & Ann rocf West Grove MM |
| 10-20-1831 | Enos & fam gct West Grove MM |
| 10-28-1834 | Lydia, a comm appt to visit with ---- |
| 11-20-1834 | Comm rpt: "We friends report no way offered to propose anything to the MM" |
| 6- 2-1836 | John, s Daniel & Charity of Wayne Co, m at Duck Creek M H to Asenath Hinshaw, dt Seth & Hannah, decd, of Henry Co, Ind |
| 9-22-1836 | Nathan & w Malinda & a bound ch under their care, H Beeson, rocf Springfield MM |
| 9-22-1836 | Asenath gct Springfield MM |
| 3-23-1837 | Nathan & fam gct Springfield MM |
| 2-26-1852 | Milton, Duck Creek P M compl for mcd dis 5-20-1852 |
| 2-22-1855 | Uriah, Duck Creek PM compl for na dis 5-24-1855 |
| 12-24-1868 | Uriah rec in mbrp |
| 3-26-1874 | Milton, Mary Ann & Corinthia rec in mbrp |
| 4-23-1874 | Virgil H rec in mbrp |
| 8-23-1874 | Virgil H dis for disunity |
| 5-23-1878 | Virgil H rec on req |
| 2-23-1899 | Virgil rel on req |

**BALES - BEALS**
| | |
|---|---|
| 6-26-1828 | John gct Milford MM |
| 7-23-1829 | Mehetable & ch Bethier, Matilda & Sarah rocf Fairfield MM |
| 6-24-1830 | Sarah Hiatt (form Bales) Duck Creek P M compl for mcd dis 9-23-1830 |
| 6-24-1830 | Bethier Hiatt (form Bales) Duck Creek P M compl for mcd dis 9-23-1830 |
| 7-22-1830 | Matilda Duck Creek P M compl for att a mcd dis 9-23-1830 |
| 1-26-1832 | John rocf Milford MM, to m Ann Hasket |

## BALES - BEALS (Cont)

|  |  |
|---|---|
| 2- 2-1832 | John, of Knightstown, Henry Co, s Jesse decd, formerly of Guilford Co, N C & w Ann (Hoskins) now Ann Jessop, w of Elias Jessop of Henry Co, m at Duck Creek M H to Ann Haskit, dt Thomas, decd, formerly of Warren Co, Oh, & w Ann, now Ann Cook the 2nd w of Levi Cook of Henry Co |

## BALLENGER

|  |  |
|---|---|
| 5-24-1832 | Henry & w Rebecca & ch Elijah, Henry & Nathan H rocf New Garden MM, N C |
| 6-24-1852 | Hannah (form Elliott) Duck Creek P M compl for mcd   dis 8-26-1852 |
| 3-26-1868 | William L rec in mbrp |
| 3-24-1892 | William L rel on req to j Meth Ch |

## BANKS

|  |  |
|---|---|
| 7-24-1924 | Chloe rocf Shirley MM |

## BARKER

|  |  |
|---|---|
| 3-23-1865 | Caleb & w Laura Ann rocf Walnut Ridge Mtg |
| 8-24-1865 | Caleb & w Laura Ann gct Deep River MM, N C |
| 8-24-1905 | Bessie May gct Knightstown MM |

## BARNARD

|  |  |
|---|---|
| 4-24-1834 | Asa & w Huldah & ch Elizabeth, Lucinda & Franklin rocf Silver Creek MM |
| 5-24-1835 | William, Salem MM req this mtg to treat w/h for mcd   offered chm 7-23-1835 & Salem so inf |
| 11-26-1835 | William rocf Salem MM |

## BARTHOLOMEW

|  |  |
|---|---|
| 5-25-1916 | Florence Copeland rel on req |

## BARTLEY

|  |  |
|---|---|
| 1-21-1892 | Rettie rec on req |

## BASEY

|  |  |
|---|---|
| 7-22-1882 | Wilson & w Ellen & ch Etheline & Miriam Artella rocf Spiceland MM |
| 1-21-1897 | William dis |
| 1-21-1904 | Ellen & ch Miriam A, Lorna C, Herman L & Howard H gct Spiceland MM |

## BEARD

|  |  |
|---|---|
| 10-20-1853 | (John) & Hannah rocf Center MM, N C |
| 10-20-1853 | David rocf Center MM, N C |
| 2-21-1867 | David, Clear Spring P M inf mcd   his mbrp was retained |

## BEESON

|  |  |
|---|---|
| 10-20-1831 | William Maudlin gct Springfield MM to m Mildred Beeson |
| 8-22-1833 | Edward & w Mary & ch Martha, Benjamin & Jemima rocf Deep River MM, N C |
| 8-24-1834 | Martha Osborn (form Beeson) compl of for mcd   dis 11-20-1834 |
| 9-22-1836 | H Beeson, a bound boy, under care of Nathan & Malinda Baldwin, rocf Springfield MM |
| 2-24-1881 | Martha rocf Raysville MM |
| 5-23-1907 | Estella James gct Spiceland MM |

## BELL

|  |  |
|---|---|
| 11-27-1833 | Jesse, s John & Lydia of Wayne Co, m at Walnut Ridge M H to Penelope N Henley, dt Elias & Jane, decd of Rush Co |
| 2-20-1834 | Penelope N gct Milford MM |
| 7-23-1846 | Jephthah rocf Milford MM |
| 5-23-1850 | Reuben Ratliff gct Milford MM to m Penelope N Bell (a wid w/ch) |
| 9-26-1850 | Penelope N Ratliff & her dt Lydia Jane Bell rocf Milford MM |
| 11- 1-1854 | Lydia Jane, dt Jesse, decd, formerly of Milford MM & w Penelope N (now Penelope Ratliff, 2nd w of Reuben Ratliff) m at Clear Springs M H to Michael Stanley, s of Aaron & Mahala, of Henry Co |
| 2-24-1859 | Jephtha gct Fairfield MM |
| 5-21-1903 | Aaron & w Georgie & ch Mabel, Howard, Laverna & Donald gct New Castle MM |

|  |  |
|---|---|
|  | (the cert was returned because they manifested no interest in mbrp) |
| 11-21-1907 | Ira C rocf Spiceland MM |
| 10-26-1927 | Maud Bond, dt of Ira & Ora S rec in mbrp |

## BENBOW

|  |  |
|---|---|
| 5-22-1879 | Enos & w Mary & ch Emma A, Josie E, Ella, Lieudoskia & Melvin rocf Pipe Creek MM |
| 7-26-1894 | Catherine gct Marion MM |

## BENNETT

|  |  |
|---|---|
| 12-25-1845 | Emeline (form Wright) mcd & j (ASF) |

## BERRY

|  |  |
|---|---|
| 8-11-1921 | John M Phelps & w Ella & dt Anna Phelps Berry gct New Castle MM |

## BINFORD

|  |  |
|---|---|
| 11- 2-1826 | Joshua & w Lydia & ch Asahel, Joshua, James, Peter, Hannah, Polly, Lydia & Sarah rocf Rich Square MM, N C end by Whitewater MM |
| 11- 2-1826 | Micajah & w Miriam & ch William, Micajah Crew, Rebecca, Anna, Sarah & Mary rocf Rich Square MM, N C, end by Whitewater MM |
| 11- 2-1826 | Benajah & w Judith & ch John, Asa, Jared, Benajah jr, Nathan, Elijah, Elisha & Angeline rocf Rich Square MM, N C |
| 11- 2-1826 | James Ladd & 2nd w, Jane & ch Robert, Joseph, Benjamin, William Ladd & Ann rocf Rich Square MM, N C end by Whitewater MM |
| 12-28-1826 | Micajah appt a Trustee to receive Title to land for use of Mtg at Walnut Ridge P M |
| 2-mo-1827 | Mirian appt an o at Walnut Ridge P M |
| 6-13-1827 | William of Rush Co, s Micajah & 1st w, Sarah, decd m at Walnut Ridge M H to Mary Jessop, of Rush Co  dt Jonathan & Elizabeth |
| 6-28-1827 | James Ladd appt an o |
| 7-26-1827 | Hannah Sr rocf Still Water MM, Ohio |
| 8-23-1827 | Joshua & Benjamin Cox appt to att funerals of Friends at burial ground at Walnut Ridge P M |
| 10- 3-1827 | Hannah, dt Joshua & Lydia, all of Rush Co, m at Walnut Ridge M H to Bethuel C White of Rush Co, s Robert & Rebecca |
| 1-22-1829 | Micajah, Duck Creek P M compl for j Hicksites |
| 12-24-1829 | Joshua appt an Elder |
| 1-20-1831 | Miriam proposed for an Elder but some objection was found |
| 2-24-1831 | Miriam, comm reported that the objection does not now exist, so she is now appt an Elder |
| 2-29-1832 | Rebecca, dt Micajah & Sarah, decd of Rush Co, m at Walnut Ridge M H to Thomas Jessop, Rush Co, s of Jonathan & Elizabeth also of Rush Co |
| 3- 7-1832 | Mary, dt Joshua & Lydia of Hancock Co, m at Walnut Ridge Mtg to Absalom Presnall of Henry Co, s Stephen, decd & Hannah |
| 5-31-1832 | Ashbel, s Joshua & Lydia of Rush Co, m at Duck Creek M H to Avice Edgerton, dt Reuben & Patience of Henry Co, Ind |
| 11-22-1832 | Samuel B rocf Upper MM at Gravely Run, Va Dinwiddie Co |
| 11-22-1832 | Martha & ch Anna & Martha rocf Upper MM at Gravelly Run, Va, Dinwiddie Co |
| 3- 3-1833 | Ann, dt Micajah & Sarah, decd, of Rush Co, m at Walnut Ridge M H to Henry Winslow of Grant Co, s Joseph & Peninah |
| 3-21-1833 | Samuel B gct Milford MM to m Ann J Butler |
| 4-30-1834 | Angelina, dt Benajah & Judith, m at Walnut Ridge M H to George Bundy of Duck Creek Mtg, Hancock Co  s George & Sarah, decd of Wayne Co, Ind |
| 6-26-1834 | Samuel B gct Milford MM |

## BLACK

|  |  |
|---|---|
| 8-23-1874 | Henry & w Elizabeth & ch Senath L & William rocf Hopewell MM |
| 6-23-1898 | Henry & w Viretta rel on req |

## BLUNT

|  |  |
|---|---|
| 11-22-1827 | Rachel rocf Springfield MM |

DUCK CREEK

## BOGUE
12-20-1888  Sarah gct Spiceland MM

## BOLEN
1-25-1894  Eugene & Viretta rec on req

## BOND
8-31-1826  William appt an o
8-31-1826  Charles appt an overseer at Flat Rock P M
8-31-1826  Charlotte appt an o at Flat Rock P M
8-31-1826  Jesse appt Trustee to hold deed to land where mtg is held at Flat Rock P M (he not having complied with appt, he is released on 11-22-1827)
1-21-1827  Thomas appt Trustee at Spiceland P M
6- 7-1827  Amor, s Thomas & Mary, of Henry Co, m at Duck Creek M H to Mary Pickett, of Henry Co, dt Joseph & Priscilla
7- 5-1827  Betsy of Henry Co, dt Thomas & Mary m at Duck Creek M H to Exum N Palin of Henry Co  s Henry & Sarah of Wayne Co
6-26-1828  Edward & w Ann & s Henry rocf Springfield MM, N C
4-28-1828  William, Duck Creek P M inf that he "hath been guilty of saying that he believes Elias Hicks was as good a man as Jesus Christ and that a certain approved minister aught to be killed off ----"  dis 8-21-1828
12-25-1828  Jesse, Duck Creek P M compl of for j Hicksites  dis 3-26-1829
12-25-1828  William jr, Duck Creek P M compl of for j Hicksites  dis 3-26-1829
12-25-1828  Charlotte, Duck Creek P M compl for j Hicksites  dis 2-26-1829
12-26-1828  Charlotte jr, Duck Creek P M compl of for j H  dis 2-26-1829
12-26-1828  Mary, w of Jesse, Duck Creek P M compl for j H  dis 2-26-1829
1-22-1829  Thomas appt o at Spiceland
5-21-1829  Edward & w Ann & fam gct Milford MM
5-21-1829  Jesse gct West Grove Mtg to m Ann Cook
8-20-1829  John & w Rebecca & ch Lavina, Hannah, Abigail, Jacob, William, Elias, Albertson, Aaron, Mannon, Sarah & Anna rocf Milford MM
1-21-1830  Anna rocf West Grove Mtg
1-20-1831  John H & w Milly & s Asa rocf New Garden Mtg
8-25-1831  John H & w Milly & s Asa gct White River MM
9-22-1831  Thomas jr gct Springfield MM to m Anna Hobson
1-26-1832  Thomas & Mary & ch Hiram, Pleasant, Asenath, Phebe & Mary gct New Garden MM
1-26-1832  Thomas jr req cert to New Garden MM
4-26-1832  Thomas jr informs mtg "that he had declined his int of m with Anna Hobson, a mbr of Springfield MM & he not having applied for a cert on that acct" He was gct New Garden MM
5-24-1832  Jesse & w Anna & ch Calvin gct New Garden MM
9-25-1834  Lydia Sarah & Jesse ch of Jesse & Mary (living in St Joseph Co) gct to Mississinewa MM
9-25-1834  John & Ja--- (living in St Joseph Co) ch of William gct Mississinewa MM
4-20-1837  John & w Mary & ch Abigail, Jacob, William, Aaron & Anna rocf Spiceland MM
9-21-1843  Jacob H, Duck Creek P M compl of for upl, gambling, dancing & spiritous liquor to excess  Mississinewa MM req to treat w/h & rpt
10-11-1843  William, of Henry Co, s John & Rebecca, decd, of Henry Co, m at Clear Spring M H to Sarah Hunt, dt Hanuel & w Eleanor, decd of Henry Co
12-21-1843  Jacob H, Mississinewa MM informs that he denies part of the charges  dis 6-26-1845 & the disownment forwarded to Mississinewa MM
10-25-1849  Anna Gibson (form Bond) Clear Spring P M compl of for mcd  dis 11-22-1849
10-23-1851  John gct Westfield MM to m Rachel Moore
10-30-1851  Elias A of Henry Co, s John & Rebecca, decd, m at Cadiz M H to Sarah Ann Bufkin, of Henry Co dt Samuel, decd & Catharine
5-26-1853  John gct Westfield MM
6-23-1853  Ann (form Ratliff), Cadiz P M compl for mcd  chm
8-25-1853  Aaron M condemns his disunity
3-26-1857  Martha Ann (form Hosier) rpt mcd  dis
5-21-1868  William gct Bangor MM, Iowa
7-25-1895  Louisa gct Fairmount MM
3-26-1896  Elizabeth rec on req

## BOON
11-25-1830  John & Dorcas & ch Charles, Betsey, Stephen & Dorcas jr rocf Milford MM
7-21-1831  Driver & w Anna & ch Rachel, Rhoda, Rebecca, Sampson & Irena rocf Milford MM
4-26-1883  Jonathan & w Mary A rocf Spiceland MM

## BOREN
4-21-1851  Nancy rocf Spiceland MM
4-23-1874  William N & w Elizabeth Jane & ch Eunice Emily, Sarah Jane, & Phebe Elmira rec in mbrp

## BOWIE
6-20-1872  T C rec on req
3-25-1875  Alice C rec in mbrp
11-26-1884  Thomas L dis

## BOWLES
2-25-1836  Martha rocf Marlborough MM & end to Walnut Ridge MM

## BOWMAN
11-21-1833  Edmond & w Sarah & ch Phebe, Anna, George, Eliza, Martha & Mary rocf Whitewater MM
7-24-1834  Richard & w Phebe & ch Sarah Ann, Elvira, Susannah & Jonathan rocf West Grove MM
11-20-1834  Jesse & w Mary & ch Lucinda rocf Dover MM, N C
11-20-1834  William & w Anna & ch George & Cyrus rocf Dover MM, N C
1-26-1837  William jr & (2nd w) Elvira & ch Milton, Martha Ann, Edmund, Sally, Emaline, Calvin W, Beulah M & William rocf West Grove MM
5-20-1841  Martha Ann gct White Lick MM
2-24-1842  Milton H con his att at mcd
3-24-1842  Mary (form Deselms), Duck Creek P M compl of for mcd  (offered ackn 4-21-1842)
6-22-1843  Richard, Duck Creek P M compl that he has consented to two of his dts accompl their m contr to our discipline  On 7-20-1843  the comm appt rptd that he has decd since the last mtg
8-24-1843  Sarah Ann Saint (form Bowman), Duck Creek P M compl of for mcd  dis 12-21-1843
8-24-1843  Elvira Newby (form Bowman), Duck Creek P M compl of for mcd  dis 11-23-1843
1-25-1844  Phebe & ch Susannah, Jonathan M, Edmund, Oliver H, Louise & Robert B gct West Grove MM
3-21-1844  Hannah (form Hosier), Duck Creek P M compl for mcd  dis 8-22-1844
5-23-1844  Milton H, Duck Creek P M compl of for mcd  dis 8-22-1844
2-20-1845  Mary, Clear Springs P M compl, j Meth dis 4-24-1845
3-20-1845  Edmund jr, Duck Creek P M compl for mcd dis 6-26-1845
4- 2-1846  Anna M, dt Edmund & Sarah of Henry Co, m at Duck Creek M H to Harmon Stanley of Henry Co, s of John & Elizabeth
6-25-1846  Mary P Elliott (form Bowman), Duck Creek P M compl for mcd  dis 8-20-1846
11-25-1847  Edmund & w Sarah & ch gct Westfield MM
3-23-1848  Phebe S gct Westfield MM
7-20-1848  Susanna M, compl of for att mcd of two mbrs, she is mbr of West Grove MM that mtg is inf  dis rec from West Grove MM 5-24-1849

DUCK CREEK

## BOWMAN (Cont)

|  |  |
|---|---|
| 2-22-1849 | George A, Duck Creek P M compl of for att a mcd & j Meth Ch  dis 5-24-1849 |
| 9-21-1848 | George, a comm appt to prepare a cert, if way is clear to Westfield MM  On 10-20-1848 comm rpt there is an obstruction they can not remove.  On 9-20-1849 Westfield MM inf they have treated with him w/out satisfaction  dis forwarded to Westfield MM |
| 3-22-1849 | Calvin req cert to White Lick Mtg  On 4-26-1849, a communication from White Lick MM, West Union Preparative, that he does not comform to plainness of dress & has been guilty of abusive conduct toward a fellowman  dis 11-22-1849 |
| 4-25-1850 | Lucinda Elliott (form Bowman), Duck Creek MM compl for mcd & j Meth Ch  dis 6-20-1850 |
| 12-26-1850 | Edmund, Louise & Oliver H, & Robert Barclay, minor ch of Phebe, now Phebe Hutton rocf West Grove MM |
| 7-22-1852 | Beulah Burris (form Bowman) Duck Creek PM compl of for mcd  dis 10-21-1852 |
| 4-21-1853 | Louiza E Swain (form Bowman)  Duck Creek P M compl for mcd  dis 7-21-1853 |
| 8-25-1853 | Anna Gilbreath (form Bowman)  Duck Creek P M compl for mcd  dis 11-24-1853 |
| 7-20-1854 | William jr, Duck Creek P M compl as "he is charged with being guilty of larceny"  dis 9-21-1854 |
| 9-25-1856 | Edmond, Duck Creek P M compl for mcd  dis |
| 11-20-1856 | Oliver, Duck Creek P M compl for "cursing & fighting a fellowman"  dis  3-26-1857 |
| 2-26-1857 | Caroline Bundy (form Bowman) rpt mcd  dis |
| 8-26-1858 | Lavina rocf West Union MM |
| 10-20-1859 | Sarah compl of for na of mtg & unchaste conduct  dis 12-22-1859 |
| 12-20-1860 | William jr & w Elvira & fam gct Greenwood MM |
| 5-23-1861 | Sheppard, Duck Creek P M compl for mcd dis |
| 11-22-1861 | Jabez H, Duck Creek P M compl for na  dis |
| 12-26-1861 | Robert Barclay, Duck Creek P M is inf has mcd  dis |
| 5-25-1865 | Levina gct Greenwood MM |
| 9-21-1871 | Tabitha M gct Tonganoxie Mtg, Kansas |
| 2-25-1875 | Robert B & fam gct Raysville MM |
| 9-25-1879 | Robert B & fam rocf Raysville MM |
| 4-26-1883 | Alma gct Whitewater MM |
| 1-22-1885 | Robert B & fam gct Spiceland MM |

## BOYLE

|  |  |
|---|---|
| 3-25-1909 | Hazel & Blanche rec on req |

## BRANSON

|  |  |
|---|---|
| 2-23-1843 | Hannah (form Holloway), Duck Creek P M inf has mcd with her 1st cousin  Offered ackn 5-25-1843 |
| 5-25-1843 | John W, Duck Creek PM compl for mcd with his 1st cousin  Offered ackn 6-22-1843 |
| 8-20-1846 | Mary (form Hinshaw), Duck Creek mtg compl for mcd & j (ASF)  dis 10-22-1846 |
| 11-21-1861 | Hannah gct Spiceland MM |

## BRATTON

|  |  |
|---|---|
| 6-25-1829 | Hannah gct West Grove MM |
| 7-22-1830 | Hannah rocf West Grove MM |
| 4-24-1845 | Hannah gct Dover MM |
| 8-21-1845 | Hannah, the cert issued to Dover MM has been returned as she has returned to Duck Creek MM |

## BRAZINGTON

|  |  |
|---|---|
| 3-23-1837 | Samuel & w Lydia & ch Joseph, William, Samuel & Hannah rocf Whitewater & end by West Grove MM |

## BREWER

|  |  |
|---|---|
| ( 9-28-1839 | Sarah & ch Elizabeth, William, Mary, Morris had been issued a cert from Spiceland MM to Milford MM, but the fam actually moved to Duck Creek) |

|  |  |
|---|---|
| 2-24-1842 | Sarah (w of John) & ch gct West Grove MM (The cert for John was withheld) |
| 2-24-1842 | Elizabeth gct West Grove MM |
| 4-20-1843 | John gct West Grove MM |
| 2-25-1858 | Morris W, Jason W, Susannah & Rebecca H, minors, rocf West Grove MM |
| 12-26-1861 | Morris, Duck Creek P M compl for mcd  dis |
| 12-26-1861 | Jason W, Duck Creek P M compl for mcd dis |
| 7-25-1867 | Jason W & w Eliza Jane & ch, Oscar rec in mbrp |
| 3-21-1869 | Susannah & s Jason Equador gct Carthage MM |
| 2-25-1869 | Jason & w Eliza req a cert to Walnut Ridge MM  On 4-22-1869 the matter was dropped |
| 6-26-1873 | Jason con mcd so he retains his mbrp |
| 6-26-1873 | Jason & fam req cert to Fairmount MM |
| 5-24-1877 | Jason W rel on req |

## BRIGHT

|  |  |
|---|---|
| 11-22-1832 | Abigail (Stafford) Small rocf Whitewater MM |

## BROOKSHIRE

|  |  |
|---|---|
| 4-24-1924 | Elizabeth rec on req |

## BROWN

|  |  |
|---|---|
| 5-21-1829 | Frederick rocf Whitewater MM |
| 12-30-1832 | Frederick gct Whitewater MM to m Sarah Morris |
| 6-20-1833 | John & w Cyrene rocf Milford MM |
| 6-20-1833 | Sarah rocf Whitewater MM |
| 6-25-1835 | William & w Celia & ch Cyrus N, Milton D, Mary, Rebecca & Henry rocf Whitewater MM |
| 11-26-1846 | James Presnall gct Springfield MM to m Anna Brown |
| 3-26-1874 | Albert & William H rec in mbrp |
| 8-20-1874 | Albert rel on req |
| 8-25-1898 | Susan W rocf Carmel MM |
| 2-25-1904 | Margaret M rec on req |
| 6-23-1904 | George H rec on req |
| 3-22-1906 | W---- & Elmer rec on req |
| 7-25-1912 | Mariam gct Muncie MM |
| 9-26-1912 | William gct Spiceland MM |

## BUCK

|  |  |
|---|---|
| 2-21-1892 | James E & w Margery E & ch Walter B rocf Walnut Ridge MM |
| 1-23-1919 | Walter & William F rel on req |
| 9-25-1924 | Walter rec on req |
| 10-23-1924 | Margaret Iris rec on req |
| 11-24-1926 | Walter drpd from mbrp |

## BUFKIN

|  |  |
|---|---|
| 6-23-1836 | Thomas req to be mbr again, he having been dis by Marlborough MM, Ohio  Comm rpts "time not come to accept" 8-25-1836 |
| 7-21-1836 | Ruth & ch Barhsheba, Gulielma, Sarah & Ruth jr rocf Marlborough MM, Ohio |
| 7-21-1836 | John rocf Marlborough MM, Ohio |
| 7-21-1836 | Warner rocf Marlborough MM, Oh |
| 6-29-1837 | Warner of Henry Co, s Thomas & Ruth of same co m at Duck Creek M H, Mary Ann Kirk dt Thomas & Sarah of Henry Co |
| 7-20-1837 | Gulielma, Clear Spring P M compl for na & j Meth  dis |
| 1-21-1841 | Bathsheba Edwards (form Bufkin) Clear Springs P M compl for mcd  2-24-1841 now residing in limits of Back Creek MM That mtg req to treat w/h 11-25-1841 Back Creek rpts treated w/out satisfaction  dis |
| 4-22-1841 | Samuel rocf Spiceland MM |
| 8-26-1841 | Warner & w Mary Ann & ch gct Sugar River MM |
| 4-22-1847 | Katharine of Clear Springs P M, w of Samuel, rec in mbrp |
| 4-22-1847 | Sarah Ann, John C, Mary, Oliver, Thirza Jane, Martha & Ezra, ch of Samuel & Catharine, rec in mbrp |

DUCK CREEK

## BUFKIN (Cont)

|  |  |
|---|---|
| 12-26-1850 | John & w Hannah & ch gct Richland MM |
| 10-30-1851 | Sarah Ann, Henry Co, dt Samuel, decd & Catharine, m at Cadiz M H to Elias A Bond of Henry Co, s John & Rebecca, decd |
| 12-25-1851 | John & w Hannah & ch Eliza, Lindley, Lydia, Elizabeth, Sarah & Calvin rocf Richland MM |
| 5- 1-1856 | John of Cadiz, Henry Co, s Thomas & Ruth both decd m at Cadiz M H to Abigail B Ellis of Cadiz, dt Joshua & Miriam, both decd |
| 10- 2-1856 | John of Cadiz, Henry Co, s Samuel, decd & Catharine m at Cadiz M H to Jane L Newby of Cadiz, dt Elias & w Lydia, decd |
| 4- 2-1857 | Mary, dt Samuel, decd & Catharine of Cadiz m at Cadiz Mtg to Joshua Moore of Walnut Ridge M H, Henry Co s James & w Rebecca, decd, of same place |
| 2-25-1858 | John C & w Jane L req Plainfield MM |
| 12- 1-1859 | Eliza C, dt John & w Hannah, decd of Cadiz m at Cadiz M H to Ezra Spencer of Cadiz, Henry Co, s John & w Elizabeth of Clear Springs Mtg |
| 12-22-1859 | Catharine Redding (wid Bufkin) rpt mcd (her mbrp is retained) |
| 5-21-1863 | Oliver, Cadiz Mtg compl for mcd   dis |
| 2-25-1864 | Lindley H gct Lynn Grove MM, Iowa |
| 11-25-1869 | John & w Abigail & fam gct Spiceland MM |

## BULLA

|  |  |
|---|---|
| 12-25-1834 | Cynthia rocf Marlborough MM, N C end by Whitewater MM |
| 1-28-1835 | Cynthia of Rush Co, dt of John & Margaret, both decd m at Walnut Ridge M H to Luke Newsom of Rush Co  s Ransom, decd & Sarah |

## BUNDY

|  |  |
|---|---|
| 5-20-1830 | Ephraim rocf Back Creek MM, N C end by Whitewater MM |
| 1-20-1831 | Samuel & w Priscilla rocf Milford MM |
| 12-22-1831 | Nancy rocf Springfield MM, N C |
| 4-26-1832 | Mary rocf Milford MM |
| 8-22-1833 | Mary gct Milford MM |
| 10-24-1833 | Elias & w Sarah & ch Ellen, Mary, Peninah, Martha & Ann rocf Milford MM |
| 11-21-1833 | George jr rocf Milford MM |
| 4-30-1834 | George of Duck Creek Mtg, Hancock Co, s George Sr & Sarah, decd, of Wayne Co  m at Walnut Ridge M H to Angelina Binford dt Benajah & Judith |
| 12-25-1834 | Josiah & w Mary & ch Huldah, Susannah, Nathan, Ruth, Henry, Mary, Caleb & Josiah jr rocf Milford MM |
| 3-26-1835 | Huldah & Phineas Lamb appeared & continued their int to m each other  They are altm |
| 4-23-1835 | The comm appt to att m of Huldah Bundy & Phineas Lamb, rpt it was accompl in an orderly manner, They produced the m cert (but thru some error, the m cert was not recorded) |
| 3-24-1836 | George & w Karon & ch Mary, Josiah & Catharine with a minor under their care Anthony Hasket, rocf Milford MM |
| 8-24-1843 | Josiah, Duck Creek P M compl he has been guilty of getting in a passion & upl & threatening a fellowman with violence & for using spiritous liquor to excess 11-23-1843 chm |
| 2- 1-1844 | Josiah of Henry Co, s George, decd & Karen m at Duck Creek M H to Maria Jane Stanley, dt John & Elizabeth of Henry Co |
| 12-26-1844 | Josiah con upl & fighting |
| 4-27-1848 | Catherine E, of Henry Co, dt George & Karen, both decd, m at Duck Creek M H to William Wales of Henry Co, s Samuel decd, formerly of Hancock Co & w Mary |
| 2-24-1853 | Josiah, Duck Creek P M compl for na & for upl & drinking spiritous liquor to excess & also has had fiddling & dancing in his house |
| 2-26-1857 | Caroline (form Bowman) rpt mcd  dis |
| 10-20-1864 | Mariah Jane & ch gct Minneapolis MM, MN |
| 4-26-1883 | Maria J & ch Charles, Lorenzo D, John F & Orelester rocf Spiceland MM |

|  |  |
|---|---|
| 2-22-1894 | John M & w Ida gct Raysville MM |

## BURCHAM

|  |  |
|---|---|
| 2-23-1893 | Julia rec on req |
| 3-25-1915 | Charley drpd from mbrp |

## BURK

|  |  |
|---|---|
| 11-24-1836 | Rachel rocf Flushing MM, Ohio |
| 3-25-1847 | Eliza Jane rec in mbrp |
| 7-20-1848 | Eliza Jane Presnall (form Burk) Clear Springs P M compl for mcd  10-26-1848 offered an ackn |
| 2-26-1885 | Thomas J & w Hannah E rec on req |
| 3-26-1895 | Frank rec on req |
| 3-26-1903 | Frank drpd from mbrp |

## BURRIS

|  |  |
|---|---|
| 2-26-1828 | Stephen rocf Fall Creek MM, Ohio |
| 5-28-1829 | Stephen of Henry Co s Daniel & Mary of Highland Co, OH m at Duck Creek M H to Hannah Hiatt, dt Absalom & Ann of Henry Co |
| 3-24-1831 | Jane (form Hiatt) Duck Creek compl for mcd dis 5-26-1831 |
| 2-28-1832 | Daniel & w Mary & dt Rebecca rocf Fall Creek MM, OH |
| 2-28-1844 | Stephen of Henry Co, s Daniel & Mary of Henry Co, m at Clear Springs M H, Margaret Lewelling, wid of Meshack of Henry Co & dt James & Julia Ann Williams, both decd, late of White Lick Mtg |
| 11-26-1846 | Stephen appt an Elder |
| 12-24-1849 | Stephen & ch req cert to Westfield MM |
| 7-22-1852 | Beulah (form Bowman) Duck Creek P M compl for mcd  dis 10-21-1852 |
| 1-22-1857 | Rebecca (form Norton) rpt mcd  dis |

## BUSHONG

|  |  |
|---|---|
| 4-20-1916 | Margaret rec on req |

## BUTLER

|  |  |
|---|---|
| 6-28-1827 | Elizabeth rec in mbrp |
| 3- 4-1830 | Jonathan & dt Sarah Ann rocf Milford MM |
| 12-23-1830 | Jonathan gct Milford MM to m Sarah P Hubbard |
| 4-21-1831 | Sarah P rocf Milford MM |
| 2-21-1833 | Lemmuel rocf Milford MM |
| 5- 2-1833 | Lemuel jr of Fayette Co, s Lemuel & Jane of same place, m at Duck Creek M H, Henry Co, to Hannah Kirk, dt Thomas & w Sarah of Henry Co |
| 6-26-1834 | Lemuel & w Hannah gct Milford MM |
| 11-20-1834 | Charlotte & dt Edna rocf Milford MM |
| 1-22-1835 | Robert B rocf Milford MM |
| 12-25-1834 | Joseph, Milford MM req this mtg to treat w/h for mcd. 1-22-1835 Duck Creek MM treated w/out satisfaction & Milford MM is so inf. 4-23-1835 a dis received from Milford MM |
| 2-25-1836 | Elisha & w Rhoda & ch rocf Marlborough MM end to Walnut Ridge MM |
| 7-20-1837 | Jonathan & w Sarah & ch gct Spiceland MM |
| 1-23-1845 | Elizabeth gct Mississinewa MM |
| 12-30-1847 | Joseph of Henry Co, s James & Deborah, m at Duck Creek M H to Sarah Ann Pickering dt Abner & Charity, decd of Henry Co |
| 5-25-1848 | Sarah Ann gct Hopewell MM |
| 3-22-1849 | Joseph & w Sarah Ann rocf Hopewell MM |
| 5-22-1856 | Joseph & w Sarah Ann & ch gct Spiceland MM |
| 1-26-1865 | Sallie B, a communication from Lynn Grove MM, Iowa, is rec to inform mtg that her cert has been received from this mtg |
| 2-23-1893 | Noble rec on req |
| 1-24-1901 | Noble & William L gct Spiceland MM |

## BUXTON

|  |  |
|---|---|
| 12-20-1906 | A J & w Minnie rec on req |

## BYERS

|  |  |
|---|---|
| 2-23-1893 | Samuel C & w Florence & ch Emma E & Estella M rec on req |
| 12-26-1907 | Samuel & w Francis rel on req |

DUCK CREEK

## BYRKETT
|  |  |
|---|---|
| 2-24-1881 | Brooks & w Margaret & s Edgar Burton rocf Raysville MM |
| 2-21-1884 | Ida S gct Spiceland MM |
| 10-25-1900 | Evangeline Benbow rec on req |
| 1-26-1905 | Edgar Burton & w Leudoska Benbow gct Knightstown MM |

## CADWALLADER
|  |  |
|---|---|
| 5-23-1850 | Joseph req to be rec in mbrp, having been dis by Lick Creek MM  6-20-1850 req not granted |
| 4-21-1853 | Ann (form White) Cadiz P M compl for mcd with a divorced man  dis  6-23-1853 |

## CAIN - CANE
|  |  |
|---|---|
| 8-22-1867 | Exaline (w of James) & her s Everett gct Spiceland MM |
| 9-26-1867 | Exaline & her s Everett, Spiceland MM informs cert was end to Hopewell MM |
| 5-20-1869 | Edwin D rec in mbrp |
| 9-23-1869 | Exalina C & her ch Everett & Orville rocf Hopewell MM |
| 6-20-1872 | Exalina C & her ch Everett, Orville & Claude gct Milford MM |

## CAMPLIN
|  |  |
|---|---|
| 8-20-1896 | Maggie  rocf West Grove MM |

## CANADAY
|  |  |
|---|---|
| 4-25-1850 | Nathan & w Ann rocf Walnut Ridge MM |
| 6-24-1852 | Nathan H, Duck Creek P M compl for na, use of spiritous liquor & upl  dis 8-26-1852 |
| 7-22-1852 | Ann, Duck Creek P M compl for na & dpl |
| 12-23-1852 | Ann offered an ackn |
| 1-26-1854 | Anna, Duck Creek P M inf has j Meth Ch  dis 3-23-1854 |

## CANON
|  |  |
|---|---|
| 6-25-1885 | Martha rec on req |

## CAREY
|  |  |
|---|---|
| 3-25-1830 | Edmund of Walnut Ridge P M rec in mbrp |

## CARLISLE
|  |  |
|---|---|
| 9-25-1890 | Jasper drpd from mbrp |

## CARMICHAEL
|  |  |
|---|---|
| 1-21-1892 | Joseph, Rebecca, Rollie & Susie rec on req |
| 10-25-1894 | Catharine & Susie req release |
| 12-23-1897 | Pearl rec on req |
| 1-25-1917 | Catharine rec on req |

## CARPENTER
|  |  |
|---|---|
| 12-21-1843 | John rec in mbrp |
| 2-28-1844 | John of Henry Co, s Jonathan & Susannah, decd, m at Clear Springs M H, Penelope Newby, dt Elias & Lydia, decd of Henry Co |
| 3-20-1845 | Ann (form Pickering), Duck Creek P M compl for mcd  dis  5-22-1845 |
| 10-26-1848 | John, Clear Springs P M compl for mcd  dis 12-21-1848 |
| 3-21-1869 | Rebecca gct Walnut Ridge MM |

## CARR
|  |  |
|---|---|
| 3-22-1894 | Thomas rec in mbrp |

## CARTER
|  |  |
|---|---|
| 5-25-1871 | Robert & w Rebecca & ch Carlton & Edward rec in mbrp |
| 6-26-1884 | Elihu & w Amanda & ch Elizabeth P, Mary L, Bertha F, Ote E & Eunice P rocf Oak Ridge MM |
| 1-23-1896 | Otis drpd from mbrp |
| 4-22-1897 | Carrie rel on req |
| 5-20-1897 | Benjamin rec on req |
| 2-20-1902 | Benjamin gct Fairmount MM |

## CASEY
|  |  |
|---|---|
| 8-23-1894 | Nora gct Raysville MM |
| 4-23-1914 | Mary & dt Rowena rec on req |
| 6- 7-1928 | Jesse & w Lucy Vera & ch Mark & Tresse Maria rocf Shirley MM |

## CHALFANT
|  |  |
|---|---|
| 10-25-1906 | F Wesley & w Melissa Jane & ch Adda, Ora, Rose, Edna & Ivan rocf Whitewater MM |
| 3-25-1909 | Ora, William & Rose gct Whitewater MM |
| 3-25-1909 | Frank & w Jane & ch Adda, Edna & Ivan gct Farmland MM |

## CHAMNESS
|  |  |
|---|---|
| 10-22-1874 | Cadwallader Pitts gct Springfield MM to m Mary Chamness |
| 10-22-1874 | Benjamin F (minor s of Caleb & 1st w, Anna decd) rocf Cherry Grove MM |

## CHAPPEL
|  |  |
|---|---|
| 8-22-1833 | Thomas S & w Peggy & ch John & Deborah rocf Marlborough MM  end by Whitewater MM |
| 8-22-1833 | Martha Ann rocf Marlborough MM, Ohio & end by Whitewater MM |
| 7-24-1834 | Thomas rocf Marlborough MM, OH |

## CHEW
|  |  |
|---|---|
| 5-25-1876 | Emeline rec on req |
| 12-23-1897 | Milton C & Martha C rec on req |
| 9-22-1904 | Mary J drpd from mbrp |
| 3-22-1917 | Martha rel on req |

## CLAMPET
|  |  |
|---|---|
| 6-20-1833 | Mary rocf Milford MM |
| 9-22-1836 | Mary gct Milford MM |
| 9-25-1890 | Charles drpd from mbrp |

## CLARK
|  |  |
|---|---|
| 1-24-1833 | John & w Nancy & ch Judiah, Daniel, Alfred, Anna, Martha Ann & Thomas rocf Back Creek MM, N C  end by White Lick MM |
| 4-26-1834 | John of Wayne Co, s John & Sarah, both decd m at Walnut Ridge MH to Jane Hamm, dt John decd, & Elizabeth of Hancock Co |
| 10-23-1834 | Jane gct Whitewater MM |
| 4-23-1835 | Mary & dt Mary rocf Center MM, N C |
| 10-22-1835 | Abigail & ch Richard Mendenhall, George Cicero, Eliza Kinzey, Daniel Addison, John Wilberforce Long, Cynthia Ann, Hezekiah Franklin, Abigail Jemima & David Worth rocf Center MM, N C |
| 10-20-1842 | Calvin gct White Lick MM |
| 4-22-1847 | Alfred gct White Lick MM |

## CLATTERBAUGH
|  |  |
|---|---|
| 3-25-1875 | Elizabeth & Mary rec in mbrp |
| 2-21-1884 | M M gct Spiceland MM |

## CLEARWATER
|  |  |
|---|---|
| 9-25-1890 | Charles drpd from mbrp |

## CLEAVER
|  |  |
|---|---|
| 4-24-1828 | Nathan, Miami MM req Duck Creek MM to treat w/h for mcd |
| 5-22-1828 | Nathan, comm rpts no satisfaction with him  Dis rec from Miami Mtg on 10-23-1828 |

## CLOUD
|  |  |
|---|---|
| 6-28-1827 | Tach rocf Whitewater MM |
| 8-23-1827 | William rocf West Grove MM |
| 6-26-1828 | Ann (form Hunt) compl of for mcd  7-24-1828 chm |
| 1-26-1832 | Joel & w Abba & ch Asenath, Ruth &-----? rocf West Grove MM |

## COATE
|  |  |
|---|---|
| 8-24-1893 | Caroline (Harris) Coate rocf New Garden MM |

## COBLE
|  |  |
|---|---|
| 7-24-1845 | William Penn, a minor rec on req |
| 1-22-1846 | Susan E (form Swain), Duck Creek PM compl for mcd  2-26-1846 chm |
| 4-25-1861 | William P, Wabash MM, inf mcd  dis |
| 3-22-1866 | Susan gct Wabash MM |

## COFFIN
|  |  |
|---|---|
| 5-24-1832 | Alfred rocf Deep River MM, N C |
| 12-20-1832 | Elihu, White River MM infs that he a mbr Milford MM, is "guilty of getting in a passion & threatening a fellow creature" |

DUCK CREEK

## COFFIN (Cont)

|  |  |
|---|---|
| 2-21-1833 | Elihu, Milford MM req this mtg to treat w/him 3-21-1833 He offered an ackn & Milford MM so informed |
| 9-26-1833 | Elihu & w Sarah & ch Isaac Newton, William Starbuck, Alfred & Phebe rocf Milford MM |
| 5-22-1834 | Moses & w Phebe & ch Elihu, Cyrus, Louisa, Mary, Jonathan, Emily, Sylvester & Lucinda rocf Salem MM |
| 9-25-1834 | Sarah & s George F rocf Salem MM |
| 9-25-1834 | Ruth rocf Salem MM |
| 1-22-1835 | Alfred gct Deep River MM, N C |
| 3-26-1835 | Moses appt o at settlement of Little Blue River |
| 6-25-1835 | Catharine, a minor, rocf Milford MM |
| 12-25-1835 | Phebe rocf Dover MM, N C |
| 2-25-1847 | Abel, Duck Creek compl for j Meth Ch dis 4-22-1847 |
| 9-22-1859 | Tirsa Ann (form Hinshaw) rpt mcd dis |

## COGGSHALL

|  |  |
|---|---|
| 6-20-1833 | Millicent & ch Eunice Worth, Rhomas Elwood, John Milton, & Joseph Newby rocf Back Creek MM, N C |
| 1-23-1834 | Tristram rocf Back Creek MM, N C |
| 3-26-1846 | Elias Palmer gct Walnut Ridge MM, to m Eunice W Coggshall |
| 12-25-1851 | Nathan Ratliff gct Walnut Ridge MM to m Penelope W Cogshall |

## COLLIER

|  |  |
|---|---|
| 1-23-1896 | Jasper N & w Malinda & ch Maude, Frank, Charles, Orville, Herley & Herbert rec on req |
| 8-22-1901 | Jasper & w Melinda & ch Frank, Charles, Orville, Herley & Herbert rel on req |

## COLLINS

|  |  |
|---|---|
| 9-25-1890 | Joel & w Mary drpd from mbrp |
| 1-26-1899 | William & Joel rec on req |
| 2-23-1899 | Mary & Catharine rec on req |
| 4-23-1903 | Raymond drpd from mbrp |
| 8-25-1904 | Hattie rec on req |
| 1-26-1905 | Joel & w Mary drpd from mbrp |
| 2-22-1906 | Hattie D rel on req |
| 4-26-1917 | Charles & w Nolah & dt Mary Adah rec on req |
| 5-23-1918 | Grace rec on req |
| 1-20-1921 | Joseph C gct Knightstown MM |
| 3-20-1924 | Emma, Elmer E, Pearl May, Franklin Edward & Edith Rosetta rec on req |

## COMMONS

|  |  |
|---|---|
| 2-21-1833 | Sarah & ch Jesse, Eleanor, Ludia Lavina, John & Isaac D rocf West Grove MM |

## COMPTON

|  |  |
|---|---|
| 8-25-1853 | Mahlon, Allen, Lydia, Evan, Sarah Ann & Levi, ch of Nathan rocf Dover MM |
| 11-20-1856 | Nancy rec in mbrp w/con of Dover MM |
| 12-25-1856 | Lydia Weaver (form Compton) rpt mcd dis |
| 10-21-1858 | Jemima R (form Ellis), Wabash MM req this mtg to treat w/her 12-23-1858 Duck Creek treated w/out satisfaction & Wabash MM so inf Dis rec from Wabash MM 3-24-1859 |
| 2-24-1859 | Mahlon, Clear Springs P M compl for mcd dis 3-24-1859 |
| 6-23-1859 | Allen gct Salem MM, Iowa to m Elizabeth Marshall |
| 8-24-1859 | Sarah Ann Crandle (form Compton) rpt mcd dis |
| 12-22-1859 | Elizabeth rocf Salem MM, Iowa |
| 2-23-1860 | Evan, Cadiz P M informs he mcd He retains his mbrp |
| 5-24-1860 | Allen & w Elizabeth gct Salem MM, Iowa |
| 7-25-1878 | Nancy rocf Bangor MM, Iowa |

## CONKLE

|  |  |
|---|---|
| 5-22-1924 | James Wilson & George, ch of Esther Bale Hardin by former m rec on req |
| 3-25-1926 | Lloyd W Harden & w Esther & ch Edith Maxine dt of Lloyd by a former m, & James Conklin, s of Esther by a former m, gct New Salem MM |

## CONKLIN

|  |  |
|---|---|
| 3-24-1881 | Mary A rec on req |
| 3-25-1920 | Louie Templeton rocf Charlottsville MM |

## CONNER

|  |  |
|---|---|
| 7-24-1884 | Sarah & ch Franklin, Lee Oran & Ethel Georgia gct Mississinewa MM |
| 4-23-1903 | Sarah gct New Castle MM |

## COOK

|  |  |
|---|---|
| 7-27-1826 | Ann appt to a comm |
| 8-31-1826 | Ann appt to comm on "poor" |
| 8-31-1826 | Ann appt to comm to have care of Indulged Mtgs |
| 8-31-1826 | Levi appt on comm to att Q M |
| 10-25-1827 | Levi appt an Elder |
| 11-22-1827 | John gct Milford MM to m Julian Saint |
| 3-20-1828 | Julian rocf Milford MM |
| 3-20-1828 | Betty rocf Miami MM, Oh |
| 4- 3-1828 | Isaac, of Henry Co, s Levi & his 1st w Ann decd, m at Duck Creek M H, to Anna Picket dt Joseph & Priscilla of Henry Co |
| 10- 2-1828 | Betty, dt Levi & his 1st w Ann (decd) of Henry Co, m at Duck Creek M H to James Hiatt of Henry Co s of Absalom & Ann of same county |
| 11-20-1828 | Levi, Duck Creek P M inf that he holds to some pernicious doctrine of the Separatists & for falsly accusing the Y M of unfairness dis 1-22-1829 |
| 5-21-1829 | Ann, Duck Creek compl for j Hicksites dis 7-28-1829 |
| 9-24-1829 | Isaac, Duck Creek Mtg compl for j Hs dis 11-26-1829 |
| 12-24-1829 | John, Duck Creek compl for j Hs dis 3-11-1830 |
| 1-21-1830 | Julian, Duck Creek compl for j Hs dis 3-25-1830 |
| 6-20-1832 | John, Sarah, Elizabeth, Nancy, Ruth Catharine, minor ch of Mary rocf Whitewater MM |
| 3-21-1833 | James S, Chester Mtg req this mtg to treat w/h for refusing to pay a debt & upl 1-23-1834 James does not make satis ackn & Chester MM so inf 4-24-1834 dis rec from Chester MM |
| 8-22-1833 | Anna, Duck Creek P M compl for na & j Hs dis 10-24-1833 |
| 9-25-1834 | Ireney rocf Fairfield MM |
| 10-23-1834 | Eunice (& dts Minerva, Ann & Elizabeth) rocf Chester MM (James not clear) |
| 6-25-1835 | Irena gct Cherry Grove MM |
| 3-23-1837 | Thomas rocf Flushing MM, Oh |
| 2-22-1844 | Mary Ann of Clear Spring P M, rec in mbrp |
| 9-21-1848 | Mary Ann Reynolds (form Cook), Duck Creek P M compl for mcd dis 7-26-1849 |
| 6-21-1849 | Eliza, Duck Creek P M compl for j Hs dis 8-23-1849 |
| 6-21-1849 | Nancy, Duck Creek P M compl for unchaste conduct dis 8-23-1849 |
| 1- 1-1851 | Jesse of Richland Mtg, Hamilton Co, s Zimri & w Lydia of Hamilton Co, m at Clear Springs M H to Abigail Stafford of Henry Co dt Eli & Elizabeth |
| 2-20-1851 | Abigail gct Richland MM |
| 5-27-1852 | Mary, dt of Isaac, decd & Anna of Henry Co m at Duck Creek M H to Whitesel D Macey of Spiceland Mtg, Henry Co, s Nathan & Jane of same co |
| 6-24-1852 | Jesse & w Abigail rocf Richland MM |
| 5- 2-1866 | Abigail, wid of Jesse Cook & dt of Eli & Elizabeth Stafford m at Clear Springs M H to Nathan P Henley of Henry Co, s Abraham, decd & Mary of N C |
| 3-23-1876 | Seth & w Minerva & ch Mary Eleanor, Wildy Brant & Holland Lee rec on req |
| 9-25-1890 | Milton drpd from mbrp |
| 1-21-1892 | Carrie rec on req |
| 3-24-1892 | Carrie, Ilie Oran & Erskin rec on req |
| 9-25-1894 | Seth dis for disunity |
| 2-20-1896 | Seth & Milton rec on req |
| 3-24-1898 | Alice Lindley rocf Bloomingdale MM |
| 5-25-1899 | Seth drpd from mbrp |

## COOK (Cont)

|  |  |
|---|---|
| 4-23-1903 | James, Clem & George drpd from mbrp |
| 3-21-1907 | Milton, Julie & Lora drpd from mbrp |
| 4-25-1912 | John C & fam gct New Castle MM |

## COON

|  |  |
|---|---|
| 7-25-1890 | Sarah rec on req |
| 1-21-1892 | Willis E rec on req |
| 3-24-1892 | Della rec on req |
| 2-23-1893 | James rec on req |
| 2-20-1896 | Arthur & w Ellen & s Floyd rec on req |
| 1-26-1899 | Lizzie rec on req |
| 2-25-1904 | Howard rec on req |
| 8-23-1906 | Job drpd from mbrp |
| 3-21-1907 | Arthur & w Ellen & s Floyd drpd from mbrp |
| 11-3-1927 | Earl & w Elsie & s Manford gct Dublin MM |

## COOPER

|  |  |
|---|---|
| 1-21-1836 | William & w Anna Star & ch Levi K & Elizabeth rocf Sadsbury MM, Pa |
| 6-24-1847 | Harriet (form Hiatt), Clear Springs P M compl for mcd dis 8-26-1847 |
| 3-13-1854 | Elizabeth, of Henry Co, dt William & Anne m at Cadiz M H to Asa Ellis of Harrison twp, Henry Co, s Joshua & Miriam of the same place |
| 2-22-1855 | Levi K, Cadiz P M inf has j Meth dis 4-26-1855 |
| 2-26-1857 | Christina (form Reese) rpt mcd dis |
| 3-31-1859 | Phebe R, dt William T & Anna S of Cadiz Henry Co, m at Cadiz M H to Lindley A Spencer of Clear Spring Mtg, Henry Co, s John & Elizabeth of same place |
| 5-25-1859 | Melvina (form Deselms) rpt mcd dis |
| 4-30-1862 | Truman, s William T & Anna S of Cadiz, Henry Co, m at Clear Springs M H to Mary H Hiatt, dt William & Martha of Clear Springs Mtg, Henry Co |
| 8-20-1863 | Jeremiah S, Cadiz P M compl for na dis 11-26-1863 |
| 6-23-1864 | Truman & w Mary gct Lynn Grove MM, Iowa |
| 5-26-1865 | William & w Anna & ch gct Lynn Grove MM, Iowa |
| 2-21-1895 | Bessie rel on req |
| 6-20-1895 | Nora rocf Raysville MM |
| 1-23-1896 | Louie drpd from mbrp |
| 4-20-1916 | Catharine rec on req |
| 2-25-1926 | Dorotha A rec on req |

## COPELAND

|  |  |
|---|---|
| 7-27-1826 | John & Susannah are appt to comms |
| 8-31-1826 | John appt Clerk of MM but was replaced on 5-3-1827 by George Evans |
| 8-31-1826 | Susannah appt to comm to att Q M |
| 8-31-1826 | Susannah appt an o at Duck Creek P M |
| 3-24-1827 | Jonathan, Duck Creek P M comp of for mcd with his 1st cousin dis 5-31-1827 |
| 3-29-1827 | John, Duck Creek P M compl that he Hath assisted his son in procuring license to accomplish his mcd 6-28-1827 John con his disunity |
| 1-24-1828 | John, Duck Creek P M inf that he hath been guilty of light, airy conduct to reproach of our Society 5-22-1828 John chm |
| 7-24-1828 | Leah, Duck Creek P M compl for mcd with 1st cousin dis 9-25-1828 |
| 6-25-1829 | John appt Trustee Duck Creek |
| 4-22-1830 | John, Spiceland P M compl for j Hs dis 6-24-1830 |
| 7-22-1830 | Susannah, Spiceland P M compl for j Hs dis 9-23-1830 |
| 7-26-1832 | Jesse, Joshua, Samuel, John jr & Nathan, ch of John, gct Milford MM |
| 4-24-1834 | Joshua, Samuel, John A & Nathan, minor ch of John & Susannah rocf Milford MM |
| 7-24-1845 | Eunice (form Hiatt) Duck Creek P M compl for mcd Eunice offered ackn on 8-21-1845 |
| 3-25-1852 | Eunice gct Spiceland MM |
| 6-6-1854 | Lucinda (form Pickering) Clear Springs P M compl for mcd & j Meth dis 8-24-1854 |
| 4-25-1878 | Sarah rec on req |
| 4-24-1879 | Sarah dis |
| 2-20-1896 | Exum & w Elizabeth & ch Jennie & Hattie rec on req |
| 11-26-1903 | J L & dt Florence rec on req |
| 3-25-1909 | James E & w Nettie & ch Merle rec on req |
| 8-11-1921 | Clyde gct New Castle MM |

## COPPOCK

|  |  |
|---|---|
| 4-23-1835 | John & w Martha & ch Aaron, Darias, Margaret Jane, Sarah, David, Lydia & John rocf Union MM, Ohio |
| 2-25-1836 | John, Fall Creek P M compl for upl dis 5-26-1836 |
| 8-24-1837 | Abraham, Fall Creek P M compl he has entirely na, upl, used spiritous liquor to excess & has offered to fight his fellowman and went so far as to say that he believed the scriptures as they read ----------- that he has a cert for himself & fam given forth by Union MM, Ohio & he refuses to forward it to the MM Union MM, Ohio is so informed (Duck Creek MM was laid down 8-mo-1837) |

## COSAND

|  |  |
|---|---|
| 12-28-1826 | William rocf Chester MM |
| 9-22-1831 | Nathan, Whitewater MM infs this mtg that he na, dpl & att a mcd & Duck Creek req Whitewater MM to treat w/h on 12-22-1831 Whitewater MM infs they've had no satis 1-26-1832 Nathan was dis & the dis forwarded to Whitewater Mtg |
| 8-23-1832 | William, Spiceland P M compl for na dis 1-24-1833 |
| 9-20-1832 | John gct Milford MM |
| 9-20-1832 | Mary & s Elisha gct Milford MM |

## COWGILL

|  |  |
|---|---|
| 4-22-1875 | Samuel C & w Caroline & ch Luzena C, S Macey & Lydia M rocf Hopewell MM, Oh |
| 2-24-1881 | Samuel & w Caroline & ch Luzena, Solomon M, Lydia M, Josephine & Clarkson D gct Fairmount MM |

## COX

|  |  |
|---|---|
| 7-27-1826 | Benjamin appt to a comm |
| 8-31-1826 | Benjamin appt an o |
| 8-31-1826 | Mary appt on comm on "poor" |
| 10-2-1826 | Mary appt to a comm |
| 8-23-1827 | Benjamin & Joshua Binford appt to att funerals of Friends at burial ground at Walnut Ridge P M |
| 1-21-1830 | Mary & ch Gulielma, Delilah, Exeline & Riley rocf West Grove P M |
| 2-23-1843 | Solomon & w Anna W & ch Milton, Cyrus, Annice, Mariah & Susan rocf Sugar River MM |
| 12-21-1843 | Solomon, Duck Creek P M compl for att Mtgs of the Separatists dis 2-2-1844 |
| 1-25-1844 | Anna, Duck Creek P M compl of for j Hs dis 3-21-1844 |
| 6-24-1858 | Milton gct New Salem MM |
| 5-24-1860 | Cyrus, New Salem MM infs this mtg, he mcd dis & dis forwarded to New Salem MM |
| 1-26-1865 | Mahlon & w Sarah & ch Luzena A, Lydia M, Barzilla W, Rebecca P, Julius M & Milton S rec in mbrp (formerly mbrs of Holly Spring MM, N C but due to war, we have been unable to receive their cert at this mtg) |
| 8-24-1865 | William B & w Elvira & ch Arthur L & Debert W rocf Bridgeport MM |
| 12-20-1866 | Joel & w Catharine rocf Bridgeport MM |
| 11-26-1868 | William B, Duck Creek P M compl he has been guilty of improper & scandalous conduct He offered an ackn 2-25-1869 |
| 4-22-1869 | William B & w Elvirah & ch gct Indianapolis MM |
| 5-20-1869 | Joel & w Catharine gct Walnut Ridge MM |
| 10-26-1871 | Elnathan & w Elizabeth & ch Letitia L, Rebecca E, Martha E, Sarah E, Melissa E, Thomas J A & Etta J rocf Deep Creek MM, NC |
| 7-25-1872 | Elnathan & w Elizabeth & fam gct Westfield MM |
| 9-17-1872 | Mahlon & fam req cert to Westfield MM 1-23-1873 comm rpts that they are not permanently located. So matter is drpd |

DUCK CREEK

### COX (Cont)
| | |
|---|---|
| 3-23-1876 | Mahlon & fam gct Honey Creek MM |
| 7-24-1919 | Robert & w Fayette & ch Mary Olive & Herbertine rocf Westland MM |
| 9-25-1920 | William Thomas & w Olive & ch Paul, Thomas rocf Westland MM |
| 2-26-1925 | Herbert & fam drpd from mbrp |

### CRAFT
| | |
|---|---|
| 1-21-1892 | Charles rec on req |
| 3-24-1892 | Nancy rec on req |

### CRAIG
| | |
|---|---|
| 9-25-1890 | Mary drpd from mbrp |
| 12-25-1890 | David, Melvina, Phillip, Sarah & Clarinda drpd from mbrp |
| 11-26-1891 | John drpd from mbrp |
| 3-24-1892 | Oren rec on req |
| 3-22-1894 | Wilson & w Clara rec on req |
| 5-24-1894 | Wilson & Clara rel on req |
| 1-23-1896 | David & w Emma & ch Mary & Phillip rec on req |
| 12-23-1897 | Jehu M, & w Eliza A & ch Alonzo M, Daniel Leroy, Claude O & Lula M rec on req |
| 8-22-1901 | David & w Emma & ch Philip & Olive rel on req |
| 5-25-1916 | Mrs Etta rec on req |
| 2-21-1924 | David & Emma rec on req |

### CRANDLE
| | |
|---|---|
| 8-24-1859 | Sarah Ann (form Compton) rpt mcd   dis |

### CRONK
| | |
|---|---|
| 10- 6-1927 | Margaret Thelma, Joseph Myron, Dorothy Jean & Horace Allen ch of Chester & Mary rec on req |
| 1- 5-1928 | Chester rec on req |

### CROOK
| | |
|---|---|
| 12-26-1844 | Eliza Anna (form Dulea) Clear Spring P M compl for mcd & j Meth   Milford MM is req to treat w/h   Milford MM rpts no satisfaction   dis 7-24-1845 |

### CROY
| | |
|---|---|
| 8-26-1869 | Lavina rec in mbrp |
| 2-23-1882 | Lavina gct Raysville MM, but she died before cert was sent.  She was buried at Duck Creek burying ground |

### CULBERTSON
| | |
|---|---|
| 10-24-1878 | Martha J Reece & her ch Ellen C & Walter T CULBERTSON rocf Honey Creek MM |

### DARLING
| | |
|---|---|
| 5-21-1914 | Ruth & Mary Lucille rec on req |
| 1-24-1924 | Murry rec on req |
| 9-25-1924 | Elsworth drpd from mbrp |

### DAVIDSON
| | |
|---|---|
| 6-22-1911 | Clessie & s Clarence B rec on req |
| 12-21-1911 | Clessie & w Ona & ch Clarence rel on req |

### DAVIS
| | |
|---|---|
| 9-28-1826 | Nathan appt to a comm |
| 3- 1-1827 | Lovey appt to a comm |
| 2-26-1830 | Thomas, of Wayne Co, s Harmon & Hannah of same county, m at Duck Creek M H to Hannah Moore, dt Abraham Henry & 1st w Susannah, decd of Henry Co |
| 4-22-1830 | Hannah gct Milford MM |
| 1-20-1831 | Tristrim & w Rebecca & ch Clarkson, Elwood, Matilda, Lucinda & Leander rocf Silver Creek Mtg |
| 1-20-1831 | Thomas & w Hannah rocf Milford Mtg |
| 10-20-1831 | Thomas & w Hannah & dt Susannah gct Milford MM |
| 7-25-1833 | Thomas & w Hannah & ch Susannah & Abraham rocf Milford MM |
| 9-25-1834 | Lovey & ch (living in St Joseph Co) gct Mississinewa MM |
| 10-23-1834 | Isaac & w Phebe & dt Lavinia rocf Milford MM |
| 12-25-1834 | Sarah (form Hosier), Clear Springs P M compl for mcd   dis 3-26-1835 |
| 9-25-1834 | Alexander, Duck Creek P M compl mcd Mississinewa declines to treat w/him |
| 1-25-1835 | Jehu & w Rebecca & s Oliver rocf Milford MM |
| 2-25-1836 | Thomas & w Hannah & ch gct West Grove MM |
| 11-24-1842 | Elizabeth rec in mbrp |
| 2-26-1846 | Elizabeth (form Ratliff) Clear Springs P M compl for mcd   3-26-1846 she offered an ackn |
| 4-23-1846 | Elizabeth gct Spiceland MM |
| 10-29-1851 | Nathan of Spiceland Mtg, Henry Co, s Elihu & Alice both decd, of Huntington Co, Pa  m at Clear Springs M H to Jane Dickey of Henry Co, dt Nimrod & w Ann, decd |
| 2-26-1852 | Jane gct Spiceland MM |
| 1-26-1870 | Jacob of Mississinewa MM, Grant Co, s Jesse & Alice, both decd, m at Clear Springs M H to Hannah Ratliff, dt Phineas & Christy Ann, decd of Henry Co |

### DAWSON
| | |
|---|---|
| 11-24-1836 | Isaac & w Sarah & ch William & Anna rocf Marlborough MM, Ohio |
| 6-23-1859 | Ann Modlin (form Dawson) rpt mcd  Anna retains her mbrp |
| 6-26-1862 | William gct Spiceland MM to m Abigail Hammer |
| 7-23-1863 | William gct Spiceland MM |
| 11-23-1871 | Isaac & dt Sinai gct Tonganoxie MM, Kas |

### DEAN - DEEN
| | |
|---|---|
| 1-21-1836 | John Schooley Pike gct Spiceland MM to m Elma Dean |
| 4-22-1841 | Uriah rocf Dover MM, N C end by Spiceland MM |
| 9-21-1843 | Uriah gct Westfield MM |

### DEEM
| | |
|---|---|
| 3-22-1894 | Mary E rec on req |

### DELON
| | |
|---|---|
| 8-23-1855 | Penina (dt of James Morgan) rocf Deep River MM, N C |
| 5-22-1924 | Horace L & w Reola L & ch Joseph Paul, Robert Horace & Douris Loucile rec on req |

### DENER
| | |
|---|---|
| 3-20-1902 | Anna rec on req |

### DENNY
| | |
|---|---|
| 4-25-1861 | Jacob L B, Springfield MM, req this mtg to treat w/h for mcd |
| 4-24-1862 | Shubel & 2nd w Dorothy & ch Lewis Marion & Mary Lucinda rocf Springfield MM |
| 7-20-1871 | Shubal & fam req trans Walnut Ridge MM |
| 8-22-1872 | Shubal & fam, comm rpt "difficulties in the way" case dismissed |

### DESELMS
| | |
|---|---|
| 3-23-1837 | Jonas rocf Flushing MM, Ohio |
| 8-24-1837 | Mary rocf Flushing MM, Ohio |
| 3-24-1842 | Mary Bowman (form Deselms) Duck Creek P M compl for mcd   On 4-21-1842 she offered ackn |
| 4-24-1845 | Jonas & w Elizabeth & fam gct Mississinewa MM |
| 3-23-1854 | Sarah (form Pickering) Clear Springs P M compl for mcd   dis 6- 6-1854 |
| 10-21-1858 | Melvina rocf Mississinewa MM |
| 5-25-1859 | Melvina Cooper (form Deselms) rpt mcd dis |

### DICKEY
| | |
|---|---|
| 11-24-1836 | Nimrod & w Ann & ch Phebe, Jane Charity, Mary Ann, James & Asenath rocf Newberry MM, Ohio |
| 2-24-1842 | Phebe Hiatt (form Dickey) Clear Springs P M compl for mcd  3-24-1842 Phebe offered ackn |

DUCK CREEK

## DICKEY (Cont)

|  |  |
|---|---|
| 9-22-1842 | James, Clear Springs P M compl for mcd 1-20-1842 chm |
| 3-23-1843 | Jane rocf Elk MM, Oh |
| 1-22-1846 | Mary Ann, Clear Springs compl for j Meth She now resides in the limits of Milford MM & req that mtg treat w/h 6-25-1846 Milford MM rpt no satis dis 7-23-1846 |
| 11-22-1849 | Jane gct Milford MM |
| 12-26-1850 | Asenath gct Milford MM |
| 6-26-1851 | James, Clear Springs P M compl for j Meth dis 9-25-1851 |
| 9-25-1851 | Jane rocf Westfield MM |
| 10-29-1851 | Jane of Henry Co, dt Nimrod & Ann, decd m at Clear Springs M H to Nathan Davis of Spiceland Mtg, Henry Co, s Elisha & Alice both decd, of Huntington Co, Pa |
| 8-26-1858 | Asenath, Cadiz P M compl for na, jas & unchastity. Being a mbr of Milford MM that mtg is informed Duck Creek is req to treat w/h No satisfaction & so rptd to Milford MM |

## DICKS

|  |  |
|---|---|
| 7-22-1830 | Job & w Hannah & ch Naomi, Elizabeth, Sally, Nathan & Levisa rocf Bloomfield MM |
| 7-22-1847 | Elizabeth (form Heston), Clear Springs MM inf mcd dis 8-26-1847 |

## DIFFIE

|  |  |
|---|---|
| 4-25-1872 | William A & w Pheraba & fam rec in mbrp |
| 5-21-1874 | William A & w Pheraba & fam gct Raysville MM |

## DILHORN

|  |  |
|---|---|
| 12-25-1856 | James, Duck Creek P M compl for upl toward his parents He is mbr of Whitewater MM which has been informed dis 7-23-1857 at Whitewater MM |

## DILLON

|  |  |
|---|---|
| 8-25-1836 | Jonathan & w Agnes & ch Elizabeth L, Jonathan jr & Sarah rocf Center MM, Ohio |
| 8-25-1836 | Richard H & w Elizabeth & s Allen rocf Center MM, Ohio |
| 10-20-1836 | Jesse & w Mary & ch Isaac, Albert, Sarah A, Mary Jane & William rocf Center MM, Ohio |
| 8-24-1837 | Joseph rocf Center MM, Ohio |
| 3-26-1896 | Nathan, Catharine & Elbert rec on req |

## DRAPER

|  |  |
|---|---|
| 11-22-1827 | Josiah jr & w Catharine & ch Huldah & Jane rocf Milford MM |
| 11-26-1829 | Josiah jr, Duck Creek P M compl that he refuses to comply with an engagement 1-21-1830 case dismissed |
| 4-22-1830 | Joshua & Huldah & dt Millicent rocf Milford MM |
| 6-24-1830 | Josiah, Duck Creek P M compl that there is a compl for refusing to comply with the judgement of the arbitrators chosen to settle a matter of interest between him and another friend. 8-26-1830 cause of complaint has been removed so case dismissd |
| 9-23-1830 | Joshua, Duck Creek P M compl for na & upl dis 11-25-1830 |
| 8-23-1832 | Joshiah Sr & 2nd w, Jemima & his dt Mary Ann, rocf Milford MM |
| 8-22-1833 | Elizabeth rocf Marlborough Mtg end by Whitewater MM |
| 4-24-1834 | Thomas req to become a mbr 5-22-1834 The comm wrote to Western Branch MM, Va for it's consent 10-23-1834 It's consent not given |
| 9-24-1835 | Mary of Walnut Ridge MM rec in mbrp |
| 10-23-1834 | Huldah & fam gct Mississinewa MM |
| 5-24-1835 | Thomas rocf Western Branch MM, Va |
| 8-20-1835 | Josiah, Clear Springs P M, inf he is out of unity with friends & manifests a -----? disposition dis 11-26-1835 |
| 1-21-1836 | Josiah informs mtg he is appealing to the Q M |
| 2-26-1845 | Jane, dt Josiah & Catharine, m at Clear Springs M H to Eli Ratliff of Henry Co, s Joseph, decd & Rebecca |
| 1-24-1850 | Hannah (form Presnall) Clear Spring P M compl for mcd 2-21-1850 an ackn offered |
| 2-21-1850 | Rachel Newby (form Draper), Clear Springs P M compl for mcd 3-21-1850 an ackn offered |
| 11-27-1850 | Martha of Henry Co, dt Josiah & Catharine m at Clear Springs M H to Thomas Clarkson Kirk of Henry Co, s Thomas & Sarah, decd |
| 5-24-1855 | Miriam Stanley (form Draper) Clear Springs P M inf mcd 7-26-1855 chm |
| 4-24-1856 | Catharine gct Spiceland MM |
| 4-24-1856 | Mary gct Spiceland MM |
| 10-23-1862 | Lydia gct Mississinewa MM |
| 3-24-1865 | Noah & w Lydia & ch Amanda M & Elmer G rocf Mississinewa MM & end by Spiceland MM |
| 9-22-1864 | Catharine & Mary gct Spiceland MM |
| 3-21-1867 | Harriet, dt of Noah & Lydia rec in mbrp |
| 5-30-1867 | Catherine of Greensboro, Henry Co, wid of Josiah jr & dt of Nathan & Huldah Pearson, both decd m at Duck Creek M H to David Palmer of Clear Springs, Henry Co, s John & Anna, both decd |
| 5-21-1868 | Nathan & w Mary Ann rec in mbrp |
| 1-21-1869 | Noah & w Lydia req Walnut Ridge MM cert 9-23-1869 req dismissed on acct of unpaid debts |
| 11-24-1870 | Nathan & fam gct Bangor MM, Iowa |
| 12-21-1871 | Noah & fam gct Tonganoxi MM, Kas |
| 2-26-1874 | Jemima E rec in mbrp |
| 4-23-1874 | Ephraim & Oliver H rec in mbrp |
| 4-23-1874 | Laura rec in mbrp |
| 2-23-1893 | Emma rocf Spiceland Mtg |
| 4-26-1894 | Luther C rec on req |
| 1-20-1898 | Luther & w Emma & dt Jessie Cleta gct Spiceland MM |
| 3-25-1915 | Leburn & w Hattie rel on req |

## DULEA

|  |  |
|---|---|
| 11-24-1836 | Lydia & ch William, Susanna, Sina Jane, Lizanna, Thomas Elwood, Lydia jr & Mary rocf Marlborough MM, Ohio |
| 1-26-1837 | Maxson, Marlborough MM req Duck Creek MM to treat w/h for intoxication & upl 2-23-1837 He denies the charges & Marlborough so informed |
| 2-25-1841 | Susannah, Sinah Jane, Elizanna, Lydia, James, T Elwood, Mary & John B, ch of Lydia rocf Back Creek MM |
| 3-25-1841 | Lydia rocf Mississinewa MM end by Back Creek MM |
| 2-24-1842 | Sina Jane Hiatt (form Dulea) Clear Springs P M compl for mcd offered ackn on 3-24-1842 |
| 5-23-1843 | Susannah Love (form Dulea) Clear Spring P M compl for mcd & j Meth dis 8-24-1843 |
| 12-26-1845 | Elizanna Crook (form Dulea) Clear Spring P M compl for mcd & j Meth dis 6-26-1845 |
| 1-22-1846 | Lydia, Clear Springs P M compl for j Meth dis 3-26-1846 |
| 6-21-1849 | Maxson's ch gct Sugar River MM |
| 3-21-1850 | Thomas Elwood's cert issued 6-mo-1849 ret by Sugar River MM with inf he had j Meth before the date of the cert dis 7-25-1850 |
| 3-21-1850 | The cert issued to Sugar River MM for the ch of Maxson has been returned with info that they had j Meth previously to the date of cert dis |

## DUNLAP

|  |  |
|---|---|
| 4-25-1844 | Phebe (form Grey) Duck Creek P M inf mcd & j Meth She being a mbr of Milford MM that MM has been informed dis by Milford MM 9-26-1844 |

## DYER

|  |  |
|---|---|
| 8-24-1837 | George & w Elizabeth & ch Mahala, Priscilla, Rebecca, Levi, Isaac & Ruth rocf Cherry Grove MM |
| 1839 | George & ch gct Westfield MM |

DUCK CREEK

## DYSART
| | |
|---|---|
| 8-25-1853 | Rachel gct Salem MM, Iowa |
| 7-24-1856 | Rachel gct Spring Creek MM, Iowa |

## EDGERTON
| | |
|---|---|
| 8-31-1826 | Patience appt to comm to att Q M |
| 8-31-1826 | Patience appt to comm to have charge of indulged Mtgs |
| 3-29-1827 | Reuben appt to a comm |
| 8-23-1827 | Reuben & Jehu Wickersham appt to att funerals of Friends at Duck Creek P M |
| 9-23-1830 | Reuben & Josiah Small, Micajah Binford appt to hold title to land for school purposes that may be deeded to the Society |
| 5-31-1832 | Avice, dt Reuben & Patience of Henry Co m at Duck Creek M H to Ashbel Binford, s Joshua & Lydia of Rush Co |
| 4-24-1834 | Samuel (a Minister) & w Elizabeth & ch Samuel & Joseph rocf Elk MM, Ohio |
| 9-25-1834 | Tabitha rocf Elk MM, Ohio |
| 9- 1-1836 | Benajah, s Reuben & Patience of Henry Co m at Duck Creek M H to Diana Hinshaw, dt Seth & Hannah, decd of Henry Co |
| 5-20-1841 | Martha rocf Whitewater MM |
| 4-22-1842 | Elizabeth, dt Reuben & Patience of Henry Co m at Duck Creek M H to Joseph Marshall of Sugar Plain MM, Boone Co, s Isaac & Ruth, both decd, of Driftwood Mtg |
| 3-20-1845 | Reuben gct Mississinewa MM |

## EDWARDS
| | |
|---|---|
| 3- 5-1827 | William & w Elizabeth & ch Jonathan & Anna rocf Miami MM, Ohio |
| 1-21-1841 | Bathsheba (form Bufkin) Clear Springs P M compl for mcd  2-25-1841 she now residing in limits of Back Creek MM & that mtg is req to treat w/h  11-25-1841 Back Creek MM rpts no satisfaction  dis |
| 7-20-1843 | Mary (form Weeks) Duck Creek MM compl for mcd  dis 9-21-1843 |
| 12-23-1880 | William & w Rebecca & ch Levi Morton & Martha P rocf Raysville MM |
| 9-22-1881 | Peninah & ch Charles Elsworth & Eunice Semira gct Raysville MM |
| 3-25-1885 | William & w Elizabeth & ch Levi M & Martha P gct Raysville MM |
| 5-21-1885 | Sarah & ch Julia, Edna, Maude, May & ----? rocf Raysville MM |
| 2-21-1892 | Charles E rocf Raysville MM |
| 12-20-1906 | Nellie gct New Castle Mtg |
| 10-24-1907 | Nellie drpd from mbrp |

## ELLIOTT
| | |
|---|---|
| 2- 1-1827 | Ann appt to a comm |
| 3-29-1827 | Elizabeth (form Hobson) compl of for mcd  dis 7-26-1827 |
| 3-27-1828 | Susannah, dt Jacob & Ann of Henry Co m at Duck Creek M H to Nathan Reece of Henry Co s John & Ann of same place |
| 8-20-1829 | Welmet Hodson (form Elliott) compl of for mcd  9-24-1829 Welmet chm |
| 12-22-1831 | Ruth rocf Milford MM |
| 4- 5-1832 | Elvy, dt Jacob & Ann of Henry Co m at Duck Creek M H to John Lewelling of Henry Co s Meshack & Jane |
| 10-24-1833 | Obadiah & w Armelia & ch Benjamin, Seth, Calvin & Clark rocf Center MM, N C end by Spiceland MM |
| 10-23-1834 | Obadiah & w Sarah rocf Centre MM, N C |
| 2-26-1835 | Obadiah & w Sarah gct Sugar River MH |
| 2-23-1843 | Isaac, Katharine, Maryann, Martha, Melissa & John jr, minor ch of John, decd, & Mary (now Mary Palmer, 2nd w of David Palmer) rocf Milford MM |
| 11-23-1843 | Obadiah, Duck Creek P M compl that he has identified himself with the Separatists  dis 1-25-1844 |
| 7-25-1844 | Armelia, Duck Creek Mtg compl for j (ASF)  dis 9-26-1844 |
| 6-25-1846 | Mary P (form Bowman) Duck Creek P M compl for mcd  dis 8-20-1846 |
| 6-25-1846 | Catharine W rocf Milford MM |
| 3-25-1847 | Richard P rocf Milford MM |
| 2-25-1847 | Isaiah, Duck Creek P M compl for na & upl  dis 6-24-1847 |
| 5-25-1848 | Jacob, Duck Creek P M compl for na & att a mcd of a mbr  dis 7-20-1848 |
| 8-24-1848 | Richard P gct Spiceland MM to m Martha E Prichard |
| 12-21-1848 | Richard P gct Spiceland MM |
| 3-28-1849 | Mary Ann of Henry Co, dt John, decd & Mary, m at Clear Springs M H to William Saint of Henry Co, s William Sr & Achsah decd |
| 11-28-1849 | Isaac of Clear Springs P M, Henry Co, s John, decd formerly of Wayne Co, & w Mary (now Mary Palmer) m at Clear Springs M H to Mary E Newby, dt of Elias & Lydia, decd of Clear Springs P M |
| 4-25-1850 | Lucinda (form Bowman) Duck Creek P M compl for mcd & j Meth dis 6-20-1850 |
| 5-23-1850 | Calvin, Duck Creek P M compl for mcd  dis 7-25-1850 |
| 6-24-1852 | Hannah Ballenger (form Elliott) Duck Creek P M compl for mcd  dis 8-26-1852 |
| 7-21-1853 | Martha N (form Elliott) Clear Springs P M compl for mcd  dis 1-26-1854  She having removed to the limits of Salem MM, Iowa a copy of the dis has been forwarded there |
| 11-24-1853 | Martha Hunt (form Elliott) rpt mcd  dis 1-26-1854 |
| 11-24-1853 | Seth, Clear Springs P M compl for mcd  dis 1-26-1854 |
| 8-21-1862 | John S gct West Union MM to m Rhoda M Johnson |
| 5-21-1863 | John S gct West Union MM |
| 1-21-1864 | Nathan, Duck Creek P M inf he has mcd  dis |
| 5-25-1865 | Melissa Jane gct Hopewell MM |
| 7-21-1870 | Isaac T & fam gct Plainfield Mtg |
| 1-25-1877 | Emily rocf Spiceland MM |
| 6-26-1884 | Job & w Margaret rocf Raysville MM |
| 3-26-1891 | Gulia A rocf Raysville MM |
| 1-25-1894 | Richard rec on req |
| 1-26-1899 | Columbus & w Evaline & ch Nellie, Milford, Clara & Mollie rec on req |
| 3-24-1904 | Albert E rec on req |
| 3-24-1910 | Catharine rocf Hopewell MM |
| 6-24-1915 | Norman Lee rec on req |
| 3-22-1917 | Carlon & Norma drpd from mbrp |
| 3-20-1919 | Carlon & Norma & ch Alta Maurine rec on req |
| 3-23-1921 | Gulia A gct New Castle MM |
| 3-23-1921 | Carlon & w Norma & ch B Alison & Alta Maurine gct New Castle MM |

## ELLIS
| | |
|---|---|
| 11-21-1833 | Thomas & w Elizabeth & ch Nancy, Jesse W & Ellis rocf New Hope MM, TN |
| 7-20-1837 | Elizabeth appt o at Fall Creek P M |
| 10-20-1842 | Thomas & ch Nancy Ann, Jesse, Jacob, Sarah, Jane, Jemima & Ruth rocf Back Creek MM |
| 5-23-1844 | Elizabeth, Back Creek MM req this mtg to treat w/h for mcd in a mtg of Anti-Slavery Friends  2-20-1845  dis rec from Back Creek MM |
| 3-27-1845 | Nancy A, dt Thomas & Elizabeth, decd m at Duck Creek M H to Pemberton Macy of Hopewell Mtg, Henry Co s Nathan & Katharine, decd |
| 11-21-1850 | Thomas, Duck Creek P M inf mcd  dis 1-23-1851 |
| 11-20-1851 | Ruth & Jemima, minors, gct Wabash MM |
| 3-24-1853 | Asa rocf Flushing MM, Ohio |
| 11-24-1853 | Joshua & dts Martha & Miriam rocf Flushing MM, Ohio |
| 11-24-1853 | Jonathan rocf Flushing MM, Ohio |
| 11-24-1853 | Lydia rocf Flushing MM, Ohio |
| 11-24-1853 | Abigail rocf Flushing MM, Ohio |
| 3-13-1854 | Asa, of Harrison twp, Henry Co, s Joshua & Miriam of same place, m at Cadiz M H to Elizabeth Cooper, dt William & Ann of Henry Co |
| 5- 1-1856 | Abigail B, of Cadiz Mtg, dt Joshua & Miriam, both decd, m at Cadiz M H to John Bufkin of Cadiz, Henry Co, s Thomas & Ruth, both decd, of same place |
| 12- 1-1856 | Lydia, of Henry Co, dt Joshua & Miriam, both decd m at Clear Spring M H to William Macy of Spiceland Mtg, Henry Co s Stephen & Sarah, decd of Guilford Co, NC |

ELLIS (Cont)
10- 1-1857    Asa, of Cadiz Mtg, Henry Co, s Joshua &
              Miriam, both decd m at Cadiz M H, to
              Asenath Ratliff, (wid of John M Ratliff)
              & dt David & Sarah, decd, Palmer
10-23-1857    Sarah Jane rpt j Meth    dis
9- 1-1859     Martha, dt Joshua & Miriam, both decd, m
              at Cadiz M H, to Stephen Gause of Elm
              Grove Mtg, Henry Co, s Nathan, decd & Mary
              of same place
10-25-1866    Asa & w Asenath & fam gct Plainfield MM
10-25-1866    Miriam gct Plainfield MM

ELZEY
4-26-1832     Jared rocf Milford MM
11-20-1834    Susannah & ch Absolom Vickery, Sarah Ann,
              John, Nancy & William Dawson rec on req

ENGLEBERTH
7-22-1841     Jane (form Newby) Duck Creek P M compl for
              mcd    dis  9-22-1841

ESTELL
4-26-1894     Francis M & w Mary rec on req
2-26-1903     Charles H & ch Ollie, Francis, Flo & John
              Reuben, rec on req
3-22-1906     Charles & w Josephine & ch Flora M & John
              R gct Carthage MM
3-22-1917     Charles H, Ollie & Flora drpd from mbrp
9-24-1925     Charles & w Ollie & s Floyd Coffin, Estell
              & Edna Levaughn & Thelma Fern Herrald, ch
              by -----? former m, rocf Knightstown MM
8- 2-1928     Charley & w Olive & s Floyd gct New Castle
              MM

EVANS
8-31-1826     George & w Mary & ch Asenath & a minor ch
              under their care, John Van Horn, rocf
              Miami MM, Ohio end by Milford MM
5- 3-1827     George appt a Clerk to fill place of John
              Copeland
(1832)        (George & Mary & fam living in the area
              of Duck Creek Mtg which became Spiceland
              MM, became charter mbrs of said Spiceland
              MM)
1-26-1848     Owen of Spiceland P M, Henry Co, s George
              & Mary of same place, m at Clear Springs M
              H to Martha Price, dt Rice jr & Susannah
              Price
11-23-1848    Martha Ann gct Spiceland MM
11-22-1849    Ann (form Moore) Clear Spring P M compl
              for mcd & unbecoming conduct  dis 1-24-1850
5-26-1853     Children of Ann gct Greenfield MM
4-28-1854     Richard of Spiceland Mtg, Henry Co, s
              George & Mary, m at Cadiz M H to Lydia
              Jane Pickering, dt David & Nancy of Cadiz,
              Henry Co
6-21-1855     Lydia Jane gct Spiceland MM
4-23-1868     Miriam rec in mbrp
2-22-1877     William H rec on req
2-20-1879     William H gct New Salem MM
11-24-1881    William H rocf New Salem MM
4-20-1882     Mary M & dt Minnie Jane rocf Hopewell MM
1-24-1884     Narcissa rocf Spiceland MM
11-22-1900    William & fam gct New Hope MM

FARQUAR
8-22-1833     David, a minor, rocf Flushing MM, Ohio

FAUST
2-21-1901     Bessie Pearl rec on req
4-23-1903     May gct Westland MM

FAWCETT
10-21-1852    Eliza Jane rocf Flushing Mtg, Ohio
1-26-1854     Nancy & ch Joseph, Alpheus, Lewelda, John,
              William & Benjamin F rocf Flushing MM, Oh
5-24-1855     Eliza Jane Small (form Fawcett) rpt mcd
              dis
12-20-1860    Alpheus, Duck Creek P M compl for using
              spiritous liquor & fighting  2-21-1861
              offered ackn
4-24-1862     Alpheus, Duck Creek rpt mcd  dis
6-21-1866     Samuel rec on req

2-23-1871     John W, Duck Creek P M inf mcd  He
              retained his mbrp
4-23-1874     J W gct Spiceland MM
2-21-1884     Nancy gct Spiceland MM

FENTRESS
8-21-1834     Susannah rocf Newgarden MM
1-25-1844     Susannah, Duck Creek compl for j (ASF)
              dis

FIELDS
2-26-1925     Olive Shugart gct Marion MM

FISHER
4- 5-1928     Orville & w Cecil & ch Eugene, Elsworth,
              William & Louise rocf Rockford MM, Ohio

FLETCHER
9-24-1903     Joel rocf Spiceland MM

FORBES
3-25-1881     Martha & dt Martha rec on req
9-25-1890     Martha drpd from mbrp
4-26-1900     William & Rebecca drpd from mbrp

FOREMAN
12-21-1893    Ida B rocf New Salem MM

FORKNER
2-23-1892     Louis, Elma & Carl Logan rec on req
3-22-1900     Raymond & Eva, ch of Lewis & Velma rec
              on req
 -23-1919     Belva, Carl & Raymond rel on req

FORREST
3-23-1922     Elsie Fay & Palmer Albertus rec on req
1-25-1923     Jesse Elsworth & w Kate May & s James
              Taylor rec on req

FORSTER - FOSTER
11-25-1830    Joseph & w Mary & ch Jemima, Samuel &
              Hester rocf New Garden MM, N C
9-21-1848     Asenath B rocf New Garden MM, N C
5-23-1850     Robert rocf New Garden MM, N C
7-24-1851     Asenath B gct Spiceland MM
3-20-1856     Sallie Ann (form Macy) rptd mcd  dis
4-20-1882     Emma rocf Raysville MM

FOWLER
11-25-1880    Eliza J gct Whitewater MM
8-20-1891     Benjamin F & w Linnie gct Indianapolis MM

FOX
1-20-1870     William P & w rec on req
11-24-1881    Lida & ch Artie & Cora rec on req
12-24-1881    Minnie, dt of Lida rec on req
10-23-1890    Parker & w Cornelia rec on req
5-25-1893     William P & w Cornelia gct Raysville MM
12-24-1896    Eliza J gct Knightstown MM but cert was
              returned
3-21-1901     Eliza J drpd from mbrp
4-23-1903     Cornelia rocf Knightstown MM

FRAMPTON
3-24-1881     Sarah A rec on req
3-24-1892     Nancy G & dt Myrtle rec on req
2-24-1898     William & Sarah drpd from mbrp

FRAZIER
1-26-1893     Eldora gct Nettle Creek MM

GANO
1-25-1923     Jennie Copeland gct Whittier MM, Ca

GARD
1-26-1899     Raymond rec on req
2-23-1899     Gresham & w Vashti & ch Alden E, Nellie O,
              Christopher H, Orville M, Eva M, Verllie
              B, Orman P & Gresham M roc
4-23-1903     Raymond drpd from mbrp
1-25-1912     Gresham gct Fairmount MM (returned he
              was in Kansas)
6-25-1914     Gresham gct Knightstown MM

DUCK CREEK

## GARNER
| | |
|---|---|
| 3-24-1881 | Phebe rec on req |
| 4-26-1900 | Daniel & Maggie rel on req |
| 5-21-1903 | Alice & ch Walter, Maud, Herman & Fannie gc |

## GARRETSON
| | |
|---|---|
| 12-21-1843 | Joel rocf Flushing Mtg, Ohio |
| 7-25-1844 | Joel, Clear Spring P M compl for mcd & jas dis 9-26-1844 |

## GAUSE
| | |
|---|---|
| 9-1-1859 | Stephen A of Elm Grove Mtg, Henry Co, s Nathan, decd, & Mary m at Cadiz M H, Martha Ellis, dt Joshua & Miriam both decd |
| 11-24-1859 | Martha E gct Spiceland MM |
| 5-26-1865 | Samuel rocf Spiceland MM |
| 3-22-1866 | Samuel gct Springfield MM to m Mary Jane Harvey |
| 7-26-1866 | Mary J rocf Springfield MM |
| 12-20-1866 | Eli C & w Elva P & ch Oliver & Seth M rocf Spiceland MM |
| 3-26-1868 | William T & w Jane M & ch Everetta Rebecca & Daniel M rocf Bridgeport MM |
| 3-26-1868 | Elva P recorded as a Minister |
| 3-21-1869 | Oliver gct Lynn Grove MM, Iowa |
| 5-20-1869 | William & w Jane & ch gct Indianapolis MM |
| 4-27-1870 | Samuel & w Mary J & ch gct Miami MM, Ohio |
| 10-26-1871 | Eli P gct Cane Creek, N C |
| 11-23-1871 | Seth M gct Lynn Grove MM, Iowa |
| 4-20-1876 | Solomon & w Celia rocf Raysville MM |
| 11-23-1876 | Solomon & w Celia gct Walnut Ridge MM |

## GIBBONS
| | |
|---|---|
| 11-22-1832 | Sophia rocf Whitewater MM |

## GIBSON
| | |
|---|---|
| 10-25-1849 | Anna (form Bond) Clear Springs P M compl for mcd dis 11-22-1849 |

## GILBERT
| | |
|---|---|
| 8-25-1859 | Joseph H Williams gct Hopewell MM to m Dorothy Gilbert |
| 3-23-1860 | Aaron rocf Milford MM |
| 3-24-1892 | Jesse & w Sarah Ann rocf New Castle MM |
| 6-23-1892 | Josiah Clarence rocf Hopewell MM |
| 6-21-1894 | Glenna Maria rocf New Castle MM |
| 5-26-1910 | Josiah & w Glenna gct Dublin MM |

## GILBREATH
| | |
|---|---|
| 9-22-1853 | Anna (form Bowman) Duck Creek P M compl for mcd dis 11-24-1853 |

## GRAHAM
| | |
|---|---|
| 8-22-1918 | Earl rec on req |

## GRAVES
| | |
|---|---|
| 8-25-1870 | Jesse, cert not accepted, clerk directed to return it to New Salem MM |

## GRAY
| | |
|---|---|
| 9-25-1834 | David & Jonathan, minors, rocf Spiceland MM |
| 10-8-1841 | Davis of Rush Co, s James & Margaret, decd m at Duck Creek M H, Ruth Ann Jay, dt Joseph of Randolph Co, N C decd & Edith Jay |
| 2-24-1842 | Ruthanna gct Walnut Ridge MM |
| 12-22-1842 | Davis & Ruth Anna rocf Walnut Ridge MM |
| 3-20-1856 | Davis, Duck Creek P M compl for cursing & j Meth dis 5-22-1856 |
| 8-21-1856 | Ruthanna dis for j Meth |
| 3-25-1858 | Ruthanna rec in mbrp |
| 7-25-1867 | Thomas, Duck Creek P M compl of using liquor, upl & na dis 10-24-1867 |
| 6-25-1868 | Hugh E, Duck Creek P M inf mcd but he retains his mbrp |
| 10-21-1869 | Hugh E, con his using intoxicating drink to excess |
| 4-24-1873 | Hugh E, Duck Creek P M compl for na dis 11-20-1873 |
| 3-26-1874 | Davis rec in mbrp |
| 4-25-1878 | Thomas rec on req |
| 8-25-1880 | Thomas rel on req |
| 11-24-1881 | Hugh E & w Rebecca Jane & ch Rosa, Ora, Ellen & Maude rocf Raysville MM |
| 8-24-1882 | Hugh E dis |
| 10-23-1884 | Jane rel on req |
| 10-20-1892 | Thomas rel on req |
| 1-26-1899 | Malissa rec on req |
| 2-23-1899 | Annis May & Docie Ruth rec on req |
| 12-20-1906 | Alice rocf New Castle MM |
| 3-24-1910 | Leroy & w Melissa & ch Docia & Abbis drpd from mbrp |
| 3-20-1913 | J Wayne rec on req |
| 4-23-1914 | Bessie M rec on req |

## GREEN
| | |
|---|---|
| 7-21-1907 | Martha Carlile drpd from mbrp |
| 3-23-1922 | Frances Emogene rec on req |

## GREGG
| | |
|---|---|
| 5-21-1829 | Hannah & ch Anna, Hannah, Achsah, Sarah, Lydia, Eliza & Mary rocf Flushing MM, Oh |
| 1-22-1835 | Hannah Williams (form Gregg), Duck Creek P M compl for mcd & j Hs dis 3-26-1835 |
| 9-26-1842 | Eliza, dt Stephen & Hannah m Jesse W Kenworthy of Spiceland MM, Henry Co s Amos & Mary, at Duck Creek M H |

## GRIEST
| | |
|---|---|
| 12-20-1891 | Dr Henry W & w Ebeline Edwards rocf Indianapolis MM |
| 2-22-1906 | Henry W & w Evalina E & ch Wishard H, Arnold E & C Elwood gct New Castle MM |
| 10-25-1906 | Nettie rec on req |

## GRIFFIN
| | |
|---|---|
| 8-23-1827 | Lydia appt to a comm |
| 9-23-1830 | Joshua & w Matilda rocf West Grove MM |
| 1-20-1831 | Ann & ch John, Mary, Jane, Eliza Ann & Lydia rocf Cherry Grove MM |
| 8-25-1831 | Joseph, West Grove MM req this mtg to treat w/h for dp & mcd Had no satisfaction treating w/h & West Grove so informed 1-26-1832 dis rec from West Grove MM |
| 5-2-1855 | John W of Spiceland, Henry Co, s Joseph & Rebecca m at Clear Spring M H, Anna C Price, dt Rice & Susannah of Henry Co |
| 8-23-1855 | Anna C gct Whitewater MM |
| 2-25-1904 | Edith J & David P rec on req |
| 9-21-1905 | Kenneth A & w Margaret rec on req |
| 4-20-1910 | Edith & Margaret rec on req |
| 1-22-1925 | David & w Eva & ch Edith, Margaret & Anna May gct Spiceland MM |

## GRIGG
| | |
|---|---|
| 9-22-1831 | Nathaniel & fam, Short Creek MM req to know what the records show concerning their rights. 10-21-1831 search was made but nothing found. Short Creek was informed that there is a recollection of the mbrs of this mtg of a cert for that fam coming to hand and being end to Short Creek MM |

## GRISSOM
| | |
|---|---|
| 9-26-1912 | Nettie gct New Castle MM |

## GRULER
| | |
|---|---|
| 11-25-1920 | Ethel Kern gct New Castle MM |

## GRUNDER
| | |
|---|---|
| 8-21-1900 | Maude gct Back Creek MM |
| 6-20-1907 | Maude Hinshaw drpd from mbrp |

## GYPE
| | |
|---|---|
| 2-20-1896 | Albert & w Rose & ch Lucy rec on req |
| 1-25-1899 | Henry rec on req |
| 4-20-1899 | Albert & w Rose & dt Lucy rel on req |
| 5-25-1899 | Sarah drpd from mbrp |
| 3-20-1902 | Maggie rec on req |
| 1-26-1905 | Henry drpd from mbrp |

## HABADIER
| | |
|---|---|
| 2-26-1885 | Amanda C rec on req |

DUCK CREEK

## HADLEY
8-9-1870    James of Fairfield Mtg, Highland Co, Ohio s James & Ann m at a Meeting held at Greensboro, Emily Saint, wid of Jonathan Saint & dt of James & Mary Johnson

1-26-1871    Emily & dt Mary Ella Saint gct Milford MM

## HAGERMAN
1-23-1913    Bradford, Lockridge & Effie rocf Spiceland MM

## HAISLEY
1-23-1851    David Kendall gct Dover MM to m Irena Ann Haisley

## HALE
11-25-1830    Derinda rocf Back Creek MM, N C & end to Arba MM

5-24-1832    Caleb & w Hannah rocf Milford MM

## HALL
1-20-1831    Benjamin & w Elizabeth & s Chalkley rocf Milford MM

5-24-1832    Hannah (w of Caleb) rocf Milford MM
7-26-1832    Rhoda rocf Milford MM
7-23-1835    Price F rocf New Garden MM
7-20-1837    Hannah (form Stanfield) mcd dis
4-23-1846    William rec on req
5-20-1847    William, Duck Creek P M inf mcd 2-24-1848 Honey Creek MM inf they treated w/h to satisfaction

3-23-1848    William gct Honey Creek MM

## HAMILTON
3-26-1896    Mary & dt Lela rec on req
4-22-1897    Thomas E rel on req
11-20-1902    Ida & Florence C rec on req
12-21-1911    Ida M & Florence gct Knightstown MM

## HAMM
7-21-1831    Elizabeth & ch Martha, Hezekiah & Elizabeth rocf Milford MM

1-23-1834    Jane rocf Milford MM
4-26-1834    Jane, dt John decd & Elizabeth of Hancock Co, m at Walnut Ridge M H, John Clark of Wayne Co, s John & Sarah, both decd

## HAMMER
4-21-1831    Isaac rocf Lost Creek MM, Tenn
3-22-1832    Elisha & w Nancy & ch Newton, Abigail & Catherine rocf Milford MM
7-26-1832    John rocf Lost Creek MM, Tenn
12-20-1832    Jonathan rocf Lost Creek MM, Tenn
10-24-1833    Nathan & w Ruth & ch Laban & Abigail rocf Springfield MM
11-21-1833    Laban rocf New Hope MM, Tenn
2-25-1836    Jonathan gct Westfield MM
3-24-1836    Nathan & w Ruth & ch gct Westfield MM
3-24-1836    Laban gct Westfield MM
5-25-1848    Elisha & w Nancy & ch gct Spiceland MM
5-25-1848    Isaac Newton, Duck Creek P M compl for upl & mcd 7-20-1848 he offered an ackn
2-21-1850    Isaac Newton gct Spiceland MM
6-26-1862    William Dawson gct Spiceland MM to m Abigail Hammer
7-21-1864    Peter rocf Spiceland MM
4-25-1867    Peter & w Sarah & fam gct Spiceland MM

## HAMMOND
11-25-1880    Sarah & dt Louisa Osborn rocf Raysville MM
3-24-1881    Joseph & w Hannah & dt Viola Frances rec on req
2-21-1884    Joseph & w Hannah & dt Viola Frances gct Mississinewa MM
12-24-1891    John & w gct Salem MM

## HAMPTON
1-24-1867    Deborah & ch Sarah, Edith, Thomas Elwood, Samuel & Haines rocf Whitewater MM
1-25-1883    Elmer gct Wabash MM
3-26-1891    Elwood gct Whitewater MM cert ret 5-21-1891
7-23-1903    Elwood gct Berkley MM, Ca

## HANSARD - HANSWARD
9-25-1890    J W, John & Mary drpd from mbrp
3-20-1902    G W rec on req
9-23-1920    George W rel on req

## HARDEN - HARDIN
10-26-1843    Lucinda (form Williams) mcd dis
3-23-1876    John C & w Ann & ch Edwin I & Horace L rec on req
3-23-1876    Mary C rec on req
3-24-1881    Jane rec on req
1-24-1907    Sarah Elma rocf Whitewater MM
3-26-1914    Margaret, J Alvin & Fred gct Spiceland MM
11-24-1921    Horace L gct Spiceland MM
5-22-1924    Lloyd Wilson & w Esther Mable & ch Edith rec on req
3-25-1926    Lloyd W & w Esther & Edith Maxine, dt of Lloyd by a former m & James Conkle, s of Esther by a former m gct New Salem MM

## HARKER
6-26-1873    Angenetta mcd dis

## HARNEY
1-21-1897    Charles B & w Martha & ch Lillian M, Edna R, Ethel S & Ruth A gct Spiceland MM

## HARRIS
11-23-1893    Phebe rel on req

## HARRISON
3-25-1847    William, a mbr of Rochester MM, N Y has mcd & that mtg has been informed
12-20-1855    Rachel rocf Balby MM held at Sheffield, Eng
4-22-1858    Rachel gct Balby MM, Eng

## HARROLD
12-24-1829    Patsey rec in mbrp w/con of New Garden MM
8-2-1928    Edna & Thelma gct New Castle MM

## HARTER
3-23-1922    Bertha S rec on req

## HARTLEY
1-21-1892    Thompson, Anna, Emma & Albert rec on req
1-21-1892    Charles, Mary J & Clara rec on req
3-24-1892    John rec on req
1-23-1896    Edward F & w Susan rec on req
11-23-1899    Mary J rel on req
8-22-1901    John rel on req
2-20-1902    Edward & w Susie gct Muncie MM
6-22-1905    Edward & w Susie rocf Muncie MM
9-20-1906    Edward & w Susie gct Whitewater MM
6-20-1907    Etta drpd from mbrp
12-23-1915    Rev Edward E & w Susie E rocf West Union MM
12-21-1928    Edward E & w Susie E rel on req

## HARVEY
2-1-1827    Elizabeth rocf New Garden MM & end by Milford MM
8-26-1830    Elizabeth gct Springfield MM cert ret 4-21-1831
8-25-1831    Elizabeth, Duck Creek P M compl for dpl & na dis 10-20-1831
10-24-1833    Elisha Hobbs gct Miami MM, Ohio to m Deborah Harvey
8-24-1843    Davis, a mbr of Miami MM, Ohio rptd to mcd & j Hs Miami MM, Oh dis him 8-22-1844
12-21-1843    Isaac, mbr of Miami MM, Ohio, rptd na & j Hs dis by Miami MM, Ohio 8-22-1844
8-24-1848    Rachel (form Elliott) rpt mcd & Milford MM, req this mtg to treat w/h 9-21-1848 she offered an ackn & Milford was so inf
1-25-1849    Rachel rocf Milford MM
8-23-1849    Henry H, s of Rachel rec on req
9-20-1849    Rachel & s Henry gct Milford MM
3-22-1866    Samuel Gause gct Springfield MM to m Mary Jane Harvey
10-20-1870    Rebecca W & dt Sarah Ellen rec on req
1-23-1896    William P & fam gct Anderson MM
8-22-1901    Dorcas rec on req
12-26-1912    Edna R rocf Spiceland MM

## HASKET
8-31-1826    Ann appt asst Clerk of Women's mtg & Phebe Macy appt Clerk

DUCK CREEK

## HASKET (Cont)

2-28-1828   Charity, dt Thomas, decd formerly of Warren Co, Ohio, & Ann m at Duck Creek M H Abner Pickering

4-23-1829   Thomas, Duck Creek P M compl for j Hs dis 6-25-1829

4-22-1830   Sarah (Pickering) (form Hasket) compl of for mcd at Hicksites Mtg dis 9-23-1830

8-26-1830   Ann, Duck Creek P M compl for att a mcd held at Hicksites Mtg 1-21-1831 she offered an ackn

11-24-1831   William compl for dpl & unbecoming conduct 1-26-1832 he offered an ackn

2-2-1832   Ann, dt Thomas, decd & Ann m at Duck Creek Mtg, John Bales of Knightstown

3-22-1832   William, Duck Creek compl for att a mcd dis 5-24-1832

10-23-1834   Morgan rocf Suttons Creek MM, N C

1-22-1835   Morgan compl of for mcd 2-26-1835 he offered an ackn

3-24-1836   Anthony, a minor, rocf Milford Mtg under the care of George & Karen Bundy

6-22-1837   Morgan & ch req a cert to Milford MM Cert had not been granted by the time Duck Creek Mtg was laid down on 8-mo-1837

8-26-1841   Morgan, Clear Springs compl for j Meth Ch He was a mbr of Milford MM dis 4-21-1842 by Milford MM

3-21-1895   Anthony gct Earlham MM, Iowa

## HASTINGS

12-20-1827   Aaron & w Margaret rocf West Grove MM
1-22-1829   Aaron & s Solomon gct West Grove MM
7-22-1830   Aaron & s Solomon rocf West Grove MM
8-26-1830   Aaron gct Milford MM to m Christian Reece
12-23-1830   Aaron & s Solomon gct Milford MM
1-21-1869   Phebe rocf Beech Grove MM,----?
9-1-1870   Phebe, wid, dt of Jesse, decd & Elizabeth George of New London MM, Howard Co, m at Cadiz M H Elwood Stanley of Dunreith
10-25-1906   Sarah C gct Knightstown MM

## HAUL

3-23-1837   Hannah (form Stanfield) Fall Creek P M compl for mcd & as she now resides in the limits of Milford MM, they are req to treat w/her Milford rpts no satisfaction dis

## HAYS

3-11-1830   John & w Susannah rocf Silver Creek MM
12-22-1836   John mcd dis

## HAYWORTH - HAWORTH

6-26-1828   Dillon & w Sarah & ch James B & Benjamin rocf West Grove MM

10-23-1828   James & w Peninah & s Ira rocf West Grove MM

3-26-1829   Richard, a minor, rocf West Grove MM
3-26-1829   James & w Peninah gct West Grove MM
4-22-1830   Richard, Walnut Ridge P M compl for mcd dis 6-24-1830

1-20-1831   Mary (form Hill) Whitewater Mtg req this Mtg to treat w/her for mcd Mtg treated w/out satisfaction Whitewater MM dis 6-23-1831

10-24-1833   Richard & ch Benjamin H & James W rec on req

1-23-1834   Mary (w of Richard) rec on req w/con of Whitewater MM

9-27-1849   Ira of Wayne Co, s James & Peninah of same place m at Duck Creek M H Asenath Hunt dt Nathan & Tamar

4-25-1850   Asenath gct West Grove MM
3-20-1851   Ira & w Asenath & dt Irena rocf West Grove MM
9-22-1853   Ira & w Asenath gct Whitewater Mtg
2-23-1865   Peninah rocf Whitewater MM

## HEACOCK

3-20-1913   Roy W & w Jessie & ch Cathleen & Maxine rec on req

2-20-1919   Roy W & w Jessie & ch Catherine & Maxine gct Dublin MM

## HEDGES

4-23-1874   John S rec on req
3-26-1908   Emmet C rec on req
7-25-1912   Emmett & w Cora & ch Odessa M, Edith V & R Wilma gct New Castle MM
4-20-1918   Nellie rec on req

## HENBY

6-25-1835   Mary (w of John decd of N C) & her minor ch John, Sarah, Ephraim B, Martha, Mary & William rocf Suttons Creek MM, N C (Her older ch settled in Milford MM, & were, Willis, Eli & Elias Henby) (It appears that Mary was a dt of John & Lydia (White) Bogue)

## HENDERSON

12-22-1904   Fannie gct Indianapolis MM

## HENDRICKS

1-21-1836   Peninnah rocf Suttons Creek MM, N C end by Milford MM & end by Duck Creek MM to Walnut Ridge MM

2-21-1907   Alfred rec on req

## HENLEY

6-25-1829   Thomas rocf Back Creek MM, N C
6-25-1829   Abigail (w of Thomas) rocf Dover MM, N C
10-21-1830   Henry & w Ruth rocf Whitewater MM
2-24-1831   Elias & ch Ann, Jabez, Judith, Penelope, William H, Thomas W, Martha Jane & Elias jr rocf Back Creek MM, N C end by Whitewater MM

2-8-1832   Judith M dt Elias Sr & Jane, decd, of Rush Co, m at Walnut Ridge M H to Joshua Lindley of Chatham Co, N C

2-6-1833   Ann E, dt Elias & Jane, decd of Rush Co, m at Walnut Ridge M H to John Morris of Rush Co

11-27-1833   Penelope N dt Elias & Jane, decd of Rush Co m at Walnut Ridge M H to Jesse Bell of Wayne Co

1-21-1841   Jabez H & w Margaret rocf Walnut Ridge MM
2-22-1855   Hannah C (form Williams) Duck Creek P M compl for mcd She has settled in limits of Walnut Ridge MM so that mtg is req to treat w/her She offered ackn on 5-24-1855

7-26-1855   Hannah C gct Walnut Ridge MM
6-26-1856   Jabez H appt an Elder
8-24-1865   Nathan P, Back Creek MM, N C req inf as to whether his conduct since he has resided within our limits, was such that they could rec him in mbrp

3-22-1866   Nathan P rocf Back Creek MM, N C
5-2-1866   Nathan P, S Abraham, decd & Mary of N C m at Clear Springs M H to Abigail Cook, wid of Jesse Cook & dt Eli & Elizabeth Stafford

3-28-1867   Ellen S, dt Jabez H & Margaret of Henry Co m at Duck Creek M H to John Symons of Spiceland Mtg, Henry Co

5-26-1870   Albert, Duck Creek P M inf has mcd but he retains his mbrp

8-25-1870   Albert gct Spiceland MM
5-20-1875   Jabez H & fam, Spiceland rpts their cert has been rec

2-23-1876   David H gct Spiceland MM
4-25-1901   Anna gct New Castle MM

## HESTER

11-22-1832   Mary (w of Robert) & ch Amos, Zimri & Louiza rocf Milford MM (Mary & ch return to Milford Mtg 1835)

3-24-1836   Mary rocf Milford MM, but when Duck Creek MM was laid down in 8-mo-1837 she was attached to Spiceland MM

## HESTON

10-2-1826   Ann appt to a comm
5-3-1827   Amos & minor ch req to be rec in mbrp at Duck Creek P M 11-22-1827 "it appeared to be the mind of the mtg to return his req"

12-25-1828   Ann, Duck Creek P M compl for disunity dis 3-26-1829

DUCK CREEK

## HESTON (Cont)

|  |  |
|---|---|
| 12-24-1829 | Mary & Mercy, Duck Creek P M compl for j Hs dis 3-25-1830 |
| 3-20-1834 | Elizabeth (form Hiatt) Clear Spring P M compl for mcd 6-26-1834 she offered an ackn |
| 7-22-1847 | Elizabeth Dix (form Heston) Clear Spring P M inf has mcd dis 8-26-1847 |
| 4-23-1868 | Amos & w Elvira & dt Laveria rec on req |

## HIATT

|  |  |
|---|---|
| 6-24-1824 | William rec in mbrp at Duck Creek P M w/con of Milford MM |
| ( 8-27-1825) | (Aaron & w Elizabeth & ch Amos & Eunice rst at Duck Creek P M w/con of Fall Creek MM, Ohio) |
| 8-31-1826 | Absalom appt to comm to see that the M H is reconditioned to make it comfortable |
| 8-31-1826 | Ann appt to a comm |
| 9-28-1826 | James appt to comm |
| 2- 1-1827 | Ruth rocf Whitewater MM end by Milford MM (w of David) |
| 6-28-1827 | John & w Rachel & ch Henry, Greenberry, Lydia & Mary rocf Fall Creek MM, Ohio |
| 8-23-1827 | Allen & w Rhoda & ch Susanna, Gulielma & John Milton rocf Milford MM |
| 9-20-1827 | James appt to comm for visiting aged & infirm persons |
| 1-24-1828 | Enoch, Fall Creek Mtg, Ohio forwarded to this mtg a dis for "training with the militia" |
| 3-20-1828 | Henry, Duck Creek P M inf mcd He offered an ackn 4-24-1828 |
| 8-21-1828 | Absalom, Duck Creek inf that " he hath spoken irreverently of our Lord & Saviour, Jesus Christ & denied the authenticity of the Holy Scriptures" dis 10-23-1828 |
| 7-24-1828 | John jr, Duck Creek P M inf that he hath been guilty of drinking spiritous liquors to excess & of paying military demands dis 1-22-1829 |
| 10- 2-1828 | James, s Absalom & Ann of Henry Co, m at Duck Creek M H Betty Cook of Henry Co |
| 12-25-1828 | Allen, Walnut Ridge P M inf na, dpl & administered oath dis 2-26-1829 |
| 2-26-1829 | Hiram, Duck Creek P M compl for mcd & j Hs dis 4-23-1829 |
| 3-26-1829 | James, Duck Creek P M compl for j Hs dis 5-21-1829 |
| 4-23-1829 | Martha (form Presnall) compl of for mcd She offered an ackn 5-21-1829 |
| 5-21-1829 | John, Duck Creek P M compl for j Hs dis 7-23-1829 |
| 5-21-1829 | Joseph, Duck Creek P M compl for j Hs dis 7-23-1829 |
| 5-21-1829 | Ann & Betty dis for j Hs |
| 5-28-1829 | Hannah, dt Absalom & Ann of Henry Co, m at Duck Creek M H Stephen Burris of Henry Co |
| 10-22-1829 | Joseph, Fall Creek MM, Ohio req this mtg to treat w/h for refusing to settle demands against him 11-26-1829 he agreed to settle & Fall Creek MM was so informed |
| 11-26-1829 | Absalom jr, Duck Creek P M compl for mcd dis 1-21-1850 |
| 12-24-1829 | Jehu, Chester MM req this mtg to treat w/h for j Hs treated w/out satisfaction & Chester so informed |
| 6-24-1830 | Greenberry, Duck Creek P M compl for mcd dis 9-23-1830 |
| 6-24-1830 | Bethier (form Beals) Duck Creek P M compl for mcd dis 9-23-1830 |
| 6-24-1830 | Sarah (form Beals) Duck Creek P M compl for mcd dis 9-23-1830 |
| 11-25-1830 | Aaron, Duck Creek P M compl for paying military demand dis 1-20-1831 |
| 3-24-1831 | Jane Burris (form Hiatt) Duck Creek P M compl for mcd dis 5-26-1831 |
| 4-26-1832 | John & w Rebecca & ch Anna Jane, Alfred & Josiah rocf Milford MM |
| 6-20-1832 | Anthony, Duck Creek P M compl for mcd dis 8-23-1832 |
| 10-24-1833 | Rhoda & ch Gulielma & Milton gct White River MM |
| 2-20-1834 | David has been na & has acted as a magistrate in performing a m accomplished by a mbr dis 7-24-1834 |
| 3-20-1834 | Elizabeth Heston (form Hiatt) Clear Spring P M compl for mcd She offered an ackn 6-26-1834 |
| 5-21-1835 | Lydia, Duck Creek P M compl for att a mcd of a mbr in a Hicksites mtg dis 7-23-1835 |
| 5-25-1837 | Joel, Clear Springs P M compl for mcd & att other mcd dis 7-20-1837 |
| 2-24-1842 | Jesse, Clear Spring P M inf mcd He offered an ackn 3-24-1842 |
| 2-24-1842 | James, Clear Spring P M inf mcd dis 5-26-1842 |
| 2-24-1842 | Phebe (form Dickey) Clear Springs P M compl for mcd She offered an ackn 3-24-1842 |
| 2-24-1842 | Sina Jane (form Dulea) Clear Springs P M compl for mcd She offered an ackn 3-24-1842 |
| 2-23-1843 | Mary, Duck Creek P M compl for j Carmelites dis 4-20-1843 |
| 3-21-1844 | Mary & dt, Sparrow Creek MM inquires if their rights had been rec |
| 5-23-1844 | Melinda (or Belinda) Allee (form Hiatt) Duck Creek P M compl for mcd dis 9-26-1844 |
| 7-25-1844 | Elizabeth Sopher (form wid Hiatt) Duck Creek P M compl for mcd She offered an ackn 9-26-1844 |
| 8-22-1844 | Mary & dt Elizabeth & Hannah rocf Sparrow Creek MM |
| 1-23-1845 | Elizabeth Wilson (form Hiatt) rpt to j AS She has removed & settled in limits of Salem, Iowa which mtg is req to treat w/her Salem inf no satisfaction dis 7-24-1845 & forwarded to Salem Mtg |
| 3-20-1845 | Hannah Hunt (form Hiatt) Duck Creek P M compl for mcd & j A S dis 5-22-1845 |
| 3-20-1845 | Henry, Duck Creek P M compl for j (ASF) dis 5-22-1845 |
| 5-25-1845 | Rebecca & ch Calvin, Daniel & Thomas rec on req |
| 7-24-1845 | Eunice Copeland (form Hiatt) Duck Creek P M compl for mcd She offered an ackn 8-21-1845 |
| 7-24-1845 | Margaret McCormick (form Hiatt) Clear Springs P M compl for mcd dis 10-23-1845 |
| 7-24-1845 | Mary, Duck Creek Mtg compl for j (ASF) dis 10-23-1845 |
| 1-22-1846 | Sina Jane, Clear Springs compl for j Meth dis 3-26-1836 |
| 11-26-1846 | Ruth, Clear Spring P M compl for j Meth dis 1-21-1847 |
| 6-24-1847 | Harriet Cooper (form Hiatt) Clear Springs P M compl for mcd dis 8-26-1847 |
| 8-26-1847 | Joshua, Clear Springs P M compl for mcd dis 11-25-1847 |
| 12-21-1848 | Cynthia Weaver (form Hiatt) Duck Creek compl for mcd dis 4-26-1849 |
| 9-26-1850 | Joel rec in mbrp again |
| 10-24-1850 | Ann rec in mbrp |
| 12-26-1850 | Asher & w Sarah M (a Minister) & ch Eleazer B, Clarkson & Charles rocf Spiceland MM |
| 7-24-1851 | Jesse & w Phebe & ch gct Salem MM, Iowa |
| 12-25-1851 | Jesse H, John H, Rebecca Jane, Robert C & Nancy Melissa, ch of Joel & Ann rec in mbrp |
| 1- 1-1852 | Rebecca, dt William & Elizabeth, both decd m at Duck Creek M H Nathan Hunt of Henry Co |
| 11-22-1852 | Gulielma Payne (form Hiatt) Clear Springs P M compl for mcd She now lives on verge of East Grove MM, Iowa, which mtg is req to treat w/her East Grove MM, Iowa inf no satisfaction dis 9-21-1853 |
| 11-22-1855 | Joshua reinstated in mbrp |
| 4-30-1856 | Abigail, dt William & Martha of Clear Springs Mtg, Henry Co, m at Clear Springs M H to Isaac Kenworthy of Raysville, Henry Co |
| 6-26-1856 | Calvin, Daniel & Thomas rocf Richland MM (under care of their mth now Rebecca Hunt w of Nathan) |

DUCK CREEK

## HIATT (Cont)

|  |  |
|---|---|
| 7-24-1856 | Asher & w Sarah & ch Eleazar & Clarkson have been rec at Winnesheick, Iowa |
| 3-25-1858 | Joel gct Walnut Ridge MM to m Isabella Parker |
| 6-24-1858 | Jesse M, Cadiz Mtg inf mcd He now resides in limits of Honey Creek MM, which mtg is req to treat w/him Honey Creek rpts no satisfaction dis 10-21-1858 |
| 9-23-1858 | Isabella rocf Walnut Ridge MM |
| 2-24-1859 | Daniel, Duck Creek compl for mcd dis 3-24-1859 |
| 11-22-1860 | Joshua gct Raysville Mtg |
| 4-30-1862 | Mary H, dt William & Martha of Clear Spring P M, Henry Co m at Clear Springs M H, Truman Cooper of Cadiz, Henry Co |
| 7-23-1863 | Rebecca Jane jas dis |
| 1-26-1865 | William & w Martha & fam gct Spring Creek MM, Iowa |
| 4-20-1865 | Daniel & ch Francis Marion, Elenor Elsworth & Roscoe J rec in mbrp |
| 5-24-1865 | John C req cert to Lynn Grove MM, Iowa |
| 9-21-1864 | Joel & fam gct Lynn Grove MM, Iowa |
| 10-25-1866 | Thomas jr, Duck Creek P M inf mcd but he retains his mbrp |
| 9-26-1867 | Robert C gct Lynn Grove MM, Iowa |
| 4-25-1867 | John C, Cadiz Mtg compl for j Free Masons Lynn Grove MM, Iowa req to treat w/him Lynn Grove Mtg rpts he has not participated with Free Masons since being in Iowa On 10-24-1867 he was gct Lynn Grove MM, Io |
| 12-22-1870 | Job & fam rocf Spiceland MM |
| 9-23-1875 | Daniel & ch gct Raysville Mtg |
| 6-20-1878 | Daniel & w Esther & ch Francis M, Elenor E, Roscoe D & James E rocf Raysville MM |
| 6-23-1881 | Matilda & ch Ora D rocf Raysville MM |
| 4-21-1892 | Roscoe D & w Rosabba & ch Laverna E, Edith M, Ethel M & Robin W rocf Fairmount MM |
| 4-26-1894 | J Edgar gct Baltimore MM, Md |
| 3-21-1895 | Seth & w rocf Spiceland MM |
| 2-25-1897 | Daniel drpd from mbrp |
| 5-21-1897 | Seth & w Zelinda gct New Castle MM |
| 6-23-1910 | Roscoe & w Rose & ch Goldie, Ethel, Edith, Lambert, Bernice Alta, Olive & Corwin gct New Castle MM |

## HIBBS

|  |  |
|---|---|
| 10-21-1852 | Jason & w Ann B & ch Abraham, William, Amasa & Rachel Ann rocf Flushing MM, Ohio |
| 6-6-1854 | Jason & w Ann B & ch gct Pleasant Plain MM, Iowa |

## HILL

|  |  |
|---|---|
| 8-31-1826 | Nathan appt on comm on "poor" |
| 12-28-1826 | Nathan appt a Trustee to receive title to land for use of Mtg at Walnut Ridge P M |
| 3-29-1827 | John & w Dinah & ch Joseph, Martha, Benjamin C, Nathan, Clark, Irvin & Sarah Ann rocf Milford MM |
| 7-26-1827 | Thomas & w Tamer & ch Milton, John Clark, & Sarah Ann rocf Milford MM |
| 2-26-1829 | Mary rocf Back Creek MM, N C end to New Garden MM |
| 5-21-1829 | Benjamin & w Anna rocf Whitewater MM |
| 7-23-1829 | Jesse & fam rocf Back Creek MM, N C & end to Whitewater MM |
| 6-24-1830 | John appt Trustee at Walnut Ridge P M |
| 1-20-1831 | Henry B & w Lucrecia rocf Back Creek MM, NC |
| 6-20-1832 | Jesse & Elizabeth rocf Whitewater Mtg |
| 10-25-1832 | Dinah, White River inf she hath paid Military demands She offered an ackn 11-22-1832 |
| 3-21-1833 | William & w Charity & ch Mary Ann, Elizabeth C, Amos H, Martha Jane & Samuel B rocf Arba MM |
| 5-23-1833 | Exum, White River MM, compl that he, a mbr of Back Creek MM, N C has mcd |
| 2-20-1834 | Benjamin & fam gct Whitewater MM |
| 2-20-1834 | Exum, a cert was presented 12-25-1833 from Back Creek MM, N C but was not accepted because of a compl & cert was returned |
| 5-22-1834 | Peninah rocf Milford MM |
| 6-26-1834 | Thomas appt an Elder |
| 6-26-1834 | Tamer appt an Elder |
| 9-13-1835 | Mary, dt Nathan & Elizabeth of Rush Co, m at Walnut Ridge M H to George Nicholson of Milford Mtg, Wayne Co |
| 6-22-1848 | Anna Phelps (form Hill) compl of for mcd She offered an ackn |
| 8-22-1861 | Henry B, a mbr of Walnut Ridge mcd so Clear Springs P M inf & White River is so informed |
| 8-25-1870 | Lucinda gct Greenwood MM |
| 12-24-1874 | Mary Jane (form Henley) gct New Garden MM |

## HINEY

|  |  |
|---|---|
| 9-24-1896 | Joseph K rocf Knightstown MM |

## HINSHAW

|  |  |
|---|---|
| 10-24-1833 | Seth & w Abigail & ch Dianna, Asenath, Hannah, Mary & Ruth rocf Marlborough MM, N C end by Spiceland MM |
| 11-21-1833 | Jabez rocf Marlborough MM, N C end by Spiceland MM |
| 11-21-1833 | Mary rocf Center MM, end by Marlborough MM, N C & end by Spiceland MM to Duck Creek |
| 4-24-1834 | John & ch Quinten & Ruth rocf New Garden MM |
| 5-22-1834 | Benjamin & w Annis & ch Benjamin F, Cyrus E, David F, Mills, Mariah & Elias rocf New Garden MM |
| 9-23-1834 | William, Fall Creek P M inf he mcd Lost Creek MM, (Tenn) was informed |
| 10-23-1834 | Seth, s of Benjamin rocf New Garden MM |
| 12-25-1834 | Charles rocf Newberry MM & end to Mississinewa MM |
| 4-23-1835 | William & w Hannah & ch James Madison rocf New Garden MM |
| 12-20-1835 | John of Henry Co, s Benjamin & Annis m at Clear Springs M H Anna Ratliff dt Joseph & Rebecca |
| 1-21-1836 | William B, Duck Creek P M inf he has used spiritous liquor to excess & was intoxicated 2-25-1836 chm |
| 6-2-1836 | Asenath, dt Seth & his w Hannah, decd of Henry Co, m at Duck Creek M H to John Baldwin of Wayne Co |
| 9-1-1836 | Diana, dt Seth & Hannah, decd of Henry Co, m at Duck Creek Mtg to Benajah Edgerton of Henry Co |
| 12-22-1836 | Jesse B & Lydia rocf Whitewater MM |
| 9-21-1843 | Abigail, Duck Creek P M compl for j A S dis 11-23-1843 |
| 10-26-1843 | Seth, Duck Creek P M compl that he has willfully neg the att of our mtgs, has been instrumental in setting up mtgs contrary to our discipline & has identified himself with the late Separatists dis 12-21-1843 |
| 11-23-1843 | Jabez, Clear Springs P M compl for identifying himself with the late Separatists dis 2-22-1844 |
| 11-23-1843 | Benjamin & Annis, Duck Creek P M compl for j A S dis 2-22-1844 |
| 12-28-1843 | Cyrus, s Benjamin & Annis of Henry Co, m at Duck Creek M H to Eliza Jane Pitts |
| 7-25-1844 | William, Clear Springs P M compl for j Separatists dis 9-26-1844 |
| 6-26-1845 | Mary & fam gct Westfield MM |
| 9-21-1845 | John & fam req a cert |
| 2-26-1846 | Anna (w of John) & ch gct Back Creek MM |
| 5-21-1846 | John gct Back Creek MM |
| 6-25-1846 | Milly Mariah, Duck Creek P M compl for j Meth dis 8-20-1846 |
| 8-20-1846 | Mary Branson (form Hinshaw), Duck Creek P M compl for misconduct & j Separatists dis 10-22-1846 |
| 8-20-1846 | Hannah Small (form Hinshaw) Duck Creek P M has mcd & j Separatists A S dis 1-20-1847 |
| 11-25-1847 | Ruth rocf Back Creek MM |
| 4-25-1850 | Henry, Seth, Elkanah & Hannah Ellen, ch of Jabez, decd, & w Mary (now Mary Morton) rocf Westfield MM |
| 2-21-1850 | David L, Walnut Ridge Mtg inf he had att a dancing frolick & danced White River MM is req to treat w/h 7-25-1850 White River MM rpt the charge was not substantiated A comm appt 8-22-1850 to prepare a cert comm learned he had mcd so subject was drpd he was dis 6-24-1852 at Duck Creek MM |

DUCK CREEK

## HINSHAW (Cont)

|  |  |
|---|---|
| 6-24-1852 | Eliza Jane, Duck Creek MM compl for na & disunity dis 9-30-1852 |
| 2-24-1853 | William rocf Lost Creek MM, Tenn |
| 4-24-1853 | Cyrus, Duck Creek P M compl for na & att a mcd dis 4-21-1853 |
| 8-23-1855 | Quinton, Duck Creek P M inf he mcd. He being a mbr of Back Creek MM, that mtg was inf Back Creek req this mtg to treat w/h but they had no satisfaction & he was dis by Back Creek MM on 4-24-1856 |
| 5-22-1856 | Elias, Duck Creek P M compl for mcd dis 7-24-1856 |
| 6-25-1857 | Annis (w of Benjamin Sr) was reinstated in mbrp |
| 4-23-1859 | Seth, Duck Creek P M compl " he has na our mtgs & consented to a m of one of our mbrs being accomp in his house" dis 6-23-1859 |
| 9-22-1859 | Terresa Ann Coffin (form Hinshaw) rpt mcd dis |
| 11-24-1859 | Sarah compl of for att a mcd of a mbr dis |
| 11-22-1860 | Seth (s of Jabez, decd) Duck Creek P M inf mcd dis |
| 11-22-1861 | Asahel, Duck Creek P M compl for na dis 1-24-1861 |
| 1-21-1864 | William Henry, Duck Creek P M compl for mcd dis |
| 8-25-1864 | Mary rec on req |
| 9-22-1864 | John jr, Jesse, Sarah J & Benjamin F, ch of John Sr rocf New Salem MM |
| 9-22-1864 | Rebecca Ann rocf New Salem MM |
| 3-23-1865 | Nathan, New Salem MM req Duck Creek to treat w/h for mcd 6-22-1865 Duck Creek rpts he is not in the limits of this Mtg & New Salem MM so informed |
| 12-21-1865 | John jr gct Bangor MM, Iowa |
| 2-21-1867 | Rebecca Ann gct Bangor MM, Iowa |
| 9-21-1871 | Emeline rec in mbrp |
| 5-23-1872 | Jesse, Duck Creek P M inf he mcd but his mbrp is retained |
| 6-20-1872 | Nathan rocf New Salem MM, ----? |
| 8-22-1872 | Mary & s rec in mbrp |
| 9-21-1876 | Mary & ch Anna & Frederick gct Carthage MM |
| 3-24-1881 | Martha & dt Alice Hosier rec on req |
| 3-24-1881 | Josephine rec on req |
| 3-24-1892 | Grant U rec on req |
| 3-22-1894 | Benton & William rec on req |
| 3-21-1895 | Robert S & w Nellie T rec on req |
| 6-20-1895 | Elsie D rec on req |
| 1-23-1896 | Isaac rec on req |
| 11-26-1896 | Benton & w Maggie rel on req |
| 2-21-1901 | Anna M rec on req |
| 8-23-1906 | William H drpd from mbrp |
| 3-21-1907 | Clinton drpd from mbrp |
| 6-20-1907 | William B & Sarah drpd from mbrp |
| 11-25-1909 | Lenora Pickett rocf Spiceland MM |
| 4-20-1911 | John Rufus gct New Castle MM |
| 1-25-1912 | Clara Burcham gct New Castle MM |
| 11-20-1913 | Grant & w Eva gct Knightstown MM |
| 10-22-1914 | Leona A gct Whittier MM, Ca |
| 3-22-1917 | William H & Sarah rel on req |
| 6- 9-1921 | Sarah rec on req |
| 8-21-1924 | Nora rec on req |

## HOBBS

|  |  |
|---|---|
| 11-22-1832 | Elisha rocf Vermilion MM, Ill |
| 10-24-1833 | Elisha gct Miami MM, Ohio to m Deborah Harvey |
| 3-20-1834 | Deborah rocf Miami MM, Ohio |

## HOBSON

|  |  |
|---|---|
| 3-29-1827 | Elizabeth Elliott (form Hobson) compl for mcd dis 7-26-1827 |
| 7-26-1827 | Mary, Duck Creek P M compl for att a mcd dis 9-20-1827 |
| 9-22-1831 | Thomas Bond jr gct Springfield MM to m Ann Hobson |
| 2-21-1833 | David compl of for na & dpl dis 4-25-1833 |
| 2-21-1833 | Allen compl of for na & dpl dis 4-25-1833 |

## HODSHIRE

|  |  |
|---|---|
| 3-23-1922 | Delmar Franklin rec on req |
| 2- 3-1927 | Delmar Franklin drpd from mbrp |

## HODSON

|  |  |
|---|---|
| 12- 9-1826 | Isaac rocf Springfield MM, N C & end to White Lick MM |
| 2- 1-1827 | Robert F & w Ann & ch Mary Ann & Susannah rocf Springfield MM, N C & end to White Lick MM |
| 6-25-1829 | Isaac, Spiceland Mtg compl for mcd dis 8-20-1829 |
| 8-20-1829 | Welmet (form Elliott) compl for mcd She offered ackn 9-24-1829 |
| 1-21-1830 | Robert, compl of for paying military demand dis 4-22-1830 |
| 3-22-1832 | Aaron & w Mary & ch Lydia, Neri, Seth, Anna, Robert B, Reuben & Sarah rocf Springfield MM, N C |
| 10-24-1833 | Jesse F & w Nancy & ch Jeffrey, Caleb, Jabez, Isabel Ann & Elizabeth rocf Springfield MM, N C & end to Spiceland MM |
| 7-20-1854 | Huldah (form Hosier) Clear Springs P M compl for mcd dis 11-23-1854 |
| 6-26-1890 | Clara G rec on req |
| 8-23-1894 | Gertrude gct Spiceland MM |
| 2-24-1898 | Moses rocf Spiceland MM |
| 3-24-1898 | Clara rec on req |

## HOGATT

|  |  |
|---|---|
| 5-31-1827 | Nathan & w Nancy & ch Rosinda & Rachel rocf New Garden MM |
| 3-11-1830 | Nathan & fam gct White River MM |

## HOLCOMB

|  |  |
|---|---|
| 1-25-1894 | James I & Eunice C rec on req |
| 3-22-1894 | Elizabeth rec on req |
| 1-25-1906 | Harrison rec on req |
| 12-21-1921 | Ethel Maddy rec on req |
| 1-25-1923 | Katharine Bell & Frances Laverne, ch of Harrison & Ethel rec on req |

## HOLLOWAY

|  |  |
|---|---|
| 9-25-1828 | Dayton, Walnut Ridge P M inf he has na & has administered oaths dis 12-25-1828 |
| 12-25-1828 | Hannah & dt Ruth, Whitewater MM req this mtg to treat w/them for j Hs Treated w/out satisfaction dis 5-21-1829 by Whitewater MM |
| 5-21-1829 | Jesse rocf Whitewater Mtg |
| 5-21-1829 | David, Whitewater req this mtg to treat w/him for j Hs Duck Creek mtg treated w/out satisfaction dis by Whitewater MM 11-26-1829 |
| 3-20-1834 | Jesse, a minor, gct Whitewater MM |
| 10-20-1836 | Joseph & w Elenore & ch Hannah, Margaret & Nancy & grandson William rocf Flushing MM, Ohio |
| 1-26-1837 | David & w Mary & ch Joseph W & Asa rocf Flushing MM, Ohio |
| 6-24-1841 | David & w Mary & ch Joseph Asa, Eliza & Hannah Ann rocf Spiceland MM |
| 2-23-1843 | Hannah Branson (form Holloway) Duck Creek P M compl for mcd with her 1st cousin She offered ackn 5-25-1843 |
| 10-25-1849 | Nancy Kindley (form Holloway) Clear Springs P M compl for mcd dis 12-20-1849 |
| 3-23-1855 | Dorotha & ch Elizabeth & Sarah Jane rocf Chesterfield MM, Ohio |
| 3-23-1855 | Ann B rocf Chesterfield Mtg, Ohio |
| 4-26-1855 | William W, Clear Springs P M compl for mcd dis 6-21-1855 |
| 2-26-1857 | Hannah rocf Walnut Ridge MM |
| 7-23-1857 | Joseph W gct Spiceland MM to m Hannah A Stanley |
| 12-24-1857 | Joseph W gct Spiceland MM |
| 3-20-1858 | Dorothy & ch Sarah Jane, Elizabeth & Anna B gct Plainfield MM |
| 12- 8-1859 | Eliza W, dt David & Mary m at Duck Creek MM to Addison White |
| 5-22-1862 | David & w Mary & ch gct Spiceland MM |
| 9-21-1876 | Cynthia W gct Spiceland MM |
| 2-26-1880 | Robert A & w Elizabeth & ch rec on req |
| 3-25-1880 | Jason W & w Cynthia rocf Spiceland MM |
| 4-20-1911 | Ella rel on req |

DUCK CREEK

## HOLT
| | |
|---|---|
| 6-24-1909 | Hattie Allison rel on req |

## HOOKER
| | |
|---|---|
| 6-26-1873 | Angenetta mcd but mbrp retained |
| 11-24-1904 | Minnie E Ratcliff gct Knightstown MM |

## HOOPS
| | |
|---|---|
| 4-24-1834 | Ellis & ch Margaret, Elizabeth, Sarah & Susannah rocf Milford MM |
| 12-24-1835 | Ellis, White River MM compl for na & for marking his neighbor's pig with a fraudulent intent  3-24-1836 Ellis denies part of the charge  4-21-1836 the complaint is dismissed |

## HOOVER
| | |
|---|---|
| 6-24-1830 | Margaret rocf West Grove MM |
| 1-21-1841 | Margaret, Duck Creek P M compl for jas dis 3-25-1841 |

## HORTON
| | |
|---|---|
| 1-21-1926 | Julia E (w of Dr F W) & dt Ruth Louise & minor ch Ellis Hadley, Francis Walter jr, Joseph Wynn, James Frederick & Blanch Windall rocf West Union MM |
| 5-20-1926 | Francis W rocf West Union MM |

## HOSEA
| | |
|---|---|
| 5-23-1916 | Robert C & w Blanch H & s Robert M rec on req |
| 1-23-1917 | Robert C & w Blanch H & s Robert M rel on req |

## HOSIER
| | |
|---|---|
| 7-27-1826 | William appt to a comm |
| 9-26-1826 | Caroline Hunt (form Hosier) Duck Creek P M compl for mcd  dis 11-30-1826 |
| 12-25-1828 | Milicent appt to a comm |
| 3-26-1829 | Henry, Duck Creek P M compl for mcd dis 5-21-1829 |
| 12-25-1834 | Sarah Davis (form Hosier) Clear Springs P M compl for mcd  dis 2-26-1835 |
| 7-23-1835 | Alice & ch Hannah, Huldah, Alfred & Martha Ann rocf Spiceland MM |
| 4-21-1842 | William gct Walnut Ridge MM to m Susanna Hunnicut |
| 1-26-1843 | Susanna rocf Walnut Ridge MM |
| 3-21-1844 | Hannah Bowman (form Hosier) Duck Creek Mtg compl for mcd  dis 8-22-1844 |
| 4-24-1845 | William & w Susannah & fam gct Mississinewa MM |
| 7-24-1845 | Lucinda Smith (form Hosier) Clear Springs P M mtg compl for mcd  Since she is residing in verge of Sand Creek MM that mtg is req to treat w/her  10-23-1845 has returned to limits of this mtg  dis 12-25-1845 |
| 6-22-1848 | Millicent gct Mississinewa MM |
| 9-20-1849 | Evan, Mississinewa MM inf that he has dpl & att pld  That mtg req to treat w/him but they rpt no satisfaction  dis 5-23-1850 and it forwarded to Mississinewa MM |
| 6-24-1847 | William, a mbr of Mississinewa MM has mcd 12-23-1847 Mississinewa MM req this mtg to treat w/him  1-20-1848 Duck Creek inf Mississinewa MM treated w/out any satisfaction |
| 7-20-1854 | Huldah Hodson (form Hosier) Clear Springs P M compl for mcd  dis 11-23-1854 |
| 3-26-1857 | Martha Ann Bond (form Hosier) rpt mcd  dis |
| 4-22-1858 | Clark, Clear Springs P M inf he is guilty of fighting a fellowman  dis 6-24-1858 |
| 10-25-1860 | Lewis, Clear Spring P M compl "he has att a music school to learn how to fiddle & has fiddled at places of diversion"  dis |
| 5-24-1860 | Allen, Clear Springs P M compl for use of spiritous liquor & for fighting  dis 11-22-1860 |
| 10-24-1861 | Alfred, Clear Spring MM inf mcd  dis |
| 4-25-1878 | Clark & w Mary M & ch Cora & Clinton rec on req |
| 1-23-1896 | Mary M rec on req |
| 8-22-1901 | Daisy Hiatt rocf Spiceland MM |
| 8-25-1915 | C H rel on req |

| | |
|---|---|
| 7-20-1922 | Clint & w Daisy & ch H R & Warren Carl drpd from mbrp |
| 4-26-1923 | Morris gct Spiceland MM |

## HOWARD
| | |
|---|---|
| 3-22-1894 | Charles rec on req |
| 4-25-1907 | Charles & w Ida rel on req |

## HUBBARD
| | |
|---|---|
| 12-23-1830 | Jonathan Butler gct Milford MM to m Sarah Hubbard |
| 4-25-1833 | Hardy & w Mary & ch Anna, Susannah, Mary & Caleb rocf Milford MM |
| 8-21-1834 | Martha rocf Milford MM |
| 12-24-1835 | Anna C rocf Milford MM |
| 4-20-1837 | Anna C gct Spiceland MM |
| 12-23-1880 | Butler rocf Raysville MM |

## HUDSON
| | |
|---|---|
| 3-22-1906 | Laura rec on req |

## HUFF
| | |
|---|---|
| 2-22-1906 | Lura B rel on req |

## HUNNICUTT - HONEYCUTT
| | |
|---|---|
| 12-20-1832 | Robert & w Elizabeth A & ch Martha, John Andrew, Sarah Ann, Susannah, Mary, Elizabeth, Robert Edwin & Emily Jane rocf Western Branch MM, Nansemond Co, Va |
| 12-26-1833 | James B rocf Milford MM |
| 11-26-1834 | Martha, dt Robert decd, & Elizabeth of Hancock Co m at Walnut Ridge M H to Eli White of Rush Co |
| 3-24-1836 | George E rocf Dover MM, Ohio & end to Walnut Ridge MM |
| 12-24-1840 | John Elwood Wright gct Springfield MM to m Jemima Hunnicutt |
| 4-21-1842 | William Hosier gct Walnut Ridge MM, to m Susanna Hunnicutt |

## HUNT
| | |
|---|---|
| 7-27-1826 | Rachel appt Clerk for the day of opening the MM |
| 8-31-1826 | John appt to comm to have care of indulged mtg at Flat Rock M H |
| 9-26-1826 | Caroline (form Hosier) Duck Creek P M compl for mcd  dis 11-30-1826 |
| 4- 5-1827 | Nathan, Henry Co, s Isom, decd of Guilford Co, N C & w Margaret of Henry Co m at Duck Creek M H to Tamar Pickett of Henry Co |
| 9-20-1827 | John appt to comm to visit aged & infirm persons |
| 6-26-1828 | Ann Cloud (form Hunt) compl for mcd 7-24-1828 chm |
| 1-20-1831 | Lucinda "produced a voluntary offering expressing sorrow for having attended a ball" |
| 2-24-1831 | Eleazar & w Susannah & ch Amiel & Eber Hunt & a bound ch Mary Hunt, under their care, rocf New Garden MM, N C end to White Lick MM |
| 2-24-1831 | Isom rocf New Garden MM, N C |
| 4-21-1831 | Isom condemns his att a place of music & joining with others in dancing |
| 9-22-1831 | William & w Elizabeth & ch John & William Allen rocf Chester MM |
| 4-26-1832 | Lucinda Reagin (form Hunt) Spiceland P M compl for mcd  dis 6-21-1832 |
| 6-20-1832 | Elizabeth appt overseer at Fall Creek P M |
| 6-20-1832 | William appt o at Fall Creek P M |
| 4-25-1833 | Allen, a minor, rocf New Garden MM |
| 1-23-1834 | Eber mcd  dis at Clear Springs P M |
| 5-22-1834 | Sarah rocf New Garden MM |
| 5-22-1834 | Francis B Macy gct Whitewater MM to m Huldah B Hunt |
| 11-20-1834 | Eleazer & w Susannah gct Mill Creek MM, Ohio (already removed) |
| 11-20-1834 | Mary, a minor, under care of Eleazer & w gct Mill Creek MM |
| 5-21-1835 | Margaret (wid of Isom of N C) rocf Whitewater MM |
| 12-24-1835 | Amiel gct Mill Creek MM |

DUCK CREEK

## HUNT (Cont)

|  |  |
|---|---|
| 10-20-1842 | William & w Elizabeth & s William rocf Back Creek MM |
| 3-23-1843 | Hanuel & w Lucinda & ch Sarah, Asenath, Ezra, Nancy, Jane, James D, Cyrus, Josiah N & Eleanor rocf Walnut Ridge MM |
| 6-22-1843 | Isom & w Susannah & ch Margaret Ann, William A & John W rocf Hopewell MM |
| 10-11-1843 | Sarah, dt Hanuel & Eleanor, decd, m at Clear Springs M H to William Bond of Henry Co |
| 3-21-1844 | Zadock James, an orphan child under the care of John & Elizabeth Stanley rec in mbrp |
| 3-21-1844 | William & w Elizabeth gct Chester MM |
| 3-21-1844 | William Allen gct Chester MM |
| 3-20-1845 | Hannah (form Hiatt) Duck Creek P M compl for mcd & j A S dis 5-22-1845 |
| 1-21-1847 | Isom & w Susannah & fam gct Honey Creek MM |
| 4-22-1847 | Asenath gct Walnut Ridge MM |
| 4-20-1848 | Nancy Jane gct Clear Creek MM, Ohio |
| 9-27-1849 | Asenath, dt Nathan & Tamar of Henry Co m at Duck Creek M H to Ira Hayworth of Wayne Co |
| 1- 1-1852 | Nathan, Henry Co, s Isom & Margaret, both decd, m at Duck Creek M H Rebecca Hiatt (wid of Anthony) |
| 8-26-1852 | Margaret Macy (form Hunt) Duck Creek P M compl for mcd 9-23-1852 chm |
| 8-26-1852 | Hanuel & w Lucinda & fam gct East Grove MM, Iowa |
| 9-23-1852 | Ezra gct Spring Creek MM, Iowa |
| 7-21-1853 | Martha N (form Elliott) Clear Springs P M compl for mcd Having removed to limits of Salem MM, Iowa A copy of her dis was forwarded there 1-26-1854 |
| 1-25-1855 | Nathan & w Rebecca & fam gct Westfield MM |
| 6-26-1856 | Nathan & w Rebecca & ch Lucinda, Louisa & Nathan jr rocf Richland MM |
| 5-21-1857 | Zadoc, Duck Creek P M compl for mcd dis |
| 10-24-1861 | Nathan & w Rebecca & fam gct Lynn Grove MM, Iowa |
| 4-24-1862 | Lucinda dis for unchaste conduct |
| 4-25-1863 | Nathan & fam rocf Lynn Grove MM, Iowa |
| 4-24-1924 | George W & Elizabeth J rec on req |
| 9-25-1924 | Nellie rec on req |
| 11-20-1924 | Clinton M rocf Shirley MM |

## HUTCHENS

|  |  |
|---|---|
| 7-21-1904 | Benjamin H & w Emma rocf Walnut Ridge MM |
| 10-25-1906 | Benjamin & w Emma gct Thorntown MM |

## HUTSON

|  |  |
|---|---|
| 12-25-1828 | Margaret & dt Sarah Ann rocf Newberry MM, Ohio |
| 3-24-1831 | Mary (form Maudlin) Duck Creek P M compl for dpl & mcd 5-26-1831 chm |
| 3-24-1831 | James, Duck Creek P M compl for unbecoming language & mcd dis 6-23-1831 |
| 8-21-1834 | Nathan, Clear Springs P M inf he has na & made contradictory statements dis 11-20-1834 |
| 10-21-1841 | Lydia, Clear Springs P M inf j Meth dis 12-23-1841 |
| 7-21-1842 | Sarah, Clear Springs P M compl for j Meth dis 9-22-1842 |
| 9-26-1844 | Margaret, Clear Springs P M compl for j Meth dis 12-26-1844 |
| 10-30-1844 | Anna, dt Daniel & Elizabeth of Henry Co m at Clear Springs M H to Enos Pearson of Henry Co |
| 5-21-1846 | Elizabeth, Clear Springs P M compl for j Meth dis 7-23-1846 |
| 5-24-1849 | Richard, Clear Springs P M compl for mcd dis 7-26-1849 |
| 4-26-1849 | Marilla (form Wright) Clear Springs P M compl for mcd dis 9-20-1849 |
| 12-25-1851 | Sarah (form Pearson) Clear Springs P M compl for mcd 5-20-1852 chm |
| 2-26-1852 | Levi, Clear Springs P M compl for mcd 5-20-1852 chm |
| 2-24-1853 | James, Clear Springs P M compl for mcd dis 5-26-1853 |
| 10-21-1858 | Sarah Wright (form Hutson) rpt mcd & j Meth dis |
| 11-22-1860 | Levi, Clear Springs P M inf mcd dis |
| 5-25-1865 | Mary Ellen dis for jas |
| 3-22-1866 | Seth & Daniel jr jas dis |
| 1-25-1866 | Joel R, Clear Springs P M compl for fighting 4-26-1866 chm |
| 1-24-1867 | Joel R, Clear Spring P M inf mcd but he retained his mbrp |
| 11-22-1874 | Lucy rec on req |
| 9-21-1876 | Mary F rocf Hopewell MM |
| 9-25-1890 | Clark drpd from mbrp |
| 1-26-1899 | Martha rec on req |
| 10-26-1922 | John & Roe drpd from mbrp |

## HUTTON

|  |  |
|---|---|
| 12-26-1850 | Edmund, Louisa & Oliver H Bowman, ch of Richard, decd, & Phebe (now Phebe Hutton) rocf West Grove MM |
| 3-23-1854 | John & w Phebe & her minor s Robert Barclay Bowman rocf Richland MM |
| 12-21-1871 | John gct Lick Creek MM |

## ICE

|  |  |
|---|---|
| 3-21-1907 | Evangeline rel on req |

## JAMES

|  |  |
|---|---|
| 9-28-1826 | Evan appt to a comm |
| 2- 1-1827 | Rebecca appt to a comm |
| 3-20-1828 | Evan, Duck Creek P M inf he hath been guilty of getting in a passion, accusing a friend in an unbecoming manner & manifesting a disposition inimical to friends 4-24-1828 chm |
| 1-21-1830 | Naomi (form Stratton) rocf Whitewater MM |
| 5-20-1830 | Evan, Duck Creek Mtg compl for drinking & upl dis 5-20-1830 |
| 7-22-1830 | Rebecca, Duck Creek P M compl for na dis 9-23-1830 |
| 1-24-1833 | Isaac, (a Minister) & w Leah rocf Whitewater MM |
| 7-24-1834 | Isaac & w Leah "being about to perform a visit to their friends & relatives in Columbiana Co, Ohio, req a few lines ---- certifying they are mbrs of our Society" 1-22-1835 the minute was returned, unused on account of their health |
| 7-24-1834 | Hannah Manlove (form James) Duck Creek P M compl for mcd 9-25-1834 chm |
| 1-22-1835 | Jesse, Duck Creek P M compl for att a mcd of a mbr & j Hs dis 3-26-1835 |
| 1-22-1835 | Jonas, Duck Creek P M compl for att a mcd of a mbr & j Hs dis 4-23-1835 |
| 8-20-1835 | Phebe compl of for j Hs dis 11-26-1835 |
| 9-24-1835 | Daniel (s of Isaac) rocf Carmel MM, Ohio |
| 5-25-1837 | Isaac & w Leah gct Whitewater MM |
| 2-21-1892 | Arthur & w & ch Claudius, Estelle, Robert, Mary M rocf Raysville MM |
| 6-26-1902 | Effie & dt Catharine Claire gct Knightstown MM |
| 11-26-1903 | Herbert L drpd from mbrp |
| 10-22-1914 | Claudius A gct Westfield MM |
| 9-23-1920 | Claudius & w Merihah & ch Earl Edward, Milton Arthur & Wilma Carrol rocf Lamong MM, Hamilton Co |
| 10-25-1923 | Claudius & w Merihah & ch Earl E, Milton A & Wilma C gct Raysville MM |
| 4-23-1925 | Robert C & w Cecil M & ch Mary Louise, Pauline, Charles L & Barbara C gct New Castle MM |
| 2- 3-1927 | Robert & w Cecil & ch Mary Louise, Pauline, Charles R & Barbara C rocf New Castle MM |

## JAY

|  |  |
|---|---|
| 10- 8-1841 | Ruth Anna, dt Joseph, decd, late of Randolph Co, N C & Edith m at Duck Creek M H to Davis Gray of Rush Co |
| 6-24-1847 | Hugh, Duck Creek P M inf of upl dis 9-23-1847 |
| 8-24-1848 | Asenath Phelps (form Jay) Duck Creek P M compl for mcd 9-21-1848 chm |
| 3-21-1895 | Mary E rocf Westland MM |

DUCK CREEK

## JESSOP

|  |  |
|---|---|
| 2- 1-1827 | Tideman & w Lydia & s Morris rocf Milford MM |
| 2- 1-1827 | Elias & w Ann & her ch John Bales & their s Jesse Jessop rocf New Garden MM, N C & end to White Lick MM |
| 3-mo-1827 | Ann appt to comm to visit aged & infirm persons |
| 6-13-1827 | Mary, dt Jonathan & Elizabeth of Rush Co, m at Walnut Ridge M H to William Binford of Rush Co |
| 8-23-1827 | Jonathan rec in mbrp w/con of West Grove MM |
| 6-25-1829 | Tidemon appt Trustee Duck Creek |
| 6- 2-1830 | Penninah, dt Jonathan & Elizabeth of Rush Co, m at Walnut Ridge M H to Henry Macy of Henry Co |
| 2-29-1832 | Thomas of Rush Co, s Jonathan & Elizabeth of same place m at Walnut Ridge M H to Rebecca Binford of Rush Co |
| 12-26-1833 | Evan rocf West Grove Mtg |

## JOHNSON

|  |  |
|---|---|
| 7-21-1831 | James & w Mary & ch Rachel, Elizabeth, Emily Grace, Caleb & John Warner rocf Milford MM |
| 8-23-1832 | William Parker gct Milford MM to m Almeda Johnson |
| 11-20-1834 | Sukey (Sookey) (wid of Zachariah, late of Branch Mtg, Isle of Wight Co, Va) rocf Milford MM |
| 11-25-1841 | Jesse & w Lydia & ch Susanna, Patience, Mary & David rocf Deep Creek MM, N C |
| 11-25-1841 | Thomas rocf Deep Creek MM, N C |
| 3-24-1842 | Jonathan Saint gct Spiceland MM to m Emily Johnson |
| 6-22-1848 | Patience Wilkerson (form Johnson) Duck Creek P M compl for mcd dis 8-24-1848 |
| 10-25-1860 | David, Duck Creek P M inf mcd dis |
| 8-21-1862 | John S Elliott gct West Union MM to m Rhoda M Johnson |

## JONES

|  |  |
|---|---|
| 6-26-1828 | Lydia rocf Milford MM |
| 4-24-1834 | Margaret Jane rocf Newberry MM, Tn |
| 6-25-1835 | William & Huldah & dt Mary Ann rocf Newberry MM, Tn |
| 11-25-1866 | Samuel N & w Jane (a Minister) & ch Emma H & Martha A rocf Elk MM, Ohio |
| 4-25-1867 | Wiley B, a copy of dis from Honey Creek MM forwarded by Elk MM, Ohio has been rec |
| 5-23-1867 | Samuel N & w Jane & fam gct Walnut Ridge MM |
| 11-21-1895 | Herbert S rec on req |

## JUDGE

|  |  |
|---|---|
| 1-25-1906 | Harry rec on req |
| 6-26-1924 | Garret rec on req |

## KEAN

|  |  |
|---|---|
| 5-31-1827 | Jacob B rocf Contentnea MM, N C |
| 12-20-1827 | Jacob B gct New Garden MM |

## KENDALL

|  |  |
|---|---|
| 5-26-1836 | Reuben Ratliff gct Whitewater MM to m Margaret Kendall |
| 12-25-1845 | Lydia rocf Hopewell MM |
| 3-26-1846 | Cyrus rocf Whitewater MM |
| 8-24-1848 | David gct Hopewell MM to m Mary Cook |
| 5-24-1849 | Mary rocf Hopewell MM |
| 10-25-1849 | Cyrus & w Lydia gct Whitewater MM |
| 1-23-1851 | David gct Dover MM to m Irena Ann Haisley (a wid) |
| 5-22-1851 | Irena Ann rocf Dover MM |
| 7-24-1851 | Dennis & w Rebecca Jane & dt Margaretta rocf Whitewater MM |
| 4-22-1852 | Cyrus & w Lydia rocf Whitewater MM |
| 5-23-1861 | Thomas rocf Chester MM |
| 8-30-1865 | Wilson of Wayne Co, s William, decd & Abigail m at Clear Springs M H to Martha S Weisner (dt William & Sarah, both decd) |
| 10-26-1865 | Irena Ann rec a Minister |
| 1-25-1866 | Martha S gct Chester MM |
| 1- 2-1868 | Dennis of Cadiz, Henry Co, s Thomas & Elizabeth, both decd, m at Cadiz M H Martha C Payne (a wid) |
| 4- 1-1869 | Irena A (wid of David Kendall & dt Isaac, decd & Ann Jessop) m at Cadiz M H to John Overman of Mississinewa Mtg, Grant Co |
| 7-22-1869 | Susannah P, Thomas C & Hannah Eliza, ch of David, decd, & Irena Ann (now Irena Ann Overman) have been rec at Mississinewa MM |
| 8-25-1870 | Silas, Cadiz P M inf has mcd dis |
| 3-23-1871 | Margaretta gct Whitewater MM |
| 5-22-1873 | Albert gct Chester MM |
| 5-24-1883 | William H gct Hopewell MM |
| 4-20-1893 | William H & w Emma & ch Jesse, Lillie, Clessie, Ida, Ada & Walter rocf New Castle MM |
| 5-25-1893 | Joel rel on req |
| 1-23-1896 | Harmon rec on req |
| 2-24-1898 | W H & w Mary Emma & ch Jesse, Lillie, Clessie, Ada, Ida, Walter & Gilbert gc |
| 12-21-1911 | Oliver L & ch Vaughn R & Earnest A gct New Castle MM |
| 12-21-1911 | Esther L & Martha gct New Castle MM |
| 11-23-1922 | Harriet rec on req |

## KENWORTHY

|  |  |
|---|---|
| 2-25-1841 | Robert & w Doughty & s William rocf Spiceland MM |
| 5-26-1842 | Robert & w Doughty & s gct Spiceland MM |
| 9-26-1842 | Jesse W of Spiceland Mtg, Henry Co, s Amos & Mary of same place m at Duck Creek M H to Eliza Gregg |
| 12-21-1843 | Jesse & w Eliza & ch Ambrose Asahel rocf Spiceland MM |
| 6-26-1845 | Jesse & w Eliza & ch Mary Elizabeth gct Spiceland MM |
| 9-23-1847 | Jesse & w Eliza & ch Mary Elizabeth & Emily G rocf Spiceland MM |
| 11-30-1848 | Willis of Spiceland Mtg, s Amos & Mary, decd, of Henry Co, m at Duck Creek M H Naomi Kirk |
| 2-22-1849 | Naomi gct Spiceland MM |
| 3-20-1851 | Amos M rocf Spiceland MM |
| 4-22-1852 | Amos M gct Spiceland MM |
| 4-20-1854 | Jesse W & w Eliza & ch gct Salem MM, Iowa |
| 4-30-1856 | Isaac of Raysville Mtg, s Amos & Mary, decd of Henry Co, m at Clear Springs M H Abigail Hiatt |
| 6-26-1856 | Abigail gct Spiceland MM |
| 3-24-1904 | Albert E rec on req |

## KERNS

|  |  |
|---|---|
| 5-26-1836 | Deborah rocf Sadsbury MM, Pa |
| 10-20-1836 | Deborah compl of for j Hs Whitewater MM req to treat w/her & they req rpt 2-23-1837 no satisfaction dis 3-23-1837 |
| 4-23-1903 | Maurine Gardner rocf Spiceland MM |
| 12-20-1906 | Nellie rec on req |
| 6-23-1910 | Amos & Laura gct New Castle MM |
| 4-20-1916 | Louisa rec on req |
| 1-25-1917 | Fanny & s Obed rec on req |
| 4-26-1917 | Robert C & w Grace & dt LaVaughn rec on req |
| 4-26-1917 | Herbert & w Georgie & dt Maxine Graves rec on req |
| 1-22-1920 | Mrs Grace rel on req |
| 7-20-1922 | Anna rec on req |
| 9-24-1922 | Maxine & dt Louise gct Spiceland MM |
| 10-26-1922 | Fannie & Obed rel on req |
| 12-24-1924 | Robert rel on req |
| 2-26-1925 | Louise gct Spiceland MM |

## KERSEY

|  |  |
|---|---|
| 1-26-1832 | Asher & w Susannah & s Benjamin V rocf Milford MM |

## KINDLEY

|  |  |
|---|---|
| 12-20-1832 | Joel & w Rachel rocf Milford MM |
| 10-25-1849 | Nancy (form Holloway) Clear Springs P M compl for mcd dis 12-20-1849 |
| 12-24-1849 | Isaac, a mbr of West Grove MM has na & mcd dis by West Grove MM 6-20-1850 |

## KING

|  |  |
|---|---|
| 4-25-1833 | Isaac & w Ann & ch Harman, Hannah, Phebe, Lydia & Deborah rocf Milford MM |

DUCK CREEK

## KINSEY
| | |
|---|---|
| 6-20-1844 | Joseph rocf Milford MM |

## KIRK
| | |
|---|---|
| 5-26-1831 | Thomas & w Sarah & ch Israel, Hannah, Elizabeth, Mary Ann, Rachel, Thomas Clarkson, Naomi & Allen rocf Center MM, Ohio |
| 9-27-1832 | Elizabeth, dt Thomas & Sarah of Henry Co m at Duck Creek M H to Milton McMillan of Clinton Co, Ohio |
| 5-23-1833 | Hannah, dt Thomas & Sarah of Henry Co, m at Duck Creek M H Lemuel Butler jr of Fayette Co |
| 5-24-1835 | Israel gct Salem MM |
| 6-22-1837 | Hannah rocf Center MM, Ohio end by Whitewater MM |
| 6-29-1837 | Mary Ann, dt Thomas & Sarah of Henry Co, m at Duck Creek M H Warner Bufkin of Henry Co |
| 11-30-1848 | Naomi, dt Thomas & Sarah, decd, of Henry Co m at Duck Creek M H Willis Kenworthy of Henry Co |
| 11-27-1850 | Thomas C of Henry Co, s Thomas & Sarah, decd, m at Clear Springs M H Martha Draper of Henry Co |
| 8-26-1852 | Lucinda (form Sanders) Duck Creek P M compl for mcd   10-21-1852 chm |
| 11-25-1852 | Allen T, Duck Creek P M compl for mcd 1-20-1853 chm |
| 8-23-1855 | Allen T & w Lucinda gct Spring Creek MM, Ia |
| 4-23-1857 | Thomas Clarkson & w Martha & ch Philander M, Julius E, gct Spiceland MM |
| 5-23-1861 | Thomas C & w Martha & ch Philander M, Julius E, Henry, Milton & Albert rocf Spiceland MM |
| 7-1-1862 | Jesse W of Henry Co, s Thomas & Sarah, decd m at Duck Creek M H Sarah M Wright |
| 2-23-1871 | Allen T & w Lucinda & ch Alice M, Anna M & Elmer E rocf Raysville MM |
| 9-17-1872 | Allen T & fam, a comm appt to produce a cert  Raysville MM 12-26-1872 drpd |
| 11-21-1872 | Philander, Clear Springs P M inf mcd but his mbrp retained |
| 3-26-1874 | A T & fam gct Raysville MM |
| 3-22-1883 | Albert gct Spiceland MM |
| 11-26-1891 | Jennie rec on req |
| 1-23-1896 | Lizzie & ch Charles E, Bessie M, Goulder L, Harvey, Thomas S & Freddie rec on req |
| 1-23-1896 | Leora rec on req |
| 12-23-1897 | Herbert rec on req |
| 2-24-1898 | Lillian rec on req |
| 2-20-1902 | Julias E & w Rebecca & ch Lee Oren & Herbert S gct Muncie MM |
| 4-24-1902 | Julias & fam cert was end back to Duck Creek |
| 12-21-1911 | Clifford gct New Castle MM |
| 12-21-1911 | Blanch Bicknell gct New Castle MM |
| 3-22-1917 | Jesse, Charles, Lillian, William E, Frederick E & Charles E drpd from mbrp |
| 2-22-1923 | Blanch Bicknell drpd from mbrp |
| 2-21-1924 | Frederick & Louise rec on req |

## KIRKMAN
| | |
|---|---|
| 3-24-1892 | William & w Cynthia rec on req |
| 3-20-1902 | Willard rec on req |
| 4-12-1903 | Willard gct Hopewell MM |

## KIRKPATRICK
| | |
|---|---|
| 3-20-1902 | Iva rec on req |
| 3-22-1917 | Iva drpd from mbrp |

## KISSEL
| | |
|---|---|
| 7-21-1883 | Anna H rocf Spiceland MM |

## KNIGHT
| | |
|---|---|
| 9-22-1831 | John & w Sarah & ch Elizabeth, Milly, James, Nancy, Martha & Lucinda rocf New Garden MM, N C |

## KOONTZ
| | |
|---|---|
| 1-21-1892 | John, Orla & Clifford rec on req |
| 1-26-1899 | George & s Russell rec on req |
| 1-26-1899 | Walter rec on req |
| 3-20-1902 | Hazel rec on req |
| 4-23-1903 | John & w Minerva & dt Ola Alice gct Knightstown MM |
| 12-20-1906 | Addie gct New Castle MM |
| 3-21-1907 | Florence drpd from mbrp |
| 5-23-1907 | George & Russell rel on req |

## LACY
| | |
|---|---|
| 4-23-1829 | Pearson rocf West Grove MM |
| 6-25-1829 | Margaret & dt Sarah Ann rocf Whitewater MM |
| 10-25-1832 | Margaret, Whitewater rptd she has paid military demands  11-22-1832 chm |
| 3-26-1835 | Josiah & w Ruth & s Louring rocf Milford MM |
| 1-21-1892 | Emory rec on req |
| 1-21-1892 | Bertha rec on req |
| 3-24-1892 | Josephine rec on req |
| 3-22-1894 | Lizzie rec on req |
| 10-25-1894 | Bertha rel on req |
| 12-21-1899 | Emory rel on req |
| 2-20-1902 | Josepheus & w Lizzie & dt Gladys gct Muncie MM |

## LAMB
| | |
|---|---|
| 12-28-1826 | Miles, Whitewater MM req Duck Creek to treat w/him for mcd  3-28-1827 forwarded inf to Whitewater MM |
| 7-26-1827 | Miles rocf Whitewater MM |
| 2-24-1831 | Miles, Duck Creek P M inf mcd  dis 5-26-1831 |
| 2-24-1831 | Nancy (form Maudlin) Duck Creek P M compl for mcd  4-21-1831 chm |
| 5-24-1832 | Sarah rocf Symons Creek, N C & end by Milford MM to Duck Creek |
| 6-20-1833 | Lydia is compl of for mcd  8-22-1833 chm |
| 10-23-1834 | Henry & w Rebecca & ch Salathiel, Benjamin & Allen rocf Center MM, N C |
| 3-26-1835 | Phineas (of Milford MM) & Huldah Bundy appeared in mtg & cont their int to m  Phineas Produced a cert from Milford to certify his clearness  They are altm |
| 4-23-1835 | The comm appt to att m of Phineas Lamb & Huldah Bundy rep it was accompl in an orderly manner (They produced the m cert but thru some error the cert was not recorded in the m cert book) |
| 6-26-1835 | Huldah gct Milford MM |
| 9-22-1836 | Henry, Clear Spring P M inf that he "has regardless & in violation to the repeated advices and entreaties of Elders & Overseers, continued to disturb our religious Meetings by making public communications therein" (but the meeting believes it was not in a suitable situation to appoint a comm so Duck Creek MM was laid down  8-mo-1837) |
| 5-26-1837 | Thomas of Whitewater Mtg, Wayne Co, s Phineas & Dorothy, of N C both decd, m at Clear Creek M H Margaret Ratliff of Henry Co |
| 8-24-1837 | Margaret gct Whitewater MM |
| 10-22-1840 | Lydia, Clear Springs Mtg compl for jas dis 12-24-1840 |
| 8-26-1841 | Martha, Clear Springs Mtg compl for j Meth  dis 11-25-1841 |

## LAFFERTY
| | |
|---|---|
| 9-25-1890 | Alfred drpd from mbrp |
| 6-24-1897 | Fanny rec on req |
| 6-21-1900 | Carrie rec on req |
| 3-20-1902 | Warner rec on req |
| 2-25-1904 | Spencer rec on req |

## LAMORE
| | |
|---|---|
| 1-24-1924 | Elmer rec on req |
| 2-21-1924 | Elmer rel on req |

## LARMORE
| | |
|---|---|
| 4-20-1911 | Frank rocf Knightstown MM |
| 10-26-1911 | Franklin rel on req |

## LARRANCE - LAWRENCE
| | |
|---|---|
| 12-25-1834 | Nathan rocf Holly Spring Mtg, N C |
| 10-1-1835 | Nathan, s Peter & Abigail, decd of N C m at Duck Creek M H Penninah Webb of Henry Co |

DUCK CREEK

## LEDWELL
| | |
|---|---|
| 6-21-1877 | Luzena gct Honey Creek MM |

## LEE
| | |
|---|---|
| 6-20-1912 | Willard rec on req |
| 5-21-1914 | Harold rec on req |
| 2-22-1923 | Clarence & w Ethel Maline & ch Dale, Alice May & James Francis Derome rec on req |

## LENOX
| | |
|---|---|
| 2- 3-1927 | Ola Burcham gct Farmland MM |

## LEWELLING
| | |
|---|---|
| 8-31-1826 | Meshack appt to comm on "poor" |
| 8-31-1826 | Jane appt to comm on "poor" |
| 3- 8-1827 | Henry of Henry Co, s Meshack & Jane m at Duck Creek M H Rachel Presnall of Henry Co |
| 11-25-1830 | Meshack hath been guilty of getting in a passion & has in an unbecoming manner, accused one of his neighbors with reproachful conduct & also threatened to strike two of his fellow creatures 1-20-1831 the comm suggests that a part of the charges be dropped. He offered an ackn on 2-24-1831 |
| 12-30-1830 | Henderson of Henry Co, s Meshack & Jane m at Duck Creek M H Elizabeth Presnall of Henry Co |
| 4- 5-1832 | John of Henry Co, s Meshack & Jane m at Duck Creek M H Elvey Elliott of Henry Co |
| 5-24-1832 | Henry, Duck Creek compl that he "has by his conduct in several particulars manifested a malicious and unchristian disposition toward one of his neighbors & has also made use of an expression shocking to Christian feelings" He offered an ackn 7-26-1832 |
| 7-27-1837 | Meshack of Henry Co, s William & Mary, decd m at Duck Creek M H Margaret Williams of Henry Co |
| 7-22-1841 | Jane jr gct Salem MM, Iowa |
| 2-28-1844 | Margaret wid of Meshack & dt James & Julia Ann Williams, both decd, m at Clear Springs M H to Stephen Burris of Henry Co |
| 8-22-1844 | Seth, Duck Creek P M compl for mcd 9-26-1844 chm |
| 11-24-1848 | Jane, dt Henry & Rachel of Henry Co, m at Clear Springs M H Jonathan Votaw of Wayne Co |
| 4-25-1850 | John P compl for att a mcd of a mbr |
| 5-23-1850 | Harrison & Jefferson gc |
| 5-22-1851 | Jehu gct East Grove MM, Iowa |
| 10-21-1852 | Rachel & fam gct East Grove MM, Iowa |
| 12-25-1852 | Jefferson W rocf Hinkles Creek MM |
| 4-20-1854 | Jefferson W gct Salem MM, Iowa |
| 3-23-1871 | James gct Spiceland MM |

## LINDLEY
| | |
|---|---|
| 2- 8-1832 | Joshua of Chatham Co, N C, s Aaron & Phebe of same place m at Walnut Ridge MM Judith M Henly of Rush Co |
| 2-21-1833 | Judith M gct White Lick MM |
| 5- 3-1849 | Henry J of Westfield MM, Hamilton Co, s Aaron & Ann, decd m at Duck Creek M H Abagail Pickering of Henry Co |
| 10-25-1849 | Henry J rocf Westfield MM |
| 12-25-1856 | Henry J & w Abigail gct Fairfield MM |

## LINNEUS
| | |
|---|---|
| 3-24-1892 | John rec on req |
| 12-21-1899 | John rel on req |

## LITTLE
| | |
|---|---|
| 10-24-1844 | Elizabeth (form Lowder) Clear Springs P M compl for mcd Back Creek MM req to treat w/her They rpt 4-24-1845 no satisfaction dis 5-22-1845 & forwarded to Back Creek Mtg |

## LOCKRIDGE
| | |
|---|---|
| 1-21-1892 | Daniel, Ulmer, Margaret, Margie H, Robert G, Albert & Charley rec on req |
| 3-24-1892 | John, Melissa, Minnie & Bessie rec on req |
| 4-21-1892 | Herbert rec on req |
| 4-26-1894 | John dis for disunity |
| 10-25-1894 | Minnie rel on req |
| 12-25-1897 | John rec on req |
| 1-26-1899 | Mary, Bert & George rec on req |
| 5-25-1899 | Albert drpd from mbrp |
| 12-20-1900 | John rel on req |
| 8-22-1901 | Melissa rel on req |
| 3-20-1902 | Nettie rec on req |
| 10-26-1922 | Nellie drpd from mbrp |

## LOWDER
| | |
|---|---|
| 1-22-1829 | Samuel & w Elizabeth & ch Sally, Thomas, Marium, Mary, Emily, Phineas, Hiram & Elizabeth rocf Deep Creek MM, N C |
| 2-20-1834 | Sarah, Clear Springs P M compl of unchastity dis 5-22-1834 |
| 6-26-1834 | Samuel compl of for na, has manifested disunity dis 9-25-1834 |
| 6-26-1834 | Thomas has been guilty of getting in a passion & beating one of his fellow creatures dis 10-23-1834 |
| 2-23-1837 | Emily Presnall (form Lowder) compl of for mcd dis 7-20-1837 |
| 8-26-1841 | Hiram, Clear Springs P M compl for striking a fellow creature dis 1-21-1841 |
| 4-25-1844 | Mary Winslow (form Lowder) Clear Springs P M inf mcd & has removed to Back Creek MM, which mtg is req to treat w/her 9-26-1844 chm |
| 10-24-1844 | Elizabeth Little (form Lowder) Clear Springs P M compl for mcd dis 5-22-1845 is forwarded to Back Creek MM |
| 11-20-1846 | Miriam Polk (form Lowder) Duck Creek compl for mcd dis 4-23-1846 |
| 3-21-1850 | Phineas, Cadiz P M compl for na & dpl & has served as a regular soldier in the late war with Mexico Comm rpts he has moved to Iowa dis |
| 1-20-1859 | Eber, New Salem Mtg inf he has offered violence to a fellowman & has sued at law a mbr of our Society, rpt to have removed somewhere in Ill dis 9-22-1859 |

## LOVE
| | |
|---|---|
| 3-23-1843 | Susannah (form Dulea) Clear Spring P M compl for mcd & j Meth dis 8-24-1843 |

## LOWE
| | |
|---|---|
| 3-26-1896 | Levi rec on req |
| 12-23-1897 | Minnie A rec on req |

## LOWERY
| | |
|---|---|
| 1-24-1884 | Angeline rocf Hopewell MM |
| 9-25-1890 | Charles & w Sarah drpd from mbrp |
| | Freeman & Leta drpd from mbrp |

## LYNN
| | |
|---|---|
| 1-21-1892 | Addie rec on req |
| 12-20-1906 | Katharine rec on req |
| 9-26-1912 | Catharine gct Indianapolis MM |

## LYTLE
| | |
|---|---|
| 3-26-1896 | Robert R rec on req |

## MACY
| | |
|---|---|
| 7-27-1826 | Phebe appt to a comm |
| 8-31-1826 | Phebe appt Clerk of women's mtg & Ann Hasket appt asst Clerk |
| 8-31-1826 | William appt to comm to have care of indulged mtg at Flat Rock M H |
| 8-31-1826 | Nathan rocf Hopewell MM, N C & end by Milford MM |
| 12-28-1826 | Phebe appt an Elder |
| 4-23-1829 | Henry rocf Bloomfield MM, Parke Co |
| 6- 2-1830 | Henry of Henry Co s Thaddeus, decd, & Catharine m at Walnut Ridge M H Peninah Jessop of Rush Co |
| 6-24-1830 | Obed & w Lydia & ch Anna Mariah & Nathaniel rocf Silver Creek MM |
| 1-20-1831 | Nathan, Duck Creek P M compl for mcd 2-24-1831 chm |
| 2-24-1831 | Solomon & w Priscilla rocf Milford MM |
| 3-22-1832 | Joseph W rocf Center MM, N C |
| 8-23-1832 | Joseph, Duck Creek P M compl for mcd dis 10-25-1832 |
| 8-23-1832 | Jane rec in mbrp |

## MACY (Cont)

| | |
|---|---|
| 1-24-1833 | Francis B rocf Whitewater MM |
| 4-25-1833 | Solomon & w Priscilla & s Edwin gct Spiceland MM |
| 5-22-1834 | Francis B gct Whitewater MM to m Huldah B Hunt |
| 9-25-1834 | Thomas & w Rebecca & ch Tristram Barnard, Lucinda Swain & Thomas Clarkson rocf Salem MM |
| 10-23-1834 | Huldah B rocf Whitewater MM |
| 6-25-1835 | Anna rocf Milford MM |
| 9-24-1835 | Stephen jr rocf Whitewater MM |
| 6-23-1836 | Stephen jr gct Whitewater MM |
| 9-22-1836 | William & w Rhoda & ch Henry, Phebe, Louisa, Jesse & Irena rocf New Garden MM |
| 6-22-1837 | Enoch & w Nancy & dt rocf Hopewell MM, N C & end to Spiceland MM |
| 7-20-1837 | Rhoda appt o at Fall Creek P M in room of Ann Morgan |
| 5-25-1843 | Francis B & w Huldah & ch Rebecca Ann, Margaret, Jane, John Lilburn & Loretta Mariah rocf Spiceland MM |
| 2-22-1844 | James Stanbrough gct Hopewell MM to m Sarah Macy |
| 11-27-1844 | Stephen of Spiceland Mtg, Henry Co, s Enoch & Ann, both decd, formerly of Guilford Co, N C, m at Clear Spring M H to Rebecca Ratliff, wid of Joseph Ratliff & dt of Jacob & Sarah Lamb, both decd, of Randolph Co, N C |
| 3-27-1845 | Pemberton, of Hopewell MM, Henry Co, s Nathan & Katharine, decd, m at Duck Creek M H Nancy Ann Ellis of Henry Co |
| 5-22-1845 | Rebecca gct Spiceland MM |
| 5-22-1845 | Nancy Ann gct Hopewell MM |
| 1-22-1846 | Stephen & w Rebecca rocf Spiceland MM |
| 2-24-1848 | Rachel, Duck Creek P M inf j Meth, she being a mbr of New Garden MM, N C that mtg has been so inf  Dis rec from New Garden MM, N C on 5-25-1848 |
| 10-25-1849 | Pemberton & w Nancy & ch Robert P & Catherine Elizabeth rocf Westfield MM |
| 9-26-1850 | Margaret rec in mbrp |
| 5-22-1851 | Francis B & w Huldah & ch gct Walnut Ridge MM |
| 11-20-1851 | Pemberton & w Nancy Ann & fam gct Wabash MM |
| 5-27-1852 | Whitesel D of Spiceland MM, Henry Co, s Nathan & Jane, m at Duck Creek M H to Mary Cook of Henry Co |
| 8-26-1852 | Margaret (form Hunt) Duck Creek P M compl for mcd  9-23-1852  chm |
| 3-24-1853 | Tyrrel rocf Spiceland MM |
| 6-23-1853 | Sally Ann, James, Lydia & Lurana, ch of Gardner & Margaret rec in mbrp |
| 1-26-1854 | Terrel & w Margaret gct Westfield MM |
| 2-28-1856 | Nathan of Spiceland Mtg, Henry Co, s Thaddeus & Caroline m at Duck Creek M H to Jennett Pickering & dt William & Achsah Saint of Henry Co |
| 3-20-1856 | Sallie Ann Foster (form Macy) rpt mcd  dis |
| 5-22-1856 | Jennetta & her ch (Martha, Thomas S, Julia Ann & William Exum Pickering) gct Spiceland MM |
| 12- 1-1856 | William of Spiceland Mtg, Henry Co, s Stephen & Sarah, decd, of Guilford Mtg, N C m at Clear Springs M H to Lydia Ellis, dt Joshua & Miriam, both decd of Henry Co |
| 2-26-1857 | Lydia gct Spiceland MM |
| 10-22-1863 | Gardner & w Margaret & fam gct Sugar Plain MM |
| 3-26-1874 | William H & Irenne rec on req |
| 2-25-1875 | William H, a comm appt to treat w/him for drunkenness, profanity & fighting  3-25-1875  chm |
| 9-21-1876 | Rachel gct Carthage MM |
| 3-24-1893 | Susan L & ch Moselene rec on req |
| 2-20-1896 | Lambert rec on req |

## MADDOCK

| | |
|---|---|
| 6-23-1881 | John C & w Rachel H rocf Elk MM, Ohio |
| 11-22-1883 | John & w Rachel gct Whitewater MM |

## MADISON

| | |
|---|---|
| 2-26-1903 | Lewis C rec on req |
| 6-25-1903 | Anna B rec on req |
| 5-23-1907 | Lewis rel on req |

## MAJORS

| | |
|---|---|
| 1-24-1901 | Charles & Susan rec on req |

## MANLOVE

| | |
|---|---|
| 7-24-1834 | Hannah (form James) Duck Creek P M compl for mcd  9-25-1834  chm |

## MARLEY

| | |
|---|---|
| 1-21-1875 | Joseph rec on req |

## MARSH

| | |
|---|---|
| 7-24-1834 | Elias & w Edith & ch William, Lydia, Jesse, Sabina, Fanny & Joseph rocf Sandy Springs MM, Ohio |
| 7-24-1834 | Martha rocf Sandy Springs MM, Ohio |

## MARSHALL

| | |
|---|---|
| 11-25-1830 | Thomas rocf Deep Creek MM, N C |
| 4-26-1832 | Jesse & w Mary & ch Jane & William rocf New Hope MM, Tn |
| 1-23-1834 | Thomas req a cert to Fairfield MM  4-24-1834 the comm is continued as "the way is not clear for him to have a cert"  9-25-1834  comm rec rpt that he is decd |
| 5-24-1835 | Jesse & w Mary gct Spiceland MM |
| 4-21-1836 | Dinah req to rec in mbrp  7-21-1836 not granted |
| 4-22-1842 | Joseph of Sugar Plain MM, Boone Co, s Isaac & Ruth of Driftwood Mtg, both decd m at Duck Creek M H Elizabeth Edgerton of Henry Co |
| 12-22-1842 | Joseph rocf Sugar Plain MM |
| 3-20-1845 | Elizabeth (a wid) & dt Ruth J gct Mississinewa MM |
| 6-23-1859 | Allen Compton gct Salem MM, Iowa to m Elizabeth Marshall |

## MAUDLIN - MODLIN

| | |
|---|---|
| 11- 2-1826 | John & w Rebecca & s Mark rocf West Grove MM |
| 12-28-1826 | George compl of for mcd  dis 3- 5-1827 |
| 12-25-1828 | Rhoda, dt George & Sarah, decd gct West Grove MM |
| 1-22-1829 | Dillon, Reuben, Elias, Mark, Leah & Jacob, ch of George & Sarah, decd, gct West Grove MM |
| 6-25-1829 | Nancy Ann, dt George & Sarah, decd gct West Grove MM |
| 11-26-1829 | Joseph & w Violet & ch Thomas, Newby, Mary, Mark, Hannah, Elwood & Elias rocf Back Creek MM, N C |
| 11-26-1829 | William rocf Back Creek MM, N C |
| 11-26-1829 | Nancy rocf Back Creek MM, N C |
| 3-11-1830 | John, cert from Back Creek MM, N C was returned because "he had laid himself liable to a complaint by att a Muster, having spiritous liquor distilled & for not fulfilling his engagements" |
| 7-22-1830 | Ann rocf West Grove MM |
| 11-25-1830 | Thomas, Duck Creek P M inf is mcd  1-20-1831  chm |
| 11-25-1830 | Newby, Duck Creek P M compl for att a mcd  dis 1-20-1831 |
| 2-24-1831 | Nancy Lamb (form Maudlin) Duck Creek P M compl for mcd  4-21-1831  chm |
| 3-24-1831 | Mary Hutson (form Maudlin) Duck Creek P M compl for mcd & dpl 5-26-1831  chm |
| 4-21-1831 | Dillon, Reuben, Elias, Mark, Jacob & Leah, ch of George & Sarah, decd, rocf West Grove MM |
| 4-21-1831 | Nancy rocf West Grove MM |
| 7-21-1831 | Nancy, Duck Creek P M compl for dancing dis 9-22-1831 |
| 7-21-1831 | Rhoda, a mbr of West Grove MM rpt to have att a place of diversion & to have danced Dis rec from West Grove MM 5-24-1832 |

DUCK CREEK

## MAUDLIN (Cont)

|  |  |
|---|---|
| 10-20-1831 | William gct Springfield MM to m Mildred Beason |
| 2-20-1834 | Dillon compl of for mcd  dis 6-26-1834 |
| 3-20-1834 | Reuben compl for att a mcd of a mbr  dis 6-26-1834 |
| 4-24-1834 | Thomas, Clear Spring P M inf "he hath been guilty of upl & telling an untruth and using an excess of spiritous liquor" dis 7-24-1834 |
| 5-22-1834 | William & w Mildred & s Calvin gct Springfield MM |
| 6-26-1834 | Mark "has been charged with fornication & using spiritous liquor to excess"  dis 9-25-1834 |
| 5-24-1835 | Richard & w Gulielma B rocf Milford MM |
| 5-21-1835 | Hannah Antrim (form Maudlin) Clear Springs P M compl for mcd  Springfield Mtg req to treat w/her  dis 9-24-1835 |
| 1-21-1836 | William & w Elizabeth & s Oliver rocf Milford MM |
| 8-24-1837 | Elwood, Clear Springs P M inf na & jas |
| 8-24-1837 | Mark, Clear Springs P M compl for mcd |
| 12-24-1840 | Martha C (form Ratliff) Clear Springs P M compl for mcd  She now resides in verge of Mississinewa MM which is req to treat w/her  No satisfaction  dis 7-25-1845 |
| 11-25-1841 | Ann & s Joseph rocf Milford MM |
| 9-21-1843 | Anna & s Joseph gct Hopewell MM |
| 12-25-1845 | Richard, Clear Springs P M compl for att mcd & j Meth  dis 2-26-1846 |
| 5-21-1846 | Jane, Clear Spring P M compl for j Meth  dis 7-23-1846 |
| 1-25-1849 | Lydia (form Osborn) Clear Spring P M compl for mcd  She now resides in limits of Hopewell MM which mtg is req to treat w/her  Hopewell rpts no satisfaction  dis 6-21-1849 |
| 3-22-1849 | Elias, Clear Spring P M compl for mcd "with a woman who has obtained a divorce from her former husb" dis 5-24-1849 |
| 3-21-1850 | Martha rec in mbrp again |
| 4-25-1850 | Elias & Martha are reinstated in mbrp |
| 1-26-1854 | Joseph, Cadiz P M compl for mcd  3-23-1854 chm |
| 1-25-1855 | Lydia, Seth & Sarah Ann, ch of Elias & Martha rec in mbrp |
| 4-21-1859 | Elias, Clear Spring P M inf mcd but he retains his mbrp |
| 5-25-1859 | Lydia Anderson (form Modlin) rpt mcd  dis |
| 6-23-1859 | Ann (form Dawson) rpt mcd but she retains her mbrp |
| 6-21-1860 | Oliver, Clear Spring P M compl for mcd  dis 9-20-1860 |
| 10-25-1860 | Luther, Clear Spring P M compl for mcd & na dis |
| 6-23-1864 | Richard, Clear Spring P M compl for mcd but he retains his mbrp |
| 6-22-1865 | Elias, Clear Spring P M compl mcd but he retains his mbrp |
| 4-23-1868 | Emily Jane & dt Mary Ann rec in mbrp |
| 12-24-1868 | Seth, Clear Spring Mtg inf mcd but his mbrp retained |
| 3-20-1873 | Lindley M produced an ackn chm |
| 9-25-1890 | Seth drpd from mbrp |
| 3-24-1898 | John D (of Grant Co) mcd |
| 4-26-1900 | John D gct Deer Creek MM |

## MAULSBY

|  |  |
|---|---|
| 11-26-1829 | Samuel Pickering gct Springfield MM to m Cynthia Maulsby |
| 6-24-1847 | Sally (form Price) Clear Springs P M inf mcd 12-23-1847 chm |
| 1-20-1848 | Sally gct Springfield MM |
| 2-20-1868 | James & w Ruth rocf Indianapolis MM |
| 12-24-1868 | James & w Ruth gct Indianapolis MM |

## McALISTER

|  |  |
|---|---|
| 2- 9-1907 | Charles E & w Sarah M rec in mbrp |
| 6-23-1910 | Emma Denny gct Anderson MM |
| 2-11-1911 | Charles E & w Sarah M rel on req |

## McCASLIN

|  |  |
|---|---|
| 6-24-1915 | Mary Pearl rocf Shirley MM |
| 6-24-1915 | Annes May & James Paul rec on req |

## McCLAIN

|  |  |
|---|---|
| 6- 9-1921 | Clifford M & w Vivian L & ch Hershel Lowell, Vergil Von & Conrad Max rec on req |

## McCLELLAND

|  |  |
|---|---|
| 8-25-1853 | Jemima (form Osborn) Clear Spring P M compl for mcd  dis 10-20-1853 |

## McCLINTIC

|  |  |
|---|---|
| 1-25-1923 | William & w Della America rec on req |

## McCONNELL

|  |  |
|---|---|
| 10-22-1891 | Joseph & fam gct Raysville MM |
| 12-10-1892 | William D rec on req |
| 4-25-1901 | Albert & w Charity & ch Moses B & Arthur gct Muncie MM |
| 8-22-1901 | Albert & fam drpd from mbrp |

## McCORKLE

|  |  |
|---|---|
| 11-22-1894 | Jennie dis for disunity |

## McCORMICK

|  |  |
|---|---|
| 9-25-1845 | Margaret (form Hiatt) Clear Spring P M compl for mcd  dis 10-23-1845 |
| 10-25-1894 | Frances rel on req |

## McCOY

|  |  |
|---|---|
| 4-21-1883 | David E & w Susannah rocf Oak Ridge MM |

## McDANIEL

|  |  |
|---|---|
| 1- 5-1928 | Ethel Hittle rec on req |

## McFADDEN

|  |  |
|---|---|
| 10-25-1849 | Amy & ch gct Mississinewa MM |

## McGREW

|  |  |
|---|---|
| 2-20-1868 | Squire J & w Lucinda & ch Wilma rec in mbrp |
| 11-20-1873 | Squire J & fam rel on req |

## McHATTON

|  |  |
|---|---|
| 2-25-1847 | Mary Ann rocf Back Creek MM |
| 3-24-1848 | Mary Ann, Duck Creek Mtg compl for j Meth  dis 5-25-1848 |
| 4-20-1848 | Anna (form Symons) Duck Creek P M compl for mcd  6-26-1848 chm |

## McKEE

|  |  |
|---|---|
| 8-24-1922 | Helen R & Vivian, ch of Ross & Massie rec on req |
| 5-22-1924 | Jennie rec on req |

## McKINLEY

|  |  |
|---|---|
| 2-26-1900 | Delie gct Muncie MM |

## McKINSEY

|  |  |
|---|---|
| 2-21-1924 | Granville Ernest & Grace Frances rec on req |

## McMILLAN

|  |  |
|---|---|
| 9-27-1832 | Milton of Clinton Co, Ohio s David & Hannah, m at Duck Creek M H to Elizabeth Kirk of Henry Co |
| 4-25-1833 | Elizabeth gct Center MM, Ohio |

## McNEAR

|  |  |
|---|---|
| 12-22-1842 | Esther (form Williams) Back Creek MM req Duck Creek to treat w/her for mcd  No satisfaction & Back Creek so inf  Dis rec from Back Creek MM 6-22-1843 |

## McNEW

|  |  |
|---|---|
| 3-25-1909 | John & w Elizabeth gct Knightstown MM |
| 9-25-1913 | Ernest & Harriet & ch Orland & Earl V gct Spiceland MM |

## MELSON

|  |  |
|---|---|
| 6-24-1915 | Ezra rec on req |

## MENDENHALL

|  |  |
|---|---|
| 1-26-1843 | Joseph & w Mariam gct Westfield MM |
| 6-24-1858 | Lydia Ann rptd mcd but her mbrp was retained |

DUCK CREEK

MENDENHALL (Cont)
8-26-1858 Lydia gct Bear Creek MM, Iowa
9-22-1864 Rachel rocf Springfield MM
6-22-1865 Taylor & w Lydia A & ch Lelia & Samuel rocf Sugar River Mtg
4-22-1869 Oliver & Lydia rec in mbrp
1-26-1871 Isaac & ch Viretta, Eliza Ann, Luella, Valentine M & Elma rocf Springfield MM
1-26-1871 Taylor & fam gct Tangonoxie Mtg, Kas
8-20-1908 Jesse O & w gct New Castle MM
11-20-1919 Luther & w Grace & s George gct Dublin MM

MEREDITH
3-27-1845 James Harvey of Spiceland, s James & Mary m at Duck Creek M H Eliza Stanley of Henry Co
5-22-1845 Eliza gct Spiceland MM
1-20-1848 James Harvey & w Eliza & ch Jane & Oliver rocf Spiceland Mtg
5-24-1849 William W rocf Spiceland MM
2-21-1850 Jesse & w Luzena & ch Charles, Franklin & Melissa Ann rocf Spiceland MM
5-23-1850 William W, Duck Creek compl for mcd 6-20-1850 chm
11-21-1850 Mary rocf Spiceland MM
7-24-1851 William gct Spiceland MM
6-24-1852 Jesse & w Luzena & ch gct Richland MM
9-22-1853 James H & w Eliza & ch Jane, Oliver, Ellen, Elizabeth, Caroline & Mary gct Spiceland MM
12-22-1853 Jesse & w Luzena & ch Charles, Franklin, Melissa Ann, Anna Jane & John rocf Spiceland MM
6-22-1854 James H & w Eliza & ch Jane, Oliver, Ellen, Caroline, Elizabeth & Mary rocf Spiceland MM
3-25-1858 Jesse & w Luzena & ch gct Spiceland MM
7-22-1858 William gct Spiceland MM
6-24-1858 James Harvey, Duck Creek MM inf he has att a ball & took part in a dance & has na dis 10-21-1858
11-21-1861 Jane, Oliver, Ellen, Caroline, Elizabeth & Mary, ch of James H (& Eliza) gct Lynn Grove MM, Iowa
7-21-1864 James H, Center MM, Iowa req permission to rec him in mbrp It was granted

MILLS
8-31-1826 Lydia appt to a comm
11-30-1826 Hugh appt to a comm
3-1-1827 Lydia appt to a comm
5-21-1827 Aaron, Duck Creek P M inf that he, a mbr of Springfield MM, has mcd Duck Creek treated w/him but he does not make satisfaction & Springfield MM is so inf
6-26-1828 Isaac & w Catharine & ch Sarah, Eli, Samuel, Rowland, Noah, Mary Ann & Joel T rocf Springborough MM, Ohio
2-20-1829 Isaac, Walnut Ridge P M compl for j Hs dis 4-23-1829
6-25-1829 Hugh, Spiceland P M compl for j Hs dis 10-22-1829
2-26-1829 Catharine, Walnut Ridge P M compl for j Hs dis 4-23-1829
2-26-1829 Sarah, Walnut Ridge P M compl for j Hs dis 4-23-1829
7-23-1829 Lydia, Spiceland P M compl for j Hs dis 9-24-1829
1-26-1832 Eli, Samuel, Rowlan, Noah, Mary Ann & Joel T, ch of Isaac gct Whitewater MM
9-26-1844 Patience rocf Union MM
5-21-1846 Peninah Pope (form Mills) Duck Creek P M compl for mcd & j Hs but she having re-moved within verge of Fairfield MM, that mtg is req to treat w/her They report no satisfaction 10-22-1846 her dis forwarded to Fairfield MM
10-20-1848 Thomas H, Duck Creek P M compl for mcd & j Hs dis 12-21-1848
4-20-1854 Elizabeth (form Stafford) Clear Springs P M compl for mcd 6-6-1854 chm
2-25-1858 Eber, Duck Creek P M compl for mcd He is rptd as being a mbr of Spiceland MM & that mtg has been informed

7-22-1858 Eber rocf Spiceland MM
4-24-1867 Susannah & dt Rosetta rec in mbrp
7-25-1878 Susannah & dt Rosetta gct Whitewater MM
9-25-1913 Seth & w Catharine & ch Edna & Edgar gct New Castle MM

MITCHELL
3-22-1894 John rec on req
2-20-1896 Fannie rec on req
12-20-1900 John rel on req

MODDY
2-25-1904 Fleming L, Martha J & Hilda V rec on req

MOFFITT
12-20-1894 Gertrude M gct Raysville MM
1-25-1923 J Earl & w Florence E & ch Robert, Mary Fay & Barbara Jane gc
1-25-1923 Victor S, s of J Earl & Florence gc

MOON
11-30-1826 Mary gct Newberry MM, Ohio
12-28-1826 Benoni Presnall gct Newberry MM, Ohio to m Mary Jane Moon
3-23-1837 Judith & ch Vashti, Abigail, Esther, Levi, Elwood & Susannah rocf Fairfield MM
3-23-1842 Eli, Newberry MM (Ohio) ackn rpt & mentioned that he has moved back within their limits
4-21-1842 Eli, Clear Springs P M compl for mcd He offered an ackn which was forwarded to Newberry MM, Ohio on 9-22-1842
3-22-1844 Thomas of Newberry MM, Ohio, s Joseph & Ann, both decd, m at Clear Springs M H to Sarah Presnall of Henry Co
5-23-1844 Sarah gct Newberry MM, Ohio
7-26-1849 Rachel (form Stanbrough) Clear Springs P M compl for mcd She having removed to Newberry MM (Ohio) that mtg req to treat w/her She offered an ackn 12-20-1849
1-24-1850 Rachel gct Newberry MM, Ohio
2-21-1850 Mary (form Stanbrough) Clear Springs P M compl for mcd She moved to limits of Newberry MM (Ohio) which mtg is req to treat w/her 7-25-1850 chm
8-22-1850 Mary gct Newberry MM, Ohio
7-24-1851 Tabitha (form Stanbrough) Clear Springs P M compl for mcd dis 9-25-1851

MOORE
12-28-1826 Rebecca rocf Milford MM
3-5-1827 Samuel appt to a comm
12-20-1827 Abraham & w Hannah & ch Hannah, Jacob & Abraham rocf Center MM, Ohio
12-20-1827 Abraham appt Trustee Duck Creek
2-26-1830 Hannah, dt Abraham & Susannah, decd, of Henry Co m at Duck Creek M H to Thomas Davis of Wayne Co
3-11-1830 William & w Ann & ch Samuel, Thomas, Achsah, Truman & Margaret H rocf Whitewater MM
5-24-1832 Charles & w Ann & ch Camm, Sarah, Addison G, Malinda G, Caroline & Emily rocf West Grove MM
12-30-1832 John & w Ann & ch Sarah & Martha Ann rocf Springfield MM, Ohio
12-25-1834 Abraham appt an Elder
11-26-1835 Jacob gct Sugar River MM
1-21-1841 Elizabeth W, Duck Creek compl for jas dis 3-25-1841
11-22-1849 Ann Evans (form Moore) Clear Springs P M compl of unbecoming conduct & mcd dis 1-24-1850
1-23-1851 Martha Ann, Clear Springs P M compl for j Meth dis 3-20-1851
1-23-1851 Sarah, Clear Springs P M compl for j Meth She resides in limits of Sugar River MM which mtg is req to treat w/her
10-23-1851 John Bond gct Westfield MM to m Rachel Moore
5-26-1853 Thomas, Elizabeth, Rebecca J, Mary, John W & Nancy E, ch of John decd, gct Greenfield MM

DUCK CREEK

MOORE (Cont)
4- 2-1857    Joshua of Walnut Ridge MM, Henry Co, s James & Rebecca, decd, m at Cadiz M H to Mary Bufkin of Cadiz, Ind
8-20-1857    Mary gct Walnut Ridge MM
3-26-1874    Elias rec in mbrp
8-20-1874    Rhoda rec in mbrp
4-26-1900    Magdeline, Camplin, Henry, Harris & Thomas drpd from mbrp

MOORMAN
11-26-1841    Thomas of Grant Co, s Uriah & Elizabeth m at Clear Springs M H, to Margaret Jane Wright of Henry Co
2-23-1843    Mary Jane & infant son gct Back Creek MM
10-20-1853    Lydia rocf Centre MM, N C

MORGAN
11-22-1832    Hezekiah & w Lydia & ch Obadiah, Henry, Isaac, Thomas, Jane, Hannah, Rebecca, Zeno & Nathan rocf Lost Creek MM, Tenn
10-24-1833    Obadiah & w Ann & ch Hezekiah, Margaret, Thomas, Sophia, Joseph & William T rocf Newberry MM, Tenn
8-21-1834    Ann appt o at Fall Creek P M
7-20-1837    Rhoda Macy appt o in room of Ann Morgan

MORLEY
1-21-1875    Joseph rec in mbrp

MORRIS
9-28-1826    Reuben & w Miriam & ch Benjamin, John, Joseph, Sarah, Levi, Samuel & Mary rocf West Grove MM
11-13-1829    Benjamin of Henry Co, s Reuben & Miriam of same place, m at Duck Creek M H to Caty Williams of Madison Co
1-20-1830    John gct Springfield MM to m Rachel Ward
8-25-1831    John, Springfield MM informs that he has joined with others in propogating a slanderous report against one of his fellow creatures dis 12-22-1831
8-25-1831    Joseph, Springfield MM infs that he has joined with others in propogating a slanderous report against one of his fellow creatures dis 12-22-1831
1-26-1832    John appealed his case to Q M
1-26-1832    Joseph appealed his case to Q M
6-20-1832    Jonathan & w Theodate & dt Ruthanna V rocf Deerfield MM, Morgan Co, Ohio
9-20-1832    Jonathan & fam gct Milford MM
9-24-1833    John rocf Whitewater MM
2- 6-1833    John of Rush Co, s Jesse & Mary of Wayne Co m at Walnut Ridge M H to Ann E Henley of Rush Co
2-21-1833    Jonathan & w Theodate & dt Ruth Ann rocf West Grove MM
8-22-1833    John & w Ann E gct Whitewater MM
12-26-1833    John, minor s of Joshua, decd, rocf Milford MM
4-24-1834    Joseph, rec in mbrp at Spiceland MM w/con of this mtg
4-24-1834    Jonathan & w Theodate & ch req our cert to join them to Milford MM
6-26-1834    Lydia rocf Deerfield MM, Ohio end to Milford MM
7-24-1834    Jonathan & w Theodate & ch gct Milford MM
12-25-1834    William & w Susannah & dts Ruth & Rachel rocf Milford Mtg
3-26-1835    Lydia rocf Milford MM
7-23-1835    John, s Joshua, decd & Mary gct Milford MM
6-23-1836    William & w Susannah & fam gct Milford MM
6-25-1885    Sarah gct Raysville MM
4-20-1893    Albert G & w Anna & ch Ward H rocf Carthage MM
1-24-1895    Albert G & fam gct Earlham MM, Iowa
3-23-1905    John T roc
11-21-1912    John & w Emily gct Carthage MM

MUNDEN - MUNDANE
5-21-1829    Joseph & w Milicent & ch Peninah & Thomas rocf Whitewater MM
12-23-1830    Mary & ch gct Vermilion Mtg, Ill

3-24-1853    Ruth (form Presnall) Clear Springs P M compl for mcd dis 4-21-1853
3-20-1902    William E & Jennie rec on req
2-22-1906    Herman rec on req
1-21-1909    Herman & w Grace rec on req
3-22-1917    William E & Jennie drpd from mbrp
6-26-1924    Howard & w Ethel & ch Erveli Munden & Margaret Lee Wise ------?

MURNAN
2- 3-1927    Celia Burcham gct New Castle MM

MURPHY
7-27-1826    Miles appt to a comm
2- 1-1827    Miles jr compl of for training with the militia dis 5- 3-1827
6-28-1827    Clement, Duck Creek P M compl for mcd dis 8-23-1827
6-25-1829    Eli, Spiceland P M compl of for upl & training in the militia dis 8-20-1829
3-25-1830    Miles, Spiceland P M compl for "not complying with his engagements, & for upl & for furnishing grain for the purpose of distillation of spiritous liquor" dis 8-26-1830
4-21-1831    Martha & David, ch of Miles gct Springfield MM
8-25-1831    William, Duck Creek P M compl that he "has complied with military requisitions & dpl" dis 10-20-1831
8-25-1831    Mary, Duck Creek P M compl for na & dpl dis 10-20-1831

MUTTERSPAUGH
3-20-1924    Rosetta Melissa rec on req

MYERS
2-22-1894    John & s Wayne rec on req
2-22-1894    Martin rec on req
11-23-1911    Martin & w & ch Mary Esther & Franklin gct Whittier MM, Ca
10-26-1916    Wayne P gct Spiceland MM
4-22-1920    J C & w Ethel & s Robert E gct Spiceland MM

NEEDAM
2-24-1898    Annetta Smith drpd from mbrp

NEWBY
12-28-1826    Elias & w Lydia & ch William P & Mary rocf Back Creek MM, N C end by Whitewater MM
2- 1-1827    Lydia appt to comm to visit aged & infirm persons
2- 1-1827    Sarah (w of Thomas) & ch William, Jane & Alfred rocf Back Creek MM, N C end by Whitewater MM
1-24-1828    Thomas & w Susannah rocf Milford MM
6-26-1828    Thomas req that Duck Creek rst him in mbrp Comm to write Back Creek MM N C for permission 5-21-1829 Back Creek MM informs "that the cause for which he was disowned has not been removed" subject dismissed
7-22-1830    William & w Elizabeth & ch Cyrus & Joseph rocf Milford MM
11-22-1832    Henry & w Sarah & ch Penelope, Abigail, Milly, Mary, William & Phebe rocf Back Creek MM, N C
11-22-1832    Penelope (wid of Joseph) rocf Back Creek MM, N C
11-22-1832    John Henley rocf Back Creek MM, N C
11-22-1832    Thomas gct Milford MM
1-29-1834    John H, s Joseph, decd, of Back Creek MM N C & Penelope of Rush Co m at Walnut Ridge MH to Harriett White
12-26-1836    Elias req cert to Walnut Ridge MM to m Ann Binford On 1-26-1827 the case was dismissed
3-23-1837    Micajah & nephew, Thomas & niece Eleanor rocf Back Creek MM, N C end by White Lick MM
7-22-1841    Jane Engleberth (form Newby) Duck Creek P M compl for mcd dis 9-22-1841
1-26-1843    John rocf Milford MM to m Rachel Pearson

DUCK CREEK

## NEWBY (Cont)

|  |  |
|---|---|
| 2-2-1843 | John of Wayne Co, s Thomas & Mary of Jackson Co, m at Duck Creek M H to Rachel Pearson of Henry Co, a wid w/ch |
| 3-23-1843 | Rachel, (now w of John Newby) & her son Reuben Pearson (by a former m) gct Milford MM |
| 8-24-1843 | Elvira (form Bowman) Duck Creek P M compl for mcd dis 11-23-1843 |
| 2-28-1844 | Penelope, dt Elias & Lydia, decd of Henry Co, m at Clear Springs MH John Carpenter of Henry Co |
| 12-26-1844 | Elias appt an Elder |
| 1-1-1845 | Lydia, dt Elias & Lydia, decd of Henry Co m at Clear Springs M H to Pearson Palmer of Henry Co |
| 11-26-1846 | Tabitha appt an Elder |
| 11-28-1849 | Mary E, dt Elias & Lydia decd of Henry Co m at Clear Springs M H to Isaac Elliott of Henry Co |
| 2-21-1850 | Rachel (form Draper) Clear Springs Mtg compl for mcd 3-21-1850 chm |
| 5-23-1850 | William B, Duck Creek P M compl for mcd 6-20-1850 chm |
| 2-26-1852 | Alfred, Duck Creek P M compl for mcd & j Meth dis 4-22-1852 |
| 10-21-1852 | William P, Cadiz P M compl for mcd 11-25-1853 chm |
| 8-22-1853 | Jemima (form White) Walnut Ridge MM req this mtg to treat w/her for mcd Treated w/out any satisfaction 12-23-1853 dis rec from Walnut Ridge MM |
| 1-26-1854 | William B, Clear Springs P M compl for "immoral & reproachful conduct by attempting to fight a fellowman" dis 4-20-1854 |
| 2-22-1855 | William P, Cadiz P M inf mcd dis 5-24-1855 |
| 3-23-1855 | Louisa (form Spencer) Cadiz P M inf mcd 4-26-1855 chm |
| 4-26-1855 | James, Clear Springs P M compl for mcd dis 7-26-1855 |
| 3-20-1858 | John, Duck Creek P M compl for mcd dis |
| 10-2-1856 | Jane L, dt Elias & Lydia, decd, of Cadiz, m Cadiz M H John Bufkin of Henry Co |
| 2-25-1858 | Zimri dis for upl & fighting a fellowman |
| 7-20-1860 | Charity Ann, compl for na dis |
| 4-23-1868 | James P & w Delphia D & ch Sarah, Ella & Joseph rec in mbrp |
| 3-26-1874 | Clinton rec in mbrp |
| 3-26-1874 | William P rec in mbrp |
| 4-22-1875 | Rachel & fam gct Spiceland MM |
| 3-23-1893 | Louisa rel on req |
| 2-20-1896 | Charles F rec on req |
| 4-22-1897 | Joseph & w Florence gct New Castle MM |
| 12-21-1899 | Joseph A & w Jenne M & ch Paul J & Harrold I gct New Castle MM |
| 2-26-1900 | Delie & ch Earnest, Verna May & Katie rel on req |
| 2-26-1914 | William H & w Mary L & ch Lowell B & Lewis M rel on req |
| 6-24-1915 | Ward rec on req |

## NEWLIN

|  |  |
|---|---|
| 12-22-1870 | Asenath J gct Plainfield MM |

## NEWSOM

|  |  |
|---|---|
| 8-20-1829 | Luke & w Elizabeth & ch Martha & Henry rocf Milford MM |
| 1-28-1835 | Luke of Rush Co, s Ransom, decd & Sarah m at Walnut Ridge M H to Cynthia Bulla of Rush Co |
| 10-22-1835 | Luke, Walnut Ridge P M inf he is "guilty of fornication" 12-24-1835 chm |
| 11-26-1835 | Cynthia, Walnut Ridge P M compl for "being guilty of unchaste conduct with a man to whom she has since been married" 1-21-1836 chm |

## NICHOLS

|  |  |
|---|---|
| 3-23-1837 | John rocf Flushing MM, Ohio |

## NICHOLSON

|  |  |
|---|---|
| 4-26-1832 | Elizabeth & George, minor ch of Daniel & Elizabeth, rocf Caesars Creek MM, Ohio |
| 2-27-1833 | Elizabeth Adamson (form Nicholson) compl of for mcd dis 4-25-1833 |
| 10-24-1833 | Peninah & ch Nathan Parker & Peninah rocf Milford MM |
| 9-13-1835 | George of Milford Mtg, Wayne Co, s Nathan decd, late of Perquimans Co, N C & Peninah of Rush Co, m at Walnut Ridge M H Mary Hill of Rush Co |
| 12-24-1835 | Thomas William & Joshua ch of John, rocf Suttons Creek MM, N C end by Milford MM |
| 3-26-1896 | Ned rocf New Castle MM |
| 12-20-1906 | Albert L rec on req |

## NIXON

|  |  |
|---|---|
| 12-23-1841 | Asenath (form Wickersham) Duck Creek P M compl for mcd 3-24-1842 chm |
| 4-21-1842 | Jacob, who had been dis by Deep Creek MM, N C req to be rec in mbrp again 10-20-1842 rec in mbrp w/con of Deep Creek |
| 9-26-1844 | Jacob, who is on a visit to his friends in N C req a few lines . . . . to certify that he is a mbr here |
| 2-26-1846 | Jacob gct Hopewell MM |
| 1-21-1847 | Asenath gct Honey Creek MM |
| 12-26-1850 | Jacob & w Anna rocf Hopewell MM |
| 5-22-1851 | Jacob & w Anna gct Hopewell MM |
| 1-21-1858 | Jacob & w Anna rocf Hopewell MM |
| 11-20-1862 | Jacob & w Anna gct Honey Creek MM |
| 10-26-1865 | Jacob & w Anna rocf Honey Creek MM |
| 9-24-1868 | Jacob gct Kokomo MM |

## NORMAN

|  |  |
|---|---|
| 10-20-1853 | Lydia rocf Centre MM, N C |

## NORTON

|  |  |
|---|---|
| 3-20-1834 | Richard & w Elizabeth rocf Whitewater MM |
| 10-23-1834 | Dennis & w Sarah & ch Anna Jane & Elizabeth Caroline rocf Dover MM, N C |
| 5-24-1835 | Edward & w Nancy & s Dennis R rocf Whitewater MM |
| 1-30-1845 | Richard, a widower & s Edward & Nancy, decd, m at Duck Creek M H to Phebe Wilson, wid of Joseph Wilson |
| 11-26-1846 | Edward, Clear Spring P M compl for mcd dis 4-22-1847 |
| 11-26-1846 | Mary (form wid Hinshaw) Clear Springs Mtg compl for mcd & j Meth Being a mbr of Westfield MM that mtg was inf 4-22-1847 Westfield req this mtg to treat w/her Treated w/out satisfaction dis rec from Westfield MM on 12-23-1847 |
| 2-28-1849 | Dennis of Henry Co, s Richard & Elizabeth decd, m at Clear Springs M H to Deborah Stanley, wid, dt of Jesse & Ann Weisner both decd |
| 3-29-1849 | Anna Jane, dt Dennis & Sarah, decd, of Henry Co, m at West Branch MH to Moses Stanley of Henry Co |
| 2-20-1851 | Elizabeth Caroline, Cadiz P M compl for j Meth dis 4-21-1851 |
| 4-26-1855 | Dennis K, Clear Springs P M inf he has "been guilty of larceny & has used violence towards a fellow being & has upl & has reproachable conduct by making an attempt on the chastity of a young woman" dis 6-21-1855 |
| 11-20-1856 | Ann Stanley (form Norton) rpt mcd dis |
| 1-22-1857 | Rebecca Burrahs (form Norton) rpt mcd dis |
| 9-22-1859 | Dennis & w Deborah & fam gct Lynn Grove MM, Iowa |

## NUGENT

|  |  |
|---|---|
| 4-25-1895 | Harry rocf Raysville MM |
| 6-20-1907 | Harry drpd from mbrp |

## OLDEN

|  |  |
|---|---|
| 4-20-1899 | Laura rocf Knightstown MM |

## OLDHAM

|  |  |
|---|---|
| 4-23-1925 | Laura rec on req |

## OLIPHANT

|  |  |
|---|---|
| 6-23-1836 | Mary rocf New Hope MM, Tenn |

DUCK CREEK

## OLIPHANT (Cont)
| | |
|---|---|
| 2-23-1893 | John rec on req |
| 4-22-1897 | John & w Ettie Newby & ch Lollus gct New Castle MM |

## O'NEAL
| | |
|---|---|
| 10-24-1850 | Mariah (form Saint) Duck Creek P M compl for mcd & j Meth  dis 1-23-1851 |

## OSBORN - OZBURN
| | |
|---|---|
| 11-21-1833 | Jane & ch Lydia N & Clayton R rocf New Hope MM, Tenn |
| 8-24-1834 | Martha (form Beeson) compl of for mcd dis 11-20-1834 |
| 7-21-1836 | Jane & ch gct Mississinewa MM |
| 7-20-1837 | Jane & ch Clayton R, Jeremiah W & Lydia Ann rocf Mississinewa MM |
| 1-25-1849 | Lydia Modlin (form Osborn) Clear Springs P M compl for mcd  She is residing in limit of Hopewell MM which mtg is req to treat w/her  Hopewell rpts no satisfaction dis & copy forwarded to Hopewell MM  6-21-1849 |
| 8-25-1853 | Jemima McClelland (form Osborn) Clear Springs P M compl for mcd  dis 10-20-1853 |
| 2-20-1862 | Clayton, Clear Springs P M inf mcd  dis |
| 11-25-1880 | Sarah Hammond & her dt Louisa Osborn rocf Raysville MM |
| 6-22-1905 | Louisa gct New Garden MM, N C |
| 5-21-1903 | Flora gct New Castle MM |

## OVERMAN
| | |
|---|---|
| 4- 1-1869 | John of Mississinewa Mtg, Grant Co, s Eli & Polly of same place, m at Cadiz M H to Irena A Kendall, wid of David of Henry Co |
| 5-20-1869 | Irena gct Mississinewa MM |

## PALIN - PALEN
| | |
|---|---|
| 6-28-1827 | Exum N rocf Milford MM |
| 7- 5-1827 | Exum N of Henry Co, s Henry & Sarah of Wayne Co m at Duck Creek M H Betsey Bond of Henry Co |
| 5-21-1829 | Exum N & w Betsey & fam gct Milford MM |
| 9-23-1830 | Nixon & w Peninah & ch William, Lucinda, Irena & Silvaneus rec in mbrp w/con of West Grove MM |

## PALMER
| | |
|---|---|
| 4-21-1842 | Henry of Clear Springs P M rec in mbrp |
| 6-23-1842 | Ann rec in mbrp again w/con of Spiceland MM |
| 7-21-1842 | David rec in mbrp |
| 11-24-1842 | David gct Milford MM to m Mary Elliott |
| 2-23-1843 | Mary & her minor ch, Isaac, Katharine, Mary Ann, Martha, Melissa & John ELLIOTT jr rocf Milford MM |
| 6-22-1843 | Pearson, Nathan, Elias, Asenath, John P & Hannah ch of David rec in mbrp |
| 1- 1-1845 | Pearson of Henry Co, s David & Sarah, decd m at Clear Springs M H to Lydia Newby |
| 6-26-1845 | Nathan, Clear Springs P M compl for mcd 8-21-1845 chm |
| 3-26-1846 | Elias gct Walnut Ridge MM to m Eunice W Coggeshall |
| 8-20-1846 | Eunice W rocf Walnut Ridge MM |
| 8-21-1846 | Nathan, Clear Springs P M compl for j Meth dis 11-26-1846 |
| 3- 3-1847 | Asenath, dt of David & Sarah, decd, of Henry Co, m at Clear Springs M H to John M Ratliff of Henry Co |
| 4-28-1852 | Hannah B, dt of David & Sarah, decd, of Henry Co m at Clear Springs M H to Ezra Spencer of Henry Co |
| 5-24-1855 | John P, Clear Spring P M compl for mcd dis |
| 5-24-1855 | Hannah L (form Ratliff) rpt to have mcd dis |
| 11-20-1856 | Elias & w Eunice W & ch gct Fairfield MM |
| 5-21-1857 | Hannah L rec in mbrp |
| 4-22-1858 | Pearson & w Lydia & fam gct Plainfield MM |
| 2-23-1860 | Pearson & w Lydia & ch Isaac E, Asenath Jane & Mary Louisa rocf Plainfield MM |
| 8-24-1865 | Lydia appt an Elder |
| 8-23-1866 | John P & s William Irvin rec in mbrp |
| 5-30-1867 | David of Henry Co, s John & Ann, both decd m at Duck Creek M H to Catharine Draper, wid of Josiah Draper jr, of Henry Co |
| 1-21-1869 | Isaac E gct Plainfield MM |
| 1-22-1880 | Joseph & w Louisa H rec on req |
| 3-25-1909 | Bell rec on req |
| 1-26-1911 | William & w Bell & s Raymond gct Whittier MM, Ca |
| 4-20-1916 | Forrest rec on req |
| 3-22-1917 | E O & w Julia & ch Forest J, Ralph & Harriett gc |

## PARKER
| | |
|---|---|
| 11-22-1826 | Samuel & w Rebecca & ch Silas, James & John rocf Rich Square MM, N C end by Whitewater MM |
| 3-26-1829 | William rocf Rich Square MM, Northampton Co, N C, end by Milford MM |
| 8-23-1832 | William gct Milford MM to m Almeda Johnson |
| 4-25-1833 | Almeda rocf Milford MM |
| 3-25-1858 | Joel Hiatt gct Walnut Ridge MM to m Isabella Parker |

## PATTERSON
| | |
|---|---|
| 4-20-1837 | Hezekiah & w Elizabeth & ch Joseph, Sarah, Eli & Levi rocf Dover MM |
| 1-20-1848 | Joseph, Duck Creek P M compl for mcd 2-24-1848 chm |
| 5-25-1848 | Joseph gct Mill Creek MM |
| 11-22-1849 | Hezekiah & w Elizabeth & ch gct Spiceland MM |

## PAYNE - PAIN
| | |
|---|---|
| 11-25-1852 | Gulielma (form Hiatt) Clear Springs P M compl for mcd  She is now living in the verge of East Grove MM, Iowa & that mtg req to treat w/her  7-21-1853 East Grove MM rpts no satisfaction dis |
| 5-23-1861 | Martha C & ch William & Emma Jane rec in mbrp |
| 7-20-1865 | Joel R & dt Rebecca Ellen rec in mbrp |
| 1- 2-1868 | Martha C, a wid & dt of William, decd & Jane Hastings, m at Cadiz M H to Dennis Kendall of Cadiz Henry Co |
| 6-22-1882 | Eliza & s gct Spiceland MM |
| 11-22-1883 | William H gct Indianapolis MM |
| 1-21-1897 | Maude S gct Spiceland MM |

## PEARSON
| | |
|---|---|
| 8-31-1826 | Peter appt Treasurer of Duck Creek MM |
| 7-26-1827 | Huldah (w of Levi) rocf New Garden MM |
| 10- 4-1827 | Bailey of Henry Co, s of Nathan & Mary, decd  m at Duck Creek M H to Jane Ratliff of Henry Co |
| 3-20-1828 | Zeno, Duck Creek P M inf mcd  dis 5-22-1828 |
| 10-23-1828 | John & w Lydia & fam gct White River MM |
| 10- 1-1829 | Levi of Henry Co, s Nathan & Mary, decd m at Duck Creek M H to Rachel Presnall of Henry Co |
| 4-22-1830 | Jonathan rocf Milford MM |
| 5-20-1830 | Nancy, Milford MM, req this mtg to treat w/her for na & dpl  6-24-1830 Milford MM inf no satisfaction |
| 8-26-1830 | David, Lydia, Jane, Eli, Zeno, Moses & Sarah, ch of Jonathan & Nancy rocf Milford MM |
| 11-24-1831 | David, Duck Creek P M compl for training in the militia & dpl dis 2-23-1832 |
| 4-26-1832 | John & w Lydia & ch Huldah, Mary, Bailey, David, Sarah, Lydia & John jr rocf White River MM |
| 7-26-1832 | Jesse & w Polly & ch Rebecca, Jesse jr & Jane rocf Milford MM |
| 1-24-1833 | Nathan, Jesse, Polly & Patty ch of Jonathan & w Anna rec in mbrp & her ch (by former M) Sarah & Lydia Small rec in mbrp |
| 4-25-1833 | Aaron, Duck Creek Mtg compl for mcd 6-20-1833 chm |
| 5-23-1833 | Anna rec in mbrp w/con of Springfield MM N C |
| 6-20-1833 | John rocf Mill Creek MM |
| 6-20-1833 | Huldah compl for mcd  8-22-1833 chm |
| 2-20-1834 | John & w Lydia gct Mississinewa MM |

DUCK CREEK

## PEARSON (Cont)

|  |  |
|---|---|
| 4-24-1834 | Rhoda Small (form Pearson) Clear Springs P M compl for mcd  Mississinewa MM req to treat w/her  7-24-1834 Mississinewa MM rpts she offered an ackn |
| 10-23-1834 | Bailey & fam gct Mississinewa MM |
| 5-21-1835 | Exum rocf Milford MM |
| 3-24-1836 | Jesse jr mcd  dis 5-26-1836 |
| 3-24-1836 | John, Clear Springs MM inf has mcd  dis 5-26-1836 |
| 1-26-1837 | Joseph, Clear Springs P M infs mcd  dis 5-25-1837 |
| 1-26-1837 | Nathan, Clear Springs P M infs mcd  dis 3-23-1837 |
| 1-21-1841 | Aaron, Clear Springs P M compl for j Meth  dis 3-25-1841 |
| 5-20-1841 | Huldah, Clear Springs P M compl for j Meth  dis 7-22-1841 |
| 11-25-1841 | Enoch gct Walnut Ridge MM to m Rachel Brown |
| 5-26-1842 | Rachel rocf Walnut Ridge MM end to Spiceland MM |
| 5-26-1842 | Peter & w Eunice & ch gct Spiceland MM |
| 6-23-1842 | Enoch gct Spiceland MM (already removed) |
| 2-2-1843 | Rachel, wid of Levi Pearson & dt Stephen, decd & Hannah Presnall of Henry Co m at Duck Creek M H John Newby of Wayne Co (a widower) |
| 5-25-1843 | Hiram & Sarah, minor ch of Levi, decd gct Mississinewa MM |
| 6-22-1843 | Enoch & w Rachel (form Brown) & ch Nathan rocf Spiceland MM |
| 1-25-1844 | Elizabeth rec in mbrp again w/con of West Grove MM |
| 1-25-1844 | Enos, Seth, Sarah, Mary & Abigail ch of Exum & Elizabeth rec in mbrp |
| 10-30-1844 | Enos of Henry Co, s of Exum & Elizabeth of same place m at Clear Springs M H to Anna Hutson of Henry Co |
| 8-21-1845 | Eli, Clear Springs P M compl for mcd  dis 10-23-1845 |
| 9-25-1845 | Zeno, Clear Springs P M compl for mcd  dis 12-25-1845 |
| 8-26-1847 | Moses, Clear Springs P M compl for mcd  dis 1-20-1848 |
| 3-23-1848 | Enoch & Rachel & ch gct Honey Creek MM |
| 12-25-1851 | Sarah Hutson (form Pearson) Clear Springs P M compl for mcd  5-20-1852 chm |
| 12-25-1851 | Mary Baker (form Pearson) Clear Springs P M compl for mcd  1-22-1852 chm |
| 11-25-1852 | Rebecca (form Ratliff) Clear Springs P M compl for mcd  1-20-1853 chm |
| 7-21-1853 | Seth gct Hopewell MM to m Sarah Bundy |
| 11-24-1853 | Enos, Cadiz P M compl for mcd 12-22-1853 chm |
| 1-26-1854 | Sarah rocf Hopewell MM |
| 6-26-1852 | Sarah gct Hopewell MM |
| 6-23-1859 | Delilah L dis for jas |
| 2-21-1861 | Joseph reinstated in mbrp |
| 5-26-1864 | Enos jr, Cadiz P M compl for j Freemasons dis 7-21-1864 |
| 5-25-1882 | Enos & fam gc |
| 4-20-1893 | Lydia N rocf New Castle MM |
| 11-21-1895 | Mary J rec on req |
| 1-23-1896 | Lydia rec on req |
| 4-26-1900 | Henderson & w Mary J rel on req |
| 1-24-1907 | Henderson & w Mary J rec on req |
| 11-25-1915 | Abigail gct Spiceland MM |

## PENNINGTON

|  |  |
|---|---|
| 7-27-1826 | Josiah appt to a comm |
| 7-27-1826 | Deborah appt to a comm |
| 8-31-1826 | Deborah appt to comm to have care of indulged mtgs |
| 8-31-1826 | Josiah appt to comm on "poor" |
| 9-28-1831 | Mary, dt Josiah & Deborah of Henry Co, m at Spiceland M H Jesse White of Henry Co |

## PERISHO

|  |  |
|---|---|
| 5-24-1832 | Nathan & w Mary & ch John, Joshua, Morris, Mary Elma & Martha Ann rocf Symons Creek Mtg, N C |

## PERRY

|  |  |
|---|---|
| 3-22-1894 | Clara & dt Eva rec on req |

## PETERS

|  |  |
|---|---|
| 8-22-1918 | George rec on req |
| 10-25-1923 | George gct Shirley MM |

## PHELPS

|  |  |
|---|---|
| 6-22-1848 | Anna (form Hill) Walnut Ridge MM req this mtg to treat w/her for mcd  7-20-1848 chm |
| 8-24-1848 | Asenath (form Jay) Duck Creek P M compl for mcd  9-21-1848 chm |
| 10-26-1848 | Anna rocf Walnut Ridge MM |
| 7-21-1853 | Asenath gct East Grove MM, Iowa |
| 8-22-1861 | Frederick of Cadiz P M rec in mbrp |
| 4-23-1874 | Elias rec in mbrp |
| 1-23-1896 | Elias rec on req |
| 8-11-1921 | John M & w Ella & dt Anna Phelps Berry gct New Castle MM |

## PICKERING

|  |  |
|---|---|
| 7-27-1826 | Jonas appt to a comm |
| 7-27-1826 | Ruth appt to a comm |
| 8-31-1826 | Jonas appt to comm to see that the mtg house is reconditioned to make it comfortable |
| 8-31-1826 | Jonas appt to comm on "poor" |
| 8-31-1826 | Priscilla appt an o for Duck Creek P M |
| 9-2-1826 | Phebe appt to comm |
| 3-29-1827 | Abner appt to comm |
| 2-28-1828 | Abner of Henry Co, s Jonas & Ruth m at Duck Creek M H Charity Haskit |
| 1-22-1829 | Jonas, Duck Creek compl for j Hs  dis 3-26-1829 |
| 4-23-1829 | Samuel req cert to Flushing MM, Belmont Co, Ohio Cert ret 5-21-1829, did not remove |
| 5-21-1829 | Phebe dis for j Hs |
| 12-26-1829 | Jacob & w Rachel & ch John H, Jonathan E, Sarah Ann, Aquilla, Elihu & Naomi rocf Short Creek MM, Ohio |
| 11-26-1829 | Samuel gct Springfield MM to m Cynthia Maulsby |
| 4-22-1830 | Sarah (form Hasket) compl for mcd at a Hicksite mtg  dis 9-23-1830 |
| 8-26-1830 | Phebe con her having att a mcd |
| 7-22-1830 | Rebecca Smith (form Pickering) Duck Creek P M compl for mcd at a Hs mtg  dis 9-23-1830 |
| 12-2-1830 | Phebe, dt Jonas & Ruth of Henry Co, m at Duck Creek M H to Exum Saint of Henry Co |
| 1-26-1832 | Mary rec in mbrp |
| 3-24-1831 | Cynthia rocf Springfield MM |
| 3-24-1831 | John, Duck Creek compl for dancing & for mcd 5-26-1831 chm |
| 3-22-1832 | Samuel, Duck Creek inf "that he had entered suit at law against two individuals, mbrs of our society"  6-20-1832 complaint dismissed |
| 8-23-1832 | William, formerly a mbr of & dis by Hopewell MM, Va, req to become a mbr of society  1-24-1832 Hopewell MM, Va writes that due to the late separation they were unable to even ascertain the cause for disownment  He is rec in mbrp |
| 10-25-1832 | Susannah & dt Lurena rec in mbrp |
| 1-23-1834 | Phineas & w Rachel & ch Nancy, Ellis & Jesse rocf New Hope MM, Tenn |
| 7-24-1834 | James, Samuel, Esther, Susanna, Phebe Ann, Mary & Leah ch of Phebe (form Kirk) & (Samuel) gct Milford MM |
| 9-25-1834 | Samuel & w Cynthia (now living in St. Joseph Co, Ind) gct to Mississinewa MM |
| 1-22-1835 | Jonathan, Duck Creek P M compl for mcd 4-23-1835 chm |
| 1-22-1835 | Jonas, Duck Creek Mtg compl for mcd & dpl 4-23-1835 chm |
| 7-23-1835 | Tirzah rec in mbrp |
| 10-1-1835 | William, s John decd, & Jane m at Duck Creek M H, Sarah Willets of Henry Co |
| 11-24-1836 | Sarah rocf Flushing MM, Ohio |
| 6-22-1837 | Samuel & w Cynthia & ch Larken, Elizabeth & Lindley rocf Mississinewa MM |
| 8-24-1837 | Jonas, Duck Creek P M infs  he mcd |
| 8-27-1837 | Abner of Henry Co, s Jonas & Ruth m at Spiceland M H Jennet Saint of Henry Co (m accomp at Spiceland Mtg as Duck Creek mtg had been laid down) |

DUCK CREEK

## PICKERING (Cont)

|  |  |
|---|---|
| 11-26-1840 | John & w Mary gct Salem MM, Iowa |
| 12-24-1840 | Lurana gct Salem MM, Iowa (already removed) |
| 5-20-1841 | Jacob & w Ruth & fam gct Salem MM, Iowa |
| 4-21-1842 | John H, Duck Creek P M infs that he "a mbr of Salem MM, Iowa during his late sojourn with us, has been unjust in his dealings & has refused to comply with an engagement" Salem MM has so been inf 2-23-1842 Salem MM inf he denies the charge A comm has been appt to examine the matter. 3-23-1842 The comm believes the complaint against him to be fully substantiated but that he has since made satisfaction to the injured parties |
| 8-25-1842 | Nancy, Clear Springs P M rec in mbrp |
| 11-24-1842 | David, who has been dis by Plainfield MM, Ohio req to be rec in mbrp Rec in mbrp 12-22-1842 |
| 5-25-1843 | Joseph gct Salem MM, Iowa (already removed) |
| 5-25-1843 | Samuel jr, Duck Creek P M compl for att a mcd of a mbr dis 8-24-1843 |
| 9-21-1843 | Mahlon, Clear Springs P M compl for mcd dis 11-23-1843 |
| 3-20-1845 | Ann Carpenter (form Pickering) Duck Creek P M compl for mcd dis 5-22-1845 |
| 8-21-1845 | Mary, Duck Creek P M compl for unchastity but being a mbr of Milford MM that mtg was inf dis 6-25-1846 by Milford MM |
| 9- 7-1845 | Sarah A, a wid, & dt of Cadwallader & Elizabeth, decd, Pitts, m at Duck Creek M H to Pleasant Unthank of New Garden Mtg, Wayne Co |
| 10-23-1845 | Leah Stanley (form Pickering) Duck Creek P M compl for mcd She being a mbr of Milford MM that mtg is inf |
| 5-21-1846 | Esther Jane with mother Sarah Ann Unthank gct New Garden MM |
| 8-20-1846 | Mary, Milford MM forwards dis |
| 1- 2-1847 | Mary Vance (form Pickering) Duck Creek P M compl for mcd dis 3-25-1847 |
| 4-22-1847 | Lydia Jane, ch of Nancy, rec in mbrp |
| 12-30-1847 | Sarah Ann, dt Abner & Charity, decd, of Henry Co m at Duck Creek M H to Joseph Butler of Henry Co |
| 2-24-1848 | Jordan, Duck Creek P M compl for mcd dis 4-20-1848 |
| 5- 3-1849 | Abigail, dt Abner & Charity, decd of Henry Co, m at Duck Creek M H Henry J Lindley of Westfield Mtg, Hamilton Co |
| 5-24-1849 | Elizabeth J & s James Irvin rocf Spiceland MM |
| 10-25-1849 | Elizabeth Sharp (form Pickering) Duck Creek P M compl for mcd, but she now lives in limits of Hopewell MM, so this mtg req that mtg to treat w/her dis forwarded to Hopewell MM on 4-25-1850 |
| 8-26-1852 | Margaret (form Reese) Cadiz compl for mcd 11-25-1852 It is rptd she is decd |
| 11-25-1852 | Elizabeth M Swain (form Pickering) Duck Creek P M compl for mcd 12-23-1852 chm |
| 3-23-1854 | Sarah Deselm (form Pickering) Clear Spring MM compl for mcd dis 5- 6-1854 |
| 4-28-1854 | Lydia Jane, dt David & Nancy of Cadiz, Henry Co m at Cadiz M H Richard Evans of Spiceland Mtg, Henry Co |
| 6- 6-1854 | Lucinda Copeland (form Pickering) Clear Springs P M compl for mcd & j Meth dis 8-24-1854 |
| 12-21-1854 | Mary (form Stanley) Clear Springs P M compl for mcd & jas dis 2-22-1855 |
| 3-22-1855 | Samuel & w Cynthia & fam gct Richland MM |
| 12-20-1855 | Samuel & w Cynthia & ch Henry, Lydia Ann, & Macy rocf Richland MM |
| 2-28-1856 | Jennet, a wid & dt of William & Achsah Saint of Henry Co m at Duck Creek M H to Nathan Macy of Spiceland MM, Henry Co |
| 3-20-1856 | Lindley M, Richland MM req this mtg to treat w/him for upl 4-24-1856 chm but on 7-24-1856 Duck Creek P M compl to Richland MM that he has upl 3-26-1857 Richland MM has been inf of no satisfac |
| 11-26-1857 | Samuel & w Cynthia & ch gct Back Creek MM, Iowa |
| 11-26-1857 | Mary & dt Mary Ann rec in mbrp |
| 5-22-1862 | Samuel & w Cynthia (a Minister) rocf Springfield MM |
| 6-26-1862 | Macy, Springfield req this mtg to visit for mcd 7-24-1862 desires to retain mbrp & Springfield MM so inf |
| 6-25-1863 | Macy rocf Springfield MM |
| 6-25-1863 | Lydia rocf Spiceland MM |
| 6-25-1863 | Samuel, Duck Creek P M compl "he has been guilty of making false charges against one of our mbrs" He denies the charges 12-24-1863 the matter dismissed |
| 5-25-1865 | Seth, Clear Springs P M inf he has jas dis |
| 4-23-1868 | Jonas rec in mbrp |
| 4-23-1868 | Mahlon rec in mbrp |
| 12- 3-1868 | Cynthia, wid of Samuel & dt John & Elizabeth Maulsby m at Cadiz MH to Eli Reece of Washington twp, Randolph Co |
| 8-20-1869 | Macy, Cadiz P M inf has j Free Masons dis 1-21-1869 |
| 2-25-1869 | Cynthia, a Minister, now Cynthia Reece gct Cherry Grove MM |
| 11-22-1874 | Jonathan & w Emeline rec on req |
| 4-23-1885 | Mary L rec on req |
| 3-24-1892 | Mary L rel on req |
| 2-23-1893 | Mahlon gct Indiola MM |
| 11-24-1904 | Victor H & Mary Malone rec on req |
| 11-21-1912 | Victor & w Florence & ch Mary Malone, Penn Wood & Seth Cummins gct Whittier MM, Ca |
| 3-25-1915 | Jonathan & w Emeline drpd from mbrp |
| 2-25-1926 | Rosa A rec on req |

## PICKETT - PIGGOTT

|  |  |
|---|---|
| 2- 1-1827 | Joseph appt to a comm |
| 7-27-1826 | Priscilla appt to a comm |
| 4- 5-1827 | Tamar, dt Joseph & Priscilla of Henry Co m at Duck Creek M H Nathan Hunt of Henry Co |
| 6- 6-1827 | Mary, dt Joseph & Priscilla of Henry Co m at Duck Creek M H to Amor Bond of Henry Co |
| 4- 3-1828 | Anna, dt Joseph & Priscilla of Henry Co m at Duck Creek M H Isaac Cook of Henry Co |
| 7-24-1828 | Lydia gct West Grove Mtg |
| 12-22-1831 | Anna & dts Rhoda & Esther rocf Chester MM |
| 12-30-1832 | James & w Mary & ch William, Elihu, Thomas & Margaret rocf White River MM |
| 1-24-1833 | William & w Sarah rocf Whitewater MM |
| 3-21-1833 | William & w Sarah gct Spiceland MM |
| 4-21-1836 | Joseph jr, Duck Creek P M compl for upl & dpl dis 8-25-1836 |
| 1-21-1869 | Joseph retained in mbrp |
| 4-27-1870 | Joseph jr gct Raysville MM |
| 5-24-1877 | Joseph rocf Raysville MM |
| 3-22-1894 | Nora rel on req |
| 3-22-1894 | Jason Albert rec on req |
| 5-26-1898 | Nancy rec on req |

## PICKNELL

|  |  |
|---|---|
| 5-25-1905 | Blanch rec on req |

## PIERCE - PEARCE

|  |  |
|---|---|
| 4-23-1874 | Walter M rec in mbrp |
| 2-23-1893 | Walter & Luther rec on req |
| 4-26-1917 | Blanch rec on req |
| 1-23-1919 | Walter M & Leota rel on req |
| 8-11-1921 | Laura gct New Castle MM |

## PIKE

|  |  |
|---|---|
| 2-21-1833 | Nathan, an infant under care of Cadwallader Pitts, rocf Union - - -, N C |
| 3-21-1833 | John & w Hannah & s John S rocf Fairfield Mtg, Ohio, end by New Garden MM |
| 1-21-1836 | John Schooley gct Spiceland MM to m Gulielma Dean |
| 6-23-1836 | Gulielma rocf Spiceland MM |
| 4-23-1846 | Nathan Weisner gct Walnut Ridge MM, to m Hannah Pike |
| 5-21-1846 | Jesse Weisner gct Walnut Ridge MM to m Phebe Pike |

## PITTS

|  |  |
|---|---|
| 2-21-1833 | Cadwallader & w Elizabeth & ch Sarah & Eliza & an infant under their care, Nathan Pike, rocf Union MM, N C end by Whitewater MM |
| 11-24-1836 | Isaac & w Charity & ch Emily, Elizabeth & Susannah rocf Cherry Grove MM |
| 12-28-1843 | Eliza Jane, dt Cadwallader & Elizabeth, decd m at Duck Creek M H to Cyrus Hinshaw of Henry Co |
| 10-24-1844 | Cadwallader gct Springfield MM to m Mary Chamness |
| 1-23-1845 | Charity, Duck Creek Mtg compl for j (ASF) dis 3-20-1845 |
| 4-24-1845 | Mary rocf Springfield MM |
| 2-20-1845 | Isaac, Duck Creek Mtg compl for j Separatists |
| 11-25-1852 | Emily Wright (form Pitts) Duck Creek P M compl for mcd dis 2-24-1853 |
| 10-20-1853 | Elizabeth Weeks (form Pitts) Duck Creek P M compl for mcd dis 12-23-1853 |
| 5-22-1856 | Mary gct Springfield MM |
| 9-21-1871 | Martha rec in mbrp |
| 4-23-1925 | Minnie rec on req |

## PLACE - PLEAS

|  |  |
|---|---|
| 7-26-1827 | William & w Priscilla & dt Naomi rocf Whitewater MM |
| 4-23-1829 | William & w Priscilla & fam gct New Garden MM |

## POE

|  |  |
|---|---|
| 12-24-1896 | Jonathan W & w Antinet rel on req |
| 4-23-1903 | Elizabeth & dt Jessie gct Spiceland MM |
| 1-26-1911 | Hattie, Elizabeth gct Spiceland MM |

## POLK

|  |  |
|---|---|
| 11-20-1846 | Miriam (form Lowder) Duck Creek P M compl for mcd dis 4-23-1846 |
| 3-20-1902 | Rose rec on req |

## POPE

|  |  |
|---|---|
| 5-21-1846 | Peninah (form Mills) Duck Creek P M compl for mcd & j Hs & being a mbr in the verge of Fairfield MM that mtg req to treat w/her They rpt no satisfaction 10-22-1846 dis is forwarded to Fairfield MM |
| 5-21-1891 | William P drpd from mbrp |

## PRESNALL

|  |  |
|---|---|
| 12-28-1826 | John & w Hannah & ch Martha, Rachel, Daniel, Mary Elizabeth, Jeremiah, John & Jehu rocf Back Creek MM N C end by Whitewater MM |
| 12-28-1826 | Benoni gct Newbury MM, Ohio to m Jane Moon |
| 2- 1-1827 | Rachel appt to a comm |
| 3- 8-1827 | Rachel, dt John & Hannah of Henry Co, m at Duck Creek M H Henry Lewelling of Henry Co |
| 5-31-1827 | Martha appt to a comm |
| 1-24-1828 | Elijah rocf Back Creek MM, N C |
| 1-24-1828 | Hannah & ch Rachel, Absalom, Christina, James & Sarah rocf Back Creek MM, N C |
| 1-22-1829 | Nathan & w Rebecca & ch Elihu & Julia rocf Back Creek MM, N C end by West Grove MM |
| 4-23-1829 | Martha Hiatt (form Presnall) compl of for mcd 5-21-1829 chm |
| 8-20-1829 | Nathan & fam gct White Lick MM |
| 9-24-1829 | Benoni, Duck Creek Mtg compl for upl & striking one of his fellowmen & for varying from the truth by falsely accusing two of his neighbors of giving false evidence He denies a part thereof 1-21-1830 the Q M is req to assist in the case dis 7-22-1830 |
| 10- 1-1829 | Rachel, dt of Stephen, decd, & Hannah of Henry Co, m at Duck Creek M H to Levi Pearson of Henry Co |
| 7-22-1830 | Jane & ch rocf Newberry MM, Ohio |
| 9-23-1830 | Daniel inf this mtg that he is aggrieved on account of (as he apprehends) the proceedings of the comm appt last year on the subject of the "poor" 10-21-1830 The comm appt to investigate rpt it groundless |
| 12-30-1830 | Elizabeth, dt John & Hannah of Henry Co, m at Duck Creek M H to Henderson Lewelling of Henry Co |
| 4-21-1831 | Christina, wid of Daniel Sr, Duck Creek P M rpts that $4.25, 9½ bu of corn, 3 bu of wheat, 8 pounds of sugar & ½ peck of peaches has been subscribed for the benefit of Jacob Lamb & fam for the taking care of (above named person) |
| 4-21-1831 | Daniel, Duck Creek P M inf "that he hath been guilty of raising & circulating a slanderous rpt on an individual, calculated to lower the credit & dignity of the society" dis 7-21-1831  8-25-1831 he appealed to the Q M |
| 5-26-1831 | Christina, wid of Daniel Sr, Spiceland P M rpts has subscribed $1.87½, 37½ pounds of bacon, 4½ pounds of flour, 3 lbs of wool, 6½ bu corn, & 2½ bu of potatoes for the benefit of the caretakers of (above named persons) |
| 9-22-1831 | Jane & ch Jeremiah & William gct Newberry MM, Ohio |
| 1-26-1832 | John, Duck Creek P M compl for giving a vague testimony & making contradictory statements 6-20-1832 case dismissed |
| 3- 7-1832 | Absalom, s Stephen, decd & Hannah of Henry Co, m at Walnut Ridge M H to Mary Binford of Hancock Co |
| 4-26-1832 | Nathan & w Rebecca & ch Elihu, Julia & Dempsey rocf White Lick MM |
| 5-24-1832 | John, Duck Creek P M inf that he joined with others in propagating a slanderous accusation against one of his fellow creatures and has partaken of a threat under circumstances very unbecoming in a mbr of our society 6-20-1832 complaint dismissed |
| 6-20-1832 | Daniel, Duck Creek P M compl for upl & using spiritous liquor dis 9-20-1832 |
| 12- 6-1832 | Christina, dt Stephen, decd & Hannah of Henry Co, m at Duck Creek M H to Elijah Thomas of Henry Co |
| 5- 9-1833 | Daniel of Henry Co, s John & Hannah, m at Duck Creek M H to Huldah Ratliff of Henry Co |
| 3-20-1834 | John jr compl of for mcd 5-22-1834 chm |
| 10-23-1834 | Jane & ch Jeremiah, William, James, Henry & Mary rocf Newberry MM, Ohio |
| 11-26-1835 | Mary Ratliff (form Presnall) Clear Springs P M compl for mcd 1-21-1836 chm |
| 4-21-1836 | Nathan mcd 7-21-1836 |
| 1-26-1837 | Henry mcd 4-20-1837 chm |
| 2-23-1837 | Emily (form Lowder) compl of for mcd dis 7-20-1837 |
| 6-22-1837 | Henry, Clear Springs P M inf he upl & drinks to excess but the mtg not being united that the complaint was in order, returned it to the P M |
| 4-20-1837 | Nathan, Clear Spring P M compl for att a mcd of a mbr 6-22-1837 chm |
| 1-20-1842 | Jeremiah L & s James rocf Westfield MM |
| 10-26-1843 | John jr, Clear Springs P M compl for mcd dis 12-21-1843 |
| 3-22-1844 | Sarah dt Daniel & Pleasant of Henry Co, m at Clear Springs M H to Thomas Moon of Clinton Co, Ohio |
| 7-25-1844 | Nathan, Clear Springs P M compl for j Meth dis 9-26-1844 |
| 11-21-1844 | Jeremiah L, Clear Springs P M compl for mcd & j Separatists He now resides in limits of Westfield MM which is req to treat w/ him Westfield MM rpts no satisfaction dis 3-20-1845 |
| 4-23-1846 | Julia gct Back Creek MM |
| 7-23-1846 | Jeremiah, Clear Springs P M compl for mcd & j Meth dis 10-22-1846 |
| 8-20-1846 | Pleasant (a female) Clear Springs P M compl for j Meth dis 11-26-1846 |
| 8-20-1846 | Henry, Clear Springs P M compl for j Meth dis 11-26-1846 |
| 11-26-1846 | James gct Springfield MM to m Anna Brown |

DUCK CREEK

PRESNALL (Cont)

|  |  |
|---|---|
| 12-24-1846 | Elihu, Back Creek MM inf upl & this mtg req that mtg to treat w/him  They rpt no satisfaction  dis 7-22-1846 & dis forwarded to Back Creek MM |
| 4-20-1848 | John M gct Hopewell MM to m Edith Wilson  But before the m could be accomplished John Presnall died |
| 5-25-1848 | Anna rocf Springfield MM |
| 5-25-1848 | Jehu, Clear Springs P M compl for mcd 6-22-1848 chm |
| 7-20-1848 | Eliza Jane (form Beik) Clear Springs P M compl for mcd   10-26-1848 chm |
| 1-24-1850 | Hannah Draper (form Presnall) Clear Spring P M compl for mcd  2-21-1850 chm |
| 6-24-1852 | James, East Grove MM, Iowa inf has mcd  This mtg req East Grove MM to treat w/him  They rpt no satisfaction  dis |
| 9-23-1852 | William, Clear Springs P M compl for mcd & j Meth  Since he now resides in limits of GreenfieldMM  they are req to treat w/him (no record of settlement) |
| 3-24-1853 | Ruth Mundane (Munden) (form Presnall) Clear Springs P M compl for mcd  dis 4-21-1853 |
| 4-20-1854 | Rebecca C, Clear Springs P M compl for unchaste conduct  dis 6-22-1854 |
| 3-22-1855 | Dempsey, Cadiz P M inf mcd (previously to the reception of new discipline) 4-26-1855 chm |
| 4-26-1855 | Eliza Jane (form Stanley) Duck Creek P M inf mcd  5-24-1855 chm |
| 5-22-1856 | Jeremiah, Richland MM req permission to rec him in mbrp  Granted |
| 7-24-1856 | Mary dis for j Meth |
| 9-24-1857 | Rebecca Jane, Lynn Grove MM, Iowa inf this mtg she att mcd of a mbr  11-26-1857 chm |
| 12-22-1859 | Elihu, Winneshiek MM, Iowa, req permission to rec him in mbrp |
| 2-25-1860 | Daniel & w Huldah & ch gct Spring Creek MM, Iowa |
| 11-24-1859 | Joseph G, Clear Spring MM inf mcd  Since he now resides in limits of Spring Creek MM, Iowa, they are req to treat w/him  5-24-1860 Spring Creek MM, Iowa inf he offers an ackn |
| 6-21-1860 | Joseph J G gct Spring Creek MM, Iowa |
| 1-26-1865 | Elihu & w Mary Ann & ch Martha, Rebecca Jane, Mary & Eunice rocf Baraboo MM, Wisc |
| 3-23-1865 | Nathan Sr rec in mbrp |
| 7-20-1865 | Hannah & dt Mary rec in mbrp |
| 7-20-1865 | Elihu & fam gct Back Creek MM |
| 8-24-1865 | Dempsey, Cadiz Mtg inf j Free Masons 11-23-1865 dis |
| 7-22-1869 | Eliza & ch John Temple & William D gct Back Creek MM |
| 7-21-1870 | Alfred, Cadiz P M inf mcd but has retained his mbrp |
| 6-26-1873 | Bowen, Clear Springs P M inf mcd but he retained his mbrp |
| 6-26-1873 | Charles, Clear Springs P M compl for fighting & using spiritous liquor to excess (no record of disposition of case) |
| 5-21-1874 | Hannah jr gct Deer Creek MM, Grant Co |
| 7-23-1874 | Hannah B & ch Alonzo L, John M, Jesse Elmer, Lydia Jane, Daniel & Joseph rocf Spring Creek MM, Iowa |
| 11-23-1876 | James & w Anna gct Fairmount MM |
| 4-25-1901 | Pheneas & w Theresa gct Muncie MM |
| 5-22-1902 | Harvey F gct Fairmount MM |

PRICE

|  |  |
|---|---|
| 7-27-1826 | Rice jr appt to a comm |
| 8-31-1826 | Rice appt an overseer |
| 9- 2-1826 | Catharine appt to a comm |
| 1- 4-1827 | Robert of Henry Co, s Rice, decd, of Preble Co, Ohio & Catharine of Henry Co, m at Duck Creek M H to Mary Ratliff of Henry Co |
| 3- 5-1827 | Rice jr appt Recorder of M Certs |
| 7-23-1846 | Rice & Susannah appt Elders |
| 6-24-1847 | Sally Maulsby (form Price) Clear Springs inf mcd  12-23-1847 chm |
| 1-26-1848 | Martha Ann, dt Rice & Susannah, m at Clear Springs M H to Owen Evans of Spiceland MM Henry Co |
| 9-26-1851 | Narcissa, dt Rice & Susannah of Henry Co, m at Clear Springs M H to Isaac K Steddom of Miami MM, Warren Co, Ohio |
| 10-26-1854 | Rice, infs mtg "that there is an unsettled difficulty existing between himself & another friend & asks the privilege to pursue a legal course at last to settle the same"  11-23-1854  not granted |
| 5- 2-1855 | Anna C, dt Rice & Susannah of Henry Co, m at Clear Springs M H to John W Griffin of Spiceland Mtg, Henry Co |
| 10-25-1855 | Rice & w Susannah & fam req cert to Winnesheik MM, Iowa  4-24-1856 Winnesheik Mtg, Iowa rpts cert was rec |

PRITCHARD - PRICHARD

|  |  |
|---|---|
| 7-24-1834 | William, who has been dis by Blue River MM & s Edwin & Calvin Wasson req mbrp  1-22-1835  they are rec in mbrp w/con of Blue River MM |
| 8-24-1848 | Richard P Elliott gct Spiceland MM to m Martha Prichard |

PRIGG

|  |  |
|---|---|
| 12-20-1906 | Myrtle gct New Castle MM |
| 10-24-1907 | Myrtle drpd from mbrp |

PUCKETT

|  |  |
|---|---|
| 6-24-1830 | Cyrus & w Betty & dt Lucinda rocf New Garden MM |
| 4-24-1834 | Cyrus & w Betty & fam gct Springfield MM |
| 4-20-1837 | Thomas & w Matilda & dt Mary Ann rocf Newberry MM, Ohio |
| 4-21-1842 | Thomas, Clear Springs Mtg compl for j Meth dis 6-23-1842 |
| 6-23-1842 | Matilda, Clear Springs P M compl for j Meth  dis 8-25-1842 |
| 1-26-1843 | Margaret & ch Samuel H & Thomas Clarkson rocf Hopewell MM |
| 4-24-1845 | Margaret & ch gct New Garden MM |

PUGH

|  |  |
|---|---|
| 8-21-1828 | Rue, Cincinnati MM, Ohio, req this mtg to treat w/him for mcd  no satisfaction 3-26-1829 dis rec from Cincinnati |
| 6-20-1832 | Rachel rocf Cincinnati MM, Ohio |
| 2-27-1833 | Rachel compl for j Hs  dis 4-25-1835 |

PURVIS

|  |  |
|---|---|
| 7-24-1851 | Rachel rocf Whitewater MM |
| 2-26-1852 | Rachel gct Whitewater MM |

RANDOLPH

|  |  |
|---|---|
| 5-21-1902 | J Farland & w Emma J rocf Cleveland MM, Oh |
| 10-12-1903 | J Farland & w Emma (a Minister) gct Sugar Plain MM |

RATLIFF

|  |  |
|---|---|
| 7-27-1826 | Joseph appt to a comm |
| 8-31-1826 | Joseph appt an overseer |
| 8-31-1826 | Phineas appt on comm to att Q M |
| 12-28-1826 | Joshua appt to a comm |
| 12-28-1826 | Letitia appt to comm to visit aged & infirm persons |
| 1- 4-1827 | Mary, dt Joshua & Letitia of Henry Co, m at Duck Creek M H to Robert Price of Henry Co |
| 2- 1-1827 | Letitia appt to a comm |
| 3- 5-1827 | Richard appt to a comm |
| 3-29-1827 | Gabriel appt to a comm |
| 8-23-1827 | Phineas gc N C (ret 1-22-1829 for mcd to Christy Ann----) |
| 9-20-1827 | Margaret rocf Whitewater MM |
| 9-20-1827 | Caroline appt to comm to visit aged & infirm persons |
| 9-20-1827 | Joshua appt to comm to visit aged & infirm persons |
| 10- 4-1827 | Jane, dt Joseph & Rebecca of Henry Co, m at Duck Creek M H Bailey Pearson of Henry Co |

DUCK CREEK

RATLIFF (Cont)

|  |  |
|---|---|
| 3-26-1829 | Phineas offered an ackn at Duck Creek P M for mcd |
| 12-24-1829 | Joseph appt an Elder |
| 5-9-1833 | Huldah, dt of Joseph & Rebecca of Henry Co, m at Duck Creek M H, Daniel Presnall of Henry Co |
| 6-20-1833 | Nathan & w Lydia & ch Mary, Alfred, Martha, Joseph, Anna, Levi & Nathan rocf Milford MM |
| 2-26-1835 | Mary, Clear Springs P M compl for unchastity  dis 4-23-1835 |
| 6-25-1835 | Richard appt an Elder |
| 11-26-1835 | Isaac rocf Newberry MM, Ohio |
| 11-26-1835 | Isaac, Clear Springs P M compl for mcd 12-24-1835  chm |
| 11-26-1835 | Mary (form Presnall) Clear Springs P M compl for mcd 1-21-1836  chm |
| 12-30-1835 | Anna, dt of Joseph & Rebecca of Henry Co, m at Clear Springs M H John Hinshaw of Henry Co |
| 5-26-1836 | Reuben gct Whitewater MM, to m Margaret Kendall |
| 6-23-1836 | John & w Sarah & ch Ann & Abner rocf Newberry MM, Ohio |
| 11-24-1836 | Moses rocf Newberry MM, Ohio |
| 11-24-1836 | Jesse rocf Newberry MM, Ohio |
| 11-24-1836 | Amos & w Elenor rocf Newberry MM, Ohio |
| 11-24-1836 | Abner & w Martha & ch John, Amos jr, Elenor, Ann, Thomas, Martha jr & Elizabeth rocf Newberry MM, Ohio |
| 12-22-1836 | Margaret rocf Whitewater MM |
| 2-23-1837 | Gabriel & w Catharine & ch gct Spiceland MM |
| 2-23-1837 | Ephraim B gct Walnut Ridge MM |
| 4-20-1837 | Joseph rptd deceased |
| 5-25-1837 | Richard, Clear Springs P M inf "he has been guilty of lewd conduct with an unmarried woman, told untruths & is charged with being the father of an illegitimate child" dis 7-20-1837 |
| 5-26-1837 | Margaret dt Thomas, decd & Hannah of Henry Co, m at Clear Springs M H to Thomas Lamb of Whitewater Mtg, Wayne Co |
| 12-24-1840 | Martha Maudlin (form Ratliff) Clear Springs P M compl for mcd  She is now living in the verge of Mississinewa MM which mtg is req to treat w/her  No satisfaction  dis 9-25-1845 |
| 10-20-1842 | Alfred, Clear Springs P M compl for mcd dis 12-22-1842 |
| 2-1-1843 | Nathan of Henry Co, s of Joseph, decd & Rebecca, m at Clear Springs M H Cynthia Stafford of Henry Co |
| 1-25-1844 | Caroline Sanders (form Ratliff) Clear Springs P M compl for mcd  She being a mbr of Hopewell MM, that mtg is informed 5-23-1844  chm |
| 11-27-1844 | Rebecca, wid of Joseph & dt Jacob & Sarah Lamb, both decd, of Henry Co, m at Clear Springs M H to Stephen Macy of Spiceland, Henry Co |
| 2-26-1845 | Eli of Henry Co, s Joseph, decd & Rebecca m at Clear Springs M H Jane Draper of Henry Co |
| 2-26-1846 | Elizabeth Davis (form Ratliff) Clear Springs P M compl for mcd 3-26-1846  chm |
| 3-3-1847 | John M of Henry Co, s Joseph, decd & Rebecca m at Clear Springs M H Asenath Palmer |
| 4-20-1848 | Joseph, Clear Springs P M compl for mcd dis 6-22-1848 |
| 7-20-1848 | Thomas C & w Rebecca & ch Sarah Jane, Elizabeth Ann, John T & Margaret H rocf Newberry MM, Ohio |
| 5-23-1850 | Reuben gct Milford MM to m Penelope N Bell |
| 5-23-1850 | Hannah rec in mbrp |
| 9-26-1850 | Penelope N & her dt Lydia Jane Bell rocf Milford MM |
| 6-26-1851 | Levi, Clear Springs P M compl for mcd dis 10-23-1851 |
| 12-25-1851 | Nathan gct Walnut Ridge MM to m Penelope N Coggshall |
| 6-26-1851 | Isaac req assistance of this mtg in settling a matter of dispute between himself & another friend |
| 4-22-1852 | Penelope N rocf Walnut Ridge MM |
| 7-22-1852 | Nathan, s of Nathan, Clear Springs P M compl for mcd  dis 9-23-1852 |
| 11-25-1852 | Rebecca Pearson (form Ratliff) Clear Springs P M compl for mcd  1-20-1853  chm |
| 6-23-1853 | Ann Bond (form Ratliff) Cadiz P M compl for mcd  7-21-1853  chm |
| 5-24-1855 | Hannah L Palmer (form Ratliff) rpt mcd  dis |
| 9-20-1855 | Nathan & w Penelope & two ch gct Spring Creek MM, Iowa |
| 5-22-1856 | Eli & w Jane & ch gct Spiceland MM |
| 6-26-1856 | Nathan & w was issued a cert to Spring Creek MM, Iowa but it was returned as they decided to remain in this vicinity |
| 6-26-1856 | Abner, Cadiz P M compl for mcd  dis |
| 9-25-1856 | Nathan & w Lydia gct Spring Creek MM, Iowa |
| 9-25-1856 | David gct Spring Creek MM, Iowa |
| 9-25-1856 | Milton gct Spring Creek MM, Iowa |
| 10-1-1857 | Asenath, wid of John M Ratliff & dt David & Sarah, decd, Palmer m at Cadiz M H, Henry Co, Asa Ellis of Henry Co |
| 2-25-1858 | Abner C, Clear Springs P M compl for mcd dis |
| 4-23-1859 | Isaac, Clear Springs P M compl for na dis 6-23-1859 |
| 7-23-1859 | Thomas C & w Rebecca & fam gct Honey Creek MM |
| 4-25-1861 | Penelope N, Sr appt an Elder |
| 6-26-1862 | Reuben appt an Elder |
| 4-21-1864 | Nathan & ch gct Fairfield MM |
| 4-21-1864 | Marcus, a minor ch under the care of Cyrus & Lydia Kendall, rec in mbrp |
| 11-24-1864 | Sarah rocf Bangor Mtg, Iowa & end to Hopewell MM |
| 7-26-1866 | Reuben & w Penelope & ch gct Spring Creek MM, Iowa |
| 7-25-1867 | John, Cadiz P M compl for mcd & na  dis |
| 6-25-1868 | S S Clear Spring P M inf he mcd but he retained his mbrp |
| 4-22-1869 | Abner C & w Mary & ch Henry & Lindsey D rec in mbrp |
| 1-26-1870 | Hannah M, dt Phineas & Christy Ann, decd of Henry Co, m at Clear Springs M H Jacob Davis of Mississinewa MM, Grant Co |
| 11-21-1872 | A C Clear Springs P M inf he mcd but he retains his mbrp |
| 2-20-1873 | John P, Clear Springs P M inf mcd & retained mbrp |
| 11-20-1879 | Marcus & w Hannah A gct Spiceland MM |
| 4-26-1883 | Fleming rocf Spiceland MM |
| 11-26-1891 | John drpd from mbrp |
| 5-20-1897 | Henry rec on req |
| 3-23-1899 | Lillian M rocf Spiceland MM |
| 2-25-1904 | Rose A rec on req |
| 7-20-1905 | Bertha W rec on req |
| 12-20-1906 | Olive rec on req |
| 5-21-1908 | Emory gct Whittier MM, Ca |
| 1-26-1911 | William, Charles, Morris, Cornelius & Anna rocf Spiceland MM |
| 10-26-1916 | Clara rec on req |
| 5-24-1917 | Vela rec on req |
| 4-22-1920 | Albert & w Bertha & ch Wayne gct New Castle MM |
| 4-7-1921 | Earl C & w Olive E & dt Pearl Marie gct Economy MM |
| 7-7-1921 | Emma & ch Forest A, Hershal H & Carl H gct New Castle MM |
| 3-26-1925 | Jesse C & w May & ch Ray & Joseph W gct New Castle MM |
| 10-26-1927 | Jean Juanita, foster ch of J Estes & Marie rec on req |

RAY

|  |  |
|---|---|
| 12-21-1899 | Lavina & Tesse drpd from mbrp |
| 10-26-1922 | Roger E & Robert B ch of Clayton & Hazel rec on req |
| 4-24-1924 | Clayton rec on req |

REAGAN

|  |  |
|---|---|
| 4-26-1832 | Lucinda (form Hunt) Spiceland MM compl for mcd  dis 6-21-1832 |
| 10-21-1852 | Thomas, Milford MM req this mtg to treat w/him for mcd  No satisfaction & Milford MM so inf  4-21-1853 dis rec from Milford |

DUCK CREEK

REDDING
12-22-1859   Catharine (form Bufkin) rpt mcd but her mbrp is retained
6-22-1865    Catharine & fam gct Walnut Ridge MM
5-23-1867    Tirzah J rocf Walnut Ridge MM & end to Hopewell MM
7-24-1884    Tirzah gct Carthage MM

REDDICK
12-26-1912   William rec on req
11-20-1913   William E & w Edna R gct Amboy MM

REECE
8-31-1826    John appt as one of Trustees to hold deed to land where mtg is held at Flat Rock M H (not having complied with appt, he is released on 11-22-1827)
5-31-1827    Lydia & dt Mary (fam of Dempsey) rec on req
5-31-1827    Abner, s of Dempsey, rec on req of parent
2-21-1828    John & w Anna & fam gct Milford MM
3-27-1828    Nathan, of Henry Co, s John & Ann of same place m at Duck Creek M H Susannah Elliott of Henry Co
12-25-1828   Lydia appt to a comm
5-21-1829    Nathan & w Susannah & fam gct Milford MM
7-21-1831    Dempsey gct Newberry MM, Ohio to m Ann Ratcliff
10-25-1832   Ann rocf Newberry MM, Ohio
10-22-1835   Charity rocf New Hope MM, Tenn
2-22-1844    Lydia rocf New Hope MM, Tenn
7-25-1844    Ruth, Clear Springs P M compl for j Separatists (ASF) dis 9-26-1844
2-26-1846    Solomon, Clear Springs P M compl for j Separatists (ASF) dis 4-23-1846
7-23-1846    Lydia compl of for j Separatists (ASF) dis 9-24-1846
4-25-1850    Abner chm which was accepted
6-20-1850    Sarah (form Terrel) Newberry MM (Ohio) req this mtg to treat w/her for mcd 7-25-1850 she chm which was forwarded to Newberry MM Ohio
12-26-1850   Sarah rocf Newberry MM, Ohio
8-26-1852    Margaret Pickering (form Reece) Cadiz P M compl for mcd on 11-25-1852 A rpt is rec that she is decd
6-6-1854     Jesse gct Back Creek MM
11-23-1854   Susannah & fam gct Hopewell Mtg
6-26-1856    Solomon & w Ruth, Back Creek MM req con to rec them in mbrp granted
7-24-1856    Lydia, Margaret & Reuben, minor ch of Solomon & Ruth gct Back Creek MM
2-26-1857    Christina Cooper (form Reece) rpt mcd dis
7-22-1858    Dempsey, Cadiz P M inf he has joined himself to the Secret Order known by the name of Free Masons 9-23-1858 the comm rpt they are united in judgement that the proceedings in this case are illegal The complaint is therefore directed back to the P M
11-25-1858   Dempsey, Cadiz P M compl for j Free Masons dis 1-20-1859
8-20-1863    Thomas, Cadiz P M inf he has j Free Masons dis 10-22-1863
12-3-1868    Eli of Washington Twp, Randolph Co, s Levi & Sarah, decd of Iowa, m at Cadiz M H Cynthia Pickering wid of Samuel
10-24-1878   Martha J & ch Ellen C & Walter T Culbertson rocf Honey Creek MM
7-21-1881    Wilson & w Pamelia & dt Lizzie rec on req
3-23-1893    Elvira T & s rec on req
3-20-1902    Mary Malissa rocf Fairmount MM
3-25-1909    Harry rec on req
11-24-1910   Ella F rel on req
1-26-1911    Oris J & w Anna & ch Everett M & Mary Elizabeth gct Whittier MM, Ca
6-22-1911    Benjamin & w Ella F & s Hoyt gct Whittier MM, Ca
4-23-1914    Maud & s Robert rec on req
6-25-1914    Elmer D rel on req
4-20-1916    Elizabeth rec on req
4-26-1917    Paul rec on req
7-20-1922    Opal Delon rec on req
10-26-1922   Carrie rec on req

REED
2-23-1893    Charley & Minnie rec on req

REEDER
8-24-1893    Zilpha roc
9-20-1908    Emma roc

RENNIX
8-22-1901    Mary Craig rel on req

REYNOLDS
9-21-1848    Mary Ann (form Cook) Duck Creek P M compl for mcd dis 7-26-1849
12-22-1859   Allen & w Mary & ch Martha Sarah, Albert Samuel, William & Josiah rocf Driftwood MM
8-22-1867    Allen & w Mary & ch gct Minneapolis MM, Mnn

RICH
1-26-1832    Moses rocf Marlborough MM, N C (originally issued to White Lick MM)
5-23-1833    Moses gct Fairfield MM

RICKET
2-24-1881    Joseph rocf Raysville MM

RICKS
12-24-1863   Eliza Ann rec on req
3-26-1874    Milton rec on req
4-23-1874    Rachel rec on req
3-24-1892    William L, Alfaretta, Orth M & Ruby rec on req
3-23-1893    William L & w Alfaretta & ch Orth M & Ruby B rel on req
4-20-1911    Lizzie rec on req
7-7-1921     Joseph & w Mary & ch Laura & Earnest rocf Shirley MM
12-21-1921   Earnest rel on req

RIDDLE
9-25-1890    Joshua drpd from mbrp
7-23-1891    Minnie gct Spiceland MM

RIDGEWAY
9-24-1829    Reece, Spiceland MM inf that he is a mbr of Short Creek MM, Ohio, now residing in our limits, has j Hs 11-25-1830 this mtg treated w/him without satisfaction 5-26-1831 dis rec from Short Creek MM, Oh

RINEHART - RINARD
5-31-1827    Jacob appt to a comm
5-26-1831    Jacob, Spiceland P M compl that he "hath refused to comply with engagement and has made contradictory statements in endeavoring to screen himself from a contract" dis 9-22-1831

RISK
4-25-1878    Rebecca rec on req
4-25-1878    Rachel rel on req
9-25-1913    Julia gct Knightstown MM

ROBERTS
3-22-1894    Kittie gct Raysville MM

ROBERTSON
11-25-1841   Thomas rocf Deep River MM, N C
6-23-1842    Thomas gct Mississinewa MM
8-22-1844    Thomas, Duck Creek P M compl for mcd 9-26-1844 chm
1-23-1845    Rebecca (form King) rpt mcd She is a mbr of Walnut Ridge MM which mtg is informed 4-24-1845 She chm which was forwarded to Walnut Ridge MM
8-21-1845    Rebecca rocf Walnut Ridge MM
7-26-1849    Thomas & Rebecca & fam gct West Grove MM

ROGERS
8-20-1835    Sarah of Clear Springs P M rec in mbrp
11-26-1835   Charles J, Sarah Ann, Hannah & Mary Ann, ch of Joseph & Elizabeth rocf Uwchland MM, Pa
1-21-1892    Lavina, Tressie W, Ray, Don, Jessie, Tennie & Edgar L rec on req

DUCK CREEK

## ROGERS (Cont)
| | |
|---|---|
| 12-23-1899 | Don, Jessie, Jennie & Edgar L drpd from mbrp |

## ROSE
| | |
|---|---|
| 3-25-1830 | Esther rocf West Grove MM |
| 3-25-1830 | Hester "having settled within the verge of this mtg without producing a cert, Hannah Moore & Hannah Gregg were appt to write to West Grove MM & req them to inf us whether her right is in that mtg" cert rec 6-24-1830 |
| 2-24-1831 | Hester, Duck Creek P M compl for being out of unity & na  dis 4-21-1831 |

## RUSSELL
| | |
|---|---|
| 3-26-1896 | Elsie rec on req |

## SAFFELL
| | |
|---|---|
| 8-23-1883 | Orlando C rel on req |

## SAINT
| | |
|---|---|
| 11-22-1827 | John Cook gct Milford MM to m Julia Saint |
| 7-22-1830 | Exum rocf Milford MM |
| 12- 2-1830 | Exum of Henry Co, s William & Achsah of Wayne Co m at Duck Creek M H, Phebe Pickering of Henry Co |
| 6-25-1835 | Alpheus rocf Milford MM, but endorsed back |
| 5-26-1836 | Alpheus & w Irena rocf Milford MM |
| 11-24-1836 | William & w Achsah & ch Jennett, Doughty, Joseph, Jonathan, Daniel, Milton, William jr & Cynthia rocf Milford MM |
| 1-26-1837 | Exum rocf Spiceland MM |
| 1-26-1837 | Mariah rocf Spiceland MM |
| 8-27-1837 | Jennet, dt William & Achsah (m accomplished under care of Spiceland MM as Duck Creek had been laid down) m to Abner Pickering |
| 3-24-1842 | Jonathan E gct Spiceland MM to m Emily Johnson |
| 8-25-1842 | Ruth Anna req to be rec in mbrp  Not granted 9-22-1842 |
| 9-22-1842 | Emily J rocf Spiceland MM |
| 6-22-1843 | William, Duck Creek P M compl for consenting to his sons att mcd  chm 8-24-1843 |
| 8-24-1843 | Sarah Ann (form Bowman) Duck Creek P M compl for mcd  dis 12-21-1843 |
| 9-21-1843 | Daniel, Duck Creek P M compl for mcd & drinking to excess  dis 11-23-1843 |
| 5-23-1844 | Alpheus, Duck Creek compl for j Separatists (ASF) dis 8-22-1844 |
| 6-26-1845 | Irena, Duck Creek compl for j Separatists (ASF) dis 8-21-1845 |
| 6-24-1847 | Milton mcd chm 7-22-1847 |
| 3- 2-1848 | Cynthia, dt William & Achsah, decd of Henry Co, m at Duck Creek M H Addison Unthank of Spiceland Mtg, Henry Co |
| 3-28-1849 | William jr, s William Sr & Achsah, decd of Henry Co m at Clear Springs M H Mary Ann Elliott of Henry Co |
| 10-24-1850 | Mariah O'Neal (form Saint) Duck Creek P M compl for mcd & j Meth  dis 1-23-1851 |
| 6-23-1853 | William jr, Duck Creek P M compl for mcd chm 8-25-1853 |
| 6-23-1853 | Mary A (form Johnson) rpt mcd  She being a mbr of Milford MM, that mtg has been inf 9-23-1853 Milford MM req this mtg to treat w/her 10-20-1853  chm which was forwarded to Milford MM |
| 1-26-1854 | Mary A rocf Milford MM |
| 5-22-1856 | William, Duck Creek P M compl for mcd  dis |
| 8-24-1865 | Mary A appt an Elder |
| 9-23-1869 | Exum & w Louisa & dt Ethel rec in mbrp |
| 8- 9-1870 | Emily, dt James & Mary Johnson of Henry Co, m at mtg held at Greensboro, to James Hadley of Fairfield Mtg, Highland Co, Ohio |
| 8-25-1870 | John S, Duck Creek P M compl mcd but he retained his mbrp |
| 9-17-1872 | John Q gct Bangor MM, Iowa |
| 3-20-1873 | Exum compl of for upl, drinking spiritous liquor to excess & offering violence to a fellowman 4-24-1873 chm |
| 3-26-1874 | Mary A rec as Minister |
| 6-20-1878 | Eliza J rec on req |
| 6-25-1885 | Sarah gct Raysville MM |
| 4-25-1895 | Florence Alberta rocf Raysville MM |
| 10-20-1898 | Martha J rec on req |

## SANDERS - SAUNDERS
| | |
|---|---|
| 5-25-1837 | Charity, Clear Springs P M compl for mcd dis 8-27-1837 |
| 1-25-1844 | Caroline (form Ratliff) Clear Springs P M compl for mcd  she being a mbr of Hopewell MM, that mtg is inf  5-23-1844 chm |
| 4-25-1844 | Anna, Clear Springs P M compl for j Separatists (ASF)  dis 6-20-1844 |
| 7-23-1846 | Miriam & dts Lucinda, Pheriba & Maria Jane rec in mbrp |
| 8-20-1846 | Caroline, Clear Springs P M compl for j Meth  dis 10-22-1846 |
| 2-20-1845 | Caroline rocf Hopewell MM |
| 9- 2-1849 | Sarah (form Wood) compl for mcd & j Hs dis 12-20-1849 |
| 3-21-1850 | Mariam, Duck Creek Mtg compl for j Meth dis 6-20-1850 |
| 8-26-1852 | Lucinda Kirk (form Sanders) Duck Creek P M compl for mcd  chm 10-21-1852 |
| 4-23-1857 | Maria Jane Stanley (form Sanders) rpt mcd dis |
| 6-25-1857 | Tobias & w Anna & ch Jonah, Sarah Jane, Calvin, Seth & Eliza Ann rec in mbrp |
| 2-20-1868 | Tobias gct Mississinewa Mtg to m Phebe Schooley |
| 5-21-1868 | Jonah W & Calvin gct Legrand MM, Iowa |
| 5-21-1868 | Tobias & ch gct Mississinewa MM |
| 11-25-1875 | Rachel Small & ch gct Deer Creek MM |
| 3-22-1877 | Seth gct Mississinewa MM |

## SCARF
| | |
|---|---|
| 10-21-1905 | Russell A rec on req |

## SCHOOLEY
| | |
|---|---|
| 5-21-1829 | William Sheridan gct New Garden MM to m Elizabeth Schooley |
| 4-21-1831 | Susannah & her youngest ch, Edith, Susannah & Rachel rocf New Garden MM |
| 3-22-1832 | John, Spiceland P M inf that he is a former mbr of & was dis by New Garden MM, but he req to become a mbr again 6-20-1832 New Garden MM does not give consent |
| 3-22-1832 | Isaac & w Celia & ch Anna & Nancy rocf New Garden MM |
| 2-20-1868 | Tobias Sanders gct Mississinewa MM to m Phebe Schooley |

## SCOTT
| | |
|---|---|
| 2-22-1917 | J Elmer & w Cora & s Paul & Willard rec on req |
| 1-26-1922 | James O rocf Charlottsville MM |
| 1-26-1922 | Mrs Esta rec on req |
| 1-26-1922 | Florence L rocf Indianapolis MM |
| 1-26-1922 | Howard Elwood & w Elizabeth B & ch James O & Esta rec on req |
| 1-26-1922 | Esther Grace dt of Elmer & Cora rec on req |
| 1-26-1927 | Ruth Maria (w of Howard) rec on req |

## SEXTON
| | |
|---|---|
| 12-28-1826 | Hannah rocf Miami MM, Ohio end by Milford MM |

## SHAFFER
| | |
|---|---|
| 11-24-1870 | Peter rec on req |
| 1-23-1873 | Peter, Clear Springs P M compl for getting in a passion & offering violence to a fellowman  chm which was rec |
| 12-22-1910 | Elizabeth gct New Castle MM |
| 4-23-1914 | Milton F rel on req |

## SHARP
| | |
|---|---|
| 4-21-1836 | Mary (form Satterthwait) Plainfield MM, Ohio req this mtg to treat w/her for mcd Since she does not reside in the limits of this mtg, the req is returned |
| 10-25-1849 | Elizabeth (form Pickering) Duck Creek P M compl for mcd  She is residing in the limits of Hopewell MM which is req to treat w/her  Hopewell gets no satis 4-25-1850 dis is forwarded to Hopewell |

DUCK CREEK

## SHAW
| | |
|---|---|
| 8-24-1882 | Rebecca rec in mbrp |

## SHELLY
| | |
|---|---|
| 7-25-1867 | Ruth A rec in mbrp |

## SHERIDAN
| | |
|---|---|
| 8-31-1826 | John appt to comm on "poor" |
| 3- 1-1827 | Margaret appt to a comm |
| 8-23-1827 | Mary rec in mbrp |
| 5-21-1829 | William gct New Garden MM to m Elizabeth Schooley |
| 10-22-1829 | Elizabeth rocf New Garden MM |
| 1-26-1831 | Mary, dt John of Henry Co & Mary, decd of Chatham Co, N C m at Spiceland M H to Ephraim Stout of Springfield Mtg, Wayne Co |
| 1-26-1832 | Rachel, Spiceland P M compl for mcd 2-25-1832 chm |
| 3-26-1874 | Rachel rec in mbrp |

## SHOWALTER
| | |
|---|---|
| 6-23-1842 | Asenith (form Gilbert) Milford MM req this mtg to treat w/her for mcd  No satisfaction 10-20-1842  Milford MM forwards copy of dis |

## SHUGART
| | |
|---|---|
| 4-23-1885 | Julia Stafford gct Deer Creek MM |
| 5-25-1893 | Julia & dt Olive rocf Deer Creek MM |
| 2-26-1925 | Olive (Shugart) Fields gct Marion MM |

## SISSON
| | |
|---|---|
| 3-26-1914 | Elva rel on req |

## SMALL
| | |
|---|---|
| 3-29-1827 | Josiah & w Jane & ch Thomas, Sarah, Elizabeth & Abigail rocf Milford MM |
| 8-21-1828 | Abraham rocf Milford MM |
| 10-23-1828 | Obadiah & w Isabel & dt Mary rocf Arba MM |
| 1-21-1830 | Obediah appt Trustee at Spiceland in room of Thomas Bond "who was about to become a grantor to the Society" |
| 5-24-1832 | Jane appt an Elder |
| 1-24-1833 | Sarah & Lydia, ch of Anna (now w of Jonathan Pearson) rec in mbrp |
| 7-25-1833 | Delilah & dt Anna rec in mbrp (dt Elizabeth not rec) |
| 4-24-1834 | Rhoda (form Pearson) Clear Springs P M compl for mcd  Mississinewa MM is req to treat w/her  7-24-1834 chm |
| 9-25-1834 | Rhoda (living in St Joseph Co) gct Mississinewa MM |
| 7-21-1842 | Elihu gct Mississinewa MM |
| 8-20-1846 | Hannah (form Hinshaw) Duck Creek P M compl for mcd & j Separatists (ASF) 12-24-1846 Walnut Ridge MM req to treat w/her  They rpt no satisfaction  dis 1-20-1847 |
| 5-24-1855 | Eliza Jane (form Fawcett) rpt mcd  dis |
| 4-26-1860 | Eliza Jane & ch Ida Lindora rec in mbrp |
| 4-23-1868 | Rhoda rec in mbrp |
| 5-21-1868 | Rachel & ch Reuben, Elkanah & Mary C rec in mbrp |
| 2-21-1884 | Elizabeth Jane gct Spiceland MM |

## SMITH
| | |
|---|---|
| 7-24-1828 | Mary & fam rocf Springfield MM, N C end to Springfield MM, Ohio |
| 7-22-1830 | Rebecca (form Pickering) Duck Creek P M compl for mcd  dis 9-23-1830 |
| 9-22-1831 | Nathan, Duck Creek P M inf he being a mbr of Whitewater MM has j Hs & that mtg so inf 12-22-1831  Whitewater req this mtg to treat w/him  No satisfaction  dis by Whitewater MM 5-24-1832 |
| 7-24-1845 | Lucinda (form Hosier) Clear Springs P M compl for mcd but she resides in verge of Sand Creek MM so that mtg is req to treat w/her  10-23-1845 moved in limits of this mtg  dis 12-25-1845 |
| 2-24-1881 | Emma rec on req |
| 3-24-1881 | Robert A & w Mary J & ch Catharine, George & Nettie rec on req |
| 5-26-1881 | Ephraim P & w Sarah Jane & ch Dorcas Ann, Rachel Jane, Mary Elizabeth, Sarah Ellen & Isaac R rocf Poplar Run MM |
| 4-20-1882 | Rebecca rec on req |
| 7-26-1894 | Philander & w & ch rel on req |
| 10-25-1894 | Mary A gets a letter to Christian Church |
| 12-25-1902 | Robert A gct Knightstown MM |
| 4-24-1919 | Mrs Cora Brooks rocf Pleasant Valley MM |

## SMOOT
| | |
|---|---|
| 3-23-1922 | Mattie Dean, Anna May & Sherman Floyd rec on req |
| 11-20-1924 | Mattie Dean, Sherman Floyd & Anna May, ch of Albert rel on req |

## SNODGRASS
| | |
|---|---|
| 3-23-1876 | Sarah E rec on req |
| 6-20-1878 | Rose Ella rocf Raysville MM |
| 2-26-1903 | Maude & Josephine rec on req |
| 3-25-1909 | Pearl, Urben & Grace rec on req |
| 8-26-1915 | Clint J & w Lucy B & ch H Gilbert & Howard J rec on req |

## SNOWDEN
| | |
|---|---|
| 1-21-1892 | Pearl rec on req |
| 2-23-1893 | Pearl rel on req |

## SOPHER
| | |
|---|---|
| 7-25-1844 | Elizabeth (form wid Hiatt) Duck Creek P M compl for mcd  9-26-1844 chm |
| 4-23-1846 | Hannah K rocf Greenfield MM |
| 9-23-1847 | Elizabeth & her son Allen Hiatt gct Spiceland MM |
| 8-22-1850 | Hannah compl for j Meth  dis 10-24-1850 |

## SPENCER
| | |
|---|---|
| 8-24-1837 | Elizabeth (w of John, a non mbr) rocf Flushing MM, Ohio |
| 8-21-1845 | Louisa, Milford MM req this mtg to treat w/her for na & att Hicksites mtg  dis rec from Milford MM 1-22-1846 |
| 5-21-1846 | John rec in mbrp |
| 3-25-1847 | Ezra, Louisa, Lindley M, David, John A & Milton, ch of John & Elizabeth rec in mbrp |
| 4-28-1852 | Ezra of Henry Co, s John & Elizabeth of same place m at Clear Springs P M Hannah B Palmer of Henry Co |
| 3-23-1855 | Louisa Newby (form Spencer) Cadiz P M inf mcd  4-26-1855 chm |
| 3-21-1859 | Lindley M of Henry Co, s John & Elizabeth m at Cadiz M H Phebe R Cooper of Henry Co |
| 12- 1-1859 | Ezra of Henry Co, s John & Elizabeth of same place m at Cadiz M H Eliza C Bufkin of Cadiz |
| 2-23-1860 | David, Clear Springs P M compl for mcd, but he retained his mbrp |
| 10-25-1860 | Lindley, Cadiz P M compl for use of intoxicating liquor  dis 1-24-1861 |
| 8-24-1865 | Ezra appt an Elder |
| 3-26-1868 | Phebe R gct Lynn Grove MM, Iowa |
| 12-25-1873 | John A, Duck Creek P M compl for drinking & fighting  2-26-1874 chm |
| 3-26-1874 | Sallie rec in mbrp |
| 3-25-1875 | Ezra rec as a Minister |
| 8-mo-1875 | David & w Mary Jane & fam gct Spiceland MM |
| 12-23-1875 | John A & fam gct Spiceland MM |
| 3-23-1876 | Milton gct San Jose MM, Ca |
| 11-21-1878 | Ezra gct Fairview MM, Kan |
| 7-24-1879 | John gct Spiceland MM |
| 8-24-1893 | C Burrett & fam gct Dublin MM |

## SPRINGER
| | |
|---|---|
| 3-22-1832 | Barnabas rocf Whitewater MM |

## STAFFEL
| | |
|---|---|
| 3-26-1874 | O C rec in mbrp |

## STAFFORD
| | |
|---|---|
| 7-27-1826 | Samuel appt to a comm |
| 8-31-1826 | Eli appt to comm to have care of indulged mtg at Flat Rock MH |
| 8-31-1826 | Samuel appt on comm to att QM |
| 2- 1-1827 | Rachel appt to a comm |
| 3- 5-1827 | Samuel appt a Minister |
| 9-20-1827 | Rachel appt to comm to visit aged & infirm persons |

DUCK CREEK

## STAFFORD (Cont)

|  |  |
|---|---|
| 4-21-1831 | Samuel "expressed concern to appoint & hold a meeting in the settlement of Friends on Fall Creek" |
| 7-21-1836 | Elizabeth, Salem MM req to know if a cert for her has been rec (no further record) |
| 6-22-1837 | Daniel req a cert to Milford MM Not granted yet when Duck Creek MM was laid down 8-mo-1837 |
| 5-26-1842 | Eli, Clear Springs P M compl that he has been guilty of fornication & detraction 9-22-1842 treated w/him & he offered an ackn but the Q M was asked for help 2-23-1843 chm |
| 2-1-1843 | Cynthia, dt Eli & Elizabeth of Henry Co m at Clear Springs M H Nathan Ratliff of Henry Co |
| 1-1-1851 | Abigail, dt Eli & Elizabeth of Henry Co m at Clear Springs M H Jesse Cook of Richland Mtg, Hamilton Co |
| 8-26-1852 | Elizabeth, Clear Springs P M compl for disunity with friends & is guilty of defamation & detraction to the injury of the reputation of some friends & calculated to lower the dignity of the society 11-25-1852 comm req help of the Q M 1-20-1853 Case dismissed by Q M comm They earnestly desire that she & all others may hereafter be more careful of the reputation & interest of others |
| 4-20-1854 | Elizabeth Mills (form Stafford) Clear Springs P M compl for mcd 6-6-1854 chm |
| 3-23-1860 | Seth, Clear Springs P M inf mcd but he retained his mbrp |
| 5-22-1862 | Rebecca Jane rec in mbrp |
| 9-21-1871 | Seth rec a Minister |
| 2-21-1895 | Elva Bell rocf Vermilion MM, Ill |
| 6-23-1910 | Merritt gct Westland MM |
| 3-20-1923 | Minnie S rec on req |

## STANBROUGH

|  |  |
|---|---|
| 1-23-1834 | Nehemiah & w Ruth & ch Ann, Thomas, Francis, James, Solomon, Mark H, Levi, Tabitha & Malinda rocf Milford MM |
| 4-20-1837 | Phebe & Elizabeth rocf Spiceland MM |
| 3-25-1841 | Francis rocf Spiceland MM |
| 9-22-1842 | Leah, Mary, Rachel, Elizabeth, Tabitha & Sarah ch of William & Rachel rocf Westfield MM |
| 9-21-1843 | Elizabeth, a minor gct Spiceland MM |
| 1-25-1844 | Leah Williams (form Stanbrough) Clear Springs P M compl for mcd dis 3-21-1844 |
| 2-22-1844 | James gct Hopewell MM to m Sarah Macy |
| 4-25-1844 | Thomas & w Abigail & fam gct Westfield MM |
| 5-23-1844 | Nehemiah & w Ruth & fam gct Back Creek MM |
| 5-23-1844 | James gct Back Creek MM |
| 7-26-1849 | Rachel Moon (form Stanbrough) Clear Springs P M compl for mcd Having removed this mtg req Newberry MM to treat w/her 12-20-1849 chm |
| 2-21-1850 | Mary Moon (form Stanbrough) compl for mcd She now resides in limits of Newberry MM which mtg is req to treat w/her 7-25-1850 chm |
| 5-22-1851 | Francis & w Huldah gct Honey Creek MM |
| 7-24-1851 | Tabitha Moon (form Stanbrough) Clear Springs P M compl for mcd dis 9-25-1851 |
| 4-21-1859 | Sarah Ann Wright (form Stanbrough) rpt mcd but she retained her mbrp |

## STANFIELD

|  |  |
|---|---|
| 11-21-1833 | David (a Minister) & w Elizabeth & ch William Williams, David S, Charles, Isaac, Samuel Vernon, Hannah Jones, Lydia Jane, Elijah & Clayton Reeves rocf New Hope MM, Tn |
| 11-26-1835 | William Williams gct New Hope MM, Tn to m Elizabeth Reece |
| 3-24-1836 | David was removed from station of Minister |
| 9-22-1836 | Elizabeth rocf New Hope MM, Tn |
| 2-23-1837 | David & fam gct Mississinewa MM |
| 2-23-1837 | William W & w Elizabeth gct Mississinewa MM |
| 3-23-1837 | Hannah Haul (form Stanfield) Fall Creek PM compl for mcd She now resides in limits of Milford MM which mtg is req to treat w/her Milford Treated without satisfaction dis |
| 10-23-1851 | Mary Ann (form Wright) Clear Springs P M compl for mcd She now resides within limits of Back Creek MM which mtg is req to treat w/her chm 3-25-1852 |
| 4-22-1852 | Mary Ann gct Back Creek MM |
| 8-20-1857 | Clayton R, a mbr of Back Creek MM, Cadiz P M inf na & j Wesleyan Meth & Back Creek is so inf |

## STANLEY

|  |  |
|---|---|
| 8-26-1830 | Aaron & w Mahalah & ch Eliza Jane & Michael rocf Milford MM |
| 1-20-1830 | Nathan rocf Dover MM, N C & end to Milford MM |
| 12-22-1831 | John & w Elizabeth & ch Wyatt, Milton, Harmon, Mariah & Eliza rocf Bloomfield MM |
| 12-22-1831 | Nathan rocf Milford MM |
| 2-23-1832 | Delana rocf Bloomfield MM |
| 3-29-1832 | Nathan of Henry Co, s Michael & Mary of Guilford Mtg, N C m at Duck Creek M H Delana Stanley dt of John & Elizabeth of Henry Co |
| 1-23-1834 | John & w Deborah & ch Moses, Elizabeth & Aaron rocf Dover MM, N C |
| 3-20-1834 | Temple & w Anna rocf Whitewater MM |
| 11-26-1835 | Richard & w Abigail & ch Rebecca, Joshua & Nathan D rocf Whitewater MM |
| 11-26-1835 | Elwood rocf Whitewater MM |
| 2-25-1836 | Sarah (wid of Samuel) rocf Dover MM, N C end by Milford MM |
| 3-23-1837 | Elwood gct Milford MM to m Martha Butler |
| 1-26-1837 | Elwood rocf Spiceland MM |
| 2-23-1843 | Delana & ch gct Spiceland MM |
| 1-25-1844 | Wyatt & w Mary gct Walnut Ridge MM |
| 2-1-1844 | Maria Jane, dt John & Elizabeth of Henry Co, m at Duck Creek M H Josiah Bundy of Henry Co |
| 3-27-1845 | Eliza B dt of John & Elizabeth of Henry Co m at Duck Creek M H James H Meredith of Spiceland Mtg, Henry Co |
| 9-25-1845 | Milton, Duck Creek P M compl for mcd He now resides in limits of Mississinewa MM which mtg is req to treat w/him 3-26-1846 Mississinewa rpts no satisfaction dis |
| 10-25-1845 | Leah (form Pickering) Duck Creek P M compl for mcd She being a mbr of Milford MM that mtg has been inf |
| 4-2-1846 | Harmon of Henry Co, s John & Elizabeth m at Duck Creek M H Anna M Bowman of Henry Co |
| 6-24-1847 | Temple B (having been dis by Spiceland MM) he is rec in mbrp again |
| 9-25-1847 | Nathan D, Duck Creek P M compl for mcd & use of spiritous liquor dis 12-23-1847 |
| 3-24-1848 | Anna (w of Temple B) & dt Mary rec in mbrp |
| 8-24-1848 | Eliza Ann, Joab G, Henry C, Huldah Ellen, Oliver H S & Anna Mariah ch of Temple B & Anna rec in mbrp |
| 2-28-1849 | Deborah, wid of John Stanley & dt Jesse & Ann Weisner, both decd, m at Clear Springs M H Dennis Norton of Henry Co |
| 3-29-1849 | Moses of Henry Co, s John, decd & Deborah, m at West Branch M H Anna Jane Norton of Henry Co |
| 10-25-1849 | Mary chm for having mcd (to Joshua Stanley) |
| 12-24-1849 | Joshua, Duck Creek P M compl for mcd chm 1-24-1850 |
| 7-20-1854 | Temple B condemned upl & na |
| 8-24-1854 | Harmon & w Anna & ch gct Hinkles Creek MM |
| 11-1-1854 | Michael of Henry Co, s Aaron & Mahala m at Clear Springs M H Lydia Jane Bell |
| 12-21-1854 | Mary Pickering (form Stanley) Clear Springs P M compl for mcd & jas dis 2-22-1855 |
| 4-26-1855 | Lydia Jane gct Spiceland MM |
| 4-26-1855 | Eliza Jane Presnall (form Stanley) Duck Creek P M compl for mcd chm 5-24-1855 |
| 5-24-1855 | Miriam (form Draper) Clear Springs P M inf mcd chm 7-26-1855 |
| 8-23-1855 | Elwood, Clear Springs P M inf mcd chm 9-20-1855 |

DUCK CREEK

## STANLEY (Cont)
|  |  |
|---|---|
| 11-20-1856 | Jesse, Cadiz P M compl for mcd  dis |
| 10-23-1856 | Aaron, Clear Springs P M compl for mcd dis 12-25-1856 |
| 11-20-1856 | Ann (form Norton) rpt mcd dis |
| 3-26-1857 | Richard, Duck Creek P M rpt mcd  dis |
| 12-24-1857 | Elwood N & w Miriam & ch gct Lynn Grove MM, Iowa |
| 4-23-1857 | Maria Jane (form Sanders) rpt mcd  dis |
| 9-22-1859 | Joshua & w Mary gct New Salem MM |
| 9-22-1859 | Abigail gct Lynn Grove MM, Iowa |
| 10-20-1859 | Anna & fam gct Lynn Grove MM, Iowa ( a cert for Temple is withheld) |
| 2-23-1860 | Temple gct Lynn Grove MM, Iowa |
| 5-24-1860 | Moses & w Anna Jane & ch gct Lynn Grove MM, Iowa |
| 5-23-1861 | Temple B & w Anna & ch gct Richland MM |
| 1-20-1870 | Milton chm for anger & offering violence to a fellowman |
| 9- 1-1870 | Elwood of Dunreith, Henry Co, s Richard & Abigail, both decd m at Cadiz M H Phebe Hastings (a wid) |
| 10-20-1870 | Phebe gc |
| 1-26-1882 | Kelita F & w Elizabeth A & ch Egenia E, Alice F, Mary J & William rocf New Garden MM, N C |
| 3-26-1891 | Jesse & w gct Raysville MM |

## STANTON
|  |  |
|---|---|
| 5-22-1834 | Zacheas & w Elizabeth & ch Mahala, Cynthia, Milton & Milo rocf Silver Creek MM |
| 9-22-1836 | Hiram & w Sarah & ch John & Joseph rocf New Garden MM |

## STARBUCK
|  |  |
|---|---|
| 7-21-1853 | Jane & ch William HH, George W, James M, Thomas C, Benjamin F & Richard W, rocf Walnut Ridge MM |
| 1-25-1866 | William HH, Clear Springs P M inf mcd but his mbrp is retained |
| 4-26-1866 | George W, Clear Springs P M inf mcd but mbrp retained |
| 12-26-1867 | James M, Duck Creek P M inf mcd but mbrp retained |
| 2-20-1868 | Thomas C, Duck Creek P M inf mcd but mbrp retained |
| 4-22-1869 | William H H & w Mary M gct Milford MM |
| 2-23-1871 | Benjamin, Duck Creek P M inf mcd but mbrp retained |
| 12-23-1880 | Rose rec on req |
| 8-25-1892 | Benjamin & s Earl rocf East Branch MM |
| 9-22-1892 | Walter B & Clinton L, ch of Benjamin rec on req |
| 8-22-1893 | Charles rel on req |
| 3-26-1896 | Bertha & Charles rec on req |
| 4-24-1902 | Mary A & dt Olive rec on req |
| 10-21-1915 | William M & dt Olive E rel on req |
| 5-23-1918 | Holbert rec on req |
| 5-22-1919 | Velva Bell rel on req |
| 4- 7-1921 | Thomas & w Mary & s Reuben gct New Castle MM |
| 10-26-1922 | Walter B drpd from mbrp |
| 1-25-1923 | Earl & w Bertha E & s Walter gct Spiceland MM |
| 2-22-1923 | Clinton drpd from mbrp |

## STEDDOM
|  |  |
|---|---|
| 9-26-1851 | Isaac K of Miami MM, Warren Co, Ohio  s Samuel & Susanna, m at Clear Springs M H Narcissa Price of Henry Co |
| 3-25-1852 | Narcissa gct Miami MM, Ohio |

## STEPHENS
|  |  |
|---|---|
| 3-22-1906 | Elizabeth rec on req |

## STEWART
|  |  |
|---|---|
| 10-20-1831 | Jehu & w Sarah & ch Beulah, Sarah, Anna, Robert, Cyrus & Ithamer rocf Whitewater MM, & end to Spiceland MM |
| 8-23-1832 | Sarah Aydelotte (form Stewart) Spiceland P M inf mcd  chm |
| 10-24-1833 | Jehu & w Sarah & ch Beulah, Anna, Robert & Ithamer rocf Spiceland MM |
| 11-20-1834 | Louhanna rocf Deep River MM, N C end by Whitewater MM |

## STOFFEL
|  |  |
|---|---|
| 3-26-1874 | O C rec on req |

## STOLP
|  |  |
|---|---|
| 11-21-1912 | Vaugh Wood gct Whittier MM, Ca |

## STONEMAN
|  |  |
|---|---|
| 6-22-1843 | Mark D rocf Deep Creek MM, N C end by Springfield MM |
| 12-26-1844 | Mark D, Duck Creek MM compl for mcd dis 3-20-1845 |

## STOUT
|  |  |
|---|---|
| 1-26-1831 | Ephraim of Springfield MM, Wayne Co, s Charles & Lydia of Randolph Co, m at Spiceland M H Mary Sheridan of Henry Co |
| 7-21-1831 | Ephraim & ch Charles, James, Robert, Elias, Anna Ruth & Ephraim jr rocf Springfield MM |
| 4-25-1833 | Solomon & w Susannah & ch Zeno & Isaac rocf White Lick MM |
| 1-25-1849 | Isaac gct Spiceland MM |
| 11-22-1849 | Charles, Westfield MM req this mtg to treat w/him for jas 1-24-1850  This mtg treated without satisfaction & Westfield is so inf |
| 4-26-1855 | Joseph req Spring Creek MM, Iowa |

## STRATTON
|  |  |
|---|---|
| 1-23-1834 | Jonathan & w Prudence & ch Millicent Ann & Samuel rocf Whitewater MM |
| 2-20-1834 | Levi & w Ruth & ch Lucinda, Albert & Hannah rocf Whitewater MM |
| 5-24-1834 | Eli & w Eunice rocf Elk MM, Ohio |
| 5-21-1835 | Joseph E rocf Elk MM, Ohio |
| 11-26-1835 | Levi H, Duck Creek Mtg compl for na, dpl & upl dis 2-25-1836 |
| 7-21-1836 | Samuel & w Rachel & ch gct Westfield MM |

## STREET
|  |  |
|---|---|
| 7-25-1844 | Samuel & w Anna & ch Jane, Lydia, Rebecca & Mary rocf Spiceland MM |
| 2-20-1845 | Samuel & fam gct Spiceland Mtg (already removed) |

## SUMNER
|  |  |
|---|---|
| 2-26-1835 | Esther rocf Fall Creek MM, Ohio |
| 12-23-1915 | Charles & w Elizabeth Wood & s Aldus L rocf Shirley MM |

## SWAIN
|  |  |
|---|---|
| 2-21-1833 | Thomas jr, a mbr of New Garden MM, N C rpt mcd & that mtg is inf |
| 2-27-1833 | Elizabeth (form Williams) compl of for mcd dis 4-25-1833 |
| 7-24-1834 | Prior, Achsah & Silas, ch of Thomas decd, & Sarah (Leonard) rocf Springfield MM |
| 9-25-1834 | Thomas & ch Elmira, Franklin F, Alonzo & Alfred rocf Salem MM |
| 12-25-1834 | John & w Ann & ch Thomas Clarkson, Elihu William, Ezra, Susannah, Sally Ann, John jr & Rachel rocf Lost Creek MM, Tn |
| 12-25-1834 | Lewis rocf Lost Creek MM, Tn |
| 9-24-1835 | Thomas, Walnut Ridge P M inf mcd with his cousin  11-26-1835  chm |
| 8-20-1835 | John Turner, Fall Creek P M inf he refuses to give up his cert of mbrp directed to this mtg from New Garden MM, Guilford Co, N C  That Mtg has been so inf |
| 9-24-1835 | Elizabeth, Walnut Ridge P M compl for mcd with 1st cousin 12-24-1835 chm |
| 1-21-1841 | William, Clear Spring P M compl for na, dpl & j Meth  dis 6-24-1841 |
| 2-23-1843 | Elihu, Clear Spring P M compl for mcd dis 4-20-1843 |
| 5-23-1844 | John, Clear Springs P M compl for j Separatists (ASF)  dis 8-22-1844 |
| 5-23-1844 | Ann, Clear Springs P M compl for j Separatists (ASF) dis 7-25-1844 |
| 4-24-1845 | Howland & w Phebe & ch Susan E, Betsey Ann, Phebe Emily, George Howland, William Henry & Thomas Moore rocf New Garden MM, N C |
| 4-24-1845 | Susan & dt Emile rocf New Garden MM, N C |

DUCK CREEK

## SWAIN (Cont)

|  |  |
|---|---|
| 1-23-1845 | Lewis, Clear Springs P M compl for j Separatists (ASF) dis 4-24-1845 |
| 1-22-1846 | Susan E Coble (form Swain) Duck Creek P M compl for mcd 2-26-1846 chm |
| 5-25-1848 | Ezra, Clear Springs P M compl for mcd & na dis 7-20-1848 |
| 7-20-1848 | Phebe Emily, Duck Creek P M compl for att a mcd of two mbrs dis 10-26-1848 |
| 3-21-1850 | Susannah Weeks (form Swain) Cadiz P M compl for mcd dis 6-20-1850 |
| 4-22-1852 | Jesse F H & w Anna & ch William N Franklin, John Henry & George Stretcher rocf New Garden MM, N C |
| 11-25-1852 | Henry, Duck Creek Mtg compl for mcd 12-23-1852 chm |
| 11-25-1852 | Elizabeth M (form Pickering) Duck Creek P M compl for mcd 12-23-1852 chm |
| 2-24-1853 | George Howland, Duck Creek P M compl for mcd dis 5-26-1853 |
| 4-21-1853 | Louiza E (form Bowman) Duck Creek P M compl for mcd dis 7-21-1853 |
| 6-23-1853 | John jr, Cadiz P M compl for na dis 8-25-1853 |
| 9-22-1853 | Howland gct Walnut Ridge MM to m Elizabeth Swain |
| 1-26-1854 | Howland gct Walnut Ridge MM |
| 2-22-1855 | Thomas, Duck Creek P M compl for mcd & na dis 5-24-1855 |
| 5-24-1855 | William Henry, Duck Creek P M compl for na & because he has opened his house for a fiddling & dancing frolic dis 7-26-1855 |
| 1-21-1858 | Elizabeth, Duck Creek P M compl for att a public ball & participating therein by joining in the dance dis 3-25-1858 |
| 2-24-1859 | Ch of William Henry gct Bear Creek MM, Ia |
| 1-26-1860 | Elizabeth, Bear Creek MM, Iowa has been given consent of this mtg to rec mbrp again |
| 2-25-1864 | Ann rec in mbrp |
| 11-22-1866 | William N F condemns his mcd |
| 4-23-1868 | Nancy rec in mbrp |
| 6-20-1872 | John R & w Sarah & ch Albertes F & Sandford M rec in mbrp |
| 4-23-1874 | Alice rec in mbrp |
| 3-25-1875 | Thomas M & w Julia E & dt Minnie C rec in mbrp |
| 3-25-1880 | Thomas M & w Julia & ch Minnie C & George H gct Spiceland MM |
| 2-23-1893 | Sarah rec on req |
| 8-24-1893 | Cinderella rec on req |
| 3-20-1902 | Bertha & Emma rec on req |
| 6-26-1902 | Charles & w Sarah F rel on req |
| 2-23-1903 | Embry M rel on req |
| 8-24-1905 | Cinderella B rel on req |
| 5-12-1921 | Mary B rel on req |
| 3-23-1922 | Sophia rec on req |

## SWEET

|  |  |
|---|---|
| 12-24-1849 | Eli M rocf Spiceland MM |
| 6-26-1851 | Eli M gct Spiceland MM |

## SWIGARD - SWEIGART

|  |  |
|---|---|
| 1-21-1892 | Ellen, Addie & Sadie rec on req |
| 1-26-1893 | Ellen gct New Castle MM |
| 12-21-1899 | Ellen, Addie & Sadie rel on req |

## SYMONS

|  |  |
|---|---|
| 11-20-1834 | Matthew rocf Milford MM |
| 5- 7-1835 | Matthew of Henry Co, s Henry & Mary, decd m at Duck Creek M H Susanna Willets of Henry Co |
| 10-22-1840 | Bethuel & w Anna & ch Hannah, Martha Ann & Milicent rocf Mississinewa MM |
| 10-26-1843 | Susannah, Duck Creek P M compl for j Separatists (ASF) dis 12-21-1843 |
| 3-25-1847 | Anna & fam gct Spiceland MM |
| 11-25-1847 | Anna & dts Hannah, Martha Ann, Lucinda & Louisa rocf Spiceland MM |
| 4-20-1848 | Anna McHatton (form Symons) Duck Creek P M compl for mcd 6-26-1848 chm |
| 3-28-1867 | John of Spiceland Mtg, Henry Co, s Josiah & Sarah of same place m at Duck Creek M H Ellen S Henley of Henry Co |
| 10-22-1868 | Ellen gct Spiceland MM |
| 1-25-1894 | Abraham rocf Poplar Run MM |
| 2-21-1895 | Louisa rec on req |

## TALBERT

|  |  |
|---|---|
| 7-21-1870 | Aaron, sojourning cert rec from Minneapolis MM, Minn |

## TAYLOR

|  |  |
|---|---|
| 1-20-1831 | Simeon & w Elizabeth & ch Elbina S, Angelina P, John M, Daniel G & Allen D rocf Somerset MM, Ohio |
| 7-25-1833 | Elbina, Walnut Ridge Mtg compl for deviating from the truth & having unbecoming conduct dis 9-26-1833 |
| 11-26-1835 | Simeon compl of for telling untruths dis 1-21-1836 |
| 5-24-1923 | Loyd M rec on req |
| 11-24-1926 | Juanita rec on req |

## TEMPLETON

|  |  |
|---|---|
| 1-23-1896 | David & Lulu rec on req |
| 3-26-1896 | Eunice gct Knightstown MM |
| 8-25-1904 | Lulu drpd from mbrp |
| 3-23-1921 | David gct New Castle MM |

## TEST

|  |  |
|---|---|
| 4-20-1893 | Samuel & w Cora gct Raysville MM |

## THOMAS

|  |  |
|---|---|
| 9-20-1827 | Simeon appt to comm for visiting aged & infirm persons |
| 1-22-1829 | Simeon appt overseer Spiceland P M |
| 11-22-1827 | Elijah rocf New Garden MM |
| 3- 5-1827 | Simeon appt to a comm |
| 12- 6-1832 | Elijah of Henry Co, s Elijah Sr & Susannah of New Garden Mtg, Wayne Co m at Duck Creek M H Christina Presnall of Henry Co |
| 3-24-1836 | Manlove & w Polly S rocf Deep River MM, N C end to New Garden MM |
| 2-23-1893 | Harrt rec on req |
| 4-20-1899 | Flora & ch gct Knightstown MM |
| 10-23-1924 | Hoyt rec on req |

## THORNBURGH

|  |  |
|---|---|
| 10-20-1831 | Joel & w Anna & ch Cyrus, William, Willis, Mary Ann, & Lydia Jane rocf Fairfield MM, Ohio |
| 8-23-1832 | Joseph & w Rachel rocf Cherry Grove MM |
| 10-23-1834 | Ezekial rec in mbrp |
| 12-24-1835 | Anna rec in mbrp |

## THORP

|  |  |
|---|---|
| 1-26-1837 | Elenor (form Adison) Fall Creek P M compl for mcd & dpl dis 5-25-1837 |

## TICE

|  |  |
|---|---|
| 8-24-1893 | R Solomon & w Amanda rocf Maryville MM |
| 7-21-1907 | R Solomon & w Amanda gct Victoria MM, Mex |

## TOMLIN

|  |  |
|---|---|
| 1-20-1842 | Mahlon & w Susanna rocf Fairfield MM |
| 3-25-1843 | Mahlon & fam gct Westfield MM |

## TOMS

|  |  |
|---|---|
| 11-24-1864 | Phebe Ann gct Milford MM |

## TRICE

|  |  |
|---|---|
| 2-21-1924 | Edna rec on req |

## TRIMBLE

|  |  |
|---|---|
| 7-21-1907 | Mary Carlile drpd from mbrp |

## TRUEBLOOD

|  |  |
|---|---|
| 2-21-1850 | Zachariah rocf Vermilion MM, Ill & end to Pleasant Plain MM, Iowa |

## TUNGATE

|  |  |
|---|---|
| 4-21-1892 | John & Luther rec on req |

## TWEEDY

|  |  |
|---|---|
| 3-25-1909 | Sarah Ann gct Dublin MM |

DUCK CREEK

## ULMER
|  |  |
|---|---|
| 3-22-1894 | Daniel N rec on req |
| 9-24-1896 | Daniel & w Margaret rel on req |
| 6-24-1897 | Daniel jr & w Louise & ch Harry H & Esther G rel on req |
| 12-26-1912 | Della rec on req |

## UNTHANK
|  |  |
|---|---|
| 1-20-1831 | William B & w Rebecca & ch Drucilla, Samuel & Addison rocf Milford MM |
| 9- 7-1845 | Pleasant of New Garden MM, Wayne Co, (s Josiah, decd, & Anna) m at Duck Creek M H Sarah A Pickering, a wid, & dt of Cadwallader & Elizabeth, decd, Pitts |
| 5-21-1846 | Sarah Ann & her dt Esther Jane Pickering gct New Garden MM |
| 3- 2-1848 | J Addison of Spiceland Mtg, Henry Co, s William & Rebecca m at Duck Creek M H Cynthia Saint of Henry Co |
| 11-23-1848 | Cynthia gct Spiceland MM |
| 3-25-1852 | Joseph Addison & w Cynthia & s Samuel Exum rocf Spiceland MM |
| 12-23-1852 | J Addison & w Cynthia & fam gct Spiceland MM |

## VANCE
|  |  |
|---|---|
| 1-21-1847 | Mary (form Pickering) Duck Creek P M compl for mcd   dis  3-25-1847 |
| 2-23-1893 | Flora rec on req |
| 2-21-1895 | Elias rel on req |

## VAN HORN
|  |  |
|---|---|
| 8-31-1826 | John, a minor under care of George Evans, rocf Miami MM, Ohio |
| 7-25-1833 | John, a minor, now living in the limits of Miami MM, Ohio gct that mtg |

## VICARS
|  |  |
|---|---|
| 2-25-1897 | Lula Weasner rel on req |

## VOTAW
|  |  |
|---|---|
| 11-24-1848 | Jonathan jr of Wayne Co, s Jonathan Sr & Elizabeth m at Clear Springs M H Jane Lewelling of Henry Co |
| 1-25-1849 | Jane B gct Salem MM, Iowa |

## WALDRON
|  |  |
|---|---|
| 1-21-1847 | Jemima gct Back Creek MM |

## WALES
|  |  |
|---|---|
| 9-23-1847 | William W rocf Deep Creek MM, N C |
| 4-27-1848 | William of Henry Co, s Samuel, decd & Mary, formerly of Hancock Co, m at Duck Creek M H Catharine E Bundy of Henry Co |
| 9-25-1852 | William W & w Catharine & ch gct Winnesheik MM, Iowa |

## WALLS
|  |  |
|---|---|
| 1-25-1894 | William F & w Josie & ch Harvey B & Mary M gct Raysville MM |

## WALTON
|  |  |
|---|---|
| 1-23-1868 | Rufus P rocf Spiceland MM |
| 1-26-1899 | Rufus drpd from mbrp |
| 9-21-1899 | Rufus P & w Theresa A gct Knightstown MM |

## WARD
|  |  |
|---|---|
| 1-20-1831 | John Morris gct Springfield MM, to m Rachel Ward |
| 1-26-1843 | Simeon P dis for j Hs |

## WARNER
|  |  |
|---|---|
| 3-20-1902 | Lula rec on req |

## WASSON
|  |  |
|---|---|
| 8-31-1826 | Jehiel appt one of Trustees to hold deed to land where the mtg is held at Flat Rock M H (not having complied with appt, he is released on 11-22-1827) |
| 8-31-1826 | Mary appt to comm to att Q M |
| 5- 3-1827 | Jehiel appt an overseer |
| 9-20-1827 | Calvin appt to comm for visiting aged & infirm persons |
| 9-20-1827 | Lydia appt to comm on "poor" |
| 12-20-1827 | Calvin & w Mary & fam gct Chester MM |
| 12-25-1828 | Lydia, Duck Creek P M compl for j Hs  dis 2-26-1829 |
| 1-22-1829 | Jehiel, Duck Creek P M compl for j Hs  dis  3-26-1829 |
| 8-20-1829 | Ch of Jehiel gct Whitewater MM |
| 3-24-1831 | Calvin, a Minister & w Mary & ch William, Nathan, Elizabeth, Sally & Mary Jane rocf Chester MM |
| 4-23-1835 | Calvin & w Mary & ch gct Spiceland MM |

## WEAVER
|  |  |
|---|---|
| 12-21-1848 | Cynthia (form Hiatt) Duck Creek MM compl for mcd  dis 4-26-1849 |
| 12-25-1856 | Lydia (form Compton) rpt mcd  dis |

## WEBB
|  |  |
|---|---|
| 3-20-1834 | Lydia, a minor, rocf Carmel MM held at Elk Run, Ohio |
| 7-24-1834 | Benjamin, a minor, rocf Upper Spring MM, Ohio |
| 8-20-1835 | Peninah rocf Salem MM, Ohio |
| 10- 1-1825 | Peninah, dt John, decd & Leah (now Leah James w of Isaac James) m at Duck Creek M H Nathan Larrance |
| 10-21-1841 | Benjamin, Clear Springs P M compl for upl 11-25-1841 He now resides in the limits of Fairfield MM & that mtg is req to treat w/him  Fairfield rpts no satis dis forwarded to Fairfield MM 7-21-1842 |
| 3-24-1881 | Joseph rec on req |
| 3-25-1885 | Joseph gct Spiceland MM |

## WEEKS
|  |  |
|---|---|
| 1-20-1830 | William rocf Whitewater MM |
| 1-20-1830 | Winifred, Duck Creek P M compl for telling untruths & for reproach of her neighbors  dis 4-22-1830 |
| 7-22-1830 | William, Whitewater MM req this mtg to treat w/him for mcd  9-23-1830 chm & Whitewater is informed |
| 2-23-1832 | Mary Ann rec in mbrp |
| 7-20-1837 | William & fam gct White River MM |
| 7-20-1843 | Mary Edwards (form Weeks) Duck Creek P M compl for mcd  dis 9-21-1843 |
| 3-31-1850 | Susannah (form Swain) Cadiz P M compl for mcd  dis 6-20-1850 |
| 10-20-1853 | Elizabeth (form Pitts) Duck Creek P M compl for mcd  dis 12-23-1853 |
| 12-22-1853 | Allen, Duck Creek P M compl for mcd  dis 6- 6-1854 |
| 2-23-1854 | Alfred, Duck Creek P M compl for att three mcd of mbrs  dis 6- 6-1854 |
| 9-25-1856 | Benjamin, Duck Creek P M compl for na  dis 12-25-1856 |
| 12-23-1880 | Allen & w Elizabeth & ch Benjamin R, Arthur N & Oscar rocf Raysville MM |
| 2-22-1894 | Ida & dt Maria rec on req |
| 7-23-1896 | Oscar rel on req |
| 5-20-1897 | Oscar rec on req |
| 5-25-1899 | Oscar drpd from mbrp |
| 4-25-1901 | Ida & ch Maurice & Pauline gct Walnut Ridge MM |

## WEISNER - WEESNER
|  |  |
|---|---|
| 11-22-1832 | Michael jr & w Hannah rocf Chester MM |
| 4-25-1833 | Jesse & (2nd w) Lydia & ch William, Jehu, Hannah, Cyrus, Ann, Seth, Nathan, Margaret & Jesse jr rocf New Garden MM |
| 12-21-1843 | Elwood & Martha, ch of William & Sarah, decd rec in mbrp by req of grandparents Jesse & Lydia Weisner |
| 2-20-1845 | Seth req cert to Walnut Ridge MM to m Ann Pike |
| 12-25-1845 | Ann rocf Walnut Ridge MM |
| 4-23-1846 | Nathan gct Walnut Ridge MM to m Hannah Pike |
| 5-21-1846 | Jesse gct Walnut Ridge MM to m Phebe Pike |
| 7-22-1847 | Hannah rocf Walnut Ridge MM |
| 2-24-1848 | Margaret gct Walnut Ridge MM |
| 1-20-1848 | Jesse & ch req cert to Walnut Ridge MM  9-21-1848 comm rpts that Jesse has decd & fam is about to return to the limits of Duck Creek |

DUCK CREEK

## WEISNER - WEESNER (Cont)
|  |  |
|---|---|
| 9-26-1850 | Elwood, a minor gct Walnut Ridge MM |
| 8-26-1852 | Seth & w Ann & fam gct East Grove MM, Iowa |
| 11-25-1852 | Jesse jr, Cadiz Mtg compl for mcd  2-24-1853 chm |
| 2-24-1853 | Mary (form Pike) Cadiz P M compl for mcd & j Meth  She being a mbr of Walnut Ridge MM that mtg has been inf  10-20-1853 Walnut Ridge MM dis |
| 12-26-1861 | Nathan, Clear Springs P M inf na  2-20-1861 chm |
| 12-25-1862 | Nathan & w Hannah & ch gct Walnut Ridge MM |
| 8-30-1865 | Martha S of Henry Co, both her parents are decd, m at Clear Springs M H Wilson Kendall of Chester Mtg, Wayne Co |
| 1-21-1892 | Frank, Alice & Cecil rec on req |
| 1-21-1892 | Thomas, Lucy, Elva, Florence & Arnal rec on req |
| 3-22-1917 | Paul drpd from mbrp |

## WELLING
|  |  |
|---|---|
| 12-25-1890 | William & fam drpd from mbrp |
| 3-24-1892 | William & w Minnie & dt Nora rec on req |

## WELLS
|  |  |
|---|---|
| 7-22-1915 | J W & w Martha F rec on req |

## WHITE
|  |  |
|---|---|
| 11- 2-1826 | Robert rec in mbrp |
| 12-28-1826 | Rebecca appt an o  at Walnut Ridge P M |
| 10- 3-1827 | Bethuel C of Rush Co, s Robert & Rebecca m at Walnut Ridge M H Hannah Binford of Rush Co |
| 11-22-1827 | Stanton & w Sary rocf Hopewell MM, N C end by Milford MM |
| 11-22-1827 | Jesse rocf Hopewell MM, N C & end by Milford MM |
| 11-22-1827 | Isaac & w Louisa & ch Micajah, Lilburn, Jesse & Martha G rocf New Garden MM, N C & end by Milford MM |
| 6-26-1828 | Phineas rocf Piney Woods MM, N C |
| 12-25-1828 | Lydia appt to a comm |
| 1-22-1829 | Isaac appt Trustee for Spiceland P M |
| 8-20-1829 | Phineas, being about to travel on business to Piney Woods MM, N C, req a few lines certifying his right of mbrp  5-20-1830 he returned his minute, end by Piney Woods |
| 12-24-1829 | Rebecca appt an Elder |
| 5-20-1830 | Robert & w Rebecca & ch gct Milford MM |
| 5-20-1830 | Eli gct Milford MM |
| 9-23-1830 | Jesse, being about to travel to N C to visit his friends, req a copy of minutes certifying his right of mbrp |
| 2-24-1831 | Robert & w Rebecca & ch Harriett, Thomas, Thaddeus, Isaac & George B rocf Milford MM |
| 2-24-1831 | Eli rocf Milford MM |
| 3-24-1831 | Isaac appt o Spiceland P M |
| 5-26-1831 | Pheneas gct Milford MM to m Sarah Bundy |
| 9-28-1831 | Jesse of Spiceland Mtg, Henry Co, s Stanton & Sarah m at Spiceland M H Mary Pennington of Henry Co |
| 11-24-1831 | Sarah rocf Milford Mtg |
| 12-30-1832 | Betsy Ann rocf Piney Woods MM, N C |
| 1-29-1834 | Harriett, dt Robert & Rebecca m at Walnut Ridge M H John H Newby of Rush Co |
| 9-25-1834 | Robert, Walnut Ridge P M compl for applying & obtaining a license to accomplish his mcd & for justifying himself therein dis 12-25-1834 |
| 11-26-1834 | Eli of Rush Co, s Robert & Rebecca, decd m at Walnut Ridge M H Martha Honeycutt (Hunnicutt) of Hancock Co |
| 3-26-1835 | George, Springfield MM req this mtg to treat w/him for mcd  Duck Creek MM treated w/out satisfaction  Springfield MM dis him 10-22-1835 |
| 8-20-1846 | Henry rocf Hopewell MM, N C & end by Walnut Ridge MM |
| 1-20-1848 | Mary & dt Abigail B & Polly Jane rocf Walnut Ridge MM |
| 5-25-1848 | Henry & w Mary gct Spiceland MM |
| 6-22-1848 | Abigail & Mary Jane gct Spiceland MM |
| 4-26-1849 | Elijah, a mbr of Walnut Ridge MM is compl of for  att a mcd  & that mtg inf |
| 4-21-1833 | Ann Cadwallader (form White) Cadiz P M compl for mcd with a divorced man  dis  6-23-1853 |
| 12-26-1850 | Nathan & w Prudence & ch William G, Moses H & Esther Ann rocf Marlborough MM, Ohio |
| 12-26-1850 | Ann (wid of Robert L) rocf Marlborough MM, Ohio |
| 12-26-1850 | Ann jr (dt Robert L & w Ann) rocf Marlborough MM, Ohio |
| 4-21-1853 | Paul & w Tabitha & ch John M, Joseph W, William, Ann Eliza, Sarah & Robert L rocf Marlborough MM, Ohio |
| 4-22-1858 | Paul & w Tabitha & fam gct Marlborough MM, Ohio |
| 6-23-1859 | Edward rocf Raysville MM |
| 12- 8-1859 | Addison of Henry Co, s Jesse & Mary m at Duck Creek M H Eliza W Holloway |
| 4-26-1860 | Eliza H gct Richland MM |
| 3-21-1861 | Paul & w Tabitha & ch William P, Sarah, Robert & Samuel rocf Marlborough MM, Oh |
| 1-25-1866 | Nathan & w Prudence & fam gct Minneapolis MM, Minn |
| 1-25-1866 | John, Cadiz P M inf mcd but he retained his mbrp |
| 4-25-1867 | John M & w Martha gct New Salem MM |
| 9-22-1870 | Martha & ch Charles & John rocf New Salem MM |
| 8-24-1871 | Paul & fam gct Tonganoxie MM, Kansas |
| 2-23-1892 | Carlie rec on req |
| 4-20-1916 | Gerald & Isabel rec on req |

## WHYBREW
|  |  |
|---|---|
| 4-24-1924 | Rev Daniel & w Harriet & ch Beverly S, Dugan K & Daniel jr rocf Arba MM |

## WICKERSHAM
|  |  |
|---|---|
| 7-27-1826 | Mary appt to a comm |
| 8-31-1826 | Jehu appt to comm to see that the M H is reconditioned to make it comfortable |
| 3- 5-1827 | Jehu appt Recorder of Births & Deaths |
| 8-23-1827 | Jehu & Reuben Edgerton appt to att funerals of Friends at Duck Creek P M |
| 12-23-1841 | Asenith W Nixon (form Wickersham) Duck Creek P M compl for mcd  3-24-1842 chm |
| 11-20-1845 | Mary & ch gct Back Creek MM |

## WILFER
|  |  |
|---|---|
| 10-23-1924 | Wilber rec on req |

## WILKERSON - WILKINSON
|  |  |
|---|---|
| 6-22-1848 | Patience (form Johnson) Duck Creek P M compl for mcd dis 8-24-1848 |

## WILLETS
|  |  |
|---|---|
| 8-25-1831 | Nathan rocf New Garden MM |
| 3-22-1832 | Gabriel & w Elizabeth & ch Joseph, Phebe, Susannah, Levi, Jesse, Ruth & Isaac rocf Union MM, Stokes Co, N C |
| 6-21-1832 | Asenath (form Schooley) rec in mbrp w/con of New Garden MM (w of Nathan) |
| 8-23-1832 | Sarah rocf Clear Creek MM, Ohio, end by New Garden MM |
| 10-25-1832 | Phebe gct Cherry Grove MM |
| 8-21-1834 | Asenath & dt Ruth rocf Spiceland MM |
| 9-25-1834 | Phebe rocf Cherry Grove MM |
| 5- 7-1835 | Susanna dt of Gabriel of Henry Co, & w Priscilla, decd, late of Stokes Co, N C m at Duck Creek M H Matthew Symons of Henry Co |
| 10- 1-1835 | Sarah, dt Gabriel of Henry Co, & w Priscilla decd, late of Stokes Co, N C m at Duck Creek M H William Pickering |
| 5-23-1844 | Phebe, Duck Creek Mtg compl for j Separatists (ASF) dis 7-25-1844 |
| 3-26-1846 | Gabriel & w Elizabeth & dt Ruth gct Westfield MM |
| 3-26-1846 | Jesse gct Westfield MM |
| 9-26-1850 | Phebe consent given by Duck Creek P M to Hinkle's Creek MM to rec her in mbrp |

## WILLIAMS
|  |  |
|---|---|
| 11-13-1829 | Caty, dt William & Hannah of Madison Co, m at Duck Creek M H Benjamin Morris of Henry Co |

DUCK CREEK

## WILLIAMS (Cont)

|  |  |
|---|---|
| 10-22-1829 | William & w Hannah & ch Caleb, Anna, Caty, Elizabeth, Esther, Hannah, Mariam, Martin & Lucinda rocf Springfield MM |
| 7-21-1831 | Ann, Duck Creek P M compl for j Hs dis 9-22-1831 |
| 11-24-1831 | Caleb, Duck Creek P M compl for j Hs dis 1-26-1832 |
| 2-21-1833 | William, Duck Creek P M compl for j Hs dis 5-23-1833 |
| 2-27-1833 | Elizabeth Swain (form Williams) compl of for mcd dis 4-25-1833 |
| 1-22-1835 | Hannah (form Gregg) Duck Creek P M compl for mcd & j Hs dis 3-26-1835 |
| 10-20-1836 | Jason & w Abigail & ch Sarah, Hannah, Joseph & Mary Ellen rocf Flushing MM, Oh |
| 4-20-1837 | Margaret & Melinda rocf Centre MM, Ohio |
| 5-25-1837 | Melinda gct Westfield MM |
| 7-27-1837 | Margaret, dt James & Julia Ann, decd, m at Duck Creek M H to Meshack Lewelling of Henry Co |
| 8-27-1837 | Miriam, Fall Creek P M compl for j Hs |
| 10-20-1842 | Hannah & dts Hannah & Lucinda rocf Back Creek MM |
| 8-24-1843 | Lucinda Hardin (form Williams) Clear Springs P M compl for mcd dis 11-23-1843 |
| 8-24-1843 | Hannah, Clear Springs P M compl for j Hs dis 11-23-1843 |
| 11-23-1843 | Darius gct White Lick MM |
| 1-25-1844 | Leah (form Stanbrough) Clear Springs P M compl for mcd dis 3-21-1844 |
| 7-21-1853 | Mary Ruhanna (form Wilson) Duck Creek P M compl for mcd 8-25-1853 chm |
| 12-22-1853 | Mary Ruhanna gct Spiceland MM |
| 2-22-1855 | Hannah C Henley (form Williams) Duck Creek P M compl for mcd She settled in limits of Walnut Ridge MM, which mtg is req to treat w/her 5-24-1855 chm |
| 6-24-1858 | Isaac rocf New Garden MM |
| 4-21-1859 | Jason & w Abigail & fam gct Spiceland MM |
| 3-24-1859 | Isaac req cert to New Garden MM but on 4-21-1859 it is rptd that he again resides in the limits of this mtg |
| 4-21-1859 | Isaac req cert to Westfield MM |
| 8-25-1859 | Joseph H gct Hopewell MM to m Dorothy Gilbert |
| 4-26-1860 | Joseph H gct Hopewell MM |
| 5-23-1861 | Mary Ruhanna rocf Spiceland MM |
| 3-22-1866 | Ruhanna gct Spiceland MM |
| 2-26-1900 | Andrew J & ch Blanch, Leslie G, Jesse & Robert J rec on req |
| 2-26-1900 | Corena rocf New Castle MM |
| 4-26-1917 | Lola May rec on req |
| 9-25-1924 | Lola Blakely rocf Shirley MM |

## WILLOUGHBY

|  |  |
|---|---|
| 1-24-1895 | Eliza rec on req |

## WILLS

|  |  |
|---|---|
| 6-20-1895 | Jacob & w Rosanna & ch Arthur, Lora & Mary M rocf Raysville MM |
| 1-26-1899 | Jacob drpd from mbrp |
| 2-23-1926 | Jacob rec on req |

## WILSON

|  |  |
|---|---|
| 12-20-1827 | Michael jr & w Rebecca rocf Fall Creek MM, Ohio |
| 2-26-1829 | Joseph & w Phebe rocf Fall Creek MM, Ohio |
| 3-26-1829 | William rocf Fall Creek MM, Ohio |
| 11-24-1831 | Sirena, David, Esther, Jane & Elias ch of Michael jr & Rebecca rec in mbrp |
| 11-22-1832 | Susannah, Catharine, Abner, Asenath & Henry ch of Joseph, decd & Phebe rec in mbrp |
| 5-23-1833 | David & w Esther & ch Margaret, Isaac & Amy rocf Flushing MM, Ohio |
| 8-22-1833 | Jonathan rocf Flushing MM, Ohio |
| 10-24-1833 | Jonathan gct Milford MM to m Drucilla Cox |
| 3-20-1834 | Jonathan gct Milford MM |
| 6-26-1834 | Esther (wid of Michael Sr) rocf Fall Creek MM, Ohio |
| 7-23-1835 | Henry rocf Deep Creek MM, N C end by Fairfield MM, Ohio & Milford MM |
| 10-26-1843 | Michael, Duck Creek P M compl for na & identifying self with Separatists (ASF) dis 12-21-1843 |
| 5-23-1844 | David, Duck Creek P M compl for mcd & j Separatists (ASF) He has removed to limits of Salem MM, Iowa & that mtg is req to treat w/him No satisfaction dis 11-21-1844 |
| 5-23-1844 | Asenath Wright (form Wilson) Duck Creek P M compl for mcd dis 7-25-1844 |
| 10-26-1844 | Rebecca, Duck Creek P M compl for j Separatists (ASF) dis 1-25-1844 |
| 1-23-1845 | Elizabeth (form Hiatt) has j Separatists (ASF) She has removed to limits of Salem MM, Iowa which mtg is req to treat w/her No satisfaction dis 7-24-1845 forwarded to Salem MM |
| 1-30-1845 | Phebe, wid of Joseph & dt David & Susannah Reece, both decd m at Duck Creek M H Richard Norton of Henry Co |
| 2-21-1850 | Henry, Duck Creek P M compl for mcd dis 4-25-1850 |
| 12-26-1850 | Calvin, Clear Springs P M compl for mcd dis 3-20-1851 |
| 1-22-1852 | Benjamin & w Sarah Caroline & s William Albert rocf Milford MM |
| 3-25-1852 | John & w Mary & s Michael rocf New Garden MM, N C |
| 4-22-1852 | David Franklin rocf New Garden MM, N C |
| 4-22-1852 | Mary Ruhanna rocf New Garden MM, N C |
| 4-22-1852 | Thomas Arnett rocf New Garden MM, N C |
| 2-24-1853 | John & w Mary & s gct Spiceland MM |
| 3-24-1853 | David D & Thomas A gct Spiceland MM |
| 7-21-1853 | Mary Ruhanna Williams (form Wilson) Duck Creek P M compl for mcd 8-25-1853 chm |
| 8-24-1854 | Benjamin A, Cadiz P M compl for mcd dis 11-23-1854 |
| 12-25-1856 | Elias gct Salem MM, Iowa |
| 12-25-1856 | Rebecca gct Salem MM, Iowa |
| 8-20-1857 | Abner, Duck Creek P M inf mcd dis |
| 11-26-1857 | Rebecca, Duck Creek P M gives con to Salem MM, Iowa to rec her in mbrp |
| 1-20-1859 | Richard, Salem MM, Iowa req con to rec him in mbrp granted |
| 4-26-1860 | Peggy rocf Spiceland MM |
| 3-22-1866 | Deborah A gct Lynn Grove Mtg, Iowa |
| 6-22-1871 | William E & w Sarah Ann rec in mbrp |
| 10-26-1876 | William F & w Sarah Ann rel on req |
| 12-23-1880 | Henry & w Rebecca rocf Raysville MM |
| 7-22-1882 | Marcus rocf Spiceland MM |
| 1-25-1883 | Marcus & dt Florence gct Dover MM |
| 1-20-1891 | Dora & ch Carrie, & Eva rocf New Castle MM |
| 1-21-1892 | Charles rec on req |
| 3-24-1892 | John, Margaret & Rosetta rec on req |
| 8-23-1894 | Franseigel & fam gct Raysville MM |
| 8-24-1899 | William gct Knightstown MM |
| 11-20-1902 | Cora Snodgrass & dt Mary Eliza rec on req |
| 12-22-1904 | Cora S & dt Mary E gct Knightstown MM |

## WILTSE

|  |  |
|---|---|
| 1-23-1834 | Simeon jr & w Rachel rocf Elk MM, Ohio |
| 4-24-1834 | Simeon Sr & w Elizabeth & ch John C, Martin, George & Elizabeth rocf Elk MM, Ohio |
| 5-24-1834 | William rocf Elk Mtg, Ohio |
| 12-25-1834 | William gct New Garden MM |
| 5-24-1835 | William, the cert to New Garden MM was end back to this mtg |

## WINSLOW

|  |  |
|---|---|
| 5-21-1829 | John & w Mary & ch Henry & John H rocf Whitewater MM |
| 3- 3-1833 | Henry of Grant Co, s Joseph & Peninah m at Walnut Ridge M H Ann Binford of Rush Co |
| 5-23-1833 | Anna gct Mississinewa MM |
| 4-25-1844 | Mary (form Lowder) Clear Springs P M inf mcd She has removed to limits of Back Creek MM which mtg is req to treat w/her 9-26-1844 chm |
| 11-21-1844 | Mary gct Back Creek MM |
| 2-20-1919 | Frank & w Dora & ch Frank jr, Joseph W & Harry rec on req |

## WINSLOW (Cont)
| | |
|---|---|
| 2-21-1924 | Freda rec on req |
| 11-24-1926 | Freda Reece drpd from mbrp |

## WINTERS
| | |
|---|---|
| 1-20-1891 | Alvin rocf Spiceland MM |

## WISE
| | |
|---|---|
| 6-26-1924 | Howard Munden & w Ethel & ch Ervell Munden & Margaret Lee Wise (a dt by a former m) |

## WISEHART
| | |
|---|---|
| 4-26-1900 | Benjamin F rec on req |

## WISSINGER
| | |
|---|---|
| 1-22-1885 | Daniel & w rec on req |

## WOOD
| | |
|---|---|
| 7-27-1826 | Phebe appt to a comm |
| 8-31-1826 | Phebe appt on comm on "poor" |
| 8-21-1826 | Jacob appt asst Clerk & John Copeland appt Clerk |
| 11-30-1826 | Jacob appt to a comm |
| 5- 3-1827 | Jacob appt asst Clerk & George Evans appt Clerk |
| 5-21-1829 | Jacob, Duck Creek P M compl for j Hs dis 8-20-1829 |
| 5-21-1829 | Phebe, Duck Creek P M compl for j Hs dis 7-23-1829 |
| 2-23-1837 | Huldah compl of for j Hs dis 4-20-1837 |
| 11-24-1842 | Simeon P, Duck Creek P M compl for na & j Hs dis 1-26-1843 |
| 9-20-1849 | Sarah Sanders (form Wood) compl of for mcd & j Hs dis 12-20-1849 |
| 12-24-1849 | Levi P, Duck Creek P M compl for mcd & j Hs dis 3-21-1850 |
| 12-24-1849 | Seth, Duck Creek P M compl for j Hs & for theft & leaving the county dis |
| 11-21-1850 | Mary rocf Milford MM |
| 4-21-1904 | Charles S & w Elizabeth Ann & ch Forest O, Julia L & Aldna L gct Knightstown MM |
| 7-21-1904 | Joseph & w Ruth gct Knightstown MM |
| 5-23-1907 | Orville gct Knightstown MM |
| 9-26-1912 | Chalkley E & w Mary gct Whittier MM, Ca |

## WOODARD
| | |
|---|---|
| 11-21-1850 | Mary rocf Milford MM |

## WORTH
| | |
|---|---|
| 7-24-1834 | William & w Sarah & his ch Belinda & Ann Worth & her ch Prior, Achsah & Silas Swain rocf Springfield MM |
| 3-20-1835 | William appt o at Settlement of Little Blue River |

## WRENNICK
| | |
|---|---|
| 2-21-1901 | May rec on req |

## WRIGHT
| | |
|---|---|
| 1-24-1833 | John & Abigail & ch Mary Jane, Nathan & Catharine rocf Fairfield MM, Ohio |
| 4-24-1834 | James & w Katharine & ch Allen, David, Joel & Jemima rocf Springfield MM, end by White River MM |
| 10-23-1834 | George, Clear Springs P M compl for mcd now resides in limits of Springfield MM which mtg is inf |
| 1-22-1835 | David compl of for att a mcd of a mbr dis 4-23-1835 |
| 5-24-1835 | James, Clear Springs P M compl for using spiritous liquor & j Hs dis 8-20-1835 |
| 10-22-1835 | Jacob & w Catharine & ch John Elwood, Moses F, Evaline & Marilla rocf New Hope MM, Tenn |
| 10-22-1835 | Ann & ch Joab, Joel & Anna rocf New Hope MM, Tenn |
| 2-23-1837 | Jesse Sr req to be again rec in mbrp 7-20-1837 rec in mbrp at Duck Creek w/con of New Hope MM, Tenn |
| 7-20-1837 | Joab gct Spiceland MM to m Mary Small |
| 12-24-1840 | John Elwood gct Springfield MM to m Jemima Hunnicut |
| 10-21-1841 | Jemima W rocf Springfield MM |
| 11-26-1841 | Margaret Jane dt John & Abigail of Henry Co m at Clear Springs M H Thomas Moorman of Grant Co |
| 9-21-1843 | Nancy, Duck Creek P M compl for j Separatists (ASF) dis 11-23-1843 |
| 11-23-1843 | Catharine, Clear Springs P M compl for j (ASF) dis 1-25-1844 |
| 11-23-1843 | Abigail, Clear Springs P M compl for j (ASF) dis 1-25-1844 |
| 12-21-1843 | John, Clear Springs P M compl for identifying with the Separatists dis 2-22-1844 |
| 12-21-1843 | Jesse, Duck Creek P M compl for att mtgs of the Separatists dis 2-22-1844 |
| 1-25-1844 | Jacob, Clear Springs P M compl for identifying with the (ASF) dis 5-23-1844 |
| 2-22-1844 | John & w Joanna & ch Isaac Vincent, Jesse W R, Samuel F, Margaret P & Zenas F rocf New Hope MM, Tn end by Spiceland MM |
| 4-25-1844 | Jemima, Clear Springs P M compl for j (ASF) dis 7-25-1844 |
| 5-23-1844 | Asenath (form Wilson) Duck Creek P M compl for mcd dis 7-25-1844 |
| 8-22-1844 | Joel, Duck Creek P M compl for j (ASF) dis 10-24-1844 |
| 6-26-1845 | Sarah & Benjamin, ch of William & Elizabeth rocf Milford MM end to Back Creek MM |
| 11-20-1845 | Emiline Bennett (form Wright) Clear Springs P M compl for mcd & j (ASF) dis 1-22-1846 |
| 2-26-1846 | John Elwood, Clear Springs P M compl for j (ASF) dis 4-23-1846 |
| 2-24-1848 | Moses, Clear Springs P M compl for mcd in a mtg set-up contrary to our discipline dis 4-20-1848 |
| 2-22-1849 | Eliza (form Swain) Springfield MM req this mtg to treat w/her for mcd no satisfaction 3-22-1849 Springfield was so inf |
| 2-22-1849 | Elizabeth (form Hollingsworth) Springfield MM req this mtg to treat w/her for mcd treated w/out satis & 3-22-1849 Springfield was so inf |
| 2-22-1849 | Charles C, a mbr of Walnut Ridge MM rpt mcd |
| 7-26-1849 | Marella Hutson (form Wright) Clear Springs P M compl for mcd dis 9-20-1849 |
| 8-23-1849 | Nathan, Clear Springs P M compl for mcd dis 10-25-1849 |
| 10-23-1851 | Mary Ann Stanfield (form Wright) Clear Springs P M compl mcd She now resides in limits of Back Creek MM which mtg is req to treat w/her 3-25-1852 chm |
| 11-25-1852 | Emily (form Pitts) Duck Creek P M compl for mcd dis 2-24-1853 |
| 7-24-1856 | Sarah j Meth dis |
| 3-26-1857 | Jacob & Catharine reinstated in mbrp |
| 3-26-1857 | William & Martha appt Elders |
| 8-20-1857 | Jacob B, Cadiz P M inf mcd dis |
| 4-22-1858 | Ann reinstated in mbrp |
| 5-20-1858 | Joel & w Eliza M & ch Marilla E, Sylvanus J, Cynthia Ann & Caroline J rec in mbrp |
| 10-21-1858 | Sarah (form Hutson) rpt mcd & j Meth dis |
| 4-21-1859 | Sarah Ann (form Stanbrough) rpt mcd but mbrp retained |
| 4-21-1859 | Nancy gct Oak Ridge MM |
| 9-22-1859 | Sarah Ann gct Back Creek MM |
| 7- 1-1862 | Sarah M dt Joel & w Ann, decd, m at Duck Creek M H Jesse W Kirk of Henry Co |
| 2-23-1865 | Jacob, Cadiz P M compl for mcd but mbrp retained |
| 10-24-1878 | Sylvanus J gct Spiceland MM |
| 7-22-1882 | Sylvanus J & w Sarah & ch Pearl Iva, Jessie Leona & Russell Lovell rocf Spiceland MM |
| 3-24-1892 | Lulu W & ch Horace, Miriam & Olive C rec on req |
| 4-25-1895 | Margaret E rec on req |
| 7-20-1905 | S J rel on req |
| 4-20-1911 | Russell gct Portland MM, Oregon |
| 4-20-1911 | Jesse gct New Castle MM |
| 11-23-1911 | Mariam E gct Spiceland MM |
| 7-25-1912 | Olive gct Whittier MM, Ca |
| 10-23-1922 | Walter drpd from mbrp |

# DUCK CREEK MONTHLY MEETING
## (Anti-slavery)
## Henry County, Indiana

Duck Creek Monthly Meeting of Anti-slavery Friends was formed in Greensboro early in 1843. The exact date is unknown. Constituent meetings were Elm Grove and Clear Spring. After Westfield (Hamilton County) was discontinued as a monthly meeting it was attached to Duck Creek.

It is not certain where the Duck Creek meetinghouse was located. Most likely it was held in the same meetinghouse as the quarterly meeting which in 1844 held meetings in "Liberty Hall."

*"In the days of anti-slavery agitation the town (Greensboro) was a noted place, being the home of many determined Abolitionists. In old Liberty Hall, many noted men from far and near made enthusiastic speeches in favor of relieving the condition of the black man."* (1884 History of Henry County.)

Duck Creek Anti-slavery meeting was discontinued in 1857 and many of the remaining members were re-attached to the larger body of Duck Creek Friends.

### Monthly Meeting Records

These records are in a collection of Anti-slavery material in the Indiana Historical Society Library.

Because of the paucity of records some additional data has been culled from the Quarterly Meeting Minutes and appear in brackets. Witnesses have been retained with the marriage records as they may serve some useful purpose. It should be noted, however, that a witness was not necessarily a Friend, but could be a neighbor who attended the ceremony.

### Women's Minutes
5-11-1850 : 3-11-1857

### Marriage Register
1843-1855

## DUCK CREEK MONTHLY MEETING
### (Anti-slavery)
### MINUTES

**ANTRIM**
( 8 mo-1844   James P to QM)

**COMPTON**
8-10-1853   Nancy (& husband) & dts Lydia & Sarah Ann rocf Newport MM

**COOK**
9-11-1852   Martha (f Tomlinson) rpt mcd.  11-13-1852 rpt now deceased

**COX**
(11 mo-1843   Solomon to QM)

**EDGERTON**
( 8 mo-1844   Walter to QM)
10- 9-1850   Rebecca app comm
11- 9-1850   Sarah appt asst clerk
7- 7-1853   Caroline (with husband) rocf Newberry MM

**ELLIOTT**
( 5 mo-1845   Obadiah to QM)

**GAUSE**
(11 mo-1843   James to QM)

**HADLEY**
12-11-1852   Mercy dis for having withdrawn from our Society

**HIATT**
( 9 mo-1846   John to QM)
( 3 mo-1847   Henry to QM)
6- 8-1850   Mary app comm
12-11-1852   Asenith (f Tomlinson) mcd dis

**HINSHAW**
( 2 mo-1844   Benjamin to QM)
( 5 mo-1844   Henry to QM)
( 6 mo-1846   Seth to QM)

**JESSOP**
(11 mo-1844   Tidemon to QM)
( 6 mo-1846   Jesse to QM)
8-10-1850   Lydia app comm
11- 9-1850   Rachel app Recorder

**JONES**
12-13-1851   William & ch gct Deer Creek MM

**MACY**
(11 mo-1843   William to QM)
( 2 mo-1844   Enoch to QM)
( 3 mo-1845   Calvin to QM)
( 3 mo-1846   Benedict to QM)
5-11-1850   Nancy app comm

**MEREDITH**
( 3 mo-1846   Jesse to QM)

**PEARSON**
( 8 mo-1845   Peter to QM)

**PLEAS**
12-11-1852   Priscilla dis for having withdrawn from our Society

**REYNARD**
( 3 mo-1850   Jacob to QM)

**ROBERTS**
12- 7-1853   Priscilla app overseer at Westfield PM

**SAINT**
( 3 mo-1846   Alpheus to QM)
6- 8-1850   Irene app comm

**SMALL**
9-14-1850   Hannah req to be rel from serving as Recorder

**SWAIN**
( 2 mo-1845   John to QM)
( 3 mo-1846   Lewis to QM)
8-14-1852   Nancy app comm

**STANFIELD**
11- 9-1853   Mary Ann (f Wright) mcd dis

**STRATTON**
(11 mo-1843   Jonathan D to QM)

**TOMLINSON**
12-11-1852   Lydia dis for having withdrawn from our Society
12-11-1852   Asenith Hiatt (f Tomlinson) mcd dis
9-11-1852   Martha Cook (f Tomlinson) rpt mcd.  11-13-1852 rpt now deceased

**WHITE**
(11 mo-1844   Jesse to QM)
6- 8-1850   Susannah app comm
8-10-1850   Mary app comm

**WICKERSHAM**
( 6 mo-1847   Caleb to QM)
6- 8-1850   Caroline dis

**WILSON**
( 9 mo-1847   Elias to QM)
5-11-1850   Rebecca app overseer in room of Abigail Hinshaw
9-14-1850   Michael & Rebecca & dts Esther & Rebecca gct Salem MM, IA

**WRIGHT**
( 2 mo-1844   John to QM)
(11 mo-1844   Jacob to QM)
( 5 mo-1845   Joel to QM)
( 3 mo-1848   Jesse to QM)
5-11-1850   Eliza M app overseer in room of Annis Hinshaw
11-13-1852   Catharine app comm
9- 7-1853   Moses T & w gct Deer Creek MM
11- 9-1853   Mary Ann Stanfield (f Wright) mcd dis
11- 9-1853   Abigail app Elder

## DUCK CREEK MONTHLY MEETING

### (Anti-slavery)

### MARRIAGE REGISTER

Jesse MEREDITH, of Spiceland, son of James & Mary
Luzina MACY, dt of William & Phebe, all of Henry County
    m 11 16 1843 at Elm Grove MH
Witnesses:

| | | |
|---|---|---|
| Phebe Macy | Anna H Macy | S K Scovel |
| Jesse White | Sarah Edgerton | Peter Pearson |
| Diana Macy | Ann Jessop | Enoch Macy |
| William Edgerton | Mary White | Walter Edgerton |
| Louisa Hiatt | Rebecca Edgerton | Wm Macy |
| Thaddeus Macy | Martha J White | Elias Jessop |


David WILSON, son of Michael & Rebecca
Elizabeth HIATT, dt of Charles & Mary (the former deceased) of Henry Co
    m 3 13 1844 at Duck Creek MH
Witnesses:

| | | |
|---|---|---|
| Benjamin Hinshaw | Thaddeus Macy | Phebe Willits |
| Henry Hiatt | Walter Edgerton | Rachel Gause |
| Seth Hinshaw | Michael Wilson | Ann M Pickering |
| Tidamon Jessop | Thomas W Hiatt | Hannah Hiatt |
| Jesse Right senr | Abigail Hinshaw | Rachel Hiatt |
| Solomon Cox | Nancy Wright | Anna Reece |
| James Gause | Annis Hinshaw | Nancy Macy |
| Obadiah Elliott | Mary Ellen Hinshaw | Jane Wilson |
| Jabez Hinshaw | Sarah Ann Saint | Esther Wilson |
| John Hiatt | Jemima A Wickersham | |
| | Hannah Jane Hinshaw | |


Thomas J MEREDITH, of Spiceland, son of James & Mary
Susannah MACY, dt of William & Phebe, all of Henry County
    m 6 19 1845 at Elm Grove MH
Witnesses:

| | | |
|---|---|---|
| William R Macy | Jesse B Jessop | Enoch Macy |
| Morris Jessop | Calvin Macy | Alfred H Macy |
| Jesse White | Elias Jessop | Rosanna Byers |
| David Jessop | Ezra Scovell | Mary Jane Byers |


William BENNETT of Clear Spring, son of John (deceased) & Catharine
Emaline WRIGHT, dt David & Catharine, all of Henry County
    m 7 16 1845 at Clear Spring MH
Witnesses:

| | | |
|---|---|---|
| M R Hull | John Wright | Abigail Wright |
| G B Rogers | Richard Modlin | Ann Tailor |
| Jacob Wright | Nancy Macy | Charity Compton |
| John T Hunnicutt | Ruth Rees | Sarah Hunnicutt |


Silas SMALL, of Rush County, son of Silas & Mary (both deceased)
Hannah Jane HINSHAW, dt of Seth & Abigail, of Henry County
    m 3 18 1846 at Duck Creek MH
Witnesses:

| | | |
|---|---|---|
| Benjamin Hinshaw | Elisha Branson | Phebe Willits |
| Saml F Schooley | Mary Ellen Branson | Susanna S Fentress |
| Obadiah Elliott | Enoch Macy | Mary C Pickering |
| Benjamin B Elliott | James Gause | Sarah Ann Saint |
| Seth H Elliott | Tidamon Jessop | Annis Hinshaw |
| Seth Hinshaw | Joel Wright | Nancy Macy |
| Abigail Hinshaw | Thomas H Mills | Mary Hiatt |
| Calvin Macy | Alpheus Saint | Mille Maria Hinshaw |
| Dianna Macy | Thaddeus Macy | |
| Henry Hiatt | Seth Wood | |

DUCK CREEK

Jesse B JESSOP, son of Elias & Ann
Catharine G MACY, dt of Enoch & Nancy, all of Henry County
    m 10 15 1846 at Elm Grove MH
Witnesses:
| | | |
|---|---|---|
| Susanna Jessop | Emaline Mundon | Tidamon Jessop |
| Phebe Macy | Jesse White | Wm T Parkhurst |
| Ruth Jessop | Mary White | Morris Jessop |
| Mary Jessop | Nancy Macy | Benedict Macy |
| Rachel Hiatt | Elias Jessop | Seth R Allee |
| Sarah Edgerton | Enoch Macy | Henry Hiatt |
| Susanna White | Elias R Wilson | Lilburn Macy |
| | William Macy | |


Nathan WRIGHT, son of John & Abigail
Lydia REECE, dt of Moses & Sarah (both deceased), of Henry County
    m 11 15 1848 at Clear Spring MH
Witnesses:
| | | |
|---|---|---|
| John Wright | John Swain | Mary Ann Wright |
| Solomon Reece | William Pressnell | Jemima W Osborn |
| William Bennett | Abigail Wright | Jemima Wright |
| John E Wright | Anna Wright | Marilla Wright |
| Seth Hinshaw | Emaline Bennett | Mary Ann McHaten |
| Benjamin Hinshaw | Lydia N Modlin | Annis Hinshaw |
| Moses Wright | Elizabeth Wright | Abigail Hinshaw |
| | Ruth Reece | Lydia M Reece |


Richard HUTSON, son of Daniel & Elizabeth
Marilla WRIGHT, dt of Jacob & Catherine, all of Henry County
    m ? 14 1849 at Clear Spring MH
Witnesses:
| | | |
|---|---|---|
| John E Wright | Nathan Compton | Nathan Wright |
| Richard Modlin | Benjamin Hinshaw | William Bennett |
| John Wright | Obadiah Elliott | John Hutson |
| Jacob Wright | Harry C Barton | James Hutson |
| Catharine Wright | Solomon Rees | Thomas Ellis |
| Ana Wright | Joel Wright | Anna Saunders |
| | Moses Wright | Eliza M Wright |
| | Rebecca Hasket | Mary Ann McHatten |
| | Sarah Haigt | Jemima Osborn |
| | Jane Hutson | |
| | Martha Hutson | |


Morris JESSOP, son of Tidamon & Lydia
Rachel HIATT, dt Henry (deceased) & Mary, all of Henry County
    m 11 14 1849 at Duck Creek MH
Witnesses:
| | | |
|---|---|---|
| Rebecca Edgerton | Priscilla Jessop | Seth Hinshaw |
| Rebecca Wilson | Lydia Jessop | Benjamin Hinshaw |
| Martha Jessop | Mary C Paxton | Michael Wilson |
| Joel Wright | Mary S Manlove | Seth R Allee |
| Obediah Elliott | Sarah J Macy | Jason W Macy |
| Catharine Macy | Jacob Reynard | Sarah Edgerton |
| Rebecca Macy | Emeline Munden | Esther Wilson |


Isaac W RAYLE, son of George & Ann
Rebecca MACY, dt William & Phebe, all of Henry County
    m 9 18 1851 at Elm Grove MH
Witnesses:
| | | |
|---|---|---|
| Walter Edgerton | Mary Hiat | Jason W Macy |
| Tidamon Jessop | William Macy | Seth Macy |
| Elias Jessop | Himelius Rayle | Asa P Rayle |
| Enoch Macy | | Phebe Macy |

Elijah C FELLOW, son of John & Abigail, of Newberry, Howard County
Susannah WHITE, dt of Jesse & Mary, of Henry County
    m 11 14 1855 at Duck Creek MH

Witnesses:
| | |
|---|---|
| Cintha E Fentress | Mary White |
| Elizabeth Macy | John P Pennington |
| Walter Edgerton | Enoch Macy |
| Annis Hinshaw | Joel Wright |
| William Edgerton | Tidamon Jessop |
| Sarah Edgerton | Jesse White |
| Sarah Jane Burket | Adison White |
| Rebecca Edgerton | Elisha Fellow |
| Gambrel White | Alfred White |
| Josiah White | Angeline Holoway |
| | Nancy Macy |
| | Jane E Hiatt |

# SPICELAND MONTHLY MEETING
## Henry County, Indiana

Spiceland Monthly Meeting was set-off from Duck Creek Monthly Meeting and first held on the 23rd of First Month 1833. The meetinghouse is located in the village of Spiceland.

Richard P. Ratliff tells the story well of **The Quakers of Spiceland, Henry County, Indiana – A History of Spiceland Friends Meeting, 1828-1968.** (Newcastle: 1968).

When Spiceland was set-off it was constituted of members residing on the east side of Blue River. There was some question among Friends in the vicinity of Knightstown as which monthly meeting they chose to be attached to. In Fourth month a committee reported that *"Friends on the west side of Blue River wish to be considered members of Duck Creek; except Jehu Stewart and Barnabas Springer, who have a choice of belonging to Spiceland."*

In 1835 *"Friends in the lower settlement of Spiceland and Duck Creek preparatives request the privilege of holding a meeting for worship and a preparative . . ."* These were the same Friends on both sides of Blue River above Knightstown. First month 1836 Elm Grove was established by both Spiceland and Duck Creek Monthly Meetings and the membership was attached to Spiceland.

In 1846 **Raysville** was established as a meeting for worship and a preparative and was set-off as a monthly meeting in 1857.

Spiceland was widely known because of the Spiceland Academy.

### Monthly Meeting Records

The volumes listed below are in the vault of the Indiana Yearly Meetinghouse in Richmond. These records have been microfilmed. The material searched for this publication is marked (*).

Men's Minutes
\* 1-23-1833 : 10-23-1844
\*11-20-1844 : 12- 2-1865 :
\* 1- 6-1866 : 1- 6-1883 (meetings held jointly after 10-14-1876)

Women's Minutes
\*1-23-1833 : 3-22-1854
\*4-19-1854 : 5- 2-1874

Joint Minutes
\*2-3-1883 : 12-4-1897
\*1-1-1898 : 12-1-1921 [1]

\* 1 Volume Births and Deaths
\* 3 Volumes Membership Records
\* 1 Volume Removal Certificates

1. Two marriage records are recorded in back of this volume.
No Marriage Register was located. Jay in 1900 lists a marriage register in his inventory, but then he notes *"lost by fire."*

SPICELAND MONTHLY MEETING

BIRTH & DEATH RECORD

ABSHIRE
Lydia (Pence)   b 2-18-1828 Rockingham, Va  dt H & S
                Pence
Ch:  Rebecca    b 4-mO-1846  Delaware Co, Ind

ADAMS
(Stephen)
Amanda (Farley? or Farlow?)  b 12- 3-1852 in Iowa
            dt John & Jane
Ch:  Hettie     b 3-14-1876

ADDISON
(Alonzo)
    m ( 9- 6-1891)  Henry Co, Ind
Jennie (Reese)  b 1-26-1868  Guilford Co, N Car
        dt Henry & Mary (Carmack)

Levi M          d 4-30-1911
Hannah E (Pike)  dt Ephraim & Beulah
Ch:  Maude A    b 2-19-1879  in Rush Co, Ind
    (m 8-25-1897, Henry Co, Ind to John Reese)

ALBERTSON
Benjamin    b 7-21-1845  s William B & Mary (Davis)
Lenora
Ch:  Dumont     b 9- 7-1870
     Lena       b 12-27-1876  Dunreith, Ind

Jordan      b 3- 2-1802  Perquimans Co, N C  d 1-21-1841
        s Francis & Caroline (Bell)
Martha N (Elliott)  b 9- 8-1813  dt James & Sarah (Toms)
Ch:  Caroline   b 4- 6-1840   d 2-23-1841
                bur Raysville Mtg

William B   b 9- 4-1814  Piney Woods MM, N C
            d 10-19-1858  bur Spiceland, Ind
    m 1st
Mary (Davis)  b 11- 1-1823  Henry Co, Ind  dt Nathan & Lydia
    (Cleaver)  d 9-27-1849  Spiceland, Ind
Ch:  Nathan D   b 7- 4-1842  Madison Co, Ind
     Eli        b 10-22-1843  d 9- 3-1858
                Spiceland, Ind
     Benjamin   b 7-21-1845
     Lydia Ann  b 6-12-1847  d 8-10-1848
                Spiceland, Ind
    m 2nd
Rebecca (Larrance)  b 10-14-1826  dt Peter & Sarah (Hinshaw)
Ch:  Josiah     b 8- 7-1856  Spiceland MM, Ind
     Sarah      b 12-31-1857

ALDRICH
Charles
    m (12-29-1891)
Rilla (Taylor)  b 4-11-1868  dt Milton & Emily (Gordon)

ALLEN
Daniel C    b 2-18-1820  Holly Spring MM, N Car
            s Harmon & Nancy (Clark)
    m 1st
Susannah (Sheridan)  b 1-15-1821  Clinton Co, Ohio
        dt John & Margaret (Osborn)  d 9- 3-1845
        bur Spiceland Mtg, Ind
Ch:  John W         b 8- 3-1843  Spiceland Mtg, Ind
     Susan Margaret b 8-20-1845  d 11- 8-1845
    twins Anna Mariah )  b 8-20-1845  d 9- 7-1845
    m 2nd
Elizabeth (Dicks)  b 11-14-1819  Guilford Co, N Car
        dt Job & Hannah (White)  d 10-11-1851  bur Spiceland
        Mtg, Ind
Ch:  Narcissa   b 8-11-1848  d age 3 days
                bur Spiceland Mtg, Ind
     Charles    b 6-13-1849
     Job D      b 7-19-1851
    m 3rd (1854  Springfield MM, Ohio)
Elizabeth (Hadley) of Springfield MM, Ohio

Harman jr   s Harman & Nancy (Clark)
    m 1st
Julianna (Wilson)  b 7- 7-1831  Decatur Co, Ind
        dt Amasa & Elizabeth  d 8-18-1856  bur Spiceland
                                            MM, Ind

Ch:  Elizabeth Ann  b 10-24-1849
     Mary Emma      b 11- 8-1852  d 11-17-1852
                    bur Spiceland, Ind
     Frank Edgar    b 12-10-1853
     Enos P         b 7-25-1856  d 8- 7-1856
                    bur Spiceland, Ind
    m 2nd (1858)
Lydia M (King)  b 7- 6-1833  dt Joseph & Mary (Morris)
        of Morgan Co, Ohio
Ch:  Lineas

Jesse P     b 2- 6-1877  Hancock Co, Ind  s John E & Lydia
    m (9- 5-1900 Henry Co, Ind)
Irene (Deem)  b 5-22-1878  Henry Co, Ind dt Sedley &
        Elizabeth (Hodson)

John Philander      s Harmon & Nancy (Clark)
    m (1843)
Rachel (Boon)  b 3- 4-1821  Springfield MM, N Car
        dt Driver & Anna (Kersey)
Ch:  Naomi J    b - - - -
     Gulielma   b 11- 4-1845

Joseph M    b 10-16-1822  Holly Spring MM N Car
        s Harmon & Nancy (Clark)
Charity W (Kersey)  b 8-20-1822  Guilford Co, N Car
        dt William & Rachel (Hiatt)
Ch:  William K  b 8-13-1846  d 12-12-1853
                bur Spiceland, Ind
     Charles F  b 5-10-1849
     Ann Eliza  b 9-20-1851
     Emma Semira b 8-25-1853

Nathan F    b 2-17-1839     s John D & Letitia
Kizzie (Milligan)

ALLISON
Frank       b 6-20-1862  s Leonadas & Marietta
    m (10-13-1894 Henry Co, Ind)
Cora (Winkler)  b 3-27-1874  Franklin, Ind  dt John &
                                            Margaret
Ch:  Nora Leona    b 5-26-1895  Ogden, Ind
     Eva Maretta   b 1-10-1897
     Roy           b 11-23-1899
     Maggie Marie  b 4- 4-1902

AMICK
Charles
    m (12-30-1883)
Mecia (Scott)  b 5- 5-1861  dt Benjamin & Martha

ANDERSON
Luther
    m ( 1-13-1883)
Lavina (Hodson)  b 5-16-1861  dt John B & Huldah (Hozier)

ANTRIM
James Clarkson  b 9-10-1844  s James P & Mary (Beard)
    m (5-21-1888 Henry Co, Ind)
Hattie L (Pierce) Carson, wid, dt James & Christin (Perry)
     Pierce         b 10-12-1854
Ch:  Mary Christina b 9-12-1892
     Earl P         b 10-22-1896

James P     b 2- 5-1800  N J  d 2-17-1873  bur Spiceland,
        Ind  s Levi & Ann of Chesterfield MM, (Burlington) N J
Mary (Beard)  b 2-12-1810  Randolph Co, N Car
        dt Thomas & Elizabeth
Ch:  Louisa         b 10- 8-1829  Hagerstown, Ind
     John Beard     b 11-25-1833
     Thomas Elwood  b 4-11-1838  d 2- 6-1859
     Eli Wright     b 8- 7-1840  d 8-20-1845
                    bur Spiceland, Ind
     James Clarkson b 9-10-1844

APPLEGATE
Ernest      b 9-20-1875  Fayette Co, Ind
Mary Emma   b 6-24-1876  Wayne Co, Ind
Ch:  Philip     b 1- 6-1905
     Robert     b - - - - - -

Nellie (Hodson)  dt William & Amanda (Scoville)
        b 6-20-1871  Henry Co, Ind  m 11-23-1904  Henry Co,
        Ind to - - - - Applegate

SPICELAND

```
APPLEGATE (Cont)
Samuel Clifford   b 4-19-1880  Fayette Co, Ind
       s Theodore & Mary (Clifford)
       m ( 9-28-1908  Henry Co, Ind)
Elsie (Bell)  b 9-28-1885  Rush Co, Ind    d 7-23-1913
       dt Archibald & Francis (Working)
Ch:    Kenneth S         b 7-27-1910

Theodore
Mary (Clifford)
Ch:    Leota May         b 4- 4-1879  Connersville, Ind
       Samuel Clifford   b 4-19-1880  Fayette Co, Ind
       Mary Ethel        b 7-mo-1881

Theodore
       m (11-23-1904  Henry Co, Ind)
Nellie G (Hodson)  b 6-20-1871  dt William & Amanda
                                            (Scoville)

ARNETT
Milton      b 2- 8-1838  s Willis & 2nd w Nancy (Scott)
                              Hockett Arnett
       mcd 1862  New Garden Mtg, Ind
Nancy L
Ch:    Willis
       Josephine E
       Mattie M
       Lola E
       Alice G

ATHERTON
Chester B
       m (11-28-1879)
Rachel Emma (Bufkin)  b 11-27-1861  dt John & Abigail
                                              (Ellis)

BAILEY
George Dillwyn  b 10-28-1845  Flushing Mtg, Ohio
       d 10-mO-1908  Whitewater MM, Ind  s Jesse & Lydia
       m 1st (8-31-1896)                     (Townsend)
Susan (Fussel) Bower, wid, dt of Morris & Sarah
       b 4- 6-1861  Chester Springs, Pa  d 10- 3-1905
       bur Circle Grove Cemetery, Spiceland, Ind
       (George D Bailey was a doctor)

Herbert T    b 6- 3-1863  s J Sydenham & Phebe W (Hoge)
       m (6- 2-1897  Henry Co, Ind)
Myrta (Barnard)  b 11- 4-1871  Clinton Co, Ohio
       dt Thomas & Jane (Hoskins)
Ch:    H Stanton         b 7-24-1907

(Jesse of Pa & Flushing MM, Ohio was s of Joseph &
       Elizabeth)      (m Middleton MM, Ohio)
(Lydia (Townsend) dt Joseph & Sinah)
Ch:    who came to Spiceland MM, Ind:
       Rachel S          b 1-21-1828
       Joseph Sydenham   b 2-10-1830
       Hannah Lavina     b 4- 6-1837
       John Quincy       b 7-23-1842
       George Dillwyn    b 10-28-1845

John Quincy  b 7-23-1842  Flushing Mm, Ohio
       s Jesse & Lydia (Townsend)
       m (5-19-1880)
Mary Anice (Wilson)  b 2-12-1856  dt William W & Caroline
Ch:    Mary              b 4- 3-1881
       Jesse             b 6-19-1883

Joseph Sydenham  b 2-10-1830  Flushing MM, Ohio
       s Jesse & Lydia (Townsend)
       m ( 9- 1-1859  Belmont Co, Ohio)
Phebe W (Hoge)  b 11- 2-1840  Flushing MM, Ohio
       dt Elisha & Lydia E (Vanpelt)
Ch:    Arthur H          b 12- 3-1860  Belmont Co, Ohio
       d 2- 1-1889  bur Spiceland, Ind
       Herbert T         b 6- 3-1863   Belmont Co, Ohio
       Lydia L           b 8-26-1867   Harrison Co, Ohio
       Jesse G           b 4-17-1872   Freeport, Ohio

BAKER
Lewis
       m  (5-23-1901  Henry Co, Ind)
Caroline (Cook)  b 1-28-1872  dt Robert & Martha (Nixon)
```

```
BALDWIN
Elwood       b 11-25-1814  New Garden MM, N Car
       s Isaiah & Elizabeth (Jessop)
Phebe (Scott)  b 10-29-1816  dt John & Rachel
Ch:    Franklin          b 12-25-1836  Henry Co, Ind
       Harriet           b 7-22-1838   d 7- 8-1839
                         bur Spiceland Mtg, Ind
       Patsey            b 4- 5-1840
       William           b 11-22-1841  d 10-29-1842
                         bur Spiceland Mtg, Ind
       Jonathan          b 11-20-1842
       Hannah            b 5-25-1844   d 7-20-1845
                         bur Spiceland Mtg, Ind
       Stephen S         b 2-13-1846
       Betsey            b 7-24-1847
       John S            b 5-15-1851
       Rachel            b 12- 9-1854

Franklin A   b 12-25-1835  at Spiceland, Ind  d 4-12-1917
       s Elwood & Phoebe (Scott)
       m 1st (5-31-1853)
Martha (Hodson)
Ch:    Lewis C           b 9- 7-1856
       m 2nd (12-26-1857
Mary Ann (Hodson) Macy, wid,  dt John & Elizabeth Hodson
       b 5-22-1830  Iowa            d 2- 4-1898
Ch:    Phebe H           b 7-27-1861
       Elizabeth         b 1-15-1864  Spiceland, Ind
       Flora A           b 9-14-1867  Tipton Co, Ind
       Elwood L          b 2- 1-1870  Spiceland, Ind
       m 3rd (6- 6-1904  Grant Co, Ind)
Julia A (Walker)  b 12-22-1838  Adams Co, Pa
       dt Isaac & Rebecca of Adams Co, Pa

Isaiah       b 2- 9-1789  N Car  d 5-14-1858 bur Spiceland
             Mtg  s Uriah & Hannah (Hunt)
       m 1st
Elizabeth (Jessop)  b 4-30-1790  Stokes Co, N Car
       d 7-30-1823  bur West Grove Mtg, Ind
       dt William & Mary
Ch:    William           b 12-22-1812 N Car  d 6-14-1833
                         bur Spiceland Mtg
       Ellwood           b 11-25-1814
       Louisa            b 10-12-1816
       Uriah             b 6-28-1818
       Hannah            b 7-14-1820
       Mary              b 1-16-1822  Ind
       m 2nd
Elizabeth (Bond)  b 1-21-1795  N Car  d 1-28-1841
       bur Spiceland  dt Samuel & Elizabeth
Ch:    Betsy             b 2-23-1826  Ind
       Ann               b 11-11-1827
       Eunice            b 8-20-1831
       Rachel            b 1-25-1834

(Jesse  s William & Elizabeth of New Garden MM, N Car)
       (b 1-26-1759)  (d prior to 1838)
       (m 1st 12-15-1779  Deep River MM, N Car)
(Hannah (Thornborough) dt Henry & Rachel, b 10-15-1760)
       (probably d 1818 Clear Creek MM, Ohio)
       (m 2nd 10-21-1820  Clear Creek MM, Ohio)
(Catherine (Sexton) dt Meschack & Hannah) (who d White-
       water MM, Ind 10-23-1823  bur Center, worship Mtg,
       (m 3rd 7- 7-1825  Milford MM, Ind)            Ind)
Miriam (Macy)  b 4-21-1781  New Garden MM, N Car
       d 9- 1-1851  bur Elm Grove Mtg, Ind  dt Enoch &
       Anna (Macy) Macy
       (Miriam was a sister to Stephen Macy of Spiceland
       MM, Ind)

Stephen S  b 2-18-1846  s Elwood & Phebe (Scott)
       m (9-11-1867)
Mary E (Wilson)  b 7-15-1841  dt Michael & Delilah from
       Greensboro, N Car
Ch:    William           b 5- 7-1868
       Delilah           b 12-23-1869
       Michael E         b 4-15-1871
       Hannah Ann        b 3- 2-1874
       Stephen Scott     b 4-19-1877
       John Richard      b 2-10-1880
```

# SPICELAND

## BALES - BEALS
John H      b 8-10-1810 New Garden MM, N Car  
     s Jesse & Anna  
Ann (Hasket) b 4- 2-1810 Warren Co, Ohio   dt Thomas & Ann  
Ch: Emily      b 12-16-1832 Henry Co, Ind  
     d 4-24-1834  
    Minerva     b 5- 8-1835   d 7-27-1837  
    Oliver H     b 9- 3-1837  
    Melissa Ann     b 7-10-1841  
    Mary     b 3-22-1843  
    Louisa     b 8-16-1846  
    Samira     b 5-11-1849  
    Jesse     b 3-23-1851  

Oliver H     b 1- 3-1837 Henry Co, Ind   s John & Ann (Hasket)  
   m (9-26-1860) Henry Co, Ind  
Martha (Hunt) b 1-14-1835 Henry Co, Ind   dt Joseph A & Ann (Gause)  

## BALLARD
Addie     b 3- 5-1892 Henry Co, Ind   dt Peyton E & Jane (Spell)  

Jesse F     b 10-10-1810   s William & Phebe  
Mary (Arnold) b 12-28-1816   dt William & Celia  
Ch: (to Spiceland with parents)  
    Loretta C     b 10-10-1850  
    Jeremiah M     b 8-10-1852  

## BALLENGER
Charles W     b 9-18-1858 Henry Co, Ind   s Nathan & Margaret (Hubbard)  
   m (6- 2-1897 Marion Co, Ind)  
Florence (Porch) b 12- 6-1866 Henry Co, Ind   dt Albert & Phoebe (Hiatt)  

Henry     b 1- 9-1772   d 11-19-1865 Elm Grove Mtg, Ind  
Rebecca (Hunt)     b 9-28-1779 New Garden MM, N C  
   d 11-19-1872 Spiceland Mtg, Ind   dt Jacob & Hannah (Brittan)  

Nathan H     b 2-13-1823   d 11-12-1905 bur old cemetery  
     at Spiceland Mtg, Ind   s Henry & Rebecca (Hunt)  
   m 1st (11-28-1849)  
Margaret (Hubbard) b 8- 3-1831   d 8-26-1880 bur old  
    cemetery at Spiceland Mtg, Ind   dt Richard & Sarah  
Ch: Mary V     b 9- 8-1850  
    Oliver H     b 3-18-1853   d 7- 1-1876  
     bur old cemetery, Spiceland Mtg, Ind  
    Emma     b 9- 5-1856  
    Charles W     b 9-18-1858  
    Albert     b 5- 6-1861  
    Myrtilla R     b 1-30-1868  
    Walter P     b 11-25-1871   d 1-31-1902  
     bur Guffey, Colorado  
    Edward L S     b 11-20-1876  
   m 2nd (11- 4-1885)  
Martha (Morris) b 5-16-1848 Howard Co, Ind  
    dt Jesse & Sarah (Lamb)  
Ch: Margaret H     b 1-31-1891 Henry Co, Ind  

## BARNARD
Elwood     b 10- 1-1860 Eden, Hancock Co, Ind  
    s Robert Y & Polly  
   m (10-18-1883) Henry Co, Ind  
Ola (Gordon) b 11-27-1863 Henry Co, Ind   dt Micajah C & Sarah (Wright)  
Ch: Olive     b 9-15-1886 Henry Co, Ind  
    Helen     b 7- 4-1888 Hancock Co, Ind  
    Anna     b 3- 9-1892  
    Robert     1893  

Malinda     b 11-19-1822 Union Co, Ind   d 8- 7-1910  
    dt William & Matilda  

William O  
   m (1- 1-1878)  
Mary V (Ballenger) b 9- 8-1850   dt Nathan & Margaret (Hubbard)  

## BARNS
Edith     b 11- 1-1888 Rochester, N Y   dt W F & A C  

## BARRETT
Lawrence  
   m (6-mo-1897)  
Alice (Hiatt) b 1-24-1871   dt Josiah & Rhoda (Sheridan)  

## BASSETT
Minnie     b 8-25-1866 at Mt Pleasant, Ohio   dt Stephen & Amanda  

## BAYSE
Wilson  
   m (4- 6-1876) Henry Co, Ind  
Mary Ellen (Test) b 12- 1-1856 Wayne Co, Ind   dt Josiah, decd & Miriam (Dennis)  
Ch: Ethaline     b - - - - -  
    Miriam O     b 3-16-1881 Henry Co, Ind  
    Lorna     b 10- 1-1887  
    Herman L     b 8- 6-1891  
    Howard H     b 10-10-1892  

## BEARD
Clarence  
   m (1911)  
Addie (Symons) b 1-27-1872   dt Seth C & Lizzie (Morris)  

## BECKETT
George W     b 2-17-1854 Watseka, Ill   d 1919  
    s James & Susanna  
   m (4-26-1879) Henry Co, Ind  
Mattie (Mary) B (Pleas) b 2-29-1859 Lake Co, Ind  
    dt Elwood & Sarah Ann (Griffin)  
Ch: Nellie L     b 9-27-1881 Dunreith, Ind  
    Mable Clare     b - - - - -  

## BEEMAN - BEAMAN
(James)  
Maria (Jackson) b 2-4-1819 Northampton Co, (Rich Square MM N Car)  
    dt John & Hester (- - -)  
Ch: Sarah Jane     b 12- 9-1838 Hertford Co, N Car  
    Mary Ann     b 5-11-1841 Northampton Co, N Car  
    Margaret Isabella     b 7- 3-1843  
    Harriet Edney     b 9-13-1845  
    William Penn     b 7-22-1848 Clinton Co, Ohio  
    Martha Olivia     b 5-11-1851 Spiceland, Ind  

## BEESON
David M     b 7-28-1850 Henry Co, Ind   s Benjamin & Rebecca  
    d 1917  
   m (11-15-1877)  
E Adaline (Lemmens) b 1-15-1858 Henry Co, Ind   d 5- 3-1901  
    dt J F & Elizabeth  
Ch: Sylvia May     b 9-13-1878  
    Josie A     b 2- 1-1882 Henry Co, Ind  
    Walter H     b 3-10-1884  

Walter H     b 3-10-1884   s David M & E Adaline (Lemmens)  
   m (1903) Henry Co, Ind  
Estella (James) b 10-26-1885 Henry Co, Ind   dt Arthur & Phebe (Garner)  
Ch: Margarette     b 3-16-1907  
    James Fred     b 11- 9-1908   d 1- 3-1909  

## BELL
Archibald  
   m (8-22-1871) Rush Co, Ind  
Francis H (Working) b 11-22-1857 Fayette Co, Ind  
    dt Samuel & Malinda (Irvin)  
Ch: Odessa     b 3-17-1876 Rushville, Ind  
    Ira     b 3- 9-1882 Sexton, Ind  
    Elsie B     b 9-28-1885 Rush Co, Ind  

Jesse     b 1-14-1846 Hopewell Mtg, Ind   s Thomas & Hannah (Mendenhall)  
   m (9-23-1886)  
S Emma (Newby) b 12-22-1858 Hopewell Mtg, Ind   d 3-18-1915  
    dt Albert & Caroline (Hubbard)  
Ch: Irene     b 8- 2-1888 Henry Co, Ind  
    Dorothy     b 8- 8-1893  
    Richard     b 12- 6-1900   d 3-19-1902  

John     b 3-31-1870 Dublin, Ind   s Jesse & Elizabeth  

Thomas  
Hannah (Mendenhall)

SPICELAND

BELL (Cont)
Ch: of Thomas & Hannah
  Jesse        b 1-14-1846
  Lydia G      b 7- 6-1848  Wayne Co, Ind  d 1924
  Enos T       b 7-18-1853  Wayne Co, Ind
               d 2-10-1914

BENNETT
Thomas       b 11- 5-1863  Henry Co, Ind  s John J &
   m (9- 8-1886 Rush Co, Ind)           Emmaline
Mary (Smear) b 9- 7-1866  Rush Co, Ind  dt John & Nancy M

BERRY
Andrew J     b 10- 2-1839  Mason Co, Ky  s James M & Juliann
Mary
Ch:  Minnie Pearl    b 1-mo-1869  Henry Co, Ind

BIRD
George
   m (11-14-1894)
Christie (Deem) b 11-17-1868 Spiceland, Ind  dt Sedley
                H & Elizabeth (Hodson)

BOGUE
Alfred       b 3- 7-1808  d 12-25-1871 bur Spiceland Mtg
             s Josiah & Elizabeth of N Car
   m 1st (1-mo-1830 Westfield MM, Ohio)
Keziah (Stubbs)  b 5- 9-1804  d 6-27-1836 bur Spiceland
             dt John & Jane (Jones)
Ch:  Elizabeth W    b 10-16-1830  Ohio
     Jane J         b 1-29-1832
     Josiah P       b 11- 3-1833  Ind
   m 2nd (12-23-1840 Henry Co, Ind)
Charity (Bogue)  b 9-11-1817 Wayne Co, N Car  d 9-10-1910
             dt Benjamin & Leah (Parker)
Ch:  Calvin W       b 9-30-1840
     Anna Emily     b 1-23-1842
     Marietta       b 8-21-1844
     Charles        b 6-26-1848
     Emira G        b 8- 3-1851
     Ignatius T     b 11-17-1855  d 1- 1-1859
                    bur Spiceland, Ind
     Sarah Ellen    b 7-31-1857
     Harriett       b 3- 4-1861

Alfred       b 4- 2-1871  Henry Co, Ind  s Josiah & Sibbie
   m (2- 6-1893 Henry Co, Ind)         J (Allen)
Bessie H (Kirk) b 12- 4-1874 Belmont Co, Ohio  dt Kersey
                              & Mary L (Wilson)
Ch:  Josiah P       b 12-23-1893  Henry Co, Ind
     Edgar Kirk     b 5- 5-1895

Anson
   m ( 5- 5-1887)
Minnie C (Swain) b 8-12-1867  dt Thomas M & Julia E
                              (Swain) Swain

Calvin       b 9-30-1840  s Alfred & Charity (Bogue)
Rachel (Pearson) dt Isaac & Rachel, both decd

John S       b 7-30-1835  Henry Co, Ind  d 4-26-1912
             s Alfred & Keziah (Stubbs), decd
   m (10-mo-1887) Henry Co, Ind
Sarah (Smiley) Edwards, wid of Benjamin Edwards, dt John
       & Elizabeth (Jackson) Smiley  b 4- 20-1849
                                     Hancock Co, Ind

Joseph E     b 2- 6-1837  d 3-10-1879 bur Spiceland, Ind
             s Charles W & Sarah
Martha Emily (Allen)  b 3- 9-1842  dt Harmon & Nancy Ann
                      (Clark) of Rush Co, Ind
Ch:  Oscar A        b 12-21-1860  d 4- 9-1865
                    bur Spiceland, Ind
     Carlos         b 2-18-1863  d 3-17-1865
     E Josephine    b 6-11-1869

Josiah       b 3-16-1772  N Car  d 7- 6-1848 bur Spiceland,
             s Joseph & Mary (Newby)                  Ind
Elizabeth (Wells) b 5- 9-1781  dt Joseph & Mary
Ch:  Alfred         b 3- 7-1808
     Charles        b 8-11-1810
     John           b 7-22-1814 Ohio  d 11-17-1839
                    bur Spiceland, Ind

Josiah P     b 11- 3-1833  d 11-21-1894  s Alfred & Keziah
   m ( 1- 1-1858 Henry Co, Ind)    (Stubbs), decd
Sibbie J (Allen)  b 2-16-1836  d 6-18-1908
             dt Harmon & Nancy (Clark) of Walnut Ridge Mtg,
                                                      Ind
Ch:  Cordelia       b 11-30-1861  Spiceland
     Oneda          b 7-29-1864
     Anna H         b 4- 4-1867
     Alfred         b 4- 2-1871
     Oscar H        b 5-15-1873

Oscar H      b 5-15-1873  s Josiah & Sibbie J (Allen)
   m (9-10-1903 Henry Co, Ind)
Cora P (Hodson)  b 1-29-1877  dt Albert & Mary E (Hiatt)

BOND
Amer         b 9-22-1805  N Car  d - - - -? bur Spiceland Mtg,
             s Thomas & Mary (Nations)                Ind
Mary (Piggott)  b 4-30-1808  N Car  d 11- 9-1858 bur
             Spiceland Mtg, Ind  dt Joseph & Priscilla (Wickersham)
Ch:  Priscilla      b 11- 1-1828  Ind
     Jonathan       b 11- 4-1831  d 12-21-1833
                    bur Spiceland, Ind
     Thomas         b 5-12-1834
     Caleb W        b 10- 3-1836
     Sarah Ann      b 8-30-1839  d 10-27-1858
                    bur Spiceland, Ind
     Mary Jane      b 9-27-1841
     Martha         b 6-27-1844
     Mahlen         b 11-30-1851
     Rhoda S        b 1-19-1853  d 5-21-1854
                    bur Spiceland, Ind

Jesse        b 10- 7-1808  Wayne Co, Ind  d 4-21-1881
             bur Spiceland, Ind  s Jesse Sr & Anna
   m 1st
Anna (Cook)
Ch:  Calvin         b 4-22-1830  Ind
     Mahala         b 7-31-1832  Ind
     William        b 10-13-1834
     Lydia          b 9- 1-1837  d 10-19-1858
                    bur Spiceland, Ind
   m 2nd
Delana (Stanley) Stanley, a wid  dt of John & Elizabeth
             b 5- 2-1810                        Stanley
             d 3-11-1883  bur Circle Grove Cemetery, Spiceland

John         b         N Car  s William, decd & Abigail (Albertson)
             who became the w of Thomas Moore, a widower,
             in 1796
   m 1st ( 4- 4-1807 Perquimans MM, N Car)
Mary (Lamb)
Ch:  Lavina         b - - - -  d 9-22-1835
                    bur Whitewater Mtg, Ind
   m 2nd (10-15-1817 Lick Creek MM, Ind)
Rebecca (Holoday)  b 12-23-1795  (d ca 1834 Spiceland Mtg)
             dt Robert, decd & Hannah (Newlin)
Ch:  Hannah         b - - - -
     Abigail
     Jacob
     William
     Elias A
     Aaron
     Sarah
     Anna
   m 3rd ( 2- 3-1836 Milford MM, Ind)
Mary (Hodgson) Stanbrough, wid of James  dt Hur &
             Elizabeth (Thornbrugh) decd
             b 7- 2-1790  New Garden MM, N Car

BOON - BOONE
Charles      b 8-29-1801  Dauphin Co, N Car  d 12- 4-1878
             bur Spiceland, Ind  s John & Dorcas

Driver       b 9- 5-1795  Dauphin Co, N Car  d 8-20-1881
             Spiceland, Ind  s John & Dorcas
   m 1st (4-22-1819 Springfield MM, N Car)
Anna (Kersey)  b 6-17-1802  N Car  d 9-12-1837
             Spiceland, Ind  dt William & Rachel (Hiatt)
Ch:  Anslem         b 10- 6-1819 N Car
                    d 12- 5-1819 Guilford Co, N Car
     Rachel H       b 3- 4-1821
     Rhoda C        b 3-26-1823  d 9-18-1839
                    bur Spiceland Mtg

SPICELAND

227

BOON - BOONE (Cont)
Ch: of Driver & Anna (Cont)
    Rebecca U         b 11-13-1824   Ind
    Samson           b 11-28-1826
    Irena H          b 12-12-1828
    Dorcas           b 10-26-1832
    Betsy Ann       b 12- 2-1834
   m 2nd
Elizabeth (Cooper) Gause, wid of Richard,  dt Jonathan &
    Esther Cooper  b 4- 6-1820  Summerville, Ohio
Ch:  Anna Jane      b 3- 7-1845  d 8-20-1846
                     bur Spiceland
    Christenia     b 2-18-1847
    Richard        b 9- 9-1849
    Jonathan       b 8-14-1852
    John William   b 1- 5-1855  d 7-22-1856
                     bur Spiceland

(John of Springfield MM, N Car & Cherry Grove MM, Ind)
Dorcas (- - - -)  b 4-12-1765 N Car  d 1-21-1846
     bur Spiceland Mtg
Ch:  Driver         b 9-15-1795  N Car
    John           b - - - - -
    Charles        b 8-29-1801
    Elizabeth      b 11-28-1803  d 9- 5-1870
    Stephen        b 2-15-1806   d 7-30-1840
                     bur Spiceland
    Dorcas          b 5-22-1808   d 11-19-1875
                     bur Spiceland

Richard G  b 9- 9-1849  s Driver & Elizabeth (Cooper)
   m (7-23-1874)               Gause Boone
Mary E (Stanley)  b 7-10-1853 Lewisville, Ind  dt Elwood
                             & Martha
Ch:  Chesire L      b 9- 7-1875  Lewisville, Ind
    Mabel G        b 11-29-1877  Frankfort, Ind
    Herbert S      b 8- 7-1881

BOREN
Lillie V  b 2-21-1865  dt Franklin & Sarah Jane

BOWEN
Thomas S  b 1- 1-1863  Ireland  s Thomas Sr & Anna
   m (3-11-1884 Henry Co, Ind)
Sarah M (Allison)  b 9- 8-1867  Ogden, Ind  dt Leonard L
                              & Marietta
Ch:  Violet          b 11-26-1889  Hamilton Co, Ind

BOWER
(Thomas C) (a doctor)   m (1882)
Susan (Fussell)  b 4- 6-1861  Chester Springs, Pa
   dt Morris & Sarrah
Ch:  Chester    b 7- 3-1883  Chester Co, Pa  d 1907
    (after the death of Thomas Bower, Susan m 2nd,
    8-31-1896 to Dr. George D Bailey)

BOWLES
John    m (3-12-1879
   Susan (Johnson)  dt Evan & Betsey A of Henry Co, Ind

BOWMAN
Robert B  b 9-11-1842  Henry Co, Ind  s Richard & Phebe
   m (9- 7-1861)
Sarah A (Risk)  b 7-2-1837 Augusta Co, Va  dt John & Martha
Ch:  Eva            b 7- 9-1862  Henry Co, Ind
    Arthur D       b 4-16-1871
    Oscar L        b 10-30-1872

BRANSON
(John)  m (1843)
Hannah (Holloway)  b 3-19-1808  Flushing MM, Ohio
  d 8-13-1879 bur Spiceland, Ind  dt Joseph & Ellinor

BRAZINGTON
Laura Ann  b 11-16-1850  Rush Co, Ind  d 9- 7-1851
   dt Joseph S & Gulielma (Davis)

Samuel    b 8-16-1797  New Jersey
Lydia (- - - -)  dt Isaac & Rebecca (Andrews) b 10- 8-1798
   Upper Eversham MM, N J
Ch:  Joseph S       b 6-16-1825
    William A      b 9-22-1828  Haddonfield, N J
    Samuel jr      b 12-31-1831  Everham, N J
    Ann           b 8-31-1834  Whitewater MM, Ind
    David         b 5- 6-1837  Duck Creek MM, Ind
    Eli           b 4- 6-1839  Spiceland MM, Ind

BREWER
(Daniel)
   m (8- 3-1882 Henry Co, Ind)
Elizabeth Ann (Baldwin)  b 1-15-1864  Hamilton Co, Ind
   dt Frank & Mary Ann (Hodson) Macy Baldwin

Horace
   m (6-29-1898)
Annie G (Kirk)  b 12- 9-1876  Belmont Co, Ohio  dt Kersey
                         & Mary L (Wilson)

Ira W    b 5-20-1879  s John W & Emily S (Carr)
   m (11- 7-1900 Henry Co, Ind)
Lydia (Poe)

(John  s Elias & Mary of Pa & Ohio) (b 9-mo-1796)
   (d 6- 5-1847 bur Whitewater Mtg, Ind)
   (mcd 1st ca 1821 in Ohio)
- - - -?  (wife may have died at Blue River Mtg, Ind)
   (m 2nd ca 1833 probably at Blue River Mtg)
Rachel (Jessop)   d ca (prior to 1836)
   (mcd 3rd in Ohio ca 1837)
Sarah (- - - -)  (after the death of John Brewer, Sarah
   m Samuel Cox & removed from Whitewater Mtg to West
   Grove Mtg)
Ch:  (by 1st wife)
    Elizabeth
    Rachel
    William H
    Elias
Ch:  (3rd wife)
    Mary
    Morris W        b - - - -  Spiceland Mtg
    (Jason W )
    (Susanna         b 2-22-1843  Whitewater Mtg)
    (John Wilson     b 12-17-1844  d 3-13-1847
                     Whitewater Mtg)
    (Rebecca H      b 1- 6-1847  Whitewater Mtg)

John W
   m (7-28-1878) Henry Co, Ind
Emily S (Carr)  b 3-15-1860  Lacona, Iowa  d 5-21-1921
   dt Daniel & Mary Ann
Ch:  Ira W          b 5-20-1874  Knightstown, Ind
    Alta Mable     b - - - - -

Susan (- - - -)  b 2-22-1849
Ch:  Jason Equador   b 7- 2-1869

BROADBENT
(Robert N)
   m (1865)
Martha J (Griffin)  b 9-11-1841  dt Samuel & Lydia
Ch:  Richard N     b 6-22-1866  Ogden, Ind
    Alice         b 10-30-1871

BROOKSHIRE
(Emsley)
Julia M (Thorp)  b 8-20-1821   d 3- 4-1911?
   dt Alfred & Rebecca (Moorman)
Ch:  Rebecca Belle   b 6- 7-1860

BROSSINS
Margaret G  b 6-26-1868  at Raysville  dt Frank &
                           Elizabeth

BROTHERS
Robert    b 4-12-1843  Perquimans Co, N Car  s Peter &
                                  Mary
   m (2-mo-1874)
Emily (Mellett)  b 12- 3-1846  dt William & Julia of
                           Henry Co, Ind
Ch:  Mary Hellen    b 5-13-1886  Dunreith, Ind

BROWN
Alfred    b 6-29-1850  Charlottesville, Ind  s Eli &
   m (6- 5-1888 Miami Co, Ohio)       Sarah
Effie Afton (Newbern)  b 11-22-1857  Richmond, Ind
   dt Paul & Eliza (Horne)
Ch:  Paul Howard    b 7-12-1889  Cleveland, Ohio
    Russell Lowell  b 10-28-1892  Knightstown, Ind
    (after the death of Alfred Brown, Effie Afton
    m 2nd on 9-10-1899 to Edwin Hall)

Elgar jr  b 11-18-1835  Rainsboro, Ohio  s Elgar &
   m (9-11-1861)                    Mary
Sarah (Bond)  b 12-16-1836  Union Co, Ind  dt Benjamin &

SPICELAND

## BROWN (Cont)
Ch: of Elgar jr & Sarah
 Emma S   b 6-11-1862 Rainsboro, Ohio
 Mary L   b 4- 4-1865
 Mattie E   b 9-17-1867 Highland Co, Ohio
 Joseph A   b 2-13-1872 d 11-29-1881
 Bessie I   b 8-21-1876

- - - -? Brown m (9-30-1917 Henry Co, Ind)
Emily J (Hiatt) b 8-29-1852 Randolph Co, Ind
 dt Daniel & Melinda (Mendenhall) Hiatt

Mercer  b 10- 3-1835 Georgetown, Ill s Joseph &
       Elizabeth (Cook)
 m 1st (1856)
Elizabeth (Mills)
Ch: Albert   b 3-24-1869 Kokomo, Ind
      d 6- 4-1911
  Clara   b 12-24-1870
 m 2nd (1-16-1881 Henry Co, Ind)
Martha J (Griffin) Broadbent, wid of Robert N dt Samuel
 & Lydia (Rinard) b 9-11-1841 Spiceland, Ind
 d 1-24-1915

Nathan  b 6-19-1845 s Eli of Walnut Ridge Mtg, Ind
Mary Ann (Maxwell) b 7-10-1845 dt Hugh & Anna (Talbert)
Ch: Anna S   b 10-15-1870
  Frank C   b 9- 9-1872
  Mable C   b - - - - -
  Leroy N   b - - - - -

## BUDD
John b 6-14-1812 Cincinnati, Ohio s John Sr & Mary
 (rec in mbrp Whitewater MM, Ind 1840)
Elizabeth (Hunt) b 10- 9-1811 Highland Co, Ohio
 dt Jonathan & Phebe
Ch: Calvin W   b 1- 6-1837 Greensborough, Ind
  Albert   b 4-22-1839 Madison Co, Ind
  Phebe Ann  b 6- 2-1841 Whitewater MM, Ind
  Charles   b 1- 6-1843
  John jr   b 3- 6-1850

## BUFKIN
John C  b 9-10-1811 Flushing Mtg, Ohio
 d - - - - bur Spiceland, Ind s Thomas & Ruth
 (Cadwalader) Dawson Bufkin
 m 1st (1840)
Hannah Weisner
 m 2nd
Abigail (Ellis) b 8-14-1822 Guernsey Co, Ohio
 dt Joshua & Miriam
Ch: Elizabeth  b - - - - -
  Calvin A   b - - - - -
  Asa E   b 2-27-1860
  Rachel Emma  b 11-27-1861

Thomas  s Samuel & Bathsheba
 m (7-26-1809) Plainfield MM, Ohio (Flushing M H)
Ruth (Cadwalader) Dawson, a wid, dt John & Sarah
 Cadwalader of Ohio
Ch: Samuel   b 5-31-1810
  John C   b 9-10-1811
  Gulielma  b 8-30-1815
  Sarah   b 4- 4-1817
  Ruth C   b 3-25-1820

## BULLEN
(- - - -)? Bullen
 m (2-14-1898 Marion Co, Ind)
Elizabeth Emma (Edmundson) b 8-27-1867 Henry Co, Ind
 dt John & Elmina (Lupton)

Martha (Marks) b 3- 3-1879 dt William & Prudence

## BUNDY
Charles  b 12-31-1800 Pasquotank MM, N Car
 s Nathan & Ruth (Morris)
Pharaba (Nixon) b 10-31-1805 Suttons Creek MM, N Car
 dt Nathan, decd, & 2nd w Margaret (Bagley)
Ch: Josiah   b 9- 3-1826 Suttons Creek MM,
         N Car
  Morris N   b 10-17-1828

Charles  b 5-19-1864 Henry Co, Ind s George &
 Caroline A (Bowman)
 m (10-30-1898 Rush Co, Ind)
Helen (Ballinger) b 3-23-1874 Henry Co, Ind dt Joseph
 & Elizabeth
Ch: Huldah M  b 7-18-1903

Charles F b 12-15-1851 Henry Co, Ind s Josiah &
 m (12- 2-1874)    Eliza (Byrket)
Martha (Guy) b 7- 3-1855 Madison Co, Ind d 1912
 dt John & Lavinia (McCarty)
Ch: Marie   b 11-16-1894 Hancock Co, Ind

Elizabeth (Marshall) b 12-26-1859 in Ohio dt Robert &
 m (1-15-1908 Wayne Co, Ind)   Sarah

Frank b 10- 3-1868 s George & Caroline (Bowman)
 m (5- 9-1889 Henry Co, Ind)
Cora A (Pickett) b 10- 5-1870 dt John & Esther (Foster)
Ch: Walter   b 1-21-1890
  Raymond   b 1-22-1891 d 8-18-1892
  Floyd C   b 8-15-1894
  Esther Carrie b 11-28-1902

George  b 8-16-1781 N Car s Josiah & Mary (Symons)
 (m 1st 10- 6-1804 Piney Woods N Car)
(Sarah (Moore)) (b - - - -) (d 5- 1-1811 N Car)
 (m 2nd 7- 1-1815 Piney Woods Mtg, N Car)
Karen (Elliott)
Ch: Mary   b 8-23-1819
  Josiah   b 4-21-1823
  Catharine  b 7-23-1826

(George)
 m (9- 4-1856 Henry Co, Ind)
Caroline A (Bowman) b 2-17-1840 dt Jesse & Mary
 (Burcham) of Greensboro, Ind
Ch: Charley   b 5-19-1864
  Frank   b 10- 3-1868
  Howard   b 5-23-1873 Spiceland, Ind
  Clinton   b 9-15-1875
  Jesse   b 3-22-1879

Ira S b 12-17-1843 s Jesse & Rachel
Sallie (- - - -) b 2- 9-1847
Ch: Charles Warner b 11-29-1864

Jesse b 8- 5-1803 Symons Creek MM, N Car d 9-26-1873
 s Benjamin & Sarah (Bell)
 m (8- 4-1825 Milford MM, Ind)
Rachel (Hester) b 1- 4-1807, Center MM, Ohio
 d 12- 2-1870 dt Francis & Mary, decd, (Hodson)
Ch: (to Spiceland with parents)
  Enos   b 11- 4-1850

Thomas & Mary (Bogue) Bundy's minor children, (the parents
 had been dis at Milford MM)
Ch: (minors)
  Morgan   b 7- 2-1830
  Sarah   b 5- 9-1832
  Charles   b 7-24-1834
  Mariah   b 7-21-1837

William P b 3-12-1833 Deep River, N Car d 4-27-1917
 s John & Mary (Moore)
 m 1st (2-11-1858 Guilford Co, N Car)
Martitia (Stewart or Stuart) b 7-16-1833 Deep River
 Mtg, N Car d 1- 7-1907 dt Amos & Matilda (Hadley)
 m 2nd (1-15-1908 Wayne Co, Ind)
Elizabeth (Marshall) b 1- 6-1859 in Ohio dt Robert &
           Sarah

## BURNETT
David b 2- 4-1803 Redstone MM, Pa d 10-18-1853 bur
 Spiceland MM, Ind s Robert & Anna (Smith) of
 Miami MM, Ohio
 m 1st (4-24-1829 Caesars Creek MM, Ohio)
(Hannah (Wilson)) dt Christopher & Mary of Caesars Creek
 MM, Ohio & Fairfield MM, Ind) b (7- 8-1805)
Ch: Christopher
  Seth
  Isaac F
  (there may have been others)
 m 2nd (5-23-1844 Spiceland MM, Ind)
Eliza (Pennington) b 11-30-1818 Barnesville, Ohio
 dt Josiah & Deborah (Talbott)

## BURNETT (Cont)
Ch: of David & Eliza
    Levi )             b 6-26-1848    d 8- 7-1848
         twins     bur Spiceland Mtg
    Jesse)           b 6-26-1848
    Anna             b 8-29-1851

Jesse   b 6-26-1848   Spiceland, Ind   s David & Eliza
     m (5-15-1874)               (Pennington)
Mary A (Osborne)   b 4- 1-1844   Center MM, N Car
     dt David & Cazah

## BUSBY
(John McA)
     m (12-28-1882)
Emma S (Brown)   b 6-11-1862   Rainsboro, Ohio
     dt Elgar jr & Sarah (Bond)

## BUTLER
Daniel W    b 7- 4-1837   s George W & Martha of Hancock
     m 1st                           Co, Ind
- - - -?
Ch:   Minnie L        b 1- 4-1862
      Leatha          b 11-13-186 ?
     m 2nd
Mary A (McPherson)   b 1- 8-1850   Fayette Co, Ind
     dt Philip & Sarah
Ch:   Herbert D       b 9-29-1886   Fayette Co, Ind

Elisha M           b 8-16-1828
   (mcd 1869)
Keziah (D   )

George W          b 4-25-1818
Martha (- - - -)   b 9-29-1814
Ch:   Daniel W        b 7- 4-1837
      Micajah M       b 11-15-1845
      Elwood )        b 5-23-1850
      Almeda ) twins   b 5-23-1850
      Elizabeth A      b 5-15-1854

Jonathan   (b 5-28-1800   Upper MM, Va)   (s William Sr &
                                      1st w Mary, decd)
     (m 1st 4-27-1826 at Duck Creek M H, Ind)
Abigail (Pickering)   (b 8-25-1806 in Ohio)   dt Jonas &
                                         Ruth (Greeg)
Ch:   Sarah Ann
     m 2nd (1- 6-1831 Milford MM, Ind)
Sarah P (Hubbard)   dt Hardy & Mary of Milford Mtg & Duck
                     Creek Mtg, Ind
Ch:   Mary Jane
      Priscilla

Joseph       b 5- 6-1824   d 4- 8-1881 bur Spiceland, Ind
     s James S & Deborah of Hopewell Mtg, Henry Co, Ind
     m (12-30-1847)
Sarah Ann (Pickering)   b 1-14-1829   dt Abner & Charity
               of Duck Creek Mtg, Ind
Ch:   Charity Ann      b 5-19-1849   Indiana
      Calvin P          b 2-14-1851
      Fredus E         b 5-26-1853
      Charles F        b 7-20-1855   d 5-2-1863
      Mary Ellen       b 5- 1-1858
      William W        b 3-21-1861
      James Abner      b 12-10-1863   Henry Co, Ind
      Thomas P         b 2-11-1867   Iowa
      Lindley H        b 1-10-1869   Iowa

Noble        b 5-30-1826 or 1828   d 6-29-1909
     s Levi & Elizabeth (Carr)
Missouri (Fisher)
Ch:   William L        b 11-22-1876   Henry Co, Ind

William     s Joseph & Miriam of Upper MM, Va & Ohio
     m 1st   Upper MM, Va
Mary (- - - -)   d (5- 7-1811 age 36 yrs, Center MM, Ohio)
Ch:   (David          b 7-27-1798)
       Jonathan        b 5-28-1800
       (Michael         b 4-10-1802)
       Elizabeth       b 5- 6-1805
       (William jr     b 9-17-1807)
     m 2nd (12- 2-1812 Fairfield MM, Ohio)
Esther (Ladd)   (dt Garrard & Sarah, decd, of Upper MM,
     Va & Fairfield MM, Ohio)

Ch:   Joseph           b 9-22-1813
      James            b 3- 5-1815   d 4-12-1822
      Jesse            b 9-29-1816   d 12- 6-1816
      Lydia            b 10-17-1817
      Priscilla        b 9- 4-1820
      Edward           b 5-28-1822
      Robert L         b 8-13-1824

William Exum   b 10-27-1823   s Stephen & Louisa of Va
Sarah (Foulk)   b 11- 5-1827   dt Samuel & Ann of Knox Co,
               Pa, and of Hopewell MM, Ind
Ch:   Joseph Coradon    b 11-15-1850

## CALHOUN
(Martin)
     m (8-21-1889)
Esther (Painter)   b 4- 6-1861   dt Samuel S & Mercy Ann
                                 (King)

## CAMMACK
Henry        b 4-28-1814   Warren Co, Ohio   d 3- 4-1898
     s John & Jane (Hollingsworth)
     m (12-23-1841)
Sally (Horner)   b 12-19-1812   Warren Co, Ohio   d 1-30-1893
     dt John & Elizabeth (Compton)
Ch:   Rachel
      Emeline
      Elwood
      John H
      Elizabeth H

## CANADAY
(Oliver)       m (11-20-1876 Wayne Co, Ind)
Eliza E (Horne) Newbern, wid of Paul & dt Wilson &
     Clarkey (Henby)   b 1- 1-1837   Wayne Co, Ind
                   d 3-24-1912

## CARR
(Daniel H)
(Mary Ann)
Ch:   Emily S          b 3-15-1860   Lacona, Iowa
      Cyntha V         b 11-14-1863   Iowa
      Emory Morton     b 3-22-1866

Ella (Swain)   b 5-12-1859   dt Thomas M & Mary M

## CARSON
(Samuel)
Hattie L (Pierce)   b 10-12-1854   dt James & Christina
                                   (Perry)
Ch:   William James    b 5- 2-1876   Knightstown, Ind
      Ray S             b 11-12-1879   Westfield, Ind

## CARTER
Ira    b 3-20-1854   Parke Co, Ind   s Joshua & Katharine
     m 1st                                (Moorman)
(Sophronia Ellis)
Ch:   Eber E           b 3-12-1888
     m 2nd (9- 5-1901 Henry Co, Ind)
Oneda (Bogue) Reece, wid of Charles   dt Josiah & Sibbie
     b 7-27-1864                       (Allen)

## CHAMNESS
Theodore E   b 3-13-1859 Wayne Co, Ind   s William S
                                 & Rebecca (Lamb)
     m (9- 3-1881)
Fannie C (McCombs)

William S   b 11- 2-1824   Randolph Co, N Car   s Nathan
     m (3- 6-1855)                       & Mary
Rebecca J (Lamb)   b 5-16-1835   Henry Co, Ind
     dt Miles & Nancy
Ch:   Theodore E       b 3-13-1859   Wayne Co, Ind
      Carrie R         b 4-12-1861
      Oscar L          b 6-12-1862
      Olinda F         b 1-18-1868   d 8-mo-1895
      Rufus E          b 10- 9-1870
      Mary E           b 4- 3-1874

## CHAPPELL
Reuben       b 8- 1-1810   Suttons Creek, N Car
     s Gabriel & Lydia (Overman)
     m 1st
Mary Ann (Johnson)   b 12-30-1813 in Va   dt Nicholas &
     Catherine from South River MM, Va   (d probably at
                                       West Grove MM, Ind)

SPICELAND

## CHAPPELL (Cont)
Ch: of Reuben & Mary Ann
    John N           b 2-16-1838 Milford MM, Ind
    Griffen A         b 4-26-1839 Union Co, Ind
    Milton K          b 8-23-1841
    Lydia M           b 8-26-1844
m 2nd (1851 Spiceland MM, Ind)
Martha M (- - - -) White (a widow)

## CHARLES
Clarkson   b 11-6-1842 Williamsburg, Ind  d 7-24-1905
  Montana  s Daniel & Miriam (Moore)
m 1st
Caroline E (Horne) b 8-10-1847 d 1-28-1882 bur Arba
  dt Jeremiah & Mazana (Griffin) of New Garden Mtg
Ch:  Oliver L        b 3-13-1867 Randolph Co, Ind
    Minnie J        b 12-3-1869
    Lillian A       b 12-30-1872
    Rose Estella    b 10-2-1875
    Bertha M        b 4-14-1879
    Cora A          b 3-4-1881
m 2nd (9-8-1883 Wayne Co, Ind)
Emily (Hill) b 4-28-1851 dt Aaron & Piety (Arnold) Hill

Henry W  b 2-4-1837 Wayne Co, Ind  d 1920
  s Daniel & Miriam (Moore)
m 1st (1863)
(Narcissa (Osborne)  dt Isaiah & Lydia (Worth) )
  (b 10-30-1840 Springfield Mtg, Ind) (d between
  1873 & 1880 ca)
m 2nd (9-26-1882 Henry Co, Ind)
Martha E (Jones) Stewart wid of Edmund dt William &
  Huldah   b 8-14-1847 Westfield, Ind

## CHEW
Ephraim G b 6-24-1790 Westfield MM, N Car d 1-27-1862
  (s Samuel & Abigail (Green) )
m 1st
Rachel (Knight) b 1-12-1792 Guilford Co, N Car
  d 8-30-1848 Henry Co, Ind dt Abel jr
Ch:  William)         b 2-14-1815  N Car
    Mary   ) twins   b 2-14-1815  N Car
    Isaac           b 6-30-1816  N Car
    Hannah         b 12-31-1817  Ohio
    Abigail)        b 10-23-1820  Ohio  d 12-mo-1897
    Lydia  ) twins   b 10-23-1820  "  d 9-10-1839
                       bur Spiceland
    Nathan         b 10-17-1822  "  d 9-17-1876
                       bur Spiceland
    John Milton     b 6-23-1827  "
    Joseph M        b 3-6-1830  "  d 9-18-1841
m 2nd (1851)
Patsey (Scott) Harrold, a wid dt of John & Rachel
  b 1-8-1805

Ephraim N
  m (6-8-1895 Henry Co, Ind)
Josie Ellen (King) b 6-15-1877 dt Calvin N & Emily A
                                      (Poe)
Ch:  Gladys Augusta   b 3-12-1896
    Donald          b 6-29-1901

Milton Harvey b 1-22-1867 Spiceland, Ind d 3-20-1917
  s John Milton & Louisa
  m (12-2-1893 Henry Co, Ind)
Bertha (Sheridan) b 3-5-1874 dt Oliver & Edith
                       (Sheridan) Sheridan
Ch:  Edith            b 4-7-1895

William
  m (8-27-1890 Henry Co, Ind)
(Regina) Ellen (Winters) b 7-7-1871 Guilford Co, N Car
  dt John W, decd & Melvina (King)

## CLARK
John
  m (3-6-1894)
Carrie S (Dawson) b 10-16-1863 dt William & Abigail
                                   (Hammer)

## CLATTERBAUGH
(James)  m (5-1-1850)
Mary (Risk) b 12-3-1832 Augusta Co, Va d 8-17-1904
  dt John & Martha

## CLEAVER
Isaac Allen  b 6-26-1835 Washington Co, Pa
  s Isaac & Susan (Shaw)
  m (4-11-1858 Chester Co, Pa)
Sarah (Maxwell) b 8-31-1840 Chester Co, Pa
  dt James & Mary (Mendenhall)

## CLEMENT
(Edgar)  s Charles A, decd & Susanna T of Camden Co, N J
  m (10-18-1899 Henry Co, Ind)
Lydia L (Bailey) b 8-26-1867 Harrison Co, Ohio
  dt Joseph Sydenham, decd & Phebe (Hoge) (now Phebe
                                 Winder)
Ch:  Wilmer Baily     b 9-11-1900 Haddonfield N J
    Charles Allen    b 1-29-1905 Camden N J
    Phebe Alice      b - - - - - -

## CLEVENGER
Sanford
Rebecca E (Tuttle) b 2-18-1837 dt J S & H Tuttle

## CLOUD
Joel  b 5-23-1800 Sevier Co, Tenn  s Jonathan &
  Elizabeth (Campbell)
Anna (Gordon) b 8-28-1798 Deep River MM, N Car
  d 9-26-1859 bur Spiceland Mtg dt Charles & Ruth
                            (Williams)
Ch:  Asenath W       b 9-25-1822 West Grove Mtg, Ind
    Ruth             b 12-7-1824
    William          b 7-5-1827
    Seth             b 11-5-1829
    Levi C           b 4-6-1832 Spiceland Mtg, Ind
    Joseph           b 1-5-1842

Joel Edgar  b 5-24-1858  s Levi & Rebecca (Hunt)
  m (10-8-1883)
Ella (Hoover) b 4-20-1859
Ch:  Carl             b 10-18-1886
                       d 5-3-1908 bur Earlham

Levi  b 4-6-1832    d 5-28-1903
  s Joel & Anna (Gordon)
  m (6-15-1854 Rush Co, Ind)
Rebecca (Hunt) b 6-5-1832 New Vienna, Ohio d 4-1-1913
  dt Libni & Jane (Hockett) of Walnut Ridge MM, Ind
Ch:  Lewis Emory     b 1-19-1857 Henry Co, Ind
    Joel Edgar      b 5-24-1858
    Emma Alice      b 9-14-1859

Lewis Emory b 1-19-1857 Henry Co, Ind s Levi &
  m (11-23-1887)             Rebecca (Hunt)
Mary Emma (Ratcliff) b 6-23-1866 Belmont Co, Ohio
  dt Edward & Julia (Lupton)
Ch:  Jessie           b 9-14-1888
    Georgia          b 1-9-1890
    Howard           b 1-19-1892
    Holman R        b 3-13-1894
    Dorris Corrine   b 1-14-1896

Mordecai  b 8-2-1808 Warren Co, Ohio
     s Jonathan & Elizabeth (Campbell)
Jemima (Baldwin) b 1-12-1809 Deep River Mtg, N Car
  dt John jr & Charlotte
Ch:  John

Seth  b 11-5-1829 West Grove MM, Ind
  s Joel & Anna (Gordon)
m 1st
Perlina (Rayle) b 7-14-1832 Guilford Co, N Car
  d 8-14-1853 Bur Spiceland Mtg, Ind
  dt Zadock & Delilah (Hunt)
Ch:  Anna Jane       b 2-2-1852
    Adison E        b 6-30-1853 d 8-15-1853
                       Spiceland Mtg, Ind
m 2nd
Mahala (Bond) b 7-31-1832 New Garden MM, Ind
  dt Jesse & Anna
Ch:  Evaline          b 1-14-1858 Spiceland MM, Ind

William  b 7-14-1805 Randolph Co. N Car
  s Jonathan & Elizabeth (Campbell)
Tacy (Moffit)  b 2-24-1810 Cane Creek Mtg, N Car
  dt Charles & Elizabeth (Cox)

SPICELAND

CLOUD (Cont)
Ch: of William & Tacy
    Jonathan        b 7- 1-1829 Spiceland Mtg
    Hannah          b 3-24-1831
    David           b 5-11-1833
    Elizabeth Ann   b 7-10-1835

William C   b 7- 5-1827 West Grove Mtg, Ind
   s Joel & Ann (Gordon)
Irena (Boon) b 12-12-1828 Milford MM, Ind  d 5-29-1851
   bur Spiceland Mtg, Ind  dt Driver & Ann (Kersey)
Ch:   Ellen         b 1-10-1850 Spiceland Mtg, Ind

COCHRAN
Francis  b 3-19-1862 Henry Co, Ind  (s James jr & his
   2nd w Mary (White))
   m (10- 9-1890 Henry Co, Ind)
Nora (Brooks) b 11-30-1870 dt Frank & Caroline
                         (Clatterbaugh) Brooks
Ch:   Mary Hazel     b 9- 6-1891
      Ruby M         b 2- 8-1893

James jr  b 6-10-1824 Washington Co, Ind  d 2-27-1894
   s James Sr & Miriam (Trueblood)
   m 1st  (10- 9-1848)
Martha Ellen (Wilson) b 3-27-1828 d 11-24-1852 Blue
   River Mtg, Ind  dt Henry & Deborah (Coffin)
Ch:   Anice         b 9- 5-1849 Spiceland Mtg, Ind
      Charles       b 12- 5-1851
   m 2nd  (6- 8-1854 Washington Co, Ind)
Mary (White)  b 12-23-1825 Washington Co, Ind  d 11-20-
   1906 bur Circle Grove Cemetery, Spiceland, Ind
   dt Toms & Millicent
Ch:   Maria         b 9- 1-1856 Spiceland Mtg
      Alida         b 6- 3-1858  d 2- 3-1860
                     bur Spiceland
      William       b 9- 2-1860
      Francis       b 3-17-1862

COFFIN
Allen M  b 5-20-1873  s William H jr & Josephine (Harris)
   m (10-14-1896)
Cora Pearl (Hawkins) b 7-16-1873 dt Nathan S & Cornelia
                         (Marsh)

Catherine (White)  (b 1- 4-1776 N Car)  d 11-25-1839
   Spiceland Mtg, Ind  (dt Isaac & Catherine (Stanton))
   (wid of Thaddeus Macy of New Garden Mtg, N Car)
   (wid of Betheul Coffin of N Car & Milford Mtg, Ind)
   d at age 63-10-21  a Minister for many years
   (several of her MACY children live in Spiceland Mtg)

Earnest H  b 5- 2-1885 Henry Co, Ind  s William &
   Josephine (Harris)
   m (12- 7-1905 Randolph Co, Ind)
Jessie Belva (Jordon) b 10-21-1885 dt James B & Ida M
                             (Bowen)
Ch:   Mable         b 8-27-1907
      Edna May      b 4-16-1909
      Clifford      b 7-19-1915

Emory D  b 9-19-1824 New Garden MM, N Car  d 7- 4-1863
   bur Spiceland Mtg, Ind  s Vestel & Aletha
Elmina H (Foster) b 12-27-1827 dt Joshua & Sarah
Ch:   Julius V       b 7-13-1846
      Laura Ellen    b 10-17-1848
      Maria Louisa   b 8- 4-1851 Spiceland
      Alice Carey    b 3-29-1856
    * Amanda F      b 5- 5-1859
      Walter E)      b 5-13-1860
      Mary E ) twins b 5-13-1860  d 8-25-1884
      accidently drowned  bur at Bonn-on-the-Rhine, Germ
   (* Amanda F was adopted by Asa C Davis & his wife
      Mary A (Foster) after the death of Emory D Coffin)
   (After Emory died, his wid Elmina m 2nd to Timothy
      Wilson)

Frank  b 10-27-1860 in Kansas  s William H & Sarah
   m(10-27-1885)
Minnie E (Wilson)  b 1-19-1864 dt Christopher &
   Margaret(Butler)
Ch:   Lena          b 8- 3-1887
      Myron         b 12-28-1889
      Irvin Wilson   b 8-11-1892

Isaac N  b 9-26-1826 Deep River MM, N Car  s Elisha &
   m (2-20-1850)                          Sarah
Martha (Bell) b 11-25-1829 Hopewell Mtg, Henry Co, Ind
   dt Thomas & Jerusha
Ch:   Albert Morris   b 5-12-1862 Sugar Plains
                                    Mtg, Ind

A Morris  b 5-20-1873 Wayne Co, Ind  s William H &
     Josephine (Harris)
   m (10-14-1896 Henry Co, Ind)
Pearl H (Hawkins) b 7-16-1873 Wayne Co, Ind
   dt Nathan S & Cornelia (Marsh)
Ch:   Otis Earnest   b 4- 7-1898 Henry Co, Ind
      William Allen  b 5-31-1899
      Mary          b 12-25-1901
      Charles Nathan b    1906

(Nathan, decd)
Sarah (Stuart) b 2- 1-1838 Guilford Co, N Car
   (d 2- 8-1922 Wayne Co, Ind)  dt Amos & Matilda
                               (Hadley)
Ch:   Vestal H       b 7-25-1860 Morgan Co, Ind
   (after the death of Nathan, Sarah m 2nd, 7-25-1867
    to Edward Y Teas)

Walter  b 12-17-1878 Wayne Co, Ind  s William H jr &
   Josephine (Harris)
Leota M (Applegate) b 4- 4-1879 Fayette Co, Ind
   dt Theodore & Mary (Clifford)
Ch:   Russell Theodore b 3-28-1904 Henry Co, Ind
      Myron          b 10-mo-1906
      Cecil Lowell   b 8- 1-1908

William H jr  b 4-29-1850 Wayne Co, Ind
   s William H Sr & Sarah N (Wilson)
   m (8-18-1872 Wayne Co, Ind)
Josephine (Harris) b 5- 7-1856 Wayne Co, Ind
   d (after 1904  ca)  dt Allen M & Rebecca (Letty)
Ch:   Allen Morris   b 5-20-1873
      Walter        b 12-17-1878
      George        b 11-15-1882 Henry Co, Ind
      Ernest H      b 5- 2-1885
      Arthur B      b 6-19-1890
      Mary          b 11-28-1894  d 3- 6-1895

COLLINS
Etta (Burt)  b 4-11-1880  d 6- 6-1921
   dt Francis & Addie (Symons)
   m (6-23-1904 Henry Co, Ind
- - - - ?
Ch:   Mary Louise    b 6-12-1905
      Dorothy E      b 12- 4-1907

Henry A  b    Dorchester Co, Md  d 4-11-1894
   s Henry Sr & Mary
   m (11-19-1861)
Harriet (Mowbray)  b 2- 2-1840 Dorchester Co, Md
   dt William & Libey (Cochran)

(Joel)
(Mary)
Ch:   Ella J         b 10-24-1863
      Charlie C      b 12- 9-1865

COMPTON
Henry Allen  b 6-19-1859  s Phares & 1st w Delitha A
   m (9-20-1883)                       (Bailey)
Florence N (Talbert) b 11-30-1858 dt Jabez & Mary
                               (Cook)

Lindley M  b 8-27-1868 Miami Co, Ohio
   s Phares & Delitha (Bailey)
   m (10- 9-1891 Henry Co, Ind)
L Elva (Elliott) b 12-17-1866 dt Jacob & Phebe
                          (McKinney)
Ch:   Donald E      b 11-26-1896 Greensboro, Ind
      Charles L     b 4-10-1906 Wisconsin
      Ruth E        b - - - - -

Phares  b 10-22-1830 West Milton, Ohio  d 6-25-1913
   s Henry & Rachel (Mendenhall)
   (m 1st 11-19-1852 Dover MM, Ohio)
Delitha Ann (Bailey)  b 4-23-1833 Wilmington, Ohio
   d 10-23-1877 bur Spiceland, Ind  (dt George &
     Lydia (Shields))

# SPICELAND

COMPTON (Cont)
Ch: of Phares & Delitha Ann
    (Lydia Ellen    b 3-14-1854)
    (Rachel Emma    b 7- 2-1855  d 12- 7-1855)
    Sylvia Jane    b 7- 5-1857  West Milton, Ohio
    Henry Allen    b 6-19-1859
    Anna Mary    b 12-29-1863
    Lindley M    b 8-27-1868
  m 2nd  (12- 4-1879 Henry Co, Ind)
Elvira (Dilley) b 6-19-1846    d 5- 19-1915
    dt Joseph & Rachel (Boren) of Knightstown, Ind
Ch:  Jennie    b 2- 9-1884  Spiceland, Ind
    Merrill P    b 9-25-1888

CONWAY
(Elihu W)
Rhoda Grace (Symons) b 8-31-1857  Carmel, Ind
    dt Thomas & Miriam
Ch:  Bertha    b 6-22-1878  Fountain City, Ind
  (after the death of Elihu W, Rhoda Grace m 2nd,
    2-13-1883 to Ira Pearson)

COOK
Charles
    m  (8-mo-1896 Henry Co, Ind)
Nora Bell (Poer) b 12-29-1873    d 10-mo-1911
    dt James & Lucinda (Byrkit)

(Isaac)  (d prior to 1834)
(Mary (- - - -) )
Ch:  John
    Sarah
    Elizabeth
    Nancy
    Ruth
    Catherine
(Mary (- - - -) Cook, wid of Isaac m 2nd to - - - -
    Chestnut a non-mbr)

Robert H b 11-10-1842 Spiceland, Ind  s Thomas & Martha
  m 1st (11-27-1861)    (Unthank)
Martha (Nixon) b 3-11-1841 Salem, Ind  d (ca after
    1893)  dt John & Deborah (Hobbs)
Ch:  Luella    b 10-15-1867  d 9-12-1896
    Caroline    b 1-28-1872
  m 2nd (7-28-1897)
Frances (Barlow) Sapp, wid of Andrew J b  1856 Tipton,
    Ind  d 8- 7-1906 bur Shiloh Cemetery
    dt S R & Mary of Tipton Co, Ind

Thomas  b 3-27-1814 Jefferson Co, Ohio  d 2- 5-1899
    Spiceland, Ind  s Ellis & Elizabeth
  m (2-26-1840 Henry Co, Ind)
Martha (Unthank) b 9-21-1821 Guilford Co, N Car
    dt Eli & Anna (Hiatt)
Ch:  Robert H    b 11-10-1840  Henry Co, Ind
    Elizabeth Ann    b 2-11-1843
    Eli    b 6-22-1845
    Ellen    b 1-18-1848
    Mary Louisa    b 8- 7-1854

(Wright  s Isaac Sr & Charity (Wright))  (b 8-27-1778
    Bush River Mtg)
    (m 2nd in Ohio) (1808)
(Anna (Hodgson) dt John & Naomi)
Ch:  (who came to Spiceland)
    (Henry    b    1814)
    (David    b    1816)
    (Rebecca    b 12-30-1818)
    (Wright jr    b 6-28-1821)
    (Anna    b 1-25-1823)
    (Naomi    b 9-11-1825)

COON
Dalles    s Eli & Mary of Knightstown, Ind
  m (7-13-1892)
Florence (Martindale)    d 8-14-1898 dt William & Mary E
Ch:  Olive Christina    b 6-13-1894  Dunreith, Ind
    Vassie Cassel    b 6-14-1898  Charlottesville,
        Ind

COOPER
Homer H b 12-22-1868 Noble Co, Ind  s Hiram & Margaret
    (Simpson)
  m (5-31-1900 Henry Co, Ind)
Mary (Bailey)  b 4- 3-1881 Henry Co, Ind
    dt J Quincy & Mary Anice (Wilson)
Ch:  Miriam    b 6- 1-1907

Minnie  b 4-10-1865 Cincinnati, Ohio

COPELAND
Albert
    m  (1903)
Alice (Hiatt) Barrett, wid of Lawrence b 1-24-1871
    dt Josiah & Rhoda (Sheridan)

John  b 9-22-1853 Henry Co, Ind  s Richard & Cynthia
    m (3-29-1893)
Eva (Chandler) b 8-30-1860 Rush Co, Ind  dt Taylor
    & Martha

CORY
William
    m  (8-27-1891)
Virginia (Griffin) b 10-10-1865 dt John W & Anna (Price)

COSAND
John jr b 6-16-1825 Perquimans Co, N Car  d 9-13-1909
    bur Raysville, Ind  s John & Mildred
    m (6- 4-1846 Perquimans Co, N Car)
Malinda (Lancaster)  b 4- 5-1825 Johnstown, N Car
    dt Lawrence & Rebecca

Lyman G  b 7- 5-1886 Howard Co, Ind  s A T & Mary M
    m (9- 9-1912 Howard Co, Ind)
Nora (Carter) b 10-22-1887 Howard Co, Ind
    dt Charles E & Millie J

COX
Edgar J  b 11- 1-1872 Goldsboro N Car  s Nathan B &
    m (6-14-1907 N Car)    Sarah (Wilson)
- - - - ?

Joseph  (he may be a son of Joseph Sr & w Dinah of West
    Grove MM, Ind)  - - - -?
Ch:  ? Delia    b 10- 1-1825  West Grove MM, Ind
    Riley    b 5- 6-1829  Duck Creek MM, Ind
    Irena    b 2- 6-1831  Spiceland Mtg, Ind
    Clark    b 3-21-1833

Joseph  b 4-15-1834 Holly Spring MM, N Car  s Simon & Ruth
Ruth E (Allen)  b 8-12-1837 Holly Spring MM, N Car
    dt Samuel & Elizabeth (Larrance)
Ch:  infant dt    b 11-22-1859  d 11-26-1859

William Penn  b 9-15-1845 Monroe Co, Ind  s W & N Cox
    m (1866)
Sarah A (Skinner)  b 7- 3-1847 Brown Co, Ind
    dt C  & A  Skinner
Ch:  Mahlon O    b 8- 7-1867  Monroe Co, Ind
    Ira E    b 6-19-1869  Delaware Co, Ind
    Ida B    b 11-11-1871
    Emma M    b 7- 3-1873
    Elnora A    b 8-21-1877
    Josie V    b 8-19-1880

CRETORS
Adolphus  b 3- 3-1851    s George & Hannah
    m (7- 30-1887)
Mary E (Forbes) b 9- 6-1861 Jamestown, N Car
    dt William & Rebecca

CRICKMORE
Joseph E    b    1859 Rush Co, Ind  s Frank & Mary
    m (1880 Rush Co, Ind)
Huldah Emma (Foster) b    1857 Rush Co, Ind
    dt John & Asenith
Ch:  Etha Pearl    b    1884 Nebraska
    Claudia Bartlett    b    1888    "

CRUM
William P
Martha (Greenstreet)  (b ca 1857) IBB  dt Albert &
    his 2nd wife Mary T (Elliott)

SPICELAND

## CUDE
John M     b 10- 7-1829  Guilford Co, N Car   s Noah &
    m  (10-16-1851 Guilford Co, N Car)Huldah (Swain)
Sarah Jane (Macy)
Ch:  Elizabeth N       b 11-13-1856  Guilford Co, N Car
                   d 4-15-1908  bur Circle Grove Cem, Spiceland
     Flora           b  5-17-1858
     Rosabell        b  3-19-1863    d 2-24-1889
                   bur Spiceland, Ind
     Ida May         b  1-26-1870
     Ora             b 10-10-1874   Wayne Co, Ind

## DARLING
William     b 8-26-1845  Salem Co, N J  s Samuel & Beulah
Sarah E (Scott)  b 8-13-1848  Henry Co, Ind  dt Henry &
                                                Abigail

## DAUGHERTY
Charles B    b       Rush Co, Ind   s John & Caroline (Taylor)
    m  (8- 2-1886 Henry Co, Ind)
Laura B (Winters)  b 4- 4-1867  Guilford Co, N Car
        dt John W, decd, & Melvina (King)
Ch:  John A           b 4-27-1888  Blackford Co, Ind

John A       b 4-27-1888  Blackford Co, Ind  s Charles B &
                                              Laura B (Winters)
    m  ( 1- 5-1910 Clinton Co, Ind)
- - - - - -?

Ross
    m  (3-26-1891)
Josephine (Unthank)  b 6-27-1868   d 4-mo-1901
        dt Josiah T & Susanna B (Hunt)
Ch:  Helen            b  8-25-1895

## DAVIS
Asa C    b 10-29-1834  Spiceland Mtg, Ind  s Nathan &
                       1st w Lydia (Cleaver)
Mary A (Foster)  b 7-24-1833  dt Joshua & Sally
Ch:
adopted dt: Amanda F Coffin   b 5- 5-1858
        (dt of Emory, decd & Elmina (Foster) Coffin)
        (thus Amanda was a niece of Asa C & Mary)

Clarkson    b 1- 7-1833   d 5-26-1883  bur Circle Grove
        Cemetery, Spiceland    s Wylliss & Ann (Coggshall)
    m  (9- 1-1862)
Hannah E (Brown)  b 11- 5-1841  Wayne Co, Ind   d 3-24-1898
    bur Spiceland    dt Benjamin & Naomi (Taylor)

Deborah D(Hare)  wid of Griffin Davis   b 11- 9-1825
        Nansemond Co, Va   d 7-29-1887  bur Fountain
        City, Ind   dt Herman & Rosilla

Eliza    b 3-21-1826  dt Thomas & Rachel

Gulielma   b 9- 2-1830  Core Sound MM, N Car  dt Thomas M
    & 1st w, Talitha (Harris)  from Core Sound Mtg, N Car

Jesse    b 1-26-1788  Core Sound MM, N Car  d 9-16-1859
        living at Raysville, Ind  s Joseph Wicker & Susanna
    m 1st ( 1810 N Car)
Alice (- - -)   d 9-11-1832  bur at New Garden MM, Ind
Ch:  Hannah           b  5-12-1811
     John R           b  8-29-1812
     James S          b  8- 5-1814
     Francis M        b  3- 6-1816
     Jacob            b  3- 1-1818
     William S        b 10-15-1819
     Abigail          b  1-17-1822
     Jonas M          b  3- 2-1824
     Rheufus W        b  7- 1-1827
     Mary Jane        b  4-20-1830
    m 2nd  (10-27-1841)
Mary (Gordon)  b 12-11-1794  Guilford Co, N Car
        d 4- 9-1888  bur Spiceland, Ind   dt Charles Sr &
                             Ruth (Williams)  his 2nd w

Nathan    b 4-12-1792 in Pa   d 1-29-1854  bur Spiceland
        Mtg   s Elisha & Alice of Center MM, Pa
    m 1st  (Ohio)
Lydia (Cleaver)  b 10-29-1801  Warren Co, Ohio  d 12-23-
        1837  bur Spiceland   dt Ezekiel & Abigail

Ch:  Elizabeth        b  7-19-1821  Ohio
     Mary             b 11- 1-1823  Ind
     John F           b  8-21-1826
     David            b 10-17-1828   d 12- 4-1829
                      bur Spiceland
     Hannah Ann       b  8-19-1831
     Asa C            b 10-29-1834
    m 2nd  (11-25-1840 Springborough Mtg, Ohio)
Mary M (Stanton)  b 7- 7-1804 Va  d 12- 2-1845 bur
        Spiceland Mtg   dt John & Michael from
                        Dinwiddie Co, Va
Ch:  James Stanton    b 11-20-1845
    m 3rd  (Duck Creek Mtg, Ind)
Jane (Dickey)  dt Nimrod & Ann   b  5- 7-1808

Rosa (Fifer)  b 8- 5-1876  Henry Co, Ind  dt Henry &
    m (5-19-1901 Wayne Co, Ind)          Mary (Burris)
- - - -?

## DAWSON
William    b 4- 3-1834  Marlboro, Ohio  s Isaac &
        Sarah of Stark Co, Ohio
    m  (7-30-1862 Henry Co, Ind)
Abigail (Hammer)  b 9-26-1829  Henry Co, Ind  d 7- 6-1910
        dt Elisha & Nancy (Larrence)
Ch:  Cora or Carrie S  b 10-16-1863  Spiceland, Ind
     Luther H          b  1-23-1868

Luther H    b 1-23-1868  s William & Abigail (Hammer)
    m  ( 4-29-1900 Hancock Co, Ind)
Charity L (Wilkinson)  b 7-23-1870  Hancock Co, Ind
        dt Hezekiah & Mary

## DEAN
(Isaac     d 11-12-1818  Dover MM, N Car)
Elizabeth (Stanley)  b 12- 7-1793  (one of twins)
        dt Michael & Mary (Gurley)
Ch:  Gulielma         b  8-20-1815
     Maria            b 12-26-1816
     Uriah            b  7-24-1818
(after the death of Isaac, Elizabeth m 2nd  1825 to
        Gabriel Willits in Union MM, N Car)

## DEEM
John A
    m  (8- 2-1862 Henry Co, Ind)
Elizabeth (Cloud)  b 6-19-1836   d 5-mo-1919
        dt Joel & Anna (Gordon)
Ch:  Nora             b  5-22-1872  Knightstown, Ind

Ernest
Minnie A (Hodson)  b 10-27-1867  dt William & Amanda
                                              (Scoville)

Sedley A    b 10-10-1836  Lunsberry, Pa   s Daniel &
        Christinia (Minneyer)
    m (10- 1-1867)
Elizabeth (Hodson)  b 11-18-1841  Jamestown N Car
        d 5-14-1906  dt John & Jane (Horney)
Ch:  Christie         b 11-17-1868  Spiceland, Ind
     Emma             b  7-11-1871
     Irene L          b  5-22-1878

## DELON
David    b 11-13-1866  Greensboro, Ind  s Jonah & Mary
    m (12-10-1887 Henry Co, Ind)
Adeline (Hodson)  b 9-20-1869  dt Jonas E & Mary A
                                              (Antrim)
Ch:  Loma             b  9-30-1888  Greensboro, Ind
     Carl             b 12-12-1893   d 3- 6-1895
     Floyd            b  3- 3-1896   d 2-22-1914

## DENNIS
Henry C    b 12- 6-1846  Wayne Co, Ind  s Mahlon &
    Louisa (Beeson)
    m  (9-28-1878 Wayne Co, Ind)
Cordelia (Chamness)

John  b 11-17-1849  Wayne Co, Ind   s Mahlon & Louisa
    m  (1872 Wayne Co, Ind)                     (Beeson)
Mary (Keener)  b 5- 6-1852  dt Nicholas & Catherine
Ch:  Clarkson         b  3-20-1873  Beunavista, Ind
     Ada V            b  8-17-1877  Winchester, Ind

SPICELAND

## DICKEY
(Nimrod (rec on req 1821 Newberry Mtg, Ohio with his w & family))
(Ann (- - - -))
Ch: (to Indiana in 1836)
    (Phebe        b - - - - )
    (Jane         b 5- 7-1808)
    (Charity      b ca 1816)
    (Mary Ann     b ca 1818)
    (James        b ca 1820)
    (Asenath      b 11-26-1822)

## DICKINSON
Charles    b 9-27-1816 County of York, old England
    d 10-20-1896 s Jonathan & Alice
    m( 2- 7-1846)
Hannah (Hiatt) b 12-24-1818 Guilford Co, N Car
    d 10-11-1894 dt Benajah & Elizabeth (White)
Ch: Henry Wilson    b 6- 1-1847 Milford, Ind
    Benajah         b 11-20-1851 d 8-mo-1884
    Joshua J        b 9-16-1855 Richmond, Ind
                    d 1923
    Harriett E      b 2-18-1860 Springdale, Kansas

Henry Wilson  b 6-10-1847 Milford, Ind s Charles & Hannah (Hiatt)
    m (10-29-1870 Leavenworth, Kansas)
Rebecca J (Ridgway) b 7- 1-1853 Miami Co, Ind
    dt Abijah & Eliza

## DICKS
Allen    b 11- 6-1860 s Nathan & Nancy C (Allen)
    m 1st (12-10-1887)
Ada (Hodson)
    m 2nd ( 3- 7-1888)
Mary A (Pennington) b 8-29-1865 Henry Co, Ind
    dt John P & Elizabeth S
Ch: Ada Virginia    b 10- 9-1889 Spiceland, Ind
    Nathan Russell  b 1- 7-1891

Job  b 8-29-1794 Guilford Co, N Car d 12- 1-1860
    bur Spiceland Mtg, Ind s Joshua & Elizabeth
                                 (Baldwin)
Hannah (White) b 5-25-1796 N Car dt Stanton & Sarah
                                   (Stanley)
Ch: Naomi W       b 1-19-1818 N Car
    Elizabeth W   b 11-14-1819
    Sally         b 12-21-1821
    Nathan        b 2-24-1826 Sullivan Co, Ind
    Louisa        b 8- 2-1828
    William       b 9-19-1831 Henry Co, Ind
    Jesse         b 11-19-1834 d 10- 4-1840
                    bur Spiceland Mtg
    Milton S      b 5-28-1840

Nathan  b 2-24-1826 Spiceland Mtg, Ind d 1- 6-1892
    bur Spiceland, Ind s Job & Hannah (White)
    m (11-30-1853)
Nancy C (Allen) b 11-25-1832 Randolph Co, N Car? or
    Walnut Ridge Mtg, Ind dt Harmon & Nancy (Clark)
Ch: Eveline       b 9-12-1855
    Gurney        b 3- 5-1859
    Allen         b 11- 6-1860
    Mary Emily    b 5-17-1867 d 9- 5-1868
                    bur Spiceland Mtg, Ind

## DILHORN
(Robert Milner, s George & Mary of Redstone MM, Pa)
(Sarah (- - - - )
Ch: (to Spiceland Mtg)
    (Joshua W     b 9- 5-1821)
    (William G    b 11-10-1823)
    (Anna Mariah  b 2-18-1826)

## DILLON
(Absalom, s Daniel jr & Ann)
    (decd)
    m (ca 4-20-1820 Springfield MM, Ohio)
Gulielma (Hiatt) b 4-27-1798 dt Joel & Mary (Unthank)
                  of New Garden MM, N C
Ch: Allen H
    Nathan
    Mary Ann
    Maria Jane
    Naomi
    Sarah

(after the death of Absalom, Gulielma mcd, 1838 2nd to
    - - - - Williams)

(Jonathan Sr, s Jesse & Hannah (Ruckman)) (b 1- 8-1783)
(Agnes (Stanley)) (b 4-11-1785)
Ch: (who came to Ind)
    (Elizabeth L  b 1-24-1816)
    (Jonathan jr  b 2-21-1818)
    (Sarah        b 1-29-1820)

## DIMMIT
John       b 5-10-1854 s Willis
Elizabeth Jane (Hendrix) b 9- 4-1854 dt John & Sarah
Ch: Charity      b 8-20-1875 Rush Co, Ind

## DOGGETT
William
    m (11-mo-1888)
Sarah Ellen (Bogue) b 7-31-1857 dt Alfred & Charity
                       (Bogue) Bogue

## DRAPER
(Josiah)
Catherine (- - - -) b 10-12-1806
Ch: Mary         b 6-11-1836

Luther Ora  b 4-25-1867 Henry Co, Ind s Oliver H &
    Jemima E (Harvey)
    m (6-13-1889 Henry Co, Ind
Emma (Griffin) b 8-18-1869 Henry Co, Ind dt Jeremiah
    & Ann (Kenworthy)
Ch: Jessie Cleta   b 5-26-1894
    Esther G      b 9-21-1906

(Samuel) decd, of N Car
(Mary (Albertson))
Ch: (under care of Samuel & Harriet Pritchard)
    Rebecca      b 1-18-1821 Perquimans Co, N Car
    William       b 3-27-1824

## EASTRIDGE
- - - -?
Eva Lena  b 12-17-1887 Spiceland, Ind dt John &
    Marcelle (Emminger)

- - - -?
    m (10-mo-1907 Henry Co, Ind)
Flora (Edwards) b 9-19-1882 dt Benjamin, decd, &
    Sarah (Smiley)

## EDGERTON
Walter    b 8- 6-1806 Stillwater MM, Ohio
    s James & Sarah (Cox)
    m 1st (Somerset MM, Ohio) (11- 9-1826)
Rebecca (Cox) b 2-23-1807 Ohio dt Joseph & Elizabeth
                                (Musgrave)
Ch: William       b 11- 4-1827 Barnesville, Ohio
    Sarah         b 8- 5-1830 Milford MM, Ind
    m 2nd (8-25-1869 Green Plain MM, Ohio)
Eliza A (Chalfont) Negus, wid of Joseph from Pa
    b 2-23-1808 d 3-13-1884 bur Circle Grove
    Cem, Spiceland dt of Abel & Hannah Chalfont

William  b 11- 4-1827 Barnesville, Ohio s Walter
    m (9-16-1850 Wayne Co, Ind) & Rebecca (Cox)
Caroline (Osborne) b 2- 4-1831 Economy, Ind d 9-8-1917
    dt Isaiah & Lydia (Worth)

## EDWARDS
Benjamin
Sarah (Smiley) b 4-20-1849 Hancock Co, Ind
    dt John & Elizabeth (Jackson)
Ch: Edna         b 9-30-1876 Henry Co, Ind
    Flora        b 9-19-1882

David    b 10- 9-1814 Warren Co, Ohio
    d 1-24-1913 "a vetran for Christ" s Nathan &
    m (11-29-1838)               Mary (Hadley)
Susanna (Pennington) b 7-18-1815 Barnesville, Ohio
    d 2-22-1911 "a good woman" (a minister)
    dt Josiah & Deborah (Talbot)
Ch: Eliza Ann     b 2-13-1842 Henry Co, Ind
    Debbiah P     b 12-15-1844
    Lindley M     b 7- 9-1846
    Henry L       b 2-28-1848

SPICELAND

EDWARDS (Cont)
Ch: of David & Susanna (Cont)
    Nathaniel    b 12-16-1850
    Josiah P    b 3-22-1852
    Levi F    b 1-29-1854
    David Wm    b 6-17-1857

Josiah P    b 3-22-1852 Henry Co, Ind  s David &
    Susanna (Pennington)
    m (6-25-1890 Jackson Co, Mo)
Ella (Bailey) b 1-31-1868 Jackson Co, Mo  dt OPW &
        Frances
Ch:  Carelton B    b 9-22-1892 Skagit, Washington
    Louise    b 9- 5-1897    "    "

Levi T  b 1-29-1854  s David & Susanna (Pennington)
    m (7- 1-1885)
Elva (Aiken)

Ruth (Mendenhall) b 5- 6-1822 Hopewell Mtg, N Car
    dt Moses & his 2nd w, Mary Benbow, both decd
    mcd 1846 to (Jairus) Edwards (s John & Nancy of
    Hopewell Mtg, N Car)

William G  b 1-11-1822 Lycoming Co, Pa  d 6-30-1900
    s Joel & Ann - an Elder
    m (7- 3-1856)
Harriett (Cummings) b 10-12-1835 Williamsport, Pa
    dt George & Elizabeth

William  b 9- 5-1802 N Car  d 6- 1-1855 bur Rays-
    ville Mtg, Ind  s Nathaniel & Mary (Hadley)
    m (Miami MM, Ohio)
Elizabeth (Newman) a minister at Spiceland 1841
    b 9-14-1802 Tenn  dt Jonathan & Anna (Cloud)
Ch:  Anna    b 12-30-1823 Miami MM, Ohio
    Jonathan J    b 6-28-1826
    David    b 6- 9-1829 Duck Creek Mtg, Ind
    Mary Jane    b 2-23-1832
    Lizzie    b 11-27-1834 Spiceland Mtg, Ind
    Milton    b 6- 4-1838
    Ruth Emily    b 11-20-1841

ELLIOTT
Charles S  b 6- 2-1869 Henry Co, Ind  s Patrick &
    his 1st w, Sarah (Ball)
    m (1899 Miami Co, Ind)
Bertha (Conway) b 6-22-1878  dt Rhoda Grace (Symons)
    Conway

Elias  b 1-23-1803 Perquimans Co, N Car  s Nixon &
    Rhoda (Scott)
    m 1st (1-11-1827 Deep River MM, N Car)
Martha (Sanders) b 8-13-1796 Guilford Co, N Car
    d  Indiana  dt David & Sarah (Brazelton)
Ch:  William Scott    b 11-11-1828
    Patrick Henry    b 2-14-1832
    David Sanders    b 12-30-1834
    James Nixon    b 10-28-1837
    Mary Jane    b 7-12-1840
    m 2nd (9-21-1853)
Jane (Cain) from N Car  b 10-17-1826  dt William & Sarah
Ch:  John B    b 6-20-1854

(Jacob  s Israel & Welnet of Lost Creek Mtg, Tenn & Ohio)
    (con mcd 7-28-1804 Lost Creek Mtg, Tenn)
(Ann (- - - -))
Ch:  (to Indiana - Duck Creek Mtg)
    (Olive    )
    (Alice    )
    (Welmet    )
    (Susannah    )
    (Elvina    )
    (Melinda    b 4- 7-1818) Indiana
    (Ann    )
    (Israel    )

(James  s Solomon, decd of Perquimans Co, N Car & w
    Miriam (Winslow))
    m (6-18-1807 Suttons Creek Mtg, N Car)
Sarah (Toms)  dt John & Mary of Perquimans Co, N Car
    b 4-23-1780 Perquimans Co, N Car
Ch:  (Benjamin Toms    b 2- 9-1809)
    (Zachariah Nixon    b 9-26-1811)
    (Martha Nixon    b 9- 8-1813)

(Miriam T    b ca 1815)
  Mary T    b 5-20-1817
  Eliza Ann    b 9-23-1825

John B  b 6-20-1854 Henry Co, Ind  s Elias & 2nd w
    m (12- 7-1876)    Jane (Cane)
Martha M (Whitely) b 8- 9-1860 Henry Co, Ind
    dt Robert & Jane (Woolen)
Ch:  Maude M    b 3-31-1878 Dublin, Ind
    J Harry    b 2-24-1880 Spiceland, Ind
    Edna J    b 8- 1-1882
    E Marvin    b 1-31-1890

Mary Eliza  b 3-21-1835  dt Zachariah & Sarah

Nathan
Eva (Bowman) b 7- 9-1862  dt Robert B & Sarah A (Risk)

(Nathan, s Thomas & Abigail (Anderson)) b 1 or 8-22-1817
    m (4-20-1837 Symons Creek M H, N Car)
(Mary Ann (Pritchard)  dt Joseph & Margaret (Jordan))
    b 8-16-1820
Ch:  Abigail P
    Lurania
    Joseph John Gurney
    William Penn
    James W

(Obadiah jr, s Obadiah Sr & Sarah (Chamness))
    b (3-28-1801)
    m (11- 1-1827 Marlborough MM, N Car)
(Armella (Hinshaw)  dt Seth & Hannah, decd) b (6-14-1810)

Patrick Henry  b 2-12-1832 Deep River MM, N Car
    s Elias & his 1st w, Martha (Sanders)
    m 1st
Sarah (Ball)
Ch:  Emily C    b 1- 1-1864 Ogden Ind d 1907
    Ida F    b 6-29-1865
    Laura B    b 6- 7-1867
    Charles S    b 6- 2-1869
    m 2nd (6-14-1884 Henry Co, Ind)
Lavina (Reeves) b 2-21-1841 Rush Co, Ind  d 4- 4-1913
    dt Asa & Rebecca (Reed)

Richard P  b 11-21-1823 Milford MM, Ind  s John &
    m (9-21-1848 Henry Co, Ind)  Mary (Ratliff)
Martha E (Pritchard) b 11-25-1828 Spring MM, N Car
    dt Samuel & Harriett (Picket)
Ch:  Mary Ann    b 7- 9-1849 Spiceland MM, Ind
    Samuel O    b 7- 6-1851  d 8-20-1853
        bur Raysville Mtg, Ind
    Edward E    b 11-20-1853
    - - - -?
    - - - -?
    - - - -?
    - - - -?
    - - - -?
    - - - -?
    John Jacob    b 10- 6-1869

(William)
Isabella (Walton) b 10-27-1813  dt George & Isabella
Ch:  Margaret Jane    b 10- 1-1850

EMMINGER
C Harry  b 2- 7-1866 Madison Co, Ind  s Henry &
    Rebecca (Trout)
    m (10-20-1894 Madison Co, Ind)
Lena M (Thomas) b 5- 6-1876 Madison Co, Ind
    dt Oliver & Josie (Windle)

James M  b 1-17-1850 Mechanicsburg, Pa  d 1925
    s Henry & Rebecca (Trout)
    m 1st ( 5-19-1883)
Josie E (Thornburg)  d 6- 4-1891
Ch:  Vera    b 7- 3-1885 Henry Co, Ind
    Jessie    b 9- 2-1887
    m 2nd (12- 1-1901 Henry Co, Ind)
Alice (Heacock)

ENGLISH
Hugh L  b 1- 1-1843 Rush Co, Ind  d 6-11-1908
    s Hugh Sr & Mary Ann (Armstrong)

SPICELAND

ENGLISH (Cont)
Hugh L    m 1st
Elvirah H
Ch:   Caroline H        b 1- 4-1877 Henry Co, Ind
    m 2nd  (4-11-1883 Madison Co, Ind)
Ruth (Jones)  b 4- 9-1862 Madison Co, Ind  dt David &
        Henrietta (Ross) Jones
Ch:   Ratie Dora        b 1-29-1885
      Freddie L         b 8- 8-1887
      Leslie E          b 8-22-1889

ERVIN
William
    m (9-10-1899)
Margaret Edna (Muffly)  b  1882 Randolph Co, Ind
    dt Daniel & Lucy J (Mills)

ESTES
Ludovice     b 3- 4-1849 Richmond, Ind  s Lewis A &
    Huldah C
    m (7- 6-1881)
Belle (Chambers)  b 10-18-1859 Newcastle, Ind
    dt Robert M & Zurilda
Ch:   Mary              b 6-28-1882  d 8-28-1884
                        bur Spiceland, Ind
      Robert Lewis      b 6-24-1884  d 8- 4-1884
                        bur Spiceland, Ind
      Lewis Alden       b 7-15-1888

EVANS
Alton
    m (6-28-1892 Henry Co, Ind)
Susanna (Griffin)  b 10-26-1867  dt John W & Anna (Price)

George  b (2-25-1802)  d 11-15-1863, an Elder
    (s Benjamin & Hannah (Smith))
    m 1st (2- 6-1822 Miami MM, Ohio)
Mary (Haskit)  b (3- 6-1798)  d 7-22-1859, an Elder
    (dt Thomas & Nancy Ann)
Ch:   Asenath           b 10-14-1822
      Owen              b 8-11-1826
      Sarah             b 3-14-1829
      Richard           b 6-15-1832
      Rebecca           b 9-30-1835  d 7-25-1849
                        bur Spiceland
      Thomas            b 7-14-1838
    m 2nd  (9-mo-1861 Raysville Mtg, Ind)
Martha N Albertson, wid of Jordan

John Hiatt   b 6-18-1878  s Thomas & Martha A (Hiatt)
    m 1st (4- 7-1900 Henry Co, Ind)
Maude (Baker)

Owen   b 8-11-1826 Duck Creek MM, Ind  s George & Mary
                                                (Hasket)
Martha Ann (Price)  b 7-29-1825 Milford MM, Ind
    dt Rice jr & Susanna
Ch:   Adaline           b 11-24-1848 Spiceland MM, Ind
      George            b 3-12-1851
      Rice              b - - - - -
      Narcissa          b - - - - -
      Mary E            b - - - - -
      Marion            b - - - - -

Thomas     b 7-14-1838  d 2- 9-1889  bur Spiceland
    s George & Mary (Haskit)
    m (10-17-1866)
Martha A (Hiatt)  b 5-19-1845  dt John & Rebecca (Unthank)
Ch:   Edgar H           b 8-20-1867 Spiceland Mtg
      Warren T          b 4-13-1871      "       "
      George            b 3- 7-1876
      John H            b 6-18-1878

FAWCETT
John W    b 11-24-1842  d - - - -?  bur Spiceland
    m (9-14-1870)              s Samuel & - - - -?
Maria E (Stanley)  b 10-11-1844  (d 11- 7-1927)
    dt Aaron & Mahala
Ch:   Erwin Earl        b 9-22-1871
      Kenneth A         b 12-30-1873

FELLOW
Alpheus  b 7-28-1858 Howard Co, Ind  s Elisha P, decd

    & Ann Eliza (- - - -?) (now Ann Eliza Beeson of
      Fairmount MM, Ind
    m (7-28-1879)
Orpha E (Cox)  b 4- 2-1859 Elwood, Hamilton Co, Ind
    dt Jeremiah T & Elizabeth
Ch:   Walter            b - - - - -
      Mary E )          b 11- 1-1880
      Anna E )  twins   b 11- 1-1880 Spiceland, Ind
                        d  1888       "      "

Elijah C    b 7-15-1833 New Garden MM, Ind
    s John & Abigail (Coleman) of Wayne Co, Ind
Susanna (White)  b 7-12-1832  dt Jesse & Mary (Pennington)
Ch:   Henry C           b - - - - -

FENTRESS
(William, decd)
Cynthia (Cook)  b 8-10-1839  dt John & Julia of Greensboro,
                                                      Ind
Ch:   Martin            b 5-27-1853
      Frank             b 6-20-1857
      Estella           b 4-14-1861
    (after death of William, Cynthia m 2nd Jesse B Jessup)

FIFER
Henry   d 11- 2-1911
Mary (Burris)  d 1-14-1914

FLETCHER
Silas R    b 12- 5-1829 Lewisville, Ind  d 2-10-1908
    s James & Elizabeth (Tackett)
    m (8-19-1876)
Jael (Holland) Ledbetter, a wid  b 8- 3-1846 N Car
    dt of Levi & Nancy Holland

Zachariah    b 2- 7-1799 Suttons Creek MM, N Car
    s Joshua & his 2nd w, Margaret (Toms)
Anna (Johnson)  b 6- 1-1813 New Garden MM, N Car
    dt James & Mary (Foster)
Ch:   William           b 4-14-1832 Milford MM, Ind
                        d 8- 5-1833      "     "   "
      Henry Francis     b 12-10-1836 Spiceland MM, Ind
      Augustus          b - - - - -
      Margaret Ann      b 10-26-1844
      James J           b 11-mo-1848

Joshua   b 9-11-1798 New Garden Mtg, N Car  s John &
    Grace (Dicks)   con mou 9-24-1825 New Garden MM,
                                                   N Car
Sarah (- - - -?)
Ch:   Elmina H          b 12-27-1827
      Mary Ann          b 7-24-1833
      Samira M          b - - - - -
      Margaret A        b - - - - -

Thomas C
    m (1- 8-1883)
Saloma F (Winslow)

William    b 6-30-1867  s Elijah & Mary M (Pickett)
    m (7-17-1890 Henry Co, Ind)
Ida (March)

FRANCIS
David H    b 2- 7-1850 Hancock Co, Ind  s Richard C
    m (2-26-1873)                    & Isabel Jane
Maria L (Sivard)  b 5- 2-1852 Belmont Co, Ohio
    dt William & Melissa
Ch:   Ida M             b 11-13-1874
      Gertie E          b 2- 3-1877
      William R         b 3-16-1879
      Odel              b 7- 2-1881  d 12-19-1883
                        bur Spiceland
      Melissa Ella      b 9-13-1888
      Sylvia Jane       b 10-12-1891

FRY
William    b 4-27-1857 Adams Co, Ind  s Eli &
    m (8- 8-1891)                      Catherine
Mary Annetta (Davy)  b 3-15-1863 Parke Co, Ind
    dt James & Mary
Ch:   Vada Lucile       b 9-13-1892 Dunreith, Ind
      Ethel Irene       b 7- 4-1897

SPICELAND

## FOREMAN
Elizabeth (Sanders) b 6-25-1806 N Car dt Joseph &
  m (ca 1825 Milford Mtg, Ind) Martha (Wells)
to - - - -? Foreman
Ch: Mary  b - - - -

## FORT
William
  m (12-28-1899 Henry Co, Ind)
Leona (Hiatt) b 1-18-1873 dt Josiah & Rhoda (Sheridan)

## FOSTER
(Caleb s Samuel & Bathsheba of New Garden Mtg, N Car)
  (b 2- 1-1799) (dis 8-31-1844 New Garden Mtg,
              N Car)
  (m 1st 4- 4-1821 New Garden Mtg, N Car)
(Hannah (White) dt Thomas & Elizabeth) (b 7- 2-1800)
Ch: (that came to Spiceland)  (d - - - ?)
  (Robert    b 6-18-1825)
  (Anna Jane  b 4-17-1828)

  (mou, 2nd, 1843 New Garden Mtg, N Car)
Sally (Rayle) b 8- 9-1809 Guilford Co, N Car
  dt Matthew & Nancy Rayle
  (rec on req New Garden Mtg, N Car 5-25-1844)

Christopher C b 4- 9-1855 Henry Co, Ind s Elijah &
            Mary M (Picket)
  m (10- 3-1877 Randolph Co, Ind)
Sarah Ellen (Nation) b 11- 8-1856 Randolph Co, Ind
  dt Hezekiah & Rachel (Pierson)
Ch: Edward   b 5-27-1880
  Walter   b 12-21-1882 Henry Co, Ind
  Harry M   b 11- 6-1884
  John C   b 10-27-1887
  Mary Ellan  b 12-22-1889
  Grace   b 12-22-1891
  Everett   b 7-20-1892
  Herschel  b 2- 7-1897
  Leslie   b 8-17-1899

Elijah C b 11- 4-1831 Spiceland, Ind d 7-mo-1889
  s Joseph & Mary H
  m (8- 7-1852)
Mary M (Pickett) b 10-30-1837 Grant Co, Ind d 1-27-1904
  dt Simon & Rebecca
Ch: Martha E  b 8-16-1853 Spiceland, Ind
  Christopher C b 4- 9-1855
  Elijah E  b 7- 2-1862
  William  b 6-30-1867
  Henry J  b 12- 8-1869 Spiceland, Ind
  Mary Effie b 9- 5-1876

Joseph b 4-17-1803 N Car d 2-26-1869 bur Spiceland,
  Ind s Samuel & Bathsheba
  m ( 2- 2-1826 New Garden MM, N Car)
Mary H (Stanley) b 10- 8-1802 Guilford Co, N Car
  d 1- 1-1882 bur Spiceland MM, Ind dt Jesse &
              Ruth (Hiatt)
Ch: Jemima   b 11- 9-1826 N Car
  Samuel   b 12-25-1827
  Esther   b 10-27-1829
  Elijah C  b 11- 4-1831 Indiana
  Daniel W  b 11-25-1833 d 10-14-1845
           bur Spiceland
  Ruth S   b 4-19-1836
  Joseph Jason b 8- 5-1838
  Mary   b 9-18-1840 d 10-24-1850
  Jenette  b 11-23-1843

## FUSSEL
(- - - -?)
  m (11-26-1874 Madison Co, Ind)
Ella (Justice) b 6- 8-1856 Madison Co, Ind
  dt John J & Linstacy (Black)

## FUSSEN
Thomas
  m (12-31-1881)
Mary Ellen (Thomas) b 1-28-1858 dt Mangum & Sarah Jane
               (Harrold)

## GANNAWAY
Robert
  m (3-11-1897)
Minnie J (Charles) b 12- 3-1869 dt Clarkson & Caroline
               (Horne)
Ch: Caroline C  b 1- 7-1898 Indiana
  Hugh Boyd  b 4- 6-1899 Montana
  Mary Louise b 9-22-1904 Choyeau, Montana

## GARDNER
Hugh b 8- 3-1844 Lotus, Union Co, Ind d 4-mo-1921
  s Thomas & Ruth (Maxwell)
  m (9-23-1868 Union Co, Ind)
Lydia M (Talbert) b 6-26-1849 Lotus, Union Co, Ind
  dt Alvin C & Rebecca (Ellis)
Ch: Ella Maurine b 8-23-1869 Lotus, Ind
  Lawrence  b 2- 5-1872
  Bertha Beatrice b 6-28-1884
  Ruth E   b 12-30-1888 Spiceland, Ind

Lawrence b 2- 5-1872 Union Co, Ind s Hugh & Lydia
  m (6-mo-1899)        (Talbert)
Ruby (Goodwin)
Ch: James Linton b 1-10-1901 Henry Co, Ind
  Eleanor Rebecca b 7-14-1902

## GARWOOD
David C b 11- 2-1842 Brownsville, Pa s Jesse R &
  m ( 3-18-1869)        Myra C
Mary E (Negus) b 1-17-1844 Redstone Mtg, Pa dt Joseph
              & Eliza
Ch: Herbert W  b 8-21-1871 Oskaloosa, Iowa
  Foster J  b 9-11-1875
  Bertha M  b 2-16-1877 Spiceland Mtg, Ind
  Anna E   b 3-24-1878

## GAUNT
Adaline (Evans) b 11-24-1848 dt Owen & Martha A (Price)

## GAUSE
Charles C  b 11-26-1830 Preble Co, Ohio s Eli &
              Martha (Pierce)
Sarah Ann (Hodson) b 3-13-1831 d 10- 2-1856 bur
  Spiceland Mtg, Ind dt Isaac & Welmet (Elliott)
Ch: Clara   b 4- 8-1854 d 8- 1-1854
          bur Spiceland
  Kasper   b - - - - - -

Eli b 11- 7-1824 Elk MM, Ohio s Eli Sr & Martha
  m 1st            (Pierce)
Martha Ann (Harrold) b 9-17-1828 Guilford Co, N Car
  d 7-30-1861 Spiceland, Ind dt John, decd,
            & Mary (Stanley)
Ch: John H   b 5-23-1848 Spiceland, Ind
  Oliver   b 1-14-1851
  Albert   b 6-15-1853
  Samuel F  b 6- 8-1855
  Isaac H  b 12-14-1857
  Seth M   b 3- 9-1860
  m 2nd (1865)
Elva (Perkins) b 2-11-1841 Contentnea Mtg, N Car
  dt John & Sally (Edgerton)

Eli b 3- 1-1786 Fayette Co, Pa d 12-18-1868
  s Solomon & Ruth
Martha (Pierce) b 1-10-1786 Chichester MM, Pa
  d 8-19-1858 bur Spiceland Mtg dt James & Miriam
Ch: James P  b 5-30-1810
  Jesse   b 12-31-1811
  Ruth   b 3-23-1816 Green Co, Ohio
       d 4-20-1840 bur Spiceland Mtg
  Richard  b 6-13-1818 Preble Co, Ohio
       d 8-17-1840
  Nathan)  b 5-18-1820
  Samuel) twins b 5-18-1820
  Hannah B  b 4-25-1822
  Eli C   b 11- 7-1824
  Aaron   b 11-25-1828
  Charles C  b 11-26-1830

Eli D b 12-23-1807 s Nathan & Mary (Ailes)
  m (Ohio)
Lydia (Cooper) b 12- 7-1813 dt Jacob & Elizabeth
Ch: William C  b 3-23-1835 d 6- 6-1836
  Jacob   b 6- 2-1837 d 6- 9-1862
  Mary E   b 10-10-1839
  Sarah T  b 11-27-1841
  Stephen  b 3- 8-1848

SPICELAND

## GAUSE (Cont)
Ch: of Eli D & Lydia (Cont)
    Amos W        b  5-20-1852
    Lydia A        b  5-17-1854
    James E        b  6- 9-1858

Isaac    b 4-21-1821  Ohio  d 11-10-1865  bur Spiceland
    Mtg, Ind  s Nathan & Mary (Ailes)
Abigail (Small) b 5-22-1824 d 5-12-1854 bur Spiceland
    Mtg, Ind  dt Josiah & Jane (Moore)
Ch:  Barclay        b  1-30-1845  d 4-26-1866
                        bur Spiceland Mtg
    Ruth           b  2-12-1848  d 2- 5-1865
                        bur Spiceland Mtg
    Elizabeth M    b  8-11-1850  d 8-15-1850
    Sarah Ann      b  1-16-1852  d 1-18-1852

James P    b 5-30-1810  Fayette Co, Pa
    s Eli G & Martha (Pierce or Pearce)
Rachel (Johnson) b 9-30-1816 New Garden, N Car
    dt James & Mary (Foster)
Ch:  Zachariah      b  2-25-1836  Spiceland Mtg, Ind
    Abigail        b  3- 1-1837
    Naomi          b  9-25-1838  d 5- 5-1839
                  bur Spiceland Mtg, Ind
    Angeline       b  11-30-1845
    Minerva        b  10-20-1848

Joseph    b 11- 2-1818  Elk MM, Ohio  s Nathan &
    Mary (Ailes)
Abigail (Moore)  b 10- 4-1830  Spiceland Mtg, Ind
    dt William & Ann (Small)
Ch:  Mary Ann      b  9- 7-1851

Nathan jr    b 10- 5-1823  s Nathan & Mary (Ailes)
Ann (Cox) b 11-30-1830 dt Joseph & Elizabeth
Ch:  Thomas         b  2- 2-1846
    Clarkson       b  12-20-1849
    Sylvester      b  12-30-1855
    Oscar          b  9-26-1859
    Joseph C       b  12-25-1863

Nathan    b 6-17-1778  Fayette Co, Pa  d 2- 8-1854
    bur Elm Grove Mtg, Ind  s Solomon & Ruth
    ✗ m (Westland MM, Pa, 6- 7-1804)
Mary (Ailes) b 12- 2-1787 Washington Co, Pa d 2-24-1883
    dt Amos & Ann (Brown)    bur Spiceland, Ind
Ch:  (Amos         b  8-30-1805)  Redstone MM, Pa
    (Eli           b  12-30-1807)
    Ann            b  4-14-1810
    Solomon        b  3-10-1813
    Ruth           b  2- 3-1816
    Joseph         b  11- 2-1818  Preble Co, Ohio
    Isaac          b  4-21-1821
    Nathan         b  10- 5-1823
    Stephen A      b  2-13-1825
    Mary           b  1-14-1828

Nathan P    b 5-18-1820  Preble Co, Ohio  d 7-28-1888
    bur Spiceland Cem, Ind  s Eli & Martha (Pierce)
    m 1st
Susanna (Mills)  b 3-22-1825  Miami MM, Ohio (probably
    d in Richland Mtg or Westfield Mtg, Ind)
    dt James & Elizabeth (Brown)
Ch:  Sarah Ann      b  5- 6-1844  Spiceland Mtg, Ind
    Nathan B       b - - - - -
    Adaline        b - - - - -
    m 2nd  (1853 Spiceland Mtg)
Eliza L (Davis)
Ch:  Mahlon         b - - - - -

Richard    b 3-13-1818  Ohio  d 8-17-1840  bur
    Spiceland    s Eli & Martha (Pierce)
Elizabeth (Cooper) b 4- 6-1820 dt Jonathan & Esther
    (Elizabeth m 2nd, Driver BOON)
Ch:  by 1st husb
    Ester Ann      b  1-22-1841  d 9-19-1855
                         bur Spiceland Mtg, Ind

Solomon    b 3-10-1813  Redstone MM, Pa  s Nathan &
    m (Milford MM, Ind)            Mary (Ailes)
Celia (Stubbs)  b 4- 9-1819  Elk MM, Ohio
    dt Joseph & Sarah (Townsend)
Ch:  Elvira         b  11- 1-1839

    William S      b  8- 6-1842
    Rachel         b  4-27-1848  d young
    Mahlon         b  12- 7-1850
    Margaret      b  12-28-1855  d 9-20-1856

Stephen A    b 2-13-1826  s Nathan & Mary (Ailes)
    m 1st
Martha (Ellis) b 6- 4-1843 Flushing MM, Ohio
    d 4-16-1865 Spiceland, Ind, dt Joshua & Miriam
                                  (Branson)
Ch:  Elmer E        b  6-24-1861
    Alma A         b  3-11-1863
    m 2nd (1866)
Rachel M (Ellis) b 6-16-1827 Flushing MM, Ohio
    dt Joshua & Miriam (Branson)

Thomas    b 2- 2-1846  s Nathan & Ann (Cox)
Christina (Boone) b 2-17-1847 dt Driver & his 2nd w
                            Elizabeth (Cooper)
Ch:  Clarendon      b  4- 4-1872  Elm Grove Mtg, Ind
    Fred Carl      b  9-29-1879  Washington, Ind

## GENAU - (GENEAUX?)
Elizabeth (Hiatt)  b 2-18-1869  dt Josiah & Rhoda
                            (Sheridan)

## GENEAUX
George    b 9-26-1868  Belgium  s Francis & Mary F
    m (11- 5-1891 Henry Co, Ind)    (George)
Annis Gertrude (Gordon) b 6- 9-1871 Henry Co, Ind
    dt Jesse & Harriet P (Unthank)

## GEORGE
Claude W    b 3-30-1881  s Washington L & Alice
    m (11-25-1902 Henry Co, Ind)    (Anderson)
Arnena ? (Shidler)

Henry    (from Hopewell MM, Va)
    m 1st
Thamer (- - - -?) d Carmel MM, Ohio, 1-29-1824? or 1828?
Ch:  Caleb          b  10-14-1815
    Mary           b  12-22-1816
    Rachel         b  5- 4-1819
    Richard        b  6-30-1822
    m 2nd    rmt 11-16-1830 New Garden MM, Ohio
Lydia (Votaw) Hoops, wid of Joseph L  dt John & Rebecca
    of Ohio, Wayne Co, Ind & Rebecca to Jay Co
    prior to 1844
Ch:  (her ch by 1st husb)
    Esther Hoops    b (ca    1824 )
    Joseph L Hoops  b (ca    1826 ) d 8-31-1835
                        bur Newgarden Mtg, Ind
Ch:  (by 2nd husb)
    John H. George    b - - - - -
(Lydia m 3rd - 1843 White River Mtg, Ind to Benjamin
    Cox, Sr)

Thomas A    b 3- 6-1883  s Washington L & Alice
    m 8-mo-1902                (Anderson)
Nellie (W-atney?)

Washington L    b 8- 8-1847  Fayette Co, Ind  s Matthew
                                  & Sabrel (Osborn)
    m (8-19-1874 Union Co, Ohio)
Barbara Alice (Anderson) b 6- 2-1857 dt Nelson &
                                  Nancy (Berger)
Ch:  Claude W       b  3-30-1881  Henry Co, Ind
    Thomas A       b  3- 6-1883
    Rossie Bell    b  7-14-1885
    Clarence Layton  b  3-16-1895  Dunreith, Ind
    Jasper Paul    b  10-11-1897

## GLIDEWELL
Robert  b 5-12-1853  Knox Co, Tenn  s Bird & Matilda
    m (8-24-1876)
Sarah (Darnall) b 5- 9-1860 Scott, Va dt Martin &
                                    Elizabeth

## GORDON
Charles Sr  b 1-11-1766  s James & Mary of Kent Co,
    m 2nd                          Delaware
Ruth (Williams) b 2- 8-1768 Guilford Co, N Car
    dt Richard & Prudence (Beals)
Ch:  (to Spiceland)
    Mary           b  12-11-1794
    Richard        b  8-22-1796
    Charles jr     b  11- 3-1804

SPICELAND

GORDON (Cont)
Charles jr   b 11- 3-1804  Guilford Co, N Car
        d 1-15-1855  bur Spiceland Mtg, Ind   s Charles Sr
        & 2nd w Ruth (Williams)
    m 1st
Lydia R (Jessop)  b 10- 9-1804  d 2- 4-1846  bur Spice-
    land Mtg, Ind  (a Minister)  dt William & Ruth
    (Thornburgh), decd  of N Car
Ch:   Micajah Collins    b 3-28-1828
      Parker             b 7-25-1830  d 3- 8-1850
                           bur Milford Mtg, Ind
      Jesse              b 8-31-1832
      Robert             b 11-11-1834
      Martha             b 12-18-1836
      Mary               b 1-29-1839  d 9-20-1862
                           bur Spiceland, Ind
      Clarkson           b 8- 4-1841
      Emily              b 11-16-1843
      Oliver C           b 11-14-1845
    m 2nd
Anna H (Macy)  b 6- 2-1814  Guilford Co, N Car
    dt Thaddeus, decd, & Catharine (White)
Ch:   Lydia              b 3-14-1851  Spiceland Mtg, Ind

Charles W    b 7- 2-1830  Salem Mtg, Ind  s James decd,
    & Ruth (Maxwell) (gr-s of Charles & Ruth (Williams)
    m (1852)
Elizabeth (Grubbs)
Ch:   - - - - -?

Herbert D   b 9- 1-1868  Henry Co, Ind   s Jesse &
    Harriett (Unthank)
    m (1-14-1904  Grant Co, Ind)
Bertha (Harden)  b 7- 6-1871  Madison Co, Ind  dt Samuel
    & Eliza Harden

Jesse   b 8-31-1832  Wayne Co, Ind   d 6-15-1917
    s Charles jr & Lydia R (Jessop)
    m (12-17-1856  Henry Co, Ind)
Harriet P (Unthank)  b 2-17-1835  d 7-24-1910
    dt William B & Rebecca
Ch:   Charles C          b 4-20-1858  d 11-23-1863
      William B          b 10-14-1861
      India              b 1-11-1865  d 9- 3-1866
      Herbert D          b 9- 1-1868  Henry Co, Ind
      Annis Gertrude     b 6- 9-1871

John        b 11-29-1879   s Charles

Micajah Collins   b 3-28-1828  Richmond, Ind
    d 2-20-1917  s Charles jr & Lydia R (Jessop)
    m (8- 6-1857  Henry Co, Ind)
Sarah (Wright)  b 5-20-1837  Henry Co, Ind  d 7-16-1904
    dt John & Martha
Ch:   M Ola              b 11- 7-1863

Richard   b 8-22-1796  Deep River MM, N Car
    s Charles & Ruth (Williams)
Susanna (Hiatt)  b 10-18-1797  at New Garden MM, N Car
    dt George & Sarah (Stanley)
Ch:   Rebecca            b 7- 2-1819
      Alfred             b 1- 7-1821
      Edwin              b 10-25-1823
      Mahalah            b 2- 1-1826  Milford MM, Ind
      Sarah Ann          b 9-19-1828
      Seth               b 7-14-1831
      Nathan             b 8-31-1833
      Phebe              b 7- 2-1841  Spiceland Mtg, Ind

Robert   b 11-11-1834  Fountain City, Ind  s Charles jr
    & Lydia R (Jessop)
    m (11-mo-1887 or 1889  Marion Co, Ind)
Margaret (Fitzgerald)

William B   b 10-14-1861  Henry Co, Ind  s Jesse &
    Harriett (Unthank)
    m (9-22-1886  Henry Co, Ind)
Harriett (Elliott)  b 2-10-1862  dt Richard & Martha
                                     (Pritchard)
Ch:   Edna Marie         b 8-15-1887  Iowa
      William Roydon     b 1-14-1897  Henry Co, Ind

GORMAN
(Charles M)

    m (11- 7-1878)
Ruth H (Whitely)  b 10-12-1850  dt Robert & Jane (Woolen)
Ch:   John               b 11-22-1879

GOTSCHALL
Oliver P   b 6-22-1845  Carleton, Carrol Co, Ohio
    s Nathaniel & Sarah (Martin)
    m (3- 7-1875)
Ida (Bennett)  b 11- 3-1856  Henry Co, Ind  dt John J &
    Eveline (Reynolds)
Ch:   Mary               b 4- 9-1876  Henry Co, Ind
      Effie              b 2- 9-1883

GRAY
Hugh E
    m (10- 5-1867)
Rebecca (Lucas)  b 5- 7-1847  Cambridge City, Ind
    d - - - -  bur Earlham Cemetery  dt William N
    & Mary A
Ch:   Flossie Bell       b 1-25-1886  Greensboro, Ind
      Elizabeth Jane     b 3-20-1890  Wilkinson, Ind

(James)  (rec on req 1820, dis 1825 New Garden Mtg, Ind)
    m (1819 New Garden Mtg, Ind)
(Margaret (Hunt)  dt Jonathan & Phebe (Macy))
    (b 4-19-1801  Guilford Co, N Car)
    (d ca 1833  Duck Creek Mtg or Spiceland Mtg, Ind)
Ch:   Davis              b - - - -  (m 1841 Duck Creek
                             Mtg - Ruth Ann Jay)
      Jonathan           b - - - -
      Phebe              b - - - -  (mcd 1844 Duck Creek
                             Mtg - to - - - -? Dunlap)

(Jesse Jerome)
    m (7- 2-1881)
Sarah E (Pearson)  b 8-23-1853  Miami Co, Ohio
    dt Jesse & Rachel

GREEN
Miriam (Trueblood) Cochran  b 2- 4-1778  Symons Creek
    MM, N Car   d 9- 1-1861  Spiceland, Ind
    dt Caleb & Ann (Delano) Trueblood   wid of James
    Cochran Sr, & wid of Robert Green Sr of Blue
    River MM, Ind

GREENSTREET
Albert     b 7-17-1816  Greene Co, Ky  s Thomas & Mary
    m 1st (1842)
Eunice B (Macy)  b 7-13-1822  in Ohio  d 8-18-1851
    (recorded in Spiceland MM, Ind records)  dt
    Stephen & Rebecca (Barnard)
    m 2nd (1852)
Mary (Elliott)  b 5-20-1817  N Car  dt Thomas &
    Sarah? or Mary? of Perquimans Co, N Car
Ch:   Franklin           b 7-27-1854
      Morris             b 9-17-1855
      Martha G           b - - - - -
      Thomas H           b 1-17-1859  Spiceland, Ind

Eli   b 6-mo-1849  Henry Co, Ind   s Albert & 1st w
    Eunice (Macy), decd
    m (1874)
Ruth (Chapman)  b 12-mo-1855  Howard Co, Ind
    dt Thomas & Phebe (Rulon)
Ch:   Nora               b 5- 4-1888
      Lloyd              b 10-15-1892

Thomas H   b 1-17-1859  Spiceland, Ind  s Albert &
    2nd w Mary T (Elliott)
    m (7-29-1880)
Jennie (Burnet)  b 11-15-1862  West Newton, Ind
    dt Isaac F & Hannah
Ch:   Ernest Leroy       b 10-13-1881
      Mary Olive         b 11-15-1883

GREGG
(Stephen   s Abner & Sarah of South River Mtg, Va & Ohio)
    (dis 1828 Flushing Mtg, Ohio)
    m (10-27-1813  Plainfield Mtg, Ohio)
(Hannah (Pickering)  dt Jacob & Hannah of Southland Mtg,
    Va & Ohio)
Ch:   (Anne              b 10- 9-1814)
      (Hannah            b 1-10-1817)
      (Asahel            b 2-28-1818)
      (Sarah             b 6-12-1819)
      (Eula              b 4-14-1821)

SPICELAND

## GREGG (Cont)
William W    b 12-28-1849
Elizabeth (Cook) Rish  wid of John Rish  b 2-1-1843
    dt Thomas & Martha Cook
Ch:    John    b (ca 1874 - 1875)

## GRIFFIN
Adam    b 1-2-1828  s Samuel & Lydia (Reynard)
Jemima (Foster)  b 11-9-1826  N Car  dt Joseph & Mary H
    (Stanley)
Ch:    Gulielma    b 12-26-1847
    Joseph Samuel    b 8-27-1854

Calvin W    b 8-23-1849  Centerville, Ind  d 8-31-1910
    s Joshua & Matilda (Cloud)
    m (8-22-1872  Grant Co, Ind)
Lucy Ann (Morris)

Elbert S    b 10-22-1864  s Jeremiah & Ann (Kenworthy)
Mamie (Pickering)

Isabelle (Poer) Rayle  wid of Zadock Rayle & Jacob
    Griffin  b 5-6-1841  Guilford Co, N Car
    d 4-15-1916  dt Absolem & Mary (Hodson) Poer
    m (10-23-1896  Henry Co, Ind) to Jacob Griffin

(James  s Jacob & Mary (Copeland))  (b 11-5-1801  N Car)
Ann (Weeks)  b 5-16-1802  N Car  dt John & Jane (Wright)
Ch:    Lydia    b 9-26-1829  d 3-8-1852
        bur Spiceland
    Hannah    b 10-4-1831
    William    b 9-11-1833
    Rebecca    b 2-1-1836

Jeremiah    b 12-25-1823  d 10-mo-1900  s Samuel &
    Lydia of West Grove Mtg, Ind
    m (10-27-1847)
Ann (Kenworthy)  b 9-4-1828  d 7-26-1896  dt Amos &
    Mary (Miller) of Sugar Creek Mtg, Ohio
Ch:    Mary Emily    b 1-1-1849  d 12-26-1853
        bur Spiceland
    Charles    b 11-3-1850  d 3-22-1851
        Wayne Co, Ind
    Martha Ellen    b 4-21-1852
    Marietta    b 8-19-1854  d 4-21-1855
        bur Spiceland
    Oliver    b 6-17-1856  d 8-9-1856
        bur Raysville Mtg
    Willis    b 9-29-1858  Spiceland
    Elbert S    b 10-22-1864
    Alice    b 10-8-1866  d 4-21-1872
    Emma A    b 8-18-1869

John S    b 7-1-1862  Henry Co, Ind  s John W & Anna
    m (6-1-1898  Henry Co, Ind)    (Price)
Ruth (Nichleson)

John William    b 3-12-1831  s Joseph & Rebecca (Burgess)
    m (5-2-1855)
Anna (Price)  b 9-30-1832  Henry Co, Ind  d 6-1-1899
    dt Rice & Susannah
Ch:    George    b 6-19-1856  d 7-28-1856
    Joseph    b 11-25-1857  d 11-19-1860
    Emily    b 11-29-1859
    John S    b 7-1-1862
    Robert    b 12-6-1863  d 1-27-1875
    Virginia    b 10-10-1865
    Susannah    b 10-26-1867
    Ernest L    b 12-19-1869  d 1-27-1872
    Rebecca J    b 10-26-1871  d 2-20-1880

Joseph    b 7-26-1806  s Jacob & Mary (Copeland)
    m (12-30-1830)
Rebecca (Burgess)  b 3-16-1811  Wayne Co, Ind
    dt John & Sarah
Ch:    John Wm    b 12-3-1831  Spiceland Mtg, Ind
    Emily Jane    b 7-30-1833
    Sarah Ann    b 4-24-1835
    Mary B    b 1-21-1837  d 9-8-1860
        Spiceland Mtg, Ind

Joshua    b 4-15-1808  Highland Co, Ohio  s Jacob & Mary
    (Copeland)

Matilda (Cloud)  b 10-18-1812  Warren Co, Ohio  dt
    Jonathan & Elizabeth (Campbell)
Ch:    Mordecai    b 11-23-1831  Spiceland MM, Ind
    Jonathan    b 6-1-1834  d 7-28-1834
        bur Spiceland

Mary Jane (Elliott) Hall  b 7-12-1840  Guilford Co, N Car
    dt Elias & Martha (Saunders) Elliott  wid of
    Alfred Hall  & wid of - - - -? Griffin
    m (12-14-1905  Wayne Co, Ind)
to - - - -? Griffin

Miriam J (- - - -?) (wid of - - - -?) (now, 1852, Miriam
    Green)
Ch:    (rec in mbrp at Spiceland MM, Ind)
    James Elliott    b 1-1-1833  Washington Co, Ind
    Parthena Jane    b 2-5-1835
    Mary Elizabeth    b 11-12-1838
    Willis    b (ca 1841)

Samuel    b 1-22-1804  s Jacob & Mary (Copeland)
    m (3-29-1823  Springfield MM, Ohio)
Lydia (Reynard)  b 2-7-1804  dt Adam & Catharine
Ch:    Jeremiah    b 12-25-1823  West Grove Mtg, Ind
    Jacob    b 1-3-1826  Spiceland Mtg, Ind
    Adam    b 1-2-1828
    Elihu    b 3-13-1830
    Maryann    b 8-25-1832
    Isom    b 8-26-1834
    William    b 11-29-1836
    Lydia    b 10-4-1838
    Martha Jane    b 9-11-1840
    Nancy    b 5-1-1843
    Samuel jr    b 8-31-1845
    Sarah Catherine    b 1-26-1850

Willis    b 9-29-1858  Spiceland, Ind  s Jeremiah &
    Ann (Kenworthy)
    m (1-27-1893)
Marietta (Odon)  b 5-30-1863  Henry Co, Ind
    dt John B & Sarah

## GRISSOM
Elmer Ellsworth  b 3-7-1864  Versailles, Ohio
    s Alfred & Sarah
    m (6-18-1892)
Bertha Estella (Hinshaw)  b 8-23-1874  Fountain City,
    Ind  dt Anselm M & Mary L

## GURLEY
(Eliza H, dt Charles & Ruth (Mendenhall), decd)
    (sister to Rhoda J (Gurley) Johnson)  (b ca
    1825 to 1829  Center Mtg, N Car)

## HAISLEY
Irvin C    b 3-1-1853  Wayne Co, Ind  d 4-30-1917
    s Josiah & Rachel
    m (6-5-1875)
Hannah (Clements)
Ch:    Pauline    b 11-11-1895

## HALL
Alfred    b 8-7-1842  d 3-19-1894 or 1895  s Caleb
    & Hannah (Saunders)
    m (5-25-1875)
Mary Jane (Elliott)  b 7-12-1840  Guilford Co, N Car
    dt Elias & Martha (Saunders)
(after the death of Alfred, Mary Jane m 2nd, 12-14-1905
    Wayne Co, Ind to - - - -? Griffin)

Benjamin    b 6-6-1767  N Car  d 9-18-1843  bur
    Spiceland, Ind  s Benjamin Sr & Sarah (Elliott)
    of Pasquotank Co, N Car
    m (12-26-1787  Center Mtg, N Car)
Elizabeth (Newby)  b 9-19-1771  N Car  d 4-14-1844
    dt Samuel & Rachel (Pearson)
Ch:    to Indiana
    Rhoda    b 10-18-1794
    Joseph    b 7-28-1797
    Benjamin jr    b 11-3-1799
    Ann    b 2-11-1802
    Caleb    b 9-7-1804
    William    b 1-22-1807
    Stephen    b 1809
    Branson    b 4-26-1811  d 11-4-1816
    Chalkley    b 9-5-1815

SPICELAND

HALL (Cont)
Caleb     b 9-7-1804   d 3-17-1881  bur Spiceland Cemetery
    s Benjamin & Elizabeth (Newby) of Randolph Co, N Car
    m 1st  (1831 Milford MM, Ind (Bethel MH))
Hannah (Saunders)  b 7-29-1810 N Car  d 9-9-1864
    bur Spiceland    dt Joseph & Martha (Wells)
Ch:  Lydia           b  2-18-1833
     Elizabeth       b  3-26-1835
     Joseph          b  5- 6-1837
     Jehu W          b 10- 2-1839
     Alfred B        b  8- 7-1842
     Nancy           b 10- 5-1845
    m 2nd  (6- 7-1866 at Bethal MH, Milford MM, Ind)
Isabella (Walton) Elliott Kennedy, a wid  b 10-27-1813 or
    1814 N Car  d 3- 8-1900  dt of George & Isabella
                                                Walton

Caleb     b 11-30-1868  s Joseph & Lucinda (Symons)
    m  (8- 2-1894 Henry Co, Ind)
Elmina (Parker) Modlin, a wid  b 3-27-1871  dt Elisha,
    decd, & Mary E (Nicholson)
Ch:  Iris E          b  6- 9-1895
     Wanita L        b  3-19-1897
     Elsie Mary      b  - - - - -
     Fay W           b  - - - - -

Clarence   b 8- 3-1875   s Edwin & Lydia E (Compton
    m  (1903 Henry Co, Ind)
Olive (Bond)

Edwin     b 1- 3-1850 Lewisville, Ind  d 10-25-1913
    s Moses & Anna M
    m 1st  (9-18-1873)
Lydia E (Compton)  b 3-14-1854 West Milton, Ohio
    d 7-15-1892  bur Circle Grove Cem, Spiceland, Ind
    dt Phares & Delitha
Ch:  Clarence        b  8- 3-1875
     Carrol          b 10-18-1880
     Clay Macy       b  8-18-1887  d 7-17-1888
                        bur Spiceland
     Arthur B        b  6-12-1892
    m 2nd  (9-20-1899 Rush Co, Ind)
Effie A (Newburn) Brown, wid of Alfred Brown  b 11-22-1857
    Wayne Co, Ind  dt Paul & Eliza (Horne) Newburn

Eli    b 3-mo-1868  Henry Co, Ind   s Obed M & Mary A
    m  (2- 6-1892)
Anna J (Whitely)  b 8-10-1871 Hancock Co, Ind
    dt Jacob & Nancy

Jehu W    b 10- 2-1839 Spiceland  s Caleb & Hannah
    m  (5-11-1864 Henry Co, Ind)         (Saunders)
Huldah (Ratliff)  b 1-20-1846  dt Eli & Jane (Draper)
Ch:  Isadore         b  8-13-1866 Henry Co, Ind
     Marybelle       b  1- 9-1871

Joseph S   b 5- 6-1837 Spiceland  s Caleb & Hannah
    m 1st  (1-11-1860)                      (Saunders)
Lucinda J (Symons)  b 3- 3-1842 Greensboro, Ind
    d 8-11-1892  bur Circle Grove Cem, Spiceland
    dt Betheul & Amy
Ch:  Eldore (Dora)   b  5- 6-1861 Spiceland
     Aldon           b  3-21-1864
     Caleb           b 11-30-1868
    m 2nd  (11- 8-1893 Wayne Co, Ind)
Mary E (Nicholson) Parker, wid of Elisha Parker
    b 5-10-1839 Wayne Co, Ind  d 8-23-1911  dt
    George & Lucinda Nicholson

HAMMER
Elisha   a Minister   b 6-19-1805 Holly Spring, N Car
    d 4-13-1893  s Abraham & Catherine (Trogden)
    m 1st  ( 6-28-1825)
Nancy (Larrance)  b 2-22-1798 Holly Spring MM, N Car
    d 11-15-1870  bur Spiceland Mtg, Ind  dt Peter &
    1st w, Abigail (Haydock)
Ch:  Abigail         b  7-26-1829 Henry Co, Ind
     Catherine       b 10-21-1831  d 8- 4-1909
     Peter           b 12-13-1833
     Mary Jane       b  5-26-1836
    m 2nd  (10-23-1872)
Elizabeth M (Heacock)  b 3-17-1814 Reichland MM, Pa
    (Bucks Co, Pa)  d 2-15-1898  dt Jonah & Abigail

Milton P  b 1- 2-1856 Wilkinson, Hancock Co, Ind
    s Isaac N & Charity
    m  (12-21-1879)
Jenesie (Castor)  b 7- 9-1859 Lynnville, Jasper Co,
    Iowa  dt S N & Rebecca

HAMMOND
Jesse   b 3- 4-1834 Back Creek MM, N Car  s Moses &
    Ruth (Larrance)
Mary (Hammer)  dt Elisha & Nancy (Larrence)
Ch:  Gurney          b  7- 2-1865 Iowa (drowned
                                      6-mo-1919)
     Martha          b  4-22-1867       "
     Harriett        b 12-29-1869       "
     Arthur          b 12-19-1871 Indiana
     Maria           b  3-11-1874
     Eunice          b  6-28-1876
     William J       b  7-10-1878   d 5- 2-1901

HARRIS
James Fremont  b 5- 1-1856 Liberty, Union Co, Ind
    s John & Emily
    m  (8-10-1879)
Mary Elizabeth (Cox)  b 3-21-1860 Dublin, Ind
    dt Joseph M & Rachel M (Terrel)
Ch:  George C        b 12-31-1880 Dunrieth, Ind
     Mary E          b  8-12-1882

Wilson    b 5-30-1805  s Stakely & Rhoda
Susannah (Davis)  b 1-30-1811  dt Benjamin & Margaret
Ch:  Asenath         b 12-11-1831
     Thomas Elwood   b  6- 6-1835
     Robert P        b 12-31-1837
     Benjamin F      b  6- 9-1840
     Martha          b 12-30-1842
     Sarah Caroline  b  5-20-1845
     Margaret Alice  b  2- 6-1848

HARRISON
Robert   from Balby, England, and by Philadelphia (Pa?)
    d 9- 4-1846 Greensborough, Ind

HARROLD
John    b 11-16-1863  s Jesse & Lucinda
Emma (Healy)  b 9-26-1862  dt Wilburn & Huldah
Ch:  Warren          b  9- 5-1887
     Hazel           b 11-29-1890
     Lillian         b 11-27-1892
     Howard          b 10-10-1902

Martha Ann    b 9-17-1828  dt John decd, & Mary
    (Stanley) Harrold of Guilford Co, N Car
    (after the death of John Harrold, Mary (Stanley)
    Harrold m 2nd, Josiah Stanley who was her double
    1st cousin)  (Mary (Stanley) Harrold Stanley,
    d 8-25-1840  bur Spiceland

Patsey (Scott)  b 1- 8-1805  wid of - - - -? Harrold
    dt John & Rachel Scott  (Patsey m 2nd, 1851
    to Ephraim G Chew)

William  b- - - -
    m  (1- 1-1884 Henry Co, Ind)
Flora (Hodson)  b 2-14-1866  dt Jonas E & Mary Ann
                                            (Antrim)

William B  b 5-16-1832 in Tenn  s Jonathan & Elizabeth
    m  (12-30-1869)
Caroline (Harrison)  b 9-26-1841 Fayette Co, Ind
    dt A B & Elizabeth
Ch:  Mary E          b  2- 4-1875 Delaware Co, Ind
     Rachel M        b  2- 7-1880

HARVEY
(Caleb, s Joshua & Mary, decd)  (b 5- 5-1803)
    (m 11- 6-1823 in Ohio)
(Bathsheba (Nicholson) (b 2-24-1802)  dt Daniel &
                                            Elizabeth)
Ch:  Asenath         b  8-20-1824
     Amos P          b  6- 6-1826
     Silas           b  2- 7-1830
     Mary            b  - - - - -
     George          b  - - - - -

SPICELAND

## HARVEY (Cont)
Charles   b 11-27-1832   s William & Sarah
Margaret (- - - -?)
Ch:  Augustus H         b  2- 7-1868
     Mahlon             b  8- 8-1871

Charles B   b  3-13-1846   s Henry B & Rebecca (Boone)
     m (5-11-1871 Henry Co, Ind)
Martha J (Shaffer)  b 10-25-1853 Hagerstown, Ind
     dt Peter & Ruth A (Bond)
Ch:  Lillian M          b 10-19-1877  Newcastle, Ind
     Edna R             b  2- 1-1880
     Ethel S            b  8-21-1884
     Ruth A             b  8-17-1893

James W    b  2-11-1846  Springfield MM, Ohio
     s Eli, decd & Ruth (Fisher)
Alice (- - - -?)   b  3-18-1848
Ch:  Blanche            b - - - -

Ruth (Fisher) b 6-29-1811 dt Joseph & Hannah of
     Columbiana Co, Ohio    wid of Eli Harvey of
     Springfield MM, Ohio  (she was his 2nd w)
Ch: (these came to Spiceland Mtg)
     James W            b  2-11-1846 Springfield MM,
     Sina Ann           b 10-28-1852

Margery Ann  b 11-10-1849  dt William L, decd & Almeda
     (Thomas) of N Car

## HASTINGS
Aaron H  b  8-29-1842  Henry Co, Ind  s William & Jane
     m (9-mo-1870)
Laura (Henley)  b  3- 3-1851  Dublin, Ind  dt Seth &
                                              Margaret
Ch:  Walter H           b  8-15-1881  Dublin, Ind

Seth G  (a Doctor in Muncie, Ind)  b  3- 1-1840  Newcastle,
     Ind  s William & Jane
     m (2- 3-1870)
Edith (Towell)  b  4-22-1845  Harveysburg, Ind
     dt Isaac & Elizabeth
Ch:  Alton P            b  8-24-1875  Wabash, Ind
     Laura E            b  7-15-1879  Decatur, Ind

## HAUGHTEN
(William, s Joshua & Mary, decd of Carlow, Ireland)
     (a Minister)
     m (3- 8-1827 Salem Mtg, Ind)
(Sally (Johnson) dt Nicholas & Martha, decd) (b 10-24-
     1804 South River Mtg, Va)
Ch: (Richard E          b ca    1828)
    (Lucy               b ca    1830 m Charles White)

## HAWKINS
Nathan S
Cornelia (Marsh)  b  8-29-1836  dt Otis & Julia (Ransom)
Ch:  Belle J            b  9-13-1859  Leavenworth, Kas
     May                b 10- 4-1866  Cambridge City, Ind
     Cora Pearl         b  7-16-1873
     Orpha              b - - - - -

## HAYS - HAYES
Daniel  b  8- 7-1847  Henry Co, Ind  s James & Nancy
     m (8-12-1875)
Zilpha (Johnson)  b 11-14-1847  Guilford Co, N Car
     dt Evan & Elizabeth

John W
     m (8-13-1874 Rush Co, Ind)
Eva (Working)  b  1-13-1854  Rush Co, Ind
     dt Samuel & Malinda (Irvin)
Ch:  Fannie             b  2-15-1876  d 8-23-1907
     Lillian            b  8-16-1880

## HECK
(Thomas)
     m (9- 6-1867)
Nancy (Ogle)  b  7-31-1846  Ross Co, Ohio  dt Erastus &
     Charlotte

## HEIFNER
Flora Frances (Talbert) b 8- 9-1875  Fayette Co, Ind
     dt Joseph & Margaret Talbert

## HENDERSON
(Luther)
Lavina (Hodson)  b  5-16-1861  dt John & Huldah

## HENLEY
David H    b 12- 6-1848  Henry Co, Ind  s Jabez H
     & Margaret S (Holloway)
     m (10-14-1874)
Mary Samantha (Painter) b 9- 1-1850 Greene Co, Ohio
     dt Samuel & Mercy Ann (King)
Ch:  Howard S           b  7-10-1877  Henry Co, Ind
     Lois M             b 11-21-1879
     Homer F            b  8-10-1886

Jabez   b  7-23-1810  Randolph Co, N Car  d 10- 4-1888
     bur Spiceland, Ind, an Elder  (s Elias & his 2nd
     w Jane (Hubbard) of N Car)
     m (5- 3-1838)
Margaret S (Holloway)  b  1-24-1817  Belmont Co, Ohio
     d  6- 8-1901  an Elder  dt Joseph & Ellinor
Ch: (who came to Spiceland)
     David H            b 12- 6-1848
     Mary Jane          b 12- 4-1853
     John Arthur        b  4-11-1859  Duck Creek Mtg

## HESTER
(Robert  s Francis & Mary (Hodgson)) (b 2-14-1803 New
     Garden MM, N Car)
     (m 9- 7-1826 Dover Mtg, Ohio)
(Mary (Starbuck) dt Gaynor & Susannah (Dillon))
     (b 2-12-1808 in Ohio)
Ch: (Amos               b  5- 9-1827)
    (Zimri              b 10- 9-1828)
    (Joel               b 10-19-1843)

## HIATT
Asher  b  6-15-1816  s Asaph & Rebecca (Hunt), decd
Sarah M (Elliott)  b  7-13-1821  dt John & Mary
Ch:  Eleazer B          b  6-24-1839
     Daniel W           b - - - - -
     Clarkson           b  2-21-1844
     Charles M          b 12-29-1846

Clarkson    b 11- 9-1839  s John & Rebecca (Unthank)
     m (10-28-1886 Henry Co, Ind)
Anna (Lowry)  b  4- 3-1850  Knightstown, Ind
     dt George S & Ruth A (Scott)

Emily J  b  8-29-1852  Randolph Co, Ind  dt Daniel &
     Melinda (Mendenhall) Hiatt
     m (9-30-1917 Henry Co, Ind)
to - - - -? Brown

George  b (6-22-1757 New Garden Mtg, N Car)
     d  4- 3-1837  bur Elm Grove Mtg, Henry Co, Ind
     s (John & Sarah (Hodson))
     m (8- 6-1794 New Garden MM, N Car)
Sarah (Stanley)  b (6-13-1765 New Garden MM, N Car)
     d  3-22-1838  Henry Co, Ind   dt William &
     Elizabeth (Walker)

Henry    b  5-28-1870  Henry Co, Ind  s William &
     Anice (Cochran)
     m (6- 5-1895 Henry Co, Ind)
Bertha M (Stafford)  b  7-13-1873  dt Freling H & Emma W

Jesse   b  9-29-1817  Guilford Co, N Car  s James & - - -?
     m (Center MM, N Car)
Achsah (Reynolds) b 12-25-1818  Randolph Co, N Car
     dt Job & Phebe (Hockett)
Ch:  Job                b  1-23-1837
     Lyndon             b  3- 9-1842  Wayne Co, Ind
     Oliver             b  6-30-1844
     Robert             b  2-14-1847
     Albert             b  7-21-1852
     Susan              b 10- 5- ?   Henry Co, Ind

Job    b  7-29-1828  s James & Betty
Lucinda (Wilson) b 7-31-1833  dt William & Sarah
Ch:  Wilson J           b 10-28-1854
     Albert F           b  3- 6-1856
     Charles D          b 10-25-1858
     Mary Jennie        b  5-12-1865

SPICELAND

HIATT (Cont)
Joel     s William, decd & Charity
    m 2nd  (11-21-1832  Newport MH, New Garden MM, Ind)
Rhoda (Davis) Mace, wid of William jr  (b 8-30-1799)
        dt Joseph & Susanna of Core Sound MM, N Car
    (for her ch by Wm Mace see Mace)

John     b 7- 9-1804  N Car    d 12-18-1893  Spiceland
    s Benajah & Elizabeth (White)
    m  (2- 4-1824)
Rebecca (Unthank)  b 5-23-1806  N Car   d 9-12-1897
    Spiceland    dt Josiah, decd & Anna
Ch:  Anna Jane          b  9- 7-1825
     Albert             b  3-28-1828
     Josiah             b  6- 4-1830  Milford Mtg, Ind
     Eliphalet          b  7- 9-1831
     Charles            b  6-17-1835
     Clarkson           b 11- 9-1839  Spiceland Mtg
     Mary Emely         b  1-12-1843
     Martha Amelia      b  5-19-1845
     William            b 10-31-1847
     Samuel P           b 12-23-1850

Josiah     b 6- 4-1830   d 1891   s John & Rebecca
    m (10-27-1860  Henry Co, Ind)         (Unthank)
Rhoda (Sheridan)  b 11-25-1839  dt William & Elizabeth
                                           (Schooley)
Ch:  Emily       b  1-30-1862  d  3- 7-1884
     Ellen       b  6-15-1863  d  7-18-1863
                 Spiceland
     Frank       b  6- 9-1864  d 10- 6-1866
                 Spiceland
     - - - -     b  - - - - -  d 11-11-1867
                 Spiceland
     Elizabeth   b  2-18-1869
     Alice       b  1-24-1871
     Leona       b  1-18-1873
     Albert      b 10-21-1875
     Daisy       b 12- 8-1877
     Grace       b  7-20-1881

Samuel     b 12-23-1850  s John & Rebecca (Unthank)
    m (12-23-1879 )
Ida J (Newby) b 12-27-1858  dt William & Rachel
Ch:  Florence M         b  4- 9-1884

Seth     b 5-29-1833  Greensboro, Ind  s James & Betsey
    m (12-19-1855)
Zalinda (James) b 11-13-1836  Greensboro, Ind
        dt Jonas & Rachel
Ch:  Alice A            b  - - - -
     Luther J           b  - - - -

William  b 10-31-1847 Henry Co, Ind  s John & Rebecca
    m (3-18-1869  Henry Co, Ind)            (Unthank)
Anice (Cochran)  b 9- 5-1849  Henry Co, Ind  (dt James
    & his 1st w, Martha Ellen (Wilson))
Ch:  Henry W           b  5-28-1870
     Martha Pearl      b 11- 5-1874  d  3-24-1879
                       Spiceland
     Charles           b  - - - - -
     Walter            b  1- 2-1881
     Lillian           b 10-23-1885

HILL
Alice Marjorie (Miles) b- 3- 9-1865 St Johns, New
    Brunswick, Canada  dt John C & Lucinda C Miles
    m (6-18-1895  Lynn, Mass)
to - - - -? Hill

Charles    b 4-17-1827  Henry Co, Ind  s J A P Hill
Eunice (Hill) b 8-13-1834  Henry Co, Ind  dt J & E Hill
Ch:  Charles M         b  - - - -
     Rebecca J         b  - - - -

Daniel   b (11-18-1817)  d (11-16-1900  Whitewater MM,
    Ind) s Henry & Achsah (Peacock)
    m (5- 6-1896 in the home of Dr George D Bailey,
        Spiceland, Ind)
Rachel S (Bailey)  b 1-21-1828  d (12- 2-1917 bur
        Luthern Cem, (see Whitewater MM records))
    dt Jesse & Lydia (Towsend) & sister to Dr. Geo D
    Bailey

Eli B     b 4-19-1852  N Car    s Thomas & Nancy B
    m  (5-20-1885)
Josephine (Buck)  b 10-20-1851  Rush Co, Ind
    dt Presley & Nancy

Jacob     b 3-25-1848  Arba, Ind   s Aaron & Piety (Arnold)
    m (10-mo-1874)
Mary Jane (Henley)  b 12- 4-1853  Spiceland
    dt Jabez & Margaret S (Holloway)
Ch:  Floy Alma         b  1-30-1876
     Myron A           b  6- 6-1880
     Cora Elsie        b  1-11-1883

Thomas
    m  (1-10-1883)
Mignonetta (Hollingsworth)  b 2-25-1864
    dt Valentine, decd & Mary F (Reed)

HINSHAW
(Albert)
Sarah C (Whitely)  b 12-11-1853  dt Robert & Jane (Woolen)
Ch:  Uva A             b  8-22-1874
     Herbert P         b  6-24-1877

Arthur M  b 4- 2-1860  Greensboro, Ind  s Benjamin F
        & Margaret (Morgan)
    m (4- 6-1887  Rush Co, Ind)
Minnie (Chandler)  b 11-22-1864  Rush Co, Ind
    dt John G & Martha A (Barnes)
Ch:  Ralph C           b  7-26-1888  Dunreith, Ind
     Bernice B         b 10-17-1891
     Howard D          b  3- 6-1898
     Franklin          b  - - - - -

(Benjamin  s Absolem & Elizabeth)  (b 10-12-1803 N Car)
    (d 5-25-1840  Cane Creek Mtg, N Car)
(Mary (Larrance) dt Peter & 1st w, Abigail (Haydock))
    (b 5-28-1800  N Car)  (d 3-24-1851  Cane Creek
    Mtg, N Car)
Ch:  their minor ch to Spiceland:
     (Elizabeth)             b 1- 1-1837)
     (Isom   ) twins         b 1- 1-1837)
     (Nathan                 b 5-22-1839)

(Benjamin)
Margaret (Morgan)  b 6- 1-1824  Camden Co, N J
        dt Michel & Mary
Ch:  Arthur M          b  4- 2-1860
     Logan             b  3-26-1864  Greensboro, Ind

(Seth  s John & Ruth (Weisner) )  (b 2-14-1789 N Car)
    (m 1st 6-21-1809  Center Mtg, N Car)
(Hannah (Beeson) dt Benjamin & Margaret (Hoggatt))
    (b 5- 2-1788  Guilford Co, N Car)  (d ca 1822)
Ch:  (to Indiana)
     (Jabez            b  8-24-1814)
     (Dianna           b  3-30-1817)
     (Asenath          b 11-21-1819)
    m 2nd (4-16-1823  Marlborough Mtg, N Car)
(Abigail (Rich)  dt Peter & Mary)
Ch:  (Hannah           b 12-15-1824)

HOBBS
Elisha    b 6- 8-1805  Randolph Co, N Car
    s William & Priscilla (Coffin)
Deborah (Harvey) b 10-28-1809? or 5-24-1809? Miami MM,
    Ohio    dt Isaac & Lydia (Dicks)
Ch:  Martha            b 10-28-1834  Rush Co, Ind
     Louisa            b  5-17-1837
     Harvey            b 10- 8-1839
     Ansalem           b 10-22-1841
     Jason             b 11-10-1844  d 6-26-1845 Ohio

William a Minister  b 1-18-1780  N Car  d 9-10-1854
    bur Spiceland Mtg, Ind - a Minister  s Elisha &
    (m 1st  N Car)                           Fanny, decd
Priscilla (Coffin)  (b 1- 8-1774) (d 1836  Blue River
    Mtg, Ind)  dt Samuel & Mary
    (m 2nd  2-20-1839  New Garden, Ind)
Anna (Britton) Unthank, wid of Josiah  b 10- 9-1779
    d 1-20-1875  bur Spiceland Mtg, Ind  dt of
    William & Rebecca Britton

SPICELAND

## HOBSON
Orlando  b 5-27-1852  Yadkin Co, N Car   s Silas & Matilda
    m  (1- 6-1881  Bedford, Ind)                (Jester)
Leannah (Henderson)  b 3-12-1861  Bedford, Ind
    dt Alexander & Amanda (Helton)

## HOCKETT - HOGGATT
Clarkson  b 10-14-1866  Marion Co, Ind  s Henry & Lavina
    m  (12-29-1905 Striker, Ohio)
Catherine (Schaffer)  b 9-30-1871  Striker, Ohio
    dt Michael & Nancy
Ch:  (Mariam)
    (Helen Maria)

Jesse Milligan  b 10-12-1820  Randolph Co, N Car
    s John & Hannah
    m (12-18-1845)
Thamasin (White)  b 12- 2-1823  Randolph Co, N Car
    (d 5-27-1907 Whitewater Mtg, Ind)  dt Isaac & Rosa

(Mary  dt Nathan, decd & Nancy (Scott) now Nancy (Scott)
    Hockett Arnet of Dover Mtg, Ind) (wife of Willis
    Arnet) (b ca 1830) New Garden Mtg, Ind  (Mary had
    a guardian in Spiceland Mtg)  (Mary's father, Nathan
    was s Samuel & Mary (Pinson))  (b 5-23-1803 Mt
    Pleasant Mtg, Va (d 10-mo-1832 New Garden Mtg, Ind)

(Phillip jr  s Phillip Sr & Alice (White))  (b 2-10-1796
    New Garden MM, N Car)
    m (7-21-1830 Arba Mtg, Ind)
Miriam (Bundy) Small, wid of Jonathan  b 1-10-1794
    Pasquotank Mtg, N Car   dt of Josiah & his 2nd w
    Miriam (Perisho) Bundy, both decd
Ch: (by 2nd husb)
    Elijah            b - - - -
    Anna Jane        b - - - -
(for Miriam's ch by 1st husb, see Jonathan Small list)

## HODGINS
(E B)
    m (5-26-1880)
Ellen M (Teas)  b 10-12-1856  Raysville, Ind
    dt Edward Y & Maria

(Joseph  s Jonathan & Deborah (Dicks))  (b 8-12-1806 N Car)
    (m 1835  Center Mtg, N Car)
(Sally (Reynolds)  dt Job & Phebe (Hockett))
    (b 9-17-1815 Guilford Co, N Car)
Ch:  (Nancy Eliza    b 3-15-1837)
    (Phebe Jane     b 9-27-1842)
    (Martha          b 2- 2-1844)
    (Margaret       b ca  1846)
    (Sarah H         b 8-22-1849)
    (David Franklin  b 6-10-1851)

## HODSON
Aaron  b 7-31-1793  Centre MM, N Car  d 11- 1-1847
    bur Spiceland Mtg, Ind  s Robert & Isabella (Frazier)
Mary (Beard)  b 1-30-1793  Deep River MM, N Car
    d 5- 5-1869  bur Spiceland Mtg, Ind  dt Reuben &
    Mary (Hoggatt)
Ch: Lydia           b 10- 9-1818  Springfield MM,
                          N Car  d 11-25-1847  bur
                          Spiceland Mtg, Ind
    Neri            b 6- 2-1820
    Seth            b 11-19-1821
    Anna            b 4-16-1824  d 1- 2-1848
                          bur Spiceland Mtg, Ind
    Robert B        b 1- 6-1826  d 11-22-1857
                          bur Spiceland Mtg, Ind
    Reuben          b 2-18-1828
    Sarah           b 10-27-1829

Albert     b 6-26-1843  d 3-mo-1920  s Isaac & Wilmett
    m (9-15-1875 Henry Co, Ind)         (Elliott)
Mary Emily (Hiatt)  b 1-12-1843  d 12-12-1909
    dt John & Rebecca (Unthank)
Ch: Cora Pearl      b 1-29-1877 Spiceland
    Elva            b 5-15-1880

Alonzo C   b 5-10-1862  s Robert & Marzilla (Antrim)
Ella (Stratton)

Caleb      b 3-27-1823  Springfield MM, N Car

    s Jesse & Nancy
Priscilla (Bond)  b 11- 1-1828  Spiceland Mtg, Ind
    dt Amer & Mary
Ch: Levi            b 1- 4-1848
    Lindsey         b 2-12-1850
    Pleasant       b 4-19-1853
    Moses          b 11-11-1855
    Emory          b 10- 9-1858
    Julius          b 11-11-1860
    Charlie         b 8-20-1863
    Arthur          b 6-17-1869
    Elmer          b 8- 1-1871

Elbert E   b 10-mo-1869  Henry Co, Ind  (s William &
    Amanda (Scoville))
    m (12-25-1895 Henry Co, Ind)
Sylvia M (Beeson)  b 9-13-1878  dt David M & E Adaline
    (Lemmens)
Ch: Orpha Ruth     b 8-19-1900
    Elberta         b 5-29-1906

Elva    b 5-15-1880  s Albert & Mary E (Hiatt)
    m (10-21-1903 Henry Co, Ind)
Carrol (Hall)  b 10-18-1880  dt Edwin & Lydia E (Compton)

Henry N  b 7-29-1859  Spiceland, Ind  s John B & Huldah
    m (6-22-1877)                        (Hozier)
Huldah L (Modlin)  b 11- 8-1856  dt Elias & Martha
Ch: Eva R          b 5-27-1878  Henry Co, Ind
    Arlington E     b 12- 7-1882
    Walter          b 1-10-1884
    Madonna        b 10- 1-1898? 1889?

Isaac  b 12-23-1795  N Car  (s Robert & Isabelle
                                 (Frazier))
Welmet (Elliott)  b 4-21-1810  d 12-10-1882  bur Circle
    Grove Cemetery, Spiceland  dt Jacob & Ann of Tenn
    & Ohio
Ch: Sarah Ann      b 3-13-1831
    Jonas E         b 5- 1-1833
    Charles         b 8-25-1835
    Albert          b 6-26-1843
    Emily J         b 4- 4-1845  d 12-16-1853
                         bur Spiceland

Jesse F    b 5- 3-1792  N Car  s Robert & Isabelle
                                   (Frazier)
    m 1st (Springfield Mtg, N Car ca 1819)
Nancy (- - - -?)
Ch: Jeffrey         b - - - -
    Caleb          b 3-27-1823  Springfield MM,
                         N Car
    Jabez          b - - - -
    Isabel Ann      b - - - -
    Elizabeth       b - - - -
    m 2nd (1853 Spiceland MM, Ind)
Albenah (Horney)  b 8- 1-1808  dt Jeffery & Elizabeth
    (Hiatt)  of N Car

John  b 8-31-1811  Guilford Co, N Car  d 3-30-1900
    s Robert & Isabelle (Frazier)
    m 1st (11-29-1831)
Jane (Horney) of Deep River MM, N Car  b 9- 6-1803
    N Car (?1808?)  d 8-15-1859  bur Spiceland, Ind
Ch: Lucinda         b 9-22-1832  Jamestown, N Car
    Robert          b 4- 7-1834
    Elizabeth       b 11-18-1841
    m 2nd (11-24-1870)
Phebe Ann (Bales)  b 12-16-1827  dt Caleb & Anna (Cook)
    of Springfield MM, N Car

John B     b 9-20-1828  s Robert F & Anna (Beals)
    m (1-10-1853)
Huldah (Hozier)  b 7- 2-1830  d 6-29-1897
    dt Nathan & Alice
Ch: Henry N         b 7-29-1859  Henry Co, Ind
    Lavina A        b 5-16-1861

Jonas E   b 5- 1-1833  Spiceland  d 3- 9-1910
    s Isaac & Welmet (Elliott)
    m (  1854  Henry Co, Ind)
Mary Ann (Antrim)  b 5- 5-1832  South Bend, Ind
    dt Daniel & Sarah (Hiatt)

SPICELAND

HODSON (Cont)
Ch: of Jonas E & Mary Ann
 Martha E   b 1- 1-1855
 Emily    b 6-15-1861 Henry Co, Ind
 Clark    b 12-27-1863 d 11-14-1874
        bur Spiceland
 Dora )    b 2-14-1866 d 9-20-1874 bur Sp
 Flora) twins b 2-14-1866
 Adaline   b 9-20-1869

Levi b 1- 4-1848 Henry Co, Ind d 6-28-1913 (fell
 from a load of wood) s Caleb & Priscilla (Bond)
 m (4-15-1884 Henry Co, Ind)
Gertrude A (Allison) b 11- 5-1862 Knightstown, Henry Co,
 Ind dt James & Rachel of Duck Creek Mtg

Lewis N b 12-12-1848
Rebecca A (Parker) b 10-29-1847 dt James & Hannah B
            (Gause)
Ch: Casper    b 5-30-1868
  Olive    b - - - - -
  Eunice   b - - - - -

Lindsey b 2-12-1850 s Caleb & Priscilla (Bond)
Mary (Arps) dt of Martha Arps
Ch: Earl     b - - - -
  Earnest   b - - - -
  Luther   b - - - -

Neri b 6- 2-1820 s Aaron & Mary (Beard)
 m (1847)
Mary (Hockett) (b ca 1830) (dt Nathan, decd & Nancy
 (Scott) now Nancy Arnett w of Willis Arnett of
 Dover Mtg
Ch: Daniel W  b 8-23-1850 Spiceland

Reuben b 2-18-1828 Springfield MM, N Car
 s Aaron & Mary (Beard)
 m (6-mo-1848 Spiceland Mtg)
Eliza (Justice) b 4- 4-1829 dt James & Malinda
Ch: Sarah Jane  b 6- 5-1849 Spiceland Mtg, Ind
  Martha Ann  b 1-31-1851
  Mary Malinda b 12- 3-1852
  Rebecca Ellen b 10- 9-1854
  Elizabeth C  b 2-15-1857
  Robert H   b 8- 7-1861
  Aaron T   b 10-22-1863
  Louisa    b 3-22-1866
  John W   b 1- 3-1868

Robert F b ca 1799 Center MM, N Car
 s Robert Sr & Isabell (Frazier)
Anna (Beals) b 4-13-1804 or 4-13-1805 Springfield MM,
 N Car d 4- 7-1870 record in Spiceland Mtg
 (dt John & Rachel (Hunt)
Ch: Mary Ann   b 7- 6-1824 Springfield MM, N Car
  Susannah   b 11- 6-1826 (probably on way to
          Indiana)
  John     b 9-10-1828 Indiana
  Eli      b 11-28-1830
  Henry    b 11-15-1835
  William   b 7-25-1838

Robert b 4- 7-1834 Jamestown, N Car (s John & Jane
 m (3- 3-1860 Henry Co, Ind)   (Horney))
Marzella J (Antrim) b 1-31-1842 South Bend, Ind
 dt Daniel & Mary
Ch: Alonzo C   b 5-10-1862 Spiceland

Rufus Perry
 m (5-23-1894)
Alice M (Pritchard) b 6-25-1868 Raysville Mtg
 d 10-22-1897 dt David T & Sarah H

Seth b 11-18-1821 Springfield MM, N Car s Aaron & Mary
 mcd 1850            (Beard)
Margaret (? Hoggatt?) b 11-24-1827 dt (R Nathan, decd
 & Nancy (Scott) now Nancy Arnett)
Ch: Jacob    b 9- 2-1850
  Ira H    b 4-12-1852
  Nancy Ellen  b 12-28-1853
  Neri     b - - - - - ?

(William)

(Amanda (Scoville))
Ch: (rec in mbrp 1886)
  Laura    b 4-14-1863 Spiceland, Ind
  Minnie A   b 10-27-1867
  Elbert E   b 10-mo-1869
  Nellie Gray  b 6-20-1871

HOFFMAN
Clarence b 5-14-1892 s Augustus & Emma S

HOLLINGSWORTH
James jr b 1-31-1799 Bush River MM, S Car
 s James & Sarah (Wright)
Lydia (Swain) b 7-31-1800 Deep River MM, N Car
 dt Silvanus & Miriam (Gardner)
Ch: Olive    b 4- 3-1829 Silver Creek MM, Ind
  Miriam   b 6-27-1831 d 9- 5-1851
        bur Raysville Mtg, Ind
  Stephen G  b 11-22-1832 Mill Creek MM, Ohio
  Valentine  b 8-26-1834
  Anderson   b 2- 7-1836
  Benjamin   b 7- 5-1839

Valentine b 8-26-1834 Mill Creek MM, Ohio d 1-13-1875
 Raysville Mtg, Ind s James jr & Lydia (Swain)
 m (6-10-1857)
Mary Frances (Reed) b 7- 7-1833 Marion Co, Ind
 dt Earl & Elizabeth
Ch: Martha R   b 4- 7-1859 Rush Co, Ind
  Willis B   b 1-19-1862
  Mignonette  b 2-25-1864
  James Earle  b 8- 2-1866 Henry Co, Ind
  Luther F   b 10-24-1870

HOLLOWAY
Arthur M b 9-26-1872 s Asa & Lizzie
 m (7-25-1894)
Louisa (Wickersham) b 6- 5-1874 dt Caleb E & Emeline
              (Stanley)
Ch: Hazel    b 6- 2-1895
  Ruth E    b 2-26-1897

Asa b 10-18-1836 Belmont Co, Ohio d 3-20-1906
 bur Circle Grove Cemetery, Spiceland s David &
 Mary S (Williams)
 m (1-20-1869 Henry Co, Ind)
Lizzie (Edwards) b 11-27-1836 Henry Co, Ind
 dt William & Elizabeth (Newman)
Ch: William L  b 12-29-1869 d 9-23-1870
  Arthur M   b 9-26-1872
  Ida Lenora  b 9-19-1874

David b 8-18-1805 d 12- 2-1881 bur Spiceland
 s Joseph & Eleanor
 (rmt, 11-21-1833 Flushing MM, Ohio)
Mary S (Williams) b 1-23-1812 Uwchlan MM, Pa
 d 9-28-1873 bur Spiceland, Ind dt (Joseph & Mary)
Ch: Joseph W   b 12-29-1834 (Flushing MM, Ohio)
  Asa     b 10-18-1836
  Eliza    b - - - - -
  Hannah Ann  b 11- 5-1840 (Duck Creek MM, Ind)
  Mary Ellen  b - - - - -
  Nancy    b 9-17-1846
  Lydia M   b - - - - -
  Jason W   b 11-10-1851

(Joseph from Southland Mtg, Va & Flushing Mtg, Ohio)
 m (ca 1802 Southland Mtg, Va)
(Eleanor (- - - -?))
Ch: (to Indiana)
  (David    b 9-19-1805)
  (Hannah   b 3-19-1808)
  (Betsy Ann)  b 8-15-1810 d 2-10-1831
        Flushing Mtg, Ohio
  (Abigail ) twins b 8-15-1810)
  (Margaret  b 4-17-1813)
  (Nancy   b 4-27-1821)

Joseph W b 12-29-1834 Flushing MM, Ohio d 3-24-1899?
 s David & Mary S (Williams)
 m (8-26-1857)
Hannah (Stanley) b 6- 8-1837 Spiceland, Ind d 6- 5-1901
 dt Aaron & Mahala (Stanley) Stanley
Ch: Emma L   b 4-14-1859 Spiceland
  Otis D    b 4-13-1863

SPICELAND

## HOLLOWAY (Cont)
Otis D    b 4-13-1863    s Joseph W & Hannah (Stanley)
    m  (7-18-1888)
Lena (Vestal)

## HOLLOWELL
(Aaron  s Thomas & Mary (Lamb))  (b 3-31-1799 Suttons
    Creek MM, N Car)  (d Spring of 1830 Perquimans MM,
    N Car)
    (rmt 12- 4-1825 Perquimans MM, N Car)
Esther (Newby)  b 4- 9-1805  dt Jesse & Elizabeth (White)
    Townsend Newby
Ch:  Nathan W          b - - - -
     Mary Jane         b - - - -
    (Esther, wid of Aaron, m 2nd 1842 Milford Mtg to
    Elijah Cox)

Edwin jr  b 8-24-1867  Indianapolis, Ind
    s Edwin & Matilda

## HOLT
Herbert C
    m  (4-19-1900)
Carrie Alberta (Newby)  b 11-13-1879  dt Albert &
    Caroline (Hubbard)

John G
    m (12-24-1874)
Martha E (Foster)  b 8-16-1853  dt Elijah & Mary
                                        (Pickett)

## HOLTSCLAW
James David  b 3- 6-1879  s Rilon & Sarah (New)
    m (5- 2-1906 Henry Co, Ind)
Bertha (Pearson)  b 8-16-1880 Miami Co, Ind  d 8-mo-
    1919     dt Charles & Lydia (Newburn)
Ch:  Paul              b        1907

Rose Ella    b 10-22-1876  dt Jehiel & Semira
    m (1895)
to - - - -? George

(Rilon)
(Sarah E (New))
Ch:  James David       b 3- 6-1879  Spiceland, Ind
     George E          b 10-18-1880  d 9-28-1905
           bur Circle Grove Cemetery  Spiceland, Ind

## HOOVER
(John)
    m (9-21-1883 Henry Co, Ind)
Anna May (Compton)  b 12-29-1863 West Milton, Ohio
    dt Phares & Delitha (Bailey)

Levi C  b 4-28-1857  Spiceland, Ind  s Henry & Ann (Cook)
    m 1st (9-30-1880)
Emma Alice (Cloud)  b 9-14-1859  dt Levi & Rebecca
                                        (Hiatt)
Ch:  Helen C           b 12-26-1881
     Everett           b 9-16-1883  d 10-26-1883
     Edna L            b 10-13-1885
    m 2nd (6-22-1912 Terre Haute, Ind)
Rachel (Sheridan)  b 2- 5-1858 N Car  dt James &
    Haseltine (Stone)

Margaret (Harvey)  b 8-16-1811  Center MM, Ohio
    dt Samuel & Rebecca (Kindley)  wid of Levi or
    Phineas Hoover

## HORNER
Amos C  b 7-10-1822 Montgomery Co, Ohio  d  1900
    s John & Elizabeth (Compton)
    m 1st (11-10-1851 Cherry Grove Mtg, Ind)
Elvira (Reece)  b 8-25-1830 Randolph Co, Ind
    dt Eli & Matilda

Ch:  Edward            b 9-18-1852  Raysville Mtg, Ind
     Luzena            b 7-27-1854
    m 2nd (9-23-1863)
Anna J (Bundy)  b 5- 7-1833 Dublin, Ind  dt Elias & Sarah

John  b 6-13-1780 Frederick Co, Va  d 10-30-1852
    bur Raysville Mtg, Ind  s Thomas & Ann
    m (Ceaser's Creek MM, Ohio 5-15-1806)

Elizabeth (Compton)  b 12-19-1779  Newberry County, S Car
    dt Samuel & Elizabeth
Ch:  Samuel       b 4-14-1807  Montgomery Co, Ohio
     Ann          b 1- 4-1809
    (Joshua       b 2-26-1810)
     Rebecca      b 9- 4-1811
     Rachel    )  b 12-19-1812
     Sally  ) twins b 12-19-1812
     E Lydia      b 9-30-1814
     Amos C       b 7-10-1822

Samuel  b 4-14-1807  Montgomery Co, Ohio
    s John & Elizabeth (Compton)
Beulah (Stuart)  b 10-14-1808  Guilford Co, N Car
    dt Jehu & Sarah

## HORNEY
Albenah    b 8- 1-1808  dt Jeffrey & Elizabeth (Hiatt)
    of Deep River MM, N Car

## HOSIER - HOZIER
Carl
    m (6-mo-1900)
Daisy (Hiatt)  b 12- 8-1877  dt Josiah & Rhoda (Sheridan)

Nathan  (s William & Milicent (Baily) of Henry Co, Ind)
    (dis 1834 Spiceland Mtg)
    m (9-29-1825  Duck Creek MH, Ind)
Alice (Elliott)  (b ca 1808)  dt Jacob & Ann
Ch:  Hannah            b - - - -
     Huldah            b - - - -
     Alfred            b - - - -
     Martha Ann        b - - - -

## HUBBARD
Charles Swain  b 9- 1-1829  Milford MM, Ind
    s Richard & Sarah (Swain)
Martha (White)  b 8- 1-1828  Blue River MM, Ind
    dt Toms & Milicent (Albertson)
Ch:  Francis           b 1- 9-1852
     Mary A            b 1- 6-1854
     Ellen             b 5-31-1856

Hardy
    m (N Car)
Mary (- - - -?)
Ch:  Joseph            b 5-27-1801  N Car
     Anna C            b 7-12-1812   "   "
     Sarah P           b - - - - -
     Simeon            b - - - - -
     Martha            b - - - - -
     Susannah          b - - - - -
     Richard           b - - - - -
     Mary              b - - - - -
     Caleb             b - - - - -

(Joseph) Butler  b 5- 7-1810  s Jeremiah & Margaret, decd
Celia (Hunt)  b 7-25-1817  N Car  dt Thomas & Sarah
                                          (Griffin)
Ch:  Eliza Ann         b 8-20-1836  N Car
    (Jeremiah          b 12-11-1827  d 10- 9-1841 N Car)
    (Eunice Emily      b 12-31-1841  d 8-25-1842 "  " )
     Delilah Caroline  b 7-23-1844  N Car
     Mary Delphyna     b 9-11-1847  Indiana
     Sarah Angeline    b 9- 4-1849  d 11-29-1849
     Horrace F         b 7-15-1851
     Electa            b 1-25-1854

Mary Jane  b 7-13-1830  Core Sound Mtg, N Car
    dt Solomon & Mary (Davis) Small Hubbard, both decd

(Mary (Davis) Small Hubbard was dt of Joseph W & Sarah
    Hubbard)  (b 7- 4-1794 Core Sound Mtg, N Car)
    (d 3-21-1836 New Garden Mtg, Ind)  (her 1st
    husb was Silas Small  s Jonas & Sarah)

Richard J  b 11- 2-1807  Guilford Co, N Car  s Jeremiah
    & Margaret, decd
    m (ca 1826 Deep River MM, N Car)
Sarah (Swain)  b 10-19-1806  Guilford Co, N Car
    d 2-20-1860 (Milford MM, Ind)  dt George &
    Deborah (Macy)
Ch:  William Edwin     b 10-24-1827  N Car
     Charles Swain     b 9- 1-1829

SPICELAND

## HUBBARD (Cont)
of Richard J & Sarah (Cont)
Ch:
- Margaret — b 8-3-1831 Indiana
- Caroline — b 10-6-1833
- Phebe Ann — b 10-17-1835  d 8-24-1854 Raysville Mtg, Ind
- Harriett P — b 12-22-1837
- Emily — b 1-12-1840  Henry Co, Ind
- Henry — b 12-7-1841  d 12-17-1864
- Joseph B — b 3-30-1844  d 5-26-1865
- George — b 4-21-1846
- Juliette — b 5-6-1848  d 12-20-1861
- Anna — b 9-17-1851

## HUDELSON
(Cephas)
m (12-21-1884)
Mary Ella (Butler) b 5-1-1859 Spiceland Mtg
   dt Joseph & Sarah A (Pickering)

Clara Elsie  b 2-22-1876  Henry Co, Ind
   dt Benjamin & Mary E

Morris  b 10-27-1851  Henry Co, Ind  s William & Lucinda
   m (6-21-1888)                             (Morris)
Flora O (True)

Samuel Harvey  b 6-15-1845  s Samuel Sr & Nancy J
   m (8-8-1871)
Hannah J (Fort)
Ch:
- Lola Bell ) — b 8-7-1876
- Irena Dell) twins — b 8-7-1876
- Hettie — b 2-15-1878

## HUFF
James  b 8-23-1811  Deep Creek MM, N Car  s John & Mary
   m 1st (11-19-1834 Newgarden MM, Ind)
Susannah (Butler) b 3-25-1812 N Car  d 3-2-1841
   (Spiceland Mtg, Ind) dt Edward, decd & Rhoda
   step-dt of Samuel Nixon
Ch:
- Caroline — b - - - -  d young
- Robert B — b 8-3-1838

Nancy - - - - -  b 1-11-1811  d - - - -  bur Spiceland
   Mtg, Ind

## HUFNER
Flora Frances (Talbert) b 8-9-1875 Fayette Co, Ind
   dt Joseph & Margaret

## HUNNICUTT
George E  b 4-4-1808 Va  (s Ephraim & Margaret, decd
   of Prince George Co, Va)
   m 1st (1837)
Martha (Pusey)  b 7-7-1816 Center MM, Ohio
   dt Joel & Hannah (Faulkner)
Ch:
- William Penn — b 3-12-1840

## HUNT
Allen  b 3-6-1783  New Garden MM, N Car  s Isom & Ann
   mou 1st ( 1805 N Car)                       (Moon)
Huldah (- - - -?)
Ch:
- Nancy C — b 9-17-1807
- Rachel — b 8-20-1813
- Abel — b 6-8-1818

Benjamin  b 11-27-1822 Burlington Co, NJ  d 8-27-1839
   bur Spiceland Mtg, Ind  s John & Ann

Joseph B  b 3-3-1807 Burlington Co, NJ  d 9-24-1839
   bur Spiceland Mtg  s John Hunt jr & Anna
Ann E (Gause) b 1-8-1814 dt Eli & Martha of Fayette Co,
   Pa  (after the death of Joseph, Ann m 2nd
   Aaron L Pleas)
Ch:
- Martha G — b 1-14-1835
- Mary — b 11-10-1836
- Susanna B — b 10-23-1839

Lafayette
   (m ca 1886-1887)
Lizzie L (McKillip) b  Summerfield, N Car
   dt James F & Melinda

(Thomas of Hopewell MM, N Car) (b 5-23-1784 probably
   d in N Car prior to 1846)
Sarah (Griffin) b 10-19-1794 N Car  d 6-2-1848
   bur Spiceland Mtg  dt Suthy & Alse
Ch: (who came to Ind with their mother)
- Jacob — b 10-25-1825
- Sally A — b 8-29-1827
- William C — b 9-26-1831
- Elmina — b 10-20-1836

## JACKSON
(William)
   m (10-4-1860)
Isabel (Guinn) b 7-2-1843 Miamiville, Ohio  dt David
   & Lydia

Hettie  b 4-3-1850 Jennings Co, Ind  dt Presley &
   m (1867)                                Nancy Ann
to J H Waymire

## JAMES
David  b 5-11-1803 in Ohio  s Isaac & Sarah, decd
   m 1st
Mary (Hunt) b 3-30-1804 N Car  dt Isom & 2nd w
   Margaret (Bundy)
Ch:
- Ruth Ann — b 10-17-1823  Ind
- Mary — b 2-18-1825  Carmel, Ohio
- Levi C — b 10-20-1828
- Atticus S — b 10-16-1830  Ind
- Alfred P — b 12-19-1832
- Jonathan H — b 4-4-1835
- Lindley M — b 1-1-1837  d 4-16-1859

## JARRET
Mabel Clair  b - - - -  d 7-8-1925
   dt John W & Rebecca (Thornburg)

Martha Lenora  b 1-21-1863 Davidson Co, N Car
   dt James & Rebecca (Secrease) Jarret &
   adopted dt of William & Elizabeth (Schooley)
   Sheridan

## JAY
James  b 11-22-1822 Silver Creek MM, Ind  s John &
   Keturah (Hollingsworth)
   (m 8-20-1846 West Branch MM, Ohio)
Susannah (Jones) b 8-23-1820 Ohio  dt Elisha & Rebecca
   (Pearson)  his 2nd w

(Joseph  s David & Ruth of Ohio) (b 11-22-1800)
Edith (Mills) b 6-16-1799 Bush River MM, S Car
   dt Marmaduke & Patience
Ch:
- Ruth Ann — b 3-3-1823
- Asenath — b 2-1-1825
- Hugh — b 2-15-1827
- Rachel — b 9-16-1830
(after the d of Joseph, Edith m 2nd  Thomas Kirk)

## JESSOP
Elias  b 8-31-1794 Stokes Co, N Car  d 7-3-1868
   Spiceland, Ind  s Pratt & Hope (White)
Ann (Hoskins) b 7-10-1788 Guilford Co, N Car
   d 3-20-1875 Spiceland, Ind  dt Joseph & Hannah
Ch:
- Jesse B — b 1-19-1824

Jesse B  b 1-19-1824 Guilford Co, N Car  s Elias &
   m 1st                                Ann (Hoskins)
Catherine (Macy) b 1-31-1831 (d ca 1850 - 1852)
   dt Enoch & Nancy (Rayl)
Ch:
- Elmina — b 1-6-1849  d 12-9-1865
   bur Elm Grove Mtg, Ind
   m 2nd
Lucinda (Mendenhall) dt Benjamin & Margaret  d 7-25-1857
Ch:
- Theodore H — b 12-27-1854
- Melissa — b 7-3-1857
   m 3rd (1858)
Milly (Newby) dt Henry & Sarah of Rush Co, Ind d 10-15-1863
Ch:
- Henry — b 11-18-1859
- Ann — b 4-10-1861  d  bur Spiceland Mtg, Ind
   m 4th (1865)
Cynthia (Cook) Fentress  wid of William & dt John &
   Julia Cook, b 8-10-1839 Greensboro, Ind

SPICELAND

## JESSOP (Cont)
Tidamon    b 9-27-1800 Stokes Co, N Car    d 4-24-1866
    bur Elm Grove Mtg, Ind   s Pratt & Hope (White)
Lydia (Morris)   b 1-15-1809 Pasquotank Co, N Car
    dt Joshua & Mary (Morgan)
Ch: Morris      b 9- 4-1826   Wayne Co, Ind
    David       b 2- 1-1828   Henry Co, Ind
    Susanah     b 9-20-1829
    Mary        b 3-15-1831
    Ruth        b 1- 2-1833
    Charles     b 12- 1-1834
    Martha      b 7- 1-1837
    Priscilla   b 12-18-1838
    Emily       b 8-22-1840
    Naomi       b 10-19-1842

## JOHNSON
Albert   b 10-17-1843 Spiceland, Ind   s Caleb &
                                        Asenath (Evans)
Martha H (Wood)
Ch: Arthur W    b - - - -
    Rothens C   b - - - -
    Gracie J    b - - - -

Caleb   b 11- 8-1820 New Garden MM, N Car  (s James &
    m 1st                                   Mary (Foster))
Asenath (Evans)   b 10-14-1822 Miami MM, Ohio
    d 7-22-1854 bur Spiceland, Ind  (dt George &
    Mary (Hasket))
Ch: Albert      b 10-17-1843  Spiceland
    Mary E      b 4- 6-1845
    Horace M    b 11-12-1850
    Josephine   b 3-21-1854   d 6-24-1858
    m 2nd
Miriam A (Wilson)   b 9- 3-1834  dt Joseph G & Hope
Ch: Louisa      b 2- 2-1860  Spiceland
    Ada         b 1-17-1861
    Caleb B     b 8-27-1866
    James H     b 12- 3-1873

Carl    b 6-28-1891 Henry Co, Ind  s Curtis & Laura
                                            (Hall)

Charles C   b 2-18-1857 Spiceland  (s Hiram & Rhoda
    m (5-13-1884)                          (Gurley))
Emma R (Timberlake)   b 7- 7-1859 Center Mtg, Ohio
    dt Alfred & Phebe
Ch: Orville H   b - - - -
    Mildred M   b - - - -

Evan
Betsy A (- - - -?)
Ch: Madison     b 3-27-1855   Henry Co, Ind
    Susan       b - - - -

Hiram   b 6- 7-1826 N Car  d 10-30-1895  bur in Oregon
    (s Joshua,decd & Sarah (Gordon))
    m (9-12-1850 Guilford Co, N Car)
Rhoda J (Gurley)   b 5-25-1831 N Car  d 2-22-1905
    Rush Co, Ind   bur Circle Grove Cem, Spiceland
    dt Charles & Ruth (Mendenhall) decd
Ch: Lindley H   b 12-22-1851  Cane Creek Mtg, N C
    Charles C   b 2-18-1857   Spiceland, Ind

James   b 3-20-1790 N Car  d 4-6-1851  bur Spiceland
    Mtg    s Caleb & Elizabeth (Rayle)
    m 1st
Mary (Foster)   b 7-24-1794  d 3-15-1835 bur Spiceland
    dt John & Grace (Dicks)
Ch: Anna        b 6- 2-1813   N Car
    Abigail     b 8- 1-1814   " "
        d 7- 1-1820  bur New Garden, N Car
    Rachel      b 9-30-1816   " "
    Elizabeth   b 10-22-1818  " "
    Caleb       b 11- 8-1820  " "
    Emily G     b 10-20-1823  " "
    John W      b 1- 7-1830   Ind
    Calvin      b 8- 2-1832   "
        d 9-18-1832  bur Spiceland
    Mary        b 2-27-1835   "
    m 2nd (1838)
Rebecca (Albertson)   White wid of Robert  b 11-10-1797
    in N Car    d 11- 4-1852 bur Raysville Mtg, Ind
    dt Francis & Caroline Albertson

John W   b 1- 7-1830   s James & Mary (Foster)
Frances (Scott)   b 3-12-1836   dt Jesse
Ch: Keotie B    b 1-31-1858
    Anna Mary   b 2-26-1860

(Joshua jr   s Joshua Sr & Mary (Hargrave))  (b 10-17-1786)
Sarah (Gordon)   b 4- 7-1789 Deep River MM, N Car
    (dt Charles & his 1st w Mary)
Ch: (who came to Spiceland with their mother)
    Susan       b 9- 9-1816   Cane Creek MM,
        N Car       d 1907
    Hiram       b 6- 7-1826   "    "    "

Lindley   b 12-22-1851 N Car   d 9-mo-1919
    (s Hiram & Rhoda (Gurley))
    m (8-23-1882 Henry Co, Ind)
Susanna (Timberlake)   b 4-17-1850 Wilmington, Ohio
    dt Alfred & Phebe (Doan)
Ch: Arthur Clarkson   b 2-12-1884  Dunreith, Ind
    Rhoda Grace       b 2-17-1887  d 2- 1-1898

Madison   b 3-27-1855 Guilford Co, N Car   s Evan &
    m 1st                                     Betsey
Mary (Hayes)   b 1- 2-1859 Henry Co, Ind  dt Joel &
                                              Lucinda
Ch: Minnie      b 7-13-1879   Henry Co, Ind
    - - - -?    b 2- 4-1883
    m 2nd
Bell (- - - -?)

Richard
    m (11-14-1900 Henry Co, Ind)
Ora E (Millikan)   b 7-10-1872  dt Thomas K & Semira
                                            (Rayle)

William A   b 12-25-1876 Rush Co, Ind  s Christopher &
                                                Alta
Maude (Dalympell)   b 4-19-1881  dt George & S- - -?
Ch: Clarence    b - - - -

## JONES
Barton E   b 7-13-1884   s Henry W & Carrie (Thornburg)
    m (9- 4-1905 Henry Co, Ind)
Anna (Johnson)   b 4- 5-1885 Terre Haute, Ind

Barclay   b 5-15-1844 Cass Co, Ind  s Henry & Susanna
Rhoda (Kendall)   b 9-30-1848 Hamilton Co, Ind
    dt Al- - -? & Rhoda

(Charles, decd  s Joseph & Mary (Overman))  b 10- 9-1791
    Suttons Creek MM, N Car  d 5-10-1826 Suttons
    Creek MM, N Car
(Nancy (Wells)  dt Joseph of Perquimans Co, N Car)
    (after Charles's death, Nancy mcd - - -Charlesbury)
Ch: (to Indiana)
    Parthena    b 4-12-1821
    Margaret    b 3-24-1823

Henry Warren   b 2-23-1845 Miami Co, Ohio  (s Samuel
    B & Rhoda (Coates))
    m (12- 9-1876)
Carrie (Thornburg)   b 9-26-1856 Charlottesville, Ind
    d 7- 4-1918  dt William W & Elizabeth (White)
Ch: Auvard Beven   b 5-23-1883   Spiceland, Ind
    Barton E       b 7-13-1884

J Chapin
    m (10- 6-1887)
Ella (Williams)   b 9-13-1855 Franklin, Wayne Co, Ind
    dt Joseph & Susan

James R   s - - - -   (rec on req 1874)
Achsah (- - - -?)
Ch: Anna L      b - - - -
    Mary F      b - - - -

Lydia (? Small?) Jones  (b 12- 8-1786 if the dt of Obediah
    decd & w Elizabeth (Symons) Small)  d 12- 7-1839
    (recorded in Spiceland Mtg, listed on the line immediate-
    ly after the record of the death of Elizabeth Newby who
    d 2-15-1842 bur Spiceland)  (This Lydia Jones probably
    is a dt of Obediah Small jr, decd & his w Elizabeth
    (Symons) Small of Pasquotank Mtg, Back Creek Mtg, Spring-
    field Mtg, N Car & Elk Mtg, Ohio White Water Mtg, New
    Garden Mtg, West Grove Mtg, Milford Mtg, Duck Creek Mtg
    & Spiceland Mtg, Ind)

SPICELAND

JONES (Cont)
Lydia (Cont)  (Elizabeth (Symons) Small, wid, m 2nd, in 1805 at Springfield Mtg, N Car to William Newby a wid  They went to Ohio & then came in to Indiana)
(Elizabeth (Symons) Small had a son Josiah Small who with the above Lydia Jones, came to Indiana and lived in the same mtgs that Elizabeth (Symons) Small Newby & her 2nd husb, William Newby, lived in)

Mourning P  b 9- 6-1817

(Stephen)
Louisa M (Coffin) b 8- 4-1851 dt Emory D & Elmina

(Sylvester H  s John D & Susannah)
(Mary A (- - - -?))
Ch:  (William C  b - - - -)
    (Maude  b - - - -)

JORDON
Maude May  b 9-12-1886 Ogden, Ind  dt William & Hannah
  m to
  - - - -? Whitsell?

JULIAN
Reno M  b 7-27-1864 Henry Co, Ind  s Emsley & Mary
  m (1892 Wayne Co, Ind)
Lillian (Fifer) b 10-22-1868 Henry Co, Ind dt Henry & Mary
Ch:  Clarice  b 7-29-1896 Hancock Co, Ind
    Jessie Mae  b 6- 6-1906 Henry Co, Ind

William A  b 3-12-1857 Henry Co, Ind  (s Amaziah & Mary (Rutledge)) of Juniata, Nebr
Grace (Russell)

KAUFMAN
Martha  b 12-24-1854 Wayne Co, Ind  d 1- 3-1910
  dt Amos & Fanny

KEARNS
Thomas  b 2-18-1818 Randolph Co, N Car  d 12-29-1881 Spiceland, Ind  s William & Margaret
  m (9-mo-1850)
Mary (Stuart) b 3-19-1828 Davidson Co, N Car
  dt Jehu & Rebecca
Ch:  Delphina J  b 9-24-1853 d 6- 6-1873
      bur Elm Grove, Ind
    Sarah E  b 5-25-1856 Salem Church, N Car
    Jehu S  b 2-15-1859 d 5-19-1880
      Spiceland, Ind
    Nereus A  b 8- 2-1861

KELLUM
Jesse
  m (2-22-1894)
Caroline E (Unthank) b 7-12-1860 dt John & Martha (Hobbs)

KENDALL
(David  s Thomas & Elizabeth of Whitewater Mtg, Ind)
  (b 7-30-1815 N Car)
  (m 1837 Spiceland Mtg, Ind)
(Charity (Dickey)  dt Nimrod & Ann) (b ca 1816)

(Wilson  s William & Abigail (Weisner)) (b 5- 7-1843 Chester Mtg, Ind)
  (m (7-30-1865 Henry Co, Ind)
Martha (Weisner) b 8- 4-1842 Henry Co, Ind
  dt William & Sarah
Ch:  Anna M  b 10-15-1875 Wayne Co, Ind
    Clara B  b 11-18-1882

KENNEDY
George F  b 12-25-1850 Neuse MM, N Car  s Thomas J & his 2nd w, Achsah (Pike)
  (George's mth, Achsah had d in N Car, 7-17-1852 & his fth, Thomas J had come to Indiana to m (in Parke Co, Ind) to Isabella Musgrave  Thomas J d in Ind on 11-17-1864)

KENWORTHY
Amos  b 7-12-1789 Pipe Creek MM, (?)  s William & Mary of Washington Co, Pa
  m 1st (3-13-1815 Redstone MM, Pa)

Mary (Miller) b 8-20-1792 Hopewell MM, Va  d 6- 2-1844 bur Raysville Mtg, Ind  dt Robert & Cassandra of Fayette Co, Pa
Ch:  William  b 1-19-1816 Pa
    Robert  b 2- 5-1819 Pa
    Jesse W  b 8- 6-1822 Ohio
    Joel  b 9-11-1824
    Willis  b 8-26-1826
    Ann  b 9- 4-1828
    Amos M  b 6-17-1830
    Isaac F  b 1-28-1834
  m 2nd (1846)
Elizabeth (Gilbert) Newby  wid Jonathan Newby  b 8- 3-1802 Randolph Co, N Car  dt Josiah & Dorothy

Amos M jr  b 6-17-1830 Ohio  s Amos Sr & Mary (Miller)
Phebe H (Reynolds) b 1-20-1828 Center MM, N Car
  dt Job & Phebe (Hockett)
Ch:  Oliver N  b 8- 1-1853
    Charles H  b 9- 2-1860
    Phebe H  b - - - - -

Charles H  b 9- 2-1860 Morgan Co, Ind  s Amos M jr & Phebe H (Reynolds)
  m (4- 7-1881)
Cynthia A (Edwards) b 9-12-1860 Grant City, Ind
  dt James & Peninah
Ch:  M Ethel  b 11-24-1882 Charlottesville, Ind

Jesse W  b 8- 6-1822 Ohio  s Amos & Mary (Miller)
Eliza D (Gregg) b 3-23-1823  dt Stephen & Hannah
Ch:  Ambrose A  b 8- 5-1843
    Mary Elizabeth  b 4-16-1845
    Emily G  b 5-11-1846

Joel  b 9-11-1824 Ohio  s Amos & Mary (Miller)
Rebecca (Spencer) b 4-25-1825 Concord MM, Ohio
  dt David & Leah (Pickering)
Ch:  Alba- -?  b 6-13-1847 Spiceland Mtg
    David Edwin  b 9-21-1848
    - - - - - -?  b 7-15-1852
    Oliver A  b 3-10-1854

Murry
  m (9-30-1902)
Ida Lenora (Holloway) b 9-19-1874 dt Asa & Lizzie (Edwards)

Robert  b 2- 5-1819 Pa  s Amos & Mary (Miller)
Doughty (Saint) b 8- 6-1818  dt William & Achsah
Ch:  Albert E  b 12-24-1842
    Mary  b 6-23-1845
    Charles M  b 9- 5-1846 d 8-28-1854
      bur Raysville, Ind
    Achsah  b 5-15-1849
    Harriett  b 8-21-1851
    John  b 8- 8-1853

Truman C  b 3-17-1863 Sugar Creek Mtg, Iowa
  s Isaac & Abigail (Hiatt)
  m (10-24-1889 Oskaloosa, Iowa)
Marianna (Thomas) b 9-17-1867 Cadiz, Ohio
  dt Peter L & Mary
Ch:  Helen  b 7- 8-1890 Hubbard, Iowa
    Mary  b 5-31-1892 Des Moines, Iowa
    Richard  b 4-14-1894
    Catherine  b 1- 3-1898 Oskaloosa, Iowa
    Eunice E  b 10-24-1900
    Isabel  b 10- 3-1902

William  b 1-19-1816 Pa  s Amos & Mary (Miller)
  m 1st
Asenath (Patterson) b - - - - d ca 1843 Walnut Ridge Mtg, Ind  dt Gerred or Jared & Angelina (Binford)
Ch:  Sarah P  b 10-26-1838
    James  b 1-26-1840
  m 2nd (1845)
Mary Ann (- - - -?) of Duck Creek Mtg
Ch:  Phebe Ann  b 2- 1-1846
    Amos  b 9-13-1848

Willis  b 8-26-1826  s Amos Sr & Mary (Miller)
  m (1848 Duck Creek Mtg, Ind)
Naomi (Kirk) b 6-19-1827 Center MM, Ohio  dt Thomas & Sarah

SPICELAND

## KENWORTHY (Cont)
Ch: of Willis & Naomi
    Sarah Ann           b  9-12-1849  Spiceland Mtg, Ind
                     d  9- 8-1850  bur Duck Creek MM, Ind
    Milton              b 12-15-1852
    Elizabeth          b  9- 1-1854

## KERSEY
Asher    b 4-22-1807  N Car  s William & Rachel (Hiatt)
    m 1st
Susanna (Morgan)  b 11- 6-1809  Ind  d 11- 2-1833 bur Beth
    bur Bethel    dt Benjamin & Naomi (White)
Ch: Benjamin V        b 8- 2-1830
    George C          b 11-15-1832  d 7- 7-1833
                           bur Spiceland
    m 2nd (1835)
Edith (Elliott)
Ch: Joel               b  5-10-1836
    Jane
    Martha
    Clarkson
    Sarah Ellen
    Elizabeth
    Albert Henry

Eli     b  3- 6-1804  Springfield MM, N Car
    s William & Rachel (Hiatt)
    mou (Springfield MM, N Car)
Sarah (- - - -?)  dt Emsley & - - - -?
Ch: Minerva Jane      b 11-20-1827
    Maria             b  1- 4-1830
    William           b 12-13-1831
    Albert H          b  4-14-1834
    Robert            b  8-25-1836
    Caroline E        b 11-27-1838
    Horace            b  3- 8-1841

Vierling  s William & Rachel (Hiatt)
    m (Springborough MM, Ohio)
Mary Emily (Butler)  dt Micajah & Ann
Ch: Anna Maria        b  8-22-1840
    Richard Wakefield  b 11- 6-1842

William  b 8-27-1781  N Car  d  8-23-1844 bur Spiceland
    s Daniel & Mary (Carter)
Rachel (Hiatt  b 3-30-1781  N Car  dt William &
    Charity (Williams)
Ch: Anna             b  6-17-1802
    Eli               b  3- 6-1804
    Asher            b  4-22-1807
    Vierling         b  9- 8-1809
    John H            b 11-24-1811
    Silas H           b 12- 9-1818
    Mary C            b 11-11-1820
    Charity W        b  8-20-1822

## KIMBREL
Andrew J  b 8-27-1843  Henry Co, Ind  s Joseph &
    m ( 4- 5-1869)                    Claracy (Hays)
Mary J (White)  b 4- 3-1851  N Car  dt William
Ch: Otis              b  7-21-1870

Otis  b 7-21-1870  s Andrew J & Mary J (White)
Ida (Francis)  b 11-13-1874  dt David & Maria (Sword)
Ch: Olen              b  - - - -

Pearl M  b 11-10-1884  Henry Co, Ind  dt Taylor & Mary
    m (11-27-1900 Henry Co, Ind)        (Adams)
to - - - -? Vickery

## KINDLEY
(Joel  s John & Betty (Wilson))  (b 1-16-1811)
    (m 1832 Milford Mtg)
(Rachel (Hunt)  dt Jonathan & Phebe)  (b 8- 7-1813)
Ch: (Charles           b  8-25-1833)

## KING
Calvin  b 3-31-1853  N Car  s Anderson & Mason (Dickins)
    m (11-12-1873 Henry Co, Ind)
Emily A (Poe)  b 8- 5-1855  N Car dt D Milton & Elizabeth L,
                                             decd
Ch: Otis Edgar        b  8-24-1874  Spiceland, Ind
    Josie Ellen        b  6-15-1877
    Florence A         b  8-26-1880
    Clarence Hildred  b  8-31-1891
    Everett Aldon     b  8- 7-1895

(Isaac  s Michael & Hannah from Nottingham MM, Md & of
    Stillwater MM, Ohio)  (b ca 1800 Nottingham Mtg,
    Md)    (m 5- 1-1822 Stillwater MM, Ohio)
(Ann (Davis)  dt Harmon & Hannah (Middleton) from Va
    & of Ohio)  (b 10-21-1804 in Ohio)
Ch: Harmon            b - - - -    in Ohio
    Hannah            b - - - -    "  "
    Phebe             b  3-25-1826    "  "
    Rebecca          b - - - -    in Indiana
    Lydia             b - - - -    "  "
    Deborah          b - - - -    "  "

(Joseph  s Michael & Hannah from Nottingham Mtg, Md to
    Ohio)  (b 1796 Nottingham Mtg, Md)  (d 1- 5-1880
    bur Pennsville Mtg, Ohio)
    (m 1st  10-28-1818 Stillwater Mtg, Ohio)
(Mary (Morris)  dt Samuel & Sally (Moore) Morris of N Car)
    (b 2-13-1800 Contentnea Mtg, N Car)  (d 9-2-1845
    bur Fairfield Mtg, Ohio)
Ch:  (to Spiceland, Ind)
    Lydia            b  7- 6-1833  Morgan Co, Ohio
    Mariam           b  6- 5-1840   "  "  "

(Maximilian)
    m (1870)
Martha (Smith)  b 5-14-1847  Raysville, Ind  dt Jackson
                                           & Mary

Rufus P  a Minister
    m 1st
Emeline H (- - - -?)  d & bur Spiceland, Ind
Ch: Nelson M          b - - - -
    William           b - - - -
    m 2nd (prior to their arrival at New Garden MM,
Alice R                                N Car)

William
    m (1890)
Olinda F (Chamness)  b 1-18-1868  d 8-mo-1895
    dt William S & Rebecca J (Lamb)

## KIRK
Albert M  b 2-23-1860  Greensboro, Ind  s Thomas C &
                                   Martha (Draper)
    m 1st (7-30-1881 Henry Co, Ind)
Amanda R (Pearson)  b 7-25-1857  West Milton, Ohio
    dt Jesse & Rachel (Furnace)
Ch: Clifford F         b  3-30-1883  Spiceland
    m 2nd (6- 9-1906 Henry Co, Ind)
Mary A (Fry)  b 3-23-1860  Holmes Co, Ohio
    dt Eli & Catherine (Crile) Fry

Elmer E  b 1- 3-1862  Flushing MM, Ohio  s Allen M &
    Mary J (Reynolds)
    m (2-14-1889 Rock Island Co, Ill)
Agnes (Fields)  b 9-10-1867  Orion, Ill  d  1924
    dt John F & Rebecca (Dillon)
Ch: Park Fields        b  4-12-1898

Kersey E  b 6-29-1849  Flushing, Ohio  s Joshua &
    m 1st (10-13-1870 in Ohio)         Hannah
Mary L (Wilson)  b 8- 4-1851  Flushing, Ohio  d  1891
    dt William & Ruth
Ch: Walter J           b  8-16-1871  in Ohio
    Bessie H           b 12- 4-1874
    Annie Gertrude    b 12- ?-1876
    Florence M         b  6-17-1881  Spiceland, Ind
    Jennie E           b 10-31-1883
    m 2nd (10-20-1900 Henry Co, Ind)
Sarah (Snavely) Taylor, wid  b 10-11-1862 Lancaster
    Co, Pa  dt Josiah & Fannie (McElheny)

Louisa B  b 3-18-1847  Near Flushing, Ohio  dt Joshua
    & Hannah

(Thomas  from Center Mtg, Pa & Center Mtg, Ohio)
    m 1st in Pa
(Sarah (- - - -?))
Ch: (Israel             b 12-26-1810)
    (Hannah           b  2- 7-1813)
    (Elizabeth        b  4- 1-1815)
    (Mary Ann          b  8-26-1817)
    (Rachel            b  1-20-1820)
    (Thomas Clarkson  b  4-12-1825)
    (Naomi             b  6-19-1827)
    (Allen             b - - - - -)

## KIRK (Cont)
### Thomas (Cont)
m 2nd   (1840 Spiceland)
Edith (Mills) Jay wid of Joseph Mills  b 6-16-1799
   Bush River Mtg, S Car   dt Marmaduke & Patience Mills

Walter J  b 8-16-1871  in Ohio  s Kersey E & Mary J
      (Wilson) decd
Edna (Edwards)  b 9-30-1876  dt Benjamin, decd & Sarah
                                              (Smiley)

## KISER
Elmer W    b 10-19-1863  Rush Co, Ind  s Joseph &
   m (2-18-1891 Henry Co, Ind)    Mary (Newkirk)
Josie Alta (Lindamood)  b 12-9-1871  dt John & Elizabeth
                                              (Lontz)
Ch:  Minnie D              b  9-26-1891
     Flossie Elizabeth     b  1-25-1894  Dunreith, Ind

(George)
Flora (Lindamood)  b  3-14-1861  dt John & Elizabeth

## KISSEL
James M
   m  (ca 1882-1883)
Anna M (Talbert)  b 9-18-1854  dt Jabez & Mary (Cook)

## KNIGHT
(Elias  s Abel jr of N Car)  (b 5-11-1779)  dis New
     Garden MM, Ind  1836
     m (10-5-1809 Mt Pleasant MM, Va)
Sarah (Carey)  b 7-7-1778  (dt Samuel & Rachel)
Ch:  (Cynthia          b  2-12-1811)
     (Solomon          b  6-20-1812)
     Hannah            b  5- 8-1814
     Samuel            b 12- 9-1815
     Rachel            b  5-15-1818
     Abel              b  2-29-1820

John  (b 11-24-1779 in N Car records)  b 11-24-1780
     in Spiceland records  s Thomas & Elizabeth (Pitts)
Sarah (Meredith)  b 6-24-1775  dt James & Mary
Ch:  Mary              b  - - - -    N Car
     Elizabeth         b  - - - -     "  "
     Amelia            b  - - - -     "  "
     James             b  6-30-1817   "  "
     Nancy             b  8-26-1821   "  "
     Martha            b 10-28-1825   "  "
     Lucinda           b 12- 4-1830   "  "

## LACY
Emory E  b 8-8-1828  Henry Co, Ind  s A D & Margaret
   m  (9-3-1904)  Henry Co, Ind
Minnie (- - - -?)
Ch:  Alpheus
     Dolores
     Paul
     Doris

## LAMB
Caleb  b (ca 4-29-1799 Perquimans MM, N Car)
     (s Restore & Milicent (Winslow))
     (rmt 3-8-1823 Suttons Creek MM, N Car)
Sarah (Nixon) dt Nathan, decd & his 2nd w Margaret
     (Bagley)  b 9-13-1800  Suttons Creek MM, N Car
Ch:  Benjamin Bagley      b 12- 7-1823  N Car
     John Anderson        b  7- 7-1826
     Edmund               b  7- 4-1828
     David                b  1-17-1831
     Margaret             b  8-13-1833
     Jonathan             b  2-22-1836

Freeman
Mary Effie (Foster)  b 9-5-1876  dt Elijah & Mary
                                              (Pickett)

Samuel  b 9-6-1828  Madison Co, Ky  s Jacob & Polly

William N  b 4-6-1857  Wayne Co, Ind  s Abiatha & Eliza
   m 1st  (5-15-1881)
Louisa (Dennis)  b 8-31-1854  d (1881)  dt Mahlon &
                                                Louisa
Ch:  Genevra             b 10- 9-1881

   m 2nd  (10-26-1882)
Eveline (Dicks)  b 9-12-1855  dt Nathan & Nancy C (Allen)
Ch:  Pearl  (a male)     b  5- 1-1884  Spiceland

## LAMBERSON
Stella  b 3-22-1891  Henry Co, Ind  dt Winson & Mary

## LAND
William C    )  non member
Kate (McMahan) )     "     "
Ch:  Elby P              b  3-11-1889  Rush Co, Ind
     Charles G           b  9-30-1891   "    "   "

## LANE
Samuel  b 9-17-1852  d 12-20-1912  s George & Melissa
   m (11-10-1875 Henry Co, Ind)            (Tucker)
Sarah Ann (Newby)  b 3-20-1856  dt Joseph & Naomi (Dicks)
Ch:  Maude               b  8-21-1876  (a non mbr)
     Nellie              b  - - - - -
     Anna or Aura        b  2-26-1886
     Roena Naomi         b  9-12-1887
     Russell Otto        b  2-22-1889
     Melissa M           b 12-20-1891
     Chester Newby       b  7-11-1895

## LARRANCE
Daniel  b 8-2-1839  Spiceland, Ind  d 7-14-1924
     s Peter & his 3rd w, Sarah (Hinshaw)
   m  (9-14-1871)
Hannah (Thorn)  b 10-5-1843  Selma, Ohio
     dt Thomas & Ruth (Greene)
Ch:  Alice Carey         b  6- 6-1873
     Ruth Elma           b  3-16-1876
     Mary Effie          b 11-26-1878
     Bertha Olive        b  6- 1-1882

Nathan  (b 8-22-1812 Cane Creek MM, N Car  He had a
     twin sister, Ruth)  (s Peter & his 1st w, Abigail
     (Haydock))
Penninah (- - - -?)
Ch:  Lucinda             b  - - - -
     Louisa Jane         b  - - - -

Peter  b 6-2-1774  Randolph Co, N Car  d 9-18-1855
     bur Spiceland MM, Ind  s John & Ann
   m 1st  (ca 1795 Cane Creek MM, N Car)
Abigail (Haydock)  ca dt John & Susanna of Grange MM,
     Charlemont, Ireland   d ca 1815-1816
Ch:  (who came to Ind)
     Nancy               b  2-22-1798  (m Elisha Hammer)
     Isaac               b  6-14-1804
     Jonathan            b  8-30-1806
     Elizabeth           b 11-27-1809  (m Samuel Allen)
     Nathan  )           b  8-22-1812
     Ruth    ) twins     b  8-22-1812  (she m in N Car)
   m 2nd  (12-10-1817 Cane Creek MM, N Car)
Abigail (Hinshaw)  dt Benjamin & Elizabeth  d 9-10-1819
     (recorded Cane Creek Mtg, but bur Holly Spring MM,
     N Car)
Ch:  William             b 11-28-1818  N Car
   m 3rd  (1-13-1822 Marlborough MM, N Car)
Sarah (Hinshaw)  b 5-20-1795  d 10-21-1856  bur Spiceland
     Mtg, Ind   dt Thomas & Rebecca (Holoday)
Ch:  Jesse               b  2-17-1823  N Car
     Thomas H            b  3- 9-1825
     Rebecca             b 10-14-1826
     Patsey (Martha)     b  2-15-1830
     Winney              b  5-13-1831
     Stephen             b  2- 2-1833
     Sally               b  6-22-1835
     Hannah              b  5-28-1837  Henry Co, Ind
                         d  6-23-1899  bur Earlham
     Daniel              b  8- 2-1839
     Eliza               b  5-25-1841
(Peter was the father of 21 children, of that number,
     the above are known to have come to Indiana, some
     after their marriage)

## LEDBETTER
Isaac Elwood  b 8-22-1856  Guilford Co, N Car  d 8-mo-
     1907     s Frank & Louisa
   m  (4-24-1892 )
Retta (Barlow)  b 5-6-1867  Tipton Co, Ind
     dt Richard & Mary (Smith)

SPICELAND

## LEDBETTER (Cont)
Ch: Isaac & Retta
    Leroy             b 10- 6-1889  Dunreith, Ind
    Frank             b 7-23-1892
    Martha G         b 10- 6-1893
    Ruby              b 5-17-1896

## LEE
Emma (Edmundson) b 8-27-1867 Henry Co, Ind
    dt John & Elmina (Lupton)
    m (2-14-1898 Marion Co, Ind)
to - - - -? Lee

## LEEKE
- - - ? - - - -? (B & D page is torn and a piece is gone)
    b 12-17-1815 (we have no clue as to whether the
    person was male or female)

## LEFTER
Ora Alonzo D b 8-29-1865 Franklin Co, Ind
    s Daniel & Mary Catharine

## LEIGHTON
Scott D b 5-20-1862 Cumberland Me s Albert & Salome
    m (11-15-1916 Henry Co, Ind)
Lena (Poer) b 11-17-1870 Jasper, Mo dt Robert & Martha

## LEONARD
Jonathan b 12-19-1816 s Obadiah & Martha

## LEWELLING
(Meshack from Back Creek MM N Car)
    m 1st
(Jane (- - - -?)) d probably in N Car prior to 1822
Ch: Henry            b - - - -
    Henderson       b - - - -
    John             b - - - -
    William         b - - - -
    Seth             b - - - -
    m 2nd
(Margaret (- - - -?))
Ch: James M         b 2- 8-1841 Henry Co, Ind
    1871 m Augusta F (Byers)

## LINDAMOOD
Albert b 12- 1-1852 s John & Elizabeth (Lontz)
    m (1-mo-1881)
Mary E (Cude)

Emory b 5-26-1855 s John & Elizabeth (Lontz)
    m (2-18-1880)
Mary Malinda (Norris)

John b 8-29-1817 Mount Jackson, Va s Michael & Mary
    m 1st
- - - -?
    m 2nd (12-12-1867)
Elizabeth (Lontz) b 9-24-1829 Dayton, Ohio
    dt Samuel & Esther
Ch: (by both wives)
    Albert           b 12- 1-1852
    Emory            b 5-26-1855
    Flora A          b 3-14-1861
    Minnie           b - - - - -
    Josie Alta       b 12- 9-1870

## LLOYD
Robert (rec on req - 1873 Newgarden Mtg, N C)
    m (Henry Co, Ind)
Phebe Ann (Baldwin) b 7-27-1861 dt Franklin & Mary
    Ann (Hodson) Macy Baldwin
Ch: Atha Dora        b 4-22-1881 Henry Co, Ind
    Leora Alice      b 1-29-1883
    Willis           b 6-26-1885
    Homer Linden     b 3-15-1893
    Loring Russell   b 1-17-1900 d 5-20-1901

## LUPTON
David W b 6-29-1815 s Joseph & Esther of Hopewell MM,
    m (1-29-1835 Springboro MM, Ohio)    Va
Ann (Miller) (b 6-20-1809 Redstone MM, Pa)
    dt Solomon & Ruth (Neal) of Montgomery Co, Ohio
Ch: Ruth Esther      b 8-14-1837 Montgomery Co, Ind
    Beulah Emily     b 10-24-1840

    Richard P           b - - - -
    Joseph M            b 9-17-1842 d 12-14-1842
        Spiceland, Ind
    Solomon M          b 11- 7-1843 Spiceland
        d 3-20-1844

Deborah Ann (Ricks) wid of Nathan jr b 2-2-1816
    Southampton Co, Va dt of Arnold & Mary Ricks
    m (8-21-1839 Short Creek MM, Ohio)

## LYKINS
Jackson Sr d 9-29-1883 bur Spiceland
    m (3-16-1876 Wayne Co, Ind)
Sarah Jane (Williams) b 1- 7-1840 Wayne Co, Ind
    dt Absalom & Mary (Cook)
Ch: Sebastian        b 12-25-1875
    Sylvester        b 5-24-1878 Spiceland
    Jackson jr       b 3-15-1880

Jackson jr b 3-15-1880 Henry Co, Ind s Jackson Sr
    & Sarah J (Williams)
    m (2-25-1910 Kenton Co, Ky)
Gertrude G (Smiley) b 10-12-1888 Henry Co, Ind
    dt John & Kate (Allison)

Sebastian b 12-25-1876 s Jackson Sr & Sarah J (Williams)
    m ( 3- 4-1901)
Myrtle (McKillip)

## MACE
Rhoda (Davis) (b 8-30-1799) dt Joseph & Susanna
    wid of William Mace jr
    m 1st (11-28-1818 Core Sound MM, N Car)
to William Mace jr (b 12-21-1796) (d prior to 1832)
Ch: James Thomas    b - - - -
    Anna Taylor     b - - - -
    Joseph Davis    b - - - -
    m 2nd (11-21-1832 New Garden MM, Ind)
to Joel Hiatt

## MACY
Anna H b 6- 2-1814 New Garden Mtg, N Car
    dt Thaddeus, decd & Katherine (White) (now Katherine
    (White) Macy Coffin, a Minister)

Benedict b 2- 9-1819 s Enoch & Nancy (Rayl)
    m 1st
Rebecca (Gorden) b 7- 2-1819 d 3-15-1850 bur Elm
    Grove Mtg, Ind dt Richard & Susanna (Hiatt)
Ch: Lambert          b 9-19-1843 Henry Co, Ind
    Bartlett         b 6-14-1847 d 3-18-1850
        bur Elm Grove Mtg, Ind
    Richard G        b 3-15-1849 d 2-18-1850
        bur Elm Grove Mtg, Ind
    m 2nd
Mary (Jessop) b 3-15-1831 dt Tidamon & Lydia (Morris)
Ch: Samira           b 4- 8-1853 d 3-19-1854
        bur Elm Grove Mtg, Ind
    Samantha         b 6-17-1854
    Ruth Ann         b 1- 6-1856
    Julia Ann        b 9-19-1858
    Lydia             b 7- 2-1862 d 5-31-1863
        bur Elm Grove Mtg, Ind

Calvin b 10- 3-1822 s William & Phebe (Hiatt)
Dianna (Edgerton)
Ch: Hannah Ellen    b 5- 9-1845
    Martha           b 4-20-1847
    Silas            b 3-24-1852
    Isaac            b 4- 2-1855
    Jabez            b 11- 1-1856 d 5-26-1857
    Franklin         b 3-26-1858

Enoch b 9-13-1797 New Garden MM, N Car d 11- 6-1870
    Elm Grove Mtg, Ind s Thaddeus, decd & Catherine
    m (4-30-1818 New Garden MM, N Car)    (White)
Nancy (Rayl) b 2-16-1800 Guilford Co, N Car
    dt William & Elizabeth (Thorp)
Ch: Benedict         b 2- 9-1819 Hopewell MM, N Car
    William R        b 12- 1-1820
    Anna Jane       b 10-23-1822 d 7-22-1823 N Car
    Thaddeus         b 6-20-1825
    Alfred           b 4-15-1827
    Betsey Ann      b 1-22-1829 d 5-11-1830 N Car

SPICELAND

MACY (Cont)
Ch:     Enoch & Nancy (Cont)
        Catharine       b  1-13-1831
        Lillburn        b  2-23-1833
        Jesse           b  6-23-1835  d  1- 3-1836  N Car
        Robert          b  9-11-1837  Spiceland MM, Ind
            d  6-23-1839  bur Elm Grove Mtg, Ind
        Elizabeth       b 11- 6-1839
        Julia Ann       b  4-23-1842  d  4-15-1850
                            bur Elm Grove Mtg, Ind

(Jabez   s Stephen & Sarah (Baldwin))  (b 10-25-1813
    d  3- 2-1853  N Car)
Isabelle (Stephenson)   dt Robert & Phebe
Ch:    (to Spiceland)
       Mary Ann         b  9-13-1840  N Car
       Ann Elizabeth    b  - - - - -

John B  b  5- 3-1846  s William R & Sally W
Lizzie A (- - - -?)
Ch:    Isadore          b  2-23-1870
       Eva Pearl        b  3-24-1872

John M   b 12-28-1806  Guilford Co, N Car
    s Stephen & Rebecca (Barnard)
    m (Milford MM, Ind   1840)
Betsy Ann (White)  b  1- 6-1806  Perquimans Co, N Car
    dt Thomas & Jemima, decd
Ch:    Henrietta Maria  b  3-23-1841
       Margaret White   b 11-16-1842
       William Allen    b  8- 4-1845
    m 2nd  (1855  Hopewell Mtg)
Lydia Bell

(Joseph D)
    m  (12-24-1866)
Jane B (Talbert)  b  6-30-1842  Union Co, Ind
    dt (Jabez & Mary (Cook))
Ch:    Anna B           b 10-22-1867  Spiceland
       Edwin S          b  1-16-1870
       Sarah E          b  1-18-1873
       Lewis W          b 12-24-1876
       Oliver P         b 11-27-1879

Julius C  b  6- 6-1853  Spiceland   s William R & Sallie W
    m  (12-24-1877)                          (Dicks)
Emma E (Poer)  b  8-12-1854  Guilford Co, N Car
    dt Absalom & Mary (Hodson)
Ch:    Gertie           b  7-14-1879  Dunreith, Ind
       William          b  - - - - -

Lilburn  b  2-23-1833  Guilford Co, N Car  (s Enoch &
    Nancy (Rayl))
Martha (Gordon)  b 12-18-1836  Wayne Co, Ind  (dt Charles
    jr & Lydia R (Jessop))
Ch:    Ida Florence     b 11- 4-1858
       Lydia Alice      b  2- 6-1860
       Emily T          b  1-13-1862
       Charles          b 10- 6-1864

Nathan   b  8-16-1803  Guilford Co, N Car   s Thaddeus,
    decd & Catherine (White)
    m 1st
Jane A (Wilson)  b 10-22-1810  Jefferson Co, Tenn
    dt Jacob & Jane
Ch:    Whitesel D       b 12-26-1833  Henry Co, Ind
            d  5-11-1853  bur Elm Grove Mtg, Ind
       Lindley H        b  6- 3-1836
       Miriam B         b  9-21-1838  d  5-20-1855
                            bur Elm Grove Mtg, Ind
       Karrissa Ann     b  1- 7-1840
       Oliver C         b  9- 5-1842  d  5-14-1852
                            bur Elm Grove Mtg, Ind
       John Wesley      b  6- 3-1845
       Nathan jr        b  3-25-1848
    m 2nd  (1856)
Jannet (Saint) Pickering   wid Abner Pickering (b 2-16-1816)
    dt William & Acsah (Elliot) Saint
Ch:    Jane A           b  3- 5-1859  Spiceland MM, Ind

Samuel H   b  6-15-1841  Spiceland   s Solomon & Priscilla
                                                 (Hamm)
Louisa (Maxwell)  b  4-19-1843  Salem Mtg, Ind   dt Hugh
    & Anna (Talbert)
Ch:    Sarah T          b  9-17-1870
       Albert           b  9-27-1876

Solomon    b 11- 3-1805  N Car   d  8-24-1898 (an Elder)
    s Thaddeus, decd & Katherine (White)
    m  (12- 2-1830  Milford MM, Ind)
Priscilla (Hamm)  b  8- 3-1809  N Car  d  7- 9-1887 Ind
    dt John, decd & Elizabeth (Hubbard)
Ch:    Edwin            b 11-24-1831  Duck Creek Mtg
       Martha Ann       b  5-19-1833  Spiceland Mtg
       Elwood           b 11-16-1836
       Samuel H         b  6-15-1841
       Caroline Elizabeth  b  6-10-1845
       Mary Jane        b  7-28-1848

Stephen jr  b  8- 8-1813  Montgomery Co, Ohio
    s Stephen & Rebecca (Barnard)
Mary (Charles)  b  3- 6-1819  Whitewater MM, Ind
    dt John & Elvira, both decd
Ch:    Samuel           b  3- 6-1840  Hamilton Co, Ind
       Rebecca          b  6-14-1841  d 12-16-1844
                            bur Raysville Mtg, Ind
       Albert           b 10-31-1842  d 12- 6-1844
                            bur Raysville Mtg, Ind
       Eli              b 11- 4-1844

Stephen Sr  b 12- 4-1778  s Enoch & Anna (Macy) Macy
    m 1st
Rebecca (Barnard)  b  6-23-1776  d  7-30-1843 Spiceland
    dt Francis & Catherine
Ch:    (who came to Spiceland)
       John M           b 12-28-1806
       Stephen jr       b  2-18-1813
       Eunice B         b  7-13-1822
    (for Stephen & Rebecca's grandchildren under their
    care, see SWEET)
    m 2nd  (1844  Duck Creek Mtg)
Rebecca (Ratliff)

William  b  1-20-1799  Guilford Co, N Car
    s Thaddeus, decd & Catherine (White)
Phebe (Hiatt)  b  6-10-1801  New Garden MM, N Car
    (an Elder)      dt George & Sarah (Stanley)
Ch:    Anna             b 11-27-1820  Indiana
            d 11-12-1840  bur Elm Grove Mtg, Ind
       Calvin           b 10- 3-1822
       Susanna          b  3-16-1824
       Louisa (Luzena?) b  8- 9-1825
       Jason            b  4-25-1827
       Tyrrel           b 12-24-1828
       Sarah Jane       b 12-11-1830
       Catherine        b  7-27-1832
       Rebecca          b  4- 9-1834
       Seth             b 11-24-1835
       Jabez            b  8-17-1837
       Asenath          b  3-17-1839
       Jesse            b  6-21-1842
       Esther May       b  - - - - -

William R  b 12- 1-1820  Guilford Co, N Car
    s Enoch & Nancy (Rayl)
    m  (11-29-1843)
Sally W (Dicks)  b 12-21-1821  Guilford, N Car
    dt Job & Hannah (White)
Ch:    John B           b  5- 3-1846  Henry Co, Ind
       Samira           b  3- 5-1849  d  5-20-1849
                            bur Spiceland Mtg, Ind
       Emily            b  8-11-1850
       - - - -?         b  5- 4-1853

MANIFOLD
Josephine (Beeson)  b  2- 1-1882  dt David & E Adeline
    m  (12- 3-1908  Henry Co, Ind)       (Lemmons)
to - - - -? Manifold

MANLY
Jane H (Rayle)  b  6-28-1809  New Garden MM, N Car
    dt William & Elizabeth (Thorp) & sister to
    Mrs. Enoch Macy (Nancy (Rayle) Macy)

MARKS
(William a non mbr)
Prudence (- - - -?)  b  9-22-1836  Chatham Co, N Car
    d  5-26-1908
Ch:    May              b 12- 6-1870  N Car
       John C           b  1-28-1873
       Martha           b  3- 3-1879  Henry Co, Ind

SPICELAND

## MARSHALL
Jesse   b 7-23-1803  Green Co, Tenn  s Abram & Martha
                                                (Doan)
Mary (Pickering) b 5-10-1805  dt Ellis & Deborah
Ch:  Jane         b 1-16-1829  Green Co, Tenn
     William      b 9-16-1830
     Calvin       b 8-17-1832  Henry Co, Ind
     Levi         b 6-22-1834
     Eli          b 8-14-1836
     Nathaniel    b 6-14-1838  d 3- 4-1839
                  bur Spiceland Mtg

## MARTIN
Simon   b 1-22-1874  s Charles & Sarah
Hettie (Adams) b 3-14-1876  dt Stephen & Amanda
Ch:  Mabel        b 5-27-1895  Lewisville, Ind

## MAUDLIN - MODLIN
(Richard  s William & Ann (Ratliff))  (b 10-10-1813)
   (m 1st  1833 Milford Mtg)
(Gulielma M (Butler) dt Joseph, decd, of Va & Charlotte)
   (m 2nd  1838 Spiceland Mtg)
(Jane (- - -?) Osborn, a wid)

Thomas   b 1-23-1804  Randolph Co, N Car
   s Benjamin & Leah (Copeland)
Hannah (Sheridan) b 2-24-1802  dt John & Margaret
                                        (Osborn)
Ch:  Sarah        b 9- 1-1823  West Grove Mtg, Ind
                  d 10-10-1823  bur Spiceland
     Elizabeth    b 2-16-1825
     Benjamin     b 2-11-1827
     Margaret     b 2-18-1829
     John         b 3-25-1831  d 10-26-1831
                  bur Spiceland
     William      b 8-25-1832
     Leah         b - - - - -

## MAXWELL
David   b 11-23-1802  Knox Co, Tenn  s Hugh Sr & Elizabeth
        d 1-26-1880  bur Spiceland MM, Ind
        m 3rd
Lydia (Worth) Osborn, wid of Isaiah  b 11- 1-1805
     Center MM, N Car  dt Job & Rhoda (Macy) Worth

## MAYS
John Wesley  b 2-28-1823  Ross Co, Ohio  s L Berry &
     m (6-10-1877)                          Mahala
Elizabeth (Wyatt)  b 10-14-1832  Putnam Co, Ind
     dt Davis & Mary

## McCLAIN
Clifford   b 1-13-1890  Henry Co, Ind  s Thomas &
           Elizabeth (Quick)

## McCOY
Henry C   b 3- 8-1843
Rachel (Wilson) b 12- 2-1846  dt John W & Margaret
                                   Winslow (White)
Ch:  Willie Rufus    b 7-18-1865
     Margaret E      b 5-20-1868
     John            b - - - - -
     James           b - - - - -

## McCRACKEN
Joseph W  b 2-20-1882  Hoxie, Kansas  s Enos H & Anna
     m (9-29-1913 Henry Co, Ind)           (Frazier)
Bertha (Larrence) b 6- 1-1882  Clark Co, Ohio
     d in Cuba   dt Daniel & Hannah (Thorne)
Ch:  Ruth Ann       b 3-19-1915  Holguin, Cuba
     Lawrence R     b 8-28-1916  Guantanama, Cuba

## McDANIEL
Alice O (Whitley) b 4-20-1858  dt Robert H & Jane
                                         (Woolen)

## McFARLAND
John W  from Greensboro, N Car & Dunreith Mtg, Ind
Mary E (Welch) b 11-30-1853  Perquimans Co, N Car  d 1911
     dt James & Hannah (Copeland)

Mary    b 8-21-1879  Jay Co, Ind  dt J William & Polly
                    of Dunreith Mtg, Ind

## McGRAW
John W  b 7-28-1842  s Thomas & Elizabeth
     m (8-10-1868)
Anna Jane (Baldwin) b 5-18-1844  dt Uriah & Orpha of Ind
Ch:  Violetta       b 7-25-1869
     Margaret       b 10-26-1873
     Minerva J      b 10- 4-1875

## McINTOSH
Viola   b 7- 8-1865  Fayette Co, Ind  dt J & A McIntosh

## McKILLIP
Oliver V  b 12-13-1866  N Car  s James F & Malinda
     m (1-27-1894)
Anna E (Cox) b 10-16-1865  Ohio  dt George & Julia
Ch:  George O       b 5-25-1896  Spiceland, Ind

## McNARY
Francis   b 3-10-1815  Guilford Co, N Car  s J & B
     m (1871)                                  McNary
Mary Jane (Heath) Grice, wid  b 8-22-1834  Delaware Co,
     Ind  dt R & A Heath
Ch:  Mamie          b 2-23-1873

## McNEW
Earnest   b 12-23-1874
Harriet (Copeland) b 5-17-1880
Ch:  Orland         b 7-12-1898
     Earl           b 8- 8-1900

Stephen G  b 4-26-1803  Deep River MM, N Car
     s Nathan & Phebe (Haworth)
Sarah (Albertson) b 6-23-1805  Symons Creek MM, N Car
     dt Phineas & Rebecca (White)
Ch:  Catherine R    b 11-22-1828  Deep River MM, NCar
     Nathan         b 3-29-1832   Blue River MM, Ind
     Albert         b 11-12-1834  Salem Mtg, Ind
     Elizabeth      b 9- 4-1838   Rush Co, Ind
     Bartlett       b 1- 8-1841    "    "    "

## MENDENHALL
(Benjamin)  (b 9-11-1808)  (s of Moses & 2nd w Mary
     (Benbow) of Hopewell MM, N Car)
     m (2-25-1828) (mou) Hopewell Mtg, N Car
Margaret (Britton) b 9-15-1808  Guilford Co, N Car
     dt of Joseph & Mary Britton of Hopewell MM, N Car
     (from Membership book #1 page 58)
     (This Margaret gct Oskaloosa MM, Iowa 1895)

(David)  (b 11- 7-1802)  (s Mordecai & Margery (Piggott))
     of Springfield MM, N Car
     (m 4-20-1826  Deep River MM, N Car)
Margaret (Moore) b 7- 6-1806  Deep River MM, N Car
     (dt Jesse Sr & Mary (Morris) Anderson Moore)
Ch:  (to Spiceland Mtg, Ind with their mth after her m)
     (Clarky         b 1-10-1827)
     (m 1855 James M Wilson in N Car)
     (This Margaret gct Greenwood MM, Ind 1865)

(Marshall)  (see mbrps book #1 Page 58)
     m (3-31-1864)
Susan C (Stanley) b 7-13-1835  Spiceland
     dt Nathan, decd & Delana (Stanley) Stanley
Ch:  George C       b 3-21-1866  Terre Haute
     Phebe Jane     b 5-10-1867  d 4-27-1876
                    Spiceland Mtg
     Delana         b 12-12-1869 d 5-18-1876
                    Spiceland Mtg
     Nathan         b 8-20-1873  d 9-20-1873
                    Bethel Mtg

(Moses, decd of Hopewell MM, N Car) (b 10-13-1778)
     (s Aaron & Miriam (Rich))  (d 5-26-1847 Hopewell
     MM, N Car)
     mou 1st
Millicent (- - -?)  (d ca 1805)
     (m 2nd  ca 1806)
(Mary (Benbow) dt Benjamin & Lydia (Reynolds))
     (b ca 1790)  (d ca 1822-1823)
     (m 3rd 7- 1-1824  Hopewell MM, N Car)
Nancy Ann (Benbow) b 11-20-1796  dt Benjamin & Lydia
                                          (Reynolds)
Ch:  (who came to Spiceland with their mother)
     Mary           b 10-16-1826
     Dinah          b 7-12-1835

SPICELAND

## MEREDITH
(James jr of Dover MM, N Car  dis)
Mary (- - - -?)
Ch: Joanna           b  6-27-1816  N Car
    Thomas Jefferson b  6-30-1817
    James Harvey     b  4-15-1819
    Rosanna          b  - - - - -
    Jabez            b 11-11-1823
    Jesse            b  3-10-1825
    William          b  3- 3-1827
    Susan            b  - - - - -

Jabez    b 11-11-1825  Dover MM N Car   d  9-18-1896
    s James jr & Mary (- - - -?)          Spiceland
    m (12-30-1846  Henry Co, Ind)
Louisa (Antrim)  b 10- 8-1829  Hagerstown, Ind
    d  8-25-1909  Spiceland (dt James & Mary (Beard))
Ch: Alfred H         b  5-21-1848
    Ann              b 10-31-1850  d  4- 1-1898
    William          b 12-18-1854
    Emmeline M       b 12-10-1856
    Elwood           b 10- 4-1861  d  7- 7-1864
    J Harvey         b  8-25-1862  Henry Co, Ind

Jesse    b  3-10-1825  Dover MM, N Car   s James jr &
    Mary (- - - -?)
Luzena (Macy)  b  8- 9-1825  dt William & Phebe (Hiatt)
Ch: Charles O        b 10-16-1844  Henry Co, Ind
    Franklin         b 10- 4-1846
    Melissa Ann      b  4-12-1848
    Joshua           b 12-16-1851
    James H          b  9- 1-1854
    Marshall         b  8-27-1856
    Elizabeth M      b  - - - - -
    Elvira           b  - - - - -

William   b 12-18-1854  Henry Co, Ind  s Jabez & Louisa
    m (9-25-1876  Henry Co, Ind)            (Antrim)
Mary Elizabeth (Harrington) b 10-23-1856  Chatham Co, N
    Car    d 12-22-1913  dt Perry & Prudence E
Ch: John             b 12- 9-1891
    Jabez            b 11-17-1894
    Alfred           b  8-11-1896

## MERKEL
(Christopher)
Sylvia (Compton) b  7- 5-1857  West Milton, Miami Co,
    Ohio     dt Phares & Delitha Ann (Bailey)

## MIDKIFF
Daisy (Allison)  b  9- 8-1867  Henry Co, Ind
    dt Leonidas & Marietta

## MILES
Alice Marjorie   b  3- 9-1865  St Johns, New Brunswick,
    Canada  dt John C & Lucinda C Miles
    m (6-18-1895  Lynn, Mass)
to - - - -? Hill

Margaret J (Brewer)  b 10-17-1859  Randolph Co, N Car
    dt William & Elizabeth (Poe)

Melissa E  b  6-26-1833  Union Mtg, Ohio  dt Samuel &
    his 1st w, Anna (Kelly) decd

Rachel E   b  8- 6-1842  Union Mtg, Ohio  dt Samuel & his
    3rd w, Elizabeth (Neal)

## MILLER
Phebe    b 11-20-1829  Springborough MM, Ohio  dt Caleb &
    Phebe, decd  (now under the care of David & Ann
    (Miller) Lupton)

Thomas Benton
    m (9-27-1882  Henry Co, Ind)
Luetta (Winters)  b 12- 4-1864  Guilford Co, N Car
    dt John W, decd & Melvina (King)

## MILLIKAN
Thomas K   b  6-26-1846  d  7- 9-1920  s William & Susan
    m (11-18-1869  Henry Co, Ind)           (Frazier)
Semira (Rayl)  b  4-14-1850  d  9-7-1913  dt Zadock &
    Delilah (Hunt)
Ch: Ora E            b  7-10-1872

William  b  9-12-1805  Springfield MM, N Car  d  5- 2-1887
    s Eli & Mary (Kersey)
    m 1st (5-13-1830  West Grove MM, Ind )
Charity (Canaday) b  9- 6-1809  (d 10- 3-1839)
    dt Charles & Sarah
    m 2nd (7- 9-1840) Flat Rock PM, Ind
Mary Russell        d  (1-20-1842)
Ch: Esther           b  4- 4-1841
    m 3rd (12- 8-1842 Flat Rock Mtg)
Susanna (Frazier)   d  7- 7-1852
Ch: (to Spiceland Mtg)
    Eli F            b  8-17-1843
    Thomas K         b  6-26-1846
    Rebecca Jane     b 12-12-1848
    William M        b  6-20-1851
    m 4th (12-10-1856)
Mary E Williams, wid of Ananias Williams  d  4- 7-1863
Ch: Priscilla E      b  2- 3-1859

William M  b  6-22-1851  s William Sr & 3rd w Susanna
Francis (Wiggs)                              (Frazier)

## MILLS
Earl S   b  9-16-1889  Henry Co, Ind  s Alonzo & Emma
    m (12-24-1909  Henry Co, Ind)       (Binford)
Blanche (Engle)  b  9-13-1889  Marion Co, Ind
    dt Perry & Margaret (Anderson)
Ch: Myron
    Lois
    Catherine

## MOFFET
Jesse
Sarah (Griffin)  b  1-26-1850  dt Samuel & Lydia (Reynard)

Reuben L  b 11-27-1856  Rush Co, Ind   s Reuben Sr &
                                            Ellen (Sears)

W S
    m (5-13-1890  Henry Co, Ind)
Emma (Kennard)  b  9-24-1856  Henry Co, Ind
    dt Jenkins & Ruth (Jessup)
Ch: Ruth             b  9-17-1891
    Essie L          b 11- 2-1893

## MOORE
(Abraham  s John & Mary of Pa, both decd) (b  6- 2-1786
    Pa) (d 12- 1-1843  bur New Garden Mtg, Ind)
    (m 1st)
(Susannah  (- - - -?))  (b  6- 7-1790)
    (d  2-13-1822  bur Center Mtg, Ohio)
Ch: (Hannah)
    (Jacob)
    m 2nd (5-17-1823  Center Mtg, Ohio)
(Hannah (Kirk)  dt Ezekiel & Hannah of Center Mtg, Pa &
    Center Mtg, Ohio)  (b  2- 9-1787) (d  2- 2-1865
    Milford Mtg, Ind)
Ch: (Abraham jr      b  7-26-1824)
    (Rachel P        b  3-22-1828)

Anna Mary  b  1- 5-1873  dt Joseph & Mary T

Charles Francis  b 11- 4-1874  d  2- 5-1894
    s Josiah & Mary

Charles   b  8-29-1788  New Garden MM, N Car
    s Camm & Sophia (Benbow)
Anna (Gregg)  b 12-14-1789  New Garden MM, N Car
    dt Moses & Martha
Ch: (who came to Spiceland Mtg)
    Caroline         b  4- 1-1827  N Car
    Emily            b  3- 4-1830  West Grove MM, Ind
    Charles H        b  7-29-1832
    Anna             b  3-17-1836  bur Elm Grove Mtg
                     d  4-14-1836

Charles Henry  b  8-29-1832  Ind  d 11-mo-1896
    m (12-19-1854)  s Charles Sr & Ann (Grigg)
Ellen (Johnson)  b  5- 9-1838  Guilford Co, N Car
    d  9-23-1902  dt Samuel B & Martha

Gideon   b  5- 4-1835  Ind  s William & Anna (Small)
Mary J (- - - -?)
Ch: Laura Emma       b  7-31-1862
    Charles B        b  4- 2-1866
    Carrie J         b  5- 7-1868

SPICELAND

MOORE (Cont)
Mary Ida (Pike) wife of William Moore  b 10-21-1866
    Rush Co, Ind   dt Ephraim & Beulah Ann

Thomas  b 7-30-1820  Wayne Co, Ind  William & Ann (Small)
Phebe (King)  b 3-25-1826  dt Isaac & Ann (Davis)
Ch: Isaac Hezekiah    b 10- 6-1844 Henry Co, Ind

William  b 12-23-1788  N Car  s Thomas & Isabel (Newby)
    m 1st (1817 Whitewater Mtg, Ind)            decd
Ann (Small)  b 4-27-1802  d 3-18-1843  bur Spiceland Mtg
    dt Gideon, decd & Sarah (Griffin)
Ch: Samuel           b 6-18-1818  Ind
    Thomas           b 7-30-1820
    Achsah           b 7-18-1822
    Truman           b 7-19-1824  d 12- 6-1839
                     bur Spiceland
    Margaret K       b 5-14-1828  d 7-30-1836
                     bur Spiceland
    Abigail          b 10-14-1830
    Gideon           b 5- 4-1835
    Josiah           b 5- 7-1838
    m 2nd  (1844 Hopewell Mtg)
Ann (- - - -?) Stretch, wid of James  b 12- 5-1790
    d 10-13-1845  Spiceland Mtg

MORGAN
Charles  b 2-18-1801  N Car (Randolph Co)  s Benjamin
    & Naomi (White), decd  (d 8- 7-1864 bur Earlham)
Michal (Butler)  b 4-10-1802  Dinwiddie Co, Va
    (d 8-19-1888  bur Earlham) dt William & Mary
Ch: Edward           b 11-19-1826  Henry Co, Ind
    Elizabeth        b 10-20-1828
    William B        b 12- 2-1830
    Benjamin         b 3-29-1834  Wayne Co, Ind
    Naomi            b 3-14-1838  Henry Co, Ind
    Mary Emily       b 12-16-1843  d 5-14-1857
                     bur Raysville Mtg

Edward  b 11-19-1826  Wayne Co, Ind  s Charles &
    Michale (Butler)
Rachel (Parker)  b 3-30-1829  Jefferson Co, Ohio
    dt Benajah & Grace (Patten)
Ch: Oliver           b 4-19-1849  Hamilton Co, Ind
    Emma             b - - - - -  Spiceland, Ind

George W  b 2-12-1848  Guilford Co, N Car  d 7-24-1912
    s William & Mariam (Taylor)
    m (10-17-1878 Henry Co, Ind)
Rose A (King)  b 12-31-1845  Guilford Co, N Car
    dt Anderson & Mason (Dickins)

Hezekiah  (b 2- 6-1796  a twin bro to Obadiah)
    (d ca prior to 1837 probably at Duck Creek Mtg, Ind)
    s Thomas & Ruth (Weisner)
    (mcd   1816 Lost Creek MM, Tenn)
(Lydia (Hammer) dt Isaac & Hannah (Mills)) (b 3-17-1799)
Ch: (Obadiah         b 2-20-1817)
    (Henry           b 4- 9-1818)
    (Thomas          b 12-24-1819)
    (Isaac           b 2- 3-1822)
    (James           b 11- 5-1824)
    (Hannah          b 1-13-1826)
    (Rebecca         b 11-24-1827)
    (Nathan          b - - - - -)
    (Hezekiah jr     b - - - - -)
    (Demarius        b - - - - -)
    (Zeno            b - - - - -)
(after the death of Hezekiah, Lydia m 2nd & was dis,
    to - - - -? Adamson)

Obadiah  (b 2- 6-1796 a twin bro to Hezekiah)
    s Thomas & Ruth (Weisner)
    (m 11- 4-1820 Newberry MM, Tenn)
(Ann (Jones) dt Thomas & Margaret (Marshall)) (b 7-21-1803)
Ch: (Hezekiah        b 11-23-1821)
    (Margaret Jane   b 7-27-1823)
    (Thomas          b 5-11-1826)
    (Sophia          b 7-27-1828)
    (Joseph          b 12-10-1830)
    (William J       b 1-13-1833)
    Mary Jane        b - - - - -

William B  b 12- 2-1830  s Charles & Michal (Butler)
    m (10-10-1855 Back Creek MM, N Car)
Sarah (Henley)  b 3- 2-1830  Back Creek MM, N Car

    dt Jesse & Margaret (Clark)
Ch: William Earl     b 9-29-1859  Wayne Co, Ind
    Jesse Henley     b 7- 6-1861

MORRIS
Benjamin  b 10-29-1808  Randolph Co, N Car
    (s Reuben & Miriam (Copeland))
- - - - -?
Ch: Hannah           b 3-24-1833
    Levi             b 1-20-1835

Benjamin  b 4-19-1800  Wayne Co, N Car  d 2-18-1892
    bur Spiceland, Ind  s William & Susannah (Copeland)
    m (10- 3-1821) (Somerset MM, Ohio)
Elizabeth (Leslie)  b - - - -  Nottingham MM, Pa
    dt Robert & Rachel of Monroe Co, Ohio
Ch: (Robert L        b 8-25-1822  Somerset MM, Ohio)
        dis in Ohio in 1844

Lydia  b 5-21-1814  Salem MM, Ohio (Columbiana Co)
    d 6-14-1882  Spiceland, Ind  dt William & Susanna
                                     (Copeland)

Martha (Pitts)  b 3-12-1853  N Car  dt Branson & Luzena
    m (11-14-1872 Shelby Co, Ind)
to - - - -? Morris

Nathan O  b 12-14-1834  Elizabeth City, N Car (Symons
    Creek MM, N Car)  s Joseph H, decd & Martha (Toms)
    m (10-26-1864 Milford MM, Ind)
Pharaba (Wilson)  b 8-19-1841  Belsidies, N Car
    dt Christopher, decd & Elizabeth
Ch: Joseph C         b 10- 5-1866  Kansas
    Edith Elizabeth  b 6-16-1868  Milford Mtg, Ind
    Francis          b 5-26-1870
    Annie M          b 12-20-1871  d 4- 3-1874
                     bur Dublin, Ind

Rachel  b 1-15-1824  Somerset MM, Ohio (Belmont Co)
    d 3-26-1909  Spiceland  dt William & Susanna
        (Copeland)

Reuben  b 11-18-1780  N Car  d 1-14-1864  bur Spiceland
    Mtg, Ind   s Benjamin & Sarah
Miriam (Copeland)  b 6-19-1786  Chowan Co, N Car
    d 8-22-1860  bur Spiceland Mtg, Ind
    dt Joshua & Susanna (Pike)
Ch: Benjamin         b 10-29-1808  Randolph Co, N Car
    John             b 2- 7-1811
    Joseph           b 9-22-1813
    Sarah            b 10-10-1816  Ind  d 8-13-1854
                     bur Spiceland Mtg, Ind
    Levi             b 1-30-1819
    Samuel           b 7-29-1821
    Mary             b 12-21-1823

MUFFLEY
(Daniel of Columbiana Co, Ohio)
    m (1881)
Lucy Jane (Mills)  b  1847  Dark Co, Ohio  dt James &
                                               Lucretia
Ch: Margaret Edna    b    1882  Randolph Co, Ind
    Daniel Lester   b    1884
    Benjamin Golden  b    1886

MUNDEN
(Jesse  s Levi & Rhoda (Albertson)) (b 7- 6-1790
    Pasquotank Co, N Car)
    (m 4-17-1817 Suttons Creek Mtg, N Car)
(Mary (Bagley) Toms, wid of Anderson Toms & dt Nathan
    & Mary (Low) Bagley)
Ch: (Asenath         b 12-17-1817)
    (Margaret        b 4-30-1820)
    (Susannah        b 3-26-1827)
    (Calvin A        b 4-26-1830)

Joseph  b 11- 5-1802  N Car  s Mark & Peninah (Albertson)
Millicent (Albertson)  b 2-10-1805  N Car
    dt Thomas & Milicent (Bagley)
Ch: Peninah          b 2-14-1827  N Car
    Thomas           b 9-27-1828  Indiana
    Jane             b 5-13-1830
    Martha           b 1- 4-1832
    Mary Ann         b 3-21-1834

## MYERS
John C  b 7- 8-1865  Henry Co, Ind  s Elijah & Sarah
    m  (10-24-1889  Henry Co, Ind)
Ethel M (Pickering)  b 6- 2-1868  Henry Co, Ind
    dt of Philander & Lydia
Ch:   Robert E           b 2- 9-1900

## NEET
George W  b 3-15-1863  Parke Co, Ind  s Warren &
    m  (8-14-1894)                 Harriett
Callie (Harlan)  b 4-26-1867  Vermillion Co, Ind
    dt Eldridge & Matilda
Ch:   Helen             b 8- 7-1895 Spiceland, Ind

## NELSON
Rosmus
    m  (10- 3-1880)
Mary Emily (Talbert)  b 1- 1-1858  dt Milo & his 2nd
    w Eliza (Paddock)

## NEVITT
Thomas    (from Ohio)
    rmt  (10-26-1821  Flushing MM, Ohio)
Keziah (Ridgeway)  dt Timothy & Michal of Little Egg-
    harbour MM, ?  & of Plainfield MM, Ohio
Ch:   Lavins          b 1-21-1823  d 9-20-1844
                     bur Spiceland Mtg, Ind
    Isaac           b 7-21-1826  d 11-18-1842
    David           b 10- 1-1828
    Mary Ann       b 7-21-1831  d 12-28-1842
                     bur Spiceland Mtg, Ind
    Thomas Johnson  b 12-13-1833
    Richard        b 2-13-1837
    Joseph K       b 9-18-1839
    Martha         b 4-20-1842

## NEWBERN
Paul
    m  (1- 1-1857)
Eliza E (Horne)  b 1- 1-1837  Wayne Co, Ind
    dt Wilson & Clarky  (after the death of Paul,
    Eliza m 2nd, 11-20-1876 to Oliver Canaday)

## NEWBY
Albert  b 2- 1-1826  d 11-25-1870  Spiceland, Ind
    (s Frederick & Sally (White))
Caroline (Hubbard)  b 6- 4-1833  dt Richard & Sally
                                 (Swain)
Ch:   Charles E      b 11-11-1854
    S Emma         b 12-22-1858 Hopewell Mtg, Ind
    Allen L        b 6-23-1860  d 6- 6-1883
    Luther G       b 3- 3-1864
    Freddie        b 7- 2-1866  d 8-26-1867
    Henry          b 5- 4-1868
    Carrie Alberta   b 11-13-1870

Cyrus  b 10-30-1809  Springfield MM, N Car  s William
    & 2nd w, Elizabeth (Symons) Small Newby

David  b 10- 6-1846  d 12-23-1908  (Spiceland)
    s Frederick & Sarah (White)
Marianna (Elliott)  b 7- 9-1849  dt Richard & Martha
                                (Pritchard)
Ch:   Mary
    Frederick E
    R Wallace
    Paul

Eli J  b 1- 5-1864  s William B & Rachel (Draper)
    m  (1-26-1901  Henry Co, Ind)
Kate (Snavely)

Elias  b 10- 6-1798  N Car  s Joseph & Penelope (Henley)
    m 1st  (4- 9-1823  Back Creek MM, N Car)
Lydia (Presnall)  (b ca 1803)  (d ca 1838 perhaps bur
    at Duck Creek Mtg, Ind)  dt John & Hannah (Littler)
Ch:   William        b ca 1824
    (there are others)
    m 2nd  (5-28-1840 Milford Mtg, Ind)
Tabitha (Bond)  b 5- 3-1808  Springfield MM, N Car
    dt Benjamin & Mary (Williams) both decd

Elizabeth  wid of William Newby  (her 2nd husb)
    wid of Obadiah Small jr  (her 1st husb)
    dt of Thomas of N Car & w Jane (Bundy)
    b 4- 5-1768 (according to Hinshaw's Vol I page
    120)  b 4- 5-1773 so recorded at Spiceland Mtg
    (Probably only a guess as her son Josiah Small
    and her dt Lydia (Small) Jones had died prior to
    her)  d 2-15-1842  bur Spiceland MM, Ind

Elton  b 2-24-1877  Henry Co, Ind  s Jason & Nancy E (Hall)
    m  (1- 9-1897  Henry Co, Ind)
Nora (Sapp)  b 1878 in Missouri  dt Andrew J & M Frances
                                 (Barlow)

Emory C  b 11-21-1851  s Joseph & Naomi (Dicks)
    m  (2-29-1880  Henry Co, Ind)
Maggie (Nixon)

Frederick  b 5-25-1794  Piney Woods MM, N Car
    s Jesse & Elizabeth (White) Townsend Newby
Sarah (White)  b 6-17-1802  dt Thomas & Jemima (- - -?)
    (she of Western Branch MM, Va)
Ch:   William Jesse   b 2- 8-1822  d 12-17-1881
                      Spiceland
    John Thomas    b 6- 1-1823
    Albert         b 2- 1-1826
    Oliver         b 9-21-1827
    Eliza Townsend  b 1-26-1829
    Lydia          b 9- 6-1830  d 8-30-1880
                      bur Raysville
    Exum           b 4-12-1833  d 10-13-1852
                      Spiceland, Ind
    Henry Francis   b 9-15-1834
    Maria Jane     b 10- 1-1836  Spiceland, Ind
    Sarah Ann      b 1-26-1838
    Mary           b 7-23-1840  d 9-21-1842
                      bur Spiceland, Ind
    David W        b 10- 6-1846

Henry
    m  (8-mo-1889)
Minnie Pearl (Berry)  b 1-mo-1869  dt Andrew J & Mary

Herbert  b 12-30-1870  Henry Co, Ind  d Kansas
    s Jason & Nancy (Hall)
    m  (3-17-1894  Rice, Kansas)
Alice (Thompson)  b 2-19-1875  Illinois  dt Joseph &
    Rebecca (Brothers)

Jason W  b 10-25-1843  s Joseph & Naomi (Dicks)
    m 1st
Nancy E (Hall)  b 10- 5-1843  dt Caleb & Hannah
Ch:   Irvin           b 2- 5-1868
    Herbert        b 12-30-1870  Spiceland
    Elton          b 2-24-1877
    Cecil          b 5- 6-1882  Sterling, Kansas
    Joseph Carl    b 8-24-1885    "      "
    m 2nd  (12-20-1894  Wayne Co, Ind)
Anna (Collins)  b 11-30-1860  Thorntown, Ind
    dt Rowland & Mary (DeVoll)
Ch:   Rowland Collins  b 8-26-1896  Henry Co, Ind
    Wister DeVoll   b 11- 1-1900

Joseph  b 10- 7-1815  Wayne Co, Ind  d 1-20-1898
    s William, decd & his 2nd w, Elizabeth (Symons)
    m  (1-29-1840)                 Small Newby
Naomi (Dicks)  b 1-19-1818  Guilford Co, N Car
    d 3-28-1898  dt Job & Hannah (White)
Ch:   Jesse          b 3-24-1841  d 8- 7-1844
                      bur Spiceland
    Jason          b 10-25-1843
    Josiah S       b 9-18-1846  d 10-30-1853
                      bur Spiceland
    Thomas A      b 4-24-1849
    Emory C       b 11-21-1851
    Sarah Ann     b 3-20-1856
    Job D          b 5-12-1858  d 7- 1-1861

Luther G  b 3- 3-1864  s Albert & Caroline (Hubbard)
    m  (10- 9-1902  Illinois)
Anabel (Graff)

Mary D (Coffin)  b 11-18-1792  dt Bethuel & Hannah
                                  (Dicks)

SPICELAND

## NEWBY (Cont)
Thomas   b 3-11-1807  Springfield MM, N Car   s William,
     decd & his 2nd w Elizabeth (Symons) Small Newby
     (m 1st    8- 2-1827  Milford MM, Ind)
Susannah (Pearson)   dt Jesse & Mary (Beeman)
     m 2nd  (1- 2-1834  Milford MM, Ind)
Millicent (Reece)  b 4- 8-1809  Back Creek MM, N Car
     dt John, decd  & Ann (Needham)
Ch:  Huldah
     Jesse
     (there may be others)

Thomas A  b 4-24-1849  s Joseph & Naomi (Dicks)
     m  (2- 7-1872)
Isabelle (Walton)  b 10-12-1851  Holly Springs, Miss
     dt George & Mary
Ch:  Otto              b 12-30-1872  Spiceland, Ind
     Bertha            b 2- 5-1878

William B  b 4-13-1824  Greensboro, N Car  s Thomas &
     m (11-11-1849)                                Sarah
Rachel (Draper)  b 4-22-1831  Newcastle, Ind
     dt Josiah & Catherine
Ch:  Adolpheus A       b 7-16-1850  Newcastle, Ind
     Ida J             b - - - - -
     Mary L            b 5- 3-1862  d - - - -
     Eli J             b 1- 5-1864
     Louissie          b 11-30-1868  Greensboro, Ind

## NEWLIN
Charles
     m  (8-28-1884)
Harriet (Bogue)  b 3- 4-1861  dt Alfred & Charity
                                      (Bogue) Bogue

Thomas  b 12-28-1855  New London, Ind  s John & Elizabeth
     m  (7-10-1884)
Olive B (Wilson)  b 6-30-1858  Milford MM, Ind
     dt Timothy & his 1st w Elizabeth Ann (Terrell)

## NICHOLS
Ann   b 4-13-1828  (d 7-29-1901  bur Arba)
Henry W Horne     b 5-14-1829

## NICHOLSON
(Nathan)
Asenath (Cloud)  b 9-25-1822  dt Joel & Ann
Ch:  Milton            b 12- 5-1858
     Hiram J           b 10-12-1861

## NIXON
(John   s Zachariah & Martha (Toms))  (b 5-22-1803)
     (d 1-28-1846  Blue River MM, Ind)
     m 3rd  (2-6-1840  Blue River MM, Ind)
Deborah (Hobbs)  b 4- 7-1810  dt William & Priscilla
                                              (Coffin)
Ch:  Martha            b 3-11-1841  Blue River Mtg
     Oliver            b 1- 5-1843  d 5- 7-1906
     bur Circle Grove Cemetery, Spiceland
     Priscilla         b 5-25-1844  d 6- 7-1864
                       bur Spiceland
     Nathan            b 11-28-1845  Blue River Mtg
(after the death of John Nixon, Deborah m 2nd William
                                              H Unthank)

## NOAH
Orville P  b 5-29-1881  Franklin Co, Ind  s John &
     m  (5-29-1900 Shelby Co, Ind)    Julia (Buttern)
Leona (Templeton)  b 5-25-1881  dt D F & Laura (Bailey)

## NOBLE
Stuart   b 4-12-1856  West Union, Iowa  s Amasa & Sarah A

## NOTTINGHAM
Peter F  b 10- 2-1844  Delaware Co, Ind  s John & Sarah
     m  (2-12-1868)
Sarah Jane (Fankboner)  b 12-13-1847  Tuscarawas Co, Ohio
     dt John & Mary
Ch:  Harry Morton      b 11-30-1872  Shelby Co, Ill

## NUGEN
Silas R  b 7- 8-1821  Wayne Co, Ind  d 11-27-1892
     s John & Mary
     m  (1-28-1845)

Martha Jane (Kennett)  b 10- 9-1829  Franklin Co, Va
     dt Joseph & Mary
Ch:  Ellen F           b 8-20-1865  Henry Co, Ind

## OAKEY
(Bryant)
     m  (Guilford Co, N Car)
Minerva (King)  b 4-14-1843  Nash Co, N Car
     dt Anderson & Mason (Dickens)

## ODGERS
William  b 6- 6-1870  Queensland, Aus  s John & Emma
     m  (3-28-1905  Indianapolis, Ind)
Anna (Kelly)  b 1-23-1874  Grant Co, Ind
     dt Alfred & Martha (Morris)
Ch:  Elizabeth         b 11-29-1906  Grant Co
     William Edward    b 6-14-1909     "      "
     Mary Emma         b 12-22-1916  Henry Co

## OELSCHLAGEL
Josephine (Bogue)  b 6-11-1869  dt Joseph & Martha
                       Emily (Allen)  m (Tipton Co, Ind)
to - - - -? Oelschlagel

## OSBORN
Arthur  b 1- 7-1859  near Economy, Ind  s Charles W &
                                       Asenath (Wood)

(John   s Jeremiah & Sarah)  (b 6-29-1808)
     (m 1st  1842)
(Beulah (Kersey)  dt Jesse & Rachel (Haworth))
     (b 9-21-1807)  (d 1843 Center Mtg, N Car)
Ch:  Beulah Luzena    b 4-11-1843
     (m 2nd 12-19-1855 Springfield Mtg, N Car)
(Sarah (Mendenhall)  dt William & Rosanna (Leach))
     (b 10-14-1821)
Ch:  William E         b - - - -
     Alexander         b - - - -
     John G            b - - - -

Laurinda  b 10- 1-1838  dt Isaiah, decd, & Lydia (Worth)
     now Lydia Maxwell, 3rd w of David Maxwell

## OVERMAN
Eli  b 10- 3-1795  Pasquotank MM, N Car  s Charles &
                                       Mary (Albertson)
Elizabeth (Albertson)  b 5- 1-1793  Suttons Creek MM,
     N Car  dt Chalkley & Elizabeth (Toms)
Ch:  Charles           b 8-29-1828
     Edwin             b 12- 9-1830
     Nixon             b 9-28-1833
     Alpheus           b 1-25-1839

## PAINTER
Alvin C  b 4- 5-1856  s Samuel S & Mercy Ann (King)
     m  (10-26-1881  Henry Co, Ind)
Harrietta (Gray)  b 5-19-1859  Indianapolis, Ind
     d - - - -  dt John & Harrietta
Ch:  Frank Floyd       b 8-23-1883  Wabash, Ind
     Myron O           b 4-25-1887
     Almira Myra       b 8-11-1890
     Harrietta Edna    b 2- 6-1900  Spiceland, Ind

Clarence D  b 6- 5-1876  s Henry & Mary V (Stubbs)
     m  ( 8- 8-1905)
Claire (Wilson)  b 10-27-1869  dt Levi C & Jane
Ch:  Agnes Etta        b 8- 4-1906

Henry W   b 10-20-1848  s Samuel S & Mercy Ann (King)
     of Paintersville, Ohio
     m  (4- 1-1875  Henry Co, Ind)
Mary V (Stubbs)  b 6-23-1853  dt Charles & America
                                              (Sample)
Ch:  Clarence D        b 6- 5-1876  Spiceland, Ind
     Walter S          b 9-30-1878  Wabash, Ind
     Laura E           b 1-18-1881
     Anna M            b 7-17-1886  Spiceland
     K Levinus         b 7-12-1889
     Herbert B         b 2-11-1893  d 12-20-1893

Mary Ethel (Applegate)  b 7-mo-1881  Fayette Co, Ind
     dt Theodore & Mary (Clifford)
     m  (3-10-1910  Hancock Co, Ind)
to - - - -? Painter

SPICELAND

PAINTER (Cont)
Samuel S   b 5- 3-1820  Green Co, Ohio, Center MM
     d 4-30-1910  s Jesse & Elizabeth (Smith)
Mercy Ann (King)  b 3-20-1829  Whitewater MM, Ind
     d 2-19-1882  bur Circle Grove Cemetery, Spiceland,
     Ind     dt Dean & Esther (Carpenter) of Center MM,
     Ohio & Wabash MM, Ind
Ch:  Henry W            b 9-25-1848
     Mary Samantha      b 9- 1-1850
     Alvin C            b 4- 5-1856
     Orange S           b 12-14-1858
     Esther C           b 4- 6-1861
     m 3rd (6- 2-1890 Henry Co, Ind
Catherine (Hubbard) Newby, wid of Albert Newby  b 6-4-
     1833   dt Richard & Sally (Swain) Hubbard of Wayne
                                                    Co

Walter S
     m 8- 2-1905  Wayne Co, Ind
Jennie (Bond)   d 5-31-1915

PALIN
Nixon  (b 4- 3-1800 Symons Creek Mtg, N Car)
     s Henry Sr & Sarah (Nixon)
Peninah (- - - -?)
Ch:  Lucinda
     William
     Irene
     Sylvanus           b 9-20-1827

Sylvanus  b 9-20-1827  s Nixon & Peninah
Mary Ann (Pike)  b 3- 7-1829  Symons Creek MM, N Car
     dt Wilson, decd & Miriam (now w of Henry Palin Sr)
Ch:  Eliza Jane         b 7-11-1847
     John W             b 5- 4-1849  d 7-18-1851
                        bur Spiceland
     James P            b 4-17-1851

PARKER
Benajah  b 3-22-1783 in N Car  (s Jacob & Rhoda (Draper))
     (m 2- 7-1810 Stillwater MM, Ohio)
Grace (Patten)  b 11- 9-1784  Loudon Co, Va
     dt William & Rachel
Ch:  Nathan             b 11-30-1810
     Emma               b 12-15-1812
     Hannah Ann         b 12- 3-1815
     Philip Draper      b 4-21-1818
     Charity            b 5-10-1821
     Isaac              b 5- 1-1823
     Benajah jr         b 1-11-1825
     Rachel             b 3-20-1829

Eli G  b 8-22-1844  s James & Hannah (Gause)
Mary M (Thomas)  b 2-27-1845  Randolph Co, Ind
     dt Frances W & Rebecca
Ch:  Violet             b 6-15-1866  Spiceland

(Elisha   s Nathan & Sarah (Outland)) (b 12-27-1833 New
     Garden Mtg, Ind) (d prior to 1883 prob at Springfield
     MM, Ind)   (m 4-24-1867 Springfield Mtg)
Mary E (Nicholson) Jessup wid Henry  b 5-10-1839 Wayne
     Co, New Garden Mtg, Ind  d 8-23-1911 (as the w of
     Joseph Hall)   dt George & Lucinda (Dennis)
Ch:  (to Spiceland, by Elisha Parker)
     Elmina             b 3-27-1871  Dalton
     Nathan Earl )         8-11-1880
     George Irwin) twins   8-11-1880

Isaac  b 5- 1-1823  Jefferson Co, Ohio  s Benajah &
     Grace (Patten)
Hannah Maria (Newby)  b 5- 1-1825  Washington Co, Ind
     dt Micah & 2nd w Mary D
Ch:  Micah N            b 10-22-1854  Raysville Mtg, Ind

James B  b 9- 8-1819  Rich Square MM, N Car
     s Samuel & Rebecca (Binford)
Hannah B (Gause)  b 4-25-1822  Preble Co, Ohio
     dt Eli & Martha (Pierce)
Ch:  Eli G              b 8-22-1844  Hancock Co, Ind
     Rebecca Ann        b 10-29-1847  Spiceland, Ind
     Charles Owen       b 6- 4-1859

(Josiah, decd, s Joseph & Sarah)  (b 10- 4-1769)
     (d prior to 1837, prb Rich Square Mtg, N Car)

     (m 3-21-1792 Rich Square)
Martha (Peele)  b 3-17-1769  Rich Square Mtg, N Car
     dt John & Mary
Ch:  (to Spiceland with their mth)
     Nathan             b 7-30-1805
     Martha jr          b 12-29-1809
     Phebe M            b 1-14-1813

(Nathan, s Benajah & Grace (Patten)) (b 11-30-1810 in Ohio)
     (d prior to 1855 at Westfield Mtg, Ind)
     (m 7-31-1834 Short Creek MM, Ohio)
(Nancy T (Crew)  dt Robert, decd & Nancy of Charles City,
     Va) (Wayne Oak MM, Va)
Ch:  Robert C           b - - - -
     Nathaniel          b - - - -
     Catherine          b - - - -
     Grace              b - - - -
     Charity            b - - - -

Nathan  b 7-27-1805  Rich Square MM, N Car
     s Josiah, decd & Martha (Peele)
Sarah Ann (- - - -?) of Western Branch MM, Va  b 1-15-1809
     Cedar Creek MM, Hanover Co, Va
Ch:  Sarah Isabelle     b 12-26-1834
     Josiah Thomas      b 11- 2-1836  d 11-10-1838
     Margaret Ann       b 9-27-1839   d 1-18-1840
     Deborah            b 7-26-1842

Philip D  b 4-21-1818  Stillwater MM, Ohio
     s Benajah & Grace (Patten)
Joanna (Morris)  b 10- 9-1822  Blue River MM, Ind
     dt Benoni & Rebecca (Trueblood)
Ch:  Ella               b 8-12-1853  Spiceland MM, Ind

PARTON
William  b 12-10-1838  Chatham Co, N Car  s Elisha &
     m (11-25-1861)                              Elizabeth
Elizabeth (Neighbors)  b 3- 4-1848  Randolph Co, N Car
     dt James & Charity

PATE
William A  b 12-22-1837  Franklin Co, Va  s John & Rhoda
     m (8-25-1859 Henry Co, Ind)
Martha (Livesey)  b 7-31-1840  Henry Co, Ind
     dt Isaac & Margaret
Ch:  Isaac              b 1-16-1874  Henry Co, Ind

PATTERSON
Hezekiah (from Union MM, N Car)
Elizabeth (Williams) (from same place)
Ch:  Joseph             b - - - -?
     Sarah E            b - - - -?
     Eli                b 10-14-1830  Wayne Co, Ind
     Levi C             b 4-17-1834
     Margaret           b 1- 5-1839  Henry Co, Ind
     Milton             b 10-10-1842
     John W             b 12- 6-1844

PAYNE
John W
     m (3-15-1860 Henry Co, Ind)
Eliza (Newby)  b 2-12-1841  d 5- 7-1915 (drowned)
     dt Elias & Tabitha B (Newby) Newby
Ch:  Olen E             b 9-22-1871  Cadiz, Ind

Olen E  b 9-22-1871  s John & Eliza (Newby)
     m (10-21-1896)
Maude (Shaffer)  b 11-10-1876  dt Nathan B & Cynthia H
Ch:  Horace             b 1- 7-1900

PEARSON
Baily  b 10- 4-1849  Henry Co, Ind  d 5- 1-1909 Wabash
     s Lydia (Thomas) Pearson

Bertha G  b 8-16-1880  Miami Co, Ind  dt Charles M &
     Lydia G (Newbern)
     m (5- 2-1906 Henry Co, Ind)
to - - - -?

Isaac  b 5-19-1798  Bush River MM, N Car  d 9-12-1856
     bur Spiceland Mtg, Ind  (s Enoch & Anna (Evans))
     (of Mill Creek Mtg, Ohio)
     (mou Mill Creek MM, Ohio ca 1823)
Rachel (- - - -?)

SPICELAND

PEARSON (Cont)
Ch: Isaac & Rachel
    Seth W             b  9-25-1824   Mill Creek Mtg, Ohio
    Henry S           b  2-12-1829
    Mary Jane        b  5-11-1831
    Sarah Ann        b 11-16-1833
    Enoch S           b  7-22-1836
    Rebecca C        b  4-18-1839
    Calvin W          b  5-17-1841
    Rachel E          b  - - - - -?
    Elvira M          b  - - - - -?
    Martha M          b  - - - - -?

Isaiah B  b  2- 4-1857
Levina E  (- - - -?)  b  7- 8-1857

Jesse  b 11- 7-1827  Mill Creek MM, Ohio  s Hiram &
    Elizabeth (Jenkins)
    m  (3-19-1851 Union MM, Ohio)
Rachel (Furnas)  b 10- 1-1830  Miami Co, Ohio
    dt Joseph & Patience (Mills)
Ch:  Amanuel Jesse       b  7-25-1857  Miami Co, Ohio

Peter  (b  4-19-1797  Back Creek Mtg, N Car)  s Nathan &
    Mary (Bailey), decd
    m  (ca 1820 West Grove Mtg, Ind)
Eunice (- - - -?)
Ch:  Enoch             b  - - - -
    Isom              b  - - - -
    Nancy             b  - - - -
    Aaron B           b  - - - -
    William           b  - - - -
    Mary              b  - - - -
    Lilburn           b  - - - -
    Irene             b  - - - -

Seth  b  9-25-1824  Mill Creek Mtg, Ohio  s Isaac &
    m  (1850 Bloomfield MM, Ind)     Rachel, decd
Nancy C (Stanley)
Ch:  Alva H            b  - - - -

PEGG
(Sarah (Griffin) Small Pegg, wid of Valentine Pegg)
    (wid of Gideon Small)  (dt of James & Hannah
    (Kenyon) Griffin)  (b 10-12-1773 Symons Creek MM,
    N Car)

PENNINGTON
Josiah  b  2-17-1780  Baltimore Co, Md  d  8-27-1850
    bur Elm Grove Mtg, Ind  s Daniel & Martha
Deborah (Talbot) a Minister b  4- 9-1782 Frederick Co,
    Md.  d 11- 3-1870  dt John & Mary
Ch:  Levi T            b  4-30-1812  Belmont Co, Ohio
    Mary              b 10- 9-1813
    Susannah          b  7-18-1815
    John P            b  3-15-1817
    Eliza             b 11-30-1818
    Rachel            b  3- 8-1821  d 11-25-1837
                      Elm Grove Mtg, Ind

John P  b  3-15-1817  Barnesville, Ohio  d  9- 4-1902
    s Josiah & Deborah (Talbot)
    m 2nd  (10-28-1861)
Elizabeth (Wiltsie)  b  3- 5-1832  d 10-28-1867  bur
    Spiceland  dt Simeon & Rachel of Rush Co, Ind
Ch:  Levi T            b  9-15-1863
    Mary A            b  8-29-1865
    George W          b  5-12-1867  d 10-24-1867
    m 3rd  (1-16-1871 Wayne Co, Ind)
Melissa (Elliott)  b 11-16-1836  Wayne Co, Ind
    d  7-15-1910  ar Fairmount, Ind but bur Spiceland,
    Ind  dt John & Mary (Ratliff)

Levi T  b  9-15-1863  Spiceland  s John & his 2nd w
    Elizabeth (Wiltsie)
    m  (10-30-1890 Henry Co, Ind)
Mary L (Brown)  b  4- 4-1865  Rainsboro, Highland Co,
    Ohio  (dt Edgar & Sarah (Bond))
Ch:  John Elgar        b  9- 9-1891
    Everatt Levi      b  3- 4-1893
    Agnes Miriam      b  3-11-1896
    Irene             b  8-30-1897
    Leslie T          b 10-30-1899

PERKINS
(Elva  dt John & Sarah (Edgerton))  (b 2-11-1841
    Contentnea Mtg, N Car)

PHELPS
Ezekiel  b  2-11-1829  d  1891 bur Circle Grove Cem
    Spiceland  s Samuel & Sarah
    m  (2-28-1850)
Sarah (Hoover)  b  8- 3-1833  d  5-28-1893
    dt Levi & Margaret
Ch:  Calvin H          b  5-16-1851  d 11-27-1859
    Mary E            b  9- 9-1852  d 11-13-1859
    Cora A            b  7- 8-1859? 1861?
    Verling           b  2-18-1866  Henry Co, Ind

PHILABAUM
(James  s Daniel & Maria)  (b  1- 7-1846)
(Sarah E (Stoker)  (b 5-30-1857)  dt Urias & Ann)
Ch:  Alonzo
    Lura

PICKERING
(Abner  s Jonas & Ruth (Gregg))  b  3- 9-1805
    (d prior to 1856)
Jannette (Saint)  b  2-16-1816  dt William & Achsah
    (Elliott)  (after the death of Abner, Jannette
    m 2nd, Nathan Macy)
Ch:  (by 1st husb)
    Martha            b  8-15-1838
    Achsah            b  9-29-1840  d 1-20-1843
                      Duck Creek MM, Ind
    Thomas S          b 12-23-1843
    Julia Ann         b 10-25-1846
    William E         b  8-28-1849

Jacob  b 11-19-1819  Ohio  s Jacob & Nancy
    m 1st  (1842)
Araminta (Cooper)  d 1856 Greensboro, Ind
    m 2nd  (1870)
Miriam C (Dennis) Test, wid of Josiah  b  8-10-1824
    West Grove Mtg, Ind  d  4- 2-1880  bur Richmond,
    Ind  dt Thomas & Elizabeth Dennis
Ch:  John              b  - - - -

(James C  s Samuel jr & Phebe jr (Kirk) of Milford Mtg)
    (m 1838 Spiceland Mtg, Ind)
(Sarah Ann (Pitts)  dt Cadwalader & Elizabeth (Stanley))
    (b  8- 8-1817 Union Mtg, N Car)

John F  s Jacob & 2nd w Miriam C (Dennis) Test Pickering
Orpha (Hawlins)  dt Nathan S & Cornelia (Marsh)
Ch:  Ralph             b  9-21-1890
    U Irene           b 11-13-1897

(Jonas Sr  s Samuel Sr & Phebe Sr  from Crooked Run MM,
    (?Va))  (m 2-23-1804 Plainfield MH, Concord MM,
    Ohio)
(Ruth (Gregg)  dt Abner & Sarah  from South River MM, Va)
Ch:  (Abner            b  3- 9-1805)
    (Abigail           b  8-25-1806)
    (Samuel            b 11-30-1807)
    (Sarah             b  4- 7-1809)
    (Phebe             b  6-30-1811)
    Jonas jr          b  9- 8-1812
    Mahlon            b  6-15-1814
    Ruth Ann          b  2-25-1816
    Joseph            b  1-27-1818
    Jordan            b  5-31-1820

PICKETT - PIGGOTT
Albert Arnet  b 10-20-1857 Henry Co, Ind  d  7-21-1908
    s John & Esther (Foster)
    m  ( 2- 5-1880 Henry Co, Ind)
Martha L (Jarret)  dt James & Rebecca (Simmons)  b 1-21-
    1863 Davidson Co, N Car  adopted dt of William
    & Elizabeth (Schooley) Sheridan

James  b  2-13-1804  Cane Creek Mtg, N Car
    s John & Rebecca (Woody)
    m 1st  (ca 1823 Cane Creek Mtg, N Car
Priscilla (Pike)  d ca 1826 N Car
Ch:  William           b 10- 7-1826

PICKETT - PIGGOTT (Cont)
James (Cont)
    m 2nd  (con mcd  3- 3-1827  White River Mtg, Ind)
Mary (Way)  b 4-22-1805  Chatham Co, N Car
    dt Abel & Margaret
Ch:  Elihu               b 4- 1-1828
      Thomas              b 3- 4-1830
      Margaret           b 3-28-1832
      Aaron                b - - - -?
      Obadiah S          b 7-18-1835
      Joel John           b 9-11-1837
      Rebecca Jane      b 1-28-1840  d 8- 1-1844
                                  bur Spiceland Mtg
      Josiah              b 5- 3-1842  d 10- 5-1842
      Samuel M           b 11- 2-1844
      James Milton      b 3-12-1849
      Priscilla Ann     b - - - -?

John
    mcd  (1853)
Esther (Foster)  b 10-27-1829  (dt Joseph & Mary (Stanley))
Ch:  Albert Arnet      b 10-20-1857
      Rosa Etta           b 4-12-1866  Henry Co, Ind
      John B              b 6-13-1868
      Cora Ann            b 10- 5-1870

(Joshua jr  s Joshua & Sarah (Davis))  (b 2-16-1805
    Orange Co, N Car)
    mcd  (1823 Chester Mtg, Ind)
(Anna (Hall)  dt Benjamin & Elizabeth (Newby))
    (b 2-11-1802  Back Creek MM, N Car)
Ch:  Rhoda H             b - - - -
      Benjamin N         b - - - -
      Esther S            b - - - -
      Elizabeth Jane    b - - - -

William  b 10- 7-1826  N Car  s James & his 1st w
    m (1846 Spiceland)         Priscilla (Pike)
Lydia (Simcox)  b 5- 3-1826  Springfield Mtg, Ohio
    dt Job & Catharine (Reynard), decd
Ch:  James Hervey      b - - - -
      Job S P             b - - - -

William jr  b 12-31-1766  Orange Co, N Car  d 12- 3-1847
    bur Raysville Mtg, Ind  s William & Sarah (Pike)
    (m 1st  1792 Cane Creek Mtg N Car)
Sarah (Jackson)  b 12- 4-1762  d 5-11-1811  Spring Mtg,
    N Car  dt Isaac & Mary (Peirson)
Ch:  (probably all the older ch were non-mbrs)
      (Harriett          b 5- 4-1805)
      (was rec in mbrp at Spring Mtg, N Car in 1823 &
      m Samuel Pritchard & came to Lick Creek Mtg, Ind
      in 1829)
    m 2nd  (1814 Spring MM, N Car)
Sarah (Thompson)  b 7-15-1790  dt Joseph & Hannah of
    Eno Mtg, N Car

William Riley  b 8-29-1853  s John & Esther (Foster)
    b Independence, Ind  (Fountain Co)
    m ( 2- 3-1876  Henry Co, Ind)
Almira H (Sheridan)  b 3-22-1852  Spiceland
    dt William & Elizabeth (Schooley)
Ch:  Carlos B            b 1-31-1877  d 11- 4-1878
                                  Spiceland
      Ethelena S         b 4-16-1879
      Evalyn              b 4-27-1882
      Elbert Ray         b 7-24-1884
      Rubie May          b 8-28-1886
      Russell             b 11-30-1888
      Ora Pearl          b 5-13-1891  d 9-10-1892
      Lenora              b 10-13-1893
      Esther Fern        b 5- 1-1896

PIDGEON
David L  b 4- 2-1857  Nettle Creek, Ind  s Jesse W &
    m (10- 2-1879)            Mary (Chamness)
Elizabeth (Hardman)  b 8-30-1861  Cambridge City, Ind
    dt Daniel & Sarah
Ch:  Nellie              b 7-18-1880
      Lillie              b 8-28-1884

PIERCE
(James)
    Christina (Perry)  b 5-12-1822  d 6-22-1873  Rich
      Square, Henry Co, Ind

Ch:  Elizabeth C        b 11- 9-1846  Perquimans Co, N Car
      Hattie L            b 10-12-1854
      Lavina Frances    b 12-27-1856  Knightstown, Ind
      Edgar M             b 2-14-1860

PIKE
Himelius  b 7-20-1822  Union Mtg, N Car  s Nathan & Mary
    m (1849 Spiceland Mtg)          (Newby)
Ruth (Cloud)  b 12-17-1824  dt Joel & Anna (Gordon)
Ch:  Levi C              b 2-24-1853  Spiceland
                              d 4-28-1854  bur Spiceland

Ida May  b 10-21-1866  Rush Co, Ind  dt Ephraim & Beulah

PINKHAM
(William P  s Thomas & Mary B of Litchfield MM, Maine)
    (b 9- 3-1843)
    (m 1860 Salem MM, Ohio)
(Emma (Curry)  dt Cornelius & Hannah of Columbiana Co,
    Ohio)  (b - - - -)
Ch:  (Mary Cornelia    b 7-28-1861)
      (Gertrude Harriett  b 12-12-1873)
      (Charles Heber     b 4-20-1871)
      (Bertha              b - - - - )

PITTS
(Cadwalader)  (rec on req 1812 Deep River Mtg, N Car)
    (m ca 1810)             (b 1-30-1787 N Car)
(Elizabeth (Stanley)  dt Samuel & Sarah (Williams))
    (b 3- 5-1788  New Garden Mtg, N Car)
Ch:  Sarah Ann          b 8- 8-1817

PLEAS
Aaron Lancaster  b 10-29-1805  Symons Creek MM, N Car
    d 2-29-1856  bur Spiceland Mtg, Ind  s Isaac, decd
    m 1st (12- 5-1827 Whitewater Mtg, Ind)    & Jane
Lydia (Gilbert)  b 4-22-1812  d 5-18-1839  (may be at
    Hopewell Mtg, Ind)  dt Josiah & Dorothy
Ch:  Elwood              b 4- 5-1831
      Maurice             b 9-10-1833
      Dorothy J          b 4-17-1836
      Achsah G            b 12-28-1838
    m 2nd  (10-26-1842  Spiceland Mtg, Ind)
Ann E (Gause) Hunt  wid of Joseph B Hunt  b 1- 8-1814
    Redstone, Pa  d 5-mo-1900  dt Eli & Martha Gause
Ch:  Lydia               b 11-25-1843
      Joseph H           b 4-21-1846
      Benjamin H         b 12-24-1848  d 2-11-1909
      Charles F          b 10-18-1852  d 2-15-1856
                               bur Spiceland

Elwood  b 4- 5-1831  s Aaron L & Lydia (Gilbert) decd
    m (4-26-1854  Henry Co, Ind)
Sarah Ann (Griffin)  b 4-24-1835  Spiceland, Ind
    dt Joseph & Rebecca (Burgess)
Ch:  Ernest              b 7- 6-1856
      Mary B              b 2-28-1859  Lake Co, Ind
      Edgar               b 1-17-1862  Spiceland
      Robert J           b 10-10-1865  Newcastle, Ind
      Charles E          b 9-10-1867
      Nellie M           b 8- 5-1873  d 11-26-1878
                               bur Spiceland

Robert J  b 10-10-1865  Newcastle, Ind  s Elwood & Sarah
    m (10-mo-1887 Henry Co, Ind)      Ann (Griffin)
Laura (Elliott)  b 6- 7-1867  Henry Co, Ind
    dt Patrick & Sarah (Ball) his 1st w
Ch:  Ida
      Ernest
      Ivanhoe             b 9-16-1893  Arkansas

POE
David Milton  b 6-28-1831  Guilford Co, N Car
    s David Sr & Abigail (Wilson)
    m 1st
Elizabeth L  (- - - -?)
Ch:  Emily A             b 8- 5-1855
    m 2nd (2-15-1878 Henry Co, Ind)
Melvina (King) Winters  wid of John W  b 8- 8-1846
    Franklin Co, N Car  d 1921  dt Anderson &
    Mason (Dickins) King

(John)
    m ( 5- 6-1899 Henry Co, Ind
Hattie Elizabeth (Koon)  b 12- 1-1871  Cadiz, Ind
    dt Jesse & Caroline
Ch:  Jessie (a dt)      b - - - -

SPICELAND

## POER
(Absalom)
    m (1835)
Mary (Hodson) b 7-15-1813 Guilford Co, N Car
    dt Robert & Isabella (Frazier)
Ch:  Isabella         b - - - -
     James R        b 12-16-1842
     Rebecca Ellen   b 6-10-1855 Spiceland, Ind

Alva
    m ( 6- 1-1898)
Florence (King) b 8-26-1880 dt Calvin N & Emily A (Poe)

James R b 12-16-1842 N Car s Absalom & Mary (Hodson)
    m (9-23-1864 Henry Co, Ind)
Lucinda (Byrkit) b 10-27-1849 dt Jonas & Sarah (Coon)
Ch:  John          b 12-13-1865 d 1-12-1914
     Arthur         b 10-25-1871
     Nora Bell      b 12-20-1873

Lena b 11-17-1879 Jasper Co, Mo dt Robert & Martha
    m (11-15-1916 Henry Co, Ind)
(to S D Leighton)

Minnie May (Reeves) b 9-10-1873 Dickinson Co, Kansas
    dt John & Mary (Vanmeter) Reeves
    m (12-24-1909 Henry Co, Ind)
to - - - -? Poer

Muratt J C b 11-20-1863 Brownsburg, Ind s Elwood &
    m (3-31-1887)                Ellen
Jennie (Courtney)

Otho
    m (12-24-1896)
Alpha Mable (Brewer) dt John W & Emily S (Carr)

## PORCH
(Albert W) b 5-mo-1845 s Samuel & Anna Jane (Unthank)
Phoeba A (Hiatt) b 7-mo-1844 Greensboro, Ind
    d 5- 7-1908 Alabama dt Simeon & Mary
Ch:  Florence      b 12- 6-1866 Spiceland, Ind

Linnius L b 7-29-1857 d 9-mo-1895 s Samuel & Anna
    m (11-14-1883)            Jane (Unthank)
Ada T (Paxson)

Robert F b 9-23-1840 Newport, Wayne Co, Ind
    s Samuel & Anna Jane (Unthank)
    m (10- 5-1871)
Emma (Vaughn) b 2-26-1848 in Ohio d 8-10-1893
    dt Thomas & Edith
Ch:  Samuel Carelton  b 7- 6-1877 d 7-27-1893

Samuel b 3-15-1816 d 5- 4-1884 bur Circle Grove Cem,
    Spiceland, Ind s Michael & Esther
    m (12-31-1839)
Anna Jane (Unthank) b 3-30-1819 d 3-11-1895
  a Minister dt Josiah & Ann (Britton) of Guilford
    Co, N Car
Ch:  Robert F       b 9-23-1840
     Albert W       b 5-mo-1845
     William A      b 9-21-1855
     Linius L       b 7-29-1857

William A b 9-21-1855 s Samuel & Anna Jane (Unthank)
    m (10- 8-1880 Henry Co, Ind)
Nancy Emma (Macy) b 12- 7-1853 dt Thaddeus & Elizabeth
                                            J

## PORTER
Orville b 5-24-1890 Rush Co, Ind s Laurine E (Kizer)
                                       Porter

## POWELL
Henry C b 3-24-1829 Butler Co, Ohio s John & Catharine
                                    (Sink)
Lucinda A (Gibson) b 11-19-1833 Stokes Co, N Car
    dt Jesse A & Mary (Vance) d - - - -

## PRESNALL
(Benoni s Daniel jr & Plesant (Maudlin))
    (m 3- 1-1827 Newberry MM, Ohio)
(Jane (Moon) dt Daniel & Ruth of Clinton Co, Ohio)
    b 2-10-1810

Ch:  Jeremiah      b 3-11-1828
     William       b 9-31-1829
     James         b 2- 4-1831
     Henry         b 5-17-1832
     Mary          b - - - -

(Jeremiah L s John & Hannah (Littler)) (b ca 1815)
    m (1838 Spiceland Mtg, Ind)
Phebe (Stanbrough) b 8-10-1818 dt James, decd & Mary
    (Hodgson), now m to John Bond

## PRITCHARD - PRICHARD
Benjamin C b 12-21-1814 N Car s Caleb & Mary (Winslow)
    (m 7-18-1839 Piney Woods MM, N Car)
Rachel W (Robinson) b 11-18-1820 N Car
    dt William & Anna (White)
Ch:  Caleb W       b 10- 1-1842
     Anna          b 5-29-1857
     Thomas R      b 6- 2-1861

Samuel b 7- 8-1801 Symons Creek, MM, N Car
    s Benjamin & Peninah (White)
Harriett (Picket) b 5- 4-1805 Orange Co, N Car
    dt William & Sarah
Ch:  William       b 2-14-1827 near Hillsborough,
     d 12-31-1828 at Eno Mtg, N Car
     Martha        b 11-25-1828
     Anna          b 1-21-1831 Wayne Co, Ind
     David         b 9-11-1833
     Sarah Jane     b 11-25-1835 Raysville Mtg, Ind
     Mary          b 1-19-1838 Elm Grove Mtg, Ind
                  d 9- 1-1839 Elm Grove Mtg, Ind
     Joseph        b 3-12-1840
     Charles       b 2-15-1845

Thomas (s Benjamin & Peninah (White)) (b 6-17-1790)
    (m 1st)
(Mary (Morris) dt Christopher & Gulielma (Bundy))
    (b 1-12-1798 N Car) (d 4-22-1822 Pasquotank
    MM, N Car)
    (m 2nd 1824 Pasquotank MM, N Car)
Elizabeth (Morris) dt Joseph b 7-19-1800 N Car
    d 10-11-1851 bur Raysville Mtg, Ind

William b 10- 4-1792 Pasquotank Co, N Car d 1-23-1837
    bur Walnut Ridge Mtg, Ind s Benjamin & Peninah
    mcd (Blue River MM, Ind 1831)     (White)
Mary (Hobbs) (b 3-19-1802) (dt Wm & Priscilla (Coffin))
Ch:  Edwin         b 12-24-1831 Washington Co, Ind
     Calvin W      b 1-24-1834 Henry Co, Ind
     William Barnabas Hobbs b ca 1837
  (after the death of William Prichard, Mary mcd 1838
    to Thomas Saint of Milford MM, Ind. They went to
    Blue River MM, Ind then returned to Milford MM, Ind)

## PUSEY
Joel b 2-13-1794 Culpeper Co, Va s Nathan decd &
    Mary m (6-21-1815 Center MM, Ohio)
Hannah (Faulkner) b 9-11-1793 Berkley Co, Va
    dt Jesse & Ruth, decd
Ch:  Martha        b 7- 7-1816 Green Co, Ohio
     Jesse F       b 10-18-1820 Warren Co, Ohio
     Rachel        b 8-15-1834 Green Co, Ohio

## RALSTON
(John W)
    m ( 2- 8-1898)
Elizabeth (Marshall) b 1-26-1859 Urbana, Ohio
    dt Robert & Sarah

## RATLIFF - RATCLIFF
Calvin W b 10-27-1848 d 1901 s Eli & Jane (Draper)
    m (11-26-1868 Henry Co, Ind)
Ary Isabelle (Williams) b 3-30-1846 Newcastle, Ind
    dt Ananias, decd & Mary E (- - - -?) (lately m
    to William Millikan)
Ch:  Harlan        b 8-16-1871 Spiceland, Ind

Charles F b 8- 4-1862 Spiceland, Ind s Eli & Jane
    m (11-11-1885 Charlottsville, Ind) (Draper)
Matilda E (Harold) b 8-22-1864 Carmel, Ind
    dt Lemuel & Jane
Ch:  Harold E      b 1- 5-1889 Westland, Ind
     Russell M)     b 10-27-1891 Greenfield, Ind
     Ralph H ) twins b 10-27-1891    "        "

SPICELAND

RATLIFF - RATCLIFF (Cont)
Cornelius  b 8-14-1846   s Jonathan & Sarah
    m  (3-28-1868  Henry Co, Ind)
Anna (Harris)   dt Davis & Jane
Ch:  Henry         b  2-23-1872  Henry Co, Ind
     William       b  2-17-1878
     Charles       b  8-27-1879
     Morris        b 11- 1-1881

Cyrus   b 1- 2-1835  d 8-mo-1904  s Phineas & Chiristy
    Ann of Greensboro, Ind
    m  (12-17-1857 Henry Co, Ind)
Elizabeth (Hoover)  b 11-16-1839  dt Phineas & Margaret
                                          (Harvey)
Ch:  Charles       b  5-21-1860
     Wilburn       b 12-21-1862
     John          b 10-12-1865
     Rufus K       b 10- 1-1869  d 9- 8-1896
     Levi S        b  4- 6-1872
     Nellie M      b  8- 9-1875  d 8-19-1896

Edward  b 10-21-1837  Belmont Co, Ohio  (s William, decd
                                          & Sarah (Wood))
    (con mcd  7-25-1866  Short Creek MM, Ohio)
    (m  4-16-1865)
Julia Ann (Lupton)  b 4-6-1846  Mt Pleasant, Ohio
    (dt Nathan & Deborah A (Ricks)
Ch:  Mary Emma     b  6-23-1866
     Freddie       b  1-23-1870  d 9- 8-1870
     Achsah E      b  3- 2-1872  Spiceland, Ind

Eli  b 10- 7-1822  Wayne Co, Ind  d  1903  s Joseph &
    m  (2-26-1845  Henry Co, Ind)              Rebecca
Jane (Draper)  b 9- 1-1827  d 10- 6-1907
    dt Josiah & Catherine (Pierson) of Henry Co, Ind
Ch:  Huldah P      b  1-20-1846
     Calvin W      b 10-27-1848
     Charles F     b  8- 4-1862

Elisha B  b 9-18-1833  Flushing, Ohio  d 1-10-1916
    (s William, decd & Sarah (Wood))
    m  (1- 1-1863)
Rebecca T (Bailey)  b 11-26-1831  Flushing, Ohio
    (dt Jesse & Lydia (Townsend))
Ch:  Loren T       b  6-15-1864  in Iowa
     Henry Herbert b  5-22-1867    "     "
     Edwin B       b  2-12-1869  Spiceland, Ind
     William       b 10-29-1870
     Dalton        b  8- 1-1872  d 8-24-1873
                                 Spiceland
     Anna Evelyn   b  4-24-1876

Fleming  b 10-17-1846  Belmont Co, Ohio  s William, decd
                                          & Sarah (Wood)
Anna (Hubbard)

Gabriel (an Elder)  b 5- 8-1802  Randolph Co, N Car
    d 10-18-1846  bur Spiceland Mtg, Ind  s Richard &
        Elizabeth (Pearson)
Catherine (Pearson)  b 1-31-1805  Back Creek, N Car
    dt Nathan & Mary (Bailey)
Ch:  Mahlon        b 11- 2-1825  Henry Co, Ind
                   d 11-20-1846  bur Spiceland Mtg, In
     Mary          b 12-16-1826  d 9-18-1846
     Benajah       b  6-15-1828  d 11-12-1846
     Huldah        b 12-25-1829
     Caroline      b  3-10-1831  d 8- 1-1833
     Sarah         b 10-10-1832
     Seth          b  9-29-1834
     Elizabeth     b  5-23-1836
     Joseph        b  3-27-1838
     Rebecca )     b  2-27-1840
     Isaac  ) twins b 2-27-1840  d 10-17-1846
                   bur Spiceland Mtg, Ind
     Martha        b  3- 6-1842
     Asenath       b 11-15-1843
     John P        b  5-12-1845

Harlan S  b 8-16-1871  s Calvin W & Ara Isabella
    m  (10- 2-1897)                     (Williams)
Lydia K (Newby)

Jesse
    m  (12-28-1898)
Lillian M (Harvey)  b 10-19-1877  dt Charles B & Martha J
                                          (Shaffer)

(Joshua)  (b ca 1780  Perquimans Co, N Car) (d ca 8-mo-1838
    Spiceland, Ind)  s Thomas & Hannah (Munden) of
        Perquimans MM, N Car
    m  (ca 1804  Back Creek Mtg, N Car)
Letitia (Branson)
    rec on req with ch  Deep Creek Mtg, Surry Co, N Car
Ch:  Ruth          b  - - - -  ca 1806
     Mary          b  - - - -
     Thomas        b  - - - -
     Samuel        b  - - - -
     Ephraim       b  - - - -
     Joseph Branson b - - - -
     Amelia        b  - - - -
     Emily         b  - - - -

Marcus  b 2-10-1857  New Lisbon, Ind (Henry Co)
    s Millicent Ratliff
    m  (8-22-1878  Duck Creek Mtg)
Hannah Adalaide (Woolen)  b 8-28-1861  Spiceland, Ind
    dt Edward L & Elizabeth
Ch:  William E     b  1-17-1880
     Herschel      b  4-30-1883
     Carl Marcus   b  8-15-1886
     Jesse Claude  b  8-21-1889
     Ruby Evelyn   b  7-13-1893

(William, decd, s Mary of Waynoak MM, Va & Flushing MM,
    Ohio)
Sarah (Wood)  b 6-17-1803  d 11- 1-1880  Spiceland, Ind
    dt Joshua & Hannah of Flushing Mtg, Ohio
Ch:  Elisha B      b  9-18-1833
     Edward        b 10-21-1837
     Hannah        b  2-24-1840
     Fleming       b 10-17-1846

RAYL
Addison Clarkson  b 11-17-1833  New Garden MM, N Car
    s Zadock & Delilah (Hunt)
    m  (8-29-1868)
Julia Ann (Morris)  b 6-25-1847  Westfield, Ind
Ch:  Ella          b  7-10-1869  Hamilton Co, Ind
     Nora W        b  7-28-1871
     Rosa D        b  2- 3-1873
     Frank M       b  8-20-1878

Alpheus  b 11- 2-1837  Guilford Co, N Car  d 7-26-1921
    bur Spiceland, old cem, Ind  s Zadock & Delilah
    m 1st  (11-27-1861)                        (Hunt)
Ruth Emily (Edwards)  b 11-20-1841  d 6- 8-1879  bur
    Spiceland, old cem, Ind  (a Minister)
    dt William & Elizabeth (Newman)
Ch:  Harmon        b  5-14-1865  Spiceland
    m 2nd  (12-27-1883  Henry Co, Ind)
A Emily (Bogue)  b 1-23-1842  Spiceland, Ind
    d 8-24-1919  dt Alfred & Charity (Bogue) Bogue

(Charles  s George & Hannah (?Canaday))
    (b 9-13-1804  N Car)
(Mahala (- - - -?))
Ch:  (to Spiceland Mtg)
     John W        b  9-28-1830
     Elizabeth Ann b  6-14-1833
     Zadock B      b  5- 5-1836

George  b 3-19-1798  s William E & Elizabeth (Thorp)
Ann (White)  b 5- 4-1791  dt Thomas & Betty
Ch:  Isaac W       b  8- 9-1824
     Himelius      b  3-25-1827
     Rebecca J     b  5- 2-1829
     Thomas Chalkley b 1- 1-1832  d 3-11-1851
                   bur Elm Grove Mtg, Ind
     Asa P         b  7-22-1834

George W  b 10-11-1846  d 10-26-1881  bur old Spiceland
    Cem   s Zadock & Delilah (Hunt)
    m  (11-24-1869)
Debbie P (Edwards)
Ch:  Florence D    b 10-22-1873  Hamilton Co, Ind

Harmon  b 5-14-1865  s Alpheus & Ruth Emily (Edwards, decd
    m  (9- 7-1890  Henry Co, Ind)
Odessa (Painter)  b 9- 7-1869  Middletown, Ind
    dt Fleming & Elizabeth (Mowes)
Ch:  Corona        b  4- 1-1898  Henry Co, Ind

SPICELAND

## RAYL (Cont)
James H   b 5- 6-1815  New Garden MM, N Car
    s William E & Elizabeth (Thorp)
    mou (ca 1839 Hopewell Mtg, N Car which mtg was laid
    down in 1849)
Margaret (Clark)  b 7- 7-1818  dt (Benjamin & Mary of
    Hopewell Mtg, N Car)
Ch: Julia Emline        b 12-22-1840
    Alpheus P           b  5- 9-1844
    Martha A            b  - - - -
    Calvin A            b  - - - -
    Laura P             b  - - - -
    William             b  - - - -
    Hannah D            b  - - - -
    Malinda C           b  - - - -

John W   b 10-31-1886  Burr Oak, Jewel Co, Kansas
    m (8-28-1916  Cleveland, Ohio)

(Matthew) (probably a son of William E & Elizabeth (Thorp))
    mou (Hopewell MM, N Car, ca 1820)
Nancy (- - - -?)
Ch: Eliza               b 11-19-1820
    (rec in mbrp 8-11-1827 Hopewell MM, N Car)

(William jr, s William E & Elizabeth (Thorp))
    (b 6-23-1804  N Car)
    m (9-23-1824  Hopewell Mtg, N Car)
(Veshti (Mendenhall) (b 2- 4-1805  N Car)  dt Moses &
    Millicent, decd)
Ch: Abulleno            b  - - - -
    Asa                 b  - - - -
    Mordecai            b  - - - -
    Ann                 b  - - - -
    Elias               b  - - - -
    Jesse               b  - - - -

William H   b 9-30-1841  Guilford Co, N Car  d 9-30-1888
    bur new cem, Spiceland, Ind  s Zadock & Delilah
                                              (Hunt)
    m (11-14-1867  Greenwood MM, Ind (Hamilton Co))
Julia (Stalker)  b 6- 3-1844  Randolph Co, N Car
    dt Thomas & Sallie (Millikan)
Ch: Walter S            b  6-16-1871  Henry Co, Ind
    Mary Lena           b  3-13-1875  d - - - -?

Zadock   b 3- 3-1809  Guilford Co, N Car  d 12-29-1886
    bur old cem, Spiceland, Ind  s George & Hannah
    m 1st (7-16-1829)  N Car           (?Canaday)
Delilah (Hunt)  b 4-12-1813  Guilford Co, N Car
    d 4- 4-1874  bur Spiceland Cemetery, Ind
    dt Thomas & Sarah (Griffin)
Ch: Perlina             b  7-14-1832
    Adison C            b 11-17-1833
    Alpheus             b 11- 2-1837
    Harmon              b 10- 4-1839  d 12-18-1863
    bur old cem, Spiceland, Ind
    William H           b  9-30-1841
    George W            b 10-11-1846
    Samira              b  4-14-1850
    m 2nd (5- 4-1876)
Isabelle (Poer)  dt Absalom & Mary (Hodson) (after the death
    of Zadock, Isabelle m 10-23-1896 to Jacob Griffin)

## REAGAN
Chester Linnus  b 9-11-1890  Hamilton Co, Ind  s John &
    m (6-18-1914  Logansport, Ind)              Mary E
Sabina (Hutton)  b 9-18-1890  Pittsburg, Pa
    dt Edward P & Alta
Ch: Alta
    Wilma
    Ina May

## REECE - REESE
Charles   d 1890  Spiceland, Ind
    m (8-20-1884)
Oneda (Bogue)  b 7-29-1864  Spiceland, Ind
    dt Josiah & Sinnie J (Allen)
Ch: Priscilla Jessie    b  6-22-1885  Henry Co, Ind
    Sibie Edna          b  4-25-1887  d 7- 4-1888
                                          Spiceland
    Charles J           b  4-14-1890
(after the death of Charles, Oneda m 2nd Ira Carter)

Henry   b Orange Co, N Car  d 8-11-1897  s Daniel &
Mary (Carmack)  dt John & Mary            Phebe
Ch: Jennie              b  1-26-1868
    (m 9- 6-1891 to Alonzo Addison)

(John)
    m (8-25-1897  Henry Co, Ind)
Maude (Addison)  b 2-19-1879  Rush Co, Ind
    dt Levi & Hannah (Pike)

Mary   b 2- 9-1829  Guilford Co, N Car  d 4-28-1908
    dt John & Mary (Carmack) Reece

(Solomon  s Moses & Sarah of New Hope MM, Tenn)
    (m 2- 2-1831  New Hope MM, Tenn)
(Ruth (Wright)  dt Jesse & Ann (Clearwater))
    (b 12- 6-1811)
Ch: Jesse               b  - - - -
    Moses               b  - - - -

## REED
Albert S   b 8- 4-1845  Richmond, Ind  (s Rowland T &
    Drusilla A (Unthank))
    m (6- 1-1868)
Ellen M (Lefevre)  b 2- 4-1847  Scipio, N Y
    (dt William M & Rebecca)
Ch: Frank Lefevre       b  7-17-1871  Richmond, Ind
    Walter C            b 12-23-1875
    Albert Rowland      b  2- 2-1878
    Hugh                b  - - - - -

Druscilla A (Unthank) wid of Rowland T Reed  b 2-14-1821
    Guilford Co, N Car  (d 5- 5-1908  bur Earlham)
    dt of William & Rebecca (Hiatt) Unthank

## REYNARD - RINARD
Jacob
    rmt (3-30-1822  Springfield MM, Ohio)
Elizabeth (Sheridan) (dt John & Margaret)
Ch: Mary                b  9-24-1829
    Elizabeth           b 12- 5-1831
    Ruth                b  2-11-1835
    Ann                 b 11-14-1837

## REYNOLDS
Job   b 5-14-1799  Randolph Co, N Car  s Francis &
    Rachel (Davis)
Phebe (Hockett)  b 8- 6-1799  Springfield MM, N Car
    dt Mahlon & Sarah (Millikan)
Ch: (that came to Spiceland)
    Achsah              b 12-25-1818
    David               b  8-21-1826
    Phebe               b  1-20-1828
    Eunice W            b  1-12-1830
    Asenath             b 11-24-1834
    Susan               b  8- 3-1837
    Jane                b  8-21-1841

## RHODES
Riley
    m (2-15-1899  Rush Co, Ind)
Hattie B (Sears)  b 8- 4-1872  dt James & Mary (Emmons)

## RICH
(Charles)
    m (4- 9-1889  Rush Co, Ind)
Olive (Ross)  b 10- 5-1879  Raleigh, Rush Co, Ind
    dt Leander & Mary

## RIFNER
Olive Ethel  b 9- 5-1879  Henry Co, Ind
    dt Charles R & Rachel C (Smith)

(Peter)
    m (1-31-1873)
Mary E (Heacock)  b 4-22-1848  dt Salathiel & Ann
                                            (Weeks)

## RISH
(John, decd)
Elizabeth (Cook)  b 2- 1-1843  dt Thomas & Martha
Ch: Emma L              b  4-11-1866
    Mary May            b  3- 7-1868

SPICELAND

## ROBERTS
Samuel  b  9- 4-1832  Fairfield MM, Ohio  (s Judah &
                                              Ruth (Pike))
Rebecca (Carey or Corey?)  b  5-16-1836
Ch:  Elizarah      b  9- 4-1856
     Emma Bell    b  12- 2-1859
     Ida May      b  9-30-1862
     Oscar        b  12-13-1868
     Austin       b  4-17-1870

## ROEGER
Violet (Bowen)  b  11-26-1889  Hamilton Co, Ind
    dt Thomas & Sarah (Allison)
    m  (9-mo-1909  Henry Co, Ind)
to - - - -? Roeger

## ROGERS
Jonathan T  b  9-17-1835  Pa  s Nathan & Atlantic (Haines)
    of Washington Co, Pa
    m  (1858  Spiceland Mtg, Ind)
Mary (Hunt)  b  11-10-1836  Indiana  dt Joseph B & Ann R
    (recorded a Minister in 1864)           (Gause)
Ch:  Geneva      b  6-26-1859  d same day, bur
                                Spiceland
     Logan M     b  7-15-1860
     Walter      b  6- 2-1865

## RUSSELL
John  of Modishia, Kansas
Emily C (Elliott)  b  1- 1-1864  d  1907  dt Patrick &
                                    1st w, Sarah (Ball)

## SAINT
Albert W
    m  (10-26-1882 )
Eliza Ann (Edwards)  b  2-13-1842  dt David & Susanna
                                           (Pennington)

(William (s of Hercules & Sarah (Barrow) of Piney Woods
    MM, N Car))  (rmt 12- 5-1807 Perquimans MM, N Car)
(Achsah (Elliott) of Piney Woods MM, N Car)
    (b 1786  d 11-29-1839)
Ch:  (Exum        b  9-10-1808  N Car)
     (Juliann     b  8- 8-1811          )
     (Alpheus     b  2-21-1813          )
     (Jennette    b  2-16-1816  N Car)
     (Doughty     b  8- 7-1818  Indiana)
     (Joseph      b  3-23-1820          )
     (Jonathan E  b  1-26-1822          )
     (Daniel      b  11-24-1823         )
     (Milton      b  1-13-1826          )
     (William jr  b  11-30-1828         )
     (Cynthia E   b  12-28-1830         )

## SANDERS - SAUNDERS
(Joseph from Suttons Creek, N Car)
    mos ca 1796  N Car
Martha (Wells)  (dt Joseph (mos 1796 Perquimans Co, N Car))
    (Martha rec on req Back Creek MM, N Car on 2-28-1807)
Ch:  (to Spiceland Mtg)
     Margaret     b  6-23-1797
     Elizabeth    b  6-25-1806
     Hannah       b  7-29-1810
     Thomas       b  11-21-1813
     Joseph Wells b  10- 6-1816

## SAPP
Andrew J  s Isaac & Elizabeth of Rush Co, Ind
    m  (3- 4-1874)
(Mary) Frances (Barlow)  b  1856  Tipton, Ind
    d 8- 7-1906  bur Shiloh Cemetery  dt S R & Mary
                                     of Tipton Co, Ind
Ch:  Nora     b       1878  Missouri
     Jacob    b       1881  Rush Co, Ind
     Isaac    b  - - - - -  d  bur Shiloh
    (after the d of Andrew, Mary m 2nd on 7-28-1897
                to Robert H Cook)

## SAUL
Francis H  b  6-30-1865  s George & Arrilda (Hooten)
    m  (12- 3-1888  Fayette Co, Ind)
Mary Frances (Daily)  b  4-11-1864  dt Oliver & Martha E
                                         (Law? Low?)

Ch:  Ruby H     b  9- 8-1890  Rush Co, Ind
     Olaf R     b  8-31-1894
     Oliver F   b  10-21-1895  Dunreith, Ind
     Gladys A   b  8- 1-1897
     Remona B   b  7- 8-1898
     Frances C  b  4- 8-1900

## SCHOOLEY
Benjamin  b  12- 2-1788  Stokes Co, N Car  s Samuel &
                                        Elizabeth (Wilson)
    m 1st  (11-29-1809 Mt Pleasant MM, Va)
Rebecca (Johnson)  b  9-29-1794  Grayson Co, Va
    d 8-31-1832  Cherry Grove Mtg, Ind  dt Thomas & Ann
Ch:  Wilson    b  6-20-1817  Clinton Co, Ohio
     Samuel    b  9-16-1820  Wayne Co, Ind
     James L   b  6-14-1822
     Milton    b  9- 5-1827
    m 2nd  (1834)
Sarah (Davis)  b  5- 2-1801  Carteret Co, N Car
    d 8- 2-1837  bur Spiceland Mtg, Ind
    dt Joseph & Susanna
    m 3rd  (1839)
Jemima DRAPER  (probably wid of Josiah (his 2nd w))
    (if so, dt of John & Jemima (Haworth) Wright of
    Bush River Mtg, S Car & Ohio)

Isaac  b  1808  s John & Susannah (Johnson)
    (m 5-24-1827  New Garden Mtg, Ind)
Celia (Thomas)  b  11-21-1808  N Car  d 1891 bur Moline,
    Kansas    dt Stephen & Hannah (Mendenhall)
Ch:  Anna     b  - - - -
     Nancy    b  - - - -
     Edith    b  - - - -
     John     b  - - - -

(John  s Samuel & Elizabeth (Wilson))  (b 2-13-1782
    Hardwick twp, W Division of N J)  (Kingwood MM, N J)
    (m 4- 4-1805  Mt Pleasant MM, Va)
Susanna (Johnson)    dt Thomas & Ann
Ch:  Isaac       b       1808
     Asenath     b  - - - - -
     Elizabeth   b  8- 2-1813
     Susannah    b  - - - - -
     Rachel      b  - - - - -

## SCOTT
Maria  b  5- 5-1861  dt Benjamin & Martha

Ophelia Ann  b  3- 3-1859  Franklin Co, Ind
    dt George & Mary Ann

## SCOVILLE
(J C F)
    m  (6-24-1886  Henry Co, Ind)
Anna M (Stuart)  b  12-10-1864  Rich Square Mtg, Henry Co,
    Ind   dt Charles & Maria (Hare)

Nathan
Sarah (Sweet)  b  ( 9-15-1824)  (dt Solomon & Catherine
                                              (Macy))
Ch:  Carrie (Caroline A) b 10-18-1849  d 9-18-1881
     Mary A     b  10-22-1853
     Eliza      b  - - - - -           Henry Co

## SEAFORD
William
    m  (9- 3-1879)
Emma (Ballenger)  b  9- 5-1855  dt Nathan & Margaret
                                          (Hubbard)

## SEARS
James W  b  7-19-1833  s David & Pauline of Rush Co, Ind
    m 1st
Mary (Emmons)  b  10-27-1843  d  - - - -
    dt William & Arminta
Ch:  Charles W   b  10- 7-1861
     Eva A       b  8-27-1863
     Omer L      b  11-23-1865  d 12- 6-1867
                                 Spiceland
     Waltin D    b  9- 4-1869
     Hattie B    b  8- 4-1872
    m 2nd  (7-10-1884)
Alice (Roberts)  b  - - - -  d  7-mo-1901

SPICELAND

## SHAFFER
Charles Elsworth  b 11-28-1867  North Manchester, Ind
   s John & Mary A
  m ( 7- 9-1893)
Anna K (Bogue)  b 4- 4-1867  dt Josiah & Sibbie J
Ch:  Elsworth Corydon  b 3-18-1895  Spiceland
     Cordelia Gretchen  b 3-10-1898

## SHEARS
Anthony jr  b 12- 3-1870  s Anthony & Lavina
Clara (Daniels)  b 8- 1-1875  dt George W & Rebecca

## SHERIDAN
Abner  b 4-22-1817  Clinton Co, Ohio  s John & Margaret
                                             (Osborn)
Matilda (Gaunt)  b 7-12-1819  Miami MM, Ohio
   d 3-13-1852  bur Spiceland Mtg, Ind  dt Nebo &
   Judith (Wright) his 2nd w
Ch:  Charles          b 6-25-1840  d 2-29-1844
                   Spiceland, Ind
    Jemima Elvina   b 6-14-1842
    Lydia Margaret  b 10-25-1844
    Beulah Ann      b 3-30-1846
    Susan Jane      b 6-12-1847

George  b 4- 6-1811  s John & Margaret (Osborn)
Mary C (Kersey)  b 11-11-1820  dt William & Rachel (Hiatt)
Ch:  Chilon          b 7-28-1839  Henry Co, Ind
    d 8-27-1839  bur Spiceland Mtg, Ind
    Henry           b 6-19-1840
    Anna K          b 11-21-1841
    Melissa Jane    b 9-16-1843
    Asher           b 5-25-1846
    Rachel Alice    b 3-17-1850
    John W          b 1- 6-1855

John  b 7-22-1775  d 10-25-1836  bur Spiceland Mtg
   s George & Hannah
Margaret (Osborn)  b 8-27-1780  N Car  d 11-25-1868
   bur Spiceland Mtg  dt Thomas & Elizabeth (Stout)
Ch:  Hannah          b 2-24-1802  N Car
    Elizabeth       b 6-10-1804
    William         b 10- 8-1806  Clinton Co, Ohio
    Rachel          b 5-26-1809
    George          b 4- 6-1811
    John jr         b 2- 7-1813
    Thomas          b 3-24-1815
    Abner           b 4-22-1817
    Margaret        b 8-27-1819  d 12-25-1820
      Clinton Co, Ohio
    Susannah        b 11-15-1821  (m Daniel Allen)
    Isaac           b 4- 9-1824  West Grove MM, Ind

Oliver  b 10-12-1835
Edith (Sheridan)  b 11- 5-1845  dt William & Elizabeth
                                    (Schooley)
Ch:  Josephine       b 8-21-1872  d Spiceland
    Bertha          b 3- 5-1874
    (Edith divorced Oliver Sheridan & m 2nd, 1-17-1884
       to Isaac N Walters)

Thomas  b 3-24-1815  Clinton Co, Ohio  s John, decd &
   Margaret (Osborn)
Hannah (Wright)  b 10-23-1818  Whitewater MM, Ind
   dt Elijah & Susanna (Hoover)
Ch:  Jane            b 8-19-1840  d 10- 3-1841
                 bur Spiceland Mtg, Ind
    Mary Ellen      b 7-16-1842
    Susan           b 8-29-1844
    Martha          b 2- 9-1847
    Emily           b 10-18-1849
    Charles         b 11-13-1851
    Elizabeth       b - - - - -
    Esther Ann      b - - - - -

William  b 10- 8-1806  d 9-23-1870  bur Spiceland
   s (John & Margaret (Osborn))
  m (6-25-1829  New Garden Mtg, Ind)
Elizabeth (Schooley)  b 8- 2-1813  Clinton Co, Ohio
   d 8-mo-1891  bur Spiceland  dt John & Susanna
                                      (Johnson)
Ch:  Isaac           b 5-27-1830  Ind  d-5-22-1852
                 bur Spiceland
    Susannah        b 4-25-1832  (m Elephalet Hiatt?)

    Eli             b 7- 2-1834
    Anna            b 7-26-1837  d 8-18-1840
                 bur Spiceland
    Rhoda           b 11-25-1839
    Asenath         b 12-22-1842
    Edith           b 11- 5-1845
    John            b 8-21-1848
    Almira          b 3-22-1852
  an adopted dt: Martha L Jarret  b 1- 2-1863  Davidson
    Co, N Car  real dt of James & Rebecca Jarrett

## SHINN
Israel  b 6-20-1812  Va  s Daniel & Mary
Cordelia Ann (Smith)  b - - - -  d 2-mo-1892

## SHIPLEY
Samuel J A
  m 11-17-1889
Eldora (Dora) (Hall)  b 5- 6-1861  dt Joseph S &
   Lucinda (Symons)
Ch:  Leah Mary       b 5- 5-1893  Fayette Co, Ind
    Esther A        b 8-29-1895   "    "    "

## SHULTZ
Samuel F  b 11- 1-1855  (may have d at Knightstown, Ind)
   s Jacob & Mary
  m (3-25-1891  Newburg, Oregon)
Eunice (Hastings)  b 7- 1-1858  Rush Co, Ind
   dt Daniel & Keziah (Brown)
Ch:  Irvin T         b 2-25-1892  Oregon
    Eva L           b 3-15-1897  Richmond, Ind

## SIMCOX
Lydia  b 5- 3-1826  dt Job & Catherine (Reynard)  decd
   of Springfield MM, Ohio & Newberry MM, Ohio

## SIMMONS - see also SYMONS
Henry Wilson  b 3- 1-1833  Ohio  d - - - -  s Matthew
  m (11- 2-1859)                           & Mary Jane
Sarah Ann (Brown)  b 11-24-1842  dt John & Mary Ann
Ch:  Eva             b 10- 8-1863  Charlottesville, Ind
    Melvin          b 8-10-1869  Knightstown, Ind
    Lora            b 7- 7-1872
    Emma Florence   b 7- 8-1875
    Minnie Ray      b 7- 9-1878
    Floyd A         b 9-28-1881
    Mattie (Nettie) b 6-25-1884

## SLEMMER
J H
  m (2-19-1895)
Laura (Hodson)  b 4-14-1863  dt William & Amanda (Scoville)

## SMALL
(Gideon  s Jonathan, decd & Miriam (Bundy) now Miriam
   Hockett)  b 7-28-1817
  m (1837)
Dinah (- - - -?)  rec in mbrp 1839 Spiceland Mtg
Ch:  Jonathan T      b - - - -
    Mary            b - - - -
    Josiah M        b - - - -

(Jonathan  s Gideon decd & Sarah (Griffin)) (b 8-12-1796)
   (d 8-12-1824  bur Arba, Ind)
   (m 10- 2-1816  Whitewater Mtg)
Miriam (Bundy)  b 1-10-1794  dt Josiah, decd & Miriam
   (Perisho)  (now Miriam Hockett)
Ch:  Gideon          b 7-28-1817
    Sarah           b 3-11-1819
    Elihu           b 2- 5-1823
    Josiah          b 7-12-1824  (bound out to
   Nathan & w Polly Small in 1837)
   (after the d of Jonathan Small, Miriam m 2nd, 7-21-1830
    Philip Hocket at Arba Mtg, Ind)

Josiah  b 10-18-1790  N Car  d 8-16-1835  bur Spiceland
   Mtg  s Obadiah, decd & Elizabeth (Symons)
Jane (Moore)  b 5-18-1797  N Car  d 2-12-1871  bur
   Spiceland  dt Thomas & Abigail (Albertson) Bond,
   Moore (2nd w of Thomas)
   (after d of Josiah Small, Jane m 2nd Jonathan Johnson
    of Cherry Grove Mtg, Ind)

SPICELAND

SMALL (Cont)
Ch: Josiah & Jane
 Thomas   b 9-27-1816 Ind d 9-24-1833
         bur Spiceland
 Sarah    b 12- 2-1818 " d 12-14-1833
         bur Spiceland
 Elizabeth  b 4-17-1822  "
 Abigail   b 5-22-1824  "
 Lydia    b 2-19-1826  " d 3-12-1827
         bur Duck Creek
 William   b 11-15-1829  "
 Anna    b 10-12-1834  " d 8- 9-1835
         bur Spiceland

(Nathan s Gideon, decd & Sarah (Griffin)) (now wid of
 Valentine Pegg) (b ca 1806)
 (mcd 1826 Whitewater Mtg, Ind)
(Polly) (- - - -?)
Ch: Samuel   b - - - -
 Martha   b - - - -
 Josiah   b - - - -

Obadiah b 10-13-1794 N Car d 8- 1-1851 bur Spiceland
 Mtg s Gideon, decd & Sarah (Griffin)
 (m ca 1815 Fall Creek Mtg, Ohio)
Isabel (Moore) b 3-13-1787 N Car d 11- 7-1854
 Spiceland dt Thomas & his 1st w Isabel (Newby), decd
Ch: Jonathan  b - - - -
 Miriam   b - - - -
 Mary    b 2-19-1819

Sarah (Griffin) Small (now wid of Valentine Pegg of
 Whitewater Mtg) b 10-12-1773 Symons Creek MM, N
 Car dt James & Hannah (Kenyon) Griffin (wid of
 Gideon Small of N Car & Ohio) (Gideon Small
 d 3- 4-1811 bur Fall Creek Mtg, Ohio)

Sophronia P b 8-11-1830 Hertford, Perquimans Co, N Car
 dt Henry & Nancy

Susannah b 11- 3-1819 Core Sound Mtg, N Car
 dt Silas & Mary (Davis) Small, both decd

(Silas Small s Jonas & Sarah) (b 1-28-1794 d ca 1821
 Core Sound Mtg N Car)
(Mary (Davis) dt Joseph W & Susannah) (b 7-18-1794
 d 3-21-1836 New Garden Mtg, Ind as the w of
 Solomon Hubbard)

William b 1-15-1829 Duck Creek MM, Ind s Josiah, decd
 d 12-14-1870        & Jane
Mary (Gause) b 1-14-1829 Preble Co, Ohio dt Nathan &
               Mary
Ch: Jane    b 12-13-1850 Spiceland, Ind
      d 8-10-1853 bur Spiceland, Ind
 Elizabeth Ann b 6-26-1854 d 8- 2-1870
      bur Spiceland, Ind
 Evaline   b 5-24-1858 d 8-25-1858
      bur Spiceland, Ind
 Abigail   b 4-28-1863

SMILEY
(John)
 m (10-12-1887 Henry Co, Ind)
Ollie Kate (Allison) b 6-22-1857 Knightstown, Ind
 dt James & Rachel

SMITH
(Fred E) b 1-26-1872 Washtenaw, Mich s of Alfred &
 Electa (Pasko?) Smith
 m (8-15-1907 Henry Co, Ind)
Mary E (Lawrence)

Wilda N b 11- 2-1873 Occident, Ind dt John W & Eliza
 Catherine Smith

Francis Joseph b 8-11-1859 Raysville, Ind s Jackson &
 m ( 4- 7-1880)        Mary
Mary E (Biddy) b 5-21-1858 Raysville, Ind
 dt James & Jennie
Ch: Jessie Evaline b 3-12-1881 Raysville, Ind
 James Monroe b 7- 1-1882 Indianapolis, Ind
 Robert Edgar b 5-11-1884 Spiceland, Ind
 Abigail W  b - - - - - "  "

William G b 8-23-1892 Henry Co, Ind s W F & Amanda
              (Cory)
William R b 9- 8-1859 Wayne Co, Ind s William & Lucy
 m ( 4-26-1884)
Martha (Sloan) b 11-21-1862 in Tenn dt William & Mary
Ch: Guy    b 9- 8-1888
 Claude   b - - - - -

SPENCER
David b 6- 1-1839 Ind d 1895 s John & Elizabeth
             (Deselms)
 m ( 9-11-1859)
Mary Jane (Grey)
Ch: John Truman  b 8-16-1860 Greensboro, Ind
 David C   b 7-31-1861 d 8-14-1882
 Lindley A  b 9-18-1865
 Louisa A   b 9-13-1866
 Milton Alonzo b 5-28-1868
 Mary Jane  b 6- 1-1872
 Florence   b 4-12-1874
 Madenmozelle b 3- 8-1877
 Bessie   b 8-31-1881 Cambridge City, Ind

John b 5-22-1802 Frederick Co, Va d 8-16-1833
 bur Duck Creek MM, Ind s Miller & Sidney
 m (5-17-1823)
Elizabeth (Dezellon)
Ch: David    b - - - -
 John Alexander b 1- 8-1845
 (m 2nd 9- 5-1874)
Sarah Seaford

John Alexander b 1- 9-1842 Ind s John & Elizabeth
              (Deselms)
Sarah (Garris) b 5-18-1848 Wayne Co, Ind
 dt Isaac & Pearcie (Howel) Garris
Ch: Edgar    b 5-18-1870 Sulphur Springs, Ind
 Montie L   b 2-13-1872 Greensboro, Ind
 Julia May  b 2- 1-1874
 Cora Elizabeth b 4-27-1876 Spiceland, Ind
 John Clemmens b 10- 3-1878 Rush Co, Ind
 William   b 7- 1-1884 Henry Co, Ind

Montie L b 2-13-1872 s John A & Sarah (Garris)
 m (3-24-1892)
Mae (Schultz)

Rebecca b 4-25-1825 dt David & Leah (Pickering) of
 Concord Mtg, Ohio

William b 7- 1-1884 Henry Co, Ind s John Alexander &
 Sarah (Garris)
 m (8- 2-1905 Henry Co, Ind)
Vera (Emminger) b 7- 3-1885 dt James & Josie
              (Thornburgh)

SPRINGER
Barnabas b 1- 9-1793 Deep River MM, N Car
 s Stephen & Sarah (Macy) of N Car & Ind
 mcd 1824 rst 1831 Whitewater Mtg, Ind

SPRONG
Andrew J b 3-19-1833 Fayette Co, Ind s Solomon &
 m (11- 5-1890)        Henrietta
Nancy (Holloway) b 9-17-1846 Henry Co, Ind
 dt David & Mary (Williams)

STAFFORD
Dora b 7-24-1874 Wayne Co, Ind dt Freling H & Emma W

STANBROUGH
Francis
 m (1850)
Rebecca (Hartley) b 6-17-1824 Butler Co, Ind dt James
              & Rebecca

Frank
Hannah (Holloway) b 11- 8-1840 Newcastle, Ind
 d 6- 5-1892 dt David & Mary

(James, decd, s Solomon & Tabitha of Center Mtg, Ohio)
 (b 5-25-1793) (d 11-22-1831 ar Bethel Mtg, Ind)
 m (ca 1813 - 1814 Ohio)
Mary (Hodgson) dt Hurr & Elizabeth (Thornbrugh) decd
 b - - - -

SPICELAND

## STANBROUGH (Cont)
Ch: of James & Mary   (came to Spiceland with mth)
    Jonathan            b  4-13-1817
    Phebe               b  8-10-1818
    Elizabeth           b  7-12-1822
  (after the d of James, Mary m 2nd at Milford Mtg, 1836
  to John Bond, a wid  w/ch)

Nehemiah  b  3-23-1792  s Solomon & Tabitha
  (m  5-24-1815  Centre Mtg, Ohio)
Ruth (Hester)  b  9-25-1798  dt Francis & Mary (Hodgin)
Ch:  (the fam was attached to Spiceland Mtg when Duck
    Creek Mtg was laid down in 1837)
    Ann                 b   3- 3-1816
    Thomas              b  ca    1818
    Francis             b  ca    1820
    James               b  ca    1822
    Solomon             b  11-19-1823
    Mary H              b  11-26-1825
    Levi                b   2-17-1828
    Tabitha             b   6- 7-1831
    Malinda             b        1833

## STANLEY
Aaron  b  5-28-1803  N Car  d  5- 4-1883  bur Circle Grove
  Cemetery, Spiceland, Ind  s Michael & Mary (Gurley)
  m  (1-19-1826)
Mahala (Stanley)  b  1- 6-1809  Stokes Co, N Car
  d  1- 9-1870  dt John & Elizabeth (Dicks) Stanley
Ch:  Eliza Jane          b  3-26-1827
    Michael             b  3- 1-1829
    Manerva             b  3-13-1831  d 10- 4-1835
      bur Spiceland
    Vierling K          b  7-28-1833
    Hannah              b  6- 8-1837
    Martha              b  5-16-1841  d 11-11-1874
      bur Spiceland
    Mariah              b 10-11-1844

(Elwood  s Richard & Abigail (Foster))  b (11-29-1814 N Car)
  (m  3-30-1837  Milford Mtg, Ind)
(Martha (Butler)  dt James S & Deborah (Johnson))
  (b  8-27-1816)
Ch:  William             b   - - - -
    Emeline             b   - - - -

Josiah  b  7- 3-1810  Guilford Co, N Car  s Michael & Mary
  m 1st                                        (Gurley)
Mary (Stanley) Harrold  a wid of John  b  9-15-1807
  Guilford Co, N Car  d  8-25-1840  bur Spiceland MM,
  Ind  dt Jesse & Lydia (Gurley)
Ch:  Jabez              b  3-21-1839  Spiceland MM, Ind
  m 2nd
Ann (Gause)  b  4-14-1810  Redstone MM, Pa  dt Nathan &
                          Mary (Ailes)
Ch:  Mary Jane          b  8-29-1844 Spiceland MM, Ind
    Amos               b  9- 1-1846  d  7-27-1847
      bur Spiceland Mtg, Ind
    Lindley Hoag       b 12- 9-1847
    Ruth Anna          b  5-11-1850  d  8-30-1851
    Amy F              b 11- 8-1852

Melvin
  m  (9-22-1901  Henry Co, Ind)
Atha Dora (Lloyd)  b  4-22-1881  dt Robert & Phebe A
                                (Baldwin)

(Michael  d 10-12-1838 Dover MM, N Car)  (s Strangeman
         & Jemima)  m (12-13-1792 New Garden Mtg, N Car)
Mary (Gurley)  b  1-27-1771  Bucks Co, Pa  d  2- 6-1858
    bur Spiceland Mtg, Ind  dt John & Lydia
Ch:  (to Indiana)
    Abigail              b  8-22-1795  N Car
                         d  2-11-1872  Bethel Mtg
    Hannah               b  8-21-1812 d 11-31-1882
    bur Nettle Creek Mtg, Ind as the 2nd w of David
    Pidgeon of Springfield Mtg

Mordecai  b  5- 2-1833  d  1877, bur Spiceland Mtg
  s Nathan, decd & Delana (Stanley)
Rebecca Jane (Hodson)  dt - - - -?  (dis 1857)
Ch:  Nancy A            b  7-29-1853
    Jessie Ann         b  4-14-1854  d  4- 9-1858
      bur Spiceland

Nathan  b  3- 5-1807  N Car  d  9-23-1837  bur Spiceland
  Mtg   s Michael & Mary (Gurley)
Delana (Stanley)  b  5- 2-1810  d 3-11-1883  bur Spiceland
  Mtg, Ind  b (Stokes Co N Car)  dt John & Elizabeth
                                (Dicks)
  (after d of Nathan, Delana m 2nd, Jesse Bond)
Ch:  Mordecai           b  5- 2-1833  d 1877 bur Spice-
                             land Mtg
    Susan              b  7-13-1835
    Naomi              b  8-10-1837  d  5-12-1838
      bur Spiceland

(Nathan  s Samuel & Sarah (Williams))  (b  8- 9-1806  Dover
  Mtg, N Car)
(Phebe (Hollingsworth)  dt Isaac & Hannah (Crew))
  (b  6- 2-1806  Dover Mtg, N Car)
Ch:  (to Spiceland)
    (Cyrus K           b  9-15-1835)
    (Gulielma          b  5-22-1837)
    (Eliza Ann (2nd)   b  - - - - -)

Solomon  b  6-18-1803  N Car  s Jesse & Lydia (Gurley)
  (d ca 1837 Spiceland Mtg, Ind)
  (m  1-10-1828  Dover MM, N Car)
Achsah (Pidgeon)  b  5- 5-1804  N Car  (d  8-23-1875 at
  Elk Mtg, Ohio as the w of Samuel Ballard)  dt Charles
  Sr & Elizabeth
Ch:  (by 1st husb)
    Elizabeth Jane     b  9-24-1830
    Lydia L            b  4-18-1833
    Mary P             b  ca  1835

Vierling K  b  7-28-1833  s Aaron & Mahala (Dicks)
Josephine (Talbert)  b  2- 1-1845  Silver Creek Mtg, Ind
  dt Jabez & Mary (Cook)
Ch:  Ora Ella           b  9-13-1867
    Martha             b  - - - - -?

William C  b  9- 2-1833  New Garden Mtg, N Car
  s William & Susannah (Moore) of Milford Mtg, Ind
  m 1st  (1863  Spiceland Mtg)
Miriam (King)  b  6- 5-1840  Morgan Co, Ohio
  dt Joseph & Mary (Morris) decd

## STANTON
Ann  b  1-23-1812  Center Mtg, Ohio  dt William & 1st w
  Ruth (Faulkner) decd

James  b  8-22-1820  Center MM, Clinton Co, Ohio
  s William & Margaret (Pusey), his 2nd w

## STEELE
Clara B  b  1-28-1856  dt Alexander & Mary (Griffin)

(Stephen)
  m  (4-15-1877)
Matilda J (Ricks)  b  1-22-1862  Guilford Co, N Car
  dt William Edward & Harriet Francis
Ch:  Charlie Edward     b  3-30-1881  Mooresville, Ind
    Mary Elizabeth     b  3-25-1883  Eden, Ind
    Stella Edna        b  9-20-1885
    Ollie Jane         b  3-19-1888  Raysville
    Verne Alberta      b  8-19-1891  Middletown,
      Shelby Co, Ind

## STEVENSON
Harry E  b  6-25-1863  Boontown, N J  s William & Phebe E
  m  (12-27-1892)
Emma V (Castor)  b  8-21-1872  Lafayette, Ind  dt Parry
                             & Mary
Ch:  Flora J            b 10-14-1893  Knightstown, Ind

## STIGLEMAN
John
  m 10- 1-1891  Henry Co, Ind
Leora (Simmons)  b  7- 7-1872  dt Henry & Sarah (Brown)
Ch:  Edith              b  7- 6-1892  Henry Co, Ind
    India              b  4-14-1894  Henry Co, Ind

## STOUT
Ephriam  b  1-14-1797  Orange Co, N Car  s Charles jr &
  Lydia (non-mbrs)  (rec on req Springfield Mtg, Ind,
  1826)
  m 1st in Ohio

## STOUT (Cont)
### Ephriam (Cont)
Ruth (Howell) b 11-10-1798 in N Car  d 10-10-1829 West
    River Mtg, Wayne Co, Ind  dt Robert & Anna (non-
                          mbrs)
Ch:  James           b  1-29-1816  Clinton Co, Ohio
     Charles         b 11-11-1817  Wayne Co, Ind
     Robert          b  2- 7-1820  Randolph Co, Ind
     Elias           b  4-17-1822
     Enoch           b  2-17-1824  d  2-20-1829
                          bur West River Mtg
     Anna            b  3-12-1825
     Ruth            b  1-14-1827  Wayne Co, Ind
     Ephraim jr      b  6- 3-1829
  m 2nd  (2-mo-1831 Duck Creek Mtg, Ind)
Mary (Sheridan) b 2-19-1800 Chatham Co, N Car
    dt John & Mary (Doan)
Ch:  Benoni          b 12- 5-1831  d same day Spiceland
     Thomas          b 10-27-1832  Spiceland Mtg
     Mary            b 12- 4-1833  d  8-21-1834
                          bur Spiceland

## STRATTON
### Albert
  m  (4-28-1884  Henry Co, Ind)
Louisa H (Unthank) b 9-23-1856 dt John & Martha A
                                        (Hobbs)

Eli  b 12-20-1772  Everham MM, Burlington Co, N J
    d  8-17-1839  bur Spiceland Mtg, Ind  s Jonathan &
                                         Sarah
Eunice (Dallas) b 10- 7-1771 Maurice River MM, Cumber-
    land Co, N J  dt William & Rebecca
    (their ch had all m)

(Levi  s Benjamin & Amy) (b ca 1801 South River MM, Va)
  (m  1822)
(Ruth (Crew)) (b ca 1802) (rec on req Springfield Mtg,
    Ohio    1819)
Ch:  Lucinda         b - - - -
     Albert           b - - - -
     Hannah           b - - - -
     Amy              b - - - -

## STREET
Samuel  b 4-18-1800  Salem MM, N J  s Aaron & Mary
  m  (4- 4-1832  Whitewater MM, Ind)
Anna (Macy) dt Stephen & Rebecca (Barnard)
    b 6-25-1802  New Garden MM, N Car
Ch:  Jane            b  3- 2-1833  Whitewater MM, Ind
     Jehu            b  9-24-1834  Spiceland MM, Ind
     Stephen         b  3-13-1836
     Lydia           b  7-31-1837
     Isaac           b  1- 9-1839
     Seth            b  9-18-1840
     Rebecca         b  4- 1-1842
     Mary            b 12-21-1843

## STUART
Amos  b 6-30-1808  (d 1-15-1905 Whitewater Mtg, bur
    Earlham)  s Jehu Sr & Sarah (Guyer)
  (m 1st  9- 8-1830  Cane Creek MM, N Car)
Matilda (Hadley) b 12- 4-1812  d 6-13-1871 Spiceland,
    Ind  (dt Jonathan & Ann (Long)
Ch:  Martitia        b  7-16-1833
     Jehu H           b  6-20-1836
     Sarah           b  2- 1-1838
     Mary E           b  7-12-1840
     Jonathan        b  8-14-1842
     Eliza           b 12- 6-1844
     Delphina        b 10- 2-1847
     John Sidney     b  3- 2-1850
     David W         b  8-19-1852  Deep River Mtg,
                         N Car
     Robert Addison    b 11-16-1854
     Amos Elbridge     b  9-12-1856
     Francis         b  8-15-1859  Deep River Mtg,
                         N Car
  m 2nd  (3-25-1875  Whitewater Mtg, Ind)
Melissa (Miles) b 6-26-1833 (d 4-17-1923 Whitewater
    Mtg, Ind bur Earlham) dt Samuel & Anna (Kelly)

Edmond  b 5-21-1841  s Samuel W of Hopewell Mtg, Ind
Martha (Jones) b 8-14-1847 dt William & Huldah of
    Madison Co, Ind
Ch:  Clyde           b  2-26-1875

Jehu jr  b 11-10-1772 Guilford Co, N Car  d 2-16-1845
    bur Raysville Mtg, Ind  s Jehu Sr & his 1st w
    Sarah (Stanley), decd
  m  (1795 Deep River Mtg, N Car)
Sarah (Cook) b 12-12-1772  dt Thomas & Mary (Mills)
Ch:  (to Spiceland with their parents)
     Beulah           b 10-14-1808  N Car
     Anna            b  2-19-1813
     Robert          b  1- 7-1815  Indiana
     Cyrus           b  7-20-1817
     Ithmer W        b  5-18-1820

John Sidney  b 3- 2-1850  s Amos & Matilda (Hadley)
  m  (8-29-1876)
Laura Alice (Davidson) b 7- 2-1849 dt Joseph & Ann of
    Springfield, Ohio
Ch:  Florence        b  5-22-1878
     Joseph E        b  3- 3-1881

Robert  b 1- 7-1815 Indiana  s Jehu jr & Sarah (Cook)
Rachel (Maudlin) b 10- 8-1821 of West Grove Mtg, Ind
Ch:  William Henry    b  4-16-1846  Raysville Mtg, Ind
     Mary            b - - - - -

## STUBBS
Charles  b 7- 5-1827  Preble Co, Ohio  s Joseph &
    Margaret (Saunders)
  m  (9- 2-1848)
America (Sample) b 8-11-1830 Hancock Co, Ind
    dt James & Mary
Ch:  Mary V           b  6-23-1853
     Joseph H        b  5-23-1855
     James W         b  4-15-1857
     John E           b  3-18-1859
     Otis A           b 12-24-1866
     Charles L       b  7-21-1868
     Samuel E        b  5- 2-1871

Charles L  b 7-21-1868 s Charles Sr & America (Sample)
  m  (9-14-1898  Henry Co, Ind)
Parthena (Nicholson)

James W  b 4-14-1857 Spiceland, Ind  d 4-mo-1907
    bur Circle Grove Cem, Spiceland  s Charles &
    America (Sample)
  m 1st  (10-19-1882)
Emma L (Holloway) b 5-14-1859 Spiceland, Ind
    d  3- 7-1890  dt Joseph & Hannah
  m 2nd  (1-19-1898  Henry Co, Ind)
Emma (Scoville)

John E  b 3-18-1859  d 8-23-1898  s Charles Sr &
    America (Sample)
  m  (2-15-1882)
Dora (Shelby)

John Sr  ( b ca 1760 Cane Creek Mtg, N Car)  s John &
    Esther of Cane Creek Mtg, N Car & Fredericksburg,
                                  S Car
  (rmt 5- 7-1785  Wrightsboro Mtg, Ga)
Jane (Jones)  (b 6-22-1764) dt Francis & Sarah

Joseph  b 10- 6-1801  Columbia Co, Ga  d 1-28-1836
    bur Spiceland  s John Sr & Jane (Jones)
  m  (8- 9-1820  Elk Mtg, Ohio)
Margaret (Sanders) b 6-23-1797 Perquimans Co, N Car
    d 2-19-1835 bur Spiceland Mtg  dt Joseph & Martha
                                    (Wells)
Ch:  John            b  3-23-1821  Ohio  d 5-24-1838
     Newton          b  4- 6-1823
     Esther Ann      b  3-17-1825
     Charles         b  7- 5-1827
     William N       b  4- 3-1830  d 2-24-1846

Joseph H  b 4-15-1855 s Charles & America (Sample)
Maria (Cochran) b 9- 1-1856 dt James & his 2nd w Mary
                                    (White)
Ch:  Ethel Blanche     b - - - -

Mahlon  b 2- 2-1825  s Joseph, decd & Sarah (Townsend)
  m  (1848 New Garden Mtg, Ind)
Rachel (Woodard) b 12- 7-1827 New Garden Mtg, Ind
    dt Cedar & Rachel (Outland)

SPICELAND

## STUBBS (Cont)
Otis A  b 12-24-1866  s Charles & America (Sample)
  m  (9-mo-1889)
Annettie (Butler) b 5-26-1867  dt Robert & Rebecca

Samuel E  b 5- 2-1871  s Charles Sr & America (Sample)
Mattie (McCray)

## SUTTON
Henry
  m  (1880)
Emma A (White)  b 11-14-1861  dt Jesse & Sarah Ann
                              (Pickett), decd

## SWAIN
(John  s Elihu & Sarah (Mills))  (b 1-10-1784 Center Mtg,
  m  (Lost Creek Mtg, Tenn)                    N Car)
(Ann (Lewis)  dt Evan & Susannah (Moon))
  (b 7-31-1789 Hopewell Mtg, Va)
Ch:  (to Indiana 1834)
     (Lewis           b  6-21-1810)
     (Huldah          b  3-20-1812  m Tenn, Wm Jones,
                         came to Ind)
     (Thomas Clarkson b  2- 6-1814)
     (Elihu           b  4-21-1816)
     (William         b 10-14-1818)
     (Ezra            b  3-10-1822)
     (Susannah        b  9-20-1824)
     (Sally Ann       b 11- 8-1826)
     (John jr         b  3- 5-1830)
     (Rachel          b  3-31-1832)

Thomas More  b 1-26-1834  Guilford Co, N Car (s Howland Sr
  m 1st                                        & Phebe)
Mary M (- - - -?)
Ch:  Ella            b 5-12-1859  Greensboro, Henry Co,
  m 2nd  (11-17-1864)                            Ind
Julia E (Swain) b 4-14-1842  Madison Co, Ind
  dt John T & Mary C
Ch:  Minnie C        b 8-12-1867  Knightstown, Ind
     George Howland  b 7-14-1877  Greensboro, Ind

## SWEET
Solomon  b 7-27-1800  Ohio    s Judith
  m  (Mill Creek Mtg, Ohio)
Catherine (Macy)  b 9-13-1804  Deep Creek Mtg, N Car
  d 7-11-1835 Whitewater Mtg, Ind  dt Stephen &
  Rebecca (Barnard)
Ch:  Anna M          b  8-18-1822
     Sarah           b  9-15-1824
     Rebecca E       b 11-27-1826
     Louisa Amelia   b  5- 8-1829
     Eli M           b  5-29-1833

## SWINDLE
Frank
  m  (10-mo-1870)
Emmeline (Meredith) b 12- 0-1856  dt Jabez & Louisa
  (Antrim)  (Emmeline divorced Frank Swindle & changed
  name back to MEREDITH)

## SYMONS - see also SIMMONS
Aaron  b 4- 3-1836  s Josiah & Sarah (Kindley)
  m  (1861)
Anna K (Sheridan)  b 11-21-1841  dt George & Mary C
                                          (Kersey)
Ch:  Vida            b 10-29-1861  d 11-19-1861
                        bur Spiceland
     Charles         b  2-26-1862
     Mary            b  9-16-1863
     Alice           b  - - - - -

Alfred H  b 11-17-1870  Spiceland, Ind  s Jehu, decd &
  Lydia (Hall) (now w of Rufus Test)
  m  (9-12-1901 Hancock Co, Ind)
Bell (Johnson)

Benjamin F  b 12-16-1837  d 7-23-1884  bur Circle Grove
  Cem, Spiceland  s Abraham jr & Achsah (Gilbert)
  m  (11- 2-1862)
Verlinda (Jenkins)  b 2- 3-1835  d 10-14-1908 as the w
  of Milo Talbert  dt Robert & Ann (Pearson) of Troy,
                                              Ohio

Ch:  Joseph Ellis    b 4- 4-1864  Dunreith, Ind
     Anna L          b 11-22-1866
     Achsah E        b 9-20-1868
     Mary J          b 7- 6-1872
     Robert M        b 7- 9-1875
  (after the d of Benjamin F, Verlinda m 2nd 10-10-1893
   to Milo Talbert)

Frank  b 11-28-1857  Spiceland, Ind  s Joel & Rebecca
  m  (6-mo-1887)
Mary C (Pinkham)  b 7-28-1861  dt William P & Emma
                                          (Curry)

Hannah (Brewer)  b (ca 1806 Pa)  w of Nathan of Drift-
  wood Mtg, & Blue River Mtg, Ind & dt Elias & Mary
  (Cadwallader) of Pa & Ohio
Ch:  Malinda         b  9-19-1832
     Sarah Jane      b  - - - - -
     Martha Ann      b  - - - - -

James M  (from Blue River Mtg, Ind 1845)
  m  (1846-1847)
Sally Ann (Hunt)  b 8-29-1827  Hopewell Mtg, N Car
  dt Thomas & Sarah (Griffin)
Ch:  Thomas Elwood   b 11-11-1847  d 12- 4-1850
                        bur Spiceland
     Lindley Lewis   b  5- 6-1851
     Morris          b 12-26-1853  d  8- 7-1854
                        bur Spiceland

Jehu  b 7-16-1832  (d probably prior to 1885 in Kansas)
  s Josiah & Sarah (Kindley)
  m  (1856)
Lydia (Hall)  b 2-18-1833  d 7- 6-1902 (as the w of
  Rufus Test)  dt Caleb & Hannah (Saunders)
Ch:  Lindley         b  9-27-1857  d  3-28-1858
                        bur Spiceland, Ind
     Elma            b 12-15-1859  d after Jan, 1865
     Flora           b  6-22-1862  d young
     Mary            b  7-27-1863  d  5-18-1864
                        bur Spiceland
     Caleb H         b  1- 1-1866  d  4- 7-1870
                        bur Spiceland
     Alfred H        b 11-17-1870
  (after the d of Jehu, Lydia m 2nd, 2- 4-1890 to
   Rufus Test)

Joel  b ca 1834  s Josiah & Sarah (Kindley)
  m  (1855)
Rebecca (- - - -?)
Ch:  Frank           b 11-28-1857  Spiceland
     Emma            b  9-23-1858
     Thomas Lincoln  b  9-23-1860

John  b 2-19-1838  Grant Co, Ind  d 10-23-1883  bur
  Circle Grove Cem, Spiceland  s Josiah & Sarah
                                          (Kindley)
  m  (3-28-1867 Duck Creek Mtg)
Ellen S (Henley)  b 1-28-1843  Henry Co, Ind
  dt Jabez & Margaret S (Holloway)
Ch:  Estella         b 10-13-1870  Spiceland, Ind
     Arthur H        b  6-24-1872
     Oscar           b  8-13-1874
     Jabez Henley    b  3- 4-1877

Joseph Ellis  b 4- 4-1864  Dunreith, Ind  s Benjamin F
  & Verlinda (Jenkins)
  m  (10-31-1894)
Nora (Deem)  b 5-22-1872  Henry Co, Ind  dt John &
  Elizabeth (Cloud)
Ch:  Elsie E         b  - - - -
     John Franklin   b 3-17-1896  Henry Co, Ind

Josiah  b 6-10-1812  Wayne Co, Ind  d 7-24-1879  bur
  Spiceland, Ind  s Thomas & Hannah (Coffin)
  m  (9- 8-1831 Milford Mtg, Ind)
Sarah (Kindley)  b 12- 7-1813  Miami MM, Ohio  d 10- 4-1893
  dt John & Betty (Wilson)
Ch:  Jehu            b  7-16-1832
     Joel            b   ca 1834
     Aaron           b  4- 3-1836
     John            b  2-10-1838
     Thomas          b 12-10-1839  d 1-20-1848
                        bur Spiceland

SYMONDS - SIMMONS (Cont)
Ch: of Josiah & Sarah (Cont)
    George            b 12- 5-1841
    Mark              b  9-12-1843
    Mary              b 10-13-1846  d 2-11-1865
                      bur Spiceland
    Seth C          b  2- 4-1849
    Josiah jr       b 12-26-1850  d 7-25-1855
                      bur Spiceland

Mark  b  9-12-1843  Spiceland  d 8-13-1909  s Josiah &
  m  (6- 7-1876  Henry Co, Ind)      Sarah (Kindley)
Algy (Applegate)  b  9- 3-1852
Ch:  Henry           b  3- 4-1877  Spiceland
    Susan           b  2-27-1879
    Leroy A         b  5-27-1881
    Albert          b  2- 5-1884

Robert M  b  7- 9-1875  s Benjamin F & Verlinda (Jenkins)
  m  (10-28-1896)
Gertie E (Francis)  b  2- 3-1877  dt David H & Maria

Seth C  b  2- 4-1849  Spiceland, Ind  s Josiah & Sarah
  m  (12-30-1869  Henry Co, Ind)      (Kindley)
Elizabeth (Morris)  b  7-26-1852  Henry Co, Ind
  d  8-mo-1920  dt Isaac & Susannah
Ch:  Maurice (Morris)  b  9-16-1870  d  1890
    Addie           b  1-27-1872
    Pearl           b 10- 8-1880

Thomas  b  2-17-1782  Pasquotank Mtg, N Car  d  9-30-1865
    bur Spiceland Mtg, Ind  s Jesse & Sarah (Bundy)
Hannah (Coffin)  b  5-15-1788  New Garden Mtg, N Car
  d  3- 6-1873  dt Bethuel & Hannah (Dicks)
Ch:  (who came to Spiceland Mtg)
    Josiah          b  6-10-1812  Indiana
    Bethuel         b  2- 7-1814
    Elijah          b  8-17-1816  d  6- 3-1859
                      bur Spiceland

TALBERT
Alvin C  b 11- 6-1825  Union Co, Ind  d 12-18-1881  bur
    Spiceland Mtg  s William & Miriam (Gardner)
  m  (1848  West Grove Mtg, Ind)
Rebecca (Ellis)  b  4-30-1830  Wayne Co, Ind
  dt Thomas & Lydia
Ch:  Martha Florence  b  8-31-1850  Union Co, Ind
    Orpheus E       b 11-27-1852  Howard Co, Ind
    Sylvanus D      b  9-20-1854  Georgetown, Ill
    Edgar           b  7- 3-1857  Union Co, Ind
                 d  1- 6-1875  Spiceland
    Mary Elma       b  1-21-1861
    Elwood          b  9- 1-1862  Howard Co, Ind
    William         b  9- 6-1865  Union Co, Ind
    Edna Blanche    b  4- 8-1876  Henry Co, Ind

Daniel  b  3- 2-1860  Salem, Ind  s Sylvanus G & Phebe
  m  (9- 9-1887)                  (Hiatt)
Caroline (Wilson)  b  4-25-1863  in Iowa  dt William
    & Caroline
Ch:  Mabel           b  7-25-1888
    Annie           b 12- 3-1889
    Ruby            b  - - - - -
    Frank           b  - - - - -

Jabez  b  2-18-1816  Union Co, Ind  s William & Miriam
  m  (3-29-1837  Salem Mtg, Ind)    (Gardner)
Mary (Cook)  b  8- 6-1815  Wayne Co, Ind  dt John & Hannah,
                                          decd
Ch:  (who came to Spiceland Mtg)
    Josephine       b  2- 1-1845
    Anna M          b  9-13-1854
    Sarah D         b  5- 3-1857
    Florence N      b 11-30-1858  Union Co, Ind

Milo  b  3-12-1823  Union Co, Ind  d  4-21-1909  Wichita,
    Kansas  s William & Miriam (Gardner)
  m 1st  (1846)
Mary D  (- - - -?)
Ch:  Sarah Caroline  b  3-21-1849
  m 2nd  (4-23-1854)
Eliza (Paddock)  b 11-12-1827  Union Co, Ind  d - - - -
    dt Reuben & Lydia
Ch:  Mary Emily      b  1- 1-1858  Union Co, Ind

  m 3rd  (10-10-1893  Henry Co, Ind)
Verlinda (Jenkins) Symons, wid of Benjamin F Symons
    b  2- 3-1835  Miami Co, Ohio  d 10-14-1908
    dt Robert & Ann (Pearson) Jenkins

Orpheus E  b 11-27-1852  s Alvin C & Rebecca (Ellis)
  m  (12-31-1874)
Jennie (Jefferson)

Sylvanus D  b  9-20-1854  Georgetown, Ill  s Alvin C
    & Rebecca (Ellis)
  m  (12- 4-1878)
Catharine (Lewis)  b 10-23-1859  Bartholomew Co, Ind
    dt Bradley C & Anna
Ch:  Carl M          b  1-18-1879  Spiceland
    Mable           b  2- 2-1883

Sylvanus G  b  5- 6-1819  s William & Miriam (Gardner)
    (m  6- 2-1842  Miami Mtg, Ohio)
Phebe (Hiatt)  b 11-21-1821  dt Isaac & Shannah D
                             (Hogue)
Ch:  (who came to Spiceland Mtg)
    Daniel H        b  3- 2-1860
    Anna Jane       b  6-18-1862

TAYLOR
Enoch  b  7-12-1850  Greensboro, Ind  d  3-24-1906
    s Frances & Amanda
Mary H (Branson)  b 12- 2-1854  Greensboro, Ind
    dt John & Annis
Ch:  Russell         b 11-12-1875  d  9-24-1907
    Herman          b 11- 3-1879
    Amanda          b 12-25-1882

Jacob  b  5- 5-1828  Center Mtg, Ohio  d  3-15-1887
    bur Richmond, Ind  s Jesse & Deborah (McMillan)
  m  (1851  Spiceland)
Sarah (Evans)  b  3-14-1829  Spiceland, Ind  (to
    Indianapolis 1898)  dt George & Mary (Haskit)
Ch:  Jesse Frank     b  3-31-1853
    Evans           b  4-11-1855  d  7-28-1855
    Ella            b  1-13-1857
    Oliver P        b  2-27-1859
    Clarence M      b  4- 6-1865  d  8-21-1866
    Walter J        b  4- 1-1870  d  7-18-1871

Jesse Frank  b  3-31-1853  Wilmington, Ohio  s Jacob
  m  (9- 4-1877)            & Sarah (Evans)
Chloe Ann (Douglas)  b  2-13-1857  Bloomington, Ohio
    dt John Henry & Miriam Carter
Ch:  Douglas         b  5-27-1880  Spiceland, Ind
    Ethel           b  2-19-1882

(Marcellus)
Rebecca Jane (White)  b  2-21-1864  Henry Co, Ind
    dt Jesse & Sarah Ann (Pickett)

Milton  b  5-13-1836  Centre Mtg, Ohio  d 4-27-1901
    s Jesse & Deborah (McMillan)
  m  (5-29-1861  Henry Co, Ind)
Emily (Gordon)  b 11-16-1843  dt Charles & Lydia
                            (Jessup)
Ch:  Addie           b  3-29-1864  d  3-29-1869
    Rilla           b  4-11-1868
    Isadore         b  4-28-1871  d  4-29-1871
    Mary Lena       b  5-31-1879
    Clinton Albert  b  3-29-1882  Spiceland

TEAS
Edward Y  b  3- 8-1830  Dunlapsville, Ind  s Thomas
    & Sarah C (Stratton)
  m 1st
Maria  (- - - -?)
Ch:  Ellen M         b 10-12-1856  Wayne Co, Ind
    William S       b  2-14-1861
  m 2nd  (7-25-1867)
Sarah (Stuart) Coffin, wid of Nathan Coffin  b  2- 1-1838
    Guilford Co, N Car  dt Amos & Matilda Stuart
Ch:  Fred E          b  8- 5-1869  Richmond, Ind
    Mary A          b  9- 4-1871
    Frances M       b  1-30-1883

Thomas S  b 11-28-1796  Pa  d 11-30-1850  bur Spiceland
    Mtg, Ind  s John & Rachel

SPICELAND

### TEAS (Cont)
Thomas S   (rmt 11-27-1826  Westfield Mtg, Ohio)
Sarah C (Stratton)  b  5-24-1800  Maurice River MM, N J
    d  2- 5-1871  Whitewater Mtg, bur Earlham
    dt Eli & Eunice (Dallas)
Ch:  John Carter       b 11-12-1827  Silver Creek Mtg, Ind
     Edward Y          b  3- 8-1830
     Martha            b  4-27-1833  Whitewater Mtg
     Rachel            b  9-15-1835  Spiceland d 9-18-1845
     Eunice            b  7- 6-1839
     Thomas S jr       b 11-14-1841

Thomas S jr  b 11-14-1841  Spiceland  s Thomas Sr & Sarah
    m (11-26-1867  Henry Co, Ind)        C (Stratton)
Marietta (Bogie)  b  8-22-1844  dt Alfred & 2nd w Charity
                                       (Bogue) Bogue
Ch:  Albert C          b  8-26-1869
     Jean Paul         b  3-25-1889  Henry Co, Ind

### TEASLE
Rebecca (Abshire)  b  4-mo-1846  Delaware Co, Ind
    w of Henry Teasle    dt S & Lydia Abshire
    (living at Keystone, Wells Co, Ind in 1878)

### TEMPLETON
Martin
    m 10-20-1884  Henry Co, Ind
Emmeline (Meredith)  b 12-10-1856  dt Jabez & Louisa
                                        (Antrim)

### TEST
(Josiah  s Samuel jr & Hannah (Jones))  (b 12- 6-1826)
    (d 10-mo-1864  Springfield Mtg, Ind)
Miriam C (Dennis)  b  9-10-1824  West Grove Mtg, Ind
    d  4- 2-1880  (as the w of Jacob Pickering)  bur
    Richmond, Ind   dt Thomas & Elizabeth
Ch:  Mary Ellen        b 12- 1-1856
     Samuel Edward     b  4-20-1859
    (Miriam, m 2nd Jacob J Pickering)

Rufus  b  1-12-1833  Dunlapsville, Ind  d 9-26-1906
    s Samuel jr & Hannah (Jones)
    m 1st  (1858  New Garden Mtg, Ind)
Margaret (Stubbs)  b  5- 7-1839  dt Joseph, decd & Sarah
                                          (Townsend)
Ch:  Zacheus           b 10- 9-1865  Wayne Co, Ind
    m 2nd  (2- 4-1890  Spiceland Mtg, Ind)
Lydia (Hall) Symons  wid of Jehu Symons  b  2-18-1833
    Spiceland  d  7- 6-1902  bur Spiceland, Ind
    dt Caleb & Hannah (Saunders) Hall

Samuel Edward  b  4-20-1859  Nettle Creek, Ind
    s Josiah, decd & Miriam (Dennis)
    m  (4-20-1881  Henry Co, Ind)
Cora A (Phelps)  b  7- 8-1861  Henry Co, Ind  dt Ezekiel
    & Sarah (Hoover)
Ch:  Everett Cecil     b  3- 6-1885  Greensboro, Ind

Zacheus  b 10- 9-1865  Wayne Co, Ind  d  5-23-1914
    s Rufus & 1st w Margaret (Stubbs)
    m  (3-29-1888  Wayne Co, Ind)
Jennie (Baldwin)  b  7- 4-1866  Wayne Co, Ind
    dt Nathan & Rachel (Reynolds)
Ch:  Ralph             b  5-23-1891  Wayne Co, Ind
     Rachel Irene      b  7-24-1894    "    "   "

### THOMAS
Charles F  b  4-18-1863  s Francis W & Rebecca (Corbit)
    m (11-19-1884  Henry Co, Ind)
Nancy (McCombs)

Charleton  b  8-19-1849  s Francis & Rebecca (Corbit)
    m  (10-30-1871  Henry Co, Ind)
Viretta (Commons)  b  2-27-1849  Rush Co, Ind  dt John &
                                                  Frances
Ch:  Walter Ray        b  4-26-1873  Dunreith
     Harry             b  1-13-1877  Fairmount
     Edna              b  1-12-1880     "

(Elijah jr  s Elijah Sr & Susannah)  (b  2-19-1809  S Car)
(Christina (- - - -?))
Ch:  Elvy
     Alfred

---

Francis W  b  1-15-1823  Wayne Co, Ind  d  3- 1-1909
    s Francis Sr & Lydia (Woodard)
    m  (7-21-1842  Randolph Co, Ind)
Rebecca (Corbit)  b  1- 7-1823  Wayne Co, Ind  d 1903
    dt Jeremiah & Mary
Ch:  Jeremiah M        b  8- 1-1844
     Mary M            b  2-27-1845
     Charleton H       b  8-19-1849
     Michael William   b  8- 5-1856
     Charles Francis   b  4-18-1863  Wayne Co, Ind
    m 2nd  (1905  Indianapolis, Ind)
Anna (Bowles) Mills, wid  b  7-14-1831  (d 12-25-1920
    Springfield Mtg, Ind)  dt George & Elizabeth (Bailey)

Isaac J  b  1- 2-1831  N Car  s Isaac & Jane
    m  (1- 2-1855)
Hannah S (Wood)
Ch:  Martha E          b 11- 1-1859  Guilford Co, N Car
     James G           b  9-27-1863

Isaac N  b  6-24-1861  s Mangum & Sarah Jane (Harrold)
    m  (4-10-1882)
Mary (Pugh)

Jeremiah M  b  8- 1-1844  s Francis W & Rebecca (Corbit)
Luzena S (Johnson)  b  1-16-1844  dt William & Ruth (Moody)
Ch:  Rhoda Emma        b  - - - -

John  b  9-27-1854  s Alfred & Mary J
    m  (12-25-1878)
Sarah E (Smith)  b  7-12-1861  dt Richard & Amanda
Ch:  Merril            b  6- 3-1889

Mangum E  b 11-24-1827  d 10-18-189?  s Isaac & Jane
Sarah Jane (Harrold)  b 12-23-1823  dt James & Nancy
Ch:  Pharaba Ann       b  5-23-1853
     Martha J          b  1- 5-1855
     William S         b 11- 8-1856
     Mary Ellen        b  1-23-1858
     Isaac N           b  6-22-1861
     Margaret L        b  7-25-1866
     Henry C           b  8-20-1869

Michael William  b  8- 5-1856  s Francis W & Rebecca
                                        (Corbit)
Flora (McFarland)
Ch:  Clide             b  7- 1-1880
     Francis W         b  1- 8-1883  Hardin Co, Iowa
     Thomas H          b  1- 8-1883
     Rebecca Pearl     b  9-27-1886     "    "   "

Simeon  b  7-29-1803  S Car  s Elijah Sr & Susannah
    m  (9- 1-1825  Duck Creek MH, Ind)
Olive (Elliott)  b  (ca 1806)  Tenn (may have d in
    Duck Creek prior to 1837)  dt Jacob & Anna
Ch:  Ruth              b  - - - -
     Henry             b  - - - -
     Susanna           b  - - - -
     Malinda           b  - - - -

### TIMMONS
Williams M  b 10- 8-1861  Cattin, Ill  s Ezekiel &
                                          Margaret
Clara M (Hiestand)  b  3-12-1862  Indianola, Ill
    dt William M & Esther

### TROUT
Anna  b  7- 2-1874  Henry Co, Ind  dt Samuel & Mary

### TRUEBLOOD
Isaac O  b 12- 8-1808  Pasquotank MM, N Car  s Aaron &
    Milicent (Clanshaid)
Sarah (White)  b  3- 2-1805  Suttons Creek Mtg, N Car
    dt Francis, decd & Miriam (Toms)
Ch:  Elizabeth Miriam  b 12-15-1836  Spiceland Mtg, Ind
     Martha W          b  9-24-1838  d  3-31-1841
                                     bur Raysville Mtg
     Harriet P         b  3-29-1840  d  4- 5-1841
     Jason             b  7-12-1842
     Miles W           b  8-25-1844
     Mary              b  5- 1-1846

SPICELAND

## TUTTLE

Abraham J  b 7-10-1833  Warren Co, Ohio  s J S & Hannah
    m (2-18-1858)
Saloma (Heath)  b 11-mo-1838  Delaware Co, Ind
    dt R & M Heath
Ch: Marson Sanford    b  3- 3-1860
    Morton L          b  9-16-1865
    Charles I         b 10-16-1867
    Cora B            b  1-29-1875


(Darlin)
    m (6-17-1858)
Susan (Lake)  b 7-10-1840  Licking Co, Ohio  dt G & N Lake

Louisa  b 9-28-1855  Delaware Co, Ind  dt Thomas W &
                                              Elizabeth

Rebecca E  b 2-18-1837  Ohio  dt J S & Hannah Tuttle

## UNTHANK

Eli  b 6-26-1799  Guilford Co, N Car  d 4-10-1881  bur
    Spiceland Mtg, Ind  s Joseph & Rebecca (Stanley)
Anna (Hiatt)  b 10-10-1801  Guilford Co, N Car  d 4-7-1881
    bur Spiceland Mtg, Ind  dt Benajah & Elizabeth
                                              (White)
Ch: Martha        b  9-14-1821  N Car
    Mordecai     b 12-10-1823
    John         b  1-27-1826
    Rebecca      b  4-16-1828
    Joseph A     b  3-28-1833
    William      b  9- 8-1835  Indiana
    Achilles W   b  3- 5-1838
    Daniel W     b  4- 1-1840
    Naomi C      b 11-12-1845


(Joseph) Addison  b 6-27-1827  s William B & Rebecca
    (m Duck Creek Mtg, 1848)                (Hiatt)
Cynthia E (Saint)  b 12-28-1830  d - - - -
    dt William & Achsah (Elliott)
Ch: Samuel Exum     b 12-24-1848  Henry Co, Ind


J Addison
    mcd (Whitewater Mtg, Ind)
Susan B (Reed)  b 2- 2-1831  dt John G & Sarah (Graves)
Ch: Harry           b  9- 7-1865  Wayne Co, Ind


John  b 1-27-1826  d 11-21-1888  bur Circle Grove Cem,
    Spiceland  s Eli & Anna (Hiatt)
    m (11-28-1855 Henry Co, Ind)
Martha A (Hobbs)  b 11-28-1834  Walnut Ridge Mtg, Ind
    d 9-24-1912  dt Elisha & Deborah (Harvey)
Ch: Louisa H        b  9-23-1856
    Caroline E      b  7-12-1860
    Rebecca H       b  4-28-1867  Henry Co, Ind


Josiah T  b 4-23-1837  Henry Co, Ind  d 7-mo-1919
    s William & Rebecca (Hiatt), decd
    m (3-27-1861 Henry Co, Ind)
Susanna B (Hunt)  b 10-23-1839  dt Joseph B & Ann (Gause)
    of Burlington, N J & Fayette Co, Pa
Ch: Eva             b 11-27-1862  d  6- 7-1863
    Minnie B        b  1-17-1867  d  1-27-1867
    Josephine       b  6-27-1868


Mordecai  b 12-10-1823  Guilford Co, N Car  s Eli & Anna
    m 1st                                       (Hiatt)
Eliza Jane (Stanley)  b 3-26-1827  Ind  dt Aaron &
    Mahala (Dicks)  (d prior to 1870, probably in Iowa)
Ch: Amanda          b 10-28-1849
    Emily C         b 10-14-1851
    Albert H        b  2- 8-1854
    Elmina C        b  9-15-1858
    Eli             b  5-12-1860
    Edgar )         b  6-11-1865
    Eva   ) twins   b  6-11-1865
    m 2nd (1874 Cherry Grove Mtg)
Ruth Jane (Hodgin) wid & 2nd w of Jesse C Reese b 2-18-1839
    dt Benjamin & Elizabeth (Johnson) Hodgin


Samuel Exum  b 12-24-1848  Spiceland, Ind  s Joseph
        Addison & Cynthia E (Saint)
    m (10- 8-1872 Henry Co, Ind)
Margaret Jane (Elliott) called Jennie b 10- 1-1850
    Woodville, N Car  dt William & Isabelle (Walton)


William  b 9- 8-1835  s Eli & Anna (Hiatt)
    (mcd Fairfield Mtg, Ohio)
Dinah K (Cowgill)  b 8-23-1843  (Hopewell Mtg, Ohio)
    d - - - -  in Iowa  dt John & Lydia (Coffin)
Ch: John C          b  3-30-1871
    Martha C        b 11-24-1872


William B  b 1-27-1802  N Car  d 4-15-18??
    s Josiah & Ann
    m 1st (2- 2-1820 New Garden Mtg, N Car)
Rebecca (Hiatt)  b 4-18-1796  N Car  d 4-15-1852
    bur Spiceland Mtg, Ind  dt William & Charity
                                              (Williams)
Ch: Drusilla A      b  2-14-1821
    Samuel N        b  3-22-1823  d 1-14-1843
                    bur Spiceland
    Naomi Jane      b 12-22-1824  d 6-26-1826
                    bur Bethel
    J Addison       b  6-27-1827
    Emaline         b  5-22-1829  d 9-25-1830
    Anna            b  1- 1-1833
    Hariett         b  2-17-1835
    Josiah          b  4-23-1837
    Mary Emily      b  2- 9-1841  d 2-17-1841
    m 2nd (2- 6-1854 Blue River Mtg, Ind)
Deborah (Hobbs) Nixon, wid of John Nixon  b 4- 7-1810
    N Car  d 2- 9-1899  dt William & Priscilla
                                     (Coffin) Hobbs
    (for a list of her ch by John Nixon see Nixon)

## VEACH

Jesse  b 3-28-1880  Henry Co, Ind  s Benjamin & Margaret

## VICKERY

David L  b 2- 7-1832  Henry Co, Ind  d 1919
    s Martin & Margaret
    m (4-26-1855 Henry Co, Ind)
Tabitha J (Fletcher)  b 2-19-1834  dt James & Elizabeth
Ch: Onias           b  2- 8-1860
    Charles F       b  - - - - -
    Isaac C         b  4- 8-1871  Lewisville, Ind


Onias  b 2- 8-1860  s David L & Tabitha J (Fletcher)
Alice (Perry)  b 11- 4-1868  Hamilton Co, Ind
    dt Jacob & Celia
Ch: Edith E
    Glenn
    Ada J

## VOTAW

William S
    m (9- 8-1891)
Lillian A (Charles)  b 12-30-1872  dt Clarkson & Caroline
                                              (Horne)

## WAGAMAN

Aaron
    m (1899)
Evalyn (Pickett)  b 4-27-1882  dt William R & Almira H
                                              (Sheridan)

## WAKE

William A
    m 1st (ca 1891)
Martha (Smith)
Ch: Cloid           b  3- 9-1893  Delaware Co, Ind
    Arlie I         b  8- 6-1894    "    "    "
    m 2nd (ca 1905)
Nettie (Lane)  dt Samuel & Sarah (Newby) Lane
Ch: Francis Maria   b 12-mo-1906
    Elsie           b  7-18-1908

## WALTERS

(Isaac)
    m (1-17-1884 Henry Co, Ind)
Edith (Sheridan) Sheridan, divorced from Oliver
    Sheridan  b 11- 5-1845  Henry Co, Ind  d 2-mo-1919
    dt William & Elizabeth (Schooley) Sheridan

## WALTON

(George)
(Mary)
Ch: Isabella E      b 10-12-1850
    Robert C        b  2- 6-1853  Mississippi

SPICELAND

WALTON (Cont)
Joseph P
Caroline (Huddleston) b 5-15-1850 dt Silas & Emily Ann
Ch: Anna B           b 7-11-1868
    George Franklin  b - - - - -

(Rufus P rec on req 1864 Springfield Mtg, N Car)
    (b 4-16-1841)

WARD
Charles A b 3-15-1852 Henry Co, Ind s Jacob M & Martha
    m ( 1- 1-1881 Henry Co, Ind)
Mary (Kaufman)

WARNER
Joseph b 10-23-1844 Green Plain Mtg, Ohio
    s Isaac & Sarah A
    m (9- 2-1868 Whitewater Mtg, Ind (H))
Mary (Mendenhall) dt Gardner & Phebe (Macy), decd

WAYMIRE
J H
    m (1867)
Hettie (Jackson) b 4- 3-1850 Jennings Co, Ind
    dt Presley & Nancy Ann

WEBB
Joseph M b 6-25-1865 Helena, Arkansas

WEBSTER
Edmond A b 6- 5-1847 s William O & Sarah (Perryman)
    m (11- 9-1872)
Sarah M (Weed)

William O b 4-21-1807 Richmond d 5-19-1883 bur
    Wabash Co, Ind s John & Ann
    m (9-11-1829)
Sarah (Perryman) b 5- 7-1815 Madison Co, Ala
    dt Alexander & Jane
Ch: Edmond A    b 6- 5-1847 Rush Co, Ind
    Joseph P    b - - - - -
    Ajalisa?    b - - - - -

WEISNER - WIESNER
Jonathan b 12- 6-1815 N Car s Michael & Rebecca
                                (Mendenhall), decd
    m (10-26-1836 Chester Mtg, Ind)
Ruth (Williams) b 10-15-1815 N Car
    dt William & Mary (Moon)
Ch: Hezekiah      b 9-14-1837 Spiceland Mtg, Ind
    Susanna       b 5-20-1839 Chester Mtg
    Clarkson      b 8-12-1841 Spiceland Mtg
    Elwood        b 11-16-1842
    Henry Grear   b 1-12-1845

Michael b 11-10-1811 Union Mtg, N Car d 10-mo-1839
    Spiceland Mtg s Jesse & Ann (Mendenhall)
    m ( 8- 1-1832)
Hannah (Barker) b 2-24-1812 dt Isaac & 2nd w Mary (Cox)
Ch: Ann       b 4- 8-1835 Spiceland Mtg
    Mahlon    b 1-25-1837

(William s Micajah & Abigail (Hinshaw)) (b 8- 1-1791
    N Car) Surry Co (dis 1835)
Rachel (Moon) (b 5-11-1794 Chatham Co, N Car)
    dt John & Rachel
Ch: Josiah      b 8- 6-1813 Stokes Co, N Car
    John        b 9-26-1815 Chatham Co, N Car
    Micajah     b 4-26-1817
    Abigail     b 2- 1-1819
    Elizabeth   b 5-13-1822
    Milicent    b 11- 3-1823
    Matilda     b 10-28-1825
    Emeline     b 11- 4-1827
    Jabez       b 2-21-1830
    Cyrenius    b 11-28-1833

WELLS
(Dudley)
    m (2-25-1903 Henry Co, Ind)
Dora (Kimbrell) b 9-17-1871 Henry Co, Ind
    dt Taylor & Mary

WELSH
(James)
    m (12-31-1850 Perquimans Co, N Car)
Hannah S (Copeland) b 11-13-1832 Perquimans Co, N Car
    d 7-30-1913 dt Jacob & Martha (Smith)
Ch: Margaret E   b - - - -
    John C       b 10-14-1866
    Julia J      b 3-27-1869 Henry Co, Ind
    James jr     b - - - -

WHEELER
John  b 8-25-1837
Elizabeth (Baldwin) b 7-24-1847 dt Elwood & Phebe
                                        (Scott)
Ch: Martha A       b 10-26-1861
    Sarah E        b 5-10-1864
    William F      b 4-29-1867
    Rose Lewellen  b - - - -
    Rachel H       b - - - -
    Lydia Emeline  b - - - -

WHITE
Augustus Edwin b 1-31-1823 s Nathan, decd & Mary
                                        (Jordon)
Margaret A (Bundy) b 3-31-1832 dt Jesse, decd &
                                Ascention (White)
Ch: John Richard   b 4-22-1850

Caleb b 11-12-1796 N Car s Francis, decd & Miriam
                                        (Toms)
Mary (White) b 9- 7-1801 d 3-31-1857 bur Raysville
    Mtg, Ind    dt Edmund & Mary
Ch: Jane            b 11-11-1822 N Car
    Charles         b 11-15-1824
    James           b 8-26-1826
    Joseph          b 9-10-1828
    Edmund F        b 12-13-1830 d 1831 N Car
    Elizabeth       b 8-23-1832 d 1832 " "
    infant          b 10- 6-1833 d 10-20-1833 N Car
    Margaret        b 4- 3-1835
    Edmund the 2nd  b 9-15-1837
    Harriett        b 11-24-1839
    Francis         b 11-19-1841 d 1-14-1842
                    bur Raysville, Ind

(Charles s Caleb & Mary) (b 11-15-1824 N Car)
    m (5-24-1852 Salem Mtg, Ind)
(Lucy (Haughton) d William & Sally (Johnson))
    b (ca 1830 Salem Mtg, Ind)
Ch: (Emma     b ca 1853)

Edmund b 1-31-1826 Symons Creek Mtg, N Car
    s Joseph M & his 1st w Margaret (White), decd

Elmina b 10-25-1835 N Car dt Borden & Agnes or
    (Agatha) White, both decd
    Elmina under the care of George & Ann (White) Rayl,
    (an aunt & uncle)

Exum b 11-24-1799 Perquimans Co, N Car s Thomas &
    Jemima (- - - -) (Jemima of Isle of Wight Co, Va)
    m (Western Branch Mtg, Isle Wight Co, Va)
Ann (Hare) b 8-15-1803 Nansemond Co, Va
    dt Jesse & Sarah
Ch: Sarah Ann        b 1-24-1826 N Car
                     d 6-21-1826 N Car
    Margaret Susan   b 3-28-1827
    Joseph Hare      b 2- 7-1830 Va
    Jesse Thomas     b 9-20-1832 Ind
    Harriet          b 4-20-1835
    John Gurney      b 3-15-1838

Gamaliel b 8-20-1846 Henry Co, Ind s Jesse & Mary
    m (1-19-1887)                          (Pennington)
Esther (Wilson) b 8-13-1853 Bridgeport, Ind
    dt Charles & Elizabeth

George B  b 7-20-1840
Sarah R (Hockett) b 9-22-1845 dt Mahlon Hockett

(Francis, decd)
Miriam (Toms) b 10-23-1773 Suttons Creek, Perquimans Co,
    N Car d 7-29-1855 bur Raysville Mtg, Henry Co,
    Ind dt John & Mary Toms & wid of Francis White

SPICELAND

**WHITE** (Cont)
Ch: of Francis & Miriam
(her ch that came to Spiceland Mtg)
| | |
|---|---|
| Caleb | b 11-12-1796 |
| John T | b 1-17-1801 |
| Rebekah | b 12-4-1802 |
| Sarah | b 3-2-1805 |
| Martha | b 9-27-1812 |

Henry b 7-16-1784 N Car d 12-mo-1853 bur Raysville
Mtg, Ind s Thomas & Elizabeth (Lamb)
Mary (Hunt) b 8-14-1792 N Car dt Jacob & Hannah
(Brittain)
| Ch: | | |
|---|---|---|
| | Asenath B | b 8-18-1814 |
| | Abigail B | b 11-5-1816 |
| | Mary Jane | b 1-26-1829 |
| | Henry H | b 8-21-1835 |

Isaac b 8-24-1798 N Car d 8-4-1840 bur Spiceland
Mtg, Ind s Stanton & Sarah (Stanley)
Louisa (Bunden) b 9-26-1797 Henry Co, Va
dt Nancy Bunden
| Ch: | | |
|---|---|---|
| | Micajah C | b 5-29-1819 N Car |
| | Lilburn | b 3-21-1821 |
| | Jesse S | b 11-19-1823 d 10-16-1825 N Car |
| | Martha G | b 8-22-1826 |
| | Mordecai | b 7-20-1829 Ind |
| | Aletha C | b 3-1-1832 |
| | Isaac jr | b - - - - - |

Jesse b 12-14-1805 New Garden Mtg, N Car
s Stanton & Sarah (Stanley)
Mary (Pennington) b 10-9-1813 Stillwater Mtg, Ohio
dt Josiah & Deborah (Talbot) from Center Mtg, Pa
& Stillwater Mtg, Ohio
| Ch: | | |
|---|---|---|
| | Susannah | b 7-12-1832 Duck Creek Mtg, Ind |
| | Adison | b 6-18-1834 Spiceland Mtg |
| | Alfred | b 11-16-1837 |
| | Joseph P | b 11-6-1840 |
| | Gamalial | b 8-20-1846 |

Jesse b Hancock Co, Ind s Phineas & Sarah (Bundy)
m 1st (1858)
Sarah Ann (Pickett) b 6-??-???? d 1873
dt Simon & Rebecca
| Ch: | | |
|---|---|---|
| | Emma A | b 11-14-1861 Grant Co, Ind |
| | Rebecca Jane | b 2-21-1864 |
| | Otis J | b 2-6-1869 d 1878 |

m 2nd
Catherine McCarter
m 3rd (7-30-1881 Henry Co, Ind)
Eliza McCombs

John T b 2-17-1801 Perquimans Co, N Car s Francis,
decd, & Miriam (Toms)
m 1st
Susanna (Morris) b 8-18-1809 N Car d 8-14-1833
bur Blue River Mtg, Ind dt Mordecai & Martha
(Winslow)
| Ch: | | |
|---|---|---|
| | Mordecai Morris | b 12-3-1830 Washington Co, Ind |
| | Francis Toms | b 6-25-1831 |

m 2nd (12-20-1837 Spiceland Mtg, Ind)
Hannah Ann (Parker) b 12-3-1815 Belmont Co, Ohio
dt Benajah & Grace (Patten)
| Ch: | | |
|---|---|---|
| | Joel | b 5-12-1839 Henry Co, Ind |
| | Benajah | b 8-26-1842 |
| | Narcissa | b 2-11-1845 d 5-6-1845 bur Raysville Mtg |
| | Elizabeth | b 4-21-1846 d 5-23-1855 bur Raysville Mtg |
| | Allen | b 9-20-1848 |

Josiah P b 11-8-1840 s Jesse & Mary (Pennington)
Elizabeth (Macy) b 11-6-1839 dt Enoch & Nancy
| Ch: | | |
|---|---|---|
| | Laura Emma | b 4-17-1862 |
| | Viola | b 7-8-1865 |
| | Julia | b - - - - - |

Lilburn b 3-21-1821 New Garden Mtg, N Car d 2-21-1900
s Isaac & Louisa (Bunden)
m 1st (4-mo-1840 Spiceland Mtg, Ind)
Elizabeth (Small) b 4-17-1822 d ---- dt Josiah, decd
& Jane (Moore)
m 2nd
Adelia R (- - - -?) b 3-21-1822 d    Spiceland Mtg

m 3rd (8-mo-1879 Henry Co, Ind)
Martha A (Macy) b 5-19-1833 dt Solomon & Priscilla
(Hamm)

(Marmaduke)
Rachel (Baldwin) b 12-19-1854 dt Elwood & Phebe
| Ch: | | |
|---|---|---|
| | Minnie L | b 9-17-1869 |
| | Henry E | b 4-9-1871 |
| | Harriet P | b 4-3-1873 |

Mordecai b 7-20-1829 s Isaac & Louisa (Bunden)
m (5-20-1850)
Phebe (Clampet) b 8-14-1831 dt William & Mary
| Ch: | | |
|---|---|---|
| | May | b 6-21-1868 |
| | Frank | b - - - - - |

(Robert, decd s John & Mourning (Cornwell))
(b 6-18-1789) (d 6-25-1830 Suttons Creek Mtg,
N Car)
Rebecca (Albertson) b 11-10-1797 N Car d 11-4-1852
bur Raysville Mtg, Ind (as the w of James Johnson)
dt Francis & Caroline (Bell)
| Ch: | | |
|---|---|---|
| | Elizabeth | b 8-18-1823 |
| | Lucinda | b 2-19-1826 |
| | William A | b 2-15-1828 |

Samuel jr b 11-19-1804 Piney Woods Mtg, N Car
s Samuel Sr & Elizabeth (Symons)
Rebecca (White) b 12-4-1802 Suttons Creek Mtg, N Car
dt Francis, decd & Miriam (Toms)
| Ch: | | |
|---|---|---|
| | Martha | b 4-8-1835 Suttons Creek Mtg N Car |

Stanton b 12-14-1767 N Car d 2-4-1837 bur Elm Grove
Mtg, Ind s Isaac & Catherine (Stanton)
Sarah (Stanley) b 3-22-1771 d 1-17-1847 (recorded in
Spiceland Mtg records) dt Micajah & Barbara of Va
& N Car
Ch: (that came to Spiceland Mtg)
| | |
|---|---|
| Isaac | b 8-24-1798 |
| Jesse | b 12-14-1805 |

Thaddeus b 6-25-1800 s Samuel & Elizabeth (Symons)
Elizabeth (Pritchard) b 12-7-1805 Pasquotank Co, N Car
dt Joseph & Margaret (Jordan)
| Ch: | | |
|---|---|---|
| | Samuel P | b 8-18-1828 N Car d 12-10-1848 bur Raysville, Ind |
| | Margaret Jordan | b 9-8-1830 |
| | Abigail | b 9-19-1833 |
| | Alpheus | b 1-17-1836 |
| | Elizabeth Ann | b 2-22-1839 |
| | Harriet Susanah | b 12-20-1841 |
| | Peninah | b 10-29-1844 Spiceland, Ind d 12-15-1844 |
| | Louisa E | b 1-10-1847 |

**WHITELY**
George C b 9-9-1841 s Robert H & Jane (Woolen)
Lydia A (Weeks) b 12-14-1845 dt Thomas
| Ch: | | |
|---|---|---|
| | Laura J | b 9-21-1866 |
| | Isador | b 9-28-1867 |
| | Jehu H | b 3-11-1868 d 8-21-1868 bur Spiceland Mtg, Ind |
| | Dendid? | b 1-17-1874 |

John A b 9-9-1855 s Robert H & Jane (Woollen)
m (9-14-1881)
Addie (Trout) b 2-25-1853 Pendleton, Ind
dt Isaac & Amelia
| Ch: | | |
|---|---|---|
| | Robert W | b 10-27-1883 |
| | Florence M | b 5-29-1885 |
| | Eva Jane | b 10-19-1887 |

Robert H b 8-27-1815 d 1-23-1894 s William & Francis
m (1-12-1837)    of Caroline Co, Md
Jane (Woollen) b 10-6-1820 d 5-22-1896
dt Jacob & Nancy of Dorchester Co, Md
| Ch: | | |
|---|---|---|
| | George | b 9-9-1841 |
| | Alexander C | b 11-25-1848 |
| | Ruth H | b 10-12-1850 Spiceland, Ind |
| | Sarah C | b 12-11-1853 |
| | John A | b 9-9-1855 |
| | Alice O | b 4-20-1858 |
| | Martha M | b 8-9-1860 |

SPICELAND

## WICKERSHAM
Abel  b 1- 8-1804  N Car  (s Caleb & 1st w Lydia (Gardner))
   m 1st  (5- 8-1828 Silver Creek Mtg, Ind)
Eliza Ann (Bailey)  b- - - -  d - - - -
   dt Exum & Tabitha, decd of Campbell Co, Va
Ch: Caroline M        b - - - -
    Caleb E           b 8-27-1834  Lewisville, Ind
    Stephen           b - - - -
   m 2nd ( 5-28-1849 Silver Creek Mtg, Ind)
Mary (Bailey)  dt Exum & Tabitha of Va, both decd
Gr-dt: Caroline Wilson  b - - - -

Caleb E  b 8-27-1834 Lewisville, Ind  s Abel & Eliza Ann (Bailey), decd
   m (1858)
Emeline B (Stanley)  b 10- 7-1839  Greensboro, Ind
   dt Elwood & Martha
Ch: Mary Annice       b - - - - -  Smyrna, Iowa
    Louisa            b 6- 5-1874  Smyrna, Iowa

Jethro  b 4- 9-1823  Union Co, Ind  s Caleb Sr & his 2nd w Eunice (Folger)
   m 2nd (12-27-1888 Henry Co, Ind)
Margaret A (Brown)  b 8-21-1845  dt Moses & Delphia
Ch: (by 1st w)
    Louisa            b 1- 6-1849

## WILCUTTS
David  b 8- 7-1805  S Car  s Thomas & Milly (both decd)
   m ( 2- 1-1865 Dover Mtg, Ind)
Rachel (Williams) Unthank, a wid  b 7-13-1809
   dt of William Williams, a Minister & w Rachel (Kemp)

## WILDMAN
Murry S  b 2-22-1868  Selma, Ohio  s John & Mary (Pugh)
   m (8-16-1893 Wayne Co, Ind)
Olive (Stigleman)  b 5- 2-1865  Wayne Co, Ind
   dt Henry & Caroline
Ch: Mary S            b 10-10-1899  Indianapolis, Ind

## WILES
Luke jr  b 12-19-1796  N Car  s Luke Sr & Francis
   m 1st (1823 N Car)
Rhoda (- - - -?)  b 5-24-17??  d 2-27-1853  (bur Flat Rock)
Ch: (by 1st w that came to Spiceland Mtg)
    Rhoda Jane        b 1-27-1839
    Luke jr           b 8-15-1841  d 7-25-1863 Spiceland
    Nancy E           b 5- 7-1843
    Ester G           b 11-14-1845
    Anna Mariah       b 6-17-1847
   m 2nd (1856 Spiceland Mtg)
Jane (Dickey) Davis, wid Nathan Davis  b 5- 7-1808
   dt Nimrod Dickey

## WILKINSON
Malinda (Ballinger)  b 1-11-1810  New Garden MM, N Car
   dt Henry & Rebecca (Hunt) of Duck Creek Mtg, Ind

## WILLETTS
Henry  b 10-11-1803  Union Mtg, N Car
   s Gabriel & Priscilla (Pike), decd
   m 1st (Deep Creek Mtg, N Car)
Mary (Mendenhall)  b 8-27-1807  N Car  d (ca 1830 New Garden Mtg, Ind)  dt Jonathan & Ann (Phillips)
Ch: Jonathan          b 2- 6-1826
    Mahlon            b 10-13-1827
    Mary              b 3-16-1830
   m 2nd
Rachel (Murphy)  b 1-26-1808  Ohio  dt Joshua & Margaret (Chamness)
Ch: William           b 12- 7-1833
    Jeremiah          b - - - - -

Levi, minor  b 2- 4-1819  N Car  s Gabriel & Priscilla (Pike) both decd

Nathan  b 9- 2-1807  N Car  s Gabriel & Priscilla (Pike), decd
   m (Indiana)
Asenath (Schooley)
Ch: Ruth              b - - - - -
    John              b - - - - -
    Rachel            b - - - - -
    Gabriel           b - - - - -

## WILLIAMS
Albert F  b 10-31-1849  Wayne Co, Ind  s Washington & Ruhama (Stevenson)
   m (9-21-1881)
Lizzie (Hill)  b 4-10-1859  Ashboro, N Car
   dt Thomas & Nancy (Davis)
Ch: Arthur H          b 6- 8-1883
    Wister P          b 3-11-1885
    Albert R          b 1-12-1891
    Elizabeth Ernestine  b 7- 7-1893
    Ross              b - - - - -

Ary Isabelle  b 3-30-1846  Newcastle, Ind  dt Mary E (- - - -?) Williams, wid of Ananias Williams (lately m to William Millikan)
   m (11-26-1868 Henry Co, Ind)
to Calvin W Ratliff

(Charles)
   m (1883)
Susan Belle (Howard)  b 1859  Grayson Co, Texas
   dt John & Carrie (Grant)

Ella  b 9-13-1855  Franklin, Wayne Co, Ind  dt Joseph & Susan

James  b 10-26-1860  Henry Co, Ind  s Gabriel & Charlotte
   m (7-23-1892 Delaware Co, Ind)
Bessie (Frymyre)  b 11- 1-1871  Augusta Co, Va
   dt Jacob & Charlotte

Jason  b 7- 5-1808  Chester Co, Pa  d 4-21-1877 (Spiceland, Ind)  s Joseph & Mary of Flushing Mtg, Ohio
   rmt (10-26-1829 Flushing Mtg, Ohio)
Abigail (Holloway)  b 8-15-1810  Flushing Mtg, Ohio
   dt Joseph & Elleanor from Southland MM, (Va?)
Ch: Sarah             b 8-17-1830  Ohio
    Hannah            b 6-23-1832
    Joseph H          b 8-19-1834
    Mary Ellen        b 6-30-1836
    Samuel D          b 7-14-1841  Ind
    William C         b 11-22-1843

Joseph  b 10- 1-1784  Pa  d 7-30-1863 age 78-10-0 an Elder at Spiceland Mtg, Ind & fth of Jason  s Daniel & Mary of Berks Co, Pa
   m 1st
Mary (- - - -?)  d 2- 4-1844  Flushing Mtg, Ohio
   m 2nd (4-29-1846 Salem Mtg, Ohio)
Lydia (Morris)  b 3-21-1801  Contentnea Mtg, N Car
   dt Sally (Moore) Cox Morris

Simon of Newcastle, Ind
Anna J (- - - -?) decd
Ch: Louring           b 6-18-1848
    Caroline V        b 1-17-1854

William C  b 11-22-1843  s Jason & Abigail (Holloway)
Anna W (Steddom)  b 9-14-1850  dt Abijah & his 1st w (rec on req of Abijah & his 2nd w Deborah (Mendenhall) Steddom)

## WILSON
Allen  b 8-14-1843  s Michael & Delilah
   m (12-21-1869)
Mary Louisa (Williams)
Ch: Anna              b 1-23-1871
    Herman            b 5- 1-1873
    Josie Irena       b 3-29-1875

Benjamin  b 7- 7-1823  N Car  s Reuben, decd & Miriam of Washington Co, Ind
   m (11- 2-1848 Milford Mtg)
S Caroline (Stanley)  b 4-10-1829  dt William, decd & Susanna (Moore)
Ch: William Albert    b - - - - -

Claire  b 10-27-1869  dt Levi C & Jane Wilson
   m (8- 8-1905)
to Clarence D Painter

David  b 12- 3-1802  (s Israel & Martha (Cadwallader) of Flushing Mtg, Ohio)  (rmt 11-24-1826)
Easther (Barrett)  b 2-12-1801  dt Thomas & Margaret

WILSON (Cont)
Ch: of David & Easther
    Margaret          b - - - -
    Isaac             b - - - -
    Amy               b - - - -

David F  b 6- 5-1819 N Car  s John & Mary (Osborn)
Betsey (Baldwin)  b 2-23-1826  d  1907  dt Isaiah &
    Elizabeth (Bond) his 2nd w
Ch:  Rachel E        b 12- 5-1854  d 11-26-18??
                        bur Spiceland
    Mary Emma      b 9-17-1858  d - - - -
    Newton H        b 5- 5-1860
    Eli E           b 7-23-1865  d 9- 9-1896

Elizabeth  w of - - - -?  b 12-15-1818  d  1877
Ch:  William R       b 4- 2-1844

Eunice (Reynolds) w of - - - -? Wilson  b 1-12-1830
    dt of Job & Phebe (Hockett)

(James M)
(Clarky (Mendenhall)  dt David & Margaret (Moore))
    b  (1-10-1827)

John  b 7-10-1796 N Car  d 6- 6-1880 bur Spiceland
    s John Sr & Elizabeth of N Car
Mary (Osborn)  b 3- 7-1795  d 3- 6-1860 bur Spiceland
    Mtg  dt David & Lydia (Davis)
Ch:  (to Ind)
    David Franklin   b 6- 5-1819
    Thomas Arnett    b 2-13-1828
    Rachel E         b 8- 8-1831  d 7- 4-1841
    Mary             b 7-28-1833
    Michael Clarkson  b 10-25-1835

Joseph G    b 2- 9-1798 N Car
    m (Core Sound Mtg, N Car)
Hope (Mace)  b 11-25-1802 N Car  dt Francis, decd &
    Pharaba (Harris)
Ch:  John B   )         b 1-23-1829
    Mary Jane) twins  b 1-23-1829
    Miriam Ann       b 9- 3-1834
    Pharaby M        b 6- 9-1836
    Rachel M         b - - - - -
    Nathan M         b 2- 2-1843
    Elias E          b 5-16-1846

Matthew T  b 1-29-1863  (s Timothy & Elizabeth (Terrell))
    m (6-22-1887) Henry Co, Ind
Isadora (Hall)  b 8-13-1866  dt Jehu W & Huldah (Ratliff)
Ch:  Lowell H        b 8-17-1888  Henry Co, Ind

Michael
Delilah (- - - -?)
Ch:  Allen           b 8-24-1843
    Richard         b 6-13-1855

Newton H  b 5- 5-1861  s David F & Betsey (Baldwin)
    m (9-26-1891) Henry Co, Ind)
Daisy J (Berry)

Richard  b 6-13-1853  (s Michael & Delilah)
    m (6-14-1888)
Ettie H (Mendenhall)  b 12-22-1862 West Newton, Ind
    dt Jesse & Elizabeth
Ch:  Perry Alva       b 3-28-1889  Bakers Corner, Ind
    Kerney Ellis     b 11- 2-1890
    Alice Ercel      b 2-15-1893  Spiceland
    Carrie          b 5-21-1900
    Dorothy         b 9-28-1904

Sylvester  b 10- 8-1852 Henry Co, Ind  s Henry & Rebecca
    m (9- 9-1875)
Abigail Sarah (Green) b 6- 6-1854 Elizabeth City, Ind
    dt Stephen & Nancy
Ch:  Izzy            b 11- 5-1876  Henry Co, Ind
    Lucy            b 2-27-1877

Terrell  b 11-28-1860 Dublin, Ind  (s Timothy & Elizabeth
    A (Terrell) decd)
    m (6-27-1881) Henry Co, Ind)
Rebecca Belle (Brookshire)  b 6- 7-1860  dt Emely
    & Julia (Thorp) of New Castle, Ind

Ch:  Lucile          b 5-20-1889  Henry Co, Ind
    Walter          b - - - -
    Russell T       b - - - -

Thomas Arnett  b 2-13-1828 Guilford Co, N Car
    s John & Mary (Osborn)
Ruth (Foster)  b 4-19-1836 Spiceland Mtg, Ind
    dt Joseph & Mary H (Stanley)
Ch:  Joseph Eli       b 7-15-1854  d 11-11-1855
                        bur Spiceland
    Nathan E         b 8- 7-1857  d 8- 1-1861
    Jesse H          b 3- 5-1860
    Anna R           b 6-11-1862
    Mary J           b 7- 8-1866

Timothy  b 1-20-1832 Perquimans Co, N Car
    (s John W & Margaret (White))
    m 1st ( 8-25-1852 Short Creek Mtg, Ohio)
Elizabeth Ann (Terrell)  b 3- 6-1832 in Ohio
    d 4-24-1865 Milford Mtg, Ind  (dt Mathew &
    Elizabeth D)
Ch:  William Nicholson b 7-30-1853
    Olive B          b 6-30-1858
    Terrel L         b 10-24-1860
    Mathew T         b 1-29-1863
    m 2nd (1866 Spiceland Mtg)
Elmina (Foster) Coffin wid of Emory D Coffin
    b 12-27-1827  dt of Joshua & Sarah Foster

William R  b 4- 2-1844  s of Elizabeth
Sara E (Reddick)  b 11-20-1843  d 11- 4-1881
Ch:  Jessie          b 3-20-1874
    Elizabeth       b - - - - -
    Louisa          b - - - - -

William W  from Hopewell Mtg, Ind
    m 1st (Hopewell Mtg)
Caroline (Wickersham) b - - - - d - - - -(Hopewell Mtg,
    Ind) (dt Abel & Eliza Ann (Bailey) decd (his 1st w))
Ch:  Marcus A         b - - - -
    Mary Annis       b 2-12-1856
    Eva Ellen        b 6-13-1859
    Caroline M       b - - - -
    m 2nd (1867 Milford Mtg, Ind)
Olive (Butler)  b 2-12-1846  dt Lemuel Butler of
    Dublin, Ind
Ch:  Lucy            b 8-28-1868
    Martha          b 3-28-1870
    Warner          b 5-24-1873

WINKLE - WINKLER
(John R)
(Margaret E (- - - -?))
Ch:  Bert            b 11-10-1872  Franklin, Ind
    Cora            b 3-27-1874    "    "

WINTERS
(John W)  (b 5-30-1846 N Car) (d 7-10-1876 Deep
    River Mtg, N Car)
    (m 2- 1-1864)
Melvina (King)  b 6- 8-1846 Franklin Co, N Car
    d 1921 as w of David M Poe  dt Anderson &
    Mason (Dickins) King
Ch:  Luetta          b 12- 4-1864  Guilford Co, N Car
    Laura B          b 4- 4-1867
    Alvin            b 7- 7-1869
    Regina Ellen     b 7- 7-1871  Deep River Mtg, N
                                          Car
    John Avery       b 12-16-1872
(after the d of John W Winters, Melvina m 2nd David
    Milton Poe)

WOODARD
Cornelius J  b 3-15-1823 N Car  s Cedar & Rachel
    m (3-29-1848 Whitewater MM, Ind)  (Outland)
Sarah (Burgess)  b 8-26-1824 Smithfield, Ohio
    dt John & Margaret, decd of Morgan Co, Ohio
Ch:  Mary E           b 10-11-1855  Wayne Co, Ind
    Herbert         b 4- 2-1873

WOOLEN
Edward L  b 6-15-1831  d 5- 9-1872 bur Spiceland
    Mtg, Ind  s John Woolen
Elizabeth (Hall)  b 4-26-1835  dt Caleb & Hannah

SPICELAND

## WOOLEN (Cont)
Edward L & Elizabeth
    (after the d of Edward, Elizabeth m 2nd to - - - -?
      Black)
Ch:  (by 1st husb)
    James A          b 4-16-1857  d 2- 5-1873
                             bur Spiceland, Ind
    William A         b 4-31-1859
    Hannah Addie      b 2-28-1867

## WORTH
Everett E  b 12- 3-1873  Rush Co, Ind  s Franklin &
    Martha (Pitts)
      m (8-29-1905 Lakeside, Ohio)
Bertha (Knight)  b 12-27-1877  Hillsdale, Mich
    dt W W & Lucinda (Rosenberger) Knight

## WRIGHT
Alpheus L  b 3-22-1845  N Car  s Micah & Edith
Mary Elizabeth (Reese)  b 1-16-1851  N Car
    dt Henry & Mary (Carmack)
Ch:  Willie A           b 10- 2-1873  d 8-24-1897

(James  s John & Jemima (Haworth))  (b ca 1771  Bush
    River MM, S Car)  (prob d Duck Creek Mtg)
    (mcd ca 1798 New Hope Mtg, Tenn)
(Catherine (Allen)  dt James Sr & Elizabeth)
Ch:  (to Duck Mtg, Ind about 1834)
    (John              b       1799)
    ( George           b - - - - - )
    (James Allen       b - - - - - )
    (Joel              b - - - - - )
    (Jemima           b - - - - - )

Joab  b 6-10-1816  Green Co, Tenn  s Jesse Sr & Anna
    (Clearwater)
    m 1st (1837 Spiceland Mtg)
Mary (Small)  b 2-19-1819  New Garden Mtg, Ind
    d 7-19-1838 bur Duck Creek Mtg, Ind  dt Obadiah
    & Isabell (Moore)
Ch:  Obadiah M         b 6-mo-1838 Duck Creek Mtg
  m 2nd (1839 Spiceland)
Malinda (Elliott)  b 4- 7-1818  dt Jacob & Ann
Ch:  Anna                b 10-14-1840
    Abijah             b 12-13-1841  d 1- 3-1843
                           bur Spiceland
    Jesse D             b 10-10-1843

John  b 5-21-1798  New Hope MM, Tenn  s Jesse & Ann
    m 1st (10-23-1822 Newhope, Tenn)  (Clearwater)
Margaret (Reese)  b - - - -  d 10-30-1838 Newhope MM,
    Tenn  dt Moses & Sarah
Ch:  (to Ind)
    Sarah              b 10-28-1826
    Isaac              b 2- 9-1829
    Vincent            b 10-10-1832
    Jesse S R         b 8- 5-1837
  m 2nd (Newhope Mtg, Tenn)
Joanna (Gaunt)  b 2-13-1814  (Bush River, Newberry Dist,
    S Car)  dt Samuel K & Susanna (Julian)
Ch:  Samuel Kelly Gaunt  b 9-28-1840 Newhope, Tenn
    Precious M        b 3-10-1842
    Zenas J             b 6- 5-1843
    Beulah Ann        b - - - - -  Ind

Russell L  b 9-16-1881  Rush Co, Ind  s Sylvanus J &
    Sarah D (Talbert)
    m (2-26-1908 Portland, Oregon)
Flossie (Ferrier)  b 3- 7-1889  Lincoln, Neb  dt William
    & Mary
Ch:  Gladys E           b - - - -
    Lowell S           b - - - -

Sylvanus J  b - - - -  s Joel & Eliza
Sarah D (Talbert)  b 5- 3-1857  dt Jabez & Mary (Cook)
Ch:  Pearl Iva
    Jessie Leona
    Russell L          b 9-16-1881  Rush Co, Ind

## WYKOFF
Ebert
    m (12-26-1895)
Marybelle (Hall)  b 1- 9-1871  dt Jehu & Huldah
                                (Ratliff)

## YATES
John F
Hannah (Ratliff)  b 2-24-1840  Flushing, Belmont Co,
    dt William & Sarah (Wood)          Ohio
Ch:  Edna                b - - - -

## YOUNG
Leonard  b 3- 8-1871  Wabash, Ind  s John D & Christiana

(William)
Lucy Jane (Hodson)  b - - - -  (prior to 1868)
    dt Jabez & Jane (Jackson)

SPICELAND

## SPICELAND MONTHLY MEETING

### MINUTES

ABSHIRE
1- 1-1876    Lydia rec in mbrp

ADAMS
3- 4-1893    Amanda & Hattie rec in mbrp
10-11-1902   Amanda gct Hopewell MM

ADAMSON
11-22-1837   Lydia (form Morgan) rpt mcd
2-21-1838    Huldah & Mary Jane minors gct Springfield MM
3-21-1838    Lydia dis mcd
3-20-1839    Rebecca (form Cook) dis mcd
3-20-1839    John, dis Somerton PM compl of for mcd
5-22-1839    dis
6-19-1839    Elizabeth Hodson (form Adamson) dis mcd
10-23-1839   Seth & w Rhoda rocf Springfield MM, endorsed to Back Creek MM
5-20-1840    Isaac appt to comm

ADDISON
3- 7-1896    Maud rec in mbrp
9- 3-1904    Hannah & dt Mary Henrietta rec in mbrp
10- 8-1904   Levi rec in mbrp
4- 1-1915    Edna rec in mbrp
9- 4-1920    Hannah rel on req

ADKINS
12- 3-1925   Esther Holloway rel on rq

ALBERTSON
3-23-1836    Jordon rocf Milford MM
8-22-1838    Jordan & Martha Elliott altm
3-24-1841    William rocf Milford MM, Ind
9-22-1841    William B & Mary Davis altm
9-22-1841    For the convenience of William B & Mary Davis for their m, a mtg has been granted at Elm Grove M H, tomorrow at 11 o'clock
6-22-1842    Wm B & w Mary gct Back Creek MM
6-23-1847    Polly rocf Blue River MM
2-19-1851    Benjamin rocf Milford MM
5-21-1851    Daniel rocf Blue River MM
11-19-1851   Benjamin gct Richland MM
9-19-1855    William B & Rebecca Larrance altm
9-25-1861    George Evans gct Raysville MM to m Martha Albertson
9-23-1863    Rebecca & Elijah Hinshaw inf mtg of int to m. A comm is appt to see that the right's of Rebecca's ch are legally secured
10-21-1863   Rebecca & Elijah Hinshaw altm
3- 7-1868    Benjamin dis mcd
4- 2-1870    Luella C dis
4- 5-1890    Nathan D & w Luella & ch Herbert & Lois Mary gct Mill Creek MM
9- 1-1891    Benjamin gct Portland MM
4- 7-1894    Lena gct Olive Branch MM

ALDRICH
3- 5-1892    Rilla? Taylor rel on rq

ALLEN
4-20-1842    Daniel C produced a certif from Walnut Ridge Mtg to m Susannah Sheridan
4-20-1842    Daniel C & Susannah Sheridan altm
2-22-1843    Rachel (form Boon) mcd
7-24-1844    Daniel C rocf Walnut Ridge MM, Ind
10-22-1845   Joseph M produced a certif from Walnut Ridge Mtg to m Charity Kersey
10-22-1845   Joseph M & Charity Kersey altm
10-21-1846   Daniel C & Elizabeth W Dicks altm
4-21-1847    John Philander rocf Walnut Ridge MM
3-24-1852    Herman jr & w Julia Ann & dt Elizabeth Ann rocf Walnut Ridge MM
9-21-1853    Nancy C rocf Walnut Ridge MM
11-23-1853   Nancy C & Nathan Dicks altm
3-22-1854    Daniel C gct Springfield MM, Oh to m Elizabeth Hadley
6- 7-1854    Daniel C & ch John W & Charles gct Springfield MM, Oh
4-25-1855    Rachel & ch gct Whitewater MM
2-25-1857    Joseph M & w Charity & ch Charles F, Ann Ellen, Emma Samira & Mary Ann gct Whitewater MM
4-22-1857    Libby J rocf Walnut Ridge MM
6-23-1858    Harmon H & Lydia M King altm
1-19-1859    Job D, a minor, gct Springfield MM, Oh
6-20-1860    John Philander dis
8-20-1862    Herman jr & w Lydia & ch Elizabeth Ann, Frank Edgar & Lineas gct Duck Creek MM
5- 4-1872    John - - - - -?
8- 1-1874    Nathan rocf New Hope MM, Va
6- 2-1883    John drpd
3- 5-1887    Anna rocf Sugar River MM, (w of F. E. Allen)
3- 1-1890    Dr F E rec on req
9- 5-1891    Frank Edgar dis
1- 2-1892    Nathan gct Indpls MM
1- 7-1893    Anna gct Whitewater MM
3- 6-1915    Jesse rec on req
?- 6-1918    Ruben & Elizabeth rec on req
8-16-1926    Helen McKee rocf Duck Creek MM
10- 1-1931   Ruben & w gct Duck Creek MM

ALLEY
9-25-1839    Catherine (form Wilson) mcd dis

ALLISON
5- 2-1895    Frank & Cora rec mbrp
6- 3-1905    Ella Pickett rel on req
12- 7-1913   Frank & w Cora & ch Nora L, Ray, Marietta & Maggie H drpd from mbrp

AMMICK
10- 9-1886   Mecia rocf Liberty MM, Ks

ANDERSON
4- 4-1891    Delana rec mbrp
6- 1-1901    Lavina Hodson gct Duck Creek MM
7- 7-1906    Elsie rec mbrp

ANTRIM
3-19-1845    Louiza, John B, Thomas Elwood & Eli, ch of James & Mary rocf Westfield MM
6-24-1846    James P & w Mary rst w/c of Westfield MM
6-24-1846    Thomas infant s of James P & Mary rec in mbrp
12-23-1846   Louisa & Jabez H Meredith altm
8-23-1847    Mary Ann, a minor, rocf Westfield MM
10-24-1849   James P Antrim, William Sheridan & John Hiatt appt overseers at Spiceland P M
3-22-1854    Mary Ann & Jonas E Hodson altm
10-11-1857   John E dis
1- 4-1868    John rec mbrp
9- 7-1872    John mcd
9- 7-1872    James C rel on req
2- 5-1876    James C rec mbrp
4- 7-1883    John B gct Raysville MM. cert was returned 6- 2-1883
1- 1-1887    J C rec mbrp
4- 5-1890    Hattie L & s Ray Carson rec mbrp
3- 7-1914    Earl rec mbrp

APPLEGATE
1- 7-1900    Samuel Clifford, Lesti May & Mary Ethel rec mbrp
4- 3-1909    Elsie Bell rec mbrp
1- 4-1913    Ernest, Mary Emma, Phillip Clifford & Robert Stafford rec mbrp
6-30-1916    Anna Thomas rocf New Garden MM
4-21-1931    Robert & w Elizabeth & s Beverly Eugene rel on req

ARNETT
5- 2-1885    Milton W & w Nancy L & ch Mattie May, Lola E & Alice G rocf New Garden MM
5- 1-1886    Willis rec mbrp
1- 5-1889    Milton & fam rel on req
3- 7-1891    Willis gct Marion MM

ARNOLD
5- 6-1871    Celia rocf Spring Creek MM
2- 7-1874    Celia gct New Garden MM

SPICELAND

## ARPS
4- 4-1868  Martha Ann, Mary Frances & William Beam rec in mbrp

## ATHERTON
4- 7-1883  R Emm B gct Rose Hill MM, Ks

## AYDELOTT
5-24-1848  Anna (form Stuart) mcd
8-21-1849  Anna S gct Whitewater MM
1-24-1855  Henry C rocf Whitewater MM

## BAILEY
8- 3-1872  George D rocf Flushing MM, Oh
8- 3-1872  Rachel S rocf Flushing MM, Oh
9- 2-1876  John Q rocf Freeport MM, Oh
11- 3-1877  Hannah Lavinia rocf Freeport MM, Oh
5- 7-1891  Phebe W & ch Arthur H, Herbert T, Lydia L & Jesse S rocf Freeport MM, Oh (family of Joseph Sydenham Bailey)
1- 4-1896  Jesse S gct Indpls MM
5- 6-1896  Rachel S m Daniel Hill
9- 4-1897  J Quincy & dt gct Knightstown MM
10-18-1899  Lydia Lavina m Edgar Clement
1- 3-1903  Hannah Lavinia gct Whitewater MM
4- 4-1903  Flossie Gray gct Duck Creek MM
10-10-1908  Dr George Dillwin gct Whitewater MM
10-10-1910  Phebe W gct Haddenfield MM, N J
12- 7-1912  Grace & Jesse drpd from mbrp

## BALDWIN
1-23-1833  Isaiah & w Elizabeth & ch original mbrs
1-23-1833  William Baldwin, James Johnson, Josiah Small & Isaac White appt to unite with a comm from women's mtg, to form a comm on Education & to rpt
1-23-1833  Isaiah Baldwin, Nathan Davis, William B Unthank, Josiah Pennington, Amer Bond & Aaron Stanley to unite with a comm from women's mtg to form a comm to inspect & relieve the poor
11-19-1834  Elwood gct New Garden MM to m Phebe Scott
4-22-1835  Phebe rocf New Garden MM
7-19-1837  Uriah dis for dp
5-23-1838  Louisa Newby (form Baldwin) mcd  dis
10-24-1838  Miriam rocf Goshen MM, Oh
4-19-1848  Eunice & Elihu Pickett  altm
10-25-1848  Josiah & Sarah Small inf mtg of int to m
11-22-1848  Josiah & Sarah Small inf mtg in writing as follows: "We,. . ., think best to discontinue our int of m with each other"
5-23-1849  Rachel & Bailey Pearson inf mtg of int to m
6-20-1849  Rachel & Bailey Pearson not appearing, the case is deferred to next mtg
7-25-1849  Rachel & Bailey Pearson not appearing, a comm appt to ascertain the cause
8-22-1849  The comm appt in case of Rachel & Bailey Pearson, is continued to next mtg
9-19-1849  The comm appt rpt that Rachel & Bailey Pearson declined proceeding in their int to m so case is dismissed
1-23-1850  Rachel Pearson (form Baldwin) mcd
1-22-1851  Ann Pearson (form Baldwin) mcd
5-21-1851  Mary Hodson (form Baldwin) mcd  dis
11-24-1852  Hannah Stanley (form Baldwin) mcd  dis
6-20-1855  Franklin mcd  dis
8-23-1857  Elwood mcd  dis
11-19-1862  Jonathan mcd  dis
12- 7-1867  Elwood rec in mbrp
5- 2-1868  Mary E rec in mbrp
6- 6-1868  Stephen mcd
2- 4-1871  John mcd
2- 7-1874  Franklin & w Mary Ann & ch Louis C, Phebe, Flora A & Elwood S rec in mbrp
4- 1-1876  Ellwood & w Phebe & dt Patsy gct West Grove MM
1- 7-1882  Stephen S rel on req
4- 7-1883  John gct Greenwood MM
10-13-1883  Lewis Clarkson gct Westfield MM
12- 6-1884  Mary Elizabeth rel on req
6- 7-1890  Ella Carr gct - - - returned by Duck Creek MM as she was has
12- 6-1890  Ella rel on req
3- 5-1892  Flora A gct Raysville MM
9- 3-1904  Julia A Sullivan roc
11- 6-1919  Edwin gct Whittier MM, Cal

## BALES - BEALS
1-23-1833  John H & w Ann original mbrs
10-25-1837  John H compl for na & dp at Elm Grove P M dis
9-19-1860  Oliver H & Martha G Hunt
9- 1-1866  Melissa A & Owen S Hill  altm
9- 1-1866  Melissa & Owen S Hill req a mtg appt at the house of John H Bales on the 13th of the present month, at 3 o'clock to accomplish their m.  Req granted
6- 6-1868  Ann appt an overseer at Elm Grove P M
8- 1-1868  Louisa & Edward Taylor  altm
8- 1-1868  Louisa & Edward Taylor req privilege of accomp their m in the retirement of home which was granted.  Meeting to be held at John Bales on next fifth day, at half after two o'clock
3- 3-1869  Oliver H & w Martha H & s Edward R gct Ash Grove MM, Ill
6- 5-1869  Mary & John T Charles  altm
6- 5-1869  Mary & John T Charles req privilege to accomp their m at home, which was granted & a mtg was appt at John Bales on next fourth day at half past 2 o'clock
2- 1-1896  Oliver H & Martha H rocf South Wabash MM
10- 1-1910  Oliver H & w rel on req

## BALLARD
2- 6-1869  Jesse F & w Mary & ch Jeremiah M & Loretta Candance rocf Plainfield MM
3- 7-1874  Jeremiah M gct Whitewater MM
1- 2-1875  Jesse F & w Mary & dt Lauretta gct Whitewater MM
4- 7-1906  Addie rec in mbrp

## BALLENGER
1-23-1833  Henry & w Rebecca original mbrs
6-25-1834  Henry dis for disunity & na
7-23-1834  Henry appeals his case to QM (he not appearing the case is drpd)
2-22-1837  Elijah compl for na & dp at Elm Grove P M dis
10-25-1837  Henry jr compl at Elm Grove P M for dp & na dis
12-19-1838  Philadelphia MM for the Northern District (Pa) req Spiceland to treat with Ellwood Ballenger for mcd.  Committee is appt
1-23-1839  The comm appt in the Elwood case, rpt that it is their judgement that he is not of the mind to make satisfaction & have so informed Philadelphia Mtg (Pa)
5-22-1839  Philadelphia MM, Northern District dis Ellwood & req a comm to hand him the copy
10-19-1842  Henry Sr mbrp restored at Spiceland MM
11-21-1849  Nathan H & Margaret Hubbard  altm
1-20-1864  Nathan H appt clerk & Jason Williams appt asst clerk
1- 2-1869  Margaret rec as Minister
7- 1-1871  Nathan H rec as Minister
4- 3-1886  Martha M rocf Raysville MM
3- 7-1891  Martha rel on req
12- 2-1893  Nathan H rel on req
8- 4-1894  Martha rec in mbrp
2- 6-1904  Nathan H rst in mbrp
5- 4-1907  Martha & dt Margarete H gct S 8th Street MM, Richmond, Ind

## BARKER
12-20-1848  Job rocf Westfield MM

## BARNARD
5- 7-1881  Malinda rocf Salem MM
6- 2-1883  Mary V gct Duck Creek MM
3- 6-1886  Elwood rec in mbrp
9- 3-1910  Anna & Robert drpd from mbrp
4- 6-1933  Emma & dt Helen rocf Knightstown MM

## BARNS
4- 7-1894  Edith rec in mbrp

SPICELAND

BARRETT
8- 5-1903        Alice (Hiatt) widow of Lawrence m Albert
                 L Copeland

BASEY
7- 5-1890        Mary gct Duck Creek MM

BASSETT
10-12-1901       Minnie rocf Cleveland MM, Oh

BAYSE
7- 1-1882        Wilson & Mary Ellen & ch Ethaline & Miriam
                 Ortella gct Duck Creek MM
2- 6-1904        Mary E (Test) & ch Lorna C, Herman L &
                 Howard H rocf Duck Creek MM
2- 6-1904        Miriam O, rocf Duck Creek MM
1- 4-1913        Murry rec in mbrp

BEACH
10- 9-1886       Lafayette rel on req

BEAMAN
11-21-1849       Maria & ch Sarah Jane, Mary Ann, Margaret
                 Isabella, Harriett Edna & William Penn rocf
                 Rich Square MM, N C (Rich Square inf that
                 cert for James is withheld)
10-mo-1850       James dis at Rich Square Mtg, N C
7- 7-1866        James B rec on req
10-10-1868       Joanna gct Raysville MM

BEARD
7-21-1858        Martha rocf Deep River MM, N C
5-21-1862        Martha gct Greenwood MM
4-20-1864        Martha rocf Greenwood MM

BEAVER
9-19-1838        Rhoda (form Hall) mcd    dis

BECKETT
5- 6-1882        George W rocf Hopewell MM, Ind
11- 6-1918       Nettie & dt Nellie gct Whittier MM, Calif

BEESON
1-23-1839        Jemima Manlove (form Beeson) mcd    dis
9-25-1839        Benjamin of Duck Creek PM dis for na &
                 att a mcd
11- 4-1876       Charles & sons Joseph, Samuel & Jonathan
                 rocf Fairmount MM
11- 2-1878       Charles & w Eliza & ch Joseph, Samuel,
                 Jonathan & Olive Beeson & Josephine Frances
                 & Ann Eliza Elmore gct Fairmount MM
6- 6-1896        David M & w Addie E & ch Josie Alma &
                 Walter H rocf Knightstown MM
7- 6-1897        Estella James rocf Duck Creek MM

BELL
10-25-1854       Michael Stanley gct Duck Creek MM to m
                 Lydia Jane Bell
11-21-1855       John M Macy gct Hopewell MM, to m Lydia Bell
12- 7-1889       Jesse & s John rocf Hopewell MM
4- 2-1892        Odessa rec in mbrp
6- 4-1892        Frances H rec in mbrp
3- 4-1893        Ira rec in mbrp
4- 4-1903        John gct Dublin MM
6- 6-1903        Enos & Lydia rocf Dublin MM
11- 2-1907       Ira E gct Duck Creek MM
3- 7-1908        Lena roc

BENBOW
6-20-1838        Leah (form Modlin)    mcd
1-25-1843        Leah (form Modlin)    dis

BENGE
10-23-1833       Elizabeth (form Knight) now residing in
                 limits of New Garden MM, mcd    dis

BENNETT
3- 2-1885        Thomas & Mary E rec in mbrp
9- 4-1930        Mary drpd from mbrp

BERRY
3- 6-1886        Andrew J & dt Pearl rec in mbrp

BINFORD
8-25-1841        James produced a cert from Walnut Ridge MM
                 to m Ruth Gause
8-25-1841        James & Ruth Gause altm
3-23-1842        Ruth gct Walnut Ridge MM
10-20-1852       Mary Ann rocf Walnut Ridge MM
2-20-1856        Mary Ann, a minor, gct Milford MM
12- 6-1923       Esther G rocf

BIRD
4- 6-1895        Christie (Deem) gct Raysville MM

BLACK
1- 1-1876        Elizabeth & ch Wm a & Hannah A Woolen gct
                 Hopewell MM
3- 4-1893        Harry rec in mbrp
12- 5-1903       Harry gct Dublin MM
5- 5-1911        Dorothy rec in mbrp
12- 7-1922       Irvin E & Ida M rec in mbrp
12- 7-1922       W Saul, Donald E, Margaret L & Maurice
                 rec in mbrp

BLACKLEDGE
5- 3-1873        Joseph rocf Deer Creek MM
1- 1-1876        Joseph gct Dover MM

BOGUE
12-25-1833       Josiah & w Elizabeth & ch John rocf
                 Westfield MM, Oh
12-25-1833       Alfred & w Keziah & ch Elizabeth & Jane
                 rocf Westfield MM, Oh
12-25-1833       Charles rocf Westfield MM, Oh
12-21-1836       John & Elizabeth Johnson altm
10-25-1837       John appt Treasurer of Spiceland School,
                 in room of Nathan Stanley, decd
11-20-1839       Alfred gct New Garden MM, Ind to m
                 Charity Bogue
11-20-1839       John is decd & Wm Unthank was appt to
                 fill his place as Spiceland School Treasurer
5-20-1840        Charity rocf New Garden MM
11-22-1843       Elizabeth Pickering (form Bogue) con mcd
8-20-1851        Charles dis
5-23-1855        Jane J & David H Reece  altm
4-21-1858        John mcd   dis
1-19-1859        Josiah P mcd
10-24-1860       Martha E rocf Walnut Ridge MM
3- 3-1866        Joseph E rec in mbrp
2- 1-1868        Calvin W con   mcd
1- 4-1873        Charles F con   mcd
5- 2-1874        Charity appt an overseer
1- 6-1877        Emery C gct Raysville MM
5- 5-1883        Josiah P appt an Elder
5- 5-1883        Sibbie appt an Elder
1- 5-1889        Sarah & ch Edna & Flora Edwards rocf
                 Duck Creek MM
3- 1-1890        John S rec in mbrp
9- 6-1890        Emma & Josephine gct Whitewater MM
10-10-1896       Minnie C gct Knightstown MM
9- 8-1898        Martha Emily rocf Whitewater MM
10- 3-1900       Alfred & w Ruth H & ch Josiah P & Edgar S
                 gct Muncie MM
4- 1-1905        Alfred & w Ruth H & ch Josiah P rocf
                 Muncie MM
5- 5-1906        Calvin & Rachel drpd from mbrp
5- 5-1921        Herman rec in mbrp
11- 6-1930       Ruth Kirk & ch Jennie, Josiah & Kirk gct
                 Dublin MM

BOND
1833             John & w Rebecca & ch living in area of
                 Duck Creek Mtg that became Spiceland Mtg
1-23-1833        Amer & w Mary & ch original mbrs
1-23-1833        Amer Bond, Nathan Davis, William B Unthank,
                 Josiah Pennington, Aaron Stanley & Isaiah
                 Baldwin to unite with a comm from women's
                 mtg, to form a comm to inspect & relieve
                 the poor
5-20-1835        Elias A & Sarah, minor ch of John gct
                 Whitewater MM
6-24-1835        Lavina gct Whitewater MM
1-20-1836        John gct Milford MM, Ind to m Mary
                 Stanbrough
4-20-1836        Mary & dts Phebe & Elizabeth Stanbrough
                 rocf Milford MM

SPICELAND

## BOND (Cont)
|  |  |
|---|---|
| 3-22-1837 | John & w Mary & minor ch Abigail, Jacob, William, Aaron & Anna Bond and Phebe & Elizabeth Stanbrough gct Duck Creek MM |
| 1-24-1838 | Abigail & Thomas Stanbrough altm |
| 5-20-1840 | Elias Newby gct Milford MM, to m Tabitha Bond |
| 7-22-1840 | Sarah & Elias A, minor ch of John rocf Whitewater MM |
| 1-20-1847 | Priscilla & Caleb Hodson altm |
| 1-19-1848 | Jesse produced cert from West Grove Mtg to m Delana Stanley |
| 1-19-1848 | Jesse & Delana Stanley (a wid w/ch) altm |
| 4-19-1848 | Delana & ch Mordecai & Susan Stanley gct West Grove MM |
| 9-19-1849 | Jesse & w Delana & ch Mahala, William, Lydia Bond & Mordecai & Susan C Stanley rocf West Grove MM |
| 8-22-1855 | William gct Walnut Ridge MM |
| 12-24-1856 | Thomas mcd dis |
| 1-21-1857 | Mahala & Seth Cloud altm |
| 4-22-1857 | Sarah rocf Walnut Ridge MM |
| 12-23-1857 | Delana appt an Elder |
| 3-23-1859 | William & w Sarah & ch gct Walnut Ridge MM |
| 11-23-1859 | Mahlen, a minor, gct Dover MM |
| 1-25-1860 | Caleb W dis |
| 8-5-1871 | Jesse appt an Elder |
| 4-6-1889 | Lavina Tuttle gct Duck Creek MM |

## BONIER
|  |  |
|---|---|
| 4-4-1896 | Susan F rec in mbrp |

## BOON - BOONE
|  |  |
|---|---|
| 1-23-1833 | Driver & w Anna & ch original mbrs |
| 3-20-1833 | Driver Boon, Isaac White, William Unthank & George Evans appt to comm to attend funerals of our members |
| 10-21-1840 | Driver appt Librarian at Spiceland PM in place of Richard Gause who is decd |
| 1-25-1843 | Rachel Allen (form Boon) con mcd |
| 1-24-1844 | Driver & Elizabeth C Gause (a wid w/ch) altm |
| 12-23-1844 | Rebecca Harvey (form Boon) mcd dis |
| 3-23-1848 | Irena H & William C Cloud altm |
| 5-25-1853 | Samson gct Whitewater MM |
| 9-1-1866 | Christena & Thomas Gause altm |
| 11-4-1871 | Charles gct Fairfield MM, Oh |
| 11-4-1871 | Dorcas gct Fairfield MM, Oh |
| 5-2-1874 | Elizabeth appt an overseer |
| 8-5-1876 | Charles rocf Hopewell MM, Oh |
| 9-1-1877 | Charles gct Duck Creek MM |
| 6-4-1881 | Mary Ann rocf Springfield MM |
| 4-7-1883 | Jonathan C & w Mary A gct Duck Creek MM |
| 2-3-1894 | Richard C & ch rel on req |

## BOREN
|  |  |
|---|---|
| 3-19-1851 | Nancy gct Duck Creek MM |
| 2-3-1883 | Lillian V rec in mbrp |
| 5-7-1887 | Lillie gct New Castle MM |

## BOSYE
|  |  |
|---|---|
| 3-2-1867 | Thomas & family rec in mbrp |

## BOWEN
|  |  |
|---|---|
| 3-2-1895 | Thomas S, Sarah M & Violet rec in mbrp |

## BOWERS
|  |  |
|---|---|
| 5-5-1906 | Chester rec in mbrp |

## BOWMAN
|  |  |
|---|---|
| 1-22-1840 | George W gct Dover MM, N C |
| 7-22-1840 | Cyrus R jas dis |
| 2-7-1885 | Robert B & w Sarah & ch Delbert & Oscar rocf Duck Creek MM |
| 6-7-1890 | Robert B, Sarah H, Arthur D & Oscar gct Duck Creek MM |
| 8-6-1892 | Robert & w Sarah & ch Arthur D & Oscar L drpd from mbrp |

## BOYD
|  |  |
|---|---|
| 6-2-1921 | Minnie Kiser gct New Castle MM |

## BRADFORD
|  |  |
|---|---|
| 12-7-1912 | Pearl Thomas gct Duck Creek MM |
| 9-4-1930 | Pearl Thomas drpd from mbrp |

## BRAITHWAIT
|  |  |
|---|---|
| 7-7-1900 | Henry M Jones & w Carrie T & ch Osward Beven Braithwait & Barton Ellwyn Jones rocf Friends Chapel MM |

## BRANDENBURG
|  |  |
|---|---|
| 4-3-1893 | Nancy gct Westfield MM |

## BRANSON
|  |  |
|---|---|
| 6-22-1838 | Hannah, Susannah, Margaret & Owen, ch of Owen, rocf New Garden MM |
| 5-25-1838 | Susanna Clifford (form Branson) mcd dis |
| 4-24-1839 | John W rocf Flushing MM, Oh |
| 12-25-1861 | Hannah rocf Duck Creek MM |

## BRAZINGTON
|  |  |
|---|---|
| (9-20-1837) | Samuel & w Lydia & ch Joseph S, William A, Samuel jr, Ann, David & Eli mbrs of Duck Creek Mtg, now laid down, attached to Spiceland Mtg |
| 11-24-1847 | William A, minor s of Samuel gct Whitewater MM, Ind |
| 5-23-1849 | Joseph S & Gulielma Davis altm |
| 2-25-1852 | Joseph & w Gulielma gct Mississinewa MM |
| 2-25-1852 | Lydia & ch Hannah Ann, David & Eli gct Mississinewa MM |
| 11-23-1853 | Samuel jr gct Pipe Creek MM |

## BREWER
|  |  |
|---|---|
| 5-20-1835 | Zachariah Fletcher & w Anne & Rachel Brewer, a minor, under their care, rocf Milford MM |
| 6-20-1838 | John & minor ch Elizabeth & William rocf West Grove MM |
| 7-25-1838 | Sarah who had been dis by Deerfield MM, Oh, req to be again rec in mbrp & that her dt Mary also be rec |
| 1-23-1839 | Sarah rst with con of Pennville MM, Oh (3rd w of John) |
| 6-19-1839 | John & w Sarah & ch Elizabeth, William, Mary & Morris gct Milford MM, (but Milford ret the cert as it appears they are going to move back)(However they went to Duck Creek Mtg) IBB |
| 2-19-1840 | Elias, a minor, rocf Milford MM |
| 2-19-1845 | Rachel gct Salem MM, Iowa |
| 12-7-1872 | Susannah & s Jason Equador rocf Carthage MM |
| 6-4-1881 | Susan & s Jason E gct Milford MM |
| 4-6-1918 | Ruby rec in mbrp |
| 3-1-1919 | Myron rec in mbrp |
| 12-7-1922 | Carl H, Christena C & L Harold rec in mbrp |
| 12-7-1922 | Forest H & Earl rec in mbrp |

## BROADBENT
|  |  |
|---|---|
| 8-5-1876 | Martha & ch Richard & Alice rocf Raysville MM |
| 10-6-1932 | Ada & Mary rec in mbrp |

## BROOKS
|  |  |
|---|---|
| 5-9-1929 | George & Irvin rec in mbrp |
|  | R E & Mary rec in mbrp |

## BROOKSHIRE
|  |  |
|---|---|
| 6-5-1897 | Julia rec in mbrp |

## BROSSINS
|  |  |
|---|---|
| 6-6-1885 | Margaret rec in mbrp |
| 6-7-1890 | Margaret gct Raysville MM |

## BROTHERS
|  |  |
|---|---|
| 3-4-1882 | Robert & w Emily rec in mbrp |
| 1-7-1893 | Robert & Emily gct Fairmount MM |

## BROWN
|  |  |
|---|---|
| 8-18-1835 | Sarah (form Moore) mcd dis |
| 5-6-1871 | Mary A & dt Anna S rocf Salem MM |
| 7-1-1871 | Nathan rocf Walnut Ridge MM |
| 4-3-1875 | Mary Jane gct Walnut Ridge MM |
| 10-9-1880 | Elger & Sarah & dt Emma & minor ch Mary, Martha, Joseph & Bessie rocf Hopewell MM, Ohio |
| 6-4-1881 | Nathan & w Mary Ann & ch Anna I, Frank C, Mabel C, & Leroy N gct Walnut Ridge MM |
| 8-8-1881 | Mercer & ch Albert & Clara rocf Stanton MM, Ill |

SPICELAND

## BROWN (Cont)

|  |  |
|---|---|
| 2- 6-1892 | John Franklin rocf Poplar Ridge MM |
| 12- 1-1894 | Alfred & w Effie Afton & ch Paul Howard & Russell Lowell rocf Walnut Ridge MM |
| 1- 2-1897 | John F gct Poplar Ridge MM |
| 3- 6-1897 | Alfred & w Effie Afton & ch Paul Howard & Russell Lowell gct Walnut Ridge MM |
| 1- 6-1900 | Effie Afton Hall & ch Paul Howard & Russell Lowell Brown rocf Walnut Ridge MM |
| 5- 3-1903 | Bessie Irene gct Anderson MM |
| 8- 3-1912 | William W rocf Duck Creek MM |
| 1- 3-1914 | Paul H gct West Richmond MM |
| 8- 1-1914 | Russell Lowell gct W Richmond MM |
| 1- 1-1931 | Harvey & w Mary & ch Lola Catherine & Wilbur rocf Dublin MM |

## BUDD

|  |  |
|---|---|
| 11-24-1852 | John & w Elizabeth & ch Calvin Albert, Phebe Ann, Charles & John B rocf White Lick MM |

## BUFKIN

|  |  |
|---|---|
| 1837 | (Gulielma, Sarah, John C & Ruth C were ch of Thomas & w Ruth. The family no doubt were mbrs of Duck Creek Mtg which was laid down 9-20-1837 & mbrs attached to Spiceland Mtg) |
| 9-20-1837 | The comm appt at Duck Creek Mtg to prepare disownment of Gulielma, are continued at Spiceland Mtg. (Duck Creek Mtg had been laid down) |
| 10-25-1837 | Gulielma dis for jas |
| 7-24-1839 | Sarah Weisner (form Bufkin) mcd |
| 2-19-1840 | John C & Hannah Weisner altm |
| 2-24-1841 | Samuel rst with con of Flushing MM, Oh |
| 3-24-1841 | Samuel gct Duck Creek MM |
| 10-19-1842 | Ruth C Charles (form Bufkin) jas & mcd dis |
| 9- 4-1869 | Hannah N & ch Orie Ann & Mary D rocf Indianapolis MM |
| 12- 4-1869 | John & Abigail B & ch Elizabeth, Calvin A, Asa E & Rachel rocf Duck Creek MM |
| 1- 1-1876 | Hannah N T & dt Mary Lee gct Indianapolis MM |
| 12- 4-1880 | Abigail gct Rose Hill MM, Kan |
| 3- 3-1883 | Asa rel on req |

## BUNDY

|  |  |
|---|---|
| 9-25-1833 | Nancy dis for na |
| 12-27-1835 | Nancy rocf New Garden MM |
| 8-24-1836 | Charles & w Pheraby & ch Josiah & Morris rocf Symons Creek MM, N C & end by Milford MM |
| 9-20-1837 | George Sr & w Karen & their ch Mary, Josiah & Catharine, mbrs of Duck Creek Mtg, now laid down, have been attached to Spiceland Mtg |
| 2-21-1838 | Karen appt to station of Elder |
| 10-24-1838 | Mary & Wiatt Stanley inf mtg of int to m |
| 11-21-1838 | Mary & Wyatt Stanley altm |
| 12-19-1838 | The comm appt to att m of Mary & Wyatt Stanley, rpt it was orderly & they have placed m cert in the hands of the Recorder |
| 11-19-1845 | Morgan, Sarah, Charles & Mariah, ch of Thomas & Mary, rocf Milford MM |
| 2-19-1851 | Josiah mcd dis |
| 4-21-1851 | Sarah rocf Symons Creek MM, N C |
| 1-19-1853 | Sarah gct Hopewell MM |
| 3-23-1853 | Henry produced a cert from Walnut Ridge Mtg to m |
| 3-23-1853 | Henry & Mary Eliza Elliott altm |
| 8-24-1853 | Mary Eliza gct Walnut Ridge MM |
| 4- 1-1865 | Jonathan N & w Anna M & ch Sarah Ellen, Mary Emily, Anna Matilda & Lewis Allen rec in mbrp |
| 5- 4-1867 | Charles & w Pheribia gct Raysville MM |
| 10-11-1867 | Jonathan N & w Anna & ch Sarah Ellen, Mary Emily, Anna Malinda & Lewis Allen gct Westfield MM |
| 1- 4-1868 | Ira S & w Sarah & s Charles W rocf Carthage MM |
| 6- 6-1868 | Jesse & w Rachel & s Enos rocf Hopewell MM |
| 6- 6-1868 | Morris N gct Raysville MM |
| 11- 6-1869 | Ira & w Sarah & s Charles Warren gct Hopewell MM |
| 8- 6-1870 | Maria J & ch Charles David, Lorenzo, John Franklin, Orlestes rocf Minneapolis MM, Minn |
| 2- 3-1872 | William P & w Martha J rocf Carthage MM |
| 6- 7-1873 | Enos con mcd |
| 4- 3-1875 | David C & w Rebecca Ellen & ch Florence gct Lynnville MM, Iowa |
| 3- 4-1878 | Enos rel on req |
| 3- 4-1882 | Carolline A & ch Frank, Howard, Clint & Jesse rec in mbrp |
| 4- 7-1883 | Maria J & s Charles, Lorenzo, John F & Orlestes gct Duck Creek MM |
| 6- 2-1883 | Morgan, Charles, Sarah & Maria drpd from mbrp |
| 11- 4-1892 | Ella & ch Florence & Maria M rocf Lynn Grove MM, Iowa |
| 1- 5-1907 | Charles T & w Martha Guy rec in mbrp |
| 5- 3-1908 | Elizabeth Ralston rocf Dublin MM |
| 8- 1-1908 | Walter rel on req |
| 1- 7-1911 | Charles rec in mbrp |
| 1- 7-1911 | Helen, w of Charles, & dt Hulda rocf ?? |
| 2- 7-1912 | Minnie Collier & ch Alice Caroline & Edna Lucile rec in mbrp |
| 4- 3-1915 | Hilda & Esther rec in mbrp |
| 4- 6-1918 | Alice rec in mbrp |
| 5- 5-1921 | Edna rec in mbrp |
| 9- 7-1925 | Elizabeth gct Dublin MM |
| 6- 4-1931 | Hilda gct West Richmond MM |

## BURGESS

|  |  |
|---|---|
| 8-19-1846 | Sarah rocf Pennsville MM, Oh |
| 10-20-1847 | Sarah gct Whitewater MM |
| 3- 3-1866 | William & s Frank rec in mbrp |
| 11-11-1884 | William rel on req |
| 4- 2-1892 | Anna gct Springfield MM |
| 4- 2-1892 | Mary Ellen gct Springfield MM |

## BURNETT

|  |  |
|---|---|
| 5-22-1844 | David produced cert from Miami MM, Oh to m Eliza Pennington |
| 5-22-1844 | David & Eliza Pennington altm |
| 5-22-1844 | For the convenience of David & Eliza Pennington, a mtg for their m is granted, for tomorrow at Elm Grove MH at 11 o'clock |
| 7-24-1844 | Eliza gct Miami MM, Oh |
| 1-19-1848 | David & w Eliza & s Isaac F rocf Miami MM, Oh |
| 4-21-1858 | Isaac F gct Fairfield MM, Oh to m Hannah Kenworthy |
| 12-22-1858 | Isaac F gct Fairfield MM, Oh |
| 8- 2-1874 | Jesse con mcd |
| 2- 4-1882 | Jesse & w Sarah rel on req |

## BUROKER

|  |  |
|---|---|
| 4- 5-1928 | Lucy rocf West Richmond MM |

## BURT

|  |  |
|---|---|
| 12- 7-1912 | Lillian Hiatt rel on req |

## BUTLER

|  |  |
|---|---|
| 2-24-1836 | William & w Esther & ch Elizabeth, Lydia, Priscilla, Edward & Robert T rocf Milford MM |
| 3-23-1836 | Elizabeth & Simeon Wiltsie altm |
| 9-21-1836 | William & w Esther & ch Lydia, Priscilla, Edward & Robert L gct Walnut Ridge MM |
| 8-23-1837 | Jonathan & w Sarah P & ch Sarah Ann, Mary Jane & Priscilla rocf Duck Creek MM |
| 10-24-1838 | Jonathan & w Sarah P & ch Sarah Ann, Mary Jane & Priscilla gct Walnut Ridge MM |
| 9-25-1839 | Vierling Kersey gct Marlborough MM, Oh to m Mary E Butler |
| 8-21-1844 | Alfred produced cert from Hopewell MM, to m Elizabeth Morgan |
| 8-21-1844 | Alfred & Elizabeth Morgan altm |
| 4-23-1845 | Elizabeth gct Hopewell MM |
| 2-23-1848 | Alfred & w Elizabeth & s Benjamin M rocf Hopewell MM |
| 2-20-1850 | Alfred & w Elizabeth & ch Benjamin M & Lindley H gct Honey Creek MM |
| 7-24-1850 | William E rocf Milford MM end by Whitewater MM |
| 6-25-1858 | Joseph & w Sarah Ann & ch Charity Ann, Calvin, Fredus Eugene, & an infant, rocf Duck Creek MM |
| 1-20-1864 | William Exum gct Rocksylvania MM, Iowa |
| 5- 6-1865 | George W & w Martha & ch Micajah, Elwood, Almeda & Elizabeth Ann rocf Walnut Ridge MM |
| 6- 2-1866 | Joseph & w Sarah Ann & ch Charity Ann, Calvin P, Fredus E, Mary Ellen, William W & James A gct Lynn Grove MM, Iowa |

SPICELAND

## BUTLER (Cont)

|  |  |
|---|---|
| 1- 5-1867 | Elisha M rocf Plainfield MM |
| 7- 6-1867 | John N rocf Walnut Ridge MM |
| 9- 1-1867 | Daniel W rocf Walnut Ridge MM |
| 11- 7-1867 | Lucinda B rocf Walnut Ridge MM |
| 7- 4-1868 | Sarah E rec in mbrp |
| 8- 1-1868 | Sybil A rocf Walnut Ridge MM |
| 11- 7-1868 | John M con mcd |
| 6- 5-1869 | Elisha con mcd |
| 6- 5-1869 | Kizzie rec in mbrp |
| 2- 3-1870 | John M dis |
| 2- 4-1871 | Elisha & w Keziah gct Clear Creek MM, Oh |
| 3- 7-1874 | Joseph & w Sarah Ann & ch Fredus E, Mary Ellen, William W, James A, Thomas P & Lindley H rocf Lynn Grove MM, Iowa |
| 5- 2-1874 | George W & w Martha & ch Almeda & Elizabeth gct Fairmount MM |
| 8- 1-1874 | John M rec in mbrp |
| 8- 1-1874 | Micajah rel on req |
| 10-10-1874 | John M & w Sylvia & ch Edgar Ernest & George Douglas gct Carthage MM |
| 5- 6-1876 | Daniel W rel on req |
| 10-11-1890 | Sarah Ann & s William gct Minneapolis MM, Minn |
| 12- 6-1890 | Lindley gct Minneapolis MM, Minn |
| 4- 7-1894 | Dr D W, Mary & Herbert rec in mbrp |
| 1- 4-1896 | Mary A & s George Herbert rel on req |
| 3- 2-1901 | Noble & s William L rocf Duck Creek MM |
| 12- 7-1912 | Alvin drpd from mbrp |
| 5- 5-1927 | Loren rec in mbrp |
| 5- 3-1928 | Dorothy rec in mbrp |

## BYERS

|  |  |
|---|---|
| 2- 4-1871 | Augusta rec in mbrp |
| 10-14-1871 | Augusta F & James M Lewelling altm (there are no surviving parents) |
| 10-14-1871 | Augusta F & James M Lewelling req a mtg apptd at Jesse B Jessup's on next First Day at 2 o'clock for the purpose of accomplishing their m. Req is granted |
| 5- 7-1887 | Margaret S gct Hopewell MM |

## CADWALLADER

|  |  |
|---|---|
| 8-25-1847 | Joseph req to be again rec into mbrp. He had been dis by Lick Creek MM. A comm appt to treat with him |
| 9-22-1847 | The comm appt to consider Joseph's req for mbrp, makes the following rpt; "We have had the subject under consideration and are united in believing that the circumstances in life in which he has placed himself are such that he can not consistently become a mbr of our Society. (He having availed himself of the privilege of a divorce by marrying again. Both of the women to whom he was married, being still living") |

## CALHOUN

|  |  |
|---|---|
| 10-12-1895 | Esther Painter gct Garden City MM, Kan |

## CAMMACK

|  |  |
|---|---|
| 12-22-1841 | Henry produced cert from New Garden MM to m Sally Horner |
| 12-22-1841 | Henry & Sally Horner altm |
| 12-22-1841 | For the accomodation of Henry & Sally Horner for their m, a mtg has been granted for tomorrow at Raysville MH at 11 o'clock |
| 11-22-1843 | Sally H gct Cherry Grove MM |
| 5-23-1849 | Henry & w Sally & ch Rachel, Emmaline & Elwood rocf Cherry Grove MM |
| 6-19-1850 | Henry & w Sally & ch Rachel, Emeline, Elwood & John rocf Cherry Grove MM |
| 12-24-1856 | Henry & w Sally & ch Rachel, Emeline, Elwood, John & Elizabeth rocf New Garden MM |
| 6-20-1860 | Henry & w Sally & ch Rachel, Emeline, Elwood, John H & Elizabeth H rocf Raysville MM |
| 9- 7-1867 | Henry & w Sally & ch Rachel, Emeline, Elwood, John & Elizabeth gct Bear Creek MM, Iowa |
| 5- 5-1877 | Henry & w Sally rocf North Branch MM, Iowa |
| 6- 3-1882 | Henry & w Sally gct Pike Creek MM |
| 2- 2-1889 | Henry & w Sally rocf Amboy MM |

## CANADAY

|  |  |
|---|---|
| 5- 5-1900 | Eliza E rocf Walnut Ridge MM |

## CANE

|  |  |
|---|---|
| 6-20-1849 | Jane rocf Deep River MM, N C & end by Cherry Grove MM |
| 8-24-1853 | Jane & Elias Elliott altm |
| 9- 1-1867 | Exelina rocf Duck Creek MM, & end to Hopewell MM |

## CANNON

|  |  |
|---|---|
| 12-23-1840 | Horace T & w Gulielma rocf New Garden MM, N C & end to White Lick MM |

## CARR

|  |  |
|---|---|
| 11-23-1842 | Thomas produced a cert from Springfield MM, Ind to m Rachel Stout |
| 11-23-1842 | Thomas & Rachel Stout altm |
| 11-23-1842 | For the convenience of Thomas & Rachel Stout, a meeting for their m has been granted for tomorrow at 11 o'clock |
| 1-25-1843 | Rachel gct Springfield MM |
| 2- 7-1874 | Emily S, Cynthia V & Emory M rec on req |
| 3- 4-1888 | Ella rocf Duck Creek MM |
| 3- 3-1892 | Emory Morton gct New Castle MM |
| 5- 5-1921 | Thelma rec in mbrp |
| 1- 7-1922 | Everett & Lillian M rec in mbrp |
| 1- 4-1923 | George rec in mbrp |
| 5- 6-1926 | Wilbur rec in mbrp |
| 12- 4-1930 | Wilbur gct Chester MM, N J |

## CARSON

|  |  |
|---|---|
| 3- 4-1893 | William J rec in mbrp |
| 11- 7-1900 | Ray S s Samuel decd, & Harriet L of Henry Co, Ind m Cora A Charles, dt Clarkson & Caroline E, decd of Spiceland |
| 1- 5-1901 | Ray S & Cora A gct Upland MM |
| 11- 7-1905 | William J gct Chicago MM, Ill |
| 8- 3-1911 | Ray & w & ch Robert Wm, Charles, Harriett Emma & Annie Caroline roc |
| 7- 6-1912 | Ray & fam gct New Garden MM |
| 4- 1-1916 | Ray gct Whitewater MM |
| 10- 6-1927 | Martha rec in mbrp |
| 12- 1-1927 | Leslie & w Yevonne & s Robert Leslie rocf Amboy MM |

## CARTER

|  |  |
|---|---|
| 12-19-1849 | Anna (form Forster) con mcd |
| 9-25-1850 | Anna gct White Lick MM |
| 6- 5-1869 | Samuel C & w Albertine & dt Lilly Mary rocf Plainfield MM, ?? |
| 2- 1-1873 | Samuel C & w Albertine & ch Lilly Mary, Claudine gct Whitewater MM |
| 12- 6-1902 | Oneida E & s Charles J Reece gct Olive Branch MM |
| 8- 6-1904 | Ira G & w Oneida & ch Eber E, Carter & Charles Reece rocf Farmland MM |
| 10-14-1905 | Ira G & w gct Stanton MM, Ill |
| 11- 4-1905 | Eber Ernest gct Whittier MM, Ca |

## CASSEN

|  |  |
|---|---|
| 9- 4-1930 | Frank & Ebbie, Carl, Gail & Violet drpd from mbrp |

## CASSITY

|  |  |
|---|---|
| 5- 5-1927 | Russell rec in mbrp |
| 11- 1-1928 | Clarence & Maude rec in mbrp |

## CHAMNESS

|  |  |
|---|---|
| 6- 1-1872 | William S & w Rebecca & ch Theodore Elbridge, Carrie Ruth, Oscar Luther, Olinda Florence & Rufus Estes, rocf Springfield MM |
| 3- 3-1877 | Mary & dt Abigail rocf Springfield MM |
| 8- 6-1892 | William & w Rebecca & dts Caroline & Mary E gct Marion MM |
| 10-10-1896 | Theodore gct Marion MM |

## CHANDLER

|  |  |
|---|---|
| 8- 4-1883 | Ellen J P & ch drpd from mbrp |
| 5- 4-1912 | Metta & Clara rec in mbrp |
| 5- 4-1912 | Albert N & w Jennie & dt Ethel rec in mbrp |
| 5- 4-1912 | Claude rec in mbrp |

SPICELAND

## CHAPPEL
| | |
|---|---|
| 4-23-1851 | Reuben produced a cert from West Grove MM to m |
| 4-23-1851 | Reuben & Martha N White altm |
| 10-22-1851 | Reuben & ch John N, Griffin A, Milton K, Lydia Matilda rocf West Grove MM |

## CHARLES
| | |
|---|---|
| 8-22-1836 | Jesse rocf Whitewater MM |
| 11-21-1838 | Lydia & ch req cert to Mississnewa MM |
| 10-10-1842 | Ruth C (form Bufkin) mcd  dis |
| 9-25-1844 | Jesse mcd  dis |
| 6-25-1845 | Eli rocf Whitewater MM |
| 1-23-1850 | Eli mcd & joined Masonic lodge  dis |
| 7-24-1850 | Eliza (form Newby) mcd  dis |
| 6- 5-1869 | John T & Mary Bales altm |
| 6- 5-1869 | John T & Mary Bales req privilege to accomplish their m at home, which was granted & a mtg was appt at John Bales on next fourth day at half past 2 o'clock |
| 4- 7-1883 | Henry rocf New Garden MM |
| 5- 3-1890 | Clarkson & w Emily & ch Minnie J, Lillian A, Rosa E, Bertha M & Cora A rocf New Garden MM |
| 5- 3-1890 | Oliver M rocf New Garden MM |
| 11- 7-1900 | Cora A m Ray Carson |
| 6- 2-1906 | Estella gct Indianapolis MM |
| 6- 1-1912 | Oliver H gct Newberry MM, Oregon |

## CHESTNUT
| | |
|---|---|
| 3-19-1834 | John & Sarah COOK, minor ch of Isaac, decd & w Mary (now Chestnut) gct Whitewater MM? |

## CHEW
| | |
|---|---|
| 10-24-1838 | Ephraim & w Rachel & ch Isaac, Hannah, Lydia, Abigail, Nathan, Milton & Joseph rocf Newberry MM, Oh |
| 1-23-1839 | Hannah Gardner (form Chew) mcd dis |
| 6-21-1843 | Isaac, Elm Grove PM compl for mcd  dis |
| 6-25-1851 | Ephraim G con mcd |
| 7-23-1851 | Patsy (form Harold) con mcd |
| 12-22-1852 | John mcd  dis |
| 10- 9-1886 | John M & w Louisa & ch John P, Thomas E, Nancy J & Lizzie P & Ira C rec in mbrp |
| 8- 3-1901 | Nancy & Lizzie R drpd from mbrp |
| 12- 7-1912 | John & Ira rel on req |
| 4- 6-1918 | Donald rec in mbrp |
| 10- 4-1928 | Josie drpd from mbrp |

## CLARK
| | |
|---|---|
| 7-22-1840 | Calvin & Arthur, minors, rocf Whitewater MM |
| 3- 3-1894 | Anna E gct New Garden MM |
| 4- 5-1902 | Caroline (form Dawson) rel on req |

## CLATTERBAUGH
| | |
|---|---|
| 4- 2-1892 | Mary rocf Duck Creek MM |

## CLEAVER
| | |
|---|---|
| 10- 8-1904 | Isaac Allen & w Sarah rocf Dublin MM |
| 11- 2-1907 | Isaac Allen & w Sarah H gct Ypsilanti MM, Mich |
| 11- 7-1908 | Allen & w Sarah rocf Ypsilanti, MM, Mich |

## CLEMENT
| | |
|---|---|
| 10-18-1899 | Edgar m Lydia Lavinia Bailey |
| 4- 7-1909 | Lavinia (Bailey) & ch Wilmer Bailey, Charles, Allen & Phebe Alice gct Haddenfield MM, N J |

## CLEVENGER
| | |
|---|---|
| 1- 1-1876 | R Ellen rec in mbrp |
| 12- 5-1885 | Sanford rec in mbrp |
| 1- 1-1887 | Rebecca E & Sanford transferred to Muncie MM |

## CLIFFORD
| | |
|---|---|
| 5-23-1838 | Susanna (form Branson) mcd dis |
| 5- 7-1870 | Cassius rec in mbrp |

## CLIFTON
| | |
|---|---|
| 6- 2-1900 | Rose rel on req |

## CLOUD
| | |
|---|---|
| 1-23-1833 | Joel & w Anna & ch original mbrs |
| 1-23-1833 | William & Tacy & ch original mbrs |
| 8-21-1833 | Joel & Ann on comm rpt on school |
| 12-25-1833 | Mordecai & w Jemima rocf West Grove MM |
| 8-19-1835 | Mordecai & w Jemima & ch John gct Fairfield MM |
| 9-20-1837 | William & w Tacy &´ch Jonathan, Hannah M, David & Elizabeth Ann gct Sugar River MM |
| 9-20-1837 | Nancy gct Westfield MM |
| 12-25-1839 | Nancy rocf Westfield MM |
| 3-23-1848 | William C & Irena H Boon altm |
| 10-24-1849 | Ruth & Himelius Pike altm |
| 10-24-1849 | Ruth & Himelius Pike req a mtg be granted at Spiceland MH, for tomorrow at 11 o'clock for them to accomplish their m, which was granted |
| 9-25-1850 | Asenath H & Nathan Nicholson altm |
| 5-21-1851 | Pauline (form Rayl) con mcd |
| 6-25-1851 | Seth con mcd |
| 6- 7-1854 | Levi gct Walnut Ridge MM to m Rebecca Hunt |
| 2-21-1855 | Rebecca rocf Walnut Ridge MM |
| 8-20-1856 | William C dis for mcd |
| 1-21-1857 | Seth & Mahala Bond altm |
| 8-19-1857 | Joel appt an overseer at Spiceland PM |
| 2-24-1858 | Nancy gct Lynn Grove MM (Iowa) |
| 4-23-1862 | Levi & w Rebecca & ch Louis Emory, Joel Edgar & Emily Alice gct Westfield MM |
| 2- 2-1867 | William C & Anna M & ch Luther Lee, Leora Bell & Ada Evelyne rec in mbrp |
| 9- 7-1867 | William C & w Anna & ch Luther Lee, Leora Bell & Ada Evelyn gct Greenwood MM |
| 12- 7-1867 | Joel gct Westfield MM |
| 3- 6-1869 | Joseph gct Westfield MM |
| 4- 3-1869 | Seth & w Mahala & ch Anna Jane, Eveline, Lydia, Josephine & Sidney E gct Westfield MM |
| 3- 7-1874 | Levi & w Rebecca & ch Lewis Emory, Joel Edgar & Emma Alice rocf Westfield MM |
| 10-11-1890 | Joel Edgar & w Ella & s Carl gct Whitewater MM |
| 10- 3-1900 | Louis E & w Minnie & ch Jessie Georgia, Howard, Holman, Davis & Louis E gct New Castle MM |
| 9- 7-1901 | Carl rocf Whitewater MM |

## COBLE
| | |
|---|---|
| 7-24-1839 | Rebecca (form Stanley) con mcd |

## COCHRAN
| | |
|---|---|
| 6-21-1848 | James rocf Blue River MM |
| 10-25-1848 | James gct Blue River MM to m Martha Ellen Wilson |
| 5-23-1849 | Martha Ellen rocf Blue River MM |
| 9-23-1852 | James & w Martha Ellen & ch Annis & Charles W gct Blue River MM |
| 7-25-1855 | James & w Mary & his dt Annis rocf New Salem MM |
| 6- 7-1873 | James appt a Trustee of Spiceland Academy |
| 3- 2-1895 | Nora Belle, Mary Hazel & Ruby Miriam rec in mbrp |

## COFFIN
| | |
|---|---|
| 1835 | Catherine, a Minister, rocf Milford MM (end by Duck Creek MM, Ind) |
| 7-20-1836 | Catherine, a Minister, accompanied by Phebe Macy, an Elder & Isaac White, an Elder, gct to visit meetings in White Lick Quarter |
| 7-24-1839 | Nathan of Elm Grove PM, dis for jas |
| 10-20-1847 | Alfred rocf Walnut Ridge MM |
| 2-21-1848 | Alfred dis |
| 12-19-1849 | Embry D & w Elmina & ch Julius Vestal & Laura Ellen rocf New Garden MM, N C |
| 10-12-1864 | Elmina H & ch Julius, Ellen, Maria L, Alice, Amanda, Walter E & Mary E rocf Raysville MM |
| 8- 4-1866 | Elmina H, a wid & Timothy Wilson altm |
| 8- 4-1877 | Edward G Teas & w Sarah & ch Ellen, William, Frederick & Mary Teas & gr-son Vestel Coffin rocf Whitewater MM |
| 5- 5-1883 | William E & s Allen Morris rocf West Grove MM |
| 8- 4-1883 | Josephine & ch Walter & George rec in mbrp |
| 8- 5-1887 | Melissa rocf Dublin MM |
| 3- 3-1888 | Frank A rocf Whitewater MM |
| 1- 7-1893 | Isaac N & w Martha & ch Albert Morris rocf Sugar Plain MM |
| 12- 2-1893 | Isaac N & w gct Elmodena MM, Calif |
| 12- 2-1893 | Albert Morris gct Elmodena MM, Calif |
| 7- 7-1894 | Frank A & w Melissa & ch Lena Margaret, Myron F & Irvin W gct Whitewater MM |

SPICELAND

## COFFIN (Cont)
| | |
|---|---|
| 3- 5-1898 | William H & w Josephine & ch Walter, George, Ernest & Arthur gct West Grove MM |
| 2- 1-1902 | Walter rocf West Grove MM |
| 3- 5-1904 | William H & w Josephine & ch George, Ernest & Arthur rocf West Grove MM |
| 3- 7-1908 | Jessie Belva rocf New Garden MM |
| 6- 5-1909 | George gct Greens Fork MM |
| 4- 3-1915 | Mary rec in mbrp |
| 5- 5-1921 | Mable rec in mbrp |
| 2- 1-1923 | Mildred gct Fairmount MM |
| 5- 1-1924 | Ernest S & w Jessie Belva & ch Mahala, Edna May, Clifford, Esther Lois & Josephine gct Fairmount MM |
| 1- 1-1925 | Morris & w & s Charles gct Mooreland MM |
| 4- 2-1925 | Ella Benton rocf Whitewater MM |
| 12- 5-1929 | Wilbur rocf Rich Square MM |

## COHN
| | |
|---|---|
| 10- 9-1886 | Sarah E rec in mbrp |
| 1-17-1888 | Leah rec in mbrp |
| 5- 4-1889 | Leon & w Sarah gct New Castle MM |

## COLLINS
| | |
|---|---|
| 1- 6-1872 | Edward H rocf Westfield MM |
| 12-25-1874 | Edward H gct Westfield MM |
| 3- 4-1882 | Henry A & w Harriet rec in mbrp |
| 3- 6-1886 | Charles & Ella rec in mbrp |
| 9- 6-1890 | Ella rel on req |
| 3- 6-1915 | Etta & dts Mary Louise & Dorothy Elaine rec in mbrp |

## COMPTON
| | |
|---|---|
| 10-14-1876 | Phares & w Delitha Ann & ch Henry A, Anna Mary & Lindley M rocf West Branch MM, Oh |
| 10-14-1876 | Sylvia rocf West Branch MM, Oh |
| 12-16-1889 | Elvira D rec in mbrp |
| 5- 3-1890 | Henry A drpd from mbrp |
| 6- 2-1900 | Elva & s Donald rec in mbrp |
| 10-12-1901 | Effie E Gotschall gct New Castle MM |
| 4- 7-1921 | Daniel gct New Castle MM |
| 5- 6-1926 | Ruth E rel on req |

## COMSTOCK
| | |
|---|---|
| 12- 5-1885 | Joseph S rec in mbrp |
| 1- 1-1887 | J S transferred to Muncie MM |

## CONWAY
| | |
|---|---|
| 2- 5-1876 | Elihu rec in mbrp |
| 1- 6-1877 | Elihu & w Rhoda G gct New Garden MM |
| 1- 6-1883 | Rhoda G & dt Bertha rocf Richland MM |

## CONRAD
| | |
|---|---|
| 5- 2-1929 | Elaine, Raymond & Gertrude rec in mbrp |

## CONNELL
| | |
|---|---|
| 3- 4-1911 | Elsie Anderson rel on req |

## COOK
| | |
|---|---|
| (1-23-1833) | John, Sarah, Elizabeth, Nancy, Ruth & Catharine, minor ch of Isaac, decd & w Mary, (of Whitewater Mtg, Cherry Grove Mtg & Duck Creek Mtg) now living in the area that is now Spiceland MM |
| 3-19-1834 | John & Sarah ch of Mary (now Chestnut) gct Whitewater MM |
| 8-19-1835 | Elizabeth Cox (form Cook) mcd dis |
| 12-20-1837 | Wright & w Anna & ch Henry, Rebecca Wright jr, Anna & Naomi rocf Springfield MM |
| 3-20-1839 | Joseph prod a cerf from West Grove MM to m Rachel Patterson |
| 3-20-1839 | Joseph & Rachel Patterson altm |
| 3-20-1839 | For the accomodation of Joseph & Rachel Patterson, a mtg is appt at Elm Grove MH for tomorrow at the usual hour |
| 4-24-1839 | Rebecca Adamson (form Cook) mcd dis |
| 7-24-1839 | Rachel gct West Grove MM |
| 2-19-1840 | Thomas's parents give consent for m |
| 2-19-1840 | Thomas & Martha Unthank altm |
| 4-21-1852 | W D Macy req cert to Duck Creek MM to m Mary Cook |
| 12-20-1854 | Mary Ann rst with con of Flushing MM, Ohio |
| 11-21-1855 | Rachel rocf West Grove MM |
| 4-23-1856 | Rachel gct Walnut Ridge MM |
| 9-24-1856 | Mary Ann gct Red Cedar MM, Iowa |
| 11-20-1861 | Robert H & Martha A Nixon altm |
| 8- 5-1865 | Martha appt an Elder |
| 6- 6-1868 | Martha appt an overseer at Spiceland PM |
| 8- 6-1870 | Elihu con mcd |
| 9- 6-1870 | Elvira rec in mbrp |
| 8- 5-1871 | Martha appt an Elder |
| 9- 7-1872 | Elihu & w Elvira gct Springdale MM, Kan |
| 3- 1-1873 | Robert H & w Martha A & ch Lewellen & Caroline gct West Branch MM, Iowa |
| 4- 3-1875 | Thomas S & w Martha gct Lynn Grove MM, Iowa |
| 1- 6-1877 | Eli M gct Centre MM, Iowa |
| 12- 3-1887 | Thomas & w Martha rocf Muscoline MM, Iowa |
| 11- 5-1892 | Caroline rec in mbrp |
| 3- 4-1893 | Robert H & w Martha A & dt Luella rocf Lynn Grove MM, Iowa |
| 8- 7-1901 | Robert drpd from mbrp |
| 8- 9-1923 | Lindley & Corona Rayl rpt m |
| 11- 5-1928 | Corona Rayl gct Westland MM |

## COON
| | |
|---|---|
| 3- 4-1893 | Dalles & Florence rec in mbrp |

## COOPER
| | |
|---|---|
| 11-20-1839 | Richard Gause gct Elk MM, Oh to m Elizabeth Cooper |
| 12-20-1848 | Mary jr rocf Elk MM, Ohio |
| 11-24-1852 | Mary gct Elk MM, Oh |
| 3- 6-1886 | Minnie rec in mbrp |
| 2- 6-1892 | Minnie gct White River MM |
| 3- 7-1903 | Mary B rocf Knightstown MM |
| 7- 1-1905 | Homer M rec in mbrp |
| 4- 6-1918 | Homer drpd from mbrp |
| 3- 1-1919 | Mary & dt Mariam gct New Castle MM |

## COPELAND
| | |
|---|---|
| ( 9-20-1837) | John & Nathan ch of John Sr & Susannah mbrs of Duck Creek Mtg, now laid down, have been attached to Spiceland MM |
| 5-25-1842 | John & Nathan, ch of John & Susannah gct Bloomfield MM |
| 7-20-1842 | Joshua, Bloomfield MM rpts mcd, upl & na dis |
| 7-24-1844 | Sarah (form Morris) con mcd |
| 4-21-1852 | Eunice rocf Duck Creek MM |
| 12-24-1856 | Eunice gct Spring Creek MM, Iowa |
| 8- 5-1903 | Albert L of Plainfield, Ind m Alice H Barrets, wid, & dt Josiah, decd & Rhoda Hiatt of Henry Co, Ind |
| 10-10-1903 | Alice H gct Bridgeport MM |
| 2- 3-1912 | Charles E & Mary Georgia & dt Vernon Louise rec in mbrp |
| 5- 4-1912 | Eva rec in mbrp |
| 5- 4-1912 | John rec in mbrp |
| 2- 4-1926 | Frederick N & Lillian B & dt Emma May rec in mbrp |
| 5- 2-1929 | Edan Addison gct New Castle MM |

## COPPOCK
| | |
|---|---|
| 12-20-1837 | Union MM, Oh, compl to Duck Creek MM, (which has been laid down & mbrp attached to Spiceland MM) that Abram has na, upl, dr & fought his fellowmen. Mtg ask he be treated with |
| 1-24-1838 | Abram not appearing in a satisfactory mind, to make amends, so Union Mtg, Oh is thus informed |
| 7-25-1838 | Abram dis by Union Mtg, Oh |
| 7-25-1838 | Margaret rocf Union MM, Oh |
| 7-25-1838 | Mary, Rebecca, Seth & William Beals, minor ch of Abraham & Lydia rocf Union MM, Oh & end to Back Creek MM |
| 8-22-1838 | Fall Creek PM rpts that Aaron has dr & upl & that he now resides in the limits of Back Creek MM & req that Mtg to treat with him & rpt |
| 9-19-1838 | Dorcas Mote (form Coppock) con mcd |
| 10-24-1838 | Martha & ch Aaron, Dorcas, Margaret, Sarah, Martha Jane, David, Lydia & John gct Back Creek MM (w & ch of John) |
| 2-20-1839 | Back Creek Mtg rpts that Aaron produced an offering which was accepted. A comm appt to make an inq & if no obstructions to prep a cert of removal to that mtg |

SPICELAND

## COPPOCK (Cont)
|  |  |
|---|---|
| 3-20-1839 | Aaron gct Back Creek MM |
| 10-19-1842 | Margaret gct Union MM, Oh (this was the elderly widow of Aaron Sr, of Union MM, Oh She was Margaret (Tucker) Coppock, dt of Abe (or Abraham Tucker of Tenn) (She d 5- 6-1848, age 78 yrs & was bur in Union MM, Oh. She was the mth of the above Abraham & John Coppock  IBB) |

## COSAND
|  |  |
|---|---|
| 2-25-1857 | Charles & w Elvy & ch rocf Deep River MM, N C & end to Hopewell MM |
| 4- 1-1882 | John & w Malinda rocf Raysville MM |
| 1- 1-1915 | Lyman G & w Nora Carter rocf Barclay MM, Neb |
| 8- 9-1915 | Lyman G & Nora C gct Georgetown MM, Ill |

## COWGILL
|  |  |
|---|---|
| 11- 7-1868 | Samuel C prod cert from Fairfield MM, Oh to m |
| 11- 7-1868 | Samuel C & Caroline Macy altm |
| 11- 7-1868 | Samuel C & Caroline Macy req priv to accomp their m at home.  Req granted & mtg appt on next fourth day at half past 3 o'clock |
| 4- 3-1869 | Caroline M gct Fairfield MM, Oh |

## COX
|  |  |
|---|---|
| (1-23-1833) | Joseph & fam living in the area that became Spiceland |
| 11-20-1833 | Mary dis for na |
| 8-19-1835 | Elizabeth (form Cook) mcd  dis |
| 11-22-1843 | Gulielma Moffitt (form Cox) con mcd with 1st cousin |
| 4-23-1845 | Nathan Gause gct Milford MM, to m Ann Cox |
| 4-22-1850 | Rily con mcd  (s of Joseph) |
| 8-21-1850 | Exelion Moffitt (form Cox) mcd dis |
| 2-23-1852 | Rily dis |
| 7-23-1856 | Joseph J & w Lydia rocf Milford MM |
| 6-23-1858 | Joseph & w Ruth rocf Holly Spring MM, N C |
| 12-22-1858 | Joseph & w Lydia Ann gct Westfield MM |
| 10-24-1860 | William not producing a cert to m Elvira T Gause, the case is cont to next mtg |
| 11-21-1860 | William prod a cert from Milford MM to m but the mtg was inf he has accomplished his m contrary to discipline |
| 5-22-1861 | Elvira T gct Bridgeport MM |
| 8-20-1862 | William Gause gct Bridgeport MM, to m Jane M Cox |
| 2-25-1863 | Jeremiah T prod a cert from Bridgeport MM to m |
| 2-25-1863 | Jeremiah T & Lydia E Street  altm |
| 7- 7-1863 | Lydia S gct Bridgeport MM |
| 7- 4-1865 | Orpha Elizabeth rocf Bridgeport MM |
| 4- 1-1865 | Ruth dis |
| 9- 2-1876 | William Penn & w Sarah & ch Mahlon, Ira Edward, Ida Bell & Emma May rec in mbrp |
| 12- 5-1885 | William P & fam gct Honey Creek MM |
| 1- 7-1888 | Abbie B rec in mbrp |
| 1- 7-1888 | H Preston & s Exum Otis rec in mbrp |
| 4- 6-1892 | Preston & w Abbie & s Otis rel on req |
| 2- 2-1895 | Edgar James rocf Neuse MM, N C |
| 6- 2-1906 | Thomas J & w Mary rec in mbrp |
| 12- 7-1912 | Thomas drpd from mbrp |
| 4- 1-1920 | Mildred Mercer rel on req |
| 5- 4-1922 | J Edgar rel on req |

## CRETORS
|  |  |
|---|---|
| 4- 3-1897 | Adolphus & w Mary rec in mbrp |
| 7- 1-1899 | Adolphus & w rel on req |

## CRICKMORE
|  |  |
|---|---|
| 3- 4-1893 | Joseph, Emma, Pearl & Claude B rec in mbrp |
| 12- 5-1896 | Pearl rel on req |
| 12- 4-1915 | Claude rel on req |

## CRUM
|  |  |
|---|---|
| 11- 3-1883 | Mattie (Greentree) rec in mbrp |
| 1- 7-1889 | William P rec in mbrp |
| 2- 6-1892 | William P & w Martha G & dt Clara gct Hopewell MM |

## CUDE
|  |  |
|---|---|
| 11- 1-1884 | John rocf Hopewell MM |
| 3- 6-1886 | Rosabell rec in mbrp |
| 3- 6-1893 | Ida M rec in mbrp |
| 4- 7-1894 | Lizzie rec in mbrp |
| 3- 2-1895 | Ora rec in mbrp |

## CULBERTSON
|  |  |
|---|---|
| 8- 3-1867 | Martha & ch Ella & Victoria gct Westfield MM |

## CUNNINGHAM
|  |  |
|---|---|
| 12- 1-1900 | Rhoda (Ballenger) gct Indianapolis MM |

## DARLING
|  |  |
|---|---|
| 3- 4-1893 | William & Sarah E rec in mbrp |
| 4- 4-1903 | William & Elizabeth gct Muncie MM |

## DAUGHERTY
|  |  |
|---|---|
| 2- 4-1893 | Charles B rec in mbrp |
| 1- 3-1914 | Helen rec in mbrp |

## DAVENPORT
|  |  |
|---|---|
| 4- 7-1883 | Sarah Butler gct Raysville MM |

## DAVIS
|  |  |
|---|---|
| 1-23-1833 | Nathan & w Lydia & ch original mbrs |
| 1-23-1833 | Nathan Davis, William B Unthank, Josiah Pennington, Amer Bond, Aaron Stanley & Isaiah Baldwin, to unite with comm from women's mtg to form a comm to inspect & relieve the poor |
| 2-20-1833 | Jesse & ch John R, James S, Francis M, Jacob A, William S, Jonas M, Rufus H, Abigail & Mary Jane rocf New Garden MM |
| 8-21-1833 | Lydia appt to a comm |
| 12-25-1833 | Clarissa rocf White River MM |
| 6-21-1834 | Sarah rocf New Garden MM |
| 6-25-1834 | Sarah altm Benjamin Schooley |
| 11-19-1834 | Jesse & minor ch, Jacob A, William S, Jonas M, Rufus W, Abigail & Mary Jane gct New Garden MM |
| 3-25-1835 | John R gct New Garden MM |
| 8-19-1835 | Nathan Davis, David James, Isaac White, Calvin Wasson, Vierling Kersey, John Hiatt, George Evans, William Edwards & Joseph B Hunt appt to comm on Education for the ensuing year |
| 8-19-1835 | James gct Milford MM |
| 7-20-1836 | Clarissa gct White River MM |
| 10-19-1836 | Francis M gct Milford MM |
| 7-12-1837 | Jesse & ch William E, Rufus W & Mary J rocf Dover MM |
| ( 9-20-1837) | Tristrum jr & w Rebecca & ch mbr of Duck Creek Mtg, now laid down, have been attached to Spiceland Mtg |
| 4-25-1838 | Rebecca gct Westfield MM |
| 4-25-1838 | Tristrum jr & w Rebecca & ch Clarkson Elwood, Malinda, Lucinda, Irena, Delana & Henry gct Westfield MM |
| 10-23-1839 | Elizabeth & Joel Johnson altm |
| 10-21-1840 | Nathan gct Springborough MM, Oh to m Mary Stanton |
| 12-23-1840 | Abigail rocf Mississinewa MM |
| 4-21-1841 | Mary S rocf Springborough MM, Oh |
| 6-23-1841 | James rocf Milford MM |
| 9-22-1841 | Mary Davis & William B Albertson  altm |
| 9-22-1841 | For the convenience of Mary Davis & William B Albertson for their m, a mtg has been granted at Elm Grove MH, tomorrow at 11 o'clock |
| 10-20-1841 | Jesse & Mary Gordon altm |
| 2-23-1842 | Gulielma rocf White River MM |
| 10-19-1842 | William S of Elm Grove PM dis for na & dp |
| 12-25-1844 | Joseph B rocf White River MM |
| 1-22-1845 | Joseph B & Parthena Jones altm |
| 8-20-1845 | Eliza & Priscilla rec in mbrp |
| 12-24-1845 | Joseph B & Parthena gct Milford MM |
| 6-24-1846 | Elizabeth rocf Duck Creek MM |
| 8-23-1848 | Jonas M rocf Milford MM |
| 6-21-1848 | Hannah Ann & John A Hunnicutt inf mtg of int to m |
| 7-19-1848 | The consent of Hannah Ann's father not being produced, a comm appt to find the reason for it being withheld & directed to rpt to next mtg |
| 8-23-1848 | Hannah Ann & John A Hunnicutt now altm |
| 5-23-1849 | Gulielma & Joseph S Brazington altm (consent of her father has been given) |

SPICELAND

## DAVIS (Cont)
|  |  |
|---|---|
| 8-22-1849 | Mary Jane Harvey (form Davis) mcd with a non-mbr, dis |
| 1-23-1850 | John mcd dis |
| 3-20-1850 | James dis |
| 11-20-1850 | Priscilla Woods (form Davis) con mcd |
| 8-20-1851 | Betsy Ann (form Rayl) jas, mcd, dis |
| 10-22-1851 | Nathan gct Duck Creek MM, to m Jane Dickey |
| 3-24-1852 | Jane rocf Duck Creek MM (3rd w of Nathan) |
| 10-19-1853 | Eliza L & Nathan P Gause altm |
| 11-24-1855 | Jonas M gct Vermillion MM, Ill |
| 10-24-1855 | Elizabeth gct Spring Creek MM, Iowa |
| 11-19-1856 | Jane, wid of Nathan, & Luke Wiles altm |
| 3-25-1857 | Rufus gct Vermillion MM, Ill to m Lydia Hornaday |
| 10-21-1857 | Asa C mcd, dis |
| 4-21-1858 | Rufus W gct Vermillion MM, Ill |
| 9-19-1860 | Mary rocf Raysville MM |
| 10-14-1865 | Clarkson & w Hannah (Brown) rocf Whitewater MM |
| 1-6-1866 | Asa C & w Mary rec on req |
| 12-6-1867 | Asa C appt an overseer at Dunreith PM |
| 6-6-1868 | Asa C appt an overseer at Dunreith PM |
| 6-3-1871 | Asa C appt an overseer |
| 6-7-1873 | Asa C reappointed as a Trustee of Spiceland Academy |
| 1-3-1874 | Asa C appt asst clerk & William Edgerton appt clerk |
| 9-2-1882 | Deborah D rocf New Garden MM |
| 10-14-1905 | Rosa rocf West Grove MM |
| 3-2-1912 | Charles Everett roc |
| 10-4-1913 | Everett gct Hopewell MM |
| 1-6-1921 | Mrs Rosa gct New Castle MM |

## DAWSON
|  |  |
|---|---|
| 7-23-1862 | William produced a cert from Duck Creek MM to m |
| 7-23-1862 | William & Abigail Hammer altm |
| 9-23-1863 | William rocf Duck Creek MM |
| 8-1-1903 | Charity Luella rocf Knightstown MM |

## DEAN
|  |  |
|---|---|
| 4-24-1833 | Gulielma rocf Union MM, N Car & end by New Garden MM |
| 2-24-1836 | Gulielma altm John S Pike |
| 12-20-1837 | Maria rocf Dover MM, N C |
| 2-19-1840 | Maria & Joseph Mendenhall altm |
| 4-21-1841 | Uriah rocf Dover MM, N C and end to Duck Creek MM |

## DEEM
|  |  |
|---|---|
| 5-21-1851 | Hannah (form Stratton) mcd dis |
| 7-7-1866 | Elizabeth gct Plainfield MM |
| 3-5-1876 | Se ley? A rec in mbrp |
| 4-7-1900 | Elizabeth & dt Nora Symons rec in mbrp |
| 6-1-1901 | Elizabeth rocf Knightstown MM |
| 5-5-1921 | Charlotte rec in mbrp |
| 5-4-1922 | Dorothy rec in mbrp |
| 8-2-1923 | Marshall gct Dublin MM |

## DELON
|  |  |
|---|---|
| 1-5-1880 | David rocf Duck Creek MM |
| 2-7-1914 | Frank rec in mbrp |

## DENNIS
|  |  |
|---|---|
| 8-4-1883 | Henry C rocf Springfield MM |
| 3-6-1886 | John & w Mary & ch Clarkson & Ada Viola rec in mbrp |
| 8-2-1890 | Henry gct New Castle MM |
| 5-5-1906 | John, Mary & Clarence drpd from mbrp |

## DENNY
|  |  |
|---|---|
| 10-6-1926 | Silas G & w rec in mbrp |

## DESELMS - DISHELMS
|  |  |
|---|---|
| 3-21-1838 | Consent of surviving parents now had Jonas & Elizabeth Hosier altm |
| 9-19-1838 | Clearsprings PM rpts that Jonas has been telling untruths & using deceptions to injure his neighbour |
| 11-21-1838 | The friends appt to investigate compl against Jonas, rpt "We. . . unite in believing the rpts to be unsubstantial" & Clearspring Mtg is so inf |

## DEULA - DULEA
|  |  |
|---|---|
| 5-23-1838 | Marlborough Mtg, Starke Co, Oh, req Spiceland to treat with Maxson for dr & upl |
| 7-25-1838 | The comm appt to treat with Maxson, rpt him not of the mind to make satisfaction & so inf Marlborough Mtg, Oh |
| 12-19-1838 | Lydia & ch William, Susan, Sina Jane, Elwood, Elizann, Mary, Lydia & John gct Mississinewa MM, Ind |
| 4-24-1839 | Maxson dis by Marlborough Mtg, Oh |

## DICKEY
|  |  |
|---|---|
| 9-20-1837 | (Nimrod & w Ann & ch Phebe, Jane, Charity, Mary Ann, James & Asenath were mbrs of Duck Creek, now laid down, whose mbrp attached to Spiceland MM) |
| 12-20-1837 | Charity & David Kendall altm |
| 4-22-1840 | Jane gct White River MM |
| 10-22-1851 | Nathan Davis gct Duck Creek MM, to m Jane Dickey |

## DICKINSON
|  |  |
|---|---|
| 1-20-1864 | Charles & w Hannah & ch Henry Wilson, Benajah, Joshua Ingle & Harriett Elizabeth rocf Kansas MM, Kan |
| 10-14-1871 | Henry, Kansas MM rpts mcd |
| 1-6-1872 | Henry con mcd |
| 4-6-1872 | Henry W gct Kansas MM, Kan |
| 3-7-1874 | Benajah H gct Whitewater MM |
| 3-2-1878 | Henry W & w Rebecca J & ch Irvin rocf Hope MM |
| 11-5-1881 | Henry W & w Rebecca J & ch Irvin & Eliza gct White River MM |
| 2-6-1909 | Henry W & w Rebecca J rocf Greentown MM |
| 2-1-1919 | Henry W & w Rebecca Jane rocf 1st Friends Church, Marion |

## DICKS
|  |  |
|---|---|
| 1-23-1833 | Job & w Hannah & ch original mbrs |
| 1-22-1840 | Naomi H & Joseph Newby altm |
| 11-22-1843 | Sally W & William R Macy altm |
| 10-21-1846 | Elizabeth W & Daniel C Allen altm |
| 12-25-1850 | Louisa McCombs (form Dix) con mcd |
| 11-23-1853 | Nathan & Nancy C Allen altm |
| 9-23-1857 | William dis |
| 12-23-1863 | Milton S gct Pipe Creek MM |
| 1-3-1885 | Allen rel on req |
| 1-1-1887 | Allen C rec in mbrp |
| 6-2-1894 | Allen C & w Mary P & ch Ada Virginia & Nathan Russell gct Fairmount MM |
| 6-1-1901 | Nancy & Gurney gct Fairmount MM |

## DILHORN
|  |  |
|---|---|
| 11-20-1839 | Robert & w Sarah & ch Joshua, William & Ann Maria rocf Whitewater MM |

## DILLIE
|  |  |
|---|---|
| 2-7-1880 | Daniel D & w Mary A rec in mbrp |
| 8-4-1883 | David D drpd from mbrp |
| 11-3-1883 | Mary A drpd from mbrp |

## DILLON
|  |  |
|---|---|
| 1-20-1836 | Gulielma (wid of Absolem) & ch Allen H, Nathan, Mary Ann, Maria Jane, Naomi & Sarah rocf New Garden MM |
| ( 9-20-1837) | Jonathan Sr & w Agnes & ch Elizabeth, Jonathan jr & Sarah, mbrs of Duck Creek Mtg, now laid down, have been attached to Spiceland Mtg |
| 2-21-1838 | Gulielma Williams (form Hiatt) (wid of Absalom) mcd, dis |
| 3-21-1838 | Samuel rocf Centre MM, Oh |
| 6-20-1838 | Jonathan appt an overseer |
| 3-20-1839 | Elizabeth Pence (form Dillon) con mcd |
| 5-22-1839 | Allen H, Nathan, Mary Ann, Maria Jane & Sarah, ch of Absalom, decd, gct Vermillion MM, Ill |
| 6-23-1852 | William rocf Blue River MM |

## DIMMIT
|  |  |
|---|---|
| 3-7-1891 | Charity rec in mbrp |
| 3-4-1893 | John & Elizabeth rec in mbrp |
| 6-2-1900 | John & w Elizabeth Jane gct Hopewell MM |

SPICELAND

DOGGETT
6- 1-1889        Sarah Ellen rel on req

DOUGHERTY - (DAUGHERTY)
2- 4-1893        Charles rec
1- 3-1914        Helen rec

DRAPER
11-19-1834       Samuel Prichard & w Harriet & their ch
                 Martha, Anna & David Prichard, and 2 minor
                 ch under their care, Rebecca & William
                 Draper (ch of Samuel decd & Mary (Albert-
                 son) Draper, of N C) rocf New Garden MM
( 9-20-1837)     Jemima & step-dt, Mary Ann, mbrs of Duck
                 Creek M, now laid down, attached to
                 Spiceland Mtg
4-25-1838        Mary Ann gct Mississinewa MM
1-23-1839        Jemima & Benjamin Schooley altm
8-19-1840        Huldah Stanbrough (form Draper) con mcd
7-19-1843        William, a minor, gct Blue River MM
                 (s of Samuel, decd)
10-23-1844       Rebecca gct Blue River MM (dt Samuel, decd)
6-25-1856        Catherine rocf Duck Creek MM
6-25-1856        Mary rocf Duck Creek MM
2-24-1864        Noah & fam rocf Mississinewa MM
9-21-1864        Catherine gct Duck Creek MM
9-21-1864        Mary gct Duck Creek MM
10-11-1890       Emily Griffin gct Duck Creek MM, returned
                 1- 2-1891 non-residence
10- 8-1892       Emma gct Duck Creek MM
3- 5-1898        Luther O & w Emma & dt Jessie Cleta rocf
                 Duck Creek MM
5- 5-1921        Esther rec in mbrp

DUGAN
2- 1-1873        Sarah J gct Oak Ridge MM

DUKE
12- 7-1907       Raymond rec in mbrp
4- 1-1911        Raymond rel on req

DUNLOP
8-23-1843        Lydia (form Soper) mcd, dis

DYER
( 9-20-1837      George H & fam were mbrs of Duck Creek M
                 now laid down) attached to Spiceland Mtg
11-22-1837       George H & ch Mahala, Rebecca, Isaac &
                 Ruth gct New Garden MM

DYSART
5-20-1840        Rachel (form Kirk) con mcd

EASTRIDGE
4- 7-1900        Eva & Lena rec in mbrp
12- 7-1912       Lena gct New Castle MM

EDGERTON
1-25-1837        Walter & w Rebecca & ch William & Sarah
                 rocf Milford MM
8- 9-1837        Walter appt to comm on Education for
                 ensuing year
10-24-1838       Susanna & Mahlon Tomlinson inf mtg of int
                 to m  Her parents have given consent
11-21-1838       Susanna & Mahlon Tomlinson altm (for the
                 accomodation of Susannah & Mahlon Tomlinson
                 in the accomplishment of their m, a meeting
                 is apptd for tomorrow at Duck Creek MH
                 at the usual hour)
7-24-1839        Walter appt asst clerk & Jason Williams
                 appt clerk
1-22-1840        Reuben appt an overseer
10-19-1842       Diana & Calvin Macy altm
11-22-1843       Walter dis, jas    (ASF)
1-24-1844        Rebecca dis, jas   (ASF)
7-22-1846        William & w Hannah & ch Mary Jane & Rebecca
                 Ann rocf Walnut Ridge MM
4-20-1853        William jas, mcd, dis
3-21-1860        William & w Hannah & dt Annetta Ellen gct
                 Red Cedar MM, Iowa
9-24-1862        Walter, William & Caroline rst on req
9- 7-1869        Walter gct Green Plain MM, Oh to m Eliza A
                 (Chalfont) Negus
11- 4-1872       Eliza A rocf Green Plain MM, Oh
1- 3-1874        William appt clerk & Asa C Davis appt asst
                 clerk
3- 4-1875        William appt an overseer in place of
                 Valentine Hollingsworth, decd
8- 5-1876        Walter dis
5- 5-1883        Caroline appt an Elder

EDMUNDSON
4- 7-1894        Lena rec in mbrp

EDWARDS
1-23-1833        William appt to comm
1-23-1833        Elizabeth appt to comm
2-25-1835        David rocf Miami MM, Oh
8-19-1835        William Edwards, David James, Isaac White,
                 Calvin Wasson, Vierling Kersey, John Hiatt,
                 George Evans, Nathan Davis & Joseph B Hunt
                 appt to comm on Education for the ensuing
                 year
2-24-1836        William Edwards, William Macy & Samuel
                 Pritchard appt at Elm Grove PM to receive
                 & hold a deed to real estate at that place
2-22-1837        William Edwards, Samuel Pritchard &
                 William Macy appt to receive and hold in
                 trust, deeds to Elm Grove PM for land on
                 which the MH now stands & the land
                 purchased from Nathan Gause for a burying
                 ground
11-21-1838       David & Susanna Pennington altm
2-24-1841        Elizabeth rec as Minister at Spiceland PM
3-23-1843        William appt overseer in room of Tidamon
                 Jessop
6-21-1843        David & Susan & dt Eliza Ann gct Miami MM,
                 Oh
4-24-1844        Anna & Nathan C Hill altm
9-25-1844        William appt an overseer
10-23-1844       William appt asst clerk & Thomas S Teas
                 appt clerk
12-25-1844       David & w Susanna & dt Eliza Ann rocf
                 Miami MM, Oh
8-25-1847        William appt an overseer at Elm Grove PM
1-19-1848        William Edwards & Nathan Macy appt to a
                 comm on burials within the limits of Elm
                 Grove PM
10-24-1849       David Edwards & Solomon Gause appt over-
                 seers at Elm Grove PM
10-24-1849       William appt asst clerk & John M Macy
                 appt clerk
10-23-1850       David appt asst clerk & Caleb Johnson
                 appt clerk
7-23-1851        Ruth rocf New Garden MM, N C
5-21-1856        David appt Treasurer in place of the decd
                 Treasurer
11-19-1856       Jonathan J dis
3-24-1858        David appt asst clerk
2- 2-1860        David reappointed Recorder of m Certifs
5-23-1860        Jonathan J dis
5-23-1860        David appt as a Trustee for real estate
                 at Elm Grove PM
11-23-1864       David reappointed a Trustee
4- 6-1867        Susannah rec as Minister
1- 1-1870        William appt asst clerk & Elisha B
                 Ratcliff appt clerk
7- 2-1870        Henry L con mcd
8- 3-1872        Lindley M con mcd
9- 5-1874        Surviving parent having consented to m of
                 Nathaniel & Margery Harvey, they have req
                 a mtg apptd at the residence of John P
                 Pennington on the 22nd of this month at
                 4 o'clock P M for the purpose of solemniz-
                 ing their m  The req was granted
3- 6-1875        Nathaniel & Margery A gct Raysville MM
1- 1-1881        William G rocf Raysville MM
5- 5-1883        William G appt an Elder
6- 6-1885        David William gct Philadelphia MM, Pa
                 Western District, to m Fanny Lytle
12- 8-1890       David W gct Indianapolis MM
12- 6-1890       Josiah P gct Whitewater MM
3- 4-1893        Harriet rec in mbrp
6- 3-1899        J P rocf Whitewater MM
11- 1-1902       Harriett gct New Castle MM
11- 2-1907       Henry L rel on req

SPICELAND

### EDWARDS (Cont)
| | |
|---|---|
| 12- 7-1918 | Josiah gct Knightstown MM |
| 7- 6-1922 | Carlton E gct 1st Friends Church, Indianapolis |

### ELLIOTT
| | |
|---|---|
| 4-24-1833 | Hannah rocf Westfield MM |
| 10-23-1833 | Obadiah jr & w Armella rocf Center MM, N C & end to Duck Creek MM |
| 7-25-1838 | Martha N, Mary T, & Eliza A rocf Blue River MM (dts of James & Sarah) |
| 8-22-1838 | Anna & Joel Wright altm |
| 8-22-1838 | Sarah's consent, the mother of Martha N is produced in writing |
| 8-22-1838 | Martha N & Jordan Albertson altm |
| 8-21-1839 | Malinda & Joab Wright altm |
| 1-19-1842 | Sarah rocf Blue River MM |
| 5-24-1843 | Mary Eliza, a minor, rec in mbrp by req of her grandmother, Sarah Elliott |
| 4-19-1848 | Mary (form Reynard) con mcd |
| 9-20-1848 | Richard P produced cert from Duck Creek MM to m Martha E Pritchard |
| 9-20-1848 | Richard P & Martha E Pritchard altm |
| 9-20-1848 | At the req of Richard P & Martha E Pritchard a mtg is granted to be held at Raysville MH tomorrow at 11 o'clock, to accomplish their m |
| 1-24-1849 | Richard P rocf Duck Creek MM |
| 6-20-1849 | Elias & w Martha & ch William Scott, Patrick Henry, David Sanders, James Nixon & Mary Jane rocf Deep River MM, N C & end by Cherry Grove MM |
| 4-23-1851 | Jane Walker (form Elliott) jas, mcd, dis |
| 2-23-1853 | William mcd dis |
| 3-23-1853 | Mary Eliza & Henry Bundy altm |
| 4-20-1853 | Mary Eliza & Henry Bundy did not produce the m cert. The comm is to produce it at next mtg |
| 5-25-1853 | The comm did produce the m cert for Mary Eliza & Henry Bundy |
| 6-22-1853 | Mary Greenstreet (form Elliott) mcd dis |
| 8-24-1853 | Elias & Jane Cain altm |
| 4-19-1854 | Nathan & w Mary Ann & ch Abigail P, Lurania, Joseph John Gurney, William Penn & James W rocf Symons Creek MM, N C |
| 10-25-1854 | Richard P appt asst clerk & John M Macy appt clerk |
| 3-21-1855 | Nathan & w Mary Ann & ch Abigail P, Lurania, Joseph John, William P & James gct Spring Creek MM, Iowa |
| 10-24-1855 | Richard P appt asst clerk & Seth W Pearson appt clerk |
| 12- 3-1870 | John P Pennington gct Milford MM, Ind to m Melissa J Elliott |
| 5- 3-1873 | Patrick Henry & ch Emma Caroline, Ida Florence, Laura Belle & Charles Sumner rec in mbrp |
| 1- 8-1877 | Emily gct Duck Creek MM |
| 8- 7-1880 | Martha & s John J rocf Raysville MM |
| 4- 7-1883 | Harriett A gct Walnut Ridge MM |
| 11- 3-1883 | Martha & s John J gct Raysville MM |
| 5- 3-1884 | John B & fam rocf Dublin MM |
| 8- 7-1886 | Lavina rec in mbrp |
| 8- 6-1892 | Eva (Bowman) drpd from mbrp |
| 2- 4-1893 | Martha E rocf Raysville MM |
| 8- 6-1898 | John B & w Martha & ch Maude M, J Harry & E Marvin gct Whitewater MM |
| 2- 2-1901 | Bertha rocf Amboy MM |

### ELLIS
| | |
|---|---|
| 12-24-1856 | William Macy gct Duck Creek MM to m Lydia Ellis |
| 8-24-1859 | Stephen A Guase gct Duck Creek MM to m Martha Ellis |
| 7- 7-1866 | Rachel M rocf Duck Creek MM |
| 8- 4-1866 | Rachel M & Stephen A Guase altm |
| 2- 2-1867 | George Symons gct Plainfield MM to m Mariam Ellis |

### ELZEY
| | |
|---|---|
| 2-24-1836 | Jared (Garard) & w Susanna & ch Absalom VICKARY & Sarah Ann, John, Nancy & William ELLZY gct Mill Creek MM |

### ELMORE
| | |
|---|---|
| 8- 7-1875 | Ann Eliza & ch Clara Viola FELLOW & Josephene Frances & Ann Eliza ELMORE rocf New Hope MM |
| 11- 2-1878 | Charles Beeson & w Eliza & ch Joseph, Samuel, Jonathan & Olive BEESON & Josephine Frances & Ann Eliza ELMORE gct Fairmount MM |

### EMMINGER
| | |
|---|---|
| 3- 6-1897 | James M & ch Vera & Jessie rec in mbrp |
| 4- 7-1906 | Charles Henry & Lena May rec in mbrp |
| 7- 2-1910 | Harry & Lena gct Winona MM, Oh |

### ENDSLEY
| | |
|---|---|
| 7- 3-1920 | Elsie Hall rel on req |

### ENGLISH
| | |
|---|---|
| 3- 4-1893 | Ruth Delia & ch Caroline, Leslie, Ratie & Freddie L rec in mbrp |
| 3- 2-1895 | Hugh L rec in mbrp |
| 12- 7-1912 | Fred L rel on req |
| 9- 4-1930 | Ruth D & Caroline drpd from mbrp |

### ESTES
| | |
|---|---|
| 10-11-1879 | Ludovice rocf Wilmington MM, Oh |
| 12- 3-1881 | Belle C rec in mbrp |
| 8- 3-1895 | Lewis Alden rel on req of parents |
| 9- 7-1895 | Ludovice & w Belle rel on req |

### ESSINGTON
| | |
|---|---|
| 4- 6-1918 | Cass rec in mbrp |

### EVANS
| | |
|---|---|
| 1-23-1833 | George appt Clerk for the day |
| 1-23-1833 | Mary appt to a comm |
| 2-20-1833 | George appt clerk with Jesse White as asst Clerk |
| 2-20-1833 | George Evans, William Unthank, Thomas Maudlin & Aaron Stanley appt as Spiceland MM's representatives to ensuing Quarterly Mtg |
| 3-20-1833 | George Evans, Isaac White, William Unthank & Driver Boon appt to comm to attend funerals of our mbrs |
| 6-19-1833 | George Evans & Isaac White appt to correct & record minutes of the mtg |
| 9-24-1834 | George appt to station of Elder |
| 8-19-1835 | George Evans, David James, Isaac White, Calvin Wasson, Vierling Kersey, John Hiatt, William Edwards, Nathan Davis & Joseph B Hunt appt to comm on Education for the ensuing year |
| 2-22-1837 | George Evans, Solomon Macy, Richard Gordon & William B Unthank appt at Spiceland Mtg, to receive & hold in trust, a deed for land on which the school house now stands |
| 6-20-1838 | George appt asst clerk & Jason Williams appt clerk |
| 4-20-1842 | Asenith & Caleb Johnson altm |
| 6-19-1844 | Mary appt to station of an Elder at Spiceland mtg |
| 1-19-1848 | Owen gct Duck Creek MM, to m Martha Ann Price |
| 1-19-1848 | George Evans, William Unthank, Solomon Macy & Aaron Stanley appt as a comm on burials within the limits of Spiceland Mtg |
| 12-20-1848 | Martha Ann rocf Duck Creek MM |
| 11-19-1851 | Sarah & Jacob Taylor altm |
| 9-20-1854 | Richard gct Duck Creek MM to m Lydia Jane Pickering |
| 1-24-1855 | Owen dis |
| 7-25-1855 | Lydia Jane rocf Duck Creek MM |
| 7-23-1856 | Martha Ann gct Winneshiek MM, Iowa (w of Owen) |
| 1-19-1859 | Richard con mcd |
| 9-25-1861 | George gct Raysville MM to m Martha Albertson, a wid |
| 12-25-1861 | Martha rocf Raysville MM |
| 2- 3-1866 | Martha Ann & ch Adaline, George, Rice, Narcissa, Mary E & Marion rocf Minneapolis MM, Minn |
| 6- 2-1866 | Richard & s gct New Salem MM |

SPICELAND

EVANS (Cont)
6- 2-1866  Martha gct Raysville MM
10-13-1866  Thomas & Martha Hiatt altm
8- 3-1872  Alfred White gct Maryville MM, Tenn to m Elizabeth Evans
11- 3-1883  Martha Ann & Mary rel on req
12- 1-1883  Narcissa gct Duck Creek MM
12- 1-1883  Marion gct Duck Creek MM
4- 3-1915  Martha rec in mbrp
4- 6-1918  Helen rec in mbrp
5- 5-1921  Helen rec in mbrp
5- 5-1921  Thomas rec in mbrp
12- 2-1926  Gayelle rec in mbrp
5- 3-1928  Virginia rec in mbrp

EWING
2- 7-1914  Varter rec in mbrp
5- 5-1921  Theresa rec in mbrp

FARRINGTON
11- 6-1869  James con mcd
11- 3-1888  James drpd from mbrp

FAWCETT
6- 6-1874  John W & w Maria E rocf Duck Creek MM
3- 6-1886  Alpheus E & Mary rec on req
9- 1-1888  Maria & ch Ervin Earl & Kenneth A gct Wichitaw MM, Kan
4- 5-1890  Alpheus rel on req
5- 5-1921  Guy & Glenn rec in mbrp

FAY
6- 4-1892  Martha (Talbert) gct Stanwood MM, Kan

FEASEL
9- 3-1881  Rebecca rel on req

FELLOW
6-23-1858  Susanna restored
8-25-1858  Elijah C rst with/con New Salem MM
3-21-1860  Henry C s Elijah & Susanna rec in mbrp
10-23-1861  Elijah C & w Susanna & ch Henry C gct Westfield MM
1- 1-1876  Alpheus rec on req
2- 6-1892  Alpheus L & w Orpha Elizabeth & ch Walter & Mary B gct Amboy MM

FENTRESS
10-14-1865  Cynthia & Jesse B Jessup inf mtg of int to m. She is not a mbr of our Society
11- 4-1865  Cynthia & Jesse B Jessup altm
12- 7-1867  Cynthia Jessop & ch Martin, Frank & Estelle Fentress rec on req
5- 5-1883  Martin gct Raysville MM

FIELDS
4- 5-1913  Cecil rec on req

FIFER
8- 6-1904  Henry & w Mary rocf West Grove MM

FINKLE
2-24-1841  Nancy (form Wright) mcd  dis

FLANNIGAN
4- 1-1920  Barney & w Maria & ch Lavira & George rec in mbrp

FLETCHER
5-20-1835  Zachariah & w Anne & Rachel BREWER, a minor, rocf Milford MM
7-22-1835  Zachariah appt to comm
1-20-1847  Zachariah & w Ann & ch Henry Francis, Augustus & Margaret Ann gct Milford MM
9-21-1853  Zachariah & w Anne & ch Henry, Margaret & James Johnson rocf Milford MM
7- 1-1889  Silas rec on req
8- 5-1890  Joel rec on req
9- 5-1903  Joel gct Duck Creek MM

FLINN
9- 5-1903  Laura Hodson drpd from mbrp

FORBIS
1- 1-1876  Mary H rec on req
12- 3-1886  Mary drpd from mbrp

FOREMAN
11-23-1836  Mary rocf Milford MM
11-23-1836  Elizabeth rocf Milford MM

FORT
1- 2-1875  Milton P & Lydia V rec on req
6- 2-1883  Milton P & Lydia V drpd from mbrp
6- 1-1901  Leone Hiatt gct Knightstown MM

FOSTER
1-23-1833  Joseph & w Mary & ch original mbrs
7-22-1835  Joseph appt to comm
5-24-1843  Spiceland PM compl of Joseph making a lewd proposition to a female. A comm appt to treat with him
6-21-1843  Joseph con his act, which mtg accepts
10-21-1846  Jemima & Adam Griffin altm
8-23-1847  Sally rocf New Garden MM, N C
10-25-1848  Anna J rocf New Garden MM, N C
12-19-1849  Anna J Carter (form Foster) con mcd
9-25-1850  Robert rocf New Garden MM, N C end by Duck Creek MM
10-25-1850  Sarah & dts Samira M & Margaret A rocf New Garden MM, N C
10-25-1850  Joshua & fam (rocf New Garden MM, N C)
8-20-1851  Asenath B rocf Duck Creek MM
12-24-1851  Robert dis
9-23-1852  Elijah dis
3-23-1853  Esther Pickett (form Foster) mcd
9-21-1853  Ruth S & Thomas A Wilson altm
8-22-1855  John H rocf New Garden MM, N C
10-24-1855  Samuel mcd  dis
11-19-1856  Asenath gct Walnut Ridge MM
4-23-1862  Phebe Ann rocf Raysville MM
12-22-1862  Jason mcd  dis
5- 6-1865  Jason rec on req
1- 4-1868  Elijah & w Mary M & ch Martha Ellen, Christopher Columbus, Elijah Ellsworth & William rec in mbrp
4- 4-1868  Robert J & w Susannah rec on req
11- 6-1869  Robert J con mcd
9- 3-1870  Robert J & ch Rollin & Jonathan Lewis gct Dover MM
2- 5-1876  John M rec on req
1- 6-1877  Jesse C gct Honey Creek MM, Iowa
12-16-1879  Sarah Ellen rocf Cherry Grove MM
6- 2-1883  John M drpd from mbrp
8- 4-1883  Jason drpd from mbrp
5- 3-1890  Ellsworth drpd from mbrp
12- 7-1912  Walter, Harry & John drpd from mbrp
4- 3-1915  Everett rec in mbrp

FOUST
11- 4-1876  Emil J gct Carthage MM

FOX
12- 1-1927  William D & w Edna & dt Jeanette rocf Amboy MM

FOXWORTHY
8- 4-1921  Theodore & w Estelle rocf Central City MM, Neb
9- 6-1923  Theodore & w Estelle gct Whitewater MM

FRANCIS
3- 4-1882  David H & Maria & ch Ida M, Gertie, William R & Odel rec in mbrp
4- 4-1891  Ida rec in mbrp

FRANKLIN
12- 7-1922  Thelma rec in mbrp

FREEMAN
12- 7-1867  Nancy (form Wiles) mcd,  dis

FRY
7- 6-1878  William rec in mbrp
3- 2-1895  Annetta & dt Vada Lucile rec in mbrp
3- 7-1914  Annetta & Ethel Irene rel on req
3- 7-1914  Vada Lucile rel on req

SPICELAND

## FURBY
4-21-1858    Mary & ch rocf Warwichshire North MM, England, end to Raysville MM

## FUSSEN
6- 4-1887    Mary gct Muncie MM

## FUSSELL
5- 5-1906    Ella rec in mbrp

## GANDY
3- 7-1908    Paul rec in mbrp

## GANNAWAY
2- 7-1903    Caroline Cornelia & Hugh Boyd, ch of Minnie J (& husb Robert) rec in mbrp
4- 7-1906    Mary Louise rec in mbrp
3- 2-1907    Minnie (Charles) & ch Caroline Cornelia, Hugh Boyd & Mary Louise rel on req

## GARD
5- 7-1870    Philander & fam rec in mbrp

## GARDNER
1-23-1839    Hannah (form Chew) rpt mcd
4- 3-1876    Francis rec in mbrp
5- 3-1876    Lydia Marcella rec in mbrp
4- 7-1883    Francis gct Salem MM
2- 2-1884    Hugh & w Lydia & ch Ella Maurine & Lawrence rocf Salem MM
12- 2-1899    Ruby rec in mbrp
4- 7-1906    Lawrence & fam gct Knightstown MM

## GARNER
7- 7-1921    Herman rocf Shirley MM

## GARWOOD
3- 3-1877    David & w Mary E & ch Herbert W & Foster J rocf Oskaloosa MM, Iowa
1- 6-1883    David C appt Recording Clerk to enter Minutes, Certificates of Removal, Births & Deaths, Resignations & Disownments All persons previously appt to care for & record the above information are now released
11- 7-1885    David & Mary his wife gct

## GAUNT
1-24-1838    Jemima Pearson (form Gaunt) mcd dis
10-24-1839    Matilda Sheridan (form Gant) con mcd
11- 3-1883    Adaline Evans rec in mbrp
6- 7-1890    Adaline gct Marion MM
8- 8-1890    Adaline drpd from mbrp

## GAUSE
4-23-1834    Eli & w Martha & ch Ruth, Richard, Nathan, Samuel, Hannah, Eli jr, Aaron & Charles rocf Elk MM, Oh
4-23-1834    Jesse rocf Elk MM, Oh
4-23-1834    James P rocf Elk MM, Oh
10-22-1834    James P & Rachel Johnson inf mtg of int to m. The parents' consent being produced
11-19-1834    James P altm Rachel Johnson
5-20-1835    Eli appt to the comm to att Quarterly Mtg
3-23-1836    Solomon rocf Elk MM, Oh
3-23-1836    Nathan Sr & w Mary & ch Joseph, Isaac, Nathan, Stephen A & Mary rocf Milford MM
3-23-1836    Ann rocf Elk MM, Oh
3-23-1836    Ruth rocf Elk MM, Oh
8-24-1836    Eli appt to comm on Education for ensuing year
8-23-1837    Eli & w Lydia rocf Elk MM, Oh
8-23-1837    Solomon gct Milford MM to m Celia Stubbs
11-22-1837    Eli appt to have care of deeds etc of Spiceland Mtg
12-20-1837    Celia rocf Milford MM
8-22-1838    Jesse & Ann Stanbrough inf mtg of int to m His parents' consent was produced in writing
9-19-1838    Jesse & Ann Stanbrough altm
11-21-1838    Nathan, a minor, s of Eli gct New Garden MM
11-20-1839    Richard gct Elk MM, Oh to m Elizabeth Cooper
1-22-1840    Richard appt Librarian at Spiceland PM in place of the former one, now decd
3-25-1840    Elizabeth rocf Elk MM, Oh
8-19-1840    Richard, Librarian at Spiceland PM rpt decd
11-25-1840    Eli appt to station of Elder
5-19-1841    Nathan rocf New Garden MM
8-25-1841    Ruth & James Binford altm
2-23-1842    Isaac & Abigail Small altm
2-22-1843    Anna & Josiah Stanley altm
5-24-1843    Nathan P gct New Garden MM, to m Susanna Mills
8-23-1843    Hannah B & James B Parker altm
11-22-1843    Susanna rocf New Garden MM
12-20-1843    Elizabeth C & Driver Boon inf mtg of int to m. A comm appt to see if the rights of Elizabeth's ch are secure
1-24-1844    Elizabeth C & Driver Boon altm
10- 3-1844    James jas (ASF) dis
4-23-1845    Nathan jr (s Nathan & Martha) gct Milford MM to m Ann Cox
6-25-1845    Rachel jas dis
8-20-1845    Ann rocf Milford MM
11-19-1845    Samuel & Mary Morris altm
12-24-1845    Nathan P (s Eli & Martha) & w Susanna & ch Sarah Ann gct Westfield MM
2-25-1846    Nathan (s Nathan & Martha) & w Ann gct Milford MM
2-25-1847    Eli jr & Martha Ann Harrold altm
8-25-1847    Solomon appt an overseer at Elm Grove PM
1-19-1848    James & w Rachel restored in mbrp
2-23-1848    Angeline, infant dt of James & Rachel rec in mbrp
2-23-1848    Joseph & Abigail Moore altm
3-21-1849    Mary (jr) & William Small altm
9-19-1849    Eli D & w Lydia & ch Jacob, Mary, Sarah & Stephen gct Walnut Ridge MM
10-24-1849    Solomon Gause & David Edwards appt overseers at Elm Grove PM
4-20-1853    Charles C & Sarah Ann Hodson altm
6-24-1853    Nathan P rocf Richland MM
10-19-1853    Nathan P & Eliza L Davis altm
9-20-1854    Sarah Ann & Nathan B, ch of Nathan rocf Westfield MM
10-25-1854    Aaron gct Walnut Ridge MM to m Elizabeth Parker
11-22-1854    Eli D & w Lydia & ch Jacob, Mary E, Sarah T, Stephen, Amos & Lydia Ann rocf Walnut Ridge MM
2-21-1855    Elizabeth rocf Walnut Ridge MM
4-25-1855    Eli jr & w Martha Ann & ch John, Oliver & Albert gct Spring Creek MM, Iowa
4-25-1855    Charles C & w Sarah Ann gct Spring Creek MM, Iowa
5-23-1855    Adaline rocf Westfield MM, minor ch of Nathan P
10-24-1855    Nathan P & w Eliza L & ch Sarah Ann, Adaline & Mahlon gct Spring Creek MM, Iowa
10-24-1855    Aaron C & w Elizabeth gct Spring Creek MM, Iowa
10-24-1855    Isaac mcd dis
6-25-1858    Isaac & Jane rec in mbrp
7-23-1856    Charles D & w Sarah & ch Kasper rocf Spring Creek MM, Iowa
4-22-1857    Joseph & w Abigail M & ch Mary Ann gct Westfield MM
6-24-1857    Charles D & ch gct Lynn Grove MM, Iowa
6-24-1857    James P & w Rachel & ch Angaline & Minerva gct Lynn Grove MM, Iowa
4-21-1858    Abigail S gct Lynn Grove MM, Iowa
4-21-1858    Zachariah F gct Lynn Grove MM, Iowa
4-21-1858    Eli D rst with/con of Walnut Ridge MM
8-24-1859    Stephen A gct Duck Creek MM to m Martha Ellis
12-21-1859    Martha E rocf Duck Creek MM
5-25-1860    Solomon appt a Trustee for real estate at Elm Grove PM
6-20-1860    Eli D & w Lydia & ch Mary Elizabeth, Sarah T, Stephen, Amos, Lydia Ann & James Edwin gct Westfield MM
10-24-1860    William Cox having not produced a cert to m Elvira T, the case is continued to next mtg
11-21-1860    Elvira T & William Cox rptd to have mcd
3-20-1861    Eli & w Martha Ann & ch John H, Oliver, Albert, Samuel P, Isaac H & Seth M rocf Lynn Grove MM, Iowa

SPICELAND

GAUSE (Cont)
|  |  |
|---|---|
| 5-22-1861 | Nathan & w Anna & ch Thomas, Clarkson, Sylvester & Oscar rocf Bridgeport MM |
| 8-20-1862 | William gct Bridgeport MM to m Jane M Cox |
| 5-20-1863 | William gct Bridgeport MM |
| 7-mo-1863 | Solomon appt an overseer |
| 8-mo-1864 | Our aged friend, Eli Gause, req to be released from having the care of holding the records and papers, of this mtg. James B Parker is appt to receive them & take charge of them in Eli's stead |
| 11-23-1864 | Solomon appt a Trustee of real estate at Elm Grove PM |
| 3- 4-1865 | Eli C & Elva P Perkins altm |
| 7- 1-1865 | Solomon appt an overseer |
| 8- 5-1865 | Eli retained as an Elder |
| 8- 5-1865 | Celia appt an Elder |
| 8- 4-1866 | Stephen A & Rachel M Ellis altm |
| 9- 1-1866 | Thomas & Christena Boon altm |
| 10-13-1866 | Jane gct Hopewell MM |
| 12- 1-1866 | Eli & Elva P & ch Oliver & Seth M gct Duck Creek MM |
| 1- 4-1868 | John H gct Lynn Grove MM, Iowa |
| 4- 4-1868 | Stephen A & w Rachel & ch Elmer F & Alma M gct Westfield MM |
| 6- 6-1868 | Solomon appt an overseer at Elm Grove PM |
| 6- 6-1868 | Celia appt an overseer at Elm Grove PM |
| 11- 6-1869 | Isaac H, a minor, gct Richland MM |
| 6- 6-1874 | Eli C rocf Cane Creek MM, N C |
| 10-10-1874 | Eli C gct Lynn Grove MM, Iowa |
| 3- 8-1875 | Nathan & w Ann & ch Sylvester Oscar & Joseph G gct Milford MM |
| 7- 3-1875 | Nathan rocf Richland MM |
| 11- 4-1876 | Thomas & w Christena & ch Clarence gct West Grove MM |
| 10-13-1883 | Christena & ch Clarendon & Fred Carl rocf West Grove MM |
| 3- 5-1892 | Clarkson gct Carthage MM |
| 8- 1-1896 | Fred Carl rel/req |
| 5- 5-1906 | Clarence drpd from mbrp |

GENEAUX
|  |  |
|---|---|
| 9- 3-1904 | George rocf Knightstown MM |
| 9- 2-1911 | George & w Gertrude rocf Independence MM, Ks |
| 10- 6-1921 | George & Gertrude rel on req |
| 4- 1-1926 | Elizabeth rel on req |
| 8- 6-1931 | George & Gertrude rec in mbrp |

GENTRY
|  |  |
|---|---|
| 4- 1-1920 | Willie Ann rec in mbrp |

GEORGE
|  |  |
|---|---|
| 4-25-1838 | Henry & w Lydia & ch Mary, Richard & Sarah rocf New Garden MM |
| 4-24-1839 | Lydia & ch Esther Hopps, Sarah & John B gct White River MM |
| 4- 7-1894 | Washington L & Alice B rec in mbrp |
| 4- 3-1897 | Claude & Thomas rec in mbrp |
| 10- 8-1904 | Rosie rec in mbrp |
| 2- 7-1929 | Claude gct Anderson MM |

GIBSON
|  |  |
|---|---|
| 10- 5-1912 | Maud Lane - - - -? |

GILBREATH
|  |  |
|---|---|
| 6- 1-1878 | Henrietta rec in mbrp |
| 8- 4-1883 | Henrietta drpd from mbrp |

GLIDEWELL
|  |  |
|---|---|
| 1- 7-1888 | Robert rec in mbrp |
| 5- 2-1891 | Sarah D rel on req |
| 8- 7-1897 | Robert rel on req |
| 5- 4-1912 | Sarah rec in mbrp |
| 10- 5-1912 | Violet rec in mbrp |

GORDON
|  |  |
|---|---|
| 7-22-1835 | Charles Sr & w Ruth rocf New Garden MM |
| 7-22-1835 | Mary rocf New Garden MM |
| 11-25-1835 | Richard & w Susanna & ch Rebecca, Alfred, Edwin, Mahala, Sarah Ann, Seth & Nathan rocf Milford MM |
| 2-24-1836 | Richard appt an overseer at Spiceland Mtg |
| 2-22-1837 | Richard Gorden, Solomon Macy, George Evans & William B Unthank appt at Spiceland Mtg, to receive and hold in trust, a deed for land on which the School House now stands |
| 4-24-1839 | Charles & w Lydia & ch Micajah Collins, Parker, Jesse, Robert, Martha & Mary rocf New Garden MM, Ind |
| 11-25-1840 | Lydia appt to station of Minister |
| 10-21-1841 | Mary & Jesse Davis altm |
| 1-19-1842 | Rebecca & Benedict Macy altm |
| 7-23-1845 | Alfred jas dis |
| 8-19-1846 | Lydia, a Minister of this mtg, decd 2- 4-1846 |
| 12-23-1847 | Charles & Anne H Macy altm |
| 5-23-1853 | Richard & w Susanna & ch Mahala, Nathan & Phebe Macy gct Back Creek MM |
| 10-19-1853 | Elizabeth rocf Elk MM, Oh |
| 9-20-1854 | Charles W rocf Salem MM |
| 9-20-1854 | Seth gct Back Creek MM |
| 4-23-1856 | Clarkson gct Spring Creek MM, Iowa |
| 1-21-1857 | Jesse mcd dis |
| 8-19-1857 | Micajah C mcd dis |
| 7-21-1858 | Charles W & w Elizabeth & ch gct Winneshick MM, Iowa |
| 10-21-1860 | Thomas Clarkson rocf Lynn Grove MM, Iowa |
| 4-24-1861 | Emily & Milton Taylor in f mtg of int to m Her guardian being present gives consent |
| 5-22-1861 | Emily & Milton Taylor altm |
| 8- 5-1865 | Edwin con mcd |
| 9- 2-1865 | Edwin gct Cedar Creek MM, Iowa |
| 4- 7-1866 | Jesse & w Harriett P & ch William H & India rec in mbrp |
| 4- 6-1867 | Oliver C con mcd |
| 10-12-1867 | Oliver C gct New Garden MM |
| 11- 2-1872 | Anna H gct Bangor MM, Iowa |
| 12- 1-1877 | Micajah Collins & w Sarah rocf Raysville MM |
| 1- 6-1883 | Micajah C appt a clerk |
| 1- 6-1883 | M Ola rec in mbrp |
| 2- 3-1883 | Thomas C rel on req |
| 1- 2-1884 | Thomas C & w & ch Luella, Jennie & Mattie rel on req |
| 4- 2-1892 | William B gct White River MM |
| 1- 6-1906 | William B & w Harriett & ch Edna Maria, William, Boydon rocf White River MM |
| 2- 7-1914 | Boydon rec in mbrp |
| 4- 6-1916 | Boydon rel on req |
| 1- 6-1922 | Edith (Collins) rec in mbrp |

GORMAN
|  |  |
|---|---|
| 3- 4-1893 | John rec in mbrp |
| 8- 6-1898 | Ruth & s John gct Fairmount MM |

GOTSCHALL
|  |  |
|---|---|
| 7- 6-1878 | Oliver & Ida rec in mbrp |
| 5- 7-1891 | Mary rec in mbrp |
| 5- 2-1914 | Oliver P & w Ida & dt Mary Gotschell Stewart gct Hopewell MM |

GRAN?
|  |  |
|---|---|
| 3- 1-1919? | Fred? roc - - - -? |
| 10- 6-1927 | Julia rec in mbrp |

GRAY
|  |  |
|---|---|
| ( 1-23-1833) | Davis, Jonathan & Phebe, minor ch of James & Margaret, mbrs of Spiceland Mtg |
| 7-26-1834 | Davis & Jonathan, minor ch of James, gct Duck Creek MM, having resided some time past in the limits of Duck Creek Mtg |
| 7-26-1834 | Phebe minor dt of James gct Milford MM, having for some time past resided within limits of Milford Mtg |
| 3-23-1836 | Henry H Macy & w Peninah & dt Anna H & a minor, Jonathan GRAY gct Walnut Ridge MM |
| 10-20-1841 | Davis gct Duck Creek MM to m Ruth Ann Jay |
| 12-22-1841 | Davis gct Walnut Ridge MM |
| 5- 5-1883 | Sarah rocf Union MM, Oh |
| 6- 7-1890 | Alice gct Raysville MM |
| 5- 4-1895 | Jane & ch Flossie & Elizabeth J roc |
| 11- 6-1904 | Alveretta Hiatt gct New Salem MM |
| 6- 5-1906 | Elizabeth Jane drpd from mbrp |

GREEN
|  |  |
|---|---|
| 2-19-1851 | Miriam rocf Blue River MM |
| 6-23-1852 | Miriam gct Blue River MM |
| 7-23-1855 | Miriam rocf New Salem MM |

SPICELAND

## GREENSTREET
|  |  |
|---|---|
| 1-25-1843 | Eunice (form Macy) con mcd |
| 6-22-1853 | Mary (form Elliott) mcd dis |
| 2- 1-1868 | Albert & w Mary E rec in mbrp |
| 12- 4-1880 | Hannah J Burnett rocf Plainfield MM |
| 2- 3-1883 | J F & Morris rel on req |
| 9- 5-1891 | Thomas & fam gct New Garden MM |
| 3- 4-1893 | Albert & Clarence roc |
| 11- ?-1912 | Eli, Ruth, Nora & Alford rocf Sycamore MM |
| 12- 7-1912 | Bertie & Clarence drpd from mbrp |
| 2- 1-1913 | Albert rocf Sycamore MM, Ind |
| 9- 7-1914 | T A gc |

## GREGG
|  |  |
|---|---|
| ( 9-20-1837) | Stephen, w Hannah, & ch, mbrs of Duck Creek Mtg, now laid down, have been attached to Spiceland Mtg |
| 2-21-1838 | Sarah & Seth Hinshaw inf mtg of int to m Consent of parents now had |
| 3-21-1838 | Sarah & Seth Hinshaw jr altm |
| 9-21-1842 | Jesse W Kenworthy gct Duck Creek MM to m Eliza Gregg |
| 2- 7-1874 | William W rec in mbrp |
| 8- 7-1875 | William W & w Elizabeth Ann & ch Emma Lee Risk, Mary May Risk & John Gregg gct Lynn Grove MM, Iowa |

## GREESON
|  |  |
|---|---|
| 6- 3-1899 | Elmer & w Stella gct Anderson MM |

## GRIFFIN
|  |  |
|---|---|
| 1-23-1833 | Samuel & w Lydia & ch original mbrs |
| 1-23-1833 | Joshua & w Matilda & s Mordecai original mbrs |
| 3-20-1833 | Samuel Griffin, John Hiatt, Aaron Stanley, Isaac Schooley & Josiah Small appt to comm to have oversight of & care of the burial ground at Spiceland Mtg |
| 8-19-1835 | Joshua & w Matilda & ch Mordecai gct West Grove MM |
| 6-20-1838 | Joseph req to again be rec in mbrp He had been dis by West Grove MM |
| 11-21-1838 | Joseph rst with con West Grove MM |
| 2-20-1839 | John William, Emily Jane, Sarahann & Mary B ch of Joseph rec in mbrp |
| 2-20-1839 | West Grove Mtg req that Spiceland Mtg treat with William for dpl & mcd |
| 3-20-1839 | The comm appt to treat with William, rpt he does not appear to be of the mind to condemn his deviation & West Grove mtg is so inf |
| 4-24-1839 | Rebecca rec in mbrp |
| 7-24-1839 | West Grove Mtg dis William |
| 5-24-1843 | Miriam J rocf Walnut Ridge MM |
| 10-25-1843 | James Elliott, Parthena Jane, Mary Elizabeth & Willis ch of Miriam rec in mbrp |
| 4-24-1844 | Mary Jane jas dis |
| 9-25-1844 | Joseph appt an overseer |
| 4-23-1845 | Miriam dis for fornication & hiding the child & telling untruths |
| 10-21-1846 | Adam & Jemima Foster altm |
| 12-23-1846 | Jacob & Anna Jane Hiatt altm |
| 10-20-1847 | Jeremiah & Ann Kenworthy altm |
| 11-21-1849 | Jacob & w Anna Jane & ch Robert Ervin gct Westfield MM |
| 11-21-1849 | Adam & w Jemima & dt Gulielma gct Westfield MM |
| 5-22-1850 | Jeremiah & w Ann & dt Emily gct West Grove MM |
| 4-23-1851 | John dis |
| 10-22-1851 | James gct Walnut Ridge MM |
| 10-22-1851 | Elihu jas mcd dis |
| 11-19-1851 | Eliza Ann Reynard (form Griffin) mcd dis |
| 12-24-1851 | Jeremiah & w Ann & dt Mary Emily rocf West Grove MM |
| 3-24-1852 | Mary Elizabeth & Willis, minor ch of Miriam now Miriam Green gct Whitewater MM |
| 5-19-1852 | Rebecca Vernon (form Griffin) mcd dis |
| 7-21-1852 | Adam & w Jemima & dt Gulielma rocf Hinkles Creek MM |
| 4-19-1854 | Sarah Ann & Ellwood Pleas altm |
| 4-25-1855 | Isom mcd dis |
| 4-25-1855 | John W gct Duck Creek MM to m Anna Price |
| 8-22-1855 | John W gct Whitewater MM |
| 4-24-1861 | John W & w Anna & dt Emily rocf Whitewater MM |
| 5-22-1861 | Joseph & w Rebecca gct Raysville MM |
| 5-22-1861 | Emily J gct Raysville MM |
| 2-24-1864 | Jeremiah & w Ann & ch Martha Ellen & Willis rocf Raysville MM |
| 11- 4-1871 | John W rel on req |
| 4- 6-1872 | Sylvia Jane rec in mbrp |
| 12- 2-1875 | Mattie rel on req |
| 6- 2-1883 | Joseph rocf Raysville MM |
| 4- 4-1885 | Lydia rocf Raysville MM |
| 1- 7-1893 | Elbert rel on req |
| 3- 4-1893 | Etta rec in mbrp |
| 2- 1-1896 | Belle Rayle gct Sheridan MM |
| 3- 7-1896 | Calvin W rec in mbrp |
| 4- 4-1896 | Emily rel on req |
| 4- 3-1897 | Willis & w Mary gct Knightstown MM |
| 12- 3-1903 | Isabella E rocf Sheridan MM |
| 5- 3-1908 | Mary Jane Hall rocf Whitewater MM |
| 2- 1-1919 | Willis & w Henrietta rec in mbrp |
| 2- 1-1919 | Mary gct Fairmount MM |
| 2- 5-1925 | David & w Eva & ch Edith, Margaret & Anne M, rocf Duck Creek MM |

## GRISSON - GRISSOM
|  |  |
|---|---|
| 5- 4-1895 | Bertha Estellia rocf Olive Branch MM |
| 5- 4-1895 | Elmer Elsworth rec in mbrp |

## GROLER
|  |  |
|---|---|
| 4- 2-1870 | John & family rec in mbrp |
| 8- 4-1883 | John & w & ch drpd from mbrp |

## GROVES
|  |  |
|---|---|
| 6- 5-1929 | Herbert Kern & w Georgia & her dt Maxina Groves rocf Duck Creek MM |

## GURLEY
|  |  |
|---|---|
| 5-21-1856 | Eliza H rocf Deep River MM, N C |

## HADLEY
|  |  |
|---|---|
| 3-22-1854 | Daniel C Allen gct Springfield MM, Oh to m Elizabeth Hadley |
| 11-23-1854 | James produced a certif from (West Union?) to m |
| 11-23-1854 | James & Catherine R Mendenhall altm |
| 11-23-1854 | James & Catherine R Mendenhall req a mtg appt to meet tomorrow at 11 o'clock at Raysville MH for them to accomplish their m. Their req is granted & mtg directed to be held accordingly |
| 12-20-1854 | The comm appt to att m of James & Catherine R Mendenhall rpt it was orderly & they produced the m cert |
| 1-24-1855 | Catherine R gct West Union MM |

## HAGGERMAN
|  |  |
|---|---|
| 4- 7-1906 | Effie rocf Hopewell MM |
| 12- 7-1912 | Effie gct Duck Creek MM |

## HAISLEY
|  |  |
|---|---|
| 5- 4-1901 | Irvin C rocf New Garden MM |
| 1- 3-1914 | Pauline rec in mbrp |

## HALL
|  |  |
|---|---|
| 1-21-1835 | Stephen rocf Milford Mtg |
| 1-21-1835 | Chalkley rocf Milford Mtg |
| 10- 3-1835 | Chalkley dis for na & disunity (he has moved to the limits of Elk Mtg, Oh) |
| 7-19-1837 | Stephen dis for disunity & na |
| ( 9-20-1837) | Benjamin Sr & w Elizabeth & dt Rhoda, mbrs of Duck Creek Mtg, now laid down, have been attached to Spiceland Mtg |
| ( 9-20-1837) | Caleb & w Hannah & ch Lydia, Elizabeth & Joseph, mbrs of Duck Creek Mtg, now laid down, was attached to Spiceland Mtg |
| 9-20-1837 | The comm at Duck Creek mtg that had been appt to prepare disownment for Hannah, not being present, a comm was appt at Spiceland Mtg, to rpt next mtg (Duck Creek mtg had been laid down) |
| 10-15-1837 | Hannah (form ?) mcd dis |
| 9-19-1838 | Rhoda Beaver (form Hall) mcd dis |
| 2-24-1847 | Achsah (form Moore) con mcd |
| 8-25-1847 | Achsah gct Honey Creek MM |
| 12-20-1854 | Achsah & ch Esther Ann, & Samuel rocf Honey Creek MM |
| 4-23-1856 | Lydia & Jehu Symons altm |

SPICELAND

## HALL (Cont)
|  |  |
|---|---|
| 4-20-1859 | Achsah & ch Esther Ann, Gideon, Branson & Josiah Francis gct Westfield MM |
| 12-21-1859 | Joseph gct Pipe Creek MM |
| 5-23-1860 | Lucinda Jane rocf Pipe Creek MM |
| 5-23-1860 | Nancy rocf Richland MM |
| 6-24-1863 | Caleb appt to the station of Elder |
| 4-20-1864 | Jehu W & Huldah P Ratliff altm |
| 8- 5-1865 | Caleb retained as an Elder |
| 3- 3-1866 | Nancy E & Jason W Newby altm |
| 6- 2-1866 | Caleb gct Milford MM to m Isabella Kennedy |
| 11- 7-1867 | Joseph S & w Lucinda & ch Eldora gct Hopewell MM |
| 5- 6-1871 | Joseph S & w Lucinda & ch Eldora, Aldon & Caleb rocf Hopewell MM |
| 10- 9-1875 | Mary J rocf Milford MM |
| 1-mo-1880 | Huldah appt a clerk |
| 8- 4-1883 | Edwin & w Lydia & ch Clarence & Carl rocf Hopewell MM |
| 12- 6-1890 | Aldon gct Long Lake MM, Mich |
| 6- 3-1893 | Anna rec in mbrp |
| 8- 5-1893 | Eli rocf Hopewell MM |
| 5- 5-1894 | Mary E & ch Nathan Earl & George Irvin Parker rocf Springfield MM |
| 7- 6-1895 | Mary J gct Whitewater MM |
| 6- 5-1897 | Elmira M rec in mbrp |
| 1- 6-1900 | Effie Afton & ch Paul Howard & Russell Lowell Brown rocf Walnut Ridge MM |
| 4- 1-1905 | Moses rocf Hopewell MM |
| 10-12-1907 | Clarence V gct New Castle MM |
| 1- 3-1914 | Wanita rec in mbrp |
| 8- 1-1914 | Effie Afton gct West Richmond MM |
| 5- 5-1921 | Donald rec in mbrp |
| 6- 5-1924 | Iris E rel on req |
| 6- 5-1924 | Arthur B gct Indianapolis MM |

## HAMMER
|  |  |
|---|---|
| 10-25-1837 | Elisha (of Duck Creek mtg, now laid down) appt an overseer by Spiceland MM |
| 6-21-1848 | Elisha & w Nancy & ch Abigail, Catherine, Peter, & Mary Jane rocf Duck Creek MM |
| 4-21-1852 | Isaac N dis |
| 8-19-1857 | Elisha rel from overseer |
| 12-19-1860 | Elisha rec as Minister |
| 7-23-1862 | Abigail & William Dawson altm |
| 11-19-1862 | Peter con mcd |
| 7-20-1864 | Peter gct Duck Creek MM |
| 5- 4-1867 | Peter & w Sarah rocf Duck Creek MM |
| 2- 6-1869 | Peter & w Sarah & ch Elizabeth A, & Emma A gct Raysville MM |
| 10-12-1872 | Elisha gct Hopewell MM to m Elizabeth M Heacock |
| 2- 1-1873 | Elizabeth M rocf Hopewell MM |
| 3- 7-1885 | Milton P rocf Lynn Grove MM, Iowa |
| 3- 7-1885 | Jenezie rec in mbrp |
| 11- 2-1901 | Jinizie rel on req |
| 4- 4-1903 | Milton gct New Sharon MM |
| 2- 5-1925 | Milton P gct New Castle MM |

## HAMMOND
|  |  |
|---|---|
| 5- 5-1866 | Mary & s Gurney gct Salem MM, Iowa |
| 6- 4-1887 | Jesse & w Mary & ch Gurney, Martha, Harriett Arthur Maria, Eunice & William rocf Grove MM |
| 12- 6-1902 | Arthur rel on req |
| 12- 7-1922 | Pearl M rec in mbrp |
| 12- 7-1922 | Jesse, Lucy M, Ralph & Lilly rec in mbrp |

## HANE
|  |  |
|---|---|
| 7- 7-1921 | Marshall & w rocf Knightstown MM |

## HARDIN
|  |  |
|---|---|
| 2- 7-1914 | Fred & Alvin rec on req |
| 4- 4-1914 | Margaret rocf Duck Creek MM |
| 12- 5-1914 | Mabel Macy rocf Hopewell MM |
| 12- 1-1921 | Horace C rocf Duck Creek MM |
| 5- 4-1922 | R Hoyt rec in mbrp |
| 10- 5-1922 | Mrs R H rec in mbrp |
| 3- 2-1933 | Alvin & fam gct Knightstown MM |
| 3- 2-1933 | Fred & fam gct Knightstown MM |

## HARRINGTON
|  |  |
|---|---|
| 5- 2-1868 | James rec in mbrp |

## HARRIS
|  |  |
|---|---|
| 4-24-1833 | Susanna rocf New Garden MM |
| 9-25-1839 | Wilson & ch Asenath C, Thomas E, & Robert P, Elm Grove PM, rec in mbrp |
| 4-25-1849 | Wilson & w Susanna & ch Asenath, Sarah C, Thomas E, Robert B, Benjamin Franklin, Martha & Margaret A gct Birch Lake MM, Mich |
| 7- 6-1879 | Henry rec in mbrp |
| 10-11-1879 | J Fremont & w Mary Lizzie rocf Milford MM |
| 2- 2-1884 | J Fremont & w Lizzie & ch George C, Edith E, gct Dublin MM (Milford now called Dublin) |
| 3- 5-1892 | Henry gct Duck Creek MM |

## HARRISON
|  |  |
|---|---|
| 6-22-1836 | Robert rocf Milford MM |
| 9-19-1838 | Robert appt Librarian at Spiceland Mtg |
| 12- 7-1922 | Thomas P rec in mbrp |

## HARROLD
|  |  |
|---|---|
| 12-25-1839 | Martha, a minor, rocf Dover MM, N C (dt of John, decd, & w Mary (Stanley)) |
| 2-25-1847 | Martha Ann & Eli Gause jr altm |
| 7-23-1851 | Patsy Chew (form Harrold) con mcd |
| 4- 6-1872 | William & w Carolline rec in mbrp |
| 6- 7-1879 | Lemuel rocf Westland MM |
| 5- 7-1881 | Lemuel & w Jane & ch Matilda Etta, Arthur Arlo, Nathan Addus & Harriett R gct Westland MM |
| 1- 1-1887 | William B & w Caroline & dt Rachel M transfered to Muncie MM |
| 3- 4-1893 | John & w Emma C & ch Warren, Rachel & Lillian rec in mbrp |
| 3- 5-1904 | Lavada rec in mbrp |
| 5- 4-1912 | Linnie, Anna, Edith & Glenna rec in mbrp |
| 12- 7-1912 | Warren drpd from mbrp |
| 9- 4-1930 | John drpd from mbrp |

## HARVEY
|  |  |
|---|---|
| 4-24-1839 | Caleb & w Bathsheba & ch Asenath H, Amos P, Silas, Mary & George rocf Miami MM, Oh |
| 12-25-1844 | Rebecca (form Boon) mcd dis |
| 6-20-1849 | Mary Jane (form Davis) mcd with non-mbr dis |
| 12-19-1849 | James J rocf New Garden MM, N C |
| 11-20-1850 | Rebecca Jane (form Rayle) mcd dis |
| 1-22-1851 | James J mcd dis |
| 7-23-1856 | James J rocf Richland MM |
| 5-25-1859 | James gct Richland MM |
| 8-22-1860 | Rebecca rst at Richland MM |
| 8-20-1862 | Margery Ann, Thomas Chalkley & William C, minor ch of Almeda, wid of William L, rocf New Garden MM, N C. Margery Ann left her mbrp here but the others were end to Raysville MM, except Thomas Chalkley who has deceased |
| 11- 1-1873 | Ruth rocf Springfield MM, Oh |
| 1- 3-1874 | Sina A rocf Springfield MM, Oh |
| 2- 7-1874 | James W & w Alice rocf Springfield MM, Oh |
| 9- 5-1874 | Surviving parent having consented to m of Margery A & Nathaniel Edwards, they have req a mtg apptd at the residence of John P Pennington on the 22nd of this month at 4 o'clock PM for the purpose of solemnizing their m. The req was granted |
| 6- 5-1875 | William C rocf Lost Creek MM, Tenn |
| 1- 6-1877 | Ruth gct West Branch MM, Oh |
| 1- 6-1877 | James & w Alice & dt Blanche gct Wilmington MM, Oh |
| 8- 4-1877 | Chas & ch Augustus & Mahlon rocf Whitewater MM |
| 12- 1-1877 | William C gct Deer Creek MM |
| 3- 5-1892 | Charles & ch Augustus & Mahlon drpd from mbrp |
| 2- 6-1897 | Charles B & w Martha J & ch Lillian May, Edna R, Ethel S & Ruth A rocf Duck Creek MM |
| 4- 6-1912 | Opha rec in mbrp |
| 12- 7-1912 | Edna P gct Duck Creek MM |
| 5- 3-1913 | Opha rel on req |

## HASKETT
|  |  |
|---|---|
| 9-20-1837 | Morgan & ch had asked for a cert of removal from Duck Creek Mtg. But since Duck Creek had been laid down, Spiceland Mtg appt a comm to investigate the rights of the ch |

SPICELAND

HASKETT (Cont)
10-25-1837   The comm appt to investigate the giving of a cert of removal for Morgan, produced one for Morgan only
12- 7-1922   Margaret O, Melbe & Lyle rec in mbrp

HASLER
5- 5-1897    Elmer & w Lena & ch Harlan, Helen Elaine & Norman rec in mbrp

HASTINGS
8- 6-1870    Elwood Stanley gct Duck Creek MM to m Phebe Hastings
3- 1-1884    Seth G & w Edith & ch Alton P & Laura rocf Van Wert MM, Oh
9- 6-1884    Aaron & w Laura & s Harold roc
6- 4-1887    Aaron & fam gct New Castle MM
1- 7-1888    Seth G & fam gct Muncie MM

HAUGHTEN - HOUGHTEN
5-19-1852    Charles White gct Salem MM to m Lucy Haughten
8-25-1852    Richard E rocf Salem MM
7-20-1853    Richard E con mcd
12-19-1855   Richard E gct Whitewater MM
11-19-1856   William & w Sally rocf Whitewater MM
4- 4-1868    Amanda Houten rec in mbrp

HAWKINS
7- 6-1886    Mary rec in mbrp
1- 6-1894    Cornelia M & ch Belle J & Cora Pearl rocf Dublin MM

HAYS
8- 1-1879    Daniel W & Zilpha rec in mbrp
3- 4-1893    Eva, Fannie & Lilly rec in mbrp
4- 1-1896    Daniel & w Zilpha rel on req
7- 5-1913    Martha rec in mbrp
9- 6-1913    John W & w Eva & dt Lillian rec in mbrp
4- 5-1923    Lillian gct Dayton MM, Oh
3- 4-1926    Lilian rocf Plainfield MM

HEACOCK
10-12-1872   Elisha Hammer gct Hopewell MM to m Elizabeth Heacock

HEALTON
4-20-1864    Jonathan & w Catherine & ch James, Simeon & Martha rocf New Salem MM
10-14-1865   Jonathan & w Catherine & ch James, Simeon & Martha gc

HECK
1- 5-1889    Nancy rec in mbrp
4- 5-1890    Nancy rel on req

HEIFNER
3- 2-1895    Flora rec in mbrp
12- 7-1912   Flora drpd from mbrp

HELM
3- 5-1870    George rec in mbrp

HENLEY
3-21-1838    Jabez H & Margaret S Holloway inf mtg of int to m  Consent of parents now had  Jabez directed to produce a cert of his clearness
4-25-1838    Jabez H produced cert from Walnut Ridge Mtg to m Margaret S Holloway
4-25-1838    Jabez H & Margaret S Holloway altm
8-22-1838    Margaret appt to Walnut Ridge MM
7-25-1855    William H Morgan gct Back Creek MM to m Sarah Henley
3- 2-1867    John Symons gct Duck Creek MM to m Ellen S Henley
10- 8-1870   Albert rocf Duck Creek MM
5- 1-1875    Jabez & w Margaret & s Arthur rocf Duck Creek MM
5- 6-1876    David rocf Duck Creek MM
5- 5-1883    Jabez H appt an Elder
5- 5-1883    Margaret appt an Elder
6- 2-1883    Albert & w Ellen & s Albert Roy gct Lawrence MM, Kan

7- 5-1890    John Arthur gct Lawrence MM, Kan
5- 7-1892    Martha gct Carthage MM
5- 2-1906    Lois gct Indianapolis MM
7- 6-1912    Homer rel on req
11- 7-1914   Samantha gct Indianapolis MM
6- 6-1919    Mary Samantha rocf Indianapolis MM
7- 6-1922    Howard gct Cherokee MM, Okla

HENRY
12- 7-1922   J Carlton rec in mbrp
11- 5-1930   Henrietta rec in mbrp

HENTHORN
4- 7-1906    Frank rec in mbrp
12- 7-1912   Frank drpd from mbrp

HESTER
1-23-1833    Mary & ch Amos & Zimri charter mbrs
8-19-1835    Mary & ch Amos, Zimri & Joel gct Milford MM (removed with husb, Robert)
10-24-1838   Mary gct Milford MM

HEWITT
10- 2-1919   Bertha Charles rel on req

HIATT
1-23-1833    John & w Rebecca & ch original mbrs
2-20-1833    Rebecca appt an overseer
3-20-1833    John Hiatt, Aaron Stanley, Samuel Griffin, Isaac Schooley & Josiah Small appt to comm to have oversight of & care of the burial ground
8-19-1835    John Hiatt, David James, Isaac White, Calvin Wasson, Vierling Kersey, George Evans, William Edwards, Nathan Davis & Joseph B Hunt appt to comm on Education for the ensuing year
1-20-1836    Rhoda & ch James, Ann Tailor & Joseph D Mace rocf New Garden MM
2-24-1836    John appt overseer at Spiceland Mtg
9-21-1836    Rebecca appt to station of elder
12-25-1839   Daniel of Duck Creek PM dis for na & att a mcd
7-22-1840    Joel rest w/con of New Garden MM
4-19-1843    Joel & w Rhoda & her s Joseph D Mace gct Salem MM, Iowa
12-23-1846   Anna Jane & Jacob Griffin altm
11-24-1847   Elizabeth Sopher & s Allen Hiatt rocf Duck Creek MM
4-12-1848    Asher & w Sarah M & ch Eleazer B, Clarkson & Charles W rocf Whitewater MM (Sarah M is a Minister)
10-24-1849   John Hiatt, William Sheridan & James P Antrim appt overseers at Spiceland PM
5-22-1850    Asher & w Sarah M gct Springfield MM, N C (Sarah M is a Minister)
12-25-1850   Asher & Sarah M & ch gct Duck Creek MM
4-20-1853    Jesse & w Achsah & ch Job, Linden, Oliver, Robert & Albert rocf New Garden MM
12-21-1853   Eliphalet & Susannah Sheridan altm
4-23-1856    Isaac Kenworthy gct Duck Creek MM to m Abigail Hiatt
9-24-1856    Allen mcd  dis
8-19-1857    Josiah dis
3-23-1859    Eliphalet & w Susanna & ch George & Ann gct Hinkles Creek MM
2-19-1862    Nancy gct Westfield MM
4-20-1864    Charles con mcd
12-24-1864   Charles gct Hinkles Creek MM
8- 5-1865    Rebecca retained as an Elder
8- 5-1865    John appt an Elder
4- 7-1866    Eliphalet & Susanna & ch George, Anna Mary & Dora rocf Hinkles Creek MM
6- 2-1866    Josiah & dt Emily rec in mbrp
10-13-1866   Martha & Thomas Evans altm
12- 7-1867   Eliphalet & w Susanna & ch George, Anna Mary, Dora & Arthur gct Hinkles Creek MM
3- 7-1868    Job & Lucinda rec in mbrp
8- 7-1869    William con mcd
12- 3-1870   Job & w Lucinda & ch Wilson J, Albert F, Charles D & Mary gct Duck Creek MM
8- 5-1871    John appt an Elder
8- 5-1871    Rebecca appt an Elder
12- 4-1875   Albert rst

SPICELAND

## HIATT (Cont)

|  |  |
|---|---|
| 1- 1-1876 | Seth & w Zalinda & ch Alice A & Luther J rec in mbrp |
| 3- 4-1876 | Albert gct West Grove MM |
| 4- 7-1883 | Samuel & w Ida gct Raysville MM |
| 5- 5-1883 | John appt an Elder |
| 5- 5-1883 | Rebecca appt an Elder |
| 6- 2-1883 | William & w Annis & ch Henry, Charles, & Walter gct Raysville MM |
| 6- 7-1884 | Malinda gct Walnut Ridge MM |
| 12- 6-1884 | Malinda rocf Walnut Ridge MM |
| 4- 4-1885 | William & fam rocf Raysville MM |
| 4- 2-1892 | Luther (?) |
| 1- 7-1893 | Samuel & w Ida & dt Florence rocf Raysville MM |
| 2- 4-1893 | Anna L rec in mbrp |
| 2- 8-1895 | Seth & w Zalinda gct Duck Creek MM |
| 3- 7-1896 | Bertha S rec in mbrp |
| 9- 4-1897 | Samuel & w Ida J & dt Florence gct Knightstown MM |
| 2- 7-1903 | Walter E rel on req |
| 4- 2-1904 | Cleotus rocf Hopewell MM |
| 10-10-1908 | Cleotus rel on req |
| 9- 3-1910 | Albert drpd from mbrp |
| 4- 6-1918 | Ruth rec in mbrp |

## HICKS

|  |  |
|---|---|
| 1- 1-1920 | Martha (Hays) gct Portland MM |

## HILL

|  |  |
|---|---|
| 4-24-1844 | Nathan produced cert from Walnut Ridge Mtg to m Anna Edwards |
| 4-24-1844 | Nathan C & Anna Edwards altm |
| 9-25-1844 | Anna gct Walnut Ridge MM |
| 9- 1-1866 | Owen S & Melissa A Bales altm |
| 9- 1-1866 | Owen S & Melissa A Bales req a mtg appt at the house of John H Bales on the 13th of the present month, at 3 o'clock to accomplish their m. Req granted |
| 2- 2-1867 | Melissa A gct Carthage MM |
| 10-18-1872 | Eliza L gct Whitewater MM |
| 12- 4-1875 | Charles & w Eunice rec in mbrp |
| 12- 5-1885 | Rebecca rec in mbrp |
| 12- 5-1885 | Charles M rec in mbrp |
| 1- 1-1887 | Charles & w Eunice, Charles M & Rebecca J transfered to Muncie MM |
| 6- 1-1889 | Jacob & w Mary Jane & ch Floy Alma, Myron A & Cora Elsie rocf New Garden MM |
| 3- 3-1894 | Jacob & w Jannie & ch Floy, Myron & Cora gct Pasadena MM, Ca |
| 8- 1-1896 | Rachel (Bailey) gct Whitewater MM |
| 4- 3-1897 | Eli B & w Josephine rocf Carthage MM |
| 1- 3-1914 | Louise rec in mbrp |
| 2- 7-1914 | Ezra rec in mbrp |
| 1- 5-1918 | Marjorie rec in mbrp |

## HINSHAW

|  |  |
|---|---|
| 10-23-1833 | Seth & fam rocf Marlborough MM, N C & end to Duck Creek MM |
| 11-20-1833 | Mary (Lamb) rocf Providence MM, N C end by Marlborough MM, N C and end by Duck Creek MM |
| 11-20-1833 | Jabez rocf Marlborough MM, N C end to Duck Creek MM |
| ( 2-20-1837) | Seth & w Abigail & ch, mbrs of Duck Creek Mtg, now laid down, have been attached to Spiceland MM |
| 12-20-1837 | Duck Creek PM compl that Seth has encouraged disunity |
| 1-24-1838 | Seth produced an offering which was read & accepted |
| 2-21-1838 | Seth jr & Sarah Gregg inf mtg of int to m Consent of parents now had |
| 3-31-1838 | Seth jr & Sarah Gregg altm |
| 9-19-1838 | William B & w Hannah & ch James M & Elmina Louise gct Springfield MM |
| 6-19-1839 | Jesse B of Elm Grove PM dis for dpl, na & being sued at law |
| 2-19-1840 | Jabez appt Librarian at Duck Creek PM |
| 1-25-1843 | Benjamin P of Elm Grove PM rpt mcd |
| 3-22-1843 | Benjamin P dis |
| 11-24-1852 | Elizabeth, Isom & Nathan, minor ch of Mary decd, rocf Cane Creek MM, N C |
| 12-24-1856 | Isom gct West Union MM |
| 4-22-1857 | Elizabeth gct West Union MM |
| 5-19-1858 | Nathan gct West Union MM |
| 10-21-1863 | Elijah produced a cert from Cherry Grove MM to m |
| 10-21-1863 | Elijah & Rebecca Albertson (a wid) altm |
| 12-23-1863 | Rebecca gct Cherry Grove MM |
| 5- 2-1874 | Albert rec in mbrp |
| 10-11-1879 | Albert & w Sarah C & ch Uva A & Herbert P gct White River MM |
| 12- 3-1881 | Sarah C & ch Uva A & Herbert P rocf White River MM |
| 4- 7-1894 | Logan, Margaret & Minnie rec in mbrp |
| 4- 7-1894 | Arthur M, Ralph C & Bernice rec in mbrp |
| 1- 4-1896 | Logan & Margaret gct New Castle MM |
| 3- 6-1897 | Herbert gct Fairmount MM |
| 11- 6-1909 | Lenora Pickett gct Duck Creek MM |
| 6- 1-1912 | Claire gct White River MM |
| 3- 7-1929 | Edith Griffin gct Indianapolis MM |
| 3- 7-1929 | Franklin rel on req |

## HOBBS

|  |  |
|---|---|
| 6-19-1850 | William & w Anna (both Ministers) rocf New Garden MM |
| 3-19-1851 | Elisha & w Deborah & ch Martha, Louise, Harvey & Ansalem rocf Miami MM, Oh |
| 11-21-1855 | Martha A & John Unthank altm |
| 4-23-1856 | Elisha & w Deborah & ch Louise, Harvey & Anselm gct White Lick MM |
| 12- 7-1878 | Elisha rocf West Union MM |
| 4- 7-1883 | Elisha gct West Union MM |

## HOBSON

|  |  |
|---|---|
| 4- 2-1904 | Orlando & w Leanah rocf Whitewater MM |
| 4- 1-1905 | Orlando & w Lennah gct Laporte MM |
| 1- 2-1909 | Orlando & w Lennah rocf Hopewell MM |
| 9- 3-1910 | Orlando & w Leannah gct Mt Airy MM, N C |

## HOCKETT - HOGGATT

|  |  |
|---|---|
| 12-23-1835 | Phillip jr & w Miriam & ch Elijah & Anna Jane Hockett & Sarah, Elihu & Josiah Small (ch of Miriam) rocf New Garden MM |
| 6-21-1837 | Mary, a minor, rocf Dover MM |
| 10-23-1844 | Miriam & ch Elijah Hockett & Elihu Small gct Mississinewa MM |
| 5-19-1847 | Mary & Neri Hodson inf mtg of int to m The consent of her guardian has been given |
| 6-23-1847 | Mary & Neri Hodson altm |
| 6-22-1853 | Benjamin rocf Walnut Ridge MM |
| 12-24-1856 | Benjamin mcd dis |
| 10-21-1857 | Rebecca rec in mbrp |
| 1- 1-1876 | Jesse Milligan & w Tamer rec in mbrp |
| 6- 2-1888 | J Milligan & w Tamar gct Whitewater MM |
| 10-11-1890 | Mary Elma gct Hinkles Creek MM |
| 4- 6-1918 | Clarkson & Katherine rec in mbrp |
| 4- 6-1918 | Mariam & Helen Maria rec in mbrp |
| 4- 5-1928 | Katherine rel on req |

## HODGINS

|  |  |
|---|---|
| 5-12-1852 | Joseph & w Sally & ch Nancy Eliza, Phebe Jane, Martha, Margaret, Sarah Hiatt & David F rocf Center MM, N C |
| 7- 6-1879 | Lenard A rocf Cherry Grove MM |
| 6- 2-1883 | Margaret drpd from mbrp |
| 7- 7-1883 | Leonard O gct Deer Creek MM |
| 8- 4-1883 | Ellen M gct Whitewater MM |
| 2- 9-1889 | Ella rocf New Garden MM |
| 10-12-1895 | Elleen M rel on req |

## HODSON

|  |  |
|---|---|
| ( 1-23-1833) | Aaron & w Mary & ch Lydia, Neri, Seth, Anna, Robert B, Reuben & Sarah (living in the area of Duck Creek, that became Spiceland MM) original mbrs |
| 11-20-1833 | Jesse F & w Nancy & ch Jeffrey, Caleb, Jabez, Isabel Ann & Elizabeth rocf Springfield MM, N C & end by Duck Creek MM |
| 5-24-1837 | Aaron appt Treasurer for ensuing year |
| ( 9-20-1837) | Isaac & w Welmet & ch, mbrs of Duck Creek Mtg, now laid down, have been attached to Spiceland |
| ( 9-20-1837) | Robert F & w Anna & ch, mbrs of Duck Creek Mtg, now laid down, have been attached to Spiceland |

SPICELAND

HODSON (Cont)
| | |
|---|---|
| 6-19-1839 | Elizabeth (form Adamson) mcd dis |
| 9-25-1839 | Aaron appt Treasurer for ensuing year |
| 6-23-1841 | Aaron appt an overseer at Spiceland PM |
| 1-19-1842 | Jeffrey dis for dpl & upl |
| 9-25-1844 | Aaron appt an overseer |
| 1-20-1847 | Caleb & Priscilla Bond altm |
| 5-19-1847 | Neri & Mary Hockett inf mtg of int to m Consent of his parents has been given & consent of her guardian is given |
| 6-23-1847 | Neri & Mary Hockett altm |
| 6-21-1848 | Reuben & Eliza Justice altm |
| 2-20-1850 | Seth con mcd |
| 4-22-1850 | Jabez mcd dis |
| 10-23-1850 | Margaret rocf Dover MM |
| 5-21-1851 | Mary (form Baldwin) mcd dis |
| 3-24-1852 | John & w Jane & ch Lucinda, Robert & Elizabeth rocf Springfield MM, N C |
| 6-23-1852 | Neri & w Mary & ch Daniel gct Back Creek MM |
| 10-20-1852 | Rebecca Jane & Mordecai Stanley altm |
| 3-23-1853 | Jesse & Albenah Horney altm |
| 4-20-1853 | Sarah Ann & Charles C Gause altm |
| 5-25-1853 | John B rptd mcd dis |
| 3-22-1854 | Jonas E & Mary Ann Antrim altm |
| 6- 7-1854 | Albert, minor s of Welmet, rec in mbrp |
| 7-23-1856 | Seth & w Margaret & ch Jacob, Ira H, Nancy Ellen & Neri gct Back Creek MM |
| 12-24-1856 | Eli mcd dis |
| 4-25-1860 | Robert con mcd |
| 10-24-1860 | Marzilla Jane rocf Walnut Ridge MM |
| 6- 1-1867 | Edwin rocf Bangor MM, Iowa |
| 10-12-1867 | Lewis con mcd |
| 3- 7-1868 | Jabez & w Jane & dt Lucy Jane rec in mbrp |
| 3- 7-1868 | John B & w Huldah rec in mbrp |
| 2- 4-1871 | John con mcd |
| 9- 7-1872 | Phebe Ann rocf Springfield MM, N C |
| 10-12-1872 | Reuben & w Eliza & ch Martha Ann, Mary Malinda, Rebecca Ellen, Elizabeth Cordelia, Robert Harvey, Thomas Aaron, Louisa & John William gct Oak Ridge MM |
| 4- 5-1873 | Linsey con mcd |
| 1- 6-1877 | Martha gct Mill Creek MM |
| 8- 4-1883 | Jane & dt Alice drpd from mbrp |
| 11- 3-1883 | Jesse drpd from mbrp |
| 12- 1-1883 | Emory dis |
| 12- 1-1883 | Julius gct Newberg MM, Ore |
| 3- 6-1886 | Laura, Minnie, Nellie & Elbert (ch of William & Amanda) rec in mbrp |
| 7- 2-1887 | Emory gct Newberg MM, Ore |
| 6- 4-1892 | Priscilla, Charles, Arthur & Elmer drpd from mbrp |
| 1- 6-1894 | Nellie gct Boston MM, MA |
| 8- 4-1894 | Gertrude rocf Duck Creek MM |
| 2- 2-1895 | Alice M rocf Raysville MM |
| 6- 6-1896 | Sylvia May rocf Knightstown MM |
| 2- 5-1898 | Moses gct Duck Creek MM |
| 6- 2-1900 | Phebe Ann gct Springfield MM, N C |
| 11- 3-1900 | Nellie G rocf Boston MM, MA |
| 4- 4-1903 | Gertrude Louisa rocf Knightstown MM |
| 12- 7-1912 | Alonzo drpd from mbrp |
| 12- 7-1912 | Elbert rel on req |
| 3- 1-1928 | Ferr & Mabel rec in mbrp |

HOFFMAN
| | |
|---|---|
| 1- 3-1914 | Maria rec in mbrp |
| 4- 6-1918 | Clarence rec in mbrp |

HOLLINGSWORTH
| | |
|---|---|
| 12-23-1840 | Cyrus & w Sarah rocf New Garden MM, N C & end to White Lick MM |
| 12-25-1850 | James & w Lydia & ch Olive, Miriam, Stephen G, Valentine, Anderson & Benjamin rocf Walnut Ridge MM |
| 4-23-1856 | Stephen G gct Western Plains MM, Iowa |
| 12- 7-1867 | Valentine appt an overseer at Dunreith PM |
| 6- 6-1868 | Valentine appt an overseer at Dunreith PM |
| 6- 6-1867 | Frances appt an overseer at Dunreith PM |
| 6- 3-1871 | Valentine appt an overseer |
| 5- 2-1874 | Valentine appt an overseer |
| 8- 2-1890 | (M) Frances gct Raysville MM |
| 3- 5-1892 | Mingnonette H drpd from mbrp |
| 4- 7-1892 | William gct Indianapolis MM |
| 5- 7-1892 | James Earl gct Carthage MM |
| 7- 2-1892 | Willis B rel on req |

HOLLOWAY
| | |
|---|---|
| ( 9-20-1837) | Joseph & w Eleanor & ch mbrs of Duck Creek Mtg, now laid down, have been attached to Spiceland Mtg |
| 3-21-1838 | Margaret S & Jabez H Henley inf mtg of int to m Consent of parents now had |
| 4-25-1838 | Margaret S & Jabez H Henley altm |
| 6-23-1841 | David & w Mary & ch Joseph, Asa, Eliza & Hannah Ann gct Duck Creek MM |
| 8-19-1857 | Joseph W produced a cert from Duck Creek Mtg to m |
| 8-19-1857 | Joseph W & Hannah A Stanley altm |
| 2- 4-1858 | Joseph W rocf Duck Creek MM |
| 6-25-1862 | David & w Mary & ch Asa, Hannah A, Mary Ellen, Nancy, Lydia M & Jason W rocf Duck Creek MM |
| 4- 1-1865 | Joseph & w Hannah & ch Emma L & Otis D gct Lynn Grove MM, Iowa |
| 10- 9-1869 | Asa con mcd |
| 3- 3-1870 | Smith rocf Wabash MM |
| 5- 7-1870 | Joseph W & w Hannah A & ch Emma L, & Otis D rocf Lynn Grove MM, Iowa |
| 2- 7-1874 | Margaret E rec in mbrp |
| 5- 2-1874 | Joseph appt an overseer |
| 1- 9-1875 | Mary E rocf Short Creek MM, Ohio |
| 5- 6-1876 | Mary E rel on req |
| 1- 6-1877 | Smith gct Raysville MM |
| 3- 3-1877 | Margaret gct Raysville MM |
| 3- 6-1880 | Jason W & w Cynthia gct Duck Creek MM |
| 1- 6-1883 | Lizzie E appt a clerk |
| 9- 5-1891 | Otis gct Raysville MM |
| 1- 2-1897 | Otis D gct Indianapolis, MM |
| 8- 6-1898 | Arthur M & w Louisa & ch Hazel & Ruth E gc |
| 6-30-1916 | Arthur & fam rocf Oskaloosa MM, Iowa |
| 12- 2-1920 | Miriam Wright gct Knightstown MM |
| 5- 5-1921 | Edna rec in mbrp |
| 11- 6-1930 | Arthur & w & s Homer gct Muncie MM |

HOLLOWELL
| | |
|---|---|
| 6-24-1840 | Esther, wid of Aaron & minor ch Nathan W & Mary Jane rocf Piney Woods MM, N C & end by Milford MM |
| 10-21-1840 | Esther & ch Nathan & Mary Jane gct Milford MM |
| 1- 7-1888 | Edwin rec in mbrp |
| 7- 2-1892 | Edwin rel on req |

HOLT
| | |
|---|---|
| 1- 6-1877 | Martha gct Carthage MM |
| 8- 3-1901 | Carrie Alberta (Newby) gct Passadena MM, CA |

HOLTSCLAW
| | |
|---|---|
| 11-23-1836 | Nancy rocf Milford MM |
| 1-23-1839 | Nancy dis for disunity, na & att a mcd |
| 4- 7-1900 | James D rec in mbrp |
| 6- 6-1900 | George E rec in mbrp |
| 4- 3-1915 | Mary E rec in mbrp |
| 5- 5-1921 | Paul rec in mbrp |

HOOD
| | |
|---|---|
| 12- 2-1905 | Mary V gct New Castle MM |
| 6- 6-1914 | Mary V rocf New Castle MM |

HOOPS
| | |
|---|---|
| 4-25-1838 | Henry George & 2nd w, Lydia & his ch Mary & Richard George & her ch Esther & Joseph L Hoops, rocf New Garden MM |
| 4-24-1839 | Lydia George & her dt Esther Hoops & Sarah & John H George gct White River MM |

HOOVER
| | |
|---|---|
| 8-23-1837 | Margaret gct Duck Creek MM |
| 5- 1-1869 | Margaret rec in mbrp |
| 10-11-1879 | Margaret rel on req |
| 2- 3-1883 | Levi & dt Hellen rec in mbrp |
| 7- 6-1890 | Levi & w Emily & ch Helen C & Edna L gct Whitewater MM |
| 1- 6-1919 | Levi C & w Rachel S gct South 8th Street MM, Richmond |
| 11- 6-1919 | Levi C & w Rachel gct South 8th Street MM, Richmond |

SPICELAND

HORNE
| | |
|---|---|
| 12-6-1873 | Henry W produced a cert from New Garden MM to m |
| 12-6-1873 | Henry W & Anna Nichols altm |
| 12-6-1873 | Henry W & Ann Nichols req a mtg appt on the 9th inst at the house of Ann Nichols in order to accomplish their m  The req was granted |
| 2-7-1874 | Ann Nichols gct New Garden MM |

HORNADAY
| | |
|---|---|
| 3-25-1857 | Rufus Davis gct Vermillion MM, Ill to m Lydia Hornaday |

HORNER
| | |
|---|---|
| 11-25-1835 | John & w Elizabeth & s Amos rocf Springborough MM, Ohio |
| 11-25-1835 | Samuel rocf Springborough MM, Oh |
| 11-25-1835 | Ann, Rebecca, Rachel, Sally & Lydia rocf Springborough MM, Oh |
| 12-19-1838 | Samuel & Beulah Stewart altm |
| 11-24-1841 | Samuel Horner, Charles Morgan, Samuel Pritchard, Caleb White & Joel Pusey appt Trustees to rec & hold titles for real estate, in trust for Raysville PM, Wayne twp, Henry Co, Ind for meeting, school & burying ground |
| 12-22-1841 | Sally & Henry Cammack altm |
| 12-22-1841 | For the accomodation of Sally & Henry Cammack, a mtg for their m has been granted for tomorrow at Raysville MH at 11 o'clock |
| 9-25-1850 | Rachel gct Cherry Grove MM |
| 10-22-1851 | Amos C gct Cherry Grove MM to m Elvira Reece |
| 3-24-1852 | Elvira rocf Cherry Grove MM |
| 12-3-1881 | Amos & w Ann J rocf Raysville MM |
| 10-9-1886 | Lydia rocf West Branch MM, Oh |
| 4-22-1892 | Lydia drpd from mbrp |

HORNEY
| | |
|---|---|
| 2-23-1853 | Albenah rocf Deep River MM, N C |
| 3-23-1853 | Albenah & Jesse Hodson altm |

HOSIER
| | |
|---|---|
| 1-23-1833 | Nathan & w Alice & ch original mbrs |
| 1-22-1834 | Nathan dis |
| 6-24-1835 | Alice & ch Hannah, Huldah, Alfred & Martha Ann gct Duck Creek MM |
| (9-20-1837) | William & w & ch mbrs of Duck Creek Mtg, now laid down, have been attached to Spiceland Mtg |
| 3-21-1838 | Elizabeth & Jonas Dishelms altm |
| 9-19-1838 | William inf mtg he has had an arbitration with another mbr of this mtg & is dissatisfied with award.  Req a new hearing |
| 10-24-1838 | The comm rpts that they believe William's award was unjust.  A new hearing has been granted |
| 11-25-1840 | William dis for disunity & refusing to abide by arbitration in another case |
| 6-1-1901 | Daisy (Hiatt) gct Duck Creek MM |
| 6-7-1913 | Maurice rocf Duck Creek MM |

HOUGH - HUFF
| | |
|---|---|
| 8-23-1837 | Hiram produced a cert from New Garden MM & the consent of his parents to m Anna C Hubbard |
| 8-23-1837 | Hiram & Anna C Hubbard altm |
| 11-22-1837 | Anna C gct New Garden MM |

HOWELL
| | |
|---|---|
| 3-7-1908 | Ira rec in mbrp |

HOWERTON
| | |
|---|---|
| 12-22-1858 | Eliza gct Lynn Grove MM, Iowa |

HUBBARD
| | |
|---|---|
| 3-24-1837 | Anna C rocf Duck Creek MM |
| 8-23-1837 | Anna C & Hiram Hough altm |
| (9-20-1837) | Hardy & ch, Martha, Susanna, Mary & Caleb who have been mbrs of Duck Creek MM, now laid down, now attached to Spiceland MM |
| 5-22-1839 | Martha, Susanna & Mary gct Walnut Ridge MM |
| 1-22-1840 | Richard J & w Sarah & ch Edwin, Charles S, Margaret, Caroline, Phebe Ann & Harriett P rocf Milford MM |
| 5-19-1841 | Caleb gct Hopewell MM |
| 2-23-1842 | Richard J appt recorder of the minutes |
| 6-22-1842 | Hardy gct Walnut Ridge MM |
| 1-24-1844 | Mary Jane rocf Cherry Grove MM |
| 3-23-1846 | Mary Jane gct Walnut Ridge MM |
| 3-25-1846 | (J) Butler & w Celia & ch Eliza Ann & Delilah Carolina rocf Whitewater MM |
| 8-25-1847 | Richard J appt an overseer at Raysville PM |
| 1-19-1848 | Richard J Hubbard, Samuel Pritchard & Amos Kenworthy appt to a comm on burials within the limits of Raysville MM |
| 7-19-1848 | Edwin mcd, dis |
| 11-21-1849 | Margaret & Nathan H Ballenger altm |
| 10-13-1850 | Charles S gct Blue River MM to m Martha White |
| 7-25-1851 | Martha rocf Blue River MM |
| 9-22-1852 | Jacob rocf New Garden MM, N C |
| 2-22-1854 | Caroline & Albert Newby altm |
| 10-24-1855 | Richard J & w Sarah & ch Harriett P, Emily, Henry, Joseph, George, Julia & Anna gct Milford MM |
| 1-21-1857 | Jacob mcd   dis |

HUCKLEBERRY
| | |
|---|---|
| 4-4-1891 | Wilburn & w Mary rec in mbrp |

HUDLESON - HUDDLESTON
| | |
|---|---|
| 4-21-1847 | Lucinda (form Morris) mcd, dis |
| 2-6-1886 | Harry rocf Salem MM |
| 6-4-1892 | Harry gct New Castle MM |
| 3-4-1893 | Irena Dell, Lola Bell, Hettie & father, Samuel Harvey rec in mbrp |
| 3-2-1895 | Morris rec in mbrp |
| 5-3-1895 | Ella gct New Castle MM |
| 12-7-1895 | Clara Elsie rec in mbrp |
| 9-4-1897 | Lola Bell & Irene Dell rel on req |
| 5-7-1898 | Hettie rel on req |
| 1-3-1903 | Clara Elsie gct Westland MM |
| 10-2-1909 | Ella Butler rocf New Castle MM |
| 2-3-1912 | Maria rec in mbrp |

HUFF - HOUGH
| | |
|---|---|
| 10-25-1837 | James & w Susannah & dt Caroline Huff & a minor nt Nathan H Coffin, under their care, rocf Newgarden MM |
| 6-28-1842 | James & s Robert B gct New Garden MM |
| 5-2-1929 | Helen, Harriet & Peggy rec on req |
| 5-2-1929 | Winifred rec on req |

HUNICUTT
| | |
|---|---|
| 9-20-1837 | George E rocf Walnut Ridge Mtg to m Martha Pusey |
| 9-20-1837 | George E & Martha Pusey altm |
| 12-20-1837 | Martha P gct Walnut Ridge MM |
| 12-19-1838 | George E & w Martha rocf Walnut Ridge MM |
| 11-22-1843 | George & w Martha & s William Penn gct Walnut Ridge MM |
| 7-22-1846 | James P & w Peninah & s William Henry rocf Walnut Ridge MM |
| 7-19-1848 | John A produced a cert from Walnut Ridge Mtg to m Hannah Ann Davis but the consent of Hannah Ann Davis's father not having been produced, a comm appt to find the reason for it being withheld & comm directed to rpt to next mtg |
| 8-23-1848 | John A & Hannah Ann Davis now altm |
| 10-25-1848 | Hannah Ann gct Walnut Ridge MM |
| 4-25-1849 | James & w Peninah & ch William H gct Duck Creek MM |
| 2-22-1854 | James & w Peninah & ch William H rocf Walnut Ridge MM |

HUNT
| | |
|---|---|
| 3-20-1833 | Allen rpt mcd,  dis 5-22-1833 |
| 3-19-1834 | Isom gct Milford MM to m Susanna Stanley (s Isom Sr, late of Guilford Co, N C) |
| 6-25-1834 | Isom gct Milford MM |
| 12-24-1834 | Joseph B & w Ann E rocf Elk MM, Oh |
| 12-24-1834 | Benjamin a minor rocf Elk MM, Oh |
| 5-20-1835 | Joseph B appt Librarian in room of Aaron Stanley |

SPICELAND

## HUNT (Cont)

|  |  |
|---|---|
| 8-19-1835 | Joseph B Hunt, David James, Isaac White, Calvin Wasson, Vierling Kersey, John Hiatt, George Evans, William Edwards, & Nathan Davis appt to comm on Education for the ensuing year |
| 8-24-1836 | Rachel dis for disunity, dpl |
| 4-19-1837 | Abel dis for na & dpl |
| 4-25-1838 | John & w Rachel gct Westfield MM |
| 4-25-1838 | William appt an overseer |
| 12-12-1838 | John of Fall Creek PM dis for na & dpl |
| 11-20-1839 | Joseph B, Librarian at Spiceland PM, rpt decd |
| 8-19-1840 | David rocf Goshen MM |
| 8-19-1840 | Phineas George Canning, a minor, rocf Goshen MM |
| 8-19-1840 | Ruth rocf Goshen MM |
| 4-20-1842 | Ruth dis |
| 6-22-1842 | David P of Elm Grove PM compl of for mcd |
| 10-19-1842 | Ann E & Aaron L Please altm  The comm rpts that the rights of her ch are secure |
| 11-23-1842 | David P now residing in limits of Fairfield MM, dis |
| 11-23-1846 | Sarah & ch Jacob, Sarah, William C & Elmina rocf Hopewell MM, N C end by Milford MM |
| 4-21-1847 | Sally Ann Symons (form Hunt) con mcd |
| 9-24-1851 | Jacob dis |
| 6- 7-1854 | Levi Cloud gct Walnut Ridge MM to m Rebecca Hunt |
| 5-19-1858 | Mary & Jonathan T Rogers altm |
| 9-19-1860 | Martha G & Oliver H Bales altm |
| 3-20-1861 | Susan B & Josiah T Unthank altm |
| 3- 6-1886 | Elizabeth rec in mbrp |
| 4- 3-1886 | Lafayette rocf Raysville MM |
| 2- 4-1888 | Lafayette & w Lizzie gct Raysville MM |

## HUNTSINGER

|  |  |
|---|---|
| 4- 6-1889 | Mary & ch William, Nellie & Nora rocf Duck Creek MM returned 5- 4-1889, jas |

## HUSTON

|  |  |
|---|---|
| 12-27-1922 | James rec in mbrp |

## HUTSON

|  |  |
|---|---|
| 11-21-1838 | Mary dis for dpl & na |
| 1- 7-1888 | John W rec in mbrp |
| 10-11-1890 | John rel on req |

## IRVIN

|  |  |
|---|---|
| 6- 2-1900 | Mary Mullin gct Indianapolis MM |

## JACKSON

|  |  |
|---|---|
| 1- 2-1886 | Hettie rec in mbrp |
| 4- 3-1886 | Isabel A rec in mbrp |
| 5- 3-1890 | Isabella drpd from mbrp |
| 8- 3-1901 | Louisa Chew drpd from mbrp |
| 5- 5-1906 | Hettie drpd from mbrp |

## JAMES

|  |  |
|---|---|
| 12-24-1834 | David & w Mary & ch Levi C, Atticus E, Ruth Ann & Alfred P rocf Whitewater MM |
| 8-19-1835 | David James, Isaac White, Calvin Wasson, Vierling Kersey, John Hiatt, George Evans, William Edwards, Nathan Davis & Joseph B Hunt appt comm on Education for ensuing year |
| 2-24-1836 | David appt an overseer at Elm Grove PM |
| 6-22-1836 | David James, Josiah Pennington & Elias Jessop appt comm to att funerals of mbrs at Elm Grove PM |
| 6-21-1837 | Naomi dis for na & dpl |
| 8- 9-1837 | David appt to comm on Education for ensuing year |
| 5-23-1838 | David & w Mary & ch Ruth Ann, Mary, Levi C, Atticus S, Jonathan H & Lindley M gct West Grove MM |
| 11-20-1839 | Joshua of Duck Creek PM compl of for na & att a mcd |
| 12-25-1839 | Joshua dis |
| 3-25-1840 | Mary dis for na & att a mcd |
| 10-21-1840 | Daniel gct West Grove MM |
| 12- 7-1922 | Betty rec in mbrp |

## JARRET

|  |  |
|---|---|
| 4- 6-1872 | Martha Lenora Isabella, a minor rec in mbrp (she was adopted by William & Elizabeth Sheridan) on req of her Guardian |
| 10- 8-1881 | John William rocf West Grove MM |
| 11- 3-1883 | J W rec in mbrp |
| 2- 7-1914 | Carl rec in mbrp |

## JAY

|  |  |
|---|---|
| 11-21-1838 | Edith & dts Asenath & Ruth Ann rocf Cherry Grove MM |
| 6-24-1840 | Edith & Thomas Kirk altm |
| 10-20-1841 | Davis Gray gct Duck Creek MM to m Ruth Anna Jay |
| 1-23-1850 | Keturah rocf Mill Creek MM, (Oh) |
| 8-21-1850 | James & w Susanna rocf Mill Creek MM, Oh |
| 3-19-1851 | James & w Susanna gct Back Creek MM |
| 3-19-1851 | Keturah gct Back Creek MM (wid of John & mth of James) |
| 5-21-1856 | Joseph W produced a cert from (?) to m |
| 5-21-1856 | Joseph W & Anna Prichard altm |
| 10-23-1861 | Eli & Mahala from West Branch MM, Oh, rptd to have been teachers for the previous 9 mths in Spiceland school |
| 2-19-1862 | Eli & w Mahala rocf West Branch MM, Oh |
| 3-25-1863 | Eli & Mahala gct West Branch MM, Oh |

## JESSUP - JESSOP

|  |  |
|---|---|
| 1-23-1833 | Tidamon & w Lydia & ch original mbrs |
| 6-22-1836 | Sarah rocf Whitewater MM |
| 6-22-1836 | Elias Jessop, David James & Josiah Pennington appt to a comm to att funerals at Elm Grove PM |
| 7-20-1836 | Evan rocf Walnut Ridge MM |
| 7-20-1836 | Tidamon appt to comm |
| 4-19-1837 | Evan gct Milford MM |
| 1-23-1839 | Sarah gct Westfield MM |
| 1-22-1840 | Tidamon appt an overseer |
| 12-10-1843 | Tidamon jas, Separatists, dis (at Elm Grove PM) |
| 5-22-1844 | Elias jas, Separatists, dis (at Elm Grove PM) |
| 8-21-1844 | Lydia jas, Separatists, dis |
| 5-19-1847 | Jesse B jas, Separatists & mcd, dis |
| 7-21-1847 | Catherine (form Macy) jas, Separatists, (ASF) mcd, dis |
| 9-24-1851 | Elias rst |
| 5-19-1852 | Mary & Benedict Macy altm |
| 4-20-1853 | Ruth Kenard (form Jessup) mcd, dis |
| 8-22-1855 | Jesse B & w Lucinda & ch Elmira & Theodore rec in mbrp |
| 8-22-1855 | William Bond gct Walnut Ridge MM to m Sarah Jessop |
| 2-25-1857 | Charles mcd dis |
| 2-24-1858 | Emily Mendenhall (form Jessup) mcd dis |
| 6-23-1858 | Tidamon & Lydia rst |
| 10-20-1858 | David mcd dis |
| 11-21-1858 | Jesse B gct Walnut Ridge MM to m Millie Newby |
| 5-25-1859 | Milly rocf Walnut Ridge MM |
| 3- 4-1865 | Jesse B appt to read marriage cert at Elm Grove PM, & place them in the hands of the Recorder |
| 7- 1-1865 | Jesse B appt an overseer |
| 11- 4-1865 | Jesse B & Cynthia Fentress a wid w/ch & not a mbr altm |
| 7- 6-1867 | Cynthia & her ch Martin Frank & Estella Fentrees rec in mbrp |
| 12- 7-1867 | Julia, with her adopted dt Ida, rec in mbrp |
| 11- 5-1870 | David rec in mbrp |
| 5- 3-1873 | Lydia gct Westland MM |
| 8- 3-1876 | Jesse B & fam gct Lynn Grove MM, Iowa |
| 6- 3-1876 | Theodore gct Lynn Grove MM, Iowa |
| 12- 1-1877 | David & w Julia & adopted dt Ida May Crawford rocf Raysville MM |
| 2- 6-1892 | Julia drpd from mbrp |

## JESTER

|  |  |
|---|---|
| 6-23-1852 | Lemuel F & w Mary rocf Mill Creek MM, Oh |
| 10-25-1854 | Lemuel F & w Mary & ch William P & Martha gct Mill Creek MM, Oh |

## JENKINSON

|  |  |
|---|---|
| 6- 7-1928 | William E & w Louisa rec in mbrp |
| 4- 6-1933 | Dr William E & Louise rel on req |

SPICELAND

## JOHNSON

|  |  |
|---|---|
| 1-23-1833 | James & w Mary & ch original mbrs |
| 1-23-1833 | James appt to a comm |
| 1-23-1833 | Mary appt to a comm |
| 1-23-1833 | James Johnson, Josiah Small, William Baldwin & Isaac White appt to unite with a comm from women's mtg, to form comm on Education & to rpt |
| 2-20-1833 | James appt an overseer at Spiceland PM |
| 11-19-1834 | Rachel & James P Gause altm |
| 8-24-1836 | James appt to comm on Education for the ensuing year |
| 12-21-1836 | Elizabeth & John Bogue altm |
| 4-25-1838 | James & Rebecca White, a wid, altm |
| 10-23-1839 | Joel produced a cert from Milford MM to m Elizabeth Davis |
| 10-23-1839 | Joel & Elizabeth Davis altm |
| 5-20-1840 | Joel rocf Milford MM |
| 10-21-1840 | Caleb appt asst clerk & Caleb White appt clerk |
| 4-25-1841 | Joel & w Elizabeth & dt Lydia Ann gct Hopewell MM |
| 11-24-1841 | Jesse & w Lydia & ch Susannah, Patience & Mary rocf Deep Creek MM, N C & end to Duck Creek MM |
| 11-24-1841 | Thomas rocf Deep Creek MM, N C & end to Duck Creek MM |
| 4-20-1842 | Caleb & Asenith Evans altm |
| 4-20-1842 | Emily & Jonathan E Saint altm |
| 10-19-1842 | Caleb appt asst clerk & Caleb White appt clk |
| 11-25-1846 | Jonathan produced cert from Cherry Grove Mtg to m Jane Small, a wid w/ch |
| 11-25-1846 | Jonathan & Jane Small altm |
| 11-25-1846 | For convenience of Jonathan & Jane Small, a mtg has been granted for tomorrow at 11 o'clock for their m |
| 12-23-1846 | The comm appt to att m of Jonathan & Jane Small rpt it was orderly & they produced the m cert |
| 1-20-1847 | Jane & s William SMALL gct Cherry Grove MM |
| 10-24-1849 | James Johnson & Samuel White appt overseers at Raysville PM |
| 10-23-1850 | Caleb appt Clerk & David Edwards appt asst Clerk |
| 5-25-1853 | Hiram & w Rhoda & s Lindley E rocf Cane Creek MM, N C |
| 5-25-1853 | Sarah & dt Susan rocf Cane Creek MM, N C |
| 12-19-1855 | William C, a Minister, & w Anna & ch Martitia E, William Elwood, Emily & Mary Ann rocf Whitewater MM |
| 12-19-1855 | Caleb & Miriam A Wilson altm |
| 3-21-1860 | John W rst at Whitewater MM, w/con of this mtg |
| 10-24-1860 | John W rocf Whitewater MM |
| 7-mo-1863 | Caleb appt an overseer |
| 3- 4-1865 | Frances H rec in mbrp |
| 3- 4-1865 | Iola Bell & Anna Mary, ch of John W & Frances H, rec in mbrp |
| 8- 5-1865 | Miriam appt an Elder |
| 4- 7-1866 | Caleb recorded as Minister |
| 7- 6-1867 | John W & w Frances & ch Iola Bell & Anna Mary gct Indianapolis MM |
| 11- 7-1867 | Jane rocf Cherry Grove MM |
| 12- 7-1867 | Rhoda appt an overseer at Dunreith PM |
| 6- 6-1868 | Rhoda appt an overseer at Dunreith PM |
| 6- 6-1868 | Albert con mcd |
| 9- 5-1868 | Mariam an Elder |
| 3- 4-1871 | Albert H appt the recorder of removals of MM |
| 8- 5-1871 | Miriam appt an Elder |
| 7- 6-1872 | Mariam rec as Minister |
| 3- 1-1873 | Mary & her s Andrew G Lewark gct New Salem MM |
| 5- 2-1874 | Hiram appt an overseer |
| 5- 2-1874 | Rhoda appt an overseer |
| 6- 1-1878 | Susan, Mathew M & Mary rec in mbrp |
| 11- 2-1878 | Caleb & fam gct Lynn Grove MM, Iowa |
| 5- 5-1883 | Hiram appt an Elder |
| 5- 5-1883 | Rhoda appt an Elder |
| 6- 2-1883 | Susan F rocf Whitewater MM |
| 6- 2-1883 | Horace M gct Lynn Grove MM, Iowa |
| 12- 1-1883 | Madison M & ch rel on req |
| 3- 7-1885 | Emma R rocf Center QM, Oh |
| 4- 4-1885 | Belle gct Sterling MM, Kan |
| 12- 5-1885 | Dorsey & William rec in mbrp |
| 1- 1-1887 | Robert A, Sarah L, William & Mary A transf to Muncie MM |
| 7- 5-1890 | Albert dropped from mbrp |
| 1- 2-1892 | Charles C & w Emma R & ch Orville & Mildred M gct Salem MM, Ore |
| 6- 4-1892 | Robert A, Sarah L & Mary A drpd from mbrp |
| 3- 5-1904 | William A & w Maude & s Clarnece rec in mbrp |
| 4- 7-1906 | Carl rec in mbrp |
| 5- 5-1906 | Arthur & Rothens drpd from mbrp |
| 3- 4-1911 | Arthur C gct Hopewell MM |
| 12- 7-1912 | William A & w Maud & s Clarence & Carl drpd from mbrp |
| 11- 1-1913 | Edith Harrold gct Hopewell MM |
| 7- 3-1915 | Albert S & w Della & ch Edna Marie & Gertrude Evelyn rocf ___?___ MM |
| 4- 6-1918 | Marie rec in mbrp |
| 4- 1-1920 | Ralph rec in mbrp |
| 7- 3-1920 | Susan E gct Whitewater MM |
| 5- 5-1921 | Evelyn rec in mbrp |
| 5- 4-1922 | Ralph rel on req |

## JONES

|  |  |
|---|---|
| 3-25-1835 | Anna rec on req |
| 8-24-1836 | Margaret, dt of Charles, decd, & Nancy (Wells) Jones Charlesbury (dis in N C) rocf Symons Creek MM, N C under the care of Charles Bundy & his w Pheraba |
| ( 9-20-1837) | Lydia, a mbr of Duck Creek MM, now laid down, attached to Spiceland Mtg |
| 5-22-1839 | Margaret Jane gct Bloomfield MM |
| 2-19-1840 | Mourning rec in mbrp |
| 11-24-1841 | Parthena, dt Charles, decd, & Nancy (Wells) Jones Charlesbury, (dis in N C) rocf Symons Creek Mtg, N C, under care of Miriam (Toms) White, a wid |
| 1-22-1845 | Parthena & Joseph B Davis altm |
| 5-20-1846 | Lucinda (form Palin) con mcd |
| 6-24-1846 | Margaret gct Milford MM |
| 12-23-1847 | Lucinda gct Salem MM, Iowa |
| 11-23-1853 | Mourning gct Westfield MM |
| 10- 8-1870 | Martha rec in mbrp |
| 2- 7-1874 | James R rec in mbrp |
| 5- 2-1874 | Sylvester rec in mbrp (s John D & Susannah) |
| 12- 4-1875 | William & w rec in mbrp |
| 11- 4-1876 | Sylvester gct Springfield MM |
| 1- 6-1877 | Sina A gct West Branch MM, Oh |
| 7- 7-1877 | James R & fam gct Milford MM |
| 6- 7-1879 | Henry W rocf Van Wert MM, Ohio |
| 6- 7-1879 | Carrie T w of Henry W rocf Walnut Ridge MM |
| 11- 3-1883 | M Louisa rec in mbrp |
| 3- 1-1884 | Elizabeth rec in mbrp |
| 4- 2-1887 | Henry W & fam gct Van Wert MM, Oh |
| 12- 3-1887 | Ella rel on req |
| 8- 7-1897 | Barclay & w Rhoda & ch Hubert rocf Scipio MM |
| 3- 4-1899 | Barclay & w Rhoda & s Hubert gct Traverse City MM, Mich |
| 7- 7-1900 | Henry W & w Carrie T & ch Osward Bevan Braithwait & Barton Ellwin Jones rocf Friends Chapel MM |
| 11- 3-1906 | Anna May rec in mbrp |

## JORDON

|  |  |
|---|---|
| 3- 2-1901 | Maud May rec in mbrp |
| 12- 7-1912 | Maud May drpd from mbrp |

## JULIAN

|  |  |
|---|---|
| 2- 5-1898 | William A of Juniata, Nebr rec in mbrp |
| 8- 4-1906 | Reno M & w Lillian V & Clarice F rocf Knightstown MM |
| 4- 1-1911 | Reno & fam gct Greenfield MM |

## JUSTICE

|  |  |
|---|---|
| 5-19-1847 | Eliza rec in mbrp |
| 6-21-1848 | Eliza & Reuben Hodson altm |

## KARSON

|  |  |
|---|---|
| 5- 4-1912 | Frank & w Abbie rec in mbrp |
| 5- 4-1912 | Carl, Pearl & Gail rec in mbrp |
| 1- 1-1916 | Mabel rec in mbrp |

## KAUFMAN

|  |  |
|---|---|
| 6- 2-1900 | Martha rec in mbrp |

SPICELAND

## KEARNS

|  |  |
|---|---|
| 10-13-1866 | Thomas & w Mary & ch William B, Delphia J, Sarah E, John S & Nerius A rec in mbrp |
| 7- 4-1874 | Thomas & w Mary & ch Sarah E, Jehu P & Nereus A, rocf Raysville MM |
| 7- 1-1882 | Mary gct Fairmount MM |
| 7- 1-1882 | Sarah E & Nereus gct Fairmount MM |
| 12- 5-1885 | Joseph & Elizabeth Agnes rec in mbrp |
| 12- 5-1885 | Walter & Heyden Arthur rec in mbrp |
| 1- 1-1887 | Joseph E, Agnes E, Walter & Heyden trans to Muncie MM |

## KEISLING

|  |  |
|---|---|
| 3- 5-1931 | James & w Alice rec in mbrp |

## KELLY

|  |  |
|---|---|
| 10- 8-1881 | Dora rocf White River MM |

## KELLUM

|  |  |
|---|---|
| 6- 2-1894 | Caroline gct Indianapolis MM |

## KELSEY

|  |  |
|---|---|
| 9- 5-1914 | Mead A & w Anna L & ch Ruth & Robert M rocf Oskaloosa MM, Iowa |
| 12- 4-1915 | Mead & w Anna L & ch Ruth & Robert M gct West Richmond MM |

## KENDALL

|  |  |
|---|---|
| 11-27-1837 | David rocf Whitewater MM |
| 12-20-1837 | David & Charity Dickey altm |
| 10- 2-1919 | Martha W, Anna M & Clara B rocf Chester MM |
| 11- 6-1930 | Richard rec in mbrp |
| 12- 4-1930 | Rebecca J rocf Duck Creek MM |
| 4- 6-1933 | Elberta Hodson gct Indianapolis MM |

## KENARD - KENNARD

|  |  |
|---|---|
| 4-20-1853 | Ruth (form Jessop) mcd dis |
| 5- 6-1876 | Rebecca rec in mbrp |
| 4- 7-1883 | Rebecca gct Raysville MM |
| 6-30-1916 | Rebecca rel on req |

## KENNEDY

|  |  |
|---|---|
| 6- 2-1866 | Caleb Hall gct Milford MM to m Isabelle Kennedy, a wid |
| 10-10-1868 | George Fox gct Neuse MM, N C |

## KENWORTHY

|  |  |
|---|---|
| 11-25-1835 | Amos & w Mary & ch William, Robert, Jesse, Joel, Willis, Ann, Amos M & Isaac F rocf Springborough MM, Ohio |
| 12-20-1837 | William gct Walnut Ridge MM to m Asenath Patterson |
| 4-25-1838 | Asenath rocf Walnut Ridge MM |
| 7-24-1839 | Robert & Doughty Saint altm |
| 11-25-1840 | William & w Asenath & ch Sarah P & James gct Walnut Ridge MM |
| 1-20-1841 | Robert & w Doughty & ch William, gct Duck Creek MM |
| 6-22-1842 | Robert & w Doughty & s William S rocf Duck Creek MM |
| 9-21-1842 | Jesse W gct Duck Creek MM to m Eliza Gregg |
| 3-22-1843 | Eliza rocf Duck Creek MM |
| 12-20-1843 | Jesse W & w Eliza & s Ambrose Asahel gct Duck Creek MM |
| 4-24-1844 | William & ch Sarah & James rocf Walnut Ridge MM |
| 2-19-1845 | William con mcd |
| 7-23-1845 | Jesse & w Eliza & ch Ambrose Asahel & Mary Elizabeth rocf Duck Creek MM |
| 12-24-1845 | Mary Ann rocf Duck Creek MM |
| 5-20-1846 | Amos Sr gct Hopewell MM to m Elizabeth Newby, a wid |
| 6-24-1846 | Joel & Rebecca Spencer altm |
| 9-23-1846 | Elizabeth rocf Hopewell MM |
| 6-23-1847 | William & w Mary & ch Sarah, James & Phebe Ann gct Hopewell MM |
| 8-25-1847 | Jesse & w Eliza & ch Ambrose A, Mary E & Emily G gct Duck Creek MM |
| 10-20-1847 | Ann & Jeremiah Griffin altm |
| 1-19-1848 | Amos Kenworthy, Sr, Richard J Hubbard & Samuel Pritchard appt to a comm on burials within the limits of Raysville PM |
| 11-22-1848 | Willis gct Duck Creek MM to m Naomi Kirk |
| 4-25-1849 | Naomi rocf Duck Creek MM |
| 12-25-1850 | William & w Mary & ch Sarah P, James, Phebe Ann & Amos rocf Hopewell MM |
| 3-19-1851 | Amos M, jr s of Amos, Sr gct Duck Creek MM |
| 5-19-1852 | Amos M rocf Duck Creek MM |
| 9-22-1852 | Amos M & Phebe Reynolds req appt at Raysville MH for tomorrow, at the usual hour, to accomp their m, on the grounds that on the next two week day meetings, their parents & some of their friends will visit at YM & the next will be PM day. Their req is granted and the mtg appt accordingly |
| 12-20-1854 | Amos M & w Phebe & ch Oliver gct Spring Creek MM, Iowa |
| 3-21-1855 | Willis & w Naomi & ch Allen, Milton, Elizabeth Caroline gct Spring Creek MM, Iowa |
| 3-21-1855 | William & w Mary Ann & ch Sarah P, James, Phebe Ann & Amos gct Spring Creek MM, Iowa |
| 4-13-1856 | Isaac F gct Duck Creek MM to m Abigail Hiatt |
| 7-23-1856 | Abigail rocf Duck Creek MM |
| 4-21-1858 | Isaac F Burnet gct Fairfield MM to m Hannah Kenworthy |
| 11-25-1863 | Amos M & w Phebe & ch Phebe H, Oliver & Charles H rocf West Union MM |
| 11- 4-1865 | Amos M & w Phebe & ch Oliver & Charles H gct New Salem MM |
| 6- 6-1868 | Elizabeth rocf Raysville MM |
| 4- 7-1883 | Charles H & w Cynthia A & dt M Ethel rocf Raysville MM |
| 11- 1-1884 | Charles H & w Cynthia A & dt M Ethel gct Long Lake MM, Mich |
| 11- 1-1902 | Ida Lenora (Holloway) gct Kokomo MM, (w of Murry) |
| 2- 5-1909 | Truman C & w Marianna & ch Helen, Mary, Richard, Catherine, Eunice Edna & Isabel rocf Damascus MM, Ohio |
| 10- 2-1909 | Truman & w Marianna & ch gct Whitewater MM |

## KEARNS - KERNS

|  |  |
|---|---|
| 4- 4-1903 | Maurine Gardner gct Duck Creek MM |
| 10- 5-1922 | Maurine Gardner rocf Duck Creek MM |
| 3- 5-1925 | Louise roc |
| 6- 5-1929 | Herbert & w Georgie & her dt Maxine Groves rocf Duck Creek MM |

## KERR

|  |  |
|---|---|
| 10- 6-1921 | Wade H rec in mbrp |

## KERSEY

|  |  |
|---|---|
| 1-23-1833 | Asher & w Susannah & s Benjamin original mbrs |
| 12-24-1834 | Vierling rocf Milford MM |
| 3-25-1835 | Asher con mcd |
| 3-25-1835 | Edith (form Elliott) con mcd (she was the 2nd w of Asher) |
| 5-20-1835 | Vierling appt to att QM |
| 8-19-1835 | Vierling Kersey, David James, Isaac White, Calvin Wasson, & John Hiatt, George Evans, William Edwards, Nathan Davis & Joseph B Hunt appt to comm on Education for the ensuing year |
| 1-25-1837 | William & w Rachel & ch Silas H, Mary C & Charity W rocf Milford MM |
| 10-25-1837 | Mary C & George Sheridan inf mtg of int to m. Parents' consent given |
| 11-22-1837 | The comm appt to investigate the proposed m of Silas H & Anna M Sweet, rpt nothing to hinder the m, but the couple not appearing, the comm is cont to next mtg |
| 11-22-1837 | Mary C & George Sheridan mcd |
| 1-24-1838 | Silas H & Anna M Sweet inf the Spiceland mtg as follows: " We, the undersigned inform friends that we have abandoned our prospect of m with each other." |
| 7-24-1839 | Silas produced an acknowledgement that he had been guilty of immoral & scandalous conduct & been in habit of upl. A comm was appt to treat with him |
| 8-21-1839 | Silas's acknowledgement is rec by mtg |
| 9-25-1839 | Vierling gct Springborough MM, Ohio to m Mary E Butler |
| 1-22-1840 | Sarah (w of Eli) rec in mbrp |

SPICELAND

## KERSEY (Cont)

|  |  |
|---|---|
| 2-19-1840 | Mary Emily rocf Springborough MM, Ohio |
| 8-19-1840 | Eli rocf Milford MM |
| 1-20-1841 | Vierling & w Mary Emily & dt Ann Mariah gct Walnut Ridge MM |
| 11-24-1841 | Minerva Jane, Maria, William, Albert H, Robert & Caroline Elizabeth, ch of Eli & Sarah rec in mbrp |
| 5-25-1842 | Vierling & w Mary Emily & dt Ann Maria rocf Walnut Ridge MM |
| 8-24-1842 | Silas H dis for dpl, upl, & unbecoming conversation & conduct |
| 3-24-1843 | William & w Rachel gct Mississinewa MM |
| 4-14-1844 | William & w Rachel rocf Mississinewa MM |
| 5-21-1845 | Vierling jas, Separatists (ASF) dis |
| 7-23-1845 | Mary Emily & ch Ann Maria & Richard W gct Milford MM |
| 10-22-1845 | Charity & Joseph M Allen altm |
| 11-19-1845 | Asher & w Edith & ch Benjamin V, Jane, Martha, Clarkson & Sarah Ellen gct Mississinewa MM |
| 3-20-1850 | Minerva Jane Kirk (form Kersey) mcd dis |
| 9-25-1850 | Edith & stepson Benjamin V & her ch Jane, Martha, Clarkson, Elizabeth & Albert rocf Mississinewa MM |
| 2-23-1853 | Edith & ch Jane, Martha, Thomas Clarkson, Elizabeth & Albert Henry gct Pipe Creek MM |
| 7-20-1853 | Benjamin V dis |

## KIMBREL

|  |  |
|---|---|
| 6- 1-1878 | Nancy rec in mbrp |
| 5- 2-1891 | Nancy rec in mbrp |
| 2- 6-1892 | Nancy gct Hopewell MM |
| 3- 2-1893 | Andrew L & Mary J & s Otis rec in mbrp |
| 4- 3-1897 | Pearl rec in mbrp |
| 3-  -1901 | Dora rec in mbrp |
| 3- 6-1904 | Mary A & Gertrude rec in mbrp |

## KINDLEY

|  |  |
|---|---|
| 8-20-1834 | Joel & w Rachel & s Charles gct Milford MM |

## KING

|  |  |
|---|---|
| ( 9-20-1837) | Isaac & w Ann & ch Herman, Hannah, Phebe, Rebecca, Lydia & Deborah, mbrs of Duck Creek Mtg, now laid down, attached to Spiceland Mtg |
| 3-23-1842 | Phebe rocf Walnut Ridge MM |
| 4-20-1842 | Phebe & Thomas Moore altm |
| 5-25-1842 | Hannah rocf Walnut Ridge MM |
| 3-22-1848 | Hannah gct West Grove MM |
| 4-21-1858 | Lydia M rocf Chesterfield MM, Ohio |
| 4-21-1858 | Marium rocf Chesterfield MM, Ohio |
| 6-23-1858 | Lydia M & Harmon H Allen altm |
| 7-22-1863 | Marium & William C Stanley inf mtg of int to m |
| 2-27-1864 | Marium, mbr of Spiceland, rptd mcd con her mcd |
| 2-27-1874 | Harriett rec in mbrp |
| 4- 4-1874 | Roseann rec in mbrp |
| 7- 4-1874 | Rufus P rocf Walnut Ridge MM |
| 10-10-1874 | Emaline H & ch Nelson M & William rec in mbrp |
| 1- 2-1875 | Nancy rec in mbrp |
| 11- 2-1878 | Rufus P gct New Garden MM, N C |
| 2- 4-1882 | Nelson M gct Baltimore MM, Md |
| 3- 4-1882 | Calvin K & w Emily & ch Otis E, Josie E & Flora A rec in mbrp |
| 3- 4-1882 | William gct Walnut Ridge MM |
| 6- 6-1896 | Mattie rec in mbrp |
| 4-12-1898 | Martha jas, M E Ch, drpd from mbrp |
| 8- 6-1898 | Martha rel from mbrp |
| 12- 7-1912 | C Kerney rel from mbrp |

## KINSEY

|  |  |
|---|---|
| 5- 6-1876 | Margaret rec in mbrp |
| 3- 7-1877 | James rec in mbrp |
| 4- 7-1883 | James & w Margaret gct Duck Creek MM (not accepted, cert returned) |

## KIRK

|  |  |
|---|---|
| ( 9-20-1837) | Thomas & w Sarah & ch mbrs of Duck Creek MM, now laid down, have been attached to Spiceland |
| 8-22-1838 | Thomas Kirk appt to a comm |
| 6-24-1840 | Thomas & Edith Jay, a wid, altm |
| 11-22-1848 | Willis Kenworthy gct Duck Creek MM to m Naomi Kirk |
| 3-20-1850 | Minerva Jane (form Kersey) mcd dis |
| 10-23-1850 | Minerva Jane jas , mcd dis |
| 5-20-1857 | Thomas C & w Martha & ch Phlander M, Julius Edward & Henry rocf Duck Creek MM |
| 4- 4-1861 | Thomas C & w Martha & ch Phlander M, Julius E, Henry Milton & Albert gct Duck Creek MM |
| 7-24-1861 | Allen T & w Lucinda E & ch Alice M, & Anna Maria rocf Lynn Grove MM, Iowa |
| 5-21-1862 | Allen T & w Lucinda E & ch Alice M & Anna Maria Jane gct Raysville MM |
| 4- 7-1883 | Albert rocf Duck Creek MM |
| 5- 5-1883 | Amanda R rocf Union MM, Ohio |
| 3- 5-1887 | Kersey E & w Mary & ch Walter, Bessie H, Annie G, Florence M & Jennie E rec in mbrp |
| 1- 7-1893 | Louisa B rec in mbrp |
| 10- 9-1897 | E E & w Agnes rec in mbrp |
| 7- 7-1900 | Louisa B rel on req |
| 4- 7-1906 | Sarah (Snavely) Taylor, rec in mbrp |
| 3- 7-1908 | Mary A rec in mbrp |
| 12- 7-1919 | Clifford drpd from mbrp |
| 11- 3-1927 | Elmer & Isadore W gct West Richmond MM |

## KISER

|  |  |
|---|---|
| 3- 4-1893 | Elmer rec in mbrp |

## KISSELL

|  |  |
|---|---|
| 6- 2-1883 | Anna gct Duck Creek MM |

## KNIGHT

|  |  |
|---|---|
| 1-23-1833 | John & w Sarah & ch original mbrs |
| 7-24-1833 | Amelia dis for na & for att a mcd |
| 10-23-1833 | Elizabeth Benge (form Knight) mcd dis |
| 7-23-1834 | Solomon rocf New Garden MM |
| 3-25-1835 | Solomon dis for dr & dpl (comm rpts he has moved to limits of New Garden MM) |
| 5-25-1836 | Sarah & ch Hannah, Rachel & Abel rocf New Garden MM |
| 10-19-1836 | James dis |
| 12-22-1841 | Abel gct Westfield MM |
| 7-20-1842 | Sarah & ch Hannah & Rachel gct Westfield MM |
| 1-22-1845 | Martha gct New Garden MM |
| 1-22-1845 | John & w Sarah & ch Lucinda gct New Garden MM |

## LACY

|  |  |
|---|---|
| 4- 3-1915 | Wilbur rec in mbrp |
| 5- 1-1919 | Emory & ch Alpheus, Dolores, Paul & Doris rec in mbrp |
| 3- 1-1923 | Anna gct Wichita MM, Kas |

## LAMB

|  |  |
|---|---|
| 9-20-1837 | The case of Henry, as deferred from Duck Creek Mtg, was contd by Spiceland Mtg. (Duck Creek MM had been laid down) |
| 12-20-1837 | Henry dis for disturbing mtgs at Duck Creek |
| 2-21-1838 | Caleb & w Sarah & ch Benjamin Bagley, John Anderson, Edmund, David, Margaret & Jonathan rocf Walnut Ridge MM |
| 7-25-1838 | Josiah s Stephen, rocf Pinney Woods, MM, N C |
| 8-25-1838 | Stephen & w Miriam & ch Timothy, Milisent E, & Esther rocf Pinney Woods MM, N C, end to Walnut Ridge MM |
| 12-19-1838 | Josiah gct Walnut Ridge MM (Cert ret & Spiceland inf he had mcd) |
| 5-22-1839 | Josiah mcd dis |
| 9-25-1839 | Clear Springs PM compl of Salathiel dr but he has moved to limits of Westfield MM |
| 11-20-1839 | Rebecca & minor ch Benjamin & Allen gct Westfield MM |
| 6-24-1840 | Nancy jas dis |
| 7-20-1842 | Henry rst at Westfield MM, w/con of this mtg |
| 9-24-1845 | Josiah rst at Walnut Ridge MM, w/con of this mtg |
| 10-22-1845 | Isom Pearson req cert to Mississinewa MM to m Naoma Lamb |
| 10-20-1847 | Nancy (form Stubbs) con mcd |
| 5-24-1848 | Nancy gct Honey Creek MM |
| 4- 7-1866 | Sarah gct Pipe Creek MM |
| 8- 6-1870 | Jefferson & w Jeriah & ch Cassius, Nancy E & Arnilda rec in mbrp |

SPICELAND

LAMB (Cont)
2- 3-1883    William N rec in mbrp
5- 5-1883    Louise rocf Springfield MM
11- 3-1883   Jefferson & fam rec in mbrp
12- 5-1883   Poline D rel on req
1- 2-1886    Jeriah & dt Nancy E & Armilda dis
6- 7-1890    William N, Louise & Pearl gct Westfield MM
6- 7-1890    Jeriah & ch Cassius & Nancy E drpd from mbrp
6- 1-1901    Effie drpd from mbrp

LANE
1- 7-1893    Samuel rec in mbrp
4- 7-1900    Russell, Otto & Roena Naomi rec in mbrp
4- 7-1906    Clifford W rec in mbrp
5- 6-1911    Melissa May rec in mbrp
4- 6-1918    Melissa drpd from mbrp

LARRANCE
2-24-1836    Peter & w Sarah & ch William, Jesse, Thomas, Rebecca, Patsey, Winney, Stephen & Sally rocf Holly Spring Mtg, N C end by White Lick Mtg
( 9-20-1837) Nathan & w Penninah & ch, mbrs of Duck Creek MM, now laid down, have been attached to Spiceland Mtg
1-22-1840    Nathan & w Penninah & ch Lucinda & Louisa Jane gct White Lick MM
11-25-1840   William gct Sugar River MM
2-24-1847    Thomas H gct Milford MM
5-22-1850    Jesse gct Rush Creek MM
9-23-1854    Stephen gct Back Creek MM
9-19-1855    Rebecca & William B Albertson altm
4-23-1856    Winnie gct Cherry Grove MM
8-19-1857    Martha & Benjamin D Pickett altm
5-19-1858    Daniel gct Oak Ridge MM
4-25-1860    Hannah gct Chester MM
6-20-1860    Mary rocf Walnut Ridge MM
5-22-1861    Mary & s William gct Spring Creek MM, Iowa
5-20-1863    Sarah & Levi Peacock altm
12- 3-1887   Daniel & Hannah T & ch Alice C, Ruth Elma, Mary Effie & Bertha O rocf Green Plain MM, Ohio
10-10-1908   Alice C gct Salem MM, Iowa
11- 7-1908   Bertha O gct Oskaloosa MM, Iowa
12- 3-1910   Bertha O rocf Oskaloosa MM, Iowa
2- 7-1914    Alice C rocf New Castle MM
12- 7-1922   Gertrude M rec in mbrp

LEDBETTER
12- 4-1869   Jael & her ch rec in mbrp
8- 1-1883    Jael & her ch drpd from mbrp
3- 2-1895    Elwood & w Rettie, & ch Leroy, Frank & Martha rec in mbrp
12- 7-1912   Ruby rel on req
12- 7-1912   Frank drpd from mbrp

LEEKA
11- 7-1868   Lucinda B gct Clear Creek MM, Oh

LEFTER
4- 7-1883    Ora A rec in mbrp
9- 4-1930    Ora A drpd from mbrp
4- 2-1931    Pansey Reece gct Lewisville MM

LEIGHTON
4- 7-1921    Scott & w Lena rec in mbrp
10- 8-1926   Scott D & w Lena rel on req

LEONARD
5- 3-1873    Jonathan rec in mbrp
6- 2-1883    Jonathan drpd from mbrp
2- 1-1905    Charity (Demit) gct Hopewell MM

LESSAULT - LESEAULT
8- 4-1911    Charles & Lena rocf Cherokee MM, Okla
12- 2-1911   Charles & Lena gct Haviland MM, Kas

LEVERING
11- 4-1911   George C & w Emily R & ch Ruth Ella, Frances Margaret, Elizabeth Bertha, & Robert George rec in mbrp
11- 1-1913   George C & fam gct Green Plain MM

LEWARK
6- 6-1868    Mary & ch rec in mbrp
3- 1-1873    Mary Johnson & her s Andrew G Lewark gct New Salem MM, ?

LEWELLING
9-20-1837    The comm which had been appt at Duck Creek MM to treat with Meshack, rpt at Spiceland Mtg, that the service had been performed (Duck Creek MM had been laid down)
1-24-1838    William & Cyrene Wilson inf mtg of int to m  Consent of parents now had
2-21-1838    William & Cyrene Wilson altm
6-20-1838    Henderson & w Elizabeth & ch Alfred, Mary Asenath & Rachel gct Vermillion MM, Ill
9-19-1838    John & w Elva & ch Sarah & Eli gct Vermillion MM, Ill
9-19-1838    William & w Cyrena gct Vermillion MM, Ill
3-25-1840    Meshack appt to a comm
4-22-1840    Henry appt to a comm
6- 3-1871    James M rocf Duck Creek MM
10-14-1871   James M & Augusta F Byers altm  (there are no surviving parents)
10-14-1871   James M & Augusta F Byers req a mtg apptd at Jesse B Jessup's on next First Day at 2 o'clock PM for the purpose of accompl their m.  Their req granted
4- 4-1903    James M gct Newberg MM, Or

LINDAMOOD
6- 4-1870    John & w Elizabeth & ch Albert, Emory, Florie & Minnie rec in mbrp

LITTLE
1- 2-1875    James & w Elizabeth rec in mbrp
11- 2-1879   James & fam gct White River MM

LLOYD
6- 2-1881    Robert rocf New Garden MM, N C

LUPTON
2-22-1843    David & w Ann & ch Ruth Esther & Beulah Emily Lupton & Phebe Miller, a relative of Ann Lupton, rocf Sugar River MM
7-22-1846    David W & w Ann & ch Ruth Esther, B Emma, Richard P Lupton, & Phebe Miller under their care, gct Walnut Ridge MM
2- 7-1880    Deborah A rocf Pleasant Grove (West) MM

LUTHER
7- 2-1870    Iwry (?) & w Sarah & ch Dorothy E, Narcissa A & James A rec in mbrp

LYKINS
1- 3-1878    Sarah Jane rocf West Grove MM
7- 5-1884    Sebastian, Sylvester & Jackson, ch of Sarah J rec in mbrp
1- 1-1887    Jackson transferred to Muncie MM
1- 4-1913    Sylvester & w Laura & s Eral Ervin rocf Knightstown MM
1- 4-1913    Gertrude rec in mbrp

LYTLE
6- 6-1885    William Edwards gct Philadelphia MM, Pa to m Fanny Lytle
5- 5-1906    Ada drpd from mbrp

MACE
1-20-1836    Rhoda Hiatt & her ch James T, Ann T & Joseph D MACE rocf New Garden MM (ch of William Mace jr, decd & Rhoda)
6-24-1840    James of Elm Grove PM dis for jas
10-19-1842   Ann t gct Salem MM, Iowa
4-19-1843    Joel Hiatt & w Rhoda & her s Joseph D Mace, gct Salem MM, Iowa

MACY
1-23-1833    William & w Phebe (an Elder), & fam original mbrs
5-22-1833    Solomon & w Priscilla & s Edwin rocf Duck Creek MM
6-19-1833    Solomon appt recorder of Births & Deaths
8-21-1833    Solomon appt clerk & Exum White appt asst clerk

SPICELAND

MACY (Cont)

|  |  |
|---|---|
| 6-25-1834 | Solomon appt clerk & Exum White appt asst clerk |
| 6-24-1835 | Solomon appt clerk & William Unthank appt asst clerk |
| 2-24-1836 | William appt an overseer at Elm Grove PM |
| 2-24-1836 | William Macy, William Edwards & Samuel Pritchard appt at Elm Grove PM to receive & hold a deed to real estate at Elm Grove PM |
| 3-23-1836 | Henry H & w Peninah & dt Ann H & Jonathan Gray, a minor under their care, gct Walnut Ridge MM |
| 7-20-1836 | Phebe, an Elder, & Isaac White, an Elder, appt to accompany Catherine Coffin, a Minister, on a trip to White Lick QMtgs |
| 8-24-1836 | William appt to comm on Education for the ensuing year |
| 2-22-1837 | William Macy, Samuel Pritchard & William Edwards appt to receive & hold in trust, the deed to Elm Grove PM for land on which the mtg house now stands & the land purchased from Nathan Gause for the burying ground |
| 2-22-1837 | Solomon Macy, Richard Gordon, George Evans & William B Unthank appt to receive & to hold in trust, the deed for land on which the school house now stands at Spiceland Mtg |
| 6-21-1837 | Stephen & w Rebecca & dt Eunice B & grandchildren Rebecca B & Eli M SWEET rocf Whitewater MM |
| 7-19-1837 | Enoch & w Nancy & ch Benedict, William R, Thaddeus, Alfred, Catherine & Lilburn rocf Hopewell MM, N C end by Duck Creek MM |
| 12-20-1837 | John rocf Salem MM |
| 2-21-1838 | Francis Macy, Rice Price, Demsey Reece, Abraham Moore, Lewis Swain & Obadiah Morgan appt by Spiceland Mtg to att funerals of friends at Duck Creek PM |
| 4-25-1838 | Stephen rocf Whitewater MM |
| 8-22-1838 | Lydia, a Minister & ch Anna Maria, Nathaniel & Susanna gct Salem MM |
| 4-24-1839 | Gardiner rocf Chester MM |
| 4-24-1839 | Elizabeth & ch Elizabeth & Isaac rocf Chester MM |
| 4-24-1839 | Stephen jr gct Whitewater MM to m Mary Charles |
| 8-21-1839 | Enoch appt to station of Elder |
| 12-25-1839 | Mary rocf Whitewater MM |
| 1-22-1840 | Solomon appt an overseer |
| 2-19-1840 | Stephen jr & w Mary gct Westfield MM |
| 1-19-1842 | Benedict & Rebecca Gordon altm |
| 10-19-1842 | Calvin & Diana Edgerton altm |
| 10-19-1842 | John M & w Betsey Ann & dt Henrietta Mariah rocf Milford MM |
| 1-25-1843 | Eunice Greenstreet (form Macy) con mcd |
| 5-24-1843 | Frances & fam gct Duck Creek MM |
| 7-19-1843 | The friends appt to att Spiceland P M of Ministers & Elders, to asst in further labour with Phebe Macy, rpt the desired effect has not been produced. - - - - unite in believing that she has lost her usefullness in the station of Elder & that the P M has fully discharged their duty toward her. The case is transmitted to the MM |
| 11-22-1843 | William R (having produced the consent of his parents) & Sally W Dicks altm |
| 11-22-1843 | Stephen jr & w Mary & ch Samuel, Rebecca & Albert rocf Richland MM |
| 12-20-1843 | Enoch & Nancy jas, Separatists (ASF) dis (Elm Grove P M) |
| 12-20-1843 | William & Phebe jas, Separatists (ASF) dis (Elm Grove P M) |
| 1-24-1844 | Phebe jas, Separatists (ASF) dis |
| 2-21-1844 | This mtg is inf that John M & his w Betsyann have made an agreement with the Yearly Mtg's comm on Indian concerns, as teachers in the school established by the Society of Friends, on the Kansas River, West of the State of Missouri. (This mtg) certifies to whom it may concer, that they are mbrs of our religious Society, with whom we have unity & with whom we feel sympathy in their undertaking - - - - |
| 7-24-1844 | Calvin jas, Separatists, (ASF) dis |
| 9-25-1844 | John M has returned the cert & brought communication from Supt of Friend's school in the Shawnee tribe of Indians, which inf this mtg that "it was on account of indisposition of body, that he was induced to return before the time of his engagement had expired." |
| 10-23-1844 | Diana jas, Separatists (ASF) dis |
| 11-20-1844 | Stephen Sr gct Duck Creek MM to m Rebecca Ratcliff |
| 11-20-1844 | John M & w Betsey Ann & ch Henrietta Maria & Margaret W gct Milford MM |
| 6-25-1845 | Rebecca rocf Duck Creek MM |
| 7-23-1845 | Luzena Meredith (form Macy) jas, Separatists (ASF) & mcd dis |
| 10-22-1845 | Thaddeus gct Westfield MM to m Elizabeth Jane White |
| 1-21-1846 | Stephen Sr & w Rebecca gct Duck Creek MM |
| 1-21-1846 | Susanna Meredith (form Macy) jas, Separatists (ASF) & mcd dis |
| 3-25-1846 | Elizabeth Jane rocf Westfield MM |
| 9-23-1846 | Calvin & Diana rst & dt Hannah rst in mbrp (Had been dis for joining anti-slavery Fr) |
| 11-25-1846 | John M & w Betsey Ann & ch Henrietta Maria, Margaret W & William Allen rocf Milford MM |
| 6-23-1847 | Solomon appt to station of Elder |
| 7-21-1847 | Catherine Jessup (form Macy) jas Separatists (ASF) & mcd, dis |
| 11-24-1847 | Stephen jr & w Mary gct Richland MM |
| 12-23-1847 | Anne H & Charles Gordon altm |
| 1-19-1848 | Solomon Macy, William Unthank, Aaron Stanley & George Evans appt as a comm on burials within the limits of Spiceland P M |
| 1-19-1848 | Nathan Macy & William Edwards appt to a comm on burials within the limits of Elm Grove P M |
| 4-19-1848 | Alfred mcd dis |
| 11-22-1848 | Nathan appt a Trustee in place of William who is released, to hold deed to real estate at Elm Grove P M |
| 10-24-1849 | John M appt clerk & William Edwards appt asst clerk |
| 12-19-1849 | Elizabeth Jane jas dis |
| 1-23-1850 | Thaddeus dis |
| 10-22-1851 | John M & w Betsey Ann & ch Henrietta Maria, Margaret W & William Allen gct Whitewater MM |
| 12-24-1851 | Jane Rayle (form Macy) con mcd |
| 4-21-1852 | W D req cert to Duck Creek MM to m Mary Cook |
| 5-19-1852 | Benedict & Mary Jessup altm |
| 5-19-1852 | William & w Phebe rst by req |
| 8-25-1852 | Sarah A & dt Mary Elma rocf New Garden MM, N C & end to Wabash MM |
| 8-25-1852 | Esther May, dt of William & Phebe rec in mbrp |
| 8-25-1852 | William & w Phebe & ch Catherine, Seth, Jabez, Asenath, Jesse & Esther gct Richland MM |
| 8-25-1852 | Terrell con mcd |
| 2-23-1853 | Terrell gct Duck Creek MM |
| 11-23-1853 | John M & w Betsey Ann & ch Henrietta Maria, Margaret W & William Allen rocf Whitewater MM |
| 10-25-1854 | John M appt clerk & Richard P Elliott appt asst clerk |
| 2-21-1855 | William rocf New Garden MM, N C |
| 3-21-1855 | Jason W dis |
| 3-21-1855 | Nancy rst on req |
| 11-21-1855 | John M gct Hopewell MM to m Lydia Bell |
| 2-20-1856 | Nathan gct Duck Creek MM to m Jannet Pickering |
| 3-19-1856 | John M & ch Henrietta Maria, Margaret W & William Allen gct Hopewell MM |
| 6-25-1856 | Jennet & her ch Martha, Thomas S, Julia Ann & William Exum Pickering rocf Duck Creek MM |
| 12-24-1856 | William gct Duck Creek MM to m Lydia Ellis |
| 5-20-1857 | Lydia rocf Duck Creek MM |
| 8-19-1857 | Solomon appt an overseer at Spiceland P M |
| 8-19-1857 | Lindley H mcd dis |

SPICELAND

## MACY (Cont)

|  |  |
|---|---|
| 10-21-1857 | Lilburn, Elm Grove P M, mcd  dis |
| 1-20-1858 | Isabelle & dt Mary Ann & Ann Elizabeth rocf New Garden MM, N C |
| 1-20-1858 | Mary Ann Baldwin (form Macy) compl of for mou |
| 6-23-1858 | Enoch rst |
| 1-19-1859 | William & w Lydia & ch Elmina gct Hinkles Creek MM |
| 6-22-1859 | Nancy appt to station of Elder |
| 7-20-1859 | Edwin con mcd |
| 4-25-1860 | Calvin & w Diana & ch Hannah Ellen, Martha, Silas, Isaac & Franklin gct Lynn Grove MM, Iowa |
| 5-23-1860 | Enoch appt a Trustee for real estate at Elm Grove P M |
| 9-19-1860 | Enoch appt to station of Elder |
| 9-19-1860 | Elizabeth & Josiah P White altm |
| 1-23-1861 | Lilburn & w Martha & ch Ida Florence & Lydia Alice rec in mbrp |
| 8-21-1861 | Elwood gct Sandwich MM, Mass to m Eliza More |
| 11-20-1861 | Elwood gct Red Cedar MM, Iowa |
| 11-20-1861 | Amelia A rec in mbrp |
| 9-24-1862 | Nathan & w Jannette & ch John W, Nathan W & Jane A gct Red Cedar MM, Iowa |
| 1-21-1863 | James H, s of Edwin & Amelia rec in mbrp |
| 8-19-1863 | Benedict & w Mary & ch Samantha, Ruth Ann & Julia gct Hinkles Creek MM |
| 8-24-1864 | Narcissa gct Springdale MM, Iowa |
| 5- 6-1865 | Edwin & w Amelia Ann & ch James, Wilber & Mary Ann gct Lynn Grove MM, Iowa |
| 8- 5-1865 | Solomon retained as Elder |
| 8- 5-1865 | Enoch retained as Elder |
| 8- 5-1865 | Nancy retained as Elder |
| 2- 3-1866 | Anna gct Hinkles Creek MM |
| 9- 1-1867 | Louiza M rocf Salem MM |
| 2- 1-1868 | Samuel con mcd |
| 6- 6-1868 | Enoch appt an overseer at Elm Grove P M |
| 11- 7-1868 | Caroline & Samuel C Cowgill altm |
| 11- 7-1868 | Caroline & Samuel C Cowgill req privilege to accomplish their m at home. Req granted & mtg appt on next fourth day at half past 3 o'clock |
| 4- 3-1869 | Samuel H & w Louisa gct Springdale MM, Iowa |
| 5- 1-1869 | Lambert con mcd |
| 2- 5-1870 | John B con mcd |
| 4- 2-1870 | Elizabeth Ann rec in mbrp |
| 11- 5-1870 | Jane B & ch Anna Bell & Edwin S rocf Salem |
| 3- 4-1871 | Solomon appt to hold books & papers of the MM |
| 8- 5-1871 | Solomon appt an Elder |
| 11- 7-1874 | Samuel H & w Louisa & dt Sarah T rocf Salem MM |
| 10-14-1876 | Lilburn & w Martha G & ch Ida Florence, Lydia Alice, Emily S, Charles G, Lenora, Horace C, Henry & Grace rocf Raysville MM |
| 5- 1-1880 | Samuel H & w Louisa & ch Sarah T & Albert gct Whitewater MM |
| 11- 6-1880 | Lilburn & w Martha & ch Ida F, L Alice, Emily T, Charles, Lenora, Horace, Henry, Grace & Walter gct Lynn Grove MM, Iowa |
| 6- 3-1882 | Emma Eliza & dt Gertie rec in mbrp |
| 5- 5-1883 | Solomon appt an Elder |
| 6- 1-1889 | Julius & w gct Westfield MM |
| 10-11-1890 | Jane B & ch Edwin, Sarah, Lewis M & Oliver gct Wichita MM, Kas |
| 10-11-1890 | Annie B gct Wichita MM, Kas |
| 11- 1-1889 | John & ch Isadore & Eva Pearl drpd from mbp |
| 2- 3-1906 | Julius C & w Emma P & ch William rocf Westfield MM |
| 2- 3-1906 | Gertrude rocf Westfield MM |
| 7- 3-1920 | Emma & dt Gertrude gct New Castle MM |
| 8- 6-1925 | Julius C rel on req |
| 11- 5-1925 | Martha & Glenn rel on req |
| 12- 4-1930 | Will & fam gct Westfield MM |

## MAHAFFY

|  |  |
|---|---|
| 4- 7-1883 | Sarah & ch Thomas C & Lillian Miles gct Union MM, Oh |

## MANLEY

|  |  |
|---|---|
| 5-22-1850 | Jane H rocf New Garden MM, N C |

## MANLOVE

|  |  |
|---|---|
| 1-23-1839 | Jemima (form Beeson) rpt mcd |
| 7- 7-1921 | O P & w Dora & ch Paul & Blanch Lyon rocf Shirley MM |
| 3- 7-1929 | Oliver P & w gct Duck Creek MM |

## MAPLE

|  |  |
|---|---|
| 7- 7-1921 | Fred M & w Dora & ch Benjamin H, Norah Bernice & Helen Katherine rec in mbrp |

## MARKS

|  |  |
|---|---|
| 1- 7-1888 | Prudence & May rec in mbrp |
| 3- 2-1895 | John & Martha rec in mbrp |
| 12- 7-1912 | May & John drpd from mbrp |

## MARSHALL

|  |  |
|---|---|
| 6-24-1835 | Jesse & w Mary & ch Jane, William, Calvin & Levi rocf Duck Creek MM |
| 8-21-1839 | Joseph rocf Driftwood MM |
| 9-25-1839 | Jesse & w & ch gct Walnut Ridge MM |
| 7-22-1840 | Joseph gct Sugar River MM |
| 10-20-1847 | Tamar rocf Sugar Plain MM |

## MARTIN

|  |  |
|---|---|
| 10-11-1890 | Benjamin E rec in mbrp |
| 3- 4-1893 | Simon rec in mbrp |
| 6- 2-1900 | Simon & w Hettie & dt Mabel gct Hopewell MM |
| 11- 5-1931 | Alice Bundy rel on req |

## MAUDLIN - MODLIN

|  |  |
|---|---|
| 1-23-1833 | Thomas & w Hannah & ch original mbrs |
| 2-20-1833 | Thomas Maudlin, William Unthank, Aaron Stanley, & George Evans appt as Spiceland MM's representatives to the ensuing Q M |
| 12-25-1833 | Caroline (form Yates) mcd  dis |
| 6-21-1837 | Thomas & w Hannah & ch Elizabeth, Benjamin, Margaret, William, Leah & Thomas jr gct Mississinewa MM |
| ( 9-20-1837) | The comm appt at Duck Creek Mtg to treat with Elwood Modlin not being present at Spiceland Mtg, a new comm is appt to the service.  (Duck Creek mtg had been laid down) |
| ( 9-20-1837) | The comm appt at Duck Creek mtg to treat with Mark Modlin, rpt but Spiceland mtg cont them for further labor with him (Duck Creek mtg had been laid down) |
| ( 9-20-1837) | Richard, a mbr of Duck Creek Mtg, now laid down, is attached to Spiceland Mtg |
| 11-22-1837 | Elwood dis for na & jas |
| 12-20-1837 | Mark dis for mcd |
| 5-23-1838 | Clearspring P M compl for Elias upl.  He now lives in the limits of Mississinewa MM.  A comm appt to treat with him |
| 6-20-1838 | Leah Benbow (form Modlin) mcd |
| 7-25-1838 | Richard & Jane Osborn, a wid, altm |
| 1-23-1839 | Mississinewa MM rpts that after treating with Elias he does not seem to be of a mind to make satisfaction. |
| 2-20-1839 | Elias dis |
| 1-25-1843 | Leah Benbow (form Modlin) dis |
| 3-20-1844 | Robert Stuart gct West Grove MM to m Rachel Maudlin |

## MAXWELL

|  |  |
|---|---|
| 11- 7-1868 | David & w Lydia rocf Salem MM |
| 4- 7-1883 | Lydia gct Springfield MM |

## MAYS

|  |  |
|---|---|
| 1- ?-1895 | John & w Elizabeth rocf Raysville MM |
| 1- 4-1896 | John W & w Elizabeth W rel on req |

## McCAN

|  |  |
|---|---|
| 3- 2-1889 | John Riley rec in mbrp |
| 8- 6-1892 | John R gct Raysville MM |

## McCLAIN

|  |  |
|---|---|
| 11- 3-1922 | Simeon B & w Clara & ch Fleta Viola & Greta rec in mbrp |
| 6- 2-1927 | Simeon & fam gct Carthage MM |

## McCOMBS

|  |  |
|---|---|
| 12-25-1850 | Louisa (form Dix) con mcd |

SPICELAND

## McCOY
2- 1-1868  Henry C & w Rachel & ch William R rocf Milford MM
5- 3-1873  Henry C & w Rachel & ch William, John & James gct Milford MM

## McCRACKEN
1- 1-1916  Joseph W & dt Ruthanna rec in mbrp
12- 6-1923  Joseph W & ch Ruthanna & Lawrence Raymond gct Scotts Mills MM, Ore

## McDANIEL
6- 7-1890  Alice rel on req
8- 6-1898  Matilda J Steele & ch Charles Elwood, Mary Elizabeth, Stella Edna, Olloe Jane & Verna Alberta Steele gc

## McFARLAND
1- 7-1889  John & Elisha rec in mbrp
3- 4-1893  Mary rec in mbrp
4- 4-1903  Elisha gct New Castle MM
9- 5-1903  Elisha drpd from mbrp
12- 7-1912  Mary drpd from mbrp
4- 9-1920  Florence gct Charlottesville MM

## McGRAW
7- 2-1892  John W & w Anna Jane & ch Violetta, Margaretta Elmina & Minerva Jane rocf Cherry Grove MM
9- 5-1906  John W & w Jannie & ch Etta, Margaret & Minerva gct Cherry Grove MM

## McINTOSH
4- 5-1879  Viola rec in mbrp

## McKILLIP
6- 6-1896  Oliver & w Anna rocf Knightstown MM
6- 6-1903  Oliver & Anna & s George O gct Duck Creek MM (cert returned for disunity)

## McNAIRY
12-23-1874  Francis rec in mbrp
5- 7-1881  Mary Jane rec in mbrp
3- 3-1883  Mamie rec in mbrp
8- 2-1884  Francis & w Mary Jane & dt Mamie gct Muncie MM

## McNEW
           Earnest & w & ch rec in mbrp

## MENDENHALL
( 9-20-1837)  Joseph, a mbr of Duck Creek MM, which is now laid down, attached to Spiceland Mtg
2-19-1840  Joseph & Maria Dean altm
4-22-1840  Ann & minor s Lewis rocf Whitewater MM
1-20-1847  Stephen & w Sarah & ch Catherine, Nathan, Albert W, Elizabeth & Bartlett rocf Walnut Ridge MM
10-20-1847  Lewis, Whitewater MM rpts he has mcd. Spiceland req Whitewater to treat w/him
5-21-1851  Nancy Ann, wid of Moses, & dts Mary & Dinah rocf New Garden MM, N C
11-24-1852  Eli E produced a cert from Hopewell MM to m Mary Jane Pearson
11-24-1852  Eli E & Mary Jane Pearson altm
3-23-1853  Eli E rocf Hopewell MM
7-20-1853  Mary Jane gct White Lick MM
10-25-1854  Nathan gct Honey Creek MM
11-23-1854  Catherine R & James Hadley altm
11-23-1854  Catherine R & James Hadley req a mtg appt to meet tomorrow at 11 o'clock at Raysville M H for them to accomplish their m. Their req is granted & mtg directed to be held accordingly
4-25-1855  Nathan produced a cert from Honey Creek MM to m
4-25-1855  Nathan & Mary Street altm
1-23-1856  Mary S gct Honey Creek MM
4-23-1856  Stephen G & w Sarah & ch Elizabeth & Bartlet gct Fairfield MM
4-23-1856  Albert W gct Fairfield MM
9-19-1857  Margaret rocf Springfield MM, N C (wid of David & mth of Clarky (Mendenhall) Wilson w of James M Wilson)
2-24-1858  Emily (form Jessup) mcd dis
9-21-1864  Susan C gct Milford MM
12- 2-
12- 2-1865  Margaret gct Greenwood MM (wid of David)
9- 3-1870  Mary gct Greenwood MM
1- 1-1876  Margaret (wid of Benjamin) rec on req
3- 4-1876  Susan C & ch George C, Phebe Jane & Delana rocf Milford MM
10-12-1895  Margaret, wid of Benjamin gct Oskaloosa MM, Iowa
8- 3-1901  George gct Fairmount MM
3- 1-1902  Susan gct Fairmount MM

## MEREDITH
6-24-1835  James H, a minor, rocf Whitewater MM
7-24-1839  James H prod an acknowledgement that he had been guilty of immoral & scandalous conduct & had evaded the truth by concealing it. Mtg receives the statement & appts a comm to inform him
10-19-1842  Thomas Jefferson rocf Whitewater MM
1-25-1843  Thomas J & Eliza Pennington inf Spiceland mtg, in writing, that they have discontinued their int to m each other
5-24-1843  Mary & ch Jabez, Jesse, Susan & William rocf Milford MM
3-19-1845  James H gct Duck Creek MM to m Eliza Stanley
5-21-1845  Jesse jas, Separatists (ASF) & mcd, dis
6-25-1845  Eliza rocf Duck Creek MM
7-23-1845  Luzene (form Macy) jas, Separatists (ASF) & mcd, dis
12-24-1845  Thomas J jas, Separatists (ASF) & mcd dis (he now resided in limits of Westfield MM)
1-21-1846  Susanna (form Macy) jas, Separatists (ASF) & mcd dis
12-23-1846  Jesse rst (had been dis for joining anti-slavery group)
12-23-1846  Jabez H & Louisa Antrim altm
1-20-1847  Luzene rec in mbrp & infant s Franklin also rec in mbrp
1-19-1848  James H & w Eliza & ch Jane & Oliver gct Duck Creek MM
10-25-1848  Susanna Mills (form Meredith) mcd dis
4-25-1849  William gct Duck Creek MM
1-23-1850  Jesse & w Luzena & ch Charles O, Franklin & Melissa Ann gct Duck Creek MM
10-23-1850  Mary gct Duck Creek MM
3-23-1853  Jesse & w Luzene & ch Charles O, Franklin, Melissa Ann, Anna Jane & John rocf Richland MM
11-23-1853  James H & w Eliza & ch Jane, Oliver, Allen, Elizabeth, Caroline & Mary rocf Duck Creek MM
11-23-1853  Jesse & w Luzene & ch Charles O, Franklin, Melissa Ann, Anna Jane & John gct Duck Creek MM
8-23-1854  James H & w Eliza & ch Jane, Oliver, Ellen, Caroline Elizabeth & Mary gct Duck Creek MM
11-19-1856  Susanna rst at Westfield MM, w/con of this mtg
5-19-1858  Jesse & w Luzene & ch Charles O, Franklin, Melissa Ann, Anna Jane, John, James & Marshall rocf Duck Creek MM
9-22-1858  William rocf Duck Creek MM
9-25-1861  William gct Lynn Grove MM, Iowa
2-24-1864  Thomas J rst at Lynn Grove MM, Iowa w/con of this mtg
3- 4-1865  Jesse & w Luzene & ch Charles O, Franklin, Melissa Ann, Anna Jane, John, James, Marshall, Elizabeth M & Elvira gct Lynn Grove MM, Iowa
4- 4-1868  Asenath gct Lynn Grove MM, Iowa
9- 4-1869  Franklin & w Asenath & s Bertram rocf Lynn Grove MM, Iowa
7- 2-1870  Franklin & w Asenath & ch Bertram & Luzena gct Hinckles Creek MM
7- 5-1890  Alfred drpd from mbrp
7- 1-1893  Mary Elizabeth rec in mbrp
6- 7-1906  Jehu rec in mbrp
5- 1-1909  Jabez rec in mbrp
12- 7-1912  Jabez rel on req

## MERKEL
4- 4-1896  Sylvia C gct Anderson MM

SPICELAND

## MICHENER
| | |
|---|---|
| 1- 4-1902 | Susan M gct Muncie MM |

## MILES
| | |
|---|---|
| 4-21-1858 | Elizabeth gct Honey Creek MM |
| 3- 6-1875 | Amos Stuart gct Whitewater MM to m Melissa Miles |
| 12- 2-1875 | Rachel E rocf Whitewater MM |
| 9- 1-1877 | Rachel gct Chester MM |
| 2- 1-1879 | Thomas & fam rocf Union MM |
| 3- 1-1919 | Alma & Pearl rec in mbrp |

## MILLER
| | |
|---|---|
| 4-20-1842 | Mary rocf Springborough MM, Ohio |
| 2-22-1843 | Phebe, dt Caleb & Phebe (Ray) Miller, both decd, rocf Sugar River MM, under the care of David Lupton & his w Ann, who is a relative of Phebe |
| 7-26-1846 | Phebe under the care of David & Ann Lupton gct Walnut Ridge MM |
| 9-22-1847 | Mary R & John Pearson altm |
| 9-22-1847 | For the convenience of Mary R & John Pearson a mtg is granted to be held at Raysville MH tomorrow at 11 o'clock for the accomplishment of their m |
| 10- 2-1920 | Rozzie G rel on req |
| 5- 2-1929 | Forestina rec in mbrp |

## MILLIKAN
| | |
|---|---|
| 6- 3-1865 | Rebecca Jane, Thomas K & William M ch of William rocf Springfield MM |
| 6- 2-1866 | William rst w/con of Springfield MM |
| 6- 2-1866 | Priscilla dt of William rec in mbrp |
| 3- 6-1869 | Eli & s Lewis V rocf Springfield MM |
| 4- 2-1870 | Thomas con mcd |
| 11- 3-1883 | Eli rec in mbrp |
| 7- 5-1890 | William & Eli drpd from mbrp |

## MILLS
| | |
|---|---|
| 1-23-1839 | Jerusha SANDERS (form Mills) compl of for mcd |
| 2-20-1839 | Jerusha dis |
| 5-24-1843 | Nathan P Gause gct New Garden MM to m Susannah Mills |
| 10-26-1848 | Susanna (form Meredith) mcd dis |
| 8-25-1852 | Elizabeth (form Reynard) con mcd |
| 4-21-1858 | Eber con mcd |
| 6-23-1858 | Eber gct Duck Creek MM |
| 3- 4-1905 | Francis W Thomas gct Indianapolis MM to m Anna Mills |
| 3- 7-1908 | Margaret J rec in mbrp |
| 4-29-1920 | Earl & w Blanch & ch Myron, Lois & Catherine rec in mbrp |
| 12- 6-1925 | Earl & fam gct New Castle MM |

## MOFFITT
| | |
|---|---|
| 11-22-1843 | Gulielma (form Cox) con mcd with her 1st cousin |
| 4-24-1844 | Gulielma gct White Lick MM |
| 8-21-1850 | Evaline (form Cox) mcd dis |
| 4- 4-1885 | Sarah rocf Raysville MM |
| 10-13-1888 | Sarah drpd from mbrp |
| 5- 4-1889 | Lycurgus & w Amanda & ch gct Raysville MM |
| 8- 6-1892 | Reuben drpd from mbrp |
| 1- 1-1915 | Edith Chew gct Knightstown MM |
| 5- 1-1915 | Ruth & Essie L rec in mbrp |
| 7- 3-1915 | Emma K rec in mbrp |
| 2- 7-1924 | Edith rel on req |
| 4- 3-1930 | Griffin & w & ch Rose Mary & Jane rec in mbrp |

## MOORE
| | |
|---|---|
| 1-23-1833 | William & w Anna & ch original mbrs |
| 6-25-1834 | Camm dis for na dpl & striking a fellow creature |
| 8-19-1835 | Sarah Brown (form Moore) mcd dis |
| 4-19-1837 | Addison dis |
| ( 9-20-1837) | Abraham & fam had been mbrs of the now laid down mtg of Duck Creek & are now attached to Spiceland |
| 10-25-1837 | Abraham appt to comm on "poor" by Spiceland MM |
| 2-21-1838 | Abraham Moore, Rice Price, Demsey Reece, Francis Macy, Lewis Swaim & Obadiah Morgan appt by Spiceland Mtg to att funerals of friends at Duck Creek P M |
| 5-23-1838 | Abraham appt to station of Elder |
| 5-23-1838 | Hannah appt to station of Elder |
| 11-21-1838 | Susanna rocf Springfield MM, Ohio |
| 2-20-1839 | Elizabeth rocf Whitewater MM |
| 2-20-1839 | Susanna gct Springfield MM, Ohio |
| 6-19-1839 | Malinda dis for na & dpl |
| 7-24-1839 | Samuel gct Milford MM |
| 10-23-1839 | Abraham & w Hannah & ch Abraham jr, & Rachel gct Dover MM |
| 4-20-1842 | Thomas & Phebe King altm |
| 10-23-1844 | William gct Hopewell MM to m Ann Stretch, a wid |
| 3-19-1845 | Ann rocf Hopewell MM |
| 7-22-1846 | Caroline Taylor (form Moore) mcd dis |
| 10-21-1846 | Emily dis for att some mcd |
| 2-24-1847 | Achsah Hall (form Moore) con mcd |
| 10-20-1847 | Thomas & w Phebe & s Isaac Hezekiah gct Honey Creek MM |
| 2-23-1848 | Abigail & Joseph Gause altm |
| 9-20-1848 | William B gct Honey Creek MM |
| 11-22-1848 | Josiah, a minor, s of William gct Honey Creek MM |
| 8-22-1849 | William rocf Honey Creek MM |
| 12-25-1850 | Josiah, a minor, s of William rocf Honey Creek MM |
| 10-22-1851 | Henry C dis |
| 4-21-1858 | Gideon gct Westfield MM |
| 7-20-1859 | Gideon rocf Westfield MM |
| 8-21-1861 | Elwood Macy gct Sandwich MM to m Eliza More |
| 1-22-1862 | Josiah con mcd |
| 2- 1-1868 | Josiah mcd dis |
| 2- 4-1882 | Charles Henry C & w Ellen rec in mbrp |
| 11- 3-1883 | Gideon rel on req |
| 12- 4-1886 | Charles H C rel on req |
| 2- 4-1893 | Francis Charles rec in mbrp |
| 3- 2-1895 | Charles H C rec in mbrp |
| 12- 7-1901 | Anna M rocf Whittier MM, Cal |
| 9- 5-1902 | Anna M gct Whitewater MM |

## MORGAN
| | |
|---|---|
| 2-24-1836 | Charles & w Michal & ch Edward, Elizabeth, William & Benjamin rocf Milford MM |
| ( 9-20-1837) | Lydia, wid of Hezekiah & her ch, mbrs of Duck Creek Mtg, now laid down, have been attached to Spiceland MM |
| ( 9-20-1837) | Obadiah & w Ann & ch, mbrs of Duck Creek Mtg, now laid down, have been attached to Spiceland MM |
| 10-25-1837 | Obadiah Sr appt an overseer by Spiceland P M |
| 11-22-1837 | Lydia Adamson (form Morgan) mcd dis |
| 1-22-1838 | Obadiah jr gct Vermillion MM, Ill |
| 2-21-1838 | Obadiah Morgan Sr, Rice Price, Dempsey Reece, Francis Macy, Abraham Moore & Lewis Swain appt by Spiceland Mtg to att Funerals of Friends at Duck Creek P M |
| 4-25-1838 | Obadiah & w Anna & ch Hezekiah, Margaret Jane, Thomas, Sophia, Joseph, William & Mary Jane gct White Lick MM |
| 12-19-1838 | Thomas mcd dis (lately of Fall Creek P M, now in limits of Westfield MM) |
| 10-23-1839 | Rebecca & Zeno, ch of Hezekiah decd, gct Walnut Ridge MM |
| 10-23-1839 | Isaac, Hannah, James, Nathan, Hezekiah jr & Demarius, ch of Hezekiah, decd, gct White Lick MM |
| 6-23-1841 | Charles appt an overseer at Spiceland P M |
| 11-24-1841 | Charles Morgan, Samuel Pritchard, Caleb White, Joel Pusey & Samuel Horner appt Trustees to rec & hold titles for real estate, in trust, for Raysville P M, Wayne twp, Henry Co for meeting, school & burying ground |
| 8-21-1844 | Elizabeth & Alfred Butler altm |
| 9-25-1844 | Charles appt an overseer |
| 6-25-1845 | Michal appt an Elder at Spiceland P M |
| 12-23-1847 | Edward & Rachel Parker altm |
| 10-23-1850 | Edward & w Rachel & ch Oliver gct Honey Creek MM (returned because they moved back) |
| 9-21-1853 | Edward & w Rachel & ch Oliver & Emma gct (New Garden MM, or East Grove MM, Iowa) |
| 7-25-1855 | William B gct Back Creek MM, N C to m Sarah Henley |
| 9-26-1856 | William B gct Whitewater MM |

SPICELAND

MORGAN (Cont)
5- 2-1866    George rec in mbrp
11- 6-1869   William B & w Sarah H & ch William Earl & Jesse Henley rocf Whitewater MM
2- 4-1871    William B & w Sarah H & ch William Earl & Jesse Henley gct Spring River MM, Kan
4- 6-1872    Jesse gct Mill Creek MM
8- 7-1872    William B & w Sarah H & ch William Earl & Jesse Henley rocf Spring River MM, Kan
11- 4-1876   William B & w Sarah H & ch Earl & Henley gct Oskaloosa MM, Iowa
10- 9-1886   William B rocf Spring River MM, Kan
6- 4-1887    William B gct Spring River MM, Kan

MORRIS
5-21-1834    Joseph rst w/con of Duck Creek MM
7-22-1835    Rachel (w of John) rocf Springfield MM, with 2 sons
9-23-1835    Joseph gct White Lick MM to m Elizabeth White
2-24-1836    Elizabeth rocf White Lick MM
1-25-1837    Katy dis for na
( 9-20-1837) Reuben & w Miriam & ch, mbrs of Duck Creek Mtg, now laid down, have been attached to Spiceland MM
4-24-1839    Reuben of Spiceland P M is rptd out of unity with friends & does not att religious mtgs
8-21-1839    Reuben produced an acknowledgement of his deviations which the mtg accepted
8-21-1839    Joseph & w Elizabeth & ch gct Mill Creek MM
2-23-1842    Levi mcd dis
7-24-1844    Sarah Copeland (form Morris) con mcd
8-20-1845    Samuel mcd dis
10-22-1845   Rachel dis for obtaining a divorce from her husband, John, and for adultery
11-19-1845   Mary & Samuel Gause altm
3-24-1847    Benjamin dis
4-21-1847    Lucinda Huddleston (form Morris) mcd dis
9-22-1847    Nathan, a minor, rocf Milford MM
1-22-1851    Louisa dis
8-29-1851    Philip D Parker gct Blue River MM to m Joanna Morris
2-22-1853    Hannah Wiggins (form Morris) mcd dis
2-25-1857    Levi mcd dis
12- 3-1870   Benjamin & Lydia & Rachel rec in mbrp (ch of William & Susannah)
11- 6-1880   Nathan O & w Pharaba & ch rocf Milford MM
11- 2-1882   Nathan & w Phariba & ch Joseph C, Edith & Francis gct Walnut Ridge MM
3- 4-1883    Obed gct Westland MM
5- 1-1915    Martha roc
12- 7-1922   Stella rec in mbrp

MORRISON
11- 7-1891   Edmund & w Mary E rocf Newberg MM, Ore
8- 6-1892    Edmund & w Mary E & dt Sarah Elizabeth gct Salem MM, Ore

MORROW
1- 4-1919    Hazel rocf Knightstown MM
2- 1-1919    Gretchel & Medeline, ch of Hazel rec in mbrp
6- 7-1928    Mrs P B rec in mbrp
3- 2-1933    Hazel & dt Madeline gct Knightstown MM

MOTE
9-19-1838    Dorcas (form Coppock) con mcd
4-24-1839    Dorcas gct Back Creek MM

MUFFLEY
12- 3-1892   Daniel & w Lucy & ch Margaret E, Daniel L & Benjamin G rocf Cherry Grove MM
9- 3-1904    Daniel dis
12- 7-1912   Dan drpd from mbrp

MUNDEN
1-23-1833    Joseph & w Millicent & fam original mbrs
6-24-1835    Joseph & w Millicent & ch Peninah, Thomas, Jane, Martha & Mary Ann gct Blue River MM
9-20-1837    Jesse & w Mary & ch Asenath, Margaret, & Calvin A rocf Milford MM, directed to Duck Creek MM, but since that mtg is laid down, has been rec at Spiceland MM

2-22-1854    Ruth (form Reynard) con mcd
4-21-1858    Ruth gct Salem MM, Iowa

MYER
4- 1-1920    John C & w Ethel & s Robert rocf Duck Creek MM

NEET
1- 5-1895    George W & Callie H rec in mbrp
12- 3-1898   George W & Callie H rel on req

NEGUS
8- 7-1869    Walter Edgerton gct Green Plain MM, Ohio to m Eliza A Negus (wid of Joseph Negus)

NELSON
7- 1-1882    Mary Emily gct Fairmount MM
11- 6-1930   Jean Ann rec in mbrp

NEVITT
1-25-1837    Thomas & w Keziah & ch Lavina, Isaac, David, Mary Ann & Thomas J rocf Flushing MM, Ohio
7-19-1848    David dis for swearing & stealing (Spiceland P M)
1-21-1852    Thomas & w Keziah & ch Thomas J, Rinnard H, Joseph H & Martha gct West Union MM

NEWBY
1-23-1833    Elizabeth (wid of William) original mbr (mother of Cyrus & Joseph & Thomas)
3-20-1833    Elizabeth appt to a comm
5-22-1833    Cyrus appt to a comm
5-21-1834    Thomas & w Millicent rocf Milford MM
11-19-1834   Cyrus dis for fornication
8-19-1835    Thomas & w Millicent & dt Huldah gct Milford MM
5-25-1836    Elizabeth gct Walnut Ridge MM
10-19-1836   Frederick & w Sarah & ch William J, John T, Albert, Oliver, Eliza, Lydia, Exum & Henry rocf Milford MM
( 9-20-1837) Elias & w Lydia & ch mbrs of Duck Creek Mtg, now laid down, are attached to Spiceland
5-23-1838    Louisa (form Baldwin) mcd dis
10-24-1838   Elizabeth rocf Walnut Ridge MM
3-20-1839    Micajah & two minor ch under his care, gct Back Creek MM
1-22-1840    Joseph & Naomi H Dicks altm
5-20-1840    Elias gct Milford MM, to m Tabitha Bond
9-23-1840    Tabitha rocf Milford MM
5-20-1846    Amos Kenworthy gct Hopewell to m Elizabeth Newby
9-22-1847    Isaac Parker gct Blue River MM to m Hannah M Newby
7-19-1848    Mary D rocf Blue River MM
7-24-1850    Eliza Charles (form Newby) mcd dis
2-22-1854    Albert & Caroline Hubbard altm
8-23-1854    John T & Martha White altm
7-23-1856    Albert & w Caroline & s Charles gct Hopewell MM
8-20-1856    Oliver mcd dis
11-24-1858   Jesse B Jessop gct Walnut Ridge MM to m Milla Newby
7- 1-1865    Joseph appt an overseer
3- 3-1866    Jason W & Nancy E Hall altm
1- 5-1867    Albert appt asst clerk & Timothy Wilson appt clerk
6- 1-1867    Thomas & Millicent & s Jesse rocf Hopewell MM
6- 6-1868    Albert appt an overseer at Spiceland PM
3- 6-1869    Sarah rocf Raysville MM
11- 6-1869   Thomas & w Millicent gct Hopewell MM
1- 1-1870    Lydia rocf Raysville MM
5- 7-1870    William rocf Raysville MM
1- 7-1871    Albert, decd, rpt to have bequeathed certain interest in his estate, to Spiceland Academy
8- 5-1871    Sarah appt an Elder
6- 1-1872    Thomas A con mcd
5- 1-1875    Margaret L & dt Laura Bell rocf Kokomo MM

SPICELAND

## NEWBY (Cont)
| | |
|---|---|
| 5- 1-1875 | Rachel & ch Adolpheus A, Ida J, Louissie, Mary L & Eli rocf Duck Creek MM |
| 1- 1-1876 | William B rec in mbrp |
| 1- 6-1877 | Margaret J gct Carthage MM |
| 3- 3-1877 | Laura Bell & Francis Ray, ch of Margaret gct Carthage MM |
| 10-13-1877 | Nathan rocf Hopewell MM |
| 3- 1-1879 | Jason W & fam gct Peace MM, Kas |
| 6- 4-1881 | Sarah gct Hopewell MM |
| 6- 7-1884 | Thomas A & w Isabelle & ch Otto & Bertha gct Sterling MM, Kas |
| 8- 1-1885 | Lorena dis |
| 8- 7-1886 | Charles F rec in mbrp |
| 6- 7-1890 | Henry & Minnie Pearl gct Pasadena, Cal |
| 12- 6-1890 | Jason W & w Nance H & ch Herbert, Ellen, Cecil & Joseph Carl rocf Sterling MM, Kas |
| 12- 1-1894 | Alice T rec in mbrp |
| 3- 2-1895 | Anna C rocf Fairview MM |
| 6- 2-1900 | Charles B gct Amboy MM |
| 8- 5-1905 | David W & w Mary Anna rocf Knightstown |
| 9- 5-1905 | Frederick M, Richard W, & Paul E & Mary M Hood, ch of David & Marianna Newby rocf Knightstown |
| 12- 2-1905 | Jason W & w Anna C & ch Joseph Carl, Rowland Collins & Wister Devall gct ____Gate MM, Okl |
| 12- 7-1912 | Fred drpd from mbrp |
| 4- 5-1923 | Paul E rel on req |
| 4- 7-1927 | Paul rel on req |

## NEWLIN
| | |
|---|---|
| 7- 2-1881 | Thomas rocf Honey Creek MM |
| 3- 2-1889 | Harriet B gct Kokomo MM |
| 5- 4-1889 | Edna B, adopted dt of Thomas & Olive rec in mbrp |
| 10-10-1891 | Thomas & w Olive & dt Edna B gct Newberg MM, Ore |

## NEWMAN
| | |
|---|---|
| 2- 7-1880 | Daniel & w Mary Ann rec on req, Mary Ann produced a letter from Christian Church of Laura, Oh |
| 12- 4-1880 | Esther & ch rocf Union MM, Ohio (returned because the fam moved back to Union MM) |

## NICHOLS
| | |
|---|---|
| 2- 1-1873 | Ann rocf Raysville MM |
| 12- 6-1873 | Ann & Henry W Horne altm |
| 12- 6-1873 | Ann & Henry W Horne req a mtg appt on the 9th inst at the house of Ann in order to accomplish their m. The req was granted |
| 6- 4-1910 | Emma Templeton gct Ludlow Falls MM, Oh |

## NICHOLSON
| | |
|---|---|
| 9-25-1850 | Nathan produced cert from Walnut Ridge Mtg to m |
| 9-25-1850 | Nathan & Asenath H Cloud altm |
| 1-29-1851 | Asenath H gct Walnut Ridge MM |
| 3- 7-1874 | Asenath & ch Milton & Hiram rocf Walnut Ridge MM |
| 4- 3-1875 | Asenath & s Milton gct Walnut Ridge MM |

## NIXON
| | |
|---|---|
| 1-25-1854 | William H Unthank gct Blue River MM to m Deborah (Hobbs) Nixon wid of John |
| 1-25-1854 | Deborah, & her ch Martha Ann, Oliver, Priscilla & Nathan Nixon rocf Blue River MM |
| 11-20-1861 | Martha A & Robert H Cook altm |
| 5- 2-1868 | Josiah rocf Milford MM |
| 5- 7-1870 | Josephine rec in mbrp |
| 1- 7-1882 | Josie rel on req |
| 4- 2-1898 | Nathan T gct Knightstown MM |

## NOBLE
| | |
|---|---|
| 1- 5-1884 | Stuart rec in mbrp |
| 7- 4-1891 | Stuart gct Goshen MM, Oh |

## NORTHUM
| | |
|---|---|
| 4- 4-1874 | Nancy Atlanta & ch gct Westfield MM |

## NORTON
| | |
|---|---|
| 4-24-1839 | Dennis compl of for "sueing at law" (he is of Clearsprings P M) |
| 6-19-1839 | Dennis produces an offering which mtg accpts |
| 3- 6-1897 | Eva (Hinshaw) gct Fairmount MM |

## NOTTINGHAM
| | |
|---|---|
| 4- 7-1883 | Peter F & Sarah Jane rec in mbrp - they produced a letter from a M E Ch in Mo |
| 12- 1-1883 | Harry, s of Peter & Jane rec in mbrp |
| 3- 6-1892 | Peter F & Sarah Jane drpd from mbrp |

## NUGEN
| | |
|---|---|
| 3- 4-1882 | Silas & w Martha Jane & Fountain Ellen & Louisa rec in mbrp |
| 11- 3-1883 | Silas & family "has been given a letter of recommendation" |
| 12- 7-1912 | Ellen drpd from mbrp |

## OAKEY
| | |
|---|---|
| 3- 6-1886 | Minerva rec in mbrp |

## OELSCHLAGLE
| | |
|---|---|
| 9- 3-1898 | Josephine rocf Whitewater MM |

## OGLE
| | |
|---|---|
| 1- 6-1878 | Mary rec in mbrp |
| 3- 4-1883 | Mary drpd from mbrp |

## OGBORN
| | |
|---|---|
| 12- 3-1887 | Daniel rec in mbrp |
| 5- 4-1889 | Daniel & w Lizzie gct West Grove MM |

## OSBORN
| | |
|---|---|
| ( 9-20-1837) | Jane & ch, mbrs of Duck Creek Mtg, now laid down, has been attached to Spiceland |
| 6-20-1838 | Jane, a wid with ch, & Richard Maudlin inf mtg of int to m. A comm appt to see that the rights of her ch are secure |
| 7-25-1838 | Jane & Richard Maudlin altm. It appears the rights of Jane's ch are secure |
| 6- 2-1866 | John & w Sarah & ch William E, Alexander, John G rocf Deep River MM, N C |
| 6- 4-1870 | Laurinda rocf Springfield MM |
| 6- 4-1870 | John & w Sarah & ch William, Alex & John G gct Pipe Creek MM |
| 4- 1-1899 | Arthur Rocf Springfield MM |

## OUTLAND
| | |
|---|---|
| 8- 6-1868 | Mary Annis & ch rocf Walnut Ridge MM |
| 11-14-1871 | Mary Annis & William Overman altm (they report there are no surviving parents) |
| 4- 6-1872 | Mary Annis Overman & her ch Oliver W & David C Outland gct Pipe Creek MM |
| 4- 6-1872 | William T gct Pipe Creek MM |
| 8- 7-1875 | Mary Annis gct Pipe Creek MM |
| 6- 3-1876 | Josiah C gct Pipe Creek MM |

## OVERMAN
| | |
|---|---|
| 5-21-1851 | Eli & w Elizabeth & ch Edwin Nixon & Alpheus rocf Blue River MM |
| 12-24-1851 | Charles rocf Blue River MM |
| 12-24-1851 | Eliza Jane, w of Charles rocf Whitewater MM |
| 11-22-1854 | Eli & w Elizabeth & s Alpheus gct White Lick MM |
| 10-24-1855 | Edwin gct White Lick MM |
| 5-19-1858 | Charles gct West Union MM to m Elizabeth J Townsend |
| 6-23-1858 | Charles & ch Oliver C & Edgar K gct Plainfield MM |
| 11-25-1861 | Nixon gct Blue River MM |
| 11-14-1871 | William produced a cert from Pipe Creek MM to m |
| 11-14-1871 | William & Mary Annis Outland altm (they report there are no surviving parents) |
| 4- 6-1872 | Mary Annis & her ch Oliver W & David C Outland gct Pipe Creek MM |

## PAINTER
| | |
|---|---|
| 6- 2-1874 | Samuel S & w Mercy Ann & ch Henry W & Mary Samantha rec in mbrp |
| 1- 1-1876 | Alvan C, Orange S & Esther C rec in mbrp |
| 7- 1-1882 | Alvin & Orange gct Wabash MM |
| 2- 3-1900 | Alvin & w Harrietta & ch Floyd, Myron & Myra rocf Wabash MM |
| 5- 6-1905 | Clarence D rel on req |
| 6- 4-1906 | Jennie P rocf 8th St MM, Richmond |
| 3- 1-1913 | Clarence D, w Claire & dt Agnes Ella rec in mbrp |

SPICELAND

## PAINTER (Cont)
| | |
|---|---|
| 8- 6-1921 | Agnes rec in mbrp |
| 12- 7-1922 | Betty Joe rec in mbrp |
| 4- 7-1927 | Agnes gct Clintondale MM, N Y |
| 11- 1-1928 | Lowell & Mildred rel on req |

## PALIN
| | |
|---|---|
| 1-23-1833 | Nixon & w Peninah & ch Lucinda, William, Irene & Sylvanus original members |
| 7-24-1839 | Peninah & ch Lucinda, William, Irene & Sylvanus gct Milford MM |
| 3-25-1840 | Peninah & ch William, Lucinda, Irene & Sylvanus rocf Milford MM |
| 2-21-1844 | William mcd dis |
| 5-20-1846 | Lucinda Jones (form Palin) con mcd |
| 11-25-1846 | Sylvanus con mcd |
| 8-25-1847 | Mary Ann rocf Milford MM |
| 5-24-1848 | Irene gct Salem MM, Iowa |
| 12-20-1848 | Nixon & Peninah gct Salem MM, Iowa |
| 11-21-1849 | William & w Sarah req mbrp for their minor ch (Sarah died after the req was made) req denied 1-23-1850 |
| 7-21-1852 | Sylvanus & w Mary & ch Eliza Jane & James P gct Salem MM, Iowa |

## PALMER
| | |
|---|---|
| 2-20-1839 | Anna (form Weisner) mcd dis |
| 11-25-1840 | Sarah dis for disunity & na |
| 5-25-1842 | Anna rst at Duck Creek MM w/con of this mtg |

## PARKER
| | |
|---|---|
| 7-22-1835 | Levi Pennington gct Short Creek MM, Oh to m Emma Parker |
| 11-23-1836 | Benajah & w Grace & ch Philip Draper, & Charity, Isaac, Benajah jr & Rachel rocf Short Creek MM, Oh |
| 11-23-1836 | Hannah Ann rocf Short Creek MM, Ohio |
| 11-27-1837 | Nathan & w Sarah Ann & ch Sarah Isabelle & Josiah Thomas rocf Rich Square MM, N C end by Walnut Ridge MM |
| 10-25-1837 | Hannah Ann & John T White inf mtg of int to m. Hannah's parents gave consent. John T was instructed to prod his mth's consent |
| 11-22-1837 | Hannah Ann & John T White altm (although his mth's consent to m has not been rec, it is supposed, to a delay in the mail) |
| 4-24-1839 | Nathan & w Nancy T rocf Short Creek MM, Oh & end to Westfield MM |
| 2-19-1840 | Charity & Isaac Williams altm |
| 2-19-1840 | For the accommodation of Charity & Isaac Williams, in accompl their m, a meeting is apptd at Elm Grove M H, tomorrow at the usual hour |
| 8-23-1843 | James B produced a cert from Walnut Ridge MM to m Hannah B Gause |
| 8-23-1843 | James B & Hannah B Gause altm |
| 11-22-1843 | Hannah B gct Walnut Ridge MM |
| 3-24-1847 | James B & w Hannah & s Eli rocf Walnut Ridge MM |
| 6-23-1847 | Martha rocf Walnut Ridge MM |
| 6-23-1847 | Martha jr rocf Walnut Ridge MM |
| 6-23-1847 | Phebe M rocf Walnut Ridge MM |
| 9-22-1847 | Isaac gct Blue River MM to m Hannah M Newby |
| 12-23-1847 | Rachel & Edward Morgan altm |
| 3-29-1848 | James B & w Hannah & ch Eli & Rebecca gct Walnut Ridge MM |
| 4-19-1848 | Hannah Maria rocf Blue River MM |
| 8-20-1851 | Philip D gct Blue River MM to m Joanna Morris |
| 7-21-1852 | Joanna M rocf Blue River MM |
| 10-25-1854 | Aaron Gause gct Walnut Ridge MM to m Elizabeth Parker |
| 12-19-1855 | Robert C, Nathaniel, Catharine, Grace & Charity, ch of Nathan, decd rocf Westfield MM |
| 4-23-1856 | James B & w Hannah B & ch Eli & Rebecca rocf Walnut Ridge MM |
| 1-28-1861 | James B appt asst clerk & Eli Ratliff appt clerk |
| 8-mo-1864 | James B is appt to receive and take charge of this mtg's records & papers that formerly have been in the possession of our aged friend, Eli Gause, who has req to be released |
| 11-23-1864 | James B appt a Trustee of real estate at Elm Grove P M |
| 1-14-1865 | James B appt clerk & John Symons appt asst clerk |
| 4- 1-1865 | Jesse rec on req |
| 7- 1-1865 | James B appt an overseer |
| 9- 2-1865 | Eli G & Mary M Thomas altm |
| 10-10-1868 | Eli G & w Mary Matilda & dt Viola Alice gct Walnut Ridge MM |
| 5- 4-1872 | Jesse B con mcd |
| 10-12-1872 | Jesse B gct Cherry Grove MM |

## PARTON
| | |
|---|---|
| 4- 4-1868 | Charles & w Jennette rec in mbrp |
| 5- 7-1870 | Jennette dis |
| 2- 3-1872 | Charles dis |
| 1- 7-1888 | William rec in mbrp |
| 5- 9-1891 | Elizabeth rec in mbrp |

## PATE
| | |
|---|---|
| 3- 4-1882 | William A & w Martha & s Isaac rec in mbrp |
| 12- 6-1890 | William dis |
| 9- 1-1906 | Martha drpd from mbrp |
| 12- 7-1922 | Ruth rec in mbrp |

## PATTERSON
| | |
|---|---|
| 11-27-1837 | Rachel rocf Stillwater MM, Oh end by Walnut Ridge MM |
| 12-20-1837 | William Kenworthy gct Walnut Ridge MM to m Asenath Patterson |
| 3-20-1839 | Rachel & Joseph Cook altm |
| 3-20-1839 | For the accommodation of Rachel & Joseph Cook, a meeting is apptd at Elm Grove M H for tomorrow at the usual hour |
| 1-23-1850 | Hezekiah & w Elizabeth & ch Sarah E, Eli, Levi C, Margaret, Milton & John W rocf Duck Creek MM |
| 1-22-1851 | Sarah Whicker (form Patterson) mcd dis |
| 9-21-1853 | Hezekiah & w Elizabeth & ch Levi C, Margaret, Milton & John W gct Westfield MM |
| 12- 2-1865 | Eli con mcd |
| 8- 2-1866 | Eli gct Westfield MM |

## PATTON
| | |
|---|---|
| 11- 4-1876 | Mary Louisa rel with a letter "to whom it may concern" |

## PAYNE
| | |
|---|---|
| 7- 1-1882 | Eliza A & s Olen E rocf Duck Creek MM |
| 2- 6-1897 | Maud S rocf Duck Creek MM |
| 2- 2-1901 | Olen E & Maud S gct New Castle MM |

## PEACOCK
| | |
|---|---|
| 5-20-1863 | Levi produced cert from New Garden MM to m |
| 5-20-1863 | Levi & Sarah Larrance altm |
| 7-22-1863 | Sarah gct New Garden MM |

## PEARSON
| | |
|---|---|
| 1-24-1838 | Jemima (form Gaunt) mcd dis |
| 4-24-1839 | Jane dis for na & dpl |
| 11-20-1839 | Zimri of Clear Springs P M, rpt mcd |
| 2-19-1840 | Zimri dis |
| 5-20-1840 | James dis for att a mcd |
| 11-25-1840 | Lydia gct Milford MM |
| 6-22-1842 | Rachel rocf Walnut Ridge MM end by Duck Creek MM |
| 7-20-1842 | Enoch rocf Duck Creek MM |
| 8-24-1842 | Peter & w Eunice & ch Isom, Nancy, Aaron B, William, Mary, Lilburn & Irene rocf Duck Creek MM |
| 1-25-1843 | Nancy & Newton Stubbs altm |
| 5-24-1843 | Enoch & w Rachel & s Nathan gct Duck Creek MM |
| 4-23-1845 | Peter jas, Separatists, dis |
| 10-22-1845 | Isom req cert to Mississinewa MM to m Naoma Lamb |
| 2-24-1847 | Eunice & ch Aaron B, William H, Mary, Lilburn, Irene & Stanton gct Honey Creek MM |
| 2-24-1847 | Isom gct Honey Creek MM |
| 6-23-1847 | Peter rst at Honey Creek MM w/con of this mtg |
| 9-22-1847 | John Produced the necessary cert from Union MM, Ohio |
| 9-22-1847 | John & Mary R Miller altm |

SPICELAND

## PEARSON (Cont)

|  |  |
|---|---|
| 9-22-1847 | For the convenience of John & Mary R. Miller, a mtg is granted to be held at Raysville M H, tomorrow at 11 o'clock for the accomplishment of their m |
| 12-23-1847 | Mary R gct Union MM, Oh |
| 5-23-1849 | Bailey & Rachel Baldwin inf mtg of int to m. He is directed to produce a cert from the mtg to which he belongs |
| 6-20-1849 | Bailey & Rachel Baldwin not appearing, the case is deferred to next mtg |
| 9-19-1849 | The comm appt rpt that Bailey & Rachel Baldwin have declined proceeding in their int to m. The case is therefore dismissed |
| 1-23-1850 | Rachel (form Baldwin) con mcd |
| 8-21-1850 | Rachel gct Mississinewa MM |
| 1-23-1851 | Ann (form Baldwin) con mcd |
| 7-23-1851 | Ann gct Mississinewa MM |
| 4-21-1852 | Seth W & w Nancy & ch Alva H rocf Mill Creek MM, Oh |
| 10-20-1852 | Isaac & ch Enoch S, Rebecca C, Calvin W, Rachel E, Elvira M & Martha M rocf Mill Creek MM, Oh |
| 10-20-1852 | Henry S rocf Mill Creek MM, Oh |
| 10-20-1852 | Sarah Ann rocf Mill Creek MM, Oh |
| 10-20-1852 | Mary Jane rocf Mill Creek MM, Oh |
| 11-24-1852 | Mary Jane & Eli E Mendenhall altm |
| 3-24-1858 | Seth W & w Nancy & s Alva & Rachel E Pearson, a minor, gct Plainfield MM |
| 3-24-1853 | Henry S gct Plainfield MM |
| 10-24-1855 | Seth W appt clerk & Richard P. Elliott appt asst clerk |
| 3-24-1858 | Elvira M & Martha M, minors, gct West Union MM |
| 5-19-1858 | Enoch S gct Plainfield MM |
| 2-22-1860 | Sarah Ann gct Plainfield MM |
| 11- 2-1867 | Jehu Stewart & w Sarah & ch Eliza Jane Pearson & Eli Stewart gct Poplar Ridge MM |
| 7- 2-1870 | Calvin W gct Adrian MM, Md to m Marthanna Taylor |
| 10- 8-1870 | Calvin W gct Whitewater MM |
| 5- 5-1883 | Amanuel Jesse rocf Union MM, Oh |
| 11- 3-1883 | Jesse & w Rachel rocf Union MM, Oh |
| 5- 2-1886 | Bailey & w Charlotte rocf Wabash MM |
| 8- 7-1886 | Nathan rec in mbrp |
| 8- 2-1890 | Grace Conway & dt Bertha gct Amboy MM |
| 12- 5-1891 | Amanuel Jesse rel on req |
| 4- 6-189? | Nathan rel on req |
| 3- 7-1896 | Isaiah B & Lavina rec in mbrp |
| 5- 1-1897 | Amanuel Jessie rec in mbrp |
| 9- 3-1898 | Isaiah & w Lavina rel on req |
| 5- 5-1900 | Bertha rocf Walnut Ridge MM |
| 6- 2-1900 | Isaiah rel on req |
| 5- 2-1903 | Sylvester & Sebastian gct Knightstown MM |
| 7- 1-1905 | Amanuel Jesse rel on req |
| 12- 4-1915 | Abigail rocf Duck Creek MM |

## PEGG

|  |  |
|---|---|
| 9-25-1833 | Sarah rocf Milford MM |
| 12-20-1848 | Sarah gct Richland MM |

## PENCE

|  |  |
|---|---|
| 3-20-1839 | Elizabeth (form Dillon) con mcd |

## PENNINGTON

|  |  |
|---|---|
| 1-23-1833 | Deborah appt to comm |
| 1-23-1833 | Josiah Pennington, Nathan Davis, William B Unthank, Amer Bond, Aaron Stanley & Isaiah Baldwin, to unite with a comm from women's mtg, to form comm to inspect & relieve the poor |
| 5-22-1833 | Levi appt to comm |
| 7-22-1835 | Josiah appt to comm |
| 7-29-1835 | Levi T gct Short Creek MM, Oh to m Emma Parker |
| 5-25-1836 | Emma rocf Short Creek MM, Oh |
| 6-22-1836 | Josiah Pennington, David James & Elias Jessop appt to att funerals of mbrs, at Elm Grove PM |
| 4-25-1838 | Levi T & w Emma gct Westfield MM |
| 11-21-1838 | Susanna & David Edwards altm |
| 5-22-1839 | Elm Grove PM rpts that John has mcd, he now resides in the limits of Elk MM, (Ohio) That mtg is req to treat with him & inf Spiceland MM |
| 11-20-1839 | Elk MM, Oh inf that John has removed to Philadelphia MM |
| 3-24-1841 | Deborah rec Minister at Spiceland P M |
| 6-23-1841 | Philadelphia MM inf that they have treated with John without any satisfaction. Spiceland MM unites to dis him |
| 12-21-1842 | Eliza & Thomas J Meredith inf mtg of int to m |
| 1-25-1843 | Eliza & Thomas J Meredith inf Spiceland mtg, in writing, that they have discontinued their int to m each other |
| 4-24-1844 | Eliza & David Burnett inf mtg of int to m |
| 5-22-1844 | Eliza & David Burnett altm |
| 5-22-1844 | For the convenience of Eliza & David Burnett, a mtg for their m is granted, for tomorrow at Elm Grove M H at 11 o'clock |
| 3-20-1861 | John P rst |
| 12- 7-1870 | John P gct Milford MM to m Melissa Elliott |
| 5- 6-1871 | Melissa J rocf Milford MM |
| 4- 6-1872 | John P rec as Minister |
| 1- 3-1914 | Agnes rec in mbrp |
| 5- 4-1922 | Louisa rec in mbrp |
| 10- 6-1927 | E? L & Louisa rel on req |

## PERKINS

|  |  |
|---|---|
| 12-24-1864 | Elva P rocf Rocky Run MM |
| 2- 4-1865 | Elva P & Eli C Gause inf mtg of int to m (on account of the national difficulties cutting off communications from N C, the consent of Elva's parents who live in that state, is waived by this mtg) |
| 3- 4-1865 | Elva P & Eli C Gause altm |

## PERRY

|  |  |
|---|---|
| 1- 7-1899 | Martha Evans gct West Grove MM |
| 4- 6-1922 | Martha Evans rocf West Grove MM |

## PHELPS

|  |  |
|---|---|
| 3- 7-1868 | Ezekiel & w Sarah & ch Cora & Virlin rec in mbrp |
| 5- 2-1874 | Ezekiel appt overseer |
| 5- 5-1883 | Ezekiel appt Elder |

## PHILABAUM

|  |  |
|---|---|
| 3- 3-1888 | James & w Sarah & ch Alonzo & Lura rocf Raysville MM, end by Duck Creek MM |
| 3- 7-1891 | Alonzo rel on req |
| 7- 4-1903 | Lura rel on req |
| 9- 5-1903 | James & Sarah gct Whitewater MM |

## PICKERING

|  |  |
|---|---|
| 8-23-1837 | Abner & Jenette Saint had inf Duck Creek MM of their int to m |
| 9-20-1837 | Abner & Jenette Saint appeared at Spiceland Mtg & continued their int to m (Duck Creek Mtg had been laid down) The comm rpts they are altm |
| 9-20-1837 | The comm at Duck Creek Mtg appt to treat with Jonas rpt no satisfactory result Comm is continued by Spiceland (Duck Creek had been laid down) |
| ( 9-20-1837) | Jonas Sr & w Ruth & ch, mbrs of Duck Creek Mtg, now laid down, have been attached to Spiceland |
| ( 9-20-1837) | Phineas & w Rachel & ch, mbrs of Duck Creek Mtg, now laid down, have been attached to Spiceland |
| ( 9-20-1837) | Jonathan & w Tersia & ch, mbrs of Duck Creek Mtg, now laid down, have been attached to Spiceland |
| 11-22-1837 | Ruth Anna Saint (form Pickering) mcd dis |
| 12-20-1837 | Jonas jr dis for dpl & mcd |
| 4-25-1838 | James C produced a cert from Milford MM to m Sarah Ann Pitts |
| 4-25-1838 | James C & Sarah Ann Pitts altm |
| 5-23-1838 | Hiram, compl of by Elm Grove P M, for mcd & na |
| 3-20-1839 | Hiram dis |
| 5-23-1839 | Jonathan & w Tersia & ch Lindley & Rachel gct Salem MM, Iowa |
| 11-22-1843 | Elizabeth (form Bogue) con mcd |
| 1-24-1844 | Phineas & w Rachel & ch Nancy, Ellis, Jane, Deborah, Rebecca, John, Enos & Mary gct Walnut Ridge MM |

SPICELAND

## PICKERING (Cont)

|  |  |
|---|---|
| 4-25-1849 | Elizabeth J & s James Erwin gct Duck Creek MM |
| 9-25-1850 | Rebecca rec in mbrp |
| 3-19-1851 | Hester rst w/con of Union MM, Oh |
| 9-20-1854 | Richard Evans gct Duck Creek MM to m Lydia Jane Pickering |
| 2-20-1856 | Nathan Macy gct Duck Creek MM, to m Jennet Pickering (a wid) |
| 6-25-1856 | Jennet Macy & her ch Martha, Thomas S, Julia Ann & William Exum Pickering rocf Duck Creek MM |
| 3-25-1863 | Lydia gct Duck Creek MM |
| 8-24-1864 | Martha gct Springfield MM, Iowa |
| 1- 1-1870 | Jacob J & Mariam C Test propose m with each other. The former, not being a mbr of our Society |
| 2- 5-1870 | Jacob J & Mariam Test altm |
| 2- 5-1870 | Jacob J req mbr in Friends Society, which req was granted |
| 7- 2-1881 | Alice H rocf Sugar River MM |
| 3- 6-1886 | John & w Orpha rec in mbrp |
| 7- 1-1893 | Jacob gct New Castle MM |
| 7- 1-1893 | John F & w Orpha & s Ralph gct New Castle MM |
| 6- 3-1906 | Orpha & ch Ralph & Nellie Irene rocf New Castle MM |
| 12- 7-1912 | Alice drpd from mbrp |
| 1- 3-1914 | Irena rec in mbrp |
| 11- 1-1928 | Kenneth rec in mbrp |

## PICKETT - PIGGOTT

|  |  |
|---|---|
| 5-22-1833 | William & w Sarah rocf Duck Creek MM |
| 2-19-1834 | Ann & ch Rhoda H, Benjamin N, Esther S & Elizabeth Jane gct Milford MM (Milford refused to rec the cert & it was returned to Spiceland Mtg) |
| ( 9-20-1837) | James & w Mary & ch William, Elihu, Thomas & Margaret having been mbrs of Duck Creek Mtg, laid down, have been attached to Spiceland |
| 10-21-1846 | William & w Lydia Simcox altm |
| 1-20-1847 | Rebecca jr rocf White River MM |
| 4-19-1848 | Elihu & Eunice Baldwin altm |
| 5-23-1849 | Elihu dis |
| 3-20-1850 | Eunice & dt gct Mississinewa MM |
| 7-23-1851 | William & w Lydia & ch James Hervey & Job S P gct Hinkles Creek MM |
| 2-25-1852 | Rebecca gct Back Creek MM |
| 3-23-1853 | Esther (form Foster) mcd |
| 4-23-1856 | James & w Mary & ch John Joel, Samuel M, James Milton & Priscilla Ann gct East Grove MM, Iowa |
| 4-23-1856 | Margaret gct East Grove MM, Iowa |
| 11-19-1856 | Rebecca rocf Back Creek MM |
| 7-22-1857 | Thomas J gct East Grove MM, Iowa |
| 8-19-1857 | Benjamin D produced a cert from Honey Creek MM to m |
| 8-19-1857 | Benjamin D & Martha Larrance altm |
| 2-24-1858 | Martha L gct Honey Creek MM |
| 12-22-1858 | Rebecca gct Back Creek MM |
| 1-22-1862 | Rebecca rocf Oak Ridge MM |
| 4- 6-1867 | Hannah H rec in mbrp |
| 2- 1-1868 | Simon & Rebecca Ellen rec in mbrp |
| 2- 3-1883 | Albert A rec in mbrp |
| 2- 3-1883 | William Riley & ch Ethaline & Evelie rec in mbrp |
| 6- 1-1901 | John drpd from mbrp |
| 9- 1-1906 | Ruby drpd from mbrp |
| 12- 7-1912 | Lenora & Esther E rel on req |

## PIDGEON

|  |  |
|---|---|
| 11- 2-1867 | David (a wid) produced a cert from Springfield MM to m |
| 11- 2-1867 | David & Hannah Stanley altm |
| 3- 7-1868 | Hannah gct Springfield MM |
| 10-11-1890 | David L & w Elizabeth & ch Nellie & Lillie rocf Springfield MM |
| 8- 6-1898 | David L & w Elizabeth & dts Nellie & Lillie gct Westland MM |
| 5- 2-1929 | Luther Albert rec in mbrp |

## PIERCE

|  |  |
|---|---|
| 1- 7-1871 | Christina rocf Hopewell MM |
| 1- 7-1871 | Lavina Frances & Edgar M, ch of Christina rec in mbrp |
| 4- 7-1883 | Edgar gct Westfield MM |
| 4- 2-1887 | Rebecca J gct New Castle MM |
| 4- 7-1900 | Frankie rec in mbrp |
| 4- 7-1906 | Obbie rec in mbrp |
| 10- 2-1919 | Abbie gct Knightstown MM |
| 2- 7-1924 | A D & w rel on req |

## PIKE

|  |  |
|---|---|
| 2-24-1836 | John S produced a cert from Duck Creek MM to m Gulielma Dean |
| 2-24-1836 | John S & Gulielma Dean altm |
| 5-25-1836 | Gulielma gct Duck Creek MM |
| 9-25-1839 | John S, Duck Creek P M, rpt to have mcd |
| 1-22-1840 | John S dis |
| 3-22-1843 | The comm appt to care of poor in the Q M, rpt that they thought the case of John Pike, an elderly friend & a mem of Duck Creek MM, should be an exception--- therefore the comm at Duck Creek Mtg should care for his case, a portion of the year, then Walnut Ridge Mtg & then Spiceland Mtg, each a like portion of the year |
| 10-24-1849 | Himelius produced cert from New Garden MM to m Ruth Cloud |
| 10-24-1849 | Himelius & Ruth Cloud altm |
| 10-24-1849 | Himelius & Ruth Cloud req a mtg be granted at Spiceland M H, for tomorrow at 11 o'clock, for them to accomplish their m, which was granted |
| 1-23-1850 | Ruth gct New Garden MM |
| 6-23-1852 | Himelius & w Ruth rocf Dover MM |
| 11-23-1853 | Anna gct Westfield MM |
| 9-19-1855 | Himelius & w Ruth gct New Garden MM |
| 4- 6-1893 | Mary Ida rec in mbrp |
| 8- 5-1893 | Peninah & ch rocf Hopewell MM |
| 4- 7-1906 | Ida rel on req |

## PINKHAM

|  |  |
|---|---|
| 10-11-1884 | William P & w Emma C & ch Gertrude Harriett, Charles Herbert & Bertha rocf Whitewater MM |
| 10-11-1884 | Mary Cornelia rocf Whitewater Mtg |
| 8- 4-1888 | William P & w Emma & ch Gertrude, Charlie & Bertha gct Salem MM, Mass |

## PITMAN

|  |  |
|---|---|
| 9-20-1837 | Robert & w Mary & ch Milton & Mary rocf Milford MM & directed to Duck Creek Mtg, but since mtg laid down, end to Spiceland MM |
| 1-19-1842 | Robert & w Mary & ch Milton & Mary gct Milford MM |

## PITTS

|  |  |
|---|---|
| ( 9-20-1837) | Cadwalder & w Elizabeth & ch, mbrs of Duck Creek Mtg, now laid down, have been attached to Spiceland |
| 10-25-1837 | Cadwallader appt an overseer by Spiceland |
| 4-24-1838 | Sarah Ann & James C Pickering altm |

## PLEAS

|  |  |
|---|---|
| 4-20-1842 | Aaron L & dt Achsah G rocf Hopewell MM |
| 10-19-1842 | Aaron L & Ann E Hunt, a wid, altm |
| 3-25-1846 | Elwood & Maurice ch of Aaron L rocf Hopewell MM |
| 12-23-1847 | Aaron L appt Treasurer |
| 4-19-1854 | Ellwood & Sarah Ann Griffin altm |
| 9-19-1855 | Maurice dis |
| 3- 3-1866 | Joseph H gct Walnut Ridge MM |
| 2- 6-1875 | Elwood rel on req |
| 12- 5-1903 | C E rel on req |
| 9- 1-1906 | Ida drpd from mbrp |
| 12- 7-1912 | R J & w & ch Ivanhoe & Ernest drpd from mbrp |
| 11- 6-1919 | Sarah gct Whittier MM, Ca |

## POE

|  |  |
|---|---|
| 3- 1-1902 | D Milton rec in mbrp |
| 5- 2-1903 | Elizabeth & dt Jessie rocf Duck Creek MM |

## POER

|  |  |
|---|---|
| 8-24-1853 | Mary rocf Springfield MM, N C |
| 2-24-1858 | Mary gct Mill Creek MM |
| 8- 4-1866 | Isabelle rec in mbrp |
| 9- 1-1866 | Mary rocf Mill Creek MM |

## POER (Cont)
| | |
|---|---|
| 5- 2-1869 | Robert rec in mbrp |
| 8- 7-1869 | Robert con mcd |
| 1- 3-1880 | Rebecca Ellen rec in mbrp |
| 3- 3-1883 | Muratt J C rec in mbrp |
| 4- 7-1883 | Robert gct Raysville MM |
| 3- 6-1886 | James & w Lucinda & ch Arthur & Nora rec in mbrp |
| 4- 4-1896 | Alice rel on req |
| 2- 6-1897 | Muratt rel on req |
| 11- 4-1905 | Lena L rocf Knightstown MM |
| 10- 2-1909 | Alta rel on req |
| 1- 4-1913 | Minnie Mae rec in mbrp |
| 2- 7-1914 | Lena L rel on req |
| 4- 3-1914 | Loucile & Dorsey Ivan rec in mbrp |
| 4- 1-1920 | Don rec in mbrp |

## PORCH
| | |
|---|---|
| 6-19-1850 | Anna Jane rocf New Garden MM |
| 5-20-1863 | Samuel rec in mbrp |
| 5-20-1863 | William & Lineas, ch of Samuel & Anna Jane, rec in mbrp |
| 4- 1-1865 | Anna Jane rec as Minister |
| 2- 7-1874 | Robert F rocf Hinkles Creek MM, end by Westfield MM |
| 3- 4-1876 | Mary Emma rec in mbrp |
| 3- 6-1886 | Phebe & dt Florence rec in mbrp |
| 4- 4-1903 | Robert gct New Castle MM |
| 12- 5-1914 | Damon rec in mbrp |
| 4- 6-1918 | Nancy Emma rec in mbrp |
| 2- 6-1930 | Damon rel on req |

## PORTER
| | |
|---|---|
| 6- 6-1868 | Ellen Jane rec in mbrp |
| 3- 5-1904 | Orville rec in mbrp |
| 12- 7-1912 | Orville drpd from mbrp |

## POWELL
| | |
|---|---|
| 9- 5-1896 | Henry C & w Lucinda A rocf Dublin MM |
| 11- 7-1903 | Henry C gct Marion MM |

## PRATT
| | |
|---|---|
| 8- 3-1912 | Leonira & dt Adrien L rec in mbrp |

## PRESNALL
| | |
|---|---|
| ( 9-20-1837) | Jeremiah L was mbr of Duck Creek mtg, now laid down, was attached to Spiceland |
| ( 9-20-1837) | Benoni & w Jane & fam mbrs of Duck Creek Mtg, now laid down, are attached to Spiceland |
| 12-20-1837 | Jeremiah L & Phebe Stanbrough inf mtg of int to m. The consent of parents' are now had |
| 1-24-1838 | Jeremiah L & Phebe Stanbrough altm |
| 5-22-1838 | Jane dis for na |
| 3-25-1840 | Daniel rst in mbrp |
| 7-22-1840 | Jeremiah L & w Phebe & ch James S gct Westfield MM |
| 6-24-1846 | Rachel (form Reynard) mcd dis |

## PRICE
| | |
|---|---|
| 2-21-1838 | Rice Price, Demsey Reece, Francis Macy, Abraham Moore, Lewis Swain & Obadiah Morgan appt by Spiceland Mtg to att funerals of friends at Duck Creek P M |
| 7-25-1838 | Robert & w Mary & ch Ann, Belinda, Zilpha, Sarah Jane & Alfred gct Vermillion MM, Ill |
| 1-19-1848 | Owen Evans gct Duck Creek MM to m Anna Price |
| 4-25-1855 | John M Griffin gct Duck Creek MM, to m Anna Price |

## PRI(T)CHARD
| | |
|---|---|
| 11-19-1834 | Samuel & w Harriet & ch Martha, Anna, & David Pritchard & Rebecca & William Draper, minor ch in their care, rocf New Garden MM (Rebecca & William Draper are ch of Samuel, decd & Mary (Albertson) Draper of N C) |
| 7-20-1835 | Samuel appt to a comm |
| 2-24-1836 | Samuel Pritchard, William Macy & William Edwards appt at Elm Grove P M to receive & hold a deed to real estate at that place |
| 2-22-1837 | Samuel Pritchard, William Edwards & William Macy appt to receive & hold in trust, deed to Elm Grove P M for land on which the Mtg House now stands and the land purchased from Nathan Gause for a burying ground |
| 5-23-1838 | Samuel appt an overseer |
| 11-24-1841 | Samuel Pritchard, Caleb White, Joel Pusey, Charles Morgan & Samuel Horner appt Trustees to rec & hold titles for real estate, in trust, for Raysville P M, Wayne twp, Henry Co, for meeting, school & burying ground |
| 6-22-1842 | Samuel appt to station of Elder |
| 8-24-1842 | Calvin W & William B ch of William, decd, gct Milford MM |
| 1-19-1848 | Samuel Pritchard, Richard J Hubbard & Amos Kenworthy appt to a comm on burials within the limits of Raysville MM |
| 2-23-1848 | Calvin W, a minor, rocf Salem MM, Iowa |
| 9-20-1848 | Martha E & Richard P Elliott altm |
| 9-20-1848 | At the req of Martha E & Richard P Elliott, a mtg is granted to be held at Raysville M H tomorrow at 11 o'clock to accomplish their m |
| 5-21-1851 | Thomas & w Elizabeth rocf Blue River MM |
| 1-24-1855 | Benjamin C & w Rachel & s Caleb W rocf Piney Woods MM, N C |
| 5-21-1856 | Edwin gct Red Cedar MM, Iowa |
| 5-21-1856 | Anna & Joseph W Jay altm |
| 9- 5-1868 | Benjamin C an Elder |
| 4- 6-1872 | Benjamin C & w Rachel & ch Thomas & Ann W gct Cottonwood MM, Kas |
| 4- 6-1872 | Caleb & ch William & Julia gct Cottonwood MM, Kas |

## PUCKET
| | |
|---|---|
| ( 9-20-1837) | Thomas & Matilda, mbrs of Duck Creek Mtg, now laid down, have been attached to Spiceland Mtg |
| 12-25-1839 | Matilda & ch Mary Ann & Lydia Margaret gct New Garden MM (fam of Thomas A, cert for him is withheld) |

## PUSEY
| | |
|---|---|
| 2-25-1835 | Joel & w Hannah & ch Martha, Jesse F & Rachel rocf Center MM, Oh |
| 11-25-1835 | Joel appt to a comm |
| 9-20-1837 | Martha & George E Hunicutt altm |
| 11-24-1841 | Joel Pusey, Samuel Pritchard, Caleb White, Charles Morgan & Samuel Horner appt Trustees to rec & hold titles for real estate, in trust, for Raysville P M, Wayne Twp, Henry Co, for meeting, school, & burying ground |
| 6-22-1842 | Jesse F & Jane White altm |
| 7-24-1844 | Joel & w Hannah & dt Rachel gct Milford MM |
| 7-24-1844 | Jesse F & w Jane & ch William gct Milford MM |
| 8-21-1850 | Joel & w Hannah & dt Rachel rocf Milford MM |
| 12-20-1854 | Rachel gct Walnut Ridge MM |
| 7-23-1855 | Joel gct Walnut Ridge MM |

## RALSTON
| | |
|---|---|
| 1- 4-1902 | Elizabeth M rocf Walnut Ridge MM |
| 11- 4-1905 | Elizabeth gct Dublin MM |

## RATLIFF
| | |
|---|---|
| 3-22-1837 | Gabriel & w Catherine & ch Mahlon, Mary, Benajah, Huldah, Sarah, Seth & Elizabeth rocf Duck Creek MM |
| 8- 9-1837 | Gabriel appt to comm on Education for ensuing year |
| ( 9-20-1837) | Joshua & w Letitia & ch mbrs of Duck Creek Mtg, now laid down, are attached to Spiceland |
| 7-25-1838 | Joshua & w Letitia & fam req cert of remov to Vermillion MM, Ill |
| 8-22-1838 | Phineas appt to comm |
| 9-19-1838 | The friends appt to prepare a cert for Joshua & fam, inf that "Joshua is decd & that the fam is yet within our limits" |
| 3-20-1839 | Thomas of Clearspring P M dis "for vending spiritous liquor" |
| 5-22-1839 | Latitia & dt Emily gct Salem MM, Iowa |
| 7-24-1839 | Richard appeared & produced an acknowledgement his deviations for which he had been dis. He req to again be rec in mbrp. |

SPICELAND

## RATLIFF (Cont)

|  |  |
|---|---|
| 7-24-1839 | Richard (Cont) A comm was appt to treat with him |
| 8-21-1839 | The comm appt believes Richard sincere in his req which mtg accepts & unites in rec him |
| 6-20-1840 | Samuel P gct Salem MM, Iowa |
| 6-23-1841 | Gabriel appt an overseer at Spiceland P M |
| 3-22-1843 | Gabriel appt to station of Elder by Spiceland P M of Ministers & Elders |
| 11-20-1844 | Stephen Macy gct Duck Creek MM to m Rebecca Ratcliff |
| 4-19-1848 | Huldah Wright (form Ratliff) con mcd |
| 12-20-1848 | Catherine & ch Sarah, Seth, Elizabeth, Joseph, Rebecca, Martha, Asenath & John gct Mississinewa MM |
| 6-25-1856 | Eli & w Jane & ch Huldah P & Calvin rocf Duck Creek MM |
| 10-21-1857 | Eli appt asst clerk |
| 3-24-1858 | Eli appt clerk |
| 1-19-1859 | Eli & w Jane & ch Huldah P & Calvin W gct Plainfield MM |
| 5-25-1859 | Eli & w Jane & ch Huldah & Calvin rocf Plainfield MM |
| 1-28-1861 | Eli appt clerk, James B Parker appt asst clerk |
| 4-20-1864 | Huldah P & Jehu W Hall altm |
| 3- 3-1866 | Sarah & s Fleming rocf Flushing MM, Oh |
| 3- 3-1866 | Hannah W rocf Flushing MM, Oh |
| 7- 7-1866 | Cyrus & w Elizabeth & ch Charlie William & John rec in mbrp |
| 6- 6-1868 | Eli appt an overseer at Spiceland P M |
| 6- 6-1868 | Jane appt an overseer at Spiceland P M |
| 1- 2-1869 | Elisha & w Rebecca & ch Loring T, Henry Herbert rocf Lynn Grove MM, Iowa |
| 3- 6-1869 | Calvin W con mcd |
| 8- 7-1869 | Calvin W appt to record the minutes of this MM |
| 9- 4-1869 | Edward rocf Flushing MM, Oh |
| 1- 1-1870 | Elisha B appt clerk & William Edgerton appt asst clerk |
| 2- 5-1870 | Julia A & dt Mary Emma rocf Short Creek MM, Oh |
| 6- 3-1871 | Eli appt an overseer |
| 8- 5-1871 | Eli appt an Elder |
| 7- 5-1873 | Jane rec as Minister |
| 12-16-1879 | Marcus & w Hannah rocf Duck Creek MM |
| 4- 7-1883 | Marcus & w Hannah Adlaide & ch William E gct Raysville MM |
| 4- 7-1883 | Fleming gct Duck Creek MM |
| 5- 5-1883 | Elisha B appt an Elder |
| 12- 7-1889 | Charles F gct Westland MM |
| 10-11-1890 | Edward & w Julia & dt Achsah E gct New Castle MM |
| 6- 4-1892 | Cornelius & w Anna & ch Henry, William, Charles & Morris rocf Hopewell MM |
| 1- 7-1893 | Marcus & w Adalaide & ch William Everett, Hershel & Edward rocf Raysville MM |
| 11- 4-1893 | Charles L rel on req |
| 3- 5-1894 | Lorin T gct Sugar Creek MM, Iowa |
| 5- 2-1896 | Marcus & w Hannah Adalaide & ch William Everett, Hershel, Edward, Earl M & Jesse Claud & Ruby Evelyn gct Carthage MM |
| 4- 2-1898 | Charles F & w Matilda & ch Harold, Russell & Ralph rocf Westland MM |
| 3- 4-1890 | Lillian May gct Duck Creek MM |
| 1- 6-1900 | Charles F & w Matilda & ch Harold, Russell & Ralph gct Anderson MM |
| 4- 4-1903 | Harlan S gct Indianapolis MM |
| 1- 6-1912 | Odelia rec in mbrp |
| 12- 7-1912 | William rel on req |
| 2- 1-1913 | Elizabeth gct Indianapolis MM |
| 2- 1-1913 | Levi S gct Indianapolis MM |
| 5- 3-1913 | John A gct Whitewater MM |
| 4- 6-1918 | Charles F & w Matilda & ch Harold & Russell rec in mbrp |
| 10- 6-1919 | Edwin gct Knightstown MM |
| 10- 6-1919 | Adella H gct Knightstown MM |
| 10- 6-1919 | Anna gct Knightstown MM |
| 1- 1-1920 | Charles & fam gct Knightstown MM |
| 4-21-1920 | Elizabeth & s Levi rec in mbrp |
| 10- 1-1925 | Elizabeth Jane gct New Castle MM |

## RAWLS

|  |  |
|---|---|
| 2-25-1847 | Centre MM req Spiceland to treat with Jonathan, a mbr of that mtg, who has mcd & rpt to them |
| 8-25-1847 | Jonathan dis by Centre MM |

## RAYL

|  |  |
|---|---|
| 8-23-1837 | Veshti & ch Abulleno, Asa, Mordecai, Ann, Elias & Jesse rocf Hopewell MM, N C, end by New Garden MM |
| 5-23-1838 | William rocf Hopewell MM, N C |
| 8-22-1838 | William & w Vashti & ch gct Mill Creek MM |
| 12-24-1845 | Zadock & w Delilah & ch Perlina, Addison Clarkson, Alpheus, Harmon & William rocf Hopewell MM, N C end by New Garden MM |
| 5-19-1847 | Nancy & dt Eliza rocf Hopewell MM, N C |
| 7-mo 1847 | Eliza Hourenton (form Rayl) rptd mou |
| 12-20-1848 | John, Elizabeth Ann, Zadock B ch of Charles rocf Hopewell MM, N C |
| 12-19-1849 | George & w Ann & ch Rebecca Jane, Thomas Chalkley & Asa P & Elmina White, a minor, under their care, rocf New Garden MM, N C |
| 12-19-1849 | Isaac W rocf New Garden MM, N C |
| 11-20-1850 | Jane Harvey (form Rayl) mcd dis |
| 3-24-1852 | Isaac con mcd |
| 10-20-1852 | Himelius & w Sarah Ann rocf Walnut Ridge MM |
| 11-24-1852 | George & w Ann & ch gct Richland MM |
| 11-24-1852 | Himelius & w Sarah Ann gct Richland MM |
| 11-24-1852 | Isaac W & Rebecca & s Chalkley gct Richland MM |
| 4-20-1853 | John jas dis |
| 11-25-1857 | George & w Ann rocf Richland MM |
| 1-20-1858 | James H & w Margaret & ch Julia E, Alpheus P, Martha A, Calvin A, Laura P, William, Hannah D & Malinda C rocf New Garden MM, N C |
| 10-20-1858 | George & w Ann gct Richland MM |
| 10-20-1858 | James H & w Margaret & ch gct Westfield MM |
| 12-22-1858 | Zadock dis |
| 3-21-1860 | Addison C con mcd |
| 7-24-1861 | Addison C gct Greenwood MM |
| 11-20-1861 | Asa P rocf Richland MM |
| 5-21-1862 | Alpheus con mcd |
| 12-24-1864 | Asa P gct Richland MM |
| 5- 2-1868 | Julia rocf Greenwood MM |
| 8- 1-1868 | William con mcd |
| 3- 5-1870 | George W con mcd |
| 5- 7-1870 | Zadock appt Treasurer of Spiceland MM |
| 6- 3-1871 | Zadock appt an overseer |
| 2- 1-1873 | George W & w Debbie gct Greenwood MM |
| 4- 4-1874 | Ruth Emily rec as Minister |
| 7- 3-1875 | George & dt Florence rocf Greenwood MM |
| 2- 5-1881 | Addison & w Julia & ch Ella, Nora, Rose & Frank M rocf Greenwood MM |
| 3- 1-1884 | Addison C & w Julia & ch Ella, Nora, Rose & Frank M gct East Branch MM |
| 12- 3-1892 | Odessa (Painter) rec in mbrp |
| 4- 3-1897 | Florence rel on req |
| 1- 7-1899 | Harman & w Odessa & dt gct Knightstown MM |
| 12- 1-1917 | John rec in mbrp |
| 8- 9-1918 | Corona & Lindley Cook rpt m |

## REAGAN

|  |  |
|---|---|
| 1- 4-1919 | Chester & w Sabina & dts Alta Mary & Wilma Lucile rocf New London MM |
| 10- 3-1929 | Sabina & dts Alta, Wilma & Ina May gct Chester MM, N J |
| 9- 4-1930 | Violet Bowen drpd from mbrp |

## REDIC - REDDICK

|  |  |
|---|---|
| 2- 6-1904 | Rupert D rec in mbrp |
| 12- 6-1913 | R D rel on req |
| 11- 6-1919 | William E & Edna gct Rockford MM, Okl |

## REDDING

|  |  |
|---|---|
| 9- 2-1871 | Sally rec in mbrp |

## REECE

|  |  |
|---|---|
| ( 9-20-1837) | Dempsey & fam, mbrs of Duck Creek Mtg, now laid down, are attached to Spiceland MM |
| 10-25-1837 | Demsey appt to comm on "poor" by Spiceland MM |

SPICELAND

REECE (Cont)
|  |  |
|---|---|
| 2-21-1838 | Demsey Reece, Rice Price, Francis Macy, Abraham Moore, Lewis Swain, & Obadiah Morgan appt by Spiceland Mtg to att funerals of friends at Duck Creek P M |
| 8-22-1838 | Solomon & w Ruth & ch Jesse & Moses rocf New Hope MM, Tenn |
| 11-23-1842 | Hiram & w Rachel & s Enos rocf Westfield MM |
| 7-19-1843 | Hiram & w Rachel & ch Enos gct Westfield MM |
| 10-22-1851 | Amos C Horner gct Cherry Grove MM to m Elvira Reece |
| 3- 4-1853 | Samuel & w Mary Ann & ch James & Mildred rocf Cherry Grove MM |
| 4-25-1855 | Samuel & w Mary Ann & ch James, Mildred & Anna Jane gct Cherry Grove MM |
| 5-23-1855 | David H produced a cert from Walnut Ridge to m |
| 5-23-1855 | David H & Jane J Bogue altm |
| 2-20-1856 | Jane J gct Walnut Ridge MM |
| 2- 6-1886 | Henry & w Mary C rec in mbrp |
| 3- 6-1886 | James rec in mbrp |
| 3- 6-1886 | Charles rec in mbrp |
| 9- 6-1890 | James rel on req |
| 12- 6-1902 | Oneida B Carter & s Charles J Reece gct Olive Branch MM |
| 12- 7-1912 | Jesse gct Long Beach MM, Ca |
| 4- 3-1915 | Pansy & Lola rec in mbrp |
| 3- 1-1919 | Russell rec in mbrp |
| 12- 7-1922 | Pearl (George), Eulala, Mildred, Lester Howard, & Alice rec in mbrp |
| 3- 5-1931 | Mallan rec in mbrp |
| 5- 7-1933 | Robert rec in mbrp |

REED
|  |  |
|---|---|
| 3-19-1845 | Drusilla (form Unthank) con mcd |
| 12-24-1845 | Drusilla gct Whitewater MM |
| 5- 3-1879 | Drusilla A rocf Whitewater MM |
| 3- 6-1880 | Albert & w Ellen M & ch Frank Lefevre, Walter C & Hugh rocf Whitewater MM |
| 6- 2-1883 | Albert S & w Ellen & ch Frank L, Walter C & Albert R gct Indianapolis MM |
| 12- 2-1905 | Drusilla rocf Sugar River MM |

REPLOGLE
|  |  |
|---|---|
| 12- 5-1885 | Charles rec on req, Clinton S rec on req |
| 8- 7-1886 | Susan rec on req |
| 1- 1-1887 | Susan, Charles & Clinton transferred to Muncie MM |

REYNARD
|  |  |
|---|---|
| 1-23-1833 | Jacob & w Elizabeth & ch original mbrs |
| 8-21-1833 | Elizabeth appt to a comm |
| 5-20-1840 | Elizabeth dis for giving way to anger, upl & encouraging music & dancing |
| 5-20-1840 | Margaret dis for dpl & att pl d |
| 11-22-1843 | Catherine jas, dis |
| 6-24-1846 | Rachel Pressnall (form Reynard) mcd dis |
| 4-19-1848 | Mary Elliott (form Reynard) con mcd |
| 11-13-1851 | Eliza Ann (form Griffin) mcd dis |
| 8-25-1852 | Elizabeth Mills (form Reynard) con mcd |
| 2-22-1854 | Ruth Munden (form Reynard) con mcd |

REYNOLDS
|  |  |
|---|---|
| 4-11-1852 | Job & w Phebe & ch David, Eunice W, Asenath C, Susan B & Jane rocf New Garden MM |
| 9-22-1852 | Phebe & Amos M Kenworthy altm & req appt at Raysville M H for tomorrow, at the usual hour, to accomp their m, on the grounds that on the next two week day mtgs, their parents & some of their friends will visit at Y M & the next will be P M day.  Their req is granted and the mtg appt accordingly |
| 12- 3-1887 | P Ellen gct Springfield MM |
| 10-11-1902 | Elizabeth rec in mbrp |

RICE
|  |  |
|---|---|
| 5- 4-1922 | John rec in mbrp |

RICH
|  |  |
|---|---|
| 3- 2-1901 | Olive rec in mbrp |

RIDDLE
|  |  |
|---|---|
| 9- 5-1891 | Minnie rocf Duck Creek MM |
| 11- 5-1892 | Minnie gct Fairmount MM |

RIFNER
|  |  |
|---|---|
| 2- 6-1897 | Mary E rec in mbrp |
| 5- 5-1900 | Olive Ethel rec in mbrp |
| 5- 5-1921 | Lowell rec in mbrp |
| 5- 2-1929 | Eugene rec in mbrp |

RILEY
|  |  |
|---|---|
| 12- 6-1909 | John A & w Nettie & ch Ruth Esther rocf University MM, Kas |
| 7- 1-1911 | John & w gct Colorado Spring MM, Co |

ROBBINS
|  |  |
|---|---|
| 11- 7-1868 | John C rec in mbrp |
| 5- 1-1869 | John C gct Mississinewa MM |

ROBERTS
|  |  |
|---|---|
| 5- 6-1871 | Samuel & w Rebecca C & ch Elizare, Emma Bell, Ida May, Oscar & Austin rocf Westfield MM |
| 11- 5-1881 | Samuel & w Rebecca & ch Oscar & Austin gct Westfield MM |
| 2- 4-1882 | Elizarah rel on req |
| 6- 1-1889 | Bell & Ida gct Westfield MM |

ROGERS
|  |  |
|---|---|
| ( 9-20-1837) | Sarah, a mbr of Duck Creek Mtg, now laid down, attached now to Spiceland |
| 10-24-1838 | Sarah & Jonathan Stanbrough altm |
| 5-19-1858 | Jonathan T produced a cert from Westland MM, Pa, to m |
| 5-19-1858 | Jonathan T & Mary Hunt altm |
| 4-29-1859 | Jonathan T rocf Westland MM, Pa end by Springfield MM, Oh |
| 3-23-1864 | Mary rec as Minister |
| 1- 4-1868 | Jonathan T & w Mary H & ch Logan & Walter gct Ash Grove MM, Ill |
| 11- 4-1876 | Jonathan & w Mary H & ch Logan M & Walter C rocf Raysville MM |
| 8- 4-1877 | Jonathan T & fam gct Barclay MM, Kas |
| 11- 3-1883 | Rebecca Jane Schooley rel on req |

SAINT
|  |  |
|---|---|
| 1-25-1837 | Exum & minor ch Maria & William gct Duck Creek MM |
| 8-23-1837 | Jennette & Abner Pickering had inf Duck Creek mtg of their int to m |
| ( 9-20-1837) | William & Achsah & fam, mbrs of Duck Creek Mtg, now laid down, are attached to Spiceland |
| 9-20-1837 | Jennette & Abner Pickering appeared at Spiceland mtg & continued their int to m (Duck Creek mtg had been laid down)  The comm rpts they are altm |
| 11-22-1837 | Ruthanna (form Pickering) mcd |
| 12-20-1837 | Exum (Duck Creek P M) compl dis mcd |
| 1-24-1838 | Ruth Ann dis |
| 2-21-1838 | Exum dis at Spiceland MM |
| 7-24-1839 | Doughty & Robert Kenworthy altm |
| 6-24-1840 | William appt to a comm |
| 4-20-1842 | Jonathan produced a cert from Duck Creek MM to m Emily Johnson |
| 4-20-1842 | Jonathan & Emily Johnson altm |
| 8-24-1842 | Emily J gct Duck Creek MM |
| 2-23-1848 | J Addison Unthank gct Duck Creek MM to m Cynthia E Saint |
| 7- 4-1868 | Daniel rocf Whitewater MM |
| 11- 2-1872 | Lydia G gct Bangor MM, Iowa |
| 4- 7-1883 | Daniel gct Whitewater MM |
| 2- 5-1887 | Lida E & ch Arthur Lee & Mary Pauline gct Raysville MM |

SANDERS
|  |  |
|---|---|
| 2-24-1836 | Martha & s Joseph rocf Milford MM |
| 11-23-1836 | Thomas rocf Milford MM |
| 9-20-1837 | Charity dis |
| 11-21-1838 | Thomas compl of for dpl & mcd |
| 1-23-1839 | Thomas dis |
| 1-23-1839 | Jerusha (form Mills) compl of for mcd |
| 1-23-1839 | Joseph, Spiceland, compl of for dpl & mcd |
| 2-20-1839 | Jerusha dis |
| 3-20-1839 | Joseph dis |
| 12-25-1839 | Anna (form Wright) con mcd |
| 11- 8-1870 | Amanda (form Wooten) mcd dis |
| 10-14-1871 | Mary H gct LeGrand MM, Iowa |

SPICELAND

## SAPP
| | |
|---|---|
| 1- 7-1888 | Andrew J & Francis rec in mbrp |
| 3- 4-1893 | Isaac, Nora & Jacob rec in mbrp |
| 11- 5-1895 | Nora rel on req |

## SAUL
| | |
|---|---|
| 3- 2-1901 | Francis H & Mary Frances rec in mbrp |
| 4- 6-1901 | Ruby H, Olaf, Oliver F, Gladys A, Ramona & Frances C, ch of Francis & w, rec in mbrp |

## SCHOOLEY
| | |
|---|---|
| 1-23-1833 | Isaac & w Celia & ch original mbrs |
| 1-23-1833 | Susannah, (w of John) & ch Susannah & Rachel original mbrs |
| 2-20-1833 | Isaac appt Treasurer |
| 3-20-1833 | Isaac Schooley, John Hiatt, Aaron Stanley, Samuel Griffin & Josiah Small appt to comm to have oversight of & care of the burial ground |
| (11-mo-1833) | Benjamin & ch Wilson, Samuel, James & Milton rocf Cherry Grove MM |
| 6- 5-1834 | Benjamin altm Sarah Davis |
| 12-21-1836 | Isaac & w Celia & ch Anna, Nancy, Edith & John gct Mississinewa MM |
| 12-21-1836 | Susanna (with husb John) & dt Susannah & Rachel gct Mississinewa MM |
| 1838 | John rst at Mississinewa MM |
| 1-23-1839 | Benjamin & Jemima Draper altm |
| 5-22-1844 | Wilson mcd dis |
| 5-22-1844 | James L con mcd |
| 9-24-1845 | Mary Ann & dt Rebecca Jane rec in mbrp through req |
| 10-25-1848 | Samuel a mbr of Spiceland, now residing in limits of Honey Creek, is rptd to have mcd dis 1-24-1849 |
| 6-20-1849 | Milton, Spiceland P M rpts has mcd (He now resides in the limits of Springfield Mtg) |
| 3-19-1851 | James dis |
| 11-21-1855 | Susanna rocf Pipe Creek MM |
| 9-24-1862 | Susanna gct Mississinewa MM |
| 6- 2-1866 | James W & Sarah C, Amanda F, Anna D & Elizabeth M, ch of Mary A rec in mbrp |

## SCHULTZ
| | |
|---|---|
| 12- 7-1918 | Eunice H & ch Irvin & Eva L rocf West Richmond MM |
| 9- 6-1928 | Eunice, Irvin & Eva gct Indianapolis MM |

## SCOTT
| | |
|---|---|
| 11-12-1834 | Elwood Baldwin gct New Garden MM to m Pheba Scott |
| 3- 4-1882 | Maria rec in mbrp |
| 4- 7-1883 | Ophelia A rec in mbrp |

## SCOVILLE
| | |
|---|---|
| 5-24-1843 | Sarah (form Sweet) mcd dis |
| 1- 1-1876 | Mary A & Caroline A rec in mbrp |
| 1- 7-1888 | Anna M rocf Hopewell MM |

## SEAFORD
| | |
|---|---|
| 1- 3-1880 | W & Emma (Ballenger) gct Fairmount MM |
| 6- 7-1926 | Gertrude rec in mbrp |
| 1- 2-1930 | Gertrude rel on req |

## SEAGRAVE
| | |
|---|---|
| 7-26-1834 | Martha rocf West Grove MM |
| 5-24-1837 | Martha dis |

## SEARS
| | |
|---|---|
| 2- 1-1868 | James W & w Mary rec in mbrp |
| 6- 4-1877 | Mary Elizabeth & ch Charles & Eva A rec in mbrp |

## SHAFFER
| | |
|---|---|
| 3- 2-1895 | Charles rec in mbrp |
| 6- 2-1900 | Charles E & Anna B rel on req |

## SHEARS
| | |
|---|---|
| 5- 3-1908 | Anthony & w Clara rec in mbrp |
| 12- 7-1916 | Anthony & w drpd from mbrp |

## SHEPHERD
| | |
|---|---|
| 2- 3-1921 | Susie & Robert rec in mbrp |

## SHERIDAN
| | |
|---|---|
| 1-23-1833 | John Sr & Margaret & ch original mbrs |
| 8-21-1833 | Margaret appt to a comm |
| 3-19-1834 | John jr dis for fornication |
| 2-22-1837 | Rachel gct Westfield MM |
| 10-25-1837 | George & Mary C Kersey inf mtg of int to m The parents' consent has been given |
| 11-22-1837 | George & Mary C Kersey altm |
| 1-24-1838 | Rachel rocf Westfield MM |
| 1-23-1839 | Pollyann rocf Springfield MM |
| 9-25-1839 | Thomas gct Whitewater MM to m Hannah Wright |
| 10-23-1839 | Abner of Spiceland P M con mcd |
| 10-23-1839 | Matilda (form Gaunt) con mcd |
| 1-22-1840 | Polly Ann gct Springfield MM |
| 9-23-1840 | Hannah rocf Whitewater MM |
| 4-20-1842 | Susannah & Daniel C Allen altm |
| 8-25-1847 | William appt an overseer at Spiceland P M |
| 1-24-1849 | Isaac con mcd |
| 10-24-1849 | William Sheridan, James P Antrim & John Hiatt appt overseers at Spiceland P M |
| 12-21-1853 | Susannah & Eliphalet Hiatt altm |
| 2-22-1854 | Abner & ch Jemima E, Lydia M, Beulah A & Susan J gct Pipe Creek MM |
| 10-21-1857 | Thomas & w Hannah & ch Mary Ellen, Susan, Martha, Emily, Charles, Elizabeth & Esther Ann gct Lynn Grove MM, Iowa |
| 5-19-1858 | Eli con mcd |
| 7-21-1858 | Isaac & w Susan Emily & ch gct Pipe Creek MM |
| 2-20-1861 | Isaac & w Susan & ch William O, Margaret Ann, Ellen J & Sarah Catherine gct Pipe Creek MM |
| 3-20-1861 | Anna K & Aaron Symons altm |
| 5- 6-1865 | George & w Mary & ch Asher, R. Alice, & John William gct Lynn Grove MM, Iowa |
| 5- 6-1865 | Henry gct Lynn Grove MM, Iowa |
| 5- 6-1865 | Melissa Jane gct Lynn Grove MM, Iowa |
| 8- 4-1866 | Eli C gct Raysville MM |
| 2- 7-1874 | Oliver & dt Josephine rec in mbrp |
| 1- 6-1877 | John gct Columbus MM, Ohio |

## SHINN
| | |
|---|---|
| 4- 4-1891 | Israel & w Ann rec in mbrp |

## SHIPLEY
| | |
|---|---|
| 4- 4-1903 | Dora Hall gct Hopewell MM |

## SIMCOX
| | |
|---|---|
| 9-24-1845 | Lydia rocf Newberry MM, Ohio |
| 10-21-1846 | Lydia & William Pickett altm |

## SIMMONS
| | |
|---|---|
| 7- 1-1893 | Henry W & w Sarah Ann & ch Emma, Minnie, Floyd & Nettie rocf Raysville MM |
| 7- 1-1893 | Melvin rocf Raysville MM |
| 7- 1-1893 | Eva rocf Raysville MM |

## SISSON
| | |
|---|---|
| 2- 6-1897 | Martha Wilson rel on req |

## SKINNER
| | |
|---|---|
| 6- 1-1878 | Benjamin F rec in mbrp |
| 11- 2-1879 | Benjamin F gct Honey Creek MM |

## SMALL
| | |
|---|---|
| 1-23-1833 | Obadiah & Isabel & ch original mbrs |
| 1-23-1833 | Josiah & w Jane & ch original mbrs |
| 1-23-1833 | Josiah Small, James Johnson, William Baldwin & Isaac White appt to unite with a comm from women's mtg, to form a comm on Education & to rpt |
| 3-20-1833 | Josiah Small, John Hiatt, Aaron Stanley, Samuel Griffin, & Isaac Schooley appt to comm to have oversight of & care of burial ground at Spiceland |
| 5-22-1833 | Polly rec on req |
| 7-24-1833 | Isabell appt to a comm |
| 8-21-1833 | Obadiah appt to the comm to att Q M |
| 11-20-1833 | Nathan rst w/con of Chester MM |
| 11-25-1835 | Sarah rec on req |
| 12-23-1835 | Sarah, Elihu & Josiah, minor ch of Jonathan decd & Miriam, now Miriam Hockett, rocf New Garden MM |

SPICELAND

## SMALL (Cont)

|  |  |
|---|---|
| 5-25-1836 | Gideon rocf New Garden MM |
| 2-22-1837 | Nathan & w Polly & ch Samuel, Martha & Josiah, and a bound boy, Josiah Small, gct Mississinewa MM |
| 8-23-1837 | Mary & Joab Wright altm (Her parents have given consent) |
| 12-20-1837 | Gideon, Spiceland P M compl for mcd |
| 1-24-1838 | Gideon con mcd |
| 5-22-1839 | Sarah rocf Walnut Ridge MM |
| 8-21-1839 | Sarah rocf Walnut Ridge MM |
| 11-20-1839 | Dinah rec in mbrp |
| 4-22-1840 | Elizabeth & Lilburn White altm |
| 8-19-1840 | Sarah gct Walnut Ridge MM |
| 10-21-1840 | Susannah rocf Milford MM |
| 2-23-1842 | Abigail & Isaac Gause altm |
| 10-23-1844 | Susan & William W Thornburgh altm |
| 10-23-1844 | Elihu gct Mississinewa MM |
| 4-22-1846 | Sarah, dt of Jonathan, decd gct Mississinewa MM |
| 4-22-1846 | Gideon & w Dinah & ch Jonathan T, Mary, & Josiah M gct Mississinewa MM |
| 10-21-1846 | Jane & Jonathan Johnson inf mtg of int to m A comm appt to see that the rights of Jane's ch are secure |
| 11-25-1846 | Jane & Jonathan Johnson altm |
| 11-25-1846 | For the convenience of Jane & Jonathan Johnson, a mtg has been granted for tomorrow at 11 o'clock, for their m |
| 1-20-1847 | Jane Johnson & s William Small gct Cherry Grove MM |
| 10-25-1848 | Sarah & Josiah Baldwin inf mtg of int to m |
| 11-22-1848 | Sarah & Josiah Baldwin inf mtg in writing as follows: "We, ----- think best to discontinue our int of m with each other" |
| 2-21-1849 | William rocf Cherry Grove MM |
| 3-21-1849 | William & Mary Gause (jr) altm |
| 11-19-1851 | Sarah Symons (form Small) con mcd |
| 10-12-1872 | Mary dis |
| 5- 4-1878 | Sophronia rocf Raysville MM |
| 8- 4-1883 | Abigail drpd from mbrp |
| 6- 3-1893 | Sophronia rel on req |

## SMILEY

|  |  |
|---|---|
| 6- 6-1896 | Ollie Kate rocf Knightstown MM |
| 5- 4-1912 | Thelma rec in mbrp |
| 1- 4-1913 | Pearl rec in mbrp |
| 4- 6-1915 | Thelma rel on req |
| 4- 5-1918 | Zela & Tivis rec in mbrp |

## SMITH

|  |  |
|---|---|
| 3- 1-1884 | Francis Joseph & w Mary Eliza & ch Jessie Evaline & James Monroe rec in mbrp |
| 3- 6-1886 | William & Martha rec in mbrp |
| 5- 5-1888 | William & Martha gct New Castle MM |
| 10-11-1890 | F. Joseph & w Mary E & ch Jessie E, James M, Robert Edgar & Abigail W gct Raysville MM |
| 4- 4-1891 | F Joseph rel on req |
| 4- 4-1891 | Mary & ch Jessie E, James M, Robert & Abigail gct Raysville MM |
| 4- 3-1893 | William R & w Martha & ch Guy rocf New Castle MM |
| 9- 2-1899 | Martha & ch Guy & Claud gct New Castle MM |
| 4- 7-1906 | Fred rocf Whitewater MM |
| 1- 2-1909 | Fred & w Mary gct Mill Creek MM |
| 8- 5-1914 | William G rec in mbrp |
| 3- 6-1918 | Eilda M rec in mbrp |
| 7- 4-1929 | Fred & w Mary L & ch Olive Geraldine & Marjorie Helen rocf Amboy MM |

## SMITHSON

|  |  |
|---|---|
| 3- 3-1877 | Julia Ann rocf Fairmount MM |
| 8- 4-1877 | Julia & ch gct Fairmount MM |

## SOPHER

|  |  |
|---|---|
| 3-24-1841 | Joseph is compl of by Providence MM, Fayette Co, Pa for absconding without satisfying his creditors, & Spiceland MM is req to treat with him |
| 4-21-1841 | Joseph appeared with an acknowledgement which Spiceland MM was free to receive. The clerk is directed to forward a copy to Providence MM, Pa |
| 7-21-1841 | A communication from Providence MM, Pa inf Spiceland that the acknowledgement of Joseph is not satisfactory to that Mtg |
| 7-21-1841 | Sarah & step-dts Hannah K & Lydia rocf Providence, Pa |
| 8-23-1843 | Lydia Dunlap (form Sopher) mcd & jas, dis |
| 11-20-1844 | Hannah gct Greenfield MM |
| 11-24-1847 | Elizabeth & s Allen Hiatt rocf Duck Creek MM |
| 10-22-1856 | Elizabeth gct Spring Creek MM, Iowa |

## SPENCER

|  |  |
|---|---|
| 5-20-1846 | Rebecca rocf Short Creek MM, Ohio |
| 6-24-1846 | Rebecca & Joel Kenworthy altm |
| 9- 4-1875 | David & w Mary Jane & ch John Truman, David Carlyle, Sidney Arthur, Louise Angennetta, Alonzo, Mary J & Florence rocf Duck Creek MM |
| 1- 1-1876 | John A & w Sarah & ch Eddie, Montie & Julia rocf Duck Creek MM |
| 8- 2-1879 | John rocf Duck Creek MM |
| 12- 6-1890 | J Alexander dis |
| 2- 6-1897 | Cora rel on req |
| 9- 5-1906 | J Truman, Lindley & Florence drpd from mbrp |
| 10- 2-1909 | Edward drpd from mbrp |

## SPITLER

|  |  |
|---|---|
| 1- 5-1933 | Donald B & Lorena & ch John Raymond & Donald Verne rocf Detroit MM, Mich |

## SPRINGER

|  |  |
|---|---|
| 1-23-1833 | Barnabas original mbr |
| 5-20-1835 | Barnabas appt to comm to att Q M |
| 3-20-1839 | Barnabas gct Walnut Ridge MM |

## SPRONG

|  |  |
|---|---|
| 6- 5-1897 | Andrew J rec in mbrp |

## STAFFORD

|  |  |
|---|---|
| 9-20-1837 | The friends appt to prepare a cert of removal for Daniel at Duck Creek mtg, are contd, by Spiceland Mtg (Duck Creek mtg had been laid down) |
| 10-25-1837 | Daniel gc |
| 1-22-1840 | Eli appt an overseer |
| 3-23-1848 | Walnut Ridge MM compl of Nathan D for mcd |
| 1-24-1849 | Nathan D dis |
| 7-20-1853 | Elizabeth & ch David, Elizabeth C, Mathew & Mary Jane rocf Walnut Ridge MM |
| 7-20-1853 | Stephen rocf Walnut Ridge MM |
| 4-21-1858 | Elizabeth & ch David B, Nathan, Mathew & Mary Jane gct Fairfield MM |
| 6- 2-1883 | Stephen drpd from mbrp |
| 1- 4-1913 | Dora rec in mbrp |

## STANBROUGH

|  |  |
|---|---|
| 1-20-1836 | John Bond gct Milford MM, to m Mary Stanbrough a wid w/ch |
| 4-20-1836 | Mary Bond & dts Phebe & Elizabeth Stanbrough rocf Milford MM |
| 3-22-1837 | John Bond & w Mary & ch Abigail, Jacob, William, Aaron & Anna Bond & Phebe & Elizabeth Stanbrough gct Duck Creek MM |
| ( 9-20-1837) | Nehemiah & w Ruth & ch, mbrs of Duck Creek Mtg, now laid down, have been attached to Spiceland |
| 10-25-1837 | Nehemiah appt an overseer by Spiceland P M |
| 1-24-1838 | Phebe & Jeremiah L Presnall (consent of parents' given) altm |
| 1-24-1838 | Thomas & Abigail Bond (consent of parents given) altm |
| 5-23-1838 | Nehemiah appt to a comm |
| 8-22-1838 | Ann & Jesse Gause inf mtg of int to m Her father being present gave his consent |
| 9-19-1838 | Ann & Jesse Gause altm |
| 10-24-1838 | Jonathan produced cert from Westfield MM to m Sarah Rogers |
| 10-24-1838 | Jonathan & Sarah Rogers altm |
| 3-10-1839 | Sarah gct Westfield MM |
| 2-19-1840 | Elizabeth gct Westfield MM |
| 8-19-1840 | Francis of Clear Spring P M rpt mcd |
| 8-19-1840 | Huldah (form Draper) mcd dis |
| 11-25-1840 | Francis con mcd |
| 2-24-1841 | Francis gct Duck Creek MM |

SPICELAND

| | | | |
|---|---|---|---|
| STANBROUGH | (Cont) | 3-24-1858 | Gulielma gct Plainfield MM |
| 11-22-1843 | Elizabeth, a minor, rocf Duck Creek MM | 3-23-1859 | Nathan & w Phebe & dt Eliza Ann gct Plainfield MM |
| 7- 3-1886 | Rebecca rec in mbrp | 7-mo-1863 | Aaron appt an overseer |
| 4- 3-1890 | Frank rec in mbrp | 8-19-1863 | Josiah & w Anna & ch Mary Jane, Lindley H & Amy F gct Richland MM |
| STANLEY | | 7-22-1863 | William C & Mirium King inf mtg of int to m |
| 1-23-1833 | Nathan & w Delana original mbrs | | |
| 1-23-1833 | Aaron & w Mahala & ch original mbrs | 11-28-1863 | William C, Bethel P M, rptd mcd, con his misconduct in Milford MM |
| 1-23-1833 | Aaron Stanley, Nathan Davis, William B Unthank, Josiah Pennington, Amer Bond & Isaiah Baldwin, to unite with a comm from women's mtg, to form a comm to inspect & relieve the poor | 5-25-1864 | Miriam gct Milford MM |
| | | 3- 4-1865 | Cyrus K gct Bloomfield MM |
| | | 3- 3-1866 | Vierling gct Salem MM to m Josephine Talbert |
| 2-20-1833 | Aaron Stanley, William Unthank, Thomas Maudlin & George Evans appt as Spiceland MM's representatives to ensuing Q M | 7- 7-1866 | Josephine A rocf Salem MM |
| | | 11- 2-1867 | Hannah & David Pidgeon altm |
| | | 8- 7-1869 | Elwood & ch Laura & Mary rocf Rich Square MM, Iowa |
| 2-20-1833 | Delana appt asst clerk of women's mtg & Rebecca Unthank appt clerk | | |
| 3-20-1833 | Aaron Stanley, John Hiatt, Samuel Griffin, Isaac Schooley & Josiah Small appt to comm to have oversight & care of the burial ground at Spiceland | 8- 6-1870 | Elwood gct Duck Creek MM to m Phebe Hastings |
| | | 11- 5-1870 | Phebe rocf Duck Creek MM |
| | | 11- 2-1872 | Laura H gct Rich Square MM |
| | | 6- 7-1873 | Veirling & Josephine A & ch Ora Etta gct Indianapolis MM |
| 10-23-1833 | Aaron appt librarian | | |
| 3-19-1834 | Isom Hunt gct Milford MM to m Susanna Stanley | 4- 4-1874 | Maria Jane gct West Grove MM, Hamilton Co, Ind |
| 5-20-1835 | Aaron resigned as librarian & Joseph B Hunt appt to replace | 3- 4-1876 | Vierling & w Josephine A & dt Ora rocf Indianapolis MM |
| 2-24-1836 | Aaron appt an overseer at Spiceland P M | 3- 5-1881 | Verling & w Josephine & ch Ora Etta & Martha gct Salem MM |
| 10-19-1836 | Nathan appt as treasurer of Spiceland school funds | | |
| 1-25-1837 | Elwood gct Duck Creek MM | 5- 3-1890 | Jesse C rec in mbrp |
| 2-22-1837 | Solomon & w Achsah & ch Betsey Jane, Lydia & Mary rocf Dover MM, N C | 11- 3-1894 | Jesse C rel on req |
| | | STANTON | |
| 11-22-1837 | Achsah & ch Betsy J, Lydia & Mary gct Springfield MM (end to Dover Mtg, N C) | 9-21-1836 | James, a minor, rocf Center MM, Ohio |
| | | 9-21-1836 | Anne rocf New Garden MM |
| 5-23-1838 | Martha rocf Milford MM | 11-21-1838 | James, a minor, gct Centre MM, Oh |
| 11-21-1838 | Wyatt & Mary Bundy altm | 10-21-1840 | Nathan Davis gct Springborough MM, Oh to m Mary H Stanton |
| 7-24-1839 | Temple of Clearsprings P M, dis for "sueing at law" | | |
| | | 2-24-1841 | Ann E gct White Lick MM |
| 7-24-1839 | Rebecca Coble (form Stanley) con mcd | | |
| 1-22-1840 | Elwood req rel from services of librarian at Duck Creek P M | STARBUCK | |
| | | 2- 1-1923 | Earl J & w Bertha & ch Harry Walter rocf Duck Creek MM |
| 3-25-1840 | Elwood & w Martha & ch William & Emeline gct Milford MM | | |
| 10-21-1840 | Josiah & w Mary rst w/con Dover MM, N C, (however Mary had d before the approval arrived) | STEELE | |
| | | 2- 4-1893 | Clara rec in mbrp |
| | | 3- 2-1895 | Matilda J & ch Charles, Mary & Stella rec in mbrp |
| 10-21-1840 | Jabez, s of Josiah rec in mbrp | | |
| 2-22-1843 | Josiah & Anna Gause altm | 3- 2-1895 | Ollie & Verna A rec in mbrp |
| 3-22-1843 | Delana & her minor ch, Mordecai & Susan rocf Duck Creek MM | 8- 6-1898 | Matilda J Steele McDaniel & ch Charles, Mary, Stella, Ollie Jane & Verna A Steele gct - - - - |
| 3-19-1845 | James H Meredith gct Duck Creek MM to m Eliza Stanley | | |
| 4-23-1845 | Nathan rocf Milford MM | STEVENSON | |
| 8-25-1847 | Aaron appt an overseer at Spiceland P M | 3- 2-1895 | Harry E & w Emma & ch Flora rec in mbrp |
| 8-25-1847 | Temple rst at Duck Creek MM, w/con of this mtg | 5- 5-1906 | Harry E & w Emma V & ch Flora drpd from mbrp |
| 12-23-1847 | Delana & Jesse Bond inf mtg of int to m A comm appt to see that the rights of Delana's ch are secured | STIGGLEMAN | |
| | | 7- 1-1893 | Leora rocf Raysville MM |
| | | 4- 7-1906 | Edith & India rec in mbrp |
| 1-19-1848 | Aaron Stanley, William Unthank, Solomon Macy & George Evans appt as a comm on burials within the limits of Spiceland Mtg | 4- 3-1915 | Hassell rec in mbrp |
| | | STINSON | |
| | | 8- 4-1883 | Ajalise V drpd from mbrp |
| 1-19-1848 | Delana & Jesse Bond altm | | |
| 4-19-1848 | Delana Bond & her ch Mordecai & Susan Stanley gct West Grove MM | STOUT | |
| | | 1-23-1833 | Ephraim & w Mary & ch original mbrs |
| 11-22-1848 | Eliza Jane & Mordecai Unthank altm | 5-22-1833 | Ephraim appt to a comm |
| 9-19-1849 | Jesse Bond & w Delana & ch Mahala, William & Lydia Bond & her ch Mordecai & Susan C Stanley rocf West Grove MM | 8-21-1833 | Ephraim appt to comm |
| | | 5-22-1833 | Ephraim appt to comm to att Q M |
| | | 4-22-1838 | Ephraim & w Mary & ch James, Charles, Robert, Elias, Ann, Ruth, Ephraim & Thomas gct Fairfield MM |
| 2-20-1850 | Nathan gct Mill Creek MM | | |
| 12-24-1851 | Mary & dts Abagail & Hannah rocf Dover MM, N C | 1-20-1841 | Rachel rec in mbrp |
| | | 11-23-1842 | Rachel & Thomas Carr altm |
| 10-20-1852 | Mordecai & Rebecca Jane Hodson altm | 11-23-1842 | For the convenience of Rachel & Thomas Carr, a mtg for their m has been granted for tomorrow at 11 o'clock |
| 11-24-1852 | Hannah (form Baldwin) mcd dis | | |
| 1-19-1853 | Nathan & w Phebe & ch Cyrus K, Gulielma & Eliza Ann rocf New Garden MM, N C | | |
| 10-25-1854 | Michael gct Duck Creek MM to m Lydia Jane Bell | 3-21-1849 | Isaac rocf Duck Creek MM |
| | | 4-25-1855 | Susanna gct Spring Creek MM, Iowa |
| 5-23-1855 | Lydia Jane rocf Duck Creek MM | 5-23-1855 | Isaac gct Spring Creek MM, Iowa |
| 12-24-1856 | Michael & w Lydia Jane & ch Eliza Ellen gct Milford MM | | |
| 8-19-1857 | Hannah A & Joseph W Holloway altm | | |
| 8-19-1857 | Rebecca dis | | |

SPICELAND

## STRATTON

|  |  |
|---|---|
| ( 9-20-1837) | Levi & w Ruth & ch Lucinda, Albert, Hannah & Amy, mbrs of Duck Creek Mtg, now laid down, have been attached to Spiceland |
| 12-20-1837 | Ruth dis for na & dpl |
| 11-21-1838 | Lucinda dis for na, dpl & jas |
| 1-23-1839 | Eli & w Eunice rocf West Grove MM |
| 3-12-1851 | Albert dis |
| 5-21-1851 | Hannah Deem (form Stratton) mcd dis |
| 6- 1-1926 | Louisa gct Knightstown MM |

## STREET

|  |  |
|---|---|
| 6-24-1835 | Samuel & w Anna & ch Jane & Jehu rocf Whitewater MM |
| 7-24-1844 | Samuel & w Anna & ch gct Duck Creek MM |
| 3-19-1845 | Samuel & w Anna & ch Jane, John, Stephen, Lydia, Isaac, Seth, Mary & Rebecca rocf Duck Creek MM |
| 12-22-1846 | Eunice rocf Walnut Ridge MM |
| 9-19-1849 | Anna appt to station of Elder |
| 6-25-1851 | Eunice & John Williams altm |
| 4-25-1855 | Mary & Nathan Mendenhall altm |
| 6-20-1855 | Samuel S & w Anne & ch Lydia, Stephen, Isaac, Seth, Rebecca B & Mary gct Pleasant Plain MM, Iowa |
| 6-20-1855 | Jane gct Pleasant Plain MM, Iowa |
| 9-24-1862 | Lydia rocf Pleasant Plain MM, Iowa |
| 2-25-1863 | Lydia E & Jeremiah T Cox altm |
| 11-23-1863 | Samuel & w Anna rocf Pleasant Plain MM, Iowa & end to Raysville MM |
| 11-23-1863 | Rebecca rocf Pleasant Plain MM, Iowa & end to Raysville MM |
| 1-20-1864 | Isaac rocf Pleasant Plain MM, Iowa |
| 6-22-1864 | Samuel & w Anna gct Hopewell MM |
| 6-22-1864 | Isaac gct Hopewell MM |
| 6-22-1864 | Rebecca gct Hopewell MM |
| 6- 5-1897 | Rebecca rocf Kokomo MM |
| 11- 6-1897 | Rebecca gct Union MM |

## STRETCH

|  |  |
|---|---|
| 10-23-1844 | William Moore gct Hopewell MM to m Ann Stretch |

## STUART

|  |  |
|---|---|
| 1-23-1833 | Jehu & w Sarah & ch original mbrs |
| 9-25-1833 | Jehu & w Sarah & ch Beaulah, Anna, Robert & Ithamer gct Duck Creek MM |
| ( 9-20-1837) | Jehu & w Sarah & ch, mbrs of Duck Creek Mtg, now laid down, have been attached to Spiceland |
| 12-19-1838 | Beulah & Samuel Horner altm |
| 3-20-1839 | Louhanna dis for dpl & jas |
| 3-20-1844 | Robert gct West Grove MM to m Rachel Maudlin |
| 12-25-1844 | Rachel rocf West Grove MM |
| 2-24-1847 | Ithamer W mcd dis |
| 5-24-1848 | Anna Aydelotte (form Stewart) con mcd |
| 10-19-1853 | Robert & w Rachel & ch William Henry & Mary gct Red Cedar MM, Iowa |
| 8-19-1857 | Zimri mcd dis |
| 9-22-1858 | Zimri rocf Back Creek MM & end to Raysville MM |
| 2- 4-1865 | Jehu & w Sarah & dt Eliza Jane rocf Hopewell MM |
| 11- 2-1867 | Jehu & w Sarah & ch Eliza Jane PEARSON & Eli Stewart gct Poplar Ridge MM |
| 5- 1-1869 | Jehu H rocf Raysville MM |
| 12- 4-1869 | Mary rocf Raysville MM |
| 12- 4-1869 | Eliza rocf Raysville MM |
| 1- 1-1870 | Amos & w Martha & ch John Sidney, David, Robert Addison, Amos Elbridge & Francis rocf Raysville MM |
| 1- 1-1870 | Jehu H con mcd |
| 3- 4-1871 | Anise rec in mbrp |
| 8- 5-1871 | Amos appt an Elder |
| 5- 4-1872 | Jehu H & w Annis gct Laurance MM, Kan |
| 2- 7-1874 | J Sidney gct Whitewater MM |
| 2- 7-1874 | Jehu & w Sarah & ch Eli Ira & Albert rocf Spicewood MM |
| 3- 6-1875 | Amos gct Whitewater MM to m Melissa Miles |
| 4- 3-1875 | Edmund & w Martha & s Clyde rocf Milford MM |
| 8- 7-1875 | Melissa E rocf Whitewater MM |
| 5- 6-1876 | John Sydney rocf Whitewater MM |
| 1- 6-1877 | Robert Addison gct Lawrence MM, Kan |
| 9- 1-1877 | Amos & Melissa gct Chester MM |
| 12- 7-1878 | Laura Alice rec in mbrp |
| 5- 7-1881 | Albert rocf Indianapolis MM |
| 6- 2-1883 | J Sidney & w Alice & ch Florence & Joseph Edgar gct Chester MM |
| 11- 3-1883 | Elbridge rec in mbrp |
| 3- 1-1884 | Jehu gct Spicewood MM |
| 3- 1-1884 | Sarah rel on req |
| 5- 3-1884 | Eli, Ira & Albert, ch of Jehu & Sarah gct Sterling MM, Kan |
| 1- 2-1885 | David W gct Minneapolis MM, MN |
| 11- 7-1885 | Jehu T gct West Grove MM |
| 6- 2-1888 | Mary E gct Whitewater MM |
| 10- 8-1898 | Elbridge rel on req |
| 1- 2-1914 | Mildred rec on req |
| 5- 2-1914 | Mary Gottschall Stewart, (with her father & mother) gct Hopewell |
| 1- 6-1926 | Margaret rocf Rich Square MM |

## STUBBS

|  |  |
|---|---|
| 12-25-1833 | John Sr & w Jane rocf Westfield MM, Oh |
| 12-25-1833 | Joseph & w Margaret & ch John, Newton, Esther Ann, Charles & William N rocf Westfield MM, Oh |
| 7-23-1834 | Joseph appt an overseer |
| 8-23-1837 | Solomon Gause gct Milford MM to m Celia Stubbs |
| 12-20-1837 | John & w Jane gct Walnut Ridge MM |
| 12-20-1837 | Newton & Charles, ch of Joseph decd, gct Walnut Ridge MM |
| 3-21-1838 | Martha gct White Lick MM |
| 9-22-1841 | Martha rocf White Lick MM |
| 1-25-1843 | Newton produced a cert from Walnut Ridge Mtg to m Nancy Pearson |
| 1-25-1843 | Newton & Nancy Pearson altm |
| 5-24-1843 | Martha Woollen (form Stubbs) mcd dis |
| 9-20-1843 | Newton rocf Walnut Ridge MM |
| 1-22-1845 | Jacob, a minor, rocf New Garden MM |
| 10-20-1847 | Mahlon rocf New Garden MM |
| 10-20-1847 | Nancy Lamb (form Stubbs) con mcd |
| 3-22-1848 | Mahlon gct New Garden MM to m Rachel Woodard |
| 6-11-1848 | Mahlon gct Chester MM |
| 1-23-1850 | Jacob gct New Garden MM |
| 4-23-1856 | Stephen & w Eliza & ch Salathiel, Clinton J & Emily rocf New Garden MM |
| 12-24-1856 | Stephen & w Eliza & ch Salathial, Clinton & Emily gct Chester MM |
| 3- 3-1866 | Charles & w America & ch Mary V, Joseph E, James M & John rec in mbrp |
| 2- 6-1875 | Alvin rocf Elk MM, Ohio |
| 1- 5-1878 | Alvan gct New Garden MM |
| 5- 1-1880 | Joseph & w Maria C & dt Ethel B gct Whitewater MM |
| 9- 6-1890 | Otis gct Hopewell MM |
| 10- 3-1900 | Everett gct Knightstown MM |

## SUTTON

|  |  |
|---|---|
| 12- 6-1890 | Emma gct Carthage MM |

## SWAIN

|  |  |
|---|---|
| 5-25-1836 | Susannah rocf New Garden MM |
| ( 9-20-1837) | John & Ann & ch, mbrs of Duck Creek Mtg, now laid down, have been attached to Spiceland |
| 2-21-1838 | Lewis Swain, Rice Price, Demsey Reece, Francis Macy, Abraham Moore & Obadiah Morgan appt by Spiceland Mtg to att funerals of friends at Duck Creek P M |
| 3-25-1840 | Thomas Clarkson of Clear Springs P M, rpt mcd |
| 4-22-1840 | Thomas C dis |
| 4- 3-1880 | Thomas M & w Julia E & ch Minnie C & George H rocf Duck Creek MM |
| 7- 1-1893 | Thomas & Julia gct Raysville MM |
| 10-10-1896 | Thomas & w Julia & s Howland gct Knightstown MM |

## SWANDER

|  |  |
|---|---|
| 11- 1-1923 | Charles W & w Etta & dt Sarah rocf Cherry Grove MM |
| 10- 6-1926 | Charles & Maritta & dt Sarah gct Westfield MM |

SPICELAND

## SWEET

|  |  |
|---|---|
| 6-22-1836 | Solomon & dt Anna M & Sarah rocf Whitewater MM |
| 6-21-1837 | Stephen Macy & w Rebecca & dt Eunice & grandch Rebecca E & Eli Sweet rocf Whitewater MM |
| 10-25-1837 | Anna M & Silas H Kersey inf mtg of int to m The parents consent has been given |
| 11-22-1837 | The comm appt to investigate the proposed m of Anna M & Silas H Kersey rpt nothing to hinder m but they not being present, the comm is cont to next month |
| 12-20-1837 | Anna M & Silas H Kersey not appearing, a comm was appt to examine the case & rpt to next mtg |
| 1-24-1838 | Anna M & Silas H Kersey notify Spiceland Mtg as follows: "We, the undersigned, inform friends that we have abandoned our prospect of m with each other" |
| 10-24-1838 | Louiza Amelia, a minor, rocf Whitewater MM |
| 2-20-1839 | Solomon gct Sugar River MM |
| 10-23-1839 | Anne M gct Sugar River MM |
| 3-24-1842 | Sarah Scovill (form Sweet) mcd dis |
| 1-24-1844 | Louisa Amelia gct Sugar River MM |
| 11-21-1849 | Eli M gct Duck Creek MM |
| 7-23-1851 | Eli M rocf Duck Creek MM |
| 3-25-1857 | Eli M dis |

## SYMONS

|  |  |
|---|---|
| 6-21-1837 | Hannah & dts Malinda, Sarah Jane & Martha Ann rocf Milford MM |
| 2-21-1838 | Duck Creek P M compl of Mathew for disunity & na |
| 4-25-1838 | Mathew dis at Spiceland MM |
| 10-21-1840 | Bethuel & w Anna rocf Mississinewa MM & end to Duck Creek MM |
| 6-21-1843 | Josiah & w Sarah & ch Jehu, Joel, Aaron, John, Thomas & George rocf Mississinewa MM |
| 9-25-1844 | Josiah appt an overseer |
| 2-19-1845 | James M rocf Blue River MM |
| 9-23-1846 | Benjamin Franklin rocf Hopewell MM |
| 2-24-1847 | James con mcd |
| 4-21-1847 | Anna & ch Hannah, Patsey, Lucinda & Louisa rocf Duck Creek MM |
| 4-21-1847 | Sally Ann (form Hunt) con mcd |
| 11-24-1847 | Ann & ch gct Duck Creek MM |
| 11-19-1851 | Sarah (form Small) con mcd |
| 9-25-1852 | Sarah, w of William, & ch Jane, Martha Ann, Alpheus & Mary Ellen gct Mississinewa MM |
| 11-24-1852 | Thomas & w Hannah rocf Richland MM |
| 10-24-1855 | Joel mcd dis |
| 4-23-1856 | Jehu & Lydia Hall altm |
| 12-21-1859 | Joseph Hall gct Pipe Creek MM to m Lucinda Symons |
| 1-25-1860 | James & w Sally Ann & s Lindley Lewis gct Plainfield MM |
| 3-20-1861 | Aaron & Anna K Sheridan altm |
| 5-22-1861 | Lydia & dt Elma gct Springfield MM |
| 6-19-1861 | Sarah rec as Minister |
| 1-14-1865 | Lydia & dt Elma rocf Springfield MM |
| 1-14-1865 | John appt asst clerk & James B Parker appt clerk |
| 3- 4-1865 | John appt to read m cert at Spiceland Mtg & to place them in the hands of the Recorder |
| 7- 1-1865 | Josiah appt overseer |
| 8- 6-1865 | Josiah appt an Elder |
| 2- 2-1867 | George gct Plainfield MM to m Mariam Ellis |
| 3- 2-1867 | John gct Duck Creek MM to m Ellen S Henley |
| 3- 1-1868 | Joel & w Rebecca rec in mbrp |
| 4- 4-1868 | Benjamin F & w Verlinda & ch Joseph E & Anna rocf Raysville MM |
| 6- 6-1868 | Josiah appt an overseer at Spiceland P M |
| 7- 4-1868 | Aaron & w Anna K & ch Charles, Mary & Alice gct Lynn Grove MM, Iowa |
| 11- 7-1868 | Ellen rocf Duck Creek MM |
| 10- 9-1869 | George & w Miriam & s Josiah gct Lynn Grove MM, Iowa |
| 3- 5-1870 | Seth C con mcd |
| 8- 5-1871 | Josiah appt Elder |
| 5- 2-1874 | Verlinda appt overseer |
| 8- 5-1876 | Jehu dis |
| 1- 6-1877 | Eliza rec in mbrp |
| 1- 6-1877 | Lydia H & s Alfred H gct Peace MM, Kan |
| 1-mo-1880 | John appt clerk |
| 6- 2-1885 | Lydia H & s Alfred H rocf Sterling MM, Kan |
| 7- 2-1887 | Lydia gct Raysville MM |
| 1- 5-1889 | Lydia H rocf Raysville MM |
| 2-24-1890 | Lydia H & Rufus Test rptd m |
| 10-11-1890 | Estella & brother Jabez Henley, gct Lawrence MM, Kan |
| 9- 5-1891 | Frank & fam gct Raysville MM |
| 8- 6-1892 | Alfred H gct Springfield MM |
| 8- 6-1892 | Frank & fam gct Falmouth MM, Me |
| 7- 5-1895 | Estella & brother, Jabez Henley rocf Lawrence MM, Kan |
| 9- 5-1896 | Mark rec in mbrp |
| 1- 2-1897 | Lincoln gct Indianapolis MM |
| 1- 2-1897 | Emma gct Indianapolis MM |
| 7- 1-1899 | Robert gct Short Creek MM, Ohio |
| 1- 6-1900 | Alfred H rocf North Branch MM, Kan |
| 4- 7-1900 | John F, s of Nora, rec in mbrp |
| 6- 2-1900 | Albert rec in mbrp |
| 2- 2-1901 | Emma & Anna gct Whitewater MM |
| 3- 7-1903 | Gertrude E (Frances) drpd from mbrp |
| 5- 5-1906 | Pearl rec in mbrp |
| 10-12-1907 | Oscar & Estella gct Minneapolis MM, Minn |
| 4- 3-1909 | Sarah Elizabeth rec in mbrp |
| 5- 7-1910 | Arthur gct Kansas City MM, Mo |
| 3- 6-1915 | Mable rec in mbrp |
| 8- 1-1919 | Joseph Ellis & w Nora & dt Elsie gct Duck Creek MM |
| 9- 7-1922 | J Ellis & w Nora & ch Elsie & John Franklin rocf Raysville MM |
| 1- 7-1926 | Frank rel on req |

## TALBERT

|  |  |
|---|---|
| 1-20-1847 | Martha (form White) mcd, j Separatists (ASF) dis |
| 3- 3-1866 | Veirling Stanley gct Salem MM to m Josephine Talbert (dt Jabez & Mary) |
| 6- 6-1868 | Sylvanus G & w Phebe H & ch Daniel H & Anne Jane rocf Plainfield MM |
| 1- 1-1870 | Milo & w Eliza & ch S Caroline & Mary E rocf Salem MM |
| 1- 1-1870 | Jabez & w Mary C & ch Sarah D, Anna M & Florence N rocf Salem MM |
| 8- 6-1870 | Charles rocf Plainfield MM |
| 12- 3-1870 | Sylvanus G & w Phebe & ch Daniel H & Anna gct Walnut Ridge MM |
| 9- 7-1872 | Charles S mcd dis |
| 2- 5-1873 | Milo appt clerk |
| 5- 2-1874 | Jabez appt overseer |
| 6- 5-1875 | Orpheus E rocf Hopewell MM |
| 6- 5-1875 | Martha F rocf Hopewell MM |
| 6- 5-1875 | Alvin & w Rebecca E & ch Sylvanus D, Mary, Elwood & William rocf Hopewell MM |
| 9- 6-1876 | Catherine L rec in mbrp |
| 9- 3-1881 | Orpheus & Martha Florence rel on req |
| 6- 7-1890 | Sylvanus D & w Katy L & ch Carl & Mable gct Sterling MM, Kan |
| 8- 2-1890 | Daniel H & w Caroline M & dt Mable rocf Hopewell MM |
| 2- 3-1892 | Elwood rel on req |
| 4- 7-1894 | Daniel & w Caroline & ch Mable, Ann, Ruby & Frank gct Raysville MM |
| 1- 2-1909 | Milo gct University MM, Kan |

## TAYLOR

|  |  |
|---|---|
| 7-22-1846 | Caroline (form Moore) mcd dis |
| 11-19-1851 | Jacob produced cert from Center MM, Oh to m |
| 11-19-1851 | Jacob & Sarah Evans altm |
| 2-25-1852 | Sarah E gct Center MM, Oh |
| 3- 7-1854 | Jacob & w Sarah & ch Jesse Frank rocf Center MM, Oh |
| 5-22-1861 | Milton produced cert from Centre MM, Oh to m |
| 5-22-1861 | Milton & Emily Gorden altm |
| 1-22-1862 | Milton M rocf Center MM, Oh |
| 8- 1-1868 | Edward produced a cert from West Union MM to m |
| 8- 1-1868 | Edward & Louisa Bales altm |
| 8- 1-1868 | Edward & Louisa Bales req privilege of accomp their m in the retirement of home which was granted. Meeting to be held at John Bales on next fifth day, at half past two o'clock |

SPICELAND

## TAYLOR (Cont)

|  |  |
|---|---|
| 7- 2-1870 | Calvin Pearson gct Adrian MM, Mi to m Marthanna Taylor |
| 8- 5-1871 | Sarah appt Elder |
| 10-12-1872 | Louise & s Henry W gct Honey Creek MM |
| 12- 1-1877 | Chloe (Douglas) rocf Wilmington MM, Oh |
| 5- 5-1883 | Jacob appt Elder |
| 5- 5-1883 | Sarah appt Elder |
| 5- 5-1883 | Emily appt Elder |
| 7- 3-1886 | Jesse F & fam gct ___?___ MM, Iowa |
| 9- 3-1887 | Sarah gct Whitewater MM |
| 10-11-1890 | Oliver P gct Minneapolis MM, Minn |
| 5- 2-1891 | Enoch E & w Mary H & ch Russell, Herman & Amanda rec in mbrp |
| 9- 5-1891 | Milton & fam gct Wichita MM, Kan |
| 10-10-1903 | Maud rocf Elk MM, Oh |
| 6- 2-1906 | Maude gct Elk MM, Oh |
| 4- 1-1911 | Mary & s Herman rel on req |
| 1- 4-1913 | Irena & Robert Milton rec in mbrp |

## TEAS

|  |  |
|---|---|
| 6-24-1835 | Thomas S & w Sarah & ch John C, Edward & Martha rocf Whitewater MM |
| 6-22-1836 | Thomas S appt clerk & Michael Wiesner appt asst clerk |
| 10-23-1844 | Thomas S appt clerk & William Edwards appt asst clerk |
| 8-25-1847 | Thomas S appt an overseer at Spiceland P M |
| 5-23-1855 | Edward mcd dis |
| 5- 1-1868 | Marietta gct Union MM, Mo ? |
| 8- 4-1877 | Edward Y & w Sarah & ch Ellen, William, Frederick & Mary Teas & Vestil Coffin rocf Whitewater MM |
| 1- 6-1883 | Thomas S & w Marietta B & s Albert C rocf Union MM, Mo ? |
| 10- 8-1887 | E Y rel on req |
| 8- 6-1892 | Sarah A & Mary gct Indianapolis MM |
| 3- 7-1896 | Fred E gct Indianapolis MM |
| 3- 5-1898 | Thomas jr & fam given a letter "to whom it may concern" |
| 2- 4-1899 | Albert rel on req |
| 3- 4-1905 | Thomas & Marietta rel on req |
| 8- 1-1908 | Edward rec in mbrp |
| 9- 3-1910 | Paul drpd from mbrp |
| 12- 7-1912 | Paul rel on req |
| 9- 4-1930 | William drpd from mbrp |

## TEASLE

|  |  |
|---|---|
| 12- 1-1877 | Rebecca rec in mbrp |
| 1- 7-1882 | Rebecca glt another society |

## TEST

|  |  |
|---|---|
| 9- 4-1869 | Miriam & ch Mary Ellen & Samuel Edward rocf Springfield MM |
| 1- 1-1870 | Mariam C & Jacob J Pickering propose m with each other. Jacob J Pickering not being a mbr of our Society |
| 2- 5-1870 | Mariam C & Jacob J Pickering altm |
| 5- 4-1889 | Samuel & w Cora & s Everett gct Duck Creek MM |
| 2-24-1890 | Rufus & Lydia Symons rptd m |
| 4- 5-1890 | Lydia H gct Springfield MM |
| 3- 3-1894 | Samuel & w Cora & s Everett rocf Raysville MM |
| 12- 2-1899 | Rufus & w Lydia rocf Whitewater MM |
| 12- 1-1906 | Zacheus & w Jennie & ch Ralph & Rachel Irene rocf Muncie MM |
| 1- 1-1915 | Lena T rec in mbrp |
| 5- 7-1926 | Everett & w Addie & ch Anna Jane & Gene gct Dublin MM |

## THOMAS

|  |  |
|---|---|
| ( 9-20-1837) | Elijah & w Christina & ch Elvy & Alfred, (mbrs of Duck Creek Mtg, which was laid down) attached to Spiceland MM |
| ( 9-20-1837) | Simeon & ch Ruth, Henry, Susanna & Malinda (mbrs of Duck Creek Mtg, which was laid down) attached to Spiceland MM |
| 12-20-1837 | Elijah & w Christina & ch Elvy & Alfred gct Mississinewa MM |
| 2-20-1839 | Simeon & ch Ruth, Henry, Susanna & Malinda gct Mississinewa MM |
| 10-12-1864 | Francis W & w Rebecca & ch Mary M, Charlton H, Michael W & Charles F rocf New Garden MM |
| 9- 2-1865 | Mary M & Eli G Parker altm |

|  |  |
|---|---|
| 12- 7-1867 | Rebecca appt an overseer at Dunreith P M |
| 5- 2-1868 | Jeremiah M & w Luzena rocf White River MM |
| 5- 1-1869 | Jeremiah M & w Luzena & ch Rhoda Emma gct Cherry Grove MM |
| 10-14-1871 | Martha J rec in mbrp |
| 3- 2-1872 | Mangum E rec in mbrp |
| 10-12-1872 | Sarah Jane rec in mbrp |
| 11- 2-1872 | Charlton con mcd |
| 2- 7-1874 | Viretta Anna rec in mbrp |
| 2- 2-1878 | Pheriba Ann gct Peace MM, Kan |
| 1- 7-1882 | Phariba Ann rocf Sterling MM, Kan |
| 2- 3-1883 | James G rec in mbrp |
| 4- 7-1883 | Martha E rec in mbrp |
| 6- 2-1883 | Isaac J rec in mbrp |
| 6- 2-1883 | Michael gct Lynn Grove MM, Iowa |
| 10- 9-1886 | James gct Hopewell MM |
| 7- 5-1890 | Isaac J drpd from mbrp |
| 8- 2-1890 | Charlton gct Fairmount MM |
| 12- 6-1890 | Isaac N dis |
| 3- 4-1893 | Clide rec in mbrp |
| 3- 4-1893 | Francis rec in mbrp |
| 7- 1-1899 | Sarah rocf Hopewell MM |
| 6- 2-1900 | Merrell, s John rec in mbrp |
| 12- 1-1900 | John & w Sarah & s Merrell gct Hopewell MM |
| 3- 2-1901 | Rebecca Pearl rec in mbrp |
| 3- 4-1905 | Francis W gct Indianapolis MM to m Anna Mills |
| 10-18-1906 | Anna Mills rocf Indianapolis MM |
| 1- 6-1912 | Anna M gct Springfield MM |
| 10- 5-1912 | Edna rel on req |

## THORNBURGH

|  |  |
|---|---|
| 2-20-1839 | Ezekiel gct West Grove MM |
| 10-23-1844 | William W produced a cert from Walnut Ridge Mtg to m Susan Small |
| 10-23-1844 | William W & Susan Small altm |
| 12-25-1844 | Susanna gct Walnut Ridge MM |
| 5- 1-1866 | Rebecca rocf Wabash MM |

## TIMMONS

|  |  |
|---|---|
| 10- 9-1897 | William W & Clara rec in mbrp |
| 9- 7-1901 | William W & Clara rel on req |

## TOMLINSON

|  |  |
|---|---|
| 11-21-1838 | Mahlon produced cert from Fairfield MM to m Susanna Edgerton along with the consent of his parents |
| 11-21-1838 | Mahlon & Susanna Edgerton altm (for the accomodation of Mahlon & Susannah Edgerton in the accomp of their m, a meeting is apptd for tomorrow at Duck Creek M H, at the usual hour) |
| 1-23-1839 | Susannah gct Fairfield MM |

## TOWNSEND

|  |  |
|---|---|
| 5-19-1858 | Charles Overman gct West Union MM to m Elizabeth J Townsend |

## TROUT

|  |  |
|---|---|
| 4- 4-1891 | Anna rec in mbrp |
| 12- 7-1912 | Anna drpd from mbrp |

## TRUEBLOOD

|  |  |
|---|---|
| 8-24-1836 | Isaac O & w Sarah rocf Symons Creek MM, N C end by Milford MM |
| 8-21-1844 | James W rocf Symons Creek MM, N C |
| 5-24-1848 | James W con mcd (he having already moved to limits of Symons Creek MM, N C) |
| 2-21-1849 | James W gct Symons Creek MM, N C |

## TUCKER

|  |  |
|---|---|
| 10-23-1850 | Eliza (form Hubbard) jas & mcd dis |

## TUTTLE

|  |  |
|---|---|
| 8- 5-1871 | Abraham & w Saloma & ch M Sanford, Morton Londora & Charles Irvin rec in mbrp |
| 12- 4-1875 | Susan rec in mbrp |
| 7- 1-1882 | Louisa rec in mbrp |
| 12- 5-1885 | Marion gct Farmland MM |
| 12- 5-1885 | Lilly Jane rec in mbrp |
| 1- 1-1887 | Abraham, Saloma, Morton, Charles I & Cora B transferred to Muncie MM |
| 1- 1-1887 | Susan transferred to Muncie MM |

SPICELAND

## UNTHANK

|  |  |
|---|---|
| 1-23-1833 | William B & w Rebecca & ch original mbrs |
| 1-23-1833 | William B Unthank, Nathan Davis, Josiah Pennington, Amer Bond, Aaron Stanley & Isaiah Baldwin, to unite with a comm from women's mtg, to form a comm to inspect & relieve the poor |
| 2-20-1833 | William Unthank, Thomas Maudlin, Aaron Stanley & George Evans appt as Spiceland MM's representatives to ensuing Q M |
| 2-20-1833 | William appt an overseer |
| 2-20-1833 | Rebecca appt clerk of women's mtg & Delana Stanley appt asst clerk |
| 3-20-1833 | William Unthank, Isaac White, George Evans & Driver Boon appt to comm to attend funerals of our mbrs |
| 6-19-1833 | William appt to Recorder of Removal Certificates |
| 3-25-1835 | Eli & w Anna & ch Martha, Mordecai, John, Rebecca & Joseph rocf New Garden MM, N C end by Milford MM |
| 6-24-1835 | William Unthank appt asst clerk & Solomon Macy appt clerk |
| 2-22-1837 | William B Unthank, Solomon Macy, Richard Gordon & George Evans appt at Spiceland Mtg, to receive and hold in trust, a deed for land on which the School House now stands |
| 11-20-1839 | William appt treasurer of Spiceland School in place of John Bogue, who is decd |
| 2-19-1840 | Martha & Thomas Cook altm |
| 3-19-1845 | Drusill Reed (form Unthank) con mcd |
| 6-23-1847 | William appt to station of Elder |
| 1-19-1848 | William Unthank, Solomon Macy, Aaron Stanley & George Evans appt as a comm on burials within the limits of Spiceland Mtg |
| 2-23-1848 | J Addison gct Duck Creek MM to m Cynthia E Saint |
| 11-22-1848 | Mordecai & Eliza Jane Stanley altm |
| 12-20-1848 | Cynthia S rocf Duck Creek MM |
| 2-25-1852 | Joseph Addison & w Cynthia & s Samuel Exum gct Duck Creek MM |
| 2-23-1853 | J Addison & w Cynthia & s Samuel Exum rocf Duck Creek MM |
| 1-25-1854 | Deborah & her ch Martha Ann, Oliver, Priscilla & Nathan Nixon rocf Blue River MM (ch of John Nixon & Deborah (Hobbs) Nixon) |
| 10-24-1855 | J Addison dis |
| 11-21-1855 | John & Martha A Hobbs altm |
| 4-23-1856 | Mordecai & w Eliza Jane & ch Amanda, Emily C & Albert H gct Spring Creek MM, Iowa |
| 3-20-1861 | Josiah T & Susan B Hunt altm |
| 12-23-1861 | Deborah appt Elder |
| 8- 5-1865 | William B retained as Elder |
| 8- 5-1865 | Deborah retained as Elder |
| 3- 3-1866 | Josiah T appt to record the minutes of this mtg |
| 8- 7-1869 | Josiah T req rel from recording the minutes of this mtg & Calvin Ratliff was appt |
| 5- 7-1870 | Dinah K rocf Fairfield MM, Oh |
| 6- 4-1870 | Mordecai & ch Emily C, Albert H, Elmina C, Eli, Edgar & Eva rocf Lynn Grove MM, Iowa |
| 8- 6-1870 | William con mcd |
| 6- 3-1871 | Mordecai appt an overseer |
| 8- 5-1871 | William B appt Elder |
| 8- 5-1871 | Deborah appt Elder |
| 2- 1-1873 | Samuel con mcd |
| 1- 3-1874 | Mordecai gct Cherry Grove MM to m Ruth Jane Reese, a wid |
| 7- 4-1874 | Mordecai & ch Albert, Elmina, Eli, Edgar & Eva gct Cherry Grove MM |
| 7- 6-1878 | Mordecai & w Ruth Jane & ch Elmina, Eli, Edgar & Eva rocf Cherry Grove MM |
| 7- 6-1878 | Joseph gct Lynn Grove MM, Iowa |
| 6- 4-1881 | Dinah K & ch John C & Martha C gct Hopewell MM, Ohio (fam of Wm - dis in 1870) |
| 5- 6-1882 | Mordecai & w Ruth Jane & dt Eva gct Deer Creek MM |
| 7- 1-1882 | Naomi gct Lynn Grove MM, Iowa |
| 7- 1-1882 | Albert & Eli gct Deer Creek MM |
| 5- 5-1883 | William B appt Elder |
| 5- 5-1883 | Deborah appt Elder |
| 6- 2-1883 | Daniel gct Indianapolis MM |
| 3- 6-1886 | Harry rec in mbrp |

## VERNON

|  |  |
|---|---|
| 5-19-1852 | Rebecca (form Griffin) mcd dis |

## VICKERY

|  |  |
|---|---|
| 2-24-1836 | Jared Ellzy & w Susanna & ch Absalom Vickery & Sarah Ann, John, Nancy & William Ellzy gct Mill Creek MM |
| 3- 4-1893 | David & w Tabitha & s Charles F rec in mbrp |
| 4- 7-1894 | Alice rec in mbrp |
| 3- 2-1895 | Isaac rec in mbrp |
| 3- 1-1902 | N F rel on req |
| 4- 3-1902 | Alice & ch Edith E, Glen, & Ada J gct Sheridan MM |
| 6- 1-1907 | Martin L rec in mbrp |
| 6- 5-1915 | Martin L & w Pearl M rel on req |
| 4- 5-1919 | Isaac gct New Castle MM |

## VOTAW

|  |  |
|---|---|
| 2- 2-1895 | Lillian gct South Wabash MM |

## WAKE

|  |  |
|---|---|
| 10-14-1905 | William A & w Nettie rec in mbrp |
| 4- 7-1906 | Cloyd & Arlie rec in mbrp |
| 2- 4-1926 | C V rel on req |

## WALDEN

|  |  |
|---|---|
| 4-24-1839 | Jemima rocf Newhope MM, Tenn |

## WALKER

|  |  |
|---|---|
| 6-20-1838 | Martha rocf Chester MM |
| 4-23-1851 | Eliza Ann (form Elliott) jas & mcd dis |

## WALTERS

|  |  |
|---|---|
| 4- 6-1901 | Sarah P rel on req |

## WALTON

|  |  |
|---|---|
| 7- 7-1866 | Rufus P rocf Springfield MM, N C |
| 5- 4-1867 | Isabelle rec in mbrp |
| 7- 6-1867 | Robert C rec in mbrp |
| 10-12-1867 | Rufus con mcd |
| 1- 4-1868 | Rufus P gct Duck Creek MM |
| 12-25-1874 | Joseph P & w Caroline & ch Anna Bell, George F rocf Milford MM |
| 11- 2-1879 | Joseph & fam gct Milford MM |

## WARD

|  |  |
|---|---|
| 6- 3-1876 | Lucinda Osborn gct Winchester MM |
| 1- 1-1887 | Charles A rocf Hopewell MM |

## WARING

|  |  |
|---|---|
| 6- 7-1890 | Emma rocf Whitewater MM |
| 2- 6-1897 | Emma given a letter of recommendation |
| 7- 4-1914 | Emma rel on req |

## WARNER

|  |  |
|---|---|
| 3- 4-1882 | Joseph rec in mbrp |
| 2- 2-1884 | Joseph S rel on req |
| 3- 7-1891 | Abigail rel on req |

## WASSON

|  |  |
|---|---|
| 5-20-1835 | Calvin (a Minister) & w Mary & ch William, Nathan, Elizabeth, Sally, Jane & Calvin jr rocf Duck Creek MM |
| 8-19-1835 | Calvin Wasson, David James, Isaac White, Vierling Kersey, John Hiatt, George Evans, William Edwards, Nathan Davis & Joseph B Hunt appt to comm on Education for ensuing year |
| 6-30-1838 | Calvin & w Mary & ch William, Nathan, Elizabeth, Sally, Mary Jane, Calvin jr & Eliza Ann gct West Grove MM |

## WAY

|  |  |
|---|---|
| 10-14-1882 | Mary A gct Springdale MM, Kan |

## WEBB

|  |  |
|---|---|
| 5- 2-1885 | Joseph rocf Duck Creek MM |
| 9- 6-1890 | J M rel on req |

SPICELAND

## WEBSTER
|  |  |
|---|---|
| 3-2-1867 | William O & w Sarah & ch Edmond A, Joseph P, & Ajalisa ? V, rec on req |
| 2-1-1873 | Joseph con mcd |
| 5-3-1872 | Linda Myra rec on req |
| 11-2-1878 | Joseph P & w Linda M gct Wabash MM |
| 7-7-1883 | Sarah D gct South Wabash MM |
| 5-3-1890 | Edmond drpd from mbrp |

## WEEDEN
|  |  |
|---|---|
| 5-25-1864 | Jane F rocf Raysville MM, Ind |
| 3-7-1868 | Jane Eliza gct Onarga (?) MM, Ill |

## WEISNER
|  |  |
|---|---|
| 1-23-1833 | Michael & w Hannah original mbrs |
| 6-22-1836 | Michael appt asst clerk & Thomas S Teas appt clerk |
| 8-24-1836 | Michael appt to comm on education for the ensuing year |
| 9-20-1837 | Jonathan & w Ruth rocf Chester MM |
| 5-23-1838 | Josiah & w Phebe rocf Cane Creek MM, N C & end to New Garden MM |
| 5-23-1838 | John rocf Cane Creek MM, N C |
| 5-23-1838 | Micajah rocf Cane Creek MM, N C |
| 5-23-1838 | Rachel & ch Abigail, Elizabeth, Millicent, Matilda, Emmaline, Jabez & Cyrenius rocf Cane Creek MM, N C |
| 7-25-1838 | John req cert to White Lick MM (s of Rachel & her husb William) |
| 8-22-1838 | The comm appt to prepare a cert for John, rpt that he has decd since last mtg |
| 8-22-1838 | Micajah gct White Lick MM |
| 8-22-1838 | Rachel & ch Abigail, Elizabeth, Millicent, Matilda, Emmaline, Jabez & Cyrenius gct White Lick MM |
| 10-24-1838 | Jonathan & w Ruth & ch gct Chester MM |
| 1-23-1839 | Jehu compl of by Clearsprings P M for mcd |
| 2-20-1839 | Anna Plamer (form Weisner) mcd dis |
| 3-20-1839 | Jehu dis |
| 6-19-1839 | William rpt by Clearsprings P M mcd |
| 7-24-1839 | Sarah (form Bufkin) mcd dis |
| 8-21-1839 | William dis |
| 12-25-1839 | Cyrus of Clearsprings P M dis (however he has left this area) |
| 2-19-1840 | Hannah (a wid) & John Bufkin altm |
| 2-19-1840 | Hannah & ch Ann & Mahlon gct Sugar River MM |
| 6-23-1841 | Jonathan & w Ruth & ch Hezekiah & Susanna rocf Chester MM |
| 12-21-1842 | Jonathan of Elm Grove P M dis for na |
| 11-24-1847 | Hezekiah, Susanna, Elwood, Clarkson & Henry, ch of Jonathan gct Mississinewa MM |
| 12-4-1869 | Leah rocf Chester MM |
| 5-6-1871 | Leah gct Chester MM |
| 3-3-1906 | Miriam Bayse rel on req |

## WELLS
|  |  |
|---|---|
| 9-4-1930 | Dora (Kimbrell) drpd from mbrp |

## WELSH
|  |  |
|---|---|
| 12-24-1856 | Hannah rocf Piney Woods MM, N C |
| 5-2-1874 | Julia Jane rec on req |
| 12-4-1919 | Julia gct Washington MM, D C |

## WHEELER
|  |  |
|---|---|
| 11-4-1865 | Mary T rocf Walnut Ridge MM |
| 12-7-1867 | John & ch Martha Ann & Sarah Elizabeth rec on req |
| 10-14-1871 | Mary T & ch Ida R & Wilkie L & Nora gct Raysville MM |
| 4-4-1874 | John & w Elizabeth & ch Martha Ann, Sarah Elizabeth, William Franklin, Rose Lewellen, Rachel Hannah & Lydia Emeline gct West Grove MM, of Hamilton Co |

## WHICKER
|  |  |
|---|---|
| 4-23-1851 | Sarah (form Patterson) mcd dis |

## WHITE
|  |  |
|---|---|
| 1-23-1833 | Isaac & w Louisa & ch original mbrs |
| 1-23-1833 | Stanton & w Sarah original mbrs |
| 1-23-1833 | Jesse & w Mary & ch original mbrs |
| 1-23-1833 | Isaac White, James Johnson, Josiah Small & William Baldwin appt to unite with a comm from women's mtg, to form a comm on Education & to report |
| 2-20-1833 | Jesse appt asst clerk & George Evans appt clerk |
| 3-20-1833 | Isaac White, William Unthank, George Evans & Driver Boon appt to comm to attend funerals of our mbrs |
| 4-24-1833 | Exum & w Ann & ch Margaret Susan & Joseph H rocf Western Branch MM, Va held at Summerton, Nansemond Co, Va, end by Milford MM |
| 4-24-1833 | Thomas Newby rocf Western Branch MM, Va |
| 6-19-1833 | Isaac White & George Evans appt to correct minutes & to record them for this mtg |
| 6-19-1833 | Exum appt Recorder of Marriage Certs |
| 6-19-1833 | Mary appt to a comm |
| 8-21-1833 | Jesse appt to comm to att Q M |
| 8-21-1833 | Exum appt asst clerk & Solomon Macy appt clerk |
| 10-23-1833 | Ann appt to comm |
| 6-25-1834 | Exum appt asst clerk & Solomon Macy appt clerk |
| 4-22-1835 | Hannah, w of John, from Md. & ch Joel, Charles, Hannah & John jr, gct Mississinewa |
| 5-20-1835 | Jesse appt to comm to att Q M |
| 6-24-1835 | Isaac appt to station of Elder |
| 8-19-1835 | Isaac White, David James, Calvin Wasson, Vierling Kersey, John Hiatt, George Evans, William Edwards, Nathan Davis & Joseph B Hunt appt to comm on Education for ensuing year |
| 9-23-1835 | Joseph Morris gct White Lick MM to m Elizabeth White |
| 12-23-1835 | Caleb & w Mary & ch Jane, Charles, James, Joseph & Margaret rocf Milford MM |
| 2-24-1836 | Betsey Ann gct Milford MM |
| 4-20-1836 | Rebecca (wid of Robert) & her ch Lucinda & William A rocf Milford MM |
| 7-20-1836 | Isaac, an Elder, appt to accompany Catherine Coffin, a Minister, on a visit to White Lick Q Mtgs |
| 6-21-1837 | John T & sons Mordecai M & Francis Toms rocf Blue River MM |
| 11-22-1837 | John T & Hannah Ann Parker altm |
| 12-20-1837 | William rocf White Lick MM |
| 4-25-1838 | Rebecca & James Johnson altm, comm rpts the rights of Rebecca's ch are secure |
| 10-24-1838 | Exum req release from services of Recorder of m certs as he is going to remove from Spiceland limits |
| 11-21-1838 | Micajah is appt Recorder of m certs in place of Exum |
| 1-23-1839 | Exum & w Ann & ch Margaret S, Joseph, Jesse T, Harriett & John G gct West Grove |
| 4-22-1840 | Lilburn & Elizabeth Small altm |
| 10-21-1840 | Caleb appt clerk & Caleb Johnson appt asst clerk |
| 10-21-1840 | Thomas N rocf Duck Creek MM |
| 1-20-1841 | Thomas N gct Milford MM |
| 11-24-1841 | Samuel & w Rebecca & dt Martha rocf Symons Creek MM, N C |
| 11-24-1841 | Miriam & dt Martha White & Parthena Jones, a minor, under the care of Miriam, rocf Symons Creek MM, N C |
| 11-24-1841 | Caleb White, Samuel Pritchard, Joel Pusey, Charles Morgan & Samuel Horner appt Trustees to rec & hold titles for real estate, in trust, for Raysville P M, Wayne twp. Henry Co, for meeting, school & burying ground |
| 6-22-1842 | Jane & Jesse F Pusey altm |
| 10-19-1842 | Caleb appt clerk & Caleb Johnson appt asst clerk |
| 9-20-1843 | Thadeus & w Betsy & ch Samuel Pritchard, Margaret Jorden, Abigail, Alpheus, Elizabeth Ann & Harriett Susan rocf Piney Woods MM, N C |
| 5-22-1844 | Mary jas, Separatists (ASF) dis |
| 5-22-1844 | Jesse & Mary jas, Separatists (ASF) dis |
| 10-23-1844 | Louisa jas, Separatists (ASF) dis |
| 6-25-1845 | Mordecai, Aletha Catherine & Isaac, ch of Isaac, decd & Louisa B gct Westfield MM |
| 7-25-1845 | Micajah C jas Separatists (ASF) dis (he having moved to limits of Westfield MM) |
| 9-24-1845 | Elizabeth jas, Separatists (ASF) dis |
| 10-22-1845 | Thadius Macy gct Westfield MM to m Elizabeth Jane White |

SPICELAND

## WHITE (Cont)

|  |  |
|---|---|
| 1-21-1846 | Lilburn jas, Separatists (ASF) dis |
| 1-20-1847 | Martha Talbert (form White) jas, Separatists (ASF) & mcd dis |
| 8-25-1847 | Samuel appt an overseer at Raysville P M |
| 9-22-1847 | Edmund Morris, a minor, rocf Milford MM |
| 6-21-1848 | Henry & w Mary rocf Duck Creek MM |
| 8-23-1848 | Abigail rocf Duck Creek MM |
| 8-23-1848 | Mary Jane rocf Duck Creek MM |
| 10-24-1849 | Samuel White & James Johnson appt overseers at Raysville P M |
| 11-21-1849 | Thadeus & w Betsy & ch Margaret J, Abigail, Alpheus, Elizabeth, Ann, Harriett L & & Louisa E gct Honey Creek MM |
| 12-19-1849 | Elmina rocf New Garden MM |
| 10-23-1850 | Betty rocf Blue River MM |
| 10-23-1850 | Charles S Hubbard gct Blue River MM to m Martha White |
| 4-23-1851 | Martha N & Reuben Chappell altm |
| 10-22-1851 | Martha rst w/con of Symons Creek MM, N C |
| 11-17-1851 | Edmund con mcd |
| 5-19-1852 | Charles gct Salem MM to m Lucy Haughton |
| 5-19-1852 | Almira & Margaret, minor ch of Martha, rec in mbrp |
| 2-22-1854 | Lucy H & dt Emma rocf Salem MM |
| 2-22-1854 | Mordecai Morris gct Cincinnati MM, Oh |
| 2-22-1854 | Francis T gct Cincinnati MM, Oh |
| 8-23-1854 | Martha & John T Newby altm |
| 10-25-1854 | Augustus & w Margaret & s John Richard rocf Piney Woods MM, N C |
| 10-24-1855 | Augustus & w Margaret Ann & ch John Richard, gct Hopewell MM |
| 1-23-1856 | Abigail dis |
| 4-23-1856 | Betty gct Fairfield MM |
| 11-19-1856 | Mary gct Walnut Ridge MM |
| 8-19-1857 | William gct Walnut Ridge MM |
| 6-23-1858 | Mary & Jesse rst |
| 12-22-1858 | Gamaliel, s Jesse & Mary rec in mbrp |
| 12-22-1858 | Louisa rst at Westfield MM |
| 11-23-1859 | Addison gct Duck Creek MM to m Eliza Holliday |
| 3-21-1860 | Addison gct Richland MM |
| 9-19-1860 | Josiah P & Elizabeth Macy altm |
| 10-24-1860 | Jesse & Mary & s gct Richland MM |
| 2-20-1861 | Josiah P & w Elizabeth gct Richland MM |
| 7-20-1864 | Addison & w Eliza & dt Annie rocf Westfield MM |
| 4- 1-1865 | Addison & w Eliza & ch Annie & Mary gct Lynn Grove MM, Iowa |
| 7- 1-1865 | Josiah P & w Elizabeth M & dt Laura rocf Richland MM |
| 8- 1-1868 | Josiah P appt to read m cert in limits of Elm Grove P M |
| 5- 1-1869 | Gamaliel rocf Richland MM |
| 3- 5-1870 | Josiah P & w Elizabeth & ch Laura Viola & Julia gct Ash Grove MM, Ill |
| 6- 3-1871 | George B & w Sarah rocf Walnut Ridge MM |
| 8- 3-1873 | Alfred gct Maryville MM, Tenn to m Elizabeth Evans |
| 3- 1-1873 | Sarah Ann & ch Emma, Otus J & Rebecca Jane rec in mbrp |
| 2- 7-1874 | Lilburn & w Adelia rec in mbrp |
| 4- 4-1874 | Adelia rec as Minister at Spiceland P M |
| 11- 4-1876 | Rachel & ch gct West Grove MM |
| 2- 6-1879 | George & w Sarah R gct Mississinewa MM |
| 6- 2-1883 | Elmina drpd from mbrp |
| 6- 2-1883 | Gamaliel gct Long Lake MM, Mich |
| 12- 5-1885 | Debbie Ann & dt Sarah Albertson rec in mbrp |
| 7- 3-1886 | Mordecai & w Phebe & ch May & Frank roc |
| 1- 1-1887 | Bertie transferred to Muncie MM |
| 8- 1-1890 | Sarah gct Muncie MM |
| 6- 6-1891 | Frank rel on req |
| 3- 5-1892 | May A rel on req |
| 3- 3-1894 | Mordecai & w Phebe gct Pasadena MM, Ca |
| 8- 7-1897 | Esther rocf Fairfield MM |
| 3- 4-1899 | Henry rec in mbrp |
| 12- 2-1905 | Gamaliel & w Esther gct Gate MM, Okla |

## WHITELY

|  |  |
|---|---|
| 2- 1-1868 | Robert & w Jane & fam rec in mbrp |
| 2- 1-1868 | George C & w Lydia A rec in mbrp |
| 4- 1-1871 | Alexander con mcd |
| 1- 6-1877 | Alexander gct Milford MM |
| 1- 6-1877 | George & w Lydia Ann & ch Laura Jane, Isadora, Josiah P & Lydia Ann gct New Salem |
| 5- 4-1895 | Addie & ch Robert W, Florence M & Eva Jane rec in mbrp |
| 8- 6-1898 | John A & w Addie & ch Robert W, Florence M, & Eva Jane gct Muncie MM |

## WICKERSHAM

|  |  |
|---|---|
| 2-21-1838 | Moses dis at Duck Creek P M for dpl & att mcd |
| 3- 5-1870 | Abel & w Mary E & grand-dt Caroline M Wilson rocf Hopewell MM |
| 3- 5-1870 | Stephen B rocf Hopewell MM |
| 9- 2-1871 | Stephen con mcd |
| 10-14-1871 | Mary rec in mbrp |
| 2- 3-1872 | Mariam rec in mbrp |
| 8- 3-1872 | Stephen B & Mary A gct Hopewell MM |
| 9- 6-1873 | Abel & w Mary & grand-dt Caroline Wilson gct Hopewell MM |
| 5- 6-1876 | Stephen & w Mary & dt Estelle rocf Hopewell MM |
| 12- 7-1878 | Stephen & w Mary & ch Estelle & Anna Pearl gct Hopewell MM |
| 1- 7-1893 | Caleb & w Emeline & dt Louisa rocf Haviland MM, Kan |
| 1- 7-1893 | Mary Annis rocf Haviland MM, Kan |
| 8- 6-1898 | Caleb E & w Emeline & Mary Annis gct Oskaloosa MM, Iowa |
| 6- 7-1913 | Jethro & Margaret A rocf Hopewell MM |
| 10- 4-1913 | Louisa roc |
| 12- 1-1917 | Louisa gct New Castle MM |

## WICKIFF

|  |  |
|---|---|
| 12- 7-1912 | Sarah gct Knightstown MM |

## WIGGINS

|  |  |
|---|---|
| 2-22-1854 | Hannah (form Morris) mcd dis |

## WILCUTTS

|  |  |
|---|---|
| 1- 6-1877 | David & w Rachel rocf New Garden MM |
| 5- 1-1880 | David gct Carthage MM |
| 9- 2-1882 | Rachel gct Whitewater MM |

## WILDMAN

|  |  |
|---|---|
| 7- 7-1894 | Olive S rocf Whitewater MM |
| 9- 1-1894 | Murray S rocf Green Plain MM, Oh |
| 1- 3-1929 | Murray S & w Olive S & dt Mary gct Green Plain MM, Oh |

## WILES

|  |  |
|---|---|
| 11-19-1856 | Luke produced a cert from Springfield Mtg to m Jane Davis |
| 11-19-1856 | Luke & Jane Davis, a wid, altm |
| 1-21-1857 | Jane D gct Springfield MM |
| 10-23-1861 | Luke & w Jane D & ch Rhoda Jane, Luke jr, Nancy E, Esther G & Anna Mariah rocf Springfield MM |
| 12- 7-1867 | Nancy Freeman (form Wiles) mcd dis |
| 1- 4-1873 | Luke & w Jane gct Plainfield MM |
| 3- 4-1873 | Anna Maria gct Plainfield MM |

## WILKINSON

|  |  |
|---|---|
| 11- 1-1884 | Malinda L rel on req |
| 1- 3-1885 | Malinda rst |
| 5- 2-1929 | Alida rec in mbrp |
| 6- 5-1929 | Alida gct ? Indianapolis MM |

## WILLETS

|  |  |
|---|---|
| 7-24-1833 | Henry & w Rachel & ch Jonathan & Mahlon rocf New Garden MM |
| 6-25-1834 | Nathan & w Asenath & ch Ruth & John rocf Duck Creek MM |
| 9-23-1837 | Nathan dis for whipping an orphan boy not under his care |
| 3-21-1838 | Joseph gct Westfield MM |
| 4-25-1838 | Henry & w Rachel & ch Jonathan, Mahlon, William & Jeremiah gct Westfield MM |
| 4-25-1838 | Asenath & ch Ruth, John, Rachel, & Gabriel gct Mississinewa MM |
| 8-22-1838 | Levi, a minor, s of Gabriel gct Mississinewa MM |

## WILLIAMS

|  |  |
|---|---|
| ( 9-20-1837) | Jason & w Abigail & ch, mbrs of Duck Creek Mtg, now laid down, have been attached to Spiceland |
| 12-20-1837 | Maria jas, dis |
| 2-21-1838 | Gulielma (form Hiatt) Dillon, wid of Absalom, compl of for mcd |
| 6-20-1838 | Jason appt clerk & George Evans appt asst clerk |
| 10-24-1838 | Gulielma dis for mcd |
| 5-22-1839 | Gulielma's ch, Allen H, Nathan, Mary Ann, Maria Jane & Sarah DILLON, ch of Absalom Dillon, decd, gct Vermillion MM, Ill |
| 7-24-1839 | Jason appt clerk & Walter Edgerton appt asst clerk |
| 2-19-1840 | Isaac produced a cert from Westfield MM to m Charity Parker |
| 2-19-1840 | Isaac & Charity Parker altm |
| 2-19-1840 | For the accommodation of Isaac & Charity Parker, in accomp their m, a mtg is apptd at Elm Grove M H, tomorrow at the usual hour |
| 4-22-1840 | Charity gct Westfield MM |
| 6-25-1851 | John produced cert from Westfield MM to m |
| 6-25-1851 | John & Eunice Street altm |
| 10-22-1851 | Eunice gct Westfield MM |
| 1-25-1854 | Mary Ruhama rocf Duck Creek MM |
| 6- 7-1854 | Joseph & w Lydia rocf Short Creek MM, Oh |
| 6-23-1858 | Joseph appt to station of Elder |
| 5-25-1859 | Jason & w Abigail & ch Sarah, Mary, Ellen, Samuel D & William C rocf Duck Creek MM |
| 5-22-1861 | Mary Ruhama gct Duck Creek MM |
| 6-19-1861 | Lydia appt Elder |
| 1-20-1864 | Jason appt asst clerk & Nathan H Ballinger appt clerk |
| 2-24-1864 | Lydia gct Plainfield MM |
| 4- 7-1866 | Ruhama rocf Duck Creek MM |
| 1- 4-1868 | Ary Isabella rec in mbrp |
| 2- 1-1868 | Loring & Caroline V rec in mbrp |
| 6- 6-1868 | William C con mcd |
| 7- 2-1869 | Anna W rocf Miami MM, Oh |
| 11- 2-1872 | Nathan rocf Pleasant Hill MM |
| 6- 7-1873 | Samuel T S con mcd |
| 5- 2-1874 | Abigail appt overseer |
| 7- 4-1874 | Martha L rec in mbrp |
| 11- 7-1874 | Nathan T gct Westfield MM |
| 11- 6-1875 | Mary Emma rocf Hopewell MM |
| 2- 5-1877 | Samuel T & w Martha L rel on req |
| 1- 5-1878 | Loring A rel on req |
| 11- 2-1878 | William C & Anna W gct Raysville MM |
| 1- 1-1881 | Mary Emma gct Raysville MM |
| 4- 7-1883 | Ruhama gct West Grove MM |
| 3- 2-1884 | Ella (dt Joseph & Susan) rec in mbrp |
| 2- 3-1887 | Abigail gct Raysville MM |
| 12- 3-1892 | Albert F & w Lizzie H & ch Arthur H, Wister P & Albert Ross rocf West Grove MM |
| 3- 2-1895 | Susie rec in mbrp |
| 3- 7-1896 | Albert F & w Lizzie H & ch Arthur, Wister P, Albert R & Elizabeth Ernestine gct Carthage MM |
| 9- 2-1905 | Albert & w Lizzie & ch Arthur H, Wister P, A Ross & Ernestine rocf Carthage MM |
| 4- 3-1909 | James & w Bessie rec in mbrp |
| 12- 5-1914 | Wister Parker rel on req |
| 10- 4-1928 | James drpd from mbrp |

## WILSON

|  |  |
|---|---|
| ( 9-20-1837) | David & w Esther & ch, mbrs of Duck Creek MM, now laid down, have been attached to Spiceland |
| ( 9-20-1837) | John & Mary & ch mbrs of Duck Creek MM, now laid down, have been attached to Spiceland |
| ( 9-20-1837) | Cyrene a mbr of Duck Creek MM, now laid down, have been attached to Spiceland |
| 1-24-1838 | Cyrene & William Lewelling inf mtg of int to m Consent of parents now had |
| 2-21-1838 | Cyrene & William Lewelling altm |
| 9-25-1839 | David & w Esther & ch gct Salem MM, Iowa |
| 9-25-1839 | Catherine Alley (form Wilson) mcd dis |
| 11-20-1839 | Susanna dis |
| 9-21-1842 | Peggy W rocf White Lick MM (w of James) |
| 10-25-1848 | James Cochran gct Blue River MM, to m Martha Ellen Wilson, a wid |
| 3-21-1849 | Benjamin & w Caroline rocf Milford MM |
| 3-20-1850 | Benjamin & w Caroline & s William A gct Milford MM |
| 3-23-1853 | John & w Mary & s Michael C rocf Duck Creek MM |
| 5-25-1853 | David F rocf Duck Creek MM |
| 5-25-1853 | Thomas Arnett rocf Duck Creek MM |
| 9-21-1853 | Reuben rec in mbrp |
| 9-21-1853 | Thomas A & Ruth S Foster altm |
| 6- 7-1854 | David Franklin mcd |
| 5-23-1855 | Michael C mcd dis |
| 10-24-1855 | Joseph & w Hope & ch Mary Jane, Miriam A, Phareba M, Rachel M, Nathan M & Elias E rocf New Garden MM, N C & end by New Garden MM |
| 12-19-1855 | Miriam A & Caleb Johnson altm |
| 6-25-1856 | James M & w Clarkie rocf Springfield MM, N C |
| 12-24-1856 | James M & w Clarkey gct Deep Creek MM, N C |
| 3-21-1860 | Peggy, w of James, gct Duck Creek MM |
| 4-25-1860 | Reuben mcd dis |
| 5- 6-1860 | James M & w Clarkey gct Richland MM |
| 7- 7-1866 | Timothy & ch William N, Olive B, Terrel, Mathew, T, rocf Milford MM |
| 8- 4-1866 | Timothy & Elmina H Coffin, a wid altm |
| 1- 5-1867 | Timothy appt clerk & Albert Newby appt asst clerk |
| 7- 6-1867 | Michael rec in mbrp |
| 4- 4-1868 | Allen L rec in mbrp |
| 12- 5-1868 | Olive rocf Milford MM |
| 1- 3-1869 | William W & ch Marcus A, Mary Annis, & Eva Ellen rocf Hopewell MM |
| 4- 3-1869 | Rebecca jas & mcd dis |
| 9- 3-1869 | Allen con mcd |
| 4- 2-1871 | Thomas A & w Ruth S & ch Jesse H, Anna P, & Mary E gct Duck Creek MM |
| 1- 4-1873 | Marcus mcd dis |
| 7- 5-1873 | William W rel on req |
| 8- 2-1873 | Thomas A & w Ruth & ch Jesse N, Anna Ruhama, & Mary Jannette gct (? West Grove MM, Hamilton Co, Ind) or (? Westfield MM) |
| 9- 6-1873 | Abel Wickersham & w Mary & grand-ch Caroline Wilson gct Hopewell MM |
| 2- 7-1874 | Richard rec in mbrp |
| 12- 4-1875 | Eunice rocf Raysville MM |
| 1- 1-1876 | Marcus A & Eliza S rec in mbrp |
| 2- 5-1876 | William N gct Whitewater MM |
| 11- 3-1877 | Ella Taylor gct Whitewater MM |
| 1-11-1879 | Richard rel on req |
| 7- 2-1881 | Sylvester & w Sarah Abigail & ch Izzie & Lucy rocf Raysville MM |
| 5- 5-1883 | Timothy appt Elder |
| 5- 5-1883 | Elmina appt an Elder |
| 7- 1-1883 | Marcus A & ch Florence gct Duck Creek MM |
| 9- 6-1884 | Timothy & w Elmina gct Maryville MM, Tenn which was returned because there was no Mtg there |
| 5- 1-1886 | Timothy & w Elmina gct Maryville MM, Tenn |
| 3- 1-1890 | Belle rec in mbrp |
| 8- 6-1892 | Eva gct Whitewater MM |
| 10- 8-1892 | Isadore H & s Lowell rocf New London MM |
| 10- 8-1892 | Ettie & ch Perry & Kearney rocf West Grove MM |
| 5- 1-1897 | Lucy C rel on req |
| 5- 5-1900 | Lucille rec in mbrp |
| 7- 2-1904 | Walter Coffin rec in mbrp |
| 3- 4-1905 | Russell T, s Terrel & Belle rec in mbrp |
| 12- 5-1908 | Walter C gct Pasadena MM, Ca |
| 5- 6-1911 | Terrell & w Rebecca Bell & ch Lucille Wilson & Julia Brookshire gct Pasadena MM, Ca |
| 1- 6-1912 | Mary Inman rocf West Grove MM |
| 1- 6-1912 | Russell T gct Whittier MM, Ca |
| 3- 1-1913 | Georgia rec in mbrp |
| 4- 3-1915 | Carrie rec in mbrp, Dorothy rec in mbrp |
| 5- 6-1916 | Perry & fam gct New Castle MM |
| 1- -1925 | Dorothy rel on req |
| 5- 3-1928 | Virginia rec in mbrp |

## WILTSE

|  |  |
|---|---|
| 3-23-1836 | Simeon produced a cert from Walnut Ridge mtg to m Elizabeth Butler, with the consent of his parents |
| 3-23-1836 | Simeon & Elizabeth Butler altm |
| 7-20-1836 | Elizabeth gct Walnut Ridge MM |
| 12-25-1850 | Elizabeth rocf Walnut Ridge MM |
| 7-20-1853 | Lydia rocf Walnut Ridge MM |

SPICELAND

SPICELAND

## WILTSE (Cont)
|  |  |
|---|---|
| 12-11-1855 | Lydia jas dis |
| 7-25-1860 | Elizabeth jr rocf Wabash MM |

## WINKLE
|  |  |
|---|---|
| 3-2-1895 | Bert rec in mbrp |
| 1-7-1899 | Bert gct Kokomo MM |

## WINSLOW
|  |  |
|---|---|
| 6-24-1840 | Jacob B & w Martha & ch Margaret Ann & Edward W rocf Piney Woods MM, N C, end by Milford MM |
| 10-21-1840 | Jacob & w Martha & ch Margaret Ann & Edward W gct Milford MM |
| 5-23-1855 | William F rocf Piney Woods MM, N C, & end to Walnut Ridge MM |
| 3-4-1882 | Saloma Florence rec in mbrp |
| 8-4-1921 | Daniel & w Cora J & ch Francis, Frederick & Esther rocf Rich Square MM |
| 12-6-1923 | John M & Adelia H roc |
| 11-7-1929 | Daniel & Cora J & ch Frederick D & Esther B rel on req |
| 11-7-1929 | Francis J rel on req |

## WINTERS
|  |  |
|---|---|
| 2-2-1878 | Luetta, Laura, Alvin, Regina E & John Avery, ch of John W, decd, & Melvina (now Poe), rocf Deep River MM, N C |
| 12-6-18__ | Alvin gct Duck Creek MM |

## WISE
|  |  |
|---|---|
| 3-7-1908 | Charley & Hubert rec in mbrp |
| 12-7-1912 | Charley & Hubert drpd from mbrp |

## WISEHART
|  |  |
|---|---|
| 10-8-1887 | Richmond & w Martha rec in mbrp |
| 5-5-1890 | Richmond & w Martha gct New Castle MM |

## WOLLAM
|  |  |
|---|---|
| 5-5-1921 | Roy & fam gct Detroit MM, Mich |

## WOODARD
|  |  |
|---|---|
| 3-22-1848 | Mahlon Stubbs gct New Garden MM to m Rachel Woodard |
| 2-22-1854 | Thomas C & w Mary Ann & ch Emily Jane, Alpheus Lindley, Vestal & Adeline rocf New Garden MM |
| 10-24-1855 | Thomas C & w Mary Ann & ch Emily Jane, Alpheus L, Vestal, Adaline & Alice gct Springfield MM |
| 12-3-1887 | Cornelius J & w Sarah B & s Herbert rocf New Garden MM |
| 8-1-1891 | Cornelius & w Sarah & s Herbert gct New Garden MM |
| 10-8-1892 | Mary E gct Westland MM |
| 2-7-1914 | Norman rec in mbrp |

## WOODS
|  |  |
|---|---|
| 11-20-1850 | Priscilla (form Davis) con mcd |
| 2-25-1852 | Priscilla jas dis |
| 4-6-1867 | Asenath rocf Flushing MM, Oh |

## WOOLEN
|  |  |
|---|---|
| 5-24-1843 | Martha (form Stubbs) mcd dis |
| 11-7-1868 | Edward L & w Elizabeth H & ch James A, William A & Adalade H rec in mbrp |
| 1-1-1876 | Elizabeth Black & her ch William A & Hannah A Woolen gct Hopewell MM |

## WOOTEN
|  |  |
|---|---|
| 11-8-1870 | Amanda Sanders (form Wooten) mcd dis |
| 12-25-1874 | Andrew rocf Whitewater MM |
| 12-7-1878 | Andrew S rel on req |

## WORTH
|  |  |
|---|---|
| 4-5-1884 | Mary E gct Argonia MM, Kan |
| 8-1-1919 | Everett & Bertha rel on req |

## WRIGHT
|  |  |
|---|---|
| 8-23-1837 | Joab produced cert Duck Creek MM to m Mary Small |
| 8-23-1837 | Joab & Mary Small altm |
| 4-25-1838 | Catharine & ch Joel & Jemima gct Mississinewa MM |
| 7-25-1838 | Abigail rocf Union MM, Oh |
| 8-22-1838 | Joel & Anna Elliott altm |
| 8-21-1839 | Joab & Malinda Elliott altm |
| 9-25-1839 | Thomas Sheridan gct Whitewater MM to m Hannah Wright |
| 12-25-1839 | Anna Sanders (form Wright) con mcd |
| 2-24-1841 | Nancy Finkel (form Wright) mcd dis |
| 10-19-1842 | Abigail gct Back Creek MM |
| 3-20-1844 | John & w Joanna & ch Isaac, Vincent, Jesse S R, Samuel K G, Precious M & Zenas J rocf Newhope MM, Tenn |
| 10-23-1844 | Joab & w Melinda & ch Obadiah, Anna & Jesse David gct Mississinewa MM |
| 1-21-1846 | John & w Joanna & ch Isaac, Vincent, Jesse S R, Samuel K G, Precious M, Beulah Ann, & Zenas J gct Back Creek MM |
| 4-12-1848 | Huldah (form Ratliff) con mcd |
| 12-20-1848 | Huldah gct Mississinewa MM |
| 11-2-1878 | Sylvanus J rocf Duck Creek MM |
| 7-1-1882 | Sylvanus & w Sarah & ch Pearl Iva, Jessie Leona & Russell Lowell gct Duck Creek MM |
| 2-6-1886 | Alpheus L & w Mary rec in mbrp |
| 1-3-1891 | John & Jemima & ch Marion S, Mary J, & Effie E rocf Raysville MM |
| 10-1-1910 | Eva rel on req |
| 12-2-1911 | Miriam E rec in mbrp |
| 12-7-1912 | John, Jemima, Marion, Mary J & Effie drpd from mbrp |
| 4-6-1918 | Cora rocf Dublin MM |
| 5-1-1919 | Russell & w Flossie & ch Gladys E & Lowell S rec in mbrp |
| 8-4-1927 | Russell & fam gct South Salem MM, Ore |
| 5-2-1929 | Margery rec in mbrp |
| 9-4-1930 | Cora drpd from mbrp |

## YATES
|  |  |
|---|---|
| 8-21-1833 | Caroline, Needham & William rocf Milford MM |
| 12-23-1833 | Caroline Maudlin (form Yates) mcd dis |
| 6-21-1837 | Needham dis for disunity & dpl |
| 2-21-1838 | William, Clear Springs P M, compl for mcd |
| 5-23-1838 | William dis |
| 12-3-1870 | John F rec on req |
| 10-9-1886 | John F & fam gct New Castle MM |

## YOUNG
|  |  |
|---|---|
| 11-3-1883 | Lucy Jane rec on req |
| 1-5-1895 | Leonard rec on req |
| 4-1-1911 | Leonard rel on req |

# WALNUT RIDGE MONTHLY MEETING
## Rush County, Indiana

Walnut Ridge Monthly Meeting was set-off from Duck Creek Monthly Meeting and first held the 16th of First Month 1836.

The meeting is located two and one-half miles southwest of Carthage, Ripley Township, Rush County. In 12th Month 1826 *"Friends in the lower settlement on Blue River"* requested of Duck Creek Monthly Meeting the privilege of holding a meeting for worship and a preparative. This was granted. Sometime previous a log meetinghouse 20 by 20 feet had been constructed near the present site of the Walnut Ridge meetinghouse.

Meetings established within the verge of Walnut Ridge were Carthage in 1839 and set-off as a monthly meeting in 1866; Little Blue River in 1842, set-off with Carthage; Westland in 1845, set-off in 1872; Pleasant View in 1850, set-off with Westland; Charlottesville in 1873, set-off in 1919; Riverside in 1875 and set-off as a monthly meeting in 1922 and was laid down in 1927.

In 1840 the log meetinghouse was replaced by a frame, which was burned Fourth Month 12th 1864 - it was thought by members of the "Knights of the Golden Circle" from below Morristown. A meetinghouse 80 by 50, a brick building on a stone foundation with a slate roof was completed in Seventh Month 1866. It still stands.

### Monthly Meeting Records

The volumes listed below are in the vault of the Indiana Yearly Meetinghouse in Richmond. The material searched for this publication is marked (*). These records have been microfilmed.

| Men's Minutes | Women's Minutes |
| --- | --- |
| *1- 16- 1836  :  3- 15- 1845 | *1- 16- 1836  :  6- 16- 1855 |
| *8- 16- 1845  :  12- 18- 1858[1] | *7- 21- 1855  :  12- 16- 1877 |
| *1- 15- 1859  :  12- 21- 1872 | *1- 20- 1872  :  3- 21- 1891 |
| *1- 18- 1873  :  12- 15- 1888[2] | |

Joint Minutes

1- 1- 1889  :  3- 16- 1907[3]
4- 20- 1907  :  3- 19- 1941
8- 21- 1946  :  6- 18- 1958

\* Book of Removals 1863- 1864 & 1864- 1881
\* Marriage Register 1836- 1863
\* 1 Volume of Births and Deaths

1. This is a reconstructed record; the original burned in 1864.
2. Meetings were held jointly after 2- 18- 1888.
3. Searched through 1899.

# WALNUT RIDGE MONTHLY MEETING

## BIRTH & DEATH RECORDS

### ADAMS
Oliver  b 4-20-1848 - s Alfred & Elizabeth
  m (7-23-1871)
Christiana (Addison)  b 12-6-1848  dt Thomas & Catharine
Ch:  Ladora     b 4-24-1872
     Letha      b 7- 1-1876

### ADDISON
Thomas James  b 11-29-1844 - s Thomas & Catharine
m 1st    (8-11-1866)
Elizabeth M (Cathen)  b 5-30-1851  dt William & M - - -
Ch:  William A    b 4-10-1867
     Delphina C   b 11-12-1869
     Orlando F    b 10-22-1872
     Charles T    b 2-19-1879
     Ruth A       b 1-29-1884

Wesley   b - - - -   m
Eliza Jane (Hasket)  b 9- 4-1839  dt Silas & Peninah
                                      (Hendricks)
Ch:  Solomon     b - - - -
     George      b - - - -
     Franklin E  b 1-17-1871
     Mary E      b 1- 7-1873
     Margaret J  b 1- 7-1875
     Simon       b - - - -
     Ann         b - - - -
William  b 3-15-1840 - s Thomas & Catharine
  m(11-14-1863 )
Miranda (Nixon)   b 8-16-1847  dt Thomas & Elizabeth
                  d 4- 6-1887
Ch:  Martha Ann    b 8-31-1864
     Elizabeth C   b 3-24-1869
     Sarah E       b 7- 3-1871
     Mariah        b 3- 4-1874
     Reuben        b 11-20-1877  d 3-16-1878
     Bertha A      b 8-15-1879   d 8-20-188?

### ALBERTSON
Benjamin  b 1-24-1826 - s Nathan & Pheraby (Nicholson)

Sabina T (Marsh)  b 6-12-1823  dt Elias & Edith
Ch:  Nathan E   b 2- 5-1849
     William    b - - - -

Nathan A  b 1- 5-1801  Perquimans Co, N Car  s Benjamin
                                                & Mary
Phariby (Nicholson)  b 5-12-1803  Perquimans Co, N Car
                                  dt Nathan & Peninnah
Ch:  Benjamin   b 1-24-1826  Perquimans Co, N Car
     Sarah      b 8-27-1828      "       "  " "
     Alpheus    b 11-25-1831     "       "  " "
     George J   b 1-25-1834  Wayne Co, Ind
     Jesse B    b 5- 9-1836  Rush Co, Ind
     Jordan P   b 2-13-1839    "    "   "
     Ezra H     b 3-30-1841  Hancock Co, Ind
     Aaron      b 8-25-1843
     Nathan W   b 11-30-1845

Thomas P  b ( 7- 2-1814) - s Nixon & Easter of Delaware
                                                Co, Pa
Hannah (Davis)   b (12-28-1816)  dt Harmon & Hannah
                                    (Mendenhall)
Ch:  Nixon     b ca (1834)

### ALEXANDER
Benjamin  d 5- 2-1866  age 82-6-0  bur Little Blue River
          Mtg, res Rush Co, Ind

### ALLEN
Harman   b 12-12-1791  N Car - s John & Rachel (Street)

Nancy Ann (Clark)  b 5-22-1796  N Car dt Daniel &
                                           Mary
Ch:  Daniel C        b 2-18-1820  Rush Co, Ind
     John Philander  b 4- 8-1821  Rush Co, Ind
     Joseph Milton   b 10-16-1822
     Samuel L        b 8-26-1824
     Harmon H        b 2-28-1826

     Julia Ann    b 5-17-1828
     Mary L       b 2-27-1830
     Nancy C      b 11-25-1831
     Jonathan T   b 4-22-1834
     Sylvia J     b 2-16-1836
     Nathan H     b 7-21-1838
     Martha E     b 3- 9-1842

Samuel   b - - - -   s John & Martha

Martha (Henley)  b 10-26-1822  dt Elias & Jane
                                  (Hubbard), decd

### ALLRED
Charles C  b - - - -
  m
Jane (Nicholson)  b 1- 2-1841  dt Nathan & Miriam
                                   (Hunt)
Ch:  Oscar Lee    b 1- 2-1872
     Adeline D    b 3-19-1873

### ANDERSON
Arabella  b 5-11-1868  dt of Nancy J

Calvin A  b 4-24-1827

Elizabeth (Haskett)  b 2-24-1824   d 8- 1-1889
                     dt John & Elizabeth

Charles B  b 11-25-1853 - s James & Mary
  m ( 3-12-1876)
Ella (Smith)  b 8-17-1859?  dt John A & Lucinda

Charles C  b 1-12-1832 - s Charles B & Martha
  m ( 8- 2-1853)
Sarah A (Munden)  b 10-20-1825  dt Christopher &
                  d 3-15-1888      Pareba
Ch:  Augustus    b 3-23-1863
     Sarah A     b 7-24-1869

### ANDREWS
Edgar J  b 4-12-1867 - s Benjamin F & Ruth

Joseph Sr  d 4-29-1868  age 81-4-11  bur Walnut Ridge Mtg,
  m 1st                                                Ind
Mary - - - -  d 8-m0-1818
Ch:  William E    b 11- 4-1817
  m 2nd
Anna Maria - - - -
Ch:  Permelia       b 11-14-1824
     Mary E         b 11-20-1826   d 10-25-1848
                    bur Westland Mtg, Hancock Co, Ind
     Caroline V     b 3- 8-1829
     Joseph Oliver  b 5-25-1831
     John R         b 3-20-1834    d 9-10-1872
                    bur Walnut Ridge Mtg
     Samuel Benjamin b 2-22-1836
     Robert D        b 1-22-1838
     Benjamin F      b 1-28-1841

Joseph Oliver  b 5-25-1831 - s Joseph Sr & 2nd w, Anna
  m 1st                                            Maria
Martha (Binford)  (d prior to 1853) dt Micajah &
                                       Miriam, decd
  m 2nd
Anna B (Jessop)   b 11-10-1833  Rush Co, Ind
                  dt Thomas & Rebecca (Binford)
Ch:  Sarah E        b 3-12-1857
     Martha J       b 12-12-1858
     Joseph Thomas  b 6- 6-1862
     John N         b 1-16-1869
     Robert Wilson  b 9-12-1871

William E  b 11- 4-1817 - s Joseph Sr & 1st w Mary, decd
  m
Mary E (Perisho)  b 12-26-1823  dt Nathan & Mary
Ch:  Pamelia A   b 5-30-1844  Hancock Co, Ind

### ATKINSON
William   b 7-18-1782  Orange Co, N Car
          s Thomas & Ruth (Harvey)

Nancy (Taylor)   (b 1- 3-1787 Jack Swamp, N Car)

WALNUT RIDGE

## ATKINSON (Cont)
Nancy (Taylor) dt Christopher & Elizabeth (Patterson)
    d 5-24-1856 Walnut Ridge MM, Ind

## AYDELOTTE
Henry C jr  b 8-2-1834 - s Henry C Sr & - - - -
    m 9-17-1864
Susannah (Parker)

Stewart    b - - - -
    m 1st 1833
Sarah S - - - -    d 8-13-1846 bur Whitewater MM,
    m 2nd    Ind
Anna (Stuart)  b 2-9-1813 dt Jehu jr & Sarah
    (Cook) of Spiceland Mtg, Ind
Ch:  Joseph Benjamin  b 1-9-1850
    Sarah L  b 12-28-1851
    Mary E  b 9-7-1853

## BAKER
James  b 12-2-1854
    m ( 8-22-1876)
Mary (Winslow)
Ch:  Cora B  b 2-1-1879

## BARNARD
Asa  b 9-17-1767  s Tristram & Margaret
    d 7-23-1852 age about 85 yrs

Huldah (Macy)  b 5-1-1770 dt Jethro & Hepsabeth
    d 10-6-1849 age 78-5-5
Ch:  Thomas  b 12-24-1804
    Lucinda  b - - - -
    Benjamin Franklin b - - - -

Benjamin Franklin - s Asa & Huldah (Macy)

Anna (Worth) dt William & Phebe (Barbard), decd
Ch:  Caroline  b 8-6-1846 Rush Co, Ind
    Louisa  b 6-22-1848  "  "  "
    Melvina  b 7-15-1854
    Mary F  b 9-20-1860

Calvin  b 10-10-1819 N Car - s John & Elizabeth (Barnard)

Lucinda S
Ch:  Thomas E  b 1-2-1846
    Adison L  b 5-7-1850
    Horace G  b 9-30-1851

Isaac b 10-20-1813 - s William & Matilda (Gardner)
Elvira
Ch:  Fernando  b 12-5-1842
    Adalaide  b 2-28-1845
    Theodore  b 12-29-1846
    Laura M  b 5-30-1849
    Julieta  b 2-27-1851
    Thomas E  b 9-28-1852
    Lydia Ellen  b 11-24-1854
    Florence Josephine b 10-5-1857

Jethro  d 9-9-1795 N Car - s Asa & Huldah (Macy)

Sally (Gardner)  b 10-12-1798 N Car dt Isaac &
      Eunice (Macy)
Ch:  Laurinda  b 7-17-1825 Union Co, Ind
    Edgehill B  b 6-17-1831
    Luzena  b 7-12-1833
    Rhoda  b 4-3-1837

John  d 2-19-1863 age 69-7-1 bur Little Blue River
    Mtg, res Shelby Co, Ind
Elizabeth (Barnard)  b 3-30-1799 N Car dt Obed & 1st
    w Elizabeth (Coffin)
Ch:  Calvin  b 10-10-1819 Guilford Co, N Car
    Anny  b 6-17-1821  "  "  "  "
    Lucinda  b 6-12-1824  "  "  "  "
    Phebe  b 8-6-1826  "  "  "  "
    William N  b 7-20-1829  "  "  "  "
    Mary  b 12-26-1832 Wayne Co, Ind
    Obed  b 6-3-1835  "  "  "
    Sophia  b 4-3-1837 Rush Co, Ind

---

Ch:  Sophia (Cont)  d 9-15-1855
    Libni F  b 3-21-1842 Rush Co, Ind
      d 8-16-1862 "was killed on the
        battle field"

Orpheus  d 2-25-1864 age 28-6-0

## BEESON
Mahlon H  b 5-15-1818 - s Isaac & Sarah, decd
    m 1st
Sarah - - - -  b 7-27-1814  d 12-18-1853
    bur Cherry Grove Mtg
Ch:  Amos C  b 7-29-1842
    Isaac A  b 8-30-1850  d 9-4-1850
    m 2nd
Mary (Reece) dt John & Abigail (Fellow) of Howard Co, Ind
Ch:  Jonathan  b 1-29-1856
    Jesse W  b 4-24-1858
    Sarah Abigail  b 11-9-1862
    Miles R  b 1-30-1866  d 2-11-1871
      bur Western Grove Mtg, res Hancock
      Co, Ind

## BENTLEY
John B  b 6-29-1823 - s Reuben & Sarah
    m 1st (1-10-1850)
Mary (Henby)  b 1-6-1831  d 6-7-1857
    dt John & Mary (Bogue)
Ch:  William Penn  b 11-4-1850
    Reuben  b 5-29-1852
    Sarah Elizabeth  b 9-5-1854
    Mary  b 6-7-1857  d 5-31-1879
    m 2nd (9-22-1859)
Mary E (Coble)  b 12-29-1841 - dt David & Martha
Ch:  Charles E  b 9-21-1860
    Ada Jane  b 8-1-1862
    Martha A  b 9-23-1864
    Olive  b 12-26-1866
    Susanna  b 7-30-1869
    Caroline  b 6-9-1872
    Naomi  b 12-20-1874

(Reuben)

Sarah - - - -
Ch:  John B  b 6-29-1823
    Ruth Anna  b 8-17-1825 Rush Co, Ind
    Thomas Ephraim  b 11-15-1829 Rush Co, Ind
    Susannah  b 4-11-1832
    Sarah Ann  b 1-21-1835  d 4-1-1843
      bur Walnut Ridge Mtg
    Benjamin Franklin b 1-21-1839

Reuben  b 5-29-1852 - s John B & 1st w Mary (Henby)

Minnie J (Stanley)  b 2-17-1862  dt John & Ann
Ch:  Mary M  b 3-28-1881
    Harry H  b 8-11-1883
    Walter B  b 4-26-1885
    Stanley  b 7-16-1891

## BINFORD
Ann  b 6-7-1793 d 2-9-1888  dt Chapel & Martha
    (m 1-20-1840 to Samuel Moore)

Asa  s Benajah & Judith (Binford)

Levina (Harrell)  b 11-1-1825  dt Charles &
      Rachel (Lamb)
    (after death of Asa Binford, Levina m 2nd to
    Ashbel Binford)
Ch: (by Asa Binford)
    Mary Jane  b 9-2-1850
    Rachel Ann  b 8-25-1853

Ashbell  b 8-6-1803  d 1-4-1860 - s Joshua &
    Lydia (Patterson)  bur Walnut Ridge Mtg,
    res Rush Co, Ind
    m 1st
Avis (Edgerton)  dt Reuben & Patience
    d 11-24-1834 age 20-5-11 bur Walnut Ridge
      Mtg

WALNUT RIDGE

BINFORD (Cont)
Ch: of Ashbell & Avis
    Jane    b 10-15-1833  Rush Co, Ind
    Jabez   b 11-17-1834  d 10-11-1859
  m 2nd
Gulielma (Symons)  b 2- 8-1805  dt Abram & Mary
Ch: Edna    b 12- 1-1837  Rush Co, Ind
    Morris  b 7-19-1841
    Joel    b 12- 4-1842
  m 3rd  1859
Lavina (Harrell) Binford b 11- 1-1825 wid of Asa & dt
        Charles & Rachel (Harrell)

Benajah jr,    s Benajah & Judith (Binford)
Ann (Moon) b 4-28-1826 dt Jeremiah & Rachel (Nixon)
Ch: Isaac   b 7-20-1845
    Emeline  b 11- 6-1846
    Rachel M  b 11-14-1848

Benajah Sr b 11- 1-1790 N Car    d 11-12-1858
    s James & Hannah (Crew)  bur Walnut Ridge Mtg
    m (his 1st cousin)  res Rush Co, Ind
Judith (Binford) b 4-24-1792 N Car  d 7-21-1871
    dt John & 2nd w Martha E. (Binford)  bur Walnut
              Ridge Mtg
Ch: John       b 3-26-1813 N Car
    Asa        b - - - - - -
    Jared B    b 5- 2-1818 N Car
    Benajah jr  b - - - - - -
    Nathan     b 10-23-1822 N Car
    Elijah)
    Elisha)  twins? b 12- 1-1824
    Jeremiah   b 2-11-1828 Ind
    Josiah     b 10-29-1830 d young
    Isaiah     b 2- 3-1833 Hancock Co, Ind d young
    Judith Ann  b 3-29-1835  "  "  "

Benjamin b 2-20-1797 s Aquilla    d 1832
Mary (Cook)  dt Josiah & Mary    d 1841
Ch: Josiah    b 6-17-1826

Benjamin  s James L & Mary (1st w) decd
Edna (Butler) b Va dt Joseph, decd, & Charlotte from
        Prince George Co, Va
Ch: Joseph O    b 1-21-1843 Hancock Co, Ind
    James L     b 6-23-1845  "  "  "
    Albert      b 6- 8-1848
    Charlotte A  b 12- 5-1858

Benjamin H b 2-12-1838 s Robert & Martha (Hill)
Lydia Ann (Johnson) b 6-27-1840 dt Joel & Elizabeth
                                   (Davis)
Ch: Amanda   b 9-29-1862
    Orlando  b 9-21-1866
    Vashti   b 11- 4-1869
    Elma     b 6- 5-18??

Isaiah  d 8- 3-1852 age 2-7-25

Jabez  d 10-11-1859 age 24-10-24 bur Walnut Ridge Mtg,
                            res Rush Co

James C  d 9-21-1843 age 1-11-27

James L  b 10- 4-1787 N Car   d 8-19-1863
    s James & Hannah (Crew)  bur Walnut Ridge Mtg,
    res Rush Co, Ind
  m 1st Wayne Oak MM, Charles City Co, Va
Mary - - - -
Ch: Robert    b 7- 2-1813
    Ann       b 3-18-1815
    Joseph    b 6-29-1817
    Benjamin  b - - - -
    William L  b 7-20-1821  d 10-28-1844
       (he never m)
  m 2nd ca Upper MM held at Burly, Prince George Co, Va
Jane - - - -  d 12-14-1867 age 79- 9-17 bur Walnut Ridge
                               Mtg, Ind
Ch: Martha    b - - - -

Jared   b 5- 2-1818         d 4-15-1877
    s Benajah Sr & Judith (Binford)
Almeda (Butler) b 11-11-1832 Ohio dt Daniel, decd, &
        Mary of Stark Co, Ohio

Ch: Lucinda Ann  b 10- 9-1851
    John Murray  b 6-26-1853
    William H    b 9- 6-1855
    Benajah D    b 11-14-1858
    Francis M    b 8- 4-1861
    Jesse C      b 11-27-1863
    Marietta     b 1-16-1867
    (Mary Etta)
    Myrtle J     b 10-22-1869

Jared P  b 12- 9-1834 s William & Mary
  m (9-26-1868)
Emily (Lamb) b 6- 3-1843 dt Phineas & Huldah
Ch: Ella      b 3-15-1869

Joel   d 9- 7-1859 age 16-9-3  bur Walnut Ridge
                          Mtg, res Rush Co

John   b 3-26-1813 Northampton Co, N Car
    s Benajah Sr & Judith (Binford)
Mary (Moon) b 3-26-1820 Highland Co, Ohio dt Jeremiah
                       & Rachel
Ch: Ruth M    b 6-27-1840 Hancock Co, Ind
    Hannah C  b 6-12-1842
    George H  b 2-25-1845

John H  b 4-13-1844 s Robert & Martha (Hill)
Lucy (Coggeshall)  b 5- 7-1852  dt John
Ch: Gertrude  b 4- 9-1874
    Edgar A   b 11-26-1875

John Murray b 6-26-1853 s Jared & Almeda (Butler)
  m (8- 9-1877)
Mary (Phelps) b 10-28-1856     d 5-27-1883
    dt Joseph & Jane
Ch: Percy    b 6-20-1878

Joseph  b 6-29-1817 N Car  s James L & Mary, decd
  m 1st
Elizabeth C (Hill) b 11- 9-1824  d 10-20-1860
    dt William & Charity (Hawkins)
    bur Walnut Ridge Mtg, res Hancock Co
Ch: Charity H   b 8-25-1846
    Anna Jane   b 8-12-1848
    Oliver T    b 7- 3-1850
    Mary Ann    b 3-23-1852
    Susanna     b 3-12-1855
    Louisa      b ca 1858
    Elizabeth C b 4-14-1860
  m 2nd (1863)
Mary Elizabeth (Hunnicutt) White, wid of William White &
    dt of Robert & Elizabeth Hunnicutt, both decd
Ch: Caroline    b 1-14-1864
    Joseph Omer  b 10-21-1866

Joseph John b 3-15-1856 s Josiah C & Mary A (Hill)
Rebecca S (Williams)  b 4- 8-1854 dt Jno A & Elizabeth
Ch: Ethel E  b 5-13-1885
    Mabel A  b 9-27-1889

Joseph
Huldah A (Moore) b 3-10-1840 N Car
    dt Samuel & Mary (Bundy)
Ch: Horace L  b 8-18-1865 Ind
    Elmer     b 9-mO-1869
    Mary E    b 12-mO-1871

Joshua jr b 3-26-1813 Northampton Co, N Car
    s Joshua Sr & Lydia (Patterson)
Sarah Ann (Hunnicutt) b - - - - Va
    dt Robert, decd, & Elizabeth (Andrews)
Ch: Elizabeth Ann b 11-21-1840 Hancock Co, Ind
    Thomas E     b 8-26-1842
    Lydia Jane   b 2-13-1845
    John H       b 10-29-1847
    Robert B     b 10-21-1849  d 3-11-1850
        bur Walnut Ridge Mtg, res Rush Co

Josiah C b 6-17-1826 s Benjamin & Mary (Cook)
Mary Ann (Hill) b 2- 6-1836 dt John & Dinah (Cox)
Ch: Joseph John b 2-15-1856
    Adaline     b 12-22-1857
    Morris      b 4- 3-1859
    Emma Jane  b 10-17-1860

# WALNUT RIDGE

**BINFORD** (Cont)
Ch: of Josiah C & Mary Ann (Cont)
    Marcia             b 12-21-1862
    Charles           b 8- 3-1864
    Irvin H           b 9-19-1866
    Walter            b 10- 9-1869
    David Warren     b 10-29-1872

Josiah     b 2-28-1841 Ind    s Micajah C & Susannah
    m (3-19-1864)                     (Bundy)
Margaret F (Hill)   b 6- 5-1843 N Car
                dt Micajah & Sarah Jane (Mendenhall)
Ch:  Gurney             b 9-15-1865
    Micajah H         b 6- 2-1868
    Bevan              b 3- 2-1872
    Rhoda J           b 1-28-1875    d 3-17-1875
                  bur Walnut Ridge Mtg
    Raymond           b 7-15-1876

Joshua     b 1- 3-1779 N Car    s James & Hannah (Crew)
Lydia (Patterson)       b ca 3- 2-1778
Ch:  Ashbell           b 8- 6-1803
    Hannah            b 2- 3-1806
    Mary (Polly)      b - - - - -
    Joshua            b 3-26-1813
    Lydia P
    James
    Peter              b 9-25-1822

Martha E (Patterson)   b (ca 9-20-1760) wid of John, decd
     of N Car & dt William & Keziah Patterson
     d 1-25-1835 age 75-4-5 bur Walnut Ridge Mtg,
     res Hancock Co, Ind  (she is mother of Judith
     (Binford) Binford, w of Benajah Sr Binford)

Mary       b 8-13-1861   dt Calvin & Peninnah

Micajah    b 3-14-1783 N Car   s James & Hannah (Crew)
     d 3-25-1865 bur Walnut Ridge Mtg, Ind
     m 1st
Sarah (Patterson)   (d prior to 1820, N Car)
Ch:  William          b 11-27-1804   (d 8-17-1885)
    Micajah Crew     b 7-14-1812
    Rebecca           b 12-25-1814   (d 9-11-1891)
    Anna              b 9-17-1816   (d 9- 9-1863)
     m 2nd
Miriam (Morris) (b 8- 1-1792 Pasquotank Co, N Car)
     dt Nathan & Mary (Bell)    d 1-26-1841
     age 48-4-25 bur Walnut Ridge Mtg, Ind
Ch:  (order of birth not recorded)
    Sarah             b 3-12-1821 Northampton Co, N Car
    Kathy             b - - - - - -
    Margaret          b - - - - - -
    Martha            b - - - - - -
    Miriam            b 5-mO-1834
    Mary              b - - - - -
     m 3rd (3-23-1842)
Charlotte A (Butler)  a wid b(8-mO-1792) d 5-26-1865
                age 72-9-15 bur Walnut Ridge Mtg,
                                          Ind

Micajah C   b 7-14-1812             d 4-26-1896
     s Micajah & Sarah (Patterson) decd
Susannah (Bundy)   b 2-18-1818     d 11th or 12th mo
     dt Josiah & Mary (Morris)             1895
Ch:  Ruth              b 8-21-1837 Rush Co, Ind
    William P         b 1- 9-1839
    Josiah            b 2-28-1841
    Levi              b 8-18-1843
    Micajah M         b 12-18-1851

Micajah M  b 12-18-1851 Rush Co, Ind    s Micajah C &
     m ( 3-19-1873)                  Susannah (Bundy)
Susannah R (Binford)   b 5-17-1851 Va
     dt Oliver & Mary (from Black Creek MM, Va)
Ch:  Edward            b 3-24-1877

Morris     d 3- 3-1842 age 7-3-11 bur Walnut Ridge Mtg,
     res Rush Co

Nathan     b 10-23-1822             d 10-19-1882
     s Benajah Sr & Judith (Binford)
Caroline V (Andrews)   b 3- 8-1829    d 4-12-1883
     dt Joseph & Anna Maria

Ch:  Emily Jane        b 7-21-1848     (d 1- 4-1891)
    Anna Maria        b 5- 3-1850
    Judith Ann        b 4- 6-1852
    Joseph T          b 1-27-1856
    Robert Baily      b 7-16-1869 ??

(Oliver of Black Creek MM, Va)
(Mary A)
Ch:   to Indiana
    Susannah R        b 5- 7-1851 Va
    Benjamin O        b 8- 7-1856 Va

Peter     b 9-25-1822              d 4-29-1887
     s Joshua & Lydia (Patterson)
     m ( 8-22-1844)
Elizabeth (Adams)   b 8-12-1826   dt Lewis & Elizabeth
Ch:  Sarah J           b 1- 9-1849
    Woodson H         b    1871

Rachel E    b 10-28-1850           d 10-31-1850
     dt of James & Rachel (Cox) Patterson Binford
     bur Walnut Ridge Mtg, res Rush Co, Ind
     (grand-dt of Joshua & Lydia (Patterson) Binford)

Robert     b 7- 2-1813    N Car    s James L & Mary
Martha (Hill)   b 1-18-1819         d 2- 2-1884
     dt John & Dinah (Cox)
Ch:  Benjamin H        b 2-14-1838
    Isaiah            b 12- 9-1839    d 8- 3-1842
                      bur Westland Mtg, res Hancock Co,
                                             Ind
    James C           b 9-24-1841    d 9-21-1843
            bur Westland Mtg, res Hancock Co, Ind
    John H            b 4-13-1844
    William P         b 2- 1-1846
    Martha J          b 8- 4-1848
    Robert Barclay     b 3- 4-1850
    Joseph L          b 3-19-1852
    Mary Ladd         b 8- 8-1855
    Nathan C          b 11-30-1859
    Alice Ann         b 12-21-1861

Sarah    (parents names not recorded)
     d 2-28-1840 bur Walnut Ridge Mtg, Ind

William    b 11-27-1804 Northampton Co, N Car
     s Micajah & Sarah (Patterson) his 1st w
Mary (Jessop)   b 4- 5-1810 Wayne Co, Ind
     dt Jonathan & Elizabeth
Ch:  Eliza              b 7- 8-1828 Rush Co, Ind
    Calvin            b 6-13-1832
    Jared P           b 12- 9-1834
    Mary              b 6-21-1837
    Michal            b 12-12-1839
    Jonathan          b 4-20-1842
    Miriam            b 12-31-1844

William H   b 9- 6-1855   s Jared & Almeda (Butler)
     m (9-15-1880)
Sarah (Phelps)  b 5-31-1859   dt Joseph & Jane
Ch:  Oren              b 8-22-1883
    Laura             b 2-24-1885
    Louis             b 9-23-1887
    Emery             b 11-11-1889

William P   b 1- 9-1839   s Micajah C & Susannah (Bundy)
     m 1st
Henrietta M - - - -     d 8- 3-1871 bur Walnut Ridge
        Mtg, res Hancock Co, Ind
Ch:  Lindley M         b 10-15-1864
    Allen Jay         b 12-22-1867
    Clark Omer        b 12- 1-1870
     m 2nd 10-23-1872 Hopewell MM, Ind
Esther (Gilbert)  (b 1-21-1852)  dt Mordecai M & Martha
                                         (Bundy)

**BOBLETT**
Isaac Marshall
     m (11- 3-1870)
Emily Jane (Binford)   b 7-21-1848    d 1- 4-1891
     dt Nathan & Caroline V (Andrews)
Ch:  Charles Nathan   b 11-25-1871    d 11-12-1873
     bur Walnut Ridge Mtg, res Hancock Co, Ind
    William Thomas   b 1-16-1873    d 8-31-1873
     bur Walnut Ridge Mtg
    Caroline E        b 1-25-1875
    Mary Annie        b 2-14-1878

WALNUT RIDGE

BOGUE
(Dilwin, s Joseph, decd, & Mary)
Ann (Jones) (b 3-1-1791 Wrightsboro Mtg, Ga)
    dt Henry & Kezia, decd
Ch: Prudence         b 1-19-1817
    Jemima           b 11-19-1818
    Dilwin R         b 9-7-1820
    Phineas          b 2-25-1823
    Mary Ann         b 5-26-1825

BOND
William    b 10-13-1834  s Jesse & Ann (Cook)
Sarah (Jessop) b 5-11-1837  dt Thomas & Rebecca (Binford)
Ch: Emily Ann        b 8-12-1856    d 10-16-1856
        bur Carthage Mtg, res Rush Co, Ind
    Thomas J         b 8-27-1857
    Franklin W       b 7-19-1860
    Jesse Irvin      b 10-7-1862    d 5-16-1864
    Micajah John     b 7-27-1865
    Charles E        b 11-5-1867
    Robert B )
    William P) twins b 11-6-1871
    Rebecca Ann      b 3-21-1876

BOYD
(Adam, decd, of Randolph Co, Ind)
Elizabeth (Hawkins)  dt Amos & Anna (Comer)
    (d prior to 1846 as the 2nd w of Elias Marsh of
        Walnut Ridge Mtg)
Ch: (by her 1st husband)
    Martha Ann       b 2-20-1828
    Jonathan Dayton  b ------
    Oliver MacKenzie b ------
    (m 1848 Mary Osborn dt Thomas, decd & Margaret)

BREWER
Morris     b 3-6-1839  Wayne Co, Ind  s John & Sarah
    m (12-1-1861)                              (Morris)
Eliza A (Starbuck) b 2-10-1842  Guilford Co, N Car
    dt Elwood & Ruhanna
Ch: Clarence         b 3-21-1863  Henry Co, Ind
    Ella C           b 1-15-1865  Rush Co, Ind
    Otis J           b 5-29-1866  Hancock Co, Ind
    Eva V            b 1-4-1868   Rush Co, Ind
    Nettie Z         b 7-25-1869
    Jennie F         b 1-25-1871  Hancock Co, Ind
    Alta E           b 8-10-1872
    Julius O         b 11-24-1873  d 10-10-1874
                                  bur Walnut Ridge
    Allen L          b 9-19-1875   d 2-10-1878
    Dellie E         b 12-21-1878

BROOKS
(Robert)
    m (9-mO-1824)
Ellen (Templeton)    b 3-22-1806  dt John & Joanna
Ch: Mary E           b 9-3-1826
    (m 9-4-1851 Henry Winslow (b 1-24-1826), probably
        s of John & Mary)
    William          b 3-3-1828
    Catharine J      b 9-28-1839 ?  d 1-25-1879
    (m 10-20-1864 William B Henby (b 5-18-1833) s John,
        decd, & Mary (Bogue))

James
    m (8-8-1872)
Mary (Woodly)        b 1-15-1855 dt Isaac & Mary
Ch: Perry F          b 7-28-1873
    Mary E           b 12-4-1874
    Alice M          b 1-16-1878

William    b 3-3-1828  s Robert & Ellen (Templeton)
Mary       b 4-14-1830
Ch: Robert           b 12-19-1854
    Amanda           b 6-26-1855
    Laura J          b 10-10-1860
    Sarah A          b 7-14-1864
    John             b 3-14-1866
    Mary E           b 2-7-1869

BROWN
Alfred     b 6-28-1850  s Eli & Sarah (Hill)
Mary Jane (Macy) b 7-28-1848          d 3-29-1878
    dt Solomon & Priscilla

Angelina B    d 1-19-1855  age 20-2-23  bur Walnut Ridge
                Mtg, res Rush Co, Ind

Eli        b 2-24-1821  s Samuel & Margaret (Stubbs)
Sarah (Hill) b 7-13-1819           d 6-8-1881
    dt Nathan & Elizabeth (Henby)
Ch: Margaret         b 11-3-1841  Rush Co, Ind
    Nathan           b 6-19-1845
    Israel           b 8-7-1847    d 4-30-1861
                     bur Pleasant View Mtg
    Alfred           b 6-29-1850
    Aaron            b 8-14-1855   d 1-7-1874

Eliza      d 9-17-1848  age 20-2-9  bur Carthage Mtg,
                res Rush Co, Ind

Frederick     s James & Rebecca of Hendricks Co, Ind
    m (1833 Whitewater Mtg, Ind)
Sarah (Morris) b 11-24-1810  dt Jesse & Mary (Moore)
Ch: Morris           b 2-18-1834  Hancock Co, Ind
    Robert B         b 11-6-1836
    John W           b 7-16-1839
    Joshua M         b 1-6-1843
    Josiah B         b 8-19-1845
    Mary Ann         b 2-21-1848
    Sarah J          b 3-25-1850
    Frederick S      b 11-6-1853   d 8-19-1859

Israel     b 4-13-1830  s Samuel & Margaret (Stubbs)
    m (9-12-1853)
Eliza (Nichols) b 1-17-1828  dt Erasmus & Elizabeth of
                Hendricks Co, Ind

John       b 12-9-1834  s William & Celia (Newby)
Sarah Ann (Coffin) b 5-25-1838  dt George & Lydia
                                           (Jessop)
    d 8-17-1862  age 24-2-23  bur Walnut Ridge Mtg,
                res Rush Co, Ind

John       b 4-15-1804  N Car  s James & Mary
                                   (Huddleston)
Cyrena (Coffin) b 11-28-1808  N Car dt Zachariah & Phebe
                                           (Starbuck)
Ch: Abigail          b 12-11-1833  Hancock Co, Ind
    Seth             b 3-13-1836
    Jesse            b 11-14-1839
    Milton C         b 10-29-1842
    Mary             b 11-17-1845
    Thomas E         b 7-24-1849

Nathan     b 6-19-1845  s Eli & Sarah (Hill)
    m (9-29-1869)
Mary A (Maxwell) b 7-10-1845  dt Hugh & Anna
Ch: Anna S           b 10-5-1870
    Frank C          b 9-9-1872
    Mabel Clara      b 4-15-1875
    Leroy N          b 10-11-1879

Oraella    b 3-21-1867  ch of Milton C & Elizabeth

Robert     b 1-27-1826  s Samuel & Margaret (Stubbs)
Martha Ann (Boyd) b 2-20-1828  dt Adam & Elizabeth,
                                       both decd
Ch: Elizabeth H      b 12-24-1847
    Rachel Ann       b 10-11-1850
    Oliver M         b 1-6-1853
    Louisa Jane      b 6-13-1857
    Eli Samuel       b 4-30-1862   d 10-10-1866
    bur Pleasant View Mtg, res Hancock Co

Robert B   b 11-6-1836  (s Frederick & Sarah (Morris))
    m 1st
Irena (Coffin) b 5-19-1841  dt Elihu & Nancy (Jessop)
Ch: Mary Etta        b 7-10-1859
    Irena Melvina    b 6-9-1861
    m 2nd  1866 Ind
Rebecca (Moore) (b 11-30-1831) dt (Samuel & Mary (Bundy))

Samuel H   b 8-22-1832  Ohio (s Samuel & Margaret
                Stubbs)  d 1-5-1860 bur Pleasant View Mtg,
                res Rush Co, Ind
(Esther) Jane (Newlin) b 9-20-1835 dt Eli & his 1st w
                                       (from Whitelick Mtg)
Ch: Charles          b 9-25-1856
    Esther Jane      b 10-23-1859

WALNUT RIDGE

BROWN (Cont)
Samuel          b 1- 3-1797              d 12-30-1881
                (s Samuel & Mary of Ohio & Ind)
        m (12-11-1816)
Margaret (Stubbs) b 6- 8-1790 Ga         d 3-19-1871
                dt John & Jane (Jones)   bur Pleasant View Mtg,
                                         res Hancock Co, Ind
    Ch:     (Kezia       b 10-17-1817)  N Car
            (Mary        b  4- 2-1819)
            (Eli         b  2-24-1821)
            (Rachel      b  1-10-1823)
            (Robert      b  1-27-1826)
            Jane         b  5-26-1828   Preble Co, Ohio
            Israel       b  4-13-1830        "    "    "
            Samuel H     b  8-22-1832        "    "    "

Seth            b 3-13-1836  s John & Cyrena (Coffin) of
                             Hancock Co, Ind
Miranda W (Rawls) dt Jesse & Elizabeth of Hancock Co, Ind
    Ch:     John M       b  9-27-1862

William         b 8-21-1802  N Car  (s James & Rebecca of
                             Hendricks Co, Ind)
                d 2-10-1872  bur Western Grove Mtg, res
                             Hancock Co
Celah (Newby) b 5- 1-1801 N Car (dt Samuel, (s of
                William) & w - - - -?)
    Ch:     Cyrus N      b 10- 9-1824   d 10- 1-1842
              bur Walnut Ridge Mtg, res Rush Co
            Milton D     b 11-27-1826
            Mary         b  5- 6-1829
            Rebecca      b  4-30-1831
            Henry        b  4-26-1833
            John         b 12- 9-1834
            Eli          b 12-18-1836
            James        b 12-29-1838
            Emily        b 11-19-1841
            Oliver       b  9- 7-1844
            Celah        b  4-17-1846

BUCK
James E         b 12-13-1863  s Robert & Ellen
        m (12-mO-1887)
Elizabeth (Cox) b 7- 5-1865  dt Enos B & Mary Ann (Swain)
    Ch:     Walter Benjamin  b 10-19-1888

BUNDY
Caleb           b 7-20-1830  s Josiah, decd, & Mary
Esther L (Butler) b 10-mO-1835 dt Daniel & Mary
    Ch:     David        b  1-21-1854
            Nathan       b  5-25-1857
            William T    b  3-25-1863
            Rebecca M    b  3-31-1869

Elias           b 4- 6-1801  N Car  s Benjamin, decd, &
                                    Sarah (Bell)
Sarah (Nicholson) b 9- 5-1801 Perquimans Co, N Car
                dt Nathan & Penninah (Parker)
    Ch:     Ellen        b  7-24-1824  Symon's Creek, N Car
            Mary         b  9-28-1826
            Penninah     b  2-22-1829
            Martha       b  9-13-1831
            Ann          b  5- 7-1833  Henry Co, Ind
            John         b  8-21-1835  Rush Co, Ind
            William      b  7-24-1837
            Ruth         b  4-20-1840
            Henry        b  5- 6-1843

George jr       b 4-24-1811  Perquimans Co, N Car
                d 10-18-1855 Ind  s George Sr & 1st w Sarah
                                         (Moore)
Angelina (Binford) b 2-18-1816 Northampton Co, N Car
                dt Benajah Sr & Judith (Binford) Binford
        (after the death of George Bundy, Angeline m 2nd
                Thomas Cook)
    Ch:     Amos B       b  9- 5-1835  Hancock Co, Ind
            Mary Ann     b  7-23-1837   d 9-26-1844
                                         res Hancock Co
            Martha Jane  b  5-16-1839
            Benajah      b  7- 1-1846

Henry C         b 5- 6-1843  s Elias & Sarah (Nicholson)
        m (7-30-1867)
Mary E (Day) b 6-29-1849  dt Dudley & Mary
    Ch:     William H    b 10-20-1868

Ch:     Nellie       b 3-11-1870
        Alice        b 8-20-1875

Henry           b 9- 2-1825  Wayne Co, Ind  s Josiah & Mary
                                            (Morris)
        m (3-31-1853)
Mary Eliza (Elliott) b 3-31-1835 Perquimans Co, N Car
                dt Zachariah & Sarah
    Ch:     Caleb        b  1-15-1854
            Huldah A     b  9-29-1855
            Sarah E      b  4-11-1857   d 8- 1-1857
            Charles R    b  2-10-1862
            Francis T    b  9-25-1865

Jordan
Nancy A (Bundy) b 8-12-1825  dt of Rex Bundy of N Car
                                    & his 1st w
    Ch:     Mary J       b  6- 6-1862

Josiah          b 11-11-1786 N Car  s Josiah Sr & Mary (Symons)
                d 4-17-1846  age 59-5-6  bur Walnut Ridge Mtg,
                                         res Rush Co, Ind
        m 1st
Huldah (Jones) b 11-15-1779 N Car        d 2-11-1811
                dt Joseph & 1st w Mary (Overman)    N Car
    Ch:     Huldah       b  1-17-1811  N Car
        m 2nd (9-22-1813)
Mary (Morris) b 9-28-1793 N Car          d 8-31-1882
                dt Nathan & Mary (Bell)           Ind
    Ch:     Miriam       b  6-30-1816
            Susannah     b  2-18-1818
            Nathan       b  3-20-1821   d 11-17-1852
                         bur Westland Mtg, res Hancock Co
            Ruth         b  8- 3-1822
            Henry        b  9-21-1825
            Mary         b  4- 4-1828
            Caleb M      b  7-20-1830
            Josiah jr    b  4-25-1833   d 11-11-1881

Josiah jr       b 4-25-1833              d 11-11-1881
                s Josiah & Mary (Morris)
        m (1- 6-1876)
Sarah Jane (Hill) b 1-29-1845 dt Micajah & Sarah
                                         (Mendenhall)
    Ch:     Miriam Pauline  b 5-12-1876
            Mary Effie      b 6- 7-1879
            Anna J          b 2-24-1882

Mary Ann        b 2-21-1859  dt of - - - -?

Nathan          b 3-20-1820  Rush Co, Ind  s Josiah & Mary
                                           (Morris)
Ann (Binford) b 3-18-1815  dt James L & Mary L
    Ch:     Mary Jane    b  2-26-1845  Hancock Co, Ind
            Ruth Ann     b 10-26-1846
            Eliza        b  4-12-1849
            Emily        b  8-19-1851

Samuel M        b 9- 2-1808              d (prior to 1845)
                s George & Sarah, decd (Moore)
Priscilla (Cox) b 5- 5-1810 Ohio  dt Joseph & Elizabeth
                                         (Musgrave)
        (after death of Samuel M Bundy, Priscilla m 2nd 1846 to
                                         David Butler)
    Ch:     (by 1st husb)
            Joseph
            Rachel
            Sarah

Thomas M        b 9-12-1838  N Car  s Rex & 2nd w, Penelope,
                                    decd, of N Car
        m (2-11-1864)
Adaline (Pool) b 10-16-1843  dt Washington & - - - -
    Ch:     George A     b 12-12-1864
            Thomas L     b  5-10-1866
            William G    b  9-21-1867
            James M      b  8-16-1869
            Charles W    b 10-22-1870
            Jesse E      b  8-28-1872
            Mary W       b 11-26-1875
            Anna         b 10-27-1877

Zenas           b 6- 1-1843  s Ellen
Rachel Ann (Brown) b 10-11-1850  dt Robert & Martha Ann
                                         (Boyd)

WALNUT RIDGE

BUNDY (Cont)
Ch: Irvin          b 8-31-1874    d 9-22-1877
                                  bur Walnut Ridge Mtg
     Edward        b 12-9-1876

BURGESS
William A (of N Car) b 2-4-1832
m (N Car)
Jane L (Johnson)  b 9-28-1834 N Car  dt David B & Fruzanah
Ch: Elizabeth C   b 10-3-1859
    Mary Jane     b 12-15-1861
    Henry         b 2-12-1864    d 10-27-1869
                                 bur Westland Mtg, res Hancock Co
    Frusanna      b 3-13-1867

BUTLER
Benjamin Pretlow  s Joseph Sr, decd & Charlotte from
    Western Branch Mtg, Va
m (probably in Ohio)
Susanna (maybe Anders or Andrews?)
Ch: William Fleming  b 10-25-1844    d 10-19-1858
    Sarah E          b 1-15-1847
    Virginia A       b 1-19-18??
    Sarah E          b 11-6-1848
    James O          b 2-11-1850
    Benjamin D       b 6-11-1853

Charlotte  b 8-mo-1792 wid of Joseph Sr, lately from
    Western Branch Mtg, Va (d 5-26-1865 as the
    wid of Micajah Binford. she had m him on
    3-23-1842 Walnut Ridge Mtg, she being his
    3rd wife)
Ch: to Indiana
    Gulielma         (m 1833 Richard Maudlin, s Wm)
    Oliver
    Benjamin Pretlow
    Edna             (m Benjamin Binford)
    Joseph jr        (m Mary Binford dt Micajah & Miriam)

Edward     b 5-22-1822          d 5-29-1879
    s William & Esther (Ladd)
m 1st
Sarah A (Lacy) b 5-12-1828      d 10-30-1856
    dt Pearson & Margaret    bur Walnut Ridge Mtg,
                             res Rush Co, Ind
Ch: Esther Ann    b 4-18-1846
    William P     b 6-9-1848
    Thomas E      b 11-18-1849
    Mary E        b 10-19-1852
    Margaret L    b 8-15-1856
m 2nd
Mary A (Pitts)  b 9-4-1830 N Car  dt James & Rebecca
                                  (Moore) his 2nd w
Ch: Rebecca Jane  b 12-31-1859   d 4-17-1861
                                 bur Walnut Ridge Mtg, res Rush Co
    Michal M      b 7-4-1861
    James P       b 7-1-1863
    Charles M     b 1-23-1865    d 10-10-1865
                                 bur Walnut Ridge Mtg
    Eunice        b 2-8-1867     d 10-4-1888
    Anna H        b 8-20-1871

Elisha    b 2-22-1785 in old Dinwidde Co, Va
    d 9-21-1843 age 58-6-29 bur Westland Mtg,
    res Hancock Co, Ind   s John & Martha of Va
m 1st
Lucinda - - - -
Ch: George W      b 5-25-1818 Southampton Co, Va
m 2nd
Rhoda (Rawls) b 3-23-1797 Southampton Co, Va  dt John &
    Tabitha of Va  (after the death of Elisha
    Butler, Rhoda m 2nd to Samuel Nixon of
    Newgarden Mtg, Ind, as his 2nd wife)
Ch: Jesse         b 9-18-1826 Stark Co, Ohio
    Elisha jr     b 8-16-1828    "    "    "
    Arthur        b 9-30-1833    "    "    "
    Lucinda       b 3-20-1836 Hancock Co, Ind

George W    b 5-25-1818 Southampton Co, Va  s Elisha &
    1st w Lucinda, decd
Martha - - - -

Ch: Daniel W      b 7-4-1837
    Mary          b 8-4-1839
    Eli           b 8-12-1841
    John Nixon    b 5-26-1843
    Micajah       b 11-15-1845
    Jesse         b 3-3-1848     d 8-13-1849
                                 bur Westland Mtg, res Hancock Co
    Elwood)
    Almeda)  twins b 5-23-1850
    Elizabeth Ann b 5-15-1854
    Charles J     b 7-28-1857    d 8-29-1862
                                 bur Westland Mtg, res Hancock Co

Joseph jr   s Joseph Sr, decd & Charlotte (now the wife
    of Micajah Binford)
Mary (Binford) dt Micajah & w Miriam, decd
    d 4-28-1861 age 37 yrs bur Walnut Ridge Mtg,
    res Rush Co
Ch: Levi          b 5-25-1849
    Margaret A    b 5-7-1853
    Micajah C     b 11-2-1855
    Nathan C      b 10-13-1858
    Joseph        b 4-20-1860

Joseph J    b 9-23-1813 s William & Esther (Ladd)
Eliza (Patterson) b 10-10-1820 dt Jared & Angelina
Ch: Miriam        b 11-26-1838 Rush Co  d 6-25-1852
                                 bur Walnut Ridge Mtg
    Angelina      b 5-1-1841 Hancock Co
                  d 8-15-1843 bur Walnut Ridge Mtg,
                  res Rush Co
    Amos          b 7-23-1843    d 5-23-1863
                                 bur Walnut Ridge Mtg, res Rush Co
    Mary P        b 7-14-1845
    Deborah A     b 11-21-1849
    Jared P       b 3-26-1850
    Hiram         b 9-21-1857

Levi    b 5-25-1849 s Joseph & Mary (Binford)
Martha (Taylor) b 12-11-1852   dt John & Nancy Ann
Ch: Joseph Riley  b 12-11-1868
    Mary Emma     b 5-22-1871
    John A        b 9-25-1873
    Charles R     b 5-16-1877
    Jesse J       b 5-7-1881     d 8-12-1886

Robert T    b 8-13-1824 Wayne Co, Ind  s William &
                                        Esther (Ladd)
Mary (Robinson)
Ch: Dempsey       b 10-4-1867

Thomas E    b 11-20-1849 s Edward & Sarah A (Lacy)
m (1-12-1871)
Thirsey Jane (Thomas) b 12-20-1850 dt Peter & Elizabeth
Ch: Minnie Alice  b 10-25-1871
    Dellie F      b 9-12-1873    d 9-27-1874
                                 bur Walnut Ridge Mtg, res Rush Co
    Hattie B      b 1-18-1877

William Sr  b (ca 1767) (s Joseph & Miriam of Upper
    MM, Va) d 1-7-1851 age 84 years bur
    Walnut Ridge Mtg, res Rush Co, Ind
m 1st - - - -
Ch: (of 1st w)
    Elizabeth     b 5-6-1805
m 2nd
Esther (Ladd)  (b ca 1780) dt Garrard & Sarah from
    Graveley Run MM, Va
    d 2-14-1844 age 63-10-25  bur Walnut Ridge Mtg,
    res Hancock Co
Ch: Joseph        b 6-19-1813
    Lydia         b 10-16-1817
    Priscilla     b 9-4-1820
    Edward        b 5-28-1822 Ohio d 5-29-1879
    Robert T      b 8-13-1824 Wayne Co, Ind
m 3rd
Margaret (Morris) Lacy wid of Pearson Lacy b 1-12-1805
    dt Jesse & Mary (Moore) Morris
(Margaret (Morris) Lacy Butler, wid m 3rd, 1854 to Abner
                                                    Blair)

WALNUT RIDGE

CARD
Phineas A      b 6-26-1840    s Jess W & Miriam
    m (5- 1-1864)
Mily Ann (Haskett) b 5-10-1843  dt Silas & Penninah
Ch:   Emma E          b 11- 3-1866
      Penina C        b  5-18-1868
      John Wesley     b  3- 5-1870
      Silas H         b  5-21-1872
      William P       b 10-17-1874
      Neda Alice      b  8-16-1877
      Milea Jane      b  2- 6-1882

CASE
G Peter      b 12- 8-1826   s Nathaniel & Lydia
    m (8- 9-1856)
Tacy M (Niles)  b 3- 8-1842    dt Reuben & Susan

CATHON
William      d 10-21-1851  age 48-8-0  s Josiah W &
                Mourning, decd, of Stark Co, Ohio
    m 1st in Ohio
Elizabeth - - - -  d 2-16-1846  bur Westland Mtg, res
                                        Hancock Co, Ind
    m 2nd
Mariah (Coffin) Davis, wid of Jesse Davis  b 12-17-1815
        dt Zachariah, decd & Phebe (Starbuck) Coffin
Ch:   Elizabeth       b 5-30-1851

CATT
Solomon      b 10-10-1818
Cyrena       b  8-18-1826
Ch:   Benjamin P      b 9-12-1846
      Eli O           b 1- 2-1849
      Lucinda         b 5-13-1851
      Harvey A        b 6- 7-1853
      Mark A          b 1- 2-1856
      Rebecca A       b 4-11-1858
      Riley A         b 7-21-1863

CHAPPELL
Elias E      b 8-16-1858    s James & Mary
Emma J (Binford) b 10-16-1860  dt Josiah C & Mary A
                                              (Hill)
Ch:   Mary B          b  3- 1-1885
      Josiah M        b 11-21-1886
      Elsie Elizabeth b  9-11-1888
      Edwin James     b 12-25-1890

James Thomas  b 4-24-1861   s James & Mary
Alice (Parker) b 1- 1-1858   dt John P & Miriam
Ch:   John Thomas     b 12-14-1890
      Leona Alice     b  3-27-1892

John W       b 3- 2-1863    s James & Mary
Marcia (Binford) b 12-21-1862  dt Josiah & Mary Ann (Hill)

Joseph J     b 9- 6-1835  Perquimans Co, N Car  s Gideon
        jr & Elizabeth, decd (Griffin)
Eliza Ann (Patterson) b 7-14-1837 Belmont Co, Ohio
        dt Amasa, decd & Lydia
Ch:   Lydia Ellen     b  4-21-1862
      Gurney G        b 10-18-1865
      Charles C       b  9-14-1870
      Anna E          b  9-17-1873

Thomas L    d 4- 8-1838  age 68-11-9  bur Walnut Ridge
        Mtg, res Rush Co, Ind
    m 1st
Martha - - - -
Ch:   William         b - - - -  Va
      Sarah M         b 4-29-1808  Southampton Co, Va
      Thomas jr       b 4-24-1810    "    "    "
                      d 4-23-1838  bur Westfield Mtg,
                                        Hamilton Co
      Martha Ann      b 5- 6-1816
      John            b 9-17-1819
    m 2nd
Margaret
Ch:   Deborah         b 3-29-1825

CLARK
(Asenith (Hunt)  wid & 2nd wife of Dougan Clark Sr &
        dt Nathan & Martha (Ruckman) Hunt, decd)
        (b 9-11-1785 N Car)
Ch:   (to Indiana with their mother)
      Nathan          b  9-10-1825  (to Westfield Mtg)
      Dougan jr       b  5-17-1828  (to Walnut Ridge
                                              Mtg)

Daniel      b 5-16-1824  Randolph Co, N Car
        s John & Nancy (Hussey)
        d 4-30-1874  bur Carthage Mtg, res Rush Co,
                                              Ind
Mary R (Hoag) b 10-11-1829  dt Nathan C & Abigail R
Ch:   Emma R          b  4-26-1850
      Nathan Hoag     b 11-27-1852  d 9-17-1857
                                bur Carthage Mtg
      Alfred Lewis    b  2-28-1855  d 12-23-1853
                                bur Carthage Mtg
      Anna Mary       b  4- 9-1859  d 7- 4-1859
                                bur Carthage Mtg
      Lindley Daniel  b  6-26-1862
      John T          b  6-23-1864
      Rowland Evans   b  3-22-1867
      Abby Maria      b  1-21-1870

Hezekiah     b 12-20-1797  Randolph Co, N Car
        s Daniel & Mary (Sanders)
Abigail G (Mendenhall) b 1-18-1795  dt George & Judith
Ch:   Richard M       b  8-24-1820  Guilford Co, N C
                      d  3-11-1838  bur Little Blue
                                River Mtg, Rush Co, Ind
      George C        b 11- 5-1821  Guilford Co, N C
      Eliza W         b  2-14-1823  Randolph Co, N C
      Daniel A        b  5- 1-1824    "      "   " "
                      d 11- 9-1849
      John L W        b  9-17-1825    "      "   " "
      Cynthia A       b  4-11-1827    "      "   " "
                      d  8-30-1836  bur Little Blue
                                River Mtg
      Hezekiah F      b  1-12-1829  Randolph Co, N C
      Abigail J       b 10-14-1830    "      "   " "
      David W S       b  4-21-1832    "      "   " "
                      d  9-28-1842  bur Little Blue
                                River Mtg
      Nathan M        b  1- 2-1834  Randolph Co, N C
                      d  1- 4-1834  bur N C
      Rhoda G         b 11- 2-1835  Rush Co, Ind
      Maria D         b  9-27-1837    "   "   "

John    b 11-24-1794  N C  s Daniel & Mary (Sanders)
Nancy (Hussey) b 3- 3-1797  N C  dt Jediah, decd, &
        Agatha (Henley)
Ch:   Jediah          b  9- 5-1822  Randolph Co, N C
      Daniel          b  5-16-1824
      Alfred          b 12-19-1825
      Anna            b 11-13-1827
      Martha A        b  9- 2-1829
      Thomas          b  8-27-1831
      Hezekiah        b  9-28-1833  Rush Co, Ind
      Lindley M       b  4-10-1836
      Nancy M         b 11- 8-1838

(John jr  s John Sr & Sarah, decd)  (b 6-29-1796 N Car)
        (d 8- 8-1836  Whitewater Mtg, Ind)
(m 1st) (Anna (Price)  dt Rice, decd & Catharine)
        (b 1-27-1798) (d ca 1831-1832)
    m 2nd
Jane (Hamm) dt John, decd, & Elizabeth of Hancock Co, Ind
        b (ca 1812)  (after the death of John Clark, Jane
        m 2nd to Samuel Hadley of Morgan Co, Ind)
minor ch, step-ch of Jane (Hamm) Clark:
      Mary Ann        b 11-21-1823
      Lydia           b 10- 2-1829

John M      b 8-16-1815  N C  s Jonathan, decd, & Ruth
                                              (Moorman)
Eunice A (Hill) b 12-9-1823  N C  dt Samuel & Mary, decd
Ch:   Mary M          b 8-14-1844

John W   (of Little Blue River P Mtg)
Rebecca Jane - - - -
Ch:   (rec in mbrp 1864)
      Lydia E
      William S
      Celia J
      Laura J
      George F
      J Martin
      Sarah A         b 10-25-1864

WALNUT RIDGE

CLARK (Cont)
Samuel     s Daniel & Mary (Sanders)
    m (1822 Back Creek MM, N Car)
Mary (Hussey)    dt Jediah, decd, & Agatha (Henley)
Ch:    Sarah
       Edwin
       Emily
       Julia
       Ascenith
       Daniel
       John

CLICK
John
Sarah
Ch:    Mariah         b  8-29-1868
       Alice          b  6- 2-1869
       Lewis          b  7-23-1871

COFFIN
Alfred    b 5-13-1812  N Car  s Zachariah & Phebe
                                    (Starbuck)
    mcd
- - - -
Ch:    Emily          b 12-23-1835  Hancock Co, Ind

Ammiel    b 6-12-1843  s Elihu & Nancy (Jessop)
Mary Jane - - - -
Ch:    Obed J         b  9-16-1869
       Isadore M      b  7-30-1871

(Edward S)
Louisa (Parker) b 3- 7-1849  dt Silas & Priscilla
                                    (Butler)
Ch:    Laura          b  5- 4-1868   d  6- 2-1871
              bur Western Grove Mtg, res Hancock Co, Ind
       Lucian         b  5-19-1870   d  9-13-1871
              bur Western Grove Mtg, res Hancock Co, Ind

Elihu     b 3-31-1807  Clinton Co, Ohio  s Zacharias
                            & Phebe (Starbuck)
Sarah (Brown) b 3- 2-1806  Guilford Co, N Car
              dt James & Mary
Ch:    Isaac Newton   b  9- 3-1826  Guilford Co, N Car
       William S      b  8-12-1828     "     "   "   "
       Alfred         b 11- 9-1830  Wayne Co, Ind
       Phebe Jane     b  4-22-1833  Hancock Co, Ind
       James B        b  7-13-1835
       Milton         b  8-29-1837
       Mary Newby     b  2-25-1839
       Abigail        b  2-15-1841

Elihu     b 2-24-1817  N Car  s Moses & Phebe
Nancy (Jessop) b 8-27-1818 (sic) dt Jonathan &
                                    Elizabeth (Hill)
Ch:    Ezekiel        b 12-31-1838
       Irena          b  5-19-1841
       Ammiel         b  6-12-1843
       Narcissa       b  9-10-1845
       Phebe Ann      b  4-28-1847
       Thomas         b  3-26-1849   d  6-28-1849
       Henry H        b 10-26-1850
       Francis M      b  3- 3-1855
       Leander        b  1-22-1857   d  2-25-1872
              bur Westland Mtg, res Hancock Co
       Luzena         b 11-11-1860

George F  b 3-20-1814  Stokes Co, N Car  s Aaron, decd
              & 2nd w Sarah (Hussey) of Shelby Co, Ind
Lydia (Jessop) b 12-22-1816  dt Jonathan & Elizabeth
                                    (Hill)
Ch:    Sarah Ann      b  5-25-1838  Rush Co, Ind
       Delfina        b 12- 2-1839
       Asenath        b  1- 2-1842   d  6-11-1844
              bur Little Blue River Mtg, res
              Rush Co
       Rebecca        b 12-23-1843
       Levi           b 10-25-1845
       Aaron          b  7-17-1847
       Mary           b 12-17-1849
       Jonathan P     b  8-28-1851
       Elizabeth J    b  6-15-1854
       Louisa J       b  6-13-1860

James     (from Howard Co)
    m 1st
Martha - - - -
Ch:    Amos           b  8- 7-1859
       Rhoda          b  8-31-1861
    m 2nd
Lucinda - - - -
Ch:    Clara  )
       Flaura ) twins b 10- 3-1872

Lydia (Swain)   d 3-26-1844  bur Little Blue River
       Mtg, res Rush Co, Ind  (Lydia may have been
       w of Alfred Coffin.  IBB)

(- - - -?)
Mary - - - -
Ch:    Iola           b  3- 4-1865
       Oliver Morton  b  9-13-1866

(- - - -?)
Miriam (Jessop)  (b 8-27-1820) (dt Jonathan & Elizabeth
                                    (Hall))
              d 8- 7-1860 age 39-10-11 bur Westland Mtg,
              res Hancock Co

Moses     (b 11-13-1788)  s Aaron, decd & 1st w Mary
              (Barnard)  d 9-10-1838 age 49-10-28 bur
              Little Blue River Mtg, res Rush Co
Phebe - - - -  (ca b 3- 8-1787)    d 12-18-1852
              age 70-9-10  bur Westland Mtg, res
              Hancock Co
Ch:    Elihu          b  2-24-1817  Stokes Co, N C
       Cyrus          b  8- 3-1819
       Louisa         b  5-21-1821
       Mary           b  5- 8-1823
       Jonathan       b  7-17-1825
       Emily          b  6-22-1827   d  4-24-1848
              bur Little Blue River Mtg, res Rush Co
       Sylvester      b 12-13-1830  Union Co, Ind
       Laurinda       b  7-28-1833  Rush Co, Ind
       Oliver         b 10-23-1835

Sarah (Hussey) wid of Aaron, decd & his 2nd wife of
              Va & N Car
Ch:    (by 1st w who came to Indiana with step-mth)
       Phebe          b  4-15-1791
       Ruth           b  4-17-1796
Ch:    (of Sarah, the 2nd w)
       George F       b  3-20-1814

Zacharias b 4- 6-1782  s Bethual & Hannah
              d 8-21-1845  bur Westland Mtg, res
              Hancock Co, Ind
Phebe (Starbuck) b 3- 8-1782  dt William & Jane
              d 12-18-1852  bur Westland Mtg, res Hancock
                                                       Co
Ch:    (to Walnut Ridge Mtg)
       Alfred         b  5-13-1812
       John           b 11-19-1813
       Maria          b 12-17-1815
       Nathan Dix     b 11-16-1818
       Phebe          b 11-12-1820

COGGSHALL
Peter     s Gayer & Hannah, both decd
Jane (Nixon) (b 2-24-1825)  dt Josiah & Mary, decd,
                                    (Newby)
Ch:    (to Walnut Ridge Mtg)
       Mary Ellen     b - - - -
       Margaret Susan b  1-24-1857

Tristram  b 9- 7-1797  N Car  s Peter & Pamela
              (Starbuck) of Surry Co, Va
Milicent (Newby) b 1-24-1801  N Car  dt Joseph &
              Penelope ( Henley)
Ch:    Eunice Worth   b  8- 8-1826  N Car
       Thomas Elwood  b  3-24-1828   d  4-21-1834
              bur Walnut Ridge Mtg, res Rush Co, Ind
       John Milton    b  6-10-1829  N Car
       Joseph Newby   b  9-28-1831   "  "
       Penelope N     b  2-23-1833  Henry Co, Ind
       Oliver         b 10- 9-1834    "    "   "
       Pamela         b  8-31-1836  Rush Co, Ind
       Clark          b  1-22-1839
       Mary           b  9-14-1842

WALNUT RIDGE

COGGSHALL (Cont)
Tristram     (b 5-30-1830)  s Edward & Sophia of Wayne
     m in Ohio                              Co, Ind
Sarah (Bruff) (b 8- 4-1834  N Y) dt James B & Sarah
                              of Mahoning Co, Ohio
Ch:   William       b ca 1860-1861

COLWELL
William F   b 12-25-1843   s Hugh & Tamar
Amanda (Harrison)  b 6-17-1842  dt Thomas & Mary

COOK
Bradley    b 3-15-1807   s John & Ann
     m (1-24-1865)
Margaret (Vanover)

Edna   d 10-30-1859  age 21-11-0  bur Walnut Ridge Mtg,
                                    res Rush Co

Jacob
Mary E
Ch:   Eva B         b 3- 6-1863

Thomas    of Hancock Co, s John & Ann, both decd
     m 1st
Ann (Hunt) b 7-10-1820  Ohio  dt Libni & Jane (Hockett)
         d 6-25-1856  bur Walnut Ridge Mtg, res Rush
                                                   Co
Ch:   Libni H       b 12-13-1848
      Phebe J       b 10-14-1850
      Amanda M      b 10-19-1852
      Elizabeth H   b  9-15-1854   d 4-15-1868
     m 2nd
Angeline (Binford) Bundy wid of George Bundy jr
         b 2-18-1816   dt Benajah & Judith (Binford)
         Northampton Co, N Car              Binford

William     b 7-13-1817 Guilford Co, N Car d 11- 5-1877
       s Abraham & his 1st w, decd
Hannah Ann (Hoover)  b 8-26-1820  Wayne Co, Ind
          dt Jacob & Catherine Hoover
Ch:   Eli H         b 12- 6-1840  Hancock Co
                                  d 11-26-1882
      Jacob H       b  2- 3-1846  Hancock Co

COX
(Benjamin   s Joseph & Dinah (Rich) of N Car & Ind)
     d prior to 1859
     m (1809 Whitewater MM, Ind)
Mary (Price)  (b 5-25-1790 N Car) dt Rice & Catherine
     d prior to 1859          (Bryant) of Ohio
Ch:   Sarah         (m 1860 to Aaron Shaw at
                       Whitewater Mtg)
      Catharine
      Lavina        (m 1840 to Samuel M Morris of
                       Wayne Co)
      Zilpha
      Mahlon        (m Sarah Jane (White))
      Rice Price    (m 1850 to Eunice S (Henley))
      Cyrus B       (m 3 times)
      Benjamin jr
      Mary

Bennet    b 1-25-1817 Wayne Co, Ind  s Joseph &
                       Elizabeth (Musgrave)
Elizabeth (Kindley) b 4-26-1815 Wayne Co, Ind
                       dt John & Betty
Ch:   Albert        b 7-10-1837  Rush Co, Ind
      Ruth Ann      b 2-26-1839
      Melissa       b 2-13-1841
      John K        b 3-23-1843
      Seth          b 7-18-1845
      Eliza         b 5-17-1847
      Catharine     b - - - - -

Cyrus B     (s Benjamin & Mary (Price))
     m 1st
Sally - - - -
Ch:   Benjamin F    b 8-13-1850  Shelby Co, Ind
      James P       b 4-17-1855
     m 2nd
Mary (Binford) (b 6-21-1837) dt William & Mary, decd
                                           (Jessop)

Ch:   Charles S     b 7-16-1860
      Anetta        b 4- 4-1862
      Sarah         b 10-10-1864
     m 3rd
Phebe (Lamb)   (from Greenfield Mtg, Ind)

Enos P    b 8-27-1841  s Obed & Margaret
Mary Ann (Swain) b 1-28-1837 dt Nathan & Elizabeth
Ch:   M Elizabeth   b 7- 5-1865
      Obed Clarkson b 9-24-1866
      William T     b 6- 5-1867
      Benjamin F    b 12-27-1872
      Enos C        b 12-23-1875   d 12-10-1879
      S Leroy       b 6-15-1879    d 12- 3-1882

Joel      b 6- 2-1805               d 10-17-1883
       s Joseph & Elizabeth (Musgrave)
     m (8- 9-1827)
Catherine (Cox)  b 6-23-1809 dt Jeremiah & Catherine
                                         (Morrison)
Ch:   Elizabeth     b 2-20-1829
      Jeremiah      b 7- 8-1830
      Joseph        b 3-11-1832
      William B     b 4-27-1834
      Rebecca E     b 12-31-1836
      Samuel        b 1-11-1839
      Jane M        b 9-20-1841
      Daniel W      b 12-28-1848

Joseph M    (b 4- 2-1827) s Joseph & Elizabeth
                                     (Musgrave)
     (m 9-21-1827  Short Creek Mtg, Ohio)
Rachel M (Terrel) (b 5- 1-1831) dt Clark & Mary
              (Jenkins) of Jefferson Co, Ohio

Joseph (rec in mbrp 1873)
     m 1st
- - - -
Ch:   Laurence
      Nathan E
     m 2nd
Sarah Ann (Hiatt) Hunt, wid of Benjamin Hunt of Westfield
     Mtg, & dt Enos & Lydia Hiatt
            b - - 1840  Hamilton Co, Ind
Ch:   Louis Bennett  b 3-24-1871  d 10- 5-1872
      Lydia C        b 7-24-1873
      Jessie L       b 2-17-1878

Mahlon    (s Benjamin & Mary (Price))
Sarah Jane (White) b 9-29-1831  N C    d 2-12-1853
          dt Thomas & Elizabeth
Ch:   Amanda A      b 10-22-1850
      Emery B       b 11- 2-1852

Rice Price  s Benjamin & Mary (Price)  chm mcd 1854
Eunice S (Henley)  (b 9- 1-1835) Rush Co, Ind
          dt Henry & Ruth (Morrow)
Ch:   Ella Jane

Warren M L
Caroline
Ch:   William       b 8-11-1858

William B   b 4-27-1834  s Joel & Catherine (Cox)
     m (10-26-1860)
Elvira T (Gause) b 11-11-1839 dt Solomon & Celia
Ch:   Delbert W     b 12-11-1861
      Mary E        b 2-14-1867
      Margaret B    b 10-24-1868
      S Bartlett    b 9-14-1871

DAVIS
Charles Henry b 7-11-1820  s John & Hannah (Anthony)
                   late of Cincinnati, O
          d 1- 7-1837 bur Rushville, Ind (reported by
                                  Walnut Ridge Mtg)

Isaac     b 4-24-1802  s Harmon & Hannah (Middleton)
Phebe (Brown) b 10-16-1811 dt James & Mary
Ch:   Louiza        b 5- 6-1834
      Mary          b - - - - -
      Ruth          b - - - - -

WALNUT RIDGE

DAVIS (Cont)
Jehu    (b 6-11-1814)  (s Harmon & Hannah (Middleton))
Rebecca (Brown)  (b 12-22-1802) dt James & Mary
Ch:   Oliver         b  8- 9-1833

Jesse    b 5-13-1812  (s William Sr & Elizabeth of
            Grayson Co, Va)  d 5-25-1848  bur Westland Mtg,
            res Hancock Co, Ind
Mariah (Coffin)  b 12-17-1815  dt Zachariah & Phebe
            (Starbuck)  (after the death of Jesse Davis,
            Mariah m 2nd Wm Cathon in 1849)
Ch:   Nancy Edna     b  1-15-1835  Henry Co, Ind
      Phebe Jane     b 10-16-1837  Hancock Co
         d 11-14-1838  bur Walnut Ridge Mtg, res Hancock Co
      Delfina        b  4-10-1839   (m - - - Hasket
         d 10-19-1862  bur Tipton, Ind)
      Martha Ann     b 10- 4-1841
      Mary E         b  9-29-1843
      Rhoda          b  8-21-1846      d 11-16-1847

(Joseph s Tristram & Love)  (b 5- 6-1797) (d 8-25-1844
         bur Salem Mtg (Silver Creek) Ind)
Judith (Macy)  b 6-18-1796  N Car  dt Timothy & Meraba
         d 12-27-1862  bur Little Blue River Mtg, res
         Shelby Co, Ind
Ch:   Eliza Ann      b  6- 7-1827
      Sally B        b 12-16-1828
      John M         b  2-12-1835

DENNIS
Benjamin F   b  3-10-1853  s William & Attilla
         m (11- 3-1873)
Marion E (Grose)  b  8- 7-1853  dt Abigail
Ch:   Raymond        b 10- 3-1875
      Leroy          b 11-19-1878
      Mary J         b  9- 9-1880
      Emma E         b  9-11-1882
      William        b  ?- 7-1884
      Atilla E       b 11- 4-1887
      Grace Olive    b 11- 4-1889

Edna     d  7-15-1845  bur Little Blue River Mtg, res Rush
                                                     Co, Ind

DIXON
Calvin       b 11-17-1842  s Phineas & Sarah (Stanley)
Mary M (Hastings)  b  6-21-1838  (dt Daniel & Kezia (Brown))
Ch:   Emery E        b  5- 3-1864    d 11- 3-1867
            bur Walnut Ridge Mtg, res Hancock Co
      Keziah J       b  2- 2-1866
      Rossey J       b  4-16-1867
      Letitia A      b 11- 7-1869
      Elmer P        b  5-25-1872
      Harley C       b - - - - -

Phineas      b  5-17-1813               d 10-13-1877
         s Joel & Mary        m (11-26-1835)
Sarah (Stanley)  b 6-14-1815            d 12-14-1878
         dt Abel & Rachel (Rayle)
Ch:   Calvin         b 11-17-1842
      Joel           b  1- 5-1845
      Naomi          b  7- 4-1853       d 10-10-1875
      Caleb          b  9- 4-1857

DRAPER
Elizabeth    d  9-22-1834  bur Walnut Ridge Mtg, res
                                Hancock Co, Ind

Thomas
Mary
Ch:   John E
      Marzilla
      Jeremiah T
      Joseph
      Margaret E

DRYSDALE
Henry F      b  9-10-1839  s William & Elizabeth
         m (3-14-1863)
Mary E (Davis)  b  9-29-1843  dt Jesse C & Mariah (Coffin)
Ch:   William F      b  9-22-1865   d 10- 5-1867
            bur Westland Mtg, res Hancock Co
      Mariah B       b  1-23-1867
      Henry O        b  3-14-1869

Gurney         b  5-14-1871
Jesse C        b  6- 1-1873
Edna Ann       b  5- 5-1877   d 11-23-1887

DUNBAR
dts of John & Sarah, both decd, of Randolph Co, N Car
      Sarah          b  6- 3-1828  N Car
      Eliza          b  5- 5-1847

EDGERTON
William      s Thomas & Mary
Hannah (Hastings)  b 8-28-1819  dt William & Sarah
Ch:   Mary Jane
      Rebecca Ann

ELLIOTT
David W      b  3- 8-1829  s Aaron & Mary (White)
         m (10- 9-1856)
Mary Ann (Hill)  b 12- 5-1832  dt Micajah & Sarah J
Ch:   Elihu Oliver   b  7-31-1857
      Micajah A      b  5- 3-1863
      Margaret Mary  b 12-22-1864   d 3-14-1891

Jonathan     b  8-31-1811  s Jacob & Mary (Peele)
Amelia (Huff)  b  8- 1-1815  dt John & Mary
Ch:   Eliza          b  7-23-1835  Hancock Co
      William B      b 10-13-1837
      Jacob C        b 10-20-1840

ENGLE
Joshua Sr  of Ohio
Hope - - - -  of Ohio     d 7-15-1847  bur Little Blue
         River Mtg, res Rush Co, Ind
Ch:   (to Walnut Ridge MM, Ind)
      Lucinda        b  5-19-1819
      Samuel         b  5-23-1824
      Elam           b  4-22-1831

FODREA
Benjamin D  b 12- 3-1841  Hamilton Co, Ind   s David &
                                                 Tamer
Sarah E (Taylor)  b  8- 3-1846  dt John & Nancy
Ch:   Horace J       b  5- 3-1865
      Ethel E        b 10-20-1866
      Rhoda A        b  3-14-1868
      Charles E      b  8-11-1871  d young
      John H         b  2-27-1874
      Nancy T        b  6- 1-1877
      Lillian C      b  2-20-1879

FOLGER
(Jethro s Latham & Matilda)
Mary (Barnard)  dt Asa & Huldah  d 12-26-1849 age 52-0-26
Ch:   Thomas S       b  2- 9-1822  Stokes Co, N Car
      Henry C        b  4-30-1826
      Lurany B       b  8- 5-1829
      Adaline  )
      Rufus    ) twins  b 7- 4-1833  Union Co, Ind
      Maria          b  3-17-1837  Rush Co

FORBIS
James M      b 10- 1-1849  s David M & Elizabeth
Sarah A (Haskett)  b 11-24-1853  dt Henry & Mariah (Coffin)
Ch:   H Leona        b  7- 6-1875
      Ada M          b 11-25-1877
      Eva            b  4-25-1881
      Henry H        b 12-29-1888

FOSTER
Anna Jane    b  4-17-1828  N Car  dt Caleb & Hannah (White)
         (m 1848 - - - - Ball)

- - - -?
Asenath - - - -  b  8-28-1814
Ch:   Anna M         b  3- 9-1847
      Huldah Emma    b  1- 3-1857

FOUST
Washington   b  5-10-1835  s Andrew & Malema?
         m (11-23-1863)
Josephine (Huggins)  b 4-27-1839  dt T - - & Sarah
Ch:   Eda O          b  9-13-1869

WALNUT RIDGE

FRIES - FRIEZE
Zachariah         b 8-26-1830   s Daniel & Mary
    m (10-27-1860)
Priscilla C (Hunt) b 11-19-1828  dt Libni & Jane (Hockett)
Ch:  Cynthia Ann       b 10- 4-1861
     Clara Ellen       b  7- 9-1863

FULGHAM
Woodward    b 4-30-1823 Wayne Co, N Car  d 9-22-1893
    s Michael & Sarah              (prob in Ohio)
    m (9-25-1845)
Anny (Stubbs)  b 3- 1-1827 Preble Co, Ohio  dt Joseph &
                                                Sarah

GARDNER
Isaac jr      (b 8-23-1787 N Car) s Isaac Sr & Eunice
                                              (Macy)
Dinah (Folger) (b 2-18-1788 N Car) (dt Latham & Matilda)
Ch:  (to Walnut Ridge Mtg)
     Asa F             b  2-13-1817  Ind
     Dorcas (the 2nd)  b  6-18-1819  Ind
     Sally             b 12- 4-1823  Ind

GATES
Ithamar       b  3-15-1851  s Isaac T & Jemima
Peninah (Haskett) b 10- 9-1856  dt Silas & Peninah
Ch:  Lora Bell        b  6-25-1884
     Harlan H         b  8- 6-1890

GAUSE
Eli D       (b 12-23-1807) (s Nathan & Mary (Ailes) of
                                  Preble Co, Ohio)
Lydia (Cooper) (dt Jacob & Elizabeth of Butler Co, O )
Ch:  (minors)
     Jacob           b - - - - -
     Mary E          b - - - - -
     Sarah T         b - - - - -
     Stephen         b - - - - -
     Amos            b  5-20-1852
     Lydia Ann       b - - - - -

Eli C
Martha Ann - - - -
Ch:  Samuel T        b  8-29-1855
         (m 8- 9-1877 to Amanda Hastings)

Mahlon        b 12- 7-1850  s Solomon & Celia (Stubbs)
    m (11- 5-1874)
Alice (Fort)  b 3- 8-1854  dt Benjamin & Eliza

Solomon       b  3-10-1813  s Nathan & Mary (Ailes)
Celia (Stubbs) b 4-10-1819  dt Joseph & Sarah
Ch:  Elvira T       b 11- 1-1839
     William        b  8- 6-1842    d 10-10-1885
     Rachel A       b  4-27-1848    d  3-17-1871
     Mahlon         b 12- 7-1850
     Margaret       b 12-28-1855    d  9-20-1856

GERBER
Isaac M       b  8-12-1846   s David
    m 1st
Anna M (Hill) b  1-17-1861              d 8-13-1888
    dt Nathan & Asenith
Ch:  Bertha         b  2- 3-1886
     Floyd          b  8-19-1887
    m 2nd  (5-11-1890)
Mary Ellen (Parnell) b  3- 5-1850  dt James & Catharine

GRAY
Albert H      b 10-10-1846  Rush Co, Ind
    s Jonathan, decd, & Sarah Ann (Hill)
    m (7-14-1867)
Mariah (Coffin) b 4- 5-1850  Hancock Co, Ind  dt John &
                                                Matilda
Ch:  Eddy A         b  7-31-1869  Rush Co, Ind
     Rosanna R      b  8-20-1872  Rush Co, Ind
     Ida M          b 11-26-1874    "    "   "

James Owen    b 10-30-1861  s Jonathan H & Sarah Ann
                                              (Hill)
Myrtle (Lacy) b  1-11-1866  dt Henry & Lavinia
Ch:  Marine Tacket   b 10-16-1884
     Blanche         b  1-22-1887

Jonathan H    b 9-30-1822  s James & Margaret, decd, of
    Shelby Co, Ind  d 3-15-1866  bur Walnut Ridge
    Mtg, res Rush Co
Sarah Ann (Hill) b 5-10-1827  dt Thomas & Tamar (Clark)
Ch:  Albert H        b 10-10-1846  Rush Co, Ind
     Mary Jane       b 11-30-1848
     Martha Ann      b 11- 3-1850  (m Josiah Taylor)
     Horace M        b  1-12-1853  (m Rosa Wirt)
     Phebe S         b  3-20-1855
     Bayard T        b  1-28-1857    d  9- 4-1858
                         bur Walnut Ridge Mtg
     Rosalie         b  7-28-1859
     James Owen      b 10-30-1861
     Lindley H       b 12-20-1863

GRIFFIN
James Cephas  b  1-31-1852   s - - - - & Elizabeth
    m (12- 1-1870)
Eliza (McDermott) b 1-30-1855  dt James & Caroline
Ch:  Minnie M        b 12-21-1871
     John W          b  8-22-1873
     Charles O       b  8-16-1875

HAINES
Levi  (s Levi & Elizabeth of Southland MM, Va & Columbiana
                                  Co, O)
    m 1st
Sarah (Hatcher)  b 4- 3-1792 Va (dt William & Mary from
                Goose Creek Mtg, Va & Columbiana Co, O )
Ch:  (to Indiana)
     Hannah          b  1-30-1818
     Hinchman        b  2- 9-1820
     William         b 12-22-1821
     Mary            b  1-27-1824
     Levi A          b 11-16-1826
     Sarah Ann       b - - - - - -
    m 2nd
Deborah W - - - -
Ch:  Enos
     Elizabeth
     Bennett

HALL
Price F       b  3- 4-1813  N Car  s Joshua & Charity
                                              (Fellow)
    m 1st
Rebecca (Mendenhall)
    m 2nd  (Ohio)
Elizabeth (Dibra) dt Daniel & Elizabeth of Ohio
Ch:  Martha Ann

HAMMER
Thomas B      b 12- 2-1848   s Newton & Charity
    m (3-17-1872)
Elmira (Craven) b 5-13-1847  dt Nathan & Zeriah
Ch:  Walter C        b  5-17-1875
     Blanche         b  7- 4-1877
     Chester         b  5-22-1885

HARRELL - HAROLD
Charles
Rachel (Lamb)  of N Car
Ch:  Levinia M       b 11- 1-1825
     Sarah Ann       b  3-16-1827
     Albertson L     b  3- 4-1830
     Mary N          b 10-14-1832    d 6-19-1852

John          b  7-18-1833  s Nathan & Betsy (Hawkins) of
                                  Hamilton Co, Ind
Sarah Ann - - - -  b  2-26-1842
Ch:  Cora Jane       b  8-29-1862
     Hannah Alice    b  9-12-1864
     Luella          b  3- 2-1866
     Lewis N         b  2-24-1868
     Henry E         b  1-10-1871

Lemuel        b  4-22-1839  s Nathan & Betsy (Hawkins) of
                                  Hamilton Co, Ind
Jane L (Hunt) b  3-19-1836  dt Libni & Jane (Hockett)
Ch:  Matilda Etta    b  8-22-1864
     Arthur O        b  5-20-1867
     Nathan Aldus    b  4-27-1872
     Harriett R      b  5-21-1880

**WALNUT RIDGE**

HASKETT
Daniel        b 3- 4-1818    s Nathan & Mary
Elizabeth (Griffin)

Delphina (Davis)    dt Jesse & Mariah Davis
    d 10-19-1862 age 23-5-29 bur at Tipton, Tipton Co, Ind

(Henry)
Mariah (Coffin) b 12-17-1815 dt Zachariah & Phebe (Starbuck)
Ch: Sarah Ann        b 11-24-1853
    John             b 8-15-1862  an adopted son

Paulina Lena  b 1-19-1870  dt Sarah Ann Hasket

Silas
Penninah (Hendricks) b 3- 9-1816 dt Solomon & Penninah
Ch: Eliza J          b 9- 4-1839
    Milly A          b 4-10-1843
    Ruth A           b 1-22-1844
    Margaret         b 4-11-1850
    Penninah         b 10- 9-1856

HASTINGS
Daniel C      b 2-19-1815           d 5-22-1893
    s William & Sarah
    m (10-22-1835)
Kezia (Brown) b 10-17-1817          d 10-30-1894
    dt Samuel & Margaret (Stubbs)
Ch: Samuel B        b 8-11-1836  Hancock Co, Ind
    Mary M          b 6-21-1838     "    "    "
    Rebecca         b 4- 5-1840
    William         b 2-20-1842
    Daniel )        b 1- 9-1845     d 1-30-1845
    Kezia  ) twins  b 1- 9-1845     d 1-24-1845
    Jesse           b 12-26-1845    d 1-15-1847
    Sarah J         b 12- 3-1847  Hancock Co, Ind
    David           b 5-17-1850
    Amanda          b 8-31-1855
    Eunice C        b 7- 1-1858

David         b 5-18-1850  s Daniel C & Keziah (Brown)
    m (2-20-1872)
Mary E (Reese) b 11-29-1852  dt John & Gulielma (Dennis)
Ch: John C          b 11-15-1874
    Clemma A        b 1- 2-1877
    Albert Owen     b 5- 6-1884

HAWORTH
Dillon    (b 11-18-1806 Tenn) (s Richard, decd, & Hannah
    (Whitlock) now Hannah Maxwell)
Sarah (Maudlin) (b 3-10-1809) (dt Benjamin & Leah)
Ch: James B         b 12-14-1826
    Benjamin        b 4-11-1828
    Solomon         b 8-28-1829
    Calvin          b - - -1831    d 1918 in N Dakota
    Cynthia A       b 5-10-1833
    Mariah          b 2- 5-1835
                    (m Albert Maxwell at Plainfield, Ind)

Richard jr (b 4-12-1809 Tenn) (s Richard Sr, decd &
    Hannah (Whitlock) now Hannah Maxwell)
Mary (Hill) b (12-27-1806) dt Benjamin & Mary (Jessop),
                                                both decd
Ch: Benjamin H
    James W

HEATHCOCK - HEDGECOCK
Samuel W   b 5-14-1835?
    m (1858 N Car)
Sarah (Pitts) b 1- 2-1832 N Car  dt James, decd, & 2nd
                                    w Rebecca (Moore)
Ch: Eliza           b 9-25-1859
    Nancy J         b 9-24-1864  Ind
    Joseph L        b 3-26-1869
    Flora B         b 5- 2-1871
    Lulla M         b 3-28-1873

HENBY
Elias      b 2-27-1813 Perquimans Co, N Car  s John decd,
                                        & Mary (Bogue)

    m 1st
Phebe (Symons)  b 4- 2-1813 Randolph Co, N Car  dt
    Abraham & Mary, both decd    d 3- 4-1852 bur
    Walnut Ridge Mtg, res Rush Co, Ind
Ch: Martha Ann      b 1-31-1840 Rush Co, Ind
    Margaret        b 8- 1-1842   d 9-12-1844 bur
                    Walnut Ridge Mtg
    John            b 7-20-1846
    Sarah           b 2-28-1849
    Phebe E         b 11-22-1851
    m 2nd  1853
Elizabeth (White) b 9- 7-1828 dt Bethuel C & Hannah
                d 3-13-1854            (Binford)
Ch: Elizabeth W     b 3- 1-1854
    m 3rd  1857
Elizabeth L (Henley) b (ca 1830) dt Elias, decd & Judith

(John, decd of N Car)
Mary (Bogue)
Ch: (to Ind)
    Willis
    Eli
    Elias           b 2-27-1813  N Car
    John jr
    Sarah           (m - - - - Layman)
    Ephraim B
    Martha          (m - - - - Coble)
    Mary            b 1- 6-1831
    William B       b 5-18-1833

John K       b 3- 8-1840  s Elijah & Elizabeth
Ruth Ann (Haskett) b 1-22-1844 dt Silas & Penninah
                                        (Hendricks)
Ch: Olive Jane      b 2-17-1870    d 1-24-1881
    Elijah A        b 5- 1-1872
    Miriam M        b 11-14-1876   d 2-17-1881
    Nora A          b 10-11-1878
    Silas           b - - - - - -
    Abbie           b - - - - - -

William B    b 5-18-1833 Perquimans Co, N Car
    m 1st           s John, decd & Mary (Bogue)
Katharine J (Brooks) b 9-28-1839 Rush Co, Ind
    dt Robert & Ellen             d 1-25-1879
Ch: Annie           b 5-17-1865
    Mary Ellen      b 2-11-1867
    Charles         b 5-27-1869
    Jennie M        b 10-14-1871
    Lydia A         b 10-11-1874   d 3-31-1878
                    bur Walnut Ridge Mtg
    Nora C          b 11-30-1878
    m 2nd
Mary Emily (Hill)

HENLEY
Charles    (b 7-17-1814) (s Joseph & Peninah (Morgan))
    m 1st
Tamar
Ch: Charles         b 11-27-1847
    Sarah           b 6-29-1850
    William C       b 4-21-1853
    Caroline        b 3-19-1855
    m 2nd  10-17-1868
Cynthia (Stanley)

Elias       b 8-11-1779  N Car  s John & Mary (Albertson)
    d 9-15-1848 age 67-1-4 bur Carthage Mtg, res
                                        Rush Co, Ind
    m 1st
Ann (Hubbard)  (b 3-29-1784 N Car) dt John & Martha
    (Sanders) (d 7-16-1807 N Car)
Ch: Mary A          b 10-23-1804
    m 2nd
Jane (Hubbard)  (b 7-24-1788 N Car) dt John & Martha
    (Sanders) (d 3- 7-1825 N Car)
Ch: (to Ind)
    Ann E           b 8-11-1808
    Jabez H         b 7-23-1810
    Judith          b 9- 6-1812  (m Joshua Lindley
                                  & rem to N Car)
    William H       b 10-30-1816
    Thomas Wilson   b 12-22-1818
    Martha Jane     b 10-26-1822
    Elias jr        b 1- 1-1825

## HENLEY (Cont)
### Elias (Cont)
m 3rd N Car
Rebecca (Allen) dt Samuel & Hannah  d N Car
m 4th (N Car)
Judith M - - - -?
Ch:  Elizabeth L      (b ca 1831)
     Jemima D         (b 5-20-1834)

Henry W    (b 1- 3-1830  Rush Co, Ind)  s Thomas &
                                          Abigail (Starbuck)
Avis Jane (Macy)  b 7-14-1838  dt James & Anna
                                          (Mendenhall)
Ch:  Franklin H        b - - - -    d 9-27-1863
     Lillie E          b 12-24-1861
     Nettie A          b 1-27-1863

Henry      b 11-19-1805  Randolph Co, N Car  s Joseph &
                                   Penninah (Morgan)
Ruth (Morrow)  b 4-19-1806   dt Mary
Ch:  Mary M            b 6-12-1831  Rush Co, Ind
     Penninah          b 2-12-1833
     Eunice S          b 9- 1-1835
     Jane              b 2- 9-1838  d 3- 2-1839  bur
                                     Walnut Ridge Mtg
     Sarah             b 5-23-1841  d 7-27-1842  bur
                                     Carthage Mtg
     Joseph            b 7-28-1843
     William Penn)
     Robert B     )twins b 8-11-1846

Hezekiah   b 2-11-1795  Randolph Co, N Car  s Henry &
                                   Martha (Sanders)
m 1st N Car
Priscilla (Ham)  b 6-12-1799  N Car  dt Hezekiah & Sarah
                 (Stuart)  d 10- 8-1823  Whitewater Mtg, Ind
Ch:  Martha S          b 2-25-1820  d 7- 9-1821 Ind
     Sarah H           b 7-16-1821
m 2nd (Lick Creek Mtg, Ind)
Ann (Maris) Lindley, wid of John T Lindley & dt Thomas &
   b 12-15-1809 Randolph Co, N Car       Jane Maris
Ch:  Cyrus             b 4-20-1841  Rush Co, Ind
     Jane              b 2-12-1844
     George            b 9- 9-1845
     Henry M           b 9-20-1847
     Alfred            b 12-29-1849 d 8-11-1851
     William           b 3-12-1852

Jesse      b 10-19-1818   s Joseph & Peninah (Morgan)
Abigail (Newby) b 10-30-1821 Randolph Co, N Car  dt Henry
                                                 & Sarah
Ch:  Enos              b 9- 6-1842
     Nancy Jane        b 1-18-1844
     Charles           b 9- 9-1845
     Sarah             b 8-20-1847
     Joseph Hill       b 5-12-1849
     Leland H          b 3-14-1854
     Phebe N           b 9-14-1855
     Pennina           b 10- 5-1858 d 8- 4-1860
                                     bur Carthage Mtg
     Mary              b - - - - -

John Milton  b 5-29-1833  s Thomas & Abigail (Starbuck)
Gulielma (Stanley) b 10-15-1839 dt Wyatt & Mary (Bundy),
                                                   decd
Ch:  Harvey G          b 4- 4-1860
     Walter C          b 9-15-1861

Joseph     b 6-16-1768  N Car  s John & Mary (Albertson)
             d 12-17-1860 age 92-6-1 bur Carthage Mtg, Ind
Penninah (Morgan) b 12-26-1779  N Car  dt Charles &
             Susannah (Nixon), both decd  d 4-30-1860 age
             80-4-4  bur Carthage Mtg, Ind
Ch:  Mary              b 2-14-1810  Randolph Co, N Car
     Nancy A           b 5-12-1812
     Charles           b 7-17-1814
     Micajah           b 9- 7-1816
     Jesse             b 10-19-1818
     Robert            b 3-17-1822

Micajah    b 9- 7-1816  s Joseph & Peninnah (Morgan)
Ruth Ann (Bentley) b 8-17-1825 Rush Co, Ind  dt Reuben
                                               & Sarah

Ch:  Reuben B          b 10-19-1845  Rush Co, Ind
     Caroline V        b 4-11-1847
     Lavina            b 1- 2-1849  d 6-16-1854
     Mary S            b 2- 3-185?
     Harlan H          b 3-27-1853
     Eva Ann           b 11- 5-1855
     Lenora            b 2- 7-1860

Reuben B   b 10-19-1845  s Micajah & Ruth Ann (Bentley)
Rachel (Young)  b 5-24-1844  dt Joseph & Sarah
Ch:  Herbert Oran      b 6-14-1873
     Sarah Lina        b 8-13-1875
     Lillian R         b 3-23-1878

Robert     b 3-17-1822  s Joseph & Penninah (Morgan)
Mary (Newby) b 8-18-1826  dt Henry & Sarah (Thornburgh)
Ch:  Hiram             b 3-28-1857
     Albert            b 4- 1-1859

Thomas     b 8-18-1803  Randolph Co, N Car  s Joseph &
                                   Penninah (Morgan)
Abigail (Starbuck)  b 8-2-1804  N Car  dt Thomas & 1st w
                                                 Eleanor
Ch:  Henry W           b 1- 3-1830  Rush Co, Ind
     Thomas Elwood     b 1- 7-1832
     John Milton       b 5-29-1833
     Ann               b 5-24-1835
     Jane              b 4-21-1837
     Eliza             b 10-11-1842
     Jason             b 6-28-1844
     Owen              b 10-20-1846

Thomas Elwood  b 1- 7-1832  s Thomas & Abigail (Starbuck)
Phebe (Newby)  b 9-20-1831  dt Henry & Sarah (Thornburgh)
Ch:  Penelope          b 7-18-1857
     John Clark        b 10-20-1859
     Abigail           b 8- 2-1862

Thomas W   b 12-22-1818  s Elias & Jane (Hubbard) decd
Hannah C (Williams)
Ch:  Rollin Edgar      b 10-10-1855
     Abigail Jane      b 6-20-1857
     Mary E            b 8- 2-1859

## HILL
Amos H     b 1- 4-1827  Randolph Co, Ind  s William &
                         Charity (Hawkins)    d 2-28-1896
Pennina (Thornburgh)  b 10-24-1826  Randolph Co, N Car
             dt Thomas & Sarah (Henley)
Ch:  Mary Alice        b 5- 6-1852
     Leora Ann         b 5- 9-1854
     William B         b 2- 6-1861
     Lucy J            b 6-11-1863

Cyrus E    b 6- 8-1850  s Nathan C & Asenath (Hunt)
  m (2-20-1872)
Gulielma (Butler)  b 5-5-1852  dt William & Priscilla
                                            (Dennis)
Ch:  Arthur O          b 1-11-1873  d 12-23-1888
     Nathan A          b 5-24-1874  d 8- 1-1874
     Mary M            b 11-18-1876
     William           b 10-11-1882
     Alice A           b 11-17-1887

Elisha  d 4-13-1854  bur Walnut Ridge Mtg, res Rush Co, Ind

Enos B     b 2-19-1842  s Thomas & Tamar (Clark)
  m (12-15-1866)
Ruth (Winslow)  b 5-30-1844            d 2-21-1873
             dt Henry & Anna
Ch:  Anna J            b 9-18-1867
     Albert T          b 1-27-1869
     Ernest            b 9-29-1871

Ezra S     b 12- 9-1851  s Nathan & Asenath (Hunt)
  m (10- 1-1874)
Louisa J (Brown)  b 6-13-1857  dt Robert & Martha Ann
                                             (Boyd)
Ch:  Elva B            b 11-27-1875  d 4-23-1877
                                     bur Walnut Ridge Mtg
     Effie A           b 9- 5-1879
     Ida L             b 11-14-1881

HILL (Cont)
Henby          b 11-11-1820  Ind  s Nathan & Elizabeth (Henby)
Lydia Jane (Thornburgh) b 12-12-1827 Highland Co, Ohio
                 dt Joel & Anna J (Willis)
Ch:  Mary Ann           b  5-18-1846
     Samuel             b  7- 5-1848
     Joel T             b  8- 6-1850
     Martha Jane        b  5- 3-1853

Henry B        b  7- 1-1807  Randolph Co, N Car
        s Samuel & Mary (Branson)
Lucretia (Henley) b  2- 4-1808  Randolph Co, N Car
                 dt Joseph & Peninnah (Morgan)
Ch:  William Penn       b 12-19-1830  Rush Co, Ind
     Allen              b 12-15-1832
     Jane               b  2-27-1835  d 10-14-1835
                         bur Walnut Ridge Mtg
     Thomas Elwood      b  9- 9-1836

John           b  2-20-1797  N Car  s Benjamin & Mary (Jessop)
        decd, d 10-20-1846  bur Walnut Ridge Mtg, res
        Rush Co
Dinah (Cox)    b (9- 4-1795  N Car)  dt Joseph & Dinah (Rich)
        d 11-30-1867  age 72-2-26 bur Walnut Ridge Mtg
Ch:  Joseph             b  2-19-1818  Wayne Co, Ind
     Mary  )            b  1- 8-1819  d young
     Martha) twins      b  1- 8-1819  d  2- 2-1884
        w of Robert Binford
     Benjamin C         b  4-19-1820  d  1-17-1837 bur
                         Walnut Ridge Mtg
     Nathan C           b 12- 3-1821
     Ervin              b  4-29-1823  d  3-19-1844
                         bur Walnut Ridge Mtg
     Sarah Ann          b  8- 7-1824
     William R          b  7-19-1827  Rush Co, d 9-27-1846
                         bur Walnut Ridge Mtg
     Miriam Jane        b  3-24-1831
     Mary Ann           b  2- 6-1836

John C         b  1- 7-1825  Wayne Co, Ind  s Thomas & Tamar
     m 1st                                           (Clark)
Mary Phelps  (d prior to 1859)
Ch:  (by 1st w)
     Allen              b  8-13-1853
     Thomas J           b  7-27-1855
Ch:  (by 2nd w)
     Luther G           b 11-23-1864? 1861? d 10-29-1894

John R         b  8-24-1834  s William & Charity (Hawkins)
Penninah (Henley) b  2-12-1833  dt Henry & Ruth (Morrow)
Ch:  Amos L             b  6- 1-1859
     Eunice             b 11-17-1860

John W         b  7-22-1857  s Nathan C & Asenath (Hunt)
Eunice (Jessop) b 11-14-1857  dt Jonathan & Mary
Ch:  Oden J             b 11-19-1880
     Elbert W           b  7-16-1883
     Howard W           b 12-18-1885
     Laura E            b  1-27-1888
     Mary Avis          b  4- 8-1889

Jonathan  b 11-21-1795  s Thomas & Ann (Haskett) both decd
        d  9-12-1844  age 48-9-21  bur Walnut Ridge Mtg,
        res Rush Co
Zilpha (Price) b  7-14-1799  Wayne Co, N Car
                 dt Rice, decd & Catharine (Bryant)
Ch:  Anna               b 10-15-1822  Rush Co, Ind
     Calvin             b  2- 1-1825  d  9- 8-1844
                         bur Walnut Ridge Mtg
     Robert             b  9- 7-1826  d  9- 6-1833
     Cynthia            b  1- 8-1829
     Matilda            b 12- 9-1830
     Elisha             b  6- 9-1833
     Joel               b  5-23-1835
     Tamar              b  4-19-1837  d  7- 8-1837
                         bur Walnut Ridge Mtg
     Henry B            b  4-12-1839

Joseph         b  2-19-1818  Wayne Co, Ind  s John & Dinah (Cox)
     m 1st
Penelope (Newby) b 10-23-1819  Randolph Co, N Car
                 dt Henry & Sarah  d  7- 3-1855  bur Walnut Ridge Mtg,
                 res Rush Co
     m 2nd
Rachel (Pussey)  dt Joel & Hannah, decd, of Hancock Co, Ind

Mary  d 12-13-1855  bur Carthage Mtg, res Rush Co, Ind

Micajah        b 10-26-1808  N Car  s Aaron & Mary
     m 1st
Naomi (Pugh)   d 10-18-1830  dt Thomas & Rebecca
     m 2nd
Sarah Jane (Mendenhall) b 12- 5-1807  N Car  dt James &
                                              Miriam (Hoggatt)
Ch:  (by 2nd w)
     Mary Ann           b 12- 5-1832
     Daniel M           b  6-14-1838
     James M            b 10- 5-1840
     Margaret F         b  6- 5-1843
     Sarah J            b  1-29-1845
     Micajah A          b  5-11-1847
     Rhoda M            b  2-21-1849

Milton  b  7-19-1822  Rush Co, Ind  s Thomas & Tamar (Clark)
Amanda (Hobbs)  b 12-29-1824  dt Samuel & Ruth
Ch:  Thomas C           b  7-15-1845  Rush Co, Ind
     Ruth               b 12-12-1846
     Sarah J            b  2-17-1848
     Susannah           b  5-29-1850
     Mary Ellen         b  4-18-1852
     Charles Summer     b 10-11-1854
     Emma               b  5-20-1857
     William H          b 12- 5-1859
     Irvin              b  1-19-1868

Nathan         b  9- 7-1788  s William & Margaret (of N Car)
Elizabeth (Henby) b  2-26-1793
Ch:  Robert             b  3- 2-1813  Hancock Co, Ind
     Mary               b  9-14-1814
     Henry              b  5- 1-1816
     Thomas             b 11-11-1817
     Sarah              b  7-13-1819
     Henby              b 11-11-1820
     Elizabeth          b  2-25-1823
     Nathan             b  4-14-1825
     William S          b 10-16-1827
     Samuel             b  5-20-1836  d  6-26-1836
                         bur Walnut Ridge Mtg
     James Hadley       b  6-15-1839

Nathan
Martha (Bundy)
Ch:  Elias              b  9-28-1853

Nathan C  b 12- 3-1821  Wayne Co, Ind  s John & Dinah
     m 1st                                        (Cox)
Ann Edwards
     m 2nd
Asenath (Hunt) b 11-22-1825  Clinton Co, Ohio
                 dt Ezra & Rebecca (Albertson)
Ch:  Cyrus E            b  6- 8-1850
     Ezra S             b 12- 9-1851
     Rebecca Jane       b 12- 3-1853
     John W             b  7-22-1857
     Anna M             b  1-17-1861

Owen S         b  2- 7-1837  s Thomas & Tamar (Clark)
     m (9-13-1866)
Melissa H (Bales) b  7-10-1841  dt Jno & Ann (Hoskins)

Robert         b  3- 2-1813  Wayne Co, Ind  s Nathan &
                                              Elizabeth (Henby)
Lydia (Binford) b 12-30-1810  Northampton Co, N Car
                 dt Joshua & Lydia
Ch:  Mary Jane          b  3- 2-1837  Hancock Co, Ind
     Joshua B           b  2- 8-1839
     Elizabeth          b  6-10-1841
     Cyrus              b 11-27-1843
     Susanna M          b  3- 1-1846
     Sarah              b  8-30-1848
     Lydia Ann          b  6- 7-1851

Samuel B  b  2-22-1832  s William & Charity (Hawkins)
     m 1st
Mary M (Henley) b  6-12-1831  Rush Co, Ind  dt of Henry
     & Ruth (Morrow)  d 8- 3-1874  bur Pleasant View
     Mtg, res Hancock Co, Ind
Ch:  Franklin           b  5-13-1855  d 11-12-1873
     bur Pleasant View Mtg, res Hancock Co
     Caroline           b  9-15-1858

**HILL** (Cont)
Ch: Samuel B & Mary M (Cont)
    Annie          b 2-29-1860
    Jane H         b 2- 1-1863   d 4-27-1863
        bur Pleasant View Mtg
    Henry H        b 8- 8-1864
    Lewis          b 8-17-1867   d 3-18-1869
        bur Pleasant View Mtg
    Ruth           b 2-15-1870
m 2nd (1875)
Mary R (Hadley) b 8-31-1843   d 3-18-1880
    dt Zeno & Rebecca Hadley
Ch:  Rowland H     b 6- 5-1878
m 3rd ( 1882)
Elizabeth (Jarrett) b 9- 5-1844  dt Daniel & Elizabeth
                                (Thomas)

Sarah Jane   d 4-30-1848  bur Carthage Mtg, res Rush Co,
                                      Ind

Thomas     b 11-30-1797 Randolph Co, N Car  d 5- 2-1879
    s Thomas & Ann (Haskett)
Tamar (Clark) b 6-17-1801 Orange Co, N Car  d 2-14-1890
    dt John & Sarah
Ch:  Milton        b 7-19-1822 Rush Co, Ind
    John Clark    b 1- 7-1825 Wayne Co, Ind
    Sarah Ann     b 5-10-1827 Rush Co, Ind
    Susannah      b 9-29-1829  d 3-31-1854
        (as the w of Joseph Phelps)
    Jane          b 7-23-1832 (d 2-21-1893 as 2nd w
        of Joseph Phelps)
    Albert        b 9-26-1835  d 8-13-1837
        bur Walnut Ridge Mtg
    Owen S        b 2- 7-1838
    Enos          b 2-19-1842

Thomas T   b 2-21-1825 N Car  s Aaron & Miriam
                          (Thornburgh)
Nancy (Davis)
Ch:  Benjamin C    b 1- 4-1848 N Car
    Miriam P      b 6-15-1850
    Eli B         b 4-19-1852
    Abby E        b 3-27-1856
    Asenath E     b 4-10-1858
    Margaret M    b 5- 2-1860

Thomas C   b 7-15-1845 Rush Co, Ind
        (s Milton & Amanda (Hobbs))
    m 1868
Esther (Parker) b 2-11-1847  d 8-28-1875
    dt Silas & Priscilla (Butler)
Ch:  Leonidas      b 9-19-1869
    Iona P        b 10-10-1871

Thomas     b 11-11-1817  s Nathan & Elizabeth (Henby)
                  of Hancock Co, Ind
    m in Ohio
Melissa (Hodson) b 6- 1-1824  dt Matthew & Hannah (Hunt)
                      of Clinton Co, Ohio
Ch:  Hannah E     b 3-23-1844 Ohio
    Sarah Ann    b 7-24-1846   "
    William W    b 11-30-1847  "
    Eunice C     b 9-11-1856

Ulyssius Grant b 1-16-1865 (s James Henley Hill, who
        served in the Civil War) (Ulyssius G's
        Aunt & Uncle, Alfred & Elizabeth (Hill)
        Hunt adopted him)

William     b 3-18-1802 N Car  s Benjamin & Mary
                            (Jessop)
    d 2-26-1861 bur Pleasant View Mtg, res Hancock Co,
                                      Ind
Charity (Hawkins) b 1-14-1794   d 3-16-1882
    dt Amos & Anna (Comer)
Ch:  Mary Ann     b 2-23-1823 Hancock Co, Ind
    Elizabeth C   b 11- 9-1824
    Amos H        b 1- 4-1827
    Martha J      b 7-10-1828
    Samuel B      b 2-22-1832
    John R        b 8-24-1834

William T
Martha ( - - - - ) from Greenwood MM, Ind

Ch:  Asenath      b 9-25-1853
    Samuel C     b 11-23-1857
    Junius Orlando  b 6- 3-1860

William B   b 2- 6-1861  s Amos H & Peninnah (Thornburgh)
    (d 12-29-1920 near Knightstown, Ind, but bur Walnut
    Ridge Mtg, Ind)
    m (2-17-1887)
Anna (Elliott) b 2-21-1861  dt Solomon & Penelope (Morris)
Ch:  Lois P        b 3- 7-1888
    Marjorie M    b 6- 1-1890

**HOAG**
Nathan C, a Minister from Ferrisburgh MM, Vt (b ca 10-13-
    1785) d 11-26-1854 age 69-1-13 bur Carthage Mtg,
    res Rush Co, Ind
Abigail R - - - - (b ca 2-28-1789) d 4-13-1855 at
    Whitewater MM, Ind, but bur at Carthage Mtg
    (Rush Co) age 66-1-16

**HOBBS**
Elisha   b 6- 8-1805 Randolph Co, N Car  s William &
    Priscilla (Coffin)
Deborah (Harvey) b 5-24-1809 Clinton Co, Ohio
    dt Isaac & Lydia
Ch:  Martha        b 10-28-1834 Rush Co, Ind
    Louisa        b 5-17-1837
    Harvey        b 10- 8-1839
    Anslem        b 10-22-1841
    Jason         b 11-10-1844

**HOCKETT - HOGGATT**
Joseph    (b 11- 2-1764 N Car) s William & Hannah (Beals)
    d 8- 1-1843 age 78-9-0 bur Walnut Ridge Mtg, res
    Rush Co, Ind (he had m Ann (Thornburgh) dt Joseph
    & Ann she had d 10-12-1832 & was bur East Fork Mtg
    in Clear Creek MM, Ohio)

Mahlon   b 5-27-1808  s Mahlon Sr & Sarah
    m 1st
Luzena S (Davis)  dt William & Elizabeth
    m 2nd (3- 4-1858)
Hannah (Barker) b 3-15-1818 dt Enoch & Elizabeth
Ch:  Sarah R
    Sybil A

**HODSON**
George  (b 1- 6-1763 in N Car)  s John & Mary
    m 1st (1784 in N Car)
Ann (Maris) (b 11-23-1766) (d 3-16-1806 N Car)
    dt John & Jane
Ch:  (Jane Ann    b 1-16-1797)
    m 2nd (1809 Ohio)
Mary (Nixon)  dt Peirce & Penninah

Gideon
Delphina - - - -
Ch:  Mary Rebecca   b 9- 4-1875

Matthew   b ( 7-29-1795 N Car)  s Jonathan & Mary
    (Frazier) d 4- 7-1874 bur Walnut Ridge
    Mtg, res Rush Co, Ind
    m in Ohio
(Hannah (Hunt) dt Asa & 2nd w, Sarah (Gifford))
    (b 1-31-1799)
Ch:  Sarah Ann    b 7-26-1822 Ohio
    Melissa      b 6- 1-1824  "
    John Milton   b - - - - -  "

**HOLDEN - HOLDING**
Thomas J   b 5-24-1847  s John & Lydia
    m (8-13-1871)
Emily (Bundy) b 8-19-1851 Hancock Co, Ind
    dt Nathan & Ann (Binford)
Ch:  Naomi         b 4-25-1872
    Samuel Raymond  b 12-29-1873
    Orpha         b 2-26-1876
    Charlotte     b 4- 3-1878

**HOLLINGSWORTH**
(James s of James Sr & Sarah of Union Co, Ind)
    (b 1-31-1799)
Lydia (Swain) (b 7-31-1808) dt Silvanus, decd & Miriam

WALNUT RIDGE

HOLLINGSWORTH (Cont)
Ch: James & Lydia
    Olive         b 4- 3-1829  Ind
    Miriam        b 6- 7-1831
    Stephen       b 11-22-1832
    Valentine     b 8-26-1834  Ohio
    Anderson      b - - - - -
    Benjamin      b - - - - -

HOSKINS
Albert M    s Joseph & Sarah Ann (Hodson)
Sarah Jane (Hastings) (b 12- 3-1847) dt Daniel & Kezia
                                                    (Brown)
Ch:  Minnie Viola    b 8-20-1868
     Emma C         b 4-22-1872

Cyrus E    s Joseph & Sarah Ann (Hodson)
Matilda (Hadley)
Ch:  Elias          b 2-22-1870  d 1870 bur Walnut
                                   Ridge Mtg
     Joycey        b 10-23-1872

Joseph          b 7- 7-1819    d (9-14-1892)
    s George & Mary, decd
    m (9-27-1841)
Sarah Ann (Hodson) b 7-26-1822 dt Matthew & Hannah
                                          (Hunt)
Ch:  Capitolia M     b - - - - -
     Josiah Lewis    b 3-25-1846
     Caroline M      b 5-15-1852  d (4- 5-1875)
     Albert M        b - - - - -
     Cyrus E         b - - - - -
     William         b - - - - -

Josiah Lewis  b 3-25-1846  s Joseph & Sarah Ann (Hodson)
    m (2-10-1876)
Mary L (Hadley) b 3-17-1850 Morgan Co, Ind dt Thomas
                                         & Lucinda (Macy)
Ch:  Anna B         b 11-11-1876
     Henry M        b 1- 4-1879

William    s Joseph & Sarah Ann (Hodson)
Margaret (- - - -)
Ch:  Edward L       b 1-13-1877
     Mollie         b - - - - -
     Charles        b - - - - -
     Jeptha         b - - - - -
     Jennie         b - - - - -

HUBBARD
(Hardy s Joseph & Ann) (b 12-23-1777 Mecklenburg Co, N
    Car) (wife Mary, decd)
Ch:  (Martha       b 2-19-1808  Pearson Co, N Car)
     (Susanna      b 2-10-1810  Guilford Co, N Car)
     (Mary         b 6-15-1816   "    "   "   " )

(John s John & Martha of N Car) (b 9-12-1796)
    (dis 1845 Deep River MM, N Car)
Abigail (Coffin) b 10-29-1805 dt Zacharius & Phebe
                                   (Starbuck)
Ch:  (to Walnut Ridge Mtg, Ind)
     Phebe C         b 4- 7-1827
     Mary H         b 11- 5-1834
     Abigail C      b 6-23-1837
     Thomas Dews     b 3- 9-1840
     William Gilman  b - - - - -

HUNNICUT
Elizabeth (Andrews) wid of Robert of Dinwiddie Co, Va,
    Upper MM & dt John & Sarah Andrews (Elizabeth
    (Andrews) Hunnicutt, m 2nd, 1843 to Nathan
    Overmann) (d prior to 1859)
Ch:  (to Walnut Ridge Mtg, Ind)
     Martha         b 8- 1-1816
     John A         b - - - - -
     Sarah Ann      b - - - - -
     Susannah       b - - - - -
     Mary Elizabeth  b - - - - -  (m 1st William White,
                                 m 2nd Joseph Binford)
     Robert E       b - - - - -

George E    s Ephraim & Margaret, decd, of Prince George
    m 1st                            Co, Va

Martha (Pussey) (b 7- 7-1816) dt Joel & Hannah
    (Faulkner) d 5- 3-1856 age 39-9-28 bur Walnut
    Ridge Mtg, res Rush Co
Ch:  William Penn    b 3-12-1840  Hancock Co, Ind
     Hannah P        b 4-23-1844
     Margaret P      b 6- 2-1846
     Mary Ann        b 7-28-1848
     Joel P          b 9-18-1850  d 9-25-1852
                       bur Walnut Ridge Mtg, res Rush Co
     Martha Jane     b 5- 8-1853  d 5-16-1854
     Rachel P        b 6- 8-1855
    m 2nd        9- 1-1858  Whitewater Mtg, Ind
Mary Ann (Barker) Winslow, a wid w/ch & dt Mathew &
    Ruth Barker from Scipio MM, N Y

James B of Hancock Co, Ind s Daniel & Mary, decd, from
    Upper MM, Va
    m (10-21-1840 New Garden MM, Ind)
Peninah (Bunton or Burton) dt James & Lydia, both decd
Ch:  William Henry   b - - - -

John A    (s Robert, decd, & Elizabeth (Andrews) now
         Elizabeth Overman w of Nathan Overman)
    m 1st
Hannah Ann (Davis) of Spiceland Mtg, Ind  d 2- 3-1854
Ch:  Delitha Ann     b 9-22-1849
     Charles E       b 5-17-1852  d 3-11-1854
     Hannah Ann     b 1-15-1854  d 3-19-1854
    m 2nd
Martha Jane (Bundy) b 5-16-1839 dt George, decd &
         Angelina of Hancock Co, Ind

William P  b 3-12-1840  Hancock Co, Ind  (s George E &
                                  1st w Martha (Pussey))
Rachel (- - - -)
Ch:  Anny           b 11-22-1877

HUNT
Alfred    b 7-25-1817 Clinton Co, Ohio  s Libni &
                                        Jane (Hockett)
Elizabeth (Hill)  b 2-25-1823 Rush Co dt Nathan &
                                        Elizabeth
Ch:  Joseph H        b 9-28-1842  Rush Co
     Eunice         b ?-13-1844
     Nathan         b 12-30-1845  d 1- 9-1846
                       bur Walnut Ridge Mtg
     Jesse L         b 4- 6-1847
     Ulyssius Grant Hill an adopted son and a nephew
       of Elizabeth (Hill) Hunt; a real son of James
       Henley Hill brother to Elizabeth, who had served
       in the Civil War  b 1-16-1865

Asa    b 5-25-1807 Highland Co, Ohio  s Asa Sr, decd
    & 2nd w Sarah (Gifford) Hunt
Lydia (Stephens)  b 6-17-1805 Guilford Co, N Car
    dt Gideon & Mary
Ch:  Mary Ann        b 3- 4-1831  Clinton Co, Ohio
     Levi Stephens   b 7-18-1833
     Cyrus Adison    b 7- 6-1836
     Gideon         b 5- 9-1840  Hancock Co, Ind
     Eunice         b 12-13-1845
     Jesse L         b 4- 6-1847

Asa    b 9-17-1828  s Ezra & Rebecca (Albertson)
Mildred (Newby)  b 9- 7-1828 dt Henry & Mary of Hancock
                                      Co, Ind
Ch:  Henry C         b 1-20-1851
     Lindley R       b 7-29-1857
     Alvin H         b 4- 7-1861
     Mary Alice      b 6-18-1863  d 3-11-1864

Benjamin  (b 6-27-1837)  (s Ezra & Rebecca (Albertson))
    d 3-mo-1866 bur Pleasant View Mtg, Ind
Sarah Ann (Hiatt)  b 1840 Hamilton Co, Ind  dt Enos
    & Lydia (after the death of Benjamin Hunt, Sarah
    Ann m 2nd to Joseph Cox at Westfield MM)
Ch:  Florence E      b 9-21-1860  Rush Co
     Nathan E        b 6-22-1862
     Asa Ludora      b 10-29-1865

Clarissa    d 11- 4-1868  (no parents' name recorded)

WALNUT RIDGE

## HUNT (Cont)
Ezra  (b 7-17-1797)  s Asa Sr & 2nd w Sarah (Gifford)
    d 9-29-1861 age 64-2-12 bur Walnut Ridge Mtg,
    res Rush Co
Rebecca (Albertson) b 11-29-1799 dt Pheraby Albertson
    Griffin of Ohio
    d 8-20-1863 age 63-8-22 bur Pleasant View Mtg,
    Ind
Ch:  James        b 8-18-1822  d 10- 9-1864
                    res near Charlottesville, Ind
     Ascenath     b 11-22-1825
     Asa          b 9-17-1828
     Priscilla    b - - - - -
     Benjamin     b 6-27-1837

Hannuel  b 1-18-1804  Ohio  s Asa Sr & 2nd w Sarah
  m 1st                           (Gifford)
Eleanor (Newby) b 8-13-1805  d 1-26-1835
  dt William & Sarah (Overman)
Ch:  Sarah        b 8-12-1824
     Ascenath     b 6-15-1827
     Ezra         b 1-12-1829
     Nancy Jane   b 1-11-1832
  m 2nd
Lucinda (Dickey) b 1-14-1815 dt Nimrod & Ann of
    Newberry Mtg, Ohio
Ch:  James D      b 1-19-1836
     Cyrus O      b 2-11-1838
     Josiah N     b 9-14-1839
     Eleanor      b 7- 9-1842
     Libni        b 7-10-1844
     Ann          b 10- 7-1846
     Hannah H    b 4- 7-1851

John  b 3-13-1823  s Libni & Jane (Hockett)
Sarah (- - - -)  b 7-23-1827
Ch:  Isaac N      b 7-12-1848
     Lucinda      b 10-26-1850
     William H    b 7-16-1852
     Mary A       b 12-31-1853
     Daniel A     b 10-22-1855  d 7-16-1867
                    bur Walnut Ridge Mtg res Rush Co
     Alfred T     b 10-10-1857
     Oliver M     b 3- 6-1860
     Levi Alvin   b 8-22-1862  d 4- 4-1863
                    bur Walnut Ridge Mtg

Joseph H  b 9-28-1842  s Alfred & Elizabeth (Hill)
  m (12- 5-1866)
Elizabeth H (Brown) b 12-24-1847 dt Robert & Martha A
                                 (Boyd)
Ch:  Elmer E      b 9-17-1870

Joseph R  b 1- 6-1834  s Libni & Jane (Hockett)
  m (12-22-1870)
Deborah A (Williams)
Ch:  Edith J      b 10-19-1871
     Esther       b 2- 8-1874

Libni  b 8- 4-1791  N Car  s Asa & 1st w Priscilla
  (Coffin)  d 1- 8-1875  bur Walnut Ridge Mtg,
  res Rush Co, Ind
Jane (Hockett) b 11- 9-1792 dt Joseph & Ann (Thornburgh)
Ch:  Alfred       b 7-25-1817
     Ann          b 7-10-1820
     Miriam       b 9-18-1821
     John        b 3-13-1823
     Priscilla    b 11-19-1828
     Isaac        b 3-16-1830  d 12-25-1837
                    bur Walnut Ridge Mtg, res Rush Co
     Rebecca      b 6- 5-1832
     Joseph R     b 1- 6-1834
     Jane L       b 3-19-1836

Sarah (Gifford) wid of Asa Hunt of Ohio & dt Jonathan &
  Eunice (Beard) Gifford of N Car  b 4-28-1776 N Car
  d 3-21-1844 age 67-10-23 bur Walnut Ridge Mtg,
  res Rush Co, Ind

William A   (parents' names not recorded)
  d 12-14-1861 age 19-0-14 bur Pleasant View Mtg

## JESSOP
Jacob  b 12- 5-1824  s Jonathan Sr & Elizabeth (Hill)
Rebecca (Brown) b 4-30-1831 dt William & Celia of
  Hancock Co, Ind
Ch:  John         b 7-17-1854
     Caroline     b 1-27-1857
     Thomas H     b 11- 8-1858
     Elwood       b 5-12-1862
     Olive  )     b 10-13-1865
     Orlando) twins b 10-13-1865
     Eliza        b 1- 1-1868

Jane  b 8-17-1813  d 3-15-1890 (she may be
  the mother of Lewis Jessop) IBB (rec in mbrp 1865)

Jonathan Sr  (b 8- 6-1785 N Car)  s Jacob & Rachel (Cook)
  d 3-25-1860 age 74-7-7 bur Carthage Mtg, res
  Rush Co, Ind
Elizabeth (Hill)  b 8- 2-1789 N Car dt Thomas & Ann
                              (Hasket)
Ch:  Mary         b 2- 5-1810
     Penninah     b 10-16-1812
     Thomas       b 9- 8-1814
     Lydia        b 12-22-1816
     Nancy        b 8-27-1818
     Miriam       b 8-27-1820
     Jonathan jr   b 3- 2-1822
     Jacob        b 12- 5-1824
     Huldah       b 10- 4-1826
     Mathew       b 3- 6-1830
     William      b 4- 9-1832  d 1-13-1834
                    bur Walnut Ridge Mtg, res Rush Co
     Samuel       b 8-27-1834

Jonathan jr  b 3- 2-1822  s Jonathan & Elizabeth (Hill)
Mary (Bundy) b 4- 4-1828 dt Josiah & Mary (Morris)
Ch:  Josiah B     b 1-29-1850
     Levi         b 10-23-1851
     Susannah     b 12-23-1853
     Elizabeth    b 9-25-1855
     Eunice       b 11-14-1857
     Mary Ann     b 2-20-1863

Levi  b 10-23-1851  s Jonathan & Mary (Bundy)
  m ( 1-22-1872)
Mary Ann (Binford) b 3-23-1852 dt Joseph & 1st w
  Elizabeth C (Hill)
Ch:  Iola         b 3-27-1883

Lewis  (rec in mbrp 1865)
Achsah (- - - -)
Ch:  Nancy Jane   b 10-25-1865
     Elldora      b 1- 8-1868
     Mary A       b 8-20-1869 d 12-15-1870
                    bur Western Grove Mtg, res Hancock
                                    Co
     Susannah E   b 5- 8-1871

Mathew  b 3- 6-1830  (s Jonathan Sr & Elizabeth
                                   (Hill))
Laurinda (Coffin) b 7-28-1833 Rush Co, Ind (dt Moses &
                                        Phebe)
Ch:  Sibern       b 5- 6-1859
     Sylvester    b 12-22-1863
     Jonathan     b 8-15-1865

Thomas  b 9- 8-1814  Wayne Co, Ind  (s Jonathan Sr
  & Elizabeth (Hill))
Rebecca (Binford) b 12- 2-1814 Northampton Co, N Car
  dt Micajah & Sarah (Patterson) decd
Ch:  Anna B       b 11-10-1833  Rush Co, Ind
     Sarah        b 5- 1-1837   "   "   "
     Elizabeth    b 10-11-1842
     Micajah B    b 10-11-1848

## JOHNSON
Richard W  s Zachariah decd & w Susannah (called Sookey)
  m 1st                           of Va
Edna (Butler) (b 3-16-1813) dt Stephen & Matilda, decd
  (d 12- 5-1836 bur Silver Creek MM, Ind)
Ch:  William S    b 4-15-1835
  m 2nd
Lucinda (Watkins) of Goshen Mtg, Ohio

# WALNUT RIDGE

## JOHNSON (Cont)
Ch: Richard & Lucinda
- John     b 6- 3-1847
- Mary J     b 11- 4-1848
- Albert     b 4-17-1851

(Zachariah decd of Western Branch Mtg, Isle of Wight Co, Va)
Susannah (called Sookey) d 8-15-1861 aged about 75 yrs bur Carthage Mtg, res Rush Co, Ind
Ch: (to Walnut Ridge Mtg, Ind)
- Almeda     b - - - -
- Richard W     b - - - -

## JONES
Isaac M     (rec in mbrp 1868)
Martha A (Hunt)
Ch:
- Annie Leora     b 10-30-1868 d 8- 2-1870 bur Walnut Ridge Mtg
- Alma E     b 7- 9-1870
- Alvin Carey     b 8-13-1878

Lemuel R
Anna M
Ch: May Emily     b 11-10-1873

## KEARNS
O Winbern
Mary (Brown)
Ch:
- Abigail Leona     b 8-12-1865
- Orval J     b 8- 2-1867
- William     b 6-10-1870

## KELLEY
William (late of Marlborough MM, Ohio) d 3-19-1868 aged about 40 years bur Walnut Ridge Mtg, res Hancock Co, Ind

## KENDALL
Charles A b 8- 6-1857 s Dennis & Rebecca J
Huldah (Bundy) b 9-29-1855 dt Henry & Mary
Ch:
- Orris D     b 9- 1-1878 d 7-23-1879
- Nora M     b 12- 9-1879

## KENWORTHY
William (b 1-19-1816 Westland Mtg, Pa) s Amos & Mary (Miller)
Asenath (Patterson) (b ca 9-17-1818) dt Jared & Angelina (Binford) d 9-18-1843 age 25-0-1 bur Walnut Ridge Mtg, res Rush Co
Ch:
- Sarah
- James
- Joseph     d 9-14-1842 age 1-0-24 bur Walnut Ridge Mtg

## LACY
(Josiah s Peter & Susanna (Price)) (b 1- 5-1803 N Car)
(Ruth (Gordon) dt Charles & Ruth (Williams)) (b 5-17-1807 N Car)
Ch:
- Lowring     b - - - -
- Phebe     b - - - -
- Lavina     b - - - -

Pearson b 10-14-1796 s Peter & Susanna (Price) d (ca 1844)
Margaret (Morris) b 1-12-1805 dt Jesse & Mary (Moore) of Wayne Co, Ind (after the death of Pearson Lacy, Margaret m 2nd to William Butler in 1846, in 1854 she m 3rd to Abner Blair)
Ch:
- John M     b 8-17-1825 d young
- Mary Jane     b 8-24-1826 Richmond, Ind
- Sarahann     b 5-12-1828 " "
- Eunice M     b 5- 1-1830 Rush Co, Ind
- Jonathan P     b 7-12-1832
- Susannah P     b 7- 9-1834 d 4- 9-1841 bur Walnut Ridge Mtg, res Rush Co
- Jesse M     b 1- 5-1837
- Asenath     b 9-22-1838
- Margaret     b 4-19-1841
- Phebe     b 6- 9-1843

## LAMB
Caleb b 4-29-1799 Perquimans Co, N Car s Restore & Milicent (Winslow)
Sarah (Nixon) b 9-13-1800 Sutton Creek MM, N Car dt Nathan decd, & 2nd w Margaret (Bagley)
Ch:
- Benjamin B     b 12- 7-1823
- John Anderson     b 7- 7-1826
- Edmond     b 7- 4-1828
- David     b 1-17-1831
- Margaret     b 8-13-1833
- Jonathan     b 2-22-1836

Joseph from Sugar River Mtg, Ind
Lydia (Marsh) b 4- 5-1818 (dt Elias & Edith (Townsend))
Ch:
- Sarah T     b 6-28-1848 d 7-26-1870 bur Western Grove Mtg, Hancock, Co
- Edith M     b 12-27-1849
- Fanny     b 12- 2-1851
- Eliza     b 5-26-1853
- Martha Ann     b 6-14-1855 d 7-27-1859
- Elias Robert     b 5-18-1857
- Lydia E     b 2-15-1860
- Joseph W     b 1-23-1863

Phineas from Piney Woods, N Car altm 3 mo 1835 Duck Creek Mtg, Ind
Huldah (Bundy) b 1-17-1811 N Car dt Josiah & 1st w Huldah (Jones) decd (d prior to 1862)
Ch:
- Martha     b 3-22-1836
- Mary     b 2-13-1840
- Phebe     b - - - -
- Emily     b - - - -

Stephen b 8-20-1786 (s Restore & Milicent (Winslow)) d 10-10-1865 bur Walnut Ridge Mtg, res Hancock Co
Miriam (Copeland) b 10- 2-1784 N Car dt Josiah & Esther (Griffin) d 4- 9-1872 bur Western Grove Mtg, res Hancock Co
Ch:
- Josiah     b 3-14-1813
- Timothy     b 11-28-1814
- Milicent     b 8-25-1819
- Elizabeth     b 12- 1-1822
- Esther     b 5- 7-1826

## LATIMORE
(- - - - - -)
Ella (- - - -) b 10-14-1853
Ch: Susan A     b 9- 7-1872

## LEDWELL
John W b 5-15-1842 s Elwood & Martha
Margaret E (Thornburgh) b 1- 8-1845 Randolph Co, N Car dt Winslow & L - - - -
Ch:
- Martha H     b 5- 1-1866
- Mary A     b 10-13-1868
- Luella     b 10-12-1869
- Rosina     b 12-11-1870
- Delphina     b 9-17-1872
- Anna J     b 9-27-1873

## LEONARD
Jesse
Belinda (Worth) b N Car dt William & 1st w Phebe (Barnard)
Ch:
- Lutitia     b - - - -
- Joseph     b - - -1844 d 1-24-1860 bur Little Blue River Mtg
- Hiram     b - - - -
- Anna Marie     b - - - -

## LINDLEY
John T b 11-20-1831 Orange Co, N Car s John T, decd & Ann (Maris) now Ann Henley, w of Hezekiah Henley

William C b 2-14-1836 (from Deep Creek MM, N Car) m ( 6-29-1859)
Melissa F (Johnson) b 1- ?-1839 (dt David & Frusanna) of Iredell Co, N Car
Ch:
- Thomas H     b 10-29-1861
- William F     b 7-22-1863 Iredell Co, N Car
- Sarah K     b 8- ?-1865
- David J     b 8- ?-1867 Hancock Co, Ind
- Martha J     b 4- ?-1869 d 6-24-1877 Westland Mtg
- Delfina M     b 8- ?-1871

WALNUT RIDGE

LINEBACK
Lewis L          b 12-29-1838   s Benjamin & Agnes
   m (1- 7-1864)
Nancy A (Woods)  b 9-22-1848    dt Conrad & Susan
Ch:   Oliver M            b  9-31-1864
      Sarah M             b 11-22-1866
      Margaret E          b  2-18-1869
      Hattie A            b 11- 2-1872  d 12-25-1874
         bur Walnut Ridge Mtg, res Rush Co
      William Wesley      b  9-18-1874
      Franklin C          b  3-15-1877
      Eldora J            b  1-27-1879


LOUDENBACK
Joseph A
Malinda (- - - -)
Ch:   Daniel              b  3-19-1849
     (Elizabeth E         b - - - - - )


LOW
Nathan B         b  2-26-1840   Randolph Co, N Car
                 s William & Grace (Hammond)


McCANN
James M          b  8-11-1854   s William
Emily Alice (Miner)  b 3- 6-1857  dt Thomas & Cyrena
Ch:   Iris Pearl          b  9- 3-1882
      Grace               b  9-13-1883
      Hazel L             b  5-27-1888


MACY
(Francis B s Stephen & Rebecca (Barnard))
  (b 9-18-1810 Montgomery Co, Ohio)
(Huldah (Hunt) dt Isom decd & Margaret (Bundy))
  (b 5-28-1807 Guilford Co, N Car)
Ch:   Rebecca Ann         b  6-20-1835
      Margaret Jane       b 10- 9-1836
      John Lilburn        b  9-27-1839
      Loretta Maria       b  3- 2-1842

Henry H          b  5-31-1801   Guilford Co, N Car
                 s Thaddeus, decd & Katharine (White)
Penninah (Jessop)  b 9-16-1811  Wayne Co, Ind
                 dt Jonah & Elizabeth (Hill)
Ch:   Ann H               b  7-11-1831  Rush Co, Ind
      Catharine           b  6-20-1836  d  9- 9-1839
         bur Walnut Ridge Mtg
      Elizabeth           b  7-11-1838  d 11-19-1839
         bur Walnut Ridge Mtg
      William P           b  8-22-1840
      Isaac H             b 11-27-1842
      Lydia               b  2- 5-1845
      Huldah              b  6-17-1847

John M           b 12-28-1806   d  5-10-1887
                 s Stephen & Rebecca (Barnard)
   m 1st (5- 7-1840)
Betsey Ann (White)  b 1- 6-1806  d 12-20-1853
                 dt Thomas & Jemima (Johnson)
Ch:   Henrietta M         b  3-23-1841
      Margaret W          b 11-16-1842
      William A           b  5- 4-1845
   m 2nd (12-20-1855)
Lydia (Bell)     b  3-11-1806   d  4-15-1891
                 dt John & Lydia (Symons)
Ch:   Josephine M         b 10-25-1856  d  5- 1-1894
         as wife of Clarkson Parker

Reuben           b  7-27-1812   Randolph Co, N Car
                 s William & Mary (Barnard)
Maria (Gardner)  b  4-13-1815   Guilford Co, N Car
                 dt Isaac jr & Dinah (Folger)
Ch:   Delphina            b  8-14-1837  Union Co, Ind
         d  7-27-1838  bur Little Blue River Mtg, res
         Rush Co
      Orlando             b  9-22-1839  d  9- 2-1839
         Little Blue River Mtg, res Rush Co
      Evander             b  7- 2-1840  Rush Co
      Lutittia            b  8-29-1842    "      "

Thomas  (b 11- 9-1780 N Car) (s Henry Sr & 1st w Sarah
   from Nantucket to N Car)  d  4-18-1855  bur
   (Rush Co or Shelby Co)
Rebecca (Barnard)  (b 7-12-1784 N Car)  dt Tristram &
   Margaret from Nantucket Mtg  d  2-16-1862  bur
   Little Blue River Mtg, res Shelby Co, Ind

Ch:   (to Indiana)
      Joseph W            b  1-30-1811  N Car
      Frederick           b  2- 6-1813
      Tristram Barnard    b 11-22-1815
      Lucinda Swain       b  1-23-1820
      Thomas Clarkson     b  3-26-1823

Tristram Barnard  b 11-22-1815  N Car  s Thomas & Rebecca
                                              (Barnard)
Dorcas (Gardner) the 2nd  b  6- 8-1819
      dt of Isaac jr & Dinah (Folger)
Ch:   Erasmus D           b  1-10-1842
      Lysander            b  5- 8-1844
      Byron               b 11-24-1846
      Isaac G             b 12- 3-1849
      Thomas B            b  4- 7-1854
      Orlando C           b  8- 2-1858


MARSH
Elias   (b ca 1785-1786)  s Elias Sr & Martha, both decd,
   of Woodbridge, Rahway & Plainfield MM, N J
   d  2- 9-1871  aged about 85 yrs, bur Westland Mtg,
   Hancock Co, Ind
   m 1st
Edith (Townsend)  (b ca 12- 7-1791)  dt Benjamin & Jemima
   of Washington Co, Pa  d  8- 5-1837  age 45-7-29
   bur Walnut Ridge Mtg, res Hancock Co, Ind
Ch:   Robert              b  2-25-1811
      Martha              b  9- 5-1812  Columbiana Co, Ohio
      William             b  2- 1-1817  Carrol Co, Ohio
      Lydia               b  4- 5-1818
      Jesse               b 10-11-1820  Columbiana Co, Ohio
      Sabina T            b  6-12-1823  Carrol Co, Ohio
      Fanny               b  6-13-1827
      Joseph              b  5- 8-1830  d 10-11-1837
         bur Walnut Ridge Mtg
   m 2nd (4-24-1839)
Elizabeth (Hawkins) Boyd  wid of Adam Boyd & dt of Amos,
   decd & Anna (Comer) Hawkins of Wayne Co, Ind
   (d ca 1844-1845)
   m 3rd
Margaret (- - - -) Osborn, wid of Thomas Osborn of Ohio,
   w/ch (b ca 3-10-1796)  d 12-15-1866  bur Westland
   Mtg, res Hancock Co, Ind

Jesse   b 10-11-1820  Columbiana Co, Ohio  s Elias & 1st
                 w Edith (Townsend)
Catharine (Osborn)  b  7- 1-1827  Ohio  dt Thomas decd, &
   Margaret, now Margaret Marsh the 3rd w of Elias
                                              Marsh
Ch:   Elias               b  1- 5-1848
      Margaret            b  9-28-1849
      George W            b  1-23-1852

William          b  2- 1-1817  s Elias & 1st w Edith (Townsend)
   d 10-12-1861  age 44-8-11  bur Westland Mtg, res
   Hancock Co, Ind
Martha A (Chappell)  b  5- 6-1816  Southampton Co, Va
                 dt Thomas L & Martha, decd
Ch:   Thomas L C          b  5-21-1839
      Edith T             b  8-29-1842  d  9-13-1848
         bur Westland Mtg
      William P           b  2-18-1844
      Elias J  )          b 11- 9-1846
      Margaret E)         b 11- 9-1846  twins
      Benjamin F          b 10-15-1856

(Martha (Chappell) wid of William Marsh m 2nd, 1866 to
   James Brown & gct Sugar Plain MM, Ind)

MARSHALL
Jesse   b  7-21-1803  Green Co, Tenn  s Abram & Martha
                                              (Doan)
Mary (Pickering)  b  5-10-1805  Green Co, Tenn  dt Ellis
                 & Deborah
Ch:   James               b  1-16-1829  Green Co, Tenn
      William             b  9-18-1830    "    "    "
      Calvin              b  8-17-1832  Indiana
      Levi                b  6-22-1834
      Eli                 b  8-14-1836  d  3- 4-1844
         res Hancock Co, Ind
      Nathaniel           b  6-14-1838  d young
      Jared               b 12-31-1839
      Ellis               b  3-20-1841  d 10-28-1841
         res Hancock Co

WALNUT RIDGE

## MARSHALL (Cont)
Ch: Jesse & Mary (Cont)
  Nathan    b 11-14-1844
  Rachel    b 11- 2-1846

Abigail S b 2-12-1848 dt of David & Zilinda from Wabash MM, Ind

## MAUDLIN
John  b 1-18-1806 s Benjamin & Leah (Copeland)
Rebecca (Elliott) b 1-31-1803 dt Exum & Catharine (Lamb)
Ch: Mark    b 9- 6-1826
  Nathan   b 12-23-1827
  Exum    b 10-11-1829
  Eliza Ann   b 2- 1-1831
  Catherine Jane  b 11-26-1832
  Sarah    b 3-12-1835

## MENDENHALL
James C b 11- 3-1817 s Richard & Polly, decd of Hendricks Co, Ind
Mary (Brown) b 4- 2-1819 dt Samuel & Margaret (Stubbs)
Ch: Robert   b 6-11-1843
  Jane    b 2-16-1844
  Thomas   b 9-22-1845
  Zeno    b 8- 3-1848

Samuel H b 3-18-1842 s Elihu E & 1st w Ann (Hill) decd

Stephen G b 4-26-1803 Guilford Co, N Car
  s Nathan & Phebe (Haworth)
Sarah (Albertson) b 6-23-1805 N Car dt Phineas & Rebecca (White)
Ch: Catharine Rebecca b 11-22-1828 Guilford Co, N Car
  Nathan   b 3-29-1832 Washington Co, Ind
  Albert W   b 11-12-1835 Butler Co, Ohio
  Elizabeth   b 9- 4-1838 Rush Co, Ind
  Bartlet   b 1- 8-1841 " " "

## MILLER
George  b 12- 5-1865 s of James & Eucebia

## MILLIKIN
William P b 10-17-1835 N Car
Rebecca J (Spencer) b 6-25-1839 N Car (dt Joseph & Rachel his 2nd w)
Ch: Sarah   b 9- 3-1860 N Car
  Quincy Monroe b 10- 6-1862
  Rachel V  b 3-30-1865
  Joseph   b - - - - -
  Benjamin  b - - - - -
  William jr  b - - - - -

## MOON
George Hodson b 4-18-1823 Ohio s Jeremiah & Rachel (Nixon)
Susanna (Osborn) b 4- 2-1821 dt Thomas, decd & Margaret (now Margaret Marsh, the 3rd w of Elias Marsh)
Ch: Thomas O  b 6- 9-1843
  Jeremiah  b 3-21-1845

Jeremiah b 1-15-1800 Tenn s Daniel & Ruth of Clinton Co, Ohio
Rachel (Nixon) b 11- 5-1803 dt George & Mary (Hodgson) of Highland Co, Ohio
Ch: Mary   b 11- 5-1820 Ohio
  George H  b 4-18-1823
  Ann   b 4-28-1826
  Jane   b 3-20-1829
  Elizabeth  b 2-27-1831
  Nixon   b 10-14-1833
  Havilah  b 8-28-1837
  Rachel   b - - - - -
  Ruth   b - - - - -

## MOORE
James  b 11-16-1828 s Silas & Sally
m (3- 4-1852)
Elizabeth (Myers) b 4- 5-1836 dt Joseph & Elizabeth

Joseph  s Mordecai & Rachel of Hamilton Co, Ind
Deborah (Chappell) b 3-29-1825 dt Thomas L & 2nd w Margaret

---

Ch: Thomas C  b 9- 4-1840
  John   b 6-12-1842
  William  b 10-29-1843
  Silas   b 9-15-1846
  Mary E  b 8- 5-1850
  Finley M  b 5-28-18??

Joseph B b 9-26-1837 s Samuel & Mary (Bundy)
Ruth Ann (Bundy) b 10-26-1846 dt Nathan & Ann (Binford)
Ch: Oliver Morton b 10-25-1866

Joshua b 12- 2-1826 s Samuel jr & 1st w Rebecca
m (4- 2-1857)
Mary (Bufkin) b 6- 5-1837 dt Samuel & Catharine
Ch: Lanorah Alice b 4-23-1858 d 9-15-1858
  Lindley Murry b 6-30-1861
  Emma Annie b 4-20-1865

Samuel jr s Samuel & Margaret (White) both decd, of Perquimans Co, N C
m 1st
Rebecca (- - - -) d 6- 7-1837 age 33-1-25 bur Walnut Ridge Mtg, res Rush Co, Ind
Ch: Joshua  b 12- 2-1826
  Jesse W  b 10-18-1828 d 12- 4-1829
  Mary   b 8- 4-1830
  Margaret  b 8-11-1832
  Sarah   b 8- 7-1834
m 2nd
Ann (Binford) b 6- 7-1793 d 2- 9-1888
 dt Chappel & Martha, both decd of Prince George Co, Va

Samuel b 10- 1-1808 N Car s Jesse & Mary (Morris)
           Anderson
Mary (Bundy) b 2- 6-1806 N Car
Ch: Abigail  b 7- 2-1830
  Rebecca  b 11-30-1831
  Morris   b 7-18-1833
  John B  b 10-22-1835
  Joseph B  b 9-26-1837
  Huldah Atwater b 3-10-1840
  Samuel jr  b 4-23-1843
  Eli J   b 1-31-1846

## MORGAN
Benjamin (b 7- 1-1772 Pasquotank Co, N Car) s Charles & Susanna, both decd d 11- 1-1859 age 87-4-0 bur Carthage Mtg, res Rush Co, Ind
m 1st
Naomi (White) (b 7-24-1773) dt Isaac & Catharine (d 7- 8-1811 bur Whitewater Mtg, Ind)
Ch: (Micajah  b 11-10-1798)
  (Charles  b 2-18-1801)
  (Isaac   b 12-31-1803)
  (Katharine b 8-10-1806 d 1808)
  (Susan  b 11- 6-1809)
m 2nd
Elizabeth (Johnson) (b 2-28-1782) dt James & Ruth decd of N Car (d 3-13-1821 bur West Union MM, Ind)
Ch: Hannah  b 4-24-1814
m 3rd
Ruth (Moffitt) (b 9-16-1780) dt Hugh, decd & Hannah of Wayne Co, Ind (d 1- 9-1852 Milford MM, Ind)
m 4th
Sarah (Hill)

## MORRIS
Jesse b 9-24-1819 N Car s Joshua & Mary
m 1st
Joanna (Cammack) b 12- 7-1821 dt John & Jane
d 5-27-1847 bur Carthage Mtg, res Rush Co, Ind
Ch: Henry  b 7-10-1842 Rush Co, Ind
  Mary Jane b 3-11-1842
  Joshua  b 6-20-1845 d 3-17-1846
    bur Carthage Mtg, res Rush Co
m 2nd
Sarah A (Macy) (a wid w/ch) dt Henry M & Rachel (- - - -)
Ch: Robert  b 12- 8-1855 Rush Co
  Abigail  b 10-10-1857

John b 4-17-1815 N Car s Joshua & Mary
Martha (Chappell) b 10-11-1806 N Car dt Gideon & Mary (Squires)

WALNUT RIDGE

MORRIS (Cont)
Ch: John & Martha (Cont)
    Francis Morgan    b 1-29-1838 Wayne Co, Ind
    David W    b 8-19-1840 Rush Co
    Caleb J    b 6-28-1842
    Anna    b 3-16-1844

NELSON
Thomas B    b 3-29-1839 s Christian & Luttetia
  m ( 6- 5-1862)
Phebe (Ball) b 3-11-1842
Ch: Catharine S    b 6- 4-1867
    Thomas C    b 12-25-1871
    James O    b 9- 5-1874
    Henry H    b 4- 1-1877
    John O    b 2-25-1880

NEWBY
Henry    b 8- 8-1795 Randolph Co, N Car
  s Joseph, decd & Penelope (Henley)
Sarah (Thornburgh) b 8-22-1800 N Car dt Thomas &
    Miriam (Winslow) (d prior to 1856)
Ch: Penelope    b 10-23-1819 Randolph Co, N Car
    Abigail    b 10-30-1821
    Milly    b 4-20-1824
    Mary    b 8-18-1826
    William    b 10-28-1828 d 6-19-1855
        bur Carthage Mtg, res Rush Co, Ind
    Phebe    b 9-20-1831
    Thomas T    b 5-16-1834 Rush Co, Ind
    Henry jr    b 2- 5-1837 d 5-30-1855
        bur Carthage Mtg
    Daniel H    b 5-16-1839 d 8-15-1847
    Ruth W    b 5-18-1843 d 8-15-1846
        bur Carthage Mtg, res Rush Co

Henry (may be s Thomas & Mary (Bogue) of Driftwood Mtg,
  Ind 1816)
Mary (- - - -) d 2-19-1853 age 43-6-10 bur Westland
  Mtg, res Hancock Co, Ind
Ch: Mildred    b 9- 7-1828
    William    b 7-15-1831
    Nathan    b 9-10-1834
    Matilda    b 12-22-1842

John H    b 5-27-1808 Randolph Co, N Car
  s Joseph, decd & Penelope (Henley)
Harriet (White) b 8- 2-1813 Guilford Co, N Car
  dt Robert & Rebecca (d 7- 2-1886 Hamilton
    Co, Ind)
Ch: Rebecca W    b 3- 7-1835 Rush Co
    Micah    b 12-18-1837
    Franklin    b 9-15-1839

NEWSOM
Jabez H    b 12-25-1830 s Luke & 1st w Elizabeth (Hill)
Margaret (Cox) b 12- 7-1834 dt Aaron & 1st w Jemima
  (Draper) of Blue River Mtg
Ch: Charles H    b 10-26-1855 d 1-14-1856
        bur Carthage Mtg, res Rush Co
    Oliver M    b 12-17-1856
    Milton D    b 5-30-1858 d 9-28-1858
        bur Carthage Mtg
    Anna J    b 1-11-1861
    Mary E    b 5- 5-1862

Luke    b 12-15-1802 s Ransom & Sarah
  m 1st
Elizabeth (Hill) b 9-20-1800 dt Jesse & Mary (Pritchard)
  d 7-17-1833 bur Walnut Ridge Mtg
Ch: Martha    b 7-24-1826
    Henry    b 9-22-1828 d 11-24-1850
        bur Carthage Mtg, res Rush Co, Ind
    Jabez H    b 12-25-1830
    Elizabeth    b 7-16-1833 d 8- 3-1833
  m 2nd
Cynthia (Bulla) rec in mbrp Marlborough Mtg, N Car 1830
  dt John & Margaret, both decd
Ch: Elizabeth B    b 9-18-1835
    Mary Ann    b 8- 8-1837
    George W    b 2-28-1839 d 10-27-1860
        bur Carthage Mtg, res Rush Co
    John Gurney    b 9- 2-1840
    Allen W    b 6- 7-1842

    William P    b 9-21-1843
    Thomas C    b 4- 8-1845
    Daniel W    b 9- 3-1847
    Allen W    b 1-31-1849
    Charles H    b 11- 9-1850 d 7-19-1854
        bur Carthage Mtg
    Melissa    b 2-18-1852

NICHOLS
(Thomas s Eramus & Elizabeth (Stanley) of Hendricks Co,
  Ind) (d 1- 7-1863 bur Mill Creek Mtg Cemetery,
  Hendricks Co, Ind)
Jane (Brown) b 5-26-1828 Preble Co, Ohio dt Samuel &
  Margaret (Stubbs) of Rush Co, Ind
Ch: Margaret    b - - - - -
    Elizabeth    b - - - - -
    Rachel    b 2-11-1856 Walnut Ridge Mtg,
        Rush Co
    Anna    b 3-26-1860 d 1-12-1863
        bur Mill Creek Mtg, Hendricks Co,
        Ind

NICHOLSON
Josiah    b 9-18-1848 s Nathan & Miriam (Hunt) decd
  m (9-22-1868)
Esther Ann (Butler) b 4-18-1846 dt Edward & Sarah A
        (Lacy)
Ch: Arminta J    b 7-18-1869 d 11- 2-1870
    Nathan Owen    b 12-22-1870 d 1-30-1871
    Edward Elsworth)b 7-18-1872
    Effie Ethel)twins b 7-18-1872 d 4-20-1879
    Naomi May    b 9-22-1874
    Elva Gertrude    b 12-19-1876
    Lemuel Earl    b 1- 6-1879
    Ernest Raymond    b 9-19-1880

Milton    b 12- 3-1858 s Nathan & Asenath (Cloud)
  m (4- 8-1880)
Annette (Cox) b 4- 4-1862 dt Cyrus & Mary
Ch: Bertha M    b 12- 4-1882
    Lillian A    b 11-22-1885

Nathan Parker b 7-21-1816 Perquimans Co, N Car
  s Nathan Sr & Penninah (Parker) d 3- 8-1868
  m 1st
Miriam (Hunt) b 9-18-1821 Clinton Co, Ohio dt Libni &
  Jane (Hockett) d 10- 5-1848 bur Walnut Ridge Mtg,
  res Hancock Co, Ind
Ch: Cynthia    b 3- 5-1839 Rush Co, Ind
    Jane    b 1- 2-1841
    Anna    b 1-25-1844 d 11-19-1844
    Mary E    b 10-23-1845
    Josiah    b 9-28-1848
  m 2nd (10- 2-1850)
Asenath (Cloud) b 9-25-1822 d 5-14-1878 dt Joel & Anna
Ch: Emily    b 10-27-1851 Rush Co d 7-22-1854
    Louisa    b 1-20-1854
    Milton    b 12- 3-1858
    Hiram P    b 10-12-1861

Penninah (Parker) wid of Nathan of Suttons Creek Mtg,
  N Car & dt of John Parker b 7-22-1781 N Car
  d 9-18-1857 age 77 yrs bur Walnut Ridge Mtg,
  res Rush Co
Ch: (to Indiana with their mother)
    Mary    b 1-24-1812 d 8-13-1837
        bur Walnut Ridge Mtg
    George    b 4- 1-1814
    Nathan Parker    b 7-21-1816

OSBORN
(Thomas decd of Springfield MM, Ohio)
Margaret (- - - -) d 12-15-1866 age 70-9-5 bur Westland
  Mtg, res Hancock Co, Ind (Margaret d as the 3rd w
  of Elias Marsh)
Ch: (by 1st husb)
    Susanna    b 4- 2-1821
    Catharine    b 7- 1-1827
    Mary    b 6-26-1829
    Margaret jr    b 3-20-1833
    Thomas jr    b 3-24-1835

WALNUT RIDGE

## OUTLAND
David           (b 11-3-1818)  s John & Martha
Margaret A (Copeland)  dt Henry & Dorothe of Northampton
        Co, N Car
Ch:     Ann C               b 11-15-1844
        John Edwin          b  3-30-1846
        James Henry         b 12-10-1847
        David Amos          b 12-12-1851
        Martitia I          b 12- 3-1853
        Mahlon H            b  7-21-1856
        Joseph              b - - - - -

William P       (s John & Martha)  d 2-24-1868  age 53-3-8
        bur Walnut Ridge Mtg, res Rush Co
Mary Annis (- - - -) of Western Branch MM, Va
Ch:     Benjamin Porter     b 9- 8-1845  d 7- 5-1849
        Mary Annis jr       b 8-17-1847  N Car
        Josiah B            b 5- 8-1849
        William Thomas      b 1-12-1851
        Oliver Winfield     b 1-17-1853
        Francis Nicholson   b 1- 2-1855  d 12-30-1860
                            bur Walnut Ridge Mtg, res Rush Co,
                                                            Ind
        David Clark         b 2-13-1861

## OVERMAN
(Nathan  s Isaac & Sarah, decd, of N Car)  (b 2- 8-1777)
        (dis Walnut Ridge Mtg, Ind 1844)
    m 2nd
Elizabeth (Andrews) Hunnicut, wid of Robert Hunnicutt
    & dt John & Sarah Andrews of Upper MM, Va
    (d prior to 1859)
Ch:     (minor ch of 1st w)
        Joseph
        Charles
        Elizabeth
        John

## PARKER
Clarkson        b 7- 9-1853  s John P & Miriam (Hill)
    m (10-25-1883)
Josephine (Macy)  b 10-25-1856    d 5- 1-1894
        dt John & Lydia (Bell)
Ch:     Howard C            b  2-15-1886
        Edna J              b  5-11-1888  d 10-12-1890

Eli G           b 8-22-1844  s James B & Hannah B (Gause)
    m (9- 6-1865)
Mary M (Thomas)  b 2-27-1845  dt Francis W & Rebecca
                                              (Corbett)
Ch:     Viola Alice         b  6-15-1866
        Lydia Francis       b  3-18-1869
        James V W           b 10-28-1870
        Marietta            b 12-29-1872

Elwood          b 3-25-1838  s William & Almeda (Johnson)
        d 6-17-1873  bur Walnut Ridge Mtg, Ind
    m (5- 2-1866)
Rachel (Johnson) b 6-16-1836  dt James & Sarah V of
        Wayne Co, Ind
Ch:     Fidelia C           b 10-19-1869

James B         b 9- 8-1819  s Samuel & Rebecca (Binford)
Hannah B (Gause)  (b 4-25-1822 Ohio)  dt Eli & Martha
                                              (Pierce)
Ch:     Eli G               b  8-22-1844  Hancock Co
        Rebecca             b 10-29-1847
        Charles Owen        b  6- 4-1859

John P          b 4-16-1823  s Samuel & Rebecca (Binford)
Miriam J (Hill)  b 3-24-1831  dt John & Dinah (Cox)
Ch:     Clarkson            b  7- 9-1853
        Almira              b  8-12-1854
        Benjamin F          b  7-13-1856
        Alice               b  1- 1-1858
        Samuel Murray       b  8-25-1860
        Hannah Ann          b  9- 5-1862  d 3- 9-1863
                            bur Walnut Ridge Mtg
        John Oscar          b  8-25-1874

Lindley M       b 3-25-1853  s Silas & Priscilla (Butler)
    m (10-16-1879)
Louisa C (Winslow)  b 2-12-1862  dt John H & Susan
Ch:     Walter S            b 11- 4-1880
        Curtis W            b 10-22-1883
        Lenora              b  7-20-1886

Martha (Peele) wid of Josiah late of Rich Square MM, N Car
        (b 3-17-1769 N C)  (d April 1850 Spiceland MM, Ind)
Ch:     (to Walnut Ridge Mtg, Ind with their mother)
        Martha jr           b 12-29-1809
        Phebe May           b  1-14-1813

Olney T         b 4- 2-1858  s Silas & Priscilla (Butler)
    m (11-20-1879)
Rilda A (Cox)  b 3-18-1855  dt Benjamin & Alice
Ch:     Ethel               b 11-17-1880
        Silas Farrell       b  5- 4-1883

Silas           (b 9-29-1817 Northampton Co, N Car)
        s Samuel & Rebecca (Binford)   d 8-27-1884
Priscilla (Butler)  (b 9- 4-1820 Clinton Co, Ohio)
        d 7-22-1889    dt William & Esther
Ch:     Oliver S            b 8-12-1839  d 2-12-1844
                            bur Walnut Ridge Mtg
        Lydia Ann           b 1- 7-1842  d 4-20-1865
        Rebecca             b 2-17-1845  d 1-19-1846
                            bur Walnut Ridge Mtg
        Esther B            b 2-11-1847  d 8-28-1875
        Louisa              b 3- 7-1849
        Samuel W            b 4-30-1851
        Lindley M           b 3-25-1853
        Albert S            b 7-20-1855
        Olney T             b 4- 2-1858
        Mary                b 8-26-1860
        Charles M           b 9-19-1862

Samuel          b 2-20-1793  s Josiah, decd & Martha (Peele)
        of Northampton Co, N Car  d 6-13-1847  age
        54-3-23  bur Walnut Ridge Mtg, res Rush Co
Rebecca (Binford)  b 6- 4-1792 N Car  d 6-27-1872
        dt James & Hannah (Crew)
Ch:     Silas               b  9-29-1817  Rush Co
        James B             b  9- 8-1819
        John P              b  4-16-1823
        Josiah              b  9-17-1827  d 8- 7-1846
                            bur Walnut Ridge Mtg
        Hannah Jane         b  2-17-1830
        Martha Ann          b  3- 5-1832
        Angelina            b 10-26-1834

Samuel Murray  b 8-25-1860  s John P & Miriam (Hill)
    m (10- 8-1890)
Margaret (Morris)  b 10- 8-1863  dt Jonathan & Patience
                                              (Hall)
Ch:     Miriam Patience  b 11-23-1891

Samuel W        b 4-30-1851  s Silas & Priscilla (Butler)
    m (2-27-1876)
Susannah H (Phelps)  b 5-18-1854  dt Joseph & Jane (Hill)
Ch:     Leroy               b 12-10-1877
        Mary L              b 10- 5-1883

(Thomas, decd  s Josiah, decd & Martha (Peele))
        (d 11-14-1845 Northampton Co, N Car)
(Rebecca (Copeland)  dt Eli & Ann)  (b 1-15-1793)
        (d ca 1852 to 1854, Ind)
Ch:     (with mother to Indiana)
        Sarah Ann           b  1-15-1825
        Asenath             b  5- 4-1830
        Isabella            b 12- 8-1832
        Elizabeth           b  3-17-1835

William         b 12- 5-1800  s Josiah, decd & Martha (Peele)
        of Northampton Co, N Car & Ind
Almeda (Johnson)  dt Zachariah, decd, late of Isle of
        Wight Co, Va & his w "Sookey" (Susanna) of
        Milford MM, & Carthage Mtg, Ind
Ch:     Albert L            b  8-22-1833  Rush Co, Ind
        Elizabeth Ann       b  8-11-1835
        Elwood              b  3-25-1838
        Robert J            b  3-19-1840
        Susanna             b  7- 1-1842
        Charles W           b  6- 9-1846
        Alfred              b 10-24-1853

## PATTEN
Joseph          b 7-10-1823  Ohio  s John & Rebecca (Stubbs)
Rachel (Macy)  b 11- 3-1829  Union Co, Ind
        dt James & Anna (Mendenhall)
Ch:     Eunice A            b  1-21-1848
        John W              b  2-17-1850  d 3-12-1852
                            bur Hopewell Mtg, Ind

WALNUT RIDGE

PATTEN (Cont)
Ch: Joseph & Rachel (Cont)
    James A        b - - - -
    Thomas C      b - - - -
    Lewis L       b - - - -
    Corella J     b - - - -

PATTERSON
Amasa  s (Jared & Angelina (Binford) of Belmont Co, Ohio)
    b  N Car   d 7-30-1862 age 55-5-18 bur Walnut
    Ridge Mtg, res Rush Co
Lydia (Starbuck)  b 2-12-1807 N Car (dt George &
    Elizabeth (Starbuck) Starbuck of Belmont Co, Ohio)
Ch:  James          b  2- 4-1834  Ohio
    Eliza Ann      b  7-14-1837
    Rachel         b  1-18-1840
    Mary Jane      b  6- 1-1843  Rush Co, Ind

Elizabeth (Ladd) wid of William of Va, N Car & Ohio &
    dt Garrard & Sarah Ladd  b 7- 5-1762 (ca Surry
    Co, Va)   d 12-30-1841 bur Walnut Ridge Mtg,
    (Rush Co, Ind)  (Elizabeth was the mother of
    Jared Patterson)

James B  s Jared & Angelina (Binford)
    m Ohio
Elizabeth (Starbuck)  dt George & Elizabeth (Starbuck)
    Starbuck of Belmont Co, Ohio
Ch:  Jared          b  9-25-1839  d 10-15-1843
                           bur Walnut Ridge Mtg, res Rush
                           Co, Ind

James      b 2- 4-1834  Ohio  s Amasa & Lydia
    m  1857                               (Starbuck)
Elizabeth Ann (Parker) b 8-11-1835 Rush Co, Ind
    dt William & Almeda (Johnson)
Ch:  Enos           b   5-13-1858
    Amasa          b  12-20-1860
    William Edgar    b   6-19-1862
    Susannah Eudora  b   3- 7-1864
    George          b - - - - -

Jared (Garrard)  (b 4- 2-1786 N Car) s William &
    Elizabeth (Ladd) from Va  d 4-26-1857 bur
    Walnut Ridge Mtg, res Rush Co, Ind
Angelina (Binford) b 7-13-1785 dt James & Hannah (Crew)
Ch:  Amasa          b (ca     1807)
    James B        b (ca     1809)
    Elihu          b - - - - -   d 10-14-1843
                      age 27-0-25 bur Walnut Ridge Mtg
    Asenath        b (ca 9-17-1818)
    Eliza          b  10-10-1820
    Mary           b - - - - -   d 9- 7-1843
                      age 20-0-16 bur Walnut Ridge Mtg
    Amos           b  3-22-1826

PEARSON
Daniel     b 6-16-1852 s Enoch & Rachel (Brown)
    m (7- 4-1872)
Elizabeth E (Loudenback)
Ch:  Louisa E       b  7-20-1873
    Frank L        b  8-16-1877

Enoch      b 6-18-1822 Wayne Co, Ind  s Peter &
    Eunice (Hastings) of Henry Co, Ind
Rachel (Brown) b 1-10-1823 dt Samuel & Margaret (Stubbs)
Ch:  Nathan         b  1- 4-1843  d 3- 7-1846
                         bur Spiceland Mtg
    Mary Jane      b  9-11-1845
    Martin         b  8- 6-1848
    Samuel         b  1- 8-1851  d 8- 9-1851
                         bur Honey Creek Mtg
    Daniel         b  6-16-1852
    David          b  1-28-1855
    Sarah          b  9-20-1857
    Peter          b  7-23-1860
    Thomas         b  4-22-1863

Martin     b 8- 6-1848 s Enoch & Rachel (Brown)
    m (11- 7-1872)
Phebe (Cook) b 10-10-1851 dt Thomas & Ann
Ch:  Leora          b  1-31-1874
    Bertha A       b  8-30-1876
    Charles        b  12-24-1879

    Stella May     b  6-20-1882
    Ada M          b  10- 9-1885
    Bessie)        b  6-12-1888  d 7-14-1888
    Jessie) twins   b  6-12-1888

Peter       b 7-23-1860 s Enoch & Rachel (Brown)
Amanda (Cook) b 10-19-1852 dt Thomas & Ann
    d 7-m0-1890
Ch:  Jennie Pearl   b  7-29-1888
    Lura A         b  5-22-1890
    m 2nd (10-25-1891)
Nellie J (Starbuck) b 9- 3-1874 dt Henry & Rebecca

PERISHO
Nathan     b 9-29-1800 N Car s Joshua & Elizabeth
    m 1st                          (Griffin)
Mary (Lamb) dt Joseph, decd & Lovey (Smith)
    d 4-17-1835 about 40 yrs of age bur Walnut
    Ridge Mtg, res Hancock Co, Ind
Ch:  Mary Elma      b  12-26-1824  N Car
    John C         b  7-11-1826
    Joshua Morris   b  3- 5-1829
    Martha Ann     b  1-18-1831
    Margaret J     b  3-21-1833
    m 2nd
Sarah M (Chappell) b 4-29-1808 Southampton Co, Va
    dt Thomas L & 1st w, Martha, both now decd
Ch:  Susannah       b  3- 4-1840
    Elizabeth      b  8- 6-1842
    Nathan )       b  1-28-1844
    Sarah M) twins b 1-28-1844  d 4- 3-1845
                  bur Westland Mtg, Hancock Co

PHELPS
(Jonathan)  b 1- 4-1801    d 1-17-1876
           bur Carthage Mtg (Rush Co, Ind)
    m 1st
Susannah (- - - -)
Ch:  Joseph         b  2-28-1829
    Mary ?         b - - - - -
    m 2nd
Mary A (Henley) b 10-23-1804 wid of John Winslow (w/ch)
    Winslow           & dt Elias & Ann Henley
    d 10-10-1893

Joseph     b 2-28-1829 s Jonathan & Susannah, decd
    m 1st
Susannah (Hill) b 9-29-1829 dt Thomas & Tamar (Clark)
    d 3-31-1854 bur Walnut Ridge Mtg, res Rush Co,
                                      Ind
Ch:  Susannah H     b  3-18-1854
    m 2nd
Jane (Hill) b 7-23-1832    d 2-21-1893
    dt Thomas & Tamar (Clark)
Ch:  Mary P         b  10-28-1856
    Sarah          b  5-31-1850
    Enos E         b  2-28-1862
    Thomas H       b  3- 4-1869  d 3- 3-1870
    Olive E        b  11-29-1871

PICKERING
Phineas    b 7-30-1807 Tenn (s Ellis & Deborah)
Rachel (Wright)  b 5- 9-1806 Tenn dt Jesse & Ann
                                (Clearwater)
Ch:  Nancy          b  1-12-1829  Hancock Co, Ind
    Ellis          b  8-18-1830
    Jesse          b  7-20-1832
    Deborah        b  8- 3-1834
    Rebecca        b  2-27-1836
    John           b  9- 7-1839
    Enos           b  8-22-1841
    Mary           b  9-22-1843
    Phineas jr     b  1-28-1846

PIKE
Himelus    b 7-20-1822 s Nathan & 1st w Mary (Newby)
                                      decd
Ruth (Cloud) b 12- 7-1824
Ch:  Levi           b  2-24-1853  d 1854 Spiceland Mtg
    Luzena         b  2-17-1856
    Emma Jane      b  5-12-1860

WALNUT RIDGE

## PIKE (Cont)
(William) (b 9-30-1782) (s Nathan & Elizabeth (Williams)
both decd) (d ca 1844 in Walnut Ridge Mtg)
m 1st
(Phebe (Macy) ) (d 12-15-1812 Clear Creek MM, Ohio)
m 2nd
Lucy (Butler) (b 10-26-1795 Upper River MM, Va) dt
Samuel & Ursula (d 6-16-1839 Clear Creek MM,
Ohio)
Ch: (by 2nd w, to Walnut Ridge Mtg with father)
Mary                b 10- 1-1824
Ann                 b  5- 9-1826
Hannah              b  7-22-1828
Samuel              b  7-29-1830
William jr          b  3-16-1834
Eli                 b  9- 3-1836
m 3rd
Phebe (Coffin) dt Aaron & 1st w Mary, decd b 4-15-1791
(Phebe (Coffin) Pike m 2nd  6-25-1846 to Jesse
Weisner of Henry Co, Ind)

## PITTS
Henry    b 8-29-1841 (s James, decd, & Rebecca (Moore))
Mary P (Butler) b 7-14-1845 dt Joseph J & Eliza
                                        (Patterson)
Ch: Eliza Ellen         b  8- 4-1864
    Amy J               b 12-28-1866

(James, decd, s John & Elizabeth of Stokes Co, N Car)
    (b 5- 7-1791)
m 2nd
Rebecca (Moore) b 11-26-1803 dt Jesse & Mary (Morris)
    d 9- 7-1873 age 69-9-11 bur Walnut Ridge Mtg,
    res Rush Co, Ind
Ch: (to Indiana with their mother)
    Jesse M             b  7-20-1829
    Mary                b  9- 4-1830
    Sarah               b  1- 2-1832
    Samuel C            b  9- 3-1833
    James               b  9-22-1836
    Jonathan B          b  3-25-1838
    Daniel W            b  1-10-1840
    Henry               b  8-29-1841

James jr b 9-22-1836 s James Sr, decd & Rebecca (Moore)
Rebecca M (White) dt Phineas & Lydia, both decd
    b - - - -                    d      1891
Ch: Ada Frances         b  9-20-1864
    Charles M           b  3-19-1866
    Martha              b  3- 4-1868
    William             b  - - - - -

Jesse b 7-20-1829 s James decd & Rebecca (Moore)
m 1st
Esther J (White) b    N Car dt Borden C & Agness, both
                                        decd
Ch: James Omer          b  4- 9-1860 d 6-10-1862
m 2nd
Miriam (Binford) b 5-mO-1834 dt Micajah & 2nd w Miriam
                                        (Morris)
Ch: Anna Elma           b  9-13-1864
    William Francis     b 10-23-1866

Samuel C b 9- 3-1833 s James Sr, decd & Rebecca (Moore)
m 1st
Lydia A (Parker) b 1- 7-1842 dt Silas & Priscilla
    (Butler) d 4-20-1865 bur Walnut Ridge Mtg,
    res Rush Co
Ch: Clara Ida           b  8- 9-1863
m 2nd ( 5- 5-1869)
Dinah Jane (Kendall) b - - - ?   d 5- 5-1870
    dt John & Sarah Ann (Hodson)
Ch: Lydia Ann           b  5- 1-1870
m 3rd (      1874)
Camilla (Fawsett) b 1-11-1841 dt Samuel & Nancy
                                        (Branson)
Ch: John F              b  4-17-1877
    Emery Junius        b  3- 5-1880
    Flora Alma          b 11- 9-1882

William W   b 2-21-1834  s Andrew & May
    m (10-11-1860)
Anny Elizabeth (Reed) b 9-28-1840 dt Charles & Sarah

Ch: Hannah E            b  6-24-1862
    William N           b  8-14-1866
    Florence C          b  9-28-1869
    Sanford C           b  6- 8-1874
    Jesse B             b  7-18-1876

## POWERS
Benjamin   b 3- 1-1822                d 11-29-1889
    s Lemuel & Nancy
    m (1-12-1848)
Margaret (Lister) b 1-12-1829   d 3-28-1888
    dt John & Keziah
Ch: William H           b  7-20-1851

John William b 9- 8-1848 s John & Judith
    m (9-22-1869)
Phebe A (Layman) b 6-22-1848   d 4- 4-1885
    dt Absalom & Sarah
Ch: Rosa L              b 10-30-1870
    John Warren         b  5-16-1872
    Stella              b  3-27-1876
    Sarah               b  4-19-1878
    Lulu                b 12-17-1879
    May                 b 10- 1-1882

## PRESNALL
(Absalom s Stephen, decd & Hannah (Reece))
    (b 10- 5-1809 Randolph Co, N Car)
Mary (Binford) dt Joshua & Lydia (Patterson)
Ch: Emily
    Sarah Jane
    Lydia

## PUSEY
Jesse F    (b 10-18-1820 Ohio) (s Joel & Hannah
                                        (Faulkner))
Jane W (- - - -)
Ch: William B           b  6- 7-1844 (d 7-29-1874 bur
    Raysville Mtg, res Henry Co, Ind)
    Caleb W             b  5-18-1846
    Mary E              b 11-18-1847
    Francis W           b  9- 7-1851
    Joel                b 12-20-1853
    Emma Jane           b  9-11-1857
    Charles Rollin      b  7-18-1861

Martha   b 7- 7-1816 Ohio dt Joel & Hannah (Faulkner)

## RAMSEY
Richard Harvey
Mary Ann (- - - -) d 8- 3-1874 bur Knightstown, Ind,
    res Henry Co, Ind
Ch: Mary Rose           b  8-30-1869 Marion Co
    Adelia Minnie       b  4- 1-1873 Rush Co

## RAWLS
(Burwell, dis in Ohio 1845)
Sarah (- - - -)  d (10-20-1849 Springborough Mtg, Ohio
    age 57-4-0, bur Center MM, Ohio)
Minor Ch to Indiana
    William             b (ca 1829) d 5-13-1846 bur
    Westland Mtg, res Hancock Co, Ind
    Esther T            b  2- 7-1831 Ohio
    John )              b  9-12-1833 Ohio
    Jesse) twins        b  9-12-1833 Ohio
    Sarah Jane          b  2-18-1836 Ohio

## RAYLE
(Asa s of - - - -) (b 3-16-1807 N Car)
Elizabeth (White) b 2- 5-1817 dt Isaac & Mahala (Hunt)
(Elizabeth (White) Rayle m 2nd 1850 to William W
                                        Thornburgh)
Ch: Emily Jane          b  1- 1-1836
    Jacob B             b  1-21-1839
    Isaac B             b       1841
    William L           b  2- 2-1842 Guilford Co, N Car

William L  b 2- 2-1842 Guilford Co, N Car
    s Asa & Elizabeth (White)
    m (12-24-1874)
Martha A (Wooten)
Ch: John H              b  4-26-1877 d 1878
    Nellie              b  2- 3-1879

WALNUT RIDGE

REDDING
Jacob
Annie (Moore)
Ch:   Mary Cecil         b  1-27-1888

REECE
Charles     b  2- 9-1829  s Nathan decd & Susannah (Elliott)
Eunice (Dennis)  b 7-19-1829  dt Benjamin decd & Clarky
                                                    (Pool)
Ch:   Edwin           b 12-17-1854  (d 4- 1-1859
                                      Whitewater Mtg)
      Oliver          b  7-22-1857  (d 10- 6-1859
                                      Whitewater Mtg)
      Elmina Cora     b  7-18-1859

Charles   b 10-12-1842  s John & Gulielma (Dennis)
          d  3-19-1887
          m  (5-11-1863?)
Martha (Harvey)  b 3- 9-1845  Morgan Co, Ind  dt David &
                                                    Mary
Ch:   Ruth Anna       b  3-18-1864
      David Oscar     b  8-18-1865
      John Wiley      b  2-12-1867
      Mary Elma       b  2-26-1869
      Harvey Morris   b  2- 4-1871
      Laura D         b  4-23-1874  (d 10-25-1878)
      Hulda E         b 11- 7-1877

Daniel    b 7- 8-1810  N Car  s John & Nancy Ann
                                             (Needham)
Sarah (Hastings)  b 4- 8-1817  dt William & Sarah (Evans)
Ch:   David           b  9- 5-1835  Henry Co, Ind
      Thomas          b  5- 6-1838  Rush Co
                      d 12- 4-1840 bur Walnut Ridge Mtg, res Rush Co
      Nathan          b  6- 4-1840

Elias     b 6-10-1857  s John & Gulielma (Dennis)
          m  (7- 4-1877)
Clementine (Barrett)  b 5-11-1856  dt Samuel & Charlotte
Ch:   Clarence L      b  8-10-1878

Elkannah  b 7-14-1830  s Jesse decd & Anna (now Anna
          Osborn, 2nd w of John Osborn)
Mary (Brown)  b 5- 6-1829  (dt William & Celah (Newby))
Ch:   Jesse           b  7- 6-1854
      Albert          b 10-25-1855
      Celah Jane      b  7-10-1858
      Nathan N        b 10- 5-1860
      Elwood O        b  9- 9-1862
      Eli B           b  7-19-1865
      Mary Ann        b  8-15-1868
      Emma A          b 12-21-1870

John      (b 1817)  (s John & Ann)  d 10-15-1888
          m  (7- 3-1839)
Gulielma (Dennis)  (b 12- 5-1822)  (dt Benjamin & Clarky
          d  9-16-1892                       (Pool))
Ch:   Anna            b  7-17-1840  (d 8-27-1847)
           bur Walnut Ridge Mtg, res Hancock Co
      Charles         b 10-12-1842
      William         b 11-23-1844  d 10-31-1862
           bur Walnut Ridge Mtg
      Benjamin D      b  8-19-1846  d  1-27-1851
           bur Walnut Ridge Mtg, res Rush Co
      Martha Ann      b 11-15-1848  d  4- 5-1850
           bur Walnut Ridge Mtg, res Rush Co
      Mary Elma       b 11-29-1852
      Elias           b  6-10-1857

Levi      b 10-29-1831   d 8- 4-1877  (s Eli &
                                            Matilda)
Sarah Ann (Herrold)  b 3-16-1827  dt Charles & Rachel
                                                  (Lamb)
Ch:   Mary M          b  1-12-1853
      Eli Charles     b  8- 1-1856

Miles     b 1-18-1827  (s Eli & Matilda) of Randolph Co,
          Ind   d 6-13-1852 bur Walnut Ridge Mtg, res
                                                  Rush Co
Mary (Fellow)  b 7- 3-1829  dt John & Abigail (Coleman)
Ch:   John            b  5- 6-1851

(Nathan  s John & Nancy Ann (Needham))  (b  5-23-1806 N Car)
          (d  9- 2-1841 bur Rich Square Mtg, Ind)

Susannah (Elliott)  b 2-25-1812  dt Jacob & Ann
Ch:   Charles         b  2- 9-1829
      Jane            b 11-11-1835
      Mary            b  5-31-1838
      Joel            b  5-24-1840

REEVES
John W
Mary E
Ch:   Walter A        b  3-17-1876
      James E         b 11- 3-1879

RHOADS
Cyrus
Mahala
Ch:   Ollie K         b  8-15-1860
      Emma            b 11-10-1863
      Bertha          b 10-23-1871

ROBINSON
Elliott   b 4-22-1843  s John & Rebecca
          m  (9-13-1868)
Elmira C (Baker)    b  2-17-1842

SHAFFER
Michael
          m (12- 4-1832)
Anna (Rickart)  b 9- 1-1811  dt Anthony & Esther
Ch:   Ira             b  2-20-1845

SKINNER
Joshua J    b 5-22-1848  s Miles & Sarah
            m  (1-18-1878)
Margaret (Haskett)  b 4-11-1850  dt Silas & Peninah
                                              (Hendrix)
Ch:   William

SMALL
Josiah
Susannah (Record?)  b 2-14-1812  dt Adam & Sarah
Ch:   William Penn    b  5-31-1843
      Zachariah T     b  7-30-1850

William Penn  b 5- 3-1843  s Josiah & Susannah (Record?)
              m (11- 8-1867?)
Rebecca (Beckner)  b 4-25-1849  dt Jacob & Harriett
Ch:   Anna F          b  8-11-1868
      Elbert          b  9-25-1869
      George W        b  2-14-1878

Zachariah T   b 7-30-1850  s Josiah & Susannah (Record?)
              m  (1- 3-1870)
Martha (Holding)  b 5-31-1853  dt John & Lydia A
Ch:   Celia           b 11-22-1870
      Estella         b  7- 8-1873
      John R          b  4- 4-1879
      Rufus K         b  9-22-1883  d  8-22-1884

STAFFORD
Joseph C   (s Joseph & Mourning of Randolph Co, N Car)
Lydia (Mendenhall)  (b 8- 9-1807)  dt Nathan & Phebe
                    (Haworth)  of Guilford Co, N Car
Ch:   Nathan D        b  6- 2-1825
      Elias Clarkson  b  5- 15-1827
      Phebe M         b  5-20-1828
      William P       b  7-15-1830
      Julius          b 10-19-1832

(Nathan, dis)  (s Joseph & Mourning of Randolph Co, N Car)
Elizabeth S (Mendenhall)  (b 4-17-1805)  dt Nathan &
                    Phebe (Haworth) of Guilford Co, N Car
Ch:   Barzillia G     b  8-20-1827  Rush Co, Ind
      Eli F           b 10-11-1828
      Martha Ann      b  7-28-1830
      Stephen         b  5- 2-1833
      David B M       b  3-12-1840
      Elizabeth C     b  7- 2-1842
      Mathew          b  - - - - -
      Mary Jane       b  - - - - -

STANLEY
Joseph H     b 9-11-1850  s Wyatt & Nancy A (Henley)
             m (11- 4-1886)
Penelope N (White)  b 9-28-1855  dt Isaac & Pamelia

# WALNUT RIDGE

**STANLEY** (Cont)
Ch: Joseph H & Penelope N (Cont)
    Ethel P         b 9-13-1887
    Leona H        b 6-24-1890

(------?)
Ruth (Hill)
Ch: Verlin          b 5-18-1870
    Ithamer        b 4-17-1872

Wyatt    b 12-18-1813    d 2-12-1883
    s John, decd & Elizabeth (Dicks)
    m 1st
Mary (Bundy) b 8-23-1819 Wayne Co, Ind  d 9-21-1846
    bur Walnut Ridge Mtg, res Hancock Co, Ind
    dt George Sr & 2nd w Karen (Elliott)
Ch: Gulielma       b 10-15-1839
    Phariba M      b 10-15-1840
    Cynthia E      b 3-20-1843
    John           b 6-26-1845
    m 2nd
Nancy A (Henley) b 5-12-1812 dt Joseph & Penniah (Morgan)
Ch: Joseph Henley   b 9-11-1850
    George Riley    b 9-20-1854

**STANTON**
(- - - -?)
    mcd
Eunice (Barnard)  (b 4-13-1810) dt William & Matilda
    (Gardner)  d 3-9-1850 aged 39-10-27

Zacheus    (b 11-6-1779) s William & Phebe of South River
    m 1st Va                       MM, Va
Sarah (- - - -) (b 4-3-1778) (d ca 1818 prob Salem MM,
    m 2nd                           Ind)
Elizabeth (Swain) b (12-6-1787) d (7-14-1868 bur
    Salem Mtg, Ind) dt Joseph & Jediah (Macy) of N
                                            Car
Ch: Mahala        b 7-31-1821
    Cynthia       b 1-13-1824
    Milton        b 2-23-1826
    Milo          b 6-5-1827

**STARBUCK**
(Bezabel  s Thomas & 2nd w Rachel) (b 2-17-1818 dis 1842)
Jane (- - - -) (she may have been Jane Temple, dt of Mary
    (Beals) Temple, wid, who m Isaac Hollingsworth in
    N Car)
Ch: Temple        b 6-16-1839  Dover Mtg N Car
    William H      b 6-26-1840
    George W       b 2-17-1842
    James M        b 9-13-1844
    Thomas C       b 4-18-1846
    Benjamin F     b 2-13-1848
    Richard W      b 5-20-1853  Rush Co, Ind

Elwood G  b 12-20-1815 N Car  s Thomas & 2nd w Rachel of
    m (2-16-1841)                       N Car
Susanna (Pitts) b 7-25-1816 dt Andrew & Mary

Henry R
    m (12-19-1867)
Rebecca (Winegardner) b 11-29-1848 dt John & Mary
Ch: Nelly J       b 9-3-1874
    Floyd         b 6-11-1878

**STEERE**
Benjamin W
Emily (Hoag) b 12-8-1824  d 5-5-1897 dt Hazael &
                                      Sarah B
Ch: (a dt)              m William P Henley
    (a dt)              m Robert B Henley

**STRATTON**
Eli (s Jonathan & Sarah from Green Street MM, Philadelphia,
    Pa) b 12-20-1772 (d ca prior to 1846) IBB
Eunice (Dollar or Dallas?) b 10-7-1771 dt William &
                                     Rebecca
Ch: (to Walnut Ridge Mtg)
    Jonathan D     b 11-8-1804
    William L      b - - - - -
    Joseph E       b 9-2-1811

Jonathan D b 11-8-1804 Maurice River, N J  s Eli &
    Eunice (Dollar or Dallas?)
Prudence (Edgerton) b 2-14-1807 Belmont Co, Ohio dt
    Samuel & Elizabeth (Wilkins)
Ch: Milicent Ann   b 7-8-1831  Westfield, O
    Samuel        b 8-30-1833
    Joseph L      b 1-23-1836  Rush Co, Ind
    Eli            b 9-6-1838
    Eunice        b 10-4-1840

**STUBBS**
John (s John Sr & Esther) d 7-17-1854 "in the 92nd year
    of his age" bur Pleasant View Mtg, res Rush Co, Ind
Jane (Jones) b 6-22-1764 dt Francis & Sarah of Wrights-
    boro Mtg, Ga  d - - - -? (Ind)

Joseph (s John & Jane (Jones)) (b 11-6-1801 Columbia Co,
    Ga) (d 1-28-1836 bur Spiceland Mtg, Ind)
Margaret (Saunders) (b 6-23-1797 N Car) dt Joseph &
    Martha (Wells) (d 2-19-1835 bur Spiceland Mtg, Ind)
Ch: (to Walnut Ridge Mtg)
    Newton        b 3-6-1823  Ohio
    Charles       b 7-5-1827  Preble Co, O

**STUMP**
John W  b 4-22-1848
Margaret E (Snyder) b 12-16-1851
Ch: Caroline Etta  b 12-16-1875
    Cora Eveline   b 10-11-1877
    Nora Alice     b 1-11-1880
    George        b 6-22-1882
    Gurney        b 8-1-1885
    Jemima        b - - - - -

**SWAIN**
David of Fayette Co, Ind  b 5-25-1790 s Sylvanus, decd
    & Miriam (Gardner)
Ruth (Coffin) of Shelby Co, Ind
Ch: Ruth          b (ca 1817)
    m 3rd
Phebe (Coffin) Weisner, a wid & dt of Aaron & Mary
    (Barnard), decd   b 4-15-1791

George  b 10-29-1805 s Sylvanus, decd & Miriam
                                  (Gardner)
Margaret (Barnard) b 10-10-1793 N Car dt Asa & Huldah
                                     (Macy)
Ch: Usebia        b 7-10-1832
    Almira        b 1-1-1835

Jethro    b 9-15-1783 (s Joseph & Jediah (Macy))
Susannah (Leonard) b 11-28-1787 (dt Joseph & Phebe (Macy))
Ch: (to Walnut Ridge Mtg, Ind)
    Susanna       b - - - -

Oliver    b 12-21-1829 s Elihu & Hannah (Stanton)
Almira (Swain) b 1-1-1835 dt George & Margaret (Barnard)
Ch: Dora Elma      b 10-6-1855  d 11-24-1860
        bur Little Blue River Mtg, res Rush Co
    Aura Eusebia   b 6-9-1859
    Linanis E      b 12-30-1861

Sarah (Leonard) wid of Thomas Swain, his 2nd w (now w of
    William Worth) & dt Joseph & Phebe, decd, Leonard
    of N Car     b 9-8-1791
Ch: (to Walnut Ridge Mtg)
    Prior
    Achsah
    Silas

Thomas    (b 7-6-1790 N Car) (s Joseph & Jediah (Macy))
    d 1-7-1841 bur Little Blue River Mtg, res Rush Co,
                                              Ind
    m 1st
(Lydia (Folger) dt Latham & Matilda) (b 8-28-1786 N Car)
    (d prior to 1834 probably at Salem Mtg, Ind) IBB
Ch: Rhoda         b - - - - -
    Elvira        b 6-5-1817  N Car
    Franklin      b 8-15-1819  Silver Creek Mtg, Ind
    Alonzo        b 7-5-1822
    Alfred        b 9-22-1825
    m 2nd
Elizabeth (Barnard) (b 2-17-1800) dt Asa & Huldah (Macy)
    decd (after death of Thomas Swain, she m 2nd, 1853 to
    Howland Swain and was his 2nd w)

WALNUT RIDGE

## SWAIN (Cont)
Ch:  Thomas & Elizabeth
    Zeno    (m Lucinda Maulsby)

## SYMONS
Mary (Morgan) Morris (wid of Joshua Morris) & dt of Charles & Lydia Morgan, decd  d 4-30-1852 age 64-3-14  d at Carthage Mtg, Rush Co, Ind but was bur at Milford MM, Wayne Co, Ind
Ch:  Eunice    b 2-27-1829  (m 1851 Evan Lewis Johnson of Wabash Co, Ind)

## TALBERT
Jesse  (the family name had been BULL until 1806 when it was legally changed to TALBERT.  see Deep River MM, N Car)  (s Richard decd & Mary of Bradford MM, Pa 1780)  (b 9- 3-1783)  d 10-22-1866 age 82-3-0 bur Little Blue River Mtg, res Rush Co, Ind
Margaret (Beeson)  dt William & Elizabeth (Norton) (b 3-11-1784)

Jesse  (s Joseph decd & Rachel (Beeson))
Hannah (- - - -?)
Ch:  Milton    b 10- 1-1826  Preble Co, Ohio
    Louisa    b 8-14-1829
    Abel    b 1-11-1832  Union Co, Ind
    Alpheus    b 1- 2-1835
    Enos    b 4-23-1837  Shelby Co, Ind
    Maria    b 12-13-1839
    Harrison    b 4-19-1842
    Hadley    b 2-23-1845

(Jonathan  s Thomas & Elizabeth (Beard))  (b 7- 3-1799 N Car)
Esther (Hart)  b 2-28-1797  dt Isaac & Sarah
Ch:  Mary    b /- 3-1818  Ohio
    Thomas    b 9-26-1819
    Rebecca    b 9-25-1821
    Sarah    b 6-13-1823
    John    b 4-28-1826
    Isaac    b 2-20-1828
    Rhoda    b - - - - -
    Elizabeth    b - - - - -

Sylbanus  b 5- 6-1819  s William & Miriam (Gardner)
Phebe (Hiatt)  b 11-21-1821  dt Isaac & Shannah of Warren Co, Ohio
Ch:  (minors)
    Daniel H    b 3- 2-1860
    Anna    b 6-18-1862

## TAYLOR
George L  (dis 1890)
  m (12- 6-1866)
Rebecca (Fodrea)  dt David & Tamar
Ch:  Joseph M    b 10-17-1867
    Mary J    b 11- 2-1868
    John D    b 4-21-1870  d 7-27-1871
    Julia Ann    b 12- 3-1871
    Laura B    b 2-24-1873
    Harvey N    b 2-11-1875
    Oliver W    b 10-30-1876
    Martha E    b 12-18-1878
    Lucy    b - - - - -
    Lena    b - - - - -
    Jennie    b - - - - -
    Ruby    b - - - - -
    Elmer    b - - - - -

Josiah N  b 6-29-1844  s John & Nancy
Martha A (Gray)  b 11- 3-1850  dt Jonathan & Sarah Ann
Ch:  Andrew    b 6-29-1870  (m Lillian B Addison)

(Simeon  s Christopher & 1st w Elizabeth (Patterson)) (b 1- 3-1785 Northampton Co, N Car)
Elizabeth Peninah (Binford)  b 9-20-1786 Henrico Co, Va  dt John & 1st w Elizabeth of Va
Ch:  Angeline P    b 9-24-1815  Belmont Co, Ohio
    John M    b 7- 4-1819
    Daniel G    b 1-24-1822
    Allen D    b 10-29-1825

## THORNBURGH
Claudius B  b 9-25-1860  s Harris W & Emily (Bowen)
Janette (Falls)  b 3-26-1868  dt Edwin & Diza
Ch:  Esther    b 11-13-1885
    Edwin    b 10- 8-1886
    Lillian    b 9-12-1891

Harris W  b 6-24-1835  s Winslow & Landy
  m (12-25-1859)
Emily (Bowen)  b 5- 2-1835  dt Hobbs & Nancy
Ch:  Claudius B    b 9-25-1860
    Franklin N    b 2-27-1863  d 3-22-1866
    William W    b 3-30-1865
    Theodosia W    b 8-12-1867
    Caroline M    b 3- 7-1872
    Landy A    b 10-15-1874
    Jesse H    b 12-10-1876

Joel  b 11-29-1789 Guilford Co, N Car  s Joseph & Rachel
Anna J (Willis)  b 9-28-1794 Guilford Co, N Car  (d 10-25-1866  Memorial at Walnut Ridge Mtg, Ind on 8- 17-1867)  dt Joel & Hannah Willis
Ch:  (to Walnut Ridge Mtg, Ind)
    Cyrus    b 3-15-1818 Highland Co, Ohio
        d 11-13-1835 bur Walnut Ridge Mtg
    William Willis    b 7- 9-1819
    Mary Ann    b 12-25-1822  d 9- 8-1838
        bur Walnut Ridge Mtg
    Lydia Jane    b 12-12-1827

Joseph  (b 2-29-1759 N Car)  (s Joseph & Ann of N Car)  d 5-13-1842 age 83-2-14  bur Walnut Ridge Mtg, res Rush Co, Ind
Rachel (Brown)  (b 10-2-1754 Orange Co, N Car)  dt William & Hannah (Moon) of N Car  d 3-31-1842 age 87-5-29  bur Walnut Ridge Mtg, res Rush Co, Ind

Thomas  b 10-16-1794 N Car  s Thomas & Miriam (Winslow) of Randolph Co, N Car
Sarah (Henley)  b 10- 8-1799  dt Joseph & Peninah (Morgan)
Ch:  Phebe    b 12-21-1820  Randolph Co, N Car
    Elizabeth    b 9-22-1822
    Diza R    b 10-16-1824
    Penninah    b 10-24-1826
    Miriam    b 9-14-1828
    Amanda    b 10-14-1830
    Luzena    b 1-11-1833
    Mary    b 2- 2-1835
    Thomas H    b 5-20-1837  Rush Co, Ind
        d 10-18-1838  bur Walnut Ridge Mtg, res Rush Co, Ind

William Willis  b 7- 9-1819 Highland Co, Ohio  s Joel & Anna J (Willis)
  m 1st (12-15-1838)
Sarah (Clark)  b 1- 9-1822 Wayne Co, Ind  dt John & Anna  d 7-13-1841 bur Walnut Ridge Mtg, res Rush Co, Ind
Ch:  John Clark    b 9-19-1839 Rush Co  d 10- 7-1862
    Sarah    b 6- 3-1841  d 10-16-1841
        bur Walnut Ridge Mtg, res Rush Co
  m 2nd (10-30-1844)
Susan (Small)  b 1820  dt Silas & Mary  d 5-13-1849  bur Walnut Ridge Mtg, res Rush Co, Ind
Ch:  Charles L    b 11-12-1846  d 4-28-1879
    Silas S    b 4-16-1849  d 12-28-1863
        bur Walnut Ridge Mtg, res Rush Co
  m 3rd
Elizabeth (White) Rayle, a wid & dt of Isaac & Mahala White  b 2- 5-1817 N Car  d 5-23-1883
Ch:  Minerva    b 9- 1-1852  d 9- 9-1854
    Caroline    b 9-26-1855
    Monroe    b 4- 1-1858  d 4-27-1881

## THORNBURRY - THORNBERRY
William J  b 8-11-1837  s Abel & Rhoda
Mary A (Davis)  b 9-29-1845  dt Jordan & Phebe
Ch:  William J    b 7-25-1871  d same day
    Josephine    b 1-29-1873  d 2-12-1873
    Risher W    b 8-13-1875
    Rhoda    b - - - - -

## TOWNSEND
(Thomas  s James & Rosannah (Smith))  (b 12- 3-1808)

WALNUT RIDGE

TOWNSEND (Cont)
(Thomas m)
Mary (Hastings) b 9-26-1810 dt William & Sarah (Evans)
Ch: (to Walnut Ridge Mtg)
 Nancy    b 1-30-1831 Ind
 Elisha    b 10-15-1834
 James    b 10- 6-1838
 Isaac    b 6- 5-1843

TRIBBY
John B  b 5- 3-1858 s James W & Minerva
Lavina (Conaway) b 8- 5-1866
Ch: Clessie   b 11-11-1883

TWEEDY
Jonathan P
Emily
Ch: William Edmund
 Albert Marion
 George Riley
 Anna J   b 11-13-1867

WHEELER
Alfred
Lydia
Ch: Alonzo L
 Lydia C

Jesse b 9-16-1831 N Car s John & Phebe of Guilford
 Co, N Car
 m (1862 Westland Mtg, Ind)
Mary J (Butler) b 2-26-1845 Hancock Co, Ind dt Nathan,
 decd & Ann (Binford)
Ch: Phebe A   b 3- 4-1864
 Nathan J   b 11-11-1868

WHITE
Aaron S
Ann (Outland)
Ch: Hannah Alice  b 9- 7-1866
 Henry Riley A  b 6- 3-1868
 Margaret Ann  b 7-20-1871

Albert b 1-24-1825 s Thomas & Elizabeth
Cynthia (Nicholson) b 3- 5-1839 dt Nathan & Miriam
Ch: Emery Alvin  b 4-29-1860 d 9- 4-1862
 Franklin   b 6-27-1863 d 10-25-1864
  bur Pleasant View Mtg
 Harvey T   b 8- 4-1865
 Annie Alice  b 10-19-1870
 Martin L   b 10-10-1872
 Ella L   b 1-20-1876

Augustus
Margaret (- - - -)
Ch: Laura A   b 6-21-1862

Bethuel C b 9- 7-1806 Guilford Co, N Car s Robert
 & Rebecca (Coffin) d 10-13-1891
 m (10-30-1827)
Hannah (Binford) b 2- 3-1806 Northampton Co, N Car
 dt Joshua & Lydia (Patterson) d 7-23-1884
Ch: Elizabeth L  b 9- 7-1828
 Aaron   b 10- 3-1830
 Ann R   b 12-31-1832
 Eli J   b 5- 4-1835
 Barclay   b 11- 9-1837 d 2-10-1859
  at Earlham College, bur Walnut Ridge Mtg
 Sarah B   b 2-29-1840 (d 8- 3-1864)
 Henry B   b 5-19-1842
 Bethuel jr  b 8- 7-1844 d 7-26-1890
 John   b 2-28-1847
 Hannah E   b 5-16-1850

Bethuel jr b 8- 7-1844  d 7-26-1890
 s Bethuel Sr & Hannah (Binford)
 m (10- 9-1873)
Emma (Burton) b 10-20-1854 dt Charles & Margaret E
Ch: John H   b 12- 6-1876 d 1- 8-1884
 Charles B  b 7- 5-1880
 M Jobin   b 4-29-1883

David O b 4-12-1857 s Thomas N & Lydia

m ( 8-31-1881)
Annie (Hill) b 2-29-1860 dt Samuel B & Mary E (Henley)
Ch: Franklin E)  b 9- 8-1882
 Floyd L )twins b 9- 8-1882
 Herbert Ellsworth b 8-28-1886

Eli b 9- 7-1808 Guilford Co, N Car s Robert &
 Rebecca (Coffin) decd
Martha (Hunnicut) b 8- 1-1816 Prince George Co, Va
 dt Robert & Elizabeth (Andrews)
Ch: Rebecca E  b 12-14-1835 Rush Co, Ind
 Robert H  b 8-26-1837
 Mary N   b 1-30-1840
 Sarah J   b 1-24-1842
 George K  b 9-15-1843
 Susannah  b 8- 3-1846
 Harriett N  b 9-26-1848
 Nathan L  b 8-25-1850
 Samuel M  b 6-25-1852

Eli J b 5- 4-1835 s Bethuel C & Hannah (Binford)
 m ( 4-14-1865)
Lucinda (Hall) b 2-22-1837 dt Silas & Sarah
Ch: Olive B   b 3-14-1866
 Silas B F  b 5-19-1867
 Charles O  b 12-19-1869
 Barclay O  b 2-26-1873

Henry (b 7-16-1784) s Thomas & Elizabeth (Lamb)
Mary (Hunt) (b 8-14-1793) dt Jacob & Hannah
 d 3-25-1863 age 69-7-11 (Recorded in Walnut Ridge
 Mtg records)
Ch: (to Ind)
 Abigail B  b 11- 5-1816 N Car
 Elijah   b 9-22-1821
 Charles C  b 5-17-1826
 Polly J   b 1-26-1829

(Isaac s Robert & Rebecca (Coffin) decd)
(Pamelia (Foster) )
Ch: (Lindley H  b 10-18-1851 d 7-12-1890)
 (George W  b 9- 3-1853)
 (Penelope N  b 9-28-1855)
 (Samira   b 9- 7-1857)

(Isaac s Thomas & Elizabeth) (b 8-28-1793 N Car)
 (d ca prior to 1844) IBB
Mahala (Hunt) b 9-27-1798 dt Jacob & Hannah
Ch: (to Ind)
 Elizabeth  b 2- 5-1817 N Car
 William C  b 10-22-1818
 John M   b 12-21-1823
 Rebecca   b 7- 3-1826
 Jemima   b 4-16-1830
 Borden C  b 10-21-1832
 Addison T  b 7-21-1835

Isaac (no parents' names recorded or age recorded at time
 of death) d 1-31-1882 bur Walnut Ridge Mtg, res
 Rush Co, Ind

Lindley H b 10-18-1851  d 7-12-1890
 s Isaac & Pamelia (Foster)
 m (9-27-1877)
Sarah A (Coble) b 12- 9-1857 dt David & Martha
Ch: Leora   b 9-30-1878
 Naomi C   b 2-21-1880
 Charles E  b 3-23-1882
 Mary A   b 9-10-1884
 William A  b 4- 6-1887

Oliver H (b 10- 9-1852) s Josiah T & Elizabeth
(Caroline (Hill) dt Samuel B & Mary E (Henley))
 (b 9-15-1858)
Ch: (Mary E   b 1- 9-1883)
 (Ione H   b 3- 8-1886)

Phineas s Jesse & Mary, both decd
 m 1st
Sarah (Bundy) b 4-24-1811 N Car dt George & Sarah
 (Moore) decd d 9-29-1843 age 32-5-5 bur Walnut
 Ridge Mtg, res Rush Co
Ch: Jesse   b 6-14-1837 Hancock Co, Ind
 George   b 7-20-1840 " " "

WALNUT RIDGE

## WHITE (Cont)
Phineas   m 2nd
Lydia (Butler)   b       1817   dt William & Esther (Ladd)
    d 1- 8-1855  age 37-2-22  bur Walnut Ridge Mtg,
        res Rush Co
Ch:   Rebecca M            b  3-28-1846

Rebecca   (no parents' names recorded)   d 1- 6-1837
    age 33-1-25  bur Walnut Ridge Mtg, res Rush Co
    (the above person may be the w of Samuel White jr
    whose family is recorded in Spiceland Mtg as Duck
    Creek Mtg had been temporarily discontinued & mbrs
    attached to Spiceland MM, until 1840) (if that
    were true, then the above Rebecca was the dt of
    Francis, decd & Miriam (Toms) White of Suttons
    Creek Mtg, N Car) IBB

(Robert s Thomas & Elizabeth (Lamb))  (b 5- 1-1781 N Car)
Rebecca (Coffin)  (b 2-27-1786 N Car) dt Bethuel & 1st
    w, Hannah (Dicks) decd  (d prior to 1834 probably
    in Rush Co, Ind)
Minor Ch to Walnut Ridge Mtg, Ind
    Thomas
    Thaddeus          (m Rhoda (- - - -?))
    Isaac             (m Pamelia (Foster))
    George B          (m Eliza(Griffin) at West Grove
                                                  Mtg)

Robert B    b 6- 1-1829  s Thomas & Elizabeth
    m ( 4-17-1856)
Nancy A (Devlin)  b 6-16-1831  dt George & Ann
Ch:   Wilson H            b 12-27-1856
      Charles E           b 11-12-1864
      Morris E            b  7-17-1866
      Alvin A             b  3- 5-1870
      Linburn M           b  1-18-1873

Thaddeus   s Robert & Rebecca (Coffin) decd
Rhoda M (- - - -?)
Ch:   Ruth Ann            b 11- 1-1847
      Anna Jane           b  7-30-1850

Thomas jr  (b 9-24-1795 N Car) (s Thomas & Elizabeth
                                              (Lamb))
Elizabeth (- - - -?)  (rec on req 8-25-1821 N Car)
Ch:   Albert              b  1-24-1825  N Car
      Robert B            b  6- 1-1829
      Sally J             b  9-29-1831
      Nancy A             b  9- 9-1833
      Semira A            b  9-24-1835
      John G              b 11- 8-1837
      Wyatt               b 12-18-1839
      Martha D            b  7-17-1842
      Eliza               b 11- 1-1844

William  (no parents' or wife's name recorded)
    d 3-15-1860 age 59-9-15  bur Walnut Ridge Mtg, res
        Rush Co

(William, decd in Iowa)
Mary Elizabeth (Hunnicut) dt Robert decd & Elizabeth
    (Andrews)
(she m 2nd 1863 to Joseph Binford, a widower at Walnut
    Ridge Mtg)
Ch:   William jr          b  4-11-1860  (Iowa)

## WIGGINS
Lawson      b 6-16-1838  s Garrett & Harriett
    m ( 2-27-1863)
Margaret J (Coble)  b 5- 7-1845  dt David & Martha A
Ch:   John R              b  1-10-1864
      Laura A             b  1-25-1865
      Arthur E            b  5-22-1867
      George J            b 11-12-1869
      Ida B               b 10-24-1872
      Marshall E          b  5-21-1874
      Clara C             b 12-10-1875
      Martha L            b 12- 7-1884

## WILLIAMS
George W
Sarah (- - - -?)
Ch:   Orlando B           b  9-29-1847

## WILSON
James       b   1826   s J & Eleanor
Grizzell (Powers)  b 10-14-1844  dt J & Martha
Ch:   William B           b  4- 3-1862
      John C              b 11-14-1863
      Phineas D           b  6-25-1865
      Angeline E          b 12-20-1866
      Norah F             b  1-24-1869
      Omer J              b  9-17-1871
      Asenath H           b  9-30-1873
      Henry I             b  1-23-1875
      Susan J             b  3- 1-1877

Joseph      b 12-16-1809  s Samuel & Ruth (Thornburgh)
Elizabeth (Stokes)   dt Samuel & Jane (from MM in Pa)
Ch:   Sarah               b 11-24-1839
      Samuel S            b 12- 7-1840
      Ruthanna            b  2-20-1842
      Isabella            b  6-10-1845
      Mary Abigail        b  2-12-1847
      Charles             b 11-14-1848

## WILTSE
Simeon Sr   b 7-10-1763 (NJ?)  d 5-26-1837  bur Walnut
    Ridge Mtg, res Hancock Co, Ind
Elizabeth (Craven)  b 4-30-1781  d 9- 1-1841  bur
    Walnut Ridge Mtg, res Rush Co, Ind
Ch:   Simeon jr           b  9-10-1808  N J
      William             b  5-11-1811  Gloucester Co,N J
      John C              b 10-12-1813
      Martin              b  2- 2-1816  d 8-20-1840
         bur Walnut Ridge Mtg, res Rush Co
      George              b  6-26-1818  Preble Co, Ohio
      Elizabeth           b 12-19-1820     "    "    "

Simeon jr  b 9-10-1808  Gloucester Co, N J  s Simeon
    Sr & Elizabeth (Craven)
    m 1st  (Ohio)
Rachel (Edgerton)  b 10-20-1808  dt Samuel & Elizabeth
    d 7- 9-1834  bur Walnut Ridge Mtg,   (Wilkins)
    res Rush Co, Ind
Ch:   Elizabeth S         b  3- 5-1834  Rush Co, Ind
    m 2nd
Elizabeth (Butler)  b 5- 6-1805  dt William & Mary
Ch:   David               b 12-29-1836  Rush Co
      Josiah              b  7- 6-1838
      William E           b  8-23-1840
      Martin              b  4-27-1842
      Rachel              b  7-24-1844

## WINSLOW
Charles S   b 6-22-1862  s William & Mary J (Patterson)
    m (11-11-1885)
Addella J (Bentley)  b 6- 1-1862  dt John & Mary E
Ch:   William H           b  6- 6-1886
      Grace V             b 10- 3-1888
      John Russell        b 12-30-1890

Henry   b 9-11-1813           d 10-20-1887
    s Joseph & Peninah (Pritchard)
    m 1st (3-23-1833)
Anna (Binford)  (b 8-17-1816)  dt Micajah & Sarah
                    (d 9- 9-1863 N Car)  (Patterson)
Ch:   Micajah B           b  3-13-1834  d 2- 8-1875
      Levi                b  7-20-1836
      Emily               b 12-30-1838
      Jonathan            b  8-16-1841
      Ruth                b  5-30-1844  d 2-21-1873
      Sarah               b  3- 7-1848  d 1-25-1850
      Joseph)             b  9-13-1849
      Josiah)  twins      b  9-13-1849
      William             b  7- 4-1852  d 9- 1-1873
      Mary                b 10-12-1857  d 12- 7-1889
    m 2nd
Sarah E (Dunbar)  b 6- 3-1828  dt John & Sarah
Ch:   Arthur L            b  7- 7-1867
      Rufus K             b  2-27-1869
      Henrietta Eliza     b  9-22-1872

James   b 2- 8-1861  s Josiah & Rachel (Patterson)
    m ( 3-14-1888)
Emma J (Pussey)  b 12-11-1857   d 12-12-1891
    dt Jesse & Jane
    Ch

WALNUT RIDGE

WINSLOW (Cont)
Ch: of James & Emma J
    Camilla E           b 12-17-1888
    Mary Anna          b 7-26-1890

John      b 9- 6-1800 Randolph Co, N Car  d 10- 9-1841
    bur Carthage Mtg, res Rush Co, Ind  s Joseph &
    m (11-12-1822)                        Penninah
Mary A (Henley)  b 10-23-1804  dt Elias & Ann (Hubbard) decd
    (after the death of John Winslow, Mary A, m 2nd
    1849 to (- - - -?) Phelps)
Ch:    Elias H           b 10-20-1823  d 5- 2-1826
        bur Walnut Ridge Mtg, res Rush Co
    Henry             b 1-24-1826
    John Hubbard      b 1-23-1827
    Judith Ann        b 4- 7-1830  Rush Co, Ind
        d 9- 4-1847  bur Carthage Mtg
    Jabez H           b 1- 6-1833  d 8-20-1847
        bur Carthage Mtg
    Penninah          b 8-25-1835
    George H          b 12-16-1837
    Jesse B           b 8-11-1840  d 12- 9-1855
        bur Carthage Mtg, res Rush Co, Ind

John Hubbard  b 1-23-1827  Randolph Co, N Car  s John &
    m 1st (6-28-1854)              Mary A (Henley)
Susan (Jenkins)  b 8- 8-1834 Coles Co, Ill  d 3-28-1865
                                  dt Noble & Ellen
Ch:    George Allen      b 10- 7-1856
    John Noble        b 3- 3-1859  d 12-16-1891
    Louisa C          b 2-12-1862
    Ellen             b 8-22-1864
    m 2nd (11- 8-1866)
Emily (Macy)  b 5- 9-1837 Guilford Co, N Car  dt Lorenzo D
                                  & Rachel
Ch:    Lorenzo          b 8-26-1867

Josiah T    b 10- 2-1831  s William & Julia Ann (Parker)
Rachel (Patterson)  b 1-18-1840  dt Amasa & Lydia
Ch:    Orlando Vornel    b 11- 6-1858
    James             b 2- 8-1861
    Julianna          b 7- 2-1863
    Mary Anna         b 4-15-1866
    Amasa E           b 1-20-1869
    Martha C          b 9-26-1871  d 12- 7-1891
    John L            b 3-11-1874
    Josiah M          b 1-29-1877
    Albert            b 9-11-1879

Orlando    b 11- 6-1858  s Josiah & Rachel (Patterson)
    m (11-20-1879)
Mary (Parker)  b 8-26-1860  dt Silas & Priscilla
Ch:    Walter F          b 10- 1-1880  d 12-29-1880
    Jewel G           b 1-12-1882  d 3-27-1887
    Rachel A          b 8-26-1884
    Esther            b 6-24-1888

William      b 9-10-1799        d 2- 5-1839
        s William & P
Julia Ann (Parker)
Ch:    Josiah            b 10- 2-1831
    William jr        b 2- 6-1833  d 5-19-1855

William F    b 2- 6-1833  s William & Julia Ann (Parker)
Mary Jane (Patterson)  b 6- 1-1843  dt Amasa & Lydia
Ch:    Charles S         b 6-22-1862
    Eunice            b 2-26-1864
    William Thomas    b 5-11-1866
    Zerie             b 3-12-1868
    Daniel            b 12- 4-1869
    Ellen             b 3-17-1873
    James A           b 10- 9-1876  d 3 weeks later
    Harriet           b 9-13-1877
    Alice P)
    Albert ) twins    b 6-10-1879

WOODLY
Isaac      d - - - -  bur Walnut Ridge Mtg, res Rush Co, Ind
Mary (- - - -?)  d - - - -  bur Walnut Ridge Mtg
Ch:    Mary Elizabeth    b 1-15-1855

WOODS
John D      b 1-27-1828  s Henry & Mary
    m (11-25-1849)

Margaret A (- - - -?)  b 5-19-1833  dt Jefferson & Rachel S
Ch:    Ruhanna          b 10-16-1869
    Nellie            b 4-10-1873

Joseph J
    m (11-20-1872)
Louisa J (Nicholson)  b 1-20-1854  dt Nathan & Asenath
                                (Cloud) his 2nd w
Ch:    Ida May           b 5-22-1876  Hancock Co
    LeRoy             b 9-29-1878

WOOTEN
Lee      b 10-10-1857  s John & Elvira
    m (3-mO-1888)
Mary Ann (Winslow)  b 4-15-1866  dt Josiah & Rachel
                              (Patterson)
Ch:    Rachel Elvira     b 2-27-1889

WORTH
William      b 7-18-1789     d 2-28-1855  s Job &
    m 1st                                      Rhoda
Phebe (Barnard)     (Walnut Ridge Mtg record)
Ch:    Belinda         (m Jesse Leonard)
    Anna
    m 2nd
Sarah (Leonard) Swain, wid of Thomas Swain & dt Joseph &
    Phebe Leonard, decd
Ch:    Thomas           b 5- 6-1834  Rush Co

YOUNG
Joseph      b 2- 7-1814 Baltimore, Md  s Robert W & Rebecca
    d 9- 6-1855 age 41-6-29  bur Carthage Mtg, res
                                      Rush Co, Ind
Sarah (Binford)  b 3-12-1821 Northampton Co, N Car
    dt Micajah & Miriam (Morris)
Ch:    George H          b 10- 1-1840  Rush Co
    Miriam B          b 8- 3-1842
    Rachel            b 3-24-1844
    Micajah           b 10-21-1846
    William           b 6-23-1851

Robert W from Philadelphia MM, Pa  d 11-11-1854 age 74-8-2
    bur Carthage Mtg, res Rush Co, Ind
Rebecca (- - - -?)  d 3-11-1854 age 63-6-2  bur Carthage
    Mtg, res Rush Co
Ch:    Joseph            b 2- 7-1814  Maryland
    Robert W jr
    Hiram
    Edward Carnegy

# WALNUT RIDGE

## WALNUT RIDGE MONTHLY MEETING
## MINUTES AND MARRIAGES

### ADAMS
| | |
|---|---|
| 5-20-1876 | Christiana rec in mbrp |
| 4-19-1879 | Oliver & ch Ledora Bell & Leatha Ora rec in mbrp |
| 2-18-1893 | Oliver & w Christiana rel on req |

### ADAMSON
| | |
|---|---|
| 12- ?-1865 | Isaac produced certif from Duck Creek MM to m Catherine Bufkin Redding & they are altm. A comm is appt to att m & rpt to next mtg |
| 2-17-1866 | The comm appt to att m of Isaac & Catherine Bufkin Redding rpts it was orderly & that the m certif has been placed in hands of the Recorder |
| 2-12-1870 | Catherine gct Duck Creek MM, Ind |

### ADDISON
| | |
|---|---|
| 4-20-1867 | Elizabeth (form Cathen)  chm for mcd |
| 6-19-1869 | Eliza Jane rec in mbrp |
| 2-15-1873 | Thomas J rec in mbrp |
| 3-21-1874 | William & w Marinda & ch Martha A, Elizabeth C, Sarah E & Mariah rec in mbrp |
| 2-19-1881 | Solomon, George, ----- rec in mbrp |
| 3-18-1882 | Wesley rec in mbrp |
| 1-21-1883 | Wesley & w Eliza Jane & ch Mary, Margaret J, Simon & Ann gct West Indianapolis MM, Ind |
| 8-17-1895 | William A & w Crilla (?) & dt Ruby gct Indianapolis MM, Ind |
| 6-19-1897 | Anna Mary  rec in mbrp |

### ALBERTSON
| | |
|---|---|
| 3-19-1836 | Nathan A & w Pheriba & ch Benjamin, Sarah, Alpheus & George J are charter mbrs |
| 3-17-1838 | Thomas & w Hannah & minor s Nixon rocf West Grove MM, Ind |
| 6-16-1838 | Hannah & minor s Nixon gct White River MM, Ind (Thomas's certif is withheld) |
| 6-15-1844 | Thomas P gct Sugar River MM, Ind |
| 11-25-1847 | Benjamin from Rush Co, Ind s Nathan & Pheraby of Hancock County, Ind, m at Westland M H (Walnut Ridge MM) to Sabina T Marsh of Hancock Co, Ind |
| 7-17-1850 | Nathan & w Pheriba & ch Sarah, Alpheus, George J, B Jordan, Ezra, Aaron & Nathan H gct Westfield MM, Ind |
| 5-15-1852 | Benjamin & w Sabina & minor ch Nathan E & William gct Westfield MM, Ind. |

### ALLEN
| | |
|---|---|
| 8-17-1838 | Daniel C rocf Dover MM, Ind |
| 10-19-1839 | Harmon & w Nancy Ann & minor ch John P, Joseph M, Samuel L, Harmon jr, Julia Ann, Mary L, Nancy C, Jonathan T, Sylvia J & Nathan H rocf West Grove MM, Ind |
| 4-16-1842 | Daniel gct Spiceland MM to m Susanna Sheridan |
| 5-21-1842 | Samuel rocf Holly Springs MM, N Car |
| 10-20-1842 | Samuel of Rush Co, Ind  s John & Martha of Randolph Co, N Car m at Walnut Ridge MM, Ind to Martha J Henley of Rush Co |
| 12-16-1843 | Samuel & w Martha J gct Westfield MM, Ind |
| 3-16-1844 | John P gct Spiceland MM, Ind |
| 6-15-1844 | Daniel C gct Spiceland MM, Ind |
| 9-18-1845 | Joseph M gct Spiceland MM, Ind to m Charity K Boone |
| 4-17-1847 | John P gct Spiceland MM, Ind |
| 8-21-1847 | Samuel L chm for mcd |
| 11-? -1847 | Harman jr chm for mcd |
| 2-16-1850 | Lydia M & infant dt Elizabeth Ann rec in mbrp |
| 7-19-1851 | Samuel L dis for j Meth Ch |
| 2-21-1852 | Harman jr & w Lydia M & minor dt Elizabeth Ann gct Spiceland MM, Ind |
| 5-15-1852 | Jonathan dis for intoxication, gambling & upl & lieing |
| 9-17-1853 | Nancy C gct Spiceland MM, Ind |
| 2-21-1857 | Sylvia J gct Spiceland MM, Ind |
| 11-24-1859 | Mary S dt Harman & Nancy Ann, decd, of Carthage Mtg, Rush Co, m at Carthage M H, Walnut Ridge MM, to Lesse Lawrence of Mahaska County, Iowa |
| 5-19-1860 | Martha Bogue (form Allen)  chm for mcd |
| 12-15-1860 | Nathan dis for fighting |
| 4-21-1866 | Charles P  rec in mbrp |
| 4-16-1870 | Charles P  drpd from mbrp |

### ALLRED
| | |
|---|---|
| 5-20-1871 | Jane (form Nicholson)  chm for mcd |
| 12-19-1885 | Jane & ch Oscar Lee & Adeline D gct Duck Creek MM, Ind |

### ANDERS  (maybe ANDREWS)
| | |
|---|---|
| 2-17-1844 | Susannah Butler (form Anders)  chm for mcd |

### ANDERSON
| | |
|---|---|
| 4-19-1879 | Charles B & w Ella rec in mbrp |
| 4-19-1879 | Charles C & w Sarah & ch Charles & Sarah A rec in mbrp |
| 4-19-1879 | Jesse F & Olive M rec in mbrp |
| 6-16-1883 | Calvin A & Elizabeth rec in mbrp |
| 7-16-1887 | West  & Arabella  rec in mbrp |
| 3-19-1892 | Jesse F & w Olive M & ch Marshall, Chester & William gct White Lick MM, Ind |

### ANDREWS
| | |
|---|---|
| 1-16-1836 | Joseph & w Ann Maria & ch Permelia, Mary E, Caroline V, Joseph O & John R are charter mbrs |
| 3-16-1836 | Joseph appt to comm to care for indigent persons |
| 3-23-1843 | William E s Joseph of Hancock Co, Ind & 1st w, Mary, decd, lately of Dinwiddie Co, Va, m at Westland M H (Walnut Ridge MM) to Mary Elma Perisho of Hancock Co, Ind |
| 9-23-1847 | Caroline V dt Joseph & 2nd w, Anna Maria of Hancock Co, m at Westland M H (Walnut Ridge MM) to Nathan Binford of Rush Co, Ind |
| 8-22-1849 | Joseph Oliver of Hancock Co, Ind s Joseph Sr & Anna Mariah of same place, m at Walnut Ridge MM, to Martha Binford of Rush Co, Ind |
| 10-20-1853 | Joseph Oliver of Rush Co, s Joseph & Anna Mariah of Hancock Co, m at Carthage M H (Walnut Ridge MM) to Anna B Jessop of Rush Co, Ind |
| 5-19-1855 | William E & w Mary Elma & minor dt Pamelia gct Pleasant Plain MM, Iowa |
| 3-20-1862 | Parmelia Jane dt Joseph & Anna Mariah of Hancock Co, m at Westland M H (Walnut Ridge MM) to Jehu Newlin of Hendricks Co, Ind |
| 12-17-1864 | Samuel B gct Bridgeport MM, Ind |
| 10-20-1866 | Ruth Rocf Bridgeport MM, Ind |
| 2-18-1871 | (Samuel) Benjamin & w Ruth & minor ch Edjar J gct  Bridgeport MM, Ind |
| 11-15-1873 | Oliver Binford gct Westland MM, Ind to m Martha Ann Andrews |

### ANTRIM
| | |
|---|---|
| 6-20-1840 | John Milton, Mary Ann & William Penn, ch of Daniel rocf Mississinewa MM, Ind (certif of Daniel has been withheld) |
| 1-15-1841 | Daniel rocf Mississinewa MM, Ind |
| 5-15-1841 | Mary & dt Sarah  rec in mbrp |
| 4-20-1844 | John Milton, Mary Ann & William Penn, minor ch of Daniel, decd, gct Westfield MM, Ind |
| 7-19-1845 | Mary Kendal (form Antrim)  dis for mcd |
| 5-19-1860 | Marzilla Hodson (form Antrim) chm for mcd |
| 5-18-1861 | Sarah (form Shorter) dis for mcd |

### ATKINSON
| | |
|---|---|
| 11-18-1854 | William & w Nancy rocf Stillwater MM, Ohio |
| 12-18-1858 | William gct Pipe Creek MM, Ind |
| 8-18-1866 | Lavinia  (form Binford) chm for mcd |

### AYDELOTTE
| | |
|---|---|
| 5-19-1860 | Stewart & w Anna S & ch Joseph B, Sarah L, & Mary E  rocf Whitewater MM, Ind |
| 10-19-1861 | Henry C rocf Raysville MM, Ind |
| 8-20-1864 | Henry C & Susanna Parker altm A comm appt to att m & rept to next mtg |
| 9-17-1864 | The comm appt to att m of Henry C & Susanna Parker rpt it was orderly & the m certif has been placed in the hands of the Recorder |
| 5-18-1895 | Carrie Thornburgh glt Meth Church, South, Ben Franklin, Texas |

WALNUT RIDGE

359

BACON
3-21-1891   Dr Charles H rolf Meth Church, of S W
            Kansas Conference

BAKER
4-18-1874   James rec in mbrp
3-15-1879   James & w Mary & minor dt Cora B gct Carthage
            MM, Ind

BALES
8-18-1866   Owen S Hill gct Plainfield MM, Ind to m
            Melissa A Bales

BALL
5-20-1848   Anna Jane Ball (form Foster) dis for mcd

BARKER
9-19-1863   Caleb from Deep River MM, N Car, unable to
            produce certif of mbrp owing to the war.
            rec in mbrp
12-17-1864  Caleb & Laura Ann Quate are altm & a comm is
            appt to att the m & rpt to next mtg
1-21-1865   The comm appt to att m of Caleb & Laura Ann
            Quate rpt it was orderly & that the m certif
            has been placed in hands of the Recorder
3-18-1865   Caleb & w Laura Ann gct Duck Creek MM, Ind
7-28-1885   Delphina rocf Raysville MM, Ind
12-17-1887  Delphina & ch gct - - - - - ?

BARNARD
1- ?-1836   Asa & w Huldah & ch Thomas, Lucinda &
            Benjamin Franklin are charter mbrs
10-15-1836  John & w Elizabeth & ch Calvin, Anny, Lucinda,
            Phebe Newton, Mary & Obed rocf West Grove MM,
            Ind
4-24-1838   Zeno & w Anna Maria & s Eudoris rocf Salem
            MM, Ind
1-19-1839   Thomas rocf Salem MM, Ind
4-20-1839   Zeno & w Anna Maria & minor s Eudorus gct
            Salem MM, Ind
1-15-1841   Anny Gardiner (form Barnard) chm for mcd
1-21-1841   Thomas of Shelby Co, Ind s Asa & Huldah of
            same place m at Little Blue River M H
            (Walnut Ridge MM) to Rhoda Swain of Rush Co
9-23-1841   Benjamin Franklin of Shelby Co, Ind s Asa
            & Huldah of same place, m at Walnut Ridge
            MM, Ind to Anna Worth of Rush Co
2-19-1842   Jethro & w Sally & ch Laurinda, Edgehill B,
            Luzena & Rhoda rocf Salem MM, Ind
2-19-1842   Isaac chm for mcd
7-16-1842   Isaac rocf Salem MM, Ind
2-15-1845   Lucinda chm for mcd
3-18-1848   Phebe Folger (form Barnard) dis for mcd
5-20-1848   Lucinda Ridgey (form Barnard) dis for mcd
9-30-1851   Mary rec in mbrp
11-15-1851  William Newton dis for att mcd & upl
1-15-1853   Laurinda Swain (form Barnard) dis for mcd
1-15-1853   Mary Riggsey (form Barnard) dis for mcd
4-17-1858   Edgehill dis for mcd & j Meth Church
6-19-1858   Obed dis for j Meth Church
1-21-1860   Calvin & w Lucinda & minor ch Thomas E,
            Addison L & Horace G gct Spring Grove MM,
            Kansas Territory
7-16-1864   Maria (form Folger) mcd drpd from mbrp
5-19-1866   Adalaid Ingold (form Barnard) mcd drpd from
            mbrp

BARRETT
7-15-1854   Priscilla (form Hunt) dis for mcd

BEEMON
4-18-1840   Abigail (form Hendricks) dis for mcd

BEESON
5-15-1858   Mahlon H & w Mary & ch Amos & Jonathan J rocf
            Cherry Grove MM, Ind
8-20-1859   Isaac rocf Cherry Grove MM, Ind
9-21-1861   Isaac chm for mcd
11-18-1865  Mehitable rec in mbrp
12-15-1866  Phebe Ann rocf Richland MM, Ind
2-15-1868   Amos mcd drpd from mbrp
3-21-1868   Margaret (form Marsh) mcd drpd from mbrp

BELL
7-18-1846   Penelope & ch Lydia Jane rocf Milford MM, Ind
8-19-1848   Penelope N & minor dt Lydia Jane gct Milford
            MM, Ind

BENNETT
4-21-1894   Otto rec in mbrp
8-17-1895   Otto rel on req

BENTLEY
1-15-1841   Ruth Ann, Thomas E, Susannah, Sarah &
            Benjamin F, ch of (Reuben) & Sarah, rec in
            mbrp
11-20-1844  Ruth Anna dt Reuben & Sarah of Rush Co, Ind,
            m at Walnut Ridge MM, Ind to Micajah Henley
            of Rush Co, Ind
2-15-1845   Sarah Hasket (form Bentley) chm for mcd
11-17-1849  Susannah Holloway (form Bentley) chm for mcd
4-20-1850   Mary (form Henley) chm for mcd
12-21-1861  John B & w Mary E & ch William Penn, Reuben,
            Sarah E, Mary & Charles rec in mbrp
1-15-1881   William Penn gct Carthage MM, Ind
6-16-1883   John B rec in mbrp
7-16-1887   Nina & ch rec in mbrp
4-21-1888   Charles E gct Barclay MM, Kansas
3-21-1896   John B & w Mary E & Susanna & Martha A gct
            Carthage MM, Ind

BIGWOOD
7-15-1876   Rachel gct Bloomindale MM, Ind

BINFORD
1-16-1836   Ashbell & minor ch Jane & Jabez are charter
            mbrs
            William & w Mary & ch Eliza, Calvin & Jared
            P are charter mbrs
            Micajah & w Miriam & ch Micajah C, Sarah,
            Mary, Margaret, Martha & Miriam jr are
            charter mbrs
            James L & w Jane & ch Robert, Ana, Joseph,
            Benjamin & William L are charter mbrs
            Benajah & w Judith & ch John, Asa, Jared,
            Benajah jr, Nathan, Elijah, Elisha, Jeremiah
            & Judith Ann are charter mbrs
            Joshua & w Lydia & ch Lydia, Joshua, Sarah,
            James & Peter are charter mbrs
1-16-1836   Micajah appt to a comm
            Benajah appt to comm on education
            James L appt to comm on education
2-20-1836   Ann appt an overseer
3-23-1836   Lydia dt Joshua & Lydia m at Walnut Ridge
            Mtg, Ind to Robert Hill of Rush Co, Ind
9-21-1836   Micajah C of Rush Co, Ind s Micajah & Sarah,
            decd, of same place m at Walnut Ridge Mtg
            to Susanna Bundy
1-21-1837   Ashbell gct Milford MM, Ind to m Gulielma
            Symons
3-30-1837   Robert of Rush Co, Ind s James L & Mary,
            decd, of Hancock Co, Ind m at Walnut Ridge
            MM to Martha Hill of Rush Co
11-18-1837  Gulielma rocf Milford MM, Ind
8-23-1839   John of Hancock Co, Ind s Benajah & Judith
            of same place m at Walnut Ridge MM to Mary
            Moon of Hancock Co
9-25-1839   Sarah dt Micajah & Miriam of Rush Co, Ind m
            at Walnut Ridge MM to Joseph W Young of
            Rush Co
1-22-1840   Ann of Hancock Co, Ind dt Chappel & Mary,
            late of Prince George Co, Va, both decd, m
            at Walnut Ridge MM to Samuel Moore jr of
            Rush Co
1-29-1840   Joshua of Rush Co, Ind s Joshua Sr & Lydia
            of same place m at Walnut Ridge MM to
            Sarah Ann Hunnicutt of Hancock Co
8-21-1841   James gct Spiceland MM, Ind to m Ruth Gause
3-23-1842   Micajah of Rush Co, Ind s James & Hannah of
            North Hamilton Co, N Car m at - - - -
            (Walnut Ridge MM) to Charlotte A Butler
4-16-1842   Ruth rocf Spiceland MM, Ind
5-25-1842   Benjamin of Hancock Co, Ind s James L &
            Mary, decd, of same place, m at Walnut Ridge
            MM to Edna Butler of Rush Co
12-17-1842  Peter dis for disorderly conduct & j Meth
            Church
12-21-1842  Ann dt James L & Mary, decd, of Hancock Co,
            Ind m at (Walnut Ridge Mtg) to Nathan
            Bundy of Rush Co, Ind
8-22-1844   Benajah jr of Hancock Co, Ind s Benajah Sr
            & Judith of same place m at Walnut Ridge
            MM to Ann Moon of Hancock Co

WALNUT RIDGE

**BINFORD (Cont)**

|  |  |
|---|---|
| 12-25-1844 | Joseph of Rush Co, Ind s James L & Mary, decd of Hancock Co, m at Walnut Ridge MM Elizabeth C Hill of Rush Co |
| 1-23-1845 | Asa of Hancock Co, Ind s Benajah of same place m at Westland M H (Walnut Ridge MM) to Lavina M Harrell of Hancock Co |
| 3-21-1846 | Rachel rocf Milford MM, Ind |
| 3-25-1846 | Mary dt Micajah & Miriam, decd, of Rush Co, Ind m at Walnut Ridge MM to Joseph Butler of Rush Co |
| 9-23-1847 | Nathan of Rush Co, Ind s Benajah & Judith of Hancock Co m at Westland M H (Walnut Ridge MM) to Caroline V Andrews of Hancock Co |
| 8-21-1848 | Eliza dt William & Mary of Rush Co, Ind m at Carthage M H (Walnut Ridge MM) to Milton Brown of Hancock Co |
| 8-22-1849 | Martha dt Micajah & Miriam, decd, of Rush Co, Ind m at Walnut Ridge MM to Joseph Oliver Andrews of Hancock Co |
| 11-17-1849 | Benajah & w Ann & minor ch Isaac, Emeline & Ashbel N gct Salem MM, Iowa |
| 11-17-1849 | Jeremiah gct Salem MM, Iowa |
| 5-23-1850 | Jared of Rush Co, Ind s Benajah & Judith of Hancock Co, Ind m at Westland M H (Walnut Ridge MM) to Almeda Butler from Stark Co, Ohio, now of Indiana |
| 11-15-1851 | John & Mary & minor ch Ruth M, Hannah C, & George H gct East Grove MM, Iowa |
| 9-18-1852 | Mary Ann a minor gct Spiceland MM, Ind |
| 11-19-1853 | Jane Bright (form Binford) dis for mcd |
| 11-21-1853 | William of Rush Co, Ind s Micajah & Sarah, decd, of same place at Carthage M H (Walnut Ridge MM) to Mary Henley of Rush Co, Ind |
| 12-16-1854 | Josiah rocf Smithfield MM Ohio |
| 2-21-1855 | Josiah C of Rush Co, Ind s Benjamin & Mary of Prince George Co, Va, m at Walnut Ridge MM to Mary Ann Hill of Rush Co |
| 3-15-1856 | Joshua & w Sarah Ann & ch Elizabeth A, Thomas E, Lydia J, John H, Martha E & Eli G gct Spring Creek MM, Iowa |
| 4-18-1856 | James & w Rachel gct Milford MM, Ind |
| 5-26-1859 | Mary dt William & Mary, decd, of Rush Co, Ind m at Carthage M H (Walnut Ridge MM) to Cyrus B Cox of Rush Co, Ind |
| 8-25-1859 | Ashbel of Rush Co, Ind s Joshua & Lydia, both decd, m at Westland M H (Walnut Ridge MM) to Lavinia M Binford, a wid, of Hancock Co |
| 8-25-1859 | Lavinia M, wid & dt of Charles & Rachel Harrel of Hancock Co, Ind m at Westland M H (Walnut Ridge MM) to Ashbel Binford of Rush Co, Ind |
| 1-19-1861 | Peninah rocf Back Creek MM, Ind |
| 12-21-1861 | Lydia Ann rocf Hopewell MM, Ind |
| 3-25-1863 | Miriam dt Micajah & Miriam, decd, of Rush Co, Ind, m at Walnut Ridge MM to Jesse M Pitts of Rush co, Ind |
| 4-23-1863 | Joseph of Hancock Co, Ind s James L & Mary, decd of same place m at Carthage M H (Walnut Ridge MM) to Mary E White, a wid, of Rush Co, Ind |
| 11-21-1863 | Thomas mcd drpd from mbrp |
| 1-16-1864 | Henrietta M recf Hopewell MM, Ind |
| 5-21-1864 | Lydia Jane (form Binford) chm for mcd |
| 1-20-1866 | Mary Jane LYMAN (Form Binford) mcd drpd from mbrp |
| 8-18-1866 | Lavinia ATKINSON (form Binford) chm for mcd |
| 6-15-1867 | Susannah R & Benjamin O, minors, rocf Black Creek MM, Va |
| 5-16-1868 | Joshua & w Sarah Ann & minor ch John H, Martha E, Eli G, Emeline & Sarah gct Richland MM, Ind |
| 9-19-1868 | James H produced a cerfif from Hopewell MM, Ind to m Hannah E White. They are altm & a Friend is appt to att m & rpt to next mtg |
| 10-17-1868 | The Friend appt to att m of James H & Hannah E White rpts service att & that the m certif has been placed in hands of the Recorder |
| 12-18-1869 | Levi gct Carthage MM, Ind to m Abigail S Marshall |
| 6-18-1870 | Abigail S rocf Carthage MM, Ind |
| 7-16-1870 | Elizabeth Ann gct Richland MM, Ind |
| 11-19-1870 | Judith Ann KERNS (form Binford) chm for mcd |
| 2-18-1871 | Hannah & dt Mary E gct Hopewell MM, Ind |
| 4-15-1871 | Anna Jane & Joseph Pritchard are altm & a Friend is appt to att m & rpt to next mtg |
| 4-15-1871 | Emily Boblet (form Binford) chm mcd |
| 5-20-1871 | The Friend appt to att m of Anna Jane & Joseph Pritchard rpts service att & the certif has been forwarded to the Recorder |
| 9-21-1872 | William P gct Hopewell MM, Ind to m Esther Gilbert |
| 9-21-1872 | Levi & w Abbie gct Carthage MM, Ind |
| 1-18-1873 | Robert B chm mcd |
| 2-15-1873 | Robert B gct Westland MM, Ind |
| 5-17-1873 | John H gct Newgarden MM, Ind to m Susy Coggshall |
| 11-15-1873 | Oliver gct Westland MM, Ind to m Martha Ann ANDREWS |
| 5-16-1874 | Josiah & w Margaret F & ch Gurney, Micajah H & Bevan rocf Westland MM, Ind |
| 6-20-1874 | Oliver S gct Westland MM, Ind |
| 12-18-1874 | Joseph L gct Westland MM, Ind to m Susannah Jessop |
| 5-15-1875 | Peter & w Elizabeth & minor ch Woodford H rocf Westland MM, Ind |
| 12-18-1875 | Joseph L gct Westland MM, Ind |
| 4-15-1876 | Joseph & w Mary Elizabeth & ch Louisa, Elizabeth, Caroline & Joseph Omer Binford & her son William White gct Westland MM, Ind |
| 6-17-1876 | Robert & w Martha & minor ch Nathan & Alice gct Westland MM, Ind |
| 6-17-1876 | William P gct Westland MM, Ind |
| 10-19-1878 | Josiah & w Margaret F & ch Gurney, Micajah H, Bevan & Raymond gct Carthage MM, Ind |
| 4-19-1879 | Jared & w Emily & a minor ch under their care, Elias Binford rocf Carthage MM, Ind |
| 1-17-1880 | Robert & w Martha & ch Mary L, Nathan C & Alice A rocf Westland MM, Ind |
| 1-15-1881 | Thomas gct Westland MM, Ind (Hancock Co) |
| 2-16-1884 | Emma J & Elias Chappel are altm Josiah & Mary A Binford req a mtg be appt to be held at their residence on 2-21-1884 at 2 o'clock, Req is granted |
| 2-21-1884 | Emma J & Elias Chappel m at residence of Josiah & Mary A Binford |
| 6-19-1886 | Rebecca S & dt Ethel rec in mbrp (w & dt of Joseph) |
| 2-19-1887 | Benjamin O gct Carthage MM, Ind |
| 4-16-1887 | Benajah gct Westland MM, Ind |
| 4-16-1887 | Robert B gct Westland MM, Ind |
| 5-21-1887 | Lindley M rocf Westland MM, Ind |
| 5-18-1839 | Benjamin rocf Westland MM, Ind |
| 9-20-1890 | By written inf this mtg is inf that Nathan C & Lucy S Hill intend m with each other, A Friend is appt to att m & rpt to next Mtg |
| 10-18-1890 | The Friend appt to att m of Nathan C & Lucy S Hill rpts service att & m certif has been forwarded to the Recorder |
| 1-17-1891 | Jared & w Emily & dt Ellen O gct Carthage MM, Ind |
| 10-17-1891 | Lindley M gct Salem MM, Mass |
| 11-21-1891 | Marcia & John W Chappell inf mtg of int to m each other, They are altm Josiah C & Mary A Binford req a mtg appt at their home on 11-26-1891 at 6 P M for the m req granted |
| 11-26-1891 | Marcia & John W Chappell m at home of Josiah C & Mary A Binford |
| 1-21-1893 | Frank & w Olive & ch Hazel & Virgil gct Westland MM, Ind |
| 1-21-1893 | Benjamin O gct Dublin MM, Ind |
| 9-15-1893 | Micajah & w Susie & s Edward gct Whitewater MM, Ind |
| 9-15-1893 | Nathan C & w Lucy gct Carthage MM, Ind |
| 9-15-1893 | William P & w Esther & dt Adella M rocf Emporia MM, Kansas |
| 2-17-1894 | Susie P rec in mbrp |
| 3-21-1896 | Benjamon O gct Hopewell MM, Ind |
| 9-19-1896 | Ruth gct Whitewater MM, Ind |
| 9-19-1896 | William P & w Esther & dt Adella M gct Hopewell MM, Ind |
| 1-16-1897 | Agnes H rocf Westland MM, Ind |

## WALNUT RIDGE

### BLAIR
3-20-1854    Abner of Hendricks Co, Ind, s Enos & Hannah, both decd, formerly of Randolph Co, N Car m at Walnut Ridge Mtg, Ind to Margaret Butler, a wid, of Rush Co, Ind

7-15-1854    Margaret & her minor ch Jesse M, Asenath & Phebe Lacey (ch of her late husb Pearson Lacy) gct Westland MM, Ind

### BOBLET
4-13-1871    Emily (form Binford) chm mcd

### BOGUE
11-19-1836    Prudence, Jemima, Dilwin, Phineas & Mary Ann (ch of Dilwin Sr & Ann) rocf Salem MM, Ind

5-20-1837    Jemima dis for mcd
11-21-1840    Lydia rocf Salem MM, Ind
9-18-1845    Lydia dis for att mcd
5-19-1855    David REECE gct Spiceland MM, Ind to m Jane J Bogue
5-19-1860    Martha (form Allen) chm mcd
9-15-1860    Martha gct Spiceland MM, Ind

### BOND
9-20-1855    William of Spiceland Mtg, Henry Co, Ind, s Jesse & Anna, decd, of same place m at Carthage M H (Walnut Ridge MM) Ind to Sarah Jessop of Rush Co, Ind
2-21-1857    Sarah gct Spiceland MM, Ind
4-16-1859    William & w Sarah & s Thomas J rocf Spiceland MM, Ind
12-21-1861    Anna rocf Spiceland MM, Ind
1-21-1882    William & fam gct Dover MM, Ind

### BOWERS
5-17-1856    Mary BOWERS (form Talbott) dis mcd

### BOYD
3-16-1839    Elizabeth (wid of Adam Boyd) rocf Whitewater MM, Ind
4-24-1839    Elizabeth, wid of Adam Boyd & dt of Amos Hawkins, decd, & w Anna of Wayne Co, Ind m at Walnut Ridge Mtg, Ind to Elias Marsh of Hancock Co, Ind
6-18-1842    Martha Ann, Jonathan Dayton, & Oliver Mackenzie Boyd, ch of Adam, decd & Elizabeth (now Elizabeth Marsh) rec in mbrp
9-23-1846    Martha Ann of Rush Co, Ind dt Adam & Elizabeth, both decd, m at Walnut Ridge MM, Ind to Robert Brown of Rush Co, Ind
2-24-1848    Oliver Mac. of Hancock Co, Ind s Adam & Elizabeth, both decd, m at Westland M H (Walnut Ridge M Mtg) Ind to Mary Osborn of Hancock Co, Ind
12-20-1851    Oliver Mac. & w Mary & minor ch Thomas E & John W gct Westfield MM, Ind
5-15-1852    Jonathan D gct Sugar Plain MM, Ind

### BRANSON
12-20-1862    John H rec in mbrp

### BREWER
4-19-1873    Morris W & w Eliza & ch rec in mbrp
9-21-1873    Janette F & dt Martha E, Stella gct Fairmount MM, Ind
7-15-1876    Morris J & w Eliza & minor ch Clarence A, Otis J, Eva V, Nettie Z, Jennie F, Allie E & Allen L gct Raysville MM, Ind
6-19-1880    Morris & w Eliza Ann & ch Clarence, Augustus Otis J, Eva, Jennie, Nettie, Alta & Dellie rocf Raysville MM, Ind
2-19-1881    Morris & w Eliza Ann & ch Clarence, Otis, Eva, Nettie, Jennie, Alta & Dellie gct Springfield MM, Ind

### BRIGHT
11-19-1853    Jane (form Binford) dis for mcd

### BROOKS
6-15-1867    Ellen rec in mbrp
11-16-1867    William & w Mary & ch Robert, Amanda, Laura, Sarah & John rec in mbrp
1-15-1881    William & w Mary & ch Robert, Amanda, Laura, Sarah & John gct Westland MM, Ind
2-15-1896    James rec in mbrp

### BROWN
1-16-1836    John & w Cerina & ch Abigail are charter mbrs
1-16-1836    William & w Celia & ch Cyrus N, Milton D, Mary, Rebecca, Henry & John are charter mbrs
12-17-1836    Samuel & w Margaret & ch Mary, Eli, Rachel, Robert, Jane, Israel & Samuel H rocf West Grove MM, Ind
9-23-1840    Eli of Rush Co, Ind s Samuel & Margaret of same place m at Walnut Ridge Mtg, Ind to Sarah Hill of Hancock Co, Ind
9-22-1841    Mary dt Samuel & Margaret of Rush Co, Ind m at Walnut Ridge Mtg, Ind to James C Mendenhall of Hendricks Co, Ind
12-22-1841    Rachel dt Samuel & Margaret of Rush Co, Ind m at Walnut Ridge Mtg, Ind to Enoch Pearson of Henry Co, Ind
9-23-1846    Robert of Rush Co, Ind s Samuel & Margaret m at Walnut Ridge MM, Ind to Martha Ann Boyd of Rush Co, Ind
8-21-1848    Milton of Hancock Co, Ind s William & Celia of same place m at Carthage M H (Walnut Ridge MM) Ind to Eliza Binford of Rush Co, Ind
12-18-1848    Jane dt Samuel & Margaret of Rush Co, Ind m at Walnut Ridge Mtg, Ind to Thomas Nichols of Hendricks Co, Ind
1-20-1853    Rebecca, dt William & Celia of Hancock Co, Ind m at Westland M H (Walnut Ridge MM) Ind to Jacob Jessop of Rush Co, Ind
8-20-1853    Israel gct Mill Creek MM, Ind to m Eliza Nichols
8-20-1853    Mary REECE (form Brown) chm mcd
9-21-1853    Milton of Rush Co, Ind s William & Celia of Hancock Co, m at Walnut Ridge Mtg, Ind to Angelina B Parker of Rush Co, Ind
12-17-1853    Eliza rocf Mill Creek MM, Ind
4-21-1855    Israel & w Eliza gct Mill Creek MM, Ind
10-20-1855    Samuel H gct White Lick MM, Ind to m Jane Newlin
2-16-1856    Jane rocf White Lick MM, Ind
11-22-1857    John of Westland PM, Hancock Co, Ind s William & Celia of same place m at Westland M H (Walnut Ridge MM) Ind to Sarah Ann Coffin of Hancock Co, Ind
2-19-1859    Irena (form Coffin) chm for mcd
2-19-1859    Robert B chm for mcd
4-16-1859    Milton mcd drpd from mbrp
9-23-1860    Seth of Westland Mtg, Hancock Co, Ind s John & Cyrena of same place m at Westland M H (Walnut Ridge MM) Ind to Miranda W Rawls of Hancock Co, Ind
6-15-1861    Jane & minor ch Charles & Esther J gct Newberry MM, Ohio
7-20-1861    Lydia HILL (form Brown) mcd drpd from mbrp
9-21-1861    Henry mcd drpd from mbrp
4-19-1864    Mary & O. Winbern Kerns are altm A comm is appt to att m & rpt to next mtg
5-21-1864    The comm appt to att m of Mary & O. Winbern Kerns rptd it was orderly & that the m certif has been placed in hands of the Recorder
5-20-1865    John chm for mcd
11-18-1865    Joshua M gct Plainfield MM, Ind
7- ?-1866    James produced a certif from Sugar Plain MM, Ind to m Martha Ann Marsh, a wid They are altm & a Friend is appt to att m & rpt to next Mtg
8-18-1866    The Friend appt to att m of James & Martha Ann Marsh rptd the service att & m certif has been placed in hands of the Recorder
9-15-1866    Robert B & Rebecca J Moore are altm A Friend is appt to att m & rpt to next mtg
10-20-1866    The Friend appt to att m of Robert B & Rebecca J Moore rpts the service att & the m certif has been placed in hands of the Recorder
10-20-1866    Martha Ann & minor s Benjamin F Marsh gct Sugar Plain MM, Ind
12-15-1866    Elizabeth (form Mills) chm for mcd
5-18-1867    Elizabeth rocf Sugar Plain MM, Ind

WALNUT RIDGE

**BROWN (cont)**

|  |  |
|---|---|
| 6-15-1867 | Elizabeth HUNT (form Brown) chm for mcd |
| 1-18-1868 | Robert B & w Rebecca J & minor ch Marrietta & Irene Melissa gct Toledo MM (Chase Co) Kansas |
| 1-16-1869 | Seth & w Maranda W & minor s Jasper M gct Sugar Plain MM, Ind |
| 3-20-1869 | Milton C & w Elizabeth & minor ch Orah Ellen gct Sugar Plain MM, Ind |
| 8-21-1869 | Frederick & w Sarah & minor ch Morris J, John, Josiah, Mary A & Sarah J gct Tonganoxie MM, Kansas |
| 10-18-1869 | Jesse gct Greenwood MM, Ind to m Lydia C Perisho |
| 7-16-1870 | Lydia C rocf Greenwood MM, Ind |
| 7-16-1870 | Nathan chm for mcd |
| 1-21-1871 | Rachel rec in mbrp |
| 6-17-1871 | Nathan gct Spiceland MM, Ind |
| 4-17-1875 | Mary J rocf Spiceland MM, Ind |
| 4-17-1880 | Oliver M & Almira Parker are altm A Friend is appt to att m & rpt to next Mtg |
| 5-15-1880 | The Friend appt to att m of Oliver M & Almira Parker, rpts service att & the m certif has been placed in hands of the Recorder |
| 7-16-1881 | Nathan & w Mary Ann & ch Anna, Frank, Mabel Clair & Leroy rocf Spiceland MM, Ind |
| 8-18-1883 | Alfred gct Wilmington MM, Ohio |
| 7-28-1885 | Nathan & w Mary & ch Anna, Frank, Mabel & Leroy gct Liberty MM, Kansas |
| 5-17-1890 | Alfred & w Effie Afton & s Paul Howard rocf Wilmington MM, Ohio |
| 11-17-1894 | Alfred & w Effie Afton & ch Paul Howard, Russell Lowell gct Spiceland MM, Ind |
| 3-20-1897 | Alfred & w Effie Afton & ch Paul H & Russell L rocf Spiceland MM, Ind |
| 12-16-1899 | Effie Afton Hall & her ch Paul H & Russell L Brown gct Spiceland MM, Ind |

**BRUNER**

|  |  |
|---|---|
| 12-19-1886 | Mary gct Westland MM, Hancock Co, Ind |

**BUCK**

|  |  |
|---|---|
| 3-17-1888 | James E rec in mbrp |
| 2-20-1892 | James & w Margery gct Duck Creek MM, Ind |

**BUFKIN**

|  |  |
|---|---|
| 3-21-1857 | Joshua Moore gct Spiceland MM, Ind to m Mary Bufkin |
| 10-20-1866 | Thirza Jane Redding (form Bufkin) chm mcd |

**BUNDY**

|  |  |
|---|---|
| 1-16-1836 | Elias & w Sarah & ch Ellen, Mary, Pennina, Martha, Ann & John are charter mbrs |
| 1-16-1836 | Josiah & w Mary & ch Susanna, Ruth, Nathan, Henry, Mary, Caleb M & Josiah jr are charter mbrs |
| 1-16-1836 | George & w Angelina & s Amos B are charter mbrs |
| 1-16-1836 | Samuel & w Priscilla & ch Joseph & Rachel are charter mbrs |
| 1-16-1836 | Josiah appt to a comm |
| 2-20-1836 | Priscilla appt to comm on Education |
| 2-20-1836 | Elias appt an overseer |
| 3-16-1836 | Elias appt to comm to care for indigent persons |
| 3-16-1836 | Samuel appt to a comm |
| 9-21-1836 | Susanna dt Josiah & Mary of Rush Co, Ind m at Walnut Ridge Mtg Ind to Micajah C Binford of Rush Co, Ind |
| 12-21-1842 | Nathan of Rush Co, Ind s Josiah & Mary of same place m at - - - - - Mtg, Ind to Ann Binford of Hancock Co, Ind |
| 9-16-1843 | Ellen dis |
| 2-19-1845 | Priscilla & minor ch Joseph, Rachel & Sarah gct Hopewell MM, Ind |
| 9-24-1845 | Mary dt Elias & Sarah of Rush Co, Ind m at Walnut Ridge MM, Ind to Nathan Pearson |
| 1-15-1848 | Henry gct Westfield MM, Ind |
| 1-24-1849 | Mary dt Josiah, decd, & Mary of Rush Co, Ind m at Walnut Ridge MM, Ind to Jonathan Jessop jr of Rush Co, Ind |
| 3-16-1850 | David Butler & w Priscilla & her ch Joseph, Rachel & Sarah Bundy & his dt Esther Butler & their s Cyrus Butler rocf Milford MM, Ind Ellen rec in mbrp |
| 5-18-1850 | |
| 6-18-1852 | Martha HILL (form Bundy) chm for mcd |
| 12-22-1852 | Caleb M of Rush Co, Ind s Josiah, decd, & Mary of same place MM, Ind to Esther L Butler of Rush Co, Ind m at Walnut Ridge |
| 3-19-1853 | Rachel & Sarah Bundy with their mother Priscilla & step-fth David Butler gct Honey Creek MM, Ind |
| 3-19-1853 | Henry gct Spiceland MM, Ind to m Eliza Elliott |
| 9-17-1853 | Mary Eliza rocf Spiceland MM, Ind |
| 10-21-1854 | John gct Pipe Creek MM, Miami Co, Ind to m Hannah Symons |
| 3-17-1855 | Joseph J gct Honey Creek MM, Ind |
| 2-16-1856 | Hannah S rocf Pipe Creek MM, Ind |
| 5-20-1857 | Ruth dt Elias & Sarah of Rush Co, Ind m at Walnut Ridge MM, Ind to Josiah Cook of Henry Co, Ind |
| 3-23-1859 | Angelina, wid of George jr, & dt Benajah Sr & Judith Binford, both decd, m at Walnut Ridge MM, Ind to Thomas Cook of Hancock Co, Ind |
| 5-25-1859 | Martha Jane dt George, decd, & Angelina of Hancock Co, Ind m at Pleasant View M H (Walnut Ridge MM) Ind to John A Hunnicutt of Rush Co, Ind |
| 1-21-1860 | John & w Hannah & minor ch Thomas E, William F, Sarah Jane gct Pipe Creek MM, Ind |
| 4-19-1862 | William gct Hopewell MM, Ind |
| 11-20-1862 | Mary Jane dt Nathan, decd, & Ann of Hancock Co, Ind m at Westland M H, (Walnut Ridge MM) Ind to Jesse Wheeler of Guilford Co, N Car |
| 9-23-1863 | Ann J dt Elias & Sarah of Rush Co, Ind m at Walnut Ridge Mtg, Ind to Amos C Horner of Henry Co, Ind |
| 8-20-1864 | William P & w Matilda rocf West Union MM, Ind |
| 10-21-1865 | William & w Mary & ch Ada Eldora & Albert Luther rocf Hopewell MM, Ind |
| 10-21-1865 | Ira S & w Sarah R & s Charles Warren rocf Hopewell MM, Ind |
| 3-17-1866 | Ruth Ann MOORE (form Bundy) chm mcd |
| 3-21-1868 | Elias, an Elder, & w Sarah & dt Penina gct Carthage MM, Ind |
| 9-19-1868 | Henry C chm for mcd |
| 10-18-1869 | Amos B dis for drinking |
| 8-19-1871 | Henry C gct Whitewater MM, Ind |
| 3-21-1874 | Zenas rec in mbrp |
| 5-15-1875 | Sarah rocf Carthage MM, Ind |
| 12-18-1875 | Josiah gct Carthage MM, Ind to m Sarah J Hill |
| 3-17-1876 | Sarah J rocf Carthage MM, Ind |
| 5-20-1876 | Penina rocf Carthage MM, Ind |
| 5-18-1878 | Henry C & w Mary & ch William, Nellie & Alsie rocf Whitewater MM, Ind |
| 1-18-1879 | Thomas M & Adaline & ch Georgianna, Florence, William, James, Charles, Jesse, Mary & Anna rec in mbrp |
| 7-17-1880 | Henry C & w Mary & ch William, Nellie & Alsie gct Goshen MM, Ohio |
| 1-15-1881 | David gct Westland MM, Ind |
| 6-18-1881 | David rocf Westland MM, Ind |
| 7-21-1883 | Charlie rel on req |
| 1-19-1884 | Sarah Jane & fam gct Carthage MM, Ind |
| 6-21-1884 | Caleb & fam gct Geneva MM, Kansas |
| 1-16-1886 | Henry & w Mary & ch William, Myrtle, Nellie & Alsie rocf Cesaer's Creek MM, Ohio |
| 2-19-1887 | Caleb gct New Castle MM, Ind |
| 4-16-1887 | David gct Westland MM, Ind |
| 1-21-1888 | Henry & w Mary Eliza gct New Castle MM, Ind |
| 6-16-1888 | Eunice A & ch rocf Carmel MM, Kansas |
| 11-16-1889 | Henry C & fam gct Raysville MM, Ind |
| 3-19-1892 | Zenos & w Rachel & ch Edwin gct Carthage MM, Ind |
| 11-17-1894 | Mary gct Carthage MM, Ind |

WALNUT RIDGE

BUNTON
1-21-1837  Penina rocf New Garden MM, Ind
5-19-1838  Penina gct New Garden MM, Ind
9-19-1840  James B Hunnicutt gcf New Garden MM, Ind to m Penina Bunton

BURGIS
1-20-1866  William A & w Jane & ch Elizabeth, Mary J & Henry rocf Deep Creek MM, N Car

BURTON
9-19-1846  Margaret dis for mcd

BUTLER
1-16-1836  Charlotte, wid of Joseph Sr, late of Western Branch Mtg, Va, & ch Gulielma, Oliver, Benjamin Pretlow, Edna & Joseph jr are charter mbrs
10-26-1836  Elisha & w Rhoda & ch George W, Jesse, Elisha & Arthur rocf Marlborough MM, Ohio endorsed by Duck Creek MM, Ind
11-19-1836  William & w Esther & ch Lydia, Priscilla, Edward & Robert rocf Spiceland MM, Ind
1-31-1837  John & w Julia & ch William Henry, John Stanton rocf Marlborough MM, Ohio
5-20-1837  Joseph J rocf Milford MM, Ind
6-17-1837  Martha (form Rawls) dis for mcd
7-15-1837  George dis for mcd
9-20-1837  Joseph J of Hancock Co, Ind s William & Esther of same place m at Walnut Ridge Mtg, Ind to Eliza Patterson of Rush Co, Ind
8-18-1838  Martha rec in mbrp
8-18-1838  George rec in mbrp
10-24-1838  Priscilla dt William & Esther of Hancock Co, Ind m at Walnut Ridge Mtg, Ind to Silas Parker of Rush Co, Ind
12-15-1838  Jonathan & w Sarah & ch Sarah Ann, Mary Jane & Priscilla rocf Spiceland MM, Ind
6-20-1840  Daniel s of George & Martha rec in mbrp
3-23-1842  Charlotte A, wid of Joseph Sr & dt James & Ann - - - ? both decd of Prince George Co, Va, m at - - - - - - - Ind to Micajah Binford of Rush Co, Ind
5-25-1842  Edna dt Joseph Sr, decd & Charlotte of Rush Co, Ind m at Walnut Ridge Mtg, Ind to Benjamin Binford of Hancock Co, Ind
6-17-1843  Benjamin P chm mcd
9-16-1843  Oliver dis for dp
2-17-1844  Susanna (form Anders) chm mcd
7-10-1844  Susanna rocf Springfield MM, Ohio
2-19-1845  Edward of Rush Co, Ind s William & Esther, decd, of Hancock Co, Ind m at Walnut Ridge Mtg, Ind to Sarah Ann Lacy of Rush Co, Ind
3-19-1845  Lydia dt William & Esther, decd, of Hancock Co, Ind m at Walnut Ridge MM, Ind to Phineas White of Rush Co, Ind
3-25-1846  Joseph of Rush Co, Ind s Joseph Sr, decd & Charlotte, formerly of Prince George Co, Va, at Walnut Ridge MM, Ind to Mary Binford of Rush Co, Ind
4-18-1846  Oliver gct Whitewater MM, Ind
10-7-1846  William of Hancock Co, Ind s Joseph & Miriam, both decd, of Dinwiddie Co, Va m at Walnut Ridge MM, Ind to Margaret Lacey, a wid, of Rush Co, Ind
10-18-1847  Rhoda, wid, & dt John & Tabitha Rawls, decd, of Starke Co, Ohio m at Westland MH (Walnut Ridge MM) Ind to Samuel Nixon of Wayne Co, Ind
4-15-1848  Arthur & Lucinda with their mother Rhoda (now Rhoda Nixon) gct New Garden MM, Ind
6-17-1848  Almeda rocf Marlborough MM, Ohio
9-16-1848  Jonathan & w Sarah & ch Sarah Ann, Mary Jane Priscilla L, William H, Hardy H & James H gct Honey Creek MM, Ind
2-20-1850  Mahlon of Montgomery Co, Ind s Lemuel, decd, & Jane of same place m at Walnut Ridge Mtg, Ind to Eunice M Lacy of Rush Co, Ind
3-16-1850  David & w Priscilla & her ch Joseph, Rachel & Sarah Bundy & his dt Esther & their s Cyrus Butler rocf Milford MM, Ind
5-23-1850  Almeda, now of Indiana, dt Daniel, decd, lately of Stark Co, Ohio & his w Mary m at Westland M H (Walnut Ridge MM,) Ind to Jared Binford of Rush Co, Ind
7-17-1850  Eunice M gct Sugar River MM, Ind
12-22-1852  Esther L dt Jared & Mary, decd, of Rush Co, Ind m at Walnut Ridge Mtg, Ind to Caleb M Bundy of Rush Co, Ind
3-19-1853  David & w Priscilla & their s Cyrus Butler & her ch Rachel & Sarah Bundy gct Honey Creek MM, Ind
5-26-1853  Joshua M of Wayne Co, Ind s William & Susanna of same place m at Carthage M H (Walnut Ridge MM) Ind to Eliza Thornburgh of Rush Co, Ind
1-21-1854  Diza gct Milford MM, Ind
3-20-1854  Margaret, a wid, of Rush Co, Ind & dt of Jesse Morris & Mary, decd of same place m at Walnut Ridge Mtg, Ind to Abner Blair of Hendricks Co, Ind
11-21-1857  Lucinda rocf New Garden MM, Ind
10-20-1858  Edward of Rush Co, Ind s William & Esther, decd, of same place m at Walnut Ridge Mtg, Ind to Mary M Pitts of Rush Co, Ind
6-15-1861  Daniel chm for mcd
11-15-1862  Eli H dis for mcd
10-1-1863  Mary P dt Joseph J & Eliza of Rush Co, Ind m at Walnut Ridge Mtg, Ind to Henry Pitts of Rush Co, Ind
11-21-1863  Elisha M gct Plainfield MM, Ind
11-19-1864  Daniel W rocf New Garden MM, Ind
4-15-1865  George W & w Martha & minor ch Micajah, Elwood, Almeda & Elizabeth Ann gct Spiceland MM, Ind
4-21-1866  Joseph & Margaret Binford are altm & a comm is appt to att m & rpt to next mtg
5-19-1866  The comm appt to att m of Joseph & Margaret Binford rpt it was orderly & the m certif has been placed in the hands of the Recorder
1-19-1867  Joseph J & w Eliza, she a Minister, & the minor ch Deborah A, Jared P & Hiram gct Raysville MM, Ind
6-15-1867  John gct Spiceland MM, Ind
8-17-1867  Daniel W gct Spiceland MM, Ind
9-21-1867  Lucinda B gct Spiceland MM, Ind
5-16-1868  Sybel (form Hockett) chm for mcd
7-18-1868  Sybel A gct Spiceland MM, Ind
7-18-1868  Levi chm for mcd
5-15-1869  Esther Ann Nicholson (form Butler) chm for mcd
8-19-1871  Thomas E chm for mcd
2-15-1873  Thirsey Jane rec in mbrp
3-15-1873  David rocf Honey Creek MM, Ind
5-16-1874  Robert rocf Carthage MM, Ind
6-16-1883  Henrietta T rocf Beech Grove MM, Ind
2-20-1886  Martha A & ch John, Charles & Jessie rec in mbrp
8-19-1893  Thomas E gct Fairmount MM, Ind
7-21-1894  Levi, Charles & Martha glt Meth Church, Carthage, Ind
7-21-1894  Jonathan glt Meth Ch, Carthage, Ind

CADWELL
4-20-1878  William F & w Amanda rec in mbrp
2-16-1884  William dis for larceny

CANADAY
11-9-1844  Nathan H & w Ann rocf Hopewell MM, N Car
3-16-1850  Nathan H & w Ann gct Duck Creek MM, Ind
5-20-1899  Eliza rocf Amboy MM, Ind

CARD
12-21-1839  Miriam rocf Blue River MM, Ind
3-21-1874  Phineas & w Mila A & ch Emma E, Penninah E, John W & Silas W rec in mbrp
5-17-1890  Phineas & w Miley & ch Emma A, Penina, John W, Ida & Jennie gct Westland MM, Ind

CARFIELD
3-19-1892  Sarah Effie rec in mbrp
3-19-1892  Alta M rec in mbrp (dt of Myrtle)
3-19-1898  Myrtle & dt Alta gct Carthage MM, Ind

## WALNUT RIDGE

**CARPENTER**
4-17-1869 — Rebecca rocf Duck Creek MM, Ind

**CARY**
7-18-1846 — Edmund dis

**CASE**
4-20-1878 — Simon P & w Tacy rec in mbrp
9-18-1880 — Simon rel on req

**CATHEN**
5-16-1840 — William & w Elizabeth rocf Marlborough MM, Ohio
8-23-1849 — William s Josiah W & Mourning, decd, of Stark Co, Ohio m at Westland M H (Walnut Ridge MM) Ind to Mariah Davis, a wid, of Hancock Co, Ind
4-20-1867 — Elizabeth ADDISON (form Cathen) chm for mcd

**CATT**
4-15-1867 — Solomon & w Cyrena & ch Benjamin, Eli, Lucinda Harvey A, Mark A, Rebecca Ann & Riley A rec in mbrp

**CHAPPELL**
1-16-1836 — Thomas L & w Margaret & ch Martha Ann, John & Deborah are charter mbrs
12-21-1836 — Martha Ann dt Thomas L & Martha, decd, m at Walnut Ridge Mtg, Ind to William Marsh of Hancock Co, Ind
2-18-1837 — Benjamin & w Mary rocf Marlborough MM, (OHIO?)
4-24-1838 — Nathan Perisho gct Whitewater MM, Ind to m Sarah Chappell
12-25-1839 — Deborah dt Thomas L, decd, & w Margaret of Hancock Co, Ind m at Walnut Ridge Mtg, Ind to Joseph Moore of Hamilton Co, Ind
7-17-1841 — John gct Westfield MM, Ind
10-18-1856 — Peggy (Margaret) gct Westfield MM, Ind
8-7-1861 — Joseph J s Gideon & Elizabeth, decd, of Perquimans Co, N Car m at Walnut Ridge Mtg, Ind to Eliza A Patterson of Rush Co, Ind
2-17-1866 — Joseph John rocf Piney Woods MM, N Car
6-16-1883 — Elias rocf Piney Woods MM, N Car
2-16-1883 — Elias & Emma J Binford are altm. Josiah & Mary Binford req a mtg to be held at their residence on 2-21-1884 at 2 o'clock for the m. Req is granted
2-21-1884 — Elias & Emma J Binford m at res of Josiah & Mary A Binford
3-21-1895 — Joseph John & w Eliza Ann & Ella, Gurney, Charles & Anna gct Greenfield MM, Ind
4-16-1887 — James Thomas rocf Piney Woods MM, N Car
12-15-1888 — James Thomas & Alice Parker are altm. A req is made for a mtg at residence of John Parker on 1-1-1889 at 6 P M. Req was granted
1-1-1889 — James Thomas & Alice Parker m at residence of John Parker
6-20-1891 — John W rocf Westland MM, Ind
11-21-1891 — John W & Marcia Binford inf this mtg of int to m each other. They are altm. Josiah C & Mary A Binford req a mtg at their home on 11-26-1891 at 6 P M for the m. Req granted
11-26-1891 — John & Marcia Binford m at Josiah C & Mary A Binfords

**CLARK**
1-16-1836 — John & w Nancy & ch Jediah, Daniel, Alfred, Anna, Martha A, Thomas & Hezekiah are charter mbrs
1-16-1836 — Abigail & ch Richard, George, Eliza, Daniel A, John L W, Cynthia A, Hezekiah F, Abigail J, David W S & Rhoda G are charter mbrs
1-16-1836 — John appt Clerk for the day
1-16-1836 — John appt to comm to make a mbrp list
1-16-1836 — John appt to comm on Education
2-20-1836 — John appt Clerk of the Mthly Mtg & Jonathan D Stratton appt asst Clerk
9-17-1836 — John appt an Elder
10-21-1837 — Jane, wid rocf Whitewater MM, Ind
8-18-1838 — Eliza dis
1-19-1839 — Samuel & w Mary & ch Sally, Edwin, Julia, Ascenith, Daniel & John rocf Deep River MM, N Car
3-11-1839 — Jane, wid of John Clark now of Rush Co, Ind, & dt of John & Elizabeth Hamm, both decd, m at Walnut Ridge Mtg, Ind to Samuel Hadley of White Lick Mtg, Morgan Co, Ind
7-20-1839 — Hezekiah rocf Centre MM, N Car
7-19-1840 — Mary Ann & Lydia rocf Whitewater MM, Ind
5-20-1843 — Lydia, a minor gct White Lick MM, Ind
12-16-1843 — Mary Ann gct White Lick MM, Ind
12-18-1847 — Samuel gct Sugar River MM, Ind
2-19-1848 — Samuel & ch Emily, Julia Ann, Asenath, Daniel W, John G, Oliver & Cyrus gct Sugar River MM, Ind
1-20-1849 — Daniel gct Fairfield MM, Ind
9-15-1849 — John M & w Eunice & dt Mary M rocf New Garden MM, N Car
11-17-1849 — Daniel gct Whitewater MM, Ind
4-17-1852 — David & w Mary R & ch Ezra R rocf West Union MM, - - -?
11-22-1852 — Anna dt John & Nancy of Rush Co, Ind m at Carthage M H (Walnut Ridge Mtg) Ind to Bowling H Winston of Sugar River MM, Montgomery Co, Ind
10-17-1853 — Abigail J dt Hezekiah S & Abigail of Rush Co, Ind m at Little Blue River M H (Walnut Ridge MM) Ind to David L Hadley of Clinton Co, Ohio
11-18-1854 — John W gct Honey Creek MM, Ind
2-17-1855 — John dis for mcd
2-21-1857 — Dougan & w Sarah & ch Charles J & William E rocf New Garden MM, N Car
6-20-1857 — Ascenith (mother of Dougan) rocf New Garden MM, N Car
7-18-1857 — Dougan & w Sarah & minor ch Charles J & William E gct Westfield MM, Ind
10-17-1857 — Ascenith, a Minister, gct Westfield MM, Ind
12-15-1860 — Hezekiah F gct Fairfield MM, Ind
6-15-1861 — Thomas gct Raysville MM, Ind to m Emily J Griffin
8-17-1861 — Thomas gct Hinkles Creek MM, Ind
5-16-1863 — Caroline A rocf Adrian MM, Mich
4-16-1864 — John W & w Rebecca Jane & ch Lydia, William, Celia, Laura, George & Martin rec in mbrp
9-21-1889 — Lindley & w Maria & ch Edward Daniel gct Maryville MM, Tenn
3-20-1897 — Rowland E glt Presby Ch, Wabash, Ind

**CLICK**
9-21-1872 — John R & w Sarah & ch Alice & Lewis rec in mbrp
1-16-1875 — John R & fam gct Salem MM, Ind

**CLOUD**
9-21-1850 — Nathan Nicholson gct Spiceland MM, Ind to m Ascenith Cloud
6-14-1854 — Levi of Spiceland Mtg, Henry Co, Ind, s Joel & Anna of same place m at Pleasant View M H (Hancock Co,) (Walnut Ridge MM) Rebecca Hunt of Hancock Co, Ind
1-20-1855 — Rebecca gct Spiceland MM, Ind

**COBLE**
2-15-1840 — Martha (form Henby) dis for mcd

**COFFIN**
1-16-1836 — Elihu & w Sarah & ch Isaac N, William S, Alfred & Phebe J are charter mbrs
1-16-1836 — Moses & w Phebe & ch Elihu, Cyrus, Louisa, Mary, Jonathan, Emily, Sylvester, Laurinda & Oliver are charter mbrs
1-16-1836 — Sarah, (wid of Aaron) & step-dts Phebe & Ruth & s George are charter mbrs
1-16-1836 — Moses appt to comm to make a mbrp list
2-20-1836 — Moses appt an overseer
3-16-1836 — Moses appt to comm to care for indigent persons
7-23-1836 — Zacharias & w Phebe & ch Nathan Dix & Phebe rocf Deep River MM, N Car
6-21-1837 — George F of Shelby Co, Ind, s Aaron & Sarah of same place m at Walnut Ridge Mtg, Ind to Lydia Jessop of Rush Co, Ind
9-16-1837 — John rocf Deep River MM, N Car
2-21-1838 — Elihu of Rush Co, Ind s Moses & Phebe, m at Walnut Ridge MM, Ind to Nancy Jessop

**WALNUT RIDGE**

COFFIN (Cont)
| | |
|---|---|
| 10-20-1838 | Alfred & ch Emily rocf Deep River MM, N Car |
| 5-18-1839 | Lydia (form Swain) chm mcd |
| 2-23-1841 | Phebe dt Aaron & Mary, decd, of Indiana, m at Walnut Ridge Mtg, Ind to William Pike of Highland Co, Ohio |
| 2-18-1843 | Cyrus gct Salem MM, Iowa |
| 12-21-1843 | Ruth dt Aaron & Mary, decd, of Shelby Co, Ind, m at Little Blue River M H (Walnut Ridge MM) Ind to David Swain of Fayette Co, Ind |
| 5-17-1845 | Louisa SWAIN (form Coffin) chm for mcd |
| 9-18-1847 | Alfred gct Spiceland MM, Ind |
| 11-17-1849 | Mary Macy (form Coffin) dis for mcd |
| 5-18-1850 | Isaac Newton gct Hopewell MM, Ind |
| 9-23-1850 | Phebe J dt Elihu & Sarah of Rush Co, Ind m at Westland M H (Walnut Ridge MM) Ind to Joel M Gilbert of Hopewell Mtg, Henry Co, Ind |
| 12-21-1850 | Miriam (form Jessop) chm for mcd |
| 3-15-1851 | Jonathan dis for mcd |
| 8-16-1851 | Sarah (w of Elihu) & ch William, Alfred, James B, Milton, Mary M, Abigail H, Alvin & Sarah Ann gct Pleasant Plain MM, Iowa (Elihu's certif withheld) |
| 4-16-1853 | John dis for jas - Universalists |
| 8-19-1854 | Elihu gct Spring Creek MM, Iowa |
| 11-22-1857 | Sarah Ann dt George & Lydia of Westland Mtg, Hancock Co, Ind m at Westland M H (Walnut Ridge MM) Ind to John Brown of Hancock Co, Ind |
| 6-19-1858 | Oliver dis for na & participating in music & dancing |
| 12-18-1858 | Laurinda JESSOP (form Coffin) mcd. drpd from mbrp |
| 8-15-1863 | Ezekiel T chm for mcd |
| 2-19-1859 | Irena BROWN (form Coffin) chm for mcd & dp |
| 5-21-1864 | George F & w Lydia & minor ch Delphina, Rebecca, Levi, Aaron, Mary, Jonathan P, Elizabeth J & Louisa J gct West Union MM, Ind |
| 5-21-1864 | Tabitha J (form Rawls) chm for mcd |
| 3-18-1865 | Elihu & w Sarah & dt Sarah Ann rocf Pleasant Hill MM, Ind |
| 1-18-1868 | Louisa (form Parker) chm for mcd |
| 4-17-1869 | Ammiel chm for mcd |
| 3-18-1871 | Ezekiel T gct Carthage MM, Ind |
| 11-18-1871 | James & w Lucinda & ch Amos & Rhoda Elmira rocf Pleasant Hill MM, (Howard Co) Ind |
| 11-18-1871 | Narcissa MACY (form Coffin) chm mcd |
| 1-20-1872 | George F & w Lydia & ch Mary, Jonathan & Louisa rocf Spring Grove MM, Kansas |
| 4-16-1887 | Louisa & ch Olga gct Carthage MM, Ind |
| 6-27-1890 | Abram & ch Lena & Sylvia rec in mbrp |
| 6-27-1890 | John rec in mbrp |
| 1-20-1894 | Abram & w Etta B & ch Lena, Sylvia, Lora & Ellis gct Westland MM, Ind |
| 4-18-1896 | George, Jonathan & Mary rocf Westland MM, Ind |

COGGESHALL
| | |
|---|---|
| 1-16-1836 | Tristram & w Millicent & ch Eunice Worth, John Milton, Joseph Newby, Penelope & Oliver are charter mbrs |
| 1-16-1836 | Tristram appt to comm on Education |
| 4-23-1846 | Eunice W dt Tristram & Millicent of Rush Co, Ind, m at Walnut Ridge MM, Ind to Elias Palmer of Duck Creek Mtg, Henry Co, Ind |
| 3-18-1848 | John Milton gct Milford MM, Ind |
| 1-22-1852 | Penelope N dt Tristram & Millicent of Rush Co, Ind m at Carthage M H (Walnut Ridge MM) Ind to Nathan Ratliff of Duck Creek Mtg, Henry Co, Ind |
| 10-18-1856 | Tristram & w Millicent & minor ch Joseph N, Pamela C & Mary gct Fairfield MM, Ind |
| 4-21-1860 | Oliver gct Fairfield MM, Ind |
| 6-10-1860 | Tristram & w Sarah H rocf Dover MM, Ind |
| 10-19-1861 | Tristram & w Sarah & minor s William gct New Garden MM, Ind |
| 7-18-1868 | Peter & w Jane & ch Mary Ellen & Margaret rocf Milford MM, Ind |
| 5-17-1873 | John H Binford gct New Garden MM, Ind to m Lucy Coggeshall |

COMMONS
| | |
|---|---|
| 10-21-1837 | Sarah dis for na & indulging her ch in the customs & manners of the world |
| 10-21-1837 | Eleanor dis for na & patterning after the fashions of the world |
| 8-12-1841 | Jesse dis for mcd & dp |
| 7-19-1841 | Charity WOLF (form Commons) dis for mcd |
| 1-16-1847 | Elbina dis for att mcd & na |

CONNER
| | |
|---|---|
| 1-18-1868 | Mary Lily rec in mbrp |

COOK
| | |
|---|---|
| 6-19-1841 | Hannah rec in mbrp |
| 7-17-1841 | William rocf West Grove MM, Ind |
| 6-17-1848 | Ann (form Hunt) chm for mcd |
| 2-18-1854 | Thomas rec in mbrp |
| 3-18-1854 | Nathan B rst w/c of West Grove MM, Ind |
| 8-19-1854 | Libni H, Phebe J, Amanda M & Elizabeth H, ch of Thomas & Ann, decd, rec in mbrp |
| 12-16-1854 | Sarah Jane rec in mbrp |
| 9-15-1855 | Nathan & w Sarah Jane gct Western Plain MM, Iowa |
| 5-17-1856 | Rachel rocf Spiceland MM, Ind |
| 8-18-1856 | Eli & w Emily rocf West Grove MM, Ind |
| 5-16-1857 | Eli & w Emily gct West Grove MM, Ind |
| 5-20-1857 | Josiah of Hopewell Mtg, Henry Co, Ind, s John & Mary, decd, of same place, m at Walnut Ridge Mtg, Ind to Ruth Bundy of Rush Co, Ind |
| 3-23-1859 | Thomas of Hancock Co, Ind, s John & Ann, both decd, m at Walnut Ridge Mtg, Ind to Angelina Bundy, wid of George Bundy jr |
| 2-28-1878 | Judith Ann gct Westland MM, Ind |
| 7-20-1878 | Bradly rec in mbrp |
| 4-16-1887 | David & ch Eva gct Westland MM, Ind |
| 12-11-1891 | Hannah gct Westland MM, Ind |

COX
| | |
|---|---|
| 1-16-1836 | Benjamin & w Mary & ch Sarah, Catherine, Lavina, Zilpha, Mahlon, Rice P, Cyrus, Benjamin jr & Mary are charter mbrs |
| 1-16-1836 | Benjamin appt to a comm |
| 7-15-1837 | Bennet & w Elizabeth rocf Milford MM, Ind |
| 9-23-1840 | Lavina dt Benjamin & Mary of Rush Co, Ind m at Walnut Ridge Mtg, Ind to Samuel M Morris of Whitewater Mtg, Wayne Co, Ind |
| 3-19-1842 | Elihu Patterson gct Milford MM, Ind to m Rachel Cox |
| 11-17-1849 | Bennet & w Elizabeth & ch Albert, Ruth A, Melissa, John K, Seth, Eliza & Catherine gct Milford MM, Ind |
| 5-18-1850 | Sarah Jane (form White) chm for mcd |
| 7-20-1850 | Mahlon chm for mcd |
| 12-20-1851 | Sarah gct Whitewater MM, Ind |
| 6-18-1853 | Cyrus B chm for mcd |
| 9-17-1853 | Benjamin T gct Whitewater MM, Ind |
| 2-18-1854 | Joseph M rocf Milford MM, Ind |
| 3-18-1854 | Cyrus B gct Whitewater MM, Ind |
| 4-15-1854 | Rachel M rocf Short Creek MM, Ohio |
| 12-16-1854 | Eunice (form Henley) chm mcd |
| 2-17-1855 | Margaret NEWSOM (form Cox) chm mcd |
| 4-11-1855 | Semira (form White) dis for mcd |
| 4-21-1855 | Rice P dis for mcd |
| 4-19-1856 | Joseph M & w Rachel M gct Milford MM, Ind |
| 10-18-1858 | Cyrus B rocf Whitewater MM, Ind |
| 4-16-1859 | Semira rst at Lynn Grove MM, Ind w/c of this mtg |
| 5-26-1859 | Cyrus B of Rush Co, Ind s Benjamin & Mary, both decd, of same place m at Carthage M H (Walnut Ridge MM) Ind to Mary Binford of Rush Co, Ind |
| 7-21-1860 | Rice P & w Eunice S & dt Ella Jane rec in mbrp |
| 12-21-1861 | Benjamin & James, ch of Cyrus B & Mary, rec in mbrp |
| 12-21-1867 | Cyrus B & w Mary & ch Benjamin F, James P, Charles S, Annette & Sarah gct Carthage MM, Ind |
| 6-19-1869 | Joel & w Catherine rocf Duck Creek MM, Ind |
| 2-18-1871 | Sarah Ann & ch Florence, Nathan E & Asa L HUNT rocf Westfield MM, Ind |
| 6-21-1873 | Joseph rec in mbrp |
| 12- ?-1874 | Cyrus B having produced a certif from Carthage MM, Ind to m Phebe Lamb, they are altm. A Friend is appt to att m and rpt to next mtg |
| 1-16-1875 | The Friend appt to att m of Cyrus B & Phebe Lamb rpts service att & m certif has been forwarded to the Recorder |
| 2-20-1875 | Phebe S gct Carthage MM, Ind |
| 7-21-1877 | William B & w Elvira T & ch Delbert W, Martha B & Bartlett S rocf Indianapolis, MM, Ind |
| 4-20-1878 | William J rec in mbrp |
| 6-18-1881 | Enos & w Mary A & ch Margery Elizabeth, Obed Clarkson, William Thomas, Benjamin Franklin & Sanford Leroy rocf Raysville MM, Ind |

WALNUT RIDGE

**COX (Cont)**
5-17-1884 William J dis for na & dishonesty
3-19-1892 William B & w Elvira & s Delbert & Bartlett gct Whittier MM, Calif
1-21-1893 William B & w Elvira rocf Long Beach MM, Calif
2-17-1894 William B & w Elvira gct Long Beach MM, Calif
12-15-1894 William B & w Elvira rocf Long Beach MM, Calif
5-18-1895 Lundy Ann & ch Joseph Enos rec in mbrp
6-15-1895 Olive & s Herbert rec in mbrp
3-20-1897 Benjamin F glt Meth Ch, Cleveland, Ohio
10-16-1897 Obed Clarkson & w Lundy Ann & ch Joseph Enos gct Knightstown MM, Ind
4-15-1899 Lottie B & dt Mary Elizabeth rec in mbrp
4-15-1899 Adelbert rec in mbrp
5-20-1899 Marcus & w Junia & ch Earnest, Iona, Presella, Ruby & Amos rocf Carthage MM, Ind

**CRANE**
11-20-1897 Ella Bell & Iona L rel on req

**CROW**
11-21-1868 Isabella T rocf Plainfield MM, Ind
11-20-1869 Isabella T dis for disunity

**CURR**
1-17-1874 William H rec in mbrp

**DAVIS**
1-16-1836 Jehu & w Rebecca & s Oliver are charter mbrs
1-16-1836 Isaac & w Phebe & ch Louisa are charter mbrs
3-18-1837 Charles H rocf Cincinnati MM, Ohio
6-17-1837 Jesse & w Maria & dt Nancy Edna rocf Springfield MM, Ind
6-18-1837 Samuel rocf Cincinnati MM, Ohio
7-15-1837 Samuel dis for mcd & dp
3-19-1838 Jehu & w Rebecca & minor s Oliver gct West Grove MM, Ind
2-18-1839 Isaac & w Phebe & minor ch Louisa, Mary & Ruth gct Sugar River MM, Ind
7-15-1848 John Hunnicutt gct Spiceland MM, Ind to m Hannah Ann Davis
8-23-1849 Mariah, wid, & dt of Zachariah, decd & w Phebe Coffin of Hancock Co, Ind, m at Westland M H (Walnut Ridge MM) Ind to William Cathon from Stark Co, Ohio
12-16-1854 Judith & ch Eliza Ann, Sally B & John M rocf Salem MM, Ind
11-15-1856 Delphina HASKET (form Davis) mcd. drpd from mbrp
11-21-1857 Martha Ann WALLIS (form Davis) mcd. drpd from mbrp
7-18-1863 Mary Drysdale (form Davis) mcd. drpd from mbrp
7-18-1868 Nancy JORDAN (form Davis) chm for mcd

**DENNIS**
6-16-1838 George Nicholson gct Springfield MM, Ind to m Lucinda Dennis
7-17-1852 Charles Reece gct Hopewell MM, Ind to m Eunice Dennis
1-15-1887 Julia gct Hopewell MM, Ind
12-16-1893 Benjamin & w Maria & ch Raymond, Leroy, Mary, Emma & William rocf Westland MM, Ind
1-20-1894 Atilla & Grace Olive ch of Benjamin & Maria rocf Westland MM, Ind

**DIBRA**
5-15-1841 Price F Hall gct Union MM, Ohio, to m Elizabeth Dibra

**DIGGS**
5-20-1871 Elizabeth (form Nichols) chm for mcd
7-15-1871 Elizabeth gct North Branch MM, Iowa

**DIXON**
12-19-1863 Calvin rocf Mill Creek MM, Ind
1-16-1864 Mary (form Hastings) chm for mcd
5-20-1865 Mary Jane (form Pearson) chm for mcd
9-16-1865 Mary J gct Mill Creek MM, Ind
12-21-1867 Calvin & w Mary & minor ch Keziah & Rosa J gct Plainfield MM, Ind
3-19-1870 Calvin & w Mary M & ch Keziah, Rosa Jane & Letittia Ann rocf Plainfield MM, Ind
3-19-1871 Phineas & w Sarah & ch Naomi & Caleb rocf Plainfield MM, Ind
3-18-1871 Joel & w Mary Jane & ch Rachel & Lewis rocf Plainfield MM, Ind
10- ?-1877 Calvin & w Mary M & ch Keziah, Rosa Jane, Letittia Ann & Elmer P gct Whitewater MM, Ind
8-16-1879 Calvin & fam rocf Whitewater MM, Ind
1-15-1881 Calvin & w Mary M & ch Keziah, Rosa J, Letittia A, Elmer P & Harley C gct Milford MM, Ind
5-17-1884 Caleb gct Hopewell MM, Ind

**DRAPER**
1-16-1836 Thomas & w Mary are charter mbrs
7-23-1836 John, Marzilla, Jeremiah, Joseph & Margaret, ch of Thomas & Mary rec in mbrp
12-17-1836 Martha (form Marsh) chm for mcd
9-18-1837 Thomas dis for na & disunity
12-17-1842 Marzilla ENNIN (EARNEST) (form Draper) dis for mcd
6-17-1848 Joseph dis for mcd
2-16-1850 Jeremiah dis
9-21-1850 Martha gct Westfield MM, Ind
12-20-1851 Martha rocf Westfield MM, Ind
11-19-1853 Aaron rocf Chester MM, Ind
11-19-1853 Martha dis for jas, a "Society called Christians"
8-21-1858 Timothy Lamb gct Raysville MM, Ind to m Rebecca Draper

**DRYSDALE**
7-18-1863 Mary (form Davis) mcd
6-15-1868 Mary Emeline & dt Maria B rec in mbrp
4-18-1874 Henry rec in mbrp

**DUBOISE**
6-15-1895 Francis & w Penelope & s Ralph rocf Westland MM, Ind
8-17-1895 Luther E s of Francis & Penelope, rec in mbrp

**DUNBAR**
10-21-1865 Sally E rocf Back Creek MM, N Car
10-21-1865 Eliza rocf Back Creek MM, N Car
8-18-1866 Sallie E & Henry Winslow are altm & a Friend is appt to att m & rpt to next mtg
9-15-1866 The Friend appt to att m of Sallie E & Henry Winslow, rpts the service att & the m certif has been placed in hands of the Recorder
6-27-1890 Anna & s Earl rec in mbrp

**DUTY**
3-20-1897 John & w Olive rolf Meth Church South, Waldron Circuit, Ill

**EATON**
2-21-1891 Dora rec in mbrp

**EDGERTON**
1-16-1836 Samuel, a Minister, & w Elizabeth & s Joseph are charter mbrs
1-16-1836 Samuel appt to a comm
6-21-1836 Samuel & w Elizabeth & s Joseph gct Salem MM, Ind
3-16-1839 William & w Hannah & ch Mary Jane rocf West Grove MM, Ind
12-18-1841 William & w Hannah & ch Mary Jane gct West Grove MM, Ind
5-20-1843 William & w Hannah & ch Mary Jane & Rebecca Ann rocf West Grove MM, Ind
6-20-1846 William & w Hannah & ch Mary Jane & Rebecca Ann gct Spiceland MM, Ind

**EDWARDS**
4-20-1844 Nathan C Hill gct Spiceland MM, Ind to m Anna Edwards

**ELLIOTT**
11-19-1836 Jonathan & w Amelia & ch Eliza rocf Milford MM, Ind
1-21-1837 Absalom & w Polly rocf West Grove MM, Ind
7-21-1838 Absalom & w Polly gct West Grove MM, Ind
3-20-1841 Jonathan & w Amelia & minor ch Eliza, William B, Jacob C gct Milford MM, Ind
3-19-1853 Henry Bundy gct Spiceland MM, Ind to m Eliza Elliott

WALNUT RIDGE

ELLIOTT (Cont)
6-21-1862    David & w Mary A & ch Elihu O & Micajah A rocf Deep River MM, N Car
5-16-1868    David W & w Mary Ann & minor ch Elihu O, Micajah & Mary E gct Carthage MM, Ind
5-20-1876    David W & fam rocf Carthage MM, Ind
9-18-1880    Martha J gct New Garden MM, Ind
5-17-1890    Emery Clarkson & w Martha J & s William E rocf Westland MM, Ind
10-17-1891   E Clarkson & w Martha J & ch William E & Mary Alice gct Westland MM, Ind
1-21-1893    David & w Mary Ann gct Carthage MM, Ind
11-17-1894   Emery Clarkson & w Martha J & ch William E & Mary A rocf Westland MM, Ind
10-16-1897   Emery Clarkson & w Martha Jane & ch William & Mary Alice gct Westland MM, Ind

ENGLE (INGLE)
4-15-1837    Joshua & w Hope & ch Samuel & Elam rocf Salem MM, Ind
10-21-1837   Lucinda POWELL (form Engle) dis for mcd
4-15-1848    Samuel dis for mcd

ENNIN
12-17-1842   Marzilla (form Draper) dis for mcd

ESTELL
11-17-1860   Mary Jane rec in mbrp

EVANS
5-15-1886    Jesse rec in mbrp
4-15-1899    Jesse glt Meth Ch, Charlottsville, Ind

FAULL
6-18-1898    Lillie & dt Fanny rec in mbrp

FLOWERS
1-16-1847    Esther (form Lamb) dis for mcd
3-15-1879    Lemuel V & w Esther rec in mbrp
5-17-1884    Lemuel C dis for drinking

FODREA
4-15-1865    David & w Tamer & ch Rebecca, Hannah, Mary M & Levi H rocf Westfield MM, Ind
5-20-1865    Benjamin D rocf Westfield MM, Ind
11-18-1865   David & w Tamer & minor ch Rebecca, Hannah, Mary M & Zeri H gct Westfield MM, Ind
3-15-1873    Sarah E rec in mbrp
7-19-1879    Benjamin D & w Sarah E & minor ch Horace J, Ethel E, Rhoda A, John H, Nancy T & Lillian C gct Raysville MM, Ind

FOLGER
5-19-1838    Mary & ch Thomas S, Henry C, Lusany, Adalina, Rufus & Maria rocf Salem MM, Ind (w & fam of Jethro Folger)
3-18-1848    Phebe (form Barnard) dis for mcd
4-15-1848    Henry B dis for att a mcd
5-29-1849    Thomas dis for mcd
7-19-1851    Adaline LEONARD (form Folger) dis for mcd
10-18-1851   Lurena B dis for att a mcd
8-18-1856    Rufus dis for mcd
7-16-1864    Maria BARNARD (form Folger) mcd. drpd from mbrp

FORBIS
4-19-1879    James M & dt Ada Mildred rec in mbrp

FOSTER
7-18-1846    Anna Jane rocf New Garden MM, N Car
5-20-1848    Anna Jane BALL (form Foster) dis for mcd
12-20-1856   Ascenith rocf Spiceland MM, Ind
11-17-1860   Anna M & Huldah E, ch of Ascenith, rec in mbrp

FOULKE
7-21-1838    Tacy Margaretta, Sarah, Jesse & Joseph minor ch of Samuel M rocf Gwynell MM, Pa
4-18-1840    Tacy, Margaretta, Sarah Jesse & Joseph ch of Samuel M gct Milford MM, Ind

FOUST
3-20-1880    Washington & w Josephine & s Alonzo rec in mbrp

5-15-1886    Clara rec in mbrp

FOUTS
3-17-1876    William & ch Sarah L, Roscoe & Mary rec in mbrp

FREDERICK
3-15-1879    Ella rec in mbrp

FRIEZE - FRIES
1-21-1860    Priscilla (form Hunt) chm for mcd
11-15-1873   Zachariah & dts Cynthia Ann & Clara Ellen rec in mbrp

FULGHUM
6-19-1880    Woodard & w Amy rocf White River MM, Ind
12-19-1885   Amy gct Raysville MM, Ind
1-16-1886    Woodard gct Raysville MM, Ind

FUSSELMAN
9-16-1848    Emeline (form Gordon) dis for mcd

GARDNER
3-16-1839    Isaac & w Dinah & ch Sally & a nephew John Jay Gardner rocf Salem MM, Ind
3-16-1839    Dorcas rocf Salem MM, Ind
3-16-1839    Asa F rocf Salem MM, Ind
1-15-1841    Amy (form Barnard) chm for mcd
3-20-1841    Asa chm for mcd
5-15-1841    Dorcas MACY (form Gardner) chm for mcd
5-18-1844    Isaac & w Dinah & minor s John J gct Salem MM, Ind
9-15-1845    Sally gct Salem MM, Ind
3-15-1845    Asa F & w Amy gct Salem MM, Ind
7-15-1865    Isaac & w Dinah rocf Richsquare MM, Iowa

GATES
2-18-1893    Delphina glt Meth Ch, Morristown, Ind
5-17-1893    Ithamer & fam rec in mbrp

GAUSE
8-21-1841    James Binford gct Spiceland MM, Ind to m Ruth Gause
5-20-1843    James B Parker gct Spiceland MM, Ind to m Hannah B Gause
11-17-1849   Eli D & w Lydia & ch Jacob, Mary Elizabeth & Sarah T rocf Spiceland MM, Ind
12-17-1853   Eli D dis for scandalous conduct
11-22-1854   Aaron C of Spiceland Mtg, Henry Co, Ind at Walnut Ridge MM, Ind to Elizabeth Parker formerly of Northampton Co, N Car
1-20-1855    Elizabeth gct Spiceland MM, Ind
4-17-1858    Eli D rst at White Lick MM, Ind w/c of this MM
12-16-1876   Solomon & w Celah rocf Duck Creek MM, Ind
4-19-1879    Mahlon rocf Raysville MM, Ind
4-19-1879    Allie rec in mbrp
5-17-1890    Mahlon & w Allie F gct Westland MM, Ind
2-16-1899    Samuel & w Amanda & ch Lucy & Myrtle gct Newburg MM, Oregon

GERBER
3-15-1884    Isaac M rec in mbrp
3-21-1891    Mary E rocf Westland MM, Ind
4-16-1892    Mary E rel on req

GILBERT
9-23-1850    Joel M of Hopewell Mtg, Henry Co, Ind, s Aaron & Margaret of same place, m at Westland M H (Walnut Ridge MM) Ind to Phebe J Coffin of Rush Co, Ind
1-18-1851    Phebe J gct Hopewell MM, Ind
5-21-1862    John of Hopewell Mtg, Henry Co, Ind, s Josiah, decd, & Abigail of same place, m at Walnut Ridge Mtg, Ind to Mary Lamb of Rush Co, Ind
7-19-1862    Mary L gct Hopewell MM, Ind
5-21-1864    Mordecai M produced a certif from Hopewell MM, Ind to m Mary Moore. They are altm & a comm is appt to att m & rpt to next mtg
6-18-1864    The comm appt to att m of Mordecai M & Mary Moore, rpts it was orderly & that the m certif has been placed in hands of the Recorder
9-17-1864    Mary gct Hopewell MM, Ind

WALNUT RIDGE

## GILBERT (Cont)
9-21-1872   William P Binford gct Hopewell MM, Ind to m Esther Gilbert

## GLUYAS
4-15-1865   James M from Deep River MM, N Car, rec in mbrp, "he being unable to obtain a certif because of the war"

## GORDON
6-21-1845   Emeline rocf Whitewater MM, Ind
9-16-1849   Emeline FUSSELMAN (form Gordon) dis for mcd
3-18-1865   Luther B & Amy & ch William & Oliver rocf Bangor MM, Iowa
10-20-1866   Luther, a Minister, & w Amy & minor ch William L & Oliver D gct Sugar Plain MM, (Boone Co) Ind
5-15-1886   Andrew rec in mbrp

## GORMAN
1-21-1893   Clara gct Westland MM, Ind

## GRAY
5-21-1836   Henry Macy & w Penina & their ch Ann H & a minor ch under their care, Jonathan Gray, rocf Spiceland MM, Ind
3-19-1842   Ruth Ann rocf Duck Creek MM, Ind
4-16-1842   Davis rocf Spiceland MM, Ind
11-19-1842   Davis & w Ruth Ann gct Duck Creek MM, Ind
12-24-1845   Jonathan H of Carthage, Rush Co, Ind, s James & Margaret, decd, of Shelby Co, Ind, m at Walnut Ridge MM, Ind to Sarah Ann Hill of Walnut Ridge MM, Ind
2-16-1867   Mary Jane & Joseph H Pleas are altm & a Friend is appt to att m & rpt to next Mtg
3-16-1867   The Friend appt to att m of Mary Jane & Joseph H Pleas, rpts the service att & m certif has been forwarded to the Recorder
4-18-1868   Martha Ann TAYLOR (form Gray) chm mcd
1-16-1869   Albert H chm mcd
4-16-1870   Sarah Ann & John T Morris are altm & a Friend is appt to att m & rpt to next Mtg
5-21-1870   The Friend appt to att m of Sarah Ann & John T Morris, rpts service att & that m certif has been forwarded to the Recorder
1-18-1873   Mariah rec in mbrp
1-15-1881   Horace M gct Westland MM, Ind

## GRIFFIN
8-16-1838   Miriam rocf Blue River MM, Ind
5-20-1843   Miriam L gct Spiceland MM, Ind
3-15-1851   George B White gct West Grove MM, Ind to m Eliza Griffin
1-17-1852   James, a minor, rocf Spiceland MM, Ind
4-18-1857   Priscilla rocf Milford MM, Ind
12-17-1859   James mcd. drpd from mbrp
6-15-1861   Thomas Clark gct Raysville MM, Ind to m Emily J Griffin
12-21-1861   Parthenia Jane rocf Raysville MM, Ind
3-17-1876   James C & Eliza & ch Minnie, John & Charles rec in mbrp
6-18-1887   James & fam gct Fairmount MM, Ind

## GURLEY
11-17-1894   Leon rocf High Point MM, N Car

## GUYER
4-15-1876   John R produced a certif from West Union MM, Ind to m Elizabeth Wiltse. They are altm & a Friend is appt to att m & rpt to next mtg
5-20-1876   The Friend appt to att m of John R & Elizabeth Wiltse, rpts service att & the m certif has been forwarded to the Recorder
6-17-1876   Elizabeth gct West Union MM, Ind

## HADLEY
3-11-1839   Samuel of White Lick MM, Morgan Co, Ind, s John & Hannah of Randolph Co, N Car, m at Walnut Ridge Mtg, Ind to Jane Clark, a wid, of Rush Co, Ind dt of John & Elizabeth Hamm, both decd
12-21-1839   Jane gct White Lick MM, Ind
10-17-1853   David L of Clinton Co, Ohio, s David, decd, & Sarah of same place, m at Little Blue River M H (Walnut Ridge MM) Ind to Abigail J Clark of Rush Co, Ind
7-15-1854   Abigail J gct Springfield MM, Ohio
2-23-1859   Addison of Mill Creek Mtg, Hendricks Co, Ind, s Joshua & Rebecca of same place, m at Pleasant View M H (Walnut Ridge MM) Ind to Martha Jane Hill of Rush Co, Ind
6-18-1859   Martha Jane gct Mill Creek MM, Ind
6-15-1867   Matilda HOSKINS (form Hadley) chm for mcd
12-19-1875   Samuel B Hill gct Mill Creek MM, Ind to m Mary P Hadley

## HALL
1-16-1836   Price F was a charter mbr
1-12-1837   Price F req a certif to West Grove MM, Ind to m Rebecca Mendenhall
5-15-1841   Price F gct Union MM, Ohio to m Elizabeth Dibra
4-16-1842   Elizabeth rocf Union MM, Ohio
12-21-1844   Price F & w Elizabeth & minor dt Martha Ann gct Mill Creek MM, Ind
4-20-1867   Elwood Weisner gct Springfield MM, Ind to m Mahala Hall
12-16-1899   Effie Afton & her ch Paul H & Russell L BROWN gct Spiceland MM, Ind

## HAMM
5-15-1841   Martha gct White Lick MM, Ind

## HAMMER
6-21-1879   (Thomas) & w Elmira & ch Walter & Blanche rocf Hopewell MM, Ind
4-18-1885   Thomas B rocf Hopewell MM, Ind
5-21-1887   Thomas B & w Elmira & ch Walter, Blanche & Chester gct Acton MM, Iowa

## HARE - HAIR
2-17-1866   David & w Rhoda rocf Springboro MM, Ohio

## HARRELL - HARROLD
8-21-1841   Charles & w Rachel & ch Albertson, Levina, Sarah & Mary rocf Piney Woods MM, N Car
1-23-1845   Lavina M dt Charles & Rachel of Hancock Co, Ind, m at Westland M H (Walnut Ridge MM) Ind to Asa Binford of Hancock Co, Ind
5-20-1852   Sarah Ann dt Charles & Rachel of Hancock Co, Ind, m at Westland M H (Walnut Ridge MM) Ind to Levi Reece of Cherry Grove Mtg, Randolph Co, Ind
4-21-1855   Albertson dis for mcd
10-19-1861   Lemuel produced a certif from Richland MM, Ind to m Jane L Hunt. They are altm & a Friend appt to att m & rpt to next Mtg
11-16-1861   The Friend appt to att m of Lemuel & Jane L Hunt, rpts it was orderly & the m certif has been placed in hands of the Recorder. (m at Pleasant View M H (Wanut Ridge MM) Ind)
1-18-1862   Jane, a Minister, gct Richland MM, Ind
5-19-1866   Lemuel & w Jane L & dt Matilda E rocf Richland MM, Ind (Hamilton Co)
3-16-1867   John & w Sarah Ann & ch Cora Jane, Hannah Alice & Luella rocf Richland MM, (Hamilton Co) Ind
9-20-1884   Lemuel & w Jane & ch Matilda, Etta, Arthur O, Nathan Aldis & - - - -? rocf Westland MM, (Hancock Co) Ind
11-21-1891   Lemuel & w Jane & dt Harriett gct Westland MM, Ind
11-21-1891   Arthur gct Westland MM, Ind

## HART
1-20-1838   Thomas rocf Elk MM, Ohio
12-19-1840   Thomas gct Elk MM, Ohio

## HARVEY
11-21-1863   Martha Reece (form Harvey) chm for mcd

## HASKET
1-19-1839   Peninah (form Hendricks) chm for mcd
2-15-1845   Sarah (form Bentley) chm for mcd
11-15-1856   Delphina (form Davis) mcd. drpd from mbrp
5-19-1860   Mary & dt Mary Jane rec in mbrp
3-16-1861   Mary & dt Mary Jane gct Hopewell MM, Ind

WALNUT RIDGE

### HASKET (Cont)
| | |
|---|---|
| 3-21-1874 | John rec in mbrp |
| 7-18-1874 | Margaret rec in mbrp |
| 10-19-1878 | Daniel rec in mbrp |
| 4-19-1879 | Abbie rec in mbrp |
| 1-21-1893 | Penina gct Westland MM, Ind |

### HASTINGS
| | |
|---|---|
| 5-21-1836 | Daniel E & w Keziah rocf West Grove MM, Ind |
| 8-18-1855 | Samuel B gct Mill Creek MM, Ind to m Matilda Nichols |
| 3-15-1856 | Matilda rocf Mill Creek MM, Ind |
| 4-17-1858 | Samuel B & w Matilda & minor s Mathew J gct Mill Creek MM, Ind |
| 2-22-1860 | Rebecca dt Daniel C & w Keziah of Hancock Co, Ind, m at Pleasant View M H (Walnut Ridge MM) Ind to Joseph B Hill of Hancock Co, Ind |
| 3-21-1863 | William chm mcd |
| 1-16-1864 | Mary DIXON (form Hastings) chm for mcd |
| 3-21-1868 | Sarah HOSKINS (form Hastings) chm for mcd |
| 7-20-1872 | David chm for mcd |
| 3-21-1874 | Mary E rec in mbrp |
| 4-15-1882 | William & fam gct Council Grove MM, Kansas |
| 4-15-1882 | Ann & dt Lola Bell HEADLY gct Carthage MM, Ind |
| 1-19-1890 | Daniel & w Keziah gct Newburg MM, Oregon |
| 11-15-1890 | Eunice C gct Newburg MM, Oregon |

### HAWORTH
| | |
|---|---|
| 1-16-1836 | Richard & w Mary & ch Benjamin & James are charter mbrs |
| 1-16-1836 | Dillon & w Sarah & ch James, Benjamin, Solomon, Calvin, Cynthia A & Mariah are charter mbrs |
| 1-16-1836 | Dillon appt to comm to make a mbrp list |
| 6-21-1836 | Dillon & w Sarah & ch James, Benjamin, Solomon, Calvin, Cynthia Ann & Mariah gct West Grove MM, Ind |
| 12-16-1837 | Richard & w Mary & ch Benjamin H & James W gct West Grove MM, Ind |
| 5-16-1868 | Ascenith rocf Vermillion MM, Illinois |

### HAYNES - HAINES
| | |
|---|---|
| 1-21-1837 | Lydia & ch William Elwood & Almeda rocf Marlborough MM, Ohio |
| 1-21-1837 | Hannah rocf Marlborough MM, Ohio |
| 1-21-1837 | Levi & w Deborah W & ch Hinchman, William, Mary, Levi jr, Sarah A, Enos, Elizabeth & Bennett rocf Marlborough MM, Ohio |

### HAZLET
| | |
|---|---|
| 8-19-1837 | Angelina (form Taylor) dis for mcd |

### HEADLY
| | |
|---|---|
| 4-19-1879 | Anna & dt Lola Bell rec in mbrp |

### HEARKLESS
| | |
|---|---|
| 4-21-1894 | James C rec in mbrp |
| 8-17-1895 | James rel on req |

### HEDGECOCK - HEATHCOCK
| | |
|---|---|
| 6-19-1858 | Sarah (form Pitts) chm for mcd |
| 3-20-1875 | Samuel W rec in mbrp |
| 3-17-1876 | Nancy, Joseph, Flora & Lulie, ch of Samuel W rec in mbrp |
| 3-17-1876 | Sarah rec in mbrp |
| 11-17-1877 | Samuel W & w Sarah & minor ch Nancy Jane, Joseph S, Flora Bell & Lulie May gct Carthage MM, Ind |
| 2-17-1883 | Benjamin rec on req |

### HENBY
| | |
|---|---|
| 1-16-1836 | Mary, (wid of John) & ch Sarah, John jr, Ephraim, Martha, Mary jr & William B are charter mbrs |
| 6-15-1839 | Elias & w Phebe rocf Milford MM, Ind |
| 2-15-1840 | Martha COBLE (form Henby) dis for mcd |
| 9-19-1840 | Sarah LAYMAN (form Henby) dis for mcd |
| 8-21-1841 | John dis for na |
| 4-20-1853 | Elias of Rush Co, Ind, s John decd of Perquimans Co, N Car & Mary of Rush Co, Ind, m at Walnut Ridge Mtg, Ind to Elizabeth White of Rush Co, Ind |
| 6-17-1854 | Ephraim gct Spring Creek MM, Iowa |
| 4-19-1856 | Elias & minor ch Martha Ann, John, Sarah, Phebe E & Elizabeth W gct Milford MM, Ind |
| 3-26-1857 | Elias of Fayette Co, Ind, s John decd, & Mary of Rush Co, Ind m at Carthage M H (Walnut Ridge MM) Ind to Elizabeth L HENLEY of Rush Co, Ind |
| 10-19-1857 | Elizabeth L gct Bethel Mtg, Milford MM, Ind |
| 8-19-1865 | Catherine J rec in mbrp (w of William B Henby & dt of Ellen Brooks) |
| 6-19-1869 | Ruth Ann rec in mbrp (w of John K) |
| 6-19-1869 | John K chm for mcd |
| 6-16-1877 | William B & w Catherine & ch rocf Westland MM, Ind |
| 5-20-1882 | Mary Emily rocf Carthage MM, Ind |
| 6-16-1883 | William B rel on req |
| 4-16-1887 | John K & w Ruth Ann & ch Elijah, Nora, John, Silas & Abbie gct Westland MM, Ind |

### HENDRICKS
| | |
|---|---|
| 2-2-1836 | Peninah rocf Suttons Creek MM, N Car end by Milford MM, Ind & Duck Creek MM, Ind |
| 8-20-1836 | Abigail rocf Suttons Creek MM, N Car |
| 1-19-1839 | Peninah HASKET (form Hendricks) chm for mcd |
| 4-18-1840 | Abigail BEOMON (form Hendricks) dis for mcd |
| 6-27-1890 | Margaret A rec in mbrp |

### HENLEY
| | |
|---|---|
| 1-16-1836 | Elias & ch Jabez H, William H, Thomas W, Martha Jane & Elias jr are charter mbrs |
| 1-16-1836 | Thomas & w Abigail & ch Henry, Thomas E, John M & Anna are charter mbrs |
| 1-16-1836 | Henry & w Ruth & ch Mary, Peninah & Eunice are charter mbrs |
| 1-16-1836 | Thomas appt to comm to procure the necessary Record Books for the MM |
| 1-16-1836 | Henry appt to comm to make a mbrp list |
| 2-20-1836 | Jabez H appt to att Qrtly Mtg |
| 2-20-1836 | Ruth appt Clerk of Women's Mtg |
| 6-17-1837 | Joseph & w Penina & ch Mary, Nancy Ann, Charles, Micajah, Jesse & Robert rocf Back Creek MM, N Car |
| 4-24-1838 | Jabez H gct Spiceland MM, Ind to m Margaret Holloway |
| 6-16-1838 | James, a minor, rocf Milford MM, Ind |
| 8-18-1838 | Hezekiah rocf Back Creek MM, N Car |
| 10-20-1838 | Margaret G rocf Spiceland MM, Ind |
| 4-18-1840 | Hezekiah gct Lick Creek MM, Ind to m Ann Lindley (a wid w/ch) |
| 12-19-1840 | Ann & her s John LINDLEY rocf Lick Creek MM, Ind |
| 1-15-1841 | Jabez H & w Margaret gct Duck Creek MM, Ind |
| 8-26-1841 | Jesse of Rush Co, Ind, s Joseph & Peninah of same place m at Carthage M H (Walnut Ridge MM) Ind to Abigail Newby of Rush Co, Ind |
| 10-20-1842 | Martha J of Rush Co, Ind, dt Elias & Jane, decd, of same place m at Walnut Ridge Mtg, Ind to Samuel Allen of Rush Co, Ind |
| 12-17-1842 | William gct White Lick MM, Ind |
| 11-20-1844 | Micajah of Carthage, Rush Co, Ind, s Joseph & Peninah of same place, m at Walnut Ridge Mtg, Ind to Ruth Anna Bently |
| 11-21-1846 | Charles chm for mcd |
| 7-20-1848 | Nancy A dt Joseph & Peninah of Rush Co, Ind m at Carthage M H (Walnut Ridge MM) Ind to Wyatt Stanley of Rush Co, Ind |
| 10-18-1848 | James gct Milford MM, Ind |
| 6-16-1849 | Elizabeth L rec in mbrp |
| 6-16-1849 | Jemima D dt Judith M rec in mbrp |
| 6-16-1849 | Louisa Jane (form Stratton) chm for mcd |
| 11-17-1849 | Louisa Jane rocf Hopewell MM, Ind |
| 4-28-1850 | Mary BENTLY (form Henley) chm for mcd |
| 11-25-1852 | Mary M dt Henry & Ruth of Rush Co, Ind m at Carthage M H (Walnut Ridge MM) Ind to Samuel B Hill of Rush Co, Ind |
| 3-19-1853 | Louisa Jane gct Hopewell MM, Ind |
| 11-21-1853 | Mary dt Joseph & Peninah of Rush Co, Ind m at Carthage M H (Walnut Ridge MM) Ind to William Binford of Rush Co, Ind |
| 12-16-1854 | Eunice COX (form Henley) chm for mcd |
| 3-17-1855 | Hannah (form Williams) chm for mcd |
| 4-21-1855 | Thomas W chm for mcd |
| 9-15-1855 | Hannah rocf Duck Creek MM, Ind |

WALNUT RIDGE

HENLEY (Cont)
| | |
|---|---|
| 4-24-1856 | Robert of Rush Co, Ind, s Joseph & Peninah of same place m at Carthage M H (Walnut Ridge MM) Ind to Mary Newby of Rush Co, Ind |
| 9-25-1856 | Thomas Elwood of Rush Co, Ind, s Thomas & Abigail of same place m at Carthage M H (Walnut Ridge MM) Ind to Phebe Newby of Rush Co, Ind |
| 3-26-1857 | Elizabeth L dt Elias decd & Judith M of Rush Co, Ind, m at Carthage M H (Walnut Ridge MM) Ind to Elias HENBY of Fayette Co, Ind |
| 5-20-1858 | Peninah dt Henry & Ruth of Rush Co, Ind m at Carthage M H (Walnut Ridge MM) Ind to John R Hill of Rush Co, Ind |
| 11-25-1858 | Jemima D dt Elias, decd & Judith M of Rush Co, Ind m at Carthage M H (Walnut Ridge MM) Ind to James White of Henry Co, Ind |
| 3-19-1859 | Henry gct Hopewell MM, Ind to m Avis Jane Macy |
| 3-23-1859 | John Milton of Rush Co, Ind, s Thomas & Abigail of same place m at Walnut Ridge Mtg, Ind to Gulielma Stanley of Hancock Co, Ind |
| 11-19-1859 | Avis Jane rocf Hopewell MM, Ind |
| 5-19-1860 | Tamar rec in mbrp |
| 4-21-1860 | Charles jr, Sarah, William & Caroline, ch of Charles & Tamar, rec in mbrp |
| 7-19-1862 | Jane HOLLOWAY (form Henley) chm mcd |
| 11-18-1865 | Henry W & w Avis Jane & minor ch Lillie, Elihu & Asenath gct Richland MM, Ind |
| 9-19-1868 | Charles M & Cynthia Stanley are altm & a Friend is appt to att m & rpt to next Mtg |
| 10-17-1868 | The Friend appt to att m of Charles M & Cynthia Stanley, rpts service att & m certif has been forwarded to the Recorder |
| 1-16-1869 | Cynthia E gct Carthage MM, Ind |
| 8-16-1873 | Henry produced a certif from Carthage MM, Ind to m Margaret Moore. They are altm & a Friend is appt to att m & rpt to next Mtg |
| 9-20-1873 | The Friend appt to att m of Henry & Margaret Moore, rpts service att & m certif has been forwarded to the Recorder |
| 10-18-1873 | Margaret gct Carthage MM, Ind |
| 2-20-1875 | Reuben B & w Rachel Y & ch Herbert rocf Carthage MM, Ind |
| 4-19-1879 | Reuben B & w Rachel Y & ch Herbert, Sarah & Lillian R gct Carthage MM, Ind |
| 1-21-1893 | Walter C & w Caroline & s Forest Milton rocf Dublin MM, Ind |
| 5-19-1894 | Walter & w Caroline & s gct Carthage MM, Ind |

HIATT
| | |
|---|---|
| 4-21-1858 | Joel of Duck Creek Mtg, Henry Co, Ind, s Richard & Sarah, both decd, m at Walnut Ridge Mtg, Ind to Isabella Parker of Rush Co, Ind |
| 6-19-1858 | Isabella gct Duck Creek MM, Ind |
| 4-20-1861 | Sarah Ann HUNT (form Hiatt) chm for mcd |
| 6-21-1884 | Zelinda rocf Spiceland MM, Ind |
| 11-15-1884 | Zelinda gct Spiceland MM, Ind |

HILL
| | |
|---|---|
| 1-16-1836 | Thomas & w Tamar & ch Milton, John C, Sarah Ann, Susanna, Jane & Albert are charter mbrs |
| 1-16-1836 | Jesse & w Elizabeth are charter mbrs |
| 1-16-1836 | Henry B & w Lucretia & ch William P & Allen are charter mbrs |
| 1-16-1836 | Nathan & w Elizabeth & ch Robert, Thomas, Sarah, Henby, Elizabeth jr, Nathan jr, & William are charter mbrs |
| 1-16-1836 | John & w Dinah & ch Joseph, Martha, Benjamin C, Nathan C, Ervin, Sarah Ann, William R & Miriam Jane are charter mbrs |
| 1-16-1836 | Jonathan & w Zilpha & ch Anna, Calvin, Cynthia, Matilda, Elisha & Joel are charter mbrs |
| 1-16-1836 | William & w Charity & ch Mary Ann, Elizabeth C, Amos H, Martha Jane, Samuel B & John R are charter mbrs |
| 1-16-1836 | Jonathan appt to comm on Education |
| 1-16-1836 | Jesse appt to comm to procure the necessary Record Books for the MM |
| 1-16-1836 | Henry B appt to comm on Education |
| 1-16-1836 | Thomas appt to comm on Education |
| 1-16-1836 | Nathan appt to a comm |
| 1-16-1836 | Elias appt to comm on Education |
| 2-20-1836 | Nathan appt to att Qrtly Mtg |
| 2-20-1836 | Thomas appt to att Qrtly Mtg |
| 2-20-1836 | John appt to a comm |
| 2-20-1836 | Jesse appt to a comm |
| 2-20-1836 | Zilpha appt to a comm on Education |
| 3-16-1836 | William appt to a comm |
| 3-23-1836 | Robert of Rush Co, Ind, s Nathan & Elizabeth, m at Walnut Ridge Mtg, Ind to Lydia P Binford of Rush Co |
| 5-21-1836 | John appt Librarian |
| 5-21-1836 | Henry B appt Treasurer of Walnut Ridge School |
| 5-21-1836 | Nathan appt a Trustee of school property |
| 5-21-1836 | Thomas appt a Trustee of school property |
| 3-30-1837 | Martha dt John & Dinah of Rush Co, Ind, m at Walnut Ridge Mtg, Ind to Robert Binford of Rush Co, Ind |
| 9-23-1840 | Sarah dt Nathan & Elizabeth of Hancock Co, Ind m at Walnut Ridge Mtg, Ind to Eli Brown of Rush Co, Ind |
| 11-26-1840 | Joseph of Rush Co, Ind, s John & Dinah of same place, m at Carthage M H (Walnut Ridge MM) Ind to Penelope Newby of Rush Co, Ind |
| 12-19-1840 | Phebe (form Thornburgh) chm for mcd |
| 4-21-1841 | Elizabeth dt Nathan & Elizabeth of Hancock Co, Ind m at Walnut Ridge Mtg, Ind to Alfred Hunt of Rush Co, Ind |
| 2-23-1842 | Mary Ann dt William & Charity m at Walnut Ridge Mtg, Ind to James Hunt of Rush Co, Ind |
| 6-18-1842 | Henry B dis for sueing another at law |
| 12-17-1842 | Henry B rst after an appeal |
| 3-18-1843 | Thomas gct Clear Creek MM, Ohio to m Melissa Hodson |
| 4-20-1844 | Nathan C gct Spiceland MM, Ind to m Anna Edwards |
| 5-23-1844 | Milton of Rush Co, Ind, s Thomas & Tamar of same place m at Carthage M H (Walnut Ridge MM) Ind to Amanda Hobbs, formerly of Washington Co, Ind |
| 10-19-1844 | Anna E rocf Spiceland MM, Ind |
| 12-25-1844 | Elizabeth C dt William & Charity of Rush Co, Ind, m at Walnut Ridge Mtg, Ind to Joseph Binford of Rush Co, Ind |
| 1-22-1845 | Henry of Rush Co, Ind, s Nathan & Elizabeth of Hancock Co, Ind m at Walnut Ridge Mtg, Ind to Lydia Jane Thornburgh |
| 9-24-1845 | Sarah Ann dt John & Dinah of Rush Co, Ind m at Walnut Ridge Mtg, Ind to Joel W Hodson of Hendricks Co, Ind |
| 11-15-1845 | Thomas s Nathan gct Clear Creek MM, Ohio |
| 12-24-1845 | Sarah Ann dt Thomas & Tamar of Rush Co, Ind m at Walnut Ridge Mtg, Ind to Jonathan H Gray of Carthage, Rush Co, Ind |
| 5-20-1848 | Anna PHELPS (form Hill) chm for mcd |
| 9-16-1848 | Cynthia dis for att a mcd & for mcd |
| 11-22-1848 | Amos H of Rush Co, Ind, s William & Charity of same place m at Walnut Ridge Mtg, Ind to Pennina Thornburgh of Rush Co, Ind |
| 2-28-1849 | Nathan C of Rush Co, Ind, s John, decd, & Dinah of same place m at Walnut Ridge Mtg, Ind to Asenath Hunt of Rush Co, Ind |
| 7-20-1850 | Thomas jr & Melissa & ch Hannah E, Sarah Ann & William W rocf Clear Creek MM, Ohio |
| 8-17-1850 | Thomas & w Tamar & minor ch Jane, Owen & Enos gct Whitewater MM, Ind |
| 4-23-1851 | Miriam J of Rush Co, Ind, dt John, decd, & Dinah m at Walnut Ridge Mtg, Ind to John P Parker of Rush Co, Ind |
| 10-18-1851 | Susanna PHELPS (form Hill) chm for mcd |
| 11-15-1851 | Thomas & w Tamar & ch Jane, Owen & Enos rocf Whitewater MM, Ind |
| 12-20-1851 | John chm for mcd |
| 2-21-1852 | Mary (form Phelps) chm for mcd |
| 5-15-1852 | Nathan jr chm for mcd |
| 6-18-1852 | Martha (form Bundy) chm for mcd |
| 11-25-1852 | Samuel B of Rush Co, Ind, s William & Charity of same place m at Carthage M H (Walnut Ridge MM) Ind to Mary M Henley of Rush Co, Ind |
| 10-15-1853 | Robert & w Lydia & ch Mary Jane, Joshua B, Elizabeth, Cyrus T, Susannah, Sarah & Lydia Ann gct East Grove MM, Iowa |
| 1-21-1854 | Jane PHELPS (form Hill) chm for mcd |
| 4-15-1854 | Thomas rocf Back Creek MM, N Car |

WALNUT RIDGE

**HILL (Cont)**

|  |  |
|---|---|
| 6-18-1854 | William dis for mcd |
| 2-21-1855 | Mary Ann dt John & Dinah of Rush Co, Ind, m at Walnut Ridge Mtg, Ind to Josiah C Binford of Rush Co, Ind |
| 12-15-1855 | Malinda MATHERS (form Hill) mcd. drpd from mbrp |
| 11-17-1855 | Mary Ann (form Newsom) dis for mcd |
| 12-10-1855 | Nathan & w Martha & minor s Elias B gct Spring Creek MM, Iowa |
| 6-20-1857 | Thomas C mcd. drpd from mbrp |
| 5-19-1858 | Joseph of Rush Co, Ind, s John, decd, & Dinah of same place m at Walnut Ridge Mtg, Ind to Rachel Pussey of Hancock Co, Ind |
| 5-20-1858 | John R of Rush Co, Ind s William & Charity of same place m at Carthage M H (Walnut Ridge MM) Ind to Peninah Henley of Rush Co, Ind |
| 2-23-1859 | Martha Jane dt of William & Charity of Rush Co, Ind m at Pleasant View M H (Walnut Ridge MM) Ind to Addison Hadley of Hendricks Co, Ind |
| 9-17-1859 | John C chm for mcd |
| 2-22-1860 | Joseph B of Hancock Co, Ind, s Aaron & Miriam of Randolph Co, N Car, m at Pleasant View M H, (Walnut Ridge MM) Ind to Rebecca Hastings of Hancock Co, Ind |
| 5-19-1860 | Thomas & w Nancy & ch Benjamin, Miriam, Eli B, Abbie E & Ascenith rocf Back Creek MM, N Car |
| 6-10-1860 | Martha & ch Ascenith E & Samuel C rocf Greenwood MM |
| 7-21-1860 | Thomas C & w Adeline B & dt Ione M rec in mbrp |
| 11-20-1860 | Allen of Carthage, Rush Co, Ind, s Henry B & Lucretia of same place m at Walnut Ridge Mtg, Ind to Ann R White of Rush Co, Ind |
| 7-20-1861 | Lydia (form Brown) mcd. drpd from mbrp |
| 12-21-1861 | Daniel M & James M certif of mbrp issued "because of present condition of the country, they are unable to get a certif of their rights of mbrp from N Car" |
| 2-15-1862 | Mary Elizabeth rocf Raysville MM, Ind |
| 4-19-1862 | Henry B gct Westfield MM, Ind |
| 6-21-1862 | Micajah & w Sarah Jane & ch Margaret F, Sarah, Micajah jr & Rhoda E rocf Deep River MM, N Car |
| 8-16-1862 | Allen dis for participating in Military Training |
| 8-16-1862 | Thomas E dis for contributing money for military purposes & participating in military training |
| 9-20-1862 | Henry B dis for accepting an appointment in the Army |
| 10-18-1862 | James H dis for participating in military training |
| 3-11-1863 | Daniel M of Rush Co, Ind s Micajah & Sarah Jane of same place m at Walnut Ridge Mtg, Ind to Phariba M Stanley of Hancock Co, Ind |
| 3-21-1863 | Joseph B & w Rebecca & minor s Daniel A gct Westfield MM, Ind |
| 8-15-1863 | Daniel M & w Phariba M gct Minneapolis MM, Minn |
| 11-21-1863 | Henby & w Lydia Jane & minor ch Mary Ann, Samuel & Joel gct Westfield MM, Ind |
| 12-19-1863 | John & w Lydia B & minor ch Mary E, Penelope T, Aaron L, Robert B, Micajah C, William G, Sarah Jane & Ruth E gct Kansas MM, Kansas |
| 1-18-1864 | William L & w Mary Ann & ch Viola J & Oliver E rec in mbrp |
| 4-19-1864 | Margaret F & Josiah Binford are altm. A Friend is appt to att m & rpt to next mtg |
| 5-21-1864 | The Friend appt to att m of Margaret F & Josiah Binford, rpts it was orderly & m certif has been placed in hands of the Recorder |
| 5-21-1864 | Samuel B who has been Recorder of m certif, req to be released |
| 5-21-1864 | Achsah rocf Back Creek MM - - - -? |
| 5-21-1864 | Joseph having been Recorder of removal certif, req to be released |
| 3-21-1865 | Rebecca & husb & fam gct Westfield MM, Ind |
| 12-16-1865 | Susan L & ch Mary Alice, Lemuel P & Luther G rec in mbrp |
| 12-18-1865 | Sarah MOORE (form Hill) chm for mcd |
| 2-17-1866 | Samuel B & w Nancy & ch Eunice Ann, Emily B & Edgar N rocf Back Creek MM, N Car |
| 5-19-1866 | Ann R & ch Horace M & Irving gct Minneapolis MM, Minn |
| 8-18-1866 | Owen S gct Plainfield MM, Ind to m Melissa A Bales |
| 4-20-1867 | Thomas H & w Melissa, she a Minister, & ch Hannah E, William W & Eunice gct White Lick MM, Ind |
| 4-20-1867 | Ruth (form Winslow) chm for mcd |
| 6-15-1867 | William T & w Martha & minor ch gct Springfield MM, Kansas |
| 7-20-1867 | Consent of parents being had, Thomas C & Esther B Parker are altm. A Friend is appt to att m & rpt to next Mtg |
| 8-18-1867 | The Friend appt to att m of Thomas C & Esther B Parker, rpts service att & m certif has been forwarded to the Recorder |
| 10-19-1867 | Enos chm for mcd |
| 12-21-1867 | Thomas & w Nancy & minor ch Benjamin C, Miriam, Eli B, Abby & Asenath Elizabeth & Martha gct Whitewater MM, Ind |
| 1-18-1868 | Ruth STANLEY (form Hill) chm for mcd |
| 3-21-1868 | James M & Charity Binford are altm (he having produced a certif from Carthage MM, Ind). A Friend is appt to att m & rpt to next Mtg |
| 4-18-1868 | The Friend appt to att m of James M & Charity Binford, rpts service att & the m certif has been forwarded to the Recorder |
| 11-19-1870 | Thomas gct Whitewater MM, Ind |
| 4-15-1871 | Ulyssius G, a minor under care of Alfred & Elizabeth Hunt, (an Aunt & Uncle) rec in mbrp |
| 6-15-1872 | Charity B & William Toms are altm & a Friend is appt to att m & rpt to next Mtg |
| 7-20-1872 | The Friend appt to att m of Charity B & William Toms, rpts service att & m certif has been forwarded to the Recorder |
| 6-15-1872 | Owen S & Melissa B rocf Carthage MM, Ind |
| 9-21-1872 | Gulielma rocf Hopewell MM, Ind |
| 12-18-1875 | Samuel B gct Mill Creek MM, Ind to m Mary R Hadley |
| 12-18-1875 | Josiah Bundy gct Carthage MM, Ind to m Sarah J Hill |
| 3-17-1876 | Mary B rocf Mill Creek MM, Ind |
| 7-15-1876 | Amos & w Penina & ch Mary Alice, Leora Ann, William & Lucy Sarah rocf Carthage MM, Ind |
| 10-20-1877 | Leonidas, Ione & Silas P ch of Thomas C, rocf Westland MM, Ind |
| 1-19-1878 | Joel & dt Lillie gct Minneapolis MM, Minn |
| 4-16-1880 | Owen & w Melissa gct Raysville MM, Ind |
| 12-18-1880 | Caroline & Oliver H White are altm & a Friend is appt to att m & rpt to next Mtg |
| 1-15-1881 | The Friend appt to att m of Caroline & Oliver H White, rpts service att & m certif has been forwarded to the Recorder |
| 1-15-1881 | Amanda & ch Charles S, William H, Emma J & Irvin gct Carthage MM, Ind |
| 4-16-1881 | Eunice rocf Westland MM, Ind |
| 4-17-1886 | Mary rocf Duck Creek MM, Ind |
| 3-19-1887 | Milton & w Amanda & ch Emma J & Irvin rocf Carthage MM, Ind |
| 1-18-1890 | Milton & w Amanda & s Irvin gct Carthage MM, Ind |
| 6-27-1890 | Fannie rec in mbrp |
| 9-20-1890 | Lucy S & Nathan C Binford, by writing, infs this mtg that they intend m with each other. They are altm & a Friend is appt to att m & rpt to next Mtg |
| 10-18-1890 | The Friend appt to att m of Lucy S & Nathan C Binford, rpts service att & m certif has been forwarded to the Recorder |
| 5-16-1891 | Samuel B & w Elizabeth & ch Ruth & Roland gct Carthage MM, Ind |
| 1-21-1893 | Albert gct Newburgh MM, Oregon |
| 1-21-1893 | Ione gct Westland MM, Ind |
| 7-18-1896 | Charles & fam rec in mbrp |
| 5-20-1899 | Allen rocf Carthage MM, Ind |

**HINSHAW**

|  |  |
|---|---|
| 10-19-1878 | Henry B rec in mbrp |
| 12-21-1878 | Henry B gct Whitewater MM, Ind |

WALNUT RIDGE

## HOAGG
| | |
|---|---|
| 5-16-1863 | Susan rocf Adrian MM, Mich |
| 2-16-1884 | Amy rocf Springdale MM, Cedar Co, Iowa endorsed by Carthage MM, Ind |

## HOBBS
| | |
|---|---|
| 1-16-1836 | Elisha & w Deborah & ch Martha are charter mbrs |
| 1-16-1836 | Elisha appt to comm on Education |
| 2-20-1836 | Deborah appt asst Clerk of Women's Mtg |
| 3-16-1836 | Elisha appt Recorder of Births & Deaths |
| 4-17-1841 | Amanda rocf Blue River MM, Ind |
| 2-17-1844 | Wilson gct Flushing MM, Ohio |
| 5-23-1844 | Amanda, dt Samuel & Ruth, both decd, of Washington Co, Ind m at Carthage M H (Walnut Ridge MM) Ind to Milton Hill of Rush Co, Ind |
| 1-18-1845 | Elisha & w Deborah & minor ch Martha, Louisa, Harvey, Anslem & Jason gct Miami MM, Ohio |
| 2-17-1866 | Wilson & w Zelinda & ch Orville W, Mary Z, Walton S, Charles M, Fanny, Robert & Harry Lincoln rocf Bloomfield MM, Ind |

## HOCKETT
| | |
|---|---|
| 9-16-1837 | Joseph rocf Clear Creek MM, Ohio |
| 4-15-1848 | Benjamin chm for mcd |
| 10-21-1848 | Benjamin rocf White Lick MM, Ind |
| 6-18-1853 | Benjamin gct Spiceland MM, Ind |
| 11-21-1863 | Mahlon & w Hannah & ch Sarah R & Sybil A rocf Raysville MM, Ind |
| 9-17-1864 | Sarah & George S White are altm & a Friend is appt to att m & rpt to next Mtg |
| 10-15-1864 | The Friend appt to att m of Sarah & George S White, rpts it was orderly & the m certif has been placed in hands of the Recorder |
| 5-16-1868 | Sybil Butler (form Hockett) chm for mcd |
| 7-17-1886 | Hannah gct Carthage MM, Ind |

## HODGE
| | |
|---|---|
| 2-17-1855 | Abigail B rocf Whitewater MM, Ind |

## HODSON
| | |
|---|---|
| 6-15-1839 | George & w Mary rocf Newberry MM, Ohio |
| 3-18-1843 | Thomas Hill gct Clear Creek MM, Ohio to m Melissa Hodson |
| 9-24-1845 | Joel W of Mill Creek MM, Hendricks Co, Ind, s Jesse, decd, & Mary m at Walnut Ridge MM, Ind to Sarah Ann Hill of Rush Co, Ind |
| 2-21-1846 | Sarah Ann gct Mill Creek MM, Ind |
| 10-19-1850 | George & w Mary, a Minister, gct East Grove MM, Iowa |
| 3-20-1852 | Matthew & w Hannah & ch John Milton rocf Clear Creek MM, Ohio |
| 3-20-1852 | Asa rocf Clear Creek MM, Ohio |
| 4-25-1855 | Joel W of Mill Creek MM, Hendricks Co, Ind, s Jesse & Mary, both decd, m at Walnut Ridge Mtg, Ind to Hannah Jane Parker of Rush Co, Ind |
| 8-18-1855 | Hannah Jane gct Mill Creek MM, Ind |
| 4-23-1856 | John M dis for mcd |
| 4-21-1858 | Newby of Spring Mtg, Hendricks Co, Ind, s Robert E & Catherine of same place, m at Walnut Ridge Mtg, Ind to Martha Ann Parker of Rush Co, Ind |
| 11-20-1858 | Martha Ann gct Mill Creek MM, Ind |
| 5-19-1860 | Marzilla (form Antrim) chm for mcd |
| 9-16-1860 | Marzilla J gct Spiceland MM, Ind |
| 12-21-1861 | John Milton chm for mcd |
| 12-21-1861 | Martha Ann (form Rawls) chm for mcd |
| 3-16-1872 | Lewis & w Rebecca & ch Casper & Oliver rocf Raysville MM, Ind |
| 2-28-1878 | Lewis & w Rebecca rel on req |
| 3-10-1878 | Casper W, Oliver E & Eunice H, ch of Lewis & Rebecca gct Milford MM, Ind |

## HOGUE
| | |
|---|---|
| 9-20-1879 | Philetha A rocf Dover MM, Ind |

## HOLDEN
| | |
|---|---|
| 2-15-1873 | Thomas J rec in mbrp |
| 1-15-1881 | Thomas J & w Emily & ch Naomi, Samuel R, Orpha & Lottie gct Westland MM (Hancock Co) Ind |
| 7-28-1885 | John & w rec in mbrp |

## HOLFORD
| | |
|---|---|
| 4-17-1897 | John O rec in mbrp |

## HOLLINGSWORTH
| | |
|---|---|
| 5-18-1850 | James & w Lydia & ch Stephen G, Valentine, Anderson & Benjamin rocf Mill Creek MM, Ohio |
| 5-18-1850 | Miriam rocf Mill Creek MM, Ohio |
| 5-18-1850 | Olive rocf Mill Creek MM, Ohio |
| 11-16-1850 | James & w Lydia & ch Oliver H, Miriam T, Stephen G, Valentine, Anderson & Benjamin gct Spiceland MM, Ind |

## HOLLOWAY
| | |
|---|---|
| 4-15-1837 | Anna & Jesse, ch of Jason & Jane rocf Marlborough MM, Ohio |
| 4-24-1838 | Jabez Henley gct Spiceland MM, Ind to m Margaret Holloway |
| 3-21-1846 | Edna HOLLOWELL (form Holloway) dis for mcd |
| 4-18-1846 | Jesse gct Mississinewa MM, Ind |
| 11-17-1849 | Susannah (form Bentley) chm for mcd |
| 3-16-1850 | Hannah rocf New Garden MM, N Car |
| 1-17-1857 | Hannah gct Duck Creek MM, Ind |
| 7-19-1862 | Jane (form Henley) chm for mcd |
| 7-18-1864 | Susanna B dis for na & dancing |
| 2-18-1888 | Sarah & ch rec in mbrp |
| 12-15-1888 | Sarah & fam gct Newburg MM, Oregon |

## HOLLOWELL
| | |
|---|---|
| 3-21-1846 | Edna (form Holloway) dis for mcd |

## HOOPS
| | |
|---|---|
| 4-?-1834 | Ellis & w & minor ch Margaret, Elizabeth, Sarah & Susan rocf Somerset MM, Ohio (to Duck Creek MM, Ind but lived in the area that became Walnut Ridge MM) |
| 9-17-1836 | Ellis & 5 minor ch, Margaret, Elizabeth, Sarah, Susanna & William gct Somerset MM, Ohio |

## HOOVER
| | |
|---|---|
| 2-15-1868 | Jennette F rec in mbrp |

## HORNADAY
| | |
|---|---|
| 4-15-1871 | Mary & s Samuel rocf Elk MM, Ohio |

## HORNER
| | |
|---|---|
| 9-23-1863 | Amos C, of Raysville Mtg, Henry Co, Ind, s John, decd, & Elizabeth, m at Walnut Ridge Mtg, Ind to Ann Bundy of Rush Co, Ind |
| 1-16-1864 | Ann gct Raysville MM, Ind |

## HOSIER
| | |
|---|---|
| 5-25-1842 | William of Henry Co, Ind, s William Sr & Milicent of same place m at Walnut Ridge Mtg, Ind to Susannah Hunnicutt of Hancock Co, Ind |
| 1-21-1843 | Susanna gct Duck Creek MM, Ind |

## HOSKINS
| | |
|---|---|
| 9-15-1866 | Sarah Ann rocf Clear Creek MM, Ohio |
| 6-15-1867 | Matilda (form Hadley) chm for mcd |
| 10-19-1867 | Matilda J rocf White Lick MM, Ind |
| 3-21-1868 | Sarah J (form Hastings) chm for mcd |
| 4-16-1870 | George & w Asenith & ch Mary Jane rocf Clear Creek MM, Ohio |
| 4-15-1871 | George & w Asenith & ch Mary Jane gct Westfield MM, Ind |
| 8-17-1872 | George & w Asenith & dt Mary Jane rocf Westfield MM, Ind |
| 4-19-1873 | Joseph rec in mbrp |
| 2-21-1874 | Albert M & William rec in mbrp (s of Joseph & Sarah Ann) |
| 2-21-1874 | Caroline M & Josiah Lewis rec in mbrp (ch Joseph & Sarah Ann) |
| 2-20-1875 | Cyrus E rec in mbrp (s Joseph & Sarah Ann) |
| 1-19-1878 | Mary L rocf White Lick MM, Ind |
| 7-20-1878 | Cyrus E & w Matilda & minor ch Joicey gct Chehalem MM, Oregon |
| 10-19-1878 | Albert M & w Sarah J & minor dt Minnie Viola gct Chehalem MM, Oregon |
| 4-19-1879 | Joseph & w Sarah Ann gct Chehalem MM, Oregon |

**HOSKINS (Cont)**

| | |
|---|---|
| 4-19-1879 | Josiah Lewis & w Mary L & ch Anna B & Henry M gct Chehalem MM, Oregon |
| 9-17-1892 | Margaret & minor ch Mollie, Charles, Jeptha & Jennie A gct Fairmount MM, Ind |

**HUBBARD**

| | |
|---|---|
| 7-20-1839 | Martha, Susanna & Mary (dt of Hardy & Mary, decd) rocf Spiceland MM, Ind.(they lived in Duck Creek area but Duck Creek Mtg has been in disunity & was laid down & mbrs attached to Spiceland Mtg until 1841) |
| 10-15-1842 | Hardy rocf Spiceland MM, Ind |
| 1-18-1845 | Abigail & ch Phebe, Mary H & Abigail C, Thomas Dews & William Gilman (fam of John) rocf White Lick MM, Ind |
| 3-17-1845 | Phebe C dt John & Abigail of Hancock Co, Ind, m at Westland M H (Walnut Ridge MM) Ind to Amos Owen of Hendricks Co, Ind |
| 6-20-1846 | Mary Jane rocf Spiceland MM, Ind |
| 12-19-1846 | Abigail (wJohn) & minor ch Martha T, Nathan, Mary H, Abigail C, Thomas Dews & William Gilman gct White Lick MM, Ind |
| 9-16-1848 | Hardy & dts Susannah, Martha W & Mary C gct Honey Creek MM, Ind |

**HUESTES**

| | |
|---|---|
| 11-15-1873 | Aaron & w Mary Ann & s Charles rocf Bridgeport MM, Ind & endorsed to Carthage MM, Ind |

**HUNNICUTT**

| | |
|---|---|
| 1-16-1836 | Elizabeth (wid of Robert Sr) & ch John A, Sarah Ann, Susanna, Mary E & Robert E are charter mbrs |
| 4-16-1836 | George rocf Dover MM, Ohio |
| 9-16-1837 | George gct Spiceland MM, Ind to m Martha Pusey |
| 1-20-1838 | Martha rocf Spiceland MM, Ind |
| 12-15-1838 | George E & w Martha gct Spiceland MM, Ind |
| 1-29-1840 | Sarah Ann dt Robert, decd, & Elizabeth of Hancock Co, Ind m at Walnut Ridge Mtg, Ind to Joshua Binford jr of Rush Co, Ind |
| 9-19-1840 | James B gct New Garden MM, Ind to m Penina Bunton |
| 1-16-1841 | Penina rocf New Garden MM, Ind |
| 5-25-1842 | Susannah dt Robert, decd, & Elizabeth m at Walnut Ridge Mtg, Ind to William Hosier jr of Henry Co, Ind |
| 4-19-1843 | Elizabeth (form Andrews) wid of Robert Hunnicutt Sr, & dt of John & Sarah Andrews, both decd, of Dinwiddie Co, Va m at Walnut Ridge Mtg, Ind to Nathan Overman, a widower, of Rush Co, Ind |
| 12-18-1843 | George & w Martha & s William Penn rocf Spiceland MM, Ind |
| 6-20-1846 | James B & w Peninah & minor s William H gct Spiceland MM, Ind |
| 7-15-1848 | John A gct Spiceland MM, Ind to m Hannah Ann Davis |
| 12-16-1848 | Hannah Ann rocf Spiceland MM, Ind |
| 8-16-1849 | James B & w Penina & ch William H rocf Spiceland MM, Ind |
| 2-18-1854 | James B & w Penina & s William H gct Spiceland MM, Ind |
| 6-20-1857 | Mary gct Lynn Grove MM, Iowa |
| 8-21-1858 | George gct Whitewater MM, Ind to m Mary Ann Winslow, a wid w/ch |
| 2-19-1859 | Mary Anna & s Robert B WINSLOW rocf Whitewater MM, Ind |
| 5-25-1859 | John A of Carthage Mtg, Rush Co, Ind, s Robert Sr, & Elizabeth, both decd, m at Pleasant View M H (Walnut Ridge MM) Ind to Martha Jane Bundy of Hancock Co, Ind |
| 6-16-1860 | George E & w Mary Anna & his ch William P, Hannah L, Margaret P, Mary A, & Rachel P gct Honey Creek MM, Iowa |
| 8-21-1897 | Martha rocf Newberry MM, Ohio |
| 8-19-1899 | Martha gct Whittier MM, Calif |

**HUNT**

| | |
|---|---|
| 9-16-1837 | Libni & w Jane & ch Alfred, Anna, Miriam, John, Priscilla, Isaac, Rebecca, Joseph & Jane rocf Clear Creek MM, Ohio |
| 4-25-1838 | Miriam dt Libni & Jane of Rush Co, Ind m at Walnut Ridge Mtg, Ind to Nathan Nicholson of Rush Co, Ind |
| 6-16-1839 | Ezra & w Rebecca & ch James, Ascenith, Asa, Priscilla & Benjamin rocf Milford MM, Ind |
| 4-20-1839 | Asa & w Lydia & ch Mary Ann, Levi S, & Cyrus A rocf Clear Creek MM, Ohio |
| 6-15-1839 | Hannuel & w Lucinda & ch Sarah, Ascenith, Ezra, Nancy Jane, James & Cyrus rocf Milford MM, Ind |
| 10-19-1839 | Sarah rocf Clear Creek MM, Ohio |
| 4-21-1841 | Alfred of Rush Co, Ind, s Libni & Jane of same place, m at Walnut Ridge Mtg, Ind to Elizabeth Hill of Hancock Co, Ind |
| 2-23-1842 | James of Rush Co, Ind, s Ezra & Rebecca C of same place, m at Walnut Ridge Mtg, Ind to Mary Ann Hill |
| 11-19-1842 | John chm for mcd |
| 2-18-1843 | Hannuel & w Lucinda & minor ch Sarah, Asenath, Ezra, Nancy J, James D, Cyrus, Josiah N & Eleanor gct Duck Creek MM, Ind |
| 12-16-1843 | John dis |
| 5-15-1847 | Asenith rocf Duck Creek MM, Ind |
| 6-17-1848 | Ann COOK (form Hunt) chm for mcd |
| 9-16-1848 | Asenith gct Clear Creek MM, Ohio |
| 9-21-1848 | Asa of Rush Co, Ind, s Ezra & Rebecca of same place m at Westland M H (Walnut Ridge MM) Ind to Mildred Newby of Hancock Co, Ind |
| 2-28-1849 | Asenath dt Ezra & Rebecca of Rush Co, Ind m at Walnut Ridge MM, Ind to Nathan C Hill of Rush Co |
| 4-20-1850 | John rec in mbrp again (having been dis) |
| 6-18-1850 | Sarah rec in mbrp |
| 7-20-1850 | Isaac N, s of John & Sarah, rec in mbrp |
| 2-15-1851 | Asa & w Lydia & ch Mary Ann, Levi S, Cyrus, Gideon, Eunice & Jesse L gct Richland MM, Ind |
| 6-14-1854 | Rebecca dt Libni & Jane of Hancock Co, Ind m at Pleasant View M H (Walnut Ridge MM) Ind to Levi Cloud of Henry Co, Ind |
| 7-15-1854 | Priscilla BARRETT (form Hunt) dis for mcd |
| 5-16-1857 | Cyrus O, Josiah N, Eleanor, Libni, Ann & Hannah minor ch of Hannuel rocf Richland MM, Ind |
| 4-16-1859 | Josiah N, Eleanor, Libni, Ann & Hannah, minor ch of Hannuel gct Westfield MM, Ind |
| 9-17-1859 | Cyrus gct Pleasant Plain MM, Iowa |
| 12-17-1859 | Benjamin chm for mcd |
| 1-21-1860 | Priscilla FRIEZE (form Hunt) chm for mcd |
| 4-20-1861 | Sarah Ann (form Hiatt) chm for mcd |
| 10-19-1861 | Sarah Ann rocf Hinkles Creek MM, Ind |
| 10-19-1861 | Jane L & Lemuel Harrell (Harold) are altm & a Friend is appt to att m & rpt to next Mtg |
| 11-16-1861 | The Friend appt to att m of Jane L & Lemuel Harrell, rpts it was orderly & the m certif has been placed in hands of the Recorder. (m at Pleasant View M H, Walnut Ridge MM, Ind) |
| 3-17-1866 | Asa & w Mildred & minor ch Henry C, Cynthia R & Alvin H gct Indianapolis MM, Ind |
| 2-16-1867 | Martha Ann JONES (form Hunt) chm mcd |
| 4-20-1867 | Sarah Ann & her minor ch Florence E, Nathan E & Asa L gct Westfield MM, Ind |
| 6-15-1867 | Joseph H chm for mcd |
| 6-15-1867 | Elizabeth (form Brown) chm for mcd |
| 11-16-1867 | Clara rec in mbrp |
| 2-18-1871 | Sarah Ann COX (wid of Benjamin Hunt) & her ch Florence E, Nathan E & Asa L HUNT rocf Westfield MM, Ind |
| 4-15-1871 | Alfred & Elizabeth have a minor under their care, Ulyssius G Hill, a nephew of Elizabeth (Hill) Hunt, & he is rec in mbrp |
| 5-11-1871 | Joseph R chm for mcd |
| 5-10-1873 | Deborah & dt Edith rocf Honey Creek MM, Iowa |
| 12-20-1873 | Joseph R & w Deborah & minor ch Edith Jane gct Indianapolis MM, Ind |
| 4-16-1887 | Henry C gct Westland MM, Ind |
| 5-21-1887 | Marianna gct Indianapolis MM, Ind |
| 3-15-1890 | Joseph R & ch Edith & Bettie rocf Indianapolis MM, Ind |
| 3-18-1893 | Ora J rocf Indianapolis MM, Ind |
| 4-20-1895 | Alfred rocf Minneapolis MM, Minn |
| 4-20-1895 | Neva F rec in mbrp |

WALNUT RIDGE

## HUNT (Cont)
| | |
|---|---|
| 7-18-1896 | Alfred T & w Ora J & ch Neva F & John gct Westland MM, Ind |
| 6-19-1897 | Hattie M rocf Westland MM, Ind |
| 6-17-1899 | Flora M rocf Westland MM, Ind |

## HUSSEY
| | |
|---|---|
| 3-20-1841 | Agatha & dt Agatha rocf White Lick MM, Ind |
| 5-20-1841 | Agatha of Rush Co, Ind s Jediah, decd, & Agatha late of Randolph Co, N Car, m at Walnut Ridge Mtg, Ind to John Street (a widower) of Milford Mtg, Henry Co, Ind |

## INGOLD
| | |
|---|---|
| 5-19-1866 | Adalade (form Barnard) mcd. drpd from mbrp |

## JACKSON
| | |
|---|---|
| 6-27-1890 | John M & ch Melia M, Earl B & Nellie rec in mbrp |

## JEFFRIES
| | |
|---|---|
| 5-15-1886 | Leonidas rec in mbrp |

## JESSOP
| | |
|---|---|
| 1-16-1836 | Jonathan & w Elizabeth & ch Lydia, Nancy, Miriam, Jonathan jr, Jacob, Huldah, Mathew, & Samuel are charter mbrs |
| 1-16-1836 | Thomas & Rebecca & dt Ann are charter mbrs |
| 6-21-1836 | Evan gct Spiceland MM, Ind |
| 6-21-1837 | Lydia dt Jonathan & Elizabeth of Rush Co, Ind m at Walnut Ridge Mtg, Ind to George F Coffin of Shelby Co, Ind |
| 2-21-1838 | Nancy dt Jonathan & Elizabeth m at Walnut Ridge Mtg, Ind to Elihu Coffin of Rush Co, Ind |
| 1-24-1849 | Jonathan jr of Rush Co, Ind, s Jonathan Sr & Elizabeth of same place, m at Walnut Ridge Mtg, Ind to Mary Bundy of Rush Co |
| 12-21-1850 | Miriam COFFIN (form Jessop) chm mcd |
| 1-20-1853 | Jacob of Rush Co, Ind, s Jonathan & Elizabeth of same place m at Westland M H (Walnut Ridge MM) Ind to Rebecca Brown of Hancock Co, Ind |
| 10-20-1853 | Anna B dt Thomas & Rebecca of Rush Co, Ind at Carthage M H, (Walnut Ridge MM) Ind to Joseph Oliver Andrews of Rush Co, Ind |
| 9-20-1855 | Sarah dt Thomas & Rebecca of Rush Co, Ind m at Carthage M H, (Walnut Ridge MM) Ind to William Bond of Henry Co, Ind |
| 8-21-1858 | Nathan chm mcd |
| 12-18-1858 | Laurinda (form Coffin) mcd |
| 12-23-1858 | Jesse B of Henry Co, Ind s Elias & Ann of same place m at Carthage M H (Walnut Ridge MM) Ind to Milly Newby of Rush Co |
| 1-15-1859 | Laurinda rec in mbrp |
| 4-16-1859 | Milly gct Spiceland MM, Ind |
| 9-17-1864 | Thomas appt an Elder |
| 1-21-1865 | Jane rec in mbrp |
| 5-20-1865 | Lewis rec in mbrp |
| 5-16-1874 | Levi rocf White Lick MM, Ind |
| 12-19-1874 | Joseph L Binford gct White Lick MM, Ind to m Susannah Jessop |
| 4-16-1881 | Mary E gct Carthage MM, Ind |

## JOHNSON
| | |
|---|---|
| 1-20-1838 | Richard & s William rocf Milford MM, Ind |
| 4-18-1840 | Richard chm for mcd |
| 11-15-1843 | Richard W gct Goshen MM, Ohio to m Lucinda Watkins |
| 6-20-1846 | Lucinda rocf Goshen MM, Ohio |
| 11-17-1851 | Evan L of Wabash MM, Wabash Co, Ind, s James & Elizabeth of Warren Co, Ohio, m at Carthage M H (Walnut Ridge MM) Ind to Eunice Symons lately of Wayne Co, Ind |
| 1-17-1852 | Eunice gct Wabash MM, Ind |
| 4-18-1868 | John rec in mbrp |
| 9-16-1876 | John rec in mbrp |

## JONES
| | |
|---|---|
| 6-15-1867 | Samuel N & w Jane & ch Emma & Martha rocf Duck Creek MM, Ind |
| 12-21-1867 | Catherine & dt Luella rec in mbrp |
| 12-21-1867 | Wiley B rec in mbrp |
| 4-18-1868 | Isaac M rec in mbrp |
| 2-16-1869 | Martha Ann (form Hunt) chm for mcd |
| 8-21-1869 | Wiley & w Catherine & ch Luella gct Lynn Grove MM, Iowa |
| 3-18-1871 | Samuel N & w Jane, a Minister, & minor ch Emeline & Martha gct Ceasar's Creek MM, Ohio |
| 11-18-1871 | Annie M chm for mcd |
| 4-16-1887 | Annie M & ch Mary gct White River MM, Ind |
| 5-21-1887 | Isaac M & w Martha Ann & ch Alma & Alvin gct Indianapolis MM, Ind |

## JORDAN
| | |
|---|---|
| 5-19-1849 | Margaret (form Weisner) dis for mcd |
| 7-18-1868 | Nancy (form Davis) chm for mcd |

## KELLEY
| | |
|---|---|
| 4-16-1864 | William rocf Marlborough MM, Ohio |
| 9-18-1880 | Martha & ch Benjamin F, Hannah J, Oliver, Anna & Samuel rocf Oak Ridge MM, Ind |
| 11-17-1883 | Martha gct Raysville MM, Ind |

## KENDALL
| | |
|---|---|
| 7-19-1845 | Mary (form Antrim) dis for mcd |
| 4-17-1869 | Samuel Pitts gct Plainfield MM, Ind to m Jane Kendall |
| 3-19-1887 | Huldah gct New Castle MM, Ind |

## KENWORTHY
| | |
|---|---|
| 1-24-1838 | William of Spiceland Mtg, Henry Co, Ind, s Amos & Mary m at Walnut Ridge Mtg, Ind to Asenath Patterson of Rush Co |
| 4-21-1838 | Ascenith gct Spiceland MM, Ind |
| 1-15-1841 | William & w Ascenith & ch Sarah & James rocf Spiceland MM, Ind |
| 2-17-1844 | William & 2 minor ch, Sarah & James, gct Spiceland MM, Ind |

## KERNS - KEARNS
| | |
|---|---|
| 7-18-1863 | Octavius Winbern rec in mbrp |
| 4-19-1864 | O Winbern & Mary Brown are altm. A comm is appt to att m & rpt to next mtg |
| 5-21-1864 | The comm appt to att m of Winbern & Mary Brown, rpts it was orderly & the m certif has been placed in hands of the Recorder |
| 11-19-1870 | Judith Ann (form Binford) chm for mcd |
| 11-21-1874 | Judith Ann & minor ch Julius Elmer & Elisha Lee gct Westland MM, Ind |

## KERR
| | |
|---|---|
| 12-20-1884 | Eliza gct Raysville MM, Ind |
| 4-17-1886 | Eliza rocf Raysville MM, Ind |

## KERSEY
| | |
|---|---|
| 2-20-1841 | Vierling & w Mary Emily & ch Ann Mariah rocf Spiceland MM, Ind |
| 5-21-1842 | Vierling & w Mary Emily & dt Ann Maria gct Spiceland MM, Ind |
| 9-18-1845 | Joseph Allen gct Spiceland MM, Ind to m Charity Kersey (form Boone) |

## KINDLE
| | |
|---|---|
| 8-16-1845 | Mary dis |

## KING
| | |
|---|---|
| 1-16-1836 | Nancy Ann & ch Harmon jr, Hannah, Phebe, Rebecca, Lydia & Deborah are charter mbrs |
| 9-17-1836 | Nancy Ann WHITE (wid King) dis for mcd |
| 2-19-1842 | Phebe gct Spiceland MM, Ind |
| 4-16-1842 | Millicent (form Lamb) dis for mcd |
| 4-16-1842 | Hannah gct Spiceland MM, Ind |
| 12-18-1847 | Harmon dis for mcd |
| 1-15-1848 | Lydia & Deborah King with their mother, now Nancy Ann White, gct West Grove MM, Ind |
| 12-21-1867 | Rufus P rocf Plainfield MM, Ind |
| 2-20-1869 | Rufus gct Greenfield MM, Ind |
| 4-16-1870 | Rufus rocf Greenfield MM, Ind |
| 6-20-1874 | Rufus P, a Minister, gct Spiceland MM, Ind |
| 3-18-1882 | William rocf Spiceland MM, Ind |

## KNIGHT
| | |
|---|---|
| 12-16-1871 | Eliza Ann rocf Dover MM, Ind |
| 1-20-1872 | Robert & w Sarah & ch Oliver & Luther rocf Deer Creek MM, Ind |
| 1-18-1873 | Eliza Ann gct Deer Creek MM, Ind |

WALNUT RIDGE

KNIGHT (Cont)
5-17-1873    Robert, a Minister, & w Sarah & ch Oliver B
             & Luther C gct Mississinewa MM, Ind

KRAMAS
5-21-1898    Robert & w Lydia & ch Robert, Nic (?) le,
             Arthur W, William & Ethel R rocf Westland
             MM, Ind

KYSER
1-18-1896    George M & w Phebe & ch rec in mbrp

LACY
1-16-1836    Josiah & w Ruth & ch Lowring are charter mbrs
1-16-1836    Pearson & w Margaret & ch Sarah Ann, Eunice
             M, Jonathan & Susanna are charter mbrs
2-20-1836    Pearson appt Treasurer of Mthly Mtg
3-17-1838    Samuel dis at Milford MM, Ind
8-20-1842    Jesse rocf Milford MM, Ind
4-20-1844    Josiah & w Ruth & ch Lowring A, Phebe &
             Lavina gct Salem MM, Iowa Territory
2-19-1845    Sarah Ann dt Pearson, decd, & Margaret of
             Rush Co, Ind m at Walnut Ridge Mtg, Ind to
             Edward Butler of Rush Co
4-18-1846    Jesse dis
10- 7-1846   Margaret (wid of Pearson Lacy) of Rush Co,
             Ind, dt Jesse & Mary Morris of Wayne Co, Ind,
             m at Walnut Ridge MM, Ind to William Butler
             of Hancock Co, Ind
2-20-1850    Eunice M dt Pearson, decd & Margaret (now
             Margaret Butler) m at Walnut Ridge Mtg,
             Ind to Mahlon Butler of Montgomery Co, Ind
12-17-1853   Miriam (form Thornburgh) chm for mcd
1-21-1854    Thomas chm for mcd
7-15-1854    Jesse M, Asenith & Phebe Lacy minor ch of
             Pearson, decd, & w Margaret (now Margaret
             Blair, w of Abner Blair) gct White Lick MM,
             Ind
8-18-1856    Margaret gct White Lick MM, Ind

LAMB
8-20-1836    Caleb & w Sarah & ch Benjamin, John A,
             Edmond, David, Margaret & Jonathan rocf
             Symons Creek MM, N Car
2-19-1838    Caleb & w Sarah & ch Benjamin Bagley, John
             Anderson, Edmond, David, Margaret & Jonathan
             gct Spiceland MM, Ind
4-21-1838    Phineas & w Huldah & dt Martha rocf Milford
             MM, Ind
7-21-1838    Sarah TOWNSEND (form Lamb) chm for mcd
12-15-1838   Stephen & w Miriam & ch Timothy, Millicent,
             Elizabeth & Esther rocf Piney Woods MM, N Car
4-16-1842    Millicent KING (form Lamb) dis for mcd
3-18-1843    Phineas & w Huldah & ch Martha, Mary & Phebe
             gct Westfield MM, Ind
11-15-1845   Josiah rst w/c of Spiceland MM, Ind
1-16-1847    Esther Flowers (form Lamb) dis for mcd
7-17-1847    Joseph rocf Sugar River MM, Ind
8-18-1847    Joseph chm for mcd
9-18-1847    Lydia (form Marsh) chm for mcd
3-17-1849    Joseph & w Lydia & dt Sarah T gct Westfield
             MM, Ind
3-18-1854    Josiah chm for mcd
8-21-1858    Timothy gct Raysville MM, Ind to m Rebecca
             Draper
12-18-1858   Mary rocf Greenfield MM, Ind
2-19-1859    Joseph & w Lydia & ch Sarah, Edith, Fanny,
             Eliza, Martha & Robert rocf Westfield MM, Ind
6-18-1859    Rebecca rocf Raysville MM, Ind
12-21-1861   Phebe & Emily rocf Greenfield MM, Ind
5-21-1862    Mary of Rush Co, Ind dt Phineas & Huldah,
             decd, m at Walnut Ridge Mtg, Ind to John
             Gilbert of Henry Co, Ind
11-18-1865   Lydia rec in mbrp
7-21-1866    Emily gct Hopewell MM, Ind
3-18-1871    Martha rocf Greenfield MM, Ind & endorsed to
             Hopewell MM, Ind
12- ?-1874   Phebe & Cyrus B Cox are altm & a Friend is
             appt to att m & rpt to next mtg
1-16-1875    The Friend appt to att m of Phebe & Cyrus B
             Cox, rpts service att & m certif has been
             forwarded to the Recorder

LATIMORE
4-16-1887    Susie gct Carthage MM, Ind

LAWRENCE
11-24-1859   Jesse of Mahaska? Co, Iowa, s Peter & Sarah,
             decd, of Henry Co, Ind, m at Carthage M H
             (Walnut Ridge MM) Ind to Mary S Allen of
             Rush Co, Ind
6-16-1860    Mary gct Spiceland MM, Ind

LAYMAN
9-19-1840    Sarah (form Henby) dis for mcd
1-20-1866    Mary Jane (form Binford) mcd. drpd from mbrp
1-21-1882    Sarah rec in mbrp
3-19-1887    Anna J rocf Carthage MM, Ind

LEDWELL
3-19-1870    John W & w Margaret & ch Martha, Mary Alice,
             Luetitia & Rosanna rec in mbrp

LEONARD
7-21-1838    Belinda (form Worth) dis for mcd
7-19-1851    Adaline (form Folger) dis for mcd
7-19-1856    Letitia, Joseph, Hiram & Ann Marie, ch of
             Jesse & Belinda rec in mbrp
8-18-1856    Jesse rec in mbrp

LEWIS
8-21-1897    Perry rocf Stanton MM, Ill

LINDLEY
4-18-1840    Hezekiah Henley gct Lick Creek MM, Ind to
             m Ann Lindley, a wid w/ch
12-19-1840   Ann & s John LINDLEY rocf Lick Creek MM, Ind
3-20-1858    John gct Sugar Plain MM, Ind to m Rachel C
             Mills
5-21-1859    John T gct Honey Creek MM, Ind
6-16-1866    William C & w Melissa & ch Thomas H,
             William jr & Sarah Robena rocf Deep Creek
             MM, N Car
1-17-1880    Thomas dis for na & fighting
1-21-1893    William & w Melissa & ch William & David
             gct Westland MM, Ind

LINEBACK
4-19-1873    Lewis C rec in mbrp
2-21-1874    Nancy A & ch Sarah M, Oliver M & Margaret
             E rec in mbrp
2-21-1874    Thompson & w Frances & ch William H, &
             Ruby L rec in mbrp
2-17-1883    Thompson & w Frances & ch William H, Ruby
             Lola, John & Annie gct Carthage MM, Ind
3-21-1885    Oliver rel on req
3-20-1886    Sarah M rel on req
11-20-1897   Wesley & Frank are rel on req
4-15-1899    Wesley is rec in mbrp

LOUDENBACK
5-21-1878    Daniel rec in mbrp

LOWE
10-15-1864   Nathan B from Back Creek MM, N Car, rec in
             mbrp "being unable to obtain his certif of
             mbrp owing to war conditions"
4-20-1867    Nathan B gct Mill Creek MM, Ind

LUPTON
9-19-1846    David & w Ann & ch Ruth Esther, B Emma &
             Richard P & a minor ch under their care,
             Phebe Miller, rocf Spiceland MM, Ind
6-19-1847    David W & w Ann & minor ch Ruth E, B Emma
             & Richard P gct Milford MM, Ind

McCANN
4-19-1879    James rec in mbrp
3-19-1892    Emily Alice rec in mbrp

McCOOL
6-18-1852    Eleanor (form Powell) chm for mcd
6-18-1854    Eleanor gct Vermillion MM, Illinois

McKINLEY
11-18-1893   Henry & w Esther rocf Olive Branch MM, Ind

WALNUT RIDGE

## McKINLEY (Cont)
11-17-1894   Henry & w Esther gct Olive Branch MM, Ind

## MACY
1-16-1836   Thomas & w Rebecca & ch Tristram B, Lucinda S & Thomas C are charter mbrs
5-21-1836   Henry H & w Penina & ch Ann H & a minor ch, Jonathan Gray, who is under their care, rocf Spiceland MM, Ind
2-17-1838   Mary rocf Salem MM, Ind
2-17-1838   Reuben & w Maria & ch Delphina rocf Salem MM, Ind
4-17-1841   Tristram B chm for mcd
5-15-1841   Dorcas (form Gardner) chm for mcd
3-18-1843   Silvanus rocf Salem MM, Ind
6-20-1846   Reuben & w Maria & minor ch Evander & Lutitia gct Salem MM, Ind
11-17-1849   Mary (form Coffin) dis for mcd
2-16-1850   Thomas dis
6-21-1851   Francis B & w Huldah & ch Rebecca Ann, Margaret Jane, John Lilburn & Loretta Maria rocf Duck Creek MM, Ind
6-18-1854   Sarah (a wid) & dt Mary Elma rocf Wabash MM, Ind
9-20-1854   Sarah (a wid w/ch) of Rush Co, Ind & dt of Henry M & Rachel - - - -? m at Walnut Ridge Mtg, Ind to Jesse Morris of Rush Co
8-18-1855   Henry H & w Peninah & ch Ann H, William, Isaac & Huldah Jane gct Western Plain MM, - - - -?
7-19-1856   Margaret Jane NEWBY (form Macy) mcd. drpd from mbrp
3-19-1859   Henry W Henley gct Hopewell MM, Ind to m Avis Jane Macy
9-20-1862   John L dis for "participating in military training" & att a mcd
4-18-1863   Samuel & w Sarah & ch Charles, Elmira, Nancy, Simpson & Daniel Clinton rec in mbrp as they're "unable to obtain certif from Deep Creek MM, N Car because of war now existing"
4-18-1863   David W & William G, mbrs at Deep Creek MM, N Car are rec in mbrp because of war conditions, they are unable to get certif of mbrp
4-21-1866   Francis B & w Huldah & dt Loretta M gct Honey Creek MM, Ind
11-18-1871   Narcissa (form Coffin) chm for mcd
10- ?-1883   Clarkson Parker gct Hopewell MM, Ind to m Josephine Macy
3-17-1888   Newton Y & fam rec in mbrp
5-19-1888   Laura B rocf Hopewell MM, Ind
5-19-1888   Margaret rocf Hopewell MM, Ind
1-21-1893   Ella gct Newburg MM, Oregon
6-18-1898   Margaret gct Hopewell MM, Ind

## MARSH
1-16-1836   Elias & 1st w Edith & ch Martha, William, Lydia, Jesse, Sebina T, Fanny & Joseph are charter mbrs
1-16-1836   Elias appt to comm to make a mbrp list
2-20-1836   Elias appt an overseer
3-16-1836   Elias appt to comm to care for indigent persons
12-21-1836   William of Hancock Co, Ind s Elias & Edith, m at Walnut Ridge Mtg, Ind to Martha Ann Chappell
12-17-1838   Martha DRAPER (form Marsh) chm for mcd
4-24-1839   Elias of Hancock Co, Ind, s Elias Sr & Martha, both decd, lately of Columbiana Co, Ohio m at Walnut Ridge Mtg, Ind to Elizabeth Boyd, a wid
6-18-1842   Dayton, Martha Ann & Oliver MacKenzie BOYD, ch of Elizabeth BOYD (now Elizabeth MARSH w of Elias MARSH) rec in mbrp
5-16-1846   Elias, a widower, gct Springfield MM, Ohio to m Margaret Osborn, (wid of Thomas Osborn)
10- ?-1846   Elias gct Springfield MM, Ohio
2-20-1847   Elias & w Margaret & her ch Mary, Margaret & Thomas OSBORN rocf Springfield MM, Ohio
3-25-1847   Fanny dt Elias & Edith, decd, of Hancock Co, Ind m at Westland M H (Walnut Ridge MM) Ind to John C Perisho of Rush Co, Ind
3-28-1847   Jesse of Rush Co, Ind s Elias & Edith, decd, of Hancock Co m at Westland M H (Walnut Ridge MM) Ind to Catherine Osborn of Hancock Co, Ind
9-18-1847   Lydia LAMB (form Marsh) chm for mcd
11-25-1847   Sabina T dt Elias & Edith, decd, of Hancock Co, Ind m at Westland M H (Walnut Ridge MM) Ind to Benjamin Albertson of Rush Co, Ind
10-21-1854   Elias & w Margaret gct Westfield MM, Ind
11-18-1854   Jesse & w Catherine & ch Elias, Margaret & George W gct East Grove MM, Iowa
9-15-1855   Elias & w Margaret rocf Springfield MM, Ohio
7- ?-1866   Martha Ann, (wid of William) & James Brown are altm & a Friend is appt to att m & rpt to next Mtg
8-18-1866   The Friend appt to att m of Martha Ann & James Brown, rpts service att & m certif has been placed in hands of the Recorder
10-20-1866   Benjamin F, minor s of Martha Ann (now Martha Ann Brown) gct Sugar Plain MM, Ind
3-21-1868   Margaret BEESON (form Marsh) mcd. drpd from mbrp
9-19-1868   Elias J dis for jas
6-18-1870   William P chm for mcd
5-17-1873   Benjamin F rocf Sugar Plain MM, Ind & endorsed to Westland MM, Ind

## MARSHALL
10-19-1839   Jesse & w Mary & ch James, William, Calvin, Levi & Eli rocf Spiceland MM, Ind
12-19-1846   Jesse & w Mary & minor ch James, William, Calvin, Levi, Jared, Nathan & Rachel gct Honey Creek MM, Ind
5-21-1853   David & w Zilinda & dt Abigail S rocf Wabash MM, Ind
4-19-1864   David appt Clerk & William P Binford appt asst Clerk
12-18-1869   Levi Binford gct Carthage MM, Ind to m Abigail S Marshall

## MATHERS
12-15-1835   Matilda (form Hill) mcd drpd from mbrp

## MAUDLIN
1-16-1836   John & w Rebecca & ch Mark, Nathan, Exum, Eliza Ann, Catherine Jane & Sarah are charter mbrs
5-21-1836   John & w Rebecca & ch gct West Grove MM, Ind

## MAYWEATHER
11-19-1887   Plummer rec in mbrp

## MENDENHALL
4-24-1838   Stephen J & w Sarah & ch Katherine Rebecca, Nathan & Albert rocf Blue River MM, Ind
9-22-1841   James C of Hendricks Co, Ind, s Richard & Polly, decd, m at Walnut Ridge Mtg, Ind to Mary Brown of Rush Co, Ind
8-20-1842   Mary gct White Lick MM, Ind
6-15-1844   James C & w Mary & ch Robert & Jane rocf White Lick MM, Ind
12-19-1846   Stephen G & w Sarah & minor ch Catharine R, Nathan, Albert, Elizabeth & Bartlett gct Spiceland MM, Ind
7-17-1852   Eli rocf Mill Creek MM, Ind
11-20-1852   Eli B gct Spiceland MM, Ind to m Mary Jane Pierson
7-16-1853   Eli B gct White Lick MM, Ind
1-15-1859   James C & w Mary & minor ch Robert, Jane, Thomas & Zeno gct Lynn Grove MM, Iowa
1-18-1862   Samuel rocf Deep River MM, N Car
1-21-1882   Samuel gct Deep River MM, N Car

## MEREDITH
2-15-1868   Elizabeth M & dt Lydia E rec in mbrp
5-15-1869   George dis

## MERRIWEATHER
4-15-1893   Elizabeth & ch rec in mbrp

## MILES
2-17-1883   David OUTLAND gct Dublin MM, Ind to m Rhoda E Miles

WALNUT RIDGE

## MILLER
|  |  |
|---|---|
| 9-19-1846 | Phebe a minor, under the care of David & Ann Lupton, rocf Spiceland MM, Ind |
| 9-18-1847 | Phebe gct Milford MM, Ind |
| 2-21-1874 | Rudolph & w Missouri rec in mbrp |
| 7-17-1886 | Foster & w Olive rec in mbrp |
| 5-21-1887 | Rudolph & w Missouri gct Indianapolis MM, Ind |
| 3-19-1892 | Foster & w Olive gct Dublin MM, Ind |

## MILLIKIN
|  |  |
|---|---|
| 10-17-1874 | William P & w Rebecca J & ch Sarah, Quincy Monroe, Rachel V, Joseph, Benjamin & William rocf Marlborough MM, N Car |

## MILLS
|  |  |
|---|---|
| 3-20-1858 | John Lindley gct Sugar Plain MM, Ind to m Rachel C Mills |
| 12-15-1866 | Elizabeth BROWN (form Mills) chm for mcd |

## MOON
|  |  |
|---|---|
| 6-15-1839 | Jeremiah & w Rachel & ch Mary, George, Ann, Elizabeth, Jane, Nixon & Havilah rocf Newberry MM, Ohio |
| 8-23-1839 | Mary dt Jeremiah & Rachel N of Hancock Co, Ind m at Walnut Ridge Mtg, Ind to John Binford of Hancock Co |
| 3-19-1842 | George H gct Springfield MM, Ohio to m Susanna Osborn |
| 2-18-1843 | Susanna rocf Springfield MM, Ohio |
| 8-22-1844 | Ann dt Jeremiah & Rachel of Hancock Co, Ind m at Walnut Ridge Mtg, Ind to Benajah Binford jr, of Hancock Co |
| 4-19-1845 | Jeremiah & w Rachel & minor ch Elizabeth, Nixon, Havilah, Rachel & Ruth gct Salem MM, Iowa Territory |
| 9-19-1850 | George H & w Susanna & minor ch Thomas O, Jeremiah, Jesse N, & Rachel Ann gct East Grove MM, Iowa |

## MOORE
|  |  |
|---|---|
| 1-16-1836 | Samuel & w Rebecca & ch Joshua, Mary, Margaret & Sarah are charter mbrs |
| 1-16-1836 | Samuel appt to comm on Education |
| 2-20-1836 | Rebecca appt to comm on Education |
| 12-25-1839 | Joseph of Hamilton Co, Ind s Mordecai & Rachel of same place m at Walnut Ridge Mtg, Ind to Deborah Chappel of Hancock Co, Ind |
| 1-22-1840 | Samuel jr of Rush Co, Ind s Samuel & Margaret, both decd, of Perquimans Co, N Car, m at - - - - - Mtg, Ind to Ann Binford of Hancock Co, Ind |
| 2-20-1841 | Deborah gct Westfield MM, Ind |
| 3-15-1845 | Joseph & w Deborah & ch Thomas C, John, & William rocf Westfield MM, Ind |
| 9-20-1856 | Joseph & w Deborah & ch Thomas C, John, William, Silas, Mary E & Lindley M gct Westfield MM, Ind |
| 3-21-1857 | Joshua gct Duck Creek MM, Ind to m Mary Bufkin |
| 9-19-1857 | Mary rocf Duck Creek MM, Ind |
| 4-20-1861 | Samuel & w Mary & ch Rebecca, Joseph, Huldah, Samuel, Eli J rocf Deep River MM, N Car |
| 5-21-1864 | Mary & Mordecai M Gilbert are altm. A comm is appt to att m & rpt to next mtg |
| 6-18-1864 | The comm appt to att m of Mary & Mordecai M Gilbert, rpts it was orderly & m certif has been placed in hands of the Recorder |
| 11-19-1864 | Huldah A & Joseph O Binford are altm & a comm is appt to att m & rpt to next mtg |
| 12-17-1864 | The comm appt to att m of Huldah A & Joseph O Binford, rpts it was orderly & m certif has been placed in hands of the Recorder |
| 3-10-1865 | John B chm for mcd |
| 6-17-1865 | John B rocf Mill Creek MM, Ind |
| 12-18-1865 | Sarah (form Hill) chm for mcd |
| 1-20-1866 | Ransom B rec in mbrp |
| 3-17-1866 | Joseph B chm for mcd |
| 3-17-1866 | Ruth Ann (form Bundy) chm for mcd |
| 9-15-1866 | Rebecca J & Robert B Brown are altm & a Friend is appt to att m & rpt to next Mtg |
| 10-20-1866 | The Friend appt to att m of Rebecca J & Robert B Brown, rpts the service att & the m certif has been placed in hands of the Recorder |
| 1-18-1868 | Samuel & w Mary & s Samuel & Eli gct Toledo MM, (Chase Co), Kansas |
| 1-18-1868 | John B & w Sarah Ann gct Toledo MM, (Chase Co) Kansas |
| 1-18-1868 | Ransom S gct Raysville MM, Ind |
| 8-16-1873 | Margaret & Henry Henley are altm & a Friend is appt to att m & rpt to next Mtg |
| 9-20-1873 | The Friend appt to att m of Margaret & Henry Henley, rpts the service att & the m certif has been forwarded to the Recorder |
| 1-18-1878 | Joseph B & w Ruth & ch gct Toledo MM, Kansas |
| 9-19-1888 | Joshua & Mary B gct Carthage MM, Ind |

## MORGAN
|  |  |
|---|---|
| 1-18-1840 | Rebecca & Zeno, ch of Hezekiah, rocf Spiceland MM, Ind |
| 4-15-1848 | Rebecca gct Mill Creek MM, (Hendricks Co) Ind |
| 4-15-1854 | Benjamin & w Sarah rocf Milford MM, Ind |
| 3-15-1862 | Sarah gct New Garden MM, Ind |

## MORRIS
|  |  |
|---|---|
| 6-16-1838 | John & w Martha & s Francis M rocf Milford MM, Ind |
| 9-23-1840 | Samuel M of Whitewater Mtg, Wayne Co, Ind, s Jesse & Mary of same place, m at Walnut Ridge Mtg, Ind to Lavina Cox of Rush Co, Ind |
| 8-21-1841 | Lavina gct Whitewater MM, Ind |
| 4-16-1842 | Lydia chm for mcd |
| 5-21-1842 | Jesse & w Joanna rocf Milford MM, Ind |
| 10-17-1842 | Lydia WHEELER (form Morris) dis for mcd |
| 5-21-1853 | John & w Martha & ch Francis M, David W, Caleb J & Ann gct Milford MM, Ind |
| 3-18-1854 | Sarah (form Townsend) chm for mcd |
| 8-19-1854 | Sarah rocf Whitewater MM, Ind |
| 9-20-1854 | Jesse of Rush Co, Ind s Joshua & Mary, m at Walnut Ridge Mtg, Ind to Sarah A Macy (a wid) of Rush Co, Ind |
| 4-16-1870 | John T & Sarah Ann Gray are altm & a Friend is appt to att m & rpt to next Mtg |
| 5-21-1870 | The Friend appt to att m of John T & Sarah Ann Gray, rpts service att & m certif has been forwarded to the Recorder |
| 8-20-1870 | John T & his ch Mary B, Luther L, Eli, Emma & Daniel rocf Onarga MM, Illinois |
| 8-21-1875 | Mary Eliza gct Oak Ridge MM, Ind |
| 3-17-1877 | Luther L, Emma & Daniel, ch of John T & Mary B gct Oak Ridge MM, Ind |
| 1-18-1879 | John T & w Sarah A gct Chehalem MM, Oregon |
| 11-18-1882 | Nathan O & w Phariba & ch Joseph, Edith & Francis rocf Spiceland MM, Ind |
| 12-20-1884 | John & Sarah rocf Chehalem MM, Oregon |
| 4-19-1890 | Joseph gct Newburg MM, Oregon |
| 9-20-1890 | S Murry Parker gct Sand Creek MM, Ind to m Margaret Morris |
| 1-21-1893 | Nathan & w Phariba & ch Edith & Frank gct Marion MM, Oregon |
| 1-19-1895 | Micajah & w Ella & ch Minnie, Clara, Charles, William, Elizabeth & Ineze rocf Deer Creek MM, Ind |
| 9-19-1896 | Frances B rocf Marion MM, Oregon |
| 8-19-1899 | Micajah & ch Charles, William, Elizabeth & Ineze gct Oak Ridge MM, Ind |

## MULLIS
|  |  |
|---|---|
| 7-19-1873 | Pennina rec in mbrp |
| 8-15-1874 | Pennina gct Carthage MM, Ind |

## MUNDANE
|  |  |
|---|---|
| 8-15-1868 | Thomas W rec in mbrp |
| 1-15-1881 | Thomas & w Margaret & ch Pharaba, Mary M, John K & Christopher gct Indianapolis MM, Ind |

## MIRES
|  |  |
|---|---|
| 4-15-1848 | Louisa (form Talbert) chm for mcd |
| 9-17-1853 | Louiza dis for jas, U B Ch |

## NAYLOR
|  |  |
|---|---|
| 3-19-1898 | Murray gct Dublin MM, Ind |

## NELSON
|  |  |
|---|---|
| 4-19-1879 | Thomas & w Phebe & ch Catherine, Thomas, Oscar & Henry rec in mbrp |
| 4-17-1897 | Maria Belle glt Meth Ch, Arlington Circuit, Ind |

WALNUT RIDGE

## NEWBY

|  |  |
|---|---|
| 1-16-1836 | Henry & w Sarah & ch Penelope, Abigail, Milly, Mary, William, Phebe & Thomas T are charter mbrs |
| 1-16-1836 | John H & w Harriett & ch Rebecca W are charter mbrs |
| 1-16-1836 | Henry appt to comm to procure the necessary Record Books for the Mthly Mtg |
| 2-20-1836 | Henry appt to a comm |
| 3-16-1836 | Henry appt to comm to care for indigent persons |
| 3-16-1838 | Henry appt Recorder of marriage certificates |
| 9-15-1838 | Sarah gct Spiceland MM, Ind |
| 11-26-1840 | Penelope dt Henry & Sarah of Rush Co, Ind m at Carthage M H, (Walnut Ridge MM) Ind to Joseph Hill of Rush Co |
| 8-26-1841 | Abigail dt Henry & Sarah of Rush Co, Ind m at Carthage M H, (Walnut Ridge MM) Ind to Jesse Henley of Rush Co, Ind |
| 5-16-1846 | Henry & w Mary & ch Mildred, William, Nathan & Matilda rocf Milford MM, Ind |
| 9-21-1848 | Mildred dt Henry & Mary of Hancock Co, Ind m at Westland M H, (Walnut Ridge MM) Ind to Asa Hunt of Rush Co, Ind |
| 6- ?-1850 | William chm for mcd |
| 12-20-1851 | John H & w Harriett & ch Rebecca W, Micah & Franklin gct Richland MM, Ind |
| 7-16-1853 | William dis for "taking an oath" |
| 9-17-1853 | Jemima (form White) dis for mcd |
| 2-18-1854 | Henry chm for mcd |
| 6-18-1854 | Nathan dis for mcd |
| 9-15-1855 | Ascenith (form Parker) dis for mcd |
| 4-24-1856 | Mary dt Henry & Sarah, decd, of Rush Co, Ind m at Carthage M H, (Walnut Ridge MM) Ind to Robert Henley of Rush Co, Ind |
| 7-19-1856 | Margaret Jane (form Macy) mcd. drpd from mbrp |
| 8-25-1856 | Phebe dt of Henry & Sarah of Rush Co, Ind m at Carthage M H, (Walnut Ridge MM) to Thomas Elwood Henley of Rush Co |
| 6-19-1857 | Matilda RICHARDSON (form Newby) mcd. drpd from mbrp |
| 8-21-1858 | Henry dis for promoting mcd of dts |
| 12-23-1858 | Milly dt Henry & Sarah of Rush Co, Ind m at Carthage M H, (Walnut Ridge MM) Ind to Jesse B Jessop of Henry Co, Ind |
| 5-16-1863 | Margaret J & dt Laura Bell rec in mbrp |

## NEWLIN

|  |  |
|---|---|
| 10-20-1855 | Samuel Brown gct White Lick MM, Ind to m Jane Newlin |
| 3-30-1862 | Jehu of Mill Creek MM, Hendricks Co, Ind, s Jacob & Ruth of Parke Co, Ind m at Westland M H, (Walnut Ridge MM) Ind to Pamelia Jane Andrews of Hancock Co, Ind |
| 6-21-1862 | Pamelia Jane gct Mill Creek MM, Ind |

## NEWSOM

|  |  |
|---|---|
| 1-16-1836 | Luke & w Cynthia & his ch Martha, Henry, Jabez H & their dt Elizabeth B are charter mbrs |
| 6-19-1847 | Martha gct Back Creek MM, Ind |
| 2-17-1855 | Margaret (form Cox) chm for mcd |
| 9-15-1855 | Margaret rocf Blue River MM, Ind |
| 11-17-1855 | Mary Ann HILL (form Newsom) dis for mcd |
| 2-16-1856 | Elizabeth RUBY (form Newsom) mcd. drpd from mbrp |
| 5-21-1864 | John dis for mcd & for Military Service |
| 1-20-1866 | Allen W chm for mcd |
| 2-15-1896 | Mary Ellen gct Carthage MM, Ind |

## NICHOLS

|  |  |
|---|---|
| 12-18-1848 | Thomas of Hendricks Co, Ind, s Erasmus & Elizabeth of same place, m at Walnut Ridge Mtg, Ind to Jane Brown of Rush Co |
| 3-17-1849 | Jane gct Mill Creek MM, Ind |
| 8-20-1853 | Israel BROWN gct Mill Creek MM, Ind to m Eliza Nichols |
| 5-19-1855 | Thomas & Jane & dts Margaret & Elizabeth rocf Mill Creek MM, Ind |
| 8-18-1855 | Samuel B HASTINGS gct Mill Creek MM, Ind to m Matilda Nichols |
| 5-16-1857 | Jane & minor ch Margaret, Elizabeth & Rachel gct Mill Creek MM, Ind |
| 1-15-1859 | Thomas gct Mill Creek MM, Ind |
| 6-17-1865 | Jane & ch Margaret, Elizabeth & Rachel rocf Mill Creek MM, Ind |
| 2-16-1867 | Margaret Osborn (form Nichols) chm for mcd |
| 5-20-1871 | Elizabeth Diggs (form Nichols) chm for mcd |

## NICHOLSON

|  |  |
|---|---|
| 1-16-1836 | Peninah, wid of Nathan, & ch Mary, George & Nathan P are charter mbrs |
| 1-16-1836 | Thomas, William & Joshua, ch of John of N Car are charter mbrs |
| 4-25-1838 | Nathan of Rush Co, Ind, s Nathan decd & Peninah, late of Perquimans Co, N Car, m at Walnut Ridge Mtg, Ind to Miriam Hunt of Rush Co |
| 6-16-1838 | George gct Springfield MM, Ind to m Lucinda Dennis |
| 1-19-1839 | George gct Springfield MM, Ind |
| 8-19-1843 | Thomas gct Salem MM, Iowa Territory |
| 3-16-1850 | William gct Salem MM, Iowa |
| 3-16-1850 | Joshua gct Salem MM, Iowa |
| 9-21-1850 | Nathan gct Spiceland MM, Ind to m Ascenith Cloud |
| 3-15-1851 | Ascenith rocf Spiceland MM, Ind |
| 9-22-1858 | Cynthia dt Nathan & Miriam, decd, of - - - -? m at Walnut Ridge Mtg, Ind to Albert White of Rush Co, Ind |
| 5-15-1869 | Esther Ann (form Butler) chm for mcd |
| 6-19-1869 | Josiah chm for mcd |
| 5-20-1871 | Jane ALFRED (form Nicholson) chm for mcd |
| 2-21-1874 | Ascenith & minor ch Milton & Hiram J gct Spiceland MM, Ind |
| 4-17-1875 | Ascenith & ch Milton rocf Spiceland MM, Ind |
| 1-19-1884 | Anetta rocf Carthage MM, Ind |
| 5-21-1887 | Josiah & w Esther & ch Edward, Naomi, Elva, Lemuel, Earnest, Pearcy, Pearl & Grace gct Back Creek MM, Ind |
| 2-16-1889 | Milton & w Nettie & ch Bertha & Lillian gct Newburg MM, Oregon |

## NIXON

|  |  |
|---|---|
| 10-17-1840 | Benjamin & w Lydia & ch John rocf Milford MM, Ind |
| 10-19-1844 | Benjamin dis for mcd & j Meth Ch |
| 12-19-1846 | Lydia WILTSE (form Nixon) chm for mcd |
| 10-18-1847 | Samuel of Wayne Co, Ind s Barnabas & Sarah, both decd, lately of Prince George Co, Va, m at Westland M H (Walnut Ridge MM) Ind to Rhoda Butler, a wid |
| 4-15-1848 | Rhoda & her minor ch Arthur & Lucinda BUTLER gct New Garden MM, Ind |

## NORTHAM

|  |  |
|---|---|
| 5-21-1853 | Matilda rocf Center MM, N Car |
| 8-16-1856 | Matilda dis for jas - Wesleyans |

## OLDHAM

|  |  |
|---|---|
| 12-21-1867 | James rec in mbrp |

## OSBORN

|  |  |
|---|---|
| 3-19-1842 | George H Moon gct Springfield MM, Ohio to m Susannah Osborn |
| 5-16-1846 | Elias Marsh (a widower) gct Springfield MM, Ohio to m Margaret Osborn (wid of Thomas Osborn, w/ch) |
| 2-20-1847 | Margaret & her ch Mary, Margaret & Thomas OSBORN rocf Springfield MM, Ohio |
| 2-20-1847 | Catherine rocf Springfield MM, Ohio |
| 3-28-1847 | Catharine of Hancock Co, Ind dt Thomas, decd, late of Clinton Co, Ohio & w Margaret (now Margaret MARSH) of Hancock Co, Ind m at Westland M H (Walnut Ridge MM) Ind to Jesse Marsh of Rush Co, Ind |
| 2-24-1848 | Mary of Hancock Co, Ind dt Thomas, decd, & Margaret (now Margaret MARSH) of same place m at Westland M H (Walnut Ridge MM) Ind to Oliver M Boyd of Hancock Co, Ind |
| 10-15-1853 | Margaret gct Springfield MM, Ohio |
| 6-18-1854 | Thomas dis for taking an oath |
| 2-16-1867 | Margaret (form Nichols) chm for mcd |
| 8-17-1867 | Margaret gct Plainfield MM, Ind |

WALNUT RIDGE

OUTLAND
10-18-1856  William P & w Mary Annis & ch Mary A, Josiah B, William T, Oliver W & Francis N rocf Rich Square MM, N Car
5-21-1859  Mary rocf Rich Square MM, N Car
6-16-1860  Mary, a Minister, gct Westfield MM, Ind
7-18-1864  David & fam from Rich Square MM, N Car, rec in mbrp, "being without a certif owing to the war"
9-16-1865  Ann WHITE (form Outland) chm for mcd
4-18-1868  Mary Annis & ch Mary A, Josiah B, William T, Oliver W & David gct Spiceland MM, Ind
12-19-1868  John dis for jas
3-20-1869  David & minor ch David A, Marticia J, Mahala & Joseph W gct Richland MM, Ind
4-20-1872  David & ch Marticia, Amos, Mahlon & Joseph rocf Richland MM, Ind
2-21-1874  James gct Westland MM, Ind
12-16-1876  David A rocf Westland MM, Ind
2-17-1883  David gct Dublin MM, Ind to m Rhoda E Miles (from Milford MM)
2-16-1884  David A gct Dublin MM, Ind
12-19-1886  James H & w Elizabeth & s Eldon rocf Westland MM, Ind

OVERMAN
5-21-1836  Isaac rocf New Garden MM, Ind
4-21-1838  Isaac gct Westfield MM, Ind
8-18-1838  Nathan & ch Joseph, Charles, Elizabeth & John rocf West Grove MM, Ind
4-18-1840  Joseph dis for mcd & dp
5-21-1842  Elizabeth dis for att a mcd & dp
4-19-1843  Nathan of Rush Co, Ind s Isaac & Sarah, decd, of Pasquotank Co, N Car, m at Walnut Ridge Mtg, Ind to Elizabeth Hunnicutt, wid of Robert Hunnicutt
1-20-1844  Charles gct Westfield MM, Ind
2-17-1844  Nathan dis for att a mcd & dp

OWEN
3-17-1845  Amos of Hendricks Co, Ind, s John & Rebecca, decd, of same place, m at Westland M H (Walnut Ridge MM) Ind to Phebe C Hubbard of Hancock Co, Ind
5-17-1845  Phebe C gct Fairfield MM, Ind

PAGE
11-14-1885  Elizabeth rocf Whitewater MM, Ind

PALMER
4-23-1846  Elias of Duck Creek Mtg, Henry Co, Ind, s David & Sarah, decd, of same place, m at Walnut Ridge MM, Ind to Eunice W Coggshall
7-18-1846  Eunice W gct Duck Creek MM, Ind

PARISH
6-27-1890  Harry & w Miriam & ch Charles, Edith, Carl Walter & Nellie rec in mbrp
4-20-1895  Henry & Miriam & ch gct Carthage MM, Ind

PARKER
1-16-1836  William & w Almeda & ch Albert J & Elizabeth are charter mbrs
1-16-1836  Samuel & w Rebecca & ch Silas, James B, John, Hannah Jane, Martha & Angeline are charter mbrs
1-16-1836  William appt to comm on Education
10-21-1837  Nathan A & w Sarah A & ch Josiah T & Sarah Isabella rocf Rich Square MM, N Car
10-21-1837  Martha & dts Martha & Phebe May rocf Rich Square MM, N Car
10-24-1838  Silas of Rush Co, Ind, s Samuel & Rebecca m at Walnut Ridge Mtg, Ind to Priscilla Butler of Hancock Co, Ind
5-20-1843  James B gct Spiceland MM, Ind to m Hannah H Gause
12-16-1843  Hannah B rocf Spiceland MM, Ind
3-20-1847  James B & w Hannah & minor ch Eli gct Spiceland MM, Ind
3-20-1847  Martha Sr gct Spiceland MM, Ind
3-20-1847  Phebe May gct Spiceland MM, Ind
3-20-1847  Martha jr gct Spiceland MM, Ind
5-20-1848  James B & w Hannah & ch Eli, Rebecca rocf Spiceland MM, Ind

4-23-1851  John P of Rush Co, Ind, s Samuel, decd, & Rebecca of same place m at Walnut Ridge Mtg, Ind to Miriam J Hill of Rush Co
9-21-1853  Angelina B dt Samuel, decd, & Rebecca of Rush Co, Ind, m at Walnut Ridge Mtg, Ind to Milton Brown of Rush Co
7-15-1854  Sarah, Ascenith, Isabel & Elizabeth ch of Thomas & Rebecca, both decd, rocf White Lick MM, Ind
11-22-1854  Elizabeth formerly of Northampton Co, N Car, dt Thomas & Rebecca, both decd, m at Walnut Ridge Mtg, Ind to Aaron C Gause of Henry Co, Ind
4-25-1855  Hannah Jane dt Samuel, decd, & Rebecca of Rush Co, Ind m at Walnut Ridge Mtg, Ind to Joel W Hodson of Hendricks Co, Ind
9-15-1855  Ascenith NEWBY (form Parker) dis for mcd
4-19-1856  James B & w Hannah B & minor ch Eli G & Rebecca Ann gct Spiceland MM, Ind
3-25-1857  Elizabeth Ann dt William & Almeda of Rush Co, Ind m at Walnut Ridge Mtg, Ind to James Patterson of Rush Co
4-21-1858  Martha Ann dt Samuel, decd, & Rebecca of Rush Co, Ind m at Walnut Ridge Mtg, Ind to Newby Hodson of Hendricks Co, Ind
4-21-1858  Isabella dt Thomas & Rebecca, both decd, of N Car, m at Walnut Ridge Mtg, Ind to Joel Hiatt of Henry Co, Ind
11-20-1858  Rebecca gct Mill Creek MM, Ind
12-21-1861  Sarah Ann gct Spiceland MM, Ind (certif returned, she is not there)
11-19-1862  Lydia Ann dt Sylas & Priscilla of Rush Co, Ind m at Walnut Ridge Mtg, Ind to Samuel C Pitts of Rush Co
5-21-1864  Elwood appt Recorder of marriage certificates
8-20-1864  Susanna & Henry C Aydelotte are altm. A comm is appt to att m & rpt to next mtg
9-17-1864  The comm appt to att m of Susanna & Henry C Aydelotte, rpts it was orderly & the m certif has been placed in hands of the Recorder
3-11-1866  Elwood gct New Garden to m Rachel Johnson
7-21-1866  Rachel J rocf New Garden MM, Ind
7-20-1867  Consent of parents being had, Esther B & Thomas C Hill are altm. A Friend is appt to att m & rpt to next mtg
8-17-1867  The Friend appt to att m of Esther B & Thomas C Hill, rpts the service att & the m certif has been forwarded to the Recorder
1-18-1868  Louisa COFFIN (form Parker) chm for mcd
10-17-1868  Eli J & w Mary M & dt Viola Alice rocf Spiceland MM, Ind
2-18-1871  Robert J gct Milford MM, Ind
7- ?-1873  Elwood who has been Recorder of m certif is rptd decd. A Comm is appt to propose a name of a person to fill his place
3-21-1874  James B & w Hannah & ch Charles C rocf Raysville MM, Ind
5-16-1874  Sarah Ann gct Carthage MM, Ind
4-17-1875  Eli & w Mary M & ch Viola Alice, Lydia Francis, James & Maryetta rocf Westland MM, Ind
3-17-1877  James B & w Hannah V & s Charles gct Milford MM, Ind
2-21-1880  Rilda rocf White River MM, Ind
4-17-1880  Almira & Oliver M Brown are altm & a Friend is appt to att m & rpt to next mtg
5-15-1880  The Friend appt to att m of Almira & Oliver M Brown, rpts service att & m certif has been forwarded to the Recorder
1-15-1881  Eli G & w Mary M, a Minister, & ch Viola Alice, Lydia Frances, James V W & Marietta gct White River MM, Ind
2-17-1883  John & w Miriam & ch John Oscar gct Whitewater MM, Ind
10- ?-1883  Clarkson gct Hopewell MM, Ind to m Josephine Macy
1-19-1884  Josephine M rocf Hopewell MM, Ind
12-19-1885  John & w Miriam J & ch John Oscar rocf Whitewater MM, Ind
5-15-1886  Mary M rec in mbrp
9- 8-1886  Benjamin Franklin gct Liberty MM, Kansas
4-16-1887  Rachel & ch Fidelia gct Westfield MM, Ind
5-21-1887  Rachel & ch Fidelia rocf Westfield MM, Ind

WALNUT RIDGE

## PARKER (Cont)

|  |  |
|---|---|
| 12-15-1888 | Alice & James Thomas Chappel are altm. Req is made for a mtg to be appt at residence of John P Parker on 1-19-1889 at 6 P M. Req is granted |
| 1-19-1889 | Alice & James Thomas Chappel m at residence of John P Parker |
| 9-20-1890 | S Murray gct Sand Creek MM, Ind to m Margaret Morris |
| 12-20-1890 | Margaret M rocf Sand Creek MM, Ind |
| 3-21-1891 | Lindley & w Louisa & ch Walter, Curtis, Lenora & Floyd gct Newberg MM, Oregon |
| 4-18-1891 | Albert S rel on req |
| 1-21-1893 | Rachel & Fidelia gct White Lick MM, Ind |
| 1-20-1894 | Charles M & w Mary & s Albert gct Mill Creek MM, Ind |
| 3-16-1895 | Charles & w Mary & ch Albert Charles & Pearl gct Mill Creek MM, Ind |
| 4-17-1897 | Nathan & dt Deborah rocf Goshen MM, Ohio |

## PATTEN

|  |  |
|---|---|
| 2-17-1855 | William dis |
| 2-17-1855 | Joseph & w Rachel & ch James A & Thomas C rocf Hopewell MM, Ind |
| 4-21-1855 | Eunice, dt of Joseph & Rachel rec in mbrp |

## PATTERSON

|  |  |
|---|---|
| 5-21-1836 | Jared & w Angeline & ch Elihu, Ascenith, Eliza, Mary & Amos rocf Stillwater MM, Ohio |
| 5-21-1836 | Elizabeth (wid of William & the mother of Jared) rocf Somerset MM, Ohio |
| 9-20-1837 | Eliza dt Jared & Angeline of Rush Co, Ind m at Walnut Ridge Mtg, Ind to Joseph J Butler of Hancock Co, Ind |
| 11-18-1837 | Rachel rocf Stillwater MM, Ohio |
| 1-24-1838 | Ascenith dt Jared & Angeline of Rush Co, Ind m at Walnut Ridge Mtg, Ind to William Kenworthy of Spiceland Mtg, Henry Co, Ind |
| 5-15-1841 | Amasa & w Lydia & ch James, Eliza Ann & Rachel rocf Stillwater MM, Ohio |
| 6-19-1841 | James B & w Elizabeth & s Jared rocf Somerset MM, Ohio |
| 3-19-1842 | Elihu gct Milford MM, Ind to m Rachel Cox |
| 3-18-1843 | Rachel rocf Milford MM, Ind |
| 11-16-1844 | Rachel gct Milford MM, Ind |
| 11-16-1850 | Amos dis for na, upl, falsifying & dishonesty |
| 1-18-1851 | James F dis for upl & dp |
| 11-15-1851 | Jared, a Minister, & w Angeline gct Rhode Island MM, R I |
| 6-19-1852 | Jared & w Angeline rocf New Port MM, R I |
| 3-25-1857 | James of Rush Co, Ind s Amasa & Lydia of same place m at Walnut Ridge Mtg, Ind to Elizabeth Ann Parker of Rush Co |
| 9-23-1857 | Rachel dt Amasa & Lydia of Rush Co, Ind m at Walnut Ridge Mtg, Ind to Josiah T Winslow of Rush Co |
| 9-19-1860 | Mary J dt Amasa & Lydia of Rush Co, Ind m at Walnut Ridge Mtg, Ind to William F Winslow of Rush Co |
| 8-7-1861 | Eliza A dt Amasa & Lydia of Rush Co, Ind m at Walnut Ridge Mtg to Joseph J Chappell of Piney Woods Mtg, N Car |
| 6-17-1876 | James & w Elizabeth Ann & minor ch Enos, Amasa, William E, Susannah Endora & George gct Lynn Grove MM, Iowa |

## PEACOCK

|  |  |
|---|---|
| 3-18-1893 | Cynthia A gct Fairmount MM, Ind |

## PEARSON - PIERSON

|  |  |
|---|---|
| 1-16-1836 | Jonathan & w Anna & ch Nathan, Jesse, Martha, Mary, Josiah & Elizabeth are charter mbrs |
| 7-17-1841 | Jonathan dis for disunity & na |
| 12-22-1841 | Enoch of Henry Co, Ind s Peter & Eunice of same place m at Walnut Ridge Mtg, Ind to Rachel Brown of Rush Co, Ind |
| 4-16-1842 | Rachel gct Duck Creek MM, Ind |
| 1-31-1843 | Newton Stubbs gct Spiceland MM, Ind to m Nancy Pierson |
| 9-24-1845 | Nathan of Rush Co, Ind s Jonathan & Anna of same place m at Walnut Ridge Mtg, Ind to Mary Bundy of Rush Co |
| 9-19-1846 | Anna & minor ch Jesse, Martha, Josiah & Elizabeth gct Mississinewa MM, Ind |
| 4-17-1847 | Nathan & w Mary gct Mississinewa MM, Ind |
| 11-20-1852 | Eli B MENDENHALL gct Spiceland MM, Ind to m Mary Jane Pierson |
| 2-16-1861 | Enoch & w Rhoda & ch Mary Jane, Martin, Daniel, David, Sarah & Peter rocf Honey Creek MM, Ind |
| 5-20-1865 | Mary Jane DIXON (form Pearson) chm for mcd |
| 5-17-1873 | Martin chm for mcd |
| 7-19-1873 | Daniel chm for mcd |
| 3-19-1887 | Mary J rocf Carthage MM, Ind |
| 1-21-1888 | Ezra gct Hesper MM, Iowa |
| 10-16-1897 | Bertha Gertrude rocf Muncie MM, Ind |

## PEEPLES

|  |  |
|---|---|
| 2-19-1853 | Elijah rocf Whitewater MM, Ind |
| 2-17-1855 | Elijah gct Richland MM, Ind |

## PERISHO

|  |  |
|---|---|
| 1-16-1836 | Nathan & w Mary & ch Mary Elma, John C, Joshua Morris, Martha Ann & Margaret Jane are charter mbrs |
| 4-24-1838 | Nathan gct Whitewater MM, Ind to m Sarah Chappell |
| 8-18-1838 | Sarah M rocf Whitewater MM, Ind |
| 3-23-1843 | Mary Elma of Hancock Co, Ind, dt Nathan & Mary, decd, m at Walnut Ridge Mtg, Ind to William E Andrews of Walnut Ridge Mtg, Ind |
| 4-20-1844 | Nathan complained of for refusing to comply with the award of an arbitration |
| 3-25-1847 | John C of Rush Co, Ind, s Nathan & Mary, decd, of Hancock Co, Ind, m at Westland M H (Walnut Ridge MM) Ind to Fanny Marsh of Hancock Co, Ind |
| 2-19-1848 | Nathan & w Sarah & minor ch Joshua M, Margaret J, Susan T, Elizabeth E & Nathan T & Lydia C gct Richland MM, Ind |
| 9-16-1848 | Martha Ann gct Richland MM, Ind |
| 5-19-1849 | John & Fanny gct Westfield MM, Ind |
| 10-18-1869 | Jesse BROWN gct Greenwood MM, Ind to m Lydia C Perisho |

## PERVIS

|  |  |
|---|---|
| 10-20-1849 | Sarah rocf West Grove MM, Ind |
| 3-19-1853 | Sarah gct Newgarden MM, Ind |

## PHELPS

|  |  |
|---|---|
| 5-20-1848 | Anna (form Hill) chm for mcd |
| 9-16-1848 | Anna gct Duck Creek MM, Ind |
| 4-21-1849 | Mary A (wid of John Winslow) chm for mcd |
| 5-19-1849 | Mary jr rec in mbrp |
| 10-18-1851 | Susanna (form Hill) chm for mcd |
| 2-21-1852 | Mary HILL (form Phelps) chm for mcd |
| 1-21-1854 | Jane (form Hill) chm for mcd |
| 10-18-1856 | Elisha (s of Henry O) rec in mbrp |
| 11-17-1860 | Joseph & w Jane & ch Susannah, Mary & Sarah rec in mbrp |
| 10-19-1867 | Louiza J rocf West Union MM, Ind |
| 3-21-1868 | Henry rec in mbrp |
| 4-18-1868 | Joseph & s Enos rec in mbrp |
| 4-16-1887 | Enos gct Carthage MM, Ind |
| 4-16-1887 | Joseph & w Jane & ch Olive gct Carthage MM, Ind |
| 1-21-1888 | Henry gct Carthage MM, Ind |
| 2-18-1888 | Henry rel on req |

## PICKERING

|  |  |
|---|---|
| 2-17-1844 | Phineas & w Rachel & ch Nancy, Ellis, Jesse, Deborah, Rebecca, John, Enos & Mary rocf Spiceland MM, Ind |
| 4-17-1847 | Phineas & w Rachel & minor ch Nancy, Ellis, Jesse, Deborah, Rebecca, John, Enos, Mary & Phineas jr gct Honey Creek MM, Ind |

## PIKE

|  |  |
|---|---|
| 2-?-1841 | William produced certif from Clear Creek MM, Ohio to m Phebe Coffin |
| 2-23-1841 | William of Highland Co, Ohio, s Nathan & Elizabeth, both decd, m at Walnut Ridge Mtg, Ind to Phebe Coffin of Indiana |
| 4-17-1841 | Phebe gct Clear Creek MM, Ohio |
| 11-20-1841 | William & w Phebe & ch Mary, Ann, Hannah, Samuel, William jr & Eli rocf Clear Creek MM, Ohio |

WALNUT RIDGE

PIKE (Cont)
4-24-1845    Ann of Rush Co, Ind, dt William & Lucy, both decd, m at Little Blue River M H (Walnut Ridge MM) Ind to Seth Weisner of Henry Co, Ind
5- 1-1846    Hannah of Rush Co, Ind, dt William & Lucy, both decd, m at Little Blue River M H (Walnut Ridge MM) Ind to Nathan Weisner of Henry Co, Ind
6-25-1846    Phebe, wid of William Pike & dt Aaron & Mary Coffin, decd, m at Little Blue River M H (Walnut Ridge MM) Ind to Jesse Weisner of Henry Co, Ind
8-21-1847    Samuel, William jr & Eli, orphan minor ch of William & Lucy, both decd, gct Newberry MM, Ohio
4-16-1853    Mary WEISNER (form Pike) dis for mcd
5-18-1867    Himelus & w Ruth & ch Luzena & Emma rocf New Garden MM, Ind
1-18-1868    Himelus & w Ruth & minor ch Luzena & Emma gct Westfield MM, Ind

PITTS
2-20-1858    Rebecca & ch Jesse, Mary, Sarah, Samuel, James, Jonathan B, Daniel W & Henry rocf Deep River MM, N Car
6-19-1858    Sarah HEDGECOCK (form Pitts) mcd. drpd from mbrp
10-20-1858   Mary M dt James, decd, & Rebecca of Rush Co, Ind m at Walnut Ridge Mtg, Ind to Edward Butler of Rush Co
5-25-1859    Jesse M of Rush Co, Ind, s James, decd, & Rebecca m at Walnut Ridge Mtg, Ind to Esther J White of Hancock Co, Ind
11-19-1862   Samuel C of Rush Co, Ind, s James, decd, & Rebecca m at Walnut Ridge Mtg, Ind to Lydia Ann Parker of Rush Co
3-25-1863    Jesse M of Rush Co, Ind s James, decd, & Rebecca m at Walnut Ridge Mtg, Ind to Miriam Binford of Rush Co
10- 1-1863   Henry of Rush Co, Ind s James, decd, & Rebecca m at Walnut Ridge Mtg, Ind to Mary P Butler of Rush Co
10-21-1863   James of Rush Co, Ind s James, decd, & Rebecca of same place m at Walnut Ridge Mtg, Ind to Rebecca M White of Rush Co
5-21-1864    Jesse M appt Recorder of removal certificates
5-20-1865    Jonathan B mcd. drpd from mbrp
10-21-1865   Catherine rec in mbrp
9-19-1868    Daniel W & w Catherine gct Ash Grove MM (Iroquois Co) Illinois
1-16-1869    James jr & w Rebecca & minor ch Ada F, Charles M & Martha Ann gct Springfield MM, Kansas
3-20-1869    Henry & w Mary & minor ch Elijah & Anny J gct Ash Grove MM, Illinois
4-17-1869    Samuel gct Plainfield MM, Ind to m Dinah Jane Kendall
1-16-1875    Camillia rocf Duck Creek MM, Ind
4-20-1878    William W & w Elizabeth & ch Hannah, Naomi, Clarinda, Sanford E & Jesse B rec in mbrp
1-21-1893    Samuel C & w Camillia & ch Franklin, Emory & Flora gct Spiceland MM, Ind
2-16-1895    Ada rocf Glen Elder MM, Kansas

PLEAS - PLACE
3-17-1866    Joseph H rocf Spiceland MM, Ind
2-16-1867    Joseph H & Mary Jane Gray are altm & a Friend is appt to att m & rpt to next mtg
3-16-1867    The Friend appt to att m of Joseph H & Mary Jane Gray, rpts the service att & m certif has been forwarded to the Recorder
3-20-1869    Joseph H & w Mary & minor s Julian gct Ash Grove MM, Illinois
11-21-1874   Joseph & w Mary Jane & s Jonathan rocf Ash Grove MM, Illinois

PORTER
4-18-1896    William H, Emma G & Guy L rec in mbrp

POWELL
5-21-1836    Jesse Talbert & w Margaret & niece Edna POWELL rocf Salem MM, Ind
10-21-1837   Lucinda (form Engle) dis for mcd

4-15-1848    Eleanor rocf Salem MM, Ind
6-19-1852    Eleanor McCOOL (form Powell) chm for mcd
11-19-1853   Mary rocf Chester MM, Ind

POWERS
3-21-1874    Phebe A & ch Rosa L & John W rec in mbrp
3-21-1874    John William rec in mbrp
3-17-1876    Benjamin & Margaret rec in mbrp
3-17-1876    William H rec in mbrp
8-20-1881    Catherine F & ch Margaret & Rufus rec in mbrp
4-16-1887    William & Catherine gct Westland MM, Ind
5-17-1890    John William & ch Rose, John Warren, Stella, Sarah, Lulu & Mary gct Raysville MM, Ind

PRESNALL
1-16-1836    Absalom & w Mary & ch Emily are charter mbrs
2-15-1840    Mary & minor ch Emily, Sarah Jane & Lydia gct Driftwood MM, Ind (Absalom's withheld)
6-20-1846    Absalom gct Driftwood MM, Ind

PRITCHARD
4-15-1871    Joseph produced a certif from Raysville MM, Ind to m Anna Jane Binford. They are altm & a Friend is appt to att m & rpt to next mtg
5-20-1871    The Friend appt to att m of Joseph & Anna Jane Binford rpts service att & m certif has been forwarded to the Recorder
10-21-1871   Anna J gct Raysville MM, Ind

PRULE
2-21-1857    Mary (form Thornburg) dis for mcd

PUSEY
9-16-1837    George HUNNICUT gct Spiceland MM, Ind to m Martha Pusey
5-17-1845    Jesse F & w Jane & s William B rocf Milford MM, Ind
1-20-1855    Rachel rocf Spiceland MM, Ind
8-18-1855    Joel rocf Spiceland MM, Ind
5-19-1858    Rachel dt of Joel & Hannah, decd, of Hancock Co, Ind m at Walnut Ridge Mtg, Ind to Joseph Hill of Rush Co
2-24-1859    Joel of Hancock Co, Ind, s Nathan & Mary, both decd, m at Carthage M H (Walnut Ridge MM) Ind to Agatha Street, (wid of John Street) of Rush Co
4-16-1887    Joel gct Westland MM, Ind
5-17-1893    Hannah rocf Westland MM, Ind

QUATE
4-16-1864    Laura Ann rec in mbrp
12-17-1864   Laura Ann & Caleb Barker are altm & a comm is appt to att m & rpt to next mtg
1-21-1865    The comm appt to att m of Laura Ann & Caleb Barker rpt it was orderly & that m certif has been placed in hands of the Recorder

RALSTON
8-20-1898    John W rocf Little Blue River MM (Rush Co) Ind

RAMSAY - RAMSEY
2-18-1871    Richard Harvey & w Mary Ann & ch Mary R rec in mbrp
5-15-1875    Richard H rel on req
10-21-1893   Mary Rosa & Adelia Minnie gct Raysville MM, Ind

RATLIFF
4-15-1837    Ephraim B rocf Duck Creek MM, Ind
9-21-1839    Ephraim P dis
2-15-1840    Anna gct Salem MM, Iowa Territory
1-22-1852    Nathan of Duck Creek Mtg, Henry Co, Ind, s Joseph, decd, & Rebecca of same place m at Carthage M H (Walnut Ridge MM) Ind to Penelope N Coggshall of Rush Co
4-17-1852    Penelope N gct Duck Creek MM, Ind
12-21-1889   Matilda & s Harold gct Westland MM, Ind

RAWLS
3-19-1836    Martha rocf Marlborough MM, Ohio, endorsed by Duck Creek MM, Ind

WALNUT RIDGE

**RAWLS (Cont)**
|  |  |
|---|---|
| 6-17-1837 | Martha BUTLER (form Rawls) dis for mcd |
| 2-21-1846 | Sarah & ch William, Esther, Jesse, John & Sarah Jane rocf Center MM, Ohio |
| 9-18-1847 | Sarah & minor ch Esther, John, Jesse & Sarah Jane gct Springboro MM, Ohio |
| 4-20-1850 | Phebe dis for j Meth Ch |
| 1-15-1853 | Jesse & w Elizabeth & ch Martha Ann, Mary C, Miranda, Tabitha Jane & Joseph M rocf Marlborough MM, Ohio |
| 2-21-1857 | Thomas C, Rufus F & Mary Jane WHITE, ch of Phebe White, now Phebe Rawls, gct Three Rivers MM, Iowa |
| 9-23-1860 | Miranda W dt Jesse & Elizabeth M of Hancock Co, Ind m at Westland M H (Walnut Ridge MM) Ind to Seth Brown of Hancock Co, Ind |
| 12-21-1861 | Martha Ann HODSON (form Rawls) chm for mcd |
| 12-21-1861 | Mary COFFIN (form Rawls) chm for mcd |
| 1-18-1862 | Jesse & w Elizabeth M & minor ch Tabitha J, Joseph M gct Richland MM, Ind |
| 9-19-1863 | Jesse & w Elizabeth M & ch Tabitha J, Joseph M & Horace Mann rocf Richland MM, Ind |
| 5-21-1864 | Tabitha J COFFIN (form Rawls) chm for mcd |

**RAYL**
|  |  |
|---|---|
| 10-18-1844 | Elizabeth & s William rocf Hopewell MM, N Car |
| 6-19-1850 | Elizabeth W, wid of Asa of Rush Co, Ind & dt of Isaac, decd, & Mahala White of Hopewell Mtg, Guilford Co, N Car, m at Walnut Ridge Mtg, Ind to William W Thornburgh of Rush Co, Ind |
| 9-18-1852 | Himelius gct Spiceland MM, Ind |
| 12-17-1881 | Martha A rec in mbrp |

**REDDING**
|  |  |
|---|---|
| 8-19-1865 | Catherine (wid of Samuel Bufkin, now w of - - - Redding) & her ch Thirza Jane, Martha, Ezra & Samuel BUFKIN jr rocf Duck Creek MM, Ind |
| 1-20-1866 | Catherine, a wid & Isaac Adamson are altm & a comm is appt to att m & rpt to next mtg |
| 2-17-1866 | The comm appt to att m of Catherine & Isaac Adamson, rpt it was orderly & that the m certif has been placed in hands of the Recorder |
| 10-20-1866 | Thirza Jane (form Bufkin) chm for mcd |
| 3-16-1867 | Thirza Jane gct Hopewell MM, Ind |

**REECE**
|  |  |
|---|---|
| 1-21-1837 | Sarah rocf Marlborough MM, - - - - |
| 2-18-1837 | Daniel & w Sarah & s Daniel jr rocf Milford MM, Ind |
| 6-20-1840 | John & w Gulielma rocf Milford MM, Ind |
| 1-19-1850 | Miles & w Mary & fam rocf Cherry Grove MM, Ind |
| 11-15-1851 | Charles rocf Hopewell MM, Ind |
| 5-20-1852 | Levi of Cherry Grove Mtg, Randolph Co, Ind, s Eli & Matilda of same place m at Westland M H (Walnut Ridge MM) Ind to Sarah Ann Harrel of Hancock Co, Ind |
| 11-20-1852 | Levi rocf Cherry Grove MM, Ind |
| 6-18-1853 | Susanna (wid of Nathan) & minor ch Jane, Mary & Joel gct Duck Creek MM, Ind (they actually went to Hopewell Mtg) |
| 7-16-1853 | Mary (wid of Miles) & s John gct Cherry Grove MM, Ind |
| 8-20-1853 | Mary (form Brown) chm for mcd |
| 9-17-1853 | Eunice D rocf Hopewell MM, Ind |
| 1-21-1854 | Elkanah chm for mcd |
| 4-15-1854 | Elkanah rocf Westfield MM, Ind |
| 5-19-1855 | David gct Spiceland MM, Ind to m Jane J Bogue |
| 3-15-1856 | Daniel & w Sarah & minor s Nathan gct Red Cedar MM, Iowa |
| 8-18-1856 | Jane J rocf Spiceland MM, Ind |
| 9-20-1856 | Charles & w Eunice & s Edwain gct Whitewater MM, Ind |
| 10-18-1856 | David & w Jane J & dt Mary Alice gct Red Cedar MM, Iowa |
| 5-16-1863 | Levi & w Sarah Ann & minor ch Mary, Matilda & Eli Charles gct Cherry Grove MM, Ind |
| 9-19-1863 | Charles chm for mcd |
| 11-21-1863 | Martha (form Harvey) chm for mcd |
| 3-19-1864 | Martha rocf White Lick MM, Ind |
| 2-20-1875 | Charles rel on req |
| 5-19-1883 | Seth C & w Huldah A & ch Byron J & Loring W rocf Cherry Grove MM, Ind |
| 12-15-1883 | Seth & fam gct Raysville MM, Ind |
| 4-16-1887 | Martha (a wid) & ch Ruth Ann, David Oscar, John Wiley, Mary Elma & Harvey Morris gct Liberty MM, Kansas |
| 9-20-1890 | David rocf Pleasant Plain MM, Kansas |

**REEVES**
|  |  |
|---|---|
| 11-19-1892 | Walter gct Wilkinson Mtg, Hancock Co, (Raysville MM) Ind |
| 11-19-1892 | James gct Wilkinson Mtg, Hancock Co, (Raysville MM) Ind |
| 11-19-1892 | Nancy gct Wilkinson Mtg, Hancock Co, (Raysville MM) Ind |
| 11-19-1892 | Minnie gct Wilkinson Mtg, Hancock Co (Raysville MM) Ind |

**REYNOLDS**
|  |  |
|---|---|
| 3-19-1864 | Josiah & w Lucretia & ch William Henry rocf Hopewell MM, Ind |
| 1-20-1866 | Josiah & w Lucretia & s William H gct Hopewell MM, Ind |

**RHODES**
|  |  |
|---|---|
| 4-20-1878 | Emma & Ollie rec in mbrp |
| 12-18-1880 | Ollie rel on req |
| 4-18-1885 | Emma rel on req |
| 5-15-1886 | Bertie rec in mbrp |
| 10-18-1890 | Emma rec in mbrp |
| 8-17-1895 | Emma gct Whitewater MM, Ind |

**RICHARDSON**
|  |  |
|---|---|
| 6-19-1858 | Matilda (form Newby) mcd. drpd from mbrp |

**RIGSBY**
|  |  |
|---|---|
| 5-20-1848 | Lucinda (form Barnard) dis for mcd |
| 1-15-1853 | Mary (form Barnard) dis for mcd |

**ROBERTS**
|  |  |
|---|---|
| 5-15-1886 | Daniel rec in mbrp |
| 4-21-1894 | Elias W rec in mbrp |
| 8-17-1895 | George W rel on req |
| 4-18-1896 | Edward W & Washington E rec in mbrp |
| 11-20-1897 | Washington & Edward rel on req |

**ROBERTSON**
|  |  |
|---|---|
| 6-21-1845 | Rebecca gct Duck Creek MM, Ind |

**ROBINSON**
|  |  |
|---|---|
| 10-19-1878 | Eliott & w Almira rec in mbrp |
| 1-17-1880 | Elliott & w Almira rel on req |
| 1-15-1881 | Elliott dis for appropriating money to his own use, money which was placed in his hands for a specific purpose |

**RUBY**
|  |  |
|---|---|
| 2-16-1856 | Elizabeth (form Newsom) mcd. drpd from mbrp |
| 4-16-1892 | Emma glt Meth Ch, Carthage, Ind |

**RULE**
|  |  |
|---|---|
| 3-19-1859 | Lewis G & w Mary & s Jesse M rec in mbrp |

**SCOTT**
|  |  |
|---|---|
| 3-17-1876 | David C & w Mary J & dt Stella rec in mbrp |
| 9-15-1877 | David C & w Mary & dt Stella S gct Indianapolis MM, Ind |
| 4-16-1887 | Nancy gct Westland MM, Ind |
| 6-16-1888 | Malinda A rec in mbrp |
| 2-17-1894 | Samuel & w Millie M & ch James, John & Jesse rocf Raysville MM, Ind |
| 2-15-1896 | John gct Eagle Creek MM, Ind |

**SHAFER**
|  |  |
|---|---|
| 1-17-1874 | Anna rec in mbrp |
| 4-18-1874 | Ira s Michael & Anna, rec in mbrp |

**SHERIDAN**
|  |  |
|---|---|
| 4-16-1842 | Daniel ALLEN gct Spiceland MM, Ind to m Susanna Sheridan |

**SHIELDS**
|  |  |
|---|---|
| 4-15-1899 | Connard (Conrad) rec in mbrp |

WALNUT RIDGE

SHINN
8-21-1880   Israel & Cornelia Ann rec in mbrp
12-16-1882  Israel dis for bringing a law-suit

SHIPLEY
1-21-1882   Nancy E rec in mbrp

SHORTER
5-18-1861   Sarah ANTRIM (form Shorter) dis for mcd

SHULTZ
6-27-1890   Samuel B rec in mbrp
11-21-1891  Samuel F gct Salem MM, Oregon
4-15-1899   Joseph glt Meth Ch, Charlottesville, Ind

SKINNER
7-18-1874   Joshua J rec in mbrp
5-17-1890   Joshua & Margaret & s William gct Westland MM, Ind

SMALL
1-16-1836   Abraham & w Delilah & ch Anna are charter mbrs
1-16-1836   Sarah & Lydia are charter mbrs
5-19-1838   Lydia dis for na & dp
4-20-1839   Sarah gct Spiceland MM, Ind
10-19-1844  William THORNBURGH gct Spiceland MM, Ind to m Susan Small
12-18-1847  Silas dis for mcd & jas
5-20-1848   Zachariah rec in mbrp
3-21-1868   Susan rec in mbrp
6-20-1868   Josiah rec in mbrp
5-20-1876   William Penn & w Rebecca rec in mbrp
7-21-1877   Josiah rel on req
3-15-1879   Annie, Elbert & George W, ch of William & Rebecca rec in mbrp
6-21-1884   William & fam gct Geneva MM, Kansas
8-18-1887   Zachariah & w Martha & ch Celia, Stella & Riley rec in mbrp

SMITH
5-19-1855   Achsah (form Swain) dis for mcd

SPRINGER
4-20-1839   Barnabas rocf Spiceland MM, Ind

STAFFORD
1-21-1837   Elizabeth & ch Barzilla, Eli, Martha Ann & Stephen rocf Salem MM, Ind (fam of Nathan who had been dis)
3-17-1838   Joseph C & w Lydia & ch Nathan, Elias, Phebe, William & Julius rocf Salem MM, Ind
7-16-1842   Joseph dis for na & dealing in spiritous liquors
7-16-1853   Elizabeth & minor ch David, Elizabeth C, Mathew & Mary Jane gct Spiceland MM, Ind
7-16-1853   Stephen gct Spiceland MM, Ind
12-17-1853  Eli dis for mcd & j Meth Ch

STANLEY
2-17-1844   Wyatt & w Mary & ch Gulielma, Phariba & Cynthia rocf Duck Creek MM, Ind
7-20-1848   Wyatt of Rush Co, Ind, s John, decd, & Elizabeth of Henry Co, Ind m at Carthage M H (Walnut Ridge MM) Ind to Nancy A Henley of Rush Co
2-15-1851   Lydia rocf Dover MM, N Car (she has decd within the limits of this Mtg since the date of certificate, dated at Dover MM, N Car, 11-28-1850) (she may have been a dt of Zimri & Betsey (Cook) Stanley, both decd, of Dover MM, N Car) IBB
3-23-1859   Gulielma dt Wyatt & Mary, decd, of Hancock Co, Ind m at Walnut Ridge Mtg, Ind to John Milton Henby of Rush Co
3-11-1863   Phariba M dt Wyatt & Mary, decd, of Hancock Co, Ind m at Walnut Ridge Mtg, Ind to Daniel M Hill of Rush Co
5-16-1863   John dis for military service
1-18-1868   Ruth (form Hill) chm for mcd
9-19-1868   Cynthia & Charles M Henley are altm & a Friend is appt to att m & rpt to next mtg
10-17-1868  The Friend appt to att m of Cynthia & Charles M Henley rpts service att & m certif has been forwarded to the Recorder

STANTON
1-16-1836   Zacheus & w Elizabeth & minor ch Mahala, Cynthia, Milton & Milo are charter mbrs
2-20-1836   Elizabeth appt an overseer
2-17-1838   Eunice rocf Salem MM, Ind
2-16-1839   Zacheus & w Elizabeth & minor ch Mahala, Cynthia, Milton & Milo gct Salem MM, Ind

STARBUCK
2-15-1851   Jane & ch William, George, James, Thomas & Benjamin rocf Dover MM, N Car ( fam of Bezabel Starbuck)
5-21-1853   Jane & ch William H, George W, James M, Thomas C & Benjamin F gct Duck Creek MM, Ind
7-15-1865   George W & w Sally & ch Endorus E, Lydia E & Dorcas Almira rocf Rich Square MM, Iowa
3-15-1873   Rebecca rec in mbrp
4-20-1878   Elwood & w Susanna rec in mbrp

STEVENSON
10-20-1894  Joseph & fam rec in mbrp

STEWART
2-15-1862   Alexander rec in mbrp

ST JOHN
12-20-1856  William dis for mcd

STRATTON
1-16-1836   Eli & w Eunice & ch Joseph B are charter mbrs
1-16-1836   Jonathan D & w Prudence & ch Millicent A, Samuel E & Joseph L are charter mbrs
2-20-1836   Eunice appt to comm on Education
2-20-1836   Jonathan D appt asst Clerk of Mthly Mtg & John Clark appt Clerk
3-16-1836   Jonathan D appt an overseer
3-16-1836   Joseph B appt to keep record of families
3-16-1836   Eunice appt an overseer
1-21-1837   Eli & w Eunice gct West Grove MM, Ind
1-21-1837   Joseph B gct West Grove MM, Ind
4-20-1844   Jonathan & w Prudence dis for na & att a mtg set up contrary to discipline
5-19-1849   Louisa HENLEY (form Stratton) chm for mcd
2-16-1850   Millicent A, Samuel, Joseph L & Eli minor ch of Jonathan gct Honey Creek MM, Ind

STREET
5-20-1841   John (a widower) of Milford Mtg, Henry Co, Ind, s Aaron & Mary, decd, of Henry Co, Iowa Territory, m - - - - - Mtg, Ind to Agatha Hussey of Rush Co, Ind
11-14-1841  John & ch Eunice, Mary & John rocf Hopewell MM, Ind
10-17-1846  Eunice gct Spiceland MM, Ind
8-18-1849   Mary gct Hopewell MM, Ind
2-24-1859   Agatha (wid of John of Carthage Mtg) Rush Co, Ind & dt Jediah & Agatha Hussey, both decd, m at Carthage M H (Walnut Ridge MM) Ind to Joel Pussey of Hancock Co, Ind
3-19-1859   John jr dis for mcd
12-16-1871  Sarah A (form - - -?) chm for mcd

STUBBS
1-20-1838   John & w Jane rocf Spiceland MM, Ind
1-20-1838   Newton & Charles, minor ch of Joseph & Margaret, both decd, rocf Spiceland MM, Ind
1-21-1843   Newton gct Spiceland MM, Ind to m Nancy Pierson
9-16-1843   Newton gct Spiceland MM, Ind
12-16-1848  Charley chm for mcd

STUMP
3-20-1886   John & w Margaret E & ch Carrie Etta, Cora Eveline, Nora Alice, George, Gurney & Jemima rec in mbrp

STUTSMAN
3-19-1892   Ann E glt Meth Ch, Greencastle, Ind

WALNUT RIDGE

## SWAIN

|  |  |
|---|---|
| 1-16-1836 | Thomas & w Elizabeth & ch Elvira, Franklin, Alonzo & Alfred are charter mbrs |
| 1-16-1836 | Prior, Achsah & Silas, ch of Sarah Swain, now w of William Worth, are charter mbrs |
| 4-16-1836 | Lydia rocf Springfield MM, Ind |
| 5-21-1836 | George & w Margaret & ch Eusebia & Almira rocf Springfield MM, Ind |
| 4-15-1837 | Rhoda rocf Springfield MM, Ind |
| 5-18-1839 | Lydia COFFIN (form Swain) chm for mcd |
| 1-21-1841 | Rhoda of Rush Co, Ind, dt Thomas & Lydia, both decd, m at Little Blue River M H (Walnut Ridge MM) Ind to Thomas Barnard of Shelby Co, Ind |
| 12-21-1843 | David of Fayette Co, Ind, s Sylvanus & Miriam of Union Co, Ind, m at Little Blue River M H (Walnut Ridge MM) Ind to Ruth Coffin of Shelby Co, Ind |
| 3-16-1844 | Ruth gct Salem MM, Ind |
| 5-17-1845 | Louisa (form Coffin) chm for mcd |
| 8-18-1845 | Prior dis |
| 7-18-1846 | Franklin dis for att a mcd |
| 10-17-1846 | Alonzo dis for mcd |
| 7-15-1848 | Alfred dis for att a mcd |
| 1-15-1853 | Laurinda (form Barnard) dis for mcd |
| 10-20-1853 | Elizabeth (wid of Thomas) of Rush Co, Ind, dt Asa & Huldah Barbara, decd, m at Little Blue River M H (Walnut Ridge MM) Ind to Howland Swain of Henry Co, Ind |
| 10-20-1853 | Howland of Henry Co, Ind, s George & Deborah, decd, m at Little Blue River M H (Walnut Ridge MM) Ind to Elizabeth Swain, a wid, of Rush Co, Ind |
| 2-23-1854 | David of Wayne Co, Ind, s Sylvanus & Miriam, decd, of Union Co, Ind, m at Little Blue River M H (Walnut Ridge MM) Ind to Phebe Weisner, a wid, of Rush Co, Ind |
| 7-15-1854 | Phebe gct Milford MM, Ind |
| 4-21-1855 | Jethro & w Susanna & dt Susanna rocf Center MM, N Car |
| 1-20-1855 | Almira SWAIN (form Swain) chm for mcd |
| 5-19-1855 | Almira gct Salem MM, Ind |
| 5-19-1855 | Achsah SMITH (form Swain) dis for mcd |
| 5-19-1855 | George & w Margaret gct Salem MM, Ind |
| 12-15-1855 | George & w Margaret rocf Salem MM, Ind |
| 12-15-1855 | Oliver & w Elmira rocf Salem MM, Ind |
| 4-15-1865 | David & w Phebe & dt Ruth rocf Milford MM, Ind |

## SYMONS

|  |  |
|---|---|
| 1-21-1837 | Ashbell BINFORD gct Milford MM, Ind to m Gulielma Symons |
| 2-16-1850 | Mary & dt Eunice rocf Milford MM, Ind |
| 11-17-1851 | Eunice, lately of Wayne Co, Ind, dt Abraham, decd, & Mary of Wayne Co, Ind, m at Carthage M H (Walnut Ridge MM) Ind to Evan Lewis Johnson of Wabash Co, Ind |
| 10-21-1854 | John BUNDY gct Pipe Creek MM, Ind to m Hannah Symons |

## TALBERT - TALBOTT

|  |  |
|---|---|
| 3-19-1836 | Jonathan & w Esther & ch Mary, Thomas, Rebecca, Sarah, John, Isaac, Rhoda & Elizabeth rocf Elk MM, Ohio |
| 5-21-1836 | Jesse & w Margaret & niece Edna POWELL rocf Salem MM, Ind |
| 8-20-1836 | Rachel (wid of Joseph) & s Joseph A rocf Elk MM, Ohio |
| 10-15-1836 | Jesse (the younger one) & w Hannah & ch Milton, Louisa, Abner & Alpheus rocf Salem MM, Ind |
| 1838 | Paris rptd mcd. dis by Silver Creek MM, Ind |
| 4-20-1839 | Jonathan & w Esther & ch Mary, Thomas, Rebecca, Sarah, John, Isaac, Rhoda, Elizabeth & Amanda gct Westfield MM, Ind |
| 4-15-1848 | Louisa MYRES (form Talbert) chm for mcd |
| 12-15-1855 | Abel dis for mcd |
| 4-19-1856 | Alpheus dis for mcd |
| 5-17-1856 | Mary BOWERS (form Talbot) chm for mcd |
| 7-21-1866 | Harrison dis for jas & serving in the army |
| 12-17-1870 | Sylvanus & w Phebe H & ch Daniel H & Anna rocf Spiceland MM, Ind |
| 12-19-1874 | Sylvanus & w Phebe, a Minister, & ch Daniel & Anna gct Salem MM, Ind |
| 2-19-1887 | Daniel gct Hopewell MM, Ind |

## TAYLOR

|  |  |
|---|---|
| 1-16-1836 | Elizabeth (w of Simeon) & ch Angeline P, John M, Daniel G & Allen D are charter mbrs |
| 8-19-1837 | Angeline HAZLETT (form Taylor) dis for mcd |
| 7-17-1847 | Simeon rst w/c of Duck Creek MM, Ind |
| 12-20-1851 | John dis for dishonesty |
| 7-21-1855 | Allen D dis for mcd |
| 4-18-1868 | Martha Ann (form Gray) chm for mcd |
| 5-21-1870 | John M rec in mbrp |
| 2-18-1871 | Rebecca rocf Westfield MM, Ind |
| 3-15-1884 | John M gct Dublin MM, Ind |
| 3-15-1884 | George L rec in mbrp |
| 3-20-1886 | Josiah M rec in mbrp |
| 12-20-1890 | George L dis |
| 1-17-1891 | Rebecca & ch Gulielma, Laura, Harvey, Oliver, Martha, Lucy, Lena, Jennie, Ruby & Elmer gct Dublin MM, Ind |
| 2-17-1894 | Lily B & ch Ethel rec in mbrp |

## THORNBURGH

|  |  |
|---|---|
| 1-16-1836 | Joel & Anna & ch William W, Mary Ann, & Lydia Jane are charter mbrs |
| 2-20-1836 | Joel appt to comm on Education |
| 2-20-1836 | Ann appt to comm on Education |
| 3-16-1836 | Joel appt to comm to care for indigent persons |
| 6-17-1837 | Thomas & w Sarah & ch Phebe Elizabeth, Dina, Penina, Miriam, Amanda, Luzenia & Mary rocf Back Creek MM, N Car |
| 2-16-1839 | William chm for mcd |
| 9-21-1839 | Sarah rocf Whitewater MM, Ind |
| 12-19-1841 | Phebe HILL (form Thornburgh) chm for mcd |
| 10-19-1844 | William gct Spiceland MM, Ind to m Susan Small |
| 1-22-1845 | Lydia Jane dt Joel & Anna of Rush Co, Ind, m at Walnut Ridge Mtg, Ind to Henby Hill of Rush Co |
| 11-22-1848 | Pennina of Rush Co, Ind dt Thomas, decd, formerly of Randolph Co, N Car & his w Sarah, now of Rush Co, Ind, m at Walnut Ridge Mtg, Ind to Amos H Hill of Rush Co |
| 6-19-1850 | William W of Rush Co, Ind, s Joel & Anna of same place m at Walnut Ridge Mtg, Ind to Elizabeth W Rayl, (a wid) of Rush Co, Ind |
| 5-26-1853 | Diza R of Rush Co, Ind dt Thomas, decd, & Sarah of Randolph Co, N Car m at Carthage M H (Walnut Ridge MM) Ind to Joshua M Butler of Wayne Co, Ind |
| 12-17-1853 | Miriam LACY (form Thornburgh) chm for mcd |
| 2-21-1857 | Mary RULE (form Thornburgh) mcd. drpd from mbrp |
| 7-30-1861 | John C gct White Lick MM, Ind |
| 4-18-1864 | Joel & w Anna, a Minister, gct Westfield MM, Ind |
| 3-21-1865 | Amanda WALTON (form Thornburgh) mcd. drpd from mbrp |
| 3-16-1867 | Joel rocf Westfield MM, Ind |
| 3-16-1867 | Anna's death is rptd & a comm is appt to prepare a Memorial |
| 6-17-1871 | Charles L chm for mcd |
| 9-16-1871 | Charles L gct Raysville MM, Ind |
| 2-15-1873 | Charles & w Ann & s Walter rocf Raysville MM, Ind |
| 7-21-1877 | Harris(on) W & w Emily & ch Claudius B, William W, Carrie M & Linda Ann rec in mbrp |
| 1-19-1878 | Charles & w Anna & ch Walter & Leona gct Spiceland MM, Ind |
| 4-20-1889 | William W gct Van Wert MM, Ohio |
| 10-19-1889 | Jeannette & ch Elsie & Harris rec in mbrp |
| 3-21-1891 | William W dis for threatening the life of a fellowman & failing to confess his error |
| 4-16-1892 | Landy A rel on req |
| 12-18-1895 | Harris(on) & Emily dis for divorcing each other |
| 12-19-1896 | William W rocf Eagle Creek MM, Ind |

## THORNBERRY - THORNBURRY

|  |  |
|---|---|
| 11-21-1874 | Will J & w Mary rocf Mill Creek MM, Ind |
| 4-16-1880 | William J & Mary & ch Risher & Rhoda gct Smithfield MM, Ohio |

# WALNUT RIDGE

## TOMLINSON
6-15-1889  Mary J gct Westfield MM, Ind

## TOMS - (TOMBS)
6-15-1872  William produced a certif from Milford MM, Ind to m Charity B Hill. They are altm & a Friend is appt to att m & rpt to next mtg
7-20-1872  The Friend appt to att m of William & Charity B Hill, rpts service att & m certif has been forwarded to the Recorder
6-21-1873  Charity B gct Milford MM, Ind

## TOWNSEND
6-16-1838  Thomas & w Mary & ch Nancy & Elisha rocf West Grove Mtg, Ind
7-21-1838  Sarah (form Lamb) chm for mcd
1-18-1845  Thomas & w Mary & minor ch Nancy, Elisha, James & Isaac gct West Grove MM, Ind
3-15-1845  Sarah gct Whitewater MM, Ind
3-18-1854  Sarah MORRIS (form Townsend) chm for mcd

## TRIBBY
3-19-1892  John & w Levina & ch Clessie rec in mbrp

## TWEEDY
6-17-1865  Jonathan P & w Emily & ch William Edmund, Albert Marion & George Riley rec in mbrp
6-19-1869  Jonathan & w Emily J & minor ch William E, Albert M, George R & Anna J gct Greenwood MM, Ind

## UNZICKER - (? HUNSICKER)
4-16-1892  Effie rocf Hopewell MM, Kansas

## UPDEGRAFF
2-20-1849  Mary J (form Stafford) dis for mcd & j Meth Ch

## VANMETER
2-15-1873  Nancy rec in mbrp
4-19-1873  Anderson rec in mbrp

## WALLIS
11-21-1857  Martha Ann (form Davis) mcd. drpd from mbrp

## WALTON
5-16-1863  Amanda dis
3-21-1865  Amanda (form Thornburgh) mcd. drpd from mbrp

## WARE
6-21-1851  Nancy (form White) dis for mcd

## WATKINS
11-15-1845  Richard W Johnson gct Goshen MM, Ohio to m Lucinda Watkins

## WATTS
3-20-1886  Harrison & fam rec in mbrp

## WEAVER
1-18-1873  Ella & dt Susie Abbie rec in mbrp

## WEISNER
4-24-1845  Seth of Henry Co, Ind, s Jesse & Lydia, decd, m at Little Blue River M H (Walnut Ridge MM) Ind to Ann Pike of Rush Co, Ind
12-20-1845  Ann gct Duck Creek MM, Ind
5-1-1846  Nathan of Henry Co, Ind, s Jesse & Lydia, decd, of same place, m at Little Blue River M H (Walnut Ridge MM) Ind to Hannah Pike of Rush Co, Ind
6-25-1846  Jesse of Henry Co, Ind, s Micajah & Abigail, both decd, m at Little Blue River M H (Walnut Ridge MM) Ind to Phebe Pike, a wid, of Rush Co, Ind
6-19-1847  Hannah gct Duck Creek MM, Ind
3-18-1848  Margaret rocf Duck Creek MM, Ind
5-19-1849  Margaret JORDAN (form Weisner) dis for mcd
12-21-1850  Elwood, a minor, rocf Duck Creek MM, Ind
4-16-1853  Mary (form Pike) dis for mcd
2-23-1854  Phebe, a wid, & dt of Aaron Coffin & w Mary, decd, of Shelby Co, Ind m at Little Blue River M H (Walnut Ridge MM) Ind to David Swain of Wayne Co, Ind
2-21-1862  Nathan & w Hannah & dt Phebe Ann rocf Duck Creek MM, Ind
4-20-1867  Elwood gct Sugar Plain MM, Ind to m Mahala Hall
1-18-1868  Elwood W gct Sugar River MM, Ind

## WHEELER
10-17-1846  Lydia (form Morris) dis for mcd
11-20-1862  Jesse, of Springfield Mtg, Guilford Co, N Car, s John & Phebe of same place m at Westland M H (Walnut Ridge MM) Ind to Mary Jane Bundy of Hancock Co, Ind
12-17-1864  Alfred & w Lydia & ch Alonzo & Lydia rocf Deep River MM, N Car
5-20-1865  Mary J & dt Phebe A gct Spiceland MM, Ind

## WHITE
1-16-1836  Eli & w Martha & ch Rebecca E are charter mbrs
1-16-1836  Bethuel C & w Hannah & ch Elizabeth, Aaron, Ann R & Eli J are charter mbrs
1-16-1836  Phineas & w Sarah are charter mbrs
1-16-1836  Thomas, Thaddeus, Isaac & George B, ch of Robert & Rebecca, decd, are charter mbrs
9-17-1836  Nancy Ann (wid King) dis for mcd
1-20-1838  Thomas dis for j Meth Ch
10-19-1844  Mahala & ch John, Rebecca, Jemima, Borden C & Addison T rocf Hopewell MM, N Car
10-19-1844  William C rocf Hopewell MM, N Car
3-19-1845  Phineas of Rush Co, Ind s Jesse & Mary, both decd, m at Walnut Ridge Mtg, Ind to Lydia Butler of Hancock Co
6-21-1845  Nancy Ann rst in mbrp
11-15-1845  Polly & ch Elijah, Abigail, Charles & Polly Jane rocf Hopewell MM, N Car
11-15-1845  Thomas & w Elizabeth & ch Albert, Robert, Sally, Nancy, Semira, John, Wyatt, Martha & Eliza rocf Hopewell MM, N Car
6-20-1846  Henry rocf Hopewell MM, N Car
7-17-1847  Rhoda M rocf White Lick MM, Ind
1-15-1848  Mary & dts Abigail B & Mary Jane gct Duck Creek MM, Ind
1-15-1848  Nancy Ann with her minor ch Lydia & Deborah KING gct West Grove MM, Ind
2-19-1848  Isaac dis
3-16-1850  Esther J dt Borden & Agness, both decd, rocf New Garden MM, N Car
3-16-1850  Thomas rst in mbrp
5-15-1850  Sarah Jane COX (form White) chm for mcd
3-15-1851  George B gct West Grove MM, Ind to m Eliza Griffin
6-21-1851  Nancy WARE (form White) dis for mcd
3-20-1852  Thaddeus M & w Rhoda H & minor ch Ruth A & Anna Jane gct Richland MM, Ind
6-19-1852  George B gct West Grove MM, Ind
12-18-1852  Thomas gct Pleasant Plain MM, Iowa
4-20-1853  Elizabeth dt Bethuel C & Hannah of Rush Co, Ind m at Walnut Ridge Mtg, Ind to Elias Henby of Rush Co, Ind
9-17-1853  Jemima Newby (form White) dis for mcd
6-17-1854  Eli & w Martha & minor ch Rebecca E, Robert H, Mary N, Sarah Jane, George K, Susanna, Harriett, Nathan L & Samuel M gct Spring Creek MM, Iowa
4-21-1855  Samira COX (form White) dis for mcd
4-21-1855  William C gct Spring Creek MM, Iowa
12-10-1855  Mahala & minor ch Isaac A & Thomas J gct Spring Creek MM, Iowa
3-15-1856  Borden C gct Spring Creek MM, Iowa
4-23-1856  Robert B dis for mcd
12-20-1856  Mary rocf Spiceland MM, Ind
2-21-1857  Thomas C, Rufus F & Mary Jane, minor ch of Phebe White, now Phebe Rawls, gct Three Rivers MM, Iowa
9-19-1857  William rocf Spiceland MM, Ind
11-21-1857  Thomas & w Elizabeth & minor ch John G, Wiett, Martha D, Eliza & Elizabeth gct Lynn Grove MM, Iowa
9-22-1858  Albert of Rush Co, Ind s Thomas & Elizabeth of Jasper Co, Iowa m at Walnut Ridge Mtg, Ind to Cynthia Nicholson

WALNUT RIDGE

## WHITE (Cont)

|  |  |
|---|---|
| 11-25-1858 | James of Raysville Mtg, Henry Co, Ind, s Caleb & Mary, decd, of same place m at Carthage M H (Walnut Ridge MM) Ind to Jemima D Henley of Rush Co, Ind |
| 2-19-1859 | James gct Raysville MM, Ind |
| 2-19-1859 | Jemima D gct Raysville MM, Ind |
| 5-25-1859 | Esther J of Hancock Co, Ind dt Borden & Agness, both decd, of N Car, m at Walnut Ridge Mtg, Ind to Jesse M Pitts of Rush Co |
| 11-20-1860 | Ann R dt Bethuel C & Hannah of Rush Co, Ind m at Walnut Ridge Mtg, Ind to Allen Hill of Rush Co, Ind |
| 3-16-1861 | Paul & w Letitia & ch William, Sarah, Robert & Samuel rocf Marlborough MM, Ohio |
| 4-18-1863 | Mary E & s William rocf Lynn Grove MM, Iowa |
| 4-23-1863 | Mary E (wid of William, w/ch) & dt Robert & Elizabeth Hunnicut, both decd, of Rush Co, Ind m at Carthage M H (Walnut Ridge MM) Ind to Joseph Binford of Hancock Co, Ind |
| 10-21-1863 | Rebecca M dt Phineas & Lydia, both decd, of Rush Co, Ind m at Walnut Ridge Mtg, Ind to James Pitts of Rush Co |
| 4-16-1864 | Rebecca gct Raysville MM, Ind |
| 6-18-1864 | Lydia Jane (form Binford) chm for mcd |
| 9-17-1864 | George S & Sarah Hockett are altm & a comm is appt to att m & rpt to next mtg |
| 10-15-1864 | The comm appt to att m of George S & Sarah Hockett rpts it was orderly & the m certif has been placed in hands of the Recorder |
| 5-20-1865 | Mary gct Spiceland MM, Ind |
| 8-19-1865 | Aaron S chm for mcd |
| 9-16-1865 | Ann (form Outland) chm for mcd |
| 11-18-1865 | Eli J chm for mcd |
| 12-21-1867 | Lucinda rec in mbrp |
| 9-19-1868 | Hannah E & James H Binford are altm & a Friend is appt to att m & rpt to next mtg |
| 10-17-1868 | The Friend appt to att m of Hannah E & James H Binford, rpts service att & m certif has been forwarded to the Recorder |
| 5-20-1871 | George B & w Sarah gct Spiceland MM, Ind |
| 6-15-1872 | Lydia Jane & minor ch Dora & Lydia gct Richland MM, Ind |
| 8-16-1873 | Eli J appt Recorder of marriage certificates in place of Elwood Parker who is decd |
| 2-21-1874 | Linley & George B rec in mbrp |
| 10-17-1874 | Emily rec in mbrp |
| 2-20-1875 | Robert B & w Nancy A & ch Wilson H, Charles, Morris E, Alvin A & Linburn M rec in mbrp |
| 4-15-1876 | William minor s of William Sr, decd & Mary Elizabeth (now Mary Elizabeth Binford, w Joseph Binford) gct Westland MM, Ind |
| 12-18-1880 | Oliver H produced a certif from Milford MM, Ind to m Caroline Hill. They are altm & a Friend is appt to att m & rpt to next mtg |
| 1-15-1881 | The Friend appt to att m of Oliver H & Caroline Hill, rpts service att & m certif has been forwarded to the Recorder |
| 2-19-1881 | Caroline H gct Piney Woods MM, N Car |
| 10-15-1881 | Ella J & dt Edna R rocf Lynn Grove MM, Iowa |
| 5-20-1882 | Oliver H & w Caroline rocf Piney Woods MM, N Car |
| 5-20-1882 | David O rocf Hopewell MM, Ind |
| 4-21-1883 | Henry B gct Westland MM, Ind |
| 4-21-1883 | Sarah Alice & ch Leora, Naomi & Earl rec in mbrp |
| 8-16-1884 | Semira & Penelope rec in mbrp |
| 3-19-1887 | William C rocf Carthage MM, Ind |
| 5-19-1888 | George B dis |
| 5-19-1888 | Laura rocf Hopewell MM, Ind |
| 12-15-1888 | George B & fam rocf Raysville MM, Ind |
| 1-17-1891 | George B & w Sarah R gct Springfield MM, Ohio |
| 5-16-1891 | Harvey T gct Salem MM, Oregon |
| 10-15-1892 | Alice & ch Leora, Naomi, Mary & Earl gct - - - - -(place not recorded) IBB |
| 2-18-1893 | Hannah H rocf Green Plain MM, Ohio |

## WHITACRE

|  |  |
|---|---|
| 7-17-1897 | Elbert & s Orpha A rec in mbrp |

## WIBBLE

|  |  |
|---|---|
| 3-16-1895 | Sallie glt Meth Ch, Mapleton, Ind |

## WIGGINS

|  |  |
|---|---|
| 12-21-1878 | Lawson & w Margaret & ch rec in mbrp |
| 3-16-1895 | Arthur E gct Westland MM, Ind |
| 3-16-1895 | George J gct Westland MM, Ind |
| 3-16-1895 | M Edward gct Westland MM, Ind |
| 3-16-1895 | Lawson & w Margaret & ch Clara & Mattie gct Westland MM, Ind |

## WILLIAMS

|  |  |
|---|---|
| 3-17-1855 | Hannah HENLEY (form Williams) chm for mcd |
| 5-20-1896 | Orlando B & w Sarah E glt Meth Ch, Casey, Illinois |

## WILSON

|  |  |
|---|---|
| 6-19-1847 | Joseph & w Elizabeth & ch Sarah, Samuel, Ruth Anna, Isabella & Mary Abigail rocf Milford MM, Ind |
| 3-15-1851 | Joseph & w Elizabeth & minor ch Sarah, Samuel, Ruth A, Isabell, Mary, Abigail, Charles & Susan gct Richland MM, Ind |
| 10-21-1865 | Joseph produced a certif from Back Creek MM, Ind to m Miriam Binford. They are altm & a comm is appt to att m & rpt to next mtg |
| 11-18-1865 | The comm appt to att m of Joseph & Miriam Binford, rpts it was orderly & the m certif has been placed in hands of the Recorder |
| 3-17-1866 | Miriam gct Back Creek MM, Ind |
| 4-20-1878 | James & w Grizzell & ch William, Phineas, Angeline, Nora F, Omer G, Ascenith, Harry & Susan rec in mbrp |
| 8-19-1892 | James rel on req |
| 5-15-1886 | James rec in mbrp |
| 5-21-1887 | James & w Grizzell & ch Dayton, Nora, Hattie, Henry & Susan J gct Dublin MM, Ind |

## WILTSE

|  |  |
|---|---|
| 1-16-1836 | Simeon Sr & w Elizabeth & ch William, John C, Martin, George & Elizabeth are charter mbrs |
| 1-16-1836 | Simeon jr a charter mbr |
| 2-20-1836 | Simeon jr req certif to Spiceland Mtg to m Elizabeth Butler |
| 2-20-1836 | William appt to comm to att Qrtly Mtg |
| 11-19-1836 | Elizabeth rocf Spiceland MM, Ind |
| 6-18-1842 | John C gct Mississinewa MM, Ind |
| 10-21-1843 | William gct Springfield MM, N Car |
| 11-15-1845 | William rocf Springfield MM, N Car |
| 1-17-1846 | Simeon jr & w Elizabeth & minor ch Elizabeth T, David, Josiah, William E, Martha & Rachel gct Mississinewa MM, Ind |
| 12-19-1846 | Lydia (form Nixon) chm for mcd |
| 4-17-1847 | George dis for mcd |
| 8-21-1847 | William chm for mcd |
| 12-21-1850 | Elizabeth gct Spiceland MM, Ind |
| 7-16-1853 | Lydia gct Spiceland MM, Ind |
| 3-21-1874 | Elizabeth rocf Raysville MM, Ind |
| 4-15-1876 | Elizabeth & John R Guyer are altm & a Friend is appt to att m & rpt to next mtg |
| 5-20-1876 | The Friend appt to att m of Elizabeth & John R Guyer, rpts service att & m certif has been forwarded to the Recorder |

## WINSLOW

|  |  |
|---|---|
| 1-16-1836 | John & w Mary & ch Henry, John H, Judith A & Jabez H are charter mbrs |
| 1-16-1836 | John appt to a comm |
| 2-20-1836 | Mary appt to comm on Education |
| 3-16-1836 | John appt Recorder of removal certificates |
| 4-21-1849 | Mary PHELPS (wid of Winslow) chm for mcd |
| 11-15-1851 | Henry chm for mcd |
| 12-17-1853 | Josiah rocf Piney Woods MM, N Car |
| 10-21-1854 | John H chm for mcd |
| 6-16-1855 | William F rocf Piney Woods MM, N Car |
| 9-23-1857 | Josiah T of Rush Co, Ind, s William, decd, & Julia Ann of Chowan Co, N Car m at Walnut Ridge Mtg, Ind to Rachel Patterson of Rush Co |
| 8-21-1858 | George Hunnicut gct Whitewater MM, Ind to m Mary Anna Winslow, a wid w/ch |
| 2-19-1859 | Mary Ann HUNNICUT & her s Robert B WINSLOW rocf Whitewater MM, Ind |
| 9-19-1860 | William F of Rush Co, Ind s William decd, & Julia Ann of Chowan Co, N Car m at Walnut Ridge Mtg, Ind to Mary J Patterson of Rush Co |

## WINSLOW (Cont)

| | |
|---|---|
| 8-17-1861 | Susan rec in mbrp |
| 12-21-1861 | George & John, ch of John & Susan rec in mbrp |
| 5-21-1864 | Henry & ch Ruth, Joseph, Josiah, William & Mary rocf Back Creek MM, Ind |
| 3-18-1865 | Levi & ch Nancy & Sarah Ellen rocf Back Creek MM, Ind |
| 5-20-1865 | Mary rec in mbrp |
| 8-18-1866 | Henry & Sallie E Dunbar are altm & a Friend is appt to att m & rpt to next mtg |
| 9-15-1866 | The Friend appt to att m of Henry & Sallie E Dunbar, rpts service was att & m certif has been placed in hands of the Recorder |
| 4-20-1867 | Ruth HILL (form Winslow) chm for mcd |
| 10-19-1867 | John chm for mcd |
| 3-21-1868 | Emily rec in mbrp |
| 9-17-1870 | Joseph chm for mcd |
| 11-19-1870 | Joseph gct Back Creek MM, Ind |
| 2-18-1871 | Levi & minor ch Nancy, Sarah, Aletha & Elizabeth gct Blue River MM, Ind |
| 7-20-1872 | Josiah gct Back Creek MM, Ind |
| 3-21-1891 | Orlando & w Mary & ch Rachel & Esther gct Evangeline MM, La |
| 5-17-1893 | Henry & w Mary glt Presby Ch, Greenup, Ill |
| 5-17-1893 | Emma J glt Presby Ch, Greenup, Ill |
| 5-18-1895 | Clara E rolf Meth Ch, Greencastle, Ind |
| 12-18-1897 | Adella B rocf Hopewell MM, Ind |

## WINSTON

| | |
|---|---|
| 11-22-1852 | Bowling H of Sugar River MM, Montgomery Co, Ind, s Pleasant & Elizabeth, decd, of same place m at Carthage M H (Walnut Ridge MM) to Anna Clark of Rush Co |
| 2-19-1853 | Anna gct Sugar River MM, Ind |

## WOLF

| | |
|---|---|
| 7-19-1841 | Charity (form Commons) dis for mcd |

## WOODLY

| | |
|---|---|
| 10-20-1855 | Mary & dt Mary Elizabeth rec in mbrp |
| 4-21-1866 | Isaac rec in mbrp |

## WOODS

| | |
|---|---|
| 5-15-1886 | Snow rec in mbrp |
| 11-19-1892 | John D & w Margaret Ann, & ch Nellie & Hannah rec in mbrp |
| 1-21-1893 | Louisa J gct Newburg MM, Oregon |
| 4-18-1896 | Emerson rec in mbrp |

## WOOTEN

| | |
|---|---|
| 2-17-1883 | Lee rec in mbrp |
| 3-19-1892 | Lee & w Mary Ann & dt Rachel E gct Carthage MM, Ind |

## WORTH

| | |
|---|---|
| 1-16-1836 | William & Sarah & ch Belinda, Anna & Thomas WORTH & Sarah's ch Prior, Acsah & Silas SWAIN are charter mbrs |
| 2-20-1836 | William appt an overseer |
| 2-20-1836 | Sarah appt an overseer |
| 7-21-1838 | Belinda LEONARD (form Worth) mcd. dis |
| 12-15-1838 | Obed B rocf Springfield MM, Ind |
| 9-23-1841 | Anna dt of William & Phebe, decd, m at Walnut Ridge Mtg, Ind to Benjamin Franklin Barnard of Shelby Co, Ind |
| 8-18-1856 | Obed dis for j Meth Ch |
| 7-17-1858 | Thomas dis for na & participating in music & dancing |

## WREN

| | |
|---|---|
| 2-18-1837 | Lydia rocf Marlborough MM, Ohio |

## WRIGHT

| | |
|---|---|
| 11-20-1880 | David & w Sarah Miriam rocf Raysville MM, Ind |
| 4-15-1882 | David & fam gct Milford MM, Ind |
| 10-21-1882 | David B & w Sarah Miriam & s Lloyd A gct Carthage MM, Ind |

## YOUNG

| | |
|---|---|
| 2-16-1839 | Joseph rocf Philadelphia MM, Pa |
| 9-25-1839 | Joseph W of Rush Co, Ind, s Robert W & Rebecca of Wayne Co, Ind m at Walnut Ridge Mtg, Ind to Sarah Binford of Rush Co |
| 2-15-1840 | Robert & w Rebecca & minor ch Robert W, Hiram & Edward C rocf Whitewater MM, Ind |
| 3-16-1844 | Hiram, a minor gct Cincinnati MM, Ohio |
| 3-16-1848 | Robert & w Rebecca gct Cincinnati MM, Ohio |
| 3-16-1850 | Robert jr dis for mcd & na |
| 3-15-1851 | Edward C gct Goshen MM, Ohio |
| 8-20-1859 | William rocf Cincinnati MM, Ohio |
| 2-19-1881 | Joseph W rocf Carthage MM, Ind |

## YOUNT

| | |
|---|---|
| 6-27-1890 | Susannah rec in mbrp |

# HOPEWELL MONTHLY MEETING
## Henry County, Indiana

Hopewell Monthly Meeting was set-off from Milford Monthly Meeting and first held the 17th of Fourth Month 1841. The meetinghouse was located in Dudley township three-fourths of a mile southeast of the present site. It was early referred to as *"the Friends of the upper settlement of Symon's Creek."*

When set-off the monthly meeting was composed of Hopewell Preparative and Rich Square Preparative which had been established in 1835. Rich Square was set-off as monthly meeting in 1920. In 1888 Lewisville was established as a preparative under Hopewell. It was set-off as a monthly meeting in 1916.

## Monthly Meeting Records

The records below will be found in the vault of the Indiana Yearly Meetinghouse in Richmond. The material for this record is based on Hinshaw abstracts. The minutes seem to be examined to about 1900. These records have been microfilmed.

| Men's Minutes | Women's Minutes |
|---|---|
| 4-17-1841 : 12-18-1858 | 4-17-1841 : 12-17-1870 |
| 1-15-1859 : 8-20-1887 | 1-21-1871 : 10-21-1893 |
| 9-17-1887 : 12-20-1919 | |

1 Volume Births and Deaths
2 Membership Records
Marriage Register 1842-1904
Removal Certificates 1841-1913

HOPEWELL MONTHLY MEETING
BIRTH AND DEATH RECORD

ADDISON
Uva Alma          b 4-29-1886  -dt Harvey & Adaline Gilbert

AILS
Emma              b 7-2-1872   -dt George & Margaret J
                                    Johnson

ATKINSON
Newman            b 2-26-1860  -s Benajah & Elizabeth
Laura             b 4-29-1860  -dt Henry & Bethiah Stokes
Ch: Earl Albert              b 3-13-1885
    Ruby E                   b 4-22-1887

BAILEY
Daniel H          b 4-8-1826, Ohio  -s Daniel Sr & Mary
Asenath H         b 11-24-1827                 (Haworth)
Ch: Amos H                   b 12-27-1851
    Nathan                   b 1-10-1854
    Edith Elma               b 6-19-1856
    David Milo               b 11-24-1859
    Mary Anna                b 8-10-1862
    Elmer E                  b 8-18-1864
    Laura                    b 10-4-1866
    Harriett                 b 10-4-1866

BAIRD
Joseph            b 10-25-1857, Henry Co, Ind  -s Joseph &
                                                  Mariam

BALDWIN
Rachel Lewis      b 4-24-1793, N C  Widow of Nathan Lewis
                  -dt Josiah & Rachel Thomas
                  d 11-21-1880  -bur Hopewell MM, Ind
                  (She m John Baldwin in 1859 -2nd m)

BALLARD
Morman            b 4-4-1807, Va  -s James & Jane
                  d 8-28-1891  -bur Lewisville, Ind
Elizabeth         b 11-10-1808  d 8-10-1893 -bur Lewisville,
                  -dt Isaac & Mercy Paul              Ind
Ch: Ira           (m Melissa J Brothers, -dt Nathan & Abigail
                                    (Moore) Brothers)

BATEMAN
John              b 10-8-1810, N Y  -s Elisha & Catherine
                  d 8-22-1897  -bur Lewisville, Ind

BATSON
(Asahel)
Rachel (1st w)
Ch: James                    b 10-5-1865
Sarah (2nd w) b 4-18-1846 (m 2nd to Thomas Boone)
Ch: John                     b 5-30-1868
    Elizabeth                b 11-19-1871
    Ezra                     b 7-20-1878

Ezra              b 7-20-1878  -s Asahel & Sarah d 2-19-1916
Mary              b 5-23-1887, Ind  -dt Edward & Rachel Dish-
Ch: Alvan E                  b 1-10-1905 d 8-20-1905  man

BEALS
Thomas            b 2-14-1791  -s John & Mary
Nancy             b 9-16-1790  -dt Samuel & Susannah Stanley
Ch: Lemuel                   b 12-20-1822
    Mary                     b 6-27-1827
    Daniel                   b 12-5-1830

BEESON
Eva Euna          b 4-23-1883, Ind -dt Elijah & Sarah E
                  m 2-26-1901, Henry Co, Ind      Johnson

BELL
Alfred W          b 8- -1859  -s John & Eliza
                  d 12-31-1906, Wayne Co, Ind
                  m 12-2-1885, Henry Co, Ind
Mary E            b 7-21-1860, Rich Square MM, Henry Co
                  -dt Benjamin & Elizabeth (Stewart) Stuart

Ch: Glenn Alice       b 7-5-1889, Dublin, Ind
    Gladys Mariam     b 8-29-1891, Dublin, Ind
    John Carlton      b 9-15-1902, Rich Square MM,
                                   Henry Co, Ind

Jesse             b 1-14-1846, Ind  -s Thomas & Hannah
                                         (Mendenhall)
Sarah E (1st w)  m 1-28-1866, Hopewell MH, Ind
                  (non-mbr) -dt Charles L & Luriah (Reems) Hood
                  d 12-1-1882,  -bur Dublin, Ind
Ch: Martha            b 3-11-1867    d 9-23-1867
    Nancy L           b 2-5-1869     d 3-12-1869
    Clorice L         b 2-5-1869     d 8-20-1869
    John              b 3-31-1870
    Edgar D           b 5-6-1875
    Lillie M          b 4-2-1877     d 9-3-1877
    Thomas R          b 1-3-1880
Emma (2nd w)  m 9-23-1886 at Spiceland MH, Ind
                  -dt Albert & Caroline (Hubbard) Newby

Lydia             b 3-11-1816

Oliver            -s John & Eliza (Elliott)
                  m 12-23-1894, Dublin, Henry Co, Ind
Martha            Widow of Val Gauker    b 5-23-1866
                  -dt Benjamin & Lydia (Gilbert) Butler
Ch: Edwin             b 8-9-1898

Thomas            b 4-17-1802, N C  -s John & Sarah
                  d 11-24-1878  -bur Hopewell MM, Ind
Jerusha (1st w)   d 7-26-1837  -ae 29yrs,6mo,1da
                  -bur Hopewell MM, Henry Co, Ind
Ch: Martha            b 11-25-1829
    Sarah             b 2-20-1832
    Margaret          b 7-8-1834
    Eliza             b 9-26-1836    d 3-14-1838
                                     -bur Hopewell MM
Hannah (2nd w)    b 12-16-1813
                  d 2-28-1873  -bur Hopewell MM, Henry Co,
                                                     Ind
Ch: Asenath           b 4-18-1842    d 10-5-1843
                                     -bur Hopewell MM
    Josiah            b 3-13-1844    d 2-17-1863
    Jesse             b 1-14-1845
    Lydia G           b 6-7-1848
    Enos Thomas       b 7-18-1853
    Jehu F            b 10- -1855    d 9-8-1856
                                     -bur Hopewell MM

BENTLY
Jehu
Martha
Ch: Matilda          b 11-28-1847
    (She m 1st ... Stout)
    (She m 2nd Charles Goodwin in 1888)

BINFORD
Arlington         b 11-20-1852, Ind
                  m 12-15-1888
                  -s Samuel B & Ann Johnson
Emma              b 9-15-1852, Ind
                  -dt Jethro & Mary Wickersham

Barclay           -s Robert & Martha (Hill)
                  of Westland, Ind
                  m at Dublin, Ind
Deborah Ann       -dt William & Priscilla (Dennis)
                                    Butler

Benjamin O        b 8-7-1856, Southampton Co, Va
                  -s Oliver & Mary F
                  d 6-21-1914
                  m 10-3-1897, Rush Co, Ind
Julia B           b 9-9-1865, Rush Co, Ind
                  -dt Enos & Caroline Pickering

HOPEWELL

### BINFORD (Cont)
Ch of Benjamin O & Julia B (Pickering):
    Mary Etta C          b 2-21-1901
    Ruby Janett          b 6-10-1903

Edward        b 3-24-1877, Rush Co, Ind
    -s Micajah & Susanna    m 8-31-1904
                                at St Louis, Mo
Emily         b 11-15-1873, Henry Co, Ind
    -dt John & Mary L Gilbert
Ch: Mary Susanna       b 2-25-1912, Henry Co, Ind

James H       b 10- 7-1845
Hannah E      b 5-16-1850
Ch: Mary E             b 12-31-1869

Micajah       m 3-19-1873, Rush Co, Ind
Susanna       -dt Oliver & Mary F Binford   b 5- 7-1851
                                   Southampton Co, Va
Ch: Edward          b 3-24-1877, Rush Co, Ind

Oliver
Mary F
Ch: Susanna         b 5- 7-1851, Southampton Co,Va
     m 3-19-1873, Rush Co, Ind, to Micajah M
                                Binford
     Benjamin O       b 8- 7-1856, Southampton Co,Va

Samuel Bailey   b 11-24-1808   d 8-23-1872   -bur Rich Square
                                          Henry Co, Ind
Anna (1st w)   b 10-13-1814   d 10-19-1856   -bur Rich Square
     -dt ... Johnson                        MM, Ind
Ch: Deborah Ann        b 12-23-1833   d 9-15-1838
                         -bur Rich Square MM, Ind
    Mary Snowden        b 8-25-1835
    William Penn         b 9-17-1837
    Oliver                b 3-14-1840
    Albert                b 2- 4-1843   d 4-24-1866
                         -bur Rich Square MM
    Deborah Ann         b 10- 8-1848   d 10- 4-1850
                         -bur Rich Square MM
    Arlington           b 11-20-1852
    Anna Maria          b 12- 4-1854
    Samuel Charles       b 9-18-1856   d 10-24-1857
                         -bur Rich Square MM, Ind
Hannah R (Stokes) Cox (2nd w)      b 1-28-1822
     -dt Samuel & Jane Stokes   Widow of William Cox
Ch: Emma                b 2- 4-1859
    Dora                  b 5-12-1861
    Susan                 b 9-12-1863

### BISH
Bertie         b 7- 5-1873

Sylvester     b 12- 3-1872

### BLACK
Henry      b 2-18-1835
Elizabeth   b 3-25-1835
Ch: Sinetha Ethel        b 6- 5-1876
Minor ch u/c Bertie & Sylvester: (1877)
    William A Woollen     b 4-11-1859
    Hannah A Woollen     b 2-28-1861

### BOGUE
Amos         b 12-31-1829     -s Newby & Hannah
Phebe        b 9- 5-1836    -dt Daniel & Margaret (Morris)
                                         Reynolds
Ch: J Albert            b 4-28-1854
    Huldah                b 11-12-1855
    Mary E                b 3-11-1858
    Abigail               b 7-22-1860
    Henry R              b 9-27-1863
    Newby                b 2- 4-1866
    Anna M                b 4-17-1868
    Josiah M             b 7-27-1871
    Nancy E              b 2-29-1873

### BOND
Cyrus       b 8- 8-1828, Ind    -s Daniel & Mary
                                         (Hussey)
Edward      b 3- 8-1800, N C    -s Benjamin & Mary
                                         (Williams)
Ann         b 10-21-1803, N C
    -dt Henry & Betsey Hayworth
Ch: Lucinda            b 6-18-1828
    Athelinda           b 6- 6-1830
    Jediah                b 4-16-1832
    Benjamin F          b 1-30-1836
    Elizabeth A          b

Elam          b 7-18-1830

Jediah      b 8-19-1804    -s Benjamin & Mary (dec)
                                         (Williams)
Elmina      b 4-12-1812, N C
    -dt Richard & Abigail (Foster) Stanley
    d 3- 3-1847    -bur Rich Square MM, Ind
Ch: Luzena S            b 10- 6-1833
    Martha Jane         b 7-14-1839
    Rebecca C           b 4-27-1841   d 9-25-1869
        m ... Lowry      -bur Rich Square MM
    Angelina             b 6-15-1843
    Elmina                b 8-13-1846

Benjamin
Mary (Williams)
Ch: Jonathan W          b 10-15-1801, N C

### BOONE
George R                  -s James W & Mary
Mattie      b 1878    -dt Thomas & Phoebe E Hooker

James White   b 12-21-1821, N C    -s Thomas & Mary
           d 2- -1910
Mary
Ch: Mary                b 11-28-1847
    Wesley                b 2- 2-1850
    John                  b 6-14-1854, N C
    Ella                  b 9-14-1857
    George R             b
    Fanny                 b 12- 5-1862, N C

Wesley      b 2- 2-1850, N C    -s James & Mary
.....
Ch: Rosetta             b 8- 2-1878

### BRADBURY
James L     b 6- 7-1829, Ind    -s Abner M & Mary
           d     1911
Annie        -dt Moses & Delphinea Brown
           b 2-29-1840, Ind   d 7-11-1909

Luther      m 5- -1888, Henry Co, Ind
Emma Jane   b 5-16-1868
     -dt Lewis W & Rebecca L Windsor

Robert      -s Thomas & Jubena (Cartright) of
            Straughn, Ind    A non-mbr   m 8-24-1892
                                   at New Castle, Ind
Abigail     b 9- 9-1870
     -dt Milton & Mary Ann (Ratliff) Stewart
       of Straughn, Ind

### BRIDGET
Frank        a non-mbr    -s Henry & Ellen (Clark)
            m 2-17-1895        of New Lisbon, Ind
            near Hopewell, Ind
Martha      b 12-29-1868    -dt Samuel & Mary Jane
                               (Haskett) Cook of New
                               Lisbon, Ind

### BROTHERS
Ira    -s Nathan & Abigail (Moore) of Lewisville, Ind
        m 3-12-1884, near Lewisville, Ind
R Ella (Lamb)     -dt Phnieas Lamb of Lewisville, Ind

HOPEWELL

BROTHERS (Cont)
Nathan          b 8-21-1822, N C    -s Durin & Sarah
Abigail         b 9- 1-1816, N C    -dt Jesse & Sarah Moore
Ch: Mary A          b 1- 8-1845, N C
    Sarah R         b 2- 9-1847
    Rebecca A       b 7- 9-1849
    Melissa J       b 1-18-1852
    Maria E         b 3-20-1854   d 9-11-1863
                        -bur Hopewell MM, Ind
    Joel G          b 1- 4-1857
        (m 8-10-1876 to Emma Bierly, -dt Levi &
        Mary Ann (Brown))
    Ira S           b 1- 4-1859
        (m 3-12-1884 to Ella Lamb)

BROWN
Charles C       b 5- 8-1862, Lewisville, Ind
                -s John & Caroline

(Moses)
Delphenia
Ch: Annie           b 2-29-1840
    Margaret        b 8-22-1845

Zimri Austin    b 12-23-1865, Henry Co, Ind
                -s Samuel & Maria
                m 5-25-1893, Henry Co, Ind
Mattie          b 12-22-1862, Henry Co, Ind
                -dt Henry & Matilda Black  d 12-   -1936
Ch: Harrold B       b 2-19-1896, Henry Co, Ind

BUNCE
James W         b 6- 5-1841     -s Richard & Sarah
                d               -bur Hopewell MM, Ind

BUNDY
Ira G           b 11-17-1843    -s Jesse & Rachel
Sarah R         b 2- 9-1847 -dt Nathan & Abigail Brothers
Ch: Christy (or Charity) b 11-19-1864

Jesse           b 8- 5-1803     -s Benjamin & Sarah
                d 9-16-1873 -bur Hopewell MM, Ind
Rachel          b 1- 4-1807 -dt Francis & Mary Hester
                d 12- 2-1872 -bur Hopewell MM, Ind
Ch: Benjamin        b 4-25-1826   d 3- 8-1844
                        -bur Hopewell MM, Ind
    Martha          b 4-16-1828
    Mary            b 3-17-1830
    Sarah           b 4-30-1832
    Jonathan        b 6-24-1834
    William H       b 10- 7-1836
    Francis A       b 4-22-1839
    Elias           b 7-18-1841
    Ira             b 12-17-1843
    Lydia           b 9- 8-1846
    Enos            b 11- 4-1850
    Achsah          b 5- 8-1853   d 4-27-1855
                        -bur Hopewell MM, Ind

Josiah          b 8-22-1773   d 1-22-1839
                -bur Hopewell MM, Henry Co, Ind
Dorothy         b 4-17-1777   d 12- 9-1852
                -bur Hopewell MM, Henry Co, Ind

Sarah           b 8- 4-1786 -bur Hopewell MM, Henry Co, Ind
                d 7- 9-1871

William         b 7-24-1837 -s Elias & Sarah of Rush Co, Ind
Mary A          b 4- 7-1840 -dt John & Martha (Stratton)
                                Stuart
Ch: Ada E           b 7-14-1862
    Albert          b 8-14-1864

William H       b 10- 7-1836
Nancy           b 4-10-1840       d 2-22-1875
Ch: Melissa         b 8-29-1858
    Catharine       b 8-17-1869

BUNKER
Ann             b 3-16-1825, N C  d 2-12-1913
                -dt Gaterey Tuttle

Carrie L        b 12-28-1871, Ind  (m Milton Hayse)
                -dt Jesse & Josephine

(John)
Ann
Ch: Rebecca         b 7-14-1855, Ind
    Rachel          b 4-23-1865, Ind

BURT
Charles E       b 10-19-1852, Ind  (a non-mbr)
                -s William & Susan (Ballard) of New Lisbon,
                m 12-24-1876 Near Hopewell, Ind   Ind
Mary Alice      b 5- 1-1860
                -dt Morris & Huldah (Ratliff) Reynolds

William
Susan           b 6- 2-1833, Ind  -dt Morman & Elizabeth
                d 9- 5-1886    -bur Lewisville, Ind
Ch: Charles E       b 10-19-1852

BUTLER
Alfred          b 5-29-1822    -s James L & Deborah
                                    (Johnson), Va
Elizabeth       b 10-20-1828   -dt Charles & Michal
                                    (Butler) Morgan
Ch: Benjamin M      b 8-28-1845
    Lindley H       b

Allen           -s Robert & Rebecca Ann (Bond) of
                Spiceland, Ind
                m 4-23-1891 at New Castle, Ind
Margaret        b 7-16-1865, Henry Co, Ind
                -dt James & Louisa (Stratton) Henley of
                Straughn, Ind
Ch: Rebecca         b

Benjamin J      b 12- 6-1833, Ind  -s Ansalom & Ruth (Cook)
                d 9-20-1901  -bur Hopewell MM, Henry Co,
                m 7-22-1857                          Ind
Lydia           b 2-22-1838, Ind    d 9- 4-1909
                -dt Aaron & Margaret (Bell) Gilbert
Ch: Charles A       b 7- 1-1858
    John A          b 1-22-1861
    Mary B          b 1-27-1864   d 10- 5-1867
                        -bur Hopewell MM, Ind
    Martha G        b 5-23-1866
    Walter J        b 1- 3-1869
    William         b 4- 4-1872
    Stacy           b 1- 1-1877   d 3-29-1879
                        -bur Hopewell MM

Charles A       b 7- 1-1858, Henry Co   m 6- 5-1881
                -s Benjamin & Lydia (Gilbert)
Flora           b 5-17-1858, Guilford Co, N C
                -dt John & Sarah J Cude
                d 12-27-1938
Ch: Nellie          b 11-14-1882
        (m 10-4-1903 to John Brenner)

Horace          b 5-28-1849  m 1-9-1881, Osawpie, Kans
                -s William & Priscilla (Dennis) of Oswapie,
Evaline         -dt ... Keener                      Kans

James E         b 10-31-1864  m 11-22-1890, Westland, Ind
                -s William & Priscilla (Dennis) of West-
                                            land MM, Ind
Ethel           -dt Perry & Jane (Binford) Lynum

James Ladd      b 7-31-1782, Va  -s Stephen & Mary
                d 2-17-1856
Deborah         b 6-21-1791, Va  -dt .. & Mary Johnson
Ch: Ann Johnson     b 11-13-1814
    Martha          b 8-27-1816
    William         b 9-19-1818
    James Edward   b 9-17-1820

HOPEWELL

## BUTLER (Cont)
Ch of James Ladd & Deborah (Cont):
- Alfred    b 5-29-1822
- Joseph    b 5- 6-1824
- Robert    b 3-29-1827
- Deborah Jane    b 2- 2-1830
- Mary Elizabeth    b 10-14-1833

John A    b 1-26-1861    m 10- 4-1883, Dublin, Ind
   -s Benjamin & Lydia (Gilbert) of Dublin, Ind
Melissa    (a non-mbr) -dt Cornelius & Nancy (Copeland)
       Gephart of Dublin, Ind

(Robert)
Rebecca Ann    b 6- 6-1837    -dt Isom & Dinah Bond
   d 9- 6-1892    -bur Rich Square MM, Ind
Ch: Leona    b 2-13-1876

(Stanton) fr West Branch MM, Va
   Dis 1833 at Milford MM, Ind
Elizabeth    b 10-31-1798, Va    d 10-19-1878
       -bur Lewisville, Ind
Ch: John Chappel    b ,
- Martha Ann    b 11-16-1821, Va
- Elizabeth Stanton    b 10-23-1823, Va
- James B    b 5- 9-1826, Va    d 12-11-1848
- Robert Binford    b 5- 2-1828, Va
- Rebecca Jane    b 8-25-1830, Va
- Julia E    b 8-17-1833, Ind    d 10-19-1863
- Mary L    b 3-13-1836, Ind

Walter    b 1- 3-1869    m 9-12-1898, Lewisville, Ind
   -s Benjamin & Lydia (Gilbert) of Dublin, Ind
Georgia    (a non-mbr)
   -dt William & Jane (Ballard) Murphy of
       Lewisville, Ind

William Jr    b 9-17-1807    m at Milford MM, Ind
   -s William Sr & Mary (dec)
Susannah    b 10-10-1810 -dt Joshua (dec) & Mary
       (Morgan) Morris
Ch: Joshua M    b 10- 3-1830
- Mary    b 6-25-1832    d 4- 5-1841
       -bur Bethel MM, Henry Co, Ind
- Margaret    b 4-13-1834
- Charles Morgan    b 1-27-1837
- Malissa    b 1-15-1839
- Mariah    b 3- 1-1841    d 3- 8-1841
       -bur Bethel MM

William    b 9-19-1818, Va
   -s James L & Deborah (Johnson)
Priscilla    b 10- 2-1824, Ind
   -dt Benjamin & Clarkie (Pool) Dennis
Ch: Horace I    b 5-28-1849
- Gulielma    b 5- 3-1851
- Deborah    b 7-10-1853
- Mary E    b 11-10-1855
- Eunice    b 2-24-1858
- William T    b 4- 3-1860
- James E    b 10-31-1864

## BYERS
John    b 5-18-1852    -s John Sr & Rebecca
   d 4- 1-1893    -bur New Castle, Ind
Margaret    b 7-25-1856 -dt Manylone & Hannah Thomas

## BYRKET
(John)
Fanny    b 12- 5-1862, N C    -dt James W & Mary Boone
Ch: Harmon    b 6-10-1885
   Maude    b 12-30-1888

## CAMPBELL
(Nicholas)    (a non-mbr) -s George & Margaret (Cress)
       of Dublin, Ind
   m 12- 5-1875 near Chicago, Ind
Mary Matilda    b 8-17-1854, Ind    d 9-10-1892
   -dt Phineas & Betsey (Ratliff) Macy of
       Dublin, Ind

## CAMELIN
John Franklin    b 9-16-1842, N C
   -s James & Irene
Carrie E    b 2-10-1847, Ind
   -dt Jabez & Caroline O Newby

## CARTER
(Elisha)
Ruth    b 9- 7-1848    -dt Samuel P & Eliza M
       Seward
Ch: Earl C    b 3- 7-1882
- Clayton H    b 9- 7-1883
- Evert    b 1-22-1886

## CATY - CATEY
William    b 5-25-1856, Wayne Co, Ind
   -s Samuel & Priscilla (Mullin) d 10-1-1939
   m 2-19-1887, Henry Co, Ind
Margaret    b 4- 7-1867, Henry Co, Ind    d 5-29-1937
   -dt George & Peninah (Gilbert) Stopher
Ch: Chester    b 1-12-1890, Wayne Co, Ind
- Gerald    b 4-16-1892, Henry Co, Ind
- Martha P    b 12- 6-1905, Henry Co, Ind

## COFFIN
Aaron    b 7-17-1847, Ind    -s George & Lydia
Emma A    b 2-17-1859    -dt William Dennis
Ch: Glenn D    b 6-12-1882
- Eva    b
- Leland    b

Isaac N    b 9- 3-1826    -s Elihu & Sarah of Hancock
       Co, Ind
Martha    b 11-25-1829    -dt Thomas & Jerusha (dec)
       Bell
Ch: Charles W    b 4-27-1851

(Oliver)
Jennie    b 9-26-1845, Ohio -dt Jesse & Elizabeth
       Rawls
Ch: Arthur A    b 5-5-1875, Ind

## COLTRAIN
Maude    b 1876    -dt Jarred & Sylvia

## COOK
Allen    b 1-27-1854    -s John & Peninah (Gilbert)
       (his 2nd w)
   m 10- 4-1873 at Hopewell MM, Ind
Elizabeth Elma (a non-mbr)
   -dt Cyrus & Mary Lutetia (Macy) Stanley
Ch: Levi    b 5-21-1875
- Eli    b 5-21-1875

Isaac Jr    b 3-22-1781, South Carolina
   -s 'old' Isaac & Charity (Wright)
   d 9- 7-1850 -bur Hopewell MM, Henry Co,
Elizabeth    b 9-22-1783        Ind
   d 8-14-1867 -bur Hopewell MM, Henry Co
Ch: John    b 8-24-1806
- Mary    b 4-11-1815
- Susannah    b 8-22-1823

John    b 8-24-1806, Ohio    d 4- 5-1891
       -bur Hopewell MM, Ind
   -s Isaac Jr & Elizabeth    m (1st) 1830
Mary (1st w)    b 2-15-1805, N C    -dt Josiah & Dorothy
   d 5- 2-1839        (Nixon) Gilbert
       -bur Hopewell MM, Henry Co, Ind
Ch: Martha    b 10- 4-1831
- Josiah    b 12-10-1833
- William    b 7- 9-1836    d 2- 6-1865
       -bur Hopewell MM
- Samuel    b 11- 7-1838
Peninah    b 10-11-1815, N C    (2nd Wife)
   -dt Joel & Lydia (Morgan) Gilbert
   d 3-31-1874 -bur Hopewell MM
Ch: Mary    b 8-15-1842    d 3-17-1853
       -bur Hopewell MM

HOPEWELL

COOK (Cont)
Ch of John & Peninah (Cont):
    Elizabeth    b 11- 7-1846  d 9- 6-1848
        -bur Hopewell MM
    Nancy    b 11-23-1849  d 3-17-1853
        -bur Hopewell MM
    Allen    b 1-27-1854
    Ellen    b 1-27-1854

Josiah    b 12-10-1833  d 1-31-1873  -bur Hopewell MM, Henry Co, Ind
Ruth    b 4-20-1840, Ind
    -dt Elias & Sarah (Nicholson) Bundy
Ch: Luzena    b 4- 6-1858
    Sarah P    b 2-16-1860
    Martha A    b 6-19-1862
    (m Andrew Amic on 11-4-1891)
    Mary E    b 6-23-1864
    Jane M    b 3- 4-1866
    (m Willis Smith on 11-1-1882)
    Marshall    b 12- 1-1868  d 12-17-1887
        -bur Hopewell MM, Ind
    (m Margaret Bennett on 9-12-1886)
    Henry    b 7-23-1871

. . . . .
Lydia    -dt Stephen & Ann Taylor  b 1- 6-1820
    d 1905

Samuel    b 11- 7-1838, Ind
    -s John & 1st w, Mary (Gilbert)(dec)
Mary Jane    -dt Henry & Mary Haskett
    b 2-13-1842, N C  d 11-16-1898
Ch: William    b 8-20-1862
    Franklin    b 9- 8-1864  d 8- 3-1865
        -bur Hopewell MM
    Peninah    b 12- 8-1865
    Mary M    b 5-20-1867
    Martha S    b 12-29-1868
    Josiah W    b 1-25-1873

William    b 8-20-1862, Hopewell MM, Ind  d 1933
    -s Samuel & Mary J (Haskett)
    m 12-23-1888, Henry Co, Ind
Alice    b 4- 5-1861, Ind
    -dt Cornelius & Nancy (Copeland) Gephart
        of Straughn, Ind
Ch: Walter J    b 9-17-1889, Henry Co, Ind

COPE
David    b 8-22-1848, Ind  -s Edmund & Margaret
Mattie J    b 9- 7-1854, Ind  -dt John B & Nancy W Guerin
Ch: Everett    b 11-30-1879

COSAND
Charles    b 10-25-1795, N C  -s John & Sarah (Morgan)
    d 11-20-1872  -bur Hopewell MM, Henry Co, Ind
Elvah    b 3-17-1799, N C
    -dt Jordon White & wife, Gurela White
    d 11-17-1864, -bur Hopewell MM, Ind
Ch: Joseph    b 4- 7-1829, N C
    Edmund    b 8-26-1831  d 8- 2-1855, NC
    Mary Ann    b 1-15-1834, N C
    Charles F    b 4-23-1841, N C

Cornelius    b 12- 7-1844, Ind  -s Gabriel & Sarah
        (Wickersham)
Jemima    b 2-13-1844, Ind
    -dt Robert & Malinda Needham

Frank    b    m 10-15-1879
Martha E    b 6- 5-1856, Ind  -dt David & Abigail Vickery

(Gabriel)    b 1-13-1799, N C  (Dis in 1821 in N C)
    -s Benjamin (dec) & Mary (Morgan)
Sarah    b 12-28-1811, N C
    -dt Caleb & Lydia (Gardner) (dec) Wickersham

    d 3- 6-1884, -bur Rich Square MM, Ind
Ch: Eunice    b 5-30-1838, Ind
    Cornelius    b 12- 7-1844
    Aaron    b 11- 9-1851, Ind

John    b 1- 2-1805, N C  d 9-22-1900, Ind
    -s Benjamin (dec) & Mary (Morgan)
Joseph    b 4- 7-1829, N C  -s Charles & Elvah (White)
    d 9-26-1887  -bur Hopewell MM, Henry Co, Ind
    m 12-21-1859, Henry Co, Ind
Sarah    b 12-14-1830, Ind
    -dt John (dec) & Rebecca (Bell) Symons

Benjamin (dec) of N C
Mary    -dt Lemuel & 1st w, Miriam (Griffin)
    b 12- 5-1775, N C
    d 12-17-1871  -bur Rich Square MM, Henry Co, Ind
Ch: (brought to Ind in 1822 with their mother)
    William    b 9-11-1797, N C
    Gabriel    b 1-13-1799, N C
    Samuel    b 11-21-1800, N C
    John    b 1- 2-1805, N C
    Nathan    b    , N C
    Elias    b    , N C

COX
Alfred    b 11-20-1843  -s William (dec) & Hannah R
    (Stokes) (now wife of Samuel B Binford)
Ruth Ann
Ch: Gertrude    b 7-23-1868
    Nellesson    b 6-23-1871

Henry    b 3-19-1847, Ind
    -s William (dec) & Hannah R (Stokes)
    (now the wife of Samuel B Binford)
    d 2-14-1879  -bur Rich Square MM, Ind
Malinda J    -dt Thomas & Jane Wilson  b 3-12-1850, Ind
Ch: William T    b 2- 2-1872
    Edwin H    b 8-16-1873
    Minetta    b 10- 1-1875
    Elnora    b 9-22-1877
    Henrietta    b 8- 7-1879

J Clark    m 9- 6-1888 at Hopewell MM, Ind
    -s Joseph M & Rachel M (Terrell) of Dublin, Ind
Harriet E    b 10- 1-1868
    -dt Jeremiah & Mary (Macy) Gilbert of Straughn, Ind

William    b 5-28-1821, Ohio
    -s Joseph & Elizabeth (Musgrave)
    d 5- 4-1854  -bur Rich Square MM, Henry Co, Ind
Hannah R    -dt Samuel & Jane Stokes  b 1-28-1822, Pa
    (Hannah R m 2nd in 1857 to Samuel B Binford)
Ch: Alfred    b 11-20-1843
    Ellen    b 7-16-1845  d 8-12-1846
    Henry    b 3-19-1847
    Elwood    b 2-25-1848
    Elizabeth Jane    b 12-12-1850
    Walter    b 5- 7-1853

CRAWFORD
William C    b 11-25-1842, Ind  -s Harrison & Olive
Amanda J    b 10- 6-1844, Ind  -dt Phineas & Mary Hall
    d 8-11-1894  -bur Hopewell MM, Henry Co
Ch: Phineas H    b 3- 5-1878  d 5-22-1889
        -bur Hopewell MM, Ind
    Mary M    b 4- 5-1879
    Ethel C    b 5- 3-1881
    (m 9-14-1902 to ... Vanderhook)
    Liban Vadia    b 9-17-1883

CUDE
John M    b 10- 7-1829, N C  -s Noah & Huldah (Swain)
Sarah Jane    -dt ... Macy  m 1851, N C

HOPEWELL

## DALYRIMPLE
Lydia (Stevenson)   -dt Charles & Eliza
            b 9-16-1868, Rush Co, Ind

## DAVITT (or Demitt)
Ella        d 6- 2-1908

## DEMITT
James       b 3- 5-1874      -s John & Jane
Belle       b 6-22-1873 -dt Thomas & Ellen Hooker
Ch: David Leroy     b 7-19-1895
    Floyd L         b 2-19-1899

## DENNIS
Benjamin    b 10-15-1795 -s John & Hannah, Ohio (non-mbrs)
            d 8- 8-1844  -bur Hopewell MM, Henry Co, Ind
Clarky      b 11-15-1801, N C
            -dt John & Elizabeth (Charles) Pool
            d 10- 4-1884 -bur Hopewell MM, Ind
Ch: John            b 3- 3-1821
    Gulielma        b 12- 5-1822
    Priscilla       b 10- 2-1824
    Elizabeth       b 12-25-1826
    Eunice          b 7-19-1829
    William Charles b 2- 9-1832
    Jethro          b 9- 2-1834
    Benjamin Stewart b 8-10-1837
    Sarah Ann       b 9- 2-1839  d 8- 4-1840
                    -bur Hopewell MM
    Thomas Pool     b 8-26-1841  d 3- 3-1865
    Albert Tell     b 4-15-1844

John        b 3- 3-1821, Ind  -s Benjamin (dec) &
                              Clarky (Pool)
Mary        -dt Jonathan & 2nd w Sarah (Bogue) Ratliff
            b 7- 6-1827
Ch: Sarah Ann       b 3- 6-1846

John        -s William & Milicent (Mills)
            b 7-14-1882

William C   b 2- 9-1832 -s Benjamin & Clarky (Pool)
Atilla (Bacon) b 7-7-1835 -dt Delzel & Rebecca Bacon

## DISHMAN
(Edward)
Rachel      b 4-23-1865, Ind  -dt John & Ann Bunker
Ch: Annie A         b 5- 2-1885
    Mary            b 5-23-1887
    Clark           b

Frank       b 11- 6-1876 -s Solomon & Rebecca (Bunker)
Eva         -dt Henry & Angelina Pervis
Ch: Edith Ilene     b 12-28-1905, Henry Co, Ind

(Solomon)
Rebecca     -dt John & Ann Bunker  b 7-14-1855, Ind
Ch: Frank           b 11- 6-1876, Ind
    Cora            b 3-12-1879
    Freddie         b 8-14-1881

## DIXON
Caleb       b 9- 4-1857, Ind  d 3-27-1911
            -s Phineas & Sarah
            m 12- 2-1881, Henry Co, Ind
Hannah Jennie b 1- 3-1854, Ind
            -dt Benjamin & Elizabeth (Stewart) Stuart
Ch: Leota           b 8-13-1891 d same day
    Oris            b 7-27-1895

Calvin      b 11-17-1842, Ind  -s Phineas & Sarah
Mary        b 6-22-1837, Ind
            -dt Daniel & Keziah Hastings
Ch: Keziah J        b 2- 2-1866, Ind
    Rosa J          b 4-16-1867
            (m Calvin Elliott)
    Letitia Ann     b 11- 7-1869
    Elmer P         b 5-25-1872
    Harley C        b 5-25-1878

## DOUGHERTY
Sarah       b 7-17-1837   (Now Sarah E Weeks)

## EAGLE
William     b 3-11-1878, Wayne Co, Ind
            -s George & Susanna

## EATON
John        (a non-mbr)
            -s Ulysus & Harriett (Hines) of Cambridge
            City, Ind
            m 2- 1-1890 near Straughn, Ind
Minnie E    b 10-13-1868
            -dt J Milton & Mary Ann (Ratliff) Stewart
            of Straughn, Ind

## ELLIOTT
......      m 2-28-1887, Hamilton Co, Ind
Catharine   -dt William & Margaret McKie
            b 8-19-1845, Scotland

## ENGLE
Perry       b 5- 7-1860  d 8- 9-1910
Maggie A    b 7-17-1862
Ch: Blanche         b 9-13-1890
    Lloyd           b 11-25-1896
    Hobart          b 3- 5-1899

## FANCHER
(Thomas)
Cora        b 3-12-1879, Henry Co, Ind
            -dt Solomon & Rebecca (Bunker) Dishman

## FORD
(William T)
Harriett    b 9-29-1867
            -dt Joshua & Sarah (Stead) Moore
Ch: Carl            b
    Clara           b
    Irvan Adolpheus b
    Blanche

## FOULKE
Samuel F (dec)
Ann H       b 12-27-1791  d 8-14-1885 in Iowa
            -bur Hopewell MM, Henry Co, Ind
Ch: Jesse H         b 4- 5-1826
            (Gct Three Rivers MM, Ia, 1856)
    Sarah H         b 11- 5-1827
    Joseph          b 7-29-1829
    Edith B         b 7- 2-1831

Jesse H     b 4- 5-1826  -s Samuel F (dec) & Anna H
Michel      b 2-13-1829  -dt Elisha & Martha Johnson
Ch: Mary E          b 9-27-1849
    Deborah J       b 6-29-1851
    Joshua          b 12-21-1853

## GAUKER
(Charles)   -s Val (dec) & Martha G (Butler)
            m 12-24-1901, Henry Co, Ind
Laura Estella -dt William & Rachel (Macy) Pearce
            b 8-23-1885   d 1930

(Val)       d prior to 1894  m 9-16-1885
Martha G    b 5-23-1866  -dt Benjamin J & Lydia
                         (Gilbert) Butler
            (Martha G m 2nd in 1894 to Oliver Bell)
Ch: Charles         b

## GAYLOR
Andy        b 6-16-1883

Joseph      b 2-21-1859, Ind  -s John
            d 12-13-1892  -bur Lewisville, Ind
Elizabeth A b 5- 1-1862  d 7- -1895
            -bur Lewisville, Ind
            -dt Isaac & Mary J Goodwin
Ch: Mary J          b 4-14-1886
    Myrtle          b 8- 7-1890
    Joseph          b 2-16-1893

HOPEWELL

GEPHART
Alice           b 4- 5-1861  -dt Cornelius & Nancy

GILBERT
Aaron           b 12- 8-1804, N C  -s Joel & Lydia (Morgan)
Margaret        b 5- 6-1810, N C
                -dt John & 2nd w, Lydia (Symons) Bell
                d 3- 1-1877 or 9-24-1896
                NOTE: Both dates given - there may be 2
                Margarets - both listed as bur at Hopewell
                MM, Ind  -may be mother & daughter
Ch: John B              b 10-24-1828
    Joel M              b 10-14-1830
    Jesse               b 4- 2-1834
    Martha              b 6-26-1836
    Lydia               b 2-22-1838
    Peninah             b 5-25-1841
    Sarah               b 4-25-1843
    Margaret            b 3-16-1845
    Aaron Jr            b 4-17-1849

Aaron Jr        b 4-17-1849, Ind
                -s Aaron Sr & Margaret (Bell)
                (Mou in 1871, Dover MM, Ohio)
Sarah Ann       b 9-22-1849, Ohio
                -dt Reuben & Emily Peele
Ch: Melvin A            b 9-12-1873, Ind

Abel            b 4- 7-1846, Henry Co, Ind
                -s Mordecai & Martha (Bundy) (dec)
                d 11-27-1928  m 2-21-1866, Henry Co, Ind
Lucinda         b 3- 1-1846, Henry Co, Ind
                -dt James & Anna (Mendenhall) Macy
                d 4-28-1924
Ch: Lucy Ann            b 5-23-1868, Henry Co, Ind
                        d 4-11-1939
    Henry W             b 10-25-1874, Henry Co, Ind
                (m Bertha Wilson, 8-2-1899)

Alfred          b 7- 5-1867  d 10-26-1915
                -s Mordecai & 2nd w, Mary (Moore)
                m 10-25-1888, Dublin, Henry Co, Ind
Ida E           b         (a non-mbr)
                -dt Jesse & Alice (Shinholt) Ballard of
                Lewisville, Ind

Charles M       b 2- 8-1854, Ind  -s Jeremiah & Mary (Macy)
                m 3- 1-1872, near West Milton, Ohio
Elizabeth       b 5-18-1852, Ohio  -dt Jonathan & Elizabeth
                (Jay) Coates of Pleasant Hill, Ohio
Ch: William J           b 3- 8-1873
    Nora Etta           b 8-28-1875
    Erastus E           b 11-26-1879
    Eva                 b 8-18-1882  d 4-25-1885
                        -bur Hopewell MM, Ind

Cyrus W         b 9- 1-1858, Henry Co, Ind
                -s Jeremiah & Mary (Macy)
                m 8-30-1876, near New Castle, Henry Co, Ind
Mary M          b 12- 4-1857 (a non-mbr)  -dt Henry &
                Matilda (Hammer) Black, Lewisville, Ind
Ch: Henry A             b 8-25-1878, Ind
    Matilda J           b 8-10-1880  d 9-17-1880
                        -bur Hopewell MM
    Orville Chester     b 11- 7-1881
    Pearly May          b 12-28-1884
    Carl J              b 6-19-1887
    Charles E           b 10-15-1889
    William Cecil       b 4-19-1891
    Luther              b 11-19-1893
    Leona Bell          b 6-18-1896
    Elroy               b 1-22-1899

Edgar J         b 8-17-1867  -s Harvey & Adeline (Stanley)
                of New Castle, Ind
                m 4-27-1887, New Castle, Ind
Belle           (non-mbr)  -dt John & Lulie (Livezey)
                           Harvey

Harvey          b 8-25-1843, Ind
                -s Joel & 1st wife, Hannah (Kendall) (dec)
Adaline         b 7-26-1849, Ind
                -dt Nathan & Mary Stanley
                d 8-30-1886  -bur Hopewell MM
Ch: Edgar J             b 8-17-1867
    Laura H             b 9-25-1869
    Leora               b 5- 5-1874  d 1-22-1886
                        -bur Hopewell MM
    Elizabeth E         b 5- 8-1876  d 9-18-1886
                        -bur Hopewell MM
    Luretta             b 7-20-1880
    Vernon              b 11- 8-1882
    Uva Alma            b 4-29-1886
Nancy (2nd w)   A widow
                -dt John & Rebecca (Bellhammer) Copeland
                m 6- 8-1887, near Hopewell, Ind

Isaiah B        b 10-23-1834, Ind  -s Josiah & Abigail (Bell)
Martha Ann      b 2- 7-1835, Ohio
                -dt Thomas & Nancy Dougherty (both dec)
                of Warren Co, Ohio
Ch: Walter J            b 2-12-1858
                (m Laura Lamb, 3-27-1887)
    Josiah W            b 3-30-1861  d 5-10-1862
    Dorothy             b 5-11-1863
    David B             b 1-20-1866
                (m Kate Huron, 7-28-1892)
    Maria Emma          b 3-15-1870
                (m L F Symons, 9-2-1890)

James Lindley   b 4-30-1856, Ind
                -s Jeremiah & Mary (Macy)
                m 12- -1878 at Westland, Ind
Martecia J      b 12- 3-1853, N C
                -dt David H & Margaret A (Copeland)
                                           Outland
Ch: Bertha M            b 10-17-1880, Ind
    Clarence            b 8-22-1885
    Raymond L           b 8-17-1887

Jeptha          b 1-27-1856, Ind  m 10- -1875, Straughn, Ind
                -s Mordecai & Martha (Bundy) (dec)
Nancy           b 7-20-1857, Va
                -dt George H & Catharine (Stover) Rott
Ch: Emma                b 12- 9-1878, Ind
    George H            b 10- 9-1882

Jeremiah        b 10-17-1819, Ind  -s Thomas & Sarah (Hill)
Euna            b 3-12-1816, S C
                -dt William & Sarah (Pemberton) Thomas
                d 9- 8-1849
Ch: William T           b 10-16-1840
    Sarah               b 12- 1-1842
    John                b 8-17-1845
    Nancy               b 1-21-1848

Jeremiah        b 10-13-1826  -s Joel & Lydia (Morgan)(dec)
                d 3-23-1871  -bur Hopewell MM, Henry Co,
Mary            b 10- 8-1835, Henry Co, Ind            Ind
                -dt James & Anna (Mendenhall) Macy
                d 12-26-1912
Ch: Lydia Ann           b 11-30-1851
    Charles M           b 2- 8-1854
    James Linley        b 4-30-1856
    Cyrus W             b 9- 1-1858
    Rebecca J           b 4-15-1861
    Luther              b 10-18-1863
    Rosanna             b 3-22-1866  d 7-14-1885
                        -bur Hopewell MM
    Harriett E          b 10- 1-1868
                (m J Clark Cox, 9-6-1888)
    Joel J              b 2-19-1871
                (m Margaret Welsh, 7- 3-1899)

Jesse           b 4- 2-1834, Ind  -s Aaron & Margaret
Sarah Ann       b 1- 2-1838, Ind               (Bell)
                -dt Morris & Elizabeth (Elliott) Gilbert
                                                   (dec)

HOPEWELL

GILBERT (Cont)
Ch of Jesse & Sarah Ann:
 Mary Elizabeth    b 11-16-1856 d 12- 8-1860
            -bur Hopewell MM
 Albert Warren    b 10-14-1858 d 4-24-1863
            -bur Hopewell MM
 Ada J       b 9- 7-1861 d 2-27-1863
            -bur Hopewell MM
 Josiah C      b 3-16-1864
 Coreni       b 10-22-1866

Joel    b 10-14-1783, N C
     -s Jeremiah & 2nd w, Rebecca (Morris)
     d 2-12-1870 -bur Hopewell MM, Henry Co, Ind
Lydia   b 11- 1-1786 -dt James & 2nd w, Millicent
             (Symons) Morgan
     d 12-15-1846 -bur Hopewell MM
Ch: Aaron      b 12- 8-1804, Guilford Co, N C
  Abigail     b 10- 7-1808, Guilford Co, N C
  Millicent    b 10- 7-1808, Guilford Co, N C
         d 5-22-1839 -bur Hopewell MM
  Peninah     b 10-11-1815, Guilford Co, N C
  Nathan     b 9-22-1817, Guilford Co, N C
  Joel Jr     b 8-15-1820, Guilford Co, N C
  Lydia      b 5-29-1822, Guilford Co, N C
  Mordecai M   b 9- 5-1824, Guilford Co, N C
  Jeremiah    b 10-13-1826, Ind

Joel Jr   b 8-15-1820, N C d 8- 3-1890
     -s Joel Sr & Lydia (Morgan)
Hannah (1st w) b 6-30-1818, Ind
     -dt Thomas & Elizabeth Kendall
     d 8- 2-1860 -bur Hopewell MM, Henry Co, Ind
Ch: Harvey     b 8-25-1843
  Elizabeth    b 10-11-1849
  Jason      b 8-12-1854 d 8-22-1855
         -bur Hopewell MM
Sarah (2nd w) b 9-10-1824, Ind d 2- 6-1885
           -bur Hopewell MM
     -dt Jehoshephat & 3rd w, Mary (Bell) Morris
Harriet (3rd w) b 8- 8-1842 m 6- 9-1887
     -dt John & Mary Harris

Joel M   b 10-14-1830 -s Aaron & Margaret (Bell)
Phebe   b 4-22-1833

John    b 2-12-1837, Ind -s Josiah (dec) &
     Abigail (Bell) - now w of Daniel Johnson
Mary   b 2-13-1840 -dt Phineas & Huldah (Bundy)
            Lamb
Ch: Levi      b 11-13-1863, Ind
  Daniel J    b 2-12-1865
   (m Linnie A Hadley, 2-4-1891)
  Huldah     b 1-18-1867 d 9-23-1873
         -bur Rich Square MM
  Abigail     b 4-10-1869
  Olive      b 9-20-1872
   (m Milo Elliott, 8-12-1891)
  John Gurney   b 6-28-1876
  Mary E     b 11-15-1878
  Annie Bell    b 10-13-1880

John Gurney b 6-28-1876, Henry Co, Ind m 10-9-1901,
     -s John Sr & Mary (Lamb)    Ohio
Elizabeth T  -dt Isaac & Hannah Lloyd
Ch: Dorothy L    b 7- 4-1902, Henry Co, Ind
  John Wendall  b 9-15-1905, Henry Co, Ind

Josiah Jr  b 11-30-1809, N C
     d 1-26-1839 -bur Hopewell MM, Henry Co, Ind
     -s Josiah Sr & Dorothy (Nixon)
Abigail  b 1-14-1814 -dt John & 2nd w, Lydia
     d 8-31-1888 (Symons) Bell
     (m 2nd in 1847, Daniel Johnson)
Ch: Josiah     b 10-23-1834
  John      b 2-12-1837
  Dorothy J    b 4-18-1839

Josiah C  b 3-16-1864 m 3-24-1886, Dublin, Ind
     -s Jesse & Sarah Ann (Gilbert)
Glenna  (a non-mbr)
     -dt Halech & Mary E (Veals) Floyd

Luther B  b 10-18-1863 m 3-26-1886, Hopewell
     -s Jeremiah & Mary (Macy), Straughn, Ind
Mary Alice b 5-24-1866
     -dt Isaac W & Elizabeth (Peele) Pidgeon
     of Dublin, Ind

Mordecai M b 9- 6-1824, N C
     -s Joel & Lydia (Morgan)
     d 9- 3-1899 -bur Hopewell MM, Henry Co,
               Ind
Martha (1st w) b 4-16-1828 d 3- 7-1863 -bur Hopewell MM
     -dt Jesse & Rachel (Hester) Bundy
Ch: Abel      b 4- 7-1846
  Rachel     b 1-23-1849 d 11-22-1855
         -bur Hopewell MM
  Esther     b 1-21-1852
  Jeptha     b 1-27-1856
  Wilson     b 6-24-1859 d 3- 3-18..
Mary (2nd w) b 8-24-1830, Ind
     -dt Samuel & Rebecca (White) Moore
     d 3-14-1880 -bur Hopewell MM
Ch: Alfred     b 7- 5-1867
  Albert     b 7- 5-1867 d 3-31-1868
         -bur Hopewell MM
Catharine (3rd w) b 10-12-1821, Ind
     -dt Jacob & Mary (Peele) Elliott
     -widow Thomas Gilbert d 12-30-1909

Morris   b 7-10-1817, Ind
     -s Josiah & Dorothy (Nixon)
Elizabeth b 3- 9-1819, Ind
(1st w)  -dt John (dec) & Mary (Ratliff) Elliott
     d 9- 2-1841 -bur Hopewell MM, Henry Co
Ch: Sarah Ann    b 1- 2-1838
  Josiah     b 2-15-1840
Eunice (2nd w) b 1- 4-1826, Union Co, Ind
     -dt James & Ann (Mendenhall) Macy
Ch: Delilah E    b 11- 3-1848
  Alvarinus    b 1- 1-1852
  Thomas Clarkson b 3-12-1854
  Morris J    b 4-25-1857
  Daniel B    b 12- 8-1859
  Samantha    b 6-12-1864 d 10- 8-1864
         -bur Hopewell MM

Nathan   b 9-22-1817, N C
     -s Joel & Lydia (Morgan)
     d 1- 8-1870 -bur Hopewell MM, Henry Co,
Rhoda   b 4- 8-1818, Wayne Co, Ind     Ind
     -dt Jacob & Mary (Peele) Elliott
     d 4- 7-1909
Ch: Solomon    b 8- 9-1841
  Mary      b 2-26-1848
  Louisa     b 3-27-1852
  Ruth Ann    b 5-12-1855

Solomon  b 2- 9-1841, Ind d 3- 2-1905
     -s Nathan & Rhoda (Elliott)
Sarah (1st w) b 3-24-1847 d 8-11-1864
         -bur Hopewell MM
     -dt Thomas E & Martha (Bell) Henley
Ch: Franklin    b 4-11-1864 d 7- -1864
         -bur Hopewell MM
Sarah (2nd w) b 12-10-1843 d 12-11-1917
     -dt John & Hannah (Gilbert) Ratliff
     m 12-30-1865, Henry Co, Ind
Ch: Albert S    b 2-10-1867, Ind
  (m Arnette Brenner, 11-3-1896)
  Alonzo     b 11-19-1871

Thomas   b 2-20-1779, N C
     -s Jeremiah & 1st w, Miriam (Overman)
     d 1-14-1849 -bur Hopewell MM, Henry Co,
Sarah   b 4-14-1788, N C        Ind
     -dt Aaron & 1st w, Sarah (Rich) Hill (dec)

## GILBERT (Cont)

Ch of Thomas & Sarah:
- Phebe    b 1- 4-1811, N C
- Miriam    b 3- 7-1813, N C
- Hannah    b 3-14-1815, N C
- Mary    b 6- 8-1817, Ind   d 1- 4-1839 -bur Hopewell MM
- Jeremiah    b 10-17-1819
- Gulielma    b 12- 7-1821
- Martha    b 2- 2-1824   d 6-22-1824 near Richmond, Ind
- George H    b 5-29-1825
- Thomas Jr    b 11-29-1827
- Aaron    b 8-29-1833

Thomas    b 8-18-1818, N C   -s Josiah & Dorothy (Nixon)
(probably died in Milford MM after 1856 & prior to 1881)

Catherine W    b 10-21-1821, Wayne Co, Ind
-dt Jacob & Mary (Peele) Elliott
(Catherine m Mordecai M Gilbert 2nd)
(m 4-27-1881)
d 12-30-1909

Ch: Jonathan    b 6-15-1840
    Oliver    b 12-21-1843
    Ann    b 3-20-1847

## GOODWIN

Charles    b 8-11-1845   -s David & Sarah   m 1888
Matilda    b 11-28-1847   -dt Jehu & Martha Bently

David    b 2-25-1838   -s David & Sarah
    d 11-19-1912 -bur Centerville, Ind

John    b 2-11-1850, N Y   -s Isaac & Jane
Elizabeth    b 2- 3-1858, Ohio
-dt William & Nancy Marsh

Ch: Mary A    b 1- 2-1875
    Bessie    b 6-25-1877
    Bertha    b 12-17-1881
    Raymond    b 6-13-1883   d 1905
    John Jr    b 1885
    Shirl    b 8- 7-1887
    Lucy    b 1-12-1892

William B    b 7-24-1863, Columbus, Ind
-s Isaac & Mary Jane

## GOTTSCHALL

Gurney    b 9- 4-1871   -s Oliver & Mary
Rosa Alice    b 9-14-1875   -dt Henry & Angelina Pervis

Ch: A Guy    b 6-25-1893
    Paul H    b 9-22-1895
    Ethel Marie    b 9-12-1897

Mabel    b 1-13-1894, Henry Co, Ind
-dt James R & Charity

## GOUGH

(Hiram)    -s Enoch & Elizabeth (Leahy) of New Lisbon
Ind (a non-mbr) m 1863 at New Lisbon, Ind
Ellen    b 6- 4-1844, Ind   -dt Robert & Lydia (White) Hall

Ch: Charles Elmer    b 5-20-1864
    Lydia J    b 3- 8-1866   d 2- 1-1867
    Martha M    b 11- 4-1870   d 12-16-1871
    Orion L    b 6- 7-1873
    Robert W    b 4-22-1876
    Chester    b 10-25-1885

## GUERIN

(Augustus)
Lizzie
Ch: Effie    b - -1876

Nancy    b 12-20-1836   -dt Joseph & Jennie Willis

## HAISLEY

Isaac E    b 8-12-1850   -s Jonathan & Susanna
    m 1- 1-1874
Martha E    b 5- 9-1854   -dt Miles & Cynthia (Dennis) Mendenhall

Ch: Edwin R    b 2-11-1875

## HALL

Albert    b 10-26-1847   m 6-18-1873, New Castle Ind
-s Robert & Lydia (White) of Lewisville, Ind
Fanny (1st w)   -dt Mordecai & Fanny (Neugen) Weekly
of Lewisville, Ind   (A non-mbr)
Olive (2nd w)   b 8-10-1847, Ohio   m 8-16-1880, Noblesville, Ind
-dt Charles & Ruth (Elliott) Edison

Charles W    b 9- 8-1854, Ind   -s Phineas & Mary
Clara Emma    b 2-18-1859   -dt Sylvanus Ware
Ch: Nettie    b 6-16-1876
    Maude J    b 1-10-1879   d 2- 3-1879
    Guy Roy    b 3-10-1881
    C Blanche    b 8-22-1884
    Ruby B    b 8- 7-1887

Edwin C    b 1- 3-1850, Ind
-s Moses & Anna (Macy) of Lewisville, Ind
Lydia E    b 3-14-1854, Ohio
-dt Tharis & Delitha (Bailey) Compton
of West Milton, Ohio

Ch: Clarence    b 8- 3-1875, Ind

Eli    m 2- 6-1892 at Balbeck, Ind
-s Obed & Mary Ann (Brothers) of Lewisville, Ind
Anna    (a non-mbr)   -dt Jacob Whitely

Elmer E    m 1-17-1891, Henry Co, Ind
-s Obed & Mary Ann (Brothers) of Lewisville, Ind
Pearl    b (a non-mbr)
-dt Margaret Semuller of Lewisville, Ind

John Jr    b 11- 9-1792, Northampton Co, N C
-s John Sr & Mariam (Grant)
d 8-27-1855 -bur Hopewell MM, Henry Co, Ind
Sarah    b 1-10-1790, Northampton Co, N C
-dt Jeremiah & Karen (Newby) Parker
d 1-25-1859   -bur Hopewell MM

Ch: Martha    b 11- 9-1812, N C
    Phineas    b 9-24-1814, N C
    Robert    b 1-19-1817, N C
    Moses    b 6-18-1819, Wayne Co, Ind
    Sarah    b 1- 8-1826   d 3- 9-1856 -bur Hopewell MM
    John    b 1-19-1828   d 4- 8-1866 -bur Hopewell MM
    Joseph    b 9- 11-1831, Henry Co, Ind

Joseph    b 9-11-1831, Ind   d 8-10-1890
-s John Sr & Sarah (Parker)
Mary Ann    b 1-15-1834, N C   d 6-22-1908
-dt Charles & Elvah (White) Cosand

Ch: William Henry    b 1-16-1866   d 7-27-1866 -bur Hopewell MM
    Elva Jane    b 2-26-1867
    Moses    b 8-14-1871

Joseph S    b 5- 6-1837, Ind
-s Caleb & 1st w, Hannah (Saunders)
m 1-11-1860, Henry Co, Ind
Lucinda J    -dt Bethuel & Amy Symons   b 3- 3-1842 at Greensboro, Ind

Ch: Eldora    b 6- 6-1861
    Aldon    b 3-21-1864
    Caleb B    b 11-30-1868

HOPEWELL

## HALL (Cont)

Luther    b 6-6-1864    -s Moses & Anna (Macy) of
     m 1-24-1884    Straughn, Ind
     at Dublin, Ind
Ida Ann    (a non-mbr)    -dt John & Rebecca (Scott) Haskett of Straughn, Ind

Mary    -dt Isaac & Sarah (Parker) (both dec), of Rich Square MM, N C    b 10-8-1834, N C
     d & -bur Rich Square MM, Henry Co, Ind
     (She may have m William Searcy in Ind)

Sarah    b 9-6-1837, N C    d 4-17-1877
     -dt Isaac & Sarah (Parker) (both dec) of Rich Square MM, N C
     (m John T Jefferies in Ind as his 2nd w)

Moses    b 6-18-1819, Wayne Co, Ind
     d 9-1-1871    -bur Hopewell MM, Henry Co, Ind
     -s John & Sarah (Parker)
Anna Maria    b 6-6-1824, N C
     -dt Obed & Lydia (Davis) Macy
     d 1-13-1899    -bur Hopewell MM, Ind
Ch: Obed M      b 11-14-1843
     Luanna      b 4-29-1845
     Edwin      b 1-3-1851
     Lydia M      b 1-27-1853
     Luther      b 6-6-1864

Moses    b 8-14-1871    m 3-15-1893
     -s Joseph & Mary Ann (Cosand) of Lewisville, Ind
Margaret J    (a non-mbr)    -dt Curtis & Jane Wiggs of Lewisville, Ind

Obed M    b 11-14-1843, Ind    d 7-25-1913
     -s Moses & Anna Maria (Macy)
Mary A    b 1-8-1845, N C
     -dt Nathan & Abigail (Moore) Brothers
Ch: Jesse M      b 3-13-1866, Ind
     Eli H      b 3-26-1868
     Elmer E      b 10-2-1870
     Alvin      b 11-13-1872
     (m Ethel Black in 1895)
     Omer      b 7-17-1875
     Eva      b 11-5-1878    d 7-13-1879
     Edna      b 7-27-1880
     Rosey      b 4-25-1885

Phineas    b 9-24-1814, N C    -s John & Sarah (Parker)
     m (ca 1839)
Mary
Ch: Amanda J      b 10-6-1844
     Charles W      b 9-8-1854

Robert    b 1-19-1817, N C    -s John & Sarah (Parker)
     d 6-6-1896    -bur Hopewell MM, Henry Co, Ind
Luanna (1st w)    b 3-21-1820, Ind
     -dt Benjamin & Anna (Curl) Stratton
     d 9-8-1841    -bur Hopewell MM, Henry Co, Ind
Lydia (2nd w)    b 2-22-1816, Va    d 3-31-1864
     -bur Hopewell MM
     -dt Thomas & Jemima White, Va (both dec)
Ch: Ellen      b 6-4-1844
     Thomas W      b 2-14-1846
     Albert N      b 10-26-1847
     Mary M      b 7-19-1850
     Sarah E      b 5-29-1852
     Robert Willard      b 10-8-1854
Martha C (3rd w)    b 3-2-1822, Ohio    d 4- -1906
     -dt Nathan (dec) & Rachel (Thomas) Lewis
     (now Rachel (Thomas) Lewis Baldwin)
     -widow of Jacob M Ward

Robert Willard    b 10-8-1854, Ind
     -s Robert & 2nd w, Lydia (White) (dec)
     m 12-12-1876 at Dublin, Ind
Alice W    b 2-12-1853    -dt James & Eliza (Brown) McCoy

Ch: Leona      b 8-13-1877

Thomas W    b 2-14-1846, Ind
     -s Robert & 2nd w, Lydia (White) (dec)
     m 9-23-1869, Lewisville, Ind
Laura    (a non-mbr)
     -dt William M & Elizabeth (Lepler) Bartlett

## HARE

Herman    b 3-12-1797    (fr Western Branch MM, Va)
     d 5-25-1862    -bur Rich Square MM, Henry Co, Ind
Rozilla (1st w)    d & bur in Va
Ch: Deborah D      b 11-9-1825, Somerton MM, Nansemond Co, Va
     Maria J      b 8-1-1828, Somerton MM, Nansemond Co, Va
Mary (2nd w)    b 9-2-1798    d 2-10-1865
     -bur Rich Square MM, Ind
Ch: Sarah E      b 7-6-1832, Somerton MM, Nansemond Co, Va
     Rebecca Ann      b 12-28-1835, Somerton MM, Nansemond Co, Va    d 3-13-1855
     -bur Rich Square MM, Henry Co, Ind
     Mary E      b 6-11-1839, West Grove MM, Wayne Co, Ind
     Sophrona P      b 11-6-1841, West Grove MM, Wayne Co, Ind
     d 9-6-1901
     -bur Rich Square MM, Henry Co, Ind

## HARVEY

William A
Lydia A
Ch: Guy Wright      b 2-23-1888, Hendricks Co, Ind
     Ruth Esly      b 12-10-1889

## HASKETT

Claude
Esther A    b 10-24-1871    -dt Isaac & Elizabeth (Peele) Pidgeon

......
Emma    b 8-12-1846, Ind    d 5-15-1889
     -dt Charles & Sarah Clanton

Henry
Mary    b 7-29-1803
Ch: Mary Jane      b 2-13-1842

Anthony Sr
Mary Ann    b 9-8-1781, N C
     d 8-25-1865    -bur Hopewell MM, Henry Co, Ind
Ch: (Came to Ind with their mother)
     Daniel Y      b 1-15-1815, N C
     William      b 3-13-1819, N C
     Anthony Jr      b 5-29-1824

## HASTINGS

Aaron    b 5-2-1808    -s William Sr & Sarah (Evans)
Margaret (1st w)    b 4-16-1801    d ca 1828-1829
     -dt Uriah & Hannah (Hunt) Baldwin
Ch: Solomon      b 10-10-1828
Christiana (2nd w)    b 5-29-1813, N C
     -dt John & Nancy Ann (Needham) Reece
Ch: Sarah      b 9-19-1831    d 12-5-1832
     William      b 7-12-1833
     Elias R      b 6-25-1835
     Eunice      b 11-19-1837    d 10-16-1838
     Letitia Ann      b 9-14-1839
     Joshua      b 12-19-1841
     Margaret J      b 3-22-1844
     John      b 8-9-1846
     Henry H      b 12-2-1848
     Emily E      b 7-29-1851    d 8-22-1851
     Mary E      b 6-28-1854    d 10-22-1856

HOPEWELL

## HASTINGS (Cont)
William Jr   b 3-10-1813  -s William Sr & Sarah (Evans)
             d 5- 2-1854  -bur Rich Square MM, Henry Co, Ind
Jane         b 1- 1-1815, N C
             -dt John & Nancy Ann (Needham) Reece
Ch: David          b 9- 4-1832
    John R         b 1- 5-1834
    Martha         b 4-30-1835
    Rebecca        b 9-24-1837
    Seth           b 3- 1-1840
    Aaron          b 8-29-1842
    Sarah Ann      b 6-30-1845
    William Clarkson b

William Sr   b 1-31-1773, N J  -s Joshua & Ann (1st w)
             d 8-30-1845  -bur West Grove MM, Ind
             (His res was at Rich Square MM)

## HAYES
(Pleasant)
Sarah J      b 1840  -dt Jesse & Charity (Sanders) d 1912
Ch: Edith          b 1-11-1882 (m Ira Jackson)

Silas        b 7-28-1862, Henry Co, Ind
             -s Pleasant & Fannie

## HAYSE
(Milton)
Carrie L     b 12-28-1871, Ind  -dt Jesse & Josephine Bunker

## HEACOCK
Edgar        b 3-31-1858  -s Hugh F & Mary
Mary E       b 4-16-1858, Henry Co, Ind
             -dt John & Hannah A (Jeffries) Parker

John F       -s Hugh F & Mary
Ella         -dt Isaac Whitely
Ch: Bertha         b

Jonah        b 2-18-1788 (Res now of Hopewell MM, Ind)
             d 6-13-1861  -bur Hopewell MM, Ind
             (late res Richland, Bucks Co, Pa)
Abigail
Ch: Elizabeth M    b 3-17-1814, Pa
    (m Elisha Hammer of Spiceland MM, Ind, 1872)

## HEAVENRIDGE
(Samuel)     -s John & Margaret from Blackwater MM at
             Burleigh, Va to New Hope MM, Tenn, 1801
             to Silver Creek MM, Ind    m 1816
Elizabeth    b 1-29-1792, N J
             -dt John & Abigail Bradway fr Greenwich MM,
             N J
Ch: Margaret A     b
    (m Greenlee Pucket at Milford MM, Ind, 1837)
    (1850 - Margaret & ch Samuel & Didema get
    Mississinewa MM, Ind)

## HENLEY
Elmer E      b 4-11-1868 m 8-24-1892, Dublin, Ind
             -s James & Louisa (Stratton), Straughn, Ind
Cora         -dt William & Jennie (Shinholt) Ballard of
             Lewisville, Ind  (Non-mbr)

Harrison B   b 9-27-1869 m 10-12-1893, New Castle, Ind
             -s Isaac & Lydia (Bundy), Straughn, Ind
Nettie       -dt Charles & Emma (Ward) Hall of New Lisbon, Ind

Isaac H      b 8- 8-1849, Ind d 7-22-1915
             -s Thomas & Martha (Bell)
             m 12- 9-1866, near Hopewell, Ind
Lydia (1st w) b 9- 8-1846, Ind
             -dt Jesse & Rachel (Hester) Bundy
             d 8- 7-1881  -bur Hopewell MM
Ch: Walter F       b 11-18-1867
    Harrison B     b 9-27-1869

Thomas E         b 11-14-1874
Oliver M         b 12-24-1876  d 5- 8-1879
Clara Pearl      b 3-12-1879
Jesse B          b 4- 1-1881  d 7-13-1881
Dora (2nd w)     m 6-22-1884, Straughn, Ind
             -widow of ..... Pratt
             -dt Eli & Mary Ann (Jacoby) Hawley

(James)      m 2-12-1849, Henry Co, Ind
Louisa J     b 10-28-1828, Ind d 11- -1916
             -dt Ephraim & Lavinia Stratton
Ch: John M         b
    Margaret E     b 7-16-1865, Ind
    Elmer E        b 4-11-1868

John M       -s James & Louisa (Stratton)
             m 7- 1-1886, Dublin, Ind
Lydia        b 1-27-1853, Henry Co, Ind
             -dt Moses & Annie M (Macy) Hall

Thomas Elwood (a minister) b 11- 2-1824, Ind
             -s Jordon & Elizabeth (Morgan)
             d 11-28-1884  -bur Hopewell MM, Henry Co, Ind
Martha       b 1-29-1818, Ind
             d 1-25-1884  -bur Hopewell MM, Ind
             -dt John & Lydia (Symons) Bell (both dec)
             (Lydia was John's 2nd wife)
Ch: Sarah          b 3-24-1847
    Isaac          b 8- 8-1849

Walter F     b 11-18-1867 m 10- 9-1890, Straughn, Ind
             -s Isaac & Lydia (Bundy), Straughn, Ind
Lola Belle   -dt Sylvanus & Lydia J (Spencer) Ward
             of Lewisville, Ind  (Non-mbr)

## HENRY
John         b 12-27-1868
Mary E       b 8-26-1868
Ch: Alta Lula      b 8- 1-1894
    Lawrence P     b 9-26-1896
    Zelma L        b 8- 6-1898
    Chester Joseph b 5-14-1900
    Mildred Anna   b 7-21-1904

## HIATT
Christopher  b 3-27-1805, Va  -s Amos & Priscilla
             m at Newberry MM, Ohio
Martha       b 3-12-1803, N C
             -dt Samuel & Susannah Stanley
Ch: Amos           b 1- 8-1825 d 3- 9-1846
                   -bur Hopewell MM, Ind
    Susannah       b 7-20-1826 d 12- 4-1834
    Lydia          b 10-16-1828 d 9-14-1829
    Emily          b 11-18-1830
    Samuel         b 9-16-1833 d 9- 4-1835
    Priscilla      b 3-17-1836
    Christopher T  b 11- 8-1838

Edwin W      b 9- 8-1842, Ind
             -s Daniel & Malinda (Mendenhall)
Catharine    b 9- 1-1842, Ind
             -dt Enos & Susan Bond
             d 4- 8-1897  -bur Rich Square MM, Ind
Ch: Cleodus        b 2-10-1870
    Ida            b 9-18-1871
    Elmer          b 3- 4-1874
    Enos           b 9-10-1877

## HILL
Cyrus        -s Nathan & Asenith (Hunt), Carthage, Ind
             m 2- -1872, Walnut Ridge, Ind
Gulielma     b 5- 3-1851
             -dt William & Priscilla (Dennis) Butler

John         b 4-20-1877, Rush Co, Ind
             -s Hadley & Ellen
Elizabeth    b 1-31-1881, Rush Co, Ind -dt .. Fodrea
Ch: Forest O       b 1-25-1906, Henry Co, Ind

HOPEWELL

## HOBSON
Orlando    b 5-27-1852, Surry Co, N C
     m 1- 6-1887
Leannah    b 3-12-1861, Hamilton Co, Ind
     -dt Alexander & Amanda H Henderson

## HODGES
Vincent Leroy   b 7- 3-1875   -s William J & Mary
Vermilla Pearl   b 12-15-1874
     -dt John J & Susanna Stanley
Ch: Velma Lenora    b 2-15-1903

## HOLLINGSWORTH
George (dec)
Hepzebah    b 2- 4-1780, N C
     -dt Nathaniel & Hepzebah Macy of Nantucket,
     New Garden MM, N C & Salem MM, Ind
     d 4-15-1851   -bur Hopewell MM, Henry Co, Ind
     (Late residence Union Co, Ind)

## HOOKER
Orlando    b 1875   -s Thomas & Phebe E (Byrkit)
     m 3-14-1900, Henry Co, Ind
Albia    -dt William & Elizabeth Reynolds
Ch: Elizabeth    b 1- 9-1902, Madison Co, Ind
     Madeline    b 6-17-1904, Madison Co, Ind

Thomas    b 1847, N C   -s Isham & Martha
Phebe Ellen   b 1844, Ind   -dt Joseph & Joanna Byrkit
Ch: Joanna Belle    b 1873
     Alonzo M    b 1875
     Orlando J    b 1875   - Twins
     Hattie L    b 1878
     (m George R Boone, 8-24-1898)

## HOWE
Charles    b 5-20-1849, N Y   -s Lewis & Eliza
Mary Jane
Ch: Joseph    b 1- 7-1872, Lewisville, Ind
     Flora    b
     Chester L    b

## HUBBARD
Joseph    b 5-27-1801, Pearson Co, N C
     -s Hardy & Mary
     m at New Garden MM, Ind
Sarah (1st w) b 2-12-1811   -dt Francis & Lydia (Woodard)
                                     Thomas
     d 9-30-1832   -bur New Garden MM, Ind
Ch: Jehiel    b 7-31-1831, Wayne Co, Ind
     William    b 5-30-1832, Wayne Co, Ind
Matilda (2nd w) b 9-23-1811 (mcd 1837)
     (She may have been a widow)
Ch: Sarah    b 11- 3-1842
     Henry    b 7-13-1845
     Gamaliel B    b 12-13-1847
     Joseph Asher    b 2- 8-1851
     Mary Matilda    b 6-16-1853

## HUDLESTON
Lavina    -dt Seth & Lydia   b 1-10-1777, Dartmouth
                                                   MM
     d 10-24-1875   -bur Hopewell MM, Henry Co, Ind
     NOTE: Her mother Lydia came to Silver Creek
     MM, Ind with Lavina in 1819   Her mother's
     dec is not recorded in the Silver Creek
     records    Lavina came to Milford MM, 1836

## HUNNICUTT
William P
Susan
Ch: Frances B    b 6-20-1886

## INGERSOL
John    b 3- 3-1856   -s Erasmus & Miriam
Josephine E
Ch: Mary Lotty    b 11-14-1884
     Ada Gertrude    b
     Edward Dozier    b

## IRVIN
William    (non-mbr)   -s John & Mary (Martaine)
     m 3-15-1883, Auburn, Ind
Laura H    b 9-25-1869
     -dt Harvey & 1st w, Adeline (Stanley)
                             Gilbert

## JAY
William D    b 6-18-1863, Preble Co, Ohio
     -s Walter D & Rebecca (Clawson)
     d 7- 4-1940   m 10- 1-1892, Henry Co, Ind
Mary E    b 10-27-1872, Henry Co, Ind
     -dt James & Miriam C (Pidgeon) Macy
Ch: Sarah R    b 8- 7-1895, Grant Co, Ind
     Mark    b 1- 3-1900, Grant Co, Ind

## JEFFERIES
Asa    b 10-13-1796    d 3-18-1858
     -bur Rich Square MM, Ind
Margaret D   b 9-17-1798    d 8-29-1863
     -bur Rich Square MM, Ind
Ch: Elijah W    b 12-23-1823
     Rebecca R    b 2- 3-1826   d 12-26-1854
         -bur Rich Square MM
     William D    b 12-13-1827   d 7-12-1845
     Asa Jr    b 4- 3-1830
     John T    b 8-15-1832
     Elizabeth    b 10-14-1834   d 12-13-1854
         -bur Rich Square MM
     Hannah Ann    b 8- 8-1838   d 12-23-1902
         -bur Rich Square MM
     Benjamin E    b 7-13-1840   d 12-20-1841
         -bur Whitewater MM

John T    b 8-15-1832, Ind      d 2-16-1904
     -s Asa & Margaret D
Martha (1st w)    -dt ... Tareman
Ch: Margaret    b 4-27-1862
     Flora B    b 3-10-1865
Sarah (2nd w) b 9- 6-1837    d 4-17-1877
     -dt Isaac & Sarah (Parker) Hall (both dec)
Ch: William H    b 8-30-1867
     Mary L    b 3-21-1869
     Joseph John    b 2- 7-1871
     Orestus Alden    b 11-28-1874   d 1- 6-1880
         -bur Rich Square MM
     An infant    b 4-16-1877   d 4-16-1877
Emily R (3rd w) b 8-29-1852   m 9- 9-1880
     -dt Daniel & Malinda (Mendenhall) Hiatt
Ch: Leroy    b 7- 5-1881
     Jessie Maude    b 12-15-1882   d 4-13-1891
         -bur Rich Square MM
     Oliver Edwin    b 5-11-1885
     Emma Lea    b 1-30-1887
     Floyd    b 1-22-1891

Joseph J    b 2- 7-1871   -s John T & Sarah (Hall)
                                              (dec)
Inez May    b 7-25-1872, Shelby Co, Ind
     -dt Amos & Anna M Crane
Ch: Lowell C    b 8-12-1896
     Marion    b 7- 9-1898

## JENKINS
William
Anna J (or Anny J)   b 4-16-1850, Dover MM, Ind
     -dt John & 2nd wife, Rebecca (Engle) Knight (both dec)

## JOHNSON
Albert    b 3-18-1859, Rich Square MM, Ind
     -s Ansalem & Rebecca (Bell)   m 4- 5-1892
Della    -dt William & Ann Johnson of Carthage, Ind
Ch: Myron B    b 7- 8-1895   d 2-28-1896
         -bur Rich Square MM
     Edna Maria    b
     Gertrude Evelyn    b 6-30-1908

Ansolom    b 9- 2-1821, Va   -s Laban & Sarah
     d 3-30-1884   -bur Rich Square MM, Ind
Rebecca    b 3- 5-1830, Ind   d 1-11-1909

## JOHNSON (Cont)

Rebecca (w of Ansolom) -dt Josiah & Abigail (Charles) Bell
Ch of Ansolom & Rebecca:
    Zelinda             b 10-10-1851, Ind
    Josiah C            b 8- 6-1854
    Mary Ann           b 10-31-1856    d 10-24-1865
                         -bur Rich Square MM
    Albert               b 3-18-1859

Arthur          b 2-12-1884, Dunreith, Ind
                 -s Lindley & Susanna (Timberlake)
Mabel V         b 9-10-1884, Henry Co, Ind
                 -dt Albert & Antionette Stewart
Ch: Russell Lindley      b 8-20-1911, Henry Co, Ind
                               d 8-26-1911
    Marjorie Edna        b 1- 7-1913, Henry Co, Ind
    Wendell Louis        b            d 5-17-1917

Barkley        b 9-12-1843   -s Joel & Elizabeth (Davis)
Sylvia Ann    b 4-10-1854
Ch: Ernest V             b 12- 9-1872
    Elizabeth A         b 3-13-1874

Daniel         b 9-22-1800, Va
                -s Elisha & Elizabeth (both dec)
                d 10-20-1872 -bur Rich Square MM, Henry Co, Ind
Maria (1st w) b 12-25-1803, Va (an Elder)
                d 3-16-1846 -bur Rich Square MM
Abigail (2nd w) b 1-14-1814     -dt John & 2nd w, Lydia Symons (both dec)
                d 8-31-1888    -widow of Josiah Gilbert Jr

Elijah          b 12-21-1851, Ind  -s Joel & Elizabeth (Davis)
                d 3- 6-1914
Sarah E
Ch: Leora                b 10- 7-1876
    Eva Elma            b 4-23-1883

Elisha          b 8- 8-1802
Martha         b 2-15-1808
Ch: Michal              b 2-13-1829
    Mary E               b 2- 6-1833
    Deborah             b 1- 7-1836
    Martha A            b 8-22-1838
    Mahlon              b 5- 9-1841    d 2- 4-1848
    Daniel H            b 1- 4-1844

Emma           b 7- 2-1872 -dt George W & Margaret J
                ( may have m William Ails)

Joel            b 2- 1-1814       d 2- 6-1871
                -s Laben & Sarah
Elizabeth      b 7-19-1821 or 1822 -dt Nathan & Lydia
                in Ohio                 Davis
                d 12- 2-1878 -bur Rich Square MM
Ch: Lydia Ann          b 6-27-1840
    Sarah C              b 6- 4-1842      d 11- 3-1860
                      -bur Rich Square MM
    Barclay             b 9-12-1843
    Marcia              b 4- 5-1845      d 11-30-1858
    John                 b 1-28-1847      d 5-26-1856
                      -bur Rich Square MM
    Mary Ann           b 11-15-1849     d 5-26-1856
                      -bur Rich Square MM
    Elijah              b 12-21-1851
    Alice               b 7-22-1854, Ind
           (m Thomas Nixon, 5-2-1883)
    Emily J              b 9- 8-1857
           (m Garney Lindley, 8-11-1881)
    Ellwood             b 5-18-1863

John            b 1-28-1847, Ind  -s Joel & Elizabeth (Davis)
Elizabeth F   b 1- 6-1852, Ind d 9- -1905
                -dt John & Anna Black
Ch: Myrton L            b 1- 4-1876
    Lulie M              b 9-30-1882     d 9-15-1898
                      -bur Rich Square MM

Josiah C        b 8- 6-1854, Ind
                -s Ansolom & Rebecca (Bell)
Matilda         b 1- 5-1863
                -dt John & Lucinda Newlin
Ch: Eunice Lucile       b 7-25-1896

Laben           b in Va
Sarah           b 12-29-1788
Ch: Eliza               b 12- 2-1811
    Joel                 b 2- 1-1814
    Robert C            b 7-22-1819
    Ansalom             b 9- 2-1821
    Elijah              b 9-25-1826

Myrton L         b 1- 4-1876, Henry Co, Ind
                -s John & Elizabeth F (Black)
Emma Lea        b 1-30-1887
Ch: John Wilmer        b
    Everett Orville     b 1- -1912
    Ralph Louis         b 8- 7-1914

Robert C        b 7-22-1819   -s Laben & Sarah
Elizabeth      b 12-25-1826
Ch: Eliza C             b 3-18-1846

William         b 3- 8-1858, Ky    -s Alexander
                d 5- -1897, Lewisville, Ind
Mary            b 2-17-1860
Ch: Martha E            b 7-16-1879
    Laura               b 4-12-1883
    Oscar               b 1-10-1886
    Simeon P            b 4-18-1888
    Pearlie May         b 12- 6-1890
    Alpha               b
    Ursa                b
    Clifford            b

William G       b 6- 1-1817, N C (a minister)
                -s Nathan & Mary (Guyer)
Anna            b 11-14-1823, N C
                -dt William (dec) & Rosanna (Leech) Mendenhall
Ch: Marticia E           b
    William Elwood      b
    Emily               b
    Mary D               b

## KATEY (or may be CATY)

William         -s Samuel & Priscilla (Mullen) of Williamsburg, Ind
                m 2-17-1887, Dublin, Ind
Margaret Susan         b 4- 4-1867
                -dt George & Peninah (Gilbert) Stopher of Dublin, Ind

## KELLER

Margaret L    b 2-27-1839, Pa -dt Samuel & Hannah

## KENDALL

Dennis         b 6-23-1827, Ind  -s Thomas & Elizabeth
Rebecca Jane b 12- 7-1831    -dt Harmon & Mary (Henley) Hill
Ch: Henry               b
    Harmon              b 7-22-1855

## KELLUM

Nathan         b 1-11-1814, N C
Nancy          b 7-16-1815, N C
                -dt Moses & 2nd w, Mary (Benbow) Mendenhall
                d 5-20-1854    -bur Hopewell MM, Henry Co, Ind
Ch: James               b 12- 8-1838, N C
    William             b 1- 8-1840, N C
    Aaron               b 8- 6-1842, N C
    Phebe A             b 11- 4-1844, N C   d 10- 6-1846
                      -bur N C
    Hermon              b 7-23-1846, N C
    Lucinda J           b 8-14-1848    d 9-15-1851
    Jesse               b 2- 4-1853

HOPEWELL

## KENDALL (Cont)
Ch of Dennis & Rebecca Jane (Cont):
- Mary E     b 4-11-1858, Ind
  - d 10- 8-1886 -bur Hopewell MM
- William H     b 1- 7-1860, Ind

Harmon     b 7-22-1855, Ind
-s Dennis & Rebecca J (Hill)
d     m 7-21-1880, New Castle, Ind
Rebecca J     -dt Jeremiah & Mary (Macy) Gilbert of Dublin, Ind    b 10-18-1863
Ch: Arthur J     b 6- 1-1881
    Mary Eva     b 9-18-1883

Henry     -s Dennis & Rebecca J (Hill) of Cadiz, Ind
m 2-26-1873, Dublin, Ind
Lydia Ann     b 11-30-1851 -dt Jeremiah & Mary (Macy) Gilbert of Dublin, Ind

William H     b 1- 7-1860, Henry Co, Ind
-s Dennis & Rebecca J (Hill) of Dublin, Ind
d 1-24-1932 m 2- 1-1882, Henry Co, Ind
Mary Emma     b 1-16-1863, Henry Co, Ind
-dt George & Peninah (Gilbert) Stopher
d 1-16-1940
Ch: Jesse     b 12- 3-1882
    (m Media Brown, 7-12-1902, Henry Co, Ind)
    Lilly     b 6-24-1884
    (m T L Gilbert, Henry Co, Ind, on 5-5-1904)
    Clessie     b 8-11-1886
    (m 10-3-1906 with Vivian Hamer, Wayne Co, Ind)
    Ada     b 7- 9-1888 (A twin)
    (m 8-31-1910 to Luke A Langston, Henry Co, Ind)
    Ida     b 7- 9-1888 (A twin)
    Walter     b 6- 3-18 ..
    (m 6-10-1911 to Lola H.., Henry Co, Ind)
    Gilbert     b 1-11-1898
    Margaretta     b 1-21-1901
    Anna M     b 11- 6-1903

## KENWORTHY
Oliver N     b 8- 1-1853 -s Amos M Jr & Phebe H (Reynolds)
Isabell     b 3-27-1855 -dt Jesse & Elizabeth (Osborn) Bell
Ch: Jesse V     b 5-31-1875
    (m 8-8-1899 to Myrtle Moffett)
    Walter C     b 1- 6-1878
    ( m 5-25-1898 to Ella Bell)
    Amon D     b 3-17-1884
    Alva E     b 8- 2-1887

William     b 1-19-1816, Westland MM, Pa
-s Amos & Mary (Miller) (dec)
Mary Ann     b 8-30-1814
Ch: Sarah P     b 10-26-1838
    James     b 1-26-1840
    Phebe Ann     b 2- 1-1846
    Amos     b 9-13-1848

## KIMBALL
Nancy     (May have been w of Hartwell Kimball)
b     d 2-10-1913

William     b 9-26-1870 -s Hartwell & Nancy

## KINNEY
Richard     b 2- 9-1848, Ky -s James & Nancy
Laura
Ch: Jennie     b 2-20-1876

## KNIGHT
Absalem     m 8-26-1884
Lydia D     b 6-19-1861 -dt Thomas N & Lydia (Parker) White
Ch: Leslie     b 8-16-1885
    Joseph Exum     b 7-27-1887    d 5-22-1895

## KOON
Eli     b 3-16-1843 -s Daniel & Hannah
Elizabeth     b 11- 1-1846
Ch: Dora     b 1- 6-1871
(m William Lefler)

## LACEY
Eliza Jane     -dt Elias & Miriam (Bogue) Ratliff
b 10- 5-1838    d 8-21-1866
-bur Hopewell MM, Henry Co, Ind

## LAMB
Martha     -dt Phineas & Huldah (Bundy) b 3-22-1836
d 1905                          Ind

## LANE
(John)     m 7- 3-1897, Henry Co, Ind
Annie     b 2-17-1878
-dt Joseph & Abbie (Hodgen) White

William     b 5- 2-1849, Ind -s James & Elizabeth
Anna E     b 1- 2-1850, Ohio
-dt Samuel & Nancy Darnell
Ch: John R     b 1- 7-1870
    Dora B     b 11- 2-1873
    James     b 7- 6-1877

## LANGSTON
(Alpha)     m 9- 2-1874, Henry Co, Ind
Emily     b 3-22-1851, Henry Co, Ind
-dt Ira & Elizabeth (Bennett) Stanley
Ch: Walter     b 6-14-1875
    Clarence     b 9-20-1883
    Luke     b     d 11- -1937
    (m 8-31-1910, Henry Co, Ind, Ada Kendall)

## LAROWE
Nathan     b     d 3-17-1906
-s Elnathan & Susannah    m 11-26-1896
Ida Matilda     b 2-14-1864    Widow of Andrew Smith
-dt Morris & Huldah (Ratliff) Reynolds
Ch: Lula Blanche     b 2- 4-1897, Henry Co, Ind

## LEONARD
E....     m 10- 4-1899, Rush Co, Ind
Charity     b 8-20-1876, Rush Co, Ind
-dt John & Jane Demitt
Ch: Clifford     b

## LEWIS
Josiah T     b 7-10-1819, Ohio
-s Nathan (dec) & Rachel (Thomas)
(Now wife of John Baldwin)
d 4- 6-1886 -bur Rich Square MM, Ind
Julia Ann     b 3-12-1830, Pa -dt Nathan & Eliza Heacock
Ch: Nathan H     b 8-25-1849    d 10- 3-1854
                       -bur Wabash Co, Ind
    Mary E     b 5-28-1851
    Marcas Anselom     b 2-13-1856, Ind
    Sarah Ann     b 1-18-1864    d 10-10-1865
                       -bur Rich Square MM
    Charley A     b 2-15-1867, Ind

Nathan (dec) -s Evan & Sarah from Goose Creek MM, Va to Ohio, to Ind    m in Ohio
Rachel     b 4-24-1793 -dt Josiah & Rachel Thomas of Ohio
d 11-21-1880 -bur Hopewell MM, Henry Co, Ind, as wife of John Baldwin
Ch: Josiah T     b 7-10-1819, Ohio
    Martha C     b 3-22-1822, Ohio
    Rachel M     b 10- 6-1823, Ind
    Susanna     b 12-25-1825, Ind
    Stephen     b 8- 1-1827, Ind
    Emaline A     b 4-23-1830, Ind
    John M     b 8-25-1831, Ind
    Tenison     b 12-31-1832    d 9-27-1842
                       -bur Hopewell MM

HOPEWELL

## LINDEL
James    (Non-mbr)    -s James Sr & Martha
     m 4-1-1894, Henry Co, Ind
Peninah    b 12-8-1865
     -dt Samuel & Mary Jane (Haskett) Cook of New Lisbon, Ind

## LISTER
Edwin    b
Eleanor    b 5-14-1875, Ind
     -dt Isaac W & Elizabeth (Peele) Pidgeon

## LONGWELL
David A    b 1-16-1850
Ophelia    b 3-3-1859
Ch: Charles Albert    b 5-8-1887
     David Alfred    b 10-4-1890
     Linnie May    b 9-4-1893

## LOVEALL
Stephen    b 9-12-1824
Gulielma    b 12-7-1821
     -dt Thomas & Sarah (Hill) Gilbert
Ch: Thomas    b 11-19-1845
     Naomi    b

## LOWRY
.....
Mary    b 5-15-1856    -dt Benjamin U & Beulah Paxson

## MACY
James    b 8-29-1805, Guilford Co, N C
     -s Zacheus & Sarah (Huddleston)
     d 10-8-1884    -bur Hopewell MM, Ind
Anna    b 3-10-1805, Ohio
     -dt Joseph & Rachel (Gardner) Mendenhall
     d 8-4-1881    -bur Hopewell MM, Ind
Ch: Lydia Ann    b 6-7-1824, Miami Co, Ohio
     Eunice    b 1-4-1826, Union Co, Ind
     Sarah P    b 12-22-1827, Union Co, Ind
         d 8-13-1828    -bur Salem MM, Union Co, Ind
     Rachel    b 11-3-1829, Union Co, Ind
     Phineas    b 8-19-1833, Union Co, Ind
     Mary    b 10-2-1835, Henry Co, Ind
     Avis    b 7-14-1838, Henry Co, Ind
     James    b 9-22-1840, Henry Co, Ind
     Lucretia    b 3-25-1843
     Lucinda    b 3-1-1846
     Malinda    b 1-2-1849    d 6-15-1866

James Jr    b 9-22-1840, Henry Co, Ind
     -s James Sr & Anna (Mendenhall)
     m 8-28-1870, Henry Co, Ind
Miriam C    b 7-3-1844, Henry Co, Ind
     -dt David & Rachel (Wilson) Pidgeon
     d 12-15-1905
Ch: Rachel Ann    b 7-13-1871
     Mary E    b 12-27-1872
     Malinda    b 5-24-1874
     Oliver L    b 11-8-1876    d 7-25-1941
     Luella    b 10-27-1878    d 4-19-1895
     Dora Etta    b 2-23-1881, Henry Co, Ind
     Roland Warren    b 11-13-1883

John M    b 12-28-1806, N C    (an Elder)
     -s Stephen Sr & Rebecca (Barnard)
     d 5-19-1887    -bur Rich Square MM, Ind
Betsy Ann (1st w)    -dt Thomas & Jemima (both dec) White of Perquimans MM, N C
Ch: Henrietta Martha    b 3-23-1841
     Margaret White    b 11-16-1842
     William Allen    b 8-4-1845
Lydia (2nd w) b 3-11-1816, N C
     -dt John & Lydia (Symons) (2nd wife), Bell
Ch: Mariah Josephine    b 10-25-1856

John W    b 5-11-1858, Henry Co, Ind
     -s Phineas & Betty (Ratliff)
     d 5-29-1931 or 1935
     m 10-18-1883, Hendricks Co, Ind

Jennie    b 8-31-1859, Ohio
     -dt Mathew & Jane (Armstrong) Green of Plainfield, Ind
Ch: Luther W    b 10-3-1884
        (m Ethel Wright, Delaware Co, Ind, 1909)
     Chester    b 2-4-1888
     Mabel    b 2-18-1894
        (m Alvin Hardin, 1914)

Joseph R    b 3-7-1860, Henry Co, Ind
     -s Phineas & Betty (Ratliff) of Dublin, Ind
     m 5-18-1879, Henry Co, Ind
Julia Elma    b 6-19-1861, N C
     -dt William & Matilda (Ross) Hendrix
Ch: Mary Louisa    b 5-28-1880, Kans
     Ross    b 5-1-1886, Henry Co, Ind
     Reuben    b 8-28-1888

Nathan    b 8-8-1802
     -s Zacheus & Sarah (Huddleston)
Catharine (1st w)    b 6-28-1800
     -dt Jeremiah & Karon (Newby) Parker
     d 2-18-1838, -bur Hopewell MM, Ind
Ch: Pemberton    b 1-29-1825
     Sarah    b 6-3-1826
     Jemima    b 4-12-1828
     Lydia    b 5-4-1830
     Hepzibah    b 4-7-1832
     Miriam    b 5-21-1835
     Nathan Parker    b 7-3-1837    d 11-8-1838
        -bur Hopewell MM, Ind
Lydia (2nd w)    b 10-5-1799
     -dt Tristram & Love Davis
     -widow of Obed Macy

Obed    b 6-29-1803, N C
     -s Robert & Elizabeth
     d    -bur Duck Creek MM, Ind
Lydia    b 10-5-1799
     -dt Tristram & Lovey Davis
     (Lyda m 2nd Nathan Macy)
Ch: Anna Maria    b 6-6-1824
     Nathaniel    b 4-11-1826
     Elizabeth    b 6-1-1830
     Susannah    b 9-22-1836

Phineas    b 8-19-1833, Ind
     -s James Sr & Anna (Mendenhall)
     d 4-12-1898    -bur Hopewell MM, Ind
Betty    b 12-16-1830, Ind
     -dt Cornelius & Abigail Ratliff
     d 4- -1905    -bur Hopewell MM, Ind
Ch: Mary M    b 8-17-1854
     Rachel    b 2-27-1856
     John Westley    b 5-11-1858
     Joseph R    b 3-7-1860

Roland Warren    b 11-13-1883, Henry Co, Ind
     m 10-2-1907, Henry Co, Ind
Muriel Elma    b 9-29-1881, Hendricks Co, Ind
Ch: Miriam Elizabeth    b 8-6-1908
     Elbert    b 9-7-1910
     Margaret Ruth    b 6-20-1914    d 10-26-1915
     Paul    b

William    b 11-8-1801, N C
     -s Robert & Elizabeth
Rhoda    b 1-13-1803, N C
     -dt William & 2nd wife, Catharine, from Va    Stanton
Ch: Henry    b 4-22-1824
     Phebe    b 7-4-1826
     Louisa    b 1-10-1829
     Jesse    b 9-23-1831
     Irena    b 7-17-1834
     Joseph    b 6-23-1838
     Catharine Elizabeth    b 8-6-1843

HOPEWELL

## MACY (Cont)
William A	b 8- 4-1845, Ind
	-s John M & Betsy Ann (White)
Zelinda J	b 10-10-1851
	-dt Ansalem & Rebecca (Bell) Johnson
Ch: Clarence	b 12- 7-1879
    Florence	b 12- 7-1879
    Everet J	b 11- 1-1881
    Ernest	b 11- 1-1881
    Owen Bevan	b 9- 7-1884
    Lucy Bell	b 9- 7-1884	d 10- 7-1884
    Reba	b 10-22-1887
    Alice Lillian	b 2- 2-1891

Zacheus	b 10-18-1773, N C
	-s Nathaniel & Hepsabath	d 8-29-1843
	-bur Hopewell MM, Henry Co, Ind
Sarah	b 5-15-1775, N C
	-dt Seth & Lydia Huddleston
	d 2-29-1858  -bur Hopewell MM, Ind

## MALLORY
William	b		d 1909

## MARLEY
Joseph	b 6-30-1854, N C  -s William B & Sarah
Henrietta	b 8-17-1860, Ind
	-dt Edmond & Barbara Rodgerson

## MARSH
Thomas	b 5-  -1839, Ind  -s William & Martha
	m at Westland, Ind
Mary E	b 11-10-1855
	-dt William & Priscilla (Dennis) Butler

## MARTIN
James Riley	b	-s Simon	d 12-18-1913
Ella	b 3-12-1851  -dt Joseph & Miriam Baird
Ch: Effie	b

Simon	b 1-22-1874
Hattie	b 3-14-1876  -dt Stephen Adams
Ch: Mabel	b 5-27-1895

Willard	b		d 1-15-1916
Ella (1st w)	b		d 3-29-1901
Ch: Edith	b		(m Elza Miles)
Elizabeth (2nd w) b 6- 2-1874, Parke Co, Ind
	-dt John & Minnie Woody  m 2-18-1902, Parke Co
Ch: Milton Simon	b 12- 6-1905, Henry Co, Ind

## MARTS
John W	m 7-21-1872
Margaret A	b 5- 2-1849  -dt Daniel H & Sarah G
		(Stretch) Stafford

## MAUDLIN - MODLIN
William	b 1782  -s John & Ann (Newby)
	d 6-  -1839  -bur Hopewell MM, Henry Co, Ind
Anna	b 3- 4-1786  -dt Richard & Betty Ratliff
Ch: Joseph	b 3- 1-1829
	NOTE: After dec of William Maudlin, Anna
		m 2nd to Jacob Nixon

## MAY
Samuel
Martha
Ch: Margaret E	b 9-17-1870

## McCARTY
Felix	b 9- 1-1820  -s Felix & Mary
Nancy	b 5- 8-1831  d 1905
	-dt Samuel & Nancy Humphries

## McWILLIAMS
Nelson	b 12-27-1850, Guilford Co, N C  d 4- 1-1937
	-s Jonathan & Lizzie
	m 9-17-1872, Henry Co, Ind
Louisa	b 3-27-1852, Henry Co, Ind
	-dt Nathan & Rhoda (Elliott) Gilbert

Ch: Ethel	b 6-13-1882, Henry Co, Ind
    Ralph	b 6- 4-1898  d 4- 6-1899

## MILLER
Frank	(Non-mbr) Of Honey Creek MM, Ind
	m 10-15-1884, New Lisbon, Ind
Mary	-dt Robert & Lydia (White) Hall of
	Lewisville, Ind

Horace	b 2-16-1874, Wayne Co, Ind  (Non-mbr)
	-s Philip & Susan (Baylor)
	m 9-15-1895, Henry Co, Ind
Rachel A	b 7-13-1871, Henry Co, Ind
	-dt James & Miriam (Pidgeon) Macy

## MILLS
Alonzo	b 1-25-1852	d 7-18-1910
	-s John D & Huldah (Mendenhall)
Emma	b 2- 4-1859
	-dt Samuel & Hannah R (Stokes) (2nd wife)
	Binford
Ch: Roscoe	b 10-20-1882
    Estella	b 4-21-1885
    Earl	b 9-16-1889
    Howard I	b 8-28-1891

Carrol	b 3-19-1882, Henry Co, Ind  d 1917
	-s William & Laura (Elliott) (2nd wife)
	m 4- 5-1906, Henry Co, Ind
Laura R	b 2-12-1883, Yam Hill, Oregon
	-dt Samuel & Ida Woodward
Ch: Keneth W	b 2-12-1907
    Olive	b 3-19-1910

John D	b 10-19-1819, Ind
	d 9- 2-1882  -bur West River MM, Wayne
	-s John & Mary		Co, Ind
Huldah	b 12-12-1826, Ind
	-dt William & Rebecca (Coffin) Mendenhall
Ch: Lorinda	b 5-11-1844, Ind  d 1914
    William M	b 8-16-1849
    Alonzo T	b 1-25-1852
    Elihu	b 4- 2-1854
    Millicent	b 4-25-1857
    Mary	b 6-17-1860
    Arthur	b 6-29-1865
	(Married Lizzie McClure, 10-21-1885)

William M	b 8-16-1849, Randolph Co, Ind
	-s John D & Huldah (Mendenhall)
Edith F (1st w) b 11- 1-1853, Ind  d 1-20-1878
	-dt Joshua & Edith F Morris
Ch: Elva	b 8-10-1875
    Lee Roy	b 8-27-1877
Laura (2nd w) b 11-13-1856, Wayne Co, Ind
	m 1- 1-1880, Henry Co, Ind
	-dt Solomon & Penelope (Morris) Elliott
Ch: Marion	b 10-31-1880
    Carrol	b 3-19-1882
    Anna Mary	b 6-24-1884
    Olive	b 3-31-1887
    Orpha	b 1-12-1892
    William R	b 10- 3-1898

## MOORE
Frank A	b 8- 9-1861, Ohio  -s Joshua & Sarah A
Ola	b 2-17-1868, Ind  -dt Peter & Nancy Wise
Ch: Harry F	b 4-20-1888
    Lora	b 6-18-1890

(Joshua)
Sarah Ann	b 2- 7-1836, England	d 1912
	-dt Gabriel & Rebecca B Stead
Ch: Harriett	b 9-29-1867
    Calvert	b 5-15-1872
    Fred	b 7-28-1873
    Walter	b -  -1876

## MOORE (Cont)
Sarah (More)  b 7-14-1814, N C
              d          -bur Walnut Ridge MM, Ind

## MORGAN
......
Fanny    b 7-17-1870, Highland Co, Ohio
         -dt Samuel & Martha J Shoemaker
         m 11-28-1888, Wilmington, Ohio

James A   b 9-21-1853

## MORRIS
Jonathan P   b 5-18-1855   -s Elias & Margaret
Laura Ellen  b 3-23-1860   -dt Daniel & Martha Foutz
Ch: Elma Elisa          b 3- 4-1880
    Florence M          b 10-16-1883
    Charles Everett     b 5- 7-1886
    Ada J               b 11- 2-1887
    Eugene              b 7-14-1989
    Martha N            b 4-17-1892
    Raymond             b
    Ruth                b 7- 7-1895

Joshua    b 7-20-1826  d 11-24-1854  -bur Hopewell MM
                                      Henry Co, Ind
          -s Jehosephat & 3rd Wife Mary (Bell)
          (both dec)
Edith F   b 10-13-1823  -dt John C & Amelia (Foulke)
                                      Wilson
          d 11- 7-1853  -bur Hopewell MM, Henry Co, Ind
Ch: Mary B           b 10- 5-1852  d 10- 2-1863
                     -bur Hopewell MM, Ind
    Edith F Jr       b 11- 1-1853

Sarah     -dt Jehosephat & 3rd wife, Mary (Bell)
          b 9-10-1824
          (m Joel Gilbert Jr in 1861 as the 2nd wife)

## MOTLEY
Samuel       b 4-10-1847, Va   -s John & Martha
Lou (1st w)
Ch: Rollin              b 7-12-1875
Sarah (2nd w) b 3- 4-1865
              -dt John & Mary Ann Williams
Ch: Arrat               b 7-12-1886
    Pearlie May         b 9-26-1888
    Edna                b 10-19-1890
    Rosa Lee            b 5- 7-1892

## MURPHY
Samuel     -s William & Jane (Ballard) of Lewisville,
           Ind     (Non-mbr)
           m 2-19-1891 at Dublin, Ind
Emily      b 7-15-1869
           -dt Isaac & Elizabeth (Peele) Pidgeon of
           Dublin, Ind

## NEWBY
Albert     b 2- 1-1826  -s Frederick & Sarah (White)
           d & -bur at Spiceland MM, Ind
Caroline   b 10- 6-1833
           -dt Richard & Sally (Swain) Hubbard
Ch: Charles E          b 11-11-1854
    Sarah Emma         b 12-25-1858
    Allen Lewis        b 6-24-1860

Jonathan   b 3- 1-1799, N C
           -s Gabriel & Elizabeth (Phelps) (dec)
           d 4- 7-1839  -bur Hopewell MM, Henry Co, Ind
Elizabeth  b 8- 3-1802, N C
           -dt Josiah & Dorothy (Nixon) Gilbert
           (After dec of Jonathan Newby, Elizabeth m
           2nd in 1846 to Amos Kenworthy of Raysville
           MM, Ind)

Mary       b 8-29-1765  d 2-18-1848  -bur Hopewell MM

Frederick (dec)
Sarah      widow of Frederick Newby
           -dt Thomas & Jemima Newby of Va & N C
           b 6-17-1802, N C
           d 3-12-1883 at Spiceland MM
           -bur Raysville MM, Ind

Thomas     b 3-11-1807, Springfield MM, N C
           -s William (dec) & 2nd w, Elizabeth
           (Symons) Small Newby
Susannah (1st w) d 7-23-1830, -ae about 23yrs
           -dt Jesse & Mary (Beaman) Pearson  -bur Spiceland MM, Ind
Millicent (2nd w) b 4- 8-1809, Back Creek MM, N C
           d 8-20-1872  -bur in Kans
Ch: Huldah           b 5- 5-1835
    Daniel           b 12- 4-1838
    Nathan           b 9-19-1841
    Abigail          b 2-25-1844
    Jesse            b 7- 4-18..

## NIXON
Jacob      b 2-28-1784, Symons Creek MM, N C
           -s Pearce & Peninah (Smith) (both dec)
Ann        b 3- 4-1786, N C
           -widow of William Medlin
           -dt Richard & Betty Ratliff (both dec)

## OGLE
Bertha     -dt Mary Ogle  b 6-  -1881
Erastus    b 7-24-1819, Va  d 12-11-1900
Charlotte  b 5-17-1825, Muskingom Co, Ohio  d 1905
           -dt John & Charlotte O'Neal

## OUTLAND
James H    b 10-12-1851
           -s David H & Margaret A (Copeland) of
           Carthage, Ind
           m 11-30-1873, Henry Co, Ind
Elizabeth  b 11-10-1849
           -dt Joel & Hannah (Kendall) Gilbert of
           Dublin, Ind
Ch: Elden J          b 8-10-1879

## PALIN
Huldah     b 12-17-1805, Ohio
           d 10-31-1852  -bur Hopewell MM, Henry
                                      Co, Ind
           -dt Jonathan & Phebe Hunt

## PARKER
Albert L   b 9-25-1862 (res in Idaho in 1915)
           -s John & Hannah A (Jefferies)
Sarah E    b 1- 1-1858
           -dt Benjamin W & Beulah (Stuart) Paxson
Ch: Lily May         b 7-28-1890
    Leslie Blanche   b 8- 8-1892

Albert     b       -s Silas & Priscilla (Butler)
                   of Carthage, Ind
           m 9-19-1878 at Westland, Ind
Eunice     b 2-24-1858
           -dt William & Priscilla (Dennis) Butler
           of Westland, Ind

Benjamin S  b 2-10-1833, Ind
            -s Isaac & Mary (Stratton)
Huldah      b 5-19-1846, Ind
            -dt Jethro & Mary Wickersham
Ch: Florence         b 3-30-1871
    Allegra          b 7-10-1873
    Jethro Jr        b 1- 4-1879

Clarkson H   -s John & Miriam (Jeffries) of Rush Co, Ind
             m 10-25-1883
Mariah Josephine b 10-25-1856
             -dt John M & 2nd wife, Lydia (Bell) Macy

HOPEWELL

## PARKER (Cont)

| | | |
|---|---|---|
| Isaac | b 9-22-1806 | -s Jeremiah & Keron (Newby) |
| | d 10-27-1866 | -bur Rich Square MM, Henry Co, Ind |
| Mary | b 10-17-1812 | d 2-21-1862 |
| | -bur Rich Square MM, Ind | |
| | -dt Benjamin & Anny (Curl) Stratton | |
| Ch: Benjamin S | b 2-10-1833 | |
| Robert | b 2- 8-1835 | d 10- 2-1835 |
| | -bur Rich Square MM | |
| Rebecca | b 8-12-1836 | d 3-11-1838 |
| Ellen | b 2-16-1839 | d 4- 7-1839 |
| | -bur Rich Square MM | |
| Edwin | b 12-11-1840 | |
| Oliver | b 4-25-1843 | d 7-19-1843 |
| | -bur Rich Square MM | |
| Mary A | b 12-16-1846 | d 2- 2-1848 |
| | -bur Rich Square MM | |
| Martha | b 12-28-1848 | d 5- 5-1858 |
| | -bur Rich Square MM | |
| Charles R | b 10-11-1851 | d 8- 8-1858 |
| | -bur Rich Square MM | |
| Flora | b 5-22-1853 | d 9- 1-1854 |
| | -bur Rich Square MM | |

| | | |
|---|---|---|
| John | b 6- 6-1835, Ind | (d rpt at MM, 9- -1916) |
| | -s Robert & Miriam (both dec) | |
| Hannah A | b 8- 8-1838, Ind | |
| | d 12-29-1902 | -dt Asa & Margaret D Jefferies |
| Ch: Mary E | b 4-16-1858 | |
| Margaret L | b 9-18-1859 | |
| Albert L | b 9-25-1862 | |
| William A | b 4-11-1864 | d 9-11-1864 |
| | -bur Rich Square MM, Ind | |
| Laura | b 3-17-1866 | |
| Annas A | b 8-17-1870 | d 10- 2-1870 |
| | -bur Rich Square MM | |
| Charles L | b 6- 8-1873 | |
| | (m 12-25-1897 to Bessie Crim) | |

| | | |
|---|---|---|
| Robert | b 3-13-1792, N C | -s Jeremiah & Karen (Newby) |
| | d 3- 8-1838 | -bur Hopewell MM, Henry Co, Ind |
| Miriam | b 8- 5-1795, N C | |
| | -dt John & 1st wife, Sarah (Bundy) Bell (dec) | |
| | d prior to 1844 | -bur Hopewell MM, Ind |
| Ch: Mary | b 3-19-1826 | d 8-27-1852 |
| | -bur Rich Square MM, Ind | |
| Lydia | b 4-15-1827 | |
| Abigail | b 7-22-1829 | d 3- 8-1846 |
| | -bur Rich Square MM | |
| William | b 12- 3-1830 | |
| Michael | b 4-12-1833 | d 1-24-1838 |
| | -bur Hopewell MM, Ind | |
| John | b 6- 6-1836 | |

| | | |
|---|---|---|
| William | b 12- 3-1830 | -s Robert & Miriam (Bell) |
| Deborah | b 1- 7-1836 | -dt Elisha & Martha Johnson |
| Ch: Marcus E | b 8-24-1854 | |

## PATTEN

| | | |
|---|---|---|
| Elihu H | b 1-18-1818, Ohio | |
| | -s William Jr & Phebe (Embre) of Stillwater MM, Ohio | |
| Eliza Jane | b 8- 6-1820 | |
| | -dt William A & Ann Talbott of Ohio | |
| Ch: William T | b 5- 8-1839 | |
| Phebe Ann | b 11-10-1840 | |
| Jesse | b 9-10-1842 | d 3-15-1846 |
| | -bur Hopewell MM, Ind | |
| Ellen J | b 3-30-1845 | |
| Mahlon H | b 6-25-1847 | d 4-25-1866 |
| | -bur Pilot Grove MM, Ill | |
| John H | b 6-25-1847 | |
| Eliza H | b 1- 5-1850 | |

| | | |
|---|---|---|
| Joseph | b 7-10-1823, Ohio | |
| | -s John & Rebecca (Stubbs) | |
| Rachel | b 11- 3-1829, Union Co, Ind | |
| | -dt James & Anna (Mendenhall) Macy | |
| Ch: John W | b 2-18-1850 | d 3-12-1853 |
| | -bur Hopewell MM, Henry Co, Ind | |
| James A | b | |
| Thomas C | b | |

## PAUL

| | | |
|---|---|---|
| Daniel | m 1- 1-1872 | |
| Mary Elma | b 8- 6-1851, Ind | |
| | -dt Daniel H & Sarah G (Stretch) Stafford | |
| Ch: Infant Son | b 10-11-1872 | d Same day |
| Josie L | b 11-19-1873 | |
| Pearl | b 10- 5-1875 | |

## PAXSON

| | | |
|---|---|---|
| Benjamin Webster | b 8- 2-1827, Belmont Co, Ohio | |
| | -s Benjamin Sr & 2nd wife, Mary (Walker) | |
| Beulah | b 8- 4-1828, Ind | |
| | -dt Samuel & Hannah Stewart from Greenwich MM, N J | |
| | d 3-26-1887 | -bur Rich Square MM, Henry Co, Ind |
| Ch: Charles A | b 12- 1-1853 | d 2-23-1854 |
| | -bur Rich Square MM | |
| Samuel W | b 12-27-1854, Ind | |
| Mary B | b 5-15-1856 | |
| | (m Stephen Sour on 9-25-1881) | |
| Sarah E | b 1- 1-1858 | |
| William E | b 2-22-1859 | |
| | (m Florence Heacock on 9-10-1884) | |
| Ada E | b 2-12-1861 | |
| | (m Nathaniel Stretch on 9-13-1884) | |

| | | |
|---|---|---|
| Samuel | b 12-27-1854, Ind | |
| | -s Benjamin W & Beulah (Stuart or Stewart) | |
| | m 10-26-1887 | |
| Margaret L | b 9-18-1859 | |
| | -dt John & Hannah A (Jefferies) Parker | |

## PEARCE - PIERCE

| | | |
|---|---|---|
| Francis | b 6-22-1882, Zionsville, Ind | |
| | -s James & 2nd wife, Jane | |
| Eliza Jane | | |

| | | |
|---|---|---|
| James | b 5-13-1846 | -s Henry C & Susan (MacGalia) |
| Eliza (1st w) | | |
| Ch: Carrie | b 6-24-1873 | |
| | (m John Copeland in 1898) | |
| Jane (2nd wife) | | |
| Ch: Francis | b 6-22-1882 | |
| Charles | b | |

| | | |
|---|---|---|
| William | b 5-27-1852, Ohio | |
| | -s Henry C & Susan (MacGalia) m 2-2-1876 | |
| Rachel | b 2-27-1856, Ind | |
| | -dt Phineas & Betty (Ratliff) Macy | |
| Ch: Lucinda | b 10-12-1876 | d 1- 8-1881 |
| | -bur Hopewell MM, Ind | |
| Elmore C | b 11-11-1877 | d 2-16-1881 |
| | -bur Hopewell MM, Ind | |
| Gertrude | b 5-16-1881 | |
| | (m William Somers, 1- -1902) | |
| Charlie | b 2-10-1883 | |
| | (m Orla Gauker, 1- -1902) | |
| Laura Estella | b 8-23-1885 | |
| Clarence W | b 9-29-1886 | d 8-25-1887 |
| | -bur Hopewell MM, Ind | |
| Myra B | b 6-22-1889 | |
| | (m ..... Boyd on 2- 1-1912) | |
| Everett | b 3- 5-1891 | |

## PEARSON

| | | |
|---|---|---|
| Seth | b 2-27-1832 | -s Exum & Elizabeth (Ratliff) |
| Sarah | b 4-30-1832 | -dt Jesse & Rachel Bundy |
| | NOTE: After d of Seth, Sarah m 2nd to John T Stuart | |
| Ch: Eliza Jane | b 7-15-1854 | |

## PEELE

| | | |
|---|---|---|
| Edmond | (a min) b 1-14-1823 | |
| | -s Robert & Phariba (both dec) of Northampton Co, N C | |

## PEELE (Cont)
(Edmond & Mary Jane)
     d 1-19-1886 -bur Rich Square MM, Ind
     m at New Hope, Tenn
Mary Jane  b 10- 5-1826
 (1st w)  -dt Jesse & Rachel (Brown) Ellis
Martha (2nd w) b 6-26-1836  d 11-23-1901
     -dt Aaron & Margaret (Bell) his 2nd wife
Ch: Lydia     b

James  b 4-21-1844, Ind -s Henry & Mary (Morris)
Adaline b 12-22-1843, Ind
    -dt Nathan & Priscilla (Morris) Cammack

## PETTY
.....
Maude  b 10- 4-1878, Fayette Co, Ind
    -dt George & Jennie Michner
    m 1-22-1896, Newport, Ky

## PIDGEON
Albert L b 10-14-1867 -s Isaac & Elizabeth (Peele)
       of Dublin, Ind
    m 2-28-1889, Rich Square, Ind
Ruth Ann (a non-mbr)
    -dt Enoch & Sarah E (Bundy) Nation of New
    Lisbon, Ind

Isaac W b 6-14-1839, Springfield MM, Ind
    -s David & Rachel (Wilson)
Elizabeth b 7-27-1841, Ind
    -dt Reuben & Emily Peele
Ch: Mary A   b 5-24-1866
  Albert L   b 10-14-1867
  Emily P   b 7-15-1869
  Esther Ann  b 10-24-1871
  Abigail Ellen  b 5-14-1875

PIERCE - PEARCE (SEE PEARCE - PIERCE)

## PIKE
John  -s Ephraim & Beulah d 4-18-1890
Peninah -dt Hamilton & Elizabeth Powers
Ch: Bertie   b 10-20-1880
  Harry   b 6- 9-1886
  Frank   b 12-13-1889

Wilson b 1- 5-1798, Pasquotank Co, N C
    -s John & Fanny of N C m in N C
Miriam -dt Mark & Nancy Dillon
Ch: Milah or Miley b 1-25-1818, N C
  Peninah   b 3- 6-1820, N C
  Jordan   b 11-21-1823, N C
  Mary Ann  b 3- 7-1829, N C
  Stanford  b
NOTE: After d of Wilson Pike, Miriam m 2nd to Henry
   Palin Jr - m 3rd, after d of Henry Palin Jr,
   to ..... Wickersham

## PITTS
Daniel
.....
Ch: Albert B  b 7- 8-1879
  Alice   b 9-20-1880

## PLEAS - PLACE
Aaron L b 10-29-1805, N C -s Isaac & Jane
Lydia (1st w) b 4-22-1812 -dt Josiah & Dorothy (Nixon)
        Gilbert
    d 5-18-1839, -ae 27yrs,26da
    -bur Hopewell MM, Ind - Henry Co
Ch: Elwood   b 5- 4-1831
  Maurice   b 10- 9-1833
  Dorothy Jane  b 4-17-1836 d 11- 6-1840
    -bur Hopewell MM, Ind
  Achsah P  b 12-28-1838

## POTTER
Clinton b 8- 7-1842, Ohio
   -s Jefferson & Susannah S
Sarah  b 9-19-1844, Ohio
   -dt Philip & Susan Ammerman
   d 7-25-1892 -bur Lewisville, Ind

## POWELL
James C -s Allen & Sarah b 4-24-1856

## PRICE
Christopher C  b 5-18-1844
Martha Ann   b 3-10-1851
Ch: Callie May  b 9-11-1867
  Walter Ward  b 1-28-1873

## RAFFENBERGER
Charles (a non-mbr) m 12- 5-1891, near Hopewell, Ind
   -s John & Sarah (Hart) of New Lisbon, Ind
Sarah E b 10-25-1871
   -dt Morris & Huldah (Ratliff) Reynolds
   of New Lisbon, Ind

## RATLIFF
Amos  b 12- 2-1848, Ind
   -s Jonathan & Sarah (Bogue)
Jane
Ch: Mary E  b 7-22-1874 d 5- -1908

Cornelius b 2-17-1810, Surry Co, N C
   -s Richard (dec) & Elizabeth (Pearson)
Abigail (1st w)  b 9-25-1806, Perquimans Co, N C
   -dt Joel & Lydia (Morgan) Gilbert
   d 6-12-1851 -bur Hopewell MM, Henry Co,
         Ind
Ch: Richard  b 10- 7-1828 d 12-28-1849
  Betty   b 12-16-1830
  Calvin  b 10-25-1832
  Reuben  b 3- 6-1834
  Milicent  b 2-25-1836
  Joel   b 5- 3-1838
  Mary Ann  b 7- 2-1840
  Exum   b 5-16-1843
  Lydia   b 6- 8-1845
Lydia Ann (2nd w) b 6- 7-1824, Miami Co, Ohio
   -dt James & Ann (Mendenhall) Macy
Ch: Abigail  b 5-18-1853
  Anna Flora  b 1-30-1856
  Seth Carson  b 9-27-1857
  James F  b 3-24-1860
  Avis L   b 11- 2-1864
  Phineas M  b 7-15-1866
  Henry H  b 8-11-1868 d 3- 7-1870
   -bur Hopewell MM, Ind

Cornelius b 8-14-1846, Ind
   -s Jonathan & Sarah (Bogue) (his 2nd w)
Anna  b 2-15-1850, Ind -dt Davis & Jane Harris
Ch: Harriett  b 3-23-1869
  (m Jacob E Hecker on 8-18-1886, Henry
    Co, Ind)
  Henry  b 2-15-1872
  Eva Bell  b 10- 1-1875
  (m ..... Haggerman)
  William C  b 2-22-1878
  Charles E  b 8-28-1879
  Morris  b 10- 1-1881

Elias  b 3- 1-1814, N C
   -s Jonathan & Sarah (dec) (1st w)
Miriam b 8- 8-1814, N C
   -dt Samuel & Elizabeth (Morgan) Bogue
   d 11- 9-1892 -bur Hopewell MM, Henry Co,
         Ind
Ch: Eliza Jane  b 10- 5-1838
  (m ..... Lacey) d 8-21-1866
  -bur Hopewell MM, Ind
  Isom B  b 1- 7-1846, Ind

HOPEWELL

## RATLIFF (Cont)

Exum     b 5-16-1843, Ind   -s Cornelius & Abigail (Gilbert)
    m 8-18-1866, Cadiz, Henry Co, Ind
Virginia E     b 9-13-1845, Ill
    -dt Joel & Elizabeth (Dempsey) Baker
Ch: Cora Etta     b 12-26-1867
    (m John Shelley on 9-30-1886)

Isom B     b 1-7-1846, Henry Co, Ind
    -s Elias & Miriam (Bogue)
    m 6-23-1897, Henry Co, Ind
Sarah Etta     b 1-27-1869
    -dt Elnathan & Susan Larrowe
Ch: James A     b 6-18-1898   d 8-11-1898
    -bur Hopewell MM

John P     b 10-12-1817, Ind
    -s Jonathan & Sarah (dec) (his 1st w)
    d 9-11-1849   -bur Hopewell MM, Henry Co, Ind
Hannah     b 3-14-1815, N C
    -dt Thomas & Sarah (Hill) Gilbert
    d 5-5-1847   -bur Hopewell MM, Ind
Ch: Manoah     b 1-18-1842
    Sarah     b 12-10-1843
    Thomas     b 12-10-1843   d 7-25-1863
    -bur Hopewell MM
    Eli     b 4-29-1847

Jonathan     b 2-8-1791, N C
    -s Richard Sr & Elizabeth (Pierson)
    d 8-23-1854   m (1st w) in N C
Sarah (1st w) d in Ind
Ch: Elias     b 3-1-1814, N C
    John P     b 10-12-1817, Ind
Sarah (2nd w) b 12-28-1807, N C   -dt Samuel & Elizabeth (Morgan) Bogue
    d 12-8-1887   -bur Hopewell MM, Henry Co, Ind
Ch: Caroline     b 10-1-1822
    Mary     b 7-6-1827
    Samuel     b 8-2-1828
    Sarah     b 8-28-1829
    Miriam     b 8-12-1831
    Jonathan Jr     b 1-17-1833
    Huldah     b 9-10-1834
    Hannah     b 12-30-1836   d 9-7-1856
    -bur Hopewell MM
    Henry     b 12-7-1838   d 12-20-1862
    Nancy     b 4-10-1840
    Margaret     b 5-15-1842
    Asa     b 3-3-1844
    Cornelius     b 8-14-1846
    Amos     b 12-2-1848

## REECE

John     b 2-18-1780, N C   -s Francis (dec) & Christiana (Stone)
Nancy Ann     b 2-15-1781, N C   -dt ... Needham
Ch: Nathan     b 5-23-1806, N C
    Needham     b 10-2-1807, N C
    Milicent     b 4-4-1809, N C
    Daniel     b 7-8-1810, N C
    Elias     b 11-16-1811, N C
    Christiana     b 5-29-1813
    Jane     b 1-1-1815
    John Jr     b 4-7-1817

Nathan     b 5-23-1806, N C
    -s John & Nancy Ann (Needham)
    d 9-2-1841   -bur Rich Square MM, Henry Co, Ind
Susannah     b 2-25-1812   -dt Jacob & Ann Elliott
Ch: Charles     b 2-9-1829
    Seth     b 4-8-1832   d 7-2-1833
    -bur Rich Square MM
    Ann     b 1-19-1834   d 7-14-1835
    -bur Rich Square MM
    Jane     b 11-11-1835
    Mary     b 5-31-1838
    Joel     b 5-24-1840

Needham     b 10-2-1807, N C
    -s John & Nancy Ann (Needham)
Celia     b 11-10-1812   -dt .. Townsend of West Grove MM, Ind
    d 9-10-1838   -bur Rich Square MM, Ind
Ch: John     b 3-12-1832
    James T     b 10-25-1834

## REED

Nathan     b 11-9-1855, Owen Co, Ky
    -s Benjamin & Jane (Holdback)
Mary Alice     b 10-3-1856, Grant Co, Ky
    -dt John M & Eliza Marquis
Ch: Charles M     b 9-22-1874, Grant Co, Ky
    Eliza Jane     b 2-28-1876, Grant Co, Ky
    Mary A     b 8-12-1878, Grant Co, Ky
    Minnie M     b 7-18-1881, Henry Co, Ind
    Bertha     b 1-25-1884, Henry Co, Ind
    Maurice     b 6-10-1897, Henry Co, Ind

## REYNOLDS

Daniel     b 10-15-1805, N Y
    -s Benjamin & Ann of Cornwall MM, N Y & West Grove MM, Ind
Margaret     b 5-12-1806, N C
    -dt Christopher & Gulielma (Bundy) (both dec) Morris
Ch: Mary     b 12-3-1828
    Milton     b 11-1-1830
    Morris     b 10-11-1832
    Thomas     b 8-15-1834
    Phebe     b 9-5-1836
    Josiah     b 9-29-1838
    Anna     b 9-7-1840
    Benjamin     b 8-17-1842   d 1-22-1844
    Henry     b 7-13-1844   d 1-12-1863
    Isaac     b 3-22-1846
    Martha     b 10-29-1848

Edwin     b 11-4-1834, Ind
    -s Isaac & Sarah (Hinshaw)
Phebe J (1st w) b     -dt .... Knight
Ch: Martha A     b 7-15-1871
    (m William C Willis on 1-20-1889)
Elvira (2nd w) (Non-mbr) Widow of ... Starr
m 3-14-1877   -dt Jackson & Elizabeth (Maltsee) Smith

Josiah     b 9-29-1838   -s Daniel & Margaret (Morris)
    m 6-22-1859, Henry Co, Ind
Lucretia     b 3-25-1843
    -dt James & Annie (Mendenhall) Macy
Ch: William H     b 4-19-1860
    Jennie Reynolds   (An adopted dt)

Milton     b 11-1-1830   -s Daniel & Margaret (Morris)
Nancy     b 2-7-1833
Ch: Samuel     b 5-24-1855   d 8-15-1855
    -bur Hopewell MM
    Newby     b 5-24-1855
    Margaret     b 4-17-1857
    William F     b 6-15-1860

Morris     b 10-11-1832, Ind   -s Daniel & Margaret (Morris)
Huldah     b 9-10-1834, Ind
    -dt Jonathan & Sarah (Bogue) (2nd w) Ratliff
Ch: Hannah M     b 3-30-1857   d 4-8-1890
    Mary A     b 5-1-1860
    Ida M     b 2-14-1864
    Adda Florence     b 10-12-1865
    Phebe Ann     b 1-15-1870
    Sarah E     b 10-25-1871

## RISH

(Alvie)     m 11-24-1907, Henry Co, Ind
Lillian Vadia     -dt William C & Amanda J Crawford
    b 9-17-1883, Henry Co
Ch: William     b

HOPEWELL

SANDS
Israel          b 10- 6-1812
Cynthia A       b 2-25-1819   d 12-14-1889
                -bur Rich Square MM, Henry Co, Ind
Ch: Cornelia            b  9- 9-1851, Ind
    Sadie T (Sarah)     b  5-26-1855
    India A             b 11-17-1857

SANDERS
Jesse           b  4-24-1810, N C        d 1- 2-1901
                -s John & Pheriba

SAUL
George          b  4-30-18..
Sarah           b 11- 5-1853, N Y
                -dt Isaac & Jane Goodwin

SCOTT
Nancy           b 10- 8-1825      d 1907

Stephen         m 8- 1-1887, near Hopewell, Ind
                -s James & Annie (Arnett) of Fairmount, Ind
Mary Etta       b 12- 9-1867
                -dt Benjamin & Margaret (Gilbert) Stratton

SHALLEY
John C          b  7-25-1853
                -s George & Patience Ann (Dufferman)
                m  9-30-1886, Henry Co, Ind
Cora Etta       b 12-26-1867
                -dt Exum & Virginia E (Baker) Ratliff of
                Straughn, Ind

SHEPHERD
Maurine         b  6-19-1896, Henry Co, Ind
                -dt Jesse & Maud (Jones)

SHIPLEY
Mary F          b  3-18-1866

(Samuel A)
Dora (Eldora)   b  6- 6-1861   -dt Joseph & Lucinda Hall
Ch: Leah Mary           b  3- 5-1893, Fayette Co, Ind
    Esther A            b  8-29-1895, Fayette Co, Ind

SHOEMAKER
(Charles)       -s Ezekiel & Margaret     b in Pa
Margaret Ann    b  1-24-1819, Ohio
                -dt Thomas & Lydia (Thornburg) Ellis
Ch: Ezekiel             b 10- 2-1840, Ind
    Elijah              b 10- 3-1842, Ind
    Anna M              b  5- 1-1859, Ind

SHOWALTER
(Thomas)        m  4-10-1892
Ella            b 10-14-1871   -dt Joseph & Abbie (Hodgen)
                                        White

William         b 12-16-1849   -s Jacob C & Anna M
Sarah           b  2-16-1860   -dt Josiah & Ruth (Bundy)
                                        Cook
Ch: Arlie               b  8-30-1877   d 11-  -1913
    Gertrude A          b  1- 7-1880   d  -  -1896
    Grace               b  8- 2-1883
    Eva Ellen           b  4- 4-1886
    Roy Allen           b  1-21-1889
    Mabel               b
    Adaline             b  2-  -1896
    George Nathan       b  1-26-1899

SIMPSON
John            (Non-mbr)  -s Benjamin & Jane (Strong)
                m  7-22-1888, near Hopewell, Ind
Mary M          b  5-20-1867
                -dt Samuel & Mary Jane (Haskett) Cook of
                New Lisbon, Ind

SMITH
Andrew          b 12-16-1865  (non-mbr)
                -s John & Jane (Ray) of New Lisbon, Ind
                m 12-17-1881, Henry Co, Ind
Ida Matilda     b  2-14-1864, Henry Co, Ind
                -dt Morris & Huldah (Ratliff) Reynolds
Ch: Clarence            b  9-14-1885, Henry Co, Ind
    Orville             b 10- 8-1887, Henry Co, Ind
    Clark               b  4-13-1895, Henry Co, Ind
(After d of Andrew, Ida Matilda m 2nd to Nathan Larrowe)

(John)          -s John & Jane (Ray)  (All non-mbrs)
                m  8- 3-1889, Hopewell, Ind
Ada Florence    b 10-12-1865, Henry Co, Ind
                -dt Morris & Huldah (Ratliff) Reynolds of
                New Lisbon, Ind

Oliver          b  6-20-1868   -s Joseph & Nancy (Oliver)
                                        Smith
Annie           -dt Isaac & Mary (Ballard) Messick
Ch: Lucy Bell           b  9-17-1896
    Margaret G          b  1-21-1899

STAFFORD
Daniel H        b  8-30-1818, Ind
                -s Samuel & Nancy (Hastings) (dec)
                d 7-29-1901   -bur Rich Square MM, Ind
Sarah G         b 10-24-1819, N J        d 1894
                -dt James & Ann Stretch
Ch: James A             b  9-28-1839
    Samuel A            b  9-14-1841   d 9-19-1843
    William H           b  4-20-1844   d 2-12-1886
                        -bur Rich Square MM, Ind
    Linley M            b  9- 6-1846   d 1- 5-1871
    Margaret A          b  5- 2-1849
    Mary Elma           b  8- 6-1851
    Charles Henry       b  6-17-1853
    Josephine           b  2- 2-1855
        (m Conwell Paul on 6-15-1875)
    John E              b  8- 6-1859
        (m Alfretta Nicholson on 12-25-1880)

James H         b  9-28-1839, Ind
                -s Daniel H & Sarah G (Stretch)
Martha E (1st w) b 3-31-1842
                d 6-11-1866   -bur Rich Square MM, Ind
Ch: William H           b  8-20-1862, Ind
        (m Lizzie Edwards on 12-28-1887)
    Charles             b  2-28-1864
        (m Anna Edwards)

STANLEY
Amy Adeline     -dt Nathan & Mary  b 7-26-1849
                (m Harvey Gilbert)

Cyrus           b 10-18-1821, N C
                -s Israel & Elizabeth (Benbow) (both dec)
                of N C       d 9-18-1874
                -bur Henry Co, Ind
Mary
Ch: Aaron Hooper        b  9-25-1868   d 8- 2-1896
                        -bur Hopewell MM, Henry Co, Ind
    William J Clinton   b  6-23-1871   d 7-27-1896
                        -bur Hopewell MM, Ind

Elwood          b  6-29-1814, N C
                -s Richard & Abigail (Foster)
Martha          b  8-27-1816, Va
                -dt James L & Deborah (Johnson) Butler
Ch: William E           b  2-16-1838
    Emaline             b 10-17-1839
    Margaret Ann        b  3- 4-1841
    Elmina              b  8-29-1843
    Louisa              b  5- 2-1846
    Edwin A             b
    Laura A             b
    Mary E              b

George          b  5-16-1795
                -s Samuel & Susanna of N C, Ohio & Ind
Jemima          b  1-27-1795
                -dt Jeremiah & Keron (Newby) Parker

HOPEWELL

STANLEY (Cont)
Ch of George & Jemima:
| | | |
|---|---|---|
| Samuel | b | 12-12-1822 |
| Jeremiah P | b | 7-13-1824 |
| Isaac | b | 12-15-1825 |
| Keron N | b | 2-11-1828 |
| John T | b | 10-14-1829 |
| Elizabeth | b | 9-25-1831 |
| Elam | b | 7- 5-1834 |
| James M | b | 4-16-1838 |

Samuel — From Deep Creek MM, N C   d 7- 7-1840
 (Supposed to be about 86 yrs of age)
Susanna — d 12-22-1838  -bur Hopewell MM
 (Supposed to be about 72yrs of age)

STEWART (See also STUART)
Albert   b 5-14-1844, Ind
  -s Samuel W & Hannah (Jeffries)
  m 7- 4-1876, Henry Co, Ind
Antoinette   b 5-28-1854, Ind   d 8-30-1907
  -dt William & Hannah Jones
Ch: Mabel V   b 9-10-1884, Ind

Charles   b 12-25-1829, Ind
  -s Samuel W & Hannah (Jeffries) of N J
Mary E (1st w) b 6-11-1839, Ind
  -dt Hermon & Mary (2nd w) Hare of West
   Grove MM
Maria J (2nd w) b 8- 1-1828 d 12-20-1864
  -bur Rich Square MM, Ind
  -dt Hermon & Rozella (dec) (1st wife) Hare,
   Somerton MM, Nansemond Co, Va
  d 12-20-1864  -bur Rich Square MM, Ind
Ch: Robert F   b 3-24-1857
  Thomas Elton   b 4- 2-1859
  Oliver E   b 3-17-1862
  Maria A   b 12-10-1864
   (m John C Scovell of Spiceland MM on
   6-24-1886)

Jasper   b 6-21-1855  -s Perry & Mary
Lousina   b 3-26-1869
  -dt Joshua & Elizabeth Smith

Oliver E   b 3-17-1862, Ind
  -s Charles & Maria J (Hare) m 4- 2-1890
Mary   b 8-16-1862, Ind  -dt John & Sarah Foulke

Robert F   b 5-24-1857, Ind   d 8- 8-1917
  -s Charles & Maria J (Hare)
Elizabeth   b 1-24-1857, Ind
  -dt Willis S & Sarah (Cosand) White
Ch: Clayton   b 5-11-1884

Samuel W   b 7-21-1798  -s James & Mary of N J
  d 4-26-1872  -bur Rich Square MM, Ind
Hannah   b 12-25-1801  -dt Asa & Elizabeth Jefferies
   of N J
  d 2-16-1855  -bur Rich Square MM, Ind
Ch: Mary   b 10-25-1823, Greenwich MM, NJ
  Elizabeth   b 7- 2-1825, Ind
  James   b 1-10-1827  d 2-28-1855
   -bur Rich Square MM
  Beulah   b 8- 4-1828
  Charles   b 12-25-1829
  John   b 10-18-1831  d 2-14-1855
   -bur Rich Square MM
  William   b 9-10-1833  d 9-20-1863
   -bur at Chickamoga (Civil War)
  Edwin   b 8- 5-1835  d 7-27-1838
  Samuel   b 5-10-1838  d 2-13-1855
  Edmond   b 5-21-1841
  Albert   b 5-14-1844

Thomas E   b 9- 2-1859, Ind
  -s Charles & Maria J (Hare)
Margaret B   b 11-17-1861, Ind
  -dt Isaac & Elizabeth Chamness

Ch: Ethel Grace   b 8- 6-1883, Ind
  (m Laban Johnson)
  Carl C   b 10-17-1890
   (m Jennie Ballard, 4-10-1909)
  Mildred Maria   b 8-23-1895

William   b 9-10-1833, Ind
  -s Samuel W & Hannah (Jefferies) (dec)
  d 9-20-1863  -bur at Chickamoga (Civil War)
Huldah   b 5- 5-1835, Ind
  -dt Thomas & 2nd wife, Milicent (Reece)
   Newby

William T   b 12-27-1867  -s Samuel & Mattie (Gentry)

STIGLEMAN
Alfred   b 8-18-1849  -s Philip & Jane

STOKES
Edmond E   b 12-10-1832, N C  -s Edwin & Susan
Elizabeth

STONESTREET
Emma   d 3-20-1915

STOPHER
(George)
Peninah   b 5-25-1841
  -dt Aaron & Margaret (Bell) Gilbert
  d 2-26-1871  -bur Hopewell MM, Henry
   Co, Ind
Ch: Mary Emma   b 1-16-1863, Ind
  Ada Jane   b 5- 7-1865  d 10-24-1870
   -bur Hopewell MM
  Margaret S   b 4- 4-1867

STOUT
Samuel S   b 4-18-1800
Anna   b 6-25-1802
Ch: Isaac   b 1- 9-1839
  Rebecca B   b 4- 1-1842

STRATTON
Benjamin   b 4-18-1773
  -s Joseph & Naomi from South River MM, Va
   & Ohio
  d 3- 2-1851  -bur Hopewell MM, Henry Co, Ind
Anna   b 9-22-1777
  -dt Joseph & Rebecca Curl of South River
   MM, Va
  d 7- 7-1864  -bur Hopewell MM, Ind
Ch: (came to Hopewell MM with parents)
  Joseph   b 2- 5-1815, Ohio
   d 5- 8-1897
   -bur Hopewell MM, Ind

Benjamin   b 11-13-1842  -s Joseph & Ann (Hawley)
  d 11-29-1869  -bur Hopewell MM, Henry Co,
Margaret   b 3-16-1845, Ind               Ind
  -dt Aaron & Margaret (Bell) Gilbert
  d 8- 1-1903
Ch: Charles H   b 1- 9-1866, Ind
  Mary E   b 12- 9-1867

Charles Hawley b 1- 9-1866
  -s Benjamin & Margaret (Gilbert) of
   Dublin, Ind
  d 10-20-1897  -bur Hopewell MM, Henry Co
  m 10-24-1893, near Hopewell, Ind
Estella   (Non-mbr)
  -dt Charles & Amanda (Nipes) Okel

Joseph   b 2- 5-1815, Ohio
  -s Benjamin & Anna (Curl)
  d 5- 8-1897  -bur Hopewell MM, Henry
   Co, Ind
Ann   b 11- 1-1819  -dt ... Hawley
  d 12- 6-1877  -bur Hopewell MM, Ind

## STRATTON (Cont)

Ch of Joseph & Ann:
- Richard H    b 1-13-1841
- Benjamin    b 11-13-1842
- Malinda    b 8-30-1844   d 5-27-1847 -bur Hopewell MM
- Mary Jane    b 9-27-1846   d 9-11-1863 -bur Hopewell MM
- Isaac N    b 7- 5-1848   d 8-18-1874
- Eli Franklin    b 6-11-1850
- Rebecca Ann    b 11-28-1855   d 8-29-1863 -bur Hopewell MM

Richard    b 1-13-1841 -s Joseph & Ann (Hawley)
   m 2-20-1861, Henry Co, Ind   d 1911
Luanna    b 4-29-1845, Ind   d 3-29-1912
   -dt Moses & Anna (Macy) Hall

## STREET

John    b 11- 9-1804 -s Aaron & Mary
Dorothy (1st w)    b 12-29-1807   d 1- 6-1839 -bur Hopewell
   -dt Josiah & Dorothy (Nixon) Gilbert

Ch: Eunice    b 5-21-1828
     Mary    b 11-28-1832
     John Jr    b

Agatha (2nd w)   -dt ... Hussey of Walnut Ridge MM, Ind

Samuel    b 4-18-1800 -s Aaron & Mary
Anna    b 6-25-1802 -dt Stephen & Rebecca (Barnard) Macy

Ch: (brought to Hopewell MM with parents)
     Isaac    b 1- 9-1839
     Rebecca    b 4- 1-1842

## STRETCH

James    b
Ann    b 12- 5-1790
   -dt Asa & Elizabeth (dec) Jefferies of Salem Co, N J

Ch: Elizabeth    b 3-12-1809, N J
     James Jr    b 7-15-1817, N J
     Sarah J    b 10-24-1819, N J
     Hannah Ann    b 2-15-1826

(Ann m 2nd to William Moore of Hopewell MM)

## STUART (See also STEWART)

Benjamin    b 10-30-1828, Ind
   -s John & Martha (Stratton)
Elizabeth    b 7- 2-1825, Ind   d 2-19-1916
   -dt Samuel W & Hannah (Jefferies) Stewart

Ch: Hannah J    b 1- 3-1854
     Martha Ann    b 5-18-1856   d 9-18-1858 -bur Rich Square MM, Ind
     Mary E    b 7-21-1860
     Henry H    b 3-24-1862
     (m Lula Crandall on 9-2-1894)
     Margaret E    b 7- 5-1865
     William R    b 4-10-1868
     (m Clara B Stafford, 12-31-1891)

Jehu T    b 3-21-1830, Henry Co, Ind
   -s John & Martha (Stratton)
Sarah    b 4-30-1832 -widow of Seth Pearson
   -dt Jesse & Rachel (Hester) Bundy

Ch: Rachel    b

John    b 10-22-1802 -s Jehu & Sarah (Cook)
Martha    b ca 1810-1811, Ohio
   -dt Benjamin & Anna (Curl) Stratton

Ch: Benjamin    b 10-30-1828
     Jehu T    b 3-21-1830
     Anny    b 1-19-1833
     Levi    b 7- 8-1836   d 9- 3-1838 -bur Hopewell MM
     Mary Ann    b 4- 7-1840
     John Milton    b 5-12-1843

---

Martha Ellen    b 5-25-1845
Albert W    b 5-26-1850   d 8-20-1853
   -bur Hopewell MM
Emma C    b

John M    b 5-12-1843, Ind -s John & Martha (Stratton)
Mary Ann    b 7- 2-1840   d 7-20-1895
   -dt Cornelius & Abigail (Gilbert) Ratliff

Ch: Lydia    b 12-26-1866   d 10-26-1868
     Lewis Clarkson    b 2-23-1867
     Minnetta    b 10-13-1868
     Abigail    b 9- 9-1870
     Lindley F    b 11- 4-1873   d 1-13-1882
     John    b 12-14-1883   d 5-25-1896

## STUBBLEFIELD

John    b 4-16-1869 -s Jacob & Malissa
Rosa    b 4- 4-1871 -dt Elwood & Mary E Cox

Ch: Hazel    b 7-30-1892
     Elwood    b 1895

## STUBBS

Otis A    b 12-10-1866, Ind
   -s Charles & America
Annette    b 5-26-1867, Ind   d 10- 1-1908
   -dt Robert & Rebecca A Butler

Ch: Mildred    b 6-10-1891
     Celia    b
     Raymond B    b 8-11-1895   d - -1916
     Elva Marie    b 12-18-1898
     Thelma    b

## SWAIM

(Charles)    m 6- 1-1897
Mary Maude    b 4- 5-1879
   -dt William C & Amanda J Crawford

## SYMONS

Abraham Jr    b 10-17-1809, N C
   -s Abraham & Mary (Charles)
   d 10- 8-1838 -bur Hopewell MM, Henry Co, Ind
Achsah    b 3-28-1815
   -dt Josiah & Dorothy (Nixon) Gilbert
   d 11- 7-1838 -bur Hopewell MM, Ind

Ch: Matilda    b 4- 2-1836   d 12-28-1838 -bur Hopewell MM
     Benjamin Franklin    b 12-16-1837

Abraham    b 11- 3-1828
   -s John (dec) & Rebecca (Bell)
Mary    b 5- 7-1834, Ind   d 4-16-1866
   -dt Wilson & Clarky Horn of Cherry Grove MM

Ch: William Elwood    b 3-28-1853   d 9- 9-1854 -bur Chester MM, Wayne Co, Ind
     Julian Oscar    b 8- 8-1855
     Luther    b 9- 2-1862, Randolph Co, Ind

Daniel    b 6-11-1827
   -s John (dec) & Rebecca (Bell)
Louisa    b 1-10-1829
   -dt William & Rhoda (Stanton) Macy

Ch: Jesse C    b 10- 8-1849
     Phebe A    b 11-13-1851
     John W    b 4- 6-1854
     Mary E    b 7- 1-1858
     Mathew M    b 1- 5-1861
     Sarah J    b 2- 2-1866

John    b 9- 2-1801, N C
   -s Abraham & Mary (Charles)
   d 8- 2-1845 -bur Hopewell MM, Henry Co, Ind
Rebekah    b 4-27-1804, N C
   -dt John & Sarah (Bundy) (dec) Bell
   d 8-13-1887 -bur Hopewell MM, Henry Co, Ind

Ch: Charles    b 11- 8-1823   d 8-19-1840 -bur Hopewell MM
     Daniel    b 6-11-1827
     Abraham    b 11- 3-1828

HOPEWELL

## SYMONS (Cont)
Ch of John & Rebekah (Cont):
| | |
|---|---|
| Sarah | b 12-14-1830 |
| Joel | b 7-18-1833 |
| Mary | b 10-22-1835 |
| Abigail | b 7-26-1839 |
| Benjamin Franklin | b 8-28-1842  d 3-17-1863 |

Luther     b 9-2-1862, Randolph Co, Ind
           -s Abraham & Mary (Horn)
Maria E  b 3-15-1870 -dt Isaiah & Martha A (Doutherty)
Ch:  Mervin      b 7-4-1893 or 4 Gilbert
     Olen G      b 3-11-1897

Samuel   b 1-6-1794 -s Abraham & Mary (Charles)
Ann      b 5-17-1794 -dt Daniel (dec) & Mary Bonine
                       from Warrenton MM, Pa
Ch: Lydia       b 6-22-1825
    James       b 1-7-1828
    John B      b 10-17-1830
    Abraham B   b 8-13-1832
    Henry       b 12-23-1834

Samuel Webster (or Ternal)  b 6-10-1868

## TALBERT
Alvin C   b 11-6-1825, Ind
          -s William & Miriam (Gardner)
Rebecca   b 4-30-1830, Ind  -dt Thomas & Lydia
          (Thornburgh) Ellis of West Grove MM, Ind
Ch: Martha     b 8-31-1850
    Orpheus    b 11-27-1852
    Sylvanius  b 9-20-1854
    Edgar      b 7-5-1857
    Hays E     b 1-20-1861
    Elwood     b 9-1-1863
    William    b 9-6-1865

Daniel    b 3-2-1860, Ind
          -s Sylvanius & Phebe (Hiatt)
Caroline M  b 4-25-1863 -dt William & Caroline Wilson
Ch: Mabel       b 7-23-1887

## TAYLOR
Mary B    Fr Springfield MM, N C    d 8-15-1842
          -bur Hopewell MM, Henry Co, Ind

## THOMAS
Henry C (Non-mbr) -s Eli & Mary Ann of Richmond, Ind
          m 4-30-1883, New Castle, Henry Co, Ind
Sarah E   b 5-29-1852 -dt Robert & 2nd w, Lydia
          (White) Hall (dec) of Lewisville, Ind

James G   b 9-27-1863 -s Isaac & Hannah

John W    b 9-27-1854 -s Alfred & Mary J
Sarah E   b 7-12-1861 -dt Richard & Amanda Smith
Ch: Verna      b 4-16-1880
    Merrill    b 6-3-1889  d 10-20-1905

William
Sarah
Ch: Euna       b 3-12-1816, Henry Co, Ind

## THOMPSON
Joseph   -s Hannah (Brown) Thompson of Buckley, Ill
          m 9-28-1874, Henry Co, Ind
Rebecca A  b 7-9-1849 -dt Nathan & Abigail (Moore)
                     Brothers of Lewisville, Ind

## THORNBURGH
Charles  -s Seth & Mahalah (Bookout), Westland, Ind
          m 9-22-1895 at Charlottesville, Ind
Ada F    -dt John & Jane (Coaltrain) Addison
          of Charlottesville, Ind  (A non-mbr)

---

Seth    b 11-26-1832, Wayne Co, Ind   d 8-4-1912
        -s Dempsey & Jane
        m 2-28-1861, Randolph Co, Ind
Mahala  -dt ..... Bookout
        b 4-28-1839, Randolph Co, Ind
Ch: Dempsey F   b 9-14-1865, Randolph Co, Ind
    John H      b 2-9-1866, Ind
    (m Martha Gunden on 4-16-1896)
    Charley G   b 9-9-1870, Randolph Co, Ind
    Oliver W    b 5-9-1872, Henry Co, Ind
    Esther      b 12-1-1873  d 1-18-1904
    Alice       b 9-14-1875, Henry Co, Ind
    (m ..... Baldwin)
    Frank       b 9-17-1877, Henry Co, Ind
    Dexter      b 10-26-1880, Henry Co, Ind
    Roscoe      b 10-6-1882, Henry Co, Ind

## VICKERY
Martha E   b 6-5-1856, Ind -dt David & Abigail
           m Frank Cosand, 10-15-1879

## WALTERS
William   -s James & Elizabeth (Straughn) of
           Straughn, Ind  (Non-mbr)
           m 6-1-1876, Dublin, Henry Co, Ind
Ruth Ann  b 5-12-1855
           -dt Nathan & Rhoda (Elliott) Gilbert of
           Dublin, Ind

## WALTHALL
Levi       b 2-12-1850, Ind
           -s William & Sarah
Elizabeth J  b 12-12-1850, Ind
           -dt William & Hannah Cox
Ch: Elma       b 9-11-1874
    Elsie      b 8-1-1876
    Dora H     b 9-29-1878
    Albert J   b 5-9-1881
    Frank J    b
    Edward     b
    Clinton B  b
    E Luella   b

## WARD
Charles A  b 3-15-1854, Ind
           -s Jacob (dec) & Martha C Lewis of
           Lewisville, Ind
           m 1-1-1881 at Hagerstown, Ind
Mary       (Non-mbr)
           -dt Amos & Fanny (Shafer) Kaufman

Jacob Jr   b 4-9-1858, Ind
           -s Jacob (dec) & Martha C (Lewis) of
           Lewisville, Ind    m 6-7-1882
Florence   -dt Levi & Mary Ann (Brown) Byerly
Ch: Orville     b

Jacob (dec)
Martha C   b 3-2-1822, Ohio
           -dt Nathan & Rachel (Thomas) Lewis
           d 4- -1906 as 3rd wife of Robert Hall,
           (dec)
Ch: (by 1st h)
    Charles A   b 3-15-1854, Ind
    Jacob Jr    b 4-9-1858

## WASSON
Calvin H   b 2-24-1832, Ind
           -s Calvin Sr & Mary (Bond)
Abigail C  b 3-9-1835, Ind
           -dt Jonathan & Abigail (Charles) (both dec)
           Morris

## WEEKS (or WERTS)
Sarah E   -dt ... Dougherty    b 7-17-1837

## WHITE
Augustus Edwin     b 1-31-1823, N C
           -s Nathan (dec) & Mary Jordon of N C
Margaret Ann  b 3-31-1832, N C

HOPEWELL

WHITE (Cont)
(Augustus Edwin & Margaret Ann)
    -dt Jesse (dec) & Ascention (White) Bundy
    d 7-28-1864  -bur Rich Square MM, Ind
    (Augustus Edwin d 7-2-1864 -bur Rich Square
    MM, Henry Co, Ind)
Ch: John Richard    b 4-22-1850
    Robert Jesse    b 5-11-1857
    Mary Alice    b 1-25-1860    d 3-20-1862
        -bur Rich Square MM, Ind
    Laura A    b 6-21-1862

Charles    b 5-23-1862    -s Willis S & Sarah (Cosand)
Mary Della    b 10-11-1862
    -dt William & Sallie (Shepherd) Stretch
Ch: Leora E    b 9- 1-1897

Daniel T    b 2-23-1835    -s Alfred & Mary
Sarah    b 4-25-1843
    -dt Aaron & Margaret (Bell) Gilbert
Ch: Annie S    b 8-27-1865
    Olive B    b 1-16-1868
    Arthur T    b 8-24-1869

Edgar    b 6- 3-1856
    -s Joseph H & Ellen M (Cosand) (dec)
Mariam T (1st w)    b 1-19-1857
    -dt Isaac & Elizabeth Chamness
Ch: Bertha E    b 11-11-1881
    Leroy    b 10-13-1883
Amanda (2nd w)    m 2- -1895

Edward    b 6-10-1867    -s Thomas N & Lydia (Parker)
    m 9-12-1894, Henry Co, Ind
Laura    -dt ... Millikan

Exum    From Western Branch MM, Va to West Grove MM,
    Ind
Ann    b 8-15-1803, Va    -dt Jesse & Sarah Hare
    d 1-26-1892
Ch: Margaret Susan    b 3-28-1827, Va
    Joseph H    b 2- 7-1830, Va
    Jesse T    b 9-20-1832, Va    d 9-25-1844
        -bur Rich Square MM, Ind
    Harriet    b 4-19-1835, Ind d 3-17-1855
        -bur Rich Square MM, Ind
    John G    b 3-15-1838, Ind d 10-3-1846
        -bur Rich Square MM, Ind
    Elizabeth    b 12- 1-1840, Ind

Francis G    b 2-12-1804, N C
Peninah    b 5-10-1810, N C
Ch: (Came to Hopewell MM, Ind with parents)
    Joseph    b 6-17-1845

George Wilson    b 6-21-1855, Perquimans Co, N C
    -s Rufus & Lydia (Wilson) of Belvidere,
    Perquimans Co, N C
    m 7- 1-1881, Henry Co, Ind
Esther Ann    b 12-24-1852    -dt Thomas & Lydia (Parker)
        White
    d 5-14-1882    -bur Rich Square MM, Henry Co,
        Ind
Ch: George Elfred    b 5- 6-1882    d 9-14-1882

Joseph    b 6-17-1845, N C
    -s Francis & Peninah
Abigail    b 12- 4-1845 -dt Asa & Elizabeth Hodgen
Ch: Mary S    b 12-29-1867
    (m George Petty on 1-1-1892)
    Ella    b 10-14-1871
    (m Thomas Showalter on 4-10-1892)
    Willie S    b 6- 5-1876
    Annie L    b 2-17-1878
    (m John Lane on 7-3-1897)
    Grace    b 11- 3-1883
    LaVern G    b 5-10-1887

Joseph H    b 2- 7-1830, Va    -s Exum & Ann (Hare)
    d 11-21-1919
Ellen M (1st w)    b 8-11-1837, Ind
    -dt Gabriel & Sarah Cosand
    d 4- 4-1878    -bur Rich Square MM, Henry
        Co, Ind
Ch: Edgar T    b 6- 3-1856
    Harriet E    b 6-13-1858
    (m Solomon Stigelman, 9-11-1879)
    Lucy E    b 8-27-1860
    (m Wilson H Cox, 4-5-1883)
    Anna L    b 4-30-1862
    (m Robert B Smith, 8-9-1884)
    Mary E    b 2-12-1864
    (m Franklin Beech, 4-16-1885)
    Albert O    b 2-16-1866, Henry Co, Ind
    Sybil    b 5-17-1868
    (m Hugh G Maxon, 9-15-1887)
    Timothy    b 12- 9-1870
    (m Grace McLean, 5-13-1896)
    Aaron    b 1-18-1873
Sophronia (2nd w) b 4-29-1845 N C -dt Gideon & Elizabeth Chappel
Lydia    b 2-22-1816    Res at Rich Square MM,
        Henry Co, Ind
    (She may be a sister to Exum White & be
    from Western Branch MM, Va)

Robert    b 2-26-1855, Ind
    -s Thomas N & Lydia (Parker)
    m 5- -1879, Grant Co, Ind
Mary    b 11- 6-1856, Ind
    -dt Cornelius & Harriet Shugart
Ch: Irving    b 4-27-1881    d 1906

Thomas N    -s Thomas Sr & Jemima (both dec)
    b 10-25-1818, N C
    d 4-28-1899    -bur Rich Square MM, Ind
Lydia    b 4-15-1827, Ind    -dt Robert & Miriam
        (Bell) Parker
    d 10-12-1898    -bur Rich Square MM, Henry
        Co, Ind
Ch: Maria J    b 7- 4-1846    d 2-25-1865
    Mary A    b 11-29-1848
    Alpheus E    b 11-27-1850
    (m Sarah Henderson, 10-15-1879)
    Esther Ann    b 12-24-1852
    Robert    b 2-26-1855
    David    b 4-12-1857
    (m Annie Hill at Walnut Ridge MM, Ind
    on 8-31-1881)
    Rebecca E    b 6-15-1859    d 6- 6-1860
        -bur Rich Square MM
    Lydia D    b 6-19-1861
    Thomas William    b 12-21-1863
    Edward    b 6-10-1867

Thomas W    b 12-21-1863    -s Thomas N & Lydia (Parker)
    m 8-17-1892
Henrietta    b 9- 7-1870, Ohio
    -dt Robert & Sarah (Tatum) Stanley
    (his 2nd wife)
Ch: Mildred Esther    b 2-24-1894, Adrian, Mich
    Everett Stanley    b 2-15-1895, Adrian, Mich
    Robert William    b 9-30-1902, Lewisville, Ind
    Rebecca Frances    b 8- 7-1906
    Lois Miriam    b 5-12-1908    d 2- 5-1910

William W    b 11- 2-1846, N C
    -s Josiah T & Elizabeth (Wilson)
    d 6-24-1891    -bur Rich Square MM, Henry
        Co, Ind
Mary A    b 11-29-1848, Ind
    -dt Thomas N & Lydia (Parker) White
Ch: Roy W    b 6- 6-1872    d 5-20-1900
        -bur Philadelphia
    Thomas R    b 8-30-1875
    (m Elizabeth Wilson, 6-12-1901)
    Mariam E    b 12-28-1877
    Lydia Florence    b 11-23-1880

HOPEWELL

## WHITE (Cont)
Ch of William W & Mary A (Cont):
- Esther Mary    b 12-30-1883, Mich
- Helen Dora    b 1-25-1888

Willis S    b 10- 4-1815, N C
     d 2- 5-1897 -bur Hopewell MM, Henry Co,
Sarah    b 12-13-1818, N C    Ind
     -dt Charles & Elvah (White) Cosand
     d 2-25-1893 -bur Hopewell MM, Ind
Ch: (There may be others):
- Elizabeth    b 1-24-1857, N C
- Charles    b 5-23-1862, Ind

## WHITSELL
Alonzo    b 2- 5-1838, Ohio
     -s Tobias & Mary Ann
Rhoda    b 6- 3-1845 -dt Daniel & Hannah Koon
Ch:
- Joseph    b 2-20-1880
- John    b 4-27-1884

## WICKERSHAM
Abel    b 1- 8-1804, N C
     -s Caleb & 1st w, Lydia (Gardner) (dec)
     d 7- 6-1878 -bur Rich Square, Henry Co, Ind
Eliza Ann (1st w) b 2- 8-1805, Va
     -dt Exum & Tabitha (dec) of South River MM,
     d 3-31-1847    Va
Ch:
- Caroline Meader    b 7- 1-1831
- Caleb Exum    b 8-27-1834
- Joshua Gurney    b 7-22-1837
- Mary Annis    b 3- 4-1844
- Stephen B    b 3-21-1847

Mary (2nd w) b 9- 1-1811, Va
     -dt Exum & Tabitha (both dec) of South
     River MM, Va
     d 10-13-1896 -bur Rich Square MM, Ind

Arthur    b 9-15-1850, Ind
     -s Jethro & Mary (Stewart) (dec)
Jennie    m 11-15-1879 -dt .....Cartwright

Caleb    b 2-10-1780, N C    -s Jehu & Mary (Kirk)
Lydia (1st w) b 10- 6-1782, N C
     -dt Eliab & Sarah (Stanton) Gardner
     d 1- 9-1820 -bur Salem MM, Ind
Ch: (Came to Hopewell MM with mother)
- Huldah    b 11-28-1815

Eunice (2nd w) b 11-14-1782, N C
     -dt Latham & Matilda (Worth) Folger of
     Stokes Co, N C
Ch:
- Jethro    b 4- 9-1823
- David    b 1- 4-1825

Jethro    b 4- 9-1823, Union Co, Ind
     -s Caleb & 2nd w, Eunice (Folger)
Mary (1st w) b 10-25-1823
     -dt Samuel & Hannah (Jefferies) Stewart
     d 8-29-1878 -bur Rich Square MM,
     Henry Co, Ind
Ch:
- Huldah    b 5- 9-1846
- Louisa    b 1- 6-1849
- Arthur    b 9-15-1850
- Emma    b 1-18-1852
- Eunice    b 9-15-1854    d 2-11-1860
       -bur Rich Square MM, Ind

Margaret (2nd w)    b 8-22-1845
     m 12-27-1888, Henry Co, Ind
     -dt Moses & Delphina Brown

Stephen B    b 3-21-1847, Ind
     -s Abel & Eliza Ann (Bailey) (dec)
Mary A    b 4-18-1849, Ind
     -dt James & Rachel Obrian
Ch:
- Estella E    b 2-17-1873
- G Pearl    b 7-13-1876

## WILES
Daniel H    b 3-25-1831 -s Luke & Rhoda (Davis)

William Davis    b 2- 4-1828 -s Luke & Rhoda (Davis)
Deborah Jane    b 2- 2-1830 -dt James L & Deborah
     (Johnson) Butler
     d 3-27-1864 -bur Rich Square MM, Henry
     Co, Ind
Ch:
- Orlando    b 3- 8-1852
- Lenora    b 11-14-1853
- Mary E    b 3-10-1860
- Corine E    b 3-20-1864    d 8-28-1864
       -bur Rich Square MM, Ind

## WILLIAMS
Andrew Jackson (Non-mbr)-s Jonathan & Elizabeth (Veach)
     m 10-25-1884 at Hopewell, Ind
Cordeni    b 10-22-1866
     -dt Jesse & Sarah Ann (Gilbert) Gilbert

Charles    -s Samuel C & Harriet (Richardson)
     d 7-25-1902 (Non-mbr)
     m 9- 7-1892, Dublin, Henry Co, Ind
Malinda J    b 5-24-1874    d 5- 3-1940
     -dt James & Miriam C (Pidgeon) Macy
Ch:
- Blanche M    b 10- 2-1894, Henry Co, Ind
  (m Virgil Huffman)

Joseph H    b 8-19-1834 -s Jason & Abigail (Holloway)
     d 3-30-1867 -bur Rich Square MM, Ind
Dorothy    b 4-18-1839 -dt Josiah Jr & Abigail (Bell)
     Gilbert
     d 5- 2-1862 -bur Rich Square MM, Ind
Ch:
- Mary E    b 8-24-1860

Nelson M    -s Jonathan & Elizabeth (Veach) of
(Non-mbr)    Dublin, Ind
     m 9-17-1877, Henry Co, Ind
Louisa    b 3-27-1852
     -dt Nathan & Rhoda (Elliott) Gilbert of
     Dublin, Ind
Ch:
- Ethel    b 6-13-1882
- Ralph    b 6- 4-1898    d 4- 6-1899

## WILLIS
William C    (a Non-mbr)
     -s Joseph & Elizabeth of Straughn, Ind
     m 1-20-1889 at Straughn, Henry Co, Ind
Martha    b 7-15-1871
     -dt Edwin & Phebe J (Knight)(dec) Reynolds

## WILSON
Alfred H    b 11-20-1842, Ind (Res Zionsville, Ind)
     -s Thomas & Jane
Lydia    b 6- 8-1845
     -dt Cornelius & Abigail (Gilbert) (1st w)
     Ratliff
Ch:
- Sybil J    b 11- 8-1868, Kans
- Mary A    b 5-20-1870    d 6-29-1873
       -bur Hopewell MM, Ind
- John C    b 6-28-1875, Ind
- Sylva Ann    b 10-18-1882

Charles F    b 4-16-1864, Nabr -s Jessie F

David    b 3-28-1823
Phebe    b 3-19-1818
Ch:
- Adaline B    b 6- 2-1851
- Emma M    b 2-13-1856    d 9- 4-1872
       -bur Hopewell MM, Henry Co, Ind

Jennie    -a widow (wife of ..... Wilson)
     -dt Joseph & Sallie Hodgins
     b 9-27-1842    d 3- -1894

John C    b 1- 5-1799, Westland MM, Pa
     -s Israel & Martha (Cadawallader)
     d 2- 2-1865 -bur Rich Square MM,
     Henry Co, Ind
Amelia    b 6- 2-1801, Pa    d 9-10-1888
     -dt Judah & Sarah Foulke of Richland MM,
     Pa & Plainfield MM, Ohio

## WILSON (Cont)
Ch of John C & Amelia:
- Edith F — b 10-13-1823, Ohio
- Mary T — b 2-5-1825, Ohio d 2-16-1863
- Martha C — b 10-8-1826, Ohio
- William W — b 7-8-1829, Ind
- Jesse — b 1-5-1831
- Joseph — b 9-15-1832
- Sarah — b 11-12-1834
- Isaac — b 9-24-1836
- Hannah — b 7-12-1838
- John Jr — b 4-24-1840
- Israel — b 3-1-1842
- Albert — b 12-21-1847  d 4-19-1848
  -bur Rich Square MM, Ind

William W    b 7-8-1829  -s John C & Amelia (Foulke)
Caroline M   b 7-1-1831  d 5-16-1865
             -dt Abel & Eliza Ann (Bailey) Wickersham
Ch: Marcus        b 6-15-1851
    Joseph W     b 12-14-1853  d 8-25-1859
                 -bur Western, Ia
    Mary M       b 5-19-1856
    Eva E        b 6-13-1859, Ia
    Caroline M   b 4-25-1863, Ia
             (m Daniel Talbert)

## WINDSOR
Lewis M     b 6-2-1837
Rebecca L   b 7-30-1832
Ch: John B      b 6-9-1860   d 3-16-1889
    James F     b 2-19-1862
    William H   b 8-28-1864
    Emma Jane   b 5-16-1868

## WISE
Peter    b 10-9-1846
Nancy    b 6-14-1841  -dt Thomas & Nancy Scott
Ch: Ola   b 2-17-1868

## WOODARD
Robert M   d 1- -1919

## WOODY
John M    b 7-25-1843, Parke Co, Ind
          -s Mahlon & Agnes  m 1-1-1867
Minnie    b 3-28-1844, Orange Co, Ind
          -dt Jesse & Elizabeth Osborn

## WOOLAN
Hannah Adalaide  b 2-28-1861
          -dt Elizabeth (a widow) - now Elizabeth Black
          (Hannah Adalaide was u/c Henry & Elizabeth Black & was gct Duck Creek MM, Ind, in 1877 with the Black fam)

Hiram   b 11-1-1849  -s Alfred & Nancy
Emma    b 6-28-1858  -dt Andrew J & Margaret Smith
Ch: Edgar A       b 9-22-1879
    Arthur J      b 1-23-1883
    Roy Hiram     b 4-6-1885
    Ruby Francis  b 4-6-1885

William A  b 4-11-1859  -s Elizabeth (a widow) now Elizabeth Black
          (He was u/c Henry & Elizabeth Black & went to Duck Creek MM, Ind with them)

## WORTS
William Winford    b 9-17-1873

## YOUNG
Omer H         Of West Elkton, Ohio
Ruby Francis   b 4-6-1885
               -dt Hiram & Emma (Smith) Woollan

HOPEWELL

## HOPEWELL MONTHLY MEETING
## MINUTES AND MARRIAGES

ADAMS
- 6- 4-1868  Rebecca rocf Deep Creek MM, N C
- 9-21-1872  Sarah Jane rec in mbrp
- 10-19-1872  Sarah Jane & fam gct San Jose MM, Calif
- 1-18-1873  Mary Ann gct Honey Creek MM, Ia
- 4-17-1875  Rebecca gct Deep River MM, N C
- 5-20-1897  Carrie rocf Muncie MM, Ind
- 11-15-1902  Amanda rocf Spiceland MM, Ind

AMICK
- 8-20-1892  Martha A gct Haviland MM, Kans

ATKINSON
- 3-16-1889  Newman A & w Laura & ch rec in mbrp

BAILEY
- 11-19-1842  Mary gct Salem MM, Ind
- 4-17-1852  Tabitha Ann & Lucy Amanda rec in mbrp
- 5-23-1854  Lucy Amanda gct Chester MM, Ind
- 11-23-1854  Tabitha Ann gct Chester MM, Ind
- 10-19-1861  Daniel H & w Asenath H & ch Amos H, Nathan H, Edith E & David Milo rocf Dover MM, Ohio
- 8-19-1871  Daniel & w Asenath & ch Amos H, Nathan H, Edith E, David Milo, Mary Anna, Elmer, Louisa & Harriet gct Chance MM, Kans

BALDWIN
- 7-16-1842  Simeon chm
- 8-19-1843  Simeon mcd & na
- 3-20-1859  John, a widower, of Chester MM, Wayne Co, Ind, -s Daniel & Mary of N C, m at Rich Square MH, Rachel (Thomas) Lewis of Henry Co, Ind, widow of Nathan Lewis & -dt Josiah & Rachel Thomas, (both dec) of Ohio
- 5-21-1859  Rachel gct Chester MM, Ind
- 6-21-1873  Rachel rocf West Branch MM, Ohio

BALL
- 12-16-1848  Anna Jane (form Foster) dis for mcd at White River MM, Ind

BARK
- 5-16-1903  Thomas & Daisy & Raymond gct Westland MM, Ind

BATEMAN
- 1-16-1892  Henry C rel fr mbrp on rq

BATSON
- 1-15-1887  James rec in mbrp
- 2-19-1887  John & Elizabeth rec in mbrp

BEALS
- 2-19-1848  Thomas & w Nancy & minor s Daniel gct Westfield MM, Ind
- 2-19-1848  Lemuel gct Westfield MM, Ind
- 2-19-1848  Mary gct Westfield MM, Ind

BEECH
- 11-20-1886  Mary rel fr mbrp on rq; jas

BEESON
- 10-15-1910  Eva gct Dublin MM, Ind

BELL
- -  -1841  Thomas & Hannah & ch are CHARTER MBRS
- 4-17-1841  Thomas appt to a comm to procure the necessary Record Books
- 5-15-1841  Thomas appt to comm to att QM
- 6-19-1841  Thomas appt to a comm
- 7-17-1841  Thomas appt recorder of Births & Deaths
- 10-  -1841  Thomas appt Asst-Clerk of MM
- 5-16-1846  Lydia rocf Milford MM, Ind
- 6-13-1847  Hannah named an Elder
- 2-20-1850  Martha, -dt Thomas & Jerusha (dec) of Henry Co, Ind, m at Hopewell MH, Isaac W Coffin of Walnut Ridge MM, Hancock Co, Ind
- 3-22-1854  Margaret, -dt Thomas & Jerusha (dec) of Henry Co, Ind, m at Hopewell MH, Christopher Morris of Milford MM, Ind, Wayne Co
- 5-23-1855  Sarah, -dt Thomas & Jerusha (dec), of Hopewell MM, Henry Co, Ind, m at Hopewell MH, Mordecai Parry of Richmond MM, Wayne Co, Ind
- 12-20-1855  Lydia of Henry Co, Ind, -dt John & Lydia, (both dec), lately of Wayne Co, Ind, m at Rich Square MH, John M Macy of Henry Co, Ind
- 4-17-1886  Mary E (form Stewart) gct Dublin MM, Ind
- 8-18-1886  Jesse chm of mcd
- 9-21-1889  Lydia gct Dublin MM, Ind
- 9-21-1889  Jesse & minor s, John, gct Spiceland MM, Ind
- 9-21-1889  Enos gct Dublin MM, Ind
- 4-20-1895  Alfred W & w Mary E & ch Glenn Alice & Gladys Marian rocf Westland MM

BERT
- 8-21-1841  Tacy (form Foulke) dis for mcd

BINFORD
- -  -1841  Samuel B & w Anna & ch are CHARTER MBRS
- 4-17-1841  Samuel B appt to a comm
- 4-17-1841  Anna J appt to comm to care for indigent persons
- 4-17-1841  Samuel B app to comm on Education
- 9-18-1841  Samuel B appt Librarian at Rich Square MM in place of Nathan Reece (dec)
- 12-24-1857  Samuel B of Rich Square MM, Henry Co, Ind -s Samuel & Mary (both dec), of Prince George Co, Va, m at Rich Square MH, Hannah R (Stokes) Cox, widow of William Cox of Henry Co, Ind
- 7-25-1861  Benjamin H of Walnut Ridge MM, Rush Co, Ind, -s Robert & Martha of Hancock Co, Ind, m at Rich Square MH, Lydia Ann Johnson of Henry Co, Ind
- 10-19-1861  Lydia Ann gct Walnut Ridge MM, Ind
- 2-15-1862  Oliver gct Rich Square MM, Ia
- 9-24-1863  William P of Walnut Ridge MM, Rush Co, Ind -s Micajah C & Susannah of same place, m at Rich Square MH, Henrietta M Macy of Henry Co, Ind
- 12-19-1863  Henrietta M gct Walnut Ridge MM, Ind
- 4-15-1865  William P gct Rich Square MM, Ia
- 9-16-1867  Jared P of Carthage MM, Rush Co, Ind, -s William & Mary (dec) of same place, m at Rich Square MH, Ind, Emily Lamb of Hopewell MM, Henry Co, Ind
- 1-18-1868  Emily L gct Kokomo MM, Ind
- 4-18-1868  Mary S Gardner (form Binford) chm for mcd
- 3-18-1871  Hannah E & dt Mary E rocf White River MM, Ind
- 10-23-1872  William P of Hancock Co, Ind, -s Micajah C & Susannah of Rush Co, Ind, m at Hopewell MH, Esther Gilbert of Henry Co, Ind
- 12-21-1872  Esther gct Walnut Ridge MM, Ind
- 5-17-1873  Deborah A (form Butler) chm for mcd
- 6-21-1873  Deborah Ann gct Westland MM, Ind
- 6-19-1875  James H & Hannah E & minor dt Mary gct Walnut Ridge MM, Ind
- 10-20-1888  Arlington & w Emma gct Westfield MM, Hamilton Co, Ind
- 4-15-1899  Julia P rocf Carthage MM, Ind
- 6-16-1900  William P & w Esther G gct Walnut Ridge MM, Ind
- 1-17-1903  Susanna R & s Edward rocf South 8th St MM, Richmond, Ind
- 3-16-1912  Susan gct Carthage MM, Ind

BIRK
- 4-18-1868  Elmina (form Bond) mcd; rel fr mbrp on rq

BLACK
- 2-19-1876  Elizabeth & dt Adalaide Woollan & s William A Woollan rocf Spiceland MM, Ind
- 7-21-1877  Henry & w Elizabeth & minor ch Sintha Ethel Black & William A & Hannah Adalaide Woollan gct Duck Creek MM, Ind

HOPEWELL

BOGUE
5-21-1849   Benjamin & w Milly & ch Huldah, Samuel, Joshua, Allen, Asenath, Newby & Mary Ellen rocf Milford MM, Ind
12-21-1850  Benjamin & w Milly & minor ch Huldah, Samuel, Joshua, Allen, Asenath, Newby, Mary Ellen & Joseph D gct Milford MM, Ind
12-21-1853  Amos of Henry Co, Ind, -s Newby & Hannah of same place, m at Hopewell MH, Phebe Reynolds of Henry Co, Ind
11-17-1860  Amos & w Phebe & minor ch John Albert, Huldah, Mary E & Abigail gct Birch Lake MM, Mich
5-16-1863   Amos & w Phebe & ch John Albert, Huldah, Mary Elizabeth & Abigail rocf Birch Lake MM, Mich
6-16-1877   Amos & w Phebe & minor ch Mary, Abigail, Henry, Newby, Anna N, Josiah M & Nancy E gct Greenwood MM, Ia
6-16-1877   Huldah gct Greenwood MM, Ia
6-16-1877   John A gct Greenwood MM, Ia

BOND
-  -1841    Edward & w Ann & ch are CHARTER MBRS
4-17-1841   Edward appt to comm to att funerals
8-21-1841   Cyrus rocf Sparrow Creek MM, Ind; -end by Milford MM, Ind
7-18-1846   Lucinda, Athelinda, Jediah, Benjamin F & Elizabeth Ann, minor ch of Edward Bond, gct Salem MM, Ia
8-15-1846   Jediah & w Elmina & ch Luzena S, Martha Jane, Rebecca & Angelina rocf Salem MM, Ia
3-20-1847   Edward gct Salem MM, Ia
11-16-1850  Jonathan dis for mcd
12-20-1851  Cyrus gct Whitewater MM, Ind
2-26-1852   Luzena S, -dt Jediah & Elmina (dec), Henry Co, Ind, m at Rich Square MH, William P Hastings of Henry Co, Ind
10-15-1859  Martha Jane Foreman (form Bond) dis for mcd
4-18-1868   Elmina Birk (form Bond) mcd & rel fr mbrp on rq
10-18-1873  Angeline Lowery (form Bond) chm of mcd

BOONE
2-19-1887   James W, Mary & Ella rec in mbrp
3-17-1894   Mary & Ella glt M E Ch, Lewisville, Ind
1-19-1895   Ella gct New Castle MM, Ind
3-19-1904   George R & Mattie gct Knightstown MM, Ind

BRADBURY
6-20-1891   Anna B rocf New Castle MM, Ind

BRIDGET
4-20-1895   Mattie rel fr mbrp on rq; jas

BROOMELL
7-11-1867   James H of Chicago, Cook Co, Ill, -s John & Esther (dec), Chester Co, Pa, m at Rich Square MH, Mary Annis Wickersham of Henry Co, Ind
1-18-1868   Mary Annis gct Chicago MM, Ill

BROTHERS
10-20-1860  Nathan & w Abigail & ch Mary Ann, Sarah R, Rebecca A, Melissa, Maria E, Joel G & Ira S rocf Milford MM, Ind
2-25-1863   Sarah R, -dt Nathan & Abigail of Henry Co, Ind, m Ira G Bundy of Hopewell MM, Henry Co, Ind
2-22-1865   Mary A, -dt Nathan & Abigail of Henry Co, Ind, m at Hopewell MH, Obed M Hall of Henry Co, Ind
1-17-1880   Joel gct Peace MM, Kans
4-18-1885   Ira S (rec in mbrp with wife) gct Sterling MM, Kans
12-18-1902  Nathan & Abigail gct Sterling MM, Kans

BUFKIN
1-19-1867   Tirza Jane Redding (form Bufkin) chm of mcd at White River MM, Ind

BUNDY
-  -1841    Jesse & w Rachel & ch are CHARTER MBRS
4-17-1841   Jesse appt to comm to have care of indigent persons
4-17-1841   Rachel appt to a comm
2-19-1845   Martha, -dt Jesse & Rachel of Henry Co, Ind, m at Hopewell MH, Mordecai M Gilbert of Henry Co, Ind
3-15-1845   Priscilla, -widow of Samuel, & her ch Sarah, Joseph & Rachel rocf Walnut Ridge MM, Ind -end to Milford MM, Ind
3-21-1849   Mary, -dt Jesse & Rachel of Henry Co, Ind, m at Hopewell MH, George H Gilbert of Henry Co, Ind
8-24-1853   Sarah, -dt Jesse & Rachel of Henry Co, Ind, m at Hopewell MH, Seth Pearson of Henry Co, Ind
10-22-1856  William H of Henry Co, Ind, -s Jesse & Rachel of same place, m at Hopewell MH, Nancy Ratliff of Henry Co, Ind
5-19-1860   Francis gct Vermilion MM, Ill
12-15-1860  William H & w Nancy & minor ch Melissa gct Vermilion MM, Ill
7-25-1861   William of Walnut Ridge MM, Rush Co, Ind, -s Elias & Sarah of same place, m at Rich Square MH, Mary A Stuart of Henry Co, Ind
5-17-1862   William rocf White River MM, Ind
2-25-1863   Ira G of Henry Co, Ind, -s Jesse & Rachel of same place, m at Hopewell MH, Sarah R Brothers of Henry Co, Ind
1-21-1865   Nancy & fam rocf Honey Creek MM, Ind; -end by Westfield & Duck Creek MM, Ind
9-15-1865   William & w Mary A & ch Ada Eldora & Albert Luther gct Walnut Ridge MM, Ind
9-15-1865   Ira & w Sarah R & minor s Charles Warren gct Walnut Ridge MM, Ind
1-17-1867   Francis A gct Vermilion MM, Ill
8-17-1867   Lydia Henley (form Bundy) chm of mcd
11-2-1869   Ira & w Sarah R & s Charles Warren rocf Spiceland MM, Ind
12-17-1870  Sarah & her minor s Charles Warren Bundy gct Ash Grove MM, Ill
4-20-1872   Ira S gct Ash Grove MM, Ill
9-20-1890   Katie rec in mbrp
7-18-1891   Katie gct New Castle MM, Ind

BURT
3-18-1876   Susan rec in mbrp (wife of William Burt)

BUTLER
-  -1841    William & w Susanna & ch are CHARTER MBRS
-  -1841    James L & w Deborah & ch are CHARTER MBRS
4-17-1841   James L appt to comm for care of indigent persons
4-17-1841   James L appt to comm to att funerals
5-15-1841   James L appt to comm to att QM
9-18-1841   James L appt a trustee at Rich Square MM, of land purchased from Edward Bond
10- -1841   James L appt an Overseer in place of Nathan Reece, dec
9-18-1841   (John) & w Julia & ch William Henry, John Stanton & Elizabeth J gct Westfield MM, Ind
8-20-1842   John C rpt na
3-16-1844   William & w Susanna & minor ch Joshua, Margaret, Charles & Melissa gct Milford MM, Ind
8-17-1844   Alfred gct Spiceland MM, Ind to m Elizabeth Morgan
6-21-1845   Elizabeth rocf Spiceland MM, Ind
9-22-1846   William of Henry Co, Ind, -s James L & Deborah, m at Hopewell MH, Priscilla Dennis of Henry Co, Ind
12-18-1847  Julia, wife of John, & ch William Henry, John Stanton & Elizabeth J rocf Westfield MM, Ind
12-18-1847  Joseph gct Duck Creek MM, Ind to m Sarah Ann Pickering
1-15-1848   Alfred & w Elizabeth & minor s Benjamin gct Spiceland MM, Ind
3-18-1848   James B dis for mcd
7-15-1848   Sarah Ann rocf Duck Creek MM, Ind

## BUTLER (Cont)

|  |  |
|---|---|
| 2-17-1849 | Joseph & w Sarah Ann gct Duck Creek MM, Ind |
| 9-20-1849 | William E of Union Co, Ind, -s Stephen (dec) & Louisa of same place, m at Rich Square MH, Sarah Foulke of Henry Co, Ind |
| 10-20-1849 | Elizabeth dis for att a mcd |
| 10-20-1849 | Martha Ann dis for att a mcd |
| 3-16-1850 | Sarah gct Whitewater MM, Ind |
| 6-26-1851 | Deborah Jane, -dt James L & Deborah of Henry Co, Ind, m at Rich Square MH, William D Wiles of Henry Co, Ind |
| 12-20-1851 | William & w Priscilla & minor ch Horace & Gulielma gct Honey Creek MM, Ind |
| 1-21-1854 | Mary L Grey (form Butler) dis for mcd |
| 3-18-1854 | Rebecca J dis for att a mcd |
| 7-15-1854 | Elizabeth Shalley (form Butler) dis for mcd |
| 7-15-1854 | William H dis for na & taking an oath |
| 10-21-1854 | Alfred & w Elizabeth & minor ch Benjamin M & Lindley H gct Whitewater MM, Ind |
| 3-19-1856 | Mary E Miles (form Butler) dis for mcd |
| 5-16-1857 | Benjamin rocf Milford MM, Ind |
| 7-22-1857 | Benjamin J of Henry Co, Ind, -s Ansalem & Ruth of Wayne Co, Ind, m at Hopewell MH, Lydia Gilbert of Henry Co, Ind |
| 8-18-1860 | Sarah, wife of William E, & son Joseph Coridon Butler rocf Whitewater MM, Ind |
| 2-21-1863 | William & w Priscilla & ch Gulielma, Deborah Ann, Mary & Eunice rocf White Lick MM, Ind |
| 11-21-1863 | Sarah, wife of William E, & s Joseph C gct Rocksylvania MM, Ia |
| 6-15-1872 | Gulielma Hill (form Butler) chm of mcd |
| 5-17-1873 | Deborah A Binford (form Butler) chm of mcd |
| 2-15-1879 | William & w Priscilla & minor ch William Thomas & J Ellis gct Westland MM, Ind |
| 1-17-1880 | Mary gct Westland MM, Ind |
| 1-17-1903 | William rel fr mbrp on rq |

## BYERS

|  |  |
|---|---|
| 3-19-1887 | John rec in mbrp |
| 6-18-1887 | Margaret L rocf Spiceland MM, Ind |
| 3-19-1894 | Margaret gct New Castle MM, Ind |

## CAIN - CANE

|  |  |
|---|---|
| 9-21-1867 | Exaline & ch Everett rocf Duck Creek MM, Ind, -end by Spiceland MM |
| 7-17-1869 | Exaline C, wife of James, & her minor ch Edward Everet & Orville gct Duck Creek MM, Ind |

## CARR

|  |  |
|---|---|
| 6-17-1893 | Joseph & w Almira & dt rocf West Grove MM, Ind |

## CARTER

|  |  |
|---|---|
| 8-17-1867 | Margaret Carter (form Ratliff) chm of mcd |

## CATEY - KATEY

|  |  |
|---|---|
| 9-21-1889 | Margaret Susan (form Stopher) gct Dover MM, Ind |

## CLANTON

|  |  |
|---|---|
| 3-21-1868 | Margaret Emma rec in mbrp |

## CLEAVER

|  |  |
|---|---|
| 11-16-1907 | William J & w Evelyn & minor ch Lowell, Allen, Abe & Marie gct Hopewell MM, Vermilion Co, Ind |

## COFFIN

|  |  |
|---|---|
| 8-19-1843 | Cyrus dis for mcd |
| 2-20-1850 | Isaac N of Walnut Ridge MM, Hancock Co, Ind, -s Elihu & Sarah of same place, m at Hopewell MH, Martha Bell of Henry Co, Ind |
| 2-17-1855 | Isaac N & w Martha & s Charles W gct Sugar Plain MM, Ind |
| 6-18-1881 | Aaron rocf Westland MM, Ind |
| 3-17-1883 | Emma A & s Glenn rec in mbrp |
| 5-21-1892 | Aaron & w Emma & minor ch Glenn, Eva & Leland gct Carthage MM, Ind |
| 5-15-1909 | Estella M & minor ch W Harrold & Wilbur M gct Greensfork MM |

## COLTRAIN

|  |  |
|---|---|
| 2-19-1887 | Maude rec in mbrp |

## CONNER

|  |  |
|---|---|
| 8-17-1907 | Francis Pearce gct Dublin MM, Ind |

## COOK

|  |  |
|---|---|
| - -1841 | Isaac & w Elizabeth & their fam are CHARTER MBRS |
| - -1841 | John & minor ch are CHARTER MBRS |
| 6-19-1841 | Isaac appt to a comm |
| 8-20-1842 | James dis for mcd |
| 9-20-1848 | Mary, -dt Isaac & Elizabeth of Henry Co, Ind, m at Hopewell MH, David Kendal of Duck Creek MM, Henry Co, Ind |
| 1-17-1857 | Susanna Foster (form Cook) dis for mcd |
| 12-19-1857 | Ruth rocf White River MM, Ind |
| 4-24-1861 | Martha, -dt John & Mary (dec) of Henry Co, Ind, m at Hopewell MH, Edmund Osborn of Mill Creek MM, Hendricks Co, Ind |
| 10-23-1861 | Samuel of Henry Co, Ind, -s John & Mary (dec) of same place, m at Hopewell MH, Mary Jane Haskett of Henry Co, Ind |
| 9-15-1883 | Lydia rec in mbrp |
| 2-17-1894 | Allen rel fr mbrp on rq; jas |

## COPE

|  |  |
|---|---|
| 10-18-1890 | Mattie rec in mbrp |

## COPELAND

|  |  |
|---|---|
| 8-17-1907 | Carrie Pearce gct Dublin MM, Ind |

## COSAND

|  |  |
|---|---|
| 3-20-1857 | Charles & w Elvah & ch Mary & Charles F rocf Spiceland MM, Ind |
| 12-21-1859 | Joseph of Henry Co, Ind, -s Charles & Elvah of same place, m at Hopewell MH, Sarah Symons of Henry Co, Ind |
| 6-15-1861 | Mary Ann Hall (form Cosand) dis for mcd |
| 2-15-1862 | Charles Jr mcd; drpd fr mbrp |
| 6-18-1863 | Sarah rst in mbrp w/c Milford MM, Ind |
| 10-15-1864 | Eunice rec in mbrp |
| 12-21-1889 | Cornelius & w Jemima rec in mbrp |
| 1-17-1891 | Martha E gct Haviland MM, Kans |
| 9-19-1891 | Aaron gct Haviland MM, Kans |

## COX

|  |  |
|---|---|
| 5-17-1845 | William & w Hannah R & ch Alfred rocf Milford MM, Ind |
| 12-24-1857 | Hannah R, widow of William Cox of Henry Co, Ind, & -dt Samuel & Jane Stokes of Wayne Co, Ind, m at Rich Square MH, Samuel B Binford of Henry Co, Ind |
| 1-16-1869 | Henry gct Kansas MM, Kans |
| 10-19-1870 | Elwood mcd; drpd fr mbrp |
| 6-17-1871 | Malinda Jane & husband, Henry, rocf Kansas MM, Kans |
| 9-21-1872 | Henry & w Malinda & ch William T gct Milford MM, Ind |
| 9-25-1873 | Elizabeth J, -dt William (dec)& Hannah R of Henry Co, Ind, m Levi Walthal of Vermilion Co, Ind |
| 12-20-1873 | Henry & fam rocf Milford MM, Ind |
| 7-21-1883 | Lucy W gct Coloma MM, Ind |
| 7-21-1883 | Alfred & minor ch Gertrude & Clissie gct Carthage MM, Ind |
| 10-19-1889 | Harriet E gct Dublin MM, Ind |
| 8-17-1890 | Matilda Jane & her ch William T, Monnetta, Edwin, Elnora & Henrietta glt M E Ch at Hastings, Nebr |

## CRUM

|  |  |
|---|---|
| 2-20-1892 | William P & w Martha G & dt Clara rocf Spiceland MM, Ind |

## CUDE

|  |  |
|---|---|
| 8-16-1884 | John gct Spiceland MM, Ind |

## HOPEWELL

**DAVIS**
- 3-18-1854   Joel & w Nancy & minor ch Betsey Ann, Jesse, Julia, Israel C, Lurana E, Winslow H & Hannah L gct Three Rivers MM
- 5-16-1868   Abigail (form Newby) chm of mcd
- 8-21-1869   Abigail gct Deer Creek MM, Ind

**DEMITT**
- 4-15-1905   James & fam gct Knightstown MM, Ind
- 10-19-1912   James & J Bell, his wife, & minor ch D Leroy, Floyd & Kenneth gct Greensfork MM, Ind

**DENNIS**
- - -1841   Benjamin & w Clarky & ch are CHARTER MBRS
- 4-17-1841   Benjamin appt to comm to procure the necessary Record Books
- 5-21-1845   Elizabeth P, -dt Benjamin (dec) & Clarky of Henry Co, Ind, m at Hopewell MH, Robert C Johnson of Henry Co, Ind
- 5-21-1845   John of Henry Co, Ind, -s Benjamin (dec) & Clarky of same place, m at Hopewell MH, Mary Ratliff of Henry Co, Ind
- 9-22-1846   Priscilla of Henry Co, Ind, -dt Benjamin (dec) & Clarky, m at Hopewell MH, William Butler of Henry Co, Ind
- 3-20-1847   John dis for dealing in spirituous liquors & upl
- 2-17-1849   Mary dis for disunity
- 8-25-1852   Eunice, -dt Benjamin (dec) & Clarky of Henry Co, Ind, m at Hopewell MH, Charles Reece of Walnut Ridge MM, Rush Co, Ind
- 8-16-1862   Sarah Ann gct Whitewater MM, Ind
- 11-15-1862   Benjamin S drpd fr mbrp
- 8-15-1863   Jethro dis
- 1-19-1867   Albert gct Honey Creek MM
- 2-17-1883   Millicent, wife of Wilson HO & her minor s John Warren gct Springfield MM, Ind
- 2-19-1887   Jethro rocf Westland MM, Ind
- 2-19-1887   Julia rocf Walnut Ridge MM, Ind
- 6-15-1889   William & w Atilla rocf Westland MM, Ind
- 2-21-1891   Jethro & w Julia gct Carthage MM, Ind
- 5-16-1891   William & w Atilla glt M E Ch, Straughn, Ind

**DIXON**
- 2-23-1884   Calvin & w Mary M & ch Keziah J, Rosa Jane, Letitia Ann, Elmer P & Harley G rocf Dublin MM, Ind
- 3-16-1889   Calvin & w Mary M & minor ch Elmer & Harley gct Newberg MM, Oregon

**DOUGHERTY**
- 6-18-1859   Sarah Ellen rec in mbrp
- 10-18-1873   Sarah Ellen Weeks (form Dougherty) chm of mcd

**EATON**
- 8-16-1890   Minnie E (form Stewart) rel fr mbrp on rq

**EDGERTON**
- 1-24-1843   Thomas & w Mary & minor ch William, Elizabeth Ann, Samuel & Sarah Jane gct Milford MM, Ind

**ELLIOTT**
- 6-17-1865   Melissa J rocf Duck Creek MM, Ind
- 2-19-1870   Melissa J gct Milford MM, Wayne Co, Ind
- 8-15-1891   Rosa J, wife of Calvin Elliott, gct Raysville MM, Ind
- 11-21-1891   Olive (form Gilbert), wife of Milo Elliott, gct Dublin MM, Ind
- 2-17-1910   Catherine (form McKie) gct Duck Creek MM, Ind

**ELLIS**
- 5-17-1845   Pemberton Macy gct Duck Creek MM, Ind to m Nancy Ann Ellis
- 10-15-1910   Ruth & dt Ethel & Rachel gct Fairmount MM, Ind

**ENGLE**
- 1-20-1912   Margaret & minor s Lloyd & Hobart glt U B Ch, Morristown, Ind

**FARMER**
- 12-17-1842   Penina (form Pike) dis for mcd
- 6-18-1847   Nathaniel Macy gct Springfield MM, Ind to m Rhoda H Farmer

**FARQUHAR**
- 1-20-1849   David & w Elizabeth rocf Milford MM, Ind
- 6-15-1850   David & w Elizabeth gct Milford MM, Ind

**FORD**
- 9-20-1902   William & w Harriett rec in mbrp

**FOREMAN**
- 10-15-1859   Martha Jane (form Bond) dis for mcd

**FOSTER**
- 12-16-1848   Anna Jane Ball (form Foster) dis for mcd at White River MM, Ind
- 1-17-1857   Susanna (form Cook) dis for mcd

**FOULKE**
- 8-21-1841   Tacy Bert (form Foulke) dis for mcd
- 3-21-1846   Ann H rec in mbrp (was dis by Gwynedd MM, Pa
- 3-20-1847   Ann H rst in mbrp w/c Gwynedd MM, Pa
- 12-21-1848   Jesse of Rich Square MM, Henry Co, Ind, -s Samuel F (dec) & Ann of same place, m at Rich Square MH, Michal Johnson of Henry Co, Ind
- 9-20-1849   Sarah, -dt Samuel (dec) & Ann of Henry Co, Ind, m at Rich Square MH, William E Butler of Union Co, Ind
- 10-18-1856   Jesse H & w Michal & minor ch Mary Ellen, Deborah Jane & Joshua gct Three Rivers MM, Ia

**GARDNER**
- 4-18-1868   Mary S Gardner (form Binford) chm of mcd
- 6-20-1868   Mary S gct Rich Square MM, Ia

**GARRETT**
- 10-12-1841   William & fam rocf White Lick MM, Ind, -end by Milford MM, Ind & -end by this to Westfield MM, Ind

**GAUSE**
- 11-17-1866   Jane rocf Spiceland MM, Ind
- 1-18-1868   Jane gct Kokomo MM, Ind

**GEPHART**
- 2-19-1887   Alice rec in mbrp

**GILBERT**
- - -1841   Joel & w Lydia & ch are CHARTER MBRS
- - -1841   Aaron & w Margaret & ch are CHARTER MBRS
- - -1841   Thomas & w Sarah & ch are CHARTER MBRS
- - -1841   Abigail, widow of Josiah Jr, & ch are CHARTER MBRS
- - -1841   Nathan & w Rhosa are CHARTER MBRS
- 4-14-1841   Joel appt to a comm
- 4-14-1841   Sarah appt to comm to care for indigent persons
- 4-14-1841   Joel appt to comm on Education
- 4-14-1841   Lydia appt to a comm
- 4-14-1841   Aaron appt to comm to att funerals
- 4-14-1841   Thomas appt to comm to att funerals
- 5-15-1841   Rhoda appt to comm to att the QM
- 5-15-1841   Lydia appt Asst-Clerk of Women's MM
- 5-15-1841   Sarah appt Overseer at Hopewell MM
- 10-19-1842   Morris of Henry Co, Ind, -s Josiah (dec) & Dorothy of same county, m at Hopewell MH, Eunice Macy of same county & state
- 2-19-1845   Mordecai M of Henry Co, Ind, -s Joel & Lydia of same place, m at Hopewell MH, Martha Bundy of Henry Co, Ind
- 8-20-1845   Lydia, -dt Joel & Lydia of Henry Co, Ind, m at Hopewell MH, Cyrus Kendal of Wayne Co, Ind
- 9-22-1847   Abigail, widow of Josiah of Henry Co, Ind, & -dt John & Lydia Bell, (both dec), Wayne Co, Ind, m at Hopewell MH, Daniel Johnson of Henry Co, Ind

## GILBERT (Cont)

|  |  |
|---|---|
| 3-21-1849 | George H of Henry Co, Ind, -s Thomas (dec) & Sarah of same place, m at Hopewell MH, Mary Bundy of Henry Co, Ind |
| 8-22-1849 | John B of Henry Co, Ind, -s Aaron & Margaret of same place, m at Hopewell MH, Jemima Macy of Henry Co, Ind |
| 8-21-1850 | Jeremiah of Henry Co, Ind, -s Joel & Lydia (dec) of same place, m at Hopewell MH, Mary Macy of Henry Co, Ind |
| 10-19-1850 | Thomas gct West Branch MM |
| 12-21-1850 | George H & w Mary & minor ch Malissa gct Westfield MM, Ind |
| 1-18-1851 | John B & w Jemima gct Mississinewa MM, Ind |
| 11-15-1851 | Sarah gct Westfield MM, Ind |
| 12-20-1851 | Aaron, a minor, gct Westfield MM, Ind |
| 12-20-1851 | William T, Sarah, John & Nancy, minor ch of Jeremiah Gilbert, gct Westfield MM, Ind |
| 9-19-1855 | Sarah Ann, -dt Morris & Elizabeth (dec) Gilbert of Henry Co, Ind, m at Hopewell MH, Jesse Gilbert, -s Aaron & Margaret Gilbert of Henry Co, Ind |
| 9-19-1855 | Jesse of Henry Co, Ind, -s Aaron & Margaret of same place, m at Hopewell MH, Sarah Ann Gilbert -dt Morris & Elizabeth (dec) of Henry Co, Ind |
| 12-20-1856 | Thomas & w Catharine & minor ch Jonathan, Oliver & Ann gct Milford MM, Ind |
| 7-22-1857 | Lydia, -dt Aaron & Margaret of Henry Co, Ind, m at Hopewell MH, Benjamin J Butler of Henry Co, Ind |
| 4-16-1859 | Joel & w Phoebe gct Milford MM, Ind |
| 9-22-1859 | Dorothy J, -dt Josiah (dec) & Abigail of Henry Co, Ind, m at Rich Square MH, Joseph H Williams of Henry Co, Ind |
| 10-24-1861 | Joel Jr of Henry Co, Ind, -s Joel Sr & Lydia (dec) of same place, m at Rich Square MH, Sarah Morris of Henry Co, Ind |
| 5-17-1862 | Mary B & her minor ch Martha E, Sarah Jane, Luany H & Amos P gct Greenwood MM |
| 5-25-1863 | Solomon of Henry Co, Ind, -s Nathan & Rhoda of same place, m at Hopewell MH, Sarah Henley of Henry Co, Ind |
| 2-24-1864 | Sarah, -dt Aaron & Margaret of Henry Co, Ind, m at Hopewell MH, Daniel T White of Henry Co, Ind |
| 2-24-1864 | Margaret, -dt Aaron & Margaret of Henry Co, Ind, m at Hopewell MH, Benjamin Stratton of Henry Co, Ind |
| 5-20-1865 | Morris & w Eunice & ch Delilah E, Alvarinius, Thomas C, Morris I & Daniel B gct Richland MM, Ind |
| 2-21-1866 | Abel of Henry Co, Ind, -s Mordecai M & Martha (dec) of same place, m at Hopewell MH, Lucinda Macy of Henry Co, Ind |
| 8-23-1866 | Harvey of Henry Co, Ind, -s Joel & Hannah of same place, m at Rich Square MH, Adaline Stanley of Henry Co, Ind |
| 10-19-1867 | Josiah B gct Whitewater MM, Ind |
| 10-23-1872 | Esther, -dt Mordecai M & Martha of Henry Co, Ind, m at Hopewell MH, William P Binford of Hancock Co, Ind |
| 11-20-1876 | Martha, -dt Aaron & Margaret of Henry Co, Ind, m at residence of Aaron Gilbert, Edmond Peele of New Hope MM, Howard Co, Ind |
| 4-18-1879 | Mary gct Milford MM, Ind |
| -    -1884 | Jeptha & w Nancy & minor ch Emma & George gct Sterling MM, Kans |
| 4-18-1889 | Luther B & w Mary Alice gct Muncie MM, Ind |
| 11-16-1889 | Walter J gct New Castle MM, Ind |
| 12-21-1889 | Levi gct Pleasant Plain MM |
| 3-15-1890 | Jesse & w Sarah Ann gct New Castle MM, Ind |
| 4-16-1892 | Daniel J gct White Lick MM, Ind |
| 5-21-1892 | Josiah C gct Duck Creek MM, Ind |
| 6-18-1892 | Isaiah B & w Martha Ann gct New Castle MM, Ind |
| 6-18-1892 | Dora gct New Castle MM, Ind |
| 9-17-1892 | Daniel B gct Danville MM, Ind |
| 6-19-1897 | James Lindley & w Marticia & minor ch Bertha, Clarence & Raymond gct Muncie MM, Ind |
| 6-19-1897 | Aaron & w Sarah Ann gct Gravely Run MM, Ohio |
| 1-18-1902 | Harvey & w Lizzie & minor ch Mary B & Elmer L Lawson gct Dublin MM, Ind |
| 1-17-1903 | Harriet gct Carthage MM, Ind |
| 1-18-1908 | Gurney & w Elizabeth & minor ch Dorothy, Lloyd & John Wendell gct 8th St MM, Richmond, Ind |
| 11-27-1908 | John J & w Mary L & Anna Bell gct Newberg MM, Ore |

## GILLINGHAM

|  |  |
|---|---|
| 5-17-1873 | Mary Elizabeth (form Lewis) mcd; rel fr mbrp on rq |

## GLUYS

|  |  |
|---|---|
| 9-17-1910 | Reba M gct West Richmond MM, Ind |

## GOODWIN - GOODIN

|  |  |
|---|---|
| 1-15-1887 | Isaac rec in mbrp |
| 2-19-1887 | John & Elizabeth & ch Mary A, Bessie, Bertha & John Jr rec in mbrp |

## GORDON

|  |  |
|---|---|
| 4-21-1894 | Luther B, a min, rocf Earlham MM, Ind |
| 4-20-1895 | Luther B gct Whitewater MM, Ind |

## GOTTSCHALL

|  |  |
|---|---|
| 3-18-1893 | Rosa Alice rec in mbrp |

## GOUGH

|  |  |
|---|---|
| 12-17-1864 | Ellen (form Hall) chm of mcd |
| 2-12-1887 | Orien, Robert & Chester V rec in mbrp |
| 10-18-1902 | Ora & Robert gct Westland MM, Ind |

## GREY

|  |  |
|---|---|
| 1-21-1854 | Mary L (form Butler) dis for mcd |

## GRUEN - GUERIN

|  |  |
|---|---|
| 1-15-1887 | Effie rec in mbrp |
| 10-18-1890 | Nancy rec in mbrp |

## HAGGERMAN

|  |  |
|---|---|
| 3-17-1906 | Effie gct Spiceland MM, Ind |

## HAISLEY

|  |  |
|---|---|
| 11-12-1876 | Isaac E rocf Dover MM, Ind |
| 12-15-1877 | Isaac gct Springfield MM, Ind |

## HALL

|  |  |
|---|---|
| -    -1841 | John & w Sarah & ch are CHARTER MBRS |
| 4-17-1841 | John appt to comm to att funerals |
| 4-17-1841 | John appt an Overseer |
| 8-24-1842 | Moses of Henry Co, Ind, -s John & Sarah of same place, m at Hopewell MH, Anna M Macy, Henry Co, Ind |
| 8-24-1843 | Robert of Henry Co, Ind, -s John & Sarah of same place, m at Hopewell MH, Lydia White of Henry Co, Ind |
| 6-18-1853 | Phineas rec in mbrp |
| 2-16-1861 | Mary rocf Rich Square MM, N C |
| 5-18-1861 | Joseph A chm of mcd |
| 6-15-1861 | Mary Ann (form Cosand) dis for mcd |
| 12-17-1864 | Ellen Gough (form Hall) chm of mcd |
| 1-21-1865 | Sarah rocf Milford MM, Ind |
| 2-22-1865 | Obed M of Henry Co, Ind, -s Moses & Anna M, m at Hopewell MH, Mary A Brothers of Henry Co, Ind |
| 4-24-1867 | Robert of Henry Co, Ind, -s John & Sarah, (both dec), m at Hopewell MH, Martha C (Lewis) Ward, widow of Jacob M Ward & -dt Nathan & Rachel Lewis, Henry Co, Ind |
| 6-15-1867 | Sarah Jefferies (form Hall) chm of mcd |
| 11-16-1867 | Joseph S & w Lucinda & minor ch Eldora & Aldon rocf Spiceland MM, Ind |
| 8-15-1868 | Luanna Stratton (form Hall) chm of mcd |
| 2-18-1871 | Joseph S & w Lucinda & minor ch Eldora, Aldon & Caleb gct Spiceland MM, Ind |
| 3-17-1877 | Charles & w Clara E & ch rec in mbrp |
| 8-17-1880 | Olive rocf Poplar Ridge MM, Ind |

HOPEWELL

**HALL (Cont)**
- 7-21-1883 — Edwin & w Lydia E & minor ch Clarence & Carle gct Spiceland MM, Ind
- 1-17-1891 — Albert & w Olive gct Indianapolis MM, Ind
- 8-15-1891 — R Willard & w Alice & dt Leona gct Dublin MM, Ind
- 2-18-1893 — Elmer E gct Fairmount MM, Ind
- 5-20-1893 — Eli gct Spiceland MM, Ind
- 6-17-1893 — Jesse glt U B Ch, Salem, Ind
- 3-16-1895 — Charles & fam rel fr mbrp on rq; jas
- 3-16-1895 — Luther rel fr mbrp on rq; jas
- 3-18-1905 — Moses gct Spiceland MM, Ind

**HAMMER**
- 10-23-1872 — Elisha of Spiceland MM, Henry Co, Ind, -s Abraham & Catherine, m at Hopewell MH, Elizabeth M Heacock of Henry Co, Ind
- 1-18-1873 — Elizabeth gct Spiceland MM, Ind
- 3-15-1879 — Thomas B & w Elmira gct Walnut Ridge MM, Ind

**HARE**
- 1-15-1842 — Herman & w Mary & ch Deborah D, Maria J, Sarah E, Rebecca A, Mary E & Sophrona P rocf West Grove MM, Ind
- 5-20-1850 — Sarah E, -dt Herman & Mary of Henry Co, Ind, m at Rich Square MH, Daniel W Mendenhall of Hendricks Co, Ind
- 8-17-1850 — Deborah D gct West Grove MM, Ind
- 8-21-1856 — Maria J, -dt Herman & Rozella (dec), Henry Co, Ind, m at Rich Square MH, Charles Stewart of Henry Co, Ind, Hopewell MM
- 5-21-1870 — Isham rec in mbrp

**HARLEY**
- 6-18-1887 — Joseph rocf Duck Creek MM, Ind

**HARRIS**
- 2-18-1887 — Jonathan P & w Laura & ch Alma, Florence & an infant rec in mbrp

**HARVEY**
- 6-18-1909 — Guy Wright & Ruth Esley gct Fowler MM, Fowler, Kans (Ch of William A & Lydia A Harvey)

**HASKETT**
- 12-17-1842 — William chm of mcd
- 3-21-1846 — Mary Ann rocf Symons Creek MM, N C
- 4-18-1846 — William dis for na
- 12-15-1849 — Daniel Y gct Westfield MM, Ind
- 3-16-1861 — Mary & dt Mary Jane rocf White River MM, Ind
- 10-23-1861 — Mary Jane, -dt Henry & Mary, Henry Co, Ind, m at Hopewell MH, Samuel Cook of Henry Co, Ind
- 10-21-1876 — Mary dis for "abusing her h & using violence on him"
- 2-28-1897 — Esther A rocf Muncie MM, Ind

**HASTINGS**
- -1841 — Aaron & w Christiana & ch are CHARTER MBRS
- -1841 — William Jr & w Jane & ch are CHARTER MBRS
- 4-17-1841 — Aaron appt to comm to procure the necessary Record Books
- 4-17-1841 — Christiana appt to a comm
- 5-15-1841 — Aaron appt to comm to att QM
- 5-15-1841 — Christiana appt to comm to att QM
- 5-15-1841 — Aaron appt an Overseer
- 9-18-1841 — Aaron appt a trustee at Rich Square MM, of land purchased from Elwood Bond
- 10-16-1841 — William rocf West Grove MM, Ind
- 11-19-1842 — William gct West Grove MM, Ind
- 4-12-1851 — Solomon dis for mcd
- 2-26-1852 — William P of Henry Co, Ind, -s Aaron & Christiana, m at Rich Square MH, Luzena L Bond of Henry Co, Ind
- 6-19-1852 — Aaron & w Christiana & minor ch Elias, Lettitia, Joshua, Margaret, Jane, John & Emily E gct Milford MM, Ind
- 9-15-1855 — Martha Pane (form Hastings) dis for mcd
- 9-15-1855 — William P & w Luzena S & minor ch Elmina Jane gct Milford MM, Ind
- 9-17-1859 — Jane & minor ch Seth, Aaron & William Clarkson Hastings gct Whitewater MM, Ind
- 9-17-1859 — John R gct Whitewater MM, Ind
- 9-17-1859 — Rebecca Jane gct Whitewater MM, Ind
- 5-19-1860 — Solomon rst in mbrp at Milford MM, Ind
- 11-16-1861 — Solomon rocf Milford MM, Ind
- 12-21-1861 — Hannah rocf Honey Creek MM
- 8-20-1864 — Solomon & w Hannah & ch (minors) George & Arthur gct Honey Creek MM
- 2-20-1864 — Phebe rocf Whitewater MM, Ind
- 8-20-1864 — Phebe, wife of John R, gct Honey Creek MM, Ind

**HAWLEY**
- 1-21-1843 — Eli dis for na, dp & att singing school
- 12-21-1844 — Charles dis for att a mcd, na & dp

**HAWORTH**
- 5-20-1876 — Ellen gct New Salem MM

**HEACOCK**
- 9-16-1843 — Jesse dis for mcd
- 1-17-1857 — Jonah rocf Frankfort MM, Pa
- 4-18-1857 — Elizabeth M rocf Philadelphia MM, Northern Dist, Pa
- 10-23-1872 — Elizabeth M, -dt Jonah & Abigail (both dec), Henry Co, Ind, m at Hopewell MH, Elisha Hammer of Spiceland MM, Henry Co, Ind
- 12-21-1889 — Hugh F & w Mary gct Newberg MM, Ore
- 11-15-1890 — John F & w Ella M & minor dt Bertha gct Middleton MM, Ore

**HEAVENRIDGE**
- -1841 — Elizabeth a CHARTER MBR
- 5-15-1841 — Elizabeth appt an Overseer at Hopewell MM
- 1-15-1842 — John dis for na & dp
- 9-17-1842 — Elizabeth Jr dis for na & dp
- 8-19-1843 — Calvin dis for na, upl & dp
- 4-20-1844 — Edmund, Allen D, William & Gideon, ch of William & Mary, gct Mill Creek MM, Ind
- 4-19-1845 — Elvin dis for na, upl & dp
- 11-18-1854 — Elizabeth gct Back Creek MM, Ind

**HEMINGTON**
- 9-25-1856 — James of Wayne Co, Ind, -s Robert (dec) & Elizabeth of Cambridgeshire, England, m at Rich Square MH, Ind, Margaret White, -dt Exum & Ann of Henry Co, Ind
- 4-18-1857 — Margaret W gct Whitewater MM, Ind

**HENLEY**
- 3-21-1846 — Thomas & w Martha rocf Milford MM, Ind
- 5-21-1849 — Louisa J (form Stratton) chm of mcd at White River MM, Ind
- 10-20-1849 — Louisa Jane gct Walnut Ridge MM, Ind (having removed with her h)
- 4-20-1859 — Henry W, Rush Co, Ind, -s Thomas & Abigail of same place, m at Hopewell MH, Avis Jane Macy of Henry Co, Ind
- 7-16-1859 — Avis Jane gct Walnut Ridge MM, Ind
- 5-25-1863 — Sarah, -dt Thomas E & Martha of Henry Co, Ind, m at Hopewell MH, Solomon Gilbert of Henry Co, Ind
- 7-18-1863 — Thomas E & w Martha & minor s Isaac gct Milford MM, Ind
- 11-19-1864 — Thomas E & w Martha & fam rocf Milford MM, Ind
- 8-17-1867 — Lydia (form Bundy) chm of mcd
- 7-21-1883 — John gct Oak Ridge MM, Ind
- 3-16-1895 — Pearl glt Meth Ch, Straughn, Ind

**HIATT**
- 5-21-1849 — Emily Spencer (form Hiatt) dis for mcd
- 12-17-1853 — Priscilla Butler (form Hiatt) dis for mcd
- 8-16-1856 — Christopher & w Martha & minor s Teneson gct Honey Creek MM, Ind
- 3-16-1867 — Martha Ellen (form Stuart) chm of mcd
- 3-15-1873 — Edwin & ch Cleodoes & Ida rocf Wabash MM, Ind

HOPEWELL

## HIATT (Cont)
- 4-19-1873 Catherine, wife of Edwin, rec in mbrp
- 3-19-1904 Cleodine gct Spiceland MM, Ind
- 3-18-1905 Enos glt Meth Ch, Palisade, Colo
- 10- -1907 Edwin gct New Castle MM, Ind

## HILL
- 4-20-1867 Martha Ellen gct Carthage MM, Ind
- 6-15-1872 Gulielma (form Butler) chm for mcd
- 7-20-1872 Gulielma gct Walnut Ridge MM, Ind
- 12-27-1898 Elva gct Indianapolis MM, Ind
- 4-15-1905 John & Elizabeth rocf Carthage MM, Ind

## HOBIDLER
- 2-16-1895 Amanda rocf New Castle MM, Ind
- 12-19-1896 Amanda gct New Castle MM, Ind

## HOBSON
- 12-19-1908 Orlando & Leannah gct Spiceland MM, Ind

## HODGIN
- 1-21-1871 Cyrus & w Emily C & dt Laura Alice rocf Whitewater MM, Ind
- 7-21-1883 Cyrus W & w, E Carrie & dt L Alice gct Whitewater MM, Ind

## HOLLINGSWORTH
- - -1841 Hepzebah, widow of George, a CHARTER MBR
- 4-17-1841 Hepsebah appt to a comm

## HOOKER
- 5-16-1903 Thomas & Phebe Ellen gct Knightstown MM, Ind
- 5-16-1903 Alonzo M gct Knightstown MM, Ind

## HORN
- 1-17-1852 Abraham Symons gct Cherry Grove MM, Ind to m Mary Horn

## HUBBARD
- 6-19-1841 Caleb rocf Spiceland MM, Ind
- 6-19-1841 Matilda rec in mbrp at Rich Square PM
- 5-17-1845 Caleb chm of mcd
- 2-19-1848 Caleb gct Honey Creek MM, Ind; cert was ret with complaint by which he was dis
- 1-17-1854 Joseph & w Matilda & minor ch Sarah, Henry, Gamiliel, Joseph Asher & Mary Matilda gct Chester MM, Ind

## HUNNICUTT
- 3-13-1887 Susan glt Meth Ch, Phelps Co, Nebr
- 9-20-1902 Irena, a min, rocf Dover MM, Ind
- 3-18-1905 Irena gct High Point MM, N C

## HUNT
- 4-15-1843 Isam & w Susannah & minor ch Margaret Ann, William A & John W gct Duck Creek MM, Ind

## HUTSON
- 8-19-1876 Mary E gct Duck Creek MM, Ind

## INGERSOL
- 8-18-1883 Josephine E rocf Dublin MM, Ind
- 5- -1885 John & w Josephine gct Salem MM, Ind
- 2-28-1897 Gertrude glt Meth Ch, Straughn, Ind
- 9-16-1899 Lottie gct Whitewater MM, Ind

## IRVIN or IRWIN
- 4-20-1895 Laura H rel on rq

## JAY
- 11-16-1872 Eli & w Mahala & dt Mary Adaline rocf West Branch MM, Ohio
- 6-20-1874 Eli & w Mahala & minor dt Mary Adaline gct Whitewater MM, Ind
- 10-20-1894 William D rocf Dublin MM, Ind

## JEFFERIES - JEFFRIES
- 7-20-1844 Asa & w Margaret & ch Elijah, William D, Asa Jr, John T, Elizabeth & Hannah Ann rocf Whitewater MM, Ind
- 7-20-1844 Rebecca R rocf Whitewater MM, Ind
- 11-22-1855 Hannah Ann, -dt Asa & Margaret of Henry Co, Ind, m at Rich Square MH, John Parker of Henry Co, Ind
- 6-15-1867 Sarah (form Hall) chm of mcd
- 1-15-1881 Emily R C rocf Springfield MM, Ind
- 7-16-1898 William H gct Sand Creek MM, Ind
- 1-19-1901 William H & w Laura rocf Sand Creek MM, Ind
- 11-19-1910 William H & w Laura gct Dublin MM, Ind

## JENKINS
- 5-23-1853 Evans H of Montgomery Co, Ohio, -s Robert & Jemima (dec) of same place, m at Rich Square MH, Emaline A Lewis of Henry Co, Ind
- 10-15-1853 Emaline A gct Mill Creek MM, Ohio
- 11-17-1877 Anna J rocf New Garden MM, Ind
- 9-19-1882 Amos gct Dover MM, Ind
- 12-17-1883 William C rec in mbrp
- 8-15-1885 William & wife, Anna J, rel fr mbrp on rq; jas

## JOHNSON
- - -1841 Daniel & w Maria are CHARTER MBRS
- 4-17-1841 Daniel appt to comm on Education
- 4-17-1841 Maria appt to comm on Education
- 4-17-1841 Maria appt Clerk of Women's MM for the day
- 5-15-1841 Maria appt Clerk for Women's MM
- 6-19-1841 Daniel appt to a comm
- 6-19-1841 Joel & w Elizabeth & dt Lydia Ann rocf Spiceland MM, Ind
- 9-16-1843 Maria appt an Elder
- 5-21-1845 Robert C of Henry Co, Ind, -s Laban (dec) & Sarah, formerly of Isle of Wight Co, Va, m at Hopewell MH, Ind, Elizabeth P Dennis of Henry Co, Ind
- 9-10-1846 Elisha & w Martha & ch Michal, Mary E, Deborah, Martha A, Mahlon & Daniel H rocf Black Creek MM, Southampton Co, Va
- 9-22-1847 Daniel of Henry Co, Ind, -s Elisha & Elizabeth (both dec), m at Hopewell MH, Abigail Gilbert, widow of Josiah Gilbert Jr, & -dt John & Lydia Bell (both dec), late of Wayne Co, Ind
- 12-21-1848 Michal, -dt Elisha & Martha of Henry Co, Ind, m at Rich Square MH, Jesse Foulke of Henry Co, Ind
- 2-17-1849 Robert C & w Elizabeth & minor ch Eliza C & Lindley M gct Honey Creek MM, Ind
- 9-20-1851 Rebecca rocf Milford MM, Ind [also Elijah P] (Wife of Ansolom Johnson)
- 10-16-1852 Sarah gct Honey Creek MM, Ind
- 10-16-1852 Eliza gct Honey Creek MM, Ind
- 9-22-1853 Deborah, -dt Elisha & Martha of Henry Co, Ind, m at Rich Square MH, William Parker of Henry Co, Ind
- 5-15-1856 Abigail appt an Elder
- 10-18-1856 Elisha & w Martha & ch Mary Elizabeth, Martha Ann & Daniel Holland gct Three River MM, Ia
- 8-15-1857 Mary rocf Springfield MM, N C
- 8-15-1857 William G, a min, & w Anna & ch Martitia E, William Elwood, Emily & Mary D rocf Raysville MM, Ind
- 1-20-1858 Mary gct Plainfield MM, Ind
- 11-20-1858 William G, a min, & w Anna & minor ch Martitia E, William E, Emily & Mary D gct Plainfield MM, Ind
- 7-25-1861 Lydia Ann, -dt Joel & Elizabeth of Henry Co, Ind, m at Rich Square MH, Benjamin H Binford of Walnut Ridge MM, Rush Co, Ind
- 6-15-1872 Barclay chm of mcd
- 4-17-1875 Barclay & w Sylvia Ann & ch gct Deer Creek MM, Ind
- 7-15-1876 Elizabeth T & s Myrton L rec in mbrp
- 1- 1-1879 Zelinda, -dt Ansalem & Rebecca of Henry Co, Ind, m at the res of Ansalem Johnson, William A Macy of Henry Co, Ind
- 7-21-1883 Elwood gct Deer Creek MM, Ind

HOPEWELL

## JOHNSON (Cont)
- 1-15-1887  William, Mary, Martha A & Laura, ch of William & Mary, rec in mbrp
- 1-20-1894  Della rocf ...... (wife of Albert Johnson)
- 3-17-1894  Eva rec in mbrp
- 4-16-1904  Herbert C rec in mbrp
- 11-26-1912 Josiah O & Matilda N & minor dt Lucile gct Dublin MM, Ind

## KELLAM - KELLUM
- 6-21-1851  Nathan & w Nancy & ch James, William, Aaron, Hermon & Jesse rocf New Garden MM, N C
- 12-17-1859 Nathan & ch William, Aaron, Hermon & Jesse gct Hinkles Creek MM, Ind
- 12-17-1859 James gct Hinkles Creek MM, Ind

## KENDALL
- 8-21-1841  Joel Gilbert Jr gct Whitewater MM, Ind to m Hannah Kendall
- 8-20-1845  Cyrus of Wayne Co, Ind, -s Thomas & Elizabeth of same place, m at Hopewell MH, Lydia Gilbert of Henry Co, Ind
- 11-15-1845 Lydia having removed with her h, gct Duck Creek MM, Ind
- 9-20-1848  David of Duck Creek MM, Ind, -s Thomas & Elizabeth of Wayne Co, Ind, m at Hopewell MH, Mary Cook of Henry Co, Ind
- 3-17-1849  Mary having removed with h, gct Duck Creek MM, Ind
- 7-21-1877  Lydia Ann gct Duck Creek MM, Ind
- 1- 1-1879  Mary rocf Duck Creek MM, Ind
- 6-18-1883  William H rocf Duck Creek MM, Ind
- 10-16-1886 Herman & w Rebecca Jane gct Duck Creek MM, Ind
- 9-21-1889  William & w Mary & minor ch Jesse, Lillie, Clessie, Addie & Ida gct New Castle MM, Ind
- 4-16-1898  William H & w Mary Emma & ch Jesse, Lillie, Clessie, Ada, Ida, Walter & Gilbert rocf Duck Creek MM, Ind

## KENWORTHY
- 6-24-1846  Amos of Raysville MM, Henry Co, Ind, -s William & Mary (both dec), m at Hopewell MH, Elizabeth Newby, a widow, of Henry Co, Ind, & -dt Josiah & Dorothy Gilbert
- 8-15-1846  Elizabeth gct Spiceland MM, Ind
- 8-21-1847  Mary Ann rocf Spiceland MM, Ind
- 11-16-1850 William & w Mary Ann & ch Sarah F, James, Phebe Ann & Amos gct Spiceland MM, Ind
- 4-15-1893  Oliver N & w Isabella, both mins, rocf Penn MM -end by Raysville MM, Ind
- 4-15-1899  Walter C gct Dublin MM, Ind
- 3-16-1901  Virgil gct Knightstown MM, Ind
- 12-20-1902 Oliver N & Isabella & minor ch Amos D & Alva E gct San Jose MM, Calif

## KERN
- 5-22-1910  Eli & Elizabeth gct Greenfield MM, Ind

## KINBALL
- 2-20-1892  Nancy rocf Spiceland MM, Ind
- 2-20-1892  William rec in mbrp

## KINNEY
- 1-15-1887  Richard & dt Jennie rec in mbrp

## KNIGHT
- 9-19-1891  Lydia D & s Leslie & Joseph E gct Westfield MM, Ind

## KOON
- 1-15-1887  Oscar & Jane rec in mbrp
- 2-19-1887  Dora rec in mbrp
- -  -1910   Eli gct Greenfield MM, Ind

## LACEY
- 3-17-1866  Eliza Jane (form Ratliff) chm of mcd

## LAMB
- 3-15-1862  John I Gilbert gct White River MM, Ind to m Mary Lamb

- 8-18-1866  Emily rocf White River MM, Ind
- 9-16-1867  Emily, -dt Phineas & Huldah (dec) of Henry Co, Ind, m at Rich Square MH, Jared P Binford of Carthage MM, Rush Co, Ind
- 4-15-1871  Miriam rocf Greenfield MM; -end by White River MM, Ind

## LANE
- 6-15-1878  William & w Anna & ch John, Dora & James rec in mbrp

## LANGSTON
- 10-20-1894 Emily & s Walter rocf Dublin MM, Ind
- 12-17-1910 Clarence gct Dublin MM, Ind
- 9-16-1911  Walter E gct Greenleaf MM, Greenleaf, Idaho

## LARROWE
- 11-20-1897 Nathan & w Etta Ratliff rolf 1st Christian Ch, Mooreland, Ind
- 3-17-1906  Nathan glt Christian Ch, Mooreland, Ind
- 8-17-1907  Lura Blanche gct Dublin MM, Ind

## LEFTER
- 4-21-1906  Omar gct New Castle MM, Ind
- 5-22-1910  William & Dora K gct Greenfield MM, Ind

## LEWIS
- 12-17-1842 Rachel & minor ch Susannah, Stephen, Emmaline, John Milton & Tennison rocf Whitewater MM, Ind
- 12-17-1842 Josiah rocf Whitewater MM, Ind
- 3-19-1843  Rachel Jr rocf Whitewater MM, Ind
- 7-20-1844  Martha C rocf Whitewater MM, Ind
- 9-21-1844  Nathan dis for ... by Whitewater MM, Ind
- 10-19-1844 Rachel Smith (form Lewis) chm of mcd
- 10-19-1844 Martha C Ward (form Lewis) mcd
- 9-15-1849  Stephen dis for att a mcd
- 9-21-1850  Julia Ann rec in mbrp
- 5-23-1853  Emaline A, -dt Nathan (dec) & Rachel of Henry Co, Ind, m at Rich Square MH, Evans H Jenkins of Mill Creek MM, Montgomery Co, Ohio
- 3-20-1859  Rachel, widow of Nathan Lewis of Henry Co, Ind &-dt Josiah & Rachel Thomas (both dec), of Ohio, m at Rich Square MH, John Baldwin of Chester MM, Wayne Co, Ind
- 5-17-1873  Mary Elizabeth Gillingham (form Lewis) mcd; rel fr mbrp on rq
- 9-17-1887  Julia A gct South Wabash MM, Ind (Cert was ret to Hopewell MM - no further information as to where she lived)

## LINDELL
- 4-20-1895  Penina (Cook) rel fr mbrp on rq; jas

## LINDLEY
- 1-21-1882  Emily Jane (form Johnson) gct Deer Creek MM, Grant Co, Ind

## LISTER
- 4-15-1905  Edwin & w Eleanor rocf Muncie MM, Ind

## LOVEALL
- 7-19-1845  Gulielma (form Gilbert) chm of mcd
- 11-15-1845 Stephen rec in mbrp
- 5-20-1848  Gulielma & minor ch Thomas & Naomi gct Westfield MM, Ind
- 3-17-1849  Stephen gct Westfield MM, Ind

## LOWRY
- 10-12-1873 Angelina (form Bond) chm of mcd
- 12-15-1883 Angelina gct Duck Creek MM, Ind

## MACY
- -  -1841   Lydia, widow of Obed, & ch are CHARTER MBRS
- -  -1841   James & w Anna & ch are CHARTER MBRS
- -  -1841   Nathan & fam are CHARTER MBRS

HOPEWELL

MACY (Cont)
- -1841    Zacheus (aged) & w Sarah are CHARTER MBRS
4-17-1841  James appt to a comm
4-17-1841  Nathan appt to comm on Education
4-17-1841  Ann appt to comm on Education
4-17-1841  Nathan appt Treasurer of the MM
4-17-1841  Lydia appt to a comm
5-15-1841  James appt Asst-Clerk with Nathan Reece as Clerk
5-15-1841  Nathan appt to att QM
5-15-1841  Nathan appt an Overseer
8-21-1841  James appt Librarian at Hopewell MM
9-18-1841  James appt Clerk for the day because of death of Nathan Reece
10- -1841  James appt Clerk of MM with Thomas Bell as Asst-Clerk
8-24-1842  Anna M, -dt Obed (dec) & Lydia of Henry Co, Ind m at Hopewell MH, Moses Hall of Henry Co, Ind
10-19-1842 Eunice, -dt James & Anna of Henry Co, Ind, m at Hopewell MH, Morris Gilbert of Henry Co, Ind
12-16-1843 (William) & w Rhoda & ch Henry, Phebe, Louisa, Jesse, Irena & Joseph rocf Back Creek MM, Ind
3-12-1844  Sarah, -dt Nathan & Catharine (dec) of Henry Co, Ind, m at Hopewell MH, James Stanbrough of Duck Creek MM, Ind
8-21-1844  Henry of Henry Co, Ind, -s William & Rhoda of same place, m at Hopewell MH, Huldah Nixon
10-19-1844 Phebe Owen (form Macy) chm of mcd
11-16-1844 Henry & w Huldah N gct Back Creek MM, Ind
5-17-1845  Pemberton gct Duck Creek MM, Ind to m Nancy Ann Ellis
6-21-1845  Nancy Ann rocf Duck Creek MM, Ind
12-19-1846 Pemberton & w Nancy Ann & minor s Robert P gct Westfield MM, Ind
4-17-1847  Rachel Patten (form Macy) chm of mcd
6-19-1847  Nathaniel gct Springfield MM, Ind to m Rhoda H Farmer at Flat Rock MH, Ind
5-20-1848  Nathaniel gct Springfield MM, Ind
5-24-1848  Louisa, -dt William & Rhoda of Rich Square MM, Henry Co, Ind, m at Hopewell MH, Daniel Symonds of Henry Co, Ind
8-22-1849  Jemima, -dt Nathan & Catharine (dec) of Henry Co, Ind, m at Hopewell MH, John B Gilbert of Henry Co, Ind
8-21-1850  Mary, -dt James Sr & Anna of Henry Co, Ind, m at Hopewell MH, Jeremiah Gilbert of Henry Co, Ind
12-21-1850 Nathan & w Lydia & minor ch Lydia, Hepzibah, Mariam & Susannah Macy & Eli Ratliff, an orphan u/c, gct Mississinewa MM, Ind
6-13-1852  Phineas of Henry Co, Ind, -s James & Anna, m at Hopewell MH, Betty Ratliff of Henry Co, Ind
11-24-1852 Lydia Ann, -dt James & Anna of Henry Co, Ind, m at Hopewell MH, Cornelius Ratliff of Henry Co, Ind
9-17-1853  William & w Rhoda & minor ch Joseph & Catharine Elizabeth gct Back Creek MM, Ind
9-17-1853  Irena gct Back Creek MM, Ind
12-20-1855 John M of Henry Co, Ind, -s Stephen & Rebecca (dec), of same place, m at Rich Square MH, Lydia Bell of Henry Co, Ind
4-19-1856  John M & dt Henrietta M & Margaret P rocf Spiceland MM, Ind
4-20-1859  Avis Jane, -dt James & Anna of Henry Co, Ind, m at Hopewell MH, Henry W Henley of Rush Co, Ind
6-22-1859  Lucretia, -dt James & Anna of Henry Co, Ind, m at Hopewell MH, Josiah Reynolds of Henry Co, Ind
9-24-1863  Henrietta M, -dt John M & Betsey Ann (dec) of Henry Co, Ind, m at Rich Square MH, William P Binford of Walnut Ridge MM, Rush Co, Ind
4-16-1864  William rocf Back Creek MM, Ind
2-21-1866  Lucinda, -dt James & Anna of Henry Co, Ind, m at Hopewell MH, Abel Gilbert of Henry Co, Ind
9-15-1868  Mary rocf West Union MM, Ind
6-17-1870  William & w Mary gct West Union MM, Ind
1-21-1871  Miriam C rocf Springfield MM, Ind
1- 1-1879  William A of Henry Co, Ind, -s John M & Betsey Ann (dec) of same place, m at the residence of Ansalem Johnson, Zelinda Johnson of Henry Co, Ind
10-25-1883 (Mariah) Josephine, -dt John M & Lydia B of Henry Co, Ind, m at residence of John M Macy, Clarkson H Parker of Rush Co, Ind
4-21-1888  Lydia B gct Walnut Ridge MM, Ind
4-21-1888  Margaret W gct Walnut Ridge MM, Ind
9-17-1898  Margaret W rocf White River MM, Ind
3-18-1905  Clarence O glt Meth Ch at Frankfort, Ind
8-17-1907  Florence O gct .... MM, New Mexico
8- 2-1908  Everett John of Lewisville, Henry Co, Ind, -s William A & Zelinda J of same place, m at residence of Charles Wiltsee of Rochester, Fulton Co, Ind, Gertrude May Wiltsee of Rochester, Fulton Co, Ind
11-18-1911 Everett J & Gertrude W gct Scott City MM, Scott City, Kans
2-17-1912  William A & w Zelinda & dt Alice & Margaret W gct West Richmond MM, Ind

MARLEY
6-18-1887  Joseph rocf Duck Creek MM, Ind

MAUDLIN - MODLIN
1-20-1844  Anna & s Joseph rocf Duck Creek MM, Ind
3-25-1846  Anna, widow of William of Henry Co, Ind, & -dt Richard & Betty Ratliff, m at Hopewell MH, Jacob Nixon of Henry Co, Ind
4-21-1849  Joseph mcd; dis
10-20-1849 Lydia (form Osborne) dis for mcd at Duck Creek MM, Ind

McCRACKIN
7-19-1873  Eunice rocf Carthage MM, Ind

McWILLIAMS
2-19-1887  Nelson rec in mbrp

MENDENHALL
6-19-1841  Jonathan appt Treasurer of the fund to care for indigent persons
9-21-1844  Asenith rocf Salem MM, Ia
9-21-1848  Asenith gct Salem MM, Ia
5-21-1849  Richard of Whitewater MM, Wayne Co, Ind, -s Obadiah & Sarah (both dec) of Hendricks Co, Ind, m at Rich Square MH, Sarah Ann Nixon of Henry Co, Ind
5-20-1850  Daniel W of Hendricks Co, Ind, -s Obadiah & Sarah (both dec), of same place, m at Rich Square MH, Sarah E Hare of Henry Co, Ind
6-15-1850  Sarah Ann & minor s Charles gct Whitewater MM, Ind
9-21-1850  Sarah E gct White Lick MM, Ind
2-19-1853  Benjamin gct Spiceland MM, Ind

MILES
3-19-1856  Mary E (form Butler) dis for mcd

MILLER
3-20-1909  Horace & Rachel Ann gct Dublin MM, Ind
2-17-1912  Emma B gct New Castle MM, Ind
10- -1912  J Elva gct West Richmond MM, Ind
11-16-1912 Mary J gct Dublin MM, Ind

MILLS
1-20-1872  John D & w Huldah & ch Lorinda, Alonzo T, Elihu, Millicent, Mary & Arthur rocf Wabash MM, Ind
1-20-1872  William M rocf Wabash MM, Ind
9-24-1874  William M of Henry Co, Ind, -s John D & Huldah of same place, m at Rich Square MH, Edith F Morris of Henry Co, Ind
6-19-1880  Laura rocf Milford MM, Ind
1-17-1903  William M & w Laura & minor ch Anna Mary, Olive P, Orpha H & William Ralph gct Dublin MM, Ind

HOPEWELL

**MOORE**
- 11-21-1844  William of Henry Co, Ind, -s Thomas & Isabel (dec), formerly of Perquimans Co, N C, m at Rich Square MH, Ind, Ann Stretch, a widow & -dt Asa & Elizabeth Jefferies (dec) late of Salem Co, N J
- 1-18-1845  Ann gct Spiceland MM, Ind
- 10-19-1861  Joseph gct Springfield MM, Ohio
- 4-15-1865  Joshua gct Center MM, Ohio
- 11- 2-1869  Sarah rocf Deep River MM, N C
- 10-16-1875  Sarah gct Westland MM
- 2-19-1887  Walter rec in mbrp
- 5-16-1891  Sarah A & ch Calvert & Walter rel fr mbrp on rq

**MORGAN**
- 8-17-1844  Alfred Butler gct Spiceland MM, Ind to m Elizabeth Morgan

**MORRIS**
- 11-19-1848  Joshua rocf Milford MM, Ind
- 9-25-1851  Joshua of Hopewell MM, Henry Co, Ind, -s Jehoshaphat & Mary, (both dec), of Dublin MM, Henry Co, Ind, m at Rich Square MH, Edith F Wilson of Rich Square MM, Henry Co, Ind
- 3-22-1854  Christopher of Milford MM, Wayne Co, Ind, -s Josiah & Abigail of same place, m at Hopewell MH, Margaret Bell of Henry Co, Ind
- 8-19-1854  Margaret B gct Milford MM, Ind
- 10-24-1861  Sarah of Henry Co, Ind, -dt Jehosaphat & Mary, (both dec), late of Wayne Co, Ind, m at Rich Square MH, Joel Gilbert Jr of Henry Co, Ind
- 9-24-1874  Edith, -dt Joshua & Edith F of Henry Co, Ind, m at Rich Square MH, William M Mills of Henry Co, Ind
- 2-19-1887  Jonathan P & w Laura & dt Alma E rec in mbrp
- 2-19-1887  Florence rec in mbrp on rq of parents

**MOTLEY**
- 2-19-1887  Sarah & her ch Arrat & her step-ch Rollin rec in mbrp

**NEEDHAM**
- 1-21-1843  Sarah rocf Back Creek MM, Ind
- 10-19-1844  Mary (form Winslow) dis for mcd at Back Creek MM, Ind
- 2-21-1846  Sarah gct Mississinewa MM, Ind
- 3-17-1849  Reece & s John & James gct Whitewater MM, Ind

**NEWBY**
- -  -1841  Elizabeth, widow of Jonathan, a CHARTER MBR
- -  -1841  Thomas & w Millicent & ch are CHARTER MBRS
- 4-17-1841  Elizabeth appt to comm to care for indigent persons
- 4-17-1841  Millicent appt to comm on Education
- 5-15-1841  Elizabeth appt to att QM
- 7-20-1844  Mary rocf Symons Creek MM, N C
- 6-24-1846  Elizabeth, a widow, -dt Josiah (dec) & Dorothy Gilbert of Henry Co, Ind, m at Hopewell MH, Ind, Amos Kenworthy of Raysville MM, Henry Co, Ind
- 5-15-1853  Mariam (form Ratliff) chm of mcd
- 4-24-1856  Huldah, -dt Thomas & Millicent of Henry Co, Ind, m at Rich Square MH, William Stewart of Hopewell MM, Henry Co, Ind
- 8-15-1856  Caroline rocf Spiceland MM, Ind
- 4-16-1859  Miriam has removed with her h, gct Whitewater MM, Ind
- 2-15-1862  Albert & w Caroline & minor ch Charles Edward, Sarah Emma & Allen L gct Raysville MM, Ind
- 4-20-1867  Thomas & w Millicent & minor s Jesse gct Spiceland MM, Ind
- 5-16-1868  Abigail Davis (form Newby) chm of mcd
- 11- 2-1869  Thomas & w Millicent & ch rocf Spiceland MM, Ind
- 9-15-1877  Nathan gct Spiceland MM, Ind
- 6-18-1881  Sarah rocf Spiceland MM, Ind

**NIXON**
- 8-21-1844  Huldah, -dt Caleb (dec) & Elizabeth of Wayne Co, Ind, m at Hopewell MH, Henry Macy of Henry Co, Ind
- 3-25-1846  Jacob of Hopewell MH, Henry Co, Ind, -s Pearce & Peninah (both dec), m at Hopewell MH, Anna Modlin, widow, of Henry Co, Ind & -dt Richard & Betty Ratliff (both dec)
- 3-17-1849  Sarah Ann rocf Center MM, Ohio
- 5-21-1849  Sarah Ann of Henry Co, Ind, -dt Thomas & Peggy (both dec) of Nansemond Co, Va, m at Rich Square MH, Richard Mendenhall of Whitewater MM, Wayne Co, Ind
- 11-16-1850  Jacob & w Anna gct Duck Creek MM, Ind
- 6-11-1851  Jacob & w Anna rocf Duck Creek MM, Ind
- 9-20-1856  Mary rocf White River MM, Ind
- 12-19-1857  Jacob & w Anna gct Duck Creek MM, Ind
- 12-18-1858  Mary gct White River MM, Ind
- 12-18-1858  William & minor s William Jr gct White River MM, Ind
- 7-21-1883  Alice Johnson gct Fairmount MM, Ind

**OSBORN**
- 10-20-1849  Lydia Maudlin (form Osborn) dis for mcd at Duck Creek MM, Ind
- 4-24-1861  Edmund of Mill Creek MM, Hendricks Co, Ind, -s Henry & Sarah of same place, m at Hopewell MH, Martha Cook of Hopewell MM, Henry Co, Ind
- 1-18-1862  Martha C gct New Salem MM, Ind

**OUTLAND**
- 1-17-1874  Elizabeth Gilbert gct Westland MM, Ind
- 6-18-1881  Mahlon (or Malinda) rocf Westland MM, Ind
- 7-18-1891  James & w Elizabeth & minor s Eldon J gct Westland MM, Ind
- 2-18-1893  James dis
- 3-16-1895  James gct Westland MM, Ind

**OWEN**
- 10-19-1844  Phebe (form Macy) chm of mcd
- 8-20-1853  Phebe gct Wabash MM, Ind

**PALIN**
- 2-24-1842  Henry of Wayne Co, Ind, -s Henry Sr & Mary, (both dec), of Pasquotank Co, N C, m at Hopewell MH, Ind, Miriam Pike, a widow of Henry Co, Ind & -dt Mark & Nancy Dillon (both dec) of Pasquotank Co, N C
- 7-16-1842  Miriam & her minor ch Mary A & Stanford Pike gct Milford MM, Ind

**PANE**
- 9-15-1855  Martha (form Hastings) dis for mcd

**PARKER**
- -  -1841  Isaac & w Mary & ch are CHARTER MBRS
- -  -1841  Miriam, widow of Robert & her ch are CHARTER MBRS
- 4-17-1841  Isaac appt to a comm
- 9-18-1841  Isaac appt Recorder of Cert of Removals
- 9-18-1841  Isaac appt a trustee at Rich Square MM, of land purchased from Edward Bond
- 4-24-1844  Lydia of Henry Co, Ind, -dt Robert & Miriam, (both dec), m at Hopewell MH, Thomas N White of same place
- 9-22-1853  William of Henry Co, Ind, -s Robert & Miriam (both dec), m at Rich Square MH, Deborah Johnson of same place
- 11-22-1855  John of Rich Square MM, Henry Co, Ind, -s Robert & Miriam (both dec), m at Rich Square MH, Hannah Ann Jefferies of Henry Co, Ind
- 10-18-1856  William & w Deborah & minor ch Marcus Elmore gct Three River MM, Ia
- 5-16-1863  Edwin E dis
- 6-16-1866  William & s Marcus E rocf Rich Square MM, Iowa
- 11-16-1867  Amanda W rec in mbrp

HOPEWELL

## PARKER (Cont)

10-21-1871 — William & w Amanda & minor s Marcus E gct Deer Creek MM
10-25-1883 — Clarkson H of Rush Co, Ind, -s John & Piriam of Wayne Co, Ind, m at residence of John M Macy, Mariah Josephine Macy of Henry Co, Ind
12-15-1883 — Josephine gct Walnut Ridge MM, Ind
10-20-1888 — Benjamin S & w Huldah & minor ch Florence, Allegra & Jethro gct New Castle MM, Ind

## PARRY

5-23-1855 — Mordecai of Richmond, Wayne Co, Ind, -s Joseph & Sarah, m at Hopewell MH, Sarah Bell of Henry Co, Ind
9-15-1855 — Sarah B gct Whitewater MM, Ind

## PATTEN

2- -1845 — Elihu H & w Eliza Jane & ch William T, Phebe Ann & Jesse rocf Pennville MM, Ohio (Deerfield MM, Ohio)
11-15-1845 — Sarah Talbert (form Patten) dis for mcd at Pennville MM, Ohio
4-17-1847 — Rachel (form Macy) dis for mcd
3-17-1849 — Rachel rst in mbrp by rq
6-16-1849 — Joseph rst in mbrp w/c Pennsville MM, Ohio
11-16-1850 — Elihu H & w Eliza Jane & minor ch William, Phebe Ann, Ellen, Mahlon H, John H & Eliza H gct Richland MM, Ind
1-20-1855 — Joseph & w Rachel & minor ch James A & Thomas C gct Walnut Ridge MM, Ind

## PAUL

6-15-1872 — Mary Ellen (form Stafford) chm of mcd

## PAXSON

2-29-1853 — Benjamin Webster of Henry Co, Ind, -s of Benjamin (dec) & Mary, m at Rich Square MH, Beulah Stuart of Henry Co, Ind
8-21-1858 — Beulah dis at Honey Creek MM for jas
11-17-1866 — Beulah S & younger ch Addie Eldora & William E rec in mbrp

## PEARCE

2-19-1898 — Eliza Jane & s Charles rec in mbrp
8-17-1907 — Eliza J & s Charles gct Dublin MM, Ind

## PEARSON

8-21-1841 — Lydia dis for na & dp
12-18-1841 — William dis for mcd at Salem MM (Silver Creek) MM, Ind
8-24-1853 — Seth, -s Exum & Elizabeth of Henry Co, Ind, m at Hopewell MH, Sarah Bundy of Henry Co, Ind
11-19-1853 — Sarah gct Duck Creek MM, Ind
3-15-1856 — Thomas B & w Mary E & minor ch rocf Dover MM, Ind
8-21-1856 — Sarah & dt Eliza Jane rocf Duck Creek MM, Ind
12-20-1856 — Thomas B & w Mary E & minor ch Charles E gct Milford MM, Ind
3-25-1857 — Sarah (form Bundy) widow of Seth Pearson & -dt Jesse & Rachel Bundy of Henry Co, Ind, m at Hopewell MH, Jehu T Stuart of Henry Co, Ind
3-19-1859 — Eliza Jane, minor dt of Seth (dec) & Sarah, (now Sarah Stuart, wife of Jehu T Stuart) gct Honey Creek MM, Ind
4-21-1860 — Sarah Stuart & her dt Eliza Jane Pearson & Rachel Stuart rocf Honey Creek MM, Ind

## PEELE

11-20-1876 — Edmond of New Hope MM, Howard Co, Ind, -s Robert & Pheraba (both dec) of Northampton Co, N C, m at residence of Aaron Gilbert, Martha Gilbert of Henry Co, Ind
1-20-1877 — Martha gct New Hope MM, Ind
5-17-1879 — James & w Adaline rocf Milford MM, Ind
10-20-1883 — Edmond, a min, & w Martha rocf New Hope MM, Ind
1885 or 1886 — James & w Adaline gct Saline MM, Ill

## PHILLIPS

2-16-1889 — Clementine & dt Laura & Verna rec in mbrp
4-13-1893 — William rec in mbrp

## PICKERING

12-12-1847 — Joseph Butler gct Duck Creek MM, Ind to m Sarah Ann Pickering
6-15-1850 — Elizabeth I Sharp (form Pickering) dis at Duck Creek MM, Ind

## PIDGEON

4-17-1869 — Isaac W & w Elizabeth & ch Mary Alice & Albert Lindley rocf Springfield MM, Ind
5-21-1892 — Isaac W & w Elizabeth P & ch Esther R & Elenor A gct Muncie MM, Ind

## PIERCE

2-19-1871 — Christian gct Spiceland MM, Ind
6-16-1906 — James W gct Carmel MM, Ind

## PIKE

2-24-1842 — Miriam, -widow of Wilson Pike of Henry Co, Ind, & -dt Mark A & Nancy Dillon (both dec) of Pasquotank Co, N C, m at Hopewell MH, Ind, Henry Palin of Wayne Co, Ind
7-16-1842 — Miriam Palin & her ch Mary A & Stanford Pike gct Milford MM, Ind
10- -1845 — Jordon gct Milford MM, Ind
6-15-1850 — Stanford, a minor, rocf Milford MM, Ind
2-19-1887 — Lydia rec in mbrp
3-18-1893 — Peninah & ch Bertie, Harry & Frank gct Spiceland MM, Ind

## PITTS

6-21-1902 — John Henry & w Mary & minor ch Alta Lulu, Clarence F, Velma L & Chester Joseph rocf Amboy MM, Ind
2-15-1908 — John H & w Mary & ch Alta L, Clarence P, Chester J & Mildred A gct Alva MM, Alva, Okla

## PLEAS - PLACE

- -1841 — Aaron L, a widower, & his ch are CHARTER MBRS
4-17-1841 — Aaron L appt to a comm
3-19-1842 — Aaron L & his minor dt Achsah G gct Spiceland MM, Ind
12-20-1845 — Elwood & Maurice, s of Aaron & Lydia (dec), gct Spiceland MM, Ind

## PLUMMER

4-16-1842 — Sophia (form Pierson) mcd; dis at Salem MM, Ind
5-17-1873 — Adaline (form Winslow) mcd; rel on rq

## POWELL

7-21-1883 — James C gct Dublin MM, Ind

## PRESNALL

4-15-1848 — John M & Edith F Wilson dec m int, 1st time
5-20-1848 — John M & Edith F Wilson dec m int, 2nd time (John M Presnall died before they could be married)

## PRICE

12-20-1884 — Christopher & dt Calla May rec in mbrp
1-16-1885 — Martha & s Walter W rec in mbrp

## PUCKETT

12-17-1842 — Margaret A (wife of Greenlee Puckett) & minor ch Samuel H & Thomas Clarkson gct Duck Creek MM, Ind
12-17-1842 — Greenlee dis for na & unbecoming language
1-16-1864 — Greenlee rst in mbrp at Back Creek MM, Ind w/c this MM

## RATLIFF

- -1841 — Jonathan & w Sarah & ch are CHARTER MBRS
4-17-1841 — Jonathan appt to a comm

HOPEWELL

**RATLIFF (Cont)**

| | |
|---|---|
| 12-16-1843 | Elias dis for stealing & falsefying |
| 7-20-1844 | Caroline Sanders (form Ratliff) chm of mcd |
| 5-21-1845 | Mary, -dt Jonathan & Sarah of Henry Co, Ind, m at Hopewell MH, John Dennis of Henry Co, Ind |
| 6-15-1850 | Samuel mcd |
| 12-21-1850 | Eli, an orphan u/c Nathan & w Lydia Macy, gct Mississinewa MM, Ind |
| 6-13-1852 | Betty, -dt Cornelius & Abigail (dec), Henry Co, Ind, m at Hopewell MH, Phineas Macy of Henry Co, Ind |
| 11-24-1852 | Cornelius of Henry Co, Ind, -s Richard & Elizabeth (both dec), m at Hopewell MH, Lydia Ann Macy of Henry Co, Ind |
| 5-15-1853 | Miriam Newby (form Ratliff) chm of mcd |
| 10-19-1853 | Huldah, -dt Jonathan & Sarah of Henry Co, Ind, m at Hopewell MH, Morris Reynolds of Henry Co, Ind |
| 2-13-1856 | Sarah Reyton (form Ratliff) dis for mcd |
| 10-22-1856 | Nancy, -dt Jonathan & Sarah of Henry Co, Ind, m at Hopewell MH, William Bundy of Henry Co, Ind |
| 11-21-1857 | Millicent dis for being mother of a ch out of wedlock |
| 6-20-1863 | Mary Ann Stuart (form Ratliff) dis for mcd & unchastity |
| 12-17-1864 | Sarah rocf Bangor MM, Ia; -end by Duck Creek MM, Ind |
| 3-17-1866 | Eliza Jane Lacy (form Ratliff) chm of mcd |
| 5-19-1866 | Sarah A Gilbert (form Ratliff) chm of mcd |
| 7-21-1866 | Lydia gct Richland MM, Ind |
| 8-17-1867 | Margaret Carter (form Ratliff) chm of mcd |
| 9-19-1868 | Monoah dis for jas |
| 4-20-1872 | Cornelius & w Lydia Ann & minor ch Abigail, Anna F, Seth C, James, Avis L & Phineas M gct Deer Creek MM, Ind |
| 4-20-1872 | Reuben gct Deer Creek MM, Ind |
| 4-18-1874 | Elizabeth rec in mbrp |
| 4-17-1875 | Asa gct Deer Creek MM, Ind |
| 5-21-1892 | Cornelius gct Spiceland MM, Ind |
| 2-19-1898 | Exum & w Virginia gct Dublin MM, Ind |
| 3-16-1912 | Isom & Etta gct Springfield MM, Ind |

**REDDING**

| | |
|---|---|
| 1-19-1867 | Tirza Jane (form Bufkin) chm of mcd at White River MM, Ind |
| 4-20-1867 | Tirza Jane rocf White River MM, Ind |

**REECE**

| | |
|---|---|
| - -1841 | Nathan & Susannah & ch are CHARTER MBRS |
| 4-17-1841 | Nathan appt Clerk for the day |
| - -1841 | Needham & his minor ch are CHARTER MBRS |
| 4-17-1841 | Nathan & Susannah appt to comm to have care of indigent persons |
| - -1841 | Ann, widowed mother of Nathan & Needham, a CHARTER MBR |
| 4-17-1841 | Ann appt to comm on Education |
| 4-17-1841 | Nathan appt to comm to att funerals |
| 5-15-1841 | Nathan appt Clerk & James Macy appt Asst-Clerk |
| 5-15-1841 | Nathan appt an Overseer at Rich Square MM |
| 5-15-1841 | Susannah appt an Overseer at Rich Square MM |
| 6-19-1841 | Needham appt to a comm |
| 8-21-1841 | Nathan appt Librarian at Rich Square MM |
| 9-18-1841 | Nathan rpt dec |
| 3-17-1849 | Needham & minor s John & James gct Whitewater MM, Ind |
| 4-19-1851 | Elias dis |
| 9-20-1851 | Susanna & her minor ch Jane, Mary & Joel gct Walnut Ridge MM, Ind |
| 9-20-1851 | Charles gct Walnut Ridge MM, Ind |
| 8-25-1852 | Charles of Walnut Ridge MM, Rush Co, Ind, -s Nathan (dec) & Susannah, m at Hopewell MH, Eunice Dennis of Henry Co, Ind |
| 8-20-1853 | Eunice D gct Walnut Ridge MM, Ind |
| 11-21-1863 | Susannah, a widow, gct Mississinewa MM, Ind |
| 11-21-1863 | Mary & Jane gct Mississinewa MM, Ind |
| 11-21-1863 | Joel gct Mississinewa MM, Ind |

**REYNOLDS**

| | |
|---|---|
| 7-15-1848 | Mary Scott (form Reynolds) dis for mcd |
| 10-19-1853 | Morris of Henry Co, Ind, -s Daniel & Margaret of same place, m at Hopewell MH, Huldah Ratliff of Henry Co, Ind |
| 12-21-1853 | Phebe, -dt Daniel & Margaret of Henry Co, Ind, m at Hopewell MH, Amos Bogue of Henry Co, Ind |
| 11-18-1854 | Nancy rec in mbrp |
| 6-22-1859 | Josiah of Henry Co, Ind, -s Daniel & Margaret of same place, m at Hopewell MH, Lucretia Macy of Henry Co, Ind |
| 11-17-1860 | Milton & w Nancy & minor ch Newby, Margaret & William F gct Birch Lake MM, Mich |
| 12-21-1861 | Anna Thomas (form Reynolds) chm of mcd |
| 2-20-1864 | Josiah & w Lucretia & minor s William Henry gct Walnut Ridge MM, Ind |
| 2-18-1865 | Daniel & w Margaret & minor dt Martha gct Milford MM, Ind |
| 2-17-1866 | Josiah & w Lucretia & s William H rocf White River MM, Ind |
| 12-15-1866 | Isaac drpd fr mbrp |
| 4-18-1874 | Jane rec in mbrp |
| 11-21-1874 | Josiah & w Lucretia & minor s William H & adopted dt Jennie Reynolds gct Milford MM, Ind |
| 9-17-1898 | Harvey & w Cynthia Ann & ch Nellie Ruth, Isaac, Herbert, Bertha & John Albert rocf Springfield MM, Ind |
| 12-21-1907 | Morris & w Huldah gct Dublin MM, Ind |

**RHODES**

| | |
|---|---|
| 6-15-1912 | Frank B & Clara gct Walnut Ridge MM, Ind |

**RUSSELL**

| | |
|---|---|
| 10-15-1892 | Perry M & Ruthanna gct West Grove MM, Ind |

**SANDERS**

| | |
|---|---|
| 7-20-1844 | Caroline (form Ratliff) chm of mcd |
| 8-17-1844 | Caroline gct Duck Creek MM, Ind |

**SANDS**

| | |
|---|---|
| 7-18-1868 | Cornelia rec in mbrp |
| 1-15-1887 | Israel & w Cynthia Ann & ch Sarah & India rec in mbrp |

**SAUL**

| | |
|---|---|
| 1-15-1887 | Sarah rec in mbrp |
| 2-19-1887 | George rec in mbrp |
| - -1896 | Sarah rel fr mbrp on rq |

**SCOTT**

| | |
|---|---|
| 7-15-1848 | Mary (form Reynolds) dis for mcd |
| 12-17-1887 | Mary Ettie Stratton gct Fairmount MM, Ind |
| 4-20-1895 | Nancy rolf Meth Ch, Lewisville, Ind |

**SCOVILLE**

| | |
|---|---|
| 12-17-1887 | Anna M (Stewart) gct Spiceland MM, Ind |

**SHALLEY**

| | |
|---|---|
| 7-15-1854 | Elizabeth (form Butler) dis for mcd |
| 9-19-1891 | John C rocf Dover MM, Ind |
| 9-17-1904 | John C gct Poplar Run MM, Ind |

**SHATIS**

| | |
|---|---|
| 6-17-1911 | Hazel glt Meth Ch, Lewisville, Ind |

**SHARP**

| | |
|---|---|
| 6-15-1850 | Elizabeth (form Pickering) dis at Duck Creek MM, Ind |

**SHIPLEY**

| | |
|---|---|
| 7-21-1883 | Mary F gct Westland MM, Ind |

**SHOEMAKER**

| | |
|---|---|
| 2-15-1873 | Charles & w Margaret Ann & dt Anna Mary rocf Salem (Silver Creek) MM, Ind |
| 2-15-1873 | Ezekiel & Elijah rocf Salem (Silver Creek) MM, Ind |
| 10-18-1879 | Elijah gct LaCrosse MM, Kans |
| 2-21-1880 | Ezekiel gct LaCrosse MM, Kans |

HOPEWELL

## SHOEMAKER (Cont)
11-20-1880  Charles & w Margaret Ann gct LaCrosse MM, Kans
11-20-1880  Anna Mary gct LaCrosse MM, Kans
4-17-1881  Alpheus gct LaCrosse MM, Kans

## SIMPSON
4-20-1895  Mary rel fr mbrp on rq to jas

## SMITH
2-18-1843  Thomas W dis for jas   U B CH)
10-19-1844  Rachel (form Lewis) chm of mcd
5-15-1856  Rachel dis for na
8-17-1907  Clarence, Clark, Ida M & Orville gct Dublin MM, Ind

## SPENCER
5-21-1849  Emily (form Hiatt) dis for mcd
9-16-1911  Mary Emma & minor s John Carlton Bell gct Knightstown MM, Ind

## STAFFORD
2-16-1861  James A dis for mcd
7-21-1866  James A & ch William H & Charles A rec in mbrp (Martha E, wife of James A, dec before rq gr)
6-15-1872  Mary Elma Paul (form Stafford) chm of mcd
8-15-1891  Charles A gct New Castle MM, Ind
9-25-1895  Hannah A rolf Meth Ch, Fairmount, Ind
7-19-1902  Hannah A gct Fairmount MM, Ind
3-19-1904  Lindley H gct Indianapolis MM, Ind

## STANBROUGH
3-12-1844  James of Duck Creek MM, Henry Co, Ind, -s Nehemiah & Ruth of same place, m at Hopewell MH, Sarah Macy of Henry Co, Ind
5-18-1844  Sarah gct Back Creek MM, Ind

## STANLEY
- -1841  Elwood & w Martha & ch are CHARTER MBRS
- -1841  George & w Jemima & ch are CHARTER MBRS
4-17-1841  Elwood appt to comm on Education
4-17-1841  Jemima appt to a comm
9-21-1844  Samuel gct Back Creek MM to m Mary C Stanbrough
5-17-1845  Mary H rocf Back Creek MM
2-21-1846  Samuel & Mary H gct Westfield MM, Ind
2-20-1847  George & w Jemima & minor ch Isaac, Karen N, John T, Elizabeth, Elam & James M gct Richland MM, Ind
5-17-1847  Jeremiah P gct Richland MM, Ind
9-16-1849  Elizabeth gct Westfield MM, Ind
8-18-1855  Elwood & w Martha & minor ch William E, Emeline B, Margaret A, Elmina, Louisa J, Edwin A, Laura A & Mary E gct Spring Creek MM, Ia
7-16-1859  Avis Jane gct Walnut Ridge MM, Ind
8-23-1866  Adaline, -dt Nathan & Mary of Henry Co, Ind, m at Rich Square MH, Harvey Gilbert of Henry Co, Ind
- -1868  Cyrus & w Mary rocf New Garden MM, N C

## STAUB
2-19-1887  Matilda rec in mbrp

## STEELE
4-15-1893  Adam & w Martha rec in mbrp

## STEWART  (See also STUART)
- -1841  Samuel W & w Hannah & ch are CHARTER MBRS
4-17-1841  Samuel W appt to a comm
7-17-1841  Samuel W appt Recorder of Marriage Certs
5-25-1843  Mary, -dt Samuel W & Hannah of Rich Square MM, Henry Co, Ind, m at Rich Square MH, Jethro Wickersham of same place
9-23-1852  Elizabeth, -dt Samuel W & Hannah of Henry Co, Ind, m at Rich Square MH, Benjamin Stuart, -s John & Martha Stuart of Henry Co, Ind
2-29-1853  Beulah, -dt Samuel W & Hannah of Henry Co, Ind m at Rich Square MH, Benjamin W Paxson of Henry Co, Ind
4-24-1856  William of Henry Co, Ind, -s Samuel W & Hannah (dec), m at Rich Square MH, Huldah Newby of Henry Co, Ind
8-21-1856  Charles of Henry Co, Ind, -s Samuel W & Hannah (dec), m at Rich Square MH, Maria J Hare of Henry Co, Ind
10-19-1861  Edmond & Albert, ch of Samuel, gct Milford MM, Ind
6-18-1881  Albert rocf Indianapolis MM, Ind
2-17-1883  Antoinette rocf Fairmount MM, Ind
7-21-1883  Margaret B rocf Springfield MM, Ind
11-20-1886  Elizabeth W & s Clayton rec in mbrp
4-15-1905  Charles & Maria J gct Dublin MM, Ind

## STIGELMAN
3-18-1893  Solomon W & w & ch Robert R, L Ethel, Warren A & O Jennette rec in mbrp
12-17-1910  Solomon W & w Harriet & dt Olive Jennette & Ethel D glt Meth Ch, Chester, Ind

## STOPHER - STOFFER
2-16-1861  Penninah (form Gilbert) chm of mcd
7-21-1866  Mary Emma, -dt George & Penninah, rec in mbrp

## STOUT
9-18-1841  Peter & minor ch Catherine, Mary & John gct Walnut Ridge MM, Ind

## STRATTON
- -1841  Benjamin & w Ann & s Joseph are CHARTER MBRS
4-17-1841  Benjamin appt to a comm
4-17-1841  Ann appt to comm on Education
11-18-1848  Louisa Jane rec in mbrp
5-21-1849  Louisa J Henley (form Stratton) chm of mcd at White River MM, Ind
2-24-1864  Benjamin of Henry Co, Ind, -s Joseph & Ann of same place, m at Hopewell MH, Ind, Margaret Gilbert of Henry Co, Ind
8-15-1868  Luanna (form Hall) chm of mcd

## STRAUGHN - STRAWN
4-16-1842  Jehu dis for na & dp
9-18-1847  James dis for na, dp & upl
2-17-1849  Milton dis for dp & na

## STREET
9-12-1841  John & ch Eunice, Mary & John gct Walnut Ridge MM, Ind
9-15-1849  Mary rocf White River MM, Ind
5-23-1854  Mary gct Spiceland MM, Ind
7-16-1863  Samuel & Anna rocf Spiceland MM, Ind
7-16-1863  Rebecca rocf Spiceland MM, Ind
7-16-1863  Isaac rocf Spiceland MM, Ind
11-18-1871  Samuel & w Anna gct Kokomo MM, Ind
11-18-1871  Rebecca gct Kokomo MM, Ind
6-10-1875  Isaac gct Peace MM, Kans (Instead of going to Kans, Isaac went to reside in Kokomo, Ind)
4-21-1877  Isaac gct Kokomo MM, Ind

## STRETCH
11-16-1844  Hannah Ann Templeton (form Stretch) dis for mcd
11-21-1844  Ann, widow of James & -dt Asa Jeffers, late of Salem Co, N J & wife Elizabeth (dec), m at Rich Square MH, William Moore of Henry Co, Ind

## STUART  (See also STEWART)
9-23-1852  Benjamin of Henry Co, Ind, -s John & Martha of same place, m at Rich Square MH, Elizabeth Stewart, -dt Samuel & Hannah of Henry Co, Ind
3-25-1857  Jehu T of Henry Co, Ind, -s John & Martha of same place, m at Hopewell MH, Sarah Pearson, widow of Seth Pearson & -dt Jesse & Rachel Bundy
3-18-1859  Jehu & w Sarah & ch Eliza Jane Pearson & Rachel Stuart gct Honey Creek MM, Ind

HOPEWELL

STUART (Cont)  (See also STEWART)
4-21-1860   Jehu & w Sarah & dt Eliza Jane Pearson & Rachel Stuart rocf Honey Creek MM, Ind
7-25-1861   Mary A, -dt John & Martha of Henry Co, Ind, m at Rich Square MH, William Bundy of Walnut Ridge MM, Rush Co, Ind
6-20-1863   Mary Ann (form Ratliff) mcd; dis
1-21-1865   Jehu T & w Sarah & dt Eliza Jane Pearson gct Spiceland MM, Ind
8-18-1866   Mary Ann rec in mbrp
3-16-1867   Martha Ellen Hiatt (form Stuart) chm of mcd
7-18-1868   John & w Martha gct Carthage MM, Ind
7-18-1868   Emma C gct Carthage MM, Ind
8-16-1890   Minnie E Eaton (form Stuart) rel fr mbrp on rq
4-21-1906   William Rollin gct Greenfield, Ind
5-19-1906   Oliver & Mary E gct Dublin MM, Ind
7-17-1909   Henry H gct Whitewater MM, Richmond, Ind

STUBBLEFIELD
3-17-1894   John & w Rosetta & dt Hazel rec in mbrp

STUBBS
9-20-1890   Annette B rec in mbrp

SURITH
7-17-1903   Mary E glt Meth Ch at Greenfield, Ind

SWAFFORD
3-17-1894   W O rec in mbrp

SWAIN
4-21-1906   Mary Maude (form Crawford) gct Knightstown MM, Ind

SWANDER
12-17-1904  James M & Franklin R, minor ch of Elain W, gct South Wabash MM, Ind

SYMONS - SYMONDS
  -  -1841  John & w Rebecca & ch are CHARTER MBRS
  -  -1841  Samuel & w Ann & ch are CHARTER MBRS
4-17-1841   John appt to comm on Education
11-18-1843  Samuel & w Ann & minor ch Lydia, James, John B, Abraham & Henry gct Westfield MM, Ind
8-15-1846   Benjamin, a minor, gct Spiceland MM, Ind
5-24-1848   Daniel of Henry Co, Ind, -s John (dec) & Rebecca of same place, m at Hopewell MH, Louisa Macy of Henry Co, Ind
1-17-1852   Abraham gct Cherry Grove MM, Ind to m Mary Horn
3-19-1853   Daniel & w Louisa & minor ch Jesse C & Phebe Ann gct Wabash MM, Ind
6-19-1853   Joel dis for na
4-19-1856   Abraham & w Mary C & minor ch Julian Oscar gct Poplar Run MM, Ind
12-21-1859  Sarah, -dt John (dec) & Rebecca of Henry Co, Ind, m at Hopewell MH, Joseph Cosand of Rich Square MM, Henry Co, Ind
1-17-1863   Benjamin F rocf ... (may be Spiceland MM, Ind)
5-16-1863   Verlinda J rocf West Branch MM
6-18-1863   Daniel & w Louisa & ch Jesse C, Phebe Ann, Jane, John W, Mary E, Sarah Elizabeth & Matthew M rocf Back Creek MM, Ind
12-19-1863  Benjamin F & w Verlinda J gct Raysville MM, Ind
7-16-1864   Rebecca, a widow, gct Milford MM, Ind
7-16-1864   Mary & Abigail gct Milford MM, Ind
12-16-1871  Daniel & w Louisa gct Deer Creek MM, Ind
4-20-1872   Jesse gct Deer Creek MM, Ind
8-21-1875   Rebecca rocf Milford MM, Ind
3-17-1894   Luther & ch Mervin rec in mbrp

TALBERT - TALBOTT
11-15-1845  Sarah (form Patten) dis for mcd at Pennsville MM, Ohio
3-20-1875   Alvin & w Rebecca & minor ch Sylvanus D, Mary E & William gct Spiceland MM, Ind

3-20-1875   Orpheus gct Spiceland MM, Ind
3-20-1875   Martha E gct Spiceland MM, Ind
3-19-1887   Daniel rocf White River MM, Ind
8-18-1888   Daniel & w Caroline M gct Spiceland MM, Ind

TAYLOR
  -  -1841  Mary B is a CHARTER MBR
4-17-1841   Mary B appt to comm on Education

TEMPLETON
11-16-1844  Hannah Ann (form Stretch) dis for mcd

THOMAS
12-21-1861  Anna (form Reynolds) chm of mcd
11-20-1887  James C rocf Spiceland MM, Ind
2-19-1898   Sarah E rec in mbrp
1-19-1901   Sarah E & s Merrel rocf Spiceland MM, Ind

THOMPSON
2-21-1874   Rebecca A (form Brothers) gct Ash Grove MM, Ill

THORNBURG
8-21-1897   John H gct Knightstown MM, Ind

THORNTON
1-21-1893   Evan C & Martha B gct Olive Branch MM

VICKERY
4-17-1875   Martha rec in mbrp

WALTHAL
9-25-1873   Levi of Vermilion Co, Ind, -s William B & Sarah of same place, m at Hopewell MH, Henry Co, Ind, Elizabeth J Cox of Henry Co, Ind
7-20-1895   Levi & w Elizabeth J & minor ch Elma, Elsie A, Dora H, Albert, Frank J, Edward, Clinton B & E Luella gct Barclay MM, Kans

WARD
10-16-1844  Martha C (form Lewis) chm of mcd
4-24-1867   Martha C, widow of Jacob Ward Sr, & -dt Nathan & Rachel Lewis, m at Hopewell MH, Robert Hall of Henry Co, Ind
3-17-1877   Charles A & Jacob Jr rec in mbrp
11-20-1886  Charles A gct Spiceland MM, Ind
9-17-1887   Jacob gct Whitewater MM, Ind

WASSON
2-20-1858   Calvin H rocf Newberry MM, Ohio
2-20-1858   Abigail C rocf Milford MM, Ind
6-17-1871   Calvin H rec a min
11-16-1889  Calvin H & w Abigail gct New Castle MM, Ind

WEEKS or WERTS
10-18-1873  Sarah Ellen (form Dougherty) chm of mcd

WEST
11-20-1909  William & w Margaret & minor gr-ch Raymond & Gladys West gct Fairmount MM, Ind

WHITE
5-15-1841   Thomas N rocf Spiceland MM, Ind; -end by Milford MM, Ind
5-15-1841   Lydia appt to att QM
10-  -1841  Thomas N appt Recorder of Certs of Removals in place of Isaac Parker who has rq to be rel
5-20-1843   Ann & ch Margaret S, Joseph H, Jesse T, Harriett, John G & Elizabeth rocf West Grove MM, Ind
8-24-1843   Lydia, -dt Thomas & Jemima (both dec), of Perquimans Co, N C, m at Hopewell MH, Ind, Robert Hall of Henry Co, Ind
4-24-1844   Thomas N of Henry Co, Ind, -s Thomas & Jemima (both dec), of Perquimans Co, N C, m at Hopewell MH, Ind, Lydia Parker of Henry Co, Ind
4-19-1845   Oliver, a minor, rocf Milford MM, Ind

HOPEWELL

## WHITE (Cont)

|  |  |
|---|---|
| 5-15-1847 | Oliver, a minor, gct Milford MM, Ind |
| 6-18-1853 | Joseph H mcd |
| 11-10-1855 | Margaret Ann rocf Spiceland MM, Ind |
| 9-25-1856 | Margaret, -dt Exum & Ann of Henry Co, Ind, m at Rich Square MH, James Hemington of Wayne Co, Ind, -s Robert (dec) & Elizabeth of Cambridgeshire, England |
| -26-1860 | Elizabeth, -dt Exum (dec) & Ann of Henry Co, Ind, m at Rich Square MH, Joshua G Wickersham of Henry Co, Ind |
| 6-15-1861 | Sarah rocf Milford MM, Ind |
| 2-15-1862 | Daniel T rocf Milford MM, Ind |
| 2-24-1864 | Daniel T of Henry Co, Ind, -s Alfred & Mary, m at Hopewell MH, Sarah Gilbert of Henry Co, Ind |
| 7-21-1866 | Joseph & w Ellen M & ch Edgar T, Harriett E, Lucy E, Anna L, Mary E & Albert O rec in mbrp |
| 1- 5-1871 | William W of Dublin, Wayne Co, Ind, -s Josiah T & Elizabeth W of same place, m at Rich Square MH, Mary A White, -dt Thomas N & Lydia White of Henry Co, Ind |
| 1- 5-1871 | Mary A, -dt Thomas T & Lydia of Henry Co, Ind, m at Rich Square MH, William W White of Dublin MM, Wayne Co, Ind |
| 7-16-1871 | Mary A gct Milford MM, Ind |
| 6-15-1872 | Daniel T & w Sarah & ch Annie S, Olive B & Arthur T rocf Milford MM, Ind |
| 3-15-1873 | Peninah rocf Deep River MM, N C (Wife of Francis) |
| 5-16-1874 | Francis G rec in mbrp |
| 2-18-1876 | Daniel T & w Sarah & minor ch Anna S, Olive B & Arthur T gct Milford MM, Ind |
| 4-21-1877 | Francis G & w Peninah gct Milford MM, Ind |
| 12-12-1880 | Mary S rocf Deer Creek MM, Ind |
| 6-18-1881 | Miriam T rocf Springfield MM, Ind |
| 7- 1-1881 | Esther A, -dt Thomas N & Lydia White of Henry Co, Ind, m at Rich Square MH, George W White of Belvidere, Perquimans Co, N C, -s Rufus & Lydia |
| 7- 1-1881 | George W of Belvidere, Perquimans Co, N C, -s Rufus & Lydia of same place, m at Rich Square MH, Henry Co, Ind, Esther A White, -dt Thomas N & Lydia White of Henry Co, Ind |
| 4-15-1882 | David O gct Walnut Ridge MM, Ind |
| 4-21-1883 | Robert J gct La Grande MM |
| 7-17-1886 | William W & w Mary A & ch Marian E, Lydia Florence & Esther Mary rocf Adrian MM, Mich |
| 2-19-1887 | Joseph & w Abigail & ch Mary S, Ella Ann, William S, Anna L & Elizabeth rec in mbrp |
| 7-16-1887 | Chappel rocf Dublin MM, Ind |
| 4-21-1888 | Laura gct Walnut Ridge MM, Ind |
| 12-16-1893 | Joseph & w Abigail glt U B Ch, Salem, Ind |
| 11-20-1897 | Mary A & her minor ch Mariam E, Lydia F, Esther, Mary & Hellen Dora gct Whitewater MM, Ind |
| 3-15-1902 | Thomas R gct Frankford MM, Philadelphia, Pa |
| 4-15-1905 | Edgar T gct New Castle MM, Ind |
| - -1907 | Albert O gct Indianapolis MM, Ind |

## WHITSELL

|  |  |
|---|---|
| 2-19-1887 | Alonzo & w Rhoda & ch Joseph & John rec in mbrp |

## WICKERSHAM

|  |  |
|---|---|
| - -1841 | Caleb & 2nd w Eunice & ch are CHARTER MBRS |
| - -1841 | Abel & w Eliza Ann & ch are CHARTER MBRS |
| 4-17-1841 | Caleb appt to comm |
| 4-17-1841 | Eunice appt to a comm |
| 5-15-1841 | Eunice appt an Overseer at Rich Square MM |
| 8-21-1841 | Oliver dis for mcd |
| 5-25-1843 | Jethro of Henry Co, Ind, -s Caleb & Eunice of same place, m at Rich Square MH, Mary Stewart, -dt Samuel W & Hannah of Henry Co, Ind |
| 1-20-1844 | Caleb & dt Huldah dis for disunity |
| 2-17-1844 | Eunice dis for disunity |
| 7-19-1845 | Jethro dis for jASF |
| 9-15-1849 | Mary B rocf Salem MM (Silver Creek) Ind |
| 12-20-1849 | Caroline M, -dt Abel & Eliza Ann of Henry Co, Ind, m at Rich Square MH, William W Wilson of Henry Co, Ind |
| 1-15-1859 | Jethro rst in mbrp by rq |
| -26-1860 | Joshua G of Henry Co, Ind, -s Abel & Eliza Ann (dec), m at Rich Square MH, Elizabeth White of Henry Co, Ind |
| 3-15-1862 | Caleb E gct Rich Square MM, Ia |
| 3-19-1864 | Joshua G & w Elizabeth W & minor ch Elnora gct Milford MM, Ind |
| 7-11-1867 | Mary Anis, -dt Abel & Eliza Ann (dec), Henry Co, Ind, m at Rich Square MH, James H Broomell of Chicago, Cook Co, Ill |
| 1-15-1870 | Abel & w Mary & gr-dt Caroline Wilson gct Spiceland MM, Ind |
| 1-15-1870 | Stephen gct Spiceland MM, Ind |
| 2-19-1870 | W B gct Honey Creek MM, Howard Co, Ind |
| 3-15-1873 | Stephen & w Mary A rocf Spiceland MM, Ind |
| 2-21-1874 | Abel & w Mary & gr-dt Caroline Wilson rocf Spiceland MM, Ind |
| 2-19-1876 | Stephen & w Mary A & minor ch Estella gct Spiceland MM, Ind |
| 1- 1-1879 | Stephen & w Mary A & dt Estella E & Anna Pearl rocf Spiceland MM, Ind |
| 1-15-1887 | Estella E glt Meth Ch, Ord, Nebraska |
| 4-16-1887 | Harry O glt Meth Ch, Ord, Valley Co, Nebr |
| 4-19-1913 | Jethro & w Margaret A gct Spiceland MM, Ind |

## WILES

|  |  |
|---|---|
| 6-26-1851 | William D of Wayne Co, Ind, -s Luke & Rhoda of same place, m at Rich Square MH, Deborah Jane Butler of Henry Co, Ind |
| 5-23-1854 | Deborah J & minor ch Orlando & Lenora gct Springfield MM, Ind |
| 6- -1855 | William & w Deborah & ch Orlando P & Lenora E rocf Springfield MM, Ind |
| 6- -1855 | Daniel rocf Springfield MM, Ind |
| 4-20-1867 | Willism dis |
| 4-20-1867 | Orlando P, Lenora E & Mary Etta, minor ch, gct Indianapolis MM, Ind |

## WILLIAMS

|  |  |
|---|---|
| 9-22-1859 | Joseph H of Henry Co, Ind, -s Jason & Abigail of same place, m at Rich Square MH, Dorothy J Gilbert of Henry Co, Ind |
| 5-19-1860 | Joseph H rocf Duck Creek MM, Ind |
| 10-16-1875 | Mary Emma, a minor, gct Spiceland MM, Ind |
| 2-19-1887 | Nelson M rec in mbrp |
| 5-21-1892 | Corina gct New Castle MM, Ind |
| 2-19-1893 | John Newton rec in mbrp |
| 6-18-1898 | Isaac Newlin rel on rq |

## WILSON

|  |  |
|---|---|
| 9-20-1845 | John C & w Amelia rec in mbrp |
| 10-12-1845 | Sarah & Hannah, ch of John C & Amelia, rec in mbrp on rq of parents |
| 10-12-1845 | Edith F, Mary T & Martha C rec in mbrp |
| 1-17-1846 | William, Jesse, Joseph, Isaac, John Jr & Israel, ch of John C & Amelia, rec in mbrp on rq of parents |
| 4-15-1848 | Edith F & John M Presnall ann m int 1st time |
| 5-20-1848 | Edith F & John M Presnall ann m int 2nd time (He did not live to accomplish marriage) |
| 12-20-1849 | William W of Henry Co, Ind, -s John C & Amelia of same place, m at Rich Square MH, Caroline M Wickersham of Henry Co, Ind |
| 9-25-1851 | Edith F, -dt John C & Amelia of Henry Co, Ind, m at Rich Square MH, Joshua Morris of Henry Co, Ind |
| 6-15-1861 | Isaac dis for mcd |
| 3-15-1862 | John Jr mcd; drpd fr mbrp |
| 1-17-1863 | David & w Phebe W & ch Adaline & Emma rec in mbrp |
| 12-16-1865 | Joseph gct Lynn Grove MM |
| 11-21-1868 | William W & minor ch Marcus A, Mary G & Eva E gct Spiceland MM, Ind |
| 1-15-1870 | Abel Wickersham & w Mary & gr-dt Caroline Wilson gct Spiceland MM, Ind |
| 2-12-1870 | Alfred & w Lydia & ch rocf Kansas MM, Kans |

HOPEWELL

## WILSON (Cont)
- 12-16-1871  Sarah E gct Cane Creek MM, N C
- 2-21-1874  Abel Wickersham & w Mary & gr-dt Caroline Wilson rocf Spiceland MM, Ind
- 12-18-1886  Alfred & w Lydia & minor ch Sybil J, John & Sylvia Ann gct Lawrence MM, Kans
- 4-16-1887  Charles F rec in mbrp
- 4-16-1887  Phebe J rocf Raysville MM, Ind
- 4-16-1892  Charles F gct Back Creek MM, N C
- 4-15-1893  William Henry rec in mbrp

## WILTSIE
- 8-2-1908  Gertrude May, -dt Charles A & Florence E of Rochester, Fulton Co, Ind, m at res of Charles Wiltsie at Rochester, Ind, Everett John Macy of Lewisville, Henry Co, Ind

## WINDSOR
- 1-15-1881  Lewis M & w Rebecca & dt Emma Jane rocf Raysville MM, Ind
- 12-19-1896  Lewis & w Rebecca gct New Castle MM, Ind

## WINSLOW
- 10-19-1844  Mary Needham (form Winslow) dis for mcd at Back Creek MM, Ind
- 5-17-1873  Adaline Plummer (form Winslow) mcd; rel fr mbrp on rq
- 10-19-1873  Phebe W dis for jas
- 11-20-1897  Adella M B gct Walnut Ridge MM, Ind

## WOOLEN - WOOLAM
- 2-19-1876  Elizabeth & her ch Hannah Adalaide & William A Woollen rocf Spiceland MM, Ind
- 7-21-1877  Henry Black & w Elizabeth & ch Lineth Ethel Black & William A & Hannah Adalaide Woollen gct Duck Creek MM, Ind
- 3-18-1905  Hiram & w Emma & ch Rubie rocf Smithfield MM, Ohio
- 11-17-1906  Hiram & w Emma gct Union MM, Ludlow, Ohio

## WORTS  (see Weeks or Werts)

## WRIGHT
- 7-17-1886  Milton & w Sarah Emma & ch Verda rocf Raysville MM, Ind
- 8-17-1889  Milton & w Sarah Emma & minor ch Verdie & Emma gct New Salem MM

## YOUNG
- 11-18-1905  Ruby Frances (form Woollam) gct West Elkton MM, Ohio

# RAYSVILLE – KNIGHTSTOWN MONTHLY MEETING
## Henry County, Indiana

Raysville Monthly Meeting was set-off from Spiceland Monthly Meeting and first held on the 25th of Fourth Month 1857. The meetinghouse stands just east of Raysville.

What few Friends lived here in the years of 1836 to 1841 attended Elm Grove Meeting some two miles north of this place. The Friends began building a meetinghouse before Raysville Meeting was established in 1841.

Meetings established by Raysville Monthly Meeting include Grant City established as a preparative in 1870; Knightstown established in 1876; Wilkinson Preparative granted 1887; Shirley Preparative, 1892. In 1912 Shirley Monthly Meeting was set-off from Raysville. It included the Preparatives of Shirley, Grant City and Wilkerson.

It is not clear but it appears that Raysville Meeting declined as Knightstown thrived. Monthly meetings were held at Knightstown and the name changed to Knightstown Monthly Meeting 25th of Fifth Month 1895. In 1919 Sixth Month 25th Raysville was re-established as a monthly meeting.

### Monthly Meeting Records

The volumes hereunder listed are found in the vault of the Yearly Meetinghouse in Richmond. These records have been microfilmed. Volumes marked (*) have been searched for this publication. Later abstractions to 1916 have been taken from Hinshaw.

| Men's Minutes | Women's Minutes |
|---|---|
| *4-25-1857 : 3-28-1868 | *4-25-1857 : 6-25-1870 |
| 4-25-1868 : 1-22-1887 | |
| 2-26-1887 : 11-24-1900 | |

Joint Minutes
12-22-1900 : 4-25-1908
5-23-1908 : 6-26-1924

Raysville Monthly Meeting Re-established

Joint Minutes  6-25-1919 : 12-28-1950

*1 Volume Births and Deaths
*3 Membership Records
*Marriage Register 1857-1908

RAYSVILLE-KNIGHTSTOWN MONTHLY MEETING
BIRTH AND DEATH RECORD

**AIKEN**
Albert W
Grace D    b 3-1-1857    -dt ... Tatnor
     (Raised by John & Catherine Morrison)

**ALBERTSON**
Edmund Junius -s Edmund P & Sophia (Morris)
     b 12-22-1859    d 11-25-1916
     -bur Glencove Cemetery, Knightstown, Ind
Mary    -dt ... Forbes

Jordan    b 3-2-1802, Perquimans Co, N C
     -s Francis & Caroline
     d 1-19-1841    -bur Raysville MM, Henry Co,
Martha    b 9-8-1813    -dt James & Sarah    Ind
                           Elliott
     d 4-20-1887 (as wife of George Evans)
     -bur Raysville MM
Ch: Caroline    b 4-6-1840, Spiceland MM, Ind

**ALLEE**
Seth R    b 2-10-1823    d 8-10-1902, near New Castle
     -bur Knightstown, Ind

**ALLEY**
Susannah    b 9-20-1826
     -dt Tidamon & Lydia Jessop

**ALLISON**
James R    b 4-25-1834    -s William & Sarah
Rachel    b 8-31-1839
     -dt Jacob & Christina Burris or Binns
Ch: Fay L    b 1-8-1876

Jay Laurence    b 1-8-1876    Of Grant City MM, Ind
Rose    b 8-14-1879
Ch: Mary    b 11-19-1899

**ALPAW**
Joseph    b 3-3-1855
Martha Ann    b 8-23-1855
Ch: Flora E    b 3-24-1877
     (m Owen Roades, 1895)

**AYDELOTTE**
Henry C Jr    b 8-2-1834, Wayne Co, Ind
     -s Hnery C Sr

**ANDERSON**
Terrell    b 12-19-1826    Of Grant City PM, Ind
Margaret A    b 8-6-1830

**APPLEGATE**
Charles W    b 8-7-1885, Cincinnati, Ohio
Emma Viola    b 2-29-1880, Loveland, Ohio
     (m 2nd to Leroy Dilkey, 3-3-1906)

Charles P    b 5-3-1863, Loveland, Ohio
Mary    b 4-20-1865, Carthage, Ind    -dt .. Estal
     d 11-4-1902    -bur Rushville, Ind Cem
Ch: Ethel Ione    b 8-18-1884
     Clara Belle    b 3-6-1888
     Pearl    b 2-26-1889, Canton, Ill
     Edward Bryon    b 8-26-1896, Sugar Grove, Ind
     Mary L    b 8-22-1901, Rushville, Ind

Elijah    b 9-19-1830, Clermont Co, Ohio
     d 4-17-1914, Shirley, Ind
     -bur Glencove Cemetery, Knightstown, Ind
     m 7-26-1905
Tressa Walton (3rd w)    b 7-23-1844
                     -widow of Rufus P
Ch: (By previous wife)
     John F    b 4-3-1861
     Elleanor Jane    b 3-25-1870, Knightstown, Ind

     (Elleanor Jane m Thomas Cox, 3-1-1906)

**ARMSTRONG**
Clara    b 7-12-1886, Indianapolis, Ind
     (m Verl Miller)
Emma C    b 11-28-1850
Pearl    b 3-1-1883, Knightstown, Ind

Oliver H    b 3-4-1874, Knightstown, Ind
Lorena    b 6-14-1879, Wilkinson

**ATKINS**
Lena B    -dt Columbus Moffitt    b 3-18-1882

**BAILEY**
John Quincy    b 7-23-1852
.....
Ch: Mary Etta    b 4-3-1881
     Jessie    b 6-19-1883

**BAKER**
Almeda    b 4-9-1826

**BALES**
Myra    -dt John Bales    b 5-10-1850
     d 7-10-1895 at White's Institute, Ind
     -bur Glencove Cem, Knightstown, Ind

**BALFOUR**
(George)
Lillian M    b 11-22-1866    -dt Edwin & Martha Hubbard

**BALLINGER**
Elbert O    b 4-24-1876

Isaac H    b 8-22-1810, N J
     -s Isaac & Hannah (Haines) of Burlington MM,
     N J & Elk MM, Ohio
Rachel Ann
Ch: Isaac    b

**BARKER**
Jacob E    b 5-31-1863, Thorntown, Ind
     d 3-9-1915 -bur Glencove Cem, Knightstown,
m                                          Ind
Stella    -dt Jabez & ... Newby

Orville C    b 7-22-1881, Henry Co, Ind
     -s Delphia M (Cox) Barker Spencer & step-s
     of Charles B Spencer
Bessie W (Kirk)    -dt Milton & Lizzie Kirk
     b 2-4-1882, Cadiz, Ind
Ch: Bethel K    b 5-25-1902
     William L    b 5-5-1904
     Milton R    b

**BARNARD**
Isaac    b 4-2-1856    d 4-24-1923
     -bur Glencove Cem, Knightstown, Ind
Mary Emma    b 8-24-1860, Rich Square MM, Ind
     -dt Joseph H & Dorothy (Gilbert) (both dec)
     Williams
Ch: Carl W    b 9-11-1889    d 5-10-1910
                                at Knightstown, Ind
     Helen    b 4-17-1892
     Joseph S    b 3-1-1895
         (m Rua Fort)

**BARRETT**
Cyrus C    b 4-13-1852    -s Addison & Nancy
Flora (1st w)    b 4-10-1854    d 1-21-1893
     -bur Glencove Cem, Knightstown, Ind
Ch: Ralph Scott    b 2-12-1876, Martinsville, Ind
         d 10-22-1909, Indianapolis, Ind
         -bur Indianapolis, Ind
     Charles Addison    b 10-16-1877, Martinsville, Ind
     L Ora    b 9-12-1879, Knightstown, Ind
         (m Fred Eugene Barrett, 6-18-1903)
     Leo Murray    b 2-28-1883, Knightstown, Ind

RAYSVILLE-KNIGHTSTOWN

## BARRETT (Cont)
Ch of Cyrus C & Flora (1st w) (Cont):
Claude Robert    b 10-27-1890, Knightstown, Ind
                   d 9- 2-1911, Indianapolis, Ind
                   -bur Glencove Cem, Knightstown, Ind
..... (2nd w)
Ch: Dean    b 1-11-1898, Knightstown, Ind

## BARTELL
Frank    b 2- 4-1871
Pearl    b 3-15-1870    -dt Joseph & Louisa McConnell
Ch: Edna    b 10-17-1897
     Hazel    b 8-10-1899
     Chester D    b

## BARTLOW
Charles    b 8-18-1863
Emma    b 12-10-1863    -dt ..... Jack
Ch: Etta Hazel    b 8-17-1888
     Francis Russell    b

## BECK
John W    b 3-30-1865, Ohio    -s Millicent
Dollie L    b 8- 2-1867
Ch: Adean    b

Millicent    b 2-28-1832    From East Goshen, Ohio
Ch: John W    b 3-30-1865, Ohio

## BEEMAN
James    b    d 1- 1-1888, Knightstown, Ind
Mariah    b 2- 4-1819, Perquimans Co, N C
     -dt John & Hester Jackson
     d 4- 8-1874
     -bur Meth Ch Burial Gr, Knightstown, Ind
Ch: Sarah Jane    b 12- 9-1839, Hartford Co, N C
         d 2- 3-1856    -bur Raysville MH, Ind
     Mary Ann    b 5-11-1841
         d 7-10-1860    -bur Raysville MH, Ind
     Margaret Isabelle    b 7- 3-1843
     Harriet Edna    b 9-13-1845
         d 4- 4-1874    -bur Knightstown, Ind
         (prob Meth Ch Burial Gr)
     William Penn    b 7-22-1848, Clinton Co, Ohio
     Martha Olivia    b 5-11-1851    d 12- 8-1856
         -bur Raysville MH, Ind

William Penn    b 7-22-1848, Clinton Co, Ohio
     -s James & Mariah (Jackson)
.....
Ch: Bernis M    b 11-12-1885, Knightstown, Ind

## BEESON
Benjamin    b 4-20-1817, Deep River MM, N C
     -s Edward & Mary
Rebecca
Ch: David M    b 7-28-1850, Henry Co, Ind

Carrie M    b 1- 2-1863

Charles M    b 2- 8-1858
Callie    b 1- 2-1863
Ch: Mamie Ermel    b 3- 9-1883

David M    b 7-28-1850, Henry Co, Ind
     -s Benjamin & Rebecca
Addie E    b 1-15-1858, Henry Co, Ind
     -dt J F & Elizabeth Lemmens
Ch: Sylvia May    b 9-13-1879
     Josie Helen    b 2- 1-1882
     Walter Henry    b 3-18-1884

Edward    b 3-15-1766, N C    From Deep River MM, N C
     -s Isaac & Phebe
Mary    b 9-15-1770, N C
     -dt David & Sarah Brooks of Deep River MM, N C
Ch: (Brought to Ind)

Benjamin    b 4-20-1817, Deep River MM, N C
     -bur Knightstown, Ind

William Wilson    b 9-10-1846 Of Grant City PM, Ind
     d 6-24-1912
Margaret Ann    b 2-12-1854
Ch: Goldina    b 7-27-1875
     Rosalta    b 8-27-1879
     William Herbert    b 2-17-1882
     Hazel Dell    b 3-20-1885
     Bennie    b 5- 3-1892
     Bonnie    b 1- 5-1895

.....
.....
Ch: Myrtle Alice    b 6-21-1871
     Harriet M    b 12-25-1875
     Clara C    b 8-16-1885

## BELL
Henry C    b 2-13-1848, Randolph Co, N C
     d 8-26-1927, New Castle, Ind
Emaline (1st w)    b 1852    -dt Joseph & Mary Wilson
     d 10-31-1874
Ch: Margaret Emeline    b 10- 1-1874
Elizabeth M (2nd w)    b 7-22-1844
     d 1- 1-1904, Rushville, Ind
     -bur Knightstown, Ind

William F    b 9-15-1832    From Back Creek MM, N C
Nancy M    b 4-30-1830
Ch: James Madison    b 3-14-1859, N C
     Mary Mariah    b 3-21-1861, N C
     Sarah Ellen    b 3-11-1864, N C
     Julia Ione    b 6-27-1871, Ind

## BENNET
.....
Sarah    b 6-28-1844 (prob in England)
     (now Sarah Frederick of Knightstown, Ind)
Ch: (by 1st h)
     William Henry    b 6-23-1871, Herfordshire
                            Co, England
     Frew Howe    b 5-31-1873, Poughkeepsie, NY
     James Hodson    b 7-21-1875, Hillsboro, Ohio
     Charles Gladstone    b 8-10-1881, Carthage, Ind
     Frank    b 5-22-1883, Carthage, Ind

## BERNARD
Thomas J    b 7- 1-1846
Jane E    b 10-30-1845

## BERT
Harry    b 12-16-1877
Cora    b 11-26-1880

## BINFORD
Rev Joseph O    b 1-21-1843    d 8-18-1910
     -bur Glencove Cem, Knightstown, Ind
Huldah A    b 10-10-1840, Guilford Co, N C
     d 11- 4-1923    -dt Samuel & Mary (Bundy)
     -bur Glencove Cem, Knightstown, Ind    Moore
Ch: Anna J    b 3-12-1873, Hancock Co, Ind
     Arthur O    b 1-20-1882, Hancock Co, Ind
     Ada C    b 5-18-1887, Hancock Co, Ind

## BIRD
George W    b 5-22-1869    -s John & Ann (Manning)
     m 11-14-1894 at Spiceland, Ind
Christie    b 11-17-1868, Spiceland, Ind
     -dt Sedley H & Elizabeth (Hodson) Deem
Ch: Harry    b 11-24-1896, Henry Co, Ind

John    b 3-14-1828
Ann    b 7- 6-1834, Suffolk Co, England
     -dt Robert & Patience Manning
Ch: George W    b 5-22-1869

## BISHOP
John Wesley    b 7-10-1847
Nannie Josephine    b 6- 8-1844
Ch: Bennie Spooner    b 12- 4-1875
     Albertie Belle    b 3- 8-1879
     Eva Preston    b 6- 4-1884

BLAKELEY
Henry            b 1867
Lola M           b 1873
Ch: Tressa D                    b 1894

BOGUE
(Anson)          m 5- 5-1887
Minnie C         b 8-12-1867    -dt Thomas M & Julia E (Swain)
                                    Swain
Ch: Paul A                      b 10- 7-1888, Spiceland, Ind

BOLINGER
Joseph           b 8-23-1834
.....
Ch: Oliver E                    b 11-29-1866
    Virginia Ellen              b 3-23-1870
    John Dave                   b 11-   -1873
                    d 4-25-1895, Carthage, Ind
                    -bur Knightstown, Ind

BOONE
George R         b 8- 9-1860, N C
Mattie           b 6- 4-1878

BOREN
Mary A           -a Widow        (mother-in-law Henry Holland)
                 b 1-12-1835    d 6-20-1913

Cora Bell        b 3-19-1880    d 1-26-1916, near Knightstown
    (m Arthur Reeves in 1899)
    -bur Glencove Cem, Knightstown, Ind

BOUSLOG
Zelma            b 7-30-1879

BRANDENBURG
Thomas           b 8-11-1832    Of Wilkinson MM
Louisa           b 12-18-1836

BRATTON
Mary L           b 9-19-1864    -dt ... Heathcoe

BRACKENRIDGE
.....
Jerutha          b 8- 7-1875, Hancock Co, Ind
                 -dt Silas & Amanda Patterson
Ch: Alfred                      b 5-27-1899, Knightstown, Ind

BREWER
Morris W         b 3- 6-1839, Milford MM, Ind   -s John & Sarah
Eliza Ann        b 2-10-1842, Greensboro, Guilford Co, N C
                 -dt Elwood & Susanna Starbuck
Ch: Clarence Augustus           b 3-21-1863, Greensboro, Ind
    Ella C                      b 1-15-1865, Carthage, Ind
            d 1-18-1865         -bur Carthage, Ind
    Otis J                      b 5-29-1866, Westland, Han-
                                    cock Co, Ind
    Eva V                       b 1- 4-1868, Carthage, Ind
    Nettie B                    b 7-25-1869, Carthage, Ind
    Jennie F                    b 1-25-1871, Westland, Han-
                                    cock Co, Ind
    Alta E                      b 8-10-1872, Charlottesville,
                                    Ind
    Julius O                    b 11-24-1873, Charlottesville,
                                    Ind
            d 10-10-1874        -bur Walnut Ridge MM, Ind
    Allen L                     b 9-19-1875, Raysville, Ind

William          b 2- 2-1822    d 7-31-1889   -bur Knights-
                                    town, Ind

BRINKMAN
Billy
Hattie (Pauline)                -dt ... Callahan
                 b 6-21-1865

BROADBENT
(John)           (non-mbr)
Nancy (1st w)    b 5- 1-1843, Spiceland MM, Ind

Ch: Arthur Owen      b 6-18-1867, Raysville MM, Ind
    Lucy Mary        b 3- 5-1869, Raysville MM, Ind
Mary (2nd w)

Robert           (non-mbr)
Martha Jane      b 9-11-1840, Spiceland MM, Henry Co, Ind
                 -dt Samuel & Lydia Griffin
Ch: Richard          b 6-22-1866, Raysville MM, Ind

BROSSIUS
(Frank)
(Elizabeth)
Ch: Margaret G       b 6-26-1868, Raysville, Ind
        (m William Porter)

BROWN
(Ethen)          From Sterling MM, Kans
.....
Ch: Oscar Otis       b 7-14-1876
    Ora Lindley      b 1-15-1878
    William Franklin b 9- 4-1880
    Leuella Wallace  b 3-18-1884

Lydia E          b 11-16-1853   (From Tipton, Ind)

BUDD
John             b 6-14-1812, Cincinnati, Ohio
                 -s John & Mary
                 (mcd, 1836, Milford MM, Ind)
Elizabeth        b 10- 9-1811, Highland Co, Ohio
                 -dt Jonathan & Phebe (Coffin) Hunt
                 -bur Raysville Cem, Henry Co, Ind
Ch: Calvin W         b 1- 6-1837, Duck Creek MM, Ind
    Albert           b 5-22-1839, Madison Co, Ind
    Phebe Ann        b 6- 2-1841, Whitewater MM, Ind
    Charles          b 1- 6-1843, Whitewater MM, Ind
    John Jr          b 3- 6-1850, Sugar River MM,
                                    Montgomery Co, Ind
            d 12- 1-1892, near Arlington, Rush Co, Ind

BUNDY
Charles          b 12-31-1800, Perquimans Co, N C
                 -s Nathan & Ruth
                 d 1-21-1868    -bur Raysville MM, Ind
                 m 11-18-1824 at Suttons Creek MH, N C
Phariba          b 10-31-1805, Perquimans Co, N C
                 -dt Nathan (dec) & 2nd w, Margaret Nixon
                 d 11- 1-1873   -bur Raysville MH, Ind
Ch: Morris N         b

Henry C          b 5- 6-1843, Ind =s Elias & Sarah (Nichol-
                 m 7-30-1867                            son)
Mary E           b 6-29-1849    -dt Dudley & Mary Day
Ch: William H        b 10-20-1868
    Nellie D         b 3-11-1870
    Alice            b 8- 2-1875
    Myrtle F         b 5-11-1881
    Orville H        b 10-25-1888

John M           b 9-20-1857, Henry Co, Ind
                 d 3-17-1909, near Kennard
                 -bur New Castle, Ind
Adaline R        b 8-20-1865, Henry Co, Ind
Ch: Charles          b 7-15-1893, Knightstown, Ind

BURGESS
William          b 6-15-1826, near Richmond, Ind
                 d 11-24-1911, Knightstown, Ind
                 -bur Spiceland, Ind
Ch: Anna P           b 6-30-1867, near Spiceland, Ind

BURNS
William G        b 1873         -s C & Lucy
Emma J           b 1878

BURT
(Sike)
Clarissa         b 11-25-1844
Ch: Harry            b 12-16-1877
    Cora             b 11-26-1880

RAYSVILLE-KNIGHTSTOWN

## BURT (Cont)
Wilson           b  4-17-1855

## BUTLER
Charles M        b  1-27-1837, Milford MM, Henry Co, Ind
                 -s William & Susannah
                 d  9-10-1912   -bur Glencove Cem, at Knightstown, Ind
Miriam           b  12-15-1833, Blue River MM, Washington Co, Ind
                 -dt Tom & Milicent White
                 d  11-15-1908  -bur Glencove Cem, Knightstown, Ind
Ch: Eleanora           b  10-28-1858, Milford MM, Ind
                       d  1- 9-1864, Raysville MH, Ind
    Coriana            b  4- 5-1861, Knightstown, Ind
                       d  11-21-1905  -bur Knightstown Cem, Ind
    Noah W             b  7-31-1864
    John T             b  11- 4-1865
    Harriet M          b  1- 2-1869   d 10- 1-1888
                       -bur Glencove Cem, Knightstown, Ind
    Emma Luretta       b  8-27-1871   d  1-12-1895
                       -bur Glencove Cem, Knightstown, Ind

Micha            b  7- 4-1865

## BUZAN
.....
Mary Ann         b  1-19-1847
                 -dt Elijah & Eliza Armstrong
Ch: Gertrude           b  8-27-1867
    Louis R            b  12- 4-1869
    Gracie Eliza       b  7- 2-1872

## BYERLEY
Wesley           b  9- 8-1838, Wayne Co, Ind
                 -s John & Catharine
                 m  12-31-1863, Knightstown, Ind
Mahala           b  11- 6-1838, Louis Co, Va
                 -dt Eskridge & Mary Hail
Ch: Emma               b  10-27-1864, Knightstown, Ind
    Mary Maud          b  2-19-1866, Knightstown, Ind
    Edgar              b  11-25-1868, Knightstown, Ind
    Nellie             b  4-25-1871, Knightstown, Ind
    Sadie M            b  5- 3-1875, Knightstown, Ind

## BYRKET
Edgar B          b  6-30-1876, Hancock Co, Ind
                 -s Brooks & Margaret
Ludoska J        b  7- 7-1875, Grant Co, Ind
                 -dt Enos & Mary (Modlin) Benbow

Jonas            b  12-20-1832, Shirley PM, Ind
                 -s Joseph & Joanna
                 d  6-  -1902   -bur Knightstown Cem, Ind
Luzena           b  5-30-1836
                 -dt Edward & Sarah Beeson
Ch: Amos E             b  2-22-1857, Henry Co, Ind
    David B            b  2-22-1857, Henry Co, Ind
    William F          b  4- 5-1863, Henry Co, Ind
    Charles E          b  1- 6-1868, Henry Co, Ind
    Benjamin L         b  8-23-1871, Henry Co, Ind

William F        b  4- 5-1863   -s Jonas & Luzena
Hattie M         b  2- 1-1868
Ch: Arista             b  7- 6-1889

## CALLAHAN
.....
.....
Ch: Sarah Emma         b  1-21-1863
    Paulla (or Pauline) b  6-21-1865
    S Elizabeth        b  2- 9-1874

Hildie Gaynell   b  10-29-1898

## CAMPBELL
(William)        b  6-10-1903
Mary E           b  8-12-1882   -dt L Fremont & Mary E Harris

## CAMMACK
Henry            b  4-28-1814, Warren Co, Ohio
                 -s John & Jane Hollingsworth
                 m  12-23-1841, Spiceland MM, Ind
Sally            b  12-19-1812, Warren Co, Ohio
                 -dt John & Elizabeth (Compton) Horner
Ch: Rachel             b
    Emeline            b
    Elwood             b
    John H             b
    Elizabeth H        b

Vestal C         b  9-22-1860
Amanda           b  3-22-1868
Ch: Noral R            b  8-15-1887
    Donald V           b  2-23-1889
    Esther Rover       b  12-11-1903, Henry Co, Ind

## CAREY
Ada M            b  5-11-1879

Vernon F                       d  9-  -1910
Harriet E        b  4- 7-1883

## CARSON
Frank E          b  7-30-1873   -s Sam

## CASEY
Mary E           b  3-24-1865

## CASS
Abel             b  8- 6-1847
Susannah         b  7-25-1845
Ch: William L          b  1-24-1878

## CATT
Albert W         b  4-22-1863
Sarah Ann        b  7-27-1869
Ch: Ross C             b  1-22-1893

George M         b  9- 9-1836
Elizabeth D      b  2- 2-1837

John K           b  12-11-1858
Luzetta Melvina  b
Ch: George S           b  5- 3-1882
    Albert O           b  2-10-1887

## CHAPPELL
Dr Milton H      b  8-23-1841, Silver Creek MM, Ind
                 -s Reuben & Mary Ann
Caroline C       b  2- 4-1844
Ch: Evaline M          b  2-10-1872
    Adrinne            b  8- 9-1873
    Vera M             b  7- 3-1875
    Robert M           b  8-23-1877
    Reuben M           b  10-30-1879   d  3-17-1883
                                       Knightstown, Ind
    Milton M           b  4- 8-1885

Reuben           b  8- 1-1810, Suttons Creek Perquimans Co, N C
                 -s Gabriel & Lydia
                 d  3-17-1883   -bur Raysville MM, Ind
                 (m 1836, Salem MM, Ind)
Mary Ann (1st w) b  12-30-1813, South River MM, Va
                 -dt Nicholas & 2nd w, Catharine Johnson
                    of Va & Ind
                 d  10-26-1849  -bur West Grove MM, Ind
Ch: John N             b  2-16-1838, Milford MM, Ind
    Griffin            b  4-26-1839, Silver Creek MM, Ind
                       d  6-17-1863
    Milton H           b  8-23-1841, Silver Creek MM, Ind
    Lydia M            b  8-24-1844, Silver Creek MM, Ind
Martha (2nd w)   b  9-27-1812, Suttons Creek MM, N C
                 m  4-  -1851, Spiceland MH, Ind
                 -bur Raysville MM, Ind
                 -dt Francis & Miriam White
Martha (3rd w)   b  6-13-1810   d  2-16-1899
                 -bur New Lisbon, Ind

## CHARLES
John T     b 2- 8-1832, Wayne Co, Ind     d 1-12-1911
Mary     b 3-22-1843     -dt ... Bales
Ch: Cora     b 10- 7-1870
       (m N Aldus Harrold)

## CLARK
...
Mary Elizabeth     b 4-17-1874
       -dt Ephraim & Sarah J Smith

## COFFIN
Emory D     b 9-19-1824, New Garden MM, N C
    -s Vestak & Altha     d 7- 4-1863
    -bur Spiceland MH, Ind
Elmira H     b 12-27-1827, New Garden MM, N C
    -dt Joshua & Sarah Foster
Ch: Julius     b 7-13-1846
       New Garden MM, N C
       d 4-17-1874     -bur Spiceland MM, Ind
    Ellen L     b 10-17-1848
       New Garden MM, N C
    Marie L     b 8- 4-1851
       Spiceland MM, Ind
    Alice     b 2-29-1856
       Spiceland MM, Ind
    Amanda     b 5- 7-1858, Raysville MM, Ind
    Walter E     b 5-13-1860, Raysville MM, Ind
    Mary E     b 5-13-1860, Raysville MM, Ind

Ezekiel T
Nancy Edna     b 10-25-1840, Springfield MM, N C
    -dt Mahlon & Luzenia Hockett
Ch: Charles Lindley     b 2- 8-1866     d 8-16-1866
    Addie Lenora     b 10-20-1867
    Mahlon Preston     b 10- 6-1869
    Chester Elihu     b 2-22-1871

Louisa     b 3- 7-1849     -dt Silas & Priscilla (Butler)
       Parker
    (She was divorced from Edward S Coffin)
Ch: Olga     b 6-24-1872

Nathan T     b 10-25-1818, Jackson Co, Ind
    -s Barnabas & Sarah
Jennie     b 1- 4-1829     -dt ..... Wickham

Stella     b 5- 1-1876     (m Frank Pitts, 7-30-1899)

## COLE
Edith C     b 10-12-1878     (m Jesse Earnest)
Eva     (m ..... Painter)

## COLEMAN
Effie     b 4- 4-1883     (Of Grant City MM, Ind)

## COLLINS
(Roy)     m 5-16-1903
Effie     b 12- 5-1872     -dt Ed & Mary Elizabeth Hays

.....
Frances     b 2- 1-1879     -dt Sarah Jane Kerr

## COMBS
Myrtle     b 6- 1-1871

## CONKLIN
David     b 4- 2-1817     d 3- 5-1887
    -bur Knightstown Cemetery, Ind

## COGGESHALL
John     b 6- 7-1814, Deep Creek MM, N C
    -s Tristrim & 2nd w, Elizabeth (Gardner)
    m 2-26-1862, Raysville MM, Ind
Lucinda (2nd w)     b 2-19-1826, Suttons Creek MM, N C
    -dt Robert & Rebecca White

## COOK
.....
Leila P     b 1876     -dt James & Mary Morris
Ch: Myrtle M     b 1898
    Russell M     b 1903

Joseph K     b 8-24-1871
Iola May     b 4-19-1874
Ch: Floyd W     b 6-19-1893

## COON
.....
Martha     b 10- 7-1825, Guilford Co, N C
    d 1- -1921, near Knightstown, Ind
    -bur Glencove Cem, Knightstown, Ind
    (Mother of Lou Pitts)

## COOPER
Margaret     d 1-20-1897     -bur Old Cemetery,
       Knightstown, Ind

## COSAND
John     b 8-18-1825, Perquimans Co, N C
    -s John & Milly
Malinda     b 2- 5-1825, Stokes Co, N C
    -dt R L & Rebecca Lancaster

## COWAN
Charles
Ella H     b 5-24-1875, Ridge Farm, Ill
    -dt Rufus Davis

## COX
Anna E     b 9-19-1845

Charles S     b 11-22-1847
Eliza E     b 7- 4-1854
Ch: Manda L     b 12-13-1874
    Cora     b 11-29-1877
    Charlie E     b 5-24-1881
    Lucretia V     b 5-24-1882
    Otto Z     b 7-20-1884

Emory J     m 10-17-1906
Florence Elizabeth     b 9-16-1886, Knightstown, Ind
    -dt Columbus C & Rebecca J (Kearns) Midkiff

Enos     b 8-27-1841, Randolph Co, N C
    -s Obed & Margery (Stout)
Mary Ann     b 1-28-1839, Guilford Co, N C
    -dt Nathan & Elizabeth Swain
Ch: Margery Elizabeth     b 7- 5-1865
    Obed Clarkson     b 9-24-1866
    William Thomas     b 6- 5-1867
    Benjamin Franklin     b 12-27-1872

Mahlon N     b 10-27-1845, Holly Spring MM, N C
    -s Obed & Margery (Stout)
Martha E     b 8- 3-1846     -Widow of Samuel S Jones
    -dt James & Agnes Slack
Ch: Lucretia V     b 5-20-1882
    George W     b 7-25-1885
    Martin L     b 7-25-1885

Obed (dec)
Margery     b 4- 2-1822, N C -dt ... Stout
Ch: (Brought to Knightstown MM, Ind)
    Penelope R     b 8- 4-1855, N C
    Delphina M     b 11-10-1858, Yadkin Co, N C
    Nerius     b

Obed Clarkson     b 9-24-1866     -s Enos & Mary Ann
Lundy Ann     b 10-15-1874
Ch: Joseph E     b 7-10-1894
    Martha J     b 6- 7-1898

.....
Rachel M     b 5- 1-1831
Ch: Hannah A     b 1-21-1862
    Thomas M     b 8-21-1872

RAYSVILLE-KNIGHTSTOWN

## COX (Cont)
Thomas M    b 8-21-1872    -s Rachel M Cox m 3-1-1906
Elleanor J    b 3-25-1870, Knightstown, Ind
     -dt Elijah Applegate

## CRANDALL
John A    (non-mbr)    m 2-21-1865
Sirena B    b 5-7-1840, Garrard Co, Ky
     -dt John & Martha Duggins
     d 11-13-1894    -bur Knightstown Cemetery, Ind
Ch: Howard    b 2-25-1866
    Margaret M    b 11-28-1867
     (Married Samuel McCarkle)

## CRANK
Mary P    b 2-20-1881

## CRUM
Scott    b 1-3-1875
Margaret    b 3-19-1880
Ch: (Birthright mbrs)
    Lucy C    b 8-31-1903
    Warren S    b 3-16-1905
    Hyle Eugene    b 2-10-1907

## CULP
William (dec)
Mary    b 1846    -widow of William Culp
     -dt Joseph Long

## CUNNINGHAM
John    b 9-12-1827    d 7-8-1904
     -bur Knightstown Cemetery, Ind
Harriet    b 3-12-1830
Ch: Grace Roseboom (Adopted dt) b 8-13-1869
     (m Luther Locke)

John Sherman    b 8- -1865

## DAVENPORT
(Charles)
Sarah    b 8-25-1839    -dt ..... Butler

## DALRYMPLE
Frank K    b 4-4-1871, Rush Co, Ind
     d 6-15-1924    -bur Glencove Cem, Knightstown, Ind
Verna    b 9-15-1873, Henry Co, Ind

## DAVIS
Jesse    b 1-26-1788, Core Sound MM, N C
     -s Joseph W & Susannah m 10-27-1841, in Ind
     d 9-16-1859    -bur Raysville MH, Ind
Mary (2nd w) b 12-11-1794, Deep River MM, N C
     -dt Charles & 2nd w, Ruth (Williams) Gordon
     d 12- -1888    -bur Spiceland, Ind

James (dec)
Sarah A    b 4-18-1825    d 12-26-1901
     -bur Cemetery at Knightstown, Ind
Ch: Jesse E    b 11-8-1857
    Della    b 1-11-1866
     (m Ed Holland)

(Rufus)
Mary Z    b 9-7-1849, Wilmington, Ohio
     -dt Dr Wilson & Zalinda Hobbs
     d 1-11-1923    -bur Glencove Cemetery, Knightstown, Ind
Ch: Ella H    b 5-24-1875 (m Chas Cowan)
    Mary B    b 8-13-1885
    Maynard R    b 10-18-1887
     d 11-3-1919, Indianapolis, Ind
     -bur Glencove Cemetery, Knightstown, Ind
    Ina B    b 9-19-1892
     d 2-27-1919, Richmond, Ind
     -bur Glencove Cemetery, Knightstown, Ind

## DAVY
Lawrence    b 6-6-1886    -s J W & Lydia
Mary M    b 2-22-1889    -dt Samuel & Lavina Raper

## DEEM
(John A)
Elizabeth    b 6-19-1836
     -dt Joel & Anna (Gordon) Cloud
     d 5- -1919, Spiceland MM, Ind
Hannah E    b 5-28-1828

## DeGOLYER
Lauren L    b 2-25-1868
Jessie M    b 1874
Ch: Zulu J    b 7-12-1896
    Howard E    b 8-23-1899

## DENT
George    b 5-8-1850
Jennie    b 7-30-1853
     d 12-24-1894
     -bur Cemetery at Knightstown, Ind
Ch: Harry O    b 8-30-1888 or 1889

## DIFFEE
William A    b 7-22-1827, Ashborough, N C
     -s John & Sylvania
Pharaba    b 8-1-1835, Ashborough, N C
     -dt Joseph & Martha Pritchard
Ch: Nancy L    b 7-16-1860, Greensboro, N C
    Martha E    b 7-6-1862, Statesville, Iradell Co, N C

## DOAN
Jane    b 1-16-1841, Hendricks Co, Ind
     d 1-25-1917, Knightstown, Ind
     -bur near Danville, Ind (Mill Creek Cem)
Mother of Rev. Doan    -dt .... Hadley

## DOUGLAS
Rev David W    b 10-15-1843, Durham MM, Durham, Maine
     -s Joseph & Phebe
     m 8-28-1868, Manchester, Maine
Lydia    b 4-21-1848, China MM, Albion, Maine
     -dt James & Emaline Myers

## DRAKE
Harriett Dulcenia    b 2-17-1874

## DRAPER
Rebecca    b 1-18-1821, Suttons Creek MM, N C
     -dt Samuel & Mary Albertson
     d 3- -1888    -bur Walnut Ridge Cem, Rush Co, Ind
     (Married Timothy Lamb, 9-1-1858)

## DUNCAN
.....
Naomi    b 10-19-1842    -dt Tidamon & Lydia Jessop

## EDWARDS
James    b 9-20-1816    -s David & Hope
Peninah    b 2-14-1822    -dt Isaac & Harriett Cook
Ch: James Monroe    b 12-27-1844
    Perry M    b
    Julia Ann    b
    Isaac Jefferson    b
    Cynthia Ann    b
    Charles E    b
    Eunice S    b

James Monroe    b 12-12-1844, Grant City, Ind
     -s James & Peninah (Cook)
Sarah J    b 3-18-1845
     -dt Alexander & Mary Younce
Ch: Cora Ellen    b 11-18-1873
    Charles Eddie    b 11-25-1879

## EDWARDS (Cont)

Nathaniel b 12-16-1849, Spiceland MM, Ind
  -s David & Susannah
Margery A b 11-10-1849, New Garden MM, N C
  -dt William L & Almeda Harvey
Ch: Everett P      b 7-13-1875, Grant City, Ind
    Roscoe D      b 12- 4-1876, Grant City, Ind
    Debbie P      b 2-25-1879, Grant City, Ind
    Mary Ethel    b 3-27-1883, Grant City, Ind
    Warren Lisle  b 9-10-1884, Grant City, Ind

Perry M
Sarah    b 5-20-1849  -dt John & Elizabeth Smiley
Ch: Julia Edna    b 9-30-1876
    Maud May      b 2- 8-1880

William  b 9- 5-1802, Cane Creek MM, N C
  -s Nathaniel & Mary
  m 11- 6-1822, Miami MM, Ohio
Elizabeth b 9-14-1802, Lost Creek MM, Tenn
  -dt Jonathan & Anna Newman
Ch: David    b 6- 9-1829, Spiceland MM, Ind
    Milton   b 6- 4-1838, Spiceland MM,
             d 12-12-1911    Ind

William G b 1-11-1822, Lycoming Co, Pa
  -s Joel & Ann
Hattie

William H b 4- 4-1841  -s James & Elizabeth
Elizabeth b 3-10-1839  -dt John & Martha Wright
          d 8-27-1916, Knightstown, Ind
Ch: Levi Martin  b 6-17-1869
    Martha P     b

## ELLIOTT
(Clarence)
Rosa Q   b 4-16-1867

Calvin   b 9- 8-1831  d 9-30-1894
                      -bur Knightstown, Ind
Mary Martitia b 9-31-1835
         d 7-29-1914  -bur Glencove Cem, Knights-
                       town, Ind
         (NOTE: Spiceland MM Record: Mary m Mr White
                in 1897)

Charles H b 1865      -s R..
Sarah J   b 1864
Ch: Hazel           b 1890

Clark    b 5-25-1860, Knightstown, Ind
Anna M   Of Carthage MM, Ind  d 12-10-1890
Ch: Russell        b 12- 6-1888

Edward E  b 11-20-1853  -s Richard P & Martha E
Alice Anna b 12-19-1857 -dt Eli & Jane E Hodson
Ch: Raymond Eli    b 7-19-1880
         d 8- 8-1902  -bur Glencove Cem, Knights-
                       town, Ind
         (Residence was Indianapolis, Ind)
    Ada May        b 9-20-1882
    Richard Russell b 7-10-1884
    Susie T        b 8-11-1886

Elias    b 1-23-1803, Suttons Creek, N C
  -s Nixon & Rhoda
Martha (1st w) b 8-13-1796, Deep River MM, N C
  -dt David & Sarah Saunders
         d 9-24-1850  -bur Raysville MH, Ind
Ch: William    b 11-11-1828, Deep River MM,
                              N C
    Patrick H  b 2-14-1832
    David L    b 12-30-1834
    James N    b 10-28-1837
    Mary Jane  b 7-12-1840, Deep River MM,
                              N C

Jane (2nd w) b 10-17-1826, N C
  -dt William & Sarah Cain
Ch: John B     b 6-20-1854, Spiceland MM, Ind
    Martha E   b 12-20-1856, Spiceland MM, Ind
    Emily Ann  b 10-15-1857, Raysville MM, Ind

Job  b 10- 7-1798, Suttons Creek MM, N C
  -s Nixon & Rhoda
Margaret b 4-18-1798, Symons Creek MM, N C
  -dt Mark & Susan Dillon
Nina b 3- 5-1870  d 7-29-1893  -bur Knightstown, Ind
     (m Charles Steele)

.....
Ola       Of Grant City MM, Ind
Ch: Claude C      b 5- 8-1885

Richard P b 11-21-1823, Milford MM, Wayne Co, Ind
          d 8- 9-1874   -bur Raysville MH,
                         Henry Co, Ind
  -s John & Mary
Martha E  b 11-25-1828, Spring MM, Orange Co, N C
  -dt Samuel & Harriett Pritchard
Ch: Mary Ann       b 7- 9-1849, Spiceland MM, Ind
    Samuel O       b 7- 6-1851
         d 8-20-1853  -bur Raysville MH, Ind
    Edward E       b 11-20-1853
    Clarence       b 3- 1-1856
    William Walter b 5- 9-1858, Raysville MM, Ind
         d 9-20-1862  -bur Raysville MH, Ind
    Samuel Francis b 3- 1-1860, Raysville MM, Ind
    Harriett P     b 2-10-1862
    Paul           b 9-29-1864
    Joseph Jay     b 11-15-1866
    John Jacob     b 10- 6-1869
    Richard Rollin b 9- 3-1874
         d 12-31-1877  -bur Raysville MH, Ind

Samuel Francis b 3- 1-1860
  -s Richard P & Martha E (Pritchard)
  m (prob at Honey Creek MM, Ind)
Estella H b 12-17-1859
Ch: Edmona        b 4-17-1883
         (m Ralph Allen, 12-29-1906)
    Paul R        b 12-12-1886
    Edith A       b 10- 5-1890
    Rupert H      b 11-20-1896
    Clara L       b 1-21-1899
    Richard F     b 7-25-1902

## ELLIS
Vincent  b 5-24-1880

William  b 4- 4-1874 or 1879
         -nephew of Will R Zion

## ENRIGHT
Winfield b 11-13-1879   Of Wilkinson MM, Ind

## ESTELL
Clarence C b 2-27-1878
Minnie May b 9- 4-1884
Ch: (Birthright mbrs)
    Elsie C       b 9-27-1901
    Kennes H      b 11-16-1903
    Clifford Leon b 1-24-1906

Westley  b 2-25-1827

## EVANS
(George) (dec)
Martha (2nd w) b 9- 8-1813
  -dt James & Sarah Elliott
  -widow of Jordan Albertson
         d 4-20-1881 or 1887
         -bur Raysville MH, Ind

## FEAR
Charles E b 7-31-1867
Della M   b 12- 3-1873

RAYSVILLE-KNIGHTSTOWN

### FINDLEY
H Marie     b 1-25-1895

### FISHER
George T O     m 3-1-1922
Ethel     b 10-20-1867, Westfield, Ind
    -a widow (Fodrea) Smith
    d 10-25-1928, Indianapolis, Ind
    -bur Glencove Cem, Kinghtstown, Ind

### FITHIAN
Frank     b 4-13-1862     -s Amos & Joanna

### FLETCHER
Zachariah     b 2-7-1799, Suttons Creek MM, N C
    -s Joshua & Margaret (Tom)
Anna     b 6-1-1813, Guilford Co, N C
    -dt James & Mary Johnson
Ch: William     b 4-14-1832, Milford MM, Ind
       d 8-5-1833 -bur Milford MM, Ind
    Henry Francis     b 12-10-1836
    William A     b 3-4-1843
       d 2-16-1847, Milford MM, Ind
    Margaret Ann     b 10-26-1844
    James J     b 11- -1848

### FORBES
Lorenzo     d 5-21-1909
Lydia A
Ch: Burtsal M     b

### FODREA
Benjamin D     b 1-23-1841, Hamilton Co, Ind
    -s David & Tamar
Sarah E     b 8-3-1846, Charlottesville, Hancock Co, Ind
    -dt John & Nancy Taylor
Ch: Horace J     b 5-3-1865, Raysville, Henry Co, Ind
    Ethel E     b 10-20-1866
    Rhoda A     b 3-14-1868
    John H     b 2-27-1874
    Nancy T     b 6-12-1877
    Lillian C     b 2-20-1879

### FORT
Brice D     b 4-10-1844
Alice A     b 10-30-1850
Ch: Charlie V     b 6-16-1871
    Minnie     b 11-10-1873
    Harry C     b 12-30-1881

Charles V     b 6-16-1871     -s Brice D & Alice A
Anna Mary     b 8-16-1870     -dt ... Parker
    (Anna Mary m 2nd, Samuel Pritchard, his 2nd w)
Ch: Ruby B     b 4-10-1894

Marshall     b 2-14-1871, near Knightstown, Ind
    d 6-2-1919, Knightstown, Ind
Alice F     b 9-14-1869, Tipton Co, Ind
    -dt Franklin A & 2nd w Mary A (Hodson) Macy Baldwin
Ch: Rua     b 6-11-1896, near Knightstown, Ind

### FOSTER
Robert J     b 8-19-1834

### FOWLER
George C E
Eliza Ellen
Ch: Oscar     b 5-5-1883
    Monta E     b 4-5-1885
    Harry B     b 9-26-1888

### FOX
William P     b 6-12-1829     d 8-29-1899, Ogden, Ind
    -bur Greensboro, Ind
Cornelia P     b 11-6-1831

### FOXWORTHY
Earl D     b 12-31-1883     -s Samuel & Clara

### FREDRICK
Mary     -dt Daniel & Mary Burns
    Step-mother of Tom Fredrick
    b 4-21-1805, Stokes Co, N C
    d 1-18-1878     -bur Glencove Cem, Knightstown, Ind

Sarah E (form Bennett) -a widow with ch, now Sarah Fredrick     b 6-28-1844

### FULGHUM
William A     b 3-8-1840, Whitewater MM, Ind
    -s Benjamin & Rhoda
    m 8-28-1861
Harriett     b 11-24-1839, Spiceland MM, Ind
    -dt Caleb & Mary White
Ch: Roscoe W     b 4-25-1863
    Benjamin F     b 4-11-1865

### GANO
Nixon H     b 4-2-1864     -s Aaron of Louisville, Ky
Elizabeth     b 10-12-1869     -dt Abraham & Edith Jefferies
Ch: Paul Jeffries     b 11-18-1892
       d 7-7-1895 -bur Earlham Cem, Richmond, Ind
    Mary     b 6-5-1898

### GARDNER
Lawrence     b 2-5-1872     d 12-27-1906
Ruba A     b 2-1-1878
Ch: James Linton     b 5-10-1901
    Elma Rebecca     b 7-14-1902

### GARNER
.....
Alice     b 4-16-1855
Ch: Walter     b 8-2-1883
    Maud     b
    C Herman     b 8-14-1891
    Fannie L     b 7-3-1895

Edmund
Elizabeth
Ch: Angaline B     b 4-10-1855
    Mary J     b 1-18-1858

John     b 4-17-1836, Northumberland Co, Pa
    d 2-21-1908, near Knightstown, Ind
    -bur Knightstown, Ind

Walter     b 8-21-1883     -s Alice Garner
Gertrude     b 8-18-1885
Ch: (Birthright mbr)
    Wilma     b 7-5-1904

### GARRIS
Rayford     b 12-21-1823, Pikesville, Wayne Co, N C
    -s Ichabod & Sarah
Mary Ellen     b 4-18-1844, Greensboro, Henry Co, Ind
    -dt John & Elizabeth Copeland
Ch: Sarah     b 12-11-1874, Raysville MM, Ind

### GAUSE
Eli     b 11-7-1824, Elk MM, Ohio -s Eli Sr & Martha (Pierce)
Martha Ann (1st w)     b 9-17-1828, Guilford Co, N C
    -dt John (dec) & Mary (Stanley) Harrold
    d 7-30-1861, Spiceland, Ind
Ch: (Born at Raysville PM)
    Albert     b 6-15-1853
    Samuel F     b 8-29-1855

Solomon     b 3-10-1813, Redstone MM, Pa
    -s Nathan & Mary (Ailes)
Celia     b 4-9-1819, Westfield MM, Ohio
    -dt Joseph & Sarah Stubbs

## GAUSE (Cont)
Ch of Solomon & Celia:
- Rachel    b 4-27-1848, Spiceland MM, Ind
  - d 3-17-1871   -bur Spiceland MM, Ind
- Mahlon    b 12-7-1850, Spiceland MM, Ind

Thomas Clarkson    b 12-20-1846, Milford MM, Ind
- -s Nathan & Ann

Christina    b 2-15-1847, Spiceland MM, Ind
- -dt Driver & 2nd w, Elizabeth (Cooper) Boon

## GENAUX
George J    b 9- -1868    Of Wilkinson MM, Ind

## GILBRETH
F....
Lillie (form Stuart) -a widow with ch
Ch: (By 1st h)
- Horace Greely Stuart    b
- Rhoda Maud Stuart

## GILLINGHAM
Sarah M    b 2-26-1833    d 7-11-1911, Rushville, Ind
- -bur Knightstown, Ind

## GORDON
David W    b 1-15-1879

## GOURLEY
(Claude)    m 4-9-1902
Carrie G    b 10-27-1879, Knightstown, Ind
(form Parker)

## GREEN
Blanche    b 11-16-1890    Of Grant City MM, Ind

Clara V    b 12-24-1860

George Taylor    b 8-15-1860
Lucy May    b 8-23-1865
Ch:
- George T Jr    b 7-27-1890
- Blanche I    b 11-16-1891
- Harold C    b 4-12-1895

Katie    b 4-21-1887

P....    m 1898
Bertha    b 4-6-1873    -dt ..... Adams
Ch: Harold Clifford    b 12-3-1898

Sarah A    b 6-13-1854, Knightstown, Ind
- -dt Stephen & Nancy

William H    b 8-7-1873

(Names of parents not recorded)
- Stella V    b 2-5-1880
- Gertie F    b 10-1-1883
- George C    b 12-30-1885
- Maggie M    b 1-4-1888

## GRIFFIN
Adam    b 1-2-1828, Spiceland MM, Henry Co, Ind
- -s Samuel & Lydia
Jemima    b 11-9-1826, Spiceland, near Ogden, Ind
- -dt Joseph & Mary Foster
Ch:
- Gulaelma    b 12-26-1847, near Ogden, Henry Co, Ind
- Joseph Samuel    b 8-27-1854    d 9- -1855
  - -bur Spiceland
- Clarietta    b 10-20-1856

Carrol    b 2-3-1888    -s Elza & Elizabeth

.....
Della    b 12-23-1871    -dt Elizabeth Moffit
Ch: Lillian    b 12-23-1896

Jeremiah    b 12-25-1823, West Grove MM, Wayne Co, Ind
- -s Samuel & Lydia    m 10-27-1847
Ann    b 9-24-1828, Springboro MM, Montgomery Co, Ohio
- -dt Amos & Mary Kenworthy
Ch:
- Mary E    b 1-1-1849, West Grove MM, Ind
  - d 12-26-1853
  - -bur Spiceland MH, Ind
- Charles    b 11-3-1850
  - d 3-22-1851    -bur West Grove MM, Ind
- Martha Ellen    b 4-21-1852, Spiceland MM, Ind
- Marietta    b 8-19-1854
  - d 4-21-1855    -bur Spiceland MM
- Willis    b 9-29-1858, Raysville MM, Henry Co, Ind

Joseph    b 7-26-1806, Clear Creek MM, Highland Co, Ohio
- -s Jacob & Mary
Rebecca    b 3-16-1811, Richmond, Ind
- -dt John & Sarah Burgess

Samuel    b 1-22-1804, Back Creek MM, N C
- -s Jacob & Mary
- d 1-13-1875    -bur Spiceland MM
Lydia    b 2-7-1804    -dt Adam & Catharine Rinard
Ch:
- Jeremiah    b 12-25-1823, West Grove MM, Wayne Co, Ind
- Jacob    b 1-3-1826, Spiceland MM, Ind
- Adam    b 1-2-1828, Spiceland MM, Ind
- Elihu    b 3-13-1830, Spiceland MM, Ind
- Mary Ann    b 8-25-1832, Spiceland MM, Ind
- Isom    b 8-26-1834
- William    b 11-29-1836
- Lydia    b 10-4-1838
- Martha Jane    b 9-11-1840
- Nancy    b 5-1-1843
- Samuel Jr    b 8-31-1845
- Sarah Catharine    b 1-26-1850, Spiceland MM, Ind

Willis    b 9-29-1858    -s Jeremiah & Ann
Mary E    b 5-30-1863
Ch: Ruth    b 10-9-1899

## GRUNDEN
Frost    b 8-16-1877

Marshall    b 5- -1877
Ethel    b 12- -1879    -dt ..... Sears
Ch: Orlutus    b 4- -1904

Walter    b 8- -1886
Malinda A    b
Ch: Martha    b

## GUARD
Philander    b 7-23-1840    -s Simeon & Eliza
Mary A    b 10-19-1842    -dt James & Ruth Binford
at Walnut Ridge MM, Ind
Ch:
- Rosie E    b 1-28-1864
- Mary A    b 4-14-1865

## HACKLEMAN
Omer E    b 1-3-1863, Greenfield, Ind
- d 12-1-1904
Olive H    b 10-13-1865, Greenfield, Ind
Ch:
- Charles D    b 12-20-1882
- Paul B    b 7-11-1888
  - d at Pascoula, Mo
- Dwight D    b 7-13-1893
  - d 6-25-1901, Pascoula, Mo
- Mary Gladys    b 12-25-1900

## HAINES
.....
Margaret I    b 7-3-1843    -dt James & Mariah Beeman
- d 7-2-1909, Knightstown, Ind

RAYSVILLE KNIGHTSTOWN

## HALL
Emily  b 8-17-1870

## HAMILTON
Stephen  b 7- 9-1878  (Names of parents not given)

James E  b 4- 5-1881  Of Shirley MM

Samuel D  b 1890  (Names of parents not given)

## HAMMER
Isaac N  b 5-19-1826, N C  -s Elisha & Nancy
Charity  b 8-18-1828  -dt Samuel & Hannah Wilkinson
 d 3- 3-1875  -bur Greensboro, Ind
Ch: Milton  b 1- 2-1856, Hancock Co, Ind

Peter  b 12-13-1833, Duck Creek MM, Ind
 -s Elisha & Nancy  d 9-25-1906
Sarah  b 10-29-1836, Deep Creek MM, N C
 -dt Jesse & Lydia Johnson
Ch: Elizabeth Alice  b 2-25-1863, Spiceland MM, Ind
 Emma Anice  b 10-28-1867
 Marietta  b 4-18-1872
 Jesse E  b 1-29-1877

## HARDIN
William C  b 8-15-1847, Guilford, N C
Elizabeth Caroline  (Sister of Robert Gilbreath)
 b 6- 1-1840, Guilford, N C  d 6- 5-1925

## HARRIS
J Fremont  b 5- 1-1856
Mary E  b 3-21-1860  d 4-22-1902, Indianapolis, Ind
 -bur Crown Hill Cem, Indianapolis, Ind
Ch: George Cox  b 12-31-1880
 d 1- -1905, Indianapolis, Ind -bur Crown Hill
 Mary E  b 8-12-1882
 (m William Campbell, 6-10-1903)
 Mabel G  b 1-14-1888

## HARRISON
Sarah J  b 2-28-1856

Timothy  b 5-12-1834, England  -s Timothy Sr & Mary
Naomi W  b 3-14-1838, Henry Co, Ind
 -dt Charles & Michal Morgan
Ch: Mary Emily  b 5-30-1859

## HARROLD
Lemuel  b 4-22-1839  -s Nathan & Betsey
Jane L  b 3- 9-1836  -dt L & Jane Hunt
Ch: Harriett R  b 5-20-1881
 (m Charles Butler, 6-28-1905)

Nathan Aldus  b 4-27-1872, Westland, Ind
 -s Lemuel & Jane L (Hunt)
Cora  b 10- 7-1870, Knightstown, Ind
 -dt John T & Mary (Bales) Charles
Ch: Mary Margery  b 1-19-1904, Knightstown, Ind

## HARVEY
(William L) (dec)  m N C
(Almeda)  -dt ..... Thomas
Ch: (Brought to Ind in 1862)
 Margery Ann  b 11-10-1849
 Mary  b 11-25-1851
 Thomas Chalkley  b 1-19-1854
 William Chalkley  b 2-24-1856

## HASTINGS
Charles A  b 8- 8-1865  Of Grant City MM, Ind
Laura A  b 11- 5-1872
Ch: Russell G  b 10-12-1890

Ida  b 3-21-1868  (prob wife of Chester Hastings)

Peter F  b 8- 9-1840
Ella E  b 7-23-1839

Ch: Chester  b 11- 5-1870
 Ralph W E  b 11-18-1880

Sarah  b 9-12-1843  Of Grant City PM, Ind

## HAUGHTON
William  b 8- 8-1803, Carlon MM, Ireland
 -s Joshua & Mary
 d 7- 1-1878  -bur Raysville MH, Ind
Sally  b 10-23-1854, South River MM, Bedford Co, Va
 -dt Nicholas & Martha Johnson
 d 8- -1884  -bur Raysville MH, Ind

## HAWKINS
Bryant  b 10-29-1878
Leatha D  b 3-22-1880  -dt ..... Holland
Ch: Virginia M  b 5- 3-1902 or 1903

## HAYS
Ed
Mary Elizabeth b 7-24-1853
Ch: Effie M  b 12- 5-1872
 (m Roy Collins, 5-16-1903)

Francis Marion  b 1-28-1832, Knightstown, Ind
 -s Ed
Tacy (1st w)  b 3-30-1830, Pa
 d 10-31-1889  -bur Raysville MM, Ind
Ch: Isaac E  b 11-12-1864, Rush Co, Ind

## HEATHCOCK
Joseph  b 3-10-1833  d 9- 4-1921
 -bur Knightstown, Ind
Elizabeth  b 12- 7-1839  d 6-12-1908
 -bur Knightstown, Ind
Ch: Franklin Immanuel  b 1- 1-1857
 Simon T  b 2-19-1859
 Mary L  b 9-19-1864
 (m Mr Bratton)

Samuel W  b 5-14-1835
 (mcd 1858, Deep River MM, N C)
Sarah M  b 12- 8-1832, Deep River MM, N C
 -dt James (dec) & 2nd w Rebecca (Moore)
  Pitts
Ch: Eliza  b 9-25-1859, N C
 Nancy Jane  b 9-25-1864, Ind
 (m Wilson Rutledge)
 Joseph L  b 9-26-1869
 Flora Bell  b 5-28-1871
 (m Jacob Ralston)
 Julia M  b 3-28-1873
 (m James Welborn)
Amanda  b 1-28-1876, Carthage MM, Ind

## HEINY
Elmer  b 5- 6-1873  -s Solomon & Anna
Nellie L  b 4- 7-1882

## HELPINSTINE
Hamilton C  b 9- 3-1846
Fannie H  b
Ch: Blanche  b  (m Mr Mills)

## HIATT
Daniel  b 4-21-1838, Duck Creek, Henry Co, Ind
 -s Anthony & Rebecca
Esther M  b 12- 3-1840, Greensboro, Henry Co, Ind
 -dt Jonas & Rachel James
Ch: Francis M  b 5-25-1859, Greensboro, Ind
 Elma E  b 6-10-1861, Greensboro, Ind
 Roscoe D  b 12-31-1862, Greensboro, Ind
 James E  b 1-26-1868, Greensboro, Ind

Jesse  b 9-29-1817, Deep River, Guilford Co, N C
 -s James & Milly
Achsah  b 12-25-1818, Center MM, N C
 -dt Job & Phebe Reynolds

## HIATT (Cont)
### Ch of Jesse & Achsah:
| | | |
|---|---|---|
| Job | b | 1-23-1837, Center MM, N C |
| Lyndon | b | 3- 9-1842, New Garden MM, Ind |
| Oliver | b | 6-31-1844, New Garden MM, Ind |
| Robert | b | 2-14-1849, New Garden MM, Ind |
| Albert | b | 7-14-1852, New Garden MM, Ind |
| Susanna | b | 10- 5-1854, Spiceland MM, Ind |
| Jane | b | 4-22-1857, Spiceland MM, Ind |
| Mary | b | 9-24-1859, Raysville MM, Ind |

Joshua    b 7-20-1826, Duck Creek MM, Ind
     -s David & Ruth

Samuel P    b 12-23-1850, Henry Co, Ind
     -s John & Rebecca (Unthank)
     d 3- 2-1921, -bur Knightstown MM, Ind
Ida J    b 12-27-1858, Henry Co, Ind
     -dt William & Rachel Newby
     d 10-11-1917 -bur Knightstown, Ind
Ch: Florence M    b 4- 9-1884
     Willard H    b 9-25-1897, Knightstown, Ind
     Raymond S    b 4-30-1901, Knightstown, Ind

Thomas
Matilda    b 10-16-1846 -dt Bowater & Elenor Burris
Ch: Ora Daniel    b 9-19-1876, Henry Co, Ind

William B    b 10-31-1847, Henry Co, Ind
     -s John & Rebecca (Unthank)
     m 3-18-1869, Henry Co, Ind
Anice    b 9- 5-1849, Henry Co, Ind
     -dt James & 1st w, Martha E (Wilson) Cochran
Ch: Henry W    b 5-20-1870
     Martha Pearl    b 11- 5-1874      d 3-24-1879
                                 Spiceland MM, Ind
     Charles J    b 5- 9-1877
     Walter E    b 1- 2-1881
     Lillian    b 10-23-1885

## HIBBENS
Laura    b 3- 8-1867

## HILL
Caroline    A person of color from the South
     d 8-16-1870 -bur Raysville Burial Gr, Ind
     Late residence was at Soldier's Home, Rush
     Co, Ind
Ch: John

Owen S    b 2- 7-1837 -s Thomas & Tamar (Clark)
Malissa (1st w) b 7-10-1841
     -dt John & Ann (Hoskins) Bales
Elizabeth (2nd w) b 10- 9-1847 -dt ..... Pierce

William B    b 2-26-1861 -s Amos H & Peninah Thornburgh
     d 12-29-1920, near Knightstown, Ind
     -bur Walnut Ridge MM, Ind
Anna    b 2-21-1861 -dt Solomon & Penelope (Morris)
                               Elliott

## HINSHAW
Mary Etta    b 9- 3-1874 -dt Samuel & Martha (Slack)
                               Jones

## HOBBS
Dr Wilson    b 8-21-1823 -s Samuel & Ruth
     d 7-24-1892 -bur Knightstown, Glencove Cem,
                                   Ind
     m 10-12-1846, West Grove MM, Ind
Zalinda    b 12-16-1824 -widow of ..... Lynch
     -dt Achilles & Beulah Williams
     d 3-23-1903 -bur Glencove Cem, Knightstown,
                                       Ind
Ch: Orville Williams b 1- 6-1848, Harveysburg, Ohio
     Mary Zalinda    b 9- 7-1849, Wilmington, Ohio
     Walton C    b 4- 2-1852, at Friends establish-
               ment among the Shawnee Indians, Kans
     Charles Milton b 10- 4-1854, Annapolis, Parke Co,
           d 1-27-1910 -bur Denver, Colo    Ind

     Fannie B    b 3-13-1856, Annapolis, Parke
                               Co, Ind
        d 5- 5-1914, Richmond, Ind
        -bur Glencove Cem, Knightstown, Ind
     Robert W    b 1-12-1858, Annapolis, Parke
                               Co, Ind
        d 11- 9-1879, Denver, Colo
        -bur Glencove Cem, Knightstown, Ind
     Harry Lincoln    b 8-20-1860

## HOCKETT
Mahlon    b 5-27-1808, Springfield MM, N C
     -s Mahlon Sr & Sarah (Millikan)
Luzena S (1st w) b 6-13-1814, Grayson Co, Va
     -dt William & Elizabeth (Huff) David
Ch: Alphonzo    b 7- 7-1836, Springfield MM, N C
     Nancy Edna    b 10-25-1840, Springfield MM, N C
     William Lindley    b 10-28-1843, Springfield MM, N C
     Sarah Rufina    b 9-22-1845, Springfield MM, N C
     Sibyl Almira    b 7- 3-1848, Springfield MM, N C
Hannah (2nd w) b 3- 5-1818, Holly Spring MM, Randolph
                                 Co, N C
     m 3- 4-1858
     -dt Enos & Elizabeth Barker

Warner M    b 8- 1-1831, Centre MM, N C
     -s William & Hannah
Matilda C    b 9-16-1835, Springfield MM, Ind
     -dt Elisha & Ruth Dennis
Ch: Adison F    b 3-13-1862, Raysville MM, Ind

## HODGINS
Jonathan Jr    b 4-14-1820, Center MM, N C
     -s Jonathan Sr & Deborah
     m 3-13-1843
Jane (1st w) b 8-29-1820, Springfield MM, N C
     -dt Benjamin & Margaret Milligan
     d 5-30-1864, Center MM, N C
Ch: Martitia M    b 9-23-1845, Center MM, N C
     Benjamin M    b 12-25-1847, Center MM, N C
     Robert L    b 9- 6-1850, Center MM, N C
     Cordelia B    b 11- 2-1852, Center MM, N C
     Francis T    b 11- 3-1854
     Isaac C    b 11-16-1856, Center MM, N C
           d 7-31-1865, N C
     Mary V    b 4- 1-1859, Center MM, N C
     Martha E    b 6-10-1861, N C
     Margaret E    b 6-10-1861, N C
Rebecca (2nd w) b 7-13-1838, Cane Creek MM, N C
     m in 1867 at Fairfield MM, Ind
     -widow of Mahlon Pickett
     -dt Isham & Lavina Cox
Ch: Norris O    b 9-23-1868

Joseph    b 8-12-1806, Center MM, N C
     -s Jonathan Sr & Deborah
Sally    b 9-17-1815, Center MM, N C
     -dt Job & Phebe Reynolds
     d    -bur Raysville MH, Ind
Ch: Nancy Eliza    b 3-15-1837, Center MM, N C
     Phebe Jane    b 9-27-1842, Center MM, N C
     Martha    b 2- 2-1844, Center MM, N C
           d 2- 4-1865 -bur Raysville, Ind
     Sarah H    b 8-22-1849, Center MM, N C
           d 3- 3-1886 -bur Raysville, Ind
     David Franklin    b 6-10-1851, Center MM, N C
         (was drowned in Calif)
     Margaret    b 2- 2-1848, Center MM, N C
           d 12- 7-1864 -bur Raysville, Ind

## HODSON
Eli F    b 11-28-1830 -s Robert
     d 11-29-1887 -bur Raysville MH, Ind
Jane    b 8-27-1841, New Garden MM, Ind
     -dt Job & Phebe Reynolds
Ch: Alice A    b 12-19-1857 (m Edward Elliott)
     Adda M    b 8-29-1865, Raysville MM, Ind
         (m William Hadley Ballard)
     Caroline C    b 4-18-1874, Raysville MM, Ind
         (m Frank K Steele)

RAYSVILLE-KNIGHTSTOWN

## HODSON (Cont)
Lewis N    b 12-12-1843, Springfield MM, Ind
    -s Nathan & Elizabeth (Ratliff)
Rebecca    b 10-29-1847, Spiceland MM, Ind
    -dt James B & Hannah Parker
Ch: Casper W    b 4-30-1868, Spiceland MM, Ind
    Olive E    b 10-18-1870

(Perry)
Mary Alice    b 6-24-1868    -dt David T & Sally H Pritchard

## HOLLAND
Charles    b 3-3-1861    -s Otis & Martha
Catharine M    b 11-23-1862
Ch: Earl Rupert    b 11-8-1888

Edwin    b 3-3-1861    -s Otis & Martha
Della (1st w)    b 1-11-1866    -dt James E & Sarah A Davis
    d 12-6-1914    -bur Glencove Cem, Knightstown, Ind
Ch: Jessie Marie    b 9-13-1890    d 9-26-1918 Santa Cruz,
    -bur Glencove Cem, Knightstown, Ind    Calif
Genoa (2nd w)    b 10-24-1867
    -widow of Albert F Trowbridge

Henry    b 12-15-1859
Mary Adda    b 7-26-1856    -dt Mary A Boren Sr
Ch: John Frederick    b 10-11-1888
    Maurice Byron    b 9-8-1890

Leatha D    b 3-22-1880    (m Bryant Hawkins)

Otis    b 11-11-1837    d 12-19-1913
    -bur Knightstown, Ind
Martha    b 3-26-1834    d 5-29-1911, Knightstown, Ind
Ch: Henry    b 12-12-1859
    Charles    b 3-3-1861
    Edwin    b 3-3-1861
    Murta    b 10-20-1866    (m L Small)
    Tiffin    b

## HOLLINGSWORTH
James    b 1-31-1799, Bush River MM, S C (Lawrence Co)
    d 4-11-1859, -bur Raysville MH, Ind
Lydia    b 7-31-1800, Deep River MM, N C
    -dt Sylvanus & Miriam Swayne or Swain
    d 5-22-1861, Raysville MH, Ind
Ch: Olive    b 4-3-1829, Silver Creek MM, Ind
    d 12-24-1859 -bur Raysville MH, Ind
    Miriam    b 6-27-1831, Silver Creek, Ind
    d 9-5-1851, Raysville MH, Ind
    Stephen G    b 11-22-1832, Mill Creek MM, Ohio
    Valentine    b 8-26-1834, Mill Creek MM, Ohio
    Anderson    b 2-7-1836, Mill Creek MM, Ohio
    Benjamin S    b 7-3-1839, Mill Creek MM, Ohio

Valentine    b 8-26-1834, Mill Creek MM, Ohio
    -s James & Sarah    d 1-13-1875
    -bur Raysville, Ind
    (Killed by being thrown off the RR between Muncie & Hartford City, Ind)
Mary Frances    b 7-7-1833
    -dt John B Earl & Elizabeth Reed
Ch: Martha R    b 4-7-1859
    Willis    b 1-19-1862

## HOLLOWAY
Smith (a doctor)    b 1-17-1810    d 1-25-1890 Knightstown, Ind
Margaret    b 1810    d 10-11-1904, Knightstown, Ind
Ch: Mary E    b 3-1-1842
    d 10-11-1915 -bur Glencove Cem, Knightstown, Ind

## HOLT
Warren F    b 6-30-1876, Rush Co, Ind
    -s John J & Martha S
Katie Licile    b 11-30-1877    -dt Jni P & Susan Owens

## HOOKER
Alonzo    b 6-25-1875, Rush Co, Ind
    -s Thomas L & Phebe Ellen
Minnie E R
Ch: Reba May    b 3-19-1906, Henry Co, Ind

Thomas L    b 9-6-1847, Randolph Co, N C
    -s Isham & Martha
    d 12-26-1903    -bur Lewisville, Ind
Phebe Ellen    b 4-12-1844    d 12-14-1905
    -dt Joseph & Joanna Byrkit    -bur Lewisville, Ind
Ch: Alonzo M    b 6-25-1875, Rush Co, Ind

William H    b 3-16-1850    -s Isham & Martha
M Elmira    b 3-5-1854    -dt Allen & Elizabeth Weeks
Ch: Louisa    b 8-3-1874, Henry Co, Ind
    Berthie    b 2-2-1876, Henry Co, Ind

## HOOTON
Paul    b 4-24-1883

## HORNER
Amos C    b 7-10-1822, Miami MM, Ohio
    -s John & Elizabeth    d 2-14-1900
    -bur Raysville, Ind
Elvina (1st w)    b 8-25-1830, Cherry Grove MM, Ind
    -dt Eli & Matilda Reece
    d 10-13-1859    -bur Raysville MH, Ind
Ch: Elwood T    b 9-18-1852, Spiceland MM, Ind
    Luzena    b 7-27-1854    d 8-19-1855
    -bur Raysville MH, Ind
    Stephen C    b 8-25-1856, Spiceland MM, Ind
    -bur 9-25-1857 at Raysville MH
    Enos Clayton    b 5-7-1859, Raysville MM, Ind
    d 10-26-1859    -bur Raysville MH, Ind
Ann J (2nd w)    b 5-7-1833, Milford MM    -dt Elias & Sarah

John    b 6-13-1780, Frederick Co, Va    Nicholson
    -s Thomas & Ann
    d 10-30-1852    -bur Raysville MH, Ind
Elizabeth    b 12-19-1797, Newberry Co, S C
    -dt Samuel & Elizabeth Compton
    d 3-20-1864    -bur Raysville MH, Ind
Ch: Samuel    b 4-14-1807, Miami MM, Ohio
    d    -bur Raysville MH, Ind
    Ann    b 1-4-1809, Montgomery Co, Ohio
    d 12-27-1877    -bur Raysville MH, Ind
    Rebecca    b 9-4-1811, Montgomery Co, Ohio
    d 10-22-1876    -bur Raysville MH, Ind
    Sally    b 12-19-1812, Montgomery Co, Ohio
    Rachel    b 12-19-1812, Montgomery Co, Ohio
    Lydia    b 9-30-1814, Montgomery Co, Ohio
    Amos A    b 7-10-1822, Montgomery Co, Ohio

## HOWARD
Clarence    b 1-18-1880

## HUBBARD
Alonzo    b 8-3-1837
    (brother-in-law to Sol Montacue)

(Joseph) Butler    b 5-7-1810, Spring MM, N C
    -s Jeremiah & Margaret
    (chm of mou in 1835 at Hopewell MM, N C)
Celia    b 7-25-1817, Guilford Co, N C
    -dt Thomas & Sarah Hunt
Ch: Eliza Ann    b 8-29-1835, Hopewell MM, N C
    Delia Caroline    b 7-23-1844, Hopewell MM, N C
    Mary Delphina    b 9-11-1847, Spiceland MM, Ind
    Sarah Angelina    b 9-4-1849, Spiceland MM, Ind
    d 11-29-1849    -bur Raysville MH, Ind
    Horace Franklin    b 7-15-1851, Spiceland MM, Ind
    Electa Catharine    b 1-25-1854
    Ida    b 5-11-1856, Spiceland MM, Ind
    Margaret Ella    b 10-26-1859, Raysville MM, Ind

Charles S    b 9-1-1829, Milford MM, Ind
    -s Richard J & Sarah
    d 6-2-1906    -bur Glencove Cem, Knightstown, Ind

## HUBBARD (Cont)
Martha (w of Charles S)   b 8-1-1828, Blue River MM, Washington Co, Ind
    -dt Thomas & Millicent White
    d 9-17-1915,  -bur Glencove Cem, Knightstown, Ind
Ch: Francis T       b 1-9-1852, Spiceland MM, Ind
    Mary A         b 1-6-1854, Spiceland MM, Ind
    Ellen          b 5-31-1856, Spiceland MM, Ind
    Henry          b 2-25-1865, Raysville MM, Ind
       d 9-12-1865 -bur Raysville MH, Ind
    Elizabeth      b 12-8-1867, Raysville MM, Ind
    Estella H      b 3-20-1870, Raysville MM, Ind

Edwin       b 10-24-1827, Milton, Wayne Co, Ind
    -s Richard & Sarah
    d 10-29-1887  -bur Raysville MH, Ind
Martha      b 8-22-1829       d 1895 in Iowa
Ch: Lillian M     b 11-22-1866  (m George Balfour)
    William S    b

Francis T    b 1-9-1852, Raysville MM, Henry Co, Ind
    -s Charles & Martha
Juliett      b 10-18-1854, Belmont Co, Ohio
    -dt Lewis & Mary V Wood
Ch: Lewis Wood     b 12-27-1876, Raysville MM, Ind
    Clara Ann      b 2-12-1879, Knightstown, Ind
    Samuel Myers   b 9-8-1888, Knightstown, Ind

S Myers     b 7-8-1858
Idella P    b 6-24-1855
    (Idella P m 2nd on 5-21-1907 to Charles Osborn)

.....
Hattie      -dt ... Bremon     b 7-3-1857
Ch: Cecil F     b 10-9-1878, Ogden, Henry Co, Ind
    Edwin F     b 10-7-1880, Charlottesville, Ind

## HUDDLESON
Ada Marie   b 5- -1883   -dt Emory Huddleson

## HUNT
George
.....
Ch: Clinton H     b 1884
    Eva           b 1887

## HURST
.....
Dorcas Ann  b 1-14-1870  -dt Ephraim & Sarah J Smith

## HUSSEY
Elijah B    b 10-5-1839, Clermont Co, Ohio
    d 6-22-1903, Knightstown, Ind
    -bur Greenville, Ohio
Mary        b 3-19-1837, Wayne Co, Ill
    d 1-20-1911, Knightstown, Ind
    -bur Greenville, Ohio

## HUTSON
James       b 7-22-1844
Mary A      b 12-8-1843
Ch: Ida     b 7-28-1873    d 7-28-1891
    -bur Glencove Cem, Knightstown, Ind
    Willie  b 11-13-1880

## JACK
Emma        b 12-10-1863  (m Charles Bartlow)

Franklin L  b 9-15-1858   -s Ras Jack

## JACKSON
(Alf)
Susan       b 3-24-1838  d 6-12-1918, Shirley, Ind
    -bur Glencove Cem, Knightstown, Ind

## JAY
Joseph W    b 1-22-1825, Mill Creek MM, Ohio
    -s Thomas & Eliza

Anna (1st w)  b 1-21-1831, New Garden MM, Ind
    -dt Samuel & Harriet Pritchard
    d 2-27-1867    -bur Raysville MH, Ind
Ch: Harriett E    b 8-13-1858, Raysville MM, Ind
    William P     b 9-29-1863, Raysville MM, Ind
Sarah Jane (2nd w)  m 4-23-1869
    b 11-25-1835, New Garden MM, Ind
    -dt Samuel & Harriet Pritchard
    d 5-3-1869    -bur Raysville MH, Ind

## JENKINS
Henry       b 4-25-1850    -s William A Jenkins
    d 6-4-1921, Knightstown, Ind
Mary S (1st w) b 10-3-1853   d 5-19-1914
    -bur Glencove Cem, Knightstown, Ind
Mary (2nd w)  d 12-10-1918, Knightstown, Ind

William A   (Father of Henry Jenkins)
    d 9-2-1919, Knightstown, Ind
    -bur Carthage, Ind

## JESSOP - JESSUP
David       b 2-1-1828, Henry Co, Ind
    -s Tidamon & Lydia (Morris)
Julia       b 12-26-1826   -dt William & Sarah Wilson
Ch: Ida May Crawford (adopted dt)

Tidamon     b 9-27-1800   -s Pratt W & Hope(White)
    m 1826 at Milford MH, Ind
Lydia       b 1-15-1809, Symons Creek MM, N C
    -dt Joshua & Mary (Morgan) Morris
    d 9-29-1875   -bur Elm Grove Cem, Ind
Ch: Morris           b 9-4-1826, Wayne Co, Ind
    David            b 2-1-1828, Henry Co, Ind
    Susannah Alley   b 9-20-1829
    Mary             b 3-15-1830
    Ruth             b 2-1-1833
    Naomi Duncan     b 10-19-1842

## JOHNS
(William H)  Of Wilkinson MM, Ind
Bertha       b 6-8-1880
    -dt John & Elizabeth Corbin
Ch: Mamie Esther   b 11-22-1896
    Martha Carol   b 4-2-19..

## JOHNSON
(Gid...)
Mary   b 8-1-1845   d 12-2-1907, Knightstown, Ind
Ch: Harvey T    b 8-6-1869
    Walter E    b 8-19-1881

Hiram       b 6-7-1826, Cane Creek MM, N C
    -s Joshua & Sarah
    m 9-12-1850, Deep River MM, N C
Rhoda J     b 5-25-1831, Center MM, N C
    -dt Charles & Ruth (Mendenhall) Gurley
    d 3-4-1905, near Dunreith, Ind
Ch: Lindley H   b 12-22-1851, Cane Creek MM, N C
    Charles C   b 2-18-1857, Spiceland MM, Henry Co, Ind

Joshua      b 10-17-1786, New Garden MM, N C
    -s Joshua Sr & Mary (Hargrave)
    m 2-16-1811, Deep River MM, N C
Sarah       b 4-7-1789, Deep River MM, N C
    -dt Charles & Mary (dec) Gordon
Ch: (Came to Indiana with their mother)
    Susan     b 9-9-1816, Cane Creek MM, N C
    Hiram     b 6-7-1826, Cane Creek MM, N C

Mary Alice  b 4-22-1855

Rosa B      b 1-27-1877   (m George Steiner)

Thomas H    b 8-6-1869

William G, a min    b 6-1-1817, Springfield MM, N C
    -s Nathan & Mary (Guyer)
Anna        b 11-14-1823, Springfield MM, N C
    -dt Mendenhall

## JOHNSON (Cont)
Ch of William G & Anna:
- Marticia E    b
- William Elwood    b
- Emily    b
- Mary D    b

## JONES
Samuel    b 4-13-1843, Chatham Co, N C
     -s Benjamin & Rebecca
Martha E    b 8-30-1846, Beallsville, Monroe Co, Ohio
     -dt James & Agnes Slack
Ch:
- Orpheus C    b 4-4-1872    d 6-21-1875
       -bur Knightstown, Ind
- Mary Etta    b 9-3-1874 (m Mr Hinshaw)
- Cora A    b 8-12-1879, Knightstown, Ind
  (m Silas Shipley, 7-19-1898)
- Samuel Jr    b 3-12-1880, Grant City, Henry Co

NOTE: Martha E (Slack) Jones m 2nd Mahlon Cox & had ch

Samuel Jr    b 3-12-1880    -s Samuel Sr (dec) & Martha E
Bernice M    b 11-12-1885      (Slack)
Ch: William P    b 5-24-1909

## KEARNS
Thomas    b 2-18-1818    d 12-29-1881    -s Wm & Margaret
Mary B    b 3-19-1828, Back Creek MM, N C    d 11-20-1891
     -dt Jehu & Rebecca Stuart
Ch:
- Emory    b 5-16-1851
- Delphina    b 9-24-1853    d 6-2-1873
- Sarah E    b 5-25-1856
- Jehu S    b 2-16-1859    d 5-19-1880
- Nerius A    b 8-2-1861

William M    b 10-4-1834, Randolph Co, N C    -s Josiah &
     d 2-26-1816      Jane
     -bur Glencove Cem, Knightstown, Ind
Elizabeth    b 5-8-1836, Davidson Co, N C
     -dt Jehu & Rebecca Stuart    d 3-12-1910
     -bur Glencove Cemetery, Knightstown, Ind
Ch:
- Flora E    b 1-17-1857, Randolph Co, N C
       d 2-24-1875    -bur Knightstown, Ind
- Rebecca J    b 8-16-1861

## KENNARD
(Jacob)
Rebecca    b 9-11-1828, Guilford Co, N C
     d 2-26-1905, Toledo, Ohio
     -bur Glencove Cem, Knightstown, Ind

## KENWORTHY
Amos    b 7-12-1789, Pipe Creek MM, Frederick Co, Md
     -s William & Mary    d 1-30-1863
     -bur Raysville Burial Gr, Ind
Mary (1st w)    b 8-20-1792, Hopewell MM, Berkley Co, Va
     -dt Robert & Cassandra Miller    d 6-2-1844
     -bur Raysville Burial Gr, Ind
Ch:
- William    b 1-19-1816, Westland MM, Washington Co, Pa
- Robert    b 2-5-1819, Westland MM, Washington Co, Pa
- Jesse    b 8-6-1822, Springboro MM, Montgomery Co, Ohio
- Joel    b 9-11-1824, Springboro MM, Montgomery Co, Ohio
- Willis    b 8-25-1826, Springboro MM, Montgomery Co, Ohio
- Ann    b 9-4-1828, Springboro MM, Montgomery Co, Ohio
- Amos M    b 6-17-1831, Springboro MM, Montgomery Co, Ohio
- Isaac P    b 3-28-1834, Springboro MM, Montgomery Co, Ohio

Elizabeth (2nd w)    b 8-3-1802, Randolph Co, N C
     -dt Josiah & Dorothy

Rev Amos M    b 6-17-1831, Montgomery Co, Ohio
     -s Amos Sr & 1st w, Mary (Miller)
Phebe H    b 1-20-1828

Ch:
- Oliver    b - - , Iowa
- Isaac F    b 3-28-1834, Montgomery Co, Ohio
       -s Amos Sr & 1st w, Mary (Miller) (dec)
  Abigail    b
  Ch: Owen    b

Robert    b 2-5-1819, Westland MM, Washington Co, Pa
     -s Amos Sr & 1st w, Mary (Miller)
Doughty    b 8-6-1818, Wayne Co, Ind
     -dt William & Achsah Saint
Ch:
- William L    b 5-24-1840, Spiceland MM, Henry Co, Ind
- Albert E    b 12-24-1842, Spiceland MM, Henry Co, Ind
- Mary    b 6-23-1845, Spiceland MM, Henry Co, Ind
- Charles M    b 9-5-1846    d 8-28-1854
       -bur Raysville MH, Ind
- Achsah    b 5-15-1849, Spiceland MM
- Harriet    b 8-21-1851, Spiceland MM
- John C    b 8-8-1853, Spiceland MM
- Morris W    b 5-8-1855, Spiceland MM

Virgil    b 5-31-1875
Myrtie R    b 1-19-1879
     -dt Christopher Columbus Moffitt
Ch: Virgil Byron    b 8-5-1900

Willis    b 8-25-1826, Springboro MM, Warren Co, Ohio
     -s Amos Sr & 1st w Mary (Miller)
     m 11-30-1848
Naomi    b 6-19-1827, Centre MM, Clinton Co, Ohio
     -dt Thomas & Mary Kirk
Ch:
- Sarah Ann    b 9-12-1849, Spiceland MM, Ind
       d 8-9-1850    -bur Raysville MH, Ind
- Allen    b 4-5-1851, Spiceland MM, Ind
- Milton    b 12-15-1852, Spiceland MM, Ind
- Elizabeth Caroline    b 9-1-1854, Spiceland MM, Ind
- Thomas Clarkson    b 9-17-1857, Raysville MM, Ind
- Mary M    b 11-29-1860, Raysville MM, Ind

## KERR
Sarah Jane    b 6-13-1830
Ch: Frances    b 2-1-1879 (m Mr Collins)

## KEYS
John E    b 1-28-1845, Centerville, Wayne Co, Ind
     -s John W & Martha W    d 2-18-1924
     -bur Glencove Cem, Knightstown, Ind
Sophia L    b 2-5-1850, Knightstown, Ind
     -dt John & Elizabeth Weaver
Ch: Harry E    b 9-19-1875, Knightstown, Ind

## KIRK
Allen T    b 11-15-1829, Centre MM, Clinton Co, Ohio
     -s Thomas & Sarah    d 5-8-1908
     -bur Glencove Cem, Knightstown, Ind
Lucinda E (1st w)    b 9-12-1831, Duck Creek MM, Ind
     -dt Richard & Miriam Saunders
     d 11-7-1897    -bur Knightstown, Ind
Ch:
- Alice M    b 3-10-1854, Duck Creek MM, Ind
  (m Frank Vestal)
- Anna M    b 8-5-1856, Spring Creek MM, Jasper Co, Ind
  (m John Sample)
- Elmer E    b 10-29-1862, Raysville MM, Ind
  d 11-30-1871    -bur Greensboro, Ind

Asenath (2nd w)    b 11-24-1834, Center MM, N C    m 12-28-1898
Widow of Jesse N Townsend    -dt Job & Phebe Reynolds
d 11-20-1906    -bur Knightstown, Ind

## KITTERMAN
John R    b 6-22-1862    Of Shirley MM, Ind
Alpha R    b 3-14-1865
Ch:
- J Vernnis    b - -1887
- Orpha    b - -1895

### KITTERMAN (Cont)
Joseph Willard    b 11- 6-1867
Laura M    b 2- 8-1870

Clayton E    b 1887    (Relationship not recorded)

### KNIGHT
John    b 11-21-1779, New Garden MM, N C
     -s Thomas & Elizabeth (Pitts)
     d 6- 4-1861 at B Boren's home near Knightstown, Ind   -bur Raysville MH, Ind
Sarah    b 6-24-1775, N C
     -dt James & Mary Meredith    d 7-24-1856
     *(May have been bur at Raysville MH, Ind)
Ch: Ira
     James
     Mary
     Elizabeth
     Amelia
     (Rec in mbrp in 1819 in N C on rq of father)

### KOONS
John A    b 1858    -s George & M E
Minerva J    b 1-17-1860, Duck Creek MM, Ind
     -dt Elias & 3rd w, Ann (Dawson) Modlin
Ch: Ola A    b 1885    (m Mr Brooks)

### LAMB
Timothy    b 11-28-1814, N C    -s Stephen & Miriam
     m 9- 1-1858    (Copeland)
Rebecca    b 1-18-1821, Suttons Creek, Perquimans Co, NC
     -dt Samuel (dec) & Mary (Albertson) Draper
     d 3- -1888    -bur Walnut Ridge Cem, Rush Co, Ind

### LARIMORE
Frank    Of Shirley MM    b 3-17-1876

Laura C E    b 1-23-1890

### LEFLER
William L    b 8-31-1863, Franklin Co, Ind
Christena Eldora    b 9- 1-1870, Henry Co, Ind
Ch: Clifford Eli    b

### LEISURE
Frank M    b 11-30-1869, Rush Co, Ind
     -s Henry & Martha
Beatrice    b 11-11-1877, Rush Co, Ind
     -dt William & Victoria Goddard

Johnson    b 5-16-1854
Hannah B    b 11-12-1864

### LIGGETT
Joseph O    b 1874    -s J R Liggett

### LIPSEY
     (-s John & Ann)
William B    b 10-20-1825, Stillwater MM, Harrison Co, Ohio
Hannah (1st w)    b 6-12-1825, Ohio
     -dt Ellis & Rachel (Lewis) Willets
     m 8-29-1849    d 11-14-1863
     -bur Blue River MM, Washington Co, Ind
Ch: Oliver G    b 9- 6-1850, Gilead MM, Morrow Co, Ohio
   Rachel Ann    b 12- 7-1852, Gilead MM, Morrow Co, Ohio
   Seneca H    b 6-24-1855, Gilead MM, Morrow Co, Ohio
   Lucius W    b 10-17-1857, Gilead MM, Morrow Co, Ohio
   Elizabeth    b 5-20-1860, Blue River MM, Washington Co, Ind
   Albertus    b 10-12-1862, Blue River MM, Washington Co, Ind
     d 8- 4-1863, Blue River MM, Ind
Hannah (2nd w)    m 10- 5-1866
     b Grant Co, Ind, Mississinewa MM
     -dt Timothy & Avis (Sleeper) Kelly
Ch: Samuel Leo    b 10- 1-1867, Raysville MM, Ind

     d 1-19-1869    -bur Raysville MH, Ind

### LISHER - LESHER
Riley    b 3-25-1847

### LITTLEWOOD
Edmund    b 8-21-1828, Norfolk Co, England
     -s Robert & Patience
Harriett M    b 9- 8-1834, Suffolk Co, England
     -dt James & Hannah S Garbald    d 1913

### LOCK
Luther
Emma Grace    b 8-13-1869
     Adopted dt of John & Harriet Cunningham Roseboom

### LOGAN
Wesley A    b 3-19-1842
.....
Ch: Mary E    b 8- 9-1880

### LOWRY
Eliza M    b 10-26-1836, Rome, Mich
     d 5- 4-1909, Spiceland, Ind
     -bur Knightstown, Ind
     (m Charles Stubbs on 9-12-1906)

### LUTHER
Ivan (or Ivy)    b 2-22-1834    -s Martin & Sarah
Sarah    b 8-21-1833    -dt Jehu & Rebecca Stuart
Ch: Dorothy E    b 2-20-1861
   Narcissa G    b 3-12-1863
   James A    b 1- 5-1866
   Emily R    b 10-18-18..

### LYKINS
Sebastian    b 12-25-1876
Myrtle    b 3- 8-1885
     -dt Henry & Martha McKillip
Ch: Charles A    b 10-19-1902

Sylvester    b 5-24-1879
Laura A    b 9-26-1885

### LYMAN
.....
Anna    b 7- 3-1870    -dt David T & Sally H Pritchard

### McCANN
John R    b 2-13-1845    d 9-12-1900
     -bur Raleigh, Ind
..... Morgan    -dt Erie Morgan
(1st w)

### McCONNELL
Joseph    b 2- 4-1840    d 12-31-1900
     Knightstown, Ind
Louisa    b 3-20-1844    d 8- 2-1912
     Knightstown, Ind
Ch: Pearl    b 3-15-1870 (m Mr Bartell)
   Freemont    b 5- 8-1872

### McCORKLE
Edna    b 2-2-1897    Of Grant City MM, Ind

Joseph    b 9-28-1855
Emma (1st w)    -dt .... Dell    b 10-18-1861
     d 12-12-1886, Knightstown, Ind
     -bur Cadiz, Ind
Ch: Willie    b 10-12-1879    d 10- 8-1889 or 98
     -bur Cadiz, Ind
   Dolphie    b 6-14-1881    d 7-24-1888
     -bur Cadiz, Ind

Marion F    b 5-24-1868    Of Grant City, Ind
Elvira L    b 11-18-1875
Ch: Orpha    b 12-14-1894

RAYSVILLE-KNIGHTSTOWN

## McCORKLE (Cont)
Samuel A    b 12-28-1859
Margaret    b 11-28-1867    -dt John & Serena Crandall
Ch: Charles H      b 8- 8-1886
    George E       b 7-29-1888
    Russell R      b 8-16-1890
    Ina B          b 2- 6-1893
    Henry Elbert   b 3-20-1897
    William C      b 11-11-1900
    Carl M         b

## McKEE
Charles    b 1890

Matilda    b 1860

## McKILLIP
Henry      b 11- 3-1855    Of Wilkinson, Ind
Martha     b 11- 7-1861
Ch: David S        b 1-12-1881
    Myrtle M       b 3- 8-1885
        (m Sebastian Lykins)
    Lena           b 6- 1-1883
    James M        b 11- 2-1888

James H    b 3- 7-1852    Of Grant City MM, Ind
Ada Q      b 2-14-1857
Ch: Lucia A        b 9-23-1874
    Anna M         b 2-15-1884

Malinda    d 6- -1898    -bur Raysville Cem, Ind

Oliver V   b 12-13-1866
Annie Eliza b 10-18-1865

## McKINNEY
Henry C    b 11-25-1853    Of Grant City MM, Ind

Jessie     b 3-20-1816    Of Grant City MM, Ind

## McNEW
John N     b 3-29-1840

Elizabeth  b 11-20-1843

Minnie     b 11-18-1873    (m Mr Melvin)

## MACY
Joseph L   b 12-31-1860
Cornelia   b 12-23-1868
           d 3-18-1911, Knightstown, Ind
Ch: Benjamin F     b 4-10-1884    d 9-27-1896
    Lindley Morton b 6- 3-1886

Lilburn    b 2-23-1833, Guilford Co, N C
           -s Enoch & Nancy (Rayl)
Martha     b 12-18-1836, Wayne Co, Ind
           -dt Charles & Lydia R (Jessop) Gordon
Ch: Ida Florence   b 11- 4-1858
    Lydia Alice    b 2- 6-1860
    Emily T        b 1-13-1862
    Charles        b 10- 6-1864

Lindley H  b 6- 3-1836, Spiceland MM, Ind
           -s Nathan & Jane A of Iowa
Sarah E (1st w)    b 9- 3-1836, Lynn Grove MM,
                   Poweshiek Co, Iowa
           -dt William & Sarah Wilson
           d 2-14-1869    -bur Iowa
Ch: Oliver W       b 3-16-1858, Poweshiek Co, Iowa
           d 2-28-1861    -bur Duck Creek MM, Ind
    Rozella        b 8-18-1859, Henry Co, Ind
    Joseph L       b 12-31-1860, Henry Co, Ind
    Lubell         b 6-19-1862, Henry Co, Ind
    Viola A        b 9-29-1864, Henry Co, Ind
    Ida            b 4-18-1866, Poweshiek Co, Iowa
    Nathan W       b 9-30-1868, Poweshiek Co, Iowa

Nancy      b 3-18-1800    Mother of Lilburn Macy
           -widow of Enoch   -dt William & Elizabeth
                                              Rayl

## MADISON
(John) Charles    b 10- 4-1863
           -s Harrison & Sallie
Mary F     b 1-16-1865    -dt Albert & Margaret
                                              Lacy
Ch: Bessie         b 12- 7-1886

## MANLOVE
Charles    b 11-11-1863    Of Grant City MM, Ind
Matilda (or Mary Alma)  b 8-29-1863
Ch: Lucy V         b 6-10-1891
    Howard A       b

Monte      b 9-23-1874    Of Grant City MM, Ind
Ch: Myrna F        b 8-10-1894
    James F        b 5-28-1901

Oliver P   b 3- 4-1860    Of Grant City MM, Ind
Lora (or Eldora)   b 8-19-1868
Ch: Blanche A      b 4- 4-1889
    Paul Morris    b 6-30-1898

Mary Alma  (Sister of Charles)    b 11-14-1867

(Relationship of following is unknown)
Caroline   b 11-19-1842

Hester A   b 2- 8-1848

Laura B    b 8- 5-1872

Lucy A     b 10-29-1869    Of Grant City MM, Ind

Walter     b 12-22-1883    Of Grant City MM, Ind

## MANNING
Henry      b 9-20-1849, Suffolk Co, England
           -s Robert & Patience    d 3-12-1907
Mary Jane  b 10-15-1856, Va
           -dt Thomas & Amanda Hatfield
Ch: Robert         b 7-27-1874, Raysville, Ind
    Edward T       b 10- 6-1876

## MAPLE
Ralph R    b 11-25-1882

## MARKLE
Mary A     b 11-14-1867    Of Grant City MM, Ind

## MARTIN
Cora       b 9- 4-1873

Guy R      b 6-28-1886    -s Henry & Elizabeth

Henry      b 10- 4-1829

Mary Ann   b 3-22-1845    d 12- 1-1907

Ira E      b 2-22-1878

## MATTOX
Elmer      b 4- 6-1871

## MAULSBY
James      b 12-15-1812    d 3- 6-1888
           -bur Knightstown, Ind
Sarah Ann  -s John & Elizabeth of New Garden MM, Ind
           From Cherry Grove MM, Ind, - 1887

## MAXWELL
(Jim)
Clara      b 11- 2-1859
Ch: Ora Navada     b 1-18-1882    (m Munson Reeves)

## MAXWELL (Cont)
(Henry)
Laura    b 3-22-1862
Ch: Mary Lola    b 11- -1884
     (m Mr Peck on 10-31-1903)

## MAYS
John W    b 2-23-1823    d 1- 4-1898
     -bur Knightstown, Ind
Elizabeth F    b 10-14-1832

## MELVIN
Minnie (form McNew)    b 11-18-1873

## MIDKIFF
Columbus C    b 7- 4-1858, Hancock Co, Ind
     d 6-12-1927 -bur Glencove Cem, Knightstown, Ind
Rebecca J    b 8-16-1861 -dt William & Elizabeth Kearns
Ch: Florence Elizabeth    b 9-16-1886, Knightstown, Ind
     (m Emory J Cox, 10-17-1906)

Jerry    m 9-21-1902
Nina    b 3-13-1865, Knightstown, Ind
     -dt ..... Steiner

## MILLER
Esta T    b 5-10-1888

## MILLS
James S    b 1-19-1836    d 1901
Serepta    b 5-27-1839
     (-s Amos & Mary E (Cook))
Rev Samuel C    b 2-21-1859, near West Newton, Ind
     d 5- 6-1900 -bur Valley Mills, Ind
Flora    b 5-11-1863 -dt Lot & Asenath (Canaday) Pickett

## MOFFITT
Asa C    b 8-25-1867, Rush Co, Ind
     -s Calvin & Elizabeth
Gertrude    b 8- 6-1875 -dt John McNew
Ch: Lowell    b 11- 6-1895
     Ralph C    b 10- 8-1898
     Naomi Irvin (foster dt) b 6-20-1910, Marion Co, Ind

(Calvin)
Elizabeth    b 4-20-1834
Ch: Asa C    b 8-25-1867, Rush Co, Ind
     Della M    b 12-23-1871 (m ... Griffin)

Christopher Columbus    b 3-22-1855, Henry Co, Ind
Elnora    b 7-31-1859
Ch: Myrtie R    b 1-19-1879
     Lena B    b 3-18-1882
     Elva D    b 10-16-1884
     Carl A    b 8- 9-1886
     Bessie P    b 2-15-1891
     Ethel Fay    b 11-22-1892
     Mary Hazel    b 11-28-1895
     Helen Iris    b 11- 9-1902

Lycurgus    b 11-26-1856
Amanda    b 10- 1-1855
Ch: Myla Leota    b 8-24-1875
     Florence Leona    b 12-14-1893

## MOON
Oscar    b 1- 9-1873, Grant Co, Ind    -s Thomas & Mary
Mary    b 1-20-1872, Marion, Ind -dt ..... Overman
     d 10- 6-1905, Pleasant Hill, Ohio
     -bur Marion, Ind
Ch: Turner F    b 5-13-1901, Marion, Ind

## MOORE
Charles    b 8-29-1788, Dover MM, N C
     -s Camm & Sophia (Benbow)
Ann    b 12-14-1789, Westfield, Stokes Co, N C
     d 9-23-1863 Late res, Logansport, Cass Co, Ind
     -dt Moses & Martha Gregg

Ransom S    b 6-13-1827, Contentnea MM, N C
     -s William & Zilpha
Rebecca B    b 3-22-1826, Hopewell MM, N C
     -dt Isaac & Mahala White
Ch: Ora W    b 6-12-1868, Raysville MM, Ind
     d 3-16-1870 -bur Raysville MH, Ind
     Ola I    b 1- 2-1870, Raysville, Ind

David W    b 12- -1887

## MORGAN
Charles    b 2-16-1801, Back Creek MM, N C
     -s Benjamin & Naomi
     d 8- 7-1864 -bur Earlham Cem, Richmond, Ind
Michal    b 4-10-1802, Gravely Run MM, Dinwiddie Co, Va
     -dt William & Mary Butler
     d 8-19-1888 -bur Earlham Cem, Richmond, Ind
Ch: Edward    b 11-19-1826, Milford MM, Henry Co, Ind
     Elizabeth    b 10-20-1828, Milford MM, Henry Co, Ind
     William B    b 12- 2-1830
     d & bur Lowell, Kans
     Benjamin    b 3-29-1834, Wayne Co, Ind
     Naomi W    b 3-14-1838, Spiceland, Henry Co, Ind
     Mary E    b 12-16-1843, Spiceland, Henry Co, Ind
     d 5-14-1857 -bur Raysville MH, Ind

H L (or A L)
Martha L    b 9-10-1865, Knightstown, Ind
     -dt Isaac & Hannah Maria Parker
Ch: Sherman P    b 9- 1-1894, Zanesville, Ohio
     Mary    b 11- 8-1898, Zanesville, Ohio
     Hannah L    b 11- 8-1898, Zanesville, Ohio

## MORRIS
Lena Marie    b 8- 7-1896
     -dt Oliver P & Anna Morris of Grant City MM, Ind

Mark    b 10- 3-1841
Sarah    b 12-29-1851
Ch: Charles Ora    b 12- 8-1885, Knightstown, Ind
     Isaac Taylor    b 8- 6-1889, Knightstown, Ind
     Claud Hurst    b 7- 3-1891, Knightstown, Ind
     Irwin Mark    b 6-21-1894, Knightstown, Ind

Nathan O    b 12-14-1834, Symons Creek MM, N C
     -s Joseph H (dec) & Martha (Toms)

## MORRISON
John I
Catharine    b 9- 1-1812, Symons Creek MM, N C
     -dt Benoni & Rebecca Morris
Ch: Sarah P    b 9- 7-1833, Salem, Ind
     d 7- 9-1919, Indianapolis, Ind
     -bur Crown Hill Cem, Indianapolis, Ind
     Grace D Tatnor (foster dt) b 3- 1-1857
     (m Albert Aikin)

.....
Laura    b 7- 4-1857
     -dt Ithamar & Margaret Stuart
Ch: Barbara    b 9-15-1888
     John Stuart    b 11-24-1890
     Alice Rebecca    b 12-17-1892
     Russel    b 12-12-1894

## MORROW
Jessie A    b 7- 2-1885

## MOYER
Edith    b 7-28-1889, Randolph Co, Ind
     -dt Daniel & Martha Moyer

RAYSVILLE-KNIGHTSTOWN

## MURRAY
Lemuel    b 6-1-1817, Worcester Co, Md
     d 1-1-1883 -bur Glencove Cem, Knightstown,
     -s Severn & Nancy      Ind
Abigail    b 1-17-1822, Cartright Co, N C
     -dt Jesse & Alice (1st w) (Mace) Davis
     d 1-29-1894, Lincoln, Nebr but -bur Glencove Cemetery, Knightstown, Ind

## NEWBY
Albert    b 2-1-1826, Piney Woods MM, N C
     -s Frederick & Sarah
Caroline    b 10-6-1834, Milford MM, Ind
     -dt Richard & Sarah Hubbard
Ch: Charles M    b 11-11-1854, Spiceland MM, Ind
   Sarah Emma    b 12-22-1858, Hopewell MM, Ind
   Allen L    b 8-3-1860, Hopewell MM, Ind

Alma P    b 6-6-1879 (Names of parents not given)
   (m William Smith)

David W    b 10-6-1846, Raysville MM, Ind
     -s Frederick & Sarah    m 12-2-1869
Sarah Marianna    b 7-9-1849
     -dt Richard & Martha Elliott
Ch: Frederick F    b 9-18-1870, Raysville MM, Ind
   Richard W    b 1-17-1873, Ash Grove MM, Ill
   Mabel Mary    b 2-23-1875
   Naurice B    b 3-17-1878, Spiceland MM, Ind
     d 9-21-1884
   Paul Elliott    b 6-18-1882, Raysville MM, Ind
   Clara Margaret    b 1-19-1887
     d 2-12-1905 or 1906

Florence    b 8-2-1861 (Names of parents not given)

Frederick    b 5-25-1794, Piney Woods MM, N C
     -s Jesse & Elizabeth (White) Townsend Newby
     d 7-13-1866 Residence East of Raysville, Henry Co, Ind
Sarah    b 6-17-1802, Perquimans Co, N C
     -dt Thomas & Jemima (White)
Ch: William Jesse    b 2-8-1822, Perquimans Co, N C
   John Thomas    b 6-1-1823, Perquimans Co, N C
   Albert    b 2-1-1826
   Oliver    b 9-21-1827
   Eliza Townsend    b 1-26-1829
   Lydia    b 9-6-1830
   Exum    b 4-12-1833, Perquimans Co, N C
     d 10-13-1852, -bur Spiceland MM, Ind
   Henry F    b 9-15-1834, Perquimans Co, N C
     d 6-2-1877 -bur Raysville MM, Ind
   Mariah Jane    b 10-1-1836, Spiceland, Henry Co, Ind
   Sarah Ann    b 1-26-1838, Spiceland, Henry Co, Ind
   Mary    b 7-23-1840, Spiceland, Henry Co, Ind
   David W    b 10-6-1846, Spiceland, Henry Co, Ind

John Thomas    b 6-1-1823, Piney Woods MM, N C
     d 3-2-1905, Lynnville, Ia
     -s Frederick & Sarah (White)
Martha    b 4-8-1835, Suttons Creek MM, N C
     -dt Samuel & Rebecca White
Ch: Samuel F    b 5-27-1855, Spiceland MM, Henry Co, Ind
   Charles H    b 4-27-1857, Spiceland MM, Henry Co, Ind
   Mary Elizabeth    b 3-4-1859, Raysville MM, Ind
   Minnie Eliza    b 3-4-1861, Raysville MM, Ind
   Thomas Edward    b 3-7-1863, Raysville MM, Ind
   Miles White    b 8-31-1865, Raysville MM, Ind
   John Earl    b 6-2-1867, Raysville MM, Ind
   Anna Maria    b 8-6-1869, Raysville MM, Ind
   Albert N    b 6-19-1872, Raysville MM, Ind

(John)
.....

Ch: Gertrude M    b 10-18-1865
   Frank    b 12-10-1870

Loren (Yank) b 10-18-1851 (Brother to John Newby)
Mary F    b 8-2-1861
(Alma, b 6-6-1879 may be their dt)

(Micah) (dec)
Mary D (2nd w) b 11-18-1792, New Garden MM, N C
     -dt Bethuek & Hannah Coffin
     d    -bur Raysville MH, Ind

## NIBARGER
Charles    b 5-13-1852 Of Grant City MM, Ind
Cordelia Ann    b 5-1-1858
Ch: Ellen    b 10-21-1871
   Elizabeth P    b 3-11-1876

John Harvey    b 12-15-1859
Violetta    b 3-28-1861
Ch: Mertie Alma    b 12-4-1881
   Laura Bell    b 2-18-1883
   Maudie Ann    b 7-31-1885
   Emma Jane    b 3-10-1888
   James S C    b 4-7-1893

(Parents names not given)
Ch: William E    b 8-4-1883
   Minnie May    b 9-4-1886

## NIXON
Nathan T    b 11-28-1845
Sophia    b 6-10-1861 -dt ..... Parker
Ch: Johanna    b 4-25-1895

## OAKERSON
(James)
Lena    b 7-17-1878 -dt Silas & Amanda Patterson
Ch: Edith Lena    b 1-30-1897
   Florence    b 10-12-1900

## OSBORN
Martin
Sarah    b 8-10-1838 -dt James & Penina Edwards
Ch: Harriett L    b 7-11-1860

## OVERMAN
Jesse C    b 11-2-1860 From Fairmount MM, Ind
Isabel H    b 6-3-1865
Ch: Edna I    b 12-5-1884
   Thurman    b 1-8-1887
   Elsie Miriam    b 9-10-1897

## PAINTER
Eva    b 10-12-1878 -dt ..... Cole

## PARKER
Anna Mary    b 8-16-1870 m 1st to Charles Fort
   m 2nd to Samuel Pritchard

Benajah Sr    b 3-22-1783, Rich Square MM, N C
     -s Jacob & Rhoda (Draper)
     d 8-27-1857 -bur Raysville MH, Ind
Grace    b 11-9-1784, Loudon Co, Va
     -dt William & Rachel Patton
     d 9-22-1866 -bur Raysville MH, Ind
Benajah Jr    b 9-11-1825, Mt Pleasant, Ohio
     -s Benajah Sr & Grace (Patton)
     d 7-18-1895, near Cleveland, Ohio
     & -bur there
Deborah Ann    b 9-13-1836, Sabdy Spring MM, Hanover, Columbiana Co, Ohio
     -dt Isaac & Martha Miller
     d 9-6-1883, Hutchinson, Kans
     -bur near Hutchinson, Kans

## PARKER (Cont)

Ch of Benajah Jr & Deborah Ann:
- Philemon           b 1-30-1859, Raysville MM, Henry Co, Ind
- William M          b 7-28-1860, Raysville MM, Henry Co, Ind
                     d 1- 8-1865  -bur Raysville MH, Ind
- Ione               b 3-30-1862
- Sarah Frances      b 2- 8-1864
                     d 3-18-1865  -bur Raysville MH, Ind
- George             b 11-23-1867, Raysville MM, Ind
- Benajah Franklin   b 6-11-1874
- Anna R             b 2-17-1877

Benoni Morris   b 12-24-1858    -s Philip D & Joanna
                d 7-10-1918  -bur Glencove Cem, Knightstown, Ind
Minnie Eliza    b 3- 4-1861, Henry Co, Ind
                -dt John Thomas & Martha Newby

(Parents names not given)
Ch: Carrie G         b 10-27-1879  (m Claude Gourley)

Isaac           b 5- 1-1823, Mt Pleasant, Jefferson Co, Ohio
                -s Benajah Sr & Grace (Patton)
                d 7-31-1902  -bur Raysville Cem, Ind
Hannah Mariah   b 5- 1-1825, Salem, Ind (Blue River MM, Washington Co, Ind)
                -dt Micah (dec) & Mary D (Coffin) Newby
                d 12-21-1903, Leatherwood Station, West Va
                -bur Raysville MH, Ind
Ch: Micah Newby      b 10-22-1854, Spiceland MM, Ind
    Mary Amelia      b 8- 2-1857, Raysville MM, Ind
    Henry Allen      b 5-22-1860, Raysville MM, Ind
    John Eberly      b 7-17-1862, Raysville MM, Ind
    Martha L         b 9-10-1865, Raysville MM, Ind

James B         b 9- 8-1819  -s Samuel & Rebecca
Hannah B        b 4-25-1822  -dt Eli & Martha Gause
Ch: Charles Owen     b 6- 4-1859

John Eberly     b 7-17-1862, near Knightstown, Ind
                -s Isaac & Hannah Maria (Newby)
Anna M (1st w)       -dt ..... Wildman
Ch: Edna Amelia      b 3-16-1895, Kansas City, Kans
    James Wildman    b 7-26-1896, Eaton, Ohio
    Priscilla        b 2-14-1899, Eaton, Ohio
    Elizabeth        b 5-14-1901, Eaton, Ohio
    John E Jr        b 6-16-1905, Eaton, Ohio
Mary M (2nd w) b    m 2-16-1910, Wayne Co, Ind
                -dt Edward Y & Sarah A (Stuart) Teas

Nathan          b 7-29-1803, Rich Square MM, Northampton Co, N C
                -s Josiah & Martha
Sarah Ann       b 1-15-1809, Cedar Creek MM, Hanover Co, Va
                -dt Thomas & Chlotilda Harris
                d 12-12-1877  -bur Raysville MH, Ind
Ch: Sarah Isabella   b 12-26-1834, Rich Square MM, N C
    Josiah T         b 10- 8-1836, Rich Square MM, N C
                     d 11-10-1838  -bur Elm Grove MH, Ind
    Margaret Ann     b 9-27-1839, Spiceland MM, Ind
                     d 1-18-1840  -bur Raysville MH, Ind
    Deborah Harris   b 7-26-1842, Spiceland MM, Ind
                     d 1-24-1905, Charlottesville, Ind
                     -bur Raysville, Ind

Philip D        b 4-21-1818, Stillwater MM, Ohio
                -s Benajah & Grace (Patton)
                d 4- 5-1889  -bur Raysville, Cem, east of Raysville, Ind
Joanna          b 10- 9-1822, Blue River MM, Washington Co, Ind
                -dt Benoni & Rebecca Morris
                d 7-18-1902  -bur Raysville Cem, Ind
Ch: Ella             b 8-12-1853, Rush Co, Ind
                     d 3-24-1869  -bur Raysville MH, Ind
    Theodore F       b 11-21-1856
    Benoni Morris    b 12-24-1858, Rush Co, Ind
    Sophia           b 6-10-1861, Knightstown, Ind

Samuel J        b 3- 5-1845  -s Samuel M & Eliza
Jennie          b 7-13-1837  d 4- -1912, -bur Moreland, Ind

NOTE: Samuel J & Jennie were parents of 3rd wife of Alex McCarty

(Parents Names not given)
Ch: Sherman          b 9- 1-1894
    Hannah L         b 11- 8-1898
    Mary             b 11- 8-1898

## PATTERSON
Frank           b 6-12-1881

Silas           b 4-25-1849
Amanda          b 2-19-1847   d 3-16-1908
                -bur Glencove Cem, Knightstown, Ind
Ch: Jerutha          b 8- 7-1875, Hancock Co, Ind
    Lena             b 7-17-1878
    Terrell          b 2-25-1880
    Clara Mabel      b 8- 9-1882  (m Mr Rockhill)

## PAXTON
Ollie Kate      b 6-22-1858    Of Grant City MM, Ind

## PEARSON
Rev Morton C    b 7-16-1867, Amboy, Ind
                -s Enos & Phebe
Cora            b 12-13-1876, Santa Fe, Ind
                -dt ..... Rees
Ch: Mildred Lorine   b 3-19-1895, Wabash, Ind
    Lyman Rees       b 10-16-1898, Sabina, Ohio

## PECK
Mary L          b 11- 1-1884

## PEELE
Caleb M         b 6-12-1843, Ind
                -s Henry E & Mary (Morris)
Maria           b 10- 7-1842, Balby, England
                -dt James & Sarah (Williams) Smith
Ch: Frances Henry    b 4-15-1870
    Walter           b 3-26-1872
    Louisa W         b

## PENNINGTON
Levi            b 8-29-1875    -s Josiah & Mary (Cook)
F Rebecca       b 9-23-1873
                -dt George & Isabel (Wynn) Kidd
Bertha (2nd w)       -dt ..... Waters
Ch: May Esther       b 6- 6-1899
    Bertha May       b 6-28-1903

## PHILABAUM
James B         b 1- 7-1846
Sarah E         b 5-30-1851
Ch: Alonzo W         b 12-30-1871
    Lura             b 9-17-1879

## PICKETT
Claude          b 10- 5-1880

Joseph Jr       b 7-24-1814, Lidles Creek MM, Ohio
                -s Joseph Sr & Priscilla

(Mahlon)(dec)
Rebecca         b 7-13-1838, Cane Creek MM, N C
                -dt Isham & Lavina Cox
Ch: Theodate         b 7-26-1861
NOTE: Rebecca (Cox) Pickett m 2nd Jonathan Hodgins, in 1867

Ola Etta        b 12- 1-1869, Henry Co, Ind
                Of Howard Co, Ind
                -dt Thomas E & Mary Pickett

William Jr      b 12-31-1766, Cane Creek MM, N C
                -s William & Sarah   d 12- 3-1847
                -bur Raysville MH, Ind
Sarah (2nd w)   b 7- 1-1790, Orange Co, N C
                -dt Joseph & Hannah Thompson
                d 2-15-1860  -bur Raysville MH, Ind

## RAYSVILLE-KNIGHTSTOWN

**PITTS**
Stella  b 5-1-1876  -dt ..... Coffin
(m Frank Pitts, 7-30-1899)

**POER**
Robert  b 2-14-1838

**PORTER**
William
Margaret G  b 6-26-1868, Raysville, Ind
-dt Frank & Elizabeth Brossius

**POWELL**
Elihu  b 10-5-1836  Of Raysville MM, 1908
d 12-31-1908

Henry C  b 3-24-1829  -s John & Catherine
Lucinda A  b 11-19-1833  -dt Jesse & Mary Wilson
d 10- -1897, Dunreith, Ind  (or Gibson)

**POWERS**
John William  b 9-8-1848  -s John & Judith
Phebe A  b 6-22-1848  -dt Absalom & Sarah Layman
d 4-4-1885  -bur Walnut Ridge MM, Ind
Ch: Rose  b 10-30-1870
John Warren  b 5-16-1872
Stella  b 3-27-1876  (m Mr Hargrove)
Sarah C  b 4-19-1878
Lulu S  b 12-17-1879
May  b 10-1-1882

.....
Louisa  b 3-7-1849
-divorced wife of Edward S Coffin
-dt Silas & Priscilla (Butler) Parker
Ch: (by 1st husband)
Olga Coffin  b 6-24-1872

**PRAY**
William  b 2-2-1836  -s Enos & Elvira
Nancy H (1st w) May have dec, Indianapolis, prior to 1894
Ch: Clara E  b 4-12-1864, Raysville MM, Ind
Bessie  b 8-27-1873, Raysville MM, Ind
Jane (Jennie) (2nd w)  b 8-27-1841
-dt Job & Phebe Reynolds  -widow Eli F Hodson

**PRITCHARD**
Benjamin C  b 12-21-1814, Symons Creek MM, N C
-s Caleb (dec) & Mary (Winslow) - now Mary
Parker, wife of Joseph Parker
Rachel W  b 11-8-1820, Piney Woods MM, N C
-dt William & Anna (White) Robinson
[Anna White Robinson now wife of Josiah Nicholson]
Ch: Caleb W  b 10-1-1842, Piney Woods MM, NC
Anna W  b 5-29-1857, Raysville MM, Ind
Thomas Robinson  b 6-2-1861, Raysville MM, Ind

Calvin W  b 1-24-1834  m 9-28-1875  -s Wm & Mary
Elizabeth Maryann  b 12-15-1836
-dt Isaac & Sarah Trueblood  d Chicago, Ill
-bur Raysville MM, Ind

Charles F  b 6-6-1876  -s Joseph & Ann J (Binford)
near Raysville MM, Ind
Zenia  b 2-17-1878  -dt ..... White
Ch: Helen Lucile  b 5-11-1903
Leland S  b 4-12-1904
Joseph Samuel  b 10-21-1906
Francis White  b 4-28-1912

David T  b 9-11-1833  -s Samuel & Harriett
d 11-24-1919, Spiceland, Ind
-bur Raysville Cem, Ind
Sally Ann  b 4-27-1838, Springfield MM, Ohio
-dt Eli (dec) & Anna (Hadley) Hale

Ch: Samuel  b 10-29-1865, near Raysville, Ind
Mary Alice  b 6-24-1868, near Raysville, Ind
(m Perry Hodson)
Anna  b 7-30-1870, near Raysville, Ind
(m Mr Lyman)
Gertrude  b 9-28-1875, near Raysville, Ind
(m Perry Hodson in 1902)
Carrie  b 3-3-1877  d 10-3-1899
-bur Raysville MH, Ind

Joseph  b 3-12-1840, near Raysville, Ind
-s Samuel & Harriett  d 1-11-1911
Anna J  b 8-12-1848, Walnut Ridge MM, Ind
-dt Joseph & Elizabeth Binford
Ch: Henry R  b 12-10-1872, near Raysville, Ind
Charles F  b 6-6-1876, near Raysville, Ind
Mary E  b 12-30-1878, near Raysville, Ind
Harriett Estella  b 4-7-1883, near Raysville, Ind
(m Vernon Carey)

Samuel  b 10-29-1865, near Raysville, Ind
-s David T & Sally (Hale)
Emma O (1st w)  b 8-13-1866  -dt ..... Montague
d 4-27-1917
-bur Glencove Cem, Knightstown, Ind
Ch: Florence Mable  b 7-3-1887  d 3-16-1905
d Los Angeles, Calif  -bur Glencove Cem,
Knightstown, Ind
David H  b 9-2-1889  d 3-12-1906
-bur Glencove Cem, Knightstown, Ind
Margaret C  b 9-22-1900
(m William Henley)
Anna Mary (2nd w)  b 8-16-1870  -dt ... Parker
-widow of ..... Fort

Samuel  b 7-8-1801, Symons Creek MM, N C
-s Benjamin & Penninah  d 5-13-1878
-bur Raysville MH, Ind
Harriett  b 5-4-1805, Orange Co, N C
-dt William & 1st w, Sarah (Jackson) (dec)
Pickett
d 3- -1886  -bur Raysville MH, Ind
Ch: William  b 2-14-1827, Orange Co, N C
d 12-31-1828  -bur Eno MH, N C
Martha  b 11-25-1828, Orange Co, N C
Anna N  b 1-21-1831, New Garden MM, Ind
d 2-27-1867  -bur Raysville MH, Ind
David  b 9-11-1833, New Garden MM, Ind
Sarah Jane  b 11-25-1835, New Garden MM, Ind
Mary  b 1-19-1838, New Garden MM, Ind
d 9-1-1839  -bur Elm Grove MH Cem
Joseph  b 3-12-1840
Charles  b 2-15-1845

Thomas  b 6-17-1790, Symons Creek MM, N C
-s Benjamin & Penninah (White)
m 1st in 1814, N C
Mary (1st w)  b 1-12-1798  d 4-1-1822
d at Symons Creek MM, N C
-dt Christopher & Gulielma (Bundy) Morris
Elizabeth (2nd w)  m 1824, N C
b 7-19-1800 at Pasquotank Co, N C
-dt Joseph & Sarah Morris
d 10-11-1851  -bur Raysville MH, Ind

**PYLE**
Olive S  b 3-8-1878, Wayne Co, Ind
-dt Joseph Pyle

**RAMSEY**
(Richard Harvey)
(Mary Ann) (dec)
Ch: Mary Rose  b 8-13-1869, Marion Co, Ind
Adeline M  b 4-1-1873, Rush Co, Ind
(m William L Williams)

**RATCLIFF - RATLIFF**
Anna E  b 4-24-1876  -sister of Edwin B

## RATCLIFF - RATLIFF (Cont)

Charles F    b 8- 4-1862, Henry Co, Ind
Matilda E    b 8-22-1864, Hamilton Co, Ind -dt .. Harrold
Ch: Harold E      b 1- 5-1889, Hancock Co, Ind
     Russell M      b 10-27-1891, Hancock Co, Ind

Edwin B    b 2-12-1869
Adella H    b 8-12-1876
Ch: Anna Roberta    b 11- 3-1919

Marcus    b 10- 2-1857   Reared by Cyrus & Lydia Kendall
     -s Millicent Ratliff
Hannah A    b 2-28-1861   -dt Edward L & Elizabeth Woolen
Ch: William E      b 1-17-1880
     Herschel E      b 4-30-1883
     Carl M      b 8-15-1886
     Jesse C      b 8-21-1889
     Ruby E      b 7-13-1893

## RAYL

Harmon H    b 5-14-1865
Odessa P    b 9- 7-1869
Ch: Corona      b 4- 1-1898

## REDDICK

Elias T    b 5- 8-1857   d 11-23-1929
     -bur Glencove Cem, Knightstown, Ind
Emma S (1st w) b 11-20-1855    d 5-10-1915
     -bur Glencove Cem, Knightstown, Ind
Martha P (2nd w) b 3-11-1895
...ormallt Parker (3rd w)

James T      b 12- 8-1868   Of Grant City MM, Ind

(Jeff)    m 11-16-1902
Mary Alma    b 8-22-1879, Holder, Kans
     -dt Mrs Mary Stites of Henderson, Ind

## REECE

Cynthia    b 11-23-1808, Tenn   -widow of Samuel Pickering
     -dt John & Elizabeth Maulsby
     d 10-23-1893   -bur Knightstown Cem, Ind

## REEVES

(Arthur)    m 1899
Cora Bell    b 3-19-1880   -dt ..... Boren
     d 1-26-1916, near Knightstown, Ind
     -bur Glencove Cem, Knightstown, Ind

.....
Nancy Ann    b 1854      d 6-22-1892
     -bur Knightstown, Ind
Ch: Jessie May      b - -1874
     (m L L Degolier)
     Ila Mills (a son)    b 6-30-1879

Munson    b 4- 9-1881
Ora Navada    -dt Jim & Clara Maxwell b 1-18-1882

## REYNOLDS

Job      b 5-14-1794, Center MM, N C
     -s Francis & Rachel   d 3-29-1862
     -bur Raysville MH, Ind
Phebe    b 8- 6-1799, Springfield MM, N C
     -dt Mahlon & Sarah   -bur Raysville MH, Ind
Ch: Sally      b 9-17-1815, Center MM, N C
     Achsah      b 7- 7-1817, Center MM, N C
     Elma      b 9-21-1820, New Salem MM,
         Randolph Co, N C
     Margaret      b 4- 9-1823, Center MM, N C
         Randolph Co
     Mary Ann      b 10-18-1825, Center MM, N C
     David      b 8-21-1826   d 2-10-1899
         -bur Raysville, Ind
     Phebe      b 1-20-1828
     Eunice      b 1-12-1830
     Asenath      b 11-24-1834
     Susan B      b 8- 3-1837
     Jane      b 8-27-1841

## RHOADES

Flora E    b 3-24-1877

Oscar W    b 1-27-1880      Gr-son Elijah Applegate

James E    b 9-21-1868

Ralph    b 4-30-1884

## RICKS

Joseph Milton    b 3-12-1856, Henry Co, Ind
     Of Grant City MM, Ind
Alice Mary    b 5-20-1856
Ch: Ernest Brian      b 12-16-1896
     Laura May      b 5-13-1902

## RISK

Alvia    b 9-11-1881      -s Percevil & Louie
Lillian Vada    b - -1883, Henry Co, Ind
     -dt ..... Crawford
Ch: William Percevil b - -1909, Henry Co, Ind

C B
Julie
Ch: Helen      b 5- 5-1893, Greensboro, Ind
       d 4-15-1926   (m Herschel Foster)
       -bur Glencove Cem, Knightstown, Ind

Percevil    b 5- 2-1852      d 6-19-1905
     -bur Glencove Cem, Knightstown, Ind
Louie    b 4-15-1856
Ch: Alvia      b 9-11-1881
     Fred      b 4-15-1887   d 4-25-1906
       -bur Knightstown, Ind
     Bertha May      b 5- 4-1889   d 9-30-1911
       -bur Knightstown, Ind
     (m Harry Watkins, 9-5-1909)

## ROBERTS

.....
Alzina S    b 11- 5-1852      d 3- 4-1907
Ch: Maude A      b 6- 7-1875
     Clarence O      b 2-10-1878
     Effie J      b 2-12-1880
     Clara Alice      b 1-10-1889
     Irene Evelyn      b 3- 2-1895

Carrie Evaline b 10-27-1868, Raysville, Ind
     (m Mr Stocton)

(Elmar)
Kittie    b 2- 9-1872

William
Della
Ch: Homer S      b - -1872
     Harry C      b - -1879
     Frank W      b - -1882

Zeikel    b 10-30-1840
Emma Bell    b 8-19-1845      d 8- 6-1928
         at Indianapolis, Ind
     -bur Knightstown, Ind
Ch: Raymond Ezekiel    b 3- 4-1880, Raysville, Ind
       d 9-13-1905
       -bur Glencove Cem, Knightstown, Ind
     Dessie Edna      b 12- 8-1881

## ROBINSON

James    b 11- -1871

## ROCKAFELLOW

Charles W    b 2- 7-1860
Minnie M    b 6- 9-1866

## ROLAND

(Edward)
Josephine    b 3- -1876, Hancock Co, Ind
     -dt Rufus & Anna Chapman

RAYSVILLE-KNIGHTSTOWN

ROLAND (Cont)
Ch of (Edward) & Josephine
    Laurence          b 1-  -1895, Hancock Co, Ind
    Emma              b 9-  -1897, Hancock Co, Ind
    Russell           b 5-  -1899, Hancock Co, Ind
    Orpha             b 6-  -1901, Hancock Co, Ind
    Ivy                b 2-  -1903
    Lucile            b 9-  -1904
    Severn            b 5-  -1906

ROSENBOOM
Emma G      b 8-13-1869  (m Luther Locke)
    -adopted dt John & Harriet Cunningham

ROUNDS
James H     b 11-26-1868, Rushville, Ind
Mary P      b 6-16-1872  -dt Joshua & Margaret C Welborn
Ch:  Elizabeth        b 8-12-1899, Knightstown, Ind
    James Welborn    b 2-26-1904, Knightstown, Ind
    Joseph B         b 5-24-1909, Knightstown, Ind

RUBY
Riley
Minnie Bell  b 11- 5-1873

SAINT
Albert W    b 8-24-1838
Lida Emily  b 2-13-1842
Ch:  Fred C          b 5-19-1868
    Grace C         b 9- 3-1876
    George A        b 3-31-1878
    Arthur L        b 9-15-1883
    Mary Pauline    b 5-13-1885

John W      b 12-11-1855  Of Grant City MM, Ind
Anna M      b 5-25-1861
Ch:  Maud B         b 11-18-1881
    Daisy T         b 8- 2-1886

Olive M     b 5- 1-1881 (Parents names not given)

SAMPLE
(John)
Anna M      b 8- 5-1856, Jasper Co, Ind
    -dt Allen & 1st w, Lucinda Kirk

SAYLOR
(James L)  m 10-17-1905  -s James Sr & Elizabeth of
                                  Preble Co, Ohio
Eleanor R  b 4- 4-1880  -dt Allen & Anna R White

SHAW
Henry C     b 7-11-1860
Emma        b 6-19-1866  -dt John Marian & Rebecca Jane
                                  Little
Ch:  Effie B         b 4- 4-1883
    Gertie E        b 8-18-1885

Joseph      b 1-29-1849
Josephine  b 6-28-1847

SHIELDS
Franklin   b 10- 4-1866
Hannah E   b 1-14-1864
Ch:  Bulah Carletta   b 8- 2-1891
    Willard Pauldon  b 11-13-1893

SHOEMAKER
Tacy        b 4-11-1844, West Grove MM, Ind
    -dt Charles & Margaret Ann Ellis

SIMMONS - SYMONS
Henry Wilson b 3- 1-1833, Ohio  -s Mathew & Mary Jane
            m 11- 2-1859
Sarah Ann    b 11-24-1842  -dt John & Mary Ann Brown
Ch:  Eva            b 10- 8-1863, Charlottesville, Ind
    Melvin          b 8-10-1869, Knightstown, Ind
    Lora            b 7- 7-1872
    Emma F          b 7- 8-1875
    Minnie R        b 7- 9-1878

Floyd A     b 9-28-1881
Nettie      b 6-25-1884

Louella     b 8- 8-1872    -dt John & Nancy

(Robert)
Gertrude    b 2- 3-1877
    -dt William C & Anne W Williams

SLACK
Jacob W     b 1- 1-1853, Dark Co, Ohio

SLAUGHTER
Minnie Bell  b 11- 5-1873    (m Riley Ruby)

SMALL
Murte       b 10-20-1866, Henry Co, Ind
           d 8-29-1921, Knightstown, Ind
    -dt ..... Holland

SMITH
Ephraim R  b 4-20-1850
Sarah J    b 5-11-1851
Ch:  Dorcas Ann      b 1-14-1870
    Rachel Jane     b 5- 8-1872
    Mary Elizabeth  b 4-17-1874
    Sarah E         b 7- 2-1876
    Isaac R         b 1- 7-1879
    Arthur R        b 11-10-1884
    Mettie R        b 6-30-1891

John W      b 5-16-1856, near Elizabeth City, Han-
                          cock Co, Ind
    -s William G & Amanda

F Joseph    b 8-11-1859
    -s Jack Smith who died at Raysville, Ind
Mary E      b -  -1858
Ch:  Jessie E        b -  -1881
    James M         b -  -1882
    Robert E        b -  -1883
    Abigail W       b -  -1886

Mary Alice  b 4-22-1855    -dt ..... Johnson

Dr Robert   b 4-13-1843    d 12-15-1913,
                                  Indianapolis, Ind
    -bur Greensboro, Ind

Thomas
Jennie      b 6-12-1864
Ch:  Robert S        b
    Sarah R         b 11-29-1902

(Tom)
Ethel       b 10-20-1867, Westfield, Ind
    -dt ..... Fodrea
    d 10-25-1928, Indianapolis, Ind
    -bur Glencove Cem, Knightstown, Ind
(Ethel m 2nd to George Thomas Fisher, 3-1-1922)
Ch: (by 1st husband)
    Anna Pearl      b 5- 6-1892, Carthage, Ind
                          d 9-22-1913, Indianapolis, Ind
    -bur Indianapolis, Ind

(William)
Alma P      b 6- 6-1879    -dt ..... Newby

SNYDER
Isaac L     b 3-23-1865    Of Grant City MM, Ind
Martha M   b 2-18-1866
Ch:  Vada           b 2-27-1900

.....
Viola M     b 2- 9-1872
Ch:  Samuel Fay      b 5- 7-1893
    Robert Guy      b 1-27-1895

## SPARKS

Samuel L     b 1860, Hancock Co, Ind
    -s William & H (Teas)
Lucy A     b 1868, Henry Co, Ind
    -dt A & L (Coon) Jackson
Ch: Flossie B     b - -1890

## SPENCER

Charles B     b 2-28-1855, Henry Co, Ind
    -s Ezra & 1st w, Sarah (Pearson)
Delphina M (2nd w) b 11-10-1858, Yadkin Co, N C
    -dt Obed & Margery (Stout) Cox
    Widow of .... Cox, widow with ch
Ch: Josie P     b 12- 5-1880, Hamilton Co, Ind
       d 2- 2-1898
    Olive Myrtle     b 5- 4-1885, Henry Co, Ind
    Francis E     b 2-17-1887, Henry Co, Ind
    Harold C     b 11-30-1894, Henry Co, Ind

## STANLEY

Jesse     b 2- 9-1834, Henry Co, Ind
    -s John & Deborah (Weisner)
Fariba W     b 6- 9-1836

## STEELE

(Max)
Carrie Isabel     b 11-24-1870

(Charles)
Nina A     b 3- 5-1870   -dt ..... Elliott
    d 7-29-1893   -bur Glencove Cem, Knightstown, Ind

Frank K     b 5- 7-1868   d 3- 6-1902
       -bur Knightstown, Ind
Caroline C     b 4-18-1874, Raysville MM, Ind
    -dt Eli F & Jane (Reynolds) Hodson
    (m 2nd to Dr O H Barrett)

George W     b 3- 9-1856
Emma A     b 1-22-18..
Ch: Maggie M     b 7- 2-1882
    Charles M     b 7-28-1885

## STEINER

Elmer     b 10-19-1861, Knightstown, Ind

Nina     b 3-13-1865, Knightstown, Ind
    (m Jerry Midkiff)

George
Rosa B     b 1-27-1877   -dt ..... Johnson
Ch: Margaret E     b 3-10-1900, Knightstown, Ind
    Carl Orien     b 12-30-1901, Knightstown, Ind
       d 11-17-1927, Woodman, Colorado
       -bur Glencove Cem, Knightstown, Ind
    Mary Louise     b 5-10-1904, Knightstown, Ind

## STITES

.....
Mary     b 5-13-1851 or 1855, Greensboro, Ind
Ch: Mary Alma     b 8-22-1879, Holder, Kans
    (m Jeff Reddick, 1902)
    Sarah E     b 11-22-1882, McClain Co, Ill
    Lulu T     b 8-22-1885, Hoopston, Ill
    George W     b 10-20-1889, East Lynn, Ill
    Anna B     b 6-17-1892, Knightstown, Ind

## STOCTON

.....
Caroline Eveline     b 10-27-1868, Raysville, Ind
    -dt ..... Roberts

## STOWHIG

Harry     b 1-17-1876
Ethel     b 7-26-1879   -dt Sam & 1st w, Lou A Williams
Ch: Marie     b 3-13-1900, Knightstown, Ind

## STRATTON

Eli     b 12-20-1772, Eversham MM, Burlington Co, N J
    d 8-17-1839   -s Jonathan & Sarah
    -bur Spiceland MH, Ind
Eunice     b 10- 7-1771, Maurice River MM, Cumberland Co, N J
    -dt William & Rebecca Dallas
    d 2-16-1859   -bur Raysville MH, Ind

(Levi)     -s Benjamin & Anna (Curl) of Va, Ohio & Whitewater MM, Ind
Ruth     b 5- 1-1804   -dt ..... Crews

## STUART

Amos     b 6-30-1808, Deep River MM, N C
    -s Jehu & 2nd w, Sarah (Guyer)
    d 1-15-1905   -bur Earlham Cem, Richmond, Ind
Matilda (1st w) b 12- 4-1812, Cane Creek MM, N C
    -dt Jonathan & Ann (Long) Hadley
    d 6-13-1871, Spiceland, Ind
Ch: Harper F     b 1-15-1832, N C
       d 7-18-1859, N C
    Martitia Jane     b 7-16-1833
    Jehu H     b 6-20-1836
    Sarah Ann     b 2- 1-1838
    Mary E     b 7-12-1840
    Jonathan H     b 8-14-1842
    Eliza M     b 12- 6-1844
    Delphina M     b 10- 2-1847
    John Sidney     b 3- 2-1850
    David W     b 8-19-1852
    Robert Adison     b 11-16-1854
    Amos Eldridge     b 9-10-1856
    Francis B     b 8-15-1859
Melissa E (2nd w)     b 6-26-1833
    m 3-25-1875, Whitewater MM, Ind
    -dt MILES - Samuel & Ann (dec) of Chester MM, Ind
    d 4-17-1923   -bur Earlham Cem, Richmond, Ind

(Greely) (dec)
Lillie     (m 2nd to F Gilbreath)
Ch: (by 1st h)
    Horace Greely     b
    Rhoda Maud     b

Ithamar W     b 5-18-1820, Wayne Co, Ind
    -s Jehu & Sarah (Cook)
    d 3- 7-1892
    -bur Glencove Cem, Knightstown, Ind
Margaret H     b 9-24-1823
    d 3- 7-1890
    -bur Glencove Cem, Knightstown, Ind
Ch: Laura     b 7- 4-1857
    (m ..... Morrison)
    Holloway I     b 8-28-1865

Zimiri     b 4-28-1823, Back Creek MM, Davidson Co, N C
    -s Jehu & Rebecca
    d 1-30-1899, Knightstown, Ind
    -bur Raysville Cem, Ind

## STUBBS

(Charles)     Of Spiceland MM, Ind     b 7- 5-1827
    -s Joseph & Margaret (Saunders)
    b Preble Co, Ohio     m 9- 2-1848
America (1st w)     b 8-11-1830, Hancock Co, Ind
    -dt James & Mary Sample
Eliza M     b 10-26-1836, Rome, Mich     m 9-12-1906
    -dt ..... Lowry     d 5- 4-1909, Spiceland
    -bur Knightstown, Ind

Samuel Everett     b 5- 2-1871, Spiceland, Henry Co, Ind
    -s Charles & 1st w, America (Sample)

## STURGESS

Amanda E     b 7-13-1872     Of Grant City MM, Ind

RAYSVILLE-KNIGHTSTOWN

## SWAIN - SWAYNE

.....
Alma D        b 11- 6-1874         -dt ..... Young

(Charley)
Mary Maud     b 4-30-1879    -dt William C & Amanda Crawford
Ch: Hazel Ellen              b 1- 9-1898
    Elizabeth A              b 2-18-1903

George Howland  b 7-12-1877   -s Thomas M & Julie
Elvira          b 3-20-1878   -dt ..... Weaver

Howland Jr      b 1-14-1832, New Garden MM, N C
                -s Howland Sr & Phebe (Kelley)
                d 2-20-1906  -bur Knightstown, Ind
Louisa E (1st w) b 10-24-1838
                d 6-24-1892  -bur Knightstown Cem, Ind
Ella H (2nd w)  b 2-25-1859   m 8- 1-1893
                -dt ..... Fithian

Nathan Carter   b 7- 5-1850, Deep Creek MM, N C
                -s Nathan W & Elizabeth (Patterson)
Penelope R      b 8- 4-1855, Randolph Co, N C
Ch: Laura M              b 3- 8-1887, Hancock Co, Ind
    Sanford O            b 8-23-1890, Henry Co, Ind

Nathan W        b 10- 3-1809, New Garden MM, N C
                -s Ruel & Miriam (Russell)
Elizabeth       b 7-19-1809, N C
                -dt Jorden & Mary (Clasby) Patterson
Ch: William Jorden       b 6-29-1837, Deep Creek MM, NC
    Mary                 b 7-28-1839
    Joseph Patterson     b 5- 9-1841
    Sarah Miriam         b 6-18-1843
                         To Ind with parents
    John R               b 3-10-1847
    Nathan Carter        b 1- 5-1850
                         To Ind with parents

Thomas          b 7-21-1867, Deep Creek MM, N C
                -s William Jorden & 1st w, Ruth (Coffin)
Jennie          b 6-12-1864
                -dt John & Sarah Smith of Chester MM, Ind
Ch: Robert Sidney        b 12-16-1900
    Sarah Ruth           b 11-29-1902

Thomas M        b 1-26-1834, New Garden MM, N C
                -s Howland & Phebe (Kelley)   m 11-17-1864
Julie E (2nd w) b 4-14-1842, Madison Co, Ind
                -dt John T & Mary C Swain
                d 11-28-1900 -bur Glencove Cem, Knightstown, Ind
Ch: Minnie C             b 8-12-1867, Knightstown, Ind
    George Howland       b 7-12-1877, Greensboro, Ind

William Jorden  b 6-29-1837, Deep Creek MM, N C
                -s Nathan W & Elizabeth (Patterson)
Ruth (1st w)    b 4-23-1833, Deep Creek MM, N C
                -dt William & Anna Coffin    d 1888
                -bur Raysville Burial Ground, Ind
Ch: Thomas               b 7-21-1867, Deep Creek MM, NC
    Sidney               b 6-18-1869, Deep Creek MM, NC
Emma J (2nd w)  b 7- 9-1838

## SWORDS
Samuel          b 3-11-1820, Bainbridge, Lancaster Co, Pa
                -s Thomas & Barbara
Frances         b 10-30-1825, Springweal, Lancaster Co, Pa
                -dt Philip & Mary Fawley or Fairby
Ch: William H            b 10-21-1856, Milton, Wayne Co, Ind
    George F             b 10- 7-1859, Milton, Wayne Co, Ind
    Joseph Seigle        b 11-23-1865, Milton, Wayne Co, Ind

## SYMONS - SIMMONS
Benjamin F      b 12-16-1837  -s Abraham & Achsah (Gilbert)
                              (both dec)
                m 1862 at West Branch MM, Ohio

Verlinda        b 2- 3-1835, Mill Creek MM, Miami Co, Ohio
                -dt Robert & Ann Jenkins
Ch: Joseph Ellis         b 4- 4-1864, Raysville MM, Henry Co, Ind
    Anna Lora            b 11-22-1866, Raysville MM, Henry Co, Ind

## TALBERT
Daniel H        b 3- 2-1860, Salem, Ind
                -s Sylvanus & Phebe (Hiatt)
Caroline        b 4-25-1863, Iowa
                -dt William & Caroline Wilson
Ch: Mabel                b 7-25-1888
    Annie                b 12- 3-1889
    Eubie                b 1-15-1892
    Frank D              b 12-16-1894
    Mary Bertha          b 1- 7-1896
    Ruth Eva             b 6-11-1898

## TATNOR
Grace           b 3- 1-1857      (m Albert Aikin)
                (Brought up by John & Catherine Morrison)

## TAYLOR
.....
Effie J         b 2-12-1880      -dt Alzina Roberts

.....
Rachel Jane     b 5- 8-1872      -dt Ephraim Smith

## TEAS
John C          b 11-12-1827, Silver Creek MM, Union Co, Ind
                -s Thomas (dec) & Sarah (Stratton)
Sarah Isabella  b 12-26-1834, Rich Square MM, N C
                -dt Nathan & Sarah Ann (Harris) Parker
Ch: Walter               b
    Anna                 b

Thomas          b 11-23-1790, Northern Dist, Philadelphia MM, Pa
                -s John & Rachel   d 10-31-1850
                -bur Spiceland MM, Ind
Sarah C         b 5-24-1800, Maurice River MM, Cumberland Co, N J
                -dt Eli & Eunice (Dallas) Stratton
                d 2- 5-1871   -bur Earlham Cem, Richmond, Ind
Ch: John C               b 11-12-1827, Silver Creek MM, Ind
    Edward               b 3- 8-1830, Silver Creek MM, Ind
    Martha               b 4-27-1833, Whitewater MM, Wayne Co, Ind
    Rachel               b 9-15-1835, Spiceland MM, Ind
                         d 9- 8-1845   -bur Spiceland MM, Ind
    Eunice               b 7- 6-1839, Spiceland MM, Ind
    Thomas Jr            b 11-14-1841, Spiceland MM, Ind

## TEMPLETON
Willie          b 7-12-1861
Eunice S        b 12-24-1866
Ch: Grace                b 8-16-1888
    Estella              b 7-29-1890

## TERRY
(Names of Parents not given)
Cora            b 7- 8-1867
Charles L       b 10-20-1869, Henry Co, Ind

## THOMAS
Virlie          Of Grant MM, Ind
Flora (or Nora) b 9-13-1879
Ch: Opal                 b 5-13-1896
                         d 2-25-1901 at Dunreith, Ind
    Inez                 b 9-20-1899

Luella          b 8- 8-1872  (Parents not given)
                Of Wilkinson MM, Ind

## THOMAS (Cont)
William D  b 1849    Of Shirley MM, Ind
Cascinda   b 1853
Ch: Lucy L         b  -  -1875

## THORNBURG
Rev Charles b 1871, Wayne Co, Ind
            -s Charles & F (Symons) Thornburg
Minnie     b 11-10-1873  -dt Brice & Alice (Woods) Fort
Ch: Brice C        b

John Henry  b 2- 9-1865 Of Grant City MM, Ind

## TICE
Nathan G   b 8-15-1868, Highland Co, Ohio
           -s Elias & Matilda
Anna Jane  b 3-31-1868, Rush Co, Ind
           -dt Albert & Mary Rhodes
Ch: Walton Elias    b 4-24-1892, Warren Co, Ohio
    Maggie Edith    b 6-16-1894, Warren Co, Ohio
    Amy Loretta     b 11-18-1896, Warren Co, Ohio
    Mary Matilda    b 1- 8-1901, Knightstown, Ind
    Pearl           b 12-28-1912
    Ethel           b 12-28-1912

## TINNY
John H    b 4- 9-1845
Mary E    b 11-13-1851
Ch: Homer         b 1-13-1872
    Franklin      b 4-16-1875
    Edwin F       b 9-30-1884
    Bessie M      b 10- 8-1887

## TOWNSEND
Eva    b 6-13-1859  (Parents not given)

Jesse N    -s William & Ann (both dec), Hendricks Co, Ind
Asenath    b 11-24-1834, Center MM, N C
           -dt Job & Phebe Reynolds
(Asenath m 2nd Allen T Kirk, a widower, 12-28-1898)

## TROWBRIDGE
Albert F   b 6-16-1864
Genoa      b 10-24-1867 (sister to Norman Reeves)
Ch: Estie         b 5-10-1888
    (m Joseph F Miller at Rushville, Ind on
                10-17-1906)
    Chester       b

## TROXELL
Jessie    b 8-26-1879, Raysville, Ind
          a widow    -dt ... Swain
          (m Charles Francis Edgerton on 6-22-1904)

## TRUEBLOOD
Isaac Overman  b 12-18-1808, Symons Creek MM, N C
               -s Aaron & Milicent (Clanshaid)
               d Blue River MM, Washington Co, Ind
               m 1-19-1832, Suttons Creek MM, N C
Sarah          b 3- 2-1805  -dt Francis & Miriam
                                       White
               d 5- 3-1865 -prob Raysville MH, Ind
Ch: Elizabeth Mariam    b 12-15-1836
    (m C W Pritchard of Chicago, Ill)
    -bur Raysville MH, Ind
    Martha W        b 9-24-1838   d 3-31-1841
    Harriet P       b 3-29-1840   d 4- 5-1841
    Jason           b 7-12-1842   d 9- 6-1873
                    -bur Raysville MH, Ind
    Miles W         b 8-25-1844
                    d 4-12-1875, Hendricks Co, Ind
                    -bur Raysville MH, Ind
    Mary            b 5- 1-1846   d 11-14-1875
                    -bur Raysville MH, Ind

Jason   b 7-12-1842, Spiceland MM, Ind
        -s Isaac O & Sarah (White)
        d 9- 6-1873, -bur Raysville MH, Ind

Matilda H

## RAYSVILLE-KNIGHTSTOWN

Ch: Orville       b 6-20-1865, Raysville MM, Ind
    Sarah Bell    b 12-23-1866, Raysville MM, Ind
        d 10-13-1867  -bur Friends Burying Gr,
                       near Raysville, Ind
    Anna Mary     b 8- 1-1868
    Pearl         b 6-17-1871
        d 3-27-1889  -bur Raysville MH, Ind

Newton A   b 10-20-1834  -s James & Martha (Albertson)
           d 1-24-1910   -bur Raysville MH, Ind
           m 3-26-1864
Susan B    b 8-13-1837  -dt Job & Phebe Reynolds
           d 12- 2-1913, Knightstown, Ind
           -bur Raysville MH, Ind

Rebecca    b 1-29-1841, Washington Co, Ind
           -dt James & Martha (Albertson)

## TWEEDY
Thomas A   b 2-25-1850
Sarah E    b 7- 4-1856
Ch: Minnie F    b 12-13-1888

## TYRE
Matthew A (or Madison A)   b 7-11-1848
Caroline S   b 7-14-1849
Ch: Ada       b 6- 2-1874
    Frank     b 9- 1-1876
        d 10- 6-1898  -bur Wilson Lake, La
    Kate      b 6- 1-1878
    Cora      b 6-22-1880
    Arthur    b 12-29-1882
NOTE: All joined Episcopal Ch at Natchez, Miss

## VANDENBARK
John Wesley  b 2- 4-1825  -s Jacob & Elizabeth
Nancy        b 2- 8-1837  -dt Moses & Jane McCray
Ch: (Grant City PM, Ind)
    Peter        b 6- 2-1862
    John W Jr    b 1-10-1866

John W Jr   Of Grant City MM, Ind   b 1-10-1866
Clara       b 7-20-1865  From Marion MM, Ind
Ch: Pauline      b 2-13-1897  d 4-14-1900
    James H      b 4-16-1900

Peter       b 6- 2-1862   Of Grant City MM, Ind
Mary Bell   b 3- 2-1862, Henry Co, Ind
Ch: Bessie       b 1-12-1884, Henry Co, Ind
    Hazel        b 1- 6-1888, Henry Co, Ind
    (m Mr Cooper on 10-20-1910)

## WAGONER
George   b 11-25-1873

Thomas Perry  b 4-12-1845
Annis         b 11-11-1849
Ch: Anna      b 6- 4-1876

William E     b 1-30-1869   Of Grant City MM, Ind
Jenetta Grace b 2-11-1887

## WALLS
William F   b 3-27-1862   m 6- 9-1881
            d 3- -1934, Knightstown, Ind
Josie E     b 5- 6-1865  -dt Enos & Mary Benbow
            d 6-24-1940, Knightstown, Ind
Ch: Harvey B     b 6- 8-1883
    Mary M       b 10-19-1893  d 5- 9-1917
    -bur Glencove Cem, Knightstown, Ind
    (m Robert Hinshaw in 1911)
    Otto F       b 8-26-1899, Knightstown, Ind
    (m Ruth Miller in 1921)

## WALSH
Clara A   b 2-12-1879

## WALTON
.....
Opal   b 1- 9-1869   -dt ..... Wysong

## WALTON (Cont)
| | | |
|---|---|---|
| Rufus P | b 4-16-1841 | d 4-25-1904, Knightstown |
| | -bur Greensboro, Ind | |
| Teressa A | b 7-23-1844 | |
| | (m 2nd on 7-26-1905 to Elijah Applegate) | |

## WARRICK
| | |
|---|---|
| Ezra M | b 1860 |
| ..... | |
| Ch: Bessie | b 1892 |

## WATTS
| | |
|---|---|
| Henry | m 1- 6-1869, Raysville, Ind |
| Mary | b 12-25-1836, New Trenton, Ohio |
| | -dt Nathan & Nancy Parker |
| Ch: Grace | b 11-23-1870 |
| George | b 10-28-1872 |

## WEAVER
.....
.....
| | |
|---|---|
| Ch: Elvira | b 3-20-1878 |
| Charles L | b 11-11-1880 |

## WEBBER
| | |
|---|---|
| Jacob | b 11-15-1864, Wilson Co, Tenn |
| Anna | b 8-16-1872, Spiceland MM, Ind |
| Ch: Edith | b |
| Darwin | b 12- 1-1904, Raysville, Ind |
| Roy | b |

## WEEKS
| | |
|---|---|
| Allen | b 10- 3-1831    -s Benjamin & Winifred |
| Elizabeth | b 3-10-1834, Duck Creek MM, Ind |
| | -dt Isaac & Charity Pitts |
| Ch: Elmira | b 3- 5-1854 |
| Alsafine | b 4-16-1855, Henry Co, Ind |
| Ellen | b 10- 7-1856, Henry Co, Ind |
| Emily J | b 10- 7-1856, Henry Co, Ind |
| Jane | b 10-21-1858, Henry Co, Ind |
| Benjamin F | b 7- 6-1864, Henry Co, Ind |
| Arthur N | b 5-26-1866, Henry Co, Ind |
| Oscar | b 5-25-1872, Henry Co, Ind |

## WELBORN
| | |
|---|---|
| Joshua D | b 2- 4-1839    d 11-20-1911 |
| | -bur Glencove Cem, Knightstown, Ind |
| Margaret C | b 10-29-1845    d 6-16-1924 |
| | -bur Glencove Cem, Knightstown, Ind |
| Ch: James E | b 10- 7-1870 |
| | (m Julia M Heathcock) |
| Mamie P | b 6-16-1872 |
| | (m James H Rounds) |
| Rozel | b 6-21-1874 |

## WEST
| | |
|---|---|
| Wiley M | b 7- 2-1878, Washington Co, Ohio |

## WHITE
| | |
|---|---|
| Allen S | b 9-20-1848, Spiceland MM, Ind |
| | -s John T & Hannah (2nd w) |
| Anna R | b 4-14-1845    d 11-20-1922, Knightstown |
| | -bur Glencove Cem    (FROM N Y MM) |
| Ch: Frederick M | b 3- 2-1878 |
| Eleanor R | b 4- 4-1880 |
| Francis Joel | b 7-28-1883 |
| Caleb | b 11-12-1796, Suttons Creek MM, N C |
| | -s Francis & Miriam |
| | d 5-10-1860    -bur Raysville MM, Ind |
| Mary | b 9- 7-1801, Symons Creek MM, N C |
| | -dt Edmond & Mary White |
| | d 3-31-1857    -bur Raysville MH, Ind |
| Ch: Jane | b 11-11-1822, Symons Creek MM, N C |
| Charles | b 11-15-1824 |
| James | b 8-26-1826 |
| Joseph | b 9-10-1828 |
| Margaret | b 4- 3-1835, Symons Creek MM, N C |

| | |
|---|---|
| Edmund | b 9-16-1837, Spiceland MM, Ind |
| Harriet | b 11-24-1839, Spiceland MM, Ind |
| Francis | b 11-19-1841, Spiceland MM, Ind |
| | d 1-14-1842    -bur Raysville MH, Ind |
| Charles | b 11-15-1824, Symons Creek MM, N C |
| | -s Caleb & Mary (White)  d 6- -1905 |
| | -bur Odessa, Texas |
| Lucy | b 8-28-1830, Silver Creek MM, Union Co, Ind |
| | -dt William & Sally Haughton |
| Ch: Emma H | b 3-27-1853, Spiceland MM, Henry Co, Ind |
| Ella | b 1-24-1856, Spiceland MM, Henry Co, Ind |
| | d 8-20-1856    -bur Raysville MH, Ind |
| Walter Warren | b 5- 1-1859, Raysville MM, Ind |
| | d 6-26-1861    -bur Raysville MH, Ind |
| Wilfred W | b 11-12-1861    Raysville MM, Ind |
| Herbert H | b 12- 5-1864 |
| Anna May | b 3-22-1868   d 1- 1-1870 |
| | -bur Raysville MH, Ind |
| Edmund | b 9-16-1837, Spiceland MM, Ind |
| | -s Caleb & Mary (White)  m 11-30-1864 |
| Emily J (1st w) | b 7- 3-1844 |
| | -dt Thomas C & Mary Woodard |
| | d 5-11-1877    -bur Raysville MH, Ind |
| Ch: Anna | b 4-24-1866  (m Alvin Wildman) |
| Walter | b 7-14-1869 |
| | d 9- 9-1869    -bur Raysville MM, Ind |
| Bertha | b 10-26-1870 |
| Evelyn | b 10- 4-1873 |
| Henry | b 11-10-1875 |
| Ada (2nd w) | b 3-27-1850 |
| Ch: Edna A | b 9-27-1881 |
| Howard W | b 11-13-1882 |
| Olive Emily | b 1-14-1885 |
| Wayne Watson | b 3-28-1887 |
| Cecil E | b 6-16-1890 |
| Edmond | b 1-31-1826, Symons Creek MM, N C |
| | -s Joseph M & Margaret (White) White (dec) |
| Herbert | b 12- 5-1864    -s Charles & Lucy |
| | d 10-13-1894 at Seymour, Ind |
| Carrie | b 4-12-1867 |
| | -dt William & Eliza Sheppard |
| Ch: Russell | b 2-23-1891 |
| James | b 8-26-1826, Symons Creek MM, N C |
| | -s Caleb & Mary (White) |
| | d 12-31-1903    -bur Raysville MH, Ind |
| Jemima D | b 5-20-1834, Walnut Ridge MM, Ind |
| | -dt Elias (dec) & Judith Henley |
| Ch: Mary Elizabeth | b 10-20-1859, Raysville MM, Ind |
| Elias H | b 6-21-1861 |
| George E | b 5-21-1863 |
| Nereus | b 4-27-1865 |
| | d 9- 5-1868    -bur Raysville MM, Ind |
| Caleb | b 7-17-1867  d 9-15-1868 |
| | -bur Raysville MH, Ind |
| Sibyl Jones | b 7-28-1869 |
| Francis C | b 7-20-1873 |
| Clara Augusta | b 8- 7-1875 |
| John T | b 2-17-1801, Suttons Creek MM, N C |
| | -s Francis & Miriam    d 1879 |
| | -bur Raysville Cem, Ind |
| Susannah (1st w) | b 8-18-1809, Symons Creek MM, N C |
| | -dt Mordecai & Martha Morris |
| | d 8-14-1833, Blue River MH, Washington Co, Ind |
| Hannah A (2nd w) | b 12- 3-1815, Stillwater MM, Ohio |
| | -dt Benajah & Grace Parker |
| | d 8- -1907 |
| Ch: (by 1st wife) | |
| Mordecai M | b 2- 3-1830, Blue River MM, Ind |
| Francis T | b 6-25-1831, Blue River MM, Ind |

## WHITE (Cont)
Ch of John T & Hannah A:
```
    Joel              b  5-12-1839, Spiceland MM, Ind
                      d 12-20-1870      -bur Raysville MH, Ind
    Benajah           b  8-26-1842, Spiceland MM, Ind
    Narcissa          b  2-11-1845, Spiceland MM, Ind
                      d  5- 6-1845      -bur Raysville MH, Ind
    Elizabeth         b  4-21-1846, Spiceland MM, Ind
                      d  5-23-1855      -bur Raysville MH, Ind
    Allen S           b  9-20-1848, Spiceland MM, Ind

Joseph Morris    b  1-14-1800   -s Edmund & Mary (Morris)
Martha (2nd w)   b 10-19-1809, Suttons Creek MM, N C
                 Widow of Joseph H Morris
                 -dt Anderson (dec) & 2nd w Mary (Bagley)
                                                     Toms
Ch: Almira            b  3-14-1843
    Milton            b  9-10-1845, Wayne Co, Ind
    Margaret          b 10- 9-1847, Rush Co, Ind
                      d  4-13-1876      -bur Raysville MH, Ind
    Albert            b  6-23-1850, Rush Co, Ind

Mary Martitia  -widow of Calvin Elliott   b  9-31-1835
               d  7-29-1914     -bur Glencove Cem, at
                                       Knightstown, Ind
(m 2nd to Mr White in 1897)

Samuel           b 11-19-1804, Piney Woods MM, N C
                 -s Samuel & Elizabeth (Symons)
                 d  8- 2-1889     -bur Raysville MH, Ind
Rebecca          b 12- 4-1802, Suttons Creek MM, N C
                 -dt Francis & Miriam (Toms) White
                 d  8-12-1881     -bur Raysville MH, Ind
Ch: Martha            b  4- 8-1835, Suttons Creek MM,
                                               N C

Toms             b 12-15-1790, Piney Woods MM, N C
                 -s Francis & Miriam     d  3-24-1875
                 -bur Raysville MH, Ind
                 m  5- 6-1819, Blue River MM, Washington
                                                 Co, Ind
Milicent         b  6- 3-1801, Back Creek MM, N C
                 -dt John & Mary Albertson
                 d  1-24-1889 at home of H C Woods, son-in-
                 law, at Knightstown, Ind
                 -bur Raysville MH, Ind
Ch: John Toms         b 10-23-1836, Blue River MM,
                                        Washington Co, Ind
    Jane              b  9-23-1839, Blue River MM,
                                        Washington Co, Ind
```

## WHITTEN
```
Ora              b  9-24-1861
Maggie           b  8-20-1867      d  4-14-1897, Knightstown,
                 -bur Cadiz, Ind                        Ind
Ch: Roy C             b  7-11-1885
```

## WHITWORTH
```
Alexander        b  4-18-1804, Guilford Co, N C
                 -s Archibald & Elizabeth   d  4-28-1896
                 -bur Raysville MH, Ind
Jemima           b  9-19-1800, Guilford Co, N C
                 -dt George & Deborah Swain
                 d  3-22-1896     -bur Raysville MH, Ind
```

## WIGGINS
```
Elizabeth        b  4-24-1869     -dt William Addison
                 Of Wilkinson MM, Ind
```

## WILCOX
```
Mahlon Morrow    b  2-22-1870      Of Grant City, MM, Ind
Ida Hester       b  1- 8-1882
Ch: Selia May         b 12-13-1901
```

## WILKINSON
```
James E          b  7-10-1832, Va  -s Lemuel & Hannah
Jane (Sisley)    b  5-26-1838, Henry Co, Ind
Ch: Ida B             b  6- 4-1870, Henry Co, Ind
    Albert L          b  8- 4-1871
    Hatty A           b  7- 2-1872
    William E         b  8- 1-1874
    Milton R          b  4-24-1876

Hezekiah         b  3-25-1835, Va  -s Lemuel & Hannah
Mary P           b  1-27-1836, Henry Co, Ind
                 -dt William & Jane Johnson
Ch: Emma A            b  4-23-1864, Henry Co, Ind
    Charity L         b  7-23-1870
    Alida L           b  1- 6-1872
    Hannah J          b  4- 3-1875
    Sarah E           b
```

## WILLEY
```
Bell M           b  8-21-1860 (parents not given)
```

## WILLIAMS
```
(Jason)
Abigail          b  8-18-1810, Belmont Co, Ohio
                 -dt Joseph & Eleanor Holloway
                 d  5- 2-1888 at Carthage, Ind
                 -bur Spiceland Cem, Ind

Jacob            b  6-12-1840, Wayne Co, Ind
                 -s Joseph & Sarah
                 d  3-23-1913, Philadelphia, Hancock Co, Ind
                 -bur Philadelphia, Hancock Co, Ind

Joseph H         b  8-19-1834      -s Jason & Abigail
                 d  3-30-1867              (Holloway)
                 -bur Rich Square MM, Ind
Dorothy          b  4-18-1839 -dt Josiah Jr & Abigail (Bell)
                                                    Gilbert
                 d  5- 2-1862     -bur Rich Square MM, Ind
Ch: Emma              b  8-24-1860 (m Isaac Barnard)

Samuel T S       b  7-14-1849  -s Jason & Abigail (Holloway)
Lou A (1st w)    b  7-24-1852      d 11-22-1894
                 -bur Glencove Cem, Knightstown, Ind
Ch: William L         b  4-17-1874
    Ethel             b  7-26-1879
        (m Harry Stowhig)
    Olen Edgar        b  1-21-1890
Arminta (2nd w)  b  3- 6-1857

William C        b 11-22-1843      -s Jason & Abigail
                 d  8- 9-1914, Adena, Ohio   (Holloway)
                 -bur Glencove Cem, Knightstown, Ind
Annie W          b  9-14-1850     -dt Abijah & 1st wife
                 d  5- 2-1919, Adena, Ohio        Steddom
                 -bur Glencove Cem, Knightstown, Ind
Ch: Gertrude          b  2- 3-1877, Ohio
        (m Robert Simmons)

William L        b  4-17-1874    -s Samuel T S & Lou A
Adelia M         b  4- 1-1873
                 -dt Richard H & Mary Ann Ramsey
```

## WILLIAMSON
```
(Amos)           Of Grant City PM in Wilkinson vicinity)
Nettie F         b  8-22-1877
Ch: Laurence          b  -  -1893
    Inez E            b 10- 3-1895

Anna M           b  9- 3-1879      (Parents not given)

Isaac            (Of Grant City PM in Wilkinson vicinity)
Basheba
Ch: Robert            b
    Charlie O         b  7- 7-1874
.....
.....
Ch: Jesse E           b  5- 4-1884
    Carl              b  3- 1-1886
```

## WILLS
```
(Jacob L)
(Rosena)
Ch: Arthur            b 1895
    Lona              b
```

RAYSVILLE-KNIGHTSTOWN

## WILLS (Cont)
Ch of Jacob L & Rosena Cont:
   Mary M                  b

## WILMOTT
Henry           b 11-23-1836       -s William & Mary of Eng
                    b Montgomery Shire, Town of Hay, Wales
     (He returned to England)

## WILSON
Abner           b 3- 1-1823, Duck Creek MM, Ind
                  -s Joseph & Phebe
Elizabeth        b 4- 8-1831
                  -dt Ichabod & Sarah Garnis
Ch: Grant City PM, Ind
    Charles F             b 5-24-1857
    Thomas Oscar         b 7- 6-1859
                     d 7- 1-1902       -bur Knightstown, Ind
    Francis Siegle       b 3- 8-1862
    Sarah A                b 8-11-1864

Bert (or Burt)   b 4-17-1855       Of Knightstown, Ind

Charles         b 6- 1-1853       -s James & Charlotte

Elizabeth        b                  -dt George Bell

Elwood          b 3- 6-1870       Of Knightstown MM, Ind

Eva Ellen        b 6-13-1859, Iowa
                  -dt William W & Caroline Wickersham
                  (m James L Townsend 1904)

Francis Siegle   b 3- 8-1862       -s Abner & Elizabeth
                                                   (Garnis)
Sarah E           b 12- 1-1867
Ch: Russel              b 6-13-1887
    Orval                b 1-23-1890
    Effie P              b 2-13-1892

Henry           b 10-21-1827, Duck Creek MM, Ind
                  -s Joseph & Phebe
Rebecca         b 7-25-1829
                  -dt Isom & Mahala Copeland
Ch: Sylvester           b 10- 8-1852
    Arlington           b 6-13-1854

(Jesse H)        b               Of Knightstown MM, Ind
Cora S           b 9-27-1867, Lee Co, Va
Ch: Mary Eliza         b 12-30-1901, Henry Co, Ind

Joseph G         b 2- 9-1798, Piney Woods MM, N C
                  -s Jacob & Miriam    d 1875
                  (May have dec in Westfield, Ind)
Hope            b 11-25-1802, Core Sound MM, N C
                  -dt Francis & Fariba Mace
Ch: John Brian          b 1-23-1829, Core Sound MM, N C
    Mary Jane           b 1-23-1829, Core Sound MM, N C
    Miriam Ann         b 9- 3-1834, Deep River MM, N C
    Phariba M           b 6- 9-1836, Deep River MM, N C
    Rachel G            b 10-23-1838, Deep River MM, N C
    Nathan Mendenhall   b 2- 2-1843, Deep River MM, N C
    Elias Elliott       b 5-16-1846, Deep River MM, N C

Reuben
Eunice           b 1-12-1830, Center MM, Randolph Co, N C
                  -dt Job & Phebe Reynolds
Ch: Clarence            b 2-28-1861, Duck Creek MM, Ind
    Nora J               b 9-18-1862, Duck Creek MM, Ind
    Edgar                b 1- 5-1866, New Salem MM,
                                   Howard Co, Ind

Dr William E   b 12-18-1843     d 11-12-1910, Wingate, Ind
                  -bur IOOF Cem, Darlington, Ind
Wilda A          b 1-25-1855      -dt Hugh & Ruth Green
                  d 2- 1-1906, Knightstown, Ind
                  -bur Knightstown, Ind

## WILTSE
Elizabeth C     b 12-19-1820       -dt Simeon & Elizabeth

## WINDSOR
Lewis William   b 6- 2-1837, Hamptonville, Athen Co, N C
                  -s James & Susannah
Rebecca Lucinda b 7-30-1832, Statesville, Iradell Co, N C
                  -dt John & Patience Johnson
Ch: John Baxter         b 6- 9-1860, Hamptonville, N C
    James Franklin      b 2-19-1862, Hamptonville, N C
    William Henry       b 8-28-1864, Hamptonville, N C
    Emma J               b 5-16-1868, Hamptonville, N C

## WINSLOW
Emily           b 5- 9-1836, Greensboro, N C
                  (m John T Morris in 1904)

## WOODARD
Horace G         b 12-10-1857, Henry Co, Ind
                  -s Thomas C & Mary Ann (Reynolds)
Mary Elizabeth b 3- 4-1859, Henry Co, Ind
                  -dt John Thomas & Martha (White) Newby
Ch: Minnie Emma        b 12-13-1879
    (m Frank Edwards in 1902)
    Edith Ann           b 10-21-1882, Henry Co, Ind
       (m Reginald Bell, 1908)
    Thomas Earl         b 9-20-1885, Henry Co, Ind

Thomas C         b 12-16-1821, N C    -s Luke & Avis (Cox)
                                       (Luke dec)
                  m 10-20-1841, Newport NH, New Garden MM,
                                             Ind
Mary Ann (1st w)    b 10-18-1824
                  -dt Job & Phebe(Hockett) Reynolds
Ch: Emily Jane         b 7- 3-1844, New Garden MM, Ind
    Alpheus Lindley    b 12-14-1846, New Garden MM, Ind
    Vestal               b 10-22-1848, New Garden MM, Ind
    Adaline             b
    Alice                b
    Horace G            b 12-10-1857, Henry Co, Ind
2nd mcd, 1865, Raysville MM, Ind

Thomas R         b 1-28-1853, Wayne Co, Ind
                  -s Cornelius & Sarah (Burgess)
                  m 8-17-1880
Caroline         b 2-26-1855, Wayne Co, Ind
                  -dt Stephen & Mary (Griffin) Townsend
                  d 12-26-1908, Knightstown, Ind
                  -bur New Garden MH, Wayne Co, Ind
Ch: Mabel L             b 6- 8-1885, Bartholomew Co, Ind

## WOODRUFF
Mary Jane        b 10-23-1845      Of Raysville MM, Ind

## WOODS
Addlebert S      b 1-29-1850, Madison Co, N Y
                  -s Joseph & Angeline
Ella (1st w)      b 10-25-1851, Jackson Co, Mich
                  -dt John & Eliza Densmore
Ch: Ruel L               b 3-18-1879, N Y
    Angeline            b 6-10-1886, Ulster Co, N Y
    Edgar J              b 9-12-1889, Ulster Co, N Y
    Adelbert Jay        b 11-27-1892, Amboy, Ind
    Joseph D            b 11-30-1898, Wichita, Kans
Ida M (2nd w)    b 1-18-1862, Adrian, Mich

Charles Summer      b 12- 3-1864
              Of Grant City PM, Ind
Elizabeth Ann b 3-10-1866
Ch: Forest O            b 7- 7-1887
    Zula L               b 4-16-1893
    Aldus L              b 11- 4-1897

Eddie W          Of Shirley MM, Ind        b 1861
Laura E          b 1863

Henry C          b 3-12-1839, Knightstown, Ind
                  -s Robert & Hannah
                  d 5-21-1918       -bur Glencove Cem, Knightstown,
                                                     Ind
Jane E            b 9-23-1839, Blue River MM, Washington Co,
                                                        Ind

## WOODS (Cont)
(Henry C & Jane E Cont)
        d 9- 3-1928    -dt Toms & Milicent White
        -bur Glencove Cem, Knightstown, Ind
Ch:  Edward T     b 9-21-1866, Raysville MM, Ind
         d 4- 3-1875    -bur Knightstown Cem, Ind
         (fell from barn loft near Grant City, Henry
          Co, Ind)
    Robert       b 10-16-1869
    Charles Earnest  b 2-15-1871, Grant City, Ind
        d 8-28-1892    -bur Knightstown Cem, Ind
    Fannie M     b 11-23-1873, Grant City, Ind

John         b 1-25-1813   d 11- 6-1887 at Knights-
         town, Ind and bur there
Jane         b 3- 4-1824   d 8- 6-1899 at Cincinnati
         -bur Knightstown, Ind
Ch:  Louvina     b 12-29-1853
        d 11-13-1898, Knightstown, Ind & bur there
    Jerry       b

Milton       b 12- 5-1829

## WRIGHT
David B      b 5- 7-1832, Knightstown, Ind
        -s William & Sarah
Sarah Miriam  b 6-18-1843, Iradel Co, N C
        -dt Nathan W & Elizabeth (Patterson) Swain
Ch:  Floyd A     b 1880
    Ella B      b 1883

Elizabeth    -mother of Milton A Wright  b 4-20-1833

Milton A    b 8- 7-1857   -s Elizabeth
Sarah Emma  b 1-21-1863   -widow .... Reece
        -dt ..... Callahan
Ch:  Verdie Reece   b 11-20-1879
    (stepson of Milton A Wright)
    Emma       b 1-22-1883

Newton      b 5-24-1825   -s William & Sarah
Emily J     b 8-15-1832, Duck Creek MM, Ind
        -dt Isaac & Charity Pitts

## WYSONG
Opal        b 1- 9-1869   (m ..... Walton)

## YATES
Laura       b 1-27-1866   d 3-25-1913, Indianapolis
        -bur Middletown, Ind
        -a niece of Mrs Martin Scoville of
         Knightstown, Ind

## YOUNGS
(Albert R)   Of Grant City, Ind
(Anna M)
Ch:  Grant City PM, Ind - 1908
    Joseph N     b 11- 6-1885
    Charles Maurice  b 9-25-1887
    Herbert C    b 4-21-1889
    Wilbur R     b 3- 8-1894

Alma D      b 11- 6-1874   (m Mr Swain)

## ZEHRING
Edwin B     b 7-13-1855
Mary E      b 6-14-1861
Ch:  Leora L     b 1882
    Franklin H   b 1884

## ZION
John         b 12-10-1828   -s Matthew
        d 7-10-1896   -bur Carthage, Ind
Maria       b 3-23-1831   -dt Benjamin Pickering
Ch:  Hester C     b 5- 5-1854, Rush Co, Ind
    (m Melville Ellis)
    Mary E      b 3-16-1857, Rush Co, Ind
    (m Joseph Hubbard)
    William R    b 1-31-1859, Rush Co, Ind

William R    b 1-31-1859   -s John & Maria (Pickering)
Laura A      b 5-30-1857
Ch:  Ruby M      b 1-10-1891, Knightstown, Ind
    (m Mark A Wilson of Redkey, Ind in 1915)

RAYSVILLE - KNIGHTSTOWN MONTHLY MEETING

MINUTES AND MARRIAGES

ADAMS
5-27-1893  Bertie rec in mbrp

AIKEN
7-24-1875  Albert W rec in mbrp
4- 2-1876  Albert W, CHARTER MBR at Knightstown PM, Ind
10-27-1877 Albert W gct Indianapolis MM, Ind
5-27-1882  Albert rocf Indianapolis MM, Ind
9-21-1895  Albert & w Grace gct Fairmount MM, Ind

ALAXANDER
4-24-1909  E W drpd fr mbrp

ALBERTSON
4-25-1857  Martha, widow of Jordan, CHARTER MBR of Raysville MM, Ind
10- 2-1861 Martha, widow of Jordan Albertson & dt of James S & Sarah Elliott, form of Perquimans Co, N C, but now dec, m at Raysville MM, Ind, George Evans of Spiceland, Henry Co, Ind
8-24-1889  Edmund rocf Blue River MM, Ind

ALLEE
4-24-1886  Seth R rec in mbrp
8-27-1892  Seth R rel on rq
4-28-1894  Seth R rec in mbrp

ALLEN
12-23-1871 Deborah Ann & minor s, Joseph W, gct Ash Grove MM, Ill
1-23-1875  Julia A rec in mbrp
3-26-1914  John Ralph & w Mona rolf M E Ch, Ogden, Ind
3-26-1914  John Francis & Estella Eliza, ch of John Ralph & Mona, rec in mbrp

ALLISON
1-28-1888  James & w Rachel & ch Faye L rec in mbrp

ALPAW
1-28-1888  Joseph & w Martha A & ch Flora E rec in mbrp

ANDERSON
10-23-1886 Amos B & w Martha & ch Bernard & Raymond rec in mbrp
12-25-1886 Terrell & Margaret rec in mbrp

APPLEGATE
3-26-1881  Elijah, John Franklin & Charles rec in mbrp
12-23-1882 Charles & w Mary gct Indianapolis MM, Ind
2-27-1886  Ella rec in mbrp at Knightstown PM
1-28-1893  Charles P & w Mary & ch Ethel Ione & Clara rocf Indianapolis MM, Ind
2-26-1898  Charles W & Emma V rec in mbrp
10-26-1912 Charles W & ch Pearl, Edward Byron & Mary Lorine jas; rel fr mbrp on rq

ARMSTRONG
2-23-1889  Emma C rec in mbrp
2-26-1898  Clara & Pearl rec in mbrp
4-24-1909  Pearl drpd fr mbrp
 - -1921   Oliver & w Lorena rec in mbrp

ATKINS
2-27-1909  Lena B glt M E Ch, Ogden, Ind

AYDELOTT
4-25-1857  Henry C Jr, CHARTER MBR of Raysville MM, Ind
7-27-1861  Henry C gct Walnut Ridge MM, Ind
6-23-1866  Henry C appt to a comm
1-26-1889  Mary S rec in mbrp
2-27-1897  Jesse & w Mary Selina drpd fr mbrp

BAILEY
9-25-1897  J Quincey & ch Mary & Jessie rocf Spiceland MM, Ind

BAKER
6-26-1886  Almeda & ch Abraham Lincoln & Hugh Latimer rocf Lost Creek MM, Tenn
6-26-1886  Almeda Rush, -dt Almeda Baker, rec in mbrp
5-23-1896  Hugh L gct Anderson MM, Ind
2-24-1916  Laura rec in mbrp

BALDWIN
12-25-1880 Hannah A gct Springfield MM, Ind
3-26-1892  Flora A rocf Spiceland MM, Ind

BALES
5-27-1893  Mira rec in mbrp

BALFOUR
4-22-1893  Lillian rec in mbrp
11-24-1900 Lillian drpd fr mbrp; jas

BALLARD
2-25-1882  Mary rocf Whitewater MM, Ind
2-25-1882  Jeremiah rocf Whitewater MM, Ind
2-25-1882  Lauretta C rocf Whitewater MM, Ind
3-28-1885  Mary & Lauretta gct Dublin MM, Ind

BALLENGER
8-25-1866  Isaac H & w Rachel Ann & s Isaac rec in mbrp
11-24-1866 Isaac H appt to a comm
7-24-1875  Hannah rec in mbrp
5-28-1881  Isaac H & w Rachel Ann gct Elk MM, Ohio
3-27-1886  Martha K gct Spiceland MM, Ind
9-24-1887  Henry & w Sarah C rec in mbrp
8-24-1889  Henry & w Sarah C rel fr mbrp on rq
4-28-1894  Elbert rec in mbrp
3-23-1895  Alice rel fr mbrp on rq; jMeth Ch

BARKER
3-24-1877  Jacob E rocf Sugar Plain MM, Ind
5-28-1881  William J rocf Greenwood MM, Ind
6-27-1896  Orvil C rocf Dublin MM, Ind
2-27-1909  Orville & Bessie & ch Bethel K, William L, & Milton R gct Spiceland MM, Ind

BARNARD
1-28-1888  Isaac rec in mbrp
           (h of Mary Emma, nee Williams)

BARRETT
4-22-1882  Cyrus C rec in mbrp
2-27-1886  Joseph H rec in mbrp at Knightstown PM
4-26-1890  Joseph M drpd fr mbrp
5-27-1893  Ora rec in mbrp
2-26-1898  Leo rec in mbrp
9-22-1900  Charles rel fr mbrp on rq
9-25-1913  Cyrus C drpd fr mbrp
2-24-1916  Dean rec in mbrp

BARTELL
3-24-1900  Frank rec in mbrp
6-23-1900  Frank & ch Ella & Hazel rec in mbrp

BARTLOW
9-26-1891  Charles C & w Emma S & ch Francis Russell & Ella Hazel rec in mbrp
5-22-1897  Emma rel fr mbrp on rq
11-24-1900 Francis drpd fr mbrp; jas

BEAN
3-23-1912  Mable & Carrie rec in mbrp

BECK
6-26-1897  John W & w Dollie S rec in mbrp
7-24-1897  Millicent rocf East Goshen MM, Ohio

BEEMAN
10-24-1868 (Beemin), James B rocf Spiceland MM, Ind

RAYSVILLE-KNIGHTSTOWN

**BEEMAN (Cont)**
- 4-2-1876    James B & ch William P CHARTER MBRS of Knightstown PM, Ind
- 1-22-1898    Bernice rec in mbrp

**BEESON**
- 9-20-1866    Rachel rq mbrp
- 10-27-1866    Rachel rpts to comm that she is about to remove & so withdraws her rq for mbrp
- 1-23-1875    Benjamin (Beason) rec in mbrp
- 1-22-1881    Martha gct Duck Creek MM, Ind
- 3-28-1885    Charles M & w Callie M & ch Mamie Ermel rec in mbrp
- 12-25-1886    David M, Addie A, Sylvia M & Josephine rec in mbrp
- 12-25-1886    Walter W, William W, Margaret A, Goldena, Rosa A, William H & Hazel rec in mbrp
- 2-26-1887    Olivia, Amanda, Jabez & Allie rec in mbrp at Grant P Mtg, Wilkinson neighborhood
- 2-26-1887    Augustus & Addie rec in mbrp at Grant P Mtg, Wilkinson neighborhood
- 11-26-1887    Mary Alice rec in mbrp
- 3-23-1895    Isaac & w Addie M rec in mbrp
- 2-22-1896    Frank rec in mbrp
- 5-23-1896    David W & w Adda & ch gct Spiceland MM, Ind
- 5-23-1896    Charles & Caroline drpd fr mbrp
- 3-27-1897    Clara C & Mariett M rec in mbrp
- 3-25-1911    J C Mogle & w Mary & adopted ch Olive C Beeson rec in mbrp

**BELL**
- 10-27-1866    William F rocf Back Creek MM, N C
- 7-27-1867    Nancy M & ch James Madison, Mary Maria & Sarah Ellen rec in mbrp
- 1-24-1874    Henry C rec in mbrp
- 3-26-1881    Lizzie rec in mbrp
- 10-22-1881    William F & w Nancy M & ch Mary M, Sarah E & Julia Ione gct Fairmount MM, Ind
- 10-22-1881    James M gct Fairmount MM, Ind
- 8-24-1889    Elizabeth M rec in mbrp
- 9-30-1911    Mary Emma Spencer & her s John C Bell rocf Hopewell MM, Ind

**BELSHAM**
- 1-25-1868    Arthur rec in mbrp
- 11-28-1868    Mary rocf Kingston MM, England
- 4-23-1870    Arthur appt asst-clerk of MM
- 3-23-1872    Mary gct Whitewater MM, Ind
- 5-25-1872    Arthur gct Whitewater MM, Ind

**BERNARD**
- 8-25-1900    Thomas & w Jane rec in mbrp

**BERRY or BUSSY**
- 1-26-1867    Mary rec in mbrp

**BINFORD**
- 3-25-1871    Samuel Horner gct Walnut Ridge MM, Ind to m Anna J Binford
- 10-22-1898    Joseph O & w Huldah A & ch Arthur O & Ada C rocf Westland MM
- 10-22-1898    Anna J rocf Westland MM
- 8-18-1910    Joseph O, a min, dec, Memorial to him
- 11-27-1914    Arthur glt Clifton Cresent Hill M E Ch, Louisville, Ky

**BIRD**
- 2-26-1887    John rec in mbrp
- 2-26-1887    George W, b 3-22-1869, m Christi D, b 11-17-1868
- 4-27-1895    Christi D rocf Spiceland MM, Ind
- 10-26-1912    George W & w Christi & ch Harry gct Pennville MM

**BISHOP**
- 2-27-1886    John W, Nancy, Benny, Alberta & Eva rec in mbrp at Knightstown PM
- 2-25-1893    John W & w & ch gct Carthage MM, Ind
- 2-24-1894    John W dis for disunity
- 2-23-1895    Benjamin gct Carthage MM, Ind
- 1-23-1897    Nannie & ch Bertie & Eva gct Carthage MM, Ind

**BLAKLEY**
- 3-23-1912    Harris rec in mbrp

**BOGESS**
- 11-26-1898    William rec in mbrp

**BOGUE**
- 11-28-1896    Minnie C & s Paul rocf Spiceland MM, Ind
- 4-24-1909    Minnie C & s Paul drpd fr mbrp
- 4-24-1909    Lowell W drpd fr mbrp

**BOLINGER**
- 2-27-1886    Joseph, Oliver, Virginia, Ellen & John D rec in mbrp at Knightstown PM
- 12-23-1893    Helen gct Carthage MM, Ind
- 9-22-1900    Joseph, Oliver & Virginia gct Carthage MM, Ind

**BOND**
- 4-22-1915    Willis & w Lelia rocf Danville MM, Ind (Pastor of Knightstown Mtg)
- 2-22-1917    Willis H & w Lelia gct Westfield MM, Ind

**BOREN**
- 3-26-1881    Mary Adeline rec in mbrp
- 2-23-1889    Cora Bell rec in mbrp
- 4-25-1896    Mary A rec in mbrp
- 3-22-1917    Nellie & dt Marguerite rec in mbrp

**BOUSELOG**
- 9-26-1896    Zelma rec in mbrp
- 3-24-1900    Zelma glt M E Ch, Knightstown, Ind

**BOWMAN**
- 6-26-1875    Barclay & w Sarah & ch Eva, Arthur D & Oscar rocf Duck Creek MM, Ind
- 5-24-1879    Barclay & w Sarah & ch Eva, Arthur D & Oscar gct Duck Creek MM, Ind

**BOYER**
- 1-25-1890    Arthur, John, Annie & Vernie rec in mbrp
- 11-26-1898    Athelinda, John E & William rec in mbrp

**BRACKENRIDGE**
- 6-23-1900    Alford, -s G & P ...

**BRANDENBURG**
- 4-24-1886    Thomas, Louisa & Earl F rec in mbrp
- 8-24-1889    Louisa rel fr mbrp on rq
- 1-25-1890    Samuel O & Frances rec in mbrp
- 4-23-1892    Thomas & Louisa rec in mbrp
- 6-26-1909    Louisa glt Christian Ch, Middletown, Ind

**BRATTON**
- 11-26-1892    Mary L gct Marion MM, Ind

**BRECKENRIDGE**
- 3-23-1916    Olive Christina (Coon) rocf Greenfield MM

**BREWER**
- 7-22-1876    Morris & w & ch Clarence A, Ottis Jay, Ava V, Nettie Z, Jennie F, Alice & Allen T rocf Walnut Ridge MM, Ind
- 5-22-1880    Morris & w Eliza Ann & ch Clarence Augustus, Ottis Jay, Eva V, Nettie Z, Jennie F, Alta E & Julius O gct Walnut Ridge MM, Ind
- 2-27-1886    William rec in mbrp at Knightstown P Mtg, Ind

**BRINKMAN**
- 3-23-1895    Hattie (or Paula) rel fr mbrp on rq to j M E Ch of Knightstown, Ind
- 3-2-1922    Pauline rolf Bethel Presby Ch, Knightstown, Ind

**BROADBENT**
- 12-23-1865    Martha (form Griffin) mou; chm
- 1-22-1876    Martha J & ch Richard & Alice gct Spiceland MM, Ind

RAYSVILLE-KNIGHTSTOWN

## BROOKS
- 2-26-1887   Charles & w Ida & ch Oran rec in mbrp at Grant P Mtg, Ind
- 2-26-1887   Dallas rec in mbrp at Grant P Mtg, Ind

## BROSSINS - BROSIUS
- 6-28-1890   Margaret rocf Spiceland MM, Ind

## BROTHERS
- 3-23-1895   Ora rec in mbrp
- 4-24-1909   Ora drpd fr mbrp

## BROWN
- 1-24-1880   Harvey F & w Martha & ch Harry E & Nellie E rec in mbrp
- 11-27-1880   Harvey F dis
- 1-22-1881   Martha H & ch Harry E & Nellie E gct Westfield MM, Ind
- 10-27-1894   Oscar Otis, Ora Lindley, William Franklin & Leuella Wallace, ch of Ethen, rocf Sterling MM, Kans
- 4-24-1909   William F drpd fr mbrp
- 4-24-1909   Lowell W drpd fr mbrp
- 4-24-1909   Oscar Ottis & Ora Lindley drpd fr mbrp

## BRUMFIEL
- 3-2-1922   Blanche & Clara rec in mbrp

## BRUSHWILER
- 4-27-1916   Margaret rocf Upland MM, Ind

## BRYANT
- 4-28-1894   Nelson rec in mbrp
- 1-23-1897   Nelson gct Westland MM, Ind

## BUDD
- 8-27-1864   Albert mcd; chm
- 4-27-1867   John appt to a comm
- 10-27-1877   John gct Indianapolis MM, Ind
- 2-28-1885   John gct Carthage MM, Ind

## BUNDY
- 8-23-1863   Amos C Horner gct Walnut Ridge MM, Ind to m Ann Bundy
- 6-22-1867   Charles & w Pharaba rocf Spiceland MM, Ind
- 9-26-1868   Morris N rocf Spiceland MM, Ind
- 2-26-1870   Morris N mcd; drpd fr mbrp
- 11-23-1889   Henry C & w Mary C & ch Nellie, Elsie Myrtle & Orcil rocf Walnut Ridge MM, Ind
- 2-28-1891   Eliza L rec in mbrp
- 9-26-1891   Henry C & fam gct Dublin MM, Ind
- 3-24-1894   John M & Adda rocf Duck Creek MM, Ind
- 8-27-1914   Adaline & s Charles gct New Castle MM, Ind
- 10-28-1915   Mrs Bessie jas, M E Ch; drpd fr mbrp

## BURGES - BURGESS
- 8-28-1909   (Burges) William & dt Emma rolf Christian Ch, Hagerstown, Ind
- 4-22-1915   (Burgess) Anna P gct Whittier MM, Calif

## BURNS
- 4-27-1912   William G & Emma J glt M E Ch, Wilkinson, Ind

## BURRIS
- 1-23-1875   Charles & Amos rec in mbrp

## BURT
- 7-28-1866   Grace (form Parker) mou; chm
- 11-28-1868   James H, of Knightstown, rec in mbrp
- 4-22-1893   Cora rec in mbrp
- 5-27-1893   Harry rec in mbrp
- 12-23-1893   Clarissa rec in mbrp
- 11-24-1900   Clarissa & dt Cora drpd fr mbrp; jas
- 4-24-1909   Harry drpd fr mbrp

## BURTON
- 3-26-1881   Elmer & w Sarah C & ch FaniEttie rec in mbrp
- 2-28-1885   Elmer gct Indianapolis MM, Ind

## BUTLER
- 10-22-1859   Charles M & w Miriam & Elinora rocf Milford MM, Ind
- 4-28-1866   Charles M dis for enlisting in Army
- 1-26-1867   Joseph J & w Eliza, a min, & ch Deborah A, Jared P & Hiram rocf Walnut Ridge MM, Ind
- 1-27-1872   Joseph J & w Eliza & s Hiram gct Ash Grove MM, Ill
- 1-27-1872   Jared rel fr mbrp on rq
- 2-27-1886   Charles M rec in mbrp at Knightstown P Mtg, Ind
- 4-26-1917   Harriet gct Indianapolis MM, Ind

## BUZAN
- 2-28-1880   Mary A & ch Gertrude, Louis Rex & Gracie Eliza rec in mbrp
- 1-24-1885   Mary A & ch Gertrude, Grace Eliza & Louis Rex rel fr mbrp on rq

## BYERLY
- 9-23-1876   Wesley & w Mahaly & ch Emma Mary, Edgar, Nellie & Sadie rec in mbrp
- 9-24-1892   Wesley & w & 5 ch rel fr mbrp on rq

## BYRKET
- 3-27-1875   Jonas & w Luzena & ch David B, Amos E, William F, Charles E & Benjamin S rec in mbrp at Grant P Mtg, Ind
- 11-24-1877   Jonas & w Luzena & ch Amos E, William F, Charles E & Benjamin S rel fr mbrp on rq
- 1-22-1881   Brooks & w Margaret & s Edgar Burton gct Duck Creek MM, Ind
- 3-26-1881   Jonas & Luzena rec in mbrp
- 2-26-1887   Benton & w Miriam & ch Erma, Olga & Alta Fay rec in mbrp at Grant P Mtg, in Wilkinson neighborhood
- 2-25-1888   William F & w Hattie M rec in mbrp
- 5-27-1893   Earnest rec in mbrp
- 1-28-1899   William F & w Hattie M & ch gct New Castle MM, Ind
- 4-24-1909   Earnest drpd fr mbrp
- 2-27-1919   Marshall & w rec in mbrp

## CALLAHAN
- 1-28-1882   Sarah Emma rec in mbrp
- 4-22-1882   Pauline J rec in mbrp
- 4-22-1893   Lizzie rec in mbrp
- 5-27-1893   Effie rec in mbrp
- 6-23-1900   Sarah E, -dt Elizabeth, rec in mbrp

## CAMPBELL
- 4-24-1909   Mary E drpd fr mbrp

## CAMMACK
- 4-25-1857   Henry & w Sally & ch Rachel, Emeline, Elwood, John H & Elizabeth H, CHARTER MBRS OF Raysville MM, Ind
- 5-26-1860   Henry & w Sally & ch Rachel, Emeline, Elwood, John H & Elizabeth H gct Spiceland MM, Ind
- 2-26-1898   Amanda, Noral B & Donald V rec in mbrp
- 2-26-1898   Vestal C rocf Amboy MM, Ind

## CANADAY
- 6-23-1866   Nathan H rec in mbrp
- 10-24-1868   Nathan C rel frm mbrp on rq

## CARY
- 1-22-1898   Ada rec in mbrp

## CARMICHAEL
- 12-25-1886   Benton, Ella, Grace Tillman, Emma Eva & Fay rec in mbrp

## CARSON
- 3-29-1865   Amos of Hinkles Creek MM, Hamilton Co, Ind, -s Jacob & Esther of same place, m at Raysville MM, Ind, Lydia Ellen Griffin of Raysville, Henry Co, Ind
- 8-26-1865   Lydia E gct Hinkles Creek MM, Ind
- 12-24-1887   Frank rec in mbrp

## CARSON (Cont)
1-23-1897 Frank E gct Dublin MM, Ind
3-27-1897 Frank E - cert to Dublin MM ret as "he does not reside there"

## CAISEY
8-25-1888 Christinia rec in mbrp

## CASEY
2-26-1887 Vinton, Nora & Ole rec in mbrp at Grant P Mtg, Wilkinson neighborhood
10-27-1894 Nora rocf Duck Creek MM, Ind

## CASS
4-23-1892 Able & w Susannah & s William L rec in mbrp

## CATT
3-28-1885 John K & w Melvina Luzetta & s George Lawrence rec in mbrp
12-25-1886 Albert rec in mbrp
11-24-1888 John dis for jas
4-27-1889 Albert W rel fr mbrp on rq
2-25-1893 George & w Elizabeth D rec in mbrp
1-23-1897 Albert W & w Sarah Ann & ch Ross rec in mbrp
1-28-1899 George & w Elizabeth drpd fr mbrp; jas
1-28-1899 Albert & w Sarah Ann & s Ross drpd fr mbrp; jas

## CHAMBERLAIN
3-23-1912 Lydia rec in mbrp

## CHAMPLIN
5-28-1914 Oliver & w Susan & ch Nellie F rocf Duck Creek MM, Ind

## CHAPPELL
4-25-1857 Reuben & 2nd w, Martha, & his ch Griffin, Milton H & Lydia M, CHARTER MBRS of Raysville MM, Ind
8-27-1864 Milton H mcd; drpd fr mbrp
4-2-1876 Mary B (wife of John T) & dt Cora, CHARTER MBRS of Knightstown P Mtg, Ind
8-23-1879 Martha Ann rec in mbrp
3-27-1880 Milton H rec in mbrp
3-26-1881 Caroline, Eva M, Ada M, Vera M, Robert M & Reuben M rec in mbrp
2-27-1886 Eva & Ada rec in mbrp at Knightstown P Mtg, Ind
8-27-1886 Milton H & fam rel fr mbrp on rq

## CHARLES
4-2-1876 Mary B & her minor dt, Cora, CHARTER MBRS of Knightstown P Mtg, Ind
2-27-1886 John F rec in mbrp at Knightstown P Mtg, Ind

## CHEW
5-28-1910 Lela Maud rec in mbrp

## CLARA
2-27-1886 Bertha, Alice, Mary & Robbie rec in mbrp at Knightstown P Mtg, Ind

## CLARK
6-26-1861 Thomas, -s John & Nancy of Ripley Twp, Rush Co, Ind, m at Raysville MM, Ind, Emily Jane Griffin of Spiceland Twp, Henry Co, Ind
9-28-1861 Emily Jane gct Hinkles Creek MM, Ind
2-25-1899 Mary Elizabeth gct Anderson MM, Ind

## COFFIN
4-25-1857 Emory D & w Elmina H & ch Julius, Ellen L, Maria L, Alice, Amanda, Walter & Mary E, CHARTER MBRS of Raysville MM, Ind
4-25-1863 Nancy E (form Hockett) mou; chm
6-25-1864 Sarah A & s rocf West Union MM, Ind
8-27-1864 Elmina & ch Julius, Ellen L, Maria L, Alice, Amanda, Walter E & Mary E gct Spiceland MM, Ind
8-24-1867 Sarah Ann Teas (form Coffin) mou; chm
10-26-1867 Sallie A Teas & her minor s, Vestal H Coffin, gct Whitewater MM, Ind
10-28-1871 Nancy Edna & ch Addie Lenora, Mahlon Preston & Chester Elihu gct Carthage MM, Ind
4-27-1872 Anna rocf Deep River MM, N C
2-28-1874 Nathan T & w Jane rec in mbrp
4-2-1876 Nathan T & w Jane, CHARTER MBRS of Knightstown Preparative Mtg, Ind
3-22-1879 Nathan T & w Jane rel fr mbrp on rq

## COGGESHALL
2-26-1862 John of New Garden Mtg, Wayne Co, Ind, -s Tristram & Elizabeth, (both dec), m at Raysville MM, Ind, Lucinda White of Raysville, Henry Co, Ind
6-28-1862 Lucinda gct New Garden MM, Ind

## COLE
4-22-1893 Eva rec in mbrp
4-28-1894 Edith rec in mbrp

## COLLIER
1-25-1890 Lillian & Emma rec in mbrp

## COLLINS
11-24-1900 Frances Kerr drpd fr mbrp
2-24-1921 Joseph C rocf Duck Creek MM, Ind
2-24-1921 Exie (wife of Joseph C) rocf West Richmond MM, Ind

## COMBS
11-26-1887 Myrtle L rec in mbrp

## CONGER
6-26-1919 Russel rec in mbrp

## CONKLING
2-27-1886 David rec in mbrp at Knightstown P Mtg, Ind

## COOK
12-23-1865 Sarah Ann (form Newby) mou; chm
1-27-1866 Sarah Ann gct Spring Creek MM
4-24-1886 Lorenzo, E J, Nile, Porter & Orva V rec in mbrp
2-26-1887 Lorenzo rec in mbrp at Grant P Mtg, in the Wilkinson neighbrohood
3-27-1897 John & w Jennie rec in mbrp
1-22-1898 May rec in mbrp
2-26-1898 Joseph R rec in mbrp
5-27-1899 John & w Jennie glt Meth Ch, Greenfield, Ind

## COON - see also Koon
4-24-1886 Kate, Sarah & Dessa rec in mbrp
2-26-1887 Frank & Lafayette rec in mbrp at Grant P Mtg in Wilkinson neighborhood
11-26-1887 Martha rocf Duck Creek MM, Ind
1-25-1890 John & Nancy rec in mbrp
8-27-1892 Lafayette rec in mbrp
5-25-1895 Frank, Sarah & Adda rel frm mbrp on rq to jas
8-25-1895 Mary rec in mbrp
5-26-1900 Lafayette drpd fr mbrp
3-23-1916 Eli rocf Greenfield MM, Ind
6-22-1916 Jane, wife of Eli, rec in mbrp

## COOPER
7-24-1886 Margaret Jane rec in mbrp
5-25-1895 Nora gct Duck Creek MM, Ind

## COPELAND
1-26-1889 Louisa rec in mbrp

## COPPER
12-30-1913 Dallis G & w Elsie V rec in mbrp

## COSSAND
8-28-1875 John & w Malinda rec in mbrp
1-22-1898 Aaron & s Verling rocf Haviland MM, Kans

RAYSVILLE-KNIGHTSTOWN

## COX
- 6-28-1873   Enos & w Mary Ann & ch Margie Elizabeth, Obed Clarkson, William Thomas & Benjamin Franklin rocf Deep Creek MM, N C
- 1-25-1879   Margery, w of Obed, & ch Penelope R, Delphina M & Nerius rocf Union Grove MM, Hamilton Co, Ind
- 5-28-1881   Enos & w Mary & ch Margery Elizabeth, Obed Clarkson, William Thomas, Benjamin Franklin & Sandford S gct Walnut Ridge MM, Ind
- 6-24-1882   Mahlon rec in mbrp
- 2-28-1885   Mahlon drpd fr mbrp
- 1-22-1887   Charles S, Eliza E, Maud L, Cora L, Charles E & Otto Z rec in mbrp
- 12-24-1887   Mahlon N & ch George Wesley & Martin Luther rec in mbrp
- 6-24-1893   Charles & fam gct Dublin MM, Ind
- 7-27-1895   Rachel M, Hannah A & Thomas M rocf Dublin MM, Ind
- 10-23-1897   Obed Clarkson & w Lundy & ch Joseph Enos rocf Walnut Ridge MM, Ind
- 12-25-1909   Anna E rec in mbrp
- 9-17-1910   William B & w Elvira T rocf Plainfield MM, Ind
- 3-22-191.   Emory J rocf Westland MM, Ind
- 4-22-1915   Hannah A gct Anderson MM, Ind

## CRANK
- 3-27-1897   Pearl rec in mbrp

## CRUM
- 3-24-1894   Scott rec in mbrp

## CUNNINGHAM
- 2-26-1887   John rec in mbrp
- 4-23-1887   Harriett rec in mbrp
- 11-26-1887   Grace rec in mbrp
- 2-24-1916   John Sherman & Anna Elora rec in mbrp

## DALRYMPLE
- 2-24-1916   Frank, Verna K & Edith rec in mbrp

## DAVENPORT
- 4-28-1883   Sarah Butler rocf Spiceland MM, Ind

## DAVIS
- 4-25-1857   Jesse & w Mary, CHARTER MBRS of Raysville MM, Ind
- 7-28-1860   Mary gct Spiceland MM, Ind
- 4- 2-1876   Mary Z, wife of Rufus, & dt Ella H, CHARTER MBRS of Knightstown Prep Mtg, Ind
- 2-27-1886   Sarah, Jesse & Della rec in mbrp at Knightstown PM
- 4-22-1893   Ella H rec in mbrp

## DAWSON
- 1-28-1915   Mrs Leslie & s Thomas Buck rec in mbrp
- 5-25-1916   Mrs Leslie & s Thomas Buck glt United Presby Ch, College Corner, Ohio

## DEAN
- 11-28-1868   Elizabeth rocf Plainfield MM, Ind

## DEEM
- 4- 2-1876   Elizabeth (wife of John A), CHARTER MBR of Knightstown Prep Mtg, Ind
- 1-24-1880   Hannah rec in mbrp
- 4-24-1909   Lucy M & Harold C drpd fr mbrp

## DEGOLYER
- 5-24-1894   Loren L rec in mbrp

## DENT
- 2-27-1886   George & Jennie rec in mbrp at Knightstown PM, Ind
- 4-28-1898   George rel fr mbrp on rq

## DIFFEE
- 6-27-1874   William A & w Pharaba & ch Margaret E, Louisa & Martha rocf Duck Creek MM, Ind
- 8-27-1881   Pharaba rec in mbrp

## DILLON
- 2-25-1888   Nathan T & w Margaret S & ch Willis Edward & Horace rec in mbrp
- 10-22-1892   Nathan T & w Margaret S & ch Willis Edward & Horace gct Indianapolis MM, Ind

## DOAN
- 9-28-1916   Zeno H, a min, & w Leona B & s Kenneth B & also Jane (form Doan) rocf Lynn Grove MM, Ia (Jane H Doan died 1-25-1917)

## DOTSON
- 1-27-1912   Alice, Emma & Omer rec in mbrp

## DOUGLAS
- 3-27-1875   David & w Lydia M rocf West Branch MM, Ohio
- 4- 2-1876   Rev David W & w Lydia M, CHARTER MBRS at Knightstown Preparative Mtg, Ind
- 5-26-1877   David W & w Lydia gct Litchfield MM, Maine

## DRAKE
- 2-27-1886   Eliza & Charles rec in mbrp - Knightstown Mtg, Ind
- 9-24-1892   Eliza & 2 ch rel fr mbrp on rq
- 4-25-1896   Delcena rocf Carthage MM, Ind
- 8-25-1900   Harriett gct Carthage MM, Ind

## DRAPER
- 9- 1-1858   Rebecca of Raysville MM, Ind, Henry Co, -dt Samuel & Mary (dec), m at Raysville MM, Ind, Timothy Lamb of Hancock Co, Ind

## DUEL or DUELL
- 6-25-1870   Keziah R rocf Pipe Creek MM, Ind
- 1-24-1874   Keziah R gct Vermillion MM, Ill

## EARNEST
- 11-24-1900   Edith (form Cole) drpd fr mbrp, jas

## EDWARDS
- 7-28-1866   William G rocf Muncy MM, Pa
- 11-28-1868   James & w Peninah & ch James Monroe, Perry M, Julia Ann, Isaac Jefferson, Cynthia Ann, Charles E & Eunice L rec in mbrp at Grant Mtg, Ind
- 11-28-1868   Jemima rec in mbrp at Grant Mtg
- 10-23-1869   William H & w Elizabeth & s Levi Martin rec in mbrp
- 4-23-1870   James M mcd; drpd fr mbrp
- 5-27-1871   William G appt recorder of removal cert at Raysville Mtg, Ind
- 11-25-1871   Jemima gct New Garden MM, N C
- 4-24-1875   Nathaniel & w Margera rocf Spiceland MM, Ind
- 4-24-1875   James M rec in mbrp
- 4- 2-1876   William G, CHARTER MBR of Knightstown PM, Ind
- 1-24-1880   James M rel fr mbrp on rq
- 11-27-1880   William H & w Elizabeth & ch Levi Martin & Martha P gct Duck Creek MM, Ind
- 12-25-1880   William G gct Spiceland MM, Ind
- 12-25-1880   Sarah M, w of Perry, & ch Julia Edna & Maude May rec in mbrp
- 8-27-1881   Peninah & 2 ch gct Duck Creek MM, Ind
- 3-28-1885   Sarah & ch Julia Edna & Maud P gct Duck Creek MM, Ind
- 1-28-1888   James M & w Sarah J & ch Cora Ellen & Charles Eddie rec in mbrp
- 12-26-1891   Charles gct Duck Creek MM, Ind
- 9-24-1892   William H & w Elizabeth & s Levi Martin rel fr mbrp on rq
- 9-12-1906   Mary Ethel, -dt Nathaniel & Margery of Grant City, Ind, m at Grant City, Ind, J Aubrey Kraimen of Newberry, Yamhill Co, Oregon
- 8-28-1909   Ethel M rec in mbrp
- 4-26-1913   Ella Bailey, Carlton Bailey & Ella Louise rec in mbrp

## ELLIOTT

| | |
|---|---|
| 4-25-1857 | Richard P & w Martha E & ch Mary Ann, Samuel O, Edward E & Clarence, CHARTER MBRS at Raysville MM, Ind |
| 4-25-1857 | Elias & his 2nd w Jane & his ch Patrick H, David L, James N, Mary Jane, John B & Martha E are CHARTER MBRS at Raysville MM, Ind |
| 4-25-1857 | Elias appt to a comm to att funerals of mbrs |
| 4-25-1857 | Richard P appt to a comm |
| 5-23-1857 | Richard P appt Clerk of MM |
| 7-25-1857 | Richard P appt Recorder of Removal Certs |
| 5-22-1858 | Richard P appt Clerk of MM |
| 11-26-1859 | David L gct Back Creek MM, Ind |
| 7-28-1860 | Richard P appt to comm to examine B & D record of Raysville MM, Ind & render any assistance necessary to complete them |
| 8-25-1860 | Elias appt to comm to care for burial ground in place of Caleb White who is dec |
| 12-27-1861 | Richard P appt an Overseer |
| 1-25-1862 | Patrick H mcd; drpd fr mbrp |
| 3-25-1865 | James Nixon gct Back Creek MM, Ind |
| 8-26-1865 | Job S & Margaret rec in mbrp |
| 5-26-1866 | Elias & w Jane & s John B gct Whitewater MM, Ind |
| 5-26-1866 | Mary Jane gct Whitewater MM, Ind |
| 6-25-1867 | Richard P rec a min |
| 12-2-1869 | Mary Ann, -dt Richard P & Martha E of Raysville, Henry Co, Ind, m at a Mtg held at res of Richard P Elliott, to David W Newby of Henry Co, Ind |
| 7-24-1880 | Martha P & s John gct Spiceland MM, Ind |
| 6-23-1883 | Francis gct Honey Creek MM, Ind |
| 11-24-1883 | Martha E & s John J rocf Spiceland MM, Ind |
| 3-22-1884 | Calvin rec in mbrp |
| 4-26-1884 | Job & w Margaret gct Duck Creek MM, Ind |
| 2-26-1887 | Nina rec in mbrp |
| 11-24-1888 | Mary Martha rec in mbrp |
| 7-27-1889 | Francis & w Estella & ch Edmond & Paul Revere rocf Honey Creek MM, Ind |
| 1-27-1891 | Julia A gct Duck Creek MM, Ind |
| 9-26-1891 | Rosa J rocf Hopewell MM, Ind |
| 11-26-1892 | Martha gct Spiceland MM, Ind |
| 2-24-1894 | John J glt M E Ch |
| 1-23-1897 | Paul gct Indianapolis MM, Ind |
| 2-17-1897 | Joseph J gct Whitewater MM, Ind |
| 8-24-1912 | Charles & w Rosa Jane & ch Wilber Elmer & Herman Joseph rocf Newberg MM, Oregon |

## ELLIS

| | |
|---|---|
| 1-27-1900 | William rec in mbrp |
| 2-24-1900 | Vincent rolf M E Ch |
| 6-23-1900 | William glt M E Ch, Knightstown, Ind |

## ELLISON

| | |
|---|---|
| 12-23-1915 | Josephine C rec in mbrp |

## ENWRIGHT

| | |
|---|---|
| 3-24-1900 | Winfield rec in mbrp |

## ESTELL

| | |
|---|---|
| 2-26-1881 | Estelle, Mary rocf Carthage MM, Ind |
| 3-26-1887 | Wesley rec in mbrp |
| 4-27-1916 | Charles & w Ollie T & ch Flora M, John Ruben, Ollie F & Floyd C rocf Carthage MM, Ind |

## EVANS

| | |
|---|---|
| 10-2-1861 | George of Spiceland, Henry Co, Ind, -s Benjamin & Hannah, form of Warren Co, Ohio but now dec, m at Raysville MM, Ind, Martha Albertson, widow of Jordan Albertson of Raysville, Ind |
| 11-30-1861 | Martha gct Spiceland MM, Ind |
| 7-28-1866 | Martha rocf Spiceland MM, Ind |

## FARLEY

| | |
|---|---|
| 10-27-1860 | John & ch Louisa G, Joseph Byres, Edith Emmeline, Francis John & Alice Maude rec in mbrp |

## FAULKNER

| | |
|---|---|
| 8-27-1910 | Abigail gct Whitewater MM, Ind |

## FEAR

| | |
|---|---|
| 6-23-1900 | Charles rec in mbrp |

## FENTRESS

| | |
|---|---|
| 7-28-1883 | Martin rocf Spiceland MM, Ind |
| 3-28-1885 | Martin rel fr mbrp on rq |

## FESLER

| | |
|---|---|
| 2-27-1909 | Hattie Josephine & Vera rec in mbrp |

## FINNEY

| | |
|---|---|
| 2-28-1891 | John rec in mbrp |
| 2-22-1896 | Mary E, Homer, Frank, Edwin L & Bessie M rec in mbrp |
| 3-23-1912 | Noble rec in mbrp |

## FITHIAM or FITHIAN

| | |
|---|---|
| 3-26-1881 | Frank rec in mbrp |
| 2-25-1882 | Frank gct San Jose MM, Calif |

## FLANNER

| | |
|---|---|
| 4-28-1866 | Albert H rec in mbrp |
| 12-26-1868 | Albert H rel fr mbrp on rq |

## FLETCHER

| | |
|---|---|
| 4-25-1857 | Henry F, CHARTER MBR at Raysville MM, Ind |
| 4-25-1857 | Zachariah & w Anna & ch Margaret Ann & James J, CHARTER MBRS at Raysville MM, Ind |
| 6-25-1859 | Zachariah & w Anna & ch Margaret Ann & James J gct Fairfield MM, Ind (But rec at Bridgeport MM, Ind) |
| 3-25-1865 | Henry gct Indianapolis MM, Ind |

## FODREA

| | |
|---|---|
| 7-26-1879 | Benjamin D & w Sarah E & ch Horace, Ethel E, Rhoda A, John H, Nancy T & Lillie C rocf Walnut Ridge MM, Ind |
| 2-28-1885 | Benjamin & w Sarah & ch gct Carthage MM, Ind |

## FORBES

| | |
|---|---|
| 4-24-1886 | Lorenzo W, Lydia A & Burtsal M rec in mbrp |
| 5-22-1909 | Lorenzo W & w Lydia rocf Indianapolis MM, Ind |

## FORT

| | |
|---|---|
| 12-24-1887 | Charley & Harry rec in mbrp |
| 8-27-1887 | Brice D & w Alice & dt Minnie rec in mbrp |
| 1-28-1911 | Leone (form Hiatt) rocf Spiceland MM, Ind |
| 12-23-1915 | Brice D & Alice gct Anderson MM, Ind |
| 2-24-1916 | Marshal rec in mbrp |
| 3-23-1916 | Ruby gct Anderson MM, Ind |
| 5-22-1919 | Reva rec in mbrp |

## FOSTER

| | |
|---|---|
| 3-22-1862 | Phebe Ann gct Spiceland MM, Ind |
| 3-26-1881 | Emma rec in mbrp |
| 1-22-1898 | Robert rocf Carthage MM, Ind |

## FOWLER

| | |
|---|---|
| 12-28-1912 | George C E, Eliza Ellen Sager & Lesha Edna Angie rec in mbrp |

## FOX

| | |
|---|---|
| 5-27-1893 | William P & w Cornelia rocf Duck Creek MM, Ind |
| 2-27-1897 | Elizabeth J rocf Duck Creek MM, Ind |

## FOXWORTHY

| | |
|---|---|
| 4-24-1909 | Earl drpd fr mbrp |

## FREDERICK

| | |
|---|---|
| 2-26-1876 | Frederic, Mary rec in mbrp |
| 4-2-1876 | Mary (step-mother of Tom Frederick) CHARTER MBR at Knightstown PM, Ind |
| 1-28-1899 | Sarah rec in mbrp |

## FRIDDLE

| | |
|---|---|
| 1-22-1887 | James rec in mbrp |
| 11-26-1892 | James gct Indianapolis MM, Ind |

RAYSVILLE-KNIGHTSTOWN

**FULGHUM**
8-28-1861  William A of Richmond, Wayne Co, Ind, -s Benjamin & Rhoda of same place, m at Raysville MM, Ind, Harriett White of Henry Co, Ind
11-23-1861  Harriet A gct Whitewater MM, Ind
12-24-1864  William A & w Harriet & s Roscoe rocf Whitewater MM, Ind
5-26-1866  William A appt Clerk of MM
2-27-1867  William & w Harriet & ch Roscoe & Benjamin F gct Whitewater MM, Ind
2-   -1886  Woodard & w Amy rocf Walnut Ridge MM, Ind
5-24-1890  Woodard & w Amy gct Springfield MM, Ohio

**FURBY**
4-24-1858  Mary & ch Mary Eliza, Sarah Ann & Ellen Bowrow rocf Warwickshire North MM, held at Dudley, England
10-27-1860  John & minor ch Louisa G, Joseph B, Edith E, Francis John & Alice Maud rec in mbrp
3-28-1863  Mary Eliza Wilson Bowrow mcd; chm
5-25-1867  John & w Mary & ch Ellen B, Joseph B, Francis I & Alice M gct Onarga MM, Ill
5-25-1867  Louisa G & Edith E, -dts of John & Mary, gct Indianapolis MM, Ind

**FURNACE**
4-24-1886  Leroy rocf Beech Grove MM, Ind

**GANO**
12-23-1893  Nixon H & w Elizabeth E & s Paul Jeffery rocf Whitewater MM, Ind
4-24-1909  Nixon & w & dt Mary drpd fr mbrp

**GARD**
7-23-1914  Cerohom rocf Duck Creek MM, Ind

**GARDNER - GARNER**
1-22-1876  (Garner) Angeline B rec in mbrp
2-26-1876  (Gardner) Mary J rec in mbrp
2-22-1896  (Garner) John rec in mbrp
4-24-1909  (Gardner) James L & Elanor R drpd fr mbrp

**GARRIS**
12-23-1871  Rafor rec in mbrp

**GAUDY**
1-24-1885  Omer drpd fr mbrp

**GAUSE**
3-25-1876  Solomon & Celia, both Elders, gct Duck Creek MM, Ind
3-22-1879  Mahlon gct Walnut Ridge MM, Ind

**GILBERT**
6-24-1911  Robert & Emily rocf Walnut Ridge MM, Ind

**GILBREATH - GILLBREATH**
1-25-1890  Oscar & Ella rec in mbrp
10-22-1892  Lille M & ch Horace G & Maud Stuart gct MM Indianapolis, Indiana

**GILLINGHAM**
5-27-1893  Sarah rec in mbrp

**GIRLEY**
5-27-1893  Hattie rec in mbrp

**GORDEN**
12-27-1873  Micajah rec in mbrp
11-24-1877  Micajah C & w Sarah gct Spiceland MM, Ind

**GORDON**
4-23-1892  Harriett E & ch Lois Irene & Edna Marie gct Winchester MM, Ind
1-28-1899  David W rec in mbrp

**GRAY - GREY**
12-23-1877  Hugh E & w Rebecca & ch Rosetta May & Flora E rec in mbrp
12-25-1880  Hugh E & w Rebecca & ch Rosetta May & Flora E gct Milford MM, Ind
5-28-1881  Hugh & fam not accepted at Milford MM, Ind because of his intemperate habits
9-24-1881  Hugh E & w Rebecca & ch Rosa, Ora Ellen & Maude gct Duck Creek MM, Ind
4-24-1886  Eva M & Herbert & "an infant yet un-named" rec in mbrp
1-26-1889  Jane rec in mbrp at Duck Creek MM, Ind
1-26-1889  Hugh & ch Maddy Athiline, Lorenza Davis & Flozzie Bell rec in mbrp
8-24-1889  Hugh dis
1-25-1890  Maud rec in mbrp
6-28-1890  Alice rocf Spiceland MM, Ind
4-23-1892  Hugh rec in mbrp
8-27-1892  Hugh rel fr mbrp on rq
4-27-1895  Nancy Jane & ch M Atheline & Elizabeth gct Spiceland MM, Ind
4-27-1895  Maud & Lorenzo D, ch of Nancy Jane, drpd fr mbrp; jas

**GRAHAM**
2-24-1912  Laura Fern rec in mbrp

**GREEN**
1-23-1875  William E rec in mbrp
5-27-1876  W E dis for unnecessary use of liquor, upl & denying the divinity of Christ
1-24-1885  Sarah drpd fr mbrp
4-27-1895  Clara V rec in mbrp
2-22-1896  Estella, Gertie F, George C & Maggie M rec in mbrp
2-22-1896  William Henry rec in mbrp
4-28-1898  Benjamin rec in mbrp
?-24-1900  Katie rec in mbrp
6-23-1900  Harold C, -s Bertie, rec in mbrp
11-24-1900  George & w May rolf Cumberland Presby Ch, Danville, Ind
4-24-1909  George Taylor drpd fr mbrp
11-24-1911  George & Clark, ch of George & May, rec in mbrp

**GRIFFIN**
4-25-1857  Jeremiah & w Ann & ch Martha Ellen & Oliver CHARTER MBRS at Raysville MM, Ind
4-25-1857  Samuel & w Lydia & ch Adam, William, Lydia, Martha Jane, Nancy, Samuel Jr & Sarah C, CHARTER MBRS at Raysville MM, Ind
5-23-1857  Samuel appt to comm to att QM
2-27-1858  Mary E rocf Whitewater MM, Ind
4-23-1859  Adam dis for striking a man in anger (Now residing in limits of Fairfield MM, Ind)
7-2-1859  Samuel appt to comm on Education
5-25-1861  Joseph & w Rebecca rocf Spiceland MM, Ind
5-25-1861  Emily Jane rocf Spiceland MM, Ind
6-26-1861  Emily Jane of Spiceland Twp, Henry Co, Ind, -dt Joseph & Rebecca, m at Raysville MM, Ind, Thomas Clark of Ripley Twp, Rush Co, Ind
9-28-1861  Jeremiah appt Recorder of Marriage Certs
11-23-1861  Parthena Jane gct Walnut Ridge MM, Ind
12-27-1861  Samuel appt overseer
8-23-1863  William gct Milford MM, Ind to m Margaret M Wilson
1-23-1864  Jeremiah & w Ann & ch Martha Ellen & Willis gct Spiceland MM, Ind
7-23-1864  Jemima & ch Gulielma, Clarietta & George W gct Bridgeport MM, Ind
3-29-1865  Lydia Ellen, -dt Samuel & Lydia of Raysville, Henry Co, Ind, m at Raysville MM, Ind, Amos Carson of Hamilton Co, Ind
12-23-1865  Martha Broadbent (form Griffin) chm of mou
12-22-1866  Raysville PM rpts that William has forsaken his wife & obtained a divorce; comm appt to investigate & rpt to next Mtg
1-   -1867  William is rpt to have left the country so can not be interviewed; comm rpts the charges are true & the Mtg unites in dis him
8-24-1867  Sarah A gct Onargo MM, Ill
2-22-1868  James rec in mbrp

RAYSVILLE-KNIGHTSTOWN

GRIFFIN (Cont)
1-23-1869  Joseph appt an Overseer at Raysville MM
6-26-1869  Samuel Jr mcd; drpd fr mbrp
3-28-1874  James gct Pleasant Hill MM, Ind
11-27-1880  Rebecca gct Spiceland MM, Ind
2-25-1882  Joseph gct Spiceland MM, Ind - ret here 6-24-1882
4-28-1883  Joseph gct Spiceland MM, Ind
2-28-1885  Lydia gct Spiceland MM, Ind
1-28-1888  John B rec in mbrp
4-24-1897  Willis & w Mary E rocf Spiceland MM, Ind
6-23-1900  Lillian, -dt Della, rec in mbrp
2-27-1909  Della (form Moffitt) & ch Lillian gct Spiceland MM, Ind

GRUNDEN
2-22-1896  Frost rec in mbrp
6-23-1900  Frost gct Back Creek MM, Ind

HACKELMAN
3-28-1891  Olive rocf Westland MM, Ind
4-22-1893  Omer E rec in mbrp
2-26-1893  Charles rec in mbrp

HAINES
4-2-1876  Margaret I, CHARTER MBR at Knightstown PM

HALE
9-24-1864  David Pritchard gct Miami MM, Ohio to m Sarah A Hale

HALL
4-24-1875  Jesse F & w Mary rec in mbrp
1-25-1879  Jesse & w rel on rq
5-27-1893  Emily rec in mbrp

HAMILTON
4-22-1882  Alice & s Floyd rec in mbrp
1-24-1885  Alice & s Floyd drpd fr mbrp
2-26-1887  William rec in mbrp, Grant Prep Mtg, in the Wilkinson neighborhood
2-26-1887  Frank rec in mbrp, Grant Prep Mtg, Wilkinson neighborhood
5-25-1895  Frank rel fr mbrp on rq; to jas
2-22-1896  Alpha O rec in mbrp
4-25-1896  Stephen H rec in mbrp
12-25-1897  James E rec in mbrp
12-23-1911  Ida & dt Floren C rocf Duck Creek MM, Ind

HAMMER
2-27-1869  Peter & w Sarah & ch Elizabeth, Alice & Emma Anice rocf Spiceland MM, Ind
4-23-1870  Charity rec in mbrp at Grant P Mtg, Ind
2-24-1872  Isaac N rec in mbrp
4-27-1872  Thomas B rec in mbrp
12-26-1874  Almira rocf Ackworth MM, Ia
1-22-1876  Milton P rec in mbrp
11-25-1876  Thomas B & w Almira & s Walter gct Hopewell MM, Ind
11-25-1876  Nancy P rec in mbrp
1-22-1881  Milton P gct Lynnville MM, Ia
4-23-1881  Mary rocf Toledo MM, Kans
3-28-1885  Thomas B gct Walnut Ridge MM, Ind
3-23-1912  Mary rec in mbrp

HAMMOND
9-25-1880  Sarah, a widow now Sarah Hammond, & dt Louisa OSBORN gct Duck Creek MM, Ind

HANKINS
5-23-1874  Sirena B, widow of Crandall & now Sirena Hankins, & her ch Howard H & Margaret CRANDALL, rec in mbrp

HARDEN
4-24-1886  William C & Caroline rec in mbrp
2-25-1893  Cicero & w Caroline gct Indianapolis MM, Ind
5-22-1909  William C & w Caroline rocf Indianapolis MM, Ind

HARDY
5-26-1900  Elizabeth & ch gct Anderson MM, Ind

HARKLESS
7-22-1893  Ora H rocf Carthage MM, Ind
4-24-1909  Ora drpd fr mbrp

HAROLD
1-22-1898  Nathan Aldus rocf Westland MM, Ind
11-23-1912  Lemuel & w Jane gct Carthage MM, Ind
3-25-1915  Nathan Aldus & w Cora & ch Marjorie glt Presby Ch, Elkhart, Ind

HARRIS
9-28-1867  Robert rocf Lower MM, held at Black Creek, Southampton Co, Va
7-28-1883  Robert T gct Lower MM, Va
11-25-1893  James F & w Mary Elizabeth C & ch George F, Mary E & Mabel G rocf Dublin MM, Ind
4-24-1909  Fremont & Mabel G drpd fr mbrp

HARRISON
10-24-1857  Timothy rocf Brighouse MM, England
5-5-1858  Timothy of Henry Co, Ind, -s Timothy Sr (dec) & Mary of Doncaster, England, m at Raysville MM, Ind, Naomi W Morgan of Henry Co, Ind
6-26-1858  Timothy appt Recorder of Marriage Certs
11-26-1859  Timothy & w Naomi & ch Mary Emily gct Whitewater MM, Ind
3-24-1866  William rec in mbrp
6-23-1894  Jane rec in mbrp

HARVEY
8-23-1862  William & Mary, ch of William L (dec) & Almeda, rocf New Garden MM, N C; -end by Spiceland MM, Ind
7-23-1863  William, a minor, gct Westfield MM, Ind
12-28-1867  Mary gct Westfield MM, Ind

HASTINGS
2-22-1862  Samuel B & w Matilda rocf Mill Creek MM, Ind
9-23-1865  Samuel & w Matilda & ch Matthew James, Robert Barclay & Arthur gct Mill Creek MM, Ind
4-27-1889  Anna Ethel rec in mbrp
4-27-1889  Ralph Waldo rec in mbrp
5-25-1889  Charles A rec in mbrp
5-27-1893  Charles drpd fr mbrp
2-22-1896  Charles A, w Laura A & s Russel Glenn rec in mbrp
2-22-1896  Peter F & Ella B & ch Ralph W E rec in mbrp
4-28-1898  Chester & w Ida rec in mbrp
1-28-1899  Peter F drpd fr mbrp
1-28-1899  Charles A & w Laura drpd fr mbrp
7-28-1900  Ella rel fr mbrp on rq
12-26-1908  Rebecca rec in mbrp

HAUGH
5-27-1893  Kate rec in mbrp
1-23-1897  Kate gct Anderson MM, Ind

HAUGHTON
4-25-1857  William & w Sally, CHARTER MBRS at Raysville MM, Ind
5-23-1857  William appt to comm-att QM

HAWORTH
7-25-1868  Asenath rocf Vermillion MM, Ill, -end by Walnut Ridge MM, Ind
10-28-1871  Asenath gct Duck Creek MM, Ind

HAYS
4-28-1877  Frances M & w Tacy & s Isaac E rec in mbrp
2-28-1880  Mary Lizzie & ch Effie rec in mbrp
12-25-1886  Marion dis

HEATHCOE
1-22-1881  Samuel H & w Sarah & ch Nancy, Joseph Leroy, Flora Bell, Lula May & Maudie rocf Carthage MM, Ind

RAYSVILLE-KNIGHTSTOWN

### HEATHCOE (Cont)
- 1-22-1881  Immanuel F rocf Carthage MM, Ind
- 3-26-1881  Simon rec in mbrp
- 8-27-1881  Elizabeth & ch Mary L rocf Carthage MM, Ind
- 5-27-1882  Joseph rocf Carthage MM, Ind

### HEATON
- 1-27-1883  Joseph rec in mbrp

### HECK
- 11-26-1898  Frank rec in mbrp

### HEINEY
- 1-26-1889  Jasper, Mary & Addie rec in mbrp
- 1-25-1890  Nora rec in mbrp
- 4-24-1909  Elmer & w Nellie drpd fr mbrp

### HELPENSTINE
- 4-22-1882  H C & Fannie B rec in mbrp
- 4-28-1883  Blanche Mills rec in mbrp
- 1-24-1885  H C drpd fr mbrp

### HENLEY
- 10-23-1858  James White gct Walnut Ridge MM, Ind to m Jemima D Henley

### HIATT
- 4-25-1857  Jesse & Achsah & ch Job, Lyndon, Oliver, Robert, Albert, Susan & Jane, CHARTER MBRS at Raysville MM, Ind
- 5-25-1861  Job dis for na
- 10-26-1861  Eleazar B rocf Winnesheik MM, Iowa
- 11-27-1861  Eleazer B of Winnesheik MM, Iowa, -s Asher & Sarah M of Grant Co, Minnesota, m at Raysville MM, Ind, Eunice S Teas of Henry Co, Ind
- 12-29-1861  Jesse & w Achsah & ch Lyndon, Oliver, Robert, Albert, Susan, Jane & Mary gct Plainfield MM, Ind
- 3-25-1865  Eleazar & w Eunice S & dt Lucy gct Whitewater MM, Ind
- 9-22-1866  Ruth rec in mbrp
- 11-24-1866  Elizabeth & ch Mary A, Ephraim R & Anna Margaret rec in mbrp
- 3-27-1875  Esther & s James E rec in mbrp
- 10-23-1875  Daniel & ch Francis M, Elmer Ellsworth & Roscoe D rocf Duck Creek MM, Ind
- 2-26-1876  Matilda C rec in mbrp
- 5-25-1878  Daniel & w Esther & ch Francis M, Elmer E, Roscoe D & James E gct Duck Creek MM, Ind
- 5-28-1881  Matilda & s Ora Daniel gct Duck Creek MM, Ind
- 4-28-1883  Samuel & w Ida rocf Spiceland MM, Ind
- 7-28-1883  William & fam rocf Spiceland MM, Ind
- 2-28-1885  William & fam gct Spiceland MM, Ind
- 3-28-1885  Matilda & ch Ora P gct Duck Creek MM, Ind
- 4-24-1886  Mary rec in mbrp
- 2-26-1887  Leonidas & w Lizzie & ch Thomas rec in mbrp at Grant P Mtg, Ind
- 2-26-1887  Susannah & ch Claudius A rec in mbrp at Grant P Mtg, Wilkinson neighborhood
- 11-26-1892  Samuel & fam gct Spiceland MM, Ind
- 10-23-1897  Samuel & w Ida J & ch Florence rocf Spiceland MM, Ind
- 4-22-1899  M Florence glt Presby Ch
- 2-24-1916  Raymond glt Presby Ch, Knightstown, Ind

### HIBBEN
- 5-25-1916  Lucile glt M E Ch, Spiceland Ind

### HILL
- 10-26-1861  Mary Elizabeth mcd; chm
- 1-25-1862  Mary Elizabeth gct Walnut Ridge MM, Ind
- 3-27-1869  Caroline & s John, people of color, rec in mbrp
- 4-24-1880  Owen S & w Melissa B rocf Walnut Ridge MM, Ind
- 1-28-1882  Owen S & w Melissa B gct Carthage MM, Ind
- 2-28-1885  John drpd fr mbrp
- 12-24-1887  Elizabeth P gct Carthage MM, Ind
- 5-22-1919  William B & w Annie E & gr-son William Gary Birch rocf Carthage MM, Ind

### HINEY
- 8-22-1896  Joseph K gct Duck Creek MM, Ind

### HINSHAW
- 7-22-1893  Etta gct Carthage MM, Ind
- 11-27-1913  Grant & w Eva rec in mbrp
- 3- 2-1922  Richard rec in mbrp

### HISINBOUGH
- 3-26-1881  Jane rec in mbrp

### HOBBS
- 11-28-1874  Wilson & w Zelinda & ch Charles M, Fannie, Robert W & Harry L rocf Carthage MM, Ind
- 1-23-1875  Walton C rocf Carthage MM, Ind
- 4- 2-1876  Dr Wilson & w Zelinda & ch Orville W, Walton C, Charles M, Robert W, Harry L & Fannie B, CHARTER MBRS of Knightstown MM, Ind

### HOCKETT
- 6-22-1862  Mahlon, w Hannah & ch Nancy, Lindley, Rufina & Sybil rec in mbrp (they were unable to gct from Springfield MM, N C, due to lack of communication between states due to the war)
- 4-25-1863  Nancy E Coffin (form Hockett) chm
- 10-24-1863  Mahlon, a min, & w Hannah & ch Sarah R & Sybil A gct Walnut Ridge MM, Ind
- 5-25-1867  Warner & w Matilda & ch Addison S & Martha C gct Springfield MM, Ind
- 10-22-1881  Celie rocf New Garden MM

### HODGIN
- 4-25-1857  Joseph & Sally & ch Nancy Eliza, Phebe Jane, Martha, Sarah H, David F & Margaret, CHARTER MBRS at Raysville MM, Ind
- 4-27-1867  Jonathan & ch Martitia, Benjamin M, Robert L, Francis T, Cordelia B & Mary V rocf Center MM, N C
- 4-27-1867  Jonathan gct Fairfield MM to m Rebecca C Picket, a widow
- 8-24-1867  Rebecca C, now 2nd wife of Jonathan Hodgin, & her dt Theodate Picket, rocf Fairfield MM, Ind
- 5-22-1869  Benjamin M rel frm mbrp on rq
- 7-24-1869  Rebecca C appt Asst-Recorder of Removal Certs
- 5-27-1871  Jonathan & 2nd w Rebecca C & ch Robert L, Frances T, Mary V, Morris O, Anna G & her dt Thdoedate L Pickett (dt by previous m) gct Springfield MM, Douglass Co, Kans
- 7-26-1871  Nancy Eliza, -dt Joseph & Sally of Henry Co, Ind, m at mtg held at residence of Joseph Hodgin of Ogden, Henry Co, Ind, to Calvin Osborn of Hendricks Co, Ind
- 4-26-1873  Cordelia gct Plainfield MM, Ind

### HODSON
- 3-28-1863  Jane & dt Alice Anna rec in mbrp
- 12-25-1869  Martitia mou; chm
- 1-22-1870  Martitia I gct Plainfield MM, Ind
- 5-28-1870  Eli F rec in mbrp at Raysville P Mtg
- 2-24-1872  Lewis N & w Rebecca M & ch Casper W & Olive E gct Walnut Ridge MM, Ind
- 1-26-1895  Alice M gct Spiceland MM, Ind
- 5-23-1896  Sylvia May gct Spiceland MM, Ind

### HOLDER
- 11-28-1868  Elizabeth rec in mbrp at Grant P Mtg, Ind
- 11-25-1871  Elizabeth gct New Garden MM, N C

### HOLLAND
- 3-26-1881  Otis, Martha & Murta rec in mbrp
- 4-22-1882  Charles, Henry & Edwin rec in mbrp
- 4-22-1893  Della rec in mbrp
- 6-23-1900  Earl R, -s Charles, rec in mbrp
- 10-27-1900  Katie rec in mbrp
- 7-24-1909  Earl R jas Christian Ch; drpd fr mbrp

## HOLLINGSWORTH
- 4-25-1857  James & w Lydia & ch Olive, Stephen G, Valentine, Anderson & Benjamin S, CHARTER MBRS at Raysville MM, Ind
- 8-22-1857  Valentine mcd; drpd fr mbrp
- 1-23-1858  Valentine & w Mary Frances rec in mbrp
- 1-28-1865  Anderson gct Bangor MM, Iowa
- 2-26-1870  Benjamin gct Bangor MM, Iowa
- 8-23-1890  Frances rocf Spiceland MM, Ind
- 10-22-1892 Mary F gct Indianapolis MM, Ind

## HOLLOWAY
- 3-3-1877   Smith & w Margaret rocf Spiceland MM, Ind
- 8-27-1886  Nellie rec in mbrp
- 9-23-1893  Mary E rec in mbrp
- 12-25-1897 Nellie glt 1st Presby Ch, Colorado Springs, Colo

## HOLLOWELL
- 5-25-1878  Mary Ann rec in mbrp

## HOOKER
- 1-24-1874  William H rec in mbrp
- 6-27-1874  Isham rec in mbrp
- 9-26-1874  Isham gct Bangor MM, Iowa
- 2-24-1877  William Harrison & w Almira & ch Laura & Bertha gct New Salem MM, Ind

## HOOTON or HOOTEN
- 2-26-1898  Paul rec in mbrp

## HOPKINS
- 11-26-1898 Pearl rec in mbrp

## HORNER
- 4-25-1857  Samuel & w Beulah, CHARTER MBRS of Raysville MM, Ind
- 4-25-1857  Elizabeth, widow of John, & dts Ann, Rebecca & Lydia, CHARTER MBRS of Raysville MM, Ind
- 4-25-1857  Amos C & w Elvina & ch Elwood T & Stephen C, CHARTER MBRS of Raysville MM, Ind
- 7-25-1857  Samuel S & w Beulah gct Whitewater MM, Ind
- 8-23-1863  Amos C gct Walnut Ridge MM, Ind to m Ann Bundy
- 1-23-1864  Ann rocf Walnut Ridge MM, Ind
- 3-25-1871  Samuel & w Beulah rocf New Garden MM, Ind
- 10-22-1881 Amos C & w Ann gct Spiceland MM, Ind
- 10-22-1881 Lydia gct West Branch MM, Ohio

## HOWARD
- 3-29-1897  Clarence rec in mbrp
- 12-28-1912 Susie & Daisy Marie rec in mbrp

## HUBBARD
- 4-25-1857  Charles S & w Martha & ch Francis T, Mary A & Ellen, CHARTER MBRS at Raysville MM, Ind
- 4-25-1857  Butler & w Celia & ch Delia C, Mary D, Horace F, Electa C & Ida, CHARTER MBRS at Raysville MM, Ind
- 4-25-1857  Charles S appt to comm to obtain MM Record Books
- 7-2-1859   Charles S appt to comm on Education
- 7-2-1859   Martha appt to comm on Education
- 5-28-1864  Butler rq Duck Creek MM, Ind, but Butler now infs mtg at Raysville that he wishes their mbrp to remain at Raysville MM, Ind The request was granted
- 12-22-1866 Charles S appt Clerk of MM in place of William Fulghum who has removed
- 5- -1867   Charles appt Clerk of Removal Records
- 1-24-1874  Edwin rec in mbrp
- 9-23-1876  Juliette rec in mbrp
- 2-28-1880  Martha & dt Lillie rec in mbrp
- 11-27-1880 Butler gct Duck Creek MM, Ind
- 3-26-1881  William & Alonzo rec in mbrp
- 2-27-1886  Hattie, Cecil & Edwin rec in mbrp at Knightstown MM, Ind
- 10-23-1886 William L rel fr mbrp on rq
- 12-25-1886 Alonzo dis for gambling
- 5-27-1893  Della rec in mbrp
- 12-24-1898 Juliette glt Methodist Ch, Benton Harbor, Mich

## HUDELSON or HUDDLESTON
- 1-22-1898  Hudelson, Ada rec in mbrp
- 3-24-1900  Hudelson, Ada glt M E Ch, Knightstown, Ind
- 7-26-1908  Huddleston, Nellie W glt M E Ch, Knightstown, Ind

## HUNNICUTT
- 7-24-1869  William gct New Salem MM, Ind; Cert was ret as he does not reside in their limits Cert ret 2-20-1870
- 3-26-1870  William H gct Springfield MM, Ind

## HUNT
- 5-25-1878  Catherine & ch Daniel L & Alice L rocf Poplar Run MM, Ind
- 4-23-1881  Lafayette W rocf Greenwood MM, Ind
- 9-24-1881  Catherine & ch Daniel L, Alice L & Charles C gct ..
- 3-27-1886  Lafayette gct Spiceland MM, Ind
- 2-26-1887  Omer L rec in mbrp
- 2-25-1888  Lafayette & w Lizzie rocf Spiceland MM, Ind
- 2-27-1897  Lafayette & w Elizabeth drpd fr mbrp

## HUNTER
- 2-27-1886  George W rec in mbrp at Knightstown MM, Ind
- 1-22-1887  George W dis for intemperance

## HURST
- 2-25-1899  Dorcas Ann gct Anderson MM, Ind

## HUSSEY
-            Elijah B & w Mary mbrs of Knightstown MM, Ind

## HUTSON
- 2-27-1886  James rec in mbrp at Knightstown MM, Ind
- 2-27-1886  Mary, Ida & Willie rec in mbrp at Knightstown MM, Ind
- 4-24-1909  James, Mary A & Will drpd fr mbrp

## JACK
- 4-22-1882  Franklin L & Emma rec in mbrp
- 11-24-1900 Franklin gct Muncie MM, Ind

## JACKSON
- 2-27-1886  Susie rec in mbrp
- 1-23-1897  Susan gct Jonesboro MM, Ind
- 4-21-1900  Susan rocf ...
- 11-27-1909 Elsie J rec in mbrp

## JAMES
- 4-24-1886  Arthur L & Stella A rec in mbrp
- 12-26-1891 Arthur & w Phoeba gct Duck Creek MM, Ind

## JAMISON
- 2-25-1915  Morton & w Maud rec in mbrp

## JAY
- 7-25-1857  Joseph W rocf Honey Creek MM, Ind
- 7-28-1860  Joseph W appt to comm to examine B & D Records of Raysville MM, Ind & render any assistance necessary to complete the records
- 5-25-1861  Joseph W appt Clerk of the MM
- 11- -1861  Joseph W appt Clerk of Removal Certs
- 5-24-1862  Joseph W appt Clerk of MM
- 3-27-1869  Joseph W & 2nd w, Sarah J, chm of mcd
- 11-25-1871 Joseph W, now a widower, gct Whitewater MM, Ind

## JENKINS
- 10-25-1862 Benjamin F Symons gct West Branch MM to m Verlinda Jenkins
- 2-26-1887  Henry rec in mbrp
- 2-24-1916  Mary rec in mbrp

RAYSVILLE-KNIGHTSTOWN

**JESSUP**
- 11-24-1877  David & w Julia & adopted dt Ida Mary Crawford gct Spiceland MM, Ind
- 6-25-1914  Walter & w Frankie & s Carl rocf Carthage MM, Ind
- 7-22-1915  Walter & w Frankie & s Carl gct Carthage MM, Ind

**JOHNS**
- 2-26-1887  William, William T, Sarah Louella & Ethel J rec in mbrp at Knightstown MM, Ind
- 1-25-1890  Rily rec in mbrp

**JOHNSON**
- 4-25-1857  William G & w Anna & ch Marticia E, William Elwood, Emily & Mary D, CHARTER MBRS at Raysville MM, Ind
- 4-25-1857  Hiram & w Rhoda J & ch Lindley H & Charles C, CHARTER MBRS at Raysville MM, Ind
- 7-25-1857  William G & w Anna & ch Martitia E, William Elwood, Emily & Mary D gct Hopewell MM, Ind
- 7- 2-1859  Rhoda appt to comm on Education
- 8-28-1869  Edmond & w Eliza S & dt Emily rocf Milford MM, Ind
- 4-27-1872  Edmond & w Eliza S & dt Emily gct Indianapolis MM, Ind
- 1-22-1887  William A, Hannah, Sarah J & Hattie L E rec in mbrp
- 2-26-1887  Hezekiah Sr rec in mbrp at Grant P Mtg, Wilkinson Neighborhood
- 1-25-1890  Lewis rec in mbrp
- 5-27-1893  Mary & s Walter E rec in mbrp
- 7-22-1893  Harvey T rec in mbrp
- 2-24-1894  Rosa rec in mbrp
- 5-25-1895  Hezekiah rel fr mbrp on rq
- 1-25-1896  Mary A rec in mbrp
- 3-23-1912  Ruth rec in mbrp
- 10-22-1914  Mrs Bessie rec in mbrp
- 2-24-1916  Floyd rec in mbrp

**JONES**
- 4-22-1871  Samuel rec in mbrp
- 1-25-1873  Harriet (form Bremon) rec in mbrp on rq
- 4-24-1886  Claudius A rec in mbrp
- 2-28-1891  Etta rec in mbrp
- 1-23-1897  Hattie Hubbard & ch Cecil & Edwin gct Muncie MM, Ind

**JORDAN**
- 3-28-1885  William Henderson & w Hannah & ch John Emery & Mary Lucy rec in mbrp
- 8-28-1919  William H & w Georgia B rolf Bethel Presby Ch, Knightstown, Ind

**JULIAN**
- 2-26-1887  Orange & Wren rec in mbrp at Grant P Mtg, Wilkinson neighborhood
- 1-26-1889  Emsley & Mary rec in mbrp
- 4-28-1894  Nellie rocf West Grove MM, Ind
- 5-23-1896  Fannie M gct Indianapolis MM, Ind

**KAMMEYER**
- 3-25-1911  Henry C & w Helena rec in mbrp

**KEARNS**
- 6-27-1874  Thomas & fam gct Spiceland MM, Ind
- 12-26-1874  William & w Elizabeth & ch Flora Ellen & Rebecca Jane rec in mbrp
- 4- 2-1876  William & w Elizabeth & dt Rebecca Jane, CHARTER MBRS at Knightstown P Mtg, Ind

**KECK**
- 1-25-1890  George rec in mbrp
- 5-25-1895  George rel fr mbrp on rq to jas

**KELLY**
- 11-24-1883  Martha rocf Walnut Ridge MM, Ind

**KENNARD**
- 5-26-1883  Rebecca rocf Spiceland MM, Ind
- 1-28-1888  Francis Marion rec in mbrp
- 4-28-1898  Frank rel fr mbrp on rq

**KENWORTHY**
- 4-25-1857  Amos Sr & 2nd w, Elizabeth, CHARTER MBRS at Raysville MM, Ind
- 4-25-1857  Joel & w Rebecca & ch Albanus, David E, Alcinda E, Oliver & Lydia A, CHARTER MBRS at Raysville MM, Ind
- 4-25-1857  Robert & w Doughty & ch William L, Albert E, Mary, Achsah, Harriett, John C & Morris W, CHARTER MBRS at Raysville MM, Ind
- 4-25-1857  Isaac F & w Abigail & s Owen, CHARTER MBRS at Raysville MM, Ind
- 4-25-1857  Amos appt on comm to att funerals of mbrs
- 4-25-1857  Robert appt to comm on Education
- 5-23-1857  Isaac appt to comm to att QM
- 7-25-1857  Joel & w Rebecca & ch Albanus, David Edwin, Alcinda Ellen, Oliver & Lydia Ann gct Lynn Grove MM, Iowa
- 7-25-1857  Doughty appt Asst-Recorder of Removal Certs
- 1-23-1858  Amos M & w Phebe & s Oliver rocf Lynn Grove MM, Iowa
- 3-27-1858  Isaac F & w Abigail & ch Owen gct Lynn Grove MM, Iowa
- 4-24-1858  Robert & w Doughty & ch William S, Albert C, Mary, Achsah, Harriett, John C & Maurice W gct Lynn Grove MM, Iowa
- 8-28-1858  Willis & w Naomi & ch Allen, Milton, Elizabeth Caroline & Clarkson rocf Lynn Grove MM, Iowa
- 7- 2-1859  Willis & Naomi appt on comm on Education
- 5-26-1860  Amos M & w Phebe H & s Oliver gct West Union MM, Ind
- 6-25-1864  Willis & w Naomi & ch Allen, Milton, Caroline, Elizabeth, Thomas Clarkson & Mary M gct Sugar River MM, Ind
- 3-28-1868  Elizabeth gct Spiceland MM, Ind
- 5-22-1880  Amos M & w Phebe H & s Charles H rocf Richland MM, Ind
- 5-28-1881  Amos M & w Phebe H gct Cottonwood MM, Kans
- 11-26-1881  Amos M & w Phebe H rocf Cottonwood MM, Kans
- 3-24-1883  Charles H & w Cinthia A & dt M Ethel gct Spiceland MM, Ind
- 1-24-1885  Amos & w Phebe H gct Long Lake MM, Mich
- 3-25-1893  Oliver N & w Isabelle & ch Jesse V, Walter C, Amos D & Alva E rocf Penn MM, Mich; -end to Hopewell MM, Ind
- 6-23-1894  Amos M & w Phebe rocf Penn MM, Mich

**KERR**
- 2-28-1885  Eliza rocf Walnut Ridge MM, Ind
- 3-27-1886  Eliza gct Walnut Ridge MM, Ind
- 2-26-1887  Sarah Jane & Francis rec in mbrp
- 7-22-1893  Eliza gct Indianapolis MM, Ind

**KEYS**
- 3-27-1875  John E & w Sophia L rec in mbrp
- 4- 2-1876  John E & w Sophia L & s Harry E, CHARTER MBRS at Knightstown P Mtg, Ind

**KING**
- 12-23-1871  Ellen & ch Isaac, Rozetta Estella, Emery Zeno, Ruth & Abner rocf Cherry Grove MM, Ind
- 5-24-1873  Ellen & ch Isaac, Rozetta Estella, Emery Zeno, Ruth & Abner gct Whitewater MM, Ind
- 8-27-1886  William F & Ella F rec in mbrp
- 8-27-1892  William & w Ella & ch Dale R, Maurice S & Russel H gct Indianapolis MM, Ind

**KIRK**
- 6-28-1862  Allen & w Lucinda & ch Alice M & Anna Maria rocf Spiceland MM, Ind
- 7-24-1869  Allen T appt Recorder of Removal Certs
- 4-23-1870  Allen T appt Clerk of MM
- 1-28-1871  Allen T & w Lucinda E & ch Alice M, Annie M & Elmer E gct Duck Creek MM, Ind

## KIRK (Cont)
- 3-28-1874   Allen T & w Lucinda & ch Alice & Anna M rocf Duck Creek MM, Ind
- 4- 2-1876   Allen T & w Lucinda, CHARTER MBRS of Knightstown PM, Ind
- 6-25-1887   Allen T & w Lucinda gct New Castle MM, Ind
- 1-26-1889   Allen T & w Lucinda rocf New Garden MM, Ind

## KITTERMAN
- 3-28-1896   J Willard & Laura M rec in mbrp

## KNIGHT
- John & w Sarah CHARTER MBRS at Knightstown MM, Ind

## KRAEMER
- 9-12-1906   J Aubrey of Newberry, Yamhill Co, Oregon, -s John & Emma of same place, m at Grant City, Ind to Mary Ethel Edwards of Grant City, Ind

## KREITZER
- 2-24-1916   Edward & Gladys rec in mbrp

## LAMB
- 9- 1-1858   Timothy of Walnut Ridge MM, Ind, Hancock Co, -s Stephen & Miriam of same place, m at Raysville MM, Ind to Rebecca Draper of Henry Co, Ind
- 3-28-1859   Rebecca gct Walnut Ridge MM, Ind
- 8-27-1859   Thomas rocf Piney Woods MM, N C
- 4-28-1860   Thomas gct Piney Woods MM, N C

## LARIMORE
- 2-26-1898   Frank rec in mbrp
- 3-25-1911   Frank gct Duck Creek MM, Ind

## LEDBETTER
- 3-27-1869   Fannie rocf Fairfield MM, Ind

## LEFLER
- 3-23-1916   William L & w Christina Eldora & ch Clifford Eli rocf Greenfield MM, Ind

## LEISURE
- Johnson & w Hannah, CHARTER MBRS Knightstown MM, Ind

## LIPSEY
- 2-23-1867   Hannah rocf Back Creek MM, Ind
- 7-27-1867   William B & his minor ch Oliver G, Rachel Ann, Seneca & Elizabeth rocf Blue River MM, Ind
- 7-25-1868   William appt to a comm
- 3-27-1869   William B & w Hannah & ch Oliver G, Rachel Ann, Seneca & Elizabeth gct Mississinewa MM, Ind

## LISHER
- 3-24-1900   (Lesher) Riley rec in mbrp
- 4-21-1900   Altha rec in mbrp

## LISTER - LIESTER
- 3-28-1896   Johnson & Anna Bell rec in mbrp (Liester)
- 4-24-1909   Rily drpd fr mbrp

## LITTLEWOOD
- 7-24-1875   Edmund & w Harriett M rec in mbrp
- 8-23-1890   Edmund rel fr mbrp on rq
- 2-25-1895   Edmund rec in mbrp

## LOCK
- 5-27-1893   Louella rec in mbrp
- 1-23-1897   Grace gct Anderson MM, Ind
- 6-23-1900   Grace Cunningham gct Anderson MM, Ind

## LOCKRIDGE
- 11-26-1898   Daisy rec in mbrp

## LOGAN
- 9-26-1896   Wesley & dt Mary E rec in mbrp

## LOWDER
- 10-23-1880   Alice & ch Florence & Martha Jane gct Salem MM, Iowa

## LOWRY
- 3-23-1895   Eliza M rec in mbrp

## LUKENS
- 5-22-1858   Elizabeth & ch Mary Ellen, Harriet Elizabeth & William Ellis rocf Short Creek MM, Ohio
- 5-22-1858   Martha rocf Short Creek MM, Ohio
- 3-23-1861   Elizabeth & ch Mary Ellen, Harriet Elizabeth & William E gct Short Creek MM, Ohio
- 3-23-1861   Martha gct Short Creek MM, Ohio

## LUTHER
- 10-26-1872   Ivy & w Sarah & ch Dorothy E, Narcissa J, James A & Emily R gct Fairmount MM, Ind

## LUTRELL
- 1-27-1894   Nancy rec in mbrp
- 9-22-1900   Nancy drpd fr mbrp

## LYKENS
- 12-28-1912   Sylvester & w Laura A gct Spiceland MM, Ind

## LYMAN
- 7-25-1886   Anna M gct Topeka MM, Kans

## McCAIN
- 9-24-1892   John R rocf Spiceland MM, Ind

## McCONNELL
- 11-28-1891   Joseph & w Louisa & ch Freemont & Pearl rocf Duck Creek MM, Ind
- 2-24-1899   Freemont glt 2nd M E Ch, Muncie, Ind

## McCARKLE
- 2-27-1886   Joseph & Samuel, Emma Dell, Willie & Dolphia rec in mbrp at Knightstown MM, Ind

## McCORKLE
- 2-22-1896   Marion F, Elvira & ch Opal rec in mbrp
- 1-28-1899   Marion F & w Elvira drpd fr mbrp; jas
- 4-24-1919   Samuel & w Margaret gct New Castle MM, Ind

## McFALL
- 2-27-1909   Mabel rec in mbrp
- 2-24-1912   Audra rec in mbrp

## McKILLIP
- 12-25-1886   James, Ada, Lucy A & Anna M rec in mbrp
- 1-26-1889   Malinda rec in mbrp
- 4-23-1892   Henry & w Mattie & ch David S, Myrtle M, Lena & James M rec in mbrp
- 2-25-1893   Omer rec in mbrp
- 3-24-1894   Anna E rec in mbrp
- 5-23-1896   Oliver & Annie gct Carthage MM, Ind
- 5-23-1896   James H drpd fr mbrp
- 6-26-1909   Sol J gct Salem MM, Ind
- 4-23-1910   Solomon J & w Martha & s gct Blue River MM, Salem, Ind

## McKINNEY
- 12-25-1886   Jessie & Henry rec in mbrp

## McNEW
- 11-24-1883   Martin & w Jane rec in mbrp
- 2-26-1887   Alice rec in mbrp
- 12-26-1891   Martin rel fr mbrp on rq
- 9-22-1894   Minnie rec in mbrp
- 1-26-1895   Martin rec in mbrp
- 3-27-1909   John & w Elizabeth rocf Duck Creek MM, Ind
- 2-24-1916   A M & Flora rec in mbrp

## MACY
- 11-26-1870   Lindley H & ch Rozella, Joseph L, Lubelle, Viola A, Ida & Nathan W rocf Linwood MM, Iowa

RAYSVILLE-KNIGHTSTOWN

## MACY (Cont)
- 2-20-1871    Lindley appt an Overseer at Grant City Prep Mtg, Ind
- 2-22-1873    Mary rec in mbrp
- 1-24-1874    Lindley H & w Mary A, his 2nd wife, & ch Rozella, Joseph L, Lubelle, Viola A, Ida J & Nathan W gct Toledo MM, Kans
- 7-22-1876    Lilburn & w Martha G & ch Ida, Florence L, Alice, Emily T, Charles G, Lenora, Horace C, Henry & Grace gct Spiceland MM, Ind
- 3-28-1885    Cornelia Jane & s Benjamin Floyd rec in mbrp
- 4-26-1890    Harriett rel fr mbrp on rq

## MADISON
- 1-28-1888    John & w Mary F & dt Bessie rec in mbrp
- 5-27-1893    John drpd fr mbrp

## MALONE
- 1-28-1871    Pleasant M Terrell gct Clear Creek MM, Ohio to m Alice E Malone

## MANLOVE
- 12-25-1886    Sallie & Charles rec in mbrp
- 2-26-1887    Mary Alma & Mary Fannie rec in mbrp
- 7-23-1887    George dis for unnecessary use of liquor
- 1-25-1890    Charles C & Lilla C rec in mbrp
- 4-27-1895    Laura Bell rec in mbrp
- 2-22-1896    Caroline J rec in mbrp
- 2-22-1896    Oliver P & Dora & ch Blanche H rec in mbrp
- 2-22-1896    Walter & Hester rec in mbrp
- 2-27-1897    Hester rocf Westland MM, Ind
- 6-26-1897    Hester cert ret to Westland MM - does not reside here
- 4-28-1898    Lucy A rec in mbrp
- 7-28-1900    Myrna & James of Monta rec in mbrp

## MANNING
- 3-27-1875    Henry & w Mary Jane rec in mbrp
- 7-27-1895    Robert rec in mbrp

## MARKLE
- 3-26-1910    Mary (form Manlove) rel fr mbrp on rq

## MARSHALL
- 1-22-1887    Caleb H rec in mbrp
- 1-25-1890    Timothy rec in mbrp
- 5-25-1895    Timothy rel fr mbrp on rq

## MARTIN
- 3-26-1887    Henry & Mary Ann rec in mbrp
- 3-26-1892    Henry dis for disunity
- 5-27-1893    Angie rec in mbrp
- 2-22-1896    Cora A rec in mbrp
- 2-26-1898    Ira C rec in mbrp

## MATTOX
- 4-28-1894    Elmer rec in mbrp
- 5-25-1895    Elmer dis for disunity
- 9-30-1911    Mary Davis gct Indianapolis MM, Ind

## MAULSBY
- 8-24-1866    James & w Ruth rq mbrp at Raysville MM, Ind
- 10-27-1866    James & w Ruth rpt to comm that they are about to remove, so withdraw their rq of mbrp
- 8-27-1887    Sarah Ann rocf Cherry Grove MM, Ind
- 10-22-1887    James rec in mbrp
- 9-22-1888    Sarah Ann gct Cherry Grove MM, Ind

## MAXWELL
- 9-26-1896    Laura rec in mbrp
- 2-27-1897    Ora Navada rec in mbrp
- 1-22-1898    Lola rec in mbrp

## MAYS
- 9-25-1886    John W & w Elizabeth rec in mbrp
- 5-25-1895    John W & w gct Spiceland MM, Ind

## MENDENHALL
- 10-23-1869    William rec in mbrp
- 8-25-1877    William gct Indianapolis MM, Ind

## MEREDITH
- 1-27-1912    Isaac H & w Sarah D & ch Basil, Edith & Elwood gct Springfield MM, Ind

## MIDKIFF
- 2-27-1886    Columbus C rec in mbrp at Knightstown MM, Ind

## MILES
- 6-27-1863    Keturah (form Pickering) mou; chm
- 7-23-1864    Union MM, Ind rpts they have rec our cert of removal for Keturah Miles

## MILLER
- 11-26-1898    Ada rec in mbrp
- 4-24-1909    Clara Armstrong drpd fr mbrp

## MILLS
- 12-23-1877    Elizabeth rocf Duck Creek MM, Ind
- 11-25-1899    Samuel C & w Flora P rocf Whitewater MM, Ind
- 7-28-1900    Flora gct Bloomingdale MM, Ind

## MOFFITT
- 2-28-1885    Sarah gct Spiceland MM, Ind
- 6-22-1889    Lucurgas & w Amanda & ch Myla rocf Spiceland MM, Ind
- 4-22-1893    C S, Ellen N & Myrtle rec in mbrp
- 5-27-1893    Elizabeth, Asa C, Della M & Lena rec in mbrp
- 12-23-1893    Reuben Z & w Amanda & ch Millia rocf Westland MM, Ind
- 3-24-1894    Effie rec in mbrp
- 12-22-1894    Gertrude M rocf Duck Creek MM, Ind
- 2-28-1898    Carl rec in mbrp
- 2-27-1909    Asa C & w Gertrude & ch Lowell & Ralph glt M E Ch, Ogden, Ind
- 2-27-1909    Columbus & w Elnora & ch Bessie P, Ethel Fay, Mary Hazel & Helen Inez glt M E Ch, Ogden, Ind
- 2-27-1909    Carl A glt M E Ch, Ogden, Ind
- 2-27-1909    Elizabeth glt M E Ch, Ogden, Ind
- 2-25-1915    Edith (form Chew) rocf Spiceland MM, Ind, her h, Lowell, rec in mbrp
- 6-24-1915    Asa C & w Gertrude M & ch Lowell & Ralph C rec in mbrp

## MOGLE
- 11-26-1898    Charles & James W rec in mbrp
- 3-25-1911    J C & w Mary & adopted dt Olive C Beeson rec in mbrp

## MOORE
- 4-25-1857    Charles & w Anna (aged people), CHARTER MBRS of Raysville MM, Ind
- 5-28-1859    Charles & w Anna gct Honey Creek MM, Howard Co, Ind
- 3-24-1866    Phebe (form White) mou; chm
- 1-25-1868    Ransom S rocf Walnut Ridge MM, Ind
- 2-20-1870    Ransom S appt Overseer at Grant City Prep Mtg, Ind
- 5-26-1877    Ransom S & w Rebecca & s Orla gct Westfield MM, Ind
- 1-27-1883    Thomas J & w Sarah A & ch Delaware, Ella May & Mary C rec in mbrp

## MORELAND
- 2-26-1898    Watson rec in mbrp

## MORGAN
- 4-25-1857    Charles & w Michal & ch Benjamin, Naomi W & Mary E, CHARTER MBRS at Raysville MM, Ind
- 4-25-1857    Charles appt to a comm
- 5-5-1858    Naomi, -dt Charles & Michal of Henry Co, Ind, m at Raysville MM, Ind, Timothy Harrison, now of Henry Co, Ind, lately of England
- 6-25-1859    Benjamin gct Whitewater MM, Ind
- 9- -1859    Whitewater MM, Ind has ret cert for Benjamin Morgan as he is not now in that Mtg
- 10-27-1860    Charles & w Michal gct Whitewater MM, Ind
- 11-24-1860    Benjamin gct Whitewater MM, Ind
- 10-26-1912    Sherman B gct Harverford MM, Pa

RAYSVILLE-KNIGHTSTOWN

MORRIS
9-24-1864   Nathan O gct Milford MM, Ind to m Phariba A Wilson
11-23-1867  Nathan O gct Milford MM, Ind
2-27-1886   Mark M & Sarah rec in mbrp at Knightstown MM, Ind
1-23-1897   Frank M & w Sarah rocf New Garden MM, Ind

MORRISON
11-27-1875  Cahterine rocf Indianapolis MM, Ind
8-26-1876   Sarah P rec in mbrp
8-26-1876   Grace D TATNOR, a minor u/c Catherine Morrison, rec in mbrp
3-24-1883   Laura S gct Indianapolis MM, Ind
2-28-1885   Catherine gct Indianapolis MM, Ind
2-22-1890   William rec in mbrp
3-24-1894   Sarah P rocf Indianapolis MM, Ind
11-26-1898  Laura S rocf Indianapolis MM, Ind
6-23-1900   Barbara, John S, Alice & Russel, ch of Laura, rec in mbrp
2-25-1911   Sarah rst in mbrp on rq

MORROW
6-22-1895   Jessie rec in mbrp
5-27-1899   Jesse jas; drpd fr mbrp

MOYER
3-27-1909   Edith gct White River MM, Ind

MURRAY
1-22-1876   Lemuel rec in mbrp at Raysville MM, Ind
4-2-1876    Lemuel & w Abigail D, CHARTER MBRS of Knightstown PM, Ind

NEWBY
4-25-1857   John T & w Martha & ch Samuel F & Charles H, CHARTER MBRS of Raysville MM, Ind
4-25-1857   Frederick & w Sarah & ch Sarah Ann, Mary & David W, CHARTER MBRS at Raysville MM, Ind
4-25-1857   Mary D, widow of Micah Newby, CHARTER MBR at Raysville MM, Ind
3-22-1862   Caroline & fam rocf Hopewell MM, Ind
4-25-1863   Albert appt Asst-Clerk of MM
12-23-1865  Sarah Ann Cook (form Newby) mou; chm
1-27-1866   Albert & w Caroline & ch Charles E, Sarah Emma, Allen L & Luther gct Spiceland MM, Ind
3-23-1867   Margaret Jane & dt Laura Bell rocf Carthage MM, Ind
7-25-1868   Sarah appt an Elder
8-22-1868   Margaret J & dt Laura Bell gct Kokomo MM, Ind
8-22-1868   Henry F gct Plainfield MM, Ind
2-27-1869   Sarah, an Elder, gct Spiceland MM, Ind
12-2-1869   David W of Raysville, Henry Co, Ind, -s Frederick (dec) & Sarah of same place, m at mtg held at residence of Richard P Elliott, Mary Ann Elliott of Henry Co, Ind
12-25-1869  Lydia B gct Spiceland MM, Ind
4-23-1870   William gct Spiceland MM, Ind
1-25-1873   David W & w Marianna & s Frederick gct Ash Grove MM, Ill
8-23-1873   Isadena I rec in mbrp
6-26-1875   David W & w Mary Anna & ch Frederick & Ricard W rocf Ash Grove MM, Ill
4-24-1880   John T & w Martha & ch Minnie E, Thomas Edward, Miles W, John Earl, Annie M & Albert N gct Lynn Grove MM, Iowa
3-26-1881   Gertie M rec in mbrp
1-24-1885   Gertie M drpd fr mbrp
4-23-1887   Minnie E rocf Lynn Grove MM, Iowa
1-28-1888   Frank rec in mbrp
7-22-1893   L Y rec in mbrp
9-23-1893   Charles H gct Lynn Grove MM, Iowa
4-28-1894   Mary & Alma rec in mbrp
4-28-1898   Lankford rel fr mbrp on rq
4-24-1909   Frank drp fr mbrp

NIBARGER
12-25-1886  Cordelia rec in mbrp
2-28-1891   Ellen & Lizzie rec in mbrp

2-25-1893   Charles rec in mbrp
3-24-1894   Harvey & w Lettie & ch Mertie Alma, Laura Bell, Maudie Ann, Emma Jane & James S Clarence rec in mbrp
3-24-1894   Minnie May & William E rec in mbrp
6-23-1894   Sarah rec in mbrp

NICHOLS
5-28-1870   Ann rocf Cherry Grove MM, Ind
1-25-1873   Ann gct Spiceland MM, Ind

NIXON
4-28-1898   Nathan T rocf Spiceland MM, Ind
5-27-1911   Nathan T & fam gct Pasadena MM, Calif

NUGENT
3-23-1895   Harry gct Duck Creek MM, Ind

OAKERSON
6-23-1900   Edith Lee, -dt Lena, rec in mbrp

OLDHAM
2-25-1899   Laura gct Duck Creek MM, Ind

OSBORN
5-26-1866   John & fam rocf Deep Creek MM, N C
11-28-1868  Sarah E, -dt James & Penina Edwards, & her minor dt Harriett L rec in mbrp at Grant City P Mtg, Ind
7-26-1871   Calvin of Hendricks Co, Ind, -s David & Anna (dec), of same place, m at a mtg at residence of Joseph Hodgins of Ogden, Henry Co, Ind, to Eliza Hodgins
9-23-1871   Eliza H gct Plainfield MM, Ind

OVERMAN
4-24-1886   R E & Anna rec in mbrp
2-26-1887   Alpheus L, Augusta & Perna Gertrude rec in mbrp at Grant P Mtg, Wilkinson neighborhood
4-24-1909   Jesse & w Isabella & ch Therman, Edna & Elsie gct Haviland MM, Kans

PAINTER
11-24-1900  Eva Cole drpd fr mbrp; jas

PARE
5-26-1883   Robert rocf Spiceland MM, Ind

PARKER
4-25-1857   Nathan & w Sarah Ann & dt Deborah, CHARTER MBRS at Raysville MM, Ind
4-25-1857   Benajah & w Grace & s Benajah Jr, CHARTER MBRS at Raysville MM, Ind
4-25-1857   Phillip D & w Joanna & ch Ella & Theodore F, CHARTER MBRS at Raysville MM, Ind
4-25-1857   Isaac & w Hannah Maria & ch Micah N & Mary Amelia, CHARTER MBRS at Raysville MM, Ind
4-25-1857   Nathan appt to a comm
4-25-1857   Isaac appt to comm to att funerals of mbrs
2-27-1858   Benajah Jr gct Newberry MM, Ohio to m Deborah A Miller
3-26-1859   Deborah rocf Newberry MM, Ohio
11- -1861   Hannah M appt Asst-Recorder of removal certs
11-27-1861  Isabella, -dt Nathan & Sarah Ann of Henry Co, Ind, m at Raysville MM, Ind, John C Teas of Henry Co, Ind
3-4-1863    Elisha of Arba, Randolph Co, Ind, -s Thomas & Margaret of same place, m at Raysville MM, Ind, Martha D Teas of Raysville MM, Henry Co, Ind
2-27-1864   Isaac appt Recorder of m certs
1-28-1865   Martha D gct Whitewater MM, Ind
7-22-1865   Isaac appt an Elder
7-28-1866   Grace Burt (form Parker) chm of mou
9-22-1866   Robert dis for Military Service
9-22-1866   Nathan W dis for participating in Military Service
6-8-1867    Mary rocf Blue River MM, Ind
7-25-1868   Isaac retained as an Elder

### PARKER (Cont)

| | |
|---|---|
| 7-25-1868 | Hannah M appt an Elder |
| 2-28-1874 | James B & w Hannah B & their s Charles O & Samuel Hause, a mbr of their fam, (brother of Hannah), gct Walnut Ridge MM, Ind |
| 4-2-1876 | Benajah Jr & w Deborah & ch Philemon, Ione, George & Benajah F, CHARTER MBRS at Knightstown Prep Mtg, Ind |
| 4-26-1879 | Nathan gct Union MM, Mo |
| 4-26-1879 | Deborah H gct Union MM, Mo |
| 8-23-1884 | Philip B gct Cleveland MM, Ohio |
| 6-22-1889 | Anna Mary rec in mbrp |
| 4-22-1893 | Carrie G rec in mbrp |
| 12-23-1893 | John E gct Kansas City MM, Kans |
| 3-26-1910 | James W rec in mbrp |
| 11-23-1916 | Henry Allen glt 2nd Presby Ch, Kansas City, Mo |
| 2-28-1918 | Nellie Chaplin glt Presby Ch, Knightstown, Ind |

### PATTERSON

| | |
|---|---|
| 2-27-1886 | Silas, Amanda, Genitha, Lenna, Mabel & Terrell rec in mbrp at Knightstown MM, Ind |
| 5-27-1892 | Frank rec in mbrp |
| 9-24-1892 | Silas rel fr mbrp on rq |
| 9-26-1908 | Clara B rec in mbrp |
| 9-26-1908 | Clara B, a widow, & Elias H White, non-resident mbr, living in Philadelphia, Pa, ann int to m 1st time |
| 11-17-1908 | Clara B, a widow of Henry Co, Ind, -dt James A & Elizabeth R Johnson (both dec), of Milton, Sussex Co, Dela, m at the Landsdown, Parkside Ave & 41st St in Philadelphia, Pa, to Elias Henly White of Philadelphia, Pa |

### PAXTON

| | |
|---|---|
| 12-25-1886 | Katie rec in mbrp |
| 1-25-1890 | Lucinda rec in mbrp |

### PEARSON

| | |
|---|---|
| 10-27-1900 | Morton & w Sarah & ch Lorene & Lyman rocf Sabina MM, Ohio |

### PEDRICK

| | |
|---|---|
| 12-22-1888 | Sarah & ch rocf Carthage MM, Ind |

### PEELE

| | |
|---|---|
| 5-22-1875 | Caleb M & w Maria W & ch Francis Henry, Walter & Louisa W rocf Milford MM, Ind |
| 4-2-1876 | Caleb M & w Maria W & ch Francis Henry, Walter & Louisa W, CHARTER MBRS at Knightstown Prep Mtg, Ind |
| 1-26-1878 | Maria W & ch Francis Henry, Walter & Louisa W gct White River MM, Ind |
| 1-26-1878 | Caleb's cert to White River MM, Ind, has been ret because of an objection in his business dealings |

### PENNINGTON

| | |
|---|---|
| 11-27-1909 | Rebecca & ch Mary & Bertha May gct South 8th St MM, Richmond, Ind |

### PERKINS

| | |
|---|---|
| 4-24-1886 | Clayton L rec in mbrp |
| 1-28-1888 | Clayton L rel fr mbrp on rq |

### PHARES

| | |
|---|---|
| 12-26-1908 | Willard & w & ch Glen & Guy rec in mbrp |
| 5-27-1911 | William & w glt M E Ch, Knightstown, Ind |

### PHILABAUM

| | |
|---|---|
| 12-25-1886 | Sarah rec in mbrp |
| 1-22-1887 | Alonzo rec in mbrp |
| 4-23-1887 | James & dt Lura rec in mbrp |
| 12-24-1887 | James & fam gct Duck Creek MM, Ind |

### PICKERING

| | |
|---|---|
| 4-25-1857 | Rebecca & Hester, CHARTER MBRS at Raysville MM, Ind |
| 11-28-1857 | Keturah rec in mbrp |
| 6-27-1863 | Keturah Miles (form Pickering) mou; chm |
| 9-21-1874 | Benjamin rec in mbrp |
| 3-27-1875 | Benjamin gct Carthage MM, Ind |
| 3-27-1875 | Rebecca gct Carthage MM, Ind |

### PICKET - PICKETT

| | |
|---|---|
| 4-25-1857 | Sarah, widow of William, CHARTER MBR at Raysville MM, Ind |
| 4-27-1867 | Jonathan Hodgin gct Fairfield MM to m Rebecca C Picket, a widow w/ch |
| 8-24-1867 | Rebecca Hodgin & her dt Theodate Picket rocf Fairfield MM, Ind |
| 4-23-1870 | Joseph rocf Duck Creek MM, Ind |
| 5-27-1871 | Jonathan Hodgin & 2nd w, Rebecca, & ch Robert L, Frances T, Mary V, Morris O & Anna G Hodgin & Theodate L Pickett, -dt Rebecca by previous m, gct Springfield MM, Douglas Co, Kans |
| 4-28-1877 | Joseph gct Duck Creek MM, Ind |
| 1-22-1881 | Joseph gct Duck Creek MM, Ind |
| 2-26-1898 | Claude rec in mbrp |

### PITTS

| | |
|---|---|
| 2-24-1900 | Estella (form Coffin) (w of Frank Pitts) gct Indianapolis MM, Ind |

### PORTER

| | |
|---|---|
| 3-25-1893 | Margaret B rel fr mbrp on rq |

### POWELL

| | |
|---|---|
| 4-25-1891 | Henry C & w Lucinda A rec in mbrp at Knightstown MM, Ind |
| 5-27-1893 | Henry & w gct Milford MM, Ind |

### POWERS

| | |
|---|---|
| 6-28-1890 | William & ch Rosa, Warren, Stella, Sarah, Lulie & May rocf Walnut Ridge MM, Ind |
| 5-27-1893 | Sadie rec in mbrp (Power) |
| 5-27-1893 | Louisa, now Louisa Powers, divorced w of Edward Coffin, & dt Olga Coffin rocf Carthage MM, Ind |
| 6-23-1900 | Lulu gct Dublin MM, Ind |
| 11-24-1900 | Stella drpd fr mbrp; jas |

### PRAY

| | |
|---|---|
| 1-27-1894 | William & dts Clara E & Bessie rocf Indianapolis MM, Ind |

### PRESNETT

| | |
|---|---|
| 9-21-1895 | Nora rel fr mbrp on rq |

### PRITCHARD

| | |
|---|---|
| 4-25-1857 | Samuel & w Harriett & ch David, Sarah Jane, Joseph & Charles, CHARTER MBRS at Raysville MM, Ind |
| 4-25-1857 | Benjamin C & w Rachel & ch Caleb W & Anna W, CHARTER MBRS at Raysville MM, Ind |
| 4-25-1857 | Benjamin C appt to comm on Education |
| 4-25-1857 | Samuel appt to a comm |
| 4-25-1857 | Benjamin C appt to comm to obtain MM Record Books |
| 7-25-1857 | Benjamin C appt Recorder of Removal Certs |
| 8-22-1857 | Benjamin C appt to att QM & rpt to next mtg |
| 5-22-1858 | Benjamin C appt Asst-Clerk of MM |
| 2-25-1860 | Thomas gct Driftwood MM, Ind |
| 5-28-1863 | Harriett appt an Elder |
| 8-23-1863 | Caleb W chm of mcd |
| 9-24-1865 | David T gct Miami MM, Ohio to m Sarah A Hale |
| 4-22-1865 | Sarah H rocf Miami MM, Ohio |
| 7-22-1865 | Samuel appt an Elder |
| 7-22-1865 | Benjamin C appt an Elder |
| 7-25-1868 | Samuel appt an Elder |
| 7-25-1868 | Harriett appt an Elder |
| 3-25-1871 | Joseph gct Walnut Ridge MM, Ind to m Anna J Binford |
| 10-28-1871 | Anna J rocf Walnut Ridge MM, Ind |
| 9-28-1875 | Calvin W of Indianapolis, Marion Co, Ind, -s William & Mary (dec), m at mtg held at res of Isaac O Trueblood, to E Miriam Trueblood |
| 3-25-1876 | Miriam T gct Indianapolis MM, Ind |
| 6-24-1876 | Isaac O gct Blue River MM, Ind |

## PRITCHARD (Cont)
- 2-26-1887  Emma O rec in mbrp (wife of Samuel)
- 1-23-1891  Maria & ch Eva, Jesse & Mattie B gct Westland MM, Ind
- 5-23-1891  Charles W gct Westland MM, Ind
- 9-26-1891  Charles W rel fr mbrp on rq
- 4-22-1915  Charles Francis & w Zenia W & ch Helen Lucile, Leland Stanford, Joseph Samuel & Francis White glt U B Ch, Sugar Grove

## RAMSEY
- 10-28-1893  Adeline Minnie & Mary Rose, -dts Richard H & Mary Ann (dec), rocf Walnut Ridge MM, Ind

## RAPER
- 11-26-1898  William rec in mbrp

## RATLIFF
- 7-28-1860  Elisha taught school for 3 mo this past winter
- 4-28-1883  Marcus & w Hannah Adelaide & ch William E rocf Spiceland MM, Ind
- 5-22-1886  Marcus & w Hannah gct Walnut Ridge MM, Ind
- 1-28-1893  Marcus gct Spiceland MM, Ind
- 2-26-1898  Marcus & w Hannah A & ch William E, Herschel E, Carl M, Jesse C & Ruby E rocf Carthage MM, Ind
- 9-26-1908  Marcus & fam gct Knoxville MM, Tenn
- 2-25-1915  Ralph rocf Anderson MM, Ind

## RAYL
- 12-24-1898  Harmon & w Odessa & dt Corana rocf Spiceland MM, Ind

## REDDICK
- 11-27-1897  Elias T & w Emma S rec in mbrp
- 4-28-1898  James T rec in mbrp
- 12-26-1908  Alma glt Christian Ch, Knightstown, Ind

## REECE
- 12-22-1883  Seth C & w Huldah H & ch Byron Johnson & Loring Walter rocf Walnut Ridge MM, Ind
- 4-26-1884  Seth C & w Huldah & ch Byron Johnson & Loring Walter gct Smithfield MM, Ohio
- 7-23-1892  Cynthia P rocf Cherry Grove MM, Ind
- 3-23-1912  Omer H rocf Vermillion MM, Ill

## REEVES
- 3-28-1874  John W & w Desdamonia rec in mbrp
- 6-27-1891  Nannie & dt Jessie rec in mbrp
- 4-28-1894  Ila rec in mbrp
- 3-24-1900  Munson rec in mbrp
- 1-27-1912  Ora Navada rec in mbrp
- 5-22-1919  Ruby rec in mbrp

## REISSENER
- 10-25-1917  Edward J rec in mbrp

## REYNOLDS
- 4-25-1857  Job & w Phebe & ch Eunice, Asenath, Susan B & Jane, CHARTER MBRS at Raysville MM, Ind
- 8-22-1857  Job appt to att QM & rpt to next mtg
- 11-26-1859  Eunice Wilson (form Reynolds) chm of mcd
- 9-28-1861  Phebe rec a min at Raysville MM, Ind
- 4-27-1864  Susan B, -dt Job (dec) & Phebe of Henry Co, Ind m at Raysville MM, Ind, to Newton A Trueblood of Marion Co, Ind
- 10-31-1872  Asenath C, -dt Job, (dec) & Phebe of Henry Co, Ind, m at a mtg held at res of Phebe Reynolds in Ogden, Henry Co, Ind, Jesse N Townsend of Hendricks Co, Ind

## RHOADES - RHODES
- 9-23-1893  Oscar W rec in mbrp
- 4-28-1894  James rec in mbrp
- 2-26-1898  Ralph rec in mbrp
- 12-25-1909  Frank B, a min, & w Clara rocf Olive Branch MM, Ind

## RICKS
- 4-27-1912  Joseph N, Mary Alice, Ernest B & Laura rec in mbrp

## RIGGS
- 3-23-1912  Georgia rec in mbrp

## RILEY
- 8-26-1915  Martin rec in mbrp

## RISK
- 3-26-1881  John rec in mbrp
- 1-24-1885  John drpd fr mbrp
- 2-24-1895  Percival & w Louie rec in mbrp
- 11-27-1913  Julia rec in mbrp
- 6-25-1914  Lillian Vada Crawford & s William rocf Hopewell MM, Ind
- 2-25-1915  Helen rec in mbrp

## ROBERTS
- 2-27-1886  Carrie E rec in mbrp at Knightstown Prep Mtg, Ind
- 3-27-1886  Ezekiel, Belle, Earl, Raymond & Dessie rec in mbrp
- 4-24-1886  Della & ch Homer S, Harry C & Frank W rec in mbrp
- 2-26-1887  William rec in mbrp
- 3-26-1887  Alzina, Clarence O & Effie J rec in mbrp
- 9-24-1892  William rel fr mbrp on rq
- 4-28-1894  Kittie rocf Duck Creek MM, Ind
- 4-28-1898  Ezekiel rel fr mbrp on rq
- 6-23-1900  Clara A & Irena E, ch of Alzina, rec in mbrp
- 7-24-1909  Kittie jas, Christian Ch; drpd fr mbrp

## ROBINSON
- 11-26-1898  James rec in mbrp

## ROCKAFELLOW
- 4-22-1882  C W & Minnie M rec in mbrp
- 8-25-1883  Charles W gct Dublin MM, Ind
- 8-25-1883  Minnie M gct Dublin MM, Ind

## ROGERS
- 9-21-1874  Jonathan T & w Mary & ch Logan N & Walter L rocf Beloit Grove MM, Ill
- 10-28-1876  Jonathan T & w Mary H, a min, & ch Logan & Walter gct Spiceland MM, Ind

## ROSENBOOM
Emma Grace, the adopted dt of John & Harriett Cunningham

## ROUNDS
- 5-26-1900  Mary (form Welborn) glt M E Ch, Knightstown, Ind

## RUSH
- 6-26-1886  Almeda, dt of Almeda Baker, rec in mbrp

## RUTLEDGE
- 3-25-1893  Nancy A rel fr mbrp on rq
- 12-26-1908  Pearl rec in mbrp

## SAINT
- 12-25-1886  John rec in mbrp
- 1-22-1887  Albert rocf....
- 2-26-1887  Lydia E & ch Arthur Lee & Mary Pauline rocf Spiceland MM, Ind
- 4-23-1887  Fred C, Grace J & George A, ch of Albert, rocf Duck Creek MM, Ind
- 7-25-1891  Albert W & fam gct New Castle MM, Ind
- 6-24-1893  Fred gct New Castle MM, Ind
- 3-23-1895  Florence Alberta gct Duck Creek MM, Ind
- 2-22-1896  Olive M & Daisy Florence rec in mbrp
- 5-28-1910  Margaret rec in mbrp

## SANDY
- 4-22-1882  Omar rec in mbrp

## SAYLER
- 10-17-1905  James Lanning of Eaton, Preble Co, Ohio, -s James Sr & Elizabeth of same place, m at Knightstown, Ind, Eleanor Rathbone White of Knightstown, Henry Co, Ind

### SCOTT
1-27-1894  Samuel & w Millia & ch James O, John E & Jesse E rocf Westland MM, Ind

### SEARS
12-23-1915  Lisha Fowler gct Muncie MM, Ind
12-27-1917  Oscar & Lisha rocf Muncie MM, Ind

### SEBASTIAN
5-27-1911  George R & w Inez rolf M E Ch, Charlottesville, Ind

### SELL
1-22-1910  Mary A Smith rel fr mbpr on rq; jas

### SEWARD
11-22-1879  Samuel rel fr mbrp on rq

### SHACKLE
4-22-1882  Ella rec in mbrp
6-24-1882  Ella rel fr mbrp on rq

### SHAW
3-25-1882  Josephine rec in mbrp
12-25-1886  Henry C, Emma L, Effa Bell & Gertie Ethel rec in mbrp
3-28-1896  Joseph & w Josephine rec in mbrp
5-23-1896  Horace C & Emma L rec in mbrp
10-27-1900  Josephine rel fr mbrp on rq
4-27-1912  Emma Luella rec in mbrp

### SHEPPARD
1-26-1884  Carrie M rec in mbrp
10-25-1888  Carrie M, -dt William & Eliza of Seymour, Ind, m at Raysville MM, Ind, Herbert H White of Raysville, Henry Co, Ind
4-25-1891  Thomas M & Martha S & dt Clara D rec in mbrp

### SHERIDAN
10-27-1866  Eli rocf Spiceland MM, Ind

### SHIELDS
10-26-1895  Frank & w Hannah & ch Beulah Carlotta & Willard Paul rocf Newberg MM, Oregon
12-24-1898  Frank & w Hannah & ch gct Muncie MM, Ind

### SHINN
4-22-1882  Newton rec in mbrp
1-24-1885  Newton drpd fr mbrp

### SHOEMAKER
9-25-1869  Tacy rocf Salem MM, Ind
4-2-1876  Tacy, a widow, CHARTER MBR at Knightstown Prep Mtg, Ind
2-28-1885  Tacy gct LaCross MM, Kans

### SIMONS - SIMMONS
8-27-1887  Lydia rocf Spiceland MM, Ind
1-28-1888  Henry Wilson & w Sarah Ann & ch Melvin, Lora, Emma Florence, Minnie, Alma & Nettie rec in mbrp
1-28-1888  Eva rec in mbrp
4-23-1892  Nancy A, Louella & John A rec in mbrp
6-24-1893  Henry N & fam gct Spiceland MM, Ind

### SIPLINGER
7-24-1875  Henry & w Desdemonia & ch Mary J, Patsy S E, William H, Meredith A & Luther T rocf Westland MM, Ind

### SLACK
4-24-1909  Jacob drpd fr mbrp

### SLAUGHTER
2-28-1891  Minnie B rec in mbrp

### SLISHMAN
3-24-1894  Rosanna rec in mbrp

### SMALL
4-24-1869  Sophrona rec in mbrp
4-27-1878  Sophrona gct Spiceland MM, Ind
3-22-1913  Edna rec in mbrp
10-22-1914  Mrs Sadie rec in mbrp
2-24-1916  Omer & w Sadie & ch Floyd & Florence rec in mbrp

### SMITH
2-24-1877  John W rec in mbrp
2-26-1887  Isabelle, Gracie & Hannah rec in mbrp at Grant Prep Mtg, Wilkinson neighborhood
12-24-1887  Jesse rec in mbrp
2-28-1891  Ephraim R & w Sarah & ch Dorcas, Rachel, Mary E, Isaac R & Arthur rocf Duck Creek MM, Ind
6-27-1891  Mary E & ch Jesse E, James M, Robert & Abigail W gct Spiceland MM, Ind
5-27-1893  F Joseph rec in mbrp
5-25-1895  Hannah L rel fr mbrp on rq to jas
8-25-1895  Joseph dis for disunity
2-27-1897  Joseph rec in mbrp
2-25-1899  Ephraim R & w Sarah Jane & s Isaac R gct Anderson MM, Ind
2-25-1899  Sarah Ellen gct Anderson MM, Ind
9-23-1899  Jesse M rel fr mbrp on rq
11-24-1900  Alma gct Carthage MM, Ind
7-23-1910  Pearl gct Indianapolis MM, Ind
4-22-1911  Oscar Z & w Rosa A rec in mbrp

### SNODGRASS
3-23-1878  Rosa Ella, Lulebella, Joseph, Viola, Nathan, Ida & Hattie Macy rocf Toledo MM, Kans
5-25-1878  Rosa Ella gct Duck Creek MM, Ind

### SNUTEY
5-23-1896  Ollie Kate gct Spiceland MM, Ind

### SNYDER
Isaac L, b 3-23-1865, m Martha M ...., b 2-18-1866
2-22-1896  Viola M, Samuel Fay & Robert Guy rec in mbrp
2-22-1896  Isaac L & Martha M rec in mbrp

### SOHN
4-24-1919  Frederick & w Grace & s Alva rocf Carthage MM, Ind

### SPELLMAN
2-24-1912  Elise May rec in mbrp
10-2-1919  Elsie rocf Raysville MM, Ind

### SPENCER
6-27-1896  Charles B & w Delphina & ch Josie, Olive M, Francis E & Harold C rocf Dublin MM, Ind
9-30-1911  Mary Emma & ch John C Bell rocf Hopewell MM, Ind
8-23-1917  C B & w Mary F & s Carlton Bell gct New Castle MM, Ind

### SPRONG
2-28-1891  Clara rec in mbrp

### STANLEY
4-25-1891  Jesse & w Feriba W rocf Duck Creek MM, Ind
11-28-1891  Jesse & w Feriba gct Westfield MM, Ind

### STEELE
1-22-1887  George W, Emma Alice, Maggie Mary & Charles Marion rec in mbrp
3-24-1894  Frank K rec in mbrp
7-25-1896  Carrie Isabelle rec in mbrp

### STEINER
3-26-1881  Elmer & Nina rec in mbrp
1-24-1885  Elmer drpd fr mbrp
6-23-1900  Margaret, -dt Rosa, rec in mbrp

### STIGGLEMAN
6-24-1893  Leora gct Spiceland MM, Ind

## STITES
- 2-22-1896   Mary & Mary E rec in mbrp
- 3-28-1896   Sarah E, Lula, Anna B & George W, ch of Mary, rec in mbrp
- 9-22-1900   Mary & dts drpd fr mbrp

## STOCKTON
- 4-28-1898   Carrie rel fr mbrp on rq
- 6-25-1914   Harold glt M E Ch

## STONE
- 4-24-1886   Alfred rec in mbrp
- 11-26-1898   Mary Ellen & Emory rec in mbrp

## STOWHIG
- 2-26-1898   Harry rec in mbrp

## STRATTON
- 4-25-1857   Eunice, widow of Eli, CHARTER MBR of Raysville MM, Ind
- 3-27-1875   Ruth rec in mbrp
- 4-2-1876   Ruth, widow of Levi, CHARTER MBR of Knightstown Prep Mtg, Ind

## STREET
- 10-24-1863   Samuel & w Anna & dt Rebecca rocf Pleasant Plain MM, Iowa; -end to Spiceland MM, Ind

## STUART - STEWART
- 10-23-1858   Zimri rocf Back Creek MM, N C
- 6-28-1862   Amos & w Matilda & ch Mary E, Jonathan H, Eliza L, Delphina M, John S, David W, Robert A, Amos E & Francis B rocf Deep River MM, N C
- 2-23-1867   Jehu H rocf Deep River MM, N C
- 8-24-1867   Henry rocf Back Creek MM
- 7-25-1868   Amos appt an Elder
- 3-27-1869   John H gct Spiceland MM, Ind
- 10-23-1869   Mary & Eliza gct Spiceland MM, Ind
- 11-27-1869   Amos & w Matilda & ch Sidney, David, Addison, Eldridge & Francis gct Spiceland MM, Ind
- 1-22-1870   Jonathan gct Whitewater MM, Ind
- 5-23-1874   Ithamer W & w Margaret rec in mbrp
- 1-23-1875   Laura rec in mbrp
- 4-2-1876   Ithamer W & w Margaret & ch Laura, CHARTER MBRS of Knightstown Prep Mtg, Ind
- 4-22-1882   Holloway I rec in mbrp
- 2-23-1884   Lillie M & dt Rhoda Maud rec in mbrp
- 12-29-1888   Holloway I gct Pasadena MM, Calif
- 11-26-1892   Zimri gct Fairmount MM, Ind
- 11-28-1896   Zimri rocf Fairmount MM, Ind

## STURGES
- 11-26-1887   Amanda L rec in mbrp

## SUTTON
- 8-25-1900   George White gct Whitewater MM, Ind to m Mary B Sutton

## SWAIN
- 8-24-1872   Sarah M rocf Deep Creek MM, N C
- 5-24-1873   William J & w Ruth E & ch Thomas M & Sidney rocf Deep Creek MM, N C
- 6-28-1873   Nathan C rocf Deep Creek MM, N C
- 10-23-1880   Nathan H gct Walnut Ridge MM, Ind
- 2-27-1886   Harvey & Louisa rec in mbrp at Knightstown Mtg, Ind
- 2-27-1886   Elihu, Elizabeth E, Claud & Maud rec in mbrp at Knightstown Mtg, Ind
- 11-26-1887   Elihu dis for excessive drinking
- 1-28-1893   Nathan C & ch Laura M & Sanford O gct Newberg MM, Oregon
- 7-22-1893   Thomas M & w Julia E & s George H rocf Spiceland MM, Ind
- 11-25-1893   Ella H rec in mbrp
- 2-22-1896   Emma J rec in mbrp
- 4-25-1896   Jennie Smith rocf Chester MM, Ind
- 5-23-1896   Nathan C & w Nettie R & ch Laura M & Sanford O rocf Newberg MM, Oregon
- 11-28-1896   Thomas M & w Julia E & ch George Howland rocf Spiceland MM, Ind
- 8-28-1897   Alma Young glt Christian Ch, Noblesville, Ind
- 1-22-1898   W Jordan & w Emma gct Westland MM, Ind

## SWORD
- 6-24-1871   Samuel & w Fannie & ch William, George & Seigle rec in mbrp

## SYMONS
- 4-25-1857   Benjamin F, a minor, CHARTER MBR at Raysville MM, Ind
- 10-25-1862   Benjamin F gct West Branch MM, Ohio to m Verlinda Jenkins
- 1-24-1863   Benjamin Franklin gct Hopewell MM, Ind
- 12-26-1863   Benjamin F & w Verlinda rocf Hopewell MM, Ind
- 1-27-1866   Benjamin F appt Asst-Clerk of MM in place of Albert Newby who has removed
- 3-28-1868   Benjamin F & w Verlinda & ch Joseph E & Anna L gct Spiceland MM, Ind
- 12-22-1888   Lydia H gct Spiceland MM, Ind
- 6-24-1889   Gertrude E gct Short Creek MM, Ohio

## TALBERT
- 12-23-1877   Sylvanus rec in mbrp
- 10-23-1880   Sylvanus gct Carthage MM, Ind
- 3-26-1881   Lizzie rec in mbrp
- 4-28-1894   Daniel & fam rocf Spiceland MM, Ind

## TATNOR
- 3-25-1876   Grace D rec in mbrp at Raysville MM, Ind (Grace D was raised by John & Catherine Morrison)
- 4-2-1876   Grace D, CHARTER MBR at Knightstown Prep Mtg, Ind (Raised by John & Catherine Morrison)

## TAYLOR
- 2-25-1899   Rachel Jane gct Anderson MM, Ind

## TEAS
- 4-25-1857   Sarah C, widow of Thomas, & her ch John C, Edward, Martha, Eunice & Thomas Jr, CHARTER MBRS at Raysville MM, Ind
- 5-23-1857   John C appt Asst-Clerk of MM
- 7-28-1860   Martha D taught a school for 3 mo this summer with 25 average attendance. The teacher reads from the Holy Scriptures at close of each day
- 5-25-1861   John C appt Asst-Clerk of MM
- 11-27-1861   John C of Henry Co, Ind, -s Thomas (dec) & Sarah C, m at Raysville MM, Ind to Isabella Parker of Henry Co, Ind
- 11-27-1861   Eunice S, -dt Thomas (dec) & Sarah C of Henry Co, Ind, m at Raysville MM, Ind to Eleazer B Hiatt of Winneshiek MM, Iowa
- 5-24-1862   John C appt asst-Clerk of the MM
- 3-4-1863   Martha D, -dt Thomas (dec) & Sarah C of Raysville, Henry Co, Ind, m at Raysville MM, Ind, Elisha Parker of Randolph Co, Ind
- 10-28-1863   Edmund Y rec in mbrp
- 8-28-1865   Edmund Y gct Whitewater MM, Ind
- 8-25-1866   Thomas S gct Whitewater MM, Ind
- 8-24-1867   Sarah Ann (form Coffin) clm of mou
- 10-26-1867   Sallie A & her minor s, Vestal H Coffin, gct Whitewater MM, Ind
- 8-28-1869   Sarah C gct Whitewater MM, Ind
- 11-27-1869   John C & w Sarah Isabella & ch Walter & Anna gct Spring River MM or Union MM, Mo

## TEMPLETON
- 2-22-1896   Willie, Grace & Estella Louisa rec in mbrp
- 3-27-1897   Eunice S rocf Duck Creek MM, Ind

## TERRELL
- 6-26-1869   Pleasant M rocf Fairfield MM, Ohio
- 1-28-1871   Pleasant M gct Clear Creek MM, Ohio to m Alice E Malone
- 6-24-1871   Pleasant M gct Clear Creek MM, Ohio

## TERRY
- 4-22-1882   Cora rec in mbrp
- 1-24-1885   Cora drpd fr mbrp

RAYSVILLE-KNIGHTSTOWN

## TERRY (Cont)
3-24-1900  Frank rec in mbrp

## TEST
4-22-1893  Samuel & w Cora & s Everette rocf...
1-27-1894  Samuel C & fam gct Spiceland MM, Ind

## THOMAS
2-26-1887  Virlie & Nora rec in mbrp at Grant Prep Mtg, Ind
1-28-1888  Dora Francis rec in mbrp
8-27-1892  William D & w Casinda & ch Lucy L rec in mbrp
2-22-1896  Aubra & Ermis rec in mbrp
1-27-1900  Perry & w Annis & ch Anna glt M E Ch, Knightstown, Ind
3-24-1900  Flora & ch rocf Duck Creek MM, Ind

## THORNBURG
8-24-1871  Anna M rocf Carthage MM, Ind
1-25-1873  Charles S & w Anna & s Arthur gct Walnut Ridge MM, Ind
8-28-1897  John W rocf Hopewell MM, Ind
11-26-1910  Charles E, a min, & w Minnie & ch Brice C gct Union Grove MM, Bethel, Ind

## TICE
12-28-1912  Pearl & Ethel rec in mbrp

## TINNEY
8-26-1865  Almira (form White) mou; chm
2-24-1912  Tinny, Edwin gct Barbers Mill MM, Ind

## TOWNSEND
10-31-1872  Jesse N of Hendricks Co, Ind, =s William & Ann (both dec), of same place, m at a mtg held at residence of Phebe Reynolds in Ogden, Ind, to Asenath C Reynolds of Henry Co, Ind
1-25-1873  Asenath C gct Plainfield MM, Ind
7-23-1892  Asenath C rocf Plainfield MM, Ind
12-28-1898  Asenath C m 2nd to Allen Kirk
7-25-1908  Eva A rq letter to Christian Science Ch, of Indianapolis, Ind; drpd fr mbrp

## TROWBRIDGE
5-27-1893  Albert F & Geneva F rec in mbrp
4-28-1894  Chester rec in mbrp
2-26-1898  Esti rec in mbrp
2-27-1909  Albert F & Genoa glt M E Ch, Ogden, Ind
12- 2-1915  Genoa rolf M E Ch, Ogden, Ind

## TRUEBLOOD
4-25-1857  Isaac O & w Sarah & ch Elizabeth M, Jason, Miles W & Mary, CHARTER MBRS at Raysville MM, Ind
4-25-1857  Isaac O appt to comm on Education
4-27-1864  Newton A of Marion Co, Ind, =s James & Martha (dec), of same place, m at Raysville MM, Ind, Susan B Reynolds of Henry Co, Ind
1-22-1864  Susan B gct Bridgeport MM, Ind
8-26-1865  Jason chm of mcd
1-23-1869  Isaac O appt an Overseer
4-23-1870  Miles W chm of mcd
9-28-1875  E Miriam, -dt Isaac O & Sarah (dec) of Raysville MM, Ind, m at a mtg held at residence of Isaac Trueblood, Calvin W Pritchard of Indianapolis, Ind
11-27-1875  Eliza H rec in mbrp
3-25-1876  Eliza H & dt Evangeline gct Mill Creek MM, Ind
6-24-1876  Isaac O gct Blue River MM, Ind
10-28-1893  Newton A & Susan B rocf Kokomo MM, Ind
12-30-1913  Rebecca rocf Kokomo MM, Ind
6-22-1916  Rebecca gct Kokomo MM, Ind

## TWEEDY
2-22-1896  Thomas A & w Sarah E & ch Minnie rec in mbrp
4-24-1909  E W & w & ch C Minnie drpd fr mbrp

## TYRE
3-27-1886  Mathew & w Carrie & ch Ada, Frank, Katie, Cora & Arthur rec in mbrp

11-24-1900  Ada, Kate, Cora & Arthur drpd fr mbrp; jas

## URST
4-24-1909  Wiley M drpd fr mbrp

## VANDERBARK - VANDENBARK
1-22-1887  Peter V & Mary Belle rec in mbrp
1-22-1887  John W Jr, rec in mbrp
1-28-1888  John Wesley & w Nancy rec in mbrp
5-27-1893  Peter & John W Jr drpd fr mbrp
3-24-1894  Bessie & Hazel rec in mbrp
2-22-1896  John W Jr rec in mbrp
10-23-1897  Clara & dt Pauline rocf Marion MM, Ind

## VANDUYNE
1-27-1912  Ruby McKinney & ch Rose L & Phillip A rec in mbrp

## VANMETER
12-24-1914  Ida May Hamilton & dt Florence Charlotte Hamilton gct New Castle MM, Ind

## WAGONER
3-23-1895  Thomas Berry & w Annis & ch Anna rec in mbrp
3-28-1896  George rec in mbrp

## WALKER
1-27-1912  Sarah Elsie rec in mbrp

## WALTON
9-23-1899  Rufus P & w Theresa rocf Duck Creek MM, Ind

## WALLS
3-24-1894  William F & w Josie E & ch Harvey B & Mary Margaret rocf Duck Creek MM, Ind
3-23-1916  Harvey B glt M E Ch, Knightstown, Ind
3-21-1921  Ruth Miller, w of Otto, rec in mbrp

## WATSON
2-25-1888  Ida rec in mbrp

## WATTS
6-26-1869  Mary mou; chm
3-26-1887  Mary rel fr mbrp on rq
9-24-1892  George & Grace rel fr mbrp on rq

## WEAVER
2-26-1898  Charles L rec in mbrp
4-24-1909  Charles drpd fr mbrp

## WEBER
4-24-1909  Emma & 3 minor ch rec in mbrp
2-25-1915  Harry J rec in mbrp
2-24-1916  Jacob rec in mbrp
10- 2-1919  Webber, Anna & ch Roy, Darwin & Edith rocf Raysville MM, Henry Co, Ind

## WEEDEN
10-24-1863  Jane Eliza rocf Lynn Grove MM, Iowa
4-23-1864  Jane E gct Spiceland MM, Ind

## WEEKS
7-22-1871  Elizabeth rec in mbrp
12-23-1871  Allen & ch Maria E, Marian A, Ellen, Emily J & Benjamin Franklin rec in mbrp
11-27-1880  Allen & w Elizabeth & ch Benjamin F, Arthur N & Oscar gct Duck Creek MM, Ind

## WELBORN
2-27-1886  Joshua P C, Margaret, James E, Mary P & Royal rec in mbrp at Knightstown Prep Mtg, Ind

## WELCH
1-28-1888  John Alexander rec in mbrp
4-26-1890  John H drpd fr mbrp

## WEST
3-24-1900  Wiley rec in mbrp

## WHEELER

| | |
|---|---|
| 9-21-1872 | Mary T & ch Ida R & Wiley L gct Fairmount MM, Ind |

## WHITE

| | |
|---|---|
| 4-25-1857 | Samuel appt to comm to att funerals of mbrs |
| 4-25-1857 | Samuel & w Rebecca & dt Martha, CHARTER MBRS at Raysville MM, Ind |
| 4-25-1857 | Caleb, a widower, CHARTER MBR at Raysville MM, Ind |
| 4-25-1857 | Edmund, CHARTER MBR at Raysville MM, Ind |
| 4-25-1857 | John T & 2nd w Hannah A & ch Joel, Benajah & Allen S, CHARTER MBRS at Raysville MM, Ind |
| 4-25-1857 | Charles & w Lucy H & ch Emma H, CHARTER MBRS at Raysville MM, Ind |
| 4-25-1857 | Lucinda, CHARTER MBR at Raysville MM, Ind |
| 4-25-1857 | John T appt to comm to obtain MM Record Books |
| 6-27-1857 | John T proposed for Recorder of Births & Deaths Records |
| 12-26-1857 | Samuel appt an Elder |
| 10-23-1858 | James gct Walnut Ridge MM, Ind, to m Jemima D Henley |
| 1-22-1859 | John T Jr rocf Blue River MM, Ind |
| 4-23-1859 | Edmund gct Duck Creek MM, Ind |
| 5-28-1859 | Joseph gct Rocksylvania MM, Iowa |
| 7-23-1859 | Samuel appt to comm on Education |
| 7-23-1859 | Hannah Ann appt to comm on Education |
| 7-23-1859 | Toms & w Milicent & dt Jane E rocf Blue River MM, Ind |
| 7-28-1860 | Toms appt to comm to examine Records of Births & Deaths & render any assistance necessary to complete records |
| 8-28-1861 | Harriet, -dt Caleb & Mary, (both dec), Henry Co, Ind, m at Raysville MM, Ind, William A Fulghum of Richmond, Wayne Co, Ind |
| 2-26-1862 | Lucinda of Raysville, Henry Co, Ind, -dt of Robert White, form of Perquimans Co, N C, & his w Rebecca (both dec), m at Raysville MM, Ind, John Coggeshall of New Garden MM, Wayne Co, Ind |
| 4-23-1864 | Rebecca rocf Walnut Ridge MM, Ind |
| 11-30-1864 | Edmund of Henry Co, Ind, -s Caleb & Mary, (both dec), m at Raysville MM, Ind, Emily J Woodard of Henry Co, Ind |
| 7-22-1865 | Samuel appt an Elder |
| 8-26-1865 | Almire Tinney (form White) chm of mou |
| 3-24-1866 | Jane Woods (form White) chm of mou |
| 3-24-1866 | Phebe Moore (form White) chm of mou |
| 7-25-1868 | Samuel appt an Elder |
| 7-25-1868 | Rebecca appt an Elder |
| 7-25-1868 | Lucy H appt an Elder |
| 9-25-1869 | Joel chm of mcd |
| 6-2-1870 | Margaret M, -dt Caleb & Mary (both dec), of Raysville, Ind, m at a mtg held at res of Charles White in Raysville, Ind, Elihu A White of Belvidere, Perquimans Co, N C |
| 6-2-1870 | Elihu A of Belvidere, Perquimans Co, N C, -s David & Elizabeth (both dec), m at a mtg held at res of Charles White in Raysville, Ind, Margaret M White, -dt Caleb & Mary, (both dec) of Raysville, Henry Co, Ind |
| 3-23-1872 | Margaret M & dt Emma gct Piney Woods MM, N C |
| 11-27-1875 | Edmund appt Recorder of Removal Certs |
| 10-27-1877 | John T gct Cincinnati MM, Ohio |
| 4-7-1880 | Anna R rocf New York MM, N Y |
| 10-23-1880 | John T gct Chicago MM, Ill |
| 10-23-1885 | Elihu Anthony of Piney Woods, Perquimans Co, N C, m at a mtg held at res of Charles White near Raysville, Henry Co, Ind, Emma Haughton White, -dt Charles & Lucy of Raysville, Henry Co, Ind |
| 10-23-1885 | Emma Haughton, -dt Charles & Lucy White of Raysville MM, Henry Co, Ind, m at mtg held at res of Charles White near Raysville, Henry Co, Ind, Elihu Anthony White of Piney Woods, Perquimans Co, N C |
| 3-27-1886 | Emma H gct Piney Woods MM, N C |
| 9-16-1886 | George Wilson of Hendricks Co, Ind, -s Rufus & Lydia of Perquimans Co, N C, m at Raysville, Ind, Mary Elizabeth White, -dt James & Jemima D White of Henry Co, Ind |
| 9-16-1886 | Mary Elizabeth, -dt James & Jemima D White of Henry Co, Ind, m at Raysville, Ind, George Wilson White of Hendricks Co, Ind, -s Rufus & Lydia of Perquimans Co, N C |
| 1-22-1887 | George B rocf ... |
| 8-27-1887 | Mary E W gct Plainfield MM, Ind |
| 10-25-1888 | Herbert H of Raysville, Henry Co, Ind, -s Charles & Lucy of Orlissa, Oder Co, Texas, m at Raysville MM, Ind to Carrie M Sheppard of Seymour, Ind |
| 11-24-1888 | George B & w Sarah gct Walnut Ridge MM, Ind |
| 8-25-1900 | George gct Whitewater MM, Ind to m Mary B Sutton |
| 10-17-1905 | Eleanor Rathbone, -dt Allen S & Anna R White of Knightstown, Henry Co, Ind, m at Knightstown, Ind, James Lanning Saylor of Eaton, Preble Co, Ohio |
| 9-26-1908 | Elias H & Clara B Patterson, non-res mbrs, inf mtg of m int; mtg has no objections & they are altm |
| 11-17-1908 | Elias Henley of Philadelphia, Pa, -s James (dec) & Jemima D of Knightstown, Henry Co, Ind, m at The Landsdown, Parkside Ave & 41st St, Philadelphia, Pa, Clara B Patterson of Philadelphia, Pa, -dt James A & Elizabeth R Johnson of Milton, Sussex Co, Dela |
| 11-26-1910 | Mabel Newsom rocf Sand Creek MM, Ind |
| 3-23-1912 | Dwight F & Prudence A rec in mbrp |

## WHITTEN

| | |
|---|---|
| 4-22-1893 | Ora rec in mbrp |
| 4-22-1893 | Maggie rec in mbrp |
| 3-23-1895 | Roy, -s Ora, rec in mbrp |

## WHITWORTH

| | |
|---|---|
| 7-24-1875 | Alexander & w Jemima rec in mbrp |

## WIGGS

| | |
|---|---|
| 9-22-1900 | Angie rel fr mbrp on rq |

## WILCOX

| | |
|---|---|
| 4-27-1912 | Mahlon M, Ida, Lalia, Maud, Guy, Opal, Ray & Samuel rec in mbrp |

## WILCOXEN

| | |
|---|---|
| 8-26-1911 | Thomas O rec in mbrp |

## WILCOXIN

| | |
|---|---|
| 9-30-1911 | Edith rec in mbrp |

## WILKINSON

| | |
|---|---|
| 1-24-1874 | Hezekiah E & w Mary rec in mbrp |
| 1-24-1874 | James E & w Jane rec in mbrp |
| 10-28-1876 | Ida B, Albert L, Hattie A, ch of James E & Sisley, rec in mbrp |
| 10-28-1876 | Emma A, Charity F & Alida F, ch of Hezekiah & Mary P rec in mbrp |
| 10-28-1901 | Margie Clayanna & Helen Elizabeth, ch of Estelle Hubbard Wilkinson, rec in mbrp |

## WILLEY

| | |
|---|---|
| 4-22-1882 | Belle rec in mbrp |
| 1-24-1885 | Belle M drpd fr mbrp |

## WILLIAMS

| | |
|---|---|
| 11-23-1878 | William C & w Anna W rocf Spiceland MM, Ind |
| 1-22-1881 | Emma rocf Spiceland MM, Ind |
| 1-22-1887 | Samuel T S & w Lou A & ch Ethel & Willie rec in mbrp |
| 2-26-1887 | Abigail rocf Spiceland MM, Ind |
| 2-26-1887 | George, Mary Ellen & ch Alfred L, Milton E & Ida May rec in mbrp at Grant Prep Mtg, Wilkinson neighborhood |
| 12-24-1887 | Anna W gct Selma MM |
| 5-27-1893 | Gertrude rec in mbrp |
| 5-25-1895 | George, Mary E, Alfred L, Milton & Ida May rel frm mbrp on rq to jas |
| 11-25-1911 | S T & w gct Whittier MM, Calif |

RAYSVILLE-KNIGHTSTOWN

**WILLIAMS (Cont)**
    Samuel T S & Lou A & ch, CHARTER MBRS of Knightstown MM, Ind

**WILLIAMSON**
| | |
|---|---|
| 2-26-1887 | Isaac & w Basheba & ch Robert & Charlie rec in mbrp at Grant Prep Mtg, Wilkinson neighborhood |
| 2-26-1887 | Amos rec in mbrp at Grant Prep Mtg in Wilkinson neighborhood |
| 6-25-1887 | Elva Ethel rec in mbrp |
| 7-23-1887 | Charles O rec in mbrp |
| 1-25-1890 | Charles rec in mbrp |
| 10-24-1891 | Amos rel fr mbrp on rq |
| 8-27-1892 | Nettie rec in mbrp |
| 11-23-1895 | Amos rec in mbrp |
| 2-22-1896 | Nettie F & ch Inez E rec in mbrp |
| 3-28-1896 | Anna M rec in mbrp |
| 3-27-1897 | Jessie & Carl rec in mbrp |
| -28-1898 | Charles rec in mbrp |
| 3-23-1912 | Dennis & Mary rec in mbrp |

**WILLS**
| | |
|---|---|
| 1-25-1890 | Jacob L, Rosena, Arthur, Lona & Mary M rec in mbrp |
| 8-22-1891 | Jacob & w Rosena dis for disunity |
| 5-25-1895 | Jacob & w Rosena & ch Arthur, Lona & Mary gct Duck Creek MM, Ind |

**WILMOTT**
| | |
|---|---|
| 10-24-1868 | Henry rocf Salem MM, Ohio |
| 7-26-1873 | Henry gct Birmingham MM, England |

**WILSON**
| | |
|---|---|
| 4-25-1857 | Joseph G & w Hope & ch Pharaba, Rachel & Elias, CHARTER MBRS. at Raysville MM, Ind |
| 4-25-1857 | Joseph appt to comm on Education |
| 8- 2-1857 | Joseph G appt to att QM & rpt to next Mtg |
| 11-26-1859 | Eunice (form Reynolds) mcd; chm |
| 1-24-1863 | Joseph G & w Hope & ch Pharaba, Rachel & Elias gct Westfield MM, Ind |
| 3-28-1863 | Mary Eliza (form Furby) mcd; chm |
| 8-23-1863 | William Griffin gct Milford MM, Ind to m Margaret M Wilson |
| 9-26-1863 | Mary Eliza gct New Castle on the Tyne MM, England |
| 9-24-1864 | Nathan O Morris gct Milford MM, Ind to m Phariba A Wilson |
| 6-24-1865 | Eunice gct New Salem MM, Ind |
| 1-23-1869 | Nathan gct Westfield MM, Ind |
| 2-27-1869 | Henry & w Rebecca & ch Sylvester & Arlington rec in mbrp |
| 3-26-1870 | Abner & w Elizabeth & ch Charles, Thomas, Francis Siegle & Sarah A rec in mbrp at Grant Prep Mtg, Ind |
| 2-25-1871 | Eunice W & ch Clarence, Nora Jane & Edgar rocf New Salem MM, Ind |
| 7-22-1871 | Joseph N & w Mary & ch Laura M, Martha J, Jesse H & Delphina O rec in mbrp |
| 1-23-1875 | Charles rec in mbrp |
| 11-27-1875 | Eunice & ch Clarence, Nora J & Edgar V gct Spiceland MM, Ind |
| 1-22-1876 | Abigail S rec in mbrp |
| 12-23-1876 | Rachel V rocf ... |
| 5-26-1877 | Abner & w Elizabeth & ch Charles, Thomas, Sarah Ann & Francis Siegle gct Westfield MM, Ind |
| 11-22-1880 | Henry & w Rebecca gct Duck Creek MM, Ind |
| 5-28-1881 | Sylvester A & w Sarah A & ch Ozzie & Suey gct Spiceland MM, Ind |
| 2-28-1885 | Charles drpd fr mbrp |
| 2-28-1885 | Elizabeth B gct Whitewater MM, Ind |
| 2-26-1887 | Phebe Jane gct Hopewell MM, Ind |
| 9-23-1893 | Burt rec in mbrp |
| 4-28-1894 | Elwood rec in mbrp |
| 10-27-1894 | Francis Siegle & w Sarah & ch Russel Orville & Effie rocf Duck Creek MM, Ind |
| 12-22-1894 | Eva E rocf Whitewater MM, Ind |
| 11-26-1898 | Olive rec in mbrp |
| 8-26-1899 | William E rocf Duck Creek MM, Ind |
| 2-24-1900 | Wilda rolf Christian Ch, Darlington, Ind |
| 10-27-1900 | Thomas Oscar rocf Westfield MM, Ind |
| 9-24-1914 | Mark A & Ruby M Zion dec m int |
| 3-25-1915 | Mark A rec in mbrp - living in Redkey, Ind |

**WILTSE**
| | |
|---|---|
| 2-28-1874 | Elizabeth gct Walnut Ridge MM, Ind |

**WINDSOR**
| | |
|---|---|
| 1-23-1879 | Lewis W & w Rebecca & ch John B, James F, William H & Emma J rec in mbrp |
| 11-27-1880 | Lewis W & w Rebecca & ch John B, James F, William H & Emma gct Rich Square MM, Ind |

**WISHARD**
| | |
|---|---|
| 9-21-1878 | Lucinda B rocf Whitewater MM, Ind |
| 9-22-1883 | Lucinda B gct Indianapolis MM, Ind |

**WOODARD**
| | |
|---|---|
| 10-25-1862 | Emily Jane, Alpheus Lindley, Vestal, Adaline, Alice & Horace G, ch of Thomas C & Mary Ann (Reynolds) Woodard, rocf New Garden MM, Ind |
| 12-26-1863 | Thomas C rocf New Garden MM, Ind |
| 11-30-1864 | Emily J, -dt Thomas C & Mary A (dec), of Henry Co, Ind, m at Raysville MM, Ind, Edmund White of Henry Co, Ind |
| 10-28-1865 | Thomas C mcd; chm |
| 11-28-1868 | Alpheus mcd; chm |
| 7-26-1873 | Thomas C rel fr mbrp on rq |
| 7-23-1898 | Thomas R & w Carrie R & Mabel Lucile rocf Sand Creek MM, Ind |

**WOODRUFF**
| | |
|---|---|
| 3-26-1887 | Mary Jane rec in mbrp |

**WOOD**
| | |
|---|---|
| 10-24-1908 | S Adelbert, a min, & w Ella D & ch Angelina, Adelbert Jay, Edgar J & Delamore gct Farnsworth MM, N H |
| 3-27-1909 | Ruel rocf Providence MM |
| 7-24-1919 | S Adelbert, a min, & w Ida M, rocf Piney Woods MM, N C |

**WOODS**
| | |
|---|---|
| 3-24-1866 | Jane (form White) mou; chm |
| 9-26-1869 | Delphina mou; chm |
| 1-23-1875 | Henry C rec in mbrp |
| 8-24-1878 | Delphina rel fr mbrp on rq |
| 3-26-1881 | John rec in mbrp |
| 2-27-1886 | Anna Bertha, Nellie Hannah & Laura Hadley, ch of Robert E & Delphina, rel fr mbrp on rq |
| 2-27-1886 | George W rec in mbrp |
| 3-27-1887 | Jane rec in mbrp |
| 3-26-1887 | Milton rec in mbrp |
| 2-25-1888 | Louvina rec in mbrp |
| 8-27-1892 | Eddie W & Laura E rec in mbrp |
| 3-24-1900 | Eddie & w gct Walnut Ridge MM, Ind |
| 3-24-1900 | Milton drpd fr mbrp |

**WOOLEN**
| | |
|---|---|
| 2-26-1887 | Eunice rec in mbrp at Grant Prep Mtg, Wilkinson neighborhood, Ind |
| 7-28-1888 | William rocf Duck Creek MM, Ind |
| 1-23-1892 | W A rel fr mbrp on rq |
| 5-25-1895 | Eunice rel fr mbpr on rq to jas |

**WRIGHT**
| | |
|---|---|
| 4-23-1870 | Newton & w Emily Jane rec in mbrp at Grant Prep Mtg, Ind |
| 1-27-1877 | David B rec in mbrp |
| 10-23-1880 | David & w Sarah Miriam gct Walnut Ridge MM, Ind |
| 2-27-1886 | Milton A & Verda rec in mbrp at Knightstown Prep Mtg, Ind |
| 5-22-1886 | Milton A & w Emma C & ch Verda R gct Rich Square MM, Ind |
| 2-25-1888 | John & w Jemima & ch Marion Sylvester, Mary Jane & Effie Etta rec in mbrp |
| 11-22-1890 | John & w Jemima gct Spiceland MM, Ind |

**WRIGHT (Cont)**
12-26-1896 David E & w Sarah M & ch Floyd A & Etta B rocf Fairmount MM, Ind
9-22-1900 David & w Sarah & ch Floyd A & Etta gct Fairmount MM, Ind

**WYSONG**
7-27-1889 Opal rec in mbrp
6-22-1895 Opal gct Dublin MM, Ind

**YATES**
1-26-1889 Louella rec in mbrp
4-22-1893 Laura rec in mbrp

**YOUNG**
4-28-1894 Alma rocf Spiceland MM, Ind

**ZEHRING**
4-22-1893 Edwin B & Mary E rec in mbrp
5-24-1894 Leora L & Franklin H rec in mbrp
6-22-1895 Edward B & w Mary E & ch Leora L & Franklin H gct West Grove MM, Ind

**ZION**
2-25-1865 John & w Maria & ch Hester E, Mary E & William R rec in mbrp
4-26-1884 William R gct Carthage MM, Ind
12-24-1887 John gct Carthage MM, Ind
8-23-1890 William & w Laura rocf Carthage MM, Ind
4-22-1893 William & w Laura B & ch Ruby gct Carthage MM, Ind
12-26-1896 William R & w Laura B & dt Ruby rocf Carthage MM, Ind
9-24-1914 Ruby M & Mark A Wilson (a non-mbr) dec m int

# CARTHAGE MONTHLY MEETING
## Rush County, Indiana

Carthage Monthly Meeting was set-off from Walnut Ridge Monthly Meeting and first held on the 4th of Eighth Month 1866. The meetinghouse is located in the village of Carthage. There is a meeting still (1972) held there.

The monthly meeting was comprised of two preparatives, Carthage and Little Blue River.

At the time Carthage Meeting was established in 1839 some Friends thought it should be located near the schoolhouse. The school at that time was southeast of the present town. It is said that the committee appointed to decide on the location was intending to report in favor of that site. But before the meeting convened, John Clark took the chairman aside and told him he would donate the site in town if they would establish the meetinghouse there.

The committee announced that it was not ready to report. By the time of the next monthly meeting the site in town was approved with little opposition. The location of the meetinghouse did not cause any depreciation of the value of Clark's other lots.

### Monthly Meeting Records

The volumes noted below will be found in the vault of Indiana Yearly Meetinghouse in Richmond. These records have been microfilmed. A concerted effort was made to locate Birth and Death records. None were found. The Hinshaw abstracts have been used. These terminate in 1897.

| Men's Minutes | Women's Minutes |
|---|---|
| 8-4-1866 : 5-6-1897 | 8-4-1866 : 7-1-1882 |

Joint Minutes 6-10-1897 : 1-8-1930

## CARTHAGE MONTHLY MEETING
### MINUTES

**ACRES**
2- 7-1885  Ludocia rec in mbrp

**ALLEN**
2- 1-1868  Joseph M & w Charity W & minor ch Charles F, Ann Eliza, Emma, Mary Anna, George Carter & Minnie rocf Whitewater MM, Ind
3- 6-1869  Joseph M & w Charity & fam gct Whitewater MM, Ind

**ANDREWS**
5- 4-1872  Samuel B & w Maggie rocf Indianapolis MM, Ind
3- 7-1891  Robert rocf ....

**AYDELOTTE**
8- 4-1866  Stuart & w Anna & ch Joseph B & Mary E, CHARTER MBRS (Carthage MM)
8- 4-1866  Henry C & w Susanna, CHARTER MBRS
9- 1-1866  Henry C appt to comm on Education
9- 1-1866  Henry C appt to comm to care for poor
9- 5-1868  Henry C appt Asst-Clerk
1- 2-1869  Henry C appt Treasurer
12- 6-1873  Henry C rec a min
6- 6-1874  Henry C re-appt an Overseer
10-14-1876  Henry C gct Swanky MM, Mass to m Phebe S Gifford
12- 1-1877  Henry C & w gct Swanky MM, Mass
2- 5-1887  Joseph B having jMeth; drpd fr mbrp

**BAKER**
6- 7-1879  James & w Mary & ch Cora R rocf Walnut Ridge MM, Ind

**BARKER**
9- 2-1871  Caleb & Laura A rocf Deep River MM, N C
5- 2-1874  Caleb & w Laura A gct Westfield MM, Ind
1- 1-1876  Sarah, a mbr of this Society, accompanied by E Barker, rocf Union Grove MM, Ind

**BARNARD**
8- 4-1866  Thomas & w Rhoda, CHARTER MBRS (Little Blue River PM)
8- 4-1866  William & w Mary, CHARTER MBRS (Little Blue River PM)
8- 4-1866  Jethro & w Sally & ch Luzena & Rhoda, CHARTER MBRS (Little Blue River PM)
8- 4-1866  Franklin & w Ann & ch Caroline, Louisa, Melvina & Mary F, CHARTER MBRS (Little Blue River PM)
8- 4-1866  Lucinda, CHARTER MBR
8- 4-1866  Isaac & w Elvira & ch Laura M, Theodore, Julietta, Thomas E, Lydia E & Florence J, CHARTER MBRS (Little Blue River PM)
8- 4-1866  Elizabeth, CHARTER MBR (Little Blue River PM)
9- 1-1866  Franklin appt to comm on Education
9- 1-1866  Thomas appt to comm to care for the poor
1- 2-1875  David E & w Jenny & minor ch Alice S & Omer P rec in mbrp
4- 3-1875  Mariah L rec in mbrp
5- 1-1876  Thomas appt an Elder
5- 4-1878  Luzena rq rel fr mbrp to jas
8- 2-1879  Franklin appt an Elder

**BARNUM**
10-11-1879  William E rocf ....... Grove MM, Ind

**BECKETT**
11- 7-1891  Abiah rocf Westland MM, Ind

**BEESON**
12- 4-1893  Elbert, minor s of William, rocf Westland MM, Ind
2- 7-1895  Mattie rec in mbrp
2- 6-1896  John V rocf Westland MM, Ind

**BENNET**
2- 3-1883  James H & w Sarah & ch William, Fred H, James & Charles G rec in mbrp
11- 3-1888  Fred H, James, Charles G & William H, minor ch of Sarah, now Sarah Frederick, gct Raysville MM, Ind

**BENTLEY**
2- 5-1881  William P rocf Walnut Ridge MM, Ind
4- 9-1896  John B & w Mary E & dt Martha A & Susannah rocf Walnut Ridge MM, Ind

**BINFORD**
8- 4-1866  William & w Mary & ch Jared P, Michal & Jonathan, CHARTER MBRS (Carthage Mtg)
9- 1-1866  Jared P appt to comm on Education
6- 1-1867  Susannah R, Zelinda A & Benjamin O, minor ch of Oliver & Mary (dec), rocf Lower MM, Va; -end to Walnut Ridge MM, Ind
9- 7-1867  Jared P gct Hopewell MM, Ind to m Emily Lamb
12- 7-1867  Jonathan gct Back Creek MM, Ind to m Anna Wilson
2- 1-1868  Emily L rocf Hopewell MM, Ind
6- 6-1868  Anna rocf Back Creek MM, Ind; Anna has dec within limits of this mtg since the issuing of said cert
11- 6-1869  Jonathan & Nancy Jane Henley inf mtg of int to m each other
12- 4-1869  Jonathan & Nancy Jane Henley are altm; a Friend is appt to read m cert & rpt to next mtg
12- 4-1869  Levi & Abigail S Marshall inf mtg of int to m each other
1- 1-1870  The Friend appt to att m of Jonathan & Nancy Jane Henley, rpts it was att & m cert has been forwarded to the Recorder
1- 1-1870  Levi prc fr Walnut Ridge MM, Ind to m Abigail S Marshall; they are altm & a Friend is appt to att m & read cert & rpt to next mtg
2- 6-1870  The Friend appt to att m of Levi & Abigail S Marshall, rpts it was att & the m cert has been forwarded to the Recorder
6- 4-1870  Abigail S gct Walnut Ridge MM, Ind
8- 6-1870  Michal & Henry Charles inf mtg of m int
9- 3-1870  Michal & Henry Charles are altm; a Friend appt to att m & rpt to next mtg; at rq of parties, a mtg was appt at home of William Binford on 2nd day next at 10 A M
12- 2-1871  Jared P rec a min
11- 8-1872  Levi & w Abbie rocf Walnut Ridge MM, Ind
5- 6-1876  Mary appt an Elder
12- 7-1878  Josiah & w Margaret F & ch Gurney, Micajah H, Bevan & Raymond rocf Walnut Ridge MM, Ind
4- 5-1879  Jared P & w Emily & ch Ella gct Walnut Ridge MM, Ind
8- 2-1879  Josiah appt an Elder
3- 5-1881  Joseph & w Mary Elizabeth & ch Elizabeth C, Caroline, Joseph Omer Binford & Willie C White rocf Westland MM, Ind
5- 2-1885  Joseph appt an Elder
5- 2-1885  Mary appt an Elder
7- 4-1885  Josiah & fam gct Liberty MM, Kans
8- 6-1887  Benjamin O rocf Walnut Ridge MM, Ind
8- 4-1888  Levi appt Clerk
5- 4-1889  Benjamin O gct Walnut Ridge MM, Ind
2- 7-1891  Jared P, a min, & w Emily L rocf Walnut Ridge MM, Ind
2- 7-1891  Ellen O rocf Walnut Ridge MM, Ind
5-11-1893  Penina gct Back Creek MM, Ind
10-12-1893  Nathan & Lucy rocf Walnut Ridge MM, Ind
7-12-1894  Nancy H gct Back Creek MM, Ind
12- 6-1894  Levi & w Eve & minor s Marshall D gct Whitewater MM, Ind (Richmond)

**BISHOP**
3- 7-1895  Ben rocf Raysville MM, Ind
2-11-1897  Nannie & minor ch Bertie & Eva rocf Knightstown MM, Ind

CARTHAGE

## BOND
- 8- 4-1866    Ann, CHARTER MBR    (Little Blue River PM)
- 4- 6-1893    Claud rec in mbrp

## BOWLINGER
- 1-11-1894    Virginia rocf Raysville MM, Ind

## BRANSON
- 8- 4-1866    John H, CHARTER MBR    (Carthage Mtg)
- 5- 7-1887    William rec in mbrp

## BREWER
- 4- 5-1869    Susannah & her minor s, Jason E, rocf Duck Creek MM, Ind

## BROWN
- 11- 5-1870    James & Mary Powell inf mtg of m int; he prc fr Spring River MM, Kans
- 12- 5-1870    James & Mary Powell are altm; a Friend is appt to att m & rpt to next mtg
- 1- 7-1871    The Friend appt to att m of James & Mary Powell rpts it was att
- 5- 3-1873    Mary B gct Sugar Plain MM, Ind

## BUDD
- 4- 4-1885    John rocf Raysville MM, Ind
- 11- 7-1885    Mary M rolf Meth Ch, Arlington, Ind

## BUNDY
- 8- 4-1866    William & w Mary A & ch Ada Eldora & Albert Luther, CHARTER MBRS (Carthage Mtg)
- 8- 4-1866    William P & w Martitia, CHARTER MBRS (Carthage Mtg)
- 8- 4-1866    Ira S & w Sarah R & ch Charles W, CHARTER MBRS (Carthage Mtg)
- 12- 7-1867    Ira S & w Sarah R & ch Charles W gct Spiceland MM, Ind
- 4- 4-1868    Elias, an Elder, & w Sarah & dt Peninnah rocf Walnut Ridge MM, Ind
- 1- 6-1872    William P & Martitia J gct Spiceland MM, Ind
- 4- 3-1875    Sarah gct Walnut Ridge MM, Ind
- 12- 4-1875    Josiah & Sarah Jane Hill inf mtg of m int; he not being a mbr of this mtg, is rq to prc
- 1- 1-1876    Josiah prc fr Walnut Ridge MM, Ind to m Sarah Jane Hill; they are altm; a Friend is appt to att m & rpt to next mtg
- 2- 5-1876    The Friend appt to att m of Josiah & Sarah Jane Hill, rpts it was att
- 3- 5-1876    Sarah J gct Walnut Ridge MM, Ind
- 4- 1-1876    Peninnah gct Walnut Ridge MM, Ind
- 2- 2-1884    Jane & her minor ch Miriam Pauline, Mary Effie & Annie Jose rocf Walnut Ridge MM, Ind
- 5- 2-1885    William appt an Elder
- 3- 7-1891    Alice & her s Roy D rec in mbrp
- 4- 2-1892    Zenos & w Rachel A & minor s Edwin rocf Walnut Ridge MM, Ind
- 1-10-1895    Mary H rocf Walnut Ridge MM, Ind

## BUTLER
- 8- 4-1866    Robert T, CHARTER MBR    (Carthage Mtg)
- 5- 2-1874    Robert T gct Walnut Ridge MM, Ind
- 11- 7-1874    John M & w Sibyl & minor ch Edgar Earnest & George D rocf Spiceland MM, Ind
- 1- 1-1881    John N & fam, having previously removed, gct..
- 5- 5-1883    Henrietta rocf Beech Grove MM, Ind; -end to Walnut Ridge MM, Ind

## CANNON
- 10- 9-1892    Solomon & w Sophrona rocf Westland MM, Ind

## CATT
- 7- 7-1884    Harry J rocf Westland MM, Ind

## CHAMBERLAIN
- 4- 5-1884    Wilson N rec in mbrp at Little Blue River PM

## CHARLES
- 8- 6-1870    Henry & Michal Binford inf mtg of m int
- 9- 3-1870    Henry rocf Fairmount MM, Ind to m Michal Binford; they are altm; a Friend is appt to att m & rpt to next mtg; at the rq of parties a mtg was appt at home of William Binford on 2nd day next at 10 A M
- 6- 3-1871    Michal B gct Fairmount MM, Ind
- 6- 1-1878    Henry & w Michal & minor ch Laura Ellen, Gulielma, Luther B & Luke W rocf Fairmount MM, Ind
- 7- 3-1886    Michal B & minor ch Luther B & Luke W gct Sterling MM, Kans

## CLARK
- 8- 4-1866    John & ch Martha A & N Maria, CHARTER MBRS (Carthage Mtg)
- 8- 4-1866    John W & w Eunice A & ch Mary M, CHARTER MBRS (Carthage Mtg)
- 8- 4-1866    Hezekiah & w Caroline A & ch Martha & Susan, CHARTER MBRS (Carthage Mtg)
- 8- 4-1866    Hezekiah S & w Abigail G & ch George C, Rhoda & Delphina, CHARTER MBRS (Little Blue River PM)
- 8- 4-1866    John W & w R Jane & ch Lydia E, William L, Celia J, Laura J, John Morton, Sarah A & George F, CHARTER MBRS (Little Blue River PM)
- 8- 4-1866    John W appt to comm to make a Mbrp List of this MM
- 8- 4-1866    John W appt to comm on Education
- 8- 4-1866    John W appt to comm to care for poor
- 12- 1-1866    Hezekiah L appt to comm to att QM & rpt to next Mtg
- 2- 6-1870    Hezekiah L dis for disunity
- 5- 7-1870    Hezekiah L inf mtg he is appealing his dis
- 7- 2-1870    N Maria dis
- 10- 6-1874    Hezekiah & w Caroline & minor ch Mattie Susan, Jediah H & John, previously removed, gct Smyrnia MM, Iowa
- 5- 6-1876    John appt to station of Elder
- 5- 6-1876    Eunice appt an Elder
- 2- 1-1879    Hezekiah & w Caroline & minor ch Martha Susan, Jediah H & John rocf Smyrnia MM, Iowa
- 10-15-1883    Celia B rq rel fr mbrp of Society
- 12- 1-1883    Celia B withdraws her rq for rel fr mbrp
- 6- 8-1893    Jediah gct Indianapolis MM, Ind
- 4-11-1895    John gct Indianapolis MM, Ind

## COFFIN
- 8- 4-1866    Jennie R & her ch J Murray Rawls, CHARTER MBRS (Carthage Mtg)
- 8- 4-1866    Phebe, CHARTER MBR (Little Blue River PM)
- 7- 6-1867    Lydia rocf Deep Creek MM, N C
- 4- 1-1871    Ezekiel T rocf Walnut Ridge MM, Ind
- 12- 2-1871    Nancy E & her minor ch Addie Lenora, Mahlon P & Chester Elihu rocf Raysville MM, Ind (Fam of Ezekiel T, who was rec on 4-1-1871)
- 4- 3-1875    Enos & w Sarah A rec in mbrp at Little Blue River PM
- 5- 6-1882    Frances M rocf Westland MM, Ind
- 6- 8-1882    Lydia gct Westland MM, Ind
- 6- 4-1887    Louisa & minor dt Olga rocf Walnut Ridge MM, Ind
- 6- 2-1888    Jennie R & minor s Arthur gct Hopewell MM, Ind
- 7- 4-1891    Francis M & w Ella J & minor dt Hazel C gct Indianapolis MM, Ind
- 6- 9-1892    Aaron & Emma & minor ch Glen, Eva & Leland rocf Hopewell MM, Ind
- 5-11-1893    Olga, -dt Louise, now Louise Powers, gct Knightstown MM, Ind
- 2- 7-1895    Ollie & Leona E rec in mbrp
- 2- 7-1895    Anna rec in mbrp
- 3- 7-1895    Enos & w Sarah A & ch Leora E, Ollie J, William S, Opher T, Merrel D, Cecil & Ethel S rocf Little Blue River MM, Ind

## COLCORD
- 6- 9-1892    Sarah (form Cox) gct...

## CONNER
- 5- 7-1870    William H H rocf Marlborough MM, N C
- 3- 4-1871    Joseph T, minor s of William H H & w Emma rec in mbrp

CARTHAGE

COONS
2- 7-1895  George rec in mbrp

COX
8- 4-1866  Rice P & w Eunice L & ch Ella Jane, CHARTER
           MBRS  (Carthage Mtg)
1- 4-1868  Cyrus B & w Mary & minor ch Benjamin F, James
           P, Charles S, Annetta & Sarah rocf Walnut
           Ridge MM, Ind
6- 6-1874  Cyrus B re-appt Overseer
12- 5-1874 Cyrus B gct Walnut Ridge MM, Ind to m Phebe
           Lamb
3- 6-1875  Phebe L rocf Walnut Ridge MM, Ind
4- 5-1879  Cyrus B appt an Elder
11- 8-1881 James B gct Westland MM, Ind to m Elizabeth
           Jessop
11- 8-1883 Alfred Y & minor ch Gertrude & Clessie rocf
           Hopewell MM, Ind
12- 1-1883 Ruth Ann rolf Meth Ch, Northern Ind Conference
5- 2-1885  Cyrus B appt an Elder
5- 2-1885  Phebe appt an Elder
1-12-1893  Clessius rq cert to Fairmount MM, Ind; rq is
           granted
4- 6-1893  Alfred & w Anna rq letter to Meth Ch, Alexand-
           ria, Ind
5-11-1893  Gertrude  glt Meth Ch, Rushville, Ind
6- 7-1894  Jennie & her minor ch Earnest A, Leona M, Ione
           N & Jessie E rec in mbrp
3-12-1896  Nereus rocf Westland MM, Ind

CRAWFORD
3-13-1892  Charles & Clara rec in mbrp

DAVIS
8- 4-1866  John M, CHARTER MBR  (Little Blue River PM)
8- 4-1866  Eliza Ann & Sally, CHARTER MBRS  (Little Blue
           River PM)
11- 5-1866 John M rptd at Little Blue River PM for mcd
12- 1-1866 John M desires to ret mbrp & manifests affection
           for the Society; rst in mbrp
3- 1-1873  John M appt one of Trustees of Little Blue
           River Mtg property
5- 6-1876  Eliza Ann appt an Elder

DELASHMIT
11- 7-1895 Minerva A rec in mbrp

DENNIS
3- 7-1891  Jethro & w Julia rocf Hopewell MM, Ind

DRAKE
2- 3-1883  Flavius J & w Josephine & minor ch Delina &
           an infant s, rec in mbrp
1-12-1893  Flavius J & w Jane & minor s Edwin glt Meth
           Ch, Knightstown, Ind
4- 9-1896  Delina gct Raysville MM, Ind

DRAPER
8- 4-1866  Mary, CHARTER MBR  (Carthage Mtg)

DUKE
4- 7-1888  Gulielma rocf Spring MM, N C

DUNBAR
8- 4-1866  Eliza, CHARTER MBR  (Carthage Mtg)

DUNN
6- 4-1881  Edward J rec in mbrp
9- 6-1884  Eunice A appt to comm on Education
8- 4-1888  Eunice appt Asst-Clerk

ELLIOTT
7- 4-1868  David W & w Mary Ann & minor ch Elihu O,
           Micajah H A & M Mary E rocf Walnut Ridge MM, Ind
4- 1-1876  David W & fam gct Walnut Ridge MM, Ind
4- 7-1888  Anna M gct Raysville MM, Ind
2- 9-1893  David & w Mary Ann rocf Walnut Ridge MM, Ind

ELLIS
4- 6-1893  Otto J & Lester G rec in mbrp

ESTELL
2- 5-1881  Mary, having previously removed, gct ...

FINNEY
7- 7-1883  Mary V & Clara B rec in mbrp

FODREA
4- 4-1885  Benjamin & w Sarah E & minor ch Ethel E,
           Rhoda A, John H, Nancy L, Lilly C & M Lizzie
           rocf Raysville MM, Ind

FOLGER
9- 6-1873  Carrie & George H Young inf mtg of m int
10-11-1873 Consent of surviving parents being produced,
           Carrie Folger, not a mbr, & George H Young
           are altm at a mtg appt at their rq to be
           held at home of Addison Folger at 10 A M on
           14th instant; a Friend is appt to att m & to
           rpt to next mtg & forward m cert to Recorder
5- 6-1882  Phebe rec in mbrp
3-13-1892  William O & Lydia A & ch Florence, Carrie A
           & Homer H rec in mbrp

FOSTER
8- 4-1866  Asenath B & ch Anna M & Huldah E Foster &
           Mary Estoll, CHARTER MBRS
2- 7-1895  Robert rec in mbrp
1- 6-1898  Robert gct Knightstown MM, Ind

FOUST
12- 2-1876 Emily rocf Spiceland MM, Ind
7- 4-1891  Emma glt Meth Ch, Carthage, Ind

FRAZIER
1- 1-1876  John & w Lydia & minor ch Lizzie & Hannah P
           rocf Dover MM, Ohio

FREDERICK
11- 3-1888 Sarah & her minor ch Fred H, James, William
           H & Charles G Bennett gct Raysville MM, Ind

GALLOWAY
3-13-1892  Estella rec in mbrp
12- 9-1897 Estella gct Kokomo MM, Ind

GAUSE
3-13-1892  Mary, Estella & Helen rec in mbrp
4- 2-1892  Clarkson rocf Spiceland MM, Ind

GILBREATH
3- 1-1873  Jesse & w Sarah S rec in mbrp at Carthage
           Mtg

GLUYS - GLUYAS
12- 6-1879 J Marmaduke & w Zalinda A gct Whitewater MM,
           Ind

GARDNER
8- 4-1866  Isaac & w Dinah, CHARTER MBRS

GARRISON
6- 2-1883  John B rocf Mill Creek MM, Ind

GREIST
12- 6-1894 Dr Henry W rocf Indianapolis MM, Ind & his
           w Elvina E rocf Miami MM, Ohio; -end to Duck
           Creek MM, Ind

GRIFFIN
8- 4-1866  Parthena Jane, ch of Mary E, now Mary E Hill,
           CHARTER MBR
10- 8-1875 Parthena Jane & Thomas T Newby inf mtg of
           m int; consent of surviving parents in
           writing is produced
11- 6-1875 Parthena Jane & Thomas T Newby are altm; a
           Friend is appt to att m & rpt to next mtg

## GRIFFIN (Cont)
12- 4-1875 The Friend appt to att m of Parthena Jane & Thomas T Newby rpts it was att

## HACKLEMAN
4-11-1895 Mary glt Meth Ch, Rushville, Ind

## HADOCK
2- 7-1895 Mary rec in mbrp

## HARE
8- 4-1866 David, CHARTER MBR (Carthage Mtg)
5- 1-1875 David appt an Overseer
9- 1-1883 David & Rhoda M Hill inf mtg of m int
10-15-1883 David & Rhoda M Hill are altm; a Friend is appt to att m & rpt to next mtg; they rq a mtg be appt at home of Micajah Hill on 10-17-1883 at 10 A M; rq granted
5- 2-1885 David appt an Elder
11-10-1892 David & w Rhoda M inf mtg they expect to spend some time in the South, perhaps at Kerr City, Fla & rq a minute of recommendation; rq is granted
5-11-1893 David & w Rhoda ret the letter of sojourn to Kerr City, Fla
11- 7-1894 Lizzie M rec a minute to go to Matamoras, Mexico, as a missionary

## HARRIS
12- 7-1867 Sarah A rocf Lower MM, Va
11- 4-1871 Sarah A & William Johnson inf mtg of m int
12- 2-1871 Sarah A & William Johnson are altm; a Friend is appt to att m & rpt to next mtg
1- 6-1872 The Friend appt to att m of Sarah A & William Johnson, rpts it att & m cert has been forwarded to the Recorder
8- 6-1887 Harriett rocf Lower MM, Va; -end to Hopewell MM, Ind

## HARROLD
3-13-1892 Fred rec in mbrp

## HAWKINS
4- 6-1893 Asa rec in mbrp

## HEADLER
5- 6-1882 Ann & minor dt Lura Bell rocf Walnut Ridge MM, Ind

## HEARKLESS
3-13-1892 Ora rec in mbrp
6- 8-1893 Ora gct Raysville MM, Ind

## HEATHCOCK - HEDGECOCK
2- 5-1876 Joseph & w Elizabeth & ch Mary L rec in mbrp at Carthage PM
3- 5-1877 Emanuel F rec in mbrp at Carthage PM
12- 1-1877 Samuel W & w Sarah & minor ch Nancy Jane, Joseph L, Flora Bell & Julia May rocf Walnut Ridge MM, Ind
8- 2-1879 Joseph & w Elizabeth & ch Mary L had rq a cert to Raysville MM, Ind but mtg's judgement is that action be suspended
1- 1-1881 Samuel & fam, having previously removed, gct Raysville MM, Ind
1- 1-1881 Emanuel F, having previously removed, gct ..
8- 6-1881 Elizabeth & minor dt Mary L gct Raysville MM, Ind

## HELMS
6- 4-1887 Angeline E Helms (form Hunnicutt) glt 2nd Presby Ch, Chicago, Ill

## HENDERSON
2- 7-1895 Harry rec in mbrp

## HENDRIX - HENDRICKS
3- 7-1891 J H & w Elizabeth rec in mbrp
2- 7-1895 Nina & Flora rec in mbrp

## HENLEY
8- 4-1866 Thomas & w Abigail & ch Ann, Jane, Eliza, Jason & Owen, CHARTER MBRS (Carthage Mtg)
8- 4-1866 Henry & w Ruth & ch Joseph J, William P & Robert B, CHARTER MBRS (Carthage Mtg)
8- 4-1866 Micajah & w Ruth Ann & ch Reuben B, Caroline V, Mary L, Harlan H, Eva A & Lenora, CHARTER MBRS (Carthage Mtg)
8- 4-1866 Charles & w Tamar & ch Charles Jr, Sarah & Caroline, CHARTER MBRS (Carthage Mtg)
8- 4-1866 Jesse & w Abigail N & ch Enos Charles, Sarah, Joseph H, Leland H, Phebe, Mary & Reu E, CHARTER MBRS (Carthage Mtg)
8- 4-1866 Robert & w Mary & ch Hiram H, Albert, Rumina & Jesse, CHARTER MBRS (Carthage Mtg)
8- 4-1866 Thomas W & w Hannah C & ch Rollin E, Abie J, Mary E, William J & John B, CHARTER MBRS (Carthage Mtg)
8- 4-1866 Ann & ch George W, Henry M & William, CHARTER MBRS (Carthage Mtg)
8- 4-1866 Elwood & w Phebe & ch Penelope, John C, Abigail & Barclay, CHARTER MBRS (Carthage Mtg)
8- 4-1866 Milton & w Julia Ann & ch Harvey & Walter C, CHARTER MBRS (Carthage Mtg)
9- 1-1866 Jesse appt to comm on Education
9- 1-1866 Henry appt to comm on Education
9- 1-1866 Thomas appt to comm to care for poor
10-13-1866 Elwood & w Phebe & fam gct Poplar Ridge MM, Ind
1- 5-1867 Milton appt Recorder of Births & Deaths
1- 5-1867 Joseph J appt Recorder of Removal Certs
4- 4-1868 Ann & Aaron B Hunt inf mtg of m int
5- 2-1868 Ann & Aaron B Hunt are altm; a Friend is appt to read m cert & rpt to next mtg
6- 6-1868 The Friend appt to att m of Ann & Aaron B Hunt, rpts the m cert has been forwarded to the Recorder
9- 5-1868 Charles M gct Walnut Ridge MM, Ind to m Cynthia Stanley
2- 6-1869 Robert appt one of Trustees of Carthage School
2- 6-1869 Milton appt one of Trustees of Carthage School
3- 6-1869 Cynthia E rocf Walnut Ridge MM, Ind
11- 6-1869 Nancy Jane & Jonathan Binford inf mtg of m int
12- 4-1869 Nancy Jane & Jonathan Binford are altm; a Friend is appt to att & read m cert & rpt to next mtg
1- 1-1870 The Friend appt to att m of Nancy Jane & Jonathan Binford, rpts m att & m cert has been forwarded to the Recorder
6- 4-1870 Joseph H rptd to have mcd
7- 2-1870 Mtg unites in permitting Joseph H to ret mbrp
7- 2-1870 Joseph J rptd to have mcd
7- 2-1870 Jason rptd to have mcd
8- 6-1870 The Mtg unites in permitting Joseph J to ret his mbrp
8- 6-1870 The Mtg unites in permitting Jason to ret his mbrp
2- 4-1871 Sarah N & Micajah Young inf mtg of m int Surviving parents will be expected at next mtg
3- 4-1871 Sarah N & Micajah Young are altm; a Friend is appt to att m & rpt to next Mtg
4- 1-1871 The Friend appt to att m of Sarah N & Micajah Young, rpts it was att
5- 6-1871 Mary rocf Deep River MM, N C
2- 5-1872 Rebecca E rocf West Branch MM, Ohio
3- 2-1872 Reuben B & Rachel Young inf Mtg of m int
4- 6-1872 Reuben B & Rachel Young are altm; a Friend is appt to att m & rpt to next Mtg
8- 2-1873 Henry gct Walnut Ridge MM, Ind to m Margaret Moore
9- 6-1873 Joseph J appt Asst-Clerk
11- 1-1873 Margaret rocf Walnut Ridge MM, Ind
11- 1-1873 William P appt Treasurer
4- 1-1874 Henry M appt Recorder of MM
2- 6-1875 Reuben B & fam obtained transfer of mbrp to Walnut Ridge MM, Ind as they now reside in limits of newly established Riverside PM
5- 6-1876 Thomas appt an Elder

CARTHAGE

### HENLEY (Cont)
|  |  |
|---|---|
| 5- 6-1876 | Henry appt an Elder |
| 5- 6-1876 | Ruth Ann appt an Elder |
| 7- 1-1876 | Owen appt Recorder of the Birth & Death Record of Carthage Mtg |
| 9- 2-1876 | Mary M rec a min |
| -  -1876 | William P gct Adrian MM, Mich to m Ida S Steere |
| 3- 5-1877 | Ida S rocf Adrian MM, Mich |
| 7- 6-1878 | Jesse dis |
| 5- 4-1879 | Elizabeth & her minor s Raymond rec in mbrp |
| 6- 9-1879 | Reuben B & w Rachel Y & ch Herbert O, Sarah L & Lillian R rocf Walnut Ridge MM, Ind |
| 4- 3-1880 | Mary B & her minor ch Earl B rocf Mississinewa MM, Ind |
| 8- 7-1880 | Jason E appt Clerk |
| 5- 7-1881 | William P appt to comm to have care of Grave Yard in place of Joseph J Henley who is rptd decd |
| 6- 4-1881 | Clara & minor s Frank D rec in mbrp |
| 8- 4-1883 | Owen S appt Clerk of MM |
| 9- 1-1883 | John C rocf Poplar Ridge MM, Ind |
| 11- 3-1883 | Jason gct West Branch MM, Ohio |
| 8- 2-1884 | Florence E rocf Adrian MM, Mich |
| 9- 6-1884 | Owen S appt to comm on Education |
| 5- 2-1885 | Jason & R Ella gc for their minor ch Anna B & Clarence J to West Branch MM, Ohio |
| 5- 2-1885 | Thomas appt an Elder |
| 5- 2-1885 | Henry appt an Elder |
| 5- 2-1885 | Ruth A appt an Elder |
| 10-  -1885 | Harvey G gct West Branch MM, Ohio |
| 3- 6-1886 | Robert B & w Florence & dt Grace F gct Archer MM, Fla |
| 3- 7-1887 | Joseph H & w Elizabeth & minor ch Lula May, Lucius, Raymond, Forest, Frank & an unnamed infant gct New Hope MM, Howard Co, Ind |
| 2- 4-1888 | Walter C & Carrie B gct Dublin MM, Ind |
| 9- 7-1889 | Elvirah rocf Westland MM, Ind |
| 10-11-1890 | Charles M & his minor ch gct Marion MM, Ind |
| 3- 7-1891 | Jennie rec in mbrp |
| 9- 4-1891 | Alma & dt Lavina rec in mbrp |
| 6- 9-1892 | Martha rocf Spiceland MM, Ind |
| 9- 8-1892 | Bert rq rel fr mbrp to jMeth; rq granted |
| 4- 6-1893 | Mattie rolf Meth Ch, Carthage, Ind |
| 4- 6-1893 | Loise & Margaret, minor ch of John & Mattie, rec in mbrp |
| 11- 9-1893 | Ida S appt an Elder |
| 6- 7-1894 | Walter C & w Carrie & minor ch Forest M rocf Walnut Ridge MM, Ind |
| 1-10-1895 | Owen S appt Recorder of Marriage Records |
| 4- 8-1897 | John C & w Mattie D & minor ch Marguerite & Loise gct Indianapolis MM, Ind |

### HILL
|  |  |
|---|---|
| 8- 4-1866 | Micajah & w Sarah Jane & ch James M, Sarah Jane, Rhoda M Hill & James M Gluyas, CHARTER MBRS |
| 8- 4-1866 | Samuel B & w Nancy H & ch Eunice A, Emily R & Edgar N, CHARTER MBRS |
| 8- 4-1866 | Thomas C & w Adeline B & ch Ione, Anna L, Joseph G & Gertrude, CHARTER MBRS |
| 8- 4-1866 | William L & w Mary Ann & ch Viola Jane & Florence, CHARTER MBRS |
| 8- 4-1866 | John C & w Susan L & ch Allen, Thomas J, Mary Alice, Lemuel P & Luther G, CHARTER MBRS |
| 8- 4-1866 | Amos H & w Peninah & ch Mary Alice, Leora A, William & Lucy L, CHARTER MBRS |
| 8- 4-1866 | Mary E & her ch Parthena Jane Griffin, CHARTER MBRS |
| 8- 4-1866 | Jesse, CHARTER MBR |
| 8- 4-1866 | Lucretia, CHARTER MBR |
| 8- 4-1866 | Phebe, CHARTER MBR |
| 8- 4-1866 | Owen S, CHARTER MBR |
| 8- 4-1866 | Amos H appt on comm to procure Record Books for the MM |
| 9- 1-1866 | Amos H appt to comm on Education |
| 3- 2-1867 | Melissa A B rocf Spiceland MM, Ind |
| 3- 2-1867 | Thomas C & Adeline & ch gct Chicago MM, Ill |
| 4- 6-1867 | Henry B rec in mbrp |
| 6- 1-1867 | Martha Ellen rocf Hopewell MM, Ind |
| 9- 7-1867 | James Hadley rst in mbrp |
| 3- 7-1868 | James W gct Walnut Ridge MM, Ind to m Charity H Binford |
| 2- 6-1869 | Daniel M & w Pharabe M & minor ch James Warren rocf Minneapolis MM, Minn |
| 2- 6-1869 | Amos H appt one of Trustees of Carthage School |
| 2- 5-1872 | Miriam rocf Back Creek MM, N C |
| 9- 3-1873 | Samuel B appt Clerk |
| 12- 4-1875 | Sarah Jane & Josiah Bundy inf mtg of m int; Consent of surviving parents is produced |
| 1- 1-1876 | Sarah Jane & Josiah Bundy are altm; a Friend is appt to att m & rpt to next Mtg |
| 2- 5-1876 | The Friend appt to att m of Sarah Jane & Josiah Bundy, rpts it was att |
| 5- 6-1876 | Micajah appt an Elder |
| 5- 6-1876 | Nancy H appt an Elder |
| 7- 1-1876 | Amos & w Penina & ch Mary Alice, Leora Ann, William & Lucy Sarah gct Walnut Ridge MM, Ind |
| 1- 4-1879 | Thomas T & Nancy D & ch Eli R, Abbie E, Elizabeth & Margaret M rocf Whitewater MM, Ind |
| 6- 7-1879 | Robert & w Elizabeth D & ch Mary Emily, Edward S, Annie Jane, John C, Mahlon R & Rebecca Jane rocf Whitewater MM, Ind |
| 2- 5-1881 | Amanda & ch Charles S, William H, Emma J & Irvin rocf Walnut Ridge MM, Ind |
| 6- 4-1881 | Benjamin F rec in mbrp at Carthage PM |
| 2- 4-1882 | Owen S & w Melissa B rocf Raysville MM, Ind |
| 3- 4-1882 | Rhoda M rec a min |
| 4- 1-1882 | William S dis |
| 2- 3-1883 | Robert H rec in mbrp |
| 9- 1-1883 | Rhoda M & David Hare inf mtg of m int |
| 10-15-1883 | Rhoda M & David Hare are altm; a Friend is appt to att m & rpt to next Mtg; they rq a mtg be appt at home of Micajah Hill on 10-17-1883 at 10 A M; rq granted |
| 2- 2-1884 | Milton rec in mbrp at Carthage PM |
| 5- 2-1885 | Micajah appt an Elder |
| 5- 2-1885 | Nancy H appt an Elder |
| 12- 5-1885 | Isaac rec in mbrp |
| 2- 6-1886 | Lydia M rolf Meth Ch, Carthage, Ind |
| 2- 6-1886 | Oliver M, Mary Gertrude & Lawrence S, minor ch of Benjamin & Lydia M, rec in mbrp |
| 1- 1-1887 | Jesse rolf Meth Ch, North Indianapolis, Ind |
| 3- 7-1887 | Milton & w Amanda J & ch Emma J & Irvin gct Walnut Ridge MM, Ind |
| 1- 7-1888 | Elizabeth P rocf Raysville MM, Ind |
| 7- 7-1888 | Aaron O rocf Back Creek MM, N C |
| 4- 6-1889 | Samuel B, who has been on comm in care of Grave Yard, has dec & a comm appt to fill his place |
| 2- 6-1890 | Milton & w Amanda & minor s Irvin rec in mbrp |
| 11- 1-1890 | Margaret McCarter (form Hill) glt Meth Ch, Topeka, Kans |
| 1- 3-1891 | Abbie E glt Meth Ch, Topeka, Kans |
| 6- 6-1891 | Samuel B & w Elizabeth J & ch Ruth M & Rowland H rocf Walnut Ridge MM, Ind |
| 3- 5-1892 | Alice P & dt Hazel rolf Meth Ch, Carthage, Ind |
| 2- 8-1894 | Abbie E rolf Meth Ch, Osawatomie, Kans |
| 6- 6-1895 | Hannah Elnora rocf Westland MM, Ind |
| 3-11-1897 | Eli & w Josie gct Spiceland MM, Ind |

### HILLIGOSS
|  |  |
|---|---|
| 3-13-1892 | Hattie rec in mbrp |
| 4- 2-1892 | Agnes, minor dt of Hattie, rec in mbrp |

### HINSHAW
|  |  |
|---|---|
| 10-14-1876 | Mary & minor ch William, Annie & Frederick rocf Duck Creek MM, Ind |
| 2- 5-1887 | William, having jMeth, rq rel fr mbrp of Friends Society |
| 8-11-1893 | Etta rocf Raysville MM, Ind |
| 3-11-1897 | Ancil & w Mary S & minor ch Eva, Luella, Eli Henry & Harry Erthel rocf Olive Branch MM, Ind |

### HOAG
|  |  |
|---|---|
| 1- 3-1874 | Susan gct Toledo MM, Kans |
| 2- 7-1880 | L Ann rocf Dover MM, Ind; -end by Walnut Ridge MM, Ind |

CARTHAGE

**HOAG (Cont)**
2- 2-1884   Anny rocf Springdale MM, Iowa; -end to Walnut Ridge MM, Ind

**HOBBS**
8- 4-1866   Wilson & w Zelinda L & ch Orville W, Mary L, Walton, Charles Milton, Fannie, Robert W & Harry L, CHARTER MBRS (Carthage Mtg)
12- 7-1872   John W rq mbrp in Society at Little Blue River PM
2- 1-1873   John W rec in mbrp
10- 6-1874   Wilson & w Zelinda & ch Charles M, Fannie, Robert W & Harry L gct Raysville MM, Ind
12- 5-1874   Mary Z gct Raysville MM, Ind
2- 6-1875   Walton gct Raysville MM, Ind
3- 6-1875   The comm appt to consider case of Orvil W, rpts his affairs are not in a condition to grant him a cert of removal, so comm is rel

**HOCKETT**
9- 4-1886   Hannah rocf Walnut Ridge MM, Ind
7- 5-1890   Hannah gct Union Grove MM, Hamilton Co, Ind

**HODSON**
8- 4-1866   Mathew & w Hannah, CHARTER MBRS (Carthage Mtg)
8- 4-1866   J Milton & w Mattie R, CHARTER MBRS (Carthage Mtg)
10- 6-1874   John Milton & w Mattie & minor ch Gertrude, having previously removed, gct White River MM, Ind

**HOLLOWAY**
8- 4-1866   Jane, CHARTER MBR (Carthage Mtg)

**HOLLINGSWORTH**
6- 9-1892   Earl rocf Spiceland MM, Ind

**HOLT**
2- 5-1877   Martha rocf Spiceland MM, Ind

**HOPKINS**
4- 6-1893   William G & Ella rec in mbrp

**HUBBARD**
2- 3-1883   Joseph L rec in mbrp
3- 6-1886   Mary L rocf Raysville MM, Ind

**HUESTES**
12- 6-1873   Aaron & w Mary Ann, a min, & minor ch Charles H rocf Bridgeport MM, Ind; -end by Walnut Ridge MM, Ind
5- 1-1875   Isador G & Samantha rocf Bridgeport MM, Ind
10-12-1878   Charles rq rel fr mbrp to jas
2- 1-1879   Aaron rq rel fr mbrp; rq granted

**HUNNICUTT**
8- 4-1866   John A & w Martha Jane & ch Tabitha Ann, Olive, Annie & Angelina E Hunnicutt & Angeline Cook, CHARTER MBRS (Carthage Mtg)
8- 1-1868   Tabitha A Stuart (form Hunnicutt) dis for mcd
6- 4-1887   Angeline, now Angeline Helms, glt 2nd Presby Ch, Chicago, Ill
11- 9-1893   Martha J appt an Elder
1-11-1894   Olive gct Chicago MM, Ill
7- 9-1896   Olive rocf Chicago MM, Ill

**HUNT**
4- 4-1868   Aaron B & Ann Henley inf mtg of m int
5- 2-1868   Aaron B prc fr Newberry MM, Ohio to m Ann Henley; they are altm; a Friend is appt to read m cert & rpt to next mtg
6- 6-1868   The Friend appt to att m of Aaron B & Ann Henley, rpts attd m & m cert has been forwarded to the Recorder
7- -1868   Ann gct Newberry MM, Ohio
6-10-1897   Ann H rocf Newberry MM, Ohio

**JEFFERSON**
7- -1883   Bartlett rq mbrp

9- 1-1883   Mtg unites in deferring action on case of Bartlett

**JENKINS**
2- 3-1883   Mary rec in mbrp
6- 6-1885   Mary S gct Raysville MM, Ind
1- 2-1886   William rec in mbrp
3- 6-1886   Elizabeth A rec in mbrp

**JESSOP**
8- 4-1866   Thomas & w Rebecca & ch Elizabeth & Micajah B, CHARTER MBRS (Carthage Mtg)
8- 4-1866   Samuel A & ch Huldah & Jane, CHARTER MBRS (Carthage Mtg)
9- 1-1866   Thomas appt an Overseer
12- 1-1866   Elizabeth & Samuel C Wilson inf Mtg of m int
1- 5-1867   Elizabeth & Samuel C Wilson are altm; Friend appt to att m & rpt to next mtg
2- 2-1867   The Friend appt to read the m cert of Elizabeth & Samuel C Wilson, rpts it was att & m cert has been forwarded to the Recorder
12- 5-1868   Micajah B rptd mcd
1- 2-1869   Micajah, having expressed a desire to ret his mbrp, the mtg unites in granting rq
3- 5-1876   Sarah E rocf Springdale MM, Kans
5- 6-1876   Thomas appt an Overseer
10-14-1876   Jane gct Westland MM, Ind
5- 7-1881   Mary E rocf Walnut Ridge MM, Ind
5- 2-1885   Thomas appt an Elder
12- 5-1885   Manone B (female) rec in mbrp

**JOHNSON**
8- 4-1866   William, CHARTER MBR
8- 4-1866   Richard W & w Lucinda W & ch John W, Mary Jane & Albert H, CHARTER MBRS
8- 4-1866   William appt to comm to procure Record Books for MM
9- 1-1866   William appt an Overseer
9- 1-1866   William appt to comm on Education
9- 7-1867   William S & w Ann B & minor ch Eva & Delia rec in mbrp
11- 4-1871   William & Sarah A Harris inf mtg of m int
12- 2-1871   William & Sarah A Harris are altm; a Friend is appt to att m & rpt to next mtg
1- 6-1872   The Friend appt to att m of William & Sarah A Harris, rpts it was att & m cert has been forwarded to the Recorder
5- 6-1876   William appt an Elder
5- 2-1885   William appt an Elder
5- 1-1886   Mary rel fr mbrp on rq
4- 2-1892   Charles glt Meth Ch, Newcastle, Ind
1-11-1894   Delia gct Hopewell MM, Ind
11- 7-1895   Frank F & w Luella & ch Oscar & Harry rec in mbrp

**JONES**
6-11-1896   Cora & Laura rocf Knightstown MM, Ind
12- 9-1897   John H & w Laura E & minor dt Laura E rocf Grove MM, Ind

**JUDY**
2- 7-1895   Celia F rec in mbrp

**KELLY**
4- 6-1893   Samuel rec in mbrp

**LACY**
8- 4-1866   Thomas & w Miriam H, CHARTER MBRS (Carthage Mtg)
2- 1-1884   Henry & w Margaret L & minor ch Ira M, Joseph F & Samuel F rec in mbrp

**LATTIMORE**
8- 6-1887   Susie rocf Walnut Ridge MM, Ind

**LAYMAN**
3- 7-1887   Anna J gct Walnut Ridge MM, Ind

CARTHAGE

### LEONARD
- 8- 4-1866  Jesse & w Belinda & ch Letitia, Hiram W & Anna M, CHARTER MBRS  (Little Blue River PM)
- 9- 1-1866  Jesse appt an Overseer
- 4- 4-1868  John rocf Centre MM, N C
- 4- 2-1870  Job W rocf Centre MM, N C
- 9- 6-1873  Jonathan rocf Centre MM, N C
- 9- 6-1873  Abigail rocf Centre MM, N C
- 6- 6-1874  Jesse re-appt an Overseer
- 5- 6-1876  Belinda appt an Elder
- 9- 2-1882  Anna M rec a min

### LINEBACK
- 3- 3-1883  Thompson & w Frances & ch William H, Ruby Lola, John & Annie rocf Walnut Ridge MM, Ind
- 9- 8-1892  Horace rq rel fr mbrp to jMeth; rq granted
- 6-10-1897  Flora H glt Meth Ch, Carthage, Ind

### MACY
- 8- 4-1866  Mary E, -dt Sarah A, now Sarah A Morris, wife of Jesse, CHARTER MBR  (Carthage Mtg)
- 8- 4-1866  Tristram B & w Dorcas & ch Lysander F, Byron R, Isaac G, Thomas B & Orlando H, CHARTER MBRS (Little Blue River PM)
- 8- 4-1866  Samuel & w Mary & ch Charles C, Elmira, Nancy, William L, David E & Lydia J, CHARTER MBRS (Little Blue River PM)
- 8- 4-1866  Mary, CHARTER MBR  (Little Blue River PM)
- 8- 4-1866  David W, CHARTER MBR  (Little Blue River PM)
- 8- 4-1866  William G, CHARTER MBR  (Little Blue River PM)
- 8- 4-1866  Erasmus D, CHARTER MBR  (Little Blue River PM)
- 2- 2-1867  David W Macy rocf Deep Creek MM, N C
- 7- 6-1867  Samuel & w Mary & minor ch Charles, Elmina Nancy & Simpson rocf Deep Creek MM, N C
- 7- 6-1867  William C rocf Deep Creek MM, N C
- 6- 3-1871  William G rptd mcd by Little Blue River PM
- 7- 1-1871  William G desires to ret mbrp; Mtg unites & grants rq
- 1- 6-1872  Lysander F rptd mcd by Little Blue River PM
- 2- 5-1872  Lysander F desires to ret mbrp; the Mtg unites in granting his rq
- 12- 7-1872  Charles rptd mcd by Little Blue River PM
- 1- 4-1873  Charles desires to ret mbrp & Mtg unites to grant rq
- 2- 6-1875  Lydia M rec in mbrp (Form Miller)
- 7- 1-1876  David W appt an Overseer in place of Nathan Weisner who is dec
- 10-14-1876  Rachel rocf Duck Creek MM, Ind
- 4- 5-1879  William rocf Deep River MM, N C
- 7- 5-1879  Parthena C rocf Centre MM, N C
- 4- 5-1884  Nancy M & her ch Deborah Ann, Samuel A, Clinton W, David A, John L, Charles S & Thomas S rec in mbrp at Little Blue River PM

### MADDOX
- 11- 7-1895  Oliver & w Nancy & minor ch Beatrice, Clarence & Roscoe rec in mbrp
- 11- 7-1895  Charles & Nora rec in mbrp

### MANLEY
- 11- 7-1874  Andrew J & w Nancy rec in mbrp

### MARIS
- 7- 7-1892  Albert J & w Anna Elizabeth rocf Rush Creek MM, Ind
- 4- 6-1893  Dr Albert & w Anna & minor s Ward Hale gct Duck Creek MM, Ind

### MARSHALL
- 8- 4-1866  David & w Zelinda M & ch Abbie L, CHARTER MBRS (Carthage Mtg)
- 9- 1-1866  David appt Clerk of MM; Thomas L Newby appt Asst-Clerk
- 9- 1-1866  David appt to comm on Education
- 12- 1-1866  David appt to comm to att QM & rpt to next Mtg
- 9- 7-1867  David appt Clerk of MM
- 9- 7-1867  David rec a min
- 12- 4-1869  Abigail S & Levi Binford inf Mtg of m int
- 1- 1-1870  Abigail S & Levi Binford are altm; a Friend appt to att m & read cert & rpt to next Mtg
- 2- 2-1870  The Friend appt to att m of Abigail S & Levi Binford, rpts it was att & m cert has been forwarded to the Recorder

### McBANE
- 11- 7-1885  Jacob F & w Lodema & minor ch Bertha D, Luly D & Robby C rec in mbrp

### McCARTER
- 11- 1-1890  Margaret (form Hill) rq letter to Meth Ch, Topeka, Kans

### McCRACKEN
- 10-10-1891  Eunice McCracken (form Patten) rq letter to Meth Ch, Ridge-water, Iowa

### McCRACKIN
- 7- 5-1873  Eunice A gct Hopewell MM, Ind

### McDANIELS
- 2- 7-1895  Allen rec in mbrp

### MILES
- 11- 6-1875  Keturah, a min, & her dt Caroline rocf Union MM, Ohio

### MILLER
- 8- 4-1866  Eusebia F & ch George S, CHARTER MBRS (Carthage Mtg)

### MILLS
- 8- 2-1873  John rocf Fairfield MM, Ind
- 12-12-1895  Olive Hare Mills gct El Modena MM, Calif

### MOORE
- 11- 3-1888  Joshua & w Mary B rocf Walnut Ridge MM, Ind

### MORRIS
- 8- 4-1866  Jesse & w Sarah A & ch Henry, Mary Jane, Robert & Abigail Morris & Mary E Macy, are CHARTER MBRS  (Carthage Mtg)
- 12- 1-1866  Jesse appt to comm att QM & rpt to next Mtg
- 3- 5-1876  Mary E rec in mbrp
- 5- 1-1886  Jesse rq assistance in his financial affairs; comm appt to give assistance
- 3-13-1892  Presley & Jessie rec in mbrp

### MULLIS
- 1- 2-1886  James H rec in mbrp
- 5- 7-1887  John & Louisa rec in mbrp

### NEWBY
- 8- 4-1866  Henry & w Sarah & s Thomas T Newby & her dt Nancy Jane Henley, CHARTER MBRS
- 8- 4-1866  Thomas appt to comm to prepare list of Mbrs of this MM (Carthage Mtg & Little Blue River PM)
- 9- 1-1866  Thomas appt Asst-Clerk; David Marshall appt Clerk
- 9- 5-1868  Thomas appt Clerk
- 9- 4-1869  Elizabeth rocf Back Creek MM, Ind
- 1- 5-1867  Thomas T appt Recorder of m Certs
- 3- 2-1867  Margaret Jane & her minor dt Laura Bell gct Raysville MM, Ind
- 9- 7-1867  Thomas T appt asst Clerk of MM
- 7- 5-1873  Mary rocf Back Creek MM, Ind
- 10- 8-1875  Thomas T & Parthena Jane Griffin inf Mtg of m int; the consent of surviving parents in writing is produced
- 11- 6-1875  Thomas T & Parthena Jane Griffin are altm; a Friend is appt to att m & rpt to next Mtg
- 12- 4-1875  The Friend appt to att m of Thomas T & Parthena Jane Griffin, rpts it was att
- 2- 5-1877  Margaret rocf Spiceland MM, Ind
- 5- 5-1877  Laura Bell rocf Spiceland MM, Ind
- 5- 5-1877  Francis R, infant ch of Oliver & Margaret J, rocf Spiceland MM, Ind
- 1- 2-1886  Mary Ella gct Back Creek MM, Ind

### NEWLIN
- 10-15-1883  Jesse rec in mbrp at Carthage PM

CARTHAGE

NEWLIN (Cont)
12- 5-1885  Jonathan rec in mbrp
 4- 7-1888  Emily rocf Spring MM, N C

NEWSOM
 8- 4-1866  Luke & w Cynthia & ch William R, David W, Thomas C & Melissa Jane, CHARTER MBRS
 8- 4-1866  Jabez H & w Margaret C & ch Oliver M, Anna Jane & Mary Ella, CHARTER MBRS
 8- 4-1866  Allen W, CHARTER MBR
 8- 4-1866  Jabez H appt to comm to make list of mbrs of this MM (Carthage & Little Blue River PM)
 2- 2-1867  Luke & Cynthia rq their gr-ch, u/c, Ada M & Oma C Ruby be rec in mbrp, with which this Mtg unites
12- 6-1873  David W rptd mcd by Carthage PM
12- 6-1873  William P rptd mcd by Carthage PM
 1- 3-1874  David W permitted to ret his mbrp
 1- 3-1874  William P permitted to ret his mbrp
 4- 2-1892  Cora glt Meth Ch, Carthage, Ind
 4- 9-1896  Mary Ellen rocf Walnut Ridge MM, Ind

NICHOLSON - NICKLESON
 1- 5-1884  Annetta gct Walnut Ridge MM, Ind

NIXON
 1-12-1893  Maryetta (Wilcutts) Nixon & her ch Florence, Bertha & John Nixon gct New Garden MM, Ind

O'NEAL
10-11-1885  Nellie rec in mbrp

PAGE
 2- 3-1883  George rec in mbrp
10-15-1883  Pariba & minor dt Mary Dell rec in mbrp

PARKER
 9- 6-1874  Sarah rocf Walnut Ridge MM, Ind
12- 7-1878  Almeda gct Lynn Grove MM, Iowa
 2- 7-1880  William & w Amanda rocf Deer Creek MM, Ind
 2- 7-1885  William gct Smyrna MM, Iowa
 4- 8-1897  Benjamin Franklin & w Elvira Hester rocf Haviland MM, Kans

PARRISH
 2- 7-1895  Henry F rec in mbrp
 5- 9-1895  Henry & w Mariam C & minor ch Charles, Edith S, Carl, Walter B & Nellie rocf Walnut Ridge MM, Ind

PATTEN
 8- 4-1866  Joseph & w Rachel & ch Eunice A, James A, Thomas C, Lewis F, Corilie J, Clara E & William O, CHARTER MBRS  (Carthage Mtg)
 6- 7-1873  James A gct Deer Creek MM, Ind
 4- 3-1886  Lewis glt Meth Ch, Monticello, Ill
 7- 6-1889  Clarkson, owing to his isolation fr the Society of Friends, jMeth; his mbrp has ceased
 7- 6-1889  Albert, owing to his isolation fr the Society of Friends, has united in mbrp with Christian Ch; his mbrp has ceased
 2- 9-1893  Clara glt Meth Ch, Bridgewater, Iowa

PATTERSON
 8- 4-1866  Elizabeth, CHARTER MBR  (Carthage Mtg)

PETERS
 3-13-1892  Ray rec in mbrp

PHELPS
12- 7-1867  Louisa J rocf West Union MM, Ind; -end by Walnut Ridge MM, Ind
 4- 4-1868  Mark rec in mbrp
 8- 4-1883  Eunice appt Asst-Clerk
 6- 4-1887  Enos rocf Walnut Ridge MM, Ind
 6- 4-1887  Joseph & w Jane & minor dt Olive rocf Walnut Ridge MM, Ind
 4- 2-1892  Mary E & ch Nevil F, Russell H & Walter J rec in mbrp

PHILLIPS
 1- 2-1875  Richard H rec in mbrp

PICKERING
 4- 3-1875  Benjamin rocf Raysville MM, Ind
 4- 3-1875  Rebecca rocf Raysville MM, Ind
 2- 5-1876  Sarah C & her ch Julia A, Charles F & Rosa J rec in mbrp
 4- 5-1879  Rebecca appt an Elder
 5- 2-1885  Rebecca appt an Elder

PIERSON
 2- 5-1887  May S gct Walnut Ridge MM, Ind

PITTS
 7- 6-1867  Branson & Luzena rocf Deep Creek MM, N C
12- 7-1867  Henry Cicero, Martha Jane, Joseph Milton, James Edwin, Lutitia Maria, Alonzo Clarkson & Rufus Emery, ch of Branson & Luzena, rec in mbrp
12- 5-1885  James S & w Marcia & minor s Harry O rec in mbrp

POGUE
 3- 5-1876  Frank H rq mbrp in Society; comm appt to consult his guardian as he is a minor, & rpt to next Mtg
 4- 1-1876  Frank H rec in mbrp

POWELL
 8- 4-1866  Mary, CHARTER MBR  (Carthage Mtg)
11- 5-1870  Mary & James Brown inf Mtg of m int
12- 5-1870  Mary & James Brown are altm; a Friend is appt to att m & rpt to next Mtg
 1- 7-1871  The Friend appt to att m of Mary & James Brown, rpts it was att

POWERS
 5-11-1893  Louisa (form Coffin) & her dt Olga Coffin gct Knightstown MM, Ind

PRICE
 2- 7-1895  Rosa rec in mbrp
 8- 6-1896  Rosa glt Meth Ch, Eliotsville, Ind

PUSSEY
 8- 4-1866  Joel & w Agatha, CHARTER MBRS (Carthage Mtg)

RATLIFF
 6-11-1896  Marcus & w Hannah A & minor ch William E, Herschel Edward, Carl M, Jesse Claud & Ruby Evelyn rocf Spiceland MM, Ind
 2-10-1898  Marcus & w & minor ch gct Knightstown MM, Ind

RAWLS
 8- 4-1866  Jesse & w Elizabeth, CHARTER MBRS (Carthage Mtg)
 8- 4-1866  J Murray, -s Jonnie (now Jonnie R Coffin), CHARTER MBR  (Carthage Mtg)
 3- 4-1871  Murray rptd mcd & jas
 4- 1-1871  Murray does not desire to ret mbrp; dis
 5- 6-1876  Elizabeth appt an Elder
 3-13-1892  J Murray rec in mbrp
 3-13-1892  Pearl rec in mbrp
 3- 7-1895  Laura rolf Meth Ch, Carthage, Ind

REDDING
 3- 1-1884  Jared B rec in mbrp
11- 3-1888  Anna & minor ch Mary Cecil rocf Walnut Ridge MM, Ind
11- 1-1890  Dr Jacob & w Emma Ann & minor ch Mary Cecil glt 1st Congregational Ch, Anderson, Ind

RIGSBY
 1- 2-1875  Lucinda & F..... rec in mbrp
 1- 2-1875  Alvason rec in mbrp

ROBISON
 1-11-1894  Ivy L  glt Meth Ch, Rushville, Ind

CARTHAGE

RUBY
2- 2-1867   Ada M & Oma C, gr-ch of Luke & Cynthia Newsom, under whose care the ch are, rec in mbrp

SAVIN
3-13-1892   Michael rec in mbrp

SCHAFFER
11- 7-1885   Milton rec in mbrp
7- 4-1891   Milton & w Dora & minor dt Essie gct Westland MM, Ind
12- 9-1897   Dora & minor dt Essie rocf Westland MM, Ind

SCOTT
6- 6-1885   Elwood, a min, & w Susannah & minor ch Orley J, Elmer, Jennie B, Frederick, Laura F & Florence L rocf Oak Ridge MM, Ind
2- 6-1886   Susannah appt an Elder
6- 9-1892   Emily R rq cert to Fairmount MM, Ind; rq is granted
1-12-1893   Orla J & Elmer gct Fairmount MM, Ind
1-12-1893   Elwood, a min, inf mtg he wishes to hold mtgs in limits of Ohio & New York YM; he is liberated to do so
5-11-1893   Elwood ret copy of minutes of sojourn
12- 4-1893   Elwood, a min, & fam gct Newburg MM, Oregon Terr

SHAFER - SHAFFER
3-13-1892   Emma rec in mbrp

SHAWCROSS
12- 6-1884   William J & w Mary J & ch William Jr, Charles, Albert & Emma Adeline rec in mbrp
5- 7-1887   William J & fam glt Meth Ch, Knightstown, Ind
3-10-1898   William J & w & ch gct Fairmount MM, Ind

SMALL
8- 4-1866   Abraham & ch Zachariah, CHARTER MBRS (Carthage Mtg)
11- 5-1866   Abraham, not in condition of mind to make an acknowledgement, the comm is continued
12- 1-1866   Zachariah appt to comm to att QM & rpt to next Mtg
1- 5-1867   Abraham is dis
6- 6-1868   Abraham rst in mbrp on rq
4- 1-1871   Abraham continues to disturb Mtg so comm thought best to take legal advice to suppress the disturbance

SMITH
2- 3-1883   John P rec in mbrp
8- 6-1887   Mary F rolf Meth Ch, Decatur, Ill
5- 6-1897   John gct Oskaloosa MM, Iowa

SOULE
5- 7-1887   Charles rec in mbrp

STANLEY
3- 7-1891   Robert Ford Sr & w Martha Ellen & minor ch Avery C, Lewis W, Oliver M, Rupert H & Robert F Jr, rec in mbrp

STARBUCK
8- 4-1866   George W & w Sally & ch Eudora E, Lydia M & Dorcas A, CHARTER MBRS (Little Blue River PM)
8- 4-1866   George W appt to comm to make List of Mbrs for this MM (Carthage Mtg & Little Blue River PM)
3- 6-1880   George & w Sally & ch Lydia & Dorcas gct Westland MM, Ind

STEER
4- 6-1893   Benjamin & w Emily & dt Grace rocf Adrian MM, Mich

STONE
3-13-1892   Jesse rec in mbrp

STUART - STEWART
8- 4-1866   Alexander, CHARTER MBR (Carthage Mtg)
5- 2-1868   Alexander gct Cincinnati MM, Ohio
8- 1-1868   Tabitha (form Hunnicut) dis for mcd
9- 5-1868   John & w Martha rocf Hopewell MM, Ind
9- 5-1868   Emma C rocf Hopewell MM, Ind
11- 7-1874   Andrew T & w Margaret & minor ch Clarence E, Gladys M & Warner Ernest rec in mbrp at Carthage PM
2- 5-1877   Nathaniel & w Delila Ann & minor ch Arthur & Blanch rec in mbrp
2- 5-1887   Nathaniel drpd fr mbrp
4- 4-1891   Delitha A rq letter to 1st Presby Ch, Logansport, Ind for her dt Blanche; rq granted on 5- 2-1891
6- 8-1893   Andrew & w Margaret & minor s Carl gct (Greenfield) Westland MM, Ind
2- 7-1895   Maud glt 1st Presby Ch, Logansport, Ind

SUTTON
1- 3-1891   Emma A rocf Spiceland MM, Ind
3- 5-1892   Emma glt Meth Ch, Carthage, Ind

SWAIN
8- 4-1866   Howland & w Elizabeth, CHARTER MBRS (Little Blue River PM)
8- 4-1866   David & w Phebe & ch Ruth, CHARTER MBRS (Little Blue River PM)
8- 4-1866   Hannah, CHARTER MBR (Little Blue River PM)
8- 4-1866   George & w Margaret, CHARTER MBRS (Little Blue River PM)
8- 4-1866   Jethro & w Susannah & dt Susannah, CHARTER MBRS (Little Blue River PM)
8- 4-1866   Oliver & w Elvira & ch Aura & Linneus, CHARTER MBRS (Little Blue River PM)
8- 4-1866   Louisa, CHARTER MBR (Little Blue River PM)
3- 1-1873   Oliver appt one of Trustees of Little Blue River property
6- 6-1874   Oliver appt an Overseer
1- 2-1875   William & w Nancy rec in mbrp
1- 2-1875   William Oliver rec in mbrp
5- 6-1876   Elizabeth appt an Elder
2- 3-1883   Alva H & w Mary A rec in mbrp
6- 2-1883   Rhoda glt Meth Ch, Rushville, Ind
4- 5-1884   William N, Cora M & Sarah E rec in mbrp at Little Blue River PM

TALBERT
8- 4-1866   Jesse & w Hannah & ch Milton, Enos, Hadley & Albert, CHARTER MBRS (Little Blue River PM)
12- 7-1867   Hadley chm; rets mbrp
2- 6-1869   Little Blue River PM rpts Albert mcd
2- 6-1869   Little Blue River PM rpts Enos mcd
3- 6-1869   Albert dis
3- 6-1869   Enos dis
10- 9-1869   Little Blue River PM rpts Hadley mcd
11- 6-1869   Hadley desires to ret mbrp; Mtg grants rq
7- 5-1873   Mary A rec in mbrp
11- 6-1880   Sylvanus rocf Raysville MM, Ind
5- 7-1887   Frank rec in mbrp
6-11-1896   Sylvanus rq rel fr mbrp; rq granted

TERRELL
10-10-1891   Nellie rq letter to U P Ch, Clayton, Ill; rq granted

THORNBURGH
8- 4-1866   Sarah & ch Elizabeth & Luzena, CHARTER MBRS (Carthage Mtg)
8- 5-1871   Anna M gct Raysville MM, Ind
5- 2-1885   Luzena appt an Elder

TRUEBLOOD
4- 9-1896   Nina H gct Whitewater MM, Ind

VESTAL
4- 5-1884   J L & w Vachel rec in mbrp

VICKORY
1- 5-1867   Harmon rocf Centre MM, N C
6- 5-1869   Harmon gct Bloomfield MM, Ind

# CARTHAGE

**VICKORY (Cont)**
- 7- 2-1870  Spring River MM, Kans rpts to Carthage MM, Ind that Harmon has been rec there as Bloomfield MM, Ind had end the cert to them

**WADKINS - WATKINS**
- 3- 5-1881  Edgar J rocf Westland MM, Ohio
- 6- 4-1881  Maggie & minor ch Zula M & an unnamed infant rec in mbrp
- 5- 9-1895  Zula glt Meth Ch, Carthage, Ind

**WARNER**
- 6- 7-1894  Ruth M gct Western Springs MM, Ill

**WEISNER**
- 8- 4-1866  Nathan & w Hannah & ch Phebe Ann, CHARTER MBRS  (Little Blue River PM)
- 9- 1-1866  Nathan appt an Overseer
- 3- 5-1875  Nathan appt an Overseer
- 6- 3-1876  A comm appt to propose a name for an Overseer to take place of Nathan who has dec

**WHITE**
- 2- 5-1887  W A gct Walnut Ridge MM, Ind
- 8- 1-1891  Caroline rocf Poplar Ridge MM, Ind
- 11-10-1892 Sarah Alice & her minor ch Lora, Naomi, Charles Earl & Mary A rocf Walnut Ridge MM, Ind

**WILCUTTS**
- 6- 5-1880  David rocf Spiceland MM, Ind
- 4- 7-1883  Billy & w Sallie & ch Mariette & Sallie rocf New Garden MM, Ind
- 10- 9-1892 Billy gct New Garden MM, Ind

**WILLIAMS**
- 7- 4-1891  Lizzie H gct West Grove MM, Ind
- 4-12-1894  Mary (form Henley) gct Greensboro MM, N C
- 3-12-1896  Albert L & w Lizzie & ch Arthur H, Wister P, Albert R & Elizabeth E rocf Spiceland MM, Ind

**WILSON**
- 12- 1-1866  Samuel C & Elizabeth Jessop inf Mtg of m int
- 1- 5-1867  Samuel C prc fr Back Creek MM, Ind to m Elizabeth Jessop; they are altm; comm appt to att m & rpt to next Mtg
- 2- 2-1867  Comm appt to read the m cert of Samuel C & Elizabeth Jessop rpts it has been att to & m cert has been forwarded to the Recorder
- 5- 4-1867  Elizabeth J gct Back Creek MM, Ind
- 1- 4-1868  Samuel C & w Elizabeth rocf Back Creek MM, Ind
- 5- 1-1869  Samuel C & w Elizabeth J gct Back Creek MM, Ind
- 7- 7-1877  Joseph & w Miriam & ch Eliza & Charley rocf Fairmount MM, Ind
- 8- 7-1880  Joseph appt Asst-Clerk
- 4- 7-1888  Joseph & w Miriam & minor ch Eliza & Charles gct Earlham MM, Calif

**WILTSE**
- 4- 2-1887  George & w Lydia rolf Meth Ch, Carthage Circuit, Ind
- 12- 3-1887  George & w Lydia gct Independence MM, Kans

**WOLF**
- 3-13-1892  Arthur rec in mbrp

**WOOTEN**
- 4- 2-1892  Lee R & w Mary A & minor dt Rachel E rocf Walnut Ridge MM, Ind

**WORTHINGTON**
- 1- 5-1867  Rhoda C gct Springfield MM, Ohio

**WRIGHT**
- 12- 2-1882  David B & w Sarah M & s Floyd A rocf Walnut Ridge MM, Ind

**YOUNG**
- 8- 4-1866  Sarah & ch George H, Miriam B, Rachel, Micajah & William J, CHARTER MBRS  (Carthage Mtg)
- 8- 4-1866  William L, CHARTER MBR  (Carthage Mtg)
- 2- 4-1871  Micajah & Sarah N Henley inf mtg of m int Surviving parents will be expected to be at next mtg
- 3- 4-1871  Micajah & Sarah N Henley are altm; a Friend is appt to att m & rpt to next mtg
- 4- 1-1871  The Friend appt to att m of Micajah & Sarah N Henley, rpts it was att
- 3- 2-1872  Rachel & Reuben B Henley inf mtg of m int
- 4- 6-1872  Rachel & Reuben B Henley are altm; a Friend appt to att m & rpt to next Mtg
- 9- 6-1873  George H & Carrie Folger inf Mtg of m int
- 10-11-1873 George H & Carrie Folger, not a mbr, are altm; a mtg is appt at their rq to be held at home of Addison Folger at 10 A M on 14th inst; a Friend is appt to att m & to forward m cert to the Recorder & to report at next Mtg
- 2- 5-1876  Theodore F & w Rebecca & minor ch Willis R, Edith, Benny & Claudius rec in mbrp at Carthage PM
- 8- 6-1876  Jenny Ann rocf Westland MM, Ind
- 9- 6-1879  Charles E rec in mbrp
- 11- 6-1880 Micajah & w Virginia A & minor ch Walter J & Oliver P gct Westland MM, Ind
- 2- 5-1881  Joseph W, having previously removed, gct ..
- 6- 4-1887  George H gct Little Blue River MM, Ind
- 5- 3-1890  William & w Laura gct Raysville MM, Ind

**ZION**
- 2- 2-1884  Mary rec in mbrp
- 5- 3-1884  William R rocf Raysville MM, Ind
- 1- 7-1886  John rocf Raysville MM, Ind
- 5-11-1893  William & w Laura & minor dt Ruby rocf Raysville MM, Ind
- 12- -1896  William R & w & dt Ruby gct Knightstown MM, Ind